The Rough Guide to

India

written and researched by

David Abram, Nick Edwards, Mike Ford, Devdan Sen and Beth Wooldridge

with additional contributions from

Daniel Jacobs, Joshua Goodman, Anil Mulchandani, Laura Stone and Caroline Sylge

NEW YORK • LONDON • DELHI

www.roughguides.com

Contents

◄◄ Leh ◄ *Sadhu* on balcony, Ujjain

CHINA
AFGHANISTAN
PAKISTAN
TIBET
AUTONOMOUS REGION
NEPAL
BHUTAN
BANGLADESH
N
Metres
6000
5000
4000
3000
2000
1000
500
200
0
JAMMU & KASHMIR
Srinagar
Leh
Jammu Tawi
Dharamsala
Manali
Pathankot
Kullu
Amritsar
HIMACHAL PRADESH
Shimla
Chandigarh
PUNJAB
Mussoorie
Rishikesh
Haridwar
UTTARANCHAL
Naini Tal
HARYANA
CORBETT NATIONAL PARK
DELHI
Bikaner
UTTAR PRADESH
Jaisalmer
RAJASTHAN
Mathura
Bharatpur
Agra
Ganges
Gorakhpur
Kushinagar
Jaipur
Yamuna
Lucknow
Jodhpur
Kanpur
Gwalior
Sarnath
BIHAR
Patna
Allahabad
Kota
Orchha
Varanasi
Mount Abu
Udaipur
Khajuraho
Gaya
JHARKHAND
BANDHAVGARH NATIONAL PARK
Bhuj
Gandhidham
Ujjain
Sanchi
Jabalpur
Ahmedabad
Bhopal
WEST BENGAL
Indore
MADHYA PRADESH
Dwarka
GUJARAT
Vadodara
Mandu
KANHA NATIONAL PARK
KOLKATA (CALCUTTA)
SIKKIM
Gangtok
Kalimpong
Darjeeling
ARUNACHAL PRADESH
Itanagar
ASSAM
Guwahati
NAGALAND
Kohima
Shillong
MEGHALAYA
Imphal
MANIPUR
TRIPURA
Agartala
Aizawl
MIZORAM

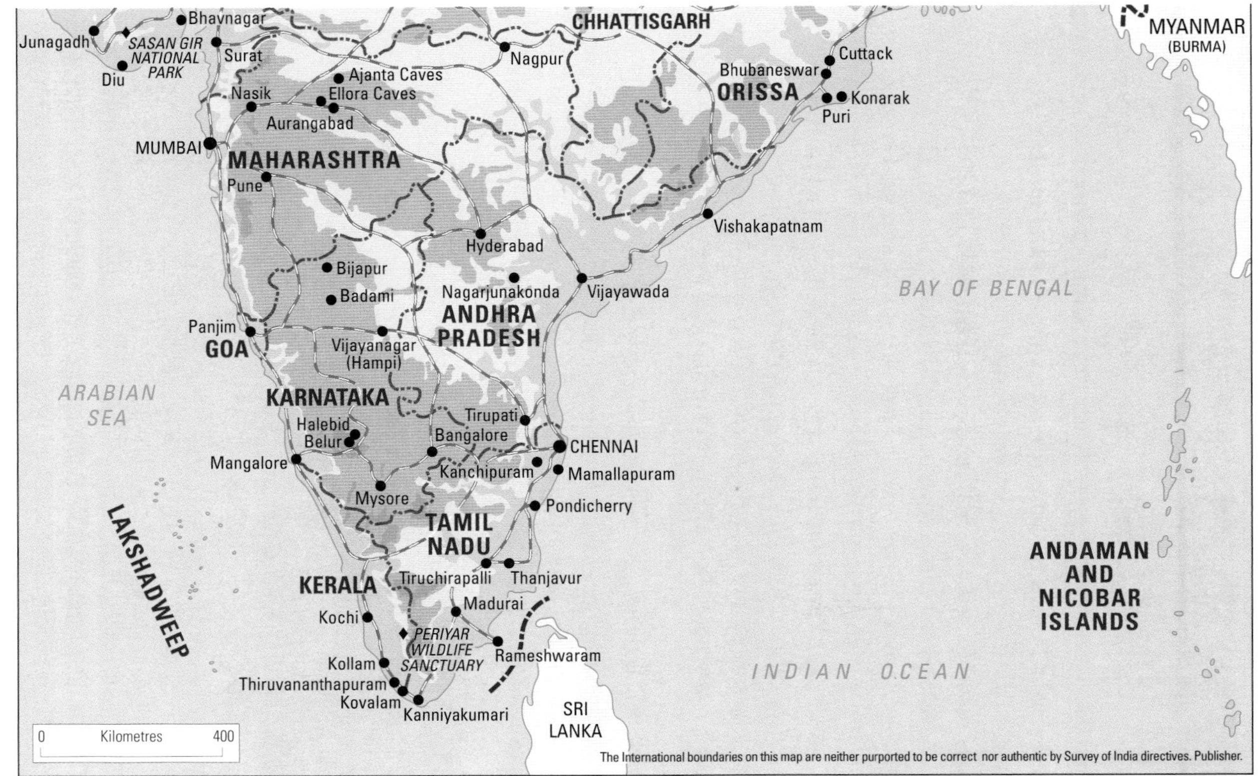

The International boundaries on this map are neither purported to be correct nor authentic by Survey of India directives. Publisher.

Introduction to India

"Unity in Diversity" was the slogan chosen when India celebrated fifty years of Independence in 1997, a declaration replete with as much optimism as pride. Stretching from the frozen barrier of the Himalayas to the tropical greenery of Kerala, and from the sacred Ganges to the sands of the Thar desert, the country's boundaries encompass incomparable variety. Walk the streets of any Indian city and you'll rub shoulders with representatives of several of the world's great faiths, a multitude of castes and outcastes, fair-skinned, turbanned Punjabis and dark-skinned Tamils. You'll also encounter temple rituals that have been performed since the time of the Egyptian Pharaohs, onion-domed mosques erected centuries before the Taj Mahal was ever dreamt of, and quirky echoes of the British Raj on virtually every corner.

That so much of India's past remains discernible today is all the more astonishing given the pace of change since Independence in 1947. Spurred by the free-market reforms of the early 1990s, the **economic revolution** started by Rajiv Gandhi has transformed the country with new consumer goods, technologies and ways of life. Today the land where the Buddha lived and taught, and whose religious festivals are as old as the rivers that sustain them, is the second-largest producer of computer software in the world, with its own satellites and nuclear weapons.

However, the presence in even the most far-flung market towns of Internet cafés and Japanese hatchbacks has thrown into sharp relief the **problems** that have bedevilled the subcontinent since long before it became the world's largest secular democracy. Poverty remains a harsh fact of life for around forty percent of India's inhabitants; no other nation

▶ Decorated truck, Thiruvananthapuram

on earth has slum settlements on the scale of those in Delhi, Mumbai and Kolkata (Calcutta), nor so many malnourished children, uneducated women and homes without access to clean water and waste disposal.

Many first-time visitors find themselves unable to see past such glaring disparities. Others come expecting a timeless ascetic wonderland and are surprised to encounter one of the most materialistic societies on the planet. Still more find themselves intimidated by what may seem, initially, an incomprehensible and bewildering continent. But for all its jarring juxtapositions, intractable paradoxes and frustrations, India remains an utterly compelling destination. Intricate and worn, its distinctive patina – the stream of life in its crowded bazaars, the ubiquitous *filmi* music, the pungent melange of *beedi* smoke, cooking spices, dust and cow dung – casts a spell that few forget from the moment they step off a plane. Love it or hate it – and most travellers oscillate between the two – India will shift the way you see the world.

Fact file

- The Republic of India, whose capital is New Delhi, borders Afghanistan, China, Nepal and Bhutan to the north, Bangladesh and Myanmar (formerly Burma) to the east and Pakistan to the west.
- The world's seventh-largest country, covering more than 3 million square kilometres, it is second only to China in terms of population, which stands at over 1.1 billion. Hindus comprise 82 percent of the population, Muslims 12 percent, and there are millions of Christians, Sikhs, Buddhists and Jains. Eighteen major languages and more than 1000 minor languages and dialects are spoken; Hindi is the language of forty percent of the population, but English is widely spoken.
- The caste system is all-pervasive and, although integral to Hindu belief, it also encompasses non-Hindus. A system of social hierarchy that holds especial sway in rural areas, it may dictate where a person lives and what their occupation is.
- Literacy extends to 76 percent of males and 54 percent of females: 65 percent of the total population.

Where to go

The best Indian itineraries are the simplest. It just isn't possible to see everything in a single expedition, even if you spent a year trying. Far better, then, to concentrate on one or two specific regions and, above all, to be flexible. Although it requires a deliberate change of pace to venture away from the urban centres, rural India has its own very distinct pleasures. In fact, while Indian cities are undoubtedly adrenalin-fuelled, upbeat places, it is possible – and certainly less stressful – to travel for months around the subcontinent and rarely have to set foot in one.

The most-travelled circuit in the country, combining spectacular monuments with the flat, fertile landscape that for many people is archetypally Indian, is the so-called "**Golden Triangle**" in the north: Delhi itself, the colonial capital; Agra, home of the Taj Mahal; and the Pink City of Jaipur in **Rajasthan**. Rajasthan is probably the single most popular state with travellers, who are drawn by its desert scenery, by the imposing medieval forts and palaces of Jaisalmer, Jodhpur, Udaipur and Bundi, and by the colourful traditional dress.

East of Delhi, the River Ganges meanders through some of India's most densely populated regions to reach the extraordinary holy Hindu city of **Varanasi** (also known as Benares), where to witness the daily rituals of life and death focused around the waterfront *ghats* (bathing places) is to glimpse the continuing practice of India's most ancient religious traditions. Further east still is the great city of **Kolkata (Calcutta)**, the capital until early last century of the British Raj and now a teeming metropolis that epitomizes contemporary India's most pressing problems.

The majority of travellers follow the well-trodden Ganges route to reach Nepal, perhaps unaware that the **Indian Himalayas** offer superlative trekking and mountain scenery to rival any in the range. With Kashmir

▲ Arambol beach, Goa

▲ Umbrella stall, Kolkata

effectively off the tourist map since the escalation of its civil war, **Himachal Pradesh** – where Dharamsala is the home of a Tibetan community that includes the Dalai Lama himself – and the remote province of **Ladakh**, with its mysterious lunar landscape and cloud-swept monasteries, have become the major targets for journeys into the mountains. Less visited, but possessing some of Asia's highest peaks, is the niche of **Uttaranchal** bordering Nepal, where the glacial source of the sacred River Ganges has attracted pilgrims for over a thousand years. At the opposite end of the chain, **Sikkim**, north of Bengal, is another low-key trekking destination, harbouring scenery and a Buddhist culture similar to that of neighbouring Bhutan. The **Northeast Hill States**, connected to eastern India by a slender neck of land, boast remarkably diverse landscapes and an incredible fifty percent of India's biodiversity.

For all its jarring juxtapositions, India remains an utterly compelling destination

Heading south from Kolkata (Calcutta) along the coast, your first likely stop is Konarak in **Orissa**, site of the famous Sun Temple, a giant carved pyramid of stone that lay submerged under sand until its rediscovery at the start of the twentieth century. Although it bore the brunt of the 2004 Asian tsunamis, **Tamil Nadu**, further south, has retained its own tradition of magnificent architecture, with towering *gopura* gateways dominating towns whose vast temple complexes are still the focus of everyday life. Of them all, Madurai, in the far south, is the most stunning, but you could spend months wandering between the sacred sites of the Cauvery Delta and the fragrant Nilgiri Hills, draped in the tea terraces that have become the hallmark of South Indian landscapes. **Kerala**, near the southernmost tip of the subcontinent on the western coast, is India at its most tropical and relaxed, its lush backwaters teeming with simple wooden craft of all shapes and sizes, and red-roofed towns and villages all but invisible beneath a canopy of palm trees. Further up the coast is **Goa**, the former Portuguese colony whose hundred-kilometre coastline is fringed with beaches to suit all tastes and budgets, from upmarket package tourists to long-staying backpackers, and whose towns hold whitewashed Christian churches that might have been transplanted from Europe.

India's sacred geography

It's hard to think of a more visibly religious country than India. The very landscape of the subcontinent – its rivers, waterfalls, trees, hill-tops, mountains and rocks – comprises a vast sacred geography for adherents of the dozen or more faiths rooted here. Connecting the country's countless holy places is a network of pilgrimage routes along which tens of thousands of worshippers may be moving at any one time – on regular trains, specially decorated buses, tinsel-covered bicycles, barefoot, alone or in noisy family groups. For the visitor, joining devotees in the teeming temple precincts of the south, on the *ghats* at Varanasi, at the Sufi shrines of Ajmer and Delhi, before the naked Jain colossi of Sravanabelagola, or at any one of the innumerable religious festivals that punctuate the astrological calendar is to experience India at its most intense.

North of here sits **Mumbai**, an ungainly beast that has been the major focus of the nationwide drift to the big cities. Centre of the country's formidable popular movie industry, it reels along on an undeniable energy that, after a few days of acclimatization, can prove addictive. Beyond Mumbai is the state of **Gujarat**, renowned for the unique culture and crafts of the barren Kutch region.

Some of India's most memorable monuments lie far inland, on long-forgotten trading routes across the heart of the peninsula – the abandoned city of Vijayanagar (or Hampi) in **Karnataka**, whose ruins are scattered across a primeval boulder-strewn landscape; the painted and sculpted Buddhist caves of Ajanta and Ellora in **Maharashtra**; the erotic temples of Khajuraho and palaces of Orchha in **Madhya Pradesh**.

On a long trip, it makes sense to pause and rest every few weeks. Certain places have fulfilled that function for generations, such as the Himalayan resort of **Manali**, epicentre of India's hashish-producing area, and the many former colonial hill stations that dot the country, from **Ootacamund (Ooty)**, in the far south, to that archetypal British retreat, **Shimla**, immortalized in the writing of Rudyard Kipling. Elsewhere, the combination of sand and the sea, and a picturesque rural or religious backdrop – such as at **Varkala** in Kerala, **Gokarna** in Karnataka, and the remoter beaches of Goa – are usually enough to loosen even the tightest itineraries.

When to go

India's weather is extremely varied, something you must take into account when planning your trip. The most influential feature of the subcontinent's climate is the wet season, or **monsoon**. This breaks on the Keralan coast at the end of May, working its way northeast across the country over the following month and a half. While it lasts, regular and prolonged downpours are interspersed with bursts of hot sunshine, and the pervasive humidity can be intense. At the height of the monsoon – especially in the jungle regions of the northwest and the low-lying delta lands of Bengal – flooding can severely disrupt communications, causing widespread destruction. In the Himalayan foothills, landslides are common, and entire valley systems can be cut off for weeks.

By September, the monsoon has largely receded from the north, but it takes another couple of months before the clouds disappear altogether from the far south. The east coast of Andhra Pradesh and Tamil Nadu, and the south of Kerala, get a second drenching between October and December, when the "northwest" or "retreating" monsoon sweeps in from the Bay of Bengal. By December, however, most of the subcontinent enjoys clear skies and relatively cool temperatures.

Kashmir

Few civil wars on earth can have been fought against a more idyllic backdrop than the current troubles in Kashmir. During the run-up to Partition in 1947, when the local Hindu maharaja threw the lot of this Muslim-majority valley in with India instead of neighbouring Pakistan, he sowed the seeds of a conflict that would erupt into a full-scale uprising forty years later, between various factions of Islamic, Pakistani-backed militants and the Indian state.

Since 1989, between 40,000 and 60,000 Kashmiri separatists, Indian troops and civilians have died in a campaign of appalling violence that has, on several occasions, brought south Asia's two nuclear powers to the brink of all-out war. Although technically open to visitors, the Kashmir Valley, for all its undeniable beauty, remains a war zone we strongly recommend you steer clear of – hence the absence of a chapter on the region in this book. For more background, see p.1386.

▲ *Ghat* on the Ganges, Varanasi

Mid-winter sees the most marked contrasts between the climates of north and south India. While Delhi, for example, may be ravaged by chill winds blowing off the snowfields of the Himalayas, the Tamil plains and coastal Kerala, more than 1000km south, still stew under fierce post-monsoon sunshine. As spring gathers pace, the centre of the subcontinent starts to heat up again, and by late March thermometers nudge 33°C across most of the Gangetic Plains and Deccan plateau. Temperatures peak in May and early June, when anyone who can retreats to the hill stations. Above the baking subcontinental land mass, hot air builds up and sucks in humidity from the southwest, causing the onset of the monsoon in late June, and bringing relief to millions of overheated Indians.

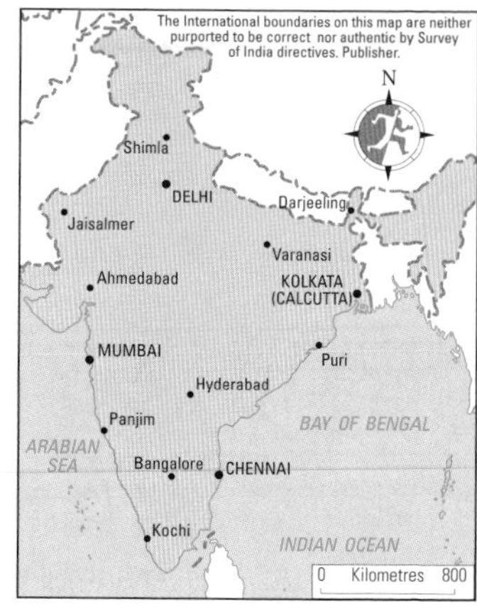

The best time to visit most of the country, therefore, is during the **cool, dry season**, between November and March. Delhi, Agra, Varanasi, Rajasthan and Madhya Pradesh, are ideal at this time, and temperatures in Goa and central India remain comfortable. The heat of the south is never less than intense

Indian railways

India's railways, which daily transport millions of commuters, pilgrims, animals and hessian-wrapped packages between the four corners of the subcontinent, are often cited as the best thing the British Raj bequeathed to its former colony. And yet, with its hierarchical legion of clerks, cooks, coolis, bearers, ticket inspectors, stations managers and ministers, the network has become a quintessentially Indian institution.

Travelling across India by rail – whether you rough it in dirt-cheap second-class, or pamper yourself with starched cotton sheets and hot meals in an air-con carriage – is likely to yield some of the most memorable moments of your trip. Open around the clock, the stations in themselves are often great places to watch the world go by, with hundreds of people from all walks of life eating, sleeping, buying and selling, regardless of the hour. This is also where you'll grow familiar with one of the unforgettable sounds of the subcontinent: the robotic drone of the chai-wallah, dispensing two-cups of hot, sweet tea. For the practical low-down on train travel see p.54.

but it becomes stifling in May and June, so aim to be in Tamil Nadu and Kerala between January and March. From this time onwards, the Himalayas grow more accessible, and the trekking season reaches its peak in August and September while the rest of the subcontinent is being soaked by the rains.

Average temperatures and rainfall

	Jan/Feb		Mar/Apr		May/Jun		July/Aug		Sept/Oct		Nov/Dec	
Ahmedabad (Guj)												
Av daily max (C°)	29	31	36	40	41	38	33	32	33	36	33	30
Rainfall (mm)	4	0	1	2	5	100	316	213	163	13	5	1
Bangalore (Kar)												
Av daily max (C°)	28	31	33	34	33	30	28	29	28	28	27	27
Rainfall (mm)	4	14	6	37	119	65	93	95	129	195	46	16
Chennai (TN)												
Av daily max (C°)	29	31	33	35	38	37	35	35	34	32	29	28
Rainfall (mm)	24	7	15	25	52	53	83	124	118	267	309	139
Darjeeling (WB)												
Av daily max (C°)	9	11	15	18	19	19	20	20	20	19	15	12
Rainfall (mm)	22	27	52	109	187	522	713	573	419	116	14	5
Delhi												
Av daily max (C°)	21	24	30	36	41	40	35	34	34	35	29	23
Rainfall (mm)	25	22	17	7	8	65	211	173	150	31	1	5
Hyderabad (AP)												
Av daily max (C°)	29	31	35	37	39	34	30	29	30	30	29	28
Rainfall (mm)	2	11	13	24	30	107	165	147	163	71	25	5
Jaisalmer (Raj)												
Av daily max (C°)	24	28	33	38	42	41	38	36	36	36	31	26
Rainfall (mm)	2	1	3	1	5	7	89	86	14	1	5	2
Kochi (Ker)												
Av daily max (C°)	31	31	31	31	31	29	28	28	28	29	30	30
Rainfall (mm)	9	34	50	139	364	756	572	386	235	333	184	37
Kolkata (Calcutta) (WB)												
Av daily max (C°)	26	29	34	36	36	34	32	32	32	31	29	27
Rainfall (mm)	13	22	30	50	135	263	320	318	253	134	29	4
Mumbai (M)												
Av daily max (C°)	31	32	33	33	33	32	30	29	30	32	33	32
Rainfall (mm)	0	1	0	0	20	647	945	660	309	17	7	1
Panjim (Goa)												
Av daily max (C)	31	32	32	33	33	31	29	29	29	31	33	33
Rainfall (mm)	2	0	4	17	18	580	892	341	277	122	20	37
Puri (Ori)												
Av daily max (C°)	27	28	30	31	32	31	31	31	31	31	29	27
Rainfall (mm)	9	20	14	12	63	187	296	256	258	242	75	8
Shimla (HP)												
Av daily max (C°)	9	10	14	19	23	24	21	20	20	18	15	11
Rainfall (mm)	65	48	58	38	54	147	415	385	195	45	7	24
Varanasi (UP)												
Av daily max (C°)	23	27	33	39	41	39	33	32	32	32	29	25
Rainfall (mm)	23	8	14	1	8	102	346	240	261	38	15	2

42 things not to miss

It's not possible to see everything India has to offer in one trip, and we don't suggest you try. What follows is a selective taste of the country's highlights: outstanding buildings, natural wonders, spectacular festivals and unforgettable journeys. They're arranged in five colour-coded categories, which you can browse through to find the very best things to see and experience. All highlights have a page reference to take you straight to the guide, where you can find out more.

01 Meherangarh Fort, Jodhpur Page **219** • The epitome of Rajput power and extravagance, its ramparts towering above a labyrinthine, blue-painted old city.

02 Classical music Page **1421** • Winter is the season for classical music in India, when recitals can last all night. Cities renowned for their music styles, or *gharanas*, include Delhi, Kolkata (Calcutta), Gwalior, Varanasi and Chennai (Madras).

03 Chauragarh Mountain, Pachmarhi Page **426** • Thousands of Shivaite tridents are carried by pilgrims to the summit of this holy peak, from where the views are stupendous.

04 Dharamsala Page **515** • Perched on the edge of the Himalayas, this is the home of the Dalai Lama and Tibetan Buddhism in exile.

05 Ashrams Page **84** • Brush up on your yoga and meditation in the holy town of Rishikesh on the Ganges, where the Beatles came to meet Maharishi Yogi.

06 Khajuraho Page **443** • Immaculately preserved temples renowned for their uncompromisingly erotic carvings.

07 Hampi/Vijayanagar Page **1331** • Deserted capital of the last great Hindu empire, scattered over a bizarre landscape of giant golden-brown boulders.

09 Ajanta caves Page **754** • Extraordinarily beautiful murals, dating from 200 BC to 650 AD, adorn the walls of caves chiselled into basalt cliffs.

08 Keoladeo National Park, Bharatpur Page **200** • Asia's most famous bird reserve, where millions of migrants nest each winter. The perfect antidote to the frenzy and pollution of nearby Agra and Jaipur.

10 Varanasi Page **329** • City of Light, founded by Shiva, where the bathing *ghats* beside the Ganges teem with pilgrims.

11 **Amritsar** Page **611** • Site of the fabled Golden Temple, the Sikhs' holiest shrine.

12 **Zanskar** Page **594** • A barren moonscape with extraordinary scenery and challenging trails over the high passes.

13 **Kathakali** Page **1258** • Kerala is the place to experience Kathakali and other esoteric ritual theatre forms.

14 **Jaisalmer** Page **224** • Honey-coloured citadel, emerging from the sands of the Thar Desert.

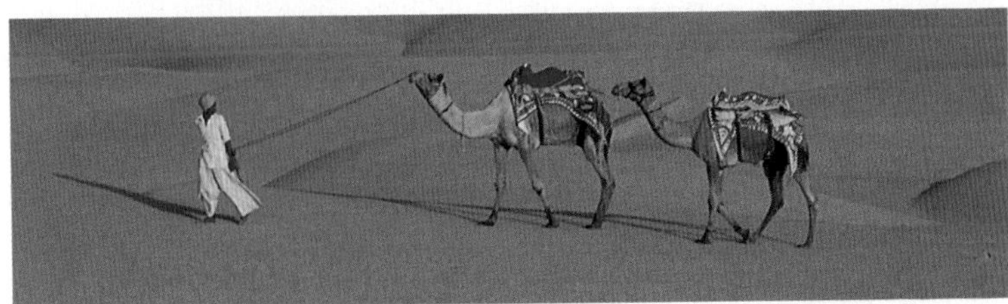

15 Camel trekking in the Thar Page **232** • A wonderfully romantic if utterly touristy way to experience the Great Indian Desert. Most visitors trek out of Jaisalmer, but Bikaner offers more variety.

16 Cricket Page **80** • The nation's favourite sport is played everywhere, from the Oval Maidan in Mumbai to Eden Gardens in Kolkata (Calcutta), the hot cauldron of Indian cricket.

17 Durga Puja Page **864** • An exuberant festival held in September or October, when every street and village erects a shrine to the goddess Durga. Kolkata (Calcutta) has the most lavish festivities.

18 Ellora caves Page **747** • Buddhist, Hindu and Jain caves, and the colossal Hindu Kailash temple, carved from a spectacular volcanic ridge at the heart of the Deccan plateau.

19 Rajasthani handicrafts Page **179** • The teeming bazaars of the Pink City in Jaipur burst with vibrant cloth, jewellery, Persian-style pottery and semi-precious stones. Simply the best place to shop in the subcontinent.

21 Kaziranga National Park Page **989** • Take a dawn elephant ride as the mists slowly lift: sightings of the one-horned rhino, symbol of Assam, are virtually guaranteed.

20 Movies Page **723** • Take in the latest Bollywood blockbuster at one of Mumbai's mega movie houses, which feature huge screens, wrap-around sound and rowdy audiences.

22 Palolem Page **846** • Exquisite crescent-shaped beach in Goa's relaxed south, famous for its dolphins and local alcoholic spirit, *feni*.

23 Gokarna Page **1325** • The beautiful beaches on the edge of this temple town are popular with budget travellers fleeing the commercialism of nearby Goa.

24 Bandhavgarh National Park Page **460** • Deep in the eastern tracts of Madhya Pradesh, this park is rich in animal and birdlife, including tigers and leopards.

25 Mysore market Page **1298** • Jaggery, incense and garlands are made and veggies and kitsch paraphernalia are sold in Mysore's covered market.

26 Manali-Leh Highway Page **550** • India's epic Himalayan road trip, along the second-highest road in the world.

27 Boating on the backwaters of Kerala Page **1234** • Lazy boat trips wind through the lush tropical waterways of India's deep south.

28 Tikse Page **577** • One of many dramatic monasteries within striking distance of Leh.

29 Kochi Page **1247** • Kochi's atmospheric harbourside is strung with elegant Chinese fishing nets.

30 Thrissur Puram Page **1266** • More than one hundred sumptuously caparisoned elephants march in Kerala's biggest temple festival, accompanied by ear-shattering South Indian drum orchestras.

31 Gangotri Page **376** • An atmospheric village on the Ganges that serves as a base for the trek into the heart of the Hindu faith – Gomukh, the source of the Ganges.

32 Taj Mahal Page **285** • Simply the world's greatest building: Shah Jahan's monument to love fully lives up to all expectations.

33 Orchha Page **438** • This semi-ruined former capital of the Bundela Rajas is an architectural gem, rising up through the surrounding jungle.

34 Pushkar camel mela Page **214** • November sees the largest livestock market on earth, where 200,000 Rajasthani herders in traditional costume converge on the desert oasis of Pushkar to trade and bathe in the sacred lake.

35 Udaipur Page **251** • Arguably the most romantic city in India, with ornate Rajput palaces floating in the middle of two shimmering lakes.

36 Rath Yatra, Puri Page **1043** • Three colossal chariots with brightly coloured canopies are pulled by crowds of devotees through the streets of eastern India's holiest town.

37 Fatehpur Sikri Page **298** • The Moghul emperor Akbar's elegant palace complex now lies deserted on a ridge near Agra, but remains one of India's architectural masterpieces.

38 Mamallapuram Page **1135** • A fishing and stone-carving village, with magnificent boulder friezes, shrines and the sea-battered Shore Temple.

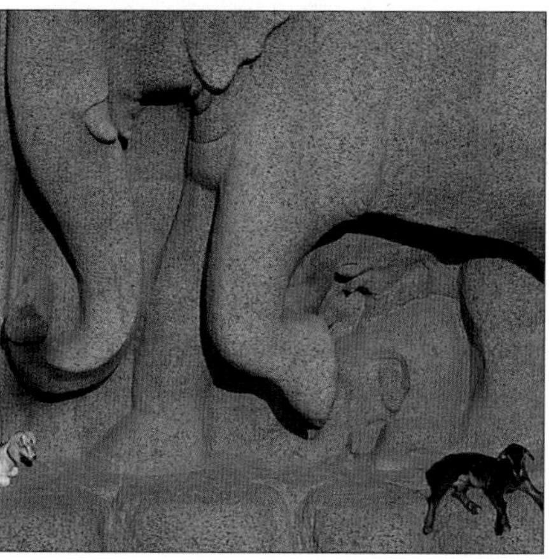

39 Varkala Page **1224** • Kerala's low-key alternative to Kovalam boasts sheer red cliffs, amazing sea views and a legion of Ayurvedic masseurs.

40 Madurai Page **1175** • Definitive South Indian city, centred on a spectacular medieval temple.

41 Konarak Page **1050** • A colossal thirteenth-century temple, buried under sand until its rediscovery by the British.

42 Rafting on the Indus Page **574** • A relatively sedate way to enjoy the grandiose scenery of the northwest Himalaya's most spectacular high-altitude valley.

Basics

Basics

Getting there

With overland routes to India effectively blocked by closed or trouble-prone borders, the only practicable way of getting to India these days is by plane. From the UK, it takes around eight and a half hours to fly to Delhi or Mumbai, and a couple hours or so more to get to Chennai in the south. Travelling from North America, you're on the opposite side of the globe and will have at least one change of plane ahead of you. Nor are there any direct flights from New Zealand or Australia; the quickest route is via southeast Asia.

Airfares worldwide always depend on the **season**, with the highest being roughly November to March, when the weather in India is best; fares drop during the shoulder seasons – April to May and August to early October – and you'll get the best prices during the low season, June and July. The most expensive fares of all are those coinciding with Diwali in November, when demand peaks as Indian emigrants travel home for holidays with their families.

You can often cut costs by going through a **specialist flight agent** – either a consolidator, who buys up blocks of tickets from the airlines and sells them at a discount, or a **discount agent**, who in addition to dealing with discounted flights may also offer special student and youth fares and a range of other travel-related services such as travel insurance or tours. Some agents specialize in **charter flights**, which may be cheaper than anything available on a scheduled service, but again departure dates are fixed and withdrawal penalties are high. For destinations such as Goa and Kerala, you may find it cheaper to pick up a bargain **package deal** from one of the tour operators listed on p.28, p.29 or p.30. Indian law prohibits the sale of flight-only tickets by charter companies, but operators sometimes get around this by tacking budget "bunk-house" accommodation to their tickets, which (if it exists at all) travellers ditch on arrival. Note also that the Indian government places restriction of 28 days on the period of time a charter ticket can cover. If you wish to stay in the country for longer than that, you technically have to take a scheduled flight. Nor is it possible to fly in on a charter and out on a scheduled, or vice versa.

If India is only one stop on a longer journey, you might want to consider buying a **Round-the-World** (RTW) ticket. Some travel agents can sell you an "off-the-shelf" RTW ticket that will have you touching down in about half a dozen cities (Delhi and Mumbai are on many itineraries); others will have to assemble one for you, which can be tailored to your needs but is apt to be more expensive. Figure on £950/$1400–£1500/$2400 for a RTW ticket including India, open for one year.

However you fly to India, bear in mind the huge distances between **gateway cities**. Plan at least the first few days of your trip in advance to avoid arriving at the opposite end of the subcontinent to the one you want to explore first – a mistake that can cost days of tedious train journeys to remedy. And shop around for the most convenient **arrival times**; nearly all of the cheaper flights land in the middle of night and it can be well worth shelling out a little extra to avoid passing through the airport in darkness, particularly if this is your first trip to India.

Also worth bearing in mind when looking for an air ticket is that economy airlines such as Aeroflot – and to a lesser extent Air Uzbekistan and Syrian Arab – are more prone to long delays and stopovers in their hub capitals than the pricier carriers.

Booking flights online

Many airlines and discount travel websites offer you the opportunity to book your tickets **online**. Good deals can often be found through discount or auction sites, as well as through the airlines' own websites.

Online travel agents

@travel.yahoo.com (US and Canada), **@travel.yahoo.co.uk** (UK) Incorporates a lot of Rough Guide material in coverage of destination countries and cities across the world, with information about places to eat, sleep and etc.
@www.cheapflights.com Bookings from the UK and Ireland only; for the US, visit @www.cheapflight .com; for Canada, @www.cheapflights.ca; for Australia, @www.cheapflights.com.au. All the sites offer flight deals, details of travel agents, and links to other travel sites.
@www.cheaptickets.com Hawaii-based discount flight specialists (US only) whose search engine claims to dig up the lowest possible fares worldwide; the one drawback is its cumbersome log-in procedure.
@www.counciltravel.com If your journey originates in the US and you've some flexibility, this site can come up with competitive deals.
@www.etn.nl/discount.htm A hub of consolidator and discount agent Web links, maintained by the nonprofit European Travel Network.
@www.expedia.com Discount airfares, all-airline search engine and daily deals (US only; for the UK @www.expedia.co.uk; for Canada @www.expedia.ca).
@www.flights4less.co.uk Does just what it says on the tin.
@www.flynow.com Simple to use independent travel site offering good-value fares.
@www.hotwire.com Bookings from the US only. Last-minute savings of up to forty percent on regular published fares. Travellers must be at least 18 and there are no refunds, transfers or changes allowed. Log-in required. If you're looking for the cheapest possible scheduled flight, this is probably your best bet.
@www.lastminute.com Offers good last-minute holiday package and flight-only deals (UK only; for Australia @www.lastminute.com.au).
@www.qixo.com A comparison search that trawls through other ticket sites – including agencies and airlines – find the best deals.
@www.skyauction.com Bookings from the US only. Auctions tickets and travel packages using a "second bid" scheme, just like e-bay. You state the maximum you're willing to pay, and the system will bid only as much as it takes to outbid others, up to your stated limit.
@www.ticketplanet.com California-based site that claims to be the first to sell consolidator fares over the web. Especially good for circle-Pacific and Round-the-World fares.
@www.travelocity.com and **@www.travelocity.co.uk** Destination guides, hot web fares and best deals for car hire, accommodation and lodging as well as fares. Provides access to the travel agent system SABRE, the most comprehensive central reservations system in the US.
@www.travelshop.com.au Australian website offering discounted flights, packages, insurance, and online bookings.

Packages

A large number of operators run **package holidays** to India, covering such activities as trekking and safaris as well as sightseeing and beach-centred holidays. Specialist minority-interest tours range from steam locomotives and textiles to religion and food. Even if you book a general sightseeing tour, most firms have a good range of options, usually including the "Golden Triangle" of Delhi, Agra and Jaipur; a tour of Rajasthan; or a southern tour taking in Bangalore, Hyderabad, Chennai and Kochi. Some also offer wildlife tours; the Palace on Wheels train journey (see p.58); take in Nepal or Bhutan; or have various combinations of all these. In addition, many companies will arrange **tailor-made tours**, and can help you plan your own itinerary.

Of course, any package holiday is a lot easier than going under your own steam, particularly if you only have a short time and don't want to use it up on making your own travel bookings. On the other hand, a typical sightseeing tour can rather isolate you from the country, shutting you off in air-conditioned hotels and buses. Specialist trips such as trekking and tailor-made tours will work out quite expensive, compared to what you'd pay if you organized everything independently, but they do cut out a lot of hassle. If you're planning to be in India for less than 28 days, it might be worth hunting for late-availability charter deals to Goa or Kerala offered by UK-based companies (normally valid for up to a month only). These can sometimes work out cheaper than a normal flight.

Specialist tour operators

In Britain

Abercrombie and Kent ⓣ0845/070 0610, @www.abercrombiekent.co.uk. Upmarket sightseeing and trekking and wildlife trips; tailor-made holidays also available.

Andrew Brock/Coromandel ⓣ01572/821330 ⓦwww.coromandelabt.com. Car itineraries, textile trips to village craft workshops, plus David Sayer's botanical and horticultural tours, Himalayan treks and luxury river cruises on the Brahmaputra.
Audley Travel ⓣ01869/276218 ⓦwww.audleytravel.com. Privately guided, tailor-made itineraries that use interesting accommodation (homestays, tented camps and heritage properties); they're also strong on wildlife.
Bales ⓣ0870/241 3208, ⓦwww.balesworldwide.com. Sixteen escorted tours covering most of India.
Blazing Trails UK ⓣ01293/533338, ⓦwww.blazingtrailstours.com. Escorted motorcycle tours (on Enfields) in Goa, Kerala and the Himalayas.
Cox & Kings ⓣ020/7873 5000, ⓦwww.coxandkings.com. Tailor-made itineraries with operators established in India since 1758.
Discovery Initiatives ⓣ01285/643333 ⓦwww.discoveryinitiatives.co.uk. Nature tour specialist offering small groups or tailor-made trips with an accent on conservation and ecology.
Essential India ⓣ01225/868544, ⓦwww.essential-india.co.uk. Courses in India on a wide range of subjects, from writing, painting, and pottery to Buddhism and outdoor pursuits, for individuals or groups. They favour low-impact travel and use local companies wherever possible.
Exodus ⓣ020/8675 5550, ⓦwww.exodustravels.co.uk. Experienced specialists in small-group itineraries, treks and overland tours.
High Places ⓣ0114/275 7500, ⓦwww.highplaces.co.uk. Sheffield-based specialists in trekking and mountaineering, who also offer biking and boating in Kerala and Aravalli walks in Rajasthan.
Himalayan Kingdoms ⓣ01453/844400, ⓦwww.himalayankingdoms.com. Quality treks in Sikkim, Garhwal, Himachal Pradesh, Ladakh and Arunachal Pradesh.
Jewel in the Crown ⓣ01293/533338, ⓦwww.jewelholidays.com. Established Goa specialist, offering a wide range of holidays across the state; they also run motorcycle tours on Enfields.
Kambala ⓣ01803/732488. One of the few operators specializing in very small group tours for the over-50s. General sightseeing and "hobby" holidays (eg textiles and painting) in rural Rajasthan, Kerala and Nepal.
Kerala Connections ⓣ01892/722440 ⓦwww.keralaconnect.co.uk. South India specialists, offering itineraries in Tamil Nadu, Karnataka and Andhra Pradesh as well as Kerala, for a wide range of budgets.
Out There Biking (no phone) ⓦwww.out-there-biking.com. Small, UK-based bicycle adventure company specialising in the Indian Himalaya. The tours are either self- or jeep-supported, with a low-impact travel philosophy and excellent local knowledge.
Pettitts India ⓣ01892/515966, ⓦwww.pettitts.co.uk. Tailor-made holidays off the beaten track.
SD Enterprises ⓣ0208/903 0392, ⓦwww.indiarail.co.uk. Run by Indian rail experts, SD Enterprises put together complex itineraries for independent travellers wanting to explore India by train, as well as budget packages to Goa and Kerala from around £499.
Soul of India ⓣ020/8901 7320, ⓦwww.soulofindia.com. Guided tours (set or tailor-made, and for individuals or groups) of sacred India, including the source of the Ganges, Sikh shrines, the Hindu and Christian south, and landmarks associated with the Buddha and Gandhi.
Trans Indus Travel ⓣ020/8566 2729, ⓦwww.transindus.co.uk. Fixed and tailor-made tours from various Indian cities: specialists in wildlife, fishing and trekking.
Voyages Jules Verne ⓣ020/7616 1000, ⓦwww.vjv.co.uk. Fourteen classic heritage tours, including some by rail.
Western & Oriental Travel ⓣ0870/499 1111, ⓦwww.westernoriental.com. Award-winning, upmarket agency with tailor-made itineraries covering all of India but favouring Goa and Rajasthan.

In the US and Canada

Above the Clouds ⓣ1-802/482-4848, ⓦwww.aboveclouds.com. Ladakh mountain treks over the Parang La range are among several India options.
Adventure Center ⓣ1-800/228-8747, ⓦwww.adventurecenter.com. Trekking and cultural tours.
Butterfield & Robinson ⓣ1-800/678-1147 or 1-510/654 1879, ⓦwww.butterfield.com. Bespoke tours, with an emphasis on bikes and walking.
Geographic Expeditions ⓣ1-800/777-8183, ⓦwww.geoex.com. Remote mountain treks and unusual tours including one of Arunachal.
Mountain Travel/Sobek ⓣ1-888/687-6235 or 510/527-8100, ⓦwww.mtsobek.com. Trekking and camel safaris, and cultural trips to Ladakh.
Myths and Mountains ⓣ1-800/670-6984 or 775-832-5454, ⓦwww.mythsandmountains.com. Special-interest trips, tailor-made or group, with an emphasis on culture, crafts, religion and traditional medicine.
Nature Expeditions International ⓣ1-800/869-0639 or 503/484-6529, ⓦwww.naturexp.com. Upscale wildlife viewing, "soft adventure" and cultural tours.
Wilderness Travel ⓣ1-800/368-2794, ⓦwww.wildernesstravel.com. Rajasthan camel safaris and elephant-research expeditions.

Worldwide Quest Adventures ⓣ1-800/387-1483, ⓦwww.worldwidequest.com. Sightseeing plus trekking, cycling, camel safaris and cultural tours.

In Australia and New Zealand

Abercrombie and Kent Australia ⓣ02/9241 3213, New Zealand ⓣ0800/441 638; ⓦwww.abercrombiekent.com.au. Specialist in individual mid- to upmarket holidays, away from the main tourist trails.

Classic Oriental Tours Australia ⓣ02/9657 2020, ⓦwww.classicoriental.com.au. Wide choice of tours ranging from three-day city breaks to 22-day itineraries, with some adventure options.

Peregrine Adventures Australia ⓣ03/9663 8611, ⓦwww.peregrine.net.au. Trekking specialists with a wide range of tailored group and individual tours.

San Michele Travel Australia ⓣ02/9299 1111 & 1800/222244, ⓦwww.asiatravel.com.au. Budget and upmarket air and accommodation packages, rail tours and tailor-made land excursions for groups or individual travellers.

Travel.com.au Australia ⓣ02/9249 6000, ⓦwww.travel.com.au. Agent for a broad range of tour operators. You can select set itineraries or tailor-make your own packages on their website.

Flights from the UK and Ireland

It takes between eight-and-a-half and eleven hours to **fly from the UK** direct to India. However, most airlines route passengers through their hub city on the way, which can double the total travelling time. By and large you get what you pay for. Economy airlines – such as Aeroflot, Syrian Arab and Uzbekistan Air – may offer rock-bottom fares from as low as £320 (or less), but you'll invariably find this means a tediously long wait at obscure airports well off the direct route, and departure and arrival times at unsociable hours of the night. At the other end of the scale, a ticket costing upwards of £600 with British Airways, Emirates, Air India or Virgin should get you there non-stop from London by a more civilized hour. Flight-only deals with charters (see p.28) go for as little as £249 low season (and sometimes even less), or £450–700 over Christmas and New Year.

Airlines

Aeroflot UK ⓣ020/7355 2233, ⓦwww.aeroflot.co.uk.

Air France UK ⓣ0845/084 5111, ⓦwww.airfrance.co.uk; Republic of Ireland ⓣ01/605 0383, ⓦwww.airfrance.com/ie.

Air India ⓣ020/8560 9996 or 8745 1000, ⓦwww.airindia.com.

Air Uzbekistan ⓣ020/7935 1899, ⓦwww.uzbekistanairways.com.

Alitalia UK ⓣ0870/544 8259, Republic of Ireland ⓣ01/677 5171; ⓦwww.alitalia.co.uk.

Biman Bangladesh Airlines ⓣ020/7629 0252, ⓦwww.bimanair.com.

British Airways UK ⓣ0870/850 9850, Republic of Ireland ⓣ1800/626747; ⓦwww.ba.com.

Egyptair UK ⓣ020/7734 2343 or 7734 2395, ⓦwww.egyptair.com.eg.

Emirates Airlines UK ⓣ0870/243 2222, ⓦwww.emirates.com.

Gulf Air UK ⓣ0870/777 1717, ⓦwww.gulfairco.com.

Jet Airwaysⓣ020/8970 1525, ⓦwww.jetairways.com

KLM Royal Dutch Airlines ⓣ08705/074074, ⓦwww.klm.com.

Lufthansa UK ⓣ0845/773 7747, Republic of Ireland ⓣ01/844 5544; ⓦwww.lufthansa.co.uk.

Pakistan International Airlines UK ⓣ020/7499 5500, ⓦwww.piac.com.pk.

Qantas ⓣ0845/774 7767, ⓦwww.quantas.com.

Royal Brunei Airlines UK ⓣ020/7584 6660, ⓦwww.bruneiair.com.

Royal Jordanian UK ⓣ020/7878 6333, Republic of Ireland ⓣ061/712874; ⓦwww.rja.com.jo.

Sahara Airlines UKⓣ0870/127 1000, ⓦwww.airsahara.net.

SriLankan Airlines UK ⓣ020/8538 2000, ⓦwww.srilankan.lk.

Syrian Arab Airlines ⓣ020/7493 2851, ⓦwww.syrianairlines.co.uk.

Swiss UK ⓣ0845/601 0956, ⓦwww.swiss.com.

Tarom Romanian Air Transport UK ⓣ020/7224 3693, ⓦwww.tarom.ro.

Thai Airways International UK ⓣ0870/606 0911, ⓦwww.thaiair.com.

United Airlines UK ⓣ0845/8444 777, ⓦwww.unitedairlines.co.uk.

Virgin Atlantic Airways UK ⓣ01293/747747, ⓦwww.virgin.com/atlantic.

Flight and travel agents

UK

Arrowguide Ltd 29 Dering St, London W1 ⓣ020/7629 9516, ⓦwww.arrowguide.co.uk. Long-established and reliable consolidator that specializes in cheap flights to India.

Bridge the World ⓣ0870/814 4400, ⓦwww.bridgetheworld.com. Specializing in Round-the-World tickets, with good deals aimed at the backpacker market.

Co-op Travel Care ⓣ0870/112 0085, ⓦwww.travelcareonline.com. Award-winning agent, offering flights and holidays around the world.

Flightbookers ⓣ0870/010 7000, ⓦwww.ebookers.com. Low fares on an extensive selection of scheduled flights.

North South Travel ⓣ01245/608291, ⓦwww.northsouthtravel.co.uk. Friendly, competitive travel agency, offering discounted fares worldwide – profits are used to support projects in the developing world, especially the promotion of sustainable tourism.

Rosetta Travel Northern Ireland ⓣ028/9064 4996, ⓦwww.rosettatravel.com. Flight and holiday agent.

STA Travel ⓣ0870/1600 599, ⓦwww.statravel.co.uk. Worldwide specialists in low-cost flights and tours for students and under-26s, though other customers welcome.

Top Deck ⓣ020/8879 6789, ⓦwww.topdecktravel.co.uk. Long-established agent dealing in discount flights.

Trailfinders ⓣ0845/0585 858, ⓦwww.trailfinders.co.uk. One of the best-informed and most efficient agents for independent travellers; they produce a very useful quarterly magazine worth scrutinizing for round-the-world routes.

Travel Bag ⓣ01/602 1904, ⓦwww.travelbag.co.uk. Discount flights to Australia, New Zealand, USA and the Far East; official Qantas agent.

Republic of Ireland

Apex Travel ⓣ01/241 8000, ⓦwww.apextravel.ie. Specialists in flights to Australia, Africa, Far East, USA and Canada.

Aran Travel International ⓣ091/562595, ⓦhomepages.iol.ie/~arantvl/aranmain.htm. Good-value flights to all parts of the world.

CIE Tours International ⓣ01/703 1888, ⓦwww.cietours.ie. General flight and tour agent.

Joe Walsh Tours ⓣ01/241 0888, ⓦwww.joewalshtours.ie. General budget fares agent.

Lee Travel ⓣ021/277111, ⓦwww.leetravel.ie. Flights and holidays worldwide.

McCarthy's Travel ⓣ021/427 0127, ⓦwww.mccarthystravel.ie. General flight agent.

Trailfinders ⓣ01/677 7888, ⓦwww.trailfinders.ie. See UK, above.

usit NOW ⓣ01/602 1600, Northern Ireland ⓣ028/9032 7111; ⓦwww.usitnow.ie. Student and youth specialists for flights and trains.

Flights from the US and Canada

India is on the other side of the planet from the **US** and **Canada**. If you live on the East Coast it's somewhat shorter to go via Europe, while from the West Coast it's quicker via the Pacific, but either way it's a long haul, involving one or more intermediate stops, and you'll arrive fresher and less jet-lagged if you can manage to fit in a few days' layover somewhere en route.

From the East Coast, you'll stop over somewhere in Europe (most often London), the Gulf, or both. Figure on at least eighteen hours' total travel time. Prices are most competitive out of **New York**, where the cheapest low-season consolidated fares to Mumbai/Delhi hover around $1250 in low season and rise to $1600 in high season. From Washington or Miami, figure on $1600 in low season to $1850 in high season; from Chicago $1600 to $2000; and from Dallas/Fort Worth $1800 to $3000.

From the West Coast, it takes about as long to fly east or west – a minimum of 22 hours' total travel time – and if you're booking through a consolidator there may not be much difference in price.

From Los Angeles or **San Francisco**, you're looking at a minimum of $1300 to fly to Delhi or Mumbai in low season, and up to $1700 in high season.

The only direct flight **from Canada** to India is Vancouver–Delhi on Air Canada (via London, and taking under 20hr). All other routeings involve a plane change and more layover time. A discount agent will probably break the journey into two, using one of dozens of carriers for the transatlantic (or trans-Pacific) leg. Typical discounted low and high season fares to Delhi or Mumbai from Montreal, Toronto and Vancouver are CDN$2000/$2600.

Airlines in North America

Aeroflot US ⓣ1-888/340-6400, Canada ⓣ416/642-1653; ⓦwww.aeroflot.com.

Air Canada ⓣ1-888/247-2262, ⓦwww.aircanada.ca.

Air France US ⓣ1-800/237-2747, ⓦwww.airfrance.com; Canada ⓣ1-800/667-2747, ⓦwww.airfrance.ca.

Air India ⓣ1-800/223-7776 or 212/751-6200, ⓦwww.airindia.com.
Alitalia US ⓣ1-800/223-5730, Canada ⓣ1-800/361-8336; ⓦwww.alitalia.com.
All Nippon Airways ⓣ1-800/235-9262, ⓦwww.fly-ana.com.
Asiana Airlines ⓣ1-800/227-4262, ⓦwww.flyasiana.com.
Biman Bangladesh Airlines ⓣ1-888-702-4626 or 212/808-4477, ⓦwww.bimanair.com.
British Airways ⓣ1-800/247-9297, ⓦwww.ba.com.
Cathay Pacific ⓣ1-800/233-2742, ⓦwww.cathay-usa.com.
Czech Airlines US ⓣ1-877/359-6629 or 212/765-6022, Canada ⓣ416/363-3174; ⓦwww.czechairlines.com.
Delta Air Lines domestic ⓣ1-800/221-1212, international ⓣ1-800/241-4141; ⓦwww.delta.com.
EgyptAir US ⓣ1-800/334-6787, Canada ⓣ416/960-0009; ⓦwww.egyptair.com.eg.
Emirates Air ⓣ1-800/777-3999, ⓦwww.emirates.com.
Gulf Air ⓣ1-888/359 4853; ⓦwww.gulfairco.com.
Jet ⓣ1-925/866 1205, ⓦwww.jetairways.com.
KLM Royal Dutch Airlines/Northwest domestic ⓣ1-800/225-2525, international ⓣ1-800/447-4747; ⓦwww.nwa.com, ⓦwww.klm.com.
Kuwait Airways ⓣ212/659-4200, ⓦwww.kuwait-airways.com.
Lufthansa US ⓣ1-800/645-3880, Canada ⓣ1-800/563-5954; ⓦwww.lufthansa-usa.com.
Malaysia Airlines ⓣ1-800/552-9264, ⓦwww.mas.com.my.
Northwest/KLM Royal Dutch Airlines domestic ⓣ1-800/225-2525, international ⓣ1-800/447-4747; ⓦwww.nwa.com, ⓦww.klm.com.
Pakistan International Airlines ⓣ1-800/221-2552 or 212/760-8484, ⓦwww.piac.com.pk.
Polynesian Airlines ⓣ1-800/644-7659, ⓦwww.polynesianairlines.com
Qantas Airways ⓣ1-800/227-4500, ⓦwww.qantas.com.
Royal Jordanian Airlines ⓣ1-800/223-0470 or 212/949-0050, ⓦwww.rja.com.jo.
Royal Nepal Airlines ⓣ1-800/266-3725, ⓦwww.royalnepal.com.
Sahara US ⓣ212/685 5456, Canada ⓣ416/966 4825; ⓦwww.airsahara.net.
Singapore Airlines ⓣ1-800/742-3333, ⓦwww.singaporeair.com.
SriLankan Airlines ⓣ1-877/915-2652, ⓦwww.srilankan.lk.
Swiss ⓣ1-877/359-7947, ⓦwww.swiss.com.
Tarom Romanian Air ⓣ212/560-0840, ⓦtarom.digiro.net/index_en.html.
Thai Airways International in US ⓣ1-800/426-5204, in Canada ⓣ1-800/668-8103; ⓦwww.thaiair.com.
TWA domestic ⓣ1-800/221-2000, international ⓣ1-800/892-4141; ⓦwww.twa.com.
United Airlines domestic ⓣ1-800/241-6522, international ⓣ1-800/538-2929; ⓦwww.ual.com.
Virgin Atlantic Airways ⓣ1-800/862-8621, ⓦwww.virgin.com/atlantic.

Travel agents, consolidators and travel clubs in the US and Canada

Air Brokers International ⓣ1-800/883-3273, ⓦwww.airbrokers.com. Consolidator and specialist in Round-the-World and Circle Pacific tickets.
Airtech ⓣ212/219-7000, ⓦwww.airtech.com. Standby seat broker; also deals in consolidator fares and courier flights.
Airtreks.com ⓣ1-877-247-8735, ⓦwww.airtreks.com. Round-the-World and Circle Pacific tickets. The website features an interactive database that lets you build and price your own round-the-world itinerary.
Educational Travel Center ⓣ1-800/747-5551 or 608/256-5551, ⓦwww.edtrav.com. Student/youth discount agent.
STA Travel US ⓣ1-800/781-4040, Canada 1-888/427-5639; ⓦwww.statravel.com. Worldwide specialists in independent travel; also student IDs, travel insurance, car rental, rail passes etc.
Student Flights ⓣ1-800/255-8000 or 480/951-1177, ⓦwww.isecard.com. Student/youth fares, student IDs.
TFI Tours ⓣ1-800/745-8000 or 212/736-1140, ⓦwww.lowestairprice.com. Consolidator.
Travelers Advantage ⓣ1-877/259-2691, ⓦwww.travelersadvantage.com. Discount travel club; annual membership fee required (currently $1 for 3 months' trial).
Travel Cuts Canada ⓣ1-866/246-9762, US ⓣ1-800/952-2887; ⓦwww.travelcuts.com. Canadian student-travel organization.
Worldtek Travel ⓣ1-800/243-1723, ⓦwww.worldtek.com. Comparison site.

Flights from Australia and New Zealand

There are no non-stop flights to India from either **Australia** or **New Zealand**; you have to make at least one change of plane in a southeast Asian hub city (usually Kuala Lumpur, Singapore or Bangkok). The choice of routes and airlines is bewildering, and most agents will offer you a combination of two or more carriers to get the best price.

Flying west, the main, and cheapest, Indian gateway city tends to be Chennai (Madras), with Mumbai (Bombay) and Delhi not far behind. As a rule of thumb, the best-value tickets from Australia are on departures from the east coast. Flying from Perth to Chennai in **low/shoulder season** (Feb 1–Nov 21) costs A$1100–1700 depending on the airline.

Flying **from New Zealand**, the cheapest fares to India range from just under NZ$2000 to around NZ$2250 if you leave from Auckland; add on approximately NZ$150 for flights from Wellington or Christchurch.

Round-the-World fares from Australia and New Zealand using the above airlines can take in India; for example, Thai Airways, Air New Zealand, Qantas and Malaysia Airlines can route you through Delhi or Mumbai as part of a RTW deal from around A$2200/NZ$2600.

Airlines in Australia and New Zealand

Air France Australia ⓣ02/9244 2100, New Zealand ⓣ09/308 3352; ⓦwww.airfrance.com.au.
Air India Australia ⓣ02/9299 2022, New Zealand ⓣ09/303 1301; ⓦwww.airindia.com.
Air New Zealand Australia ⓣ13 24 76, New Zealand ⓣ0800 247 764; ⓦwww.airnewzealand.com.
British Airways Australia ⓣ1300/767177, New Zealand ⓣ09/966 9777; ⓦwww.ba.com.
Cathay Pacific Australia ⓣ13 17 47, New Zealand ⓣ09/379 0861; ⓦwww.cathaypacific.com.
KLM Royal Dutch Australia ⓣ1300/303747, New Zealand ⓣ09/302 1792; ⓦwww.klm.com.
Lufthansa Australia ⓣ1300/655727, New Zealand ⓣ09/303 1529 or 008/945220; ⓦwww.lufthansa.com.
Malaysia Airlines Australia ⓣ13 26 27, New Zealand ⓣ0800/777747 or 649/379 3743; ⓦwww.malaysiaairlines.com.
Qantas Australia ⓣ13 13 13, New Zealand ⓣ09/357 8900 or 0800/808767; ⓦwww.qantas.com.
Singapore Airlines Australia ⓣ13 10 11 or 02/9350 0262, New Zealand ⓣ09/379 3209; ⓦwww.singaporeair.com.
SriLankan Airlines Australia ⓣ02/9244 2234, New Zealand ⓣ09/308 3353; ⓦwww.srilankan.lk.
Swiss Australia ⓣ1300/724666, New Zealand ⓣ9/977 2238; ⓦwww.swiss.com.
Thai Airways Australia ⓣ1300/651960, New Zealand ⓣ09/377 3886; ⓦwww.thaiair.com.

Travel agents in Australia and New Zealand

Flight Centre Australia ⓣ13 31 33 or 02/9235 3522, ⓦwww.flightcentre.com.au; New Zealand ⓣ0800/243544 or 09/358 4310, ⓦwww.flightcentre.co.nz. Discount flight agents.
Holiday Shoppe New Zealand ⓣ0800/808480, ⓦwww.holidayshoppe.co.nz. General travel agent with deals updated daily.
STA Travel Australia ⓣ1300/733035 or 02/9212 1255, ⓦwww.statravel.com.au; New Zealand ⓣ0508/782 872 or 09/309 9273, ⓦwww.statravel.co.nz. Worldwide specialists in independent travel; also student IDs, travel insurance, car rental, rail passes etc.
Trailfinders Australia ⓣ1300/780 212, ⓦwww.trailfinders.com.au. One of the best-informed and most efficient agents for independent travellers; especially strong on round-the-world routes.

Visas and red tape

Gone are the days when Commonwealth nationals could stroll visa-less into India and stay for as long as they pleased: today, everyone except citizens of Nepal and Bhutan needs a visa.

If you're going to India on business or to study, you'll need to apply for a special student or business visa; otherwise, a **standard tourist visa** will suffice. These are **valid**

Indian public holidays: a warning

Wherever you intend to get your visa from, bear in mind that your nearest High Commission, Embassy or Consulate will observe **Indian public holidays** (as well as most of the local ones), and that it might therefore be closed. Always check opening hours in advance by phone, or via the website, beforehand.

for six months from the date of issue (not of departure from your home country or entry into India), and cost £30/US$60/CDN$62/A$55/NZ$90. As you're asked to specify whether you need a single-entry or a **multiple-entry visa**, and the same rates apply to both, it makes sense to ask for the latter, just in case you decide to make a side trip to Nepal or another neighbouring country.

Much the best place to get a visa is in your country of residence, from the embassies and high commissions listed opposite; you should be able to download forms from the embassy and consulate websites. In Britain and North America, you'll need a passport valid for at least six months, two passport photographs and an application form, obtainable in advance by post or on the day; address applications to the Postal Visa Section of the consulate in question. In Australia and New Zealand, one passport-sized photo and your flight/travel itinerary are required, together with the visa application form. As a rule, visas are issued in a matter of hours, although embassies in India's neighbouring countries often drag their feet, demand letters of recommendation from your embassy (expensive if you are, for example, British), or make you wait and pay for them to send your application to Delhi. In the US, postal applications take a month as opposed to a same-day service if you do it in person – check with your nearest embassy, high commission or consulate. Make sure that your visa is signed by someone at the embassy, as you may be refused entry into the country otherwise.

In many countries it's also possible to pay a **visa agency** (or "visa expediter") to process the visa on your behalf, which in the UK costs £30–35 (plus the price of the visa). This is an option worth considering if you're not able to get to your nearest Indian High Commission, embassy or consulate yourself. Prices vary a little from company to company, as do turnaround times. Two working weeks is about standard, but you can get a visa in as little as 24 hours if you're prepared to pay premium rates (typically £60 on top of the cost of your visa). For a full rundown of services, check the company websites below, from where you can usually download visa application forms and confirm requirements. In **Britain**, try The Visa Service (Ⓣ08708/900185, Ⓦwww.visaservice.co.uk); Gold Arrow (Ⓣ0870/165 7412, Ⓦwww.goldarrow.info); or Visa Express (Ⓣ020/7251 4822, Ⓦwww.visaexpress.com). In **North America**, where you can expect to pay anywhere between US$140–260 to obtain a visa within two weeks, reliable expediters include Travel Document Systems (Ⓣ202/638 3800, Ⓦwww.traveldocs.com), and Visa Connection (Ⓦwww.visaconnection.com) – the latter have offices in Vancouver, Calgary, Ottawa and Toronto, as well as in the States.

Visa extensions

It is no longer possible to **extend a visa** in India, though exceptions may be made in special circumstances. Most people whose standard six-month tourist visas are about to expire head for Bangkok or neighbouring capitals such as Colombo in Sri Lanka or Kathmandu in Nepal, and apply for a new one. However, in recent years this has been something of a hit-and-miss business, with some tourists having their requests turned down for no apparent reason. The Indian High Commission in Kathmandu is particularly notorious for this; you can telephone them or visit their website to check their current policy, but the online advice is confused and you shouldn't, in any case, expect the story to be the same when you arrive. Try to find out from other travellers what the visa situation is, and always allow enough time on your current permit to re-enter India and catch a flight out of the country in case your request is refused.

If you do stay more than 180 days, you are supposed to get a **tax clearance certificate** before you leave the country, available at the foreigners' section of the income-tax department in every major city. They are free, but you should take bank receipts to show you have changed your money legally. In practice, tax clearance certificates are rarely demanded, but you never know.

For details of other kinds of visas – five-year visas can be obtained by foreigners of Indian origin, business travellers and even students of yoga – contact your nearest Indian embassy.

Indian embassies

Afghanistan Embassy: Malalai Wat, Shahre-Nau, Kabul, Afghanistan Ⓣ 873-76/309 5560, Ⓔ indembkabul@nic.in.

Australia High Commission: 3–5 Moonah Place, Yarralumla, Canberra, ACT 2600 Ⓣ 02/6273 3999, Ⓔ hcicouns@bigpond.com. Consulates: Level 27, 25 Bligh St, Sydney, NSW 2000 Ⓣ 02/9223 9500, Ⓦ www.indianconsulatesydney.org; 15 Munro St, Coburg, Melbourne, Vic 3058 Ⓣ 03/9384 0141. Honorary Consulates: Level 1, Terrace Hotel, 195 Adelaide Terrace, East Perth WA 6004, Australia (mailing address: PO BOX 6118 East Perth WA 6892, Australia) Ⓣ 08/9221 1485, Ⓔ india@vianet.net.au.

Bangladesh High Commission: House 120, Rd 2, Dhanmondi Residential Area, Dhaka Ⓣ 02/865373, Ⓦ www.hcidhaka.org. Consulate: 1253–1256 Nizam Rd, Mehdi Bagh, Chittagong Ⓣ 031/654201.

Bhutan Embassy of India, India House Estate, Thimphu Ⓣ 09752/22162, Ⓔ loplg@druknet.net.bt.

Burma (Myanmar) Embassy: Oriental Assurance Building, 545–547 Merchant St (PO Box 751), Yangon (Rangoon) Ⓣ 01/82550.

Canada High Commission: 10 Springfield Rd, Ottawa, ON K1M 1C9 Ⓣ 613/744 3751, Ⓦ www.hciottawa.ca. Consulates: 2 Bloor St W, #500, Toronto, ON M4W 3E2 Ⓣ 416/960 0751, Ⓦ cgitoronto.ca; 325 Howe St, 2nd floor, Vancouver, BC V6C 1Z7 Ⓣ 604/662 8811, Ⓦ www.cgivancouver.com.

China Embassy: Ri Tan Dong Lo, Beijing Ⓣ 01/532 1908, Ⓦ www.indianembassy.org.cn. Consulate: 1008, Shanghai International Trade Centre, 2200 Yan An (WEST) Rd, Shanghai Ⓣ 021/275 8885, Ⓦ www.indianembassy.org.cn.

Japan Embassy: 2–11, Kudan Minami 2-Chome, Chiyoda-ku, Tokyo 102 Ⓣ 03/3262 2391, Ⓔ indembjp@gol.com.

Malaysia High Commission: 2 Jalan Taman Dlita (off Jalan Duta), PO Box 10059, 50704 Kuala Lumpur Ⓣ 03/253 3504, Ⓔ hoc@po.jaring.my.

Nepal Embassy: Lainchaur (off Lazimpath), PO Box 92, Kathmandu Ⓣ 01/441 0900, Ⓦ www.south-asia.com/Embassy-India.

The Netherlands Embassy: Buitenrustweg-2, 2517 KD, The Hague Ⓣ 070/346 9771, Ⓦ www.indianembassy.nl.

New Zealand High Commission: 180 Molesworth St, PO Box 4005, Wellington Ⓣ 04/473 6390, Ⓦ www.hicomind.org.nz.

Pakistan High Commission: G-5, Diplomatic enclave, Islamabad Ⓣ 051/2206 9501. Consulate: India House, 3 Fatima Jinnah Rd, PO Box 8542, Karachi Ⓣ 021/522275.

Singapore Embassy: India House, 31 Grange Rd, PO Box 9123, Singapore 0923 Ⓣ 6737 6777, Ⓦ www.embassyofindia.com.

Sri Lanka High Commission: 36–38 Galle Rd, Colombo 3 Ⓣ 01/242 1605, Ⓦ www.indiahcsl.org. Consulate: 31 Rajapihilla Mawatha, PO Box 47, Kandy Ⓣ 08/224563.

Thailand Embassy: 46 Soi 23 (Prasarn Mitr), Sukhumvit Rd, Bangkok 10110 Ⓣ 02/258 0300, Ⓔ indiaemb@mozart.inet.co.th. Consulate: 113 Bumruangrat Rd, Chiang Mai 50000 Ⓣ 053/243066, Ⓕ 247879.

UK High Commission: India House, Aldwych, London WC2B 4NA Ⓣ 020/7836 8484, Ⓦ www.hcilondon.net. Consulates: 20 Augusta St, Jewellery Quarter, Hockley, Birmingham B18 6GL Ⓣ 0121/ 212 2782, Ⓦ www.cgibirmingham.org; 17 Rutland Square, Edinburgh EH1 2BB Ⓣ 0131/229 2144.

USA Embassy of India (Consular Services): 2107 Massachusetts Ave NW, Washington DC 20008 Ⓣ 202/939-7000. Consulates: 3 East 64th St, New York, NY 10021 Ⓣ 212/774-0600, Ⓦ www.indiacgny.org; 540 Arguello Blvd, San Francisco, CA 94118 Ⓣ 415/668-0683, Ⓦ www.indianconsulate-sf.org; 455 North Cityfront Plaza Drive, Suite 850, Chicago Il 60611 Ⓣ 312/595 0405 (ext 22 for visas), Ⓦ chicago.indianconsulate.com; 201 St Charles Ave, New Orleans, LA 70170 Ⓣ 504/582-8106; 2051 Young St, Honolulu, HI 96826 Ⓣ 808/947-2618.

Vietnam Embassy of India, 58–60 Tran, Hung Dao, Hanoi Ⓣ 04/824 4989, Ⓔ india@netnam.org. Consulate General of India, 49 Tran Quoc Thao St, 3rd District, Ho Chi Minh City Ⓣ 08/231539.

Special permits

In addition to a visa, **special permits** may be required for travel to certain areas of India – notably Sikkim, parts of Ladakh, the Andaman Islands, Lakshadweep, the far west of the Thar desert beyond Jaisalmer, the fringes of Kutch in Gujarat near the Pakistani border, and the northeastern hill states of Meghalaya and Manipur.

There are two types of permits: those for **restricted areas** such as Sikkim, and the **Inner Line Permit** required by both foreigners and Indians intending to visit politically sensitive border areas of Ladakh, parts of the northeast, and north and east Sikkim. Inner Line Permits are usually issued by the District Magistrate (see chapters for more detail). Some areas (parts of Sikkim, and the Indo–Chinese–Pak border region in Jammu–Kashmir for example) remain completely out of bounds to tourists. If you have some special reason for going to any of these latter areas, apply for a permit to the Ministry for Home Affairs Foreigners' Section, Lok Nayak Bhawan, Khan Market, New Delhi 110003, at least three months in advance.

Permits for those areas of Sikkim that are open to tourists are easily available at all foreigners' registration offices, immigration offices at the main international airports, all Indian embassies, consulates and high commissions abroad and at offices in Darjeeling and Siliguri; a two-day permit is instantly available at the checkpoint on the Sikkim border. Sikkim is the only place where you need a special **trekking permit** (see p.953).

Should you get your hands on a visa for Bhutan, you'll also need a transit permit for the border area from the Ministry of External Affairs.

For details of permit requirements to other areas, see the relevant chapters of this book.

Information, websites and maps

The Indian government maintains a number of tourist offices abroad, whose staff are usually helpful and knowledgeable. Other sources of information include the websites of Indian embassies and tourist offices, travel agents (who are in business for themselves, so their advice may not always be totally unbiased), and the Indian Railways representatives listed on p.58.

Inside India, both national and local governments run **tourist information offices**, providing general travel advice and handing out an array of printed material, from city maps to glossy leaflets on specific destinations. The Indian government's tourist department, whose main offices are on Janpath in New Delhi and opposite Churchgate railway station in Mumbai (see p.117 & p.698), has branches in most regional capitals. These, however, operate independently of the **state government information counters** and their commercial bureaux run by the state tourism development corporations, usually referred to by their initials (eg MPTDC in Madhya Pradesh and RTDC in Rajasthan), which offer a wide range of travel facilities, including guided tours, car rental and their own hotels (which we identify with the relevant acronyms throughout this book). A list of state tourist office **websites** appears below.

Just to confuse things further, the Indian government's tourist office has a corporate wing too. The **Indian Tourism Development Corporation (ITDC)**, is responsible for the Ashok chain of hotels, and operates tour and travel services, frequently competing with its state counterparts.

Indian government tourist offices

International website ⓦ **www.india-tourism.com**

Australia Level 2, Piccadilly, 210 Pitt St, Sydney NSW ⓣ02/9264 4855, ⓔindtour@ozemail.com.au; Level 1, 17 Castle Reagh, Sydney, NSW 2000 ⓣ02/9232 1600.

Canada 60 Bloor St (West), #1003, Toronto, Ontario M4W 3B8 ⓣ416/ 962-3787, ⓔindiatourism@bellnet.ca.
Netherlands Rokin 9–15, 1022 KK, Amsterdam ⓣ020/620 8991, ⓦwww.indiatourismamsterdam.com.
Singapore 20 Karamat Lane, 01–01A United House, Singapore 0922 ⓣ065/235 3800, ⓔsingapore@tourismindia.com.
Thailand Singapore Airlines Bldg, 3rd floor, 62/5 Thaniya Rd (Silom), Bangkok ⓣ02/235 2585 & 235 6670, ⓕ236 8411.
UK 7 Cork St, London W1X 2LN ⓣ020/7437 3677, ⓦwww.incredibleindia.org.
USA 3550 Wilshire Blvd, Suite #204, Los Angeles, CA 90010 ⓣ213/380-8855, ⓔla@tourismindia.com; Suite 1808, 1270 Ave of Americas, New York NY 10020 ⓣ212/586 4901, ⓔny@itony.com.

Indian state tourist office websites

For addresses and telephone numbers of State tourist offices in Delhi, see p.154. States not listed below do not yet have a website.

Andhra Pradesh ⓦwww.aptourism.com
Arunachal Pradesh ⓦwww.arunachaltourism.com
Assam ⓦwww.assamtourism.org
Bihar ⓦbihar.nic.in/depts/tourism/tourism.htm
Chandigarh ⓦcitco.nic.in
Chhattisgarh ⓦwww.cgtourism.nic.in
Delhi ⓦdelhitourism.nic.in
Goa ⓦwww.goatourism.org
Gujarat ⓦwww.gujarattourism.com
Haryana ⓦwww.haryanatourism.com
Himachal Pradesh ⓦwww.hptdc.nic.in
Jammu and Kashmir ⓦwww.jktourism.org
Jharkand ⓦjharkhand.nic.in/tourism/tour.htm
Karnataka ⓦkstdc.nic.in
Kerala ⓦwww.keralatourism.org
Lakshadweep ⓦwww.lakshadweeptourism.com
Madhya Pradesh ⓦwww.mptourism.com
Maharashtra ⓦwww.maharashtratourism.gov.in
Meghalaya ⓦwww.meghalayatourism.com
Nagaland ⓦnagalandtourism.com
Orissa ⓦwww.orissatourism.com
Pondicherry ⓦwww.tourisminpondicherry.com
Punjab ⓦwww.ptdc.nic.in
Rajasthan ⓦwww.rajasthantourismindia.com
Sikkim ⓦsikkim.nic.in
Tamil Nadu ⓦwww.tamilnadutourism.org
Tripura ⓦtripura.nic.in/ttourism1.htm
Uttaranchal ⓦwww.gmvnl.com
West Bengal ⓦwww.wbtourism.com

India online

India has one of the highest levels of IT awareness on the planet, and this has helped fuel the growth of home-grown resources on the **Internet**. There are several excellent India-specific **websites** and portals, or gateway sites, covering a vast range of topics. We list relevant websites throughout the Guide; the recommendations below are more general, and are a good place to start your navigating.

General

ⓦ**www.britannicaindia.com** Highly informative general site on India, part of the famous encyclopedia chain.
ⓦ**www.indiamike.com** Popular travel forum run out of a bedroom in New Jersey by inveterate India-phile Mike Szewczyk. Lively chat rooms, bulletin boards, photo archives and banks of members' travel articles, as well as a daily news feed.
ⓦ**www.rediff.com** Another leading India-specific portal with great search facilities and a site plan that stretches from news to travel.
ⓦ**www.travelintelligence.net/wsd/articles/artbyplce_143.html** A huge selection of top quality, inspiring travelogues by India experts including William Dalrymple, Sue Carpenter and Justine Hardy.

News and media

ⓦ**www.guardian.co.uk/india** High quality news features are the meat of this "Special Report" section of the Guardian's award-winning website, which also has links to its archived India articles and an excellent dossier on Kashmir. Access is free.
ⓦ**http://in.news.yahoo.com** India-related news from Yahoo.
ⓦ**www.samachar.com** One of the best news gateway sites, featuring headlines and links to leading Indian newspapers.
ⓦ**www.tehelka.com** Alternative news magazine (in)famous for exposing corruption scandals in government.
ⓦ**timesofindia.indiatimes.com; ⓦwww.hinduonline.com; ⓦwww.hindustantimes.com; ⓦwww.deccanherald.com** Websites of some of India's leading daily papers, with detailed national coverage. *The Deccan Herald* site has a fast-loading text-only format.

Travel advice

ⓦ**www.fco.gov.uk/travel** The British Foreign Office website is useful for checking potential or actual dangerous areas.

Ⓦ **travel.state.gov** The US State Department's travel advice regarding potential hot spots.

Culture

Ⓦ **www.artindia.net** Portal for India's performing arts.
Ⓦ **www.themusicmagazine.com** A music "e-zine" with an incredible range, from Bob Dylan to ghazal.
Ⓦ **www.carnaticmusic.com** Very well-organized site which explores Carnatic (South Indian) classical music.
Ⓦ **www.odissi.com** Site dedicated to Orissan arts and culture, in particular Odissi dance.
Ⓦ **www.planetbollywood.com** Bollywood portal where you can gorge yourself on gloss from the Hindi film world.
Ⓦ **www.sruti.com** The online version of a very informative and in-depth music and dance magazine devoted to India's performing arts.
Ⓦ **www.stardustindia.com** First stop for Bollywood gossip.
Ⓦ **www.geocities.com/Athens/Acropolis/1863/kolam.html** Tutorial that teaches you how to draw *kollam* (or *rangoli* as they're known in the north) – the rice-flour patterns with which women decorate floors and thresholds. For further inspiration, go to Ⓦ www.angelfire.com/cantina/visithra ("Vortex of Kollams").

Religion

Ⓦ **www.sacredsites.com** The India section of this website features scholarly background on India's most holy places, with quality images.
Ⓦ **www.sikh-heritage.co.uk** History, art and the lives and times of the Sikh Gurus explained.
Ⓦ **www.hinduweb.org** Amazingly comprehensive site featuring diverse topics such as Hindu art, history, religion and philosophy, with links to other sites created by users.
Ⓦ **www.hindulinks.org** Portal with nearly 30,000 links to a multitude of India-related matters.
Ⓦ **www.jainnet.com** Site dedicated to Jainism, featuring a concise introduction, devotional songs and e-cards.

Sport

Ⓦ **sify.com/sports** India's best web-based sports site, especially strong on cricket – as you'd expect.

Maps

Getting good **maps** of India, in India, can be difficult; the government – in an archaic suspicion of cartography – forbids the sale of detailed maps of border areas, which include the entire coastline. In theory, certain maps, especially detailed ones of border areas skirting Tibet and Pakistan, are illegal, so use them very discreetly. These maps are available outside India, and useful if you are going to be trekking in places like Ladakh, Spiti, Sikkim and Garhwal.

It makes sense to bring a basic map of India with you, such as Bartholomew's 1:4,000,000 map of South Asia, which has coloured contours and serves as a reliable route map of the whole country; a handful of other publishers, including the Daily Telegraph World Series, produce a similar map, while the Lascelles map on the same scale is also good. Geocentre produces an excellent three-set map of India at a scale of 1:2,500,000, showing good road detail.

Rough Guides, in conjunction with the World Mapping Project, recently published a regional map of South India at a scale of 1:1,200,000. Clearly designed and printed on un-tearable, water-resistant plastic paper, it's bang up-to-date and roadtested by the authors of this book. Nelles also covers parts of the country with 1:1,500,000 regional maps. These are generally excellent, with colour contours, road distances, inset city plans and even the tiniest places marked, but cost a fortune if you buy the complete set. Their double-sided map of the Himalayas is useful for roads and planning and has some detail but is not sufficient as a trekking map. Ttk, a Chennai-based company, publishes basic state maps which are widely available in India, and in some specialized travel and map shops in the UK such as Stanfords; these are poorly drawn but useful for road distances. The Indian Railways map at the back of the publication *Trains at a Glance* (see p.56) is useful for planning railway journeys.

If you need larger-scale **city maps** than the ones we provide in this book – which are keyed to show recommended hotels and restaurants – you can sometimes get them from tourist offices. Both Ttk and the official Indian mapping organization, the Survey of India (Janpath Barracks A, New Delhi 110001; Ⓣ011/2332 2288), have town plans at scales of 1:10,000 and 1:50,000, but they're on the whole far less accurate and up to date than the excellent Eicher series of glossy, A–Z-style books (Delhi, Mumbai, Kolkota, Chennai and Bangalore only), produced in India and available at all good bookstores.

As for **trekking maps**, the US Army Map Service produced maps in the 1960s which, with a scale of 1:250,000, remain sufficiently accurate on topography, but are of course outdated on the latest road developments. Most other maps that you can buy are based on their work. Their maps of Kanchenjunga, Leh, Palampur (including Bara Bangal, Manali and Lahaul), Tso Moriri (including Tabo, Kaza and Kibber) and Chini (including Kinnaur and the Baspa valley) are some of the best you can get. One exception is the superb Swiss Stiftung für Alpine Forschunger map of the Sikkim Himalayas at a scale of 1:150,000. The Survey of India, recognizing the competition, has come out with a version of the Sikkim map that is not particularly accurate. Leomann Maps (1:200,000) cover Srinagar, Zanskar, West Ladakh, Leh and around, Dharamsala, Kulu with Lahaul and Spiti, Garhwal and Kumaon. These are not contour maps and are therefore better for planning and basic reference than as reliable trekking maps. The Survey of India publishes a rather poor 1:250,000 series for trekkers in the Uttaranchal Himalayas; they are simplified versions of their own infinitely more reliable maps, produced for the military, which are absolutely impossible for an outsider to get hold of.

Book and map outlets

In the US and Canada

Book Passage 51 Tamal Vista Blvd, Corte Madera, CA 94925 ⓣ1-800/999-7909, ⓦwww.bookpassage.com.
Complete Traveller Bookstore 199 Madison Ave, New York, NY ⓣ212/685-9007, ⓦwww.completetravellerbooks.com.
Distant Lands 56 S Raymond Ave, Pasadena, CA 91105 ⓣ1-800/310-3220, ⓦwww.distantlands.com.
Elliot Bay Book Company 101 S Main St, Seattle, WA 98104 ⓣ1-800/962-5311, ⓦwww.elliotbaybook.com.
Globe Corner Bookstore 28 Church St, Cambridge, MA 02138 ⓣ1-800/358-6013, ⓦwww.globecorner.com.
Map Link 30 S La Patera Lane, Unit 5, Santa Barbara, CA 93117 ⓣ805/692-6777 or 1-800/962-1394, ⓦwww.maplink.com.
Rand McNally ⓣ1-800/333-0136, ⓦwww.randmcnally.com. Three US stores; check the website for the nearest location.
The Travel Bug Bookstore 3065 W Broadway, Vancouver V6K 2G2 ⓣ604/737-1122, ⓦwww.travelbugbooks.ca.
World of Maps 1235 Wellington St, Ottawa, ON K1Y 3A3 ⓣ1-800/214-8524, ⓦwww.worldofmaps.com.

In the UK and Ireland

Blackwell's Map and Travel Shop ⓦmaps.blackwell.co.uk/index.html. Branches all over the UK; check the website for details.
Easons Bookshop 40 Lower O'Connell St, Dublin 1 ⓣ01/858 3800, ⓦwww.eason.ie, plus other branches around Ireland; call or check the website for details.
John Smith & Son Glasgow Caledonian University Bookshop, 70 Cowcaddens Rd, Glasgow G4 0BA ⓣ0141/332 8173, ⓦwww.johnsmith.co.uk. For details of other branches in Scotland and England, call or check the website.
The Map Shop 30a Belvoir St, Leicester LE1 6QH ⓣ0116/247 1400, ⓦwww.mapshopleicester.co.uk.
National Map Centre 22–24 Caxton St, London SW1H 0QU ⓣ020/7222 2466, ⓦwww.mapstore.co.uk.
Ordnance Survey Ireland Phoenix Park, Dublin 8 ⓣ01/8025 300, ⓦwww.irlgov.ie/osi.
Ordnance Survey of Northern Ireland Colby House, Stranmillis Ct, Belfast BT9 5BJ ⓣ028/9025 5755, ⓦwww.osni.gov.uk
Stanfords 12–14 Long Acre, London WC2E 9LP ⓣ020/7836 1321, ⓦwww.stanfords.co.uk. For details of branches in Manchester and Bristol, call or check the website.
The Travel Bookshop 13–15 Blenheim Crescent, London W11 2EE ⓣ020/7229 5260, ⓦwww.thetravelbookshop.co.uk.

In Australia and New Zealand

The Map Shop 6–10 Peel St, Adelaide, SA 5000 ⓣ08/8231 2033, ⓦwww.mapshop.net.au.
Mapland 372 Little Bourke St, Melbourne, Victoria 3000, ⓣ03/9670 4383, ⓦwww.mapland.com.au.
MapWorld 173 Gloucester St, Christchurch ⓣ03/374 5399 or 0800/627967, ⓦwww.mapworld.co.nz.

Travel insurance

In the light of the potential health risks involved in a trip to India – see opposite – travel insurance is too important to ignore.

In addition to covering medical expenses and emergency flights, travel insurance also insures your money and belongings against **loss** or **theft**. Before paying for a new policy, however, it's worth checking whether you are already covered: some all-risks home insurance policies may cover your possessions when overseas, and many private medical schemes include cover when abroad. In Canada, provincial health plans usually provide partial **medical cover** for mishaps overseas, while holders of official student/teacher/youth cards in Canada and the US are entitled to meagre accident coverage and hospital in-patient benefits. Students will often find that their student health coverage extends during the vacations and for one term beyond the date of last enrolment.

After exhausting the possibilities above, you might want to contact a specialist **travel insurance company**, or consider the travel insurance deal we offer (see box). A typical travel insurance policy usually provides cover for the loss of baggage, tickets and – up to a certain limit – cash or cheques, as well as cancellation or curtailment of your journey. Most of them exclude so-called dangerous sports unless an extra premium is paid: in India this can mean scuba-diving, whitewater rafting, windsurfing and trekking with ropes, though probably not jeep safaris. Many policies can be chopped and changed to exclude coverage you don't need – for example, sickness and accident benefits can often be excluded or included at will. If you do take medical coverage, ascertain whether benefits will be paid as treatment proceeds or only after return home, and whether there is a 24-hour medical emergency number. When securing baggage cover, make sure that the per-article limit – typically under £500 – will cover your most valuable possession. If you need to make a claim, you should keep receipts for medicines and medical treatment, and in the event you have anything stolen, you must obtain an official statement from the police.

Rough Guides travel insurance

Rough Guides has teamed up with Columbus Direct to offer you **travel insurance** that can be tailored to suit your needs.

Readers can choose from many different travel insurance products, including a low-cost **backpacker** option for long stays; a **short break** option for city getaways; a typical **holiday package** option; and many others. There are also annual **multi-trip** policies for those who travel regularly, with variable levels of cover available. Different sports and activities (trekking, skiing, etc) can be covered if required on most policies.

Rough Guides travel insurance is available to the residents of 36 different countries with different language options to choose from via our website – Ⓦwww.roughguidesinsurance.com – where you can also purchase the insurance.

Alternatively, UK residents should call Ⓣ0800/083 9507; US citizens should call Ⓣ1-800/749-4922; Australians should call Ⓣ1-300/669999. All other nationalities should call Ⓣ+44 870/890 2843.

Health

You might have heard a lot of scare stories about the health risks of travelling in India, but rest assured that these are the exceptions rather than the rule. Standards of hygiene and sanitation have increased greatly over the past decade or so and, if you're careful, you should be able to get through with nothing worse than a mild dose of "Delhi belly". It's crucial, however, to keep your resistance high and to be very aware of the dangers of untreated water, mosquito bites and undressed open cuts.

What you **eat** and **drink** is crucial: a poor diet lowers your resistance. Ensure you eat a balance of protein and carbohydrates, as well as making sure you get enough vitamins and minerals. Meat and fish are obvious sources of protein for non-vegetarians in the West, but not necessarily in India: eggs, pulses (lentils, peas and beans), rice and curd are all protein sources, as are nuts. Overcooked vegetables lose a lot of their vitamin content; eating plenty of peeled fresh fruit helps keep up your vitamin and mineral intake. With all that sweating, too, make sure you get enough salt (put extra on your food) and drink enough water. It's also worth taking daily multi-vitamin and mineral tablets with you. Above all, make sure you eat enough – an unfamiliar diet may reduce the amount you eat – and **get enough sleep** and rest: it's easy to get run down if you're on the move a lot, especially in a hot climate.

It's worth knowing, if you are ill and can't get to a doctor, that almost any medicine can be bought over the counter without a prescription.

Precautions

The lack of sanitation in India can be exaggerated. It's not worth getting too worked up about it or you'll never enjoy anything, but a few **common-sense precautions** are in order, bearing in mind that things such as bacteria multiply far more quickly in a tropical climate, and your body will have little immunity to Indian germs.

For details on the **water**, see the box on p.42. When it comes to **food**, it's quite likely that tourist restaurants and Western dishes will bring you grief. Be particularly wary of prepared dishes that have to be reheated – they may have been on display in the heat and the flies for some time. Anything that is boiled or fried (and thus sterilized) in your presence is usually all right, though meat can sometimes be dodgy, especially in towns or cities where the electricity supply (and thus refrigerators) frequently fails; anything that has been left out for any length of time is definitely suspect. Raw unpeeled fruit and vegetables should always be viewed with suspicion, and you should avoid salads unless you know they have been soaked in an iodine or potassium permanganate solution. Wiping down a plate before eating is sensible, and avoid straws as they are usually dusty or secondhand. As a rule of thumb, stick to cafés and restaurants that are doing a brisk trade, and where the food is thus freshly cooked, and you should be fine.

Be vigilant about **personal hygiene**. Wash your hands often, especially before eating, keep all cuts clean, treat them with iodine or antiseptic, and cover them to prevent infection. Be fussier than usual about sharing things like drinks and cigarettes, and never share a razor or toothbrush. It is also inadvisable to go around barefoot – and best to wear flip-flops even in the shower.

Advice on avoiding **mosquitoes** is offered under "Malaria" below. If you do get bites or itches try not to scratch them: it's hard, but infection and tropical ulcers can result if you do. Tiger balm and even dried soap may relieve the itching.

Finally, especially if you are going on a long trip, have a **dental check-up** before you leave home – you don't want to go down

What about the water?

One of the chief concerns of many prospective visitors to India is whether the water is safe to drink. To put it simply, it's not, though your unfamiliarity with Indian micro-organisms is generally more of a problem rather than any great virulence in the water itself.

As a rule, it is not a good idea to drink **tap water**, although in big cities it is usually chlorinated. However, you'll find it almost impossible to avoid untreated tap water completely: it is used to make ice, which may appear in drinks without being asked for, to wash utensils and so on.

Bottled water, available in all but the most remote places these days, may seem like the simplest and most cost-effective solution, but it has some major drawbacks. The first is that the water itself might not always be as safe as it seems. Independent tests carried out in 2003 on major Indian brands revealed levels of **pesticide** concentration up to 104 times higher than EU norms. Top sellers Kinley, Bisleri and Aquaplus were named as the worst offenders.

The second downside of bottled water is the **plastic pollution** it causes. Visualize the size of the pile you'd leave behind you after getting through a couple of bottles per day, and imagine that multiplied by millions, which is the amount of non-biodegradable land-fill waste generated each year by tourists alone.

The best solution from the point of view of your health and the environment is to purify your own water. **Chemical sterlilization** is the cheapest method. **Iodine** isn't recommended for long trips, but **chlorine** is completely effective, fast and inexpensive, and you can remove the nasty taste it leaves with neutralizing tablets or lemon juice.

Alternatively, invest in some kind of **purifying filter** incorporating chemical sterilization to kill even the smallest viruses. An ever increasing range of compact, lightweight produces are available these days through outdoor shops and large pharmacies, but anyone who's pregnant or suffers from thyroid problems should check that iodine isn't used as the chemical sterilizer.

with unexpected tooth trouble in India. If you do, and it feels serious, head for Delhi, Mumbai or Kolkata (Calcutta), and ask a foreign consulate to recommend a dentist.

Vaccinations

No **inoculations** are legally required for entry into India, but meningitis, typhoid, and hepatitis A jabs are recommended, and it's worth ensuring that you are up to date with tetanus, polio and other boosters. All vaccinations can be obtained in Delhi, Mumbai and other major cities if necessary; just make sure the needle is new. If you're arriving in India from a country infected with Yellow Fever, you'll be asked for an inoculation certificate.

Hepatitis A is not the worst disease you can catch in India, but the frequency with which it strikes travellers makes a strong case for immunization. Transmitted through contaminated food and water, or through saliva, it can lay a victim low for several months with exhaustion, fever and diarrhoea, and may cause liver damage. The Havrix vaccine has been shown to be extremely effective; though expensive, it lasts for up to ten years. The protection given by gamma-globulin, the traditional serum of hepatitis antibodies, wears off quickly and the injection should therefore be given as late as possible before departure: the longer your planned stay, the larger the dose. Symptoms by which you can recognize hepatitis include a yellowing of the whites of the eyes, nausea, general flu-like malaise, orange urine (though dehydration could also cause that) and light-coloured stools. If you think you have it, avoid alcohol, try to avoid passing it on, and get lots of rest. More serious is **hepatitis B**, passed on like HIV through blood or sexual contact. There is a vaccine, but it is only recommended for those planning to work in a medical environment.

Typhoid, also spread through contaminated food or water, is endemic in India, but rare outside the monsoon. It produces a persistent high fever with malaise, headaches and abdominal pains, followed by diarrhoea. Vaccination can be by injection (two shots are required, or one for a booster), giving three years' cover, or orally – tablets are more expensive but easier on the arm.

Cholera, spread the same way as hepatitis A and typhoid, causes sudden attacks of watery diarrhoea with cramps and debilitation. It is endemic in the Ganges basin, but only during periodic epidemics. If you get it, take copious amounts of water with rehydration salts and seek medical treatment. There is currently no effective vaccination against cholera.

Most medical authorities now recommend vaccination against **meningitis** too. Spread by airborne bacteria (through coughs and sneezes for example), it attacks the lining of the brain and can be fatal. Symptoms include fever, a severe headache, stiffness in the neck and a rash on the stomach and back.

You should have a **tetanus** booster every ten years whether you travel or not. Tetanus (or lockjaw) is picked up through contaminated open wounds and causes severe muscular spasms; if you cut yourself on something dirty and are not covered, get a booster as soon as you can.

Assuming that you were vaccinated against **polio** in childhood, only one (oral) booster is needed during your adult life. Immunizations against **mumps**, **measles**, **TB** and **rubella** are a good idea for anyone who wasn't vaccinated as a child and hasn't had the diseases.

Rabies is a problem in India. The best advice is to give dogs and monkeys a wide berth, and not to play with animals at all, no matter how cute they might look. A bite, a scratch or even a lick from an infected animal could spread the disease; wash any such wound immediately but gently with soap or detergent, and apply alcohol or iodine if possible. Find out what you can about the animal and swap addresses with the owner (if there is one) just in case. If the animal might be infected or the wound begins to tingle and fester, act immediately to get treatment – rabies is invariably fatal once symptoms appear. There is an (expensive) vaccine, which serves only to shorten the course of treatment you need, and is only effective for a maximum of three months.

Medical resources for travellers

For up-to-the-minute information, make an appointment at a **travel clinic**. These clinics also sell travel accessories, including mosquito nets and first-aid kits. Information about specific diseases and conditions, drugs and herbal remedies is provided by the websites below; you could also consult the *Rough Guide to Travel Health* by Dr Nick Jones.

Health-related websites

Ⓦ **www.cdc.gov/travel** US Department of Health and Human Services travel health and disease control department, listing precautions, diseases and preventive measures by region, as well as a summary of cruise ship sanitation levels.

Ⓦ **health.yahoo.com** Information on specific diseases and conditions, drugs and herbal remedies, as well as advice from health experts.

Ⓦ **www.fitfortravel.scot.nhs.uk** UK NHS website carrying information about travel-related diseases and how to avoid them.

Ⓦ **www.istm.org** The website of the International Society for Travel Medicine, with a full list of clinics worldwide specializing in travel health.

Ⓦ **www.tmvc.com.au** Contains a list of all travellers medical and vaccination centres throughout Australia, New Zealand and Southeast Asia, plus general information on travel health.

Ⓦ **www.travelvax.net** Everything you ever wanted to know about diseases and vaccines.

Ⓦ **www.tripprep.com** Travel Health Online provides an online-only comprehensive database of necessary vaccinations for most countries, as well as destination and medical service provider information.

Travel clinics

In the UK and Ireland

British Airways Travel Clinics 213 Piccadilly, London W1G 9HQ (Mon–Fri 9.30am–5.30pm, Sat 10am–4pm, no appointment necessary); 101 Cheapside, London EC2 (Mon–Fri 9am–4.30pm, appointment required; Ⓣ 0845/600 2236); Ⓦ www.britishairways.com/travel/healthclinintro. Vaccinations, tailored advice from an online database and a complete range of travel healthcare products.

Glasgow Travel Clinic 3rd floor, 90 Mitchell St, Glasgow G1 3NQ ⓣ0141/221 4224. Advice and vaccinations; walk-in clinics Wed–Fri 10 am–6pm, otherwise appointments.
Hospital for Tropical Diseases Travel Clinic 2nd floor, Mortimer Market Centre, off Capper St, London WC1E 6AU (Mon–Fri 9am–5pm by appointment only; ⓣ020/7388 9600, ⓦwww.masta.org). A consultation costs £15 which is waived if you have your injections here. A recorded Health Line (ⓣ0906/133 7733; 50p per min; fax-back service ⓣ0906/991992; £1.50 per min) gives hints on hygiene and illness prevention as well as listing appropriate immunizations.
Liverpool School of Tropical Medicine Pembroke Place, Liverpool L3 5QA ⓣ0151/708 9393 or premium-rate helpline ⓣ09067/010095, ⓦwww.liv.ac.uk/lstm. Walk-in clinic (Mon–Fri 9am–noon); appointment required at other times.
MASTA (Medical Advisory Service for Travellers Abroad) 40 regional clinics – call ⓣ0870/606 2782 for the nearest; ⓦwww.masta.org. Also operates a pre-recorded 24hr Travellers' Health Line (UK ⓣ0906/550 1402, £1 per min), giving written information tailored to your journey by return of post.
Nomad Pharmacy ⓦwww.nomadtravel.co.uk, surgeries 52 Grosvenor Gdns, Victoria, London SW1W 0AG ⓣ020/7823/5823; 43 Bernard St, London, WC1N 1LE ⓣ020/7833 4114; and 3–4 Wellington Terrace, Turnpike Lane, London N8 0PX ⓣ020/8889 7014; all have walk-in and appointment clinics from Monday to Saturday.
Trailfinders Immunization clinic (no appointments necessary) at 194 Kensington High St, London W8 7RG (Mon–Fri 9am–5pm, Thurs till 6pm, Sat 10am–5.15pm; ⓣ020/7938 3999).
Travel Medicine Services 16 College St, Belfast BT1 6BT ⓣ028/9031 5220. Offers pre-trip medical advice and help afterwards in the event of a tropical disease.
Tropical Medical Bureau Grafton Buildings, 34 Grafton St, Dublin 2 ⓣ01/671 9200, plus locations all around Ireland; call ⓣ1850/487 674 or visit ⓦtmb.exodus.ie for details. Advice and vaccinations.

In the US and Canada

Canadian Society for International Health 1 Nicholas St, Suite 1105, Ottawa, ON K1N 7B7 ⓣ613/241-5785, ⓦwww.csih.org. Distributes a free pamphlet, Health Information for Canadian Travellers, containing an extensive list of travel health centres in Canada.
Centers for Disease Control 1600 Clifton Rd NE, Atlanta, GA 30333 ⓣ1-800/311-3435 or 404/639-3534, ⓦwww.cdc.gov. Publishes outbreak warnings, suggested inoculations, precautions and other background information for travellers. There's also an International Travelers Hotline on ⓣ1-877/FYI-TRIP.
International Association for Medical Assistance to Travellers (IAMAT) 1623 Military Rd, #279, Niagara Falls, NY 14302, ⓣ716/754-4883, ⓦwww.iamat.org, and 1287 St Clair Avenue West, Suite #1, Toronto, ON M6E 1B8 ⓣ416/652-0137. A non-profit organization supported by donations, it can provide a list of English-speaking doctors in the Caribbean, climate charts and leaflets on various diseases and inoculations.
International SOS Assistance 3600 Horizon Blvd, Suite 300, Trevose, PA 19053, USA

A travellers' first-aid kit

Below are items you might want to take, especially if you're planning to go trekking – all are available in India itself, at a fraction of what you might pay at home:

- ❒ Antiseptic cream
- ❒ Insect repellent and cream such as Anthisan for soothing bites
- ❒ Plasters/band aids
- ❒ A course of Flagyl antibiotics
- ❒ Water sterilization tablets or water purifier
- ❒ Lint and sealed bandages
- ❒ Knee supports
- ❒ Imodium (Lomotil) for emergency diarrhoea treatment
- ❒ A mild oral anaesthetic such as Bonjela for soothing ulcers or mild toothache
- ❒ Paracetamol/aspirin
- ❒ Multi-vitamin and mineral tablets
- ❒ Rehydration sachets
- ❒ Hypodermic needles and sterilized skin wipes

19053-6956 ⓣ 1-800/523-8930, ⓦ **www.intsos.com**. Members receive pre-trip medical referral info, as well as overseas emergency services designed to complement travel insurance coverage.

MEDJET Assistance ⓣ 1-800/963-3528, ⓦ **www.medjetassistance.com**. Annual membership program for travellers that, in the event of illness or injury, will fly members home or to the hospital of their choice in a medically equipped and staffed jet.

Travel Medicine ⓣ 1-800/TRAVMED, ⓦ **www.travmed.com**. Sells first-aid kits, mosquito netting, water filters, reference books and other health-related travel products; there's a travel clinic directory, too.

In Australia and New Zealand

Travellers' Medical and Vaccination Centres ⓦ **www.tmvc.com.au**. Vaccination and general travel health advice, and disease alerts; call ⓣ **1-300/658 844** for details of travel clinics countrywide.

Malaria

Protection against **malaria** is absolutely essential. The disease, caused by a parasite carried in the saliva of female **Anopheles mosquitoes**, is endemic everywhere in India except high-altitude regions of Ladakh, Himachal Pradesh, Kashmir and Sikkim, and is nowadays regarded as the big killer in the subcontinent. It has a variable incubation period of a few days to several weeks, so you can become ill long after being bitten. Programmes to eradicate the disease by spraying mosquito-infested areas and distributing free preventative tablets have proved disastrous; within a short space of time, the Anopheles develop immunities to the insecticides, while the malaria parasite itself constantly mutates into drug-resistant strains, rendering the old cures ineffective.

It is vital for travellers to take **preventative tablets** according to a strict routine, and to cover the period before and after your trip. The drug used is **chloroquine** (trade names include Nivaquin, Avloclor and Resochin), usually two tablets weekly, but India has chloroquine-resistant strains, and you'll need to supplement it with daily **proguanil** (**Paludrine**) or weekly **Maloprim**. In India chloroquine is easy to come by but proguanil isn't, so stock up before you arrive. **Malarone** is the newest addition to the armoury against the deadlier *Plasmodium falciparum* strain, and is increasingly prescribed for people travelling to areas of the world, such as India, where chloroquine- and other drug-resistant forms of Malaria are present. Being a relative newcomer, there's less evidence on its long-term effects, but initial studies have claimed it to be 98 percent effective and to have relatively few side-effects. The main drawback is that it's expensive and is only licensed for use for 28 days. Malarone is taken once-daily with food or milk, starting two days before entering a malaria and continuing for seven days after leaving the area. Children can also take it.

A weekly drug, **mefloquine** (Lariam) was supposed to replace chloroquine and proguanil, but during it's first year on the market many travellers complained of serious side-effects, notably acute depression, and few doctors now recommend it.

As the malaria parasite can incubate in your system without showing symptoms for more than a month, it is essential to continue to take preventative tablets for at least four weeks after returning home: the most common way of catching malaria is by forgetting to do this.

Side-effects of anti-malaria drugs may include itching, rashes, hair loss and sight problems. In the case of Larium some people may experience disorientation, depression and sleep disturbance; if you're intending to use Larium you should begin to take it two weeks before you depart to see whether it will agree with your metabolism, though normally you only need to begin taking anti-malaria medication a week before your departure date. If you plan on diving, you should perhaps avoid Mefloquine, as there is a worry about possible side effects for divers.

Malarial symptoms

The first **signs of malaria** are remarkably similar to a severe flu, and may take months to appear: if you suspect anything go to a hospital or clinic for a blood test immediately. The shivering, burning fever and headaches come in waves, usually in the early evening. Malaria is not infectious, but some strains are dangerous and occasionally even fatal when not treated promptly, in particular, the chloroquine-resistant **cerebral malaria**. This virulent and lethal strain of the disease, which affects the brain, is treatable, but has to be diagnosed early. Erratic body temperature, lack of energy and aches are the first key signs.

Preventing mosquito bites

The best way of combating malaria is of course to stop yourself getting bitten: malarial mosquitoes are active from dusk until dawn and during this time you should use **mosquito repellent** and take all necessary precautions. Sleep under a **mosquito net** if possible – one which can hang from a single point is best (you can usually find a way to tie a string across your room to hang it from), burn **mosquito coils** (widely available in India, but easy to break in transit) or electrically heated repellents such as All Out. An Indian brand of repellent called Odomos is widely available and very effective, though most travellers bring their own from home, usually one containing the noxious but effective compound **DEET**. DEET can cause rashes and a strength of more than thirty percent is not advised for those with sensitive skin. A natural alternative is **citronella** or, in the UK, Mosi-guard Natural, made from a blend of **Eucalyptus oils**; those with sensitive skin should still use DEET on clothes and nets. Mosquito "buzzers" – plug-in contraptions that smoulder tablets of DEET compounds slowly overnight – are pretty useless but wrist and ankle bands are as effective as spray and a good alternative for sensitive skin. Though active from dusk till dawn, female Anopheles mosquitoes prefer to bite in the evening, so be especially careful at that time. Wear long sleeves, skirts and trousers, avoid dark colours, which attract mosquitoes, and put repellent on all exposed skin.

Dengue fever and Japanese encephalitis

Another illness spread by mosquito bites is **dengue fever**, whose symptoms are similar to those of malaria, plus aching bones. There is no vaccine available and the only treatment is complete rest, with drugs to assuage the fever. **Japanese encephalitis**, a mosquito-borne viral infection causing fever, muscle pains and headaches, has been on the increase in recent years in wet rural rice-growing areas. However, there have been no reports of travellers catching the disease, and you shouldn't need the vaccine (which is expensive and has several potentially nasty side effects) unless you plan to spend much time around paddy fields during and immediately after the monsoons.

Intestinal troubles

Diarrhoea is the most common bane of travellers. When mild and not accompanied by other major symptoms, it may just be your stomach reacting to unfamiliar food. Accompanied by cramps and vomiting, it could well be food poisoning. In either case, it will probably pass of its own accord in 24–48 hours without treatment. In the meantime, it is essential to replace the fluids and salts you're losing, so take lots of water with oral **rehydration salts** (commonly referred to as ORS, or called Electrolyte in India). If you can't get ORS, use half a teaspoon of salt and eight of sugar in a litre of water, and if you are too ill to drink, seek medical help immediately. Travel clinics and pharmacies sell double-ended moulded plastic spoons with the exact ratio of sugar to salt.

While you are suffering, it's a good idea to avoid greasy food, heavy spices, caffeine and most fruit and dairy products. Some say bananas and pawpaws are good, as are *kitchri* (a simple dhal and rice preparation) and rice soup and coconut water, while curd or a soup made from Marmite or Vegemite (if you happen to have some with you) are forms of protein that can be easily absorbed by your body when you have the runs. Drugs like Lomotil or Imodium simply plug you up – undermining the body's efforts to rid itself of infection – though they can be useful if you have to travel. If symptoms persist for more than a few days, a course of antibiotics may be necessary; this should be seen as a last resort, following medical advice.

Sordid though it may seem, it's a good idea to look at what comes out when you go to the toilet. If your diarrhoea contains blood or mucus and if you are suffering other symptoms including rotten-egg belches and farts, the cause may be **dysentery** or giardia. With a fever, it could well be caused by **bacillic dysentery**, and may clear up without treatment. If you're sure you need it, a course of antibiotics such as tetracycline should sort you out, but they also destroy gut flora in your intestines (which help protect you – curd can replenish them to some extent). If you start a course, be sure to finish it, even after the symptoms have gone. Similar symptoms, without fever, indicate **amoebic dysentery**, which is much more serious, and can damage your gut if untreated. The usual cure is a course of Metronidazole (Flagyl) or Fasigyn, both antibiotics which may themselves make you feel ill, and must not be taken with alcohol. Symptoms of **giardia** are similar – including frothy stools, nausea and constant fatigue – for which the treatment is again Metronidazole. If you suspect that you have either of these, seek medical help, and only start on the Metronidazole (750mg three times daily for a week for adults) if there is definitely blood in your diarrhoea and it is impossible to see a doctor.

Finally, bear in mind that oral drugs, such as malaria pills, and the Pill, are likely to be largely ineffective if taken while suffering from diarrhoea.

Bites and creepy crawlies

Worms may enter your body through skin (especially the soles of your feet), or food. An itchy anus is a common symptom, and you may even see them in your stools. They are easy to treat: if you suspect you have them, get some worming tablets such as Mebendazole (Vermox) from any pharmacy.

Biting **insects** and similar animals other than mosquitoes may also aggravate you. The obvious suspects are bed bugs – look for signs of squashed ones around beds in cheap hotels. An infested mattress can be left in the hot sun all day to get rid of them, but they often live in the frame or even in walls or floors. Head and body **lice** can also be a nuisance, but medicated soap and shampoo (preferably brought with you from home) usually see them off. Avoid scratching bites, which can lead to infection. Bites from ticks and lice can spread typhus, characterized by fever, muscle aches, headaches, and, later, red eyes and a measles-like rash. If you think you have it, seek treatment (tetracycline is usually prescribed).

Snakes are unlikely to bite unless accidentally disturbed, and most are harmless in any case. To see one at all, you need to search stealthily – walk heavily and they usually oblige by disappearing. If you do get bitten, remember what the snake looked like (kill it if you can), try not to move the affected part, and seek medical help: anti-venoms are available in most hospitals. A few **spiders** have poisonous bites too. Remove **leeches**, which may attach themselves to you in jungle areas, with salt or a lit cigarette: never just pull them off.

Heat trouble

The sun and the heat can cause a few unexpected problems. Before they've acclimatized, many people get a bout of **prickly heat** rash, an infection of the sweat ducts caused by excessive perspiration that doesn't dry off. A cool shower, zinc oxide powder (sold in India) and loose cotton clothes should help. **Dehydration** is another possible problem, so make sure you're drinking enough liquid, and drink rehydration salts frequently, especially when hot and/or tired. The main danger sign is irregular urination (only once a day for instance); dark urine definitely means you should drink more (although it could also indicate hepatitis).

The **sun** can burn, or even cause sunstroke, and a high-factor sun block is vital on exposed skin, especially when you first arrive, and on areas newly exposed by haircuts or changes of clothes. A light hat is also a very good idea, especially if you're doing a lot of walking around in the sun.

Finally, be aware that overheating can cause **heatstroke**, which is potentially fatal. Signs are a very high body temperature, without a feeling of fever but accompanied by headaches and disorientation. Lowering body temperature (taking a tepid shower for example) and resting in an air-conditioned room is the first step in treatment; also take in plenty of fluids, and seek medical advice if the condition doesn't improve after 24 hours.

Altitude sickness

At high altitudes, you may develop symptoms of **acute mountain sickness (AMS)**. Just about everyone who ascends to around 4000m or more experiences mild symptoms, but serious cases are rare. The simple cure – descent – almost always brings immediate recovery.

AMS is caused by the fact that at high elevations there is not only less oxygen, but also lower atmospheric pressure. This can have all sorts of weird effects on the body: it can cause the brain to swell and the lungs to fill with fluid, and even bring on uncontrollable farting. The syndrome varies from one person to the next, but symptoms include breathlessness, headaches and dizziness, nausea, difficulty sleeping and appetite loss. More extreme cases may involve disorientation and loss of balance, and the coughing up of pink frothy phlegm.

AMS strikes without regard for fitness – in fact, young people seem to be more susceptible, possibly because they're more reluctant to admit they feel sick and they dart about more energetically. Most people are capable of acclimatizing to very high altitudes but the process takes time and must be done in stages. The golden rule is not to go too high, too fast; or if you do, spend the night at a lower height ("Climb High, Sleep Low"). Above 3000m, you should not ascend more than 500m per day; take mandatory acclimatization days at 3500m and 4000m – more if you feel unwell – and try to spend these days day-hiking higher.

The general symptoms of AMS can be **treated** with the drug acetazolamide (Diamox) but this is not advised as it will block the early signs of severe AMS, which can be fatal. It is better to stay put for a day or two, eat a high-carbohydrate diet, drink plenty of water (three litres a day is recommended), take paracetamol or aspirin for the headaches, and descend if the AMS persists or worsens. If you fly direct to a high-altitude destination such as Leh, be especially careful to acclimatize (plan for three days of initial rest); you'll certainly want to avoid doing anything strenuous at first.

Other precautions to take at high altitudes include avoiding alcohol and sleeping pills, drinking more liquid, and protecting your skin against UV solar glare.

HIV and AIDS

The rapidly increasing presence of **HIV/AIDS** has only recently been acknowledged by the Indian government as a national problem. The reluctance to address the issue is partly due to the disease's association with sex, a traditionally closed subject in India. As yet only NGOs and foreign agencies such as

Ayurvedic medicine

Ayurveda, a Sanskrit word meaning the "knowledge for prolonging life", is a five-thousand-year-old holistic medical system that is widely practised in India. Ayurvedic doctors and clinics in large towns deal with foreigners as well as their usual patients, and some **pharmacies** specialize in Ayurvedic preparations, including toiletries such as soaps, shampoos and toothpastes.

Ayurveda assumes the fundamental sameness of self and nature. Unlike the allopathic medicines of the West, which depend on finding out what's ailing you and then killing it, Ayurveda looks at the whole patient: disease is regarded as a symptom of **imbalance**, so it's the imbalance that's treated, not the disease. Ayurvedic theory holds that the body is controlled by three forces, which reflect the forces within the self: *pitta*, the force of the sun, is hot, and rules the digestive processes and metabolism; *kapha*, likened to the moon, the creator of tides and rhythms, has a cooling effect, and governs the body's organs; and *vata*, wind, relates to movement and the nervous system. The healthy body is one that has the three forces in balance. To diagnose an imbalance, the Ayurvedic **vaid** (doctor) responds not only to the physical complaint but also to family background, daily habits and emotional traits.

Imbalances are typically treated with herbal remedies designed to alter whichever of the three forces is out of whack. Made according to traditional formulae, using indigenous plants, Ayurvedic medicines are cheaper than branded or imported drugs. In addition, the doctor may prescribe various forms of yogic cleansing to rid the body of waste substances. To the uninitiated, these techniques will sound rather off-putting – for instance, swallowing a long strip of cloth, a short section at a time, and then pulling it back up again to remove mucus from the stomach. Ayurvedic **massage** with herbal oils is especially popular in Kerala where courses of treatments are available to combat a wide array of ailments.

the WHO have embarked on awareness and prevention campaigns. As elsewhere in the world, high-risk groups include prostitutes and intravenous drug users. It is extremely unwise to contemplate casual sex without a condom – carry some with you (preferably brought from home as Indian ones may be less reliable; also, be aware that heat affects the durability of condoms), and insist upon using them.

Should you need an injection or a transfusion in India, make sure that new, sterile equipment is used; any blood you receive should be from voluntary rather than commercial donor banks. If you have a shave from a barber, make sure he uses a clean blade, and don't undergo processes such as ear-piercing, acupuncture or tattooing unless you can be sure that the equipment is sterile.

Getting medical help

Pharmacies can usually advise on minor medical problems, and most doctors in India speak English. Also, many hotels keep a doctor on call; if you do get ill and need medical assistance, take advice as to the best facilities around. Basic medicaments are made to Indian Pharmacopoea (IP) standards, and most medicines are available without prescription (always check the sell-by date). Hospitals vary in standard: **private clinics** and mission hospitals are often better than state-run ones, but may not have the same facilities. Hospitals in the big cities, including university or medical-school hospitals, are generally pretty good, and cities such as Delhi, Mumbai and Bangalore boast state-of-the-art medical facilities, but at a price. Many hospitals require patients (even emergency cases) to buy necessities such as medicines, plaster casts and vaccines, and to pay for X-rays, before procedures are carried out. Remember to keep receipts for insurance reimbursements.

However, **government hospitals** provide all surgical and after-care services free of charge and in most other state medical institutions, charges are usually so low that for minor treatment the expense may well be lower than the initial "excess" on your insurance. You will, however, need a companion to stay, or you'll have to come to an arrangement with one of the hospital cleaners, to help you out in hospital – relatives are expected to wash, feed and generally take care of the patient. Beware of scams by private clinics in tourist towns such as Agra where there have been reports of overcharging and misdiagnosis by doctors to claim insurance money. Addresses of foreign consulates (who will advise in an emergency), and of clinics and hospitals, can be found in the Listings sections in the accounts of major towns in this book.

Costs, money and banks

For visitors, India is still one of the least expensive countries in the world; a little foreign currency can go a long way. You can be confident of getting good value for your money, whether you're setting out to keep your budget to a minimum or to enjoy the opportunities that spending a bit more will make possible.

While we attempt below to suggest the kind of sums you can expect to pay for varying degrees of comfort, it is vital not to make a rigid assumption at the outset of a long trip that whatever money you bring to India will last for a certain number of weeks or months. On any one day it may be possible to spend very little, but cumulatively you won't be doing yourself any favours if you don't make sure you keep yourself well rested and properly fed. As a foreigner in India, you will find yourself penalized by double-tier entry prices to museums and historic sites (see box) as well as in upmarket hotels and air fares, both of which are levied at a higher rate and in dollars.

What you spend depends on you: where you go, where you stay, how you get

Entrance fees

In 2000, the Archeological Survey of India announced a **double-tiered entry system**, with foreign visitors (including non-resident Indians) required to pay $5–20 or its rupee equivalent to enter major archeological sites. This means that foreigners can find themselves paying forty times the entrance fee levied to domestic visitors.

Charges may be in either dollars or rupees; where, as is the case at some sites, foreigners are charged in dollars at that day's exchange rate, we give the dollar rate current at the time of going to press, so bear in mind that this may fluctuate. Throughout the Guide, we list the price for Indian visitors in square brackets.

around, what you eat and what you buy. On a budget of as little as $11/£6 (Rs500) per day, you'll manage if you eat in local *dhabas* and don't move about too much; double that, and you'll be able to afford comfortable mid-range hotels, as well as meals in smarter restaurants, regular rickshaw or taxi rides and entrance fees to monuments. If you're happy spending $30–35/£15–18 (around Rs1500) per day, however, you can really pamper yourself; to spend much more than that, you'd have to be doing a lot of air-conditioned travelling, flying instead of taking trains, consistently staying in swish hotels and eating in the top restaurants.

Five-star luxury in India is cheap by Western standards but, particularly with all the extra government taxes it incurs, can soon send your budget spiralling.

Accommodation ranges from a basic $3/£2 per night upwards (see p.64), while a no-frills vegetarian meal in an ordinary restaurant will typically cost less than half that. Long-distance transport can work out to be phenomenally good value if you stick to state buses and standard second-class non-a/c trains, but soon starts to add up if you opt for air-conditioned carriages on the superfast intercity services. The four-hour, 200-km trip from Delhi to Agra, for example, can cost anywhere from Rs50 ($1.15/60p) and Rs300 ($6.50/£4), depending on the level of comfort.

Where you are also makes a difference: Mumbai is notoriously pricey, especially for accommodation, while tourist enclaves like the Goa beaches will not be cheap for things like food, and there will be more souvenirs to tempt you. Delhi, too, is substantially more costly than most parts of the country. Out in the sticks, on the other hand, and particularly away from your fellow tourists, you will find things incredibly cheap, though your choice will obviously be more limited.

Some independent travellers tend to indulge in wild and highly competitive **penny-pinching**, which Indian people find rather pathetic – they know how much an air ticket to Delhi or Mumbai costs, and they have a fair idea of what you can earn at home. Bargain where appropriate, but don't begrudge a few rupees to someone who's worked hard for them: consider what their services would cost at home, and how much more valuable the money is to them than it is to you. Even if you get a bad deal on every rickshaw journey you make, it will only add a minuscule fraction to the cost of your trip. Remember too, that every pound or dollar you spend in India goes that much further, and luxuries you can't afford at home become possible here: sometimes it's worth spending more simply because you get more for it. At the same time, don't pay well over the odds for something if you know what the going rate is. Thoughtless extravagance can, particularly in remote areas that see a disproportionate number of tourists, contribute to inflation, putting even basic goods and services beyond the reach of local people.

Currency

India's unit of currency is the **rupee**, usually abbreviated "Rs" and divided into a hundred **paise**. Almost all money is paper, with notes of 10, 20, 50, 100, 500 and, recently, 1000 rupees: a few notes of 1, 2 and 5 are still in circulation. Coins start at 10 paise range up to 20, 25 and 50 paise, and 1, 2 and 5 rupees.

Banknotes, especially lower denominations, can get into a terrible state, but don't accept **torn banknotes**; no one else will be prepared to take them, so you will be left saddled with the things, though you can change them at the Reserve Bank of India and large branches of other big banks. Don't pass them on to beggars; they can't use them either, so it amounts to an insult.

Large denominations can also be a problem, as change is usually in short supply. Many Indian people cannot afford to keep much lying around, and you shouldn't necessarily expect shopkeepers or rickshaw-wallahs to have it (and they may – as may you – try to hold onto it if they do). Paying for your groceries with a Rs100 note will probably entail waiting for the grocer's errand boy to go off on a quest to try and change it. Larger notes – like the Rs500 note – are good for travelling with and can be changed for smaller denominations at hotels and other suitable establishments. A word of warning – the Rs500 note looks remarkably similar to the Rs100 note.

At the time of writing, the **exchange rate** was approximately Rs80 to £1, or Rs46 to $1.

Travellers' cheques, credit cards and ATMs

In addition to your cash, carry some **travellers' cheques** to cover all eventualities, with a few small denominations for the end of your trip, and for the odd foreign-currency purchase such as tourist-quota rail tickets which can be bought with American Express travellers' cheques. US dollars are the easiest **currency** to convert, with pounds sterling a close second. Major hard currencies can be changed easily in tourist areas and big cities, less so elsewhere. If you enter the country with more than $10,000 or the equivalent, you are supposed to fill in a currency declaration form.

Travellers' cheques aren't as liquid as cash, but obviously more secure (and you get a slightly better exchange rate for them at banks). Not all banks, however, accept them, and those that do can be quirky about exactly which ones they will change. Well-known brands such as Thomas Cook and American Express are your best bet, but in some places even American Express is only accepted in US dollars and not as pounds sterling.

A **credit card** is a handy back-up, as an increasing number of hotels, restaurants, large shops and tourist emporia as well as airlines and train companies now take plastic; American Express, Mastercard and Visa are the most commonly accepted brands. If you have a selection of cards, take them all. You'll get much the same exchange rate as you would in a bank, and bills can take a surprisingly long time to be charged to your account at home. The Bank of Baroda (Bobcards) and Standard Chartered Grindlays issue rupees against a Visa card at all their branches. Remember that all cash advances are treated as loans, with interest accruing daily from the date of withdrawal; there may be a transaction fee on top of this. However, you can also withdraw cash from **ATMs** in India using your **debit card**, which is not liable to interest payments, and the flat transaction fee is usually quite small – your bank will be able to advise on this. Make sure you have a personal identification number (PIN) that's designed to work overseas. Larger branches of all the main Indian banks now have ATMs, though the amount you can withdraw from them in any 24-hour period varies. The other downside of relying on plastic as your main access to cash, of course, is that cards can easily get lost or stolen, so take along a couple of alternative ones in case; and make a note of your home bank's telephone number and website addresses for emergencies.

A compromise between travellers' cheques and plastic is **Visa TravelMoney**, a disposable pre-paid debit card with a PIN which works in all ATMs that take Visa cards. You load up your account with funds before leaving home, and when they run out, you simply throw the card away. Up to nine cards can be purchased to access the same funds – useful for couples or families travelling together – and it's a good idea to buy at least one extra as a back-up in case of loss or theft. The card is available in most countries from branches of Thomas Cook and Citicorp. For more information, check the Visa TravelMoney website at Ⓦwww.usa.visa.com/personal/cards/prepaid/visa_travel_money.html.

It is illegal to carry rupees (besides spending money) into India, and you won't get them at a particularly good rate in the West anyhow (though you might in Thailand, Malaysia or Singapore). It is also illegal to take any rupees out of the country.

Travellers' cheques and credit card contacts

Both American Express and Thomas Cook have offices in major cities throughout India in addition to the ones listed below; see the relevant accounts in the Guide and collect a full list when you purchase your travellers' cheques.

American Express
Ⓦ www.americanexpress.com.
Lost and stolen cards/cheques Ⓣ 011/2614 5920 or 2687 5050 (open 24hr).
Bangalore Janardhan Tower, 2 Residency Rd Ⓣ 080/2248 1800.
Chennai G-17, Spencer Plaza, 768–769 Anna Salai, Ⓣ 044/2851 5800.
Delhi Wenger House, "A" Block, Connaught Place Ⓣ 011/2280 1800 or Gurgaon branch Ⓣ 98/109 0800.
Kolkata (Calcutta) 21 Old Court House St Ⓣ 033/2210 5151.
Mumbai Regal Cinema Building, Chhatrapati Shivaji Maharaj Rd, Colaba Ⓣ 225/638 5406.

Thomas Cook
Ⓦ www.thomascook.co.in
Lost and stolen cards/cheques Ⓣ 0044-1733/318949.
Bangalore 70 Mahatma Gandhi Rd and 55 Mahatma Gandhi Rd Ⓣ 080/2558 8028.
Chennai Ceebros Centre, 45 Montieth Rd, Egmore Ⓣ 044/2855 3276 or 2336 8560.
Delhi G-33 Connaught Place, Inner Circle Ⓣ 011/2341 8571; *Hotel Imperial*, Janpath Ⓣ 2332 8468.
Jaipur Mirza Ismail Rd Ⓣ 0141/236 0940.
Kolkata (Calcutta) 19/B Shakespeare Sarani, 1st Floor Ⓣ 033/2282 4711.
Mumbai Dr Dadabhai Naoroji Rd, Fort Ⓣ 022/2204 8556–7.

Banks

Changing money in regular **banks**, especially government-run banks such as the State Bank of India (SBI), can be a time-consuming business, involving lots of form-filling and queuing at different counters, so change substantial amounts at any one time. Banks in main cities are likely to be most efficient, though not all change foreign currency, and some won't take **travellers' cheques** or currencies other than dollars or sterling (banks usually charge a percentage of the transaction while Grindlays charge a flat Rs200). You'll have no such problems with **private companies** such as Thomas Cook and American Express who have offices in most state capitals.

In the major cities and the main tourist centres, there are usually several **licensed currency exchange bureaus** where the rates are not usually as good as at a bank but where there's generally a lot less hassle. In small towns, the SBI is your best bet but you may want to ask around for an alternative. Note that if you arrive at a minor airport you may not be able to change anything except cash US dollars or sterling.

Outside **banking hours** (Mon–Fri 10am till 2–4pm, Sat 10am–noon), large hotels may change money, probably at a lower rate, and exchange bureaux have longer opening hours. Banks at Delhi, Mumbai, Kolkata (Calcutta) and Chennai **airports**, and at the *Ashok Hotel* in Delhi, stay open 24 hours but none of these is very conveniently located. Otherwise, there's always the black market if you're desperate.

Hold on to **exchange receipts** ("encashment certificates"); they will be required if you want to change back any excess rupees when you leave the country, and to buy air tickets and reserve train berths with rupees. The State Bank of India now charges for tax clearance forms (see p.35 to find out if you'll need one.)

Wiring money

Having money **wired from home** using one of the companies listed below is never convenient or cheap, and should be considered a last resort.
Thomas Cook Ⓦ www.thomascook.com US Ⓣ 1-800/287-7362; Canada Ⓣ 1-888/823-4732; Great Britain Ⓣ 01733/318922; Northern Ireland Ⓣ 028/9055 0030; Republic of Ireland Ⓣ 01/677 1721.
Travelers Express MoneyGram Ⓦ www.moneygram.com. US Ⓣ 1-800/955-7777; Canada Ⓣ 1-800/933-3278; UK Ⓣ 0800/018 0104; Republic of Ireland Ⓣ 1850/205800; Australia

Ⓣ1800/230100; New Zealand Ⓣ0800/262263.
Western Union Ⓦwww.westernunion.com. US and Canada Ⓣ1-800/325-6000; UK Ⓣ0800/833833; Republic of Ireland Ⓣ1800/395395; Australia Ⓣ1800/501500; New Zealand Ⓣ0800/270000.

Baksheesh

As a presumed-rich sahib or memsahib, you will, like wealthy Indians, be expected to be liberal with the **baksheesh**, which takes three main forms.

The most common is **tipping**: a small reward for a small service, which can encompass anyone from a waiter or porter to someone who lifts your bags onto the roof of a bus or keeps an eye on your vehicle for you. Large amounts are not expected – ten rupees should satisfy all the aforementioned. Taxi drivers and staff at cheaper hotels and restaurants do not necessarily expect tips, but always appreciate them, of course, and they can keep people sweet for the next time you call. Some may take liberties in demanding baksheesh, but it's often better just to acquiesce rather than spoil your mood and cause offence over trifling sums.

More expensive than plain tipping is paying people to **bend the rules**, many of which seem to have been invented for precisely that purpose. Examples might include letting you into a historical site after hours, finding you a seat or a sleeper on a train that is "full", or speeding up some bureaucratic process. This should not be confused with bribery, a more serious business with its own risks and etiquette, which is best not entered into.

The last kind of baksheesh is **alms giving**. In a country without a welfare system, this is an important social custom. People with disabilities and mutilations are the traditional recipients, and it seems right to join local people in giving out small change to them. Kids demanding money, pens, sweets or the like are a different case, pressing their demands only on tourists. In return for a service it is fair enough, but to yield to any request encourages them to go and pester others.

Getting around

Inter-city transport in India may not be the fastest or the most comfortable in the world, but it's cheap, goes more or less everywhere, and generally gives you the option of train or bus, sometimes plane, and occasionally even boat. Transport around town comes in even more permutations, ranging in Kolkata (Calcutta), for example, from rickshaws still pulled by men on foot to a spanking new metro systems.

Whether you're on road or rail, public transport or your own vehicle, India offers the chance to try out some classics: narrow-gauge railways, steam locomotives, the Ambassador car and the Enfield Bullet motorbike. Some people come to India for these alone.

Travel details

At the end of each chapter in this book, you'll find a **Travel details** section summarizing major transport connections in the relevant state. In addition, boxes at the end of each major city detail **moving on** from that city.

By train

Travelling by train is one of the great experiences of India. It's a system which looks like chaos, but it works, and well. Trains are often late of course, sometimes by hours rather than minutes, but they do run, and with amazing efficiency too: when the train you've been waiting for rolls into the station, the reservation you made halfway across the country several weeks ago will be on a list pasted to the side of your carriage, and when it's time to eat, the packed meal you ordered down the line will be ready at the next station, put on the train and delivered to your seat.

It's worth bearing in mind, with journeys frequently lasting twelve hours or more, that an **overnight train** can save you a day's travelling and a night's hotel bill, assuming you sleep well on trains. While sleeper carriages can be more crowded during the day, between 9pm and 6am anyone with a bunk reservation is entitled to exclusive use of their bunk. When travelling overnight, always padlock your bag to your bunk; an attached chain is usually provided beneath the seat of the lower bunk.

Routes, classes and fares

India's rail network covers almost the entire country; only a few places (such as Sikkim, Ladakh, Uttaranchal and most of Himachal Pradesh, all mountainous) are inaccessible by train. **Inter-city** trains, called "express" or "mail", vary a lot in the time taken to cover the same route. Slow by Western standards, they're still much faster than **local "passenger" trains**, which you need only use to get right off the beaten track. Note that express and mail trains cost a fair amount more than ordinary passenger trains, so if travelling unreserved you must buy the right ticket to avoid being fined. There are also an increasing number of special **"super-fast"** air-conditioned trains – the Rajdhani expresses link distant cities to New Delhi, while the Shatabdi expresses are daytime trains which connect major cities within an eight-hour travelling distance. Bottled water, snacks and good meals are included in the ticket price of these services.

Most lines are either metre-gauge or broad-gauge (1.676m, or 4'6"), the latter being faster; many metre-gauge lines are now being converted to broad-gauge. There are also a few narrow-gauge lines (often referred to as "toy trains"), notably to the hill stations of Darjeeling (now a World Heritage line), Shimla, Matheran and Ootacamund. Although being phased out, **steam locomotives** are still used on the first and last (the latter on Sundays only) of these, and you may well see some in use in shunting yards, but they are fast disappearing. Almost all trains nowadays are diesel-hauled, although some main and suburban lines are electric.

Classes of train travel

Indian Railways (IR, Ⓦ **www.indianrail.gov.in**) distinguishes between no fewer than seven **classes** of travel, though you'll seldom have more than four to choose from on mainline services: second-class unreserved, second-class sleeper, first, and air-conditioned first (or air-conditioned sleeper with two or three bunks, referred to as two- or three-tier: pronounced "tyre"). In general, most travellers (not just those on low budgets) choose to travel second class, and prefer not to be in a/c compartments; an open window keeps you cool enough, and brings you into contact with the world outside, while air-conditioning by definition involves being sealed away behind glass, often virtually opaque. Doing without a sleeper on an overnight journey is, however, a false economy. **Bed rolls** (sheet, blanket and pillow) are available in first class and a/c second for that extra bit of comfort – book these with your ticket, or before you board the train.

Second-class unreserved is painfully crowded and noisy with no chance of a berth overnight, but incredibly cheap: Rs103 (that's just over $2 or around £1.30) for a thousand-kilometre journey. However, the crush and hard wooden seats (if you are lucky or nifty enough to get one) make it viable only for short hops or for the extremely hardy. Far more civilized and only around fifty percent more expensive is **second-class sleeper** (from Rs190 for 1000km, or Rs300 for a berth rather than a slatted bench), which must be booked in advance even for daytime journeys. If you have an unreserved ticket and travel in a sleeper carriage, even if it is not full, you will be charged a Rs60 fine

Rail records

Comprising 42,000 miles (over 60,000km) of track and 14,000 locomotives that daily transport an average of 12 million passengers, India's **rail network** is the second largest in the world. It's also the biggest employer on the planet, with a workforce of around 1.6 million.

One record the country's transport ministers are somewhat less proud of, however, is the **accident rate**. Four to five hundred crashes occur annually in India, causing between seven and eight hundred fatalities, which makes this the most dangerous rail network in the world, by a long chalk.

The world's worst rail disaster took place in Ferozabad, near Delhi, in 1995, when a cyclone blew a train off a bridge, killing 800. In August 1999, another 350 passengers died when two trains – carrying a total of 2500 people – collided head on in West Bengal. On both occasions, as in sixty percent of Indian rail accidents, human error was cited as the cause. In reality, lack of adequate training, maintenance and investment at government level are the real roots of the problems facing India's ageing network.

Train passengers, however, can take solace in the fact that travelling by rail in India is considerably safer than using the buses. According to official statistics, an average of 233 people die on the country's roads every day (that's 85,000 annually).

as well as the difference in fare. Second-class sleepers can be pretty crowded during the day but never lack activity, with peanut-, chai- and coffee-sellers, travelling musicians, beggars or sweepers passing through the carriages. Overnight trips in second-class sleeper compartments are reasonably comfy (provided the berths are foam and not wooden).

First class, in comfortable if ageing compartments of two to four berths, used mainly by English-speaking business travellers, costs about 3.5 times as much as sleeper class (from Rs990 for 1000km on express and mail trains). Not always available on passenger trains and gradually being phased out, first class insulates you to a certain extent from the chaotic hustle and bustle.

Air-conditioned travel, unavailable on "passenger trains", falls into five categories but only one or two will be available on any particular service, except for the Rajdhani which has three. The best value is the **a/c chair car** (often denoted as CC), with comfortable reclining seats at only twice the price of second-class sleeper class. The "super-fast" Shatabdi expresses are exclusively chair car but come in two classes – ordinary a/c chair car and, for double the price, an executive a/c chair car. Very occasionally, a/c chair cars appear on express or mail trains. **Air-conditioned three-tier sleepers** (3AC) cost slightly less than normal first class but cost more on the Rajadhani. Three-tier can feel a bit cramped, especially with loads of luggage, but represents good value (Rs845 for 1000km); they are, however, not as common as the **a/c two-tier sleepers** (2AC) which cost half as much again as first class – Rs1350 for 1000km, and more for Rajdhani. Top of the tree is **a/c first class** (1AC), which offers shared compartments for two or four and has a little more luxury with carpeting and more presentable bathrooms, but at Rs2630 for 1000km and more on the Rajdhani, this is not much cheaper than flying. Bed linen is provided free on most a/c services while meals are also included on Rajdhani and Shatabdi trains.

Ladies' compartments exist on all overnight trains for women travelling on their own or with other women; they are usually small and can be full of noisy kids, but can give untold relief to women travellers who otherwise have to endure incessant staring in the open section of the carriage. They can be a good place to meet Indian women, particularly if you like (or are with) children. Some stations also have ladies-only waiting rooms.

Timetables and tickets

Indian Railways publish an annual **timetable** of all mail and express trains – in effect, all the trains you are likely to use. Called *Trains at a Glance*, it is available from information counters and newsstands at all main stations, and from IR agents abroad. You can also consult rail timetables and fares, and check availability at Ⓦwww.indianrail.gov.in.

All rail fares are calculated according to the exact **distance** travelled. *Trains at a Glance* prints a chart of fares by kilometres, and also gives the distance in kilometres of stations along each route in the timetables, making it possible to calculate what the basic fare will be for any given journey.

Each individual train has its own **name and number**, prominently displayed in station booking halls. When buying a second-class ticket, it makes sense to pay the tiny extra fee to reserve a seat or sleeper (the fee is already included in the price of the higher classes). To do so, you fill in a form specifying the train you intend to catch, its number, your date of travel, and the stations you are travelling to and from, plus, amusingly to most travellers, your age and sex (this helps conductors to determine who you are). Most stations have **computerized booking counters** (these are listed in *Trains at a Glance*), and you will be told immediately whether or not seats are available.

Reserving tickets

Reservation offices in the main stations are often in a separate building and generally open from Monday to Saturday from 8am to 8pm, and on Sunday to 2pm. In larger cities, the major stations have special **tourist sections** to cut the queues for foreigners and Indian citizens resident abroad, with helpful English-speaking staff; however, if you don't pay in pounds sterling or dollars (travellers' cheques or cash), you must produce an encashment certificate to back up your rupees. Elsewhere, buying a ticket can often involve a long wait, though women get round this at ticket counters which have **"ladies' queues"**; travelling in a mixed group or couple, a woman will find it easier to get a ticket. Some stations also operate a number system of queuing, allowing you to repair to the chai stall or check the timetable until your number is called. Alternatively, many travel agents will secure tickets for a reasonable Rs25–50 fee. Failure to buy a ticket at the point of departure will result in a stiff penalty when the ticket controller (known as the "TC") finds you.

It's important to plan your train journeys in advance, as the demand often makes it impossible to buy a long-distance ticket on the same day that you want to travel (although the new **Tatkal** quota system – see box – has made life a little easier if you're happy to pay extra). Travellers following tight itineraries tend to buy their departure tickets from particular towns the moment they arrive, to avoid having to trek out to the station again. At most large stations, it's

Tatkal tickets

Indian Railways recently introduced a late-availability reservation system for train travellers called **Tatkal**, which has been controversial in India, but looks set to be a great help for foreign tourists. A quota of ten percent of places on most trains is reserved under this scheme, bookable at any computerized office. Tickets are released from 8am on the day before the train departs, and there's an extra charge of Rs150 in Sleeper or Chair Car, Rs300 in First or a/c sleepers. The real catch, however, is that you also have to pay for the entire length of the journey from originating to terminating station, however much or little of the ride you do, so Tatkal is obviously not worth it if you want to get on the Guwahati–Kanniyakumari Express between Trichy and Madurai. If you're covering most of the route, though, you're pretty well guaranteed to find a place, especially if you get in the day before, as a lot of resident Indians have been put off by the price hike. One of the routes on which Tatkal is most likely to assist foreign travellers is **Mumbai–Goa**, on the Konkan Railway, where standard tickets sell out weeks in advance and are thus not available to tourists newly arrived in the country (unless they've booked at premium rates via Indian Railways agents abroad).

Indrail passes

Indrail passes, sold to foreigners and Indians resident abroad, cover all fares and reservation fees for periods ranging from half a day to ninety days. Even if you travel a lot, this works out considerably more expensive than buying your tickets individually (especially in second class), but it will save you queuing for tickets, allow you to make and cancel reservations with impunity (and without charge), and generally smooth your way in, for example, finding a seat or berth on a "full" train: passholders get priority for tourist quota places. Indrail passes are available, for sterling or US dollars, at main station tourist counters in India, and outside the country at IR agents (see p.58). If you're travelling **from Britain**, Dr Dandapani of **SD Enterprises Ltd** (see p.58) is an excellent contact, providing information on all aspects of travel on Indian railways.

	a/c First Class Sleeper, or a/c Chair Car		First Class or a/c		Second Class	
	Adult	**Child**	**Adult**	**Child**	**Adult**	**Child**
1 day*	$95	$48	$43	$22	$19	$10
4 days*	$220	$110	$110	$55	$50	$25
7 days	$270	$135	$135	$68	$80	$40
15 days	$370	$185	$185	$95	$90	$45
21 days	$396	$198	$198	$100	$100	$50
30 days	$495	$248	$248	$125	$125	$63
60 days	$800	$400	$400	$200	$185	$95
90 days	$1060	$530	$530	$265	$235	$120

Children under 5 travel free

*For sale outside India only; half-day and two-day pass also available.

possible to reserve tickets for journeys starting elsewhere in the country. You can even book tickets for specific journeys before you leave home, with Indian Railways representatives abroad (see p.58). They accept bookings up to six months in advance, with a minimum of one month for first class, and three months for second.

If there are no places available on the train you want, you have a number of choices. First, some seats and berths are set aside as a "**tourist quota**" – ask at the tourist counter if you can get in on this, or else try the stationmaster. This quota is available in advance but usually only at major or originating stations. Failing that, other special quotas, such as one for "emergencies", only released on the day of travel, may remain unused – however, if you get a booking on the emergency quota and a pukka emergency or VIP turns up, you lose the reservation. Alternatively, you can stump up extra cash for a **Tatkal** ticket (see above), which guarantees you access to a special ten percent quota on most trains, though certain catches and conditions apply.

RAC – or "Reservation Against Cancellation" – tickets are another option, giving you priority if sleepers do become available – the ticket clerk should be able to tell you your chances. With an RAC ticket you are allowed onto the train and can sit until the conductor can find you a berth. The worst sort of ticket to have is a **wait-listed** one – identifiable by the letter "W" prefixing your passenger number – which will allow you onto the train but not in a reserved compartment; in this case go and see the ticket inspector as soon as possible to persuade him to find you a place if one is free: something usually is, but you'll be stuck in unreserved if it isn't. Wait-listed ticket holders are not allowed onto Shatabdi and Rajdhani trains. Finally, and as a last resort if you get on where the train starts its journey, **baksheesh** may persuade a TC (ticket controller) to

Indian Railways online

Online ticket reservation is now available across the network via Indian Railways' website, Ⓦ **www.indianrail.gov.in**. However, at the time of writing, you need an Indian bank account (with HFDC, Citibank or the SBI) to make payments. Other disincentives include a lengthy sign-up and login process, and the overall unreliability of the Indian postal system by means of which tickets are delivered. Basically, foreign travellers are better off either purchasing tickets in person or paying a travel agent to so on their behalf. That said, the website is extremely useful as a means of **checking fares, timetables** and **availability of berths** – information that you would normally have to travel to a station and queue to obtain. A fast connection and good pop-up blocker are needed to browse the site comfortably, but all in all it's an essential, time-saving tool.

"reserve" you an unreserved seat or, better still, a luggage rack where you can stretch out for the night. You could even fight your way on and grab one yourself, although your chances are slim. As for attempting to **travel unreserved**, for journeys of any length it's too uncomfortable to be worth considering on any major route.

Tourist trains

Inspired by the Orient Express, Indian Railways runs two luxury **tourist trains** on packaged holidays with exorbitant prices charged in dollars. The flagship of the scheme is the **Palace on Wheels**, with luxurious ex-maharajas' carriages updated into modern air-conditioned coaches, still decorated with the original designs. The all-inclusive, one-week whistle-stop tour (Sept–April weekly) starts from Delhi and tours through Jaipur and Jodhpur to the sands of Jaisalmer before turning south to Udaipur and returning via Agra; prices start at around £1458/US$2450 per person for the full trip, with discounts off season (Sept & April).

Other alternatives include the **Fairy Queen**, driven by the oldest working steam engine in the world, which travels through eastern Rajasthan to Alwar and the Sariska tiger reserve (Oct–Feb twice monthly; around £835/US$1400); while the **Royal Orient**, with thirteen lavishly decorated saloon cars, travels from Delhi through southern Rajasthan to Gujarat (Oct–March, £835/US$1400).

The *Palace on Wheels* can be booked through RTDC, Bikaner House, Pandara Road, New Delhi (Ⓣ011/2338 1884); the *Fairy Queen* through the Tourism Directorate, Rail Bhawan, New Delhi (Ⓣ011/2338 3000); and the *Royal Orient* through the Tourism Corporation of Gujarat, II Floor, A–6, State Emporia Complex, Baba Kharak Singh Marg, New Delhi (Ⓣ011/2336 4724). Alternatively, book online at Ⓦwww.indiarailtours.com.

Indian railways sales agents abroad

Australia Adventure World, 73 Walker St (PO Box 480), N Sydney, NSW 2059 Ⓣ02/9956 7766, Ⓦwww.adventureworld.com.au.
UK SD Enterprises Ltd, 103 Wembley Park Drive, Wembley, Middx HA9 8HG Ⓣ020/8903 3411, Ⓦwww.indiarail.co.uk.

Cloakrooms

Most stations in India have "**cloakrooms**" (sometimes called parcel offices) for passengers to leave their baggage. These can be extremely handy if you want to go sightseeing in a town and move on the same day. In theory, you need a train ticket or Indrail pass to deposit luggage, but staff don't always ask; they may, however, refuse to take your bag if you can't lock it. Losing your reclaim ticket causes problems; the clerk will be assumed to have stolen the bag if he can't produce it, so there'll be untold running around to obtain clearance before you can get your bag without it. Make sure, when checking baggage in, that the cloakroom will be open when you need to pick it up. The standard charge is currently Rs10 per 24 hours.

By air

Considering the huge distances involved in getting around the country, **flying** will come as an attractive option until you consider the cost. Leaving aside the new no-frills airlines, India has some of the highest domestic **air fares** in the world, which is why a lot of wealthier Indians now actually find it cheaper to fly abroad on a package holiday than to see their own country.

On top of that, **foreigners** and non-resident Indians are penalized by some airlines through having to pay in dollars (or show equivalent exchange receipts), and the foreigners' price is invariably higher than for Indians – around fifteen percent. There are no return flight deals, and while short flights can cost as little as $50, longer ones prove exorbitant. For example, a Delhi–Chennai flight costs over $270 (though it takes a mere 2hr 30min by plane compared to 36 hours' hard train travel). Delays and cancellations can whittle away the time advantage, especially over small distances, but if you're short of time and plan to cover a lot of ground, you should definitely consider flying for longer journeys.

India's national domestic carrier is **Indian Airlines** or IA (Ⓦwww.indian-airlines.nic.in), which serves over 140 routes. In addition, Air India (Ⓦwww.airindia.com) runs feeder services between several major cities and its hub, Mumbai, to connect with its international flights. **Jet Airways** (Ⓦwww.jetairways.com) flies many of the major routes covered by IA, and generally provides a more efficient, dynamic and slicker service than the national airline. Amongst the smaller private airlines, **Sahara** (Ⓦwww.airsahara.net) operates a reliable, expanding network that now reaches most corners of the country (and beyond). The real success story of the past few years, however, has been India's first low-cost airline, **Air Deccan** (Ⓣ080/3900 8888, Ⓦwww.airdeccan.net) which has slashed fares across the board by adopting the "no-frills" approach. They fly to 35 destinations in India, often for ludicrously small amounts of money: you can, for example, pick up tickets for Delhi–Mumbai for as little as Rs500, though these special deals tend to be in short supply and sell out well in advance. The rock-bottom fares mean all their flights tend to be fully booked, so you'll have to buy your tickets well ahead of departure; this is easy enough to do, even from abroad, via the Air Deccan website, which accepts foreign credit and debit cards.

Hot on the heels of Air Deccan, other private, low-cost carriers have joined the fray, notably **Kingfisher** airlines (Ⓦwww.flykingfisher.com), launched in May 2005 by flamboyant beer tycoon Vijay Mallya. With the slogan "Fly the Good Times", Kingfisher offers a flashier experience than the competition, calling its planes "funliners" and kitting them out with designer white and red upholstery and exclusively female cabin crews of so-called "flying models". Based in Delhi, **Spicejet** (Ⓦwww.spicejet.com) is more in the mould of Air Deccan, prioritizing low prices over frills.

The domestic airlines all have a number of **special deals** that are worth knowing about. IA offers 25 percent discount for under-30s and students, and 50 percent for over-65s, while Jet and Air Deccan offer multi-flight passes and discounts (see box below).

Unless you book online, one major drawback with flying inside India (particularly with the less efficient Indian Airlines) is that

Multi-flight deals

For details of deals offered by low-cost airlines, go to their respective websites.

Indian Airlines
Ⓦwww.indian-airlines.nic.in
Discover India Fare Unlimited travel on all internal flights: 7 days $400; 15 days $600; 21 days $850 (no single route twice)
India Wonderfare Seven days' travel in one given region; $320

Jet Airways
Ⓦwww.jetairways.com
Visit India Fare Unlimited travel on their routes: 7 days $400; 15 days $630; 21 days $895; 7 days regional fare (either north or South India) $320

Air Deccan
Ⓦwww.airdeccan.net
Value Flier Multi-ticket discount: 14 flights for Rs24,000 (£276/$520).

Air Sahara
Ⓦwww.airsahara.net
Sixer Six tickets for Rs36,000 (£445/$780).

you tend to have to spend a considerable amount of time queuing at the airline office to get a **reservation**; it's often quicker to book through a hotel or travel agent, which is the norm for booking on private carriers. If you haven't got a confirmed seat, be sure to get to the airport early and keep checking your position in the queue; even if you have got a confirmed seat, always reconfirm 72 hours before your flight.

Airlines have offices or representatives in all the places they fly to, listed in this book in the relevant city sections. IA tickets must be paid for in hard currency or with a **credit card** (not accepted in smaller towns like Leh). Children under twelve pay half fare, and under-twos (one per adult) pay ten percent. There are no **cancellation charges** if you pay in foreign currency, but tickets are not replaceable if lost. **Timetables** for all internal flights (with fares) are published in city listings magazines and newspaper supplements, shown on teletext, and posted on the airlines' websites.

By bus

Although trains are the definitive form of transport in India, and generally more comfortable than **buses**, there are places (such as most Himalayan valleys) where trains don't go, where they are inconvenient, or where buses are simply faster (as in most of Rajasthan and other places without broad-gauge track). Buses go almost everywhere, more frequently than trains (though mostly in daylight hours).

Services vary somewhat in price and standards. Ramshackle government-run affairs, packed with people, livestock and luggage, cover most routes. In addition, popular trunk routes between large cities, towns and resorts are usually covered by **private buses**. These tend to be more comfortable, with extra legroom, tinted windows and padded reclining seats. In some states, notably Rajasthan, they are also considerably cheaper. Smaller private bus companies may be only semi-legal and have little backup in case of breakdown.

The description of the service usually gives some clue about the level of comfort. "Ordinary" buses usually have minimally padded, bench-like seats with upright backs. "Deluxe" or "luxury" are more or less interchangeable terms but sometimes the term deluxe signifies a luxury bus past its sell-by date; occasionally a bus will be described as a "2 by 2" which means a deluxe bus with just two seats on either side of the aisle. When applied to government services, these may hardly differ from "ordinary" buses, but with private companies, they should guarantee a softer, individual seat. It's worth asking when booking if your bus will have a video or music system (a "video bus"), as their deafening noise ruins any chances of sleep. Always try to avoid the back seats – they accentuate bumpy roads.

Luggage travels in the hatch of private buses – for which you will have to part with about Rs5 as "security" for the safekeeping of your bags. On state-run buses, you can usually squeeze it into an unobtrusive corner, although you may sometimes be requested to have it travel on the roof (you may be able to travel up there yourself if the bus is too crowded, though it's dangerous and illegal); check that it's well secured (ideally, lock it there) and not liable to get squashed. Baksheesh is in order for whoever puts it up there for you.

Buying a bus ticket is usually less of an ordeal than buying a train ticket, although at large city bus stations there may be twenty or so counters, each assigned to a different route. When you buy your ticket you'll be given the registration number of the bus and, sometimes, a seat number. As at railway stations, there is usually a separate, quicker, ladies' queue, although the sign to indicate it may not be in English. You can always get on ordinary state buses without a ticket, and at bus stands outside major cities you can usually only pay on board, so you have to be sharp to secure a seat. Prior booking is usually available and preferable for express and private services, and it's a good idea to check with the agent exactly where the bus will depart from. You can usually pay on board private buses too, though doing so reduces your chances of a seat.

By boat

Apart from river ferries, few **boat services** run in India. The Andaman Islands are connected to Kolkata (Calcutta) and Chennai by boat – as well as to each other. Kerala has a regular passenger service with a number of services operating out of Alappuzha and Kollam, including the popular "backwater trip" between the two. The Sunderbans in the delta region to the south of Kolkata (Calcutta) is only accessible by boat.

By car

It is much more usual for tourists to be driven in India than it is for them to drive themselves; **car rental** firms operate on the basis of supplying **chauffeur-driven vehicles**, and taxis are available at cheap daily rates. Arranged through tourist offices, local car rental firms, or branches of Hertz, Budget or Europcar, a chauffeur-driven car will run to about £22/$38 per day. On longer trips, the driver sleeps in the car. The big international chains are the best bet for self-drive car rental; in India they charge around thirty percent less than chauffeur-driven, with a Rs1000 deposit against damage, though if you pay in your home country it can cost a whole lot more.

Driving in India is not for beginners. If you do drive yourself, expect the unexpected, and expect other drivers to take whatever liberties they can get away with. **Traffic** circulates on the left, but don't expect **road regulations** to be obeyed; generally the vehicle in front seems to have right of way, so at busy intersections or roundabouts (rotaries) drivers try and get out in front as soon as possible with prudence. Another unstated law of the road is that might is right.

Traffic in the cities is heavy and undisciplined; vehicles cut in and out without warning, and pedestrians, cyclists and cows wander nonchalantly down the middle of the road. In the country the roads are narrow, in terrible repair, and hogged by overloaded Tata trucks that move aside for nobody, while something slow-moving like a bullock cart or a herd of goats can take up the whole road. To overtake, sound your **horn** (an essential item on Indian roads) – the driver in front will signal if it is safe to do so; if not, he will wave his hand, palm downwards, up and down. A huge number of potholes don't make for a smooth ride either. Furthermore, during the monsoon roads can become flooded; rivers burst their banks and bridges get washed away. Ask local people before you set off, and proceed with caution, sticking to main highways if possible.

You should have an **international driving licence** to drive in India, but this is often overlooked if you have your licence from home. **Insurance** is compulsory, but not expensive. Car **seat belts** are not compulsory in most cities (they are now mandatory in Delhi, Mumbai and a few other cities) but are very strongly recommended. Accident rates are high, and you should be on your guard at all times. It is particularly dangerous to drive at night – not everyone uses lights, and bullock carts don't have any. If you have an **accident**, it might be an idea to leave the scene quickly and go straight to the police to report it; mobs can assemble fast, especially if pedestrians or cows are involved.

Fuel is reasonably cheap compared to home, but the state of the roads will take its toll, and mechanics are not always very reliable, so a knowledge of **vehicle maintenance** is a help, as is a checkup every so often. Luckily, if you get a flat tyre, puncture-wallahs can be easily found almost everywhere.

To import a car or motorbike into India, you'll have to show a **carnet de passage**, a document intended to ensure that you don't sell the vehicle illegally. These are available from foreign motoring organizations such as the AA. It's also worth bringing a few basic spares, as parts for foreign makes can be hard to find in India, although low-quality imitations are more widely available. All in all, the route is arduous, and bringing a vehicle to India something of a commitment.

The classic Indian automobile is the **Hindustan Ambassador** (basically a Morris Oxford), nowadays largely superseded by more modern vehicles such as the Maruti Suzuki. Renting a car, you'll probably have a choice of these two or others such as the Land Rover-like Tata Sumo, popular in hill regions. Worth knowing if you're interested in buying one is that the Ambassador is not famed for its mod cons or low mpg, but has a certain style and historical interest; later models make little sense as prices are higher and quality lower than in the West.

By motorbike

Riding a motorbike around India has become increasingly popular but is not without its hazards. Beside the appalling road conditions (see above) and the ensuing fatigue, **renting a bike**, unless you are well versed in maintenance, can be a bit of a nightmare, with breakdowns often in the most inconvenient places. If you do break down in the middle of nowhere, you may need to flag down an empty truck to transport the bike to the nearest town for repairs. Motorbike rental is available in some tourist towns and useful for local use, but the quality of the bikes is never assured. You could bring your own, but then you'll need to consider spares. Helmets are best brought from home.

Buying a motorbike in India is a much more reasonable proposition, and again, if it's an old British classic you're after, the Enfield Bullet (350 model), sold cheapest in Pondicherry, on the Tamil Nadu coast, leads the field (check one of several motoring magazines for details and reviews). If low price and practicality are your priorities, however, a smaller model, perhaps even a moped or a scooter, might better fit the bill. Many Japanese bikes are now made in India, as are Vespas and Lambrettas, and motorcycles of various sorts can easily be bought new or **secondhand**. Garages and repair shops are a good place to start; see Delhi Listings (p.153) for details of the city's Karol Bagh area, renowned for its motorcycle shops. Obviously, you will have to **haggle** over the price, but you can expect to pay half to two-thirds the original price for a bike in reasonable condition. Given the right bargaining skills, you can sell it again later for a similar price – perhaps to another foreign traveller – by advertising it in hotels and restaurants. A certain amount of bureaucracy is involved in transferring vehicle ownership, but a garage should be able to put you on to a broker ("auto consultant") who, for a modest commission (around Rs300), will help you find a seller or a buyer, and do the necessary paperwork. A motorbike can be taken in the luggage car of a **train** for the same price as a second-class passenger fare (get a form and pay a small fee at the station luggage office).

Some knowledge of mechanics is necessary to ensure that you are not being sold a pup, so if you aren't too savvy yourself, make sure you take someone who is to give the once-over to important parts like the engine, forks, brakes and suspension. Experienced overlanders often claim that making sure the seat is comfy is the crucial element to an enjoyable trip.

If you are unsure of negotiating your own bike or travelling around on your own you may consider joining one of several **motorbike tours** offered by the companies below:

Blazing Trails UK ⓣ01293/533338, ⓦwww.jewelholidays.com.

Classic Bike Adventure "Casa Tres Amigos", Assagao (near Anjuna) 403 507 ⓣ0832/224 4467, ⓦwww.classic-bike-india.de.

Ferris Wheels Motorcycle Safaris Australia ⓣ(61)02/9918 8900, ⓦwww.ferriswheels.com.au.

HC Travel UK ⓣ01256/770775, ⓦwww.hctravel.com.

Himalayan Roadrunners UK ⓣ01233/733001, ⓦwww.ridehigh.com.

By bicycle

Ever since the publication of Dervla Murphy's *Full Tilt*, a trickle of travellers have either themselves done the trip **by bicycle**, or else bought a bike in India and ridden it around the country. In many ways a bike is the ideal form of transport, offering total independence without loss of contact with local people. You can camp out, though there are cheap lodgings in almost every village – take the bike into your room with you – and, if you get tired of pedalling, you can put it on top of a bus as luggage, or transport it by train.

Bringing a bike from abroad requires no carnet or special paperwork, but spare parts and accessories may be of different sizes and standards in India, and you may have to improvise. Bring **basic spares** and **tools**, and a **pump**. **Panniers** are the obvious thing for carrying your gear, but fiendishly inconvenient when not attached to your bike, and you might consider sacrificing ideal load-bearing and streamlining technology for a backpack you can lash down on the rear carrier.

Buying a bike in India presents no great difficulty; most towns have cycle shops and even cycle markets. The advantages of a local bike are that spare parts are easy to get, locally produced tools and parts will fit, and your bike will not draw a crowd every time you park it. Disadvantages are that

Indian bikes tend to be heavier and less state-of-the-art than ones from abroad; mountain bikes are beginning to appear in cities and bigger towns, but with insufficient gears and a low level of equipment, they're not worth buying. Selling should be quite easy: you won't get a tremendously good deal at a cycle market, but you may well be able to sell privately, or even to a rental shop.

Bicycles can be **rented** in most towns, usually for local use only: this is a good way to find out if your legs and bum can survive the Indian bike before buying one. Rs10–25 per day is the going rate, occasionally more in tourist centres, and you may have to leave a deposit, or even your passport as security. Several adventure tour operators such as Exodus (see p.29) offer bicycle tours of the country with most customers bringing their own cycles.

As for **contacts**, International Bicycle Fund, 4887 Columbia Drive S, Seattle, WA 98108-1919 (Ⓣ206/767-0848, Ⓦwww.ibike.org), publishes information and offers advice on bicycle travel around the world, and maintains a useful website. In India, the Cycle Federation of India, C-5A/262, DDA Flats, Janak Puri, New Delhi 110058 (Ⓣ011/2255 3006), is the main cycle-sports organization.

City transport

Transport around towns takes various forms, with **buses** the most obvious. These are usually single-decker, though double-deckers (some articulated) exist in Mumbai and elsewhere. City buses can get unbelievably crowded, so beware of pickpockets, razor-armed pocket-slitters, and "Eve-teasers" (see p.96); the same applies to **suburban trains** in Mumbai (Chennai is about the only other place where you might want to use trains for local city transport). Any visitor to Delhi or Kolkata (Calcutta) will be amazed by the clean efficiency of India's two **metro systems**.

You can also take **taxis**, usually rather battered Ambassadors (painted black and yellow in the large cities) and Maruti omnivans. With luck, the driver will agree to use the **meter**; in theory you're within your rights to call the police if he doesn't, but the usual compromise is to agree a **fare** for the journey before you get in. Naturally, it helps to have an idea in advance what the fare should be, though any figures quoted in this or any other book should be treated as being the broadest of guidelines only. From places such as main stations, you may be able to find other passengers to share a taxi to the town centre; many stations, and certainly most airports, operate prepaid taxi schemes with set fares that you pay before departure; more expensive prepaid limousines are also available.

The **auto-rickshaw**, that most Indian of vehicles, is the front half of a motor-scooter with a couple of seats mounted on the back. Cheaper than taxis, better at nipping in and out of traffic, and usually metered (again, in most places they probably won't use them and you should agree a fare before setting off), auto-rickshaws are a little unstable and their drivers often rather reckless, but that's all part of the fun. In major tourist centres rickshaw-wallahs can, however, hassle you endlessly on the street, often shoving themselves right in your path to prevent you from ignoring them, and once you're inside they may take you to several shops before reaching your destination. Moreover, agreeing a price before the journey will not necessarily stop your rickshaw-wallah reopening discussion when the trip is underway, or at its end. In general it is better to hail a rickshaw than to take one that's been following you, and to avoid those that hang around outside posh hotels.

One or two cities also have larger versions of auto-rickshaws known as **tempos** (or Vikrams), with six or eight seats behind, which usually ply fixed routes at flat fares. Here and there, you'll also come across horse-drawn carriages, or **tongas**. Tugged by underfed and often lame horses, these are the least popular with tourists.

Slower and cheaper still is the **cycle rickshaw** – basically a glorified tricycle. Foreign visitors often feel uncomfortable about travelling this way; except in the major tourist cities, cycle rickshaw-wallahs are invariably emaciated pavement dwellers who earn only a pittance for their pains. In the end, though, to deny them your custom on those grounds is spurious logic; they will earn even less if you don't use them. Also you will invariably pay a bit more than a local would. Only in Kolkata (Calcutta) do the rickshaw-wallahs continue to haul the city's pukka rickshaws on foot.

If you want to see a variety of places around town, consider hiring a taxi, rickshaw or auto-rickshaw for the day. Find a driver who speaks English reasonably well, and agree a price beforehand. You will probably find it a lot cheaper than you imagine: the driver will invariably act as a guide and source of local knowledge, and tipping is usually in order.

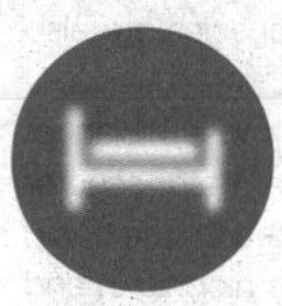

Accommodation

There are far more Indians travelling around their own country at any one time – whether for holidays, on pilgrimages, or for business – than there are foreign tourists, and a vast infrastructure of hotels and guesthouses caters for their needs. On the whole, accommodation, like so many other things in India, provides good value for money, though in the major cities, especially, expect to pay international prices for luxury establishments that provide Western-style comforts and service.

Inexpensive hotels

While accommodation prices in India are generally on the up, there's still an abundance of **cheap hotels**, catering for backpacking tourists and less well-off Indians. Most charge Rs150–250 for a double room, and some outside the big cities have rates below Rs100 (£1.50/$2.50). The rock-bottom option is usually in a dormitory of a hostel or hotel, where you'll be charged anything from Rs30 to 100. Even cheaper still are *dharamshalas*, hostels run by religious establishments and pilgrim guesthouses (see p.67).

Budget accommodation varies from filthy fleapits to homely guesthouses and, naturally, tends to be cheaper the further you get off the beaten track; it's most expensive in

Accommodation price codes

All **accommodation prices** in this book are **coded** using the symbols below. The prices given are for a double room; in the case of dorms, we give the price in rupees. Most mid-range and all expensive and luxury hotels charge a luxury tax of around ten to fifteen percent, and a local tax of around five percent. All taxes are included in the prices we quote.

India doesn't have a **tourist season** as such, and most accommodation keeps the same prices throughout the year. Certain resorts however, and some spots on established tourist trails, do experience some variation and will be more expensive, or less negotiable, when demand is at its peak. For the hill stations, this will be in the summer (April–July); for Goa and other beach resorts in the south, it'll be the winter, especially around Christmas and New Year. We indicate such fluctuations where appropriate.

- ❶ up to Rs150
- ❷ Rs150–300
- ❸ Rs300–500
- ❹ Rs500–700
- ❺ Rs700–1000
- ❻ Rs1000–1500
- ❼ Rs1500–2000
- ❽ Rs2000–3000
- ❾ Rs3000 and upwards

Delhi and Mumbai, where prices are at least double those for equivalent accommodation in most other cities.

Cold showers or "bucket baths" are the order of the day – not really a problem in most of India for most of the year – and it's always wise to check out the state of the bathrooms and toilets before taking a room. Bed bugs and mosquitoes are other things to check for – splotches of blood around the bed and on the walls where people have squashed them are tell-tale signs.

If a taxi driver or rickshaw-wallah tells you that the place you ask for is full, closed or has moved, it's more than likely that it's because he wants to take you to a hotel that pays him commission – added, in some cases, to your bill. **Hotel touts** operate in some major tourist spots, working for commission from the hotels they take you to; this can become annoying, but sometimes paying the little extra can be well worth it, especially if you arrive alone in a new place at night. One way to avoid the hassle is to stay put – some of the airports have retiring rooms and so do most of the larger railway stations.

Mid-range hotels

Even if you value your **creature comforts**, you don't need to pay through the nose for them. A large clean room, freshly made bed, your own spotless (often sit-down) toilet, and hot and cold running water can still cost under Rs400 ($7/£5). Extras that bump up the price include local taxes, TV, mosquito nets, a balcony, and, above all, **air-conditioning**. Abbreviated in this book and in India itself as **a/c**, air-conditioning is not necessarily the advantage you might expect – in some hotels you can find yourself paying double for a system that is so dust-choked, wheezy and noisy as to preclude any possibility of sleep – but providing it entitles a hotel to consider itself mid-range. Some also offer a halfway-house option known as **air-cooled** – noisy and not as effective as full-blown a/c, but better than nothing in severe heat – which is found only in drier climes as coolers do not work in areas of extreme humidity such as along the coasts of South India and the Bay of Bengal. Many medium-priced hotels also have attached restaurants, and even room service.

New hotels tend to be lined inside, on floors and walls, with marble (or some imitation), which can make them feel totally characterless. They are, however, much cleaner than older hotels, where dirt and grime clings to cracks and crevices, and damp quickly devours paint. Some mid-range hotels feel compelled to furnish their rooms with wall-to-wall carpeting which often smells due to humidity and damp.

Most state governments run their own **"tourist bungalows"**, similar to mid-range hotels, but often also offering pricier a/c rooms and cheaper dorms. They are usually good value, though they vary a lot from state to state and even within states. Rajasthan's, for example, tend to be rather run-down, whereas Madhya Pradesh's are, as a rule, very well kept, and some of those in Kerala are positively luxurious. We've indicated such places throughout this guide by including the state acronym in the name – eg *MPTDC Palace*. The "TDC" stands for Tourist Development Corporation and most states have one. Bookings for state-run hotels can be made in advance by telephone, or through the state tourist offices throughout the country.

Upmarket hotels

Most **luxury hotels** in India fall into one of two categories: old-fashioned institutions brimming with class, and modern jet-set chain hotels, largely confined to large cities and tourist resorts.

The faded grandeur of the **Raj** lingers on in the venerable edifices of British imperial hangouts such as Kolkata (Calcutta) and the hill stations. These can be well worth seeking out for their old-world charm, and their knack of being somehow more quintessentially British than the British ever managed. In addition, in states such as Rajasthan, Uttar Pradesh and Madhya Pradesh, magnificent **old forts** and **palaces** (*thikanas*) from feudal estates, and **havelis**, the former homes of aristocratic families, have been designated **heritage hotels**. Some old stately homes and forts in Himachal Pradesh have also been converted into hotels.

Modern deluxe establishments – slicker, brighter, faster and far more businesslike

Accommodation practicalities

Check-out time is often noon, but confirm this when you arrive: some expect you out by 9am, but many others operate a 24-hour system, under which you are simply obliged to leave by the same time as you arrived. Some places let you use their facilities after the official check-out time, sometimes for a small charge, others won't even let you leave your baggage after check-out unless you pay for another night.

Unfortunately, not all hotels offer **single rooms**, so it can often work out more expensive to travel alone; in hotels that don't, you may be able to negotiate a slight discount. It's not unusual to find rooms with three or four beds, however – great value for families and small groups.

In cheap hotels and hostels, you needn't expect any additions to your basic bill, but as you go up the scale, you'll find **taxes** and **service charges** creeping in, sometimes adding as much as a third on top of the original tariff. Service is generally ten percent, but taxes are a matter for local governments and vary from state to state.

Like most other things in India, the price of a room may well be open to **negotiation**. If you think the price is too high, or if all the hotels in town are empty, try haggling. You may get nowhere – but nothing ventured, nothing gained.

– tend to belong to **chains**, as often Indian as international. The *Taj Mahal Palace and Tower* in Mumbai, for example, the country's grandest hostelry, is part of a chain that includes former palaces in Rajasthan; some Taj hotels rank amongst the best and certainly the most expensive in the world. Other chains include Oberoi, Hilton, Hyatt, Marriott, Sheraton and the Indian Tourism Development Corporation's Ashok chain. You'll find such hotels in most state capitals and some resorts favoured by rich Indian and foreign tourists. It's becoming more common for these to quote tariffs in US dollars, starting at $80, but sometimes bringing the price for a double room up to an astonishing $500. In palaces and heritage hotels, however, you'll still get excellent value for money, with rates only just beginning to approach those of their counterparts back home.

Bookings for many of the larger hotel chains can be made in offices around the world and via the Internet; we've included website addresses for hotels that have them throughout the Guide. Note that when it comes to five-star and other high-end hotels, websites provide access to rates that may be far lower than the standard rack rates you'll be quoted over the phone or if you walk in. You may also find **discounts** through travel agencies such as the Travel Corporation of India who offer up to sixty percent off certain luxury hotels, depending on the season.

Other options

Many **railway stations** have **"retiring rooms"** where passengers can sleep – if they can put up with station noises. These rooms can be particularly handy if you're catching an early morning train, but tend to get booked up well in advance. They vary in price, but generally charge roughly the same as a budget hotel, and have large, clean, if somewhat institutional rooms; dormitories, where you can bank on being woken at the crack of dawn by a morning chorus of throat-clearing, are often available. Occasionally you may come across a main station with an air-conditioned room, in which case you will have found a real bargain. Retiring rooms cannot be booked in advance and are allocated on a first-come-first-serve basis; just turn up and ask if there's a vacancy.

In one or two places, it's possible to rent rooms in people's **homes**. In Rajasthan, Mumbai and Kerala the local tourist offices run **"paying guest"** or **"homestay schemes"** to place tourists with families offering lodging. Servas (Ⓦ www.servasindia.org), established in 1949 as a peace organization, is now devoted to providing homestays, representing some 626 hosts in India; you have to join before travelling by applying to the local Servas secretary (located via the website) – you then get a list of hosts to contact in the place you are visiting. Some people provide free accommodation, others are just day hosts. There is no guarantee a bed will be provided – it's up to the individual.

Camping is possible too, although in most of the country it's hard to see why you'd want to be cooped up in a tent overnight when you could be sleeping on a cool *charpoi* (a sort of basic bed) on a roof terrace for a handful of rupees – let alone why you'd choose to carry a tent around India in the first place. Except possibly on treks, it's not usual simply to pitch a tent in the countryside, though many hotels allow camping in their grounds. The YMCA runs a few sites, as do state governments (Maharashtra in particular), and the Scouts and Guides.

YMCAs and **YWCAs**, confined to big cities, are plusher and pricier than mid-range hotels. They are usually good value, but are often full, and some are exclusively single-sex. Official and non-official **youth hostels**, some run by state governments, are spread haphazardly across the country. They give HI cardholders a discount, but rarely exclude non-members, nor do they usually impose daytime closing. Prices match the cheapest hotels; where there is a youth hostel, it usually has a dormitory and may well be the best budget accommodation available – which goes especially for the **Salvation Army** ones.

Finally, religious institutions, particularly Sikh **gurudwaras**, offer accommodation for pilgrims and visitors, and may put up tourists; a donation is often expected, and certainly appreciated, but some of the bigger ones charge a fixed, nominal fee. Pilgrimage sites, especially those far from other accommodation, also have **dharamshalas** where visitors can stay – very cheap and very simple, usually with basic, communal washing facilities; some charitable institutions even have rooms with simple attached bathrooms. *Dharamshalas*, like *gurudwaras*, offer accommodation either on a donations system or charge a nominal fee, which can be as low as Rs20.

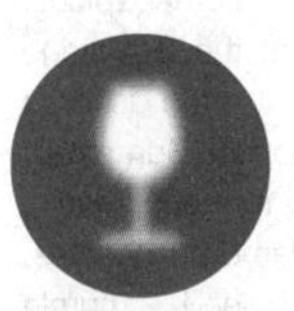

Eating and drinking

Indian food has a richly deserved reputation throughout the world for being aromatic and delicious. If you're a vegetarian, you've come to the right place. Indians are used to people having special dietary requirements: yours will be respected, and no one will think you strange for having them. Indeed, some of the very best food India has to offer is vegetarian, and even confirmed meat-eaters will find themselves tucking into delicious dhals and veg curries with relish.

Most religious Hindus, and the majority of people in the south, don't eat meat or fish, while some orthodox Brahmins will not eat food cooked by anyone outside their household (or onions or garlic, as they inflame the baser instincts), and Jains are even stricter. **Veganism** is not common, however; if you're vegan, you'll have to keep your eyes open for eggs and dairy products.

Many eating places state whether they are vegetarian or non-vegetarian either on signs outside or at the top of the menu. The terms used in India are **"veg"** and **"non-veg"**, and we have adopted these throughout our eating reviews. You'll also see "pure veg" which means that no eggs or alcohol are served. As a rule, meat-eaters should exercise caution in India: even when meat is available, especially in the larger towns, its quality is not assured except in the best restaurants, and you won't get much in a dish anyway – especially in railway canteens where it's mainly there for flavouring. Hindus, of course, do not eat beef and Muslims shun pork, so you'll only find those in a few Christian enclaves such as the beach areas of Goa, and Tibetan areas. Note that what is called "**mutton**" on menus is in fact goat.

Broadly speaking, there are four types of eating establishment: *dhabas*, *bhojanalayas* and *udipis*; restaurants; tourist restaurants; and fast-food joints. **Dhabas** and **bhojanalayas** are cheap Indian diners, where food is basic but often good, consisting of vegetable curry, dhal (a lentil soup pronounced "da'al"), rice or Indian bread (the latter more standard in the north) and sometimes meat. Often found along the sides of highways, *dhabas* traditionally cater to truck drivers, and one way of telling a good *dhaba* from a distance is to judge from the number of trucks parked outside. *Bhojanalayas* are basic eating places, usually found in towns (especially around bus stands and train stations) in the north and centre of the country; they tend to be vegetarian, especially those signed as "Vaishno". Both *dhabas* and *bhojanalayas* can be grubby – look them over before you commit yourself. The same is rarely true of their southern equivalent, *Udipi* canteens, which serve cheap, delicious snacks such as masala dosa, *iddli, vada* and rice-based dishes, all freshly cooked to order and dished up by uniformed waiters.

Restaurants as such vary in price and quality, and can be veg or non-veg, offering a wide choice of dishes, much like Indian restaurants anywhere else in the world. Deluxe restaurants such as those in five-star hotels can be very expensive by Indian standards, but they offer a chance to try classic Indian cooking of very high quality: rich, subtle, mouthwatering, and still a fraction of the price you'd pay for such delights at home – assuming you could find Indian food that good. Try a meal in one at least once.

The third type of eating place caters specifically for foreign travellers with unadventurous tastebuds: the **tourist restaurant**, found in beach resorts, hill stations and travellers' meccas across India. Here you can get pancakes and fritters, omelettes and toast, chips, fried prawns, cereal and fruit salad. The downside is that they tend to be pricey, some miss the mark by a long way, and they are not, of course, authentically Indian.

The fourth type is international **fast food** including burgers (without beef) as well as pizzas, which have taken cosmopolitan India by storm with familiar household names available in most major cities.

Finally, should you be lucky enough to be invited into someone's home, you will get to taste the most authentically Indian food of all. Most Indian women are professional cooks and housewives, trained from childhood by mothers, grandmothers and aunties, and aided by daughters and nieces. They can quite easily spend a whole day cooking, grinding and mixing the spices themselves, and using only the freshest ingredients.

For advice on **drinking water** in India, see p.42.

Indian food

What Westerners call a **curry** covers a variety of dishes, each made with a different masala, or mix of spices. Curry powder does not exist in India, the nearest equivalent being garam masala ("hot mix"), a combination of dried ground black pepper and other spices, in theory added to a dish at the last stage of cooking to spice it up, but often used as a substitute for other aromatics. Commonly used **spices** include chilli, turmeric, garlic, ginger, cinnamon, cardamom, cloves, coriander – both leaf and seed – cumin and saffron. These are not all added at the same time, and some are used whole, so beware of chewing on them. The spice that gives British and Caribbean curry powder its distinctive taste, fenugreek, is actually used much more sparingly in India.

It's the Indian penchant for **chilli** that alarms many Western visitors. The majority of foreigners develop a tolerance for it; if you don't, you'll just have to stick to mild dishes such as *korma* and biriyani where meat or vegetables are cooked with rice, and eat plenty of chapati. Indians tend to assuage the effects of chilli with chutney, *dahi* (curd) or raita (curd with mint and cucumber, or other herbs and vegetables). Otherwise, **beer** is one of the best things for washing chilli out of your mouth; the essential oils that

For a **glossary** of food items, see p.1446.

cause the burning sensation dissolve in alcohol, but not in water.

Vegetarian curries are usually identified (even on menus in English) by the Hindi names of their main ingredients. Terms like "curry" and "masala" don't really tell you what to expect; meat curries are more often given specific names such as *korma* or *dopiaza*, to indicate the kind of masala used or the method of cooking.

Regional variety is vast: **Bengalis** love fish and cook a mean *mangsho* (meat) curry as well as exotic vegetable dishes such as *mo-cha* – cooked banana flower. They also like to include fish bones for added flavour in their vegetable curries – a nasty surprise for vegetarians. **Biharis** were known for their *satu* – a staple flour used instead of rice – but *satu* has become unfashionable outside the rural communities. **Tibetans** and **Bhotias** from the Himalayas have a simple diet of *thukpa* (meat soup), and *momo* (meat dumplings), as well as a salty tea made with either rancid yak butter where available, or with ordinary butter. In **Punjab** and much of **northern India**, home cooking consists of dhal and vegetables along with roti (bread) and less rice than the Bengalis. Food in **Gujarat**, predominantly veg, is often cooked with a bit of sugar.

In the north of India especially, but as far south as Hyderabad, the influence of the Moghuls lives on in the form of **Mughlai** cooking. Mostly non-veg, the food is extremely rich, using ingredients such as cream, almonds, sultanas and saffron. Mughlai, as the name of a masala, normally indicates a mild, creamy one. *Mughlai paratha* is spicy fried bread with egg.

The other big northern style is **tandoori**. The name refers to the deep clay oven (tandoor) in which the food is cooked. Tandoori chicken is marinated in yoghurt, herbs and spices before cooking. Boneless pieces of meat, marinated and cooked in the same way are known as tikka; they may be served in a medium-strength masala (tikka masala), one thickened with almonds (*pasanda*), or in a rich butter sauce (*murg makhani* or butter chicken). Breads such as naan and roti are also baked in the tandoor.

Certain combinations are traditional and seasonally repeated, such as *makki ki roti* (fried corn bread) with *sarson ka sag* (mustard-leaf greens) around Punjab and other parts of north India. *Baingan bharta* (puréed roast aubergine) is commonly eaten with plain yoghurt and roti (plain bread). In good Muslim cooking from the north, delicately thin *rumali roti* (handkerchief bread) often accompanies rich meat and chicken dishes. Dhal is a safe bet with almost any meat or vegetable dish, and easy to eat with rice or bread.

Set meals are quite common in the north, and even more so in **the south**, where they are generally referred to simply as **"meals"**. They generally consist of a mound of rice surrounded by various delicious vegetable curries, *sambar* dhal, chutney and curd, and usually accompanied by poppadums, *vadas* and *rasam*, a hot pepper water. Traditionally served on a round metal tray or **thali** (also found in north India), with each side dish in a separate metal bowl, set meals are sometimes served up on a rectangle of banana leaf instead. In most traditional restaurants, you can eat as much as you want, and staff circulate with refills of everything. In the south even more than elsewhere, eating with your fingers is *de rigueur* (you want to feel the food as well as taste it) and cutlery may be unavailable.

Wherever you eat, remember to use only your right hand, and wash your hands before you start. Try and avoid getting food on the palm of your hand by eating with the tips of your fingers.

Snacks and street food

Feeling peckish should never be a problem, with all sorts of **snack meals** and finger food to choose from. Of the sit-down variety, *chana puri*, a chick-pea curry with a *puri* (or sometimes other breads) to dunk, is a great favourite in the north of the country; *iddli sambar* – lentil and vegetable sauce with rice cakes to dunk – is the southern equivalent. But the great snack meal of the south is masala dosa, a potato and vegetable curry wrapped in a crispy rice pancake.

Street finger food includes *bhel puris* (a Mumbai speciality of small vegetable-stuffed

Paan

You may be relieved to know that the red stuff people spit all over the streets isn't blood, but juice produced by chewing **paan** – a digestive, commonly taken after meals, and also a mild stimulant, found especially in the northeast where it is fresh and much stronger.

A paan consists of chopped or shredded nut (always referred to as betel nut, though in fact it comes from the areca palm), wrapped in a leaf (which does come from the betel tree) that is first prepared with ingredients such as *katha* (a red paste), *chuna* (slaked white lime), *mitha masala* (a mix of sweet spices, which can be ingested) and *zarda* (chewing tobacco, not to be swallowed on any account, especially if made with *chuna*). The triangular package thus formed is wedged inside your cheek and chewed slowly, and in the case of *chuna* and *zarda* paans, spitting out the juice as you go.

Paan, and paan masala, a mix of betel nut, fennel seeds, sweets and flavourings, are sold by paan-wallahs, often from tiny stalls squeezed between shops. Paan-wallahs develop big reputations; those in the tiny roads of Varanasi are the most renowned, asking astronomical prices for paan made to elaborate specifications including silver and even gold foil. Paan is an acquired taste; novices should start off, and preferably stick with, the sweet and harmless *mitha* variety, which is perfectly alright to ingest.

puris with tamarind sauce), *pani puris* (the same *puris* dunked in peppery and spicy water – only for the seasoned), *bhajis* (deep-fried cakes of vegetables in chick-pea flour), samosas (meat or vegetables in a pastry triangle, fried), and pakoras (vegetables or potato dipped in chick-pea flour batter and deep-fried). Kebabs are common in the north, most frequently seekh kebab, minced lamb grilled on a skewer, but also shami kebab, small minced lamb cutlets. Kebabs rolled into griddle-fried bread, known as *kathi* rolls, originated in Kolkata (Calcutta) but are now available in other cities as well. With all street snacks, though, remember that food left lying around attracts germs – make sure it's freshly cooked. Be especially careful with snacks involving water, such as *pani puris*, and cooking oil, which is often recycled. Generally, it's a good idea to acclimatize to Indian conditions before you start eating street snacks.

You won't find anything called "Bombay mix" in India, but there's no shortage of dry spicy snack mixes, often referred to as *channa chur*. Jackfruit chips are sometimes sold as a savoury snack – though they are rather bland – and cashew nuts are a real bargain. Peanuts, also known as "monkey nuts" or *mumfuli*, usually come roasted and unshelled. Look out for gram vendors who sell dry roasted chickpeas.

Non-Indian food

Chinese food has become widespread in large towns, where it is generally cooked by Indian chefs and not what you'd call authentic. However in a few cities, like Kolkata (Calcutta), that have large Chinese communities, you can get very good Chinese cuisine.

Western food is often dire, and expensive compared to Indian food, although the international chains serve the same standard fare as elsewhere in the world at much cheaper prices. Branches of *Pizza Hut*, *Domino's*, *KFC* and *McDonald's* can be found in Delhi, Mumbai, Kolkata (Calcutta), Chennai, Pune and Bangalore in ever-increasing numbers. *Wimpy*, home-grown chains such as *Nirula's* and *Kwality* and independently owned fast-food cafés can be found in any town. Tourist centres such as Leh, Goa and Kovalam offer a fair choice of Western food, from patisseries serving cakes and croissants to restaurants serving lasagne on candle-lit terraces. Small cheese factories are beginning to emerge, providing an alternative to the dreary processed cheese produced by Amul. Delhi and Mumbai also offer a choice Tex-Mex, Thai, Japanese, Italian and French cuisine – usually in restaurants of luxury hotels.

Breakfast

Unreconstructed Westerners seem to get especially homesick around **breakfast** time, but getting fry-ups and hash browns is likely to be a problem outside the Brit-dominated resorts of Kovalam and Goa. *Chana puri* is an option in the north, if a little spicy for some, and *alu paratha* with dhal is another traditional start to the day. *Iddli sambar* and masala dosa is the most common equivalent in the south, where branches of the *India Coffee House* chain can be depended upon for some decent coffee and toast.

In those towns which have established a reputation as hang-outs for "travellers", budget hotels and restaurants serve up the usual hippy fare – banana pancakes, muesli, etc – as well as omelettes, toast, porridge (not always oatmeal), cornflakes, and even bacon and eggs.

Sweets

Most Indians have rather a sweet tooth and Indian **sweets**, usually made of milk, can be very sweet indeed. Of the more solid type, *barfi*, a kind of fudge made from milk which has been boiled down and condensed, varies from moist and delicious to dry and powdery. It comes in various flavours from plain creamy white to *pista* (pistachio) in livid green and is often sold covered with silver leaf (which you eat). Smoother-textured, round *penda* and thin diamonds of *kaju katri*, plus *moist sandesh* and the harder *paira*, both popular in Bengal, are among many other sweets made from *chhana* or boiled-down milk. Crunchier *mesur* is made with chick peas; numerous types of gelatinous halwa, not the Middle Eastern variety, include the rich *gajar ka halwa* made from carrots and cream.

Getting softer and stickier, those circular orange tubes dripping syrup in sweet-shop windows, called *jalebis* and made of deep-fried treacle, are as sickly as they look. *Gulab jamuns*, deep-fried cream cheese sponge balls soaked in syrup, are just as unhealthy. Common in both the north and the south, *ladu* consists of balls made from semolina flour with raisins and sugar and sometimes made of other grains and flour, while among Bengali sweets, widely considered to be the best are *rasgullas*, rosewater-flavoured cream cheese balls floating in syrup. *Ras malai*, found throughout north India, is similar but soaked in cream instead of syrup.

Chocolate is improving rapidly in India and you'll find various Cadbury's and Amul bars. None of the various indigenous brands of imitation Swiss and Belgian chocolates appearing on the cosmopolitan markets are worth eating.

Among the large **ice cream** vendors, Kwality (now owned and branded as Walls), Vadilal's, Gaylord and Dollops stand out. Uniformed men push carts of ice cream around and the bigger companies have many imitators, usually quite obvious. Some have no scruples – stay away from water ices unless you have a seasoned constitution. Ice cream parlours selling elaborate concoctions including sundaes have really taken off; Connaught Circus in Delhi has several. Be sure to try kulfi, a pistachio- and cardamom-flavoured frozen sweet which is India's answer to ice cream; bhang kulfi (not available everywhere but popular during the festival of Holi) is laced with cannabis and has an interesting kick to it, but should be approached with caution.

Fruit

What **fruit** is available varies with region and season, but there's always a fine choice. Ideally, you should **peel** all fruit including apples (*sev*), or soak them in strong iodine or potassium permanganate solution for half an hour. Roadside vendors sell fruit which they often cut up and serve sprinkled with salt and even masala – don't buy anything that looks like it's been hanging around for a while.

Mangoes (*aam*) of various kinds are usually on offer, but not all are sweet enough to eat fresh – some are used for pickles or curries. Indians are picky about their mangoes, which they feel and smell before buying; if you don't know the art of choosing the fruit, you could be sold the leftovers. Among the species appearing at different times in the season, which lasts from spring to summer, look out for Alphonso and Langra. Bananas (*kela*) of one sort or another are also on sale all year round, and oranges and tangerines are generally easy to come by, as are sweet melons and thirst-quenching watermelons.

Tropical fruits such as coconuts, papayas (pawpaws) and pineapples are more common in the south, while things such as lychees and pomegranates are very seasonal. In the north, temperate fruit from the mountains can be much like that in Europe and North America, with strawberries, apricots and even rather soft apples available in season.

Among less familiar fruit, the *chiku*, which looks like a kiwi and tastes a bit like a pear, is worth a mention, as is the watermelon-sized jackfruit, whose spiny green exterior encloses sweet, slightly rubbery yellow segments, each containing a seed. Individual segments are sold at roadside stalls.

Soft drinks

India sometimes seems to run on **tea** or **chai**, grown in Darjeeling, Assam and the Nilgiri Hills, and sold by chai-wallahs on just about every street corner. However, although it was introduced from China by the East India Company in 1838, its use was only popularized by a government campaign in the 1950s.

Tea is usually made by putting tea dust, milk and water in a pan, boiling it all up, straining it into a cup or glass with lots of sugar and pouring back and forth from one cup to another to stir. Ginger and/or cardamoms are often added. If you're quick off the mark, you can get them to hold the sugar. English tea it isn't, but most travellers get used to it. Sometimes, especially in tourist spots, you might get a pot of European-style "tray" tea, generally consisting of a tea bag in lukewarm water – you'd do better to stick to the pukka Indian variety, unless, that is, you are in a traditional tea-growing area.

Instant coffee is becoming increasingly common, and in some cases is more popular than tea. At street stalls and on trains the familiar cry of "garam chai" (hot tea) is giving way to "kofi", while the *bhand* or *kulhad*, a disposable mud teacup, is gradually disappearing in preference to inferior plastic cups. In the north, most coffee is instant, even that advertised as "espresso". Good vacuum-packed filter coffee from Coorg (Kodargu) in Karnataka is now available but is yet to have an impact in cafés and restaurants. Café society has finally arrived in the major cities, and Delhi and Mumbai now have a fair share of trendy coffee shops serving real cappuccino and espresso.

In the south, **coffee** (**kofi**) is just as common as tea, and far better than it is in the north. One of the best places to get it is in outlets of the *India Coffee House* chain, found in every southern town, and occasionally in the north. A whole ritual is attached to the drinking of milky Keralan coffee in particular, poured in flamboyant sweeping motions between tall glasses to cool it down.

Soft drinks (known as cold drinks in India) are ubiquitous. Coca Cola and Pepsi returned to India in the early nineties after being banned from the country for seventeen years. That policy was originally instigated, in part, to prevent the expatriation of profits by foreign companies; since their return, militant Hindu groups such as the RSS have threatened to make them the focus of a boycott campaign against multinational consumer goods. The absence of Coca Cola and Pepsi spawned a host of Indian colas such as Campa Cola (innocuous), Thums Up (not unpalatable), Gold Spot (fizzy orange), and Limca (rumoured to have dubious connections to Italian companies, and to contain additives banned there). All contain a lot of sugar but little else: adverts for Indian soft drinks have been known to boast "Absolutely no natural ingredients!" None will quench your thirst for long.

More recommendable are straight water (see also p.42), either treated, boiled or bottled; bear in mind though, the recent reports of high concentrations of pesticides in bottled water (see p.42). There's also cartons of Frooti Jumpin, Réal and similar brands of fruit juice drinks, which come in mango, guava, apple and lemon varieties. If the carton looks at all mangled, it is best not to touch it as it may have been recycled. At larger stations, there will be a stall on the platform selling Himachali apple juice. Better still, **green coconuts**, common around coastal areas especially in the south, are cheaper than any of these, and sold on the street by vendors who will hack off the top for you with a machete and give you a straw to suck up the coconut water (you then scoop out the flesh and eat it). You will also find street stalls selling freshly made sugar-cane juice: delicious, and not in fact too sweet, but not always as safe healthwise as you might like.

India's greatest cold drink, **lassi**, is made with beaten curd and drunk either sweetened with sugar, salted, or mixed with fruit. It varies widely from smooth and delicious to insipid and watery, and is sold at virtually every café, restaurant and canteen in the country. Freshly made milkshakes are also commonly available at establishments with blenders. They'll also sell you what they call a fruit juice, but which is usually fruit, water and sugar (or salt) liquidized and strained; also, street vendors selling fresh fruit juice in less than hygienic conditions are apt to add salt and garam masala. With all such drinks, however appetizing they may seem, you should exercise great **caution** in deciding where to drink them: find out where the water is likely to have come from.

Alcohol

Prohibition, once widespread in India, is now only fully enforced in Gujarat and some of the northeastern hill states, although Tamil Nadu, Andhra Pradesh and some other states retain partial prohibition in the form of "dry" days, high taxes, restrictive licences, and health warnings on labels ("Liquor – ruins country, family and life," runs Tamil Nadu's). Even in areas where alcohol is readily available, dry days are often observed once a week (usually Thursday), and liquor shops remain shut.

Most Indians drink to get drunk as quickly as possible, and this trend has had a terrible toll on family life especially among the working classes and peasantry. Because of this, politicians searching for votes have from time to time played the prohibition card. The government in Haryana introduced prohibition in 1996 which, in a state that produces huge amounts of liquor, led to lost revenue and, as is common in all prohibition areas, the rapid growth of a highly organized illicit trade, but no evidence of less drinking. Haryana is no longer dry, but in states like Tamil Nadu, which persist with these policies, every now and then papers report cases of mass contamination from illicit stills that have led tragically to an extraordinary number of deaths.

Alcoholic enclaves in prohibition states can become major drinking centres: Daman and Diu in Gujarat, and Pondicherry and Karaikal in Tamil Nadu are the main ones. Goa, Sikkim and Mahé (Kerala) join them as places where the booze flows especially freely and cheaply. Interestingly, all were outside the British Raj. **Liquor permits** – free, and available from Indian embassies, high commissions and tourist offices abroad, and from tourist offices in Delhi, Mumbai, Kolkata (Calcutta) and Chennai, and even at airports on arrival – allow those travellers who bother to apply for one to evade certain restrictions in prohibition states like Gujarat.

Beer is widely available, if rather expensive by local standards. Price varies from state to state, but you can usually expect to pay Rs50–80 for a 650ml bottle. A pub culture, not dissimilar to that of the West, has taken root amongst the wealthier classes in cities like Bangalore and Mumbai and also in Delhi. Kingfisher, King's Black Label and Fosters are the leading brands, but there are plenty of others. All lagers, which tend to contain chemical additives including glycerine, are usually pretty palatable if you can get them cold. In certain places, notably unlicensed restaurants in Tamil Nadu, beer comes in the form of "special tea" – a teapot of beer, which you pour into and drink from a teacup to disguise what it really is. A cheaper, and often delicious, alternative to beer in Kerala and one or two other places is *toddy* (palm wine). In Bengal it is made from the date palm, and is known as *taddy*. Sweet and nonalcoholic when first tapped, it ferments within twelve hours. In the Himalaya, the Bhotia people, of Tibetan stock, drink *chang*, a beer made from millet, and one of the nicest drinks of all – *tumba*, where fermented millet is placed in a bamboo flask and topped with hot water, then sipped through a bamboo pipe.

Spirits usually take the form of "Indian Made Foreign Liquor" (IMFL), although the recently legitimized foreign liquor industry is expanding rapidly. Some Scotch, such as Seagram's Hundred Pipers, is now being bottled in India and sold at a premium, as is Smirnoff vodka amongst other known brands. Some of the brands of Indian whisky are not too bad and are affordable in comparison; gin and brandy can be pretty rough, while Indian rum is sweet and distinctive. In Goa, *feni* is a spirit distilled from coconut or cashew fruit. Steer well clear of illegally distilled *arak* however, which often contains methanol (wood alcohol) and other poisons. A look through the press, especially at festival times, will soon reveal numerous cases of blindness and death as a result of drinking bad hooch (or "spurious liquor" as it's called). Licensed country liquor, sold in several states under such names as *bangla*, is an acquired taste. Unfortunately, the Indian **wine** industry, though slowly improving with vineyards such as Grovers, is not up to scratch and the wines are pricey, while foreign wine available in upmarket restaurants and luxury hotels comes with an exorbitant price-tag.

Telephones, mail and Internet access

There's no need to be out of touch with the rest of the world while you're in India. International phone calls are surprisingly easy, the mail service is pretty reliable, if a little slow, and cybercafés are common in the major cities and in many tourist centres.

Telephones

Privately run **phone services** with international **direct dialling** facilities are very widespread. Advertising themselves with the acronyms **STD/ISD** (standard trunk dialling/international subscriber dialling), they are extremely quick and easy to use; some stay open 24 hours. Both national and international calls are dialled direct. To call abroad, dial the international access code (00), the code for the country you want – 44 for the UK, for example – the appropriate area code (leaving out any initial zeros), and the number you want; then you speak, pay your bill, which is calculated in seconds, and leave. Prices vary between private places and are slightly cheaper at official telecommunications offices; many have fax machines too. Calling from hotels is usually more expensive. "Call back" (or "back call", as it is often known) is possible at most phone booths and hotels, although check before you call and be aware that, in the case of booths, this facility rarely comes without a charge of Rs3–10 per minute.

Direct dialling **rates** are very expensive during the day – Monday to Saturday 8am to 7pm – but this falls to half rate on Sundays, national holidays, and daily from 7am to 8am and 7pm to 8.30pm, after which the charge is reduced further.

Home country direct services are now available from any phone to the UK, the USA, Canada, Ireland, Australia, New Zealand, and a growing number of other countries. These allow you to make a collect or telephone credit card call to that country via an operator there. If you can't find a

Net2Phone

Internet joints in India's big metropolitan cities have started to offer **Net2Phone** services, which allow you to make telephone calls over the web for incredibly low rates: Rs2–3 for calls to the UK/US. At the time of writing, services were limited to international calls. We've listed where you can access Net2phone in the guide, but more providers are popping up each month, so keep you eyes peeled for the logo.

International dialling

	From India	To India
UK	ⓣ00 44	ⓣ00 91
Irish Republic	ⓣ00 353	ⓣ00 91
US and Canada	ⓣ001	ⓣ011 91
Australia	ⓣ00 61	ⓣ0011 91
New Zealand	ⓣ00 64	ⓣ00 91

phone with home country direct buttons, you can use any phone toll-free, by dialling 000, your country code, and 17 (except Canada which is 000-127).

To **call India** from abroad, dial the international access code, followed by 91 for India, the local code minus the initial zero, then the number you want.

Mobile Phones

Call charges to and from **mobile phones** are far lower in India than Western countries, which is why lots of foreign tourists opt to sign up to a local network while they're travelling. To do this you'll need to buy an Indian SIM card from a mobile phone shop; these cost around Rs150, plus the price of a top-up card (varying from Rs150–500). Your retailer will help you get connected. They'll also advise you on which company to use. Different states tend to be dominated by one or other of the main firms – Airtel, BPL or !dea (formerly AT&T). If you intend to stay inside their designated coverage area, charges for texts and calls are cheap. However, to use your phone outside your company's coverage you'll need to shell out extra for a roaming facility – otherwise, you'll have to buy a new SIM card each time you change states. Note that when roaming, both you and your caller pay for incoming calls.

Internet and email

In all the large cities and in many tourist towns there are **Internet** and **email** facilities accessible to the general public, usually at **cybercafés**, though many hotels and STD booths offer this service as well. Charges for Internet use range from Rs10 to Rs60 per hour for reading mail and browsing, and extra for printing; most centres offer membership deals which can cut costs. You should make constant checks to see whether your connection is still alive; in the main cities and resorts faster connections through ISDN/broadband are now common, though they cost twice the price of standard dial-up connections. The shops that advertise email alongside unrelated business concerns are cheaper, but you have to send and receive mail through their own private account, which means your messages are open to public scrutiny, and the service is invariably slow.

Mail services

Mail can take anything from three days to four weeks to get to or from India, depending largely on where you are; ten days is about the norm. Stamps are not expensive, and aerogrammes and postcards cost the same to anywhere in the world. Ideally, you should have mail franked in front of you. Most post offices keep the same opening hours (Mon–Fri 10am–5pm & Sat 10am–noon), but big city GPOs, where the poste restante is usually located, are open longer (Mon–Fri 9.30am–6pm, Sat 9.30am–1pm). You can also buy stamps at big hotels.

Poste restante (general delivery) services throughout the country are pretty reliable, though exactly how long individual offices hang on to letters is more or less at their own discretion; for periods of longer than a month, it makes sense to mark mail with your expected date of arrival. Letters are filed alphabetically; in larger offices, you sort through them yourself. To avoid misfiling, your name should be printed clearly, with the surname in large capitals and underlined, but it is still a good idea to check under your first name too, just in case. Have letters addressed to you c/o Poste Restante, GPO (if it's the main post office you want), and the name of the town and state. In Delhi, you will probably want to specify "GPO, New Delhi", since "GPO, Delhi" means Old Delhi GPO, a lot less convenient for most tourists. Sometimes too, as in Kolkata (Calcutta) and Chennai, local tourist offices might be more convenient than the GPO. Don't forget to take ID with you to claim your mail. American Express offices also keep mail for holders of their charge card or travellers' cheques.

Having **parcels** sent out to you in India is not such a good idea – chances are they'll go astray. If you do have a parcel sent, have it registered.

Sending a parcel out of India can be quite a performance. First you have to get it cleared by customs at the post office (they often don't bother, but check), then you take it to a tailor and agree a price to have it wrapped in cheap cotton cloth (which you may have to go and buy yourself), stitched up and sealed with wax. In big city GPOs, people offering this service will be at hand. Next, take it to the post office, fill in and attach the relevant customs forms (it's best to tick the box marked "gift" and give its value as less than Rs1000 or "no commercial value", to avoid bureaucratic entanglements), buy your stamps, see them franked, and dispatch it. Parcels should not be more than 1m long, nor weigh more than 20kg. Surface mail is incredibly cheap, and takes an average of six months to arrive – it may take half, or four times that, however. It's a good way to dump excess baggage and souvenirs, but don't send anything fragile this way.

As in Britain, North America and Australia and New Zealand, books and magazines can be sent more cheaply, unsealed or wrapped around the middle, as **printed papers** ("book post"). Alternatively, there are numerous **courier** services. These are not as reliable as they should be and there have been complaints of packages going astray; it's safest to stick to known international companies such as DHL. Remember that all packages from India are likely to be suspect at home, and searched or X-rayed: don't send anything dodgy.

The media

With over one billion people and a literacy rate of around fifty percent, India produces a staggering 4700 daily papers in over 300 languages, and another 39,000 journals and weeklies. There are a large number of English-language daily newspapers, both national and regional. The most prominent of the nationals are The Hindu, The Statesman, the Times of India, The Independent, the Economic Times and the Indian Express (usually the most critical of the government). All are pretty dry and sober, and concentrate on Indian news; the Independent and Kolkata's Telegraph tend to have better coverage of world news than the rest. Asian Age, published simultaneously in India, London and New York, is a conservative tabloid that sports a motley collection of the world's more colourful stories. All the major Indian newspapers have websites (see p.37), with the Times of India, The Hindu and the Hindustan Times providing the most up-to-date and detailed news services.

India's press is the freest in Asia and attacks on the government are often quite outspoken. However, as in the West, most papers can be seen as part of the political establishment, and are unlikely to print anything that might upset the "national consensus".

In recent years, a number of *Time/Newsweek*-style **news magazines** have hit the market, with a strong emphasis on politics. The best of these are *India Today* and *Frontline*, published by *The Hindu*. Others include *Outlook*, which presents the most readable, broadly themed analysis, *Sunday* and *The Week*. As they give more of an overview of stories and issues than the daily papers, you will probably get a better insight into Indian politics, and most tend to have a higher proportion of international news too. *Business India* is more financially oriented and The *India Magazine* more cultural. Film **fanzines** and gossip mags are very popular (*Screen* and *Filmfare* are the best, though you'd have to be reasonably au fait with Indian movies to follow a lot of it), but magazines and periodicals in English cover all sorts of popular and minority interests, so it's worth having a look through what's available.

Foreign publications such as the *International Herald Tribune*, *Time*, *Newsweek*, *The Economist* and the international edition of the British *Guardian* are all available in the main cities (though bear in mind that most of the papers have websites where you can read that day's edition for free). For a read through the British press, try the British Council in Delhi, Mumbai, Kolkata (Calcutta) and Chennai; the USIS is the American equivalent. Expat-oriented bookstalls, such as those in New Delhi's Khan Market, stock slightly out-of-date and expensive copies of magazines like *Vogue* and *NME*.

BBC World Service radio can be picked up on short wave on 15.31MHz (19.6m) between about 8.30am and 10.30pm (Indian time). Alternative frequencies if reception is poor include 17.79MHz (16.9m), 15.56MHz (19.3m) and 11.96MHz (25.1m).

The government-run **TV** company, Doordarshan, which broadcasts a sober diet of edifying programmes, has tried to compete with the onslaught of mass access to **satellite TV**. The main broadcaster in English is Rupert Murdoch's Star TV network, which incorporates the BBC World Service and Zee TV (with Z News), a progressive blend of Hindi-oriented chat, film, news and music programmes. Star Sports and ESPN churn out a mind-boggling amount of cricket with an occasional sprinkling of other sports. Others include CNN, some sports channels, the Discovery Channel, the immensely popular Channel V, hosted by scantily clad Mumbai models and DJs, and a couple of American soap and chat stations. There are now several local-language channels as well.

Festivals and holidays

Virtually every temple in every town or village across the country has its own festival. The biggest and most spectacular include Puri's Rath Yatra festival in June or July, the Hemis festival in Ladakh, also held in June or July, Pushkar's camel fair in November, Kullu's Dussehra, Madurai's three annual festivals, and of course the Kumbh Mela, held at Allahabad, Haridwar, Nasik and Ujjain. While mostly religious in nature, merrymaking rather than solemnity are generally the order of the day, and onlookers are usually welcome. Indeed, if you are lucky enough to coincide with a local festival, it may well prove to be the highlight of your trip.

There isn't space to list every festival in every village across India here, but local festivals are listed throughout the body of the Guide. The following pages feature a list of the main national and regional celebrations, which requires a little explanation. Hindu, Sikh, Buddhist and Jain festivals follow the Indian **lunar calendar** and their dates therefore vary from year to year against the plain old Gregorian calendar. Determining them more than a year in advance is a highly complicated business best left to astrologers. Each lunar cycle is divided into two *paksa* (halves): "bright" (waxing) and "dark" (waning), each consisting of fifteen *tithis* ("days" – but a *tithi* might begin at any time of the solar day). The *paksa* start respectively with the new moon (*ama* or *bahula* – the first day of the month) and the full moon (*purnima*). Lunar festivals, then, are observed on a given day in the "light" or "dark" side of the month. The lunar calendar adds a leap month every two or three years to keep it in line with the seasons. Muslim festivals follow the **Islamic calendar**, whose year is shorter and which thus loses about eleven days per annum against the Gregorian.

You may, while in India, have the privilege of being invited to a **wedding**. These are jubilant affairs with great feasting, always scheduled on auspicious days. A Hindu bride dresses in red for the ceremony, and marks the parting of her hair with red *sindur* and her forehead with a *bindi*. She wears gold or bone bangles, which she keeps on for the rest of her married life. Although the practice is officially illegal, large dowries often change hands. These are usually paid by the bride's family to the groom, and can be contentious; poor families feel obliged to save for years to get their daughters married.

Principal Indian holidays

India has only four national public holidays as such: Jan 26 (Republic Day); Aug 15 (Independence Day); Oct 2 (Gandhi's birthday); and Dec 25 (Christmas Day). Each state, however, has its own calendar of public holidays; you can expect most businesses to close on the major holidays of their own religion (marked with an asterisk below).

The Hindu calendar months are given in brackets below, as most of the festivals listed are Hindu. **Key: B=Buddhist; C=Christian; H=Hindu; J=Jain; M=Muslim; N=nonreligious; P=Parsi; S=Sikh.**

Jan–Feb (Magha)

H Pongal (1 Magha) Tamil harvest festival celebrated with decorated cows, processions and *rangolis* (chalk designs on the doorsteps of houses). Pongal is a sweet porridge made from newly harvested rice and eaten by all, including the cows. The festival is also known as Makar Sankranti, and celebrated in Karnataka, Andhra Pradesh and the east of India.

H Ganga Sagar: Pilgrims come from all over the country to Sagar Dwip, on the mouth of the Hooghly 150km south of Kolkata (Calcutta), to bathe during Makar Sankranti.

H Vasant Panchami (5 Magha): One-day spring festival in honour of Saraswati, the goddess of learning, celebrated with kite-flying, the wearing of yellow saris, and the blessing of schoolchildren's books and pens by the goddess.

N Republic Day (Jan 26): A military parade in Delhi typifies this state celebration of India's republichood, followed on Jan 29 by the "Beating the Retreat" ceremony outside the presidential palace in Delhi.

N Goa Carnival: Goa's own Mardi Gras features float processions and feni-induced mayhem in the state capital, Panjim.

N International Kite Festival at Aurangabad (Maharashtra).

H Teppa Floating Festival (16 Magha) at Madurai (Tamil Nadu). Meenakshi and Shiva are towed around the temple tank in boats lit with fairy lights – a prelude to the Tamil marriage season.

N Elephanta Music and Dance Festival (Mumbai). Feb–March (Phalguna). Classical Indian dance performed with the famous rock-cut caves in Mumbai harbour as a backdrop.

B Losar (1 Phalguna): Tibetan New Year celebrations among Tibetan and Himalayan Buddhist communities, especially at Dharamsala (HP).

H Shivratri (10 Phalguna): Anniversary of Shiva's *tandav* (creation) dance, and his wedding anniversary. Popular family festival but also a sadhu festival of pilgrimage and fasting, especially at important Shiva temples.

H Holi (15 Phalguna)*: Water festival held during Dol Purnima (full moon) to celebrate the beginning of spring, most popular in the north. Expect to be bombarded with water, paint, coloured powder and other mixtures; they can permanently stain clothing, so don't go out in your Sunday best.

N Khajuraho (Madhya Pradesh) Dance Festival. The country's finest dancers perform in front of the famous erotic sculpture-carved shrines.

C Carnival (Mardi Gras): The last day before Lent, 40 days before Easter, is celebrated in Goa, as in the rest of the Catholic world.

March–April (Chaitra)

H Gangaur (3 Chaitra): Rajasthani festival (also celebrated in Bengal and Orissa) in honour of Parvati, marked with singing and dancing.

H Ramanavami (9 Chaitra)*: Birthday of Rama, the hero of the *Ramayana*, celebrated with readings of the epic and discourses on Rama's life and teachings.

C Easter (movable feast)*: Celebration of the resurrection of Christ. Good Friday in particular is a day of festivity.
P Pateti: Parsi new year, also known as No Ruz, celebrating the creation of fire. Feasting, services and present-giving.
P Khorvad Sal (a week after Pateti): Birthday of Zarathustra (aka Zoroaster). Celebrated in the Parsis' Fire Temples, and with feasting at home.
H Chittirai, Madurai (Tamil Nadu): Elephant-led procession.

April–May (Vaisakha)

HS Baisakhi (1 Vaisakha): To the Hindus, it's the solar new year, celebrated with music and dancing; to the Sikhs, it's the anniversary of the foundation of the Khalsa (Sikh brotherhood) by Guru Gobind Singh. Processions and feasting follow readings of the *Granth Sahib* scriptures.
J Mahavir Jayanti (13 Vaisakha)*: Birthday of Mahavira, the founder of Jainism. The main Jain festival of the year, observed by visits to sacred Jain sites, especially in Rajasthan and Gujarat, and with present giving.
H Puram Festival, Thrissur (Kerala): Frenzied drumming and elephant parades.
B Buddha Jayanti (16 Vaisakha)*: Buddha's birthday. He achieved enlightenment and nirvana on the same date. Sarnath (UP) and Bodh Gaya (Bihar) are the main centres of celebration.

May–June (Jyaishtha)

H Ganga Dussehra (10 Jyaishtha): Bathing festival to celebrate the descent to earth of the goddess of the Ganges.

June–July (Ashadha)

H Rath Yatra (2 Ashadha): Festival held in Puri (and other places, especially in the south) to commemorate Krishna's (Lord Jagannath's) journey to Mathura.
H Teej (3 Ashadha): Festival in honour of Parvati, to welcome the monsoon. Celebrated particularly in Rajasthan.
B Hemis Festival, Leh (Ladakh): Held sometime between late June and mid-July, this spectacular festival features chaam (lama dances) to signify the victory of Buddhism over evil.

July–Aug (Shravana)

H Naag Panchami (3 Shravana): Snake festival in honour of the naga snake deities. Mainly celebrated in Rajasthan and Maharashtra.
H Raksha Bandhan/Narial Purnima (16 Shravana): Festival to honour the sea god Varuna. Brothers and sisters exchange gifts, the sister tying a thread known as a rakhi to her brother's wrist. Brahmins, after a day's fasting, change the sacred thread they wear.
N Independence Day (15 Aug): India's biggest secular celebration, on the anniversary of independence from Britain.

Aug–Sept (Bhadraparda)

H Ganesh Chaturthi (4 Bhadraparda): Festival dedicated to Ganesh, especially celebrated in Maharashtra. In Mumbai, huge processions carry images of the god to immerse in the sea.
H Onam: Keralan harvest festival, celebrated with snake-boat races. The Nehru Trophy snake-boat race at Alappuzha (held on the second Saturday of August) is the most spectacular, with long boats each crewed by 150 rowers.
H Janmashtami (23 Bhadraparda)*: Krishna's birthday, an occasion for fasting and celebration, especially in Agra, Mumbai, Mathura (UP) and Vrindaban (UP).
H Avani Mula festival, Madurai (Tamil Nadu): Celebration of the coronation of Shiva.

Sept–Oct (Ashvina)

H Dussehra (1–10 Ashvina)*: Ten-day festival (usually two days' public holiday) associated with vanquishing demons, in particular Rama's victory over Ravana in the *Ramayana*, and Durga's over the buffalo-headed Mahishasura (particularly in West Bengal, where it is called Durga Puja). Dussehra celebrations include performances of the Ram Lila (life of Rama). Best in Mysore (Karnataka), Ahmedabad (Gujarat) and Kullu (Himachal Pradesh). Durga Puja is best seen in Kolkata (Calcutta) where it is an occasion for exchanging gifts, and every locality has its own competing street-side image.
N Mahatma Gandhi's Birthday (2 Oct): Solemn commemoration of Independent India's founding father.

Oct–Nov (Kartika)

H Diwali (Deepavali) (15 Kartika)*: Festival of lights, and India's biggest, to celebrate Rama and Sita's homecoming in the *Ramayana*. Festivities include the lighting of oil lamps and firecrackers, and the giving and receiving of sweets and gifts. Diwali coincides with Kali Puja, celebrated in temples dedicated to the wrathful goddess, especially in Bengal, and often accompanied by the ritual sacrifice of goats.
J Jain New Year (15 Kartika): Coincides with Diwali, so Jains celebrate alongside Hindus.
S Nanak Jayanti (16 Kartika)*: Guru Nanak's birthday marked by prayer readings and

processions, especially in Amritsar and in the rest of the Punjab, and at Patna (Bihar).

Nov–Dec (Margashirsha, or Agrahayana)

H Sonepur Mela: World's largest cattle fair at Sonepur (Bihar).
N Pushkar (Rajasthan) Camel Fair. Camel herders don their finest attire for this massive livestock market on the fringes on the Thar Desert.
N Hampi Festival (Karnataka): Government-sponsored music and dance festival.

Dec–Jan (Pausa)

CN Christmas (Dec 25)*: Christian festival celebrated throughout the world, popular in Christian areas of Goa and Kerala, and in big cities.
N Posh Mela (Dec 27): Held in Shantiniketan near Kolkata (Calcutta), a festival renowned for baul music.

Movable

H Kumbh Mela: Major three-yearly festival held at one of four holy cities: Nasik (Maharashtra), Ujjain (MP), Haridwar (UP), or Prayag (Maharashtra) as well as at Allahabad (UP). The Maha Kumbh Mela or "Great" Kumbh Mela, the largest religious fair in India, is held every twelve years in Allahabad (UP); the next festival is due to take place in 2013.
M Ramadan: The start of a month during which Muslims may not eat, drink or smoke from sunrise to sunset, and should abstain from sex.
M Id ul-Fitr: Feast to celebrate the end of Ramadan, after 28 days.
M Id ul-Zuha: Pilgrimage festival to commemorate Abraham's preparedness to sacrifice his son Ismail. Celebrated with slaughtering and consumption of sheep.
M Muharram: Festival to commemorate the martyrdom of the (Shi'ite) Imam, the Prophet's grandson and popular saint, Hussain.

Sports

India is not perhaps a place that most people associate with sports (the country achieved only one silver medal in the Athens Olympics in 2004), but cricket, hockey and football (soccer, that is) all have their place.

Cricket is by far the most popular of these, and a fine example of how something quintessentially British (well, English) has become something quintessentially Indian. Travellers to India will find it hard to get away from the game – it's everywhere, especially on television. Cricketing heroes such as the batting maestro **Sachin Tendulkar** live under the constant scrutiny of the media and public; expectations are high and disappointments acute; India versus Pakistan matches are especially emotive.

Test matches are rare, but interstate cricket is easy to catch – the most prestigious competition is the Ranji Trophy. Besides spectator cricket, you'll see games being played on open spaces all around the country. Occasionally, in cities like Kolkata (Calcutta), you may even come across a match blocking a road, and will have to be patient as the players begrudgingly let your vehicle continue.

Horse racing can be a good day out, especially if you enjoy a flutter. The racecourse at Kolkata (Calcutta) is the most popular, often attracting crowds of over 50,000, especially on New Year's Day. There are several other racecourses around the country, mostly in larger cities such as Mumbai, Delhi, Pune, Hyderabad, Mysore, Bangalore and Ooty. Other (mainly) spectator sports include **polo**, originally from upper Kashmir, but taken up by the British to become one of the symbols of the Raj. Princes of Rajasthan, such as the late Hanut Singh of Jodhpur, were considered in the thirties, forties and fifties to be the best polo players in the world, but since the sixties, when the privy purses were cut, they have been unable to maintain their stables, and the tradition of polo has declined. Today, it is mainly the army who plays the game; the best place to catch a match is at the Delhi Gymkhana during the winter season. Polo, in more or less its original form, is still played on tiny mountain ponies in Ladakh; a good place to see a game played in traditional style is in Leh during the Ladakh Festival in early September.

After years in the doldrums, Indian **hockey**, which used to regularly furnish the country with Olympic medals, is making a strong comeback. The haul of medals dried up in the sixties when international hockey introduced Astro-turf which was, and still is, a rare surface in India. However, hockey is still very popular, especially in schools and colleges and, interestingly, amongst the tribal girls of Orissa, who supply the Indian national team with a regular clutch of players. Indian **athletics** are improving all the time and, today the country can boast some world-class women sprinters.

Volleyball is very popular throughout India, and you may even see army men playing at extraordinary altitudes on the road to Leh. Standards aren't particularly high and joining a game should be quite easy. **Football** (soccer) is similarly popular with a keenly contested national championship. The best teams are based in Kolkata (Calcutta) and include three legendary clubs – Mohan Bagan, East Bengal and Mohamadan Sporting – who all command fanatical support. Unlike most of the league, these teams employ professional players and even include some minor internationals mostly from Africa. International soccer tournaments are becoming increasingly common.

Tennis in India has always been a sport for the middle classes. The country boasts a player or two of world-class standing, such as the duo of Bhupati and Paes who briefly achieved a world number-one ranking in the mens' doubles in 1999. Motorsport is popular in the south and there is a race-track on the outskirts of Chennai. **Golf** is extremely popular and relatively inexpensive in India, again amongst the middle classes; the second-oldest golf course in the world is in Kolkata (Calcutta), and one of the highest in the world at Shimla.

One indigenous sport you're likely to see in north India is **kabadi**, played on a small (badminton-sized) court, and informally on any suitable open area. The game, with seven players in each team, consists of a player from each team alternately attempting to "tag" as many members of the opposing team as possible in the space of a single breath (cheating is impossible; the player has to maintain a continuous chant of kabadikabadikabadikabadi etc), and getting back to his/her own side of the court without being caught. The game can get quite rough, with slaps and kicks in tagging allowed, and the defending team must try to tackle and pin the attacker so as not to allow him or her to even touch the dividing line. Tagged victims are required to leave the court. Although still an amateur sport, kabadi is taken very seriously with state and national championships, and now features in the Asian Games.

Popular with devotees of the monkey god, Hanuman, Indian **wrestling**, or **kushti**, has a small but dedicated following. Wrestlers are known as *pahalwaans* or "strong men" and can be seen exercising early in the morning with clubs and weights along river *ghats* such as those in Varanasi or Kolkata (Calcutta).

Trekking and outdoor pursuits

India offers an increasing number of opportunities for adventure sports, including trekking, mountaineering, whitewater rafting, caving and diving. A word of warning though – if you plan to do any of these activities during your trip, make sure you take out a comprehensive insurance policy (see p.40).

Trekking

Though **trekking** in India is not nearly as commercialized as in neighbouring Nepal, the country can claim some of the world's most spectacular routes, especially in the Ladakh and Zanskar Himalayas, where the mountain passes are frequently in excess of 5000m. Himalayan routes are not all extreme, with relatively gentle short trails exploring the Singalila range around Darjeeling, low-level forest walks through the rhododendron-clad hillsides of Sikkim and the well-beaten pilgrim trails of Garhwal.

Hiring a **guide**-cum-cook is recommended whenever possible, especially on more difficult and less frequented routes, where the consequences of getting lost or running out of supplies could be serious. **Porters** (with or without ponies) can also make your trip a lot less arduous, and on longer routes where a week or more's worth of provisions have to be carried, they may be essential. You'll usually be approached in towns and villages leading to the trailhead by men touting for work. Finding out what the going day rate is can be difficult, and you should expect to have to haggle.

If the prospect of organizing a trek yourself seems too daunting, consider employing a **trekking company** to do it for you. Agencies exist at such places as Manali, Leh, Darjeeling and Gangtok and are detailed in the Guide, while specialist **tour operators** offering trips based around trekking are listed in the various "Getting There" sections of Basics.

Himachal Pradesh is the most efficient state in which to trek; the Mountaineering Institute is on hand in Dharamsala to offer advice. **Uttaranchal** sees fewer trekkers, but there are plenty of opportunities to wander off the beaten track and escape the hordes of pilgrims or join them on their way to the sacred sites of Badrinath, Gangotri, Joshimath and Kedarnath. It is not advisable to venture into Kashmir at present, but there are exciting and exotic high-mountain trekking opportunities in the ancient Buddhist kingdoms of **Ladakh** and **Zanskar**, where trails can vary in length from short four-day excursions to epics of ten days or more. At the eastern end of the Himalayas, **Darjeeling** makes a good base from which to explore the surrounding mountains. Neighbouring **Sikkim** has the greatest variations in altitude, from steamy river valleys to the third highest massif in the world; there are a number of high-altitude treks here which require a permit, readily available in the capital Gangtok through government-recognized guides charging fees in dollars. Shorter and less strenuous treks are available in the Ghats and the Nilgiri hills of southern India, although access to the best of these – around Ooty – has been limited over the past few years by the presence in the forest of India's most-wanted criminal, the late bandit Veerapan (see p.1191).

Having the right **equipment** for a trek is important, but high-tech gear isn't essential – bring what you need to be comfortable but keep weight to a minimum. You can rent equipment in places such as Leh and Darjeeling, but otherwise, you'll have to buy what you need or bring it with you. Make sure everything (zips for example) is in working order before you set off. Clothes should be lightweight and versatile, especially considering the range of temperatures you might encounter: dress in layers for maximum flexibility.

Mountaineering

Mountaineering is a more serious venture, requiring planning and organization; if you've never climbed, don't start in the Himalayas. Mountaineering institutes at Darjeeling, Uttarkashi and Dharamsala run training **courses**. The one at **Uttarkashi** in Uttaranchal (ⓦuttarkashi.nic.in/nim/courses.htm) is popular with foreigners: you can learn rock- and ice-climbing skills and expedition techniques for a fraction of what you'd pay in the west, but the 28-day basic mountaineering course run by Siachen Glacier veterans of the Indian army is extremely gruelling. Permission for mountaineering **expeditions** should be sought at least six months in advance from the Indian Mountaineering Federation, Anand Niketan, Benito Juarez Road, New Delhi 110021 (ⓣ011/2467 7935, ⓦwww.indmount.org). Peak fees range from $1500 to $4000, according to height, and expeditions must be accompanied by an IMF liaison officer equipped to the same standard as the rest of the party. The IMF can also supply lists of local mountaineering clubs; climbing with such clubs enables you to get to know local climbers, and obtain permits for otherwise restricted peaks.

Skiing

Despite the mammoth spread of the Himalayas, **skiing** in India remains relatively undeveloped. The only option for organized skiing is the western Himalayas, in particular Uttaranchal and Himachal Pradesh; the eastern Himalayas have unreliable snowfall at skiing altitudes. At the time of writing, thaws in relations between India and Pakistan had also seen the re-opening of ski stations in Kashmir, one of which includes the world's longest gondelbahn.

The ski area at **Auli**, near Joshimath in Uttaranchal, has had money poured into it with a gondola lift system and a handful of surface tows but it suffers from a short season, limited (though cheap) skiing and non-existent après-ski activity. Auli also lies in a "dry zone", so you won't find a bar after a hard day on the slopes.

In Himachal Pradesh, the skiing in the vicinity of **Shimla** is far too underdeveloped to warrant a detour, but the possibilities around Manali are more enticing because of the prospect of virgin powder: two or three surface tows operate in the **Solang Nala** for three months every winter.

There are two options for back-country skiing – the first is to plan your own ski-tour and bring your own equipment, but you should never go alone. The other way to float down trackless slopes is to go heli-skiing but at around US$500 a day, you'd have to be pretty well off to explore what aficionados describe as some of the best powder in the world.

Whitewater rafting

Though not as well known as some of the mighty rivers of Nepal, the rivers Chenab and Beas in **Himachal Pradesh**, Rangit and Teesta in **Sikkim**, Zanskar and Indus in **Ladakh**, and Ganges in Uttaranchal all combine exciting waters with magnificent scenery. Kullu, Manali, Leh, Gangtok and Rishikesh are among the main rafting centres. Prices start at around Rs500 per day including food, but it's worth sounding out a few agents to find the best deals. For more details see the relevant accounts in the Guide.

Caving

Meghalaya has the best caving potential of all the Indian states. Tucked away in the northeast of India, it offers extensive limestone regions and boasts the two wettest places on earth – Mawsynram and Cherrapunjee. The three main areas for caving are: the **East Khasi hills**, the **Jainta hills** and the **South Garo hills**. Krem Umlawan, 60km from Jowai in the Jainta hills, used to be considered the longest (6381m) and deepest (107m) cave in India. That is, until cavers found a link from this cave to the nearby Krem Kotsati (another interesting cave with eight entrances, the main one being through a deep pool with some beautiful river passages), making the combined Krem Kotsati–Umlawan cave the longest system in mainland Asia, measuring 21.4km. A small cave entrance in Nengkhong village (South Garo hills) leads to a 5330m cave which is the second longest in India. The third largest system, near the village of Siju, has some of the best river sections anywhere in the world, and is the most explored cave in India. Half a kilometre west of Cherrapunjee, Krem Mawmluh (4500m) measures up in fourth place. For potholing contacts in Meghalaya, see p.996.

Diving and snorkelling

Because of the number of rivers draining into the sea around the subcontinent, India's coastal waters are generally silt-laden and too murky for decent **diving** or **snorkelling**. However, in many areas abundant hard coral and colourful fish make up for the relatively poor visibility. India also counts two beautiful tropical island archipelagos in its territory, both surrounded by exceptionally clear seas. Served by well-equipped and reputable diving centres, the Andaman islands and Lakshadweep offer world-class diving on a par with just about anything in Asia. Don't come here expecting rock-bottom prices though. Compared to Thailand, India's dive schools are pricey, typically charging around Rs15,000 ($350) for a four-day PADI-approved open-water course.

For independent travellers, the most promising destination for both scuba-diving and snorkelling is the **Andaman Islands** (see p.1102) in the Bay of Bengal, around 1000km east of the mainland. Part of a chain of submerged mountains that stretch north from Sumatra to the coast of Burma (Myanmar), this isolated archipelago is ringed by gigantic coral reefs whose crystal-clear waters are teeming with tropical fish and other marine life. Given the high cost of diving courses, most visitors stick to snorkelling, but if you already have your PADI permit, it's well worth renting equipment from one of the two dive schools in the capital, Port Blair, and joining an excursion to an offshore dive site such as Cinque Island or the Mahatma Gandhi Marine Reserve. If you want to do an open-water course, book ahead as places tend to be in short supply especially during the peak season, between December and February.

Lakshadweep (see p.1262) is a classic coconut palm-covered atoll, some 400km west of Kerala in the Arabian Sea. The shallow lagoons, extensive coral reefs and exceptionally good visibility make this a perfect option for both first-timers and more experienced divers.

As with other countries, qualified divers should take their current certification card and/or logbook; if you haven't used it for one year or more, expect to have to take a short test costing around Rs300 ($7).

Yoga, meditation and ashrams

Most first-time visitors to India opt for a cocktail – temples, trekking, palaces, wildlife parks, beaches, and, to balance the indulgences and hedonism, a spiritual element in whatever form. From basic yoga and pranayama classes to residential meditation retreats, India has no equal in terms of tradition and opportunity.

Yoga is taught virtually everywhere in India and there are several internationally known centres where you can train to become a teacher. **Meditation** is similarly practised all over the country and specific courses are available in temples, meditation centres, monasteries and ashrams. **Ashrams** are communities where people work, live and study together, drawn by a common, usually spiritual, goal. Adopting a guru is a completely different experience to simply attending a few classes, and whether you choose to do so will ultimately depend on your deep personal commitment and on how comfortable you feel being around a specific guru, but be careful in your choice.

Details of yoga and meditation courses and ashrams are provided throughout the Guide section of this book. Most centres offer courses that you can enrol on at short notice, but many of the more popular ones, listed on p.86, need to be booked well in advance.

Yoga

The word **yoga** literally means "to unite" and the aim of the discipline is to help the practitioner unite his or her individual consciousness with the divine. This is achieved by raising awareness of one's self through spiritual, mental and physical discipline. **Hatha** yoga is based on physical postures called **asanas**, and although the most popular form in the West, it is traditionally just the first step leading to more subtle stages of meditation which commence when the energies of the body have been awakened and sensitized by stretching and relaxing. Other forms of yoga include *raja* yoga, which includes moral discipline and *bhakti* yoga, the yoga of devotion, which entails a commitment to one's guru or teacher. *Jnana* yoga (the yoga of knowledge) is centred around the deep philosophies that underlie Hindu spiritual thinking; the greatest body of Hindu philosophic treatises are known as the Upanishads (c.1000 BC) which came to be embodied in the philosophical discipline of Vedanta.

Rishikesh, in Uttar Pradesh, is India's yoga capital, with a bumper crop of ashrams offering all kinds of courses. The country's two most famous teachers, however, work from institutes further south. In Pune, Yogacharya **BKS Iyengar** is the man widely credited with revolutionizing modern yoga and giving it a Western anatomical grounding. Distinguished by its use of "props" such as blocks and belts to assist learners to attain the correct alignment in poses, Iyengar yoga is taught worldwide by teachers strictly trained by Iyengar himself (now in his eighties) or one of his children in the Pune institute (which you won't be able to get into without seven years Iyengar experience). Iyengar's teacher, Sri Tirumalai Krisnamacharya, taught in Mysore, Karnataka, where another of his illustrious ex-pupils, Yogacharya **Pattabhi Jois**, is still based. Jois re-discovered the ancient science of **Ashtanga** yoga, a more dynamic (at times acrobatic) form which emphasizes movement through various series of poses.

Both styles, and their many offshoots, are taught in schools and ashrams around the country. One popular place with foreigners is the Shivanada Yoga Vedanta Dhanwanthari ashram in Neyyar Dam, Kerala (see listings below and p.1124), though in the past couple of years we've received mixed reviews of their courses. Further north, Goa boasts several less formal establishments where the standard of teaching is world-class (see p.821). In many other tourist centres you'll see ads for lessons and courses; always ask for a trial first if possible.

Meditation

Meditation is often practised after a session of yoga, when the energy of the body has been awakened, and is an essential part of both Hindu and Buddhist practice. In both religions, meditation is considered the most powerful tool for understanding the true nature of mind and self, an essential step on the path to enlightenment. In **Vedanta**, meditation's aim is to realize the true self as non-dual Brahman or godhead – the foundation of all consciousness and life. *Moksha* (or liberation – the Nirvana of the Buddhists), achieved through disciplines of yoga and meditation, eventually helps believers release the soul from endless cycles of birth and rebirth.

Vipassana meditation is a technique originally taught by the Buddha, whereby practitioners learn to become more aware of physical sensations and mental processes. Courses last for a minimum of ten days and are austere – involving 4am kick-offs, around ten hours of meditation a day, no solid food after noon, segregation of the sexes, and no talking for the duration (except with the leaders of the course). Courses are free for all first-time students, to allow everyone an opportunity to learn and benefit from the technique. Vipassana is taught in more than 25 centres throughout India including in Bodhgaya, Bangalore, Chennai, Hyderabad and Jaipur.

Tibetan Buddhist meditation is attracting more and more followers around the world. With its four distinct schools, Tibetan Buddhism incorporates a huge variety of meditation practices, including Vipassana, known as **shiné** in Tibetan, and various visualization techniques involving the numerous deities that make up the complex and colourful Tibetan pantheon. India, with its large Tibetan diaspora, has become a major centre for those wanting to study Tibetan

Buddhism and medicine. Dharamsala in Himachal Pradesh, home to the Dalai Lama and Tibetan government-in-exile, is the main centre for Tibetan studies, offering numerous opportunities for one-on-one study with the Tibetan monks and nuns who live there. Other major Tibetan diaspora centres in India include Darjeeling in West Bengal and Bylakuppe near Mysore in Karnataka. For further details of courses available locally, see the relevant chapters of the Guide.

Ashrams

Ashrams can range in size from several thousand people to just a handful, and their rules, regulations and restrictions vary enormously. Some offer on-site accommodation, others will require you to stay in the nearest town or village. Some charge Western prices, others local prices, and some operate on a donation basis. Many ashrams have set programmes each day, while others are less structured, teaching as and when requested.

Courses and ashrams

Astanga Yoga Nilayam 235 8th Cross, 3rd stage, Gokulam, Mysore 570002, Karnataka ⓦwww.ayri.org. Run by Pattabhi Jois, one of the great innovators of Yoga in India, courses in dynamic yoga affiliated with martial arts last at least a month and need to be booked in advance.

Divine Life Society PO Shivanandanagar, Muni ki Reti, Rishikesh, District Tehri Garhwal, Uttaranchal ⓣ0135/430040, ⓦwww.sivanandadlshq.org. The original Sivananda ashram – well organized if institutional, with several retreats and courses on all aspects and forms of yoga. The strength of Sivananda's yoga, however, was his deep understanding of Advaitya Vedanta – the philosophy of non-duality.

International Society for Krishna Consciousness (ISKCON) 3c Albert Rd, Kolkata (Calcutta) ⓣ033/247 3757; Bhaktivedanta Swami Marg, Raman Reti, Vrindavan ⓣ0565/442478, ⓦwww.iskcon.org. Large well-run international organization with major ashrams and temples in Mayapur, north of Kolkata (Calcutta) in West Bengal, Vrindavan in west UP and centres in several major Indian cities and abroad. Promotes bhakti yoga (the yoga of devotion) through good deeds, right living and chanting – a way of life rather than a short course.

Osho Commune International 17 Koregaon Park, Pune, Maharashtra 411001 ⓣ020/612 6655, ⓦwww.osho.com. Established by the enigmatic Osho, who generated a huge following of both Western and Indian devotees, this centre is set in 31 acres of beautifully landscaped gardens and offers a variety of courses in personal therapy, healing and meditation. For full details see p.781. There are numerous other Indian and international centres.

Prasanthi Nilayam Puttaparthi, Andhra Pradesh ⓣ08555/87236, ⓦwww.saionline.org. The ashram of Satya Sai Baba, one of India's most revered and popular gurus who has a worldwide following of millions despite the deaths of four followers in mysterious circumstances in 2000. The ashram is four or five hours by bus from Bangalore. Visitors sometimes comment on the strict security staffing and rigid rules and regulations. Cheap accommodation is available in dormitories or "flats" for four people. There is no need to book in advance though you should phone to check availability; see p.1083 for more details. Sai Baba also has a smaller ashram in Bangalore and one in Kodaikanal.

Root Institute for Wisdom Culture Bodhgaya, Bihar ⓣ0631/400714, ⓦwww.rootinstitute.com. An important meditation and teaching centre linked to the Foundation for the Preservation of the Mahayana Tradition (FPMT). Regular seven- to ten-day courses are held here and there are facilities for individual retreats. Accommodation for longer stays should be booked well in advance. See p.940 for further details.

Saccidananda Ashram Thanneepalli, Kullithalai, near Tiruchirapelli, Tamil Nadu ⓣ04323/22260, ⓦwww.bedegriffiths.com. Also known as Shantivanam (meaning Peace Forest in Sanskrit), it is situated on the banks of the sacred River Cauvery. Founded by Father Bede Griffiths, a visionary Benedictine monk, it presents a curious but sympathetic fusion of Christianity and Hinduism. Visitors can join in the services and rituals or just relax here. Accommodation is in simple huts dotted around the grounds and meals are communal. Very busy during the major Christian festivals.

Sivananda Yoga Vedanta Dhanwanthari Ashram PO Neyyar Dam, Thiruvananthapuram Dist, Kerala 695576 ⓣ0471/273493, ⓦwww.sivananda.org. An offshoot of the original Divine Life Society, a yoga-based ashram where yoga postures (asanas), breathing techniques (pranayama) and meditation are taught. They also run teacher-training programmes. There are two other branches in India: Sivananda Kutir (near Siror bridge), PO Netala (ⓣ01374/2624), and Sivananda Guha, Gangotri. Both are in the Himalayan state of Uttaranchal.

Tushita Meditation Centre McLeod Ganj, Dharamsala 176219, Himachal Pradesh ⓣ01892/21866, ⓦtushita.info. Offers a range of Tibetan meditation courses. A ten-day course costs in the region of Rs3500; book well in advance.

Vipassana International Academy The Vipassana movement (Ⓦ www.dhamma.org) has three regional centres in South India: Dhamma Khetta, Nagarjan Sagar Rd, Kusum Nagar Vanasthali Puram, Hyderabad 500070, Andhra Pradesh Ⓣ 040/402 0290; 73 Netaji Subhashchandra Bose Rd, Sowcarpet, Chennai 600079, Tamil Nadu Ⓣ 044/2535 8316; Bangalore Vipassana Centre, Dhamma Sumana, C/o Bharat Silks, no. 185, I floor, 4th Cross, Lalbagh Rd, Bangalore 560027, Karnataka Ⓣ 080/2222 4330.

Crime and personal safety

In spite of the crushing poverty and the yawning gulf between rich and poor, India is, on the whole, a safe country in which to travel. As a tourist, however, you are an obvious target for the tiny number of thieves (who may include some of your fellow travellers), and stand to face serious problems if you do lose your passport, money and ticket home. Common sense, therefore, suggests a few precautions.

If you can tolerate the encumbrance, carry valuables in a money belt or a pouch around your neck at all times. In the latter case, the cord should be hidden under your clothing and not be easy to cut through. Beware of **crowded locations**, such as packed buses or trains, in which it is easy for pickpockets to operate – slashing pockets or bags with razor blades is not unheard of in certain locations, and itching powder is sometimes used to distract the unwary. Don't leave valuables unattended on the beach when you go for a swim; backpacks in dormitory accommodation are also obvious targets.

Budget travellers would do well to carry a **padlock**, as these are usually used to secure the doors of cheap hotel rooms and it's reassuring to know you have the only key; strong combination locks are ideal. You can also use them to lock your bag to seats or racks in trains, for which a length of chain also comes in handy. Don't put valuables in your luggage for bus or plane journeys: keep them with you at all times. If your baggage is on the roof of a bus, make sure it is well secured. On trains and buses, the prime time for theft is just before you leave, so keep a particular eye on your gear then, beware of deliberate diversions, and don't put your belongings next to open windows. Remember that routes popular with tourists tend to be popular with thieves too; knife-point muggings are on the increase in Goa. Druggings leading to theft and worse are rare but not unheard of and so you are best advised to politely **refuse food and drink** from fellow passengers or passing strangers, unless you are completely confident it's the family picnic you are sharing or have seen the food purchased from a vendor.

However, don't get paranoid; the best way of enjoying the country is to stay relaxed but with your wits about you. Crime levels in India are a long way below those of Western countries, and violent crime against tourists is extremely rare. Virtually none of the people who approach you on the street intend any harm: most want to sell you something (though this is not always made apparent immediately), some want to practise their English, others (if you're a woman) to chat you up, while more than a few just want to add your address to their book or have a snap taken with you. Anyone offering wonderful-sounding moneymaking schemes, however, is almost certain to be a con artist.

If you do feel threatened, it's worth looking for help. Tourism police are found sitting in clearly marked booths in the main railway stations, especially in big tourist centres, where they will also have a booth in the main

Drugs

Future is black if sugar is brown

Indian anti-drugs poster

India is a centre for the production of **cannabis** and to a lesser extent **opium**, and derivatives of these drugs are widely available. **Charas** (hashish) is produced all along the Himalayas. The use of cannabis is frowned upon by respectable Indians – if you see anyone in a movie smoking a chillum, you can be sure it's the baddie. Sadhus, on the other hand, are allowed to smoke **ganja** (marijuana) legally as part of their religious devotion to Shiva, who is said to have originally discovered its narcotic properties.

Bhang (a preparation made from marijuana leaves, which it is claimed sometimes contains added hallucinogenic ingredients such as datura) is legal and widely available in bhang shops: it is used to make sweets and drinks such as the notoriously potent bhang lassis which have waylaid many an unwary traveller. Bhang shops also frequently sell ganja, low-quality charas, and opium (*chandu*), mainly from Rajasthan and Madhya Pradesh. Opium derivatives morphine and heroin are widespread too, with addiction an increasing problem among the urban poor. "Brown sugar" that you may be offered on the street is grade three heroin; Varanasi is becoming notorious for its heroin problem. Use of other illegal drugs such as LSD, ecstasy and cocaine is largely confined to tourists in party locations such as Goa.

All of these drugs except bhang are strictly controlled under Indian **law**. Anyone arrested with less than five grams of cannabis which they are able to prove is for their own use is liable to a six-month maximum, but cases can take years to come to trial (two is normal, and eight not unheard of). Police raids and searches are particularly common at the following places: Manali, the Kullu valley and Almora, and on buses from those places to Delhi, especially at harvest time; buses and trains crossing certain state lines, notably between Gujarat and Maharastra; budget hotels in Delhi's Paharganj; the beach areas of Goa; and around Idukki and Kumily in Kerala. "Paying a fine now" may be possible on arrest (though it will probably mean all the money you have), but once you are booked in at the station, your chances are slim; a minority of the population languishing in Indian jails are foreigners on drugs charges.

bus station. They may also have a marked booth outside major tourist sites.

Be wary of **credit card fraud**; a credit card can be used to make duplicate forms to which your account is then billed for fictitious transactions, so don't let shops or restaurants take your card away to process – insist they do it in front of you or follow them to the point of transaction. Even **monkeys** rate a mention here – it is not unknown for them to steal things from hotel rooms with open windows, or even to snatch bags from unsuspecting shoulders.

It's not a bad idea to keep $100 or so separately from the rest of your money, along with your travellers' cheque receipts, insurance policy number and phone number for claims, and a photocopy of the pages in your passport containing personal data and your Indian visa. This will cover you in case you do lose all your valuables.

If the worst happens and you get robbed, the first thing to do is **report the theft** as soon as possible to the local police. They are very unlikely to recover your belongings, but you need a report from them in order to claim on your travel insurance. Dress smartly and expect an uphill battle – city cops in particular tend to be jaded from too many insurance and travellers' cheque scams.

Losing your passport is a real hassle, but does not necessarily mean the end of your trip. First, report the loss immediately to the police, who will issue you with the all-important "complaint form" that you need to be able to travel around and check into hotels, as well as claim back any expenses incurred in replacing your passport from your insurer. A complaint form, however, will not allow you to change money or travellers' cheques. If you've run out of cash, your best bet is to ask your hotel manager to help you out (staff will have seen your passport when you checked in, and the number will be in the register). The next thing to do is telephone your nearest embassy or consulate in India. Normally, passports have to be applied for and collected in person, but if you are stranded, it is usually possible to arrange to receive the necessary forms in the post. However, you still have to go to the embassy or consulate to pick up your new passport. "Emergency passports" are the cheapest form of replacement, but are normally only valid for the few days of your return flight. If you're not sure when you're leaving India, you'll have to obtain a more costly "full passport"; these can only be issued by embassies and larger consulates in Delhi or Mumbai, and not those in Chennai, Kolkata (Calcutta) or Panjim.

Cultural hints and etiquette

Cultural differences extend to all sorts of little things. While allowances will usually be made for foreigners, visitors unacquainted with Indian customs may need a little preparation to avoid causing offence or making fools of themselves. The list of do's and don'ts here is hardly exhaustive: when in doubt, watch what the Indian people around you are doing.

Eating and the right-hand rule

The biggest minefield of potential faux pas has to do with **eating**. This is usually done with the fingers, and requires practice to get absolutely right. Rule one is: **eat with your right hand only**. In India, as right across Asia, the left hand is for wiping your bottom, cleaning your feet and other unsavoury functions (you also put on and take off your shoes with your left hand), while the right hand is for eating, shaking hands, and so on.

Quite how rigid individuals are about this tends to vary, with brahmins (who at the top of the hierarchical ladder are one of the two "right-handed castes") and southerners likely to be the strictest. While you can hold a cup or utensil in your left hand, and you can usually get away with using it to help tear your chapati, you should not eat, pass food or wipe your mouth with your left hand. Best is to keep it out of sight below the table.

This rule extends beyond food. In general, do not pass anything to anyone with your left hand, or point at anyone with it either; and Indians won't be impressed if you put it in your mouth. In general, you should accept things given to you with your right hand – though using both hands is a sign of respect.

The other rule to beware of when eating or drinking is that your lips should not touch other people's food – *jhutha* or sullied food is strictly taboo. Don't, for example, take a bite out of a chapati and pass it on. When drinking out of a cup or bottle to be shared with others, don't let it touch your lips, but rather pour it directly into your mouth. This custom also protects you from things like hepatitis. It is customary to wash your hands before and after eating.

Temples and religion

Religion is taken very seriously in India; it's important always to show due respect to religious buildings, shrines, images, and people at prayer. When entering a temple or mosque, remove your shoes and leave them at the door (socks are acceptable and protect your feet from burning-hot stone ground). Some temples – Jain ones in particular – do not allow you to enter wearing or carrying leather articles, and forbid entry to menstruating women. When entering a religious establishment, dress conservatively (see below), and try not to be obtrusive.

In a mosque, you'll not normally be allowed in at prayer time and women are sometimes not let in at all. In a Hindu temple, you are not often allowed into the inner sanctum; and at a Buddhist stupa or monument, you should always walk round clockwise (ie, with the stupa on your right). Hindus are very superstitious about taking **photographs** of images of deities and inside temples; if in doubt, desist. Do not take photos of funerals or cremations.

Funeral processions are private affairs, and should be left in peace. In Hindu funerals, the body is normally carried to the cremation site within hours of death by white-shrouded relatives (white is the colour of mourning). The eldest son is expected to shave his head and wear white following the death of a parent. At Varanasi and other places, you may see cremations; such occasions should be treated with respect, and photographs should not be taken.

Dress

Indian people are very conservative about **dress**. Women are expected to dress modestly, with legs and shoulders covered. Trousers are acceptable, but shorts and short skirts are offensive to many. Men should always wear a shirt in public, and avoid shorts (a sign of low caste) away from beach areas. These rules go double in temples and mosques. Cover your head with a cap or cloth when entering a *dargah* (Sufi shrine) or Sikh *gurudwara*; women in particular are also required to cover their limbs. Men are similarly expected to dress appropriately with their legs and head covered. Caps are usually available on loan, often free, for visitors, and sometimes cloth is available to cover up your arms and legs.

Never mind sky-clad Jains or *naga sadhus*, **nudity** is not acceptable in India. The mild-mannered people of Goa may not say anything about nude bathing (though it is in theory prohibited), but you can be sure they don't like it.

In general, Indians find it hard to understand why rich Western sahibs should wander round in ragged clothes or imitate the lowest ranks of Indian society, who would love to have something more decent to wear. Staying well groomed and dressing "respectably" vastly improves the impression you make on local people, and reduces sexual harassment too.

Other possible gaffes

Kissing and **embracing** are regarded in India as part of sex: do not do them in public. In more conservative areas (ie outside westernized parts of big cities), it is not even a good idea for couples to hold hands, though Indian men can sometimes be seen holding hands as a sign of "brotherliness". Be aware of your feet. When entering a private home, you should normally remove your shoes (follow your host's example); when sitting, avoid pointing the soles of your feet at anyone. Accidental contact with one's foot is always followed by an apology.

Indian English can be very formal and even ceremonious. Indian people may well call you "sir" or "madam", even "good lady" or "kind sir". At the same time, you should be aware that your English may seem rude to them. In particular, swearing is taken rather seriously in India, and casual use of the F-word is likely to shock.

Meeting people

Westerners have an ambiguous status in Indian eyes. In one way, you represent the rich sahib, whose culture dominates the world, and the old colonial mentality has not completely disappeared. On the other hand, as a non-Hindu, you are an outcaste, your presence in theory polluting to an orthodox or high-caste Hindu, while to members of all religions, your morals and your standards of spiritual and physical cleanliness are suspect.

As a traveller, you will constantly come across people who want to strike up a **conversation**. English not being their first language, they may not be familiar with the conventional ways of doing this, and thus their opening line may seem abrupt if at the same time very formal. "Excuse me good gentleman, what is your mother country?" is a typical one. It is also the first in a series of questions that Indian men seem sometimes to have learnt from a single book in order to ask Western tourists. Some of the questions may baffle at first ("What is your qualification?" "Are you in service?"), some may be queries about the ways of the West or the purpose of your trip, but mostly they will be about your family and your job.

You may find it odd or even intrusive that complete strangers should want to know that sort of thing, but these subjects are considered polite conversation between strangers in India, and help people place one another in terms of social position. Your family, job, even income, are not considered "personal" subjects, and it is completely normal to ask people about them. Asking the same questions back will not be taken amiss – far from it. Being curious does not have the "nosey" stigma in India that it has in the West.

Things that Indian people are likely to find strange about you are lack of religion (you could adopt one), travelling alone, leaving your family to come to India, being an unmarried couple (letting people think you are married can make life easier), and travelling second class or staying in cheap hotels when, as a tourist, you are relatively rich. You will probably end up having to explain the same things many times to many different people; on the other hand, you can ask questions too, so you could take it as an opportunity to ask things you want to know about India. English-speaking Indians and members of the large and growing middle class in particular are usually extremely well informed and well educated, and often far more *au fait* with world affairs than Westerners.

Shopping

So many beautiful and exotic souvenirs are on sale in India, at such low prices, that it's sometimes hard to know what to buy first. On top of that, all sorts of things (such as made-to-measure clothes) that would be vastly expensive at home are much more reasonably priced in India. Even if you lose weight during your trip, your baggage might well put on quite a bit – unless of course you post some of it home.

Where to shop

Quite a few items sold in tourist areas are made elsewhere and, needless to say, it's more fun (and cheaper) to pick them up at source. Best buys are noted in the relevant sections of the Guide, along with a few specialities that can't be found outside their regions. India is awash with **street hawkers**, often very young kids. Although they can be annoying and should be dealt with firmly if you are not interested, do not write them off completely as they sometimes have decent souvenirs at lower than shop prices and are open to hard bargaining.

Virtually all the state governments in India run handicraft "**emporia**", most with branches in the major cities such as Delhi, Mumbai, Chennai and Kolkata (Calcutta). There are also Central Cottage Industries Emporiums in Delhi, Chennai, Kolkata (Calcutta) and Mumbai. Goods in these places are generally of a high quality, even if their fixed prices are a little expensive, and they are worth a visit to get an idea of what crafts are available and how much they should cost.

Bargaining

Whatever you buy (except food and cigarettes), you will almost always be expected to **haggle** over the price. Bargaining is very much a matter of personal style, but should always be lighthearted, never acrimonious. There are no hard and fast rules – it's really a question of how much something is worth to you. It's a good plan, however, to have an idea of how much you want, or ought, to pay. "Green" tourists are easily spotted, so try and look like you know what you are up to, even on your first day, or leave it till later; you could wait and see what an Indian might pay first.

Don't worry too much about the first quoted prices. Some guidebooks suggest paying a third of the opening price, but it's a flexible guideline depending on the shop, the goods and the shopkeeper's impression of you. You may not be able to get the seller much below the first quote; on the other hand, you may end up paying as little as a tenth of it. If you bid too low, you may be hustled out of the shop for offering an "insulting" price, but this is all part of the game, and you'll no doubt be welcomed as an old friend if you return the next day.

Don't start haggling for something if you know you don't want it, and never let any figure pass your lips that you are not prepared to pay. It's like bidding at an auction. Having mentioned a price, you are obliged to pay it. If the seller asks you how much you would pay for something, and you don't want it, say so.

Sometimes rickshaw-wallahs and taxi drivers stop unasked in shops; they get a small commission simply for bringing customers. In places like Jaipur and Agra where this is common practice, tourists often strike a deal with their drivers – agreeing to stop at five shops and splitting the commission for the time wasted. If you're taken to a shop by a tout or driver and you buy something, you pay around fifty percent extra. Stand firm about not entering shops and getting to your destination if you have no appetite for such shenanigans.

Metalware and jewellery

Artisans have been casting **bronze statues** of Hindu gods for more than a thousand years. The images are produced by the lost-wax process, in which a model is first carved out of wax, then surrounded in clay, and finally fired. The wax melts to leave a terracotta mould. Small pieces can be cast from a single mould, but larger ones have to be assembled from up to a dozen pieces, the joins concealed by ornate ornamentation. The best-quality images will have carefully detailed fingers and eyes, and the metal should not have pits or spots. The south is one major area for them (dancing Shivas, known as Nataraj, are a favourite here – check out the quality in the palace art gallery at Thanjavur), the Himalayas another. Dokra, a speciality of West Bengal and Orissa, uses this very same lost-wax technique to produce charming figurines, often depicting animals.

Brass and copperware can be very finely worked, with trays, plates, ashtrays, cups and bowls among products available. The best trays – which should be forty years old or more – are from Varanasi. In the north, particularly in Rajasthan, enamel inlays (*meenakari*) are common. *Bidri* work, named after Bidar (Karnataka), where it originated, is a method of inlaying a gunmetal alloy with fine designs in brass or silver, then blackening the gunmetal with sal-ammoniac, to leave the inlay work shining. *Bidri* jewellery boxes, dishes and hookah pipes, among other things, are widely sold, especially in Karnataka and Andhra Pradesh; while the Orissan filigree *tarakashi* is worth looking out for. **Stainless steel** is less decorative and more workaday: thali sets and spice tins are among the possible buys, available throughout the country.

Among precious metals, silver is generally a better buy than **gold** but is difficult to distinguish from cheap white metal often palmed off in curio shops as silver. Gold is usually 22 carat and very yellow, but relatively expensive due to taxes (smuggling from the Gulf to evade them is rife) and to its popularity as a form of investment – women traditionally keep their wealth in this form, and a bride's jewellery is an important part of her dowry. **Silver** varies in quality, but is usually reasonably priced, with silver jewellery generally heavier and rather more folksy than gold. Rajasthan and Bengal are its main centres, and Tibetan silver jewellery is also popular. Gold and silver are usually sold by weight, the workmanship costing very little.

Buying **gemstones** can be something of a minefield; scams abound, and you would be most unwise to even consider buying gems for resale or as an investment without a basic knowledge of the trade. That said, some precious and semiprecious stones can be a good buy in India, particularly those which are indigenous, such as garnets, black stars and moonstones. Jaipur is a major centre for gems (and con tricks), while Hyderabad specializes in sorting pearls, which can therefore be picked up at low prices.

Woodwork, ceramics and stone

Wooden furniture, if a little heavy to carry with you, can be a real bargain, and is especially good in the mountainous areas of the north. Carvings of gods (often in sandalwood) are particularly common in the south, and those of elephants are always a favourite. Old wooden carvings from houses or temples that are being refurbished are usually available at reasonable prices, if sometimes a little weathered.

Terracotta figures are a speciality of Bengal and Bihar, but the finest **ceramic** work is the glazed pottery of Jaipur and Delhi. Brightly painted clay and plaster gods are another souvenir possibility, while marble and soapstone are both used for sculpture (though big pieces weigh a ton), and marble items inlaid in the style of the Taj Mahal are popular souvenirs in Agra. The stone carvings of Mahabalipuram prove excellent value for small pieces, which are all you will want to carry. Somewhat less weighty than these are papier-mâché items sold in Kashmiri shops that have sprung up around the country (most of which seem to get their supplies in Delhi).

Carpets and rugs

If you get dragged into a Kashmiri arts shop, chances are it's a **carpet** they really want to sell you. Kashmiri rugs are among the best in the world (up there with those from Iran) and, given a little caution and scepticism, you can get yourself a bargain in India (though you can also get shafted if you're not careful). A pukka Kashmiri carpet should have a label on the back stating that it is made in Kashmir, what it is made of (wool, silk, or "silk touch", the latter being wool combined with a little cotton and silk to give it a sheen), its size, density of knots per square inch (the more the better), and the name of the design. To tell if it really is silk, scrape the carpet with a knife and burn the fluff – real silk shrivels to nothing and has a distinctive smell. Even producing the knife should cause the seller of a bogus silk carpet to demur.

The best way to ensure a carpet reaches home is to take it away and post it yourself; a seller may offer to post it to you and bill you later, which is fair enough, but your carpet will be sent immediately, whatever you say (will someone be there to receive it?), and if you use a credit card, your account will also be billed immediately, whatever is said. Be aware of import tax being levied on arrival. Choose your shop carefully as there have been complaints of shipped carpets never arriving (or perhaps never having been shipped in the first place).

Dhurries (woven carpets or kilims), traditionally made of wool, are an older art form, and a less expensive one. UP is the main centre for these, particularly Agra and Mirzapur, but they are also made in Rajasthan, Gujarat, the Punjab, and Andhra Pradesh. Recent revelations have exposed the widespread use of child labour, especially in Mirzapur, but NGOs are proving successful in providing education and other basic facilities in the mills.

Tibetan rugs are available in areas with a large Tibetan community, such as Himachal Pradesh. Many foreigners prefer carpets in "tasteful" earthy colours, assuming them to be traditional and therefore "ethnic". In fact, Indian carpets traditionally come in bright colours, though the synthetic dyes used nowadays are of course newfangled.

Textiles and clothing

Textiles are so much a part of Indian culture that Gandhi wanted a spinning wheel put on the national flag. The kind of cloth he had in mind was the plain white homespun material worn by Nehru, whose hat, jacket and *dhoti* remain a mark of support for the Congress Party to this day. Homespun, handloom-woven hand-printed cloth is called **khadi**, and is sold in the government shops called Khadi Gramodyog that are found all over India. Methods of dyeing and printing this and other cloth vary from the tie-dyeing (*bandhani*) of Rajasthan to block printing and screen printing of calico (from Calicut – now Kozhikode – in Kerala) cotton, and of silk.

Saris are normally made of cotton for everyday use, although **silk** is used for special occasions, and quite common in the south. Western women are notoriously inept at wearing this most elegant of garments – it takes years of practice to carry one properly – but silk is usually a good buy in India, provided you make sure it is the real thing (the old test was to see whether it was possible to pull the whole garment straight through a wedding ring; however, some synthetics apparently go through too, so burn a thread and sniff it to be sure). Though Varanasi silk is world famous, the best nowadays comes from Kanchipuram and Madurai in Tamil Nadu; silk from Mysore is also prized but has recently had a bad press due to accusations concerning child labour.

Other popular fabrics include the heavy mirror-embroidered cloth of Rajasthan, Bengali *baluchari* brocade, and Indonesian-style ikat and batik from Orissa, Madhya Pradesh and Gujarat, while clothing to take home includes *lunghis* in the south (as much sheets as garments), thick Tibetan sweaters from Darjeeling, and *salwar kamise*, the elegant pyjama suits worn by Muslim women, with trousers (pyjamas) of various styles. Long loose shirts – preferably made of *khadi*, and known as *kurta* or *panjabi* – are practical in the heat of India, and traditionally worn, by men, with white pyjamas. Tourist shops sell versions in various fabrics and colours. Block-printed bedsheets, as well as being useful, make good wall-hangings, as do Punjabi *phulkari* (originally wedding sheets), but every region has its own fabrics and its own methods of colouring them and making them up – the choice is endless.

On top of this, with **tailoring** so cheap in India, you can choose the fabric you want, take it to a tailor, and have it made into whatever you fancy. For formal Western-style clothes, you'll want to see quite a posh tailor in a big city, but tailors in almost every village in the country can run you up a shirt or a pair of pyjama-type trousers in next to no time. Many tailors will also copy a garment you already have.

Paintings and antiques

Art and antiques are another field where only experts should look for an investment, but where a souvenir hunter is very likely to find a bargain. Silk and cotton paintings are popular in Rajasthan and the north, but vary vastly in quality, so check out a few before you buy. The village of Kishangarh (Rajasthan) is known for them; they are also sold in Udaipur. The striking black lines and primary colours depicting mythological and religious themes easily distinguish Madhubani paintings, also known as Mithila paintings after the district in Bihar where they are made; the folk art, which makes ideal gifts, first started as decoration on huts but is now marketed widely through emporia, using handmade paper.

Most Tibetan **thangkas** (Buddhist religious paintings mounted on brocaded silk) are mass produced (usually in Nepal) and modern, whatever the seller says, but even the cheapest boast the dense Buddhist symbolism inherent in the form. You'll find them in the north, where there are Tibetan communities, and a little investigation of the range of styles is well worthwhile.

Leaf skeleton paintings, originally from southern Kerala, are much cheaper and widely available, though they too vary somewhat in quality. **Miniatures** in the traditional style, often masquerading as antiques, are common in tourist shops too, but subject to the same provisos as *thangkas*.

When it comes to **antiques**, if they really are genuine – and, frankly, that is unlikely – you'll need a licence to export them, which is virtually impossible to get. The same applies to "art treasures". Age and status can be verified by the Archeological Survey of India, Janpath, New Delhi 110011 (☎011/2301 8614); Sion Fort, Sion, Mumbai 400022 (☎022/2407 1102); 4th floor, Block DF, Sector 1, Salt Lake City, Kolkata (Calcutta) 700064 (☎033/2334 3775); Fort St George, Chennai 600009 (☎044/2556 0397); Old Town, Bhubaneshwar 751002, Orissa (☎0674/243 0590); 5th floor, F Wing, Kendriya Sadan, 17th Main Rd, Keramangala, Bangalore 560034 (☎080/553 7348). These offices also issue export clearance certificates.

Miscellaneous

Of course, not everything typically Indian is old or traditional. **CDs, tapes or records** of classical, bhangra, *filmi* and Western music are very cheap and popular. **Videos** too are widely available; Tamil or Telugu films are more likely to be subtitled than Hindi ones.

Publishers thrive in India and **books** are excellent buys, whether by writers from India or the rest of the English-speaking world. International publishers market books in India at discounted prices and they are likely to be much cheaper than at home. Books printed and published in India tend to be not so well printed or bound, but there is a growing market for upmarket coffee-table books and old rare books. Hardback volumes of Indian sacred literature are particularly good value.

Leatherware can be very cheap and well-made, though the leather doesn't normally come from cows, of course. Rajasthani camel-hide *mojadi* slippers go down well, as do *chappal* (sandals) and the distinctive *kolhapuri* slippers, which need to be broken in; pointed *jootis*, popular around Delhi and the Punjab, also need some perseverance. Otherwise, buffalo-hide belts and bags can be very reasonable compared to similar items made of cowhide in the West; Chennai and Pondicherry are good places to go looking. Upmarket shops offer a range of good-quality leather goods, from handbags and briefcases to clothes at reasonable prices. Recent campaigns in the West have called for the boycotting of Indian leather goods due to poor treatment of animals.

Bamboo flutes are incredibly cheap, while other **musical instruments** such as tabla, sitar and sarod are heavy to carry and available in the West anyway, though usually of lower quality and higher price. The quality is crucial; there's no point going home with a sitar that is virtually untuneable, even if it does look nice. Students of music purchase their instruments from master craftsmen or established shops; get advice before you buy, and never buy one from a tourist shop.

Other possibilities include kitchen implements such as tiffin boxes, wind-up clockwork tin toys, film posters, tea (especially from Darjeeling, Assam and Nilgiri), coffee, spices, peacock feather fans (though these are considered unlucky), and anything which reminds you of India – which needn't be expensive or arty.

Things not to bring home include ivory and anything made from a rare or protected species, including snakeskin and turtle products. As for drugs – don't even think about it.

Women travellers

India is not a country that provides huge obstacles to women travellers, petty annoyances being more the order of the day. In the days of the Raj, upper-class eccentrics started a tradition of lone women travellers, taken up enthusiastically by the flower children of the hippy era. Women today still do it, but few get through their trip without any hassle, and it's good to prepare yourself to be a little thick-skinned.

Indian streets are almost without exception male-dominated – something that may take a bit of getting used to, particularly when you find yourself subjected to incessant staring, whistling and name calling. This can usually be stopped by ignoring the gaze and quickly moving on, or by firmly telling the offender to stop looking at you. Most of your fellow travellers on trains and buses will be men who may start up most unwelcome conversations about sex, divorce and the freedom of relationships in the West. These cannot often be avoided, but demonstrating too much enthusiasm to discuss such topics can lure men into thinking that you are easy about sex, and the situation could become threatening. At its worst in larger cities, all this can become very tiring. You can get round it to a certain extent by joining women in public places, and you'll notice an immense difference if you join up with a male travelling companion. In this case, expect Indian men to approach him (assumed, of course, to be your husband – an assumption it is sometimes advantageous to go along with) and talk to him about you quite happily as if you were not there. Beware, however, if you are (or look) Indian with a non-Indian male companion: this may well cause you harassment, as you might be seen to have brought shame on your family by adopting the loose morals of the West.

In addition to staring and suggestive comments and looks, **sexual harassment**, or "Eve teasing" as it is bizarrely known, is likely to be a nuisance, but not generally a threat. North Indian men are particularly renowned for their disregard of women's rights, and it is on the plains of Uttar Pradesh and Bihar that you are most likely to experience physical hassle. Expect to get groped in crowds, and to have men "accidentally" squeeze past you at any opportunity. It tends to be worse in cities than in small towns and villages, but anywhere being followed can be a real problem.

In time you'll learn to gauge a situation – sometimes wandering around on your own may attract so much unwanted attention that you may prefer to stay in one place until you've recharged your batteries or your male fan club has moved on. It's always best to dress modestly – a *salwar kamise* is perfect, as is any baggy clothing – and refrain from smoking and drinking in public, which only reinforces prejudices that Western women are "loose" and "easy".

Returning an unwanted touch with a punch or slap is perfectly in order (Indian women often become aggressive when offended), and does serve to vent a little frustration. It should also attract attention and urge someone to help you, or at least deal with the offending man – a man transgressing social norms is always out of line, and any passer-by will want to let him know it. If you feel someone getting too close in a crowd or on a bus, brandishing your left shoe in his face can be very effective.

To go and watch a Bollywood movie at the cinema is a fun and essential part of your trip to India, but unfortunately such an occasion is rarely without hassle. The crowd is predominantly male and mostly young at that. If you do go to the cinema, go with a group of people and/or sit in the balcony area – it's a bit more expensive but the crowd is much more sedate.

Violent sexual assaults on tourists are extremely rare, but the number of reported cases of rape is rising. Though no assault can be predicted, you can take precautions: avoid quiet, dimly lit streets and alleys at night; if you find a trustworthy rickshaw/taxi driver in the day keep him for the night journey; and try to get someone to accompany you to your hotel whenever possible. While Indian women are still quite timid about reporting rape – it is considered as much a disgrace to the victim as to the perpetrator – Western victims should always report it to the police, and before leaving the area try to let other tourists, or locals, know, in the hope that pressure from the community may uncover the offender and see him brought to justice. At present there's nowhere for tourists who've suffered sexual violence to go for sanctuary; most victims seek support from other travellers, or go home.

The **practicalities of travel** take on a new dimension for lone women travellers. Often you can turn your gender to your advantage. For example, on buses the driver and conductor will often take you under their wing, watch out for you and buy you chai at each stop, and there will be countless other instances of kindness wherever you travel. You'll also be more welcome in some private houses than a group of Western males, and may find yourself learning the finer points of Indian cooking round the family's clay stove. Women frequently get preference at bus and railway stations where they can join a separate "ladies' queue", and use ladies' waiting rooms. On overnight trains the enclosed ladies' compartments are peaceful havens (unless filled with noisy children); you could also try to share a berth section with a family where you are usually drawn into the security of the group and are less exposed to lusty gazes. In hotels watch out for "peep-holes" in your door (and in the common bathrooms), be sure to cover your window when changing and when sleeping, and avoid the sleazy permit-room hotels of the southern cities.

Lastly, bring your own supply of tampons, which are not widely available outside Indian cities.

Womens' organizations in India

All India Democratic Women's Association (AIDWA) 121 VP House, Rafi Marg, New Delhi 110001 ⓣ011/2371 0476 or 2331 9566, ⓦwww.aidwa.org. Women's organization committed to achieving democracy, equality and women's emancipation.

Centre for Women's Development Studies 5 Bhai Vir Singh Marg, New Delhi 110001, ⓣ011/2336 6930 or 011/2334 5530. Trains Santhal tribal women of Bankura, West Bengal, in collective and individual livelihood skills.

Forum against the Oppression of Women 29 Bhatia Bhawan, Babrekan Rd, Gokale Rd (North), Dadar, Mumbai 400028 ⓣ022/2422 2436. Support centre which also organizes workshops.

Indian Council of Social Science Research (ICSSR) 3 Feroze Shah Rd, New Delhi 110001 ⓣ011/2617 9838, ⓦwww.icssr.org. Organizes workshops and symposia on feminist themes and runs a women's studies programme.

Kali for Women B1/8 Hauz Khas Bagh, New Delhi, 110006 ⓣ011/2685 2530. Feminist publisher that produces a range of very readable books on the Indian women's movement.

SANHITA c/o Sanlaap, 89B Raja Basanta Roy Rd, Kolkata (Calcutta) 700029 ⓣ033/2466 2150 or 2216 1471. Very prominent association spearheading women's empowerment in eastern India.

Self-Employed Women's Association (SEWA) Textile Workers' Union Building, opposite Victoria gardens, Ahmedabad, Gujarat ⓦwww.sewa.org. Self-help union that helps rural women organize income-generating projects; see also p.634.

Streelekha (International Feminist Bookshop and Information Centre), 15/55, 1st floor, Cambridge, Jeevan Kendra Layout, Bangalore 560 008, Karnataka. Stocks books, journals and posters, and provides space for women to meet.

Gay and lesbian travellers

Homosexuality is not generally open or accepted in India. "Carnal intercourse against the order of nature" (anal intercourse) is a ten-year offence under article 377 of the penal code, while laws against "obscene behaviour" can be used to arrest gay men for cruising or liaising anywhere that could be considered a public place. The same law could in theory be used against lesbians.

The homosexual scene in India was brought into the spotlight in 1998 with the nationwide screening of the highly controversial film *Fire* by Deepa Mehta, about two sisters-in-law living together under the same roof who become lesbian lovers. Flying in the face of the traditional emphasis on heterosexual family life, the film created a storm and was banned in some states. Right-wing extremists attacked cinemas that showed it, and in the wake of the attacks, many gay men and lesbians came out into the open for the first time to hold candle-lit protest vigils in Delhi, Mumbai, Kolkata (Calcutta), Chennai and Bangalore – all cities known for their more open-minded younger generations.

For **lesbians**, making contacts is rather difficult; even the Indian women's movement does not readily promote lesbianism as an issue that needs confronting. The only public faces of a hidden scene are the organizations listed below and a few of the nationwide women's organizations (see above).

For **gay men**, homosexuality is no longer solely the preserve of the alternative scene of actors and artists, and is increasingly accepted by the middle-line urban middle and upper classes. If you keep your finger on the social pulse of the larger cities, especially Bangalore and Mumbai, you will soon discover which nightclubs and bars have a gay scene. Also, the organizations listed below can tell you about gay events and parties.

Bombay Dost (Rs50; Ⓦwww.bombaydost.com) is a quarterly with news, views and useful information on gay and lesbian issues. The magazine is available in Delhi at The People Tree; and in Mumbai at Danai Bookshop at Khar-Danda Road and at 105A Veena-Beena Shopping Centre.

Lesbian-Gay contacts and resources

Write in advance for information – most addresses are PO boxes:

Bombay Dost 105A Veena-Beena Shopping Centre, Bandra Station Rd, Bandra (West), Mumbai 400050, Ⓦwww.bombaydost.com. Publishes a newsletter and has contacts nationwide.

Gay Bombay Ⓦwww.gaybombay.org. Informal support, chat, background and guides to gay Mumbai.

Gay Info Centre c/o Owais, PO Box 1662, Secunderabad HPO 500003, Andhra Pradesh. Provides literature, contacts and resources on homosexuality in India.

Good As You 201 Samaraksha, 2nd Floor Royal Corner, 1–2 Lalbang Rd, Bangalore Ⓣ080/547 5571, Ⓦwww.geocities.com/goodasyoubangalore. Gay support group.

Humrahi Ⓦwww.geocities.com/WestHollywood/Heights/7258. Forum for gay men in New Delhi.

Humsafar Trust Ⓦwww.humsafar.org. Set up to promote safe sex among gay men, but the website has lots of links and up-to-date information.

Saathi PO Box 571, Putlibowli PO, Hyderabad, Andhra Pradesh. Gay support group.

Sangini Naz Foundation, PO Box 3910, Andrews Gunj, New Delhi 110049. Sangini is a group for women attracted to women with information, support, and to meet one another. Helpline Friday 6 to 8pm and Saturday 4 to 6pm at 011/2685 1970

Sappho Lesbian Support Group, C/o A.N, PO Box No. EC-35, Kolkata 700010, Ⓔmalvi99@hotmail.com. A collective of lesbian and bisexual women, established in 1999 and still going strong.

Shakhi PO Box 3526, Lajpat Nagar, New Delhi 110065. Lesbian guesthouse and resource centre.

The Counsel Club PO Bag 10237, Kolkata (Calcutta) 700016. India's first support group for lesbians, gay men, bisexuals and transsexuals.

Disabled travellers

Disability is common in India; many conditions that would be curable in the West, such as cataracts, are permanent disabilities here because people can't afford the treatment. Disabled people are unlikely to get jobs (though there is a famous blind barber in Delhi), and the choice is usually between staying at home being looked after by your family, and going out on the street to beg for alms.

For the **disabled traveller**, this has its advantages: disability doesn't get the same embarrassed reaction from Indian people that it does from some able-bodied Westerners. On the other hand, you'll be lucky to see a state-of-the-art wheelchair or a disabled loo (major airports usually have both, though the loo may not be in a useable state), and the streets are full of all sorts of obstacles that would be hard for a blind or wheelchair-bound tourist to negotiate independently. Kerbs are often high, pavements uneven and littered, and ramps nonexistent. There are potholes all over the place and open sewers. Some of the more expensive hotels have ramps for the movement of luggage and equipment, but if that makes them accessible to wheelchairs, it is by accident rather than design.

If you walk with difficulty, you will find India's many street obstacles and steep stairs hard going. Another factor that can be a problem is the constant barrage of people proffering things (hard to wave aside if you are, for instance, on crutches), and all that queuing, not to mention heat, will take it out of you if you have a condition that makes you tire quickly. A light, folding camp-stool is one thing that could be invaluable if you have limited walking or standing power.

Then again, Indian people are likely to be very helpful if, for example, you need their help getting on and off buses or up stairs. Taxis and rickshaws are easily affordable and very adaptable; if you rent one for a day, the driver is certain to help you on and off, and perhaps even around the sites you visit. If you employ a guide, they may also be prepared to help you with steps and obstacles.

If complete independence is out of the question, going with an able-bodied companion might be on the cards. Contact one of the specialist organizations listed below for further advice on planning your trip. Otherwise, some package tour operators try to cater for travellers with disabilities – Bales and Somak among them – but you should always contact any operator and discuss your exact needs with them before making a booking. You should also make sure you are covered by any insurance policy you take out.

Contacts for disabled travellers

Britain and Ireland

Irish Wheelchair Association Blackheath Drive, Clontarf, Dublin 3 ⓣ01/818 6400, ⓦwww.iwa.ie. Useful information provided about travelling abroad with a wheelchair.
RADAR (Royal Association for Disability and Rehabilitation) 12 City Forum, 250 City Rd, London EC1V 8AF ⓣ020/7250 3222, minicom ⓣ020/7250 4119, ⓦwww.radar.org.uk. A good source of advice on holidays and travel
Tripscope The Vasapll Centre, Gill Ave, Bristol BS16 2QQ, ⓣ08457/7585641 ⓦwww.tripscope.org.uk. This registered charity provides a national telephone information service offering free advice on UK and international transport for those with a mobility problem.

US and Canada

Access-Able ⓦwww.access-able.com. Online resource for travellers with disabilities.
Directions Unlimited 123 Green Lane, Bedford Hills, NY 10507 ⓣ1-800/533-5343 or 914/241-1700. Travel agency specializing in bookings for people with disabilities.
Mobility International USA 45 W Broadway, Eugene, OR 97401 ⓣ541/343-1284, ⓦwww.miusa.org. Information and referral services, access guides, tours and exchange programmes. Annual membership $35 (includes quarterly newsletter).
Society for the Advancement of Travelers with Handicaps (SATH) 347 5th Ave, New York, NY 10016 ⓣ212/447-7284, ⓦwww.sath.org. Non-profit educational organization that has actively represented travellers with disabilities since 1976.
Wheels Up! ⓣ1-888/38-WHEELS, ⓦwww.wheelsup.com. Provides discounted airfare, tour and cruise prices for disabled travellers, and publishes a free monthly newsletter. Comprehensive website.

Australia and New Zealand

ACROD (Australian Council for Rehabilitation of the Disabled) PO Box 60, Curtin ACT 2605; Suite 103, 1st floor, 1–5 Commercial Rd, Kings Grove 2208; ⓣ02/6282 4333, TTY ⓣ02/6282 4333, ⓦwww.acrod.org.au. Provides lists of travel agencies and tour operators for people with disabilities.
Disabled Persons Assembly 4/173–175 Victoria St, Wellington, New Zealand ⓣ04/801 9100 (also TTY), ⓦwww.dpa.org.nz. Resource centre with lists of travel agencies and tour operators for people with disabilities.

India

India Rehabilitation Co-ordination A–2 Rasadhara Co-operation Housing Society, 385 SVP Rd, Mumbai 400004 ⓣ040/2402 2143.
Timeless Excursions 9 Bhikaji Cama Place, New Delhi ⓣ011/2616 1198, ⓦwww.timelessexcursions.com.

Travelling with children

Travelling with kids can be both challenging and rewarding. Indians are very tolerant of children so you can take them almost anywhere without restriction, and they always help break the ice with strangers.

However the main problem with children, especially small children, is their extra vulnerability. Even more than their parents, they need protection from the sun, unsafe drinking water, heat and unfamiliar food. All that chilli in particular may be a problem, even with older kids, if they're not used to it. Remember too, that diarrhoea, perhaps just a nuisance to you, could be dangerous for a child: rehydration salts (see p.46) are vital if your child goes down with it. Make sure too, if possible, that your child is aware of the dangers of rabies; keep children away from animals, and consider a rabies jab.

For babies, **nappies** (diapers) are available in most large towns at similar prices to the West, but it's worth taking an additional pack in case of emergencies, and bringing sachets of Baby Calpol, which aren't available easily in India. A changing mat is another necessity. And if your baby is on powdered milk, it might be an idea to bring some of that: you can certainly get it in India, but it may not taste the same. Dried baby food could also be worth taking – any café or chai-wallah should be able to supply you with boiled water.

For touring, hiking or walking, child-carrier backpacks are ideal; some even come with mosquito nets these days. When it comes to **luggage**, bring as little as possible so you can manage the kids more easily. If your child is small enough, a fold-up buggy is also well worth packing, even if you no longer use a buggy at home, as kids tire so easily in the heat. If you want to cut down on long journeys by flying, remember that children under 2 travel for ten percent of the adult fare, and under-12s for half price.

For a lively account of a successful trip to India with kids in tow, complete with advice on packing and other essentials, go to ⓦtravel.guardian.co.uk/activities/family/story/0,7447,511603,00.html.

Voluntary organizations

While in India, you may consider doing some voluntary charitable work. Several charities welcome volunteers on a medium-term commitment, say over two months.

If you do want to spend your time working for an **NGO (Non-Government (voluntary) Organization)**, you should make arrangements well before you arrive by contacting the body in question, rather than on spec. Special visas are generally not required unless you intend to work for longer than six-months.

Voluntary work resources

The following organizations provide useful resources:

Charities Aid Foundation (CAF) Kings Hill, West Malling, Kent ME19 4TA, UK ⓣ01732/520000, ⓦwww.cafonline.org/cafindia/i_search.cfm. CAF is a gateway to the contact details and objectives of 2350 voluntary organizations in India.

India Development Information Network The British Council, 17 Kasturba Gandhi Marg, New Delhi 110 001 ⓣ011/2371 1401, ⓦwww.indev.org. INDEV is another huge databank, accessed through their website, with over 1000 Indian NGOs.

Peace Corps of America ⓣ1-800/424 8580, ⓦwww.peacecorps.gov. The US-government sponsored aid and voluntary organization, with projects all over the world.

Voluntary Service Overseas (VSO), 317 Putney Bridge Road, London SW15 2PN, UK ⓣ020/8780 7200, ⓦwww.vso.org.uk. A British government-funded organization that places volunteers on various projects around the world and in India.

Voluntary Service Overseas (VSO) ⓦwww.vsocanada.org. Canada 806-151 Slater Street, Ottawa ON K1P 5H3 Canada (ⓣ1-888-VSO-2911 (1-888-876-2911). Canadian-based organization affiliated to the British VSO.

Charities

Here are just some of the charities that accept voluntary workers:

Denjong Padma Choeling Academy c/o Sonam Yongda, Pemayengtse Gompa, West Sikkim 737113 ⓣ03595/50760 or 50141. The academy, with around 200 orphans and destitute children, relies on donations and welcomes voluntary teachers. Sikkim is a restricted area, so you will have to make arrangements with the academy to get a special permit.

The Farm Project International Society for Ecology and Culture (ISEC), Apple Barn, Week, Totnes, Devon TQ9 6JP, UK ⓣ01803/868650, ⓦwww.isec.org.uk The Farm Project is part of the Ladakhi Women's Alliance and set up by ISEC to help promote the rehabilitation of traditional Ladakhi agriculture. The project uses volunteers on two- to three-month agricultural projects; experience helps but is not a prerequisite.

The Missionaries of Charity International Committee of Co-Workers, 41 Villiers Rd, Southall Middlesex UB1 3BS, UK ⓣ020/8574 1892; or the Mother House, 54A AJC Bose (Lower Circular) Rd, Kolkata (Calcutta). Mother Teresa's Missionaries of Charity has numerous charitable institutions throughout India, some of which use casual volunteers. Contact the International Committee of Co-Workers to find out more.

SECMOL (Students' Educational and Cultural Movement of Ladakh), Leh, Ladakh ⓣ01982/52421, ⓦwww.secmol.org. SECMOL was set up to protect Ladakh's culture against the detrimental effects of modernization and strives to increase awareness of developmental issues amongst the young. Qualified English teachers are welcome, especially during their summer schools.

SOS Children's Villages of India A-7 Nizamuddin (West), New Delhi 110 013 ⓣ0111/2435 5835, ⓦwww.soscvindia.org. SOS has 32 villages and numerous allied projects in different parts of India, including Karnataka and Rajasthan, giving shelter to distressed children by providing a healthy environment and education including vocational training. Volunteers are welcomed at some of their centres – contact them first.

Directory

Cigarettes Indian cigarettes, such as Wills, Gold Flake, Four Square and Charms, are OK once you get used to them, and hardly break the bank (Rs10–30 per pack), but if you find them too rough, stock up on imported brands such as Marlboro and Benson and Hedges, or some rolling tobacco, available in the bigger towns and cities. One of the great smells of India is the *beedi*, the cheapest smoke, made of a single low-grade tobacco leaf. If you smoke roll-ups, stock up on good papers as Indian Capstan cigarette papers are thick and don't stick very well, and Rizlas, where available, are pretty costly.

Duty free allowance Anyone over 17 can bring in one US quart (0.95 litre – but nobody's going to quibble about the other 5ml) of spirits, or a bottle of wine and 250ml spirits; plus 200 cigarettes, or 50 cigars, or 250g tobacco. You may be required to register anything valuable on a tourist baggage re-export form to make sure you can take it home

Things to take

Most things are easy to find in India and cheaper than at home, but here is a list of **useful items** worth bringing with you bearing in mind that your bags should not get too heavy:

- ❒ A padlock and chain (to lock rooms in budget hotels, and attach your bag to train fittings); cheaper in India, of course, but you may need one on your first night.
- ❒ A universal sink plug (few sinks or bathtubs have them)
- ❒ A mosquito net; a double one with a central hanging point, impregnated with DEET-based insect repellent, is best.
- ❒ A pillowcase
- ❒ A small flashlight and spare bulbs
- ❒ Earplugs (for street noise in hotel rooms and music on buses)
- ❒ High-factor sunblock (difficult to find in India)
- ❒ A pocket alarm clock (also cheaper in India).
- ❒ A multipurpose penknife
- ❒ A needle and some thread (but dental floss is better than cotton for holding baggage together)
- ❒ Plastic bags (to sort your baggage, make it easier to pack and unpack, and keep out damp and dust)
- ❒ A small umbrella (available in Indian cities)
- ❒ Tampons
- ❒ Condoms
- ❒ Multi-vitamin and mineral tablets

with you, and to fill in a currency declaration form if carrying more than $10,000 or the equivalent. There is a market for duty free spirits in big cities: small retailers are the best people to approach.

Electricity Generally 220V 50Hz AC, though direct current supplies also exist, so check before plugging in. Most sockets are triple round-pin (accepting European-size double round-pin plugs). British, Irish and Australasian plugs will need an adaptor, preferably universal; American and Canadian appliances will need a transformer too, unless multi-voltage. Power cuts and voltage variations are very common; voltage stabilizers should be used to run sensitive appliances such as laptops.

Initials and acronyms Widely used in Indian English. Thus, the former Prime Minister, Vishwa Pratap Singh, was always "VP", and many middle-class Indian men bear similar monikers. The United Provinces, renamed Uttar Pradesh after independence, have always been UP. More recently, and less universally, Himachal Pradesh is HP, Madhya Pradesh MP, and Andhra Pradesh (not Arunchal Pradesh) AP. State and national organizations such as ITDC, RTDC and so on are always known by their acronyms. MG Road means Mahatma Gandhi Road, CST Terminus in Mumbai is Chhatrapathi Shivaji Terminus, and the only reason Kolkata (Calcutta) has come to accept the new name for Dalhousie Square is because they can call it BBD Bagh (that's Benoy Badal Dinesh).

Laundry In India, no one goes to the laundry: if they don't do their own, they send it out to a *dhobi*-wallah. Wherever you are staying, there will either be an in-house *dhobi*-wallah, or one very close by to call on. The *dhobi*-wallah will take your dirty washing to a *dhobi ghat*, a public clothes-washing area (the bank of a river for example), where it is shown some old-fashioned discipline: separated, soaped and given a damn good thrashing to beat the dirt out of it. Then it is hung out to dry in the sun and, once dried, taken to the ironing sheds where every garment is endowed with razor-sharp creases and then matched to its rightful owner by hidden cryptic markings. Your clothes will come back from the *dhobi*-wallah absolutely spotless, though this kind of violent treatment does take it out of them: buttons get lost and eventually the cloth starts to fray. If you'd rather not entrust your Savile Row made-to-measure to their tender mercies, there are dry-cleaners in large towns.

Name changes There is a growing politically motivated trend to rename some of the major Indian cities and towns to eradicate anglicized spellings and names. In the 1990s, Bombay became Mumbai, Madras became Chennai, Poona became Pune, Shimla became Simla and Banaras became Varanasi. In the latest major name change, which came into effect in early 2001, Calcutta became Kolkata.

Numbers A hundred thousand is a *lakh* (written 1,00,000); ten million is a *crore* (1,00,00,000). Millions, billions and the like are not in common use.

Opening hours Standard shop opening hours in India are Mon–Sat 9.30am–6pm. Most big stores, at any rate, keep those hours, while smaller shops vary from town to town, religion to religion, and one to another, but usually keep longer hours. Government tourist offices are open Mon–Fri 9.30am–5pm, Sat 9.30am–1pm, closed on the third Sat of the month, and occasionally also the second Sat of the month; state-run tourist offices are likely to be open Mon–Fri 10am–5pm.

Photography Beware of pointing your camera at anything that might be considered "strategic", including airports and anything military, but even at bridges, railway stations and main roads. Remember too that some people prefer not to be photographed, so it is wise to ask before you take a snapshot of them. More likely, you'll get people, especially kids, volunteering to pose. Camera film, sold at average Western prices, is widely available in India (but check the date on the box, and note that false boxes containing outdated film are often sold – Konica have started painting holograms on their boxes to prevent this). It's fairly easy to get films developed, though they don't always come out as well as they might at home; Konica and Kodak film laboratories are usually of a good standard. If you're after slide film, slow film or fast film, buy it in the big cities, and don't expect to find specialist brands such as Velvia; it is rare to find a dealer who keeps film refrigerated. Also, remember to guard your equipment from dust – reliable repair is extremely hard to come by in India.

Time India is all in one time zone: GMT+5hr 30min. This makes it 5hr 30min ahead of London, 10hr 30min ahead of New York, 13hr 30min ahead of LA, 4hr 30min behind Sydney and 6hr 30min behind NZ; however, summer time in those places will vary the difference by an hour. Indian time is referred to as IST (Indian Standard Time, which cynics refer to as "Indian stretchable time").

Toilets A visit to the loo is not one of India's more pleasant experiences: toilets can be filthy and stink. They are also major potential breeding grounds for disease. And then there is the squatting position to get used to; the traditional Asian toilet has a hole in the ground and two small platforms for the feet, instead of a seat. Paper, if used, often goes in a bucket next to the loo rather than down it. Indians use instead a jug of water and their left hand, a method you may also come to prefer, but if you do use paper, keep some handy – it isn't usually supplied, and it might be an idea to stock up before going too far off the beaten track as it is not available everywhere. Travelling is especially difficult for women as facilities are limited or nonexistent, especially when travelling by road. However, toilets in the a/c carriages of trains are usually kept clean, as are those in mid-range and a/c restaurants. In the touristy areas, most hotels offer Western-style loos, even in budget lodges. The latest development is tourist toilets at every major historical site. They cost Rs2 and you get water, mirrors, toilet paper and a clean sit-down loo.

Guide

Guide

CHAPTER 1 Highlights

* **Rajpath** The centrepiece of Lutyens's imperial New Delhi, this wide boulevard epitomizes the spirit of the British Raj. See p.126

* **Paharganj Bazaars** Frenetic market and hotel district opposite New Delhi railway station. See p.129

* **National Museum** The country's finest museum, with exhibits from over 5000 years of Indian culture. See p.130

* **Red Fort** Delhi's most famous monument, this imposing sandstone fort is a ghostly vestige of Moghul splendour. See p.133

* **Jama Masjid** Shah Jahan's great mosque, with huge minarets offering birds' eye views over the old city. See p.134

* **Hazrat Nizamuddin** A Sufi shrine in a deeply traditional Muslim quarter, where hypnotic *qawwali* music is performed every Thursday. See p.138

* **Humayun's Tomb** An elegant red-brick forerunner of the Taj Mahal, whose lovely gardens offer an escape from the heat. See p.139

* **Qutb Minar** The ruins of this twelfth-century city are dominated by the Qutb Minar or Victory Tower. See p.142

△ Street scene, Old Delhi

Delhi

Delhi is the symbol of old India and new . . . even the stones here whisper to our ears of the ages of long ago and the air we breathe is full of the dust and fragrances of the past, as also of the fresh and piercing winds of the present.

Jawaharlal Nehru

On first impressions, **DELHI**, with its jam-packed streets, tower blocks and temples, forts, mosques and colonial mansions, can be both disorienting and fascinating. It certainly takes a while to find your feet, as you attempt to weave a path through buses, trucks, nippy cars, mopeds, rickshaws, cows, bullock carts, hand-pulled trolleys and even the occasional elephant being ridden along with the flow of traffic. You'll find unlikely juxtapositions are everywhere you look: suit-and-tie businessmen rub shoulders with traditionally dressed orthodox Hindus and Muslims; groups of young Delhi-wallahs pile into glitzy bars and discos while turbaned snake charmers tease hypnotizing moans out of curved pipes; pundits pontificate while *sadhus* smoke their *chillums*; and ragged beggars clutching dusty children plead for a little help towards a meal.

Delhi's daunting scale becomes more manageable as you start to appreciate that, geographically as well as historically, it consists of seven successive cities, with British-built New Delhi making an eighth. Home to a crore of people (ten million, that is), it's big and, due partly to a tremendous economic boom, it's growing, but tucked away inside its modern suburbs and developments you'll stumble across tombs, temples and ruins that date back centuries; in some cases, the remains of whole cities from the distant past sit happily amid homes and highways built in the last decade or two, if that. The result is a city full of fascinating nooks and crannies that you could happily spend weeks or even months exploring.

From a tourist's point of view, Delhi divides into two main parts. **Old Delhi** is the city of the Moghuls, created by Shah Jahan and dating back to the seventeenth century. It's the capital's most frenetic quarter, and its most Islamic, a reminder that for more than seven hundred years Delhi was a Muslim city, ruled by Muslim sultans, with a mixed but predominantly Muslim population. While many of the buildings that enclose Old Delhi's teeming bazaars have a tale to tell, its greatest monuments are undoubtedly the magnificent constructions of the Moghuls, most especially the mighty **Red Fort**, and the **Jama Masjid**, India's largest and most impressive mosque.

To the south, encompassing the modern city centre, is **New Delhi**, built by the British to be the capital of their empire's key possession. A city of tree-lined

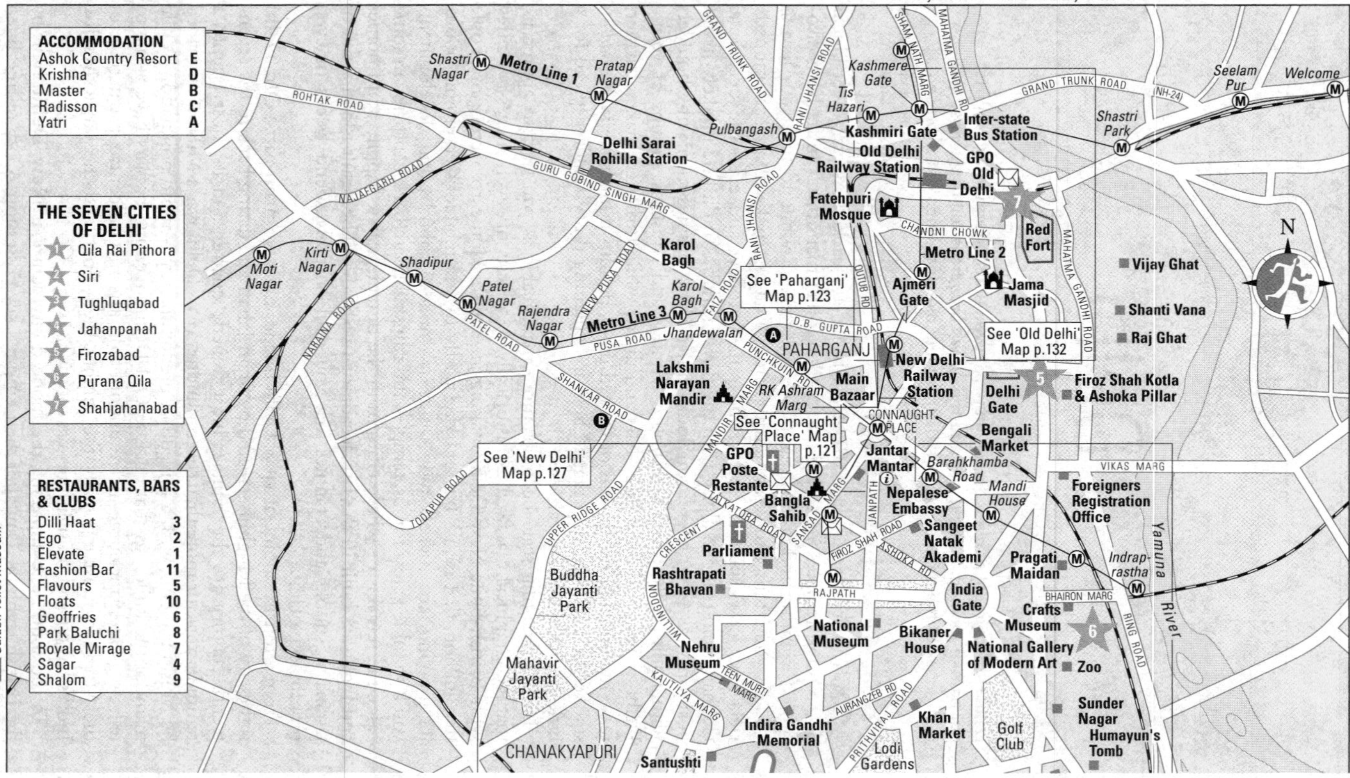
Majnu Ka Tilla Tibetan colony & hotels
Anand Vihar ISBT
Noida & 1
Sulabh Toilet Museum
ACCOMMODATION
Ashok Country Resort E
Krishna D
Master B
Radisson C
Yatri A
THE SEVEN CITIES OF DELHI
1 Qila Rai Pithora
2 Siri
3 Tughluqabad
4 Jahanpanah
5 Firozabad
6 Purana Qila
7 Shahjahanabad
RESTAURANTS, BARS & CLUBS
Dilli Haat 3
Ego 2
Elevate 1
Fashion Bar 11
Flavours 5
Floats 10
Geoffries 6
Park Baluchi 8
Royale Mirage 7
Sagar 4
Shalom 9
See 'Paharganj' Map p.123
See 'Old Delhi' Map p.132
See 'Connaught Place' Map p.121
See 'New Delhi' Map p.127
Metro Line 1
Metro Line 2
Metro Line 3
Shastri Nagar
Pratap Nagar
Pulbangash
Tis Hazari
Kashmere Gate
Kashmiri Gate
Inter-state Bus Station
Shastri Park
Seelam Pur
Welcome
Delhi Sarai Rohilla Station
Old Delhi Railway Station
GPO
Old Delhi
Red Fort
Fatehpuri Mosque
Chandni Chowk
Jama Masjid
Ajmeri Gate
Karol Bagh
Kirti Nagar
Moti Nagar
Shadipur
Patel Nagar
Rajendra Nagar
Jhandewalan
Paharganj
New Delhi Railway Station
Main Bazaar
Lakshmi Narayan Mandir
RK Ashram Marg
Connaught Place
Jantar Mantar
Barahkhamba Road
Mandi House
Delhi Gate
Bengali Market
Firoz Shah Kotla & Ashoka Pillar
Vijay Ghat
Shanti Vana
Raj Ghat
GPO Poste Restante
Bangla Sahib
Nepalese Embassy
Sangeet Natak Akademi
Pragati Maidan
Indraprastha
Foreigners Registration Office
Yamuna River
Parliament
Rashtrapati Bhavan
India Gate
Crafts Museum
National Museum
Bikaner House
National Gallery of Modern Art
Zoo
Nehru Museum
Buddha Jayanti Park
Mahavir Jayanti Park
Chanakyapuri
Santushti
Indira Gandhi Memorial
Khan Market
Lodi Gardens
Golf Club
Sunder Nagar
Humayun's Tomb
Rohtak Road
Grand Trunk Road (NH-24)
Sham Nath Marg
Mahatma Gandhi Road
Rani Jhansi Road
Guru Gobind Singh Marg
Najafgarh Road
New Pusa Road
Faiz Road
Qutub Rd
D.B. Gupta Road
Pusa Road
Patel Road
Naraina Road
Shankar Road
Punchkuin Rd
Mandir Marg
Todapur Road
Upper Ridge Road
Crescent
Talkatora Road
Sansad Marg
Janpath
Firoz Shah Road
Ashoka Rd
Rajpath
Willingdon
Teen Murti Marg
Kautilya Marg
Aurangzeb Rd
Prithviraj Road
Vikas Marg
Bhairon Marg
Ring Road

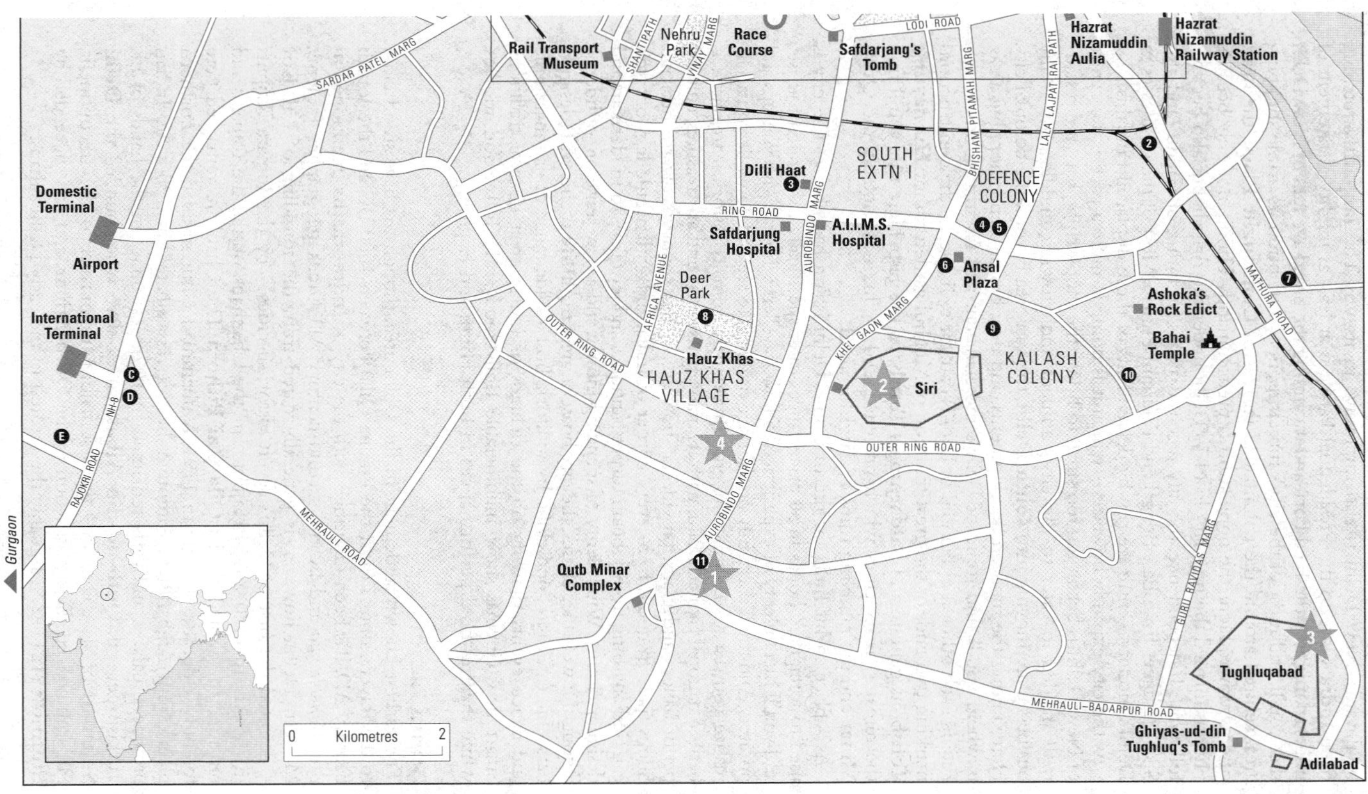
Rail Transport Museum
Nehru Park
Race Course
Safdarjang's Tomb
Hazrat Nizamuddin Aulia
Hazrat Nizamuddin Railway Station
LODI ROAD
SARDAR PATEL MARG
SHANTIPATH
VINAY MARG
SOUTH EXTN I
Dilli Haat
DEFENCE COLONY
BHISHAM PITAMAH MARG
LALA LAJPAT RAI PATH
RING ROAD
Domestic Terminal
Airport
Safdarjung Hospital
A.I.I.M.S. Hospital
AUROBINDO MARG
Ansal Plaza
MATHURA ROAD
Deer Park
AFRICA AVENUE
Ashoka's Rock Edict
International Terminal
Bahai Temple
KHEL GAON MARG
OUTER RING ROAD
Hauz Khas
KAILASH COLONY
HAUZ KHAS VILLAGE
Siri
NH-8
RAJOKRI ROAD
MEHRAULI ROAD
Gurgaon
GURU RAVIDAS MARG
Qutb Minar Complex
Tughluqabad
MEHRAULI–BADARPUR ROAD
0 Kilometres 2
Ghiyas-ud-din Tughluq's Tomb
Adilabad

boulevards, New Delhi is also impressive in its way. The **Janpath**, stretching from **India Gate** to the Presidential Palace is at least as mighty a statement of imperial might as the Red Fort, and it's among the broad avenues of New Delhi that you'll find most of the city's museums, not to mention its prime shopping area, centred around the colonnaded facades of **Connaught Place**, the heart of downtown. Here, the population is predominantly Hindu, not only because Hindus formed the majority in New Delhi under the British, but also because, following Independence, the city received a massive influx of Hindu (and also Sikh) refugees from East Bengal and Pakistani Punjab. Most of the businesses in Delhi's modern centre are run by descendants of those displaced Punjabis.

As the city expands, however – which it is doing at quite a pace – the centre of New Delhi is becoming too small to house the shops, clubs, bars and restaurants needed to cater to the city's affluent and growing middle class. Many businesses are moving into **south Delhi**, the vast area beyond the colonial city. Here, among the modern developments, and new business and shopping areas, is where you'll find some of Delhi's most ancient and fascinating attractions. Facing each other at either end of Lodi Road, for example, lie the constructions marking two ends of the great tradition of Moghul garden tombs: **Humayun's Tomb**, its genesis, and **Safdarjung's Tomb**, its last gasp. Here too, you'll find the remains of six cities which preceded Old Delhi, most notably the **Qutb Minar** and the rambling ruins of **Tughluqabad**.

As a place to hit India for the first time, Delhi isn't a bad choice. The city is used to foreigners: hotels in all price ranges cater specifically for foreign tourists, and you'll meet plenty of experienced fellow travellers who can give you tips and pointers. And there's certainly no shortage of things to see and do while you acclimatize yourself to the subcontinent. Quite apart from its historical treasures, as befits a national capital, Delhi, with its many **museums** and art treasures, cultural performances and crafts, provides a showcase of the country's diverse heritage. Shops trade in goods from every corner of India, and with a little legwork you can find anything from Tibetan carpets, antiques and jewellery to modern art and designer clothes. With plenty of spending money and a new sense of confidence among the wealthier classes, the city boasts a great **nightlife** scene, with designer bars, chic cafés and good clubs. Its auditoria host a wide range of national music and dance events, drawing on the richness of India's great classical traditions. Smart new cinemas show innumerable Bollywood and Hollywood movies, while theatres hold performances in both Hindi and English.

Some history

The earliest known settlement in the Delhi area, thought to have stood close to the River Yamuna (near the Purana Qila) between 1000 BC and the fourth century AD, has been identified with the city of **Indraprastha**, mentioned in the *Mahabharata* and by the second-century AD Greek geographer Ptolemy. Modern Delhi, however, is generally dated from the founding of **Lal Kot** – counted the first of Delhi's seven historical cities – by the Tomara Rajputs in 736 AD. In 1180, a rival Rajput clan, the Chauhans, ousted the Tomaras and renamed the walled citadel **Qila Rai Pithora**. The Chauhans remained here for only a decade, though; in 1191, Muhammad Ghur invaded the northern plains from Afghanistan. Although he was assassinated in 1206, his Indian provinces, palaces and forts remained more or less intact in the hands of his Turkish general, **Qutb-ud-din Aibak**, an ex-slave who founded the **Delhi Sultanate** or Slave Dynasty – the first major Muslim rulers of the subcontinent. He commenced the construction of the **Qutb Minar**, and was succeeded by **Iltutmish** (1211–27), arguably the greatest of the early Delhi sultans.

In 1290, another group of Turks, the **Khaljis**, came to power, extending their dominion to the Deccan plateau of central India. Under their most illustrious king, **Ala-ud-din Khalji** (1296–1316), **Siri**, the second city of Delhi, was built in 1303 – a flourishing commercial centre of characteristically ornate marble and red sandstone.

Ghiyas-ud-din Tughluq built Delhi's third city, a fortress, at **Tughluqabad**, 8km east of Qutb. It was occupied for just five years from 1321, when the capital was shifted 1100km south to Daulatabad in Maharashtra at great human cost. Water scarcity drove the Tughluqs back to Delhi in 1327, and the fourth new city, **Jahanpanah**, was built. The energies of the next sultan, Firoz Shah, were taken up with suppressing rebellion, as the Sultanate began to disintegrate, but he left his mark by moving the Ashokan pillars of Meerut and Topra to the new capital, the fifth city of **Firozabad**, built beside the river in 1354.

The Tughluq line came to an end in 1398, when Timur (Tamerlane), a Central Asian Turk, invaded Delhi. His successors, the **Sayyids** (1414–44), were in turn ousted by **Buhlul Lodi** who established a dynasty that left behind the fine tombs and mosques still to be seen in the beautiful Lodi Gardens. The Lodi dynasty ended when Sultan Ibrahim Lodi died in battle, fighting the brilliant and enigmatic **Babur** (a descendent of Genghis Khan) in 1526. Babur's victory marked the dawn of the Moghul (a derivative of Mongol) dynasty, whose lengthy sojourn in power led to the eventual realization of the dream of an Indian empire that had so eluded the earlier Delhi Sultans.

Babur was succeeded in 1530 by his son, **Humayun** who, in 1540, was pushed back to Persia by the Afghan king **Sher Shah** of Ser, and remained in exile there for fifteen years. King Sher Shah built the Din-Panah fort at Shergarh, which became Delhi's sixth capital, known today as **Purana Qila**. Humayun retook Delhi in 1555, but died the following year and was succeeded by his son **Akbar**, who then moved the capital to Agra. However, it was under **Shah Jahan** ("Ruler of the Universe"), that Delhi again became a magnificent imperial capital following the move of the court back here from Agra. Behind the ramparts of Delhi's seventh city, the walled city of **Shahjahanabad**, the mighty Red Fort, with its opulent palaces, and vast Jama Masjid, India's greatest mosque, rose to become the epitome of Moghul power. Shah Jahan was eventually deposed and imprisoned by his ruthless son, **Aurangzeb**, who ruled from Delhi until 1681, and then transferred the capital to the Deccan plateau.

Following the death of Aurangzeb in 1707, the city fell victim to successive invasions. In 1739, Nadir Shah, the emperor of Persia, sacked the city and salughtered an estimated 15,000 of its inhabitants. The massacre hastened the demise of Moghuls, who by the end of the eighteenth century had been reduced by successive marauders – Jats, Hindu Marathas and Afghans – to puppet kings presiding over decaying palaces. By the time the **British** (who had already established toeholds in Calcutta, Madras and Bombay) appeared on the scene in 1803, Delhi was a remote outpost of a spent empire, at the mercy of lawless tribes. The British swiftly took control, leaving the Moghul ruler, **Bahadur Shah**, with his palace and his pension, but no power. British forces fended off a number of Maratha attacks in the next decade, and faced determined opposition during 1857 when the city strongly supported the **Mutiny** (or First War of Independence – see p.1379), forcibly evicting the British, killing many of them, and proclaiming Bahadur Shah Hindustani emperor in the Red Fort. When the British finally recaptured the city, after a long siege, they went on a rampage of destruction, desecrating mosques and executing some three thousand people in bloody **reprisals** for the uprising. Bahadur Shah was sent off to exile in Burma, his family shot, and the city's entire population turfed out, the Muslims not allowed to return for two years.

After abolishing "John Company" (as the East India Company was known), following the Mutiny, the British, in their new incarnation as the **Raj**, at first kept their administration in Calcutta, but when George V came to India for his coronation as emperor in 1911, they decided to make Delhi India's new **capital**. Fervent construction of bungalows, parliamentary buildings and public offices followed, and in 1931 Delhi was officially inaugurated as the capital of Britain's most important colonial possession, with British-built New Delhi as the city's eighth incarnation.

With **Independence** in 1947, it was in Delhi that the British handed over power to India's first democratically elected government under **Jawaharlal Nehru**. In the wake of **Partition** however, Hindu mobs turned on Delhi's Muslim population, nearly half of whom fled to Pakistan, ending centuries of Muslim dominance in the city. They were replaced by an influx of Hindu and Sikh refugees from the Pakistani sectors of Punjab and Bengal, to the extent that whole new districts had to be created to house them (Chittaranjan Park in south Delhi, for example, was originally EBDPC – East Bengal Displaced Persons' Colony).

Indira Gandhi's **Emergency** in 1976 saw violent evictions of Old Delhi's predominantly Muslim slum-dwellers, who were sent to live in disease-ridden jerry-built housing out of town, an event recalled by Salman Rushdie at the end of his novel *Midnight's Children*. Following Indira's 1984 assassination by her Sikh bodyguards, it was the turn of the city's Sikh population to fall victim to **sectarian riots** – Khushwant Singh, in his novel *Delhi*, records that evil episode in fiction.

In 1992, having previously been a **Union Territory**, administered directly by the federal government, Delhi gained a status similar to that of Washington DC or Canberra ACT, with its own government, but lesser powers than those of a state. The Hindu sectarian BJP won power that year in the first **Capital Territory** election, but lost in 1998 to Congress, who have controlled the administration ever since.

Arrival

Delhi is India's main point of arrival for overseas visitors, and the major transport hub for destinations in the states of Rajasthan, the Punjab, Himachal Pradesh and Ladakh as well as central north India. The **airport**, 15km southwest of the centre, has two separate terminals – one handling international flights, the other domestic services; although adjacent, they're 6km apart by road. The capital is served by four long-distance **railway stations**; the vast majority of services used by tourists arrive and depart from either Old Delhi or New Delhi stations, although a few useful services use Hazrat Nizamuddin in the southeast and Sarai Rohilla in the northwest. State **buses** from all over the country pull into the Maharana Pratap Inter-state Bus Terminal in Old Delhi, while a few destinations in Uttar Pradesh and Uttaranchal are served by the Anand Vihar ISBT in the east of the city.

By air

International flights land at **Indira Gandhi International (IGI) Airport** Terminal 2, while domestic services land at the adjacent Terminal 1. There are no ATMs at the airport as yet (though this may change), but State Bank of India and Thomas Cook in the arrivals lounge offer 24-hour

Delhi scams

Delhi can prove a headache for the first-time visitor because of the numerous **scams** designed to entrap the unwary – one of the dirtier dodges is to dump dung onto visitors' shoes, then charge extortionate amounts to clean it off. The most common scheme, though, is for taxi drivers or touts to convince you that the hotel you've chosen is full, closed or has just burned to the ground. More sophisticated scammers will pretend to phone your hotel to check for yourself, or will take you to a travel agent (often claiming to be a "tourist office") who will do it, dialling for you (a different number); the "receptionist" on the line will corroborate the story, or deny all knowledge of your reservation. The driver or tout will then take you to a "very good hotel" – usually in **Karol Bagh** market – where you'll be pressured into parting with a hefty sum of money for one night's accommodation – rates vary according to how gullible/stressed/tired/affluent you seem to be. To **reduce the risk of being caught** like this, write down the registration number of your taxi (make sure the driver sees you doing it), and absolutely insist on going to your hotel. If you're heading for Paharganj, your driver may well attempt to take you to a hotel of his choice rather than yours. To prevent such conflict, you could ask to be dropped at New Delhi railway station and walk to your hotel of choice from there. You may even encounter fake "doormen" outside hotels who'll tell you the place is full; check at reception first, and even if the claim turns out to be true, never follow the tout back to anywhere he may recommend. Bear in mind, though, that most problems can be avoided by **reserving a room in advance**; many hotels will arrange for a car and driver to meet you at your point of arrival.

New Delhi railway station is the worst place of all for touts; assume that anyone who approaches you here – even in uniform – with offers of help, or to direct you to the foreigners' booking hall, is trouble – most are trying to lure travellers to the fake "official" tourist offices opposite the Paharganj entrance, where you'll end up paying way over the correct price, often for unconfirmed tickets. Similarly, steer clear of all offices along Janpath that falsely claim to be "government authorized". The Government of India tourist office, 88 Janpath, is the exception here, but be warned that touts prowl the streets outside this and other official offices.

Finally, be aware that numerous shops pretend to be official "government" shops, and that taxi, auto and rental-car drivers get a commission just for taking you there – a hefty percentage will be added on to anything you buy to pay off the touts.

Should you fall victim to a new scam, please let us know and we'll warn other readers in future editions.

money-changing facilities; be sure to get some small change for taxis and rickshaws. For those seeking **accommodation**, 24hr desks here, including ITDC and Delhi Tourism (DTTDC), have a list of approved hotels and will secure reservations by phone. **Retiring rooms** (double Rs650, a/c dorm bed Rs250, non-a/c dorm bed Rs90) at both the international and domestic terminals are convenient if you need to make an early connection, but are issued on a first-come, first-served basis. A free AAI **shuttle** bus (every 20min) runs between the two terminals.

From the international airport, the cheapest way to get into Delhi is by **bus** (Rs50); there are 18 services daily. Tickets for the ex-servicemen's shuttle (EATS) and the Delhi Transport Corporation (DTC) buses are available from their respective counters in the arrivals hall. Both services go via the domestic terminal and take around thirty minutes to the drop-off point at Connaught Place F-block in the city centre.

Taxis are faster and more comfortable, and are advisable if you arrive late at night. There are several official pre-paid taxi kiosks in the restricted area outside the arrival hall; it'll cost around Rs250 to the city centre, with a 25 percent surcharge between 11pm and 5am. It's worth noting, however, that even some of these pre-paid taxi drivers may try to take you to hotels not of your choice, and in extremely convincing ways (see the box on p.115 on ways to avoid being scammed).

The **auto-rickshaws** that wait in line at the departure gate are less expensive than taxis (Rs100–150), but constitute the most precarious and least reliable form of transport from the airport, especially at night. Many hotels, including some of the Paharganj budget options, now offer pick-up services from the airport, where you will be met with a driver bearing your name on a placard. Prices vary considerably, starting from as little as Rs200 or less for the cheaper places, and this is by far the most comfortable and hassle-free way to reach the hotel of your choice.

By train

Delhi has two major **railway stations**. **New Delhi Station** is at the eastern end of Paharganj Main Bazaar, within easy walking distance of many of the area's budget hotels. The station has two exits: take the Paharganj exit for Connaught Place and most points south, and the Ajmeri Gate exit for Old Delhi. Cycle rickshaws ply the congested main bazaar toward Connaught Place – which is just 800m down the road – but cannot enter Connaught Place itself. Auto-rickshaws start at Rs20 for Connaught Place, or Rs35 to Old Delhi – agree a price before getting in. **Old Delhi Station**, west of the Red Fort, is also connected to the city hotels by taxis, auto-rickshaws and cycle-rickshaws; you'll pay around Rs80 for a taxi to Connaught Place, and half that for an auto-rickshaw. Both stations are notorious for **theft**: don't take your eyes off your luggage for a moment. The other long-distance stations are **Hazrat Nizamuddin**, south of the centre, for trains from Agra (except the Shatabdi Express); and **Sarai Rohilla**, west of Old Delhi station, for some Rajasthan services such as the Chetak Express from Udaipur. Hazrat Nizamuddin has a pre-paid auto booth – an auto to Connaught Place is Rs50, and it should be about Rs40 from Sarai Rohilla. If you're lucky (especially during morning and evening rush hours) you may connect with a local train into New Delhi, but these do tend to be sardine-can packed.

By bus

State buses pull in at the **Maharana Pratap Inter-state Bus Terminal (ISBT)**, north of Old Delhi railway station. Auto-rickshaws to New Delhi or Paharganj take about fifteen minutes (around Rs50), cycle rickshaws twice that (around Rs30). There's a pre-paid auto-rickshaw booth at the terminal, and also a metro station (Kashmiri Gate). **Private buses** from all over India pull up in the street outside New Delhi railway station; some also drop passengers in Connaught Place. A few services, mainly from Uttaranchal, leave you at **Anand Vihar ISBT**, across the Yamuna towards Ghaziabad in east Delhi, which also has a pre-paid auto-rickshaw booth (an auto into town should cost around Rs60), and is served by buses #73 and #85 to Connaught Place. Buses from Agra and some from Rajasthan may leave you at **Sarai Kale Khan ISBT** by Hazrat Nizamuddin train station (cross over by the footbridge for pre-paid autos). Buses from Jaipur, Ajmer, Jodhpur and Udaipur may drop you at **Bikaner House** near India Gate, Rs30 from Connaught Place by auto.

Information

There are reasonably helpful tourist offices at the international and domestic airports, railway stations and bus terminals, and the **Government of India (GOI) tourist office** at 88 Janpath, just south of Connaught Place (Mon–Fri 9am–6pm, Sat 9am–2pm; ⓣ011/2332 0005 or 0008, ⓦwww.tourismofindia.com), is a good place to pick up information on historical sites, city tours, shopping and cultural events, as well as free city maps. You can change money, book trains and reserve accommodation at the extremely useful **DTTDC** (Delhi Tourism and Transport Development Corporation) office, Bombay Life Building, Middle Circle, Connaught Place (Mon–Sat 10am–5pm; ⓣ011/2331 4229, ⓦdelhitourism.nic.in). The second DTTDC office, with longer hours (daily 7am–9pm) in Coffee House 1 Annexe, Emporium Complex, Baba Kharak Singh Marg (opposite the Hanuman Mandir), does not have money-changing facilities. Beware of any other firms that look like or claim to be tourist offices – **imitators** abound, especially around Connaught Place, opposite New Delhi railway station and near the genuine tourist offices, and obviously, if they are trying to trick you into thinking that they are in some way official (even down to being decorated with GOI tourist posters), then their intentions are not going to be honest; mostly, their aim is to sell sub-standard tours at inflated prices.

Exhibitions and cultural events are listed in local **magazines** such as the weekly *Delhi Diary* and fortnightly *Delhi City*; both also have comprehensive directories and reasonable maps. The monthly *First City* is similar but also features some editorial. All three are available from bookshops and street stalls. Should you need a more detailed map, Eicher's *Delhi Road Map* (Rs30 from bookshops or newsstands) is one of the best, and if you require more detail still, the same firm produce a *Delhi City Map* in book form, with street index, for Rs270.

City transport

Public transport in Delhi is pitifully inadequate for the city's population and size, and increased car ownership is adding to the general chaos; on a positive note, however, you'll see far fewer cows on the road these days (the city's government is actually trying to round up and evict them). Furthermore, a host of newly built flyovers and underpasses have greatly improved Delhi's suburban ring-roads, while the first section of the eagerly awaited **metro** is now up and running. In an effort to reduce **pollution**, the city's buses, taxis and auto-rickshaws have all now been converted from petrol and diesel to run on compressed natural gas (CNG).

The metro

Delhi's brand new **metro system** opened in December 2002, with the capacity to carry 200,000 passengers daily. This is just the first of several ongoing phases that will continue to the year 2021. There are currently three lines, two traversing the city from east to west, and a shorter one running north to south. The only one open for business at the time of writing was **Line 1**, which runs from Rithala in the northwestern suburbs to Shahdara across the Yamuna river in the northeast. **Line 2** will run between Vishwa Vidyalaya (Delhi University) in the north to the Central Secretariat, interchanging with Line 1 at Kashmiri

City and regional tours

The **Government of India tourist office** (see p.117) organizes a/c bus **tours** of New Delhi (daily 8am–1pm; Rs200), Old Delhi (daily 2–5.15pm; Rs200), and a combined tour of Old and New Delhi (daily 8am–5.15pm; Rs300); all start at *Hotel Janpath* on Janpath. You can also hire guides at the tourist office; they charge Rs400 a day within Delhi; day-trips to Agra are also available (Rs850). Similarly, along with long-distance tours, the **DTTDC** (see p.117) also offer city tours. Their half-day Delhi tours (9am & 2.15pm) cost Rs104, while the whole-day option (9am–5.30pm) is Rs203; they start from outside the DTTDC office opposite the Hanuman Temple on Baba Kharak Singh Marg. **Delhi Transport Corporation** (Ⓣ011/2331 7445) run one-day tours starting from New Delhi railway station at 9.15am, Scindia House in Connaught Place (corner of Janpath) at 9.30am, or the Red Fort at 9.45am, for Rs100. All the five-star **hotels** offer their own, more expensive door-to-door packages, and many hotels in and around Paharganj, such as *Namaskar*, *Metropolis* and *Ajanta*, can arrange city tours by taxi for Rs500–600; very good value when shared between three or four people.

Gate (by the main Inter-state Bus Terminal), and continuing to Old Delhi and New Delhi railway stations and Connaught Place. **Line 3** will start in the southwest and terminate at Barakhamba Road, interchanging with Line 2 at Connaught Place. Altogether 50 stations should be open by the end of 2005, including Dwarka at the western end of Line 3, which will serve Indira Gandhi International Airport. The minimum fare is currently Rs6, and tickets can only be bought at metro stations. For progress updates, ask at the tourist offices (see p.117) or visit Ⓦwww.delhimetrorail.com. The metro is wheelchair accessible, and each station should have an ATM.

Buses

With auto- and cycle-rickshaws so plentiful and cheap, only hardened shoestring travellers will want to use Delhi's confusing and overcrowded **buses**. If you do, buy a **route guide** from magazine vendors in Connaught Place or Paharganj. The first digit of each three-digit **route number** shows the direction of each bus – thus routes starting with "5" head south from the centre towards Mehrauli, and those starting with "4" travel southeast towards Kalkaji through Nizamuddin, while those starting with "1" go north through Old Delhi. Two bus routes you may find useful are the #505 from New Delhi station (Chelmsford Road) and Connaught Place (Super Bazaar and the corner of Kasturba Gandhi Marg) to Safdarjung's Tomb and the Qutb Minar, and the #459 from the same stops in central New Delhi to Nizamuddin and Badarpur.

Auto-rickshaws and cycle rickshaws

Auto-rickshaws ("autos") – India's three-wheeler taxis – are the most effective form of transport around Delhi, although their drivers are notoriously anarchic. Some auto-wallahs will offer to use the meter, but in general you'll need to negotiate a price before getting in, and try and have the exact change ready; prices for foreigners vary considerably according to your haggling skills and the mood of the driver, but as a sample fare, it should cost about Rs40 from Connaught Place to Old Delhi. Auto stands, which dot the city, are the best places to pick up auto-rickshaws, though they can also be hailed in the street. In Connaught Place itself, there's a pre-paid auto-rickshaw kiosk on the innermost circle between the two halves of Palika Bazaar, and another on

Janpath outside the Government of India tourist office, where you can be sure of a certified official fare.

Cycle rickshaws are not allowed in Connaught Place and parts of New Delhi, but are handy for short journeys to outlying areas and around Paharganj. They're also nippier than motorized traffic in Old Delhi. Rates should be roughly half that demanded by autos.

Rickshaws and auto-rickshaws that hang around major tourist centres tend to do so with the intention of **overcharging** – even crossing the road from a hotel entrance can make for a better price, and it is best to get away from places like Paharganj Main Bazaar or the entrance to the Red Fort before hailing a rickshaw. Rickshaws and autos that hustle you for business on the street are worth avoiding. On the other hand, bear in mind that cycle rickshaw-wallahs in particular are among the city's poorest residents, and it really isn't worth haggling them down to the absolute minimum fare or arguing with them over what will amount in the end to a trifling sum. Indeed, when you see how hard your rickshaw-wallah has to work, you may well feel they deserve a hefty tip.

Taxis

Delhi's **taxis**, (white, or black and yellow) cost around fifty percent more than auto-rickshaws and are generally safe and reliable (at least, once you're free of the airport). Drivers belong to local taxi stands, where you can make bookings and fix prices; if you flag a taxi down on the street you're letting yourself in for some hectic haggling. A surcharge of around 25 percent operates between 11pm and 5am. A new service, **Dial-a-Cab** (Ⓣ1920), offers convenience and luxury, with air-conditioned cars (in summer at least) and tamper-proof digital meters, though their fares are higher than the going rate for an ordinary cab.

From New Delhi (Connaught Place) to Old Delhi (eastern end of Chandni Chowk, opposite the Red Fort), there's a **shared jeep taxi** service costing Rs6 and leaving when full.

Car and cycle rental

For local sightseeing and journeys beyond the city confines, chauffeur-driven **cars** are very good value, especially for groups of three to four. Many budget hotels offer cars and drivers, as does the GOI tourist office (see p.117), and the booths at the southern end of the Tibetan Market on Janpath. GOI rates are Rs655 for an eight-hour day within Delhi, which includes 80km mileage; if you want an a/c vehicle, the rate is Rs945. Private travel agencies throughout Delhi usually charge more. Driving yourself in Delhi can be nerve-wracking and dangerous, so renting a car is not a good idea.

Cycling in the large avenues of New Delhi takes some getting used to and can be dangerous for those not used to chaotic traffic. **Bicycle rental** is surprisingly difficult to come by; try Mehta Cycles at 5109–10 Main Bazaar, Paharganj, a few doors east of the *Khosla Café*, who rent pushbikes for Rs50 a day.

Accommodation

Delhi has a vast range of **accommodation**, from dirt-cheap lodges to extravagant international hotels. Bookings for upmarket hotels can be made at airport and railway station tourist desks; budget travellers will have to hunt around independently.

The hotels in **Connaught Place** cover all price ranges, are handy for banks, restaurants and shops, and have good transport connections to all the main sights. North of Connaught Place, the busy market area of **Paharganj** and the adjacent **Ram Nagar**, close to New Delhi railway station, feature the best of the budget accommodation. There will always be budget rooms available in Paharganj – don't believe anyone who tells you otherwise, and **avoid** all hotels in Karol Bagh that are recommended by touts (see box on p.115). The main youth hostel is in the **south**, where you'll also find most of Delhi's top **luxury hotels**. Fifteen minutes north of Old Delhi by auto-rickshaw, the Tibetan colony of **Majnu Ka Tilla** also has a few good places to stay.

Finally, for those leaving on early flights, we've included reviews of dependable hotels out near the international airport.

Connaught Place and central Delhi

The curved colonial lanes of **Connaught Place** hold moderately priced hotels of varying standards; further south, grander hotels on and around **Janpath** and along **Sansad Marg** cater mainly for business travellers and tourist groups. Most of these have plush restaurants and swimming pools – all add heavy taxes to their bills, which we have included in our price codes, and many require non-Indian residents to pay in foreign currency. A number of inexpensive, cramped and friendly **lodges**, huddled around the north end of Janpath near the Government of India tourist office, offer basic rooms and dorms; however, they're often full, so book ahead.

Unless otherwise stated, the hotels listed below appear on the Connaught Place **map** (see opposite).

Alka 16/90 P-Block, Connaught Place ⓣ011/2334 4328, ⓦwww.hotelalka.com. Well turned-out rooms, carpeted and en-suite with a/c, that are actually pretty poky – the cheaper rooms don't even have a window, though they do try to make up for it with mirrors round the walls. Doubles start at $70, and there's an annex on M-block if the main hotel is full. ⑨

Central Court N-Block, Connaught Place ⓣ011/2331 5015 to 7. Rooftop establishment with a nice terrace overlooking Connaught Place. The rooms, most of them en suite, are large but rather drab, with fridge and a/c. Rooms at the back are quieter; those on the balcony can be very noisy, though some have an additional sitting area. Reservations may not always be honoured. ⑥

Imperial Janpath, Connaught Place end ⓣ011/5150 1234, ⓦwww.theimperialindia.com. Delhi's classiest hotel, in a beautiful 1931 Art Deco building set amid large, palm-shaded gardens. The rooms are stylish, as is the cool lobby done out in cream and gold, and there are some excellent restaurants including the *Spice Route* (see p.145). The staff are just the right degree of friendly and courteous, and the corridors double as a fascinating gallery of eighteenth- and nineteenth-century prints of India. Doubles from $250. ⑨

InterContinental Off Barakhamba Avenue and Tolstoy Marg, southeast of Connaught Place ⓣ011/2341 1001, ⓦwww.intercontinental.com. Brash and business-oriented monolith, all opulence and mod cons with a choice of restaurants, bars and a disco, lots of shops, conference meetings and general comings and goings. Doubles from $280. ⑨

Janpath Janpath ⓣ011/2334 0070. Like an upmarket hotel in a provincial Indian town, and catering for reasonably well-heeled Indian out-of-towners rather than for foreigners, this place is too ramshackle to really be deluxe, though the services are all there. Its large carpeted rooms are comfortable enough but showing their age. The incense-laden lobby has some good restaurants, foreign exchange facilities, shops and a travel counter. Doubles from $67. ⑨

Le Meridien Windsor Place, Raisna Rd (see New Delhi map, p.127) ⓣ011/2371 0101, ⓦwww.lemeridien-newdelhi.com. Busy, futuristic-looking five-star with glass-walled elevators taking you up to bedrooms set around a massive atrium. The rooms are spacious and comfortable, and there's a swimming pool, health club and a choice of restaurants and bars. Doubles from $205. ⑨

Master R-500 New Rajendra Nagar (see Delhi map, pp.110–111) ⓣ011/2874 1089, ⓦwww.master-guesthouse.com. A lovely little guesthouse

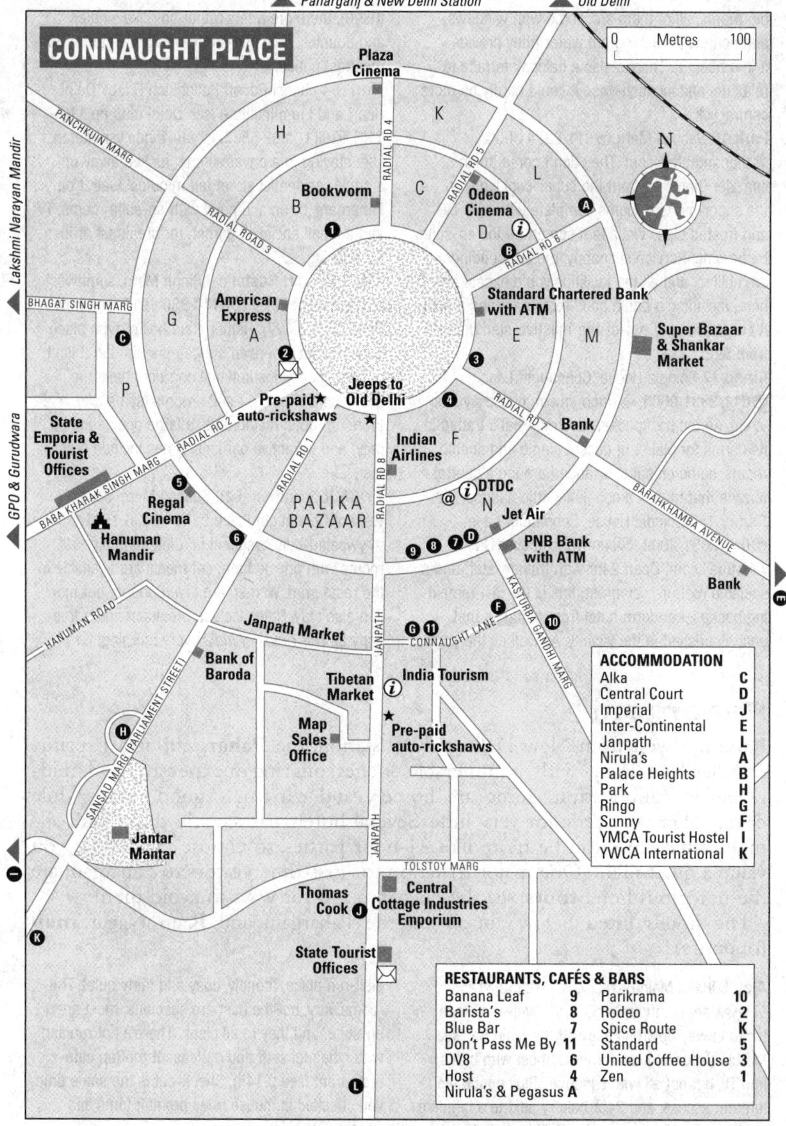

on the edge of the green belt just 10min by auto-rickshaw from Connaught Place. Comfortable, secure and family-run, with just four a/c double rooms of different sizes (a bathroom between each pair) and a secluded roof terrace. Veg meals are available. Book ahead. ⑤

Nirula's 135 L-Block, Connaught Place ⓣ011/2341 7419, ⓦwww.nirulas.com. Small and smart describes both the hotel and its cosy rooms, all with a/c and TV. Facilities include a variety of restaurants and bars, including a cyber-bar with Internet access. On the downside, windows all face onto the interior terrace, which though it keeps out the noise, can make the rooms a bit dark. Doubles from $94. ⑨

Palace Heights 26/8 D-Block, Connaught Place ⓣ011/2341 5419. Pleasantly run-down place with big rooms, all of them a/c, some with windows, and none with running hot water (they provide it in a bucket). There's also a balcony terrace to relax on, and location-wise it could hardly be more central. ❺

Park 15 Sansad Marg ☎011/2374 3000, ⓦtheparkhotels.com. They don't come much snazzier than this, from the super-cool lobby to the super-modern rooms complete with LCD TV and frosted glass walls that screen off the en-suite bathrooms. Service is snappy, the surroundings are chilled, and all the facilities you'd expect are here, including a bar, a good restaurant and a pool. A cut above your run-of-the-mill five-star. Doubles from $281. ❾

Ringo 17 Scindia House, Connaught Lane ☎011/2331 0605, ⓔringo_guest_house@yahoo.co.in. An old backpacker favourite that's traded in its dorms for plain but decent single and double rooms, some en suite, arranged around a central terrace that makes a congenial little hangout. ❷

Sunny 152 Scindia House, Connaught Lane ☎011/2331 2909, ⓔsunnyguesthouse123@hotmail.com. Open 24hr with friendly staff and a sociable rooftop restaurant, this is the last remaining backpacker dorm hotel from a gaggle that once flourished in the vicinity. As well as the dorms (Rs90), there are a few rather box-like singles and doubles, some en-suite, with hot water at 20 minutes' notice. ❷

Yatri 3/4 Jhansi Rd, off Punchkuin Rd, by Delhi Heart and Lung Institute (see Delhi map pp.110–111) ☎011/2362 5563, ⓔyatri@nde.vsnl.net.in. Like staying in a private home, tucked away up a small residential street ten minutes' walk from Paharganj, clean and quiet with en-suite rooms, TV and a small enclosed garden for breakfast or just for relaxing. ❼

YMCA Tourist Hostel Jai Singh Marg, southwest of Connaught Place ☎011/2336 1915 (see New Delhi map, p.127). Rather staid hostel-type place popular with American budgeteers (though it isn't all that cheap). Institutional corridors belie the spacious if simple en-suite rooms (some a/c), and there are good restaurants, a large pool (summer only) and attractive gardens. Rates include breakfast. ❻

YWCA International 10 Sansad Marg, southwest of Connaught Place ☎011/2336 1561, ⓔywcaind@del3.vsnl.net.in. Clean and airy a/c rooms with private bath; set meals are available in the restaurant. Women are given priority but men can also stay. Rates include breakfast and a free copy of *The Times of India* every morning. ❻

Paharganj

Running west from New Delhi railway station, the **Paharganj** area is prime travellers' territory, with innumerable lodges offering inexpensive and mid-range accommodation. Some are homely and extremely good value, while others offer very little for very little. Several hotels, particularly those with all-night restaurants, can be more like 24-hour parties, so choose carefully if you value a quiet night. One major irritation for first-time visitors to Paharganj are the notorious hotel **touts**; see the box on p.115 for ways to avoid them.

The hotels listed below appear on the Paharganj and Ram Nagar **map** (opposite).

Ajay 5084-A Main Bazaar ☎011/2358 3125, ⓦwww.anupamhoteliersltd.com. Well-run place tucked away down an alley off the Main Bazaar. Marble decor and clean rooms, most with baths and TV, but not all with windows. Plus pool table, Internet access, and 24hr bakery next to a big café area for breakfast or snacks. Popular with Israeli travellers. ❷

Camran 1116 Main Bazaar ☎011/3097 4474, ⓔsubhashthakur@yahoo.com. Small lodge in part of a late-Moghul period mosque, with some character despite being dim and a little poky. Some rooms are en suite, and there are dorm beds (Rs80) and a panoramic rooftop terrace. ❷

Hare Krishna 1572–3 Main Bazaar ☎011/5154 1340 or 1341, ⓔharekrishnagh@hotmail.com. A well-run place, friendly, cosy and fairly quiet. The rooms vary, but the best are spacious, most are en-suite, and they're all clean. There's hot running water, helpful staff and a pleasant rooftop café-restaurant (see p.146). Check-out is the same time you checked in; house rules prohibit touts and *charas*. ❷

Major's Den 2314 Lakshmi Narain Rd ☎011/2358 9599. Not the best value in town, but quiet, safe and off the main road, run by a cheerful ex-army officer. Taller travellers may appreciate the two-metre-long beds. All rooms are en suite, but the cheaper ones have no outside window. ❸

Metropolis 1634 Main Bazaar ☎011/2358 5766, ⓦwww.metropolistravels.com. Main Bazaar's most upmarket and comfortable hotel. Some doubles

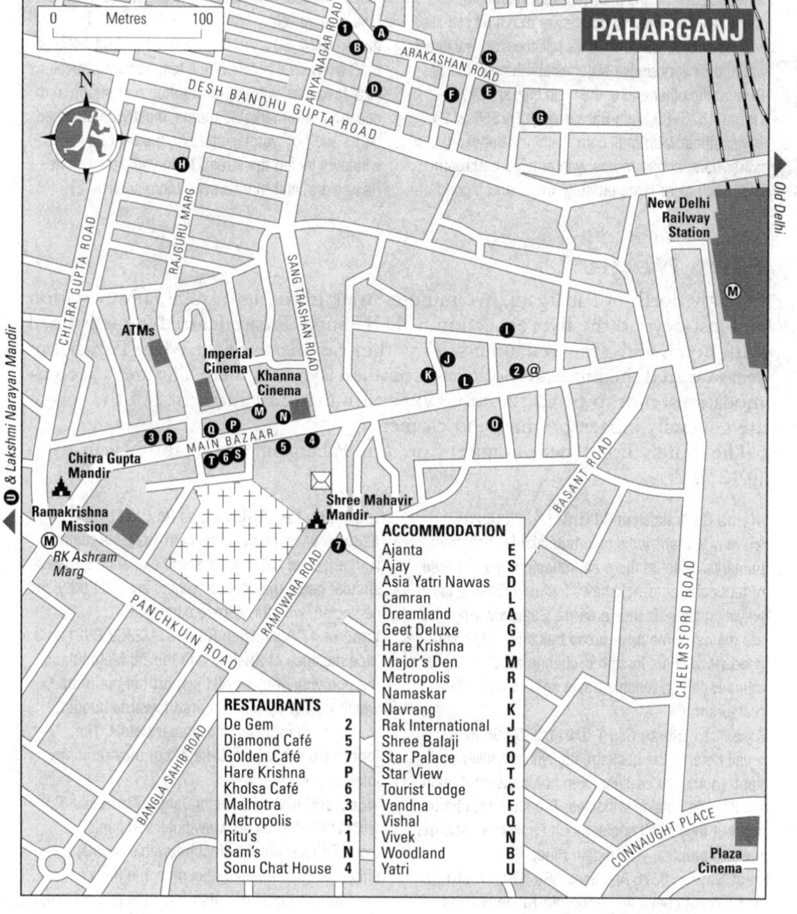

have a/c, large windows, constant hot water and bathtubs. Two good restaurants. ❺

Namaskar 917 Chandiwalan, Main Bazaar ⓣ011/2358 2233, ⓔnamaskarhotel@yahoo.com. Popular and well-kept family-run budget hotel off the main bazaar with a variety of en-suite rooms, all a/c but not all with outside windows. They also run tours, which they are rather pushy about selling, and are not happy with guests who admit to buying tours elsewhere. Airport pickups are pricey at Rs400. ❷

Navrang Tooti Chowk, 820 Main Bazaar ⓣ011/2352 1965. More like a down-at-heel lodge in some remote small town than a city hotel in the middle of Delhi, it's friendly enough, but rather basic. On the other hand, you get what you pay for, and it isn't bad value. As well as the rather grubby rooms, en-suite but without hot water, there are Rs50 dorm beds. ❶

Rak International Tooti Chowk, 820 Main Bazaar ⓣ011/2358 6508, ⓔhotelrakint@yahoo.com. One of Paharganj's best choices, in a small square off the main bazaar. Very good value with large, cool rooms, a/c, TV, fridge and hot water, and a nice rooftop too. ❸

Shree Balaji 2204 Rajguru Marg, Chuna Mandi ⓣ011/2353 2212. Between the Main Bazaar and Ram Nagar, this is one of the better hotels along this street in terms of comfort and cleanliness. All rooms have en-suite bathrooms with hot water on tap, but no shower. ❷

Star Palace 4590 Main Bazaar ⓣ011/2358 4849, ⓦwww.stargroupofhotels.com. The rooms are well-equipped for the price (en-suite bathroom, phone, a/c, satellite TV), but they're also a bit cell-like, with no outside windows. If it's full, the staff will direct you to their very similar sister establishment, the *Star View*, at the other end of the main bazaar. ❸

Vishal 1575–80 Main Bazaar ⓣ011/2356 2123, ⓔvishalhotel@hotmail.com. A choice between rather bare, cheap rooms with outside bathroom, and much nicer large en-suite ones, and a good restaurant too – but check the sheets before you take a room. ❷

Vivek 1534–50 Main Bazaar ⓣ011/5154 1435 or 6, ⓦwww.vivekhotel.com. A longstanding travellers' favourite, with a 24hr rooftop restaurant, and decent if unremarkable rooms, most with attached baths and hot water, some a/c; the best have windows facing the street. TV in your room costs Rs50 extra, and there's even room service. ❸

Ram Nagar

Directly north of Paharganj, five minutes' walk from New Delhi railway station and just beyond the flyover section of D.B. Gupta Road, **Ram Nagar** is lined with hotels and a few restaurants. It's within easy reach of the Main Bazaar, but you're spared the incessant noise and commercial atmosphere. The area's accommodation tends to be a little more expensive than in Paharganj, but the rooms are generally bigger, brighter and cleaner.

The hotels listed below appear on the Paharganj and Ram Nagar **map** (p.123).

Ajanta 36 Arakashan Rd ⓣ011/2362 0925, ⓦwww.tourism-india.com/hotelajanta. The most upmarket hotel in the area, reflected by the posse of touts and auto-rickshaws loitering outside to waylay guests as they emerge. Spacious, en-suite, a/c rooms; some have broad balconies affording good views. Plus foreign exchange facilities, an Internet café, a reliable travel agency and a good restaurant. ❻

Asia Yatri Niwas Gali 1 ⓣ011/2352 9805. A small hotel in the backstreets, with smallish, well-kept rooms, all en-suite with hot showers though not all with outside windows. The staff are charming, but they don't speak much English, so you may need to practice your pidgin Hindi. ❸

Geet Deluxe 8570 Arakashan Rd ⓣ011/2361 6140. A cut above the other mid-range options hereabouts; well-kept with nice touches and a certain charm. The clean, decent-sized rooms all have TV and either a/c or air-cooling. ❹

Tourist Lodge 26 Arakashan Rd ⓣ011/2352 5289; ⓦwww.touristlodge.com. Sizeable rooms with attached bathrooms, some a/c, and some with circular beds; the cheaper rooms are a bit tatty and neglected, with threadbare carpets. ❸

Vandna 47 Arakashan Rd ⓣ011/2362 8821 to 3. Nice mosaics of Krishna and the Taj Mahal flank the doorway of this hotel just off the main road, which is slightly more geared towards budget travellers than other Ram Nagar hotels. The rooms are not that well-kept, but they're comfy enough. ❸

Woodland 8235/6 Multani Danda, Arakashan Rd ⓣ011/5154 1304, ⓦwww.hotelwoodland.com. Popular hotel with comfortable rooms, either tiled or carpeted, though some have a mattress on the floor rather than a bed. If you want a cheaper room, they'll send you to their sister establishment, the *Dreamland* (❸), just across the street. ❹

Old Delhi

Few tourists stay in **Old Delhi**: it's less central than Connaught Place and Paharganj, and it's dirtier, noisier and more crowded, with hotels geared mostly to Indian visitors rather than foreigners. On the other hand, there are a couple of good upmarket options on the area's fringes, and some reasonable budget hotels around the Jama Masjid. And of all the areas in town, this is the most colourful, with the most character, which can be a reason in itself to stay here.

The hotels listed below appear on the Old Delhi **map** (p.132).

Amber 6477 Katra Bariyan ⓣ011/2396 5081. This newish, tourist-friendly hotel behind Fatehpuri Mosque is one of the area's better offerings, although hot water comes in buckets rather than out of the shower, and the windows all face an internal courtyard. ❸

Broadway 4/15A Asaf Ali Rd ⓣ011/2327 3821, ⓔbroadway@oldworldhospitality.com. On the southern edge of Old Delhi, close to Delhi Gate, this great mid-range hotel has loads of old-fashioned charm, an excellent restaurant specializing in Kashmiri feasts (see p.146), plus two bars. Some rooms look out over the Jama Masjid, and tours through Old Delhi are available. Prices include breakfast. ❼

New City Palace 725 Jama Masjid Motor Market ⓣ011/2327 9548. Though it doesn't quite live up to its billing of "a home for palatial comfort", this budget hotel is clean and well situated, directly behind the Jama Masjid (though you'll need to boook ahead for a room with a view). Showers are hot and the best rooms have a/c, though not all the cheaper ones have outside windows. ❸

Oberoi Maidens 7 Sham Nath Marg, Civil Lines ⓣ011/2397 5464, ⓦwww.oberoihotels.com. A nice bit of understated luxury in a lovely old colonial mansion dating from Company days; quiet and relaxing with comfortable period rooms, big bathrooms and leafy gardens as well as a swimming pool and a good restaurant. Doubles from $168. ❾

South Delhi

Most of the accommodation **south of Connaught Place** lies firmly in the luxury category, although there are a few guesthouses in Sundernagar, the odd mid-range hotel tucked away in a residential area and a modern youth hostel near the exclusive diplomatic enclave in Chanakyapuri.

The hotels listed below appear on the New Delhi **map** (p.127).

Ambassador Sujan Singh Park, off Subramaniam Bharti Marg ⓣ011/2463 2600, ⓦwww.tajhotels.com. Low-key, well-run and classy, this friendly place has comfortable-sized rooms and huge bathrooms, plus a couple of good restaurants and free use of the pool and health club at the *Taj Mahal*. Doubles from $175. ❾

Claridges 12 Aurangzeb Rd ⓣ011/2301 0211, ⓦwww.claridges.com. One of Delhi's oldest and finest establishments, oozing elegant 1930s style from its facade to its rooms and even its bathrooms. Facilities include tennis courts, restaurants and a swimming pool. Doubles from $205. ❾

La Sagrita 14 Sundar Nagar ⓣ011/2435 1249, ⓦwww.lasagrita.com. Tucked away down a quiet side street in an exclusive colony, opposite a small park and next door to the Grenadian high commission, this small guesthouse might suit if you want to escape the din of central Delhi. Rooms are small but cosy, carpeted, en suite and tastefully done out, and there's a little garden out front to relax in. ❽

Youth Hostel 5 Nyaya Marg, off Kautilya Marg, Chanakyapuri ⓣ011/2611 6285, ⓦwww.yhaindia.com. Away from the bustling city centre, this ultramodern grey concrete building, with dorms (Rs70) and a/c or non-a/c singles and doubles, is the showpiece-cum-administration centre of the Indian YHA. You need to be an HI member to stay here but you can join on the spot (Rs250 and two passport photos). ❸

Majnu Ka Tilla

The New Tibetan colony at **Majnu Ka Tilla** offers excellent-value hotels with immaculately kept rooms. The area has a very Tibetan feel, with Tibetan shops, and restaurants serving Tibetan food, as well as Internet facilities and money changers and rooms here are much nicer than what you would get for the same price in Paharganj; on the other hand, beggars and sob-story artists tend to be persistent, and it isn't very convenient for central Delhi (Connaught Place is Rs80 away on an auto, and the auto- and rickshaw-wallahs waiting at the colony exit are keen to overcharge). Old Delhi isn't so far away however (Rs40–60 by auto). Book ahead if you intend to stay here as hotels are often full up.

Lhasa House 16 New Camp ⓣ011/2393 9888, ⓔlhasahouse@rediffmail.com. Well-kept en-suite rooms with TV in a clean Tibetan-run hotel with a restaurant. ❸

White House 44 New Camp ⓣ011/2381 3888, ⓔwhitehouse02@rediffmail.com. Clean, tidy rooms with bathroom and TV, and a restaurant serving Tibetan, Chinese and Indian food. ❷

Wongdhen House 15-A New Camp ⓣ011/2381 6689, ⓔwongdhenhouse@hotmail.com. Friendly guesthouse with en-suite rooms, some overlooking the River Yamuna and all with TV. Restaurant and rooftop terrace. ❷

Near IGI Airport

There are **retiring rooms** at both airport terminals, but if you are in for a long wait between flights and don't want to head into town, you could try the hotels near the **international airport** in Mahipalpur, most of them on the Gurgaon Road, which is part of NH-8, the main highway to Jaipur. Several good *dhabas* can be found around there too, and the *Radisson* boasts a cake shop and seven cafés, bars and restaurants where you can while away the time agreeably. Mahipalpur is 4km from IGI airport, or about Rs50 by auto.

The hotels listed below appear on the Delhi **map** (pp.110–111).

Ashok Country Resort Rajokri Rd, Kapashera ⓣ011/2506 4590, ⓦwww.ashokcountryresort.com. Elegant, stylish establishment just off the NH-8, set amid spacious gardens (ask for a room with a garden view), with a 24hr restaurant and a pool. Overall service could be better for the price. From $120. ❾

Krishna M.R. Complex, NH-8, Mahipalpur ⓣ011/2678 4266. Lower end of mid-range, with clean en-suite doubles but no restaurant. ❹

Radisson NH-8, Mahipalpur ⓣ011/2677 9191, ⓦwww.radisson.com. The most luxurious choice in the area, aimed at businesspeople flying in and out of IGI, and equipped with all mod cons including pool and health club, squash courts, bowling alley, bars and Italian and Indian restaurants – even exhibitions of contemporary Indian art in the lobby. Doubles from $253; free airport transfers. ❾

The City

Delhi is both daunting and alluring, a sprawling metropolis with a stunning backdrop of ancient architecture. Once you've found your feet and got over the initial impact of the commotion, noise, pollution and sheer scale of the place, the city's geography slowly slips into focus. Monuments in sandstone and marble, which stand in assorted states of repair, are dotted around the city, concentrated in **Old Delhi** and in **southern** enclaves such as **Hauz Khas**. Delhi today, however, as experienced by its many thousands of visitors, centres very much around the imperial city built by the British from 1911 onwards. Most foreign travellers to India find it necessary to call in at some of the myriad of administrative offices that fill the formal buildings of **Connaught Place**, the heart of **New Delhi**. From here it's easy to visit one of many outstanding **museums**, stocked with artistic treasures from all over the country and recording the lives of India's political figureheads.

Central New Delhi

The modern area of **CENTRAL NEW DELHI**, with its wide tree-lined avenues and solid colonial architecture, has been the seat of central government since 1931. At its hub, the royal mall, **Rajpath**, runs from the palatial **Rashtrapati Bhavan**, in the west, to the **India Gate** war memorial in the east. Its wide grassy margins are a popular meeting place for families, picnickers and courting couples. The **National Museum** is located just south of the central intersection. At the north edge of the new capital lies the thriving business centre, **Connaught Place**, where neon advertisements for restaurants, bars and banks adorn the flat roofs and colonnaded verandas of the white buildings that circle its central park.

Rashtrapati Bhavan and Rajpath

After George V, king of England and emperor of British India, decreed in 1911 that Delhi should replace Calcutta as the capital of India, the English architect **Edwin Lutyens** was commissioned to plan the new governmental centre. **Rashtrapati Bhavan**, the official residence of the president of India, is one of the largest and

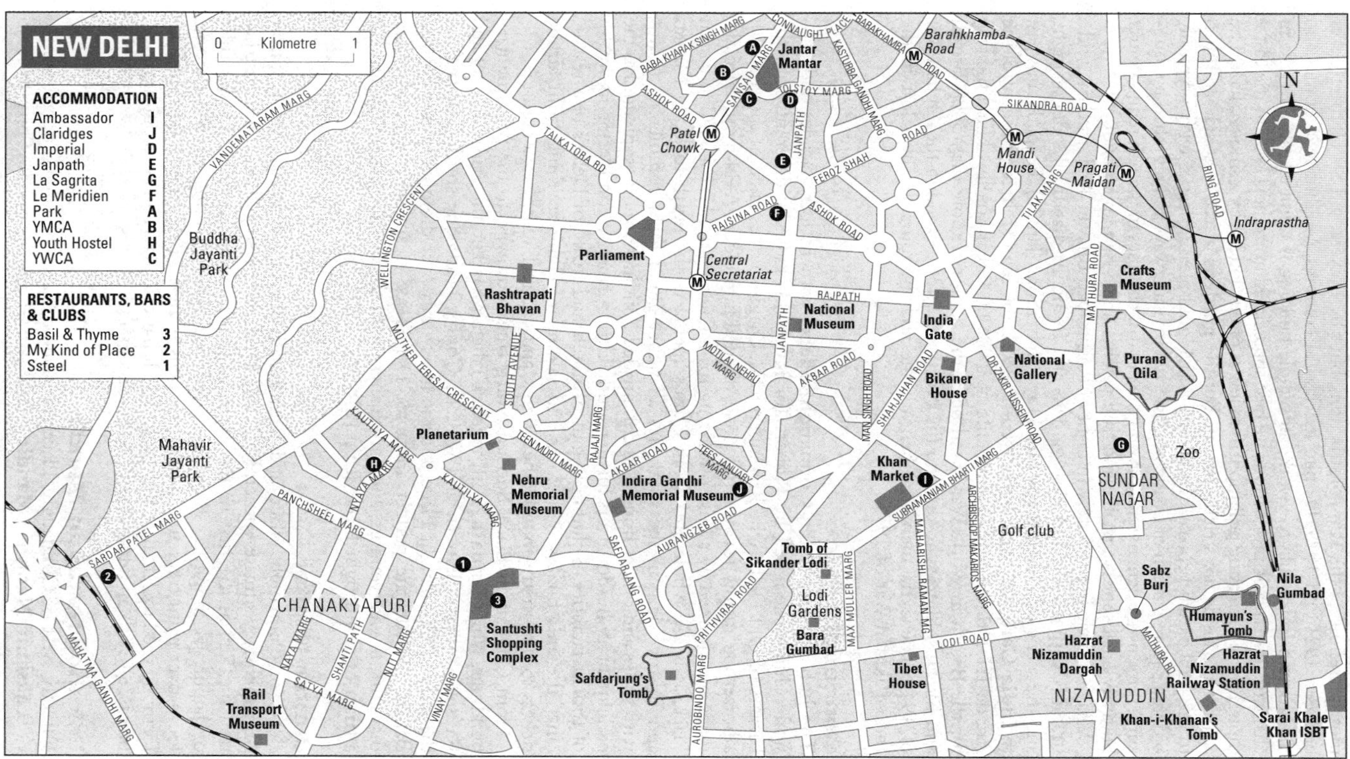
NEW DELHI
0 Kilometre 1
ACCOMMODATION
Ambassador I
Claridges J
Imperial D
Janpath E
La Sagrita G
Le Meridien F
Park A
YMCA B
Youth Hostel H
YWCA C
RESTAURANTS, BARS & CLUBS
Basil & Thyme 3
My Kind of Place 2
Ssteel 1
N
Jantar Mantar
Barahkhamba Road
Patel Chowk
Mandi House
Pragati Maidan
Indraprastha
Central Secretariat
Parliament
Rashtrapati Bhavan
National Museum
India Gate
Crafts Museum
National Gallery
Purana Qila
Bikaner House
Zoo
SUNDAR NAGAR
Planetarium
Nehru Memorial Museum
Indira Gandhi Memorial Museum
Khan Market
Golf club
Tomb of Sikander Lodi
Lodi Gardens
Bara Gumbad
Tibet House
Sabz Burj
Nila Gumbad
Humayun's Tomb
Hazrat Nizamuddin Dargah
Hazrat Nizamuddin Railway Station
NIZAMUDDIN
Khan-i-Khanan's Tomb
Sarai Khale Khan ISBT
Safdarjung's Tomb
Santushti Shopping Complex
CHANAKYAPURI
Rail Transport Museum
Buddha Jayanti Park
Mahavir Jayanti Park
VANDEMATARAM MARG
BABA KHARAK SINGH MARG
CONNAUGHT PLACE
BARAKHAMBA ROAD
KASTURBA GANDHI MARG
TOLSTOY MARG
SANSAD MARG
ASHOK ROAD
JANPATH
SIKANDRA ROAD
TALKATORA RD
FEROZ SHAH ROAD
RAISINA ROAD
TILAK MARG
RING ROAD
MATHURA ROAD
RAJPATH
WELLINGTON CRESCENT
MOTHER TERESA CRESCENT
SOUTH AVENUE
MOTILAL NEHRU MARG
AKBAR ROAD
MAN SINGH ROAD
SHAHJAHAN ROAD
DR ZAKIR HUSSEIN ROAD
KAUTILYA MARG
TEEN MURTI MARG
RAJAJI MARG
TEES JANUARY MARG
SUBRAMANIAM BHARTI MARG
ARCHBISHOP MAKARIOS MARG
NYAYA MARG
PANCHSHEEL MARG
SARDAR PATEL MARG
SAFDARJANG ROAD
AURANGZEB ROAD
PRITHVIRAJ ROAD
MAX MULLER MARG
MAHARISHI RAMAN MG
LODI ROAD
MATHURA RD
AUROBINDO MARG
VINAY MARG
NITI MARG
SHANTI PATH
SATYA MARG
NAYA MARG
MAHATMA GANDHI MARG

most grandiose of the Raj constructions, built by Lutyens and Sir Herbert Baker between 1921 and 1929. Despite its classical columns, Moghul-style domes and *chhatris*, and Indian filigree work, the whole building is unmistakeably British in character. Its majestic proportions are best appreciated from India Gate to the east – though with increasing pollution, the view is often clouded by a smoggy haze. The apartments inside are strictly private, but the **gardens** at the west side are open to the public each February. Modelled on Moghul pleasure parks, with a typically ordered square pattern of quadrants dissected by waterways and refreshed by fountains, Lutyens' gardens extend beyond the normal confines to include tennis courts, butterfly enclosures, vegetable and fruit patches and a swimming pool.

Vijay Chowk, immediately in front of Rashtrapati Bhavan, leads into the wide, straight **Rajpath**, flanked with gardens and fountains that are floodlit at night, and the scene of annual **Republic Day** celebrations (Jan 26). Rajpath runs east to **India Gate**. Designed by Lutyens in 1921, the high arch, reminiscent of the Arc de Triomphe in Paris, commemorates 90,000 Indian soldiers killed fighting for the British in World War I, and bears the names of more than 3000 British and Indian soldiers who died on the Northwest frontier and in the Afghan War of 1919. The extra memorial beneath the arch honours the lives lost in the Indo-Pakistan War of 1971.

Connaught Place

The hub of New Delhi, **Connaught Place**, with its lofty facades and classical columns designed by Robert Tor Russell, is radically different from the bazaars of Old Delhi which it superseded. Originally designed in the shape of a horseshoe, it now forms a full circle, divided into blocks A–N by seven radial roads and rimmed by a busy outer ring road. The ring road is called Connaught Place, as is the whole area, from Plaza Cinema in the north to Jantar Mantar and Tolstoy Marg in the south. It's all rather grand for a commercial centre, with shops and offices housed in colonnaded buildings almost as splendid as the parliamentary headquarters further south. Unsurprisingly, considering its wealth of tourist facilities, including a glut of hotels and many of Delhi's best restaurants, the area buzzes with touts and salesmen, selling anything from airline tickets to five-metre-long leather whips, and can feel a bit disorientating.

From Connaught Place, **Sansad Marg** runs southwest to the parliamentary buildings, while **Janpath**, with its busy Tibetan Market, the *Imperial* hotel and Russell's majestic Eastern and Western Courts, heads due south. The park at the core of Connaught Place, and the grassy area over the underground Palika Bazaar, provide the perfect arena for Delhi's ice-cream sellers, shoe-shiners, masseurs, flower-vendors, and ear-cleaners with their grubby metal spikes. For a **map** of Connaught Place, see p.121.

Jantar Mantar

Between Connaught Place and Rashtrapati Bhavan on Sansad Marg, **Jantar Mantar** (daily sunrise–sunset; $2 [Rs5]) stands little changed since its construction in 1725 as the first of five open-air observatories designed by the ruler of Jaipur, Jai Singh II. Huge deep-red and white slanting stone structures loom over palm trees and neat flower beds – these giant sundials cast shadows formerly used to calculate time, solar and lunar calendars and astrological movements, all with an admirable degree of accuracy.

Lakshmi Narayan Mandir

Directly west of Connaught Place on Mandir Marg, the large modern temple of **Lakshmi Narayan Mandir** (daily 4am–1.30pm & 2.30–9pm; free; no photography) is also known as Birla Mandir after its sponsors, the wealthy Marwari Birla merchants. With its striking white, cream and brown domes, the extravagant building makes for a good introduction to modern Hinduism. There's a special reception room for foreigners to leave their shoes and an adjacent shop selling statues and some nice devotional music. The main shrine is dedicated to Lakshmi, the goddess of wealth, who is seated on a lotus flower. The rest of the complex, spread over several raised tiers, includes smaller shrines to Hanuman (the monkey god) and Ganesh (the elephant-headed god). At the back of the second-largest carpeted hall, you'll hear music and chanting in a tiny, ornate chamber decorated with coloured stones and mirrors and dedicated to Krishna. Various quotations from the *Bhagavad Gita* and *Upanishads*, some translated into English, adorn the walls, alongside murals of Hindu deities.

Bangla Sahib Gurudwara

Southeast of Lakshmi Narayan Mandir, just off Ashoka Road near the GPO, the huge white marble structure of **Bangla Sahib Gurudwara**, Delhi's principal *gurudwara*, topped by golden onion-shaped domes, is visible from some distance. As in all Sikh places of worship, visitors of all denominations are welcome. You can deposit shoes, collect brochures, and enlist the services of a free guide in the information centre near the main entrance. Cover your head and dress conservatively. Live devotional music (vocals, harmonium and tabla) is relayed throughout the complex, and visitors are invited to share a simple meal of dhal and chapatis, served three times daily in the communal dining hall. Follow the crowd, sit in line and wait to be served.

Paharganj

Immediately west of New Delhi railway station, **Paharganj**, centred around the Main Bazaar, provides the first experience of the subcontinent for many budget travellers. Packed with cheap hotels, restaurants, cafés and *dhabas*, and with a busy fruit and vegetable market halfway along, it's also a paradise for shoestring shoppers seeking psychedelic clothing, *bindis*, bags and bronzes and essence of patchouli and sandalwood. A constant stream of cycle and auto-rickshaws, handcarts, cows and the odd taxi squeeze through impossible gaps without the flow ever coming to a complete standstill – the winding alleys where children play among chickens and pigs seem worlds away from the commercial city

The street children of Paharganj

As you wander through the mayhem of Paharganj, you may well find your clothes being gently tugged by some of the local **street kids** begging for rupees. Most of them are runaways who've left difficult homes, often hundreds of kilometres away, and the majority sleep on the street and inhale solvents – any money given directly to them is likely to further their fixes. A (non-registered) charitable organization working in the main bazaar, the **Ujala Project**, run by a Mizo-Swiss couple, is dedicated to helping street children attain a brighter future. Their main achievement so far has been the establishment of a **centre** in the heart of the bazaar where the children can meet, study, bathe and wash their clothes in a caring, drug-free space. They also offer informal counselling and teaching, and advice on hygiene and nutrition, and they try to wean the kids away from potentially harmful activities such as glue-sniffing and petty crime. The charity is sustained entirely by donations, and they welcome gifts of secondhand clothes for three- to eighteen-year-olds, coloured pens, pencils and paints, and of course money. They can be contacted at 5099 Gali Sakkan Wali, off Paharganj Main Bazaar (Ⓣ011/5539 8967, Ⓔujalapaharganj@netscape.net).

centre only just around the corner. Beware of opportunist thieves here, though, and the attentions of touts (see p.115), offering dubious hotels, overpriced tours and spurious *charas*. For a **map** of Paharganj and neighbouring Ram Nagar, see p.123.

National Museum

The **National Museum**, just south of Rajpath at 11 Janpath (Tues–Sun 10am–5pm; English-language guided tours daily 10am; Rs150 [Rs10], plus Rs300 for camera) provides a good general overview of Indian culture and history. Packed with exhibits ranging across five thousand years, it can take several hours to get around – confirmed museum lovers should set aside the whole day. A small shop in the entrance hall sells postcards, books and souvenirs, and has details of daily English-language film shows (12.30pm, 2.30pm & 4pm).

The **ground floor** is dominated by architectural displays, including **Neolithic** tools (3000–1500 BC), and shell and bone jewellery excavated from **Indus Valley civilization** sites, featuring the emperor Ashoka's lion motif and common Buddha symbols – lotus blossoms, *bodhi* trees, stupas, footprints and wheels. Other exhibits include **South Indian** figures from Pallava temples, dominated by Shiva and his consort, and some extraordinarily detailed Tibetan manuscripts.

Another gallery on the ground floor holds a superb collection of bejewelled clothes, dark-wood boxes inlaid with mother-of-pearl, silk tapestries, ivory ornaments and fierce swords, daggers and spears, all of which belonged to the powerful **Moghul** rulers, who combined art forms from Persia, Afghanistan and India to create a unique and elaborate style. The Moghul theme is continued on the **first floor**, which houses Persian and Arabic manuscripts and paintings from several Indian schools, the most distinctive of which are the **Pahari** miniatures of the Himalayan regions of Garhwal and Kangra – simple yet striking scenes of courtly life and loving couples, whose fine lines were often drawn using a single hair. Another section is devoted entirely to models and masks made in **Nagaland**, whose long straight noses, square-set faces and slanted eye-slits evoke Peruvian art; the assorted masks and religious statues from Morocco, Peru and Costa Rica on the second floor make for interesting comparison. Several thick-set and intricately carved wooden doors, lintels and window shutters from **Gujarat** are on display on the upper floor next to a gallery housing three hundred musical instruments, which represent only part of India's vast musical tradition.

Nehru Memorial Museum

Built in 1930 as the residence for the British commander-in-chief, the grand and sombre Teen Murti House on Teen Murti Marg later became home to India's first prime minister, Jawaharlal Nehru, and is now the **Nehru Memorial Museum and Library** (Tues–Sun 9.30am–5.30pm; free). The rooms are laden with photographs recording Nehru's life, from his childhood and student years at Harrow and Cambridge to his formal appointment as leader of India's government in the presence of the king and queen of England in 1948.

Astronomy was one of Nehru's passions; a **planetarium** (Rs2; daily astronomy shows in English 11.30am & 3pm; Rs15) in the grounds of the house features the descent module used by the first Indian cosmonaut in 1984, its heat-shield charred by re-entry into the atmosphere. Next to the planetarium is an old hunting lodge dating back to the time of Tughluq (early fourteenth century), which you can also explore.

Indira Gandhi Memorial Museum

Despite the excesses of the Emergency, Indira Gandhi had a strong bedrock of support during her long years of leadership, and she's remembered with deep respect at the **Indira Gandhi Memorial Museum** (Tues–Sun 9.30am–4.45pm; free), 1 Safdarjung Road. It was in this house that she was assassinated by her own Sikh bodyguards in 1984; her bloodstained sari, which has been chemically preserved, is on display. The collection of letters, press cuttings, photos (many taken by her son Rajiv) and possessions is both informative and moving. It's supplemented by a section devoted to Rajiv, including the clothes he was wearing when he was assassinated in 1991, that winds up the exhibition on a rather tragic note. The tastefully decorated and furnished study, drawing room and dining room conjure up images of how the family must have lived, in great style but not overt opulence. So popular is the former Gandhi home that you may well find yourself caught up in a fast-moving line of Indian tourists, especially at weekends; arrive early so you can view the exhibition at a leisurely pace.

National Gallery of Modern Art

Once the residence of the Maharaja of Jaipur, the extensive **National Gallery** (Tues–Sun 10am–5pm; Rs150 [Rs10]) housed in Jaipur House near India Gate, is a rich showcase of Indian contemporary art. The permanent displays, focusing on post-1930s work, have many of India's best exhibits, including pieces by the "Bengali Renaissance" artists Abanendranath Tagore and Nandalal Bose, the great poet and artist Rabindranath Tagore, and Jamini Roy, whose work, reminiscent of Modigliani, reflects the influence of Indian folk art. Also on show are the romantic paintings and etchings of Thomas Daniell and his nephew William, British artists of the Bombay or Company School. The ground-floor galleries are used for temporary exhibitions of contemporary art from all over the subcontinent, and also houses the **Art Reference Library**, which has a good collection of art books, journals and periodicals.

Crafts Museum

Immediately north of Purana Qila on Bhairon Marg, the **Crafts Museum** (Tues–Sun 10am–5pm; free) is a uniquely dynamic exhibition of the rural arts and crafts of India. Its village complex displays an assortment of building traditions, bringing together cultures from across the subcontinent to provide a unique, if artificial, insight into rural life. Authentically constructed mud huts are beautifully decorated with folk art, and exhibits include woodcarvings, paintings, papier-mâché, embroidery and a full-sized wooden *haveli* from Gujarat. Live demonstrations by the artisans offer close-up glimpses of the folk arts that can be all too difficult to obtain elsewhere in the country. You can buy ritual objects, ornaments, rugs, shawls and books from the craftsmen and women or from the excellent museum **shop**.

Old Delhi (Shahjahanabad)

Although it's not in fact the oldest part of Delhi, the seventeenth-century city of **Shahjahanabad**, built by the Moghul emperor, Shah Jahan, is known as **OLD DELHI**. The original city walls spread for seven miles, enclosing the sprawling fort, **Lal Qila**, and the formidable **Jama Masjid**, or "Friday Mosque". Old Delhi's main thoroughfare, **Chandni Chowk**, a seething mass of hooting, pushing cars, autos, cycle rickshaws and ox carts, was once a sublime canal lined

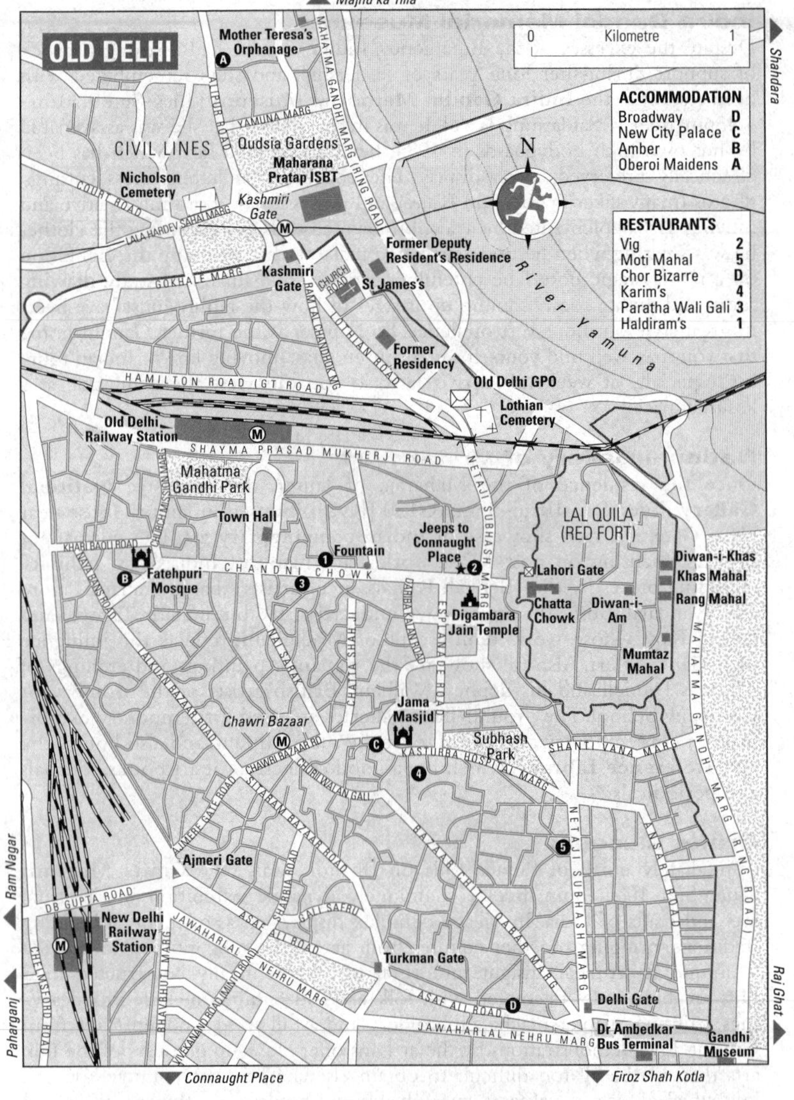

with trees and some of the most opulent bazaars of the East. If you take a walk along it, look out for numbered "heritage buildings" signposted at intervals, with placards outside explaining their historical significance – many featured in the fighting for Delhi during the 1857 Mutiny. Today the city walls have crumbled, and of the fourteen old gates only five remain. It's a fascinating area, but you'll need stamina, patience and time to endure the crowds and traffic. An easy way to get to Old Delhi from Connaught Place is on one of the shared **jeep taxis** from the inner circle by Palika Bazaar (Rs6 a place), which drop you on Chandni Chowk opposite the Red Fort.

Lal Qila (Red Fort)

The largest of Old Delhi's monuments is **Lal Qila**, or Red Fort (Tues–Sun dawn–dusk; $2 [Rs5]), whose thick red sandstone walls, bulging with turrets and bastions, rise above a wide dry moat in the northeast corner of the original city of Shahjahanabad. The fort covers a semi-octagonal area of almost 2km, its longest walls facing the town in the west and the River Yamuna in the east. Work was started on the complex – modelled on the royal citadel in Agra – in 1639, and was completed by 1648. It contains all the expected trappings of the centre of Moghul government: halls of public and private audience, domed and arched marble palaces, plush private apartments, a mosque, and elaborately designed gardens. Today the Yamuna no longer flows close to the east wall, the "Stream of Paradise" no longer trickles through each palace, copper-plated domes have been replaced with plainer marble domes, and there are few signs of the precious stones and gems once set into the marble walls. Nevertheless, the fort remains an impressive testimony to Moghul grandeur, despite being attacked and plundered by the Persian emperor Nadir Shah in 1739, and by British soldiers during the battles of 1857 – as well as being rubbed, touched and worn down by thousands of marvelling tourists.

Entrance to the fort is through the mighty three-storey **Lahori Gate** in the centre of the west wall, where tickets are sold. Once inside, eager **guides** will offer their services at negotiable prices (Rs30–50). The main entrance opens onto **Chatta Chowk**, a covered street flanked with arched cells that used to house Delhi's most talented jewellers, carpet-makers, goldsmiths and silk-weavers, but now stocks souvenirs.

Beyond the Naubhat Khana, or Musicians' Gallery, a path runs east through wide lawns to the Hall of Public Audience, the lofty **Diwan-i-Am**, where the emperor used to meet commoners until the custom was curtailed by Aurangzeb. Once strewn with silk carpets and partitioned with hanging tapestries, it houses "the seat of the shadow of God", a marble throne surrounded by twelve panels inlaid with precious stones. The seat was designed by an artist from Bordeaux, whose frieze of the Greek god Orpheus with his lute makes a surprising departure from the more usual floral designs of the Moghuls. Lord Curzon, viceroy of India from 1898 to 1905, restored the hall and returned the imperial throne from the British Museum in 1909.

The **palaces** in the fort along the east wall face spacious gardens in the west and overlook the banks of the Yamuna, once the scene of elephant fights laid on to entertain the royal occupants. Immediately east of the Diwan-i-Am, **Rang Mahal**, the "Palace of Colour", housed the emperor's wives and mistresses. It was surmounted with gilded turrets, delicately painted and decorated with intricate mosaics of mirrors, and with a ceiling overlaid with gold and silver that was reflected in a central pool in the marble floor. Unfortunately, it was greatly defaced when the British used it as an Officers' Mess after the Mutiny, and today is a shadow of its former glory. The similar **Mumtaz Mahal**, south

Sound-and-light shows

Each night except Monday, a **sound-and-light show** takes place in the **Red Fort**: the palaces are dramatically lit, and a historical commentary blares from crackly loudspeakers. The show starts after sunset and lasts an hour (in Hindi Feb–April & Sept–Oct 7pm, May–Aug 7.30pm, Nov–Jan 6pm; in English Feb–April & Sept–Oct 8.30pm, May–Aug 9pm, Nov–Jan 7.30pm; Rs50; ⓣ011/2327 4580). The mosquitoes are ferocious, so bring repellent. Heavy monsoon rains may affect summer shows.

of the main *zenana*, or women's quarters, and probably used by princesses, is now a **museum** (Tues–Thurs & Sat–Sun 10am–5pm; Rs2, pay when you buy your entrance ticket) housing weaponry, textiles, carpets, ornate chess sets and hookahs.

On the northern side of Rang Mahal, the marble **Khas Mahal** was the personal palace of the emperor, divided into separate apartments for worship, sleeping and sitting. The southern chamber, **Tosh Khana** ("Robe Room"), has a stunning marble filigree screen on its north wall, carved with the scales of justice. The octagonal tower projecting over the east wall of the Khas Mahal was used by the emperor, who would appear here daily before throngs gathered on the riverbanks below. In 1911, when Delhi was declared capital, King George V (emperor of India) and Queen Mary sat here before the citizens of Delhi.

North of Khas Mahal, in the large **Diwan-i-Khas** ("Hall of Private Audience"), the emperor would address the highest nobles of his court. Today it's the finest building in the fort, a marble pavilion shaded by a roof raised on stolid pillars embellished with amber, jade and gold, meeting in ornate scalloped arches. On the north and south walls you can still make out the Persian inscription attributed to Shah Jahan's prime minister, which translates as: "If there be paradise on the face of earth/It is this, Oh, it is this, Oh, it is this". A marble and gold peacock throne inlaid with rubies, sapphires and diamonds once stood on the central pedestal, bypassed by a "Stream of Paradise" that gurgled through the cool chamber. It took seven years to construct, and was the pride of the fort, but the Persian Nadir Shah took it back to his kingdom as booty after a raid in 1739.

A little further north are the **hammams**, or baths, sunken into the marble floor inlaid with delicate patterns of precious stones, and dappled in jewel-coloured light that filters through stained-glass windows. The western chamber contained hot baths while the eastern apartment, with fountains of rose-water, was used as a dressing room.

Jama Masjid

Old Delhi's red-and-white **Jama Masjid** (8.30am–12.15pm & 1.45pm till half an hour before sunset; opens 7am in summer; closed for 30min in the afternoon for prayers; free, plus Rs150 for camera), 500m southwest of the Red Fort, is India's largest mosque. Soaring above the narrow streets of the old city, it may look huge from a distance, but feels nothing short of immense once you've climbed the wide staircases to the arched gateways and entered the open courtyard, large enough to accommodate the bending bodies of 25,000 worshippers. It was designed by Shah Jahan and built by a workforce of 5000 between 1644 and 1656. Originally called Masjid-i-Jahanuma ("mosque commanding a view of the world"), this grand structure stands on Bho Jhala, one of Shahjahanabad's two hills, and looks east to the sprawling Red Fort, and down on the seething streets of Old Delhi all around. Broad red sandstone staircases lead to gateways on the east, north and southern sides, where worshippers and visitors alike must remove their shoes (the custodian will guard them for you for a small tip). Dress conservatively.

Once inside the courtyard, your eyes will be drawn to the three bulbous marble domes crowning the **main prayer hall** on the west side (facing Mecca), fronted by a series of high cusped arches, and sheltering the mihrab, the central niche in the west wall reserved for the prayer leader. The pool in the centre is used for ritual ablutions. At each corner of the square yard a slender minaret crowned with a marble dome rises to the sky, and it's well worth climbing the **tower** south of the main sanctuary (Rs20) for an unrivalled view over Delhi. In the northeast corner a white shrine protects a collection of Muhammad's relics, shrouded in rose petals and watched over by keepers who will, in exchange for a tip, reveal the contents: two sections of the Koran written on deerskin by relatives of the prophet, a red beard-hair of Muhammad's, his sandals, and his "footprint" miraculously embedded in a marble slab.

Digambara Jain temple and Jain Bird Hospital

Delhi's oldest **Digambara Jain temple**, opposite the entrance to the Red Fort at the east end of Chandni Chowk, was built in 1526 and remains a haven of tranquillity amid the noise and chaos of the main street. Though not as ornate as the fine temples in Gujarat and Rajasthan, it does boast detailed carvings, and gilded paintwork in the antechambers surrounding the main shrine to Parshvanath, the twenty-third *tirthankara*. Remove your shoes, and leave any leather articles at the kiosk before entering.

The **Jain Bird Hospital** (free but donations are appreciated), in the temple courtyard, puts into practice the Jain principle that all life is sacred, and serves as a rescue sanctuary for partridges, caught and wounded by fowlers and bought in bulk by Jain merchants who bring them here to recover. There are also wards for pigeons, parrots and sparrows (notoriously vulnerable to whirring ceiling fans). Birds of prey are seen on a strictly outpatient basis, as they are not vegetarian.

Raj Ghat

When Shah Jahan established his city in 1638, its eastern edges bordered the River Yamuna, and a line of *ghats*, or steps leading to the water, was installed along the riverbanks. *Ghats* have been used in India for centuries, primarily for worship, but also for washing clothes and bathing, and for the final ritual, cremation. **Raj Ghat**, the site of the cremations of three of modern India's most revered figures, Mahatma Gandhi (1948), Indira Gandhi (1984) and her son Rajiv (1991), is more of a park than a *ghat*, lying well away from the river bank. Rajiv is honoured by a striking frieze and his mother marked by a red-grey stone monolith. The Mahatma's *samadhi*, a low black plinth, receives a steady stream of visitors, and he is remembered through prayers here every Friday evening, and on the anniversaries of his birth and death (Oct 2 & Jan 30). Opposite Raj Ghat's southwest corner, the small **Gandhi Memorial Museum** (daily except Mon and every second Sun, 9.30am–5.30pm; free) houses some of Gandhi's photographs and writings, and at weekends you can watch a film on his political and personal life (English Sat 4pm; Hindi Sun 4pm).

Firoz Shah Kotla

The prosperous fifth city of Delhi, Firozabad, founded in 1354, stretched from the north ridge to Hauz Khas in the south; today few traces survive save the remains of the palace of **Firoz Shah Kotla** (also called Kotla Fort), set amid ornamental gardens 500m east of Delhi Gate, and accessed from BS Zafar Marg, which is the southern continuation of Netaji Subhash Marg. Its most incongruous and distinctive element is the single polished sandstone **Ashokan Column** (third century BC), carried down the Yamuna by raft from Ambala to grace a palace that is now a crumbling ruin. The 14m-high column, the second brought to Delhi, continues to protrude above the surroundings, withstanding the ravages of time and dominating the ill-kept gardens. Next to a *baoli* (stepwell) lie the ruins of a massive mosque which once accommodated over 10,000 worshippers; Timur (Tamerlane) is said to have been so impressed by it that it served as the model for his great mosque in Samarkand.

North of the Red Fort

Netaji Subhash Marg leads north from the Red Fort and under a railway bridge to Old Delhi GPO. Just before the post office, on the east side of the road, **Lothian Cemetery**, the burial ground for officers of the East India Company from 1808 until just after the Mutiny of 1857, is now in a state of disrepair, and occupied by squatters. In the middle of the road in front of the post office, and still topped by an old cannon, the remains of the East India Company's **Magazine** or arsenal is now used mainly as an unofficial public toilet, so watch your step if you cross the street to explore it. Another part of the magazine, with a memorial plaque, stands on a second traffic island just to the north.

Continuing north along Lothian Road, you'll pass another remnant of Company days on your right in the form of the old **Residency**, now the Dara Shikoh Library of Guru Gobind Singh Indraprastha University. A couple of hundred metres further is the rather fine cream and white baroque facade of **St James's Church** (daily 8am–noon & 2–5pm, or whenever you can find the caretaker), built in 1836 on the orders of **James Skinner**, the son of a Scottish Company-wallah and a Rajput princess. Because of his mixed ancestry, and the increasing racism of the British regime, Skinner was refused a commission in the Company's army, but set up his own irregular cavalry unit (Skinner's Horse, also called the Yellow Boys after their uniform) and made himself indispensable to the Company in northern India. Though he was continually snubbed over pay and rank, his astounding victories over the forces of the Maharaja of Jaipur and the great Sikh leader Maharaja Ranjit Singh eventually forced the Company to begrudgingly grant him the rank of Lieutenant Colonel and absorb his cavalrymen into its ranks. Skinner died in 1842 and is buried just in front of the altar.

The side street immediately north of the church (Church Road) leads to the offices of the Northern Railway, where the East India Company's **Deputy Resident's Residence** is now the office of the railway's chief engineer. If you ask at the gate, you'll probably be allowed in to admire the bow-fronted veranda and balustrades, but you probably won't be permitted to take photos or to venture inside. A plaque to the left of its front door explains the building's history.

The double-arched **Kashmiri Gate**, on the west side of Lothian Road just 300m north of the church, was where the Moghul court would leave Delhi every summer bound for the cool valley of Kashmir. To its north is Maharana Pratap Inter-state Bus Terminal, beyond which, on the left, the peaceful **Qudsia Gardens** are a fading reminder of the magnificent pleasure parks commissioned in the mid-eighteenth century by Queen Qudsia, favourite mistress of Muhammad Shah, and mother of Ahmed Shah. Some 400m north, on Commissioner's Lane, **Mother Teresa's Orphanage** (daily 8am–noon & 3–6pm) welcomes volunteers; contact Missionaries of Charity, 12 Commissioner's Lane, Shishu Bhavan, Delhi 110054, or call ⓣ011/2395 0181.

Just west of Qudsia Gardens, on Qudsia Road, is Delhi's oldest burial ground, **Nicholson Cemetery**, named after Brigadier General John Nicholson, who led the British attack to regain Delhi from the Mutineers/freedom fighters in 1857. The graveyard is still used, but most of the headstones bear British names from the nineteenth and early twentieth centuries. The area immediately to the north, the **Civil Lines**, came into being after the Mutiny, when the British no longer felt safe living among the residents of Old Delhi and moved up here for a more secluded location.

South Delhi

Most of the early settlements of Delhi, including its first cities, are to be found not in "Old Delhi" but in **SOUTH DELHI**, the area south of Connaught

Place and Rajpath. While the first Muslim kingdoms built their cities on the foundations of those settlements they conquered, shaping the **Qutb Minar Complex**, later dynasties created their own capitals at **Siri**, **Tughluqabad**, **Jahanpanah** and **Shergarh**. Nowadays many of these ancient monuments lie isolated deep within modern urban enclaves created in response to increasing congestion in the centre of Delhi. While the rash of housing developments, fashionable bars and glitzy shopping precincts is fast swallowing up the countryside, pockets of almost untouched rural peace do still exist, making south Delhi a fascinating blend of the contemporary, the pastoral and the historic.

Purana Qila

The majestic fortress of **Purana Qila** (daily dawn–dusk; $2 [Rs5]), whose crumbling ramparts dominate busy Mathura Road, 4km southeast of Connaught Place, is rumoured to stand on the site of Indraprastha, the Pandava city of *Mahabharata* fame. More certainly, it was the centre of the sixth city of Delhi, created by Humayun, the second Moghul emperor, as Din-Panah, and renamed Shergarh by Sher Shah, who briefly displaced him. Purana Qila is served by buses between Delhi Gate and Sunder Nagar, such as #423 and #438 (ask for the zoo, which is served by the same stop).

Two principal buildings survive to hint at the former glories of the fortress. The Qila-i-Kuhna Masjid is one of Sher Shah's finest monuments. Constructed in 1541 in the Afghan style, it consists of five elegant arches, embellished with white-and-black marble to complement the red sandstone. The **Sher Mandal**, a red sandstone octagonal observatory and library, was the scene of the death of Humayun, just a year after he defeated Sikander Sur and returned to power. He stumbled down its treacherously steep steps in 1556 as he answered the *muezzin*'s call to prayer; visitors today can climb to the top for panoramic views of Delhi and the River Yamuna to the east. The fortress is entered through the lofty south gate, Lal Darwaza, just inside which a small museum houses sculpture from the Mauryan era (daily except Fri, 10am–5pm; free).

The Yamuna formerly flowed along the eastern base of Purana Qila but the moats it fed are now dry. During Partition in 1947, Muslim refugees gathered within the confines of the fort to await transportation to the newly created nation of Pakistan; tens of thousands of them were slaughtered en route.

Lodi Gardens

Some 4km south of Connaught Place off Lodi Road, the leafy, pleasant **Lodi Gardens** (daily 5am–8pm; free) form part of a belt of fifteenth- and sixteenth-century monuments that now stand incongruously amid golf greens, large bungalows and elite estates. The park is especially full in the early mornings and early evenings, when middle-class fitness enthusiasts come for brisk walks or to jog through the manicured gardens against a backdrop of much-graffitied medieval monuments. The gardens, a Rs40 auto ride from Connaught Place, also contain the **National Bonsai Park**, which has a fine selection of diminutive trees. The best time to come is at sunset, when the light is soft and the tombs are all lit up.

Near the centre of the gardens, the imposing **Bara Gumbad** ("Large Dome"), is a square late-fifteenth-century tomb capped by its sizeable dome, its monotonous exterior relieved by grey and black stones and its interior adorned

The sights covered in this section appear on the New Delhi **map** on p.127.

with painted stuccowork. **Shish Gumbad** ("glazed dome"), a similar tomb 50m north, still bears a few traces of the blue tiles liberally used to form friezes below the cornice and above the entrance. Inside, plasterwork is inscribed with ornate Koranic inscriptions.

The octagonal **tomb of Muhammad Shah** (1434–44) of the Sayyid dynasty, stands 300m southwest of Bara Gumbad, surrounded by verandas and pierced by arches and sloping buttresses. Enclosed within high walls and a square garden, 300m north of Bara Gumbad, the **tomb of Sikandar Lodi** (1517–18) repeats the octagonal theme, with a central chamber encircled by a veranda. **Athpula** ("eight piers"), a sixteenth-century ornamental bridge, lies east, in the northwest corner of the park.

Nizamuddin

Now engulfed by a busy road network and plush suburbs, the *muhalla* (neighbourhood) of **Nizamuddin** is almost isolated from the rest of the city; to enter it is like passing through a time warp into the Middle Ages. The heart of the village is just off the busy Mathura Road, 6km south of Connaught Place, and easily accessible by public transport such as the #459 bus from New Delhi station and Connaught Place. At Nizamuddin's heart, surrounded by a tangle of narrow alleyways, lies one of Sufism's greatest shrines, pulsating with life and drawing devotees from far and wide.

The marble **Hazrat Nizamuddin Dargah**, tomb of the fourth saint of the Chishtiya order, Sheikh Nizamuddin Aulia (1236–1325), was built the year the sheikh died, but has been through several renovations, and the present mausoleum dates from 1562. Lattice screens and arches in the inner sanctum surround the actual tomb, enclosed by a marble rail and a canopy of mother-of-pearl. Religious song and music play an important role among the Chishtiyas, and

Qawwali

Of all Indian art forms, **qawwali**, whose prime purpose is to gain *hal* (spiritual ecstasy) through devotional song, is among the most adaptable and versatile, appearing as popular entertainment at modern weddings and on concert platforms. The form has been embraced by the world music scene: the late Nusrat Fateh Ali Khan gained an international reputation with a *qawwali* repertoire that ranged from the traditional to experimental fusion. Musically, *qawwali* is linked to the north Indian classical form of vocal music, *khyal*, deriving its melody from such sources as classic *ragas* (modal compositions) and its own modal systems based on central Asian roots. Comprising a chorus led by solo singing accompanied by clapping and usually a harmonium combined with *dholak* (double-membraned barrel drum) and tabla (paired hand-drums), the resulting hypnotic rhythm can inspire its audience into a state of *mast* (spiritual intoxication), manifested by wild swaying and swinging of the head. The simple but effective drum patterns used include *qawwali tal*, *dadra* and *keherwa* – respectively four-, six- and eight-beat rhythmic cycles.

Most performers, or *qawwals*, are hereditary musicians who trace their lineage back to **Amir Khusrau**, to whom several songs are attributed. Some compositions have become universal hymns, such as the haunting *Dam-a-dam mast Qalandar* (constantly intoxicated Qalandar) and the robust *hamd* (a eulogy in praise of God, the Prophet, or a saint), *Allah Hu*. Musical gatherings, or *Mehfil-e Sama*, are held regularly, usually on Thursday evenings, in the main *dargahs* of Delhi such as Nizamuddin and Mehrauli, with especial poignancy during the *urs* (anniversary) of the saint in question. *Qawwali* in front of the shrine is rarely as elaborate as that on stage, but far more moving in its powerful and simple devotion.

qawwals (bards) gather to sing in the evenings (especially on Thursdays and feast days). Sheikh Nizamuddin's disciple, the poet and chronicler **Amir Khusrau** – considered to be the first Urdu poet and the founder of *khyal*, the most common form of north Indian classical music – lies in a contrasting red sandstone tomb in front of his master's mausoleum.

The oldest building in the area, the red sandstone mosque of **Jam-at Khana Masjid**, looms over the main *dargah* on its western side (closed to women). It was built in 1325 by Khizr Khan, the son of Ala-ud-din Khalji. Enclosed by marble lattice screens next to Amir Khusrau's mausoleum, the tomb of **Princess Jahanara**, the favourite daughter of Shah Jahan, is topped by a hollow filled with grass in compliance with her wish to have nothing but grass covering her grave. At the north gate of the *dargah*'s compound is a holy *baoli* (step-well), next to the mosque called **Chini-ka-Burj** ("tower of tiles") for its profusely decorated upper chamber.

Humayun's Tomb

Close to the medieval Muslim centre of Nizamuddin and 2km from Purana Qila, **Humayun's Tomb** (daily sunrise–sunset; $5 [Rs10]) stands at the crossroads of the Lodi and Mathura roads, 500m from Nizamuddin railway station (one stop from New Delhi station on the suburban line), or Rs50 by auto from Connaught Place. Delhi's first Moghul mausoleum, it was constructed to house the remains of the second Moghul emperor, Humayun, who had lost Delhi and most of his father Babur's empire at the start of his reign to the Bihari ruler Sher Shah Sur. He finally managed to regain it all from Sher Shah's son Sikander just before his untimely death in 1564. The tomb was built under the watchful eye of Haji Begum, Humayun's senior widow and mother of Akbar, who camped here for the duration, and is now buried alongside her husband. The grounds were later used to inter several prominent Moghuls, and served as a refuge for the last emperor, Bahadur Shah II, captured here by the British in 1857.

The tomb's sombre, Persian-style elegance marks this as one of Delhi's finest historic sites. Constructed of red sandstone, inlaid with black and white marble, on a commanding podium looking towards the Yamuna, it stands in the centre of the formal *charbagh*, or quartered garden. The octagonal structure is crowned with a double dome that soars to a height of 38m. Though it was the very first Moghul garden tomb – to be followed by Akbar's at Sikandra (see p.294) and of course the Taj Mahal at Agra (see p.285), for which it can be seen as a prototype – Humayun's mausoleum has antecedents in Delhi in the form of Ghiyas-ud-din Tughluq's tomb at Tughluqabad (see p.141), and that of Sikandar Lodi in Lodi Gardens (see p.137). From the second of those it adopted its octagonal shape and the high central arch that was to be such a typical feature of Moghul architecture – you'll see it at the Taj, and in Delhi's Jama Masjid (see p.134), for example.

Within the grounds southeast of the main mausoleum, another impressive square mausoleum, with a double dome and two graves bearing Koranic inscriptions, is that of Humayun's barber, a man considered important because he was trusted with holding a razor to the emperor's throat. Nearby, outside the compound (you'll have to walk right round for a closer look) stands the **Nila Gumbad** ("blue dome"), an octagonal tomb with a dome of blue tiles, supposedly built by one of Akbar's nobles to honour a faithful servant, and which may possibly predate Humayun's Tomb. On your way round to the Nila Gumbad, you'll probably pass the **tomb of Khan-i-Khanan**, a Moghul general who died in 1626 (daily sunrise–sunset; $2 [Rs5]); unfortunately, the tomb looks rather ragged as the facing was all stripped for use in Safdarjung's tomb, and the garden that surrounded it has mostly gone. The blue-domed structure in the middle of the road junction in front of the entrance to Humayun's tomb is a seventeenth-century tomb called **Sabz Burj** – the tiles on its dome are not original, but the result of a recent restoration.

Safdarjung's Tomb

The tomb of **Safdarjung** (daily dawn to dusk; $2 [Rs5]), the Moghul viceroy of Avadh under Muhammad Shah (1719–48), stands at the junction of Lodi Road and Aurobindo Marg, 5km southwest of Connaught Place; served by bus #505 from New Delhi station or Connaught Place, or bus #560 from Jantar Mantar. Constructed between 1753 and 1774, the double-storeyed mausoleum, built of red and buff sandstone and relieved by marble, rises on a dramatic platform overlooking the adjacent airport of the Delhi Flying Club. It was the very last of India's great Moghul garden tombs, dating from the period after Nadir Shah's sacking of the city, by which time the empire was reduced to a fraction of its former size and most of the capital's grander buildings lay in ruins. Emblematic of the decadence and degeneracy that characterized the twilight of the Moghul era, the double-storeyed mausoleum sports an elongated, tapered dome and absurdly ornate interior filled with swirling plasterwork. In *City of Djinns*, William Dalrymple aptly describes its quirky design as "blowzy Mughal rococo" typifying an age "not so much decaying into impoverished anonymity as one whoring and drinking itself into extinction".

Rail Transport Museum

The cream of India's royal coaches and oldest engines are on permanent display at the **Rail Transport Museum** in the Embassy enclave of Chanakyapuri, southwest of Connaught Place (Tues–Sun: April–Sept 9.30am–7.30pm, Oct–March 9.30am–5.30pm; Rs10); take bus #620 from Connaught Place. Some 27 locomotives and 17 carriages – including the ornate gold-painted saloon car of the Maharaja of Baroda (1886), the teak carriage, trimmed in gold and ivory, of the Maharaja of Mysore, and the cabin used by the Prince of Wales in 1876 – are kept in the grounds. A steam-hauled miniature "Joy Train" does a circuit of the grounds (Rs10) whenever there are enough passengers to make it worthwhile.

The covered section of the museum houses models of famous engines and coaches, displays of old tickets, and even the skull of an elephant hit by a train near Calcutta in 1894. The pride of the collection, however, is a model of India's very first train, a steam engine which made its inaugural journey of 21 miles from Mumbai to Thane in 1853. Trainspotters who wish to delve deeper can ask the curators to open the library.

Hauz Khas

Set amid parks and woodland, the wealthy suburban development of **Hauz Khas**, 12km southwest of Connaught Place, is typical of south Delhi in being a thoroughly modern area dotted with remnants of antiquity. The modern part takes the form of Hauz Khas village, a shopping area packed with chic boutiques and smart restaurants, the latter mostly packed into what is called the "Village Bistro". There's also a very pleasant deer park and a rose garden, but of most interest to visitors, apart from the upmarket shopping possibilities (see p.147), are the ruins of a fourteenth-century reservoir at the western end of the village.

Ala-ud-din Khalji had the reservoir (or "tank") built to supply water to the inhabitants of Siri, Delhi's second city, and it was known after him as **Hauz-i-Alai**. Half a century later, it was expanded by Firoz Shah Tughluq, who added a two-storey *madrasa* (seminary), and a mosque at its northern end. Among the anonymous tombs scattered throughout the area is that of Firoz Shah himself, situated on the edge of the tank. Its high walls, lofty dome, and doorway spanned by a lintel with a stone railing outside, are fine examples of Hindu Indian traditions effectively blended with Islamic architecture. At dawn every day, the surrounding woodlands and the bed of the immense tank, once the site of Timur's camp, come alive with Delhi-ites out walking, practising yoga and jogging.

Siri itself was located a couple of kilometres east of Hauz Khas, and the remains of its ramparts can be seen from Khel Gaon Marg. Much of the site has been given over to parkland, which makes it pleasant enough to visit, but part of it has been subsumed by a village built to house athletes competing in the 1982 Asian Games.

Baha'i Temple

Often compared to the Sydney Opera House, Delhi's modern **Baha'i Temple** (Tues–Sun: April–Sept 9am–7pm; Oct–March 9.30am–5.30pm; you may be asked to wait briefly outside during services, which are on the hour 9am–noon & 3–5pm), on open ground atop Kalkaji Hill 12km southeast of Connaught Place, has become yet another symbol of the city and attracts a steady stream of visitors. Dominating the surrounding suburban sprawl, 27 spectacular giant white petals of marble in the shape of an unfolding lotus spring from nine pools and walkways, to symbolize the nine unifying spiritual paths of the Baha'i faith; each petal alcove contains an extract of the Baha'i holy scriptures. You're welcome to meditate in silence inside the impressive central hall, which rises to a height of 34 metres. Set amid well-maintained gardens, the temple is at its most impressive at sunset.

Kalkiji is a major bus depot – the #440 runs from here to Connaught Place.

Ashoka's Rock Edict

The emperor **Ashoka's Rock Edict** was discovered in 1966, engraved on a rock overlooking the Yamuna near Srinivaspuri, 11km southeast of Connaught Place. A ten-line epigraph in the ancient Brahmi script, one of many such placed at important sites and crossroads throughout Ashoka's vast empire, the inscription proves that Delhi was occupied during the Mauryan period (321 BC–184 BC), prior to both Muslim and Rajput settlement. It states that the emperor's exertions in the cause of *dharma* had brought the people of India (Jambudvipa) closer to the gods; and that through their efforts, irrespective of their station, this attainment could be increased even further.

Tughluqabad

Fifteen kilometres southeast of Connaught Place on the Mehrauli–Badarpur Road (the entrance is 1km east of the junction with Guru Ravidas Marg), a rocky escarpment holds the crumbling 6.5-kilometre-long battlements of the third city of Delhi, **Tughluqabad** (daily sunrise–sunset; $2), built during the short reign of Ghiyas-ud-din Tughluq (1321–25). After the king's death the city was deserted, probably due to the lack of a clean water source nearby. The Cyclopean ruins are almost entirely abandoned, overgrown with scrubland and home to nomadic Gujars and rhesus monkeys – which is seen by some as a fulfilment of a curse by the Sufi saint, Sheikh Nizamuddin Aulia. The most interesting area is the high-walled **citadel** in the southwestern part of the site, though only a long underground passage, the ruins of several halls and a tower now remain. The grid pattern of some of the city streets to the north is still traceable. The palace area is to the west of the entrance, and the former bazaar to the east.

The southernmost of Tughlaqabad's thirteen gates still looks down on a causeway, breached by the modern road, which rises above the flood plain, to link the fortress with **Ghiyas-ud-din Tughluq's tomb** (same hours and ticket as Tughlaqabad). The tomb is entered through a massive red sandstone gateway leading into a courtyard surrounded by cloisters in the defensive walls. In the middle, surrounded by a well-kept lawn, stands the distinctive mausoleum, its sloping sandstone walls topped by a marble dome, and in its small way a precursor to the fine series of garden tombs built by the Moghuls, which began here in Delhi with that of Humayun (see p.139). Inside the mausoleum are the graves of Ghiyas-ud-din, his wife, and their son Muhammad Shah II. Ghiyas-ud-din's chief minister Jafar Khan is buried in the eastern bastion, and interred in the cloister nearby is the sultan's favourite dog.

The later fortress of **Adilabad** (free), built by Muhammad Shah II in much the same style as his father's citadel, and now in ruins, stands on a hillock to the southeast.

Tughluqabad is awkward to get to by **bus**; from New Delhi station or Connaught Place either take #459 to Badarpur, and change onto a Mehrauli-bound #34, #430, #525 or #717, or else take #505 to Mehrauli/Qutb Minar Complex, and catch a #34, #525 or #717 going east. An auto-rickshaw from Connaught Place should cost around Rs100.

Qutb Minar Complex

Above the foundations of **Lal Kot**, settled in the eighth century by the Tomara Rajputs and developed in the twelfth century by the Chauhans, the first monuments of Muslim India are now known as the **Qutb Minar Complex** (daily sunrise–sunset; $5 [Rs10]), and stand in well-tended grounds 13km south of Connaught Place off Aurobindo Marg; to get here take bus #505 from Ajmeri Gate, Chelmsford Road, Connaught Place (Super Bazaar) or Kasturba Gandhi Marg. One of Delhi's most famous landmarks, the fluted red sandstone tower of the Qutb Minar tapers upwards from the ruins, covered with intricate carvings and deeply inscribed verses from the Qur'an, to a height of 72.5m. In times past it was considered one of the "Wonders of the East", second only to the Taj Mahal – in the words of the Victorian historian, James Ferguson, "the most beautiful example of its class known anywhere"; but historian John Keay was perhaps more representative of the modern eye when he claimed that the tower had "an unfortunate hint of the factory chimney and the brick kiln; a wisp of white smoke trailing from its summit would not seem out of place".

Work on the Qutb Minar started in 1199; it was Qutb-ud-din Aibak's victory tower, celebrating the advent of the Muslim dominance of Delhi (and much of the subcontinent) that was to endure until 1857. For Qutb-ud-din, who died four years after gaining power, it marked the eastern extremity of the Islamic faith, casting the shadow of God over east and west. It was also a minaret, from which the *muezzin* called the faithful to prayer. Only the first storey has been ascribed to Qutb-ud-din's short reign; the other four were built by his successor Iltutmish, and the top was restored in 1369 by Firoz Shah, who used marble to face the red sandstone.

Adjacent to the tower lie the ruins of India's first mosque, **Quwwat-ul-Islam** (the "Might of Islam"), built by Qutb-ud-din using the remains of 27 Hindu and Jain temples and the help of Hindu artisans – their influence can be seen in the detail of the masonry and the indigenous corbelled arches. Steps lead to an impressive courtyard flanked by cloisters and supported by pillars unmistakably taken from a Hindu temple and adapted to accord with strict Islamic law forbidding iconic worship – all the faces of the decorative figures carved into the columns have been removed. Especially fine ornamental arches, rising as high as 16m, remain of what was once the prayer hall. Beautifully carved sandstone screens, combining Koranic calligraphy with the Indian lotus, form a facade immediately to the west of the mosque, facing Mecca. Iltutmish and his successors extended the building, enlarging the prayer hall and the cloisters and introducing geometric designs, calligraphy, glazed tiles set in brick, and squinches (arches set diagonally to a square to support a dome).

In complete contrast to the mainly Islamic surroundings, an **Iron Pillar** (7.2m) stands in the corner of the mosque, bearing fourth-century Sanskrit inscriptions of the Gupta period attributing it to the memory of King Chandragupta II (373–413). Once topped with an image of the Hindu bird god, Garuda, the extraordinary and virtually rust-free pillar, made of 98 percent pure iron, is a puzzle to metallurgists. It must have been transplanted here, but its origins remain hazy. Tradition has it that anyone who can encircle the column with their hands behind their back will have their wishes granted, but as you are not allowed to go right up to the pillar you won't be able to test this out.

Ala-i-Darwaza, a mausoleum-like gateway with stone lattice screens, was added by Ala-ud-din Khalji (1296–1316). Its inlaid marble embellishments are ascribed to an influx of Pathan artisans from Byzantine Turkey, and the import of Seljuk influences – the true arches were the first in India. The south entrance to the complex is marked by yet another tower, **Alai Minar**, which was planned as grander and larger than the Qutb Minar but left abandoned after the construction of its first storey.

On a plinth west of Quwwat-ul-Islam, the **tomb of Iltutmish**, built in 1235 by the ruler himself, is said to be the first Muslim mausoleum in India (Hindus cremate their dead rather than bury them). A relatively plain exterior blending Indian and Muslim styles, with three ornate arches, hides an interior 9m square with geometric arabesque patterns combined with calligraphy and lotus and wheel motifs.

Perched above the scrubland 150m southeast of the Qutb Minar, the octagonal Moghul **tomb of Muhammad Quli Khan**, one of Akbar's courtiers, was somewhat bizarrely occupied by **Sir Thomas Metcalfe**, resident at the Moghul court, as a country house – the first floor above the sepulchre room was converted into a living apartment, and the chamber beneath the dome became a dining room. The building now lies in ruins. Another crumbling Raj-era house nearby still boasts a very ornamental English fireplace and swimming tank. Outside the complex, north of the Qutb Minar, **Adham Khan's tomb** stands on the remains of the walls of Lal Kot. A general in Akbar's army, Khan was hurled from the ramparts of Agra Fort on the orders of the emperor after some murderous court feuding. You can get good views of both the tomb and the Qutb complex from the roof of the Church of St John, an incongruous little chapel with an Anglican nave, monastic cloisters and a Hindu *chhatra* (tower), tucked down a lane opposite the tomb entrance.

Sulabh International Museum of Toilets

The lighthearted nature of the **Sulabh International Museum of Toilets**, on Palam Dabri Marg in Mahavir Enclave I, in Delhi's western suburbs (Mon–Sat 10am–5pm; free), belies the importance of the organization which runs it. Basing itself soundly on Gandhian principles, the Sulabh Movement aims to free members of the lowest rank of outcastes from the demeaning job of cleaning out non-flush latrines and carrying away the excrement, and to end the insanitary practice of open-air defecation by promoting hygienic, eco-friendly toilets in towns, cities and villages across India – you'll no doubt see some of their "toilet complexes" around Delhi.

The museum illustrates lavatorial history from Harappan times through to the modern day, and its grounds house examples of easy-to-build hygienic flush latrines for use in communities without sewerage or running water. Pride of place goes to the movement's machine for converting human excrement into fertilizer and fuel, an average poo yielding a cubic metre of methane gas that can be used for cooking, heating or lighting.

Coronation Park and Shalimar Bagh

Now just a windblown piece of waste ground on the city's northern fringes, **Coronation Park** once showpieced the pomp and might of the British Raj. The British held three **durbars** (huge imperial pageants) here: in 1887 on Queen Victoria's assumption of the title "Empress of India", in 1903 to mark the coronation of her successor Edward VII, and in 1911 when George V came to be crowned in person as emperor. The high point of the durbar was a procession of elephants bearing all the princes of India, headed by the Nizam of Hyderabad, to pay homage to the British ruler, in the same way that they had previously to the Moghuls. All but forgotten nowadays (your auto-wallah or taxi driver won't have heard of the place so they'll need clear instructions on how to get here), the park is centred around a **granite obelisk** commemorating the 1911 coronation. In an enclosure close by, a grandiose statue of the king-emperor George, which once graced what is now Rajpath, stands Ozymandias-like among likenesses of other nameless and forgotten rulers from an empire fast receding into history. The park is located on Nirankari Marg, just south of the Outer Ring Road NH-1 by-pass (Dr K.B. Hedgewar Marg). It costs Rs60 by pre-paid auto from Connaught Place, but around Rs100 by auto from town if you don't pre-pay.

Four kilometres to the west, on Maharaja Agrasen Marg, is an old Moghul pleasure garden, **Shalimar Bagh**, at the northern end of a modern district that also bears its name. The garden is the site of another long-forgotten coronation, that of the Moghul emperor Aurangzeb in 1658. As his father Shah Jahan fell ill and looked like dying, Aurangzeb moved quickly to seize the throne, having all his four brothers killed, and his father, whose illness proved not to be fatal, imprisoned in the Agra Fort. He then had himself crowned in this formally laid-out garden, constructed on the orders of Shah Jahan some 26 years ealier. At its heart, now crumbling and overgrown, the **Shish Mahal** was the garden's pavilion, and traces of the plasterwork still remain to give an idea of its former glory, though it was already recorded as being in a state of decay by the mid-nineteenth century.

Eating

Middle-class Delhi-ites love to eat out, and have a large variety of **restaurants** and worldwide cuisine to choose from. There's something for every budget: delicious Indian snacks at **roadside** stalls in Paharganj, Palika Bazaar and Janpath; traditional Indian cuisine at one of Delhi's many celebrated restaurants; **Western** food at the likes of *Wimpy*, *TGIF* and *Pizza Hut*, and the vast **buffets** and superlative à la carte menus of the luxury hotels.

Most restaurants close around 11pm, but those with bars usually stay open until midnight. If you're looking for a late-night meal, you can either eat in a top hotel, try a snack in Paharganj's round-the-clock rooftop cafés, or head to the markets of south Delhi.

Connaught Place

Connaught Place has local *dhabas*, upmarket restaurants and plenty of Western-style fast-food places. Even if you can't afford a meal in an expensive restaurant, it's sometimes nice to step into air-conditioned comfort just for a silver-service tea, cool milkshake or filter coffee; you can also get the latter at the coffee shops that have recently sprung up in the area.

The restaurants below appear on the Connaught Place **map** (p.121).

Banana Leaf N-12 Connaught Place. Excellent South Indian veg food, with thalis, a huge selection of *dosas*, and a few north Indian veg curries for good measure, at around Rs40–65 a plate.

Barista's N-18 Connaught Place. Popular coffee bar, the first of a nationwide chain that claims to do the best espresso in India, with a range of blends as well as snacks. Popular amongst trendy Delhi-ites.

Don't Pass Me By 79 Scindia House. Small, cheap, friendly restaurant next to *Ringo* hotel, with the usual backpackers' menu (omelettes, pancakes, toasties and the like).

Host F-8 Connaught Place. Popular a/c restaurant serving Indian kebabs and non-veg dishes, plus Chinese and some European food, as well as beer, silver-service tea, and strong filter coffee. Main dishes are around Rs180.

Nirula's 135 L-Block, Connaught Place. Choose from the downstairs snack bar (burgers, pizzas, sandwiches, or bread and curry), the Chinese or tasty multi-cuisine rooms upstairs, or sample some of the 21 flavours of delicious ice cream in the parlour. There's also a ground floor pub, *Pegasus* (see p.150).

Parikrama Kasturba Gandhi Marg. Novel and expensive Indian (mainly tandoori) and Chinese cuisine in a revolving restaurant affording superb views over Delhi; a single rotation takes ninety minutes; main dishes cost Rs150–450.

Spice Route *Hotel Imperial*, Janpath. This beautifully decorated restaurant specializes in spicy southeast Asian and Keralan cuisine, and is widely considered to be one of the best restaurants in Asia, if perhaps a little over-priced (main dishes Rs350–750).

Standard 44 Regal Building, Connaught Place. Two doors from the Regal Cinema, entered through a cake shop and instant coffee stand, serving mainly north Indian and tandoori specials such as a *raha* mutton platter, but also Goan fish curry or Hyderabadi chicken (mains Rs130–190), with chilled beer to accompany it.

United Coffee House E-15 Connaught Place. Rather an elegant coffee room, and also a restaurant, serving Indian and European dishes (including fish and chips) at around Rs180–200 a throw, as well as great coffee and cold beer.

Zen B-25 Connaught Place. Excellent Chinese meals (plus a few Thai and Japanese dishes) served in a leisurely and traditional style, plus Western snacks (3–7pm), and a broad selection of wines, spirits and beers.

Paharganj and Ram Nagar

Though most of the restaurants in **Paharganj** offer typically poor imitations of Western, Israeli, Japanese, and even Thai dishes, or under-spiced versions of Indian curries, they are nevertheless popular places to hang out. Many overlook the bazaar or are set on roof terraces that afford great city views. Most cafés serve tame breakfasts of toast, porridge, muesli and omelettes; alternatively, join the locals in the small *dhabas* dotted through the bazaar for excellent *aloo parathas* and curd. Eating options in **Ram Nagar** are more limited, with local *dhabas* and the popular *Ajanta* hotel restaurant being the best bets. If you decide to eat in any of the *dhabas* opposite New Delhi station or at the eastern end of Paharganj Main Bazaar, especially those with waiters trying to hustle you in, unless you can read the price list in Hindi always ask the price of a dish before ordering, or you're likely to be overcharged.

The restaurants below appear on the Paharganj and Ram Nagar **map** (p.123).

De Gem 1050 Main Bazaar. Good Indian cuisine (north and south, veg and non veg) and some Chinese dishes, mostly in the Rs50–100 range. There's an extensive drinks menu, and widescreen TV on the second floor, but it gets a bit beery as the night wears on.

Diamond Café Main Bazaar. Small, friendly restaurant with a good if typical backpackers' menu (main dishes around Rs50), a choice of set breakfasts (Continental, Indian, American, Israeli; Rs40–70), and Indian/fusion music on the sound system.

Golden Café Ramdwara Rd, opposite Sri Mahavir Mandir. Cheap and cheerful café popular with Korean and Japanese travellers, serving Chinese, European and Korean food with dishes at Rs30–80.

Hare Krishna *Hare Krishna Hotel*, 1572–3 Main Bazaar. Pleasant 24-hour rooftop café-restaurant where passable Italian and Thai dishes supplement the usual backpackers' menu. The Tom Yam soup isn't at all bad.

Khosla Café Main Bazaar. Popular but poky meeting place (be prepared to squeeze in) serving simple Indian snacks, Western breakfasts and drinks, with an indoors section as well as pavement seating.

Malhotra Laksmi Narain Rd. One of the best in Paharganj, offering very good tandoori and Mughlai dishes, and Chinese food too, at extremely reasonable prices (Rs60–100 for non-veg dishes). There's a basement, and an a/c upstairs section.

Metropolis 1634 Main Bazaar. Cosy a/c ground-floor restaurant in the hotel of same name. Paharganj's priciest venue serves full breakfasts, great curries and tandoori specials, plus Western dishes and beer. Main dishes Rs100–275.

Ritu's Arakashan Rd, below *Delhi Continental Hotel*. Cheap, popular *dhaba* serving excellent Indian breakfasts and South Indian snacks. A great place for *chana puri* or *iddli sambar*.

Sam's Café *Vivek Hotel*, 1534–50 Main Bazaar. A small, bright café at street level and a terrace restaurant on the roof, with the usual travellers' fare (Rs50–80), plus bakery products that go for half price after dark.

Sonu Chat House Main Bazaar. Popular cheap diner serving noodles, soup, samosas and red-hot curries in cramped but clean surroundings. Also good for South Indian dishes such as masala dosa.

Old Delhi

Old Delhi's crowded streets contain numerous simple food halls that serve surprisingly good, and invariably fiery, Indian dishes for as little as Rs20. There are few upmarket restaurants this side of town.

The restaurants below appear on the Old Delhi **map** (p.132).

Chor Bizarre *Hotel Broadway*, 4/15 Asaf Ali Rd. Wide selection of excellent Indian cuisine including specialities from around the country, but above all from Kashmir. Eccentric, delightful decor featuring a 4-poster bed, sewing table and a servery made from a 1927 vintage Fiat. Main dishes go for Rs100–400; set meals Rs325. Groups of eight or more can opt for a Rs585 Kashmiri feast.

Haldiram's Chandni Chowk. Super-hygienic snack-bar and take-away with sweets and samosas downstairs, drinks, snacks and light meals upstairs, with excellent *puris*, lime sodas, thalis and even toasties.

Karim's Matya Mahal. A perennial favourite, in a passage 10m on the left down the side street opposite the south gate of the Jama Masjid, consisting of four eating halls (same kitchen) offering the best and widest range of meat dishes (as well as the usual veg) in the city: delicious fresh kebabs, hot breads and curries. Full dishes cost Rs100–400, but half portions are also available.

Moti Mahal Netaji Subhash Marg. Renowned for its tandoori chicken, this place is another local favourite with both indoor seating and a large open-air courtyard. Main dishes go for around Rs100.

Paratha Wali Gali Off Chandni Chowk opposite the Central Bank. Head down the alleyway that leads behind Kanwarji Raj Kumar Sweet Shop, and you'll be rewarded with *parathas* filled with anything from *paneer* and *gobi* to *mutter* and *mooli*. All are cooked to order and served with a small selection of curries; you'll pay around Rs30.

Vig Chandni Chowk. A small café opposite the Jain temple, serving inexpensive South Indian snacks (*iddli sambar*, *dosas*, *uttapams*) at Rs17–40, thalis (Rs32) and excellent coffee.

South Delhi

The enclaves and villages spread across the vast area of **south Delhi** offer countless eating options. Trendy **Hauz Khas**, with its *Village Bistro* restaurant complex comprising a variety of different eateries, is renowned as one of the capital's best areas for dining out, while the **Defence Colony** boasts more than twenty trendy restaurants and coffee shops to indulge the increasingly affluent southern suburbanites. **Ansal Plaza**, one of south Delhi's most popular shopping complexes, also has several good restaurants and bars. **Chanakyapuri market** holds a cluster of Tibetan *dhabas* selling excellent *momos* (dumplings) and *thukpa* (soup), while the alleys and lanes of the medieval village of **Nizamuddin** conceal cafés and a range of restaurants. **Pandara Road Market**'s restaurants and snack bars, close to India Gate, stay open until 2am, and the expensive coffee shops in the five-star hotels are all 24hr.

Unless otherwise stated, the restaurants below appear on the Delhi **map** (pp.110–111).

Basil & Thyme Santushti Shopping Complex (see New Delhi map p.127). Tasty Mediterranean and Italian eating with mains (Rs285–355) like shiitake risotto, lamb couscous or asparagus tart, and blueberry crêpes or tiramisu to round it off. The big minus with this place is its 6pm closing time.

Dilli Haat Aurobindo Marg (1.5km south of Safdarjung's tomb). Large open-air market with small, inexpensive restaurants offering food from every state in India, although standards vary; head for the busier places.

Ego Community Centre, Friend's Colony, Mathura Rd. A saloon-style bar serving authentic and imaginative Italian food, with good beer, cocktails and loud music. Main dishes go for around Rs300.

Flavours Defence Colony Market. Run by a Mizo-Italian couple, this is a well-kept Delhi secret, where you'll find excellent Italian food including risotto and delicious tiramisu. Pizzas, pasta and main dishes cost Rs150–300.

Park Baluchi Deer Park, Hauz Khas. Baluchi, tandoori and Mughlai dishes (Rs130–270) amid pleasant woodland surroundings, with a choice of smoking (and drinking) or non-smoking (and alcohol-free) areas.

Sagar Defence Colony Market. Delicious, inexpensive South Indian veg food. A few doors away, the non-veg branch *Swagath* specializes in seafood, and there's also a branch specializing in north Indian and Chinese veg dishes. You'll pay around Rs50 per dish.

Shopping

Although the traditional places to **shop** in Delhi are around **Connaught Place** (particularly the underground Palika Bazaar) and **Chandni Chowk**, a number of suburbs are emerging as fashionable shopping districts. **Hauz Khas Village**, 12km southwest of Connaught Place, has numerous boutiques, jewellery shops and galleries, while artists and artisans from all over India sell their products at the enjoyable open-air **Dilli Haat** craft centre. **Ansal Plaza**, one of Delhi's most popular shopping precincts, is geared more towards the local middle-class than tourists.

If you're looking for hand-spun cotton clothes, **Greater Kailash Colony** and **South Extension I & II**, in Delhi's deep suburban south towards the Baha'i temple, are the hot spots for designer "ethnic chic" as well as Western chain brand names. Elsewhere, self-contained local precincts ranging from bookshops to European imported food include **Khan Market**, 1km south of India Gate, and **Bengali Market**, off Barakhamba Road, which is especially renowned for its sweet shops and large bustling cafés. Unlike the markets of Old Delhi, most shops in New Delhi take credit cards. Wherever you end up, beware of touts who'll try to drag you into false "government shops" for a commission; and bear in mind that in all of the bazaars and street markets, the rule is to **haggle** – it's even worth asking for a discount at shops which display "fixed price" notices.

Art, antiques, crafts and jewellery

Sunder Nagar Market near Purana Qila is a good upmarket place to shop for **art, antiques** and **jewellery**; try shops 5, 6, 9, 13, 14 and 26 for the best variety. **Hauz Khas Village** also has some interesting art and antiques shops and galleries. Remember that it's illegal to take art objects more than one hundred years old out of the country.

The **Tibetan Market** at the north end of Janpath remains popular with tourists, though only a few of the stalls are still run by Tibetans. You can find statues, incense, shawls, paintings and Tibetan artefacts including jewellery and semi-precious stones. Remember that not all white metal is silver, and drive a hard bargain. A number of **state government emporiums** with fixed but fair prices can be found along Baba Kharak Singh Marg near Connaught Place, where artisans sell their own wares.

Central Cottage Industries Emporium Jawahar Vyapar Bhawan, near the *Imperial* hotel, Janpath. Popular and convenient multistorey government-run complex, with handicrafts, carpets, leather and reproduction miniatures at fixed (if fractionally high) rates. Jewellery ranges from tribal silver anklets to costume jewellery and precious stones.

Cottage of Arts and Jewels 50 Hauz Khas Village. Interesting, eccentric mix with jewellery, curios and papier-mâché. The best of the collection, including miniatures and precious stones, is not on display: you'll have to ask to see it.

Neemrana Shop Upper floor, 12 Khan Market. Run by the renowned hotel group of the same name, the shop has a chic clientele and offers a range of lifestyle products as well as a small collection of antiques and *objets d'art*.

The Village Shop 10 Hauz Khas Village. An attractively presented shop selling replicas, bronzes and an assorted collection of silver and gold jewellery. Ethnic Silver two doors down at 9A, has a nice selection of silverware that's worth a browse.

Books

Delhi has a wide selection of places to buy **books**. **Connaught Place** and **Palika Bazaar** have many good bookshops, including Amrit (N-21), Galgotia & Sons (B-17), New Book Depot (B-18) and Bookworm (B-29). There are also several very good bookshops at **Khan Market**, 4km south of Connaught Place, including Bahrisons (21, opposite the main gate), The Bookshop (14-A), Faqir Chand (15-A) and Full Circle (5-B). At South Extension, check out Teksons Bookshop, 1st floor, G-4 South Extention I, and Timeless (see below). **Upmarket hotels** such as the *Imperial* often have their own bookshops, which usually tend towards the coffee-table market. Secondhand bookstalls include Jacksons on Paharganj Main Bazaar, and Anil Book Corner by the Plaza Cinema on Connaught Place. Some budget hotels have multilingual collections of used books for sale, swap or part exchange.

Corner Book Store Barista 15 Gyaandeep, Defence Colony Market, New Delhi. Popping up at cafés and other outlets all over town, this hip and happening new chain has all the latest titles.

Rajiv Book House Shop 30, Palika Bazaar. Expensive photo-packed hardbacks, great for gifts and collections, and often reduced in price, as well as cheaper novels and paperbacks.

Timeless 46 Housing Society, South Extension I. A beautiful shop with tasteful piles of coffee-table books. Complementary herbal tea or coffee for customers.

Fabrics and clothes

Delhi's **fabric** and **clothes** shops sell anything from high-quality silks, homespun cottons, Kashmiri shawls and traditional *kurta* pyjamas and saris to multicoloured tie-dyed T-shirts and other hippy gear. For Western-style trousers, skirts and shirts, try **Paharganj**, the **Tibetan Market** or the export-seconds market (watch out for "Kevin Clein" and "Ralphe Lawren" labels) at **Sarojini Nagar** near Chanakyapuri. Roadside stalls behind the Tibetan Market off Janpath sell lavishly embroidered and mirrored spreads from Rajasthan and Gujarat, but silks and fine cotton are best bought in the **government emporiums**, most of which are on Baba Kharak Singh Marg.

Delhi also holds a few upmarket boutiques, trading in designer labels and furnishings.

Anokhi Santushti Shopping Complex and upper floor, 9 Khan Market. Soft cotton and raw silk clothes and soft furnishings; particularly renowned for hand-block printed cottons combining traditional and contemporary designs.

Fabindia 14-N, N-Block Market, Greater Kailash. Spread through several shops in the market, with a range from furnishings and interiors to chic cotton clothing for men, women and children and wearable block-printed cottons.

Handloom House A-4 Connaught Place. An all-India co-operative with exquisite silks; assured quality and fixed prices, but not cheap.

Khadi Gramodyog Bhawan 24 Regal Building, corner of Sansad Marg and Connaught Place. Great place to pick up hardy, lightweight travelling clothes. Reasonably priced, ready-made traditional Indian garments include *salwar kamise*, woollen waistcoats, pyjamas, shawls and caps, plus rugs, material by the metre, incense, cards and tablecloths.

People Tree 8 Regal Building, Sansad Marg, CP. Alternative Delhi, with an emphasis on T-shirts, ethnic chic and jewellery.

Musical instruments, cassettes and CDs

Delhi is a good place to buy classical Indian **instruments** as well as **recorded music**. The listings below comprise the better options amongst the huge array of outlets.

Lahore Music House Netaji Subhash Marg, Old Delhi (next door to *Moti Mahal* restaurant). Long-established north Indian musical instrument-makers with a reputation for quality.

The Music Shop 18 Khan Market. Wide range of CDs, cassettes and videos, featuring both Indian and Western music, with helpful, well-informed staff.

Planet M E-3 South Extension II. Trendy four-storey outlet with wide-ranging stock, especially strong on Western rock and dance music. There's a pleasant café on the top floor.

Rangarsons K-Block, Outer Circle, Connaught Place. Extraordinary shop that once boasted regiments of the British Indian army among its patrons. A collection of brass and other marching band instruments as well as contemporary tablas and sitars.

Rikhi Ram G-9, Outer Circle, Connaught Place. Once sitar makers to the likes of Ravi Shankar, and still maintaining an exclusive air, with prices to match. Check out the display of their own unique instrumental inventions.

Nightlife and entertainment

With an ever-increasing number of pubs and clubs, Delhi's **nightlife** scene is in full swing. During the week the central restaurants and bars are your best bet, but come the weekend the discos really take off. Most, if not all, of the **discos** popular with Delhi's young jet-set are in the luxury hotels – some operate couples-only policies, others are free for women but not for men, and many don't allow "stag entry" (men unaccompanied by women); one place that is not in a hotel and does not restrict entry is Delhi's biggest nightclub, *Elevate*. India Gate and Rajpath attract nightly "**people's parties**" where large crowds mill about, snacking and eating ice cream; these are not great for women on their own, as hassle is likely.

For **drinking**, the five-star hotels all have plush and expensive bars – the *Patiala Peg* in the *Imperial* is perhaps the pick of the bunch. *Djinns* at the *Hyatt Regency* often puts on live music. Lounge bars have become very popular of late – but who knows how long that trend will last. Cheaper beers can be bought in many of the restaurants in Connaught Place, or in a few hotels and restaurants in Paharganj, including *De Gem* (see p.146). Note that the **legal drinking age** in Delhi is 25.

The capital also fares well on the cultural front. A range of indoor and outdoor venues host performances of **classical dance**, such as Bharatnatyam and Kathakali, and regular **classical music** concerts – check the listings magazines detailed on p.117 to see what's on. The **India International Centre** is a good place to catch art exhibitions, lectures and films on all aspects of Indian culture and environment, while the colossal **India Habitat Centre**, the **British Council** and the **art** and **theatre auditoriums** around India Gate are all renowned for their innovative shows and high-standard drama in both Hindi and English.

Finally, Bollywood hits are shown all over the capital, and there are several centrally located **cinemas**. The Chanakya in Chanakyapuri shows both Bollywood and Hollywood blockbusters.

Bars

Unless otherwise stated, the bars below appear on the Connaught Place **map** (p.121).

Blues Bar N-17 Connaught Place. Snazzy bar and restaurant offering an eclectic range of loud music (rock Thursday, retro Sunday). Extravagant cocktails expertly mixed.

DV8 Regal Building, Connaught Place. Central, popular place with an old fashioned, pub-like feel; music from 8pm and live bands on Tues.

Fashion bar Tavern by the Greens, Aurobindo Marg, Lado Sarai Rd (see Delhi map, pp.110–111). Fashion TV's trendy lounge bar down near the Qutb Minar, decked out with screens big and small. Music till midnight and the occasional fashion show; unsurprisingly, it attracts rather a glam crowd.

Geoffries Ansal Plaza (see Delhi map, pp.110–111). Very popular, supposedly English-style pub (really a bar-restaurant) in a modernistic shopping centre just south of the Ring Road, with bar meals and beer on tap. Happy hour 4–7pm (two beers for the price of one).

Pegasus Pub L-135 Connaught Place. A plush a/c pub, part of *Nirula's* hotel, with draught beer, daily happy hour (3–7pm) and good bar snacks.

Rodeo A-12 Connaught Place. Saloon-style bar with Wild West waiters, swinging-saddle bar stools, pitchers of beer, tequila slammers, and Mexican bar snacks (tacos, enchiladas, fajitas, quesadillas).

Shalom N-18, N-Block Market, Greater Kailash (see Delhi map, pp.110–111) ⓣ011/5163 2280 or 2283. A trendy lounge bar with laid-back music, a Mediterranean theme, Spanish and Lebanese food (tapas meets mezze), hookah pipes, and tables for all; but you'll need to book, especially at weekends.

Ssteel *Ashok*, 50-B Chanakyapuri (see Delhi map, pp.110–111). A sophisticated dance-bar with two dance spaces and three bars, including one just for beers, and one for wine and cocktails. There's a huge range of spirits, including all sorts of vodkas and malt whiskies, with music and dancing from around 9pm till midnight.

Discos

Unless otherwise stated, the discos below appear on the Delhi **map** (pp.110–111).

Elevate 6th floor, Center Stage Mall, Sector 18, Noida ⓣ0120/251 9905, ⓦwww.elevateindia.com. Across the river, and indeed just across the state line in UP, this is the biggest and kickingest club in town, a proper nightclub rather than a hotel disco, modelled on London's Fabric, with three floors (dancefloor, chillout and VIP), a roof terrace, and British and Aussie DJs playing the latest electronic and dance sounds. Fri and Sat nights only (check the website for what's on), but open till 4am, and "stag entry" is permitted.

Floats *Park Royal*, Lala Lajpat Rai Path, Nehru Place ⓣ011/2622 3344. Located near the Baha'i Temple, this is a bar-restaurant until around 10pm, when the dancefloor opens up and it really gets going. Open till 1 or 2am, but it's best to arrive by 11pm, as you may not be allowed in thereafter. Most popular on Wed, Fri and Sat.

My Kind of Place *Taj Palace*, 1 Sardar Patel Marg (see New Delhi map, p.127) ⓣ011/2611

0202. One of Delhi's most popular clubs, especially among expats, tending to attract a slightly older crowd than the other discos. Entry is free, but men aren't allowed in without a female companion. Wed is rock and retro night, Fri hip-house, and Sat Delhi-style music (with some bhangra and even filmi numbers).

Royale Mirage *Crowne Plaza Surya*, New Friends Colony ⓣ011/2683 5070. A long-time favourite, now revamped, with a French-Arab theme (hummus is among the snacks available), dancing podiums, state-of-the-art light show and a hip, young crowd. Open Wed–Sat only, happy hour 5–8pm, music 8pm–1am.

Dance and drama

Dances of India Parsi Anjuman Hall, Bahadur Shah Zafar Marg, near Delhi Gate ⓣ011/2328 9464. Excellent classical, folk and tribal dance. Daily 6.45pm.

Habitat World India Habitat Centre, Lodi Rd ⓣ011/2468 2222. Popular venue for dance, music and theatre as well as talks and exhibitions.

India International Centre 40 Lodi Estate ⓣ011/2461 9431. Films, lectures, dance and music.

Kamani Auditorium Copernicus Marg ⓣ011/2338 8084. Bharatnatyam and other dance performances.

Sangeet Natak Akademi Rabindra Bhavan, 35 Feroz Shah Rd ⓣ011/2338 7246, ⓦwww.sangeetnatak.com. Delhi's premier performing arts institution.

Triveni Kala Sangam 205 Tansen Marg ⓣ011/2371 8833. Bharatnatyam dance shows, also art exhibitions.

Cultural centres and libraries

British Council 17 Kasturba Gandhi Marg, south-east of Connaught Place ⓣ011/2371 1401. Talks, film shows and concerts, plus a good library and reading room.

Lalit Kala Galleries Rabindra Bhawan, 35 Firoz Shah Rd, by Mandi House Chowk ⓣ011/2338 7241 to 7243. Delhi's premier art academy, with an extensive collection of paintings, sculpture, frescoes and drawings. Also films, seminars and photographic exhibitions.

Sahitya Akademi Rabindra Bhawan, 32 Firoz Shah Rd, by Mandi House Chowk ⓣ011/2338 6626. An excellent library devoted to Indian literature through the ages, with some books and periodicals in English.

Tibet House 1 Institutional Area, Lodi Rd ⓣ011/2461 1515. A library on all aspects of Tibetan culture, plus a small museum of Tibetan artefacts. Mon–Fri 9.30am–5.30pm.

Cinemas

Bollywood movies are shown at the Odeon (ⓣ011/2332 2167), Plaza (ⓣ011/2332 2784) and Regal (ⓣ011/2336 2245) **cinemas**, all in Connaught Place, or the Shiela (ⓣ011/2367 2100) on DB Gupta Road, near New Delhi railway station. Check whether the films have subtitles. For more on Indian film, see the box on p.723.

Suburban cinemas, such as the **Priya** (ⓣ011/2614 0048) in Vasant Vihar, the **Chanakya** (ⓣ011/2467 0423) in Chanakyapuri and the **PVR Anupam** (ⓣ011/2686 5999) in Saket, provide a diet of relatively recent **Hollywood** films (in English, with Hindi subtitles) with digital surround sound and superb popcorn. In addition, many of the cultural centres listed above run international film festivals.

Sports and outdoor activities

The recreational activity most likely to appeal to visitors in the pre-monsoon months has to be a dip in one of Delhi's **swimming pools**. The main public baths are the NDMC Pool, Nehru Park & Sarojini Nagar and the Talkatora Pool, Talkatora Road. Most luxury hotels have now restricted their pools for residents only.

Other local diversions include **bowling**, **golf**, and even, during the cooler months, **rock climbing** on the outskirts of the city.

Delhi Golf Club Dr Zakir Hussein Marg ☎011/2436 2768. Busy and beautiful 220-acre golf course on the fifteenth-century estate of the Lodi dynasty; with more than two hundred varieties of trees, it also acts as a bird sanctuary. Monuments and mausoleums, such as the ruined *barakhamba* on a hillock next to the seventh green, dot the grounds. Temporary membership is available.

Delhi Lawn Tennis Association Africa Avenue ☎011/2619 3955. The DLTA's deco-turf tennis courts are now part of a sports complex that includes a swimming pool and gardens, but it still hosts India's top tennis tournaments.

Delhi Riding Club Safdarjung Rd ☎011/2301 1891. Rides at 6.45am, 7.45am, 8.45am, 3.45pm, 4.45pm and 5.45pm; open to the public by prior arrangement through the Club Secretary.

Delhi Tourism N-36 Bombay Life Building, Middle Circle, Connaught Place ☎011/2331 5332. Local activities such as rock climbing, paragliding and watersports, plus treks as far afield as Sikkim.

Indian Mountaineering Foundation Benito Juárez Marg ☎011/2467 7935. Official organization governing mountaineering and permits throughout India, with a library and an outdoor climbing wall. Some equipment can be rented here, and you can get information on local crags and climbing groups.

Listings

Airport enquiries International ☎011/2569 6021; domestic ☎011/2567 5181.

Airlines, domestic Air Deccan ☎080/3900 8888 or 98/1817 7008; Air Sahara, 102 Gopal Dass Bhawan, Barakhamba Rd ☎011/2332 6851; Archana Airways, 41-A Friends Colony East, Mathura Rd ☎011/2684 2001; Indian Airlines, Malhotra Building, Janpath, F-Block Connaught Place (daily except Sun 10am–5pm; ☎011/2331 0517), Safdarjung Airport ☎011/2462 2220 (open 24hr), general enquiries ☎1400, pre-recorded information ☎1402, departures ☎1403; Jagson Airlines, 12-E Vandhana Building, 11 Tolstoy Marg ☎011/2372 159; Jet Airways, Jetair House, 13 Community Centre, Yusuf Sarai ☎011/5164 1414, N-40 Connaught Place (Mon–Fri 9am–9pm; Sat & Sun 9am–6pm), Airport ☎011/2567 5404.

Airlines, international Aeroflot, N-1 Tolstoy House, 15–17 Tolstoy Marg ☎011/2331 0426; Air Canada, 1st floor, ALPs Building, 56 Janpath ☎011/2372 0014 or 0015; Air France, 7 Atma Ram Mansion, Scindia House, Janpath ☎011/2373 8004 or 0015; Air India, Jeevan Bharati Building, Sansad Marg ☎011/2373 6446; Air Lanka, G-55, Connaught Place ☎011/2373 1473; Alitalia, 2H, DCM Building, 16 Barakhamba Rd ☎011/2372 1006; Air New Zealand, 66 Janpath ☎011/2371 3366; American Airlines, C-38 Connaught Place ☎011/2332 5876; Bangladesh Biman, Upper Ground Floor, World Trade Centre, Babar Rd, Connaught Place ☎011/2341 4401; British Airways, DLF Plaza Tower, DLF Qutab Enclave, Gurgaon, Haryana ☎95124/512 0747 from Delhi, or ☎0124/512 0747 from outside Delhi, Airport ☎011/2565 2077; Cathay Pacific, 107–110, 1st Floor, Kanchenjunga Building, 18 Barakhamba Rd ☎011/2332 1286; Egypt Air, c/o Sphinx Travels, 101 Ansal Bhawan, Kasturba Gandhi Marg ☎011/2335 4493; El-Al, 303 Prakash Deep Building, 7 Tolstoy Marg ☎011/2335 7965; Emirates, DLF Centre, Sansad Marg ☎011/5531 4444; Gulf Air, G-12 Marina Arcade, Connaught Place ☎011/2335 1353; Japan Airlines, 36 Chandralok Building, Janpath ☎011/2332 7104; KLM, 7 Prakash Deep, Tolstoy Marg ☎011/2335 7747; Kuwait Airways, 309 Ansal Bhawan, 16 K.G. Marg ☎011/2335 4373 or 4377; Lufthansa, 56 Janpath ☎011/2372 4222; Malaysian, 10th floor, Ashoka Estate Building, 24 Barakhamba Rd ☎011/2331 3448; PIA, Kailash Building, 26 Kasturba Gandhi Marg ☎011/2373 7791; Royal Jordanian, G-56 Connaught Place ☎011/2331 9890; Royal Nepal Airlines, 44 Janpath ☎011/2332 1164; SAS, Amadeep Building 14 Kasturba Gandhi Marg ☎011/2335 2299; Saudi Arabian Airlines, Arunanchal Building, Barakhamba Rd ☎011/2331 0464; Singapore Airlines, 9th Floor, Ashoka Estate Building, Barakhamba Rd ☎011/2335 6283; Swiss, Fifth Floor, World Trade Tower, New Barakhamba Lane ☎011/2341 5000; Thai Airways, *Park Royal Hotel*, American Plaza, Nehru Place ☎011/5149 7777; United, 14 Kasturba Gandhi Marg ☎011/2335 3377; Uzbekistan Airways, 3 Prakash Deep Building, 7 Tolstoy Marg ☎011/2335 8687; Virgin Atlantic, 8th Floor, DLF Centre, Sansad Marg ☎011/5150 1300.

Archeological Survey of India 11 Janpath (☎011/2301 5954, Ⓦasi.nic.in) is responsible for the maintenance of India's numerous heritage sites and for the entry tariffs.

Banks and currency exchange At the international airport, you can exchange money at the 24hr State Bank of India and at Thomas Cook. Changing money in the city is relatively easy, with lots of ATMs which take Visa and Mastercard – almost every block on Connaught Place has one, as do metro stations, with several along Chandni Chowk and Asaf Ali Rd in Old Delhi. There's an HFDC ATM opposite the *Metropolis Hotel* on Paharganj Main Bazaar, and a couple more just up Rajguru Marg beneath the *Roxy Hotel*. Otherwise, there are branches of Thomas Cook in New Delhi station, at C-33 Connaught Place, and in the *Hotel Imperial* on Janpath (Mon–Fri 9.30am–8pm, Sat 9.30am–6pm) and American Express on A-Block, Connaught Place (Mon–Sat 9.30am–6.30pm). You can also change money at the DTTDC office, Middle Circle, Connaught Place, and there are numerous authorized exchange outlets in Paharganj (but if you're changing travellers' cheques, make sure before signing that they're not going to mess you around demanding receipts and such like, or sting you with unmentioned commissions). All major hotels have exchange facilities; the *Ajanta* (see p.124) has a 24hr bureau.
Bus enquiries Haryana Roadways ⓣ011/2386 1262; Himachal Roadways ⓣ011/2386 3473; Punjab Roadways ⓣ011/2386 7842; Rajasthan Roadways ⓣ011/2386 1246; UP Roadways ⓣ011/2386 8709. Delhi Transport Corporation (ⓣ011/2331 7445) can provide enquiry numbers for other state transport corporations.
Embassies & consulates Call ahead for opening hours before you visit. Afghanistan, 5/50F, Shanti Path, Chanakyapuri ⓣ011/2410 3331; Australia, 1/50-G Shanti Path, Chanakyapuri ⓣ011/5139 9900; Bangladesh, E-39, D Radha Krishan Marg, Chanakyapuri ⓣ011/2687 8956; Bhutan, Chandragupta Marg, Chanakyapuri ⓣ011/2688 9230; Burma, 3/50-F Nyaya Marg, Chanakyapuri ⓣ011/2688 9007; Canada, 7/8 Shanti Path, Chanakyapuri ⓣ011/5178 2000; China, 50-D Shanti Path, Chanakyapuri ⓣ011/2611 2345; Denmark, 11 Aurangzeb Rd ⓣ011/2301 0900; European Commission, 65 Golf Links ⓣ011/2462 9237 or 9238; Indonesia, 50A Chanakyapuri ⓣ011/2611 8643; Iran, 5 Barakhamba Rd ⓣ011/2332 9600; Ireland, 230 Jor Bagh-3 (near Safdarjung's tomb) ⓣ011/2462 6733; Malaysia, 50-M Satya Marg, Chanakyapuri ⓣ011/2611 1291 to 1293; Maldives, 702–3 Deepali, 92 Nehru Place ⓣ011/2622 9336; Nepal, Barakhamba Rd by Mandi House Chowk, southeast of Connaught Place ⓣ011/2332 7361; Netherlands, 6/50-F Shanti Path, Chanakyapuri ⓣ011/2688 4951; New Zealand, 50-N Nyaya Marg ⓣ011/2688 3170; Norway, 50-C Shanti Path, Chanakyapuri ⓣ011/2687 4469; Pakistan, 2/50-G Shanti Path, Chanakyapuri ⓣ011/2467 6004; Singapore, E6 Chandragupta Marg, Chanakyapuri ⓣ011/2688 5659; South Africa, B-18 Vasant Marg, Vasant Vihar, ⓣ011/2614 9411; Sri Lanka, 27 Kautilya Marg, Chanakyapuri ⓣ011/2301 0201; Sweden, Nyaya Marg, Chanakyapuri ⓣ011/2419 7100; Thailand, 56-N Nyaya Marg, Chanakyapuri ⓣ011/2611 8103; UK, Shanti Path, Chanakyapuri ⓣ011/2687 2161; USA, Shanti Path, Chanakyapuri ⓣ011/2419 8000.
Hospitals All India Institute of Medical Sciences (AIIMS), Ansari Nagar, Aurobindo Marg (ⓣ011/2658 8500) has a 24hr emergency service and good treatment, as does Lok Nayak Jai Prakash Hospital, Jawaharlal Nehru Marg, Old Delhi (ⓣ011/2323 3400) near Delhi Gate. Dr Ram Manohar Lohia Hospital, Baba Kharak Singh Marg (ⓣ011/2336 5933) is another government hospital. Private clinics include East West Medical Centre, B-28 Greater Kailash Part 1 (ⓣ011/2629 3701).
Internet access Reliable options include *Cyber Café*, N-9/II Connaught Place (Mon–Sat 9am–8pm); *Friends Internet Café*, in the small alley by 1083–6 Paharganj Main Bazaar (daily 8am–midnight), and *Ajanta Hotel*, Ram Nagar (24hr). There are lots of places on and around Paharganj Main Bazaar. You'll pay around Rs20/hr.
Left luggage Rs10–15/day at the railway stations. In addition, most hotels in Paharganj offer a left luggage service.
Money transfers Western Union agents include post offices, both small and large, plus branches of Indian Overseas Bank, Punjab National Bank and Canara Bank, and BTI Sita, F-12 Connaught Place (ⓣ011/2335 3722); if having money sent to a post office, be sure to specify the name correctly (note that "Delhi GPO" means Old Delhi GPO, but you should specify "Old Delhi" if having anything sent there, just to be sure). MoneyGram's agents include branches of Thomas Cook (for example in the *Hotel Imperial*, in New Delhi station or at C-33 Connaught Place), and Trade Wings at 60 Janpath or K-43 Connaught Place.
Motorcycles The Karol Bagh area holds many good motorcycle shops selling new or used Enfields. Reliable dealers include Inder Motors, 1744/55 Hari Singh Nalwa St, Abdul Aziz Rd (ⓣ011/2572 8579).
Opticians Bon-Ton, 13 Janpath Market, and Lawrence & Mayo, 76 Janpath, both offer good, expensive glasses and sunglasses; R.K. Oberoi, 14-H Connaught Place, will make up prescription lenses and spectacles at low prices based on thorough eye tests.

Permits and tax forms Permits for restricted states can be requested at the Ministry of Home Affairs, 26 Jaisalmer House, Man Singh Rd (Mon–Fri 10am–noon; ⓣ011/2307 4127, extn 216). If you've been in India more than 120 days, you'll need to fill in a tax clearance certificate, obtainable from the Foreign Section, Income Tax Office, Central Revenue Building, Indraprastha Estate (Mon–Fri 10am–1pm & 2–5pm; ⓣ011/2331 7826), before you can leave; have your foreign exchange certificates to hand.

Pharmacies Nearly every market has at least one pharmacy. Apollo, G-8 Connaught Place, and the pharmacy at the All India Medical Institute, Ansari Nagar, Aurobindo Marg, are open 24hr.

Photography Delhi Photo Company, 78 Janpath, offers high-quality developing, printing, and slide processing. It's second only to Kinsey Brothers beneath the *India Today* offices at 2-A Block, Connaught Place.

Police ⓣ100 (national number). Delhi now has a dedicated squad of tourist police based at the airport, main stations and major tourist sights and hotel areas, whose aim is specifically to help tourists in trouble. If you have a problem that needs to involve the police, your hotel reception or the Government of India tourist office will direct you to the appropriate station.

Postal services Poste restante (Mon–Sat 10am–5pm) is available at the GPO (known as Gole PO) on the roundabout at the intersection of Baba Kharak Singh Marg and Ashoka Rd and the Foreign Post Office, nearby on Bhai Vir Singh Marg, about fifteen minutes' walk from Connaught Place. You must show your passport to claim mail, and check the register for parcels. Letters sent to "Poste Restante, Delhi", rather than to New Delhi, may end up in Old Delhi GPO, north of the railway line on Mahatma Gandhi Rd. Reliable courier services include Overnite Express, Kanishka Shopping Plaza, Janpath (ⓣ011/2332 7921 or 7922).

State tourist offices Andaman and Nicobar Islands, 12 Chanakyapuri ⓣ011/2687 1443; Andhra Pradesh, Andhra Bhawan, 1 Ashoka Rd ⓣ011/2338 1293, ⓦwww.aptourism.com; Arunachal Pradesh, Arunchal Bhawan, Kautilya Marg ⓣ011/2301 3915, ⓦwww.arunachaltourism.com; Assam, State Emporia Complex, B-1 Baba Kharak Singh Marg ⓣ011/2334 4587, ⓦwww.assamtourism.org; Bihar, 216 Kanishka Shopping Plaza, 19 Ashoka Rd ⓣ011/2336 8371, ⓦbihar.nic.in/Depts/Tourism/Tourism.htm; Chandigarh, 21-B Telegraph Lane, behind Max Muller Bhawan ⓣ011/2335 3359, ⓦcitco.nic.in; Daman and Diu, F-308 Curzon Road Hostel, Kasturba Gandhi Marg ⓣ011/2338 5369; Goa, Goa Saear, Khan Market ⓣ011/2462 9967 or 9968, ⓦwww.goatourism.org; Gujarat, A-6 State Emporia Building, Baba Kharak Singh Marg ⓣ011/2374 4015, ⓦwww.gujarattourism.com; Haryana, Chandralok Building, 36 Janpath ⓣ011/2332 5320, ⓦwww.haryanatourism.com; Himachal Pradesh, Chanderlok Building, 36 Janpath ⓣ011/2332 5320, ⓦwww.hptdc.nic.in; Jammu & Kashmir, 201 Kanishka Shopping Plaza, 19 Ashoka Rd ⓣ011/2334 5373, ⓦwww.jktourism.org; Jharkand, B-5/2 Safdarjung Enclave ⓣ011/2618 0767, ⓦjharkhand.nic.in/tourism/tour.htm; Karnataka, C-4 State Emporia Building, Baba Kharak Singh Marg ⓣ011/2336 3863, ⓦkstdc.nic.in; Kerala, Information Centre, 219 Kanishka Shopping Plaza ⓣ011/2336 8541, ⓦwww.keralatourism.org; Lakshadweep, 301 Curzon Road Hostel, Kasturba Gandhi Marg ⓣ011/2338 6807; Madhya Pradesh, 204–205 Kanishka Shopping Plaza, Ashok Rd ⓣ011/2334 1187, ⓦwww.mptourism.com; Maharashtra, A-8 State Emporia Building, Baba Kharak Singh Marg ⓣ011/2336 3773, ⓦwww.maharashtratourism.gov.in; Manipur, C-7 State Emporia Building, Baba Kharak Singh Marg ⓣ011/2336 4026; Meghalaya, Meghalaya House, 9 Aurangzeb Rd ⓣ011/2301 4417, ⓦwww.meghalayatourism.com; Mizoram, Mizoram Bhawan, Circular Rd, Chanakyapuri ⓣ011/2301 2677; Nagaland, Government of Nagaland, 29 Aurangzeb Rd ⓣ011/2301 5638, ⓦwww.nagalandtourism.com; Orissa, B-4 State Emporia Building, Baba Kharak Singh Marg ⓣ011/2336 4580, ⓦwww.orissatourism.com; Pondicherry, 3 Sardar Patel Marg, Chanakyapuri ⓣ011/2611 1302, ⓦwww.tourisminpondicherry.com; Punjab, 214–215 Kanishka Shopping Plaza, Ashoka Rd ⓣ011/2334 3055, ⓦwww.ptdc.nic.in; Rajasthan, Bikaner House, Pandara Rd, near India Gate ⓣ011/2338 3837, ⓦwww.rajasthantourismindia.com; Sikkim, New Sikkim House, 14 Panch Sheel Marg, Chanakyapuri ⓣ011/2611 5171, ⓦsikkim.nic.in/sws/tour_off.htm; Tamil Nadu, C-1 State Emporia Building, Baba Kharak Singh Marg ⓣ011/2373 5427, ⓦwww.tamilnadutourism.org; Tripura, Tripura Bhavan, Kautilya Marg, Chanakyapuri ⓣ011/2301 5157, ⓦtripura.nic.in/ttourism1.htm; Uttar Pradesh, Chanderlok Building, 36 Janpath ⓣ011/2332 2251; Uttaranchal, 103 Indraprakash Building, 21 Barakhamba Rd ⓣ011/2371 2246, ⓦwww.gmvnl.com; West Bengal, A-2 State Emporia Building, Baba Kharak Singh Marg ⓣ011/2374 2840, ⓦwww.wbtourism.com.

Moving on from Delhi

Delhi has good international and domestic **travel connections**. Anyone heading from the south to the **western Himalayas** (Himachal Pradesh, Kullu, Manali, Ladakh) will pass through Delhi; it seldom takes more than a day to arrange the onward journey. Scores of **travel agents** (see box on below) sell bus and air tickets, while many hotels (budget or otherwise) will book private buses for you; **touts**, concentrated at the top of Janpath, waylay tourists with promises of cheap fares, but rarely give a good deal. Buses leave Delhi extremely frequently, and tourists are usually ensured places on trains in a reserved **tourist quota**. There's an ever-expanding network of internal flights, but it's still best to book as far ahead as possible; bear in mind that at peak times such as Diwali, demand is very high.

If leaving India for a country that requires a **visa** (including Pakistan, Nepal and Bangladesh), make sure you have obtained the necessary documentation from the embassy concerned (see p.153); call in advance, or visit their website, to check opening hours, specific requirements (such as how many photos you'll need), and the likely waiting period.

By air

Indira Gandhi International Airport is 15km southwest of the city centre. Most tourists on night flights book a **taxi** to the airport in advance (around Rs250) through their hotel. You can get there by **auto-rickshaw** for around Rs100–150. Otherwise, **airport buses** run from outside the Indian Airlines office at the top of Janpath (Rs50, plus Rs10–20 per item of baggage; 40min); departures are at 4am, 7.30am, 11.30am, 2pm, 3.30pm, 6pm, 7pm, 9.30pm and 10.30pm. You can book tickets in advance at the small office next to Indian Airlines.

Internal flights leave from Terminal 1 (ⓣ011/2567 5181). **Indian Airlines** have the largest number of flights, though private carriers such as **Jet Airways** serve more destinations. Tickets can be bought through travel agents or direct from the airlines. For a summary of flights, see the "Travel details" on p.158.

Travel agents and tour operators

It's a bad idea to book flights and excursions through street-side touts, particularly along Janpath and around the DTTDC office; instead, head for a **travel agent or tour operator**. Cox and Kings, Indira Palace, H-Block, Connaught Place (ⓣ011/5129 7900) offer expensive and exclusive **tailor-made tours** all over India. For competitively priced car tours around Rajasthan try *Hotel Namaskar*, Paharganj (ⓣ011/2358 2233, ⓔnamaskarhotel@yahoo.com). The Rajasthan Tourism Development Corporation, Bikaner House, Pandara Road (ⓣ011/2338 9525) organize **package tours** including wildlife and trips on the legendary *Palace on Wheels* train. For **trekking**, **mountaineering** and **rafting**, try Rimo Expeditions, 229 DLF Galleria, DLF Phase IV, Gurgaon (ⓣ0124/280 6027 or 6028). The Student Travel Information Centre, STIC Travels, 1st floor, Chandralok Building, opposite *Imperial Hotel*, Janpath (ⓣ011/2332 1487, ⓦwww.stictravel.com) can issue or renew **ISIC** cards.

For **ticketing**, established operators specializing in international and domestic flights include BTI Sita, F-12 Connaught Place (ⓣ011/2331 1122) and Capital City Travels and Tours, *Hotel Ajanta*, 36 Arakashan Rd, Ram Nagar (ⓣ011/2354 8264, ⓔccity@nda.vsnl.net.in). Travel Corporation of India, C-35 Connaught Place (ⓣ011/ 2341 6082 to 6085) can book train tickets as well. Readers' recommendations include Aa Bee Travel, 298-T off Main Bazaar, Paharganj, opposite *Hotel Ajay* (ⓣ011/2358 0172, ⓔaabee@mail.com).

Recommended trains from Delhi

The trains below are recommended as the fastest and/or most convenient for specific cities. Daily unless marked.

Destination	Name	No.	From	Departs	Total time
Agra	Shatabdi Express*	#2002	ND	6am	2hr 10min
	Mangala Express	#2618	HN	9.50am	2hr 53min
	Taj Express	#2180	HN	7.15am	2hr 52min
	A.P. Express	#2724	ND	5.45pm	2hr 53min
Ahmedabad	Ashram Express	#2916	OD	3.05pm	16hr 55min
	Rajdhani Express	#2958	ND	19.35pm	14hr 25min (except Tues)
Ajmer	Shatabdi Express*	#2015	ND	6.10am	6hr 35min (except Wed)
	Ahmedabad Mail	#9106	OD	10.50pm	8hr 35min
Chandigarh	Himalayan Queen	#4095	ND	6am	4hr 20min
	Shatabdi Express*	#2011	ND	7.40am	3hr 22min
	Shatabdi Express*	#2005	ND	5.15pm	3hr 5min
Chennai	Tamil Nadu Express	#2622	ND	10.30pm	32hr 35min
	Chennai Rajdhani	#2434	HN	3.30pm	28hr 35min (Wed & Fri only)
Haridwar	Shatabdi Express*	#2017	ND	6.55am	4hr 28min
	Mussoorie Express	#4041	OD	10.15pm	7hr 20min
Jaipur	Shatabdi Express*	#2015	ND	6.10am	4hr 30min (except Wed)
Jhansi	Shatabdi Express*	#2002	ND	6am	4hr 40min
Kolkata (Calcutta)					
	Rajdhani Express*	#2302	ND	5pm	17hr 45min (except Fri)
	Rajdhani Express*	#2306	ND	5pm	20hr 30min (Fri only)
	Howrah–Poorva Express	#2382	ND	4.15pm	24hr 30min (Mon, Tue, Fri)
	Howrah–Poorva Express	#2304	ND	4.15pm	24hr 30min (Wed, Thurs, Sat, Sun)
Mumbai	Rajdhani Express*	#2952	ND	4pm	16hr 35min
Udaipur	Chetak Express	#9615	SR	2.10pm	18hr 55min
Varanasi	Kashi Vishwanath Express	#4258	ND	1.30pm	16hr 30min
	Varanasi Express	#2560	ND	6.25pm	12hr 35min
Vasco da Gama	Goa Express	#2780	HN	3pm	40hr 05min

OD Old Delhi **ND** New Delhi **HN** Hazrat Nizamuddin **SR** Sarai Rohilla

*A/c only

International flights leave from Terminal 2 (☎011/2569 6021). If you don't already have a ticket for a **flight** out of India, you'll have little trouble finding one, except between December and March when it may be difficult at short notice. While you can buy tickets directly from the airlines (addresses are given on p.152), it saves time and leg-work to book through an **agency** (see p.155); there are many in Paharganj, Arakashan Road, Connaught Place and Janpath. Remember that most airlines require you to reconfirm your flight between a week and 72 hours before leaving.

By train

New Delhi station has regular departures to all corners of India, and a very efficient **booking office** (Mon–Sat 8am–8pm, Sun 8am–2pm) for foreign tourists, on the first floor (above ground) of the main departure building. Staff will give you advice on the fastest trains, and you should have little difficulty finding a seat or berth: **women** travelling alone in second class may prefer to ask for a berth in the ladies' carriage. Foreigners must show passports, and pay in foreign currency or in rupees backed up by exchange certificates. Ignore roadside advice to book train tickets elsewhere, and don't try buying one at the reservations building down the road – you'll be faced with a confusion of queues and crowds. Also, ignore warnings that the tourist booking office is closed during the above hours; see p.115 for more on these kind of scams.

Most southbound trains leave from New Delhi, but all trains to Rajasthan, except those to Bharatpur, Kota and Sawai Madhopur, leave from either **Old Delhi** or **Sarai Rohilla** station. A few trains to south and central India leave from **Hazrat Nizamuddin station**, so check carefully when you buy your ticket. Bookings for all trains can be made in New Delhi station.

See the box opposite for recommended trains from Delhi, and the "Travel details" at the end of this chapter for a summary of the main train services from the capital.

By bus

Delhi is the central hub of an extensive **bus** network covering much of north India's neighbouring states. On some shorter routes, buses are often quicker than trains; on long-distance routes there's usually a choice between the ramshackle state-run buses and smart soft-seated coaches run by tourist offices, hotels and private agents. Some travellers feel that these are well worth the extra handful of rupees, while others see these faster buses as potentially more dangerous. Away from the major cities, all buses are state-run.

The vast majority of **state-run buses** depart from the **Maharana Pratap ISBT** (☎011/2386 8836; see the Old Delhi map on p.132) by Kashmiri Gate metro and Rs50 from Connaught Place by auto. Be sure to arrive up to an hour before departure to allow time to find the correct counter (there are thirty or so) and book your ticket. Ask for the numbers of both platform and licence plate to ensure you board the right bus.

Services for Uttaranchal hill stations like Nainital, Almora and Ramnagar (for Corbett National Park) leave from **Anand Vihar ISBT** in East Delhi (☎011/2214 9089; buses #73 or #85, or Rs100 by auto from Connaught Place). Buses to Agra, Mathura, Bharatpur, Vrindavan, Gwalior, Jaipur, Ajmer and Pushkar leave from the **Sarai Kale Khan ISBT** (☎011/2463 8092; see the New Delhi map on p.127) east of Hazrat Nizamuddin station. However, for Jaipur, Udaipur, Jodhpur and Ajmer, the **Rajasthan Roadways terminal** at Bikaner House, India Gate (☎011/2338 3469; see the New Delhi map on p.127) has by far the best service, with a range that includes comfortable deluxe buses.

Private **deluxe buses** usually depart from near the Ramakrishna Mission at the end of Main Bazaar, Paharganj, but some pick up passengers at hotels. Popular destinations include Kullu, Manali, and Dharamsala, which are not accessible by train, as well as Pushkar and Uttaranchal hill stations. You can book tickets a day or two in advance at the agencies in Paharganj or Connaught Place.

The only **international service** from Delhi is DTC's four-times-weekly bus to Lahore in Pakistan, which leaves from Dr Ambedkar terminal on Jawaharlal Nehru Marg by the Gandhi Memorial Museum (Ⓣ011/2331 8180; see the Old Delhi map on p.132).

Travel details

Trains

To **Rajasthan**: Abu Road (1–4 daily; 10hr 50min–14hr); Ajmer (5–8 daily; 6hr 35min–10hr 45min); Bharatpur (5–6 daily; 2hr 32min–4hr 18min); Bikaner (3 daily; 10hr 20min–11hr); Chittaurgarh (2 daily; 15hr 10min–15hr 55min); Jaipur (6–10 daily; 3hr 40min–11hr 20min); Jodhpur (2–3 daily; 11hr 10min –12hr); Kota (10–11 daily; 4hr 40min–9hr 55min); Sawai Madhopur (7–8 daily; 3hr 43min–7hr 35min); Udaipur (2 daily; 18hr 55min–21hr 10min).

To **Uttar Pradesh**: Agra (21–23 daily; 2hr 8min–4hr 35min); Allahabad (18–20 daily; 7hr 5min–16hr 40min); Dehra Dun (4–6 daily; 5hr 40min–9hr 45min); Gorakhpur (5–7 daily; 13hr 5min–17hr 40min); Kanpur (28–31 daily; 4hr 35min–12hr 30min); Lucknow (11–14 daily; 6hr 15min–10hr 20min); Mathura (32–35 daily; 1hr 49min–3hr 40min); Varanasi/Moghulsarai (22–24 daily; 8hr–20hr 25min).

To **the east**: Bhubaneshwar (4–5 daily; 24hr 35min–40hr 35min); Cuttack (3–4 daily; 23hr 45min–40hr 5min); Gaya (5–7 daily; 13hr 5min–16hr 40min); Guwahati (4–5 daily; 28hr 5min–44hr 45min); Kolkata (Calcutta)–Howrah/Sealdah (5–7 daily; 17hr 45min–39hr 35min); Puri (3 daily; 31hr 10min–42hr 10min); Vijayawada (3–5 daily; 22hr 40min–35hr).

To **Punjab and Himachal Pradesh**: Amritsar (9 daily; 5hr 45min–11hr 40min); Chandigarh (5–7 daily; 3hr 5min–6hr 35min); Kalka, for Shimla (5 daily; 4hr–6hr 10min); Pathankot (4–6 daily; 10hr 30min–12hr 55min).

To **Central India**: Bhopal (18–21 daily; 8hr–14hr 20min); Gwalior (18–22 daily; 3hr 29min–6hr 35min); Indore (2–3 daily; 13hr 35min–19hr 10min); Jhansi (18–22 daily; 4hr 24min–8hr 25min).

To **Gujarat and Maharashtra**: Ahmedabad (2–4 daily; 16hr 55min–31hr 35min); Mumbai (6–7 daily; 16hr 35min–31hr 15min); Pune (2–3 daily; 25hr 45min–27hr 45min).

To **the south**: Bangalore (1–3 daily; 32hr 35min–47hr 40min); Chennai (2–4 daily; 28hr 35min–45hr 25min); Ernakulam (1–3 daily; 41hr 30min–50hr); Hyderabad/Secunderabad (3–4 daily; 22hr 20min–34hr 40min); Thiruvananthapuram (1–2 daily; 42hr 45min–54hr 50min); Vasco Da Gama (1 daily; 40hr 5min).

Buses

Only state buses are included in this summary; for details of private buses see above.

In the listings below, for points of departure, **A** means Anand Vihar ISBT in East Delhi, **B** is the Rajasthan Roadways terminal at Bikaner House, **M** is Maharana Pratap ISBT at Kashmiri Gate, and **S** is Sarai Kale Khan ISBT at Nizamuddin.

To **Rajasthan**: Ajmer (B & S, every 30min; 9hr); Jaipur (B & S, every 30–45min; 6hr); Jodhpur (B & S, 4 daily; 12hr); Pushkar (S, 1 daily; 10hr); Udaipur (B, 1 daily; 20hr).

To **Uttar Pradesh and Uttaranchal**: Agra (S, every 30min; 5hr); Almora (A, 3 daily; 12hr); Dehra Dun (M, hourly; 7hr); Haridwar (M, every 30min; 5hr 30min); Mussoorie (M, 2 daily; 8hr 30min); Nainital (A, 3 daily; 9hr); Ramnagar, for Corbett National Park (A, 11 daily; 7–8hr); Rishikesh (M, hourly; 6hr 30min).

To **Haryana & Punjab** and **Himachal Pradesh**: Amritsar (M, 10 daily; 10hr); Chandigarh (M, every 10min; 5–6hr); Dharamsala (M, 6 daily; 12–14hr); Manali (M, 8 daily; 16–18hr); Shimla (M, 11 daily; 10hr).

Flights

In the listings below, **AI** represents Air India, **IA** is Indian Airlines, **JA** Jet Airways, **AD** is Air Deccan, **SA** Air Sahara, and **JGA** is Jagson.

Delhi to: Agra (IA, AD 2–3 daily; 35min); Ahmedabad (IA, SA, JA 4–5 daily; 1hr 25min); Amritsar

(AI, IA, AD 2 daily; 55min); Bagdogra, for Siliguri and Darjeeling (JA, IA 1–2 daily; 1hr 50min–4hr); Bangalore (IA, AD, JA, SA 14 daily; 2hr 30min); Bhubaneshwar (IA 1 daily; 2hr); Chandigarh (IA, JA 2 daily; 40min–1hr); Chennai (IA, AD, JA, SA 14 daily; 2hr 25min–4hr 5min); Goa (IA, SA 2 daily; 2hr 25min–3hr 45min); Guwahati (IA, AD, JA, SA 4–5 daily; 2hr 15min–3hr 40min); Hyderabad (IA, AD, JA, SA 8 daily; 2hr); Indore (JA 2–3 daily; 2–3hr); Jaipur (IA, AD, JA, SA 6 daily; 40–45min); Jodhpur (JA 2 daily; 1hr 20min–1hr 50min); Khajuraho (IA, JA 1–2 daily; 1hr 45min–2hr 30min); Kochi (IA, SA, JA 3 daily; 4hr 25min); Kolkata (Calcutta) (IA, AD, JA, SA 9 daily; 2hr–2hr 20min); Kullu (JGA daily; 1hr 20min–1hr 50min); Leh (IA, JA 1–2 daily; 1hr 15min); Lucknow (IA, AD, JA, SA 8–9 daily; 55min–1hr 25min); Mumbai (IA, AD, JA, SA 32 daily; 1hr 55min–3hr 50min); Patna (IA, JA, SA 5–6 daily; 1hr 25min–2hr 10min); Pune (IA, JA, SA 5 daily; 2hr–3hr 5min); Thiruvananthapuram (IA daily; 5hr); Udaipur (IA, JA 3 daily; 1hr 10min–3hr); Varanasi (IA, JA, SA 3–4 daily; 1hr 20min–3hr).

CHAPTER 2

Highlights

* **Keoladeo National Park, Bharatpur** Flocks of rare cranes – and serious bird-watchers – travel across continents each winter to this amazing wetland sanctuary, one of the world's most important. See p.198

* **Ranthambore National Park** India's most visited wildlife park, where tiger sightings are an everyday occurrence. See p.203

* **Savitri Temple, Pushkar** For optimum views of the famous lake and white-washed holy town, climb to the hilltop Savitri temple at sunset. See p.213

* **Meherangarh Fort, Jodhpur** Rajasthan's showcase citadel, offering maximum impact views of the blue city below and an unparalleled museum. See p.219

* **Jaisalmer Fort** India's greatest inhabited fort with more than 2000 people still occupying its golden sandstone homes. See p.229

* **Camel trekking** There's no better way to experience the Thar desert than by riding a camel through it. See p.232

* **Udaipur** Who cares if the lake is only half-full? Fabulous palaces surrounded by spectacular countryside still have the power to inspire. See p.250

△ Jaisalmer Fort

2

Rajasthan

The state of **RAJASTHAN** emerged after Partition from a mosaic of twenty-two feudal kingdoms, known in the British era as **Rajputana**, "Land of Kings". Running northeast from Mount Abu, near the border with Gujarat, to within a stone's throw of the ruins of ancient Delhi, its backbone is formed by the bare brown hills of the Aravalli Range, which divide the fertile Dhundar basin from the shifting sands and *khejri*-covered flats of the mighty Thar Desert, one of the driest places on earth. As the site of India's recent nuclear tests, this western flank of the country, forming the sensitive border with Pakistan, has become one of the world's most notorious geopolitical hotspots. However, the flat terrain, combined with the lure of the lucrative trans-Thar trade routes, rendered it vulnerable to invasion long before Partition. By taxing the movement of silk, spices and precious stones across their territories, successive rulers – from the Hindu **Rajputs** to their medieval Muslim overlords, the Moghuls – amassed vast fortunes, which they poured into ever more ambitious building projects.

Rajasthan's extravagant **palaces**, **forts** and finely carved **temples** today comprise one of the country's richest crop of historic monuments, visited in greater numbers than any other apart from Agra. But these exotic buildings are far from the only legacy of the region's prosperous and militaristic past. Centuries of Rajput rule created a hierarchy of rigid **caste** distinctions as monolithic as any in the country, bound by codes of chivalry and honour powerful enough to have driven the female population of whole cities to mass suicide, or *johar*. The Rajputs remain the landowners, dominating the state's political and economic life, while the lot of the lower castes has altered little since feudal times. In recent years, these disparities have led to violent inter-caste confrontations across Rajasthan, sparked off by Rajput resentment at the government's introduction of job and university place quotas for members of oppressed castes.

For visitors, however, Rajasthan's strong adherence to the traditions of the past is precisely what makes it a compelling place to travel. Swaggering moustaches, heavy silver anklets, bulky red, yellow or orange turbans, pleated veils and mirror-inlaid saris may be part of the complex language of caste, but to most outsiders they epitomize India at its most exotic. Nowhere is this traditional flamboyance more vividly expressed than at the annual camel fair at **Pushkar**, when hundreds of thousands of lavishly dressed villagers converge on a sacred lake in the Aravalli Hills to buy and sell livestock.

Colour also distinguishes Rajasthan's most important tourist cities. Because of the reddish colourwash applied to its ornate facades and palaces in the nineteenth century, **Jaipur**, the chaotic state capital, is known as the "Pink

The International boundaries on this map are neither purported to be correct nor authentic by Survey of India directives. Publisher.
PAKISTAN
Kali Bangan
Indira Gandhi Canal
Thar Desert
(Great Indian Desert)
Bikaner
Gajner
Kolayat
Deshnok
Nokha
NH-15
Kishangarh
Bhuttewala
Ramgarh
Lodurva
Phalodi
R A J
Jaisalmer
Sam
Khuhri
Pokaran
Osian
Dechhu
Mandor
Jodhpur
Shiv
Balotra
Barmer
Luni
Pali
Marwar
Sanderav
Jalor
Ranakpur
Sirohi
KUMBALGARH SANCTUARY
Nagda
Sanchor
Mt Abu
Udaipur
Abu Rd
Palanpur
Rishdeo
Rann of Kutch
GUJARAT
Dungarpur
Himatnagar
Little Rann of Kutch
Ahmedabad
Bhuj
Mumbai

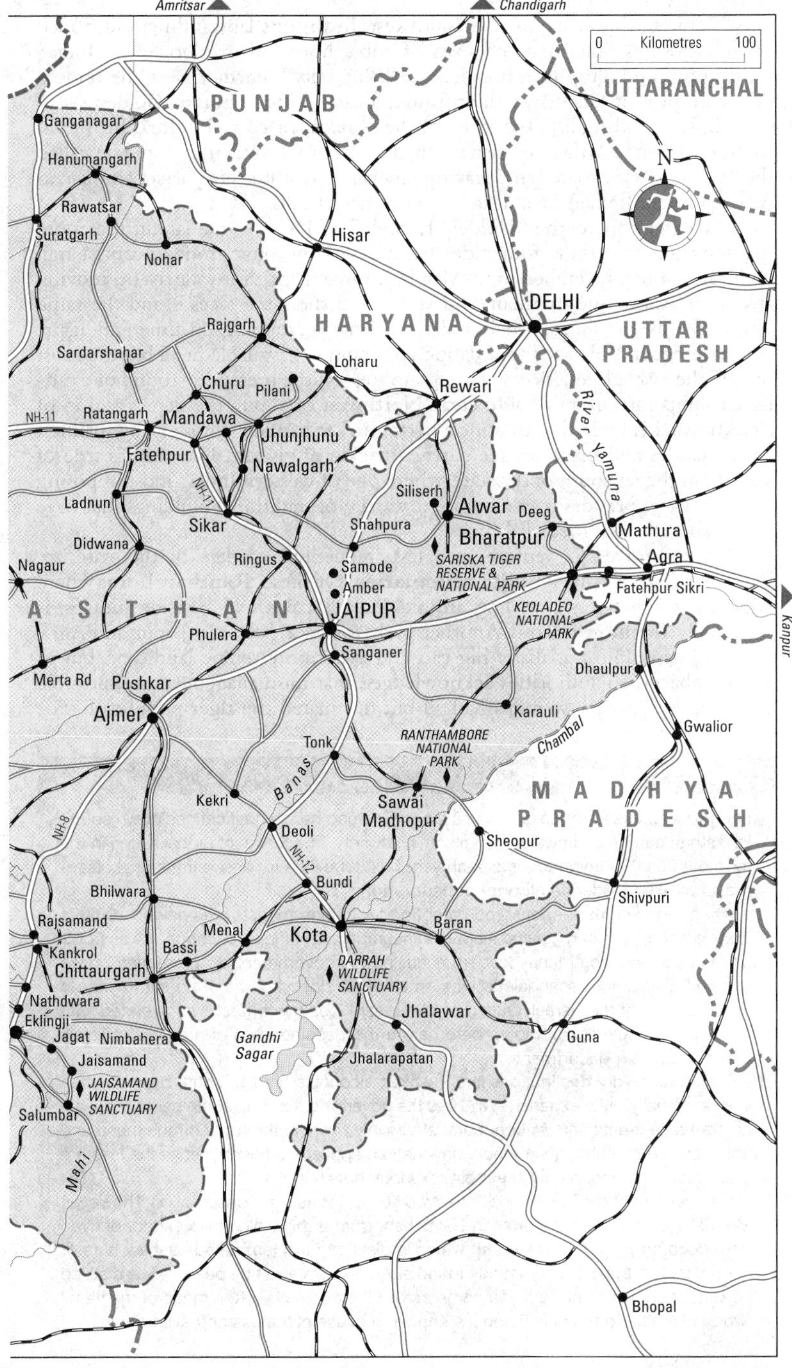
Amritsar
Chandigarh
0 Kilometres 100
PUNJAB
UTTARANCHAL
N
Ganganagar
Hanumangarh
Rawatsar
Suratgarh
Nohar
Hisar
DELHI
HARYANA
UTTAR PRADESH
Rajgarh
Sardarshahar
Loharu
Churu
Pilani
Rewari
NH-11
Ratangarh
Mandawa
Jhunjhunu
River Yamuna
Fatehpur
Nawalgarh
NH-11
Siliserh
Ladnun
Alwar
Deeg
Sikar
Shahpura
Mathura
Didwana
Bharatpur
Ringus
Samode
SARISKA TIGER RESERVE & NATIONAL PARK
Agra
Nagaur
Amber
Fatehpur Sikri
ASTHAN
JAIPUR
KEOLADEO NATIONAL PARK
Kanpur
Phulera
Sanganer
Merta Rd
Dhaulpur
Pushkar
Ajmer
Karauli
Chambal
Gwalior
Tonk
RANTHAMBORE NATIONAL PARK
Banas
Sawai Madhopur
MADHYA PRADESH
Kekri
NH-8
Deoli
Sheopur
NH-12
Bundi
Bhilwara
Shivpuri
Rajsamand
Menal
Kota
Baran
Kankrol
Bassi
Chittaurgarh
DARRAH WILDLIFE SANCTUARY
Nathdwara
Jhalawar
Eklingji
Jagat
Nimbahera
Gandhi Sagar
Guna
Jaisamand
Jhalarapatan
JAISAMAND WILDLIFE SANCTUARY
Salumbar
Mahi
Bhopal

2 RAJASTHAN

City". One day's journey to the southwest, **Jodhpur**'s labyrinthine old walled town, whose sky-blue painted mass of cubic houses is overlooked by India's most imposing hilltop fort, is called the "Blue City". Further west, the remote desert outpost of **Jaisalmer**, built from a local sandstone, is the "Golden City" – birthplace, and undisputed king, of the Rajasthani **camel safari**. In the far south of the state, **Udaipur** hasn't gained a colour tag yet, but it could be called the "White City": coated in decaying limewash, its waterside palaces and *havelis* (mansions) are framed by a distant vista of desert hills.

As an extension to the "Golden Triangle" of Delhi–Agra–Jaipur, the route stringing together these four cities has become the most trodden tourist trail in India. From November until March, thousands of visitors may be moving around it at any one moment, and you'll find the same faces – and the same kinds of souvenir shops, hotels and restaurants – cropping up time and again. But with dependable accommodation and transport available in all but the most out-of-the-way places, it's easy enough to step off the merry-go-round of established sights into more remote areas. Northwest of Jaipur, the desert region of **Shekhawati** is littered with atmospheric market hamlets whose richly painted *havelis*, castles and mausolea see barely a trickle of visitors. The same is true of **Bundi**, in the far south of the state, where one of western India's most imposing hilltop palaces presides over a compact warren of traditional buildings that have barely altered since medieval times.

Other incentives to venture into less frequented corners of the state are Rajasthan's wonderful **wildlife sanctuaries**. Of these, **Ranthambore**, where you can watch tigers prowling around Rajput ruins and lakeside jungles, is deservedly the most famous. Another park, **Sariska**, between Jaipur and Agra, used to boast almost as many big cats and even more serene landscape, but in 2005 embarrassed authorities acknowledged that mismanagement and possible poaching by corrupt wardens had all but decimated the tiger population. For

Boozers not welcome

For foreigners used to the soused scene in Goa and beach destinations down south, Rajasthan can be an unwelcome lesson in sobriety. The arrival of globalization in the form of 600,000 foreign tourists each year has done little to loosen traditional disapproval of even moderate **alcohol consumption**.

When a government-sponsored reception for foreign tourists was held in 2004, in violation of a state ban against alcohol consumption at official functions, it was front-page news, with community leaders accusing the government of "promoting booze culture." Even more scandalous was an all-night slosh fest held the same year in Pushkar, part of the "Israeli Queen of the Desert" beauty contest, which ended with the besotted beauties stripping bare before the peeping eyes of mid-level officials from the tourism department.

Even outside dry destinations like Pushkar, alcohol is hard to come by, and when you do, usually quite expensive. In 1999 the government of Rajasthan banned its sale at state restaurants and 74 beer bars, effectively pushing the trade off the menu and under the table. Although in theory anyone can apply for a liquor license the fees are prohibitively high for all but the most luxurious hotels.

The censure hasn't extended to traditional forms of consumption, however. Moonshine takes several forms in Rajasthan, from a milky alcoholic extract derived from coconut palm flower to **feni**, which is distilled from fermented cashew nuts or coconuts. But the most commonly found elixir, one preferred by peasants, is distilled rice liquor known as **arak**. If you come across it stay away – often made of methanol (wood alcohol), to the uninitiated it's known to cause blindness and even death.

sheer profusion, however, the **Keoladeo National Park** at **Bharatpur**, on the eastern border of Rajasthan near Agra, is unmatched in South Asia. Literally hundreds of species of birds, from giant saras cranes to tiny scarlet finches and incandescent kingfishers, feed here in the winter months, creating an unforgettable spectacle and a welcome respite from the frenetic cities that inevitably dominate most visitors' itineraries in this state.

Visiting Rajasthan

Rajasthan's **climate** reaches the extremes common to desert regions. Temperatures can top 45°C between May and June before the monsoon breaks over central and east Rajasthan. The fierce summer heat lingers until mid-September or October, when night temperatures drop considerably. The best time to visit is between November and February, when daytime temperatures rarely exceed 30°C; in midwinter, you'll still venture to take a mid-day dip in whatever swimming pools you can find open, but at night you'll need a shawl or thick jumper if you're outdoors, and a thin sleeping bag for train journeys and hotels that don't provide blankets.

Getting around the state is rarely problematic, though there's no avoiding some tedious long hauls. The state-run bus company, RSTDC, has regular services between cities, although **private operators** are a more popular option, offering cheaper fares and greater comfort. For those who don't want to subject themselves to sleepless nights on buses, **trains** connect all major cities and many smaller towns – always book ahead for night journeys. The most luxurious way to travel in Rajasthan, however, has to be the **Palace On Wheels** (Ⓦwww.palaceonwheels.net; see also p.58 in Basics), a rolling five-star train hotel that takes in the state's highlights over a week-long whistle-stop tour.

Thanks to massive government tax incentives, **luxury accommodation** is big business in Rajasthan. Cashing in on the kudos of their royal connections, local maharajas have opened up their family homes as "heritage" or **palace hotels**. While some have been insensitively converted under the auspices of large chains, others retain their former charm and, by comparison with the cost of five-stars in other parts of the world, offer excellent value for money. At the opposite end of the scale, the state's laudable **paying guest scheme**, Rajasthan's equivalent of B&B accommodation, provides a great opportunity to get to know an Indian family. Tourist offices across the state keep names and addresses of local families who take part in the scheme, along with details of family members, languages spoken and diet (veg or non-veg). Prices range from Rs150 per night to around Rs750, depending on the location and levels of comfort offered. For itinerary suggestions, bookings and information the government's tourist bureau has a well-organized **website**: Ⓦwww.rajasthantourism.gov.in.

Some history

The turbulent history of Rajasthan, characterized by courtly intrigue and interstate warfare, only really begins in the sixth and seventh centuries AD, with the emergence of warrior clans such as the Sisodias, Chauhans, Kuchwahas and Rathores – the **Rajputs** ("sons of princes"). Never exceeding eight percent of the population, they were to rule the separate states of **Rajputana** for centuries. Their code of honour set them apart from the rest of society – as did the genesis myth that they descended from the sun and moon – but did not invite excessive hostility. The Rajputs provided land, employment and trading opportunities for their subjects, and are still praised as gods in some communities.

Festivals in Rajasthan

Rajasthan's vibrant local costumes are at their most dazzling during the state's **festivals**. Some, such as Jaisalmer's Desert Festival, are geared particularly towards foreign visitors, and many of the most important celebrations fall in the tourist season (the cool months between November and March). For dates of specific events, ask at tourist offices; most festivals fall on days determined by the lunar calendar. Also held during the winter, **weddings** in Rajasthan tend to be ostentatious, noisy affairs whose most conspicuous feature is the raucous groom's procession, or *baraat*. Led by marching bands and lines of urchins carrying mobile strip-lights, dancing male relatives process through the streets waving wads of rupees ahead of the gold-turbaned bridegroom, seated on a white horse.

Desert Festival (Feb). Jaisalmer's own two-day event, when camel races, folk dances and competitions are laid on primarily to attract tourists and promote local handicrafts.

Elephant Festival (March). Parades of caparisoned, brightly painted elephants process through the streets of Jaipur into the City Palace. The event concludes with an extraordinary elephant versus *mahout* tug of war.

Mewar Festival (March & April). The ranas of Udaipur celebrate Holi with the lighting of a sacred fire, traditional dance from local tribals and music by the city's famous bagpipe orchestra, followed by a swish society bash in the *Shiv Niwas Palace* hotel.

Gangaur (April). A festival unique to Rajasthan, when women pray for their husbands, and unmarried girls wish for good ones. Excellent in Jaisalmer, when the local raja heads the procession amid an entourage of camels, and in Mount Abu, where effigies of Gauri (Parvati) and Isa (Shiva) – the ideal couple – are carried through the streets.

Rani Sati Mela (Aug). Vast crowds gather for this day of prayers and dances in Jhunjhunu (northern Shekhawati), in memory of a merchant's widow who committed *sati*, sacrificing her life on her husband's pyre, in 1595.

Urs Mela (Oct). Tens of thousands of Muslims converge on the Dargah in Ajmer for the subcontinent's largest Islamic festival, commemorating the life of the Sufi saint and teacher Muin-ud-din Chishti, who died here in 1236. Worship in the shrine culminates in performances by India and Pakistan's top *qawwali* singers.

Pushkar Camel Fair (Nov). Rajasthan's largest and most colourful festival attracts an estimated 200,000 people and 50,000 camels. Still an unmissable spectacle, despite the vastly inflated accommodation prices and tourist deluge.

The Rajput codes of chivalry that lay behind endless clashes between clans and family feuds found their most savage expression in battles with Muslims. **Muhammad of Ghori** was the first to march his troops through Rajasthan, eventually gaining a foothold that enabled him to establish the **Sultanate** in Delhi. During the 350 years that followed, much of central, eastern and western India came under the control of the sultans, but, despite all the Muslims' efforts, Rajput resistance precluded them from ever taking over Rajputana.

Ghori's successors were pushed out of Delhi in 1483 by the Moghul Babur, whose grandson **Akbar** came to power in 1556. Aware of the futility of using force against the Rajputs, Akbar chose instead to negotiate in friendship, and married Rani Jodha Bai, a princess from the Kuchwaha family of Amber. As a result, Rajputs entered the Moghul courts, and the influence of Moghul ideas on art and architecture remains evident in palaces, mosques, pleasure gardens and temples throughout the state.

When the Moghul empire began to decline after the accession of Aurangzeb in 1658, so too did the power of the Rajputs. Aurangzeb sided with a new force, the **Marathas**, who plundered Rajput lands and extorted huge sums of protection money. The Rajputs eventually turned for help to the Marathas' chief rivals, the **British**, and signed formal treaties as to mutual allies and enemies. Although in theory the residents who represented British authority in each state were supposed to be neutral communicators, they soon wielded more power than the Rajput princes. However, the Rajputs were never denied their royal status, and relations were so amicable that few joined the Mutiny of 1857. Wealth from overland trade enabled them to festoon their palaces with silks, carpets, jewels and furnishings far beyond the imagination of most ordinary citizens, while the prosperous **Marwari** merchants of the northwest built and decorated stylish mansions, temples and meeting halls.

The nationwide clamour for Independence in the years up to 1947 eventually proved stronger in Rajasthan than Rajput loyalty; when British rule ended, the Rajputs were left out on a limb. With persuasion from the new Indian government including the offer of "privy purses", they agreed one by one to join the Indian Union, and in 1949 the 22 states of Rajputana finally merged to form the state of **Rajasthan**.

But for three brief years of Janata domination from 1977 onwards, Congress held sway over Rajasthan from its first democratic elections in 1952 until 1994, when the **BJP** won a decisive victory. Central control soon exposed the Rajputs' neglect of their subjects, whom they had entrusted to power-thirsty landowners (*jagirdars*), and village councils (*panchayats*) were set up to organize local affairs.

Drought in Rajasthan

For nearly a decade, ever since the failure of the 1997 rains, **drought** has brought the already parched desert regions of Rajasthan to their knees, affecting some 32 million people and 40 million cattle. Signs of the never-ending dry spell are everywhere, from the steady evaporation of the famed Lake Pichola in Udaipur to the constant flow of emaciated farmers to Jaipur and other big cities. As of 2004, 24 of Rajasthan's 32 districts – some 19,000 villages in all – were in a state of emergency.

The government has spent hundreds of millions trying to mitigate the human costs of the disaster, even while international figures like Prince Charles have lent their voice – convening corporate donors for a $20,000 per table Christmas fundraiser in 2004 – to the relief effort. But the situation, borne of the Thar's status as the world's most densely populated desert, simply gets worse. In 2004, clashes between police and angry protestors resulted in the death of six farmers. Meanwhile public suicides are on the rise as debt-laden farmers attempt anything to draw attention to their plight and stave off certain starvation for their families.

To be sure, water was never abundant in Rajasthan. India's largest state by size holds less than 1 percent of its fresh water resources and erratic rainfall has been a constant for centuries. That's why observers almost unanimously agree that bad government water policies, not mother nature, is the real killer. Since Independence, huge dam and canal projects have been pushed forward by successive administrations to irrigate the dry regions. When rainfall levels were good, these lived up to expectations, but when the monsoons failed in the late 1990s, the expensive irrigation network was found wanting. The problem was compounded by the effect that the advent of seemingly inexhaustible supplies of piped water had on villagers who, instead of remaining self-reliant, relaxed their traditionally frugal attitude to water and relied on the government to meet their needs. Thus, when the drought struck, poor farmers had to rely on supplies tanked in by private hauliers, borrowing money at usurious rates and putting up their fields and homes as security to pay for it – which is why so many thousands have ended up on the road in recent years.

Since 1991 no state has come even close to matching Rajasthan's tripling of the male literacy rate – though the situation for many Rajasthani women is rather less rosy (see p.174). Several universities have also been established. New industries benefit from an increased electricity supply that once only met the needs of palaces, but now reaches most villages, while irrigation schemes such as the Indira Gandhi Canal, which brings water from Punjab across the northern deserts to Bikaner and Jaisalmer, have improved crop production, and provided relief in times of inadequate monsoon. **Tourism**, which continues to rise, is another important flank of Rajasthan's expanding economy.

Nonetheless, Rajasthan remains among the poorest and most staunchly traditional regions of India, and although the need for economic development is modernizing the state faster than ever, the state's firmly held attitudes and customs are unlikely to disappear anytime soon. As Rajasthanis themselves are apt to remind you: *Delhi door ast* – "Delhi is far away."

Jaipur and around

A flamboyant showcase of Rajasthani architecture, the **Pink City** of **JAIPUR**, just 260km southwest of Delhi and 230km west of Agra, has long been established on tourist itineraries as the third corner of India's "Golden Triangle". Though the "Pink City" label applies specifically to the old walled quarter in the northeast of town, exuberant eighteenth- and nineteenth-century palaces are scattered throughout the whole urban area. The orderly **bazaars** of the old town rank among the most vibrant in Asia, renowned above all for hand-dyed and embroidered textiles, jewellery, and the best selection of precious stones and metals in India. For all its colour, however, Jaipur's heavy traffic, combined with the aggression of over-eager traders and touts, makes it a taxing place for recent arrivals to India and many stay just long enough to catch a train to more laid-back destinations like Bharatpur or the Thar Desert towns. Equally disappointing for anyone who has read of Jaipur's marvels is the run-down state of many of the better known monuments. But with a little adapting, the city's urban edge, and the dual Eastern/Western identity of its on-the-move residents, can be beguiling and constantly stimulating.

If you're anywhere near Jaipur in March, don't miss the **Elephant Festival**, one of India's most flamboyant parades, celebrated with full Rajput pomp during Holi (March).

Some history

Jaipur is one of Rajasthan's younger cities, founded in 1727. In 1700, **Jai Singh II** succeeded at the tender age of thirteen to the throne of the **Kuchwaha Rajputs** in Ajmer, inheriting a realm that encompassed Shekhawati to the north, and spread east to the borders of the kingdom of the Jats at Bayana, south to Aligarh, and west to Kishangarh. Although the Kuchwaha Rajputs had been the first to ally themselves with the Moghuls, in 1561, thereby inviting contempt from other Rajput clans, the free flow of trade, art and ideas had by this time won them great prosperity. Jai Singh himself excelled in battle, politics and learning, and showed an aptitude for astronomy and an extraordinary passion for symmetry.

When Jai Singh decided to move his capital south from the cramped hilly area of Amber, he drew up ambitious plans for the new city of Jaipur, named after himself, in accordance with the ancient Hindu treatise *Vastu Sashtra*, a formal

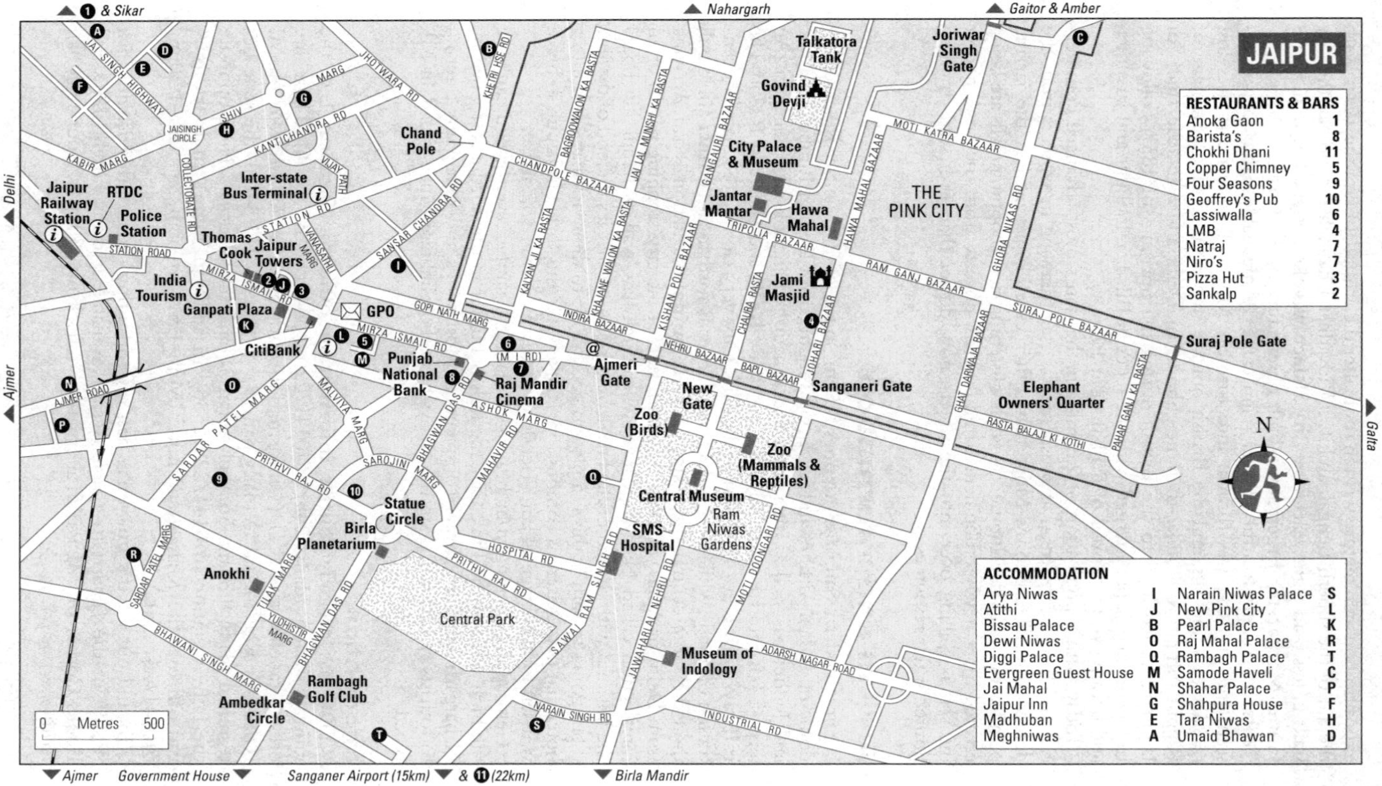

JAIPUR
RESTAURANTS & BARS
Anoka Gaon 1
Barista's 8
Chokhi Dhani 11
Copper Chimney 5
Four Seasons 9
Geoffrey's Pub 10
Lassiwalla 6
LMB 4
Natraj 7
Niro's 7
Pizza Hut 3
Sankalp 2
ACCOMMODATION
Arya Niwas I
Atithi J
Bissau Palace B
Dewi Niwas O
Diggi Palace Q
Evergreen Guest House M
Jai Mahal N
Jaipur Inn G
Madhuban E
Meghniwas A
Narain Niwas Palace S
New Pink City L
Pearl Palace K
Raj Mahal Palace R
Rambagh Palace T
Samode Haveli C
Shahar Palace P
Shahpura House F
Tara Niwas H
Umaid Bhawan D
1 & Sikar
Nahargarh
Gaitor & Amber
Delhi
Ajmer
Galta
Ajmer
Government House
Sanganer Airport (15km) & 11 (22km)
Birla Mandir
THE PINK CITY
Talkatora Tank
Govind Devji
Joriwar Singh Gate
City Palace & Museum
Jantar Mantar
Hawa Mahal
Jami Masjid
Chand Pole
Inter-state Bus Terminal
Jaipur Railway Station
RTDC
Police Station
Thomas Cook
Jaipur Towers
India Tourism
Ganpati Plaza
GPO
CitiBank
Punjab National Bank
Raj Mandir Cinema
Ajmeri Gate
New Gate
Sanganeri Gate
Suraj Pole Gate
Elephant Owners' Quarter
Zoo (Birds)
Zoo (Mammals & Reptiles)
Central Museum
Ram Niwas Gardens
SMS Hospital
Statue Circle
Birla Planetarium
Central Park
Museum of Indology
Anokhi
Rambagh Golf Club
Ambedkar Circle
JAI SINGH HIGHWAY
JAISINGH CIRCLE
KABIR MARG
SHIV MARG
JHOTWARA RD
KANTICHANDRA RD
VIJAY PATH
COLLECTORATE RD
STATION RD
STATION ROAD
VANASATHLI MARG
MIRZA ISMAIL RD
SANSAR CHANDRA RD
KHETRI HSE RD
GOPI NATH MARG
(M I RD)
AJMER ROAD
CHANDPOLE BAZAAR
BAGROOWALON KA BASTA
JAI LAL MUNSHI KA BASTA
GANGAURI BAZAAR
KALYAN JI KA BASTA
KHAJANE WALON KA BASTA
KISHAN POLE BAZAAR
INDIRA BAZAAR
NEHRU BAZAAR
BAPU BAZAAR
CHAURA RASTA
TRIPOLIA BAZAAR
JOHARI BAZAAR
HAWA MAHAL BAZAAR
RAM GANJ BAZAAR
MOTI KATRA BAZAAR
GHORA NIKAS RD
SURAJ POLE BAZAAR
GHAT DARWAJA BAZAAR
RASTA BALAJI KI KOTHI
PAHAR GANJ KA BASTA
ASHOK MARG
MALVIYA MARG
BHAGWAN DAS RD
MAHAVIR RD
SARDAR PATEL MARG
PRITHVI RAJ RD
SAROJINI MARG
HOSPITAL RD
SAWAI RAM SINGH RD
JAWAHARLAL NEHRU RD
MOTI DOONGARI RD
ADARSH NAGAR ROAD
INDUSTRIAL RD
NARAIN SINGH RD
TILAK MARG
YUDHISTIR MARG
BHAWANI SINGH MARG
N
0 Metres 500

exposition on architecture written soon after the compilation of the *Vedas*. With the aid of the superb Bengali architect Vidyadhar Bhattacharya, he had the city built in less than eight years. The **City Palace** was also designed by him, as was **Jantar Mantar**, the largest stone-built observatory in the world.

After Jai Singh's fruitful 43-year reign came an inevitable battle for succession, and the state was thrown into turmoil. Much of its territory was lost to Marathas and Jats, and the British quickly moved in to take advantage of Rajput infighting. Unlike their neighbours in Delhi and Agra, the rulers of Jaipur remained loyal to the British during the uprisings of 1857. Following Independence, Jaipur merged with the states of Bikaner, Jodhpur and Jaisalmer, and became **state capital** of Rajasthan in 1956.

Today, with a population of 2.3 million, the state's most advanced commercial and business centre is as prosperous as ever, drawing in workers from the depressed rural economy. More than other cities Jaipur evinces the jarring paradox of India's development – while glistening new shopping malls are being erected for a newly emboldened middle class, poverty from the city's poorer districts is spilling over into the streets, now dirtier than ever, and straining limited water resources.

Arrival and information

Jaipur's modern Sanganer **airport**, 15km south of the centre, is served by domestic Indian Airlines and Jet Airways flights from Delhi, Mumbai, Udaipur, and Jodhpur as well as international destinations Bangkok and Singapore. An airport bus into town costs Rs30, a rickshaw Rs70, and taxis cost Rs250. The **railway station** lies 1km west of the Pink City, very close to the main concentration of hotels, while state buses from all over Rajasthan and further afield pull in at the more central **Inter-state Bus Terminal** on Station Road. Arriving from Delhi or Agra, you skirt the south side of the city, stopping briefly at an intersection called Narayan Circle, where rickshaw-wallahs frequently board the bus, and with the aid of the bus driver, announce that it's the end of the line ("bus going to yard"); this is a ploy to get you on to their rickshaws and into a hotel that pays generous commission. Rackets like this thrive in Jaipur, so brace yourself for a barrage of auto-rickshaw drivers wherever you arrive.

Getting and keeping your bearings in Jaipur is simple; even if you can't see the high walls of the Pink City, the hills behind it in the northeast, topped by Nahargarh Fort, are always conspicuous. Most shops and restaurants catering to tourists can be found on the always busy thoroughfare Mirza Ismail, or MI, Road.

Information

RTDC has a handy **tourist information office** on Platform 1 of the railway station (daily 24hr; ⓣ0141/220 1364 or 237 5466). There are other branches and RTDC information outlets at the *Tourist Hotel* on MI Road opposite the GPO (daily 8am–8pm; ⓣ0141/237 5466), the state bus terminal (daily 9.30am–5pm, platform 3), and the *Swagatam Hotel* opposite the railway station (ⓣ0141/220 2586). In addition, there's an India Tourism office at the *Khasa Kothi* hotel (Mon–Fri 9am–6pm, Sat 9am–1.30pm; ⓣ0141/237 2200).

To find out **what's on**, you're best off consulting the monthly *Jaipur Vision* (Rs20) or the *Jaipur City Guide* (Rs30), available at many hotels, shops and Books Corner on MI Road; alternatively check out ⓦwww.jaipur-rajasthan.com.

Internet access throughout town costs Rs30–50 per hour. The majority of hotels listed overleaf are online, and there are many cybercafés: try *Modern Internet*, down an alley off MI Road near Ajmeri Gate.

City transport and tours

Jaipur, particularly its modern part, is very spread out, and although it's pleasant to walk around the Pink City, you may need some form of transport to get you there. It's best to avoid the morning and evening rush hours. Unmetered yellow-top **taxis** have stands on MI Road, and there are countless auto-rickshaws buzzing around at all times of day and night. **Radio taxis** offer the convenience of fixed, metered rates (Rs8–10/km; Rs20 minimum charge) and rarely take more than ten minutes for a pick-up; try Pink City (Ⓣ0141/222 5000). Given Jaipur's chronic pollution problems, however, it makes sense to opt for **cycle rickshaws** while travelling in the city, which travel no slower through the congestion than autos, and are much cleaner and cheaper. Many budget hotels rent **bicycles** out to their guests, or you can rent one for Rs25–30 a day from a place in the passage by 286 Kishan Pole Bazaar, about 100m north of the Ajmeri Gate, and from the Muslim cycle repair-shop just off Nirwan Marg, near the *Jaipur Inn*.

Cars with drivers can be rented most cheaply and reliably through hotels such as the *Pearl Palace*, *Arya Niwas*, or, through any RTDC office. Typical costs are around Rs375 return to Amber, or Rs675 to Samode. For destinations not covered by fixed fares, expect to pay between Rs4–7 per kilometre, depending on the make of the car, plus another Rs100 per extra hour of wait.

One efficient, though somewhat rushed, way to see Jaipur's main attractions is on a **guided tour**. Government-run half-day tours, starting from the railway station and the RTDC *Tourist Hotel* on MI Road, take in Hawa Mahal, the Observatory, the City Palace and Museum, Amber Fort, Laxminarayan Temple and the Central Museum (daily 8am, 11.30am & 1.30pm; 5hr; Rs100; book the day before). The full-day tour (daily 9am–6pm; Rs150 or Rs180 for a/c bus) skips the Central Museum, but crams in visits to Birla Mandir, Jaigarh Fort and a lunch stop at Nahargarh Fort – getting to the fort alone costs more than the tour itself, unless you walk.

Accommodation

As a major tourist and business centre, Jaipur has a wide range of **hotels**, many of them offering exceptional value. For once this is especially true at the bottom of the range, thanks largely to the **paying guest scheme** which enables you to stay in small, friendly family guesthouses. That said, the city also boasts some of India's most impressive and opulent **palace hotels**, as well as a batch of thoroughly dilapidated former mansions offering more atmosphere than creature comforts. Few places are located in the Pink City itself, but most are an easy walk from the City Palace and other sights. If you want to stay somewhere a little special, the RTDC-operated buildings next to **Nahargarh** rent out for Rs500 what could be Jaipur's most romantic lodging: a bare-bones, hexagonal-shaped room with near 360° views of the city below (Ⓣ0141/514 8044; ❹).

Wherever you choose to stay, you should **book ahead**, particularly around the Pushkar camel *mela* (early Nov) and the Elephant Festival (first half of March).

Budget

Arya Niwas Behind Amber Complex, Sansar Chandra Rd ⓣ0141/237 2456, ⓦwww.hotelaryaniwas.com. Short on character, but efficiently run and deservedly popular hotel with 100 or so varying rooms. All are clean with attached bath and hot water. Plus a large garden where you can eat breakfast or read free papers, and one of the best gift /bookstores in Jaipur. A good bet for long stays; book ahead. ❸–❺

Atithi 1 Park House Scheme, opposite All India Radio ⓣ0141/237 8679, ⓔatithijaipur@hotmail.com. Clean, friendly family-run hotel. All rooms have recently renovated bathrooms, soap and towels; the pricier ones have balconies. Internet facilities and restaurant. Recommended, despite the loud prayer call from the mosque next door. ❸–❺

Dewi Niwas Near Dhuleshwar Garden, Sardar Patel Marg, C Scheme ⓣ0141/236 3727. Guesthouse in 300-year-old yellow-washed *haveli*, marooned amid Jaipur's concrete southern suburbs. Large rooms, sunny courtyard (with incongruous grass huts for candlelit meals), and cold beers. Mrs Singh also serves home-cooked food. ❷

Diggi Palace Diggi House, Shivaji Marg, Hospital Rd ⓣ0141/237 3091, ⓦwww.hoteldiggipalace.com. A lofty 200-year-old *haveli*, one of the few heritage hotels to accommodate all budgets. Rooms in older, B-block are dark and cramped, but good value for budget travellers. The pricier, richly decorated cottage rooms have private balconies overlooking a beautiful garden. Friendly Goan manager. Internet access. ❸–❻

Evergreen Guest House Chameliwala Mkt, just off MI Rd ⓣ0141/236 3446 or 236 2415, ⓔevergreen34@hotmail.com. The cell-like rooms in this three-storey, prison-like budget hotel are totally seedy or cool, depending on your point of view. Tranquil leafy garden with a basic pool in summer (Rs100 for non-guests), café restaurant and tandoori grill. Free parking. ❶–❹

Jaipur Inn B-17 Shiv Marg, Bani Park ⓣ0141/220 1121, ⓦwww.jaipurinn.com. A cut above other backpacker hostels in town; you'll need to book ahead. Some rooms have balconies, but the dorm (Rs150) is stuffy. There's an OK restaurant, Internet access and gift shop, plus a terrace popular at sunset. ❶–❸

New Pink City Opposite GPO, Pink City Lane ⓣ0141/236 3774. A quieter and slightly dingier alternative to *Evergreen* – you may be able to haggle – accessed by a lane leading from Copper Chimney at MI Rd. Nice garden. Bring a mosquito net. ❷–❸

Pearl Palace Hathroi Fort, Ajmer Rd ⓣ0141/237 3700, ⓦwww.hotelpearlpalace.com. The gold standard for budget lodging in Rajasthan with spotless rooms, adorned with ethnic Rajasthani crafts, from Rs150. Dependable owner Mr. Singh can take care of all your travelling needs, from mailing postcards to booking bus tickets. The colorful rooftop restaurant offers choice food (thalis from Rs45) and affordable beer. Internet access. Book at least a few days ahead. ❷–❺

Shahar Palace Off Ajmer Rd, Barwada Colony ⓣ0141/222 1861, ⓦwww.shaharpalace.com. Excellent, family-run guesthouse with just six rooms on a verdant estate. Lots of personal attention, and a cute Shih-tzu to play with. Recommended. ❹–❺

Tara Niwas B-22-B Shiv Marg, Bani Park ⓣ0141/220 6823, ⓦwww.aryaniwas.com. Professionally run place aimed at longer-staying visitors, with sliding rates that offer excellent value (Rs7000/month for non-a/c doubles); daily tariffs are comparable with *Arya Niwas*, but you get a lot more personal attention and tranquillity here. The huge rooms (all en-suite; some a/c) are spotless. ❹–❺

Mid-range

Bissau Palace Khetri House Rd, outside Chand Pole ⓣ0141/230 4371, ⓦwww.bissaupalace.com. The well-stocked, antiquey library perfectly evokes this mansion's past glory as summer home of the Thakurs of Bissau. Rooms are comfortable and the main house has oodles of character, but is sadly not well cared for; the restaurant is overpriced. Swimming pool. ❻–❽

Madhuban D-237 Behari Marg, Bani Park ⓣ0141/220 0033 or 220 5427, ⓦwww.madhuban.net. Large standard rooms at the back around a lovely garden, or plusher deluxe ones in the main building (one with Jacuzzi); the Rajput decor could use a refresher, but it's still a very comfortable option at this price. Small pool. ❻–❽

Meghniwas C-9 Sawai Jai Singh Highway, Bani Park ⓣ0141/220 2034–6, ⓦwww.meghniwas.com. The attentive Mrs. Singh cares for this family-run hotel, which despite its uninspiring exterior has good rooms and a nice, pool-side garden out back. Hot water takes time. They're adding new rooms. ❻–❽

Shahpura House D-257 Devi Marg, Bani Park ⓣ0141/220 2293 or 220 3069, ⓦwww.shahpurahouse.com. Recently renovated suburban hotel well furnished with Shekhawati frescoes, colonial-era arms and modern amenities. As good as any luxury hotel but a fraction of the price (from Rs1800). Run by a descendant of the Shahpura royal family. Small pool and attentive staff. ❼–❾

Umaid Bhawan D1-2A Bani Park ⓣ0141/220 6426 or 231 6184, ⓦwww.umaidbhawanpalace.com.

Small, tastefully decorated rooms decked out with royal trimmings – 26 of the 28 have a private balcony. The owner is helpful and there are rickshaws on hand that charge fair, fixed prices. Internet and money exchange. Excellent value. ❺–❼

Expensive

Jai Mahal Jacob Rd, Civil Lines ⓣ0141/222 3636, ⓦwww.tajhotels.com. Palatial former residence of the Jaipur state PM, now run as a plush hotel by the Taj Group. Regal atmosphere, restaurant, swimming pool (Rs200 for non-guests), and gardens that come alive with festive galas during wedding season. Unless you go for superior rooms ($180) you're better off breaking your budget at *Rambagh Palace*, which feels more like the real thing. ❾

Narain Niwas Palace Kanota Bagh, Narayan Singh Rd ⓣ0141/256 1291, ⓦwww.hotelnarainniwas.com. Gaudily restored grand *haveli*, 2km from the Pink City, with individually styled rooms (Rs2700–3350) and a classy pool (Rs100 for non-guests) in huge, shady gardens. A comfortable option if you want Victorian England charm, but less expensive suites at *Diggi Palace* are better value. ❽–❾

Raj Mahal Palace Sardar Patel Marg ⓣ0141/510 5665, ⓦwww.royalfamilyjaipur.com. Elegant former palace of Jai Singh's favourite maharana, converted into a Neoclassical-style pad by the British for their agent general. Lawns, peacocks, a pool (Rs150 for non-guests) and all the trimmings, though an air of neglect hangs over the place. Rooms start at $50. ❽–❾

Rambagh Palace Bhawani Singh Marg ⓣ0141/221 1919, ⓦwww.tajhotels.com. Indisputably the grandest palace hotel in Jaipur, if not in India. A vast, thoroughly Rajasthani complex set amid 47 acres of beautiful gardens. Prince Charles and Princess Diana stayed here, and it's a favourite with Bollywood stars. Even if you can't afford a room, call in for a tea (Rs125) – accompanied by excellent sitar music – and a walk around the grounds. At night the popular disco *Steam*, housed in converted rail carriage, is Rs600 for couples, free to women. Rooms $320–1500, plus 8 percent tax. ❾

Samode Haveli Gangapole ⓣ & ⓕ0141/263 2407 or 263 2370, ⓦwww.samode.com. Exquisite old *haveli* on the northeastern edge of the Pink City, within walking distance of the City Palace. No longer the bargain it used to be, but service is still top-flight and the pool is the most Baroque in town. All rooms are individually decorated with Rajput-era antiques; rooms in the *zenana* portion of the building are newer. Ask to see the richly mirrored *sheesh mahal* suites. If you ask for a discount, they may offer a face-value conversion of their Euro-quoted rates into dollars – a considerable saving. ❾

The Pink City

Jaipur's most famous monuments – the **Hawa Mahal** and **Jantar Mantar Observatory** – both lie within the **City Palace Complex**, at the heart of the **Pink City**. For anyone familiar with Indian cities, the grid-plan may come as a surprise. Instead of a maze of narrow winding alleys, the spacious streets of the quarter are completely straight and laid out at right angles in accordance with the *Vaastu Shastras*, ancient Hindu architectural manuals, carefully adapted and applied by the local maharaja in the eighteenth century. However, the city's single most striking feature, its **pink colour**, did not form part of Jai Singh's original design. Originally a sallow yellow, the buildings were first given a rose pink wash – traditionally the colour of hospitality in Rajasthan and a good absorbent of the sun's blazing rays – when the city was spruced up for the visit of Prince Albert from England in 1876; the wash is now regularly reapplied. The visit of Bill Clinton in 2000 inspired another face-lift: shop fronts now sport regulation black Hindi graphics on white backgrounds, and a couple of streets (notably Bapu Bazaar) are permanently closed to traffic – unheard of in India.

In keeping with the prescriptions of the *Shastras*, each quarter, or *chokri*, in the Pink City is home to a particular centre of activity or commerce. **Nehru Bazaar** (closed Tues) and **Bapu Bazaar** (closed Sun) are special centres for textiles, perfumes and locally styled camelskin shoes; shops in **Tripolia Bazaar** and **Chaura Rasta** sell textiles and household utensils; and **Suraj Pole Bazaar** traditionally houses elephants and their owners – though a plan is underway to pack the pachyderms off to more spacious quarters in Amber. For more on **shopping** in Jaipur, see p.179.

Hawa Mahal

Jaipur's most acclaimed landmark, the tapering **Hawa Mahal**, or "Palace of Winds" (daily 9am–4.30pm; Rs5, plus Rs30 for camera, Rs70 video), stands to the east of the City Palace. Largely gutted, it is best appreciated from the outside during the early morning hours, when it exudes an orangey-pink glow in the rays of the rising sun. Built in 1799 to enable the women of the court to watch street processions while remaining in strict purdah, its five-storey facade, decked with no less than 593 finely screened windows and balconies, makes the building seem far larger than it really is; in fact it is little more than one room thick in most parts. Though the primary source of its appeal is undoubtedly the fantastic honeycomb pink-and-white face, visitors can go inside (enter from the back) to see exactly where the women sat, and take a close look at the detailed stonework.

City Palace

The magnificent **City Palace** (daily 9.30am–5pm; Rs180, plus Rs200 for video; same ticket also valid for Jaigarh Fort at Amber if used within 24hr), open to the public as the **Sawai Man Singh Museum**, stands enclosed by a high wall in the centre of the city amid fine gardens and courtyards. The royal family still occupies part of the palace, advancing in procession on formal occasions through the grand **Tripolia Gate** in the centre of the southern wall. Less regal

Out from under the veil

You don't have to be long in Rajasthan to realize that **women** are rarely seen or heard. As part of the state's feudal legacy, the purdah system, by which married women are kept isolated and under veil by their husbands, is still widespread in rural areas. Ditto for the dowry system and the age-old practice by which girls are denied an education. But it's not all chauvinism and second-class status. In India's male-dominated political system, where women have an abysmally low representation, it's striking that the state's top three **political offices** – Chief Minister, Governor, and Speaker of the Rajasthan Assembly – are all held by women.

Of the three, the most prominent is Chief Minister **Vasundhara Raje,** who hails from a politically powerful family that has long monopolized power in the state. Key to her 2003 victory as the head of the BJP slate was her marriage to the former ruler of Dholpur. Her decision to play the role of maharani during the campaign – trading in her chiffons for bright ethnic garb and a *rath* (chariot) – certainly endeared her to a local populace nostalgic for Rajputana's glorious past. But many feminists were uncomfortable with Raje's actions and asserted that she, Governor Pratibha Patil and Assembly speaker Simitra Singh rose to the top of their field by playing as rough and dirty as the boys and carefully avoiding the suicidal tag of "feminist".

Still, there is modest hope that the triumvirate will circumspectly and in their own way elevate the political agenda of Rajasthani women. Certainly they have their work cut out for them. The literacy rate of women in Rajasthan is one of the worst in India: 25 percent, versus more than double that for men. Women living in the state's rural areas are arguably the most relegated in all of India. By one account half are forced into marriage by the age of fifteen, and despite the intense work of internationally supported NGOs like Urmul Trust and The Barefoot College (@www.barefootcollege.org), which work to valorize the contributions of women to rural life, economic independence remains at best a distant dream for most.

visitors must enter through **Atish Gate** left of the main gate or **Nakkar Gate** in the west, passing the peanut vendors and souvenir shops in Jalebi Chowk. Official guides wait outside the ticket booth offering 1hr tours of the complex for Rs150 for up to four people.

The palace was conceived and built by Jai Singh, but many of the apartments and halls were added by his successors. The exhibits and interior design have lost none of the pomp and splendour of their glory days. Each door and gateway is heavily decorated, each chandelier intact and each hall guarded by turbaned retainers decked in full royal livery, so that Jaipur's palace impresses upon the visitor the continuity of a living royal presence.

An ornate gateway in the southwest corner of the complex leads into the first courtyard, with the solid marble **Mubarak Mahal** in its centre. This elegant palace, built as a reception hall in 1899, holds the **textile section** of the museum, whose treasures include throne carpets, antique *pashmina* shawls from Kashmir and even the maharaja's pyjamas. But the real highlight is the former maharani's richly gilded black Diwali outfit, covered in elaborate *gota* appliqué work. The first floor of the building next to the Mubarak Mahal, once the harem, houses the royal **arsenal**.

As you enter the second courtyard you're confronted by the raised **Diwan-i-Khas**, the Hall of Private Audience, built in sandstone and marble. Open-sided, with its roof raised on marble pillars, the hall contains two silver urns, or *gangajalis*, listed in the *Guinness Book of Records* as the largest crafted silver objects in the world, each more than 1.5m high with a capacity of 8182 litres. When Madho Singh II went to England to attend the coronation of King Edward VII in 1901, he was so reluctant to trust the water in the West that he had these urns filled with Ganges water and took them along with him.

In the centre of the compound, with balconies and windows studding its seven-storey facade, **Chandra Mahal** is the residence of the royal family. You can see it best from **Pritam Niwas Chowk**, known as Peacock Courtyard, to the west of the Diwan-i-Khas.

The largest section of the museum is housed in the ornate **Diwan-i-Am**, once the Hall of Public Audience. The intricately painted walls provide perfect mounts for immense medieval Afghan and Persian carpets. Miniatures from the Moghul and Jaipur schools, and Jai Singh's translations in Arabic and Sanskrit of the astronomical treatises of ancient scientists such as Euclid and Ptolemy, are displayed in glass cases.

Jantar Mantar

Unique throughout Rajasthan and an unforgettable showcase for medieval Indian astronomy is Jai Singh's astronomical **observatory** (daily 9am–4.30pm; Rs10, plus Rs50 for camera, Rs100 video). The odd-shaped trapezoids, soaring brick circles and giant-sized pillar, overlaid with sherbet-yellow gypsum and looking like futurist sculptures, are solidly planted in the southern courtyard of the palace complex. A total of eighteen instruments were erected between 1728 and 1734 by Jai Singh, many of them his own inventions.

It's a good idea to pay (Rs75–150) for the services of a **guide** to explain how the observatory works. Using Greek and Arabic brass instruments as a model, the instruments were designed so that shadows fall onto marked surfaces, identifying the position and movement of stars and planets, telling the time, and even predicting the intensity of the monsoon. The time calculated is unique to Jaipur, between ten and forty-one minutes (depending on the time of year) behind Indian standard time, but is used to calculate the Hindu (lunar) calendar.

Probably the most impressive of Jai Singh's constructions is the sundial, **Samrat Yantra**, which has a 27-metre-high centrepiece (*gnomon*), and can calculate the time to within two seconds. A more original device, the **Jaiprakash Yantra**, consists of two hemispheres laid in the ground, each composed of six curving marble slabs with a suspended ring in the centre, whose shadow marks the day, time and zodiac symbol. This is vital for the calculations of auspicious days for marriage; when unfavourable planets are in influential positions, for example between August and October, marriages have always been avoided.

Outside the Pink City

A handful of museums, temples and cenotaphs scattered around Jaipur's less congested suburbs offer welcome respite from the relentless traffic and crowds of the Pink City. The **Albert Hall museum**, housed in a grand British building that somewhat eclipses the collection inside, presides over a swathe of formal parkland, the **Ram Niwas Public Gardens**, south of the centre near the **Museum of Indology**, home to a hoard of quirky artefacts. As a target for day walks out of town, the hilltop "Tiger Fort" at **Nahargarh**, overlooking Jaipur from the rocky ridge north of the Pink City, is a strenuous option. Offering equally impressive views over the eastern fringes of the city, the old pilgrims' path to **Galta**, passing the "monkey temple" en route to a famous Hindu bathing tank, is more popular. **Gaitor**, where Jaipur's royal family has erected marble memorial *chhatris*, is best visited on the way to Amber.

Ram Niwas Public Gardens

South of the Pink City, on the road leading out of New Gate, the lush, 36-acre **Ram Niwas Gardens** were named after the planner, Ram Singh, who ruled Jaipur from 1835 to 1880 and made many successful efforts to improve public services. The gardens now house a number of institutions, most notably the **Albert Hall**, in which you'll find the **Central Museum** (daily except Fri 10am–4.30pm; Rs5), designed by the British architect Sir Samuel Jacob. This remarkable stately construction, built over several years from 1867, drew heavily on contemporary British models, but its arched verandas and rooftop domed pavilions hint at the Moghul background of its artisans. The exhibits within, which include miniature paintings, rocks, clothes and ornamental wooden boxes, may not be quite as inspiring as the building itself, but it's worth seeking out the highly original display of yoga postures demonstrated by tiny clay *sadhus*. Also within the gardens is a **zoo**, whose animals are kept in the usual grim conditions.

To the south of these, off Jawaharlal Nehru Road, the **Museum of Indology** (daily 10am–4pm; Rs40 including guided tour) holds assorted curiosities maintained by writer and painter Acharya Vyakul, including a map of India painted on a grain of rice, letters written on a hair, a glass bed and what is purported to be the largest collection of Tantric art in the world. Sadly, it's all looking a bit dishevelled, and could use a good dusting.

Nahargarh

Teetering on the edge of the hills 3km northeast of Jaipur, **Nahargarh**, or "Tiger Fort" (10am–5pm; Rs5), was built by Jai Singh II in 1734 as a retreat for his wives, the maharanis. Its unique design, regular and repetitive, stands in contrast to the other royal dwellings in Jaipur, though most of the apartments and courtyards are now in a state of near ruin. What hasn't changed over the centuries is the unrivalled view the palace affords of Jaipur and the desert beyond.

Vehicles of any kind can only get to the fort along a road that branches off Amber Road, a fifteen-kilometre journey from Jaipur. If you're feeling energetic, it's possible to **walk** there along a two-kilometre footpath that starts northwest of the City Palace. Although generally safe, it's best to avoid going alone or returning in the dark. Despite the incredibly scenic views few tour groups make the journey up here and you can enjoy a reasonably placid sunset from the ramparts just beyond the parking lot. A rundown café inside the fort serves meals and snacks.

Gaitor

A short distance north of the City Palace, and just over 6km from central Jaipur on the road to Amber, the walled complex of **Gaitor** contains the stately marble *chhatris* of Jaipur's ruling family. Built by Jai Singh II, the complex contains self-congratulating memorials to his ancestral lineage, with a room set aside for a future memorial to the present head of the family. Unless a ruler should happen to die an untimely death, the construction of his cenotaph is normally well under way during his lifetime, and traditionally each ruler takes exceptional pains to ensure that the marble carving on his own tomb is of a high standard. That of Jai Singh is inlaid with scenes from Hindu mythology and processions from his reign, depicting among other things the Hawa Mahal.

Galta-Monkey Palace

Nestling in a steep-sided valley 3km east of Jaipur, **Galta** (daily sunrise–sunset, free, plus Rs30 for camera, Rs50 video) is a picturesque collection of 250-year-old temples grouped around a sacred water tank.

Galta owes its sacred status in large part to a freshwater spring that seeps constantly through the rocks in the otherwise dry valley, keeping two **tanks** full. Traditionally humans bathe in the upper water tank, but except during the holy month of Kartika (usually Nov), the putrid-smelling reservoirs are the domain of the 5000-plus monkeys that call the place home – and earned it its nickname. Indeed, for many tourists the sight of splashing monkeys outstrips the attraction of the temples themselves. But it's worth hunting down the knowledgeable head priest, who'll gladly lead you to an inner temple that's been lit by a candle since a visit by Akbar more than four centuries years ago. Tourists wishing to **stay** overnight can do so in basic quarters for a nominal fee.

The best way **to reach Galta** is by rickshaw, or better yet, taxi, following along the road to Agra for 10km as it winds around the hills. Some rickshaws try to save time by taking a shorter, less scenic route – to avoid this, ask them to take you past Gaitor and the royal gardens at **Sisodia Rani-ka-Bagh** (daily 8am–6pm; Rs5). Landscaped with fountains and painted pavilions, these gardens are part of a palace complex built in the eighteenth century by Jai Singh II for the Udaipur princess he married to secure relations with his neighbouring Sisodia Rajputs. Temples at the back of the gardens, coated with the sherbet-yellow wash that covers the whole compound – the original colour of the Pink City – are open midday and early evening for worship. Shortly before Galta you'll come across a sign for the **Dhammathali Vipassana Centre** (Ⓣ0141/268 0220), one of fifty centres across the world set up to promote the practice of Vipassana **meditation** (see Basics, p.85). You can also **walk** to Galta (45min), leaving by **Suraj Pole** and climbing steeply up to the Surya temple on the crest of the hill above the main temple complex.

Eating, drinking and entertainment

Jaipur has an excellent choice of quality **restaurants**, both veg and non-veg, although options are more limited at the bottom of the range. If you're staying at a small or family-run guesthouse, eat in, or hop over to the *Pearl Palace* or *Arya Niwas*, where the food is fresh and less expensive than most other places catering to tourists' sensitive taste buds.

In town

Barista's Bhagwan Das Rd, across from Raj Mandir cinema. Smart, Starbucks-styled coffee house that's as popular with Jaipur's well-heeled as it is among caffeine-crazed foreigners; a bit pricey, but the best place for a real espresso. Pastries, however, are better at competitor chain *Mr. Bean's*, located at Sardar Patel Marg.

Copper Chimney MI Rd. Swish glass-fronted restaurant renowned for its top-notch Mughlai cuisine (including a friey *rogan josh*); they also offer Western and North Indian standards. If you want to spend less than Rs250, you can forego the trimmings and try *Handi*, a less expensive sister restaurant, next door.

Four Seasons D-43A Subhash Marg, C-Scheme. The most popular veg restaurant in town, in a modern two-storey building that's well off the tour group trail. Its South Indian *dosas* and *uttapams* are as good as you'll eat anywhere, and they serve a full selection of top north Indian specialties, Chinese food, and desserts. Huge portions cater to local tastes and can be a bit spicy. Expect a short wait for a table. Free delivery.

Lassiwalla Opposite *Niro's*, MI Rd. A Jaipur institution (in summer you have to wait 30min to be served) for its sublime lassis, served stand-up in old-style, hygienic terracotta mugs. Its popularity has sparked a small lassi wallah-war, with impostors setting up shop to the right (as you face it) of the original. Closes early afternoon.

LMB Johari Bazaar. Scrupulously pure-veg, high-caste cooking served in a large, cool dining hall with flashy neon decor. This has long been regarded as the best restaurant in town, but the food is not what it was, drenched in sickly *desi ghee* and too spicy for most tastes. However, their famous *paneer ghewar* (honeycomb cake soaked in treacle) and potato-and-cashew nut *tikkis* dished up piping hot (in spicy mango sauce) at the sweet counter outside are unforgettable.

Natraj MI Rd. Pure veg restaurant famed for its *paneer* dishes and superb sweets (try their melt-in-the-mouth *rasmalai*, flavoured with cardamom and saffron).

Niro's MI Rd. Along with *Copper Chimney*, this place gets the local vote for best non-veg food in Jaipur, but it's not cheap. The *sula* lamb dish is well seasoned and the other Rajasthani specialties are recommended. Usually there's a long wait.

Sankalp MI Road. Slip into one the comfortable booths at this modern South Indian restaurant and let your taste buds take over. The special *dosa* stretches four-feet long; more manageable, and out of this world, is the *uttappam*.

Out of town

Anokha Gaon 14 Vishwakarma Rd, opposite Jodla Power House, 12km north of town along Sikar Rd. Unquestionably the most authentic Rajasthani restaurant in these parts. The approach (through an industrial estate) is unpromising and the furniture rudimentary (you sit in rows on the floor and eat with your hands from leaf plates set on low plank tables) but the food, prepared on wood fires and old clay ovens, is out of this world. Rs110 for the full works, including four kinds of *rotis* and wonderful *kheer* (saffron-flavoured rice pudding).

Chokhi Dhani 22km south of Jaipur on the Tonk Rd ⓣ0141/277 0554. Well-heeled Jaipuris flock here in droves to sit on the floor and eat a rushed, mediocre thali with their hands. Luckily the Rs210 entrance fee includes access to the amusement park atmosphere – elephant rides, folk dance cabaret, puppet shows and handicraft vendors. Worth the effort if you're in a festive mood and looking for some hokey fun. A radio taxi charges Rs350 for the round trip, including wait (auto-rickshaw Rs250). Open Mon–Sat 6–11pm & Sun from 11am.

Drinking and entertainment

Several of the big five-star hotels, including the *Rambagh Palace* and *Sheraton Rajputana Palace*, host nightly culture **shows**, featuring folk dance, music and traditional puppetry. These can be a lot of fun, especially if they're held outdoors. Expect to pay around Rs150. Another music and dance venue is *Chokhi Dhani*, 22km south of the city (see above). If you're just after a quiet

drink and a chat, *Geoffrey's Pub* in the *Hotel Park Plaza* on Prithviraj Road is an English-styled pub complete with oak bar, sporting green booths and foxhunt memorabilia. They have a good range of imported and domestic beers as well as spirits, though they're not particularly cheap. It's open late.

If you go to the **cinema** just once while you're in India, it should be at the Raj Mandir on Bhagwan Das Road just off MI Road, which boasts a stunning Art Deco lobby and 1,500-seat auditorium. Most movies have four daily showings, and there's always a long queue, so get your tickets an hour or so before the show starts.

Shopping

If you come across an Indian **handicraft** object or garment abroad, chances are it will have been bought in Jaipur. Foreign buyers and wholesalers flock to the Pink City to shop for textiles, clothes, jewellery and pottery. In keeping with Maharaja Jai Singh's original city divisions, different streets are reserved for purveyors of different goods (see p.173). As a regular tourist, you'll find it harder to hunt out the best merchandise, but as a source of souvenirs, only Delhi perhaps can surpass it. The stores on MI Road and inside the City Palace tend to be pricey.

It's worth knowing that any stuff you've bought in Jaipur, but don't wish to cart around, can be **sent ahead** at nominal cost to Delhi or Mumbai. Silverwing Roadways, Mandawa House, Sansar Chandra Road, 200m north of *Hotel Arya Niwas* (Ⓣ0141/236 7542 or 237 6151), will truck parcels securely bound in cotton (which you can have done in the lobby of the Head Post Office on MI Road) to their warehouses in Kamla Market, Delhi and Clive Road, Mumbai, where you can collect them weeks (or months) later.

Clothes and cloth

For clothes and cloth, including Jaipur's famous **blockprint** work and *bandhani* **tie-dye**, recently pedestrianized **Bapu bazaar**, on the south side of the Pink City, is the best place. On the opposite side of town, along Amber Road just beyond Zorawar Gate, rows of emporia are stacked with gorgeous patchwork wallhangings, **embroidery** and traditional Rajasthani costumes; these places do a steady trade with bus parties of wealthy tourists, so be prepared to haggle hard.

For only a little more money, and a lot less hassle, head to the famous Anokhi showroom, 2 Tilak Marg, southwest of the city centre in the Civil Lines area (Ⓣ0141/238 1247, Ⓦwww.anokhi.com). Started by a British designer, it's the place to buy high-quality "ethnic" Indian evening wear, tastefully patterned *salwar kamise* and block-printed or batik men's shirts. They also do lovely bedspreads and cushion covers. Anokhi now exports, and there are outlets across India, but this is the flagship store and has the widest selection. Slightly less expensive, but similar in quality, is Soma, 5 Jacob Rd (Ⓣ0141/222 2778, Ⓦwww.somashop.com).

One of the best **tailors** in town, patronized by no less than the maharaja himself, is Jodhpur Tailors, behind *Neelam Hotel*, near Ganpati Plaza (MI Rd). A hand-stitched wool suit will run to just $160, less if you buy the fabric elsewhere.

Pottery

For old-style Persian-influenced vases, plus tiles, plates and candleholders, visit the outlets of the city's renowned **blue potteries** along Amber Road. For top-quality blue pottery, Jaipur's most famous ceramist, Kripal Singh, has a shop at B-18A Shiv Marg, Bani Park near the *Jaipur Inn* (☎0141/220 1127). Bear in mind that Jaipur's blue pottery is essentially decorative; none of it – in spite of what some shop owners tell you – may be used for hot food as the glazes are unstable and poisonous.

Jewellery and gemtones

For silver **jewellery** and **gemstones**, **Chameliwala Market**, southwest of the old city, is in a league of its own. It is also one of the hardest places to shop in peace, thanks to a particularly slippery breed of scam merchant, known locally as *lapkars* – usually smartly dressed young men speaking excellent English – whose offers of trips to local beauty spots are invariably followed by a stop at a "relative's" art studio, pottery or carpet-weaving workshop, with accompanying credit card fraud should you buy anything. If buying gemstones, be extremely suspicious of anyone offering an address in your own country where, it is claimed, you'll be able to sell them at a huge profit. This is nonsense, of course, but by the time you realize this you'll be thousands of miles away wondering where the mysterious entries on your credit card bill came from. If you're paying for gemstones or jewellery with a credit card in Jaipur, don't let it out of your sight, and certainly don't agree to leaving a docket as security.

Listings

Airlines Air India, Ganpati Plaza ☎0141/236 8569; British Airways, G-2 Usha Plaza, MI Rd ☎0141/237 0374; Indian Airlines, Nehru Place, Tonk Rd, the southward continuation of Sawai Ram Singh Rd ☎0141/274 3500; Jet Airways, opposite Ganpati Plaza on MI Rd ☎0141/511 2222; Lufthansa, Saraogi Mansion, MI Rd ☎0141/257 6360; Royal Nepal Airlines, D-46 Subash Marg ☎0141/237 6485. The others – American Airlines ☎0141/237 5430; Air France ☎0141/237 0509; Austrian Airlines ☎0141/237 7695; Gulf Air ☎0141/236 7409; KLM ☎0141/236 7772; Royal Jordanian ☎0141/237 7053 and United ☎0141/237 7062 – are all based in Jaipur Towers, on MI Rd.

Banks and exchange Changing money can be time-consuming at the city's banks, although ATM machines are common. There are plenty of private exchange places in Jaipur offering more or less the same rates, where you can cash travellers' cheques quickly and easily. The best of the bunch is Thomas Cook, ground floor, Jaipur Towers, MI Rd (Mon–Sat 9.30am–6pm); American Express, in the next building down MI Rd from Ganpati Plaza (Mon–Sat 9.30am–7pm); and LKP Merchant Financing, Sunil Sadan, first floor, 2 MI Rd (Mon–Sat 9.30am–6pm). CitiBank has an office on MI Rd, close to the GPO.

Beauty parlours Jaipur is renowned for its herbal beauty parlours, where you can pamper yourself with a massage or facial. The most famous is the Shahnaz Hussain Institute, S-55 Ashok Marg, C Scheme (☎0141/237 8444), which has separate clinics for men and women; if it's fully booked, try VLCC Beauty Parlour & Health Clinic, Ashok Marg, C Scheme (☎0141/236 3251).

Bookstores The boutique in *Hotel Arya Niwas* stocks a good selection of titles in English, especially with regards to India. Books Corner, on MI Rd just past *Niro's* has up-to-date magazines, papers and books in all major European languages. Ganpati Books at Ganpati Plaza is another option. Several guesthouses also have a second-hand stall.

Hospitals For emergencies, the government-run SMS Hospital (☎0141/256 0291 or 256 4222), on Sawai Ram Singh Rd, is best; treatment is usually free for foreigners. The largest hospital is Santokba Durlabhji Memorial Hospital (SDMH), Bhawani Singh Marg ☎0141/256 6251.

Music lessons A recommended sitar teacher is Mr Brij Mohan Sharma, who lives in Bani Park (☎0141/232 1682).

Photography Sentosa Colour Lab, Ganpati Plaza, can develop slides within 24hr, but aren't as reliable for downloading digital images. Goyal Colour Lab, next to *Lassiwalla* on MI Rd, is another good choice.

Police stations The main police post is on Station Rd opposite the railway station ☎0141/220 6324.

Post For poste restante, go to the GPO on MI Rd (Mon–Sat 10am–6pm). Parcels and registered mail are kept at the sorting office behind the main desks; packages are cotton-wrapped and sewn at the concession by the main entrance. It's preferable to bring your own box.

Swimming pools *Evergreen Guest House* charge nonresidents Rs100 for use of their pool; posher establishments such as the *Nairan Niwas* (Rs100), *Jai Mahal* (Rs200), or *Raj Mahal* (Rs150) have lawns, deck chairs and refreshments.

Travel agents For international and domestic flights, try Pinkey Forex Tours & Travels, Shop #2, Ganpati Plaza, MI Rd ⓣ0141/237 2216, ⓕ236 0437 or Rajasthan Travel Service, ground floor, Ganpati Plaza ⓣ0141/237 4344 ⓔrtsjaipur@bhaskarmail.com.

Visas For visa renewals go at least a week before expiration to the Foreigners' Registration Office (Rajasthan Police), behind the Hawa Mahal.

Yoga Jaipur has several reputable yoga schools, among them are: Rajasthan Swasth Yog Parishad, New Police Academy Rd (ⓣ0141/239 7330); Rajasthan Yoga Centre, 2km north of Bani Park in Shastri Nagar; and Madhavanand Ashram (ⓣ0141/220 0317), also in Bani Park.

Around Jaipur

Forts, palaces, temples and ruins from a thousand years of Kuchwaha history adorn the hills and valleys near Jaipur. As big a draw as Jaipur's more modern palace complex, the superb palaces of **Amber** provide the most obvious destination for a day-trip, but you can also visit **Amber Fort** – or Jaigarh – which crowns the hills to the north of the city. Many tourists also choose to travel south to search out the traditional potters, block printers and dyers of **Sanganer**. Organized tours (see p.171) visit Amber and Jaigarh in a day; Amber is accessible by public transport, and minibuses run to Sanganer.

Amber

On the crest of a rocky hill behind Maota Lake, 11km north of Jaipur, the Rajput stronghold of **AMBER** (or Amer) was the capital of the Kuchwaha Rajputs from 1037 until 1728. Fortified by natural hills, high ramparts and a succession of gates along a cobbled road, Amber's magnificent palaces are distinctly Rajput, but it's clear that Moghul ideas crept in to influence the design. The practice of covering walls with mirrored mosaics is pure Moghul, first introduced to India at Agra and Fatehpur Sikri.

It's worth visiting Amber independently, as there's so much to see; tour groups rarely get enough time to view the entire compound, let alone to scramble into the village behind it, dotted with fascinating temples and ruins. To avoid the big bus parties, get here early in the day. Regular **public buses** to Amber (#29 or #201) leave from outside Jaipur's Hawa Mahal, stopping on the main road below the palaces, where there's a **tourist office**. From there you can either enjoy a pleasant twenty-minute uphill walk, take a Jeep for Rs150 (up to six people), or waddle up the 425m slope on the back of an elephant (Rs400 for four people) – though some tourists have complained that the *mahouts* are unnecessarily cruel to their animals.

The palace complex

Entering the **palace complex** (daily 9am–4.30pm; Rs50, plus Rs75 for camera, Rs100 video) from the east through Suraj Pole (Sun Gate), you step into the main courtyard, **Jaleb Chowk**, where more elephant rides are on offer (Rs200) and official guides can be hired for about Rs200. In its southwest corner, the Shri Sila Devi temple is the Kuchwaha shrine to the goddess of war, Sila, an aspect of Kali; the image inside was brought to Amber from Bengal in 1604. Next to this, at the head of a flight of steps, **Singh Pole** ("Lion Gate") provides access to the palaces.

The lofty Hall of Public Audience, **Diwan-i-Am**, used by Raja Jai Singh I and his successors from 1639, stands in the entrance courtyard, while opposite, in the south wall of the yard, the exquisitely painted **Ganesh Pole** leads through narrow passages into the charming royal apartments. Here,

Moving on from Jaipur

Jaipur is Rajasthan's main **transport hub** and has daily air and train services to most major Indian cities. Buses are also frequent to destinations in and around the state. If your nerves are up to it, short journeys to destinations like Agra, Bharatpur, Ajmer (for Pushkar) and towns in Shekhawati are best made by road; one exception is Sawai Madhopur, the jumping-off place for Ranthambore National Park, which is most easily reached by train. For a full summary of transport services from Jaipur, giving departure frequencies and journey times, see the "Travel details" at the end of this chapter.

By bus

Frequent **RSRTC buses** leave from the Inter-state Bus Station on Station Road. For longer routes, faster (but less frequent) "deluxe" services guarantee seats. Enquiries for deluxe services can be made by phone (℡0141/511 6031) but for express services it's less hassle to turn up at the bus stand and head for the relevant booking office (destinations are listed outside each cabin). The deluxe services have their own separate booking hatch behind platform 3 (open 24hr).

Private bus services are slightly cheaper, although they tend to cram too many passengers on board and make unnecessary stops at *dhabas* along the way. You can book tickets for these at the string of agents on Station Road, but avoid the desperately uncomfortable video buses. A reliable company for direct buses to **Pushkar** is Jai Ambay Travels, next door to the Bank of Punjab on Station Rd (℡0141/220 5177), whose comfortable super deluxe coach leaves at 9.30am; you can buy tickets (Rs150) just prior to departure, but it's a good idea to get them in advance. The same outfit also runs buses to Ajmer (6 daily; 2hr 15min; Rs70), Jodhpur (3 daily, including 10.30pm sleeper; 6hr; Rs150–200), Jaisalmer (1 daily; 11hr; Rs250), Udaipur (1 nightly; 9hr; Rs220) and Agra (hourly, but making frequent stops; 5hr 30min; Rs100).

By train

Some **train** services from Jaipur have been disrupted over the past few years by track work, so check your departure and arrival times when you buy your ticket. Bookings should be made at least a day in advance at the computerized reservations hall just outside the main station (Mon–Sat 8am–8pm, Sun 8am–2pm; ℡0141/220

protruding from the east wall, the dazzling **Sheesh Mahal** houses what were the private chambers of the maharaja and his queen. Shards of mirror and coloured glass form an intricate mosaic that entirely covers the inner and outer walls and ceilings of the rooms. Above the Sheesh Mahal, the small chamber of the **Jas Mandir**, decorated with similar mosaics and guarded from the sun by delicate marble screens, served as a cool refuge in summer. A fountained garden separates the mirrored palace from the "pleasure palace" opposite, **Sukh Mahal**, where marble rooms are cooled by water cascading through fine perforations in the centre of the wall – an early and very efficient system of air-conditioning. The doors are inlaid with ivory and sandalwood.

The oldest part of the complex, the **Palace of Man Singh I**, lies south of the main quadrangle. The pillared *baradari* in the centre of the courtyard was once a meeting area for the maharanis, shrouded from men's eyes by flowing curtains. Narrow passages and stairwells connect small rooms and open balconies on all sides. Walking down the hill behind the palace complex brings you to the temples and ruined mansions of **Amber village**.

1401); there's a special "Foreign Tourist and Freedom Fighter" counter. The following daily trains are **recommended** as the fastest and/or most convenient from Jaipur. Bear in mind that timetables change, so check the departure time when you buy your ticket (it'll be printed on it).

Destination	Name	No.	Departs	Total time
Ajmer	Shatabdi Express	#2015	10.45am	2hr
	Aravali Express	#9008	8.40am	2hr 35min
Agra	Marudhar Express	#4864/4854	1.10pm	6hr 55min
	Jodhpur–Howrah Express	#2308	11.10pm	6hr 25min
Bikaner	Jaipur–Bikaner Intercity Express	#2468	3.25pm	6hr 50min
Delhi	Jodhpur–Delhi Express	#4060	5.25am	5hr 20min
	Shatabdi Express*	#2016	5.45pm	4hr 35min
Jaisalmer	Delhi–Jaisalmer Express	#4759	12.05am	12hr 40min
Jodhpur	Delhi–Jaisalmer Express	#4759	12.05am	5hr 55min
	Intercity Express	#2465	5.10pm	5hr 30min
Mumbai	Superfast Express	#2956	2.05pm	18hr 5min
	Aravali Express	#9008	8.40am	21hr 30min
Sawai Madhopur (for Ranthambore National Park)	Superfast Express	#2956	2.05pm	2hr 5min
Udaipur	Chetak Express	#9615	8.40pm	12hr 20min
Varanasi	Marudhar Express	#4864/4854	1.10pm	18hr 50min

* a/c only

Amber Fort/Jaigarh

Perched high on a hill behind Amber, offering incredible vistas over the hot plains, the mighty **Amber Fort**, or **Jaigarh** (daily 9am–5pm; Rs20, plus Rs20 for camera, Rs100 video; same ticket also valid for Jaipur City Palace if used within 24hr), was built in 1600. As the Kuchwahas were on friendly terms with the Moghuls, the fort saw few battles, and its immense cannon – the largest in Asia, needing one hundred kilos of gunpowder for one shot, which could purportedly send a ball 35km – was never fired in anger. The small museum collection displaying artillery, old maps, medals, stamps and photographs, plus the odd fifteenth-century spittoon, is unspectacular, but has an interesting hand-drawn floor plan of the palaces at Amber. The fort is also renowned as the most likely hiding place of the Kuchwahas' famous **lost treasure**. A huge hoard of gemstones and jewellery disappeared after Independence, probably to prevent its confiscation by the government. Income tax officials scoured the building with metal detectors in 1977 but found nothing.

Most people walk to Amber Fort from the village, but it's quite a long climb; the alternative is to descend to the valley and follow by vehicle the much longer road that leads to both Jaigarh and Nahargarh.

Samode

Hidden among the scrubby Aravalli Hills, **SAMODE**, on the outskirts of Shekhawati, is notable for its impeccably restored eighteenth-century **palace**. Actually a *haveli*, it became famous in the 1980s as the setting for the hit Raj-romance movie *The Far Pavilions*, and is now an award-winning heritage **hotel**, the *Samode Palace* (ⓣ01423/240014; ⓦwww.samode.com; ❾; rates drop by 40 percent May–Sept). It's possible to come here on a day-trip from Jaipur, 42km southeast, but if your budget can stretch to it, spend a night in one of the palace's uncompromisingly romantic rooms, plastered with murals and filled with antiques and ornate stonework. Non-residents have to shell out a hefty Rs100 to visit, but it's worth it just to see the beautiful **Sheesh Mahal**, or Hall of Mirrors, on the south side of the building. Three hundred steps lead up from the palace to a hilltop **fort**, the maharaja's ruined former residence, with impressive views over the surrounding countryside. Samode village itself is a centre for block printing and lacquered bangle making.

The owners of the hotel also have fifty richly appointed tents, 3km southeast of Samode at *Samode Bagh* (❾), with their own swimming pool, croquet lawns and tennis courts. **Bookings** for this and the palace can be made in Jaipur through *Samode Haveli*, Gangapole (ⓣ0141/263 2370).

Sanganer

SANGANER, 16km south of Jaipur, is the busiest centre for handmade **textiles** in the region, and the best place to watch traditional block printers in action (much of what's on offer can be bought in Jaipur). There are a couple of large factories here, but most of the printing is done in family homes as a cottage industry. Sanganeri craftsmen and women also decorate **pottery** in Rajasthan's distinctive style – floral designs in white or deep sea-green on a traditional inky-blue glaze.

Within the town itself, there are ruined palaces and a handful of elegant Jain **temples**, most notably the Shri Digamber temple near the Tripolia Gate. Mini-buses and tempos (Rs7) leave for Sanganer from Chand Pole, or you can take city bus #113 from Ajmeri Gate.

North of Jaipur: Shekhawati

North of Jaipur lies the easternmost extent of the Thar Desert, where small sand-blown towns nestle between dunes and sprawling expanses of parched land. Before the rise of Bombay and Calcutta (and the arrival of railways) diverted the trans-Thar trade south and eastwards, this region, known as **Shekhawati**, lay on an important caravan route connecting Delhi and Sind (now in Pakistan) with the Gujarati coast. Having grown rich on trade and taxes from the through traffic, the merchant Marwari and landowning *thakur* castes of its small market towns spent their fortunes competing with each other to build grand, ostentatiously decorated **havelis** (see box opposite). Many have survived, and now collectively comprise one of the richest artistic and architectural legacies in all India, if not the world: an incredible concentration of mansions, palaces and cenotaphs plastered inside and out with elaborate and colourful **murals**, executed between the 1770s and the 1930s.

Considering the wealth of traditional art here, and the region's proximity to Jaipur, Shekhawati feels surprisingly far off the tourist trail – English is rarely heard, accommodation is thin, and there's little prospect of enjoying Western

The havelis of Shekhawati

The magnificent houses built by the rich merchants of Shekhawati were called **havelis** after the Persian word for "enclosed space". Each house would be entered from the street through huge arched porches with carved brass or wooden doors. Inside, you come into the forecourt, where visitors were received. Beyond, through the most ornate doorway of the house, is the main courtyard, where the women of the family could live in purdah, shielded from the eyes of the street. The forecourt is flanked by large pillared reception areas called *baithak*, each surmounted by a gallery where the women could sit if they wanted, privy to the business conducted below. The most extravagant Marwari mansions might have four large courtyards, but three is more typical. The tradition of woodcarving that produced the imposing doors and window shutters is still strong, particularly in Churu.

The meticulous interior **murals** were painted by craftsmen from outside the region, using a vast array of intense hues, often highlighted with gold or silver leaf and mirrored designs. Like the early Catholic churches in Europe, religious themes, especially episodes from the life of Krishna, were often depicted along the lintels above the main doors to cultivate faith among the uneducated masses. The outer walls were usually decorated by the masons who built the *haveli*, employing bolder designs and weather-hardy green, maroon and yellow ochres, with the occasional flash of blue. However, what set the Shekhawati murals aside from virtually all others in India are the seemingly incongruous, naive depictions of machines, events and contemporary fashions they invariably include, from scenes of British Redcoats marching into battle against the Moghuls to eccentric Victorian flying devices, steam trains and Edwardian memsahibs in big hats. When painted, these were all features of a faraway world that the women and poor townsfolk of Shekhawati had never seen with their own eyes. The wealthy men of the region wanted to share with their compatriots the extraordinary phenomena encountered on their travels trading in the great cities of the Raj, and commissioned artists to paint these images, even though the artists had probably never seen the newfangled European novelties they were asked to depict.

Nowadays, most of the murals are faded, defaced, covered with posters or even just whitewashed over. In some ways this simply adds to their melancholy, haunting appeal, and there are so many – and the towns are so small – that you cannot fail to see a work of art virtually everywhere you look.

food or Internet access. Precisely for these reasons it ranks among the most rewarding parts of Rajasthan to explore, and of the few independent travellers who find their way up here, most invariably stay longer than planned, using **Nawalgarh** or **Mandawa** as a base for day-trips or leisurely walks into the desert.

Shekhawati is crossed by a mainline railway, linking the major towns with Delhi, Jaipur and Bikaner, but services are hopelessly slow, unreliable and inconvenient, and you're better off travelling into the region by bus. **Travelling around Shekhawati** is also far more convenient by bus than rail. Fairly regular local buses, always overcrowded, usually stop on the outskirts of town, though rarely operate after dark; Jeeps run according to demand, picking up as many passengers as physically possible. For less congested and precarious transport, you can rent a Jeep or **taxi**, starting at around Rs1500 a day, including the services of a knowledgeable guide. Travel agents in Jaipur also promote overnight excursions to the area.

Only the main towns have been covered in the following account, but you should be able to find interesting sites in any town or village you pass through. Ilay Cooper's excellent *The Painted Towns of Shekhawati* makes an ideal guide, but

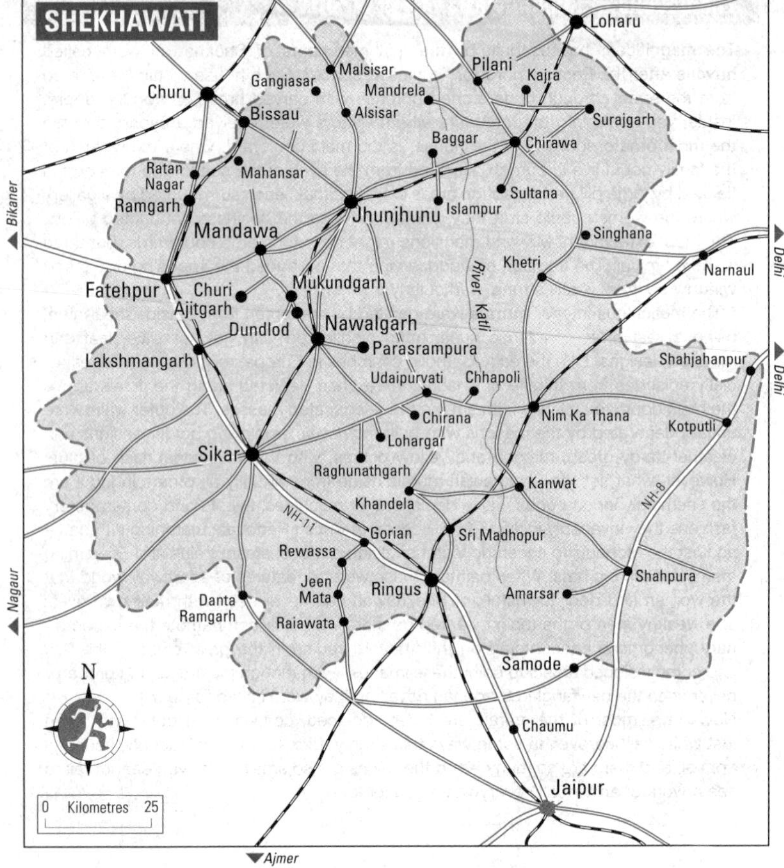

unfortunately remainder copies of its last printing are hard to find. Most of the buildings are still privately owned, and many of them are homes; ask permission to enter any house, and respect the custom of removing your shoes before you do so. A nominal baksheesh is usually expected.

Some history

The first people to settle the lands north of Jaipur, the Muslims of the Khaimkani clan, established two small states based at **Jhunjhunu** and **Fatehpur** in 1450. Their hold on the region was broken in 1730, when the Rajput **Sardul Singh** of the **Shekhawat** clan took over Jhunjhunu. Two years later he consolidated Shekhawati rule by helping his brother (already ruler of Sikar) to seize Fatehpur from its Muslim Nawab.

The local **Marwari** merchants were rivals in influence to the Rajputs, and it was this that led the Shekhawats to turn a blind eye to, and even sponsor, brigandry against them. In response, the merchants formed an alliance with the British (ever eager to get a foothold in the region), and in 1835 a small force of cavalry called the Shekhawati Brigade was set up under the command of Henry

Forster and based in Jhunjhunu to control the brigands. This gave the Marwaris the security they needed to build their magnificent *havelis*, and though many of them moved, encouraged by the British, to Bombay, Madras and especially Calcutta, they continued to send their profits back to Shekhawati, erecting elaborate buildings either to prove their worth as prospective bridegrooms, or simply as aid projects during times of famine. When the British left India, a number of Marwaris bought British industries, and such names as Birla and Poddar remain prominent in business today. Although many merchant families have relocated to major urban centres, allowing their former haunts to fall into a state of disrepair, renewed tourist interest in the region's heritage has encouraged many of late to embark on **restoration** work.

Nawalgarh

NAWALGARH, 30km north of Sikar, came into its own in 1737, when the Shekhawat Nawal Singh claimed what was then a small village as the site for a fort. Thick stone walls, pierced by four gateways, were erected to encircle Nawalgarh, now a lively little market surrounded by miles of yellow desert and *khejri* scrub. For tourists, this town of 57,000 is by far the most congenial base for the Shekhawati region, with a bumper crop of painted *havelis* and a picturesque, relatively traffic-free bazaar, along with good transport connections and budget rooms.

Arrival and information

Nawalgarh's **bus** and **Jeep** stand, about 2km west of town, is served by buses from Jhunjhunu (every 30min; 1hr) via Dundlod (15min) and Mukundgarh (20min); Sikar (every 15min; 40min); Jaipur (every 15min; 3hr 30min), and Ajmer (1 daily at 10am; 5hr). The **railway station** is about 500m west, with four daily services in each direction from Sikar to Jhunjhunu (three from Jaipur). The Shekhawati Express #9733 from **Delhi** departs from Sarai Rohilla station at 11pm and arrives just after 6am. In the opposite direction, the Shekhawati Express #9734 departs Nawalgarh at 9.24pm, arriving in Delhi eight hours later.

For trips around the region, you can either jump on and off cheap, cramped village-to-village **Jeeps** (which leave when they're full), or rent a vehicle for the day at very reasonable rates through Ramesh Jangid at *Apani Dhani* (see below). Ramesh also runs socially responsible **tours** throughout Rajasthan and India (Ⓦ www.alternativetravels-india.com). **Cycles** can be rented at *Apani Dhani* or from the small repair shop just north of the big Doordarshan transmitter mast on the northwest edge of town.

Accommodation and eating

Although plentiful compared with most towns in Shekhawati, **accommodation** can be in short supply in winter and should be booked a day or two in advance. Most tourists take **meals** at their guesthouses – otherwise, there are a few *dhabas* near the main market.

Hotels and guesthouses

Apani Dhani Northwest edge of town, on the main Jhunjhunu road Ⓣ 01594/222239, Ⓦ www.apanidhani.com. Crusading owner Ramesh relies on solar energy, compost toilets and recyclable materials to create an exemplary eco-farm; he also runs tours (see above). Traditional-style round huts, Shekhawati crafts and awesome organic cooking in bougainvillea-strewn garden add class and comfort. Excellent value; book ahead. ❺

DS Bungalow Near *Roop Niwas*, on the eastern edge of town Ⓣ 01594/222703. A good mid-range option with a friendly family atmosphere;

comfortable rooms set around a sandy courtyard are jazzed up with carpets and old wine bottles. ❹

Ramesh Jangid Tourist Pension On the west edge of town, just north of Maur Hospital ⓣ01594/224060, ⓦwww.apanidhani.com. Inexpensive rooms opening onto a sunny roof terrace, in a warm brahmin family home. Delicious pure-veg food available, as well as Jeep transport and expert advice on day-trips. Henna painting and tie-dye classes upon request. A cheaper, though less unique alternative to Ramesh's *Apani Dhani*. ❸

Roop Niwas 1km east of the bazaar ⓣ01594/222008, ⓕ223388. Nawalgarh's closest thing to an upscale resort is a rambling Raj-era mansion with grandiose rooms that upon closer inspection belie a certain faded elegance. Beds can be a bit hard. Wonderful sepia photos from the 1930s hang on the walls, along with moth-eaten hunting trophies; non-guests can saddle a Marwari thoroughbred for hour-long rides (Rs450). ❼–❽

The Town

Nawalgarh is the home town of the wealthy and influential Poddar family, merchants who emigrated south to become Bombay-based industrialists and who have, over the years, sponsored the construction of schools and colleges across the country, including here. **Nansa Gate** is the first you come to when approaching the town from the bus stand: turn left just inside it and follow the street round for about 250m, and you'll come to an enclosure on your left, surrounded by painted walls. These form part of **Aath Haveli**, a complex of eight *havelis* decorated with murals featuring trains, carts, false windows (very common in Nawalgarh) and barbers at work. Taking a right turn just inside Nansa Gate and then the second right, brings you to the **Surajmal Chhauchharia Haveli**, where murals include a picture of Europeans floating past in a hot-air balloon. The painter took some playful licence as to the mechanics involved: the two passengers blow into the balloon to power their journey.

The third right turn after entering Nansa leads to the **fort** (Bala Qila), which houses banks and offices around a central yard crowded with vegetable vendors. The dilapidated building left of the Bank of Baroda boasts the magnificent mirrored **Sheesh Mahal**, with a ceiling mural that includes maps of Nawalgarh. The spectacular room is accessed through the bedroom of a private residence; you'll need to pay a baksheesh. Heading straight on from Nansa Gate takes you, after 300m, to a little square, beyond which stands the colourful **Laxminarayan temple**. A right turn at the square brings you to the **eastern gateway**, called Poddar Gate.

Other *havelis* in Nawalgarh include **Goenka Haveli**, in the north of town near Bowri Gate, and the magnificent **Anandi Lal Poddar Haveli**, east beyond Poddar Gate (follow the main road, bearing left and then round to the right after 50m, pass a trio of rather run-down *havelis*, and it's down a turning on your right). Built in 1920 and now a school, this is one of the few *havelis* in Shekhawati to have been restored to its original glory. Among its features is a 3D-like panel of a bull's head that transmogrifies into an elephant's as you move from left to right. Admission costs Rs75, which includes a short tour; all proceeds go towards maintenance of the building.

Dunlod and Parasrampura

The most obvious target for a day-trip from Nawalgarh is **DUNLOD**, 7km north and the site of an old fort and some large *havelis*. It's possible to get there by bus, but most people walk across the fields – a leisurely amble that's enjoyable save for the last two kilometres, which you have to cover via a rough sandy track linking the village with the main road. The **fort** (Rs20), like most others in the region, has been converted into a luxury **hotel**, the *Dunlod Castle* (ⓣ01594/252519 or 0141/211275; ❽), but its murals are mediocre and the rather shabby rooms, which have been tackily restored, lack the atmosphere of those at Mandawa and Mahansar. Radiating from its southeastern walls, the village streets harbour several interesting *havelis*, painted around the turn of the twentieth century, and the delicate *chhatri* of Ram Dutt Goenka, a cenotaph erected in 1888 with vibrant friezes lining its dome.

More painted buildings are dotted around the serene hamlet of **PARASRAMPURA**, 20km southeast of Nawalgarh, set amid rolling hills dotted with janti trees that makes for some of the most attractive desert scenery in Rajasthan. Buses run every thirty minutes or so, or you could cycle (although be warned that several stretches of the track degenerate into soft sand). Monuments include the **Gopinath temple**, built in 1742, whose murals include depictions of the torments of hell (a common theme in the eighteenth century), and images of the local Rajput ruler, Sardul Singh, with his five sons. Some of the paintings are unfinished, as the artists were diverted to decorate the *chhatri* of Rajul Singh, who died that same year. The large dome of his exquisite **cenotaph**, supported by twelve pillars, contains a flourish of lively and well-preserved murals, once again including images of hell, and of Sardul Singh with his sons. Parasrampura's modest **fort**, in reasonable repair, is on the west bank of the dry riverbed.

Jhunjhunu

JHUNJHUNU, taken over by the Shekhawats in 1730 as the capital of their newly formed territory, is the principal entry point to Shekhawati if you're travelling from Delhi. Spreading in a mass of brick and concrete from the base of a rocky hill, it's a busy, unprepossessing town of 100,000, but its commercial importance – and its location, within 60km of most major sites in the region – makes it a convenient (if less tranquil) base. Although its *havelis* are less heralded than those elsewhere, in reality they are no less impressive than any others.

Arrival, information and accommodation

Buses from the chaotic government stand in the south of town run to Nawalgarh (every 30min; 40min–1hr) and towns throughout Shekhawati, as well as to Bikaner (hourly; 5hr 30min), Jaipur (every 30min; 5hr) and Delhi. Buses to Mandawa (every 30min; 30min) stop briefly near the RTDC *Tourist Bungalow*. The stand for private buses is east of the main bazaar; tempos and shared auto-rickshaws run between the two via Gandhi Chowk. Two **train** services arrive at the station on the southern edge of town from Sikar via Nawalgarh (three of them from Jaipur), and the Shekhawati Express runs in the other direction, making a stop at Jaipur, daily at 5.13am.

The local **tourist office** (Ⓣ01592/232909), attached to the RTDC *Tourist Bungalow* at Mandawa Circle, occupies a large new building on the western outskirts – it offers little other than maps of other places. Jhunjhunu is quite spread out, and walking around can be tiring, but many of the streets of the old town are too narrow for cars; **rickshaws** operate as taxis, picking up as many passengers as they can. **Bicycles** can be rented from a small shop near the park in the south. **Taxis** gather at a rank outside the bus stand, costing around Rs4 per kilometre. Laxmi Jangid (see below) offers a full-day **tour** of the region by car or Jeep for Rs1500.

Budget **accommodation** is hard to come by, but the clean *Hotel Sangam* (Ⓣ01592/232544; ❷–❹), quietly set back from the bus stand, is acceptable. If you have a little extra money to spend, head east to *Shiv Shekhawati* (Ⓣ01592/232651 or 512695, Ⓦwww.shivshekhawati.com; ❸–❻), a well-maintained hotel with large, clean rooms, restaurant and Internet access. Its knowledgeable owner, Laxmi Jangid, a government-authorized guide and avid promoter of Shekhawati's cultural heritage, has also partnered with a German friend to develop the spirited *Jamuna Resort* (Ⓣ01592/232651; Ⓦwww.shivshekhawati.com; ❹–❽). On the eastern edge of town, staying here is an unforgettable experience, with ten thatch-roofed cottages set amid extensive grounds featuring a pool and garden restaurant. Even if you can't afford them, ask to see the two "golden" rooms, which have been painstakingly plastered with Shekhawati murals by one of the art's last living practitioners. They also run **courses** in Indian cooking, art and yoga.

The Town

Jhunjhunu's most striking mansions are grouped around **Nehru bazaar**, five minutes by rickshaw north of the main bus stand along Station Road. Setting off from Gandhi Chowk, at the far east end of the market, walk west until you reach a pair of *havelis* facing each other on a lane running north. Known as the **Modi Havelis**, they contain some of the finest murals and woodcarving in town, including a depiction of Queen Victoria. Above the nearby vegetable stalls, the **Kaniram Narsinghdas Tibrewala Haveli** (built 1883) boasts coloured-glass windows around the top of its *baithak*, or pillared reception area, and depictions of steam trains and a European holding his dog. Further up the same lane, the **Bihari temple** features some of the oldest Shekhawati murals, painted in 1776 in vegetable pigments. Dating to a time before the Marwaris took over from the Rajputs as the dominant social class, they feature Sardul Singh's five sons, each of whom built a fort in the town.

Further west, the **Khetri Mahal**, built in 1760, is ageing and empty, but there's no mistaking the originality of its design: sandstone pillars stand in place of walls wherever possible, and a covered ramp, wide enough for horses, winds up to the roof. Views over Jhunjhunu from here stretch to the old Muslim quarter, **Pirzada Mahalla**, where a grand mosque is surrounded by tombs dating back to 1500. Many of Jhunjhunu's Muslims – still an important sector of the population – were wealthy merchants who built painted *havelis* of their own. A wander through Pirzada Mahalla leads past mosques, *dargahs* and meat markets, as well as neat rows of shops painted in pastel greens, blues and pinks unlike anywhere else in Shekhawati.

West of the Khetri Mahal, at the foot of the conical **Kana Pahar** hill, lie **Badalgarh** – the only fort remaining from the Nawab period – and the **Dargah of Kamaruddin Shah**, with a mosque, *madrasa* and collection of tombs enclosed in a small complex. Behind the *madrasa* stands a monument to the infant son of Henry Forster, commander of the British-run Shekhawati Brigade, who died in 1841. Only one of the five gates of "Forster Gunge", the Shekhawati Brigade's cantonment, survives.

In the north of Jhunjhunu, the **Mertani Baori** is the region's most impressive step-well. If you head up there, make the short detour east to the extraordinary **Rani Sati Mandir**. Few foreigners ever visit this shrine, but, as the centre of a phenomenally popular Sati Mata cult, it is reputedly the richest in the country after Tirupati (in Andhra Pradesh), receiving hundreds of thousands of pilgrims each year and millions of rupees in donations. Its immense popularity bears witness to the enduring awe with which **satis** – women who commit ritual suicide by climbing on the funeral pyre of their husband – are viewed in the state. Although banned by the British in 1829, the practice has survived in parts of rural Rajasthan; forty cases are known to have occurred since Independence – the latest, and most infamous, being that of Roop Kanwar, an 18-year-old Rajput girl who committed self-immolation in 1987 in the village of Deorala, near Jaipur. The *sati* commemorated here was performed by a merchant's wife in 1595. Her image, rendered in tile- and mirror-work, adorns the ceiling of the main prayer hall, while a sequence of panels on the north wall relates the legend surrounding the events of her death.

Eating and drinking

For the best food in town head for the **restaurants** at the *Shiv Shekhawati* or *Jamuna Resort*. More basic sit-down joints include *Nehru's Hotel* in Gandhi Chowk, and there are also the usual rows of cheap food stalls concentrated around the bus stand.

Mandawa

Rising from a flat, featureless landscape roughly midway between Jhunjhunu and Fatehpur, **MANDAWA** was founded by the Shekhawats in 1755, though most of its paintwork dates from the early nineteenth century. The town's imposing **fort**, right in the centre, now houses a luxury **hotel** (see p.192), whose prominence on the upmarket tour-group trail has made this the most tourist-oriented place in Shekhawati. However, the handicraft shops, touts and guides clustered around its cannonball-chipped walls detract very little from the dilapidated beauty of the profusion of mansions.

Taking a **walking tour** to see Mandawa's scattered *havelis* is recommended; Ashok at Classic Shekhawati Tours (☎01592/223144), just outside the castle gates, charges Rs250 for a two-hour tour of the city and outlying villages. Tours usually begin with the **Naveti Haveli** (now the State Bank of Bikaner & Jaipur) on the main bazaar in the centre of town. Duck through the metal gate to the right of the bank for a look at the well-preserved images of flying contraptions, a boy using a telephone and a strongman pulling a car. Over in the northwest of town, the patterns and paintings decorating the sun-faded **Goenka Double Haveli** range from traditional Rajasthani women and religious motifs to Europeans in stylish hats and Victorian finery. In the **Nand Lal Murmuria Haveli** next door, the paintings of trains, cars, George V, and Venice were executed during the 1930s by Balu Ram, one of the last working artists of the region.

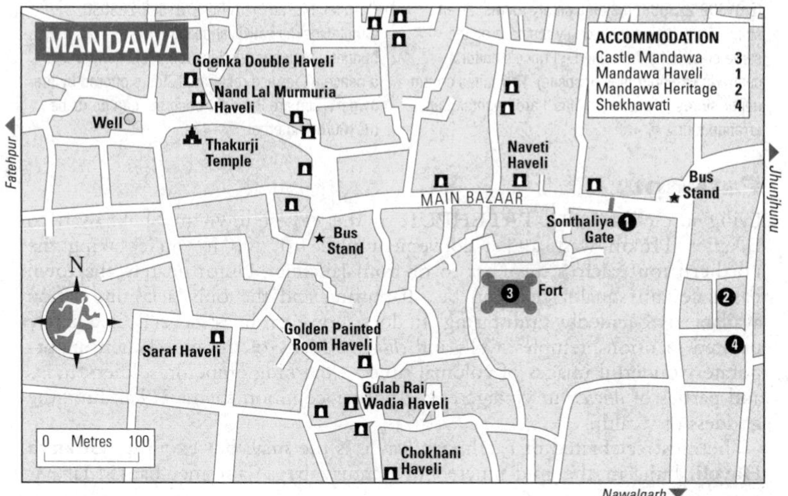

Murals in the **Thakurji temple** opposite include soldiers being shot from the mouths of cannons. Further west are a couple of *chhatris*, and a step-well, still used today and bearing paintings inside its decorative corner domes.

Another *haveli* worth asking for by name is **Gulab Rai Wadia Haveli**, in the south of town, where the decoration of the outer and inner walls is perhaps the finest in Shekhawati. Blue washes here and there betray twentieth-century censorship of the erotic scenes that had been commonly acceptable one hundred years earlier. Just south, the **Chokhani Haveli** (Rs10) is unique in the region for having twin wings. Its murals are particularly beautiful and well preserved; look for the miserable British soldiers and *chillum*-smoking *sadhu* on the walls in the recess of the facade.

Practicalities

Buses from Jhunjhunu and Nawalgarh (at least hourly), as well as Jaipur and Bikaner (10 daily) stop at Sonthalia Gate in the east of town. From Fatehpur, most buses pull in at a stand in the centre, just off the main bazaar. **Jeeps** ply the same routes. The town is so small that either bus stand is within walking distance of most hotels. For **Internet**, try Gayatri Art Gallery in the main bazaar. Most **eating** is done at hotels or guesthouses, where meals are served alondside tackier-than-average puppet shows and folk dancing.

Accommodation

Mandawa harbours a better-than-average batch of **hotels**, but not much in the budget range.

Castle Mandawa ⓣ01592/223124, ⓦwww.castlemanadawa.com. The castle is the real thing, and the rooms (Rs2650-4400), complete with alcoved sitting areas, murals and period furniture, are luxurious enough, but it feels somewhat contrived and is grossly overpriced for lacklustre amenities. Turbaned Nepali waiters perform nightly Rajasthani cabarets for tour groups. Will exchange travellers' cheques. ❽–❾

Mandawa Haveli Near Sonthaliya Gate ⓣ01592/223088. Tasteful, comfy rooms, all en suite, in a *haveli* painstakingly restored by the same crew behind Nadine Le Prince's cultural centre in Fatehpur (see opposite). The suites on the upper storey (especially "Nilas") are brighter. Can arrange tours. ❺–❽

Mandawa Heritage Mukandgarh Rd ⓣ01592/223742, ⓦwww.hotelheritagemandawa.com. A turn-of-the-century mansion on the quiet south side of town with attractively furnished rooms of varying standard; the quoted tariffs are a bit ambitious, but you should be able to bargain them down. Fine for the price, but a bit scruffy. Courtyard restaurant with puppet show and music at night. ❹–❼

Shekhawati Near Government Veterinary Hospital, Mukandgarh Rd ⓣ01592/223036, ⓔhotelshekhawati@yahoo.com. Mandawa's only budget option has spotless rooms, hot water and a peaceful, terrace restaurant. Tours offered by the owner's son are the right price but can be rushed (Rs100/hr). Internet. ❷–❹

Fatehpur

Lying just off NH-11, **FATEHPUR** is the closest town in Shekhawati to Bikaner, 116km west, and a convenient place to stop if you're taking the northern route across the Thar to or from Jaisalmer. Unfortunately, the town has a certain squalor that can be off-putting and the only accommodation available is decidedly uninspiring. It does, however, boast several elaborately painted mansions, temples, wells and *chhatris*. Many of the murals here incorporate wonderful images of colonial times – the king emperor, soldiers, trains and parties of *angrez* in vintage cars. Another common theme is Lakshmi, the goddess of wealth.

The most celebrated of Fatehpur's *havelis* is the small but exquisite **Goenka Haveli**, built in the mid-nineteenth century by a Jain merchant, Mahavir

Prasad, and currently being restored. It's reached by following the main road north from the bus stand and turning left at the first main crossroads. While the inner courtyard is beautifully painted, the first-floor room is dazzling, its walls and ceiling decorated in the finest detail with a myriad of colours, gold leaf and mirrors. Panels to either side of the door show Krishna riding an elephant (on the right) and a horse (on the left), each animal made up of contorted female figures. Nearby is **Nadine le Prince Haveli** (daily 8am–7pm; Rs100), an 1802 mansion restored to its original splendour by its current owner and namesake, a French artist. Some modern details, like the Italian marble fountain, feel out of place, but taking the tour to see how the laborious, six-year restoration was carried out is fascinating. There's also a café and gallery exhibiting local and French artists. If you rejoin the main northbound road at the crossroads, and turn right after 20m, you'll come to **Nand Lal Devra Haveli**, whose splendid ceiling panels in the reception area were copied by many other merchant families. The murals on the courtyard walls, and the complex carving of the wooden doors and shutters, are equally impressive. To the north of town, distinctive Shekhawati **wells** (*baolis*) stand raised on square platforms, with domed shelters on each corner, so they could be seen from afar.

Practicalities

Fatehpur has two **bus stands**, near each other in the centre of town on the main Sikar–Churu (north–south) road. Buses from the government Roadways stand, furthest south, serve Jaipur (every 30min; 3hr 30min), Ramgarh (hourly) and Bikaner (14 daily; 3hr 30min–4hr), as well as Delhi (5 daily; 6hr). Private buses run from the stand further north along the bazaar to Mandawa (every 30min; 30min), Jhunjhunu (every 30min; 1hr), Mahansar (4 daily; 45min) and Ramgarh (hourly; 30min). For arrivals, note that many buses drop passengers off on the NH-11 intersection, about 1km south of town. The **railway station**, east of town, has two daily **trains** to Churu (the 1.30am one continues on to Bikaner), and two pre-dawn trains to Jaipur and Sikar.

Just off NH-11, the modern RTDC *Hotel Haveli* (Ⓣ01571/220293; ❹–❺) is the town's only plausible **hotel**, though its large and light rooms, some with a/c, don't quite compensate for the dodgy plumbing and less-than-helpful staff. It's also a fair walk from the bazaar and bus stand; if you aim to catch the early morning (6.30am) express service to Bikaner, note that you can flag the bus down from the roadside next to the hotel. For **food**, you've a less than inspiring choice between the RTDC *Hotel Haveli*'s hit-and-miss overpriced menu, or the row of basic *dhabas* near the bus stand.

Mahansar, Ramgarh and Lakshmangarh

Some of the most outstanding murals and Hindu monuments in the region are scattered across three small towns in the far north and west of Shekhawati: **Mahansar**, **Ramgarh** and **Lakshmangarh**. Of these, only Mahansar has any accommodation, but you can reach the other two easily enough on day-trips from Fatehpur.

Mahansar

The relative inaccessibility of **MAHANSAR**, marooned amid a sea of scrub and drifting sand 27km northeast of Fatehpur, has ensured that its monuments, which include a fortress and some of the most accomplished interior paintings in Shekhawati, rank among the least visited in the region. A ribbon of hopelessly potholed tarmac leads out here from Mandawa, and another runs due west to Ramgarh, but aside from sporadic buses, the only traffic along them are camel carts and herds of goats. This makes Mahansar a peaceful place to hole up for a day or two, and a much more enticing prospect than touristy Mandawa, a forty-minute Jeep ride south.

Another reason to come is to **stay** at the quirky *Narayan Niwas Castle* (Ⓣ01595/264322; ❸–❺), a destination in itself. Managed by Mahansar's royal family in their crumbling 1768 abode, it consists of twelve rooms of varying standards; #1 is the most romantic, with old rugs, bolsters, ancient carved wooden doors and raised sitting alcoves with views. It's a more informal, slapdash establishment than other heritage hotels in the area, but this lends it a certain charm – and affordability. Be sure to peruse the family heirlooms and sample the royal moonshine. The food is excellent, too.

Once you've explored the fort, there's little more to do other than wander around the village looking for painted buildings. Mahansar's most beautiful murals are locked away out of sight in the **Sona Ki Dukan Haveli**, next to the main crossroads (ask around the shops for the key). The ceiling of the entrance hall to this mansion is exquisitely decorated with painted and richly gilded scenes from the *Ramayana* and *Gita Govinda*. To fully appreciate the colours and mass of detail, you'll need a pocket light. *Narayan Niwas* can arrange tours.

Ramgarh

RAMGARH, 20km north of Fatehpur, was founded in 1791 and developed as something of a status symbol by the Poddar merchant family, who made every effort to outshine nearby Churu, which they left following a dispute with the local *thakur* over wool tax. They succeeded in their aim; there's hardly a bare wall in town, even among the shops in the bazaar. Most of the grand Poddar **chhatris** beside the main Churu–Sikar road preserve vibrant turquoise and vermillion murals depicting scenes from the *Ramayana*, but to see them you'll have to ask for the key at the sweet shop just outside (communal tensions have resulted in some of the paintings being defaced in recent years). The Poddar family *havelis* in the north of town, west of Churu Gate, are decorated with scenes from local folk stories, and a three-fish motif that is unique to Ramgarh. Temples such as Natwar Niketan, Ram Lakshman and Ganga Mandir harbour accomplished depictions of scenes from the Hindu epics and local legends; the **Shani temple** in the northwest of town also holds some elaborate mirror work.

Lakshmangarh

The most imposing feature of **LAKSHMANGARH**, 20km south of Fatehpur, is the nineteenth-century **fort** that dominates the west side of town. It is now empty and dim inside, though you can climb the ramp to the summit to enjoy a spectacular view. Lakshmangarh is easy to explore, thanks to a street grid inspired by that of Jaipur. Just below the fort, near the bus stand, the huge **Char Chowk Haveli** is built around four large courtyards (*chowks*); it remains in private ownership, so access is restricted, but in any case it's best seen from the fort, from where its peculiar design can be appreciated. To see other excellent – and amusing – frescoes in Lakshmangarh search out the heavily painted **Kyal** and **Naria** *havelis* in the southeast of town, the scenes of European women on walls near the clock tower, and **Sanganeeria Haveli**, east of the Radha Murlimanohar temple. In the far east of town, near a *chhatri* and a well, the bright but dilapidated **Pansari Haveli** shelters a semi-permanent settlement of *lohars*, nomadic ironworkers.

East of Jaipur

The fertile area **east of Jaipur**, interspersed with the forested slopes of the Aravalli Hills, holds an inviting mixture of historic towns and wildlife sanctuaries. To the northeast is the fortified town of **Alwar**, jumping-off point for the **Sariska Tiger Reserve and National Park**. Further east are the former princely capitals of **Deeg** and **Bharatpur**, and India's finest bird sanctuary, **Keoladeo National Park**, worth a visit even for novice birders. The wildlife sanctuary at **Ranthambore**, in idyllic scenery southeast of Jaipur, offers the best chance in India of spotting wild tigers.

Alwar

Roughly 140km northeast from Jaipur towards Delhi, **ALWAR** rests peacefully in a valley, overlooked by a **fortress** that stretches along a high craggy ridge to the northwest. Alwar was not always so calm. Traditionally the northern gateway to Rajasthan, its strategic position on the Rajput border resulted in incessant warfare from the tenth to the seventeenth century between the Jats of Bharatpur and the Kuchwahas of Amber. Jai Singh, the flamboyant, eccentric great-grandfather of the present incumbent, became notorious during the British era for his outrageous behaviour. Official reports in the 1930s describe him burying his luxury Hispano-Suiza cars when he tired of them, and dousing his favourite polo pony in petrol and setting fire to it; rumours also circulated suggesting a predilection for young boys.

Arrival and information

The **bus stand** in the west of Alwar sees services to and from Deeg and Bharatpur (every 15min), and Sariska (every 30min or so). Frequent buses also run north to Delhi and south to Jaipur (under 4hr). There's a **bike rental** shop close by, 100m down Hope Circus Road, across from the Star Studio. The **railway station**, receiving trains from Delhi, Jaipur, Jodhpur, Ahmedabad, Deeg and Ajmer, is a few kilometres away on the east side of town, and has retiring rooms. The world's oldest working **steam train**, the 60-seater *Fairy Queen*, rolls to Alwar, using its original 1855 locomotive, on a two-day weekend journey from Delhi that includes a safari at Sariska. For bookings, contact RTDC in Jaipur ⓣ0141/511 0595). Just south of the station exit on the opposite side of Nehru Marg, the **tourist office** (Mon–Sat 10am–5pm; ⓣ0144/234 7348) has dusty piles of aged leaflets but little else. You can **change** currency and travellers' cheques at the State Bank of Bikaner & Jaipur, in the centre of town. For **Internet** access, try Meherwal's Cyber Café, Nagli Circle, halfway between the train station and the cinema.

Accommodation

Your best bet for budget **rooms** is the group of five hotels huddled together on the corner of Manu Marg, ten minutes' rickshaw ride from the railway station or a five-minute walk from the bus station. The *Ankur* (ⓣ0144/233 3025; ❷–❺) is just about the best of the bunch, but there's little to choose between them and all invariably have vacancies. For more comfort, try the *Aravalli*, a couple of doors down from the railway station on Nehru Marg (ⓣ0144/233 2883, ❷–❻), which has seen better days, but boasts an atmospheric bar with a real tap, a pool in summer, and helpful staff that can arrange tours and exchange travellers' cheques. Standard rooms with cable TV start at Rs450, but there are also basic dorms and more expensive a/c options. A more upscale choice is the *Hill Fort Kesroli*, 12km east of town (Ⓣ01468/289352, Ⓦwww.neemranahotels.com; ❼–❾), where a seven-turreted fourteenth-century fort has been impeccably restored and converted into a hotel. Centred on a lush inner courtyard filled with palms and bougainvillea, its rooms have great views over Kesroli village and the surrounding countryside.

The Town

Alwar's **fort**, now a radio station, can only be visited with police permission (easily obtained from the SP office next to the palace; Mon–Fri 10am–5pm); the buildings within are in any case unspectacular, but the forty-minute climb is worthwhile for the views. A twenty-minute taxi ride from town will cost Rs100. Construction of Alwar's Indo-Islamic **Vinay Vilas Palace**, below the fort, began under Bhaktawar Singh, Pratap Singh's successor. Although time has worn away much of its glory, it remains flamboyant, with domed roofs, lavish verandas decorated in gold leaf, and delicate balconies facing a huge tank flanked by symmetrical *ghats* and pavilions. The stately sandstone and marble **Moosi Maharani Chhatri** here was built in memory of Bhaktawar Singh's mistress, who sacrificed her life on his funeral pyre. A **museum** on the top floor of the palace (daily except Fri 10am–4.30pm; Rs3) houses a collection of courtly memorabilia. Much of the palace is now taken up with government offices; in the main courtyard – used as the venue for the local courts – paper-pushing typists, lawyers and advisers huddle round rickety tables under banyan trees.

A must for anyone spending at least one night in Alwar is the little visited **Siliserh Palace**, 15km south along the road to Sariska. Although the whitewashed structure lacks refinement nothing can compare to its Xanadu-like setting, on the edge of a ten-square-kilometre lake ringed by uninhabited, jungle-laden hills. The lake is Alwar's water source – look out for the crumbling, sandstone aqueducts built more than a century ago. Maharaja Vijay Singh had the palace (now the RTDC *Lake Palace Hotel*) built in 1845 to win over beautiful commoner Sheela, who agreed to marriage on the condition she live within sight of her family's modest home, across the lake. An ideal spot to while away an afternoon, it also rents paddle boats out for Rs60 per half hour. The lake is briefly included on *Aravalli*'s tours of Sariska, or you get there by taxi.

Eating

Aravalli's basement **restaurant** serves up spicy, moderately priced dishes, but for crispy *dosas*, tasty *channa batura* and other hot snacks, the *South India* café, opposite the State Bank of Bikaner & Jaipur, is hard to beat. The only competition comes from the clean and pleasant *Siddartha* veg restaurant, just south of the *Imperial Hotel* on Manu Marg. Several food stalls at the bus stand sell drinks and fiery curries. Alwar is famous throughout Rajasthan for its cavity-causing **milk cakes**, which you can buy at the stalls near the clock tower.

Sariska Tiger Reserve and National Park

Alwar is the access point for **Sariska Tiger Reserve and National Park**, a former maharaja's hunting ground managed since 1979 by Project Tiger (see p.1416). Accustomed to being overshadowed by the more famous Ranthambore, Sariska was unwittingly thurst into the headlines in 2005 when it was discovered that its tiger population, estimated at around 28 in 2003, had all but vanished. Conservation authorities initially blamed mismanagement and a lack of resources, but after rumours surfaced that a famed taxidermist, in collusion with corrupt wardens, orchestrated a mass poisioning, Prime Minister

Manmohan Singh ordered a high profile police investigation. Regardless of where blame lies, activists see the decimation of Sariska's tiger population as one of India's biggest conservation scandals.

One silver lining from the whole affair is that the number of visitors to the sanctuary is likely to dwindle, and for birders and wildlife enthusiasts disgusted by the hectic pace and hustling of Ranthambore, Sariska's reputation for serenity will come as a welcome relief. The 881-square-kilometre sanctuary encompasses abundant woodland dotted with evocative ruins, including the old **Kankwari Fort**; a popular Hanuman temple within the reserve grounds is also accessible. **Wildlife** here inclides sambar, *nilgai* and *chital*, wild boar, mongooses, monkeys, peacocks, parrots and other birds.

Practicalities

Sariska lies 35km from Alwar on the main Alwar–Jaipur road; express **buses** between the two will stop briefly to drop off and pick up passengers if requested. The *Aravalli Hotel* in Alwar can organize a round-trip **taxi** to the park for Rs1000, which includes stops at the Alwar museum and the Lake Palace at Siliserh.

Entrance to the park costs Rs200 per person plus Rs125 per vehicle (plus Rs200 for a video camera). **Tours** of Sariska, organized at the **park headquarters** (daily 6am–3.30pm) ⓣ0144/284 1333), located on the road near the RTDC hotel, depart according to demand. The park HQ will rent out Gypsy Jeeps with a guide for around Rs700, plus Rs1800 extra for a ride to Kankwari Fort. Because Sariska gets so few visitors, lone travellers should be prepared for a long wait if looking for a ride-share. Although not advertised, the knowledgeable booking office agent will lead short nature walks – ideal for bird watching – after the booking office closes, charging around Rs150.

Most travellers **stay** in Alwar, where rooms are more fairly priced. All the same, two options exist in Sariska: the RTDC *Hotel Tiger Den* (ⓣ0144/284 1342; ❺–❻), whose only thing going for it is its peaceful garden, right next to the park entrance, and the overpriced *Sariska Palace* (ⓣ0144/284 1322, ⓕ284 1322; ❾). The latter, the former maharaja's hunting lodge, charges Rs5000 per night for would-be luxurious rooms (ask for one in the main block or you'll find yourself in the far less appealing converted stable annexe). The hotel has a gorgeous pool (Rs500 for non-guests) and manicured lawns, but is otherwise hoary and service can be poor.

Deeg

DEEG, 30km northwest of Bharatpur, is a dust-choked little market town which, as the second capital of the local ruling Rajputs, was the scene of bloody encounters with the Moghul overlords in the mid-1700s. The only reason you might want to come here these days is to see the town's much-photographed **palace** en route between the Bharatpur bird sanctuary and the Sariska tiger reserve. Fusing Moghul and Hindu elements, it's an undeniably beautiful building, but doesn't really warrant a special day-trip.

Construction of the royal retreat began in 1730, when the Jat ruler Badan Singh established Deeg as the second capital of Bharatpur state. The delicate design of the palaces or *bhawans* (daily 8am–5pm; Rs100) is typical of the Jats, with arches, pillars and domes reflected in surrounding water tanks, and leafy gardens interspersed with two thousand fountains. Most were built by the king Surajmal in 1756, and even the oldest, **Purana Mahal**, still bears traces of wall paintings. The largest, **Gopal Bhawan**, near the entrance to the complex, was

Surajmal's summer residence. Its spacious, plushy furnished hall is gracefully proportioned, with majestic archways, sculpted pillars and intricate balconies overlooking the tank, or **Gopal Sagar**. In the east of the complex, **Kesav Bhawan** is an open-sided square pavilion, designed to re-create the freshness of the monsoon; in Surajmal's time, fountains played within it, while cooling water showered from the roof to the accompaniment of artificial rolls of thunder. The reservoir for the fountains took a week to fill and only a matter of hours to empty, and nowadays they are only switched on during local festivals.

Deeg fell into decline along with the Jat rulership at the beginning of the nineteenth century, and remains very small, though it is served by **bus** (every 15min; 1hr 30min) and **train** (daily; 2hr) from Alwar. Bharatpur is a one-hour (Rs13) bus ride away. If you get stuck, the better of the two unappealing **accommodation** options is RTDC's featureless *Motel Deeg* (☎05641/221000; ❸), on the main road near the bus stand.

Bharatpur and Keoladeo National Park

The walled town of **BHARATPUR** is just a stone's throw from the border with Uttar Pradesh, 150km east of Jaipur, and a mere 18km from Fatehpur Sikri, Akbar's deserted capital. It's fun to explore by bike or on foot, with traditional markets, mosques, temples and a massive fort, but the real reason to come here is to visit India's most famous bird sanctuary, the **Keoladeo National Park**, just a short way south of the town. Few places in the world, let alone ones so easily accessible, boast such a profusion of wildlife in so confined an area. Though serious birders and repeat visitors will tell you that recent droughts have led to a noticeable decline in the park's population, this is less than obvious to neophytes. Cycling around the sanctuary's quiet, shady paths, you're almost certain to glimpse several species of large mammals such as black buck and deer, as well as lizards and pythons, and, of course, some startlingly exotic birds.

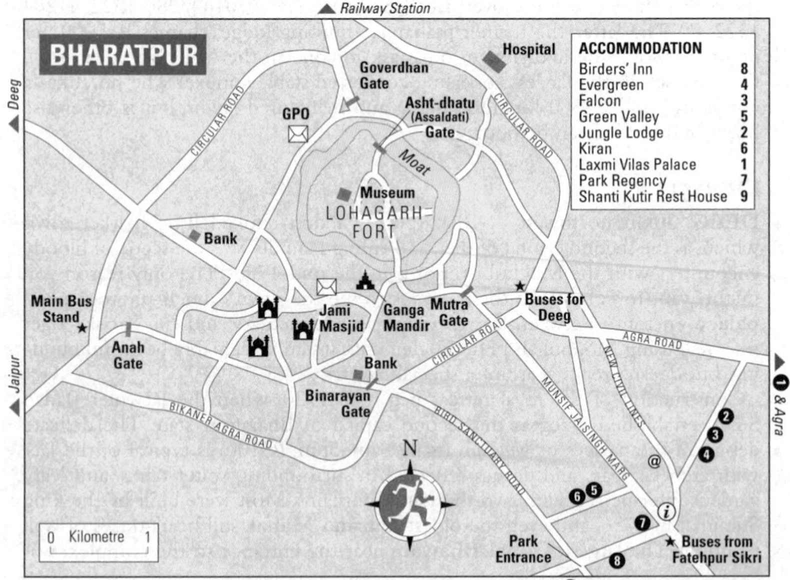

Arrival and information

Bharatpur's **bus stand** is in the west of town near Anah Gate, just off NH-11. If you're arriving from Fatehpur Sikri, get off well before, when the bus stops at the crossroads on the opposite side of town near the park gates, as this is nearer the hotels and guesthouses. From the main bus stand, services run to all major centres in Rajasthan (including Jaipur) and to Delhi, Agra (1hr, first bus at 4.45am) and Fatehpur Sikri. Two kilometres northwest, the **railway station** lies on the main Delhi–Mumbai line; at the time of research the line to Agra and Jaipur was closed but scheduled to be re-opened as part of broad gauge. A full-day taxi to Agra and back should run about Rs900. Trains also run to and from Sawai Madhopur (4 daily; 2hr 30min), though delays are common; call ⓣ131 for current timings. The park entrance, and the guesthouses, are 7km south of the railway station. Cycle rickshaws are the main form of transport within the city, but for visiting the park and getting around it makes sense to rent a **bicycle**, either from your hotel (around Rs30/day) or the shop on NH-11 outside the *Spoonbill Restaurant*.

The town's **tourist office** (Mon–Sat 10am–5pm; ⓣ05644/222542, ⓦwww.bharatpur.nic.in), where you can pick up good state maps (Rs10) and information on Bharatpur and the sanctuary, stands at the crossroads near the park entrance where Fatehpur Sikri buses pull in. Nearby, on New Civil Lines, both The Perch and Royal Forex have **Internet** and **money exchange** facilities.

Accommodation

Few people stay in Bharatpur proper – to be well placed for an early start wildlife-viewing it's a better idea to spend the night in one of several, generally welcoming **hotels** and **guesthouses** along or near NH-11, which skirts the northern edge of the park. Many of Bharatpur's hotel managers are skilled ornithologists. Bharatpur's reputation as a tourist-friendly oasis has made it an attractive base for day trippers to Agra and the Taj Mahal. It's therefore advisable, especially in peak season (mid-Nov to late Feb), to **book rooms** in advance.

Budget

Evergreen Near the tourist office ⓣ05644/225917. Congenial family-run guesthouse near the highway junction; slightly dingy rooms (most with bathroom), relaxing roof terrace and excellent home cooking. Bikes (Rs30) and binoculars (Rs20) available. ❷–❸

Falcon 100m northeast of tourist office ⓣ05644/ 225306. Set back from the main road junction on a quiet suburban street, this modern guesthouse has a range of spotless, comfortable rooms on two floors (those on the upper storey are best, with more space and thick mattresses) and a small lawn-side restaurant with an open fire in the back garden. Along with *Jungle Lodge*, the best choice in this bracket. Internet access. ❷–❹

Jungle Lodge Gori Shankar ⓣ05644/225622, ⓦwww.junglelodge.dk. Run by a knowledgeable naturalist, this friendly place has simple rooms overlooking Bharatpur's loveliest flower-filled garden. Restaurant and evening fires give it a communal feel. Cycles and binoculars for rent. Internet available. ❷

Kiran 364 Rajendra Nagar ⓣ05644/223845. Tucked away 300m northeast of the park gates on a peaceful suburban backstreet. Five large, clean and comfortable rooms, plus superb home cooking served on an intimate rooftop terrace. Unbeatable personal service includes complimentary town pickup and drop off. If full, walk a few steps to *Green Valley* guesthouse, which has similar facilities and the added gimmick of fresh milk from water buffalos parked out front. Both ❶–❸

Mid-range and expensive

Shanti Kutir Rest House 1km inside the park, ⓣ05644/222777. Available only when not occupied by government officials. Its unrivalled location and five spacious rooms make this far better value (full board doubles Rs600) than the drab government-run *Forest Lodge* next door, which charges Rs3200 for dirty rooms. No reservations, but call to check availability. Guests pay park entrance fee once only. ❹

Birders' Inn NH-11 ⓣ05644/227346, ⓦwww.birdersinn.com. Best value in town, filled with serious bird watchers, who gather nightly to compare checklists over the fire and watch slideshows by the enthusiastic owner. Large, tastefully decorated rooms set well back from the traffic and buffet meals served in an inviting, thatch-roofed restaurant. "Jungle plan" for two (Rs3650) includes park entry, boat ride, rickshaw service, knowledgeable guide and meals. Internet access. 6

Park Regency NH-11 ⓣ05644/224232, ⓔhotelparkregency@yahoo.co.uk. The newest and cleanest of the mid-range hotels along the busy thoroughfare. Prices are a bit ambitious but can be haggled down to Rs500 for a spotless room with TV and huge bath. Excellent food prepared by retired 5-star chef. 4–6

Laxmi Vilas Palace Kakaji ki Kothi ⓣ05644/223523, ⓦwww.laxmivilas.com. Former prince's palace, set amid fifty acres of grounds and mustard fields on the eastern edge of town. Although somewhat garishly converted, it's still a romantic place to stay, with a secluded inner courtyard and colourful details like tiger trophies in the buffet restaurant. The paradise-like pool is a great addition. 8

The Town

Bharatpur was founded by the Jat king Surajmal, who built the virtually impregnable **Lohagarh Fort** at its heart in 1732; known as the eastern gateway to Rajasthan, it soon developed into a busy market centre. Although the original moat, 45m wide and up to 15m deep, still encircles the town, time and modern construction have worn down the thick eleven-kilometre walls that protected it – the British spent four months in 1805 trying in vain to penetrate them, before suffering their heaviest defeat in Rajasthan. As you enter the fort from the north, through Assaldati Gate, you'll see a jumble of old and new buildings, among them the three palaces built by the Jats between 1730 and 1850. Of these, the **Maharaja's Palace** with its stone lattice windows, painted walls and a curious collection of *hammams* (sunken baths) on the ground floor, is the most aesthetically appealing. The **Kamra Palace** in the west of the fort now houses the government **museum** (daily except Fri 10am–4.30pm; Rs3, plus Rs10 for camera), with a well-stocked gallery of Jain sculptures, lots of weaponry and graphic manuscripts in Arabic and Sanskrit.

South of the fort, in the main market area, lie the **Jami Masjid**, fronted by a magnificent arched portal, and **Ganga Mandir**, a large, elaborate temple of pure sandstone.

Keoladeo National Park

Keoladeo National Park (daily 6am–6pm; Rs200 per visit, plus Rs200 for video) was for sixty years a royal hunting reserve, a glorious past marked inside the park by a plaque recounting the gunning exploits of its "illustrious" visitors. (On one particularly gruesome day, in 1938, viceroy Lord Lilinthgow bagged 4273 birds.) This had the unintended consequence of allowing the avian population, protected from encroaching farmers, to thrive. The area became a sanctuary in 1956 and was recognized as a national park in 1981. The park was declared a UNESCO World Heritage Site in 1985.

Today, Keoladeo's 29 square kilometres of swamp and lakes constitute one of the most important breeding and migratory areas in the world. **Bird species** include the majestic saras crane and a staggering two thousand painted storks, whose nesting cries create a constant background din to wanderings around the park. Other residents include snake-like darters, spoonbills, pink flamingos, white ibis, grey pelicans and around thirty species of birds of prey, among them vultures, marsh harriers, peregrine falcons and ospreys. From October to March the 200-plus residents are joined by a further 130 species from as far afield as the Russian steppes and Central Asia. Despite the abundance of bird life, overall numbers have been shrinking in recent years as a result of an enduring drought and the angry opposition of farmers to a Supreme Court-ordered irrigation of the park's fragile wetlands. Large **mammals**, however, have barely been affected by the changing environment, and you stand a good chance of glimpsing wild boar, mongoose, *chital*, *nilgai* and sambar along the paths, and spotting elusive jungle cats, hyenas, jackals and otters. Rock pythons sun themselves at Python Point, just past Keoladeo temple, and in the bush land off the main road close to the entrance barrier. Since the summer of 2000, villagers and park staff have reported sightings of a large female **tiger** in the more remote grassland areas of the park: you're unlikely to spot her, but in her presence around the Colar Dehar zone it's best to stick to the path.

Park practicalities

The park entrance lies 7km south of Bharatpur railway station. Free **maps** are available at the entrance, and at the time of writing a new **information centre** was due to open near the first checkpoint inside. A single metalled road passes through the park; numerous small paths lined with *babul* trees cut across lakes and marshes and provide excellent cover for birdwatching. If you need help identifying the birds, or finding vantage points, you can hire a **guide** at the gate (Rs70/hr for up to 5 people), who will probably have binoculars. The best way to get around is by **bike** (Rs25/hr), available at the main entrance if you haven't hired one in Bharatpur itself, or by cycle rickshaw (Rs50/hr) – drivers are very clued up, trained by the park authorities. Tongas (Rs100/hr) carry up to six people. Noisy vehicles (Rs50/car, Rs10/motorbike) are allowed up to the second checkpoint, but hardly practical when watching birds. During the winter, when water levels are normal, gondola-style **boats** (Rs100) provide a superb opportunity to get really close to the birds.

Planning **when to visit** Keoladeo can make all the difference. It is at its most picturesque at dawn and dusk, and fullest between October and March. In summer you miss the migratory flocks, but should catch some busy nesting activity.

Sawai Madhopur and Ranthambore National Park

No Indian nature reserve can guarantee a tiger sighting, but at **Ranthambore National Park**, 14km west of the rail junction and market town of **Sawai Madhopur**, the odds are probably better than anywhere else. This has less to do with the size of the population, which is perilously small due to poaching, than because the tigers themselves are famously unperturbed by humans, hunting in broad daylight and rarely shying from cameras or Jeep-loads of tourists. Combine the big cats' bravado with the park's proximity to the Delhi–Agra–Jaipur "Golden Triangle", and you'll understand why Ranthambore attracts the numbers of visitors it does.

Three kilometres beyond the turning for the park, near the village of Kutalpura, it's worth popping into the excellent **Dastkar Crafts Centre**, which trains local low-caste woman to make patchwork quilting and appliqué. Most of the pieces they produce are sent off to be sold in Delhi, but a small shop on site showcases their exceptional work – prices are very fair. The scheme is a laudable attempt to combat poverty in villages bordering the park, lessening the hardships that, in the past, have pushed villagers into illegal poaching. While you're in the area, have a wander around the houses on the opposite side of the road, whose walls are decorated with some wonderful traditional murals.

Sawai Madhopur

SAWAI MADHOPUR is served by **trains** on the main Mumbai–Delhi line, and is thus easily accessible from Bharatpur, Agra, Jaipur and Delhi, as well as destinations further south, such as Kota. The train tracks divide the main residential side of town to the north from the industrial zone, known as **Sawai Madhopur City**, to the south (where you arrive when travelling from Shivpuri). The **station** is midway between the two, close to the **bus stand** and bustling Bazriya market area, near the cheapest lodges. The very helpful **tourist office** (Mon–Sat 10am–5pm; ⓣ07462/220808) in the station hands out free fold-up **maps** of town and is a good place to check transport timings. The **Tourist Reception Centre** – where you can book **park tours** (see p.204) directly instead of through your hotel – is located at the RTDC *Hotel Vinayaka*, about 7km along Ranthambore Road. There are **exchange** facilities at many hotels and in the State Bank of Bikaner & Jaipur in the old city. **Internet** is available only at upscale hotels or, unreliably, at Tiger Track gift shop near the *Ankur* hotel.

Accommodation and eating

Hotels in Sawai Madhopur are famously opportunistic (bargaining is a must) and budget accommodations are almost non-existent except for the few dingy options in town. Most visitors will fork out the extra bucks for a room in one of the hotels dotting the road leading to the park; the more upscale options lie closer to the entrance. Though the **food** isn't special in the cheaper lodges, there aren't many alternatives. Unspectacular *dhabas* are located along the main bazaar, between the train and bus stations.

Budget

Ganesh 14 Indira Colony, Civil Lines ⓣ07462/220340 or 222642. Similar quality to *Vishal* with slightly larger, quieter rooms in a suburban hotel on the southwest side of town. Language barrier a problem. ❶

Vishal Main road, market area, about 500m north-east of the railway station ⓣ07462/220504. Only hardened backpackers will dare battle the noise and general dinginess of this, the best of the low-priced options close to the railway station. Rooms are small but reasonably clean; those upstairs are the best. ❶

Mid-range

Ankur Resort Ranthambore Rd, 1.5km from town ⓣ07462/220792, ⓕ223303. Despite average service, spotty showers and unkempt rooms, this modern, 40-room complex keeps packing foreigners in. Maybe it's the hefty commissions they pay to rickshaws – if you're savvy you can get a lift from the railway station for free. The spacious garden is good for a sundowner and the restaurant serves filling, if overpriced, meals. You may be able to bargain down to Rs300 for a double. ❷–❻

Hammir Wildlife Resort Ranthambore Rd, 7km from town ⓣ07462/220562, ⓦwww.hammirwildliferesort.com. Similar to *Ankur*, but more popular with Indian tourists; the rooms are far better value than the outside "cottages". ❸–❻

RTDC Castle Jhoomar Baori On a hillside 7km out of town ⓣ07462/220495. Former royal hunting lodge on a great hilltop site inside the park, with views from a roof terrace over woodland and escarpment. The plain rooms are good value, but the food is a lot less inspiring than the location. Book ahead; discounts April–June. ❺–❼

Tiger Safari Ranthambore Rd, 2.5 km from town ⓣ07462/221137, ⓦwww.tigersafariresort.com. The cleanest of the mid-range hotels in this area, with helpful service and modern furnishings, including TV in every room. Bargain for discounts. ❸–❺

Expensive

Sawai Madhopur Lodge Ranthambore Rd, 2km from town ⓣ07462/220541, ⓕ220718, ⓦwww.tajhotels.com. Stylish 1930s hunting lodge, formerly belonging to Maharaja Sawai Man Singh II but now run as a luxury heritage hotel by the Taj Group. Although tastefully decorated with authentic period decor the entire experience is a little hollow compared to its up-and-coming rival the *Vanyavilas*. Prices start at $200 for luxury tents (full board). ❾

Vanyavilas Ranthambore Rd, about 7km from town ⓣ07462/223999, ⓦwww.oberoihotels.com. Richly decorated, modern interiors that re-create the aristocratic, hunting lodge feel amid picture-perfect grounds. A decked-out, wooden-floored tent will set you back $570. Romantic, terrace dinner around open fire costs Rs750 for non-guests. Receives reservations up to a year in advance. ❾

Moving on from Sawai Modhopur

Sawai Madhopur straddles the main railway line, but many of the services from here are painfully slow passenger ones, so check timings at the tourist office before you book. For **Jaipur**, take the Mumbai–Jaipur Express #2955 at 10.20am (2hr 25min). There are also direct services to **Bharatpur**, of which the quickest is the Golden Temple Mail #2903 leaving at 12.40pm (2hr 40min), and daily departures to **Jodhpur** (2.40pm & 12.25am; 9hr 30min). Of the six trains to Kota, the fastest departs at 1.10pm.

Buses, slower and less comfortable, run to Jaipur every ninety minutes (5hr), Kota (4 daily; 4hr), and Ajmer (2 daily; 8hr) from a stand on the market area's main street, just before the bridge. For Shivpuri (Madhya Pradesh), however, you'll have to trek out to the city bus stand in Sawai Madhopur City.

Ranthambore National Park

In comparison to the tranquillity of the tiger sanctuaries in Madhya Pradesh, the crowds at **RANTHAMBORE NATIONAL PARK** can be off-putting, to say the least – the park is one of India's most popular, with more than 80,000 visitors a year. And for good reason; even without the wildlife, the landscape alone would make it worth a visit. One of the last sizeable swathes of verdant bush in Rajasthan, Ranthambore is fed by several rivers that have been dammed to form **lakes**, dotted with delicate pavilions and decaying, creeper-covered Rajput palaces. At sunset or in the mists of early morning, these can be ethereal, while the ruined tenth-century Chauhan **fort**, towering above the forest canopy from atop a dramatic crag, is straight out of Kipling's *Jungle Book*.

The fort was conquered by Ala-ud-din Khalji's army in 1031, and Akbar in 1569, but for most of its existence Ranthambore has been controlled by the Rajputs, and was set aside by the rulers of Jaipur for royal hunting jaunts. Soon after Independence the area was declared a sanctuary, becoming a fully fledged national park under **Project Tiger** (see p.1416) in 1972. Over time, Ranthambore became world-renowned for its "friendly tigers", unperturbed by humans. Its reputation as Project Tiger's flagship operation, however, took a severe dent a decade later when it transpired that some of Ranthambore's own wardens were involved in **poaching**, and that, as a result, the tiger population here had plummeted to single figures. (To this day, park staff deny the allegations.) Since then, more rigorous policing is said to have brought the problem under control, and numbers have recovered to 41.

In addition to tigers, Ranthambore is still home to very healthy populations of *chital*, *nilgai*, jackals, panthers, jungle cats and a wide array of birds, among which you may see crested serpent eagles, paradise flycatchers and more common peacocks and painted storks. One of the best places for birdwatching is the fort, which is also the site of a temple to Ganesh; people from all over the country write to the elephant-headed god to invite him to their weddings.

Ranthambore is open from October to June, but the **best time to visit** is during the dry season (Oct–March), when the lack of water entices the larger animals out to the lakeside. During and immediately after the monsoons, they are more likely to remain in the forest. More information can be gleaned from Project Tiger's excellent booklet, *The Ultimate Ranthambore Guide* (Rs175), on sale in local souvenir shops.

Park practicalities

Traditionally, Project Tiger managed reservations according to a strict quota system of 35 vehicles per day. But in a precedent-setting first for India's National

Parks, access to the park is now controlled by the Rajasthani tourism officials, who are more bent on accommodating deep-pocketed tourists than tigers. As a result it's now impossible to reserve in advance a five-passenger Jeep (referred to as a Gypsy) – by far the best way to spot furtive wildlife. Instead, rich and poor, Indian and foreign, nature lover and boisterous teenager alike, are thrust into cramped, twenty-seater open trucks called **Canters** (Rs350, includes park entry fee). Although licensed, the Canters are run by private contractors and the quality of the vehicle and the driving varies considerably. In general all are on the trail of tigers and don't stop for lesser creatures. You can **book** a Canter at any of the hotels listed below – one day's notice is enough – though going to RTDC *Vinayak* yourself will save you the Rs25–50 surcharge. **Safari times** vary slightly depending on sunrise, but generally they leave in the early morning and mid-afternoon, and last around three hours. **Dress** in layers: mornings can be surprisingly cool.

If you do want to try your luck at **hiring a Gypsy**, your only alternative at present – check upon arrival to see if the procedure has changed – is to line up early (around 5am, or noon for the afternoon safari) at the Tourist Reception Centre (no phone) at the RTDC *Vinayak* hotel to see if any are departing that day. Be prepared for a chaotic scene, with many hotel "boys" competing ruthlessly to commandeer for their guests whatever Gypsies might become available that day. Your chances drop considerably closer to Diwali and New Year as well as on Sundays, when the *Palace on Wheels* pulls into town. You're looking at paying Rs1050 for a Jeep that seats up to five, plus Rs325 per person for entry, and vehicle fees on top of that.

To **visit the fort**, book an early morning safari and ask to be dropped at the main park entrance on the way out, from where you can climb an old paved path to the ruins. After spending the middle of the day exploring, it's possible to meet up with your Canter or Gypsy back at the entrance gates for the evening tour (although note that you'll have to pay for your afternoon admission ticket in advance to do this). If you bring your own vehicle you won't be charged a park entrance fee if you're only heading to the fort.

Ajmer

As you head west from Jaipur, or north from Chittaur and Bundi, the flat, arid expanse of the Dhundar plains are dramatically interrupted by the Aravallis, running in a bare brown ridge towards Mount Abu and the Gujarat border. Known locally as the Nag Pahar ("Snake Mountain"), this steeply shelving spur forms an appropriately epic backdrop for **AJMER**, famous throughout India as the former home of the Sufi **Khwaja Muin-ud-din Chishti**, founder of the Chishtiya order. To this day, the Chishti's tomb, or **Dargah**, remains one of the holiest Muslim shrines in the entire world – during his 2001 visit to India even Pakistan's President, General Pervez Musharraf, scheduled a visit. The streams of pilgrims and dervishes (it is believed that seven visits here are the equivalent of one to Mecca), especially picks up during Muharram and Id, and for the Chishti's anniversary day, or **Urs Mela** in October/November.

For Hindus and foreign travellers, Ajmer is important primarily as a jumping-off place for **Pushkar**, a twenty-minute bus ride away across the hills. Generally lacking a tourist infrastructure, you're unlikely to want to pause here for longer than it takes to catch a bus out of town. But as a day-trip from Pushkar it's a worthwhile excursion and window into the lives of India's Muslim minority.

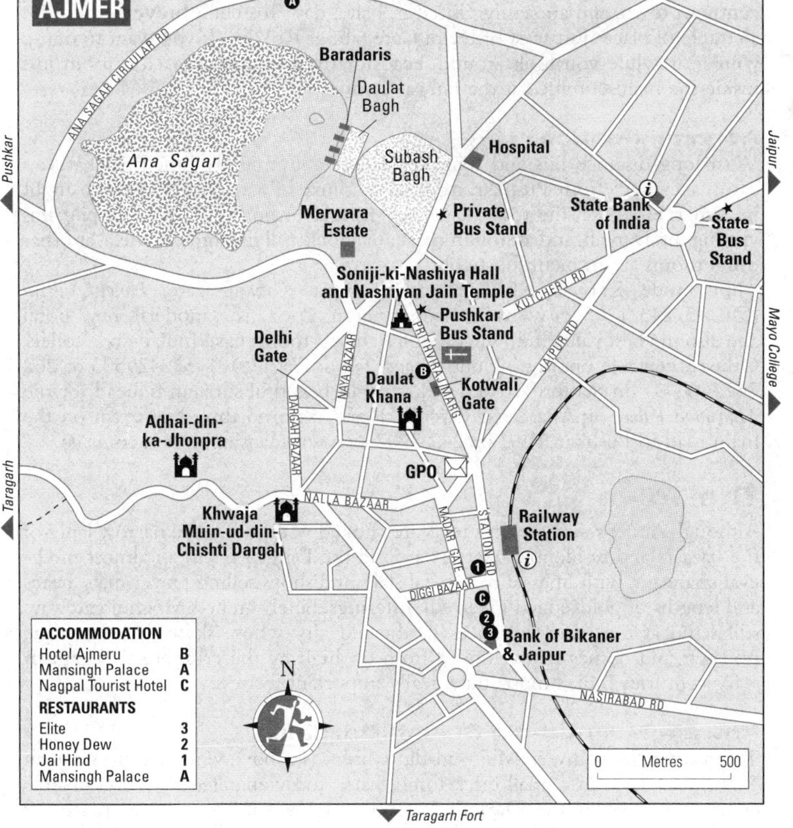

Arrival, information and accommodation

Ajmer's **railway station** is in the centre of town, with regular services from Delhi, Jaipur, Ahmedabad, Udaipur, Chittaurgarh and Kota. The state **bus stand**, with an exhaustive array of routes, is inconveniently situated on the northeast edge of town, 2km from the railway station. Tempos and auto-rickshaws connect the two; auto-rickshaws cost around Rs25. Buses to **Pushkar** leave every fifteen minutes or so from a bus stand near the Jain Temple – a Rs30 rickshaw ride from the state bus stand; buy a ticket on the bus. Seats on private buses – many of which have connecting services from Pushkar – can be reserved at Ajmer bus station, Pushkar hotels, or at any of the travel agents along Kutchery Road between the state bus stand and railway station.

The RTDC **tourist office** at the railway station (Mon–Sat 10am–5pm; no phone) is more convenient than the main office (Mon–Sat 9am–2pm & 2.30–6pm; ⓣ0145/262 7426) adjoining the RTDC *Hotel Khadim*. The State Bank of India, between the main tourist office and state bus stand, will **change** Thomas Cook, Visa and American Express travellers' cheques. A more central place to change money is the Bank of Bikaner & Jaipur, on Station Road.

Ajmer's chief attractions lie within walking distance of each other, in the centre of town, and are easily visited in half a day. To rent a **bicycle**, there are a couple of places just west of Delhi Gate (about Rs3/hr). If you want to dump your gear while you look around, head for the **left luggage** cloakroom just inside the main entrance at the railway station.

Accommodation

With long-distance bus and train departures conveniently timed so that you can make them from Pushkar, it's hard to think of a reason to spend a night in Ajmer. However, the town has many **hotels** to house the flow of pilgrims visiting the Dargah, and although most are chock-full during Urs Mela, at other times rooms are in plentiful supply.

Just inside Kotwali Khailana market, near Kotwali gate, *Hotel Ajmeru* (Ⓣ0145/243 1103, Ⓦwww.hotelajmeru.com; ❸–❺) is a modern, new hotel and also the best value in town, though standard rooms have Indian-style toilets. Other acceptable options include *Nagpal Tourist Hotel* (Ⓣ0145/2429503 or 262 7427; ❸–❺) on Station Road. For luxury in beautiful surrounds, head for the *Mansingh Palace* on Ana Sagar Circular Road, 3km northwest of town on the main road to Pushkar (Ⓣ0145/242 5702; Ⓦwww.mansinghhotels.com; ❾).

The Town

Although Ajmer's dusty main streets are choked with traffic, the narrow lanes of the bazaars and residential quarters around the Dargah retain an almost medieval character, with lines of rose-petal stalls and shops selling prayer mats, beads and lengths of gold-edged green silk offerings. Finely arched Moghul gateways still stand at the main entrances to the old city, whose skyscape of mosque minarets and domes is overlooked from on high by the crumbling **Taragarh** – for centuries India's most strategically important fortress.

Khwaja Muin-ud-din Chishti Dargah

The revered Sufi, Khwaja Muin-ud-din Chishti (see box), who died in Ajmer in 1236, was buried in a small brick tomb that is today engulfed by a large marble complex known as the **Dargah**, reached via the bazaars winding north off Station Road and west from Delhi Gate. Founded in the thirteenth century and completed under the sixteenth-century Moghul emperor Humayun, the Dargah contains structures erected by many Muslim rulers. But it was under the imperial patronage of the three great Moghuls – Shah Jahan, Jahangir and, most crucially, Akbar – that this became the most important Muslim shrine in India. It remains massively popular, with thousands of pilgrims passing through the gates every day.

Entering the Dargah via the mighty blue-and-white **Buland Darwaza** gateway, donated by the Nizam of Hyderabad, you're likely to be stopped by stern-looking young men claiming they are "official guides". In fact, they are *khadims*, hereditary priests operating in much the same way as Hindu *pujaris*, leading pilgrims through rituals in the sacred precinct in exchange for donations. Despite their assurances to the contrary, their services are not compulsory, although you may wish to employ one to point out the features of religious and historical significance inside.

The first of these are the two immense cauldrons, known as **degs**, resting on raised platforms to the right of the gateway. Continuing the saint's tradition of giving succour to the needy, pilgrims throw money into them to be shared among the poor. The two pots, able to hold 6500kg of rice between them, are also the focus of an extraordinary ritual during Urs Mela, in which a huge

Khwaja Muin-ud-din Chishti

At the height of the communal troubles in 1992–3, Ajmer – considered a prime flash-point – escaped unscathed. No one had any doubt that peace prevailed because of the enduring influence of the Sufi saint enshrined at the heart of the city, **Khwaja Muin-ud-din Chishti**.

Born in 1156, in Afghanistan, Muslim India's most revered saint, also known as Khwaja Sahib or Garib Nawaz, began his religious career at the age of 13, when he distributed his inheritance among the poor and adopted the simple, pious life of an itinerant Shia *fakir* (the equivalent of the Hindu *sadhu*). On his travels, he soaked up the teachings of the great Central Asian Sufis, whose emphasis on mysticism, ecstatic states and pure devotion as a path to God were revolutionizing Islam during this period. By the time he came to India with the invading Afghan armies, Khwaja Sahib had already established a following, but his reputation as a divinely inspired prophet only really snowballed after he and his disciples settled in Ajmer at the beginning of the thirteenth century.

Withdrawing into a life of meditation and fasting, he preached a message of renunciation, affirming that personal experience of God was attainable to anyone who relinquished their ties to the world. More radically, he also insisted on the fundamental **unity of all religions**: mosques and temples, he asserted, were merely material manifestations of a single divinity, with which all men and women could commune. In this way, Khwaja Sahib became one of the first religious figures to bridge the gap between India's two great faiths. With its wandering holy men, emphasis of mysticism and miracles, and devotional worship involving music, dance and states of trance, Sufism would have been intelligible to many Hindus. Moreover, it readily absorbed and integrated aspects of Hindu worship into its own beliefs and rituals. After Khwaja Sahib died at the age of 97, his followers lauded the *Bhagavad Gita* as a sacred text, and even encouraged Hindu devotees to pray using names of God familiar to them, equating Ram with "Rahman", the Merciful Aspect of Allah. The spirit of acceptance and unity central to the founder of the Chishti order's teachings explains why his shrine in Ajmer continues to be loved by adherents of all faiths.

gruel is cooked, paid for by wealthy patrons. When it is ready, a mad scramble begins as the devout, dressed in heat-protective plastic bags, dive head first into the bubbling *degs* to fill their buckets with the porridge, regarded by the faithful as *tabarruk* (equivalent of the Hindu *prasad*, or Christian "consecrated"). The best place from which to view this spectacle is the platform above the main entrance archway, which you can usually gain a place on by slipping a tip to one of the *khadims*.

To the right of the *degs* is the marble mosque donated by Akbar, and to the left stands an assembly hall for the homeless. Other subsidiary shrines inside the enclosure include those of Khwaja Sahib and Shah Jahan's daughters, a handful of generals and governors, and Afghani companions of the saint. Near the mosque of Shah Jahan, **Khwaja Sahib's final resting place** is impossible to miss, surrounded by silver railings and surmounted by a large gilt dome. Devotees file past with brilliant *chadars*, gilt-brocaded silk covers for the saint's grave, carried on beds of rose petals in flat, round head-baskets. Visitors are asked by the *khadims* for donations, offered blessings, lightly brushed with peacock feathers and given the chance to touch the cloth covering the tomb. In March 2002, the *khadims* reported the image of Khwaja himself mystically appearing to them on the inner dome, with the aim of "spread(ing) the message of goodwill and peace after the recent rioting in Gujarat state". Police were deployed at the site to prevent a stampede when huge numbers of pilgrims arrived soon after, although many dismissed the claims as a gimmick. Things are quieter now, but the continual murmur of prayer and the heady scent of rose attar, and uplifting **qawwali music** being performed before the shrine (from an hour or so before sunset until 9pm), exactly as it has been for seven hundred years, still create an unforgettable atmosphere.

Islamic monuments

Often overlooked by visitors, the **Adhai-din-ka-Jhonpra**, or "two-and-a-half-day mosque", 400m north of the Dargah, is the oldest surviving monument in the city and unquestionably one of the finest examples of medieval architecture in Rajasthan. Originally built in 1153 as a Hindu college, it was destroyed forty years later by the Afghan Ghors, who later renovated it. Tradition holds that the mosque's name derived from the speed with which it was constructed, but in fact the reconstruction took fifteen years, using bricks and finely sculpted panels plundered from Hindu and Jain temples. Motifs of pre-Muslim origin are still clearly discernible on the pillars and ceilings. However, the mosque's most beautiful feature is the bands of Koranic **calligraphy** decorating its arched facade.

A more recent Islamic relic is the squat sandstone **Daulat Khana**, a massive rectangular palace at the heart of the city that was used by Akbar and his son Jahangir during their visits to the Dargah. A panel outside it records that here, in 1616, **Sir Thomas Roe** became the first British ambassador to be granted an official audience, after four years of trailing between the emperor's encampments. In 1818 the palace came under British control, and after being fortified during the 1857 Mutiny, earned the nickname **Magazine** for its housing of the Rajputana Arsenal. Today, the old palace houses a small **museum** (daily except Fri 10am–4.30pm; Rs3, free on Mon, plus Rs10 for camera, Rs20 video), displaying mainly Hindu Rajasthani statues dating from the eighth century.

Laid out in the twelfth century, the artificial lake northwest of Ajmer, known as **Ana Sagar**, is today little more than a pond – a legacy of overuse in the 1980s, and drought over the past five years. There is usually enough water to keep boat-wallahs busy, but the real reason to come out here is to stroll along the long embankment, or *bund*, on its southwest shore, which moderated the flow of the river through the city. It was on top of this parapet, exposed to the cooling breezes off the water, that Shah Jahan chose to erect a line of exquisite white marble pavilions as summer shelters. Modelled on the Diwan-I-Am in Delhi's Red Fort, four of the five **Baradaris** remain beautifully preserved, standing in the shade of trees and ornamental gardens (the former **Daulat Bagh**) planted by Jahangir. To find them, turn left at the bottom of the hill as you arrive in Ajmer from Pushkar, and left again 400m later, through the park. The best time to come is an hour or so before sunset, when the colours on the lake and polished stone of the Baradaris are sublime.

The Taragarh

Just visible on the ridge high above the city, the **Taragarh** was for two thousand years the most important *point d'appui* for invading armies in northwest India. Any ruler who successfully breached its walls, rising from a ring of forbidding escarpments, effectively controlled the region's trade. Few, however, were able to do so by mounting a siege; the fortress even repulsed the indomitable Mahmud Ghazni in 1024. It's now badly ruined, but is still visited in large numbers by pilgrims, who come to pay their respects at what must be one of the few shrines in the world devoted to a tax inspector, the **Dargah of Miran Sayeed Hussein Khangsawar** – Mahmud of Ghori's chief revenue collector was one of many slain in the Rajput attack of 1202 when, following one of the fort's rare defeats, the entire Muslim population of the fort was put to the sword. Today, a vestigial Muslim community still survives in a tumbledown village inside the walls, clustered around the whitewashed Dargah.

Getting to the Taragarh entails an exceptionally rewarding ninety-minute **hike** along the ancient paved pathway from Ajmer; there are superb **views** across the plains and neighbouring hills. To pick up the trailhead, follow the lane behind the Khwaja Sahib Dargah, past the Adhai-din-ka-Jhonpra and on towards the saddle in the ridge visible to the south. Bring **food**; the only places to eat inside the battlements are a handful of fly-infested non-veg cafés. To return to Ajmer, you can either follow the path back downhill, or catch a **Jeep** (Rs20) from the lot at the northeast side of the village, near the Dargah. Heading in the other direction, the Jeeps leave from a *chowk* on the western edge of Ajmer; ask for the "Ta-ra-garh jeeps", pronouncing all the syllables clearly, or you'll end up at the main Khwaja Sahib Dargah.

Other attractions

When Ajmer came under British control, it was one of the few cities in Rajputana outside the hegemony of the princely states. Monuments still standing as echoes of its colonial past include the **Jubilee clock tower** opposite the railway station, the **King Edward Memorial Hall** a little to the west and the famous **Mayo College**, originally built as a school for princes, and now a leading educational institution known in society circles as the "Eton of the East".

Perhaps the most bizarre sight in Ajmer is the mirrored **Soniji-ki-Nashiya** hall adjoining the **Nashiyan Jain temple**, or "red temple" (daily 9am–4pm; Rs3, photography forbidden). Constructed in the 1820s by an Ajmeri diamond magnate, the hall commemorates the life of Rishabha (or Adinath), the first Jain *tirthankara*, believed to have lived countless aeons in the past. From the uppermost of the three storeys that surround it, you can look down on musicians flying above the sacred Mount Sumeru on swans, peacocks and elephants suspended on rods and strings. The display, sealed behind glass, is made from 1000kg of gold. Admission to the main temple alongside is restricted to Jains.

Moving on from Ajmer

Ajmer is on the main Delhi–Ahmedabad **train line**, but there are considerable variations between the journey times of services passing through here. The computerized **reservations** hall is on the first floor of the railway station's south wing; get there early in the morning to avoid long queues, or shell out a little extra for a travel agent.

For **Delhi**, by far the fastest and most comfortable option is the air-conditioned Ajmer–New Delhi Shatabdi Express (#2016; daily except Wed), which departs at 3.50pm, arrives at 10.20pm. There's also a slower overnight service, the Ahmedabad–Delhi Mail (#9105), leaving at 8.28pm and arriving at 4.36am, but the easiest train to get a reservation for at short notice is Porbander–Delhi Express (#9263; Wed & Sun only), which leaves at 11.20am and reaches Delhi Sarai Rohilla at 8.26pm. Of the seven or eight daily trains to **Jaipur**, the Shatabdi Express is once again the quickest, taking just under two hours; alternatively, catch the cheaper Ashram Express (#2915) at 1.55pm, which takes just thirty minutes longer. Heading in the opposite direction, the best day train for **Udaipur** is the Delhi Sarai Rohilla–Ahmedabad Express (#9943) starting from Ajmer at 7.50am and arriving at 6pm. A fast night train, #9671, departs at 8.20pm and arrives at 7.50am.

Ajmer has frequent express and deluxe **bus connections** to Jaipur (16 daily; 3hr), Delhi (8 daily; 9hr), Pushkar (every 15min; 30min), Bundi (10 daily; 5hr), Bharatpur (6 daily; 7hr) and Jodhpur (5 daily; 5hr).

Eating

In addition to the snack and fruit juice places around Dargah Bazaar and Delhi Gate, Ajmer has a handful of larger **restaurants**.

Elite Station Rd, next to *Nagpal Tourist Hotel*. White tablecloth dining room and garden restaurant, each serving moderately priced South Indian, Chinese and pure veg options.

Honey Dew Station Rd, next to the King Edward Memorial. Garden restaurant with a good mixed menu (veg, non-veg and pizza) at middling prices, as well as shakes and ice cream. Similar to *Elite*.

Jai Hind Station Rd, tucked in an alley next to the green-and-white mosque and directly opposite the station's main exit. Very good veg food, including delicious *alu-paratha-curd* breakfast thalis and *dosas*.

Mansingh Palace Hotel Ana Sagar Circular Rd. Pricey international cuisine served in a/c comfort by the lakeside. Live music.

Pushkar

According to the *Padma* (Lotus) *Purana*, **PUSHKAR**, 15km northwest of Ajmer, came into existence when Lord Brahma, the Creator, dropped his lotus flower (*pushpa*) to earth from his hand (*kar*) to kill a demon. At the three spots where the petals landed, water magically appeared in the midst of the desert to

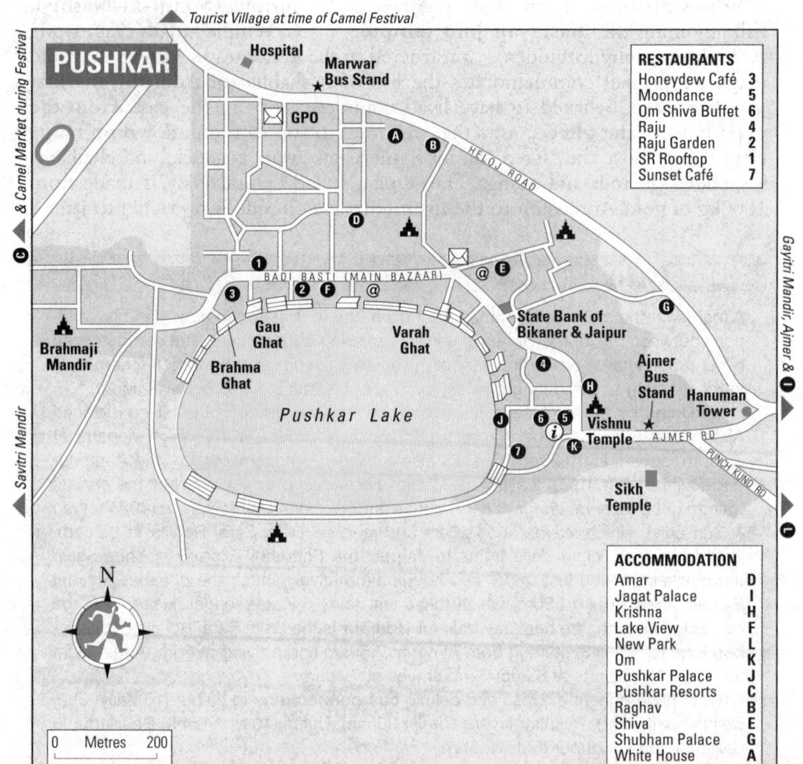

form three small blue lakes, and it was on the banks of the largest of these that Brahma subsequently convened a gathering of some 900,000 celestial beings – the entire Hindu pantheon. Surrounded by whitewashed temples and bathing *ghats*, the lake is today revered as one of India's most sacred sites: *Pushkaraj Maharaj*, literally "Pushkar King of Kings". During the auspicious full-moon phase of October/November (the anniversary of the gods' mass meeting, or *yagya*), its waters are believed to cleanse the soul of all impurities, drawing pilgrims from all over the country. Alongside this annual religious festival, Rajasthani villagers also buy and sell livestock at what has become the largest **camel market** (*unt mela*) in the world, when more than 150,000 dealers, tourists and traders fill the dunes to the west of the lake.

The legendary colour of the camel *mela*, combined with the beautiful desert scenery and heady religious atmosphere of the temples and *ghats* have inevitably made Pushkar a prime tourist destination. In fact, it's hard to think of anywhere else in India, apart from perhaps Manali, Kovalam and the resorts of Goa, that has been so thoroughly transformed by **mass tourism** over the past decade. The main bazaar, which just fifteen years ago comprised a string of stalls selling traditional puja paraphernalia, is now a kilometre-long line of shops crammed with hippy trinkets, full-moon-party fluoro outfits, jewellery and fusion CDs, while the streetside cafés churn out banana pancakes and mind-blowing *bhang lassis*. Arriving from less budget-traveller-oriented parts of the country, this may come as a welcome break, but if you've travelled here hoping for a taste of the east, the ravers and relentless didgeridoo music can be a stark disappointment.

That said, Pushkar has not been entirely spoilt. Wander away from the bazaar to the more tranquil fringes of the lake, or into the surrounding hills, and the magical atmosphere that attracted travellers here in the first place survives undiminished. At sunset, with the sound of temple bells and drums drifting across the water, this can still feel like one of the most exotic places on earth.

Arrival and information

Most long-distance journeys to and from Pushkar have to be made via Ajmer. Pushkar does not have a railway station. The **Ajmer bus stand** in the east of town is served by buses from Ajmer and Jaipur, while travellers from destinations further a field, such as Delhi, Jodhpur and Bikaner, arrive in the north of town at **Marwar bus stand**, to be besieged by accommodation touts. The lack of rickshaws means that you'll have to walk to your hotel (though there are **bicycles** for rent right by the Ajmer bus stand, and hand carts for transporting luggage).

Pushkar's **tourist office** (daily 10am–5pm; 24hr during camel fair; ⓣ0145/277 2040) is conveniently located inside the main gate of the RTDC *Sarovar Hotel*, a short walk from the Ajmer bus stand. The **GPO** for parcels and poste restante is in the north of town, and there's a smaller branch on the market square. The State Bank of Bikaner & Jaipur (Mon–Fri 11am–2pm) in the square near Varah Ghat offers **currency exchange**, but you can cash travellers' cheques and change cash more quickly at any of the private money-changers in the main bazaar. For **Internet** access, try the *Sunset Café* or *Shree Nath Cyber Zone* near *Hotel Shiva*, both of which stay open late.

Accommodation

Pushkar has numerous *dharamshalas* for pilgrims. For the ever-growing influx of Western tourists, there's a wide choice of **hotels** and **guesthouses**, many of them in family homes. Views over the lake are rare, but many have rooftops looking across Pushkar to the distant hills. Note that **prices** double or triple during the camel fair when there is considerable pressure amongst hotel managers, especially at budget hotels, to pre-pay for your entire stay or risk having your reservation lost – you should resist doing this as you won't get your money back if the fair disappoints and you decide to beat a hasty retreat back to Ajmer.

Budget

Amar In the centre of town ⓣ0145/230 5022 or 277 2809. A delightful, family-friendly little place, with 20 ground-floor rooms – more are being added – facing a jasmine-filled garden, and a secluded terrace restaurant. Maintains reasonable prices during camel fair. ❶–❷

Krishna Main bazaar near Vishnu temple, ⓣ0145/277 2461. Blue-painted compound set back from the main bazaar with the cleanest shared bath option in Pushkar (Rs150) and a large garden. Family guesthouse feel, though the owner's English is quite basic. Massages on offer. Excellent, affordable choice during camel fair, and you can reserve without paying a deposit. ❶–❸

Lake View Main Bazaar ⓣ0145/277 2106, ⓦwww.lakeviewpushkar.com. Small, run-down rooms, but a stunning view from the rooftop restaurant – it gets crowded at sunset. Management a bit pushy. ❶–❷

Om Ajmer Rd ⓣ0145/277 2672, ⓔom_deepak2004@yahoo.com. Basic rooms, with or without bathroom, close to the bazaar and Vishnu temple. Those overlooking the relaxing back garden are quieter, more spacious and within view of Sikh temple. Hammocks for lounging and friendly management, but the pool is about as inviting as the lake. Pricey during camel fair. ❶–❹

Raghav Near the Marwar bus stand ⓣ0145/277 2207, ⓦwww.lakeviewpushkar.com. Modern building set in a huge garden on the north side of town. The rooms are plain but large and clean, with narrow balconies and comfy mattresses, and there's a cool rooftop terrace shaded by a sprawling tree canopy. Quiet, and good value. ❶–❸

Shiva On the road leading off the market square by the post office ⓣ0145/277 2120. The most popular and dependable cheapie in this cramped quarter, with small rooms, a leafy courtyard, rooftop restaurant and resident tortoises. If full, try the similarly priced *Sai Baba* and *Shanti Palace* nearby. ❶

Shubham Palace near Sub Tahseal off Heloj Rd above the bazaar ⓣ0145/277 3695. Another scruffy budget choice with basic rooms and laid-back garden, a bit quieter than others. Excellent home-cooked food. ❶–❷

White House Near the Marwar bus stand ⓣ0145/277 2147, ⓦwww.pushkarwhitehouse.com. Neat, clean and well run, with attached bathrooms, good rooftop restaurant, Internet and ISD phone facilities, and a warm family atmosphere. Mango tea from rooftop herb garden upon arrival. Prices increase ten-fold during camel fair – a much bigger hike than lesser known budget hotels charge for similar rooms. ❷–❹

Mid-range and expensive

Jagat Palace Ajmer Rd ⓣ0145/277 2953, ⓦwww.hotelpushkarpalace.com. Huge luxury hotel on the outskirts, incorporating masonry plundered from an old fort, but superbly reconstructed with elaborate wall paintings, gilt inlay and period fittings. Sweeping views, huge pool, steam bath, Jacuzzi and walled garden. ❽

New Park Punch Kund Rd ⓣ0145/277 2464, ⓦwww.newparkpushkar.com. An idyllic sanctuary from the bustle of the main bazaar, but still close enough to walk there in ten minutes. Thirty-two spacious rooms and suites overlooking rose gardens tended by women in traditional dress. Pool in summer and affordable restaurant, Internet and ISD. ❸–❺

Pushkar Palace ⓣ0145/277 3001, ⓦwww.hotelpushkarpalace.com. The most stylish option in town, a former maharaja's palace on the east side of the lake. Tastefully furnished rooftop suites with verandas. The panoramic views are the same from the nearby *Sunset Café* but the terrace restaurant is good enough – and more peaceful – to warrant the splurge on a meal for non-guests. Avoid room 202, which is more affordable but cramped and noisy. ❽–❾

Pushkar Resorts Motisar Rd, Ganehara village ⓣ0145/277 2017 or 277 2944, ⓦwww.pushkarresorts.com. Modern resort, 5km out of town in the desert, comprising 40 swish a/c chalets set around a kidney-shaped pool in 15 acres of grounds. Optional extras include nocturnal camel rides (with candles and telescopes) and golf. Their top-notch restaurant is the only one hereabouts with a non-veg menu, and an alcohol licence. Booking recommended. ❽

The Town

There are more than five hundred **temples** in and around Pushkar; many had to be rebuilt after pillaging during the merciless rule of Moghul emperor Aurangzeb (1656–1708), while others are recent additions. Some, like the splendid **Vishnu Mandir**, on your right as you enter the village from Ajmer, are out of bounds to non-Hindus. Pushkar's most important temple, **Brahmaji Mandir**, houses a four-headed image of Brahma in its main sanctuary. Raised on a stepped platform in the centre of a courtyard, the always crowded chamber is surrounded on three sides by smaller subsidiary shrines topped with flat roofs providing views across the desert west to **Savitri Mandir** on the summit of a nearby hill. The one-hour climb to the top of that hill is rewarded by matchless vistas over the town, surrounded on all sides by desert, and is best done in the evening, to reach the summit for sunset. **Gayitri Mandir**, on the other hand, set on a hill east of the town, faces east and should ideally be visited at sunrise.

The lake and ghats

Pushkar **lake** is ringed by five hundred beautiful whitewashed temples, connected to the water by 52 *ghats* – one for each of Rajasthan's maharajas, who built separate guesthouses and employed their own private *pujaris* (priests) to perform rituals during their stays here. Each is named after an event or person, and three in particular bear special significance. Primary among them is **Gau Ghat,** sometimes called Main Ghat, where visiting ministers and politicians come to worship, and from which ashes of Mahatma Gandhi, Jawaharlal Nehru and Shri Lal Bahadur Shastri were sprinkled into the lake. **Brahma Ghat** marks the spot where Brahma himself is said to have worshipped, while at the large **Varaha Ghat**, just off the market square, Vishnu is believed to have appeared

Brahma, Savitri and Gayitri

Revered as the Creator from later Vedic times onwards, **Brahma** was seen as one of the most important Hindu gods, together with Shiva (Destroyer) and Vishnu (Preserver). The three served to represent the powerful, non-conceptual Brahman – an unchanging force associated with cosmic unity. As the concept of *samsara* came to the forefront of Hindu philosophy – and life was envisaged as endless transmigration with no beginning – Brahma's role as Creator was questioned. His importance dwindled in the nineteenth century, though he is still regarded as a major divinity.

Stories of Brahma's exploits are still told in Pushkar, site of a temple dedicated exclusively to the deity. One such tale reveals the significance of the temples named after Brahma's wives, **Savitri** and **Gayitri**. At the great *yagya* gathering of deities, Lord Brahma was to marry Savitri, but she was busy dressing for the ceremony and failed to show up on time. Without a wife, the Creator could not perform the *yagya* at the auspicious moment, so he had to find another consort. The only unmarried woman available was a shepherdess of the untouchable Gujar caste named Gayitri, whom the gods hastily purified by passing her through the mouth of a cow; *gaya* means "cow", and *tri*, "passed through". When Savitri finally arrived, she was furious that Brahma had married someone else and cursed him, saying that henceforth he would be worshipped only at Pushkar. She also pronounced that the Gujar caste would gain liberation after death only if their ashes were scattered on Pushkar lake – a belief which has persisted to this day. After casting her curses, disgruntled Savitri flew off to establish a temple on the highest hill above the town, while Gayitri occupied the lower hill on the opposite, eastern side of the lake.

Kartika Purnima and Pushkar camel fair

Hindus visit Pushkar year-round to take a dip in the redemptory waters of the lake, but there is one particular day when bathing here is believed to relieve devotees of all their sins, and ultimately free them from the bonds of *samsara*: the full moon (*purnima*) of the **Kartika** month (usually Nov). For five days leading up to and including the full moon, Pushkar hosts thousands of celebrating devotees, following prescribed rituals on the lakeside and in the Brahma Mandir. To add to the flurry of colour and activity, a large **camel fair** is held at around the same time in the sand dunes west of the town, with hordes of herders from all over Rajasthan gathering to parade, race and trade over 25,000 animals. The transformation of Pushkar from a peaceful, if touristy, desert town is overwhelming – the streets are packed with swarms of pilgrims, hawkers and thousands of tourists; hotels and restaurants are chock-a-block, and prices soar.

Once trading is under way, camels and cattle are meticulously groomed and auctioned, while women dressed in mirrored skirts and vivid shawls lay out embroidered cloth, jewellery, pots and ornaments beside the herds. Cattle, poultry, sheep and goats are entered for competitions, and prizes given for the best displays of fruit and vegetables. Away from the main activity, the dusty ground is stirred up by vigorous **camel races**, urged on by gamblers. Aside from its overwhelming size, the most striking feature of the fair from a foreign visitor's point of view is that it is attended by equal numbers of men and women. With the harvest safely in the bag and the surplus livestock sold, the villagers, for this brief week or so, have a little money to spend enjoying themselves, which creates a lighthearted atmosphere that's generally absent from most other Rajasthani livestock fairs.

The popularity of Pushkar's fair has – inevitably – had an effect on the event. The number of foreign tourists crossed the 10,000 mark for the first time in 2004, zoom lens-saddled package tourists now bumping elbows with the event's traditional backpacker crowd. But while the commercialism can be off-putting, the festive environment and coming together of cultures does produce some spontaneous mirth: the second prize in the 2004 moustache contest was won by a bloke from Manchester. To avoid the worst of the tomfoolery **come at least a week before the final weekend**, when most of the buying and selling is done. By the full moon, the bulk of the herders have packed up and gone home (unless the government has managed to induce them to stick around with the lure of free fodder, as it has done for the past few fairs), leaving Pushkar with the stale feeling of a party the morning after.

Practicalities

Hotels hike their rates at least a fortnight before the full moon and still fill up quickly. Though it's best to book a room as far ahead as possible, if you arrive early in the day – and with a bit of hunting – securing **accommodation** shouldn't be a problem. RTDC usually sends its package guests out to **tented compounds** close to the fairgrounds, where there's a choice between dormitory beds (❸), deluxe tents (❾), or huts (❾) complete with private bathrooms. Book well ahead by contacting the RTDC office in Jaipur (Ⓣ & Ⓕ0141/511 0595). The tent village has an information counter, exchange facilities, safes, shops, medical centre, and a **Shilpgram**, artisans' village, where you can buy crafts directly from the artists. Check RTDC's website for more details: Ⓦwww.rajasthantourism.gov.in. Additional luxury camping, complete with carpets, furniture, running water and Western toilets, is offered by the local maharaja's *Royal Desert Camp*, out on the Motisar Road (❾); for reservations, contact the *Hotel Pushkar Palace* (see "Accommodation").

The **dates** of the next few camel fairs are: Oct 29–Nov 5 2006 and Nov 17–24 2007. Bear in mind our earlier advice and get here for the first two or three days to see the *mela* in full swing.

in the form of Varaha (a boar), one of his nine incarnations. At all the *ghats*, it is a respected and unspoken request that visitors should remove their shoes at a reverential distance from the lake, and refrain from smoking and taking photos.

Indian and Western tourists alike are urged by local brahmin priests to worship at the lake; that is, to make **Pushkar Puja**. This involves the repetition of prayers while scattering rose petals into the lake, and then being asked for a donation, which usually goes to temple funds, or to the priest who depends on such benefaction. On completion of the puja, a red thread taken from a temple is tied around your wrist. Labelled the "Pushkar passport" by locals, this simple token means that you'll no longer attract pushy Pushkar priests and can wander unhindered onto the *ghats*. Indians usually give a sum of Rs21 or Rs31; Rs51 should suffice. Be vigilant about anyone demanding large sums. Most likely they are fake priests, and although otherwise harmless, should be reported to the tourist police at the RTDC office.

In years past, the lake used to be prowled by dozens of man-eating **crocodiles** that would often pick off unwary pilgrims. Elderly brahmins can still recall the days when they regularly had to beat the rapacious reptiles on the head with long sticks before entering the water, but their strict vegetarian principles prevented them from doing anything about the problem. Eventually, the British intervened by fishing the crocodiles out with nets and transporting them to a nearby reservoir. Nart Singh Ghat, a few steps down from Varaha Ghat, still has on display one rather dusty stuffed crocodile.

Eating

As Pushkar is sacred to Lord Brahma, all food within city limits is strictly veg: meat, eggs and alcohol are banned, and taking drugs is considered highly offensive. However, its **restaurants** cater for both Indian and foreign palates, offering national dishes as well as pizza, spaghetti and apple pie. Be wary of the many buffets offering tempting all-you-can-eat menus; with the highly recommended exception of *Om Shiva*, most are likely to consist of terribly unhealthy reheated food. One other word of **warning**: think twice before downing a **bhang lassi** at one of the stalls in the bazaar. Although *bhang* (ground cannabis leaves; see p.88) is legal here, it can cause intense, and protracted, psychological distress if you're not used to its mind-altering properties.

Honeydew Café Main Bazaar. Hole-in-the-wall place with tinny Western tunes playing from a battered radio. Very good pasta, plus a selection of breakfast options. It's a hippie-era hangout that hasn't altered its facade since those heady days.

Moondance Opposite the Vishnu temple. Nepali-run, with scant Indian food on the menu. Eat at table or on floor mattresses which are ideal for reclining after a filling pizza or pasta – the best in town. Attempts at Thai and "Maxican" too. Great bakery.

Om Shiva On lane heading down to *Pushkar Palace* from main bazaar. This dirt-floored buffet restaurant feels like a beach and the loyal, hippie clientele hangs out all day as if it were one. All-you-can-eat buffets are superb considering the Rs50 price tag, unchanged in over a decade. The owner studied cooking in Libya. Yoga classes in the morning. Avoid copycats with similar names like *Omshiva*.

Raju Ajmer Rd. Not to be confused with *Raju Garden Restaurant*, this small, basic place serves very cheap curries and good thalis.

Raju Garden Restaurant Main Bazaar near Ram Ghat. Delicious Indian, Chinese and Western food of a standard rarely matched by other restaurants, though service could be improved. Particularly renowned for its veg shepherd's pie and baked potatoes with peanut butter, garlic cheese or Marmite.

SR Rooftop Restaurant Main Bazaar. Grimy but atmospheric *dhaba*-style place, whose walls are hung with philosophical musings. Serves delicious north Indian thalis, and can get crowded.

Sunset Café East side of the lake near the *Pushkar Palace*. As its name implies, an ideal spot from which to enjoy Pushkar's legendary lakeside sunsets; big crowds gather here for this nightly ritual, usually accompanied by techno music. Non-alcoholic beer on offer. Service a little rushed.

Moving on from Pushkar

In addition to the state **buses**, a number of **private firms** run daily buses to Delhi, Agra, Jaipur, Mount Abu, Bikaner, Udaipur and Jodhpur. Many more destinations and frequencies are served from Ajmer. That said, we've had numerous letters from readers who, after buying tickets at agencies in Pushkar advertising "hassle-free travel", found their seats double-booked when they tried boarding in Ajmer. To avoid mishaps, make any necessary bookings for bus journeys from Ajmer in Ajmer itself. Services to Delhi in particular are often reserved days ahead. When leaving Pushkar, use the Ajmer bus stand for Ajmer train station, and the Marwar bus stand for Ajmer bus station.

A list of recommended trains from Ajmer appears in the "Moving on" box on p.209. Agencies and hotels can arrange tickets for onward **train** journeys from Ajmer for a small charge, and book, cancel or confirm air tickets (check carefully before you leave the office and make sure there's no "W/L", for "Waitlist" in front of your seat number).

Jodhpur and around

On the eastern fringe of the Thar Desert, **JODHPUR**, dubbed "the Blue City" after the colour-wash of its old town houses, sprawls across the arid terrain, overlooked by the mighty Meherangarh Fort, whose ramparts rise from a sheer-sided sandstone outcrop. It was once the centre of Marwar, the largest princely state in Rajputana, and today has a population of 1.2 million. Despite its size and importance, Jodhpur is barely a pit-stop for most travellers en route

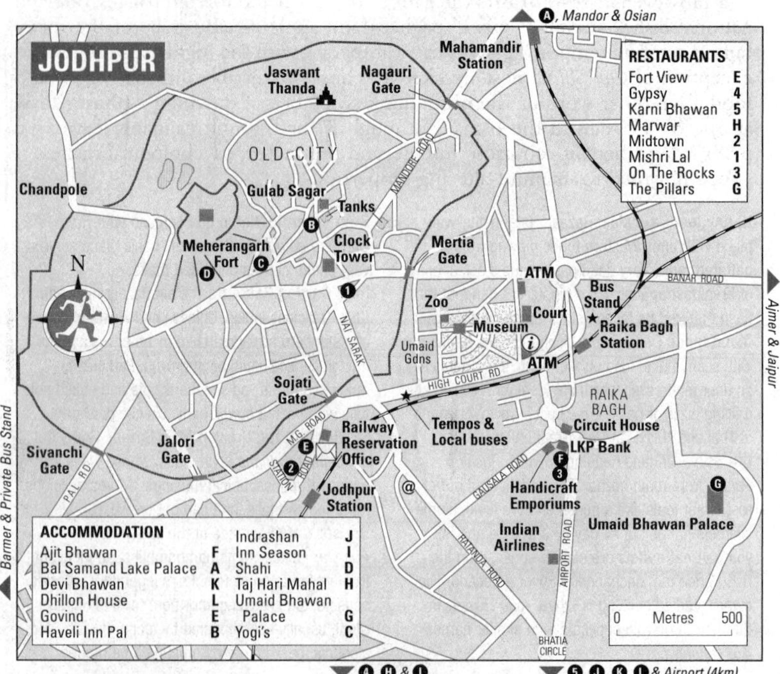

between Jaisalmer, 300km to the west, and Udaipur or Jaipur to the east, and only that by virtue of its must-see **fort** – the best maintained in Rajasthan, with a museum to rival any. It's a shame to rush the place, though. Getting lost in the blue maze of the old city you'll stumble across Muslim tie-dyers, puppet-makers and traditional spice markets, while Jodhpur's famed cubic roofscape, best viewed at sunset, is a photographer's dream. In addition, the encroaching desert beyond the blue city is dotted with small settlements where you can escape the congestion for a taste of rural Rajasthan.

Some history

In 1459, Rao Jodha of the Rathore clan moved the capital of Marwar state several kilometres from the exposed site of **Mandor** to a massive steep-sided escarpment, where he named his new capital after himself. The high barricaded **fort** proved virtually impregnable, and the city soon amassed great wealth from trade. The Moghuls, keen to take over Jodhpur but realizing there was little prospect of that, chose to negotiate peacefully instead and a marriage alliance between Udai Singh's sister and Akbar in 1561 ensured the most friendly of terms.

However, the tide turned in the mid-seventeenth century, after Jaswant Singh joined Shah Jahan's forces in an unsuccessful bid for power against his fellow Moghul Aurangzeb. Aurangzeb set out to purge his enemies, and Jodhpur was sacked in 1678 and its inhabitants forcibly converted to Islam. Jaswant Singh's son, Ajit Singh, eventually recaptured his rightful kingdom after thirty years in hiding. The eighteenth century saw many bloody battles between Jodhpur, Jaipur and Udaipur, despite their policy of unification against the Moghuls. At its close, Jodhpur passed first into the hands of the Marathas and then the British; the signing of a friendship treaty with the East India Company in 1818 guaranteed its safety, albeit at great cost to Rathore honour.

The last maharaja before Independence, **Umaid Singh**, is commemorated by his immense Umaid Bhawan Palace; he set 3000 citizens to work for sixteen years on its construction, in part to alleviate problems during a severe famine by creating employment. Jodhpur is now a democratic union within the independent India, but its social fabric remains tinged with feudalism and a medieval atmosphere prevails.

Arrival and information

Jodhpur's main **railway station** is in the south of town, a couple of kilometres southwest of the state **bus stand**. Private buses drop you at an inconvenient (and somewhat dodgy) location 4km west of town; take a rickshaw the rest of the way (Rs50). From the **airport**, 4km south, an auto-rickshaw into town costs Rs50; taxis charge a fixed Rs120. In town, these are supplemented by tempos that follow fixed routes along the main roads. **Bicycles** can be rented from shops near the railway station (Rs15/day).

The excellent **tourist office** (daily 8am–8pm; ⓣ0291/254 5083), in the RTDC *Goomar Tourist Bungalow* on High Court Road, has timings for private bus services, keeps lists of families offering homestays, and can organize city tours at far cheaper prices than most agencies – Rs150 by auto-rickshaw or Rs300 for a taxi. They also run their own **village safaris** (see p.224).

The State Bank of India has an ATM next to the tourist office and also behind the Collectorate, off High Court Road, but you can **change money** more quickly at LKP, 1 Mahavir Place, opposite the Circuit House, or at any of the agencies located near the clock tower in the old city. The **GPO**, for poste restante and parcel packing, is opposite the *Govind Hotel* on Station Road. **Internet access** is widely available, even amid the medieval labyrinth of the old city. One convenient and competitive choice is Telco operator Reliance's downstairs cyber café on Ratanda Road, which has seven fast PCs at Rs30/hour. Jodhpur's best English-language **bookstore** is Khazana Books, in the *Taj Hari Mahal* on Residency Road.

Accommodation

Jodhpur has plenty of pleasant places to stay in all brackets, but getting to most of them involves breaking through a particularly vociferous posse of touts, *lapkars* (see p.222) and rickshaw-wallahs. The best way around this problem is to phone ahead to **book a room**, in which case some guesthouse owners will pick you up from your arrival point – not a bad idea in any case as the **old city** is almost impossible to navigate on your first visit. If you are determined to go it alone, keep an eye out for the numerous signs scrawled on the town walls, pointing to the various small hotels and *haveli* guesthouses. In addition to the places listed below, there is a growing number of budget guesthouses just beyond the clock tower, and among the maze of lanes. If looking for a particular hotel, watch out for imitators: whenever one place gets popular, five more appear on the same block with nearly identical names.

With the exception of the *Govind*, where most backpackers in transit end up, the hotels outside the **railway station** on Station Road are grim and best avoided. Although farther from the action, the mid-range hotels in the **suburbs** offer greater tranquillity and are among some of the best in Rajasthan.

Budget

Dhillon House 3 Central School scheme ⓣ0291/243 4257. Clean homestay, run by a friendly university hydrologist, a 10-minute rickshaw ride south of town. Will provide TV on request. Excellent food and negotiable rates. ❸–❺

Govind Station Rd ⓣ0291/262 2758, ⓦwww.govindhotel.com. Clean budget hotel opposite the GPO (look for the tree in front), near the station. Management is helpful and there's a rooftop restaurant, but the location suffers from traffic noise and pollution. Good if you need to catch an early train, but don't expect the ambience of the old city lodges. ❷–❺

Yogi's Rajpurohitji ki Haveli, Manak Chowk, Nayabas ⓣ0291/264 3436, ⓔyogiguesthouse@hotmail.com. The mosaic-laid rooftop terrace affords excellent views of the fort and sunrise and is among Rajasthan's best chill-out spaces. Rooms are small but clean and with comfy beds. Great value. ❷–❺

Mid-range

Devi Bhawan Near Ratanada Circle, 2km south of town ⓣ0291/251 2215, ⓦwww.devibhawan.com. Individual bungalows exquisitely decorated with rustic-elegant wood and leather furniture, all designed by the young owner. Take drinks in a sophisticated, Art Deco lounge before a candlelight dinner on the garden terrace that overlooks a veritable jungle. At Rs800–1000, perhaps the best value in all of Rajasthan. Internet access. Book ahead. ❺

Haveli Inn Pal Near Gulab Sagar Lake, 200m from the clock tower ⓣ0291/261 2519, ⓦwww.palhaveli.com. The classiest mid-priced option in the old city, boasting large, well-appointed rooms (ask for new rooms with lake views) in a yellow, eighteenth-century *haveli* still owned by the same family. Ask for a tour to check out family curios. Currently adding more luxurious rooms as a separate, pricier hotel called *Pal Haveli*. Nice rooftop terrace. ❸–❻

Indrashan 593 High Court Colony, 3km south of town ⓣ0291/244 0665, ⓔrajdisk@datainfosys.net. Five thoroughly comfortable rooms in an authentic homestay. The husband/wife team offer sumptuous food and cooking classes that draw amateur chefs from around the world. Dinner guests are welcome if you call ahead. The owner also arranges homestays in other parts of the state. ❺

Inn Season PWD Rd ⓣ0291/261 6400, ⓦwww.innseasonjodhpur.com. Similar boutique hotel quality to *Devi Bhawan* but with higher prices and a modern, sun-soaked pool. Rooms, decked out in Art Deco, pay homage to the owner's love affair with vintage cars. A loyal clientele of handicraft exporters chill out at night to vinyl on a vintage gramophone. One drawback: it's noisy during wedding season due to the wedding ground next door. Book ahead. ❺–❼

Shahi Gandhi St, City Police district, opposite the Nursing Temple ⓣ0291/262 3802. Quirky 350-year-old *haveli* buried deep in the warren of lanes beneath the fort's southwest wall. Three cavernous, atmospheric rooms offer little in the way of plush comfort but a whole lot of tranquillity. Queen Palace room can sleep up to five comfortably. Call for directions. ❸–❺

Expensive

Ajit Bhawan Airport Rd ⓣ0291/251 1410, ⓦwww.ajitbhawan.com. Don't be put off by Flintstones-like theme park design. This self-contained resort – built to resemble a *dhani* village – gets rave reviews for its try-hard attitude and relaxing environment. Canvas tents start at Rs3000, but it's worth spending more for a luxury tent or rustic stone-built cottage. All guests have access to waterfall-fed pool, thatch-roofed outdoor restaurant and spa. Far better than *Ranbanks Palace* next door. ❾

Bal Samand Lake Palace Mandor Rd, 8km north of town ⓣ0291/257 2321, ⓦwww.welcomheritage.com. Among the most attractive heritage hotels of its kind in the state, converted from the maharaja's lakeside summer palace. The standard rooms are nothing special, but if your budget can stretch to Rs7000 go for one of the nine suites in the main building: they're huge, airy and exquisitely furnished. You get the run of a lush, monkey-infested garden, pool and croquet lawn. ❽–❾

Taj Hari Mahal 5 Residency Rd, less than 1km south of town ⓣ0291/243 9700, ⓦwww.tajhotels.com. All the luxury you'd expect from a 5-star Taj hotel, but given the plethora of authentic, boutiquish alternatives, there's something vacuous about the whole "ethnic" Rajasthani look the owners are trying to achieve. Huge outdoor pool. Rooms from $180. ❾

Umaid Bhawan Palace southeast of town ⓣ0291/251 0101, ⓦwww.jodhpurheritage.com. The Maharaja of Jodhpur's princely pile (see p.221) ranks among the world's grandest hotels, with eminent movie star guests. But being the king for a day can be a solitary experience – some find the oversized suites, stately salons and dark, marbled passageways a bit foreboding. Still, it's worth the Rs330 cover charge to visit the veranda café (see p.222), from where you can peak into the adjacent salons decorated with hunting trophies and royal memorabilia. It's soon to be taken over by the Taj group, but currently rooms start at $150, or $500 for the former royal apartment. ❾

The City

Life in Jodhpur focuses very much around the fort, still almost completely encircled by the strong walls erected by Rao Maldeo in the 1500s. The blue wash applied to most of the houses huddled like a Cubist painting beneath it is often erroneously said to denote high-caste brahmin residences. In fact, it originally resulted from the addition of indigo to white limewash, thought to protect the buildings from termites and other insect pests. Over time the distinctive colour caught on – there's now even a blue-wash mosque on the road from the Jalori Gate, west of the fort.

The bazaars of the old city are gathered around the tall **clock tower**, with different areas assigned to different trades. Locally made goods include tie-dye, puppets and lacquered jewellery. **Jalori Gate** and **Sojati Gate** lead out of the old city to the south, near the railway station, GPO and hospital. Beyond the walls, more modern buildings spread east and west of the old boundaries, the domes of **Umaid Bhawan** dominating the scene to the southeast.

Meherangarh Fort

Described by Kipling as the work of angels and giants, Jodhpur's **Meherangarh Fort** (daily: summer 8.30am–5.30pm; winter 9am–5pm; Rs250 entry includes audio tour if you leave ID as deposit; plus Rs50 for camera, Rs200 video; elevator Rs15; ⓦwww.maharajajodhpur.com), provides what must be the most authentic surviving taste of the ceaseless round of war, honour and extravagance that characterized Rajputana. It wasn't always so stunning, however. For decades it was locked up, caked in bat droppings, until in 1972, the current, Oxford-educated maharaja – who was born a midnight child in the year of India's Independence and took office at the age of four – created a foundation to rescue the derelict edifice. Unlike the fort in Jaisalmer it is uninhabited, its paths trodden only by visitors to the temples and palaces within its high crenellated walls.

On the wall next to **Loha Pole**, the sixth of seven gates designed to hinder the ascent of charging enemy elephants up a steep winding cobbled road, you can see the handprints of Maharaja Man Singh's widows. Following the Rajput code of honour, they voluntarily ended their lives in 1843 on their husband's pyre, in defiance of the law against *sati* passed in 1829 by the British. Beyond the massive **Suraj Pole**, the final gate, lie the palaces that now serve as the superb **Meherangarh Museum**. From the courtyards, you can see the fantastic *jali* (lattice) work that almost entirely covers their sandstone walls and balconies, as well as a portrait of Rao Jodha himself. Solid silver *howdahs* (elephant seats) and palanquins are on display, as well as daggers and photos of the maharajas' coronations. One prize exhibit is a 250-year-old pure silk tent seized during a raid on the Moghul court in Delhi. In the **Jhanki Mahal**, or "Queen's Palace", there's a colourful array of cradles of former rulers, while **Moti Mahal** ("Pearl Palace") holds the nine cushions reserved for the nine heads of the Jodhpurian state (and one central cushion for the maharaja). Outside, in **Shangar Chowk** ("King's Coronation Courtyard"), is the majestic marble coronation seat upon which all the rulers apart from Jodha have been, and still are, crowned. Nearby, the royal **astrologer** provides consultations for a Rs150–300 fee. The most elaborate of the apartments is **Phool Mahal** ("Flower Palace"), a dancing hall for the entertainment of the maharaja and his guests. Pictures of dancers, deities and rulers look out from its walls and wooden ceilings.

Fort practicalities

The **walk** up to the fort from the old city passes through busy bazaars, with some streets so narrow that pedestrians must advance in single file. You can also get there by **taxi** or rickshaw along the much longer road (5km) that enters the old city at Nagauri Gate. The outstanding self-guided audio **tour** takes a couple of hours to complete, and finishes with a stroll out to the Durga temple, perched on the far southern tip of the precipice. The fort's café **restaurant** gets busy during the day and is only really worth a refresher. But be sure to leave time to explore the first rate **gift shop**, which sells expensive, high-quality crafts, vintage jewellery and even Jodhpur riding britches, which were the height of fashion in Europe when brought over in 1887 by a royal emissary.

Jaswant Thanda

Some 500m north of the fort, and connected to it by road, **Jaswant Thanda** (daily 9am–5pm; Rs20, plus Rs25 for camera, Rs50 video) is a pillared marble memorial to the popular ruler Jaswant Singh II (1878–95), who purged Jodhpur of dacoits, initiated irrigation systems and boosted the economy. The cenotaphs of members of the royal family who have died since Jaswant are close to his memorial; those who preceded him are remembered by *chhatris* at Mandor (see p.222). This southwest-facing spot is also the best place from which to photograph the looming fort.

Umaid Bhawan Palace

Dominating the city's southeast horizon is the **Umaid Bhawan Palace**, a colossal Indo-Saracenic pile commissioned by Maharaja Umaid Singh in 1929 as a famine relief project. One of the largest and most opulent royal abodes in

Asia, it kept three thousand labourers gainfully employed for sixteen years and remains a potent symbol of Rajput authority, lording over the modern city from a scrub-covered hill on the outskirts. When it was completed in 1944, the building boasted 347 rooms, among them a cinema and indoor swimming pool. The maharaja had little time to savour his achievement, however; only three years after the work was finished he died.

The present incumbent, Maharaja Gaj Singh, occupies only one-third of the palace; the rest is given over to a luxury **hotel** (see p.219), restaurant/café (see p.222), and a small **museum** (daily 9am–5pm; Rs50; no photography), housed in the old, mural-lined Durbar Hall. Although packed with royal curios and stately garb, the museum is far less interesting then the palace itself, which is accessed through the adjacent hotel, whose furniture and fittings are nearly all original 1930s Art Deco, enlivened with lashings of typically Rajasthani gilt and sweeping staircases.

Shopping

Jodhpur's first-rate **antique reproductions** – everything from inlaid-ivory opium boxes to brass lamps – justifiably attract dealers from around the world. Among the most reliable vendors, with a warehouse-sized supply to boot, is Lalji Handicrafts, at the start of the long driveway to Umaid Bhawan Palace. Shringanesham, just behind the clock tower, sells embroidered **fabrics**, *dhurries* and other textiles at good prices without a lot of hustle. For custom-made suits, or **Jodhpur riding britches**, none can beat India Tailors, High Court Rd (Ⓣ0291/255 0214) – the tailor used by the maharaja. If you want to send **spices** home, Mohanlal Verhomal's **spice shop**, with a stand near the fort entrance and at 209-B Kirana Merchant Vegetable Market near the clock tower (Ⓣ0291/261 5846, Ⓦwww.mvspices.com) has a reliable pay-on-receipt mail-order service.

Eating and drinking

Jodhpur's **restaurants** cater for all tastes and all budgets, though most of the action is located outside the Blue City, particularly at hotels and buffet-style outdoor venues. Local **specialities** include *mawa* sweets and *doodh fini*, a sweet mixture of wheat strands and milk. Try them at *Janta Sweet* and *Poker Sweet*, both on Nai Sarak near the corner of High Court Road (look for the crowds). These places also sell *mirchi bada*, a chilli in wheatgerm and potato, deep-fried like a *pakora*, available at samosa stalls elsewhere in Rajasthan, but originally from here.

Fort View On the roof of the *Govind* hotel, Station Rd. A cut above the usual tourist places, with good veg curries, thalis, Chinese food and great views of the fort. It's open 24hr, and you can hang out here while waiting for the bus or train (baggage storage facilities available).

Gypsy PWD Rd, next to *Inn Season* hotel. The terrace at this new suburban restaurant gets busy at night with well-heeled Jodhpur residents. The lunchtime thali for two is outstanding, and even the Mexican dishes are passable.

Karni Bhawan Palace Rd, near Ratanda Circle. Dependable, moderately priced buffet located in a hotel garden. Dinner is served in thatch-roofed huts and usually accompanied by folk dancing and puppet shows. Popular with tour groups.

Marwar At the *Taj Hari Mahal* hotel. The best place in town to sample traditional Marwari cuisine, such as *Jodhpuri mas* (a spicy mutton dish) or *gatta di subzi* (its veg equivalent), rounded off with *kulfi*. Count on Rs400–600 per head for two courses.

Midtown Opposite the railway station. Bright, clean and friendly, with an exhaustive menu of pure-veg options: Gujarati, South Indian, Rajasthani specialities, thali (Rs70), pizza and pasta. Open late.

Mishri Lal In the gateway just south of the clock tower. The most famous purveyor of *makhania lassi*, made with cream, saffron and cardamom.

On the Rocks Next to *Ajit Bhawan* hotel, Airport Rd ⓣ0291/230 2701. Though the service is slow, and the buffet no great shakes, it's fun and festive at night, when tourists and locals flock to the night-club. Lunch crowd is mostly tour groups.

The Pillars *Umaid Bhawan Palace.* The veranda café (Rs330 minimum purchase, payable on entry) at the maharaja's palace gives you the excuse to wander around the hotel's opulent interior. It's also an ideal place for a sundowner, with peacocks on the well-manicured lawn and sweeping views of the distant city. Sandwiches are available all day and there's a dinner menu of mostly Western food from 7.30pm. You could also sit yourself down on an elephant foot footstool and have a drink in the *Trophy Bar*.

Around Jodhpur

Should you stay in Jodhpur for longer than a day, and be tempted to see more than the Fort and the bazaars, you can visit the gardens in the old capital of **Mandor** on the northern outskirts of town, where former maharajas are remembered by elaborate temple-like constructions. A remarkable collection of early Jain and Hindu temples lies further afield at **Osian**, an hour's drive away.

Mandor

Jodhpur's minibuses and city buses #7–15 from the railway station or Sojati Gate head for the royal cenotaphs, or *dewals*, in **MANDOR**, set in fertile gardens

Moving on from Jodhpur

Jodhpur stands at the nexus of Rajasthan's main **tourist routes**, with connections northeast to Jaipur, Pushkar and Delhi, south to Udaipur and Ahmedabad, and west to Jaisalmer – buses for most destinations are faster than the train. The five-hour journey to **Jaisalmer** is certainly more rewarding by road, as it allows for stops at Osian (see opposite), Keechen (see p.237) and Pokaran (see p.236), though most travellers end up on the freezing cold sleeper rail service across the Thar instead. If you do end up taking the train, take plenty of warm clothing and a blanket, and stay alert for thieves and con merchants – well-spoken *lapkars* from Jaisalmer routinely bribe the conductors to be allowed on board, where they attempt to recruit customers for their "uncle's" dodgy hotels and desert safaris.

By bus

Private buses depart year round from Jodhpur to Delhi, Agra and major Rajasthani destinations; the bus station is 4km west of town near Barakuttulah Stadium in Sindhi Colony. Most hotels listed above can book **tickets** for a Rs50 commission. Be extra vigilant of your valuables on night buses and around the bus stand, as **theft** has been a problem. **Government buses** tend to be slower and less comfortable but safer; turn up at the bus stand an hour or so before departure to buy a ticket. For timetable information, ask your hotel or guesthouse to ring on your behalf (ⓣ0291/254 4686).

By plane

Indian Airlines operate daily flights from Jodhpur to Delhi ($115), Mumbai ($160), Jaipur ($90) and Udaipur ($75). The IA office (Mon–Sat 10am–5pm; ⓣ0291/251 0757) is at Circuit Road. Jet Airways (Mon–Sat 9.30am–6pm; ⓣ0291/510 3333), at the Osho Apartments on Residency Road in Surya Colony, close to the *Taj Hari Mahal Hotel*, flies daily to Delhi and Mumbai. Closer to town try Friends Tours and Travels (ⓣ0291/262 7886, ⓔftt@hotelcitypalace.com), in the *Hotel City Palace*, 32 Nai Sarak, on the main avenue south of the clock tower.

By train

Train tickets should be booked at least a day in advance at the computerized **reservations office** (Mon–Sat 8am–8pm, Sun 8am–2pm), just north of the station behind

9km north of the city. The capital of the Parihar Rajputs between the sixth and fourteenth centuries, little remains of the fortified city; the Parihars were ousted by Rathore Rao Chauhan in 1381. The dark red sandstone *chhatris*, memorials to Jodhpur's rulers, grew in size and grandeur as the Rathore kingdom prospered, culminating with the last and largest, dedicated to **Maharaja Dhiraj Ajit Singh** (died 1763). By the *chhatris*, opposite a rather dull museum, you'll find the **Hall of Heroes**, a strange display of life-sized gods and Rajput fighters that were hewn out of the rock face early in the eighteenth century.

A path leads over the hill behind the gardens to another set of cenotaphs, seemingly neglected on a sandy slope among twisted cacti. These commemorate the ranis of Jodhpur and, though smaller, are more stately than those of the men, with exquisitely detailed carving on the pillars and domed roofs.

Osian

Rajasthan's largest group of early Jain and Hindu temples lies on the outskirts of the small town of **OSIAN**, 64km north of Jodhpur. Half-hourly buses (2–3hr) take a scenic route that drops you on the main road south of town; the railway station (served by the Jodhpur–Jaisalmer train, 2hr 30min trip from Jodhpur) is 1km west. Alternatively, get a group together and book a Jeep

the GPO, or at the **Northern Railways bookings counter** at the tourist office on High Court Road (Mon–Sat 10am–5pm). If you're a foreigner, you're entitled to use the musty International Tourist Waiting Room on the ground floor of the main station building. Jodhpur's tourist office will hold luggage free of charge, useful if you're lucky enough to catch a daytime train.

Recommended trains from Jodhpur

The following trains from Jodhpur are recommended as the fastest or most convenient for the destinations listed on the left; all are daily services. Departure times were correct at the time of writing, but do check when you buy your ticket. Note that there is no direct train to **Udaipur**; take the #1JM (10.45am), and change to the #221 at Marwar (departs 2.30pm, arrives 9.30pm).

Destination	Name	No.	Departs	Total time
Abu Road	Jammutawi–Ahmedabad Express	#9112	6.05am	6hr
Agra	Bikaner–Howrah Express	#2308	5.15pm	13hr 10min
	Marudhar Express	#4864/4854	7am	13hr
Ahmedabad	Jammutawi–Ahmedabad Express	#9112	6.05am	10hr 25min
Delhi	Jaisalmer–Delhi Express	#4060	10.30pm	12hr 40min
	Mandor Express	#2462	7.30pm	10hr 15min
Jaipur	Jaipur Intercity Express	#2466	5.45am	4hr 55min
	Jaisalmer–Delhi Express	#4060	10.30pm	6hr 45min
Jaisalmer	Jodhpur–Jaisalmer Express	#4810	11.15pm	6hr
	Delhi–Jaisalmer Express	#4059	6.40am	6hr
Varanasi	Marudhar Express	#4864	7am	26hr

Village safaris

Jodhpur's surroundings can be explored on organized "**village safaris**", which take small groups of tourists out into rural Rajasthan, usually stopping at four or five villages of the local **Bishnoi** tribe where you can taste traditional food, drink opium tea, and watch crafts such as spinning and carpet-making. The Bishnois are among the world's earliest tree huggers, believing that the life of an individual tree or animal is as sacrosanct as that of a human. At Khejadali, a small temple marks the place where, in 1730, 363 villagers were killed after tying themselves to a forest of *khejri* trees to prevent their felling by the maharaja. On most safaris you'll spot *nilgai*, gazelles, and countless bird species living in close company with their trusted human neighbours. Overall, though, the tours are a mixed bag: although almost always fascinating, the invasiveness of it all can prove unsettling. A lot depends on the integrity of the operators and the relations they have with the villagers. Three inexpensive, commendable **companies** are: RTDC, based at the tourist office on High Court Road; the *Govind Hotel* on Station Road (Ⓣ0291/254 5083); and *Yogi's Guest House* (Ⓣ0291/264 3436). Rates start at around Rs400 per head and usually include a home-made meal, though sharing a jeep tour booked by RTDC (Rs1200 for up to 7 people, including guide) brings down the cost considerably. Book at least one day in advance.

through Jodhpur's tourist office (Rs750 for up to five people, or Rs1050 for four people and a guide).

The oldest group, the **Vishnu and Harihara temples**, built in the Pratihara period of the eighth and ninth centuries, are right by the bus stop. All three retain a considerable amount of decorative carving. Where the main road from Jodhpur to Phalodi bends round to the right, the smaller road straight ahead leads to the town centre, where you'll find the twelfth-century **Sachiya Mata temple**, overlooking the whole of Osian, and still used for worship. The main shrine, to Sachiya, an incarnation of Durga, is surrounded by smaller, earlier ones to Ganesh and Shankar (an aspect of Shiva), and, on the right, to Surya and Vishnu.

As you leave the Sachiya Mata temple, the third group of temples lies roughly straight ahead. The first is the **Mahavira Jain temple** (Rs10, plus Rs30 for camera, Rs100 video), built in the eighth century, and renovated in the tenth. Currently under restoration, its main portico is held up by twenty elegantly carved pillars. The usual rules (no leather, don't enter during menstruation) apply. Fifty metres beyond is the **Surya temple**, surrounded by gargoyle-like projecting elephants. Its inner sanctum contains an image of Surya, flanked by Ganesh and Durga. Another 50m brings you to the **Sun temple**, and a little way behind it is a massive Pratihara period step-well, currently under restoration.

For **accommodation**, most people stay at the very basic *Priest Bhanu Sarma Guesthouse* (Ⓣ02922/274232; ❷), opposite the Mahavira temple, a welcoming place that can provide information and set up camel safaris; guests dine at the nearby *Maishuri Bhajnale* restaurant. More upmarket is the luxury *Camel Camp*, which straddles a sand dune on the village outskirts (book in advance through the *Safari Club* in Jodhpur on Ⓣ0291/243 7023; Ⓦwww.camelcamposian.com; ❾).

Jaisalmer and around

In the remote westernmost corner of Rajasthan, a good 100km beyond its closest neighbour Pokaran, **JAISALMER** is a desert town *par excellence*, its

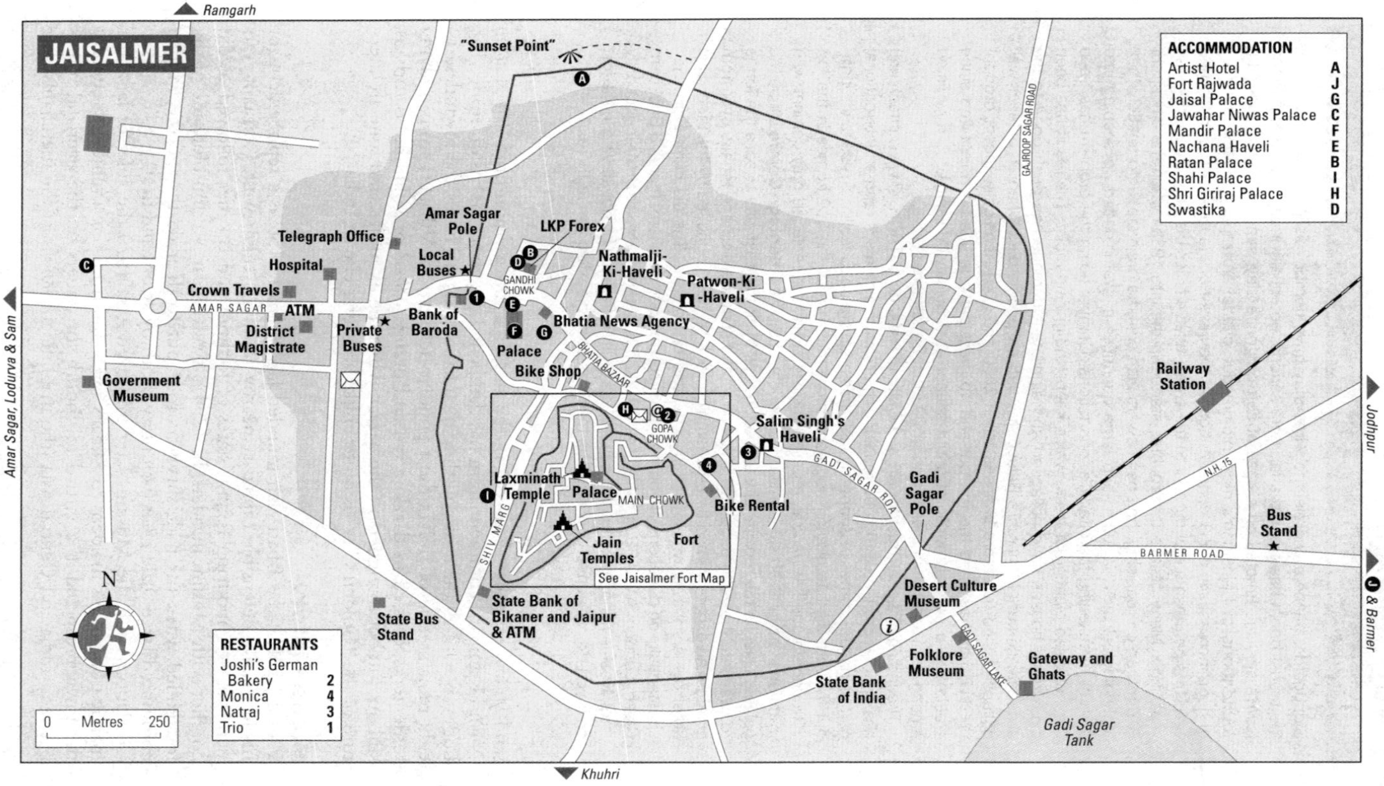

JAISALMER

ACCOMMODATION

Artist Hotel	A
Fort Rajwada	J
Jaisal Palace	G
Jawahar Niwas Palace	C
Mandir Palace	F
Nachana Haveli	E
Ratan Palace	B
Shahi Palace	I
Shri Giriraj Palace	H
Swastika	D

RESTAURANTS

Joshi's German Bakery	2
Monica	4
Natraj	3
Trio	1

Ramgarh
"Sunset Point"
Amar Sagar, Lodurva & Sam
Telegraph Office
Hospital
Crown Travels
AMAR SAGAR
ATM
District Magistrate
Private Buses
Government Museum
Amar Sagar Pole
Local Buses
Bank of Baroda
LKP Forex
GANDHI CHOWK
Nathmalji-Ki-Haveli
Patwon-Ki-Haveli
Bhatia News Agency
Palace
Bike Shop
BHATIA BAZAAR
GOPA CHOWK
Salim Singh's Haveli
Laxminath Temple
Palace
MAIN CHOWK
Bike Rental
Jain Temples
Fort
See Jaisalmer Fort Map
SHIV MARG
GADI SAGAR ROA
Gadi Sagar Pole
GAJROOP SAGAR ROAD
Railway Station
Jodhpur
NH 15
Bus Stand
BARMER ROAD
J & Barmer
State Bus Stand
State Bank of Bikaner and Jaipur & ATM
Desert Culture Museum
Folklore Museum
GADI SAGAR LAKE
Gateway and Ghats
State Bank of India
Gadi Sagar Tank
Khuhri
N
0 Metres 250

Jaisalmer in jeopardy

Signboards, banners and electric wires may have horribly disfigured Jaisalmer, but the tourist boom has created a far more serious, potentially irreversible threat to the town's survival. Erected on a base of soft bantonite clay, sand and sandstone, the **foundations** of Rajasthan's most picturesque citadel are rapidly eroding because of huge increases in water consumption. At the height of the tourist season, around 120 litres per head are pumped into the area – twelve times the quantity used fifteen years ago. Many believe the troubles started in the late 1980s when the city spent Rs9 million on replacing the open sewers with covered drainage; unfortunately their technological trick backfired and large quantities of water ended up seeping into the soil, weakening the citadel's foundations. Compounding the problem has been the increased planting of trees, which keeps the ground moist. The result has been disastrous; houses have collapsed and significant damage has been done to the sixteenth-century Maharani's Palace. In 1998 six people died when an exterior wall collapsed, and five more bastions fell in 2000 and 2001. (Ironically, recent drought in Rajasthan has dried the fort out and no great damage has been reported since – although a normal monsoon could change that quickly.) Jaisalmer is now listed among the World Monument Fund's 100 Most Endangered Sites.

The Indian National Trust for Art and Cultural Heritage (INTACH: Ⓦwww.intach.net) has spent more than $100,000 repairing the Maharani's Palace, and an international campaign, **Jaisalmer in Jeopardy** (JiJ), has been set up to facilitate repairs throughout the fort. JiJ has already upgraded more than half of the 350 homes in the fort with underground sewerage, repaired their facades and replaced grey cement with traditional material. To see some of its work, visit the new **Heritage Centre** inside the palace. Despite the repairs, city authorities still think the best way to save the fort is to evacuate the 2000 people who live there and start the drainage repairs over from scratch, an expensive and time-consuming venture much opposed by the thirty-plus hotel owners inside whose earnings depend on tourism. The JiJ campaign relies substantially on donations. If you'd like to help, contact Sue Carpenter at 3 Brickbarn Close, London SW10 0UJ (Ⓣ & Ⓕ+44(0)20/7352 4336, Ⓦwww.jaisalmer-in-jeopardy.org). Bear in mind, too, that you can make a small difference by not staying in the fort or, if you do, by conserving water as much as possible while you're there.

sand-yellow ramparts rising out of the arid Thar like a vision from *The Arabian Nights*. Rampant commercialism has dampened the romantic vision somewhat, but even with all the touts, hustling merchants and tour buses, the town deservedly remains one of India's most popular destinations. Villagers from outlying settlements, dressed in dazzling red and orange *odhnis* or voluminous turbans, still outnumber foreigners in the bazaar, while the exquisite sandstone architecture of the "Golden City" is quite unlike anything else in India.

Some history

Rawal Jaisal of the Bhati clan founded Jaisalmer in 1156 as a replacement for his less easily defensible capital at nearby Loduvra, 16km west. Constant wars with the neighbouring Rajput states of Jodhpur and Bikaner followed, as did conflict with Muslim invaders. In 1294, a twelve-year Muslim blockade of the fort ended when the male survivors rode out to their deaths and the women committed large-scale *johar* (voluntary death by sword and fire).

Relations with the Muslims later improved – in 1570 the ruler of Jaisalmer married one of his maidens to Akbar's son – and from the seventeenth century the town prospered as a virtual toll booth for traders on the overland routes between India and Central Asia (the magnificent *havelis* of the merchants bear witness to those times). However, the emergence of Bombay and Surat as major ports meant that overland trade diminished, and with it Jaisalmer's wealth. The financial problems were compounded by the usurious taxes imposed on merchants by a particularly greedy prime minister, **Salim Singh Mehta**, in the nineteenth century. The death blow came with Partition, when its life-line trade route was severed – along with several desert clans – by the new, highly sensitive Pakistani border. It took on renewed strategic importance during the Indo-Pak wars of 1965 and 1971, and it is now a major **military outpost**, with jet aircraft roaring past the ramparts at intervals throughout the day.

The area's other main source of income, of course, is **tourism**, which grew dramatically in the 1990s as its reputation as a backpacker's destination grew. Today the booming camel safari and guesthouse business has transformed Jaisalmer almost beyond recognition and the city's future as a relaxed oasis very much hangs in the balance. Its saving grace, so far, has been its relative inaccessibility. A local adage holds that you need a horse made of wood, legs of stone and a cart of iron to reach Jaisalmer. Although an uncomfortable train journey through the desert is, by comparison, a minor obstacle for modern tourists in search of Shangri La, the much promised re-opening of the civilian airport would throw the floodgates open even further.

Arrival, information and accommodation

Jaisalmer's **railway station** is 2km east of the city. Thanks to a concerted crackdown by local authorities, touts and rickshaw drivers are now held at bay outside the terminal. Instead of being accosted by aggressive hawkers, reservation-less travellers can calmly enquire among the sandwich-board toting hoteliers lined up in the parking lot. The majority offer free rides; an auto-rickshaw into town will cost around Rs20–30. **Government buses** stop briefly at a stand near the railway station before continuing to the more convenient new **RSRTC bus stand** south of the fort. The **private bus stand** is at Hanuman Circle in the west of town, within easy walking distance of most accommodation. RTDC's **tourist office,** southeast of town near Gadi Sagar Pole (Mon–Sat 10am–5pm; ⓣ02992/252406) is of little use, and its "recommended" operators pay for the privilege.

Accommodation

Jaisalmer has plenty of places to stay in all categories. Almost all offer **camel treks**, which vary in standard and price, and some managers at even the recommended hotels can be uncomfortably pushy if you don't want to arrange a safari through them, suddenly hiking room rates or turfing you out in the middle of the night. Shop around and bargain before committing.

Traditionally, visitors preferred the atmospheric guesthouses among the jumble of sandstone houses and *havelis* within the **Fort**, whose roofs offer splendid desert vistas. But that's changing fast, in response to campaign to sensitize tourists and hoteliers alike to the structural problems to the citadel caused by increased water consumption. Fearing their days are numbered, many hoteliers inside the Fort have neglected upkeep of their properties. Meanwhile, stylish hotels with lovely terraces offering majestic, panoramic views of the Fort are cropping up on the Fort's **perimeter**. Look-alike **luxury resorts** have also appeared on the fringes of Jaisalmer to service tour groups. Stiff competition between them has kept tariffs in check, so you can now enjoy five-star poolside luxury in the desert for around $70 per double room (or less off-season).

In the Fort

Desert Northwest side of the Fort ⓣ02992/250602, ⓔajitdeserthotel@hotmail.com. Tiny, friendly budget place with just six clean and comfortable rooms (2 doubles). Rooms on the second floor are newer. ❶–❷

Desert Haveli Near Jain temples ⓣ02992/251555. A slightly grungy but popular budget guesthouse. Variously sized, cavernous stone-walled rooms, with old *dhurries* on the floor, tiny windows and some attached bathrooms. The friendly owner offers free pick-ups from bus or railway station. ❷

Jaisal Castle Southwest corner of Fort ⓣ02992/252362. One of the best preserved havelis in the Fort offering somewhat small but fairly priced rooms, some a/c. Well furnished, brightly painted rooms (a few are lopsided), a big courtyard and lovely sandstone screens and balconies. ❹–❻

Killa Bhawan 445 Kotri Badda ⓣ02992/251204, ⓦwww.killabhawan.com. Stylish place created by a French fashion designer, with tasteful decor (silk bed-covers, embroidered wall hangings, antique ornaments and furniture) and a perfect roof terrace. The cheaper rooms share a (beautifully appointed) bathroom. The best upscale choice inside the Fort – if you're lucky enough to get one of the six rooms. ❽

Moti Palace Above Surya gate ⓣ02992/254693, ⓔkailash_bissa@yahoo.co.uk. One of the friendliest, most laid back budget choices inside the Fort, with unbeatable views over the main gate. Rooms all have hot showers. Five new rooms across the street, in a family-shared annexe, are better equipped and larger, but lack views. ❶–❸

Paradise Off the Main Chowk ⓣ02992/252674. Well-run, comfortable hotel in an old *haveli* with a leafy courtyard and 23 rooms covering all price ranges. The larger ones have views and bathrooms; budget options with common baths on the ground floor. Large roof terrace with live folk music each evening at sunset. ❷–❺

Simla North corner of Fort ⓣ02992/253061 or 252825, ⓔsimlahaveli@yahoo.co.in. The latest *haveli* inside the Fort to be restored is also the most beautifully done. Six rooms (some with shared bath) decked in sandstone with divan-like beds and lots of light. Room #31 is the most romantic. Rooftop terrace. Good value. ❷–❺

Suraj Near the Jain temples ⓣ02992/251623, ⓔhotelsurajjaislamer@hotmail.com. Superbly carved sandstone *haveli* – one of Jaisalmer's finest, with a simple, tasteful interior and a family atmosphere. An excellent choice if you get one of the five spacious rooms upfront, all with hot shower and some with original wall paintings – avoid the cheaper rooms in annexe across street. Excellent rooftop view of temples. Internet. ❸–❺

Suraja Southeast corner of Fort ⓣ02992/253836. Simple, budget rooms, some with shared bath. Relaxing rooftop terrace with alcove seating area is among the best in Jaisalmer. Not to be confused with the initially alluring but ultimately disappointing *Surya* next door. ❷–❹

In town

Artist Hotel Artist colony at Suly Dungri ⓣ02992/252082. Hotel run by an Austrian expat as a co-op for former Rajasthani court musicians, who live among the guests and host evening jam sessions. Rooms with balcony view of Fort go for Rs400. ❸

Jaisal Palace Behind the royal palace ⓣ02992/252717 or 251417, ⓔhoteljaisalpalace@yahoo.com. Modern and a bit bland, but the smallish, simply furnished rooms are immaculate and the beds comfortable. Upstairs rooms are better, and have balconies. Internet. ❹–❺

Mandir Palace Gandhi Chowk ⓣ02992/252788 or 252951, ⓔmandirpalace@hotmail.com. Richly carved former palace with lots of character, whose most prominent feature is the striking Badal Vilas tower – one of the town's main landmarks. However, the overpriced musty rooms offer only a faded glimpse of former grandeur. Service is slow and the hotel usually empty. Worth a try if you can negotiate a discount. ❼–❾

Nachana Haveli Gandhi Chowk ⓣ02992/252110 or 251910, ⓔnachana_haveli@yahoo.com. A recent refurbishment makes this atmospheric *haveli*, run by a cousin of the maharaja, one of the best choices in its class. Rooms are dark but lit up by funky details and period antiques. ❺–❽

Ratan Palace Off Gandhi Chowk ⓣ02992/251119 or 253615, ⓔhotelrenuka@rediffmail.com. Among the best budget options in this part of town, with a friendly owner who takes great pride in spotless, hassle-free accommodation for foreigners. Spacious rooms with large, marble-lined bathrooms. Internet. They also run the slightly less expensive (and older) *Renuka* across the street, where all rooms have attached baths. Good camel treks. ❶–❸

Shahi Palace Shiv Marg ⓣ02992/255920, ⓦwww.shahipalacehotel.com. It can be hard to find this spanking new hotel, ten minutes from the Fort gate – once you do, you'll never want to leave. High-ceilinged rooms are richly dressed with patchwork tapestries and sandstone carved beds, some which literally sit on sandboxes. The rooftop terrace restaurant with stunning views is alternately festive or romantic, depending on guests. Owner Jora and his brothers cater to all your needs – including good camel rides, Internet, and transport. Book ahead. ❷–❺

Shri Giriraj Palace Near Gopa Chowk ⓣ02992/252268 or 251519. Small, ornately carved *haveli* near the first Fort gate, with pleasant rooms and courteous management. A dependable budget choice in the (noisy) heart of the bazaar. Rs75 for basic room with shared bath. ❶–❷

Swastika Off Gandhi Chowk ⓣ02992/252483. Similar high standards of cleanliness as the nearby *Ratan Palace*, with a name that could only be politically correct in India. Helpful owner. ❶–❷

Out of town

Fort Rajwada Jodhpur–Barmer Rd ⓣ02992/253533, ⓦwww.fortrajwada.com. Among the new resort hotels on the outskirts, this place is in a league of its own. Its massive marble lobby includes chunks of richly filigreed sandstone plundered from the old city. All the facilities of a five-star (huge pool, bar, gourmet restaurant and coffee shop), but at lower rates (rooms start at Rs3100 or 30 percent less off season) that make it one of the best deals in the world. ❾

Jawahar Niwas Palace Bada Bagh Rd ⓣ02992/252208, ⓦwww.jawaharniwaspalace.com. Century-old royal guesthouse with turreted sandstone exterior straight out of a Kipling novel. The Art Deco rooms (Rs2600–4000) are graceful and comfy, if slightly cobwebby. Pool Rs200 for non-guests. ❽–❾

The Town

Getting lost in the narrow winding streets of Jaisalmer is both easy and enjoyable, and the town is so small that it never takes long to find a familiar landmark. Main roads lead around the base of the Fort from the central market square, **Gopa Chowk**, east to **Gadi Sagar Tank**, and west to **Gandhi Chowk**. Within the Fort the streets are narrower still, but orientation is simple: head west from the main *chowk* and **Maharawal's Palace** to reach the **Jain temples**. Finally, for optimum **views**, head for "Sunset Point" north of the main bazaar area, or the rooftop of the *Paradise Hotel*, where you can watch the sunset accompanied by live folk music.

Jaisalmer Fort

Every part of Jaisalmer **Fort**, from its outer walls to the palace, temples and houses within, is made of soft yellow Jurassic sandstone. The narrow winding streets are flanked with carved sandy facades, and from the barrel-sided bastions, some of which still bear cannons, you can see the thick walls that drop almost 100m to the town below. Two thousand people live inside it; seventy percent of them are brahmins and the rest, living primarily on the east side, predominantly Rajput.

A paved road punctuated by four huge gateways winds up to the Fort, built when the city was founded in 1156. Traitors and criminals were thrown into the "death well" by the second gate. The fourth gateway leads into **Main Chowk**, where terrible acts of *johar* once took place, women choosing death rather than dishonour for themselves and their children after their husbands left for the battlefield. The *chowk* is dominated by the old **palace of the Maharawal** (daily: summer 8am–6pm; winter 9am–6pm; Rs70, plus Rs50 for camera, Rs150 video; guided tour Rs100-200), whose five-storey facade of balconies and windows displays some of the finest masonry in Jaisalmer. The monarch would address his troops and issue orders from the large ornate marble throne to the left of the palace entrance. The interior, painted and tiled in typical Rajput style, has been converted into a **museum**. Displays are quite minimal, but look for the family tree showing the maharaja's 21 different wives and their respective lineages. You'll also see an assortment of royal garbs, weapons, thrones, and most curiously, Raj-era royal stamps. Thanks to restoration work supported by

Shopping in Jaisalmer

Jaisalmer's flourishing tourist trade has made it one of the best places in India to shop for **souvenirs**. Prices are comparatively high and the salesmen notoriously hard at work, but the choice of stuff on sale puts the town on a par with Pushkar and Jaipur. As well as embroidered **patchwork tapestries**, good buys include woven jackets, tie-dyed cloth, puppets, wooden boxes and ornaments, camel-leather slippers (*jutties*) and Western-style clothes. Most items can be found at Shree Art Palace and the adjacent stores inside the first Fort gate.

Every conceivable kind of traditional Rajasthani **textile** is sold at shops in and around the Fort. Most of the pieces on offer are specially made for the tourist trade, but you can occasionally find older garments, or patches worked into wall-hangings, at the more established dealers. A good place to start looking is the Barmer Embroidery House, near the Patwon-ki-Haveli, Gangana Para, in the north of town. Stock here ranges from standard Jaipuri block-printed bedspreads and mirror work or appliqué cushion covers to rare door-hangings (*torans*), ornately embroidered cradle covers, sari blouses (*choli*), Lamani *chillum* pouches and silk-woven *mashru* skirts from the remote Muslim villages of Kutch. Also worth a visit is Light of the East, near Kund Para Chowk, which sells high quality emeralds, amethysts and other rare minerals, along with crystals. One item is not for sale – the football-sized apophyllite, which the knowledgeable owner keeps under lock in a glass case.

Jaisalmer in Jeopardy (see p.226), the *zenana* (women's) quarter known as **Rani ka Mahal** was recently reopened. The fact that this richly filigreed edifice is standing – it was little more than a pile of rubble a few years ago – is a minor miracle.

Although the Fort holds temples dedicated to Surya, Lakshmi, Ganesh, Vishnu and Shiva, none is as impressive as the complex of **Jain temples** (daily 7.30am–12.30pm; Rs10, plus Rs50 for camera, Rs100 video; usual restrictions on leather and menstruation apply). Built between the twelfth and fifteenth centuries in the familiar Jurassic sandstone, with yellow and white marble shrines and exquisite sculpted motifs covering the walls, ceilings and pillars, the temples are connected by small corridors and stairways. In a vault beneath the Sambhavnath temple, the **Gyan Bhandar** (daily 10–11am) contains Jain manuscripts, paintings and astrological charts dating back to the eleventh century, among them one of India's oldest surviving palm-leaf books, a copy of Dronacharya's *Oghaniryaktivritti* (1060).

The havelis

The streets of Jaisalmer are flanked with numerous honey-pale facades, covered with latticework and floral designs, but the city's real showpieces are its **havelis**. Each of these extravagant mansions, comprising three or more storeys around a central courtyard, was commissioned by a wealthy merchant during the eighteenth or nineteenth century. Their stonework was the art of *silavats*, a community of masons responsible for much of Jaisalmer's unique sculpture.

The large **Patwon-ki-Haveli** (daily 9.30am–5pm; Rs20), in the north of town, was constructed over fifty years ago by the Patwa merchants – brocade and opium traders. Five separate suites with individual entrances facing a narrow street are connected from within, and all have flat roof areas – the views are excellent. Traces of stylish wall paintings survive in some rooms, but the building's most striking features are its exuberantly carved *jharokhas*, or protruding balconies.

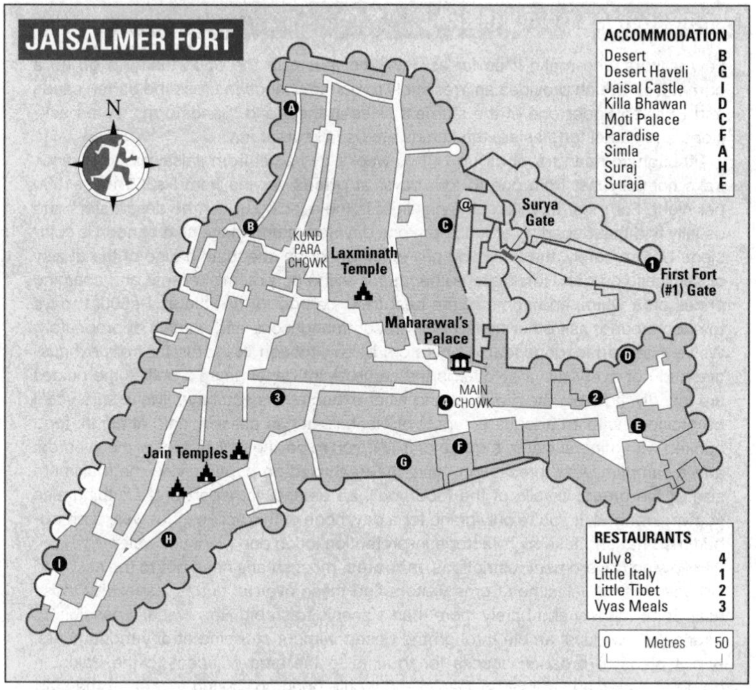

Salim Singh's small *haveli* provides Jaisalmer's only favourable memory of the tyrannical Salim Singh Mohta, who became prime minister in 1800 after his father was murdered for publicly challenging a Rajput prince to repay a loan. From an early age, Salim seemed hell-bent on avenging this crime, impoverishing Jaisalmer's citizens through vigorous taxation and extortion rackets, and holding the royal family to ransom by raising interest rates on their huge loans. He was eventually stabbed by a furious Rajput, and his wife made sure the wound wouldn't heal by infesting it with poison. Their curious family home is topped with small bluish domes; its upper floor, enclosed by a protruding balcony, is best seen from the roof of *Natraj Restaurant*. The house is still lived in, but you can go inside for Rs15. On the road to Malka Pole, you pass the decorative facade of the late-nineteenth-century **Nathmalji-ki-Haveli**, also built for a prime minister of Jaisalmer. It's free to visit but expect a hard sell at the overpriced gift shop.

Gadi Sagar Tank and the Folklore Museum

South of town through an imposing triple gateway, **Gadi Sagar Tank**, built in 1367 and flanked with sandstone *ghats* and temples, was once Jaisalmer's sole water supply. This peaceful place staring out on the desert hosts the festival of **Gangaur** in March, when women fling flowers into the lake and pray for a good husband, and the maharawal heads a procession amid a pomp and splendour unchanged for generations. It's possible to rent boats the rest of the year for Rs100 per hour.

The delightful little **Folklore Museum** near the tank's main gate (daily 8am–sunset; Rs10) has informative displays of folk art, much of it religious. The locally styled wooden statues of Krishna and Radha, musical instruments,

Camel safaris from Jaisalmer

Few visitors who make it as far as Jaisalmer pass up the opportunity to go on a **camel trek**, which provides an irresistibly romantic chance to cross the barren sands and to sleep under one of the starriest skies in the world. Sandstorms, sore backsides and camel farts aside, the safaris are usually great fun.

Although you can travel for up to two weeks by camel from Jaisalmer to Bikaner, treks normally last from one to four days, at **prices** varying from Rs350 to Rs1500 per night. For most travellers, the highlight is the evening under the desert stars and usually find that departing around 3pm one day and returning the next at noon is sufficient. Unfortunately, the price you pay is no longer an adequate gauge of the quality of services you get. Hotels are notorious for sizing up potential clients and charging prices on a whim, and some of the best treks can go for as little as Rs500. It pays to shop around, ask other travellers for recommendations and bargain appropriately. We've listed a few dependable operators below, though the list is far from exhaustive and not every trip they offer is the same. A lot depends on whether the guides are friendly, how big the group is, and what expectations you have. Make sure you'll be provided with an adequate supply of blankets (it can get very cold at night); food cooked with mineral water; a quota of fruit if you're paying anything over the average; and a campfire. As a precaution, have the deal fixed on paper, giving the maximum size of the group, details of the food you'll be getting, transport and anything else you've arranged. If you're only going for a day, none of this applies, but wear a broad-brimmed hat and take high-factor sun-protection lotion and plenty of water.

Following government restrictions on **routes**, most safaris head out to the assorted villages west of Jaisalmer. Some visitors find these overrun dunes, especially those near Sam, touristy and barely more than a scenic trash pit. However, it's possible to arrange a few days' amble through the desert without stopping at any monuments. And if plans to broaden access for tourists to the area adjacent to the Pakistan border prosper, a veritable no-man's land would open up. Taking a **Jeep** at the start or end of the trek enables you to go further in a short time, and some travellers prefer to begin their trek at Khuhri (see p.235). Longer treks to Pokaran, Jodhpur or Bikaner can also be arranged. Firms running treks into restricted areas (see "Around Jaisalmer", p.234) should fix the necessary permits for you, but check in advance.

However much you intend to spend on a trek, don't book anything until you get to Jaisalmer. Touts trawl the train from Jodhpur, but they, and the barrage of operators combing the streets, usually represent dodgy outfits, most of which are based at one or other of the small budget hotels north of the Fort. Some offer absurdly cheap rooms if you agree to book a camel trek with them, but guesthouse notice boards (not to mention our postbags) are filled with sorry stories by tourists who accepted.

Recommended operators

Adventure Travel (Ⓣ02992/252558, Ⓦwww.adventurecamel.com), just south of the first Fort gate, gets rave reviews for seeking out remote locations and providing fringe amenities, like real mattresses and sheets, for low prices. More expensive, but equally dependable, is **Sahara Travels** in Gopa Chowk (Ⓣ02992/252609, Ⓦwww.mrdesertjaisalmer.com), run by the instantly recognizable "Mr. Desert," a former truck driver turned Rajasthani model and movie star. "Don't make a booking until you see the face," is his motto. **Thar Safari** (Ⓣ02992/254296, Ⓔtharsafari@hotmail.com) in Gandhi Chowk is one of the oldest and most reputable agencies, and among the few genuinely concerned about protecting the desert environment.

Of the **hotels** which organize camel safaris, *Shahi Palace* has a deservedly good reputation and virtually guarantees you won't see another tourist, though their prices are known to fluctuate. Among the budget alternatives, the friendly *Ratan Palace* offers excellent value for money. They've been running trips for more than a decade into a stretch of drifting dunes south of Sam that only a couple of other operators are allowed into.

paintings and travelling temples (*kavad*) are all from the personal collection of its proprietor, a one-time school teacher, who still happily leads most tours. You'll find much the same selection of local curiosities, but with little explanation, at the **Desert Culture Museum** (daily 8am–7pm; Rs10), opened by the same family at larger premises next to the tourist office on the main road. One ticket is good for both museums.

Eating

Being so popular with foreign tourists, Jaisalmer offers peanut butter, Vegemite, Marmite, pizza, pancakes, apple pie and cakes on its menus alongside typical Indian dishes, usually served up on rooftop restaurants. If you're on a tight budget, a good place to fill up on freshly cooked, spicy food is the little *pao bhaji* stall on Gopa Chowk (opposite the *bhang* lassi-wallah), which does a roaring trade in the evening. Afterwards, stroll through the bazaar for a glass of hot *badam* (milk flavoured with cardamom and whole almonds), from the huge bubbling vats on the roadside between Amar Sagar Pole and Hanuman Circle.

Joshi's German Bakery Gopa Chowk.One of the few European-inspired pastry shops in Rajasthan to live up to its name. Roadside stall serving tasty *makhani* lassis and fresh croissants and cakes. Service is fast too. Best for early breakfast, before the bazaar hits full volume.

July 8 Main Chowk. Recommended for its privileged terrace view of the bustling chowk and palace rather than for its service or overpriced food. It's good for breakfast, when you can watch the city wake up before it's invaded by tourists.

Little Italy Above first Fort gate. Possibly the best Italian food in Rajasthan, served in heaped portions at reasonable prices. It's run by the same family behind the recommended lassi shop *Baba Bhang Shop* in Gopa Chowk, and geared toward foreigners, with an eastern techno soundtrack, dim lighting and pillow seating. It's new, so it remains to be seen whether they'll maintain the high standards.

Little Tibet In the Fort. Travellers' café-restaurant run by a team of smart young Tibetans. Their extensive menu includes all the usual Indian/Chinese choices, plus tasty enchiladas, pasta and Tibetan *momos*. Careful, hygienic cooking (their veg are washed in iodized water), and a good venue for breakfast. Slow service a drawback. It's the "in" place, so expect long waits

Monica Near the first Fort gate. Moderately priced Rajasthani and tandoori dishes. The "Special Kotha" is a festival of flavours.

Natraj Facing the top floor of Salim Singh's *haveli*. Pleasant rooftop and indoor non-veg restaurant, famous for its Moghlai chicken and *malai kofta*. The quality food is soft on spices and moderately priced.

Trio Gandhi Chowk ⓣ02992/252733. The granddaddy of Jaisalmer's upscale choices is no longer unrivalled. But it retains a loyal clientele for its sumptuous Moghlai food, antique decor, nice terrace and live folk music. Book early for the best tables overlooking *Mandir Palace* and the Fort.

Vyas Meals In the Fort by the handicraft shops on the way to the Jain temples. Hole-in-the-wall place run by an elderly couple who do superb home-style veg thalis and snacks at unbeatable prices. Expect a long wait. Eat in or takeaway.

Listings

Banks and exchange You can change money at the State Bank of Bikaner & Jaipur, near the state bus stand. Otherwise, Gandhi Chowk has several foreign exchange bureaux that also exchange travellers' cheques. There's also an ATM, though it can be unreliable. The Bank of Baroda can give cash advances against credit cards (1 percent plus Rs100) at their Gandhi Chowk branch.

Bike rental Atlas, south of Gopa Chowk where tour buses park alongside the Fort's ramparts, charges Rs3/hr.

Bookshops Book and magazine shops are scattered about town: Bhatia News agency on Court Rd, just beyond Gandhi Chowk, has guidebooks and English-language novels. Look out for the excellent book *Jaisalmer: Folklore, History and Architecture*, by local shopkeeper L.N. Khatri.

Doctor Dr SK Dube (ⓣm02992/9414 149500) is well liked and speaks good English; he charges Rs300 for a consultation at your hotel.

Internet access Internet is widely available but slow. The *Chai Bar*, inside the Fort just beyond

Ganesh gate, has the best PCs of the bunch. In town, try *Joshi Cyber Café* (Rs40/hr) in the *German Bakery* at Gopa Chowk.

Post office The main post office, with poste restante, is west of town, 100m south of the private bus stand; a more convenient office stands shaded by a huge banyan tree in Gopa Chowk.

Yoga Run by Dr Vyas and his wife, Ayurveda Hub (☎02992/254692) gets rave reviews, though purification therapy takes precedence over massages. They charge Rs200 for a first consultation or Rs4000 for a 5-day *Vamanam* vomit marathon.

Around Jaisalmer

The sandy, barren terrain around Jaisalmer harbours some unexpected monuments, dating from the Rajput era when this area lay on busy caravan routes. Infrequent buses negotiate the dusty roads, or you can rent a Jeep through RTDC, who also offer inexpensive **tours** (Rs300–450) to the main sights; the best way to visit these places, however, and see villages and abandoned towns inaccessible by road, is on a **camel trek**. Being close to the Pakistani border, the area west of Highway NH-15 is **restricted**, though authorities are considering lifting restrictions to at least some of the area as crossborder relations improve. Tourists are currently allowed to visit Amar Sagar, Sam, Bada Bagh, Lodurva and Khuhri without a **permit**, but if you want to travel more than 50km beyond Jaisalmer you should apply to the District Magistrate's Office (☎02992/252201), just west of the private bus stand in Jaisalmer (Mon–Fri & sometimes Sat 10am–5pm). On the few camel treks where this is necessary, however, the organizers will usually get permits for you.

Moving on from Jaisalmer

Jaisalmer's **airport**, 8km west of town on the Sam road, has been closed for years to civilian traffic, but is perennially slated for re-opening, at which time flights to Delhi and/or Mumbai would likely resume. **Taxis** charge around Rs2500 to Jodhpur (250km west).

By train

A daily **train** for Delhi departs Jaisalmer at 4.15pm, reaching Jodhpur at 10pm, Jaipur at 5.30am and Delhi at 11.30am. Two other trains to Jodhpur depart at 7.30am and 11.15pm, arriving at 4.30pm and 5.15am respectively. Buying your own tickets is not advised, especially for the night train; lines are notoriously long and you will save a lot of time by getting your ticket through your hotel (*Shahi Palace* is particularly efficient) or an agent. If you catch the night train, take along plenty of **warm clothes** and a sleeping bag if you have one as temperatures drop to almost freezing point in the winter. At the time of research plans were underway to restore links to **Pakistan** in 2005 for the first time since 1965; keep an eye on developments.

By bus

If you have travelled to Jaipur by train, consider taking a **bus** out, as this allows the opportunity to make stops at several Thar desert towns, including Phalodi and Osian. **State buses** run to Jodhpur (5–6hr) and Barmer almost hourly; there are also services to Bikaner (6am & 8.30pm), Jaipur (5pm; 12hr), and Mount Abu (5.30pm). **Private buses** leave to the same destinations from Hanuman Circle near Amar Sagar Gate. Hanuman Travels (☎02992/250340) has daily buses to Udaipur (3.15pm, with stop in Jodhpur), as well as a sleeper bus to Delhi (2pm). Other agents at the Circle include Chouhan Travels (☎02992/255925) and Swagat Travels (☎02992/252057). Frequent but much slower **local buses**, which can't be booked, use the stand a little northeast of the crossroads. They include three daily buses to Khuhri (1hr 30min).

Amar Sagar, Sam and Bada Bagh

A short distance northwest of Jaisalmer, **AMAR SAGAR** is a peaceful small town set around a large lake (empty during the dry season). A former palace and large complex of two-hundred year old Jain temples (Rs10 entry, plus Rs50 for camera), recently restored to their former magnificence, stand on the lake edges.

The huge, rolling sand dunes 40km west of Jaisalmer are known as **SAM**, though strictly this is the name of a small village further west. The dunes are a prime tourist attraction, and though sunset at Sam can be breathtaking, the drink-sellers, musicians, piles of plastic rubbish and numerous camel trains and bus parties somewhat dilute the romance. Most camel safaris decamp nearby, but there are a few **accommodation** options inside the town itself. A RTDC tourist bungalow, the *Hotel Sam Dhani* (Ⓣ02922/252392; ❸), offers simple rooms without a/c, plus bucket hot water. Even more rustic, but away from the tourist racket, are the mud-and-straw huts of the nearby *Gandwi Resort* (mobileⓉ94142/20062; ❸), where you can also see nightly dance performances. In contrast, the *Royal Desert Camp* is decidedly plush (❾; book through Royal Safari on Gandhi Chowk; Ⓣ02922/252538, Ⓔrsafari@sancharnet.in); the $90 nightly rate includes meals, evening performances and a camel ride. Three **buses** run to Sam (11am, 3pm & 5pm); the last one returns in the morning but it's easy enough to hitch a ride back after the ritual sunset viewing.

Six kilometres north of Jaisalmer, in the fertile area of **Bada Bagh** (Rs20, plus Rs20 for camera), a cluster of cenotaphs built in memory of Jaisalmer's rulers stands on a hill juxtaposed against a collection of modern windmills. Domed roofs shade small marble or sandstone slabs bearing inscriptions and equestrian statues. The green oasis below is where most of the fruit and vegetables of the region used to be grown – a surreal sight amid the sand and scrub.

Lodurva

Another 10km north of Bada Bagh, **LODURVA** was the capital of the Bhati rulers until the foundation of Jaisalmer in the twelfth century. Of the city's fine buildings, only a few **Jain temples**, rebuilt in the 1970s, remain (sunrise to sunset; Rs10, plus Rs50 for camera, Rs100 video). The *toran*, an eight-metre colonnated archway at the entrance to the temple compound, is the most exquisite in the Jaisalmer area. The main structure has detailed tracery work in the stone walls and a finely carved exterior. A smaller temple, built on a series of diminishing square platforms, stands to its right. There are several daily **buses** to Lodurva (10.30am, 12.30pm, 3.30pm & 5.30pm), but taking a **taxi** is a better, more leisurely option (Rs300 including stops at Amar Sagar and Bada Bagh). More intrepid tourists might consider getting here by **bike**.

Khuhri

Though most camel treks start in Jaisalmer, a handful of travellers prefer to begin their safari out in the desert at the village of **KHUHRI**, just 1km from the dunes. Most safaris time their arrival so tourists can see women, dressed in flamboyantly coloured dress, arriving with large jugs on their heads to fill up with water at caste-specific wells. Many of the villages' homes are still made of mud and thatch instead of concrete, and their exterior surfaces are beautifully decorated with ornate white murals. If you're lucky enough to be invited inside one, you'll see some superb moulded mud shelves and fireplaces, inlaid with mica and mirror work.

Khuhri can be reached on three daily **buses** (10.30am, 2pm & 5.30pm; 90min) from the local bus stand in Jaisalmer. The village harbours a handful of basic **guesthouses**. The oldest is *Mama's* (☎953014/274023; ❸–❻), run by Khuhri's friendly mayor, which offers "traditional" huts with common bathrooms or plainer, cheaper rooms for Rs300. *Khuhri Guest House* (☎935014/274044; ❶–❸), near the bus stand, is a better budget option, offering shared or en-suite shower-toilets. Note that the **phone code** if calling from Jaisalmer is ☎935014; from anywhere else it is ☎03014.

Pokaran

POKARAN, with its red-sandstone fort and superb *havelis*, is a quiet, seldom-visited desert pit stop 110km east of Jaisalmer, situated at the road and rail junctions between Jodhpur, Bikaner and the west. Once included in the territory of Jodhpur, it passed into the huge state of Jaisalmer after Independence. Pokaran became the unlikely object of world attention in May 1998, when five nuclear bombs were detonated at the army test range 20km northwest of town (see box below). Despite this unlikely fifteen minutes of fame, Pokaran remains something of an outpost, which is a shame given the excellent **accommodation** on offer at the **fort** (☎02994/222274; ❻–❾), where meals are served in a lovely old dining hall. The sixteenth-century fort now houses a **museum** (daily 8am–1pm & 2–6pm; Rs50, plus Rs30 for camera, Rs50 video) featuring a dusty collection of medieval weapons and clothing, as well as a Krishna shrine.

The Pokaran N-tests

At around 3.45pm on May 11, 1998, three massive explosions erupted 200m beneath the sands of Thar Desert, 20km northwest of **Pokaran**, a stone's throw north of the main Bikaner–Jaisalmer highway. The bombs were small by modern standards – 20 kilotonnes, Hiroshima-sized – but their political shockwaves resounded from western Rajasthan to Islamabad, Beijing and Washington. By May 13, after two more detonations, India's transition from so-called "threshold state" to fully-fledged atomic power was complete.

In the vehemently anti-Pak Indian press, the tests were hailed as "A Moment of Pride", and celebratory fireworks lit the skies of the capital. The widespread euphoria, however, temporarily faltered when the scale of the international outcry became apparent. Caught completely unawares by the explosions, the US immediately announced that it was suspending all aid to India, and recommended a freeze in IMF and World Bank loans. These threats alone were enough to sober up the Delhi government, which owes $40 billion to the US, and had been promised a further $3 billion in aid that year. The country's barely disguised triumphalism took a further battering when, two weeks after the tests at Pokaran, Pakistan detonated its own thermo-nuclear devices. India was suddenly locked into a spiralling nuclear arms race in one of the most geopolitically sensitive parts of the world. The rupee took a severe tumble, plummeting to an all-time low against the dollar, as did tourist bookings.

Yet within India, few dissenting voices were heard. Among the only high-profile critics of the government was Booker-prize winner Arundhati Roy, who compared India's pride at the tests with its poor track record on tackling poverty. Lesser-known opponents of the N-tests are to be found in the villages surrounding the site of the explosions, where hundreds of poor farmers and their families fell ill soon after the detonations. Although no fatalities have been directly attributed to the blast, scientists warn public health and environmental hazards may take years to materialize.

Phalodi and Keechen

The main highway and broad-gauge train wind in tandem east from Jaisalmer across the desert, separating at the small junction settlement of **PHALODI**, almost exactly midway between Jaisalmer and Bikaner. This scruffy salt-extraction colony would be entirely forgettable were it not the jumping-off place for one of Rajasthan's most beautiful natural sights, one that shouldn't be missed if you're passing. Sheltered by a swathe of soft yellow dunes, the village of **Keechen**, 4km east on the opposite side of the main road, hosts a 4000-strong flock of **demoiselle cranes** (*Anthropoides virgo*), who migrate here each winter from their breeding grounds on the Central Asian steppes. Known locally as *kurja*, the birds are encouraged to return by the villagers, who scatter specially donated grain for them to feed on twice each day – a custom which has persisted for 150 years or more. At feeding times (6.30am & 3.30–4pm), the flock descends en masse on a fenced-off area just outside the village, where you can watch and photograph them at close quarters. At other times, the birds usually congregate just outside the fenced-off area on the dunes nearby, or at a small reservoir north of town; they're easy to spot. More information can be found at Ⓦwww.savingcranes.org.

From Phalodi, the best way to **get to Keechen** is to rent a bicycle from one of the stalls near the bus stand – a pleasant, mostly flat four-kilometre ride on well-surfaced roads. Alternatively, jump in a taxi (Rs200) or auto-rickshaw (Rs100); Ambassador taxis queue outside the railway station. If you don't want to take your gear with you while you're crane-watching, try asking the well-meaning *Hotel Chetnya Palace* (Ⓣ02925/223945; ❷–❹), next to the bus stand serving Jaisalmer, to watch it for you. The hotel also allows people who are waiting for transport connections to take a room for an hour or two for Rs100. Its bright, clean **restaurant** is the most hygienic place in town to **eat**, serving inexpensive *parathas* and rice-plate veg meals to order, as well as the usual hot and cold drinks. Your only other option is the highly recommended *Lal Niwas* (Ⓣ02925/223813, Ⓦwww.lalniwas.com; ❼–❽), a 300-year-old red-sandstone *haveli* recently converted into a top-notch heritage hotel aimed at birdwatchers, with a pool and fifteen luxury suites that start at Rs1800. If you're only stopping for a couple of hours, **check bus times** before you head off to Keechen, as services can be sporadic, though theoretically there's a bus every hour to Jaisalmer and Bikaner. For Jaisalmer, **trains** depart at 9.10am and 1.45pm; to Jodhpur departure times are 6.50pm and 2.30am.

Bikaner and around

The smog-filled commercial city of **BIKANER** has none of the aesthetic magic of its more venerable neighbour, Jaisalmer, over 300km southwest, but travellers who make it here are usually surprised by the abundance of attractions. In addition to a spectacular **fort**, Bikaner boasts an atmospheric old city dotted with *havelis* and artisan shops and enclosed by 7km of high walls. And because Rajasthan's fourth largest city receives fewer visitors than other major settlements, it has a certain unspoilt feel – most residents go out of their way to be friendly, their curiosity not yet stamped out by mass tourism. Most foreign tourists only spend one night here en route to or from Jaisalmer, but extend your stay and you can visit the unforgettable **rat temple** at nearby Deshnok – one of India's most intriguing attractions – and the government **camel-breeding farm**, 10km south. If you're around in January, Bikaner's **camel fair** – smaller than Pushkar's – is an added attraction.

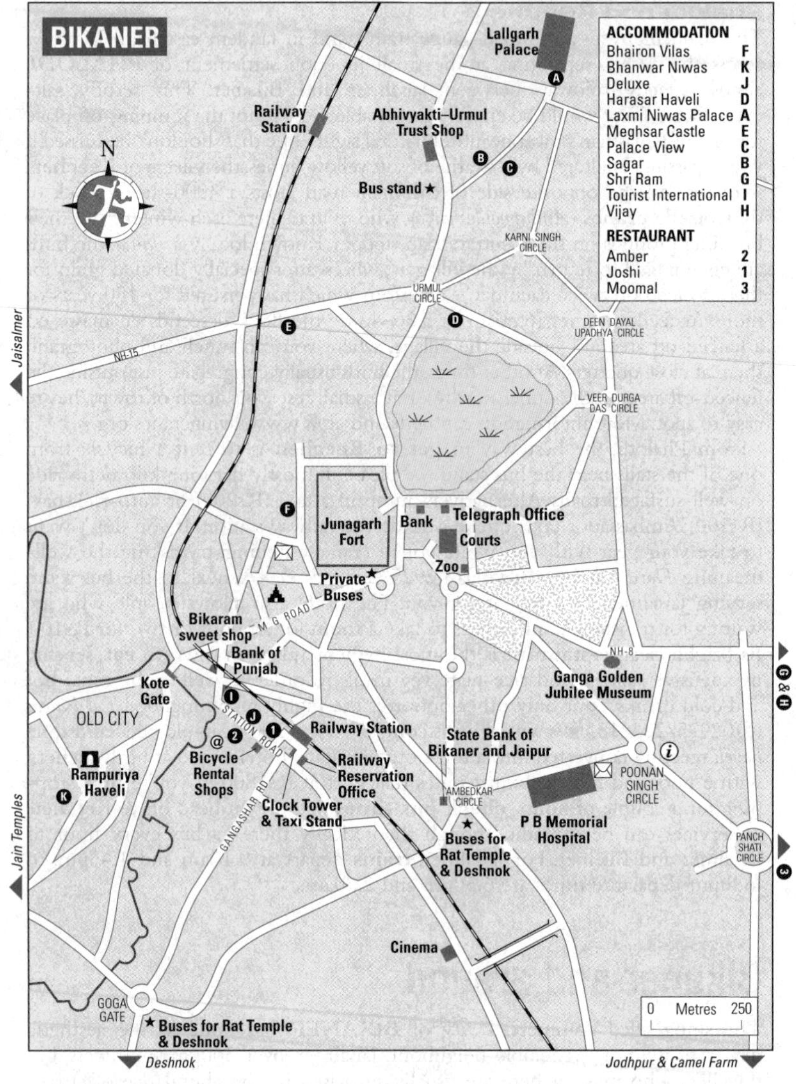

The city was founded in 1486 as a link in the overland trading route by **Bika**, one of fourteen sons of Rao Jodha, the Rathore king who established Jodhpur. Under Rai Singh, who came to the throne in 1573, **Junagarh Fort** was built and closer ties were forged with the Moghuls; Rai Singh gave his daughter in marriage to one of Akbar's sons. In the early 1900s, new agricultural schemes, irrigation work, town planning and the construction of a rail link with Delhi helped Bikaner's economic advance; it has long since outgrown the confines of the city wall, and the population has more than tripled in size since 1947 to over 600,000.

Arrival and information

Rickshaw drivers working on commission are a nuisance in Bikaner and are borderline hostile to weary travellers arriving on the evening bus from Jaisalmer. A ride across town from the **bus stand**, near Lalgarh Palace a few kilometres north of the centre, to the **railway station** should cost around Rs30. The helpful **tourist office** (daily 10am–5pm; ⓣ0151/222 6701), in the RTDC *Dholamaru Hotel* at Pooran Singh Circle, can suggest **homestays**. There's **online information** on Bikaner, including its hotels, at ⓦwww.realbikaner.com. For trips around town, use any of the cycle or auto-rickshaws, or rent a bike. You'll find two **cycle rental** shops outside the red-coloured school building (formerly the post office) on Station Road.

Travellers' cheques can be changed at the State Bank of Bikaner & Jaipur (Mon–Fri 10am–2pm), opposite the entrance to the fort, or the LKP Forex office inside the fort entrance. The SBBJ branch at Ambedkar Circle **changes money** from 2pm to 4pm. Booths all over town offer **Internet** access, but the best-equipped cyber café is New Horizons behind the *Amber Restaurant* on Station Road.

Accommodation

Bikaner boasts a surprisingly large selection of **hotels**, and because competition is cut-throat, some of the best-value accommodation in Rajasthan. The shoestring-priced flophouses along the heavily congested and trash-strewn Station Road are best avoided. Air-conditioning in summer tends to jack the prices up slightly.

Budget

Deluxe Station Rd, ⓣ0151/252 8127. A last resort for penny-pinchers, this cramped hotel is clean enough and located a stone's throw from the railway station. 24hr check out and restaurant. ❶–❷

Tourist International 200m from railway station on Gangashar Rd ⓣ0151/ 252 4267, ⓦwww.hoteltouristinternational.com. Newish hotel offering modern amenities like cable TV and 24hr room service in otherwise neglected Station Road area. Excellent value. ❸–❹

Vijay Opposite Sophia School, 5km east of centre along the Jaipur Highway ⓣ0151/223 1244, ⓦwww.camelman.com. Slightly eccentric, pleasantly scruffy and affordable family guesthouse that's been serving backpackers since 1983. Seven rooms, some huge, all have attached shower-toilets, and there's camping/parking space, plus a nice garden. ❶–❷

Mid-range

Bhairon Vilas Next to Junagarh Fort ⓣ & ⓕ0151/254 4751. Delightful owner Harsh, cosmopolitan cousin of the maharaja, has stylishly employed family curios and Art Deco antiques to convert this terracotta- and ochre-coloured royal *haveli* into a funky, lounge-like hotel – one of Rajasthan's most unique. Evening bonfires and the occasional dance party take place in the lovely garden. Room 101 has great view of the fort. Book ahead. ❹–❺

Harasar Haveli 500 meters east of Urmul Circle ⓣ0151/ 220 9891 or 252 7318. Much scorned by jealous hoteliers for paying out hefty commissions to rickshaws, there's no denying the ambition of this pink skyscraper or its politician owner. Thirty-eight stylish rooms from Rs300 to Rs2000 run the gamut from basic to garish, but all are spotless and offer excellent value. Terrace restaurant serves good veg and non-veg food and has panoramic views and live music in evening. *Desert Winds* next door is a respectable, though less lively alternative. ❸–❼

Meghsar Castle 9 Gajner Rd ⓣ0151/252 7315, ⓦwww.hotelmeghsarcastle.com. Well-equipped, comfortable rooms and a very friendly owner who goes out of his way to assist independent travellers. Well worth the hike from the city centre, even if the location on the busy Jaisalmer road (NH-15) lacks tranquillity. Buses from Jaisalmer will drop you off upon request. Excellent value. ❷–❻

Palace View Lallgarh Palace Campus ⓣ0151/254 3625, ⓔopnain_jp1@sancharnet.in. Quiet location and clean rooms with unrivalled palace views from the veranda. Owners speak superb English. ③–⑤

Sagar Lallgarh Palace Campus ☎0151/252 0677, ⓦwww.sagarhotelbikaner.com. Attractive hotel with well-appointed rooms and several conveniences (TV, exchange, travel agency, credit card advances). Service can be spotty, and it's a little overpriced, but it's generally dependable. You'll need a mosquito net for the more economical Rajasthani cottages (Rs600) in rear garden. The adjoining budget hotel is loud and unpleasant. ④–⑥

Shri Ram Sadul Ganj, 1.5 km from city centre ☎0151/252 2651 or 252 1320, ⓦwww.hotelshriram.com. This suburban guesthouse is well-liked for its friendly owner, a retired camel battalion brigadier who's a wealth of local knowledge. Second-floor suite rooms are preferable to the cramped rooms out back. Free pick up from railway station and bus stand. ②–④

Expensive

Bhanwar Niwas In the old city ☎0151/220 1043 or 252 9323, ⓕ220 0880, ⓦwww.bhanwarniwas.com. The run-down exterior makes it easy to miss Bikaner's most ostentatious *haveli*, built for a textile tycoon in the late 1920s and now run as an independent heritage hotel. Crammed with original fittings and furniture, it's a Versailles-like kitsch piece, complete with Italian tiles and two vintage cars in the lobby. Rs350 for veggie meal in the *fin-de-siècle* restaurant. Rooms Rs3200. ⑨

Laxmi Niwas Palace Lallgarh Palace ☎0151/220 2777, ⓦwww.laxminiwaspalace.com. The better and more tranquil choice of two palatial hotels in the Lallgarh Palace complex boasts large rooms with period English furniture – the best is #108, which once hosted King George V, Queen Victoria and Queen Elizabeth. Rooms cost from $100, good value compared to other heritage hotels in the state and far quieter than *Bhanwar Niwas*. ⑨

The City

It's worth spending a day or two just wandering around Bikaner, watching dyers at work, visiting the ancient **Jain temples**, and exploring **Junagarh Fort**. Bikaner is famous for its skilled lacquer work and handicrafts, sold in the bazaar for a fraction of Jaisalmer's inflated "tourist prices", and for its hand-woven woollen shawls and blankets. The best place to buy the latter is the **Abhivyakti** handicrafts shop, established with the aid of funding from the local Urmul Trust and from Oxfam in England. There's a small outlet at the camel-breeding farm, but serious shoppers will want to visit the main store (☎0151/252 2139) on Ganganar Road, near the bus station. The store manager can arrange worthwhile visits to villages to see how the textiles are woven by the charity-supported women's co-ops. **Vichitra Arts**, at *Bhairon Vilas*, sells vintage royal garb and miniature paintings, including a stamp-sized pastoral picture featuring 1220 leaves, seventy flowers and fifty animals.

Junagarh Fort

Built on ground level, defended only by high walls and a wide moat, **Junagarh Fort** (daily 10am–4.30pm; Rs100, plus Rs50 for camera, Rs100 video) is not as immediately imposing as the mighty hill forts elsewhere in Rajasthan. But the decorative interiors and sculpted stone of the palaces, temples and 37 pavilions within its walls are almost unrivalled in their magnificence. Tourist police have largely driven away the "guides" offering their services outside the main guide, and any lingering touts should be ignored – a guided tour lasting about two hours is included in admission.

The fort was built between 1587 and 1593 during the rule of Rai Singh, and embellished by later rulers, who added their own palatial suites, temples and plush courtyards. Although never conquered, the bastion was attacked – handprints set in stone near the second gate, **Daulat Pole**, bear witness to the voluntary deaths of royal women, remembered as *satis*, whose menfolk had lost their lives in battle.

Opening onto the main courtyard, the **Karan Mahal**, with gold-leaf paintings adorning its pillars and walls, was built in the seventeenth century

Camel safaris from Bikaner

Although lacking Jaisalmer's edge-of-the-desert feel, **camel treks** in Bikaner can be just as rewarding. This eastern part of the desert, while just as scenic as the western Thar, is not nearly as congested with fellow trekkers, with the result that local people in the villages along the route don't wait around all day for the chance to sell Pepsi to tourists. Wildlife is also abundant, and during a three-day safari you can be pretty sure of spotting demoiselle cranes, blackbuck, *nilgai*, desert foxes, monitor lizards and the odd chameleon.

Since safaris are less established here your choices of **operator** are somewhat limited, but the same advice applies as that outlined in the "Camel safaris from Jaisalmer" box on p.232. Most hotels work with a single guide, who usually hails from one of the villages you'll visit. Currently offering the best all-round value safaris out of Bikaner is Vijay Singh Rathore (aka "Camel Man"), based at *Vijay Guest House*, 5km out of town along the Jaipur Road (ⓣ0151/223 1244, ⓦwww.camelman.com). His basic daily rate, which includes all meals, mattresses and travel to and from starting and finishing points, is Rs400. Another similarly affordable and dependable operator is Dilip Singh Rathore's Thar Camel Safari (contacted via the Meghsar castle or ⓣ0151/9351 206093). Both offer itineraries ranging from half-day trips and village visits to full-blown fourteen-day treks to Jaislamer, complete with camel carts for carrying luggage and mattresses. One operator to watch out for is Vino Desert Safari – several readers report getting fleeced by the ubiquitous Vino, a previously recommended guide who combs the main tourist attractions in search of clients who unsuspectingly fork over triple or more what the competition charges for the same service.

to commemorate a victory over the Moghul emperor Aurangzeb, while the dazzling **Phool Mahal** was erected by Gaj Singh a hundred years later. Stained-glass windows, finely carved stone and wood balconies, and brightly painted walls and ceilings around the fort demonstrate the extravagant tastes of these rulers. The **Anup Mahal** is the grandest construction, with wooden ceilings inlaid with mirrors, Italian tiles and delicate latticework on the windows and balconies. The huge carpet is one of many made by inmates of Bikaner jail, a manufacturing tradition that has only recently ceased. Upon request (or sometimes *baksheesh*), your guide will unlock the door of the **Chandra Mahal**, the most opulent room in the fort, filled with gilded deities and precious-stone encrusted paintings. The tour generally winds up in the stately **Ganga Singh Hall**. The most recent part of the fort, dating from 1937, it houses exhibits including the inevitable weaponry and an unexpected World War I aeroplane, still in tip-top condition.

Before leaving the fort, it's worth looking at the **Prachina Museum**, separate from the main museum and located close to the car park (daily 9am–6pm; Rs25, plus Rs20 for camera, Rs75 video). It houses plenty of memorabilia and crafts owned by the royal family, but the main attractions are the Raj-era silver and gold thread dresses, embroidered in *zardozi* style, displayed in the main hall.

The old city

As you enter Bikaner's labyrinthine **old city** through Kote Gate, the main entrance at the west end of MG Road (also called KEM Road), keep an eye out for women panning for flakes of precious metals dumped in the sewers by the many goldsmiths and artisans who have their workshops here. The main attractions, though, are a profusion of extraordinary **havelis** whose idiosyncratic architecture is an unlikely fusion of indigenous sandstone carving with turn-of-the-twentieth century red-brick municipal Britain. Adorned with busts of the British king and queen emperors, the most impressive specimens can be found in the heart of the old city, about twenty minute's walk from Kote Gate. Most of the big houses, including the famous Rampuriya Haveli, have been boarded up and left in a state of neglect by absentee merchant owners. But at **Bhanwar Niwas Haveli**, now a plush hotel, it's still possible to peer inside and marvel at the ostentatious wealth (see "Accommodation", p.240).

Continue south past the colourful Barra Bazaar, the old city's only sign of commerce, and you'll eventually reach Bikaner's two **Jain temples** (daily 5am–7pm). Built by two merchant brothers, both are remarkable for the sheer mass of colour and intricate wall paintings. The ground floor of **Bhandreshwar temple** (1571) has a cluster of pillars; some are decorated with gilded floral designs known as *usta*, typical of Muslim artisans, others with embossed male and female sculptures common in medieval India. Porcelain tiles imported from Victorian England decorate the main altar and contribute to the temple's 40,000kg weight. Steps lead up the tower, from where you get a great view over the old city. **Sandeshwar temple**, dedicated to Neminath (the 22nd *tirthankara*) and dated to 1536, houses rows of saints shaped from solid marble, and has enamel and gold-leaf paintings on the walls. The sixteenth-century **Laxminath temple** nearby was built by Lunkaran Singh, the third ruler of Bikaner, on the edge of the high city wall.

Lallgarh Palace and Ganga Golden Jubilee Museum

The sturdy red-sandstone **Lallgarh Palace** in the north of the town is home to the royal family of Bikaner, although parts now serve as a hotel. It was built during the reign of Ganga Singh, who lived there from 1902, and despite some detailed carving, its modern aspect makes it fairly mundane compared to other Rajasthani palaces. The **Shri Sadul Museum** (Mon–Sat 10am–5pm; Rs20) houses an enormous collection of old photographs showing various viceregal visits, pictures of Ganga Singh at the signing of the Versailles Treaty and royal processions that will fascinate Raj-ophiles. If you still have reserves left, the small **Ganga Golden Jubilee Museum** (daily except Fri 10am–4.30pm; Rs3), east of the centre on NH-8, offers much of the same, plus terracottas from the Gupta period (fourth and fifth centuries).

Eating

Most visitors eat at their hotels or guesthouses while in Bikaner, although there are a few good **restaurants** scattered around town. Locals line up all day long at *Bikaram Sweet Shop*, just off Station Road when you reach the railroad crossing, to try its deep-fried *firnis* and other cavity-causing delicacies.

Amber Station Rd. A cleaner than average (though dark) Indian place that's popular with Westerners. Full veg menu and refreshing masala chai.

Joshi Station Rd. The most salubrious of the eating places near the station. Filling, cheap rice-plate meals and arguably the town's best-value thalis (Rs60), served in a busy ground-floor restaurant (12.30–3pm & 7.30–10pm); also recommended for *paratha*-curd breakfasts, from 6am.

Moomal Tucked away on an alley behind Panch Shati circle, this white linen restaurant serves sumptuous South Indian veg food that's popular with well-heeled locals. The punchy cashew and cherry Moomal Special alone is worth the trip.

Around Bikaner

Several places of interest close to Bikaner can be visited in a day. Most tourists spending any more than a day do so to visit the **camel-breeding farm** and **Karni Mata temple**, a scurrying mass of sacred rats.

Moving on from Bikaner

RSTRC buses operate out of the main bus stand on the north side of town. **Private buses** leave from MG Road, just below the Fort. The dependable Chandra Travels, on Gajner Road near *Meghsar Castle*, provides daily deluxe buses to most destinations across the state. The inexplicably popular night bus to Jaisalmer is an exhausting, uncomfortable journey best done in daylight hours. **Trains** include three to Delhi (8.40am, 5.50pm & 7.50pm; 10hr 30min); the morning train arrives in Delhi at a reasonable hour and allows you a chance to sightsee en route. The 7.50pm train, the Bikaner Mail #4792, is a reasonable night journey and arrives in Delhi at 6am. Services to Jaipur include the fast 5am Intercity Express #2467 (7hr) and the slow overnight 8.15pm Bikaner–Jaipur Express #4738 (9hr 30min). The latter train also serves Churu, Fatehpur and Sikar. The best train to Jodhpur is the Kalka Express #4887, leaving around noon and taking less than six hours.

What claims to be Asia's largest **camel-breeding farm** (daily 2–5pm; Rs10, plus Rs20 for camera; guided tours Rs100) lies out in the desert 10km south of Bikaner, an easy round trip by rickshaw that should cost around Rs80 (including 30min waiting time). Although Bikaner has long been renowned for its famously sturdy beasts – the camel corps was a much-feared component of the imperial battle formation – growing proliferation of the internal combustion engine has severely reduced the "desert ship's" traditional role as a means of rural transport. Although its propagation programme still provides fifty percent of India's camels, researchers at the farm now devote more of their energies to studying the properties of camel milk – purportedly effective in staving off tuberculosis and diabetes – and alternative uses for camel hair. It's best to take a guided tour of the farm; aim to be here at 4pm, when you'll be wowed by the sight of 300 stampeding dromedaries arriving from the desert for their daily chow.

Although not for the faint of heart (or the sockless), the **Karni Mata temple** (daily 4am–10pm; free; plus Rs20 for camera, Rs50 video; Ⓦwww.karnimata.com) in **DESHNOK**, 30km south of Bikaner, is definitely one of India's more bizarre attractions. Step inside the Italian marble arched doorway and within seconds you'll be accosted by teeming hordes of free-roaming holy rodents, known as *kabas*, who devotees believe are reincarnated souls saved from the wrath of Yama, the god of death. For newlyweds, the sick and other pilgrims, it's customary to eat *prasad* (blessed food from the main shrine) after it has been nibbled by the *kabas* and many spend hours hunting on their hands and knees for a glimpse of the auspicious white rat. It's also considered a blessing for a rat to run over your feet, but whatever you do don't step on one, or you'll have to donate a gold model of a rat to placate the deity.

Made of rough stone and logs cut from sacred *jal* trees, the rustic innermost shrine houses the yellow-marble image (*pratima*) of the folk hero turned goddess Karniji (see box on p.244), which in turn is encased by a much grander marble building erected by Rao Bika's grandson after he defeated the Moghuls. Directly in front of the temple, the easily overlooked **Shri Karni Sixth Centenary Auditorium** contains a worthwhile collection of oil paintings which recount the major events in Karniji's divine sojourn, with English captions. A few kilometres away on the edge of town, the rarely visited **Nahrij Temple**, although lacking in rodents, has encased in marble the tree where Karniji in her last years came to make butter and await nirvana.

Buses from Bikaner leave every fifteen minutes for Deshnok from the southwest exit at the large roundabout near the PB Memorial Hospital, or at Goga Gate Circle, just outside the southeast corner of the old city.

The Deshnok Devi

Regarded by Hindus as one of India's most potent *shakti* shrines, the **Karni Mata temple** at Deshnok is unusual for being dedicated not to a conventional Puranic deity, but to a historical figure. **Karniji** was a female bard – a *charani* – born into a wealthy landowning family at a village near Phalodi in 1387. Members of the *charan* caste believe that incarnations of the goddess Durga periodically appear among them, sometimes as *sagats*, who are blessed with healing powers, and less commonly as more powerful *purn avatars*, who are said to emerge only in times of crisis. From birth, Karni exhibited many of the traits associated with this latter incarnation of the *devi*, and she went on to perform such miracles as water divination and bringing the dead back to life, eventually becoming the region's most powerful cult leader, worshipped primarily by the Jats and low-caste farmers.

The rise in Karniji's popularity, dating from her family's move north to Deshnok, mirrored that of the Rathore clan, whose constant raids were causing great instability in the region at the end of the fourteenth century. **Rao Bika**, the founder of Bikaner, realized that he and Karniji could forge a formidable alliance, and wooed her with promises of tax exemptions and tutelary deity status if she gave his clan her stamp of approval. When her eventual endorsement came it turned Bika's fortunes, quadrupling the size of his army. After he finally defeated the local warlords, Karniji was accorded the honour of laying the foundation stone of Junagarh fort, and Bika regularly consulted her throughout his reign – a connection with the ruling family that has endured to this day. The Bikaner flag sports Karniji's colours, and she is the patron goddess of the Bikaner camel corps, who still march into battle crying "Shree Karniji!".

Mount Abu

As Rajasthan's only bona fide hill station, **MOUNT ABU** (1220m), sprawling over the sides of a wooded basin, is a major resort, popular above all with honeymooners who flock here during the winter wedding season. Although the main strip's hokey commercialism appeals more to the Indian middle-class holidayers than foreign tourists, the fresh air is exhilarating. One attraction that draws foreigners and Indians alike are the **Jain Temples** at **Dilwara**. Hidden in thick woodland north of the town, the temples are decorated with what is thought to be the most intricate marble carving in the world. Anyone happy to rock hop and follow unmarked trails will also find plenty of scope for **hikes** and scrambles amid the granite boulders and wooded ridges high above the town, where dozens of tiny caves, connected by a tangle of dirt paths, shelter a transient community of semi-nomadic, *chillum*-smoking *sadhus* – a reminder of the area's great religious importance.

According to Hindu mythology, the focal point of Mount Abu, **Nakki Lake**, was formed when the gods scratched away at the mountain with their fingernails (*nakh*). These days, the waterside is cluttered by far more pedalos and ice cream parlours than pilgrims, but the temple marking the site of the famous *yagna agnikund* – a powerful fire ceremony conducted in the eighth century AD, which Rajasthan's ruling caste, the "twice-born" Rajputs, trace their mythological origins back to – at Gaumukh, 7km south of Mount Abu, still sees streams of devotees. In addition, around Mount Abu itself you'll come across many white-clad **Brahma Kumaris**, members of an international spiritual movement whose headquarters are situated in a quiet valley behind the lake.

In order to get the most benefit from Mount Abu's scenery and climate, it's essential to **time your visit** carefully. During the peak months of April–June,

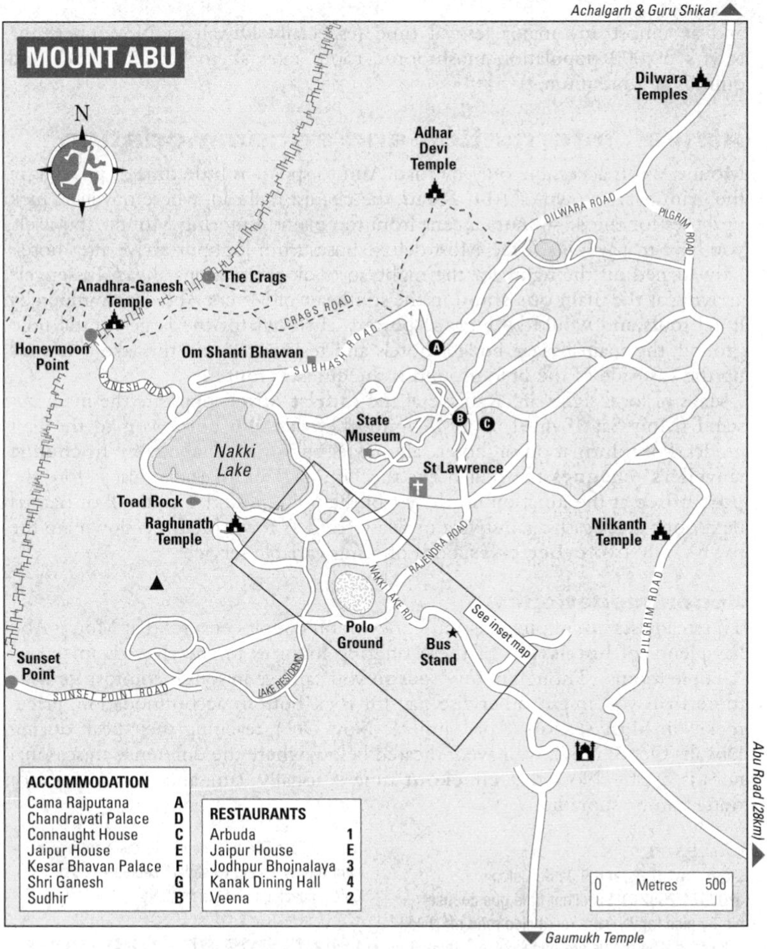

MOUNT ABU
N
Achalgarh & Guru Shikar
Dilwara Temples
Adhar Devi Temple
DILWARA ROAD
PILGRIM ROAD
The Crags
Anadhra-Ganesh Temple
CRAGS ROAD
Honeymoon Point
Om Shanti Bhawan
SUBHASH ROAD
GANESH ROAD
A
B
C
State Museum
Nakki Lake
St Lawrence
Toad Rock
Raghunath Temple
Nilkanth Temple
RAJENDRA ROAD
NAKKI LAKE RD
Polo Ground
Bus Stand
See inset map
PILGRIM ROAD
Sunset Point
SUNSET POINT ROAD
LAKE RESIDENCY
Abu Road (28km)
Gaumukh Temple
0 Metres 500

ACCOMMODATION

Cama Rajputana	A
Chandravati Palace	D
Connaught House	C
Jaipur House	E
Kesar Bhavan Palace	F
Shri Ganesh	G
Sudhir	B

RESTAURANTS

Arbuda	1
Jaipur House	E
Jodhpur Bhojnalaya	3
Kanak Dining Hall	4
Veena	2

@ Bank
GPO
Bank
MARKET
RAJENDRA ROAD
D
1
NAKKI LAKE RD
NAKKI LAKE RD
Bank
Railway Reservation Office
NAKKI LAKE RD
Boats
Private Buses
Pony Hire
Polo Ground
2
3
Taxis & Dilwara Jeeps
i
Abu Road Jeeps
4
Bus Stand
Brahma Kumaris Museum
N
E
F
G
0 100m
AROUND NAKKI LAKE ROAD

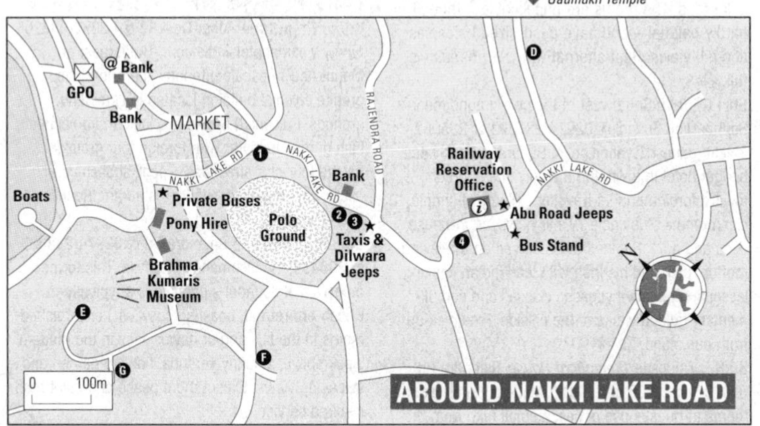

and at almost any major festival time (especially Diwali in November) the town's 30,000 population mushrooms, room rates skyrocket and peace and quiet is at a premium.

Arrival, information and accommodation

Mount Abu is accessible only by road. Aim to spend as little time as possible in the grim bazaar town of **Abu Road**, the nearest railhead, where travellers pick up buses for the 45-minute ascent from the plains. Entering Mount Abu itself, you have to pay a Rs10 fee. Most deluxe buses from Jodhpur arrive after hotels have turned off the lights for the night, so book reservations ahead. Passengers arriving at the main **bus stand** in the southeast of Mount Abu are swamped by hotel touts and would-be luggage porters. Turn left for the large central polo ground, the main bazaar, budget hotels and restaurants, and the lake (the road up the east side of the polo ground is the quickest route).

Maps of local sights are available at the **tourist office**, opposite the main bus stand (Mon–Sat 10am–1pm & 2–5pm); they can also direct you to the best guides. For information on hotels, also try Ⓦwww.mountsabu.com. To **change travellers' cheques** the best bet is the Union Bank of India, just before the **post office** at the junction northwest of the polo ground. The Bank of Baroda next door gives cash against Visa or Mastercard. A few storefronts down are the town's only two **cyber cafés**, both offering variable service.

Accommodation

The steady stream of pilgrims and honeymoon couples ensures that Mount Abu has plenty of **hotels**, lots of them offering luxuries for newlyweds in special "couple rooms". Though in **low season** you can live in stylish comfort for little more than you might otherwise pay for rock-bottom accommodation, prices rocket in **high season** (April–June & Nov–Dec), reaching their peak during Diwali (Oct & Nov). We have indicated below where the difference in seasonal rates is drastic. Note that **checkout** time is usually 9am, and the flow of hot water can be sporadic.

Budget

Chandravati Palace 9 Janta Colony Ⓣ02974/238219. Excellent little guesthouse run by nice family, on a quiet side road off Nakki Lake road. The rooms are impeccable – though hardly palatial – and have good-sized balconies and hill views. Best alternative if *Shri Ganesh* is full. ❷

Shri Ganesh Southwest of the polo ground, near Sophia High School Ⓣ02974/237292 or 235062, Ⓔlalit_ganesh@yahoo.co.in. By far the best-value budget hotel in town and the only one geared toward foreign budget travellers. Plenty of simple, clean rooms plus cable TV, hill views, an in-house shop and home-cooked thalis served on a relaxing rooftop. Lalit and his Irish wife lead Indian cooking lessons, meditative yogasan classes and complimentary guided walks of the hillside. Free pick up from bus stand. ❶–❸

Sudhir Opposite *Connaught House*, Rajendra Rd Ⓣ02974/235120 or 235311. Modern, hotel-like rooms at guesthouse prices, a small hike from the main bazaar. The best deals are the eight upper-floor rooms, facing west with separate balconies. Clean, spacious and efficient. ❸

Mid-range and expensive

Cama Rajputana Adhar Devi Rd Ⓣ02974/238205, Ⓦwww.camahotelsindia.com. The largest of Mount Abu's upscale offerings is a refurbished granite colonial building located in sprawling grounds. Balconied rooms overlook an immaculate, lush garden. Popular with foreign tour groups for the four-star amenities – pool, squash court, health club and high-quality restaurant. Rooms $60–200. ❾

Connaught House Rajendra Rd Ⓣ02974/238560 or 235439, Ⓔbalsamand_1@sify.in. This former maharaja of Jodhpur's bolthole is a typically British-era retreat, boasting cosy, wicker-furnished rooms in the building or newer ones in the modern block above, a sunny veranda, flowery garden and sweeping views. Expect more peace and quiet than inspired service. ❽

Jaipur House South of the lake ⓣ02974/235176, ⓕ235002, ⓦwww.royalfamilyjaipur.com. Refurbished princely summer palace owned by the Maharaja of Jaipur. Tastefully decorated suites with wood furnishings and high ceilings. New junior suites below the garden are larger, but lack the sweeping views of the Royal Suite (Rs40,000) and adjacent rooms. Non-guests should try the moderately priced restaurant for the best views in town. From Rs2800. ❽–❾

Kesar Bhavan Palace Sunset Rd ⓣ02974/238647, ⓕ238551, ⓦwww.mountsabu.com. Overpriced for average service, but the sun-soaked rooms are spacious and well furnished, if a bit musty. Large individual sit outs have green views over the tree tops. Avoid the overpriced rooms in the stable annexe. ❼–❽

The Town and around

Mount Abu has a significant number of religious sites, but all are some way out of town. Nearer the centre, **Nakki Lake** is where everyone converges in the late afternoon for pony and pedalo rides. Of several panoramic viewpoints on the fringes of town above the plains, **Sunset Point** is the favourite – though with its hordes of holiday-makers, peanut sellers, camel drivers, cart pushers and horse owners, it has to be the noisiest and least romantic place imaginable to watch the sunset. **Honeymoon Point**, also known as Ganesh Point (after the adjacent temple), and **Anadhra Point** offer breathtaking views over the plain at any time of day, and tend to be more peaceful; 4pm is a good time to be there.

Dotted around the plateau outside town are several Hindu shrines and the spectacular Jain **Dilwara temples**. Forget the rushed tours touted by the tourist office and make your own way up there, allowing a good one or two hours to pick your way through the extraordinary wealth of intricate carving.

Hiking in Mount Abu

The views over the plains from the hilltops around Mount Abu town are a revelation. Down in the market area, you gain little sense of the wonderfully wild **landscape** enfolding the town, but head for a few minutes up one of the many trails threading through the rocks and undergrowth around the sides of the plateau, and it is easy to see why the area has inspired sages, saints and pilgrims for centuries.

In recent decades, the forest has been decimated by woodcutters, but a recently imposed, and strictly enforced, ban on wood gathering seems to be heralding a recovery. Abu's other **environmental menace** is the lantana plant, an introduced flower that has squeezed out many of the eighteen highly prized medicinal herbs listed as growing here in ancient Hindu scriptures. Also under pressure are the fragile populations of bear and leopard. Sightings of both, however, are still not uncommon and you should take great care while trekking not to disturb any encountered along the trails. **Bears**, in particular, can be dangerous if surprised, or when with young. In 1997, two unwary French tourists were mauled during an evening scramble around the rocks above Nakki Lake.

Unfortunately **hiking alone** is no longer recommended and tourist police will turn back anyone spotted heading out on their own. The cause for alarm is well founded. The same, extended drought that has pushed emaciated bears towards the city has also denied peasant farmers of their traditional livelihood. With their forced entry into the cash economy a few unscrupulous characters have taken to highway robbery. In 2002 a group of foreign tourists were seriously injured after being barraged by stone-throwing bandits. As a result, more remote locations are considered off limits even by locals. However, closer sights can be visited safely with Lalit Kanojia at the *Shri Ganesh Hotel*, a nature enthusiast and keen trekker. He charges a one-time payment of Rs20 per person.

Dilwara temples

Jains consider temple building to be an act of devotion, and without fail their houses of worship are lovingly adorned and embellished, but even by Jain standards, the **Dilwara temples**, 3km northeast of Mount Abu (daily noon–6pm; free; no leather, cameras, transistors, tape recorders, or menstruating women), are some of the most beautiful in India. All five are made purely from marble, and the carving, especially in the two main structures, is breathtakingly intricate, unparalleled in its lightness and delicacy. For sheer aesthetic splendour, only the temples at Ranakpur 200km northwest (see p.263) come close.

The oldest temple, **Vimala Vasahi**, named after the Gujarati minister who funded its construction in 1031, is dedicated to Adinath, the first *tirthankara*, whose image sits cross-legged in the central sanctuary guarded by tall statues of Parshvanath (the 23rd *tirthankara*). Although the exterior is simple, inside not one wall, column or ceiling is unadorned; the work, carried out by almost 2000 labourers and sculptors, took fourteen years to complete. Eight of the forty-eight pillars in the front hall form an octagon that supports a domed ceiling arranged in eleven concentric circles, alive with dancers, musicians, elephants and horses.

The later **Neminath temple** (1231 AD) imitates the one dedicated to Adinath, but its carvings are yet more precise and detailed. The large dome over the entrance hall is unprecedented. Friezes etched into the walls depict cosmological themes, stories of the *jinas* (saints) and grand processions. Sculptures near the entrance porch commemorate the temple's patrons, the two brothers Vastupala and Tejapala. Said in legend to have discovered a huge treasure, they were advised by their wives – also portrayed here – to build temples, and funded many on the holy hill of Shatrunjaya in Gujarat.

The remaining three fifteenth-century temples are less spectacular. The **Adinath temple** – not to be confused with Vimala Vasahi – which houses a four-and-a-half-ton brass image of the *tirthankara*, has some fine carving,

Brahma Kumaris

The spiritual sect **Brahma Kumaris** ("children of Brahma") preach that all religions reach for the same goal, but label it differently. Based at about 5000 centres around the world they teach *raja* yoga – meditation that directs people to knowledge of an inner light, the "divine spark" or soul, that is part of, and one with, the all-encompassing soul, Shiva. Belief in the five evils – anger, ego, attachment, greed and lust – is shared with Buddhism and Hinduism, with the ultimate goal being their elimination, and the advent of a **Golden Age** of peace, prosperity and purity.

The **Brahma Kumaris Spiritual University** at **Om Shanti Bhawan** to the north of Nakki Lake (☎02974/238268) aims to foster awareness, tolerance, love and "God-consciousness" in a meditative atmosphere where smoking, alcohol, meat and sex are avoided. Classes range from three-day *raja* yoga camps to advanced six-month courses; lectures are translated into eighteen languages. The **Brahma Kumaris Museum** by the private bus stand between the polo ground and the lake (daily 8am–noon & 4–8pm; free) holds daily meditation classes. If you can endure the aggressive book-pushing by the curmudgeonly caretaker, the museum makes a worthwhile detour. Once through the "Gateway to Paradise," you'll be greeted by freakish, life-size mannequins including blue monsters wielding long knives. Each personifies greed, sex-lust and other vestiges of the so-called "iron age" that temple leaders promise deliverance from. If it all sounds somewhat cultish you'll understand why many locals try to keep foreigners from entering into the sect's clutches.

much of it unfinished; the one consecrated to Parshvanath has ornate ceilings and *jinas* etched into the outer walls, and is topped by a high grey stone tower.

To **get to Dilwara**, you can charter a Jeep (Rs40), or take a place in a shared one (Rs4), from the main junction at the southeastern end of Mount Abu's polo ground. The hour-long walk up there is also pleasant, though many prefer to save their energies for the downhill walk back into town. *Shri Ganesh* will allow non-guests to join their Jeep tours, space permitting.

Hindu temples

Beyond the Brahma Kumaris University, about 3km northeast of town, a flight of more than four hundred steps climbs up to **Adhar Devi temple** (dedicated to Durga), cut into the rocky hilltop. The milk-coloured water of the **Doodh Baori** well at the foot of the steps is considered to be a source of pure milk (*doodh*) for gods and sages.

A further 8km northeast, the temple complex at **ACHALGARH** is dominated by the **Achaleshwar Mahadeo temple**, believed to have been created when Lord Shiva placed his toe on the spot to still an earthquake. Its sanctuary holds neither an image of Shiva nor a *lingam*, only a *yoni* with a hole in it said to reach into the netherworld, watched over by figures of Parvati and Ganesh on the walls. Statues of Parvati flank the entrance, faced by an unusually large metal Nandi bull. Subsidiary shrines include one dedicated to Vishnu, in which detailed plaques depict the familiar reclining Vishnu and his nine incarnations. The large tank lined with stone buffaloes outside the temple, intended to contain purifying water, is the legendary scene of the slaying of demons disguised as buffaloes who stole purifying ghee from the tank. Nearby, the **Jamadagni Ashram** is site of the **Agnikund**, where the sage Vashishtha presided over the fire ritual that produced the four Rajput clans (the Parmars, Parihars, Solankis and Chauhans).

The lesser visited, but more dramatically situated, **Gaumukh temple** lies 7km south of the market area. Reached via a steep flight of 750 steps, the small pool inside the shrine – flowing even during drought times – is believed to hold water from the sacred Sarawati Ganga River. Pilgrims come here to perform *gauda* puja, to invoke the blessings of India's two greatest *rishis* (sages), Vashishtha and Vishwamitra, who are thought to have meditated and conducted a famous metaphysical debate on the spot.

The last important Hindu pilgrimage site on Mount Abu is the Atri Rishi temple at **Guru Shikar**, 15km northeast of town, which at 1772m above sea level marks the highest point in Rajasthan. Depending on how energetic you're feeling, you can enjoy superb panoramic vistas either from the temple itself, or from the drinks stall at the bottom of the steps that lead up to it.

Eating and drinking

Mount Abu's predominantly middle-class Gujarati visitors are typically hard to please when it comes to food, so standards are exceptionally high and prices low in the numerous **restaurants** dotted along Nakki Road. Competition is stiffest between the squeaky-clean pure-veg Gujarati thali joints, most of which have indoor seating, but you can eat top-notch South Indian snacks and spicy rice-plate meals alfresco at the terrace cafés between the bazaar and the lake, and there are plenty of busy ice cream stalls towards the waterfront. The classier hotels serve **alcohol**, also available at the wine and beer shops opposite the *Veena* at the bottom of town.

Moving on from Mount Abu

By train

For train travellers, there's a **computerized booking office** (Mon–Sat 8am–noon & 1–2pm, Sun 8am–noon) upstairs at the tourist office. Buses leave Mount Abu for **Abu Road**, the nearest railhead, every hour until 9pm; Jeeps leave when full (from opposite the bus stand), and taxis are available on request (from the junction at the southeastern corner of the polo ground; Rs250 for a full car).

The most convenient train service to **Ahmedabad** is the daily Delhi–Ahmedabad Mail #9106, which passes through at 1.10pm and arrives 4hr 20min later. In the other direction, of the three trains to **Delhi**, by far the fastest is the Ashram Express #2915, which leaves Abu Road at 9.20pm and arrives in New Delhi at 9.40am the following morning. For **Ajmer** (6hr) and **Jaipur** (9hr), take the Aravali Express #9007 which departs at 10.30am; for **Jodhpur** the Jammu Tawi #9111 (departs 3.25pm, arrives 8.15pm); and for **Mumbai** the Aravali Express #9008 (departs 5.20pm; 13–14hr) or the Ranakpur Express #4707 (departs 8.30pm; 13–14hr).

By bus

Government **buses** run services from the state bus stand, about 200m southeast of the polo ground on the main road. Most buses to Ahmedabad go via Palampur (3hr, change for Bhuj) and Mehsana (4hr). Other destinations include Udaipur, Jaipur via Ajmer (10hr) and Chittaurgarh (2 daily; 10hr), with morning departures to Delhi, Jodhpur, and Jaisalmer via Barmer (8hr).

Mount Abu's **private buses** run to Ahmedabad (3 daily; 6hr), Udaipur (2 daily; 4hr 30min), Jaipur (1 nightly; 11hr 30min), Ajmer (1 nightly; 9hr 30min), and Jodhpur (1 daily; 9hr 30min). For timings and information, go to Gujarat Travels in the main bazaar, just along from the state bus stand, or *Shrl Ganesh* guesthouse.

You can a;sp get to **Palampur**, in Gujarat, by crowded shared **Jeeps** (Rs25; 1hr).

Arbuda Arbuda Circle. A huge veggie menu ranging from continental to Gujarati make this a busy lunch spot. Lightning-fast, friendly service and a popular, airy terrace. The fresh juices are a must.

Jodhpur Bhojnalaya Near the taxi stand. The only place in town where you can eat authentic Rajasthani food, very heavy on *ghee* and spices. It's famous for its definitive *dal batti*, which comes with full veg thali and *churma* (crumbly, sweet wheat-flour balls flavoured with cardamom) for Rs40. Highly recommended.

Kanak Dining Hall Near the bus stand. Friendly place offering arguably the best Gujarati thalis in town; at Rs45 per head, also one of the least expensive options. Come hungry – portions are literally limitless.

Veena Nakki Lake Rd. Open-air seating next to the main road. Quintessentially tacky Mount Abu (bright lights and the latest *filmi* hits blaring out), but the fast food is second to none, and they have a welcome open fire on the terrace most evenings. Try their tangy *pao bhaji* or melt-in-the-mouth paper *dosas*.

Udaipur

The valley of Oodipur, the most diversified and most romantic spot on the continent of India

Col. James Tod, *Annals and Antiquities of Rajasthan* (1829)

It's hard to reconcile most people's first view of **UDAIPUR** with James Tod's assessment. Its famed **Pichola Lake**, from which the city derives its centuries-old reputation as Rajasthan's most romantic city, has been for several years now a trash-strewn, mosquito-infested puddle of what it once was. Rajasthan's always temperamental monsoon is only partly to blame; other factors include

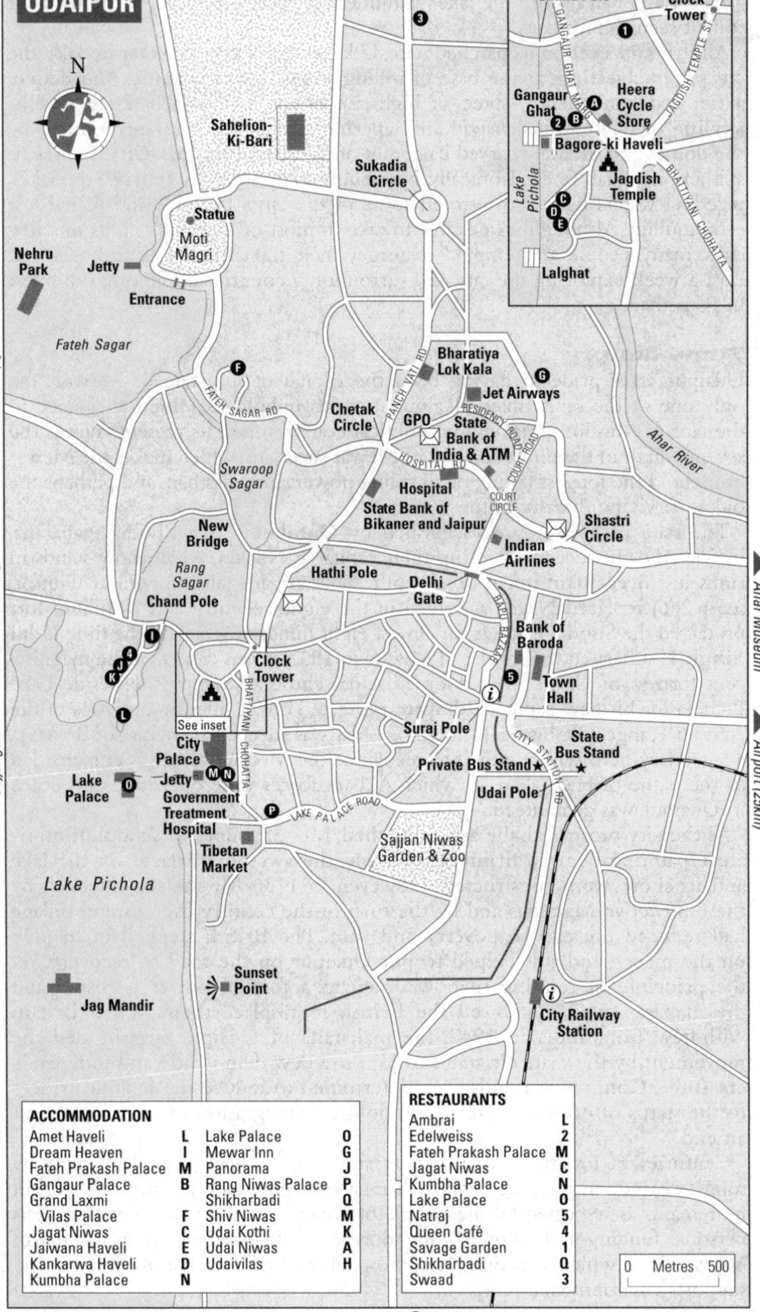
Eklingji & Mount Abu
UDAIPUR
N
Sahelion-Ki-Bari
Sukadia Circle
Statue
Moti Magri
Nehru Park
Jetty
Entrance
Fateh Sagar
Shilpgram
FATEH SAGAR RD
PANCH VATI RD
Bharatiya Lok Kala
Jet Airways
Chetak Circle
GPO
State Bank of India & ATM
RESIDENCY ROAD
COURT ROAD
HOSPITAL RD
Hospital
State Bank of Bikaner and Jaipur
COURT CIRCLE
Swaroop Sagar
New Bridge
Shastri Circle
Indian Airlines
Ahar River
Rang Sagar
Chand Pole
Hathi Pole
Delhi Gate
BAPU BAZAAR
Bank of Baroda
Town Hall
Clock Tower
BHATTIYANI CHOHATTA
See inset
Suraj Pole
CITY STATION RD
State Bus Stand
Private Bus Stand
Udai Pole
City Palace
Jetty
Lake Palace
Government Treatment Hospital
LAKE PALACE ROAD
Sajjan Niwas Garden & Zoo
Tibetan Market
Lake Pichola
Sunset Point
Jag Mandir
City Railway Station
Sajjangarh "Monsoon Palace"
Ahar Museum
Airport (25km)
Q & Ahmedabad
Chand Pole
Clock Tower
GANGAUR GHAT MARG
JAGDISH TEMPLE ST
Gangaur Ghat
Heera Cycle Store
Bagore-ki Haveli
Jagdish Temple
BHATTIYANI CHOHATTA
Lake Pichola
Lalghat
ACCOMMODATION
Amet Haveli L
Dream Heaven I
Fateh Prakash Palace M
Gangaur Palace B
Grand Laxmi Vilas Palace F
Jagat Niwas C
Jaiwana Haveli E
Kankarwa Haveli D
Kumbha Palace N
Lake Palace O
Mewar Inn G
Panorama J
Rang Niwas Palace P
Shikharbadi Q
Shiv Niwas M
Udai Kothi K
Udai Niwas A
Udaivilas H
RESTAURANTS
Ambrai L
Edelweiss 2
Fateh Prakash Palace M
Jagat Niwas C
Kumbha Palace N
Lake Palace O
Natraj 5
Queen Café 4
Savage Garden 1
Shikharbadi Q
Swaad 3
0 Metres 500

Udaipur's swelling population of 800,000. Officials hope that construction of a new canal will restore the lake's shimmering waters and with it the hard-hit tourist sector's prospects.

All that said, even in its parched state, Udaipur still shines. Lake or no lake, the city's scenic **setting**, at the base of rolling scrub hills, is majestic. And despite a frenzied construction spree of high-rise hotels and terrace restaurants, its **skyline** of whitewashed *havelis* and tapering temple *shikharas*, surmounted by the domes and ornately carved balconies of the famous Rajput **City Palace**, is still among Asia's finest. Ironically, by turning away so many tourists, the lake's receding waters have also restored some of the city's famed – and feared lost – tranquillity. Although it's possible to take in most of Udaipur's sights in a few days, many people are tempted to forget their tight itineraries and spend at least a week exploring the city and surrounding countryside, among the finest in Rajasthan.

Some history

Udaipur takes pride in having been the capital of the state of **Mewar**, the only one of the seven major Rajput states to uphold its Hindu allegiance in the face of Muslim invasions and political compromises. Its present ruler is the seventy-sixth in the unbroken line of Mewar suzerains, which makes the Mewar household the longest lasting of all ruling powers in Rajasthan, and perhaps the oldest surviving dynasty in the world.

The state of Mewar was established by **Guhil**, the first Sisodia maharana, in 568 AD. His successors set up their capital at **Nagda**, which now stands in ruins just over 30km north of Udaipur. Chittaurgarh (also known as Chittor; see p.266) replaced Nagda as capital in the eighth century, and its hilltop fort protected the Sisodia Rajputs for almost eight hundred years. By the time **Udai Singh II** inherited the throne of Mewar in 1537, it was clear that the magnificent fortress of Chittor was doomed. Udai chose a swampy site beside Lake Pichola for his new capital, **Udaipur**, protected on all sides by outcrops of the Aravalli Range. On his death in 1572 Udai was succeeded by his son **Pratap**, a legendary hero whose refusal to recognize the Moghul Akbar as emperor led to the battle of Haldighati, in which Akbar's forces were outwitted and peace in Udaipur was guaranteed.

As the city prospered, the arts flourished; Mewar's superior school of miniature painting became firmly rooted and the awesome palaces on the lake and its shore were constructed. However, in 1736 Mewar was attacked by the destructive Marathas and by the turn of the century the ensuing pillage had reduced the city to poverty and ruin. The British stepped in to pick up the pieces, and this helped to put Udaipur on the road to recovery. Yet the principle of refusing to bow down to a foreign power persisted and the maharanas never allowed the British to displace them. When Britain withdrew from India in 1947, the maharana of Udaipur spearheaded the movement by the princely states to join the new democratic and independent India. Congress was, however, determined to reduce the Rajput princes to the status of normal citizens, and political recognition of royalty came to an end.

Centuries of loyalty between rulers and subjects have been kept alive by songs, stories and paintings; the maharana may now lack political power, but he remains as respected by the people of Udaipur as were his forefathers. His personal funding and income from tourism are invested in the Maharana of Mewar Trust, which subsidizes local hospitals and educational institutions, and supports environmental projects.

△ Tiled doorway, Udaipur

Arrival, information and city transport

Daily flights connect **Dabok Airport** (☎0294/265 5453), 25km east of Udaipur, with Mumbai, Delhi, Jaipur and Jodhpur. Taxis run to the city itself for around Rs200. **Trains** from Delhi and Ahmedabad pull in at **Udaipur City Station** a little to the south of the town centre (don't get off at Udaipur Station, much further north). The **bus stand** is a few hundred metres north of here, directly opposite **Udai Pole**, the easternmost gate of the old city. The easiest way to get into town from either is to jump in a rickshaw or tempo.

The town's grand but largely ineffectual **tourist office** (Mon–Sat 10am–5pm; ☎0294/241 1535) is situated well away from the main tourist sights, on the east side of the city in the Fateh Memorial building at Suraj Pole, but there are also branch offices next to Bagore-ki-Haveli (10am–5pm Mon–Sat), the airport, and railway station. A number of free **publications** available at hotels list valuable tourist information and events calendars.

City transport and tours

Auto-rickshaws and **taxis** are the usual means of transport. Rickshaw prices are relatively high and it's worth renting a **bicycle** as traffic in Udaipur is terrible: try Heera Cycle Store, 86 Gangaur Ghat Marg, whose rates are the lowest at Rs25 per day. The same firm also has a fleet of well-maintained Scooty 60cc mopeds (Rs150/day) and a couple of 150cc Vespa-style motorcycles (Rs300/day) – ideal for trips outside the city. Wear a helmet!

RTDC, based at the tourist office, offers car rental and **tours** around the city (daily 8am–1pm; Rs78 plus museum entrance fees); to Haldighati, Nathdwara and Eklingji (daily 2–7pm; Rs110); to Ranakpur and Kumbalgarh (Rs350); and to Chittaurgarh (Rs350). In addition, some of Udaipur's **travel agencies** – mostly located around Lalghat, Lake Palace Road and Chetak Circle (a selection is listed on p.262) offer city tours (Rs40–50), airport transfer (Rs200), private car rental, and booking services for trains and buses. All offer "fixed rates" to most destinations around the city, listed on handouts, but you can nearly always negotiate a reduction on these. Count on around Rs1000 for a full-day or long-haul trip.

Accommodation

Sandwiched between the City Palace and Jagdish temple on the **east side of Lake Pichola**, countless guesthouses vie with elegant *havelis* and royal palaces for views of the water. Cut-throat competition has meant perennially low tariffs for punters in most categories, but it has also sparked off a destructive building boom as hoteliers scramble to attract custom with better views from ever loftier tower blocks; the result is a mass of hideous concrete that threatens to engulf the very skyline tourists flock here to see. The 1999 High Court ruling that no further building should take place in the area seems to have had little effect. The only sure way of slowing down the degradation is for tourists to boycott the offending hotels.

Dotted along the busy main road running due east (inland) from the foot of the City Palace, **Lake Palace Road**'s hotels have larger rooms and gardens but lack the views. Those on the **northern side of Lake Pichola**, by contrast, occupy prime spots with optimum views of the palace complex. Note that most of the cheaper hotels in Udaipur have 10am **checkout**.

Jagdish temple area/ east side of Lake Pichola

Fateh Prakash Palace City Palace ⓣ0294/252 8016, ⓦwww.hrhindia.com. Seven royal suites and nine "deluxe" rooms, crammed with miniature paintings and traditional furniture, on the lake-facing side of the City Palace, all with spellbinding views. Green carpet and period decor of the chandeliered Durbar Hall could use a refresher, and generally rooms are dark. Guests can use facilities (including pool) at sister-hotel *Shiv Niwas*. Rooms start at $200. ❾

Gangaur Palace 3 Gangaur Ghat Marg ⓣ0294/242 2303. A popular budget hotel in this densely developed tourist enclave, in spite of its insensitive rooftop expansion. Prices are overly ambitious, but you can negotiate down to Rs150 for shared bath. Ochre-washed rooms – 4 with original, 250-year-old frescoes – in traditional *haveli*, some lake facing. ❶–❸

Jagat Niwas 23–25 Lalghat ⓣ0294/242 2860, ⓦwww.indianheritagehotels.com. Beautifully restored seventeenth-century *haveli* right on the lakeside, entered down a narrow alley. A feast for the eyes, with shady courtyards, rooftop and well-regarded restaurant, but not as peaceful or as good value as the *Kankarwa* next door. Popular with groups. ❻–❽

Jaiwana Haveli 14 Lalghat ⓣ0294/241 1103, ⓔhjaiwanahaveli@yahoo.com. The affordable standard rooms (from Rs300) lack only the views of their upper-floor counterparts. Both, however, are spotless and have double linen on comfy beds. Rooftop restaurant and Internet. Excellent choice. ❷–❻

Kankarwa Haveli 26 Lalghat ⓣ0294/241 1457, ⓔkhaveli@yahoo.com. Romantically restored *haveli* slap on the waterfront. Incredible value for colourful, antiquey rooms that look straight out of an interior design magazine. Less expensive rooms start at Rs450 and only lack the views. Superb rooftop veg restaurant. Internet. ❸–❻

Lake Palace Lake Pichola ⓣ0294/252 8800, ⓦwww.lake-palace-udaipur.com or www.tajhotels.com. *Lake Palace's* romantic reputation is decidedly injured by the continuing drought – instead of being escorted by gondola from the City Palace you can now just walk across the dry lakebed. But for jet-setting tourists nostalgic for the 1970s, the Octopussy-era white-themed decor is still a draw. Prices, $475-$2000 per room, seem excessive, but you may be able to get discounts and freebies due to the low lake levels. Mere mortals are welcome to join guests for a Rs900 cocktail on the terrace or a Rs1500 buffet dinner. ❾

Shiv Niwas City Palace ⓣ0294/252 8016 or 7, ⓕ252 8016, ⓦwww.hrhindia.com. Former guesthouse of Marwar royal family, and now the luminous flagship of Maharaja Arvind Singh Marwar's HRH hotel chain. Opulently furnished rooms and even more luxurious "historic suites", overlooking the lake or city, and a dreamy pool in the courtyard (open to non-residents for Rs300). Count on at least $350 for a lakeview room. Ask for a peek at the "Imperial Suite". ❾

Udai Niwas Gangaur Ghat Marg ⓣ0294/512 0789, ⓦwww.hoteludainiwas.com. Spanking new high-rise hotel with accommodating staff and all mod cons – TV, money exchange and cyber café. Rooms start at Rs200. The three-tier rooftop restaurant is the highest in town, with sweeping views. ❷–❺

Along Lake Palace Road

Kumbha Palace 104 Bhatiyani Chohatta ⓣ0294/242 2702. Friendly, Dutch-owned hotel, hidden under the east walls of City Palace. Large rooms with attached bath for Rs150, with views and access to bougainvillea-strewn garden. Rooms are basic, but generally quieter than other budget places. ❶–❷

Rang Niwas Palace Lake Palace Rd ⓣ0294/252 3890, ⓦwww.rangniwaspalace.com. Again, an unpromising, view-less location next to the main road, but inside is a palatial old building with attractively furnished rooms and suites. The less expensive rooms (Rs350) are cramped, with shared bath. Small pool (Rs125 for non-guests). Attentive staff. ❸–❽

North side of Lake Pichola

Amet Haveli Chand Pole ⓣ & ⓕ 0294/243 1589 or 243 1085, ⓔregiudr@datainfosys.net. Old *haveli* which, when the lake is full, wins the prize for best lakefront property. At other times the six en-suite rooms, with marble floors and stained glass to reflect the building's original character, are still good value; all have lake views. Six rooms being added at time of research. Quality restaurant. ❼–❽

Dream Heaven Chand Pole ⓣ0294/243 1038. The best, budget alternative in this area if *Panorama* is full, with a real homestay feel. Rooms are a bit small and not as clean as they could be, but the rooftop restaurant has excellent views and is a great place to relax. ❷

Panorama Chand Pole ⓣ0294/243 1027, ⓔkrishna2311@rediffmail.com. New budget hotel that's quickly risen to the top of its class. Eleven rooms, each with hot water and decorated with murals, and a relaxing rooftop restaurant with superb views and an alcove seating area. Owner Krishna is laid back but his dedication to guests is commendable. Book ahead. ❶–❷

Udai Kothi Chand Pole ⓣ0294/243 2810, ⓦwww.udaikothi.com. The high prices charged for soft drinks and the like is a problem, but otherwise this modern hotel could be the best find among Udaipur's luxury options. Rooms (Rs2000–3000) are decorated with lovely adornments, marble floors and alcoved windows – perfect for catching lake views. A private lawn and rooftop pool (non-residents Rs200) set it apart. ❽–❾

Around Fateh Sagar

Grand Laxmi Vilas Palace Off Fateh Sagar Rd ⓣ0294/252 9711, ⓔgmlvp_jp1@sancharnet.in. Gopal Singh's nineteenth-century hilltop guesthouse, overlooking Fateh Sagar Lake, is marginally less pricey than other palace hotels. Recently restored, it's sumptuously furnished, has a pool (Rs200 for non-residents), and exudes a bucolic feel lacking at the luxury hotels in town. Ask to see the Maharaja's suite – its bed is big enough to fit the king's entire harem. Rooms $175–600 per night, but staff will discount meals or tax upon request. ❾

Outside the city centre

Mewar Inn 42 Residency Rd ⓣ0294/252 2090, ⓔmewarinn@hotmail.com. Backpackers' hostel north of the lake and city centre; a bit grimy, and too close to the main road for comfort, but it's far from the hustling tourist trade. There's a rooftop restaurant and cheap dorm beds go for Rs20. ❶

Shikharbadi Goverdhan Vilas ⓣ0294/258 3201 or 258 4842. Former royal hunting lodge set in the lower Aravallis (5km south on Ahmedabad road, NH-8), with own pool, lake, deer park and stud farm. Less ostentatious and more peaceful than the palaces in town. Suites in the 1930s block have more character than the newer a/c "cottages". ❽

Udaivilas ⓣ0294/243 3300, ⓦwww.oberoihotels.com. Udaipur's newest luxury resort, erected over ten years on the west side of Lake Pichola, is more regal even than anything the Rajputs ever built, consisting of a multi-domed palace, colonnades flanked by 450 hand-carved stone and acres upon acres of marble. It's an over-the-top resort aimed at jet-setters, world leaders and the ultra-rich. A magnificent courtyard and lobby lead to a wonderful Sheesh Mahal. The rooms (87 in all) start at $475, climbing up to a cool $2500 for the Kohinoor Suite. Suites come with private balconies, small swimming pools and sumptuous bathrooms with Victorian-style bathtubs. The spa is pure pampering. ❾

The City

The original settlement of Udaipur focused around the grand **City Palace**, bordering the east shore of **Lake Pichola**. Immediately north is the maze of tightly winding streets that constitute the **old city**. It takes a few hours of wandering before this labyrinth becomes intelligible; start by getting acquainted with the gates and circles that form traffic islands at the major crossroads. From the **clock tower** that marks the northern edge of the old city, roads lead east to the tourist office and Ahar, west to the lake, and north to the GPO at Chetak Circle. Continuing north, the road passes the **Bharatiya Lok Kala** folk art museum, and heads to **Sahelion-ki-Bari**, the gardens of the royal ladies.

The road that encircles **Lake Fateh Sagar** north of Lake Pichola carries on west to the crafts village of **Shilpgram**, a touristy showcase for all types of traditional Indian art. It's a good cycling route, with stop-offs at **Pratap Memorial Gardens** at Moti Magri on the eastern shore of the lake, and **Nehru Park** in its centre – you can take your bike across on the boat. In the far west of the city, **Sajjangarh** – the "Monsoon Palace" – commands superb views, while to the east both the royal cenotaphs and **Ahar museum** with its fifth-century BC relics can be visited in a morning.

Lake Pichola

The serene lakeside location chosen by Udai for his new capital made a welcome change from the craggy heights of Chittaurgarh. He enlarged the lake, which drew water from mountains up to 160km away, and when full covers eight square kilometres. Later rulers added dams and canals to prevent flooding during the monsoon.

The two **islands** in the lake, topped with the ivory-white domes and arches of private **palaces**, are the most familiar and photogenic features of Udaipur. **Jag Niwas**, now the *Lake Palace* hotel, is the larger of the two, built in amalgamated Rajput–Moghul style as a summer palace during the reign of Jagat Singh (1628–52). If you aren't staying here, you can pay a hefty price to visit for lunch, dinner or afternoon tea (booking advised; see p.255). The larger **Jag Mandir**, on the island to the south, has changed little since its construction by Karan Singh in 1615, its beauty established ever since Shah Jahan purportedly used it as a model to build the Taj Mahal. Intended as a small Rajput palace, it was never used as such; Karan Singh offered refuge here to the Moghul prince Khurum (later Emperor Shah Jahan), exiled by his father, Emperor Jahangir, in the 1620s. Khurum succeeded his father while still in Udaipur, and the Moghul gathering for the occasion defied the established code of Rajput–Moghul emnity. During the 1857 Mutiny the island once again served as a safe haven, this time for European women and children. The main building facing the City Palace has detailed stone inlay work within its domed roof. In front of it a green marble *chhatri* carved with vines and flowers is the centrepiece of a garden guarded by stone elephants. Jag Mandir's only inhabitants other than flocks of birds are three royal servants who tend the gardens and grow flowers for the maharana's celebrations.

Subject to the return of water, half-hour **boat rides** around the lake depart from Bansi Ghat behind the City Palace, below the *Fateh Prakash Palace* hotel (hourly: 10am–5pm; Rs75), while a 45-minute trip (Rs150) includes a stop at Jag Mandir. The view of the palaces and shoreline from the lake at sunset is an unforgettable image of Rajput splendour. To make the most of them by boat, sit on the side facing the palace (they usually run anticlockwise around the lake, so check when you get on).

City Palace

Udaipur's fascinating **City Palace** stands moulded in soft yellow stone on a rocky promontory on the northeast shore of Lake Pichola, its thick windowless base crowned with ornate turrets and canopies. Eleven constituent *mahals* (palaces), constructed by successive maharanas during the three hundred years that followed the foundation of Udaipur in 1559, together form the largest royal complex in Rajasthan.

Part of the palace is now a museum (daily 9.30am–4.30pm; Rs75, plus Rs100 for camera, Rs300 video), entered through **Toran Pole** from the massive courtyard where elephants once lined up for inspection before battle. Although **guided tours** (Rs100–150 for a non-Indian language) are not compulsory, they do serve to illuminate the chronology of the palaces, the significance of the paintings, and details of the lives of the maharanas.

Everywhere you look the marble and granite walls are laden with brilliant miniature paintings, decorated with tiles or overlaid with spangling mosaics of coloured glass and mirrors, and each room glows with sunlight filtering through stained-glass windows. Narrow low-roofed passages connect the different *mahals* and courtyards, creating a haphazard effect, designed to prevent surprise intrusion by armed enemies.

Each of the three large peacocks (*mor*) set into the walls of the seventeenth-century **Mor Chowk**, placed there by Sajjan Singh two hundred years after the palace was built, is composed of 5000 pieces of glass, glittering in green, gold and blue. The pillared apartments that face Mor Chowk are adorned with scenes from Krishna legends. Corridors lead to another chamber called **Kanch-ki-Burj**, decorated throughout with a mosaic of mirrors, and to **Chandra Chowk** ("Moon Square"), which encloses its own garden on the crest of a hill in the heart of the palace.

More hallways, some with good views of Lake Pichola, continue to the **Zenana Mahal**, the women's quarters, decorated with more legends of Krishna. With alcoves, balconies, coloured windows, tiled walls and floors, these are amongst the most splendid rooms in the palace. Krishna Vilas, an apartment full of miniatures, honours a nineteenth-century Udaipur princess who poisoned herself to avoid the dilemma of choosing a husband from the two rival households of Jodhpur and Jaipur.

Jagdish temple and Bagore-ki-Haveli

Raised above the main crossroads a little north of the City Palace, **Jagdish temple** is a centre of constant activity. Built in 1652 and dedicated to Lord Jagannath, an aspect of Vishnu, its outer walls and towering *shikhara* are heavily carved with figures of Vishnu, scenes from the life of Krishna, and dancing *apsaras* (nymphs). The spacious *mandapa* leads to the sanctuary where a black stone image of Jagannath sits shrouded in flowers, while a small raised shrine in front of the temple protects a bronze Garuda, the half-man, half-bird vehicle of Vishnu. Smaller shrines to Shiva and Hanuman stand to either side of the main temple.

To the right of the temple, a lane leads past a series of guesthouses to **Gangaur Ghat** and the **Bagore-ki-Haveli**, a 138-room manor built in 1751 by the prime minister, Mewar Amachand Badwa. It was taken over by the West Zone Cultural Centre (WZCC: Ⓦwww.udaipurplus.com/wzcc) in 1986 and has now been nicely restored and converted into a worthwhile museum (daily 10am–7pm; Rs25, plus Rs10 for camera, Rs50 video) housing antiques, musical instruments and a modern art gallery downstairs.

Bharatiya Lok Kala

Since the opening of Shilpgram, the **Bharatiya Lok Kala** on Panch Vati Road just north of Chetak Circle (daily 9am–5.30pm; Rs10, plus Rs20 for camera), has been squarely upstaged and the museum of folk handicrafts, traditional costumes and musical instruments is really only of marginal interest. Short, amusing **puppet shows** (free) are staged throughout the day as per demand, and a longer show, with music and dancing, takes place at 1pm & 6pm (Rs50).

Sahelion-ki-Bari and Fateh Sagar

The "garden of the maids of honour", **Sahelion-ki-Bari**, roughly 2km north of Hathi Pole (daily 9am–7.30pm; Rs5), was laid out by Sangram Singh early in the eighteenth century for the diversion and entertainment of the ladies of the royal household. Surrounding a shady courtyard, the fountained garden must once have made a delightful retreat, but today the fountains only play at the request of visitors, and the focus of attention is the wide range of indigenous trees and flowers. During the monsoon the lotus pond behind the courtyard is ablaze with colour.

West of Sahelion-ki-Bari is **Fateh Sagar**, a lake fringed by sharp hills and connected to Lake Pichola by a canal built in the early 1900s. At the jetty on the eastern shore, you can hop on the boat that ferries tourists across the water to **Nehru Park** in the centre of the lake (daily: April–Oct 8am–6.30pm; Nov–March 8am–6pm; Rs3). The park, closed at the time of writing due to drought and a lack of lake water, is nothing special, but pleasant enough if you want to get away from the bustle of the town.

Shilpgram

The road running around the north of Fateh Sagar leads to the rural arts and crafts centre of **Shilpgram** (daily 11am–7pm; Rs25, plus Rs10 for camera, Rs50 video), near the village of Havala, 5km out from town. It was set up by Rajiv Gandhi as a crafts village to promote and preserve the traditional architecture, music and crafts of the tribal people of western India, and holds displays of the diverse traditional lifestyles and customs of India's rural population. Twenty-six traditional Gujarati huts, adobe dwellings from the desert and Goan potters' huts are arranged in a village-like compound. Musicians and dancers – *hijras* (eunuchs) among them – perform around the houses, while weaving, potting, puppetry and embroidery continue as they would in their original localities.

Despite its honourable origins, many tourists find the whole atmosphere contrived, the crafts on sale unexceptional and resent the hustling by musicians and their ilk at what's supposed to be a non-commercial venue. But the scenic journey to get there by bike is a definite plus, and the week-long **crafts festival** taking place around Christmas gets quite festive, drawing more than 600 artisans from across India. It's possible to breeze through the village in less than half an hour; a guide costs Rs50.

Sajjangarh

High on a hill 5km west of the city, the "**Monsoon Palace**", **Sajjangarh** was abandoned by the royal family soon after its construction in 1880. Built to house an observatory and planned as a 19-storey structure, it was found to be impossible to pump water to the palace, which is now used as Udaipur's police radio station and closed to visitors. The views over Udaipur from the courtyards of the derelict palace are unrivalled, however, especially if you can make it there for sunrise, when the surrounding countryside looks its most magical. That said, getting up the hill requires a bit of effort, as the climb is too steep to tackle by bicycle. The journey takes a good fifteen minutes by rickshaw or taxi, and costs Rs150 for the round trip; if you can handle the traffic, rent a moped or motorcycle from Heera Cycles, just down the hill from the Jagdish temple on Gangaur Ghat Marg. Because it's located in a nature reserve, entry to the grounds, payable at the bottom of the hill, is Rs80, plus Rs20 per rickshaw or Rs100 per car.

Royal cenotaphs and Ahar museum

Across the narrow River Ahar, 2km east of Udaipur, domed **cenotaphs** huddle together on the site of the royal cremation ground. Raised on platforms, some of which are decorated with *shivalingams*, many of the *chhatris* are falling into disrepair, and the site is pretty dirty. Even so, it's a good place to pick up on local history, featuring an ornate memorial to the prodigious builder Jagat Singh (1628–52) and the cenotaph, embellished with friezes depicting the immolation of his wives, of Amar Singh (died 1620) who contributed so much to the City Palace.

Less than 1km south of here, archeological exhibits at the **Ahar museum** (daily except Fri 10am–5pm; Rs5) include locally unearthed pottery from the Ahar Civilization, which is believed to have come into existence around 2000 BC, making it one of India's earliest civilizations. Among more recent statues is a handsome tenth-century Surya image.

Eating, drinking and entertainment

The place to eat in Udaipur has long been the *Lake Palace's* romantic dining terrace. The closest most visitors get to it, however, are the rooftop **restaurants** stacked behind Lal and Gangaur *ghats*, whose gastronomic shortcomings and generally inflated prices are more than offset by spellbinding views over Pichola Lake to the distant Aravallis. Many of them also have free screenings (*ad nauseam*) of the James Bond movie *Octopussy*, with its manic boat and auto-rickshaw chases around the city's landmarks, beginning every evening, sharply at 7pm.

Live music can be found at many of the more expensive restaurants in town and everyday at 7.30pm at the Sunset View Terrace overlooking Lake Pichola, near the *Fateh Prakash Palace*. Folk **dances** are staged at Meera Kala Mandir, Meera Bhawan, Sector 11, on the Ahmedabad Road (Mon–Sat 7pm; Rs60; ⓣ0294/258 3176); call ahead for tickets. Bagore-ki-Haveli also has nightly dance performances at 7pm (Rs60). Shilpgram (see p.259) routinely invites out-of-town performers, though most of the time you'll see acts only marginally better than the street performers in town.

Restaurants

Ambrai *Amet Haveli hotel*, Chand Pole. One of the few lakeside restaurants whose cooking lives up to its location, on a spit of land facing the City Palace. Perfect for a sundowner, and their tandoori, prepared by the royal family's former chef, is second to none. Rs300 for buffet dinner.

Edelweiss 71 Gangaur Ghat Marg, next to *Gangaur Palace*. Excellent, hole-in-the-wall bakery and pastry shop that receives a steady stream of customers. Apple pie, chocolate cake, real coffee and friendly staff. Owned by the same people as *Savage Garden*.

Fateh Pakash Palace City Palace. English-style "high tea" served in an elegant, sunny gallery (3–5pm daily), with live Indian classical music and sublime lake views. Count on Rs175–250 for the full Monty – hotel-made jam, cream, tiny scones and sandwiches. An absolute must for cream-tea addicts.

Jagat Niwas In the hotel of the same name, 23–25 Lalghat. Popular restaurant in a beautiful lakeside *haveli*, with nice views over the lake from its comfy window seats. The quiet sitar and tabla music is a nice, non-intrusive touch.

Kumbha Palace 104 Bhatiyani Chotta. Better-than-average budget tourist grub (pizzas, baked potatoes, Marmite, homemade cakes), dished up on a rooftop terrace below the town-facing east wall of the City Palace. Pleasant views, big portions and very reasonable prices.

Lake Palace Lake Pichola ⓣ0294/252 8800. Non-residents can visit the *Lake Palace* for a candlelit buffet dinner (Rs1500) or slightly less for lunch (Rs1200) at what must rank among the world's most romantic restaurants. Reserve a table in advance and dress smartly – they'll say they're fully booked if you don't. As a one-off extravagance, the whole experience is hard to beat, and may well be the highlight of your time in Udaipur.

Natraj New Bapu Bazaar, behind Ashok Cinema. Udaipur's top thali joint for over twenty years, but well off the tourist trail because it's fiendishly hard to find (head down Barra Bazaar from the clock tower, and ask the way when you get to Suraj Pole). Easily the best cheap meal in town: Rs45 for unlimited portions of five different vegetables, dhal, rice, *papad*, fresh chapatis and pickle.

Queen Café Chand Pole ⓣ0294/243 0875. A good place to experience Indian food family-style. Meenu and her mother put out a spread of homemade Indian dishes each evening around 7.30pm. Dinner is communal and it's a good place to meet other travellers. If you're taken by the atmosphere, rooms are available for rent upstairs (❶). Call ahead to book.

Savage Garden On the east side of Chand Pole bridge. No longer as reputed as it once was for its Western-styled dishes, this trendy restaurant in a converted *haveli* is still a worthwhile, though pricier, option, if only for its attractive, modern decor. Fusion and pasta dishes are the mainstay at dinner, but the sandwiches make a more dependable lunch option.

Shikarbadi Goverdhan Vilas, 5km south along NH-8. Top-notch Mewari cuisine served on the terrace of the maharaja's former hunting lodge, on the slopes of the Aravallis. If you can, get here for 4.30pm when hordes of deer, bluebuck (*nilgai*), langur monkeys and wild boar mass to be fed. Lunch Rs250; dinner Rs350 per head; drinks cost extra.

Swaad Bedlar Rd, Fatehpura. The food distributor owner has plucked his best imported olive oil and fine ingredients to create one of Rajasthan's best Italian restaurants. They also serve elaborate Rajasthani dishes. A Rs30 rickshaw from Jagdish temple, but worth it for dinner when you're craving something from home.

Listings

Airlines Indian Airlines, LIC Building, opposite *Hotel Air Palace*, Delhi Gate (Mon–Sat 10am–5pm; ⓣ0294/241 0999); Jet Airways, Blue Circle Business Centre, 1C Madhuban (Mon–Sat 9.30am–6pm, Sun 9.30am–3pm; ⓣ0294/256 1105).

Banks and exchange The most efficient place to change money is LKP Forex, next to *Rang Niwas* hotel on Lake Palace Rd. Closer to Jagdish temple, there are several agencies – Mewar International, 35 Lalghat, is a good choice that's open late. For Visa withdrawals, go to Bank of Baroda, opposite the Town Hall on Bapu Bazaar; card transactions (on the mezzanine upstairs) are charged at one percent. There are several ATMs spread across the city and at the State Bank of India off Court Circle.

Bookshops The best-stocked bookstore in town is just inside the City Palace complex (no ticket required). For general India-related paperbacks and fiction in English, browse the shops around the Jagdish temple and along Lake Palace Rd, especially Mewar International, which accurately bills itself as a "one-stop shop" for travellers.

Hospital The (private) Aravalli Hospital, 332 Ambamata Rd (ⓣ0294/242 0222 or ⓣmobile98290/44155), has a 24hr emergency room and a doctor permanently on call. The government-sponsored Naturopathy Hospital at Bhattiyani Chohtta (near *Rang Niwas Palace* hotel) offers free mud treatments and steam bath.

Internet access Most of the hotels we list offer Internet access for Rs30/hr, and there are plenty of privately run cybercafés around Lalghat and Gangaur Ghat. Again, Mewar International tops the list, with ten fast computers.

Music Sitar and tabla lessons are offered to beginners on a weekly or hourly basis by the enthusiatic and experienced Rajesh Prajapat, contactable through the Prem Musical Instrument shop, opposite Hotel Gangaur Palace, Gangaur Ghat (ⓣ0294/243 0599). He charges Rs150 for a 90-minute appreciation course.

Pharmacies Bansal Department Stores, inside Suraj Pole (20m west of the gate); Vijay Medical Store, opposite the hospital entrance on Hospital Rd. Laxmi General Store, Bhattiyani Chohatta (coming from Jagdish temple, 300m on the right), is a useful general pharmacy selling almost anything you could need, including Marmite, tiger balm and rizlas.

Moving on from Udaipur

Indian Airlines **flies** to Jaipur, Jodhpur, Delhi and Mumbai. Jet Airways also fly to Jaipur ($90), Delhi ($119) and Mumbai ($138), but not to Jodhpur. See above for airline addresses. Be sure to ask for the 25 percent discount if you're under 30. At the time of research Air Deccan, which currently only operates out of Ahmedabad, was planning to expand service to Udaipur.

By train

Udaipur is poorly served by **trains**, with just one daily departure to Ahmedabad (#9943; departs 7.45pm), where you can pick up connecting services to Mumbai. Heading north, two trains run to Delhi each day. The fastest is the #9616 Chetak Express (departs 6.15pm), but for Jaipur you're better off taking the Lake City Express at 8.50pm. For Chittaurgarh, take the Chetak Express #9616 at 6.15pm.

By bus

Government **buses** from the main RSTRC bus stand at Udai Pole serve most destinations in Rajasthan as well as Dehli and Agra. Make sure when you buy your ticket that you're booked on an express bus, not a slow passenger service. More comfortable, cheaper **private buses** operate daily services to the same range of destinations (also Pushkar), departing from Udai Pole; for ticket information, ask an agent in town or Kamesh Travels (ⓣ0294/248 5823 or 248 5280) at Udai Pole – the latter has services to Mount Abu (8am & 3.30pm), Jodhpur (8am, 2pm & 9.30pm), Ahmedabad (8.30am, 11.30am, 2pm & 10pm), and Jaisalmer (10pm) among other destinations. Most night buses are sleepers. **Local buses** to destinations such as Nagda, Eklingi, Nathdwara, Kankroli and Kumbalgarh leave from the main government bus stand at regular intervals throughout the day.

Post office Parcels are best sent from the GPO, located at Chetak Circle, rather than the sub-post office. Note that parcels may only be posted Mon–Fri 10am–4pm & Sat 10am–1pm. Poste Restante can be addressed to the Postmaster at Shastri Circle. Mewar International, 35 Lalghat, sells stamps and will mail postcards at no charge.

Travel agents Reliable travel agents to choose from include the very efficient Mewar International, 35 Lalghat (☎0294/241 9810) and Gangaur Tours and Travels, 28 Gangaur Ghat Marg (☎0294/241 1476).

Volunteer work Animal Aid Unlimited is a pet hospital near Shilpgram run by a friendly American ex-pat couple. Volunteers and visitors are encouraged and no special skills are required – just a willingness to pet and talk to animals (☎35/251 1435, Ⓦwww.animalaidunlimited.org).

Yoga Ashtanga Yoga Ashram (aka "Raiba House"), Chand Pole (☎0294/252 4872, Ⓔjaswanttank@yahoo.com).

Around Udaipur

The Aravalli hills surrounding Udaipur are some of Rajasthan's most scenic, and you'd need a lot of time on your hands to see more than a fraction of the ruins, palaces, temples, forts, lakes and wildlife sanctuaries that abound here. Day-trips northeast of the city can take in the important historic temples of **Nagda**, **Eklingji**, **Nathdwara** and **Kankroli** along NH-8 towards Bhilwara, or the peaceful wooded surroundings of **Ranakpur** and **Kumbalgarh**, which also make appealing stopovers before you join NH-15 en route to Jodhpur. Renting a car or motorcycle saves time and roads are generally empty, but regular and efficient local buses, as well as private tour companies, serve both routes.

Nagda and Eklingji

The ragged remnants of the ancient capital of Mewar, **NAGDA**, which date back to 626 AD, stand next to a lake 20km northeast of Udaipur, a couple of kilometres short of Eklingji. Buses from Udaipur set down passengers for Nagda shortly before the road drops into the valley that shelters the Eklingji temple, beside a chai stall and bicycle shop (bike rental Rs5/hr). Nagda itself is about 1km away, west of the lake. Most of the buildings were either destroyed by Moghul zealots or submerged by the lake, which has naturally accumulated over the centuries. All that survives is a majestic pair of tenth-century Vaishnavite temples, known as **Saas-Bahu** – literally "mother-in-law" and "daughter-in-law". The larger (mother-in-law) has an astounding wealth of carving in its interior. Within the *mandapa*, a marriage area is marked by four pillars bearing images of the gods to which a couple must pay homage: Brahma, Vishnu, Shiva and Surya. On the northeast pillar you can make out representations of Sita's trial by fire, a favourite episode from the *Ramayana*, while scenes from the *Mahabharata* cover the ceilings. The outer walls of both temples display images of the entire Hindu pantheon, nubile *apsaras* (heavenly maidens), and even a few couples engaged in erotic acts.

Returning to the main road, you can continue down to **EKLINGJI** via the paved road or along a path that leads behind the old protective walls and downhill, passing shaded tanks and half-preserved muddy-brown temples. Ask the bike shop to point out the trailhead. The god **Eklingji**, a manifestation of Shiva, has been the protective deity of the rulers of Mewar ever since the eighth century, when Bappa Rawal was bestowed with the title *darwan* (servant) of Eklingji by his guru. To this day, the Maharana of Udaipur still visits the 108-temple complex every Monday evening – the day traditionally celebrated all over India as being sacred to Shiva. Lesser mortals can make the straightforward half-hour trip northeast of Udaipur by taxi, or on very frequent buses from the main bus stand. The milky-white marble main temple (daily 5.30am–8.30pm), dominating the compound with an elaborate two-storey *mandapa* guarded by stone elephants, surrounds a four-faced black marble *lingam* that marks the precise spot where Bappa Rawal received his accolade. Images of Shiva and his fellow deities, *apsaras* and musicians are etched into the walls both outside and within. The temple had to be rebuilt under Maharana Raimal at the end of the fifteenth century, and again two hundred years later after the ravages of Aurangzeb's iconoclastic forces.

Nathdwara

The temple dedicated to Krishna – known also as **Nath**, the favourite *avatar* (incarnation) of Vishnu – at **NATHDWARA**, "Gateway to God", is said to be the second-richest temple in India after Tirupati (in Andhra Pradesh). The site was known as Sihar until the moment in the seventeenth century when a chariot laden with an image of Krishna became stuck in the mud 26km north of Eklingji. The idol was being carried from Krishna's birthplace Mathura to Udaipur to spare it almost certain destruction by Aurangzeb; its bearers interpreted the event as a divine sign and established a new temple where it had stopped.

Nathdwara is on NH-8, and sees a constant flow of buses en route north and south. Although the area around the bus stand is grim, a short ride west on a rickshaw brings you to narrow streets where stalls display incense, beads, perfumes and small Krishna statues. In the centre of town the **Shri Nathji temple** opens for worship eight times daily, when the image is woken, dressed, washed, fed and put to bed. The most elaborate session, *aarti*, takes place between 5pm and 6pm. Don't miss the radiant *pichwai* paintings in the main sanctuary, made of hand-spun cloth and coloured with strong vegetable pigments; these original hangings possess a brilliance unmatched by the numerous copies available all over Rajasthan. You could also ask a guide to show you the "footsteps of Krishna", a process that requires rubbing rose petals on the marble floor.

Kankroli and Rajsamand

Northeast of Nathdwara, NH-8 winds through another 17km of undulating scrub before reaching **KANKROLI**, 65km from Udaipur. This dusty little market town stands on the shores of the vast **Rajsamand Lake**, whose construction was commissioned by Maharana Raj Singh in the seventeenth century after a terrible drought swept Rajasthan. On the lake's western shore, a few kilometres out of town, is **Nauchowki**, a collection of nine *chowks* (pavilions) erected by Raj Singh on platforms above the steps leading to the water. The **Dwarkadish temple** overlooking the southern shore houses an image of Krishna installed by Raj Singh in 1676, and has a sanctuary similar to that at Nathdwara. Beside the lake you can buy grain to feed the flocks of pigeons, which survive on the charity of pilgrims. The best views of the lake are to be had from the **Digambara Jain temple**, dedicated to Adinath, which crowns a steep hill between Nauchowki and the bus stand. From here you can see the Dwarkadish temple, Nauchowki, scattered old palaces on the nearby hills, and the Aravalli landscape rolling south as far as the eye can see.

With your own car or a lot of patience (local buses are painfully slow), it's possible to travel for two hours on empty country roads to **Kumbalgarh** (see p.265).

Ranakpur

Even "templed out" travellers find much to marvel at the four **Jain temples** at **RANAKPUR**, 90km north of Udaipur. The largest complex of its kind in

India, Ranakpur boasts marble work on a par with that of the more famous Dilwara shrines at Mount Abu (see p.248) and Shatrunjaya near Palitana in Gujarat (see p.677). Unlike the latter two hilltop sites, however, this sacred spot is hidden at the base of a glorious, wooded valley. The land, deep in the Aravalli Range, was originally gifted to the Jain community in the fifteenth century by Rana Kumbha, the Hindu ruler of Mewar. Ranakpur's isolated position has long kept it well off the foreign tourist trail, but word is spreading fast about the area's bucolic beauty and a new proliferation of hotels is converting it into a destination in its own right. If you're working your way between Jodhpur and Udaipur on country buses, it's an excellent place to break the journey.

The **main temple** (noon–5pm) was built in 1439 according to a strict system of measurement that had the number 72 at its core. Rising four storeys in parts, the entire temple sits on a pedestal measuring 72 by 72 yards and is held up by 1440 (a divisor of 72) individually carved pillars. Inside, there are 72 elaborately carved shrines, some octagonal in shape, and the main deity encased in the central sanctum, the four-faced Adinath, the first *tirthankara*, measures 72 inches tall. The carving on the walls, columns and the domed ceilings is superb. Friezes depicting the life of the *tirthankara* are etched into the walls, while musicians and dancers have been modelled out of brackets between the pillars and the ceiling.

Two smaller temples dedicated to **Parshwanath** and **Neminath** nestle among the trees close by; the sculptures within are of a similarly high standard. Also in the compound is a contemporary Hindu temple dedicated to **Surya**.

Practicalities

Ranakpur is a bumpy three-hour journey on regular buses from Udaipur. You can also get here from Jodhpur (4hr 15min), via the market town of Falna (the nearest railway station) on NH-14, and there are a couple of express connections to Abu Road. If you're intending to visit Kumbalgarh as well, though, think about **trekking** between the two sites, which are separated by one of the few remaining forested areas in the Aravallis. As Kumbalgarh is on the top of the range, it's much easier to hike from there down to Ranakpur (for more on this route see opposite), but guides may be arranged through any of the hotels listed below for the six-hour uphill climb in the other direction.

For budget **accommodation** in Ranakpur, you can stay for a Rs10 donation with the Jain pilgrims at the temple complex, but don't expect anything more than a mattress on a cold, cement floor; dinner, costing Rs17, is served at 5pm to satisfy Jain proscription from eating after sunset. Among the limited budget choices, the best is *Shivika Lake Hotel* (Ⓣ02934/285078; Ⓦwww.indiaoverland.com ❸–❻), 2km south of the temples, which is run by a former wildlife warden who arranges local treks and jeep safaris. Farther down the road, the more comfortable *Ranakpur Hill Resort* (Ⓣ02934/286411; Ⓦwww.ranakpurhillresort.com; ❻) offers a pool, quality buffet restaurant and nine ensuite rooms. Of the three five-star resorts along Ranakpur Road, *Fateh Bagh* (Ⓣ02934/286186, Ⓦwww.hrhindia.com; ❾), the latest addition to the Maharaja of Udaipur's HRH chain, is the best. Unique among typically plush Rajasthani castles, this 200-year-old palace was painstakingly disassembled piece by piece, transported 50km and then rebuilt here with all the corresponding pomp you'd expect. About 15km away, near the village of Maga, the new *Aranyawas* (Ⓣ0294/258 3148, Ⓔaranyawas@hotmail.com; ❽) is a jungle lodge with five rustically elegant cottages (Rs2100) that overlook a watering hole frequented by leopards – an ideal place to recharge your batteries in complete and total isolation.

Kumbalgarh

The remote hilltop fort of **KUMBALGARH**, 80km north of Udaipur, is the most formidable of the 32 constructed by Maharana Kumbha in the fifteenth century. Protected by a series of seven thick ramparts, it was only successfully besieged once, when a confederacy led by Akbar poisoned the Sisodias' water supply. Aside from the impressive fortifications and ancient monuments they enclose, the main reason to venture out here is to experience the idyllic Aravalli countryside. Winding through a string of tribal villages and picturesque valleys, the Udaipur road alone more than repays the effort, and once you've reached the top of the range the views are superb.

The most memorable panorama of all is seen from the pinnacle of Kumbalgarh **palace** (daily 9am–6pm; Rs100), crowning the summit of the fort. A guide will show you through the series of gateways and residential quarters to the room where Udai Singh was raised by his nurse after fleeing Chittaurgarh in 1535, and the topmost Cloud Palace (so named because during the monsoons it sits in the clouds), restored and furnished by Udaipur's Fateh Singh in the early twentieth century. From the rooftops, you gain striking birds' eye views over the Jain and Hindu **temples** scattered across the plateau. The oldest are thought to date from the second century; the **tombs** of Kumbha (murdered by his eldest son) and his grandson Prithviraj (poisoned by his brother-in-law) stand to the east.

Provided you're equipped with good shoes and ample provisions, the best way to explore these more remote monuments is on foot, via the old walls. Some 36km of crenellated ramparts wind around the rim of the hilltop, and it is possible to complete a circuit in two comfortable days, sleeping rough midway around. You won't need a guide, but be sure to take food and water as there are no permanent settlements.

Lining the deep valley that plunges west from the fort down to the plains, the **Kumbalgarh Wildlife Sanctuary** comprises a dense swathe of woodland that's a stronghold for wolves, leopards and panthers. With a local guide, you can trek through it to Ranakpur, a rewarding and easy hike of between four and five hours (the alternative is a long journey on an infrequent country bus). Entry to the sanctuary costs Rs80 (plus Rs200 for camera); foreigners need **permits**, obtainable from the District Forest Officer at nearby **Kelwara.** Local guides, contactable through the hotels listed below, can also obtain your permit for you – and stop you getting lost – for around Rs600-1000. To save money you can try to find a guide on your own – it's not easy, but if you ask around at the café just inside the fort gates you might get lucky.

Practicalities

Taxis regularly run tourists out to Kumbalgarh and Ranakpur as a day-trip from Udaipur (around Rs1000), but it's best to take your time and travel at a more leisurely pace, staying for a night or two. An express **bus** leaves Udaipur's RSRTC stand at 5.30am (3hr 30min) and private buses three times daily from Chetak Circle (7.30am, 11.30am & 3pm). Competent motorcyclists could consider riding out here on a rented **bike**.

Of the **accommodation** on offer, the only budget option is *Ratna Deep* (ⓣ02954/242057 or 242217; ❹–❺), 7km from the fort in the town of Kelwara; they have basic doubles and an inexpensive, musty smelling dorm. *Aodhi*, on the left side of the road as you approach the Kumbalgarh bus stop (ⓣ02954/242341, ⓦwww.hrhindia.com; ❽–❾), is a swish heritage hotel complete with a nice outdoor restaurant and pool, run by the Maharana of Udaipur's HRH chain. They can also arrange expensive guides (Rs500/hr) and

Jeep safaris (Rs2000). Nearby, the *Kumbhal Castle* (ⓣ02954/242171, Udaipur 0294/2423356, ⓦwww.kumbhalcastle.com; ❻) has good doubles and hires out scooters. The more modern *Kumbalgarh Fort Hotel* (ⓣ02954/242057, ⓔhilltop@bppl.net.in; ❽–❾; 50 percent discounts April–July), 5km along the Kelwara road, has superb hill views from its garden terraces and pool; they also rent out cycles.

Chittaurgarh, Kota and Bundi

The belt of hilly land east of Udaipur is the most fertile in Rajasthan, watered by several perennial rivers. Although you need your own vehicle to penetrate the countryside, the historic town of **Chittaurgarh**, with an impressive fort that preceded Udaipur as the seat of Mewar's rulers, is easily accessible by bus. Further east, clusters of crumbling temples mark the sites of still older cities, many of them with idyllic, but little publicized heritage hotels that are within reach of most travellers. In the far southeast, the heartland of the princely state of Kota, the tranquil village of **Bundi** is a relaxing place, with a dilapidated but atmospherhic fort that stand sentinel over fields of wheat, groundnut, and castor-oil plants. Less than an hour away by bus, **Kota** also boasts impressive palace architecture, but little else. A prime crop in this are a for centuries has been **opium.** Although grown for the pharmaceutical industry according to strict government quotas, the legal cultivation masks a much larger illicit production overseen by Mumbai drug barons. An estimated one in five men in the area are addicts.

Chittaurgarh

Of all the former Rajput capitals, **CHITTAURGARH** (or Chittor), 115km northeast of Udaipur, was the strongest bastion of Hindu resistance against the Muslim invaders. No less than three mass suicides (*johars*) were committed over the centuries by the female inhabitants of its **fort**, whose husbands watched their wives, sisters and mothers burn alive before smearing ash from the sacred funeral pyres over their bodies and riding to their deaths on the battlefield below. A Pompeii-like air of desolation still hangs over the honey-coloured ramparts, temples, towers and ruined palaces of the old citadel. It seems impossible to fathom that such an imposing structure, towering 180m over the Mewar valley on a rocky plateau, could have ever been taken, yet alone three times. As a symbol of Rajput chivalry and militarism only Jodhpur's Meherangarh Fort compares.

Below the fort, the modern **town**, whose population of 90,000 is spread over both banks of the River Ghambiri, holds little to detain travellers beyond the narrow bazaars of its old quarter, and some tourists choose to squeeze a tour of Chittaurgarh into a day-trip, or en route between Bundi and Udaipur. A one-night stop, however, leaves time for a more leisurely visit to the fort and a stroll through the town.

Some history

The uncompromising policy of death before submission followed by Chittor's **Sisodia** overlords ensured that its history is replete with tales of loyalty and terrible sacrifice. In 1303, during the reign of **Rana Ratan Singh**, a devastating attack was launched by **Ala-ud-din-Khalji**, the fiercest of the Delhi sultans. Having besieged the city, he offered to withdraw on condition that he be permitted to glimpse Ratan's legendarily beautiful queen, **Padmini**. After admitting him alone into the palace to view the queen's reflection in a lotus lake, however, the sultan contrived to have Ratan ambushed just as he was showing him out of the door. Padmini devised a plan to recapture him. Sending word that she would give herself up to the sultan, the queen left the fort accompanied by troops disguised as maids of honour. As in the Greek story of the Trojan horse, once inside the Muslim camp the sari-clad commandos unveiled themselves and managed to rescue Rana Ratan, but not before 7000 of them were killed in the process. As a result, the defence of the fort foundered and the Rajputs lost the ensuing battle. Thirteen thousand women, led by Padmini, committed *johar* by throwing themselves and their children onto a huge funeral pyre, whereupon the angry sultan destroyed most of the fort's temples and palaces.

After returning to Rajput hands in 1326, Chittaurgarh enjoyed two hundred years of prosperity. However, in 1535, an unexpected onslaught led by **Sultan Bahadur Shah** from Gujarat once again decimated the Rajput ranks, and the women surrendered their lives in another ghastly act of *johar*. Aware of Chittaurgarh's vulnerability, the young Rajput heir, **Udai Singh**, searched for a new site for his capital, and in 1559 founded Udaipur on the shore of Lake Pichola. This proved to be a prescient decision. **Akbar** laid siege to Chittaurgarh in 1567. His forces killed 30,000 of the fort's inhabitants; the women once again sacrificed themselves on a raging pyre, and many of the buildings within the fort were devastated. Although Chittaurgarh was ceded back to the Rajputs in 1616, the royal family never resettled there.

Arrival and information

Chittaurgarh's **railway station** is in the western corner of the city. From here it's about 2km north to the **Roadways** (aka "**Kothwali**") **bus stand** on the west bank of the Ghambiri, and a further 2km east to the base of the fort. RTDC's forlorn **tourist office**, where you can obtain free maps of the town (but little else), stands just north of the railway station on Station Road (daily 10am–5pm; ⓣ01472/241089).

Tours of the fort are most easily made by rickshaw (Rs150), complete with jangly pop music and silky curtains. Many hang out at the bus station awaiting tourists. Tours tend to take in only the most famous monuments rather than the entire fort, which is 5km long and 1km wide. The best way to see the whole thing – which takes a good three hours – is to rent a **bike** from the shop on the road leading west from the crossroads outside the station. The initial climb is steep, but most of the roads on the plateau itself are flat.

The fort

The ascent to the fort (daily 7am–6pm), protected by massive bastions, begins at **Padan Pole** in the east of town and winds upwards through a further six gateways (*poles*). Close to the second *pole* stand the *chhatris* of Jaimal and his cousin Kalla, who carried the injured Jaimal piggyback into battle in the final sacking of 1567. The houses of the small community that still inhabits the fort are huddled together near the final gate, **Rama Pole**, where the Rs100 entry fee is payable (plus Rs5 extra for rickshaw, Rs25 video; camera free).

As you enter the fort you pass the fifteenth-century **Shingara Chauri Mandir**, a highly adorned Jain temple dedicated to Shantinath, the sixteenth *tirthankara*. Ahead of this, the slowly deteriorating fifteenth-century **Palace of Rana Kumbha** – built by the ruler who presided over the period of Mewar's greatest prosperity – remains a classic example of Rajput architecture, and is immortalized as the scene of Padmini's *johar*. Nearby, the modern **Fateh Prakash Palace**, built for the Maharana in the 1920s, is the site of a small, dimly lit **archeological museum**, filled with weapons (daily except Fri 10am–5pm; Rs3). Also in the palace compound is the **Kumbha Shyama temple**, crowned by a pyramidal roof and lofty tower, whose eighth-century sanctuary enshrines an image of Varaha, the boar incarnation of Vishnu. Slightly to the south, a smaller temple with a delicate curved tower, also constructed by Rana Kumbha, is dedicated to **Meerabai**, a Jodhpur princess and poet famed for her devotion to Krishna.

The main road within the fort continues south to its focal point, **Vijay Stambh**, the soaring "tower of victory", erected by Kumbha to commemorate his 1440 victory over the Muslim Sultan Mehmud Khilji of Malwa. This magnificent sand-coloured tower, whose nine storeys rise 36m, took a decade to build; its walls are lavishly carved with mythological scenes and images from all Indian religions, including Arabic inscriptions in praise of Allah. You can climb the dark narrow stairs to the very summit for free.

A path leads from the tower through more fine but ruined temples to **Gaumukh Kund**, a large reservoir fed by an underground stream that trickles through carved mouths (*mukh*) of cows (*gau*). This quiet spot, away from the main road, commands superb views across the plains. Buildings further south include the **Kalika Mata temple**, originally dedicated to **Surya** in the eighth century, but rededicated to the Mother Goddess after renovations in 1568. Carvings on the outer wall include images of Surya, the guardians of the eight directions, and friezes depicting the churning of the ocean by the gods and demons, a popular creation myth. An image of Surya guards the main entrance to the temple. **Padmini's Palace**, now rather dilapidated, stands opposite, in the centre of the pool that allegedly revealed the queen to Ala-ud-din Khalji.

The road continues south past the deer park to the point used for hurling traitors to their deaths, and returns north along the eastern ridge to **Surajpol** gate, with spectacular vistas across a patchwork of farmland. Several temples line the route, but the most impressive monument is **Kirti Stambh**. The inspiration for the tower of victory, this smaller "tower of fame" was built by Digambaras as a monument to the first *tirthankara* Adinath, whose unclad image is repeated throughout its six storeys.

Accommodation and eating

While Chittaurgarh's mid- and upper-range **hotels** cost a little more than elsewhere, places at the lower end of the price scale are pretty dingy – this is one place budget travellers might want to splash out. The best of the bunch immediately outside the railway station is *Chetak*, Neemuch Road (Ⓣ01472/241589; ❸–❹), with a busy little restaurant downstairs. *Pratap Palace*, opposite the GPO on Shri Gurukul Road (Ⓣ01472/240099, Ⓦwww.castlebijaipur.com; ❸–❺), lacks hot water, but is otherwise acceptable, with a relaxing garden and Internet. Their "deluxe" rooms boast raunchy Krishna murals and plum-coloured satin bed covers, but the "ordinary" ones are much better value. A better, if still average choice is *Meera*, 500m south on Neemuch Road (Ⓣ01472/240266 or 240934; ❸–❻); rooms are larger, and the excellent facilities include an inexpensive restaurant, bar, Internet access, billiards and laundry services. Standard rooms have Indian toilets.

As for **food**, both the *Pratap Palace* and *Meera* have non-veg restaurants, the latter less expensive. A more respectable, and cheaper, option is the *Ratu*

Moving on from Chittaurgarh

Travellers to **Udaipur** do best to take the #9615 Chetak Express at 6.40am (3hr 30min) or the Ahmedabad Express #9943 departing at 1.40pm (4hr 30min). Fast trains to **Ajmer** leave at 5.30am, 1.50pm and 9.50pm. For **Delhi** (15–16hr) and **Jaipur** (8hr), the Chetak Express #9616 departs around 10pm. For **Jaipur**, fast trains depart at 5.50am and 9.50pm, or you could also take the slightly faster #9770 Purna–Jaipur Express, which leaves early in the morning at 5.30am. Travelling east to **Bundi**, you're better off catching the 7am or 2.45pm train (3hr 30min), which follows a far more scenic route (try for a window seat on the north/left side of the carriage) and takes ninety minutes less than the bus. Roads are notoriously poor in this area and buses therefore incredibly slow.

Raj Vatika across town, who have an excellent little pure veg restaurant serving a range of delicious thalis for less than Rs50. To find it, head up the insalubrious-smelling lane opposite the bus stand and follow the signboards in red Hindi writing.

Kota

KOTA, 230km south of Jaipur on a fertile plain fed by Rajasthan's largest river, the Chambal, is one of the state's dirtier and less stimulating cities. With a population nudging 700,000, it is one of Rajasthan's major commercial and industrial hubs, with hydro, atomic and thermal power stations lining the banks of the Chambal, alongside Asia's largest fertilizer plant. The nuclear plant of Rawat Bhata, protected by stringent security 60km southwest, is notorious for its impact on local villagers. Foreign visitors are sufficiently unusual here to attract stares in the streets, but Kota does have some beautiful gardens, and its old palaces house one of the best museums in Rajasthan.

Greatly prized saris from the village of **Kaithoon**, 20km southeast of Kota, are sold in all the bazaars. Made of tightly woven cotton or silk, and often highlighted with golden thread, they are known here as *masooria* and elsewhere as *Kota doria* saris.

The City

The residential areas, bazaars, fort, City Palace and museum east of the Chambal face harsh buildings and factory smokestacks across the river. **Kishor Sagar**, an artificial lake built in 1346, gives picturesque relief. The red-and-white palace in its centre, **Jag Mandir**, was commissioned by Prince Dher Deh of Bundi in 1346 and can be visited only with permission from the Superintendent Engineer of Kota; ask at the tourist office. In the Brijvilas Palace on the northern edge of the lake, the **Government Museum** (daily except Mon 10am–5pm; Rs5) has a small collection of clothes, weapons and miniature paintings and a fascinating hand-drawn plan of Kota's manoeuvres during the Mutiny of 1857.

Kota's **fort**, raised above the flat bank of the Chambal 2km south of the bus stand, was built in 1264 by Rajkumar Jait Singh of Bundi. Construction of the **City Palace** and offices of state within the fortifications began in 1625, and continued sporadically until the early years of this century. Although the older fort ramparts are falling into disrepair, the palaces are still in excellent condition. Apartments in the heart of the palace house the excellent **Maharao Madho Singh Museum** (daily except Mon 10am–5pm; Rs50, plus Rs75 for camera, Rs100 video). Among a vast collection of carefully decorated weapons, the size and severity of which is out of this world, you'll see shields adorned with the solar symbol of the Hadachauhan Rajputs, large enough to protect an elephant. Solid silver artefacts and fading sepia photographs of viceroys, maharajas, polo teams and Queen Victoria record the extravagance of royalty, and there are some outstanding examples of *Kota Kamba*, miniatures from Kota's school of painting. The most spectacular apartment is **Raj Mahal**, which contains the royal throne.

On the edge of the river a few kilometres south of the fort, crocodiles and gharial sun themselves in a shallow pond in the **Chambal Gardens** (Rs2); boats depart from here for fifteen minute tours (Rs15) of the crocodile-infested River Chambal.

Practicalities

Kota's **railway station** is in the north of town, a few kilometres from the central **bus stand** on Bundi Road. The unnervingly incompetent **tourist office** (Mon–Sat 10am–5pm; ⓣ0744/232 7695) is in the RTDC *Chambal Hotel*, Nayarpura, southeast of the bus stand. The Punjab National Bank on Aerodrome Circle will change travellers' cheques: other **banks** do not. The **post office** is northeast of the bus stand on Station Road.

Kota's **hotels** cater mainly for passing business travellers, and the cheaper resthouses reflect the neglect that prevails in the town. Among the best inexpensive dives is *Pankaj* (ⓣ0744/232 0577; ❶–❸) smack in the middle of town at Vivekanand Circle. Rooms are clean, have hot water and a hygienic restaurant serves good food. Closer to the bus stand, in the area known as Civil Lines, the hotels get dingier and louder. A cut above the competition for cleanliness and service is *Navrang* (ⓣ0744/232 3294; ❸–❼) which has an ATM next door. The best mid-range option is *Sukhdam*, Civil Lines (ⓣ0744/232 0081 or 233 2661, ⓔsukhdam@datainfosys.net; ❻), a guesthouse located in a hundred-year-old mansion set amid three acres of gardens. *Umed Bhawan Palace*, Station Road, Khelri Phatak (ⓣ0744/232 5262, ⓦwww.welcomeritage.com; ❾), is a grandiose former royal residence, but not nearly as inviting as other properties in the Welcom Heritage chain; rooms start at $55. In addition to the hotel **restaurants**, try the cheap and good veg *Barkha Restaurant* on Nayapura Circle.

Moving on from Kota

Kota is well connected by **bus** to destinations in Rajasthan and across the state border to Bhopal and Indore. Services to Bundi leave more or less every thirty minutes from the stand near Nayapura Circle, taking around one hour.

Travellers heading northeast towards **Agra** often pass through Kota to pick up the main broad-gauge line, which is also the most straightforward approach to **Sawai Madhopur**, jumping-off place for Ranthambore National Park. The recommended service here is the Paschim Express #2955, which leaves at 8.50am and arrives ninety minutes later. There are also six fast daily **trains** to **Delhi** (most of them via Jaipur and Bharatpur). The easiest one to get a seat on at short notice is the Golden Temple Mail #2903, leaving daily at 11.25am, but the Rajdhani Express services #2953 (5.30am) and #2431 (8.20am) are quicker. To **Mumbai** (via Ujjain and Indore), the fastest trains are the Rajdhani Express trains #2432 (3.40pm), #2952 (8.50pm) and #2954 (9.55pm). For **Jaipur** you'll probably find it easier to book a seat on the Mumbai–Jaipur Superfast #2955, which departs at 8.50am and takes four hours.

Bundi

Jeypore Palace may be called the Versailles of India; Udaipur's House of State is dwarfed by the hill round it and the spread of the Pichola Lake; Jodhpur's House of strife, grey tower on red rock, is the work of giants, but the Palace of Bundi, even in broad daylight, is such a palace as men build for themselves in uneasy dreams – the work of goblins rather than of men.

Rudyard Kipling

The walled town of **BUNDI**, 37km north of Kota, lies in the north of the former Hadaoti state, shielded on the north, east and west by jagged outcrops of the Vindhya Range. Visible only from the south and guarded by the tremendous **Taragarh** or "star fort" high in the north of town, the site made a perfect capital for the Hadachauhans, perched in their immense turreted **palace** beneath the lofty walls of the fort. Although settled in 1241, 25 years before Kota, Bundi never amounted to more than a modest market centre, and remains relatively untouched by modern developments. Yet its palace alone ranks among the most spectacular monuments in Rajasthan, while the almost complete absence of intrusive modern structures within the **old walled town**, site of several impressive step-wells and crumbling stucco *havelis*, make this a far more appealing destination than other more famous landmarks in the state.

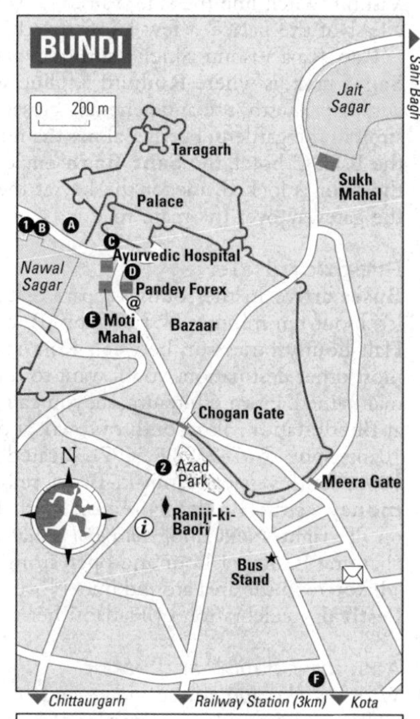

The Town

Walking north through the bazaar, you'll see the creamy stone domes, cupolas and bleached walls of Bundi's **palace** (daily 7am–5pm, Rs50; plus Rs50 for camera, Rs100 video) spilling down the hillside ahead. Built during the sixteenth and seventeenth centuries in authentic Rajput style, it was one of the few royal abodes in Rajasthan untainted by Moghul influence. Its appearance is surprisingly homogeneous considering the number of times it was added to over the years, although some wings are virtually derelict now, including the one that harbours Bundi's greatest art treasures: its famous **murals**.

A short steep path winds to the entrance, **Hathi Pole**, flanked by the elephants that are so common in the Hadaoti region. From the small courtyard within, steps lead to **Ratan Daulat**, the early seventeenth-century Diwan-i-Am or Hall of Public Audience, with its simple marble throne. Shrine rooms and the womens' quarters above it contain the cream of Bundi's murals, some which survive in remarkably good condition from the early seventeenth century and depict scenes of invading British armies as well as visiting Chinese and Persian artists. Most are located inside the previously closed quarter known as **Badal Mahal**, or Cloud Palace which also contains a curious, 30-foot carved-stone swing used by the queen for recreation. Although the palace caretaker will unlock any doors and grant access for free, it's better to hire the services of a guide; Keshav Bhati, an ex corporal in the Indian Air Force (Ⓣ0747/244 5985 or 242 3879) charges Rs150 for a **tour** of the entire palace.

Other wall paintings may be viewed in the **Chittra Shala**, a courtyard enclosed by cloisters whose sides swirl with elaborate blue, green, ruby, turquoise and white images of battles, court scenes and religious tableaux. Views over Bundi from the projecting balconies take in the **Nawal Sagar** tank with its half-submerged temple. The best views of all are from the monkey-infested **Taragarh**, though it's a steep twenty-minute climb to see them.

A walk from the palace south through the walled bazaar and old gateways takes you to Rajasthan's most spectacular step-well, **Raniji-ki-Baori**, built in 1699 by Nathwati, wife of Rao Raja Singh. One of fifty such wells in Bundi, it lies deep beneath the surface of a small plaza just beyond Azad Park, reached by a flight of steps punctuated by platforms and embellished pillars. As you descend, look for the beautifully carved panels showing the ten *avatars* of Lord Vishnu which line the side walls. The well is closed at lunchtime.

East of the palace, a few kilometres by rickshaw, the beautiful **Sukh Mahal** – Rao Raja Vishnu Singh's summer palace – on the southern shore of **Jait Sagar** tank, is where Rudyard Kipling wrote *Kim*; it's now the regional water authority's resthouse and generally closed to visitors, but you can take a pleasant stroll in the gardens. Further along the northwest side of the lake, 1.5km beyond the RTDC hotel, the **Sahr Bagh** encloses sixty crumbling royal cenotaphs. If the door is locked, ask for the key at the *chowkidar*'s hut on your left just after the gateway over the main road.

Practicalities

Buses arrive in the southeast part of town near the post office, from where it's about ten minutes by rickshaw (Rs25) to the palace and most guesthouses. Half-hourly buses run between Kota and Bundi (1hr). Coming and going to most other destinations you'll want to travel by train, as roads tend to be poorly maintained. From Chittaurgarh, you can catch the 2.55pm **train**, which arrives at Bundi station, 3km south of town, at 5pm. Bundi's **tourist office** (Mon–Sat 10am–5pm; Ⓣ0747/244 3697), located on the second floor of an old home 100m southwest of Raniji-ki-Baori, sells good maps of town. You can **change money** at the Pandey Forex on Garh Palace Road, 100m before the palace on the right. Next door, *Shri Balaji* has the best Internet connection in town, charging Rs60 per hour and open from sunrise until 9.30pm.

If you're in the area around mid-November try to arrive for the annual **Bundi Festival**, a celebration of Hadaoti heritage with a very local, country fair feel.

Accommodation and eating

With its lake and palace views, and traffic- and tout-free back streets, Bundi makes a relaxing place to **stay**, and many travellers find themselves staying for a while. Much of the accommodation is in old *havelis* that for once offer a good choice of budget rooms. Most visitors enjoy the cultural exchange that comes from eating in with their host families, which is also usually the most affordable option. Otherwise, the best **restaurant** is the modest *Garden*, next to the *Lake*

Moving on from Bundi

Buses cover the journey **to Chittaurgarh** (5hr) three times a day, two of them continuing to Udaipur; better still, jump on the 9.30am train (2hr 30min). Bundi is also connected by hourly buses to Ajmer (4hr) and Jaipur (7hr), and less frequently, to Jodhpur (10hr). For **Pushkar**, there are three daily direct buses (7hr 30min); **Sawai Madhopur** (for Ranthambore National Park) can also be reached by road (5hr), but it's quicker to travel down to Kota and pick up a Golden Temple Express at 11.30am or the 8pm train (#9019) to Delhi.

View, whose speciality is "Rajasthani Pizza", served on a lakeside lawn. The only other option is the run-of-the-mill *Diamond*, just south of Chogan Gate in the bazaar, which serves cheap rice and veg meals.

Haveli Braj Bhushanjee Below the palace ⓣ0747/244 2322, ⓦwww.kiplingsbundi.com. This 150-year-old *haveli* is full of character, with original murals and family portraits on the walls. But prices have risen of late and given the plethora of good alternatives budget travellers will want to look elsewhere. Delicious home-cooked food, served in the dining hall or an outside terrace with superb views of the palace. Internet. ❺–❽

Haveli Katoun Near Gopal Mandir Balchand para ⓣ0747/244 4311, ⓔraghunandansingh@yahoo.com. Four immaculate, newly furnished rooms overlooking a leafy garden. Real homestay feel and good thalis. Recommended. ❸–❹

Ishwari Niwas 1 Civil Lines ⓣ0747/244 3541, ⓦwww.angelfire.com/amiga/inheritage/. Well-appointed rooms (some a/c) in a period building on the south side of town. Comfortable enough, and they serve passable food, but a little far from the palace. ❹–❺

Kasera Paradise Below the palace near Surang Gate ⓣ0747/244 4679. Newly restored *haveli* with small, tastefully appointed rooms and a rooftop restaurant. Hot water 24hr. Mostly aimed at tour groups, but a few backpacker rooms go for Rs350. ❸–❻

Lake View Bohra Meghwahan Ji-ki-Haveli, opposite Nawal Sagar tank ⓣ0747/244 2326, ⓔlakeviewbundi@yahoo.com. The best of two adjoining, slightly scruffy *havelis* owned by feuding relatives who trace descent from the Diwan of Bundi. By far the best view in town, with a huge sun-soaked terrace overlooking Nawal Sagar tank. Popular choice. Home-made thalis Rs50. ❷

RN Haveli Behind Laxmi Nath temple, Rawle Ka Chow, ⓣ0747/512 0098, ⓔrnhavelibundi@yahoo.co.in. By some accounts the best guesthouse in Rajasthan, if only because it's run entirely by women – the delightfully cheeky sisters Rachna and Archna and their brave mother – who aren't afraid to speak their mind or, gasp, go shopping in the bazaar with foreign men! The 200-year-old haveli itself is a bit run-down and six rooms have bucket showers only, but there's never a dull moment and the home-cooked meals are excellent. ❶–❷

Travel details

Trains

Jaipur to: Agra (2 daily; 7hr); Ahmedabad (7 daily; 9–14hr); Ajmer (8 daily; 2–3hr); Alwar (7 daily; 2hr 35min–4hr); Bikaner (4 daily; 8–10hr); Chittaurgarh (2 daily; 7hr 40min–8hr 15min); Churu (3 daily; 5hr 20min); Delhi (10 daily; 4hr 20min–6hr 30min); Jhunjhunu (3 daily; 4hr 40min–6hr); Jodhpur (5 daily; 5hr–6hr 10min); Kolkata (Calcutta; 1 daily; 29hr); Kota (3 daily; 3hr 30min); Mount Abu (3 daily; 7–8hr); Mumbai (2 daily; 18–22hr); Sawai Madhopur (2–3 daily; 2hr–3hr 20min); Udaipur (2 daily; 12hr).

Jodhpur to: Abu Rd (2 daily; 6hr); Agra (1 daily; 13hr); Ahmedabad (2 daily; 12hr); Bikaner (5 daily; 5–7hr); Delhi (2 daily; 11–13hr); Jaipur (5–6 daily; 5–7hr); Jaisalmer (2 daily; 6hr); Osian (1 daily; 2hr 30min); Udaipur (2 daily, change at Marwar; 12hr 30min).

Udaipur to: Ahmedabad (2 daily; 12hr); Ajmer (2 daily; 7hr 15min–12hr 40min); Chittaurgarh (2 daily; 3hr 30min–4hr 30min); Delhi (2 daily; 17–23hr); Jaipur (2 daily; 10–11hr); Jodhpur (2 daily, change at Marwar; 12hr 30min).

Buses

Jaipur to: Abu Rd (1 daily; 11hr); Agra (hourly; 5hr); Ahmedabad (1 daily; 16hr); Ajmer (hourly; 1hr 55min–2hr 30min); Alwar (hourly; 4hr); Bharatpur (every 30min; 4hr 30min); Bikaner (11 daily; 7hr 30min); Chittaurgarh (7 daily; 7hr 15min); Churu (every 30min; 4hr 30min); Delhi (every 15min; 6hr); Jaisalmer (2 daily; 13–15hr); Jhunjhunu (every 30min; 5hr); Jodhpur (every 30min; 7–8hr); Kota (12 daily; 6hr); Kolkata (Calcutta; 4 weekly; 24hr); Nawalgarh (hourly; 3hr); Pushkar (9 daily; 3hr 30min–4hr); Sawai Madhopur (2 daily; 4hr 30min); Sikar (every 15min; 3hr); Udaipur (hourly; 10hr).
Jaisalmer to: Ajmer (1 daily; 12hr); Barmer (hourly; 3hr 30min); Bhuj (3 weekly; 16hr); Bikaner (4 daily; 7hr); Jaipur (2 daily; 13–15hr).
Jodhpur to: Agra (1 daily; 10hr); Ahmedabad (4 daily; 11hr); Ajmer (hourly; 5hr); Bharatpur (3 daily; 10hr); Bikaner (hourly; 6hr); Delhi (3 daily; 11–12hr); Jaipur (10 daily; 7hr); Jaisalmer (hourly; 5hr 30min); Mount Abu (1 daily; 9hr 30min); Osian (every 30min; 2hr); Ranakpur (5–6 daily; 4hr 15min); Udaipur (9 daily; 9–10hr).
Udaipur to: Agra (1 daily; 14hr); Ahmedabad (hourly; 7hr); Ajmer (hourly; 7hr); Bikaner (2 daily; 12hr); Bundi (10 daily; 7hr); Chittaurgarh (hourly; 3hr–3hr 30min); Delhi (4 daily; 15hr); Jaipur (hourly; 10hr); Jaisalmer (1 daily; 15hr); Jodhpur (11 daily; 9–10hr); Kota (10 daily; 6hr); Mount Abu (10 daily; 7hr); Mumbai (1 daily; 2hr 15min); Ranakpur (6 daily; 3hr).

Flights

Jaipur to: Ahmedabad (2 weekly; 1hr); Delhi (4 daily; 40min–1hr); Jodhpur (1 daily; 40min); Kolkata (Calcutta; 4 weekly; 2hr–3hr 40min); Mumbai (3 daily; 1hr 35min); Udaipur (3 daily; 45min–1hr 50min).
Jodhpur to: Delhi (2 daily; 1hr 20min); Jaipur (3 daily; 40min–1hr 35min); Mumbai (2 daily; 2hr 20min); Udaipur (2 daily; 40min–4hr 25min).
Udaipur to: Delhi (3 daily; 1hr 10min–3hr); Jaipur (2 daily; 45min–1hr 50min); Jodhpur (2 daily; 40min–4hr 20min); Mumbai (3 daily; 1hr 15min).

CHAPTER 3

Highlights

* **Taj Mahal** The highest expression of Moghul culture, and one of the most stunning buildings in the world. See p.285
* **Akbar's mausoleum, Sikandra** The great Moghul's tomb looks just as it does in old miniatures, with tame monkeys and deer wandering in its ornamental gardens. See p.294
* **Fatehpur Sikri** An awesomely grand deserted palace complex, straddling an arid ridge near the Rajasthani border. See p.298
* **Kalinjar Fort** Remote fortifications in UP's dusty badlands, far from the tourist trail. See p.328
* **Varanasi** Take a boat on the Ganges before dawn to watch the sun rise over India's most ancient and sacred city. See p.329
* **Sarnath** Evocative ruins on the site where the Buddha gave his first sermon. See p.344

△ Bathers at a Ganges *ghat*, Varanasi

3

Uttar Pradesh

Known as **UP** since the Raj days of the United Provinces, **UTTAR PRADESH**, or "the Northern State", is the heartland of Hinduism and Hindi, dominating the nation in culture, religion, language and politics. A vast, steamy plain of the Ganges, its history is very much the history of India, and its temples and monuments – Buddhist, Hindu and Muslim – are among the most impressive in the country.

Not far from Delhi, in the west of the state, **Agra** (home of the Taj Mahal) and deserted **Fatehpur Sikri** stand as poignant reminders of the great Moghuls. Nearby, somehow sheltered from successive waves of Muslim conquest, the much-mythologized Hindu land of **Braj** – centred on **Mathura** and **Vrindavan** – was the childhood playground of the god Krishna.

Central UP, and especially **Lucknow**, the state capital, is redolent with memories of the lavish and ultimately decadent last days of Muslim rule, when the Kingdom of Avadh faded away before the advance of the British imperialists in the nineteenth century. The scars of the First War of Independence or "Mutiny", a despairing reaction to the British usurpation of power, have in places yet to heal. To the southeast, **Allahabad** is the site of one of the world's largest religious fairs, when millions congregate at the confluence of the Ganges and the Yamuna rivers to mark the auspicious occasion of **Kumbh Mela**. Along the southern borders of the state, the rugged Vindhya Mountains mark the end of the Deccan plateau. Once the domain of the Chandela Rajputs, the belt known as **Bundelkhand** harbours forgotten fortresses such as gigantic **Kalinjar**; the fort at **Jhansi** remains a symbol of the struggle for Independence.

The Ganges meanders across the vast plains of **Eastern UP** to the holiest Hindu city of all – the sacred *tirtha* (crossing-place) of **Varanasi**, where death transports the soul to final liberation. Even before Hinduism, this land was sacred; the Buddha himself, and the founder of Jainism, Mahavira, frequented Varanasi, while the whole state – from Mathura to **Sarnath** on the outskirts of Varanasi, and beyond to the great schools of learning in Bihar – was long under the influence of Buddhism.

Although UP was once a thriving centre of Islamic jurisprudence and culture, many Muslims departed during the painful years after Independence, and the Muslim population now comprises just sixteen percent. In recent years, **Gangetic UP**, known derisively elsewhere as the "cow belt", has been plagued by caste politics and is dominated by the right-wing Hindu BJP, who control its government. The state acquired an unfortunate reputation as the focus of bitter communal tensions, most notoriously in the wake of the destruction of the Babri Masjid mosque in Ayodhya in 1992, and there have been further incidents of communal violence in recent years.

With an efficient if basic state bus system and an excellent railway network, **travelling around** the state is generally straightforward (except in Bundelkhand in the south). The major tourist cities, Agra and Varanasi, have been coping with visitors and pilgrims for centuries, and today have good transport connections and all the facilities the traveller could require.

Western UP

On the fringes of Delhi and serving as the gateway to the heartland of the subcontinent, **Western Uttar Pradesh** has always been close to the centre of power in India. Once the Moghul capital, **Agra** is renowned for the most stunning mausoleum in the world – the **Taj Mahal** – as well as the stupendous battlements and palaces of the **Agra Fort**. Not far away, the sandstone pavilions of **Fatehpur Sikri**, built by the Moghul emperor Akbar and abandoned after only fifteen years, remain perfectly preserved in the dry desert-like air.

The earliest records of the area date back 2500 years, when Gautama Buddha visited the ancient city of **Mathura**, whose strategic position at the junction of several major trade routes had already earned it the prosperity that was to attract numerous adventurers and conquerors. Later, Mathura was incorporated at the centre of the Hindu mythological landscape of **Braj**, associated with the childhood of Krishna.

Agra

The splendour of **AGRA** – capital of all India under the Moghuls – remains undiminished, from the massive fort to the magnificent **Taj Mahal**. Along with Delhi, 204km northwest, and Jaipur in Rajasthan, Agra is the third apex of the "Golden Triangle", India's most popular tourist itinerary. It fully merits that status; the Taj effortlessly transcends all the frippery and commercialism that surrounds it, and continues to have a fresh and immediate impact on all who see it. That said, Agra city itself can be an intense experience, even for seasoned India hands. Years of corruption and political neglect have reduced its infrastructure to a shambles: filthy water and open sewers are ubiquitous, power cuts routine and the traffic pollution appalling (some mornings you can barely see the sun through the fog of fumes). Moreover, as a tourist you'll have to contend with often overwhelming crowds at the major monuments, absurdly high admission fees, and some of Asia's most persistent touts, commission merchants and rickshaw-wallahs. Don't, however, let all this put you off. Although it's possible to see Agra on a day-trip from Delhi, the Taj alone deserves so much more – a fleeting visit would miss the subtleties of its many moods, as the light changes from sunrise to sunset – while the warren of old streets and bazaars around it offers glimpses of an Indo–Muslim way of life that, in many respects, has altered little since the time of the Moghuls.

Some history

Little is known of the pre-Muslim history of Agra; one of the earliest chronicles, dated to the Afghan invasion under Ibrahim Ghaznavi in 1080 AD, describes a robust fort occupying a chain of hills, with a flourishing city strategically placed at the crossroads between the north and the centre of India. However, Agra remained a minor administrative centre until 1504, when the Sultan of Delhi, **Sikandar Lodi**, moved his capital here so as to keep a check on the warring factions of his empire. The ruins of the Lodis' great city can still be seen on the eastern bank of the Yamuna. After defeating the last Lodi sultan, Ibrahim Lodi, at Panipat in 1526, **Babur**, the founder of the Moghul empire, sent ahead his son **Humayun** to capture Agra. In gratitude for their benevolent treatment at his hands, the family of the Raja of Gwalior rewarded the Moghul with jewellery and precious stones – among them the legendary **Koh-i-noor Diamond**, now among the crown jewels of England.

Agra's greatest days arrived during the reign of Humayun's son, **Akbar the Great** (1556–1605), with the construction of Agra Fort. The city maintained its position as the capital of the empire for over a century; even when **Shah**

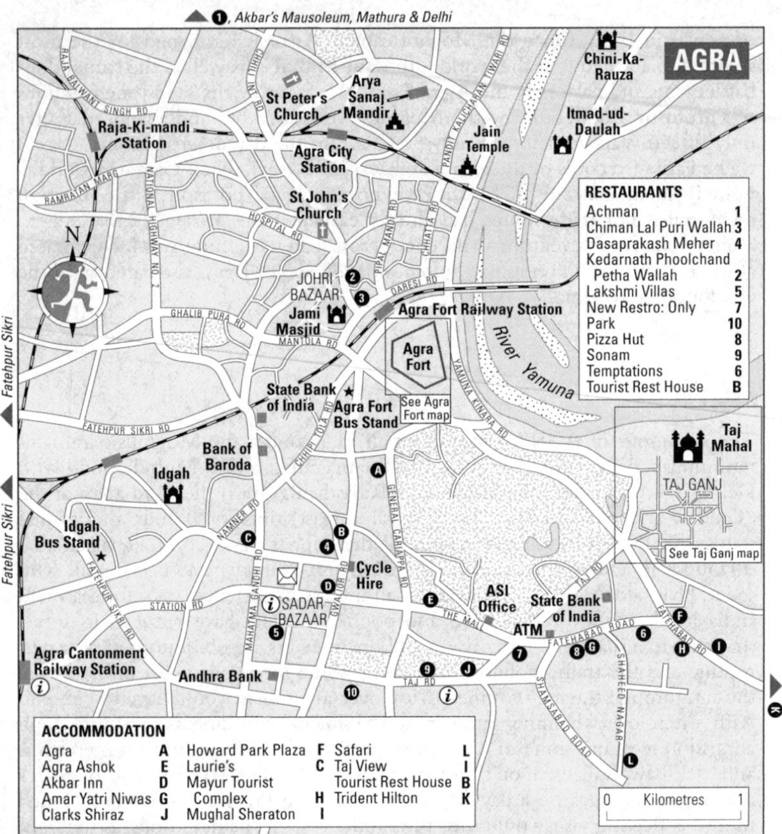

Jahan, Jahangir's son and successor, built a new city in Delhi, his heart remained in Agra. He pulled down many of the earlier red-sandstone structures in the fort, replacing them with his hallmark – exquisite marble buildings. Although the empire flourished under his heir Aurangzeb (1658–1707), his intolerance towards non-Muslims stirred a hornets' nest. Agra was occupied successively by the Jats, the Marathas, and eventually the British.

After the uprising in 1857, the city lost the headquarters of the government of the Northwestern Provinces and the High Court to Allahabad. Agra began to decline, but its medieval treasures ensured its survival, and today the city is once again prospering, as an industrial and commercial centre as well as a tourist destination.

Arrival and information

Agra has no less than six **railway stations**, though visitors are only likely to use two of them. The busiest is **Agra Cantonment** (Cantt), in the southwest, which serves Delhi, Gwalior, Jhansi and points south, has a tourist information counter and is near most hotels. Trains from Rajasthan pull in close to the Jami Masjid at **Agra Fort station**, further from the main hub of hotels. Although

Agra City station may sound centrally located, don't be persuaded to get off here, as it's an expensive rickshaw ride away from the town (and most of Agra's accommodation).

To get to a hotel, use the prepaid auto-rickshaw/taxi booth at Agra Cantonment station (Rs45/125) or flag down one of the cycle rickshaws (Rs25) that wait in the forecourt outside; avoid the drivers who dash onto the platform to find passengers. They invariably demand an inflated price and can get quite aggressive. Bear in mind, too, that most cycle rickshaw and auto-rickshaw drivers will try and gain commission by taking you to a hotel, and may tell you (falsely) that the hotel of your choice is closed.

Buses usually stop at **Idgah bus stand** close to Agra Cantonment station, though services from Mathura arrive at the more chaotic **Agra Fort bus stand**, just west of the fort. Some buses from Delhi stop outside the fort gate, where you'll have no trouble finding a rickshaw.

Kheria Airport is 7km west from the city centre. Pre-paid taxis charge Rs200 to most of the hotels.

Information

Agra has two **tourist offices**, one run by the Government of India at 191 The Mall (Mon–Fri 9am–5.30pm, Sat 9am–1pm; ⓣ0562/236 3959), and another run by UP Tourism at 64 Taj Road (Mon–Sat 10am–5pm,; ⓣ0562/222 6378, ⓦwww.up-tourism.com); there is also an information booth (Mon–Sat 8am–8pm, closed second and last Sat of each month; ⓣ0562/236 8598) at Cantonment station. The Government of India office is better organized and provides information about other destinations, though both supply information on hotels and local sights as well as details of **tours** that start and end at Agra Cantonment railway station.

City transport

Plans are being considered to create a two-kilometre pollution-free exclusion zone around the Taj, banning the petrol and diesel-powered vehicles which choke the city and spoil its architecture. At present, however, only a 500-metre ban is enforced (on scooters, auto-rickshaws and taxis). The only environment-friendly initiative in operation is an **electric bus** for tourists connecting the fort to the Taj (Rs4), and the fleet of green-painted tempos and auto-rickshaws, whose exhaust fumes are no less noxious for the "Clean Agra, Green Agra" slogans daubed across their backs. Although becoming fairly scarce, **tongas** (horse-drawn carriages) may also be encouraged as part of the pollution-control scheme, but the sight of skinny near-lame horses often covered in open sores tends to put most people off.

Tours in and around Agra

There are currently two official **tours** (daily except Friday) of Agra run by UP Tourism, designed to coincide with the main train connections on the Taj Express to and from Delhi. Pickup for both starts at 10.15am at the Government of India tourist office on The Mall, with the second stop at Agra Cantonment railway station at 10.20am. The main tour (Rs1650 including all admission charges and guide) then proceeds to Fatehpur Sikri before returning to the *Taj Kheema* hotel for lunch (not included in the price) at 2pm; the other tour just goes to Fatehpur Sikri at 3.00pm before returning to Agra in time to catch the Taj Express to New Delhi Nizamudddin at 6.25pm. Though useful for those with limited time, the tours are rather rushed and don't cover Akbar's mausoleum and the tomb of Itmad-ud-Daulah ("Baby Taj").

Another alternative is the city's dwindling fleet of **cycle rickshaws**, whose persistent drivers invariably offer their services for day tours; more often than not, they'll have a book full of encouraging comments from delighted tourists. Apart from being cleaner and greener than autos, they provide a livelihood for some of the city's poorest inhabitants. An American-backed NGO has been attempting to improve the lot of Agra's rickshaw-wallahs by introducing new, lightweight, super-strong cycle rickshaws, complete with raised passenger seats and two-speed gears. You'll come across these in the more touristy areas of town, where their drivers are encouraged to buy them using zero-interest bank loans, paid back at a manageable rate of Rs5 per day – considerably less than the rental fees most rickshaw-wallahs have to pay to their bosses.

Auto-rickshaws are faster, but contribute in no small part to Agra's traffic and pollution problems. Fares, including waiting time, are reasonable as long as you bargain hard, although the trip out to Akbar's tomb and other monuments on the outskirts of the city can cost up to Rs100. **Taxis** are handy for longer trips to the airport or Fatehpur Sikri. Expensive hotels have their own fleet of vehicles, and there are taxi ranks at the stations and airport.

Whichever form of transport you choose, expect to have to haggle hard. Agra sees so many "fresh" tourists that the drivers will always quote high prices. Also, note that many rickshaw- and taxi-drivers will stop at jewellers, marble shops and the like to earn **commission**; some will even quote you a lower fare if you agree to visit a couple of emporiums en route. Don't consent to this (their commission will only be added to your bill should you buy something).

The best way to sidestep the hassle of public transport is to rent a **bicycle** and do everything at your own pace. Try the rental shop near the *Taj View Hotel* or the Raja Cycle Stall near the tonga stand in Taj Ganj; charges should be around Rs4 per hour, and no more than Rs35 per day. If you **walk**, expect an unending stream of offers from cycle- and auto-rickshaw-wallahs. Whatever form of transport you opt for, an early start for the Taj is essential; book rickshaws and taxis the night before.

Accommodation

Taj Ganj, the grid of narrow lanes immediately south of the Taj, is where most budget travellers end up in Agra. With their matchless rooftop views, laid-back terrace cafés and rock-bottom room rates, the little guesthouses here can be great places to stay. Their downside is the constant hassle at street level, and the fact that the whole Taj Ganj tourist "scene" can completely eclipse the traditional feel of the area. In this case, you may be happier in the more modern **Tourist Complex** district, southwest of Taj Ganj, or the leafier, greener **Cantonment**, near Agra Cantonment railway station, which has places to suit every budget from overlanders' campsites to luxurious five-star hotels.

The Taj Ganj hotels and guesthouses listed below are marked on the **map** of Taj Ganj on p.285; all others appear on the map of Agra, p.280.

Taj Ganj

Host West Gate ⓣ0562/233 1010. Simple, small rooms, most of them with air-coolers, cable TV and a view of the Taj from the roof. Holes in the sheets, but otherwise a well-maintained place that's ideal as an overspill for the *Siddhartha* next door. ❷

India South Gate ⓣ0562/233 0909. Tiny, ultra-basic place whose rudimentary rooms (the one on the upper storey is best) are worth enduring for the warm hospitality of the proprietor, Mrs Nirmal. ❶

Indo 2/9 South Gate ⓣ0562/223 2638. Another pint-sized family guesthouse with rock-bottom rates, small, very basic rooms and friendly (mostly female) management. ❶

Kamal Chowk Kagzi, South Gate ⓣ0562/233 0126, ⓔhotelkamal@hotmail.com. Run-of-the-mill rooms with attached bathrooms in a dull concrete building, but right in the thick of things and with a great view from the rooftop restaurant. ❷–❹

Noorjahan South Gate (no phone). Closest to the south gate of the Taj, the rooms here are small and very basic (some with shared bathrooms). To sample the acclaimed view, you'll have to climb a ladder to the roof. ❶–❸

Shah Jahan South Gate ⓣ0562/233 1159. Variously priced, mostly clean and cosy rooms with tiny marble bathrooms, run by a well-travelled, elderly Muslim gentleman. The best are on the top floor, and there's a café with great views on the roof. ❶

Shanti Lodge Chowk Kagzi, South Gate ⓣ0562/233 1973. One of the most popular backpackers' places in Taj Ganj: avoid the poky rooms with smelly shower-toilets in the old block, and ask for one in the new annexe around the back – these are large, well ventilated and have clean tiled bathrooms. Views of the Taj from the rooftop restaurant are the best in this area. ❸

Sheela East Gate ⓣ0562/233 1973, ⓔhotelsheela@yahoo.com. Easily the best budget hotel in Taj Ganj: secluded, impeccably clean rooms only 200m from the Taj (inside the "no pollution zone"), ranged around a lovely little garden; the air-cooled options are larger and only slightly more expensive. Dependably hygienic restaurant (see p.296) and a friendly Alsatian dog add to its charm. Advance telephone bookings accepted. ❷–❸

Shyam Palace Next to the Central Bank ⓣ0562/233 1599. Large, marble-floored rooms opening onto a peaceful courtyard garden that doubles as a low-key restaurant; in need of lick of paint, but generally clean. All rooms come with fresh linen, attached bathrooms and 24hr hot-water power showers. Good value, but check your bill carefully for extra "service charges". ❶–❷

Siddartha West Gate ⓣ0562/233 0001. A clean and popular guesthouse with plain, spacious rooms set around a leafy courtyard café that includes fragments of medieval walls. The best rooms on the top floor come with air-coolers. ❶–❷

Cantonment

Agra General Cariappa Rd ⓣ0562/236 3331, ⓔagrahotel@yahoo.co.in. Former British *burra sahib*'s bungalow that's retained some of its old-world charm in spite of general shabbiness. The rooms (some a/c) are dim and musty but spacious, with large bathrooms and hot-water showers. ❸–❺

Agra Ashok 6B The Mall ⓣ0562/236 1233, ⓦwww.hotelagraashok.com. Undergoing refurbishment at the time of writing, this is one of the least expensive five stars in town. Facilities include pool, health club/spa, bar, snazzy Chinese restaurant and reasonably priced car rentals. Doubles from $80. ❾

Akbar Inn 21 The Mall ⓣ0562/222 6863, ⓔhotel_akbar_inn@yahoo.com. Deep in the cantonment green-belt, with deservedly popular budget rooms surrounding a lawn. The rock-bottom options are some of the cheapest in Agra (Rs60); the pricier ones are much larger (some with a/c), and open onto a long veranda where simple, freshly prepared meals are served. ❶–❸

Clarks Shiraz 54 Taj Rd ⓣ0562/222 6221, ⓦwww.hotelclarksshiraz.com. Huge tower-block five-star in a pleasant cantonment setting, with extensive grounds, swimming pool, golf green, restaurants, bar, shopping arcade, banks and travel services on the premises. Rooms start at around $95. ❾

Laurie's Mahatma Gandhi Rd ⓣ0562/236 4536, ⓕ226 8045. One of Agra's legendary hotels, dating from the British era, though it has definitely seen better days. Open-air swimming pool (filled intermittently and in a poor state) and pleasant grounds and gardens where you can camp. ❻

Tourist Rest House Katcheri Rd, Baluganj ⓣ0562/236 3961, ⓔdontworrychickencurry@hotmail.com. The best-value, most welcoming budget hotel in this area, if not in all Agra: some rooms are on the small side, but are immaculately clean, with attached bathrooms and 24hr running hot water; there's also a few new, much larger rooms with TV, fridge and a/c. Meals are served in the sociable, leafy ground-floor courtyard or in new dining hall. There's also a phone booth, Internet facilities and back-up generator. Rickshaw-wallahs don't get commission here, so will try to take you to one of the "soundalikes". ❶–❷

South of Taj Ganj

Amar Yatri Niwas Fatehabad Rd ⓣ0562/223 3030, ⓔamaragra@sancharnet.in. Popular and good-value multistorey hotel that's central and well maintained, if a bit bland. All mod cons, including a health club and swimming pool. ❻

Howard Park Plaza Fatehabad Rd ⓣ0562/233 1870, ⓔhppi@nde.vsnl.net.in. Smart and central, with a pool and an appealing restaurant that overlooks gardens. Aimed primarily at business clients, its large rooms with all mod cons are a good deal at this price (from $65). ❽–❾

Mayur Tourist Complex Fatehabad Rd ⓣ0562/233 2302, ⓕ233 2707. Clusters of large, semi-detached huts with TV, a/c and attached bathrooms, arranged around a large peaceful garden. Facilities include a multi-cuisine restaurant, dingy bar and swimming pool. ❺–❻

Mughal Sheraton Fatehabad Rd ⓣ0562/233 1701, ⓦwww.sheraton.com. Opulent chain five-star on the edge of town with gourmet restaurants, a bar and a large pool, but the fake Moghul splendour feels overdone. Rooms start at $90. ❾

Safari Shaheed Nagar, Shamsabad Rd ⓣ0562/233 3029. Friendly and relaxed hotel. Most rooms are clean and spacious, with attached bathrooms (with bath), and there are views of the distant Taj from the rooftop café. If it's full, don't be tempted into the shabby and overpriced *Gypsy* next door. ❷–❸

Taj View Fatehabad Rd ⓣ0562/233 1841, ⓦwww.tajhotels.com. All the hallmarks of the *Taj* group of luxury hotels, including an inlaid-marble lobby and swish rooms (the pricier ones have views of distant Taj – just about). Rooms from $120. ❾

Trident Hilton Tajnagri, Fatehabad Rd ⓣ0562/233 1818, ⓦwww.trident-hilton.com. Among the most attractive of the modern upscale hotels, in mock-Moghul style with a large pool and multi-cuisine brasserie. Usually swamped with tour groups. Recommended for disabled travellers. Rooms start at $125. ❾

The City

Agra's densely populated heart is the sprawling labyrinth of bazaars, alleys and cramped, crumbling tenements clustered around the onion domes of the **Jami Masjid**, but the most useful landmark in the city is the **fort** immediately south of the mosque, rising above the sharp bend in the River Yamuna where it changes its course to flow past the **Taj Mahal**, 2km east. Directly south of the Taj is the budget travellers' enclave of **Taj Ganj**, while most of the mid- and

Kabootars

Look up from any Taj Ganj roof terrace around 4pm, when the sun is low and the city's bulbous onion domes and minarets glow pale orange, and you'll see a side of local life of which few tourists are aware. Pigeons, or **kabootars**, wheel above clusters of men and boys staring skywards from their flat rooftops, shouting, whistling and waving sticks at the birds. Agra's pigeon fanciers, known as *kabootar baz*, don't race their pigeons, but fly them in flocks, controlling them with a code of high-pitched whistles and calls that are as much a feature of Muslim districts like Taj Ganj as the *muezzin*'s call to prayer. The waving of sticks is supposed to keep the lazier pigeons in the air, although a couple of sleepy specimens can usually be spotted hiding on nearby satellite dishes, waiting for their owners to scatter soaked grain for them to feed on. When this happens, the rest of the flock drops back to ground in a cloud, and pecks around the roof of their coop, or *kabootar khana*, for the grain. This five- or ten-minute cycle is then repeated for an hour or so until the pigeons have been well exercised.

Pigeon fancying is an established tradition in Agra, and in cities such as Old Delhi and Lucknow, where there are sizeable Muslim communities (Hindus rarely indulge in the sport). Its techniques were set down by Akbar's poet laureate, Abu'l Fazl, for the Moghul court who considered it a noble pastime, and to this day men and boys across Urdu-speaking parts of India still take their *kabootar* flying very seriously. Thoroughbred birds change hands for more than Rs5000, a fortune considering the average income of most *kabootar baz*. Owning a large flock brings with it a certain cachet, and the coveted title of *Barra Kabootar Baz*, literally "Big Pigeon Fancier". Once a man is deemed to have mastered the plethora of tricks and subtleties of this ancient sport, he may even be known among his peers as a *Khalifa*, or "Great Master". Only *Khalifas* can direct their flocks in perfect parabolic curves, or single files across the sky, or command them to encircle a neighbours' flock and drive it to ground.

Four or five flocks fly above Taj Ganj each day. You can watch them from your guesthouse rooftop, but if you'd like to get closer to the action, ask around for an introduction to a *kabootar baz* – the manager of the *Shah Jahan Lodge* on South Gate can arrange for you to meet his neighbour, Danesh Khan, a *Barra Kabootar Baz* who keeps his birds on an adjacent roof.

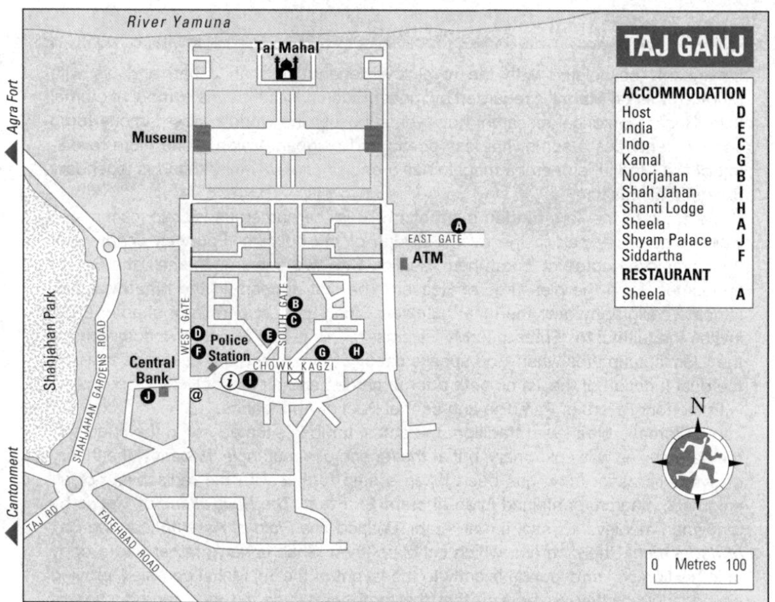

upper-range hotels, restaurants and other tourist amenities are dotted around the leafier commercial centre of **Sadar Bazaar** and the old British military **Cantonment** area, insulated from the mayhem of the centre by a swathe of open parkland.

Of the city's monuments, **Agra Fort** provides the best insight into the private lives of the Moghuls, its high sandstone ramparts crowded with golden pavilions and richly inlaid marble apartments. Immediately across the river, the tranquil tomb of **Itmad-ud-Daulah** is even more ornately decorated, while **Akbar's mausoleum** at Sikandra, 10km northwest, and the abandoned capital of **Fatehpur Sikri**, 40km west, are further unforgettable echoes of the most grandiloquent chapter in Indian history.

The Taj Mahal

Described by the poet Rabindranath Tagore as a "tear on the face of eternity", the **Taj Mahal** (daily 6am–7pm, closed Fri; Rs750 [Rs20]) is undoubtedly the zenith of Moghul architecture and quite simply one of the world's most marvellous buildings. Volumes have been written on its perfection, and its image adorns countless glossy brochures and guidebooks; nonetheless, the reality never fails to overwhelm all who see it, and few words can do it justice.

The glory of the monument is strangely undiminished by the crowds of tourists who visit, as small and insignificant as ants in the face of this immense and captivating structure. That said, the Taj is at its most alluring in the relative quiet of early morning, shrouded in mists and bathed with a soft red glow. As its vast marble surfaces fall into shadow or reflect the sun, its colour changes, from soft grey and yellow to pearly cream and dazzling white; it's well worth visiting at different times. This play of light is an important decorative device, symbolically implying the presence of Allah, who is never represented in anthropomorphic

The secret symbolism of the Taj Mahal

Inextricably associated with the royal love legend of Shah Jahan and his wife Mumtaz, the **Taj Mahal** is regarded by most modern visitors as *the* symbol of eternal love. Recent historical research, however, suggests the world's most famous tomb complex encodes a somewhat less poetic and poignant vision – one more revealing of the Moghul emperor's megalomania and unbridled vanity than his legendary romantic disposition.

The clues to the Taj's **hidden symbolism** lie in the numerous Islamic inscriptions which play a key part in the overall design of the building. Fourteen chapters of the Koran are quoted at length here, dealing with two principal themes: the Day of Judgement, and the pleasures of Heaven. The first appears in the broad band of intricate calligraphy over the main gateway. Citing the last phrase of chapter 89, it invites the faithful to "Enter thou My Paradise". This is one of only two occasions in the Islamic scriptures when God speaks directly to man, and the quotation stresses the dual function of the Taj as both a tomb garden and replica of Heaven, complete with the four Rivers of Paradise and central Pool of Abundance.

In a dramatic break with tradition, the actual tomb is situated not in the middle of the gardens, as was customary, but at the far end of a rectangle. Recently, the theory of symbolic association has been taken a step further with the rediscovery of an enigmatic diagram contained in an **ancient Sufi text**, *The Revelations of Mecca* by renowned medieval mystic, Ibn al 'Arabi. Entitled *The Plain of Assembly on the Day of Judgement*, the diagram, which scholars know Shah Jahan's father had a copy of in his library, corresponds exactly to the layout of the Taj Mahal complex, proving beyond doubt, they now claim, that the tomb was intended as a reproduction of God's throne. Given that the emperor's remains are enshrined within it, the inevitable conclusion is that, aside from being an extravagant romantic, Shah Jahan possessed an opinion of his own importance that knew no bounds. While scholars continue to debate the symbolism of the Taj, they are united in disbelieving the popular, but wholly apocryphal, image of Shah Jahan's last days as propounded by the tour guides. Far from spending his old age gazing whimsically down the river to the tomb of his beloved wife, the Moghuls' most decadent emperor expired after a protracted bout of sex and drug-taking. His death in 1666, at the ripe old age of 74, was brought about not by grief, but by a massive overdose of opium and aphrodisiacs.

form. The Taj is also particularly beautiful after dark, when the moonlight shimmers on the facade; at the time of writing, has been opened to visitors in 30min slots (8pm–midnights) on the night of the full moon, two days preceding and two days following it. Tickets have to be purchased a day in advance from the Archeological Survey of India office, 22 Mall Rd (Mon–Sat 10am–5pm; ⓣ0562/222 7261).

Overlooking the River Yamuna, and visible from the fort in the west, the Taj Mahal stands at the northern end of vast gardens enclosed by walls. Though its layout follows a distinctly Islamic theme, representing Paradise, it is above all a monument to romantic love. **Shah Jahan** built the Taj to enshrine the body of his favourite wife, Arjumand Bann Begum, better known as **Mumtaz Mahal** ("Elect of the Palace"), who died shortly after giving birth to her fourteenth child in 1631. The Shah was devastated by her death, and set out to create an unsurpassed, eternal monument to her memory. Of all the Moghuls, only Shah Jahan, who had been designing palaces and forts since the age of sixteen, could have come up with such a magnificent design. The name of the chief architect is unknown, but Amanat Khan, who had previously worked on Akbar's tomb, was responsible for the calligraphic inscriptions that adorn the gateways, mosque and tomb. Construction by a workforce of some 20,000 men from all over Asia commenced in 1632, and the mausoleum was completed in 1653. Marble was brought from Makrana, near Jodhpur in Rajasthan, and precious stones for decoration – onyx, amethyst, lapis lazuli, turquoise, jade, crystal, coral and mother-of-pearl – were carried to Agra from Persia, Russia, Afghanistan, Tibet, China and the Indian Ocean. The story is given an exquisite poignancy by the fate of Shah Jahan himself, who became a tragic and inconsolable figure. Eventually, his devout and austere son Aurangzeb seized power, and Shah Jahan was interned in Agra Fort, where as legend would have it he lived out his final years "gazing wistfully at the Taj Mahal" in the distance (although the truth is somewhat less poetic: see opposite). He died there in January 1666, with his daughter, Jahanara Begum, at his side; his body was carried across the river to lie alongside his beloved wife in his peerless tomb.

The complex

The walled **complex** is approached from the south through a red sandstone forecourt, Chowk-i Jilo Khana, whose wide paths, flanked by arched kiosks, run to high gates in the east and west. The original entrance, a massive arched gateway topped with delicate domes and adorned with Koranic verses, stands at the northern edge of Chowk-i Jilo Khana, directly aligned with the Taj, but shielding it from the view of those who wait outside.

Once beyond the southern wall, you'll see the mighty marble tomb at the end of superb gardens designed in the *charbagh* style so fashionable among Moghul, Arabic and Persian architects. Dissected into four quadrants by waterways, they evoke the Islamic image of the Gardens of Paradise, where rivers flow with water, milk, wine and honey. The "rivers" converge at a marble tank in the centre that corresponds to *al-Kawthar*, the celestial pool of abundance mentioned in the Koran. Today only the watercourse running from north to south is filled, and then only for special occasions, and its precise, glassy reflection of the Taj is a favourite photographic image. Views from the paths lining the east–west canal, lined with lofty trees, ferns and deep red and pink flowers, are equally sublime. To the west of the tomb is a domed red-sandstone mosque, and to the east a replica (*jawab*), probably built to house visitors, and necessary to achieve perfect symmetry.

Essentially square in shape, with peaked arches cut into its sides, the Taj Mahal surmounts a square marble platform marked at each corner by a high minaret. Topped with a huge central dome, it rises for over 55m, its height accentuated by a crowning brass spire, itself almost 17m high. Steps lead to the platform, and visitors must remove their shoes before climbing to the tomb. The marble floor can be icy cool in the morning, but at midday it gets extremely hot – you may want to wear socks, or rent a cloth foot-cover from the shoe attendants. On approach, the tomb looms ever larger and grander, but not until you are close do you appreciate both its awesome magnitude and the extraordinarily fine detail of relief carving, highlighted by floral patterns of precious stones. Carved vases of flowers – including roses, tulips and narcissi – rise subtly out of the marble base, a pattern repeated more colourfully and inlaid with precious stones around the four great arched recesses (*pishtaqs*) on each side. Arabic verses praising the glory of Paradise fringe the archways, proportioned exactly so that each letter appears to be the same size when viewed from the ground.

The south face of the tomb is the main entrance to the **interior**: a high, echoing octagonal chamber flushed with pallid light reflected by yellowing marble surfaces. A marble screen, cut so finely that it seems almost translucent and decorated with precious stones, scatters dappled light over the cenotaph of

Pollution threatening the Taj Mahal

Although the Taj Mahal may appear to the untrained eye almost as perfect as the day it was completed, the marble is undeniably sullen and yellow in parts, and empty casings here and there betray lost precious stones. These are the early effects of the threat posed by **pollution** from traffic and industry, and the millions of tourists who visit the tomb year-round. While marble is all but impervious to the onslaught of wind and rain that erodes softer sandstone, it has no natural defence against the sulphur dioxide that lingers in a dusty haze and shrouds the monument; sometimes the smog is so dense that the tomb cannot be seen from the fort. Sulphur dioxide mixes with atmospheric moisture and settles as sulphuric acid on the surface of the tomb, making the smooth white marble yellow and flaky, and forming a subtle fungus that experts have named "**marble cancer**".

The main sources of pollution are the continuous flow of vehicles along the national highways that skirt the city, and the 1700 **factories** in and around Agra – chemical effluents belched out from their chimneys are well beyond safety limits laid down by environmental committees. Despite laws demanding the installation of pollution-control devices, the imposition of a ban on all petrol- and diesel-fuelled traffic within 500m of the Taj Mahal, and an exclusion zone marking 10,400 square kilometres around the complex that should be free of any new industrial plants, pollutants in the atmosphere have continued to rise (many blame the diesel generators of nearby hotels), and new factories have been set up illegally. In 1993, the Supreme Court finally took action and ordered nearly three hundred plants to shut down until emissions fell to legal limits.

Cleaning work on the Taj Mahal rectifies the problem to some extent, but the chemicals used will themselves eventually affect the marble, while the doubtful methods of the Archeological Survey of India, such as scrubbing with toothbrushes, may prove disastrous in the long term. Attendants already shine their torches on repaired sections of marble to demonstrate how they've lost their translucency. Hopes for proper care of the Taj Mahal have been raised since the government turned its attention to the plight of India's greatest monument, while entry fees for foreign visitors have been increased, supposedly to regulate the flow of tourists and generate much needed income. However, the UP government have more than just the threat of pollution damage to worry about. In early 2005, they launched an investigation into claims that decreased water levels in the Yamuna have led to dangerous **tilts** in the Taj's minarets, and fears that unless something is done to restore the Yamuna to previous levels, the entire building could collapse. It would seem that for the moment, the fate of the Taj Mahal hangs in the balance.

(For more on the admission fee controversy, see Viewing Practicalities, opposite).

Mumtaz Mahal in the centre of the tomb, and that of Shah Jahan next to it. Inlaid stones on the marble tombs are the finest in Agra; attendants gladly illuminate the decorations with torches. No pains were spared in perfecting the inlay work – each petal or leaf may comprise up to sixty separate stone fragments. Ninety-nine names of Allah adorn the top of Mumtaz's tomb, and set into Shah Jahan's is a pen box, the hallmark of a male ruler. These cenotaphs, in accordance with Moghul tradition, are only representations of the real coffins, which lie in the same positions in an unadorned and humid crypt below that's heavy with the scent of incense and rose petals. Have a few coins ready as a respectful donation to an attendant priest, who will lay the offering on the graves.

If you're spending a full day at the Taj and want a break from the sun, make a small detour to the **museum** (daily 10am–5pm; included in Taj entrance fee), in the western wall of the enclosure. The collection features exquisite miniatures, two marble pillars believed to have come from the fort, and portraits of Moghul rulers including Shah Jahan and Mumtaz Mahal. Further into the building a gallery shelters architectural drawings of the Taj Mahal, a display of elaborate porcelain, seventeenth-century coins and examples of stone inlay work, though you'll more than likely have seen enough of that in the Taj.

Taj Mahal viewing practicalities

India's most famous monument became the centre of heated controversy in December 2000, when the Agra Municipality and Archeological Survey of India (ASI) jointly imposed a hike in **admission charges** for foreign visitors from Rs15 to a whopping Rs960 for a day ticket; it's since been reduced to its present level of Rs750.

Further disputes followed the announcement, in January 2001, that the Taj would be **closed on Fridays** (instead of Mondays, as it had been previously) – a move strongly resisted by Agra's vociferous Muslim community, many of whom visit the Taj to pray on the Islamic Sabbath. The profit-boosting measures would, it was claimed, generate revenue for "essential renovation work". However, most in the local tourist industry point out that little has been done to beautify the green belt around the complex in order to reduce the damaging effects of traffic pollution. In a city renowned throughout India for its corrupt politicians, little of the extra cash has been "ploughed back into the upkeep of the Taj" (or any other of the 3606 monuments on India's critical list).

Galling though the price increase is, comparatively few visitors refuse to pay it; fewer still regard the expense as money wasted once they are inside. That said, foreign tourists these days rarely visit the Taj on several consecutive days. To appreciate the famous play of light on the building, you'll have to stick around from dawn until dusk (ticket valid all day, but only for one entrance). Thankfully, the gardens are the most blissful place to spend a day in Agra. Hawkers and salesmen are not allowed in, and official guides are not available on site, so no one is likely to pester you while you're dozing or reading on the lawns.

The only ways to **see the Taj for free** are by climbing onto a Taj Ganj hotel rooftop or, better still, by heading across the Yamuna to **Katchpura** village. From the opposite bank of the river, the view is breathtaking, especially at dawn. **Boats** ferry foot passengers across from the *ghats* just east of the Taj at first light, charging what they can get away with (anything from Rs100 to Rs1000, depending on the size of your camera). Alternatively, hire a rickshaw-wallah for the trip, or cycle there yourself. You cross the river on the road bridge north of Agra Fort, and turn right when you reach the far bank, following the metalled road until it enters the village of Katchpura; here, it becomes a rough track that eventually emerges at a small Dalit shrine on the riverside, directly opposite the Taj and next to the entrance of the Mehtab Garden (daily dawn to dusk; Rs100). You can see the Taj from the garden's floodlit walkways, and from outside the gardens on the riverbank.

Agra Fort

The high red-sandstone ramparts of **Agra Fort** (dawn to dusk; Rs300 [Rs20]) dominate a bend in the River Yamuna 2km northwest of the Taj Mahal. Akbar laid the foundations of this majestic citadel, built between 1565 and 1573 in the form of a half moon, on the remains of earlier Rajput fortifications. The structure developed as the seat and stronghold of the Moghul empire for successive generations: Akbar constructed the walls and gates, his grandson, Shah Jahan, had most of the principal buildings erected, and Aurangzeb, the last great emperor, was responsible for the ramparts.

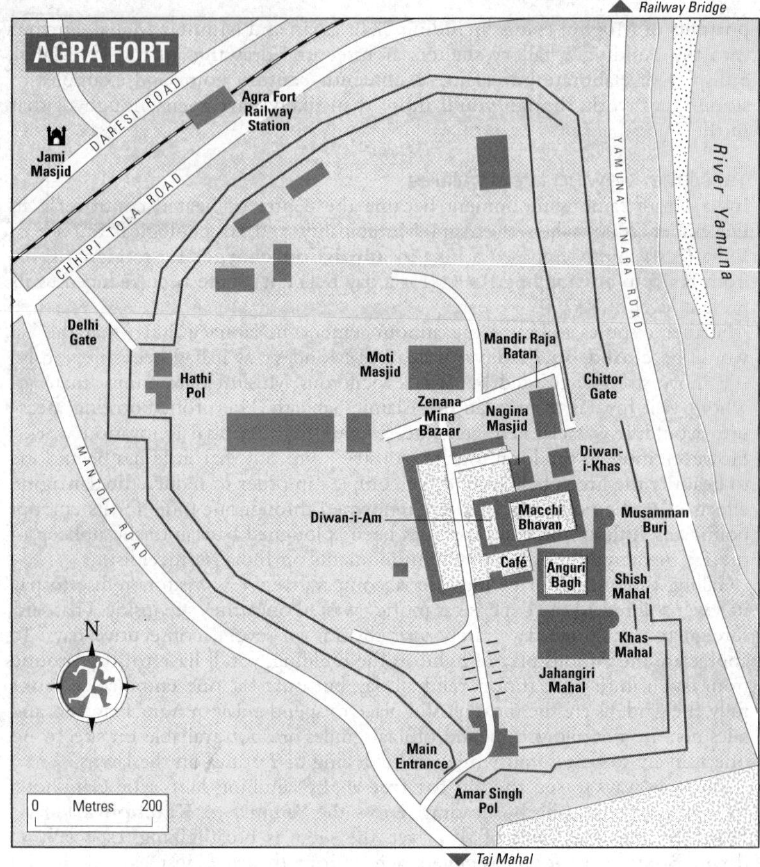

The curved bastions of the sandstone battlements are interrupted by massive gates, of which only the **Amar Singh Pol** is open to the public. Ornamented with glazed tiles, and boasting impressive double walls and a forecourt, it was used by the victorious General Lake when he entered the fort in 1803. The original and grandest entrance, however, was through the western **Delhi Gate**, leading to the inner portal, **Hathi Pol** or "Elephant Gate", now flanked by two red-sandstone towers faced in marble, but once guarded by colossal stone elephants with riders – destroyed by Aurangzeb in 1668.

Access to much of the fort is restricted, so masterpieces of Moghul architecture such as Shah Jahan's beautiful **Moti Masjid** ("Pearl Mosque") are out of bounds to visitors. Only those parts open to the public are described in detail below, working in an anticlockwise direction from Shah Jahan's Hall of Public Audience to the private apartments.

Diwan-i-Am and the great courtyard

Once through the Amar Singh Gate, ignore, for the time being, the complex of ornately carved buildings on your right and continue straight ahead through a second gate to a spacious enclosure dominated by the graceful **Diwan-i-Am**

("Hall of Public Audience"). Open on three sides, the sandstone pillared hall, which replaced an earlier wooden structure, was constructed by Shah Jahan in 1628 and, after use as an arsenal by the British, was restored in 1876 by Sir John Strachey. Three rows of white polished stucco pillars topped by peacock arches support a flat roof; the elegance of the setting would have been enhanced by the addition of brocade, carpets and satin canopies for audiences with the emperor. The ornate throne alcove is inlaid in marble decorated with flowers and foliage in bas-relief, and connects to the royal chambers within. Encrusted with diamonds, rubies and emeralds, the **Peacock Throne** which it was built to house was removed to the Red Fort in Delhi when Shah Jahan shifted his court there; it eventually ended up in Persia after the fort was looted by Nadir Shah in 1739. Adjacent to the alcove, the Baithak, a small marble block, is where ministers would have sat to deliver petitions and receive commands. This is also where trials would have been conducted, and justice speedily implemented. The East India naval commander William Hawkins, who attended Jahangir's court between 1609 and 1611, noted the presence next to the emperor of his "master hangman, who is accompanied with forty hangmen, with an hatchet on their shoulders; and others with sorts of whips being there, readie to do what the King commandeth".

An incongruous intrusion in the centre of the great courtyard is a Gothic Christian tomb marking the **grave of John Russel Colvin**, the Lieutenant-Governor of the Northwestern Provinces who died here during the Mutiny of 1857.

The royal pavilions

Clustered around a high terrace overlooking the river, the **royal pavilions** were designed to catch the cool breezes blowing across the Yamuna – and for ease of access to a water supply. The **Macchi Bhavan** ("Fish Palace"), approached through the alcove in the Diwan-i-Am, has suffered through the ages. During the period of Jat control, the Maharaja of Bharatpur removed some of its marble fixtures to his palace in Deeg; later, the zealous evangelist Lord William Bentinck (governor-general from 1828–35) auctioned off much of the original mosaic and fretwork, including parts of the **Hammam-i-Shahi**, the royal bath. The palace was once strewn with fountains and flowerbeds, interspersed with tanks and water channels stocked with fish for the angling pleasure of the emperor and courtiers. In the northwest corner of the enclosure, the exquisite little **Nagina Masjid** ("Gem Mosque") is entirely made of marble. Capped with three domes and approached from a marble-paved courtyard, it was built by Shah Jahan for the ladies of the *zenana* (harem). Below it, overlooked by a beautiful marble balcony with carved lattice screens and peacock arches, is the **Inner** or **Zenana Mina Bazaar**, where ladies of the court could look at goods such as silk, jewellery and brocade offered by merchants, without being seen themselves.

Salvaged by Akbar as a trophy from the horrific sacking of the Rajput stronghold of Chittor (now Chittaurgarh in southeast Rajasthan; see p.266), the **Old Water Gate** (also known as the **Chittor Gate**), was installed in 1568, and leads to the **Mandir Raja Ratan**, erected in 1768 during the Jat occupation of the fort. Past this is the Hall of Private Audience, the **Diwan-i-Khas**, where the emperor would have received kings, dignitaries and ambassadors, and where recently completed paintings or architectural plans were submitted for his approval. Erected in 1635, the building was badly damaged when it came under bombardment by General Lake in 1803, but the hall – with its ornate pillars and arches inlaid with lapis lazuli and jasper – survives. Two thrones adorn the large terrace in front of the Diwan-i-Khas, one of black slate and the other of white marble. Shah Jahan apparently took his evening repose in the white throne; from the black one, the emperor would amuse himself by watching elephant fights in the eastern enclosure.

A doorway from the rear of the Diwan-i-Khas leads to a two-storeyed pavilion or tower known as **Musamman Burj**, famous in Moghul legend as the spot where, in the open octagonal chamber atop the highest of the riverside bastions, Shah Jahan caught his last glimpse of the Taj Mahal before he died. Surrounded by a veranda, the elegant pavilion has a lattice-screen balustrade with ornamental niches; exquisite *pietra dura* inlay covers almost every surface, and a marble *chhatri* adds the finishing touch. In front of the tower a courtyard, paved with marble octagons, centres on a *pachisi* board where the emperor, following his father's example at Fatehpur Sikri, played a rather bizarre version of the game (a form of backgammon) using dancing girls as pieces.

To the south of Musamman Burj lies the marble building known as **Khas Mahal** ("Private Palace"), possibly used as a drawing room or the emperor's sleeping chamber. Designed essentially for comfort, it incorporates cavities in its flat roofs to insulate against the searing heat of an Agra summer, and affords soothing riverside and garden views. The palace is flanked by two Golden Pavilions, their curved roofs covered with gilded copper tiles, in a style inspired by the thatched roofs of Bengali village huts. Stretching in front of the Khas Mahal to the west is **Anguri Bagh** ("Grape Garden"), a miniature *charbagh*, with its quarters delineated by wide marble pavements. In the northeast corner, the **Shish Mahal** ("Palace of Mirrors") was where royal women bathed in the soft lamplight reflected from the mirror-work mosaics that covered the walls and ceiling. Connected to the Khas Mahal by an extensive corridor, the **Shah Jahani Mahal** ("Shah Jahan's Palace") is supported by wooden beams; its four chambers were originally painted in bright colours and embossed in gold.

The palaces of Jahangir and Akbar

Immediately southwest of the Shah Jahani Mahal is the robust, square **Jahangiri Mahal**. This red-sandstone palace, built either by Jahangir or by Akbar on his son's behalf, is almost entirely Hindu in its interior design. In the Assembly Hall, carved ornamental brackets support beams, wide eaves and ceilings with struts; the serpentine form being emitted from a dragon's mouth is reminiscent of a Gujarati temple.

Rooms to the west are thought to have been the temple and drawing room of Akbar's Rajput wife Jodhabai. Below the palace, three storeys of basement chambers were used to escape the heat. **Jahangir's Hauz** or cistern, a giant bowl made in 1611 from a single block of porphyry and inscribed in Persian, was unearthed in the nineteenth century and stands in the courtyard in front of the Jahangiri Mahal. Filled with rosewater, it would have been used by the emperor as a bathtub.

Returning towards Amar Singh Gate to the left, an assembly hall, a veranda overlooking the river and excavations are all that remain of the southernmost palace, the once extensive **Akbari Mahal**, built in 1571.

Jami Masjid and the bazaars

Opposite the fort and overlooking Agra Fort railway station, the **Jami Masjid** or "Friday Mosque" was built by Shah Jahan in 1648 and dedicated to his favourite daughter, Jahanara Begum. Standing on a high plinth approached by stairs, and with five arched entrances to the courtyard, the mosque is crowned by three large sandstone domes distinguished by their zigzag bands of marble. Along the wings of the main prayer wall, panels of beautifully inlaid sandstone similar to those decorating the main gateway of the Taj Mahal add an appropriately feminine touch. Still in use today, the mosque is one of the city's main landmarks, and serves as a useful reference point when exploring the crowded **bazaars** that sprawl from its base. These are laid out in a street plan that has barely altered since Moghul days, and are best negotiated on foot. Opposite the northeast corner of the complex, look out for the **petha-wallahs**, purveyors of Agra's most famous sweets, which are made from crystallized pumpkins (and devoured with relish by the wasps living in the eves of the mosque *mihrab* arches).

The Jami Masjid can be reached from Mantola Road, which runs northwest from the fort; alternatively, avoid the traffic by approaching through the station, taking a short cut through the mail office on the far platform. For photography, the optimum time to visit is between 7am and 8am, when the morning sun accentuates the warm reds of the stonework.

Itmad-ud-Daulah

Standing on the east bank of the Yamuna less than 3km from the city, amid gardens replete with scampering monkeys, the beautiful **Itmad-ud-Daulah** (daily dawn to dusk; Rs110 [Rs15]) is the tomb of Mirza Ghiyath Beg, an important member of Akbar's court and later *wazir* (chief minister) to, and father-in-law of, Emperor Jahangir. The first building to be built of white inlaid marble in Moghul India, this charming two-storey mausoleum, which Agra's rickshaw-wallahs misleadingly call the "**Baby Taj**", is small but perfectly executed, with translucent stones set into its walls and tracery-work. It's unmistakeably feminine, having been designed by Ghiyath Beg's daughter, the favourite queen of Jahangir and the most powerful woman in Moghul history – she was named Nur Jahan, "Light of the World", by Jahangir. He respected her intellect and talent so much that he ordered coins to be minted in her name, and by the time of her father's death in 1622 she had substantial control over the empire.

The square mausoleum, with an octagonal turret at each corner, foreshadows the Taj Mahal in its exclusive use of marble, but is more daintily proportioned and has a pavilion on its roof rather than a dome. However, recent "restoration" work has resulted in poor-quality plaster obscuring some of the exquisite detail, and in other places semiprecious stones that were once embedded into the marble have been winkled out and stolen. Ghiyath Beg's grave is underground, next to his wife's sarcophagus, shrouded in flowers. A pierced and intricately carved wall in front of the entrance to the grave casts a soft hazy light over paintings of flowers, cypresses, vases and wine vessels, all symbols of paradise.

Chini-ka-Rauza and Ram Bagh

Less than 1km north of Itmad-ud-Daulah is **Chini-ka-Rauza**, built in 1635 and reputed to be the mausoleum of Afzal Khan, a Persian poet and Shah Jahan's prime minister. Neglected and decaying, its soft brown stone is victim to the elements and is now crumbling away into the riverbank. Topped with an Afghan-style bulbous dome, the dull, earth-coloured tomb is a far cry from Nur Jahan's delicate work, but is distinctive as Agra's sole Persian construction. Parts of the walls are still covered with the coloured enamel tiles (*chini*) that once enhanced the whole of the exterior and gave the tomb its name, while traces of paintings and Islamic calligraphy can still be made out on the high domed ceiling.

Akbar's mausoleum: Sikandra

Given the Moghul tradition of building magnificent tombs for men and women of high status, it comes as no surprise that the mausoleum of the most distinguished

Moghul ruler was one of the finest and most ambitious structures of its time. A majestic composition of deep-red sandstone and cool marble designed by the emperor himself and modified in 1605 by his son, Jahangir, **Akbar's mausoleum** (daily dawn to dusk; Rs110 [Rs15]) borders the roadside at **SIKANDRA**, 10km northwest of Agra. Rickshaws charge at least Rs100 to make the round trip, or you could hop on any bus bound for Mathura from the Agra Fort bus stand.

Although neither as grand nor as awesome as the indomitable Taj, this stately structure possesses a serenity sometimes absent among the throngs of tourists at Agra's most visited monument. It also marks the important transition in Moghul design after Akbar's death, when his bold, masculine red-stone monuments were superseded by more ethereal and sensuous marble buildings, epitomized and perfected in the Taj Mahal itself. The most overwhelming feature of the complex is its huge south gate, **Buland Darwaza** or "Gateway of Magnificence" – so high that it obstructs any view to the tomb beyond. Surmounted by four tapering marble minarets, and overlaid with marble and coloured tiles set in repetitive geometrical patterns, it bears the Koranic inscription "These are the gardens of Eden, enter them and live forever". Buy a ticket at the office set into the left face of the gate, then walk through to the gardens, divided by wide paved walkways into four equal quadrants in typical Moghul fashion, and enclosed by high walls. Along the paths, friendly long-tailed langur monkeys laze in the sunshine and groom one another, and black buck roam through the tall grasses, just as they do in the Moghul miniature paintings dating from the era when the tomb was constructed.

In the centre of the gardens, directly in front of Buland Darwaza, the broad-based square **mausoleum** has arcaded cloisters along each side and pavilions enhanced by delicate marble domes rising above its centre. A high marble gateway in the southern face draws attention to meticulous lattice screens shielding a small vestibule, once painted with rich sea-blue frescoes and Koranic verses. From here a ramp leads to a subterranean crypt, where Akbar's grave lies sprinkled with rose petals and bathed in a cool yellow light.

Eating

Considering the number of tourists that pass through, Agra suffers from a dearth of good **places to eat**. With a few notable exceptions, the best restaurants are all in the upscale hotels, where, at a price, you can sample the city's speciality, **Mughlai cooking**. Imitated in Indian curry houses throughout the world, Agra's traditional Persian-influenced cuisine is renowned for its rich cream- and curd-based sauces, kebabs, naan and tandoori breads roasted in earthen ovens, *pulao* rice dishes and milky sweets such as *kheer*. However, you'll be hard pushed to find more than pale imitations in the cramped cafés and rooftop terrace restaurants of **Taj Ganj**. These places may serve much cheaper meals than you'll find further south in **Sadar Bazaar** and the **Tourist Complex** area, but the overall **poor standards of hygiene** in this district, combined with a spate of poisoning incidents (see box opposite), and the fact that most "restaurants" are merely set up as a means for touts and shop owners to hook customers, we strongly recommend you steer clear of them. The one exception is the *Sheela*, near the East Gate, reviewed below. Other than *Sheela*, which is shown on the Taj Ganj map (p.285), all the places listed here are marked on the Agra map, p.280.

Local specialities of Agra are the *petha* (crystallised pumpkin) with the best being the Panchi brand, available at various outlets all over Agra; there's also

Taj Ganj restaurants

Agra has long been renowned for its con-tricksters, but in the late 1990s some dodgy operators in **Taj Ganj** have come up with a scam so cynical it makes phoney policemen and fake gemstone peddlers look pedestrian.

The first sign of something amiss is when, shortly after a meal at a Taj Ganj café, you suddenly fall ill. As luck would have it, the rickshaw-wallah taking you back to your hotel, or some other seemingly sympathetic person such as your hotel manager, happens to know a good doctor nearby, who makes a prompt diagnosis, checks you into his private "clinic" and prescribes some pills. While you're throwing up with a drip in your arm, he faxes your medical insurers and starts claiming a huge sum of money for daily health-care costs. What you don't know, though, is that the drugs you're taking are the reason why, days later, you're still ill, and that the "doctor" has all along been in cahoots with both the rickshaw driver and restaurant.

In November 1998, dozens of so-called "clinics" were raided and their records scrutinized after a young British couple who'd been poisoned went to the Agra press with their experience. The story was soon picked up by the national dailies in Delhi and an investigation began, leading to the arrests of several doctors and co-conspirators, but no-one was convicted. No further inclidents have been reported since then, but nonetheless it remains a good idea to avoid the restaurants in Taj Ganj (unless they're listed in our Eating reviews). Failing that, stick to your hotel restaurant (although some tourists were poisoned in their own hotels) and if you do get sick, go to a reputable hospital, not a backstreet clinic (see Listings on p.296).

ghazak, a rock-hard candy with nuts that's available all over the Taj Ganj area, and *dalmoth*, and a crunchy mix made with black lentils best bought at Sadar and Johri bazaars.

Achman By-Pass Rd, Dayal Bagh. Among Agra-wallahs, this is the most rated restaurant in the city, famous for its *navratan korma* (a mildly spiced mix of nuts, dried fruit and *paneer*), *malai kofta* and chickpea masala, as well as wonderful stuffed naans. Well off the tourist trail in the north of the city, but ideally placed for dinner on your way home from Sikandra. Most mains around Rs75.

Chiman Lal Puri Wallah Opposite northeast wall of Jami Masjid. An Agra institution for five generations, this much-loved little café-restaurant looks a touch grubby from the outside, but serves delicious *puri*-thalis, with two veg dishes and melt-in-the-mouth saffron-flavoured *kheer* (Mughlai rice pudding) – all for Rs20. Ideal pit-stop after visiting the mosque.

Dasaprakash Meher Theatre Complex, 1 Gwalior Rd, close to the *Hotel Agra Ashok*. Offshoot of the famous Chennai restaurant, serving a limited menu of superb South Indian food (their onion *rawa* masala dosas and cheese *uttapams* are sublime), and an extensive ice cream menu (the "hot fudge bonanza split" wins by a nose). Count on Rs200 per head for the works.

Kedarnath Phoolchand Petha Wallah Johri Bazaar, five minutes' walk north of Jami Masjid. One of Agra's many famous sweet and *namkeen* shops for *petha* and *dalmoth*.

Lakshmi Villas Sadar Bazaar. Unpretentious South Indian café on the posh side of town, offering the usual *iddli-dosa-uttapam* menu, with delicious *chatni-sambar*, and much lower prices than *Dasaprakash*.

Only Corner of The Mall and Taj Rd. One of Agra's most popular north Indian restaurants, usually packed with local families and tourist groups and known for its Tandoori and rich Mughlai dishes like the butter chicken and malai kofta. There's seating in an indoor a/c dining room, or in a pleasant courtyard in the evenings. Mains Rs80–100.

Park Restaurant Taj Rd, Sadar Bazaar. Delicious Mughlai food and a reputation for careful cooking ensure popularity with both locals and tourists. The dining hall is sparsely furnished but immaculately kept, and blissfully air-conditioned. Dishes come in three gravies: ultra-mild "white" cashew, medium "onion", and red-hot "tomato", served with delicious garlic naans and cold Kingfishers. Main dishes Rs70–120; half portions available.

Pizza Hut Fatehabad Rd ☎0562/233 3051. Usual pizza and pasta from this Western chain (with Western prices); deliveries to hotels available.

Sheela East Gate, Taj Ganj. One of the few genuinely dependable, inexpensive and pleasant places to eat near the Taj. The menu features a good choice of simple (mostly vegetarian) Indian dishes, as well as drinks and snacks, and the fruit-and-nut lassis are a must. Seating outside in shady garden, or inside the narrow café.

Sonam 51 Taj Rd. This mid-priced garden restaurant and bar is another infamous tourist trap, but at least the food is good. The Indian options are best, attempting to re-create medieval Mughlai cuisine. There's a budget section featuring thalis, and buffets are put on in winter. Credit cards accepted.

Temptations Fatehabad Rd. Trendy little place, complete with fibre optic wall and MTV, serving huge and somewhat expensive portions of good quality Indian classics.

Tourist Rest House Baluganj. Atmospheric, candle-lit garden restaurant serving a modest selection of (large) breakfasts and tasty Indian dishes to a sedate clientele of foreign backpackers. Try the tasty cheese *malai kofta*, rounded off with fruit custard like you never ate at school. All mains under Rs50.

Shopping

Agra is renowned for its **marble** tabletops, vases and trays, inlaid with semi-precious stones in ornate floral designs, in imitation of those found in the Taj Mahal. It is also an excellent place to buy **leather**: Agra's shoe industry supplies all India, and its tanneries export bags, briefcases and jackets. **Carpets** and **dhurries** are manufactured here too, and traditional embroidery continues to thrive. *Zari* and *zardozi* are brightly coloured, the latter building up three-dimensional patterns with fantastic motifs; *chikan* uses more delicate overlay techniques.

There are several large emporiums such as the official-sounding Cottage Industries Exposition on the Fatehabad Road, which is well presented but outrageously expensive; it is one of the places you're likely to be taken to by a commission-seeking driver. Shops in the big hotels may be pricey, but their quality and service are usually more reliable. UP Handicrafts Palace, 49 Bansal Nagar, has a wide selection of marble; other state emporia round the Taj include UP's Gangotri, which has fixed prices. Close to the East Gate, Shilpgram is an extensive crafts village with arts and handicrafts from all over India, and occasional live music and dance performances.

Shopping or browsing around The Mall, MG Road, Munro Road, Kinari Bazaar, Sadar Bazaar and the Taj Complex is fun, but you need to know what you're buying and be prepared to haggle; you should also be wary of ordering anything to be sent overseas. It's advisable never to let your credit card out of your sight, even for the transaction to be authorized, and you should make sure that all documentation is filled in correctly and fully so as not to allow unauthorized later additions. A large number of serious cases of **credit-card fraud** have been reported in Agra, even in some of the most popular tourist restaurants. A list of emporia against whom complaints have been lodged is maintained by the local police department.

Listings

Banks and exchange The State Bank of India is just south of Taj Rd in the Cantonment (Amex travellers' cheques not accepted); Andhra Bank is over in Sadar Bazaar; and the Allahabad Bank is in the *Hotel Clarks Shiraz*. Money transfers can also be arranged through Sita World Travel, on Taj Rd (☎0562/236 3013). If you get caught out by a public holiday, you could always try one of the private exchange offices in the Tourist Complex Area, around *Pizza Hut* (LKP Forex, opposite the *Amar Hotel* on the Fatehabad Rd, are always reliable and fast). For those with Mastercard or Visa, ICICI Bank maintain a few ATMs (see maps on p.280 & p.285).

Hospitals Essar (☎0562/226 5587), Namner Cross Roads; GG Nursing Home (☎0562/226 5587) at Sanjay Place; Pushpanjali (☎0562/255 2981) at Delhi Gate; and the Upadhyay Hospital, Shahid

Nagar Crossing (☎0562/236 8844) are clean and dependable, with English-speaking doctors.
Internet access There are an ever-growing number of hotels, guesthouses and email booths around town, despite the notoriously undependable connection in Agra. At the time of writing, the lowest rates (Rs35/hr) and fastest connection in Taj Ganj were offered by Cyberlink on the corner of West Gate, and the main street (South Gate) through the bazaar.

Moving on from Agra

By air

Indian Airlines' **flights** to Delhi depart four times a week from Kheria airport, 7km out of town. Indian Airlines have a ticket counter at the airport (☎0562/230 2274), or you can book and re-confirm tickets at the company's office in the *Clarks Shiraz* hotel (daily 10am–1.15pm & 2–5pm; ☎0562/222 6820).

By train

Train tickets, especially to the capital, should be booked well in advance at either Agra Cantonment or Agra Fort stations, which both have fully computerized booking offices with separate tourist counters. The fastest and most expensive service to **Delhi** is the fully a/c Shatbadi Express #2001 (8.10am; 2hr 30min); in the other direction, as #2002 (8am), it travels to **Gwalior** (1hr 15min) and on to **Jhansi** (2hr 25min) from where you can catch a bus to **Khajuraho**. A convenient early-morning service to New Delhi is the A.P. Express #2723 (5.45am; 3hr 10min); the fastest midday train is the Kerala Express #2625 (12.38pm; 3hr 25min). For **Kolkata** (Calcutta), the Jodhpur–Howrah Express #2308 (5.45am; 22hr) is one of the fastest. The best train for **Varanasi** is the nightly #4854/4864 Marudhar Express (9.15pm; 13hr 30min). You can also pick up trains to **Chennai** and **Thiruvananthapuram**. For **Goa**, return to Delhi and catch the superfast #2432 Trivandrum Rajdhani (departs 11am; 25hr).

Agra's principal **Rajasthan** train is the #4853/4863 Marudhar Express, which leaves Agra Cantonment daily at 6.25am for Jaipur (7hr) and Jodhpur (13hr). From Agra Fort, the daily #5311 Lalkuan Kumaon Express (9.30pm; 11hr) travels to Lalkuan, where you can change for **Kathgodam**, the nearest railhead to the hill station of Nainital in Uttaranchal. Regular daily trains connect Agra Fort with Kanpur and Lucknow.

By bus

Travelling by **bus** along the main highways, especially to the capital on the Grand Trunk road and to Jaipur on NH-11, is considerably more hair-raising than travelling the same routes by train. Accidents, most of them head-on collisions with other buses or trucks, are disconcertingly frequent.

For those unable to get hold of a rail ticket, seats on Rajasthan Roadways buses, which leave from **Idgah bus stand** in the southwest of town, should be booked at the bus stand itself: for any destinations further afield than Jaipur, take a bus to **Jaipur** (via **Bharatpur**) and pick up a connecting service. One exception is **Ajmer**, jumping-off town for **Pushkar**, which has its own direct service (10hr). Deluxe and a/c services for Jaipur (5hr) leave from the forecourt of *Hotel Shakpura*, next to the bus stand. There's a booking office in the lodge for fast and direct private buses to **Delhi** (5–6hr) and **Gwalior** (3hr 30min), and early morning departures for **Khajuraho** (12hr), **Lucknow** (9hr 30min) and **Nainital** (10hr). Additional buses to the same destinations leave from the tourist office on Taj Road: book a day in advance at the office. If you're heading southwest towards **Bharatpur** via **Fatehpur Sikri**, catch one of the regular services from the Idgah bus stand (1hr).

Chaotic **Agra Fort bus stand** has frequent services (several each hour) on rickety, often windowless buses heading for Delhi, Mathura, Haridwar, Rishikesh and Dehra Dun, and as afar afield as Lucknow. Tickets are sold on the buses. Unless you fly, getting to **Khajuraho** involves a twelve-hour bus journey (daily; 5am), or a train to Jhansi (2hr 45min–3hr 50min), and then a six-hour bus ride from there.

Photography Agra Color Lab, E6–7 Shopping Arcade, Sadar Bazaar, and 34/2 Sanjay Place, opposite Soor Sadan, offer one-hour processing.
Post The Head Post Office is on The Mall, near the Government of India tourist office; there are smaller sub-post offices in the Taj Mahal complex and in Taj Ganj. Poste restante at the Head Post Office is inefficient and you may be better off using the Government of India tourist office's address on The Mall.
Swimming Agra's exclusive hotels sometimes let non-residents swim in their pools, for daily fees. Best of the bunch are the *Agra Ashok* (Rs300), *Clarks Shiraz* (Rs200) and the *Mughal Sheraton* (Rs200), followed by the *Park Plaza* and the *Mayur* (both Rs150).

Fatehpur Sikri

The ghost city of **FATEHPUR SIKRI**, former imperial capital of the great Moghul emperor **Akbar**, straddles the crest of a rocky ridge 40km southwest of Agra. Built between 1569 and 1585, it has lain silent for almost four centuries; by 1600, its meagre water supply had proved incapable of sustaining the population, and Akbar shifted the court to Lahore. Now deserted, it's almost perfectly preserved – a masterpiece in sandstone, glowing in subtly changing shades of pink and red as the day progresses and the light fades.

The plan to move the court here was conceived by a ruler who, tired of the crowds and congestion of Agra, wanted to create a new capital that was both an appropriate symbol of imperial power, and a sympathetic backdrop for the philosophical debates and artistic pursuits that were his passion. An astute diplomat as well as a gifted military strategist, Akbar consolidated his territorial gains in the north and west by promoting a policy of religious tolerance developed through discussions with representatives of the major faiths. He abolished the much hated poll-tax on non-Muslims (*jizya*), and was the first Moghul ruler to marry a Hindu (a Rajput princess from Jaipur). By gaining the allegiance of local rulers (often through marriage), he was also able to install the most efficient system of revenue collection ever seen in the empire, and it was this that enabled Akbar to build Fatehpur Sikri – a palace complex that would become the very embodiment of his unorthodox court, fusing Hindu and Muslim artistic traditions. Hindu buildings such as **Birbal's Palace** and **Jodhabai's Palace** mingle with the pavilions and halls of the grand court, while the **Jami Masjid**, the only building of exclusively Muslim derivation, houses one of the most exquisite mausoleums of the Moghul period, the marble **Tomb of Sheikh Salim Chishti**.

Fatehpur Sikri was originally intended to be joint capital with Agra; although it receives only a fraction of the visitors of its rival, the stunning elegance of its palace, mosque and courts ensure that it remains as powerful a testimony to Moghul grandeur. As long as you don't mind modest amenities (and salty water), it's also an enjoyably atmospheric place to stay, with a scattering of simple guesthouses huddled in the village below the ruins. The one drawback is the overall filthiness of the bazaar area, which many travellers find too high a price to pay for the awesome sight of the Buland Darwaza at sunrise.

The Royal Palace

Shunning the Hindu tradition of aligning towns with the cardinal points (as dictated by ancient canonical texts on architecture, the *Shilpa Shastras*), Akbar chose to construct his new capital following the natural features of the terrain. This is why the principal thoroughfare, town walls, and many of the most important buildings inside it (including the mint, treasury, baths and caravanserai) face

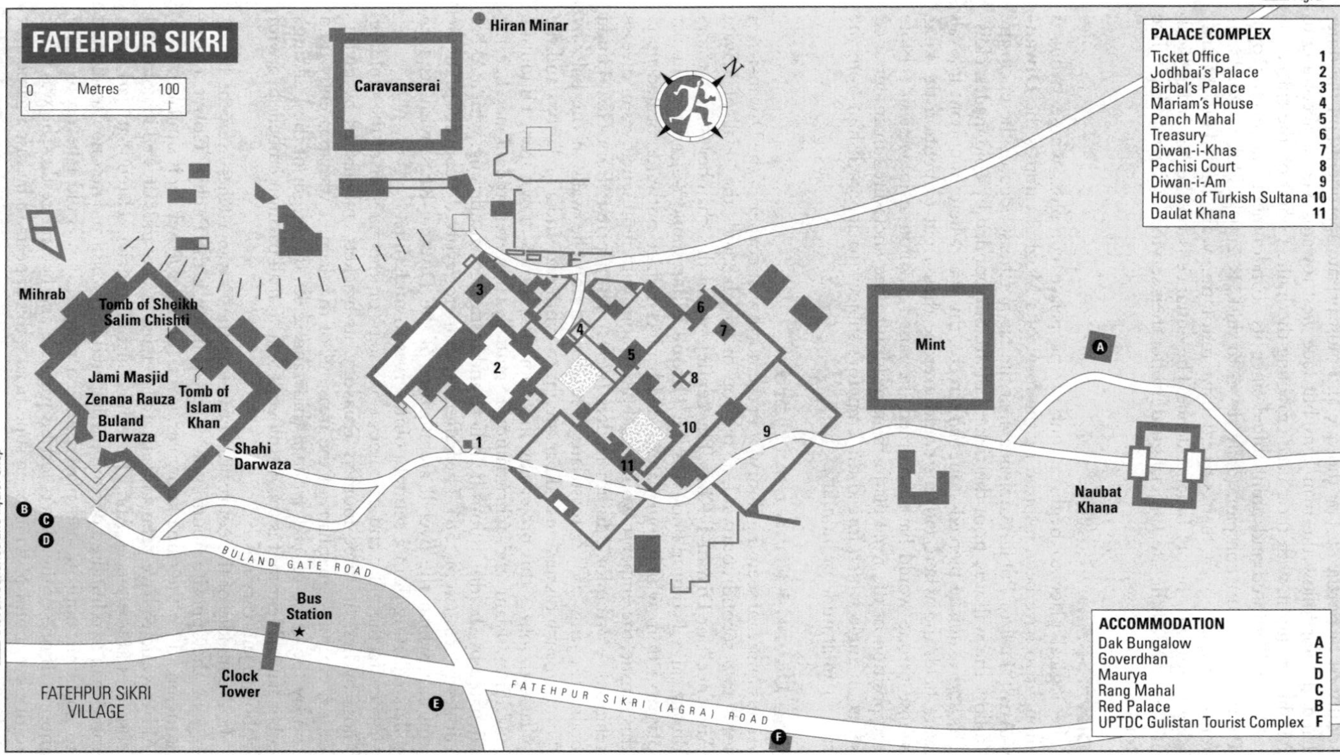
FATEHPUR SIKRI
0 Metres 100
Agra
Hiran Minar
Caravanserai
PALACE COMPLEX
Ticket Office 1
Jodhbai's Palace 2
Birbal's Palace 3
Mariam's House 4
Panch Mahal 5
Treasury 6
Diwan-i-Khas 7
Pachisi Court 8
Diwan-i-Am 9
House of Turkish Sultana 10
Daulat Khana 11
Mihrab
Tomb of Sheikh Salim Chishti
Jami Masjid
Zenana Rauza
Tomb of Islam Khan
Buland Darwaza
Shahi Darwaza
Mint
Naubat Khana
Biscuit bakeries and liquor shop
BULAND GATE ROAD
Bus Station
Clock Tower
FATEHPUR SIKRI VILLAGE
FATEHPUR SIKRI (AGRA) ROAD
ACCOMMODATION
Dak Bungalow A
Goverdhan E
Maurya D
Rang Mahal C
Red Palace B
UPTDC Gulistan Tourist Complex F
Agra & Bharatpur
Railway station

southwest or northeast. The mosque and most private apartments, on the other hand, do not follow the main axis, but face west towards Mecca, according to Muslim tradition, with the palace crowning the highest point on the ridge.

Although unused and uninhabited since its abandonment, the main **Royal Palace** and court complex (daily dawn to dusk; Rs260 [Rs20], video Rs25), remains largely intact, thanks to extensive restoration work carried out by British archeologists before Independence. The entrance is via the ASI ticket kiosk at the centre of the site. Official **guides** offer their services at the booking office for Rs75–100.

Diwan-i-Am

The logical place to begin a tour of the palace complex, whose layout is thought to have been inspired by the form of a Moghul camp, is the **Diwan-i-Am** ("Hall of Public Audience"), at the far northeast edge of the enclosure (follow the walkway from the ticket booth). Surrounded by colonnades, cloisters and exquisite pierced-stone *jali* screens, this was where important festivals were held, and where citizens could exercise their right to petition the king, whose throne would have occupied the raised pavilion at its west side. Note the position of the royal platform in relation to the enclosure's main entrance, set at an angle which forced the emperor's subjects to approach him from the side in an attitude of humility.

The Diwan-i-Khas courtyard

An insignificant seeming doorway in the northwest corner of the Diwan-i-Am leads to a second courtyard, at the top of which stands the "Hall of Private Audience", or **Diwan-i-Khas**. The centrepiece of this chamber is an extraordinary carved column known as the **Throne Pillar**, supporting a large circular platform from which four balustraded bridges radiate outwards. Seated upon this throne, the emperor would hold discussions with representatives of diverse religions – orthodox Muslim leaders (*ulema*), Jesuit priests from Goa, Hindu brahmins, Jains and Zoroastrians – ranged around the walls of the balcony. Through such discussions, Akbar sought to synthesize India's religions and the pillar symbolizes this project by incorporating motifs drawn from Hinduism, Buddhism, Islam and Christianity. Eventually, however, the *ulemas* became alienated by the discussions held here and instigated an uprising, which Akbar ruthlessly crushed in 1581. Thereafter, the emperor evolved a concept of divine kingship, which the overall architecture of the Diwan-i-Khas, with its axial pillars radiating from a central point, serves to underline.

Access to the pillar and balconies is via steps on the exterior of the building. Close by lies the three-roomed **Treasury**, its brackets embellished by mythical sea creatures, guardians of the treasures of the deep; it was apparently used to play the game of *ankh michauli* (hide and seek), the origin of the building's other name. Next to it is the Astrologer's Seat, a small pavilion embellished with elaborate Jain carvings.

In the middle of the courtyard, separating the Diwan-i-Khas from the buildings on the opposite (south) side of the complex, is the **Pachisi Court**, a giant stone board for the game known as *pachisi* (or *chawpai*), which is similar to ludo. Akbar is said to have been a fanatical player, using slave girls dressed in colourful costumes as live pieces. Abu'l Fazl, the court chronicler, related that "[at] times more than two hundred persons participated in [*pachisi*] and no one was allowed to go home until he had played sixteen rounds. This could take up to three months. If one of the players lost his patience and became restless, he was made to drink a cupful of wine. Seen superficially, this appears to be just a game. But

His Majesty pursues higher objectives. He weighs up the talents of his people and teaches them to be affable."

House of the Turkish Sultana

Immediately southeast of the *pachisi* board, the **Anup Talao Pavilion**, also known as the **House of the Turkish Sultana**, is thought to have been the palace of one of Akbar's favourite wives, the Sultana Ruqayya Begum. With balconies and Kashmiri-style woodcarvings, this exquisite building betrays Persian, Turkish and even Chinese influences, and may have been a *hammam* (bath) or pleasure pavilion. Legend has it that the great musician **Mian Tansen** once sang *Deepak*, the *raag* of fire, on its central dais. So effective was his performance that he grew hotter and hotter, until his daughter had to come to the rescue by performing the rain *raag*, *Malhar*. Understandably nervous at this great responsibility, she faltered on the seventh note of the scale, thereby creating one of the most famous and stirring *raags* of north India – *Mian ki Malhar*. Happily, the *raag* had the desired effect; rain fell, and Tansen was saved. The southern aspect overlooks the Anup Talao or "Peerless Pool" where, on a central dais surrounded by perfumed water, Akbar is believed to have taken repose.

The Daulat Khana and Panch Mahal

Facing the Turkish Sultana's house from the other side of the gardens are Akbar's private quarters, the **Daulat Khana** ("Abode of Fortune"). These comprise a series of buildings distinguished by exquisite stone *jali* screens, elaborate brackets, broad eaves, and columns mounted on carved bell-shaped pedestals. The room on the ground floor with alcoves in its walls was the emperor's library, where he would be read to (he himself was illiterate) from a collection of 50,000 manuscripts he allegedly took everywhere with him. Behind the library, the beautiful imperial sleeping chamber, the **Khwabgah** ("House of Dreams"), is decorated with faded inscriptions of Persian verse.

One of Fatehpur Sikri's most famous structures, the **Panch Mahal** or "Five-Storeyed Palace", looms northwest of here. The palace tapers to a final single kiosk and is supported by 176 columns of varying designs; the ground floor contains 84 pillars – an auspicious number in Hindu astrology. At one time, the Panch Mahal also had stone lattice screens, which would have been augmented by layers of dampened *khas*, a scented grass still harvested and used to cool verandas throughout northern India.

The women's quarters

Next to the Daulat Khana, a courtyard garden reserved for the *zenana*, the ladies of the harem, signals the start of the **women's area** of the palace complex. The adjoining **Sunahra Makan** ("Golden House") is variously thought to have been the home of the emperor's mother or the palace of one of Akbar's wives – hence its alternative names of the **Palace of the Christian Queen** and **Mariam's House** – although no record exists of Akbar's marriage to a Christian called Mariam. Once adorned with gilded murals, the only ornamentation that survives are some inscriptions of verse penned by Abu'l Fazl.

Solemnly presiding over the whole complex, the main harem, known as **Jodhabai's Palace**, blends elements of traditional Islamic architecture with Hindu influences from Gujarat and Gwalior, incorporating an elegant tulip motif characteristic of Fatehpur Sikri. Surrounding the central courtyard are four self-contained raised terraces; those on the north and south sides are

Akbar's harem

Although remembered primarily for his liberal approach to religion, Akbar was typically Moghul in his attitudes to women, whom he collected in much the same way as an obsessive philatelist amasses stamps. At its height of splendour, the **royal harem** at Fatehpur Sikri held around five thousand women, guarded by a legion of eunuchs. Its doors were closed to outsiders, but rumours permeated the sandstone walls and several notable travellers were smuggled inside the Great Moghuls' seraglios, leaving for posterity often lurid accounts of the emperors' private lives.

The size of Akbar's harem grew in direct proportion to his empire. With each new conquest, he would be gifted by the defeated rulers and nobles their most beautiful daughters, who, together with their maidservants, would be installed in the luxurious royal **zenana**. In all, the emperor is thought to have kept three hundred wives; their ranks were swollen by a constant flow of concubines (*kaniz*), dancing girls (*kanchni*) and female slaves (*bandis*), or "silver bodied damsels with musky tresses" as one chronicler described them, purchased from markets across Asia. Screened from public view by ornately pierced stone *jali* windows were women from the four corners of the Moghul empire, as well as Afghanis, Turks, Iranis, Arabs, Tibetans, Russians and Abyssinians, and even one Portuguese Christian, sent as presents or tribute.

The **eunuchs** who presided over them came from similarly diverse backgrounds. While some were hermaphrodites, others had been forcibly castrated, either as punishment following defeat on the battlefield, or after having been donated by their fathers as payment of backdated revenue – an all too common custom at the time.

Akbar is said to have consumed prodigious quantities of Persian wine, local *araq* distilled from sugar cane, *bhang* (prepared from cannabis) and opium in the drinkable form known as *majun*. The lavish dance recitals held in the harem, as well as sexual liaisons conducted on the top pavilion of the Panch Mahal and in the *zenana* itself, would have been fuelled by these substances. Over time, Akbar's hedonistic ways incurred the disapproval of his highest clerics – the *Ulema*. The Koran expressly limits the number of wives a man may take to four, but one verse also admits a lower form of marriage, known as *muta*, which was more like an informal pact, and could be entered into with non-Muslims. Akbar's abuse of this long-lapsed law was heavily criticized by his Sunni head priest during their religious disquisitions.

What life must actually have been like for the women who lived in Akbar's harem one can only imagine, but it is known that alcoholism and drug addiction were widespread, and that some also risked their lives to conduct illicit affairs with male lovers, smuggled in disguised as physicians or under heavy Muslim veils. If the reports of a couple of foreign adventurers who secretly gained access to Jehangir's seraglio are to be believed, the eunuchs were also required to intercept anything (other than the emperor) that might excite the women's passion.

In fact, the notion that the harem was a gilded prison whose inmates whiled their lifetimes away in idle vanity and dalliance is something of a myth. Many of the women in the *zenana* were immensely rich in their own right, and wielded enormous influence on the court. Jahangir's wife, Nur Jahan, virtually ran the empire from behind the screen of *purdah* during the last five years of her husband's ailing reign, while her mother-in-law owned a ship that traded between Surat and the Red Sea, a tradition continued by Shah Jahan's daughter, who grew immensely wealthy through her business enterprises.

Partly as a result of the money and power at the women's disposal, jealousies in the harem were also rife, and the work of maintaining order and calm among the thousands of foster mothers, aunties, the emperor's relatives and all his wives, minor wives, paramours, musicians, dancers, amazons and slaves, was a major preoccupation. As Akbar's court chronicler wryly observed, "the government of the kingdom is but an amusement compared with such a task, for it is within the (harem) that intrigue is enthroned".

surmounted by unusual roofs, thought to imitate the shape of bamboo and thatch, with traces of blue-glazed tile that forms a striking, distinctly Persian counterpoint to the building's beautiful local red sandstone. The **Hawa Mahal** ("Palace of the Winds"), a small screened tower with a delicately carved chamber, was designed to catch the evening breeze, while a covered walkway gave the imperial ladies of the court access to a lake which has now dried up.

The third women's palace, part of the **Haram Sara** ("Imperial Harem") is called **Birbal's Palace** – a misnomer, as Birbal, Akbar's favourite courtier, was a man and would have been most unwelcome in this area. It may in fact have been the residence of two of Akbar's senior wives. The palace's profuse carvings include a ceiling crafted to resemble a canopy of blossoms.

Jami Masjid

At the southwestern corner of the palace complex, with the village of Fatehpur Sikri nestling at its base, stands the **Jami Masjid** (daily dawn to dusk; free) or Dargah Mosque. The alignment of the entire palace complex, which faces west instead of following the ridge, was determined by the orientation of the mosque's *mihrab* (prayer niche) towards Mecca. Housing the tomb of Sheikh Salim Chishti, the mosque is unusual in that it is also a living Sufi shrine.

The main approach is through the imposing **Buland Darwaza** ("Great Gate"), though you may choose to use the Shahi Darwaza to escape the attentions of touts, unofficial guides and hawkers. Built around 1576, possibly to commemorate Akbar's brilliant campaign in Gujarat, the spectacular gate reaches a height of 54m and is scaled by an impressive flight of steps. Flanked by domed kiosks, the archway of the simple sandstone memorial is inscribed with a message from the Koran: "Said Jesus Son of Mary (peace be on him): The world is but a bridge – pass over without building houses on it. He who hopes for an hour hopes for eternity; the world is an hour – spend it in prayer for the rest is unseen."

Before entering the mosque itself, visitors are required to remove their shoes, but cloth sandals can be borrowed for a small fee. The gate leads into a vast cloistered courtyard containing the **Zenana Rauza** ("Tomb of the Royal Ladies"), and the lattice-screen **Tomb of Islam Khan**, one of many nobles buried here. The focus of the Sufi shrine or *dargah* is the relatively small but exquisite **Tomb of Sheikh Salim Chishti**, much of which was originally crafted in red sandstone and only later faced in marble: the lattice screens are among the most intricate and beautiful in the world, with striking serpentine brackets supporting the eaves.

Sheikh Salim played a crucial role in the founding of Fatehpur Sikri by prophesying the birth of a son to the emperor. When one of Akbar's wives Rani Jodhabai, a Hindu Rajput princess from Amber, became pregnant she was sent here until the birth of her son Salim, who later became the Emperor Jahangir. Fatehpur Sikri was constructed in the saint's honour. The *dargah* still attracts women who come here to pray for offspring, tying string onto the marble screen; when entering the main chamber, visitors cover their heads with cloth as a mark of respect. During Ramadan, an *urs* is held here, attracting *qawwals* (singers of Sufi songs; see p.138) from all over the country.

Practicalities

Buses to and from Agra run every half-hour from about 5.45am until 7pm, and take between one and one and a half hours. Regular buses also leave for

Bharatpur (approx every 30min; 30min); if you're in a rush, consider renting one of the Jeeps that wait outside the bus stand for Rs350–450.

Though it's well worth spending a day or two here, Fatehpur Sikri has a limited choice of places to **stay**. Unless you've pre-booked a room in the *Dak Bungalow* (see below), by far the best of the bunch is the *Goverdhan Guest House*, just east of the bus stand on Buland Gate Road (Ⓣ05619/288 2643; ❷–❸), whose spacious en-suite rooms open onto a lawn – good value, if a little grubby. This is also a dependable place to eat; unlike every other restaurant in the village, the food and hot drinks here are all made with filtered or mineral water (Fatehpur Sikri's ground water is extremely salty). Just over 1km further out of town on the Agra Road, the best fallback is the UPTDC *Gulistan Tourist Complex* (Ⓣ05619/288 2490; ❹–❺), a slightly impersonal state-run complex with en-suite rooms and a run-of-the-mill restaurant. Fatehpur Sikri's three budget guesthouses are all grouped immediately below the Buland Darwaza. The *Maurya* (Ⓣ05619/288 2348; ❷–❸) makes the most of the prime location with its atmospheric roof terrace; rooms are clean and basic, with bathrooms and hot water. In a similar mould is the *Rang Mahal* (Ⓣ05619/228 3020; ❶), next to the car park below the Buland Darwaza, and the very basic *Red Palace* (Ⓣ05619/228 8311; ❶), immediately behind it. In this bracket, however, you won't do better than the *Dak Bungalow* (no phone; ❶), located 2km northeast of the bazaar on a hill overlooking the old road into the palace complex, whose large, comfortably furnished rooms are an unbelievable bargain at Rs10; the one drawback is that you have to book ahead through the Archeological Survey, at 22 Mall Rd in Agra (Ⓣ0562/222 7261); although if you arrive late in the day and slip the chowkidar a tip, he may offer a booking on spec.

For **food**, eat either at the *Goverdhan*, UPTDC *Gulistan* or the *Maurya*, Fatephur Sikri's delicious **biscuits** are not to be missed – you can savour them hot out of the oven each evening at the bakeries on the lane leading up from the bazaar to the Jami Masjid. Nearby, next to the fork in the lane, is the **liquor shop** which, aside from the UPTDC *Gulistan*, is this predominantly Muslim village's only source of chilled beers.

Braj: Mathura, Vrindavan and around

The holy land of **BRAJ** can be precisely located on the map – centred around the city of **Mathura**, it lies in the southwestern corner of the Gangetic valley, extending 75km north to south and 50km east to west, with its northern boundary roughly 80km south of Delhi. However, its prime significance is metaphysical, as the mythological land where the Hindu god **Krishna** spent his idyllic childhood.

Early texts mention only Mathura itself – Krishna's birthplace – the forest tract of **Vrindavan**, the hill of **Govardhan**, and the **River Yamuna**. However, in the sixteenth century, Bhakti saints (Krishna devotees) such as Chaitanya and Vallabha "rediscovered" the geographical features and boundaries of the holy area and identified it with "Braj", Krishna's legendary pastoral playground. By then Vrindavan had already been decimated by deforestation, but they gave the myths a new spatial reality by mapping out the sites of Krishna's youthful adventures, pinpointing twelve smaller "forests", various woods, and assorted lakes and ponds that he might have played in. The fact that Braj lay between Delhi and Agra, and thus had borne the brunt of the Muslim conquests, provided a historical explanation for the previous "loss" of these sacred sites.

Braj became, and remains, one of the most important pilgrimage centres for devotees of Krishna, who tour the twelve forests – now reduced to groves on the outskirts of towns and villages – on foot. This great circular pilgrimage, known as the **Ban Yatra** (forest pilgrimage), or the **Chaurasi Kos Parikrama** (which refers to the circumambulatory distance of 84 *kos*, equivalent to 224km), can take several weeks. Less energetic or devout visitors may prefer to explore the major sites by bus.

Mathura

The sprawling city of **MATHURA**, 141km south of Delhi and 58km northwest of Agra, is celebrated above all as the place where Krishna was born, on the banks of the River Yamuna that features so prominently in tales of his boyhood. Hindu mythology claims that it was founded by Shatrugna, the youngest brother of Rama – hero of the *Ramayana* and incarnation of the godhead Vishnu. However, Mathura's earliest historical records date back around 2500 years, before the conquests of Alexander. Buddha himself founded monasteries here, in what was known to later Greeks as Madoura ton Theon (Mathura of the Gods). The city reached an early peak under the Indo-Bactrian Kushan people, whose greatest ruler Kanishka came to power in 78 AD. Fa Hian, the Chinese pilgrim, reported that in 400 AD it held twenty Buddhist monasteries with about three thousand resident monks. The enduring prosperity and sophistication of Mathura, which lay on a busy trade route, attracted such adventurers as the Afghan Mahmud of Ghazni in 1017, whose plundering and destruction signalled the death knell of Buddhism. Sikandar Lodi from Delhi wrought further havoc in 1500, as did Aurangzeb.

With a current population of around 460,000, Mathura has expanded rapidly in recent years, incorporating the teeming old city with its many Krishna-associated sites, a vast British military cantonment known as the **Civil Lines** to the south, and haphazard industrial development on the outskirts.

The Town

Despite its prominent history and its religious heritage, Mathura must be one of the most crowded and dusty cities in India today. The sandstone **Holi Gate** at the entrance to the old city is Mathura's major landmark, surrounded by similarly decorative temples boasting Moghul cusped arches and intricate carvings of flowers and deities. To the east, the riverfront, with its many temples haphazardly crowding the *ghats*, is minute compared with Varanasi. Flanking each temple are shops selling Krishna dolls and assorted outfits to dress them in, and other equipment necessary for devotional activities. Along the river towards the north lie the remains of **Kans Qila**, a fort built by Raja Man Singh of Jaipur and rebuilt by Akbar – little is left apart from the foundations.

To the south, the brightly coloured **Vishram Ghat** is the "*ghat* of rest", where Krishna is said to have recuperated after killing his evil uncle Kamsa. You must remove your shoes before entering the temple complex or visiting the *ghats*, no matter how muddy they are. **Boats** for river excursions (Rs25 per head) can be rented here.

Heading through the network of lanes from Vishram Ghat you come to Radha Dhiraj Bazaar and Mathura's most popular shrine, the large and ostentatious **Dwarkadhish temple**, dating from 1815. A little way north on a plinth raised above street level, **Jami Masjid** was completed in 1661 by Aurangzeb's governor Abd-un-Nabi. It has long since lost its original vivid glazed tiles, but remains surrounded by four minarets and assorted outer pavilions. Around 500m west stands another of Aurangzeb's mosques, the impressive red-sandstone **Katra Masjid**. This was erected on the foundations of the once-famous Kesava Deo temple, destroyed by the Moghul emperor, which had itself been built on the ruins of a Buddhist monastery. Some traces of the Hindu temple can be seen around the back, where the **Shri Krishna Janmasthan** or Janmabhoomi complex (summer dawn to dusk; winter 3am–8pm; free) now stands. Directly behind the mosque, approached through a corridor, a shrine marks Krishna's exact birthplace (*janmasthan*); its cage-like surround signifies that he was born in captivity, when his parents were prisoners of the tyrant king Kamsa. Inside the adjacent **Bhagwat Bhawan** – a flamboyantly modern, towering hulk also known as **Gita Mandir** – a garishly painted ceiling depicts scenes from Krishna's life. No cameras are allowed into the complex, where, although the shops and shrines combine to produce a park-like atmosphere, nothing obscures the heavy paramilitary presence – a reminder of underlying Hindu–Muslim tensions. Nearby, the impressive stepped sandstone tank of **Potara Kund** is believed to have been used to wash Krishna's baby clothes.

Close to the centre of Mathura in Dampier Park, the **Archeological Museum** (Tues–Sat 10.30am–4.30pm; free) places a particular emphasis on Buddhist and Jain sculpture dating from the Kushan (first–third centuries AD) and Gupta periods (fourth–sixth centuries). Known collectively as the **Mathura School**, it is characterized by its spotted red sandstone and reflects the assimilation of early primitive cults within the successive Jain, Buddhist and Hindu pantheons. The museum's highlight, one of the finest examples of Gupta art, is a miraculously intact standing Buddha. Shown with a beautifully benign expression, an ornate halo and delicate fluted robes, he is making the *Abhaya mudra* (fearless) hand gesture. Both this and a seated Buddha, this time depicted as the Enlightened One, are thought to have been created by the monk Dinna around 434 AD. Kushana art on display includes a headless image of King Kanishka in a central Asian tunic and boots, and some exquisite railings carved with floral motifs and human figures.

Practicalities

The city's principal **railway station**, Mathura Junction, lies south of the centre, around 4km from Holi Gate and the old city. It's on the main Delhi–Agra line, an hour and fifteen minutes from Delhi Nizamuddin on the fast Taj Express #2180, and only fifty minutes short of Agra; Mathura is also served by several Delhi–Mumbai trains such as the Golden Temple Mail #2904 and the fast Kerala Express #2626; the Pashchim Express #2926 stops at Sawai Madhopur (for the wildlife park of Ranthambore; see p.203). Mathura has two bus stands; the **Old Bus Stand** near Holi Gate has hourly connections to Agra and serves **Govardhan**, 25km west, while the **New Bus Stand**, a little way west, is used by Delhi and Jaipur, Bharatpur and Deeg buses as well as regular services to Agra. Cycle and auto-rickshaws are always on hand for local journeys, and shared tempos and horse-drawn tongas are also available. The **tourist office** (Mon–Sat 9.30am–5pm) at the Old Bus Stand is not worth seeking out; **foreign exchange** is handled by the State Bank of India, Railway Station Road.

Accommodation

Despite being an important pilgrimage centre and a large industrial and military city, Mathura offers a very limited choice of **accommodation**, and none of its upmarket hotels is especially worthy of recommendation. Neighbouring Vrindavan (see p.309) also has a small, basic range of accommodation.

Agra Bengali Ghat ⓣ0565/240 3318. Charming but small place established in 1930, overlooking the river in the old city and redolent of the atmosphere of the *ghats*. Bengali food, and a choice of clean air-cooled rooms; some have a/c. ❸–❹

International Guest House Shri Krishna Janmasthan ⓣ0565/224 3888. Large, institution-like building set in beautiful gardens beside the temple. Very affordable and clean, with a good veg café. ❶

Madhuvan Krishna Nagar ⓣ0565/242 0064, ⓕ242 0684. The top hotel in the city centre, with air-conditioned rooms and a pool (non-residents Rs200). ❺

Mansarovar Palace State Bank Crossing ⓣ0565/240 8686. Twenty-two well-appointed rooms, most with a/c and TV. Facilities include a good multi-cuisine restaurant. ❺

Radha Ashok Masani By-Pass Rd ⓣ0565/253 0395, ⓦwww.mathura-vrindavan.com/radhashok. Swish but cosy four-star, 4km northeast of town on the Delhi road. The most comfortable option in the area, with a/c rooms, garden and a pool. ❽

Eating

Due to the city's spiritual significance, restaurants and cafés in Mathura tend to serve **vegetarian** food only – the only option for non-veg is the *McDonald's*, just outside town on the road to Agra. Aside from the hotel restaurants, which are all fairly safe bets, the numerous sweetshops and *dhabas* around Holi Gate and the Shri Krishna Janmasthan serve snacks and thalis. The *Prakash dhaba* near Holi Gate is one of the best, offering delicious thalis and Thai-style *chana masala*. With branches at Shri Krishna Janmasthan and all over the city, *Brijwasi Mithai Wala* offers a huge range of fresh sweets and snacks in a clean environment; alternatively, the *Kwality Restaurant* near the Old Bus Stand, though poorly maintained and run by indifferent management, has retained much of its typical look and feel and serves decent food from an extensive menu.

Around Mathura

At the very heart of Braj, Mathura is the obvious base for peregrinations into the pastoral landscape associated with the adolescent Krishna, where the sacred temple-crowned hills of **Govardhan**, **Barsana** and **Nandagaon** stand in striking contrast to the prevailing flatness. Very little survives of its idyllic legendary forests, and only serious pilgrims would choose to walk rather than catch one of the numerous local buses.

Mahaban and Gokul

Across the Yamuna from Mathura, 10km southeast of the city and reachable by boat, rickshaw or bus, **Mahaban** and **Gokul** are associated with Krishna's foster parents, Nanda and Yashoda. There is a cluster of temples at **MAHABAN**, "the Great Forest", of which the most interesting is **Nanda's Palace**, also known as **Assi Khamba** or "Eighty Pillars", an amalgam of several influences including Buddhist. Rebuilt as a mosque under Aurangzeb, the temple's pillars resemble the Qutb Minar in Delhi, and probably date back to the tenth century.

On a high bank overlooking the river 2km from Mahaban, **GOKUL**, the cowherd encampment to which the newborn Krishna was smuggled, is the headquarters of the followers of the sixteenth-century saint Vallabha. This is where Krishna first revealed his divinity to his foster mother Yashoda – she made him open his mouth after catching him eating earth, only to peer in and see the entire universe. All of Gokul's sixteenth- and seventeenth-century temples are in a very bad state of repair.

Govardhan

GOVARDHAN, 25km west of Mathura, is significant as Krishna is said to have lifted the hill of the same name on the tip of one finger, to shelter the inhabitants of Braj from a deluge caused by the wrath of the god Indra. A popular Vaishnavite icon, the entire hill is circumambulated by thousands of pilgrims each year. The eponymous town is clustered close to a masonry tank known as Mansi Ganga, in a gap towards the hill's northern end. Two impressive **cenotaphs** immediately opposite the tank commemorate Randhir Singh and Baladeva Singh, two of the Bharatpur rajas, while the temple of **Hari Deva**, founded during the reign of Akbar, lies nearby.

Barsana and Nandagaon

The hill sites of **Barsana** and **Nandagaon**, 25km and 32km north of Govardhan respectively, were originally dedicated to Brahma and Shiva before being appropriated into the Krishna myth. An impressive stone staircase leads from the town at the base of the hill at **BARSANA** to an extensive ridge, where temples include that of **Lali ji**, a local name for Krishna's mistress, Radha.

The eighteenth-century temple of **Nand Rae** dominates the smaller hill and town of **NANDAGAON**, identified as the village of Krishna's foster father Nanda. A curious local ritual takes place each year during the spring festival of Holi. First the menfolk of Nandagaon invade Barsana, to taunt the women with lewd songs and be beaten with long wooden staffs for their pains; then on the next day the procedure is reversed, and the men of Barsana pay courting calls to the women of Nandagaon.

Vrindavan

A dusty little town on the banks of the Yamuna, 11km north of Mathura, **VRINDAVAN** is among the most important pilgrimage sites in Braj, attracting an estimated 500,000 pilgrims each year. In practice, most of these come during the spring Holi festival, which hereabouts is extended for up to a month, and during the two months of celebrations for the birthdays of Krishna and Radha, his mythical mistress, starting in August.

Although Vrindavan is in theory a *tirtha* or holy crossing place on the Yamuna, the town has in fact been progressively abandoned by the river, as it meanders away from the original two-kilometre-long waterfront – all but five of its 38 *ghats* are now without water. Neither is there much trace of the forests of the Krishna legend, and only a few sacred basil groves remain at the spot where he cavorted with the *gopis* (female cow herders). Nevertheless, as a *tirtha*, the town attracts elderly Vaishnavas who believe that to die here earns them instant *moksha* or liberation. Along with its many *dharamshalas*, Vrindavan holds several "**widow houses**", maintained by wealthy devotees, which provide food and shelter for

The widows of Vrindavan

Walk around the bazaars and temples of Vrindavan and you cannot fail to notice the overwhelming numbers of shaven-headed women dressed in ragged white-cotton saris, shuffling between shops, shrines and ashrams with their begging bowls. These are the **widows of Vrindavan** – women who, after the death of their husbands, have left home so as not to be a burden on their families, or who have been forced into destitution by cruel relatives.

Based on the tenets of the ancient *Shastras* and *Manu-Smirti*, Hindu tradition accords no status to a widow. If she outlives her husband, a Hindu woman is regarded as a curse; she is expected to destroy her marriage bangles and jewellery, abstain from wearing colour and *kohl* under her eyes, *kunkum* vermilion in her hair parting and *mehendi* on her hands, and to spend the rest of her days in fasting and prayer for her deceased spouse.

When the ostracization and ignominy of life among the in-laws gets too much, Vrindavan is one of the religious centres to which widows travel in search of succour. Here, by chanting in ashrams and begging for alms from pilgrims, they can at least expect to obtain a bowl of rice and a few rupees. It is estimated that as many as nine thousand women subsist in this way in Vrindavan alone, living off the charity of ashrams, in whose huge halls you can see them intoning mantras and *kirtans* for eight-hour shifts. The widows are becoming increasingly vulnerable to unscrupulous landlords and the sex industry, and it is also rumoured that some of the ashrams are little more than fronts for money laundering.

Women's rights and support groups from the capital have tried alleviate the suffering of Vrindavan's widows, but their efforts are swamped by the ever-increasing numbers of women pouring in.

the widows (see box on p.309) who find solace in devotion to Krishna. Two thousand of them congregate in the Mirabai Ashram twice a day to sing *bhajans* (devotional songs).

Though it may not boast the several thousand temples of popular exaggeration, the town does hold numerous shrines, many of them now neglected and crumbling or overrun with monkeys. Close to the centre, on the main Mathura–Vrindavan road, **Govinda Deva**, known locally as "Govindji", is one of northern India's most impressive medieval Hindu edifices, though worship here is low-key in comparison to some of the other shrines of Vrindavan. Erected by Raja Man Singh in 1590, its main tower is said to have once been seven storeys high; the three storeys that survived the depredations of Aurangzeb leave it with a squat and truncated look.

Although of much later design, and rebuilt in the nineteenth century, **Banke Bihari** (winter 8.45am–1pm & 4.30–8.30pm; summer 7.45am–noon & 5.30–9pm; free), off Purana Bazaar, is the town's most popular shrine, renowned for impressive floral decorations inside the temple. Stalls on the corner of the lane leading to it serve excellent *malai* (cream) and *kesar* (saffron) *lassis* in *bhands* (unfired clay cups).

Opposite Govinda Deva, across the main road, lies the lavish new South Indian-style temple of **Shri Ranganatha**, also known as **Rangaji Temple**, where ostentatious displays include the numerous gold-plated embellishments that crown its lofty *shikhara*, and the gold-plated **Dhwaja Stambha** column in the inner courtyard (no admittance to non-Hindus). An electronic puppet show of the Hindu epics enlivens the entrance gate, and a small museum inside houses processional images and chariots (Rs1).

ISKCON, the International Society of Krishna Consciousness, also has a lavish new temple complex in Vrindavan, the **Krishna Balaram Mandir**, around 3km west of town at Raman Reti. Built in Bengal Renaissance style with bright frescoes depicting episodes from Krishna's life, the temple incorporates a marble mausoleum in honour of the society's founder, Swami Prabhupada, who died in 1977.

Among the new temples springing up along the Mathura–Vrindavan road is the **Gita Mandir** which houses the Gita Stambh, a pillar with the entire *Bhagavad Gita* carved on its surface. The imposing temple, built by one of the country's leading industrial families, the Birlas, is overshadowed by the outrageous multistoreyed, spaceship-like edifice known as the **Pagal Baba Mandir** just down the road.

Practicalities

Buses, shared tempos and taxis run out to Vrindavan from Mathura for about Rs70 per head one-way. Three local **trains** also cover the same route, leaving from Mathura Junction (6.30am, 3.40pm & 7.40pm) for the station in the south of Vrindavan (they return at 7.30am, 4.35pm & 8.05pm). Besides the numerous *dharamshalas*, several ashrams offer good-value **accommodation** at fixed rates, as well as **food**. Many, however, open only to Indian pilgrims, though the places listed below are fine for foreigners. In the centre of town, around Ahir Para, try the large, friendly *Jaipuriya Guest House* (ⓣ0565/244 2388; ➌), with clean, light and airy rooms built around a pleasant garden courtyard; and the *Bankey Bihari Guest House* (ⓣ0565/244 3529, ⓕ244 2189; ➌–➍), where the large rooms (some with a/c) have bathrooms and 24-hour hot water. Rooms at the ISKCON's *Guest House* (ⓣ0565/254 0024; ➋–➌), immediately behind their temple, get booked up quickly, so reserve in advance. The vegetarian restaurant serves decent meals, pitched at the Western palate.

Central UP

Large tracts of **CENTRAL UP**, along the fertile flood plains of the Doab, constituted the nineteenth-century **Kingdom of Avadh**. Destined eventually to become little more than puppets of the British, its wealthy nawabs (governors) focused their attentions on the arts, and created a unique civilization centred around **Lucknow**. Monuments from those days, and traces of the bitter fighting of the "Mutiny" or "First War of Independence" that coincided with the final eclipse of Avadh, are scattered throughout both city and region. Today, central UP is a Hindu stronghold, with the BJP extending its grip from its seat in the state capital, Lucknow. East of here, the Ganges flows towards **Allahabad**, and the sacred confluence at **Prayag**, where it meets the Yamuna and the mythical Saraswati that flows from heaven.

Lucknow

In the approximate centre of Uttar Pradesh, 516km east of Delhi, the state capital **LUCKNOW** is best remembered for the ordeal of its British residents during the five-month **siege** of 1857. However, the city had earlier witnessed the last heady days of Muslim rule in India, before the final capitulation to the British. In fact the summary British deposition of the

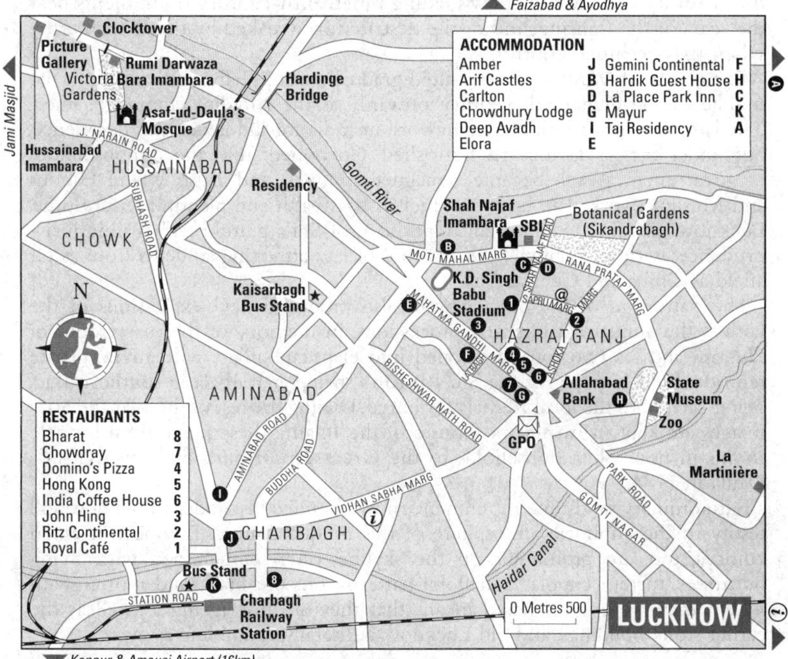

The performing arts of Lucknow

In the eighteenth and nineteenth centuries – considered a Golden Age of artistic achievement – Muslim Lucknow saw the emergence of an astounding range of **music and dance forms** that remain prominent in the performing arts of north India.

Apart from the musicians of the court, and courtiers – among them some of the nawabs themselves – **tawwaif** (courtesans) took on a vital role in the cultural life of the city, becoming proficient as poets and in dance and song. While *khyal* and *dhrupad* remained the mainstay of classical music, **thumri** – love songs amalgamating classical *ragas* and folk melodies – developed a high degree of sophistication, and forms such as *dadra*, *tappa* and *hori*, influenced by folk traditions, also became widely popular. Often referred to as "semi" or "light" classical music, these latter forms are fading from the repertoire of modern musicians.

Kathak, the main genre of north Indian classical dance, developed under nawabs such as Shuja-ud-Daula (1756–75) and Asaf-ud-Daula (1775–97). The theme of Krishna cavorting with the milkmaids (*gopis*) became especially important within performances that otherwise rely on strong and energetic footwork around *laikari*, intricate rhythmic compositions accompanied by *tabla* or hand-drums. Some of Avadh's great **Gharana** (schools) of dance and music – including those at Lucknow, Farrakhabad and Rampur – are gradually being assimilated into a new system of patronage, now dependent on the middle classes.

The **Lucknow Festival**, held in February, gives visitors an excellent opportunity to sample the city's vibrant traditions of music and dance. For information, contact UP Tourism

incompetent last Nawab of **Avadh** – or of Oudh, the British name for the kingdom – Wajid Ali Shah, is usually numbered among the root causes of the "Mutiny". Today, Lucknow's fading nineteenth-century monuments bear the scars of the fighting, and of the destruction wreaked by the British army when they regained control.

The centre of Muslim power shifted gradually from Delhi to Avadh from the middle of the eighteenth century onwards, as the Moghul empire declined. The later nawabs of Avadh are a byword in India for indolence and decadence, but under their rule the arts flourished. Cocooned from the responsibilities of government, Avadh became a magnet for poets and artists where Hindus and Muslims worked in harmony, fuelled by wealth and plentiful leisure time. Lucknow was also an important repository of Shi'a culture and Islamic jurisprudence, with its Farangi Mahal school of law attracting students from as far afield as China and Central Asia.

The patronage of the Shi'a nawabs also produced new expressions of the faith – the annual **Muharram** processions, in memory of the martyrdom of Hussain and his two sons, developed into elaborate affairs with **tazia**, ornate reproductions in paper of the Shi'a Imam's shrine at Karbala in southern Iraq, being carried to the local Karbala for burial. During the rest of the year the *tazia* images are kept in Imambara (houses of the Imam); these range from humble rooms in poor Shi'a households to the **Great Imambara** built by Asaf-ud-Daula in 1784.

Extraordinary sandstone monuments, now engulfed by modern Lucknow, still testify to the euphoric atmosphere of this unique culture. European-inspired edifices, too, are prominent on the skyline, often embellished with flying buttresses, turrets, cupolas and floral patterns, but the brick and mortar with which they were constructed means that they are not ageing as well as the earlier stone buildings, and old Lucknow is, literally, crumbling away.

Arrival, information and transport

From **Amausi airport**, 16km south on the Kanpur Road, a taxi to the centre of Lucknow costs around Rs240. Airport buses connect with flights.

Lucknow's extremely busy **Charbagh railway station** (ⓣ0522/263 5841 for computerized reservations), 4km southwest of the central hub of Hazratganj, is itself a remarkable building, with prominent *chhatris* above the entrance arcade and a roof inspired by chess pieces. Most **buses**, including those from Varanasi, Allahabad, Agra and Jhansi, arrive at the main **Charbagh Bus Stand** alongside, while some buses from the Nepal border at Sonauli and from Gorakhpur, Faizabad and Ayodhya pull in at the **Kaisarbagh stand**, near Hazratganj.

Information

The national government's **regional tourist bureau**, 2km northeast of the railway station at 10 Station Rd (Mon–Sat 10am–5pm, closed second Sat of each month; ⓣ0522/263 8105), provides information only; there's also a stand at the railway station. The **UP Tourism office**, southwest of the centre on Gomti Nagar (ⓣ0522/230 8017), has an information counter. Lucknow's **GPO** is on Vidhan Sabha Marg. For **foreign exchange**, there's Allahabad Bank on Park Road in Hazratganj and the State Bank of India, Moti Mahal Marg. Top-range hotels such as the *Taj Mahal* also have foreign exchange facilities at slightly lower rates. Both IDBI and ICICI Banks on Ashoka Marg have **ATM**s that accept Visa and Mastercard. For fast **Internet** connection in a/c surroundings, try Sify, in the building next to UP Tours' *Gomti* hotel on Sapru Marg, or Cyber Junction near Tulsi Theatre.

City transport and guided tours

Multi-seater **tempos** and **Vikrams**, their diesel engines sounding like hundreds of loud rattles, have more or less taken over from city buses, plying regular routes such as from Charbagh to the GPO, with depots at Janpath Market, Clarks Avadh Crossing and the Chowk. Adding to the chaos are legions of reasonably priced cycle rickshaws, more common than auto-rickshaws and charging around Rs15 from the station to Hazratganj. **Cars** can be rented from various operators, including *Hotel Clarks Avadh*, UP Tours at the *Hotel Gomti*, 6 Sapru Marg (ⓣ0522/261 2659), and Aliza Tours, 4A Saran Chambers, 5 Park Road (ⓣ0522/223 8357). Comprehensive daily **city tours** (Rs500 including most entry fees), which must be booked in advance through UP Tours, leave the *Hotel Gomti* at 9.30am and return at 2.30pm. You can also be picked up from the station (at 9.00am) and from various other hotels. Guide and entrance fees are included in the price except for the Residency (Rs100).

Accommodation

Budget and mid-range **hotels** are concentrated in the **Charbagh** area, around the bus and railway stations, and along Vidhan Sabha Marg, the main artery feeding into the city centre around the GPO. The more cosmopolitan **Hazratganj** district holds a few bargains.

Amber Naka Hindola ⓣ0522/221 5658 or 0522/268 3201, ⓕ268 3404. Spacious air-cooled rooms (some have a/c), with clean Indian-style toilets. ❷–❺

Arif Castles 4 Rana Pratap Marg ⓣ0522/221 1313, ⓕ221 1360. Comfortable but ostentatious place that's dripping with chandeliers and reminiscent of a Hindi film set. The standard business class rooms have central a/c and cable TV, and there's a good multi cuisine restaurant. ❻–❼

Carlton Shah Najaf Rd ⓣ0522/222 4021, ⓕ223 1886. Fabled Lucknow address, a *fin-de-siècle* Euro-Avadhi edifice with big rooms, ancient plumbing and musty hunting trophies. The non-a/c rooms are good value, but otherwise it's expensive for what it is. ❹–❻

Chowdhury Lodge 3 Vidhan Sabha Marg ☎0522/222 1911. Close to the GPO, *Chowdhury* is well-priced, pleasant, and justifiably popular. The cheapest rooms are a bit grubby, but very good value. ❶–❷

Deep Avadh Aminabad Rd, Naka Hindola ☎0522/268 4381, Ⓔdeep@lw1.vsnl.net.in. Huge range of rooms from sparse and simple to a/c, as well as two restaurants, bar and travel desk, in an interesting part of town close to the station. 24hr checkout. ❸–❻

Elora 3 Lalbagh ☎0522/221 1307. Friendly, popular place with a good range of clean rooms, including some with a/c. Facilities include cable TV in all rooms, 24hr room service and a multi-cuisine restaurant. ❸–❻

Gemini Continental 10 Rani Laximbai Marg ☎0522/221 2155, Ⓦwww.geminicontinental.com. Snazzy upscale hotel in the centre of town. Spacious, modern rooms with great views, mini bar, credit card locks, cable TV and a/c, and a 24hr coffee shop and a great Mughlai restaurant on site. ❽

Hardik Guest House 16 Rana Pratap Marg, near Jopling Rd Crossing ☎0522/220 9497. A range of rooms in this clean and comfortable family-run guesthouse, away from the hustle and bustle of the main roads. Friendly, helpful staff and good home cooking. ❹–❻

La Place Park Inn 6 Shah Najaf Rd, Hazratganj ☎0522/228 2201, Ⓦwww.sarovarparkplaza.com. Brand new upscale hotel, smart and efficient, on a quiet street off the main road. Comfortable rooms with all mod cons, and a good restaurant and coffeeshop. ❻–❽

Mayur Charbagh ☎0522/245 1824. Opposite the station, next to the Charbagh Bus Stand and above the *Bharat Restaurant*. Unattractive cheaper rooms, but those at the other end of the range are much better value. Very handy for early morning getaways and late-night arrivals. ❷–❹

Taj Residency Vipin Khand, Gomti Nagar ☎0522/239 3939,Ⓕ2392282 Ⓦwww.tajhotels.com. Built in Avadhi style, this is easily Lucknow's most elegant and comfortable hotel, with a swimming pool and a range of restaurants, but inconveniently situated 3km out of town. Doubles from US$155. ❾

The Town

Most of Lucknow's monuments are spread along or near the southern bank of the Gomti River, which is sluggish weed-covered except at monsoon time, when its waters swell enough to accommodate hordes of local fishermen's dugout boats. Close to the main central bridge lies the modern commercial centre of **Hazratganj**, with the **Shah Najaf Imambara** to its north near the riverbank. Further west, beyond the ruins of the **Residency**, the road passes the majestic **Bara Imambara**, leading through the large gate of **Rumi Darwaza** to the **Hussainabad Imambara**. South of Hussainabad, between Hazratganj and Charbagh, the old city sector of **Aminabad** holds a maze of busy streets and fascinating markets.

Hussainabad

In the west of the city, in the vicinity of Hardinge Bridge around "old" Lucknow, lie several crumbling relics of the nawabs of Avadh. Chief among them is the Great or **Bara Imambara** (daily 8am–6.30pm, closed during Muharram; Rs300, ticket includes Hussainabad Imambara and Picture Gallery), which boasts one of the largest vaulted halls in the world – 50m long and 15m high. Flat on top, slightly arched inside, and built by Asaf-ud-Daula in 1784 without the aid of a single iron or wooden beam, the roof was constructed using a technique known as *kara dena*, in which bricks are broken and angled to form an interlocking section and then covered with concrete – here several metres thick. The arcaded structure is approached through what must have been an extravagant gate, now pockmarked and on the verge of collapse. Two successive courtyards lead from the gates to the unusually festive-looking Imambara itself. Steps lead up to a labyrinth of chambers known as *bhulbhulaiya* – the "maze". Adjacent to the Bara Imambara and overlooking it is **Asaf-ud-Daula's**

△ Hussainabad Imambara, Lucknow

Mosque, set upon a two-tiered arcaded plinth with two lofty minarets. Closed to non-Muslims, it can be readily viewed from the Victoria Gardens that adjoin it to the west (daily except Fri dawn to dusk; free).

Straddling the main road west of the main gates, the colossal **Rumi Darwaza** is an ornamental victory arch modelled on one of the gates to Asia Minor in Istanbul (known to the Islamic world in Byzantine times as "Rumi"). Now decaying, it sports elaborate floral patterns and a few extraordinary trumpets; steps lead up to open chambers that command a general prospect of the monuments of Hussainabad.

A short distance further west, the lavish **Hussainabad Imambara** (same hours and ticket as Bara Imambara) is also known as the Chhota (small) Imambara, or the Palace of Lights, thanks to its fairy-tale appearance when decorated and illuminated for special occasions. The raised bathing pool in front of it, which is approached via a spacious courtyard, adds to the overall atmosphere. A central gilded dome dominates the whole ensemble, busy with minarets, small domes and arches and even a crude miniature Taj Mahal. Built in 1837 by Muhammad Ali Shah (1837–42), partly to provide famine relief through employment, the Imambara houses a silver-faced throne, plus the tombs of important Avadhi personalities. The dummy gate opposite the main entrance was used by ceremonial musicians, while the unfinished watchtower is known as the Satkhanda or "Seven Storeys", even though only four were ever constructed. West of the Imambara, and surrounded by ruins, are the two soaring minarets and three domes of the **Jami Masjid**, completed after the death of Muhammad Ali Shah, which does not admit non-Muslims.

Beyond the Hussainabad Tank, east of the Hussainabad Imambara, the isolated 67-metre-high **Hussainabad Clocktower**, an ambitious Gothic affair completed in 1887 which carries the largest clock in India. Close to this bizarre monolith lies **Taluqdar's Hall**, built by Muhammad Ali Shah to house the offices of the Hussainabad Trust and the dusty **Picture Gallery**, also known as the **Muhammad Ali Shah Art Gallery** (same hours and ticket as Bara Imambara). Arranged chronologically, the portraits of Nawabs graphically demonstrate the decline of their civilization, as the figures become progressively portlier. In a famous image, the androgynous-looking last nawab, Wajid Ali Shah (1847–56), is shown in a daringly low-cut top that reveals his left nipple.

The Residency

The blasted **Residency** (daily dawn to dusk; Rs100 [Rs5], video cameras Rs25) rests in peace amid landscaped gardens southeast of Hardinge Bridge – a battle-scarred ruin left exactly as it stood when the siege was finally relieved by Sir Colin Campbell on November 17, 1857. Its cannonball-shattered tower became a shrine to the tenacity of the British in India, and continued to be maintained as such even after Independence.

During the siege, every building in the complex was utilized for the hard-fought defence of the compound. The **Treasury**, on the right through the **Baillie Guard Gate**, served as an arsenal, while the sumptuous **Banqueting Hall**, immediately west, was a makeshift hospital, and the extensive single-storey **Dr Fayrer's House**, just south, housed women and children. Most of the original structures, such as **Begum Kothi**, were left standing to impede direct fire from the enemy. On the lawn outside Begum Kothi, a large cross honours the astute Sir Henry Lawrence, responsible for building its defences, who died shortly after hostilities began.

The pockmarked Residency itself holds a small **museum** (daily 9am–4.30pm). On the ground floor, the **Model Room**, the only one with its roof

The siege of the Residency of Lucknow

The mutinous sepoys who poured across the River Gomti into Lucknow on June 30, 1857 found the city rife with resentment against the recent British takeover of the kingdom of Avadh. The tiny and isolated **British garrison**, under the command of Sir Henry Lawrence, took refuge in the **Residency**, which became the focus of a fierce struggle for survival.

Less than a thousand of the three thousand British residents and loyal Indians who crammed into the Residency survived the relentless war of attrition. So unhygienic were their living conditions that those who failed to succumb to gangrenous and tetanus-infected wounds were liable to fall victim to cholera and scurvy. While a barrage of heavy artillery was maintained by both sides, a simultaneous **subterranean** battle was being fought. The sepoys pinned their hopes of breaching the defences on tunnelling and laying mines, but the British were far more adept at such methods. The skills of the ex-miners of the 32nd (Cornish) Regiment enabled them to follow the sounds of enemy chipping and defuse mines, and even blow up several sepoy-controlled buildings on the peripheries of the complex.

Morale remained high among the 1400 **noncombatants**, who included fifty schoolboys from La Martinière, and class distinctions were upheld throughout. While the wives of European soldiers and noncommissioned officers, children and servants took refuge in the *tikhana* (cellar), the "ladies" of the Residency occupied the higher and airier chambers, until the unfortunate loss of one Miss Palmer's leg on July 1 persuaded them of the gravity of their predicament. Sir Henry Lawrence was fatally wounded the next day. The wealthier officers managed to maintain their own private hoard of supplies, living in much their usual style. Matters improved when, after three months, Brigadier General Sir Henry Havelock arrived with reinforcements, and the normal round of visits and invitations to supper was resumed despite the inconvenient shortage of good food and wine. Not until November 17 was the siege finally lifted by the forces of Sir Colin Campbell. When the Highlanders liberated the Residency, their offers of tea were turned down by the women; they were used to taking milk in their tea, which the soldiers could not supply.

intact, houses a large model of the defences and of the Residency and a small but excellent collection of images, including etchings showing wall breaches blocked up with billiard tables and a soldier blacking up in preparation for a dash across enemy lines.

Hazratganj

Along the river, opposite the *Carlton Hotel* on Rana Pratap Marg, squats the huge dome of the **Shah Najaf Imambara** (daily except Fri dawn to dusk; donations), named after the tomb of Ali in Iraq and at its best when adorned with lights during Muharram. Its musty interior holds some incredibly garish chandeliers used in processions, several *tazia*, and the silver-faced tomb of the decadent and profligate Ghazi-ud-din-Haidar (1814–27), buried with three of his queens.

The Imambara was commandeered as a sepoy stronghold in 1857, and the crucial battle that enabled the British to relieve the Residency was fought in the adjacent pleasure gardens of **Sikandrabagh** on November 16. It took one and a half hours of bombardment by Sir Colin Campbell's soldiers to breach the defences of the two thousand sepoys; then the Sikhs and 93rd Highlanders poured through. There was no escape for the terrified sepoys, some of whom are said to have believed the bloodstained, red-faced, kilted Scots to be the ghosts of the murdered European women of Kanpur. Driven against the north wall, they were either bayoneted or shot, and the dead and dying piled shoulder-high. Tranquil once again, Sikandrabagh is now home to the National Botanical Research Institute and the beautiful **Botanical Gardens** (daily 5.30am–9pm; free), with manicured lawns, conservatories, nurseries and herb, rose and bougainvillea gardens.

Towards the east of Lucknow, an extraordinary chateau-like building has become almost a symbol of the city – **La Martinière** remains to this day an exclusive public school in the finest colonial tradition. It was built as a country retreat by Major-General Claude Martin, a French soldier–adventurer taken prisoner by the British in Pondicherry in 1761. The enigmatic Martin later joined the East India Company, made his fortune in indigo, and served both the British and the nawabs of Avadh. The building is an outrageous but intriguing amalgam, crowned by flying walkways; Greco-Roman figures on the parapets give it a busy silhouette, gigantic heraldic lions gaze across the grounds, and a large bronze cannon graces the front. Martin himself is buried in the basement. During the siege, La Martinière was occupied by rebels, while its boys were evacuated to the Residency.

Close to the centre of Hazratganj, its grounds dotted with derelict Avadhi monuments, Lucknow's small **zoo** also serves as an amusement park with a miniature train to view the animals (Tues–Sun dawn to dusk; Rs10). Head through the large zoo gardens to reach the **State Museum** (Tues–Sun 10.30am–4.30pm; Rs100, camera Rs5), with its delicate, speckled-red-sandstone sculpture from the Mathura school of the Kushana and Gupta periods (first to sixth centuries AD). Besides sculpture from Gandhara, Mahoba, Nalanda and Sravasti, it boasts a gallery of terracotta artefacts and even an Egyptian mummy. Musical instruments, paintings and costumes provide atmosphere in the Avadh Gallery, while the natural history section is a taxidermist's dream.

Eating

The rich traditional **Lucknavi cuisine** – featuring such Mughlai dishes as *shami kebabs*, *mughlai parathas*, *sheekh kebabs*, chicken *musallam*, *boti* kebabs, biryanis and sweets such as *phirni* – is available from food stalls throughout the city, in places such as Shami Avadh Bazaar, near the K.D. Singh Babu Stadium, the Chowk, Aminabad and behind the Tulsi Theatre in Hazratganj. The bazaars are also the place to get Lucknow's popular breakfast speciality *paya-khulcha*, a spicy mutton soup served with hot breads. Standard a/c **restaurants** are found mostly in Hazratganj, while, predictably, hotel restaurants such as the expensive *Clarks Avadh* and the *Taj Mahal* serve excellent but pricey food.

Bharat Charbagh. Cheap open-air *dhaba* opposite the station serving good *dosas* and thalis.

Chowdray MG Marg, Hazratganj. Excellent Lucknavi cuisine in a busy restaurant; locals say that this is *the* place to come to for lunch. The sweetshop at the front serves delicious lemon and cardamom *rasgulla*.

Domino's Pizza MG Marg ☎0522/227 4554. Pizzas from 11am to 11pm, and they'll deliver to your hotel room.

Hong Kong MG Marg, Hazratganj. Popular restaurant with standard Indian versions of Chinese food.

India Coffee House Ashoka Marg. Once a hotbed of Lucknow's political intelligentsia, and nicknamed the "maternity ward" for the ideas it has given birth to. Still popular with the faithful – who complain that these days their politicians are more likely to haunt bars or brothels – but now dingy and a bit run-down. Serves south and north Indian snacks, and coffee that you can sit over for an afternoon. Take a paper.

John Hing MG Marg, Hazratganj. One of the few genuine Chinese restaurants in Lucknow. Now a little run down, but the food is adequate. Opposite Sahu Cinema.

Ritz Continental Ashoka Marg. An upmarket place, popular with middle-class families. Western food is available but the local cuisine is much better. Try the baked vegetables.

Royal Café Shahmajaf Rd. Lively place that's popular amongst Lucknavi families, offering coffee, sandwiches and pizzas, alongside local and Western main meals, from about Rs60.

Shopping

Chikan is a long-standing Lucknavi tradition of embroidery, in which designs are built up to form delicate floral patterns along edges on saris and on necklines and collars of *kurtas*. Workshops can be found around the Chowk, the market area of old Lucknow, and shops and showrooms in Hazratganj, Janpath Market, Nazirabad and Aminabad. **Bhagwat Das & Sons** are reputable dealers with two shops – one at the Chowk and the other at Husseinganj Chaurhai; **Tandon's**, 17/1 Ashok Marg, Hazratganj, is another good outlet. **Tradition** at Subhash Marg is a family-run establishment where women can be seen at work. The fixed prices at **Gangotri**, the UP government emporium in Hazratganj, are more expensive than those in the markets, but the quality is assured and you don't have to haggle.

Lucknow is also renowned for its **ittar** (or *attar*), concentrated perfume sold in small vials – an acquired (and expensive) taste. Small balls of cotton wool are

Moving on from Lucknow

Indian Airlines **flights** from Lucknow include daily services to **Mumbai** and **Delhi**. Indian Airlines has offices at *Hotel Clarks Avadh*, 8 Mahatma Gandhi Marg (☎0522/222 0927), and at the airport at Amausi (☎0522/243 6132). Sahara Airlines, Sahara India Tower, 7 Kapoorthala Complex (☎0522/237 7675) also flies daily to **Mumbai**, **Kolkata**, **Allahabad** and **Delhi**; the latter is also served by daily flights from both Jet Airways on Park Rd in Hazratganj (☎0522/223 9662), and Air Deccan (☎0522/395 9129) at the airport.

By **train**, the excellent all a/c Shatabdi Express #2003 goes to **Delhi** (daily 3.35pm; 6hr); cheaper alternatives include the Gomti Express #2419 (daily except Sun 5.30am; 8hr), and the slower overnight Lucknow Mail #4229 (10pm; 9hr 45min). The best choice to **Agra** is the Gorakhpur Express #5046 (9.40pm; 7hr). The fast Pushpak Express #2134 travels to **Mumbai** (daily 7.50pm; 23hr). **Kolkata** (Calcutta) is served by several trains, such as the Amritsar–Howrah Mail #3006 (daily 10.55am; 22hr 15min) and the slower Amritsar–Howrah Express #3050 (daily 11.40am; 28hr). Trains to **Varanasi** include the fast, all a/c Jan Shatabdi Express (daily except Sun 7am; 5hr 15min), the overnight Kashi–Vishwanatha Express #4258 (11.15pm; 8hr), the Dehra Dun–Varanasi Express #4266 (7.40am; 8hr 30min) and the Doon Express #3010 (8.45am; 8hr); the last two in the opposite direction head for **Dehra Dun** (14hr) via **Haridwar**. Satna, the jumping-off point for **Khajuraho**, is serviced by trains such as the Chitrakoot Express #5010 (5.25pm; 11hr).

Trains such as the Vaishali #2554, Kushinagar #1015 and Gorakhpur #5045 expresses travel to **Gorakhpur** (5hr), where you can catch a bus to the Nepal border at **Sonauli** – the choice of buses to **Kathmandu** and **Pokhara** is better on the Nepalese side. This may seem a convoluted way to get to Nepal, but is more comfortable than a long and gruelling direct bus. If you're content to make the eleven- to twelve-hour journey by road, several buses leave from **Kaisarbagh** and **Charbagh** bus stands, from where buses also go to Gorakhpur and to Faizabad. Kaisarbagh also offers **Delhi** buses, and an efficient night service to **Nainital**.

Agents for air, rail and bus tickets include Travel Corporation of India, Videocon Building, 1st Floor, Jopling Road (☎0522/220 7550); and the efficient, friendly UP Tours, *Hotel Gomti*, 6 Sapru Marg (☎0522/221 2659).

Finally, if you're heading for Uttaranchal, Lucknow holds offices of both **GMVN**, at Khushnuma Complex, Old Hyderabad (☎0522/220 7844), and **KMVN**, near Kirpa Automobiles, 2 Gopal Khera House, Sarojini Naidu Marg (☎0522/223 9434), who organize tours of, and accommodation in, **Garhwal** and **Kumaon** respectively.

For more on public transport from Lucknow, see "Travel details", p.351.

daubed with the scent and placed neatly within the top folds of the ear; musicians believe that the aroma heightens their senses. Popular *ittar* are *ambar* from amber, *khus* from a flowering plant and rose-derived *ghulab*.

Allahabad and around

The administrative and industrial city of **ALLAHABAD**, 135km west of Varanasi and 227km southeast of Lucknow, is also known as **Prayag** ("confluence"): the point where the rivers Yamuna and Ganges meet the mythical Saraswati. Sacred to Hindus, the **Sangam** (which also means "confluence"), east of the city, is one of the great pilgrimage destinations of India. Allahabad comes alive during its *melas* (fairs) – the annual **Magh Mela** (Jan/Feb), and the colossal **Maha Kumbh Mela**, held every twelve years (the next is due to take place in 2013).

Allahabad is a pleasant city to visit, with vast open riverside scenery and good amenities, but is without major temples or monuments. At the junction of the fertile Doab, the "two-river" valley between the Yamuna and the Ganges, it did however possess a crucial strategic significance; its massive **fort**, built by the Emperor Akbar in 1583, is still used by the military. Another Moghul, Jahangir's son Khusrau, was murdered here by his brother Shah Jahan, who went on to become emperor and build the Taj Mahal.

Allahabad played a vital role in the emergence of modern India. After the Mutiny of 1857, the British moved the headquarters of their Northwestern Provinces here from Agra, and the formal transfer of power from the East India Company to the crown took place here the following year. Well-preserved relics of the British impact include **Muir College** and **All Saints' Cathedral**. The city also witnessed the first Indian National Congress in 1885, and the inauguration of Mahatma Gandhi's Non-Violent Movement in 1920. **Anand**

The Kumbh Mela

Hindus traditionally regard river confluences as auspicious places, and none more so than the **Sangam** at Allahabad, where the Yamuna and the Ganges meet the River of Enlightenment, the mythical subterranean Saraswati. According to legend, Vishnu was carrying a *kumbha* (pot) of *amrita* (nectar), when a scuffle broke out between the gods, and four drops were spilled. They fell to earth at the four *tirthas* of Prayag, Haridwar, Nasik and Ujjain. The event is commemorated every three years by the **Kumbh Mela**, held at each *tirtha* in turn; the Allahabad Sangam is known as Tirtharaja, the "King of *tirthas*", and its *mela*, the **Maha Kumbh Mela** or "Great" Kumbh Mela, is the greatest and holiest of all.

The largest religious fair in India, Maha Kumbh Mela was attended by an astonishing **seventeen million** pilgrims in 2001. The vast flood plains and riverbanks adjacent to the confluence were overrun by tents, organized in almost military fashion by the government, the local authorities and the police. The *mela* is especially renowned for the presence of an extraordinary array of religious ascetics – *sadhus* and *mahants* – enticed from remote hideaways in forests, mountains and caves. Once astrologers have determined the propitious bathing time or *kumbhayog*, the first to hit the water are legions of Naga Sadhus or Naga Babas, the ferocious-looking members of the "snake sect" who cover their naked bodies with ash and wear their hair in dreadlocks. The *sadhus*, who see themselves as guardians of the faith, approach the confluence at the appointed time with all the pomp and bravado of a charging army.

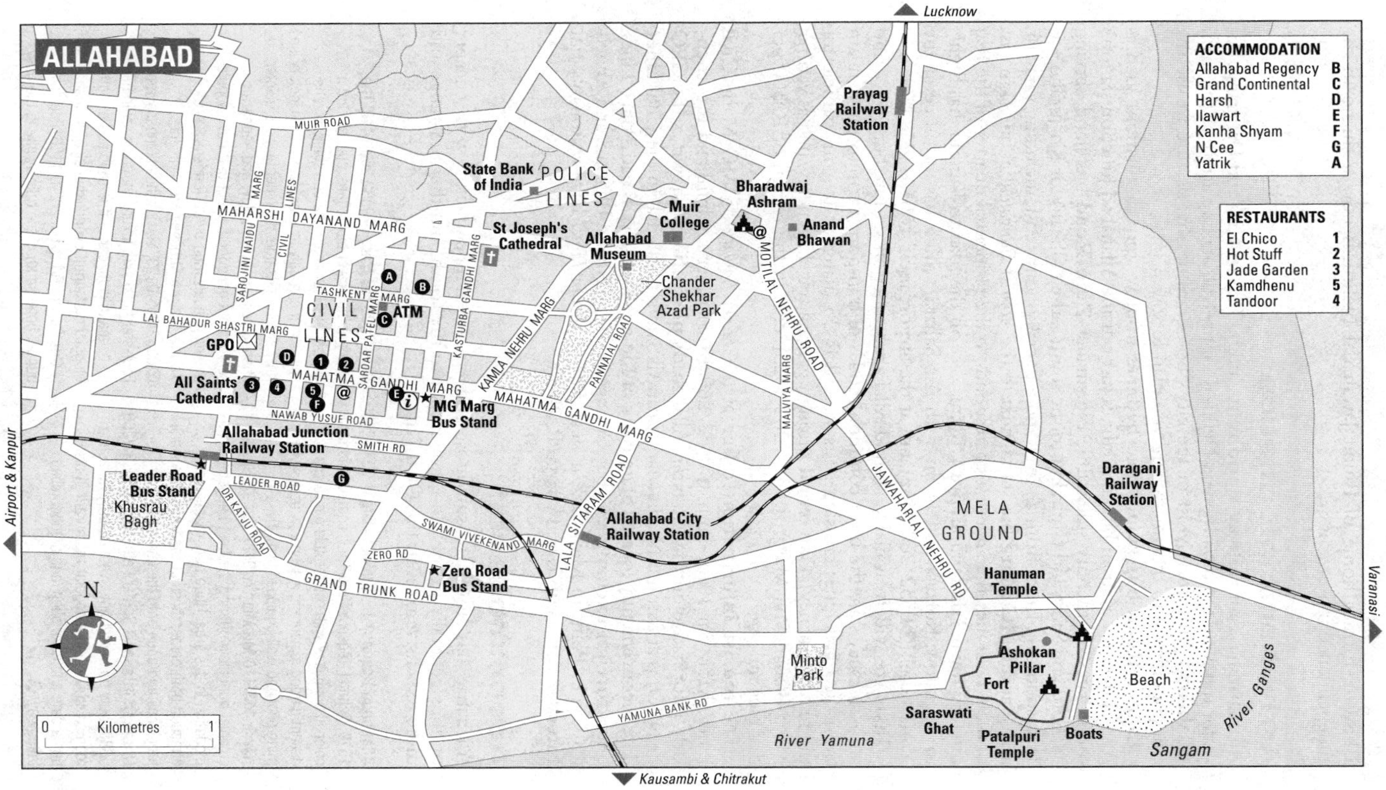

ALLAHABAD

ACCOMMODATION

Allahabad Regency	B
Grand Continental	C
Harsh	D
Ilawart	E
Kanha Shyam	F
N Cee	G
Yatrik	A

RESTAURANTS

El Chico	1
Hot Stuff	2
Jade Garden	3
Kamdhenu	5
Tandoor	4

Lucknow
Varanasi
Airport & Kanpur
Kausambi & Chitrakut
Prayag Railway Station
State Bank of India
POLICE LINES
Bharadwaj Ashram
Muir College
Anand Bhawan
St Joseph's Cathedral
Allahabad Museum
Chander Shekhar Azad Park
MUIR ROAD
MAHARSHI DAYANAND MARG
SAROJINI NAIDU MARG
CIVIL LINES
TASHKENT MARG
ATM
LAL BAHADUR SHASTRI MARG
CIVIL LINES
GPO
All Saints' Cathedral
MAHATMA GANDHI MARG
SARDAR PATEL MARG
KASTURBA GANDHI MARG
KAMLA NEHRU MARG
PANNAIAL ROAD
MOTILAL NEHRU ROAD
MALVIYA MARG
MG Marg Bus Stand
NAWAB YUSUF ROAD
Allahabad Junction Railway Station
SMITH RD
Leader Road Bus Stand
LEADER ROAD
Khusrau Bagh
DR KATJU ROAD
SWAMI VIVEKENAND MARG
ZERO RD
Zero Road Bus Stand
GRAND TRUNK ROAD
LALA SITARAM ROAD
Allahabad City Railway Station
JAWAHARLAL NEHRU RD
MELA GROUND
Daraganj Railway Station
Hanuman Temple
Ashokan Pillar
Fort
Patalpuri Temple
Saraswati Ghat
Boats
Beach
Minto Park
YAMUNA BANK RD
River Yamuna
River Ganges
Sangam
N
0 Kilometres 1

Bhawan, former home of Pandit Jawaharlal Nehru, is now a shrine to the Independence movement.

Arrival and information

Allahabad has four **railway stations** (including Prayag, City and Daraganj), but major trains on the broad-gauge Delhi–Kanpur–Kolkata line arrive at the main **Allahabad Junction**. Most of the city's hotels are nearby; be sure to use the exit appropriate to the area where you plan to stay.

Leader Road bus stand, used by buses from western destinations such as Agra, Lucknow, Kausambi and Delhi, is just outside Allahabad Junction station's south gates on the city side, while the smaller **Zero Road** bus stand, serving Mahoba and Satna and Chitrakut to the south – the railheads for Khajuraho – is 1km southeast. Buses from all over and especially points east, including Varanasi, arrive at the **MG Marg** bus stand, next to the *Tourist Bungalow*, about 1km east of the Civil Lines, the area that corresponds to the residential quarter of the Raj military town. Bamrauli **airport**, 18km west on the road to Kanpur, has flights to Lucknow, Kolkata and Delhi with Air Sahara, which has an office at the *Yatrik* hotel (Ⓣ0532/260 8533) and at the airport itself (Ⓣ0532/258 0796).

Taxis are widely available around Allahabad Junction station, but cycle- and auto-rickshaws are the most common modes of transport; a trip to the Sangam from the Civil Lines crossing costs around Rs35 (hang on to your vehicle for the return journey). **Car rental** through general travel agencies such as Varuna, Maya Bazaar, MG Marg (Ⓣ0532/262 4323), cost in the region of Rs500 per day plus mileage.

The **tourist information office** at the *Hotel Ilawart*, 35 MG Marg, Civil Lines (Mon–Sat 10am–5pm; Ⓣ0532/260 1873) is very helpful and is particularly informative during the *melas*. Allahabad's **post office** (known as the GPO or HPO) is at Sarojini Naidu Marg, near All Saints' Cathedral in the Civil Lines. The inconveniently located State Bank of India at Kutchery Road, Police Lines, offers **foreign exchange**. Cyber Cottage opposite Anand Bhawan, and Angelica Cyber Point in Maya Bazaar near *Kanha Shyam Hotel* have reasonably fast **Internet** connections and charge Rs20/hr.

Accommodation

Allahabad has **hotels** to suit most budgets and temperaments, with cheaper options generally in the old Chowk area to the south, and the mid-range and more expensive ones in the Civil Lines.

Allahabad Regency 16 Tashkent Marg Ⓣ0532/260 1519, Ⓔhotel_regency@rediffmail.com. Comfortable colonial bungalow with comfortable a/c rooms, a decent garden restaurant, a sauna, jacuzzi, swimming pool and well-equipped gym. ❻–❼

Harsh 118/116 MG Marg Ⓣ0532/22197. Shabby colonial bungalow offering the best budget accommodation in this area. Huge tatty rooms with attached bathrooms; those at the front have small fireplaces and open onto the lawn. ❷

Grand Continental Sardar Patel Marg Ⓣ0532/260 5888. New upmarket hotel with smartly furnished rooms with TV, and a popular restaurant. It also has a café and cake shop, and a good kebab takeaway. ❽

Ilawart 35 MG Marg Ⓣ0532/260 1440. The comfortable newer block here, built around a central well, overlooks the bus stand, so choose your room carefully to avoid round-the-clock noise. Now showing its age, the older block is quieter. Friendly restaurant with slow and haphazard service, but good food, and a bar that's popular amongst locals. Run by UP Tourism. ❹–❻

Kanha Shyam Strachey Rd, Civil Lines Ⓣ0532/256 0123, Ⓦwww.hotelkanhashyam.com. Four-star hotel with luxurious rooms, swimming pool, health club, bar, coffee shop and a rooftop Mughlai restaurant overlooking all of Allahabad. ❽

N Cee Leader Rd Ⓣ0532/240 1166. Popular budget hotel south of the railway line in the busy bazaar area. The rooms are small, but it's a pleasant and friendly place. ❷

Yatrik 33 Sardar Patel Marg ⓣ0532/260 1713, ⓕ260 1434. Never mind the ugly name, or that of its restaurant, *The Bhoj*, this is the best of the upmarket places, with fewer facilities but more character than its rival the *Kanha*. Popular, well run and with a beautiful garden graced with elegant palms. Sometimes booked out by tour groups. 24hr check-out. ❼

The Town

Central Allahabad is split in two by the railway line, with the chaotic and congested **Old City** or **Chowk** south of the main Allahabad Junction station, and the well-defined grid of the **Civil Lines** to the north.

One kilometre north of Allahabad Junction station, the yellow-and-red sandstone bulk of the Gothic **All Saints' Cathedral** dominates the surrounding avenues. Designed by Sir William Emerson, architect of the Victoria Memorial in Kolkata (Calcutta), the cathedral retains much of its stained glass, and an impressive altar of inlaid marble. Plaques provide interesting glimpses of Allahabad in the days of the Raj, while flying buttresses and snarling gargoyles on the exterior add to the effect of an English county town – though the impression is subverted by the palm trees in the garden. Sunday services continue to attract large congregations; so too do Masses at the flamboyant **St Joseph's Roman Catholic Cathedral**, a short distance northwest.

On the edge of the pleasant **Chandra Shekhar Azad Park**, also in the Civil Lines, the grounds of the **Allahabad Museum** (Tues–Sun 10am–5pm, closed second Sat each month; Rs100) are dotted with pieces of ancient sculpture. Inside, you'll find early terracotta artefacts, eighth-century sculptures from the Buddhist site of Kausambi, and a striking twelfth-century image from Khajuraho of Shiva and Parvati. A copious collection of modern Indian art includes work by Haldar, Sajit Khastgir and Rathin Mitra, as well as Jamini Roy, who was inspired by folk art. European paintings concentrate on spiritual themes, with bright, naive canvases by the Russian artist Nicholas Roerich, and pieces by the Tibetologist Lama Angarika Govinda. A natural history section features stuffed animals and birds, while photographs and documents cover the Independence struggle.

North of the museum rise the nineteenth-century sandstone buildings of **Allahabad University**, and the Gothic **Muir College**, built in 1870. A 61-metre-high tower accompanies domes clad with blue and white glazed tiles (some of which are missing), and a quadrangle with tall and elegant arches. Just beyond the college, in beautiful grounds roughly 1km northeast of the museum, is **Anand Bhawan** (Tues–Sun 9.30am–1pm & 1.30–5pm; Rs5 allows entry to the first floor). This ornate Victorian building, crowned by a *chhatri* and with Indo-Saracenic effects finished in grey-and-white trim, was the boyhood home of the first prime minister of an independent India, **Jawaharlal Nehru**. It's now maintained as a museum, allowing queues of visitors to peer through plate glass into the opulent interior and see how well the first family lived. More diverting than Nehru's spoons and trousers is the stuffy English court document recording his trial for making salt. Nehru was the father of one assassinated prime minister, Indira Gandhi, who was born here, and the grandfather of another, Rajiv Gandhi; Mahatma Gandhi (no relation of the family) stayed here when he visited the city. Also within the grounds, as at the Nehru Memorial Museum in Delhi, is a **planetarium**, which puts on four shows per day (Rs15; 1hr 15min, all in Hindi with a 30min lecture prior to the show).

A short way south of Allahabad Junction railway station, a lofty gateway leads to the attractive walled gardens of **Khusrau Bagh**, where the remains of Jahangir's tragic son Khusrau rest in a simple sandstone mausoleum, completed in 1622. Khusrau made an unsuccessful bid for power that ended in death at the hands of his brother Shah Jahan, and is buried far from the centre of Moghul power. His mother's two-storeyed mausoleum is a short way west, beyond a tomb reputed to be that of his sister. Once Jahangir's pleasure garden, today much of Khusrau Bagh has been made into an orchard, famous for its guavas, and a rose nursery, but parts are unkempt and overgrown.

The river frontage

Most of Allahabad's river frontage is along the Yamuna, to the south, where women perform *arati* or evening worship at **Saraswati Ghat** by floating *diya*, small oil-filled lamps, downstream. Immediately to the west, in **Minto Park**, a memorial marks the exact spot where the British Raj came into being, when India was taken away from the East India Company in 1858 and placed under the auspices of the Crown.

East of Saraswati Ghat, close to the Sangam, loom the huge battlements of Akbar's **Fort** – best appreciated from boats on the river (see box, below). Much of the fort remains in military occupation, and public access is restricted to the leafy corner around the **Patalpuri Temple**, approached through any one of the three massive gates that puncture the fort's defences. Much of the superstructure of the fort is neglected; the **Zenana** with its columned hall does survive, but can only be viewed with prior permission. At the main gates to the fort stands a poorly restored polished stone **Ashoka Pillar**, inscribed with the emperor's edicts and dated to 242 BC.

Where the eastern battlements of the fort meet the river, a muddy *ghat* is busy with boatmen jostling for custom from the steady stream of pilgrims heading to the Sangam. Inland along the base of the fort, with the vast flood plain of the Sangam to the right, a road leads past rows of stalls catering to pilgrims to the brightly painted **Hanuman Temple**. Unusually, the large sunken image of the monkey god inside is reclining rather than standing erect; the story goes that during the annual floods the waters rise to touch his feet before once again receding.

The Sangam

Around 7km from the centre of the Civil Lines, overlooked by the eastern ramparts of the fort, wide flood plains and muddy banks protrude towards the sacred **Sangam**. At the point at which the brown Ganges meets the greenish Yamuna, *pandas* (priests) perch on small platforms to perform puja and assist the devout in their ritual ablutions in the shallow waters. Beaches and *ghats* here are littered with the shorn hair of pilgrims who come to offer *pind* for their deceased parents, and women sit around selling cone-shaped pyramids of bright red and orange *tilak* powder.

Boats to the Sangam, used by pilgrims and tourists alike, can be rented at the *ghat* immediately east of the fort, for the recommended government rate of Rs12 per head. However, most pilgrims pay around Rs36 and you can be charged as much as Rs150. Official prices for a whole boat are between Rs100 and Rs120 but can soar to more than Rs250 during peak seasons and Rs1000 during the *melas*. On the way to the Sangam, high-pressure aquatic salesmen loom up on the placid waters selling offerings such as coconuts for pilgrims to discard at the confluence. Once abandoned, the offerings are fished up and sold on to other pilgrims.

Eating

Most of the better **cafés** and **restaurants** are in the Civil Lines area, within walking distance from each other close to the main crossing. In the early evening, the snack stalls along MG Marg entice the populace with their individual and often legendary specialities.

El Chico MG Marg. One of the city's best, a smart place with good Indian, Chinese and Western cuisine, including tasty fried chicken.
Hot Stuff 15 Elgin Rd. Popular hang-out for Allahabad's young and trendy, offering burgers, shakes, Chinese food and ice creams.
Jade Garden MG Marg. Small thatched garden restaurant, strong on Chinese food.
Kamdhenu MG Marg. Famous Allahabad sweet-shop, where the delicious local specialities include milk cakes stuffed with almonds.
Tandoor MG Marg. Tucked into a shopping precinct opposite *El Chico*, this comfortable, upmarket restaurant preserves its reputation as one of the best places in the city for Indian food.

Around Allahabad

Just 63km south of Allahabad, on the banks of the Yamuna, are the extensive ruins of **Kausambi**, a major Buddhist centre where the Buddha himself came to preach. The city flourished between the eighth century BC and the sixth century AD; archeological evidence suggests even earlier habitation. According to legend, it was founded by descendants of the Pandavas, after floods destroyed their city of Hastinapur. Mud ramparts (originally faced with brick) tower over the fields, running along an irregular 6km perimeter, and sections remain of a defensive moat. Within the complex, excavations have revealed a paved road, brick houses, wells, tanks and drains, a monastery with cloisters and a large stupa, and the remains of a palace in the southeast corner. The only standing feature is a damaged sandstone column ascribed to **Ashoka** – a second column, moved by the Moghuls, now graces the gates of the fort at Allahabad. If you have your own vehicle or hire a taxi (around Rs900), Kausambi is a straightforward day-trip from Allahabad. Otherwise, there is a direct bus every day from Leader Road bus station (Rs25).

Allahabad also makes a good base from which to venture into the remoter parts of **Bundelkhand** to the south. The pilgrimage town of **Chitrakut** (see p.329) is 132km south, and easily accessible by both train and bus; the hilltop fort of **Kalinjar** (see p.327) is 150km away.

Southern UP: Bundelkhand

BUNDELKHAND – the area defined by the craggy Vindhya Mountains, which stretch across southern UP – was carved by the ninth-century Chandella Rajputs into a mighty kingdom that included **Khajuraho** in Madhya Pradesh (see p.443). Today, it abounds in relics of the past – the colossal astrologically aligned fortress at **Kalinjar** that was the Chandella capital of Mahoba, the Vaishnavite pilgrimage centre of **Chitrakut**, and the fortified town of **Jhansi**, scene of epic nineteenth-century resistance to the British. However, the sheer harshness of the terrain, and the all but unbearable heat in the summer, make this the most difficult, if intriguing, region of the state to explore.

In fact, the labyrinthine hills and valleys along the border with Madhya Pradesh are also the most difficult region to govern, and even today are home to infamous bands of outlaw **dacoits**. Many of these brigands have become folk-heroes among local villagers, who shelter them from the almost equally brutal police force. The most celebrated in recent years was **Phoolan Devi**, the "Bandit Queen", who was kidnapped by a dacoit gang, became the leader's lover, and took over from him after he was killed. She eventually surrendered to the police, was released in 1994, and then became an MP; she was assassinated in 2001.

Jhansi

Unless you harbour a passion for seventeenth-century forts, you'll find the rail- and road-junction town of **JHANSI**, located in an anomalous promontory of UP that thrusts south into Madhya Pradesh, unremittingly dull. Most visitors only stop long enough to catch a connecting bus to **Khajuraho**, 175km further southeast in Madhya Pradesh.

In common with many former British cities, Jhansi is divided into two distinct areas: the wide tree-lined avenues, leafy gardens and bungalows of the **Cantonment** and **Civil Lines** to the west, and the clutter of brick and concrete cubes, narrow lanes, minarets and *shikharas* of the **old town** to the east. Dominating it all from a bare brown craggy hill, **Jhansi fort** (daily dawn to dusk; Rs100 [Rs5], video camera Rs25) was built in 1613 by one of the Orchha rajas, Bir Singh Joo Deo, and is worth visiting primarily for the **views** from the lofty ramparts – down to the densely packed old town on one side, and out across a dusty *maidan* and the Cantonment to the other. The legendary **Rani of Jhansi**, one of the great nationalist heroines of pre-Independence India, was supposed to have leapt over the west wall on horseback when she escaped from the British – if so, she must have had a very athletic horse. Inside the fort are a couple of unremarkable temples, plus an old cistern and the ruins of a palace. Incidentally, be careful of the vicious monkeys as you explore.

Two minutes' walk from the roundabout directly below the fort, the **Rani Lakshmi Mahal** (daily 9.30am–5.30pm; Rs100 [Rs5], video camera Rs25 extra) is a small stately home in "Bundela style" (lots of ornate balconies and domed roofs), built as the palace of the Rani of Jhansi. It was the scene of a brutal massacre in 1858, when British troops bayoneted all its occupants. These days, the building is a memorial museum-cum-archeological warehouse, with unlabelled fragments of antique stone sculpture littered around its attractive interior courtyard.

The grounds of a pleasant seminary in the Cantonment area hold one of the most important Catholic pilgrimage sites in India, **St Jude's Shrine**. A bone belonging to Jude the Apostle, the patron saint of hopeless causes, is said to be buried in the foundations of the sombre grey and white cathedral. On his feast day, October 28, thousands come to plead their own special causes.

Practicalities

Trains on both of the Central Railway branches that converge on Jhansi pull in at the station on the west side of town, near the Civil Lines area. Both the UP and MP **tourist information** kiosks on platform 1 are pretty much useless, but the MP one (daily 9am–6pm; ⓣ0517/244 2622) does give out leaflets on the most up-to-date methods of transport on to Khajuraho. In town, the **Regional Tourist Office** at the *Hotel Veerangana* (see below; Mon–Sat 10am–5pm, closed every second Sat; ⓣ0517/244 1267) provides literature and information on Bundelkhand and the route to Khajuraho.

Jhansi is the most convenient main railway station for Khajuraho, Orchha and Deogarh. From the railway station, the **express semi-deluxe bus** (daily 5.30am & 11am; 4hr 30min; Rs85) and local buses (3 daily starting at 5.30am), leave for **Khajuraho**. One local bus for Khajuraho departs from the Kanpur Road bus stand (daily 1.15pm). This is also the place to pick up buses for Datia, Deogarh and Gwalior; **tempos** for **Orchha** (faster than local buses, at 45min, and more frequent) wait alongside. **Car rental** is available through the larger hotels, as well as the helpful and efficient Baghel Travels, Nehru Market (ⓣ0517/244 1255). If you need to **change money**, head for the State Bank of India on Jhokan Bagh Road beside the busy intersection in the centre of town, exactly halfway between the railway station and the bus stand.

Accommodation

With Orchha just down the road, it's hard to see why you might stay in Jhansi unless you arrive too late to move on. The cheaper **hotels** operate 24-hour check-out, as opposed to noon in the mid-price and more expensive hotels.

Jhansi Shastri Marg ⓣ0517/247 0360, ⓕ247 0470. Former haunt of British *burra-sahibs*, with a well-stocked and atmospheric colonial bar and restaurant, and a small garden. The comfortable rooms, with satellite TV and verandas, have lost a little of their sparkle. ❹

Prakash Station Rd, Civil Lines ⓣ0517/244 8822. Pleasant if basic bungalow accommodation, including some a/c rooms, set around a small garden. Very handy for the station. ❷–❹

Raj Palace Shastri Marg, near the GPO ⓣ0517/247 0554. Clean, comfortable and handy for the bus stand. Rooms have attached bathrooms and hot water. Some a/c. 24hr check-out. ❸

Sita Shivpuri Rd ⓣ0517/244 2956, ⓕ244 4691. Comfortable international-style hotel close to the station, with well-appointed rooms and a good restaurant. Credit cards accepted. Some a/c. ❺–❻

Eating

With the exception of the cheaper lodges, nearly all of Jhansi's hotels have their own **restaurants**. For a cheap alternative, try the *Railway Refreshment Rooms* in the station, which serve freshly cooked twenty-rupee thalis and budget breakfasts.

Holiday Shastri Marg. Posh but not all that expensive a/c restaurant, east of the *Jhansi Hotel*. Low light, tablecloths, attentive service and classy Indian and Western food.

Nav Bharat Shastri Marg. Western-style fast food and Indian snacks behind the post office, and a proper restaurant greatly patronized by locals just down the road. Both closed Tuesday.

Sharma Sweets Shastri Marg. Hygienic sweet-shop selling delicious take-out *rasgulla*, *gulab-jamun*, *jalebi* and *barfi*.

Sita Shivpuri Rd. Spotlessly clean, upmarket hotel restaurant with a wide selection of Indian (and some Continental) dishes. The place for a splurge.

Kalinjar

Deep in the heart of Bundelkhand, in a remote region 150km west of Allahabad and 53km south of Banda, the abandoned star-shaped fortress of

KALINJAR looks down on the Gangetic valley from the final escarpments of the craggy Vindhya hills. Little remains of its huge fortifications, save sections of battlements around the rim of the high forested plateau. Overlooking the dusty town of the same name, much of the fort has been reclaimed by dry shrubby forest, populated by monkeys, while once-grand avenues are now rocky footpaths that wind through the few crumbling yet ornately carved buildings that remain. Kalinjar has no tourist facilities to speak of – most of those who do come are either on day-trips from Chitrakut or Allahabad, or stay in Banda, which is on major train and bus routes and is connected to Kalinjar by local buses.

Possibly one of the oldest forts in India, referred to by Ptolemy as Kanagora, Kalinjar may have started life as a hill shrine before it was converted into a fortress; now devoid of military significance, it's once again becoming a place of worship. It is known to have been a stronghold of the Chandellas (ninth to twelfth centuries AD), the creators of Khajuraho, who left their mark in stone sculptures around the temple of Nilkantha, below the western battlements. Its strategic location attracted repeated Muslim onslaughts; Mahmud of Ghazni laid unsuccessful siege in 1023, Qutb-ud-din-Aibak destroyed several temples in his conquest of 1202, and Humayun spent fifteen years trying to capture the fort. After Sher Shah Sur, who temporarily wrested power from the Moghuls, died when an exploding shell ignited gunpowder as he attacked Kalinjar in 1545, his son went on to take the fortress. Even the British occupied it for a while, before its strategic importance was finally exhausted, and it was left to decay.

The fortress

Sheltered by barbicans, each of the seven gates that pierce the walls of Kalinjar symbolizes one of the seven planets. Steep steps lead straight up for 3km from Kalinjar village, in the valley at the northern base of the fort, to the main gate, known as the **Alam Darwaza**. To the southeast, an unkempt boulder-strewn road gradually climbs across the hillside to approach the southernmost **Panna Gate**, where rock carvings depict seven deer. Beyond Lal Darwaza to the east, the **Bara Darwaza** or "Large Gate" is flanked by two large cannons; beneath it, in the artificial cave of **Sita Sej**, a stone couch dating from the fourth century holds some of Kalinjar's earliest inscriptions.

Colossal rambling battlements provide sweeping views of the Gangetic plain to the north and the Vindhya hills to the south, hiding the crumbling remains of a fortress that is almost 1.5km long. Tracing the faint marks of the old avenues, you arrive at its heart, littered with roofless and devastated buildings. **Kot Tirth**, a ceremonial tank with stone steps, is the largest of several bodies of water on the plateau, and still in frequent use by villagers and pilgrims. Above it, beyond a small and very beautiful Hanuman shrine, stands the well-preserved, palace-like **Raja Mansingh Mahal**. Further west, paths through desultory woodland head to a gate overlooking the fort's western side, where steep steps flanked by rock carvings wind down from the massive stone battlements to the temple of **Nilkantha** – the "Blue Throated One", an epithet of Shiva. To the left of the main shrine, within the temple compound, a five-metre-high low-relief rock carving, of primeval intensity, portrays Bhairava, the wrathful emanation of Shiva as Destroyer, sporting four arms and brandishing weapons. A gap in the retaining wall provides access to the steps back down to the village.

Chitrakut

The large sprawling town of **CHITRAKUT** stands on the banks of the Mandakini, 128km southwest of Allahabad and 116km east of Mahoba. Together with its twin town of **Karbi**, 8km east, Chitrakut, known also as Sitapur or Chitrakut Dham, is a major Vaishnavite pilgrimage centre. Most of Chitrakut's religious and leisure activity revolves around the charming central **Ramghat**, where boats with electric-blue mattresses and pillows create a pretty picture against a backdrop of ashrams and *ghats* to either side of the narrow, slow-moving river. Half-hour boat trips cost around Rs5 per person or Rs20 per boat.

Chitrakut serves as a centre for catching connecting **buses** and **trains** between Allahabad, Kalinjar and Khajuraho. Long-distance transport connections are best made via **Karbi**. From the main Karbi Bus Stand numerous daily buses run to Allahabad (3–4hr), passing through Serai Akil, 15km from the Buddhist ruins of Kausambi, and also to historic Mahoba, a possible stop-off en route to Khajuraho. The **railway station** at Karbi has services to Allahabad and Mahoba, as well as Varanasi, 374km northeast (9hr). From the **Satna Bus Stand** in Chitrakut, buses head south into Madhya Pradesh; connecting buses from Satna itself can also carry you to Khajuraho.

Eastern UP

Flowing beyond Allahabad across the plains of **EASTERN UP**, the Ganges turns sharply north at **Chunar** and traces a great arc through ancient **Varanasi**. Even before the Hindus declared this to be the most sacred spot on earth, it stood at the centre of the Buddhist universe, linked by trading routes from Rajgir in Bihar to Mathura near Delhi. It was on the outskirts of Varanasi, at the deer park at **Sarnath**, that the Buddha delivered his first sermon. North of Varanasi, the much-travelled road to **Nepal** passes through the large administrative town of **Gorakhpur**, not far from **Kushinagar**, where the Buddha achieved final enlightenment.

Varanasi

Older than history, older than tradition, older even than legend, and looks twice as old as all of them put together.

Mark Twain

The great Hindu city of **VARANASI**, also known as **Banaras** or **Benares**, stretches along the crescent of the River Ganges, its waterfront dominated by long flights of stone *ghats* where thousands of pilgrims and residents come for their daily ritual ablutions. Known to the devout as **Kashi**, the Luminous – the City of Light, founded by Shiva – Varanasi is one of the oldest living cities in the world. It has maintained its religious life since the sixth century BC in one

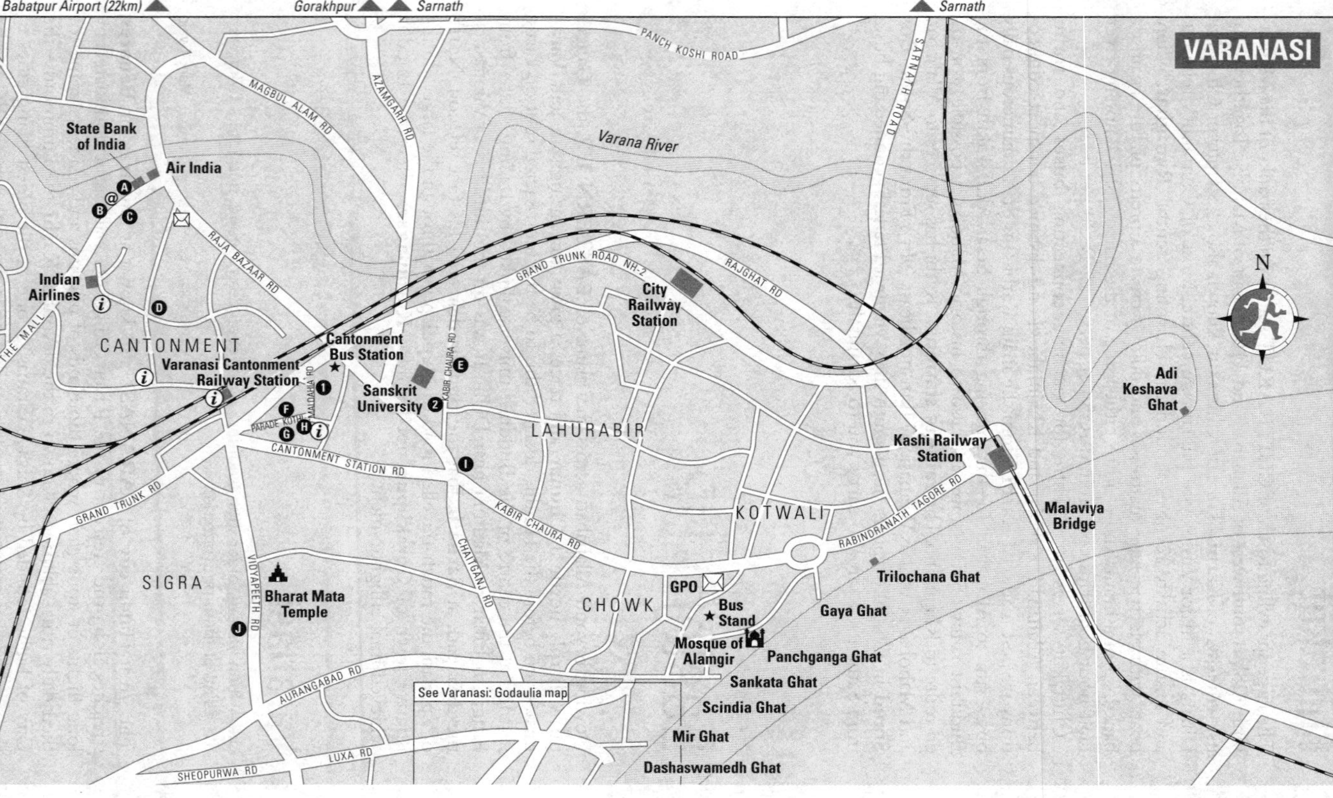
VARANASI
N
Babatpur Airport (22km)
Gorakhpur
Sarnath
Sarnath
Mughal Sarai Bus Station (17km)
PANCH KOSHI ROAD
SARNATH ROAD
MAGBUL ALAM RD
AZAMGARH RD
Varana River
RAJA BAZAAR RD
THE MALL
GRAND TRUNK ROAD NH-2
RAJGHAT RD
KABIR CHAURA RD
MALDAHIA RD
PARADE KOTHI
CANTONMENT STATION RD
GRAND TRUNK RD
KABIR CHAURA RD
CHAITGANJ RD
VIDYAPEETH RD
AURANGABAD RD
LUXA RD
SHEOPURWA RD
RABINDRANATH TAGORE RD
State Bank of India
Air India
Indian Airlines
CANTONMENT
Varanasi Cantonment Railway Station
Cantonment Bus Station
Sanskrit University
City Railway Station
LAHURABIR
Kashi Railway Station
Adi Keshava Ghat
Malaviya Bridge
KOTWALI
SIGRA
Bharat Mata Temple
CHOWK
GPO
Bus Stand
Mosque of Alamgir
Trilochana Ghat
Gaya Ghat
Panchganga Ghat
Sankata Ghat
Scindia Ghat
Mir Ghat
Dashaswamedh Ghat
See Varanasi: Godaulia map

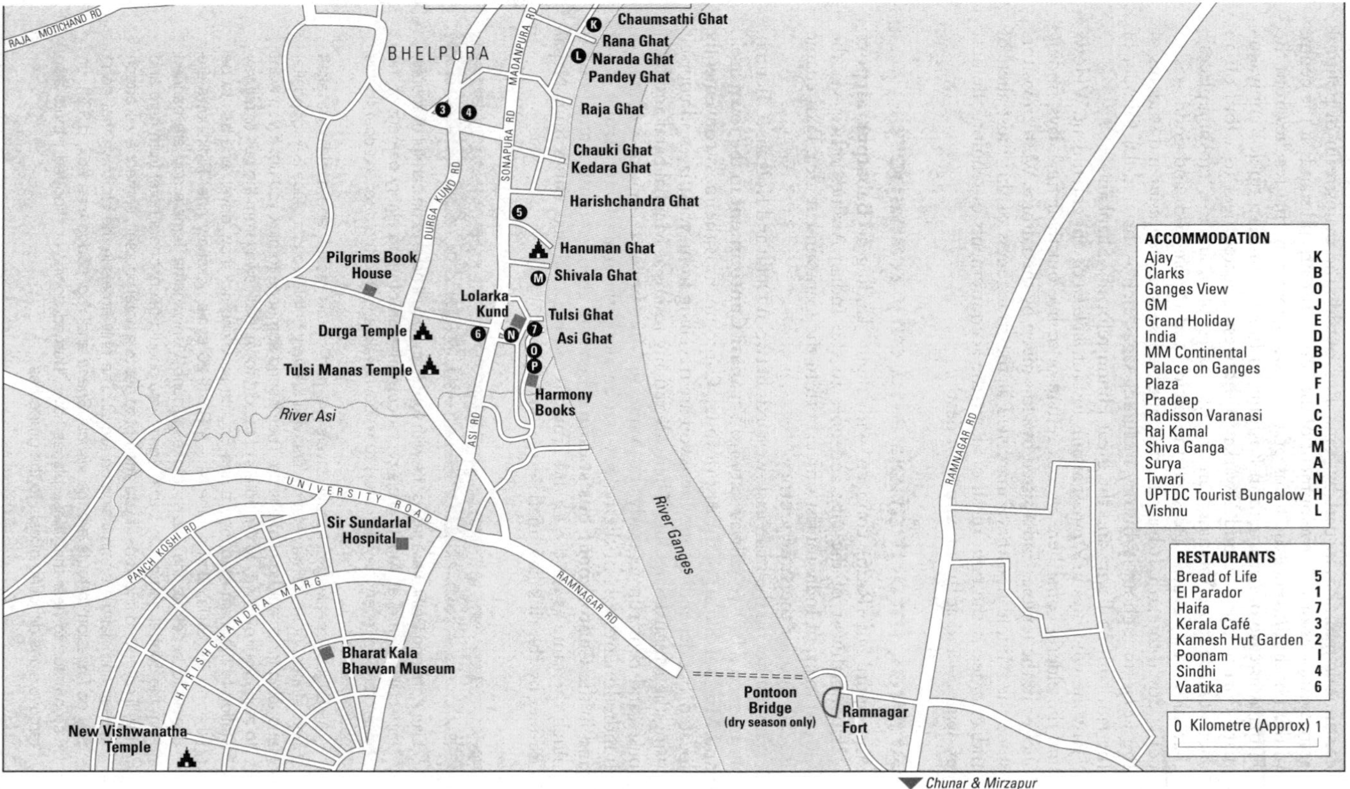
Allahabad
RAJA MOTICHAND RD
BHELPURA
MADANPURA RD
SONAPURA RD
DURGA KUND RD
ASI RD
UNIVERSITY ROAD
RAMNAGAR RD
PANCH KOSHI RD
HARISHCHANDRA MARG
Chaumsathi Ghat
Rana Ghat
Narada Ghat
Pandey Ghat
Raja Ghat
Chauki Ghat
Kedara Ghat
Harishchandra Ghat
Hanuman Ghat
Shivala Ghat
Tulsi Ghat
Asi Ghat
Lolarka Kund
Harmony Books
Pilgrims Book House
Durga Temple
Tulsi Manas Temple
River Asi
River Ganges
Sir Sundarlal Hospital
Bharat Kala Bhawan Museum
New Vishwanatha Temple
Pontoon Bridge (dry season only)
Ramnagar Fort
Chunar & Mirzapur
ACCOMMODATION
Ajay K
Clarks B
Ganges View O
GM J
Grand Holiday E
India D
MM Continental B
Palace on Ganges P
Plaza F
Pradeep I
Radisson Varanasi C
Raj Kamal G
Shiva Ganga M
Surya A
Tiwari N
UPTDC Tourist Bungalow H
Vishnu L
RESTAURANTS
Bread of Life 5
El Parador 1
Haifa 7
Kerala Café 3
Kamesh Hut Garden 2
Poonam I
Sindhi 4
Vaatika 6
0 Kilometre (Approx) 1

continuous tradition, in part by remaining outside the mainstream of political activity and historical development of the subcontinent, and stands at the centre of the Hindu universe, the focus of a religious geography that reaches from the Himalayan cave of Amarnath in Kashmir, to India's southern tip at Kanniyakumari, Puri to the east, and Dwarka to the west. Located next to a ford on an ancient trade route, Varanasi is among the holiest of all *tirthas* – "crossing places", that allow the devotee access to the divine and enable gods and goddesses to come down to earth. It has attracted pilgrims, seekers, *sanyasins* and students of the *Vedas* throughout its history, including sages such as the Buddha, founder of the Jain faith Mahavira and the great Hindu reformer Shankara.

Anyone who dies in Varanasi attains instant *moksha* or enlightenment. Widows and the elderly come here to seek refuge or to live out their final days, finding shelter in the temples and assisted by alms given by the faithful. Western visitors since the Middle Ages have marvelled at the strangeness of this most alien of Indian cities: at the tight mesh of alleys, the accoutrements of religion, the host of deities – and at the proximity of death.

Arrival, information and city transport

An airport bus (Rs25) connects with flights landing at **Babatpur airport**, 22km northwest of the city, and goes to the Indian Airlines office, via the Government of India tourist office, both in the Cantonment area. Taxis charge Rs250–300 for the same journey.

Varanasi lies on the main east–west axis between Delhi and Kolkata (Calcutta), and is served by two railway stations: **Varanasi Cantonment** in the town itself, and **Mughal Sarai**, 17km east of town. Cantonment is the most conveniently located, but depending on where you are travelling from, you may find yourself using the Mughal Sarai line. There are retiring rooms at Mughal Sarai and local buses and taxis run regularly into Varanasi. Most **buses** terminate a couple of hundred metres east of the railway station along the main Grand Trunk Road and in the **Cantonment bus station** where the chaos, confusion and noise is much the same as on the Grand Trunk Road but enclosed. Buses from Nepal are met by the rickshaw mafia – see box, below

Tout dodging

Like Agra and Delhi, Varanasi is rife with **touts**, and you'll have to be careful of scams, especially on arrival. Most hotels pay a **commission** of up to eighty percent of the room rate (for every day you stay) to whoever takes you to the door – a cost that is passed on to you.

All English-speaking rickshaw drivers are part of this racket, and avoiding it takes persistence. At the railway station, first visit the very helpful tourist office (see opposite) and telephone your hotel of choice. They'll send someone to pick you up. If you want to make your own way to the hotels of the old town, walk away from the bus or railway station to the main road, find a non-English-speaking rickshaw driver, and ask to be taken to Godaulia, 3km southeast – a Rs15–20 cycle rickshaw ride. Rickshaws are unable to penetrate the maze of lanes around Vishwanatha Temple and are banned from the central part of Godaulia. Again, you should telephone a hotel from here and they'll come and find you – if you attempt to get to a hotel yourself, someone will attach himself and claim a commission on arrival. The only hotels in the old town that don't pay commission to touts are the *Vishnu*, *Shanti* and *Yogi Lodge* (see box, p.334), so it's common to hear that these places have "burned down" or "flooded"; touts also remove signs directing guests to the properties.

Information

The main **UPTDC tourist office** is at their *Tourist Bungalow*, on Parade Kothi 500m southwest of Cantonment railway station (daily 9am–5.30pm; ⓣ0542/220 8162), though their **tourist information counter** (daily 7am–8pm; ⓣ0542/234 6370) inside the railway station is far more efficient and on the ball – the boss, Uma Shankar, seems to regard the protection of tourists as a personal crusade. Both book accommodation and provide free maps. The shabby **Bihar Government tourist office** at Englishia Market, Sher Shah Suri Marg, Cantonment (ⓣ0542/234 3821), is useful if you're heading east towards the Buddhist centres.

The **India tourist office** languishes in the leafy suburbs of the Cantonment, a long way from the main attractions of the Old City and the *ghats*, at 15B The Mall (Mon–Fri 9am–6pm, Sat 9am–2pm, closed every second Sat; ⓣ0542/234 3744, ⓦwww.india-tourism.com). Its primary function is to dish out information on the whole of India, but the staff can assist with booking accommodation and car hire. They also maintain a booth at the airport during flight times.

To experience the *ghats* at sunrise, or the peace of Sarnath, you're best off eschewing guided tours and making your own arrangements. If your time is very limited, official tour **guides** can be organized through the India tourist office.

City transport

Cycle rickshaws are the easiest way to get around Varanasi, and often defy death and traffic jams by cycling up the wrong side of the road; a ride from Godaulia to Cantonment railway station costs Rs15–20. Auto-rickshaws should be faster, but due to the volume of traffic they rarely are for short rides across town. Godaulia to the railway station should cost Rs40. **Taxis** and an inadequate and overcrowded city bus system offer further options, while shared auto-rickshaws or tempos are a cheap and efficient alternative for the trip to Sarnath.

Accommodation

Most of Varanasi's better and more expensive hotels lie on its peripheries, either in the leafy **Cantonment** area in the north or around Cantonment Station Road, south of the train tracks. However, to experience the full ambience of the city, stay close to the *ghats* and the lanes of the **Old City**. The little guesthouses here were originally geared towards budget travellers, but are increasingly offering more comfortable rooms and attracting customers away from the classier places, which have responded by trying to get all hotels near the riverbank banned for bogus environmental reasons. The top floors of Old City places, with views and more light, generally offer better value; however some are almost impossible to find during and shortly after the monsoons, when the swollen Ganges waters render them inaccessible from the waterside. Long-term tourists tend to stay around Asi *ghat* – rooms here are usually simple and cheap, and the atmosphere is laid-back.

Note that places listed below under the Godaulia heading appear on the Godaulia map (p.336); all others appear on the main Varanasi map (pp.330–331).

Godaulia

Alka D3/23 Mir Ghat ⓣ0542/232 8445, ⓔhotelalka@hotmail.com. Often booked up by tour groups, this is one of the few riverside hotels with clean, well maintained quality rooms. Spacious courtyard overlooking the river. ❷–❺

What's in a name?

The **Yogi Lodge** (near Vishwanatha temple), **Vishnu Rest House** (overlooking the river) and **Shanti Guest House** (near Manikarnika Ghat) are three of the oldest and best-run places in the Old City. Unfortunately they are all facing dubious competition from other hotels copying their names and paying rickshaw-wallahs to divert customers. Four other "Vishnu" lodges have sprung up – the *Old Vishnu Lodge, the Vishnu Guest House, the Real Vishnu Guest House* and the *New Vishnu Guest House*. And several more "Shanti" lodges and "Yogi" lodges are playing the same name game. Legal battles are being fought between some of these similarly named hotels although the outcome is uncertain as no one owns the copyright to such universal Indian words as "Yogi", "Vishnu" and "Shanti". Only the original hotels are listed below.

Ganga Fuji D7/21 Sakarkand Gali ⓣ0542/232 7333, ⓕ232 0676. Well-run family guesthouse near the Golden Temple, with tastefully decorated rooms, some with a/c, clean bathrooms and hot showers. ❷–❺

Ganpati D3/24 Mir Ghat ⓣ0542/239 0059, ⓔgghouse@satyam.net.in. Rooms here overlook the Ganges or are arranged around a courtyard, and there's a restaurant and a sociable balcony overlooking the river. Has a slight edge over the neighbouring *Alka*. ❷–❹

Golden Lodge D8/35 Kalika Gali ⓣ0542/232 878. Clean and tidy, with a wide range of rooms (with and without bathrooms and a/c) arranged around a central courtyard. ❶–❸

La-Ra India Dashaswamedh Rd ⓣ0542/240 0805, ⓔlaraindia@satyamonline.com. In the heart of Godaulia, this small place is a typical shabby-genteel mid-range hotel, with smart a/c rooms and a restaurant serving Varanasi food. ❷–❹

Puja D1/45 Lalita Ghat ⓣ0542/232 6102. Ugly concrete building overlooking the Nepali temple, with excellent rooftop views and a restaurant. Offers a range of rooms in a new upmarket wing; those on the top floor have balconies (surrounded by anti-monkey mesh), and are the best value. ❶–❺

Scindhia Scindia Ghat ⓣ0542/232 0319. Near Manikarnika Ghat, this guesthouse is easy to find at low tide but well hidden after the monsoon, when the riverside path is closed. Clean rooms, some with balconies and river views. ❷–❸

Shanti Manikarnika Ghat ⓣ0542/239 2568. An old favourite – though in need of a lick of paint – tucked away near the burning *ghats*. Large building with loads of (generally) clean rooms with attached bathrooms, as well as Varanasi's cheapest dorm beds (Rs50). Excellent views from the lively rooftop restaurant. ❶–❹

Sri Venkateswar D5/64 Dashaswamedh Rd ⓣ0542/239 2357, ⓔvenlodge@yahoo.com. Simple but clean and close to the *ghats* and to Vishwanatha Temple, capturing the ambience of the Old City. Nice courtyard, friendly staff and a strict no drugs policy. ❶–❷

Yogi Lodge D8/29 Kalika Gali ⓣ0542/239 2588, ⓔyogilodge@yahoo.com. An old favourite with budget travellers in the heart of the Old City; very well run, with a safe for valuables. Spotless restaurant, clean rooms and attractive dorms. ❶

South of Godaulia, near the river

Ajay D21/11 Rana Ghat ⓣ0542/245 0970, ⓔajaykumar35@yahoo.com. A couple of superb rooms that are in need of a facelift, but there's an extraordinary banyan tree growing through the buildings and a lovely terrace for yoga. ❷–❹

Ganges View Asi Ghat ⓣ0542/231 3218. A great veranda looking out onto the river, a lobby full of good books, a pleasant ambience and an interesting landlord mean this popular place is often booked up. The rooms are small but tastefully and stylishly decorated. ❸–❼

Palace on Ganges B1/158 Asi Ghat ⓣ0542/231 5050, ⓔpalaceonganges@indiatimes.com. The only luxury hotel on the Ganges, with 22 individually decorated rooms representing the states of India – Gujarati is particularly colourful. Facilities include central a/c, TV, minibar, tour desk and rooftop restaurant. Doubles from US$70. ❾

Shiva Ganga B3/155 Niranjani Akhara, Shivala Ghat ⓣ0542/231 4689. Peaceful place with simple rooms, a veranda and a lush enclosed garden. Next to the Shiva temple and affording great river views. ❶

Tiwari Lodge Asi Ghat ⓣ0542/231 5129. Appealing family-run place, built around a shrine and aimed at long-term guests. The simple rooms have kitchen spaces attached. ❶

Vishnu Rest House D24/17 Pandey Ghat ⓣ0542/245 0206. One of the nicest of the riverside lodges, with a lovely patio and café overlooking the Ganges; popular and often booked up. Best approached via the *ghats*, south of Dashaswamedh. ❶–❷

Cantonment and the peripheries

Clarks The Mall, Cantonment ⓣ0542/234 8501, ⓦwww.clarkshotels.com. Plush and well-presented five-star, with all mod-cons including a swimming pool, bar and a wide range of restaurants. Doubles from US$95. ❾

GM 1 Chandrika Colony, Sigra ⓣ0542/222 2638, ⓔbhagatmehra@rediffmail.com. Away from the old town, but easy to reach nonetheless. Large, good-value air-cooled rooms with clean bathrooms, plus decent food. ❷–❺

Grand Holiday Dhoopchandi, Jagatganj ⓣ0542/234 3792. Near the Sanskrit University, this is a small, homely and good-value hotel run by an eccentric family. Large, clean rooms, lovely garden and home cooking. 24hr check-out. ❸–❹

India 59 Patel Nagar ⓣ0542/250 7593, ⓦwww.hotelindiavns.com. Smart, comfortable and modern rooms with attached bathrooms and a/c; and a health and fitness centre, a rooftop bar and four restaurants, including the excellent *Palm Springs*. ❻

MM Continental The Mall, Cantonment ⓣ0542/234 5272. Tucked away between Clarks and Ideal Tops. Ordinary rooms with baths and deluxe rooms without, plus a restaurant and rooftop coffee shop. ❼

Plaza Inn Parade Kothi, Cantonment ⓣ0542/234 8210. Two hundred metres from the railway station, this is a new hotel with 63 rooms, all with a/c, baths and TV. ❻

Pradeep Kabir Chaura Rd, Jagatganj ⓣ0542/220 7231, ⓔhotelpradeep@satyam.net.in. Comfortable, quite smart and popular with tour groups; away from the *ghats* but within striking distance. Enticing multi-cuisine restaurant on site. ❸–❺

Radisson Varanasi The Mall, Cantonment ⓣ0542/250 1515, ⓦwww.radisson.com/varanasiin. This plush new hotel is one of the best-value of Varanasi's luxury places, with classy and well-appointed rooms, swimming pool, restaurant and coffee shop. Rates (doubles from US$80) include a huge buffet breakfast. ❾

Raj Kamal Parade Kothi, Cantonment ⓣ0542/250 1229. Budget option near the railway station, just outside the *Tourist Bungalow* gates. No atmosphere, but useful for early and late train departures. ❷

Surya S20/51, A5 Nepali Kothi, Varuna Bridge, Cantonment ⓣ0542/234 3014, ⓦhotelsuryavns.com. Well run, comfortable and relaxing hotel arranged around a beautiful garden that doubles up as an alfresco restaurant. All rooms are spotless with modern bathrooms; many have balconies. Facilities include Internet, tour desk, foreign exchange and a decent restaurant. ❸–❻

UPTDC Tourist Bungalow Parade Kothi, Cantonment ⓣ0542/220 8413. Large institutional complex with a garden, bar, restaurant and a wide range of rooms including a dorm (Rs150). Handy for the bus and railway stations. ❷–❹

The ghats

The great riverbanks at Varanasi, built high with eighteenth- and nineteenth-century pavilions and palaces, temples and terraces, are lined with a chain of stone steps – the **ghats** – progressing along the whole of the waterfront and altering in appearance with the dramatic seasonal fluctuations of the river level. Each of the hundred *ghats*, big and small, is marked by a *lingam*, and occupies its own special place in the religious geography of the city. Some have crumbled over the years while others continue to thrive, visited by early-morning bathers, brahmin priests offering puja, and people practising meditation and yoga. Hindus regard the Ganges as *amrita*, the elixir of life, which brings purity to the living and salvation to the dead. In reality, though, the river is scummy with effluent, so don't be tempted to join the bathers; never mind the chemicals and human body parts, it's the level of heavy metals, dumped by factories upstream, that are the real cause for concern. Whether Ganga water still has the power to absolve sin if sterilized is a contentious point; current thinking has it that boiling is acceptable but chemical treatment ruins it.

For centuries, pilgrims have traced the perimeter of the city by a ritual circumambulation, paying homage to shrines on the way. Among the most popular routes is the **Panchatirthi Yatra**, which takes in the *pancha* (five)

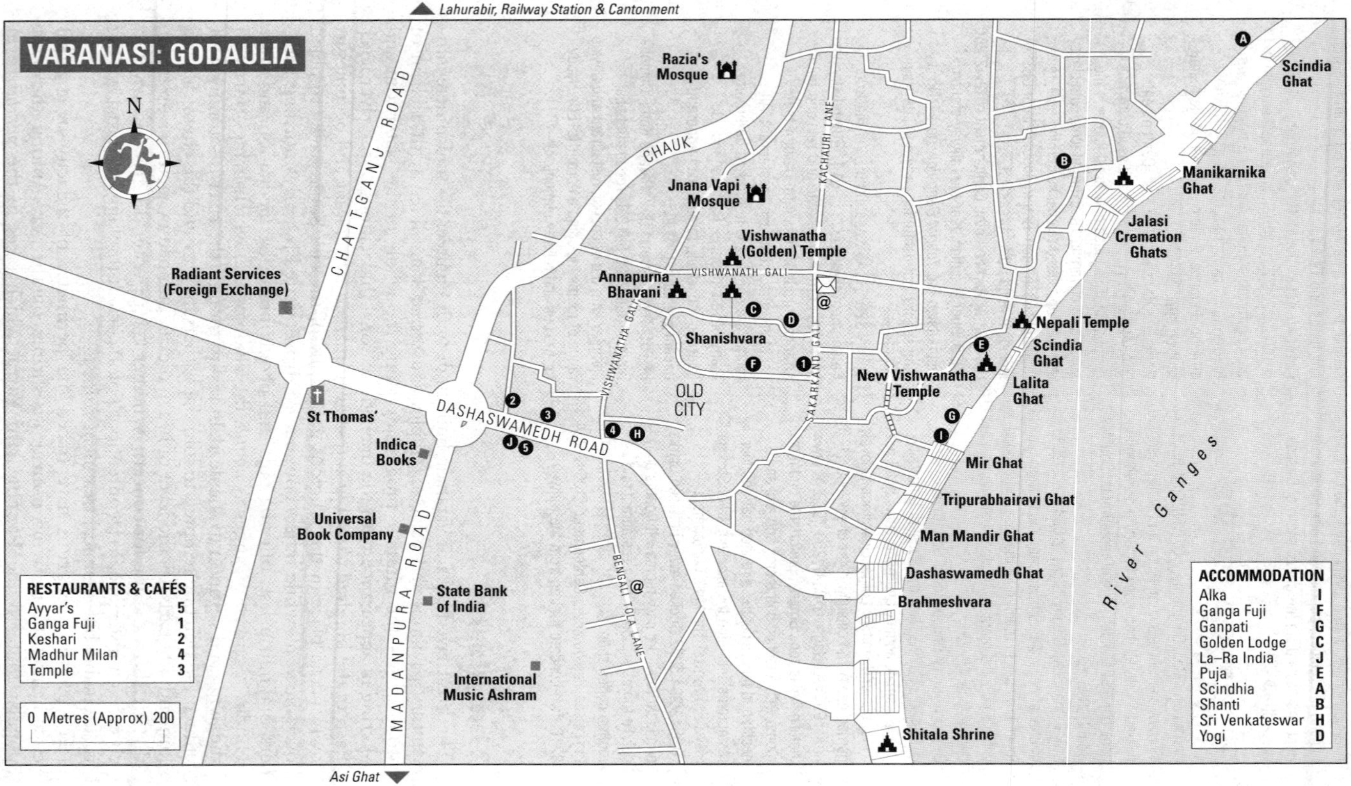

VARANASI: GODAULIA

Lahurabir, Railway Station & Cantonment

Asi Ghat

N

Razia's Mosque
Jnana Vapi Mosque
Vishwanatha (Golden) Temple
Annapurna Bhavani
Shanishvara
OLD CITY
New Vishwanatha Temple
Nepali Temple
Manikarnika Ghat
Jalasi Cremation Ghats
Scindia Ghat
Scindia Ghat
Lalita Ghat
Mir Ghat
Tripurabhairavi Ghat
Man Mandir Ghat
Dashaswamedh Ghat
Brahmeshvara
Shitala Shrine
River Ganges
Radiant Services (Foreign Exchange)
St Thomas'
Indica Books
Universal Book Company
State Bank of India
International Music Ashram
CHAITGANJ ROAD
MADANPURA ROAD
DASHASWAMEDH ROAD
CHAUK
VISHWANATH GALI
VISHWANATHA GALI
KACHAURI LANE
SAKARKAND GALI
BENGALI TOLA LANE

RESTAURANTS & CAFÉS	
Ayyar's	5
Ganga Fuji	1
Keshari	2
Madhur Milan	4
Temple	3

ACCOMMODATION	
Alka	I
Ganga Fuji	F
Ganpati	G
Golden Lodge	C
La–Ra India	J
Puja	E
Scindhia	A
Shanti	B
Sri Venkateswar	H
Yogi	D

0 Metres (Approx) 200

Boat trips on the Ganges

All along the *ghats*, and especially at the main ones such as Dashaswamedh, the prices of **boat** (*bajra*) **rental** are highly inflated, with local boatmen under pressure from touts to fleece tourists and pilgrims. There's a police counter at the top of Dashaswamedh, but the lack of government tourist assistance means that renting a boat to catch the dawn can be a bit of a free-for-all, and haggling is essential. A few boatmen operate on a fixed rate, determined by UP Tourism, of about Rs50 per hour; this is a fair price to aim for when negotiating with other operators.

tirthi (crossings) of Asi, Dashaswamedh, Adi Keshava, Panchganga and finally Manikarnika. To gain merit or appease the gods, the devotee, accompanied by a *panda* (priest), recites a *sankalpa* (statement of intent) and performs a ritual at each stage of the journey. For the casual visitor, however, the easiest way to see the *ghats* is to follow a south–north sequence either by boat or on foot.

Asi Ghat to Kedara Ghat

At the clay-banked **Asi Ghat**, at the confluence of the Asi and the Ganges, pilgrims bathe prior to worshipping at a huge *lingam* under a peepal tree. Another *lingam* visited is that of **Asisangameshvara**, the "Lord of the Confluence of the Asi", in a small marble temple just off the *ghat*. Traditionally, pilgrims continued to **Lolarka Kund**, the "Trembling Sun", a rectangular tank 15m below ground level, approached by steep steps. Now almost abandoned – except during the Lolarka Mela fair (Aug/Sept), when thousands come to propitiate the gods and pray for the birth of a son – Lolarka Kund is among Varanasi's earliest sites, one of only two remaining sun sites linked with the origins of Hinduism. Equated with the twelve *adityas* or divisions of the sun, which predate the great deities of modern Hinduism, it was attracting bathers in the days of the Buddha.

Much of the adjacent **Tulsi Ghat** – originally Lolarka Ghat, but renamed in honour of the poet Tulsi Das, who lived nearby in the sixteenth century – has crumbled. Continuing north, above **Shivala Ghat**, **Hanuman Ghat** is the site of a new temple built by the *ghat*'s large South Indian community. Considered by many to be the birthplace of the fifteenth-century Vaishnavite saint, Vallabha, who was instrumental in the resurgence of the worship of Krishna, the *ghat* also features a striking image of **Ruru**, one of the eight forms of the dog **Bhairava**, a ferocious and early form of Shiva.

Named after a legendary king who gave up his entire kingdom in a fit of self-abnegation, **Harishchandra Ghat**, the next set of steps northwards, is one of Varanasi's two cremation or burning *ghats* and is easily recognizable via the smoke of its funeral pyres.

Further north, the busy **Kedara Ghat** is ignored by pilgrims on the Panchatirthi Yatra. Above its steps, a red-and-white-striped temple houses the **Kedareshvara lingam**, an outcrop of black rock shot through with a vein of white. Mythologically related to Kedarnath in the Himalayas, Kedara and its *ghat* become a hive of activity during the sacred month of Sravana (July/Aug), the month of the rains.

Chauki Ghat to Chaumsathi Ghat

Northwards along the river, **Chauki Ghat** is distinguished by an enormous tree that shelters small stone shrines to the *nagas*, water-snake deities, while at the unmistakeable **Dhobi** ("Laundrymen's") **Ghat**, clothes are still rhythmically pulverized in pursuit of purity. Past smaller *ghats* such as **Manasarovara**, named after the holy lake in Tibet, and **Narada**, honouring the divine musician and sage, lies **Chaumsathi Ghat**, where impressive stone steps lead up to the small temple of the **Chaumsathi** (64) **Yoginis**. Images of Kali and Durga in its inner sanctum represent a stage in the emergence of the great goddess as a single representation of a number of female divinities. Overlooking the *ghats* here is Peshwa Amrit Rao's majestic sandstone *haveli* (mansion), built in 1807 and currently used for religious ceremonies and occasionally as an auditorium for concerts.

Dashaswamedh Ghat

Dashaswamedh Ghat, the second and busiest of the five *tirthas* on the Panchatirthi Yatra, lies past the plain, flat-roofed building that houses the shrine of **Shitala**. Extremely popular, even in the rainy season when devotees have to wade to the temple or take a boat, Shitala represents both benign and malevolent aspects – ease and succour as well as disease, particularly smallpox.

Dashaswamedh is Varanasi's most popular and accessible bathing *ghat*, with rows of *pandas* sitting on wooden platforms under bamboo umbrellas, masseurs plying their trade and boatmen jostling for custom. Its name, "ten horse sacrifices", derives from a complex series of sacrifices performed by Brahma to test King Divodasa: Shiva and Parvati were sure the king's resolve would fail, and he would be compelled to leave Kashi, thereby allowing them to return to their city. However, the sacrifices were so perfect that Brahma established the **Brahmeshvara** *lingam* here. Since that time, Dashaswamedh has become one of the most celebrated *tirthas* on earth, where pilgrims can reap the benefits of the huge sacrifice merely by bathing.

Man Mandir Ghat to Lalita Ghat

Man Mandir Ghat is known primarily for its magnificent eighteenth-century observatory, built for the Maharaja of Jaipur and equipped with ornate window casings. Pilgrims pay homage to the important *lingam* of Someshvara, the lord of the moon, alongside, before crossing **Tripurabhairavi Ghat** to **Mir Ghat** and the **New Vishwanatha Temple**, built by conservative brahmins who claimed that the main Vishwanatha *lingam* was rendered impure when Harijans (untouchables) entered the sanctum in 1956. Mir Ghat also has a shrine to **Vishalakshi**, the Wide-Eyed Goddess, on an important *pitha* – a site marking the place where various parts of the disintegrating body of Shakti fell as it was carried by the grief-stricken Shiva. Also here is the **Dharma Kupa**, the Well of Dharma, surrounded by subsidiary shrines and the *lingam* of **Dharmesha**, where it is said that Yama, the Lord of Death, obtained his jurisdiction over all the dead of the world – except here in Varanasi.

Immediately to the north is **Lalita Ghat**, renowned for its **Ganga Keshava** shrine to Vishnu and the **Nepali Temple**, a typical Kathmandu-style wooden structure which houses an image of **Pashupateshvara** – Shiva's manifestation at Pashupatinath, in the Kathmandu Valley – and sports a small selection of erotic carvings.

Manikarnika Ghat

North of Lalita lies Varanasi's pre-eminent cremation ground, **Manikarnika Ghat**. Such grounds are usually held to be inauspicious, and located on the fringes of cities, but the entire city of Shiva is regarded as **Mahashamshana**, the Great Cremation Ground for the corpse of the entire universe. The *ghat* is perpetually crowded with funeral parties, as well as the **Doms**, its Untouchable guardians, busy and preoccupied with facilitating final release for those lucky enough to pass away here. Seeing bodies being cremated so publicly has always exerted a great fascination for visitors to the city, but photography is strictly taboo; even having a camera visible may be construed as intent, and provoke hostility. Wood touts descend on tourists at the *ghat* explaining the finer metaphysical points of transmutation ("cremation is education") before subtly shifting to the practicalities of how much wood is needed to burn one body, the never-ending cycle of inflation and would you like to give a donation. The amounts written down in their "ledgers" are unbelievable.

Lying at the centre of the five *tirthas*, Manikarnika Ghat symbolizes both creation and destruction, epitomized by the juxtaposition of the sacred well of **Manikarnika Kund**, said to have been dug by Vishnu at the time of creation, and the hot, sandy ash-infused soil of cremation grounds where time comes to an end. In Hindu mythology, Manikarnika Kund predates the arrival of the Ganga and has its source deep in the Himalayas. Vishnu carved the *kund* with his discus, and filled it with perspiration from his exertions in creating the world at the behest of Shiva. When Shiva quivered with delight, his earring fell into this pool, which as Manikarnika – "Jewelled Earring" – became the first *tirtha* in the world. Every year, after the floodwaters of the river have receded to leave the pool caked in alluvial deposits, the *kund* is re-dug. Its surroundings are cleaned and painted with bright folk art depicting the presiding goddess, **Manikarni Devi**.

Scindia Ghat

Bordering Manikarnika to the north is the picturesque **Scindia Ghat**, its tilted Shiva temple lying partially submerged in the river, having fallen in as a result of the sheer weight of the *ghat's* construction around 150 years ago. Above the *ghat*, several of Varanasi's most influential shrines are hidden within the tight maze of alleyways of the area known as **Siddha Kshetra** (the "Field of Fulfilment"). Vireshvara, the Lord of all Heroes, is especially propitiated in prayer for a son; the Lord of Fire, Agni, was supposed to have been born here.

Panchganga Ghat to Adi Keshava Ghat

Beyond Lakshmanbala Ghat, with its commanding views of the river, lies one of the most dramatic and controversial *ghats*, **Panchganga**, dominated by Varanasi's largest riverside building, the great **Mosque of Alamgir**, known locally as Beni Madhav-ka-Darera. With its minarets now much shortened, the mosque stands on the ruins of the **Bindu Madhava**, a Vishnu temple that extended from Panchganga to Rama Ghat before it was destroyed by Aurangzeb and replaced by the mosque. Panchganga also bears testimony to more favourable Hindu–Muslim relations, being the site of the initiation of the medieval saint of the Sufi-Sant tradition, Kabir, the son of a humble Muslim weaver who is venerated by Hindus and Muslims alike. Along the riverfront lies a curious array of three-sided cells, submerged during the rainy season, some with *lingams*, others with images of Vishnu, and some empty and used for meditation or yoga. Above **Trilochana Ghat**, further north, is the holy ancient *lingam* of the three (*tri*)-eyed (*lochana*) Shiva. Beyond it, the river bypasses some of Varanasi's oldest precincts, now predominantly Muslim in character; the *ghats* themselves gradually become less impressive and are usually of the *kaccha* (clay-banked) variety. At **Adi Keshava Ghat** (the "Original Vishnu"), on the outskirts of the city, the Varana flows into the Ganga. Unapproachable during the rainy season, when it is completely submerged, it marks the place where Vishnu supposedly landed as an emissary of Shiva, and stands on the original site of the city before it spread southwards; around Adi Keshava are a number of Ganesha shrines.

The Old City

At the heart of Varanasi, between Dashaswamedh Ghat and Godaulia to the south and west and Manikarnika Ghat on the river to the north, lies the maze of ramshackle alleys that comprise the **Old City**, or Vishwanatha Khanda. The whole area rewards exploration, buzzing with the activity of pilgrims, *pandas* and stalls selling offerings to the faithful, and boasting shrines and *lingams* tucked into every corner. Watch for cow jams in the narrow lanes, and if you get lost head for the river.

Approached through labyrinthine alleys and the **Vishwanatha Gali** (or Lane), the temple complex of **Vishwanatha** or **Visheshwara**, the "Lord of All", is popularly known as the **Golden Temple**, due to the gold plating on its massive *shikhara* (spire). Hidden behind a wall, the opulent complex is closed to non-Hindus, who have to make do with glimpses from adjacent buildings. Vishwanatha's history has been fraught. Sacked by successive Muslim rulers, it was repeatedly rebuilt and destroyed; in 1785, Queen Ahilyabai Holkar of Indore built the temple that stands today. Its simple white domes tower over the **Jnana Vapi** ("Wisdom Well"), immediately north, housed in an open-arcaded hall built in 1828, where Shiva cooled his *lingam* after the construction of Vishwanatha. Adjacent to the temple, guarded by armed police to protect it from Hindu fanatics, stands the **Jnana Vapi Mosque**, also known as the Great Mosque of Aurangzeb. Close by, the temple of **Annapurna Bhavani** is dedicated to Shakti, the divine female energy. Manifest in many forms, including the awesome Kali and Durga with their weapons and gruesome garlands of skulls, she's seen here as the provider of sustenance and carries a cooking pot. Nearby is a stunning image, faced in silver against a black surround, of **Shani** or Saturn. Slightly north, across the main road, the thirteenth-century **Razia's Mosque** stands atop the ruins of a still earlier Vishwanatha temple, destroyed under the Sultanate.

The rest of the city

Varanasi holds a few other sites of interest, especially in the area south of Godaulia, just beyond Asi Ghat. The **Durga Temple** here, and **the Bharat Kala Bhawan museum of Benares Hindu University** (BHU) are easily accessible, while just across the river, **Ramnagar** and its impressive fort continue to play an important role in the life of the city.

Bharat Mata

About 3km northwest of Godaulia, outside the Old City, the modern temple of **Bharat Mata** ("Mother India"), inaugurated by Mahatma Gandhi, is unusual in that it has a huge relief map in marble of the whole of the Indian subcontinent and the Tibetan plateau, with mountains, rivers and the holy *tirthas* all clearly visible. Pilgrims circumambulate the map before viewing it in its entirety from the second floor. The temple can be reached by rickshaw from Godaulia for Rs10–15.

South of the Old City: the Durga Temple and the Hindu University

The nineteenth-century **Durga Temple** – stained red with ochre, and known among foreign travellers as the Monkey Temple, thanks to its aggressive and irritable monkeys – stands within a walled enclosure 4km south of Godaulia, not far from Asi Ghat. It was built in a typical north Indian style, with an ornate *shikhara*, consisting of five segments symbolizing the elements and supported by finely carved columns. The whole ensemble is best seen from across Durga *kund*, the adjoining tank. Permeated by a stark primeval atmosphere, it is devoted to Durga, the terrifying aspect of Shiva's consort, Parvati, and the embodiment of **shakti** or female energy. A forked stake in the courtyard is used during festivals to behead sacrificial goats.

Non-Hindus are admitted to the courtyard, but not the inner sanctum, of the Durga temple, but access to the **Tulsi Manas Temple** alongside is unrestricted (daily 5am–noon & 3pm–midnight). Built in 1964 of white-streaked marble, its walls are inscribed with verses by the poet and author of the *Ramcharitmanas*, the Hindi equivalent of the great Sanskrit epic *Ramayana*.

A little further south, the **Bharat Kala Bhawan** museum (Mon–Sat: May & June 7.30am–12.30pm; July–April 11am–4.30pm; Rs100, camera Rs10) has a fabulous collection of miniature paintings, sculpture, contemporary art and bronzes. Dedicated to the city of Varanasi, a gallery with a stunning nineteenth-century map has a display of the recent Raj Ghat excavations and old etchings of the city. Along with Buddhist and Hindu sculpture and Moghul glass, further galleries are devoted to foreign artists who found inspiration in India, such as Nicholas Roerich and Alice Boner; Jamini Roy, the Bengali renaissance painter so influenced by folk art, is also well represented.

Bharat Kala Bhawan forms part of BHU, the campus of which also holds the **New Vishwanatha Temple** (daily 4am–noon & 1–9pm), distinguished by its lofty white-marble *shikhara*. The brainchild of Pandit Malaviya, founder of the university and a great believer in an egalitarian and casteless Hindu revival, it was built by the Birlas, a wealthy Marwari industrial family. Although supposedly modelled on the original temple destroyed by Aurangzeb, the building displays characteristics of the new wave of temple architecture, amalgamating influences from various parts of India with a garish interior. Teashops, flower-sellers and other vendors in the small market outside the gates cater for a continuous flow of visitors.

Ramnagar fort

The residence of the Maharaja of Varanasi, **Ramnagar Fort** looks down upon the Ganges not far south of the Asi Ghat. The best views of the fortifications – especially impressive in late afternoon – are to be had from the rickety pontoon bridge that crosses the river to the fort on the south bank, which is reached by a road heading south from the BHU area. During the monsoon the bridge is dismantled and replaced by a ferry, still preferable to the long main road that crosses the main Malaviya bridge in the north before heading down the eastern bank of the river. It can also be reached by chartering a boat from Dashaswamedh Ghat.

Inside, the fort bears testimony to the wealth of the maharaja and his continuing influence. A dusty and poorly kept **museum** (daily 8.30am–noon & 2–6pm; Rs7) provides glimpses of a decadent past: horse-drawn carriages, old motor cars, palanquins, ornate gilded and silver *howdahs* (elephant seats), *hookahs*, costumes and old silk in a sorry state are all part of the collection, along with an armoury, some minute ivory carvings, an astronomical clock and hunting trophies. Some visitors have reported having tea with the affable maharaja after chance encounters.

Across the courtyard, a section is devoted to the **Ram Lila** procession and festivities, held during Dussehra (Oct). Varanasi is renowned for its Ram Lila, during which episodes from the *Ramayana* are re-enacted throughout the city and the maharaja sponsors three weeks of elaborate celebrations.

Eating

Most of the Old City **cafés** are veg, and alcohol is not tolerated, but the newer Cantonment area is less constrained by religious mores, and some of the more expensive hotels have bars. After a trip on the boats in the early morning, try the traditional snack of *kachori*, savoury deep-fried pastry bread sold in the Old City next to the *ghats* – but avoid the chai stalls here as the cups are washed in the river. Varanasi is also renowned for its sweets and *paan* (betel leaf).

Stomach disorders are a common phenomenon in Varanasi, so stick to bottled or treated water and be careful when choosing where you eat. In December 1998, two young Irish travellers died from **food poisoning** here, and allegations have been made suggesting that they were victims of a scam involving unscrupulous restaurateurs and medical staff poisoning customers in order to claim medical costs from the victim's insurance company. For more details on a similar scam in Agra, see the box on p.295. There are some excellent places to eat, though, and your hotel restaurant (if it has one) should be fairly safe if only because an entire guesthouse full of dying travellers may arouse suspicion. The *Vishnu Rest House* on Pandey Ghat does excellent thalis; the *Shanti* has an extensive menu including a host of Israeli food; and the *Yogi Lodge* near Vishwanatha temple must have the cleanest kitchen in the Old City – all the travellers' favourites but not a lot of spice. Places listed below under the Godaulia heading appear on the Godaulia map (p.336); all other appear on the main Varanasi map (pp.330–331).

Godaulia

Ayyar's Dashaswamedh Rd. Small, inexpensive café at the back of a shopping arcade, serving South Indian food, including masala dosas, filter coffee and delicious milk drinks.

Ganga Fuji D5/8 Kalika Gali, Dashaswamedh. Pleasant little restaurant near Vishwanatha, with a friendly host who guides diners through the multi-cuisine menu – north Indian dishes are particularly good. Live classical music every evening from 7.30pm.

Keshari Dashaswamedh Rd. Down a small alley beyond the Bank of Baroda building, as you approach from the river, this cool and clean place is very popular with locals, so arrive early. Paneer dishes, good-value thalis and pizza.

Madhur Milan Dashaswamedh Rd, just past Vishwanatha Lane. Cheap café that's very popular with locals. Good for samosas, *dosas*, sweets and *kachoris*.

Temple *Hotel Ganges*, Bank of Baroda Building, Dashaswamedh Rd. Familiar multi-cuisine menu, and tables on a balcony overlooking the busy main drag.

The rest of the town

Bread of Life B3/322 Sonapura Rd. Bakery providing brown bread, cinnamon rolls, muffins and confectionery, with a small, clean restaurant serving Western food such as tuna burgers and crème caramel. It's not cheap at around Rs200 a head, but it's good for a splurge and the profits go to charity.

El Parador Maldahia Rd. Remarkable restaurant round the corner from the *Tourist Bungalow*, serving outstanding Mexican, Italian, Greek and French cuisine in a bistro atmosphere. All the pasta is home made, main dishes around Rs90.

Haifa 1/108 Asi Rd. Popular with locals and travellers alike, this laid-back place serves excellent Middle Eastern dishes – including hummous, fresh-baked pittas and falafel – as well as the more usual Indian fare in a congenial atmosphere.

Kamesh Hut Garden C27/111 Jagatganj, near the *Hotel Pradeep*. Reasonably priced Indian, Chinese and Continental food served either indoors or in a pleasant garden.

Kerala Café Durga Kund Rd, Bhelpura Thana. A very popular South Indian restaurant with good snacks and Keralan specialities.

Poonam *Hotel Pradeep*, Kabir Chaura Rd, Jagatganj. Good, if expensive, Mughlai food served in a comfortable air-conditioned environment.

Sindhi Durga Kund Rd, Bhelpura Thana. One of Varanasi's most popular restaurants, 1.5km from Godaulia. The rickshaw ride (Rs10–15) is rewarded by excellent veg food; try the yoghurt-based Sindhi curry.

Vaatika Asi Ghat. A leafy terrace right on the *ghat*, serving good pizza and pasta at reasonable prices.

Shopping

With hustlers and rickshaw drivers keen to drag tourists into stores offering commission, **shopping in Varanasi** can be a nightmare – but it's worth seeking out the city's rich silk-weaving and brasswork. The best **areas to browse** are the Thatheri Bazaar (for brass), or Jnana Vapi and the Vishwanatha Gali with its Temple Bazaar (for silk brocade and jewellery). State-run emporia in Godaulia, Lahurabir and the Chowk – the three UP Handlooms outlets at Lahurabir, Nadesar and Neechi Bag, and Mahatex in Godaulia – offer fixed prices and assured quality. Housed in a former palace opposite the *Taj Hotel* in the Cantonment, the CIE has a large and impressive selection but, despite its official-sounding name, is an outrageously expensive Kashmiri-run chain aimed exclusively at the five-star market.

Sales pitches tend to become most aggressive when it comes to **silk**, and you need to be wary of the hard sell. Qazi Sadullahpura, near the Chhavi Mahal Cinema, lies at the heart of a fascinating Muslim neighbourhood devoted to the production of silk. Upica, the government-run emporium, has the advantage of fixed prices, with outlets at Godaulia and opposite the *Taj Hotel*, Cantonment. Handloom House, D64/132K Sigra, another government-sponsored chain, is one of the best and safest places to buy silk, while nearby Paraslakshmi Exports, 71 Chandrika Colony offer a wide range of silk fabrics as well as scarves, shawls and bedspreads at fixed prices. Mehrotra silk factory near the railway station is also recommended; ask at the station tourist office for precise directions.

Listings

Airlines Air India, The Mall ⓣ0542/234 6326; Indian Airlines, The Mall, Cantonment ⓣ0542/250 2527, and the airport ⓣ0542/234 3742; Sahara Airlines, Mint House, The Mall ⓣ0542/250 7872. Jet Airways (ⓣ0542/262 2542) has an office at the airport.

Banks and exchange Most foreign-currency branches of the major banks are located in the Cantonment area. The State Bank of India behind *Best Western Hotel* on The Mall will change travellers' cheques but doesn't advance cash on Visa cards; there's another branch in Dashaswamedh, past the *Garden Restaurant* on Madanpura Rd, which changes Thomas Cook, but not American Express, cheques. Radiant Services, near the main Godaulia junction and St Thomas' church, changes travellers' cheques and cash – they charge a higher commission than banks but stay open long hours (daily 9am–8pm; six percent commission on Visa). ICICI Bank operates an ATM on Mall Rd, Cantonment, that accepts Visa and Mastercard. Most of the top hotels also have foreign exchange facilities.

Bookshops Indica Books, D40/18 Madanpura Rd, Godaulia, have a good selection of religion and philosophy and also provide a useful parcel mailing service. Almost next door, Universal Book Company has a large selection of fiction, reference and art books. Pilgrims Book House on Durgakund Rd has a good range of books especially on Buddhism and Hinduism. Harmony, B1/158 Asi Ghat, have a superb selection of books on all things Indian as well as fiction and philosophy.

Car rental Rental at around Rs800-1000 per day from: Travel Corporation of India ⓣ01542/234 6209; *Clarks Hotel* on The Mall ⓣ0542/234 8501; Government of India tourist office ⓣ0542/234 3744.

Hospitals Sir Sunderlal Hospital, Benares Hindu University (ⓣ0542/231 2542–45); Shiv Prasad Gupta Hospital (government-run), Kabir Chaura (ⓣ0542/233 3723); Marwari Hospital, Godaulia (ⓣ0542/232 1456); Ram Krishna Mission Hospital, Luxa (ⓣ0542/232 1727).

Internet access Internet cafés aimed at travellers cluster around Kachauri Lane and Bengali Tola Lane in the Godaulia area, and across the road from the *Taj Ganges Hotel* in the Cantonment; they all charge Rs20–25/hr.

Motorcycles Mechanics and workshops specializing in Enfields are clustered in the Jagatganj area, near the Sanskrit University; ask around for a secondhand bike.

Music The International Music Ashram, D33/81 Kalishpura in the Old City, is an excellent place to get a few lessons in tabla, sitar and theory.

Pharmacies The 24hr Singh Medical pharmacy is near the Prakash Cinema, Lahurabir, a couple of kilometres north of Godaulia.

Photography Bright Studio, Godaulia; Passi Studio, Lahurabir; Veer Studio, Jagatganj, in front of Queen's College.

Moving on from Varanasi

Indian Airlines fly three times a week to Kathmandu; there are also two daily **flights** to Delhi and Mumbai. Sahara India Airlines fly daily to Bangalore, Chennai, Pune and Mumbai via Delhi, as well as a daily direct flight to Delhi. Jet Airways fly to Delhi and Khajuraho. Allow at least ninety minutes to get from the Old City to the airport due to gridlock.

Most of the super-fast **trains** on the main east–west line between Delhi and Kolkata, such as the Rajdhani, bypass Varanasi but stop at Mughal Sarai, an arduous 45 minutes away by road or a short train ride. Varanasi station has a reservations desk (daily 8am–2pm & 2.30–7pm; ⓣ0542/234 3404). The daily Mahanagri Express #1094 is the fastest service to Mumbai (11.35am; 28hr). The best service for Rajasthan is the Marudhar Express #4853 and #4863 (daily 5.25 pm or 6.35pm; 27hr). For Kolkata via Patna, the daily choice is between the Amritsar–Howrah Express #3050 (7.25pm; 20hr) or the Amritsar–Howrah Mail #3006 (4.45pm; 15hr). The #3010 Dehra Dun–Howrah train leaves at 4.25am and arrives in Kolkata at 7am. Two good trains run to Delhi: the A.C. Poorvah Express #2381 (Wed, Thurs & Sun 7.45pm; 14hr), and the Neelachal Express #8474 (Mon, Wed & Sat 6.35am; 14hr). For the mountains of UP, the Dehra Dun–Varanasi Express #4265 (8.30am; 24hr) and the Doon Express #3009 (10.40am; 20hr) are the best options. Three trains daily leave for Nepal via Gorakhpur (6–8hr); they're not mainline services, so are subject to infuriating delays. For Khajuraho, take a train to Satna (best is the #0154 Gorakhpur–Pune Express; 9.30pm; 8hr), and change onto a bus (6am, 7am, 12 noon and 3pm) for the four-hour journey. From the Cantonment Bus Stand, UPSRTC run morning and evening **buses**, including overnight services, to the Nepal border at Sonauli (10hr) via Gorakhpur.

Several buses depart for Gaya, near Bodhgaya (7hr) after 6am. Regular services ply the Grand Trunk Road east to Patna, and there are good deluxe buses for Allahabad, which is an excellent rail link. There are also regular bus services to Lucknow (9hr), Ayodhya (7hr) and Jaunpur (2hr).

For more details of public transport from Varanasi, see "Travel details", p.351.

Post The main post office is near Kotwalii police station at the top end of the chowk. Other branches are located in *Clarks* hotel and the *Madhur Milan* café in the Cantonment; and down by the river off the Dashaswamedh Rd, 100m beyond Vishwanatha Lane.

Travel agencies General travel agencies, selling train, plane and bus tickets, include the friendly Nova International on Shubhash Nagar, near Parade Kothi ⓣ0542/234 6903; Travel Corporation of India at The Mall ⓣ0542/234 6209; and Varuna Travels, Pandey Haveli ⓣ0542/232 3370.

Visa extensions The Foreigners' Registration Office is in Srinagar Colony, Sigra ⓣ0542/235 1968.

Yoga There is a yoga institute at the Benares Hindu University, but the Yoga Ashram Academy (D5/4 *Ganesha Guest House*, Saraswati Phatak) in Godaulia is more central. Vag Yoga Consciousness Institute (ⓣ0542/231 1706), is based near Shivala Ghat. Many traveller-oriented hotels and cafés have leaflets advertising classes and venues.

Sarnath

Ten kilometres north ofVaranasi, the cluster of ruins and temples at **SARNATH** is a place of pilgrimage for Buddhists, and has also become popular with day-trippers from Varanasi who picnic among the ruins and parklands. It was in a quiet grove here, in the sixth century BC, that Siddhartha Gautama – who came to be known as the **Buddha**, the "Awakened One" – gave his first sermon, and set in motion the "Wheel of Law", the *Dharmachakra*. During the rainy season, when the Buddha and his followers sought respite from their round of itinerant

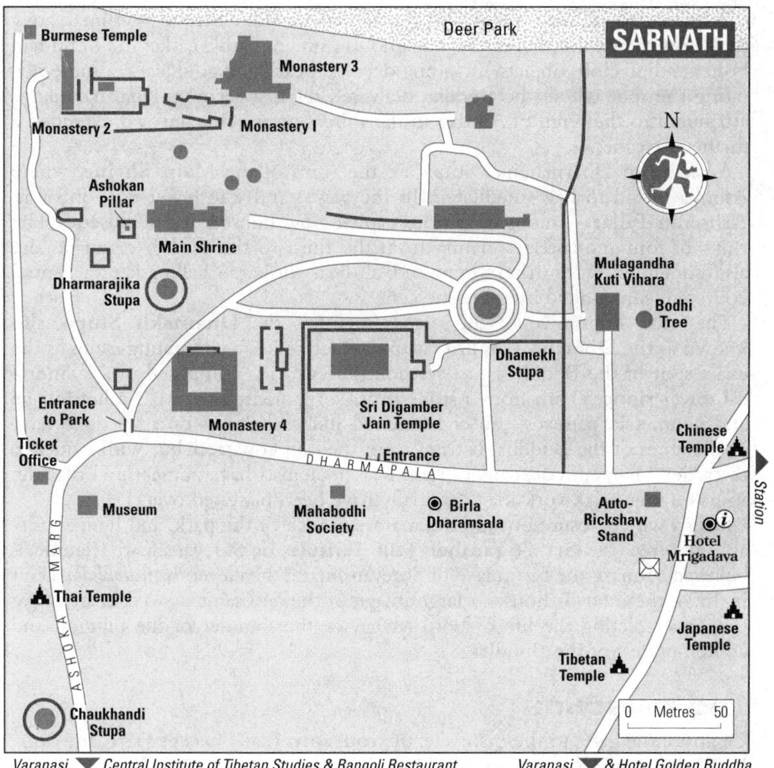

teaching, they would retire to Sarnath. Also known as **Rishipatana**, the place of the *rishis* or sages, or **Mrigadaya**, the deer park, Sarnath's name derives from *Saranganatha*, the Lord of the Deer.

Over the centuries, the settlement flourished as a centre of Buddhist art and teaching, particularly for **Hinayana** Buddhism (the "Lesser Vehicle"). In the seventh century, the Chinese pilgrim Xuan Zhang recounted seeing thirty monasteries, supporting some 3000 monks, and a life-sized brass statue of the Buddha turning the Wheel of Law. Buddhism in India floundered under the impact of Muslim invasions and the rise of Hinduism, and Sarnath's expanding Buddhist settlement eventually dissolved in the wake of this religious and political metamorphosis – except for the vast bulk of the Dhamekh Stupa, much of the site lay in ruins for almost a millennium. Prey to vandalism and pilfering, Sarnath remained abandoned until 1834, when it was visited by Major-General Sir Alexander Cunningham, the head of the Archeological Survey. Today it is once more an important Buddhist centre, and its avenues house missions from all over the Buddhist world.

The main site and the Dhamekh Stupa

Dominated by the huge bulk of the Dhamekh Stupa, the extensive archeological excavations of the main site of Sarnath are maintained within an immaculate park (daily 9am–5pm; Rs100 [Rs5], video camera Rs25). Entering from the southwest, the pillaged remains of the **Dharmarajika Stupa** lie immediately to the north: within its core the stupa holds a green marble casket full of human bones and precious objects, including decayed pearls and gold leaf. Commemorating the spot where the Buddha delivered his first sermon, Dharmarajika is attributed to the reign of Ashoka in the third century BC, but was extended a further six times.

Adjacent to Dharmarajika Stupa are the ruins of the **Main Shrine**, where Ashoka is said to have meditated. To the west stands the lower portion of an **Ashokan Pillar** – minus its famous capital, now housed in the museum. The ruins of four monasteries, dating from the third to the twelfth centuries, are also contained within the compound; all bear the same hallmark of a central courtyard surrounded by monastic cells.

The most impressive of the site's remains is the **Dhamekh Stupa**, also known as the **Dharma Chakra Stupa**, which stakes a competing claim as the exact spot of the Buddha's first sermon. The stupa is composed of a cylindrical tower rising 33.5m from a stone drum, ornamented with bas-relief foliage and geometric patterns; the eight-arched niches halfway up may once have held statues of the Buddha. It dates from the Gupta period, but with evidence of earlier Mauryan construction; some archeologists have conjectured that the stupa's upper brickwork may originally have been plastered over.

In its own enclosure outside the main entrance of the park, and hence visitable for free, the **Sri Digamber Jain Temple**, or Shreyanshnath Temple is believed to mark the birthplace of Shreyanshnath, the eleventh *tirthankara*. Built in 1824, the interior houses a large image of the Jain saint, as well as attractive frescoes depicting the life of Lord Mahavira, the founder of the religion and contemporary of the Buddha.

The museum

Opposite the gates to the main site, the **museum** (daily except Fri 10am–5pm; Rs2), designed to look like a *vihara* (monastery), has a small but renowned collection of Buddhist and Brahmanist antiquities consisting mostly of sculpture made from Chunar sandstone. The most famous exhibit is the **lion capital**, removed here from the Ashokan column on the main site. Constructed by Ashoka (273–232 BC), the great Mauryan king and convert to the *dharma*, it has become the emblem of modern India: four alert and beautifully sculpted lions guard the four cardinal points, atop a circular platform. Belonging to the first and second centuries AD are two impressive life-size standing *bodhisattvas* – one has a stone parasol with fine ornamentation and emblems of the faith. Among the large number of fifth-century figures is one of the **Buddha**, cross-legged and with his hands in the *mudra* gesture. Perfectly poised, with his eyes downcast in deep meditation and a halo forming an exquisite nimbus behind his head, the Buddha is seated above six figures, possibly representing his companions, with the Wheel of Law in the middle to signify his first sermon. Later sculptures, dating from the tenth to twelfth centuries, include an exceptionally delicate image of the deity **Avalokiteshvara** with a lotus, and another of **Lokeshvara** holding a bowl.

Chaukhandi Stupa, Mulagandha Kuti Vihara and the modern sites

The dilapidated brick remains of the **Chaukhandi Stupa**, 1km south of the main site along Ashoka Marg. Dating from the Gupta period (300–700 AD), they are said to mark the spot where the Buddha was reunited with the Panchavargiya Bikshus, his five ascetic companions who had previously deserted him. Standing on a terraced rectangular plinth, the stupa is capped by an incongruous octagonal Moghul tower, built by Akbar in 1589 AD to commemorate his father's visit to the site.

To the east of the Dhamekh Stupa, the lofty church-like **Mulagandha Kuti Vihara** monastery (no set hours; free) was built in 1931 with donations from the international Buddhist community. Run by the Mahabodhi Society, it drew devotees from all over the world to witness its consecration, and has become one of Sarnath's greatest attractions for pilgrims and tourists alike. The entrance foyer is dominated by a huge bell – a gift from Japan – and the interior houses a gilded reproduction of the museum's famous image of the Buddha, surrounded by fresco-covered walls depicting scenes from his life.

A little way east, shielded by a small enclosure, Sarnath's **bodhi tree** is an offshoot of the tree at Bodhgaya in Bihar, under which the Buddha attained enlightenment. Sangamitra, Emperor Ashoka's daughter, took a branch from the original tree in 288 BC and planted it in Anuradhapura, in Sri Lanka, where its offshoots have been nurtured through the ages.

Buddhist communities from other parts of the world are well represented in Sarnath. In addition to the long-established **Mahabodhi Society**, the **Central Institute of Tibetan Studies** (Ⓣ0542/238 5142), just out of Sarnath toward Varanasi, offers degree courses in Tibetan philosophy and the ancient language of Pali. Close to the post office is the traditional-style **Tibetan Temple** with frescoes and a good collection of *thangkas* (Tibetan Buddhist paintings): its central image is a colossal Shakyamuni, or "Buddha Calling the Earth to Witness" (his enlightenment). The **Chinese Temple** lies 200m east of the main gates; to the northwest, the **Burmese Temple** houses a white marble image of the Buddha flanked by two disciples. Behind the *Hotel Mrigadava* are the **Japanese Temple**, run by the Mrigdayavana Mahavihara Society.

Practicalities

Sarnath is easily reached by road from Varanasi. Blue **buses** depart regularly from outside Varanasi Cantonment railway station and cost Rs5, but can get very crowded. Shared auto-rickshaws also run from the station for around Rs8 per person and are quicker and more comfortable. The main sites can be quite easily – and pleasantly – explored on foot; the so-called guides who linger outside the main gates and near the museum aren't really necessary.

Opposite the post office, southeast of the park, the UPTDC-run *Hotel Mrigadava* (Ⓣ0542/259 5965; ❸–❹) has reasonable **rooms** and a **dorm** (Rs50), and also houses the UP **tourist bureau** (Mon–Sat 10am–5pm). Some of the monasteries, such as the pleasant Burmese Vihara, northwest of the main site, have basic rooms where visitors can stay for a donation. Right in front of the Mahabodhi Society gates, the *Birla Dharamsala* (no phone; ❶) is a central option with very basic facilities. Further out of town, a ten-minute walk south from the Japanese temple, *Hotel Golden Buddha* (Ⓣ0542/258 7933 Ⓕ236 9695; ❸–❺) is the most comfortable option in the area, with some very chic rooms and a decent restaurant serving good home cooking. There are a few simple **cafés** and **restaurants** outside the main gates near the Mulagandha Kuti Vihara, and a rather institutional restaurant serving thalis at the *Hotel Mrigadava*. *Rangoli*, just past Chukhandi Stupa, at the cross-road on the approach road from Varanasi is popular for inexpensive Indian food and has an outdoor sitting area.

Gorakhpur

Some 230km north of Varanasi, **GORAKHPUR** rose to prominence as a waystation on a pilgrims' route linking Kushinagar (the place of Buddha's enlightenment) and **Lumbini** (his birthplace, across the border in Nepal), and is now known primarily as a gateway to Nepal. It was named after the Shaivite yogi **Gorakhnath**, and holds a large ashram and temple dedicated to him. Tourists and pilgrims tend to hurry through, their departure hastened by the town's infamous flies and mosquitoes; if you do get stranded, there's a bustling bazaar, adequate amenities and a few passable hotels.

Practicalities

Gorakhpur has three **bus** stands – the main Railway bus stand, 1km north of the centre, for services from the Nepalese border at **Sonauli** and **Kushinagar**; the Kacheri bus stand, 1km southwest of the station, for buses from **Allahabad**, **Lucknow** and **Varanasi**; and the main bus stand for **Varanasi** (6hr) and **Nepal–Varanasi** buses, which is 2km southeast of the railway station at Pedleyganj.

Major daily **trains** servicing Gorakhpur include the fast Vaishali Express #2553 to **Lucknow** and **Delhi** (5.10pm) and the Gorakhpur–Dadar Express #1028 for **Mumbai** via Varanasi (5am); among trains to **Varanasi** (6hr) are the fast Kashi Express #1028 (5am) and the Chauri–Chaura Express #5004 (10.30pm) Station facilities include pleasant retiring rooms, a basic restaurant and a tourist information booth (theoretically Mon–Sat 9am–5pm, but usually closed).

The airport is 7km east of Gorakhpur towards Kushinagar. Air Sahara (Ⓣ0551/227 2482) operates four flights a week to Kolkata (Calcutta) and to Lucknow. Taxis at the stand charge Rs100 into town.

Cycle-rickshaws are the main means of **transport**, with few hotels more than 2km from the station. **Car rental** can be arranged through India Tours

Getting to Nepal

Gorakhpur is a convenient jumping-off point for western **Nepal**, offering access to Pokhara and even Kathmandu. Direct buses to Kathmandu and Pokhara are not a very good deal – your best bet is to enter Nepal at the 24-hour crossing at Sonauli where there's a better choice of transport.

Buses for Sonauli (3hr) depart from the bus stand near Gorakhpur railway station between 4.30am and 9pm: deluxe buses leave from in front of the railway station. Take one of the earliest if you want to get a connecting bus to **Pokhara** (10hr) or **Kathmandu** in daylight, to enjoy the views; night buses also ply the routes. Private buses leave Sonauli almost hourly in the mornings, between 5am and 11am. The most popular service for Kathmandu, the government-run Saja, actually operates from **Bhairawa**, 5km away in Nepal; the booking office is near Bhairawa's *Yeti Hotel*. Local buses cover the 24km from Bhairawa to Lumbini (Nepal), the birthplace of the Buddha. If you want to **break your journey**, UPTD's *Hotel Niranjana* (❶–❺) in Sonauli, 1km short of the border, has air-cooled rooms and a dorm (Rs50). There's more choice over the border in Nepal; and in Bhairawa, 5km up the road from the border, the Yeti and the *Himalayan Inn are* popular.

Nepalese visas (valid for one month), are available at the border for US$30. There is a State Bank of India on the Indian side of the border; moneychangers across the border will also cash travellers' cheques. Note that Indian Rs500 notes are illegal in Nepal; yours may be "confiscated".

and Travels (☎0551/203201) in the Ellora Building, opposite the railway station; beware of ticket touts and poor service from most of the travel agents around here. The main **GPO** is in Golghar, to the southwest. The State Bank of India on Bank Road is the only place able to exchange travellers' cheques. **Foreign exchange** facilities can also be found at some of the more expensive hotels.

Accommodation and eating

Gorakhpur has a wide range of **hotels**, from the budget-type near the station to the mid-range in the dull commercial hub around Golghar, 1km southwest. During the hot months, air-cooled or the more expensive air-conditioned rooms are welcome, especially if you've just come down from the mountains. Cheap *dhabas* can be found in the vicinity of the station; a row of them stand outside the station gates. Elsewhere, the best eating is in the more expensive hotels or the new multi-cuisine *Bobis* restaurant in Golghar. Unless otherwise stated, all the following hotels have 24hr check-out.

Accommodation

Bobina Nepal Rd, ☎0551/233 6663. A pleasant hotel, with a little garden out front, offering a/c rooms with TV. ❺

Ellora Station Rd, opposite the railway station ☎0551/220 0647. One of the best of the station hotels, with a range of rooms (including some with a/c) and a cheap dorm (Rs40). The best rooms are at the back, away from the station. ❷–❸

Ganges Tarang Cinema crossing, towards Gorakhnath Temple ☎0551/233 3530. Pronounced "gang-ez", this is one of Gorakhpur's better hotels, though the decor isn't hugely inspired. All the mod cons, including two good restaurants and friendly staff. ❸–❺

Ganges Deluxe Cinema Rd, Golghar ☎0551/233 6330. Spacious a/c rooms with clean bathrooms. ❹

Marina Golghar ☎0551/233 7639. Tucked away behind the *President Hotel* in the same compound, this place is older, less ostentatious and more pleasant. Clean rooms – some of those with a/c are real bargains. ❷–❸

Retiring Rooms Gorakhpur railway station. Good value, offering rooms with or without a/c; recommended if you need to catch an early train. Noon check-out. ❷–❹

Yark Inn M.P. Building, Golghar ☎0551/233 8233. One of several similarly and reasonably priced establishments along this busy stretch of road, offering clean and well-kept rooms with TV.. ❷–❸

Upvan Nepal Rd ☎0551/233 6503. Generally neat and tidy rooms with hot water for the winter and a/c for the summer, arranged around a central garden courtyard. One of the few places that will accommodate very late night arrivals. ❷–❹

Kushinagar

Set against a pastoral landscape 53km west of Gorakhpur, the small hamlet of **KUSHINAGAR** is revered as the site of Buddha's **Mahaparinirvana**, his death and cremation that marked his final liberation from the cycles of death and rebirth. During the Buddha's lifetime, **Kushinara**, as it was then called, was a small kingdom of the Mallas, surrounded by forest. It remained forgotten until the late nineteenth century, when archeologists rediscovered the site and began excavations based on the writings of the seventh-century Chinese pilgrims, including Xuan Zhang.

Set in a leafy park in the heart of Kushinagar, the **Nirvana Stupa**, dated to the reign of Kumaragupta I (413–455 AD), was extensively rebuilt by Burmese Buddhists in 1927. Within the accompanying shrine lies a large gilded **reclining Buddha**, reconstructed from the remains of an earlier Malla image, while the surrounding area is strewn with stupas erected by pious pilgrims, as well as the ruins of four monasteries. At a crossing immediately southwest, excavations continue at the **Mathakunwar** shrine, where a stunning tenth-century blue schist Buddha has been unearthed. About 1.5km southeast of the main site – surrounded by fields of rice, wheat and cane – the crumbling bricks of the **Ramabhar Stupa** are thought to be the original **Mukutabandhana Stupa** erected to mark the spot of the Buddha's cremation.

Today Kushinagar is rediscovering its roots as a centre of international Buddhism, and is home to many *viharas* (monasteries), including a Tibetan *gompa* devoted to Shakyamuni (the historical Buddha), a Burmese *vihara*, and temples from China and Japan. The strikingly simple **Japanese Temple**, built by Atago Isshin World Buddhist Cultural Association, consists of a single circular chamber housing a great golden image of the Buddha, softly lit through small, stained-glass windows. In stark contrast, the recently constructed **Thai Monastery** is a large complex of lavish, traditionally styled temples and shrines.

Practicalities

Regular **buses** link Kushinagar with **Gorakhpur** (2hr) and **Varanasi** (8hr). Shared **taxis** and Jeeps also travel to and from Gorakhpur, but are a lot less comfortable. The airport is closed to commercial flights. **UP Tourism** maintains a low-key office and information desk at the tourist bungalow, *Pathik Niwas* (Mon–Sat 10am–5.30pm; ⓣ05564/271038). Both the Government of India and UP Tourism run comprehensive tours of the whole "Buddhist Circuit" of Uttar Pradesh, which can be booked either at the tourist office in Kushinagar or in Delhi (see p.117 & p.154). There is no foreign exchange here, the nearest being Gorakhpur.

Some of the temples offer **accommodation** for visiting pilgrims in return for a donation (in the region of ❶): try rooms at the Myanmar Buddhist Temple; the *Birla Dharamshala* opposite, is similarly basic while the *International Buddhist Guest House*, opposite the Tibetan gompa, is poorly maintained but otherwise quiet and pleasant. Other **dharamshalas** offer rooms for a "suggested donation", which in reality equates to Rs250 per double; of these, the *Chinese Buddhist Temple* has clean, spacious doubles with attached baths and hot water. Note that none of the above have a phone. The relatively expensive state-run tourist bungalow, *Pathik Niwas* (ⓣ05564/271038; ❷–❼), has a/c rooms, luxury cottages called "American Huts", a canteen-like restaurant and a rather unkempt budget accommodation block. *Lotus Nikko* (ⓣ05564/272250, ❽–❾), next to the Japanese Temple is a three-star with a/c rooms and money changing facilities, but it is usually booked solid by tour groups.

Good **restaurants** are scarce, the exception being the pleasant and clean *Yama Kwality Café* near the Chinese Temple, which has a small menu of home-cooked Indian, Tibetan and Chinese food – the vegetable or chicken-noodle soup is particularly recommended. It opens for breakfast but closes early at night when power-cuts are frequent. Food stalls at the Kasia crossing also provide inexpensive snacks.

Travel details

Trains

Note that most important trains to Varanasi stop at Mughul Sarai, requiring a change of trains or a connecting bus or taxi.

Agra to: Ahmedabad (4 weekly; 27hr 45min); Alwar (1 daily; 4hr); Bhopal (15–19 daily; 6hr 10min–10hr 15min); Bhubaneshwar (1–2 daily; 39hr–42hr); Chennai (1–2 daily; 33hr–38hr 30min); Delhi (21–29 daily; 2hr 30min–6hr); Gwalior (20–28 daily; 1hr 10min–2hr 20 min); Indore (1–2 daily; 14hr 30min–16hr); Jaipur (3–4 daily; 6hr 45min–7hr 50min); Jalgaon (3–4 daily; 14hr 20min–19hr); Jhansi (15–19 daily; 2hr 25min–5hr); Jodhpur (2 daily; 14hr 15min–15hr 20min); Kanpur (4–5 daily; 5hr–11hr 35min); Kolkata (Calcutta) (2–3 daily; 27hr 10min–30hr); Lucknow (2–3 daily; 6hr 30min–15hr 30min); Mathura (12 daily; 1hr 30min–2hr); Mumbai (4–5daily; 23hr–27hr); Nainital (1 daily; 11hr); Puri (1 daily; 40hr); Satna (1 daily, 10hr 30min); Thiruvananthapuram (1–2 daily; 50hr 30min–52hr 40min); Ujjain (1–2 daily; 10hr 40min–13hr); Varanasi (1–2 daily; 10hr 20min–12hr 30min).

Varanasi to: Agra (1–2 daily; 10hr 20min–12hr 30min); Allahabad (12–15 daily; 2hr 45min–4hr); Ahmedabad (4 weekly; 41hr); Bhubaneshwar (3 weekly; 23hr); Chennai (2 weekly; 40hr 10min); Dehra Dun (2–3 daily; 20hr–24hr 30min); Delhi (5–10 daily; 14–16hr); Gaya (6–8 daily; 3hr 30min–5hr); Gorakhpur (4 daily; 5–10hr); Gwalior (1 daily; 19hr); Haridwar (2 daily; 19hr); Jabalpur (4–7 daily; 10hr 45min–11hr 45min); Jalgaon (4 daily; 18–22hr); Jhansi (1 daily; 18hr 30min); Kanpur (4 daily; 8–9hr); Kolkata (Calcutta) (5–8 daily; 10hr 30min–18hr); Lucknow (13–16 daily; 4hr 50min–7hr); Mumbai (7–8 daily; 27hr 20min–32hr); New Jalpaiguri (3 daily; 12–17hr); Patna (9 daily; 8hr); Puri (3 weekly; 24hr); Ujjain (3 weekly; 31hr 35min).

Jhansi to: Agra (15–19 daily; 2hr 25min–5hr); Chennai (3–5 daily; 24–38hr); Delhi (15–19 daily; 4hr 35min–9hr); Goa (1 daily; 35hr); Indore (1 daily; 11hr 35min); Kolkata (Calcutta) (4 weekly; 23hr 25min); Mumbai (6 daily; 19–24hr 30min); Orchha (3 daily; 15min); Ujjain (2–4 daily; 9–10hr).

Lucknow to: Agra (1–2 daily; 6hr 30min–15hr 30min); Dehra Dun (3–4 daily; 14–18hr); Delhi (7–12 daily; 6hr 10min–9hr 45min); Gorakhpur (8–13 daily; 4hr 45min–6hr 40min); Haridwar (3–4 daily; 10–12hr); Kanpur (15–20 daily; 50min–2hr 5min); Kolkata (Calcutta) (7–9 daily; 21hr 45min–28hr); Kulu (1 daily; 3hr 15min); Kathgodam for Nainital (1 daily; 8hr 30min); Mumbai (6–8 daily; 24hr 50min–29hr); Patna (2–4 daily; 9hr–12hr 20min); Varanasi (13–16 daily; 4hr 15min–7hr).

Buses

Agra to: Ajmer (for Pushkar; 2 daily; 10hr); Delhi (hourly; 5–6hr); Dehra Dun (2 daily, 13hr); Fatehpur Sikri (every 30min; 1hr–1hr 30min); Gwalior (3 daily; 3hr 30min); Haridwar (8–10 daily; 12hr); Jaipur (every 15min; 5–6hr); Kanpur (1 daily; 10hr); Khajuraho (1 daily; 12hr); Lucknow (4 daily; 9hr 30min); Mathura (hourly; 1hr 30min); Nainital (1 daily; 10hr); Rishikesh (2 daily, 12hr).

Varanasi to: Allahabad (every 30min; 2hr 30min); Delhi (1 nightly; 18hr); Gaya (4 daily; 6hr); Jaunpur (8 daily; 2hr); Kanpur (7 daily; 10hr); Lucknow (frequent; 8hr); Patna (7 daily; 6hr).

Jhansi to: Orchha (hourly; 30min).

Lucknow to: Agra (2 daily; 10hr); Delhi (2 daily; 9hr); Dehra Dun (2 daily, 10hr 30min); Haridwar (4 daily; 10hr); Kanpur (hourly; 2hr); Nainital (4 daily; 10hr).

Flights

Agra to: Delhi (4 weekly; 40min).

Allahabad to: Delhi (1 daily, 2hr 20min); Kolkata (3 weekly; 1hr 20min), Lucknow (3 weekly; 40min).

Gorakhpur to: Kolkata (Calcutta) (4 weekly; 1hr 2min); Lucknow (4 weekly; 40min).

Lucknow to: Allahabad (3 weekly; 40min); Gorakhpur (4 weekly; 40min); Delhi (2–4 daily; 1hr); Kolkata (Calcutta) (1–2 daily; 2hr 20min–3hr 40min); Mumbai (1–2 daily; 2hr–3hr 30min); Panaji (Goa) (1 daily; 2hr); Patna (1–2 daily; 1hr).

Varanasi to: Delhi (3–4 daily; 1hr min–2hr 55min); Kathmandu (3 weekly; 1hr 10min); Khajuraho (1–2 daily; 40min).

CHAPTER 4

Highlights

* **Char Dham** The pilgrim circuit around the four holy sites of Garhwal, coverable by bus, reveals a cross-section of the Indian Himalayas' most superb scenery. See p.356
* **Rishikesh** This busy pilgrimage place on the banks of the turquoise Ganges is a renowned yoga and meditation centre. See p.368
* **Gangotri** Hole up at the source of the Ganges, high in the mountains, where *sadhus* offer accommodation for spiritual retreats. See p.376
* **Valley of the Flowers** A hidden valley, discovered by Europeans only in 1931, whose lush meadows are a botanist's dream: hike here after the monsoons. See p.384
* **Curzon Trail** A ten-day trail over the Kuari Pass, offering stunning views of the Great Himalayan Watershed. See p.385
* **Corbett Tiger Reserve** Established in the 1930s, India's most famous nature reserve is renowned for its population of tigers. See p.390
* **The Panchulis** The magnificent "Five Cooking Pots" peaks, plumes of snow perennially blowing from them, are visible from Munsiyari. See p.401

△ Mountains, Gangotri

Uttaranchal

Northeast of Delhi, bordering Nepal and Tibet, the mountains of Garhwal and Kumaon rise from the fertile sub-Himalayan plains. Together they form the new state of **UTTARANCHAL**, also known as Uttarakhand, which was shorn free from lowland Uttar Pradesh in 2000 after years of agitation. The region has its own distinct languages and cultures, and successive deep river valleys shelter fascinating micro-civilizations, where Hinduism meets animism and the Buddhist influence is never too far away. Although not as high as the giants of Nepal, further east, or as the Karakoram, the snow peaks here rank among the most beautiful mountains of the inner Himalayas, forming an almost continuous chain that culminates in **Nanda Devi**, the highest mountain in India at 7816m.

Garhwal is the more visited region, busy with pilgrims who flock to its holy spots. At **Haridwar**, the Ganges thunders out from the foothills on its long journey to the sea. The ashram town of **Rishikesh** nearby is familiar from one of the classic East-meets-West images of the 1960s; it was where the Beatles came to stay with the Maharishi. From here pilgrims set off for the high temples known as the Char Dham – **Badrinath**, **Kedarnath**, **Yamunotri** and **Gangotri**, the source of the Ganges. Earthier pursuits are on offer at **Mussoorie**, a British hill station that's now a popular Indian resort. The lesser-visited **Kumaon** region is more unspoilt, and boasts pleasant small towns famed for mountain views and hill walks, such as **Kausani** and **Ranikhet**, as well as its own Victorian hill station, **Nainital**, whose promenade throngs with refugees from the heat of the plains. Further down, the forests at **Corbett National Park** offer the chance to go tiger-spotting from the back of an elephant. Both districts abound in classic **treks**, many leading through the high alpine meadows known as *bugyals* – summer pastures, where rivers are born and paths meet.

Facilities are good in the big towns of the foothills, and if you're aiming to ascend you should make the most of foreign exchange services, Internet cafés and satellite TV here as there's little chance of any of that elsewhere in the state. In the mountains, roads are good – maintained by the army, which has a large presence up here thanks to the proximity of the Tibetan border – but **getting around** is not always easy as the monsoon (Aug–Sept) causes landslides and avalanches which block the roads; similar troubles occur during the winter snow season (Dec–Feb). There are buses, but, especially high up, most locals get around by shared Jeep, with many vehicles crammed to bursting (women and foreigners inside, local youths hanging off the back). Compared to the plains, there's little caste strife (most mountain people are high-caste rajput or brahmin) and you'll see few beggars other than religious mendicants. A few words of Hindi are certainly handy as the mountain people usually speak little English.

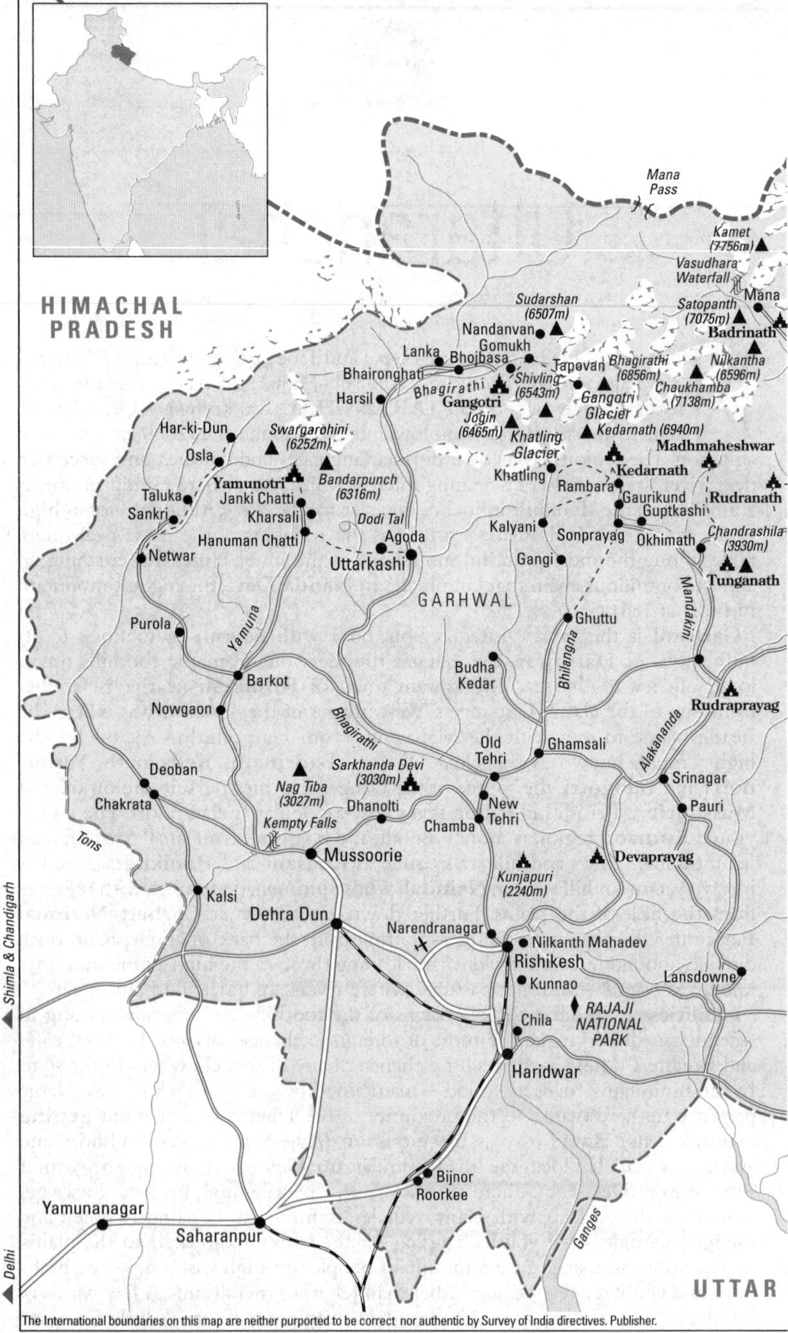

The International boundaries on this map are neither purported to be correct nor authentic by Survey of India directives. Publisher.

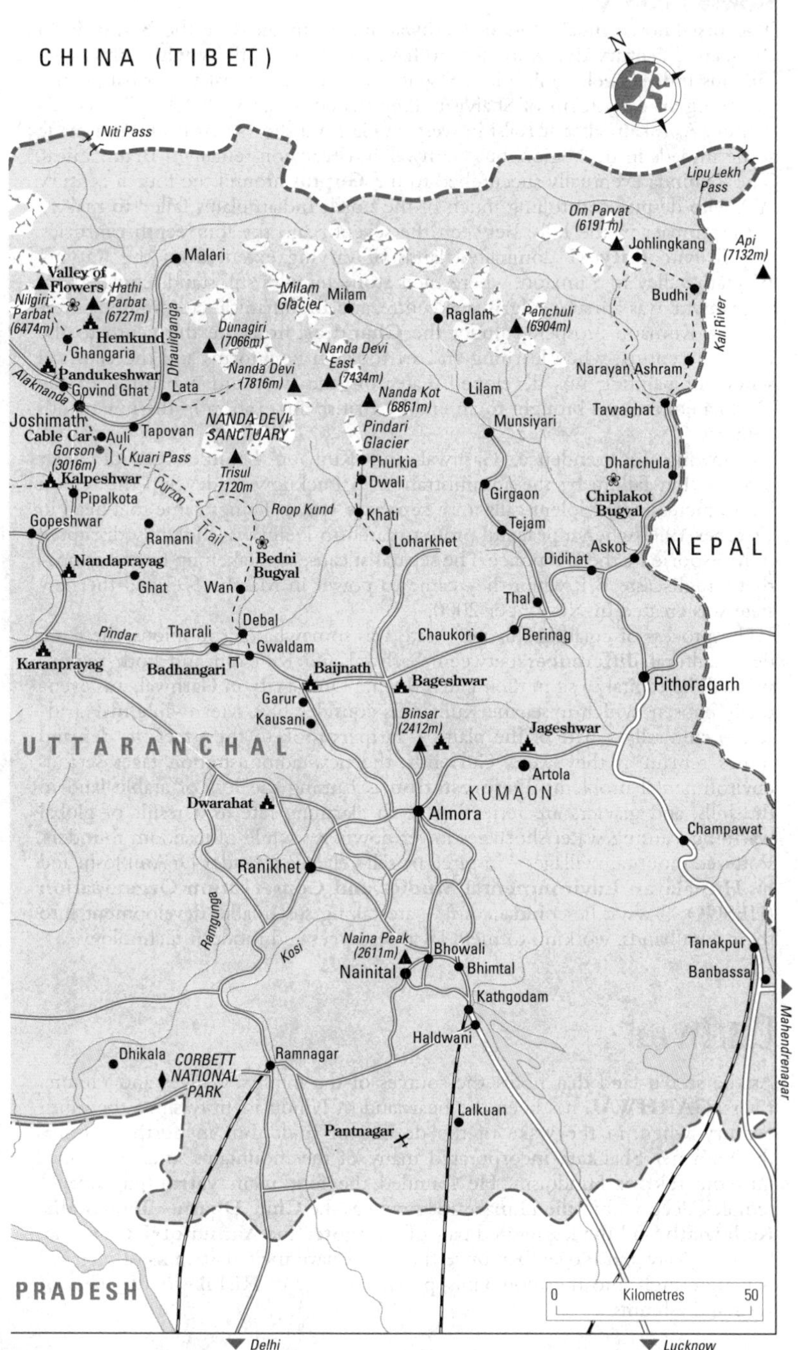

4 UTTARANCHAL

Some history

The first known inhabitants of Garhwal and Kumaon were the **Kuninda** in the second century BC, who seem to have had a close affinity with contemporaneous Indo–Greek civilization. Essentially a central Himalayan tribal people, practising an early form of Shaivism, they traded in salt with Tibet. A second-century Ashokan edict at Kalsi in western Garhwal shows that Buddhism made some inroads in the region, but Garhwal and Kumaon remained Brahmanical. The Kuninda eventually succumbed to the **Guptas** around the fourth century AD, who despite controlling much of the north Indian plains failed to make a lasting impact in the hills. Between the seventh and the fourteenth centuries, the Shaivite **Katyuri** dominated lands of varying extent from the Katyur-Baijnath valley in Kumaon, where their stone temples still stand. Under them **Jageshwar** was a major pilgrimage centre, and Brahmanical culture flourished. Eastern Kumaon prospered under the **Chandras**, from the thirteenth to the fifteenth century, when learning and art took on new forms and the Garhwal school of painting was developed. Later on, the westward expansion of the Gurkha empire was brought to an end by British annexation in the nineteenth century.

Following Independence, Garhwal and Kumaon became part of Uttar Pradesh, but failure by the administration in Lucknow to develop the region led to increasingly violent calls for a **separate state**. Things came to a head in October 1994 when a peaceful protest march to Delhi was violently disrupted in Mussoorie by the UP police. The separatist cause was taken up by the sympathetic high-caste BJP when they came to power in March 1998 and the new state was created in November 2000.

The process of creating this new state was somewhat acrimonious; there are deep cultural **differences** between Garhwal and Kumaon and both regions wanted the capital to sit in their patch (Dehra Dun, a city in Garhwal, was eventually chosen, which upset the Kumaonis considerably). Meanwhile in Haridwar – culturally a part of the plains – farmers took to the streets to demand things remain as they were. Currently, the new administration faces serious environmental problems. **Deforestation** is causing the loss of arable land in the hills, and glaciers are retreating at an alarming rate as a result of global warming, causing water shortages lower down. Yet while officialdom founders, scattered mountain villages – inspired by self-reliance crusader Dr Anil Joshi and his **Himalayan Environmental Studies and Conservation Organization** (HESCO; Ⓦwww.hescoindia.com) – are taking sustainable development into their own hands, working to meld local resources and modern technology.

Garhwal

As the sacred land that holds the sources of the mighty Ganges and Yamuna rivers, **GARHWAL** has been the heartland of Hindu identity since the ninth century when, in the wake of the decline of Buddhism in northern India, the reformer Shankara incorporated many of the mountains' ancient shrines into the fold of Hinduism. He founded the four main **yatra** (pilgrimage) temples, deep within the Himalayas, known as the **Char Dham** – **Badrinath**, **Kedarnath**, and the less-visited pair of **Gangotri** and **Yamunotri**. Each year, between May and November, once the snows have melted, streams of pilgrims penetrate high into the mountains, passing by way of **Rishikesh**, the land of *yogis* and ashrams.

For more than a millennium, the *yatris* (pilgrims) came on foot. However, the annual event has been transformed in the last few years; roads blasted by the military through the mountains during the war against China in the early 1960s are now the lifelines for a new form of motorized *yatra*. Eastern Garhwal in particular is getting rich, and the fabric of hill society is changing rapidly – visitors hoping to experience the old Garhwal should spend at least part of their time well away from the principal *yatra* routes. In addition to their spiritual significance, the hills are now becoming established as a centre for **adventure sports**, offering all levels of trekking, white-water rafting, paragliding, skiing and climbing.

Not far north of Delhi is the buzzing cantonment town of **Dehra Dun**. The pleasant hill station of **Mussoorie** rises behind, affording the traveller first sight of the Himalayan snows. Further south, near Rishikesh, holy **Haridwar** marks where the Ganges emerges from the hills onto the Indian plains.

Garhwal is a challenging place to **travel** around, with extremely long and often nerve-wracking bus and Jeep rides being the order of the day. However, you are rewarded with spectacular views of snowy peaks offset by gaudily painted Garhwali villages in deep valleys. All the tourist bungalows are operated by Garhwal Mandal Vikas Nigam – **GMVN** (Ⓦwww.gmvnl.com). Most are concentrated along the pilgrimage routes, although their network has been expanding both in areas right off the beaten track and in new destinations such as the ski resort of **Auli**. Standards vary widely, but most bungalows offer a range of rooms and dorms to suit most budgets, along with a restaurant. GMVN also organizes Char Dham **tours** (often overpriced and inefficient), and offers expensive **car rental**. The GMVN headquarters is in Dehra Dun (Ⓣ0135/274 6817), although you will get more help from their office in Delhi (Ⓣ011/2332 2251). The GMVN Trekking and Mountaineering Division, based in Rishikesh (Ⓣ01364/243 0799), is the office to contact for adventure sports packages such as skiing and trekking.

Dehra Dun

Capital of Uttaranchal since 2000, **DEHRA DUN**, 255km north of Delhi, tends to be seen simply as a staging post on the way to the hill station of Mussoorie, 34km north, and the Garhwal interior. Pleasantly located at just below 700m, as the Himalayan foothills begin their dramatic rise, Dehra Dun never gets too hot in summer, and snows only rarely appear in winter. With its vast open spaces and colonies such as the Cantonment, this popular retirement spot is renowned for its elite public schools and prestigious institutions. Although occupied in turn by Sikhs, Moghuls, and Gurkhas, it's clearly an overgrown British town, with its Raj roots very apparent.

Dehra Dun stands at the centre of the 120km-long **Doon Valley** (*dun* or *doon* literally means "valley"), famous for its long-grain rice – basmati – and unique in being hemmed in by the Yamuna to the west and the Ganges at Rishikesh to the east. Also in the east is **Rajaji National Park**, known for its wild elephants, while the low-forested Shivalik hills separate the valley from the dusty plains to the south. Thanks to local endeavours against the devastating effects of encroaching deforestation the springs are returning to life and with them the dry riverbeds that criss-cross the valley. Those tracts of forests that remain are best seen at its eastern and western extremities.

Arrival and information

The **Inter-state Bus Terminal** (ISBT) is located in the far southwest of town, a Rs45 auto-rickshaw ride from the **railway station** and the budget hotels on

Gandhi Road. Gandhi Road doglegs east then north at Princes Chowk towards the **post office** and Clock Tower in the centre of town, from where Rajpur Road heads north, with the Astley Hall area branching off to the east. The State Bank of India on Convent Road changes travellers' cheques, as do several of the state **banks** that line Rajpur Road. Dehra Dun is the best place in the state for **Internet** access as Garhwal's only server is here. The helpful **regional tourist office**, 45 Gandhi Road (Mon–Sat 10am–5pm; ⓣ0135/265 3217), covers Dehra Dun; in the same complex, Drona Travels (ⓣ0135/265 3309) books GMVN accommodation and tours throughout Garhwal, and also rents cars. Another helpful source of information is the GMVN Head Office, 74/1 Rajpur Rd (ⓣ0135/274 6817; ⓔgmvn@gmvnl.com), who can also advise about trekking. Abundant local transport includes cycle- and auto-rickshaws and multi-seater Vikrams.

If you're looking to fix up a **trek**, try Garhwal Tours and Trekking, 193 Araghar (ⓣ0135/267 7769, ⓔgarhwaltrekking@rediffmail.com), an established and experienced organization used to working with tour groups such as Exodus. Paramount, behind Paltan Bazaar at 16 Moti Market, and the nearby Mountain Equipment are the best trekking and mountaineering **equipment** dealers in the entire region.

Accommodation

Dehra Dun has a good selection of mid-range **hotels**, many of them strung along Rajpur Road as it heads north to Mussoorie. What little budget accommodation there is can be found between the railway station and the Clock Tower – or in the old-fashioned railway retiring rooms.

Ashrey 10 Tyagi Rd ⓣ0135/262 3388, ⓔinfo@hotelashrey.net. In a quiet, but still central spot, three minutes' walk south of Princes Chowk; the private lawn in front complements the spotless, spacious and well-furnished new rooms. Good value. ❹–❼

Best Western Madhuban 97 Rajpur Rd ⓣ0135/274 9990, ⓦwww.hotelmadhuban.com. A large, imposing upmarket hotel with a popular restaurant, bar, steam room and gym; some consider it Dehra Dun's best and it's certainly the most expensive at $75–130. A favourite with the few tour groups that come through. ❾

Embassy 18 Dhamawala ⓣ0135/265 5790. Down a series of lanes, not far from the centre and well worth seeking out. A good range of rooms. ❸

Great Value 74C Rajpur Rd, 2.5km north of the Clock Tower ⓣ0135/274 4086, ⓦwww.greatvaluehotel.com. Large, well-run chain hotel with good facilities including a nice garden, bar and in-room broadband Internet connections. Rooms from $45–110. ❽–❾

Kwality 19 Rajpur Rd ⓣ0135/657230. A central landmark, established in the motel-influenced 1960s, with large, refurbished rooms (avoid the stuffy, cheaper ones), and a good restaurant. ❹–❻

Victoria 70 Gandhi Rd ⓣ0135/262 3486. Simple lodge near the railway station, with a courtyard and bucket hot water. ❷

White House 15/7 Subhash Rd (aka Lytton Rd) ⓣ0135/265 2765. Rambling old Raj residence near Astley Hall, with huge verandas, lofty ceilings, sturdy furniture and moody plumbing. A peaceful retreat from the centre of Dehra Dun, yet only a few minutes' walk away. ❸

The Town and around

Driven by Dehra Dun's status as state capital, increasing local investment has resulted in a mini-boom – and the accompanying noise and traffic problems – within the city centre. Most of Dehra Dun's bustling markets lie near the tall Victorian **Clock Tower**, from where Rajpur Road, the lifeline to Mussoorie, stretches northwards. Four kilometres along is the vast leafy colony occupied by the **Survey of India**, founded in 1767. Its greatest achievement was to determine the height of Mount Everest, and name it after the surveyor general, Sir George Everest, but the Survey isn't a place to shop for **maps**; stock is paltry and the 1:250,000 scale trekking maps pretty useless.

Moving on from Dehra Dun

Jolly Grant **airport** is 24km east of Dehra Dun; Deccan Airways (®www.airdeccan.net) fly daily to Delhi for $40.

Major daily **trains** down to the plains include the Dehra Dun–Varanasi Express #4266 through **Lucknow** to **Varanasi**; the Howrah Express #3010 through Varanasi to **Kolkata (Calcutta)**; the Mussoorie Express #4042 to **Delhi**; the Mumbai Express #9020; and the Ujjain–Dehra Dun Ujjaini Express #4310, which runs on Tuesdays and Wednesdays and stops at **Agra**. **Train reservations** are available at the computerized booking office opposite the railway station.

Hourly **buses** from the **Inter-state Bus Terminal (ISBT)** head to Mussoorie (Rs23) via the old bus stand at the railway station, while a deluxe bus to Delhi from ISBT costs around Rs200. You can also get buses to **Shimla**, **Dharamsala**, **Chandigarh**, **Kullu**, **Manali**, as well as numerous services to **Rishikesh** and **Haridwar**, and one early morning bus to **Nainital**.

See the "Travel details" at the end of this chapter for more information on journey frequencies and durations.

Crossing the rainy-season riverbed of Bindal Rao, Kaulagarh Road progresses northwest past Dehra Dun's top private school, the **Doon School**, to the expansive grounds of the chateau-like **Forest Research Institute** (Mon–Fri 10.30am–5pm; free), devoted to the preservation of India's much-threatened woodlands. There's a large and interesting **museum** here holding wood samples, insects, furniture, pickled animal embryos and the like. A second museum, also in the institute, holds an anthropological exhibition on **hill tribes**. The curator knows his stuff and is happy to show visitors around. The **Botanical Survey of India**, in the next building, is only of interest to the specialist.

Somewhat further afield, **Rajpur**, 12km to the north, past the Survey of India and accessible by motorized three-wheel Vikrams, has a sizeable Tibetan community. Its striking *gompa* – the **Shakya Centre** – decorated with ornate frescoes, stands next to a centre of Tibetan medicine next door. There's another *gompa* on the main road around 5km towards Mussoorie.

Eating

Dehra Dun has several commendable mid-priced **eating places** and a bunch of adequate cheaper cafés around the bus and train stations. Several chain restaurants have opened, including *Barista* coffee shop next to *Kumar Veg*, *Baskin-Robbins* in Astley Hall and *Domino's* pizza, 800m further along Rajpur Road.

Garry's 25 Rajpur Rd. Tasty pizzas (Rs50–90) and fast food in a wannabe US atmosphere.

Kumar Veg 15B Rajpur Rd. Excellent veg cooking at reasonable prices, and comfortable surroundings. Very popular.

Kundan Palace Rajpur Rd, opposite the *Madhuban* hotel. Open-air multi-cuisine place, popular with locals.

Tirupati 27B Rajpur Rd. Clean and friendly multi-cuisine which is particularly strong on South Indian dishes.

Yeti 55A Rajpur Rd. Interesting Chinese and Thai veg and non-veg menus, including spicy Szechuan cuisine; expect to pay around Rs150 per head.

Mussoorie

Spreading for 15km along a high serrated ridge, **MUSSOORIE** is the closest hill station to Delhi, just 278km north of the capital and 34km north of Dehra Dun (from where it is clearly visible). At an altitude of 2000m, it gives

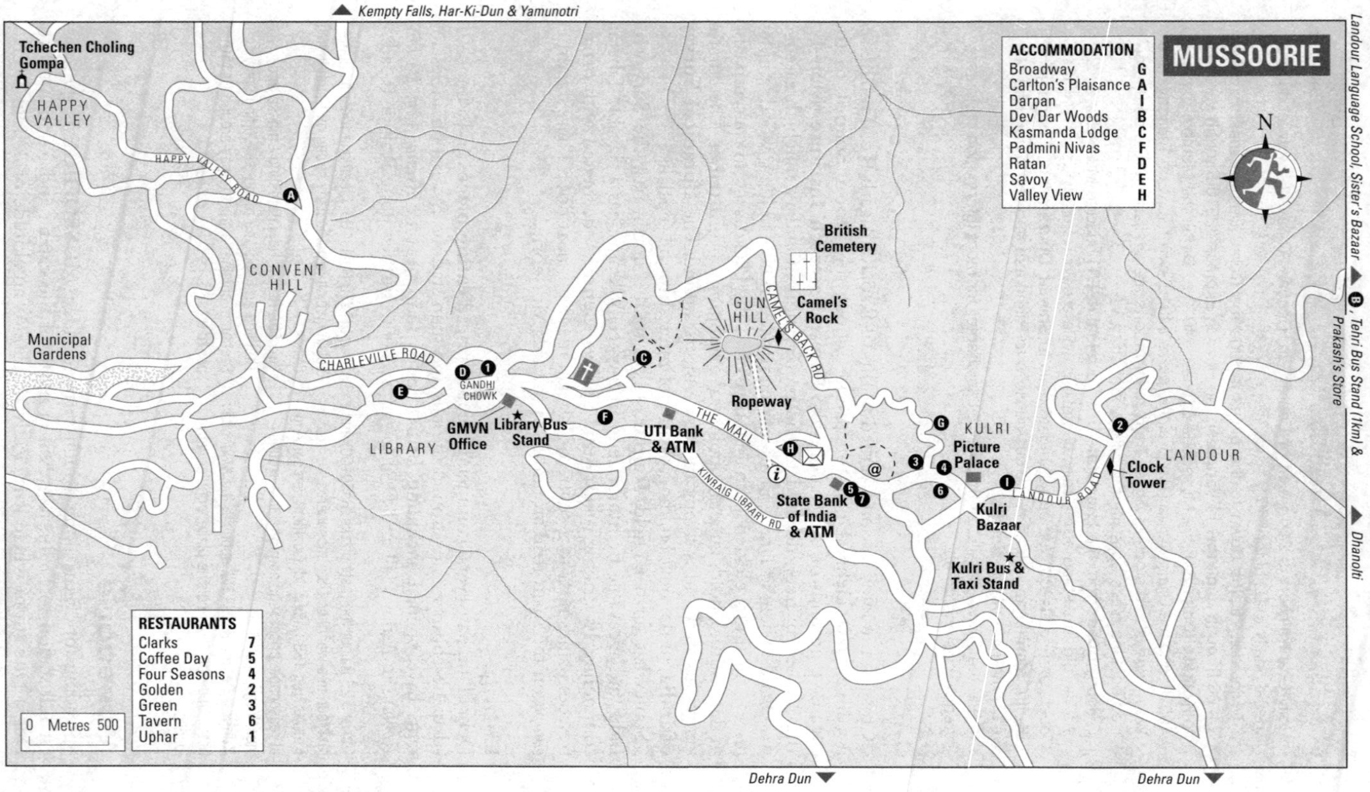

MUSSOORIE

ACCOMMODATION

Broadway	G
Carlton's Plaisance	A
Darpan	I
Dev Dar Woods	B
Kasmanda Lodge	C
Padmini Nivas	F
Ratan	D
Savoy	E
Valley View	H

RESTAURANTS

Clarks	7
Coffee Day	5
Four Seasons	4
Golden	2
Green	3
Tavern	6
Uphar	1

0 Metres 500

N

Kempty Falls, Har-Ki-Dun & Yamunotri

Landour Language School, Sister's Bazaar, B, Tehri Bus Stand (1km) & Prakash's Store

Dhanolti

Dehra Dun

Dehra Dun

Tchechen Choling Gompa

HAPPY VALLEY

HAPPY VALLEY ROAD

CONVENT HILL

Municipal Gardens

CHARLEVILLE ROAD

GANDHI CHOWK

LIBRARY

GMVN Office

Library Bus Stand

UTI Bank & ATM

THE MALL

KINRAIG LIBRARY RD

State Bank of India & ATM

Ropeway

GUN HILL

CAMEL'S BACK RD

Camel's Rock

British Cemetery

KULRI

Picture Palace

Kulri Bazaar

Kulri Bus & Taxi Stand

LANDOUR ROAD

Clock Tower

LANDOUR

travellers from the plains their first glimpse of the snow-covered Himalayan **peaks** of western Garhwal, as well as dramatic views of the Dehra Dun valley below. Established in 1823 by a certain Captain Young, Mussoorie soon became a typical Victorian resort, centring on its long promenade – the **Mall** – and boasting an Anglican church, library and club.

These days, Mussoorie is a very popular weekend retreat for middle-class Indians up from the plains. The centre is cluttered with souvenir shops, but it's easy to escape the bazaars and ramble around the atmospheric cantonment of Landour or head to the surrounding woods. Most foreign visitors come to Mussoorie to **study** Hindi at the excellent Landour Language School, but the town is also a useful base camp for **treks** into the western interior of Garhwal. Dominated by the long Bandarpunch Massif (6316m), with Swargarohini (6252m) in the west and the Gangotri group in the east, Mussoorie's mountain panorama may not be as dramatic as some other hill stations, but it forms a pleasant backdrop to the busy holiday town.

Arrival and information

As Mussoorie's two-kilometre-long **Mall** is closed to motor vehicles during the tourist season, its two ends – the **Library** area at the west end, and the **Kulri** area in the east – serve as **transport hubs**. Cycle rickshaws operate mostly on the flat Library end. Buses (Rs23) and shared taxis (about Rs70) from Dehra Dun, the plains and the rest of Garhwal arrive either at the **Library Bus Stand** at Gandhi Chowk, or the **Kulri** or **Masonic Lodge Bus Stand**. At the smaller **Tehri Bus Stand**, east of Landour 5km from the Mall, buses pull in from New Tehri, Chamba and Uttarkashi. Shared taxis and cars are available at the bus stands, while ponies and hand-drawn carriages – glorified rickshaws – run along the Mall itself. Ponies can also carry you around the Camel's Back Road.

Facilities along the Mall include the **tourist bureau** (Mon–Sat 10am–5pm; ⓣ0135/263 2863) next to the cable car, where you can get a small booklet of local information; a **post office** at the Kulri end, and a **GMVN transport office** next to the Library bus stand, which runs tours of the town and further afield. The State Bank of India near the Ropeway has an **ATM** which accepts Maestro and Cirrus cards. The Bank of Baroda in the Picture Palace area is less crowded and gives cash advances on Visa and Mastercard. The ATM at the UTI Bank on the Mall will accept Visa cards. **Internet** access is available at FastTrack across the Mall from *Clarks* restaurant (daily 10am–10pm; Rs60/hr) and at the *Tavern* restaurant. Neelu at Trek Himalaya Tourism (ⓣ0135/263 0491, ⓦwww.trekhimalaya.com), on the steep street opposite the cable car, is an extremely experienced and helpful local guide, who can put together trekking packages starting from $45 per day, while Kulwant Travels (ⓣ0135/263 2717) at Kulri bus stand are approved tour and **car rental** operators, offering services to Dehra Dun (Rs350), Haridwar (Rs900), Delhi (Rs2800), Gangotri and Yamunotri (both Rs3500).

Accommodation

Mussoorie is packed with **hotels** to suit all budgets – most of them strung along the Mall. Room rates fluctuate between three rather vague **seasons**; low (Jan–March & July–Sept, when the rains come), shoulder or mid-season (Christmas, April and the "Bengali season" of Oct & Nov), and peak (May–early July), when prices quadruple and a dingy room can cost over Rs1000. The prices below reflect low season with an indication of high-season fluctuations. The town suffers from severe **water shortages**, which may affect some of the cheaper hotels.

Porters from either the Library or the Kulri bus stands charge under Rs50 to carry luggage to most locations along the Mall.

Broadway Camel's Back Rd ⓣ0135/263 4423. Rambling old guesthouse perching on the edge of Kulri Bazaar, charming bright window boxes, lovely views and a friendly atmosphere. A good bet for budget travellers, although the more commercial *Hotel Deep* (ⓣ0135/263 2470) next door has some better-value rooms out of season. ❷

Carlton's Plaisance Happy Valley Rd ⓣ0135/263 2800, ⓔcarltons@rediffmail.com. A Raj-era house plus a more modern building, both stuffed full of Victorian drapes and memorabilia. Sir Edmund Hillary stayed here and recommended it. Lovely gardens and an ideal base for gentle rambles away from the town. Rates up to $50. ❻–❽

Darpan Landour Rd, near Picture Palace, Kulri ⓣ0135/263 2483. Reasonable and clean, though no hot showers, with mountain views and a good Gujarati veg restaurant. ❹

Dev Dar Woods Sister's Bazaar ⓣ0135/263 2644, ⓔanilprakash56@yahoo.com. Large, refurbished old hotel, with a huge restaurant. Situated on a high and secluded site, it's often full due to its proximity to the language school, so book well in advance – you may even get picked up from the bus stop. Rates include breakfast. ❸–❹

Kasmanda Lodge The Mall ⓣ0135/263 2424, ⓦhttp://indianheritagehotels.com. A short, stiff climb up from the Mall leads to this ex-maharaja's summer palace, now opened as a period hotel. Comfortable and quiet with beautiful gardens and rhino heads on the walls. Better value than the *Carlton's Plaisance* or the *Savoy*, book one month ahead. Rooms $45–65. ❽–❾

Padmini Nivas Library ⓣ0135/263 1093 ⓦwww.hotelpadmininivas.com. Just below the Mall, with a beautiful rose garden and orchard plus excellent views, this is one of Mussoorie's more established and classier addresses. Large, comfortable rooms with antique furniture and decor. ❻–❼

Ratan Gandhi Chowk ⓣ0135/263 2719. In the busy Library area, clean and friendly, with a terrace and two grades of rooms. ❸

Savoy The Mall ⓣ0135/263 2010. Reached via a long driveway, this collapsing Victorian pile above the Library is atmospheric and steeped in history. Agatha Christie based her first novel, *The Mysterious Affair at Styles*, on a celebrated poisoning that took place here. The rooms aren't great value, but you might take a look around or have a cocktail at the bar. Rates up to $50. ❺–❽

Valley View The Mall ⓣ0135/263 2324. Friendly, clean place towering over the Mall and close to all amenities, with a good restaurant and sunny terraces overlooking the Doon Valley. ❷–❸

The Town

Surprisingly, the Mall and the main hub face away from the snows towards Dehra Dun; the distant peaks can best be seen from the flat summit of **Gun Hill**, which rises like a volcano from central Mussoorie. This can be ascended on foot or pony on a bridle path that forks up from the Mall, or on the 400-metre "Ropeway" **cable car** from the Mall (Rs50 return). Alternative prospects of the mountains can be seen on a peaceful stroll or ride around the three-kilometre-long **Camel's Back Road**, which girdles the northern base of Gun Hill, passing by the distinctive Camel's Rock and an old **British cemetery** (closed to visitors). Another vantage point, the highest in the immediate vicinity, is **Childer's Lodge**, 5km east of the Mall above Landour.

At the eastern end of the Mall, beyond the bustling Kulri Bazaar, the road winds steeply upwards for 5km through the fascinating market of **Landour**, where you'll find shops overflowing with relics of the Raj, silver jewellery and books. At the top of Landour bazaar, a square surrounded by cafés attracts both travellers and the local intelligentsia. Nearby, the lovely forested area of **Sister's Bazaar** is excellent for walks, especially to the **Haunted House**, a deserted Raj-era mansion, and around the famous **Landour Language School** (ⓣ0135/263 1487, ⓔlls@nde.vsnl.co.in; one-on-one Hindi lessons Rs150 per hour; open Feb–Dec).

Away from the noise and bustle, close to Convent Hill and 3km west of the Library, the Tibetan settlement of **Happy Valley** holds a large school, a shop selling hand-knitted sweaters and the small but beautiful **Tchechen Choling**

Har-ki-Dun Valley trek

A relatively undemanding but superb trek **from Mussoorie** takes three days (plus one on the bus) to reach the sparsely populated "Valley of the Gods", **HAR-KI-DUN**, in the **Fateh Parvat** region of northwestern Garhwal. The valley trails are open from mid-April until mid-November, but the mountain passes only in mid-June. All the trails on the trek are clear, and villagers will happily point you in the right direction. Recommended maps of the trail and region include those published by Leomann – sheet 8 covers Garhwal – and the Ground Survey of India map of the area available from any major Uttaranchal tourist office. In the valley itself, if not higher in the mountains, accommodation is widely available, and food can usually be bought. This area is being developed as a National Park, so there are **fees** to be paid if you pass the forest checkpoint at Netwar: Rs175 in total for the first three days, plus Rs175 for each extra day, and a daily camping fee of Rs100.

The rivers and streams of Har-ki-Dun drain the glaciers and snowfields of the peaks of **Swargarohini** (the "Ascent to Heaven"; 6252m) and **Bandarpunch** (the "Monkey's Tail"; 6316m). Local people trace their lineage back to the *Mahabharata*, claiming descent from Duryodhana and his followers. Like the Pandavas of the epic, they practise a form of polyandry and follow intriguing religious customs, including witchcraft. Worship at Taluka's Duryodhana temple, for example, consists of throwing shoes at the idol; at Pakola, the image has its back to the congregation. Their distinctive alpine buildings have beautifully carved wooden doors and windows, with the mortar construction punctuated by wooden slats.

The trek to Har-ki-Dun

Starting out from Mussoorie on **Day 1**, catch a Yamunotri bus (1 daily; 10am) at the Library Bus Stand and change at Nowgaon (9km short of Barkot, from where a road climbs to Hanuman Chatti) to **Purola** and onto Netwar – a total of 148km. Set amid a patchwork of wheat and rice terraces in Netwar is a **PWD** bungalow with rooms; you can also obtain permission here to stay at the forest bungalows further on. Simple cafés can be found around the bus stand.

Early the next morning – **Day 2** – take the bus to the roadhead at **Sankri**, which also has a bungalow. A jeepable road from here leads 12km through *deodar* and sycamore woods to **Taluka** (1900m), where there is another bungalow serving simple food.

On **Day 3**, the trail descends to follow the River Tons through beautiful forests. Although you can get tea at the hamlet of Gangar, no food is available until you've walked the full 11km to **Osla** (2259m). The forest bungalow, GMVN hotel and *dhaba* stalls are all on the main trail in an area known as Seema, below Osla; from here on you have to carry your food, so stock up.

A steep climb of 14km from Osla on **Day 4** brings you finally to the campground at **Har-ki-Dun** (3560m) – an excellent base from which to explore the *bugyals* below the Swargarohini to the east, and the Jaundhar Glacier (3910m) at the head of the valley.

gompa overlooking the Doon valley and surrounded by gardens. It makes an enjoyable walk from the Mall along wooded roads, but you can also catch a taxi (around Rs120 return).

Eating

Cafés and **restaurants** all along the Mall and around Kulri serve everything from hotdogs to Chinese specialities; in addition to those recommended below, there are good restaurants in many of the hotels including the *Kasmanda Lodge*, the *Padmini Nivas*, the *Valley View* and the crumbling *Savoy*. Prakash's Store, in

Sister's Bazaar, is a wonderful place to shop if you're in the neighbourhood, with home-made breads, jams, peanut butter, cheddar cheese and even Marmite.

Café Coffee Day The Mall, Kulri. Lattes, cappuccinos and expressos served up in a fast-food atmosphere; snacks include apple pie, chocolate cake and sandwiches.

Clarks The Mall, Kulri. Multi-cuisine restaurant and bakery that is continually being expanded, yet maintains its period atmosphere.

Four Seasons The Mall. Not as much fun as the *Tavern* across the street, but locals claim its mostly Indian menu is the best in town. Free delivery to your hotel.

Golden Landour Bazaar. A popular if unremarkable local place next to the Clock Tower, serving Tibetan, Chinese and Indian dishes.

Green The Mall, Kulri. Justifiably popular restaurant serving Indian and Chinese food; go early at mealtimes or you'll have to queue.

Tavern The Mall. Hip and recently renovated place near the Picture Palace, offering pricey Western, Thai, Chinese and Indian dishes and the only seafood in town. There's a small bar and live music and dancing on some Saturdays. Billiards hall and Internet café upstairs.

Uphar Gandhi Chowk. Clean, friendly South Indian joint with an ice cream bar. One of the best in the Library area.

Haridwar

At **Haridwar** – the Gates (*dwar*) of God (*Hari*) – 214km northeast of Delhi, the **River Ganges** emerges from its final rapids past the Shivalik Hills to start the long slow journey across northern India to the Bay of Bengal. Stretching for roughly 3km along a narrow strip of land between the craggy wooded hills to the west and the river to the east, Haridwar is especially revered by Hindus, for whom the **Har-ki-Pairi** *ghat* (literally the "Footstep of God") marks the exact spot where the river leaves the mountains. As you look north along the vast Doon Valley, the faint lines of the Himalayan foothills can be discerned rising above Rishikesh in the distance, while Haridwar itself faces east across the river to the Rajaji National Park. A major road and rail junction, Haridwar links Delhi and the Gangetic plains with the mountains of Uttaranchal and their holy pilgrimage (*yatra*) network. Along with Nasik (see p.763), Ujjain (see p.472), and the holiest of them all, Prayag in Allahabad (see p.320), Haridwar is one of the four holy *tirthas* or "crossings" that serve as the focus of the massive **Kumbh Mela** festival (see p.320). Every twelve years, thousands of pilgrims come to bathe at a preordained moment in the turbulent waters of the channelled river around Har-ki-Pairi. Haridwar's next Kumbh Mela is due to take place in 2010.

Arrival and information

Haridwar's **railway station** and **Station Bus Stand**, southwest of the centre, face each other across the main thoroughfare that channels all the traffic through to meet the river at Har-ki-Pairi. **Trains** and **buses** connect Haridwar with Rishikesh, Dehra Dun and the mountains, and run back down to Delhi. You can also get to Rishikesh in shared taxis, while Vikrams and tempos ply the few roads in town. To arrange a **tour** of Garhwal by bus or car, call in at Konark Tourist Service, Jassa Ram Road (Ⓣ0133/242 4240.

Spotty **tourist information** is available at a booth inside the railway station (daily 8am–2.30pm) or from the more helpful Mr Raturi at the **GMVN tourist office** (Mon–Sat 10am–5pm; Ⓣ0133/242 4240) near Lalita Rao Bridge on Upper Road. A better idea is skip officialdom and enlist the aid of knowledgeable local guide Sumit Nath who charges a reasonable Rs300–500 per day rate for city or state tours. He can be reached via the *Midtown Hotel* (see below).

There's a **post office** on Upper Road, opposite Ram Panjawani (Ⓣ0133/242 7266), the local agents for Indian Airlines. You can change

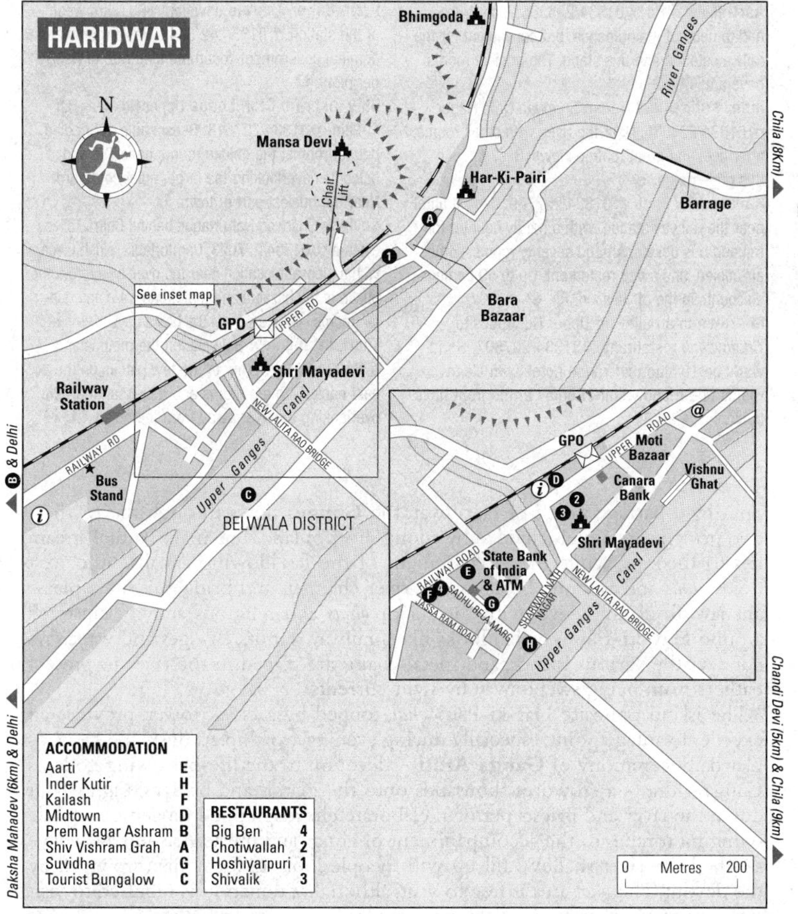

cash up to $200 at the State Bank of India on Sadhu Bela Marg, which also has an **ATM**. Canara Bank, on Railway Road, changes travellers' cheques and cash. There are small **Internet cafés** dotted all over town, some charging as much as Rs120 per hour. The best value is Cyber Zone (Rs40/hr), which is set back from Upper Road in the *Hotel Mansarover International* complex.

Accommodation

Although it has no luxury hotels, Haridwar has **accommodation** to suit most budgets, including a number of ashrams – two of which are included in the list below. None of it, however, is very good value compared to Rishikesh, 24km north (see p.368). The rates below are subject to change with seasonal discounts and hard bargaining. It's a small place, so wherever you stay the river and the bazaars are never too far away. Most hotels are a Rs5 rickshaw ride northeast of the station; some are within walking distance.

Aarti Railway Rd ☎01334/226365. A bit grubby and in need of maintenance, but convenient for the railway station and bus stand. The priciest rooms have a/c. 3–6

Inder Kutir Guest House Sharwan Nath Nagar ☎01334/226336. Near the river, with small rooms, a terrace, and great rooftop views. Best value in this price range. 2

Kailash Shiv Murti ☎01334/227789. Central hotel near the railway station, with a handy counter for rail and bus tickets. Around seventy rooms, some air-cooled, and a veg restaurant. Up to 50 percent discounts in the off-season. 4–5

Midtown In an alley off Upper Rd, opposite *Chotiwallah* restaurant ☎01334/227507. Haridwar's best-value mid-range hotel, with clean rooms and friendly staff. Rooms at the front have balconies. 3–4

Prem Nagar Ashram Jawalapur Rd, 2km west of the station ☎0133/242 6345. Basic rooms at a nominal government-recommended rate of Rs50 per night. 1

Shiv Vishram Grah Lodge Upper Rd, near Har-ki-Pairi ☎01334/227618. Reasonable, air-cooled, budget rooms; the deluxe rooms have TVs and balconies overlooking the large, quiet courtyard. Near the busiest part of town. 3–5

Suvidha Sharwan Nath Nagar, behind Chitra Talkies cinema ☎01334/227023. Comfortable, plush place with a pleasant location near the river, away from the bustle of the bazaars and main roads. A/c and non-a/c rooms – make sure yours has a geyser. 5–7

Tourist Bungalow Belwala, on the main island ☎01334/226379. One of the few places on the east bank, with a/c rooms and a pleasant garden overlooking the river away from the noise. 6–7

The Town

Split by a barrage north of Haridwar, the **Ganges** flows through the town in two principal channels, divided by a long sliver of land. The main natural stream lies to the east, while the embankment of the fast-flowing canal to the west holds *ghats* and ashrams. Promenades, river channels and bridges create a pleasant riverfront ambience, with the major *ghats* and religious activity clustered around **Har-ki-Pairi**, which looks like a railway station. Bridges and walkways connect the various islands, and metal chains are placed in the river to protect bathers from being swept away by swift currents.

The island opposite Har-ki-Pairi *ghat*, topped by a clock tower, provides an excellent vantage point, especially during evening worship. At dusk, the spectacular daily ceremony of **Ganga Arati** – devotion to the life-bestowing goddess Ganga – draws a crowd of thousands onto the islands and bridges. Lights float down the river and priests perform elaborate choreographed movements while swinging torches to the accompaniment of gongs and music. As soon as they've finished the river shallows fill up with people looking for coins thrown in by the devout. The *ghat* area is free to visit, although a donation is required to visit the section at the bottom of the first staircase.

Haridwar's teeming network of **markets** is the other main focus of interest. **Bara Bazaar**, at the top of town, is a good place to buy a *danda* (bamboo staff) for treks in the mountains. Stalls in the colourful **Moti Bazaar** in the centre of town on the Jawalapur road sell everything from clothes to spices.

High above Haridwar, on the crest of a ridge, the gleaming white *shikhara* of the **Mansa Devi** temple dominates both town and valley. The temple is easily reached by **cable car** (daily: April–Nov 6.30am–8pm, Dec–March 8am–6pm; Rs39 return), from a base station off Upper Road in the heart of town, though the steep 1.5-kilometre walk is pleasant enough early in the morning. None of the shrines and temples up top holds any great architectural interest, but you do get excellent views along the river. An elaborate queuing system leads pilgrims to a *darshan* of the main image, showing Mansa Devi – a triple-headed image of Shakti as the goddess Durga. Photography is forbidden.

The modern, seven-storeyed **Bharat Mata** temple, 5km north of Haridwar and reachable in shared Vikrams for around Rs15, is dedicated to "Mother India". A temple with a similar name and purpose can be found in Varanasi,

Moving on from Haridwar

Major **trains** passing through Haridwar include the Mussoorie Express #4042 between Dehra Dun and **Delhi**, which leaves town at 11pm and takes 7hr to reach Delhi. Other trains to Delhi include the costly but air-conditioned and fast Dehra Dun Shatabdi Express #2018, which leaves at 6.10pm and takes 4hr 35min (food is included in the price), and the Dehra Dun–Mumbai Express #2020; the Ujjain–Dehra Dun Express #4310 stops at **Agra**. The Dehra Dun–Varanasi Express #4266 covers the 850km to **Varanasi** in 22hr. Local trains on the branch line to **Rishikesh** aren't that useful in view of the excellent and more frequent road connections.

Buses to **Delhi** leave from **Station Bus Stand** almost every thirty minutes (5–6hr; roughly Rs100). Five or six buses per day leave for **Agra**, 368km south (10hr; around Rs170). Similarly, numerous buses leave for **Rishikesh**, 24km north (Rs15), and **Dehra Dun**, 57km northwest, as well as **Shimla**, **Nainital** and **Almora**. The **Taxi** Association near the railway station sets prices slightly higher than those quoted elsewhere; a taxi to Delhi costs Rs1500, and Rs350 to Rishikesh. Shared Vikrams or tempos ply the route to Rishikesh and provide a cheap if cramped alternative for Rs15. Travellers heading into the **mountains** should go to Rishikesh to pick up onward transport.

See the "Travel details" at the end of this chapter for more information on journey frequencies and durations.

but this one is much newer and much more garish. Each of its various floors – connected by lifts – is dedicated to a celestial or political theme, and populated by lifelike images of heroes, heroines and Hindu deities.

Eating

Haridwar is a strictly **vegetarian** town and the food is very good, whether in the **cafés** around Har-ki-Pairi or the **restaurants** of Upper Road and Railway Road.

Big Ben Railway Rd, next to the *Kailash* hotel. Stylish hotel-style restaurant with a mixed menu including veg sizzlers.

Chotiwallah Upper Rd. Established in 1937, this comfortable, dimly lit place is still one of the best around, offering famed Indian food and good thalis.

Hoshiyarpuri Upper Rd. Legendary, busy and friendly *dhaba*-like restaurant close to Har-ki-Pairi. Delicious Indian (especially Punjabi) and Chinese mains as well as *kheer* (pudding).

Shivalik Railway Rd. One of a row of three good restaurants. The chef prides himself on his small selection of Chinese dishes (try the chop suey). Tasty South Indian snacks, including *dosas*, are also on offer.

Rajaji National Park and around

Around 830 square kilometres of the Himalayan foothills immediately east of Haridwar are taken up by **RAJAJI NATIONAL PARK** (mid-Nov to mid-June; Rs350 for three days, Rs175 each additional day, plus Rs500 per vehicle, Rs500 with still camera, Rs5000 with video camera; Ⓦ www.rajajinationalpark.com), which belongs to the same forest belt as Corbett National Park, 180km east. Although not geared up to tourism to the same extent as Corbett, the park is absolutely beautiful, with a similar range of **wildlife** – most notably elephants, but also antelope, leopard and even a rare species of anteater – although no tigers. A nomadic tribe that has been slowly relocated outside the park over the past two decades, the native **Van Gujjars** have long been engaged in a land-rights dispute with the government over designation of the forest for wildlife use. Tribal leaders assert that the housing and agricultural land they were issued in the 1990s is inadequate, and periodically threaten to re-take the forest if their situation is not improved. While talks to resolve the matter stagnate, the remaining Van Gujjars are being pressured to leave the woods, despite a law that allows anyone to remain if they had lived there before 1980.

There are eight **entry gates** into the national park, including **Kunnao** close to Rishikesh and the main gates at **Chila**, 9km east of Haridwar by road and across the Ganges. **Accommodation** is available at nine forest rest houses within the park and is bookable through the Rajaji National Park Office, 5/1 Ansari Marg, Dehra Dun (☎0135/262 1669). However, visitors don't have to go into the core area to experience the jungles, as it's possible to venture in from Chila or Rishikesh, or from the road between the two, which runs parallel to the canal marking the boundary of the huge fringe forest.

Chila

To get to **CHILA** from Haridwar, catch one of the Rishikesh-bound GMOU buses, which leave daily from 7am to 2pm from the bus stand, and travel via Chila, or take a shared **Jeep** from Chandi Ghat opposite Har-ki-Pairi. You could even **walk**; Chila is visible from Haridwar, and taking a short cut from Har-ki-Pairi via the riverbeds and a bridge makes it a journey of just 4km east. The town itself is neither attractive nor interesting, located right beside the Ganges barrage and its massive electricity pylons. However, it makes a good base for explorations of the park, and **Chila Beach** – occasionally used by large river turtles – lies within walking distance through the woods, 1km north along the Ganges. **Elephant rides** from here cost around Rs100 per head for two hours; to arrange one, just ask the trainers who tout for business.

Accommodation is available at the large GMVN *Chilla Tourist Bungalow* (☎0138/266678; ❺–❻), which has an overpriced dorm (Rs150), deluxe and a/c rooms, huts and grassy camping facilities. Rooms here can also be reserved through the Haridwar GMVN office.

Rishikesh and around

RISHIKESH, 238km northeast of Delhi and 24km north of Haridwar, lies at the point where the wooded mountains of Garhwal rise abruptly from the low valley floor and the Ganges crashes onto the plains. The centre for all manner of New Age and Hindu activity, its many ashrams – some ascetic, some opulent – continue to draw devotees and followers of all sorts of weird, wonderful and occasionally fraudulent gurus, with the large **Shivananda Ashram** in particular renowned as a yoga centre. Rishikesh is also emerging as an **adventure sports** hub, with rafting, trekking and mountaineering all on offer.

Rishikesh has one or two ancient shrines, but its main role has always been as a way-station for sannyasin, yogis and *sadhus* heading for the high Himalayas. The arrival of the Beatles, who came here to meet the Maharishi in 1968, was one of the first manifestations of the lucrative expansion of the *yatra* pilgrimage circuit; these days it's easy to see why Ringo thought it was "just like Butlin's". By far the best times to visit are in winter and spring, when the mountain temples are shut by the snows. In the absence of the *yatra* razzmatazz, you can get a sense of the tranquillity that was the original appeal of the place. At other times, a walk

> The **telephone code** for Rishikesh is ☎0135 unless you're dialling within a 75km radius of Rishikesh, in which case the ☎0135 code changes to ☎95135.

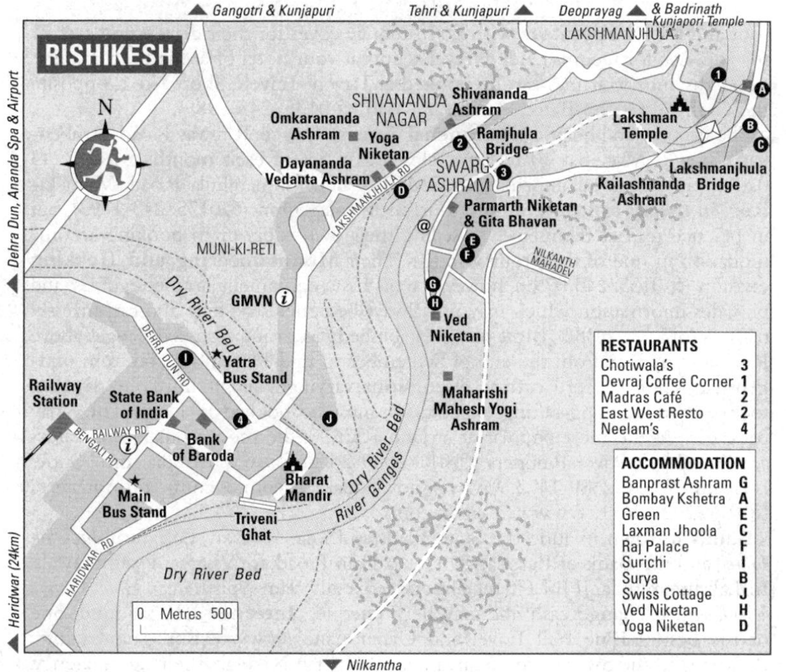

upriver leads easily away from the bustle to secluded spots among giant rocks ideally suited for yoga, meditation or an invigorating dip in the cold water.

Confusingly, the name Rishikesh is applied to a loose association of five distinct areas, encompassing not only the town but also hamlets and settlements on both sides of the river: **Rishikesh** itself, the commercial and communications hub; sprawling suburban **Muni-ki-Reti**; **Shivananda Nagar**, just north; the assorted ashrams around **Swarg Ashram** on the east bank, and the riverbank temples of **Lakshmanjhula**, a little further north.

Arrival and information

Far more visitors arrive in Rishikesh by road or rail than at the airport, 18km west. The **Main Bus Stand**, used by Haridwar and Dehra Dun government buses, as well as direct services to and from Delhi (6hr), is on Bengali Road, close to the centre; buses for the Garhwal hills use the **Yatra Bus Stand**, also known as the **Tehri Bus Stand**, off the Dehra Dun Road. Rishikesh is at the end of a small branch **railway** line, served by trains to and from Haridwar. Advance reservations can be made from the station, which only has a small quota of seats.

Local transport connecting the main areas includes cycle and auto-rickshaws and shared Vikrams; the fare from Rishikesh to Lakshmanjhula is Rs25 (Rs5 shared ride). Some head south towards Haridwar, but few go all the way. **Cars** and **taxis** can be rented through the reliable Ajay Travels, at the *Hotel Neelkanth*, Haridwar Road (Ⓣ0135/243 0644), or through the Uttaranchal Tourism-approved Mahayama Travels, Urvasi Complex, Dehra Dun Road (Ⓣ0135/243 2968). Rishikesh, like many of the hill towns, is increasingly turning to seasonal tourism, and a negative impact of this has been the dramatic rise of unregulated tour and **travel operators** with no insurance cover for their drivers and cars, or for you. Ask for recommended travel agents at your hotel or at the tourist office. Long-distance journeys can be booked at Triveni Travels, Shop No 1, opposite the Garhwal Co-op Bank, Haridwar Road (Ⓣ0135/243 0989).

The friendly and helpful **Uttaranchal Tourist Office**, Railway Road, Ambedkar Chowk (Mon–Sat 10am–5pm, closed 2nd Sat of each month; Ⓣ0135/243 0209), provides local information. **GMVN** on Lakshmanjhula Road, Muni-ki-Reti, in theory exist to promote tourism in the region (Ⓣ0135/243 1793), but in practice restrict themselves to selling their own tours or to booking accommodation in one of their tourist lodges. Their **Mountaineering and Trekking** division (Ⓣ0135/243 0799), however, rents basic equipment, arranges guides, and provides information which may not always be conclusive; they also organize ski trips to Auli (see p.382). Most of the established river camps on the Ganges above Rishikesh operate from the end of September to mid-December, and from mid-February until late April; **rafting excursions**, varying in length from one-day runs to extended camping-rafting expeditions, must be booked in Delhi. Three-day packages are the most popular at around Rs5000; the most reputable operators are Himalayan River Runners (Ⓣ011/2685 2602, Ⓦwww.hrrindia.com), Snow Leopard (Ⓣ011/2689 1473, Ⓦwww.snowleopardadventures.com) and Aquaterra (Ⓣ011/2921 2641, Ⓦwww.treknraft.com).

Banks in town include the State Bank of India, Railway Lok, near *Inderlok Hotel*, and the Bank of Baroda, 70 Dehra Dun Road, for Visa card withdrawals. In Lakshmanjhula, JPJN Financial Services (daily 9am–9pm), near *Hotel Ganga View*, will exchange cash and travellers' cheques. **Internet** cafés abound; one of the best is Blue Hill Travel and Cyber Café (Ⓦwww.rishikeshindia.com; Rs20/hr) in the Swarg Ashram area near Parmarth Niketan; their travel agency, however, has a bad reputation.

Accommodation

Rishikesh town has plenty of hotels but it's a noisy and polluted place and the only reason to stay here is to be near the bus station and amenities. **Muni-ki-Reti** is not too far and slightly more pleasant. New Agers tend to stay around **Swarg Ashram** and the east bank of the river, away from the noise and near the ashrams, while backpackers head for the cheap little guesthouses of **Lakshmanjhula**.

Banprast Ashram next to Ved Niketan, Swarg Ashram Ⓣ0135/243 0811. Well-maintained, reasonably priced rooms and a/c bungalows for four (Rs3000), in attractive grounds within a walled enclosure that's quiet and close to the river. ❷–❹

Bombay Kshetra Lakshmanjhula Ⓣ0135/244 0200. Basic, dark accommodation with shared baths off a leafy courtyard. Handy for exploring the unspoilt upper reaches of this stretch of the river. For ascetics only. ❶–❷

Green Swarg Ashram Ⓣ0135/243 1242. Popular little travellers' hotel tucked behind Gita Bhavan ashram. All rooms have attached baths, there's a roof terrace, and a restaurant serves under-spiced Indian and Italian food. The sister-hotel *Green View* behind is a slightly more upmarket option and also recommended. ❶–❹

Laxman Jhoola Guesthouse Lakshmanjhula Rd Ⓣ9897/443920. Friendly, basic place with hot showers. One of many, all pretty similar, small budget hotels in the area. ❶–❷

Raj Palace Swarg Ashram behind Parmarth Niketan Ⓣ0135/244 0117. New, well-managed hotel popular with yoga students due to its location near the ashrams and large, sunny yoga room. Rooftop café. Discounts up to 45 percent off-season. ❷–❻

Surichi Yatra Bus Stand Ⓣ0135/243 2602. Modern, slightly grubby, hotel with a good restaurant and helpful staff. A bit far from the river, but convenient for early Char Dham buses. ❷–❺

Surya Lakshmanjhula Rd Ⓣ0135/243 3211. New, immaculately clean and marble-floored double rooms, the newest (and priciest) with river views. Internet café and restaurant on ground floor. Excellent value. ❷–❹

Swiss Cottage Chandra Bhaga (no phone). Run by the affable Swami Brahmananda, once one of Swami Shivananda's inner group of disciples. Near the bridge and down unnamed lanes towards the river, it's a small but peaceful haven with nine rooms in a motley selection of buildings. Not an ashram, but popular with long-term visitors, and extremely good value, so often booked up. ❷

Ved Niketan Swarg Ashram ⓣ0135/243 0279. Enormous orange ashram on the east bank of the river, which is very popular with low-budget Westerners. Single rooms Rs50/80. ❶

Yoga Niketan Guesthouse Lakshmanjhula Rd ⓣ0135/243 3537. You don't have to involve yourself in any of the ashram activities to stay here, though guests are asked to obey an 10pm curfew and not to smoke. Light, airy, spotless, good-value rooms with balconies, right next to the river, plus a small lawn. Promixity to noisy road a minus. ❸

The Town

Most of the pilgrims who pass through Rishikesh on their way to the Himalayan shrines of the Char Dham pause for a dip and puja at what is left of the large sandy expanse of **Triveni Ghat**, close to the centre of town. The river here looks especially spectacular during *arati* (evening worship), when diya lights float on the water. Nearby, at **Bharat Mandir**, Rishikesh's oldest temple, a black stone image ofVishnu is supposed to have been consecrated by Shankara in the ninth century; the event is commemorated during Basant Panchami, to mark the first day of spring.

The dense-knit complex of cafés, shops and ashrams collectively known as **Swarg Ashram**, opposite Shivananda Ashram, backs on to forest-covered hills where caves are still inhabited by *sadhus*. The river can be crossed at this point either on the Ramjhula footbridge, or on **ferries**, which operate between 8am and 7pm according to demand (Rs5 one-way, Rs8 return). Put away any thoughts about swimming across; reports of people drowning in these swift waters are not uncommon. Swarg Ashram itself, popularly referred to as Kale Kumbli Wale, was founded in honour of Swami Vishudhanand, who came here in 1884 and habitually wore a black (*kala*) blanket (*kumble*). The most conspicuous of the other ashram-temples is **Parmarth Niketan**, whose large courtyard is crammed with brightly clad gods and goddesses. **Gita Bhavan** runs an Ayurvedic dispensary here (Tues–Sat 10.30am–noon, first 3 days of medicine free), as well as selling books and *khadi* handloom cloth.

Around 2km north of Swarg Ashram, a path skirts the east bank of the river, and beautiful sandy beaches sheltered by large boulders, en route to **Lakshmanjhula**. A footbridge spans the river here as it negotiates its final rocky course out of the mountains. It's the most appealing part of Rishikesh, featuring the enormous, gaudy **Kailashnanda Ashram**.The attractive landscape and turquoise river are best appreciated from the *Devraj Coffee Corner* on the west side where travellers spend days watching daredevil monkeys cavorting on the bridge and pouncing on unsuspecting passers-by.

Eating

Rishikesh has plenty of worthy **restaurants** and *dhabas*, many with pleasant river views and tourist orientated menus. Expect only vegetarian food in this holy town.

Chotiwala's Swarg Ashram. Two neighbouring establishments with the same name vie for custom and constantly attempt to outdo each other; their latest marketing gimmick is to have a man outside dressed as the mythical *choti wallah* and ringing a bell. The one closest to the river has slightly better service and a congenial roof terrace. Both places are large, busy and open at 7am for breakfast; the extensive menus include ice cream, sweets and cold drinks, while a thali costs around Rs60.

Devraj Coffee Corner Lakshmanjhula, just above the bridge on the town side of the river. An

Ashrams, yoga and meditation

Due to an ongoing dispute with the government, Maharishi Mahesh Yogi's beautifully situated ashram, home to the Beatles in 1968, stands empty on a high forested bluff above the river. Although there are no classes here, it's a wonderfully atmospheric place to wander around – but don't come alone, as there have been reports of muggings. Plenty of other ashrams in Rishikesh welcome students of yoga, offering courses of varying duration – from one day to several months – and cost.

Ananda Spa ⓣ0137/822 7500, ⓦwww.anandaspa.com. Not an ashram but an internationally renowned luxury resort on the outskirts of Rishikesh, offering yoga, spa and Ayurvedic-based beauty treatments. Rooms from $330 to $1550 per night.

Brahma Niwas (no phone). Towards the river near Kailash Gate in Muni-ki-Reti, Swami Kaivalyananda delivers a no-nonsense, shoot-from-the-hip interpretation of Vedanta that may not agree with some.

Dayananda Vedanta Ashram ⓣ0135/243 0769. Irregular courses on Vedanta as well as yoga classes. Near Shivananda Ashram.

Omkarananda Ashram (Durga Mandir) ⓣ0135/243 2413. On the hill above Yoga Niketan, offering classes including classical Indian music and dance. Morning and evening tours.

Parmarth Niketan Ashram ⓣ0135/244 0088, ⓦwww.parmarth.com. In association with Uttaranchal Tourism, the ashram sponsors a yoga week in late Feb/early March. There are a range of courses to choose from, costing between $40 and $120 per day including food and accommodation at a variety of hotels throughout Rishikesh.

Shivananda Ashram ⓣ0135/243 0040, ⓦwww.divinelifesociety.org. Large institution, with branches all over the world, run by the Divine Life Society and founded by the remarkable Swami Shivananda (who passed into what his followers refer to as *maha samadhi*, final liberation, in 1963). It places an emphasis on the philosophy of Advaitya Vedanta, based on the belief of the non-dual Brahman, or godhead as the undivided self, and has a well-stocked library, a forest retreat, and a charitable hospital. Sessions in meditation and yoga, plus other activities, are always going on. To arrange a long-term stay, contact the Secretary two months in advance (Divine Life Society, PO Shivanandanagar 249192, Tehri District, Garhwal, Uttaranchal).

Ved Niketan Ashram ⓣ0135/243 0279. Across the river south of Swarg Ashram. Month long courses run by the charismatic Swamiji Dharmananda, introducing students to all aspects of yoga. He also holds daily drop-in lectures on yoga from 10.30am–12.30pm. Hatha yoga classes held every morning and evening.

Yoga Niketan ⓣ0135/243 0227, ⓦwww.yoganiketanashram.com. Reached by a path adjacent to Shivananda Ashram. Meditation centre with a good library in peaceful grounds overlooking the river, founded by the late Swami Yogeshwarananda. Accommodation available for a minimum of 15 days; Rs250 per day includes all meals as well as yoga and meditation classes.

Yoga Study Centre ⓣ0135/243 3837. Reputable school for the Iyengar form of Hatha yoga, 1km south of central Rishikesh at Ganga Vihar.

outlet of the *German Bakery* chain (and also a New Age bookshop), where you can enjoy cinnamon rolls, muesli fruit curd and superb cakes as you watch the Ganges and the pilgrims flow past.

East West Resto Directly opposite ferry quay, Ramjhula. Tiny, cheap café serving up strong filter coffee and healthy, tasty lunches such as brown basmati rice with veg.

Madras Café Directly opposite ferry quay, Ramjhula. Busy, welcoming restaurant, strong on reasonably priced South Indian food.

Neelam's Off Haridwar Rd. Towards the bridge and Muni-ki-Reti, this legendary Sikh-run *dhaba* is always filled with tourists hungry for its Western-orientated food such as macaroni. It's easy to miss – look for the small sign on the left between Dehra Dun Rd and Lakshmanjhula Rd.

Char Dham buses

During the April to October pilgrimage season, when the **Char Dham** temples are open in the Garhwal hills, direct buses connect Rishikesh's Yatra Bus Stand with **Badrinath** (297km), **Kedarnath** (210km, via Gaurikund), **Gangotri** (250km) and **Yamunotri** (280km, via Hanuman Chatti). Book at least a day in advance as buses start to leave around 4am and few complete the journey in a day; the roads are treacherous and tedious, so you might prefer to break the journey along the way.

GMVN in Muni-ki-Reti (see p.370) organizes **package tours** (a four-day trip to Badrinath, including bus, food and lodging, costs around Rs3300), as well as very expensive car rental. Sharma Travels, 86 Haridwar Road (☎0135/243 0364), has a fleet of press cars leaving around 5am to carry newspapers to various points in the mountains including Joshimath and Uttarkashi. Slightly more expensive (Rs200 to Joshimath) and often cramped and uncomfortable, this is nevertheless a much faster way of getting to the interior than by bus. For an extra Rs50 the driver will pick you up from your hotel – money well spent considering the early departure time and the press car driver's tendency to turn up late.

Around Rishikesh: local treks

Although a road has now been blasted through the forest to the small Shiva shrine in the hamlet of **Nilkanth Mahadev** (Nilkantha), east of Rishikesh, it's still possible to walk there along the older and shorter pilgrim path. This beautiful forest track rises through the forests behind Swarg Ashram, passes Mahesh Yogi's ashram, and eventually crosses a spur before descending to Nilkantha. There's a chance you may encounter wildlife along the way; keep a safe distance from wild elephants. Nilkantha itself is changing, as an ever-growing number of pilgrims travel along the new road that has cut a swathe through the forests.

You can also follow the river along the motorable track north of Lakshmanjhula, passing several good beaches before arriving at the beautiful ashram of **Phulcchatti** (10km), which lies on a bend in the river and has giant boulders and excellent swimming.

Another hike leads high above Lakshmanjhula for 10km to the small white Shakti temple of **Kunjapuri**, at the sharp point of an almost perfectly conical hill with stupendous views of the Himalayas to the north and towards Haridwar to the south. Try to catch the sunrise from the top, before the haze seeps into the atmosphere. A less strenuous alternative is to take the bus to Hindola Khal on the road to Tehri and walk the remaining 3km to the temple. Bring a guide or partner in any of these areas as incidents of **robbery** along the trails have been reported.

The trek to Yamunotri

Cradled in a deep cleft in the lap of Bandarpunch, and thus denied mountain vistas, the temple of **Yamunotri** (3291m), 223km northeast of Rishikesh, marks the source of the Yamuna, India's second holiest river after the Ganges. The least dramatic but most beautiful of the four *dhams* (temples) of Garhwal, it's also the least spoiled and commercial. **Access** has become easier following road improvements; from the roadhead at Janki Chatti it's a mere 5km along a trail that follows the turbulent ice-blue river as it runs below rocky crags, with snowy peaks in the distance. The walk can also be combined with the **Dodi Tal trek** linking nearby Hanuman Chatti to Uttarkashi (see the box on p.375).

Janki Chatti and around

The enchanting little village of **JANKI CHATTI** marks the end of a motorable road connected by bus with Dehra Dun, Mussoorie and Rishikesh. Some routes require a change at **BARKOT**, a four-hour bus ride (Rs60) beyond Mussoorie, which has a GMVN *Tourist Bungalow* (☎0137/252 4236; ❸–❹). Jeeps and buses (Rs25) travel another two and a half hours to reach the small riverside hamlet of **Hanuman Chatti**, which has an excellent GMVN *Tourist Bungalow* (no phone; ❺) with river-facing rooms and a comfortable dorm (Rs130). Crossing a bridge at the edge of town, a brand new road weaves into the mountains for 9km until it reaches Janki Chatti, home to yet another GMVN *Tourist Bungalow* (no phone; ❸–❹), a friendly institution with its own café. GMVN also runs a simpler hostel with dorms (Rs150), down by the river. Also along the main trail, the *Ganga Jamuna* (❸) and the renovated *Arvind Ashram* (❶–❷) are alternatives, and there are a number of decent **restaurants** offering thalis, cold drinks and snacks. While you're in Janki Chatti, it's worth making the one-kilometre detour across the river to the traditional Garhwali village of **KHARSALI**, home to the *pandas* (pilgrim priests) of Yamunotri. Amongst the drystone buildings with their beautifully carved wooden beams stands a unique three-storey Shiva temple – dedicated to Someshwar, lord of the mythical intoxicant Soma. A 5.30am bus departs daily for **Gangotri**; make sure to find out if it departs from Janki Chatti or Hanuman Chatti.

Yamunotri

A short way beyond Janki Chatti, the trail becomes much steeper but increasingly dramatic and beautiful as it passes through rocky forested crags to **YAMUNOTRI**. Sited near the river, around three piping-hot sulphur springs, Yamunotri's temple is new and architecturally uninteresting; it has to be completely rebuilt every few years due to the impact of heavy winter snows and monsoon rains. Its main shrine – actually part of the top spring, worshipped as the source of the river – holds a small silver image of the goddess Yamuna, bedecked with garlands. The daughter of Surya, the sun, and Sangya, consciousness, Yamuna is the twin sister of Yama, the lord of death; all who bathe in her waters are spared a painful end, while food cooked in the water is considered to be *prasad* (divine offering). Most pilgrims also bathe in the **hot spring** (free); both male and female pools have been built. If you choose to **stay** in Yamunotri, there's a simple dormitory (Rs150) at the GMVN *Tourist Bungalow* near the temple. Probably the best of the few *dharamshalas* is the *Ramananda Ashram* (❶), commanding good views from the hill above the temple, and owned by the head priest. Simple **food** arrangements can be made through the ashrams and the bungalow.

Technically, the source of the Yamuna is the glacial lake of **Saptarishi Kund**. This is reached via a hard twelve-kilometre trek, which heads straight up the mountain alongside the river until finally easing towards the base of Kalinda Parbat. Both this trek, and the route over the challenging Yamunotri Pass to Har-ki-Dun (see p.363) necessitate at least one day's acclimatization, adequate clothing, supplies and a guide.

Uttarkashi

The largest town in the interior of Garhwal, **UTTARKASHI** was little-known to the outside world until its unhappy association with the massive nearby earthquake in 1992. Previous to the earthquake was a flood in 1978; then a massive landslide in 2003 wiped out several hotels on the main road, the tourist office and the bus stand. By December 2004, these still hadn't been rebuilt, though it is rumoured that the new bus stand and tourist office will be located 3km out of town. In the meantime, buses are stopping on the main road and there is no tourist office.

The town occupies the flat and fertile valley floor of the Bhagirathi; most pilgrims and tourists stop here to break the long journey between Rishikesh, 148km south, and Gangotri, 100km northeast. Uttarkashi's busy and well-stocked **market** is ideal for picking up supplies before high-altitude treks, and the town is also a good place to contact experienced **mountain guides** – mostly graduates of its highly esteemed Nehru Institute of Mountaineering (Ⓣ01374/222123, Ⓦwww.nimindia.com). The going rates stand at around Rs150 per porter and Rs200–300 for a guide. Specialist operators include Mount Support, PO Box 2, B.D. Nautial Bhawan, Bhatwari Road

The Dodi Tal trek

The relatively short **Dodi Tal trek**, which links the Gangotri and Yamunotri regions without straying into high glacial terrain, is one of Garhwal's all-time classics. It's not a difficult hike, but local villagers are keen to offer their services as porters or guides, and you should definitely avail yourself of their help if you want to wander off the beaten track and visit the villages. Carry as much of your own food as possible, and also your own tent. The best maps for this trek are the Ground Survey map of Garhwal, and Leomann map (sheet 7 in the India Series), both available from major Uttaranchal tourism offices.

The trek is described below from east to west, starting from **Uttarkashi** on the way to Gangtori, and ending at **Hanuman Chatti**, 14km south of Yamunotri.

On **DAY 1**, catch one of the three daily buses or an hourly Jeep from Uttarkashi to **Kalyani** (1829m) via Gangori (the first is at 7am; 1hr). From Kalyani, a road is being pushed through to **Agoda** (2286m), 7km on, but frequent landslides mean you'll probably have to walk this section anyway. Stop for the night at the basic *Tourist Bungalow* (❶), at the far end of the village, however tempted you may be to press on. You'll need a carry-mat to sleep on.

On **DAY 2**, the trail from Agoda climbs beside a river and then zigzags steadily upwards through lush pine and spruce forests, with a couple of chai shops en route. After 14km and a final undulation, it arrives at **Dodi Tal** (3024m), a lake set against a backdrop of thickly forested hills. Near the basic forest bungalow in the clearing are chai shops and areas for camping.

Some trekkers consider the full 18km from Dodi Tal to Shima on **DAY 3** too long and arduous, and prefer to split it into two days. Follow the well-marked path along (and often across) the stream that feeds Dodi Tal, which can get steep and entail scrambling; continue straight ahead, ignoring tracks that cross the trail, until you emerge above the treeline. After a further 1.5km the trail heads left to a small pass then zigzags up scree to **Darwa Pass** (4130m). This is the highest point of the trek, providing superb panoramas of the Srikanta Range. If you're ready to rest here, a leftward path beyond the top leads to camping and water. The main route goes down to a valley and then climbs sharply again. **Shima**, where you rejoin the treeline, has basic hut accommodation; bring your own food.

The beautiful twelve-kilometre trail down from Shima on **DAY 4** kicks off with a steep 1.5km scramble alongside a stream, then eases past forest and *bugyal*, where shepherds have their huts. A well-defined rocky path drops steadily through two villages and zigzags down to the Hanuman Ganga river. It emerges at **Hanuman Chatti** (see opposite) from where buses run via Barkot to Uttarkashi, Mussoorie and other points in Garhwal. The Dodi Tal trek can easily be tied in with hikes in the **Har-ki-Dun** and **Yamunotri** areas; see also p.363.

(☎01374/222419, ✉mountsupport@rediffmail.com), on the main road, who also has equipment for rent and porters for hire.

Practicalities

All **buses** to and from Uttarkashi – which has hourly services to both Gangotri (until 2pm) and Rishikesh between May and November – currently stop on the main road. **Taxis** can be picked up in the market area; a seat in a shared Jeep to Gangotri costs Rs100 per person. There is nowhere to change **money**, but **Internet** access is available next to the petrol station on the main drag (Rs35/hr).

On the main road, the *Bandhari* (☎01374/222203; ❷–❸) has a range of double **rooms**, some with hot water and TV. Their new annexe (❸–❹), 300m up the road on the left, is cleaner and brighter, with balconies overlooking the road. In the lanes by the market you'll find the reasonable *Meghdoot* (☎01374/222150; ❸) and the better GMVN *Tourist Bungalow* (☎01374/222271; ❷–❺), with spacious rooms and a dorm (Rs150), set around a small lawn. If you're staying in Uttarkashi for longer than a night, then by far the best accommodation and food is at the delightful, family-run *Monal Tourism Home* (☎01374/222270, ✉monal22270@rediffmail.com, ❹–❺), 2km from the centre. The friendly owner, a graduate of the Nehru Institute of Mountaineering, will pick you up from the bus stand if you phone in advance, and is more than happy to provide information (and company) if you're interested in trekking in the region.

Among the many *bhojanalaya* (veg **cafés**), in central Uttarkashi, *Roopam* on the main road serves healthy local cuisine with dhal and fresh roti.

Gangotri and around

Set amid tall *deodar* pine forests at the head of the Bhagirathi gorge, 248km north of Rishikesh at 3140m, **Gangotri** is the most remote of the four *dhams* (pilgrimage sites) of Garhwal. Although the wide Alaknanda, which flows past Badrinath, has in some ways a better claim to be considered the main channel of the Ganges, Gangotri is for Hindus the spiritual source of the great river, while its physical source is the ice cave of **Gomukh** on the Gangotri Glacier, 14km further up the valley. From here, the **River Bhagirathi** begins its tempestuous descent through a series of mighty gorges, carving great channels and cauldrons in the rock and foaming in white-water pools.

From Uttarkashi, frequent buses, taxis and Jeeps head up to Gangotri. A shared Jeep (3hr 30min) should cost no more than Rs100 per head and is probably the most enjoyable way of making the journey; buses stop frequently and can take more than five hours to make the trip. Parts of the road beyond Gangnani, where the vast and fertile Bhagirathi flood plain is famous for its apple orchards, were damaged by the earthquake in 1992; gigantic blocks of rock almost dammed the river and created a lake. Ten kilometres beyond the uninspiring village of **Harsil**, the road crosses the deep Bhagirathi gorge at **Lanka**, on a dramatic bridge said to be among the highest in the world. This is an army area, so don't take any photographs. At the hamlet of **Bhaironghati**, 3km further on and 11km short of Gangotri, the Rudragaira emerges from its own gorge to meet the Bhagirathi. A small temple stands in towering *deodar* forests, and there are a few teashops as well as a barely used GMVN *Tourist Bungalow* (❸–❺).

Gangotri

Although most of the nearby snow peaks are obscured by the desolate craggy mountains looming immediately above **GANGOTRI**, the town itself is

Gangotri ashrams

Although most of the so-called "ashrams" in Gangotri are in reality boarding houses, a few *sadhus* offer rooms on a donation basis for visitors looking for a quiet retreat. The simple, atmospheric **Kailash Ashram**, overlooking the confluence of the Kedar Ganga and the Bhagirathi, is run (along with a small Ayurvedic clinic) by the affable Bhim Yogi, who welcomes guests for medium- and long-term stays. Nearby, **Nani Mata's Ashram** belongs to an English *mataji* (female *sadhu*), who has lived in Gangotri for many years and is held in high esteem. Above Kailash Ashram, the larger **Yoga Niketan Ashram**, set in an attractive garden, operates along much more regimented lines, with fixed meal times and meditation periods, and a fixed fee of Rs200, which includes morning yoga classes.

redolent of the atmosphere of the high Himalayas, populated by a mixed cast of Hindu pilgrims and foreign trekkers. Its unassuming **temple**, overlooking the river just beyond a small market on the left bank, was built early in the eighteenth century by the Gurkha general Amar Singh Thapa. Capped with a gilded roof, consisting of a squat *shikhara* surrounded by four smaller replicas, it commemorates the legend that the goddess Ganga was enticed to earth by acts of penance performed by King Bhagirath, who wanted her to revitalize the ashes of his people. Inside the temple is a silver image of the goddess, while a slab of stone adjacent to the temple is venerated as **Bhagirath Shila**, the spot where the king meditated. Steps lead down to the main riverside *ghat*, where the devout bathe in the freezing waters of the river to cleanse their bodies and souls of sin.

Across the river, a loose development of ashrams and guesthouses dwarfed by great rocky outcrops and huge trees leads down to **Dev Ghat**, overlooking the confluence with the Kedar Ganga. Not far beyond, at the impressive waterfall-fed pool of **Gaurikund**, the twenty-kilometre-long gorge starts to get into its stride. Beautiful forest paths lead through the dark *deodar* woods and past a bridge along the edge of the gorge to a flimsy rope-bridge, commanding great views of the ferocious torrent below.

GMVN's *Tourist Bungalow* (Ⓣ013772/22221; ❸–❺), over the footbridge from the bus stand, offers rooms and a reasonably cheap dorm (Rs140). Next to the main cantilever bridge, the large and popular *Ganga Niketan* (Ⓣ013772/22219; ❷) has a café and supplies shop overlooking the river, while the *Himalaya* (no phone; ❷), along the riverside opposite the temple, offers basic, friendly accommodation with fantastic views up the valley to the snow peaks. A number of *dhabas* and cafés on both sides of the river serve thalis, good breakfasts and much-needed, warming chai. For pilgrims heading toward Gomukh, the market area also marks the last chance to buy gloves and woolly hats.

Gomukh and Gangotri Glacier

A flight of steps alongside the temple at Gangotri leads up to join a large pony path that rises gently, providing gorgeous mountain vistas, towards the **Gangotri Glacier**, long regarded as one of the most beautiful and accessible glaciers in the inner Himalayas. Sadly, it is retreating hundreds of metres per year. Two kilometres into the trek, the forest **checkpoint** demands Rs50 and confiscates any potential plastic rubbish you may be carrying in your rucksack.

Approaching the oasis of **Chirbasa**, 7km out of Gangotri, the skyline is dominated by magnificent buttresses and glass-like walls, culminating in the sharp pinnacles of Bhagirathi 3 (6454m) and Bhagirathi 1 (6856m). Chirbasa amounts to no more than a few chai stalls, which can also provide you with a roof and simple food. The path then climbs above the treeline, continuing along the widening valley to enter a high mountain desert. Just beyond Chirbasa, the trail across a cliff face has badly deteriorated and gusts of wind can send small rocks cascading down onto the narrow path, so great care is called for. Soon after crossing a stream, the path rounds a shoulder to offer a glimpse of the glacier's snout near **Gomukh** ("the cow's mouth"), the ever-present Bhagirathi peaks, and the huge expanse of the Gangotri Glacier – 23km long, and up to 4km wide – sweeping like a gigantic highway through the heart of the mountains.

Down below on the flat valley bottom, 5km from Chirbasa, is the cold grey hamlet of **Bhojbasa**, cowering in the shadow of the beautiful **Shivling Peak** (6543m), where most visitors spend the night before heading on to Gomukh and beyond. If you're planning on trekking any further than Gomukh, this is a good point at which to stop and acclimatize. The GMVN *Tourist Bungalow* here (no phone; ❷) provides a **dorm** (Rs200). Guests huddle in the evening in the small, friendly café, which is the place to arrange a mountain guide if you plan to cross the glaciers. Accommodation is also available at *Lal Baba's Ashram* (no phone; ❶) which offers only sheets and the odd floor mattress – though food is included in the price. There is a good **campground** down by the river if you have your own tent.

If you've stayed in Bhojbasa, it really is worth braving the cold to walk to Gomukh for **sunrise**. A good track continues from Bhojbasa for 5km to Gomukh, where the river emerges with great force from a cavern in the glacier. The ice is in a constant state of flux, so the huge greyish-blue snout of the glacier continually changes appearance as chunks of ice tumble into the gushing water. Be careful of standing above or below the cave; many pilgrims have been crushed to death by falling ice while attempting to collect water. Two or three chai shops near here provide food and basic shelter, and there are many flat areas for camping.

Tapovan and Nandanvan

The campsites of **Tapovan** and **Nandanvan**, 6km beyond Gomukh on slightly divergent glacier-side routes, are popular objectives for lightweight trekking and mountaineering, and as a rule best attempted using guides engaged from Gangotri or Bhojbasa.

A difficult track leads past the last teashop at Gomukh to ascend the moraine on the left edge of the glacier, following it for 1km before crossing the glacier diagonally towards a high point in the middle, in line with Shivling. Depending on the season, this stage can be confusing and dangerous; heavy snow can conceal deep crevasses and the cairns that mark the way. From the high point, you should be able to see a stream coming down the high bank opposite. Use this as a marker; an extremely steep and strenuous climb up unstable ground runs to its left, to top out eventually on the grassy meadow of **TAPOVAN**, where you're greeted by the fantastic sight of Shivling (6543m) towering above. With its herds of grazing, almost tame *bharal* (mountain goats), and a tranquil stream, the meadow makes a bizarre contrast to the sea of ice below.

Many trekkers arrive in Tapovan without camping equipment, expecting to shelter in either of its two ashrams. However, although Mataji, a female *sadhu* who lives here throughout the year, and Shimla Baba do indeed have small hermitages with blankets, and are prepared to feed visitors, their resources are greatly stretched. Whether or not you stay with them, carry supplies, which will always be welcome, and bring camping and cooking equipment if you plan to be here more than a day or two.

NANDANVAN lies on a similar but less frequented meadow below the Bhagirathi Peaks, at the junction of the glacier known as the Chaturang Bamak and the Gangotri Glacier. From here you get magnificent views of Bhagirathi, Shivling, and the huge snowy mass of **Kedar Dome** (6831m), hiding a steep sheer rocky face. The trail up follows the same path from Gomukh, but instead of the diagonal slant towards Tapovan, continues across the Raktaban Glacier and follows the left bank of the Gangotri Glacier. If you do get confused and find yourself in Nandanvan by mistake, an indistinct 3km trail across Gangotri Glacier leads back to Tapovan.

The route to Kedarnath

It's hard to imagine a more dramatic setting for a temple than **Kedarnath**, 223km northeast of Rishikesh, close to the source of the Mandakini at 3583m above sea level, and overlooked by tumbling glaciers and huge buttresses of ice, snow and rock. Kedarnath – the "field" (*kedara*) where the crop of *moksha* (liberation) is sown – is the most important shrine in the Himalayas, and among the major Shiva temples of all India. According to the *Puranas* (Hindu tales), when the Pandavas were searching for Shiva to grant them absolution, they succeeded in tracking him down to Kedarnath, where he disguised himself as a bull in a herd of cattle. One of the brothers, Bhim, then straddled the valley and allowed the herd to pass beneath him, reasoning that the only bull to refuse must be Shiva himself. When Shiva was unmasked, he dived into the ground; Bhim grabbed him from behind, and held on tight. However, all that remained of the god was his rear; his *lingam* appeared in Varanasi (Kashi), while assorted other pieces of his anatomy are commemorated by the **Panch Kedar temples**. Kedarnath is the third of the sacred Char Dham sites, and as one of India's twelve *jyotrilinga* – *lingams* of light – attracts hordes of Hindu pilgrims (*yatri*) in the summer months. The area makes a refreshing change from the rocky and desolate valleys of west Garhwal, with lush hanging gorges, immaculately terraced hillsides and abundant apple orchards. Kedarnath is also a good base for short treks to the beautiful lakes ofVasuki Tal and Gandhi Sarovar.

Gaurikund

GAURIKUND, a friendly and bustling small town perched above the road-head for Sonprayag, marks the starting point of the trek up to the **temple of Kedarnath**, although there are plans to extend the road as far as Rambara.

Direct **buses** run to Gaurikund all the way from Rishikesh, but most visitors arrive on local buses and taxis from the larger bus terminal at **Guptkashi**, 29km lower down. This receives services from **Rudraprayag**, 109km south on the busy main Rishikesh–Joshimath–Badrinath route, and **Gopeshwar**, 138km southeast.

Inexpensive *dharamshalas* and **hotels** in Gaurikund itself include the *Vijay Tourist Lodge* (☎01364/269242; ❶), which is on the main bazaar road and has clean if basic rooms. Opposite, the *Annapurna* (☎013764/269209; ❶), has large carpeted doubles with sunny balconies and dorms. The squat GMVN *Tourist Bungalow* (☎01364/269202; ❹), has pricier but cosy doubles, a cheap dorm (Rs150) and a **restaurant** offering soup and salad.

The trail from Gaurikund

So popular is Kedarnath on the *yatra* trail that the path up from Gaurikund is being slowly stripped of its vegetation, used for fuel and to feed the ponies that carry wealthier pilgrims. You can hire a horse for the trip for Rs300 – a bargain compared to the Rs2500 that some pilgrims pay to be hauled up by a four-man team of *doli*-wallahs.

Dotted with chai shops, the large pony track climbs from Gaurikund, traversing the hillside through the disappearing forests to the village of **Rambara**, 7km up and halfway to Kedarnath. With its many cafés and rest houses (and open sewers), Rambara signals the end of the treeline and the start of the alpine zone. Several conspicuous short cuts scar the hillside as the track rises steeply to **Garur Chatti**, then levels off roughly 1km short of Kedarnath. Suddenly, rounding a corner, you come face to face with the incredible south face of the peak of Kedarnath (6940m) at the end of the valley, with the temple town dwarfed beneath it and almost insignificant in the distance.

Kedarnath: town and treks

KEDARNATH is not a very attractive town – in fact it's almost unbearable at the height of the pilgrimage season (May, June & Sept). It's a grey place, consisting of a central thoroughfare stretching for 500m between the temple and the bridge, lined with rest houses and *dharamshalas*, pilgrim shops and administrative offices. However, the sheer power of its location tends to sweep away any negative impressions, and it's always possible to escape to explore the incredible high-altitude scenery.

At the head of the town, the imposing **temple** is constructed along simple lines in stone, with a large *mandapa* (fore-chamber) housing an impressive stone image of Shiva's bull, Nandi. Within the inner sanctum, open to all, *pandas* (pilgrim priests) sit around a rock considered to be Shiva's upraised arse, left here as he plunged head-first into the ground. Mendicant *sadhus* congregate in the elevated courtyard in front of the temple.

A solid path from near the main bridge, before the town, crosses the Mandakini to the left of the valley, and ends 4km away at the **glacier**. At its edge, the **Chorabari Tal** lake is now known as **Gandhi Sarovar**, as some of the Mahatma's ashes were scattered here. Close by, around 800m before the lake, is the source of the Mandakini; it emerges from a hole in the moraine on extremely suspect ground, which should not be approached. You could also cross the river by the small bridge behind the temple, and scramble up the rough boulder-strewn moraine to meet the main track.

East of town, a well-marked path rises diagonally along the hillside to the prayer flags that mark a small shrine of the wrathful emanation of Shiva – **Bhairava**. The cliff known as **Bhairava Jhamp** is said to be somewhere nearby; until the British banned the practice in the nineteenth century, fanatical pilgrims used to leap to their deaths from it in the hope of gaining instant liberation.

Practicalities

Kedarnath's new GMVN *Tourist Bungalow* (☎01364/263228; ❸–❻), located close to the centre of town, offers large anonymous double **rooms** and a dorm (Rs150). Alternatives include the clean, comfortable *Bharat Seva Ashram* (☎01364/27213; ❶), a large red building beyond the temple on the left; and the pleasantly located bungalow of *Modi Bhavan* (no phone; ❷), behind and above the temple near the monument, which has large rooms and kitchenettes.

Food in the cafés along Kedarnath's main street is simple but expensive, as all supplies have to be brought up from the valley on horseback. The one most familiar with the needs of the western palate is *Kedar Mishthan Bhandar*, which can rustle up passable salads and potato dishes. The canteen run by the temple committee, *Shri Badrinath Kedarnath Mandi Samiti*, behind the temple, serves meals and *aloo paratha*.

Joshimath and Auli

The scattered administrative town of **JOSHIMATH** clings to the side of a deep valley 250km northeast of Rishikesh, with tantalizing glimpses of the snow peaks high above and the prospect, far below, of the road disappearing into a sunless canyon at Vishnu Prayag, the confluence with the Dhauli Ganga. Few of the thousands of pilgrims who pass through en route to Badrinath linger, but Joshimath has close links with **Shankara**, the ninth-century reformer, who attained enlightenment here beneath a mulberry tree, before going on to establish **Jyotiramath**, one of the four centres of Hinduism (*dhams*) at the four cardinal points. In winter, when Badrinath is closed, the Rawal, the head priest of both Badrinath and Kedarnath, resides at Joshimath. The town itself consists of a long drawn-out **upper bazaar**, and, around 1km from the main square on the Badrinath road, a **lower bazaar** which holds the colourful Narsingh, Navadurga, Vasudev and Gauri Shankar **temples**.

Practicalities

Most **buses** and **Jeeps** up to Joshimath stop in the upper bazaar. All motorized transport onwards to Badrinath – and there are plenty of buses during the *yatra* season – is obliged to move in **convoys**. A gate system controls traffic in each direction, in two equal 24-kilometre stages – the first between Joshimath and Pandukeshwar, the second between Pandukeshwar and Badrinath. Several convoys leave Joshimath each day, the first at 6.30am and the last at 4.30pm from the Narsingh temple complex in the lower bazaar. At night the road remains closed.

For **trekking** and skiing advice, head for Eskimo Adventure Company (Ⓣ01389/222864, Ⓔaeskimoadventures@rediffmail.com), opposite *Hotel Sriram*, which is run by two graduates of the Nehru Institute of Mountaineering who can organize treks, rock climbing, skiing and river rafting, as well as provide permits, guides and equipment. They also have **Internet** access (Rs100/hr), as does KCE Uniyal Infotech (Rs60/hr), another 200m further along upper bazaar. The enthusiastic Forestry Officer, Mr A.K. Banerjee, will show tourists slide shows of Nanda Devi and the Valley of the Flowers, while explaining his **eco-tourism** drive in the region - his office (daily 10am–5pm) is up two sets of steps next to the *Dronagiri*, then to the right.

Rooms at the grim GMVN *Tourist Rest House* (Ⓣ01389/222118; ❸–❹), up a short lane at the north end of the upper bazaar, include a dorm (Rs130); a café serves simple meals. The new block, immediately above the old (accessed by the lane opposite the GMOU office), is much better but still not great value (Ⓣ01389/222226; ❹). Next to the old GMVN block the *Hotel Sriram* (Ⓣ01389/222332; ❸–❹) has good-value, clean rooms; the deluxe includes a TV and hot water geyser while standard rooms have hot bucket. Up the lane, the *Shailja* (Ⓣ01389/222208; ❶–❷) is pretty dumpy but popular with budget travellers as rates are negotiable. All of these hotels are regaled by the bus horns from 4am in the morning onwards. Further south of the centre, *Dronagiri* (Ⓣ01389/222254; ❺–❽) is the most comfortable hotel in town, with good views, a clean restaurant and satellite TV. **Food** options in Joshimath are not exciting: the restaurants at the *Dronagiri* and *Sriram* are the best; of the *dhabas* the busy *Marwari* on the main square has a good special thali (Rs50), while the *New Star*, on Upper Bazaar near the GMVNs and *Sriram* opens early for breakfast.

Auli

A rough road winds 15km up through the *deodar* forest from Joshimath to **AULI**, which has recently been developed as a **ski** resort, partly in the hope of replacing the ski areas rendered inaccessible by the war in Kashmir. To get there, you can either walk 4km straight up the hill, or take a 22-minute ride on India's highest and longest cable car (made in Austria), or the **ropeway** as it is known locally, which connects Joshimath (1906m) with **Gorson** (3016m), above Auli (every 25min 8am–7.15pm; May–June Rs300 return, July–April Rs200; no singles). You can also hire a jeep (Rs25, Rs300 when the ropeway isn't working). Energetic skiers haul themselves up Gorson Top, a nearby hill, to increase their ski runs - in summertime, this makes for a pleasant walk with excellent views of the Nanda Devi, Kamet and Dunagiri mountain peaks.

As a ski destination, Auli actually has little to offer – a short season (Jan–March), a solitary chairlift and one long T-bar to cover 3km of beginner and intermediate runs; but if you're interested, GMVNL offers various ski packages (a 7-day course is Rs5500). Equipment can be hired through Eskimo Adventure Company in Joshimath. For up-to-date information contact the GMVN **Mountaineering and Trekking** division in Rishikesh (ⓣ0135/243 0799). For skiers it's just as convenient to **stay** in Joshimath as Auli, and take advantage of the ropeway. At mid-mountain, below cable car Tower 8, the *Cliff Top Club Resort* (ⓣ01389/223217, ⓦwww.nivalink.com/clifftop; ❽–❾) offers huge wood-panelled en-suite rooms with kitchenettes for $70–140 per night. Indian and Chinese meals are outrageously priced at Rs700–900. The GMVN *Tourist Centre* (ⓣ01389/223305; ❺–❻) near the base of the chairlift has comfortable double rooms and huts, and two large dorms with lockable cubicles (Rs150). The friendly staff in the dining hall try their best, but don't expect any après-ski activity.

Badrinath

BADRINATH, "Lord of the Berries", 298km northeast of Rishikesh and just 40km south of Tibet, is the most popular of the four main temples of Garhwal. One of Hinduism's holiest sites, it was founded by Shankara in the ninth century, not far from the source of the Alaknanda, the main tributary of the holy Ganga. Although the temple boasts a dazzling setting, deep in a valley beneath the sharp snowy pyramid of Nilkantha (6558m), the town that has grown up around it is grey, grubby and unattractive.

Until a few years ago, Badrinath was a remote and evocative place, where legends spoke of mysterious *sadhus*. Now, however, it has grown out of all proportion to its infrastructure. The army-built road up from Joshimath, 48km south, brings endless convoys of **buses** and **taxis**, and the temple turns over astronomical amounts of money. Pilgrims crowd in, the streets are lined with mendicant *sadhus* and beggars, and roadside stalls sell all sorts of religious paraphernalia.

Badrinath is still presided over by a Nambudiri brahmin from Kerala – the Rawal, who also acts as the head priest for Kedarnath. According to myth, the two temples were once close enough together for the priest to worship at both on the same day. The **temple** itself, also known as **Badri Narayan**, is dedicated to Vishnu, who is said to have done penance in the mythical Badrivan ("Forest of Berries"), that once covered the mountains of Uttaranchal. Unusually, it is made of wood; the entire facade is repainted each May, once the snows have receded and the temple opens for the season. From a distance, its bright colours, which contrast strikingly with the concrete buildings, snowy peaks and deep blue skies, resemble a Tibetan *gompa*; there's some debate as to whether the temple was formerly a Buddhist shrine. Inside, where photography is strictly taboo, the black stone image of **Badri Vishal** is seated like a *bodhisattva* in the lotus position (some Hindus regard the Buddha as an incarnation of Vishnu). *Pandas* (pilgrim priests) sit around the cloisters carrying on the business of worship and a booth enables visitors to pay in advance for *darshan* (devotional rituals) chosen from a long menu.

This site, on the west bank of the turbulent Alaknanda, may well have been selected because of the sulphurous **Tapt Kund** hot springs on the embankment right beneath the temple, which are used for ritual bathing. Immediately south of the temple, the old **village** of Badrinath is still there, its traditional stone buildings and a small market seeming like relics from a bygone age. The main road north of Badrinath heads into increasingly border-sensitive territory, but visitors can normally take local buses and taxis 4km on to the end of the road where the intriguing Bhotia village of **Mana** nestles – check the current situation before setting out. It's also possible to walk to Mana along a clear footpath by the road. The village itself consists of a warren of small lanes and buildings piled virtually on top of each other; the local Bhotia people, Buddhists of Tibetan origin who formerly traded across the high Mana Pass, now tend livestock and ponies and sell yak meat and brightly coloured, handmade carpets. Past the village and over a natural rock bridge, a path leads up the true left bank of the river towards the mountain of Satopanth (7075m) on the divide between the Mana and Gangotri regions, to the base of the impressive high **waterfall** of **Vasudhara**. Dropping from a hanging valley, this is considered to be the source of the Alaknanda, where it falls from heaven. Walking time is just 1hr 30min but, unusually, there are no chai stalls en route so bring some snacks.

Practicalities

Badrinath is awash with rough, flea-bitten budget **hotels** strung along the main road, the least unpleasant being *Gujarat Bhavan* (☎01381/22266; ❶), which overlooks the river and temple but gets its loudspeaker noise. A better choice is the GMVN *Devlok* (☎01381/22212; ❸–❺), behind the post office, with pleasant rooms, a dorm (Rs50), restaurant and excellent local advice. There are two other GMVN establishments near the bus stand, both contactable via the *Devlok*: *Yatri Niwas* (aka the *Tourist Hotel*), has 500 dorm beds (Rs50), while the *Travellers Lodge* has cosy and carpeted doubles (❷). *Hotel Narayan Palace* (☎01381/22380; ❼–❽) stands alone in both price and ostentatious decor; it's not bad, but the worn carpets and lack of heating don't quite merit the price (up to $65). The most atmospheric area for **cafés** and chai shops is the old section close to the temple, but the more commercial east bank holds a few more upmarket neon-lit restaurants, such as *Laxmi* and *Saket*, along with numerous *dhabas*, none of them very special.

Traffic back down to Joshimath, including the regular local **buses**, moves in the same convoy system as on the way up (see p.381), the last one departing at 3.30pm. Long-distance buses run direct to Rishikesh – the nearest railway station – with an overnight halt en route, and to Gaurikund near Kedarnath (14hr), bookable at the bus stand office above the town.

Hemkund and the Valley of the Flowers

Starting from the hamlet of **Govind Ghat**, 28km south of Badrinath on the road to Joshimath (local buses will stop on request), an important pilgrim trail winds for 21 steep kilometres up to the snow-melt lake of **Hemkund** (4329m).

In the Sikh holy book, the *Guru Granth Sahib*, Govind Singh recalled meditating at a lake surrounded by seven high mountains; only in the twentieth century was Hemkund discovered to be that lake. A large *gurudwara* (Sikh temple), and a small shrine to Lakshmana, the brother of Rama of *Ramayana* fame, now stand alongside. However, to protect the *deodar* forests along the trail, visitors can no longer spend the night.

Instead, the overgrown village of **Ghangaria**, 6km below Hemkund, serves as a base for day-hikes. It has several chai shops, a small tourist information centre, basic lodges, *gurudwaras* and a GMVN *Tourist Bungalow*, complete with dormitory (Ⓣ01391/226228; mid-April to Oct; ⑤). Camping will incur a Rs50 fee, and a Rs60 "eco-fee" which is valid for 7 days. Govind Ghat also has a large *gurudwara*, run on a donations system.

An alternative trail forks left from Ghangaria, climbing 5km to the mountain *bugyals* of the Bhyundar valley – the **Valley of the Flowers**. Starting at an altitude of 3352m, the valley was discovered in 1931 by the visionary mountaineer, Frank Smythe, who named it for its multitude of rare and beautiful plants and flowers. The meadows are at their best towards the end of the monsoons, in early September; they too have suffered at the hands (or rather feet) of large numbers of visitors, so camping is not allowed here either. As a result, it is not possible to explore the ten-kilometre valley in its entirety in the space of a day's hike from Ghangaria. At the entrance of the valley, foreigners must pay Rs350 for a three-day **permit**.

Nanda Devi National Park

East of Joshimath and visible from Auli, the majestic twin peaks of **Nanda Devi** – at 7816m, the highest complete mountain in India – dominate a large swathe of northeastern Garhwal and Kumaon. The eponymous goddess is the most important deity for all who live in her shadow, a fertility symbol also said to represent Durga, the virulent form of Shakti. Surrounded by an apparently impenetrable ring of mountains, the fastness of Nanda Devi was long considered inviolable; when mountaineers Eric Shipton and Bill Tilman finally traced a way through, along the difficult **Rishi Gorge**, in 1934, it was seen as a defilement of sacred ground. A string of catastrophes followed, and in 1976 an attempt on the mountain by father and daughter team Willi and Nanda Devi Unsoeld ended in tragedy when Nanda Devi died below the summit after which she was named.

The beautiful wilderness around the mountain now forms the **Nanda Devi Sanctuary**. This is the core zone of the 5860 kilometre square **Nanda Devi National Park**, which was declared a UNESCO biosphere reserve in October 2004. Access into the core zone has been prohibited since 1982 for environmental reasons, and trekking in the National Park is restricted to one route from the roadhead village of Lata to Dharansi Pass, which has fabulous views over to the twin peaks of Nanda Devi. Contact Mr Banerjee, the District Forestry Officer at Joshimath (see p.381), for further information on acquiring permits to visit this region, trekking regulations and current eco-tourism fees.

Gwaldam

Straddling a pass between Garhwal and Kumaon, surrounded by pine forests 61km east of Karnprayag, the peaceful hamlet of **GWALDAM** looks down upon the beautiful valley of the Pindar, a world away from the hectic *yatra* trails. This picturesque spot, with fabulous views of the triple-pointed peak, **Trisul** (7120m), used to be a tea plantation; now, thanks to its position on the main road to Almora, 90km southeast, it makes an ideal base for treks, especially following the ten-day **Curzon Trail** across the high mountain *bugyals* of northeastern Garhwal, over **Kuari Pass** to Tapovan and Joshimath. The unassuming little Buddhist **Khamba Temple**, or **Drikung Kagyu**

Kuari Pass and the Curzon Trail

Named after a British Viceroy who trekked parts of the **Curzon Trail**, and renamed after Independence as the **Nehru Trail**, the long route over **KUARI PASS** (4268m) in northeastern Garhwal provides some stunning mountain views. Traversing the high ranges without entering the permanent snowline, the ten-day trail starts on the border with Kumaon at Gwaldam above the River Pindar and ends around 150km north, at the hot springs of Tapovan in the Dhauli Ganga valley near Joshimath. Numerous variations and shorter trails approaching the pass include one of around 24km from Auli. The whole route, and connected hikes, is mapped out on the Leomann map of Kumaon–Garhwal (sheet 8 in the India Series). The best time to go is from May to June and mid-September to November.

An ideal expedition for those not equipped to tackle glacial terrain, the trail over Kuari Pass follows alpine meadows and crosses several major streams, skirting the outer western edge of the Nanda Devi National Park. Along the way you'll get excellent views of Trisul (7120m), the trident, Nanda Ghunti (6309m), and the elusive tooth-like Changabang (6864m), while to the far north on the border with Tibet rises the unmistakeable pyramid of Kamet (7756m).

On a major bus route between Karnaprayag and Almora and with comfortable accommodation, **Gwaldam** makes a good base for the start of the trek. Camping equipment is needed, especially on the pass. Guides can be negotiated here or at several points along the route. You can either take local transport from Gwaldam, including shared Jeeps via Tharali, or trek down through beautiful pine forests and cross the River Pindar to **Debal** 8km away, where there is a forest rest house and a tourist lodge. Motorized transport is available from Debal to **Bagrigadh**, just below the beautiful hamlet of Lohajung, which has a pleasant tourist lodge. Also here is the shrine of *lohajung* – a rusted iron bell suspended from a cypress tree and rung to announce your arrival to the *devta* or local spirit.

Following the River Wan for 10km the trail arrives at the large village of **Wan**, where there's a choice of accommodation, including a GMVN *Tourist Bungalow* (1) and a forest rest house. The small village of **Sutol** is 14km from Wan, along a trail following pleasant cypress and *deodar* forests. From Sutol to **Ramani**, a gentle 10km trail passes through several villages. A steep trail rises for 4km through dense forest from Ramni to the pass of **Sem Kharak** before descending for a further 9km to the small village of **Jhenjhenipati**, from where a rough track continues to the village of Panna 12km away, passing the beautiful **Gauna Lake**. From Panna a relentlessly steep trail rises for 12km to **Kuari Pass** (4298m) on the high divide between the lesser and the greater Himalayas, with rewarding views of Nanda Devi and Trisul.

Using Kuari Pass as a base, a climb to the peak of **Pangerchuli** (5183m), 12km up and down, is thoroughly recommended – the views from the summit reveal almost the entire route, including breathtaking mountain vistas. Although snow may be encountered on the climb, it is not a technical peak and no special equipment is necessary, save a good stick. From Kuari, a gruelling, knee-grinding 22-kilometre descent brings you straight down to the small village of **Tapovan**, overlooking the Dhauli Ganga, which has a hot-spring-fed tank. From here, local buses run to Joshimath, 11km away with several bus connections back down towards Karnaprayag and Rishikesh. An alternative descent from Kuari Pass is the long but picturesque route through forest to the ski centre of **Auli** via Chitrakantha – a trek of 24km – that avoids the dramatic decrease in altitude to Tapovan.

Lhundrup Ling, stands alongside orchards in the middle of a Tibetan settlement about 1.5km from Gwaldam's main crossroads. On the ridge above the village, the small shrine of **Badhangari**, dedicated to the goddess Durga and not far from the remnants of a Chand stone fort, commands superb views of the mountains of Kumaon and Garhwal. To reach it, take a bus for 4km to the village of Tal, then trek another 4km – some of which is quite steep – through rhododendron forests.

The GMVN *Tourist Rest House* (ⓣ01363/274244; ❷–❹), above the crossroads in Gwaldam, has an old cottage equipped with two exceptionally comfortable suites, as well as ordinary **rooms** and dorms (Rs100); only limited food is available. Alternatively try the good-value and traveller-friendly *Trishul* (ⓣ05962/280609; ❶–❸), where a sunny terrace offers views of the snows, if you sit in the right place. The helpful owner also operates the nearby *Mid Point Sweet and Fast Food Centre*, which is a good place for a bite to eat or to stock up on post-trekking goodies, such as beer and soya ice cream. If you're passing through Gwaldam en route to Almora, Pithoragarh or Munsiyari, better value rooms, with even better views of Trisul, are available just 20km further down the road, at **Baijnath** (see p.400).

Kumaon

The Shaivite temples of **Kumaon**, such as **Jageshwar**, **Bhageshwar** and **Baijnath**, do not attract the same fervour as their equivalents in Garhwal. Instead they remain frozen in time, undisturbed by the throngs who stick to Uttaranchal's main routes around Garhwal. In fact, the Kumaon's comparative unholiness is probably an advantage – there is far less tourist traffic, so villages are largely unspoilt and trekking routes unlittered. Hill towns like **Almora**, **Ranikhet** and **Kausani** have a charm of their own, with views towards the snows, while in **Corbett National Park**, southeast of the resort of **Nainital**, vast jungles continue to protect tiger and huge herds of wild elephant. To the east, Kumaon's border with Nepal follows the Kali valley to its watershed with Tibet; threading through it is the holy trail (closed to foreigners) to the ultimate pilgrimage site, Mount Kailash in Tibet, the abode of Shiva and his consort Parvati. Kumaon Mandal Vikas Nigam, or **KMVN** (ⓦwww.kmvn.org), are in charge of tourism in Kumaon, providing a similar (and equally patchy) range of services to GMVN in Garhwal. Unlike Garhwal, the KMVN hotels only quote season-time rates – they publish an annual tariff leaflet, which you should be able to pick up from any of their offices. There's talk that the fixed three-tier tariffs will be reintroduced in 2006.

Kumaon's **electricity** supply is capricious, with cuts occurring daily, so hotels without generators are listed as such. Note too that the only places to **change money** are Nainital and Almora (which won't change cash).

Nainital

The dramatic, peanut-shaped crater lake of Nainital (*tal* means lake), set in a mountain hollow at an altitude of 1938m, 277km north of Delhi, gives its name to the largest town in Kumaon. Discovered for Europeans in 1841 by Mr Barron, a wealthy sugar merchant, **NAINITAL** swiftly became a popular escape from the summer heat of the lowlands, and continues to be one of India's main hill stations. Throughout the year, and especially between March and July, hordes of tourists and honeymooners pack the **Mall**, the promenade that links

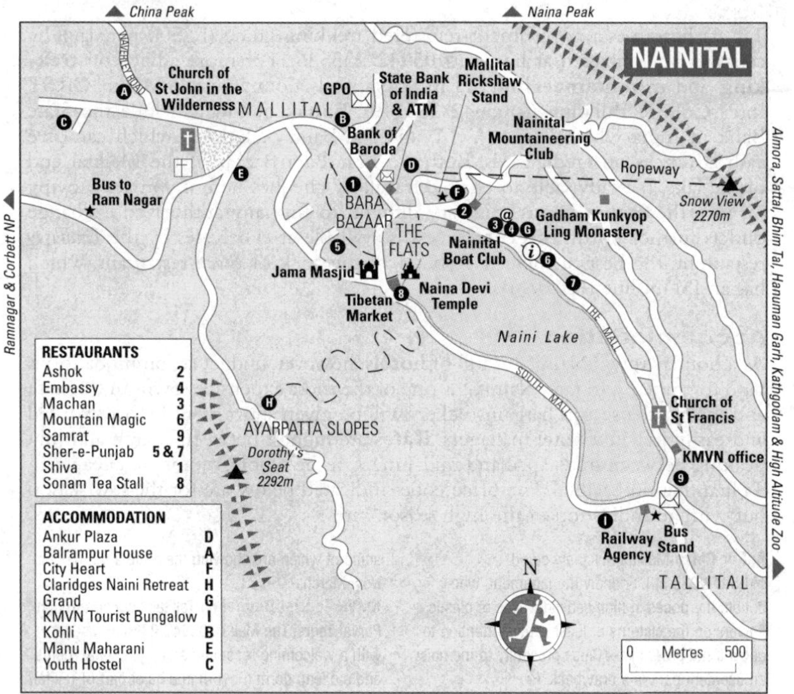

Mallital (head of the lake), the older colonial part of Nainital at the north end, with **Tallital** (foot of the lake).

Nainital's position within striking range of the inner Himalayas – the peaks are visible from vantage points above town – makes it a good base for exploring Kumaon: Corbett National Park, Almora and Ranikhet are all within easy access. When the town's commercialism gets a bit much, it's always possible to escape into the beautiful surrounding country, to lakes such as **Sat Tal** where the foothills begin their sudden drop towards the plains to the south, or to the forested ridges around **Kilbury**.

Arrival and information

Two main highways approach Nainital from opposite ends; one arrives at Mallital from Ramnagar and Corbett National Park, the other, which brings in most of the traffic, comes in at Tallital in the south. **Buses** and **taxis** from Tallital travel with great frequency to the closest railhead at **Kathgodam** near Haldwani, 40km south. The nearest airport, at **Pantnagar**, 72km south, is rarely used and best reached by taxi.

Parvat Tours and Tourist Information Centre, Tallital (Ⓣ05942/235656), a **KMVN** representative, organizes tours, car rental and books accommodation at all KMVN lodges. Cars can also be rented from agencies along the Mall, such as Hina Tours & Travels (Ⓣ05942/235860). The **Uttaranchal tourist office**, on the Mall near the Mallital end (Mon–Sat 10am–5pm; Ⓣ05942/235337), hands out leaflets and has a KMVN representative who books tours; for local info, you can also visit Ⓦwww.nainitaltourism.com. You'll often find Anil

Tiwari here too, a government-registered trekking guide (Rs500 per day), he can also be contacted at home (☎05942/235526). For more advice on **trekking** and **mountaineering**, call in at Nainital Mountaineering Club, CRST Inter College Building (☎05942/235119). **Banks** in town include the State Bank of India which has an ATM, and the Bank of Baroda, which can give cash advances on credit cards. Both are near Bara Bazaar, at the Mallital end of the lake. It is advisable to change travellers' cheques here if you are moving on into the mountains, as it is very difficult to find any authorized exchange outlets further north. **Internet** access is available at cybercafés by the *Embassy* restaurant; the best of these is Cyberia, at the back of *Swad* restaurant, which has an ISDN line (Rs20/hr).

Accommodation

As a holiday town, Nainital is full of **hotels**; however, budget accommodation is hard to come by. In fact, Nainital is one of the most expensive towns in the state and during the season bargain-seekers will be given short shrift by overworked and easily irritated hotel managers. **Rates** are highest between March and July, peaking between mid-April and mid-June. On the whole, rooms are cheaper in Tallital than in Mallital. The price codes indicated below are for the low season but with an indication of the high season rates.

Ankur Plaza Mallital rickshaw stand ☎05942/235448. Friendly management, who double the prices in high season. Vases of plastic flowers on the cisterns at least shows attention to detail if not great taste. Close proximity to the noisy amusement park is a drawback. ❷–❺

Balrampur House Waverley Rd, Mallital ☎05942/236236. Period mansion oozing with character and still owned by the Maharaja of Balrampur, whose sepia pictures hang in the hallways. The rooms ($25–100) are large and the food fairly priced, but food preparation can be slow. ❻–❾

City Heart Mallital rickshaw stand ☎05942/235228. The upper rooms are overpriced in high season, but have superb lake views. No food, but it's close to amenities, and worth coming to just to meet the eccentric manager, a wildlife photographer and bass guitarist in a local band. ❹–❻

Claridges Naini Retreat Ayarpatta Slopes ☎05942/235105. Beautifully situated high above the lake, with extensive and immaculate grounds and a great terrace for barbecues. The best rooms in town ($45-55). ❽

Grand The Mall ☎05942/235406. One of Nainital's oldest establishments, where time seems to stand still. A good location, and plenty of period atmosphere in the large, high-ceilinged rooms, some of which are showing their age a bit. Closed Nov–March. ❺–❼

KMVN Tourist Bungalow Tallital, booked through Parvat Tours, The Mall ☎05942/235656. Lodge with a welcoming reception area, functional rooms and a cheap dorm (Rs100) in a quiet part of Tallital, but not far from the bus stand. ❻

Kohli Bara Bazaar, Mallital ☎05942/236368. Budget place about ten minutes' walk from the lake. Rooms have satellite TV, hot showers and a common balcony decorated with pot plants – unusual for the price range. Rooms at the top overlook the lake and are a little more expensive. Excellent value. A sister hotel, *Kohli Cottage* (☎05942/233279; ❸–❹) is being built on the road to the zoo. ❸–❹

Manu Maharani Grasmere Estate ☎05942/237341. Luxury hotel with all mod cons, including the only bar in town, a disco, and good Szechuan food in the *Lotus Garden* restaurant. Excellent buffet breakfasts. Rooms from $60–85. ❾

Youth Hostel Mallital ☎05942/236353. Fifty dorm beds (Rs40 for YHA members, otherwise Rs60) in a charming, secluded spot with a lovely garden 1.5km above Mallital; likely to be either deserted or jammed with schoolkids. Friendly staff and excellent value – but no generator. ❶

The Town

Most of the activity around the lake of Nainital takes place along the 1.5-kilometre-long **Mall**, a promenade of restaurants, hotels and shops selling souvenirs and jumpers. Cycle rickshaws charge a standard Rs5 to go from one end to the other. A favourite pastime for day-trippers is to rent a boat for a **tour of the lake**; rates start at around Rs80 per hour out of season but can shoot up to Rs200 per hour in the summer; head for the boat club on the northeast corner of the lake in Mallital. The boat club stands on the large plain known as the **Flats**, the result of a huge landslide in 1880, which buried the *Victoria Hotel* along with 150 people. The Flats now hosts sporting events and a **Tibetan Market**. Overlooking the town is Nainital's excellent **High Altitude Zoo** (Tues–Sun 10am–4.30pm; Rs20, Rs25 for camera), a 1.5km walk uphill from the *Evelyn* hotel and home to all sorts of exotic creatures such as Siberian tigers, Tibetan wolves, leopards and Himalayan black bears. It's well managed, with detailed explanations in English and a tiny Shiva temple tucked away at the top.

A ropeway climbs from near the *Mayur* restaurant on the Mall to **Snow View** (2270m); the return ticket covers a one-hour stay (daily: summer 7am–7pm, winter 10am–5pm; Rs65 return, Rs40 single). Otherwise it's a two-kilometre hike along a choice of steep trails, which can also be undertaken on ponies for Rs100. At the top, which gets overcrowded in season, you'll find a promenade, cafés and a viewpoint; views of the snow peaks are most assured early in the morning. Trails lead on for five kilometres to **Naina Peak** (2611m) one of the best vantage points around, and to the isolated **China Peak** (pronounced "Cheena"), the craggy rise to the west. About halfway up to Snow View, conspicuous thanks to its abundant prayer flags, lies the small Tibetan *gompa* (temple) of **Gadhan Kunkyop Ling**, which has recently been rebuilt in traditional *gompa* style. Three kilometres out of town along the Almora Road, **Hanuman Garh**, a temple teeming with monkeys and young priests monkeying around, is a popular place to watch the sunset.

Moving on from Nainital

Shared taxis and **Jeeps** regularly ply the route between Tallital, Haldwani and Kathgodam, the latter being the main railway station for Nainital. **Buses** leave every thirty minutes and take around 1hr 30min to Haldwani. The **Road cum Railway Out Agency** (Mon–Sat 9am–noon & 2–5pm, Sun 9am–2pm; ⓣ05942/231010), at the Tallital bus stand, handles railway reservations. Among the trains that depart from Kathgodam are the Delhi–Kathgodam Express #5014 to **New Delhi**, the Kathgodam–Howrah Express #3020 passing through **Lucknow** to **Kolkata (Calcutta)**, and the Kumaon Express #5312 to **Agra**; the Nainital Express #5307 is a convenient overnight train to **Lucknow** leaving from Lalkuan, 14km south.

Delhi is an eight-hour ride away with either Uttaranchal government **buses** (5am, 5.30am, 7am, 8.45am & 8pm) or the Delhi Transport Corporation (8am & 7.30pm), while private operators run more comfortable coaches at around twice the price (you'll have to put up with non-stop videos). **Almora**, 67km northeast, is served by hourly direct buses (2hr 30min) and shared taxis from **Bhowali** (Rs40), 11km from Nainital. In Almora, you can catch onward services for **Pithoragarh** (9hr) and **Kausani** (5hr). There is one direct bus to Kausani at 8am (7hr) and another to **Dehra Dun** (11hr) and **Mussoorie** (13hr), with a stop at **Haridwar** (9hr). To get to Song – the start of the route to Pindari Glacier – there's a direct bus from Bhowali. For **Corbett National Park**, 113km southwest, buses run almost hourly from 7.30am until 5pm to **Ramnagar** (66km; 3hr), from where local transport is available (see p.387).

See the "Travel details" at the end of this chapter for more information on journey frequencies and durations.

Eating

Nainital has plenty of places to **eat**, with restaurants and fast-food options along the Mall geared to tourists (some close in the low season), and everyday *dhabas* (which serve cheap and tasty fish curry) in the bazaars at either end.

Ashok The Mall, Mallital. Good veg *dhaba*; cheap considering its location near the Boat Club.

Embassy The Mall, Mallital. One of Nainital's better restaurants (although many meals look better than they taste), with a wood-panelled interior. Strongest on Mughlai cooking, as well as pizzas and sizzlers.

Machan The Mall. Just west of the *Embassy*, boasting "Bronze Age chic" decor and good service, this is a well-run upstairs restaurant that's good for people-watching on the promenade below as well as excellent Indian cuisine, some of it cooked in a clay oven.

Mountain Magic The Mall. New café with sunny terrace overlooking the lake. Enjoy lattes, big salads and desserts like hot chocolate fudge from the discomfort of a wicker chair.

Samrat Hotel Tallital. A rare multi-cuisine restaurant on this *dhaba*-dominated part of the lake. Good rooftop views to go with chicken and Chinese dishes.

Sher-e-Punjab The Mall. Good Indian food, halfway along between Mallital and Tallital. A second, bigger branch, near Bara Bazaar, is just as good, a bit cheaper, and popular with locals.

Shiva Bara Bazaar, Mallital. Cheap, good and popular *dhaba* with tasty *palak paneer* and the usual casual attitude to electrical safety. The next-door clone is equally good.

Sonam Tea Stall Tibetan Market, Mallital. Roadside café in the covered section of the market selling veg *momos* (steamed dumplings) and *thukpa* (soup).

Corbett Tiger Reserve

Based at **Ramnagar**, 250km northeast of Delhi and 63km southwest of Nainital, **Corbett Tiger Reserve** is one of India's premier wildlife reserves. Established in 1936 by Jim Corbett (among others) as the Hailey National Park, India's first, and later renamed in his honour, it is one of Himalayan India's last expanses of wilderness. Almost the entire 1288-square-kilometre park, spread over the foothills of Kumaon, is sheltered by a buffer zone of mixed deciduous

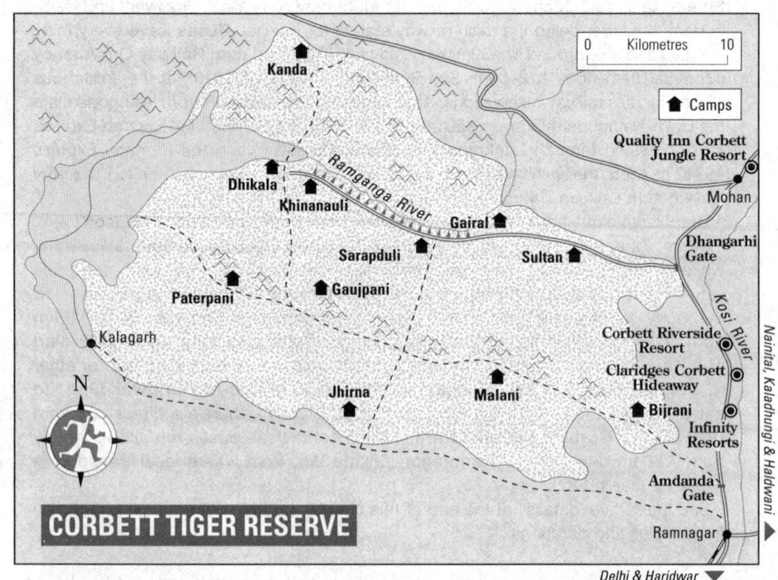

Organizing entry into Corbett Tiger Reserve

All visitors to Corbett Tiger Reserve have to obtain **permits** from the **Ramnagar reception centre** (daily 8am–noon & 1.30–4.30pm; ⓣ&ⓕ05947/251489), and are advised to **book accommodation** at least 30 days in advance (20 days for Indian nationals). If you've turned up on the off-chance of getting accommodation, poor communication between the tourist zones in the reserve, the Delhi booking office and the HQ means you may be told that rooms (and dorms) are fully booked, when they are in fact empty. No accommodation means no visiting permit, so booking thirty days ahead saves a lot of hassle. To get a permit, you have to pay at the reception centre for your entry fee, the vehicle and driver entry fees, and your accommodation. A tariff sheet spells out the various **costs**; foreigners pay up to nine times as much as Indian nationals.

Jeeps, the most convenient way to travel to and around the reserve, can only be rented at Ramnagar. Reckon on Rs1200 per day from the KMVN *Tourist Lodge* (ⓣ05947/251225), or from Girish at *Govind* restaurant (ⓣ05947/251615). Although not as reliable, **private Jeeps**, readily available outside the bus stand, are better value, costing from around Rs1000 for 24hr. As none of the traffic into the park is regulated, shop around and be clear about what you're getting for your money (fuel, a 3hr safari and driver camping fee should all be included). A Petrol 4WD, such as a Maruti Gypsy, is best as it is quiet (if the brakes are well maintained) and built for the terrain. All jeep safaris must be accompanied by a **guide** (another Rs125) – who may or may not be able to identify wildlife and speak English, and is allotted to your jeep by a rota system. If you require a guide with specific knowledge (eg for birding), write or fax the Field Director one month in advance with your request (Corbett Tiger Reserve, Ramnagar 244715, Nainital, Uttaranchal).

Note that Corbett is only **open** between 15 November and 15 June. Between June and November the monsoons flood the riverbanks, and cut the fragile road links.

and giant *sal* forests, which provide impenetrable cover for wildlife. Most of the core area of 520 square kilometres at its heart remains out of bounds, and safaris on foot are only permissible in the fringe forests.

Corbett is most famous for its big cats, and in particular the **tiger** – this was the first designated Project Tiger Reserve, in 1973 – but its 143 tigers are extremely elusive. Sightings are very far from guaranteed, and should be regarded as an unlikely bonus. Nonetheless, although there have been problems elsewhere with the project, and the very survival of the tiger in India is in serious jeopardy (see Contexts, p.1416), Corbett does at least seem to be prioritizing the needs of tigers over those of other wildlife and of tourists. Still, **poaching** is not unheard of – five tigers were killed in the Himalayan foothills in early 2001, two inside the Corbett boundaries. It's Corbett's **elephants**, however, that face a more serious threat. Around two dozen are killed each year in and around the park; poisoned by plantation workers or shot by farmers for hide, meat and, most importantly, their valuable tusks. The park's 627 elephants – 100 of them males with tusks – have been confined within its boundaries since the construction of the Ramganga reservoir in 1974 blocked migratory routes that formerly ranged as far as Rajaji National Park, 200km west. The best place to see them is around the picturesque Dhikala camp near the reservoir; spring is the best time, when the water level drops and the animals have more space to roam. The reservoir also shelters populations of **gharial**, a long-snouted, fish-eating crocodile, and **maggar**, a large marsh crocodile, as well as other reptiles. Jackal are common, and wild boar run through the camps in the evenings. The grasslands around Dhikala are home to deer species such as the spotted **chital**, hog and barking

△ Bengal tigers, Corbett Reserve

deer and the larger **sambar**, while rhesus and common langur, the two main classes of Indian **monkeys**, are both abundant, and happy to provide in-camp entertainment. Bird life ranges from water birds such as the pied kingfisher to **birds of prey**, including the crested serpent eagle, Pallas's fishing eagle and Himalayan greyheaded fishing eagle.

The closest of the various **gates** into the park, 1km from central Ramnagar, is Amdanda on the road to **Bijrani camp**, 11km away, a base for day-trips. **Dhangarhi Gate**, 18km along the highway north to Ranikhet, provides access to the northern and northwestern portion of the park along the Ramganga river valley, and to the main camp of **Dhikala**.

Ramnagar

Situated in the rich farm-belt of the *terai*, on the southeastern fringes of the great forests, the busy market town of **RAMNAGAR** is the administrative hub for **Corbett Tiger Reserve**. **Permits** and **accommodation reservations** are issued at the **reception centre**, about 200m north of the bus stand towards Nainital (see box on p.389). There's little to do around Ramnagar itself except go **fishing** (Oct 1–June 30). At Lohachaur, 15km north along the River Kosi, good anglers are in with a chance of landing the legendary *mahseer*, a redoubtable battling river carp. Fishing permits must be sought from the Corbett Tiger Reserve reception centre; most resorts also arrange all-inclusive fishing trips.

Ramnagar is served by frequent **buses** to and from Nainital and Ranikhet, 112km north. Buses arrive every half-hour or so after the eight-hour trip from **Delhi**; Delhi Transport Corporation run a semi-deluxe service (Rs120), and most of the alternatives are pretty basic. Although most tourists head straight to Dhikala in the park as soon as they arrive, Ramnagar does have some **accommodation**. The KMVN *Tourist Lodge* (Ⓣ05947/251225; ❸–❺), next to the Corbett Tiger Reserve reception, is as institutional as usual, with a dorm (Rs60) as well as spartan doubles. A further 200m south on the main road, down the lane opposite *Govind* restaurant, the basic *Everest* (Ⓣ05947/251099; ❷) has sunny balconies, but no running hot water in the attached bathrooms; a little further still is the cheaper, less salubrious *Rameshwaram* (Ⓣ05947/252664; ❶–❸), whose only advantage is that it's the quietest. On the main road, *Govind* is a good multi-cuisine **restaurant**, strongest on Indian food.

There is no official **currency exchange**, though Anuradha confectionary store, 400m south of *Govind*, will change sterling, euros and dollars if you're really stuck.

Moving on from Ramnagar, there are six daily government buses to Haridwar, three to Nainital and ten to Delhi. The only direct **train** to Delhi leaves at 9.10pm and arrives at 6.30am, with interminable stops along the way. For faster trains and connections to other parts change at Moradabad. The nearest **airport**, at Pantnagar, 80km southeast, is rarely used.

Dhikala

Beautifully situated overlooking the Ramganga reservoir and the forested hills beyond, Corbett's main camp, **DHIKALA**, lies 49km northwest of Ramnagar. As you can only stray beyond the confines of the camp on elephant-back or in a car or Jeep, the whole place has something of the air of a military encampment. **Accommodation**, all bookable via the Corbett Tiger Reserve reception in Ramnagar, ranges from the 24 bunk beds in the *Log Huts* (Rs200) to more comfortable bungalows and cabins (❻–❽) which sleep two. Indian and Western **food** is available in the KMVN-run *Parvat* restaurant, which also has a reading room and outdoor area where you can watch film shows on wildlife (in Hindi).

The same quality food is served at cheaper prices and minus the 8 percent sales tax at a *dhaba* at the other end of the camp, which is frequented by the park staff and drivers. **Entry fees** into the park, payable at the Ramnagar reception centre, are higher here than at Ramnagar.

It's normally possible to see plenty of animals and birds from the Dhikala **watchtower,** which is a 1km wander down the path near the restaurant (turn left at the crossroads of tracks); bring binoculars, remain quiet, and don't wear bright colours or perfume. Chital, sambar, and various other deer species find refuge in the savannah grasslands known as the *chaur*, behind the camp to the south, and tigers are occasionally drawn in looking for prey. Two-hour **elephant rides** (Rs250 per person; first-come-first-served) explore this sea of grass, rarely penetrating far into the deep jungles beyond; try to convince your *mahout* (elephant driver) to venture in, as they can be quite magical.

On the way to Dhikala from the Dhangarhi gate, the road passes through magnificent forest – if you have your own transport, stop at the **High Bank** vantage point, and try to spot crocodile or even elephant on the river below. If it's late, you can stop for a night halt en route at the *Sultan* (❺), *Gairal* (❻) and *Sarapduli* (❻) forest rest houses, bookable through the Reserve reception centre. The bungalows are surrounded by deep forest; as movement on foot is prohibited, you'll only see wild animals that stray close to or into the compound.

Resort accommodation around Corbett

A number of self-contained **resorts** are springing up on the fringes of Corbett, providing a higher standard of accommodation than in Dhikala or Ramnagar

Jim Corbett (1875–1955)

Hunter of man-eating tigers, photographer, conservationist and author, **Jim Corbett** was born in Nainital of English and Irish parentage. A childhood spent around the Corbett winter home of Kaladhungi (halfway between Nainital and Ramnagar, and now a rather disappointing memorial to him) brought young Jim into close communion with nature and to an instinctive understanding of jungle ways. After working on the railways, he joined the Indian army in 1917 at the age of 40, rising to the rank of Lieutenant Colonel, and seeing action in Flanders at the head of the 70th Kumaon Company.

Known locally as "Carpet Sahib", a mispronunciation of his name, Jim Corbett was called upon time and time again to rid the hills of Kumaon of **man-eating tigers** and leopards. Normally shy of human contact, such animals become man-eaters when infirmity brought upon by old age or wounds renders them unable to hunt their usual prey. Many of those killed by Corbett were found to have suppurating wounds caused by porcupine quills embedded deep in their paws; tigers always seem to fall for the porcupine's simple defensive trick of walking backwards in line with its lethal quills.

One of Corbett's most memorable exploits was the killing of the **Champawat tiger**, which was responsible for a documented 436 human deaths, and was bold enough to steal its victims from the midst of human habitation; he also terminated the careers of the Chowgarh tigress, the Talla Des and the Mohan man-eaters. By the mid-1930s, though, Corbett had become dismayed with the increasing number of hunters in the Himalayas and the resultant decline in wildlife, and diverted his energies into conservation, swapping his gun for a movie camera and spending months capturing tigers on film. His adventures are described in books such as *My India*, *Jungle Lore* and *Man-Eaters of Kumaon*; Martin Booth's *Carpet Sahib* is an excellent biography of a remarkable man. Awarded the Order of the British Empire in recognition of his lifelong work with nature, Jim Corbett was unhappy in post-Independence India, and left to retire in East Africa. He continued his conservation efforts until his death at the age of eighty.

– at a price – as well as guides for expeditions in the neighbouring forests, which can be as rich in wildlife as the park, without the restrictions.

Claridges Corbett Hideaway Garija, Ramnagar ⓣ05947/284132 or 011/2641 3303, ⓦwww.corbetthideaway.com. Luxurious terracotta-coloured huts ($200–220) with all mod cons, dotted around a pleasant orchard on a bluff overlooking the river and pretending to be rustic without success. Safaris and the usual tours arranged. ⑨

Corbett Riverside Resort Garija, Ramnagar ⓣ05947/284125, ⓦwww.corbettriverside.com. A picturesque setting, 10km north of Ramnagar looking across the River Kosi to forest-covered cliffs. Some buildings on a ledge above the extensive beach area. Rooms $55–85; off-season discounts available. ⑧–⑨

Infinity Resorts Garija, Ramnagar ⓣ05947/2804103 ⓦwww.tigercorbettindia.com. Corbett's most ostentatious resort overlooks the Kosi and the forested hills beyond, with large comfortable rooms ($135–155), a library, a well-stocked bar and a swimming pool. Activities include nature trails with the resort's own naturalists, jungle rides, fishing, trekking and films. ⑨

Quality Inn Corbett Jungle Resort Kumeria Reserve Forest, Mohan ⓣ05947/287820, ⓔqicjr@hotmail.com. Wood-panelled stone cottages ($100) in a leafy mango orchard above the Kosi, 29km from Ramnagar on the road north to Ranikhet, 9km beyond the Dhangarhi gate. Elephant rides into the forest and safaris into the park itself; food is included in the rates, and there are good off-season discounts. ⑨

Ranikhet

The small and deliberately undeveloped hill station of **RANIKHET**, 50km west of Almora, is essentially an army cantonment, the home of the Kumaon Rifles. New construction is confined to the **Sadar Bazaar** area, while the rest of the town above it, climbing up towards the crest of the hill, retains atmospheric leafy pine woods. Beautiful forest trails abound, including short cuts from the bazaar to the Mall; leopards still roam some of the more remote areas within the town boundaries, despite efforts by army officers to prove their hunting skills. There's little to do in Ranikhet, and that's its attraction – if you need to take time out from India, in a peaceful environment, this is a good place.

Ranikhet's "Mall", 3km above the town (Rs50 in a taxi), is something of a misnomer; it is simply a quiet road running along the wooded crest of the ridge, with few buildings apart from officers' messes. For a taste of Indian military life, men and women can join the **Ranikhet Officers' Club** (ⓣ05966/220611; Rs50/day), half-way up the hill, which has a rather fine bar, restaurant and billiards room, and features men with grand moustaches calling each other chaps.

Above the Narsingh Stadium Parade Ground, the **KRC Shawl and Tweed Factory and Outlet** (summer Mon–Sat 9am–7pm, Sun 10am–5pm; winter Mon–Sat 10am–6pm, Sun 10am–5pm), located in an old church equipped with looms and wheels, offers the opportunity to watch the weavers in action, a fascinating display of concentration, dexterity and counting. The herringbone and houndstooth tweeds are sold in the shop next door.

Practicalities

Buses from all over Kumaon, including the railhead at Kathgodam, 84km away, arrive at the bazaar, at either of two bus stops. The KMOU stand, on the Haldwani road, is the base for buses to Haldwani (10–12 daily; 4hr), the nearest town to Kathgodam; the Kausani–Pithoragarh bus also departs (2 or 3 daily; 4hr) from this stand. There are three buses daily direct to Nainital (9am, 11am and noon), or else you can change at Bhowali; frequent shared Jeeps also ply this route (Rs60). The Roadways (Almora) Bus Stand, 500m on, is used by regular bus and shared Jeep services to Almora (2hr). The **taxi rank** is just above the KMOU bus stand.

The **Uttaranchal tourist bureau**, above the Almora Bus Stand (Mon–Sat 10am–5pm; ⓣ05966/220227), has very little information to offer. The **post office** is at the top of the Mall.

Accommodation and eating

If you're just passing through Ranikhet, **hotels** in the busy bazaar are sufficient, while the Mall is better for an extended stay. Bear in mind that seasonal fluctuations can double prices, especially around June and July; the prices listed here apply to low season. **Eating** choices are pretty limited; the best food is found in the better hotels, but there are a few simple cafés and *dhabas* in the market area.

KMVN Tourist Bungalow The Mall ⓣ05966/220893. A well-kept complex of bungalows and a cheap dorm (Rs60) in a beautiful wooded spot. Follow the sign 1km from the *Meghdoot* and it's 0.5km down the forest track. ❺–❻

Meghdoot The Mall ⓣ05966/220475. Comfortable suites set back from balconies full of potted plants and flowers, with running hot water, parking and room service, plus a good mid-price restaurant that serves up a range of tasty biriyani and *pulao*. Off season discounts up to 50 percent. ❻

Norton's The Mall ⓣ05966/220377. Spacious family-run hotel established in 1880, with a cosy lounge featuring paintings by previous guests. The friendly manager still remembers the Raj and the atmosphere is very Anglo-Indian; the architecture and furniture is English in style but the bright colour schemes and toilets are decidedly local. ❸–❹

Rajdeep Bazaar ⓣ05966/220017. The best budget hotel in the bazaar area and nearly always busy. A bit noisy, but clean, with long verandas facing the snow peaks. The arrival of room service is announced by a spooky door buzzer that chimes "may I come in?" ❷–❺

Rosemount The Mall ⓣ05966/220989 or ⓣ011/2275 3151. Converted Raj-era mansion, 2km from the main road, deep in the woods. Lavishly restored rooms ($45), restaurant, and gardens complete with lawn tennis, croquet, badminton and snow views. There's also a four-person cottage ($70). Up to 50 percent discounts off-season. ❽–❾

Almora and around

ALMORA, 67km north of Nainital, is one of the rare Kumaoni towns which, with its cobbled alleyways and wood and stone buildings, conspicuously predates the Raj. Founded by the Chand dynasty in 1560, and occupied successively by the Gurkhas and the British, it remains a major market town, and is considered the cultural capital of the region. Set at a pleasant altitude of 1646m on rambling ridges that look towards the inner Himalayan snows, Almora's peaceful environs have attracted an eclectic assortment of visitors over the years, including Swami Vivekananda, Timothy Leary and the Tibetologist author of *The Way of the White Clouds*, Lama Angarika Govinda.

Arrival and information

Almora has regular **bus** connections with Nainital (1 daily; 3hr), Ranikhet (5 daily; 2hr 30min), Kathgodam, the nearest railhead (hourly; 4hr), and Kausani (6 daily; 2hr 30min). Most buses use either of two adjacent stands on the Mall, which has a **taxi stand** close by if you're heading for the *Deodar Holiday-Inn*. Another bus stand at Dharanaula, on the other side of the market above the Mall, is for buses to the interior of Kumaon; distant destinations such as Munsiyari and Pithoragarh have early morning departures. Access to much of the centre, including the market area, is restricted to pedestrians.

Uttaranchal Tourism maintains a **tourist office**, dishing out local info, next to the *Savoy Hotel* above the GPO (Mon–Sat 10am–5pm; ⓣ05962/230180). There are two KMVN offices - one is at the *Holiday*

Home hotel on the Mall 2km west of the centre (ⓣ05962/230250), the other next to the Gandhi statue at Chaudhan Pata, the Mall (ⓣ05962/230706). Technically, the latter covers a wider area, though both will book KMVN packages and accommodation throughout Kumaon; the *Holiday Home* also houses Almora's computerized **railways reservation centre** (9am–noon & 2–5pm). The best places to find out about taxi excursions, **treks** or equipment hire and guides are Discover Himalaya (ⓣ05962/236890; ⓔdiscoverhimalaya@sancharnet.in) and High Adventure (ⓣ05962/232277, ⓔhighadventure@rediffmail.com), both on the Mall. Discover Himalaya also offer yoga meditation packages (from Rs300 per day) at their holiday camp at Jalna, 25km east of Almora, and rock-climbing courses. The State Bank of India (Mon–Sat 10am–2pm & 3–4pm) on the Mall will only change American Express travellers' cheques. Nainital is the nearest town that will **change currency** and other cheques.

A few places along the Mall offer **Internet** access - the going rate is around Rs35 - but the nearest server is in Dehra Dun and the connection is tortuously slow. All but Joshi PCO, next to Discover Himalaya (daily 7am–10pm) close around 8pm.

Should you need a **doctor**, there's a good clinic run by Dr Gusain (daily: summer 8.30am–3.30pm & 5–7.30pm, winter 9.30am–3pm & 4–6.30pm; ⓣ05962/231423) just west of Punjab National Bank on the Mall. The sign is in Hindi, so ask if you can't find it; a consultation costs Rs50.

Accommodation

Accommodation in Almora itself is largely centred along the Mall. However, there's a thriving long-term travellers' scene around Kasar Devi (nicknamed "hippyland" by some locals); enquire about rooms to rent at the chai shops in Kalimath nearby.

Bansal Hotel Lala Bazaar ⓣ05962/230864. At the top of the lane opposite *Hotel Shikhar*, and next door to the expresso bar (see below). Spotless, simple rooms with en-suite bath (free hot bucket water), fantastic rooftop views and very friendly management, who'll deliver lassis to your room. The top room is the best. Fixed price year round. ❶

Deodar Holiday-Inn Sister Nivedita Cottage, the Mall ⓣ05962/231295. Time seems to have forgotten this friendly place, home to Swami Vivekananda and his disciple Nivedita between 1890 and 1898. The rooms are simple – the pricier ones have geysers and a TV – and there's a lovely sunny terrace and tranquil patio with a log fire at night. Fixed prices year round. ❸

Konark The Mall ⓣ05962/231217. The lobby may be full of disco-era furniture but the rooms are simple, clean and tasteful. Good value – one of the best in its price range, especially with off-season discounts – and well located. ❸

Savoy Police Line, above the GPO ⓣ05962/230329. A quiet place, away from the noise of the Mall but still central, and with pleasant gardens, a veranda and good restaurant. Spacious, dim rooms; if you go for a deluxe room, make sure it has a geyser. ❸–❺

Shikhar The Mall ⓣ05962/230253, ⓔhotelshikar@rediffmail.com. Don't be put off by the exterior or expensive reputation at what is Almora's central landmark. There's a wide range of rooms, some at very reasonable prices, most with balconies. The welcoming, cavernous restaurant serves good breakfasts, and there's an Internet café (Rs60/hour). Fixed prices year round, and a generator. ❶–❼

Shyam LR Sah Rd, 100m beyond the *Shikhar*, visible from the Mall ⓣ05962/235467, ⓦwww.hotelshyam.com. Clean en-suite rooms with cable TV, a great rooftop restaurant, dorm (Rs50) and generator. Off-season discounts up to 50 percent. ❹

The town

Although most of Almora's official business is conducted along the **Mall**, the **market area**, immediately above and parallel to it along the crest of the saddle, holds much more of interest. Exploring its well-stocked bazaars, knitted together with lanes flanked by beautifully carved wooden facades, at times you feel as though you're drifting into the distant past. Among items you might want to buy are *khadi* (home-spun) cotton textiles and ready-mades from the Gandhi Ashram near the bus stands, and local woollens from Garur Woollens or Kumaon Woollens on the Mall. However, the great local tradition is the manufacture of **tamta**, beaten copper pots plated with silver, which are sold in the busy Lala Bazaar and the Chowk area at the northeast end of the market.

Towards the top of town, beyond Chowk, a compound holds a group of Chand-period stone **temples**. The main one, a squat single-storey structure, is dedicated to **Nanda Devi**, the goddess embodied in the region's highest mountain. More typical of Kumaoni temple architecture are two larger Shaivite painted stone temples, capped with umbrella-like wooden roofs covering their stone *amalaka* (circular crowns). During September a large fair is held here in honour of Nanda Devi.

Eating

Cafés and **restaurants** are strung along the Mall, especially around the bazaar area; locally grown and prepared Kumaon rice and black dhal are particularly delicious. Hotels such as the *Savoy* can produce a feast of Kumaoni dishes, if given plenty of advance warning.

Bansal Expresso Bar Lala Bazaar. Italian-style café, complete with marble-topped tables, serving up the best chai and shakes in town, plus frothy Nescafé and freshly made snacks. The banana lassis are legendary.

Dolma Kalimath, 5km west of the town. A café run by Tibetans that shows the locals how it's done. Located at a beauty spot with a view of the Himalayas. *Momos*, beer and outdoor seating.

Glory The Mall, near *Shikhar Hotel*. Multi-cuisine café-cum-restaurant, strong on north Indian cooking.

Madras Café The Mall, opposite the *Glory*. The name is misleading, as the emphasis is on good-value north Indian food. Tasty coffee, too.

Soni Dhaba The Mall bus stand. Excellent, Sikh-run *dhaba*: famed for its chicken dishes, it can get crowded.

Swagat The Mall. Large café a few doors down from the *Shikhar*, with *dosas* and other snacks as well as meals.

Binsar and Jageshwar

Both **Binsar** and **Jageshwar** are in easy reach of Almora and can be visited as a day-trip (around Rs450 return for a taxi) although it's well worth overnighting at both places, as they are lovely spots. **BINSAR**, known locally as Jhandi Dhar (hill top), 34km north of Almora, rises in isolation to a commanding 2412m. A steep road leads 11km up from the main Almora–Bageshwar highway to a tourist complex near the top of the hill (Ⓣ05962/280176; ❹–❺), offering bland but comfortable **accommodation**. This was the summer capital of Kumaon's kings, the Chandras, but today little remains in the area except the bulbous stone Shiva temple of **Bineshwar** 3km below the summit. Most visitors come to see the 300-kilometre panorama of Himalayan peaks along the northern horizon, including, from west to east Kedarnath, Chaukhamba, Trisul, Nandaghunti, Nanda Devi, Nandakot and Panchuli. Closer at hand, you can enjoy quiet forest walks through oak and rhododendron woods. Recently designated a nature reserve, Binsar is rich in alpine flora, ferns, hanging moss and wild flowers.

JAGESHWAR, 34km northeast of Almora, is the very heart of Kumaon, a place where language and customs seem to have resisted change. An idyllic small river meanders through dark pines for 3km off the main road from **Artola** (Rs22 bus from Almora), stumbling onto a complex of 124 ancient shrines and temples which cluster at the base of venerable *deodar* trees. Jageshwar village retains much of its traditional charm, with stone-paved lanes and beautifully carved wooden doors and windows painted in green, turquoise and other striking colours. **Accommodation** can be found either in the large, comfortable KMVN *Tourist Bungalow* (☎05962/263028; ❸–❹), which also has a dorm (Rs60), or up the hill at *Tara Guesthouse* (☎05962/263068; ❶); there is also a sprinkling of simple **dhabas**. Good local **walks** include the steep three-kilometre ascent through beautiful pine forests to the small hamlet and stone temples of **Vriddha** or **Briddh Jageshwar** (Old Jageshwar), with an extensive panorama from the mountains of Garhwal to the massifs of western Nepal. A trail from here leads 12km along an undulating ridge to Binsar (see opposite); the trail finally emerges from the woods near the stone temple of **Bineshwar**.

Kausani and around

Spreading from east to west along a narrow pine-covered ridge, 52km northwest of Almora, the village of **KAUSANI** has become a popular resort thanks to its spectacular Himalayan panorama. It's a simple day-trip from Almora, though as the peaks – Nanda Choti, Trisul, Nanda Devi and Panchol – are at their best at dawn and dusk, it's worth staying overnight. The tourist scene is growing and a number of new hotels and restaurants have sprung up in recent years to cater for the very seasonal demand. There are several **ashrams**, including one that once housed Mahatma Gandhi, who walked here in 1929, thirty years before the road came through. Gandhi-ism continues to be a major influence in these hills and his symbol of self-reliance, the spinning wheel, is still used in homes in the area. There are numerous possibilities for short **day-hikes** in the woods and valleys around Kausani, as well as longer excursions to the important pilgrimage sites of **Baijnath** and **Bageshwar**. Kausani is well connected by **bus** to Almora and Ranikhet, and Bageshwar and Gwaldam further north.

Practicalities

The Global Cyber Café near Snow View Point above town offers **Internet** access (Rs40/hr), telescopes for admiring the peaks and the stars, and a knowledgeable owner who bills himself as Kausani's unofficial **tourist officer**.

As for **eating**, the *Ashok* **restaurant** near Snow View Point above town and the *Uttarkhand Tourist Lodge* serve inexpensive multi-cuisine dishes – the latter also has local Kumaoni specialities, a wonderful terrace and imported goodies like olive oil and parmesan. You can get snacks at the *Global Cyber Café*.

Accommodation

The prices below are for the **low season**, but go up by fifty percent in high season (April 15–June 15 & Oct 1–Nov 15). Rooms with views are much more expensive than those without.

Anashakti Ashram Snow View Rd, looking down on the Mall ☎05962/258028. Guests prepared to observe ashram rules, such as attending prayers and not smoking, are welcome to stay at Gandhi's pleasant but spartan former ashram. Even if you don't stay it's worth visiting the main prayer hall which doubles as a Gandhi museum. Good views, but no generator. ❶

Himalaya Mount View 1km north of town towards Baijnath ☎05962/258080. Very quiet and rather pleasant, with chunky but elegant wooden furnishings and tile floors. Little English is spoken. ❹–❼

Krishna Mountview ☎05962/258008, Ⓦwww.kumaonindia.com. Huge place next to the Gandhi Ashram with lovely gardens, comfortable rooms, a gym and an expensive restaurant. Friendly management, and good views of the snows through the telescope in the garden. ❺–❼

Uttarkhand Tourist Lodge Up the steps that head north from the bus stand ☎05962/258012. Foreigner-friendly place that can offer good hiking advice and makes a great place to hang out. Clean doubles and a great terrace with Himalayan views; the second-storey rooms with satellite TV and flush bidet toilets are the best value. ❷–❸

Baijnath and Bageshwar

BAIJNATH is halfway between Kausani, 20km southeast, and Gwaldam to the west. The road (served by occasional buses) drops down to a broad valley and to eleventh-century stone temples, standing at a bend in a beautiful river. This was once an important town of the Katyurs, who ruled much of Garhwal and Kumaon; now it's more like a park. Unusually, the main temple is devoted to Parvati, the consort of Shiva, rather than Shiva himself; its 1.5-metre image of the goddess is one of the few in the complex to have withstood the ravages of time. The only **amenities** are KMVN's modern *Tourist Rest House* (Ⓣ05963/254101; ❶–❷) – which has large en-suite rooms, a dorm (Rs50), a garden and great views of Trishul – and a couple of simple cafés.

BAGESHWAR, nestled in a steamy valley 90km north of Almora, is one of Kumaon's most important pilgrimage towns. The lush Gomti River valley around is lovely, the market is a good place to stock up on provisions, and it's used by hikers as the base for the trek to Pindari. Most foreigners stay at the rooms or dorm (Rs50) at the large, ugly, KMVN *Tourist Bungalow* (Ⓣ05963/222034; ❷–❹), 2km south of the bus station across a bridge; there are basic *dharamshalas* and *dhabas* around the temple.

Pithoragarh

Occupying the beautiful sprawling Sore valley, 188km northeast of Nainital, **PITHORAGARH** is the headquarters of the easternmost district of Kumaon and a busy administrative and market town which acts as a gateway to the mountains. While the town itself is not attractive, and only worth stopping at to stock up on provisions for expeditions, the fringes remain charming with terraced cultivation at an altitude of around 1650m offering glimpses of Panchuli and the remote mountains of western Nepal. Above Pithoragarh, in the pine-wooded slopes of the **Leprosy Mission** at Chandag 7km north, a large cross overlooks the valley, commanding views of the Saipal and Api massifs in western Nepal. It makes a pleasant walk up from the *Tourist Bungalow*, or you can take local buses en route for Bans.

Despite Pithoragarh's proximity to **Nepal**, the official border crossing for foreigners is a four-hour drive south at **Banbassa**, where 60-day visas are available for $30 and public transport can shuttle you across the frontier.

Practicalities

Uttaranchal Tourism's low-key **tourist office**, toward the top of the town, just beyond the BRO roundabout at Siltham (Mon–Sat 10am–5pm;

Trekking restrictions in eastern Kumaon

With the gradual shrinking of the Inner Line and the removal of restrictions, the mountains of Pithoragarh District are being opened up to trekkers. Ironically, while foreigners do not require **permits** on certain routes, Indians – including trekking agents – still do. Starting at Tawaghat, the trail via Nue to Johlingkang near the base of Om Parvat (6191m) aka Chotta ("small") Kailash, is currently open. Although the main Kailash trail to Tibet also starts at Tawaghat, access is allowed, via the idyllic Narayan Ashram, only as far as Budhi. Milam Glacier (see opposite) north of Munsiyari has also been derestricted. If the local tourist office and local trekking agencies can't provide the necessary information regarding current regulations, contact the Sub-Divisional Magistrates (SDM) at Pithoragarh, Dharchula or Munsiyari, who are responsible for issuing permits.

☎05964/225527), has information on current trekking restrictions. Hill **buses** and shared **taxis** stop at the main **Roadways Bus Stand**, near the centre below the bazaar; the smaller **KMOU Bus Stand**, 1km to the north, also services hill destinations. Private bus companies and USRTC buses connect the town with **Nainital** (8hr; 1 daily) and **Almora** (6hr; 3 daily), as well as the railheads of **Tanakpur**, 151km south, and **Kathgodam**, 212km southeast. Although amenities in town remain limited, Pithoragarh's busy markets are worth a browse for trek supplies.

Hotel **accommodation** is basic and, for once, the KMVN *Tourist Lodge* (☎05964/225434; dorm Rs50; ❸), tucked away in the woods 1.5km above the bazaar on the Chandag Road, comes out tops. The more central *Ulka Priyadarshani* (☎05964/225596; ❷–❸), in the top bazaar between the Roadways bus stand and BRO roundabout, is a decent, clean budget hotel. A couple of doors down Pithoragarh's best **restaurant**, the first-floor *Shagun*, serves wonderful Indian food and is a respite from the crowded bazaar. *Meghna*, in Simalgair Bazaar, a large, popular, noisy snack bar, specializes in sweets and masala dosa. There's an **Internet** café next door (Rs20/hr), though both the power and the connection are erratic.

Munsiyari

The sprawling village of **MUNSIYARI** stands at the threshold of the inner Himalayas, 154km north of Pithoragarh, looking down on the Gori River gorge and deep valleys branching up into the high mountains. Vantage spots throughout the area offer breathtaking views of the five almost-symmetrical **Panchuli Peaks**, which owe their name – the "five cooking pots" – to their plumes of wind-blown snow. These are notorious for their bad weather, but on clear days at Munsiyari you feel you could almost reach out and touch them.

Among spectacular local high-mountain walks, which are being increasingly derestricted (see box, opposite), is the gentle 11km trail up to the **Kalika Pass** (2700m), where a small Shakti temple stands amid dark pines. More difficult trails lead, via the small village of **Matkot**, 12km away, to the glaciers in the Panchuli group, and 30km away to the large alpine meadows of **Chiplakot Bugyal**, dotted with tiny lakes, as well as up to the Milam Glacier and the Johar valley.

Many of the local people are **Bhotias** of Tibetan stock. They've absorbed Indian religious and cultural practices over the ages, though their origins can be seen in their weaving of carpets, adorned with the ubiquitous dragon motif, and in cultural practices such as animal sacrifice – a festive and bloody picnic for all and sundry. Carpets are sold by Pratpsing Pangtey, an elderly man who runs a small factory just below the bus stand.

Practicalities

Munsiyari is at the end of the road, so few **buses** come this way and those that do are very basic; there are daily departures to **Pithoragarh** (5.30am; 8hr) and **Almora** (4am; 11hr). Most people arrive here by shared Jeep; you'll have to change at Thal for the last four hours of the journey. Along with KMVN's *Tourist Lodge* (☎05961/22339; ❹), which has dorms (Rs60) as well as rooms, there are a couple of simple **lodges** near the bus stand, the best of which is the *Hansling* (☎05961/222321; ❷–❸). Great views, friendly owners and a range of comfy and recently renovated rooms has made this a popular choice with foreign trekkers. A handful of **trekking agencies** are cropping up around the bazaar, including Panchuli Trekking (☎059612/262554), while Prem Ram, of Gram Bunga, Tala, Nayabasti, is a recommended guide who can organize treks, including cooks and porters, from around Rs150 per head per day. He's contactable via all local hotels.

Travel details

Trains

Haridwar to: Dehra Dun (8 daily; 2hr); Delhi (4 daily; 4hr 30min–8hr); Kathgodam (3 daily; 4hr 30min–8hr); Kolkata (Calcutta) (1 daily; 33hr); Mumbai (1 daily; 40hr); Rishikesh (2 daily; 30min).
Kathgodam (railhead 3hr from Nainital) to: Delhi (2 daily; 8hr); Kolkata (Calcutta) (1 daily; 40hr).

Buses

Almora to: Delhi (3 daily; 11hr); Nainital (1 daily; 3hr).
Dehra Dun to: Delhi (hourly; 7hr); Kullu/Manali (1 daily; 14hr); Mussoorie (every 30min; 1hr); Nainital (5 daily; 11hr); Rishikesh (every 30min; 1hr 30min).
Haridwar to: Dehra Dun (hourly; 1hr 15min); Delhi (4–6 daily; 5–6hr); Rishikesh (20 daily; 30min).
Mussoorie to: Dehra Dun (every 30min; 1hr); Delhi (2 daily; 9hr); Haridwar (every 30min; 3hr); Rishikesh (every 30min; 4hr); Uttarkashi (2 daily; 7hr).
Nainital to: Almora (4 daily; 3hr); Dehra Dun (1 daily; 10hr 30min); Delhi (4 daily; 8hr); Kausani (4 daily; 5hr); Ramnagar (4 daily; 3hr 30min); Ranikhet (4 daily; 3hr).
Rishikesh to: Dehra Dun (every 30min; 1hr 30min); Haridwar (every 30min; 1hr); Janki Chatti for Yamunotri (4 daily; 10hr); Joshimath (3 daily, 10hr); Nainital (1 daily; 9hr).

Flights

Dehra Dun to: Delhi (6 weekly; 1hr).

Highlights

CHAPTER 5

Highlights

* **Sanchi** A finely restored Buddhist stupa complex, complete with intricately carved gateways. See p.417

* **Pachmarhi** The only hill station in central India, where you can trek to the top of a sacred Shiva peak, hunt out prehistoric rock art or just relax in the cool air. See p.425

* **Orchha** Central India at its most exotic: crumbling riverside tombs and ornate Rajput palaces amid lush, tranquil countryside. See p.438

* **Khajuraho** Two groups of temples swathed in blatantly erotic sculpture, lost for centuries in thick jungle but now beautifully restored. See p.443

* **Kanha and Bandhavgarh national parks** Archetypal Kipling country, teeming with wildlife, including tigers and leopards. See p.457 & p.460

* **Mandu** A medieval fort atop a plateau where the emperor got down to serious pleasure-seeking in his vast harem, theatre, steam baths and pavilions. See p.467

△ Orchha

5

Madhya Pradesh

Hot, dusty **MADHYA PRADESH** is a vast landlocked expanse of scrub-covered hills, sun-parched plains and dense tree cover that accounts for one third of India's forests. Stretching from beyond the headwaters of the mighty **River Narmada** to the fringes of the Western Ghats, it's a transitional zone between the Gangetic lowlands in the north and the high dry **Deccan plateau** to the south.

Despite its diverse array of exceptional attractions, ranging from ancient **temples** and hilltop **forts** to some of India's best **tiger reserves**, Madhya Pradesh receives only a fraction of the tourist traffic that pours between Delhi, Agra, Varanasi and the south. For those that do make the effort, this gem of a state is both culturally rewarding and largely hassle-free – a welcome break after Rajasthan, for example. While interest from tour groups is rising, the only place you're likely to meet more than a handful of **tourists** is the palace at Orchha, at Khajuraho, one of India's most celebrated temple sites, and at the tiger reserves of Kanha and Bandhavgarh.

Any exploration of central India will be illuminated if you have a grasp of its long and turbulent **history.** Most of the marauding armies that have swept across the peninsula over the last two millennia passed along this crucial corridor, leaving in their wake a bumper crop of monuments. The very first traces of settlement in Madhya Pradesh are the 10,000-year-old paintings on the lonely hilltop of **Bhimbetka**, a day-trip south of the sprawling capital **Bhopal**. Aboriginal rock art was still being created here during the Mauryan emperor Ashoka's evangelical dissemination of Buddhism, in the second century BC. Nearby, the immaculately restored stupa complex at **Sanchi** is the most impressive relic of this era, ranking among the finest early Buddhist remains in Asia, while the rock-cut Jain and Hindu caves at **Udaigiri** recall the dynasties that succeeded the Mauryans, from the Andhras to the Guptas in the fourth century.

By the end of the first millennium AD, central India was divided into several kingdoms. The Paramaras, whose ruler Raja Bhoj founded Bhopal, controlled the southern and central area, known as **Malwa,** while the **Chandellas**, responsible for some of the subcontinent's most exquisite temples, held sway in the north. Lost deep in the countryside, equidistant from Agra and Varanasi, their magnificent erotica-encrusted sandstone shrines at Khajuraho were erected sufficiently far from the main north–south route to have been overlooked by the iconoclastic warriors who marched past in the eleventh and twelfth centuries. Today, the site is as far off the beaten track as ever; its many visitors either fly in, or make the five- to six-hour bus journey from the nearest railheads at **Satna**, to the east, or **Jhansi**, in an anomalous sliver of Uttar Pradesh to the

west. Just south of Jhansi, the atmospheric ruined capital of the Bundella rajas at **Orchha** merits a short detour from the highway.

Monuments associated with the long Muslim domination of the region are much easier to visit. The romantic ghost town of **Mandu**, capital of the Malwa sultans, can be reached in a day from the industrial city of Indore, in western Madhya Pradesh. Meanwhile **Gwalior**, whose hilltop fort-palace was the linchpin of both the Delhi Sultanate's and the Moghuls' southward expansion, straddles the main Delhi–Mumbai railway in the far north.

Under the **British**, the middle of India was known as the "Central Provinces", and administered jointly from Nagpur (now in Maharashtra), and the summer capital **Pachmarhi** near Bhopal, the state's highest hill station. Madhya Pradesh, or "**MP**", only came into being after Independence, when the Central Provinces were amalgamated with a number of smaller princedoms. Since then, the 93-percent-Hindu state, with a substantial rural and tribal population, has remained more stable than neighbouring Uttar Pradesh and Bihar. Major civil unrest was virtually unheard of until the Bhopal riots of 1992–93, sparked off by events in Ayodhya, Uttar Pradesh. Despite this sudden assertion of Hindu fundamentalism, a subsequent backlash against the BJP-led central government in 1998 resulted in Congress reasserting itself as the leading local party. Now that Hindu-Muslim relations in MP are relatively cordial again, the state has turned to focus on the latest enemy – recurring **drought** across the poverty-stricken plains and the social and environmental consequences of the damming of the great River Narmada. In November 2000, the boundaries of Madhya Pradesh were redrawn; its elongated eastern resource-rich portion, which is bereft of sights and does not feature in this guide, became **Chhattisgarh**.

In addition to its historic sites, Madhya Pradesh boasts a number of **wildlife reserves**. In the sparsely populated east, remote savannah grasslands are an ideal habitat for deer and bison, while the shady sal forests and tarai swamplands that surround the *maidans* provide perfect cover for larger predators such as the tiger. Of the **national parks** hidden away in this area, **Kanha** is deservedly popular, though there are more chances of seeing the big cats at the smaller **Bandhavgarh national park** to the north.

Visiting Madhya Pradesh

Getting around Madhya Pradesh without your own vehicle normally involves a lot of bone-shaking bus journeys, usually under the auspices of MPSRTC, the state road transport authority, although deluxe buses ply the main tourist routes too. For longer distances, **trains** are the best way to go. The Central Railway, the main broad-gauge line between Mumbai and Kolkata (Calcutta), scythes straight through the middle of the state, forking at **Itarsi** junction. One branch veers north towards Bhopal, Jhansi, Gwalior and Agra, while the other continues northeast to Varanasi and eastern India via Jabalpur. In the far west, at Indore and the holy city of **Ujjain**, you can pick up the Western Railway, which heads up through eastern Rajasthan to Bharatpur and Delhi.

The **best time to visit** Madhya Pradesh is during the relatively cool winter months (Nov–Feb). In April, May and June the region heats up like a furnace, and daytime temperatures frequently exceed 40°C, but if you can stand the heat, this is the best time to catch glimpses of tigers in the parks. The increasingly meagre rains finally sweep in from the southeast in late June or early July.

Central Madhya Pradesh

All roads through the **central Madhya Pradesh** lead to the state's capital, **Bhopal**. Although synonymous in most minds with 1984 Union Carbide gas disaster, the state's largest and fastest growing city is an upbeat cultural centre these days, whose museums, galleries and nineteenth-century Islamic architecture, as well as its parks, lakes and markets, provide ample incentive to break any long journey across central India. Moreover, only a couple of hours away is one of South India's most famous archeological sites, the Buddhist stupa complex at **Sanchi**, and there are numerous other ancient monuments scattered around the area. The prehistoric site of **Bhimbetka** lies just 45km south of Bhopal, while further southeast, at the attractive but rarely visited hill station of **Pachmarhi**, enjoyable hikes lead through craggy mountains and thick forests littered with ancient rock art.

Bhopal

With well over a million inhabitants, **BHOPAL**, the capital of Madhya Pradesh, sprawls from the eastern shores of a huge artificial lake, its packed old city surrounded by modern concrete suburbs and green hills. In addition to the nineteenth-century **mosques** that bear witness to its enduring Muslim legacy, the packed **bazaars** of the walled old city are well worth a visit. Elsewhere, a couple of good archeological **museums** house hoards of ancient sculpture, while **Bharat Bhavan**, on the lakeside, ranks among India's premier centres for performing and visual arts, with an unrivalled collection of contemporary painting, sculpture and *adivasi* (tribal) art. In the **Museum of Man** on the city's outskirts, you can also visit the country's most comprehensive exhibition of *adivasi* houses, culture and technology, spread around an open-air hilltop site.

Some history

Bhopal's name is said to have come from the eleventh-century **Raja Bhoj**, who was instructed by his court gurus to atone for the murder of his mother by linking up the nine rivers flowing through his kingdom. A dam, or pal, was built across one of them, and the ruler established a new capital around the two resultant lakes – **Bhojapal**. By the end of the seventeenth century, **Dost Mohammed Khan**, an opportunistic ex-soldier of fortune and erstwhile general of Aurangzeb, had occupied the now-deserted site to carve out his own kingdom from the chaos left in the wake of the Moghul empire. The Muslim dynasty he established eventually became one of central India's leading royal families. Under the Raj, its members were among the select few to merit the accolade of a nineteen-gun salute from the British – a consequence of the help given to General Goddard in his march against the Marathas in 1778. In the nineteenth century, Bhopal was presided over largely by women rulers. Holding court from behind the wicker screen of purdah, successive begums revamped the city with noble civic works, including the three sandstone **mosques** which still dominate the skyline.

Today, Bhopal carries the burden of the appalling Union Carbide factory gas disaster of 1984 (see p.412), with residents still quick to remind you of their continuing legal and medical plight. In 1992, Hindu-Muslim rioting broke out following the destruction of the Babri Masjid in Ayodhya, leading to a record eleven-day curfew being imposed. In spite of the inter-communal violence, however, the many tales of Hindus sheltering their Muslim friends from the mobs at this time and vice versa demonstrate the long tradition of religious tolerance which exists in the city. In the last few years, Bhopal – and Madhya Pradesh in general – has remained true to its tolerant nature and has seen little of the political and religious intolerance that bedevils many other north Indian states.

Arrival, information and city transport

Bhopal's **airport**, served by daily Indian Airlines and Jet Airways flights from Delhi and Mumbai, and Indian Airlines from Indore, is around 12km by taxi (Rs180) or auto-rickshaw (Rs100) from the city. The main **railway station**, by

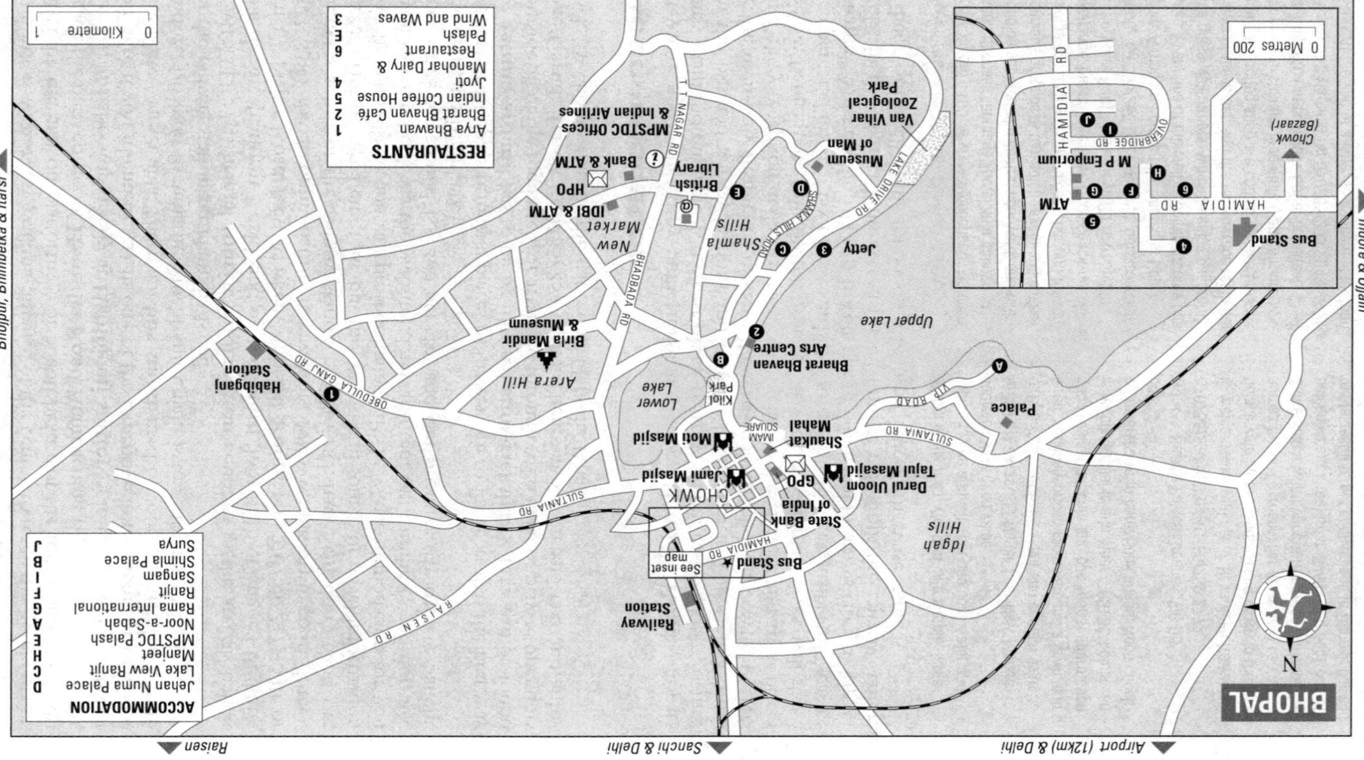
BHOPAL
ACCOMMODATION
Jehan Numa Palace D
Lake View Ranjit C
Manjeet H
MPSTDC Palash E
Noor-a-Sabah A
Rama International G
Ranjit F
Sangam I
Shimla Palace B
Surya J
RESTAURANTS
Arya Bhawan 1
Bharat Bhavan Café 2
Indian Coffee House 5
Jyoti 4
Manohar Dairy & Restaurant 6
Palash E
Wind and Waves 3
0 Kilometre 1
0 Metres 200
Bhojpur, Bhimbetka & Itarsi
Raisen
Sanchi & Delhi
Airport (12km) & Delhi
Indore & Ujjain
Habibganj Station
Railway Station
See inset map
Bus Stand
HAMIDIA RD
State Bank of India
GPO
Darul Uloom Tajul Masajid
Shaukat Mahal
IMAM SQUARE
CHOWK
Jami Masjid
Moti Masjid
Lower Lake
Kilol Park
Bharat Bhavan Arts Centre
Arera Hill
Birla Mandir & Museum
New Market
IDBI & ATM
HPO
Bank & ATM
MPSTDC Offices & Indian Airlines
British Library
Shamla Hills
SHAMLA HILLS ROAD
Jetty
Museum of Man
Van Vihar Zoological Park
LAKE DRIVE RD
Upper Lake
Palace
VIP ROAD
SULTANIA RD
Idgah Hills
RAISEN RD
OBEDULLA GANJ RD
BHADBADA RD
T T NAGAR RD
ATM
M P Emporium
OVERBRIDGE RD
Chowk (Bazaar)

contrast, is within easy walking distance of the centre; to reach the hotel district, leave by the exit on platforms 4 or 5, and head past the tonga rank until you reach the busy corner of **Hamidia Road**. Approaching Bhopal from the south, most trains also stop briefly at **Habibganj station**, a long way out – only get off here if you intend to stay in one of the expensive hotels in Shamla Hills or the New Market area. The main **bus stand**, used by long-distance buses from Indore, Jabalpur, Pachmarhi, Sanchi and Ujjain is ten minutes' walk southwest of the railway station on Hamidia Road.

MPSTDC has helpful **tourist information** counters in the arrivals hall at the station (platform 1 exit), and on the fourth floor of the Gangotri Building on TT Nagar Road, New Market (Mon–Sat 10am–5pm; ⓣ0755/277 4340, or 277 8383 for accommodation reservations, ⓦwww.mptourism.com), fifteen minutes south of the railway station by auto-rickshaw. Staff don't hand out street maps or run a city tour, but they're a useful source of travel information for the whole state, and can pre-book any MPSTDC accommodation for you (you can also book via the website). They also rent out minibuses and non-a/c diesel cars for around Rs1200 per day, and can organize day-trips to Sanchi, Bhojpur and Bhimbetka.

Most of Bhopal's principal places of interest are so far apart that the best way of **getting around** has to be by metered **auto-rickshaws**. Taxis can be found outside all of the top hotels, or arranged through MPSTDC or private operators like Garuda Travels (ⓣ0755/254 0609). There's also a prepaid taxi and auto-rickshaw booth outside the station on Hamidia Road.

Accommodation

If you're not bothered by traffic noise and fumes, **Hamidia Road**, Bhopal's busy main thoroughfare, is the best **place to stay**, within easy walking distance of the bus and railway stations and crammed with hotels. These range from grim, men-only fleapits to modern Western-style establishments with porters and glitzy reception desks; we have only included the cleanest and safest places below. Bargains are thin on the ground; all, even the dingiest dives, will slap a ten percent "luxury" tax onto your bill – some will add an equally stiff "service charge". Most of Bhopal's **top hotels** favour congenial locations close to Upper Lake in the Shamla Hills area, a fifteen-minute ride from the railway station. Check-out in all of the following is 24 hour unless otherwise stated.

Jehan Numa Palace 157 Shamla Hills Rd ⓣ0755/266 1100, ⓦwww.hoteljehanumapalace.com. Bhopal's "heritage" hotel, in a palazzo-style building set around a central courtyard, and with spacious grounds. A top-notch restaurant, coffee and pastry shop, Internet access, bar and foreign exchange, but no lake view. Noon check-out. ❽–❾

Lake View Ranjit Lake Drive Rd ⓣ0755/266 0600, ⓕ0755/266 0321 ⓔranjit_bpl@sancharnet.com. A modern hotel on the shores of Upper Lake. Every one of the well-appointed rooms has one glass wall through which to enjoy panoramic views of the water, and the roof-terrace restaurant and 24hr coffee shop are cooled by lake breezes. Currency exchange. Free station and airport pick-up/drop-off. Rates include buffet breakfast. ❻–❽

Manjeet 3 Hamidia Rd ⓣ0755/253 2949, ⓕ253 6490. At the end of a lane, so a little quieter than others in the area. Well run with simple, large rooms (some a/c) with hot and cold water and cable TV. Very good value. ❷–❹

MPSTDC Palash TT Nagar, near New Market ⓣ0755/255 3006. Pleasant and popular, with 33 large, variously priced rooms around a lawn, and a good restaurant, café and bar. Tourist information is readily available and other MPSTDC hotels can be reserved from here. Book ahead. Noon check-out. ❹–❻

Noor-a-Sabah Palace Grounds, VIP Rd ⓣ0755/522 3333, ⓕ0755/252 2777, ⓔwelcom@ndf.vsnl.net.in. Revamped Nawab's palace with large rooms looking down to the lake across tropical gardens. For those who can afford it, the suites with period furniture and private balconies are a real treat. Swimming pool, one of the fastest Internet connections in Bhopal, bar and good Indian and Continental food; ask to be served dinner in the garden. ❾

Rama International Hamidia Rd ☎0755/253 5542. Walk through a courtyard off the main road to this relatively peaceful and rambling hotel. The rooms are simple, clean and inexpensive; some have a/c. ❷–❹

Ranjit Hamidia Rd ☎0755/253 3511. One of many good-value hotels along the stretch, with light and clean rooms (all with bath and TV), as well as a terrace bar and a popular restaurant downstairs. ❷–❸

Sangam Overbridge Rd ☎0755/254 2382. Big building with variously priced, clean rooms on different floors. All are of a good standard, with TV, but the deluxe rooms aren't worth the extra. ❷

Shimla Palace 31 Shamla Rd ☎0755/254 6987. Very pleasant, family-run place in a quiet suburban backstreet overlooking the lake. The rooms, some with views, are neat and spacious. ❷–❸

Surya Hamidia Rd ☎0755/274 1701. Better, and pricier, than most in the area; the large, clean standard rooms are the best value. Rooms at the front suffer from road noise. Noon check-out. ❸–❹

The City

Bhopal has two separate centres. Spread over the hills to the south of the lakes, the **New Market** area comprises a modern mix of shopping arcades, cybercafés, ice cream parlours, cinemas and modern office blocks. Once you've squeezed through the strip of land that divides the Upper and (smaller) Lower lakes, sweeping avenues, civic buildings and pleasure gardens quickly give way to the more heavily congested **old city.** Focused around the **Jami Masjid**, the bazaar, north of the lakes, centres on the area known as **Chowk,** which occupies the dense grid of streets between **Moti Masjid Square** to the south and Hamidia Road in the north. The art **galleries** and **museums** are all tucked down side-roads off New Market, or along the hilly southern edge of the Upper Lake.

Chowk

Bhopal's lively **bazaar** (Tues–Sat) provides a welcome splash of colour after the dismal, traffic-filled streets around the railway station. Famous for "*zarda, purdah, garda and namarda*" (tobacco, veils, dust and eunuchs), it retains a strong Muslim ambience, with overhanging balconies intricately carved with Islamic geometric designs. Each of the narrow streets radiating from the central square specializes in a different type of merchandise. One has a monopoly on brocaded "Chanderi" silk saris, another, west of the square, is given over to the bass drums and wailing clarinets of Bhopali wedding bands. Particular specialities of the bazaar include tussar silk, silver jewellery and the gaudily beaded women's purses for which Bhopal is renowned.

At the heart of the market loom the rich red sandstone walls and stumpy minarets of the **Jami Masjid**. Built in 1837 by Kudsia Begum, the mosque boasts neither age nor great architectural merit, but its whitewashed domes and gleaming gilded pinnacles lend an exotic air to proceedings in the square below.

Imam Square to the Tajul Masajid

A short way southwest of Chowk, **Imam Square** was once the epicentre of royal Bhopal. Nowadays, it's little more than a glorified traffic island, only worth stopping at to admire the **Moti Masjid** on its eastern edge. The "Pearl Mosque", erected in 1860 by Sikander Begum, Kudsia's daughter, is a diminutive and much less imposing version of Shah Jahan's Jami Masjid in Old Delhi, notable more for its slender, gold-topped minarets and sandstone cupolas than its size.

Lining the opposite, northern side of the square near the ceremonial archway is a more eccentric nineteenth-century pile. An unlikely fusion of Italian, Gothic

The Bhopal gas tragedy

Bhopal is notorious as the site of the world's worst industrial disaster. Late at night, on December 2, 1984, a lethal cloud of Methyl Iso-Cynate (MIC), a toxic chemical used in the manufacture of pesticides, exploded from a tank at the huge, US-owned **Union Carbide** (UCIL) plant on the northern edge of the city.

MIC is a highly reactive chemical that has to be kept under constant pressure and at a temperature of 0°C, but regardless of the hazard, cost-conscious officials had reduced the pressure in order to save some $40 a day. The danger was heightened when water entered Tank 610 through badly maintained and leaking valves to contaminate the MIC, and a massive reaction was triggered. Cool wind dispersed the gas throughout densely populated residential districts and shanty settlements. There was no warning siren and no emergency procedures to put in place, leaving the thick cloud of burning gas to blind and suffocate its victims. The leak killed 1600 instantly (according to official figures) and between 7000 and 10,000 in the aftermath, but the figure now totals over 20,000 in the years since the incident. More than 500,000 people were exposed to the gas, of whom about one-fifth have been left with chronic and incurable health problems, often passed on to children born since the tragedy. As if the suffering was not already enough, the water in the community pumps of the affected residential areas continues to be contaminated with dangerous toxic chemicals that seeped out from the now-deserted factory.

Though the incidence of TB, cancers, infertility and cataracts in the affected area remains way above the national average, the factory officials and their "medical experts" initially said that the effect of MIC was akin to tear gas, causing only temporary health problems. They accepted moral responsibility for the accident, but blamed the Indian government for inadequate safety standards when it came to the issue of compensation. Only in 1989 did UCIL agree to pay an average of Rs15,000 to each adult victim – a paltry sum that didn't even cover loans for the medical bills in the first five years, let alone compensate for the loss of life and livelihoods, and other consequences of the disaster. Relatives of only 6000 of the victims who died have received compensation; the rest have been rejected on grounds that the death was not related to gas exposure but was a result of "personal injury". Finally, in 2001, the Bhopal Memorial Hospital and Research Centre (set up from the proceeds of Union Carbide's sale of its shares in UCIL) opened to treat patients.

Government and factory authorities have been keen to sweep the whole catalogue of mistakes and failures under the carpet – both US and Indian officials charged with serious offences, including manslaughter, have escaped their sentences to date. In 2002, a Bhopal court directed the Central Bureau of Investigation to pursue the extradition of Warren Anderson, the CEO of Union Carbide in the US; since then, however, Mr Anderson has gone "missing" from his home in the US. The Union Carbide factory now stands desolate and overgrown; UCIL has reinvented itself elsewhere in the country under the name of Eveready Industries India Ltd.

If you're interested in learning more about the disaster or **volunteering** your services in the affected communities, contact the Sambhavna Trust at 44 Sant Kanwar Ram Nagar, Berasia Rd, Bhopal 462018 Ⓣ0755/273 0914, Ⓔsambavna@bom.6.vsnl.net.in. *Five Past Midnight in Bhopal* by Dominique Lapierre and Javier Moro is recommended for further reading.

and Islamic influences, the **Shaukat Mahal** palace was originally designed by a French architect (allegedly descended from the Bourbon royal family). Unfortunately, both it and the elegant **Sadar Manzil** ("Hall of Public Audience") have been converted into government offices and are closed to visitors.

Leaving Imam Square by the archway to the west, a five-minute walk brings you to the foot of Bhopal's most impressive monument. With its matching pair of colossal pink minarets soaring high above the city skyline, the **Darul Uloom Tajul Masajid** (daily except Fri and during Id-ul-Fitr) certainly lives up to the epithet of "mother of all mosques", as denoted by the extra "a" in its name. Whether it also deserves to be dubbed the biggest in India, as locals claim, is rather less certain. Work on the building commenced under the auspices of Sultan Jehan Begum (1868–1901), the eighth ruler of Bhopal. After the death of her domineering husband, the widow queen embarked on a spending spree that left the city with a postal system, new schools and a railway, but which all but impoverished the state – and the Tajul Masajid was never actually completed.

The Birla Mandir museum

To the east of Lower Lake, the **Birla Mandir** collection (Tues–Sun 9am–noon & 2–6pm; Rs3) comprises some of the finest stone sculpture in Madhya Pradesh, informatively displayed with explanatory panels in English in the main galleries. The museum is housed in a detached mansion beside Birla Mandir, the garish modern Hindu Lakshmi Narayan temple that stands high on the hill overlooking Lower Lake. Aside from the museum itself, the **temple gardens**, which overlook the city sprawl, are a fine place to watch the sun setting behind the minarets.

The exhibition is divided between Vishnu, the mother goddesses and Shiva. The **Vishnu** section contains some interesting representations of the god's diverse and frequently bizarre reincarnations (avatars), while in the **Devi** gallery next door, a cadaverous Chamunda (the goddess Durga in her most terrifying aspect) stands incongruously amid a row of voluptuous maidens and fertility figures. Note the dying man writhing at her feet. The **Shiva** room, by contrast, is altogether more subdued. Many of the beautifully carved bas-reliefs show the god of preservation and destruction enjoying moments of marital bliss on Mount Kailash with his consort Parvati – an icon known as Uma-Maheshwar.

Finally, have a look at the replicas of the 3500-year-old **Harappan** artefacts encased under the stairs. One of the seals bears an image of the pre-Aryan god Rudra, seated in the lotus position; archeologists believe he was the ancient forerunner of Shiva.

Bharat Bhavan

Inaugurated in 1982, **Bharat Bhavan** (Tues–Sun: Feb–Oct 2–8pm; Nov–Jan 1–7pm; Rs10, Rs20–50 for stage plays) was set up as part of a wider government project to promote visual and performing arts in state capitals throughout the country. The initiative fizzled out after Indira Gandhi's death, but Bhopal's contribution has become established as provincial India's most outstanding arts centre.

Inside Goan architect Charles Correa's campus of concrete domes and dour brickwork are **temporary exhibitions** as well as a large split-level **permanent collection** of modern Indian painting and sculpture. Rather incongruously placed in the midst of the latter, look out for an eighteenth-century gilt-framed "landscape" by the Daniells' – the uncle-nephew duo employed as a part of the "Company School of Painting" during the Raj. Company artists had to churn out beautiful and romantic paintings of India for those back home in Britain who could not imagine the nature of the subcontinent. Bharat Bhavan has a gallery devoted exclusively to **adivasi art**, in search of which talent scouts spent months roaming remote regions. Among their more famous discoveries was the Gond painter **Jangarh Singh Shyam**, featured by veteran BBC correspondent Mark Tully in his book *No Full Stops In India*. A number of Jangarh's works are on display here, along with a colourful assemblage of masks, terracottas, woodcarvings and ritual paraphernalia. The absence of background information is intentional – the exhibition is intended to represent the objects as works of art in their own right, rather than merely anthropological curios.

If you're wondering how to spend an evening in Bhopal, scan the posters in the foyer for forthcoming **performances** at Bharat Bhavan. The pleasant café, to the right of the main building, is just the place to pen a couple of the tribal art **postcards** on sale in the office next to the gate.

The Museum of Man

The story of India's indigenous minorities – the *adivasis*, literally "original inhabitants" – is all too familiar. Dispossessed of their land by large-scale "development" projects or exploitative moneylenders, the "tribals" have seen a gradual erosion of their traditional culture – a process hastened by proselytizing missionaries and governments that tend, at best, to regard tribal people as anachronistic and, at worst, as an embarrassment. The **Museum of Man**, properly known as the Rashtriya Manav Sangrahalaya (Tues–Sun: March–Aug 11am–6.30pm; Sept–Feb 10am–5.30pm; Rs10, plus Rs50 for video), is an enlightened attempt to redress the balance, setting out to provide genuine insights into ways of life few see at first hand. The aim is twofold: to expose city people to the overall richness and ingenuity of India's tribal culture and to foster greater respect for their heritage among the *adivasis* themselves.

Overlooking New Market on one side and the majestic sweep of Upper Lake on the other, the two-hundred-acre hilltop site includes a reconstructed Keralan coastal village, and a winding, mythological trail where each tribal group from the state has contributed their own interpretation of the creation (with clear English translations). A large exhibition hall draws on all the daily and ritual elements in the *adivasi* lifestyle, although the focus is on one group at a time. Dotted amongst the forest scrub are botanical trails, a research centre and, as its centrepiece, a permanent open-air exhibition of traditional *adivasi* houses, compounds and religious shrines collectively known as the "**tribal habitat**". Specialist *adivasi* craftsmen and women from all corners of India were brought in to construct them, using only tools and materials available in their home environments.

Before tackling the exhibition, have a quick look at the **introductory gallery** in the small building opposite the main entrance (the approach from New Market). From here, a flight of steps leads underneath a thatched gateway (a structure adapted from the "youth dormitory" of the Ao-Naga from Nagaland) up to the top of the hill, where the seventeen or so dwelling complexes are scattered. On a quiet day, the empty mud huts, coral and beaten-earth courtyards form a striking contrast to the teeming city all around. Nearly all the interiors contain original tools, cooking utensils, baskets and musical instruments, while some are beautifully decorated with intricate murals, mouldings and carved beams. Of particular note are the multicoloured paintings of horses adorning the walls of the Rathwa huts (look out for the picture of the train that carried the artists from their village in Gujarat); the ochre, red, black and yellow rectangular designs inside the Gadaba buildings (from Orissa); and the famous Worli wedding paintings of northern Maharashtra, which show the tribal fertility goddess Palghat framed by complex geometrical patterns.

The only way to **get to the museum** without your own vehicle is by auto-rickshaw; drivers will probably insist on double the meter rate for the twenty-minute ride from the railway station as they're unlikely to pick up a return fare, so negotiate a flat rate for the round trip, including at least an hour's waiting time. A cheaper option is to take a bus or *tempo* from the railway station to New Market and pick up a rickshaw there. The museum has nowhere to buy snacks or drinks, so come with an ample supply as it can be hot work.

Van Vihar Zoological Park

If you haven't made it to Madhya Pradesh's bona fide national parks, or if you have but missed the big cats, it's well worth visiting **Van Vihar Zoological Park** (daily 7–11am & 2–5.30pm; Rs100 [Rs10]; plus Rs25 for camera, Rs200 for video; for transport around the park, a rickshaw is Rs150 plus Rs10 entrance fee for the driver, bicycle Rs10). A trip round the five-square-kilometre sanctuary ties in nicely with a visit to the Museum of Man next door – keep the same rickshaw for the whole trip. The star of the park is a regal **white tiger**, but you can also see tortoises, long-nosed gharial, leopards, Himalayan bears, Indian tigers, deer and antelopes. The best chance of sightings is from 4pm onwards, when the mighty felines pad and drool close to the boundaries of their enclosures, waiting for their daily feed. Sambar (deer) munch the grass nearby, while egrets, herons, cormorants and ducks take in the evening light on the lake shore. You can get a longer and more peaceful look at the birds by taking a boat from the jetty half a kilometre northeast of the park gate (9am–sunset; pedal and rowing boats Rs30–35/30min).

Eating

Restaurants in Bhopal's larger hotels serve uniform multi-cuisine menus; the strip-light-and-formica cafés opposite the bus stand do thalis and hot platefuls of *subzi*, rice and dhal for next to nothing. For breakfast try the state's favourite food, *poha* – a light steamed rice cake served piping hot in newspaper from every street corner, followed by *katchoris* (a fried snack stuffed with lentils) and a chai.

Arya Bhawan Behind Sargam Cinema, MP Nagar. One of the most popular restaurants near Habibganj Railway Station, this a/c dining room has main courses and North Indian thalis for around Rs60–80.

Bharat Bhavan Café Bharat Bhavan Arts Centre. A refreshingly mixed crowd of artists, workers and visitors lounge around in this friendly, relaxed café, which serves up hot and cold drinks and light snacks at reasonable prices. The terrace is a great place to watch the sunset (bring mosquito repellent).

Indian Coffee House Hamidia Rd. Bhopal's big breakfast venue for South Indian snacks, eggs and filter coffee served with great style at rock bottom prices. Plus a large selection of north and South Indian veg and non-veg dishes. Open 7.30am until late evening.

Jyoti 53 Hamidia Rd. Popular hotel-restaurant specializing in traditional (mild, pure-veg) Gujarati food. Lunchtime thalis are particularly good value.

Manohar Dairy & Restaurant Hamidia Rd. Clean and cool with a varied menu including north and South Indian snacks, *namkeen*, speciality sweets (try the milk cake and dried fruit *mithai*), a juice bar and a full range of ice cream. Good value.

Palash TT Nagar, New Market ☎0755/255 3006 or 255 3076. Inexpensive, tasty South Indian café upstairs; downstairs, the menu at the popular multi-cuisine restaurant may be standard, but the food is absolutely delicious – try the Indian veg and fish dishes. Reserve at weekends.

Wind and Waves Lake Drive Rd. Sample the same old MPSTDC menu in a better than usual setting conveniently close to the lakeside museums and the boat-rental jetty. Open 11am until late.

Listings

Airlines Indian Airlines has an office in the Gangotri complex on TT Nagar Rd, New Market (Mon–Sat 9am–5pm, Sun 9am–noon; ☎0755/255 0480), and a booking counter at the airport. Jet Airways, Ranjit Towers, MP Nagar (☎ 0755/276 0371) also has a booking counter at the airport (☎0755/264 5676)

Banks and exchange Apart from the top hotels, only the main banks in New Market offer foreign

Moving on from Bhopal

Bhopal is on one of the two broad-gauge train lines between Delhi and Mumbai. If you're heading **north** via Jhansi (for Orchha/Khajuraho), Gwalior or Agra, you have a choice between a good twelve or so regular services, and the super-fast, completely a/c Shatabdi Express #2001 which leaves Bhopal daily at 2.50pm and arrives in Delhi a mere eight hours later. The one train to avoid on this route is the super-slow Amritsar–Dadar Express #1457. In the other direction, the 4pm Punjab Mail #2138 is the best for **Mumbai** (14hr 55min). The nightly service to **Jabalpur**, Narmada Express #8233, leaves at 10.45pm and gets in at 5.30am, leaving time to pick up a connecting bus to Kanha. Other services to Jabalpur include the excellent a/c Jan Shatabdi Express #2061 (daily 5.40pm; 5hr 15min), which departs from Habibganj Station and calls at **Itarsi Junction**, 92km south, where you can pick up a connection for Kolkata (Calcutta) and Varanasi.

Most journeys from Bhopal are easier and quicker by train, but the city's good **bus** connections are especially useful for Indore, which can be reached either on frequent state buses or the daily MPSRTC super-fast luxury service, which connects with the arrival of the Shatabdi Express (**for Ujjain**, get off at Dewas and pick up a local bus for the remaining 37km); tickets are sold at the MPSTDC counter in the railway station. There are several daily buses to Pachmarhi (6–8hr), which leave from the state bus stand on Hamidia Road, the fastest of which departs at 7am.

exchange. IDBI has ATMs which accept Visa and Mastercard. In the Chowk, the ICICI in the petrol station on the corner of Hamidia Rd has an ATM, while the State Bank of India is next to the GPO.
Bookstores Variety, and other English-language bookstores at the top of Bhadbada Rd in New Market stock a reasonable range of paperbacks (mostly popular fiction and Indian authors in translation). A more limited selection is available from the newsstand on platform 1 at the railway station.
Hospital Bhopal's main Hamidia hospital (☎0755/254 0222) is on Sultania Rd, between Imam Square and the Darul Uloom Tajul Masajid. The small, private Hajela Hospital (☎0755/277 3392) on TT Nagar is excellent. Doctors are best arranged through the top hotels.
Internet access By far the best email and Internet facilities are available at the British Library (see below). The service is extremely fast and efficient, although a steep Rs60/hr for non-members. Cybercafés at Chowk and New Market area are cheaper (Rs25/hr).
Library The British Council has a library in the GTB Complex on Roshanpura Naka, New Market (Tues–Sat 11am–7pm). Non-members are welcome to peruse their collection of British newspapers, magazines and periodicals, and to use the Internet facilities (see above).
Post office Have poste restante mail sent to the Head Post Office on TT Nagar in New Market well in advance; the GPO on Sultania Rd near the Darul Uloom Tajul Masajid is less reliable.
Shopping Chowk (Mon–Sat) is the best place for silk and silver; New Market (Tues–Sun) has some bigger stores, including Mrignayani for handicrafts, men's calico shirts and trendy ethnic *salwar kamises*. The MP State Emporium on Hamidia Rd is the place to buy batiks, dokra metalwork, khadi clothes, bedspreads and silk saris, although the fixed prices are not cheap. Check the street stalls on Overbridge Rd for bargains.

Around Bhopal

A wealth of impressive ancient monuments lie within a couple of hours' journey from Bhopal. To the northeast, the third-century BC stupas at **Sanchi** can be seen in an easy day-trip, or as a stopover as you head north on the Central Railway. Sanchi's peaceful setting makes it an ideal base for visits to more stupas at **Satdhara**, or to **Udaigiri**'s rock-cut caves and the nearby Column of Heliodorus at **Besnagar**.

Close to the main road south towards Hoshangabad and the Narmada Valley, the prehistoric cave paintings at **Bhimbetka** can be visited in a day by bus.

Sanchi

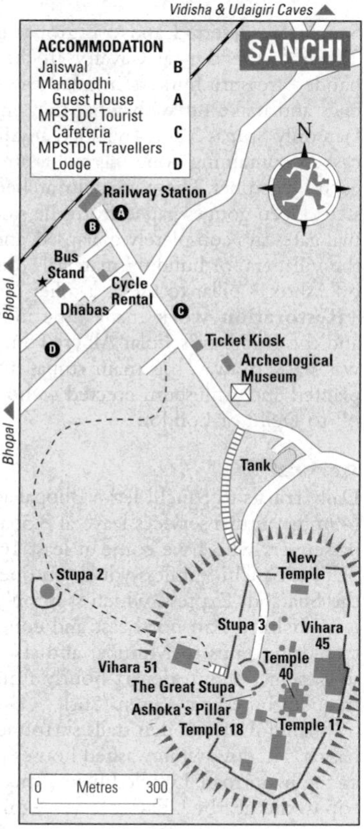

From a distance, the smooth-sided hemispherical object that appears on a hillock overlooking the main train line at **SANCHI**, 46km northeast of Bhopal, has the surreal air of a space station or an upturned satellite dish. In fact, the giant stone mound stands as testimony to a much older means of communing with the cosmos. Quite apart from being India's finest surviving Buddhist monument, the **Great Stupa** is one of the earliest religious structures in the subcontinent. It presides over a complex of ruined temples and monasteries that collectively provide a rich and unbroken record of the development of Buddhist art and architecture from the faith's first emergence in central India during the third century BC, until it was eventually squeezed out by the resurgence of Brahmanism during the medieval era.

A visit to Sanchi, however, is no dry lesson in South Asian art history. The main stupa is surrounded by some of the richest and best-preserved ancient **sculpture** you're ever likely to see in situ, while the site itself, floating serenely above a vast expanse of open plains, has preserved the tranquillity that must have attracted its original occupants. Most visitors find a couple of hours more than sufficient to explore the ruins, although you could spend several days poring over the four exquisite gateways, or **toranas**, that surround the Great Stupa. Paved walkways and steps lead around the hilltop enclosure (daily 8am–6pm; Rs250 [Rs5], plus Rs25 for video, Rs10 for car), dotted with interpretative panels and shady trees.

The site is connected to the small village at the foot of the hill by a metalled road. Once you've bought an entrance **ticket** from the roadside booth outside the museum, head up the stone steps on the right, past the welcoming posse of postcard-wallahs, to the main entrance. From here, the central walkway runs alongside the new Sri Lankan Buddhist temple and a cold drinks stall, before leading straight to the Great Stupa.

Some history

Unlike the other famous Buddhist centres in eastern India and Nepal, Sanchi has no known connection with the life of Buddha himself. It first became a place of pilgrimage when the Mauryan emperor **Ashoka**, who married a woman from nearby Besnagar (see p.424), erected a polished stone pillar and brick-and-mortar stupa here midway through the third century BC. The complex was enlarged by successive dynasties, but after the eclipse of Buddhism

Sanchi lay deserted and overgrown until its rediscovery in 1818 by General Taylor of the Bengal Cavalry. In the years that followed, a swarm of heavy-handed treasure hunters invaded the site, eager to crack open the giant stone eggs and make off with what they imagined to be their valuable contents. In fact, only Stupas 3 and 4 yielded anything more than rubble; the soapstone relic caskets containing bone fragments are displayed in the new temple for one day each December. These amateur archeologists, however, left the ruins in a sorry state. Deep gouges gaped from the sides of stupas 1 and 2, a couple of ceremonial gateways completely collapsed, and much of the masonry was plundered by the villagers for building materials (one local landlord is alleged to have carted off Ashoka's pillar to use as a roller in his sugar cane press).

Restoration work made little impact until the archeologist John Marshall and the Buddhist scholar Albert Foucher took on the job in 1912. The jungle was hacked away, the main stupas and temples were rebuilt, lawns and trees planted and a museum erected to house what sculpture had not been shipped off to Delhi or London.

Arrival

Daily **trains** to Sanchi leave Bhopal at 8am (41min), 3.15pm (28min) and 6pm (49min); return services leave at 8.50am, 10am, 3.59pm and 4.25pm. First-class passengers who have come at least 161km can also arrange to make a "special halt" at Sanchi – unless you're on one of the "superfast" a/c chair services, like the Shatabdi Express, which stop only at Bhopal. The nearest mainline station is **Vidisha**, 10km northeast and connected by plenty of local buses; there are two daily trains to Mumbai and six to Delhi from here. **Buses** from Bhopal to Sanchi (90min) depart hourly from the main city bus stand; there are also frequent buses via Raisen (2hr).

A handful of wooden stalls surround the bus stand, constituting Sanchi's tiny bazaar. The low, whitewashed houses of the village proper are on the other side of the main road, huddled below the stupa-covered hill. **Bicycles** – good for a trip to the nearby Udaigiri caves – can be rented for around Rs20 per day from a small shop in the bazaar.

Power cuts are a daily occurrence in Sanchi, often stretching through the day and night, so make sure you have a good torch and spare batteries; otherwise, stock up with candles from the bazaar.

Accommodation

Inexpensive **accommodation** can be found in the unusually good *Retiring Room* at the railway station (❶–❷), or at the nearby *Sri Lanka Mahabodhi Society Guest House* (Ⓣ07482/262739; ❶) which has basic doubles facing into a peaceful flower-filled courtyard. There is a communal bathroom, but no restaurant. Opposite, the friendly *Jaiswal* (Ⓣ07482/266746; ❶) has six simple rooms with bucket hot water in a family house. Moving up the scale, the MPSTDC *Tourist Cafeteria* (Ⓣ07482/262743; ❸), near the museum, has two plain, clean rooms with attached shower-toilets. By far the most comfortable option in Sanchi, however, has to be the MPSTDC *Travellers Lodge* (Ⓣ07482/262723; ❹–❺), five minutes' walk south of the crossroads. Their eight spacious, spotless rooms (two with a/c) are excellent value, but often booked; try to reserve at least five days in advance through any MPSTDC office or hotel, or in Delhi (see p.154).

The Great Stupa

Stupa 1, or the **Great Stupa**, stands on a stretch of level ground at the western edge of the plateau. Fragments of the original construction, a much smaller

Stupas

The hemispherical mounds known as **stupas** have been central to Buddhist worship since the sixth century BC, when Buddha himself modelled the first prototype. Asked by one of his disciples for a symbol to help disseminate his teachings after his death, the Master took his begging bowl, teaching staff and a length of cloth – his only worldly possessions – and arranged them into the form of a stupa, using the cloth as a base, the upturned bowl as the dome and the stick as the projecting finial, or spire.

Originally, stupas were simple burial mounds of compacted earth and stone containing relics of the Buddha and his followers. As the religion spread, however, the basic components multiplied and became imbued with **symbolic significance**. The main dome, or **anda** – representing the sacred mountain, or "divine axis" linking heaven and earth – grew larger, while the wooden railings, or **vedikas**, surrounding it were replaced by massive stone ones. A raised ambulatory terrace, or **medhi**, was added to the vertical sides of the drum, along with two flights of stairs and four ceremonial entrances, carefully aligned with the cardinal points. Finally, crowning the tip of the stupa, the single spike evolved into a three-tiered umbrella, or **chhattra**, standing for the Three Jewels of Buddhism: the Buddha, the Law and the community of monks.

The *chhattra*, usually enclosed within a low square stone railing, or **harmika** (a throwback to the days when sacred *bodhi* trees were surrounded by fences) formed the topmost point of the axis, directly above the reliquary in the heart of the stupa. Ranging from bits of bone wrapped in cloth to fine caskets of precious metals, crystal and carved stone, the reliquaries were the "seeds" and their protective mounds the "egg". Excavations of the 84,000 stupas scattered around the subcontinent have shown that the solid interiors were also sometimes built as elaborate **mandalas** – symbolic patterns that exerted a beneficial influence over the stupa and those who walked around it. The ritual of circumambulation, or **pradhakshina**, which enabled the worshipper to tap into cosmic energy and be transported from the mundane to the divine realms, was always carried out in a clockwise direction from the east, in imitation of the sun's passage across the heavens.

Of the half-dozen or so giant stupa sites dotted around ancient India, only **Sanchi** has survived to the present day. To see one in action, however, you have to follow in the footsteps of Ashoka's missionaries southwards to Sri Lanka, northwards to the Himalayas and the Tibetan plateau, or across the Bay of Bengal to Southeast Asia, where, as "**dagobas**", "**chortens**" and "**chedis**", stupas are still revered as repositories of sacred energy.

version built in the third century BC by Ashoka, still lie entombed beneath the thick outer shell of lime plaster added a century later. The **Shungas** were responsible for the raised processional balcony, and the two graceful staircases that curve gently around the sides of the drum from the paved walkway at ground level, as well as the aerial-like *chhattra* and its square enclosure which crown the top of the mound. Four elaborate gateways were added by the **Satavahanas** in the first century BC, followed by the four serene meditating **Buddhas** that greet you as you pass through the main entrances. Carved out of local sandstone, these were installed during the Gupta era, around 450 AD, by which time figurative depictions of Buddha had become acceptable (elsewhere in Sanchi, the Master is euphemistically represented by an empty throne, a wheel, a pair of footprints or even a parasol).

As you move gradually closer to the stupa, the extraordinary wealth of sculpture adorning the **toranas** slips slowly into focus. Staring up at these masterpieces from below, you can see why archeologists believe them to have been the work of ivory craftsmen. Every conceivable nook and cranny of the eight-metre upright posts and three curving cross-bars teems with delicate figures of humans, demigods and goddesses, birds, beasts and propitious symbols. Some of the larger reliefs depict narratives drawn from the lives of Gautama Buddha and his six predecessors, the *Manushis*, while others recount Ashoka's dissemination of the faith. In between are purely decorative panels and illustrations of heaven intended to inspire worshippers to lead meritorious lives on earth. Start with the *torana* on the south side, which is the oldest, and, as is the custom at Buddhist monuments, proceed in a clockwise direction around the stupa.

Southern torana

Opening directly onto the ceremonial staircase, the **southern torana** was the Great Stupa's principal entrance, as is borne out by the proximity of the stump of Ashoka's original stone pillar. Over the years, some of the panels with the best sculpture have dropped off the gateway (and are now housed in the site museum), but those that remain on the three crossbeams are still in reasonable condition. A carved frieze on the middle architrave shows Ashoka, complete with royal retinue, visiting a stupa in a traditional show of veneration. On the reverse side, the scene switches to one of the Buddha's previous incarnations. For the **Chhaddanta Jataka**, the *bodhisattva* adopts the guise of an elephant who, in extreme selflessness, helps an ivory hunter saw off his own (six) tusks.

Western torana

The **western torana** collapsed during the depredations of the nineteenth century, but has been skilfully restored. Some of Sanchi's liveliest sculpture appears around its two square posts. In the top right panel, a troupe of monkeys scurries across a bridge over the Ganges, made by the *bodhisattva*, their leader, from his own body to help them escape a gang of soldiers (seen below). According to the **Mahakapi Jataka**, the troops were dispatched by the local king to capture a coveted mango tree from which the monkeys had been feeding. You can also just about make out the final scene, where the repentant monarch gets a stern ticking-off from the *bodhisattva* under a *peepal* tree.

One of the most frequently represented episodes from the life of the Buddha features on the first two panels of the left-hand post facing the stupa. In the **Temptation of Mara**, the Buddha, who has vowed to remain under the *bodhi* tree until he attains enlightenment, heroically ignores the attempts of the evil demon Mara to distract him with threats of violence and seductive women (Mara's beautiful daughters). Notice the contrast at the end between Mara's agitated troops and the solemn-faced procession of angels who accompany the Buddha after he has achieved his goal.

Northern torana

Crowned with a fragmented Wheel of the Law and two tridents symbolizing the Buddhist trinity, the **northern torana** is the most elaborate and best-preserved of the four gateways. Scenes crammed onto its two vertical posts include Buddha performing an aerial promenade – one of many stunts he pulled to impress a group of heretics – and a monkey presenting the Master with a bowl of honey. Straddling the two pillars, a bas-relief on both faces of the lowest crossbeam depicts the **Vessantara Jataka**, telling of a *bodhisattva*-prince banished by his father for giving away a magical rain-making elephant. A better view of the inner, south-facing side of the plaque can be had from the balcony of the stupa's raised terrace. Note the little tableau on the far right showing the royal family trudging through the jungle; the prince's son is holding his father's hand, while his daughter clings to her mother's hip.

Eastern torana

Leaning languorously into space from the right capital of the **eastern torana** is Sanchi's most celebrated piece of sculpture, the sensuous **salabhanjika**, or wood-nymph. The full-breasted fertility goddess is one of several such figures that once blessed worshippers as they entered the Great Stupa. Only a few, however, still remain in place, others having been removed to Los Angeles and London.

Panels on the inner face of the pillar below the *salabhanjika* depict scenes from the life of the Buddha, including his conception when the *bodhisattva* entered the body of his mother, Maya, in the form of a white elephant, shown astride a crescent moon. The front face of the middle architrave picks up the tale some years later, when the young Buddha, represented by a riderless horse, makes his **Great Departure** from the palace where he grew up to begin the life of a wandering ascetic. The reverse side shows the fully enlightened Master, now symbolized by an empty throne, with a crowd of celestial beings and jungle animals paying their respects.

Elsewhere around the enclosure

Of the dozens of other numbered ruins around the 400-metre enclosure, only a handful are of more than passing interest. Smaller, plainer and graced with only one ceremonial gateway, the immaculately restored **Stupa 3**, immediately northeast of Stupa 1, is upstaged by its slightly older cousin in every way but one. In 1851, a pair of priceless reliquaries were discovered deep in the middle of the mound. Turned on a lathe from fine marble-like soapstone called steatite, the caskets were found to contain relics belonging to two of Buddha's closest disciples. In one, fragments of bone were encased with beads made from pearls, crystal, amethyst, lapis lazuli and gypsum, while on the lid, the initial of the saint they are thought to have belonged to, Sariputra, was painted in ink. Once in London's British Museum, along with other treasures pilfered from Sanchi, both are now safely locked in the new Buddhist temple outside the stupa enclosure, and are brought out for public view for one day each December (ask at any MPSTDC tourist office for details). On this day, Sanchi is transformed from a lonely open-air museum into a bustling pilgrimage site, with devotees from as far afield as Sri Lanka and Japan.

From Stupa 3, pick your way through the clutter of pillars, small stupas and exposed temple floors nearby to the large complex of interconnecting raised terraces at the far **eastern edge** of the site. The most intact monastery of the bunch, **Vihara 45**, dates from the ninth and tenth centuries and has the usual layout of cells ranged around a central courtyard. Originally, a colossal, richly decorated sanctuary tower soared high above the complex, but this collapsed, leaving the inner sanctum exposed. The river goddesses Ganga and Yamuna number among the skilfully sculpted figures flanking the entrance to the shrine itself – testimony to the mounting popularity of Brahmanism at the start of the medieval era. Inside, however, Buddha still reigns supreme. Regally enthroned on a lotus bloom, his right hand touches the ground to call upon the earth goddess to witness the moment of his enlightenment.

The enclosure's tenth-century eastern **boundary wall** is the best place from which to enjoy Sanchi's serene **views**, especially at sunset. To the northeast, a huge, sheer-sided rock rises from the midst of Vidisha, near the site of the ancient city that sponsored the monasteries here (traces of the **pilgrimage** trail between Besnagar and Sanchi can still be seen crossing the hillside below). South from the hill, a wide expanse of well-watered wheat-fields, dotted with clumps of mango and palm trees, stretches off towards the angular sandstone ridges of the Raisen escarpment on the distant horizon.

The southern area

The **southern area** of the enclosure harbours some of Sanchi's most interesting temples. Pieces of burnt wood dug from the foundations of **Temple 40** prove that the present apsidal-ended *chaitya* was built on top of an earlier structure contemporary with the Mauryan Stupa 1. **Temple 17** is a fine example of early Gupta architecture and the precursor of the classical Hindu design developed later in Orissa and Khajuraho. Its small, flat-roofed sanctum is entered via an open-sided porch held up by four finely carved pillars with lion capitals.

Before leaving the enclosure, hunt out the stump of **Ashoka's Pillar** on the right of Stupa 1's southern *torana*. The Mauryan emperor erected columns such as this all over the empire to mark sacred sites and pilgrims' trails (see p.1364 in "Contexts"). Its finely polished shaft (made, like all Ashokan pillars, with a sandstone known as Chunar after a quarry on the Ganges near Varanasi) was originally crowned with the magnificent lion capital now housed in the site museum. The inscription etched around its base is in the Brahmi script, recording Ashoka's edicts in Pali, the early Buddhist language and forerunner of Sanskrit.

The western slope

A flight of steps beside Stupa 1 leads down the **western slope** of Sanchi hill to the village, passing two notable monuments. The bottom portions of the thick stone walls of **Vihara 51** have been carefully restored to show its floorplan of 22 cells around a paved central courtyard. Further down, the second-century BC **Stupa 2** stands on an artificial ledge, well below the main enclosure – probably because its relics were less important than those of Stupas 1 and 3. The ornamental railings and gateways around it are certainly no match for those up the hill, although the carvings of lotus medallions and mythical beasts (including some bizarre horse-headed women) that decorate them are worth close scrutiny. The straps that dangle from some of the horse riders' saddles are believed to mark the first appearance in India of stirrups.

The archeological museum

Sanchi's small **archeological museum** (daily except Fri 10am–5pm; Rs5), to the left of the road up to the hilltop, houses a modest collection of artefacts, mostly fragments of sculpture, jewellery, pottery, weapons and tools recovered during successive excavations. Its **main hall** contains the most impressive pieces, including the famous Ashokan lion-capital (see above) and two damaged *salabhanjikas* from the gateways of Stupa 1. Also of note are the distinctive Mathuran red-sandstone Buddhas, believed to have been sent to Sanchi from Gandhara in the far northwest of India – source of the first figurative representations of the Master.

Eating

MPSTDC has the monopoly on good places to **eat** in Sanchi. If you're staying in the *Travellers Lodge* you can take your dinner at leisure in the courtyard, otherwise the *Tourist Cafeteria* offers the same menu and garden ambience. This is also a good base for toast-and-egg breakfast. The *Jaiswal* serves up tasty home-cooked thalis in the evenings (order in advance), as do the rather less hygienic *dhabas* at the far south end of the bus stand – a generous thali at *Gopal's* here will set you back Rs35. Steaming chai, *puri, sabzii* and *jalebi* are dished up in the stalls by the bus stand from 7am, as well as the local speciality – sweet samosa stuffed with coconut.

Satdhara

Perched on the edge of a dramatic ravine amid rolling hills 30km north of Bhopal, **SATDHARA** ("seven streams") is well worth the detour for stupa enthusiasts, although you'll need your own vehicle to get there. Heading north from Bhopal, a signpost about 13km south of Sanchi points west down a motorable seven-kilometre dirt-track leading to the excavated site. There are no less than 34 **stupas** dating from the Mauryan period in the third century BC, and fourteen monasteries, three of which have substantial foundations still visible. Under the auspices of UNESCO, a number of the stupas and two of the **monasteries** have now been reconstructed using original methods and materials, and others are currently under excavation and renovation.

A path down to the left of the makeshift car park leads directly the site. No human bones have been discovered in any of the stupas, the most impressive of which is **stupa 1**, standing 13m high and with a *medhi* (broad circumambulatory path) around the base. Some of its sculpted **toranas** (gateways) have been moved a short distance away for restoration work, but remain on view. Immediately behind it is the imposing three-metre-tall foundation platform of **Monastery 1**, while to the right are two circular **mills**, where oxen still push a great stone around a rut to crush the lime, sand and stone rubble for cement – the technique used by the original architects.

Alongside the numerous subsidiary stupas and monasteries, the remains of **apsidal temples** from the second century BC Gupta period bear inscriptions in Brahmi script. A multitude of coins, tools and terracotta objects have been unearthed and removed for cataloguing and eventual display. If you do make it here, you're virtually guaranteed to have the atmospheric site all to yourself.

Vidisha

The main reason to call in at the bustling railway and market town of **VIDISHA**, a straightforward 56-kilometre train or bus ride from Bhopal, and also served by buses from nearby Sanchi, is to hop on a tonga to the archeological sites at **Udaigiri** and **Besnagar**. However, if you're not pushed for time, the place merits a closer look. Head first for the small **museum** (Tues–Sun 10am–5pm; free), hidden away behind the railway station in the east of town. The majority of its prize pieces, such as Kubera Yaksha, the three-metre, pot-bellied male fertility figure in the hallway, are second-century Hindu artefacts unearthed at Besnagar. Attractive Jain *tirthankaras* and lumps of masonry salvaged from the district's plethora of ruined Gupta temples litter the garden. Otherwise, occupy yourself with a wander into the brightly painted **Hindu temple** opposite the station, or take a meander through the cheerful **bazaar**, which spreads out in front of the whitewashed houses of the old town.

Vidisha is also known for having financed a prolific third-century BC spate of stupa construction, including much of the work at Sanchi. By the sixth century AD however, it lay deserted and in ruins, remaining so until the arrival of the Muslims three hundred years later when a settlement, called Bhilsa, was founded around the flat-topped hill in the centre of the modern town. Vidisha's other rather tenuous claim to fame is that the bricks of a nearby second-century BC Vishnu temple were stuck together with lime mortar, believed to be the world's oldest cement.

Udaigiri and Besnagar

A modest collection of ruined temples and fifth-century rock-cut caves stand just 6km west of Vidisha at **UDAIGIRI**. The caves, many decorated by Hindu and Jain mendicants, lie scattered around a long, thin outcrop of sandstone surrounded by a patchwork of wheat fields. It's a congenial area to explore, particularly on one of the tongas that hang around outside Vidisha's bus stand (Rs40–50 round trip), though the site is also an easy cycle ride from town (bikes are available from shops on the outskirts of the bazaar) or, if your legs are up to it, from Sanchi (1–2hr). It's a good idea to bring supplies of food and water as there are no shops after Vidisha.

Heading out from town, a left turn just after crossing the River Betwa leads along a gently undulating tree-lined avenue for 2–3 km. As it approaches the hillside, the road takes a sharp left turn towards the village. Stop at this corner, at the base of the near-vertical rock face, to climb a steep flight of steps to **Cave 19**, which has worn but attractive reliefs of gods and demons around the doorways, and a **Jain cave temple** on the northern edge of the ridge. An ASI *chowkidar* should be around to unlock the doors for you.

The site's *pièce de résistance*, a four-metre image of the boar-headed hero Varaha, stands carved into **Cave 5.** Vishnu adopted the guise of this long-snouted monster to rescue the earth-goddess, Prithvi (perched on a lotus next to his right shoulder) from the churning primordial ocean – depicted by delicate wavy lines. Varaha's left foot rests on a Naga king wearing a hood of thirteen cobra heads, while the river goddesses Ganga and Yamuna hold water vessels on either side. In the background you can see Brahma and Agni, the Vedic fire-god, plus sundry sages and musicians. The scene, prominent in many contemporary Hindu monuments, is seen as an allegory of the emperor Chandra Gupta II's conquest of northern India.

The ruins of ancient **BESNAGAR**, known locally as **Khambaba**, lie couched in a tiny village down the main road from Vidisha, 5km after the Udaigiri turn-off. During the time of the Mauryan and Shunga empires, between the third and first centuries BC, a thriving provincial capital overlooked the confluence of the Beas and Betwa rivers. The emperor Ashoka himself was governor here at one time, and even married a local banker's daughter. Nowadays, a few mounds and some scattered pieces of masonry are all that remain of the houses, stupas, temples and streets. One small monument, however, makes the short detour worthwhile. According to the inscription etched around its base and sixteen-sided column, the stone pillar in an enclosed courtyard, known as the **Column of Heliodorus**, was erected in 113 BC by a Bactrian-Greek envoy from Taxila, the capital city of Gandhara (now the northwest frontier region of Pakistan), who converted to the local Vaishnavite cult during his long diplomatic posting here. The shaft, dedicated to Krishna's father Vasudeva, was originally crowned with a statue of Vishnu's vehicle Garuda. Most of the other archeological finds dug up on the site – including a colossal fertility god, Kubera Yaksha – are now at the museum in Vidisha and the archeological museum in Gwalior.

Bhimbetka

Shortly after NH-12 peels away from the main Bhopal–Hoshangabad road, 45km southeast of the state capital, a long line of boulders appears high on a scrub-covered ridge to the west. The hollows, overhangs and crevices eroded over the millennia from the crags of this malleable sandstone outcrop harbour one of the world's largest collections of **prehistoric rock art**. Discovered accidentally in 1957 by the Indian archeologist Dr V.S. Wankaner, **BHIMBETKA** (sunrise–sunset; free) makes a fascinating day-trip, although you'll need to rent a car to get there (and take along a supply of food and drink). From Bhopal, take NH-12; 7km beyond the market town of Obaidullaganj take a left when you see a sign in Hindi with "3.2" written on it. Cross the railway line and the caves are 3km further along the road.

Of the thousand **shelters** so far catalogued along the ten-kilometre hilltop, around half contain rock paintings. These date from three different periods, each with its own distinctive style. The oldest fall into two categories: green outline drawings of human figures, and large red images of animals. Lumps of hematite (from which the red pigment was manufactured) unearthed amid the deepest excavations on the site have been carbon-dated to reveal origins in the Upper Paleolithic era, around 10,000 years ago. The second and more prolific phase accounts for the bulk of Bhimbetka's rock art, and took place in the **Late Mesolithic** era – the "Stone Age" – between 8000 and 5000 BC. These friezes depict dynamic hunting scenes full of rampaging animals, initiation ceremonies, burials, masked dances, sports, wars, pregnant women, an arsenal of different weapons and even what seems to be a drinking party. No one is sure why these sophisticated communities of hunter-gatherers decorated their temporary abodes in this way. One theory is that the cave art served the ritual or **magical** function of ensuring a plentiful supply of game; but while abundant depictions of bison, wild boar, antelope and deer lend credence to that notion, animals that were not on the Mesolithic menu, such as tigers and elephants, also appear. Shards of pottery found amid the accumulated detritus on the rock-shelter floors show that Bhimbetka's third and final spate of cave painting took place during the early historic period, after its inhabitants had begun to trade with settled agriculturalists. Their stylized, geometric figures bear a strong resemblance to the art still produced by the region's *adivasi*, or tribal groups.

From the car park at the top of the hill, a paved pathway winds through the jumble of rocks containing the most striking and accessible of Bhimbetka's art. Some of the paintings can be difficult to find and decipher, but the *chowkidars* sitting at the entrance will show you around for a bit of baksheesh. As you progress through the site, look out for the Paleolithic images in green, the wonderful "X-ray" animals filled in with cross-hatching and complex geometric designs, and the recurrent image of a bull chasing a human figure and a crab – a motif believed to represent a struggle between the totemic heroes of three different tribes.

Pachmarhi

Halfway between Bhopal and Jabalpur, a forbidding wall of weird, blackened sandstone peaks and impenetrable forest rears along the south side of the Narmada Valley. Among the last tracts of central India mapped by the British, the **Mahadeo Hills** weren't explored until 1857, when big-game hunter Captain J. Forsyth and his party of Bengal Lancers stumbled upon an idyllic saucer-shaped plateau at the heart of the range, strewn with huge boulders and crisscrossed by perennial clear-water streams. Five years later a road was cut from the railhead at **Piparia**, and by the end of the century **PACHMARHI** had become the summer capital of the entire Central Provinces, complete with a military sanatorium, churches, clubhouses, racecourse and inevitable polo pitch.

Aside from the faded Raj atmosphere and walks to waterfalls and viewpoints around the hill station itself, the main incentive to travel up here is the chance to scramble around the surrounding forest in search of **prehistoric rock art**. Dozens of sites lie scattered across the remote hills and valleys of the plateau: finding them isn't always easy without the help of a guide but can be great fun and gives you a chance to explore the 600-square-kilometre **Satpura National Park**, home to Indian bison (*gaur*), barking deer, sambar, *barasingha* swamp deer, jackals, wild dogs and a handful of elusive tigers and leopards.

Popular during the summer, mainly with Bengali, Gujarati and Maharashtrian families who come here to escape the heat of the cities, Pachmarhi remains sleepy for the rest of the year. In winter, things liven up during the annual **Shivratri mela** (Feb/March), when *lakhs* of pilgrims pour through en route to the top of nearby Chauragarh mountain. Out of season, the *yatra* route they follow, which many regard as worth the journey from the plains in itself, makes one of Central India's classic **hikes**.

The best **time to visit** Pachmarhi is between October and March, when the cool, clear mountain air makes a refreshing change from the heat and dust at lower elevations. It's especially worth trying to be here for Shivratri, although the bus journeys up from the plains can be nightmarish when the *mela* is in full swing. It is also best to avoid long holiday weekends, when popular spots such as **Bee Falls** and **Dhupgarh** (famed for its sunsets) attract crowds.

Arrival and accommodation

The nearest railhead for Pachmarhi is the busy market town of **Piparia**, 52km northeast and one hour away by bus (frequent services). Piparia is on the Mumbai–Howrah (via Allahabad,Varanasi and Itarsi) line. If you're coming from the north, Bhopal or the south, you will need to get off at **Itarsi junction** and then catch a bus (3hr) or train (several daily; 1-2hr) to Piparia. To arrive in time to get the last bus up the hill, you'll need to catch the Itarsi–Bina Express #1271 (daily 4.20pm). If you arrive after the last bus (6pm) has left, the only decent **place to stay** is the MPSTDC *Tourist Motel* (Ⓣ07576/222299; ❶) behind the station. However, shared taxi-Jeeps usually keep running till later. Buses also connect Pachmarhi with Bhopal (4 "Express direct" daily; 6hr), Chindwara (2 daily; 4–5hr) en route to Nagpur, and Indore (2 daily; 12hr).

Pachmarhi's small bus stand has an MPSTDC **information** counter (Mon–Sat 10.30am–2.30pm; Ⓣ07578/252098) which is often closed during its official opening hours; their **maps** are wildly inaccurate. The best place to rent a **car** with driver (around Rs850 per day) is at the hotels or at the main MPSTDC office (Mon–Sat 10am–5pm, closed every second and third Sat; Ⓣ07578/252100), next to the *Amaltas Hotel*, 1.5km south of the bus stand. Some hotels, like *Hotel Pachmarhi* arrange tours of main points (Rs650 for 4WD petrol jeep); the reception will ask other guests if they want to share the cost of the vehicle.

Neither the State Bank of India (which has an ATM) nor any of the hotels have foreign exchange facilities. The nearest places to **change money** are in Bhopal, Jabalpur or Nagpur. Bagri Internet Centre (Rs30/hr) is opposite *Khalsa Restaurant* and there are also Internet centres near the mosque, but the connections are extremely slow and unreliable.

Accommodation

Accommodation in Pachmarhi is in short supply during the *melas*, over the Christmas and New Year period, and through May and June, during which times you'd be well advised to book in advance. The tourist information counter at the bus stand can tell you which of the eight MPSTDC hotels have vacancies;

otherwise several pleasant and friendly private places in the bazaar make good alternatives. These independent establishments will all negotiate good discounts outside the October to March high season; MPSTDC offers a twenty percent "monsoon discount". Most budget accommodation lies a short walk up the hill in the bazaar and in a cluster close to the bus stand, but a few of the more comfortable MPSTDC hotels are a five-minute Jeep or rickshaw ride south on the far side of a lotus-filled lake, near the military training area, Tehsil.

Amrapali 200m south of the bus stand ⓣ07578/252195, ⓕ252217. Good-value hotel in a quiet location. The semi-deluxe rooms are a bit on the small side, but all rooms are well maintained and very clean, with 24hr hot water and Star TV. Room service and a decent rooftop restaurant. ❸–❺

Evelyn's Own Near MPSTDC *Satpura Retreat* ⓣ07578/252056, ⓔsamirarao@hotmail.com. Homely rooms in a beautiful colonial bungalow, set in gardens with a tennis court, indoor games room and pool. Run by an ex-army officer and his wife who are both a mine of information, it also has a fascinating library. The owner plays golf and tennis with guests. Room standards vary considerably so ask to see and select. Delicious meals served by prior arrangement. ❺–❻

MPSTDC Amaltas Near Tehsil ⓣ07578/252098. Small hotel in an old British-built house with a range of rooms, each with attached bath and fans. Room no.5 is particularly grand, with circular walls, marble fireplace and a sweeping private veranda. Mediocre restaurant and bar. ❹–❺

MPSTDC Holiday Homes Near SADA Barrier, about 600m before the bus stand ⓣ07578/252099. No-frills cottages with private verandas and little gardens. The attached bathrooms across a courtyard are extremely chilly in the winter. ❸

MPSTDC Panchvati Cottages Near Tehsil ⓣ07578/252096. Five pricey, self-contained two-bedroom chalets in their own gardens, aimed mainly at honeymooners. ❺

MPSTDC Panchvati Huts Near Tehsil ⓣ07578/252096. Good-value, well-run hotel set in pleasant grounds. Spacious rooms with attached shower-toilets, and an on-site restaurant and bar. ❹

MPSTDC Rock End Manor Above *Panchvati Huts* ⓣ07578/252079. Pachmarhi's top hotel, in a well-restored, pukka British bungalow. Six very comfortable, old-fashioned rooms with huge tiled bathrooms. Easy chairs on the veranda give views over the hills and of a flower garden. Very popular with visiting VIPs, so book in advance. ❽

Pachmarhi Patel Marg, opposite *Saket* ⓣ07578/252170. One of the better choices among a batch of budget hotels on the same road. Large, institutional place offering unexciting, clean rooms with bath at assorted prices, plus a restaurant and their own taxis for sightseeing. ❷–❹

Saket Patel Marg ⓣ07578/252165, ⓕ252317. Close to the State Bank in the heart of the bazaar, five minutes from bus stand. Friendly, clean and very good value; the carpeted rooms have fan, cable TV and attached bath with hot water. ❷–❹

The town and hikes

At over 1000m above sea level, Pachmarhi **town** is clean, green and relaxed, despite the presence of a large military cantonment in its midst. Like India's better-known hill stations, it has retained a distinctly colonial ambience enhanced by the elegant British bungalows and Victorian church spires that nose incongruously above the tropical tree line. In the evenings families stroll and picnic in the parklands, while army bands and scout troupes march around the *maidans*.

The web of forest tracks and pilgrim trails that thread their way around Pachmarhi's widely dispersed archeological and religious sites make for excellent **walking**. However, few, if any, of the paths are marked in English, and if you aim to attempt any routes more ambitious than those outlined below, consider employing a local **guide**. One reliable agency is the Tola Trekking Club (ⓣ07578/252256, ⓔtrekpachmarhi@hotmail.com), run by Vinay Sahu from *Hotel Saket*, which will organize day treks for Rs150 per person (extra for Jeep hire to trailheads). The guides are all young tribal men with expert knowledge of the area, and the fees go directly to them and their villages. Kamal Dhoot from *Hotel Kachnar* (☎07578/252547), is another reliable source of information on trekking and the area's flora and fauna. **Bikes**, rentable from the bazaar or the repair shop just below the Government Gardens for around Rs35 per day, are an alternative (and cheaper) way of getting to the trailheads, but make sure you carry a chain and padlock and hide the bicycle in the bushes while you are trekking.

Visitors are required to buy **permits** (Rs200/day; vehicle Rs40; Rs300 extra for video) to enter any sites in Satpura National Park. These, and the separate permit required for overnight halts in the forest, are issued (Mon–Sat 10am–5pm) at the office of the Director of the Forestry Commission, next to the MPSTDC *Amaltas* hotel. The small forestry museum (9am–1pm & 3–7pm; free) in the office gives a good introduction to the flora and fauna of Satpura National Park.

Pachmarhi Hill and the Jatashankar cave

Two popular short excursions you can safely attempt without a guide include the fifteen-minute climb up from the whitewashed Muslim shrine in the Babu Lines area of town (1km southwest of the bus stand) to the top of **Pachmarhi Hill**. From here you have a fine panoramic view over Pachmarhi town on one side, and the thickly forested valley of **Jambu Dwip** on the other. The craggy cliffs lining the north side of the uninhabited gorge below are riddled with hidden rock-shelters and caves.

Alternatively, a thirty-minute walk follows a well-beaten track from the bus stand, twisting north from the main bazaar into the hillside through a narrow steep-sided canyon to **Jatashankar**, a sacred cave that's a prominent point in the Shivratri *yatra*. En route, in a small cluster of prehistoric rock-shelters just off the path, look out for **Harper's cave**, named for its naturally formed seated figure of a man playing a harp. Beyond it, at the head of a dark chasm, the Jatashankar cave itself lurks at the foot of a long flight of stone steps. Lord Shiva is said to have fled here through a secret passageway under the Mahadeo range to escape the evil demon Bhasmasur. The grotto's name, which literally means "Shiva's hairstyle", derives from the rock formation around a natural *lingam* on the cave floor, supposed to resemble the god's matted dreadlocks.

Pandav caves, Fairy Pool and Big Falls

A two- to three-hour walk around the eastern fringes of the plateau strings together a small cluster of interesting sights. First head up to the **Pandav caves** (40min), which occupy a knobbly sandstone hillock just east of the road between the ATC cantonment and the petrol pump. Hindu mythology tells that these five (*panch*) simple cells (*marhi*) sheltered the famous Pandava brothers of *Mahabharata* fame during their thirteen-year exile. Archeologists, however, maintain that the bare stone chambers and pillared verandas were excavated by a group of Buddhist monks around the first century BC.

Rejoin the metalled road in front of the caves and head around the back of the hill to the melancholy **British cemetery**. Beyond that, the road becomes a dirt track leading to a small car park. From here, take the footpath down the hill through the woods for about twenty minutes till the trail flattens out, and turn right at a fork to descend to **Apsara Vihar**, or "Fairy Pool" – an often crowded bathing place and picnic spot at the foot of a small waterfall. Troupes of black-faced langur monkeys crash through the canopy overhead as you approach the 150-metre **Rajat Prapat**, or "Big Falls", about a five-minute scramble over the boulders downstream from the Fairy Pool. If you walk back to the fork and continue along the trail, a five-minute walk brings you to a railing facing the 105-metre-high falls. Beyond this point you will need a guide to find the two-kilometre trail down to the deep cold pool at the bottom, best swum in when the sun is directly on it in the mornings.

Chauragarh

The 23-kilometre climb to the sacred summit of **Chauragarh mountain**, on the south rim of the plateau, follows the main *yatra* trail used by pilgrims during the Shivratri *mela*. The first 8km of this route can be covered by bike. From the bazaar, head south across the lake towards the crossroads in front of the MPSTDC *Amaltas*. From here, take the road to **Mahadeo Cave**, passing a vantage point above the narrow **Handi Kho** ravine, and leave your bike hidden in the bushes just before the road makes its first sharp descent at the turn-off for **Priyadarshini**, or "Forsyth's Point".

The **footpath** proper begins at the very bottom of the valley, after the road has plunged down a sequence of hairpin bends. Before setting off, make a brief diversion up the *khud* behind the modern **temple** to the Mahadeo cave, where pilgrims take a purifying dip in the cool perennial springwater that gushes through its pitch-black interior. From here, a strenuous two-hour climb follows an ancient trail to the top of the holy mountain, crammed with tens of thousands of worshippers and *sadhus* during the Shivratri festival. At the summit, where a temple houses the all-powerful Chauragarh *lingam*, a thicket of orange tridents surrounds a bright blue statue of Shiva. The view over the verdant Satpuras, to the scrubland and distant flat-topped mountains, is suitably sublime.

Eating

All the **MPSTDC** hotels have **restaurants** serving the same unimaginative but reliable Indian and Chinese menus at reasonable prices; *Amaltas* also has a bar. The charming *Rock End Manor* has the edge if you've come here in search of Raj-era atmosphere; book a table in advance. Less expensively, the *dhabas* along the main road serve generous and very cheap thalis, although hygiene is not always a priority. If you plan to trek all day, get a *dhaba* to prepare some *aloo parathas* and pickle for a picnic lunch.

Bombay Hotel Gandhi Chowk. A locally popular choice for mutton, chicken, egg and *paneer* curries – some dishes are very oily and fiery, but the prices are unbeatable.
China Bowl Near *Panchvati Huts*. Good mutton, chicken, *paneer* and *kofta* dishes with a few soups, chop sueys and chow meins thrown in. Open for breakfast, too: cutlets, eggs and South Indian snacks.
Indian Coffee House Main Rd, just before the bus stand. Open from 8.30am for *dosas* and coffee, and South Indian fast food lunches.
Khalsa Bottom end of bazaar, off the main road. Inexpensive, delicious Punjabi and Chinese dishes served inside in a frantic, strip-lit atmosphere, or in the calmer garden. Beer available in a side room.
Mrignayani Gandhi Chowk. The most hygienic of the cheap thali joints in the bazaar, serving fiery, no-nonsense pure-veg curries and piping hot *rotis* from large vats at rock-bottom prices.

Northern Madhya Pradesh

The remoteness of the famous temples at **Khajuraho**, with their superbly carved erotic sculptures, means that many visitors find themselves passing through a large tract of **northern Madhya Pradesh**. Few choose to linger in the region, however, preferring to return to the main Delhi–Agra artery or move onto Varanasi. Yet this much-trodden trail passes within striking distance of several other sights which are well worth taking time out to see. Foremost among them is the spectacular hill-fort at **Gwalior**, below which an extravagant European-style palace is crammed with quirky art treasures and curios.

To the east, Jhansi, in UP (see p.326), is the main jumping-off point both for Khajuraho and the medieval ghost-village of **Orchha**, a wonderfully atmospheric former capital whose decaying monuments rise from the banks of the Betwa River. Looming above a lively little market town, the multistorey fort-palace at **Datia**, 27km northwest of Jhansi, is another forgotten architectural treasure.

The region's major rail and road routes arc north from Bhopal, passing through the jigsaw joint with neighbouring Uttar Pradesh at Jhansi, before heading north to Agra and Delhi. In the east, the Central Railway connects the state capital with **Satna**, the nearest railhead to Khajuraho, then veers northeast towards Varanasi and the Ganges basin. Cutting between the two train lines on the busy back-country road to Khajuraho enables you to take in Orchha on the way.

Gwalior

Straddling the main Delhi–Mumbai train line, **GWALIOR** is the largest city in northern Madhya Pradesh and the site of one of India's most magnificent hilltop forts. The old sandstone citadel, with its temples and palaces, peers down from the edge of a sheer-sided plateau above a haze of petrol fumes, busy streets and cubic concrete houses. Once you've done a round of the **archeological museum**, and the rock-cut **Jain colossi** at the foot of the cliff, the city's other unmissable attraction is the extraordinarily flamboyant **Jai Vilas palace**, owned by the local ruling family, the **Scindias**. Their personalities and influence are everywhere, from the grand hospital and the **chhatris** (memorial halls) north of Jayaji Chowk to the excellent **Sarod Ghar** museum that celebrates the long tradition of royal patronage of classical music in the city.

Despite its proximity to Agra, 119km north, Gwalior sees few foreigners; in truth, with its drab modern centre and gritty bazaar, it lacks the charm of its counterparts in nearby Rajasthan. Nevertheless, it can be a worthwhile place to pause for a day, particularly around late November and early December, when the old **Moghul tombs** in the Muslim quarter host one of the premier Indian classical **music festivals**.

Some history

A donative inscription unearthed in a now-defunct sun temple proves that Gwalior was first occupied in the sixth century BC by Hun invaders from the north. Local legend, however, attributes the founding of the fort to the Kuchwaha prince **Suraj Sen**, said to have been cured of leprosy during the tenth century by the hermit **Gwalipa** after whom the city is named. The Kuchwahas' successors, the Parihars, were brutally overthrown in 1232 by **Iltutmish**, following an eleven-month siege. Before the fort eventually fell to the Muslim army, the Rajput women trapped inside committed mass suicide by self-immolation.

A third Rajput dynasty, the **Tomars**, retook Gwalior in 1398, and ushered in the city's "golden age". Under **Man Singh**, who ascended to the Tomar *gadi*

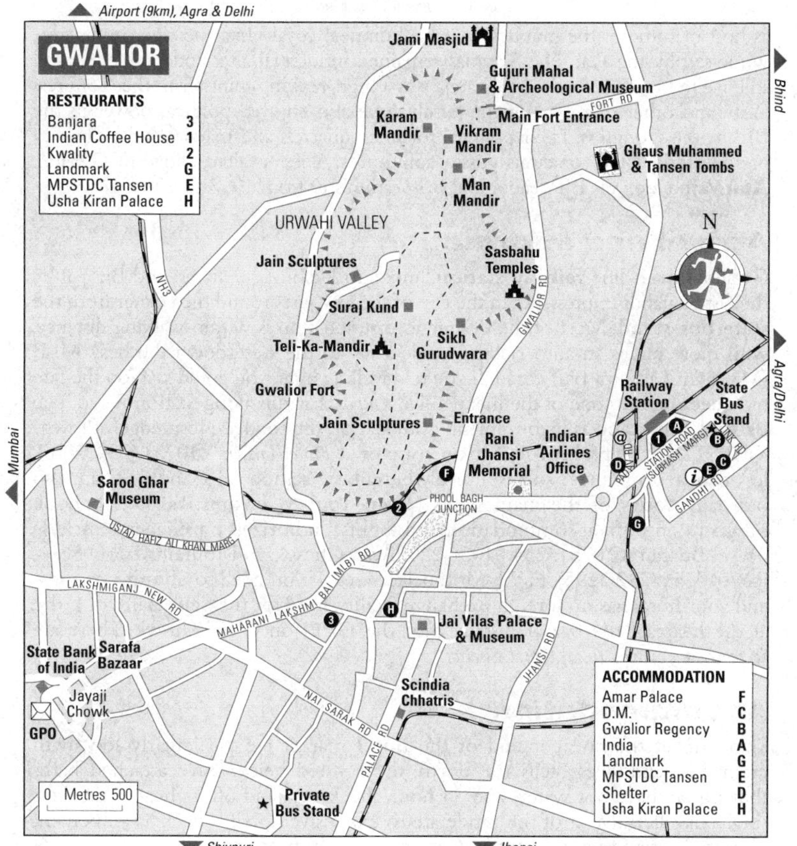

(throne) in 1486, the hilltop gained the magnificent palaces and fortifications that were to earn it the epithet "the pearl in the necklace of the castles of Hind". Skirmishes with neighbouring powers dogged the Rajputs' rule until 1517, however, when the **Lodis** from Delhi besieged the fort for a second time. On this occasion they were successful. Man Singh was slain, and his son, who managed to fend off the attackers for another twelve months, finally surrendered. Thereafter, Gwalior was ruled by a succession of Muslim overlords, including Babur, Humayun and Sher Shah, before falling to Akbar.

With the decline of the Moghuls, Gwalior became the base of the most powerful of the four Maratha clans, the **Scindias**, in 1754. Twenty-six years later, wily British East India Company troops conquered the fort in an audacious night raid, using rope ladders and socks stuffed with cotton to muffle the sound of their approach. Within hours, the citadel was overrun, and Gwalior became a British feudatory state ruled by a succession of puppet rajas. The most famous of these, the immensely rich Jayaji Rao Scindia (1843–86), remained loyal to the British during the 1857 Mutiny, although 6500 of his troops joined the opposing forces led by Tantia Tope and the infamous **Rani Lakshmi Bai** of Jhansi (see p.326). Both rebel leaders were killed in the ensuing battle, and the maharaja quickly resumed his role as host of some of the grandest viceregal dinners, royal visits and tiger hunts ever witnessed by the Raj. The Scindias remained influential after Independence, and still live in Gwalior; the late Maharaja was a high-ranking minister in the Congress Party and other members of the family have also enjoyed political power in the BJP or the Congress. Their political fortunes, quarrels and marriages continue to provide fodder for voracious gossip columnists. A less exalted native of Gwalior, **Atal Vajpayee**, was BJP leader and prime minister from 1998 to 2003.

Arrival and information

Gwalior's main-line **railway station**, linked to Delhi, Agra, Jhansi and Bhopal by the fast Shatabdi Express, lies in the east of the city, just around the corner from the **state bus stand**. Most of the decent accommodation is within walking distance, with more places an auto-rickshaw ride away to the west, down the busy MLB (Maharani Lakshmi Bai) Road. If you're travelling light, you could save on the fare by squeezing into one of the inexpensive *tempos* that run along Station Road. The **private bus stand** is inconveniently situated on the southwestern edge of town.

MPSTDC's helpful **information** counter at *Hotel Tansen* (Ⓣ0751/234 0370), less than ten minutes' walk south of the railway station on Gandhi Road, also has daily **tours** of the main sights (10am–1pm & 4-7pm; Rs100). To book onward transport, accommodation and flights, authorized travel agents include Travel Bureau (Ⓣ0751/234 0103), 220 Jiwaji Chowk, and Touraids Travel Service (Ⓣ0751/242 3293), in the Moti palace area. If you need to **change money**, and your hotel has no foreign exchange facility, head for the State Bank of India, at the heart of the bazaar district near the **GPO** on Jayaji Chowk. There are **Internet** centres near *Hotel Shelter*.

Accommodation

Standards at the cheaper end of the **hotel** market are particularly low, with cramped windowless cells the norm; those listed below have attached baths (but not all have hot water) and 24 hour check-out, and offer cheaper rates for single travellers. Most of the moderate to expensive hotels whack a ten percent "luxury" tax and ten percent service charge on top of the tariff.

Amar Palace Phoolbagh Circle, Station Rd Ⓣ0751/232 5843. Modern, friendly and well-run hotel. Clean rooms have marble floors and small balconies, some with views of the fort. ❸–❹

D.M. Near state bus stand Ⓣ0751/234 2083. Quiet, clean and friendly, this lodge is the most pleasant of the budget options in the area. The rooms all have attached baths and 24hr hot water; the slightly more pricey "deluxe" rooms are particularly good value. ❶–❷

Gwalior Regency Link Rd, near state bus stand Ⓣ0751/234 0670, Ⓔgregency@hotmail.com. Modern and ritzy, with Star TV in all rooms, foreign exchange, nightclub, health club (with jacuzzi) and a pool. ❺–❼

India Station Rd Ⓣ0751/234 1983. Friendly, no-frills lodge run by the Indian Coffee Workers' Co-op. Clean, but the rooms overlook the noisy main street; deluxe units have Western toilets. ❷–❹

Landmark Manik Vilas Ⓣ0751/234 5780, Ⓦwww.hotellandmarkgwalior.com. The best accommodation in the station area, with comfortable rooms and central a/c, Internet access, foreign exchange facilities, bar and restaurant. Noon check-out. ❺–❻

MPSTDC Tansen 6A Gandhi Rd Ⓣ0751/234 0370. Large, efficient hotel in its own gardens near the station, with plain rooms that are showing their age (some with a/c) and a good restaurant and bar. Popular with tour groups, so advance booking is recommended. Noon check-out. ❸–❺

Shelter Padav Rd Ⓣ0751/232 6209. Smart hotel near the station, with comfortable rooms, a smart bar and a very welcome swimming pool. A/c rooms are only slightly pricier. ❺–❻

Usha Kiran Palace Jayendraganj, Lakshar Ⓣ0751/232 3993, Ⓦww.tajhotels.com. Former maharaja's guesthouse now run by the Taj group as an opulent five-star. Recent renovations in the chain's usual style haven't removed the historic charm – resplendent, spacious rooms feature period 1930s furniture. A swimming pool and spa are among the many facilities. ❽–❾

The fort

Gwalior's imposing **fort** (daily 9am–5pm; Rs100 [Rs5]) sprawls over a 3km-long outcrop of sandstone to the north of the modern city. Its mighty turreted battlements encompass no less than six palaces, three temples and several water tanks and cisterns, as well as a prestigious public school and a shiny new Sikh *gurudwara*.

Two routes wind up the hill. In the west, a motorable track climbs the steep gorge of the **Urwahi valley**, passing a line of rock-cut Jain statues along the way. The other, more accessible entrance is on the northeast corner of the cliff, at the head of a long, stepped ramp. The two can be combined by taking a rickshaw to the Urwahi side, then walking up and across the plateau and dropping down via the northeastern entrance to the museum and Jami Masjid, from where it's easier to pick up a rickshaw or *tempo* back into town.

Official **guides** (approximately Rs180 for a 3hr tour) tout for trade at the Urwahi gate and the cold drinks shop at the entrance to the palace complex. You can also mug up on the fort's history via the nightly 45-minute **son-et-lumière** show (English show starts at 7.30pm Nov–Feb, 8.30pm March–Oct; Rs150 [Rs40]) at the Man Mandir.

The northeastern approach and museum

The **northeastern approach** to the fort leads under several fortified **gateways**. After the second, you arrive at the modest **Gujuri Mahal**, built by Man Singh to woo his favourite rani, Mrignayani, when she was still a peasant girl. The elegant sandstone palace now houses Gwalior's **archeological museum** (Tues–Sun 10am–5pm; Rs35 [Rs5]), where the large exhibition of sculpture, inscriptions and painting is well worth a look, even if the labels are woefully uninformative. Highlights include the twin Ashoka lion capitals from Vidisha in gallery two; and gallery nine's erotic bas-relief, in which a prince is shown gently removing the top of his beloved's sari. However, the most famous piece here is the exquisite **Salabhanjika**, a small, exquisitely carved female figurine found in the ruins of the temple at Gyaraspur. Noted for her sensuous curves and sublime facial expression, the statue is often dubbed "India's *Mona Lisa*", and crops up in books on local art the world over.

The Man Mandir

Entered via the **Hathiya** ("elephant") **Paur** gateway, with its twin turrets and ornate blue tilework, the **Man Mandir** (daily 8am–5pm; Rs100 [Rs5]) is one of the finest early Hindu palaces in India. Built between 1486 and 1517 by the Tomar ruler Man Singh, it's also known as the Chit Mandir, or "painted palace", for the rich ceramic **mosaics** that encrust its facade. The best-preserved fragments of tilework, on its south side, can be seen from the bank left of the main Hathiya Paur gateway. Spread in luxurious bands of turquoise, emerald green and yellow across the ornate stonework are tigers, elephants, peacocks, banana palms and crocodiles brandishing flowers.

By contrast, the **interior** of the four-storeyed palace is very plain. Some of the larger halls, however, do contain fine pierced-stone *jali* screens, behind which the women of the palace would assemble to receive instruction from Gwalior's great music gurus. The circular chambers in the lower storeys were formerly the palace dungeons. Prisoners incarcerated here in Moghul times were fed on a preparation made with boiled poppy heads called *poust* – a cruelly ingenious form of torture that ensured a protracted and painful death from malnourishment and drug addiction.

The Teli-ka-Mandir and Suraj Kund

The thirty-metre-tall **Teli-ka-Mandir**, on the south side of the plateau, is the oldest surviving monument in the fort. Dating from the mid-eighth century, it consists of a huge rectangular sanctuary tower capped with an unusual vaulted-arch roof, whose *peepal*-leaf shape derives from the *chaitya* windows of much earlier rock-cut Buddhist caves. In the aftermath of the Gwalior Mutiny in 1858, the temple, dedicated to Vishnu, was used by the British as a soda factory. The Archeological Survey of India is now carrying out extensive restoration work.

Set back from the road at the head of the Urwahi ravine, just north of the Teli-ka-Mandir, the **Suraj Kund** is the hundred-metre-long tank whose magical waters are supposed to have cured the tenth-century ruler Suraj Sen, later Suraj Pal, of leprosy.

The Sasbahu mandirs and Sikh gurudwara

The **Sasbahu**, or "mother- and daughter-in-law", temples overlook the city from the eastern edge of the fort, near the unsightly TV mast. The larger of the pair has a three-storey *mandapa* (assembly hall), supported by four intricate pillars, while the smaller one consists of an open-sided porch with a pyramidal roof. Both were erected late in the eleventh century and are dedicated, like the Teli-ka-Mandir, to Vishnu.

The huge, gold-tipped, white-domed marble building to the south is a modern **Sikh gurudwara**. Built to commemorate a Sikh hero who was imprisoned in the fort, the temple attracts a constant stream of pilgrims. Along the road leading to it, you'll pass groups of men clad in the traditional garb of Sikh warriors – long blue *kurtas*, bulky turbans, daggers, and spears held over their shoulders – filing along like foot-soldiers from a bygone era. The gurudwara's cool marble courtyard, filled with the strains of devotional music, makes an atmospheric place to escape the heat. Before entering, make sure you cover your arms, legs and head, remove your socks and shoes, and wash your feet in the tank at the bottom of the steps. Tobacco is strictly prohibited inside the complex.

The rock-cut Jain sculptures

The sheer sandstone cliffs around the fort harbour some imposing **rock-cut Jain sculpture**. Carved between the seventh and fifteenth centuries, most of the large honey-coloured figures depict the 24 Jain teacher-saviours – the *tirthankaras*, or "Crossing Makers" – in characteristic poses: standing with their arms held stiffly at their sides, or sitting cross-legged, the palms of their hands upturned, staring serenely into the distance. Many lost their faces and genitalia when Moghul emperor Babur's iconoclastic army descended on the city in 1527.

The larger of the two main groups lines the southwestern approach to the fort, along the sides of the **Urwahi** ravine. The largest image, to the side of the road near Urwahi Gate, portrays Adinath, 19m tall, with decorative nipples, a head of tightly curled hair and drooping ears, standing on a lotus bloom beside several smaller statues. A little further from the fort, on the other side of the road, another company of *tirthankaras* enjoys a more dramatic situation, looking over a natural gorge. All have lost their faces, save a proud trio sheltered by a delicate canopy.

The third collection stands on the southeast corner of the plateau, overlooking the city from a narrow ledge. To get there, follow Gwalior Road north along the foot of the cliff from Phool Bagh junction, near the **Rani Jhansi memorial**, until you see a paved path winding up the hill from behind a row of houses on the left. Once again, the *tirthankaras*, which are numbered, occupy deep recesses hewn from the rock wall. One of the few not defaced by the Muslim invaders, no. 10 is still visited by Gwalior's small Jain community as a shrine.

The old town and south of the fort

A number of interesting Islamic monuments are tucked away down the narrow, dusty backstreets of Gwalior's predominantly Muslim **old town**, clustered around the north and northeast corners of the hill. The **Jami Masjid** stands close to the Gujuri Mahal, near the main entrance to the fort. Erected in 1661 by Mohammad Khan, using sandstone quarried from the plateau above, the beautifully preserved mosque sports two slender minarets and three bulbous onion domes crowned with golden spires.

The city's most famous Muslim building, however, is set amid balding lawns 1km further east. The sixteenth-century **Tomb of Ghaus Mohammed**, an Afghan prince who helped Babur take Gwalior fort, is a fine specimen of early Moghul architecture, and a popular local shrine. Elegant hexagonal pavilions stand at each of its four corners; in the centre, the large central dome retains a few remnants of its blue-glazed tiles. The tomb's walls are inlaid with exquisite pierced-stone *jali* screens, whose complex geometric patterns are best admired from the incense-filled interior.

The second and smaller of the tombs in the gardens is that of the famous Moghul singer-musician **Tansen**, one of the "Nine Jewels" of Emperor Akbar's court. Every year, performers and aficionados from all over India flock here for Gwalior's annual **music festival** (Nov–Dec). At other times, impromptu recitals of *qawwali*, Islamic devotional singing accompanied on the harmonium, take place on the terrace outside. Local superstition holds that the leaves of the **tamarind tree** growing on the plinth nearby have a salutary effect on the singing voice, which explains why its bottom branches have been stripped bare. **To get there** from the station, take a rickshaw (Rs20) or a *tempo* bound for Hazira (Rs2).

The Jai Vilas palace

Due south of the fort, in the heart of Gwalior's upper-class neighbourhood, the **Jai Vilas palace** (daily except Wed 9.30am–5pm; Rs200 [Rs30], plus Rs25 for camera, Rs75 video) is one of India's most grandiose and eccentric nineteenth-century relics, although the steep entry fee and lack of labelling and information make it an unsatisfactory experience. **Guides** hang out by the entrance, however, and charge about Rs50 per tour.

The palace was built in 1875 during the reign of Maharaja Jayaji Rao Scindia. Wanting his residence to rival those of his colonial overlords in Britain, he dispatched his friend Colonel Michael Filose on a grand tour of Europe to seek inspiration. A year or so later, Filose returned with a vast shipment of furniture, fabric, paintings, tapestries and cut glass, together with the blueprints for a building that borrowed heavily from Buckingham Palace, Versailles, and a host of Greek ruins and Italian-Baroque stately homes. The result is an improbable and shamelessly over-the-top blend of Doric, Tuscan and Corinthian architecture.

The Scindias, who still occupy a part of the palace, have opened two wings to the public. Eager to maintain the sense of a family home, they have placed innumerable photographs of their richly clad clan members on every available surface throughout the first wing, a **museum** of the more valuable and extraordinary artefacts accumulated by the rulers of Gwalior. Collecting dust in the dozens of rooms and creaky wood-panelled corridors are countless Moghul paintings, Persian rugs, gold and silver ornaments, and antique furniture that had originally belonged to the estate of Louis XVI before the French Revolution. Elsewhere, you'll come across a swing made from Venetian cut glass which the royal family used to celebrate Krishna's birthday, and, upstairs, a room full erotica.

A still more extravagant wing lies across the courtyard from the museum. The **durbar hall** was where the maharaja entertained important visitors, among them the Prince of Wales (later Edward VII), who descended on Gwalior in 1875 with an entourage of a thousand people. Displayed in the banquet hall on the ground floor is a silver toy train used by Jayaji Rao Scindia to dispense brandy and cigars after dinner; the maharaja would tease anyone he didn't like by not stopping the electric locomotive when it reached them. A sweeping Belgian glass staircase leads from the lobby to the gargantuan assembly hall upstairs. Suspended from its ceiling are the world's biggest chandeliers. At over three and a half tonnes apiece, they could not be installed until the strength of the roof had been tested with eight elephants – a feat that necessitated the construction of a 500-metre-long earth ramp. The rug lining the floor of the hall is equally enormous. Woven by inmates of Gwalior jail, it took twelve years to complete and, at over 40m in length, is the largest handmade carpet in Asia.

Sarod Ghar

Tucked away in the west of the city, the **Sarod Ghar** music museum (Tues–Sun 10am–1pm & 2–4pm; free; Ⓦwww.sarod.com) is on Ustad Hafiz Ali Khan Marg, Jiwaji Ganj. Either take a rickshaw directly to the house, or a *tempo* (Rs3) to Jiwaji, a five-minute walk north of Jayaji Chowk. The museum occupies the beautiful ancestral home of the Bangash family, with its rose sandstone walls aligned in pure symmetry and delicate sculptural detail around a marble courtyard, still used for musical recitals (check newspaper listings or at the MPSTDC tourist office). The Bangash ancestors were originally Afghan horse traders who settled in India and produced a dynasty of musical virtuosos, including **Ustad Hafiz Ali Khan** and his son **Ustad Amjad Ali Khan**.

The museum traces Gwalior's rich musical legacy from Tansen, who performed in the court of Moghul emperor Akbar, to the invention by Gulam Ali Khan Bangash of the **sarod** (for more on which, see Contexts, p.1422), whose ethereal tones accompany you as you progress through the galleries. The exhibition culminates with a display of instruments donated by famous musicians, and you can buy books, cassettes and CDs of classical Indian music in the small shop.

The Scindia Chhatris

Two typically ostentatious tombs belonging to the Scindia family stand a short rickshaw ride north of Jayaji Chowk. Enclosed inside a walled courtyard, the **chhatris** (mausoleums) are worth a look for their intricate stone work and ornately painted scenes of life inside the Maratha royal court in the nineteenth century. Built in 1817 to commemorate Maharaja Jiyaji Rao Scindia, the larger of the pair is most remarkable for the intricate outside panelling of interwoven flowers. The interior is a large hall traditionally used for musical recitals.

The second *chhatri* is reached through a yellow-and-white arch to the left of the courtyard, and is a more compact and finely detailed version of the former. Constructed in 1843 for the newly departed Maharaja Janakaji Scindia, sculptures and carvings depict the hectic lifestyle of a king. There are little stone elephants, each bejewelled and covered with a unique silk canopy, plodding in a line around the platform to symbolize the power of the maharaja, and the door is guarded by two solemn soldiers in full Maratha regalia. As an antidote to the warring reputation of the Maratha rulers, numerous panels outside depict the life of Krishna surrounded by his many pleasure-seeking beauties, while inside the *chhatri* are painted frescoes of princesses and court dances, as well as life-size marble effigies of the maharaja and his three wives.

Eating

With a couple of exceptions, all the **best places to eat** in Gwalior are in the mid- and top-of-the-range hotels, where main dishes set you back anywhere between Rs30 and Rs100. More basic and much cheaper dhal, *subzi* and *roti* are doled out on stainless-steel plates at the row of *dhabas* outside the railway station. Look out too for the **juice bars** dotted around the station and Jayaji Chowk, over in the west end of town, which serve glasses of refreshing, freshly squeezed fruit juice (ask for no ice).

Banjara Old High Court Lane. Very dim lighting, but a good range of mainly Indian dishes as well as imaginative daily specials and western and South Indian breakfasts. Efficient service.

Indian Coffee House Station Rd. Delicious *dosas* and other South Indian snacks, plain or with nut and veg fillings. Opens 7.30am for breakfasts of *iddlis* and large omelettes with good coffee and the newspapers.

Kwality MLB Rd. Part of the north Indian restaurant chain, serving tasty veg and non-veg Indian dishes from a particularly long menu. It's one of the best restaurants in town, specially known for its *chicken makhani* and *malai kofta*.

Landmark Manik Vilas. The usual modestly priced multi-cuisine menu with an emphasis on Mughlai specialities; the main attraction however, is the live Indian classical music every evening.

MPSTDC Tansen 6A Gandhi Rd. Good Western breakfasts and the standard, safe MPSTDC Indian/Chinese menu; the biriyanis are particularly good.

Usha Kiran Palace Jayendraganj, Lakshar. Modest selection of (expensive) gourmet Indian and Western food, with lots of mouthwatering Mughlai-style dishes. The buffet lunches are good for a splurge.

Datia

Constructed by Bir Singh Deo at the height of the Bundela's "golden age", the majestic palace at **DATIA**, 30km northwest of Jhansi, is regarded as one of the finest Rajput buildings in India. Although few of the visitors who spy the exotic hulk of yellow-brown ramparts, cupolas and domed pavilions from the nearby train line actually stop here, those that do are rarely disappointed. Presiding over a mass of white- and blue-washed brick houses from its seat atop a rock outcrop, the **Nrsing Dev Palace** (dawn to dusk; free) stands in the north of town. Half the fun of visiting the labyrinthine palace is trying to find a path from its pitch-black subterranean chambers, hewn out of the solid base of the hill for use during the hot season, to the rani's airy apartment on the top floor. In between, a maze of cross-cutting corridors, flying walkways, walls encrusted with fragments of ceramic tiles, latticed screens and archways, hidden passages, pavilions and suites of apartments lead you in ever-decreasing circles until you eventually run out of staircases. The views from the upper storeys are breathtaking.

Practicalities

Datia, on the main Delhi–Mumbai train line, is most often visited as a day-trip from Jhansi, or as a break in the journey to Gwalior, 71km to the northwest. Buses run from both cities every thirty minutes and there are ten trains daily. If you're coming from Shivpuri, 97km west, you'll have to change buses at Karera. Tongas and cycle rickshaws ferry passengers into town from the small **railway station**, 2km southwest, while **buses** pull in at a lot on the south side of the centre. Bicycles can be hired at minimal cost from a shop on the corner of the main road and the road to the bus stand, near Raj Garh Palace. You can get simple **food** and cold drinks in the *dhabas*.

Orchha

An essential stop en route to or from Khajuraho, **ORCHHA** ("hidden place") certainly lives up to its name, languishing amid a tangle of scrubby dhak forest 18km southeast of Jhansi. In spite of its generally tumbledown state, the deserted medieval town is a former capital of the Bundela rajas and remains an architectural gem, its guano-splashed temple *shikharas*, derelict palaces, *havelis* and weed-choked sandstone cenotaphs floating serenely above the banks of the River Betwa. Clustered around the foot of the exotic ruins, the sleepy village of neatly painted houses, market stalls and a couple of attractive hotels makes an excellent spot to unwind after the hassle of northern cities. However, it's firmly established on the tour group trail these days, and it's worth spending a night or two here to see Orchha after the bus parties have moved off.

Some history

After being chased by several generations of Delhi Sultans from various capitals around central India, the Bundela dynasty finally settled at the former Malwan fort of **Orchha** in the fifteenth century. Work on Orchha's magnificent fortifications, palaces and temples was started by Raja **Rudra Pratap** soon after the move, and continued after he was killed in 1531 trying to wrestle a cow from the clutches of a tiger. Thereafter, the dynasty's fortunes depended on the goodwill of their mighty neighbours, the **Moghuls**. After being defeated in battle by Akbar, the proud and pious **Madhukar Shah** nearly signed his clan's death warrant by showing up at the imperial court with a red *tilak* smeared on his forehead – a mark at that time banned by the emperor. Luckily for the Bundelas, however, Madhukar's bold gesture earned Akbar's respect, and the two became friends – an alliance fostered in the following years by Orchha's most illustrious raja. During his 22-year rule, **Bir Singh Deo** erected a total of 52 forts and palaces across the region, including the citadel at Jhansi, the rambling Nrsing Dev at Datia, and many of Orchha's finest buildings. In 1627, he was killed by bandits while returning from the Deccan with a camel train full of booty. Afterwards, Bundelkhand's relations with the Moghuls rapidly deteriorated. Attacks by the armies of Shah Jahan, Aurangzeb, and the Marathas ensued, and a spate of eighteenth-century Jat peasant uprisings finally forced the Bundelas to flee Orchha for the comparative safety of **Tikamgarh**. Apart from the *Sheesh Mahal*, now converted into a small hotel, the magnificent monuments have lain virtually deserted ever since.

Arrival and information

Tightly packed **tempos** from Jhansi bus station run frequently to Orchha's main crossroads, 18km away, or there are five daily **buses**. Both take twenty to forty minutes (depending on the number of stops), and cost Rs10 (plus Rs10 for luggage in a *tempo*). An **auto-rickshaw** from Jhansi railway or bus station will set you back around Rs150; it costs more at night. Coming from **Khajuraho**, you can ask to be dropped at the Orchha turning on the main road and pick up a *tempo* for the remaining 7km.

If you're heading in the other direction, **towards Khajuraho**, don't bank on being able to flag down the express MPSRTC buses on the highway, as they're often full. Instead, get to Jhansi early and arrange a ticket before the Delhi/Agra trains pull in; the Shatabdi Express semi-deluxe coach leaves Jhansi railway station at 11am and takes four and a half hours. More comfortable **private Jeeps** (with drivers) cut the journey time to Khajuraho – they cost upwards of Rs1200 (one-way), and can be rented at the bus station, or through the manager of the MPSTDC *Sheesh Mahal* (ⓣ07680/252624), who can also arrange day-trips (Rs1500–1700). You can change **travellers' cheques** only at Canara Bank in the main square; Jhansi also has moneychanging facilities. There are **Internet** centres near Canara Bank, but the connection is unreliable.

Accommodation

Orchha has an increasing number of **places to stay**. Budget accommodation ranges from the extremely cheap and soulless state-run rest houses in the main bazaar to the typical backpacker hangouts with communal and/or attached bathrooms, 24-hour hot water and even generators for the frequent power cuts.

Amar Mahal ⓣ07680/252202, ⓦwww.alsisar.com. Impressive new hotel built in the style of the Orchha palaces, with Moghul domes, turrets and murals. Large a/c rooms set around a Moghul-style formal garden, a smart restaurant with good Indian food, swimming pool, and Internet. ❻–❼

Fortview Rest House Main Rd ⓣ07680/252701. An excellent option with a peaceful little garden on the banks of the river. Airy and clean doubles with hot water; one faces the palace. ❷–❸

MPSTDC Betwa Cottages ⓣ07680/252618. Cheerful place by the river, with cottages, set in the garden, boasting double bedroom, modern bathroom and some a/c. The interior design celebrates Moghul tradition with period painting and furniture. ❹–❺

MPSTDC Sheesh Mahal ⓣ07680/252624, ⓔmptorcha@sify.com. The local raja's former country bolt hole is now a friendly small hotel with one single (Rs390) and five non-a/c doubles (Rs690–790). If you can afford it, treat yourself to a romantic night in the royal suite – perks include candlelit dinner on your private veranda, a vast marble bathtub, and the ultimate loo with a view. Advance booking recommended. ❹–❾

Orchha Resort ⓣ07680/252222, ⓕ252677. Attractive, if garishly painted, riverside resort with all mod cons including foreign exchange, health club and pool. The luxury a/c tents with bath are slightly more affordable. ❼–❾

Sharma Main Rd, no phone. Just past the bazaar, this is a pleasant and relaxing lodge with spotless sunny yellow rooms around a quiet, shady courtyard; you pay more for a private bathroom. ❶–❷

Shri Mahant ⓣ07680/252715. The best option in the bazaar area, offering clean, simple rooms with attached bath; go for a room on the top storey, where a small roof terrace gives good views of the fort. ❷

The monuments

The best-preserved of Orchha's scattered **palaces**, **temples**, **tombs** and **gardens** (daily 9am–5pm; "day passport" for all monuments Rs30 [Rs5], plus Rs20 for camera, Rs50 video) lie within comfortable walking distance of the village and can be seen – at breakneck speed – in a day, but to get the most out of a trip you should plan on staying the night. English-speaking guides can be hired at the main gate for Rs100 for a short tour of the fort or near the main square for about Rs200-250 for a half-day tour of Orchha.

The Raj Mahal and the Rai Praveen Mahal

The first building you come to across Orchha's medieval granite bridge is the well-preserved ruin of the royal palace, or **Raj Mahal** (unrestricted access; free), started by Rudra Pratap and completed by one of his successors, the indomitable Madhukar Shah. From the end of the bridge, bear left at the main entrance, and then right before reaching the *Sheesh Mahal* hotel. Of the two rectangular courtyards inside, the second, formerly used by the Bundela ranis, is the most dramatic. Opulent royal quarters, raised balconies and interlocking walkways rise in symmetrical tiers on all four sides, crowned by domed pavilions and turrets; the apartments projecting into the quadrangle on the ground floor belonged to the most-favoured queens. As you wander around, look out for the fragments of mirror inlay and vibrant **painting** plastered over their walls and ceilings. Some of the friezes are still in remarkable condition, depicting Vishnu's various outlandish incarnations, court and hunting scenes, and lively festivals involving dancers, musicians and jugglers. The resident *chowkidar* is an excellent guide.

Reached via a path that leads from the Raj Mahal around the northern side of the hill, the **Rai Praveen Mahal** is a small, double-storeyed brick apartment built by Raja Indramani for his concubine in the mid-1670s. The gifted poetess, musician and dancer, Rai Praveen, beguiled the Moghul emperor Akbar when she was sent to him as a gift, but was eventually returned to Orchha to live out her remaining days. Set amid the well-watered lawns of the **Anand Mahal gardens** (unrestricted access; free), it has a main assembly hall on the ground floor (used to host music and dance performances), a boudoir upstairs, and cool underground apartments.

The Jahangir Mahal

Orchha's single most admired palace, the **Jahangir Mahal** was built by Bir Singh Deo as a monumental welcome present for the Moghul emperor when he paid a state visit here in the seventeenth century. Jahangir had come to invest his old ally with the sword of Abdul Fazal – the emperor's erstwhile enemy whom Bir Singh had murdered some years earlier. Entered through an ornate ceremonial gateway, the main, east-facing facade is still encrusted with turquoise tiles. Two stone elephants flank the stairway, holding bells in their trunks to announce the arrival of the raja, and there are three storeys of elegant hanging balconies, terraces, apartments and onion domes piled around a central courtyard. This palace, however, has a much lighter feel, with countless windows and pierced stone screens looking out over the exotic Orchha skyline to the west, and a sea of treetops and ruined temples in the other direction.

The Sheesh Mahal

Built during the early eighteenth century, long after Orchha's demise, the **Sheesh Mahal** ("Palace of Mirrors") was originally intended as an exclusive country retreat for the local raja, Udait Singh. Following Independence, however, the property was inherited by the state government, who have converted it into a hotel. The rather squat palace stands between the Raj Mahal and the Jahangir Mahal, at the far end of an open-sided courtyard. Covered in a coat of whitewash and stripped of most of its Persian rugs and antiques, the building retains little of its former splendour, though it does offer stunning views from its upper terraces and turrets. The only rooms worth a peep – assuming they're not occupied (check with reception) – are the palatial nos. 1 and 2, which contain original bathroom fittings.

Around the village

Dotted around the **village** below the hill are several other interesting monuments. The **Ram Raja Mandir** stands at the end of the small bazaar, in a cool marble-tiled courtyard. Local legend has it that Madhukar Shah constructed the building as a palace for his wife, Rani Ganesha, and it only became a temple after a Rama icon, which the queen had dutifully carried all the way from her home town of Ayodhya, could not be lifted from the spot where she first set it down; it remains there to this day, and the temple is a popular pilgrimage site.

△ Jahangir Mahal, Orchha

With its huge pointed *shikharas* soaring high above the village, **Chatturbuj Mandir** is the temple originally built to house Rani Ganesha's icon. In cruciform shape, representing the four-armed Vishnu, with seven storeys and spacious courtyards ringed by arched balconies, it epitomizes the regal Bundelkhand style inspired by the Moghuls, but is also influenced by Rajput, Persian and European tastes. It's unusual for a Hindu temple, with very few carvings and a wealth of space – perhaps to accommodate followers of the **bhakti** cult (a form of worship involving large congregations of people rather than a small elite of priests). You can climb up the narrow staircases between storeys to the temple's roof, pierced by an ornate *shikhara* whose niches shelter nesting vultures.

On the other side of Ram Mandir, a path leads through the Moghul-style **Phool Bagh** ornamental garden to **Hardaul ka Baithaka**, a grand pavilion where Bir Singh Deo's second son, Hardaul, ally of Jahangir and romantic paragon, once held court. Newlyweds come here to seek blessing from Hardaul; he was poisoned by his jealous brother who accused him of intimacy with his sister-in-law. The tall towers rising above the gardens like disregarded bridge supports are *dastgirs* (literally "wind-catchers"), Persian-style cooling towers that provided air-conditioning for the neighbouring palace, Palkhi Mahal; they're thought to be the only ones of their kind surviving in India.

A solemn row of pale brown weed-choked domes and spires, the riverside **chhatris** are Orchha's most melancholy ruins. The fourteen cenotaphs, memorials to Bundelkhand's former rulers, are best viewed from the narrow road bridge or, better still, from the boulders on the opposite bank, where you get the full effect of their reflection in the still waters of the Betwa.

The Lakshminarayan Mandir

The lone **Lakshminarayan Mandir** crowns a rocky hillock just under 1km west of Orchha village, at the end of a long, paved pathway. From the square directly behind the Ram Raja temple, a leisurely fifteen-minute stroll is rewarded with fine views, and excellent seventeenth- and nineteenth-century paintings. For a small tip, the resident *chowkidar* will lead you through the galleries inside the temple. Look out for the frieze depicting the battle of Jhansi, in which the rani appears in an upper room of the fort next to her horse, while musket-bearing British troops scuttle about below. Elsewhere, episodes from the much-loved Krishna story crop up alongside portraits of the Bundela rajas and their military and architectural achievements, while, a side pillar bears a sketch of two very inebriated English soldiers.

Eating

A smart **place to eat** and to hang out in the evenings is the colonnaded dining hall in the *Sheesh Mahal* hotel, which serves a good mix of veg and non-veg food, and tandoori specials at lunch time. Alternatively, *Betwa Cottages* cooks up delicious Indian veg dishes (order an hour in advance) and *Amar Mahal* is good for mutton and chicken curries. *Betwa Tarang* on the Fort Bridge near the main market is one of the most popular travellers' hang-outs, serving delicious Indian veg dishes, thalis and lassis in cool a/c comfort or alfresco on a rooftop; it opens early for breakfast. There are also a few simple *dhabas* in the bazaar, serving very cheap thalis, and a congenial café on the corner of the junction between the track to the Sheesh Mahal the main road through the bazaar, which serves great pancakes, thalis and lassis. The delicious local speciality, Orchha *kalakand* (milk cake), can be bought from the small stalls around the gate to the Ram Raja temple forecourt.

Khajuraho

The resplendent Hindu temples of **KHAJURAHO**, immaculately restored after almost a millennium of abandonment and neglect, are among the most essential stops on any itinerary of India's historic monuments. Famed above all for the delicate sensuality – and forthright **eroticism** – of their sculpture, they were built between the tenth and twelfth centuries AD as the greatest architectural achievement of the **Chandella** dynasty. Mysteriously, the Chandellas appear to have forgotten about the temples soon afterwards, and it took "rediscovery" by the British before these masterpieces were fully appreciated in India, let alone internationally. Excavations are ongoing.

Some 400km southeast of Agra and the same distance west of Varanasi, Khajuraho might look central on maps of the subcontinent, but remains as **remote** from the Indian mainstream as it was when the temples were built – which is presumably what spared them the depredations of the marauders, invaders and zealots who devastated so many early Hindu sites. No train routes cross this extended flood plain, set against the backdrop of the jagged Dantla hills, and visitors who don't fly straight here are faced with a long bus journey from either of the nearest railheads.

The exquisite intricacy of the temples themselves – of which the most spectacular are **Kandariya Mahadeva**, **Vishvanatha** and **Lakshmana**, all in the conglomeration known as the **Western Group** – was made possible by the soft buff-coloured sandstone used in their construction. Considering the propensity of such stone to crumble, they have withstood the ravages of time remarkably well. Much of the ornate **sculpture** that adorns their walls is in such high relief as to be virtually three-dimensional, with strains of pink in the stone helping to imbue the figures with gentle flesh-like tones. The incredible skill of the artisans is evident throughout, with friezes as little as 10cm wide crammed with naturalistic details of ornaments, jewellery, hairstyles and even manicured nails. A huge congregation of gods and goddesses are everywhere in attendance. To add to the beauty of the whole ensemble, the temples subtly change hue as the day progresses, passing from a warm pink at sunrise, to white under the midday sun, and back to warm pink at sunset. Dramatic floodlights pick them out in the evening, and they glow white when the moon is out.

The sheer splendour of the temples rather overshadows **Khajuraho village**, where most local people live and which is increasing in hotels and trinket shops fed by the daily tourist invasion. However, if you stay around a night or two, you'll discover a relaxed pace of life that exists apart from the temple scene, especially in the evening when the local market and open-air restaurants create a very social atmosphere.

Arrival and information

The easiest way to get to Khajuraho is on an Indian Airlines **flight** from Delhi (via Agra), or Varanasi (4 weekly). Jet Airways also fly daily from Delhi via Varanasi. The local **airport** is 5km south of the main square of Khajuraho village; the taxi ride in costs Rs100. The two nearest railheads are at **Jhansi** to the northwest (see p.326), and **Satna** to the southeast; both are connected by bus. All **buses** terminate less than 1km southeast of the main square at the bus stand, within walking distance of most central hotels; a cycle rickshaw will set you back Rs10, an auto-rickshaw Rs15.

The Government of India **tourist office**, on the main square, is efficient (Mon–Fri 9am–5.30pm, Sat 8am–noon; ⓣ07686/272347). The MP tourism

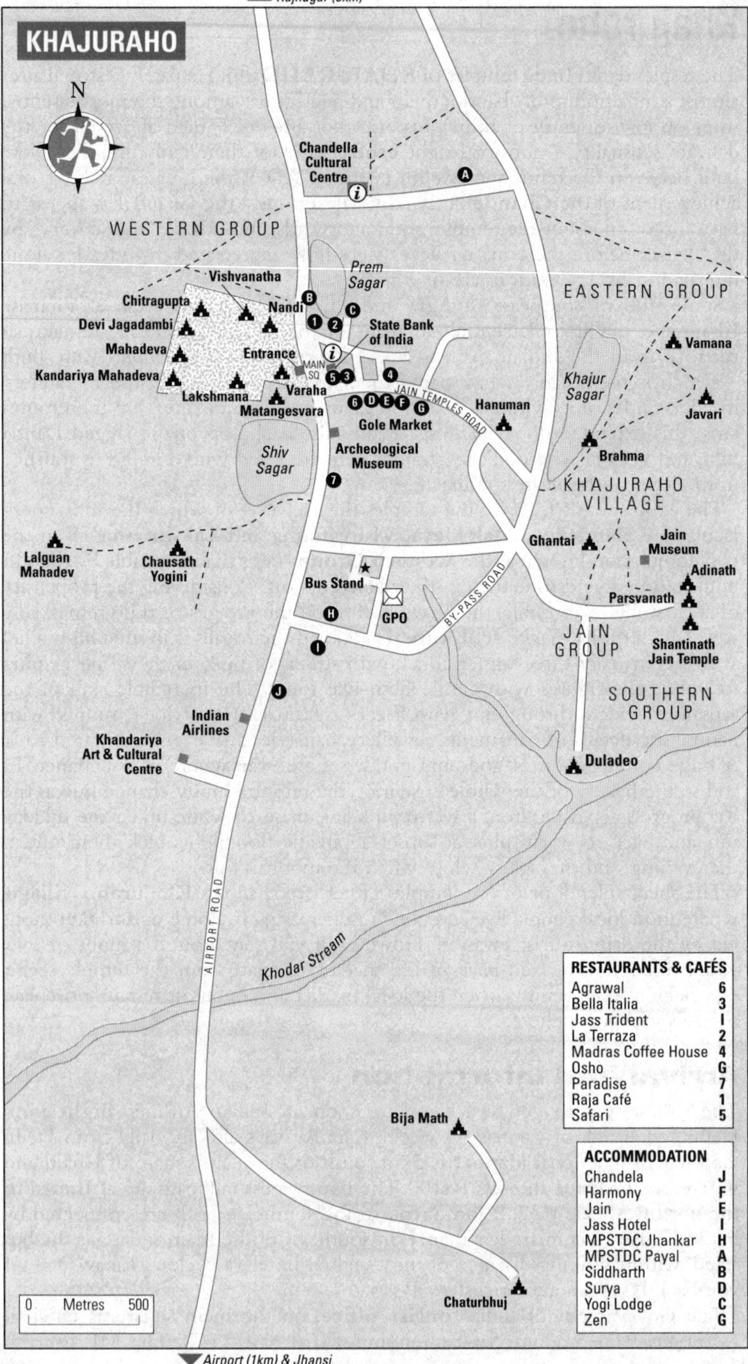
Rajnagar (5km)
KHAJURAHO
N
Chandella Cultural Centre
WESTERN GROUP
Vishvanatha
Prem Sagar
EASTERN GROUP
Chitragupta
Nandi
Devi Jagadambi
State Bank of India
Vamana
Mahadeva
Entrance
MAIN SQ
Khajur Sagar
Kandariya Mahadeva
Lakshmana
Varaha
JAIN TEMPLES ROAD
Hanuman
Javari
Matangesvara
Gole Market
Shiv Sagar
Archeological Museum
Brahma
KHAJURAHO VILLAGE
Lalguan Mahadev
Chausath Yogini
Ghantai
Jain Museum
Bus Stand
Adinath
BY-PASS ROAD
Parsvanath
GPO
JAIN GROUP
Shantinath Jain Temple
SOUTHERN GROUP
Indian Airlines
Khandariya Art & Cultural Centre
Duladeo
AIRPORT ROAD
Khodar Stream
RESTAURANTS & CAFÉS
Agrawal 6
Bella Italia 3
Jass Trident I
La Terraza 2
Madras Coffee House 4
Osho G
Paradise 7
Raja Café 1
Safari 5
Bija Math
ACCOMMODATION
Chandela J
Harmony F
Jain E
Jass Hotel I
MPSTDC Jhankar H
MPSTDC Payal A
Siddharth B
Surya D
Yogi Lodge C
Zen G
Chaturbhuj
0 Metres 500
Airport (1km) & Jhansi

office, in the Chandella Cultural Centre 2km northeast of the main square (Mon–Sat 10am–5pm; closed second and third Sat of the month), can book accommodation and car rental. **Money** can be changed at the efficient State Bank of India on the main square (Mon–Fri 10.30am–2.30pm & 3–5pm; Sat 10.30am–2.30pm); there's a **post office** near the bus stand. **Internet facilities** (Rs40/hr) are available near *Raja Café* and around the Jain Temples, but the connection is painfully slow and often unreliable.

Getting around

Khajuraho is no more than an overgrown cluster of tiny villages, with no public **transport**, and visitors are dependent on the various rented vehicles in competition with each other. **Taxis** and **rental cars** are available at the main square; through *Raja Café* or the nearby Gems & Handicrafts shop; or from operators such as the reliable Sanjay Jain of *Hotel Jain*, Khajuraho Tours (ⓣ07686/272343) in the Maqbara building, Tour Aids (ⓣ07686/274060) in the Khandariya Art and Cultural Centre, or Travel Bureau (ⓣ07686/274037), on Jain Temples Road, near the square. Typical costs are Rs500 for half a day, and Rs600 plus Rs6 per km for longer journeys. **Cycle rickshaw** drivers ask around Rs30 per hour; trips to the Eastern or Southern groups from the main square are Rs40, and a tour of all the temples costs Rs100. **Auto-rickshaws** charge Rs150 for a half-day, or Rs250 for a full day of temple-spotting. With virtually empty roads, a **bicycle** is by far the most enjoyable way of getting around; most budget hotels rent them, as do some restaurants (try *Assi* on Jain Temples Road), charging around Rs15-20 per day.

Among recommended and highly experienced **guides** who can help you make sense of Khajuraho are Ganga, the owner of the *Harmony* hotel; the reputable Mr D.S. Rajput, Mr Mama and Mr Chandel, all three of whom can be contacted through the *Raja Café*, and Raghuvir Singh, who can be contacted at the Tour Aids office. Guide rates are set by the government at Rs375 for one to four people for a half-day, Rs500 for a full day; there's a Rs180 surcharge for tours in languages other than Hindi and English.

Accommodation

There's a **hotel** in Khajuraho to suit every budget, and not a single fleapit in sight. The exclusive, deluxe places are virtually identical and a bit secluded, whereas the mid-range and budget accommodation is around the village centre, near the Western Group. In the slow summer season, you can negotiate a good **discount** at all hotels (MPSTDC offers twenty percent). There's a daily power cut from 8am to noon.

Chandela Airport Rd ⓣ07686/272355, ⓔchandela.khajuraho@tajhotels.com. Khajuraho's grandest address, with every amenity and all the hallmarks of the Taj Group, from the superb restaurant, pool and beautiful gardens to the glamorous shops. Non-residents can use the pool for Rs150. ❾

Harmony Jain Temples Rd ⓣ07686/274135. Claims to be "a real substitute to the five stars", which is an exaggeration, but the Mediterranean influence in the design lends an air of spaciousness. The rooms are neat and clean – ask for one facing the small courtyard garden. Run by Ganga, an expert local guide. ❷–❹

Jain Jain Temples Rd ⓣ07686/272352, ⓔhoteljain1964@yahoo.com. Close to the heart of Khajuraho, a popular family-run hotel with reasonable air-cooled rooms, good-value singles, and reliable veg food. ❶–❷

Jass Hotel By-Pass Rd ⓣ07686/272344, ⓔtjokjr@sancharnet.in. Elegant, understated and pleasantly friendly top-of-the-range place, with tennis courts, swimming pool, a quality shopping arcade, and a good restaurant. Rooms $75-85. ❾

MPSTDC Jhankar By-Pass Rd ⓣ07686/274063. The best of the MPSTDC options: clean doubles, some a/c, with attached bath, plus a good restaurant and bar. ❸–❹

MPSTDC Payal Across the fields northeast of the centre ⓣ07686/274064. Typical, mid-range government place. Rooms are spacious with efficient a/c, and a veranda that opens onto gardens. The campsite alongside can be booked through reception. ❸–❹

Sidharth Opposite the Western Group ⓣ07686/274627. Good hotel with clean, comfortable rooms, all with TV and hot water, and some with temple views. Breakfast can be eaten on galleries or on the rooftop facing the temples; there's a good Indian restaurant with rooftop and interior seating. ❺

Surya Jain Temples Rd ⓣ07686/274145, ⓔhotel_surya2001@yahoo.co.in. Good-value place with variously priced, immaculate rooms. Free yoga classes held daily in the large, lush garden (residents only) and tasty meals served alfresco under the stars. ❶–❸

Yogi Lodge In a small cul-de-sac between the row of shops behind *Raja Café* ⓣ07686/274158. Very popular, excellent-value budget option with a small courtyard, terrace restaurant and Internet facilities. Rooms are small and a little frayed around the edges but clean, and the owner offers free yoga instruction. ❶–❷

Zen Jain Temples Rd ⓣ07686/274228, ⓔoshozed62@hotmail.com. Ultra-cool, clean marble hotel managed by a friendly Osho devotee, who will also take you on tours. The comfortable doubles look down over the peaceful Zen-influenced courtyard where they serve great home-cooked food. Very good value. ❶–❸

The village

Facilities for visitors are concentrated in the uncluttered avenues of the small village of **Khajuraho**; the gates of the Western Group of temples open immediately onto its main square, which is surrounded by budget hotels, cafés and curio shops where you should brace yourself for some hard selling. If you aren't up to the haggling, head instead for the **Khandariya Art and Cultural Centre**, 1km south of the centre, an upmarket emporium offering quality goods at fixed price; in the same complex, an auditorium hosts evening dance shows at (daily 7 & 8pm; Rs300). On the south side of the main square, the small **Archeological Museum** (daily except Fri 10am–5pm; Rs5) is principally noteworthy for a remarkable sculpture of a pot-bellied dancing Ganesh.

Khajuraho is transformed into a bustling epicentre during **Phalguna** (Feb/March), when the festival of **Maha Shivratri** draws pilgrims from all over the region to commemorate the marriage of Shiva. It also sees one of India's premier dance events, the **Khajuraho Festival of Dance** – a showcase for all forms of classical dance with some performances staged against the stunning backdrop of the Western Group (though most take place at the more prosaic Chandella Cultural Centre). Precise dates for the festival tend to be confirmed late, so check with Government of India tourist authorities, and book early. Tickets for specific events cost between Rs40 and Rs200. A season ticket costs Rs500.

The Western Group

Stranded like a fleet of stone ships amid pristine lawns and flowerbeds fringed with bougainvillea, Khajuraho's **Western Group** of temples (daily sunrise–6.45pm; Rs250 [Rs10]) seem oddly divorced from their past. With the exception of Matangesvara, just outside the main complex, all are now virtually devoid of religious significance, and only spring back to life during Shivratri (see above). Visitors must remove their shoes before entering individual temples. MPSTDC offers informative **Walkman tours** of the Western Group (around 45min; Rs50 plus Rs500 deposit), which are available from any of their hotels, the tourist offices or at the temple booking office.

An excellent **son-et-lumière** show in the grounds of the Western group uses Indian classical music and impressive technicolour floodlighting to give ambience to the history of the temples, as narrated by the "master sculptor" (nightly English show: March–Aug 7.30pm; Sept–Feb 6.30pm; 50min; Rs200).

Varaha

Just inside the complex a small open *mandapa* pavilion, built between the tenth and eleventh centuries, houses a huge, highly polished sandstone image of **Vishnu** as the boar – **Varaha**. Carved in low relief on its body, 674 figures in neat rows represent the major gods and goddesses of the Hindu pantheon. Lord of the earth, water and heaven, the alert boar straddles Shesha the serpent, accompanied by what T.S. Burt (see p.448) conjectured must have been the most beautiful form of **Prithvi**, the earth goddess – all that remains are her feet, and a hand on the neck of the boar. Above the image the lotus ceiling stands out in relief.

Lakshman

Beyond Varaha, adjacent to the Matangesvara temple across the boundary wall, the richly carved **Lakshmana** temple, dating from around 950 AD, is the oldest of the Western Group. It stands on a high plinth covered with processional friezes of horses, elephants and camels, as well as soldiers, domestic scenes, musicians and dancers. Among explicit sexual images is a man sodomizing a horse, flanked by shocked female onlookers. The sheer energy of the work gives the whole temple an astounding sense of movement and vitality.

While the plinth depicts the human world, the temple itself, the *adhisthana*, brings one into contact with the celestial realm. Two tiers of carved panels decorate its exterior, with gods and goddesses attended by *apsaras*, "celestial nymphs", and figures in complicated sexual acts on the lower tier and in the recesses. Fine detail includes a magnificent dancing Ganesh on the south face, a master architect with his students on the east, and heavenly musicians and dancers.

Successive pyramidal roofs over the *mandapa* and the porch rise to a clustered tower made of identical superimposed elements. Small porches with sloping eaves project from the *mandapa* and passageway, with exquisite columns, each with eight figures, at each corner of the platform supported by superb brackets in the form of *apsaras*. The inner sanctum, the *garbha griha*, is reached through a door whose lintel shows Vishnu's consort **Lakshmi**, accompanied by **Brahma** and **Shiva**; a frieze depicts the **Navagraha**, the nine planets. Inside, the main image is of Vishnu as the triple-headed, four-armed Vaikuntha, attended by his incarnations as boar and lion.

Kandariya Mahadeva

Sharing a common platform with other temples in the western corner of the enclosure, the majestic **Kandariya Mahadeva** temple, built between 1025 and 1050 AD, is the largest and most imposing of the Western Group. A perfect consummation of the five-part design instigated in Lakshmana and Vishvanatha, this Shiva temple represents the pinnacle of Chandellan art, its ornate roofs soaring dramatically to culminate 31m above the base in a *shikhara* that consists of 84 smaller replicas.

Kandariya Mahadeva is especially popular with visitors for the extraordinarily energetic and provocative erotica that ornaments its three tiers, covering almost every facet of the exterior. Admiring crowds can always be found in front of a particularly fine image of a couple locked in **mithuna** (sexual intercourse) with a maiden assisting on either side. One of Khajuraho's most familiar motifs, it seems to defy nature, with the male figure suspended upside down on his head; only when considered as if from above do the sinuous intertwined limbs begin to make sense.

The erotic art of Khajuraho

Prurient eyes have been hypnotized by the unabashed **erotica** of Khajuraho ever since the "rediscovery" of the site in February 1838. A young British officer of the Bengal Engineers, **T.S. Burt**, alerted by the talk of his *palki* (palanquin) bearers, had deviated from his official itinerary when he came upon the ancient temples all but engulfed by jungle – "They reared their sun-burnt tops above the huge trees by which they were surrounded, with all the pride of superior height and age. But the chances are, the trees (or jungle rather) will eventually have the best of it."

Frank representations of oral sex, masturbation, copulation with animals and such acts may have fitted into the mores of the tenth-century Chandellas, but, as Burt relates, were hardly calculated to meet with the approval of the upstanding officers of Queen Victoria:

I found . . . seven Hindoo temples, most beautifully and exquisitely carved as to workmanship, but the sculptor had at times allowed his subject to grow a little warmer than there was any absolute necessity for his doing; indeed some of the sculptures here were extremely indecent and offensive, which I was at first much surprised to find in temples that are professed to be erected for good purposes, and on account of religion. But the religion of the ancient Hindoos can not have been very chaste, if it induced people under the cloak of religion, to design the most disgraceful representations to desecrate their ecclesiastical erections. The palki bearers, however, appeared to take great delight at those, to them, very agreeable novelties, which they took care to point out to all present.

Burt found the inscription on the steps of the Vishvanatha temple that enabled historians to attribute the site to the Chandellas, and to piece together their genealogy, but it was several more years before Major General Sir Alexander Cunningham produced detailed plans of Khajuraho, drawing the distinction between "Western" and "Eastern" groups that is still applied today. For Cunningham, "all [the sculptures] are highly indecent, and most of them disgustingly obscene".

An elaborate garland at the entrance to the temple, carved from a single stone, acts as a *torana*, the ritual gateway of a marriage procession. Both inside and out, lavish and intricate images of gods, goddesses, musicians and nymphs celebrate the occasion; within the sanctuary a dark passage leads to the *garbha griha* and its central *shivalingam*. Niches along the exterior contain images of **Ganesh**, **Virabhadra** and the **Sapta Matrikas**, the Seven Mothers responsible for dressing the bridegroom, Shiva. Wrathful deities and fearsome protectors, the seven consist of Brahmi, a female counterpart of Shiva, seated on the swan of Brahma; a three-eyed Maheshvari on Shiva's bull Nandi; Kumari; Vaishnavi, seated on the bird Garuda; Varahi, the female form of Vishnu as the boar; Narasimhi, the female form of Vishnu as lion; and the terrifying Chamunda, the slayer of the *asuras* or "demons" Chanda and Munda, and the only one of the Sapta Matrikas who is not a female representation of a major male god.

Devi Jagadambi

North of Kandariya Mahadeva along the platform, the earlier **Devi Jagadambi** temple is a simpler structure, whose outer walls lack projecting balconies. Originally dedicated to Vishnu, its prominent *mandapa* is capped by a massive pyramidal roof. Three *bhandas* (belts) bind the *jangha* (body), adorned with exquisite and sensuous carvings; the erotica on the third is arguably the finest in Khajuraho.

The erotic images remain the subject of a disproportionate amount of controversy and debate among academics and curious tourists alike. The task of explanation is made more difficult by the fact that even the Chandellas themselves barely mentioned the temples in their literature, and the very name "Khajuraho" may be misleading, simply taken from that of the nearby village.

Among attempts to account for the sexual content of the carvings have been suggestions of links with **Tantric** cults, which use sex as a pivotal part of worship. Some claim that they were inspired by the **Kama Sutra**, and similarly intended to serve as a manual on love, while others argue that the sculptures were designed to entertain the gods, diverting their wrath and thus protecting the temples against natural calamities. Alternatively, the geometric qualities of certain images have been put forward as evidence that each represents a *yantra*, a pictorial form of a mantra, for use in meditation.

The sixteen large panels depicting sexual union that appear along the northern and southern aspects of the three principal temples – Kandariya Mahadeva, Lakshmana and Vishvanatha – are mostly concerned with the junction of the male and the female elements of the temples, the *mandapa* and the *garbha griha* (the "womb"). They might therefore have been intended as a visual pun, elaborated by artistic licence.

A radical new approach that ties history and architecture with living traditions has been proposed by Shobita Punja in her book *Divine Ecstasy*. Citing historic references to Khajuraho under the name of Shivpuri – the "City of Shiva" – she uses ancient Sanskrit texts to suggest that the dramatic temples and their celestial hordes represent the **marriage party of Shiva and Parvati**, taking place in a mythical landscape that stretches along the Vindhya hills to Kalinjar in the east. Thus Punja argues that the lower panel on Vishvanatha's southern walls shows Shiva as a bridegroom accompanied by his faithful bull, Nandi, while the intertwined limbs of the panel above – the couple locked in *mithuna*, assisted by a maiden to either side – show the consummation, with the lustful Brahma a pot-bellied voyeur at their feet.

Vishnu appears throughout the panels, all decorated with sinuous figures of nymphs, gods and goddesses, some in amorous embrace. Some consider the image in the temple sanctum to be a standing Parvati, others argue that it is the black goddess Kali, known here as Jagadambi.

Between Kandariya Mahadeva and Jagadambi, the remains of **Mahadeva** temple shelter a metre-high lion accompanied by a figure of indeterminate sex. Recurring throughout Khajuraho, the highly stylized lion motif, seen here rearing itself over a kneeling warrior with drawn sword, may have been an emblem of the Chandellas.

Chitragupta

Beyond the platform, and similar to its southern neighbour, Jagadambi, the heavily (and in places clumsily) restored **Chitragupta** temple is unusual in being dedicated to **Surya**, the sun god. Once again its design emphasizes the *mandapa* rather than the main temple. Ornate depictions of hunting scenes, nymphs and dancing girls accompany processional friezes, while on the southern aspect a particularly vigorous ten-headed Vishnu embodies all his ten incarnations. Within the inner chamber, the fiery Surya rides a chariot driven by seven horses.

The small and relatively insignificant temple in front of Chitragupta, also heavily restored and now known as **Parvati**, may originally have been a

Vishnu temple, but holds an interesting image of the goddess Ganga riding on a crocodile.

Vishvanatha

Laid out along the same lines as Lakshmana, **Vishvanatha**, in the northeast corner of the enclosure – the third of the three main Western Group shrines – can be precisely dated to 1002 AD as the work of the ruler Dhangadeva. Unlike some other temples at Khajuraho, which may have changed their presiding deities, Vishvanatha is most definitely a Shiva temple, as confirmed by the open *mandapa* pavilion in front of the main temple, where a monolithic seated **Nandi** waits obediently. Large panels between the balconies once more show *mithuna*, with amorous couples embracing among the sensuous nymphs. Idealized representations of the female form include women in such poses as writing letters, playing music and fondling babies. Decorative elephant motifs appear to the south of Vishvanatha, and lions guard its northern aspect.

Matangesvara

The simplicity of the **Matangesvara** temple, outside the complex gates, shows it to be one of Khajuraho's oldest structures, but although built early in the tenth century it remains in everyday use. Deep balconies project from the walls of its circular sanctuary, inside which a pillar-like *shivalingam* emerges from the pedestal *yoni*, the vulva – the recurring symbol of the union of Shiva. During the annual festival of Shivratri, the great wedding of Shiva and Parvati, the shrine becomes a hive of activity, drawing pilgrims for ceremonies that hark back to Khajuraho's distant past.

Chausath Yogini

Southwest of Shiv Sagar lie the remains of the curious temple of **Chausath Yogini** – the "Sixty-Four Yoginis". Dating from the ninth century, it consists of 35 small granite shrines clustered around a quadrangle; there were originally 64 shrines, with the presiding goddess's temple at the centre. Only fourteen other temples, all in northern India, are known to have been dedicated to these wrathful and bloodthirsty female attendants of the goddess Kali; art historians surmise that the site was used by an esoteric Tantric group. Around 1km further west lie the ruins of Lalguan Mahadev, a small temple dedicated to Shiva.

The Eastern Group

The two separate networks of temples that make up Cunningham's **Eastern Group** (daily sunrise–sunset; free) are reached via the two forks of the road east of town. One is the tightly clustered **Jain Group**, while slightly north there are a number of shrines and two larger temples, **Vamana** and **Javari**.

On the north side of Jain Temples Road a comparatively new temple holds a two-metre-high image of the monkey god **Hanuman** that may predate all of Khajuraho's temples and shrines. As the road forks left along the eastern shore of the murky Khajur Sagar lake, at the edge of Khajuraho village, it passes the remains of a single-room temple erroneously referred to as the **Brahma** temple. Often considered to be a Vishnu temple, it is in fact a shrine to Shiva, as demonstrated by its *chaturmukha* – "four-faced" – *lingam*. While the eastern and western faces carry benign expressions, and the north face bears the gentler aspect of Uma, the female manifestation of Shiva, the ferocious southern face is surrounded by images of death and destruction. Crowning the *lingam* is the rounded form of **Sadashiva**, Shiva the Infinite at the centre of the cosmos.

The dirt road continues to the small **Javari** temple. Built late in the eleventh century, it may not have the exuberance seen elsewhere but nevertheless contains some fine sculpture, including nymphets in classic Khajuraho style.

The largest of the Khajuraho village temples, **Vamana**, stands alone in a field 200m further north. Erected slightly earlier than Javari, in a fully evolved Chandella style, Vamana has a simple uncluttered *shikhara* that rises in bands covered with arch-like motifs. Figures including seductive celestial nymphs form two bands around the *jangha*, the body of the temple, while a superb doorway leads to the inner sanctum, which is dedicated to Vamana, an incarnation of Vishnu. On the way to the Jain Group, the road runs near what survives of a late-tenth-century temple, known as **Ghantai** for its fine columns sporting bells (*ghantai*), garlands and other motifs.

The temple of **Parsvanath**, dominating the walled enclosure of the **Jain Group**, is probably older than the main temples of Khajuraho, judging by its relatively simple ground plan. Its origins are a mystery; although officially classified as a Jain monument, and jointly administered by the Archeological Survey and the Jain community, it may have been a Hindu temple that was donated to the Jain community which settled here at a later date. Certainly, the animated sculpture of Khajuraho's other Hindu temples is well represented on the two horizontal bands around the walls, and the upper one is crowded with Hindu gods in intimate entanglements. Among Khajuraho's finest work, they include Brahma and his consort; a beautiful Vishnu; a rare image of the god of love, **Kama**, shown with his quiver of flower arrows embracing his consort **Rati**; and two graceful female figures, one applying kohl to her eyes and another removing a thorn from her foot. A narrow strip above the two main bands depicts celestial musicians (*gandharvas*) playing cymbals, drums, stringed instruments and flutes. Inside, beyond an ornate hall, a black monolithic stone is dedicated to the Jain lord Parsvanath, inaugurated as recently as 1860 to replace an image of another *tirthankara*, Adinath.

Immediately north of Parsvanath, **Adinath**'s own temple, similar but smaller, has undergone drastic renovation. Three tiers of sculpture surround its original structure, of which only the sanctum, *shikhara* and vestibule survive; the incongruous *mandapa* is a much later addition. Inside the *garbha griha* stands the black image of the *tirthankara* Adinath himself. The huge 4.5-metre-high statue of the sixteenth *tirthankara*, **Shantinath**, in his newer temple, is the most important image in this working Jain complex. With its slender beehive *shikharas*, the temple attracts pilgrims from all over India, including naked *sadhus*.

Sculpture in the small circular **Jain Museum**, at the entrance to the Jain temples, includes representations of all twenty-four *tirthankaras* (Mon–Sat 7am–6pm; Rs5).

The Southern Group

Khajuraho's **Southern Group** consists of three widely separated temples. The nearest to town, **Duladeo**, is down a dirt track south of the Jain Group, 1.5km from the main square. Built early in the twelfth century, Duladeo bears witness to the decline of temple architecture in the late Chandellan period, noticeable above all in its sculpture that lacks Khajuraho's hallmark fluidity. Nonetheless, its main hall does contain some exquisite carving, and the angular rippled exterior of the main temple is unique to Khajuraho.

Across the Khodar stream and south along Airport Road, a small road leads left to the disproportionately tall, tapering **Chaturbhuj** – the *shikhara* is visible for miles above the trees. A forerunner to Duladeo, built around 1100 AD and bearing some resemblance to the Javari temple of the Eastern Group, Chaturbhuj is plainer than Duladeo and devoid of erotica. A remarkable 2.7-metre-high image of Vishnu graces its inner sanctum.

To reach the third temple, **Bija Math**, return to the cluster of houses before Chaturbhuj and take a right along the dirt track through the hamlet. The structure lay below a suspiciously large mound of mud (*tela*) until 1998, when the ASI undertook an excavation project and discovered the delicately carved platform. Unfortunately, the temple itself has disintegrated into the debris of ornate sculpture lying strewn around the site. You can go and watch the archeologists at work, patiently brushing the mud away to reveal parading elephants, intertwined lovers and rearing horses.

Eating

Khajuraho has an abundance of **restaurants**, from simple and cheap rice and *sabzi* joints to more sophisticated and expensive multi-cuisine and Italian places. At the top of the range, hotels like *Taj Chandela*, *Holiday Inn*, *Jass Trident* and *Usha Bundela* offer fine dining for very reasonable prices. We've given phone numbers only for places where you'll need to book.

Moving on from Khajuraho

The first daily express MPSTRC **bus** leaves at 9am for Jhansi (4hr 30min), 175km west, then moves directly on to Gwalior and Agra (8hr). Alternatively, the most comfortable bus leaves for Jhansi at 11.15am to connect with night trains north and express trains running to Delhi and Agra, or Bhopal and Mumbai. The super-fast a/c Shatabdi Express #2001 **train** via Gwalior and Agra to Delhi departs from Jhansi at 5.55pm. A number of private buses also run the Jhansi route, departing at 5.30am, 12.30pm, 3.15pm and 4.15pm and a MPSTRC bus leaves at 7pm daily for Bhopal. Agents and hotels all display bus timetables.

Between 7.30am and 3.30pm daily, six buses set out for **Satna** (4hr 30min), 125km east, which is served by trains on the Mumbai–Varanasi–Kolkata network, as well as to **Gorakhpur**, from where buses head for the Nepal border. If you're heading to **Varanasi**, 415km east, either take the 4.30pm overnight bus from Khajuraho, or expect a long wait in Satna: night trains (8hr) leave daily at 7.50pm, while the daily morning departure (7–8hr) leaves at 7.05am. The best train for Jabalpur is the Mahanagiri Express #1094, which leaves Satna daily at 5.55pm (3hr). An alternative route to Varanasi is to take one of the eleven daily buses north to Mahoba (first bus 6am, last 10.30pm; 3hr), from where the Bundelkhand Express #1107 train to Varanasi departs at 10.35pm (12hr).

There is an extremely efficient computerized **train booking office** at the bus stand (daily 8am–5pm). All train tickets can be reserved up to five days in advance, and it saves the long queues in Jhansi, Mahoba or Satna.

Indian Airlines (☎07686/274035, airport ☎07686/274036) has four **flights** a week to Varanasi at 4.10pm (45min), as well as to Agra at 6.25pm (40min) continuing to Delhi (1hr 45min). There are fewer services in the monsoon season. Jet Airways (☎07686/274407), whose office is in the airport, run one daily flight to Delhi via Varanasi, leaving at 1.35pm. Flights can be heavily booked, and note that with a late reservation you may be promised a confirmation, but can only be sure of a place on the flight at the airport, shortly before departure; allow a little leeway in case your flight is delayed, and be patient.

Agrawal Gole Market, Jain Temples Rd. If you eat just one thali in north India, do so here. The delicious unlimited "special thali" combines a vast array of *kofta*, fresh veg, tandoori *roti* and *pulao*.
Bella Italia Jain Temples Rd. Pleasant, leafy roof terrace café and beer bar preparing fresh pasta and wood-fired pizza – a welcome change from the norm.
Jass Trident By-Pass Rd ⓣ07686/272344. Comfortably stylish multi-cuisine restaurant in this luxury hotel. Attentive service and very reasonable prices.
La Terraza Just off the main square near Prem Sagar. A standard mish-mash of Eastern and Western cuisine, with good Kashmiri home cooking. The rooftop has a fine view.
Madras Coffee House Jain Temples Rd. Reliable South Indian food at (more expensive) north Indian prices – great *dosas*. Opens at 7.30am for pre-bus journey breakfasts.
Osho Jain Temples Rd. Italian and Korean specialities and exquisite home-cooked Indian food; eat in the very chilled-out courtyard café, with its pretty garden, or the roof-terrace restaurant.
Paradise Airport Rd. Typical pancake and non-spicy thali menu, with little tables and lanterns on a roof terrace that overlooks the waterlily-covered Shiv Sagar lake.
Raja Café Main Square. Where it all happens in Khajuraho; there's a bookstore and curio shop, too. Good tandoori, rosti, pancakes, chocolate cake and waffles; cold beers also available.
Safari Jain Temples Rd. Travellers' hangout, serving chicken and chips, extensive breakfasts, and a big range of lassis to the strains of Bob Marley.

Eastern Madhya Pradesh

The so-called "tribal belt" of **eastern Madhya Pradesh**, homeland of the Gond and Barga *adivasi* minorities, holds few historic sites of note but is justifiably famous for the **Kanha** and **Bandhavgarh national parks**. In the few remaining fragments of a forest that, until 150 years ago, extended right across central India, the reserves are among the last strongholds for many endangered species of birds and mammals, including the **tiger** – reason enough for thousands of visitors each year to make the long journey across the area's rolling terraced plains.

Two major **rail networks** cut through the region. The **Central Railway** heads straight up the Narmada Valley from Bhopal to Jabalpur, the springboard for Kanha National Park, before veering north to Satna (4hr from Khajuraho) and the Gangetic plains. The other main route, traced by the **Southeastern Railway**, skirts the top of Bastar district (the remote and poor southern extension of the state, dovetailing with Maharashtra, Andhra Pradesh and Orissa), passing through the grim industrial cities of Raipur and Bilaspur at the head of the Chhattisgarh Valley.

Jabalpur and around

After running in tandem across an endless expanse of wheat fields and tribal villages, the main Kolkata (Calcutta) to Mumbai road and train line converge on eastern Madhya Pradesh's largest city. Though an important provincial capital, **JABALPUR**, 330km east of Bhopal, harbours little of interest, and is only really worth visiting en route to the **Marble Rocks**, gouged by the River Narmada nearby, or to the national parks and tiger reserves, Kanha and Bandhavgarh, both half a day's journey to the east.

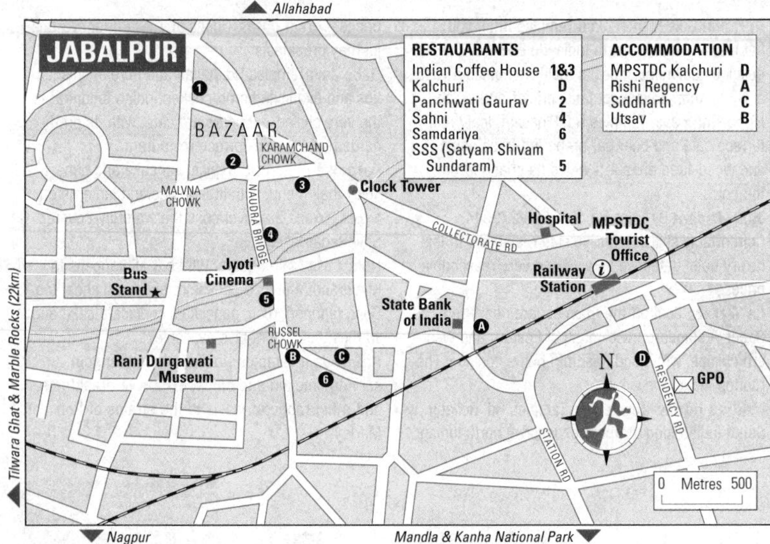

If you do have some time to kill in Jabalpur, jump in an auto-rickshaw to the **Rani Durgawati Museum** (Mon–Sat 10am–5pm; free), about 2km west of the railway station, which houses a predictable assortment of ancient temple sculpture, bronze plates and seals recording regional dynastic histories. It also boasts a better than average display on the state's *adivasi* minorities. Three kilometres further west in the direction of the Marble Rocks, the main highway skirts a large moraine of enormous granite boulders, on the top of which stand the ruins of the **Madan Mahal** – a fortress-cum-pleasure-palace built by the Gond ruler Madan Shah in 1116. Another kilometre west, you reach an impressive bridge spanning the River Narmada. Known locally as **Tilwara Ghat**, the handful of shrines near the water's edge below marks one of the sacred places where Mahatma Gandhi's ashes were scattered.

Arrival and information

Central Railway trains arrive at Jabalpur's **railway station**, 2km east of the centre. From here, it's a five-minute auto-rickshaw ride into town. The shambolic city **bus stand** is more in the thick of things, a short way south of the bazaar and west of Naudra Bridge, site of several cheaper hotels.

MPSTDC's friendly and efficient **tourist office**, inside the main arrivals hall at the railway station (Mon–Fri 6am–10pm; ⓣ0761/232 2111), can provide the usual range of hand-outs, give advice on travel arrangements, and inform you of vacancies in their hotels in Kanha or Bandhavgarh. The **post office** is a five-minute walk south of the railway station. If you need to **change money** (there are no exchange facilities in either national park), you can cash travellers' cheques at the State Bank of India, just under 1km west of the railway station, or at the *Rishi Regency* hotel opposite, which has a 24-hour exchange counter.

Jabalpur teems with **auto-** and **cycle rickshaws**, while the rarer Ambassador taxis can usually be found on Russel Chowk in front of the *Samdariya* hotel. Vehicles for day-trips can be rented through the top hotels. The dilapidated **tempos** and **minibuses** that chug through the centre of town serve outlying suburbs and are only useful for travelling out to the marble rocks.

Moving on from Jabalpur

Kanha National Park is most travellers' next stop after Jabalpur. Direct MPSRTC services leave the central bus stand twice daily for the main gate at Kisli: the first, at 7am, is faster (5–6hr); the second (6–7hr) leaves at 11am. **Buses** to Mandla, halfway to the park, leave hourly. Bandhavgarh is harder to reach; you need to catch a train (4–6 daily; 1hr 20min) or bus (1–2 hourly; 2hr) to Murwara, then travel down the Eastern Railway line to Umaria, where you can pick up a local bus to the park gate.

To get to **Khajuraho**, you can catch either the 4am express (3hr) or the later slow **passenger train** to Satna, from where you can pick up direct state buses. Alternatively, take one of the more frequent afternoon express trains and stay overnight in Satna. **Varanasi** is on the main Mumbai–Kolkata (Calcutta) line; aim for the daily Dadar-Gorakhpur Express #1027 (departs 1.25am, arrives 12.55pm). Daily trains from Jabalpur to Patna help travellers en route to **Nepal**.

Of the five or six daily **express trains** to Mumbai, the Howrah–Mumbai Mail #2321 is the most convenient (departs 5.35pm; 16hr). For Delhi, take the daily Gowndwana Express #2411 (3.40pm; 16hr) or the daily all-a/c Jan Shatabdi Express #2062 (departs 5.35am, arrives Bhopal 11.30am) and then catch the 2.50pm daily Shatabdi Express #2001 arriving in Delhi at 10.50pm. There are also 1–2 daily trains to Chennai (23hr 45min–32hr).

Accommodation

The majority of Jabalpur's **hotels** are within easy reach of the bus stand – handy for early departures to Kanha. Watch out for "luxury taxes" and "service charges" levied by the pricier places. The railway station has retiring rooms (❶–❷) and cheap dorms.

MPSTDC Kalchuri Residency Rd ☎0761/232 1491. Welcoming hotel around the corner from the railway station, with a pleasant restaurant and bar. The rooms are spacious and the deluxe ones have a/c. ❹–❺

Rishi Regency Civil Lines ☎0761/232 1804. Three-star hotel with smart communal areas and rooms, foreign exchange and a speciality barbecue restaurant. ❻–❽

Siddharth Off Russel Chowk ☎0761/240 9247. Well-run and central, with simple, light, good-value "standard" rooms, some of which have a/c. ❸–❹

Utsav Russel Chowk ☎0761/241 4038. Large, friendly hotel bang in the centre of town. The mostly a/c rooms all have satellite TV, attached bathrooms and hot water, and range from excellent-value "economy" to "super-deluxe" with bath-tubs. Avoid the restaurant. ❷–❻

Eating

With a few exceptions, the best places to eat in Jabalpur are the **hotels**. Prices are reasonable and most menus varied, though not everywhere serves alcohol.

Indian Coffee Houses Bazaar district. Two branches in the bazaar, both great for cheap *dosas*, *iddlis*, *uttapams* and other light snacks. Both open at 8.30am for breakfast.

Kalchuri Residency Rd. Dimly lit, with starched table cloths and the usual MPSTDC menu: a selection of their standard meat, veg and Chinese dishes. Tandoori after 7.30pm only. A cold beer makes the place markedly more cheerful.

Panchwati-Gaurav Civic Centre, Civil Lines. Cool, well-lit a/c restaurant known for its all-you-can-eat Gujarati thalis (Rs50–70).

Sahni Naudra Bridge. Bustling, unpretentious and cheap, serving generous heaps of spicy Punjabi food to a mainly office crowd. The more relaxed a/c family room next door is alcohol-free.

Samdariya Off Russel Chowk. The place to splash out on top-notch Indian and Chinese veg food – their unlimited thalis are particularly great value at Rs70 for an array of their best dishes. A Western-style coffee shop also does delicious South Indian snacks.

SSS (Satyam Shivam Sundaram) Near Jyoti Cinema, Naudra Bridge. Don't be put off by the bizarre Rococo Interior. The inexpensive, strictly veg food, including thalis and some set menus, is excellent value. Some tables overlook the street.

The Marble Rocks

In a bustling, dusty, Oriental land, the charm of coolness and quiet belonging to these pure cold rocks, and deep and blue yet pellucid waters, is almost entrancing.

Captain J. Forsyth, *The Highlands of Central India* (1889).

West of Jabalpur, the River Narmada suddenly narrows, plunges over a series of dramatic waterfalls, then squeezes through a seam of milky-white marble before continuing on its westward course across the Deccan. The thirty-metre cliffs and globulous shapes worn by the water out of the rock may not exactly rank as one of the seven wonders of the natural world, but the **Marble Rocks**, known locally as Bheraghat, are as good a place as any to while away an idle afternoon.

BHERAGHAT village itself, overlooking the gorge, is a sleepy little place, with few signs of activity beyond the ringing of chisels in the workshops of its many **marble-carvers**. Most pieces on display in the shop fronts are heavy-duty Hanumans, *shivalingams* and other deities, destined for sites around India – the local translucent white marble is much in demand for new temples and shrines.

From the main street, a flight of steps leads down to the river and the **ghats**, where **rowing boats** (Rs210 per boat, Rs10 per head on a shared basis) are on hand to ferry visitors up the gorge, although these don't run during the monsoon (July to mid-Oct). Trips take thirty to forty minutes, depending on the water level (if the dams upstream are open, the current can be too strong for boats to pass), though you're more likely to spend at least that long waiting for a minimum of fifteen passengers to show up. Avoid the boatmen who try and squeeze in twenty-five: the boats are old and are theoretically designed only for ten people. Once underway, the boatman begins his spiel, pointing out the more interesting **rock formations**. The most appreciative noises from the other passengers are not reserved for the "footprint of the celestial elephant", however, or even the "monkey's leap" (jumped over by Hanuman on his way to Lanka), but for the places where Hindi movie-stars posed in well-known films shot on location here. Look out for the enormous **bees' nests** dangling from the crevices in the rock. One nineteenth-century guidebook urged its readers to refrain from "smoking or firing guns" in the gorge, as an angry swarm once attacked a party of English army engineers who were carrying out survey work for a new railway here. A memorial plaque, still visible on top of the cliffs, was erected to one of their number who drowned trying to shake the bees off. The formations are floodlit after dark.

Bheraghat is also something of a **religious site**. From the fork in the river, 107 stone steps lead up to the tenth-century **Mandapur temple**, a circular building known for the 64 beautifully carved Tantric goddesses, or Chausath Yogini, which stand in its enclosure. Beyond the temple, at the far end of the gorge, the Dhuandhar, or "Smoke Cascade" waterfall, is particularly dramatic when shrouded in spray after the monsoons. It's reached either by following the main street out through the village, or else via the goat-track that twists along the top of the cliffs below the MPSTDC motel. Just above the waterfall, you pass a string of stalls loaded with locally carved marble goods.

Practicalities

Getting to Bheraghat from Jabalpur involves picking up a **tempo** (Rs10) from the bus stand next to the museum. The 45-minute stop-and-start trip on a tempo can be excruciating; you need to clamber off when you see a row of cold drink and souvenir stalls lining a sharp left-hand bend in the main street. Auto-rickshaws (Rs350 return) can be negotiated anywhere in Jabalpur, or a private taxi can be arranged in any of the hotels, at a rate of Rs500 for up to five people.

If you want to **stay** the night, head for the pleasant MPSTDC *Motel Marble Rocks* (☎0761/283424; ③), a converted four-room colonial bungalow just off the road out to the falls, complete with veranda, well-kept lawn and easy chairs. The garden looks out over the gorge and a small **restaurant** serves a standard veg and non-veg menu. The only other option is at the slightly cheaper *Shagun Resorts* (no phone; ③), a motley collection of little huts, each with a veranda, air-cooler and attached bath, in a scrubby garden opposite the brightly painted Jain temple on the main street (sign in Hindi). There is a basic veg restaurant in the garden, if you don't mind being surrounded by adolescent couples escaping here for some privacy.

From Jabalpur towards Kanha

From Jabalpur, the four-hour bone-shaking bus ride to Kanha takes you into some of eastern Madhya Pradesh's most isolated rural districts. When Captain J. Forsyth and his Bengal Lancers pushed through en route to the uncharted interior at the end of the nineteenth century, this landscape was a virtually unbroken tract of *sal* forest teeming with Indian bison, deer and tigers. Since then, the local Barga tribals have taken up the plough, and all but a few patches of forest clinging to the ridges of nearby hillsides have been logged, cleared for farmland or simply burned as firewood by the burgeoning populations of sharecroppers.

The only major town en route to Kanha is **MANDLA**, worth a brief pause to visit the sacred confluence of **Triveni Sangam**, at the bottom of town beyond the bazaar. Said to form the shape of the auspicious "Om" symbol, it's a magical spot, distinguished by a couple of temples (among them one with oddly tapering towers dedicated to Rama). If you're rushing through en route to Kanha, note that the last bus to the park departs at 2pm. Heading in the opposite direction, buses to Jabalpur leave every thirty minutes throughout the day. The State Bank of India will exchange cash only, and is the nearest place to Kanha with this facility.

Kanha National Park

Widely considered the greatest of India's wildlife reserves, **KANHA NATIONAL PARK** encompasses some 940 square kilometres of deciduous forest, savannah grassland, hills and gently meandering rivers – home to literally hundreds of species of birds and animals, including **tigers**. Despite the arduous overland haul to the park, few travellers are disappointed by its beauty, particularly striking at dawn, though many feel hard-done-by when it comes to tiger-spotting: you will need several forays into the park to ensure a chance of at least one good sighting.

Central portions of the Kanha Valley were designated as a wildlife sanctuary as long ago as 1933. Prior to this, the whole area was one enormous viceregal hunting ground, its game the exclusive preserve of high-ranking British army officers and civil servants seeking trophies for their colonial bungalows. Not until the 1950s though, after a particularly voracious hunter bagged thirty tigers in a single shoot, did the government declare Kanha a bona fide national park. Kanha was one of the original participants in Indira Gandhi's **Project Tiger** (see p.1416), and since then, animal numbers have recovered dramatically and the forest department claims figures in excess of 200 tigers. As part of the long-term project, the park has expanded to encompass a large protective buffer zone – a move not without its opponents among the local tribal community, who depend on the forest for food and firewood. Over the years, the authorities have had a hard time reconciling the needs of the villagers with the demands of conservation and tourism; but for the time being at least, an equitable balance seems to have been struck. The **poaching** record has been successfully reduced – although not completely stopped – and Kanha upholds its reputation as a model in wildlife management and research. Even if you don't spot a cat, it's a congenial environment in which to enjoy some of central India's most unspoilt and quintessentially Kiplingesque countryside.

The park

From the main gates, at **Kisli**, in the west, and **Mukki**, 35km away in the south, a complex network of motorable dirt tracks fans out across the park, taking in a good cross-section of its diverse terrain. Which animals you see from your open-top Jeep largely depends on where your guide decides to take you. Kanha is perhaps best known for the broad sweeps of grassy rolling meadows, or **maidans**, along its river valleys, which support large concentrations of deer. The park has several different species, including the endangered "twelve-horned" **barasingha** (swamp deer), plucked from the verge of extinction in the 1960s, and a handful of **hiran** (black buck antelope), now perforce enclosed by tall jackal-proof fences. The ubiquitous **chital** (spotted deer – the staple diet of Kanha's tigers), congregates in especially large numbers during the rutting season in early July, when it's not uncommon to see 4000 at one time.

The **woodlands** carpeting the spurs of the Maikal Ridge that taper into the core zone from the south consists of *sal*, teak and moist deciduous forest oddly reminiscent of northern Europe. Troupes of black-faced langur monkeys crash through the canopy, while **gaur**, India's tallest wild buffalo, forage through the fallen leaves. Years of exposure to snap-happy humans seem to have left the awesome, hump-backed bulls impervious to camera flashes, but it's still wise to keep a safe distance. Higher up, you may catch sight of a spiky-horned **nilgai** (blue cow), as well as porcupines, pythons, sloth bears, wild boar, mouse deer or the magnificent **sambar** – the latter a favourite snack for the nocturnal predators that prowl through the trees. You might even spot a **leopard**, although these shy animals tend to steer well clear of motor vehicles.

Kanha also supports an exotic and colourful array of **birds**, including Indian rollers, bee-eaters, golden orioles, paradise flycatchers, egrets, some outlandish **hornbills** and numerous kingfishers and birds of prey. Enthusiasts should head for the **River Banjar** area near the Mukki entrance, where the majority of the different species of water birds hang out.

Kanha's **tigers**, though, are its biggest draw, and the Jeep drivers, who are well aware of this, scan the sandy tracks for pug marks and respond to the agitated alarm calls of nearby animals. After an hour or so of mooching around, every jeep congregates at Kanha, a purpose-built centre in the heart of the park. While visitors can check out the excellent museum (free), spot a few birds on the nearby lake and have a chai, the drivers wait for the call of a tiger sighting by field scouts on elephants. A rush for the Jeeps ensues and the car park empties in seconds in a whirlwind of dust. When a tiger is seen sleeping or sitting, a **tiger show** (Rs600) is declared. Elephants wait nearby, and visitors disembark from their Jeeps to take a short elephant ride to see the big cat. If you're intent on **seeing a tiger**, reckon on spending three nights at the park and taking around five excursions; the cats are most often spotted lounging among camouflaging brakes of bamboo or in the tall elephant grass lining streams and waterholes. The one place you're guaranteed to see them, however, is on film, at the nightly audiovisual show at the **visitor centre** by the park gate in Kisli (6.30pm; free).

Park practicalities

Kanha is **open** from 6am–noon & 3–5.30pm (Rs500 [Rs20], vehicle Rs150, compulsory guide Rs100, plus Rs40 for camera, Rs300 video) from November 1 until the monsoon arrives at the end of June. During peak season (Nov–Feb), the nights and early mornings can get very **cold**, and there are frequent frosts, so bring warm clothing. The heat between March and June keeps visitor numbers down, but tiger sightings are more common then, when the cats are forced to come out to the waterholes and streams.

The most straightforward way to **get to Kanha** is via Jabalpur, which is well connected by **rail** to most other parts of the country. If you're coming from **Orissa**, take a direct train to Katni on the main Mumbai–Kolkata (Calcutta) line and change there onto one of the many southbound services such as the Howrah–Mumbai mail #2321 (daily 3.57pm; 1hr 30min) to Jabalpur, the park's nearest railhead. The nearest airport with scheduled domestic flights is at Nagpur, 226km away. Daily **buses** leave Jabalpur for **Kisli** (via Mandla) at 7am (5–6hr) and 11am (6–7hr). Both stop briefly at the barrier in **Khatia**, 4km down the road from Kisli; you must register with the park office here. Buses back to Jabalpur leave Khatia at 8am and 12.30pm. You can arrange to visit the park by car (around Rs2500 for the round trip from Jabalpur, with a night halt) via the MPSTDC tourist office in Jabalpur (see p.454).

The main way to **get around the park** is by open-top Jeep; these leave from Kisli every day at dawn (usually 6am) and in the afternoon. The fare, worked out according to distance travelled, usually comes to about Rs900 for the morning drive and Rs700 for the shorter evening round. Most of the moderate to expensive hotels in Khatia have jeeps for the exclusive use of their residents. If you're staying at a budget hotel, try and get a group (up to a maximum of five, though four is more comfortable) together and book a Jeep direct at the park gate a day in advance. Walking inside the park is strictly forbidden, but you can ask at the gates about arranging an evening **elephant ride**; rangers occasionally allow a maximum of four people to spend an hour tracking tigers for Rs600 per head.

Accommodation and eating

MPSTDC has two **lodges** in **Kisli**, both of them atmospherically situated inside the park proper. They can be booked in advance either by calling into a regional MPSTDC tourist office (in Delhi, Mumbai, Kolkata (Calcutta), Jhansi, Jabalpur and most of the other major towns in Madhya Pradesh), or through Central Reservations, Tours Division, MPSTDC Ltd, Fourth Floor Gangotri, TT Nagar, Bhopal 462003 (Ⓣ0755/277 8383); you can also book online at Ⓦwww.mptourism.com. If you haven't booked in advance, check availability at the MPSTDC office in Jabalpur on the off-chance that something is available.

Private hotels outside the west gate, in and around the village of **Khatia**, range from walk-in budget lodges to high-end resorts that should be booked at least five working days before arrival. At any standard of hotel it's worth asking about possible discounts; if the hotel is having a lean patch they may negotiate a good reduction.

The hotels are scattered along a six-kilometre stretch of road that sees very little traffic during the day, so make sure you are dropped off at the right place.

Kipling Camp 4km south of Khatia (book through Tollygunge Club Ltd, 120 DP Sasmal Rd, Kolkata (Calcutta) 700033; ⓣ033/2473 3306) ⓦwww.kiplingcamp.com. British-run cottage complex in a pleasant forest location offering a rustic experience with five-star comfort – and the company of Tara, the elephant made famous by Mark Shand's book (see Contexts, p.1435). "Ethnic" rooms, alfresco meals in a beautiful Barga-style restaurant, and evenings around the fire. Full board, safari and guides included. 9

Krishna Jungle Resort 4.5km south of Khatia ⓣ0761/240 1263, ⓔhotelkhrishna@hotmail.com. An attractive complex oozing rustic charm and a jungle ambience, with a swimming pool, evenings spent around the log fire with the enthusiastic manager (a wildlife expert), and one of the few restaurants in Kanha open to non-residents. 6

Machan Complex Khatia ⓣ07649/277584. Around half a kilometre before the park gate, this established backpackers' hotel, with spartan rooms and a dorm (Rs50), boasts a family atmosphere, cosy log fires in the evening, very cheap, home-cooked thalis and an à la carte menu. Jeep hire available. 1–2

Motel Chandan Khatia ⓣ07649/277220. Just before the barrier on the roadside. Rooms are overpriced and slightly shabby, with scarily garish lino, but it's clean and dependable with 24hr hot water. The attached *dhaba* specializes in pancakes smothered with local honey. 3–4

MPSTDC Baghira Log Huts Kisli ⓣ07649/277227. Spacious chalets with attached bath in the heart of the forest; nos 1–8 overlook a meadow where animals come to graze. Good restaurant, with a varied menu and beer. 4–5

MPSTDC Youth Hostel (no phone). Opposite Kisli's main gate. The in-park location is excellent, and the dorm beds good value; rates include an evening veg thali. 2

Van Vihar Backpackers Retreat Khatia (no phone). A friendly, family-run place well off the road at Khatia Gate. The ultra-basic rooms all have attached bath and hot water, and open into a flower-filled garden. The little outdoor restaurant serves thalis and pancakes. Jeeps available with excellent drivers. 2

Wild Chalet Resort Khatia (book through IAWR, 257 SV Rd, Bandra, Mumbai 400050; ⓣ022/2640 8742, ⓦwww.indianadventures.com). A similar "all-in" package to *Kipling Camp*, even further from the park gate. The luxury chalets, with hot-water bathrooms, overlook the river. There's a library, resident wildlife and birdwatching expert, and an alfresco restaurant/bar where occasional dance performances are staged. 9

Bandhavgarh National Park

With Kanha becoming ever more popular, Madhya Pradesh's second national park, **BANDHAVGARH**, tucked away in the hilly northeast of the state, is receiving increasing attention from tourists. The draw is that it has the highest relative density of **tigers** of any of India's reserves, shelters a collection of fascinating ruins, and offers the chance of trekking through the jungle on elephant-back. It's a long haul to Bandhavgarh from either Jabalpur (195km) or Khajuraho (237km), but worth it – not only to track tigers and deer but also, as all the accommodation is close to the park gates, to watch the array of birdlife without even entering the park.

Bandhavgarh may be one of India's newer national parks, but it claims a long history. Legend dates the construction of its hilltop **fort** to the time of the epic *Ramayana*, when monkey architects built Rama a place to rest on his return from his battle with the demon king of Lanka. Excavations of caves tunnelled into the rock below the fort have revealed inscriptions scratched into the sandstone in the first century BC, from which time Bandhavgarh served as a base for a string of dynasties, among them the **Chandellas**, responsible for the temples at Khajuraho. They ruled from here until the **Bhagels** took over in the twelfth century, staking a claim to the region that is still held by their direct descendant, the Maharaja of Rewa. The dynasty shifted to Rewa in 1617, allowing Bandhavgarh to be slowly consumed by forest and by the bamboo and grasslands that provided prime hunting ground for the Rewa kings. The present maharaja ended his hunting days in 1968 when he donated the area to the state as parkland. In 1986, two more chunks of forest were added to the original core zone, giving the park a total area of 448 square kilometres.

The park

Though there are flat grassy *maidans* in the south of the park, Bandhavgarh is predominantly rugged and hilly, clad in *sal* trees in the valleys, and mixed forest in the upper reaches, which shelter a diverse avian population. Bandhavgarh's headquarters are in the tiny village of **Tala**, a stone's throw from the main gate in the north, connected to Umaria, 32km southwest, by a road slicing through the park's narrow midriff. Jeep tracks wind through the park from the north gate in Tala, circling below the central **fort** through forest and grassland, and passing watering holes and streams – good spots for viewing wildlife.

On the whole, Jeep safaris tend to stick to the core area where the chances of spotting one of the fifty or so **tigers** are high, and glimpses of deer and monkeys guaranteed. Deer species include shy but animated gazelle and small barking deer, as well as the more common *nilgai* (blue cow) and *chital* (spotted deer). Sloth bears, porcupines, sambar and muntjac also hide away in the forest, while hyenas, foxes and jackals appear occasionally in the open country. If you're very fortunate, you may catch sight of an elusive leopard. Look out too for some very **exotic birds** like red jungle fowl, white-naped woodpecker, painted spurfowl, long-billed vultures, lesser adjutant stork, brown fish owl, jungle owlet, Malabar pied hornbill, eagles, falcons and flycatchers. Perhaps the most enjoyable way of viewing game is to take an **elephant ride** in the misty dawn, tramping through the undergrowth as the *mahout* hacks through spider webs and overhanging branches.

The crumbling ramparts of the **fort** crown a hill in the centre of the park, 300m above the surrounding terrain. It was off-limits at the time of writing, but check the situation when you arrive as the ramparts offer spectacular views over the valley and by far the best birdwatching in the park. Even if the fort is out of bounds, it's still possible to take in a few modest temples around its base, the rock-cut cells of monks and soldiers, and a massive stone Vishnu reclining on his cobra near a pool that dates from the tenth century and still defies the undergrowth. The exotic plant life hereabouts attracts numerous species of insects that may make your skin crawl, but not as much as the thought that tigers may be watching you as you wander the sites. They're more likely to stick to the lower levels nearer their favourite prey, and there are no instances of people actually being harmed by tigers or even suddenly coming across them – but the risks are real nonetheless.

Park practicalities

Bandhavgarh is **open** from November to June (6.15–10am & 2.15–5.45pm; R500 [Rs20], plus Rs40 for camera, Rs300 video; private vehicle Rs150, obligatory guide Rs100). For wildlife-spotting the **best time to visit** is during the hotter months between March and June, when thirsty tigers and their prey are forced out to the waterholes and the park's three perennial streams; the heat can be trying at this time, however, all the more so because Tala's sporadic electricity supply precludes the use of fans or air-conditioning between 6am and 2pm. Visiting in the cooler months, when wildlife viewing is still good, is more comfortable.

Without your own vehicle, **getting there** can be tricky. The easiest option by rail is to catch the daily overnight Narmada Express #8233 which goes through Indore, Bhopal, Jabalpur and Bilaspur (if you are coming from Orissa) to Umaria, the nearest railhead. Three daily **buses** (7.30am, 1.30pm, 6.00pm; 45min–1hr) leave Umaria for **Tala**, 33km northeast. Alternatively, a shared jeep from Umaria to Tala costs Rs15 per head, a private taxi about Rs350. Approaching from Khajuraho or Varanasi, make your way to **Satna** on the main train line and pick up a train straight to Umaria (there is currently no bus service between Satna and Umaria). If you're coming from Delhi (or Agra), the best train is the Utkal Express #8478, which leaves Delhi's Nizamuddin station at 12.50pm and arrives in Umaria early the next day. Travelling by rented car either from Khajuraho or Jabalpur takes roughly five hours, and will cost upwards of Rs2500 for the round trip, plus an extra Rs250–300 for each night you stay.

To cover a reasonable distance within the park, book a **Jeep** at the headquarters at the park gate (around Rs500) or through your hotel. Up to five people can share a jeep (though four is more comfortable). **Elephant rides** can also be arranged at the park office or your hotel (Rs600/hr, maximum four people). Elephants also wait in any area where a tiger or two has been spotted lurking deep in the forest; the lure of a quick jaunt into the jungle to get a virtually guaranteed sighting is hard to resist. The charge of Rs600 still applies, although you only get about half an hour at most; your Jeep will await your return and then continue the tour.

For the serious wildlife enthusiast, there are a few very experienced naturalists in Tala, all of whom can be contacted through your hotel. S.K. Tiwari of Skay's Camp (Ⓣ07653/265355, Ⓕ265309) specializes in nature photography, and has an impressive knowledge of Indian flora and fauna.

Accommodation and eating

Most of Bandhavgarh's hotels, all of which are in **Tala**, cater for travellers on a higher budget, and offer "jungle-plan" prices – all-inclusive deals including meals and two Jeep safaris per person. However, there are a few mid-priced hotels and budget lodges for those on a lower budget. The only places to eat outside the hotels are the friendly, cheap *dhabas* on Tala's main road.

Bandhavgarh Jungle Lodge Close to the river; book through Tiger Resorts Ltd, Suite 206 Rakesh Deep, 11 Commercial Complex, New Delhi 110049 Ⓣ011/2685 3760, Ⓦwww.welcomheritage.com. Characterful, comfortable huts finished in mud coating and tribal-style painting. Residents eat set multi-cuisine meals alfresco in the pleasant garden. Enthusiastic manager and wildlife experts. Jungle plan $150. ❾

Kum Kum Umaria Rd, next to *White Tiger Forest Lodge* Ⓣ07653/265324. Welcoming hotel with excellent-value rooms, each with tribal designs on the walls and attached bath with 24hr hot water. The Rs25 unlimited thalis, eaten around the fire, are hard to beat. ❷

MPSTDC White Tiger Forest Lodge Umaria Rd, next to the barrier over the main road Ⓣ07653/265308. Large complex with friendly staff, a good restaurant and bar, and clean, cosy rooms, all with attached bath and hot water. Rooms 17–21 are in bungalows with large verandas overlooking the river – an excellent place for birdwatching, and tigers occasionally come here to drink in the height of summer. ❹–❺

Royal Retreat Umaria Rd Ⓣ07653/265322. The Maharaja's former lodge, with its museum of hunting trophies and Rewa princely relics, is a little rundown. Each room is simple but atmospheric, with large bathrooms; the dorm is great value at Rs150. There's a ten percent discount for walk-in guests. ❺

Tiger Den Umaria Rd; book at Nature Safari, 106–107, A-3, Sector 11 Rohini, Delhi 110 085 Ⓣ011/2704 9446 Ⓔinfo@naturesafariindia.com.

Clean, comfortable rooms in a neatly laid out cluster of individual cottages in flower-filled gardens. Efficient and friendly. ❼

Tiger Lodge Umaria Rd. Small, very friendly and basic lodge and *dhaba*. The bare rooms have fans, and some have attached bathrooms. ❷

Tiger Trails 2.5km beyond Tala; book through Indian Adventures, C257, SV Rd, Bandra West, Mumbai 400050 ⓣ022/2640 8742, ⓦwww.indianadventures.com. Not cheap, but the most tastefully decorated place in Tala. The alfresco dining room overlooks a little lake that is great for birdwatching, and the cottages, with attached bathrooms and hot water, are comfortable and peaceful – a total escape. Jungle plan $150, discounts available for lengthy stays. ❾

V. Patel Jungle Resorts Close to the main Tala gate ⓣ07653/265323 or in Jabalpur at 212 Abhaykunj, Narmada Rd ⓣ0761/241 0736. Excellent-value, welcoming resort whose four clean rooms have attached bath with hot water and a communal veranda. Plus a flower-filled garden and alfresco restaurant. Jungle plan $155 per person, or accommodation only. ❾

Western Madhya Pradesh

The geography of **western Madhya Pradesh** is dominated by the River Narmada, which drains westwards through a wide alluvial valley, bounded in the south by the Satpura hills and the Maharashtran border, and in the north by the rugged Vindhya Range. Forming the major trade corridor between the Ganges plains and the west coast, the region – known as **Malwa** – was for nearly a thousand years an independent princely state ruled from the sprawling hilltop fort complex at **Mandu**. The former capital, now deserted, is the area's outstanding tourist attraction, with its ruined mosques, tanks and palaces, and its spectacular panoramic views.

Most visitors travel to Mandu via the industrial city of **Indore**, then continue northeast to Bhopal, or south on the main Delhi–Mumbai train line towards Jalgaon, the jumping-off point for the Ellora and Ajanta caves. The sacred city of **Ujjain**, 55km north of Indore, boasts a bumper crop of modern Hindu temples, but little else. You could, nevertheless, choose to pause here on your way to or from southern Rajasthan on the Western Railway, the most direct land link with Delhi. Alternatively, head south to the Narmada and the fascinating Hindu pilgrimage centres of **Omkareshwar** and **Maheshwar.**

Indore and around

The second largest city in Madhya Pradesh, **INDORE** is huge, modern, heavily industrialized and generally dull. If you find yourself with time to kill en route to or from **Mandu**, 98km southwest, however, a couple of worthwhile sights lie hidden among its tangle of ferroconcrete flyovers, expressways and crowded bazaars.

Situated at the confluence of the Kham and Saraswati rivers, the city was for centuries merely a stopover on the pilgrimage trails to Omkareshwar and Ujjain, 55km north. In the eighteenth century, however, it became the capital of the **Holkar** dynasty, whose chief, Malhar Rao, had previously managed to scrounge several choice scraps of land from the Marathas during their northward advance against the Moghuls. Later, Rao's daughter-in-law, **Ahilya Bai**, took over control of the state, which at its height stretched as far as the

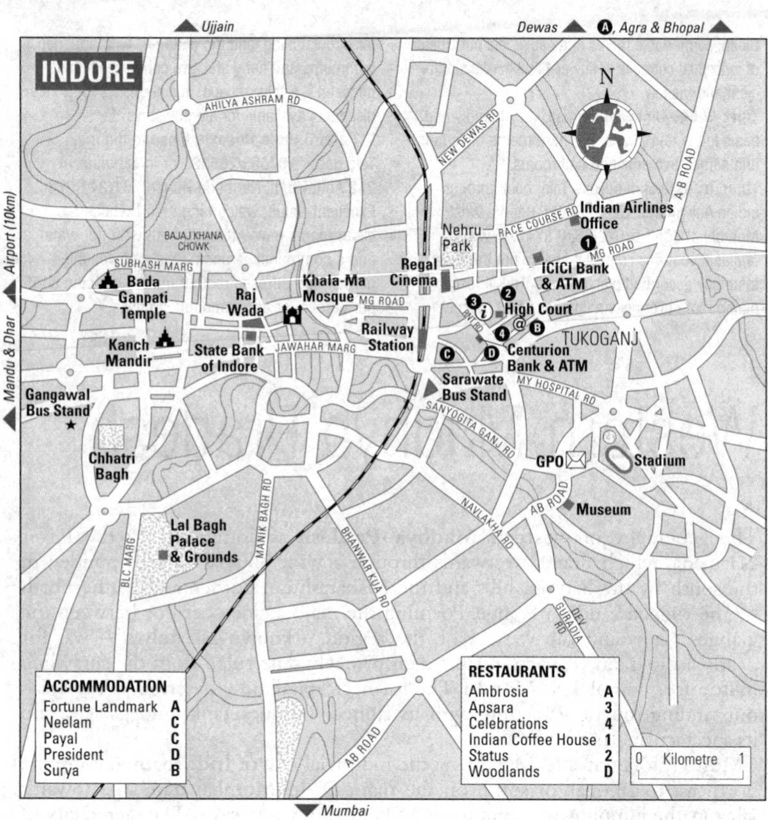

Ganges and the Punjab. Described by a contemporary British diplomat as "the most exemplary ruler that ever lived", the rani was a kind of central Indian Queen Victoria, who, in addition to founding the modern city of Indore, built palaces, temples, *dharamshalas* and charitable institutions all over the country. When she died in 1795, her four grandsons dragged the state into a bloody civil war. A series of skirmishes with the Marathas and East India Company followed, ending in the Treaty of 1818, which secured for the dynasty a small but rich dominion with Indore as the capital. The city's expansion gained momentum in the nineteenth century, fuelled by a lucrative trade in cotton and opium. Despite remaining loyal to the British in the Mutiny, the maverick Holkar maharajas stayed firmly under the thumb of their colonial overlords until Independence, when they were finally relieved of their powers by the Congress.

Indore is the region's biggest business and commercial centre today. The nearby industrial estate of **Pithampur**, hyped as "the Detroit of India", hosts numerous giant steel and auto manufacturers, including Honda, Bajaj, Hindustan Motors and Pratap Steel. The resulting **affluence** has made a big impact: satellite dishes, luxury hotels and American-style shopping malls are popping up all over, while the nouveaux riches swan ostentatiously around town on brand-new cars and Japanese scooters. Even the auto-rickshaws seem shinier.

Arrival and information

Trains arriving on the Central Railway pull in at the mainline station in the middle of the city. The principal **bus stand**, "Sarawate" (Ⓣ0731/246 5688), is a short walk south from platform 1, beyond the overpass. Buses for **Mandu** use the less convenient "Gangawal" bus stand (Ⓣ0731/248 0688), a three-kilometre auto-rickshaw ride west towards the domestic **airport**, 10km out of town. Taxis and auto-rickshaws wait at the airport.

MPSTDC's helpful **information** office (daily 10am–5pm; closed second and third Sat of the month; Ⓣ0731/252 8653, Ⓔmptindore@sify.com), in the MPSTDC Tourist Bungalow behind the R.N. Tagore Natya Griha Exhibition Hall on Rabindranath Tagore Road (RNT Road), hands out the usual glossy leaflets and a better-than-average city map. They also have a car for rent (with driver), available for two-day **tours** to Mandu and for trips to Omkareshwar and Maheshwar (all Rs5/km plus Rs250 per night halt).

The State Bank of Indore has a **foreign exchange** office opposite their main branch on Raj Wada. ICICI Bank, 576 MG Road, is an efficient alternative and has an ATM accepting both Visa and Mastercard. Another ATM can be found at Centurion Bank on RNT Road. There's a 24-hour **pharmacy** (Ⓣ0731/252 8301) in the MY Hospital compound, off AB Road. **Internet cafés** are rife; the best is Dishnet, RNT Road, in Silvermall, 2nd floor (daily 9am–11pm; Rs30/hr), with central a/c and fast connection, the ones in the basement of the same building are cheaper at Rs25/hr.

The most convenient means of **getting around** is by metered auto-rickshaw; or rather more cheaply by the ancient *tempos* that ply defined routes.

Accommodation

The majority of Indore's **hotels** cater for business visitors and are scattered around the prosperous suburb of **Tukoganj**, 1km east of the railway station. Competition here is stiff, so standards tend to be high and prices reasonable. The same can't be said of the cheaper accommodation, most of which is in the noisy area between Sarawate and the railway station. Ignore the touts who try to drag you off to the dire lodges opposite the bus stand, and head instead for the better-value budget hotels along **Chhoti Gwaltoli**, a lane just east of the railway station beneath the big Patel flyover. The railway retiring rooms dorms are cleaner and slightly more expensive than usual (Rs100). All but the absolute rock-bottom lodges levy a mandatory ten percent **luxury tax**.

Fortune Landmark Vijaynagar, 3km from the centre of town off AB Rd near Meghdoot Gardens Ⓣ0731/255 7700, Ⓕ255 5355, Ⓦwww.fortuneparkhotels.com Indore's top hotel, aimed at international business clientele with smooth and efficient staff and service, luxury rooms, a pool, fitness centre and several dining choices, including a swanky open-air terrace grill and a sports pub. Rooms $65–80. ❾

Neelam 33/2 Patel Bridge Corner Ⓣ0731/246 4616. Despite the dingy exterior, this is good value and near the station, with welcoming staff, clean rooms and cable TV. 24hr check-out. ❷–❸

Payal 38 Chhoti Gwaltoli Ⓣ0731/504 5151. One of the best deals among the row of inexpensive hotels near the station – all rooms are smart and have attached shower-toilets. It's worth shelling out an extra Rs50 for an airy deluxe room with Star TV. ❷

President 163 RNT Rd Ⓣ0731/252 8866, Ⓕ251 2230. Comfortable a/c rooms, plus a health club, excellent veg restaurant, rooftop café, and reputable in-house travel agent. ❻

Surya 5/5 Nath Mandir Rd Ⓣ2517701, Ⓕ251 8774. Friendly, well-run hotel with immaculate, spacious, tasteful rooms with all mod cons. Plus a good multi-cuisine restaurant and a pleasant bar. Good value. ❺

The City

Indore's sights lie west of the train line, in and around the **bazaar**. Two broad thoroughfares, MG Road and Jawahar Marg, form the north and south boundaries of this cluttered and chaotic district, which is interrupted in the east by the confluence of the Saraswati and Kham rivers. The city's principal landmark is the former Holkar palace of **Raj Wada**, an eighteenth-century mansion that presides over a palm-fringed square in the heart of the city and boasts a lofty, seven-storey gateway. Its upper four floors were originally made of wood, which made it particularly prone to fire; most of the palace collapsed after the last one, in 1984. Only the facade and the family temple, immediately inside the main courtyard, survive.

Indore's **bazaars** are great for a stroll, with rows of stalls and open-fronted shops jammed beneath picturesque four-storeyed houses with overhanging wooden balconies. The Jain **Kanch Mandir** or "Mirror Temple" (daily 10am–5pm; no photos), tucked away deep in the bazaar district, is one of the city's more eccentric religious monuments; surprisingly, for a faith renowned for its austerity, the interior is decked with multi-coloured glass **mosaics**. If you're in a shopping mood, the Sarafa Bazaar, around the corner from the Mirror Temple, has gold and silver **jewellery**; cloth is sold by weight at the massive wholesale textile market nearby. Also worth seeking out are shops on Bajaj Khana Chowk that specialize in traditional embroidered and beadwork costumes, and the atmospheric fruit and vegetable market on the riverbank beneath the lime-green **Khala-Ma mosque**.

The Lal Bagh palace

Set in its own grounds on the banks of the River Kham, the **Lal Bagh palace** (Tues–Sun 10am–5pm; Rs5) is another of those extravagant Neoclassical creations so beloved of rich maharajas of the nineteenth and early twentieth centuries. The building took two generations of the Holkar family around thirty years to complete, and was, in its day, rivalled only by the Scindias' Jai Vilas palace in Gwalior. Granted carte blanche and a limitless budget, its British architects and interior decorators produced a vast stately home dripping with Doric columns, gilt stucco, crystal chandeliers, and piles of replica Rococo furniture.

Lal Bagh's main entrance is via a pair of grandiose wrought-iron gates, modelled on those at Buckingham Palace, which bear the Holkar family arms – note the wheat and poppies in the background, symbolizing the two main sources of the dynasty's prosperity. **Inside**, a vast array of family heirlooms is housed in the former durbar hall, banquet rooms and the ballroom, with its specially sprung herringbone dance floor. Check out the jewel-encrusted portrait of Tukoji Rao (1902–25) – the ruler responsible for completing the palace – in the billiards room, and the underground passage leading down to the kitchens. One of the rooms hidden away in this vault contains a modest but very colourful collection of **tribal artefacts**, including terracotta votive statues, clothes, jewellery, murals and brass sculpture. At the Maharaja's private **planetarium** (Rs5) visitors are shown the position of planets, important stars and constellations in the Indore night sky on the day of their visit.

Eating

Eating out is popular among Indore's middle classes, and there are plenty of quality restaurants around the city centre to choose from. Most are in the larger hotels, and serve the usual Indian and Chinese dishes. Inexpensive meals are available in canteens and *dhabas* near Sarawate bus stand; stick to those doing brisk business and you shouldn't go far wrong. **Snack stalls** near Raj Wada and in the markets serve local favourites like *parathas*, *poha*, *chaat*, samosas and *kachoris*, and sweets including

Moving on from Indore

Tickets for daily Indian Airlines flights to Delhi, Bhopal and Mumbai from **Indore airport** (☎0731/241 1758) can be booked at the office (☎0731/243 1595) on Race Course Road, 2km northeast of the station. Jet Airways also fly twice daily to Delhi and Mumbai; tickets can be booked at their airport office (☎0731/262 0454). There's no airport bus, but there are plenty of taxis (Rs175) and auto-rickshaws (Rs90).

As for **trains**, two broad-gauge branches of the Western Railway connect Indore to cities in northern India. The fastest service to Delhi, the daily Indore–Nizamuddin Express #2416 (departs 4.25pm; 14hr) heads north via Ujjain, Kota and Bharatpur. The other branch, serviced by the daily Malwa Express #9367 (departs 1pm, arrives 6.40am next day), runs east to Bhopal, then north to New Delhi on the Central Railway via Jhansi, Gwalior and Agra. Trains to Rajasthan leave twice daily on the metre-gauge line for Chittaurgarh and Ajmer, and once to Jaipur on the Purna–Jaipur Express #9770 (departs 9.30pm, arrives 1.40pm next day). Getting to Ellora and Ajanta means catching the 4.15am Jaipur–Purna Express #9769 to Kandhwa, arriving at 9.40am in time to pick up the 11.45am Lashkar Express #2162 for Jalgaon (arrives 2.15pm). The daily 4.40pm Narmada Express #8233 is the only train to Jabalpur, for connections to Kanha and Bandhavgarh.

To get to Mandu by **bus** from Indore, take one of two daily direct services (4hr) from Gangawal bus stand; or the 3.20pm direct bus from the more convenient Sarawate bus stand. Failing that, take any of the frequent services from Gangawal bus stand to Dhar (2–3hr), which is connected to Mandu by half-hourly buses (1hr). Less frequent services run to Dhar from Sarawate bus stand. MPSRTC operates "luxury" buses to Bhopal four times daily (6am, noon, 2.45pm & 9pm; 5–6hr); you have to catch the 6am bus if you want to make the 2.50pm daily Delhi-bound Shatabdi Express.

Reliable **travel agents** in town include the excellent President Travels at *Hotel President*, 163 RNT Rd (☎0731/253 3472).

jalebi and *gulab-jamun*. Indore is also known for its salty nibbles called *namkeens* – some, like the Ratlami Sev, are fiery and spicy so choose carefully.

Ambrosia *Fortune Landmark*. Indore's smartest restaurant is a large a/c dining hall, subtly lit and well-furnished, with smart uniformed waiters. The extensive Indian, Continental and Chinese menu is strong on rich creamy dishes like mutton *rogan josh* and *malai kofta* but the grilled chicken and fish are also good; main courses run to about Rs125. The adjacent pub-like bar is lively with Western music, pool and indoor games.

Apsara RNT Rd. Popular, inexpensive family place just in front of the tourist office, serving great veg food inside and alfresco. For a snack, try the delicious stuffed naan and kulcha breads.

Celebrations RNT Rd, in the annexe to the right of *Hotel Shreemaya*. Spotless and ultra-modern coffee shop serving all things naughty, from cream cakes and ice cream to pizzas.

Indian Coffee House next to Rampura Building, off MG Rd. The usual South Indian snacks served by waiters in turbans and cummerbunds. Opens at 7.30am for big breakfasts and the papers. There's another branch set in peaceful grounds behind the high court.

Status 565 MG Rd, below *Hotel Purva*. Superb eat-till-you-burst Rajasthani lunchtime thalis, with varied veg dishes, dhal, breads and chutneys – all for Rs60. Rather disappointing veg à la carte later on.

Woodlands 163 RNT Rd. *Hotel President*'s swanky pure-veg a/c restaurant claims to offer "scrumptious food of international fame", and serves stylish, pricey South Indian specialities.

Mandu

Set against the rugged backdrop of the Vindhya hills, the medieval ghost-town of **MANDU**, 98km southwest of Indore, is one of central India's most atmospheric

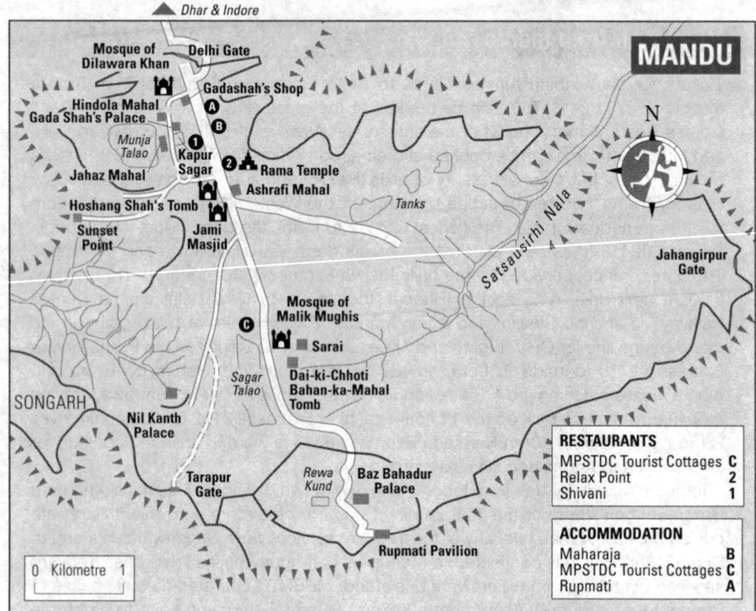

historical monuments. Come here at the height of the monsoons, when the rocky plateau and its steeply shelving sides are carpeted with green vegetation, and you'll understand why the Malwa sultans christened their capital **Shadiabad**, or "City of Joy". Even during the relentless heat of the dry season, the ruins make an exotic spectacle. Elegant Islamic palaces, mosques and onion-domed mausoleums crumble beside large medieval reservoirs and precipitous ravines, while below, an endless vista of scorched plains and tiny villages stretches off to the horizon. Mandu can be visited as a day-trip from Indore, but you'll enjoy it more if you spend a couple of nights, giving you time not only to explore the ruins, but to witness the memorable sunsets over the Narmada Valley.

Some history

Archeological evidence suggests that the remote hilltop was first fortified around the sixth century AD, when it was known as Mandapa-Durga, or "Durga's hall of worship" – in time corrupted to "Mandu". Four hundred years later, the site gained in strategic importance when the powerful **Paramaras** moved their capital from Ujjain to Dhar, 35km north. The plateau's natural defences proved, however, unable to withstand persistent attacks by the Muslim invaders during the twelfth century and the fort eventually fell to the sultans of Delhi in 1305.

While the Sultanate had its hands full fending off the Mongols on their northern borders a century or so later, Malwa's Afghan governor, Dilawar Khan Ghuri, seized the chance to establish his own independent kingdom. He died after only four years on the throne, however, leaving his ambitious young son at the helm. During **Hoshang Shah**'s illustrious 27-year reign, Mandu was promoted from pleasure resort to royal capital, and acquired some of the finest Islamic monuments in Asia, including the Jami Masjid, Delhi Gate and the sultan's own tomb.

Mandu's golden age continued under the **Khaljis**, who took over from the Ghuri dynasty in 1436, when Mahmud Shah Khalji poisoned Hoshang Shah's grandson. Another building boom and several protracted wars later, Mandu settled down to a lengthy period of peace and prosperity under **Ghiyath Shah** (1469–1500). Famous for his love of cooking and beautiful women, Ghiyath amassed a harem of 15,000 courtesans, and a bodyguard of a thousand Turkish and Abyssinian women, whom he accommodated in the appropriately lavish Jahaz Mahal. The sybaritic sultan lived to a ripe old age, but was poisoned by his son shortly after his eightieth birthday. His successor, Nasir Shah, died of guilt ten years later, and Mandu, dogged by feuds and the threat of rebellion, became an easy target for the militaristic Sultan of Gujarat, who invaded in 1526. In the centuries that followed, control over the fort and its rapidly decaying monuments passed between a succession of independent rulers, and the Moghuls. By the time King James I's ambassador, **Sir Thomas Roe**, followed the mobile court of Emperor Jahangir here in 1617, most of the city lay in ruins, its mansions and tombs occupied by Bhil villagers whose descendents continue to scratch a living from the surrounding fields. Mandu today is a tranquil backwater that sees far fewer visitors than it deserves, save for the busloads of exuberant Indian day-trippers who breeze in from Indore at weekends.

The monuments

Mandu's monuments derive from a unique school of Islamic architecture that flourished here, and at the region's former capital, Dhar, between 1400 and 1516. Much admired for their elegant simplicity, the buildings are believed to have exerted a considerable influence on the Moghul architects responsible for the Taj Mahal. Mandu's platform, a 23-kilometre square plateau, is separated from the body of hills to the north by the **Kakra Khoh**, literally "deep ravine". A narrow causeway forms a natural bridge across the gorge, carrying the present road across and up via a series of subsidiary gates to the fort's modern entrance, beside the original, and very grand, Delhi Gate.

If you don't have your own vehicle, the most pleasant way of getting around the fort and its widely dispersed monuments is to rent a **bicycle** (Rs30/24hr) from your hotel or one of the hire shops near the *Shivani Hotel*. Alternatively, squeeze into the village's decrepit old **tempo**, which runs regularly between the village square (near the village group of monuments) and the Rewa Kund group (in the far south of the site). You can also rent one of the town's two **auto-rickshaws** for a complete tour.

The Royal Enclave

Reached via the lane that leads west off the village square, **the Royal Enclave** (daily sunrise–sunset; Rs100 [Rs5], plus Rs25 for video) is dominated by Mandu's most photographed monument, Ghiyath Shah's majestic **Jahaz Mahal** or "Ship Palace". The name derives from its unusual shape and elevated situation on a narrow strip of land between two large water tanks. A breezy rooftop terrace, crowned with four domed pavilions, overlooks **Munja Talao** lake to the west, and the square, stone-lined **Kapur Sagar** to the east. From the northern balcony, you also get a good view of the geometric sandstone bathing pools where the palace's inhabitants would have whiled away their long incarceration.

The next building along the lane is the **Hindola Mahal**, or "Swing Palace" – so-called because its distinctive sloping walls supposedly look as though they are swaying from side to side. The design was, in fact, purely functional, intended to buttress the graceful but heavy stone arches that support the ceiling inside.

At the far end of the T-shaped assembly hall, a long stepped ramp allowed the sultan and his retinue to reach the upper storey on elephant-back.

Sprawling over the northern shores of Munja Talao are the dilapidated remains of a second royal pleasure palace. The **Champa Baodi** boasts an ingeniously complex ventilation and water-supply system, which kept its dozens of *tykhanas* (subterranean chambers) cool during the long Malwan summers. Immediately to the north stands the venerable **Mosque of Dilawara Khan**, dating from 1405. The chunks of Hindu temple used to build its main doorway and colonnaded hall are still very evident.

The **Hathi Pol**, or "Elephant Gate", with its pair of colossal, half-decapitated elephant guardians, was the main entrance to the Royal Enclave but is now closed. To reach the edge of the plateau and the grand **Delhi Gate** you will have to return to the bazaar and follow the road out of Mandu. Built around the same time as Dilawara Khan's mosque, this great bastion, towering over the cobbled road in five sculpted arches, is the most imposing of the twelve that stud the battlements along the fort's 45-kilometre perimeter.

The village group

Some of the fort's best-preserved buildings are clustered **around the village** (all daily sunrise–sunset; Rs100 [Rs5]). Work on the magnificent pink sandstone mosque, the **Jami Masjid** on the west side of the main square, commenced during the reign of Hoshang Shah and took three generations to complete. Said to be modelled on the Great Mosque at Damascus, it rests on a huge raised plinth pierced by rows of tiny arched chambers – once used as cells for visiting clerics. Beyond the ornate *jali* screens and bands of blue-glaze tiles that decorate the main doorway, you emerge in the Great Courtyard, where a prayer hall at the far end is decorated with finely carved inscriptions from the Koran.

Hoshang Shah's tomb (c.1440), behind the Jami Masjid, is this group's real highlight. It stands on a low plinth at the centre of a square-walled enclosure, and is crowned by a squat central dome and four small corner cupolas. Now streaked with mildew and mud washed down from the bats' nests inside its eaves, the tomb is made entirely from milky-white marble – the first of its kind in the subcontinent. The interior is very plain, except for the elaborate pierced-stone windows that illuminate Hoshang's sarcophagus.

The **Ashrafi Mahal**, or "Palace of Coins", was a theological college (*madarasa*) that the ruler Muhammad Shah later converted into a tomb. The complex included a giant marble mausoleum and a seven-storey *minar*, or victory tower, of which only the base survives.

Around the Sagar Talao

En route to the Rewa Kund group, a further handful of monuments are scattered around the fields east of Sagar Talao lake. Dating from the early fifteenth century, the **Mosque of Malik Mughis** is the oldest of the bunch, once again constructed using ancient Hindu masonry. Note the turquoise tiles and fine Islamic calligraphy over the main doorway. The high-walled building opposite was a *caravanserai*, where merchants and their camel trains would rest during long treks across the subcontinent.

A short way south, the octagonal tomb known as the **Dai-ki-Chhoti Bahan-ka-Mahal** looms above the surrounding fields from a raised plinth, still retaining large strips of the blue ceramic tiles that plastered most of Mandu's beautiful Afghan domes. Young couples from the nearby village creep off here during the evenings for a bit of privacy, so make plenty of noise as you approach.

The Rewa Kund group

The road to the **Rewa Kund group** (daily sunrise–sunset; Rs100 [Rs5]) heads past herds of water buffalo grazing on the muddy foreshores of the lake, then winds its way gently through a couple of Bhil villages towards the far southern edge of the plateau; stately old baobabs line the roadside, like giant upturned root vegetables. The **Rewa Kund** itself, an old stone tank noted for the curative properties of its waters, lies 6km south of the main village. Water from it used to be pumped into the cistern in the nearby **Baz Bahadur Palace**. Bahadur, the last independent ruler of Malwa, retreated to Mandu to study music after being trounced in battle by Rani Durgavati. Legend has it that he fell in love with a Hindu singer named Rupmati, whom he enticed to his hilltop home with an exquisite palace that she could admire from the window of her father's house on the Nirmar plains below. The couple eventually married, but did not live happily ever after. When Akbar heard of Rupmati's beauty, he dispatched an army to Mandu to capture her and the long-coveted fort. Bahadur managed to slip away from the ensuing battle, but his bride, left behind in the palace, poisoned herself rather than fall into the clutches of the attackers.

The romantic **Rupmati Pavilion**, built by Bahadur for his bride-to-be, rests on a ridge high above the Rewa Kund; beneath its lofty terrace, the plateau plunges a sheer 300m to the Narmada Valley. The view is breathtaking, especially at sunset or on a clear day, when you can just about make out the sun-bleached banks of the sacred river as it winds west towards the Arabian Sea.

Practicalities

Although there are a couple of direct private **buses** to Mandu from Indore, it's often quicker to travel to Dhar and pick up the half-hourly local service to the fort from there – a bone-shaking 35-kilometre journey that takes over one hour. Direct services back to Indore run twice a day. **Taxis** can be arranged at all hotels in Indore (see p.463), and charge around Rs800 for the round trip, plus a hefty Rs250 waiting charge if you stay overnight – which still works out cheaper than an MPSTDC rental car from their office in Indore (see p.465).

There is nowhere to **change money**; the nearest bank is in Indore. You can make **STD/ISD calls** from several booths dotted around the village square. The disorganized post office, on the main road near the Rama temple, is not recommended for poste restante.

Of the many places to **stay** inside the fort, the *Hotel Rupmati* (Ⓣ07292/263270; ❹), at the north end of the plateau near the Nagar Panchayat barrier, has good-value a/c rooms, each with a private balcony overlooking the ravine; there is a decent restaurant in the garden and a bar that serves reasonably priced cold beers. It's a one-kilometre hike from the main square where the buses pull in, however, so ask to be dropped off en route. Round towards the Royal Enclave, the *Maharaja Hotel* (Ⓣ07292/263288; ❶–❷) is the best budget deal, with ten simple, clean rooms and a restaurant around a courtyard. The MPSTDC *Tourist Cottages* (Ⓣ07292/263235, Ⓔmptmandu@sify.com; ❸–❺), 2km south of the square, is Mandu's most comfortable and expensive hotel; book ahead. The campus of chalets, in gardens overlooking the Sagar Talao lake, has twenty large rooms with attached shower-toilets and hot water; some have a/c. The semi-open-air restaurant is the smartest **place to eat** in the fort, with a moderately priced menu fairly limited to Indian veg dishes. The *Shivani* hotel, halfway between the square and the Nagar Panchayat barrier, has a fairly extensive menu of north and South Indian dishes. The *Relax Point* on the square offers chai, cold drinks, samosas and delicious all-you-can-eat thalis. Wherever you eat, avoid meat and *paneer*, as frequent power cuts mean that even places with refrigerators can have problems keeping perishables fresh.

Ujjain

Situated on the banks of the sacred River Shipra, **UJJAIN**, 55km north of Indore, is one of India's seven holiest cities. Like Haridwar, Nasik and Prayag (near Allahabad), it plays host every twelve years to the country's largest religious gathering, the **Kumbh Mela** (see p.320), which in 2004 drew an estimated thirty million pilgrims here to bathe; naked *sadhus* are among the millions jamming the waterfront, waiting to wash away several lifetimes of accumulated bad karma. Outside festival times, Ujjain is a great place for people-watching, as pilgrims and locals alike go about the daily business of puja, temple visiting and chai drinking. Around the main temples, you see modern Hinduism at its most kitsch, with all types of devotional paraphernalia, gaudy lighting and plastic flower garlands for sale. Down at the *ghats*, women flap wet saris dry while their soapy children splash in the water, and sleepy *pujaris* ply their trade beneath the rows of orange- and whitewashed riverside shrines. A mini-Varanasi Ujjain is not, but nonetheless the temples rising behind the *ghats* are majestic at dusk, and with the ringing of bells and incense drifting around, this atmospheric place can feel timeless.

Some history

Excavations north of Ujjain have yielded traces of settlement as far back as the eighth century BC. The ancient city was a major regional capital under the Mauryans (Ashok was governor here for a time during the reign of his father), when it was known as **Avantika** and lay on the main trade route that linked northern India with Mesopotamia and Egypt. According to Hindu mythology, Shiva later changed its name to **Ujjaiyini**, "He Who Conquers With Pride", to mark his victory over the demon king of Tripuri. Chandra Gupta II, renowned for his patronage of the arts, also ruled from here in the fourth and fifth centuries AD. Among the Nava Ratna, or "Nine Gems", of his court was the illustrious Sanskrit poet **Kalidasa**, whose much-loved narrative poem *Meghduta* ("Cloud Messenger") includes a lyrical evocation of the city and its inhabitants.

Ujjain was sacked in 1234 by Iltutmish, of the Delhi Slave Dynasty, who razed most of its temples. Thereafter, the Malwan capital was governed by the sultans of Mandu, by the Moghuls, and by **Raja Jai Singh** from Jaipur, who designed, along with many renovation projects elsewhere in India, the Vedha Shala observatory (Ujjain straddles the Hindu first meridian of longitude). Ujjain's fortunes declined from the early eighteenth century onwards, except for a sixty-year renaissance between the arrival of the Scindia dynasty in 1750 and their departure to Gwalior. These days, nearby Indore sees the lion's share of the region's industrial activity, leaving Ujjain's 367,000-strong population to make its living by more traditional means.

Arrival, city transport and information

Trains arriving in Ujjain on both broad-gauge branches of the Western Railway pull in at the station in the centre of town; Ujjain is on a link line between Indore and Bhopal, with regular intercity trains shunting between the three. Two minutes' walk northeast of the station is the **Dewas bus stand**, where

UJJAIN

ACCOMMODATION	
Ashray	E
Atlas	C
Girnar	B
MPSTDC Shipra	D
MPSTDC Yatri Niwas	G
Rama Krishna	A
Surana Palace	F

RESTAURANTS	
Ashnoi	4
Chanakya	1
Indian Coffee House	2
Nauratan	D
New Raj Kumar	3
White House	F

Chausath Yogini Temple
Kalideh Mahal, Siddavath & Bhartrihari Caves
Govardhan Sagar
Ksheer Sagar
Shipra River
VEER DURGADAS MARG
PATEL MARG
LALA LAJPAT RAI MARG
CHANDRASHEKER AZAD MARG
Gopal Mandir
Scindia Statue
GOPAL MANDIR MARG
CHATTRI CHOWK
BAZAAR
ARYA SAMAJ MARG
ASHOK MARG
TILAK MARG
LAMI SAI MARG
Footbridge
Harsiddhi Mandir
Rudra Sagar
HARSIDDHI MARG
Ram Ghat
MAHAKALESHWAR MARG
Mahakaleshwar Mandir
N
SAKHYA RAJA MARG
KALIDAS MARG
TATIA TOPE MARG
GPO
Dewas Bus Stand
STATION ROAD (SUBHASH MARG)
Railway Station
VIKRAM MARG
Madhav Clock Tower
Khwara Shakeb Ki Masjid
AHILYA BAI MARG
JAI SINGH PURA MARG
KHAWAJAHAN MARG
UNIVERSITY ROAD
DHANVANTRI MARG
BHAKTAWAR GANJ
ATM
GDC ROAD
0 Metres 500
BHAGAT SINGH MARG
Vedha Shala Observatory
G & P.D.V. Bus Stand
Bhopal & Dewas

buses for Gwalior, Agra, Rajasthan and Bhopal depart. The inconvenient **PDV Bus Stand**, next to the MPSTDC *Yatri Niwas* 2km south of town, serves Indore, Bhopal and Mandu. The city is fairly spread out, so you'll need to **get around** by auto-rickshaw or by renting a **bicycle** from the shop opposite the bus stand. Frequent **tempos**, #2 and #9, connect the station to the main temple area. **Taxis** can be arranged through the MPSTDC *Hotel Shipra* in the cantonment area, which is also where the **tourist office** (Mon–Sat 10am–5pm, closed every second Sat; ⓣ0734/255 1495) is located. The nearest place to **change money** is in Indore, although IDIBI Bank have an ATM on University Road and ICICI Bank maintain has another at the *Ashray* hotel on Dewas Road; both accept Visa and Mastercard.

Accommodation

Most of Ujjain's limited **accommodation** is within easy walking distance of the railway station, so ignore the auto-rickshaw-wallahs when you arrive, unless you plan to stay in one of the two upmarket hotels, both 2km southeast in the cantonment area. Luxury tax of between ten and fifteen percent is charged on all rooms costing more than Rs100. If you plan to stay a while, you could try an **ashram**; Shri Ram Mandir (no phone; ❶) close to Rudra Sagar, is one of the best.

Ashray 77 Devas Rd ⓣ0734/251 9301. Well-managed, friendly hotel with clean, comfortable rooms, some a/c, and all with hot water. ❸–❻

Atlas Station Rd (Subhash Marg), Indore Gate ⓣ0734/501 3084. Respectable, well-managed hotel with a goldfish pond in the reception area. All rooms have windows, bathrooms and comfortable beds. 9am check-out. ❷–❺

Girnar Station Rd (Subhash Marg), Indore Gate ⓣ0734/255 4161. Clean, quiet hotel next door to the *Atlas*, with comfortable, good-sized rooms, some with attached shower-toilets. ❷–❸

MPSTDC Shipra University Rd ⓣ0734/255 1495. Immaculately tidy, leafy and peaceful place, with large and comfortable rooms, some with a/c, a good restaurant and an information counter. ❸–❺

MPSTDC Yatri Niwas Off Lal Bahadur Shastri Marg ⓣ0734/251 1398. Large, institutional block almost 2km out of town, near the bus station for Mandu. The immaculate partitioned dorms (Rs75) have comfortable beds and clean sheets, and there are four simple doubles. Plus a good restaurant on site. ❷

Rama Krishna Station Rd (Subhash Marg), opposite the railway station ⓣ0734/255 3017. Large, well-presented rooms (some a/c) with Star TV and attached bathrooms with hot water. The rooms at the back suffer less road noise. Handy for late arrivals or early morning departures. ❸–❹

Surana Palace 23 GDC Rd, Dushera Maidan ⓣ0734/253 0045, ⓔsuranaujm@satya.net.in. Large, characterless block that's showing its age and is certainly not a palace, but the rooms and suites are comfortable and clean with attached hot-water bathrooms (the more expensive ones have a/c and TV), and there's a good restaurant. Check-out 9am. ❹–❼

The City

The Western Railway cuts straight through the **centre** of Ujjain, forming a neat divide between the spacious and affluent residential suburbs to the south and the more interesting, densely packed streets northwest of the station. Unless you spend all day wandering through the **bazaar**, sightseeing in Ujjain usually means treading the **temple** trail, with a brief foray south of the *ghats* to visit the **Vedha Shala observatory**.

The Mahakaleshwar and the Harsiddhi mandirs

Ujjain's chief landmark, the **Mahakaleshwar Mandir**, crowning a rise above the river, is the logical place to start a tour of the town. Its gigantic saffron-painted sanctuary tower, a modern replacement for the one destroyed by Iltutmish in 1234, soars high above a complex of marble courtyards, water tanks and fountains, advertising the presence below of one of India's most powerful *shivalingams*. Housed in a claustrophobic subterranean chamber, the deity is one of India's twelve **jyotrilingam** – "*lingam* of light" – whose essential energy, or *shakti*, is "born of itself", rather than from the rituals performed around it, and is considered particularly potent, especially by Tantric followers, due to its unusual south-facing position.

From the Mahakaleshwar Mandir, head west down the hill past the Rudra Sagar tank to the auspicious **Harsiddhi Mandir**, which Hindu mythology identifies as the spot where Parvati's elbow fell to earth while Shiva was carrying her burning body from the *sati* pyre. Its main shrine, erected by the Marathas in the eighteenth century, houses (from left to right) images of Mahalakshmi (the goddess of wealth), Annapurna (an incarnation of Durga), and Saraswati (the goddess of wisdom).

The Gopal Mandir

Northwest of **Chattri Chowk**, a chaotic market square in the heart of the bazaar, the picturesque **Gopal Mandir** was erected by one of the Scindia ranis in the early nineteenth century. With its distinctive blend of Moghul domes, Moorish arches and lofty Hindu sanctuary tower, the temple is a fine example of late Maratha architecture. Inside, the sanctum's silver-plated doors were placed here by Mahaji Scindia, who rescued them from Lahore after they had been carried off by Muslim looters. The shrine room itself, lined with marble, silver and mother-of-pearl, contains icons of the presiding deity, Gopal (Ganesh), together with his parents, Shiva and Parvati.

The Vedha Shala

In addition to being a major religious centre, Ujjain was the birthplace of mathematical astronomy in India, research into the motion of the stars and planets having been carried out here since the time of Ashok. Later, Hindu astronomers fixed both the **first meridian** of longitude and the Tropic of Cancer here – the reason why Raja Jai Singh of Jaipur, governor of Malwa under the Moghul emperor Mohammad Shah, chose it as the site for another of his surreal open-air observatories. Built in 1725, the **Vedha Shala observatory** (daily sunrise–sunset; Rs2) lies 1km southwest of the railway station, overlooking a bend in the River Shipra. The complex is nowhere near as large as its more famous cousins in Delhi and Jaipur, the Jantar Mantars, but remains in excellent condition with very informative guides (their service is free but they may expect a tip) and labelling. Local astronomers continue to use its five instruments, or *yantras*, to formulate ephemeredes (charts predicting the positions of the planets), which you can buy at the site.

Eating

Ujjain suffers from a dearth of decent **places to eat**. Most visitors either stick to their hotel restaurant, or opt for a plate of veg curry, rice and chapatis in one of the cheap *dhabas* opposite the railway station. Hygiene levels vary, though, and we've reviewed the better places below.

Ashnoi University Rd. Ujjain's nicest place to eat, with a/c, wicker chairs and lots of plastic flora; the moderately priced menu is excellent pure veg, with a few Chinese dishes thrown in for good measure.

Chanakya Station Rd (Subhash Marg). The best of several no-frills restaurants opposite the station. Spicy, inexpensive veg food, and chilled beer. The popular *Ankur* next door offers more of the same.

Indian Coffee House Durga Plaza, Dewas Rd. Good-value South Indian snacks and inexpensive Indian main courses.

Nauratan *Shipra Hotel*, University Rd. Typical MPSTDC restaurant offering tasty veg, Mughlai, tandoori and Chinese dishes, plus some Western options (even fish and chips) and a wide choice of beers and spirits.

New Raj Kumar 20 Bhaktawar Ganj, Dushera Maidan. Small, spotless and unpretentious pure-veg joint, with mains averaging at Rs50. A little difficult to find, tucked away down a suburban backstreet off Waktahwa Marg near *Surana Palace*.

White House *Surana Palace*, 23 GDC Rd. Wide range of carefully prepared Indian and Chinese vegetarian dishes at moderate prices, served indoors or on the lawn. There's also a fast food outlet for pizza, veggie-burgers and ice cream.

Maheshwar

Overlooking the north bank of the mighty River Narmada, 91km southwest of Indore, **MAHESHWAR** has been identified as the site of King Kartvirajun's ancient capital, **Mahishmati**, a city mentioned in both the *Mahabharata* and *Ramayana*. In the eighteenth century, Maharani **Ahilya Bai** built a palace and several temples here, giving the town a new lease of life. Today, it's a prominent port of call on the Narmada Hindu pilgrimage circuit, but well off the region's tourist trail.

The waterfront **ghats** that line the river below an old sandstone palace, however, make a quintessentially Indian spectacle. Parties of *yatris* take holy dips, drying their clothes in the breeze blowing off the river, while *pujaris* and groups of *sadhus* sit around murmuring prayers under raffia sunshades. For the best view of them, head for the overhanging balcony of the eighteenth-century **Ahilya Bai Mandir**, reached via the steps under the facade of the palace behind.

The palace and fort complex itself, further up the steps, houses the workshops of the Rewa Society, established by the maharani 250 years ago to promote the local handloom industry. Maheshwari **saris** are famous all over India for their distinctive patterns and superior quality; check out the designs for yourself by visiting the weavers' workshops (Mon–Fri 10am–5pm), which are sponsored by a German aid project. Though descendants of the old ruling family still occupy parts of the building, a couple of rooms around the entrance courtyard have been given over to a small and eminently missable museum.

Practicalities

All roads leading to Maheshwar are in a terrible state, so allow extra time if you are in a private car – the journey from Mandu can take up to four hours, and from Indore, at least three. There is a shady car park in the fort area (Rs10), just near the entrance to the museum. **Buses** also run from Dhar (every 20min; 2hr). From Indore, services are fairly frequent, taking three and a half hours, with a change at the market town of Dhamnod, 76km southwest of Indore on the NH-3. The nearest railhead is at **Barwah**, 39km west.

A recent spate of building means that finding decent **accommodation** is relatively easy. On the main Dhamnod–Barwah Road, 100m north of the bus stand, the *Ajanta Lodge* (☎07283/273226; ❶) offers huge, simple and spotless rooms with attached bath; the sign is in Hindi, but the building, with its distinctive circular-fronted concrete balconies, is easy to pick out. A little further out on the same road, *Hotel Kumal* (☎07283/273853; ❷) has five passably clean rooms with attached bathrooms and cable TV, all facing onto a small lawn. Conveniently situated in the centre of town, the *Aakashdeep Rest House* (☎07283/273326; ❶), to the right of the fort car park, offers five basic, scruffy rooms with attached bathrooms.

Places to eat are thin on the ground, as the majority of visitors are pilgrims who cook their own food. The best option is the *Cottage Garden*, although it is inconveniently situated 1km from the fort, next to *Hotel Kumal* on the main road.

Omkareshwar

East of the main river crossing at Barwah, the Narmada dips southwards, sweeps north again to form a wide bend, and then forks around a two-kilometre-long wedge-shaped outcrop of sandstone. Seen from above, the island, cut by several deep ravines, bears an uncanny resemblance to the "Om" symbol. This, coupled with the presence on its sheer south-facing side of a revered *shivalingam*, has made **OMKARESHWAR**, 77km south of Indore, one of the most sacred Hindu sites in central India. Since ancient times, pilgrims have flocked here for *darshan* and a holy dip in the river, but in recent years, the town's remoteness and loaded religious feel have made it a favourite with hard-core Western and Israeli dope heads, vying with local *sadhus* in the chillum-smoking and dreadlock-growing stakes. However, a more authentic atmosphere is preserved among the temples, wayside shrines, bathing places and caves strung together by an old paved pilgrims' trail.

From the bus stand at the bottom of the village on the mainland, Omkareshwar's only street runs 400m uphill to a ramshackle square, where you'll find most of the *dharamshalas* and chai shops, and a handful of stalls hawking lurid puja paraphernalia (including the excellent stylized **maps** taken home by pilgrims as souvenirs of their visits). To get to the island itself, cross the high concrete footbridge or take one of the flat-bottomed ferries that shuttle between the *ghats* crouched at the foot of the river gorge. Once across, you're soon swallowed up by the crowded narrow lane leading to the main temple.

The prominent white *shikhara* that now soars above the **Shri Omkar Mandhata Mandir** is a relatively new addition to the dense cluster of buildings on the south side of the island. Below it, the ornate pillars in the assembly hall, or *mandapa*, are more representative of the shrine's great antiquity. Myths relating to the origins of the deity in the low-ceilinged sanctum date back to the second century BC. Another of India's twelve **jyotrilingams** ("*lingams* of light"), it is said by Hindus to have emerged spontaneously from the earth after a struggle between Brahma, Vishnu and Shiva.

Around the island

Traditionally, the *parikrama* (circular tour) of Omkareshwar begins at the *ghats* below Shri Mandhata and proceeds clockwise **around the island**. The walk takes at least a couple of hours, so carry plenty of water if you plan to do the whole thing in one go.

The first section of the trail is a leisurely half-hour stroll from the footbridge to the pebble-strewn western tip of the island, where you'll find a small chai stall and a couple of insignificant shrines. The **Triveni Sangam**, or "Three-rivers Confluence", is an especially propitious bathing place where the Narmada forks as it merges with the Kaveri. From here, the path climbs above the fringe of fine white sand lining the northern shore until it reaches level ground. The ruins of the **Gaudi Somnath temple** stand in the middle of the plateau, surrounded by a sizeable collection of sculpture mounted on concrete plinths. The sanctuary houses a colossal *shivalingam*, attended by an equally huge Nandi bull. At this point, drop down a steep flight of steps to the village, or continue east towards the old fortified town that crowned the top of the island before it was ransacked by Muslims in the medieval era. Numerous chunks of temple sculpture, lying discarded among the rubble, include a couple of finely carved gods and goddesses, used for shade by families of black-faced langur monkeys.

After scaling the sides of a gully, the trail leads under the large ornamental archway of the **Surajkund Gate**, flanked by three-metre figures of Arjun and

Bheema, two of the illustrious Pandava brothers. The tenth-century **Siddhesvara temple** stands five minutes' walk away to the south, on a patch of flat ground overlooking the river. Raised on a large plinth decorated with rampaging elephants, it has some fine *apsaras*, or female fertility figures, carved over its southern doorway.

Of the two possible routes back to the village, one takes you along the top of the plateau before dropping sharply down, via another ruined temple and the **maharaja's palace**, to the Shri Mandhata temple. The other follows a flight of steps to the riverbank, and then heads past a group of *sadhus*' caves to the main *ghats*.

Practicalities

Omkareshwar is connected by state **bus** to Khandwa (4 daily; 2hr 30min) and Indore (3 daily; 4–6hr). You can also get here by catching the Indore to Khandwa bus as far as **Omkareshwar Road**, a junction and chai stop on NH-3, from where a beaten-up local bus runs the remaining 15km. Omkareshwar Road is also the nearest railhead, but only slow passenger services stop here. Barhawa, on the north bank of the Narmada, is the closest main-line railway station.

The State Bank of India on the main street changes US dollars only (at abysmal rates) so the best option is to **change money** before you arrive; Indore is the nearest place with foreign exchange facilities. A small **post office** on the main street offers reliable poste restante.

Omkareshwar has a good range of **accommodation**. For those seeking the ascetic experience, the central *dharamshalas* in the mainland village are inexpensive (Rs20–50), and offer close-hand experience of pilgrim culture. On the down side, *dharamshala* rooms tend to be windowless cells, with washing facilities limited to a standpipe in the yard (to encourage people to use the river) and communal toilets. One of the best is *Jat Samaj*, facing the river, to the right of the bridge on the main square – look for the rooftop figure on horseback. Another favourite is *Ahilya Bai*, tucked away behind the Vishnu temple off the road to Mamaleshwar temple and the *ghats*. This and its close neighbour, *Tirole Kunbi Patel*, have great views over the river to the Om island from their balconies and roof terraces. If you can't face a spell in a *dharamshala*, there are a few alternatives. The peaceful *Yatrika Niwas* (no phone; ❷), behind the bus stand, has spartan, clean rooms, some with bathrooms; the distance from the *ghats* reduces the impact of devotional music played there early each morning. Just off the square before it joins the bridge, a flight of stone steps leads to *Maharajah Guest House* (☎07280/271237; ❷–❸), a delightful family house shaded by bougainvillea; each of the ten rooms has attached bath. Quiet and cosy, it's a long-established bastion for hard-core charas smokers. Opposite the Shri Omkar Mandhata Mandir, the *Hotel Ashwaria* (☎07280/271325; ❷–❸) has simple, clean doubles with attached bathrooms, and a restaurant. *Geeta Shree Guest House* (☎07280/271560; ❶–❷) has good-value doubles with attached baths in the main market area.

Long-stay visitors and pilgrims tend to opt for cooking their own **meals** using stoves provided by the *dharamshalas* or bought at minimal cost in the bazaar, where you can also get basic provisions. The alternatives are the good, pure-veg restaurant at *Hotel Ashwaria*, or the garden restaurant of *Ganesh Guest House*, directly behind the *Tirole Kunbi Patel*, which offers travellers' favourites including good egg-free pancakes, pizza, hummus and felafel.

Travel details

Trains

Bhopal to: Agra (18–24 daily; 5hr 20min–9hr 30min); Chennai (3–7 daily; 19hr 25min–32hr); Delhi (18–24 daily; 8hr–13hr 35min); Goa (2 daily; 34hr–40hr 30min); Gwalior (17–21 daily; 4hr 5min–6hr 40min); Indore (3–6 daily; 5hr–8hr 15min); Jabalpur (2–6daily; 6–7hr 20min); Jalgaon (2–3 daily; 7–9hr); Jhansi (22–26 daily; 3hr–5hr 40min); Manmad (for Aurangabad) (7–10 daily; 9hr–11hr 30min); Mumbai (6–12 daily; 14hr 55min–18hr); Nagpur (12–28 daily; 5hr 20min–9hr 30min); Pune (2 daily; 16–17hr); Sanchi (3 daily; 38–55min); Ujjain (3–6 daily; 3–5hr); Vidisha (3–4 daily; 40–50min).
Gwalior to: Agra (20–28 daily; 1hr 10min–2hr 20min); Bhopal (18–25 daily; 3hr 40min–7hr); Chennai (2–3 daily; 28–40hr); Delhi (20–28 daily; 3hr 50min–9hr); Goa (2 daily; 30hr 30min–36hr 35min); Indore (3daily; 13hr); Jabalpur (2 daily; 11hr 12min–13hr 20min); Jalgaon (2–3 daily; 12hr 30min–16hr 30min); Jhansi (22–26 daily; 1hr 10min–2hr 45min); Kolkata (Calcutta) (4 weekly; 24hr 20min); Mumbai (5–6 daily; 20hr–25hr); Pune (2–3 daily; 21–24hr); Puri (1 daily; 38hr); Satna (1–2 daily; 10hr); Ujjain (1–2 daily; 11hr); Vidisha (5–6 daily; 4hr 30min–6hr).
Indore to: Agra (1–2 daily; 14hr 30min–16hr); Ajmer (2 daily; 13hr 30min–16hr); Bhopal (2–4 daily; 4hr 45min–8hr); Chennai (1 weekly; 34hr); Chittaurgarh (2 daily; 7hr 30min–8hr 35min); Delhi (2–3 daily; 10hr–18hr 20min); Gwalior (3 daily; 13hr); Jabalpur (1 daily; 15hr 35min); Jaipur (1–2 daily; 12–16hr); Jhansi (1 daily; 11hr 35min); Kolkata (Calcutta) (3 weekly; 34hr); Kota (1–2 daily; 6hr 30min–7hr 40min); Mumbai (1 daily; 15hr); Ujjain (4–6 daily; 1hr 30min–2hr).
Jabalpur to: Bhopal (2–6 daily; 6hr–7hr 20min); Chennai (1–2 daily; 23hr 45min–32hr); Delhi (2 daily; 15hr 40min–19hr 40min); Gwalior (2 daily; 11hr 12min–13hr 20min); Indore (1 daily; 15hr 35min); Jhansi (2 daily; 8hr 50min–11hr); Kolkata (Calcutta) (2 daily; 23–25hr); Mumbai (3–5 daily; 18–20hr); Patna (2–4 daily; 12hr 30min–18hr 30min); Satna (3–4 daily; 3hr); Ujjain (1–2 daily; 10hr 40min–13hr); Varanasi (4–7 daily; 10hr 40min–11hr 45min).
Ujjain to: Agra (2–3 daily; 12hr 10min–16hr); Ahmedabad (daily; 9hr 30min); Bhopal (3–6 daily; 3–5hr); Chennai (6 weekly; 32hr 30min–33hr 30min); Delhi (2–3 daily; 12hr–21hr 30min); Gwalior (1–2 daily; 11hr); Indore (4–6 daily; 1hr 30min–2hr); Jabalpur (1–2 daily; 10hr 40min–13hr); Jaipur (6 weekly; 8hr 45min–10hr); Jhansi (2–4 daily; 9–10hr); Kolkata (Calcutta) (3 weekly; 32hr); Nagpur (4 weekly; 12hr); Varanasi (3 weekly; 31hr 35min).

Buses

Bhopal to: Indore (every 15min; 5–6hr); Jabalpur (3 daily; 8–10hr); Nagpur (5 daily; 10–11hr); Pachmarhi (4 daily; 6–8hr); Sanchi (hourly; 1hr 30min–2hr); Ujjain (hourly; 5–6hr); Vidisha (hourly; 2hr–2hr 30min).
Gwalior to: Agra (hourly; 2–3hr); Datia (every 30min; 1hr 40min–2hr); Delhi (4 daily; 8hr); Jhansi (every 30min; 3hr); Khajuraho (4 daily; 7–9hr); Shivpuri (every 30min; 2hr–2hr 30); Ujjain (3 daily; 12hr).
Indore to: Agra (1 daily; 16hr); Aurangabad (3 daily; 14hr); Bhopal (hourly; 5–6hr); Chittaurgarh (1 daily; 10hr); Dhar (every 30min; 2–3hr); Jaipur (3 nightly; 15hr); Kota (4 daily; 8–9hr); Mandu (3 daily; 4hr); Mumbai (2 daily; 20hr); Nagpur (1 daily; 14hr); Omkareshwar (3 daily; 4–6hr); Udaipur (6 daily; 15hr); Ujjain (every 15min; 1hr 30min–2hr).
Jabalpur to: Khajuraho (5 daily; 7–9hr); Kisli (for Kanha; 2 daily; 5–7hr); Mandla (hourly; 3hr); Murwara (for Bandhavgarh; every 30min; 2hr); Nagpur (12 daily; 7hr); Satna (6–8 daily; 8hr).
Khajuraho to: Agra (2 daily; 6hr 30min–9hr 30min); Bhopal (2 daily; 12hr); Gwalior (4 daily; 6hr–9hr); Jhansi (8 daily; 4hr 30min–5hr 30min); Mahoba (11 daily; 3hr); Panna (4 daily; 1hr); Satna (6 daily; 4hr); Varanasi (2 daily; 12hr 30min).
Ujjain to: Agra (2 daily; 15hr); Delhi (1 daily; 21hr); Dhar (5 daily; 4hr); Gwalior (2 daily; 12hr); Kota (10 daily; 8hr); Maheshwar (4 daily; 5hr); Omkareshwar (3 daily; 6–7hr).

Flights

Bhopal to: Delhi (1–2 daily; 1hr 10min–2hr); Indore (1 daily; 30min); Mumbai (2–3 daily; 2hr 5min).
Indore to: Bhopal (1 daily; 30min); Delhi (3–4 daily; 2hr 10min); Mumbai (3–4 daily; 2hr 5min).
Khajuraho to: Agra (4 weekly; 40min); Delhi (1–2 daily; 1hr 50min); Varanasi (1–2 daily; 40min).

CHAPTER 6

Highlights

* **Narrow-gauge railway** A rattly ride through stunning mountain scenery to the Raj-era hill station of Shimla. See p.485

* **Rewalsar** Buddhist pilgrimage site based around a sacred lake, with monasteries, temples, caves and hermitages. See p.502

* **Dharamsala** This relaxing hill station, home of the Dalai Lama, is an ever-popular place for rest, meditation retreats and trekking. See p.507

* **Dharamsala trek** A fantastic five-day trek leading through Dhauladhar forest to the Indrahar pass, visiting traditional villages. See p.515

* **Manikaran hot springs** Sacred to Sikhs and Hindus, this steamy settlement stands at the gateway to the spectacular Parvati Valley. See p.528

* **Manali** Travellers en route to Ladakh chill out at this honeymoon capital, enjoying Himalayan panoramas from flower-filled gardens. See p.532

* **Spiti Valley** Tiny Tibetan villages and beautiful white gompas dot Spiti's lunar landscape. See p.545

* **Manali–Leh highway** The second-highest road in the world, passing through a vast wilderness. See p.550

△ Spiti Valley

6

Himachal Pradesh

Ruffled by the lower ridges of the Shivalik Range in the far south, cut through by the Pir Panjal and Dhauladhar ranges in the northwest, and dominated by the great Himalayas in the north and east, **HIMACHAL PRADESH** (HP) is India's most popular and easily accessible hill state. Sandwiched between the Punjab and Tibet, its lowland orchards, subtropical forests and maize fields peter out in the higher reaches where pines cling to the steep slopes of mountains whose inhospitable peaks soar in rocky crags and forbidding ice fields to heights of more than 6000m.

Together with deep gorges cut by rivers crashing down from the Himalayas, these mountains form natural boundaries between the state's separate districts. Each has its own architecture, from rock-cut shrines and *shikhara* temples to colonial mansions and Buddhist monasteries. Roads struggle against the vagaries of the climate to connect the larger settlements, which are way outnumbered by remote villages, many of which are home to semi-nomadic **Gaddi** and **Gujjar** shepherds.

An obvious way to approach the state is to head north from Delhi to the state capital, **Shimla**, beyond the lush and temperate valleys of **Sirmaur**. The former summer location of the British government, Shimla is a curious, appealing mix of grand homes, churches and chaotic bazaars, with breathtaking views. The main road **northeast** from Shimla tackles a pass just north of **Narkanda**, then follows the River Sutlej east to **Sarahan**, with its spectacular wooden temple, and enters the eastern district of **Kinnaur**, most of which is accessible only to those holding **Inner Line permits** (see p.484). Alpine and green in the west, Kinnaur becomes more austere and barren as it stretches east to the Tibetan plateau, its beauty enhanced by delicate timber houses, temples and fluttering prayer flags.

Another road from Shimla climbs slowly northwest to **Mandi**, a major staging post for the state. To the north is Himachal's most popular tourist spot, the **Kullu Valley**, an undulating mass of terraced fields, orchards and forests overlooked by snowy peaks. Its epicentre is the rapidly expanding tourist town of **Manali** – long a favourite hangout of Western hippies – set in idyllic mountain scenery and offering trekking, white-water rafting and relaxing hot springs in nearby **Vashisht**. The sacred site of **Manikaran** in the Parvati Valley also has hot sulphur-free springs.

Beyond the Rohtang Pass in the far north of Kullu district, the high-altitude desert valleys of **Lahaul and Spiti** stretch beneath massive snowcapped peaks and remote settlements with Tibetan *gompas* dotting the landscape. **Permits** are needed for travel through to Kinnaur, but **Ki**, **Kaza**, and **Tabo** are open, as is the road through Lahaul to Leh in Ladakh.

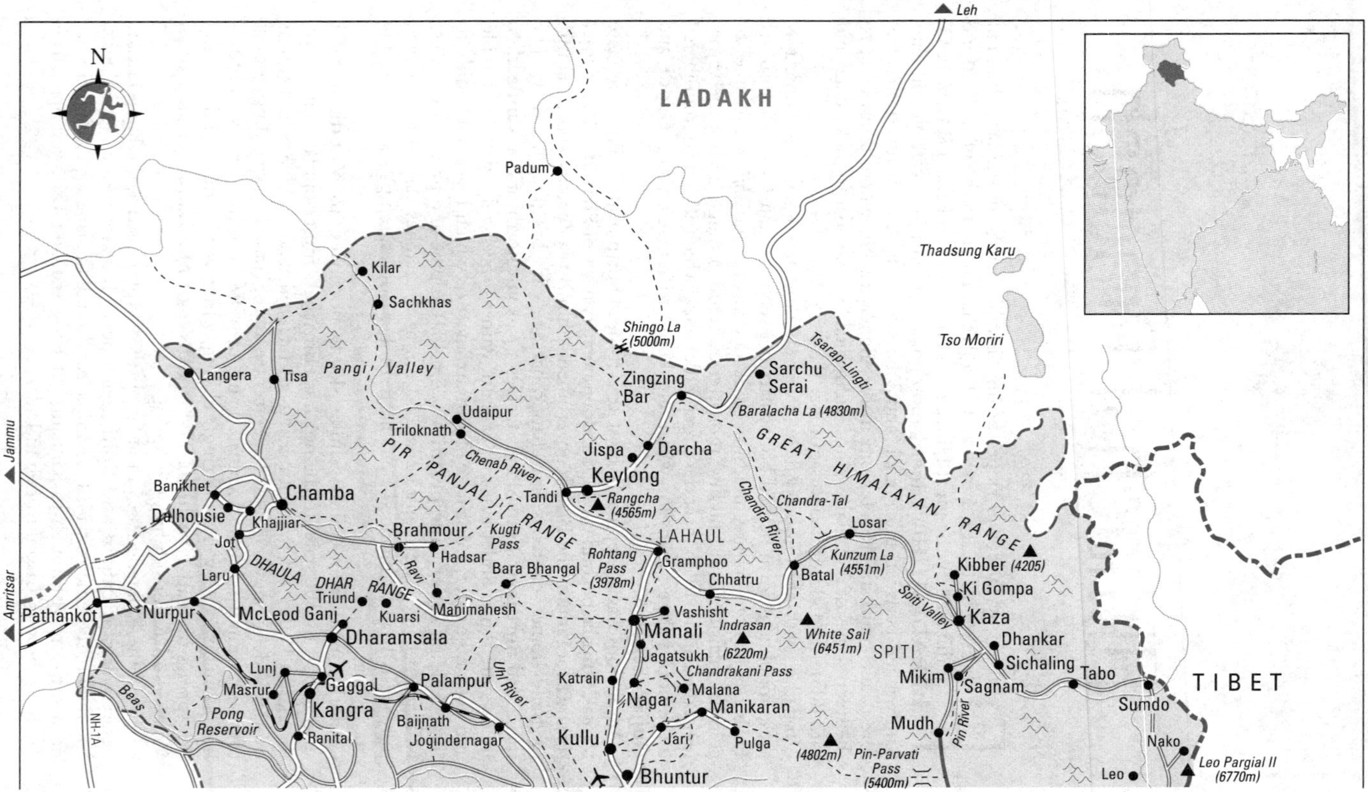

N
LADAKH
Leh
Padum
Thadsung Karu
Tso Moriri
Kilar
Sachkhas
Shingo La (5000m)
Langera
Tisa
Pangi Valley
Zingzing Bar
Sarchu Serai
Tsarap-Lingti
Baralacha La (4830m)
Udaipur
Triloknath
PIR PANJAL RANGE
Chenab River
Jispa
Darcha
GREAT HIMALAYAN RANGE
Keylong
Rangcha (4565m)
Tandi
Chandra River
Chandra-Tal
Losar
Banikhet
Chamba
Dalhousie
Khajjiar
Jot
Brahmour
Kugti Pass
LAHAUL
Kunzum La (4551m)
Kibber (4205)
Ki Gompa
Hadsar
Ravi
Rohtang Pass (3978m)
Gramphoo
Batal
Laru
DHAULA DHAR RANGE
Triund
Kuarsi
Bara Bhangal
Manimahesh
Chhatru
Spiti Valley
Kaza
Jammu
Amritsar
Pathankot
Nurpur
McLeod Ganj
Dharamsala
Vashisht
Manali
Indrasan (6220m)
White Sail (6451m)
SPITI
Dhankar
Sichaling
Lunj
Masrur
Gaggal
Kangra
Palampur
Uhl River
Jagatsukh
Chandrakani Pass
Katrain
Malana
Nagar
Manikaran
Mikim
Sagnam
Tabo
TIBET
Sumdo
Beas
Pong Reservoir
NH-1A
Ranital
Baijnath
Jogindernagar
Kullu
Jari
Pulga
(4802m)
Pin-Parvati Pass (5400m)
Mudh
Pin River
Nako
Leo
Leo Pargial II (6770m)
Bhuntur

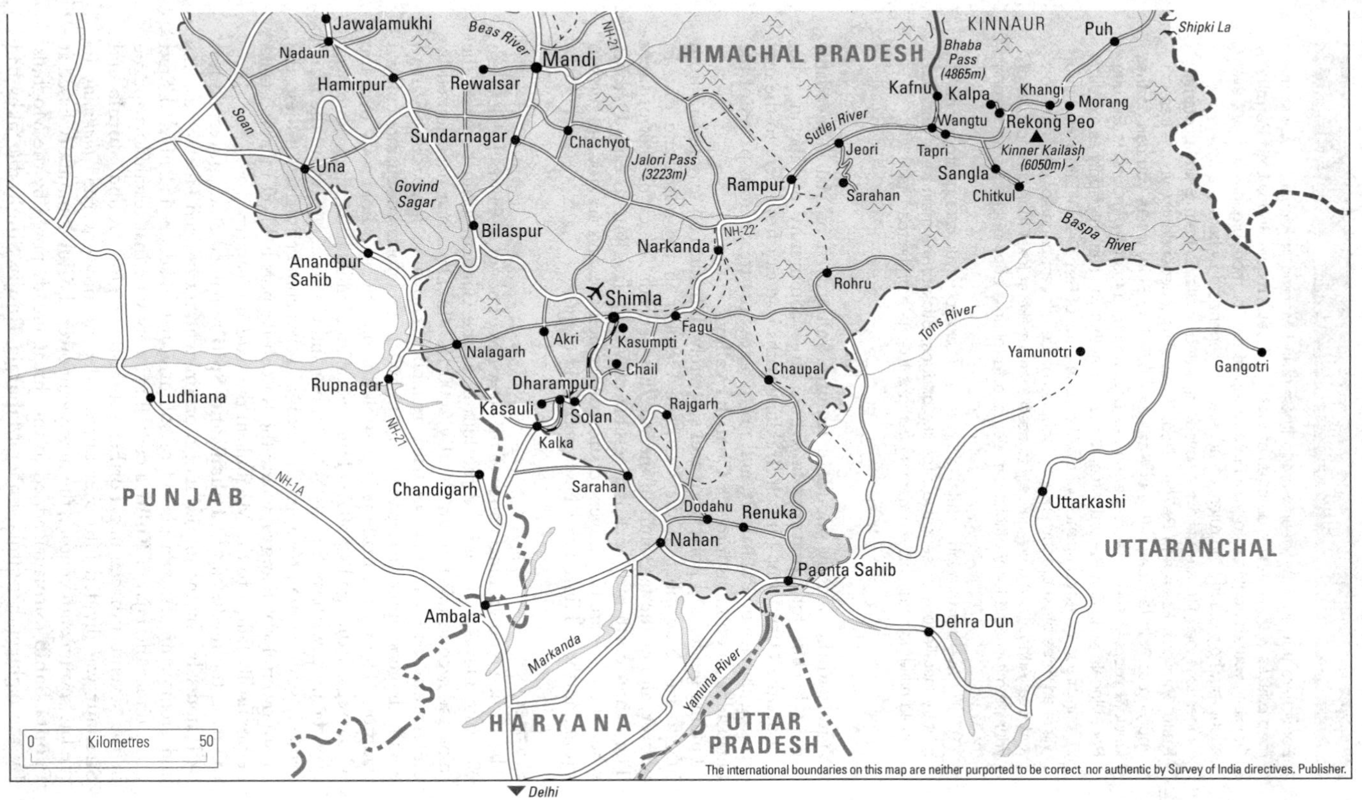

The international boundaries on this map are neither purported to be correct nor authentic by Survey of India directives. Publisher.

Restricted areas and Inner Line permits

Foreigners travelling between Sumdo in Spiti and Morang in Kinnaur – where the road passes within a few kilometres of Western Tibet – require **Inner Line Permits**. Officially you are required to travel in a group of four or more organized by a travel agent, but how strictly the rules are adhered to depends on where you apply.

Inner Line permits are valid for seven days and available from **Shimla**, **Manali**, **Kullu**, **Rampur**, **Kaza** and **Rekong Peo**. If travelling independently, you're best off applying at **Shimla** (see p.492), or **Kaza** (see p.545) in Spiti, where you can do the legwork yourself and obtain a permit free of charge in a matter of hours. In Rekong Peo, Manali, Kullu and Rampur officials may insist that you can only apply as a group of four through a travel agent – who will charge a fee of Rs100–200. Either way, you will need three photographs and photocopies of the relevant pages of your passport and visa. Although you are unlikely to need them, make at least four photocopies of your permit should local officialdom demand to retain a copy at checkpoints along the way.

When travelling through restricted areas, you should never take photographs of military installations or sensitive sites like bridges. Stick to the main route and you should have no problems – excepting perhaps the state of the road itself.

Visitors to the densely populated **Kangra Valley** west of Manali invariably make a beeline for **Dharamsala**, whose large community of Tibetan exiles includes the Dalai Lama himself. Trekking paths lead east from here to the tea-growing district of **Palampur**, and north across the treacherous passes of the Dhauladhar mountains into the **Chamba Valley**.

Finding guides and porters for **treks** is rarely difficult. The season runs from July to late November in the west, late October in the north and east. In **winter**, all but the far south of the state lies beneath a thick blanket of snow. The region north of Manali is accessible only from late June to early October when the roads are clear. Even in **summer**, when the days are hot and the sun strong, northern Himachal is beset with cold nights.

Some history

The earliest known inhabitants of the area now known as Himachal Pradesh were the **Dasas**, who entered the hills from the Gangetic plain between the third and second millennium BC. By 2000 BC the Dasas had been joined by the **Aryans**, and a number of tribal republics, known as *janapadas*, began to emerge in geographically separate regions, where they fostered separate cultural traditions. The terrain made it impossible for one ruler to hold sway over the whole region, though by 550 AD Hundu Rajput families had gained supremacy over the northwestern districts of Brahmour and Chamba, just two of the many princely states created between the sixth and sixteenth centuries. Of these, the most powerful was **Kangra**, where the Katoch Rajputs held off various attacks before finally falling to the Moghuls in the sixteenth century.

During the medieval era, **Lahaul and Spiti** remained aloof, governed not by Rajputs, but by the Jos of Tibetan origin, who introduced Tibetan customs and architecture. After a period of submission to Ladakh, Lahaul and Spiti came under the rajas of **Kullu**, a central princely state that reached its apogee in the seventeenth century. Further south, the region around **Shimla** and **Sirmaur** was divided into over thirty independently governed *thakurais*. In the late seventeenth century, the newly empowered **Sikh** community, based at **Paonta Sahib** (Sirmaur), added to the threat already posed by the Moghuls. By the eighteenth century, under **Maharaja Ranjit Singh**, the Sikhs had gained strongholds in much of western Himachal, and considerable power in both Kullu and Spiti.

Battling against Sikh expansion, Amar Singh Tapur, the leader of the **Gurkha** army set on extending his own Nepalese dominion, failed to take Kangra, but consolidated power in the southern Shimla hill states. The *thakurai* chiefs turned to the **British** for help, and forced the last of the Gurkhas back into Nepal in 1815. Predictably, the British assumed power over the south, thus tempting the Sikhs to battle in the **Anglo-Sikh War**. With the signing of a treaty in 1846 the British annexed most of the south and west of the state, and in 1864 pronounced Shimla the summer government headquarters.

After Independence, the regions bordering present-day Punjab were integrated and named Himachal Pradesh ("Himalayan Provinces"). By 1956, HP was recognized as a Union Territory, and in 1966 the state as it exists today was formed, with Shimla as its capital. Despite being a political unity, Himachal Pradesh is hardly culturally homogeneous. With more than ninety percent of the population living outside the main towns, and many areas remaining totally isolated during the long winter months, Himachal's separate districts maintain distinct customs, architecture, dress and agricultural methods. Though Hinduism dominates, there are substantial numbers of Sikhs, Muslims and Christians, and Lahaul, Spiti and Kinnaur have been home to Tibetan Buddhists since the tenth century.

Shimla and around

Shimla, Himachal's capital, is India's largest and most famous hill station, where much of the action in Rudyard Kipling's colonial classic *Kim* took place. While the city is a favourite spot for Indian families and honeymooners, its size does little to win it popularity among Western tourists who tend to pass through on their way to Manali. It is however, a perfect halfway house if you're heading to the Kullu Valley, or back in the other direction towards the plains of Haryana and Punjab. It's also the starting post for forays into the remoter regions of Kinnaur and Spiti.

The southernmost area of the state, **Sirmaur**, is Himachal's most fertile area. **Nahan**, the capital, holds little of interest, but the major Sikh shrine in **Paonta Sahib** and **Renuka wildlife sanctuary** are worth visiting if you have your own transport. Southeast of Shimla, **Kasauli** is a peaceful place to break your journey from Chandigarh in Punjab, whilst nearby **Nalagarh Fort** has been converted into the finest hotel in the state.

Northeast of Shimla, **Sarahan**, site of the famous **Bhimakali temple**, set against a backdrop of the majestic Himalayas, can be visited in a two- or three-day round trip from Shimla, or en route to Spiti.

Shimla

Whether you travel by road or rail from the south, the last stretch of the climb up to **SHIMLA** seems interminable. Deep in the foothills of the Himalayas, the

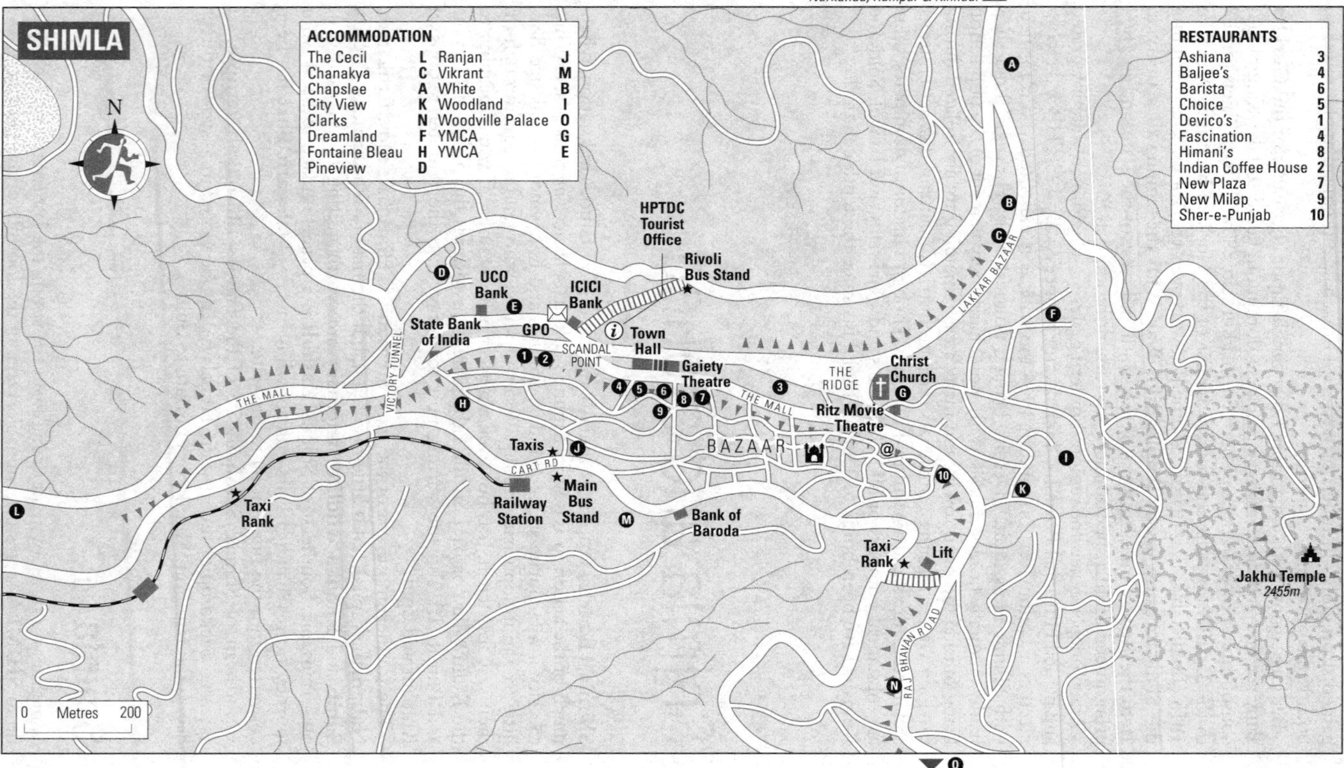
SHIMLA
N
ACCOMMODATION
The Cecil L
Chanakya C
Chapslee A
City View K
Clarks N
Dreamland F
Fontaine Bleau H
Pineview D
Ranjan J
Vikrant M
White B
Woodland I
Woodville Palace O
YMCA G
YWCA E
RESTAURANTS
Ashiana 3
Baljee's 4
Barista 6
Choice 5
Devico's 1
Fascination 4
Himani's 8
Indian Coffee House 2
New Plaza 7
New Milap 9
Sher-e-Punjab 10
Narkanda, Rampur & Kinnaur
Kufri
Kalka, Chandigarh, Delhi & Airport
(21km)
Museum & Viceregal Lodge
HPTDC Tourist Office
Rivoli Bus Stand
ICICI Bank
UCO Bank
State Bank of India
GPO
Town Hall
SCANDAL POINT
Gaiety Theatre
THE RIDGE
Christ Church
Ritz Movie Theatre
THE MALL
LAKKAR BAZAAR
VICTORY TUNNEL
BAZAAR
Taxis
CART RD
Main Bus Stand
Railway Station
Bank of Baroda
Taxi Rank
Lift
RAJ BHAVAN ROAD
Jakhu Temple
2455m
0 Metres 200

hill station is approached via a sinuous route that winds from the plains at Kalka across nearly 100km of precipitous river valleys, pine forests, and mountainsides swathed in maize terraces and apple orchards. It's not hard to see why the British chose this inaccessible site as their summer capital. At an altitude of 2159m, the crescent-shaped ridge over which it spills is blessed with perennially cool air and superb **panoramas** across verdant country to the snowy peaks of the Great Himalayan range.

Named after its patron goddess, Shamla Devi (a manifestation of Kali), the tiny village that stood on this spot was "discovered" by a team of British surveyors in 1817. Glowing reports of its beauty and climate gradually filtered to the imperial capital, Calcutta, and within two decades the settlement had become the subcontinent's most fashionable summer resort. The annual migration was finally rubber-stamped in 1864, when Shimla – by now an elegant town of mansions, churches and cricket pitches – was declared the Government of India's official hot-season HQ. With the completion of the **Kalka–Shimla Railway** in 1903, Shimla lay only two days by train from Delhi. Its growth continued after Independence, when, following the reorganization of the Punjab in 1966, Shimla became state capital of Himachal Pradesh.

Today, Shimla is still a major holiday resort, popular mainly with nouveau riche Punjabis and Delhi-ites who flock here in their thousands during the May–June run-up to the monsoons, and then again in September and October. Its jaded colonial charm also appeals to foreigners looking for a taste of the Raj. The *burra-* and *memsahibs* may have moved on, but Shimla retains a decidedly **British feel**: pukka Indian gentlemen in tweeds stroll along the Mall smoking pipes, while neatly turned-out schoolchildren scuttle past mock-Tudor shop-fronts and houses with names like *Braeside*. At the same time, the pesky monkey troupes and chaotic mass of corrugated iron rooftops that make up Shimla's **bazaar** lend an unmistakably Indian aspect to the town.

The **best time to visit** is during October and November, before the Himachali winter sets in, when the days are still warm and dry, and the morning skies are clear. From December to late February, heavy snow is common, and temperatures hover around, or below zero. The spring brings with it unpredictability: warm blasts of air from the plains, and flurries of freezing rain from the mountains. Accommodation can be scarce and expensive during the first high

The Viceroy's toy train

Until the construction of the **Kalka–Shimla railway**, the only way to get to the Shimla hill station was on the so-called **Cart Road** – a slow, winding trail trodden by lines of long-suffering porters and horse-drawn tongas. By the time the 96-kilometre narrow-gauge line was completed in 1903, 103 tunnels, 24 bridges, and 18 stations had been built between Shimla and the railhead at Kalka, 26km northeast of Chandigarh. These days, buses may be quicker, but a ride on the "toy train" is far more memorable – especially if you travel first-class, in one of the glass-windowed rail cars. Hauled along by a tiny diesel locomotive, they rattle at a leisurely pace through stunning scenery, taking between five-and-a-half and seven hours to reach Shimla.

Along the route, you'll notice the guards exchanging little leather pouches with staff strategically positioned on the station platforms. The bags they receive in return contain small brass discs, which the drivers slot into special machines to alert the signals ahead of their approach. **"Neal's Token System"**, in place since the line was first inaugurated, is a fail-safe means of ensuring that trains travelling in opposite directions never meet face to face on the single-track sections of the railway.

For information about train times and ticket booking, see p.492.

season (mid-April to the end of June), less so during the second high season of mid-September through mid-November. Expect larger crowds on weekends and holidays, notably Christmas and New Year. Whenever you come, bring warm clothes as the nights can get surprisingly chilly.

Arrival, information and local transport

Buses arriving on the main Chandigarh and Manali highways approach Shimla from the west, via Cart Road, and pull in at the chaotic main **bus stand**, halfway around the hill. Buses from Narkanda, Rampur and Kinnaur arrive at the **Rivoli** (or "Lakkar Bazaar") **bus stand** on the north side of the Ridge, unless they are continuing to the plains – in which case they too pull in at the main bus stand. Shimla's **airport** lies 21km southwest of town on the Mandi road at Jubarhati.

The HPTDC main **tourist office** (daily: high season 9am–7pm; low season 9am–6pm; ⓣ0177/265 2561, ⓦwww.hptdc.nic.in) is located on the Mall near Scandal Point. They organize whistle-stop **sightseeing tours** to destinations around Shimla, including Kufri, Chail, and Narkanda, as well as local walks (2–3hr; Rs50), and helicopter rides. To venture into the more remote and challenging regions such as Kinnaur and Spiti, check out the many mountaineering and trekking agencies on the Mall. For a list of recommended operators see p.493.

Wherever you arrive in Shimla, you'll be mobbed by **porters**. Most of the town is pedestrianized, and seriously steep, so you may be glad of the extra help to carry your gear, but bear in mind that most porters double as touts and demand a commission which will increase the cost of your room.

Local transport

Taxis are the best way to get to the pricier hotels on the outskirts. The main Vishal Himachal Taxi Union rank (ⓣ0177/265 7645) is 1km east of the bus stand, at the bottom of the **elevator** (Rs7 each way) that connects the east end of Cart Road with the Mall. The list of set fares they publish applies to high season; at other times, you should be able to negotiate discounts. Another, more central, taxi rank can be found just above the main bus stand on Cart Road.

Accommodation

Most travellers only spend a couple of nights in Shimla – just long enough to see the sights and to book an onward ticket. There's little to detain you any longer, and **accommodation** is, in the main, phenomenally expensive. In May and June it's essential to book in advance. At other times, it may be possible to negotiate a discount of up to fifty percent. Bear in mind that period buildings, such as the *YWCA* and the *Woodville Palace*, get numbingly cold during the winter months.

Budget

Chanakya Lakkar Bazaar ⓣ0177/265 4465. Cosy, clean and friendly. The cheaper rooms are small but good value, especially off-season when rates drop by as much as 50 percent. ❸–❺

Dreamland The Ridge, above the church ⓣ0177/280 6897, ⓦwww.hoteldreamlandshimla.com. Good value during the low season; all rooms are clean (though some are damp), with hot showers and Star TV. Cheaper rooms have squat toilets; the pricier rooms fantastic views over to the Himalayas. Pleasant restaurant on the top floor. ❹–❻

Fontaine Bleau Near the green-roofed army HQ, below the Mall ⓣ0177/265 3549. This eccentric place is not very clean, with yapping dogs and thin walls, but it's undeniably cheap, and near the train station. Don't arrive with a porter as they won't pay a commission. ❷–❸

Ranjan Just above the main bus stand ⓣ0177/265 2818. Originally built in 1907, this large white building is showing its age. The en-suite rooms are large and basic, with some original fittings and a sunny balcony. Good if you can't face the climb with your bags from the bus stand. ❸

Vikrant Cart Rd, near the bus stand ⓣ0177/265 3602. Large hotel with clean doubles and some singles. The cheaper ones have a common bathroom with hot bucket water. There's also a dorm (Rs100). ❸–❹

YMCA The Ridge. Take the steps to the left of the Ritz movie theatre ⓣ0177/280 4085, ⓔymcashimla@yahoo.co.in. Large rooms, including seven en-suites. In-house dining hall (breakfast is included) and sun-terrace, along with Star TV, snooker tables (Rs85), weights (Rs50), table tennis (Rs40), Internet café (Rs45/hr) and ISD/STD phone. Membership Rs40; low-season rates negotiable. ❷–❹

YWCA Constantia, the Mall ⓣ0177/280 3081. A hostel for local girls as well as foreigners, in a rambling old building set in grounds on the Ridge – great views of the Himalayas. Basic, unheated rooms and hot water by the bucket. ❸

Mid-range

City View US Club Rd, east of Christ Church ⓣ0177/281 1666. Not the cleanest, but the owners are friendly, offer good trekking advice and are flexible on the room rates. All rooms are en suite with hot showers and colour cable TV. Good sunset views from the small balcony. ❹–❺

Pineview Mythe Estate, on the far side of the Victory tunnel ⓣ0177/265 8604. A good location facing north, with a wide choice of comfortable rooms, some en suite. ❹–❻

White Lakkar Bazaar ⓣ0177/265 5276, ⓦwww.hotelwhiteshimla.com. Well-managed hotel with light rooms overlooking the Himalayas. Cleanliness can vary. The deluxe suite (Rs1540) is excellent. Fixed prices all year. ❹–❼

Woodland Daisy Bank Estate ⓣ0177/281 1002. Quiet place tucked away above the eastern end of the Mall in a concrete jungle. Attentive staff and a range of clean rooms, the pricier ones with bathtubs. Good bazaar views and easy access to Jakhu Peak. ❸–❺

Expensive

The Cecil The Mall ⓣ0177/280 4848, ⓦwww.oberoihotels.com. Raj-era building, frequented by Rudyard Kipling among others, bought and revamped by the Oberoi group in 1939. It is now opulent but devoid of character, with little but the facade as a reminder of its past. $195–475. ❾

Chapslee Lakkar Bazaar ⓣ0177/280 2542, ⓦwww.chapslee.com. Exclusive, beautiful old manor house set in its own grounds on the edge of town and stuffed with antiques. Five luxurious suites, one single room, plus a library, card room, tennis court, and croquet lawn. You'll need to book in advance; meals are also available to non-guests if booked in advance. $125–190. ❾

Clarks The Mall ⓣ0177/265 1010. Period building converted into a very comfortable, formula five-star. Double rooms $128, plus 10 percent tax. All meals, which vary in quality, are included. ❾

Woodville Palace Raj Bhavan Rd ⓣ0177/262 3919. Twenty mintues' walk south from Christ Church, this elegant 1930s mansion lies on the peaceful western side of town, with huge rooms, period furniture, lawns and a badminton court. Members of the former local royal family still live upstairs. Rooms are from $45; the showpiece Royal Suite goes for $135. ❽–❾

The Town

Although Shimla and its satellite districts sprawl over the flanks of five or more hills, the centre is fairly compact, on and immediately beneath a shoulder of high ground known as the "**Ridge**". Shimla's busy social scene revolves around the broad and breezy piazza that straddles the Ridge, overlooking rippling foothills with the jagged white peaks of the Pir Panjal and Great Himalayan ranges on the horizon. During high season the Ridge is a hive of activity, with entertainment provided by brass bands and ponymen offering rides. The Victorian-Gothic spire of **Christ Church** is Shimla's most prominent landmark. The **stained-glass windows**, the finest in British India, depict (from left to right) Faith, Hope, Charity, Fortitude, Patience and Humility. At the other end of the Ridge, **Scandal Point** is the focus of Shimla's famous mid-afternoon meet when crowds gather here to gossip.

From the Ridge, a tangle of roads and lanes tumbles down in stages, each layer connected to the next by stone steps. **The Mall**, the main pedestrian

The hike to Jakhu temple

The early-morning hike up to the **Jakhu**, or "monkey", **temple** is something of a tradition in Shimla. The top of the hill (2455m) on which it stands offers a superb panorama of the Himalayas – particularly breathtaking before the cloud gathers later in the day. The relentlessly steep climb takes twenty to forty minutes – or you could arrange a horse (a couple usually hang around in the main square opposite the Gandhi statue). The path starts just left of Christ Church; during the season, all you need do is follow the crowds.

After the hard walk up, the temple itself, a red-and-yellow-brick affair crammed with fairy lights and tinsel, comes as something of an anticlimax. The shrine inside houses what are believed to be the footprints of **Hanuman**, commander-in-chief of the monkey army that helped Rama in his struggle against the archdemon Ravana – the subject of the *Ramayana*. Legend has it that the monkey god, adored by Hindus for his strength and fidelity, rested on Jakhu after collecting healing Himalayan herbs for Rama's injured brother, Lakshmana. Watch out for the troupes of mangy monkeys around the temple. Pampered by generations of pilgrims and tourists, they have become a real pest; hang on to your bag and don't flash food.

thoroughfare, curves around the south slope of the hill. Flanked by a long row of unmistakeably British half-timbered buildings, Shimla's main shopping street was, until World War I, strictly out-of-bounds to all "natives" except royalty and rickshaw-pullers. These days, rickshaws, man-powered or otherwise, are banned, and non-Indian faces are in the minority. The quintessentially colonial **Gaiety Theatre** is still the venue for performances by the Shimla Amateur Dramatic Company; within the same premises is a gentlemen's club where the talk revolves around cricket and share prices.

Walk down any of the narrow lanes leading off the Mall, and you're plunged into a warren of twisting backstreets. Shimla's **bazaar** is the hill station at its most vibrant – a maze of dishevelled shacks, brightly lit stalls, and minarets, cascading in a clutter of corrugated iron to the edge of Cart Road. Apart from being a good place to shop for authentic souvenirs, this is also one of the few areas of town that feels Himalayan: multicoloured Kullu caps (*topis*) bob about in the crowd, alongside the odd Lahauli, Kinnauri or Tibetan face.

The state museum

The HP state **museum** (Tues–Sun 10am–1.30pm & 2–5pm, closed 2nd Sat of month; free) is a 1.5-kilometre hike west from the centre, but well worth the effort. The ground floor of the elegant colonial mansion is given over largely to temple sculpture, and a gallery of magnificent **Pahari miniatures** – examples of the last great Hindu art form to flourish in northern India before the deadening impact of Western culture in the early nineteenth century. An offspring of the Moghul painting tradition, the Pahari or "Hill" school is renowned for subtle depictions of romantic love, inspired by scenes from Hindu epics. Among the museum's **paintings** are dozens of Moghul and Rajasthani miniatures and a couple of fine "Company" watercolours. Produced for souvenir-hunting colonials by the descendants of the Moghul and Pahari masters, the *fakirs*, itinerant *sadhus* and mendicants they depict could have leapt straight from the pages of Kipling. One room is devoted to Mahatma Gandhi, packed with photos of his time in Shimla and amusing cartoons of his political relationship with the British.

To get there, follow the Mall past the post office and downhill, passing *Dalziel* and *Classic* hotels, then take the right fork at the first intersection and left at the second, where a signpost guides you up the last, short ascent.

The Viceregal Lodge and Prospect Hill

Shimla's single most impressive colonial monument, the old **Viceregal Lodge** (daily 9am–1pm & 2–7pm; Rs10, guided tours every 30min), summer seat of British government until the 1940s and today home to the **Institute of Advanced Studies**, is a fifteen-minute walk west of the museum. The lodge is Shimla at its most British. The solid grey mansion, built in Elizabethan style with a lion and unicorn set above the entrance porch, surveys trimmed lawns fringed by pines and flowerbeds. Inside is just as ostentatious, though only sections of the ground floor are open to the public: a vast teak-panelled entrance hall, an impressive library (formerly the ballroom), and the guest room. The **conference room**, hung with photos of Nehru, Jinnah and Gandhi, was the scene of crucial talks in the run-up to Independence. On the stone terrace to the rear of the building, a plaque profiles and names the peaks visible in the distance.

The short hike up to **Prospect Hill** (2176m), a popular picnic spot, ties in nicely with a visit to the lodge. By cutting through the woods to the west of the mansion, you can drop down to a busy intersection known as **Boileauganj**, from where a tarmac path climbs steeply up to the small shrine of Kamana Devi. The summit gives fine views across the south side of Shimla ridge, and over the hills and valleys of southern HP towards the plains of the Punjab.

Eating

Few **restaurants** in Shimla retain the colonial ambience you might expect, and standards are generally poor and variety disappointingly lacking. Catering mainly for Indian visitors, they are heavily Punjabi-oriented, with an emphasis on rich, spicy, meat-based menus. At the top of the range, try the restaurants at *The Cecil* or *Clarks*. Apart from the new (and usually empty) branch of *Domino's Pizza* at Scandal Point, several other "**fast food**" restaurants along the Mall offer everything from *dosas* and Chinese food to Mughlai cooking; some have adjoining bars. For a really cheap and filling meal, try the fried potato patties (*tikki*) or chickpea curry and puris (*channa batura*) at one of the snack bars that line the steps opposite the Gaiety Theatre. Alternatively the bazaar is good for cheap *dhabas*. The Mall's many **bakeries** and ice-cream parlours offer comfort for the sweet-toothed.

Ashiana The Ridge. HPTDC restaurant in a converted bandstand offering mainly non-veg Indian food, including tasty chicken *makhanwalla*, pizzas and a few Chinese dishes.

Baljee's 26 the Mall. A landmark on Shimla's culinary and social map, this hectic smart-set coffee house does a roaring trade in snacks, sweets and ice cream in the evenings, but serves no alcohol. Try the piping hot *gulab jamuns*, served to after-dinner strollers at their takeaway counter.

Barista The Mall. Western-style coffee bar, complete with excellent lattes, muffins, chocolate brownies and chirpy service, for a fraction of the price back home.

Choice Middle Bazaar. Tiny, no-nonsense Chinese restaurant with an exhaustive menu of cheap and delicious dishes.

Devico's The Mall. Lively Western-style fast food joint with South Indian snacks, veggie-burgers, and shakes. There's an additional restaurant downstairs and a plush bar upstairs.

Fascination 26 the Mall. This swish à la carte restaurant upstairs at *Baljee's* offers a good selection of Indian and Chinese dishes, including non-veg options such as curried brains, or sausage, egg and chips.

Himani's 48 the Mall. Something for everyone, with the ground floor taken up by a flashy video game arcade, a lively (mostly male) bar on the first

Moving on from Shimla

The **toy train** leaves Shimla for **Kalka**, where you can change onto the main broad-gauge line for **Chandigarh** and **New Delhi**. The 10.20am departure (Himalayan Queen #4096) gets you into Kalka just in time to catch the Shatabdi Express at 4.50pm, arriving in New Delhi just after 10pm. The other toy train services depart at 8.30am, 1.30pm, 2.25pm, 5.30pm, and 5.45pm, arriving in Kalka at 1.30pm, 6.15pm, 8.15pm, 10.15pm, and 10.55pm respectively. **Reservations** for onward journeys from Kalka can be made at Shimla station (ⓣ0177/265 2915, enquiries ⓣ131). Alternatively, you can catch a bus to Chandigarh and continue to Delhi by train from there.

The **main bus stand** (ⓣ0177/265 8765), on Cart Road below the bazaar, serves Chandigarh, Delhi, Mandi, Kullu, Dharamsala, Manali, and elsewhere, while the Rivoli (or Lakkar Bazaar) bus stand, reached via the path dropping behind ICICI Bank on Scandal Point, handles departures to Narkanda, Ani, Rampur, Sarahan, and Kalpa (for Kinnaur). Passengers for **Manali** or **Delhi** can choose between luxury a/c, deluxe non-a/c, or Himachal's standard bone-shaking state buses. Tickets for the former two should be booked a day in advance at travel agents on the Mall, while state bus tickets can be reserved at the ticket counter (daily except Sun 10am–4.30pm) outside the HPTDC tourist office near Scandal Point; alternatively, head to the counters at the main bus stand. For **Chandigarh**, services are so frequent there's no need to book.

Flights between Delhi and Shimla (1hr 10min) are operated by Jagson Airlines (Tues, Thurs & Sat) on seventeen-seater planes for around $125. Tickets are available through the HPTDC tourist office.

See the "Travel details" at the end of this chapter for more information on journey frequencies and durations.

floor, and a family-style restaurant, pool den and sundeck on the top floor. Menu includes tandoori dishes and South Indian.

Indian Coffee House The Mall. Atmospheric, faded café with colonial ambience, offering the usual *Coffee House* package of veg snacks and attentive waiter service to the predominantly male clientele.

New Milap Middle Bazaar. Small and friendly *dhaba* below *Himani's*. Big portions of Indian food as well as porridge at excellent prices.

New Plaza 60/1 Middle Bazaar, down the steps opposite the *Gaiety*. Popular family restaurant. Good-value food including tasty meat sizzlers.

Sher-e-Punjab Upper Bazaar. The best of the *dhabas* just below the Mall. Hearty portions of spicy beans, chickpeas, and dhal.

Listings

Airlines Indian Airlines, Air Sahara and Jagson Air, c/o Ambassador Travels, The Mall ⓣ0177/265 8014.

Banks and exchange ATM at UCO Bank, close to the GPO; ICICI at Scandal Point; Punjab National Bank on the Mall and the State Bank of India, between Scandal Point and the railway station. Only the SBI will cash travellers' cheques. Visa encashments can be made at the Bank of Baroda on Cart Rd, five minutes' walk east of the main bus stand. Mr Sood, next door to Sindh Tours and below the church on the Mall, keeps longer hours but offers a less favourable rate of exchange.

Bookshops Maria Brother, an antiquarian bookshop on the Mall, sells old maps and etchings as well as a limited selection of new books – but don't expect a bargain. Asia Bookhouse and Minerva, also on the Mall, both stock paperbacks.

Golf Naldera Golf Club, 22km (1hr drive) from Shimla, is served by public bus every 30min (Rs30); a taxi is Rs700 return. Green fees and club rental $15, caddy Rs60. Accommodation here includes the *Hotel Golf Glade* (ⓣ0177/248 7739) with rooms and log huts for Rs1000–5000.

Hospitals Indira Gandhi Medical College Hospital ⓣ0177/280 4251; Deen Dayal Hospital, near the ISBT ⓣ0177/265 4071.

Internet access There are several places along the Mall, but the fastest is Mr Sood's internet café (Rs30/hr) on the Mall, next door to Sindh Tours and below the church.

Laundry Band Box, Snowhite and Whiteway, all on the Mall.

Permits Inner Line permits (see p.484) are issued at the Additional District Magistrate's

office (Mon–Sat 10am–5pm; closed 2nd Sat of the month; ⓣ0177/265 7005) on the first floor of the modern courthouse, one street below the Mall, opposite Sheel SJ Jewellers.
Pharmacies Indu Medical, the Mall (9am–8pm).
Post The green-painted, Swiss-chalet-style GPO (Mon–Sat 10am–6pm), with its poste restante counter, is near Scandal Point on the Mall.
Travel agents Reliable operators include the adventurous Vicky Negi at Eagle Himalayan Tours, 23 Tashkent Annex, near AG Office below the Mall (ⓣ0177/265 2880, ⓦwww.eaglehimtours.com), and Anil Bhardwaj at Band Box, 9 the Mall, near Scandal Point (ⓣ0177/265 8157, ⓔbboxhy@satyam.net.in, who specializes in tailor-made itineraries. Other recognized agencies are White Height Himalaya Travels ⓣ0177/265 6242 and Great Himalayan Travels ⓣ0177/265 8934, ⓦwww.ghtravels.com. The *YMCA* (ⓣ0177/280 4085) also organizes treks and safaris.

South of Shimla

On the border with Uttaranchal, the town of **PAONTA SAHIB**, where pastel-yellow houses are packed tightly into the cobbled streets, holds an important shrine dedicated to **Guru Gobind Singh**, the tenth Sikh guru, who lived here. Paonta Sahib provides good bus connections for travel to Shimla from points such as Mussoorie, Dehra Dun, Haridwar and Rishikesh. Should you decide to stay, the HPTDC *Hotel Yamuna* (ⓣ01704/222341; ❸–❻), on the banks of the River Yamuna, has pleasant rooms, a restaurant and bar. From Punjab or Haryana, the first town on the road is **NAHAN**, connected by bus to Ambala, 105km southwest, and the hill stations further north. There are a few unspectacular places to stay around the cricket pitch, including the basic *Regency Hotel* (ⓣ01702/223302; ❷–❹). Six daily buses (2hr) make the journey 45km east to Dodahu, 2km from the secluded lake at **Renuka**, where a **wildlife sanctuary** protects rare deer plus a magnificent pride of Asiatic lions, introduced in the hope of creating a stable breeding population. Tropical forests reach the lakeside, along which trees and reeds shelter colonies of herons, kingfishers and bee-eaters. The HPTDC *Hotel Renuka* (ⓣ01702/267339; ❸–❺), in sloping gardens on the western shore, has rooms opening onto a shady veranda, as well as dorm beds (Rs75).

Kasauli

Though it sees few Western tourists, the small, slow-paced town of **KASAULI**, cradled by pine forests 77km southwest of Shimla (3hr by bus), and with a touch of Raj architecture, makes a good stopoff point on the way to or from Delhi. Criss-crossed by spindly cobbled streets, spreading along low ridges carpeted with forests and flower-filled meadows, Kasauli abounds in gentle short strolls; the hike to the summit of nearby Monkey Point (4km) is popular, though as it's on airforce land there's a police checkpoint, complete with metal detector, en route.

The nearest railway station is Dharampur on the Kalka–Shimla line, from where buses travel the 11km up to Kasauli; there are also direct buses from Shimla. From Kasauli, an easy and scenic twelve-kilometre trek leads through forests to **Kalka**, railhead for the **toy train** to Shimla. There is no tourist office in Kasauli but the manager at the HPTDC *Ros Common* will provide information on paths, and train and bus times. You can **change money** at the Bank of Baroda (Mon–Fri 11am–3pm) on Lower Mall.

Aside from the cheaper lodges, most of Kasauli's **hotels** have high-ceilinged rooms with fireplaces, carpets and balconies, in true Raj style. Few have built-in water heaters but supply hot water in buckets. Apart from the larger hotels, **food** options are limited to *dhabas* serving *aloo mutter*, *aloo gobi* and dhal, and fresh *puris* in the morning.

Accommodation

Alasia Lower Mall ⓣ01792/272008. One of Kasauli's better hotels; a Raj-era house with large rooms, balconies, a bar and Internet facilities, plus a couple of suites facing north towards the distant mountains. ❹–❼

Gian Post Office Rd ⓣ01792/272244. Unremarkable, but homely. Some private bathrooms and balconies. ❷–❸

HPTDC Ros Common Lower Mall ⓣ01792/272005. Period bungalow converted into a comfortable hotel almost 1km east of town, with beautiful gardens and silver-service tea and coffee all day. Its six well-maintained rooms are often full, so call ahead or book through HPDTC in Shimla (ⓣ0177/265 2561) or Delhi (ⓣ011/2332 5320). The restaurant has an extensive menu and, along with the lawn, is open to nonresidents. ❻–❼

Maurice Lower Mall ⓣ01792/272074. Rambling Raj house run by Osho devotees, with towering ceilings and airy balconies. ❼

Nalagarh Fort

If you can afford it, the eighteenth-century **fort** of **Nalagarh**, converted into probably the finest **hotel** in Himachal Pradesh, is an excellent place to break the journey between Delhi and Kullu. Towering above the town with the Himachal foothills rising steeply behind, the fort – lying 60km from Chandigarh and 12km off the main Chandigarh–Mandi road – played a key role in the Gurkha wars of the early nineteenth century, and is today filled with memorabilia evoking its military past. Accommodation (❽) is in beautifully maintained suites, each with period furniture. An atmospheric lounge bar overlooks terraced grounds with a tennis court, croquet lawn and swimming pool, and an Ayurvedic clinic offers massage. Book in advance (ⓣ01795/223009, ⓔfortresort@satyam.net.in).

Northeast of Shimla: from Narkanda to Sarahan

A three-hour (65km) bus ride northeast of Shimla, the scruffy hill town of **NARKANDA** (2725m) makes a good resting point on the bumpy, six-hour journey to Sarahan. This former staging post on the Hindustan–Tibet caravan route acts as the roadhead and main market town for the area's widely dispersed apple and potato growers, and is a popular **ski area** (Jan–March) for Indian holidaymakers, although the lone ski hill – little more than a lopsided cricket pitch – is hardly worth a special trip. A couple of places in town rent skis, including Highlands Travel & Adventure (ⓣ01782/242444, ⓔhta30@hotmail.com), overlooking the bus stand. There are some good rambles through the cedar forests that surround the town, and great **views** of the Himalayas. **Hatu Peak** (3143m), crowned by a lonely hilltop **Durga temple**, 7km east of town, looks out over the River Sutlej winding far below, and a string of white-tipped mountains to the north and east.

Accommodation options include HPTDC's quietly situated *Hotel Hatu* (ⓣ01782/242430; ❺–❻), with large well-appointed rooms, great views from the lawns, and a restaurant; and the large en-suite north-facing rooms at the ski centre (ⓣ01782/242426; ❷–❸). For a little more comfort, *Mahamaya Palace* (ⓣ01782/242448; ❹) has reasonable en-suites and a restaurant.

Rampur

Once over the pass at Narkanda, the highway winds steadily down the Sutlej Valley towards **RAMPUR**, a major transport hub 132km northeast of Shimla.

Formerly the capital of the princely state of Bhushar, the town today is a gritty and cheerless cluster of concrete houses hemmed in by a forbidding wall of rock. During the local **Lavi mela** festival (late Oct or early Nov), hill-people gather to trade bundles of wool and sacks of dried fruit and nuts. The gabled **Padam Palace**, built in 1919, is the home of the Bahadurs, the local ruling family; it's closed to the public. Across the main road from the bus stand, a small Buddhist **gompa** houses a huge metal prayer wheel and a rock reputedly bearing ten million minute inscriptions of the mantra "Om Mane Padme Hum".

Rampur has **bus** connections to Rekong Peo and onward all the way to Kaza in Spiti, and – when the Jalori Pass road is open – to Kullu. **Inner Line permits** for Kinnaur can be obtained from the Sub-Divisional Magistrate's office opposite the fire station on the main road, or else in Rekong Peo (see p.498). As you head down the steps from the bus stand, the first of the budget **lodges** is the poky *Rama* (ⓣ01782/233136; ❶). Better value is the *Amar Jyoti* (ⓣ01782/233185; ❶) further down the lane, which has comfortable en-suite doubles with balconies facing the river, a restaurant, and ISD/STD phone in reception. The plusher *Bhagwati* (ⓣ01782/233117; ❶–❸) is nearby, but top of the range is the HPTDC *Bushehar Regency* (ⓣ01782/234103; ❹–❻), on the Shimla-facing edge of town. For **food**, the *Bhagwati* has the best restaurant; *Café Sutluj*, 200m west of town, makes up for its lack of atmosphere with air-conditioning, a bar and a great terrace overlooking the river.

Sarahan

Secluded **SARAHAN**, erstwhile summer capital of the Bhushar rajas, sits astride a 2000-metre ledge above the River Sutlej, near the Shimla–Kinnaur border. Set against a spectacular backdrop, the village harbours one of the northwestern Himalaya's most exotic spectacles – **Bhimakali temple**. With its two multi-tiered sanctuary towers, elegantly sloping slate-tiled roofs, and gleaming golden spires, it is the most majestic early timber temple in the Sutlej Valley – an area renowned for housing holy shrines on raised wooden platforms. Although most of the structure dates from the early twentieth century, parts are thought to be more than eight hundred years old.

A pair of elaborately decorated metal doors lead into a large courtyard flanked by rest rooms and a small carved-stone **Shiva shrine**.Visitors should leave shoes and any leather articles at the racks, before heading up the steps to a second,

Blood sacrifice in Sarahan

The **Bhima Kali** deity, a local manifestation of the black-faced, bloodthirsty Hindu goddess Kali (Durga), has for centuries been associated with **human sacrifice**. Once every decade, until the disapproving British intervened in the 1800s, a man was killed here as an offering to the *devi*. Following a complex ceremony, his newly spilled blood was poured over the goddess's tongue for her to drink, after which his body was dumped in a deep well inside the temple compound. If no victim could be found, it is said that a voice would bellow from the depths of the pit, which is now sealed up.

The tradition of blood sacrifice continues in Sarahan to this day, albeit in less extreme form. During the annual **Astomi** festival, two days before the culmination of **Dussehra**, a veritable menagerie of birds and beasts are put to the knife, including a water-buffalo calf, sheep, goat, fish, chicken, crab, and even a spider. The gory spectacle draws large crowds, and is a memorable alternative to the Dussehra procession in Kullu, which takes place at around the same time in mid-October.

smaller yard. Beyond another golden door, also richly embossed with mythical scenes, the innermost enclosure holds the two **sanctuary towers**. The one on the right houses musical instruments, flags, paladins and ceremonial weapons used in religious festivals, a selection of which is on show in the small "museum" in the corner of the courtyard. Non-Hindus who want to climb to the top of the other more modern tower (no photography) to view the highly polished gold-faced deity have to don a saffron cap. Bhima Kali herself is enshrined on the top floor, decked with garlands of flowers and tended not by ordinary villagers, as is normally the case in Himachal, but by bona fide *brahmin* priests.

Practicalities

Buses from Shimla to Sangla and Rekong Peo pass through the small town of Jeori, from where several buses a day (Rs10) and taxis climb the 17km up the mountainside to Sarahan. There's also a direct bus service from Rampur. Keen walkers might fancy ambling along the well-worn mule track to Sarahan from Jeori (90min). **Accommodation** at Sarahan itself is fairly limited. HPTDC's *Hotel Srikhand* (Ⓣ01782/274234; ❹–❻) is a concrete monster, but has a delightful garden and a restaurant serving good veg meals on a relaxing terrace. The clean, comfortable rooms come with hot water and valley views, though they are a little overpriced; there's also a dorm (Rs75) and a cheaper annexe. The *Temple Guest House* (❶–❷), inside the Bhimakali courtyard, has a range of pleasant, albeit noisy, rooms – those with bath in the new wing are excellent value – and a basement dorm (Rs75). When the temple kitchens aren't dishing up their usual cheap and delicious meals, try one of the several *dhabas* around the square outside. Watch out for the *New Friends*, however – they may indeed be friendly, but the mutton *momos* can be dangerous.

Kinnaur

Before 1992, the remote backwater of **KINNAUR**, a rugged buffer zone between the Shimla foothills and the wild western extremity of Chinese-occupied Tibet, was strictly off-limits to tourists. Although visitors are now allowed to travel through the "**Restricted Area**", and on to Spiti, Lahaul and the Kullu Valley, permits are still required (see p.484). Other areas of Kinnaur – notably the **Baspa Valley**, and the sacred **Kinner-Kailash** massif visible from the mountain village of **Kalpa** are completely open.

Straddling the mighty River Sutlej, which rises on the southern slopes of Mount Kailash, Kinnaur has for centuries been a major trans-Himalayan corridor. Merchants travelling between China and the Punjabi plains passed through on the **Hindustan–Tibet caravan route**, stretches of which are still used by villagers and trekkers. The bulk of the traffic that lumbers east towards the frontier, however, uses the newer fair-weather road, veering north into Spiti just short of the ascent to Shipki La pass, on the Chinese border, which remains closed.

In the well-watered, mainly Hindu west of the region, the scenery ranges from subtropical to almost alpine: wood-and-slate villages, surrounded by maize

Trekking in Kinnaur

Unfrequented mountain trails criss-cross Kinnaur, offering **treks** ranging from gentle hikes to challenging climbs over high-altitude passes. The routes along the **Sutlej Valley**, punctuated with government rest houses and villages, are feasible without the aid of ponies, but away from the main road you need to be completely self-sufficient. **Porters** can usually be hired in Rampur, Rekong Peo and the Baspa Valley except in early autumn (Sept/Oct), when they're busy with the apple harvest.

The Kinner-Kailash circuit

The five- to seven-day *parikrama* (circumambulation) of the majestic Kinner-Kailash massif, a sacred pilgrimage trail, makes a spectacular trek for which you won't need an Inner Line permit. The circuit starts at the village of **MORANG**, on the left bank of the Sutlej, served by buses from Tapri or Rekong Peo. A Jeepable track runs southeast from here to **Thangi**, the trailhead, and continues through Rahtak, over the **Charang La** pass (5266m) to **Chitkul** in the Baspa Valley. The trail then follows the river down to the beautiful village of **Sangla**, from where a couple of worthwhile day hikes can be made – to **Kamru fort** behind the village, or the steep ascent to the **Shivaling La** pass, from where there are superb views of Raldang (5499m), the southernmost peak on the Kinner-Kailash massif. The final stage passes through the lower Baspa Valley, via Shang and Brua to **Karcham**, which overlooks the NH-22 highway. The best time for the Kinner-Kailash *parikrama* is between July and October; August is the most poplar month for local pilgrims to complete the circuit.

Wangtu to Kaza, via the Pin Valley

This challenging route across the Great Himalayan range, via the Kalang Setal glacier and the Shakarof La pass, is a dramatic approach to Spiti and the **Pin Valley**, and no restrictions apply. The trail, which is very steep, snow-covered, and hard to follow in places, should definitely not be attempted without ponies, porters, adequate gear, and a **guide** – preferably one arranged through a reputable trekking agency. It starts at **WANGTU** on the main highway, passing through Kafnoo village, Mulling, Phustirang (3750m), and over the **Bhaba Pass** (4865m), a gruelling slog through snowfields, before dropping down into the beautiful and isolated **Pin Valley**. **Kaza** (see p.545), the district headquarters of Spiti, lies a further three or four days' hike to the north. On its way to the main road, the trail winds through remote settlements including **Kharo**, from where the ancient Buddhist *gompa* at **Khungri** can be reached. This route, however, is under threat by road builders who are ploughing over the trail; it's expected to be accessible for motor vehicles by 2006.

Chitkul to Har-ki-Dun

This ten-day trek to **Garhwal** passes along the edge of the Inner Line and is subject to restrictions. Starting from **Chitkul** and crossing the River Baspa to Doaria, the route then climbs up a side valley to follow a lateral moraine up to the Zupika Gad and then a steep ascent – the final section of which is up a crevassed glacier – to the **Borsu Pass** (5300m). The other side of the pass is down a steep snow and boulder field requiring some scrambling; you arrive a few days later in the beautiful valley of **Har-ki-Dun** in Garhwal. You should be able to link the trek with one over the Yamunotri Pass and Dodi Tal (see p.375) to Uttarkashi but this depends on conditions around the roadhead of Har-ki-Dun and Yamunotri. A guide is essential.

The old Hindustan–Tibet road from Kalpa to the Rupa Valley

Another route to consider is the relatively easy five-day trek starting at **Kalpa** and following the old Hindustan–Tibet road through the remote hamlets of upper Kinnaur (permits needed), past Shi Asu to the Rupa Valley. The views along the route are superb and the villagers are extremely hospitable. The road, now crumbling in places, is also ideal for mountain biking. Although there is a route from the Rupa Valley over the Manirang Pass into Spiti, few locals know it or are willing to guide you across.

terraces and orchards, nestle beneath pine forests and vast blue-grey mountain peaks. Further east, beyond the reach of the monsoons (June–Sept), it grows more austere, and glaciers loom on all sides. **Buddhism** arrived in Kinnaur with the tenth-century kings of Guge, who ruled what is now southwestern Tibet. When **Rinchen Zangpo** (958–1055), the "Great Translator" credited with the "Second Spreading" of the faith in Guge, passed through here, he left behind several monasteries and a devotion to a pure form of the Buddhist faith that has endured here for nearly one thousand years. In the sixteenth century, after Guge had fragmented into dozens of petty fiefdoms, the **Bhushar kings** took control of Kinnaur. They remained in power throughout the British Raj, when this was one of the battlegrounds of the espionage war played out between agents of the Chinese, Russian and British empires – the "Great Game" evocatively depicted in the novels of Rudyard Kipling.

Rekong Peo

East of Jeori, the road climbs high above the Sutlej into ever more remote territory, traversing sheer ravines on cable bridges, while tiny wooden villages, each with a pagoda-roofed temple, cling to the mountainsides. At **Wangtu** bridge, the old Inner Line, and trailhead for the Kinnaur–Pin Valley–Kaza trek, the highway switches to the north bank of the river. Beyond the village of **Tapri**, a right fork leads to **Sangla** in the Baspa Valley, while the main highway continues to **REKONG PEO**, district headquarters of Kinnaur, 7km above the main road. Its batch of concrete houses and government buildings around a small *maidan* gives it the air of an upstart frontier settlement. The only reason to stop is to buy trekking supplies, pick up the trail to Kalpa, or obtain an Inner Line **permit** (see p.484) from the District Commissioner's office (Mon–Sat 10am–5pm) in the large red-roofed building near the main bazaar bus stop. Stop at the tourist office on the ground floor to double check the application procedure – chances are that you'll be told to apply through a travel agent as a group of four. Recommended travel agents are Sanjeev at the *Cafeteria on the Roof* (☎01786/222883), and Bhagwan Singh of the nearby National Travellers (☎01786/223271). You'll need three passport-sized photos, and photocopies of the picture and visa pages in your passport.

The Rekong Peo **bazaar** is good for crowd-watching, particularly in late afternoon when it fills up with villagers waiting for the bus home. Many of the women don traditional Kinnauri garb for their trip to town – green velvet jackets, heavy home-spun blankets with intricate borders, raw-silk cummerbunds and stacks of elaborate silver jewellery. Around 2km above the bazaar behind the All India Radio complex stands the **Mahabodhi Kinnaur Buddhist temple**, with its large yellow Maitreya statue overlooking an orchard. The temple was consecrated during the Kalachakra ceremony performed here by the Dalai Lama in 1992.

Practicalities

Rekong Peo's **buses** are fairly frequent, considering its relative isolation. Buses drop off and pick up at the bend in the main bazaar before proceeding up the hill on the Kalpa road for 2km to the **main bus stand**. There are several daily services to Shimla, an early morning departure direct to Mandi, direct buses to Chandigarh, Delhi and nearby Sangla, two buses daily to Puh and a morning departure for Kaza. Alternatively you can flag down the Tapri–Kaza bus as it passes Poberi, the Rekong Peo turn-off on the main road far down the valley. West of Rekong Peo, towards the Sangla turnoff, the fragile road is frequently blocked or washed away by landslides and floods. When this happens you'll have to wait for road crews to clear away the debris or walk over the affected area to catch a bus on the other side.

Accommodation in town is overpriced for what you get; the best options around the bazaar are the *Hotel Fairyland* (Ⓣ01786/222477; ❸), on the road behind the *Cafeteria on the Roof*, which has modest but clean rooms, some with private baths; and the four musty rooms with baths above the *Cafeteria on the Roof* (Ⓣ01786/222883; ❷). Both places have great views over the bazaar to Kinner Kailash. About 1km up the road to the main bus stand is the new *Hotel City Heart* (Ⓣm94180/18615; ❸), which has immaculate, spacious doubles with bath; the pricier rooms have the best views. Proximity to the bus stand is the only reason to stay in the shabby *Shivling Guest House* (Ⓣ01786/222421; ❶–❸); the **restaurant** is good but is also the local whisky-drinking den. Food options in Peo itself are pretty much limited to the *Cafeteria on the Roof*, 100m east of the lower bus stand, which has sizzlers, pizza, a couple of Kinnauri dishes and a small terrace for people-watching. Also on the bazaar, opposite the Sharma Boot House, is a good, unsigned *dhaba* which serves up cheap mutton *momos* and veg *thukpa*. The only Internet access is at Raj **Internet** café (Rs60/hr), 100m beyond the main bus stand.

Kalpa (Chini)

Almost 250km northeast of Shimla and 9km along a twisting road from Rekong Peo, **KALPA** can be reached by road, or on foot along various steep tracks. Its narrow atmospheric lanes and dramatic location astride a rocky bluff, high above the right bank of the Sutlej, make the hike worthwhile. The ancient Tibetan *gompa* here was founded by Rinchen Zangpo; there is also a small Shiva temple. Facing the village, the magnificent **Kinner-Kailash** massif sweeps 4500m up from the valley floor. The mountain in the middle, Jorkaden (6473m), is the highest, followed by the sacred summit of Kinner-Kailash (6050m) to the north, and the needle point of Raldang (5499m) in the south. Up the valley you'll see remains of the Hindustan–Tibet road.

Kalpa is a far more attractive place to stay than Rekong Peo, although finding **accommodation** can involve some walking. On the upper road, the *Kinner Villa* (Ⓣ01786/226006, Ⓔkinnervilla@rediffmail.com; ❻) is the most tasteful place around, with sleek, refurbished rooms, spotless bathrooms and a grassy pitch out front. On the same road is the HPDTC *Kinner Kailash Cottage* (Ⓣ01786/226159; ❺–❽), a huge new chalet under construction at the time of writing; the original rustic but comfortable four-bed cottages lie further behind. About 1km north, set in an apple orchard, is the traditional *Aucktong Guest House* (Ⓣ01786/226019; ❷), which has four basic rooms, shared bathrooms and a long balcony perfect for enjoying the views and simple food. Set behind an ugly concrete house, it's easy to miss – look for the sign hanging in the trees. In Kalpa itself, the *Blue Lotus Guest House* (Ⓣ01786/226001; ❸–❺), a concrete block 100m beyond the lower bus stand, has a reasonable restaurant, good-value dorm (Rs100), and rooms priced according to their view. Apart from the hotels and local *dhabas* there are few **places to eat** in Kalpa. Buses and taxis between Kalpa and Rekong Peo run every thirty minutes or so until 6pm; convenient connections include buses to Shimla (6.30am) and Sangla (9.30am).

The Baspa Valley

Hemmed in by the pinnacles of Kinner-Kailash to the north and the high peaks of the Garhwal range to the south, the seventy-kilometre **River Baspa** rises in the mountain wilderness along the Indo-Tibetan border to flow through what was until recently one of Kinnaur's most beautiful and secluded areas. The lower reaches of the valley below Sangla are now dominated by a massive and ugly 300MW hydroelectric plant, but beyond Sangla the scenery remains unspoilt. Although the head of the valley is closed to tourists, there are still plenty of walking opportunities exploring side valleys.

The valley's largest settlement, **SANGLA**, is served by daily **buses** from Shimla, Rampur, Rekong Peo and Tapri, and makes an excellent base to visit nearby **Kamru** village, 25 minutes' walk above Sangla, with its warren of lanes and slate-roofed stone houses, and its wood-and-stone gable-roofed **fort**. Tibetan prayer flags flutter in the breeze and the inhabitants retain Buddhist funerary rites, although they are now mostly Hindu and no longer read Tibetan. The inner sanctums of the **temple** below the fort are off limits to visitors unless a goat is paid for and sacrificed. In September and October Sangla fills up with Bengali holidaymakers, and hotel options are increasing every year. Currently the best place to **stay** is the renovated *Monal Regency* (Ⓣ01786/242922; ❸–❺), 500m before town, which has pleasant rooms with a well-tended lawn out front. The next bend in the road leads up a short path to the friendly *Sangla Resorts* (Ⓣ01786/242401; ❷–❹), offering clean doubles, a dorm (Rs75) and a good restaurant – a better option than the pink *Mount Kailash* opposite. The rather spartan *Baspa Guest House* (Ⓣ01786/242206; ❷) is on the main road near the village centre. **Eating** options are limited to hotel restaurants and a couple of small cafés in the centre, including the *Dumer Cafeteria* below the *Trekker's Lodge*, which offers valley views, *momos*, pancakes and *thukpa*.

A daily **bus** heads further up the increasingly dramatic Baspa Valley to Chitkul each day at 11.30am, though it's often late or cancelled, in which case you'll need to hitch or hire a Jeep (Rs500). Eight kilometres beyond Sangla there's a wonderful campsite on the banks of the river, the *Banjara Camp* (Ⓣ01786/242536, Ⓦwww.banjaracamps.com; ❾), with luxurious tents, attentive service and meals included for $75. At quiet **RAKCHAM**, 14km and forty minutes by bus from Sangla, the *Rupin River View Guest House* (Ⓣ01786/244225; ❷) – offering pleasant wood-panelled rooms with shared bath and hot water – can organize **porters** and **guides** for treks such as the tough three-day hike to Thangi on the Kinner-Kailash circuit.

On a rise with dramatic views of the opening valley, **CHITKUL**, 25km from Sangla, is as far up the valley as you can go without an Inner Line permit (see p.484) – a gate and checkpoint at the far end of the village marks the start of the Inner Line. The bright, friendly *Amar Guesthouse* (❷), in the upper part of the village west of the fort, redefines basic – there's not even a bucket shower – but is far cosier than the dingy *Thakur Guesthouse* (❸; dorm Rs50), which boasts great views and can give trekking advice. A couple more guesthouses were under construction in late 2004, which should increase the options. The nameless **restaurant** has pleasant outside seating and can put together food picnics for trekking.

Visible above the village, a trail winds steeply up to a huge saddle below the **Charang La pass** – the route of the Kinner-Kailash *parikrama*, or pilgrimage circuit, described on p.497. Throughout the Baspa Valley and especially past Sangla, trekkers and campers need to be self-sufficient in food and fuel so as not to overburden the local subsistence-oriented economy.

Upper Kinnaur

Inner Line permits are required for **upper Kinnaur**, the remote region east of Kalpa. Five to six hours by Jeep from Rekong Peo, within a day's hike of the frontier, the tiny hamlet of **Pooh** is the area's main settlement. Evidence from inscriptions suggest that Pooh was, in the eleventh century, an important trading centre that fell under the influence of the Tibetan kingdom of Guge when the Great Translator, Rinchen Zangpo travelled through the area. The temple here is devoted to Sakyamuni, with wooden columns supporting a high ceiling and a circumambulatory path around the altar.

Beyond Pooh, the road bends north, crossing the muddy Sutlej for the last time at **Khabo**, where it meets the turquoise waters of River Spiti. To the northeast, Kinnaur's highest peak, **Leo Pargial II** (6770m), rises in a near-vertical 4000-metre wall which marks the border with Tibet and overlooks the old Indo–Tibet road at the **Shipki La pass** (5569m). The NH-22 continues north through the barren wastes of the Hanglang Valley, very similar to parts of Ladakh with its small settlements of dry-stone houses piled high with fuel and fodder. At **Yangthang**, little more than a string of roadside chai stalls, a road leads off to **NAKO**, the valley's largest village, nestling high above the river at 2950m around a small **lake**. In the northwest corner, the eleventh-century complex of the **Nako Chokhor** is attributed to Rinchen Zangpo; although it's in desperate need of restoration, its exquisite interior paintings are comparable to those of Alchi. The finest building of all is the Serkhang or "Golden Hall", dedicated to the Tathagatas or Supreme Buddhas. There are some basic **accommodation** options – a couple of guesthouses near the bus stand and a simpler, friendlier one near the lake, plus the *Naygo Adventure Camp*, which has tents for Rs200. Frequent public **Jeeps** (Rs5) run up from Yangthang to Nako; going the other way, three **buses** a day (6am, 6.30am & 2pm) head for Rekong Peo from Yangthang.

Just north of Yangthang, all transport comes to a halt at the notorious **Malling Slide**, a high-risk landslide zone. A team of labourers has struggled since 2000 to re-open the road, only to find the collapsing hillside mercilessly burying their efforts. While the road remains impassable, a wire trolley transports your luggage over the gorge (Rs5 per bag); you can scramble over the affected area in about 35 minutes. The slide is occasionally too dangerous to walk over, in which case you will need to follow the path down the gorge to the river and up the opposite side (1hr 30min). Both routes are steep and can be treacherous – wear shoes with a good tread, and only come this way if you're fully mobile. If travelling on public transport, you can pick up another bus on the far side; those travelling in private vehicles should enquire about the state of the road before proceeding too far, and make arrangements for a vehicle pick-up on the other side if necessary. Once beyond Sumdo, the rest of Spiti is open, Inner Line Permits are not required and you have more freedom to explore and get off the beaten track.

Northwest Himachal

From Shimla the main road winds west and north to the riverside market town of **Mandi**, an important crossroads linking the Kullu Valley and the hills to **the northeast**. The rolling foothills in the northwest are warmer and more accessible than Himachal's eastern reaches, though less dramatic and considerably lower. The area sees little tourism outside **Dharamsala**, the British hill station turned Tibetan settlement, home to the Dalai Lama. Dharamsala is an excellent base for treks over the soaring Dhauladhar Range to the **Chamba Valley**, harbouring uniquely styled Hindu temples in **Brahmour** and **Chamba**. South of Chamba, the fading hill station of **Dalhousie** still has a certain ex-Raj charm, and is popular with Indian tourists who arrive in droves during the hot season.

Mandi to Dharamsala

The following section traces the River Beas and NH-21 as they weave from Mandi to Dharamsala, linking a string of quiet mountain towns and villages. While most visitors make the six-hour journey to Dharamsala in one go on one of the nine daily **buses**, those with more time can pause at sacred **Rewalsar**, just outside Mandi, or the small towns of **Baijnath** and **Palampur**. Stop at **Jogindernagar** to pick up the narrow-gauge train that trundles through patchwork fields and light forest to **Kangra** in the **Kangra Valley**, just an hour away from Dharamsala.

Mandi

The junction town of **MANDI**, 158km north of Shimla, straddles the River Beas, its riverside *ghats* dotted with stone temples where *sadhus* and pilgrims pray. Once a major trading post for Ladakhis heading south – *mandi* means market – the town still bustles with commercial activity, now centred on the attractive **Indira Market** and its sunken garden, in the centre of the town square. A collection of sixteenth-century Nagari-style temples sits above the town on **Tarna Hill**. To get there, climb the 160 steps facing the market square, or take the road which winds up from the bridge close to the Bank of Baroda. On the summit is the main Kali temple, decorated with garish paintings of the fierce mother goddess draped in skulls and blood.

The frenetic **bus stand** is across the river on the east bank; its café does delicious veg food. There are departures every half hour or so for Kullu, Manali, Dharamsala and Shimla, as well as longer-distance services. Buses for Rewalsar leave from here, and also pick up passengers from the central square. The town has plenty of **hotels**, most of them an auto-rickshaw- or taxi-ride away across the river. The nicest place to stay is the ramshackle *Raj Mahal* (Ⓣ01905/222401; ❸), above the town square, a period-furnished palace set in spacious shady gardens, with a good restaurant and atmospheric gentlemen's bar. Also on the square is the *Shiva* (Ⓣ01905/224211; ❷–❸), less atmospheric but cheaper, and the government-approved *Evening Plaza* (Ⓣ01905/225123, Ⓔmalhotralalji@hotmail.com; ❷–❹), which has a range of rooms, some with a/c. The government-run *Café Shiraz*, at the edge of the main square, serves South Indian snacks and can book **bus tickets**. Indira Market is handy for fast food joints, **Internet cafés** and the computerized **railway ticketing office** on the north end. Both the Bank of Baroda and the Overseas India Bank can change money and cash travellers' cheques, but the most convenient exchange is at the *Evening Plaza*.

Rewalsar

If you've any interest in Buddhism it's worth taking a detour 24km southeast of Mandi to **REWALSAR**, where three Tibetan monasteries (Nyingma, Drikung

Kagyu and Drukpa Kagyu) mark an important place of pilgrimage. There are also Sikh and Hindu temples here, all of which draw a steady stream of pilgrims and tourists. Most complete a *chora* around the small sacred lake (nouveau riche tourists plump for the comfort of a car) and along narrow lanes full of shrines and stalls selling Tibetan curios, before lounging beneath the prayer flags on the lake's grassy fringes.

It's believed that Padmasambhava left many footprints and handprints in rocks and caves up in the hills around the lake, and steep paths lead up from the lake to **caves** that are used today as isolated meditation retreats. Of the three monasteries around the lake, **Tso-Pema Ogyen Heruka Gompa**, below the tourist lodge, is the most venerated and atmospheric; check out the tree planted in 1957 by the Dalai Lama, who visited India that year to celebrate the 2500th anniversary of the Buddha's birth (his flight into exile occurred two years later). Towering dramatically over the lake and visually dominating the Rewalsar setting is the large but much newer **Drukpa Kagyu Zigar Gompa**.

For **Hindus**, Rewalsar is regarded as the abode of the sage Lomas, for whose sake the lake was created with waters from the Ganga and Yamuna. Three small temples dedicated to Krishna, Lomas and Shiva, along with a Nandi bull statue and lakeside *ghats*, reflect Rewalsar's Hindu connections. On the west shore, the Sikh **gurudwara** attracts pilgrims retracing the steps of Guru Gobind Singh, who came here in 1702; this is one of the few sites associated with his life in Himachal. To the south a small **sanctuary** protects deer and Himalayan black bears.

The HPTDC *Rewalsar* (Ⓣ01905/280252; ❷–❸), a short way back from the north shore, has comfortable rooms with hot showers, and a small dorm (Rs75) in the older block. Visitors who plan to stay for a while may well prefer the pleasant **monastery accommodation** at the Nyingma Gompa (Ⓣ01905/280226; ❶–❷), or the more comfortable Drukpa Kagyu Gompa (Ⓣ01905/280210; ❶). Local families are also keen to rent out rooms; ask Mr Jalal at the *Zigar Tibetan Food Corner* restaurant. **Eating** is limited to several small but reasonable Tibetan restaurants near the lake which serve *thukpa*, *momos* and noodles, and the *dhabas* along the main road serving north Indian food.

Jogindernagar

JOGINDERNAGAR, 63km northwest of Mandi, is an uninviting little town: little more than two streets flanked by wooden-fronted houses and a crowded bus stand. The main reasons to stop here are to pick up the Kangra Valley **trains** (8am & 12.20pm) to Pathankot (see box on p.506), and to visit the Tibetan settlement at **BIR**, 15km to the west, which along with its monasteries is also home to a **paragliding** centre that hosted the Paragliding World Cup in 2004. The bus stand and railway station are 500m apart, and the smart HPTDC *Hotel Uhl* (Ⓣ01908/222002; ❸–❹) is at the eastern end of town; enquire here about paragliding.

Palampur and around

Further into the Kangra Valley, tree-clad slopes give way to rolling deep-green fields, as the westbound road enters Himachal's prime tea-growing area, around the small town of **PALAMPUR**, 16km northwest of Baijnath. Few travellers stop here, though the area has a couple of exceptional places to stay as well as a few sights of interest. Among them, **Tashi Jong**, 12km to the east just off the main highway, is a Tibetan settlement whose mural-filled monastery is dedicated to Sakyamuni. A recent addition to Tashi Jong is the **Dongyu Gatsal**

Trekking from Palampur district

With its lush tea gardens and alpine meadows, Palampur makes a good base for some lesser-known **treks**; the passes north of town offer unrivalled views of the Kangra Valley. Trek & Tour Himachal, opposite the bus stand and at the *Country Cottage Tea Garden Resort* (see below), offer all-inclusive tailor-made packages with most equipment provided except sleeping bags. See opposite for a **map** of some of the hiking routes described below.

Treks from Palampur

An easy four-day hike leads from Palampur over **Waru Pass** (3850m), the "gateway of the wind", via Satchali, Thanetar and Dhog to **Holi**; continuing for two more testing days to the sacred **Manimahesh Lake** near Brahmour. From Dhog it's possible to continue east to Barabhangal and as far as Manali.

A pleasant but difficult seven- or eight-day trek from Palampur starts by crossing **Sunghar Pass** (4473m), then leads back across the Dhauladhar ranges at **Jalsu Pass** (3600m) and south to Baijnath. **Baijnath** itself, only 40km from Palampur by road, is a good trailhead for treks to Chamba or Bharabhangal, following paths that traverse glaciers, waterfalls, the high Thamsar Pass (4665m) and the River Ravi.

Other routes

Treks from **Billing** lead via Rajgunda, Palachak, and over the Thansar Pass to **Marhu** from where you can continue west to **Chamba** (3 days) and **Manimahesh** (3 days), or southeast to **Manali** over the Kalihan ("black ice") Pass. The latter is a strenuous route requiring six days and is suitable only for experienced trekkers.

Ling Nunnery, instigated by the Venerable Tenzin Palmo, a British-born nun who spends much of her time on worldwide lecture tours but often returns to Palampur; for more information visit Ⓦwww.tenzinpalmo.com. Palampur is also the trailhead for walks to nearby hills and gorges, such as the hike 2km north of the *Hotel T-Bud* to the spectacular 300-metre-wide **Neugal Gorge** on the River Bundla, and treks into the Kullu and Chamba valleys (see box above).

The best of the town's **hotels** is HPTDC *Hotel T-Bud* (Ⓣ01894/231298; ❹–❺), surrounded by lawns and pine trees 1km north of town, with immaculate, spacious rooms and an excellent restaurant. Along the main road close to the old bus stand, the dimly lit *Pines Hotel* (Ⓣ01894/232633; ❷–❸) houses a popular bar and restaurant, while further down at the new bus stand the better *Highland Regency* (Ⓣ01894/231222; ❷–❸) has good-value doubles with balconies. To sample the delights of life on a **tea estate**, head for *Country Cottage Tea Garden Resort*, Chandpur Tea Estate (Ⓣ01894/230647, Ⓦwww.countrycottageindia.com; ❻–❼), 4.5km east of Palampur, set in fifty acres of tea plantations, orchards and forest. The most luxurious place to stay in the region, however, is the 1930s *Taragarh Palace* (Ⓣ01894/242034, Ⓦwww.taragarh.com; ❻–❾), set in a fifteen-acre wooded estate in **Taragarh**, 8km east towards Baijnath. Home to the Raja of Kashmir, the palace has period furnishings, a swimming pool, a new wing with luxury suites (US$80) and a campsite geared to visiting tour groups. Book ahead either directly or through their office in New Delhi at 15 Institutional Area, Lodhi Road (Ⓣ011/2469 2317).

Kangra

Although **KANGRA** is bypassed by most travellers on their way to Dharamsala, 18km further north, it's worth a brief detour. Buses from all over the Kangra

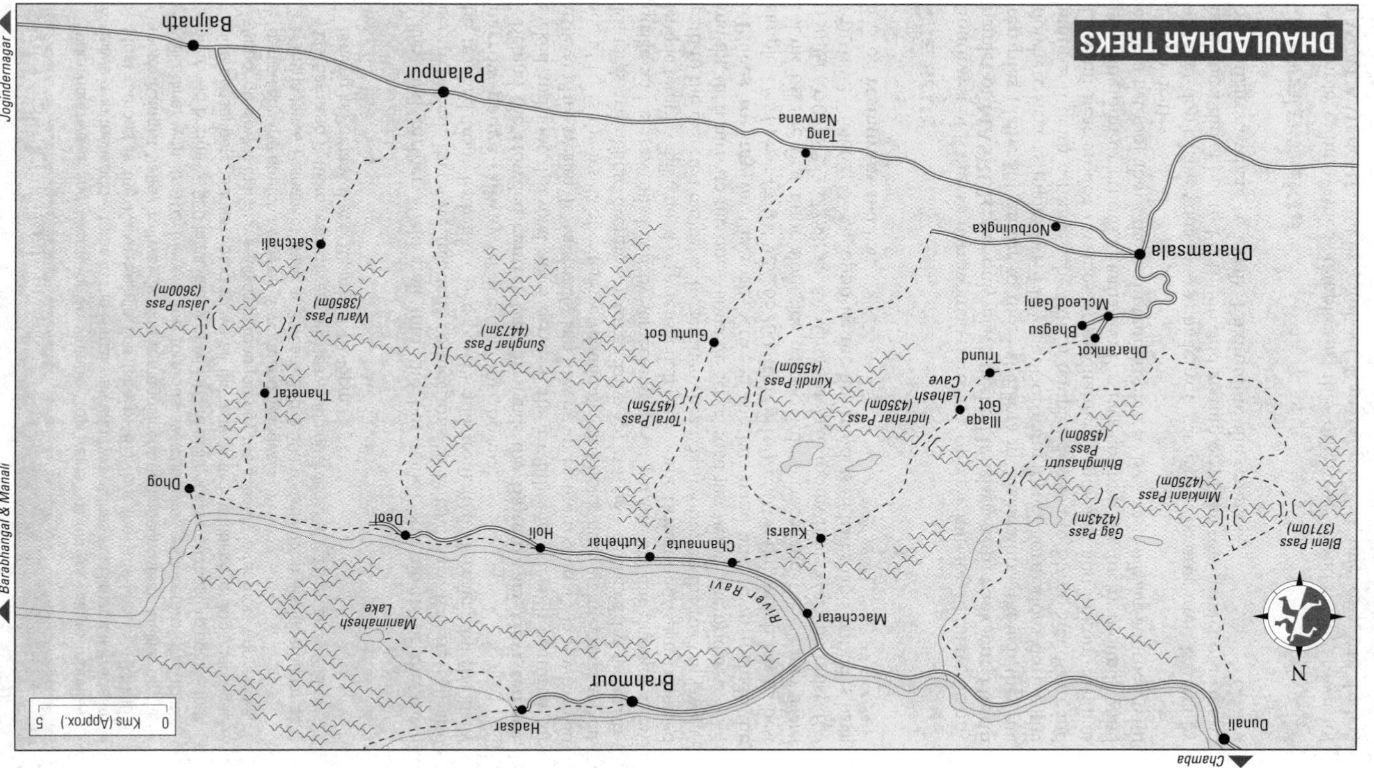
DHAULADHAR TREKS
Barabhangal & Manali
Jogindernagar
Chamba
0 Kms (Approx.) 5
N
Baijnath
Palampur
Tang Narwana
Norbulingka
Dharamsala
McLeod Ganj
Bhagsu
Dharamkot
Triund
Illaqa Got
Lahesh Cave
Satchali
Jalsu Pass (3600m)
Waru Pass (3850m)
Sunghar Pass (4473m)
Guntu Got
Kundli Pass (4550m)
Indrahar Pass (4350m)
Thanetar
Toral Pass (4575m)
Bhimghasutri Pass (4580m)
Minkiani Pass (4250m)
Gag Pass (4243m)
Bleni Pass (3710m)
Dhog
Deol
Holi
Kuthehar
Channauta
Kuarsi
River Ravi
Macchetar
Manimahesh Lake
Brahmour
Hadsar
Dunali

The Kangra Valley railway

India has five of the twenty or so vintage "toy trains" or narrow-gauge mountain railways in the world – three in the Himalayas and two of these in Himachal Pradesh. Most famous is the Kalka–Shimla line (see p.487), but the little-known 163-kilometre **Kangra Valley railway** is also a magnificent engineering feat. Unlike on the Kalka line, with its 103 tunnels and tortuous switchbacks, engineers of this route preferred bridges – 950 in all, many of which are still considered masterpieces – that give passengers uninterrupted views all the way from Pathankot to Jogindernagar. Although slower than the equivalent road journey the scenery is far more impressive, particularly the stretch between Kangra and Mangwal.

Trains leave Pathankot daily at 2.40am and 9.50am, arriving in Jogindernagar at 11.15am and 7.40pm respectively, and leave Jogindernagar at 7.20am and 12.20pm, arriving in Pathankot at 5.10pm and 10.45pm.

Valley and further afield pull into the bus stand 1km north of the town centre, where there are frequent connections to Dharamsala. Kangra can also be reached from Pathankot (see p.610) and from Jogindernagar by the daily **narrow-gauge railway** service (see box above).

Behind the crowded **central bazaar** stands the **Bajreshwari Devi temple**, sacked and looted several times between the twelfth and fifteenth centuries for its legendary wealth. It was finally laid low by an earthquake in 1905 – what you see today is the result of extensive rebuilding, and holds little architectural appeal. Kangra's crumbling, overgrown **fort** (daily; $5) was also damaged by the earthquake and is now inhabited by screeching green parrots that flit through a few simple temples still tended by priests. High gates, some British-built, span a cobbled path to the deserted ramparts. To get there, head 3km south on the road to Jawalamukhi, then turn up the one-kilometre access road just before the bridge.

Places to stay on the road between the bus stand and town include the simple *Hotel Preet* (Ⓣ01892/265260, Ⓣm98160/60049; ❷), which has its best rooms on the first floor alongside a cosy little terrace, and the cleaner *Hotel Yatrika* (Ⓣ01892/262258; ❸–❺) whose deluxe rooms have a/c. The noisy *Raj* (Ⓣ01892/264062; ❹–❺), opposite the bus stand, is in bad shape, but does have a good **restaurant** and bar.

Masrur

Southwest of Kangra a narrow road skirts low rippling hills for 30km to the tiny hamlet of **MASRUR**, the only place in the Himalayas with **rock-cut Hindu temples** (daily; $5) similar to those at Ellora in Maharashtra, though they are nowhere near as impressive. Hewn out of natural rock formations during the ninth and tenth centuries, the fifteen temples devoted to Shiva, Sita, Ram and Lakshmi bear eroded carvings of meditating mendicants and buxom maidens guarding dim cavernous sanctuaries. Passages cut into the rocky mounds wind up to a flat roof above the main temple, pierced by a vast *shikhara* adorned with Hindu deities.

If you don't have your own vehicle, you can get to Masrur from Kangra by catching a direct bus to Pir Bindu, and getting off at the tiny hamlet of Nagrota Suriyan, from where you walk 1.5km up to the temples.

Jawalamukhi

A simple whitewashed temple in the otherwise nondescript town of **JAWALAMUKHI**, 35km south of Kangra, protects one of north India's most important Hindu shrines. The sanctuary, crowned with a squat golden spire, contains a natural blue gas flame emitted from the earth, revered as a manifestation of the goddess of fire, Jawalamukhi. Priests are eager to light emissions of gas in smaller chambers for expectant devotees, but only the main flame is kept alight continuously. A three-kilometre *parikrama*, or circumambulation, starts from the temple, climbing steeply up into the wooded hills and taking in several shrines on the way.

Frequent **buses** (1hr; Rs20) depart from Kangra, but it's quicker to hitch or take a taxi. In the other direction several buses travel direct to Dharamsala, 53km north. The best **accommodation** is the new *Mata Vaishno Devi Hotel* (Ⓣ01970/222135; ④–⑥), 250m north of the bus stand, though a basic cell at the Geeta Bhawan Ashram (Ⓣ01970/222242; ①) is much cheaper.

Dharamsala and McLeod Ganj

Home to the Dalai Lama and Tibetan government in exile, and starting point for some exhilarating treks into the high Himalayas, **DHARAMSALA**, or more correctly, its upper town **McLEOD GANJ**, is one of Himachal's most irresistible destinations. Spread across wooded ridges beneath the stark rock faces of the Dhauladhar Range, the town is divided into two distinct and separate sections, separated by 10km of perilously twisting road and almost a thousand metres in altitude. Originally a British hill station, **McLEOD GANJ** has been transformed by the influx of **Tibetan refugees** fleeing Chinese oppression in their homeland. Tibetan influence here is very strong, their achievements including the construction of temples, schools, monasteries, nunneries, meditation centres, and the most extensive library of Tibetan history and religion. As well as playing host to hordes of foreign and domestic tourists, McLeod Ganj is a place of pilgrimage that attracts Buddhists and interested parties from all over the world, including Hollywood celebrities Richard Gere, Uma Thurman and Goldie Hawn. Many people visit India specifically to come here, and its relaxed and friendly atmosphere can make it a difficult place to leave.

Despite heavy snows and low **temperatures** between December and March, McLeod Ganj receives visitors year round. Summer brings torrential rains – this being the second wettest place in India – that return in bursts for much of the year. Daytime temperatures can be high, but you'll need warm clothes for the chilly nights.

Arrival and information

State-run **buses** from Shimla, Manali, Mandi, Pathankot, Kangra and Delhi pull into the bus stand in the very south of the lower town, though some continue after a short stop all the way up to McLeod Ganj – the usual arrival point for private and deluxe buses from Delhi and Manali. Dharamsala's **airport**, 11km south at Gaggal, has three Jagson Airlines' flights a week to Delhi, but the flights cost around $200 (no youth concessions), are frequently cancelled and have a luggage limit of just 10kg. McLeod Ganj's **tourist office** (Mon–Sat 10am–5pm), on South End, opposite Bookworm, provides basic accommodation and transport information. A good source of entertainment and other local listings is the free monthly magazine *Contact*, available in restaurants.

From 7.45am onwards numerous **buses** run between Dharamsala and McLeod Ganj (40min), though a **shared taxi** (Rs7) from the McLeod Ganj bus stand is much quicker; both McLeod Ganj and Dharamsala have unions with

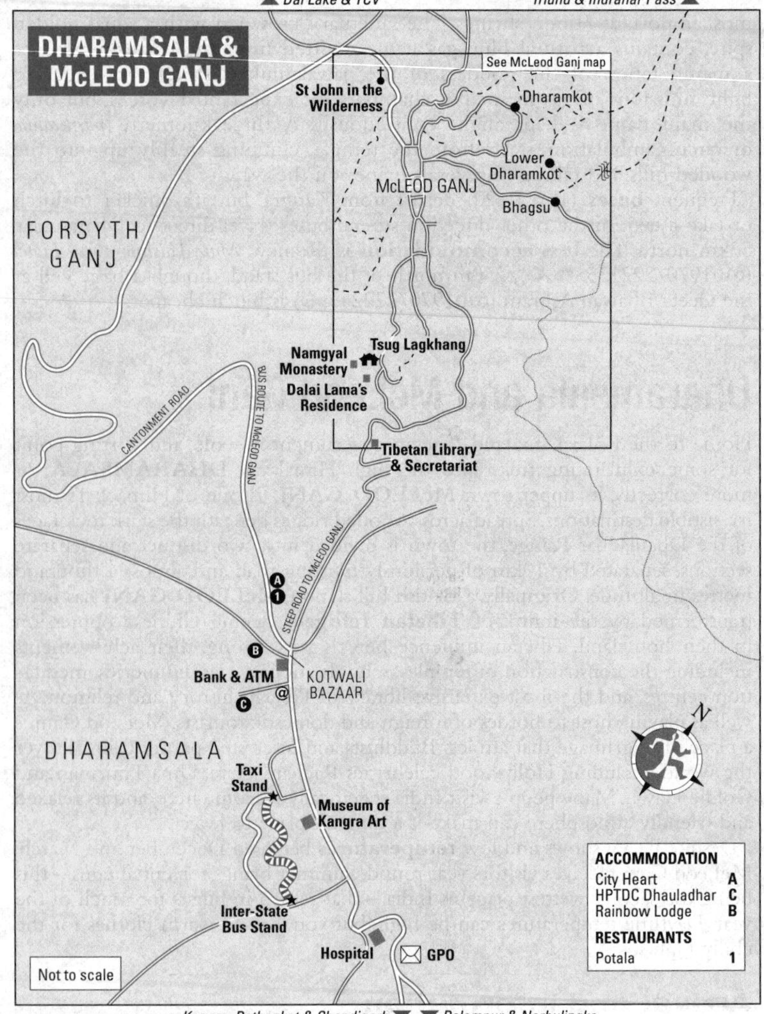

fixed prices clearly displayed. An ordinary taxi from McLeod Ganj to Dharamsala costs Rs100. Auto-rickshaws travel frequently from McLeod Ganj bus stand to Bhagsu (Rs20) and the chai shop at Dharamkot (Rs30).

Accommodation

Accommodation tends to fill up during Losar, the Tibetan New Year (Feb/March). Most visitors stay in the upper town, **McLeod Ganj**. If you have an early bus to catch, however, or arrive late, you might prefer to stay the night in **Dharamsala**, although options are fewer and the standards lower. Those planning long-term stays usually head to the small settlements of **Bhagsu** or **Dharamkot**, ten minutes' walk north or east of McLeod Ganj respectively,

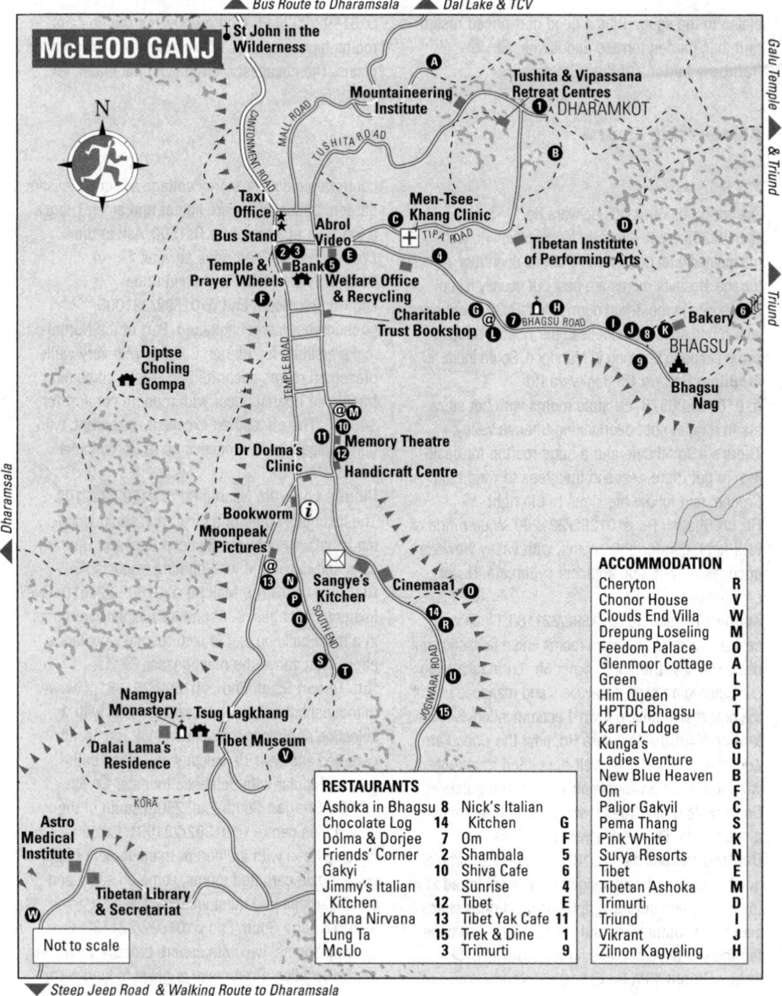

where you can rent simple self-catering rooms in family houses. Dharamkot is extremely popular with young Israeli travellers; Bhagsu is a better bet for peace and quiet.

A handful of rooms in the **Tibetan Library** are available to students taking courses here, and for dedicated Buddhists, there's always the possibility of staying at a **monastery** or nunnery.

Dharamsala

City Heart Off Kotwali Bazaar ☎01892/223761. Reasonable rooms with views, sandwiched between a popular local restaurant/beer bar and a "party hall". ❸

HPTDC Dhauladhar Off Kotwali Bazaar, near the bank ☎01892/224926. Institutional-feeling place with spacious en-suite rooms with constant hot water and balconies giving superb views over the plains to the south. Plus a good mid-priced restaurant, bar, garden terrace and lawns. ❹–❼

Rainbow Lodge Off Kotwali Bazaar ☎01892/222647. A bit grubby, but the upstairs rooms have balconies with great views towards the plains. The cheapest room has no hot water. ❷

McLeod Ganj

Budget

Drepung Loseling Off Jogiwara Rd ☎01892/221087. Standard lodge, plain and well maintained with good views from an open roof terrace. Upstairs rooms are best but usually fill up first; space in the 3-bed dorm is just Rs30. Fixed rates year round and all proceeds to the Tibetan refugee camp Drepung Loseling in Mundgod, South India. ❷

Freedom Palace Off Jogiwara Rd ☎01892/220378. En-suite rooms with hot showers in a quiet spot overlooking Bhagsu Valley. There's a small café and a huge rooftop for basking. To get there descend the steps to Yong Ling Creche, and follow the signs to the right. ❷

Green Bhagsu Rd ☎01892/221200. Wide range of well-kept, comfortable rooms, with valley views, a good restaurant, and adjacent cybercafé. Deservedly popular. ❶–❸

Kunga's Bhagsu Rd ☎01892/221180. Clean and centrally located with plain rooms and a fantastic sun deck. The down-to-earth owner Mr Tenzin (aka Nick) can cater to a range of travellers and manages one of the best restaurants in town. Recommended. ❶–❸

Ladies Venture Jogiwara Rd, past the *Chocolate Log* ☎01892/221559. Well-appointed rooms of varying size in a welcoming Tibetan-run hotel. Dorm beds Rs50. Quiet location, with a garden and a small café. Fixed price year round. ❷–❸

Om Near the bus stand ☎01892/221322. Simple, quiet and very friendly lodge on the western edge of town. A variety of rooms; the cheapest ones share squat toilet bathrooms and hot showers. The upper terrace is a popular place for a sundowner. ❷

Paljor Gakyil TIPA Rd ☎01892/221443. Immaculate lodge with plain or carpeted rooms, dorm beds (Rs25) and great views over McLeod Ganj. To get there climb the steps between the *Seven Hills* and *Kalsang* guest houses. ❶–❷

Tibetan Ashoka Jogiwara Rd ☎01892/221763. Friendly, congenial and popular place. Rooms vary from simple with shared facilities to deluxe with hot shower en suite. Superb views from the balcony. ❶–❸

Zilnon Kagyeling Monastery Bhagsu Rd ☎01892/220581. Basic and extremely cheap single and double rooms with shared facilities in an active *gompa*. ❶

Mid-range and expensive

Cheryton Jogiwara Rd, in the grounds of the *Chocolate Log* ☎01892/221237. Cute and comfortable double-storey cottage set in a pleasant garden. Upper rooms are lighter and airier. There's a top-floor apartment for Rs1500. Ask at the *Chocolate Log*. Fixed rates all year. ❸–❻

Chonor House Near Thekchen Choeling Gompa, South End ☎01892/221006, ⓔchonorhs@norgulingka.org. Part of the Norbulingka Institute for Tibetan Culture, with very well-presented rooms decorated by artists, combining traditional Tibetan decor with modern comfort for $45–60. There's also an excellent restaurant, with garden seating. All proceeds go to Norbulingka. ❽–❾

Clouds End Villa Naoroji Rd ☎01892/222109. The luxurious home of a local raja, set in woodlands halfway between McLeod Ganj and Dharamsala, and decorated with hunting trophies. ❻

Glenmoor Cottage Mall Rd ☎01892/221010. Five luxurious cottages ($70) and less expensive rooms in a main building, set in picturesque woodlands about 1km above the main bazaar. ❻–❾

Him Queen South End ☎01892/221861, ⓦwww.himqueenhotel.com. Ostentatious hotel with a selection of ordinary, deluxe and VIP rooms, all carpeted and with TV, balcony and small bathrooms. Popular with domestic tourists. ❺–❽

HPTDC Bhagsu South End, 250m south of the information centre ☎01892/221091. Large flagship hotel with indifferent management but comfortable carpeted rooms, some en suite, and small gardens in a quiet location. ❺–❼

Kareri Lodge South End ☎01892/221132. Five spotless rooms, two with superb balcony views, in a quiet location. Preference is given to long-term guests, who are also offered discount rates. ❹–❺

Pema Thang South End ☎01892/221871. Friendly hotel, the best maintained on South End. Rooms all have the same facilities (heaters, hot showers, ISD/STD phones); you'll pay more for a good view. Popular with well-off Westerners interested in Buddhism. ❹–❺

Surya Resorts South End ☎01892/221418, ⓦwww.suryarestorts.com. Big, brash, modern hotel, with some large glass-fronted rooms facing west over the plains, aimed at businessmen and domestic tourists. ❻–❽

Tibet Bhagsu Rd ☎01892/221587. Excellent hotel with a superb restaurant; the downstairs valley-facing rooms offer the best value. Popular and central. Fixed prices all year. ❹–❺

Dharamkot

New Blue Heaven Off the main path below the teashop ⓣ01892/221005. Small family house with garden. A bit tricky to get to after dark. ❶–❷

Trimurti Guest House Between Dharamkot and Bhagsu ⓣ01892/221364. A few rooms in a quiet family place with a lawn and small shrine. The owner runs a small music school; see p.514. ❷

Bhagsu

For cheap, long-term, self-catering accommodation in **Bhagsu** ask at the row of shops or in the cafés, or check out the guesthouses on the path towards Dharamkot. Hotels in Bhagsu are brash and ugly, aimed squarely at domestic tourists. Options include the *Triund* (ⓣ01892/221122; ❹–❺); the *Pink White* (ⓣ01892/221209; ❸–❹) which is mouldy but spacious, with ensuite rooms, some with balconies; and the new *Vikrant* (ⓣ01832/555034; ❸–❹), whose cheapest rooms have shared bathrooms.

Dharamsala

It's easy to see why most visitors bypass Dharamsala itself, a haphazard jumble of shops, offices and houses. The only place of interest is the **Museum of Kangra Art** (Tues–Sun 10am–5pm), with a small collection of Kangra miniatures and some modern art. From the bus stand at the bottom of town, a road winds through the crowded bazaars and continues through 10km of hairpin bends to McLeod Ganj. On foot, the quickest route is a shorter (3km) but much steeper track winding up to McLeod Ganj's southern end from behind the vegetable market, passing the Tibetan Library and Secretariat.

McLeod Ganj

The ever-expanding settlement of **McLeod Ganj** extends along a pine-covered ridge with valley views below and the near vertical walls of the Dhauladhar range towering behind. Despite being named after David McLeod, the Lieutenant Governor of Punjab when the hill station was founded in 1848, little evidence of British occupation remains. Intersected by two narrow potholed roads, the focal point of McLeod Ganj is its Buddhist **temple**, ringed with spinning red and gold prayer wheels. Today Indian residents are outnumbered by Tibetans, who bedeck their ramshackle buildings with fluttering prayer flags: McLeod Ganj is not simply a political haven for them, but also home to their spiritual leader, the Dalai Lama, and to the Tibetan government in exile.

It's easy to **find your way around** McLeod Ganj. At its northern end, the road up from the lower town arrives at a small square that serves as the bus stand. Roads radiating from here head south to the Dalai Lama's residence and the Library of Tibetan Works and Archives, north to the village of Dharamkot, the Tushita Retreat Meditation Centre and to the Tibetan Children's Village next to Dal Lake, and east to the hamlet of Bhagsu.

You may not notice it, but efforts are being made to clean up McLeod Ganj. The **Welfare Office** in particular has initiated several schemes to tackle environmental issues, including a **Green Shop** on Bhagsu Road, which sells boiled filtered water in an effort to deal with the plague of plastic bottles.

The Dalai Lama's Residence and the Tibet Museum

The Dalai Lama settled temporarily in McLeod Ganj in 1960; four decades later he's still there, and his **residence** on the south edge of town has become his permanent home in exile. His own quarters are modest, and most of the

Meeting His Holiness the Dalai Lama

The **Dalai Lama** is in great demand. Tibetans fleeing their homeland come to him for blessing and reassurance; monks and nuns from all over India and Nepal look to him for spiritual guidance; and an ever-increasing number of Westerners arrive in Dharamsala hoping for a moment of his attention. Twenty years ago it might have been possible for people to meet His Holiness on an individual basis; now casual visitors should count on attending a **public audience**, when he greets and shakes the hands of several hundred people. These are held every few weeks if His Holiness is in town, though there are no fixed dates or timings. Ask the Branch Security Office (Ⓣ01892/221560; above the Welfare Office on Bhagsu Road) when the next audience will be, but note that they themselves only know a couple of days in advance. You'll need to register here too; bring a passport and some passport photos, and expect to wait. If you're interested in attending His Holiness's **public teachings**, check Ⓦwww.tibet.com for dates, locations and what to expect.

Private audiences are granted to a select few, and can only be arranged by writing at least four months in advance. The Dalai Lama's secretary receives hundreds of such letters each day, and each case is reviewed on its merits. Spiritual enquiries are referred to a resident lama who can give advice on specific points, and secretaries and community leaders are usually able to answer queries about Tibetan issues. The **17th Karmapa Lama**, meanwhile, holds an audience daily at 2pm at Gyuto Monastery, 2km from the Norbulingka Institute (see p.514). Call first to make sure he is available (Ⓣ01892/236637) and arrive fifteen minutes beforehand in order to register at the security desk.

walled compound overhanging the valley is taken up by government offices. In front of the private enclosure, Dharamsala's main Buddhist temple, **Tsug Lakhang**, shelters images of Sakyamuni (the historical Buddha), Padmasambhava (who introduced Buddhism to Tibet) and Avalokitesvara (the *bodhisattva* of compassion) seated in meditation postures, surrounded by offerings from devotees. After paying homage to the Buddha inside, devotees complete a *kora*, a circumambulation of the temple complex (clockwise, starting at the trailhead below the monks' quarters), turning the numerous prayer wheels to send prayers out in all directions. Every afternoon monks from the nearby **Namgyal monastery** hold fierce but disciplined debates in the courtyard opposite the temple. The small Namgyal café provides quality meals and snacks (Tues–Sun 11am–8.30pm).

Next to the monastery, the **Tibet Museum** (Tues–Sun: summer 10am–6pm; winter 9am–5pm; Ⓦwww.thetibetmuseum.org) displays in graphic detail the plight of the Tibetan people since China invaded Tibet in 1949. Using photographs and video clips, the self-guided tour describes how Tibetan freedom fighters, backed by the CIA, waged an impossible guerrilla war against China that lasted into the 1970s. The upstairs hall features profiles of the museum curators – all refugees and ex-political prisoners – and a memorial to the 1.2 million Tibetans who have died in the conflict.

Library of Tibetan Works and Archives

The **Library of Tibetan Works and Archives** (Mon–Sat 9am–1pm & 2–5pm; closed 2nd & 4th Sat of month; Ⓣ01892/222467) has one of the world's most extensive collections of original Tibetan manuscripts of sacred texts and prayers, books on all aspects of Tibet, information on Indian culture and architecture, and a rich archive of historical photos. Decorated with bright Tibetan motifs, it is housed in the Tibetan Central Administration compound, below

Lhamo: the folk opera of Tibet

Lhamo originated from the masked dance drama of Tibet, dating from the sixth to ninth centuries. In the fourteenth century, Lama Thangtong Gyalpo recognized the potential of this art form to teach the morals and philosophy of Tibetan Buddhism to ordinary people. *Lhamo* performances traditionally last a whole day and are accompanied by musicians playing cymbals, drums and horns. Before each performance the arena is purified in a complex procedure involving seven Ngonpa characters in flat black masks and six dancing fairies, or Ringas. They give thanks to Thangtong Gyalpo, and place his statue centre stage. The narrator, Shung Shangen, then enters and offers a resumé of the opera in classical Tibetan (now understood by very few), culminating in a high shout.

The performers enter to the sound of music introducing the various characters – the **hero** (a prince or king), dressed in dragon-patterned brocade and a wide-brimmed hat; the **heroine**, draped in golden silk and wearing a hat of flowers; the **villain**, often a witch, dressed in black and hiding behind a black-and-white mask, followed by a retinue of ghoulish **demons** whose masks show wide staring eyes, blood-red lips and sharp fangs. Each character has a special dance, and sings in a drawn-out, droning manner known as *namthar*. The plots revolve around tales from early Buddhist texts, re-enactments of the Buddha's life and the deeds of great Tibetan saints, or stories from the courts of the emperor Songsten Gampo, under whom Buddhism was established in Tibet. Even if you don't know what's going on, you should be able to catch the drift of it from the bursts of laughter in the audience.

the southern end of McLeod Ganj. Tibetan language and philosophy **courses** are held each weekday (see "Listings", p.516), and a small **museum** on the first floor of the library (Rs10) displays Buddhist statues, finely moulded bronzes, and mandalas (symmetrical images, used in meditation to symbolize spiritual journeys and the pattern of the universe).

An information centre in the **Tibetan Secretariat**, beside the entrance to the compound, provides up-to-date news about the Tibetan community in Tibet and around the world. Just outside, the small **Astro Medical Institute** (daily 9am–1pm & 2–5pm) is staffed by monks who diagnose symptoms by examining the eyes, pulse and urine, and prescribe pills made of herbs, precious stones and sometimes animal products, mixed on particularly auspicious lunar dates. You can also have your horoscope prepared here.

North and east of McLeod Ganj

A minor road winds northwards from the McLeod Ganj bus stand to the **Mountaineering Institute** (Mon–Sat 10am–1.30pm & 2–5pm; closed 2nd Sat of month; ⓣ01892/221787), which provides information on the region, including books and maps on the Dhauladhar Range, and organizes trekking expeditions. Continuing up the road you approach two Buddhist retreat centres, both beautifully situated in the midst of forests: the **Tushita** Tibetan Buddhist Centre was founded in 1972 by Lama Thubten Zopa Rinpoche, while just around the corner is **Dhamma Sikhara**, a Theravadan Vipassana centre (see under "Meditation" on p.516 for details of courses at both centres). From here the road continues to Dharamkot, starting point for walks to **Triund** (2975m) and treks over the high passes to the Chamba Valley. Taking a path down through the wooded slopes from Dharamkot brings you to the small, murky **Dal Lake**, the scene of an animal fair and Shaivite festival in September. It stands behind the **Tibetan Children's Village** (TCV), a huge complex providing education and training in traditional handicrafts for around 2000 students, many of whom are orphans or have been brought to safety by parents who have returned to Tibet.

Bhagsu Road heads east from McLeod Ganj's main square, skirting the hillside for 2km before reaching the village of **Bhagsu** with its ancient Shiva temple. The last few years have seen big changes here, with the construction of several hotels catering primarily for the domestic tourist market. However it's still a pleasant enough place, with a few cafés near the temple complex. Beyond the temple a path meanders up the boulder-strewn slopes of a small stream up to a **waterfall** where the *Shiva Café* offers food, chai and a weekly all-night rave. If you're interested in studying tabla, contact Ashoka at the *Trimurti Guest House* (see p.511); he runs the **Trimurti International Music School** from his home. Note: there have been several **attacks** in the past few years on women walking between Bhagsu and McLeod Ganj. Don't walk it alone.

Tibetan Institute of Performing Arts

The **Tibetan Institute of Performing Arts** was founded in 1959 to preserve the Tibetan identity in exile. Around 150 people live on its campus, in the forests above McLeod Ganj overlooking Bhagsu, including artists, teachers, musicians and administrators. The TIPA troupe perform traditional *lhamo* operas (see box on p.513) and have played a morale-building role at Tibetan refugee camps throughout India, while also sharing Tibet's cultural heritage with international audiences. Visit its office for information on upcoming events and tours (Mon–Sat 9am–noon & 1–5pm, closed 2nd & 4th Sat of month; ⓣ01892/221478, ⓦwww.tibetanarts.org).

South of McLeod Ganj: the Norbulingka Institute

Eight kilometres (30min) from Dharamsala, near the village of Sidpur, the **Norbulingka Institute** (Mon–Sat 8am–5pm; ⓣ01892/246402, ⓦwww.norbulingka.org) is dedicated to preserving literary and artistic Tibetan culture. The complex of Tibetan-style buildings, built in 1985, is set amidst peaceful Japanese gardens, and centres on the two-storey **Deden Tsuglakhang temple**, which houses 1173 images of the Buddha and frescoes of the fourteen Dalai Lamas in the upper gallery. The gilded copper statue of Sakyamuni in the hall downstairs is the largest of its kind outside Tibet. Elsewhere in the complex, the **Losel Doll Museum** shows colourful dioramas packed with traditionally clothed dolls. If you'd like to **stay**, the *Norling Guest House* in the gardens (ⓣ01892/246406; ❻–❼) is clean and well decorated; even if you don't stop over it's worth a look for its upstairs gallery of fifty drawings that chronicle the life of the 14th Dalai Lama.

Eating

McLeod Ganj is one of those places where sitting, chatting and philosophizing in **restaurants** is the favoured activity. Tibetan dishes such as *thukpa* and *momos* are prominent, along with Chinese egg noodles, *chow mein* and stir frys. Fresh-baked Tibetan bread and cakes are widely available, and you'll also come across omelettes, chips, toast, veggie-burgers and plenty of Israeli dishes. If you fancy making some Tibetan food, *Sangye's Kitchen* near the Post Office on Jogiwara Road holds **cooking lessons** (daily 11am–1pm & 5–7pm; Rs150). In **Dharamsala**, there's no shortage of snack stalls, but less choice of cuisine: your

Trekking from Dharamsala

Dharamsala is one of the most popular starting points for **treks** over the rocky ridges of the Dhauladhar Range, which rise steeply from the Kangra Valley to 4600m. Trails pass through forests of deodar, pine, oak and rhododendron, cross streams and rivers and wind along vertiginous cliff tracks passing the occasional lake waterfall and glacier. Unless you are very experienced, you'll need a guide as the routes are steep and memorial stones testify to those who didn't make it. The **Mountaineering Institute** on Dharamkot Road (see p.513) can help arrange guides and porters and has maps. Despite the availability of rough huts and caves, it's best to take a tent. The best **season** to trek here is September to November, when the worst of the monsoon is over and before it gets too cold. Winter climbing should only be attempted by mountaineers experienced in the use of crampons and ice axes. See p.505 for a **map** of the hiking routes described below.

Dharamsala to Chamba over Indrahar Pass

The most frequented route from Dharamsala to the Chamba Valley, over the **Indrahar Pass** (4350m), is arduous in places, but most trekkers manage it in around five days. The first section, from Dharamkot, winds through thick forest and steep rocky terrain for 9km to a grassy plateau at **Triund**. From here the path climbs to **Laqa Got**, and then on a seriously steep section up to the knife-edged Indrahar Pass where, weather permitting, you'll enjoy breathtaking views south to the plains and north to the snowy Pir Panjal peaks and Greater Himalayas. The descent is difficult in places and will take you via the Gaddi villages of **Kuarsi** and **Channauta** to the main road, from where you can pick up transport to Brahmour and Chamba by road.

Other routes from Dharamsala to Chamba

Several **other routes** cross the Dhauladhar Range, including the **Toral Pass** (4575m) which starts from **Tang Narwana** (1150m), 10km from Dharamsala. The most difficult route north is the five- or six-day trek across **Bhimghasutri Pass** (4580m), covering near-vertical rocky ascents, sharp cliffs and dangerous gorges. A much easier four- or five-day trek from Dharamsala crosses **Bleni Pass** (3710m) in the milder ranges to the northwest, weaving through alpine pastures and woods and crossing a few streams, before terminating at **Dunali**, on the Chamba road.

best bets for Indian and Western dishes are the *Hotel Dhauladhar* and the *City Heart* hotels. For Tibetan food, try the *Potala*, a small but clean café with a simple menu. In **Dharamkot**, *Trek and Dine* is a good place to grab a bite to eat while organizing trekking guides and equipment; a ten-minute walk uphill along the village paths will bring you to the locally famous wood-fired pizza restaurant, which has pleasant outdoor seating and tremendous banoffee pie. In **Bhagsu**, the *Ashoka* serves up some of the best Indian food in town to cushion-seated diners; the great-value *Trimurti*, next to the temple (and not in the guest house of the same name), is an excellent Indian veg café with a rooftop terrace. Past the Bhagsu Nag temple, a path winds up to the popular *Shiva Café*, situated next to a waterfall and the scene of many an all-night rave.

Chocolate Log Jogiwara Rd. Delicious cakes, pies and truffles plus savouries such as spinach pizza. Eat inside or laze on deck chairs in a pleasant garden. Reasonably priced. Daily except Tues.

Dolma & Dorjee Bhagsu Rd. Tiny, family-run place dishing up tofu burgers, delicious banana bread and filtered water refills (Rs5).

Friends' Corner Temple Rd. Popular, comfortable place by the bus stop, with a range of food and beers, a good sound system and a roller skating rink upstairs.

Gakyi Jogiwara Rd. Humble and homely, with great Tibetan and Western veg dishes, plus the town's best fruit muesli and Tibetan bread.

Jimmy's Italian Kitchen Jogiwara Rd. Snug café decorated with classic film posters. Good salads, baked potatoes, lattes and home-made desserts.
Khana Nirvana Temple Rd. Great hang-out place above Stitches in Time, popular with the ex-pat volunteer crowd. Wonderful views over the plains, with healthy tofu burgers and fresh juices. Wed night jam sessions; movies on Thurs.
Lung Ta Jogiwara Rd. Japanese vegetarian place with a constantly changing menu that usually includes miso soup, sushi, tempura vegetables and tofu steak. Profits go to assisting former Tibetan political prisoners. The Korean restaurant next door, *Dokebi Nara*, offers hot-pot dishes in a cozy atmosphere.
McLlo Central Square. Massive neon-lit monstrosity overlooking the bus stop. Large, overpriced selection of good Western food, an official *Baskin-Robbins* ice cream parlour and a second-floor drinking den which is pleasant early evening but can get very rowdy later on.
Nick's Italian Kitchen *Kunga's*, Bhagsu Rd. The affable Tenzin (aka Nick) is an excellent cook with a large repertoire including great pasta, to-die-for brownies and lemon-curd cake which is apparently a favourite with Richard Gere. The sunny back deck is one of McLeod's best.
Om *Om Hotel*, near the bus stand. Friendly, comfortable restaurant jutting out over the hillside with the town's only west-facing roof terrace. Generous, good-value portions of good Tibetan and Chinese veg food and a few Western-style snacks.
Shambala Jogiwara Rd. Cramped seating but good veg food, with fresh cakes and filled pancakes.
Sunrise Bhagsu Rd. Small, friendly and popular travellers' café and late-night hang-out place, with a mixed menu.
Tibet *Tibet* hotel, Bhagsu Rd. One of the best venues in Dharamsala for Tibetan and Chinese food, veg and non-veg. High prices, but worth every rupee.
Tibet Yak Cafe Jogiwara Rd. Tiny, simple restaurant, popular with locals, serving good Tibetan food.

Listings

Banks and exchange The Punjab National Bank (Mon–Fri 10am–2pm, Sat 10am–noon) in McLeod Ganj near the bus stand will change travellers' cheques and cash, as will the upper branch of State Bank of India in Dharamsala, which also has the town's only ATM. The lower SBI branch will not handle foreign currency. There are several authorized private foreign exchange agencies in McLeod Ganj, such as Paul Merchants by the bus stand and LKP Forex on Temple Rd, who provide cash advances on credit and debit cards for a 3 percent commission.
Bookshops The Tibetan Bookshop and Information Office is a good place to browse for books on Tibetan Buddhism, as is the Charitable Trust Shop, both on Jogiwara Rd in McLeod Ganj's main bazaar. Bookworm, opposite the tourist office, South End, is small but has a very good selection, especially on Buddhism, and also stocks second-hand books. Other bookshops include Sagar and Hill's, both on Bhagsu Rd.
Cinema Cinemaa1, Abrol Video and Memory Theatre, all on Jogiwara Rd, show Hollywood flicks, often with a Tibetan or Indian theme.
Courses Numerous courses are available in McLeod Ganj, including *dharma* teachings, Tibetan language, Hindi, ancient Thai massage, yoga, tabla, karate, Xi Gung, Tai Chi, Reiki, and Indian vegetarian and Tibetan cooking. Check listings in *Contact* for further details. Free classes on *dharma* are given in translation by Buddhist monks from 11am until noon most weekdays at the Library of Tibetan Works and Archives. Philosophy courses and three-month Tibetan language courses (beginning March, June & Sept) are also run from the Library (contact the Secretary for Tibetan Studies ⓣ01892/222467).
Hospitals The Tibetan Delek Hospital (ⓣ01892/222053), above the Astro Medical Institute, is one of the best hospitals in the state and has Western physicians on call; also excellent is the Men-Tsee-Khang clinic on Tipa Rd (ⓣ 01892/221484; 9am–1pm & 2–5pm, closed every 2nd & 4th Sat & Sun). A former physician of the Dalai Lama, Dr Yeshi Dhondhen, has a clinic off Jogiwara Rd in the main bazaar; the Dr Lobsang Dolma Khangkar Memorial Clinic (daily except Thurs 9am–noon & 2–5pm; ⓣ01892/221668) lies between Jogiwara and Temple roads.
Internet access The *Green* hotel's cybercafé is the largest of many Internet cafés, but the Aroma cybercafé next to *Gakyi's* restaurant stays open until 11pm. Awasthi, close to Moonpeak Pictures, has a pretty good connection as well as a photocopy machine and DHL service. Down in Dharamsala, the first-floor *Cyber World* boasts an ISDN line, and, at Rs20/hr, the cheapest rates in town.
Meditation Tibetan Buddhist meditation courses are held at the Tushita Meditation Centre in Dharamkot (office Mon–Sat 9.30–11.30am & 1–4.30pm; ⓣ01892/221866, ⓦwww.tushita.info). Courses range from short retreats of eight to ten days to an intensive three-month summer purification retreat (Vajrasattva). Accommodation is available

Moving on from Dharamsala

Indian Airlines **fly** thrice weekly to Delhi (Mon, Wed & Fri 3pm), but flights are often cancelled so don't book your onward trip from Delhi on the same day. HRTC run numerous **buses** to destinations in Himachal Pradesh, Delhi and Chandigarh. Most travellers prefer to book "deluxe" buses through operators in McLeod Ganj near the bus stand. Try Himachal Travels on Jogiwara Rd (Ⓣ01892/221428), or Potala Tours & Travels on Bhagsu Rd, opposite *Hotel Tibet* (Ⓣ01892/221378). Buses to Pathankot, handy for train connections, leave every thirty minutes from the main bus stand in the lower town. Three buses per day (6am, 8am & 8pm) travel to Manali and two run to Delhi (6pm & 7pm) via Chandigarh, although more are put on according to demand. Two government buses per day (8am & 11.30am) travel to Dalhousie, and a few private buses depart from Gaggal (connected to Dharamsala by half-hourly buses). The most direct route to Chamba is over the mountains via Laru and Jot; a 9am bus from Gaggal arrives by 4pm. It's worth inquiring about a private bus which periodically operates between McLeod Ganj and Banikhet, where you can catch connections to Chamba or Dalhousie, 6km away.

See the "Travel details" at the end of this chapter for more information on journey frequencies and durations.

in simple rooms and dorms and there's also an excellent library. Book well in advance. The Vipassana Centre, next door, follows teachings more akin to Theravada Buddhism. They run ten-day silent retreats and daily sittings (register in person Mon–Sat 4–5pm or contact Ⓣ01892/221309, Ⓦwww.sikhara.dhamma.org). Courses are free, although donations are accepted.

Photography Moonpeak Pictures on Temple Rd (Ⓣ01892/220375, Ⓔmoonpeak@rediffmail.com) sells slide film and can develop prints. They also print from digital memory cards (Rs35) and burn CDs (Rs50).

Post office McLeod Ganj's post office, on Jogiwara Rd, has a poste restante counter that holds letters for up to one month. Letters not addressed to McLeod Ganj, Upper Dharamsala, end up in the GPO in the lower town. STD and ISD telephones are widely available.

Shopping Stalls and little shops along the main streets stock Tibetan trinkets, inexpensive warm clothing, incense, prayer bells, rugs and books. The large handicrafts shop on Jogiwara Rd sells *thangkas* of all sizes, along with prayer flags, and you can have a *bakku* (a Tibetan women's dress) stitched here for around Rs600 plus the cost of the cloth. The Green Shop, Bhagsu Rd, sells recycled painted cards, hand-painted T-shirts, books on the environment and filtered boiled water for Rs5.

Teaching The Yong Ling School, Jogiwara Rd on the left past the post office, welcomes volunteer teachers. An excellent resource for jobs is Volunteer Tibet (Ⓦwww.volunteertibet.org), whose office is opposite the school.

Tibetan settlement For enquiries about the Tibetan settlement, call in either at the Welfare Office on Bhagsu Rd in McLeod Ganj or directly at the Reception Centre below the post office, where donations of clothes, books, blankets and pens for new Tibetan arrivals are always gratefully accepted. Another good place for information is the Tibetan Bookshop and Information Office on Jogiwara Rd near McLeod Ganj's main bazaar.

Travel agents Himachal Travels, Jogiwara Rd (Ⓣ01892/221428) books local and private buses, trains from Pathankot and domestic flights, and confirms or alters international flights. You can also rent taxis for journeys within Himachal Pradesh or beyond, and enquire about treks. Ways Tours & Travels, Temple Rd (Ⓣ01892/221910, Ⓦwww.earthville.net/ETA/ways), is a well-organized agency that handles international flights, organizes tailor-made itineraries around India and changes money. Yeti Trekking, on the road to the Mountaineering Institute (Ⓣ01892/221032), offers treks and has plenty of equipment for rent.

Dalhousie and around

The quiet, relaxed hill station of **Dalhousie** spreads over five low-level hills at the western edge of the Dhauladhar Range. While the town itself, mostly modern hotels interspersed with Raj-era buildings and low-roofed stalls, is unremarkable, the pine-covered slopes around it are intersected with paths and tracks ideal for short undemanding walks.

From Dalhousie the road east zigzags through forests to **Khajjiar**, a popular local day out, before descending through terraced mountain slopes to **Chamba**, perched above the rushing River Ravi. It's a slow and relaxed place with some fascinating temples and a small art museum. **Brahmour**, three hours further east by bus and the final settlement on the road into the mountains, holds more Hindu temples – both towns make good bases for **treks** into the remote **Pangi Valley**.

In the summer of 1998, the region gained unfortunate notoriety after the **massacre** of 34 road workers by Kashmiri separatists. The killings fuelled a mistrust of Gujjar shepherds who apparently guided the perpetrators across remote mountain passes into Chamba. Although a one-off incident, it's worth being cautious in this area near the Jammu/Kashmir border.

Dalhousie

DALHOUSIE owes its name to Lord Dalhousie, Governor General of Punjab (1849–56), who was attracted by the cool climate to establish a sanitorium here for the many British, who, like himself, suffered ill health. Early in the twentieth century, it made a popular alternative to crowded, expensive Shimla, but thereafter declined. Today Dalhousie is a favourite summer retreat for holidaying Punjabis, but receives only a handful of Western tourists, few of whom stay longer than a day or two. A small population of Tibetans has lived here since the Chinese invasion of Tibet in 1959.

The town is spread over a series of hills with winding roads connecting the two focal points, the chowks. **Gandhi Chowk**, with its restaurants and post office, is the busiest section. From here the Mall and Garam Sarak dip and curve to **Subhash Chowk**, at the top end of the largely Muslim Sadar Bazaar. North of here, the bus stand and information office mark the main road out of town.

Practicalities

Dalhousie is usually approached by **bus** from Pathankot in the Punjab, 80km southwest, or Chamba, 30km north; the journey through the Himalayan foothills from Dharamsala (6hr) and Shimla (18hr) is quicker than the usual route via Nurpur. Transport to Chamba (2hr 15min) usually goes via Banikhet, though four buses also travel via Khajjiar. The **tourist information office** (Mon–Sat 10am–5pm; ⓣ01899/242136), close to the bus stand, provides transport information. A steep path leads up from the bus stand to the Mall; if you don't fancy the walk, local Maruti taxis (Rs50) ply the route. The State Bank of India at the bus stand has foreign **exchange** facilities.

Numerous **hotels** cater for Dalhousie's summer hordes, but many offer substantial **discounts** in the off-season. The *Silverton*, above the Circuit House on the Mall (ⓣ01899/240674, ⓦwww.heritagehotels.com/silverton; ❺–❽), is an old-world manor house with large rooms and immaculate lawns set within private woodlands. *Aroma N Claire's* (ⓣ01899/242199; ❺–❻), a rambling 1930s building south of Subhash Chowk on Court Road is atmospheric, cluttered and eccentric, with a library and leafy patios. Close to Subhash Chowk, *Hotel Crags* on Garam Sarak Road (ⓣ01899/242124; ❸–❺) is a quiet and exceptionally friendly hotel with a large terrace, tasty food and great views down to the plains. The **youth hostel** (ⓣ01899/242189, ⓔyh_dalhousie@rediffmail.com; ❷), five minutes' walk west of the bus stand, has dorm beds (members Rs30, non-members Rs50) and doubles – all of which need fumigating.

Apart from the hotel restaurants and scattered *dhabas*, **places to eat** include *Food Junction* at the bus stand, *Kwality's* at Gandhi Chowk, and *Moti Mahal* and *Sher-e-Punjab* at Subhash Chowk. You can access the **Internet** at Richa's Cyber Sync, next to the *Napoli* restaurant on Garam Sarak (Rs75/hr).

Khajjiar

Heading east towards Chamba, the road descends through deodar forests to the meadow of **Khajjiar** where the small twelfth-century temple of **Khajjinag** looks down over a vast rolling green with a small lake cupped in the centre. Khajjiar is a popular day-trip from Dalhousie for Indian tourists who come to have their pictures taken and to take pony rides. If you want to stay, the *Mini Swiss* (Ⓣ01899/236364, Ⓦwww.miniswiss.com; ❺–❽), beyond the meadow towards Chamba, has good food and views, and a range of en-suite rooms. The road past Khajjiar dips across denuded and terraced hillsides down towards Chamba. Prince Travels at the bus stand in Dalhousie runs a tourist **bus** to Khajjiar and Chamba, departing at 10am and returning to Dalhousie at 6.30pm; alternatively, two Chamba-bound buses travel via Khajjiar everyday.

Chamba

Shielded on all sides by high mountains, and protected by forces in Kangra to the south, **CHAMBA** was ruled for more than a millennium by kings descended from Raja Sahil Varma, who founded it in 920 AD and named it after his daughter Champavati. Unlike Himachal states further south it was never formally under Moghul rule, and its distinct Hindu culture remained intact until the first roads were built to Dalhousie in 1870. When the state of Himachal Pradesh was formed in 1948, Chamba became the capital. Today, only a handful of visitors make it out here, passing through before or after trekking, or stopping off to see the unique **temples,** but those that do make it are usually enchanted by the slower pace of life; a world away from the tourist hot spots of Manali and Dharamsala.

The *chaugan*, a large green used for sports, evening strolls and festive celebrations, marks the centre of town, overlooked by the **Rang Mahal** palace, now a government building. At the south end of the *chaugan*, the **Bhuri Singh**

Chamba festivals

Chamba's annual four-day **Suhi Mata Festival**, in early April, commemorates Rani Sunena, the wife of the tenth-century Raja Sahil Verma. A curious legend relates that when water from a nearby stream failed to flow through a channel supposed to divert it to the town, local brahmins advised Raja Verma that either his son or his wife would have to sacrifice themselves. The queen obliged; she was buried alive at the head of the channel, and the water flowed freely. Only women and children participate in the festival, dancing on the *chaugan* before processing with an image of Champavati (Rani Sunena's daughter who gave her name to the town) and banners of the Rajput solar emblem to the Suhi Mata temple in the hills behind the town.

Minjar, a week of singing and dancing at the start of August to celebrate the growth of maize, is also peculiar to Chamba. Its climax comes on the last day, when a rowdy procession of locals, Gaddis and Gujjars, dressed in traditional costumes, leaves the palace and snakes down to the riverbank, where bunches of maize are thrown into the water. Before Independence, locals had the custom of pushing one male buffalo into the river; its drowning was an auspicious sign but if the beast managed to swim to the opposite bank bad fortune was expected for the coming year.

museum (Tues–Sun 10am–5pm; free) holds a reasonable display of local arts and crafts. Its eighteenth- and nineteenth-century **Kangra miniature paintings**, depicting court life and amorous meetings, and men and women smoking elaborate hookahs, are much bolder than their Moghul-influenced Rajasthani equivalents. The museum's best feature is its small cache of **rumals**. Made by women since the tenth century, used in ceremonial exchanges to cover gifts, *rumals* are like embroidered paintings, depicting scenes from popular myth. Today only a few women continue this tradition, but a weaving centre in the old palace is attempting to revitalize the art.

The temples

The intimate complex of **Lakshmi Narayan temples**, behind Dogra Bazaar west of the *chaugan*, is of a style found only in Chamba and Brahmour. Three of its six earth-brown temples are dedicated to Vishnu and three to Shiva, all with profusely carved outer walls and curious curved *shikharas* (spires), topped with overhanging wooden canopies and gold pinnacles added in 1678 in defiance of Aurangzeb's order to destroy all Hindu temples in the hill states. Niches in the walls contain images of deities, but many stand empty, some statues lost in the earthquake of 1905 and others looted more recently.

Entering the compound, you're confronted by the largest and oldest temple, built in the tenth century and enshrining a marble idol of Lakshmi Narayan (Vishnu). The buxom maidens flanking the entrance to the sanctuary, each holding a water vessel, represent the goddesses Ganga and Yamuna, while inside a frieze depicts scenes from the *Mahabharata* and *Ramayana*. Temples dedicated to Shiva fill the third courtyard. In the inner sanctuary, you'll see sturdy brass images of Shiva, Parvati and Nandi, inlaid with silver and copper brought from mines nearby. Outside the temple complex, **coppersmiths** manufacture curved ceremonial trumpets and brass hookahs.

Of Chamba's other temples, the most intriguing is the tenth-century **Chamunda Devi temple** high above the town in the north, a steep half-hour climb up steps that begin near the bus stand. Decorated with hundreds of heavy brass bells and protecting a fearsome image of the bloodthirsty goddess Chamunda, the temple is built entirely of wood, and commands an excellent view up the Ravi gorge. Back in town, south of the *chaugan* near the post office, the small, lavishly carved eleventh-century **Harirai temple** contains a smooth brass image of Vaikuntha, the triple-headed aspect of Vishnu.

Practicalities

Buses arrive at the cramped bus stand in the north of town, close to several lodges, the best of which is the slightly shabby *Chamunda View* (ⓣ01899/222478; ❸–❹). *Jimmy's Inn* (ⓣ01899/224748; ❸), opposite the bus stand, has comfortable if noisy rooms and hot water by the bucket. Chamba's best **hotel** is the HPTDC *Hotel Iravati* (ⓣ01899/222671; ❹–❻) on the northwest edge of the *chaugan*, with comfortable carpeted en-suites; the deluxe rooms have bathtubs, but the economy ones are best value. Their cheaper annexe, *Champak* (ⓣ01899/222774; ❷), has reasonable doubles and a dorm (Rs75).

Some 12km from Chamba on the road to Sahu, the *Himalayan Orchard Hut* (ⓣ01899/222607, ⓣm94180/20401, ⓔorchardhut@hotmail.com; full board; ❹–❺) provides a taste of village life amongst rolling hills and terraced fields, and gets excellent reviews from travellers. Three-person tents (Rs150–200) are available, as well as large comfortable rooms, and they also organize treks and gentler walks into the hills around Chamba. Book through Mani Mahesh Travels near the Lakshmi Narayan complex (ⓣ01899/222507, ⓔprakashdhami@sancharnet.in).

Treks around Chamba and Brahmour

The most popular treks from Chamba lead south over the **Dhauladhar** via the Minkiani or Indrahar pass to Dharamsala. **Equipment** can be rented and porters and **guides** hired in Chamba and Brahmour. Mani Mahesh Travels in Chamba (☎01899/222507), organizes and equips treks.

Treks in the Pangi Valley to Lahaul

Few trekkers make it to the spectacular, all but inaccessible **Pangi Valley**, between the soaring Greater Himalayan Range in the north and the Outer Himalayan Range in the south. Several peaks within it have never been climbed, and onward paths lead to Kashmir, Lahaul and Zanskar. The trek to Lahaul takes nine or ten days from **Traila** (90km north of Chamba) via Satraundhi (3500m) over the Sach pass to Killar, Sach Khas, and finishing in Purthi from where you can take a bus via Tindi to **Udaipur**. Buses run from here to Keylong, capital of Lahaul and northwards to Leh or south over the Rohtang Pass and down to Manali.

Treks from Brahmour

Trekking routes lead north from **Brahmour** (2130m) over the Pir Panjal range across passes covered with snow for most of the year. The challenging six- to seven-day trek over **Kalichho Pass** (4990m), "The Abode of Kali", ends in the village of **Triloknath**, whose ancient temple to three-faced Shiva is sacred to both Hindus and Buddhists. Buses run from here to Udaipur, and on to Keylong and Manali.

Another demanding five- to six-day route crosses the **Kugti Pass** (5040m). From **Hadsar**, an hour by bus from Brahmour, the path follows the River Budhil for 12km to **Kugti**, then up to **Kuddi Got**, a vast flower-filled meadow (4000m). The next stage, over the pass, requires crampons and ice axe for an incredibly taxing six-hour climb. Having enjoyed views of the towering peaks of Lahaul and Zanskar from the summit, you plummet once again to the head of a glacier at **Khardu**, continuing down to Raape, 7km from **Shansha**, which is linked to Udaipur and Keylong by road.

Finally, a delightful three-day trek to the sacred lake of **Manimahesh** (4183m) starts from and returns to Hadsar. The awesome Manimahesh Kailash massif, with its permanent glaciers and ice fields, overlooks the lake.

The best **food** can be found at the *Iravati*, though the *Rishi* in Dogra Bazaar and *Park View* on Museum Road are decent alternatives. Try the local speciality, *madhra*, a rich, oily and slightly bitter mix of beans and curd. The **tourist office** (Mon–Sat 10am–5pm; ☎01899/224002) is next to the *Iravati*. **Internet** access is available at Mani Mahesh Travels. The Punjab National Bank on Hospital Road cannot change **money** but will cash American Express travellers' cheques.

From Chamba three buses a day leave for Dharamsala (6am, 11.30am & 9.30pm; 10hr), and two for Shimla (10.45am & 5pm; 15hr). There are buses every half hour to **Banikhet** and hourly to **Pathankot**, and a daily departure to **Amritsar** (noon; 8hr).

Brahmour

BRAHMOUR is a one-horse town of slate-roofed houses, apple trees and small maize fields, shadowed on all sides by high snowy peaks. The **temples**, whose curved *shikharas* dominate the large, neatly paved central square, are more dramatic and better preserved than their rivals at Chamba. The sanctuaries are unlocked only for puja in the mornings and evenings, permitting a glimpse of bold bronze images of Ganesh, Shiva and Parvati, unchanged since their installation in the seventh and eighth centuries when Brahmour was capital of the surrounding mountainous region.

Except during the September *yatra* or pilgrimage when everywhere is booked up, you can find **rooms** at a handful of guesthouses. Best choices are *Divya Cottage* (Ⓣ01090/275033; ❷) – probably the best in Brahmour – and *Shanti Guesthouse* (Ⓣ01090/225018; ❶) nearby. There isn't much choice of **food**; the *Chourasi* restaurant is a notch above the handful of stalls lining the main road between the bus stand and the square. The efficient Mountaineering Institute has details of local **treks**, reliable guides and porters, and equipment for rent.

The Kullu Valley

The majestic **KULLU VALLEY** is cradled by the Pir Panjal to the north, the Parvati Range to the east, and the Barabhangal Range to the west. This is Himachal at its most idyllic, with roaring rivers, pretty mountain villages, orchards and terraced fields, thick pine forests and snow-flecked ridges.

Known in the ancient Hindu scriptures as **Kulanthapitha**, or "End of the Habitable World", the Kullu Valley extends 80km north from the mouth of the perilously steep and narrow **Larji Gorge**, near Mandi, to the foot of the **Rohtang Pass** – gateway to Lahaul and Ladakh. For centuries, it formed one of the major trade corridors between Central Asia and the Gangetic plains, and local rulers, based first at **Jagatsukh** and later at **Nagar** and Sultanpur (now **Kullu**), were able to rake off handsome profits from the through traffic. This trade monopoly, however, also made it a prime target for invasion, and in the eighteenth and early nineteenth centuries the Kullu rajas were forced to repulse attacks by both the Raja of Kangra and by the Sikhs, before seeing their lands annexed by the British in 1847. Over the following years, colonial families crossed the Jalori Pass from Shimla, making the most of the valley's alpine climate to grow the **apples** that, along with **cannabis** cultivation, today form the mainstay of the rural economy. The first road, built in 1927 to export the fruit, spelled the end of the peace and isolation, prompting many settlers to pack up and leave long before Independence. The population expanded again in the 1950s and 1960s with an influx of **Tibetan refugees**.

In spite of the changes wrought by roads, immigration and, more recently, mass tourism, the Kullu Valley's way of life is maintained in countless timber and stone villages. Known as **paharis** ("hill people"), the locals – high-caste landowning Thakurs, and their (low-caste) sharecropping tenant farmers – still sport the distinctive Kullu cap, or *topi*. The women, meanwhile, wear colourful headscarves, and *puttoos* fastened with silver pins and chains. Venture into the lush meadows above the tree line, and you'll cross paths with nomadic **Gaddi** shepherds.

Most tourists make a beeline for **Manali** after a gruelling bus ride from either Leh or Delhi. With its vast choice of hotels and restaurants, there is something here for everyone. Still an evergreen hippy hangout, it's India's number one honeymoon spot too, and is also popular with outdoors enthusiasts taking advantage of the fine **trekking** opportunities – everything from day-hikes up the River Beas's side valleys (or *nalas*) to challenging long hauls over high-altitude passes and glaciers.

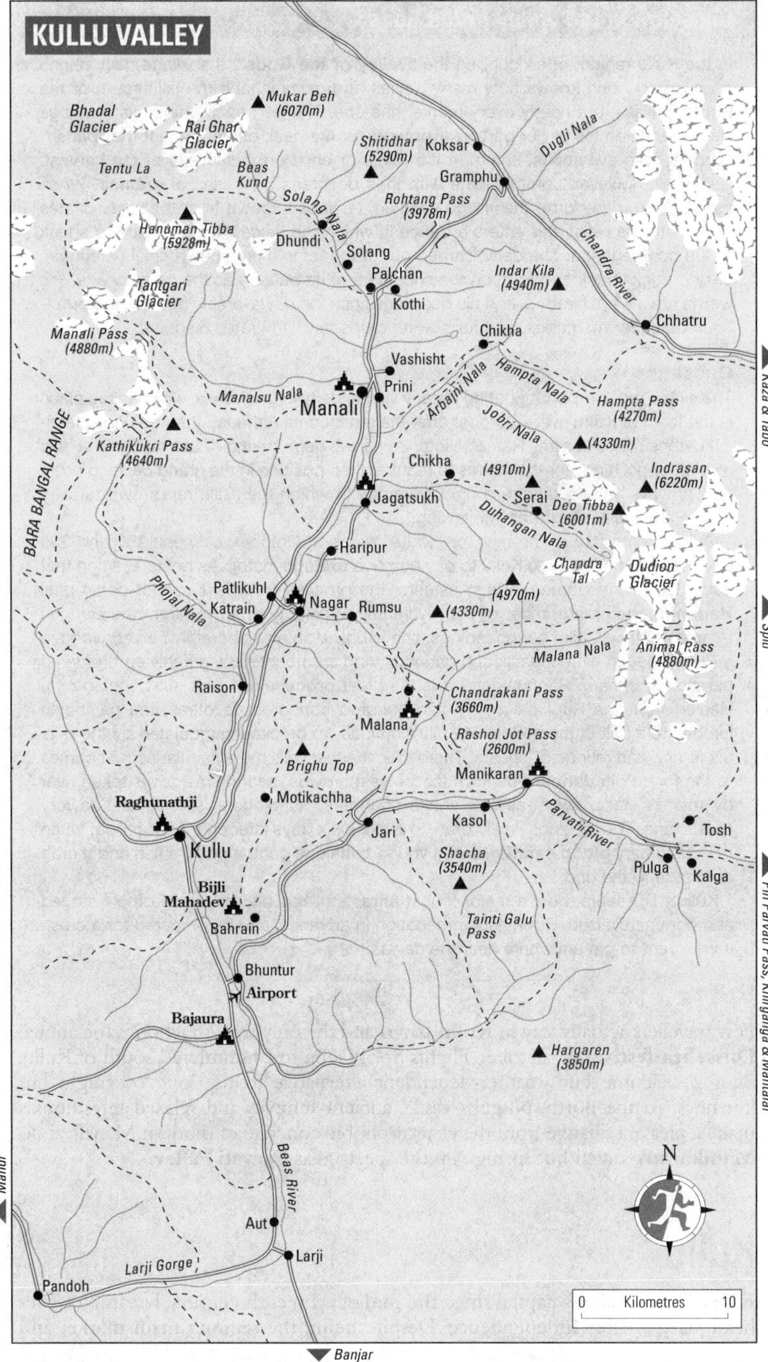
KULLU VALLEY
Leh & Lahaul
Bhadal Glacier
Mukar Beh (6070m)
Rai Ghar Glacier
Shitidhar (5290m)
Koksar
Dugli Nala
Tentu La
Beas Kund
Gramphu
Solang Nala
Rohtang Pass (3978m)
Hanuman Tibba (5928m)
Dhundi
Chandra River
Solang
Palchan
Indar Kila (4940m)
Tantgari Glacier
Kothi
Chhatru
Manali Pass (4880m)
Chikha
Vashisht
Hampta Nala
Kaza & Tabo
Prini
Manalsu Nala
Manali
Arbaini Nala
Hampta Pass (4270m)
BARA BANGAL RANGE
Jobri Nala
(4330m)
Kathikukri Pass (4640m)
Chikha
(4910m)
Indrasan (6220m)
Jagatsukh
Serai
Deo Tibba (6001m)
Duhangan Nala
Haripur
Chandra Tal
Dudion Glacier
Phojal Nala
Patlikuhl
(4970m)
Katrain
Nagar
Rumsu
(4330m)
Spiti
Malana Nala
Animal Pass (4880m)
Raison
Chandrakani Pass (3660m)
Malana
Rashol Jot Pass (2600m)
Brighu Top
Manikaran
Motikachha
Raghunathji
Kasol
Parvati River
Tosh
Jari
Kullu
Shacha (3540m)
Pulga
Kalga
Pin Parvati Pass, Khirganga & Mantalai
Bijli Mahadev
Bahrain
Tainti Galu Pass
Bhuntur
Airport
Bajaura
Hargaren (3850m)
Beas River
Mandi
N
Aut
Larji
Larji Gorge
Pandoh
0 Kilometres 10
Banjar

Dussehra in the Valley of the Gods

In the Kullu region, often dubbed the **"Valley of the Gods"**, the village deity reigns supreme. No one knows how many *devtas* and *devis* inhabit the hills south of the Rohtang Pass, but nearly every hamlet has one. The part each one plays in village life depends on his or her particular **powers**; some heal, others protect the "parish" borders from evil spirits, summon the rains, or ensure the success of the harvest. Nearly all, however, communicate with their devotees by means of **oracles**. When called upon to perform, the village shaman, or **gaur** – drawn from the lower castes – strips to the waist and enters a trance in which the *devta* uses his voice to speak to the congregation. The deity, carried out of the temple on a ceremonial palanquin, or *rath*, rocks back and forth on the shoulders of its bearers as the *gaur* speaks. His words are always heeded, and his decisions final; the *devta*-oracle decides the propitious dates for marriages, and for sowing crops, and arbitrates disputes.

Dussehra

The single most important outing for any village deity is **Dussehra**, which takes place in the town of **Kullu** every October after the monsoons. Although the week-long festival ostensibly celebrates Rama's victory over the demon-king of Lanka, Ravana, it is also an opportunity for the *devtas* to reaffirm their position in the grand pecking order that prevails among them – a rigid hierarchy in which the Kullu raja's own tutelary deity Rama, alias **Raghunathji**, is king.

On the tenth day of the new, or "white" moon in October, between 150 and 200 *devtas* make their way to Kullu to pay homage to Raghunathji. As befits a region that holds its elderly women in high esteem, the procession proper cannot begin until **Hadimba**, the grandmother of the royal family's chief god, arrives from the Dunghri temple in Manali. Like her underlings, she is borne on an elaborately carved wooden *rath* swathed in glittering silk and garlands, and surmounted by a richly embroidered parasol, or *chhatri*. Raghunathji leads the great **procession** in his six-wheeled *rath*. Hauled from the Rupi palace by two hundred honoured devotees, the palanquin lurches to a halt in the middle of Kullu's *maidan*, to be circumambulated by the raja, his family, and retinue of priests. Thereafter, the festival's more secular aspect comes to the fore. **Folk dancers** perform for the vast crowds, and the *maidan* is taken over by market stalls, sweet-sellers, snake charmers, astrologers, *sadhus* and tawdry circus acts. The revelries finally draw to a close six days later on the full moon, when the customary **blood sacrifices** of a young buffalo, a goat, a cock, a fish and a crab are made to the god.

Kullu's Dussehra, now a major tourist attraction, has become increasingly staged and commercialized. Book accommodation in advance, and be prepared for a crush if you want to get anywhere near the *devtas*.

Few travellers actually stay in **Kullu town** and the only real attraction is the annual **Dussehra festival** in October. Flights from Delhi to Bhuntur, just south of Kullu, offer a welcome but weather-dependent alternative to the long overnight bus journeys. To the north, **Nagar**'s castle, ancient temples and relaxed guesthouses make a pleasant change from the claustrophobic concrete of modern Manali, as do **Manikaran**'s sacred hot springs, up the spectacular **Parvati Valley**.

Kullu

KULLU, the valley's capital since the mid-seventeenth century, became district headquarters after Independence. Despite being the region's main market and transport hub it has been eclipsed as a tourist centre by Manali, 40km north. Kullu is noisy, polluted, and worlds away from the tranquil villages that peer down from the surrounding hillsides. Hopefully a bypass, due for completion in 2006, will divert the worst of the traffic. Kullu makes a handy **transport hub** if you're travelling onwards to the Parvati Valley, and there are several **temples** dotted around town, some of which provide fine valley views. In October, when the entire population of the valley comes to town to celebrate **Dussehra**, the city takes on a life of its own.

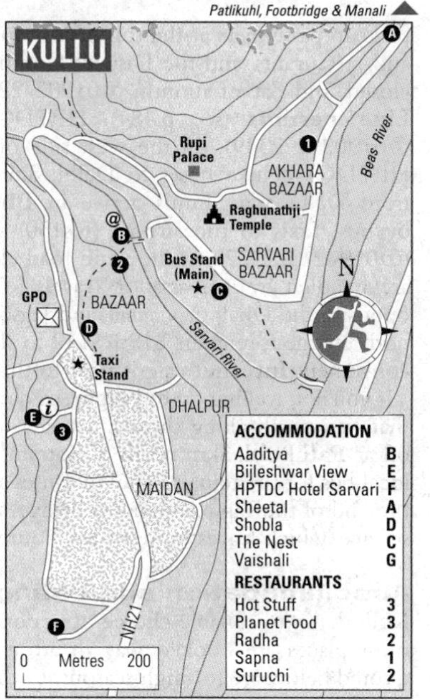

The temples

Kullu's most famous temple, the **Raghunathji Mandir** is home to a sacred statue of Lord Raghunathji, a manifestation of Rama, brought to Kullu by Raja Jagat Singh in the mid-seventeenth century. The raja had been advised by his priests to install the sacred icon here and crown it king in his place, and to this day the Kullu rajas consider themselves mere viceroys of Raghunathji, the most powerful *devta* in the valley and the focus of the Dussehra procession. The temple is tucked away behind the Kullu raja's **Rupi Palace** above the bus station. Half an hour's walk further up, the paved trail leads beyond Sultanpur to a high ridge, with excellent views over the Beas to the snow peaks in the east. **Vaishno Devi Mandir**, a small cave-temple that houses an image of the goddess Kali (Durga), is a stiff 3km further on.

Another important temple, the **Bijli Mahadev Mandir**, stands 8km southeast of town, atop the bluff that overlooks the sacred confluence of the Beas and Parvati rivers. Although it's closer to Bhuntur than Kullu, you have to approach the temple via the Akhara Bazaar–Tapu suspension bridge and a well-worn track south along the left bank of the Beas. Bijli Mahadev is renowned for its extraordinary **lingam**. Bolts of lightning, conducted into the inner sanctum by means of the twenty-metre, trident-tipped pole, are said periodically to shatter the icon, which later, with the help of invocations from the resident *pujari*, magically reconstitutes itself. From the temple there are superb panoramic views of the Parvati and Kullu valleys and Himachal's highest peaks. You can **stay** in the temple rest house (donations welcome), a simple affair with a single cold tap and no toilets, and walk down into the Parvati Valley the next day.

Practicalities

Long-distance **buses** heading up and down the valley pull in at the **main bus stand** in **Sarvari Bazaar**, on the north side of the Sarvari River, which flows through the town from the west. Local services heading north drop and pick up passengers at the top of **Dhalpur maidan**, close to most of the hotels and restaurants, and the District Commissioner's office (Mon–Sat 10am–5pm, closed 2nd Sat of month; ⓣ01902/222727) – the place to apply for **Inner Line permits** (see p.484). HPTDC's **tourist office** (daily 10am–7pm; ⓣ01902/222349), on the west side of Dhalpur *maidan*, can book tickets on HPTDC's deluxe buses to Delhi, Shimla and Chandigarh. **Flights** to Kullu from Delhi and Shimla arrive in **Bhuntur**, thirty minutes south of Kullu by bus. Taxis to the airport (Rs150) should be booked in the union office (ⓣ01902/222322) on the main road close to the tourist office. Indian Airlines are handled by Ambassador Travels (ⓣ01902/225286) in the LAC Building opposite the Dhalpur *maidan*, and Jagsons (ⓣ01902/265222) in Bhuntur, who both charge foreigners $186/$142 to fly one-way to or from Delhi. The most convenient **Internet** café is next to the *Aaditya*.

If you're travelling on to **Nagar**, catch one of the frequent Manali-bound buses that run north along the main road, on the west side of the valley, and jump off at **Patlikuhl**, 5km north of Katrain, where you can pick up a shared taxi or local bus for the remaining 6km. Buses also run direct to Manali via Nagar, from the end of the Tapu suspension bridge, across the river from Akhara Bazaar. This service, which leaves more or less hourly, is slower, but far more scenic.

Accommodation and eating

Kullu has a reasonable choice of **accommodation**, although during Dussehra most places are booked way in advance and costs can quadruple. The rates quoted below are for high season; at other times discounts of up to fifty percent may be given. Apart from hotel **restaurants**, the best places to eat are at *Planet Food* and *Hot Stuff*, two similarly priced mixed-menu joints close to the tourist office. *Sapna*, an inexpensive sweets shop in Akhara Bazaar, also offers South Indian dishes, as does *Suruchi*, on the town side of the footbridge near *Radha*, the cleanest *dhaba* Kullu has to offer.

Aaditya Lower Dhalpur ⓣ01902/224263. Centrally located with en-suite rooms; the basic rooftop double is a steal at Rs165. ❷–❹

Bijleshwar View Behind the tourist office ⓣ01902/222677. Quiet, clean, central and friendly; large en-suite rooms with fireplaces, and cheaper bungalow accommodation. ❷–❹

HPTDC Hotel Sarvari South of the *maidan* and up a small lane ⓣ01902/222471. Quiet location with wide range of rooms in old and new blocks. Good views down the valley, Ayurvedic massage and a restaurant and bar. ❸–❻

The Nest Next to the main bus stand ⓣ01902/222685, ⓔhotelnest@rediffmail.com. The best option near the bus stand, with clean, very good-value doubles. The cheapest ground-floor rooms have bucket hot water; two of the pricier second-floor rooms have en-suite bath tubs. Fixed rates all year. ❷–❸

Sheetal Akhara Bazaar ⓣ01902/224548. Pleasant little guesthouse with rooms overlooking the river. Excellent value. ❷

Shobla Dhalpur ⓣ01902/222800, ⓦwww.shoblainternational.com. Kullu's top hotel, which has recently had a major revamp. Large rooms, a good mixed-cuisine restaurant (expensive by Kullu standards), and a relaxing lawn. ❺–❽

Vaishali Gandhi Nagar ⓣ01902/224225, 1km south of town. Sizeable, comfortable rooms, and a pleasant garden restaurant with dramatic views of the river. Fixed rates all year. ❹–❺

The Parvati Valley

Hemmed in by giant-pinnacled mountain peaks, the **Parvati Valley**, which twists west from the glaciers and snowfields on the Spiti border to meet the Beas at Bhuntur is the Kullu Valley's longest tributary. It's a picturesque place,

Parvati disappearances

The last decade has seen the mysterious **disappearance** of nearly two dozen travellers in the Parvati Valley. Most were travelling alone, although the most recent incident in August 2000 involved three campers who were brutally attacked in their tent, thrown into the gorge and left for dead – one survived. Several theories have been put forward to explain these disappearances, from drug-related accidents on the treacherous mountain trails, to attacks by bears or wolves or foul play by the numerous cannabis cultivators in the region; some even claim that the disappeared may have joined secret cults deep in the mountains. The most recent case, however, suggests they have most likely been victims of bandit attacks, motivated solely by money, with the wild waters of the River Parvati conveniently placed for disposing of bodies. To add to the concern, some posters placed around Manikaran of the missing people have been ripped down and relevant pages from hotel registers have also vanished. This steamy place of pilgrimage is at the heart of the mystery, being the last place most of the travellers were seen alive. Individual travellers should **take heed** and only use recognized guides on treks across the mountains. Don't attempt solo treks – even along the relatively simple trail over the Chandrakhani Pass between Nagar and Malana and the straightforward trek to the hot springs at Khirganga. There are many trekking agencies in Kullu and Manali who can put you in touch with a reputable guide.

with quiet hamlets perching precariously on its sides amid lush terraces and old pine forests; the landscape around **Jari** has certainly been scarred by the recent completion of the **Malana hydro project**, but there is strong local pressure to at least camouflage the site. Visitors to the valley are an incongruous mix – a combination of Western hippies (there's a big Israeli scene here) and van-loads of Sikh pilgrims bound for the *gurudwara* at **Manikaran**, 32km northeast of the Beas-Parvati confluence. Crouched at the foot of a gloomy ravine, this ancient religious site, sacred to Hindus as well as Sikhs, is famous for the **hot springs** that bubble out of its stony river banks.

To make the most of Parvati's stunning scenery you'll have to **hike**. Two popular trails thread their way up the valley: one heads north from the fascinating hill village of **Malana** (see box on p.539), over the Chandrakani Pass to Nagar; the other follows the River Parvati east to another sacred hot spring and *sadhu* hang-out, **Khirganga**. The trail continues from Khirganga to **Mantalai** with its Shiva shrine and over the awesome 5400m Pin–Parvati pass into **Spiti**. This serious snowfield is riddled with crevasses and takes several hours to cross. A guide is absolutely essential (see box on pp.538–539).

Jari, Mateura and Kasol

Spilling over the main road and down the south side of the Parvati Valley, **JARI**, 15km from Bhuntur, looks across to the precipitous Malana *nala* in the north, and to the snow-flecked needles of the Baranagh Range on the eastern horizon. It used to be the starting point for a 15km trail up to **Malana** (see p.539), but the access road built to the Malana hydro project has reduced the trek to a mere 4km from the new roadhead. Like many of its lookalike cousins, the tatty settlement supports a small transient population of stoned Westerners, attracted by the top quality *charas*. For basic **accommodation**, the *Dharma Guest House* (☎01902/276059; ❶), just above the bus stand, and the cleaner *Om Shiva* (☎01902/276202; ❶–❷), on the left hand side as you enter the village, are simple and welcoming. The best place to eat is *Deepak restaurant* at the bus stand.

Just ten minutes walk up the hill from the bus stand is the unspoilt hamlet of **MATEURA**, which has spectacular views over the Parvati Range. The *Village Guest House* (Ⓣ01902/276070; ❶) is a traditional wooden-balconied house with immaculate rooms, satellite TV and an STD/ISD phone line; set in a wonderful garden, it's popular year-round. The roof terrace of the nearby *Rooftop Restaurant & Guest House* (Ⓣ01902/275434; ❶) overlooks the village. All the Mateura guesthouses offer food.

Beyond Jari, the road winds down towards the rushing grey-green Parvati, which it meets at **KASOL**, a pleasant village straddling a mountain stream and surrounded by forest. A mere 4.5km from Manikaran and a nice walk along a wooded road, Kasol has grown in popularity, and now has a large resident population of *charas*-smoking Westerners – earning it the nickname of "little Israel" from the locals. A trickle of trekkers also plod through on their way to or from the pass of Rashol Jot (2440m), a hard day's climb up the north side of the valley which provides an alternative approach to Malana and the Chandrakani route to the Kullu Valley. You can **change money** here at Swagtam Tourism, who will also give cash advances against credit cards for a three percent fee. **Accommodation** ranges from basic rooms in village houses and simple guesthouses such as the *Bhoj Guest House* (❶) on the roadside, to the plush *Hotel Sandhya Kasol*, 300m beyond the village (Ⓣ01902/273074; ❹–❺), with comfortable rooms and discounts up to 70 percent in the off-season (Oct–April). Just beyond the bridge, the best value is offered by *Deep Forest* (Ⓣ01902/273048; ❷–❸), with spacious, clean and peaceful rooms; those at the front have balconies overlooking the river. The terrace and open-plan restaurant make it a popular place to hang out, so check there are rooms before heading up the hill. Kasol's **travellers' cafes** are cheap and plentiful. The *Moondance Restaurant and German Bakery* has an excellent location near the bridge; it faces the pleasant *Sasi Café* on the opposite bank. The *Italiano Pizzeria* gets better reviews than its neighbour *Little Italy*, while further down the road to Manikaran is the popular *Evergreen* whose dope-free restaurant is less popular than its fragrant floor-cushioned backroom, which has a varied international menu. *Sadhus* and Western hippies pass *charas* round at the *Nutan Tea Stall*.

Manikaran and around

A short distance beyond Kasol, clouds of steam billowing from the rocky riverbank herald the Parvati Valley's chief attraction. Hindu mythology identifies **MANIKARAN** as the place where the serpent king Shesha stole Parvati's earrings, or *manikara*, while she and her husband Shiva were bathing in the river. When interrogated, the snake flew into a rage and snorted the earrings out of his nose. Ever since, boiling water has poured out of the ground. The site is also venerated by Sikhs, who have erected a massive concrete *gurudwara* over the springs.

Boxed in at the bottom of a vast, sheer-sided chasm, Manikaran is a damp, dark and claustrophobic place where you're unlikely to want to spend more than a night. Most of the action revolves around the springs themselves, reached via the lane that leads through the village from the footbridge. On the way, check out the finely carved pale-grey stone **Rama temple** just beyond the main square, and the pans of rice and dhal cooking in the steaming pools on the pavements. Down at the riverside **Shiva shrine**, semi-naked **sadhus** sit in the scalding waters smoking chillums. Sikh pilgrims, meanwhile, make their way to the atmospheric **gurudwara** nearby, where they take a purifying dip in the underground pool, sweat in the hot cave and then congregate upstairs to listen to musical recitations from the Sikhs' holy book, the *Guru Granth Sahib*. If you visit, keep your arms, legs and head covered; tobacco is prohibited inside the complex.

Practicalities

Buses leave Bhuntur every couple of hours for Manikaran (1hr 30min). The last bus for Kullu, via Bhuntur, leaves around 5.30pm. You can also hire Maruti-van **taxis**. Except during May and June, when Manikaran fills up with Punjabi visitors, **accommodation** is plentiful and inexpensive. All the hotels listed here have a steaming indoor hot tub but the abundance of moisture has left many of them feeling rather damp and dirty. *Hotel Shivalik* (Ⓣ01902/273817; ❸–❺), on the main road at the turn-off to the bus stand, has large rooms, TV and river views. Overlooking the bus stand itself, the *Amar Palace* (Ⓣ01902/273740; ❸–❺) is a comfortable mid-range place catering mainly for domestic tourists, with a smart new wing built in 2005. Crossing the footbridge brings you to a clutch of cheap guesthouses and overcrowded temple dorms. First up is the *Sharma Sardar Guest House* (Ⓣ01902/273703; ❷) which has the best-value doubles in town and great river views. At the far end of the bazaar near the *gurudwara* the *Sharma Guest House* (Ⓣ01902/273742; ❸) is slightly better than the nearby *Padha Family Guest House* (Ⓣ01902/273728; ❷–❹). The best **restaurant** is the *Holy Palace*, in the lane between the Rama Temple and the *gurudwara*; it has a small enclosed garden at the rear. Down a lane towards the bridge, the tiny *Iris Café*, a smokers' hang-out, also has good food (and rooms upstairs if you can't stagger home).

East of Manikaran

Fourteen kilometres beyond Manikaran the paved road swivels up the valley and peters out just beyond **Barshani**, from where it's a thirty-minute walk to the villages of Tulga, Pulga and Kalga, all visible across the river. Bridging the dramatic gorge is an ugly hydroelectric dam – still a few years away from completion, but already dominating the once pristine landscape. Despite this, the trio of beautiful villages remain relatively unscathed, resembling Manali in the late-1960s.

PULGA, the westernmost of the three, is lined with narrow stone-covered lanes and rickety wooden houses, most of which sport "room for rent" boards. The *Blue Diamond* (❶–❷), on the far edge of the village nudging against the woods, is the most secluded option. **KALGA**, perched above the dam project, already has more guesthouses than local homes; the *Pink House* (❶), run by a friendly *sadhu*, is popular. It's not uncommon to see Nepali porters hauling giant speakers up and down the mountain trail in summertime for forest raves. At **TULGA**, really just a hamlet of private homes between the aforementioned villages, you can stay at the woodsy *Peace Place Hotel* (❶).

On the Barshani side of the valley up a side canyon, **Tosh** is another traditional village turned hippie colony that can be reached on foot in an hour from the main road. Three or four hour's walk east of Kalga is **KHIRGANGA**, a resplendent alpine meadow and hamlet where you can soak in more hot springs. A couple of tea houses here provide simple food, while an ashram offers very basic **accommodation**. There are great **hiking** opportunities around this part of the valley, but they should not be attempted alone (see boxes on p.527 & p.539).

Nagar

Stacked up the lush terraced lower slopes of the valley as they sweep towards the tree line from the left bank of the Beas, **NAGAR**, 6km from the main road junction at Patlikuhl, is the most scenic and accessible of the hill villages between Kullu and Manali. Clustered around an old **castle**, this was the regional capital before the local rajas decamped to Kullu in the mid-1800s. A century or so later, European settlers began to move in.

Seduced by the village's ancient **temples**, peaceful setting and unhurried pace, visitors often find themselves lingering in Nagar – a far less hippified village than those further north – longer than they intended. Sadly, however, by 2006 Nagar's tranquillity may be shattered; the main road from Patlikuhl to Manali is due to be diverted along this side of the river so as to avoid the terrible landslides that plague the existing road. The effects of change are already being felt, with more and more construction eating into the orchards surrounding the village. However, numerous tracks wind up the mountain to more remote settlements, providing a choice of enjoyable **hikes**.

Arrival and information

Nagar is equidistant from Kullu and Manali (21km) and connected to both by regular **buses**. The direct services that ply the left-bank road, on the eastern side of the valley, are slower (1hr 30min from Manali or Kullu), but more scenic and straightforward than the more frequent services along the main highway on the opposite, west side. The latter drop at **Patlikuhl** (3km north of Katrain), from where taxis, auto-rickshaws and hourly buses cross the Beas to climb up to Nagar (6km). If you arrive in daylight and are not weighed down with bags, you can also walk from Patlikuhl on the old mule track – a hike of up to an hour. The last direct bus from Manali leaves around 5pm; if you miss it, take any bus on the main road to Patlikuhl and change there.

Most of Nagar's sights and accommodation lie a way above the small bazaar where the buses pull in. If you have your own vehicle, you can drive all the way up to the Roerich Gallery at the top of the village. If you are thinking of **trekking** around Nagar, you are advised to use guides, especially if crossing the **Chandrakhani Pass** to Malana (see p.539). Himalayan Mountain Treks at *Poonam Mountain Lodge* (☎01902/248248), have equipment, will arrange porters and guides, and can fix up Jeep trips to Lahaul and Spiti. Local guides are also easy to find, though make sure that they are reputable.

Accommodation

Alliance Guest House Halfway between the Tripuri Sundri temple and the Roerich Gallery ☎01902/248263. Popular guesthouse with simple, clean rooms (four new in 2005), a small lending library and a warm family atmosphere. ❷–❹

HPTDC Hotel Castle ☎01902/248316. Atmospheric castle with well-furnished en-suite doubles, some offering superb views from spacious wooden balconies, plus dorm beds (Rs75). Book in advance at any HPTDC tourist office to secure one of the more expensive rooms in the west wing. Not Nagar's best value accommodation, but certainly unique. ❸–❻

Karbo Shin Guesthouse Ghourdor village ☎01902/248342, ⓦwww.easytrekkingindia.com. Dutch-owned guesthouse with four rooms, a shared bathroom with hot shower, excellent food and superb views. They can also arrange local and long-distance treks. To get there follow the forest road from Nagar to Bijli Mahadev Mandir temple; the guesthouse is down the path signed off the road (10–15min). ❶

Poonam Mountain Lodge ☎01902/248248. Around the corner from the *Sheetal*, but with far more character. Cosy doubles, three with fireplaces for winter stays, Internet access, a lovely outside seating area and a good veg restaurant serving local specialities such as red rice. Recommended. ❷

Sheetal Guest House Ⓣ01902/248250. An alternative to the *Castle*, offering better-value rooms of similar standard, with balconies, a roof-top restaurant and reduced rates off-season. The nearby *Hotel Ragini* (Ⓣ01902/248185, Ⓔraginihotel@hotmail.com; ❸) is similar. ❸–❻

Snow View Guest House next to the Tripuri Sundri temple Ⓣ01902/248235. Friendly guesthouse with en-suite rooms opening onto a pleasant garden. Also cheaper shared-bath rooms (bucket hot water) and dorm beds (Rs80) available. ❷

Tree House Cottage On the opposite bank of the River Beas, 8km from Nagar, 1km up a paved road from Katrain Ⓣ01902/240365. Set in a beautiful, quiet pomegranate and apple orchard, offering a range of accommodation including self-catering cottages. ❸–❻

The castle

Since it was erected by Raja Sidh Singh (c.1700), Nagar's central **castle**, astride a sheer-sided bluff, has served as palace, colonial mansion, courthouse and school. It is now a hotel, but non-residents can wander in for Rs10 to admire the views from its balconies. Built in the traditional "earthquake-proof" *pahari* style (layers of stone bonded together with cedar logs), the castle has a central courtyard, a small shrine and a shop selling local handicrafts downstairs. The **Jagti Patt temple**'s amorphous deity, a triangular slab of rock strewn with rose petals and rupee notes, is said to have been borne here from its home on the summit of Deo Tibba by a swarm of wild honeybees – the valley's *devtas* in disguise.

The Nicholas Roerich Gallery

Perched on the upper outskirts of the village, the **Nicholas Roerich Gallery** (Tues–Sun: May–Aug 10am–1pm & 1.30–6pm; Sept–March 10am–1pm & 1.30–5pm; Rs20, Rs20 extra for camera, Rs50 extra for video) houses an exhibition of paintings and photographs dedicated to the memory of its former occupier, the Russian artist, writer, philosopher, archeologist, explorer and mystic. Around the turn of the twentieth century, Roerich's atmospheric landscape paintings and esoteric philosophies – an arcane blend of Eastern mysticism and *fin-de-siècle* humanist-idealism – inspired a cult-like following in France and the United States. Financed by donations from devotees, Roerich was able to indulge his obsession with Himalayan travel, eventually retiring in Nagar in 1929 and dying here eighteen years later. The on-site caretakers of the museum have a wealth of information about the site; ask for Mr Tsenrengdorje, whose father was employed by Roerich as a translator.

A path winds further up above the road through the forest for around 100m to **Urusvati-Himalayan Folk Art Museum** (same ticket). Founded by Madame Roerich in 1928, the museum features a collection of local folk art, costumes, more of Roerich's paintings, several paintings by his Russian followers, and a gallery of Russian folk art. Those interested in Roerich's paintings and philosophy can contact the International Centre (Ⓔicr.moscow@mtu.net.ru).

The temples

The largest and most distinctive of Nagar's ancient Hindu **temples** and shrines, the wooden pagoda-style **Tripuri Sundri**, stands in a small enclosure at the top of the village, just below the road to the Roerich Gallery. Like the Dunghri temple in Manali, it is crowned with a three-tiered roof, whose top storey is circular. Its *devta* is the focus of an annual *mela* (mid-May) in which deities from local villages are brought in procession to pay their respects.

Ten minutes' walk further up the hill – follow the stone steps that lead right from the road – brings you to a clearing where the old stone **Murlidhar** (Krishna) **Mandir** looks down on Nagar, with superb views up the valley to the snow peaks around Solan and the Rohtang Pass. Built on the ruins of the ancient town of Thawa, the shrine, set in a large courtyard, is strictly off-limits to non-Hindus.

Finally, on your way to or from the bus stand at the bottom of the village, look out for the finely carved stone *shikharas* of the **Gaurishankar Mandir**. Set in its own paved courtyard below the castle, this Shiva temple, among the oldest of its kind in the valley, houses a living *lingam*, so slip off your shoes before approaching it.

Eating

The *Cinderella* **restaurant**, above the *Sheetal Guest House*, serves good food, including grilled trout if ordered a few hours in advance. Other options include the seasonal *Chandrakhani Café*, set in a pleasant orchard above Tripuri Sundri and offering standard Western dishes. Down at the main bazaar overlooking the bus stand, *La Purezza* serves excellent Italian cuisine in a grassy yard underneath a parachute canopy.

Manali and around

Himachal's main tourist resort, **MANALI**, stands at the head of the Kullu Valley, 108km north of Mandi. Despite lying at the heart of the region's highest mountain ranges, it remains easily accessible by road from the plains; after one hour on a plane and a short hop by road, or sixteen hours on a bus from Delhi, you could be staring from your hotel veranda across apple orchards and thick pine forests to the snowfields of Solang Nala, which shine a tantalizing stone's throw away to the north. With the continuing troubles in Kashmir, Manali has become increasingly popular with domestic tourists, giving rise to an eclectic mix of honeymooners, holiday-makers, hippies, trekkers and traders.

The Manali that lured travellers in the 1970s has certainly changed, although the majestic mountain scenery, thermal springs and quality *charas* can still be enjoyed. **Old Manali** retains some of its atmosphere, and the village of **Vashisht** across the valley, with its increasing choice of guesthouses and cafés, has become a popular place to chill out. For those preferring to venture into the mountains, Manali makes an ideal **trekking** base for short hikes and serious expeditions, and countless agencies can help put a package together for you. The relaxing hotels in Manali's cleaner, greener outskirts, and dozens of sociable cafés and restaurants ranged around a well-stocked **bazaar**, provide a welcome relief from the rigours of the mountain trails. For more on treks around Manali and the Kullu Valley, see p.538.

Arrival and information

Coming from Delhi, most private buses pull into the bus stand 100m south of the State Bank of India at the bottom of town; government buses pull in to Manali's **bus stand** in the middle of the Mall, a short walk from the friendly **tourist office** (daily 10am–1.30pm & 2–5pm; ⓣ01902/252175). You can make reservations for the town's state-run hotels at the HPTDC offices, two doors down. Manali's **Taxi Operators' Union kiosk** (ⓣ01902/252450) lies just up from the tourist office. The taxis have fixed rates which are negotiable off-season. If you need to **change money**, the State Bank of India is on the main road 250m south of the Mall. There are also a handful of authorized private agencies open longer hours but these usually offer lower rates. The main **post office**, off Model Town Road, has a reliable poste restante counter

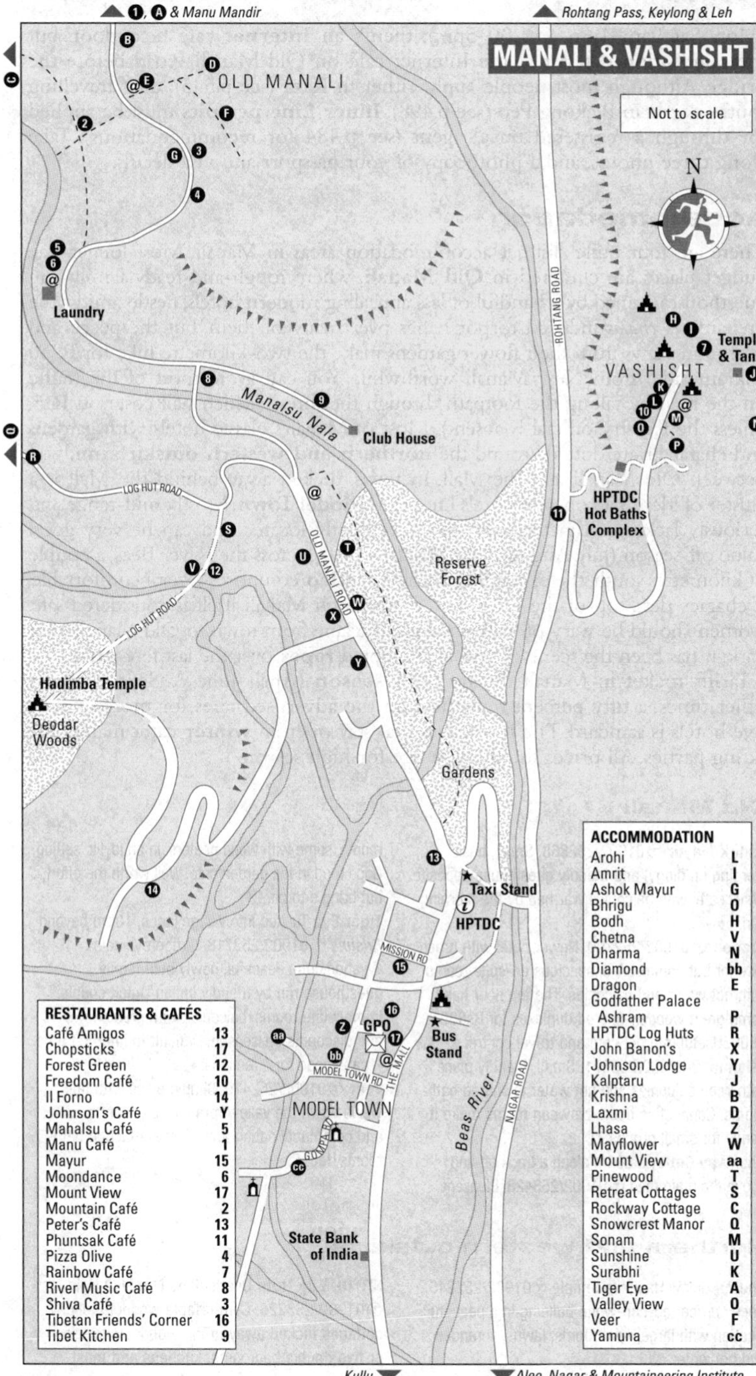

MANALI & VASHISHT
Not to scale
1, A & Manu Mandir
Rohtang Pass, Keylong & Leh
OLD MANALI
VASHISHT
Laundry
Temple & Tank
Manalsu Nala
Club House
ROHTANG ROAD
LOG HUT ROAD
OLD MANALI ROAD
HPTDC Hot Baths Complex
Reserve Forest
Hadimba Temple
Deodar Woods
Gardens
Taxi Stand
HPTDC
MISSION RD
GPO
Bus Stand
MODEL TOWN RD
THE MALL
MODEL TOWN
GOMPA RD
Beas River
NAGAR ROAD
State Bank of India
Kullu
Aleo, Nagar & Mountaineering Institute
RESTAURANTS & CAFÉS
Café Amigos 13
Chopsticks 17
Forest Green 12
Freedom Café 10
Il Forno 14
Johnson's Café Y
Mahalsu Café 5
Manu Café 1
Mayur 15
Moondance 6
Mount View 17
Mountain Café 2
Peter's Café 13
Phuntsak Café 11
Pizza Olive 4
Rainbow Café 7
River Music Café 8
Shiva Café 3
Tibetan Friends' Corner 16
Tibet Kitchen 9
ACCOMMODATION
Arohi L
Amrit I
Ashok Mayur G
Bhrigu O
Bodh H
Chetna V
Dharma N
Diamond bb
Dragon E
Godfather Palace Ashram P
HPTDC Log Huts R
John Banon's X
Johnson Lodge Y
Kalptaru J
Krishna B
Laxmi D
Lhasa Z
Mayflower W
Mount View aa
Pinewood T
Retreat Cottages S
Rockway Cottage C
Snowcrest Manor Q
Sonam M
Sunshine U
Surabhi K
Tiger Eye A
Valley View O
Veer F
Yamuna cc

(Mon–Sat 9am–1pm & 1.30–5pm); there's an **Internet** café next door, but the connection is faster at the Internet café on Old Manali Road before the bridge. Although most people apply either in Kaza (see p.545), or if travelling south–north, in Rekong Peo (see p.498), **Inner Line permits** must be applied for through a registered travel agent (see p.484 for recommendations). Take along three photos, and a photocopy of your passport and visa details.

Accommodation

There are four quite distinct accommodation areas in Manali. Most longer-stay budget places are clustered in **Old Manali**, where rough-and-ready family-run guesthouses, joined by a handful of less appealing modern hotels, nestle amidst the orchards. A *charas*-induced torpor hangs over many of them, but the peace and quiet and views from their flower gardens make the two-kilometre hike (or Rs30 Vikram ride) from New Manali worthwhile. You can avoid most of the traffic on the road by taking the footpath through the forest (which will cost you Rs5, unless the forestry official is absent). Most of Manali's classic hotels with gardens and character are dotted around the **northern and western outskirts**, midway between Old Manali and the Mall. In town, tucked away behind the Mall is a cluster of identikit concrete hotels known as **Model Town**. Mostly mid-range and seriously lacking character, they are conveniently located and can be very good value off-season (July, Aug & Nov–March). Finally, across the River Beas, a couple of kilometres south, the expanding enclave of **Aleo** comprises several comfortable, if characterless, top-of-the-range hotels. Although Manali itself is considered safe, women should be wary of walking along the lane from town to Old Manali after dark; it has been the scene of several attempted **rapes** over the last few years.

Tariffs rocket in Manali during **high season** (April–June & Sept–Oct). At other times, a fifty percent reduction on the advertised rates for more expensive hotels is standard. The few hotels that stay open in **winter** cater mainly for skiing parties. All prices listed below are for high season.

Old Manali

Ashok Mayur ⓣ01902/252868. Small, basic (verging on dingy) and friendly guesthouse opposite *Shiva* café, with balconies warmed by the morning sun. ❶–❷

Dragon ⓣ01902/252790. Newer hotel with brash exterior but comfortable, spacious en-suite rooms with hot water and balconies. The top floor has some great wooden-floored duplexes for Rs800–1500. Useful Internet café and travel centre. ❸–❻

Krishna ⓣ01902/253071. Small, friendly place with wide balconies and hot water in shared bathrooms. Connecting doors between rooms make it handy for small groups. ❷

Rockway Cottage 500m along a track off and above the main road ⓣ01902/253428. Pleasant rooms, some with wood heaters, in an idyllic setting. Good food in the garden café. Well worth the effort, but bring a torch. ❷

Tiger Eye Tucked into village lanes, 100m beyond *Krishna* ⓣ01902/252718, ⓔtigereyeindia@yahoo.com. Peaceful, newly built family guesthouse run by friendly Indian/Dutch couple. Immaculate rooms, balconies with great views and discounts off-season. Difficult to find first time – call ahead for directions. ❸

Veer ⓣ01902/252410. Simple place with fine views down the valley from a lovely leafy garden and communal eating area. Some attached bathrooms, too. ❸

Northern and western outskirts

Chetna Below Hadimba temple ⓣ01902/252245. Once spruce red-and-white building in a peaceful location with large, neat rooms, lawns, verandas and hot water. ❹

HPTDC Log Huts Overlooking Manalsu Nala ⓣ01902/253225. Comfortable wooden holiday cottages tucked away in the woods, with one or two double bedrooms, kitchens and most comforts including Star TV; a bit overpriced at $65–90. ❾

John Banon's Old Manali Rd ☎01902/252335. Old guesthouse with large, slightly run-down rooms. Pleasant orchard with valley views. ❹

Johnson Lodge Old Manali Rd ☎01902/253023. Three-star comfort in an old colonial building. Spacious and neat wooden-floored rooms overlook the garden; the carpeted downstairs rooms are cheaper, with wood-burning heaters for winter. Separate cottages in the garden sleep 4 for $70. Recommended. ❼–❽

Mayflower Old Manali Rd ☎01902/252104, Ⓦwww.negismayflower.com. One of Manali's most agreeable hotels. The large rooms are new, but feel traditional with wood-panelling and views over the pine forests. Balconies out front catch the afternoon sun. ❹–❼

Pinewood Old Manali Rd ☎01902/250118. Colonial building with furniture, fireplaces and garden to match. All rooms with balcony. Up to 50 percent discounts off-season. ❺

Retreat Cottages Log Hut Rd ☎01902/252042. Immaculate, good-sized self-catering two- and three-bedroom suites with baths ($105) in a tastefully designed building. Recommended for groups of 6–8. Meals can also be ordered. ❾

Snowcrest Manor Above the *Log Huts* ☎01902/253351, Ⓔsnowcrestmanor@hotmail.com. Aimed at business-class tourists, with luxury rooms from $50 to $75, central heating and a large terrace overlooking the valley. ❽–❾

Sunshine Off Old Manali Rd ☎01902/252320. Old double-storey wooden building with period furniture, fireplaces, and magnificent views from spacious balconies. Meals served on request in the dining room, large garden full of flowers and fixed price all year. Recommended. ❸

Model Town

A number of carbon-copy hotels are clustered in the grid of narrow streets immediately behind the Mall, in a quarter known as **Model Town**. Though bland, boxed-in and often dirty, these low- to mid-range places make good bases from which to hunt for other rooms once you've found your feet, and have flushing toilets and TV as standard. Recommended accommodation includes: *Diamond* (☎01902/253058; ❺), *Lhasa* (☎01902/252134; ❸), *Mount View* (☎01902/252465; ❸–❹), with rooftop terrace and views, and *Yamuna* (☎01902/252506; ❹) on Gompa Road. All offer discounts of up to 75 percent off-season.

Aleo

Situated a couple of kilometres south of Manali on the left bank of the Beas, the developing strip of hotels in **Aleo**, primarily aimed at Indian honeymooners, include the *Holiday Inn* (☎01902/253312; ❾), *Honeymoon Inn* (☎01902/253234; ❻–❽), *Imperial Palace* (☎01902/253330; ❻–❽), *Evergreen* (☎01902/253038; ❺–❼) and *Sunpark* (☎01902/253959; ❺–❻).

The Town

Manali's main street, **the Mall**, quite unlike its namesake in Shimla, is a noisy scene of constant activity, fronted by the bus stand, several shopping markets, a line of hotels and restaurants, and travel agents. It's a great place to watch the world go by – locals in traditional caps, Tibetan women in immaculate rainbow-striped pinafores, Nepali porters, Buddhist monks, the odd party of Zanskaris swathed in fusty woollen *gonchas*, souvenir-hunting Indian tourists and a curious mix of Westerners.

Manali's days as an authentic *pahari* bazaar ended when the mule trains were superseded by Tata trucks, but it's still great for souvenir **shopping**. Woollen goods are the town's real forte, particularly the brilliantly patterned **shawls** for which Kullu Valley is famous. Genuine pure-wool handloom shawls with embroidered borders start at around Rs500, but those made from finest pashmina cost several thousand rupees. Shop around and check out the fixed-price factory shops to get an idea of what's available: the government-sponsored

Tours and adventure sports around Manali

Weather and road conditions permitting, HPTDC (ⓣ01902/252116), two doors down from the tourist office, run daily bus **tours** to the **Rohtang Pass** (10am–6pm; Rs200) and day-trips to **Manikaran** in the Parvati Valley (9am–7pm; Rs225). Tickets can be bought in advance from their transport counter.

Considering the fierce white water that thrashes down the Kullu Valley during spring melt, Manali's **rafting** scene is surprisingly low-key. Raft trips down the River Beas are offered between the end of May and early July, when water levels are highest, beginning at Bhuntur (just south of Kullu) and ending 16km downstream at the mouth of the Larji gorge. The price should include meals, lifejackets, helmets, and return travel; check exactly what you're paying for, as some unscrupulous operators expect you to make your own way back after the trip.

The **heli-skiing** around Manali is great, but costs $6500 a week. Regular **skiing** in the Solang Valley is popular from January to April – but the slope isn't much bigger than a cricket pitch. The valley was also one of the biggest **paragliding** centres in India, though in 2004 paragliding was banned pending new safety and insurance regulations. One of the best ways to explore Kullu is by **mountain biking**, which is possible from mid-June to mid-October. The best local guide is Raju Sharma (ⓣm98160/56934, ⓦwww.magicmountainadventures.com), who can arrange bike hire (Rs300 per day for a European bike, Rs500 with Raju as guide), and suggest routes around Manali as well as expeditions up to Leh. Popular routes include the descent from Rohtang, the forest trail to the Bijli Mahadev Temple and the back road to Nagar.

If you're planning a trekking or rafting trip, shop around to compare prices and packages; many agencies are fly-by-night operators who make their money from mark-ups on long-distance bus tickets to Delhi, Chandigarh and Leh. Long-established, **reputable agents** include the very experienced Rup Negi at Himalayan Adventurers (ⓣ01902/253050), opposite the tourist office, and Himanshu Sharma at Himalayan Journeys (ⓣ01902/252365, ⓔhimalayajourneysindia.com), next to *Café Amigos*. They can organize rafting, ski packages at Solang, and heli-skiing in the thick of winter. Other recommended agents include Chandertal Treks & Tours (ⓣ01902/252665) and Shambhala West Himalayan Exploration (ⓣ01902/252690) both at the New Shopping Centre, and Nirvana Travels (ⓣ01902/253222, ⓦwww.nirvanamanali.com) on Old Manali Road before the bridge. Most agents also operate **Jeep safaris** to remote regions such as Spiti.

Bhutico on the Mall opposite the tourist office, the Bodh Shawl factory shop just off the Mall south of the bus stand and The Great Hadimba Shop & Factory next to the Manu Temple in Old Manali are recommended; the NSC (New Shopping Centre) market near the bus stand also has a good selection.

Elsewhere around the bazaar, innumerable stalls are stacked with handwoven goods and pillbox Kullu **topis**. Those with gaudy multicoloured up-turned flaps and gold piping are indigenous to the valley, but you can also pick up the plain-green velvet-fronted variety favoured by Kinnauris. Manali's other speciality is **Tibetan curios** such as prayer wheels, amulets, *dorjees* (thunderbolts), masks, musical instruments, jewellery and **thangkas**. Few of the items hawked as antiques are genuine, but it takes an expert eye to spot a fake. The same applies to silver **jewellery** inlaid with turquoise and coral, which can nonetheless be attractive and relatively inexpensive.

The Hadimba temple

Resting on a wide stone platform fifteen minutes' walk northwest of the bazaar, the **Hadimba temple** is Manali's oldest shrine and the seat of Hadimba (or

"Hirma Devi"), wife of Bhima. Considered to be an incarnation of Kali, Hadimba is worshipped in times of adversity, and also plays a key role in the Dussehra festival (see p.524). Hadimba is supposed to have given the kingdom of Kullu to the forefathers of the rajas of Kullu, and in veneration and affection the family to this day refer to her as "grandmother". The massive triple-tiered wooden pagoda crowned by crimson pennants and a brass ball and trident (Shiva's *trishul*), dates from 1553, and is a replica of earlier ones that burned down in successive forest fires. The facade writhes with wonderful woodcarvings of elephants, crocodiles and folk deities. Entered by a door surmounted by wild ibex horns, the gloomy **shrine** is dominated by several large boulders, one of which shelters the stone on which goats and buffalo are sacrificed during important rituals. The hollow in its middle, believed to be Vishnu's footprint, channels the blood to Hadimba's mouth.

Soft-drinks stands, curio stalls and yak rides cater for visitors while the presiding deity looks on. The nearby **Kullu Cultural Museum** (Rs10) displays detailed models of the valley's temples.

Old Manali

Old Manali, the village from which the modern town takes its name, lies 2km north of the Mall, on the far side of the Manalsu *nala*. Built in the old *pahari* style, most of the houses of Old Manali have heavy stone roofs and wooden balconies hung with bushels of drying herbs and tobacco. Unlike its crowded, concrete offspring, the settlement retains an unhurried and traditional feel – out of season. In summer, travellers on throaty Enfields roar through its lanes, guesthouses blare trance music and the cafés are thick with *chillum* smoke. In the wake of the tourists come the Kashmiris, Rajasthani tailors and other opportunists, eager to make good business before returning to Goa in the autumn.

To get there, head north up Old Manali Road, bear right at the fork in the road, and keep going through the pine woods until you reach the iron bridge across the river. A bit of leg work will bring you to the village proper, clustered on top of a steeply shelving ledge of level ground above the *nala*. It is also known as **Manaligarh** after its ancient citadel – a ruined fort surrounded by a patchwork of maize terraces and deep-green orchards. At the centre of the village is an unusual, brash new temple dedicated to **Manu**, who laid the foundations of Hindu law that continues to today, as well as *varna* or "colour" – the basis of the caste system. Inscribed stones dating from the Middle Ages embedded into the concrete paving reveal the site's antiquity.

The gompas

Manali harbours the highest concentration of **Tibetan refugees** in the Kullu Valley, hence the prayer flags fluttering over the approach roads into town, and the presence, on its southern edge, of two shiny new **gompas**.

Capped with polished golden finials, the distinctive yellow corrugated-iron pagoda roof of the **Gadhan Thekchhokling gompa** is an exotic splash of colour amid the ramshackle huts of the Tibetan quarter. Built in 1969, the monastery is maintained by donations from the local community and through the sale of **carpets** handwoven in the temple workshop. When they are not looking after the **shop**, the young *lamas* huddle in the courtyard to play *cholo* – a Tibetan dice game involving much shouting and slamming of wooden *tsampa* bowls on leather pads. Beside the main entrance, a roll of honour recounts the names of Tibetans killed during the violent political demonstrations that wracked China in the late 1980s.

The smaller and more modern of the two *gompas* stands nearer the bazaar, in a garden that in late summer blazes with sunflowers. Its main shrine, lit by dozens

Treks around Manali and the Kullu Valley

The Kullu Valley's spectacular alpine scenery makes it perfect for **trekking**. Trails are long and steep, but more than repay the effort with superb views, varied flora and the chance to visit remote hill stations. Within striking distance of several major trailheads, **Manali** is the most popular place to begin and end treks. While **package deals** offered by the town's many agencies can save time and energy, it is relatively easy to organize your own trip with maps and advice from the tourist office and the Mountaineering Institute at the bottom end of town. Porters and horsemen can be sought out in the square behind the main street. Always take a reliable **guide**, especially on less-frequented routes, as you cannot rely solely on **maps**. Some trekkers have reported difficulties when descending from the Bara Bangal Pass as maps don't do the terrain justice.

The optimum trekking **season** is right after the monsoons (mid-Sept to late Oct), when skies are clear and pass-crossings easier. From June to August, you run the risk of sudden, potentially fatal snow, or view-obscuring cloud and rain.

Manali to Beas Kund

The relatively easy trek to Beas Kund, a glacial lake at the head of Solang *nala*, is the region's most popular short hike. Encircled by 5000-metre-plus peaks, the well-used campground beside the lake, accessible in two days from Manali, makes a good base for side-trips up to the surrounding ridges and passes.

From **Palchan**, a village 30min north of Manali by bus, follow the Jeep track up the valley to **Solang**, site of a small ski station, rest house, and the Mountaineering Institute's log huts. The next two hours take you through pine forests and grassy meadows to the campground at **Dhundi** (2743m). A more strenuous walk of 5–6hr the next day leads to **Beas Kund**. The hike up to the **Tentu La** Pass (4996m) and back from here can be done in a day, as can the descent to Manali via Solang.

Manali to Lahaul, via the Hampta Pass

The three-day trek from the Kullu Valley over the Hampta Pass to Lahaul, the old caravan route to Spiti, is a classic. Rising to 4330m, it is high by Kullu standards; do not undertake it without allowing good time to acclimatize. **Day 1**, from the trailhead at **Prini** (near Manali) through Hampta village to the campground above **Sethen**, is an easy hike of 4–5hr up the verdant, forested sides of the valley. **Day 2**, another 5hr, brings you to **Chikha**, a high Gaddi pasture below the pass; stay put for a day or so if you're feeling the effects of altitude. The ascent (700m) on **Day 3** to the **Hampta Pass** (4330m) is gruelling, but the views from the top – of Indrasan and Deo Tibba to the south, and the moonscape of Lahaul to the north – are sublime recompense. It takes 6–7hr of relentless rock-hopping and stream-crossing to reach **Chhatru**, on the floor of the Chandra Valley. From here, you can turn east towards Koksar and the **Rohtang Pass**, or west past the world's largest glacier, **Bara Shigri**, to **Batal**, the trailhead for the Chandratal–Baralacha trek (see p.543).

of bare electric bulbs and filled with fragrant Tibetan incense, houses a colossal gold-faced Buddha, best viewed from the small room on the first floor.

Eating and drinking

Manali's wide range of **restaurants** reflects the town's melting-pot credentials: Tibetan *thukpa* joints stand cheek-by-jowl with South Indian coffee houses, Gujarati thali bars, and Nepalese-run German pastry shops. Whatever their ostensible speciality, though, most offer mixed menus that include Chinese and Western dishes alongside standard north Indian favourites. Virtually every café in Manali serves serious "**tourist breakfasts**"

Nagar to Malana via the Chandrakani Pass and onwards

The trek to Jari in the Parvati Valley from Nagar, 21km south of Manali, is quintessential Kullu Valley trekking with superb scenery and fascinating villages. The round trip can be completed in three days, but you may be tempted to linger in **Malana** and explore the surrounding countryside. A **guide** is essential for several reasons: the first stage of the trek involves crossing a maze of grazing trails; Malana is culturally sensitive and requires some familiarity with local customs; and several people have **disappeared** in the Parvati Valley over the last few years in suspicious circumstances (see p.527). The descent to the Parvati Valley is too steep for pack ponies, but porters are available in Nagar through the guesthouses, including Himalayan Mountain Treks at *Poonam Mountain Lodge*.

The trail leads through the village of Rumsu and then winds through wonderful old-growth forests to a pasture just above the tree line which makes ideal camping ground. From here, a climb of 4km takes you to the **Chandrakani Pass** (3660m), which has fine views west over the top of the Kullu Valley to the peaks surrounding Solang *nala*, and north to the Ghalpo mountains of Lahaul. Some prefer to reach the base of the pass on the first day and then camp below the final ascent.

The inhabitants of **MALANA**, a steep 7km descent from the pass, are known for their frostiness and staunch traditions. Plans by regional developers to extend a paved road here are vehemently opposed by the insular locals. Although notions of **caste pollution** are not as strictly adhered to as they once were, you should observe a few basic "**rules**" in Malana: approach the village quietly and respectfully; stick to paths at all times; keep away from the temple; and above all, don't touch anybody or anything, especially children or houses. If you do commit a cultural blunder, you'll be expected to make amends: usually in the form of a cash payment for a sacrificial offering of a young sheep or goat to the village deity, **Jamlu**, one of the most powerful Kullu Valley gods. His **temple**, open to high-caste Hindus only, is decorated with lively folk carvings, among them images of soldiers – the villagers claim to be the area's sole remaining descendants of Alexander the Great's army. Popular **places to stay** include the *Renuka Guesthouse* (❶), which has hot water, and the *Himalaya Guesthouse* (❶), run by the former village headman. The owner of *Santu Ram's* (❶) is an authority on local trails. All the guesthouses offer simple meals. The official camping ground lies 100m beyond the village spring.

The **final stage** of the trek takes you down the sheer limestone sides of Malana *nala* to the floor of the Parvati Valley – a precipitous 12km drop that is partially covered by a new switchback road. From the hamlet of **Rashol**, you have a choice of three onward routes: either head east up the right bank of the river to **Manikaran** (see p.528); follow the trail southwest to the sacred **Bijli Mahadev Mandir**; or climb the remaining 3km up to the road at **Jari**, from where regular buses leave for Bhuntur, Kullu and Manali.

of porridge, pancakes, toast and jam. The laid-back Brit-run *Alchemy Bar* (Ⓣ01902/236110; 6km away in Jagatsukh, Rs50 by auto-rickshaw), is a home from home, serving health-conscious Western food along with creature comforts such as sofas, videos, world music and a pool table. It's good for lazy afternoons and late-night dancing. For rock-bottom budget food, head for one of the *dhabas* opposite the bus stand.

Stock up on energy-rich **trekking food** at the local produce stores and bakeries in the bazaar. The state-sponsored co-op, near the temple on the Mall, sells sacks of nuts, dried fruit and pots of pure honey at fixed prices. Chai and omelette-wallahs appear on the Mall before dawn if you need to steel yourself for a long and bumpy bus journey.

The Mall and around

Café Amigos The Mall. Wooden tables, colourful pottery, chilled out music and a fantastic range of cakes and brownies, as well as proper food.

Chopsticks The Mall. Very popular Tibetan-run restaurant with a pleasant atmosphere and varied menu. Try the filter coffee and a great muesli, fruit and curd.

Forest Green Café Off Log Hut Rd. Small local restaurant, serving the best *momos* in Manali.

Il Forno Hadimba Rd. A traditional building that has been successfully converted into an Italian-run restaurant serving excellent pizzas, pasta, salads and tiramisu. Good views.

Johnson's Café Part of *Johnson Lodge*. A great café, with garden seating and an inviting menu including beer, fresh trout and crème caramel. It's pricier than some places, but worth it.

Mayur Mission Rd, just off the Mall. Exciting and extensive Indian menu at very reasonable prices. Candles, serviettes and classical Indian music. Recommended.

Mount View The Mall. Chinese, Japanese, and authentic Tibetan food in Chinese-style restaurant decorated with paper lanterns.

Peter's Café Off Old Manali Rd, near the Mall and behind *Café Amigos*. A legendary throwback to the days of hippie yore, Peter and his excellent

Moving on from Manali

Manali is well connected by **bus** to other Himachali towns and major cities on the plains. HPSRTC run luxury, deluxe and ordinary buses, all of which can be booked at the bus stand. During the summer, demand invariably outstrips supply, particularly for the faster services, so book as far in advance as possible. The numerous travel agents dotted around town also sell tickets for **private** "deluxe" services to Delhi, Shimla and Dharamsala. Consider breaking your journey in Mandi (for Rewalsar) or using the **Kangra valley railway** to reach Dharamsala or Pathankot from where you can pick up trains for Amritsar, Delhi and Rajasthan. The **Rohtang Pass** at the head of the Kullu Valley is only open from June to October when buses travel to Keylong, capital of Lahaul. It can be difficult to book onward transport from Keylong to Leh as buses nearly always arrive full, so try to reserve a seat in advance. Buses also cross the Rohtang La to Kaza, capital of Spiti, from where you can continue to Shimla, although **permits** are required to travel beyond Tabo. Harrisons Travels (Ⓣ01902/253519), Monal Himalayan Travels (Ⓣ01902/254215), Swagtam (Ⓣ01902/253990) and Valleycon (Ⓣ01902/253776), at the bus stand and at *Mayur* restaurant, all sell tickets.

Transport to Leh

If you can afford to split the Rs12,000 fare, mini-vans and Maruti Gypsy taxis are the most comfortable way to get to **Ladakh** from Manali – you might get a cheaper deal from a returning vehicle. However, backpackers usually travel the 485km to Leh by bus – an arduous but unforgettable two-day trip (28hr), involving a night halt under canvas en route. HPTDC's daily "luxury" bus, bookable through the tourist office, costs around Rs1200, which includes accommodation at the tent colony near Sarchu. The journey can take three days, with two nights on the road. Otherwise, choice is limited to the beaten-up buses operated by HPSRTC and their J&K equivalents, which despite their discomfort are faster.

Officially, the **Manali–Leh Highway** (see p.550) is open from mid-June until September 15, after which the state services are suspended and emergency services aren't available for civilian traffic. Some of the private companies, however, continue to operate until late September. 4WD taxis continue to ply the route well into October, but again you risk getting stuck and having to spend a few extra freezing cold nights on the road. Whenever and however you travel, avoid the bumpy back seat of the bus and take food and lots of water (at least 2–3 litres) to reduce the risk of dehydration and **altitude sickness**.

See the "Travel details" at the end of this chapter for more information on journey frequencies and durations.

breakfasts are a Manali legend. The café makes for a good, centrally located hangout if you don't mind the whiff of dope.

Old Manali

Mahalsu Café Popular eatery overlooking the river, with the usual mixed menu but the benefit of satellite radio, English-language magazines and Internet access.
Manu Café A local house with a small upstairs café, which despite the usual travellers' menu is best for local food.
Moondance Popular garden café and meeting place above the river with a varied menu that includes Mexican and Italian dishes.
Mountain Café Set away from most of the guesthouses, with extensive views. Simple yet varied menu; open 24hr in season or when there's sufficient demand.
Pizza Olive Great pizzas and delicious snacks like bruschetta, without the walk to *Il Forno*.
River Music Café Hang-out place by the bridge with tables on the terrace or floor-cushion seating under shelter. Usual menu and a good sound system.
Shiva Café Sociable, lazy balcony, an open fire most evenings, and Chinese, Indian and pasta dishes make this popular among budget travellers.
Tibet Kitchen Near the Club House. A comfortable and popular restaurant with a mixed menu serving great Tibetan food as well as the odd Japanese dish.

Vashisht

Famous for its sweeping valley views and sulphurous hot-water springs, the ever-expanding village of **VASHISHT**, 3km north of Manali, is an amorphous jumble of traditional timber houses and modern concrete cubes, divided by paved courtyards and narrow muddy lanes. It is the epicentre of the local budget travellers' scene, with a good choice of guesthouses and cafés; the tranquil and traditional atmosphere is only interrupted by the occasional rave that takes place in the woods, or if the weather is poor, in one or two obliging hotels.

You can get to Vashisht from Manali by road, or along the footpath from the main highway that passes the **HPTDC hot baths complex** – which has been closed for several years now due to a dispute between the villagers and the Himachal government. In the meantime, the only place for a **hot soak** is in the bathing pools of Vashisht's ancient temple (free), which is far more atmospheric anyway. Divided into separate sections for men and women, they attract a decidedly mixed crowd of Hindu pilgrims, Western hippies, semi-naked *sadhus*, and gangs of local kids.

Vashisht boasts two old stone **temples**, opposite each other above the main square and dedicated to the local patron saint Vashishta (guru of Raghunathji). The smaller of the two opens onto a partially covered courtyard, and is adorned with elaborate woodcarvings. Those lining the interior of the shrine, blackened by years of oil-lamp and *dhoop* smoke, are worth checking out.

If you're up for more than just leaning back with a *chillum*, the **Himalayan Extreme Centre** (Ⓦ www.himalayan-extreme-center.com), on the road into the village, organizes days out snowboarding, kite-surfing and rock-climbing.

Accommodation

Vashisht is packed with budget **guesthouses**, many of them old wooden buildings with broad verandas and uninterrupted vistas up the valley. If you don't mind primitive plumbing, grungy beds and dope smoke, the only time you'll not be spoilt for choice is during high season (May–June & Sept–Oct), when even floor-space can be at a premium. On the outskirts, a couple of larger **hotels** offer good-value, comfortable rooms. The places below are marked on the Manali & Vashisht map on p.533.

Amrit The uppermost hotel, tucked away behind the temple ⓣ01902/254209. Turquoise wooden house with basic facilities, including bucket hot water (Rs5). Grubby but atmospheric with rickety balconies affording fine views. ❶
Arohi Just up from the *Bhrigu* ⓣ01902/254421. Immaculate rooms with cable TV, intercom and balconies overlooking the river. The ex-army owner speaks excellent English, and gives up to 50 percent discounts off-season. ❺
Bhrigu Hotel On the main road into the village ⓣ01902/253414. Large hotel whose west-facing rooms all have attached bathrooms and superb views from their spacious balconies. ❸
Bodh 50m past the village square ⓣ01902/254165. Superb views from the roof terrace. Shared bathrooms. ❶
Dharma Five minutes' walk up the lane behind the temples ⓣ01902/252354. The rooms have fantastic views, as does the marble terrace with a swing and loungers. There's even a tiny swimming pool, filled by the hot springs. A new wing was under construction in autumn 2004. ❸
Godfather Palace Ashram 50m before the village square, signed off the road ⓣ01902/254069. Large en-suite rooms with hot showers, cannabis growing in the garden and a basement for raves. ❷
Kalptaru Overlooking the temple tanks ⓣ01902/253443. You can't get any closer to the baths – with reasonable rooms, all en-suite, with hot bucket water. Small garden and veranda from which to watch the world go by. ❶
Sonam Just before the square ⓣ01902/251783. Small and noisy but packed with character. The painter owner shows arthouse movies in the evenings. An old favourite. ❶
Surabhi On the main road, underneath the *World Peace Café* ⓣ01902/252796. Airy, large, clean rooms, all with views of Kullu. The cheaper ground-floor rooms are colder and darker. ❸–❺

Eating

A backpackers' paradise, Vashisht has numerous **cafés** serving the typical fried rice, noodles, omelettes, pancakes and lassis. In addition, bakeries provide wholemeal bread, apple pies and a variety of sticky things. Most of the cafés are hang-out places, and several have open-air terraces with views, but there is little to choose between them.

Freedom Café On the main road past *Bhrigu Hotel*. Floor seating and a grassy deck with good views; food is Mexican, Tibetan and Italian.
Phuntsok Café On the river banks, on the outskirts of the village. Outdoor café serving delicious and wholesome home-cooked Tibetan food. One of Vashisht's best.
Rainbow Café Near *Kalptaru* hotel. Traveller-friendly offerings such as pancakes, pasta and spring rolls, with terrace views of the temple tanks.

Lahaul and Spiti

Few places on earth can mark so dramatic a change in landscape as the **Rohtang Pass**. To one side, the lush green head of the Kullu Valley; to the other, an awesome vista of bare, chocolate-coloured mountains, hanging glaciers and snowfields that shine in the dazzlingly crisp light. The district of **Lahaul and Spiti**, Himachal's largest, is named after its two subdivisions, which are, in spite of their numerous geographical and cultural similarities, distinct and separate regions.

Lahaul

Lahaul, sometimes referred to as the Chandra-Bhaga Valley, is the region that divides the Great Himalayas and Pir Panjal ranges. Its principal river, the

Chandra, rises deep in the barren wastes below the **Baralacha Pass**, a major landmark on the Manali–Leh road, and flows south towards its confluence with the River Bhaga near Tandi. Here, the two rivers become the Chenab, and crash north out of Himachal to Kishtwar in Kashmir. Lahaul's **climate** is very similar to that of Ladakh and Zanskar, which border it to the north. The valley

Trekking in Lahaul and Spiti

Although the old trade routes to Ladakh and Tibet are now sealed with tarmac, most of this remote and spectacular region is still only accessible on foot. Its trails, though well frequented in high season, are long, hard and high, so you must be self-sufficient and have a guide. Packhorses and provisions are most readily available in **Manali**; or in **Keylong** and **Darcha** (Lahaul) and **Kaza** (Spiti) if you can afford to wait a few days. A good rope for river crossings will be useful on many of the routes, particularly in summer when the water levels are at their highest.

The **best time** to trek is July to early September, when brilliant blue skies make this an ideal alternative to the monsoon-prone Kullu Valley. By late September, the risk of snowfall deters many visitors from the longer expeditions. Whenever you leave, allow enough time to acclimatize to the **altitude** before attempting any big passes: AMS (Acute Mountain Sickness) claims victims here every season (see Basics, p.47).

Lahaul: Darcha to Padum via the Shingo La pass

The most popular trek is from **Darcha** over the **Shingo La** pass (5000m) to **Padum** in Zanskar. The trail passes through **Kargyak**, the highest village in Zanskar, and follows the Kargyak valley down to its confluence with the Tsarap at **Purne**. There is a small café, shop, and camping ground here and it's a good base for the side trip to **Phuktal gompa**, one of the most spectacular sights in Zanskar. During the high season (July & Aug), a string of chai stall-tent camps spring up at intervals along the well-worn trail through the Tsarap valley to Padum, meaning that you can manage without a guide or ponies from here on. Do not bank on finding food and shelter here at the start or end of the season.

Lahaul: Batal to Baralacha Pass

Lahaul's other popular trekking route follows the River Chandra north to its source at the **Baralacha Pass** (4830m), and makes a good extension to the Hampta Pass hike described on p.538. Alternatively, catch a Kaza bus from Manali to the trailhead at **Batal** (3960m) below the **Kunzum La** (4551m). The beautiful milky-blue **Chandratal** ("Moon") **Lake** is a relentless ascent of 7hr from Batal, with stunning views south across the world's longest glacier, **Bara Shigri**, and the forbidding north face of the **White Sail** massif (6451m). The next campground is at **Tokping Yongma** torrent. **Tokpo Yongma**, several hours further up, is the second of the two big side torrents and is much easier to ford early in the morning; from here it is a steady climb up to the **Baralacha Pass**. You can then continue to Zanskar via the Phirtse La, or pick up transport (prearranged if possible) down to Keylong and Manali or onwards to Leh. Alternatively, if you're biking down from Leh and are confident off-road, this is a fantastic detour.

Spiti: Kaza via the Pin Valley to Manikaran or Wangtu

One of the best treks in **Spiti** is up the **Pin Valley**. The track is under threat by road builders (it's expected to be accessible for motor vehicles by 2006), so take advantage of it while you can. Starting 24km southeast of Kaza, a (motorable) dirt trail heads south along the right bank of the River Pin past a string of traditional settlements and monasteries to **Mudh**, where it forks into two walking paths; the northern path over the Pin-Parvati Pass (5400m) to **Manikaran** in the Parvati Valley (see p.528), and the southern one to Wangtu in **Kinnaur** via the Bhaba Pass (4865m).

receives precious little rain, and during the summer the sun is very strong and the nights cool. Between late October and late March, heavy snow closes the passes, and seals off the region. Even so, its inhabitants, a mixture of Buddhists and Hindus, enjoy one of the highest per capita incomes in the subcontinent. Using glacial water channelled through ancient irrigation ducts, Lahauli farmers manage to coax a bumper crop of **seed potatoes** from their painstakingly fashioned terraces. The region is also the sole supplier of **hops** to India's breweries, and harvests prodigious quantities of wild herbs, used to make perfume and medicine. Much of the profit generated by these cash crops is spent on lavish jewellery, especially seed-pearl necklaces and coral and turquoise-inlaid silver plaques, worn by the women over ankle-length burgundy or fawn woollen dresses. Lahaul's traditional costume and Buddhism are a legacy of the Tibetan influence that has permeated the region from the east.

State **buses** run from Manali up the Chandra and Bhaga valleys to Keylong and Darcha from whenever the Rohtang Pass is cleared, usually in late June, until it snows up again in late October. You can also travel through Lahaul on private Leh-bound buses if there are free seats.

Keylong

Lahaul's largest settlement and the district headquarters, **KEYLONG**, 114km north of Manali, is a good place to pause on the long road journey to Ladakh. Although of little interest itself, the village lies amid superb scenery, within a day's climb of three Buddhist **gompas**, one visible on the opposite (south) side of the grandiose Bhaga Valley. A couple of **stores** in the busy market sell trekking supplies if you are heading off to Zanskar.

Lahauli Buddhists consider it auspicious to make a clockwise circumambulation – known as the **Rangcha Parikarma** – of the sacred **Rangcha mountain** (4565m), which dominates the confluence of the Bhaga and Chandra rivers. A well-worn trail that makes a long day-hike from Keylong, the route is highly scenic, and takes in the large **Khardung gompa** along the way. Rising over 1000m from its base elevation (3348m), the trail is a hard slog if you haven't acclimatized. Carry plenty of food, water, and warm clothing, and be prepared to turn back if you start to feel dizzy and/or acutely short of breath. A rough motorable road leads to Khardung *gompa* (10km), but closer to Keylong and on the same side of the valley are two quiet and picturesque *gompas* high up the mountainside, **Shasher Gompa** (3km) and **Gungshal Gompa** (5km).

Practicalities

Keylong is connected by regular state **buses** to Manali, and (in summer) by private buses to all points north and south along the main highway. Note that onward **transport to Leh** can be difficult to arrange in high season (July & Aug), as most buses are full by the time they get there. Travellers frequently find themselves having to ride on the roof, or hitch a lift on one of the trucks that stop at the *dhabas* on the roadside above the village – neither legal, nor particularly safe. There are eight buses daily to Manali (6hr; Rs70), the first one leaving at 5.30am and the last at 1.30pm.

Keylong's **hotels** can be found along the main road above the town and strung out along the Mall that runs through the bazaar below the main highway. A steep path leads down to the bazaar from the main road just past where the buses pull in. The *Tashi Deleg* (Ⓣ01900/222450; ❸–❹) on the Mall has a range of clean and comfortable en-suite rooms with hot showers. The *Gyespa*, also on the Mall (Ⓣ01900/222207; ❷–❸), has en-suite rooms with hot showers, a dorm (Rs50), and a small *chorten* in the garden, but isn't as clean; both hotels have inspiring views of Khardung Gompa. Further down the Mall, the *Lamayuru* (☎01900/222202; ❷) has just four rooms – pleasant and clean with hot showers – and the best restaurant in town, while back on the main road 2km towards Darcha, the newly opened HPTDC *Chander Bhaga* (☎01900/222393; ❹, dorms Rs150) is comfortable but bland. The ramshackle batch of **lodges** strung along the bus stand, including the *Mentokling* (☎01900/222488; ❶), are somewhat more attractive on the interior, especially those on the valley side.

The **post office** is on the main road a little way beyond the bus stand. Down on the Mall, Global Info Tech and Cyber Media Services offer slower and more expensive **Internet** access than in Manali. There are no official foreign **currency facilities** here, but *Tashi Deleg* will change money for a poor rate.

Spiti

From its headwaters below the **Kunzum Pass**, the River Spiti drains 130km southeast to within a yak's spit of the border of Chinese-occupied Tibet, where it meets the Sutlej. The valley itself, surrounded by huge peaks and with an average altitude of 4500m, is one of the highest and most remote inhabited places on earth – a desolate, barren tract scattered with tiny mud-and-timber hamlets and lonely lamaseries. Until 1992, Spiti in its entirety lay off-limits to foreign tourists. Now, only its far southeastern corner falls within the **Inner Line** – which leaves upper Spiti, including the district headquarters **Kaza**, freely accessible from the northwest via Lahaul. If you are really keen to complete the loop through the restricted area to or from Kinnaur (see p.496), you will need a **permit** (see p.484). The last main stop before reaching the restricted zone is the famed **Tabo** *gompa*, which harbours some of the oldest and most exquisite Buddhist art in the world.

In summer, once the **Rohtang La** and **Kunzum La** (4550m) are clear of snow, two buses leave Manali for Spiti every morning. It is also possible to hire **Jeeps** from Manali (through HPTDC or any other travel agency) and to trek in from the Kullu Valley or south from the Baralacha La. Soon after crossing the Kunzum La the road passes through the tiny village of **LOSAR**, where there is a police checkpoint and a couple of basic hotels: the *Sam Song* (❶–❷) and the *Serchu* (❶). From here Kaza is a mere 58km further down the Spiti Valley. A great portion of the road from the Rohtang La to Kaza is unsealed and makes for a bumpy, gruelling ride.

Kaza and around

KAZA, the subdivisional headquarters of **Spiti**, lies 76km southeast of the Kunzum Pass, and 201km from Manali. Overlooking the left bank of the River Spiti, it's Spiti's least picturesque town, but it is the region's main market and roadhead, and a good base from which to head off on two- or three-day treks to monasteries and remote villages such as Kibber. Rates for porters and ponymen are comparable to those in Kullu. It is also possible to trek to Dhankar (32km) and on to Tabo (43km). Those planning to continue on to Kinnaur can pick up **Inner Line permits** from the Additional Deputy Commissioner's office in the new town. You will need three passport-sized photos and copies of the relevant pages in your passport, as well as a police stamp, obtainable from the police station down the hill from the DC office towards the river (look for the green roof near the stadium). Government regulations stipulate that travellers must be in a group of four, and be "recommended" by a travel agent (just ask for a permit and expect to pay around Rs100) – how strictly this is followed is down to the whim of the ADC. The only photocopy machine in town is at the Ashok photocopy store in the Old Market; a couple of photo studios are on the same street. The Inner Line starts at Sumdo, beyond Tabo. The road past Sumdo has been wiped out since 2000 by frequent and devastating landslides at Malling (see p.501), so if you have your own vehicle check to see whether you can get through. The alternative route via Kafni and Mudh wil not be open until 2010.

Most **places to stay** overlook the (usually dry) creek that divides the new and old quarters. On the main road, *Sakya's Abode* (Ⓣ01906/222254; ❸–❹) is a good-looking place offering a wide range of rooms and a cheap dorm (Rs80). Nearby, in the same compound as the Sakya Monastery, the *Banjara Khunphen Retreat* (Ⓣ01906/222236; ❻), has twelve comfortable double rooms and a good restaurant. Still on the new side, and a few steps down the creek, *Phuntsok Palbar* (Ⓣ01906/222360; ❶) and the adjacent *Khangre* (❶) are the best value in town, with spotless rooms and hot bucket showers; *Phuntsok Palbar* also has a warm sitting room, sunny yard and free luggage storage. Old Kaza, connected by a footpath across the riverbed, has a few more budget choices, including the *Zangchuk Guest House* (Ⓣ01906/222510; ❶), with basic facilities but excellent views from its terrace and a quiet location on the creek, the spotless *Kelsang* (Ⓣ01906/222388; ❶) next door and, on the lane leading up to the main road, the *Snow Lion* (Ⓣ01906/222525; ❷), with large, pleasant rooms. Apart from the hotel **restaurants** (best of which are the *Banjara Khunphen Retreat* and *Sakya's Abode*), and a couple of tourist cafés such as *Little Italy* next to the *Snow Lion* and *Echi Wan* in the Old Market, Kaza's food options are limited to cheap Indian and Chinese *dhabas*.

Two daily **buses** depart for Tabo (2hr; Rs35) at 9.30am and 2pm, and a lone bus leaves for Mudh in the Pin Valley at around 11am (2hr 30min; Rs40), returning at 2pm. Double check the bus times for Pin, Kibber and Tabo – they change frequently. Hiring a **Jeep** in Spiti – where the roads are dangerous and public transport unreliable – is a good idea. You can pick them up near the bus stand; expect to pay Rs700 return for the Pin Valley, Rs900 for Tabo or Rs4500 for Manali.

Ki Gompa

Set against a backdrop of snow-flecked mountains and clinging to the steep sides of a windswept conical hillock, **Ki Gompa** is a picture-book example of Tibetan architecture and one of Himachal's most exotic spectacles. Founded in the sixteenth century, Ki is the largest **monastery** in the Spiti Valley, supporting a thriving community of lamas whose Rinpoche, Lo Chien Tulkhu from Shalkar near Sumdo, is said to be the current incarnation of the "Great Translator" Rinchen Zangpo. His glass-fronted quarters crown the top of the complex, reached via stone steps that wind between the lamas' houses below. A labyrinth of dark passages and wooden staircases connect the prayer and assembly halls, home to collections of old *thangkas*, weapons, musical instruments, manuscripts, and devotional images (no photography). Many of the rooms have seen extensive renovation since an earthquake struck in 1975; a new prayer hall, dedicated by the Dalai Lama, was also added in 2000. During the new moon towards late June or early July, Ki plays host to a large **festival** celebrating the "burning of the demon" when *chaam* dances are followed by a procession that winds its way down to the ritual ground below the monastery where a large butter sculpture is set on fire.

Ki village lies 12km northwest of Kaza on the road to Kibber, and Ki Gompa is a steep 1km walk up from the town. The most scenic approach is to get off the 7am bus from Kaza to Kibber at Ki village, and walk the last section to appreciate the full effect of the *gompa's* dramatic southern aspect. Alternatively, the 9am bus from Kibber detours to the monastery on its way down to Kaza. **Accommodation** in Ki is scant: you could stay at the monks' quarters for Rs100 (including food), or try the welcoming *Tashi Khangsar Guesthouse* (❶), located after the first bend in the road and marked with a small green sign.

Kibber

KIBBER (4205m) is reputedly the highest settlement in the world with a motorable road and electricity. Jeep tracks, satellite dishes and the odd tin-roofed government building aside, its smattering of a hundred or so old Spitian houses is truly picturesque. Surrounded in summer by lush green barley fields, Kibber also stands at the head of a trail that picks its way north across the mountains, via the high **Parang La** pass (5578m) to Ladakh. Before the construction of roads into the Spiti Valley, locals used to lead ponies and yaks this way to trade in Leh bazaar. Some Manali-based trekking companies offer a seventeen-day trek from here to the lake of **Tso Moriri** in Ladakh.

The 7am **bus** (1hr; Rs15) from Kaza to Kibber is often delayed, and only waits until 9am before returning to town. Alternatively you could hire a **Jeep**, hitch with a tour group, or forego transport altogether and walk the 16km of trails (although the outbound trip is nearly all uphill). Kibber's fabulous location makes for a great overnight, and it's easy to end up staying longer than you planned in one of the congenial **guesthouses**. Opposite the school at the start of the village the adjoining *Norling* (Ⓣ01906/226242; ❶) and *Rainbow* (Ⓣ01906/226234; ❶) have similar rooms; the *Norling* has a better restaurant. Further into the village itself, the *Sargong* (Ⓣ01906/226222; ❶) has scruffy charm and is usually full.

Dhankar and the Pin Valley

Midway between Kaza and Tabo, near the meeting of the Pin and Spiti rivers, a rough road veers off to the east for 8.5km to the village of **DHANKAR** (3890m). The **Dhankar Gompa** on the uppermost peak behind the village is famed for its brilliant murals, probably painted in the seventeenth century, depicting the life of the Buddha. Although some of the work has been vandalized, the scenes depicting the Buddha's birth, re-birth and life in Kapilavastu and his rejection of worldly ways are spectacular. The *gompa* also affords superb views down to the confluence of the main River Spiti and the Pin tributary. Dhankar is not on a bus route so you will have to arrange your own transport (a taxi from **Sichaling** on the main road is Rs150) or walk – the shortcut starts from the storm shelter by the main road under the *gompa* 3km before Sichaling. Visitors are welcome to **stay** at the monastery for a donation but bring your own sheets – Dhankar's bed bugs are merciless.

The Pin Valley

Thirty minutes east of Kaza a bridge at Attargu crosses the Spiti and begins a sixteen-kilometre run up the **Pin Valley** to **GULLING**, above which stands the important Nyingma *gompa* of Gungri, believed to date back to the eighth or ninth centuries. There's a simple hotel here, the *Himalaya* (❶), a couple of cafés serving *thukpa* and *momos*, and a camping ground. Tiny **Mikim** lies 3km beyond Gulling at the confluence of the Pin and Parahio rivers; the slightly

△ Mudh

larger settlement of **SAGNAM** across the river has a few basic places to stay including a *PWD Resthouse*, the *Norzang Guesthouse* (❶) and the *Snowland Guesthouse* (❶), next to the bus stop.

Beyond Sagnam the road deteriorates rapidly, but vehicles can push ahead another 14km to **MUDH**, an enchanting hamlet with a tiny nunnery that peers over a breathtaking valley, the end of which is flanked by the pyramid-shaped Tordang Mountain. Several local families rent out **rooms** to the increasing number of trekkers passing through, though conditions remain pretty rough. The *Dawa* (❶) is the nicest, and offers a huge dorm (Rs50); food is served in the main house. Also recommended is the friendly *Pin Parvati Guest House* (❶) – if you don't mind the livestock out front. One crowded and oft-delayed **bus** departs Kaza for Mudh daily at 7am, returning at 9am. A motorable road beyond Mudh is being plowed through the virgin landscape and by 2010 should cross the Bhaba Pass down to Wangtu, thus diverting the journey from Kaza to Rekong Peo away from the landslide at Malling, and shortening it by six hours.

Tabo

One of the main reasons to brave the rough roads of Spiti is to get to **Tabo Gompa**, 43km east of Kaza. The mud and timber boxes that nestle on the steep north bank of the Spiti may look drab, but the multi-hued murals and stucco sculpture they contain are some of the world's richest and most important ancient Buddhist art treasures – the link between the cave paintings of Ajanta and the more exuberant Tantric art that flourished in Tibet five centuries or so later. According to an inscription in its main assembly hall, the monastery was established in 996 AD, when **Rinchen Zangpo** was disseminating *dharma* across the northwestern Himalayas. In addition to the 158 Sanskrit Buddhist texts he personally transcribed, the "Great Translator" brought with him a retinue of Kashmiri artisans to decorate the temples. The only surviving examples of their exceptional work are here at Tabo, at Alchi in Ladakh, and Toling and Tsaparang *gompas* in Chinese-occupied western Tibet.

Enclosed within a mud-brick wall, Tabo's **Chogskhar**, or "sacred enclave", contains eight temples and 24 *chortens* (stupas). The largest and oldest structure in the group, the **Sug La-khang**, stands opposite the main entrance. Erected at the end of the tenth century, the "Hall of the Enlightened Gods" was conceived in the form of a three-dimensional *mandala*, whose structure and elaborately decorated interior functions as a mystical model of the universe complete with deities. There are three distinct bands of detail – the lower level paintings depict episodes in the life of the Buddha and his previous incarnations; above are stucco gods and goddesses; and the top of the hall is covered with meditating Buddhas and *bodhisattvas*. Bring a torch to see the full detail of the murals.

The other temples date from the fifteenth and eighteenth centuries. Their contents illustrate the development of Buddhist iconography from its early Indian origins to the Chinese-influenced opulence of medieval Tibetan Tantricism that still, in a more lurid form, predominates in modern *gompas*. The new *gompa*, inaugurated by the Dalai Lama in 1983, houses nearly fifty lamas and a handful of *chomos* (nuns), some of whom receive training in traditional painting techniques under a *geshe*, or teacher from eastern Tibet. Visitors are welcome to attend daily 6.30am puja. It's also worth exploring the caves across the main road, one of which houses more paintings, but you need to ask for a key from the *gompa* caretaker.

Practicalities

There are a number of **accommodation** options in Tabo. The friendly, atmospheric *Millennium Monastery Guest House*, outside the main monastery gates (☎01906/223315; ❶–❷), has simple rooms, some en suite, and a dorm (Rs70). Behind the monastery near the river, the well-located *Tashi Khangsar Hotel* (☎01906/233346; ❷) is bland but good value, while the *Banjara Serkong Retreat* on the main road 200m before the bus stand (☎01906/223381; ❻), closed at the time of research, is run by the luxury Banjara chain – which usually means a comfortable stay and good food (with the option of all-inclusive meals). The *Millennium Monastery Restaurant* and the *Tibetan Dish*, down the lane towards the bus stand, offer basic Tibetan and Indian **food**; the former also provides good trekking advice and organizes recycling and eco-projects. A useful STD/ISD office is located at the back of the *Tenzin Restaurant*, which is behind the *Zion Café* and *Millennium Monastery Guest House*. Three **buses** per day travel to Kaza, the 4am departure going all the way to Manali. Another bus passes through at around 11am on its way from Kaza to the landslide at Malling, where a bus on the far side continues to Rekong Peo in Kinnaur.

The Manali–Leh Highway

Since it opened to foreign tourists in 1989, the famous **Manali–Leh highway** has replaced the old Srinagar–Kargil route as the most popular approach to Ladakh. In summer, a stream of vehicles set off from the Kullu Valley to travel along the second-highest road in the world, which reaches a dizzying altitude of 5328m. Its surface varies wildly from fairly smooth asphalt through potholes of differing depths to dirt tracks sliced by glacial streams, traversing a starkly beautiful lunar wilderness. Depending on road conditions, the 485-kilometre journey can take anything from twenty-six to thirty hours. Bus drivers cover more distance on the first day than the second, stopping for a short and chilly night in one of

Cycling the Manali–Leh Highway

Motorbikers and **cylists** revere Manali–Leh as one of the most spectacular rides in the world. And after cycling the second-highest road in the world, the highest one awaits you in Leh... Every summer, two-wheeled adventurers set off on a range of contraptions from thousand-dollar mountain bikes to single-geared local steeds, in groups or solo. While the **gradients** are rarely steep, the rough road **conditions** and, most crucially, **altitude** demand respect and some preparation. Hauling a fully laden bike up climbs of 50km isn't everyone's idea of fun, especially at over 5000m, but the rewards for your efforts are outstanding – especially if you bring camping equipment and sufficient food and water supplies for the remoter stretches. To enjoy yourself, you'll need waterproof clothing for freezing passes, a warm fleece, sunglasses and a good supply of chocolate bars. Check the bike has a suitably easy gear for grinding up the passes, enough wear left in the brake pads for bombing down them, and make sure that you can attach your belongings securely. As for clothing, loose cotton trousers and T-shirts are more suitable than Lycra. Most people start from Manali and take eight to ten days to cover the 485km, though it has been done in as little as four. Don't fret about you, or your bike, packing up half way though – as remote as it feels, you'll always be able to hitch a lift during the day. If riding solo is a daunting prospect, see p.536 for **mountain bike tour operators** in Manali. For more information see Ⓦwww.pocketsprocket.com.

the overpriced **tent camps** along the route. These, however, are few and far between after September 15, when the highway officially closes; in practice, all this means is that the Indian government won't airlift you out if you get trapped in snow, and consequently some companies run regardless until the passes become blocked in mid to late October. For more details on **transport** between Manali and Leh, see opposite.

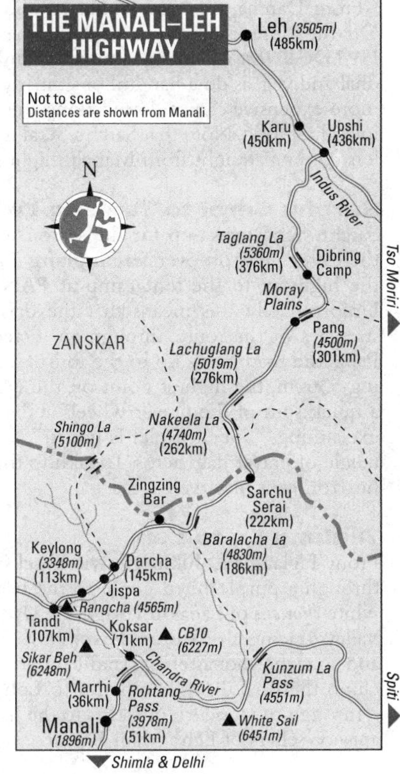

Manali to Keylong

Once out of **Manali**, the road begins its long ascent of the **Rohtang Pass** (3978m). Buses pull in for breakfast 17km before the pass at a row of makeshift *dhabas* at Marhi (3360m). Though not all that high by Himalayan standards, the pass itself is one of the most treacherous in the region and every year Gaddis and mountaineers are caught unawares by sudden weather changes – hence Rohtang's name, which literally means "piles of dead bodies". The road descends from Rohtang to the floor of the **Chandra Valley**, finally reaching the river at **Koksar**, little more than a scruffy collection of chai stalls with a **checkpoint** where you have to enter passport details in a ledger – one of many such stops on the road to Leh. The next few hours are among the most memorable on the entire trip. Bus seats on the left are best, as the road runs across the northern slopes of the valley through the first Buddhist settlements, hemmed in by towering peaks and hanging glaciers towards **Keylong** (see p.544).

Keylong to Sarchu Serai

Beyond Keylong, the Bhaga Valley broadens, but its bare sides support very few villages. By the time you reach **Darcha**, a lonely cluster of dry-stone huts and dingy tent camps, the landscape is utterly denuded. All buses stop here for passengers to grab a hot bowl of Tibetan *thukpa* from a wayside *dhaba*. There's little else to do in Darcha, though the Shingo La trailhead – the main trekking route north to Zanskar (see p.594) – is on the outskirts. If you are not on one of the through Manali–Leh buses, you're better off stopping at **JISPA** 7km south, a pleasant little hamlet with ample camping along the river as well as the upmarket *Hotel Jispa* (ⓣ01900/233203; ❻), whose breakfasts are legendary among passing cycle tourists; they also have dorm beds for Rs200. One kilometre before the *Jispa*, the Mountaineering Institute arranges mountaineering and rescue courses in summer through tour agencies in Manali, and may also provide accommodation.

From Darcha, the road climbs steadily northeast to the **Baralacha La** pass. On the other side, buses stop for the night at **SARCHU SERAI**, where HPTDC's *Tent Camp* (❸), a rather ordinary affair, serves steaming plates of rice, dhal and veg, as do a handful of similarly priced *dhabas* nearby. There are several more expensive camps dotted along the road charging up to Rs800 per person including food. Note that Sarchu Serai is 2500m higher than Manali, and travellers coming straight from Manali might suffer from the higher altitude here.

Sarchu Serai to Taglang La

Sarchu Serai packs up for the season from September 15. Northbound buses thereafter press on over **Lachuglang La** (5019m), the second highest pass on the highway, to the tent camp at **PANG** (4500m), which stays open longer. Unfortunately, this means that the drive through one of the most dramatic stretches of the route, through an incredible canyon, is in darkness. North of Pang, the road heads up to the fourth and final pass, the **Taglang La**, a dizzying 5360m, the highest point on the Manali–Leh highway. Drivers pull in for a quick spin of the prayer wheels and a brief photo session alongside the sign exclaiming "Unbelievable! Is not it?". Staring north beyond the multicoloured tangle of prayer flags across Ladakh to the Karakoram Range, just visible on the horizon, you may well agree.

Taglang La to Leh

From Taglang La, 40km of switchbacks deliver you from the windswept pass through a purple-hued gorge to the neat, kidney-shaped barley fields and the white *chortens* of Ladakhi villages. At **Upshi**, the road reaches the dramatic Indus Valley, tracing the **Indus River** past slender poplars, sprawling army camps and ancient monasteries. Traffic builds as you approach **Choglamsar**, then climb the final dusty kilometres to **Leh** – past the world's highest golf course – through the modern outskirts to the haberdashers, canny traders and wrinkled apricot-sellers of Leh's Main Bazaar.

Travel details

Trains

Jogindernagar: to Pathankot (2 daily; 7hr 30min–9hr 10min).
Shimla to: Kalka (6 daily; 4hr 45min–5hr 45min).

Buses

Chamba to: Amritsar (1 daily; 8hr); Brahmour (7 daily; 3hr); Dalhousie (10 daily; 2hr 30min); Delhi (1 nightly; 18hr); Gaggal (1 daily; 5hr 30min); Kangra (2 daily; 6hr); Khajjiar (3 daily; 1hr 30min); Mandi (1 daily; 15hr); Pathankot (10 daily; 5hr).
Dalhousie to: Amritsar (1 daily; 5hr 30min); Jullundhar (1 daily; 6hr); Khajjiar (3 daily; 1hr); Pathankot (hourly; 3hr 30min).
Dharamsala to: Baijnath (hourly; 3hr 30min); Chamba (1 daily; 6hr); Chandigarh (6 daily; 7–8hr); Dalhousie (1 daily; 6–7hr); Delhi (6 daily; 12hr); Dehra Dun (1 daily; 9hr); Haridwar (1 daily; 14hr); Jawalamukhi (8 daily; 2hr 30min); Kangra (every 15min: 45min–1hr); Kullu (4 daily; 8hr); Manali (3 daily; 10hr); Mandi (7 daily; 6hr); McLeod Ganj (every 20min; 40min); Nahan (1 daily; 12hr); Pathankot (every 30min; 3hr).
Kangra to: Delhi (every 30min; 12hr); Jawalamukhi (every 15min; 1–2hr); Mandi (4 daily; 6hr); Masrur (3 daily; 2hr); Pathankot (10 daily; 3–4hr).
Kasauli to: Chandigarh (5 daily; 2hr 30min); Delhi (3 daily; 7hr 30min); Kalka (3 daily; 1hr 30min); Solan (5 daily; 40min).
Kullu to: Amritsar (1 daily; 16hr); Bhuntur (every 10min; 30min); Chandigarh (8 daily; 6hr 30min); Dehra Dun (1 daily; 14hr); Delhi (7 daily; 14hr); Haridwar (1 daily; 14hr); Manali (every 10min; 1hr 15min–2hr); Mandi (every 30min; 3hr); Manikaran (every 30min; 2hr); Nagar (hourly; 1hr 30min).

Manali to: Amritsar (1 daily; 16hr); Chandigarh (hourly; 8–11hr); Dehra Dun (1 daily; 16hr); Delhi (8 daily; 16–17hr); Haridwar (2 daily; 16hr); Kangra (7 daily; 12hr); Kaza (2 daily; 12hr); Keylong (11 daily; 6hr); Mandi (every 30min; 4hr); Manikaran (every 30min; 4hr); Nagar (hourly; 1hr 30min); Pathankot (1 daily; 12hr); Udaipur, Lahaul (1 daily; 7hr).

Mandi to: Dharamsala (9 daily; 6hr); Kullu (every 30min; 3hr); Manali (every 30min; 4hr); Shimla (8 daily; 6hr).

Shimla to: Chail (3 daily; 3hr); Chandigarh (every 15min; 4hr); Dalhousie (1 daily; 14hr); Dehra Dun (3 daily; 9hr); Delhi (hourly; 10hr); Dharamsala (6 daily; 10hr); Haridwar (3 daily; 10hr); Kalka (every 30min; 3hr); Kangra (8 daily: 8hr); Kasauli (hourly; 2hr 30min); Kullu (7 daily; 7–8hr); Manali (7 daily; 9–10hr); Mandi (7 daily; 6hr); Nahan (3 daily; 6hr); Narkanda (6 daily; 3hr); Pathankot (4 daily; 13hr); Rampur (hourly; 6hr); Rekong Peo (5 daily; 9–11hr); Sarahan (2 daily; 7hr); Solan (every 30min; 1hr 30min).

Flights

Dharamsala (Gaggal) to: Delhi (3 weekly; 1hr 30min).

Kullu (Bhuntur) to: Delhi (daily; 1hr 20min).

Shimla to: Delhi (3 weekly; 1hr 10min); Kullu (daily; 30min).

CHAPTER 7 Highlights

* **Leh** Medieval streets, a Tibetan-style palace, bazaars and looming snowy peaks. See p.561

* **Tikse** Along with Lamayuru, the Indian Himalayas' most impressive monastery complex. See p.577

* **Hemis** Ladakh's largest monastery hosts its annual masked-dance ritual and *thangka* unveiling at the height of the summer. See p.579

* **Chemrey & Thak Thok** Neighbouring but strikingly different monasteries – one on a near-perfect conical hill and the other built into a catacomb. See pp.579–580

* **Tso Moriri** This exquisite high-altitude lake inhabited by nomadic herders features snow-fringed desert mountains and rare migratory birds. See p.580

* **Alchi** Wonderful painted murals and stucco images are hidden behind the simple exterior of this ancient monastery. See p.587

* **Lamayuru** An awesome walled *gompa* rising above a mass of weirdly eroded rock. See p.589

* **Zanskar** Walled in by the Himalayas, during the winter Zanskar can only be reached by following the frozen river route. See p.594

△ Alchi murals

7

Ladakh

LADAKH, the far-flung eastern corner of troubled Jammu and Kashmir state, is India's most remote and sparsely populated region, a high-altitude snow desert cradled by the Karakoram and Great Himalayas ranges, and criss-crossed by a myriad razor-sharp peaks and ridges. To the many thousands of military personnel charged with guarding its fragile frontiers with China and Pakistan, this barren, breathless land is a punishment posting – and a dangerous one at that. For tourists, however, it offers a window on a unique Himalayan landscape and culture that, until 1974, had only been glimpsed by a few intrepid Western travellers.

Variously described as "Little Tibet" or "the last Shangri-La", **La-Dags** – "land of high mountain passes" – is one of the last enclaves of Mahayana **Buddhism**, Ladakh's principal religion for nearly a thousand years, now brutally suppressed by the Chinese in its native Tibet. Except near the Kashmiri border, the outward symbols of Buddhism are everywhere: strings of multicoloured prayer flags flutter from the rooftops of houses, while bright prayer wheels and white-washed *chortens* (the regional equivalent of stupas; see p.566) guard the entrances to even the tiniest settlements. More mysterious still are Ladakh's medieval **monasteries**. Perched on rocky hilltops and clinging to sheer cliffs, **gompas** are both repositories of ancient wisdom and living centres of worship. Their gloomy prayer halls and ornate shrines harbour remarkable art treasures: giant brass Buddhas, *thangkas*, libraries of antique Tibetan manuscripts, weird musical instruments and painted walls that writhe with fierce Tantric divinities.

The highest concentration of monasteries is in the **Indus Valley** near **Leh**, the region's capital. Surrounded by sublime landscapes and crammed with hotels, guesthouses, and restaurants, this atmospheric little town, a staging post on the old Silk Route, is most visitors' point of arrival and an ideal base for side trips. North of Leh across one of the highest motorable passes in the world, **Khardung La**, lies the valley of **Nubra**, where sand dunes carpet the valley floor in stark contrast to the towering crags of the Karakoram Range. It is also possible to visit the great wilderness around the lake of **Tso Moriri** in **Rupshu**, southeast of Leh, and to glimpse Tibet from the shores of **Pangong Tso** in the far east of Ladakh. For these areas you will, however, need a permit (see p.558). West of Leh, beyond the windswept **Fatu La** and **Namika La** passes, Buddhist prayer flags peter out as you approach the predominantly Muslim district of **Kargil**. Ladakh's second largest town, at the mouth of the breathtakingly beautiful **Suru Valley**, marks the halfway stage of the journey to or from Srinagar, and is the jumping-off point for **Zanskar**, the vast wilderness in the far south of the state that forms the border with Lahaul in Himachal Pradesh.

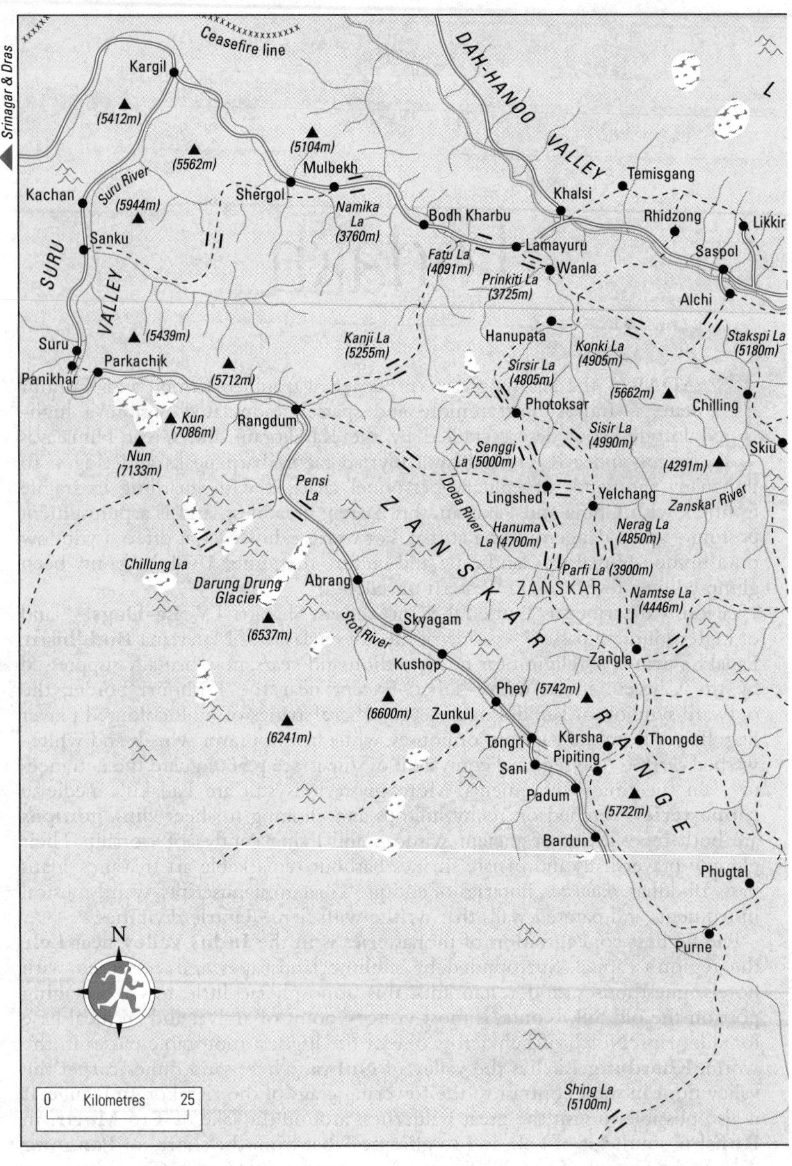

Far beyond the reach of the monsoons, Ladakh receives little snow, especially in the valleys, and even less rain (just four inches per year). Only the most frugal methods enable its inhabitants to **farm** the thin sandy soil, frozen solid for eight months of the year and scorched for the other four. Nourished by meltwater channelled through elaborate irrigation ditches, a single crop of barley (roasted to make the staple *ngamphe*) is sown and harvested between late June and

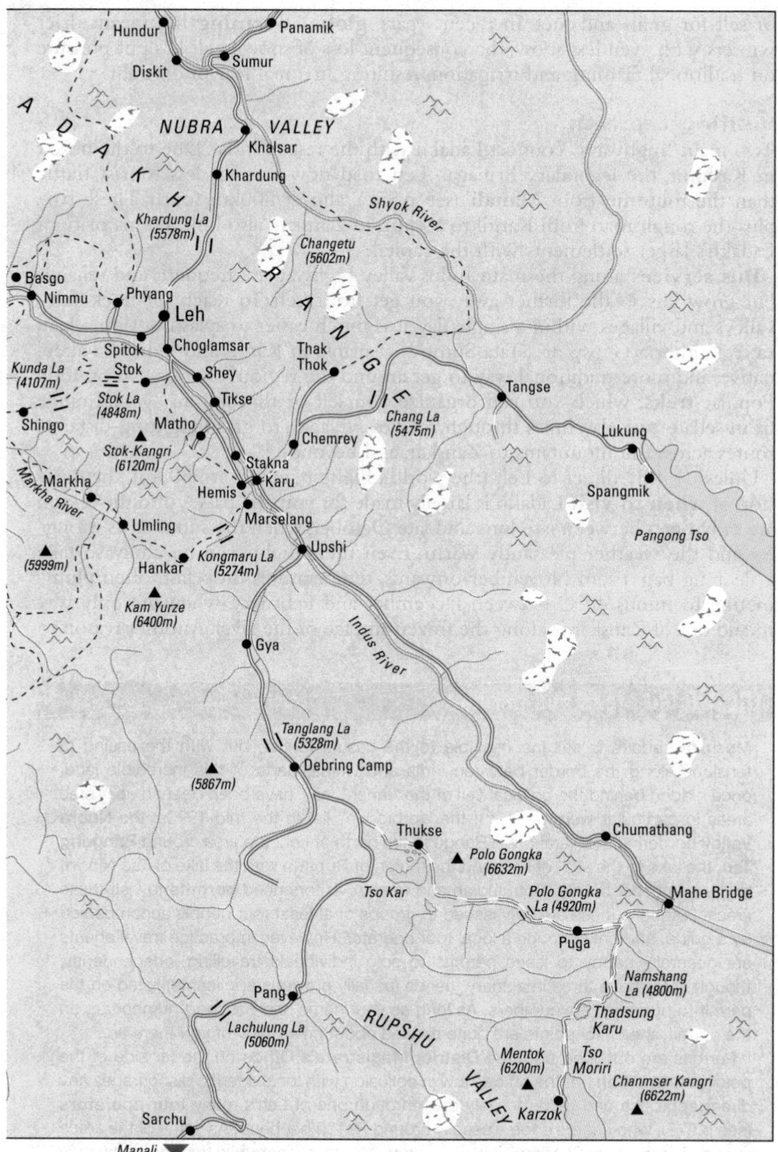

the first October frosts. At lower altitudes, where neat terraced fields provide vivid green splashes against the bare rock and mica-flecked scree slopes, this is supplemented by fast-growing strains of wheat, garden vegetables, apricots and walnuts. Higher up, the relentless chill and steep gradients render agriculture impossible, and villagers depend on **animals** – yaks, goats, sheep and *dzo* (a hybrid of the yak and the domestic cow) – for wool, milk and butter to barter or sell for grain and fuel. In recent years, **global warming** has meant drier winters with even less snow; the consequent loss of snow-melt has put pressure on traditional farming and irrigation, resulting in a real fear of drought.

Visiting Ladakh

Two main "highways" connect Ladakh with the rest of India. Due to the unrest in Kashmir, the legendary Srinagar–Leh road now sees far less tourist traffic than the route up from **Manali** (see p.550), almost 500km south. These two, plus the rough road from Kargil to Padum in Zanskar, also link the majority of Ladakh's larger settlements with the capital.

Bus services along the main Indus Valley highway are frequent and reliable, but grow less so the further away you get from Leh. To reach off-track side-valleys and villages within a single day, it is much easier to splash out on a Jeep **taxi** – either a Gypsy or a Tata Sumo – available in Kargil and Leh. The alternative, and more traditional way to get around the region, of course, is on foot. Popular **treks**, which you can organize yourself or through an agency, range from sedate two-day hikes through roadless villages, to gruelling long-distance routes across the mountains to Zanskar, and beyond.

Unless you fly direct to Leh (the world's highest airport at 3505m), the decision of **when to visit** Ladakh is largely made for you: the passes into the region are only open between late June and late October, when the sun is at its strongest and the weather pleasantly warm. Even then, nights can be chilly, so take a sleeping bag. From November onwards, temperatures drop fast, often plummeting to minus 40°C between December and February, when the only way in and out of Zanskar is along the frozen surface of the river. Another reason to

Restricted areas and permits

Much of Ladakh is still inaccessible to the casual tourist, but with the easing of tensions along the border between India and China, parts of this incredible land, once hidden behind the political veil of the "Inner Line", have been opened up. Three areas in particular were taken off the "forbidden" list in the mid-1990s: the **Nubra Valley** bordering the Karakoram Range to the north of Leh; the area around **Pangong Tso**, the lake to the east of Leh; and the region of **Rupshu** with the lake of **Tso Moriri**, to the southeast of Leh. Both Indian and foreign visitors need **permits** to visit these areas. In theory, these are only issued to groups of at least four people accompanied by a guide, and only through a local tour operator. However, in practice travel agents are generally happy to issue permits to solo individuals travelling independently, though you'll have three imaginary friends (usually previous applicants) listed on the permit to bump up the numbers. As long as your name and passport number are on the permit, the checkpoints are quite relaxed about how many of you there are.

Permits are obtained from the **District Magistrate's Office** on the far side of the polo ground in **Leh** but the office, now in collusion with local agents, discourages any direct approach and tends to only deal through one of Leh's many **tour operators** (see p.572), who charge a **fee** – usually around Rs100 per head. As some of the areas in question (such as Pangong Tso) are served by infrequent public transport, you may well find yourself using a tour operator anyway, in which case they will include your permit in the package. You will need two photocopies of the relevant pages of your passport and visa. Provided you apply in the morning, permits are usually issued on the same day. Once you have your permit, usually only valid for a maximum period of seven days, make at least five copies before setting off, as checkpoints like to keep a copy when you report in. They may also occasionally spot-check to see the original copy.

come in summer is to make arguably the most spectacular road journey in the world. The hour-long flight over the Himalayas may be memorable, but is no substitute for the two-day-plus trip from Manali (see p.550) – a crash course in just how remote and extraordinary this lonely mountain kingdom really is.

Some history

The first inhabitants of Ladakh are thought to have been a mixture of nomadic herdsmen from the Tibetan plateau and a small contingent of early Buddhist refugees from northern India called the Mons. Some time in the fourth or fifth century, these two groups were joined by the **Dards**, a tribe of Indo-Aryan origin who migrated southeast along the Indus Valley, bringing with them irrigation and settled agriculture.

The first independent kingdom in the region was established in the ninth century by the maverick nobleman Nyima Gon, taking advantage of the chaos after the collapse of the Guge empire of western Tibet. **Buddhism**, meanwhile, had also found its way across the Himalayas from India. Disseminated by the wandering sage-apostles such as Padmasambhava (alias "Guru Rinpoche"), *dharma* gradually displaced the pantheistic shamanism of the Bon cult (which still holds sway in remote villages north of Khalsi, near Lamayuru). The eastward expansion of the faith towards the Tibetan plateau continued in the tenth and eleventh centuries – the period later dubbed the "**Second Spreading**". Among its key proselytizers was the "Great Translator" **Rinchen Zangpo**, a scholar and missionary associated with the foundation of numerous monasteries in Ladakh and in neighbouring Spiti (see p.545).

Around the fourteenth century, Ladakh passed through a dark age during which, for reasons that remain unclear, its rulers switched allegiance from Indian to Tibetan Buddhism, a form of the faith deeply invested with esoteric practices drawn from the **Tantra** texts, and possibly influenced by the animated celebrations common to Bon (see Contexts, p.1407). This coincided with the rise to prominence in Tibet of **Tsongkhapa** (1357–1419), who is accepted as founder of the **Gelug-pa** or "Yellow Hat" school. With the Dalai Lama at its head, Gelug-pa is today the most popular school in Ladakh. Under **Tashi Namgyal** (1555–70), who reunified the kingdom, Ladakh became a major Himalayan power, and the ascent to the throne of the "Lion", **Sengge Namgyal**, in the seventeenth century, signalled further territorial gains. After being routed by the Moghul-Balti army at Bodh Kharbu in 1639, he turned his energies to civil and religious matters, founding a new capital and palace at Leh, as well as a string of monasteries that included Hemis, seat of the newly arrived **Brugpa** sect.

Sengge's building spree created some fine monuments, but it also drained the kingdom's coffers, as did the hefty annual tribute paid to the Moghuls after the Bodh Kharbu debacle. Finances were further strained when Deldan, Sengge's successor, picked a quarrel with his ally, Tibet. The fifth Dalai Lama dispatched an army of Mongolian horsemen to teach him a lesson, and three years of conflict only ended after the Moghul governor of Kashmir intervened on Ladakh's behalf. This help, however, came at a price: Aurangzeb demanded more tribute, ordered the construction of a mosque in Leh, and forced the Ladakhi king to convert to Islam.

Trade links with Tibet resumed in the eighteenth century, but Ladakh never regained its former status. Plagued by feuds and assassinations, the kingdom teetered into terminal decline, and was an easy target for the **Dogra** general Zorawar Singh, who annexed it for the Maharaja of Kashmir in 1834. The Ladakhi royal family was banished to Stok Palace, where their descendants reside to this day.

Ladakh became a part of independent India in 1948, following the first of the four Indo-Pak wars fought in the region. However, both the international frontier and the so-called "**Ceasefire Line**" that scythes through the top of Jammu and Kashmir remain "unauthenticated" and a source of continued tension both locally and between Delhi and Islamabad. In the spring of 1999 Pakistani-backed militants occupied a ridge on India's side of the so-called "Line of Control" just outside the Muslim town of **Kargil**. The ensuing battle, in which around one thousand Pakistani and Indian soldiers died, brought the world's two newest nuclear powers to the brink of all-out war. The incursion was eventually repulsed, but in May and June 2002 alone, some 5000 rounds of ammunition were exchanged across the Ceasefire Line. While the situation around Kargil has improved since, India and Pakistan continue to take pot-shots at each other across the disputed Siachen Glacier, 100km north in the Karakorams. When you consider the proximity of China, another old foe who annexed a large chunk of Ladakh in 1962, it's easy to see why this is India's most sensitive border zone.

Today, Ladakh comprises around seventy percent of the state of Jammu and Kashmir as it stands. Long dissatisfied with the state government based in Srinagar, and after years of agitation, the Ladakhis finally saw the establishment in their region of an **Autonomous Hill Development Council** in September

Festivals in Ladakh

Most of Ladakh's Buddhist **festivals**, in which masked **chaam** dance dramas are performed by lamas in monastery courtyards, take place in January and February, when roads into the region are snowbound. This works out well for the locals, for whom they relieve the tedium of the relentless winter, but it means that few outsiders get to experience some of the northern Himalayas' most vibrant and fascinating spectacles. Recently, however, a few of the larger *gompas* around Leh have followed the example of **Hemis**, and switched their annual festivals to the **summer** to attract tourists. Proceeds from ticket sales go towards maintenance and restoration work, and the construction of new shrines. The precise dates of these monastic events over a five-year period, which vary according to the Tibetan lunar calendar, are published in the useful local guide, *Reach Ladakh*, available from most bookshops in Leh; the description of the Hemis festival programme is also very useful in providing an insight into the proceedings. Alternatively, the tourist office in Leh produces a listings booklet called *Ladakh*.

Gompas that hold their *chaams* (dance festivals) in winter or spring include **Matho** (mid-Feb to mid-March), **Spitok** (mid-Jan), **Tikse** (late Oct to mid-Nov) and **Diskit** (mid-Feb to early March) in Nubra. Other important festivals in Ladakh include **Losar** (the Tibetan/Ladakhi New Year) which falls any time between mid-December and early January.

Summer festivals

Hemis Tsechu July 6–7, 2006; June 25–26, 2007; July 12–13, 2008. See p.579.

Karsha Gustor July 22–23, 2006; July 11–12, 2007; July 29–30, 2008. See p.597.

Thak Thok Tsechu Aug 4–5, 2006; July 24–25, 2007; Aug 11–12, 2008. See p.580.

Sani Nasjal Aug 8–9, 2006; July 29–30, 2007; Aug 15–16, 2008. See p.597.

Phyang Tsedup July 27–28, 2006; July 16–17, 2007; Aug 3–4, 2008. See p.580.

Festival of Ladakh Sept 1–15. This popular J&K Tourism-sponsored two-week event, held principally in Leh, is designed to extend the tourist season, featuring archery contests, polo matches, Bactrian camels from Nubra and traditional Ladakhi dance accompanied by some tedious speeches.

1995, localizing – in theory – government control. Local politicians and religious leaders of Leh, however, spent the late 1990s accusing the state government of manipulation and the purposeful mismanagement of the AHDC, and in 2002 created a new body called the **Ladakh Union Territory Front**, the goal of which is to split from Jammu and Kashmir and gain Union Territory recognition from Delhi. A victory of sorts occurred later that year when the newly elected government in Jammu agreed to give more internal decision-making power to the AHDC, thus ending a six-year stand-off and paving the way for UT status. Meanwhile, the Muslims of Kargil and Drass – heavily influenced by politics of the Kashmir Valley, seeking relations with their Balti cousins across the border in Pakistan and demanding a Hill Council of their own – are vehemently opposed to any separation of Ladakh from Jammu and Kashmir.

Fuelled by the competition for urban jobs, land disputes and the fighting in Kashmir, relations between **Muslims** and **Buddhists** in the region are tense. In July 2000 Muslim terrorists (their exact identity remains in dispute) shot dead three Buddhist monks outside a monastery in Rangdum in the remote area between the Suru Valley and Zanskar. A German traveller who had the misfortune of hitching a ride on the same truck as the perpetrators was also executed. That, along with the threat of nuclear exchange with Pakistan in the spring of 2002, led tourism to plummet in Ladakh. More recently, however, a change of government in Delhi, resulting in renewed talks with Pakistan over Kashmir, and the initiation of an Indo-Pak bus service between Srinagar and Muzaffarabad in 2005, is restoring confidence. That is not to say that the Kashmir Valley is no longer unpredictable – in June 2004, several Indian tourists were killed when a hotel in Pahalgam was attacked – and anyone planning to travel in that region should check on the current situation before they leave.

Leh

As you approach **LEH** for the first time, via the sloping sweep of dust and pebbles that divide it from the floor of the Indus Valley, you'll have little difficulty imagining how the old trans-Himalayan traders must have felt as they plodded in on the caravan routes from Yarkhand and Tibet: a mixture of relief at having crossed the mountains in one piece, and anticipation of a relaxing

Health in Leh: altitude sickness and dirty water

As Leh is 3505m above sea level, some travellers, and especially those who arrive by plane from Delhi, experience mild **altitude sickness**. The best way to avoid the symptoms – persistent headaches, dizziness, insomnia, nausea, loss of appetite or shortness of breath – is to rest for at least 48 hours on arrival. Drink 3–4 litres of water a day, avoid alcohol, and don't exert yourself. Overdo it in the first few days and you'll feel off-colour for up to a week. For more information, see p.47, or contact the SNM hospital (ⓣ01982/252014 or 252360).

A health problem that affects far more travellers, however, is diarrhoea. **Dirty water** is invariably the culprit – a consequence of Leh's grossly inadequate sewage system, which can't cope with the massive summer influx of visitors. Redouble your normal health precautions while you are here: take extra care over what you drink, and avoid salads and raw vegetables unless you know they have been cleaned in sterilized water. Many hotels now filter their own water, making it perfectly safe to drink, and the Dzomsa Laundry provides safe water in recycled plastic bottles (see p.563).

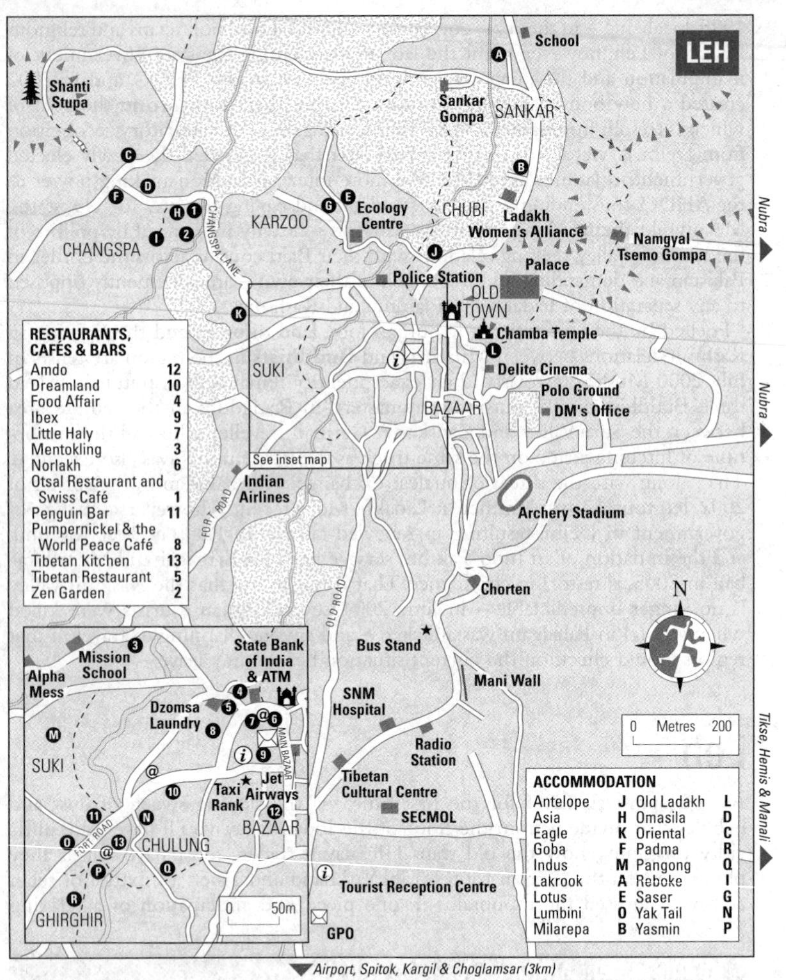

spell in one of central Asia's most scenic towns. Spilling out of a side-valley that tapers north towards eroded snow-capped peaks, the Ladakhi capital sprawls from the foot of a ruined Tibetan-style palace – a maze of mud brick and concrete flanked on one side by cream-coloured desert and on the other by a swathe of lush irrigated farmland.

Leh only became regional capital in the seventeenth century, when Sengge Namgyal shifted his court here from Shey, 15km southeast, to be closer to the head of the Khardung La–Karakoram corridor into China. The move paid off: within a generation the town had blossomed into one of the busiest markets on the Silk Road. During the 1920s and 1930s, the broad bazaar that still forms its heart received more than a dozen pony- and camel-trains each day. Leh's prosperity, managed mainly by the Sunni **Muslim** merchants whose descendants live in its labyrinthine old quarter, came to an abrupt end with the closure of the Chinese border in the 1950s. Only after the Indo-Pak wars of 1965 and 1971, when India rediscovered the hitherto forgotten capital's strategic value, did its fortunes begin to look up. Today, khaki-clad *jawans* (soldiers) and their families from the nearby military and air force bases are the mainstay of the local economy in winter, when foreign visitors are few and far between.

Undoubtedly the most radical shake-up, however, ensued from the Indian government's decision in 1974 to open Ladakh to foreign **tourists**. From the start, Leh bore the brunt of the annual invasion, as busloads of backpackers poured up the road from Srinagar. More than thirty years on, Leh has doubled in size and is a far cry from the sleepy Himalayan town of the early 1970s. The provision stores and old-style outfitters on the main street have been squeezed out by Kashmiri handicraft shops, Internet cafés, art emporiums and Tibetan restaurants. A rapid increase in the number of Kashmiri traders, who have little choice but to seek business outside Kashmir, has in recent years led to unrest in Leh's bazaar, the first communal violence ever seen in normally peaceful Ladakh.

Leh does, nonetheless have a tranquil side, and is a pleasant place to unwind after a long bus journey. Attractions in and around the town itself include the former **palace** and **Namgyal Tsemo gompa**, perched amid strings of prayer flags above the narrow dusty streets of the **old quarter**. A short walk away north across the fields, the small monastery at **Sankar** harbours accomplished modern Tantric murals and a thousand-headed Avalokitesvara deity. Leh is also a good base for longer **day-trips** out into the Indus Valley. Among the string of picturesque villages and *gompas* within reach by bus are **Shey**, site of a derelict seventeenth-century palace, and the spectacular **Tikse gompa**. Until you have adjusted to the altitude, however, the only sightseeing you'll probably feel up to will be from a guesthouse roof terrace or garden, from where the snowy summits of the majestic **Stok-Kangri massif** (6120m), magnified in the crystal-clear Ladakhi sunshine, look close enough to touch.

Arrival, information and local transport

A taxi from Leh **airport**, 5km southwest of town on the main Srinagar highway, will set you back a fixed fare of around Rs100 to the bazaar, or Rs150 to

Environmental issues

Damage to the **environment** has become an issue of paramount importance in Ladakh. Although plastic bags are banned in Leh, as they clog up the vital river systems that the state so depends on, shopkeepers continue to use them. Plastic mineral water bottles are a particular headache; you are advised to bring your own filtration system (see p.42) with you, or recycle your plastic water bottles at Leh's Dzomsa Laundry (see below). You are also advised to leave all unnecessary packaging behind before arriving in Ladakh.

Situated on a strategic corner between Upper Thaka Road and Old Fort Road at one end of the market square, the **Dzomsa Laundry** provides a vital service in ecology-sound washing, using biodegradable detergent and water at a safe distance from habitation. It also serves as a co-op for rural, semi-illiterate people. *Dzomsa*, which literally means "meeting point", serves delicious fresh apricot and seabuckthorn juices which you can drink while sitting outside watching the world go by. You can also recycle your plastic bottles and refill them with **safe drinking water** here.

For more on environmental issues in Ladakh, see the accounts of the **Ecology Centre** (see p.567) and local **voluntary organizations** (see p.568). For tips on **trekking** sensitively, see p.576.

Changspa, in the northwest of town, where many of the hotels are located. State and private **buses** pull into the dusty town bus stand, fifteen minutes' walk or a short taxi ride (Rs50) south of the bazaar and most of the hotels. Manali buses terminate on Fort Road, near the *Hotel Dreamland*.

The J&K **tourist reception centre** (Mon–Sat 10am–4pm; ⓣ01982/252094), 3km from the bazaar on the airport road, is too far out of town and hardly worth visiting. The summer-only **tourist information centre** on Fort Road in the bazaar (May–Sept Mon–Sat 10am–4pm) is a bit more helpful. Two banks offer **money-changing** facilities: try the Foreign Exchange Service Centre of the J&K Bank, 1st Floor, Himalaya Shopping Complex, Main Bazaar; or the State Bank of India on the main market square, which also has an ATM. Elsewhere, private licensed foreign exchange, including some hotels such as *Khangri* and travel agents around Fort Road, invariably offer rates around five percent lower but are accessible after hours and on weekends.

The **taxi operators' union** rank (daily 6am–7pm; ⓣ01982/253039) is almost directly opposite the tourist information centre. Each driver carries a list of fixed fares to just about everywhere you might want to visit in Ladakh, taking into account waiting time and night halt charges. These rates apply to peak season; reductions of up to forty percent can be had at other times. Deal directly with the drivers, or their boss in the union office will take a cut (payable by you). Prices are high as the season is so short. Expect to pay around Rs110 for a return trip to Changspa, Rs950 to Hemis, and Rs6585 to Nubra, with an additional Rs275 for a night's stay. Hunt around the tour operators in the bazaar and you can get cheaper deals for long-distance rides, especially if you don't mind a Maruti (Suzuki) Gypsy which is a bit more cramped and bumpy on Ladakh's rough roads.

Accommodation

Leh is glutted with **accommodation**, most of it refreshingly neat, clean and excellent value. Budget travellers in particular are in for a treat. Most of the town's **cheap guesthouses** are immaculately whitewashed traditional houses, set on the leafy outskirts, with sociable garden terraces that look onto green fields. Simple double rooms go from around Rs150, even in high season. For a little more, you can often find a sunny en-suite "glass room" with a view all to yourself. Breakfasts are usually included in the price, served in the garden or at low Tibetan tables (*chogtse*) in the family kitchen. If you're after peace and quiet, head for **Changspa** village, fifteen minutes' walk west of the bazaar. More in the thick of things are the mainly Muslim houses of the **old town**. Crouched in the shadow of Leh palace, these are cheap and full of atmosphere, but finding your way home after dark through the maze of narrow, unlit and not particularly clean lanes can be a trial.

Rooms in Leh's **mid-range hotels** come with en-suite shower-toilets and piped hot water, while **upmarket** accommodation is limited and poor value for money by Indian standards. Aimed primarily at tour groups, the rates of these hotels usually include full board. The prices below are for high season, when hotels tend to be block-booked by package tour groups. Off-season, prices can be slashed by as much as sixty percent.

Budget

Antelope Chubi ⓣ01982/252086. A short walk from the centre, this is a quiet spot, with a pleasant garden and plain rooms under the shadow of the palace. ❷

Asia Changspa ⓣ01982/253403. Large riverside guesthouse with a spanking new block. Sociable terrace-cum-café and meditation classes, but limited views. ❸

Eagle Changspa, across from the Mahabodhi centre ⓣ01982/253074. The friendly and helpful owner Motuup runs a pleasant guesthouse with a large garden and can arrange excellent trekking tours. ❶

Goba Changspa ⓣ01982/253670. Well-maintained traditional house with a pleasant garden. Rooms are immaculate, and those in the new block have attached bathrooms. ❷–❸

Indus Suki, off Fort Rd ⓣ01982/252502. Cheap singles and a few doubles, with some attached bathrooms and solar-heated water. Central, pleasant and open in winter. ❸–❹

Lakrook Sankar ⓣ01982/252987. Traditional, welcoming family house 20min walk from the main bazaar, with a huge organic garden, traditional Ladakhi kitchen and solar-heated water. ❷

Old Ladakh Old town ⓣ01982/252951, ⓔold_ladakh@rediff.com. Ladakh's first-ever guesthouse is homely and central, and offers a choice of rooms: the kitsch "deluxe" one (pink pillows and Tibetan rugs) is a real winner. On the downside, the management has been known to take advantage of its good reputation to sell overpriced trekking trips through its sister concern Little Tibet Expeditions. *Tak*, across the lane, handles overflow. ❷–❸

Oriental Below the Shanti Stupa, Changspa ⓣ01982/253153. Congenial, extremely popular guesthouse with spotless rooms (some with attached bath), free filtered water, an Internet café, superb views, nourishing home-cooked meals and a genuinely warm welcome even in winter. ❶–❸

Reboke Changspa ⓣ01982/253230. Small, simple, friendly guesthouse which also has a couple of rooms with attached baths, at the far end of a narrow lane past the ugly *Sun & Sand*. If full try the simple rooms at *Chunka* (ⓣ01982/253382) next door. ❷

Mid-range

Milarepa Lakrook, Chubi ⓣ01982/253218. Quiet place, owned by a well-informed local politician and with an extensive garden. About 10 mins' walk from the bazaar. ❷–❺

Padma Ghirghir, off Fort Rd ⓣ01982/252630, ⓦwww.reachladakh.com/padma.html. There are two parts to this hotel: a traditional old building with immaculate rooms with shared baths, a beautiful kitchen, a garden and mountain views; and a modern annexe with comfortable doubles and attached baths and a rooftop restaurant. ❹–❽

Pangong Chulung ⓣ01982/254655, ⓔpangong@sancharnet.in. Pleasant hotel built around a courtyard garden with spacious, well-priced rooms and an inviting balcony. ❼

Saser Karzoo, up the path from the Ecology Centre ⓣ01982/250162. Modern hotel which successfully embraces elements of traditional architecture, with a pleasant garden courtyard and comfortable rooms with baths – a bargain off-season. Rates include full board. ❹–❻

Yasmin Off Fort Rd ⓣ01982/252405. Clean, comfortable rooms in a custom-built guesthouse with a sunny garden. It's convenient, owned by one of Ladakh's literary figures, and impeccably managed. Good value. ❸–❹

Expensive

Lotus Upper Karzoo ⓣ01982/250265, ⓔhotellotus@vsnl.net. The laid-back staff and leafy location make this a relaxing and welcome option, although the rooms are better at the *Omasila*. It's done in a traditional style and the more expensive rooms ($55) have mountain views. Rates include full board. ❼–❽

Lumbini Fort Rd ⓣ01982/252528. Owned by one of the abbots of Phyang, this well-designed building has airy, pleasant rooms (up to $85) and a lovely courtyard that makes for excellent lounging. Rates include full board. ❼–❾

Omasila Changspa ⓣ01982/252119. Friendly, accommodating 35-room hotel, including five suites ($85) and six centrally heated rooms ($45) which stay open over winter. The large terrace offers sweeping views of the mountains and the lovely dining room serves excellent dishes featuring vegetables grown in the garden outside. ❽–❾

Yak Tail Fort Rd ⓣ01982/252118. The most central but least aesthetically pleasing in this category. Still, the rooms ($40–55) are of high standard, eight have cable TV and there's a doctor on call. ❽

The Town

With the mighty hulk of the **palace** looming to the north, it's virtually impossible to lose your bearings in Leh. The broad **main bazaar** runs north to south through the heart of town, dividing the labyrinthine **old town** and nearby polo ground from the greener and more spacious residential districts of **Karzoo** and **Suki** to the west. **Fort Road**, the other principal thoroughfare, turns west off the main street and then winds downhill past the taxi rank, the *Hotel Dreamland*,

and the arrival and departure point for Manali buses, towards the Indian Airlines office on the southern outskirts.

The bazaar and old town

After settling into a hotel or guesthouse, most visitors spend their first day in Leh soaking up the atmosphere of the **bazaar**. Eighty or so years ago, this bustling tree-lined boulevard was the busiest market between Yarkhand and Kashmir. Merchants from Srinagar and the Punjab would gather to barter for pashmina wool brought down by nomadic herdsmen from western Tibet, or for raw silk hauled across the Karakorams on Bactrian camels. These days, though the street is awash with kitsch curio shops and handicraft emporiums, it retains a distinctly Central Asian feel. Even if you're not shopping for trekking supplies, check out the **provision stores** along the street, where bright pink, turquoise, and wine-red silk cummerbunds hang in the windows.

When you've had enough of the bazaar, head past the new green-and-white-painted **Jami Masjid** at the top of the street, and follow one of the lanes that lead into the **old town**. Apart from the odd electric cable and concrete path, nothing much has changed here since the warren of flat-roofed houses, crumbling *chortens* and *mani* walls (see box, below) was laid down late in the sixteenth century – least of all the plumbing. One place definitely worth walking through the putrid-smelling puddles to visit, however, is the **Chamba temple**. It's not easy to find on your own; when you get to the second row of shops on the

Chortens and mani walls

Among the more visible expressions of Buddhism in Ladakh are the chess-pawn-shaped **chortens** at the entrance to villages and monasteries. These are the Tibetan equivalent of the Indian stupa (see p.1456) – large hemispherical burial mounds-cum-devotional objects, prominent in Buddhist ritual since the third century BC. Made of mud and stone (now also concrete), many *chortens* were erected as acts of piety by Ladakhi nobles, and like their southern cousins, they are imbued with mystical powers and **symbolic significance**: the tall tapering spire, normally divided into thirteen sections, represents the soul's progression towards nirvana, while the sun cradled by the crescent moon at the top stands for the unity of opposites, and the oneness of existence and the universe. Some contain sacred manuscripts that, like the *chortens*, wither and decay in time, illustrating the central Buddhist doctrine of impermanence. Those enshrined in monasteries, however, generally made of solid silver and encrusted with semiprecious stones, contain the ashes or relics of revered *rinpoches* (incarnate lamas). Always pass a *chorten* in a clockwise direction: the ritual of circumambulation mimics the passage of the planets through the heavens, and is believed to ward off evil spirits. The largest array is to be found in the desert east of **Shey** (see p.575), the former capital, but look out for the giant brightly painted specimen between the bus station and Leh bazaar, whose red spire stands out against the snowy Stok-Kangri mountains to the south.

A short way downhill from the big *chorten*, near the radio station, stands an even more monumental symbol of devotion. The 500-metre **mani wall**, erected by King Deldan Namgyal in 1635, is one of several at important religious sites around Ladakh. Ranging from a couple of metres to over a kilometre in length, the walls are made of hundreds of thousands of stones, each inscribed with prayers or sacred mantras – usually the invocation *Om Mani Padme Hum*: "Hail to the Jewel in the Lotus". It goes without saying that such stones should never be removed and visitors should resist the urge to climb onto the walls to have photographs taken.

left beyond the big arch ask for the key-keeper (*gonyer*), who will show you the way. Hemmed in by dilapidated medieval mansions, the one-roomed shrine houses a colossal image of Maitreya, the Buddha to come, and some wonderful old wall paintings.

The palace

Lording it over the old town from the top of a craggy granite ridge is the derelict **palace** (daily sunrise to sunset; Rs100) of the sixteenth-century ruler Sengge Namgyal. A scaled-down version of the Potala in Lhasa, it is a textbook example of medieval Tibetan architecture, with gigantic sloping buttressed walls and projecting wooden balconies that tower nine storeys above the surrounding houses. Since the Ladakhi royal family left in the 1940s, damage inflicted by nineteenth-century Kashmiri cannons has caused large chunks of it to collapse. Take a torch, and watch where you walk: in spite of restoration work, holes gape in the floors and dark staircases.

Namgyal Tsemo gompa

Once you are acclimatized to the altitude, the stiff early-morning hike up to **Namgyal Tsemo gompa** (daily 7–9am & 5–8pm), the monastery perched precariously on the shaly crag above Leh palace, is a great way to start the day. Two trails lead up to "the Peak of Victory", whose twin peaks are connected by giant strings of multicoloured prayer flags; the first and most popular path zigzags across its south side from the palace road, while a second scales the more gentle northern slope via the village of Chubi (the route followed by the lama from Sankar *gompa* (see below) who tends to the shrine each morning and evening). Alternatively, you could drive there along the dirt track that turns left off the main Khardung La highway, 2km north of the bus stand.

Approaching the *gompa* from the south, the first building you come to is the red-painted **Maitreya temple**. Thought to date from the fourteenth century, the shrine houses a giant Buddha statue flanked by *bodhisattvas*. However, its wall paintings are modern and of less interest than those in the **Gon-khang** (temple of protector deities) up the hill.

The Shanti Stupa

A relatively new addition to the rocky skyline around Leh is the toothpaste-white **Shanti Stupa** above Changspa village, 3km west of the bazaar. Inaugurated in 1983 by the Dalai Lama, the "Peace Pagoda", whose sides are decorated with gilt panels depicting episodes from the life of the Buddha, is one of several such monuments erected around India by a "Peace Sect" of Japanese Buddhists. It can be reached by car, or on foot via a steep flight of more than 500 steps, which winds up from the end of Changspa Lane to the café just below the stupa – a welcome respite for those not fit or acclimatized. Its broad terrace makes an excellent spot to watch the sunrise, and is popular with early morning *yogis*.

The Ecology Centre

Five minutes' walk north of the main bazaar, the **Ecology Centre** (Mon–Sat 10am–4.30pm; ⓣ01982/253221) is the headquarters of LEDeG (the Ladakh Ecological Development Group) – a local nongovernmental organization that aims to counter the negative impact of Western-style "development" by fostering economic independence and respect for traditional culture. This involves promoting "appropriate" technologies such as solar energy, encouraging organic farming and cottage industries, and providing education on environmental and social issues through village drama, workshops and seminars. A garden hosts an

Voluntary organizations

With limited resources at their disposal, a handful of **voluntary organizations**, including LEDeG (see p.567), battle to protect Ladakh's delicate environment and ancient culture.

SECMOL (Students' Educational and Cultural Movement of Ladakh), founded in 1988 by Ladakhi university students, strives to increase awareness of developmental issues and guide younger students through an educational system fraught with chronic inadequacies. In the hope of maintaining pride in Ladakh's traditions, SECMOL teaches local history and runs workshops on handicrafts, agriculture and technology. **Volunteer** help from TEFL-qualified visitors is especially appreciated at the summer schools run just outside Leh. If you'd like to meet members of SECMOL, either email in advance (ⓔinfo@secmol.org), or drop into their office on the southern outskirts of town, 200m down the road that leads to Hemis (Mon–Sat 9am–5pm; ⓣ01982/226115).

LEHO (Ladakh Environment and Health Organization) places its emphasis on the proper utilization of land and water resources and the management of livestock on a sustainable basis. Their office and showroom is on the first floor of the Himalaya Complex, beneath the *Amdo* restaurant, on Main Bazaar (Mon–Sat 10am–5pm; ⓣ01982/253691, ⓔsultanaleho@yahoo.com).

Helena Norberg Hodge, the Swedish-born founder of LEDeG, is also behind the International Society for Ecology and Culture (**ISEC**) website (ⓦwww.isec.org.uk), devoted to promoting sustainable ways of living in both "developing" and "developed" countries. ISEC employs **volunteers** in Ladakh on the **Farm Project** to help local farmers maintain traditional farming methods. Closely aligned to the Farm Project, the co-operative Women's Alliance of Ladakh (**WAL**), based in Chubi, north of central Leh, works to reinforce traditional Ladakhi culture. One of their more noticeable achievements was to ban plastic bags from Leh in 1998; the alliance now boasts more than 5000 members in 100 villages. The best time to visit them is during one of their **fêtes**, where you can sample local produce, pick up handicrafts and catch exhibitions of colourful traditional costume and folk dance performances. They also show a number of **videos**, including *Ancient Futures: Learning From Ladakh* (Mon–Sat 3pm), which gives an insightful account of Ladakhi culture and the sweeping changes of the past thirty or so years, many of them direct results of tourism. The film is an excellent introduction to Ladakh, though some of the political issues – including the proxy war on the borders of Jammu & Kashmir and the huge military presence in the area – are skirted, and the film has its detractors among local Ladakhis. On Wednesdays, when she's in town, Norberg Hodge leads the discussion that follows the video. Other screenings are *Paradise with Side Effects* (Mon & Thurs, 4.30pm), a documentary which follows two Ladakhi women on a tour of London, *Local Futures* (Tues, 4.30pm) and *The Future of Progress* (times vary), a thirty-minute series of interviews with leading critics of globalization.

Norberg Hodge has written an excellent **book** on Ladakh, *Ancient Futures*, available at the Women's Alliance and the Ecology Centre handicraft shop.

open-air exhibition of solar gadgets, hydraulic pumps, water mills and other ingenious energy-saving devices that have proved successful throughout Ladakh. There's also a small **library**, and a **handicraft shop**, selling locally made clothes, *thangkas*, T-shirts, books and postcards. Try to catch a screening of LEDeG's **video**, *Ladakh: the Forbidden Wilderness* (Fri 4.30pm), a well-made documentary focusing on Tso Moriri Lake and the plants, animals and people that live around it.

There's a second branch of the centre in Ribook, just below the Shanti Stupa, which also has a workshop, training centre and basic, solar-heated accommodation; email ⓔledeg@vsnl.net for details.

Sankar gompa

Nestled amid the shimmering poplar coppices and terraced fields of barley that extend up the valley behind Leh, **Sankar gompa**, 2km north of the town centre, is among the most accessible monasteries in central Ladakh – hence its restricted visiting hours for tourists (daily 7–10am & 5–7pm; Rs15). You can get there either by car or on foot: turn left at the *Antelope Guesthouse*, and then right onto the concrete path that runs alongside the stream. Sankar appears after about fifteen minutes' walk, surrounded by sun-bleached *chortens* and a high mud wall.

The monastery, a small under-*gompa* of Spitok, is staffed by twenty monks, and is the official residence of the **Kushok Bakula**, Ladakh's head of the Gelug-pa sect. The *rinpoche*, born a prince in 1914, has had an active career, serving in the Indian Parliament in the 1960s and later being posted to Mongolia as an ambassador. Though he now spends most of his days in a new house behind the *gompa*, the *rinpoche*'s glass-fronted former quarters enjoy pride of place on top of the main building, crowned with a golden spire and a *dharma chakra* flanked by two deer (symbolizing the Buddha's first sermon in Sarnath). Above the **Du-khang** (main prayer hall) stands the *gompa*'s principal deity, Tara, in her triumphant, 1000-armed form as Dukkar, or "Lady of the White Parasol", presiding over a light, airy shrine room whose walls are adorned with a Tibetan calendar and tableaux depicting "dos and don'ts" for monks – some of which are very arcane indeed. Another flight of steps leads to the *gompa* **library** and, eventually, a roof terrace with fine views towards the north side of Namgyal Tsemo hill and the valley to the south.

Eating

As Leh's thriving restaurant and café scene has been cornered by the refugee community, **Tibetan food** has a high profile alongside tourist-oriented Chinese and European dishes. Tibetan specialities include *momos* – crescent-shaped dumplings stuffed with meat, cheese or vegetables, and (if you're lucky) ginger, then steamed and served with hot soup and spicy sauce. Fried *momos* are called *kothays*. *Thukpa*, another wholesome favourite, is broth made from fresh pasta strips, meat and vegetables. These, and dozens of variations, are dished up in swanky tourist restaurants (where the meat is usually fresh); you can tuck into bigger portions of the same (for a fraction of the price) at modest, although not always hygienic, backstreet *momo* kitchens.

Most visitors have **breakfast** in their hotel or guesthouse, where the host family cook small round loaves of Ladakhi wheat-flour bread (*tagi shamos*), eaten piping hot with butter and honey or jam. For a truly authentic Leh breakfast, grab a couple of flat-breads from the clay-oven bakeries on the narrow lane at the top of the bazaar; the Tibetan restaurateurs don't mind you turning up with your own. Trekkers and cyclists will appreciate the slow energy release of *tsampa* (barley) porridge, which is often sweetened with honey, and makes a fantastic start to the day. Apple pie and chocolate brownie **pastry shops**, most of them owned by the Sikh-run *German Bakery* chain, are dotted all over town; pop in for filled baguettes, croissants and muesli breakfasts. **Beer** is widely available in most of Leh's tourist restaurants while **chang**, a local barley brew, is harder to come by: ask at your guesthouse if they can get some in for you. A handful of bars cater to the tourist trade, including the *Ibex* near the taxi stand on Fort Road.

Amdo Main Bazaar. Popular Tibetan restaurant, with freshly prepared food that is generally excellent but can take up to an hour to appear. There's a second Amdo across the street, which catches the morning sun and serves hearty *tsampa* porridge.
Dreamland Fort Rd, near the hotel of the same name. One of the most popular late night haunts in town for a mixed menu of food or beer. The chicken platter is recommended.
Food Affair Main Bazaar. A great outdoor café on the square with a mix of baked and cooked food. It's especially good for breakfast and snacky lunches.
Ibex Fort Rd (opposite taxi stand). Good Indian food plus a bar for beer and generous measures of spirits.
Little Italy Goji Complex (opposite the State Bank of India). Good for breakfast or for a beer in the evenings, with a great rooftop location in the centre of town. The mixed menu includes wood-fired pizzas and tandoor dishes. It's one up on the next door *La Terrasse*.
Mentokling Changspa Lane, near Mission School. One of the best of the garden cafés along this road, with a fine all-round menu that's especially strong on Indian food.
Norlakh Main Bazaar. First floor Tibetan-run restaurant, with excellent *momos* and filling *tsampa* porridge.
Otsal Restaurant and Swiss Café Changspa Lane. The Chinese, continental, Indian and Tibetan dishes served on the roof are fairly standard, but the place is most useful as a daytime hangout, frequented by budget travellers who while the hours away on the floor cushions, reading or catching up on their diaries. If it's packed, try the *Magpie Garden Café* across the road.
Penguin Bar Fort Rd. A great place for a beer, *German Bakery* snacks or a meal in a leafy garden setting. The *Dolphin* next door by the river is similar.
Pumpernickel & the World Peace Café Main Bazaar. A long-term travellers' haunt strong on Western food and with a useful notice board. The adjoining *German Bakery* is good for bread, pies and rolls.
Tibetan Kitchen *Hotel Tso-Kar*, Fort Rd. Considered by many, locals and visitors alike, to be the best Tibetan food in town. Large parties are advised to book.
Tibetan Restaurant New Market, Main Bazaar Square. Friendly, popular little café with a limited menu, but convenient as a meeting point.
Zen Garden Changspa Lane. Seasonal, open-air restaurant with a barbecue under willow trees. Varied menu of Indian, Chinese and Western food, including pasta and Israeli dishes.

Shopping

Between June and September, Leh is swamped by almost as many transient Tibetan and Kashmiri **traders** as souvenir-hungry tourists. Most of the merchandise hawked in their temporary boutiques and stalls comes from outside the region: papier-mâché bowls, shawls and carpets from Srinagar, jewellery and miniature paintings from Jaipur, and "Himalayan" handicrafts, including *thangkas*, churned out in Nepal and by Tibetan refugees in Old Delhi. Prices tend to be high, so haggle hard, and don't be conned into shelling out for cleverly faked "antiques". Much of the "silver" on sale is in fact cheap white metal.

Tibetan and Ladakhi **curios** account for the bulk of the goods on sale in Leh's emporiums, though most of these are run by Kashmiris from the Srinagar Valley. The Ladakh Art Palace off the main bazaar, one of the very few locally run souvenir stores, is a good place to browse. If money is no object, you could splash out on a **perak**, a long Ladakhi headdress, encrusted with turquoise, which cost upwards of Rs5000. **Turquoise** is sold by the *tolah* (there are eighty *tolahs* to a kilogram), and quality and age determine the price. You'll find vendors sitting on the main road; otherwise try the locally owned Potala – an atmospheric old-world shop well worth a rummage – down Nowshara Lane, off the main road close to the Jami Masjid. Next door, Himalayan Art is also locally owned, with an extensive selection of curios, ranging from stones to *thangkas*.

For **authentic Ladakhi souvenirs**, try the outfitters and provision stores dotted along the main bazaar. Worth browsing is Konchok Lobzang's shop, a few doors north of the Lehling bookshop, which makes its own Ladakhi-style handicrafts, including wonderfully carved tables and *thangkas*.

The lanes running off the bazaar towards old town offer hole-in-the-wall seamstress shops that can produce custom-fit **local clothing**, including the dapper stovepipe hats (*tibi*), hand-dyed *gonchas*, raw silk cummerbunds, tie-dyed rope-soled shoes (*pabbu*) and Bhutanese cross-button shirts. Try the Lonpo Shop up the lane across from *Amdo* restaurant, or around the corner to the right at the *Namgail* Dorjey and Tsereng Yangskit shops. The handicraft shops at the **Ecology Centre** and **Women's Alliance** (see p.568) are other sources of quality traditional clothing, including hand-knitted woollen jumpers, hats and socks. Most of the wool gathered in Ladakh lands up in the Kashmir Valley for milling and weaving, and few of the **pashmina shawls** on offer in the shops along Fort Road are genuine. However, a couple of Ladakhi co-operatives are trying to break the Kashmiri monopoly of the business and are producing pashmina shawls in Ladakh itself. Try the Ladakh Environment and Health Organization (LEHO; see p.568) for plush but plain shawls for around Rs5000.

Of the **bookshops** in Leh, Otdan, up the road from Dzomsa Laundry (see p.563), is one of the best, stocking a fair selection of Indian Penguin classics, plus dozens of more expensive titles on Ladakh and the Himalayas. Lehling, near the post office in the main bazaar, has a similar selection including maps. Second-hand paperbacks are sold or part-exchanged at Parkash Stationers opposite the vegetable market. Fairdeal Stationers near the Jami Masjid, Main Bazaar Square, has only a small selection of books but is good for **newspapers**.

Listings

Bike rental Mountain bikes can be rented from Again Adventures, Hemis Complex, Zangsti Rd (just up from Dzomsa Laundry). Rates are around Rs200/day for a local Hero "mountain bike".

Hospital Leh's overstretched, poorly equipped SNM Hospital (☎01982/252014), is 1km south of the centre on the main road. For urgent medical treatment, contact a doctor through any upmarket hotel.

Internet access Despite the sporadic electricity supply (expect a trickle in the evenings) and overloaded telephone exchange, Internet cafés are popping up all over Leh; the fastest connection is at eCafe next to *Tibetan Kitchen*; others to try include Gypsy World, Fort Rd, and Silk Route Travels opposite the State Bank, Main Bazaar. Charges start at Rs2/min.

Laundry Dzomsa Laundry (see p.563).

Libraries The Ecology Centre's excellent library (Mon–Sat 10am–4pm) keeps books on everything from agriculture to Zen Buddhism, as well as periodicals, magazines, and files of articles on Ladakh and development issues. Students of Buddhism should check out the collection of books at the Chokhang Vihara Monastery, across from the State Bank of India, or the Tibetan Cultural Centre in the south of town.

Meditation, yoga and alternative therapy In high season small classes are run by the Mahabodhi Society in Changspa which specializes in Vipassana ☎01982/253689; their extensive complex in Devachan (☎01982/244155, ⓦwww.mahabodhiladakh.org) near Choglamsar, 3km south of Leh, includes a meditation centre with courses ranging from three to seven days. The *Asia Guesthouse*, Changspa Lane, houses a German-run Vajrayana Meditation and Healing Arts Centre. Numerous posters and flyers advertise classes and sessions in yoga, reiki, shiatsu and other alternative therapies.

Motorbikes Although several places now hire motorcycles, with the going rate of around Rs800/day for an Enfield, you should check the bikes carefully. By far the most reliable of the agencies is Enntrax Tours (☎01982/250603), a few doors down from the *Khangri Hotel*; mopeds here are Rs650/24hr.

Paragliding Try Indus Himalayan Explorers, Fort Rd (☎01982/252788), across from the *Yak Tail Hotel*.

Pharmacy Het Ram Vinay Kumar at the top of the main bazaar sells a range of allopathic pills and potions, as well as batteries and tampons. For Tibetan medicine, two *amchis* at the LSTM Amchi Clinic, Changspa Lane (daily: July–Sept 8am–8pm, Oct–June 10am–4pm) speak English and charge Rs40 for a consultation using traditional diagnostic techniques.

Photography The Sonu Color Lab next to the Tibet Handicraft Emporium on the main street sells transparency and print film. Also look around the area beside the Jami Masjid; check the cases for expiry dates.

Moving on from Leh

As befits India's remotest Himalayan town, Leh is singularly hard to get to, and even harder to leave. Fragile road and air links mean visitors all too often find themselves stranded waiting for passes to open or planes to appear. Wherever and however you travel, book your onward ticket as far in advance as possible, be prepared for delays if the weather changes, and allow plenty of time to connect with onward flights.

By air

The quickest way out of Leh is **by plane**. During the summer, weather permitting, Indian Airlines and Jet Airways fly to **Delhi** (daily). IA also flies to **Jammu** (Mon & Fri), **Chandigarh** (Wed) and **Srinagar** (Sun). The rest of the year, flights are less reliable. Tickets can be booked and confirmed at the Indian Airlines/Tushita Travels office beyond *Hotel Lumbini* on Fort Road (daily 10am–5pm; ⓣ01982/252076), but you may have to wait. The computer is "down" a lot more than it's "up", and excessive demand for seats contributes to long queues, especially at the start and end of the tourist season before the passes open, and after the summer festival. It's a good idea to arrive thirty minutes before the office opens. The Jet office, located in the main bazaar (Mon–Sat 10am–5pm, Sun 10am–3pm; ⓣ01982/250999, ⓦwww.jetairways.com), across from Lehling Bookstore, is far more efficient. To Delhi, both IA and Jet Airways charge $117/$90 for passengers over/under 30.

Because Indian Airlines flights to Delhi and Chandigarh (but not Jammu or Srinagar) can only depart with 92 passengers (there are 126 seats but only a limited number of oxygen masks), some people inevitably get stuck. If you can, have your seat **confirmed** as soon as (or even before) you arrive in Leh. Note too that takeoffs require good visibility and the slightest scrap of cloud in the wrong place can result in last-minute cancellations.

By bus and 4WD

The overland route to **Manali** in Himachal Pradesh (see p.532) is officially open until September 15, but invariably a sense of panic sets in towards the end of the season, and some bus operators such as HPTDC fold up earlier. Private buses continue to ply the route through to early October as long as the weather holds, as do 4WD Gypsies and Sumos. The 485km journey across the Himalayas generally takes two days, with

Police ⓣ01982/252018 or 252200. ⓣ100 for the operator.

Post The post office is in the main bazaar (Mon–Sat 10am–1pm & 2–5pm). For parcels, go to the GPO (Mon–Sat 10am–4.30pm), out of town on Airport Rd, whose unreliable poste restante counter is tucked around the back. You can also receive letters through the Tourist Information Centre on Fort Rd.

Sauna and massage The sauna at the Sauna and Body Care Centre, Changspa Lane (ⓣ01982/253350) operates on demand during the season (9am till late) and charges Rs300; they also offer Ayurvedic massage sessions.

Telephones Most of the telephone facilities are to be found around the main bazaar and along Fort Rd. Though many shops have STD/ISD facilities, trunk and international telephone connections are poor, and prices higher than elsewhere in India.

Tour operators Reliable agents recommended for trekking and Jeep safaris include: Cold Desert Adventures, Fort Rd ⓣ01982/252516; Explore Himalayas, opposite the State Bank of India, Main Bazaar ⓣ01982/252727, ⓔexplorehimalayas@vsnl.com; Rimo Expeditions, *Hotel Kanglhachen* ⓣ01982/253348, ⓔrimo@vsnl.com; The Nomadic Way, Changspa Lane (ⓣ01982/255155) and Footprints, Fort Rd ⓣ01982/251799, and Dreamland Trek & Tours, Fort Rd (ⓣ01982/250784, ⓦwww.dreamladakh.com). K2 Adventure, Main Bazaar (ⓣ01982/252980) offers competitive rates for Jeep rental. Alternatively, you could try smaller agencies such as Oriental Travels, at the *Oriental Guest House*, below the Shanti Stupa, Changspa (ⓣ01982/253153), for a more personalized service. A recent initiative involves homestays in remote villages, which offer a dinner, bed and breakfast for Rs350/person (Rs600/couple), with 10 percent of the proceeds going a night halt in a tent camp en route – though if the road has been recently cleared of snow or landslides the journey can take three or four days. A full account of the route, starting at Manali, is given on pp.550–552. Tickets for **HPTDC**'s tri-weekly "deluxe" buses (Rs800 including overnight stop) can be booked at their office upstairs on Fort Road; be prepared for the journey taking a day longer. Several agencies along Fort Road, including Dreamland Trek & Tours (☎01982/250784) sell tickets for **private buses** to Manali for around Rs800. They will also help arrange a Sumo or Gypsy **4WD** to Manali from Rs11,000 one-way, or find you a seat in a shared Jeep (four in all). This is by far the most comfortable option and, if you leave before dawn, there's a good chance you can avoid the tented camps and reach the relative luxury of Keylong that evening. You may be lucky and find a Jeep returning to Manali, in which case expect to pay around Rs8000. Travellers who prefer to organize the trip themselves can march down to the long-distance bus stand where the Jeeps wait in line, and deal with the drivers directly a day before departure; pay Rs700 for a seat to Keylong and Rs1000 to Manali, and expect cramped conditions as drivers will ram in as many passengers as possible. Your position in the jeep will affect the price – the front seats can be Rs200–300 more expensive than those at the back. Cheaper options include the ramshackle **state transport** corporation buses run by HPSRTC and J&KSRTC, bookable the day before departure at the town bus stand.

J&KSRTC buses to **Srinagar** run from mid-June to late October, stopping overnight at Kargil before grinding up the bleak Zoji La pass (3540m), the threshold of Ladakh and Kashmir, and descending steeply into an alpine scene of birch, fir and flowers – the fabled Vale of Kashmir. It's a scenic route, and one which is becoming more and more popular with travellers, but you must check the current situation before you decide to visit (see p.11 for more on Kashmir).

If you want to **hitch** (unadvisable for lone women travellers) to either Manali or Srinagar, the truck park in Leh is between the old bus stand and the polo ground. Bear in mind you'll be expected to pay your way (around two-thirds of the current bus fare), and chip in for toll charges at police checkpoints. Trucks are also liable to break down more frequently than buses, and have more accidents.

For information regarding **local bus services** to destinations in Ladakh, see the relevant account, or see the "Travel details" at the end of this chapter.

towards village development programmes. The scheme is currently running in the areas between Likkir and Temisgang and Stok and Chilling. For more information contact Snow Leopard Trails (☎01982/252188, Ⓦwww.snowleopardtrails.com) in the *Hotel Kanglhachhen* Complex (on the road to Chubi). Several of these agents also offer rafting on the River Indus (see p.574).

Southeast of Leh

Southeast of Leh, the Indus Valley broadens to form a fertile river basin. Among the spectacular Buddhist monuments lining the edges of the flat valley floor are **Shey**, site of a ruined palace and giant brass Buddha, and the stunning monastery of **Tikse**. Both overlook the main highway and are thus served by regular buses.

With the exception of **Stok Palace**, home of the Ladakhi queen, sights on the opposite (south) side of the Indus, linked to the main road by a relatively infrequented and partly surfaced road, are harder to reach by public transport. South of Stok, **Matho** *gompa* is more famous for its winter oracle festivals than its art treasures, but is well worth a visit, if only for the superb views from its

Rafting on the River Indus

While water levels are high, between the end of June and late August, Leh's more entrepreneurial travel agents operate **rafting** trips on the River Indus. The routes are tame in comparison with Nepal's, but floating downstream in a twelve-seater rubber inflatable is a hugely enjoyable way to experience the valley's most rugged and beautiful landscape. Two different stretches of the river are used: from **Spitok** to the Indus-Zanskar confluence at **Nimmu** (3hr), and from Nimmu to the ancient temple complex at **Alchi** (2hr 30min). Experienced rafters may also want to try the more challenging route between Alchi and Khalsi, which takes in the kilometre-long series of rapids at **Nurla**. The annual multi-day expedition down the River Zanskar to the Indus is by far the most rewarding as it also includes the spectacular road approach to Padum.

Several adventure tour operators in Leh offer white-water rafting on the Indus, but all act as agents for Delhi-based operators who bring the equipment up during the season. **Tickets** should be booked at least a day in advance. The best established of the operators is Rimo Expeditions, *Hotel Kanglhachen* (ⓣ01982/253348, ⓔrimo@vsnl.com) near the central police station; **prices** start from Rs900. Make sure when you book that the price includes transport to and from the river, rental of life jackets and helmets, and meals, and that the raft has a waterproof strongbox for valuables.

roof terrace. Further south still, either cross the Indus and rejoin the highway, calling in at **Stakna** *gompa* en route, or continue down the left bank to **Hemis**, Ladakh's wealthiest monastery and the venue for one of the region's few summer religious festivals. To side-step your fellow tourists without spending a night away from Leh, head up the austerely beautiful tributary valley opposite Hemis to the *gompas* of **Chemrey** and **Thak Thok**, the latter built around a fabled meditation cave.

Further east and south, the easing of restrictions has opened up new areas. East of Thak Thok, the road crosses the Chang La and then veers east to the high mountain lake of **Pangong Tso**, most of which lies in Tibet. Far more relaxing and inviting is the vast wilderness of **Rupshu** with trekking possibilities around the shores of **Tso Moriri**. Permits are required for all these areas; for full details see the box on p.558.

Stok

Just beyond the Tibetan refugee camp at **Choglamsar**, at the head of a huge moraine, the elegant four-storey **Stok Palace** stands in the shadow of an intrusive TV mast, overlooking barley terraces studded with whitewashed farmhouses. Built early in the nineteenth century by the last ruler of independent Ladakh, it has been the official residence of the Ladakhi royal family since they were ousted from Leh and Shey two hundred years ago.

The present Gyalmo or "queen", Deskit Angmo, a former member of parliament, still lives here during the summer, and has converted one wing of her 77-roomed palace into a small **museum** (daily 8am–6pm; Rs30). The fascinating collection comprises some of the royal family's most precious heirlooms, including exquisite sixteenth-century **thangkas** illuminated with paint made from crushed rubies, emeralds and sapphires. The *pièces de résistance*, however, are the Gyalmo's **peraks**. Still worn on important occasions, the ancient headdresses, thought to have originated in Tibet, are encrusted with slabs of flawless turquoise, polished coral, lapis lazuli and nuggets of pure gold. **Stok gompa** (dawn–dusk; Rs10), twenty minutes' walk up the valley, boasts a collection of dance-drama masks, and some lurid modern murals painted by lamas from Lingshet *gompa* in Zanskar, the artists responsible for the Maitreya statue in Tikse (see p.578).

If you have time, it's also worth exploring the beautiful **side-valley** behind the village, which is the trailhead for the Markha Valley trek (see pp.576–577).

Practicalities

A half-day in **Stok** is enough to do it, and its side-valley, justice. **Buses** leave Leh for Stok (40min, Rs10) at 8am, 2pm, 4pm and 6pm. The last bus returning to Leh leaves at 5pm; if you miss it or are tempted to **stay**, try the *Hotel Highland* (Ⓣ01982/242005; ❻), a palatial two-storey house with fine views from its well-furnished en-suite rooms. About 2km down the road towards Leh is the imposing *Hotel Skittsal* (Ⓣ01982/242049, Ⓔhotelskittsal@vsnl.net; ❸–❻), with panoramic views over the Indus Valley. Both of these close in early September, unlike the small and basic *Kalden Guest House* (Ⓣ01982/242057; ❷) at the foot of the palace.

Shey

SHEY, 15km southeast of Leh and once the capital of Ladakh, is now all but deserted, the royal family having been forced to abandon it by the Dogras midway through the nineteenth century. Only a semi-derelict palace, a small *gompa* and a profusion of *chortens* remain, clustered around a bleached spur of rock that juts into the fertile floor of the Indus Valley. The ruins overlook the main highway, and can be reached on the frequent minibuses between Leh bus stand and Tikse. Alternatively, you could walk to Shey from Tikse monastery along a winding path that passes through one of Ladakh's biggest *chorten* fields with hundreds of whitewashed shrines of varying sizes scattered across the surreal desert landscape.

The **palace**, a smaller and more dilapidated version of the one in Leh, sits astride the ridge below an ancient fort. Crowned by a golden *chorten* spire, its pride and joy is the colossal metal Shakyamuni Buddha housed in its ruined split-level temple (daily 6–9am); if it's closed a key-keeper will let you in for Rs20. Installed in 1633, the twelve-metre icon allegedly contains a hoard of precious stones, mandalas and powerful charms. Entering from a painted antechamber, you come face to face with the Buddha's huge feet, soles pointing upwards. Upstairs, a balcony surrounding the statue's torso surveys the massive Buddha in better light. Preserved for centuries by thick soot from votary butter lamps, the gold-tinted murals coating the walls are among the finest in the valley.

Five minutes' walk from the *Shikhar Restaurant* at the base of the palace, and past an area of walled-in *chortens*, stands a **temple**, enshrining another massive Shakyamuni statue (daily 7–9am & 5–6pm). Best viewed from the mezzanine veranda on the first floor, it is slightly older than its cousin up the hill. The descendants of the Nepali metalworkers who made it, brought here by Sengge Namgyal, still live and work in the isolated village of **Chilling** (on the River Zanskar), famous for its traditional silverware.

Easily missed as you whizz past on the road is Shey's most ancient monument. The **rock carving** of the five Tathagata or "Thus gone" Buddhas, distinguished by their respective vehicles (*vahanas*) and hand positions (*mudras*), appears on a smooth slab of stone on the edge of the highway; it was probably carved soon after the eighth century, before the "Second Spreading" (see p.559). The large

Trekking in Ladakh and Zanskar

The ancient footpaths that crisscross **Ladakh** and **Zanskar** provide some of the most inspiring **trekking** in the Himalayas. Threading together remote Buddhist villages and monasteries, cut off in winter behind high passes whose rocky tops bristle with prayer flags, nearly all are long, hard and high – but never dull. Whether you make all the necessary preparations yourself, or pay an agency to do it for you, **Leh** is the best place to plan a trek (see p.561); the **best time** to trek is from June to September.

Trekking **independently** is straightforward if you have a copy of *Trekking in Ladakh* (see below), don't mind haggling, and are happy to organize the logistics yourself. To find ponies and guides, head for the Tibetan refugee camp at Choglamsar, 3km south of Leh. Count on paying around Rs200 per horse and Rs100 per donkey each day – two people trekking through the Markha Valley for example would pay around $20 each for the entire week. By contrast, a **package trek** sold by a trekking agent in Leh will cost around $45 per day, and more if your group is less than four people.

You can **rent equipment**, including high-quality tents, sleeping bags, sleeping mats and duck-down jackets, either through your chosen agency or at places like **Frontier Adventure Company**, across from the taxi stand on Fort Road (☎01982/253011) or **MERO** (Mountaineering Expeditions & Rescue Operations), across Fort Road (☎01982/253070), which is cheaper but has poorer equipment. Both also act as trek operators, supplying guides, porters, transport and food. Expect to pay Rs100 a day for a tent, Rs70 for a sleeping bag and Rs30 for a gas stove; if you're intending to climb Stok-Kangri you may need to dish out Rs40 for an ice axe. Independent trekkers might consider buying Indian equipment in the bazaar, which could be resold.

Minimize your impact in culturally and ecologically sensitive areas by being as **self-reliant** as possible, especially with food and fuel. Buying provisions along the way puts an unnecessary burden on the villages' subsistence-oriented economies, and encourages strings of unsightly "tea shops" (often run by outsiders) to sprout along the trails. Always burn kerosene, never wood – a scarce and valuable resource. Refuse should be packed up, not disposed of along the route, no matter how far from the nearest town you are, and plastics retained for recycling at the Ecology Centre in Leh. Always bury your faeces and burn your toilet paper afterwards. Finally, do not defecate in the dry-stone huts along the trails; local shepherds use them for shelter during snow storms. For more details about environmental issues in Ladakh see p.563.

An excellent **book** covering everything you need to know to undertake an expedition in the region is Trailblazer's *Trekking in Ladakh* (3rd edn), by Charlie Loram, on sale in bookstores in Leh. For information about trekking to **Zanskar** from the south, see "Trekking in Lahaul and Spiti" (p.543).

The Markha Valley

The beautiful **Markha Valley** runs parallel with the Indus on the far southern side of the snowy Stok-Kangri massif, visible from Leh. Passing through cultivated valley

central figure with hands held in the gesture of preaching (turning the wheel of *dharma*), is the Buddha Resplendant, Vairocana, whose image is central in many of the Alchi murals (see p.587).

Practicalities

Rooms are available at the *Besthang Hotel*, a converted traditional Ladakhi house (❷) with a pleasant garden and simple home cooking, located a few minutes walk down the lane behind the roadside *Shilkhar Restaurant*. The only floors, undulating high-altitude grassland, and snow-prone passes, the winding trail along it enables trekkers to experience life in a roadless region without having to hike for weeks into the wilderness – as a result, it has become the most frequented route in Ladakh. Do not attempt this trek without adequate wet- and cold-weather gear: snow flurries sweep across the higher reaches of the Markha Valley even in August.

The circuit takes six to eight days to complete, and is usually followed anticlockwise, starting from the village of **Spitok** (see p.585), 10km south of Leh. A more dramatic approach, via **Stok** (see p.574), affords matchless views over the Indus Valley to the Ladakh and Karakoram ranges, but involves a sharp ascent of **Stok La** (4848m) on only the second day; don't try it unless you are already well acclimatized to the altitude.

Likkir to Temisgang

A motorable road along the old caravan route through the hills between **Likkir** and **Temisgang** makes a leisurely two-day hike, which takes in three major monasteries (Likkir, Rhizong and Temisgang) and a string of idyllic villages. It's a great introduction to trekking in Ladakh, the perfect acclimatizer if you plan to attempt any longer and more demanding routes. Ponies and guides for the trip may be arranged on spec at either Likkir or Temisgang villages, both of which have small guesthouses and are connected by daily buses to Leh.

Lamayuru to Alchi

Albeit short by Ladakhi standards, the five-day trek from **Lamayuru** to **Alchi** is one of the toughest in the region, winding across high passes and a tangle of isolated valleys, past a couple of ancient *gompas*, and offering superb panoramic views of the wilderness south of the Indus Valley. It's very hard to follow in places, so don't attempt it without an experienced guide, ponies, and enough provisions to tide you over if you lose your way.

Padum to Lamayuru

The trek across the rugged Zanskar Range from **Padum** to **Lamayuru** on the Srinagar–Leh highway, usually completed in ten to twelve days, is a hugely popular but very demanding long-distance route, not to be attempted as a first-time trek, nor without adequate preparation, ponies and a guide.

Stok-Kangri

Visible from most of Leh, **Stok-Kangri** (6120m) is reputed to be the easiest 6000+m peak in the world. Several agents in Leh advertise five-day **climbing expeditions** via the village of Stok with a nontechnical final climb for around $35 per head per day for a group of four. If you've got *Trekking in Ladakh* in your rucksack, it's straightforward to walk up it independently, though you'll need to carry enough food for three or four days.

eating option in Shey, the *Shilkhar,* opposite the path leading up to the palace, has a varied menu of Indian and Western food. Buses arrive every couple of hours from Leh (30min), the last one at around 6.30pm. Returning to Leh, buses pass by every hour until 6.15pm, or you can hitch.

Tikse

Ladakh's most photographed and architecturally impressive *gompa* is at **TIKSE**, 19km southeast of Leh. Founded in the fifteenth century, its whitewashed *chortens* and cubic monks' quarters rise in ranks up the sides of a craggy bluff, crowned by an imposing ochre- and red-painted temple complex whose gleaming golden finials are visible for miles in every direction.

Tikse's reincarnation as a major tourist attraction has brought it mixed blessings: its constant stream of summer visitors spoils the peace and quiet necessary for meditation, but the income generated has enabled the monks to invest in major refurbishments, among them the **Maitreya temple** immediately above the main courtyard. Inaugurated in 1980 by the Dalai Lama, the shrine is built around a gigantic fourteen-metre gold-faced Buddha-to-come, seated not on a throne as is normally the case, but in the lotus position. The bright murals on the wall behind, painted by monks from Lingshet *gompa* in Zanskar, depict scenes from Maitreya's life.

For most foreign visitors, however, the highlight of a trip to Tikse is the view from its lofty **roof terrace**. A patchwork of barley fields stretches across the floor of the valley, fringed by rippling snow-flecked desert mountains and a string of monasteries, palaces, and Ladakhi villages. To enjoy this impressive panorama accompanied by primeval groans from the *gompa*'s gargantuan Tibetan trumpets – played on the rooftop at the 7am puja – you'll have to stay overnight or arrange an early Jeep from Leh.

Practicalities

A metalled road cuts up the empty west side of the hill from the main highway to the monastery's small car park. If you arrive by **minibus** from Leh (hourly, from the town bus stand), pick your way across the wasteground below the *gompa* and follow the footpath up through its lower buildings to the main entrance, where monks issue tickets (Rs20). The last bus back to Leh leaves at 6pm. The village's *Chamba Hotel* (April–Sept; ⓣ01982/267005; ❷–❸), run by the monastery, offers **accommodation** and flexible rates, with a good garden **restaurant** serving a varied menu from Tibetan food to pancakes.

Matho

MATHO, 27km south of Leh, straddles a spur at the mouth of an idyllic side-valley that runs deep into the heart of the Stok-Kangri massif. Though no less interesting or scenically situated than its neighbours, the *gompa*, the only representative in Ladakh of the **Sakyapa** sect (which held political power in thirteenth-century Tibet), sees comparatively few visitors. As it's relatively isolated from the main highway, **buses** aren't all that frequent: services leave Leh daily at 7.30am, 8am and 4pm, returning at 7am, 9am and 6pm. By car, Matho also makes an ideal halfway halt on the journey along the little-used left-bank road between Stok and Hemis.

Despite its collection of 400-year-old *thangkas*, the monastery is best known for its **oracle festival**, Matho Nagran, held on the twenty-fifth and twenty-sixth day of the second Tibetan month (around Feb/March). Two oracles, known as *rongzan*, are elected by lot every three years from among the sixty or so resident lamas. During the run-up to the big days, the pair fast and meditate in readiness for the moment when they are possessed by the spirit of the deity. Watched by crowds of rapt onlookers, they then perform all manner of death-defying stunts that include leaping blindfold around the *gompa*'s precipitous parapets while slurping kettle-fulls of *chang*, and slashing themselves with razor-sharp sabres without drawing blood. The events are rounded off with colourful *chaam* dances in the monastery courtyard, and a question-and-answer session in which the *rongzan*, still under the influence of the deity, make prophecies about the coming year.

You can admire the costumes and masks worn by the monks during the festivals in Matho's small **museum**, tucked away behind the Du-khang. Men are also permitted to visit the eerie **Gon-khang** on the roof (strictly no photography), where the oracles' weapons and ritual garb are stored. The floor of the tiny temple lies under a deep layer of barley brought as harvest offerings by local villagers.

Hemis

Thanks to its famous festival – one of the few held in summer, when the passes are open – **HEMIS**, 45km southeast of Leh, is visited in greater numbers than any other *gompa* in Ladakh. Every year in mid-July (see p.560 for dates), hundreds of foreigners join the huge crowds of locals, dressed in their finest traditional garb, that flock to watch the colourful two-day pageant. However, at other times, the rambling and atmospheric seventeenth-century **monastery** (entrance Rs20) can be disappointingly quiet. Although one of the region's foremost religious institutions, only a skeleton staff of monks and novices are resident off-season.

The main entrance opens onto the large rectangular courtyard where the festival **chaam dances** are performed. Accompanied by cymbal crashes, drum rolls and periodic blasts from the temple trumpets, the culmination of the event on the second day is a frenzied dismemberment of a dummy, symbolizing the destruction of the human ego, and thus the triumph of Buddhism over ignorance and evil. Once every twelve years, the Hemis festival also hosts the ritual unrolling of a giant *thangka*. The *gompa*'s prize possession, which covers the entire facade of the building, it was embroidered by women whose hands are now revered as holy relics. Decorated with pearls and precious stones, it was last displayed in 2004.

Practicalities

By car, Hemis is an easy day-trip from Leh. By **bus**, services are only frequent during the festival; at other times a single daily service leaves Leh at 9.30am and returns at noon, leaving barely enough time to poke your head inside the temple chambers. Another bus leaves Leh at 4pm but stays the night at Hemis, returning the next morning at 7am. An overnight stay means you can attend the 7am puja, although **accommodation** in Hemis is limited. You can camp below nearby Chomoling village for free or at the *Hemis Restaurant* (Rs50), located below the *gompa* and run by young *carrom*-playing monks. Alternatively, basic rooms (❶) are available in local houses, some let by monks – ask at either the *Hemis Restaurant* or the *Parachute Restaurant* in Chomoling. Both restaurants serve simple **food**; the latter is cheaper, has a selection of pancakes and is a useful stop-off for trekkers heading for the Markha Valley. Pause here for last-minute tips and a weather update; day hikers can enquire about guides to explore the mountains around Hemis.

Chemrey

Clinging like a swallow's nest to the sides of a shaly conical hill, the magnificent *gompa* of **CHEMREY** (Rs20) sees very few visitors because of its location – tucked up the side-valley that runs from Karu, below Hemis, to the Chang La pass into Pangong. If you don't have your own vehicle, you'll have to be prepared to do some walking to get here. It takes around fifty minutes to follow the dirt track down to the river and up to the monastery after the Leh–Thak Thok bus drops you off beside the main road.

Founded in 1664 as a memorial to King Sengge Namgyal, the monastery is staffed by a dwindling community of around twenty Drugpa monks and their young novices. Its main **Du-khang**, off the courtyard on the lower level, boasts a fine silver *chorten* and a set of ancient Tibetan texts whose title pages are illuminated with gold and silver calligraphy. Upstairs in the revamped **Guru-La-khang** sits a giant brass statue of Padmasambhava.

Thak Thok

A few kilometres up the valley from Chemrey above the village of **Sakti**, **THAK THOK** (pronounced *Tak-Tak* and meaning "rock roof") *gompa* shelters a cave in which the apostle Padmasambhava is said to have meditated during his epic eighth-century journey to Tibet. Blackened over the years by sticky butter-lamp and incense smoke, the mysterious grotto is now somewhat upstaged by the monastery's more modern wings nearby. As well as some spectacular 35-year-old wall paintings, the **Urgyan Photan Du-khang** harbours a collection of multicoloured yak-butter candle-sculptures made by the head lama. For a glimpse of state-of-the-art Buddhist iconography, head to the top of Thak Thok village, where a shiny new temple houses a row of huge gleaming Buddhas, decked out in silk robes and surrounded by garish modern murals.

Apart from during the annual **festivals** (see p.560), the village of Sakti is a tranquil place, blessed with serene views south over the snowy mountains behind Hemis. Accommodation is available in the J&K *Tourist Bungalow* (❷) on the road directly below the *gompa*. There are also plenty of ideal camping spots beside the river, although as ever you should seek permission before putting up a tent on someone's field. Nine buses a day leave Leh for Sakti, the first at 8am and the last at 4.30pm. The last bus back to Leh departs at 4pm.

Pangong Tso

Pangong Tso, 154km southeast of Leh, is one of the largest saltwater lakes in Asia, a long narrow strip of water stretching from Ladakh east into Tibet. Only a quarter of the 134-kilometre-long lake is in India, and the army, who experienced bitter losses along its shores in the war against China in 1962, jealously guard their side of the frontier. Until the mid-1990s, it was off limits to visitors, and tourists still need a permit to come here (see the box on p.588). The lake, at an altitude of 4267m, with the dramatic glacier-clad Pangong Range to its south and the Changchenmo Range reflected in its deep blue-green waters to the north, measures 8km across at its widest point and provides a tantalizing view of Tibet in the distance, although the bitter winds blowing over the brackish water make it one of the coldest places in Ladakh. Occasional public **buses** from Leh (Rs144) will drop off visitors at the village of **Spangmik** before continuing to the restricted border area; return buses come through the next morning at around 7.30am. There is basic **accommodation** (Rs100) and food at Spangmik, but most tourists come here on an organised two-day **Jeep safari**. Tour operators in Leh (see pp.572–573) provide all the necessary facilities, including camping and food at **Lukung**, 15km north of the lake, and will also arrange your permit. Jeep safari prices start at around Rs5500 for up to four people plus a driver and guide. To add further interest to the trip, take in the monasteries of Chemrey and Thak Thok en route.

Tso Moriri

Famous for the large herds of *kiang*, or wild ass, which graze on its shores, the lake of **Tso Moriri**, 210km southeast of Leh, lies in the sparsely populated region of **Rupshu**. You need a permit to travel here (see the box on p.558), which most visitors do via a Jeep safari out of Leh.

Nestling in a wide valley flanked by some of the highest peaks in Ladakh – **Lungser Kangri** (6666m) and **Chanmser Kangri** (6622m) – the twenty-kilometre-long lake is home to flocks of migratory *nangpa* or bar-headed geese, as well as occasional herds of pashmina goats and camps of nomadic herders. Located on the shores of the lake at an altitude of 4595m, **Karzok** – the only large village in the area – is a friendly place with a small *gompa*. To help protect the fragile ecosystem against the influx of tourists, a new directive stipulates that no habitation can be built within 700m of the shoreline. Visitors should bring their own food supplies and make sure they take all their rubbish away.

The open spaces around Tso Moriri make for some pleasant **trekking**, including the relatively easy – if you are acclimatized – three-day, forty-kilometre circuit of the lake. Another route gaining popularity is the trail from Rumtse near Upshi via Tso Kar to Tso Moriri. Some trekking operators in Manali and Leh can arrange more ambitious routes such as the ancient trade route linking **Spiti** to Tso Moriri and Leh via Kibber. Treks start from around $40 per person per day in a group of four, which usually includes transport, food and tents.

Practicalities

From Leh, three **buses** depart for Tso Moriri on the 10th, 20th and 30th of each month at 6am (Rs158), returning the following day. Another option is to hitch a ride on a truck, or to visit on a **Jeep safari** (see pp.572–573 for details of tour operators in Leh), which start at around Rs7000 for a two-day trip. These usually follow a circular itinerary through Upshi and Mahe Bridge, winding up at Karzok. From there they then continue on towards the Manali–Leh Highway, passing the lake of Tso Kar and Thukse village along the way. **Accommodation** is available in local homestays (❷) – you may have to ask around – and in Karzok, at the Delhi-run and fairly grotty *Lake View* (❺), just below the bus stand. Similarly overpriced is the tent colony, where a bed costs a whopping Rs1000. Anyone headed this way should first check out the **video** on Tso Moriri, *Forbidden Wilderness*, shown at Leh's Ecology Centre (see p.567).

North of Leh: Nubra Valley

Until 1994, the lands north of Leh were off limits to tourists, and had been unexplored by outsiders since the nineteenth century. Now, the breathtaking **Nubra Valley**, unfolding beyond the world's highest stretch of motorable road as it crosses the **Khardung La** (5602m), can be visited with a seven-day **permit** (see p.558), which gives you enough time to explore the stark terrain and trek out to one or two *gompas*. The valley's mountain backbone looks east to the Nubra River and west to the Shyok River, which meet amid silver-grey sand dunes and boulder fields. To the north and east, the mighty Karakoram Range marks the Indian border with China and Pakistan. In the valley it's relatively mild, though **dust storms** are common, whipping up sand and light debris in choking clouds above the broad riverbeds.

Before the region passed into the administrative hands of Leh, Nubra's ancient kings ruled from a palace in **Charasa**, topping an isolated hillock opposite Sumur, home to the valley's principal monastery. Further up the Nubra River, the hot springs of **Panamik**, once welcomed by footsore traders, are blissfully refreshing after ten hours on a bus. By the neighbouring Shyok River, **Diskit**, surveyed by a hillside *gompa*, lies just 7km from **Hundur**, known for its peculiar high-altitude double-humped Bactrian camels.

The route north to Nubra, a steep and rough road that forces painful groans from buses and trucks, keeps Leh in sight for three hours before crossing the Khardung La, and ploughing down more gently towards the distant Karakoram Range. Due to its strategic importance as the military road to the battlefields of the Siachen Glacier, the road to Nubra is kept open all year round but conditions can be treacherous at any time.

Practicalities

Buses (Rs95) leave Leh at 6am for Panamik via Sumur (Tues & Sat; 8hr) and Hunder via Diskit (Tues, Thurs & Sat; 6hr). The buses return to Leh the next day and you should book your return journey on arrival. Alternatively, **Jeeps** for a maximum of five people can be rented from Leh taxi rank or any tour operator (see pp.572–573). A complete three-day itinerary, including a visit to Diskit and Panamik, costs in the region of Rs6500 for the Jeep plus driver. Once in the valley, **hitching** on military or road-builders' trucks is an option, though it's inadvisable for lone travellers. The few **taxis** at Diskit charge from around Rs1000 for a day's exploration of the valley, with trips to Sumur and Panamik adding up. **Buses** between Diskit and Panamik travel daily, leaving Panamik at 7am and returning at 4pm.

Sumur

Beyond the confluence of the Shyok and Nubra rivers, **SUMUR**, a sleepy oasis spread over a large area, is home to the valley's most influential monastery, **Samstem Ling gompa**, a pleasant forty-minute walk behind the village. Built in 1841, the *gompa* accommodates just under a hundred Gelug-pa monks, aged between 7 and 70. To catch the morning or evening pujas, you'll have to **stay** in Sumur. Most of the guesthouses are on the sand lane which leads off from the bus stop at the prayer wheel. Closest to the main road is the *AO Guesthouse*, which has basic doubles including six with attached baths (ⓣ01980/223506; ❶–❷), a garden, vegetarian café and camping; as a fallback option, head further down the lane to the *Galaxy Guesthouse* (ⓣ01980/223503; ❷), where you can also camp for Rs60. A further ten minutes up the lane, in the village proper, the friendly *Stakray Guesthouse* (ⓣ01980/223518; ❷) has basic double rooms overlooking a huge vegetable garden and a traditional Ladakhi kitchen. It's a 1.5km trek to the *gompa*; equally convenient for catching the pujas, but overpriced, the *Yarab Tso* (Leh ⓣ01980/223544; ❻ full board) is at Teggar village, twenty minutes walk up the main road to Panamik.

Buses leave from the prayer wheel on the main road for Leh (Wed & Sun 7am; 5hr), Panamik (daily 4pm; 1hr), and Diskit (daily 8am; 1hr 30min).

Panamik

A one-hour bus journey (22km) up the valley from Sumur, **PANAMIK** (aka Pinchimik), a dusty hamlet overlooked by the pin-point summit of Charouk Dongchen, marks the most northerly point in India accessible to tourists. A kilometre past the **hot springs**, beyond the stone walls that line the pitted road, is the village proper. Splitting into wide rivulets at this point, the sapphire Nubra seems shallow and tame, but it's not – heed local advice not to ford it as there have been several reported accidents involving travellers.

Don't expect much from Panamik's hot springs – they're no more than a stone shack on the hillside, 100m past the J&K tourism hut. In fact, once you're here, there's little to do but walk. A dot on the mountainside across the river, **Ensa gompa** makes an obvious excursion. The route, three hours each way, passes through the village and crosses a bridge beyond the vast boulder field 3km upstream, then joins a wide Jeep track above the river for 3 or 4km. The final haul up a precipitous gorge hides the *gompa* from view until you stumble upon it, couched in an unexpected valley of willow and poplar trees fed by a perennial sweet-water stream. Though the *gompa* is usually locked, the views from rows of crumbling *chortens* nearby make the climb worthwhile. If one of the few semi-resident monks is there, however, you'll be shown inside to see the old wall paintings in the temples, and the footprint of Tsong-kha-pa, allegedly imprinted at this spot when he journeyed from Tibet to India in the fourteenth century.

The *Hot Spring Guesthouse* (❷) just beyond the hot springs themselves, and the unsigned *Bangka Guesthouse* (❷), 600m further along, comprise Panamik's unexciting **accommodation** options. All **buses** passing through Sumur originate from or terminate in Panamik. Direct buses to Leh depart Wednesday and Sunday at 6am.

Diskit and Hundur

DISKIT feels rather dull on first impressions, but it does possess an appealing old town, whose low, balconied houses lie below the main road before the diversion to the centre. For the guesthouses, get off at the first bus stop, next to the prayer wheel, from where a road runs down through the old quarter to the bazaar. The other road climbs the hillside above the town to Diskit's picturesque **gompa**, built in 1420. If you're on foot, follow the long *mani* wall, which continues on the other side of the road, and trace the path that winds upwards from its end to the monastery – a steep walk of around thirty minutes. The *gompa*'s steps climb past the monks' quarters to the first of a group of temples (Rs20; a monk may offer his services as a guide). Local legend has it that a Mongol demon, a sworn enemy of Buddhism, was slain nearby, but his lifeless body kept returning to the *gompa*. What are reputed to be his wrinkled head and hand are now clasped by a pot-bellied protector deity in the spooky **Gon-khang**.

The diminutive **Lachung temple**, higher up, is the oldest here. Soot-soiled murals face a huge Tsong-kha-pa statue, topped with a Gelug-pa yellow hat. In the heart of the *gompa*, the **Du-khang**'s remarkable mural, filling a raised cupola above the hall, depicts Tibet's Tashilhunpo *gompa*, where the Panchen Lama is receiving a long stream of visitors approaching on camels, horses and carts. Finally, the **Kangyu Lang** (bookroom) and **Tsangyu Lang** temples act as storerooms for hundreds of Mongolian and Tibetan texts.

HUNDUR, a tiny village in a wooded valley, 7km north, is as far as one is allowed to go along this part of the Nubra Valley. The village is renowned for its herd of Bactrian camels (a vestige of its days on the old trans-Karakoram trade route) which you may encounter during the walk up here. The main monastery lies just below the main road, near the bridge and the end of the route. Further down and across the brook is a creaky, cobweb-filled old manor that once belonged to the local Zimskhang royal family, and is now occasionally unlocked by a key-keeper at the *Goba Guesthouse*. Abdul Razzaq, an ex-teacher, organizes **camel rides** around Hundur starting around Rs800: ask at the *Snow Leopard Guesthouse*. A similar deal can be struck at the *Sangam View Guesthouse* in Diskit.

Practicalities

Buses stop on Diskit's main road by the prayer wheel where the road descends through the old quarter to the bazaar, and then again on the new road to the bazaar, before continuing to Hundur.

Accommodation in Diskit is simple but ample. By the upper bus stop close to the prayer wheel on the main road, *Olthang Guest House* (ⓣ01980/220025; ❶–❺) has a wide range of rooms, including five with bath; home-grown vegetables from the picturesque garden are served for dinner in the dining hall, which doubles as a bar in the evenings. You can camp here for Rs80. Follow the road down from the prayer wheel and along the *mani* wall on your right through a *chorten* gate to cosy *Sun Rise* (ⓣ01980/220011; ❷) which has cheap beds, shared bathrooms and a pleasant garden. Further down the road, behind a set of *chortens*, is the homely *Karakoram Guest House* (ⓣ01980/220024; ❶–❷) which has good food in the traditional Ladakhi kitchen and camping spots in the garden for Rs30. Another 100m down the lane the pleasant *Thachung* (ⓣ01980/220002; ❶–❷) has beautiful sunny glass rooms and clean bathrooms. All the guesthouses will provide food.

Accommodation in **Hundur** is even more laid back; the most popular hangout is the friendly *Goba Guesthouse* (ⓣ01983/221083; ❶–❷), 400m down from the roadside *gompa*, a quaint, low-key affair with a sunny yard and hundreds of flowers. Closer to the road and catering to group tours is the overpriced *Chamba Camp* (ⓣ01980/221140; ❽), a group of luxury tents ($55) set up on the grounds of Zimskhang Manor. More secluded, but excellent value, the *Snow Leopard* (ⓣ01980/221097; ❷–❸), set in a beautiful vegetable garden, has great views and offers some rooms with bath. To get there, follow the metalled road past *Chamba Camp* and the new *Jamshed Guesthouse* toward Diskit; you'll reach the *Snow Leopard* in around ten minutes.

Buses return to Leh from Diskit at 9am (Wed, Fri & Sun; 6hr). Make sure you buy a ticket from the driver the day before, otherwise you're unlikely to be let on. There's a daily bus to Sumur and Panamik at 3pm, except on Sundays when the bus departs at 8am and returns at 2pm. If you're not alone, **hitching** is a good alternative. You can usually get a lift with one of the slow military vehicles running up and down the valley.

West of Leh

Of the many *gompas* accessible by road **west of Leh**, only **Spitok**, piled on a hilltop at the end of the airport runway, and **Phyang**, which presides over one of Ladakh's most picturesque villages, can be comfortably visited on day-trips from the capital. The rest, including **Likkir** and the temple complex at **Alchi**, with its wonderfully preserved eleventh-century murals, are usually seen en route to or from **Kargil**. The 231km journey, which takes in a couple of high passes and some mind-blowing scenery, can be completed in a single eight-hour haul. To do this stretch of road justice, however, you should spend at least a week making short forays up the side-valleys of the Indus, where idyllic settlements and *gompas* nestle amid barley fields and mountains.

One of the great landmarks punctuating the former caravan route is the monastery of **Lamayuru**. Reached via a nail-biting sequence of hairpin bends as the highway climbs out of the Indus Valley to begin its meandering ascent of **Fotu La**, it lies within walking distance of some extraordinary lunar-like rock formations, at the start of the main trekking route south to Padum in Zanskar.

The Kargil War

After three years of cross-border artillery exchanges over the "Ceasefire Line", in the spring of 1999 conflict between India and Pakistan escalated into the full-blown **Kargil War**. The conflict was to shatter the Indo-Pakistani dialogue which seemed to be gradually improving after years of impasse, and resulted in the dramatic overthrow of the Pakistani prime minister Nawaz Sharif, followed by the re-establishment of military rule by General Musharraf. Pakistani intentions were to cut the Srinagar–Leh Highway and capture the Muslim-dominated areas of western Ladakh, putting further pressure on Indian Kashmir.

In early May, the Indian army realized that infiltrators across the disputed 150-kilometre Line of Control, who had followed the high ridges snaking into Indian territory, were not disparate bands of separatists but Pakistani regulars. The ensuing conflict to dislodge the Pakistanis involved intense artillery battles and raids by an initially dispirited Indian army up from the valley floors to near inaccessible positions, many on peaks in excess of 5000m. Some of the heaviest fighting, involving regiments from all over India, including the newly formed Ladakh Scouts, took place in the Drass sector where Pakistani positions came as close as 3km to the strategic highway. The battles for the peaks of Tololing and Tiger Hill above Drass proved crucial in turning the tide of a war which was the first between the neighbours to be fully televised. After nearly three months of bitter fighting, the war came to a close towards the end of July 1999, with Pakistan having to retreat from the heights, by which time over a thousand Indian and Pakistani soldiers had lost their lives.

The Line remained relatively quiet until the spring of 2002 when tensions over a possible nuclear exchange were relieved by heavy shelling around Kargil and Drass – some 5000 rounds in eight weeks. Pakistan delivered its heaviest onslaught of shells a week prior to the J&K state elections in September 2002, hoping to prevent voters from reaching the polls, though unexpected media pressure laid upon Pakistani President Musharaf, touring the US at the time, were perhaps the reason further strikes were called off on polling day.

Further west still, beyond the dramatic **Namika La** pass, **Mulbekh** is the last Buddhist village on the highway. From here on, *gompas* and *gonchas* give way to onion-domed mosques and flowing *salwar kamises*.

There is, on average, an accident a day on the narrow, high and twisting Leh–Kargil road. Tata trucks are the most prone to toppling off the tarmac, and it can take hours for the rescue vehicles from Leh and Kargil to arrive and then clear the road. In summer, **transport** along the highway is straightforward; ramshackle state and private buses ply the route; getting to more remote spots, however, can be hard. Some travellers resort to paying for a ride on one of the countless Tata trucks that lumber past, or hitch with an army convoy, but getting a group together to rent a **Jeep** from Leh (pp.572–573), while expensive, will be safer, save time and give more access to the side-valleys.

Spitok

SPITOK gompa, rising incongruously from the end of the airport runway, makes a good half-day foray from Leh, 10km up the north side of the Indus Valley. If you can't afford the taxi fare, the easiest way to get there is to stroll down to the crossroads above the GPO and J&K's tourist reception centre, and then flag down any of the **buses** heading west along the main Srinagar highway. Travellers who walk the whole way invariably regret it, as the route is relentlessly dull, passing through a string of unsightly military installations hemmed in by barbed-wire fences. A break in the monotony appears

1km before Spitok in the form of the **Museum of Ladakh, Culture and Military Heritage** (Rs20), a self-congratulatory montage of Indian military achievements in Ladakh, with tributes to the heroic road builders who risked their lives to open Ladakh to the world. A couple of token rooms cover the other 2000 years of Ladakhi history.

The fifteenth-century **monastery**, which tumbles down the sides of a steep knoll to a tight cluster of farmhouses and well-watered fields, is altogether more picturesque. Approached by road from the north, or from the south along a footpath that winds through Spitok village, its spacious rooftops command superb views. The main complex is of less interest than the **Palden Lumo** chapel, perched on a ridge above. Although visiting soldiers from the nearby Indian army barracks consider the deity inside the temple to be Kali Mata, the key-keeper will assure visitors that what many consider to be the black-faced and bloodthirsty Hindu goddess of death and destruction is actually **Yidam Dorje Jigjet**. Coloured electric lights illuminate the cobwebbed chamber of veiled guardian deities whose ferocious faces are only revealed once a year. If you have a torch, check out the 600-year-old paintings on the back wall, partially hidden by eerie *chaam* masks used during the winter festival season.

Phyang

A mere 17km west of Leh, **PHYANG gompa** looms large at the head of a secluded side-valley that tapers north into the Ladakh Range from the Srinagar highway. Eight daily **buses**, including three battered government buses (7.30am, 2pm & 5pm; Rs11), serve the *gompa*; if you miss your return bus, just walk down the paved access road to the main highway (30min) and flag down a vehicle bound for Leh.

The *gompa* itself houses a fifty-strong community of lamas, but few antique murals of note, most having recently been painted over with brighter colours. Its only treasures are a small collection of fourteenth-century Kashmiri bronzes (locked behind glass in the modern Guru-Padmasambhava temple), and the light and airy **Du-khang**'s three silver *chortens*, one of which is decorated with a seven-eyed **dzi stone**. The gem, considered to be highly auspicious, was brought to Phyang from Tibet by the monastery's former head lama, whose ashes the *chorten* encases. Tucked away around the side, the shrine in the *gompa*'s gloomily atmospheric **Gon-khang** (Rs20) houses a ferocious veiled protector deity and an amazing collection of weapons and armour plundered during the Mongol invasions of the fourteenth century. Also dangling from the cobweb-covered rafters are various bits of dead animals, including most of a vulture and several sets of yak horns, believed to be 900-year-old relics of the Bon cult (see p.1407).

Phyang's annual **festival**, Phyang Tsedup, held in summer (between mid-July and early Aug; see p.560) to coincide with the tourist season, is the second largest in Ladakh after Hemis. Celebrated with the usual masked *chaam* dances, the event is marked with a ritual exposition of a giant ten-metre brocaded silk *thangka*.

Likkir

Five kilometres to the north of the main Leh–Srinagar highway, shortly before the village of Saspol, the large and wealthy *gompa* of **LIKKIR**, home to around one hundred monks, is renowned for its new 23-metre-high yellow statue of the Buddha-to-come which towers serenely above the terraced fields. A pleasant break from the bustle of Leh, the village of Likkir offers a small but adequate choice of accommodation which, along with the sheer tranquillity of the surroundings, tempts many travellers to linger a few days.

The *gompa*, 3km up the valley from the village, was extensively renovated in the eighteenth century and today shows little sign of the antiquity related to the site. It overlooks the starting point for the popular two-day hike to Temisgang via Rhizong, which provides a comparatively gentle introduction to trekking in Ladakh.

The direct **bus** from Leh (4pm) goes past the village and makes the 3km haul up the valley to the *gompa*, returning to Leh at 7am the next morning. If you miss the regular bus, take any west-bound vehicle, get dropped off on the main Leh–Kargil highway (by the solitary chai stall) and walk the short but treeless one-kilometre road to the village, where you can hire a taxi for the *gompa*. Simple **rooms** are available at the *gompa* itself and next door at the monastic school; both ask for a donation. The pleasant *Gaph-Chow*, in the lower village (Ⓣ01982/252748; ❷), has simple, comfortable rooms with attached baths, camping space in the lovely vegetable garden, email facilities, a garden café and traditional Ladakhi kitchen. The other option is the friendly *Norboo Spon* (❸), easily spotted from the road to the monastery; accommodation is full-board and the owner offers woodcarving and *thangka*-painting lessons to his guests. He can also give good trekking advice – aided by the scale model of the Likkir-Temisgang trek in his garden.

Alchi

Driving past on the nearby Srinagar–Leh highway, you'd never guess that the cluster of low pagoda-roofed cubes 3km across the Indus from **Saspol**, dwarfed by a spectacular sweep of wine-coloured scree, is one of the most significant historical sites in Asia. Yet the *Chos-khor*, or "religious enclave", at **ALCHI**, 70km west of Leh, harbours an extraordinary wealth of ancient wall paintings and wood sculpture, miraculously preserved for more than nine centuries inside five tiny mud-walled temples. The site's earliest murals are regarded as the finest surviving examples of a style that flourished in Kashmir during the "Second Spreading". Barely a handful of the monasteries founded during this era escaped the Muslim depredations of the fourteenth century; Alchi is the most impressive of them all, the least remote and the only one you don't need a special permit to visit. Nestled beside a bend in the milky-blue River Indus amid some dramatic scenery, it's also a serene spot to break a long journey to or from the Ladakhi capital.

Legend tells that Rinchen Zangpo, the "Great Translator" (see p.559), stuck his walking stick in the ground here en route to Chilling and upon his return found it had become a poplar, an auspicious sign that made him build a temple on the spot. One tree near the entrance to the *Chos-khor*, denoted with a signboard, is symbolic of this event. The *Chos-khor* itself consists of five separate temples, various residential buildings and a scattering of large *chortens*, surrounded by a mud-and-stone wall. If you are pushed for time, concentrate on the two oldest buildings, the **Du-khang** and the **Sumtsek**, both in the middle of the enclosure. Entrance **tickets** (Rs25) are issued by a caretaker lama from nearby Likkir *gompa*, who will unlock the doors for you. Newly installed lights mean you can no longer use a torch to examine the paintings' vibrant colours close up, nor are you allowed to take photographs (even without flash).

The Du-khang

An inscription records that Alchi's oldest structure, the **Du-khang**, was erected late in the eleventh century. Its centrepiece is an image of Vairocana, the "Buddha Resplendent", flanked by the four main Buddha manifestations that appear all over Alchi's temple walls, always presented in their associated colours: Akshobya ("Unshakeable"; blue), Ratnasambhava ("Jewel Born"; yellow), Amitabha ("Boundless Radiance"; red) and Amoghasiddhi ("Unfailing Success"; green). The other walls are decorated with six elaborate mandalas, interspersed with intricate friezes.

The Sumtsek

Standing to the left of the Du-khang, the **Sumtsek** marks the high watermark of early-medieval Indian-Buddhist art. Its woodcarvings and paintings, dominated by rich reds and blues, are almost as fresh and vibrant today as they were 900 years ago, when the squat triple-storey structure was built. The heart of the shrine is a colossal statue of **Maitreya**, the Buddha-to-come, his head shielded from sight high in the second storey. Accompanying him are two equally grand **bodhisattvas**, their heads peering serenely down through gaps in the ceiling. Each of these stucco statues wears a figure-clinging *dhoti*, adorned with different, meticulously detailed motifs. Avalokitesvara, the *bodhisattva* of compassion (to the left), has pilgrimage sites, court vignettes, palaces and pre-Muslim style *stupas* on his robe, while that of Maitreya is decorated with episodes from the life of Gautama Buddha. The robe of Manjushri, destroyer of falsehood, to the right, shows the 84 masters of Tantra, the *mahasiddhas*, adopting complex yogic poses in a maze of bold square patterns.

Among the exquisite **murals**, some repaired in the sixteenth century, is the famous six-armed green goddess Prajnaparamita, the "Perfection of Wisdom". Amazingly, this, and the multitude of other images that plaster the interior of the Sumtsek, resolve, when viewed from the centre of the shrine, into a harmonious whole.

Other temples

The *Chos-khor*'s three **other temples** all date from the twelfth and thirteenth centuries, but are nowhere near as impressive as their predecessors. Tucked away at the far, river end of the enclosure, the **Manjushri La-khang** is noteworthy only for its relatively recent "Thousand Buddha" paintings and gilded four-faced icon of Manjushri that fills almost the whole temple. Next door, the **Lotsawa La-khang**, with its central image and mural of Shakyamuni, is one of a handful of temples dedicated to Rinchen Zangpo; his small droopy-eared image sits on the right of Shakyamuni. The lama may need to be cajoled into unlocking the **La-khang Soma**, the small square shrine south of the Sumtsek, which is decorated with three large mandalas and various figures including an accomplished *yab-yum*: the Tantric image of the copulating deities symbolizes the union of opposites on a material and spiritual level.

Practicalities

An alternative to hiring a taxi from Leh is to catch the 8am or 4pm private **bus** (Rs38) which takes three hours to cover the 70km and returns at 3.45pm or 7am the next day. Other buses heading in that direction leave Leh at 5.30am (for Kargil) and 9am (for Dah-Hanoo) – you can catch one of these, get off at the turn-off past **Saspol**, and walk up the remaining 6km via the motorable suspension bridge west of the village.

Of the growing selection of **guesthouses** in Alchi, the *Lotsava* (☎01982/227129; ❷), left of the main road as you approach the taxi stand, is pleasant and simple with good views; the landlady serves filling breakfasts and evening meals in the small garden if you give her enough warning. On both sides of the lane that leads to the *gompa*, the *Zimskhang* (Ⓣ01982/227086; ❷–❺) has two identities; to the right a modern hotel, and to the left a cheaper guesthouse with a pleasant garden. More upmarket is the purpose-built *Sam Dubling* (Ⓣ01982/221704; ❼), 100m above the taxi stand, approached by following the stream behind the *Potala Guesthouse*. The *Alchi Resort* (Ⓣ01982/252520; ❽) near the taxi stand consists of luxurious cabins aimed at tour groups.

Lamayuru

If one sight could be said to sum up Ladakh, it would have to be **LAMAYURU gompa**, 130km west of Leh. Hemmed in by a moonscape of scree-covered mountains, the whitewashed medieval monastery towers above a scruffy cluster of tumbledown mud-brick houses from the top of a near-vertical, weirdly eroded cliff. A major landmark on the old silk route, the *gompa* numbers among the 108 (a spiritually significant number, probably legendary) founded by the Rinchen Zangpo in the tenth and eleventh centuries. However, its craggy seat, believed to have sheltered Milarepa during his religious odyssey across the Himalayas, was probably sacred long before the advent of Buddhism, when local people followed the shamanical Bon cult (see p.1407). Just thirty lamas of the Brigungpa branch of the Kagyu school are now left, as opposed to the four hundred that lived here a century or so ago. Nor does Lamayuru harbour much in the way of art treasures. The main reason visitors make a stop on this section of the Srinagar–Leh road is to photograph the *gompa* from the valley floor, or to pick up the trail to the Prikiti La pass – gateway to Zanskar – which begins here.

The steep footpath from the highway above town brings you out near the main entrance to the monastery, where you should be able to find the lama responsible for issuing entrance tickets (Rs20), and unlocking the door to the **Du-khang**. Lamayuru's newly renovated prayer hall houses little of note other than a **cave** where Naropa, Milarepa's teacher, is said to have meditated, and a collection of colourful yak-butter sculptures. If you're lucky, you'll be shown through the tangle of narrow lanes below the *gompa* to a tiny **chapel**, whose badly damaged murals of mandalas and the Tathagata Buddhas date from the same period as those at Alchi (see p.587).

Practicalities

Lamayuru lies too far from either Leh or Kargil, 107km west, to be visited in a day-trip, so you either have to call in en route between the two, or spend the night here. The daily Leh–Kargil and Kargil–Leh **buses** both depart at 5.30am from their respective towns of origin, and pass through Lamayuru at around 9am – either by the chai shops next to the *Dragon Guest House*, or on the road high above the *gompa* – so check locally before you sit down to wait. Alternatively, a private bus (Mon, Tues & Thurs 7am; Rs76) leaves Leh for Lamayuru, passing through Lamayuru at 10.30am before continuing to Kargil. **Trekkers** in search of reliable guides and ponies could ask at the *Dragon Guest House*; give a couple days advance notice or enquire with their office in Leh (Ⓣ01982/253164).

Dominating the village skyline, the four-storey *gompa*-style *Niranjana Hotel* (❺–❻) has twenty plain concrete **rooms** with good views of the surrounding valleys; shared bathrooms have hot running water. Dorms cost Rs100, and there are meditation rooms and a veg restaurant. Prices double during the **festival** (late June/early July). Alternatively, the welcoming family-run *Dragon Guest House* (❷) has a range of rooms, including one coveted glass room, and a

△ Lamayuru

pleasant garden restaurant which is the best place to eat in Lamayuru. For rock-bottom price and cleanliness, there are a couple of traditional family homestays (❶); the best is the *Tashi Guesthouse* at the foot of the cliff under the *gompa*.

Mulbekh

West of Lamayuru, the main road crawls to the top of **Fotu La** (4091m), the highest pass between Leh and Srinagar, then ascends **Namika** ("Sky-Pillar") **La** (3760m), so called because of the jagged pinnacle of rock that looms above it to the south. Once across the windswept ridge, it drops through a dramatic landscape of disintegrating desert cliffs and pebbly ravines to the wayside village of **MULBEKH** – the last sizeable Buddhist settlement along the road before the Muslim Purki settlements around Kargil. The village is scattered around the banks of the River Wakha, lined with poplars and orchards of walnut and apricot trees.

Formerly an outpost of the Zangla kingdom of western Ladakh (the deposed monarchs, King Nyima Norbu Namgyal Dey and his queen, Tashi Deskit Angmo, still live in a dilapidated four-storey mansion on the western outskirts of the village), Mulbekh would be a sleepy hamlet were it not for the endless convoys of trucks and tourist buses that thunder through while the passes are open. Those visitors who stop at all tend only to stay long enough to grab a chai at a roadside *dhaba*, and to have a quick look at the seven-metre-high **Maitreya** ("Chamba" in Tibetan) **statue** carved from the face of a gigantic boulder nearby. The precise origins of the shapely four-armed Buddha-to-be are not known, but an ancient inscription on its side records that it was carved between the seventh and eighth centuries, well before Buddhism was fully established in Tibet. The single-chambered *gompa* (Rs10), in front of the statue and decorated with particularly beautiful murals, is dedicated to the thousand-armed Chenrazig (Avalokiteshvara).

Another incentive to prolong your stay in Mulbekh is the brace of village **gompas**, perched atop a smooth 200-metre rock 1km west of the Chamba statue. A steep flight of steps winds up to the whitewashed temples; one Kargyu-pa and the other Gelug-pa, each maintained by a lone caretaker monk. Neither houses any great treasures, but the views down the Wakha Valley from their terraces make the climb (a very stiff one if you're not yet acclimatized to the altitude) well worthwhile. Some 2.5km east of the Chamba statue, on the road to Leh, lies the small Gelug-pa nunnery of **Jangchup Choeling**, founded in 1987, which has a school and pleasant garden courtyard.

Accommodation in Mulbekh is limited to shabby rooms above tea shops such as the *Paradise* (❶) and the *Tsomo Riri* (❶) on the main road opposite the Chamba statue; serving *thukpa*, dhal, rice, *momos* and butter tea during the day, they later turn into cheap drinking dens. The *Tourist Bungalow* (❶), 800m down the road towards Leh, though poorly maintained is a better bet, with attached baths.

Kargil

Though it is surrounded by awesome scenery, most travellers don't spend more than a few hours in **KARGIL**, capital of the area dubbed "Little Baltistan", which rises in a clutter of corrugated iron rooftops from the confluence of the Suru and Drass rivers. As a half-way point between Leh and Srinagar, its grubby hotels fill up at night-time with weary bus passengers, who then get up at 4am and career off under cover of darkness. While Kargil has no attractions, it is an atmospheric place to pass a day or more while waiting for a bus to Zanskar.

Woolly-hatted and bearded old men and slick youths stroll the streets past old-fashioned wholesalers with their sacks of grains, spices and tins of ghee, Tibetans selling Panasonic electricals and butchers displaying severed goats' heads on dusty bookshelves. The town feels more Pakistani than Indian, and the faces (nearly all male) and food derive from Kashmir and Central Asia. Tourists are unusual, and Western women should keep their arms and legs covered; those walking around alone will probably encounter both giggling teenage boys and curious elderly Kargili gentlemen.

The majority of Kargil's 5500 inhabitants, known as Purki, are strict **Muslims**. Unlike their Sunni cousins in Kashmir, however, the locals here are orthodox **Shias**, which not only explains the ubiquitous Ayatollah photographs, but also the conspicuous absence of women from the bazaar. You might even spot the odd black turban of an Agha, one of Kargil's spiritual leaders, who have outlawed male-female social practices such as dancing and still go on pilgrimage to holy sites in Iran. Descendants of settlers and Muslim merchants from Kashmir and Yarkhand, Purkis speak a dialect called **Purig** – a mixture of Ladakhi and Balti. Indeed, had it not been for the daring Indian reconquest of the region during the 1948 Indo–Pak War (the Indian army forced their Pakistani adversaries out of town after transporting an entire tank division over the Zoji La pass), Kargil would today be part of Baltistan, the region across the Ceasefire Line which it closely resembles. Indeed, Kargil is so close to the Ceasfire Line and Pakistani positions that it served as the logistics centre in the 1999 War, and was repeatedly targeted by Pakistani artillery. Aside from the odd building destroyed, however, much of the town escaped unscathed as the army bases and airport lie on the outskirts of town. The tense summer of 2002 saw further conflict, and a civilian road worker was killed during a heavy raid of more than 200 shells. Now the dust has settled somewhat, the cautiously friendly dialogue between India and Pakistan on Kashmir will hopefully diminish the border tensions here, and already tourist numbers are starting to increase. You should still, however, check the current situation before setting out.

Practicalities

Buses arriving in Kargil from Leh, Srinagar and Padum either pull in to the main bus stand, immediately below the top (west) end of the bazaar, or at the truck park above the river, two minutes' walk downhill from the main street. If you plan to head off early in the morning, check when you buy your ticket where the bus leaves from. Buses for Mulbekh leave at 3pm, 3.30pm and 4pm (Rs20) every day. In the mornings you may be able to catch a shared Matador minibus. If you're wanting to head south, the government has recently suspended its service to Padum in Zanskar, citing lack of demand, so you'll need to try your luck with the private buses. These are patchy at best, and generally run three times a week (but not on fixed days) – and, due to the lack of alternatives, tend to be very busy. If you don't mind hitching, you could catch a bus to Panikhar (daily 7am & 2pm; Rs45) and wait by the *Kayoul*. Hiring a taxi is much less hassle; the one-way fare to Padum is Rs7900 (Rs1300 per person). For **Leh**, a reliable J&K state bus departs on Mondays at 4.30am (Rs180), but the quick and easy option is to book a seat (a day in advance) in a Tata Sumo (Rs400), which run daily from the taxi stand.

The J&K **tourism reception centre** (Mon–Sat 10am–4pm; ⓣ01985/232721) is on the east side of town, around the corner from the **taxi stand** and most of the hotels. As well as the usual leaflet on Ladakh, they rent out Norwegian **trekking equipment**, including four-season sleeping bags, tents, coats and boots. The State Bank of India will not change money or travellers' cheques, but the *Siachen Hotel* can exchange sterling or dollars. Kargil's mercurial **Internet** connection (Rs50/hr) can be accessed at the Kargil Computer Institute, under the arch of the Jami Masjid.

Accommodation

The Kashmir crisis, which reduced tourist traffic to a trickle, squeezed half of Kargil's **hotels** out of business, and most of those that remain are either geared towards tour groups or are total dives. Room tariffs soar in July and August, when a flea-infested windowless hovel without running water can cost as much as Rs250. The rates quoted below apply to peak season; discounts are usually available at other times. Most of the more salubrious hotels offer meals, with substantial discounts if you don't take the option.

Crown Next to the bus stand. Rambling old budget hotel that's seen better days but somehow still attracts backpackers. Some rooms come with attached bathrooms and there's a dirt cheap dorm (Rs20). Running water on request. ❶–❷

Greenland At the end of the lane heading east from the taxi stand ⓣ01985/232324. A notch above rock-bottom, with a restaurant and reasonable rooms (some with bath); those on the first floor are more spacious. ❸

J&K Tourist Bungalow no.1 A 5min walk uphill from the crossroads above the bus stand ⓣ01985/232328. Clean rooms, clean sheets and peaceful atmosphere, with a small dining room. By far the best budget deal in town. If the *chowkidar* says it's full, get a "chit" from the tourist reception centre. ❶

Kargil Continental Next to the *Greenland*, past the tourist office ⓣ01985/232304. Open all year, with large comfortable rooms and a pleasant garden, but it's a bit soulless and expensive. ❻

Siachen Below the west side of the taxi stand ⓣ01985/233055, ⓔhotel-siachen-kargil@rediffmail.com. Large, comfortable, and one of the best of the downtown hotels, with en-suite rooms, a few budget options on the first floor, a good restaurant and STD phones. The friendly management will exchange foreign currency. ❺–❻

Eating

Besides upmarket hotels like the *Siachen*, finding somewhere to **eat** in Kargil is a toss-up between the small tourist-oriented cafés on the lane from the truck park to the bazaar, or a *dhaba* on the main street. All the restaurants are closed for **breakfast**, but the street food can be delicious - chai, chapatis and omelettes, with hot Kashmiri bread slathered with butter. From 7am try the chai stall just up from the *Naktul*.

Karan Singh Punjabi Janata East end of Main St. One of the town's better *dhabas*: spicy Indian sauces spooned onto groaning platefuls of rice.

Naktul On the lane from the bus stand to Main Bazaar. Delicious Kashmiri *kawa* tea, as well as a range of Kashmiri and Chinese dishes. Better at lunchtime; they run out of food in the evening.

Rubby Main bazaar. Popular restaurant serving local specialities including *yakhani* (meat boiled in yoghurt) and *gustaba* (meat balls), both of which can be daunting if you're not adjusted to Central Asian cuisine.

Shashella Main bazaar. Kashmiri and Chinese dishes, as well as *momo thukpa*.

Zojila Bakery Main bazaar. A good place to stop for a morning tea, or to pick up bread and cookies.

The Suru Valley

Dividing two of the world's most formidable mountain ranges, the **Suru Valley** winds south from Kargil to the desolate Pensi La – the main entry point for Zanskar. The first leg, usually undertaken in the pre-dawn darkness by bus, leads through the broad lower reaches of the Suru Valley, strewn with Muslim villages clustered around metal mosque domes. As you progress southwards, the pristine white ice-fields and pinnacles of **Nun-Kun** (7077m) nose over the horizon. Apart from a brief disappearance behind the steep sides of the valley at **Panikhar**, this awesome massif dominates the landscape all the way to Zanskar.

Shortly beyond Panikhar, the Suru veers east around the base of Nun-Kun, passing within a stone's throw of the magnificent **Parkachik Gangri** glacier. Having wound across a seemingly endless boulder field, closed in on both sides by sheer mountain walls, the road then emerges at a marshy open plain surrounded by snow peaks and swathes of near-vertical strata. **Juldo**, a tiny settlement whose fodder-stacked rooftops are strung with fluttering prayer flags, marks the beginning of Buddhist **Suru**.

The climb to the pass from **Rangdum gompa**, across the flat river basin from Juldo, is absolutely breathtaking. One glistening 6000-metre peak after another appears atop a series of side-valleys, many lined with gigantic folds of rock and ice. The real high point, though, is reserved for the dizzying descent from **Pensi La** (4401m), as the road's switchbacks swing over the colossal S-shaped **Darung Drung Glacier**, whose milky-green meltwaters drain southeast into the Stod Valley, visible below.

Panikhar

Although by no means the largest settlement in the Suru Valley, **PANIKHAR**, three hours' bus ride south of Kargil, is a good place to break the long journey to Padum. Before the Kashmir troubles, it was a minor trekking centre, at the start of the Lonvilad Gali–Pahalgum trail. These days, the scruffy collection of roadside stalls and poor mud-brick farmhouses sees very few tourists, even in high season.

The main reason to stop is to hike to nearby **Parkachik La**, for panoramic views of the glacier-gouged north face of the mighty **Nun-Kun massif**. The **trail** up to the pass begins on the far side of the Suru, crossed via a suspension bridge thirty minutes south of the village. It may look straightforward from Panikhar, but the four-hour round-trip climb to the ridge gets very tough indeed towards the top, especially for those not used to the altitude. However, even seasoned trekkers gasp in awe at the sight that greets them when they finally arrive at the cairns. Capped with a plume of cloud and with snow streaming from its huge pyramidal peak, Nun sails 3500m above the valley floor, draped with heavily crevassed hanging glaciers and flanked by its sisters, multi-pinnacled Kun and saddle-topped Barmal.

There are only two **places to stay** in Panikhar. The *Kayoul* (☎01985/259080, ❶), directly opposite the bus stand, has a couple of very basic rooms with fold-away *charpois* and shared "earth" latrines, plus a ramshackle roadside café. For a bit more comfort, try the modest J&K *Tourist Bungalow* (❶), 100m further down the road on the left, where a large en-suite room with running water sets you back a mere Rs80. **Buses** to Kargil leave from the *Kayoul* at 7am and 11am. If you're looking for a lift to Padum, collar the truckers as they leave the *dhaba* after their lunch; the one-way fare costs around the same as the bus (Rs170).

Zanskar

Walled in by the Great Himalayan Divide, **ZANSKAR**, literally "Land of White Copper", has for decades exerted the allure of Shangri-La on visitors to Ladakh. The region's staggering remoteness, extreme climate and distance from the major Himalayan trade routes has meant that the successive winds of change that have blown through the Indus Valley to the north had little impact here. The annual influx of trekkers and a motorable road have certainly quickened the pace of development, but away from the main settlement of Padum, the

Zanskaris' way of life has altered little since the sage Padmasambhava passed through in the eighth century.

The nucleus of the region is a Y-shaped glacial valley system drained by three main rivers: the **Stod** (or Doda) and the **Tsarap** (or Lingit) join and flow north as the **Zanskar**. Lying to the leeward side of the Himalayan watershed, the valley sees a lot more snow than central Ladakh. Even the lowest passes remain blocked for seven or eight months of the year, while midwinter temperatures can drop to a bone-numbing minus 40°C. Ten thousand or so tenacious souls subsist in this bleak and treeless terrain – among the coldest inhabited places on the planet – muffled up for half the year inside their smoke-filled whitewashed crofts, on a winter's-worth of fodder piled on the roof.

Until the end of the 1970s, anything the resourceful Zanskaris could not produce for themselves (including timber for building) had to be transported into the region over 4000 to 5000-metre passes, or, in midwinter, carried along the frozen surface of the Zanskar from its confluence with the Indus at Nimmu – a ten- to twelve-day round trip that's still the quickest route to the Srinagar–Leh road from Padum. Finally, in 1980, a motorable dirt track was blasted down the Suru and over Pensi La into the Stod Valley. Landslides and freak blizzards permitting (Pensi La can be snowbound even in August), the bumpy journey from Kargil to Padum can now be completed in as little as thirteen hours.

Most visitors come to Zanskar to **trek**. Numerous trails wind their way north from Padum to central Ladakh, west to Kishtwar, and south to neighbouring Lahaul – all long hard hikes (see box on pp.576–577). If you're travelling down here hoping to use the district headquarters as a comfortable base from which to make short day-trips, you'll be disappointed. Only a handful of Zanskar's widely scattered *gompas* and settlements lie within striking distance of the road. The rest are hidden away in remote valleys, reached after days or weeks of walking.

Improved communications may yet turn out to be a mixed blessing for Zanskar. While the new road has undoubtedly brought a degree of prosperity to Padum, it has already forced significant changes upon the rest of the valley – most noticeably a sharp increase in tourist traffic – whose long-term impact on the region's fragile ecology and traditional culture has yet to be fully realized. Increased tourism has, in fact, done little to benefit the locals financially, with agencies in Leh, Manali, Srinagar and even Delhi pocketing the money paid by trekking groups. Zanskaris, weary of seeing their region come second to Kargil (which lies in the same administrative district), have been campaigning for several years for a sub-hill council status with more control over development, and a road following the Zanskar river gorge to Nimmu; the road project is going ahead, but painfully slowly. Buddhist concerns have also been heightened in the face of state government mismanagement and communal tensions that followed the massacre of the three monks at Rangdum in July 2000.

Padum

After a memorable trek or bus ride, **PADUM**, 240km to the south of Kargil, comes as a bit of an anticlimax. Instead of the picturesque Zanskari village you might expect, the region's administrative headquarters and principal roadhead turns out to be a desultory collection of crumbling mud and concrete cubes, oily truck parks and tin-roofed government buildings. The settlement's only real appeal lies in its superb location. Nestled at the southernmost tip of a broad, fertile river basin, Padum presides over a flat patchwork of farm land enclosed on three sides by colossal walls of scree and snow-capped mountains.

Straddling a nexus of several long-distance trails, Padum is an important **trekking hub** and the only place in Zanskar where tourism has thus far made much of an impression. During the short summer season, you'll see almost as many weather-beaten Westerners wandering around its sandy lanes as locals – a mixture of indigenous Buddhists and Sunni Muslims. Even so, facilities remain very basic, limited to a small tourist office and a handful of temporary tea-shops and guesthouses, as well as the inevitable rash of Kashmiri handicraft stalls. Nor is there much to see while you are waiting for your blisters to heal. The only noteworthy sight within easy walking distance is a small **Tagrimo gompa** fifteen minutes' walk to the west.

Practicalities

Arriving in Padum by **bus**, you'll be dropped in the dusty square at the far south end of the village, close to the old quarter and a couple of the cheaper guesthouses. Going the other way, a bus ticket for Leh costs around Rs390. The J&K **Tourist Complex** (July–Sept Mon–Sat 10am–4pm; ☎01983/245017) lies 1km north of the square in Mane Ringmo, on the side of the main road, two minutes' walk from the other main concentration of guesthouses; it's good for general advice, though it doesn't rent out trekking gear. Due to the short season and the limited tourist trade, renting a car in Padum (through the Padum Taxi Union office near the bus stand) is expensive: a trip to Karsha and back costs around Rs2000. As yet, there is nowhere in Padum to change money, although you can mail letters from the **post office** next door to the tourist centre. STD **telephone** facilities are available nearby at the Zanskar Telecom Service.

Basic **trekking supplies** are sold at the hole-in-the-wall stores above the bus stand. Prices are much higher than elsewhere, so it pays to bring your own provisions with you from Kargil. Most trekkers arrange **ponies** through the tourist office or guesthouse owners, or you could try Zanskar Trek (☎01983/245053), who also supply guides (Rs500 per day). Expect to pay Rs200–300 per pony per day, depending on the time of year (ponies transport grain during the harvest, so they're more expensive in early September). If you have trouble finding a horse-wallah in Padum, ask at a neighbouring village, such as Pipiting, a thirty-minute walk north across the fields from Padum, where many of them live.

Accommodation

Accommodation in Padum is limited to a handful of grotty guesthouses and rooms in private family homes. In both cases, bathrooms are usually shared, and toilets are of the "long-drop" variety. One exception is the simple but comfortable J&K *Tourist Complex* (☎01983/245017; ❶), whose well-maintained en-suite doubles have running cold water. The *Hotel Ibex* (☎01983/245012; ❸), with doubles set around a courtyard, could be much improved if fumigated. Other options, both near the bus stand, include the friendly French-run *Mont Blanc* (❷–❸, tent pitch Rs50) and the *Chorala* (☎01983/245035; ❶), which offers reasonable doubles and even has a travel desk. The least shambolic of the budget guesthouses in the village proper is the *Greenland* (❷), near the mosque, which boasts a couple of light and airy rooms. Alternatively, **camping** pitches near the tourist centre cost Rs50 per night, though don't leave valuables in the tent – there have been recent reports of theft. Trekkers arriving from Shingo La sometimes camp beside the stream in the Tsarap Valley.

Eating

Finding **food** in Padum only tends to be a problem towards the end of the trekking season; by mid-October, stocks of imported goods (virtually everything except barley flour and yak butter) are low, and even a fresh egg can be a cause for celebration. Earlier in the year, temporary teashops and cafés ensure a supply of filling and inexpensive meals - one of the best is the *Lhasa*. For cheap Chinese and Tibetan food, try the *Changthang* near the *Tourist Bungalow*, or the *Gakyi Café* near the post office. Most guesthouses also provide half-board if given enough warning; the *Hotel Ibex* has the best restaurant.

Around Padum

Public transport around the Zanskar Valley is erratic, although one public bus travels from Padum to Zangla (Rs35) on Wednesday and Friday, leaving in the morning and returning the same afternoon. Otherwise you will have to shell out for the vastly inflated fares demanded by Padum's taxi union. Determined trekkers can alternatively set out on foot; the hike across the fields to **KARSHA gompa**, Zanskar's largest Gelug-pa monastery, is the most rewarding objective. This cluster of whitewashed mud cubes clinging to the rocky lower slopes of the mountain north of Padum dates from the tenth to the fourteenth century. Of the prayer halls, the recently renovated Du-khang and Gon-khang at the top of the complex are the most impressive, while the small *Chukshok-jal*, set apart from the *gompa* below a ruined fort on the far side of a gully, contains Karsha's oldest wall paintings, contemporaneous with those at Alchi (see p.587).

The quickest way to get to Karsha on foot is to head north from Padum to the cable bridge across the Stod, immediately below the monastery. Set off early in the morning; the violent icy storms that blow in from the south across the Great Himalayan Range around mid-afternoon make the ninety-minute hike across the exposed river basin something of an endurance test. Karsha is a far more pleasant place to stay than Padum and some villagers rent **rooms** to tourists. Try the wonderful glass room belonging to Thuktan Thardot in Sharling Ward just below the *gompa* (❶).

Karsha can also be reached by road, via the bridge at **Tungri**, 8km northwest of Padum. En route, you pass another large *gompa*, **SANI**, lauded as the oldest in Zanskar, and the only one built on the valley floor. Local legend attributes its foundation to the itinerant Padmasambhava (Guru Rinpoche) in the eighth century. Set apart from the temples a little to the north is a two-metre-high Maitreya figure, carved out of local stone some time between the eighth and tenth centuries.

Travel details

Buses

The bus details here apply during the **tourist season** between July 1 and September 15 only, after which date the Manali–Leh highway is officially closed. Most other roads, including the highway from Leh to Srinagar via Kargil, remain open until the end of October. Despite heavy snow falls, the road from Leh to the Nubra Valley over the incredibly high Khardung La is kept open all year.

Leh to: Alchi (1 daily; 3hr); Chemrey (9 daily; 2hr); Diskit (Nubra) (1 weekly; 6hr); Hemis (2 daily; 1hr 45min); Kargil (1 daily; 8hr); Lamayuru (1 daily; 6hr 30min); Likkir (2 daily; 3hr); Manali (4 daily; 28hr); Matho (3 daily; 1hr); Panamik & Sumur (Nubra) (2 weekly; 10hr); Phyang (5 daily; 1hr 15min); Shey (hourly; 30min); Spitok (4 hourly; 20min); Srinagar (1–2 daily except Sun; 20hr); Stok (2 daily; 40min); Temisgang (2 daily; 5hr); Thak Thok (9 daily; 2hr 30min); Tikse (hourly; 45min).

Kargil to: Drass (2 daily; 2hr); Leh (1 daily; 8hr); Mulbekh (2–3 daily; 1hr 30min); Padum (3 weekly; 13hr); Panikhar (2 daily; 3hr); Sankhu (3 daily; 1hr 30min); Srinagar (1–2 daily; 12hr).

Flights

Leh to: Delhi (IA, JA daily, 2 daily in high season; 1hr 15min–3hr); Chandigarh (IA 1 weekly; 1hr); Jammu (IA 2 weekly; 50min); Srinagar (IA 1 weekly; 45min).

CHAPTER 8

Highlights

* **Rock Garden, Chandigarh** This bizarre and seemingly haphazard sculpture garden, assembled from industrial debris by a local eccentric, offers curious contrast to the ordered city that surrounds it. See p.602

* **The Golden Temple, Amritsar** One of the great sights – and sounds – of India; *kirtan* (devotional songs) are performed throughout the day and into the night. See p.614

* **Border ceremony, Wagha** Shorter and more colourful than a cricket match, the border ceremony is a highly charged event, especially on Sundays, when hundreds of people gather. See p.617

△ Golden Temple, Amritsar

8

Haryana and Punjab

The prosperous states of **HARYANA** and **PUNJAB** occupy the flat and fertile tract of river plain that extends northwest from Delhi, towards the mountains of Kashmir and the border with Pakistan. Divided by the Partition of August 1947, Punjab has been systematically shorn of its once vast territory: losing the Punjab Hills to Himachal Pradesh and later sacrificing a further chunk to create Haryana. Crossed by the five major tributaries of the **Indus**, the former British-administered region of Punjab ("Land of Five Rivers") was split down the middle at Independence. Indian Muslims fled west into Pakistan, and Hindus east, in an exodus accompanied by horrific massacres. The Sikhs, meanwhile, threw in their lot with India, which they considered a safer option than the homeland of their Muslim arch-enemies. In 1966 prime minister Indira Gandhi, in response to Sikh pressure, further divided the state into two semi-autonomous districts: the predominantly Sikh Punjab, and the 96-percent Hindu Haryana, both governed from the newly built capital of **Chandigarh**.

There is little of tourist interest in the two states other than the beautiful Golden Temple in Amritsar and the wacky Rock Garden of Chandigarh, but the region – known as India's "bread basket" – is very important to the nation's **economy**. Punjabi farmers produce nearly a quarter of India's wheat, and one-third of its milk and dairy foods, while Ludhiana churns out ninety percent of the country's woollen goods. Helped by remittance cheques from millions of expatriates in the UK, US and Canada, the state's per capita income is now almost double the national average.

The Sikh faith encourages economic self-reliance and strong family ties, and their temples or **gurudwaras** are very welcoming, being open to all castes and creeds. Although you'll see full-bearded orthodox *sardars* strolling around the **Golden Temple** in the holy city of **Amritsar**, most Sikhs today are liberal. Known as *sahajdharis*, less devout members of the faith are frequently stereotyped as *bon viveurs*, and with some justification: Punjab boasts both India's richest regional cuisine, and its highest per capita consumption of alcohol.

Most travellers simply pass through the region en route to Himachal Pradesh, or to the Indo-Pak border at **Wagha**, but a visit to the Golden Temple is well worth the effort. If you want to linger longer, there's also Le Corbusier's experimental city of **Chandigarh**, the Moghul monuments at **Sirhind** and **Pinjore**, the great *gurudwara* at **Anandpur Sahib**, the European-inspired **Kapurthala** or any of the countless brick villages. You'll find the inhabitants, many of whom seem to have a cousin in Toronto or Southall, extremely hospitable. Crossing Haryana and Punjab en route to, or from, Delhi, you're bound to travel at some stage along part of the longest, oldest and most famous highway in India – the

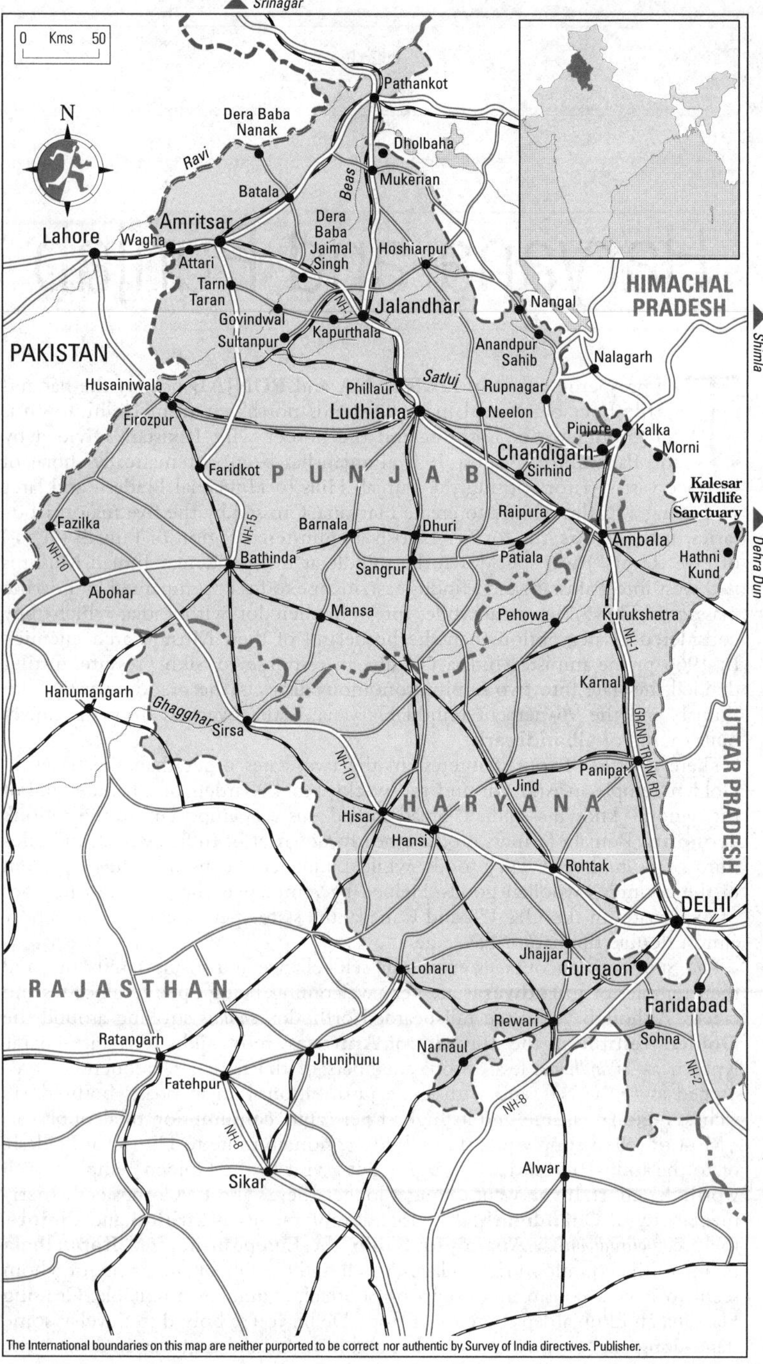

8

HARYANA AND PUNJAB

NH-1, alias the **Grand Trunk Road**, stretching 2000km from Peshawar near the rugged Afghan–Pakistan frontier to Kolkata (Calcutta) on the River Hooghly. The first recorded mention of this trade corridor dates from the fourth century BC, when it was known as the Uttar Path (the "North Way").

Some history

Punjab's first urban settlement, dating back to 3000 BC and now known as the **Harappan** Civilization, was invaded by the Aryans around 1700 BC. Among the Sanskrit scriptures set down in the ensuing **Vedic** age was the **Mahabharata**, whose epic battles drew on real-life encounters between the ancient kings of Punjab at Karnal, 118km north of Delhi. Conquered by the Mauryans in the third century BC, it saw plenty more action as various invading Moghul armies passed through on their way from the Khyber Pass to Delhi – including Babur, who routed Ibrahim Lodi at Panipat in 1526.

Meanwhile, further north, **Sikhism** was beginning to establish itself under the tutelage of Guru Nanak (1469–1539). Based on the notion of a single Formless God, the guru's vision of a casteless egalitarian society found favour both with Hindus and Muslims, in spite of Moghul emperor Aurangzeb's attempts to stamp it out. Suppression actually strengthened the Sikh faith in the long run, inspiring the militaristic and confrontational tenth guru **Gobind Singh** to introduce the Five Ks, part of a rigorous new orthodoxy called the **Khalsa**, or "Community of the Pure" (see also Contexts, p.1410).

Having survived repeated seventeenth-century Afghan invasions, the Sikh nation emerged to fill the power vacuum left by the collapse of the Moghuls. Only in the 1840s, after two bloody wars with the British, was the Khalsa army finally defeated. Thereafter, the Sikhs played a vital role in the Raj, helping to quash the Mutiny of 1857. The relationship only soured after the **Jallianwalla Bagh massacre** of 1919 (see p.614), which also ensured that the Punjab's puppet leaders (who hailed the general responsible as a hero) were discredited, leaving the way open for the rise of radicalism.

After the Partition era and Independence, things calmed down enough to allow the new state to grow wealthy on its prodigious agricultural output. As it did, militant Sikhs began to press for the creation of the separate Punjabi-speaking state they called Khalistan. A compromise of sorts was reached in 1966, when the Hindu district of Haryana and the Sikh-majority Punjab were nominally divided. However, the move did not silence the separatists, and in 1977 Indira Gandhi's Congress was trounced in state elections by a coalition that included the Sikh religious party, the **Akali Dal**.

A more sinister element entered the volatile equation with the emergence of an ultra-radical separatist movement led by **Sant Jarnail Singh Bhindranwale**. Covertly supported by the national government (who saw the group as a way to defeat the Akali Dal), Bhindranwale and his band waged a ruthless campaign of sectarian terror in the Punjab which came to a head in 1984, when they occupied the Golden Temple; Indira's brutal response, **Operation Blue Star** (see p.612), plunged the Punjab into another ugly bout of communal violence. Four years later, history repeated itself when a less threatening occupation of the temple was crushed by **Operation Black Thunder**. Since then, the Punjabi police have gone on to make considerable advances against the terrorists – helped, for the first time, by the Punjabi peasant farmers, the **Jats**, who had grown tired of the inexorable slaughter. Most Akali Dal factions boycotted the 1992 elections, which saw Congress returned on a 22 percent turnout. Chief minister **Beant Singh** was killed by a car bomb in 1995, but this was the militants' last gasp. Public support had ebbed, and the police, using strongarm tactics, were able to wipe out the paramilitary groups that had burgeoned during the 1980s. Subsequent state elections have seen a **return to normality**. In 2002, Congress wrested control from an Akali Dal/BJP coalition that had run Punjab for the previous five years. Voter turnout was back up to 69 percent, and paramilitary violence was notable by its absence. From a tourist point of view, Punjab has regained its political stability, and is quite safe to travel in.

Chandigarh

Chandigarh is jointly the state capital of both Punjab and Haryana, but oddly, it is part of neither, being a Union Territory administered by India's federal government. Its history begins with Partition in 1947, when the Punjab's main city of Lahore fell on the Pakistani side of the border, leaving the Indian state of Punjab without a capital. Nehru saw this as a golden opportunity to realize his vision of a city "symbolic of the future of India, unfettered by the traditions of the past, [and] an expression of the nation's faith in the future". The job of designing it went to controversial Swiss-French architect Charles-Edouard Jeanneret, alias **Le Corbusier**.

Begun in 1952, **CHANDIGARH** was to be a ground-breaking experiment in town planning. Le Corbusier's blueprints were for an orderly grid of sweeping boulevards, divided into 29 neat blocks, or **Sectors**, each measuring 800 by 1200 metres, and interspersed with extensive stretches of green. However, the resulting city has been a source of controversy since its completion in the 1960s. Some applaud Le Corbusier's brainchild as one of the great architectural achievements of the twentieth century, but detractors complain that the design is self-indulgent and un-Indian. They have a point: Le Corbusier created a city for fast-flowing traffic at a time when few people owned cars, while the concrete buildings turned into ovens during the summer – completely uninhabitable without expensive air-conditioning. The city has expanded from the first phase comprising Sectors 1 to 30 (there is no Sector 13), through a second phase – sectors 31 to 47 – and is now into the third phase with (half-size) sectors 48 to 61. Satellite towns emulating Chandigarh's grid plan and sterile concrete architecture have also sprung up on either side, with Panchkula in Haryana and Mohali in Punjab easing the pressure on a city left with nowhere else to grow.

Despite Chandigarh's infrastructural and aesthetic shortcomings, its inhabitants are very proud of their capital, which is cleaner, greener and more affluent than other Indian cities of comparable size, and boasts a Rock Garden said to be India's second most visited tourist site after the Taj Mahal.

Arrival, information and city transport

Most buses pull into the **Inter-state Bus Terminus** (**ISBT**) on the south edge of the main commercial and shopping district, Sector 17. Exceptions are services from Punjab and Himachal Pradesh (Shimla excepted), which may leave you at Sector 43 bus stand, connected to the ISBT by regular local buses. Chandigarh's **airport** is 11km south of the city centre, its **railway station** 8km southeast. Both have prepaid auto-rickshaw counters with fixed rates, as does the ISBT (in a the booth is at its western corner). A prepaid auto to the ISBT from the airport costs Rs83 (a taxi is around Rs200), or Rs50 from the railway station; a prepaid auto from the ISBT to the Rock Garden is Rs30.

The **tourist office** at the ISBT (daily 9.30am–1pm & 1.30–5.30pm; ⓣ0172/270 4614) is helpful, friendly and a good place to check bus and train times as well

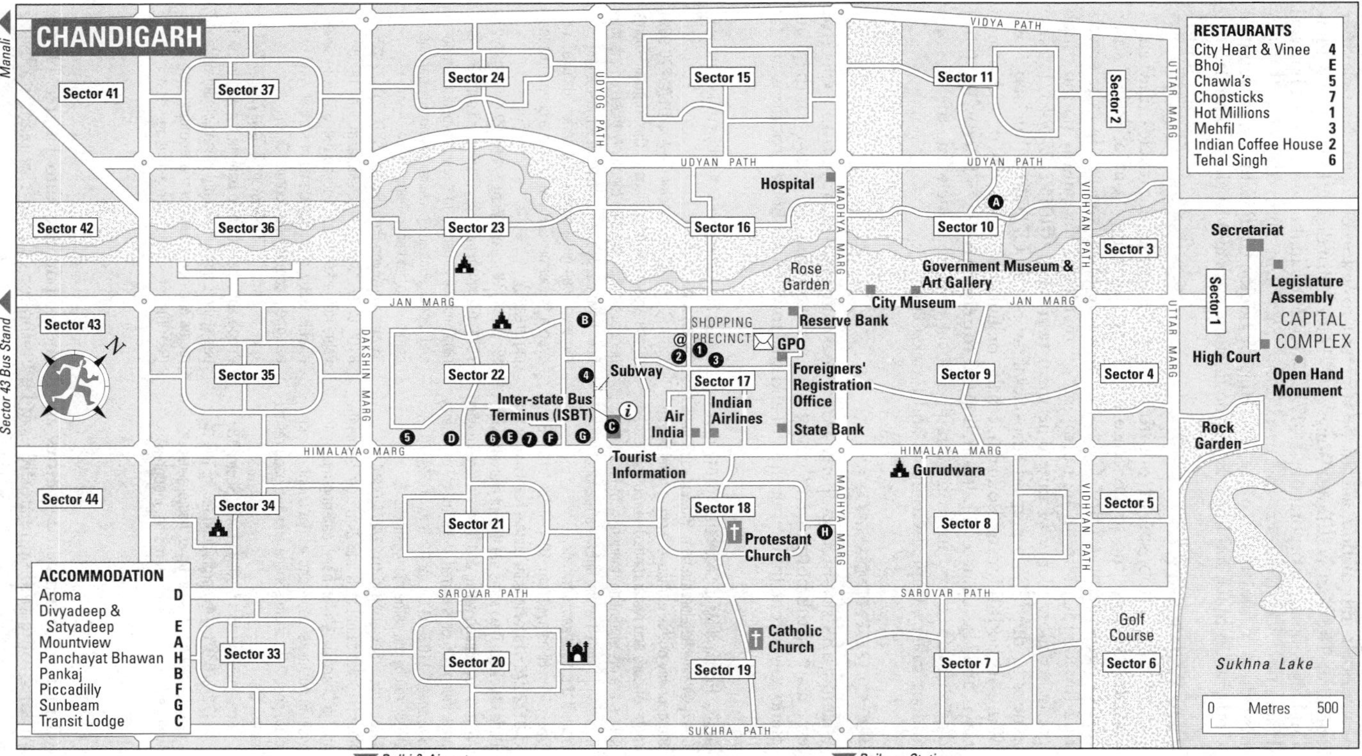
CHANDIGARH
RESTAURANTS
City Heart & Vinee 4
Bhoj E
Chawla's 5
Chopsticks 7
Hot Millions 1
Mehfil 3
Indian Coffee House 2
Tehal Singh 6
ACCOMMODATION
Aroma D
Divyadeep & Satyadeep E
Mountview A
Panchayat Bhawan H
Pankaj B
Piccadilly F
Sunbeam G
Transit Lodge C
Sector 1
Sector 2
Sector 3
Sector 4
Sector 5
Sector 6
Sector 7
Sector 8
Sector 9
Sector 10
Sector 11
Sector 15
Sector 16
Sector 17
Sector 18
Sector 19
Sector 20
Sector 21
Sector 22
Sector 23
Sector 24
Sector 33
Sector 34
Sector 35
Sector 36
Sector 37
Sector 41
Sector 42
Sector 43
Sector 44
VIDYA PATH
UTTAR MARG
UDYAN PATH
VIDHYAN PATH
JAN MARG
MADHYA MARG
UDYOG PATH
DAKSHIN MARG
HIMALAYA MARG
SAROVAR PATH
SUKHRA PATH
Secretariat
Legislature Assembly
CAPITAL COMPLEX
High Court
Open Hand Monument
Rock Garden
Sukhna Lake
Golf Course
Hospital
Rose Garden
Government Museum & Art Gallery
City Museum
Reserve Bank
SHOPPING PRECINCT
GPO
Foreigners' Registration Office
State Bank
Indian Airlines
Air India
Subway
Inter-state Bus Terminus (ISBT)
Tourist Information
Gurudwara
Protestant Church
Catholic Church
0 Metres 500
Manali
Sector 43 Bus Stand
Delhi & Airport
Railway Station

as any other information, and to get a permit to visit the Capital Complex (see opposite). The Tour and Travel Wing of CITCO (Chandigarh Industry and Tourism Development Corporation; ⓣ0172/270 3839) is in the same office. Himachal Pradesh's office (Mon–Fri and every other Sat 10am–5pm; ⓣ0172/270 8569), next door to the tourist office, is useful for booking HP Tourist Development Corporation tours, and buses to HP destinations such as Manali and Shimla.

City transport

Chandigarh is too spread out to explore on foot, but cycle- and auto-**rickshaws** cruise the streets. Auto meters are invariably "out of order" so be sure to negotiate prices first. Cycle rickshaws are much cheaper, but the drivers find the long haul up to the north end of town or to the railway station tough going, so allow plenty of time. The main **taxi** stand (ⓣ0172/270 4621; 24hr) is next to the ISBT's prepaid auto-rickshaw booth. CITCO's Tour and Travel Wing at the ISBT can also arrange half- or full-day excursions in and around town, and also operates a hop-on, hop-off **tourist bus** (Rs75 full day, Rs50 half day) that runs every hour on a circuit of local attractions including the museum and art gallery, Capital Complex and Rock Garden.

Accommodation

Chandigarh's sky-high property prices make its **accommodation** expensive, especially at the bottom end where choice is very limited. However, there are plenty of decent mid-range hotels, and the town's two budget options are far from terrible.

Aroma Himalaya Marg, Sector 22-C ⓣ0172/270 0047, ⓦwww.hotelaroma.com. Vintage cars flank the doorway of this attractive-looking hotel with a range of bars and restaurants. The rooms themselves are disappointing, though, with laminated floors and scuffed walls, but it's a reasonable fall-back if the *Sunbeam*'s full. ❼

Divyadeep Himalaya Marg, 1090–1 Sector 22-B ⓣ0172/270 5191. Pleasant budget hotel run by Sai Baba devotees. The rooms are decent enough, with a/c and hot running water, and there's a large rooftop area, though liquor is barred. If it's full, try the nearby *Satyadeep*, 1102–03 Sector 22-B (ⓣ0172/270 3103), run by the same management. ❸

Mountview Sector 10 ⓣ0172/274 0544, ⓔhmv10@glide.net.in. Some 2km from the centre, this is Chandigarh's top hotel, catering mostly for visiting businesspeople and with a sauna, health club, pool, 24hr room service and two good restaurants. ❾

Panchayat Bhawan Madhya Marg, Sector 18 ⓣ0172/278 0701, ⓔdprpb@chd.nic.in. The cheapest place to stay in town, hostel-like but well-kept, with large, clean rooms, though not always hot running water. If you're really strapped, there's a dorm (Rs40). ❷

Pankaj Udyog Path, Sector 22-A ⓣ0172/270 9891 ⓔcolharsharan@hotmail.com. The "regular" rooms here are rather box-like (and only those on the top floor have outside windows), but for just a little more you can get a bigger and better "deluxe", or even a "super deluxe" room, with a separate seating area. ❻

Piccadilly Himalaya Marg, Sector 22-B ⓣ0172/270 7571 to 3, ⓔthepiccadilly@rediffmail.com. Rather plush establishment with thickly carpeted corridors and rooms, central a/c, classy restaurant, bar and coffee shop, and an in-house travel agent. ❽

Sunbeam Udyog Path, Sector 22-B ⓣ0172/270 8100 to 07, ⓦwww.hotelsunbeam.com. Good-value upmarket hotel opposite the ISBT with swish marble lobby, good standards of service, and well-designed, comfortable rooms. ❻

Transit Lodge ISBT, Sector 17 ⓣ0172/271 2419. Cheap and cheerful, slap bang in the middle of the bus station, institutional but clean with en-suite rooms and hot water. Dorm accommodation too (Rs100). Rates include breakfast and dinner. ❸

The City

Chandigarh's numbered **sectors** are further subdivided into lettered blocks, making route-finding relatively easy. Le Corbusier saw the city plan as a living organism, with the imposing **Capital Complex** to the north as a "head", the shopping precinct, **Sector 17**, a "heart", the green open spaces as "lungs", and the crosscutting network of roads, separated into eight different grades for use by various types of vehicles (in theory only), a "circulatory system".

The museums

Situated in the green belt known as the Leisure Valley, five minutes by rickshaw north of the city centre, Chandigarh's museums form part of a cultural complex which includes the adjoining Rose Garden and open-air theatre where free concerts are occasionally staged. The **Government Museum and Art Gallery** (Tues–Sun 10am–4.30pm; Rs2, camera Rs5), in Sector 10, houses a sizeable and informatively displayed collection of textiles, Harappan artefacts, miniature paintings and contemporary Indian art, including a couple of A.N. Tagore's atmospheric watercolours and five original Roerichs. The ancient sculpture are the compelling exhibits, notably the Gandhara Buddhas with their delicately carved "wet-look" *lunghis* and distinctly Hellenic features – a legacy of Alexander the Great's conquests. A hundred metres down the road, the small but appropriately modernist **City Museum** (Tues–Sun 10am–4.45pm; free) illustrates the planning and construction of Chandigarh, with the models and photographs in a concrete pavilion based on one of Le Corbusier's designs.

The Capital Complex

Tight security following the 1995 assassination (in front of the Assembly building) of Punjab chief minister Beant Singh by Sikh nationalist hardliners, you'll need a letter of permission from the tourist office at the ISBT (see p.603) to visit the **Capital Complex** in Sector 1. The Complex's most imposing edifice is the eleven-storey **Secretariat**, Chandigarh's highest building, which houses ministerial offices for both Haryana and Punjab, and has a roof garden with good views over the city. The resemblance of the **Legislature Assembly Building**, or Vidhan Sabha (home to the legislatures of both states) to a power station is no coincidence: Le Corbusier was allegedly inspired by a stack of cooling towers he saw in Ahmedabad. Opposite the Secretariat is the most colourful building in the Complex, the **High Court** (also serving both states), which is said to incorporate elements of the Buland Darwaza in Fatehpur Sikri, and is decorated inside with huge woollen tapestries. North of the this is the black, thirteen-metre-high **Open Hand monument**, Chandigarh's adopted emblem. Weighing all of 45 tonnes, it revolves on ball-bearings like a weather vane and stands for "post-colonial harmony and peace".

The Rock Garden

Close to the Capital Complex, the **Rock Garden** (daily 8am–6pm; Rs5) is a surreal fantasyland fashioned from fragments of shattered plates, neon strip lights, pots, pebbles, broken bangles and assorted urban-industrial junk. The open-air exhibition is the lifelong labour of retired Public Works Department road inspector **Nek Chand**. Inspired by a recurrent childhood dream, he began construction in 1965 intending it to be just a small garden, but when it was discovered in 1973, by then covering 12 whole acres, it caused astonishment – although completely illegal, it was recognized as a great artistic endeavour. An enlightened decision awarded Nek Chand a salary to continue his work, and a workforce of fifty labourers to help. Opened to the public in 1976, the garden now covers 25 acres and contains several thousand sculptures.

Now 80, Nek Chand continues to oversee expansion of the site, a labyrinth of more than a dozen different enclosures interconnected by narrow passages,

△ Rock Garden, Chandigarh

arched walkways, streams, bridges, grottos, waterfalls, battlements and turrets. Stick to the path, or you could end up wandering the maze until the *chowkidar* finds you at closing time. Nek Chand's ideas about turning unwanted waste into a work of great imagination and beauty are promoted by the Nek Chand Foundation in the UK (Ⓣ+44-020/7359 1747, Ⓦwww.nekchand.com).

Eating

Chandigarh has no shortage of **places to eat**. As everywhere in Punjab, the most popular foodstuff is chicken, cooked in a variety of ways. Pastry shops like Monica's, in Sector 8-B, produce excellent cheesecake and gateau. Sai Sweets, below the *Satyadeep* hotel in Sector 22-B, and Sindhi Sweets in Sector 17-B, are two of the best sweet shops in town. Takeaway is very popular and most restaurants provide a service. Alcohol is widely available, and there are many bars around Sector 17 serving draught and bottled beer.

Bhoj *Hotel Divyadeep*, 1090–1, Sector 22-B. Classy pure-veg joint run by Sai Baba devotees, serving only thalis at Rs75 and Rs80.
Chawla's Himalaya Marg, Sector 22-C. Small tandoori restaurant renowned for its rich cream chicken (Rs200 for a whole one; half and quarter chickens are also available).
Chopsticks Near *Hotel Piccadilly*, Himalaya Marg, Sector 22. A reasonable Chinese restaurant offering mains, including some pork dishes, at Rs95–160.
City Heart and **Vinee** Udyog Path, Sector 22-B, opposite the bus stand. Inexpensive, clean, *dhaba*-like restaurants serving excellent South Indian food. *City Heart* should not be confused with its sister concern *City Heart 2* (a few doors down), which is more of a pub.
Hot Millions Sector 17-D (upstairs). Part of the successful fast-food chain, selling everything from *dosas* to pizzas. This branch also has a good salad bar, and there's an all-you-can-eat lunch and dinner buffet (Rs145 veg/Rs175 non-veg). *Hot Millions 2* in Sector 17-C near *Mehfil* has a popular pub – *Down Under*.
Indian Coffee House Sector 17-E. Clean budget chain with a limited but predictable menu, including *dosas*, sandwiches and coffee. All dishes are under Rs30.
Mehfil SCO 183–5, Sector 17-C. The exclusive preserve of Chandigarh's smart set, and *the* place to sample rich Mughlai and Punjabi cuisine in a/c comfort. Main dishes are Rs80–180. For desert, *Baskin-Robbins* is well placed across the street.
Tehal Singh Himalaya Marg, 1116–7 Sector 22-B. Very popular tandoori restaurant (main dishes Rs120–180). *Singh's Chicken* right next door provides competition.

Listings

Airline offices Air India, SCO 107–8, Sector 17-B Ⓣ0172/270 3510; Indian Airlines, #171–2, Sector 17-C Ⓣ0172/270 4539. Bajaj Travels, SCO 96–7, Sector 17-C (Ⓣ0172/270 4500) are agents for other international airlines, as well as domestic outfits Archana and Jagson.
Ambulance Ⓣ102
Banks and exchange Several of the banks ranged around Bank Square on the northwest side of Sector 17 change money, including the UCO Bank, Punjab National Bank, the State Bank of India and Andhra Bank. ATMs are common at major banks.
Bookshops Capital Book Depot, Sector 17-E.
Doctors Dr S.P. Bedi, 69 Sector 8 Ⓣ0172/278 0708.
Hospitals Chandigarh's General Hospital is in Sector 16 (Ⓣ0172/278 1876), but is not as good as the PGI, Sector 12 (Ⓣ0172/274 6018).
Internet access Net Vision, Sector 17-E (next to the *Indian Coffee House*).
Left luggage There is a 24hr cloakroom in the bus stand (Rs5/day).
Pharmacies Apollo Pharmacy, Sector 34-A Ⓣ0172/260 4386 (24hr).
Police Ⓣ0172/274 6437.
Shopping Several states run handicraft emporiums in the Sector 17 shopping complex, among them Punjab, whose Phulkari store (Sector 17-B) stocks a good range of embroidered silk, woodwork and traditional pointed Punjabi shoes. For quality handloom products, try the UP emporium in the building opposite (SCO 139–41 Sector 17-C), or the Khadi Gramodyog in the arcade at the *Shivalikview* hotel just to the west of the shopping area: both are strong on block-printed calico garments, especially *salwar kamise*.

Moving on from Chandigarh

The **railway station**, 8km southeast of the centre, has direct services to Delhi, Jodhpur, Mumbai, Kolkata (Calcutta), and even, once a week, to Chennai. The superfast a/c Shatabdi Express runs to Delhi (#2006 & #2012 departing at 7.10am & 6.20pm). Second-class tickets cost Rs430, four times the bus price, but the journey is far more comfortable and almost twice as fast. Other useful trains include the #4096 Himalayan Queen (dep 5.28pm, arr New Delhi 10.15pm), the daily #4535 Kalka–Amritsar Express (dep 4.58pm, arr Amritsar 11.20pm) and the daily #4887 Kalka–Jodhpur Express (dep 10.10pm, arr Jodhpur 5.55pm next day).

Most travellers move on from the city by **bus** from the Inter-state Bus Terminus (ISBT) in Sector 17. Tickets can be pre-booked at the counters on the ground floor, or just pay on the bus. Daytime departures to Punjab and Himachal Pradesh (except Shimla) leave from bus station no. 2 in Sector 43, which is connected to the ISBT by city bus #8.

The **airport** is 11km south of town (Rs83 by prepaid auto from the ISBT, Rs200 by taxi). Indian Airlines fly to Leh, Delhi (also served by Jet Air) and Mumbai.

Chandigarh is an important transport hub for **Shimla**. The quickest way to get to Shimla is by bus (4hr): either with the direct Himachal Pradesh or Haryana Roadways ordinary "express" buses or with more comfortable deluxe buses, departing every 15min from the ISBT. You can also get there on the slower but more congenial Viceroys' "Toy Train" (see p.487) from **Kalka** 26km to the northeast, and connected to Chandigarh by trains and frequent buses. The scenic 75-kilometre journey from Kalka to Shimla takes around 5hr (dep 4am, 5.30am, 6.30am & 12.10pm). See p.492 for Shimla–Kalka times.

See "Travel details", p.619, for more information on journey frequencies and durations.

Around Chandigarh

While Chandigarh's architecture may be of limited interest to most travellers, the ornamental Moghul gardens in **Pinjore**, on the northern outskirts of the city, have a much more universal appeal. Southwest of Chandigarh, there are further Moghul ruins at **Sirhind**, a good place to stop overnight between Delhi and Amritsar. **Anandpur Sahib**, the home of the Khalsa movement and one of Sikhism's most venerated shrines, lies just off the Chandigarh–Mandi highway and makes a worthwhile detour, especially during the festival of Holi.

Pinjore

PINJORE, 22km north of Chandigarh and 7km south of Kalka on the Shimla road, is best known for its walled **Yadavindra Gardens**, one of many sites associated with the exile of the Pandavas as chronicled in the *Mahabharata*. The gardens originally belonged to the rajas of Sirmaur, but under the Moghuls, Pinjore was taken over by Aurangzeb's foster brother, Fidai Khan, who erected three pleasure palaces for his wife amid the cypress trees. Legend tells that the raja reclaimed his summer retreat by sending a female fruit-seller with a goitre to the imperial impostors. On being told that the woman's unsightly swelling was caused by the local water, the begum and her entourage fled.

These days, the walled gardens harbour a small otter sanctuary, aviary, and zoo, and are popular places for a picnic. One of the three palaces has been converted by Haryana Tourism into a comfortable **hotel** (Ⓣ01733/230759; ❻), which boasts a range of rooms including a dorm (Rs150). Frequent local **buses** connect Pinjore with Chandigarh and Kalka.

Sirhind

Close to the Grand Trunk Road (NH-1) and Northern Railway, **SIRHIND** (the name derives from *Sir-i-Hind*, "the Head or Frontier of Hind or Hindu India"), 48km southwest of Chandigarh, was the capital of the Pathan Suri sultans and the site of an important *caravansarai*. Today, only a couple of minor-league Moghul palaces, hot baths and pleasure pavilions remain from the illustrious past, but it's still a pleasant overnight stop between Delhi and Amritsar.

The site of the Moghul ruins, **Aam-Khas-Bagh**, lies 2.5km north of the town proper. Here you'll see Sirhind's best-preserved monuments, encircled by the high walls of Sher Shah Suri's sixteenth-century fort. Approached via a tree- and fountain-lined walkway, the ruins of the old baths, or **hammam**, enclose a giant circular well whose water was channelled into geometric bathing pools outside. Nearby stand the ruins of Emperor Shah Jahan's residence, the **Daulat Khana**. Just behind the tourist complex, in much better shape, is the seventeenth-century **Sheesh Mahal** or "Palace of Mirrors". **Fatehgarh Sahib**, a pristine white *gurudwara* 1.5km north of the tourist complex, stands in memory of Guru Gobind Singh's two youngest sons who were bricked up alive in the fort by the Moghul emperor Aurangzeb for not embracing Islam. Cover your head to enter the *gurudwara*. Next door to Fatehgarh Sahib, the fourteenth-century *dargah* (burial shrine), dedicated to a Sufi saint, attracts busloads of Muslim pilgrims and provides a sharp reminder of the friction caused by the proximity of religions so fundamentally opposed.

Practicalities

Regular **buses** run between Chandigarh and Sirhind, a stopping-point on the main Delhi–Amritsar **railway**. The railway station lies 5km from the tourist complex. Buses from Amritsar usually drop passengers at the Grand Trunk Road intersection, 7km south of Aam-Khas-Bagh – catch a local bus into town or take a shared auto-rickshaw (Rs10).

Housed in a small eighteenth-century summer palace, the **PTDC Maulsarai Tourist Complex** (Ⓣ01763/222250; ❸) overlooks gardens and the Sheesh Mahal. Inexpensive **food**, chilled beers and cold **drinks** are served in the dining room, or alfresco on the tank-side terrace. Mosquitoes can be a problem, so keep the repellent handy. The **PTDC Bougainvillea Tourist Complex** (Ⓣ01763/229170; ❸), 3km up the GT Road towards Amritsar, has ordinary, air-cooled and a/c rooms, as well as a restaurant. Visitors are welcome to stay overnight at the *gurudwara* on a donation basis.

Anandpur Sahib

The gleaming-white, citadel-like *gurudwara* at **ANANDPUR SAHIB** ("The City of Bliss"), stands 75km north of Chandigarh. Known as the **Gurudwara Kesgarh Sahib**, it is one of the holiest Sikh shrines, commemorating the birth of the Khalsa movement by Guru Gobind Singh three hundred years ago. With surrounding citadels, gates and ramparts, its fortress-like appearance hints at its difficult past and the long years of struggle against Muslim domination and jealous Hindu kingdoms.

Guru Gobind Singh's father, Guru Tegh Bahadur, laid the foundations in 1664, but was beheaded by the zealous Moghul emperor Aurangzeb in Delhi for refusing to convert to Islam. His head was brought back to Anandpur Sahib and cremated at the spot now marked by the shrine of **Gurudwara Sis Ganj**. Guru Gobind Singh built the fortifications which withstood a string of onslaughts from hostile neighbours, and, on March 30, 1699, initiated five disciples into the Khalsa, whose goals were to support the poor, fight oppression, discard dogma, superstition and caste, and be warriors of their faith.

All are welcome inside the *gurudwara* (cover your head and remove shoes) to listen to the devotional singing (*kirtan*) and accompanying readings by *granthis* from the Sikh holy book, the *Guru Granth Sahib*. Every year around March, the festival of **Hola Mohalla** takes place below Kesgarh Sahib, attracting thousands of people. It celebrates Khalsa and reinterprets the Hindu festival of colour, Holi; the festivities include displays of horsemanship and swordsmanship by the *nihangs* – an orthodox sect devoted to the great guru.

Practicalities

Accommodation at Anandpur Sahib is limited to the *gurudwara*, though further afield at Rupnagar (also called Ropar), 45km south on the Chandigarh–Mandi highway, there's the *Pinkcassia Tourist Complex* (☎01881/222097; ❸), set in pleasant riverside grounds. There is no tourist information in Anandpur Sahib, but the English-speaking owner of the Gurmat Literature House, a bookshop near the *gurudwara* courtyard, can provide local information and checks visitors into the *gurudwara*. Local **buses** run between Chandigarh, Rupnagar and Anandpur Sahib, and a new high-speed railway line between Anandpur Sahib and New Delhi via Sirhind is "in the pipeline".

Pathankot

The dusty town of **PATHANKOT**, 270km north of Chandigarh and 101km to the northeast of Amritsar, is an important cantonment and railway junction, close to the frontier with Pakistan and near the borders with Himachal Pradesh and Jammu. Many travellers pass through to pick up bus connections to Dharamsala, Dalhousie, Chamba and Kashmir, or to take the slow train east through the picturesque Kangra Valley.

Pathankot can rustle up a few **hotels**, should you need to spend the night. The *Atlas Guest House*, 50m east of the station on Railway Road (☎0186/222 1397; ❷), is a good budget option with clean but bare rooms, failing which, the *Tourist Hotel* (☎0186/222 0660; ❷), a few metres further along Railway Road, has reasonable rooms including some tiny singles. The well-kept railway retiring rooms (☎0186/222 0046; ❶) are better value, with a choice of ordinary or a/c rooms, the latter containing sofas, carpets and private bathrooms with hot water. Two kilometres northeast of the railway station, PTDC's *Gulmohar Tourist Complex*, Shimla Pahari, Mission Road (☎0186/222 0292; ❷), has a wide choice of rooms, plus a restaurant, bar and pleasant gardens. The *Venice*, south of the station on Dhangu Road (☎0186/222 5061; ❺), is Pathankot's top business hotel, but lacks atmosphere.

Himachal Pradesh Tourism has a downbeat but friendly **tourist office** at the railway station (Mon–Fri and every other Sat 10am–5pm; ☎0186/222 0316). The slow narrow-gauge passenger **trains** to Jogindernagar (daily 2.20am & 9.50pm; 7hr 30min–9hr) wind through the scenic Kangra Valley, and make a pleasant alternative to the busy road to both Dharamsala (change at Kangra) and the Kullu Valley (bus from Jogindernagar). Other useful trains include the daily #3152 Jammu–Sealdah Express terminating in Kolkata (Calcutta), and the overnight #4646 Shalimar Express to New Delhi. **Taxis** to Dharamsala cost around Rs1000 (3hr). Pathankot also has a busy **bus station**, on Railway Road, 300m west of the rail station, with frequent departures to Amritsar, Jammu and various parts of Himachal Pradesh (see "Travel details", p.619).

Amritsar

The Sikhs' holy city of **AMRITSAR**, site of the fabled **Golden Temple**, is the largest city in Punjab: noisy, dirty and hopelessly congested. Its one saving grace is the Golden Temple, whose domes soar above the teeming streets. Amritsar is also an important staging post for those crossing the Indo–Pakistani frontier at Wagha, 29km west (see p.617).

Some history

Amritsar was founded in 1577 by **Ram Das**, the fourth Sikh guru, beside a bathing pool famed for its healing powers. The land around the tank was granted in perpetuity by the Moghul Akbar to the Sikhs (who paid off the local Jat farmers to avoid any future dispute over ownership). When merchants moved in to take advantage of the strategic location on the Silk Route, Amritsar

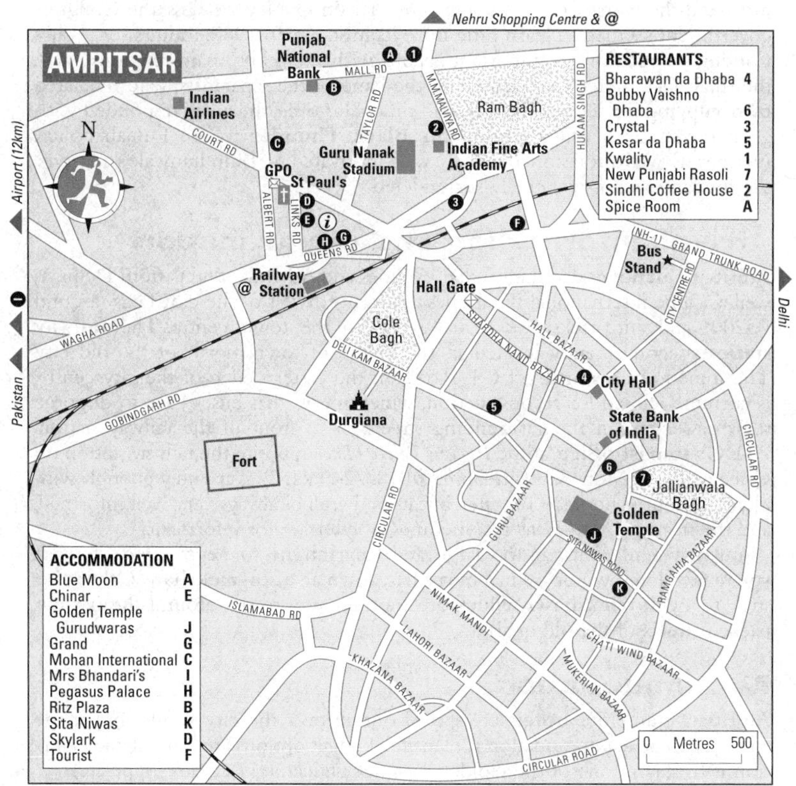

expanded rapidly, gaining a grand new temple under Ram Das' son and heir, **Guru Arjan Dev**. Sacked by Afghans in 1761, the shrine was rebuilt by the Sikhs' greatest secular leader, **Maharaja Ranjit Singh**, who also donated the gold used in its construction.

Amritsar's **twentieth-century** history has been blighted by a series of appalling **massacres**. The first occurred in 1919, when thousands of unarmed civilian demonstrators were gunned down without warning by British troops in **Jallianwalla Bagh** (see box on p.614) – an atrocity that inspired Gandhi's Non-Co-operation Movement. Following the collapse of the Raj, Amritsar experienced some of the worst communal blood-letting ever seen on the subcontinent. The Golden Temple, however, remained unaffected by the volatile politics of post-Independence Punjab until the 1980s, when as part of a protracted and bloody campaign for the setting up of a Sikh homeland, heavily armed fundamentalists under the preacher-warrior Sant Jarnail Singh **Bhindranwale** occupied the Akal Takht, a building in the Golden Temple complex that has traditionally been the seat of Sikh religious authority. The siege was brought to an end in early June 1984, when prime minister Indira Gandhi ordered an inept paramilitary attack on the temple, code-named **Operation Blue Star**. Bhindranwale was killed along with 200 soldiers and 2000 others, including pilgrims trapped inside.

Widely regarded as an unmitigated disaster, Blue Star led directly to the assassination of Indira Gandhi by her Sikh bodyguards just four months later, and provoked the worst riots in the city since Partition. Nevertheless, the Congress government seemed to learn little from its mistakes. In 1987, Indira's son, Rajiv Gandhi, reneged on an important accord with the Sikhs' main religious party, the Akali Dal, thereby strengthening the hand of the separatists, who retaliated by occupying the temple for a second time. This time, the army responded with greater restraint, leaving **Operation Black Thunder** to the Punjab police. Neither as well provisioned nor as well motivated as Bhindranwale's martyrs, the fundamentalists eventually surrendered.

Arrival, information and city transport

Amritsar's **airport**, served by Indian Airlines and Air India flights from Delhi, as well as some international flights, lies 12km northwest of the city. Taxis (around Rs200) and auto-rickshaws (Rs100) run to the town centre. The **railway station** is conveniently located in the centre of town, north of the old city. The frenetic **bus stand**, off GT Road on the eastern edge of the city centre, is currently closed for reconstruction, which means that buses have to disgorge their passengers in the surrounding streets, or in front of the railway station. PTDC's **tourist office**, at the *Pegasus Palace Hotel* opposite the railway station on Queens Road (Mon–Sat 9am–5pm; ⓣ0183/240 2452), is friendly enough with plenty of tourist booklets on offer, but its staff are not always very well informed, and the nearby *Grand Hotel* is sometimes a better bet for information.

You may find Amritsar too large and labyrinthine to negotiate on foot; if you're crossing town or are in a hurry, flag down an **auto-rickshaw**. Otherwise, stick to **cycle rickshaws**, which are the best way to get around the narrow, packed streets of the old quarter.

Accommodation

Amritsar's numerous **hotels** are spread out all over the city. While mid-range and upmarket accommodation is plentiful, budget options are limited; one solution is to stay in one of the Golden Temple's *gurudwaras* (see box, opposite).

The Gurudwaras

Undoubtedly the most authentic places to stay in Amritsar are the Golden Temple's five **gurudwaras**. Intended for use by Sikh pilgrims, these charitable institutions also open their doors to foreign tourists, who are sometimes limited to a maximum of three nights. Lodging at *gurudwaras* is free, as is the Sikh custom, but donations are expected. The first building as you approach the *gurudwaras*, which are on the east side of the temple, is the *Guru Arjan Dev Niwas*, which has the check-in counter for all the *gurudwaras* and simple but spacious rooms. The most comfortable of the five *gurudwaras* is the new, clean and excellent-value *Guru Hargobind Niwas*. The *Sri Guru Nanak Niwas* was where Bhindranwale and his men holed up prior to the Golden Temple siege in 1984.

Apart from the inevitable dawn chorus of throat-clearing, the downside of staying in a *gurudwara* is that facilities can be basic (*charpoi* beds and communal wash-basins in the central courtyard are the norm) and **security** can be a problem. During festivals, rooms and beds are at a premium and tourists are less likely to find space here.

Blue Moon Mall Rd ⊕0183/222 0759. Friendly, helpful place, much better value than its more expensive competitors. There's a decent restaurant (see p.617) open to non-residents. ❻

Chinar Links Rd ⊕0183/256 4655. Clean and reasonably priced place that's handy for railway station; the rooms are en suite and have TV, but don't get palmed off with a windowless one on the ground floor. ❸

Grand Queens Rd, opposite the railway station ⊕0183/256 2977, ⓦwww.fhrai.com. Neat, clean, convenient and central with rooms around a pleasant garden courtyard, though windows all face inward. There's an adjacent bar/restaurant replete with Hollywood movie paraphernalia. The friendly manager can organize a share-taxi to Wagha for the border ceremony. ❺

Mohan International Albert Rd ⊕0183/222 7801–8 ⓔhotel@jla.vsnl.net.in. One of Amritsar's top hotels but overpriced, though it does have a/c, room service and a pool. Popular for Punjabi wedding receptions which are colourful spectacles but very noisy. 24hr coffee shop. ❽

Mrs Bhandari's Guest House 10 Cantonment ⊕0183/222 8509, ⓦbhandari_guesthouse.tripod.com. Wonderful old-fashioned rooms with wood fires and bathtubs in a colonial home with lawns, gardens and a small swimming pool. "British-style" three-course meals are available but pricey. You can camp in the grounds for Rs165 per person. Popular with overlanders, it's become an Amritsar institution, as has the centegenarian Mrs Bhandari. ❻

Pegasus Palace Opposite the railway station ⊕0183/256 5111. This place has seen better days, but it's conveniently located and reasonably priced. Rooms are en suite, but hot water comes in a bucket. ❷

Ritz Plaza 45 Mall Rd ⊕0183/256 2836, ⓦwww.sarovarparkplaza.com. Low-key but quite classy establishment, modernized with central a/c, good-sized rooms and a relaxed atmosphere surrounded by lawns; facilities include a pool, a lounge bar and a restaurant serving international cuisine. Doubles from US$80. ❾

Sita Niwas 61 Sita Niwas Rd ⊕0183/254 3092. A good-value and popular budget option near Guru Ram Das Niwas and the Golden Temple, with wide range of rooms, most en suite, and 24hr hot water. ❷

Skylark 79 Links Rd ⊕0183/222 2353. One of the best options along this short road opposite the railway station, with huge rooms, comfortable beds and hot water round the clock. ❹

Tourist Guest House Hide Market, near Bhandari Bridge, GT Rd ⊕0183/255 3830, ⓔbubblesgoolry@yahoo.com. Popular with budget travellers since the "hippy trail" days, offering a variety of rooms. The cheapest are rather dingy with shared bathrooms; en suite ones with hot water are quite nice and still not pricey. Ignore commission-hungry rickshaw-wallahs telling you it's full. ❷

The City

The Golden Temple stands in the heart of the **old town**, itself a maze of narrow lanes and bazaars. Eighteen fortified **gateways** punctuate the aptly named

Circular Road, of which only one (to the north) is original. Skirting the edge of the old quarter, the railway line forms a sharp divide between the bazaar and the more spacious British-built side of the city. Most of the hotels and restaurants are located in this district, around the Maginot-Line-style **railway station**. Further north, long straight tree-lined streets eventually peter out into leafy residential suburbs. The neat military barracks of the **cantonment** form the northwestern limits of the city.

The Golden Temple

Even visitors without a religious bone in their bodies cannot fail to be moved by Amritsar's resplendent **Golden Temple**, spiritual centre of the Sikh faith and open to all. Built by Guru **Arjan Dev** in the late sixteenth century, the richly gilded **Harmandir** rises from the middle of an artificial rectangular lake, connected to the surrounding white marble complex by a narrow causeway. Every Sikh tries to make at least one pilgrimage here to listen to the sublime music (*shabad kirtan*), readings from the *Adi Granth* and also to bathe in the purifying waters of the temple tank – the **Amrit Sarovar** or "Pool of Immortality-Giving Nectar".

The best time to visit is early morning, to catch the first rays of sunlight gleaming on the bulbous golden domes and reflecting in the waters of the

The Jallianwalla Bagh massacre

Only 100m northeast of the Golden Temple, a narrow lane leads between two tall buildings to **Jallianwalla Bagh** memorial park (daily: summer 6am–7pm, winter 7am–6pm), site of one of the bloodiest atrocities committed by the British Raj.

In 1919, a series of one-day strikes, or *hartals*, was staged in Amritsar in protest against the recent **Rowlatt Act**, which enabled the British to imprison without trial any Indian suspected of sedition. When the peaceful demonstrations escalated into sporadic looting, the lieutenant governor of Punjab declared martial law and called for reinforcements from Jalandhar. A platoon of infantry arrived soon after, led by **General R.E.H. Dyer**.

Despite a ban on public meetings, a mass demonstration was called by Mahatma Gandhi for April 13, the Sikh holiday of Baisakhi. The venue was a stretch of waste ground in the heart of the city, hemmed in by high brick walls and with only a couple of alleys for access. An estimated 20,000 people gathered in Jallianwalla Bagh for the meeting. However, before any speakers could address the crowd, Dyer and his 150 troops, stationed on a patch of high ground in front of the main exit, opened fire without warning. By the time they had finished firing, ten to fifteen minutes later, hundreds of unarmed demonstrators lay dead and dying, many of them shot in the back while clambering over the walls. Others perished after diving for cover into the well that still stands in the middle of the *bagh*.

No one knows exactly how many people were killed. Official estimates put the death toll at 379, with 1200 injured, although the final figure may well have been several times higher. Indian sources quote a figure of 2000 dead. Hushed up for over six months in Britain, the Jallianwalla Bagh massacre caused an international outcry when the story finally broke. It also proved seminal in the Independence struggle, prompting Gandhi to initiate the widespread civil disobedience campaign that played such a significant part in ridding India of its colonial overlords.

Moving first-hand accounts of the horrific events of April 13, 1919, and contemporary pictures and newspaper reports, are displayed in Jallianwalla Bagh's small **martyrs gallery**. The **well**, complete with chilling bullet holes, has been turned into a memorial to the victims.

Golden rules

Visitors of all nationalities and religions are allowed into the Golden Temple provided they respect a few basic **rules**, enforced by patrolling guards. Firstly, tobacco, alcohol and drugs of any kind are forbidden. Before entering, you should also leave your shoes at the free cloakrooms, cover your head (cotton scarves are available outside the main entrance – or wear your Kullu hat), and wash your feet in the pool below the steps. **Photography** is permitted around the pool, but not inside any of the shrines.

Amrit Sarovar. Sunset and evenings are an excellent time to tune in to the beautiful music performed in the Harmandir. The helpful information office (daily 7am–8pm) to the right of the main entrance organizes **guided tours**, provides details on temple accommodation and has books and leaflets about the temple and Sikh faith.

The Parikrama

The principal north entrance to the temple, the **Darshini Deori**, leads under a Victorian **clocktower** to a flight of steps, from where you catch your first glimpse of the Harmandir, floating serenely above the glassy surface of the Amrit Sarovar. Dropping down as a reminder of the humility necessary to approach God, the steps end at the polished marble **Parikrama** that surrounds the tank, its smooth white stones set with the names of those who contributed to the temple's construction.

The shrines on the north edge of the enclosure are known as the **68 Holy Places**. Arjan Dev, the fifth guru, told his followers that a visit to these was equivalent to a pilgrimage around all 68 of India's most sacred Hindu sites. Several have been converted into a **Gallery of Martyrs**, in which paintings of glorious but gory episodes from Sikh history are displayed.

Four glass-fronted booths punctuate the Parikrama. Seated in each is a priest, or **granthi**, intoning verses from the *Adi Granth*. The continuous readings are performed in shifts; passing pilgrims touch the steps in front of the booths with their heads and leave offerings of money.

At the east end of the Parikrama, the two truncated **Ramgarhia Minars** – brick watchtowers whose tops were blasted off during Operation Blue Star – overlook the Guru-ka-Langar and the main bathing **ghats**. Hang around here long enough, and you'll see a fair cross-section of modern Sikh society parade past: families of Jat farmers, NRIs (Non-Resident Indians) on holiday from Britain and North America, and the odd group of fierce-looking warriors carrying lances, sabres and long curved daggers. Distinguished by their deep-blue knee-length robes and saffron turbans, the ultra-orthodox **nihangs** (literally "crocodiles") are devotees of the militaristic tenth guru, Gobind Singh.

The Guru-ka-Langar

For Sikhs, no pilgrimage to the Golden Temple is considered complete without a visit to the **Guru-ka-Langar**. The giant communal canteen, which overlooks the eastern entrance to the temple complex, provides **free food** to all-comers, regardless of creed, colour, caste or gender. Sharing meals with strangers in this way is intended to reinforce one of the central tenets of the Sikh faith, the **principle of equality**, instigated by the third guru, **Amar Das**, in the sixteenth century to break down caste barriers.

Some 10,000 chapati and black dhal dinners are dished up here each day in an operation of typical Sikh efficiency, which you can witness for yourself by joining the queues that form outside the hall (open 24hr). Thousands of pilgrims at a time pile in to take their places on the long coir floor mats. The meal begins only after grace has been sung by a volunteer, or *sevak*, and continues until everyone has eaten their fill. By the time the tin trays have been collected up and the floors swept for the next sitting, another crowd of pilgrims has gathered at the gates, and the cycle starts again. Although the meals are paid for out of the temple's coffers, most visitors leave a small donation in the boxes in the yard outside.

The Akal Takht

Directly opposite the ceremonial entrance to the Harmandir, the **Akal Takht** is the second most sacred shrine in the Golden Temple complex. A symbol of God's authority on earth, it was built by Guru Hargobind in the seventeenth century and came to house the Shiromani Gurudwara Parbandhak Committee, the religious and political governing body of the Sikh faith founded in 1925.

During the 1984 siege, **Bhindranwale** and his army used this golden-domed building as their headquarters, fortifying it with sandbags and machine-gun posts. When Indian paratroopers tried to storm the shrine, they were mown down in their hundreds while crossing the courtyard in front of it: the reason why the army ultimately resorted to much heavier-handed tactics to end the siege. Positioned at the opposite end of the Amrit Sarovar, tanks pumped a salvo of high-explosive squash-head shells into the delicate facade, reducing it to rubble within seconds. The destruction of the Akal Takht offended Sikh sensibilities more than any other aspect of the operation. The shrine has been largely rebuilt and now looks almost the same as it did before June 6, 1984. Decorated with elaborate inlay, its ground floor is where the *Adi Granth* is brought each evening from the Harmandir, borne in a gold and silver paladin.

The Jubi Tree

The gnarled old **Jubi Tree** in the northwest corner of the compound was planted 450 years ago by the Golden Temple's first high priest, or *Babba Buddhaya*, and is believed to have special powers. Barren women wanting a son hang strips of cloth from its branches, while marriage deals are traditionally struck in its shade for good luck – a practice frowned upon by the modern temple administration.

The Harmandir

Likened by one guru to "a ship crossing the ocean of ignorance", the triple-storey **Harmandir**, or "Golden Temple of God" was built by Arjan Dev to house the *Adi Granth* (Original Book), which he compiled from teachings of all the Sikh gurus; it is the focus of the Sikh faith. The temple has four doors indicating it is open to people of all faiths and all four caste divisions of Hindu society. The large dome and roof, covered with 100kg of gold leaf, is shaped like an inverted lotus, symbolizing the Sikhs' concern for temporal as well as spiritual matters.

The long causeway, or "**Guru's Bridge**", which joins the *mandir* to the west side of the Amrit Sarovar, is approached via an ornate archway, the **Darshani Deorh.** As you approach the sanctum check out the amazing Moghul-style inlay work and floral gilt above the doors and windows.

The **interior** of the temple – decorated with yet more gold and silver, adorned with ivory mosaics and intricately carved wood panels – is dominated by the enormous **Adi Granth**, which rests on a sumptuous throne beneath a jewel-encrusted silk canopy. Before his death in 1708, Guru Gobind Singh, who revised the *Adi Granth*, declared that he was to be the last living guru, and that the tome

Bedlam at the border

Every evening as sunset approaches, the **India-Pakistan border** closes for the night with a spectacular and somewhat Pythonesque show. It takes place at a remote little place 27km west of Amritsar called **Wagha** (the nearest town, 2km away, is Attari), connected by frequent minibuses to Amritsar. Hundreds if not thousands of Indians make their way westwards to Wagha (and Pakistanis eastwards) to watch the popular tourist attraction from specially erected stands.

Indian guards sporting outrageous moustaches and outlandish hats perform synchronized speed marching along a 100-metre walkway to the border gate where they turn and stomp back. Raucous cheering, clapping and much blowing of horns accompanies the spectacle. Guards on the Pakistan side then emulate their neighbours' efforts to much the same sort of cacophony on the other side of the gate. Several times the guards strut their military catwalk and then vanish into the guardhouse. Flags are simultaneously lowered, the gates slammed shut and the crowds on either side rush forward for a massive and congenial photo session. On both sides, more empathy than ever occurs on a cricket pitch permeates the air; photos are taken with the stone-faced guards and then everyone heads home – back to business as usual.

would take over after him – hence its full title, the *Guru Granth Sahib*. *Granthis* intone continuous readings from the text as the worshippers file past, accompanied by singers and musicians – all relayed by loudspeakers around the complex. Known as *Shri Akhand Path*, a single continuous reading of the *Guru Granth Sahib* is carried out in three-hour shifts and takes around 48 hours to complete.

Eating

Amritsar boasts a clutch of a/c **restaurants**, mostly located in the modern end of town north of the railway. For cheaper food, try the simple vegetarian **dhabas** around the Golden Temple and bus stand, which serve cheap and tasty *puris* and *chana* dhal. Local specialities include **Amritsari fish** (fillets of a river fish, called "sole fish", fried in a spicy batter and sold on the street), as well as *dal pinni* and *matthi*, sweets made from lentils that are sold at places such as *Mahajan* on Hall Bazaar.

Bharawan da Dhaba Near the City Hall. One of the best *dhabas* in Amritsar, serving simple and inexpensive but good veg curries (Rs20–45).

Bubby Vaishno Dhaba Opposite the Golden Temple main entrance. A handy place for veg curries (Rs30–60), thalis (Rs35–65) and breakfast options such as parathas or puris, plus a few South Indian dishes for good measure.

Crystal Crystal Chowk. One of the city's most popular restaurants, with Indian, Chinese and Western dishes (Rs90–160) served in comfortable surroundings, or from "fast-food" outlets on the street.

Kesar da Dhaba Between Golden Temple and Durgiana Temple. A limited menu of basic veg curries (Rs20–30) in an establishment that's been going since 1916.

Kwality Lawrence Rd, at the corner with Mall Rd. Tandoori and Chinese dishes (Rs60–200) in the main restaurant, as well as South Indian snacks, and sweets and ice-cream from counters on either side.

New Punjabi Rasoli By Jallianwalla Bagh. Chinese and Indian vegetarian dishes at reasonable prices (Rs35–55). Most of the Indian dishes involve paneer (the paneer tomato is good), but there's also a delicious mushroom tikka.

Sindhi Coffee House Opposite Ram Bagh. Tinted windows and tablecloths, and a menu that includes thalis, biryanis and some Sindhi specialities, with dishes in the Rs60–100 range.

Spice Room *Blue Moon Hotel*, Mall Rd. Mainly Chinese dishes, with the accent on spicy, plus some Indian and Western options. Main dishes go for Rs75–150.

Moving on from Amritsar

Amritsar is a major hub for traffic heading northeast to Jammu & Kashmir, southeast towards Delhi via Chandigarh (the main jumping-off place for Shimla and central HP), and west to India's only land-border crossing point with Pakistan at Wagha.

The bus station located on GT Road (NH-1) is currently closed for reconstruction, so buses leave from the streets to its east. Private buses, including a/c services, leave from around the railway station or outside Hall Gate (that is, on the street just north of Hall Hate/Gandhi Gate). Agencies outside Hall Gate and on Queens Road operate deluxe and a/c buses to **Delhi** (8hr) and **Chandigarh** (225km; 4–5hr). For **Pathankot** (101km) and other connections to Himachal Pradesh, you are restricted to state transport buses. Delhi, 475km away, is a long and tiring road journey – most travellers prefer to go by train.

The best **trains** for Delhi are the daily superfast all a/c chaircar Amritsar–New Delhi Shatabdis – the #2014 (dep 5.15am, arr 10.50am) and the #2030 (dep 5.05pm, arr 11.05pm). If you prefer to travel overnight, there's the #2904 Golden Temple Mail (dep 9.30pm, arr 7.25am), which continues to Mumbai (arr 6.05am the following day). Other trains include the daily #3050 Amritsar–Howrah Express via Varanasi, and the twice-weekly (Wed & Sun) #9772 Amritsar–Jaipur Express. **Flights** to Delhi are run by Indian Airlines (Tues, Wed, Fri & Sun) and Air India (Wed & Sun).

A full rundown of destinations reachable by train and bus from Amritsar is given in "Travel details" on p.619.

To Pakistan

For **Pakistan**, take one of the frequent buses to **Attari**, from where it's just 2km to the border at **Wagha**, or hire a taxi or auto from Amritsar. Rickshaws are available between Attari and Wagha. You'll have to cross into Pakistan by foot – it can take up to two hours to complete formalities. Tourists just wishing to watch the bizarre border spectacle can rent taxis (Rs400) or auto-rickshaws (Rs250) for the round trip. Depending on the political situation, **cross-border train** operations are sometimes suspended, but if all is well, the #4607 Amritsar–Lahore Samjhauta Express train (Mon & Thurs) leaves Amritsar for Lahore at 7am, reaching Wagha at 7.40am. It is then scheduled to leave Wagha at 11.30am, to reach Lahore at 4.15pm but is invariably delayed. In the other direction, the #4608 Lahore–Amritsar Express (Tues & Fri) departs at 8am, reaching Wagha at 12.30pm, and is scheduled to depart from Wagha at 2.20pm, arriving in Amritsar at 3pm.

Listings

Airlines Indian Airlines, 39A Court Rd ⓣ0183/221 3392 ; Air India, *MK International Hotel*, Ranjit Ave ⓣ0183/250 8133.

Ambulance ⓣ102.

Banks and exchange ATMs and exchange facilities are available at several banks across town, including the State Bank of India near the Golden Temple, the Punjab National Bank next to *Bharawan da Dhaba* and on Mall Rd, and the Indian Overseas Bank, ICICI and HFDC, all on Hall Bazaar. Authorized agencies such as Narang Travels at the *Amritsar International Hotel* arcade, near the bus stand, also change money, as can a clutch of exchange facilities on Links Rd near the train station.

Hospitals The best in the city are: Kakkar Hospital, Green Avenue ⓣ0183/250 6075; Sri Guru Nanak Dev, Majhita Rd ⓣ0183/242 2805; and Munilal Chopra Hospital, Mall Rd ⓣ0183/222 2072.

Internet access @Internet (Rs30/hour), 100m from the railway station towards Wagha on the second floor of a white building (entrance in the alleyway); i-way, Lawrence Rd, opposite Nehru Shopping Centre (Rs25/hour, but you have to guess how much time you're going to use and pay in advance).

Left luggage Baggage can be left for short periods at the Golden Temple's *gurudwaras*, or at the railway station cloakroom.

Police ⓣ100

Shopping Tablas (hand-drums), harmonia and other musical instruments are available at the shops outside the Golden Temple, where you can also buy cheap cassettes of the beautiful *kirtan* played in the shrine itself. Other possible souvenirs include a pair of traditional *Arabian Nights*-style Punjabi leather slippers, sold at stalls east of the temple's main entrance. Modern art paintings are available at the Indian Fine Arts Academy on M.M. Malviya Rd.

Swimming pools Both the *Mohan International* and *Ritz* hotels allow non-residents discretionary use of their outdoor pools (Rs150–200, towels not included).

Travel agents Narang Travels, *Amritsar International Hotel* (Ⓣ0183/255 4902) are good for most air ticketing.

Travel details

Trains

Amritsar to: Agra (2 daily; 11hr 10min–17hr); Ambala (for Chandigarh 13 daily; 3hr 14min–7hr 20min); Delhi (10 daily; 5hr 45min–12hr); Jaipur (2 weekly; 19hr 10min); Kolkata (Calcutta; 2 daily; 37hr 30min–46hr 55min); Mumbai (2 daily; 32hr 35min–43hr 55min); Pathankot (8 daily; 2hr 30min–3hr); Varanasi (2 daily: 22hr 15min–25hr 25min).
Chandigarh to: Ambala (for Amritsar 7 daily; 38min–1hr); Chennai (1 weekly; 45hr 15min); Delhi (6 daily; 3hr 10min–5hr 15min); Jodhpur (1 daily; 19hr 45min); Kalka (5 daily; 45–55min) Kolkata (Calcutta) (1 daily; 30hr 15min); Mumbai (1 daily; 27hr 45min).
Pathankot to: Amritsar (8 daily; 2hr 30min–3hr); Delhi (4 daily; 10hr 15min–12hr); Jodhpur (1 daily; 28hr 25min); Jogindernagar (2 daily; 7hr 30min–9hr); Kolkata (Calcutta 1 daily; 42hr 30min); Varanasi (1 daily; 27hr 10min).

Buses

Amritsar to: Chandigarh (every 30min; 5–6hr); Delhi (10 daily; 8–10hr); Pathankot (every 15min; 3hr); Wagha/Attari (hourly; 45min).
Chandigarh to: Agra (2 daily; 10hr); Amritsar (every 30min; 5–6hr); Anandpur Sahib (8 daily; 2–3hr); Chamba (6 daily; 12hr); Dehra Dun (5 daily; 4hr); Delhi (every 5–25min; 6hr); Dharamsala (19 daily; 7–8hr); Haridwar (7 daily; 6hr); Jaipur (8 daily; 11hr); Kalka (every 20min; 40min); Kasauli (3 daily; 2hr 30min); Kullu (10 daily; 9hr); Manali (9 daily; 10hr); Pinjore (every 20min; 30min); Rishikesh (2 daily; 6hr); Shimla (28 daily; 4hr–4hr 30min); Sirhind (hourly; 1hr 30min).
Pathankot to: Ambala (every 20min; 8hr); Amritsar (every 15min; 3hr); Chamba (hourly; 5hr); Dalhousie (hourly; 3hr 30min); Delhi (18 daily; 11hr); Dharamsala (10 daily; 4hr); Jammu (every 30min; 3hr); Jullundhar (every 10min; 3hr); Kangra (10 daily; 3–4hr); Manali (2 daily; 12hr); Mandi (7 daily; 8hr); Shimla (3 daily; 12hr).

Flights

Amritsar to: Delhi (1–3 daily; 55min).
Chandigarh to: Delhi (daily; 2hr); Leh (1 weekly; 1hr); Mumbai (daily; 3hr 30min).

CHAPTER 9

Highlights

* **Ahmedabad** Superb Indo-Islamic architecture and bustling bazaars; outlying sights include Mahatma Gandhi's Sabarmati ashram. See p.634

* **Sun Temple, Modhera** A beautiful eleventh-century temple, set in peaceful gardens: the finest example of Solanki architecture. See p.642

* **Kutch** Distinct from the rest of Gujarat; traditional embroidery, costume and culture still thrive in this harsh and remote landscape. See p.643

* **Dwarkadish temple** Important pilgrimage centre as the westernmost holy town, famed in legend as Krishna's capital. See p.659

* **Sasan Gir** The protected forest here is the last remaining habitat of the rare Asiatic lion. See p.668

* **Diu** This relaxed island is west India's most congenial beach venue, with a Portuguese flavour in its colonial architecture. See p.669 & p.670

* **Palitana temples** Shatrunjaya Hill bristles with sumptuously carved marble shrines and provides stunning views. See p.677

* **Champaner** A Solanki fortress and Jain temples are among the attractions around this ancient Muslim city. See p.679

△ Palitana temples

Gujarat

Heated in the north by the blistering deserts of Pakistan and Rajasthan, and cooled in the south by the gentle ocean breeze of the Arabian Sea, the industrial state of **GUJARAT** forms India's westernmost bulkhead. The diversity of its topography – which encompasses forested hilly tracts and fertile plains in the east, vast tidal marshland and the desert plains of the Rann of Kutch in the west, with a rocky shoreline jutting into its heartland – is challenged only by its diversity in politics and culture. Home to significant populations of Jains, Muslims, Hindus and Christians, as well as tribal and nomadic pastoral groups, the state boasts a patchwork of religious shrines and areas steeped in Hindu lore. Gujarat is the homeland of **Mahatma Gandhi**, the father of the modern state of India, who was born in Porbandar and worked for many years in Ahmedabad. Having long lived by his credo of self-dependence, Gujaratis are consistently at or near the top of the chart in terms of India's economic output. Like Punjabis, they have also fanned around the world to settle abroad. The region's **prosperity** dates as far back as the third millennium BC, when the Harappans started trading shell jewellery and textiles. The Jain-dominated textile industry remains an important source of income to the state, as do crafts to villagers on a smaller scale. Gujarat also boasts some of the subcontinent's biggest oil refineries; thriving cement, chemicals and pharmaceutical manufacturing units; and a vast and lucrative ship-breaking yard at Alang near Bhavnagar. Kandla, one of India's **largest ports**, handles about one third of the country's imports, while most of the country's diamond cutting and polishing takes place in centres such as Surat, Ahmedabad, Bhavnagar and Palanpur.

However, Gandhi's primary mission – to instigate political change through non-violent means – has not always been adhered to in his home state, and Muslim-Hindu tensions boil over to violence on a cyclical basis. The latest spate of such **rioting** made world headlines in 2002 when hundreds of people, mostly Muslims, died in communal violence. The fighting came on the heels of an equally traumatic and deadly event, the January 2001 **earthquake** centred in Kutch, which levelled whole towns. These events added to the woes of a state already beleaguered by severe **water shortages** and **drought**. Measures adopted to combat that problem – the import of water by train and longer-term solutions like the construction of bore-wells, desalination plants and the world's largest canal system – had already taxed state coffers before the earthquake struck. That said, Gujarat's wealth places it in a better position for recovery than other parts of the country might have been; in spite of the troubles, some economists predict 10.2 percent growth between 2002 and 2007, more than in any other state.

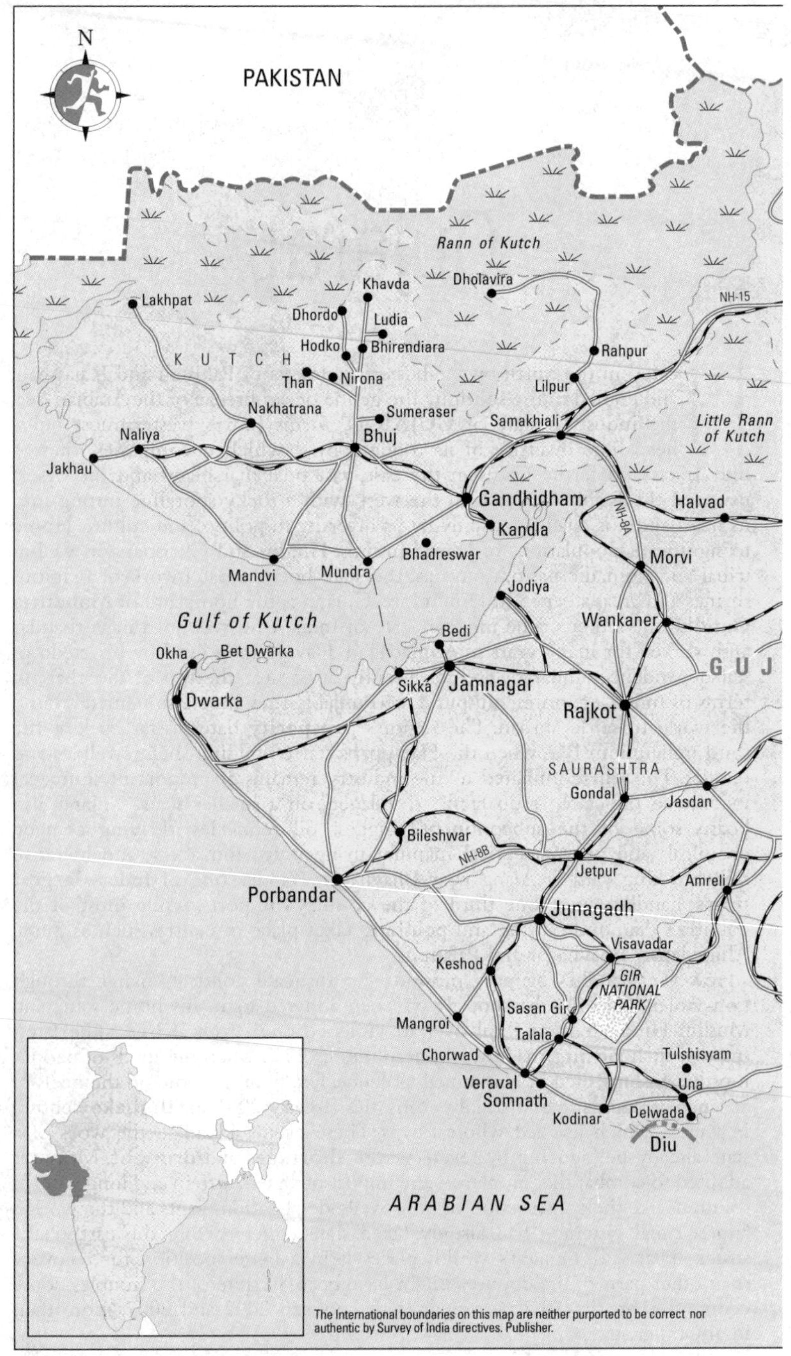
N
PAKISTAN
Rann of Kutch
Little Rann of Kutch
KUTCH
Gulf of Kutch
SAURASHTRA
GUJ
ARABIAN SEA
NH-15
NH-8A
NH-8B
Lakhpat
Khavda
Dholavira
Dhordo
Ludia
Hodko
Bhirendiara
Rahpur
Than
Nirona
Lilpur
Nakhatrana
Sumeraser
Samakhiali
Naliya
Bhuj
Jakhau
Gandhidham
Halvad
Kandla
Bhadreswar
Morvi
Mandvi
Mundra
Jodiya
Wankaner
Bedi
Okha
Bet Dwarka
Sikka
Jamnagar
Dwarka
Rajkot
Gondal
Jasdan
Bileshwar
Jetpur
Amreli
Porbandar
Junagadh
Visavadar
Keshod
GIR NATIONAL PARK
Sasan Gir
Mangroi
Talala
Chorwad
Tulshisyam
Veraval
Somnath
Una
Kodinar
Delwada
Diu
The International boundaries on this map are neither purported to be correct nor authentic by Survey of India directives. Publisher.

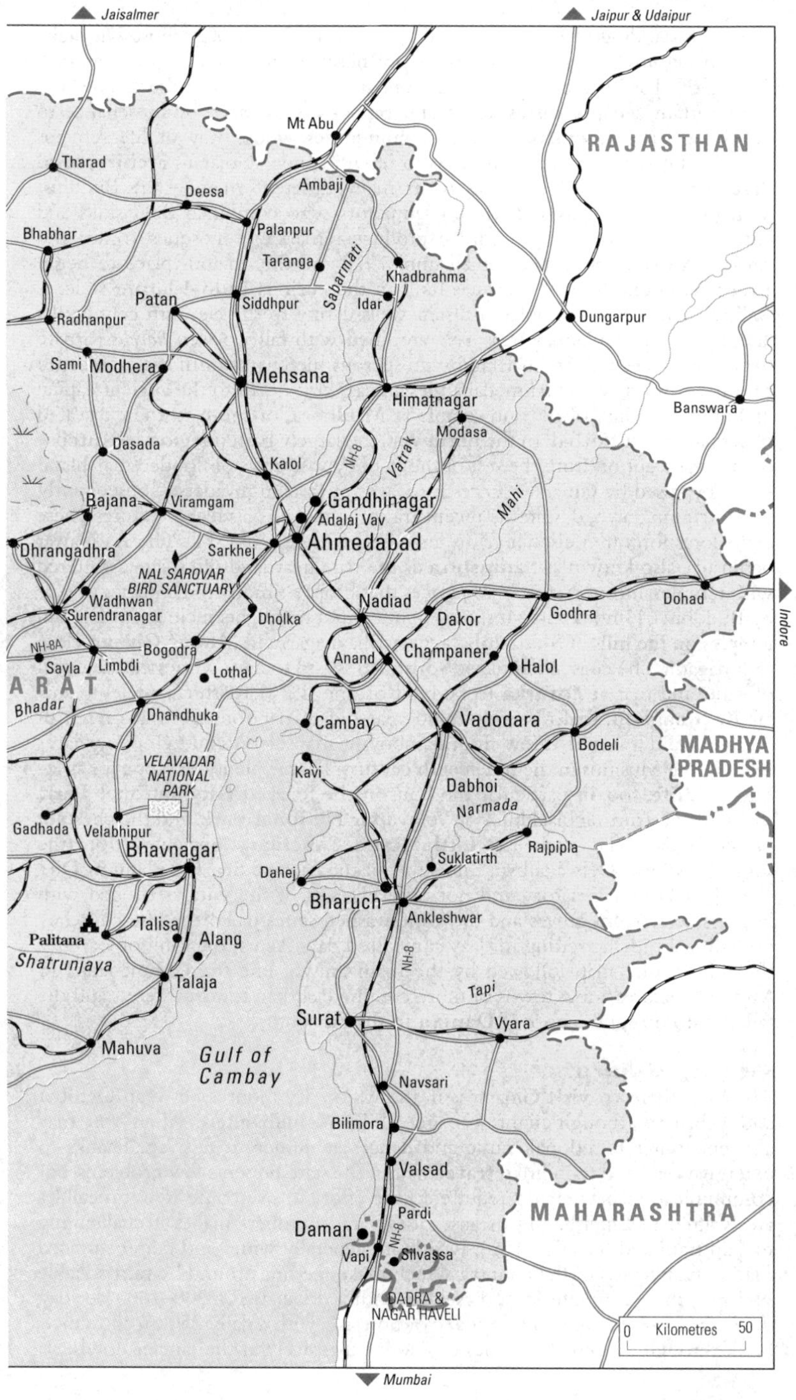

Jaisalmer
Jaipur & Udaipur
RAJASTHAN
Mt Abu
Tharad
Ambaji
Deesa
Palanpur
Bhabhar
Taranga
Sabarmati
Khadbrahma
Patan
Siddhpur
Idar
Radhanpur
Dungarpur
Sami
Modhera
Mehsana
Himatnagar
Banswara
Modasa
Vatrak
NH-8
Dasada
Kalol
Mahi
Bajana
Viramgam
Gandhinagar
Adalaj Vav
Ahmedabad
Dhrangadhra
Sarkhej
NAL SAROVAR BIRD SANCTUARY
Wadhwan
Surendranagar
Dholka
Nadiad
Dakor
Godhra
Dohad
Indore
NH-8A
Sayla
Limbdi
Bogodra
Anand
Champaner
Halol
Lothal
ARAT
Bhadar
Dhandhuka
Cambay
Vadodara
Bodeli
MADHYA PRADESH
VELAVADAR NATIONAL PARK
Kavi
Dabhoi
Narmada
Gadhada
Velabhipur
Rajpipla
Bhavnagar
Suklatirth
Dahej
Bharuch
Ankleshwar
Talisa
Palitana
Alang
Shatrunjaya
NH-8
Talaja
Tapi
Surat
Vyara
Mahuva
Gulf of Cambay
Navsari
Bilimora
Valsad
Pardi
MAHARASHTRA
Daman
NH-8
Vapi
Silvassa
DADRA & NAGAR HAVELI
0 Kilometres 50
Mumbai

9 GUJARAT

Notwithstanding recent tragedies, Gujarat has plenty to offer those who take time to detour from its more famous northerly neighbour Rajasthan, and it's free of the hard-sell and hassle that tourists often encounter there. The lure of important **temple cities**, **forts** and **palaces** is balanced by the chance to search out unique **crafts** made in communities whose way of life remains scarcely affected by global trends. As so often in India, Gujarat's **architectural diversity** reflects the influences of its many different rulers – the Buddhist Mauryans, Hindu rajas and Muslim emperors who combined their skills and tastes with Hindu craftsmanship to produce remarkable mosques, tombs and palaces. **Ahmedabad**, state capital until 1970 and the obvious place to begin a tour, harbours the first mosques built in the curious **Indo-Islamic** style, as well as richly carved temples and step-wells dating to the eleventh century. Its fascinating old residential areas, *pols*, are lined with tall wooden *havelis* (ornate mansions), carved in finest detail by prosperous merchants from the eighteenth century onwards. From Ahmedabad it's an easy trip north to the ancient capital of **Patan** and the Solanki sun temple at **Modhera**, or south to the excavated Harappan site at **Lothal**. In the northwest, the largely barren region of **Kutch** – occasionally cut off from the rest of the state by vast tracts of flooded marshland – was bypassed by Gujarat's successive waves of foreign invaders. Consequently, this intriguing area, despite its recent travails, preserves a village culture where crafts long forgotten elsewhere are practised with age-old skill. The Kathiawar peninsula, also known as **Saurashtra**, is the true heartland of Gujarat, scattered with temples, mosques, forts and palaces that bear testimony to centuries of rule by Buddhists, Hindus and Muslims. Architectural highlights include superb Jain temples on the hills of **Shatrunjaya**, near Bhavnagar, and **Mount Girnar**, close to Junagadh. The coastal temple at **Somnath** is said to have witnessed the dawn of time, and that at **Dwarka** to be built on the site of Krishna's ancient capital. At **Junagadh**, rocks bearing 2000-year-old inscriptions from the reign of Ashoka stand a stone's throw from flamboyant mausoleums and Gothic palaces built by the Muslims in the nineteenth century. There's plenty of scope for spotting **wildlife**, too, in particular the lions in the forested **Gir National Park**, the herds of strutting blackbuck at **Velavadar National Park**, and the chestnut brown Indian wild ass in the **Little Rann Sanctuary**. Separated from the south coast near Delwada by a thin sliver of the Arabian Sea, the island of **Diu**, actually a Union Territory and not officially part of the state, is fringed with beaches, leafy palm groves and the whitewashed spires of Portuguese churches, providing an idyllic setting for lazy sun-kissed days. Across the Gulf of Cambay, the thin coastal strip followed by the main railway line from Ahmedabad to Mumbai features a few towns of more commercial than tourist interest and the faded old Portuguese port of **Daman** in the far south.

Visiting Gujarat

The **best time to visit** Gujarat is in the warm, dry months between October and February (though nights can get chilly in midwinter), when you may also encounter traditional music and dances at numerous festivals. Thanks to extensive road and train links, **travel** within the state presents few problems, but communication barriers do require a little effort to overcome (few timetables are written in English, and the use of Gujarati numbers makes it challenging to find train and bus platforms). Roads are generally wider and better surfaced than in many parts of the country, which makes getting around by **taxi** a viable option – the going rate for a diesel car with a driver is Rs1200–1600 per day, depending on whether you want a/c or non-a/c, with a daily 250km allowance; book through car rental agencies or, more expensively, at the fancier hotels.

You'll be hard pushed to find a luxury **hotel** outside cities like Ahmedabad, Vadodara, Surat and Rajkot, but following Rajasthan's example a number of local maharajas and nawabs have opened their family homes as heritage hotels offering good-value accommodation. **Food** throughout the state is predominantly vegetarian, and Gujarat's good-value thalis are renowned for their size and sweetness. Note that Gujarat is India's only **dry state**: to enjoy a cold beer, you'll have to get a permit at Ahmedabad's International Airport (ask the Gujarat Tourism counter near the domestic arrival lounge for assistance) or one of the hotels allowed to stock liquor, or else head to the Union Territory enclaves of Daman and Diu.

Some history

The first known settlers in what is now Gujarat were the **Harappans**, who appeared from Sindh and Punjab in around 2500 BC and established more than a hundred towns and cities. Despite their skilful craftsmanship and trade links with Africans, Arabs, Persians and Europeans, the civilization fell into decline in 1900 BC, largely because of severe flooding around the Indus delta; some of its most mature remains, dating to 1900–1600 BC, can be seen at Lothal. From 1500 to 500 BC, little is known about the history of Gujarat but it is popularly believed that the **Yadavas**, Krishna's clan, held sway over much of the state, with their capital at Dwarka.

Gujarat's political history begins in earnest with the powerful **Mauryan empire**, established by Chandragupta with its capital at Junagadh, then known as Girinagar, and reaching its peak under Ashoka. After his death in 226 BC, Mauryan power dwindled; the last significant ruler was Samprati, Ashoka's grandson, a Jain who built fabulous temples at *tirthas* (pilgrimage sites) such as Girnar and Palitana.

Throughout the first millennium AD, control of the region passed between a succession of warring dynasties and nomadic tribes, including the **Gurjars**, from whom the state eventually derived its name, and the Kathi warriors of Saurashtra. Gujarat eventually came under the sway of the **Solanki** or **Chalukyan** dynasty in the eleventh and twelfth centuries; this is considered a golden period in the state's architectural history as the rulers commissioned splendid Hindu and Jain **temples** and **step-wells**. Many of these structures suffered during the raids of Mahmud of Ghazni in 1027, but Muslim rule was not actually established until the Khalji conquest in 1299. Eight years later, Muzaffar Shah's declaration of independence from Delhi marked the foundation of the **Sultanate of Gujarat**, which lasted until its conquest by the Moghul emperor Akbar in the sixteenth century. In this period Muslim, Jain and Hindu styles were melded to produce remarkable **Indo-Islamic** mosques and tombs. Contrary to impressions encouraged by recent sectarian violence, particularly in Ahmedabad, Islam never eclipsed Hinduism or Jainism, and the three have lived side by side for centuries.

In the 1500s, the **Portuguese**, already settled in Goa, turned their attention to the Gujarati coast, aware of the excellent potential of its ports and its long history of trade. Having captured Daman in 1531, they took Diu four years later, building forts and typically European towns. Fending off Arab and Muslim attacks, the Portuguese governed the ports until they were subsumed under the Indian Union in the 1960s.

The **British East India Company** set up its original Indian headquarters in Surat in 1613, and soon established their first "factory", a self-contained village for labourers' and merchants' houses and warehouses, sowing the seeds of a prospering textile industry. When British sovereignty was established in 1818,

Godhra and Gujarat's communal violence

When the BJP shocked India with its landslide victory over its Congress rivals in the December 2002 election, analysts needed only to point to a single word to find an answer for the victory – **Godhra**. Godhra had previously been just another anonymous train depot until February 27, 2002, when a Muslim mob set fire to train cars filled with enthusiastic Hindu pilgrims returning from the controversial temple at Ayodhya. Four cars were burned, and 59 people killed.

The incident sparked huge **riots** across Gujarat in areas where Hindus and Muslims live side by side. Muslim neighbourhoods burned while sword- and stick-wielding Hindus rampaged and looted. Muslims who fought back were largely unsuccessful, and in many cases police forces allegedly stood by and watched. Officially, more than 1000 people died in the weeks following the Godhra incident, although human rights organizations estimate the real figure at more than 2000, most of them Muslims, while thousands more moved to refugee camps, too frightened to go back to their own homes.

The unending violence was politicized after Sonia Gandhi's Congress Party accused the government of not doing enough to ensure the safety of Muslim citizens. Gujarat's BJP chief minister **Narendra Modi** earned the moniker "Muslim killer" for his seemingly passive attitude as the violence continued, and his lack of support for the survivors. Just days after the New York-based Human Rights Watch reported that Gujarat state officials "were directly involved in the killings of hundreds of Muslims since Feb 27 and are now engineering a massive **cover-up** of the state's role in the violence", Parliament attempted to censure the BJP government. At the end of the sixteen-hour debate Prime Minister Atal Bihari Vajpayee apologized for not having "tried harder" to end the riots and eventually announced a $31 million rehabilitation package to restore the riot victims' businesses and homes.

When election time neared, Modi intensified his *Hindutva* rhetoric and campaign "to prevent" another Godhra. While he avoided any direct anti-Muslim statements, it was clear that the minister was battling to haul in as many Hindu votes as possible in the midst of so much ethnic tension. Yet it wasn't until the December 12 election that his cult status among ordinary Gujaratis was at last verified by his surprising landslide win.

The 2004 elections, however, saw a turnaround, ushering in the Congress-led UPA government with Manmohan Singh of Congress as Prime Minister. Though BJP retained the majority in Gujarat, the elections were closely contested. Following protests that the violence had been government-supported and that the authorities were biased, the Supreme Court ruled that the cases of the violence-affected families be moved to courts in other states for their safety and ordered investigations into the riots. As yet, none of the investigations have been able to come to any conclusion regarding the train burning at Godhra.

governor-generals moved into some of Gujarat's main cities and signed treaties with about two hundred princely and petty states of Saurashtra. British rule brought mixed results: while machinery upgraded textile manufacture and brought substantial wealth to the region, many manual labourers were put out of business. Their cause was valiantly fought by Gujarat-born **Mahatma Gandhi** (see box on p.661), whose campaigns for Independence and social equality brought international attention to his ashram in Ahmedabad. After Partition, due to its position bordering the new Muslim state of Pakistan, Gujarat received an influx of Hindus from Sind and witnessed terrible sectarian fighting as Muslims fled to their new homeland.

In 1960, after the Marathi and Gujarati **language riots** (demonstrators sought the redrawing of state boundaries according to language, as had happened in the south), Bombay state was split and Gujarat state created. The Portuguese enclaves, along with Goa, were forcibly annexed by the Indian government in 1961. After Independence Gujarat was a staunch Congress stronghold, apart from a brief defeat by the Janata party in 1977, until the fundamentalists of the BJP took control in 1991. The communal violence of 2002, which tallied death tolls well into the hundreds, re-opened an old chapter of history by pitting Muslim and Hindu neighbours against one another. The tensions and violence started suspiciously near the start of the state election campaign; theories that the problems were politically generated appeared to be verified when the BJP rode a dramatic wave of Hindu nationalism to victory over Congress by a margin of 126 seats to 51.

Ahmedabad

A mass of factories, mosques, temples and high-rise offices, Gujarat's commercial hub, **AHMEDABAD**, sprawls along the banks of the River Sabarmati some 90km from its mouth in the Bay of Cambay. First impressions can be poor: the state's largest city is an appallingly polluted place, renowned throughout the subcontinent for its dreadful congestion and repeated outbreaks of communal violence. Give it a little time, however, and the mix of medieval and modern – along with the coexistence of thriving Hindu, Muslim and Jain communities – makes the city a compelling place to explore. Although it suffered badly in the 2001 earthquake, damage was sustained more in outlying residential areas than the parts that attract visitors.

A wander through the bazaars and *pols* (residential areas) of the bustling **old city** is rewarding enough, but Ahmedabad is also packed with diverse architectural styles, with over fifty **mosques** and **tombs**, as well as Hindu and Jain **temples** and grand **step-wells** (*vavs*). In addition, assorted **museums** provide a good introduction to Gujarati culture: the extensive **Calico Museum of Textiles** in the northern district of Shahi Bagh rates as one of the world's finest, while Mahatma Gandhi's **Sabarmati Ashram** has an exhibition on his life and the Indian Freedom Movement.

Particularly in the old city, it's advisable to cover your mouth and nose with a bandana or handkerchief to reduce inhalation of **carbon monoxide** – Ahmedabad ranks in the world's ten most polluted cities, largely because of kerosene-fuelled rickshaws. Around 60,000 new vehicles (most two- and three-wheelers) are added to the city's roads per year, resulting in horrific traffic jams. Free **oxygen bars** for public and police use are located at the crossroads near Kalupur Gate, Income Tax Circle and Panchvati Crossroads; and at the time of writing there are talks of converting the rickshaws to Compressed Natural Gas (CNG) following the success of pollution-control in Delhi. Smog notwithstanding, locals can at least rejoice in the high waters of the Sabarmati River. Since time immemorial the river had practically dried up outside the monsoon months, but in 2002, a controversial **canal project** brought in water from the River Narmada, giving it life year round. The rejuvenated river has brought a cooler feel to the city, but Ahmedabad has a long way to go before it can breathe easily.

If you are anywhere near the city on January 14, it's worth checking out the famed **International Kite Festival**, which draws kite-flyers from as far afield as America and Japan. It's a colourful two-day affair, the largest of its kind in the world, and features a frenzied battle in which kite strings coated with ground glass are set to duel with one another.

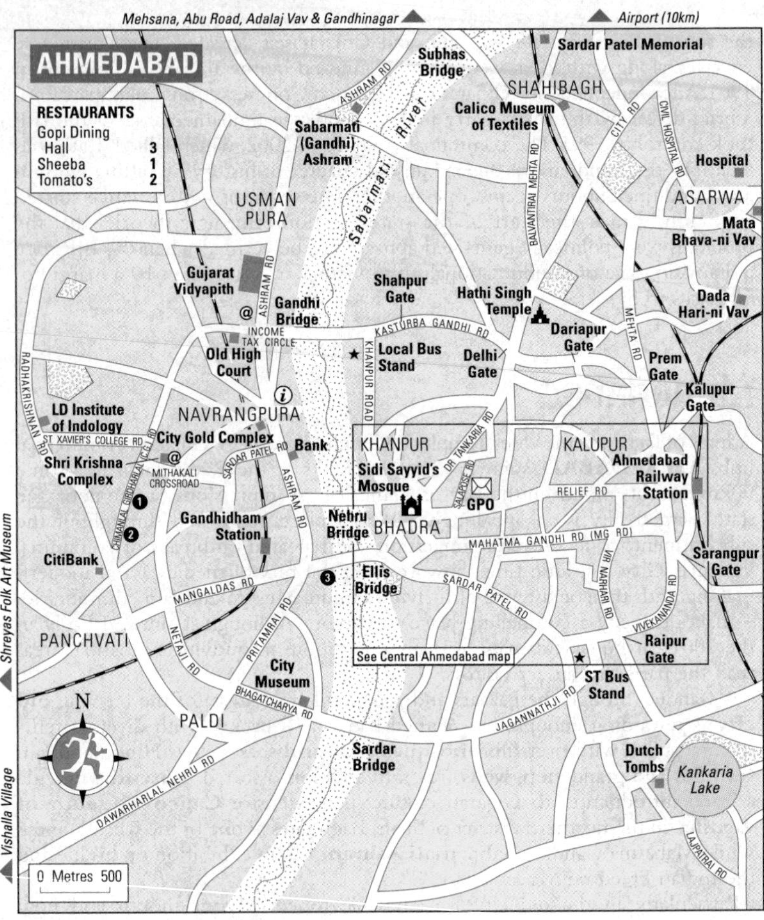

Some history

When **Ahmed Shah** inherited the Sultanate of Gujarat in 1411, he chose to move his capital from Patan to the site of Asawal village, a small settlement on the east bank of the Sabarmati, renaming it after himself. The city quickly grew as skilled artisans and traders were invited to settle. Its splendid mosques were clearly intended to assert Muslim supremacy, and heralded the new **Indo-Islamic** style of architecture, which, though best displayed here, is a marked feature of many Gujarati cities.

In 1572, Ahmedabad became part of the growing Moghul empire and was regarded as India's most handsome city. It profited from a flourishing **textiles trade** which exported velvets, silks and shimmering brocades as far afield as Europe. But after a devastating famine in 1630 and a period of political instability when government passed between the Muslims and the Hindu Marathas, the city went into **decline**. Another famine in 1812 left it almost crippled, but the merchants and traders who had left during Maratha rule were encouraged to return five years later when taxes were lowered by the newly arrived British.

Trade in opium grew – the British needed something to offer the Chinese in return for silk and tea – and the introduction of modern machinery re-established Ahmedabad as a textile exporter that came to be known as the "Manchester of the East". In the run up to Independence, while **Mahatma Gandhi** was revitalizing small-scale textile production, the city became an important seat of political power, and a hotbed for communal tension as parties vied for pre-eminence. **Communal rioting**, and in particular a series of ugly attacks on the tiny Christian minority, have sullied Ahmedabad's reputation in recent years. Periodic curfews are set in place when fighting breaks out, but these are generally confined to outlying areas and rarely affect visitors in the centre of town.

Arrival, information and city transport

Ahmedabad's **international airport** (Ⓣ079/286 9266) is linked to the city, 10km south, by prepaid taxi (Rs250–300), auto-rickshaw (Rs150) and city bus #101, which terminates at **Lal Darwaja**, the station for local buses in the west of the old city, near most of the hotels. Long-distance buses arrive at the **ST Bus Stand** in the southeast of the old city, 1km from the hotels, while the **Ahmedabad railway station** is to the east, at the far end of Relief Road and MG Road. Some trains arrive at the **Gandhidham station** in the west of the city. City buses to Lal Darwaja run from both the railway station (#37, #56, #135, #122 and #133) and the bus stand (#13/1, #32 and #52/2) – if you can't read numbers in Gujarati, simply ask at the information booth. **Taxis** and metered **auto-rickshaws** are in abundance at the airport, the railway station and both bus stands – both will generally negotiate a day rate. Although most of the tourist interest is on the east bank of the Sabarmati, the main **tourist office** is across the river in HK House, just off Ashram Road, 1km north of Nehru Bridge (Mon–Sat 10.30am–1.30pm & 2–6pm, closed 2nd & 4th Sat of month; Ⓣ079/2658 9683). **City tours** (9am & 1.30pm; Rs60; Ⓣ079/2550 7739) depart from the bus stand at Lal Darwaja, but to see Jami Mosque, Manek Chowk and the *pols* not accessible by bus, take the informative **Heritage Walk** (8.30–10.30am; Rs50), which departs from Swaminarayan Temple at Kalupur and ends at the Jami Masjid. It can be fun to amble the narrow backstreets of the old city on foot, but to cover wider distances along the main roads you'll need to use auto-rickshaws or **public transport** – which can be difficult, except at the main bus stations, as **bus** numbers and destinations are written in Gujarati.

Accommodation

Most of Ahmedabad's **hotels** are conveniently located in the **west end of the old city**, within walking distance of the bazaars, the local bus station and many of the sights. Others are clustered around the **railway station**, while north of Nehru Bridge, in the rather classy **Khanpur** area, accommodation tends to be more upmarket.

Lal Darwaja

Ajanta Dr Tankaria Rd, near Jansatta Press, Mirjapur Circle Ⓣ079/2550 6992, Ⓕ2550 6522. Colourfully decorated, comfortable hotel with good facilities. ❸–❹

Balwas 6751 Relief Rd, opposite Relief Cinema Ⓣ079/2550 7135, Ⓕ2550 6320. Modern, well-kept place with the best rooms in a separate back building. Most have a/c and TV, and all have clean private bathrooms with hot water. ❹

Cadillac Advance Cinema Rd, near Sidi Sayyid's Mosque Ⓣ079/2550 7558. Small, colourful rooms, some with private bath. The dorm (Rs50) is men only. ❶–❷

Good Night Dr Tankaria Rd, opposite Sidi Sayyid's Mosque Ⓣ079/2550 6997, Ⓕ2550 6998. Spick and span modern rooms with TV and private bathroom. ④–⑤

House of Mangaldas Dr Tankaria Rd, opposite Sidi Sayyid's Mosque ⓣ079/2550 6946, ⓕ2550 6535. Friendly heritage hotel in a 1920s building with large rooms and all mod cons. Courtyards are decorated with period furniture, while old photos of eminent visitors to the family home – including Mahatma Gandhi – line the walls. Good restaurant on site. ④–⑤

Rahil just off Dr Tankaria and Mirjapur roads ⓣ079/2551 0442. Friendly place perched above a row of shops. Good value rooms with cable TV. ③

Around the railway station

Manila Lalbhai Chambers, Kapasia Bazaar ⓣ079/212 5894. Clean place with the usual marble decor and some a/c rooms. ③–⑥

Moti Mahal Kapasia Bazaar ⓣ079/212 1881, ⓕ213 6132. Very well-kept, clean hotel offering identikit rooms with bathroom and cable TV, some a/c. ③–④

Khanpur district

Cama Khanpur Rd ⓣ079/2550 1234, ⓦwww.camahotels.com. Luxurious rooms ($95–225) overlooking the River Sabarmati, and there's a garden terrace with pool. Restaurant, coffee shop and one of the few permit rooms in the state where you can buy alcohol. Inconvenient 9am checkout. ⑨

Le Meridien Khanpur Rd ⓣ079/2550 5505, ⓦwww.lemeridien.com. A smiling doorman greets you at the entrance to this hotel, which features a large open lobby and sitting area. The service and standards are as high as you'd expect from this international chain, with an excellent restaurant, indoor pool and gym. 9am check out. Rooms $155–210. ⑨

King Palace Khanpur Rd ⓣ079/550 0280, ⓕ550 0275. Smart, comfortable rooms, all with cable TV and a/c. Good value for this bracket. ⑤–⑨

The City

The historic heart of Ahmedabad is the **old city**, an area of about three square kilometres on the east bank of the river, dissected by the main thoroughfares of Relief Road (also called Tilak Road) and Mahatma Gandhi (MG) Road, and reaching its northern limits at **Delhi Gate**. It's best to start exploring in Lal Darwaja, taking in the squat buildings of the original citadel, **Bhadra**, the **mosques** and tombs of Ahmedabad's Muslim rulers, as well as vibrant bazaars and *pols* – labyrinths of high wooden *havelis* and narrow cul-de-sacs that still house families all belonging to the same caste or trade. In the north of town, don't miss the **Calico Museum of Textiles**, one of the best of its kind in the country.

Bhadra, Sidi Sayyid's Mosque and around

The solid fortified citadel, **Bhadra**, built of deep red stone in 1411 as Ahmedabad's first Muslim structure, is relatively plain in comparison to the later mosques. The palace inside is now occupied by offices and its courtyard packed with typists and advocates who use it like an open-air office, whacking out documents and contracts for Ahmedabad's business community. Most of the building is off-limits to tourists, but you can climb to its roof via a winding staircase just inside the main gateway and survey the streets below from behind its weathered bastions. In front of the citadel is a small public garden and **Alif Shah's Mosque**, gaily painted in green and white. Further east, beyond the odoriferous meat market in **Khas Bazaar**, is **Teen Darwaja**, a thick-set triple gateway built during Ahmed Shah's reign that once led to the outer court of the royal citadel. A trio of pointed arches engraved with Islamic inscriptions and detailed carving spans the busy road below and shelters cobblers and peddlers.

A prominent feature on the front of glossy city brochures, **Sidi Sayyid's Mosque** (1573), famed for the ten magnificent *jali* (lattice-work) screens lining its upper walls, sits in the centre of a busy traffic circle to the east of Nehru Bridge. The two semicircular screens high on the western wall are the most spectacular, with floral designs exquisitely carved out of the yellow

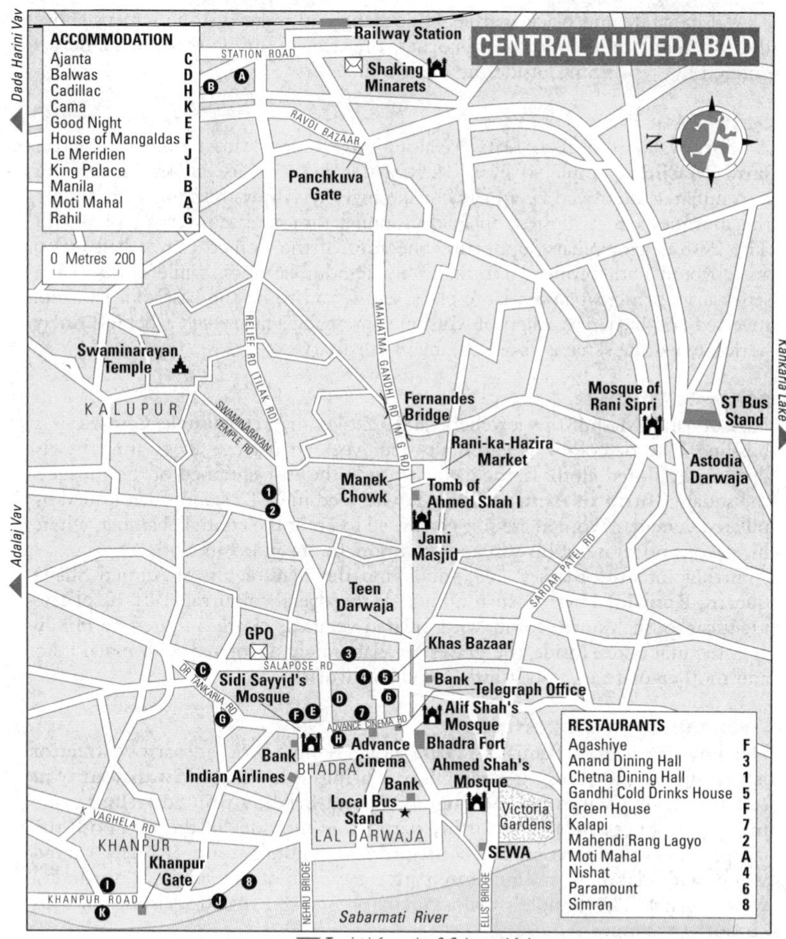

stone so common in Ahmedabad's mosques. The eastern face is open, revealing a host of pillars that divide the hall into fifteen areas, each with skilfully sculpted domed ceilings. Stonework within depicts heroes and animals from popular Hindu myths – one effect of Hindu and Jain craftsmanship on an Islamic tradition that rarely allowed the depiction of living beings in its mosques. Women cannot enter this mosque, but the gardens around it afford good views of the screens.

Ahmed Shah's Mosque

West of Bhadra, not far from Victoria Gardens, **Ahmed Shah**'s small and attractively simple **mosque** was the private place of worship for the royal household. Sections of an old Hindu temple, perhaps dating back to 1250 AD, were used in its construction – hence the incongruous Sanskrit inscriptions on some of the pillars in the sanctuary. The *mihrabs* are particularly ornate, the central one carved in white and black marble. Hidden behind pierced stone screens above the sanctuary in the northeast corner, the *zenana*, or women's chamber, is entered by steps from outside the main wall.

Jami Masjid

A short walk from Teen Darwaja along MG Road leads to the spectacular **Jami Masjid**. Completed in 1424, it stands today in its entirety, except for two minarets destroyed by an earthquake in 1957. Always buzzing with people, the mosque is at its busiest on Fridays, when thousands converge to worship. The 260 elegant pillars supporting the roof of the domed prayer hall (*qibla*) are covered with profuse, unmistakeably Hindu, carvings, while close to the sanctuary's principal arch a large black slab is said to be the base of a Jain idol inverted and buried as a sign of Muslim supremacy. The *zenana* is behind finely perforated stone screens above the main sanctuary.

Manek Chowk

East of Jami Masjid, the jewellery and textiles market **Manek Chowk** is a bustling hive of colour where craftsmen work in narrow alleys amid newly dyed and tailored cloth. Immediately outside the east entrance of the mosque, the square **Tomb of Ahmed Shah I**, who died in 1442, stands surrounded by pillared verandas. Women are not permitted to enter the central chamber, where his grave, and those of his son and grandson, lie shrouded in cloth.

Further into the market area, you'll find the mausoleum of Ahmed Shah's queens, **Rani-ka-Hazira**, surrounded by the dyers' colourful stalls. Its plan is identical to Shah's own tomb, with pillared verandas clearly inspired by Hindu architectural tastes. Inside, the graves are elaborately decorated with metal inlay and mother-of-pearl, now a little faded and worn.

Swaminarayan temple

Heading north from Rani-ka-Hazira along Temple Road, a narrow street of fabric shops, and crossing Relief Road brings you to the **Swaminarayan temple**, which stands behind huge gates and brightly painted walls. Forming a delicate contrast to the many hard stone mosques in the city, both the temple and the houses in the courtyard surrounding it are of finely carved wood, with elaborate and intricate patterns typical of the *havelis* of north and west Gujarat. The temple's main sanctuary is given over to Vishnu and his consort Lakshmi.

Mosque and Tomb of Rani Sipri

Near Astodia Darwaja in the south of the city, the small and elegant **mosque of Rani Sipri** was built in 1514 at the queen's orders. Her grave lies in front, sheltered by a pillared mausoleum. The stylish mosque shows more Hindu influence than any other in Ahmedabad, with several Hindu carvings and an absence of arches. Its pillared sanctuary has an open facade to the east and fine tracery work on the west wall.

Shaking minarets

South of the railway station, opposite the large gate of Sarangpur Darwaja, **Sidi Bashir's minars** are all that remain of the mosque popularly named after one of Ahmed Shah's favourite slaves. More than 21m high, these are the best existing example of the "**shaking minarets**" – built on a foundation of flexible sandstone, probably to protect them from earthquake damage – that were once a common sight on Ahmedabad's skyline. At least two European visitors,

Robert Grindlay (1826) and Henry Cousens (1905), reported climbing to the top storey of one minaret, shaking it hard, and causing its twin to shake, but as entry is restricted you'll be lucky to be able to try this yourself.

Dada Hari-ni Vav and Mata Bhava-ni Vav

Northern Gujarat abounds in remarkable **step-wells** – deep, with elaborately carved walls and broad flights of covered steps leading to the shaft – but **Dada Hari-ni Vav**, in the northeast of the city just outside the old boundaries, is among the very finest. It can be reached by taking bus #111 to Asarwa; ask to be dropped nearby, and either walk or take an auto-rickshaw to the well. An auto-rickshaw from Lal Darwaja should cost around Rs25. While it's a Muslim construction, built in 1500 for Bai Harir Sultani, superintendent of the royal harem, the craftsmen were Hindu, and their influence is clear in the lavish and sensuous carvings on the walls and pillars. The best time to visit is an hour or so before noon when the sculpted floral patterns and shapely figurines inside are bathed in sunlight. **Bai Harir**'s lofty mosque and lattice-walled tomb stand west of the well.

A couple of hundred metres north, the neglected **Mata Bhava-ni Vav** was probably constructed in the eleventh century, before Ahmedabad was founded. It's profoundly Hindu in character, and dedicated to Bhava-ni, an aspect of Shiva's consort Parvati, whose modest shrine is set in the back wall of the well shaft.

Hathi Singh Temple

The Svetambara **Hathi Singh Temple** (daily 10am–noon & 4–7.30pm), a few hundred metres north of Delhi Gate, is easily distinguished by its high carved column, visible from the road. Built entirely of white marble embossed with smooth carvings of dancers, musicians, animals and flowers, this serene temple is dedicated to Dharamnath, whose statue stands in the main sanctuary. He is the fifteenth *tirthankara*, or "ford-maker", one of twenty-four great teachers sanctified by the Jains. Other *tirthankaras* peer out with jewelled eyes from smaller shrines in the pillared cloisters around the courtyard.

Calico Museum of Textiles

Nobody should leave Ahmedabad without taking a tour of the **Calico Museum of Textiles**, in the Sarabhai Foundation, 3km north of Delhi Gate in Shahibagh (bus #101, #101/1, #103, #105); it's simply the finest collection of textiles, clothes, furniture, and crafts in the country. Highlights of the **morning tour** (10.30am–12.30pm; free) include a number of exquisite pieces made for the British and Portuguese, while from India's royal households there's an embroidered tent and the robes of Shah Jahan. Look out too for the *patola* saris, woven in Patan (see p.642), as well as the extravagant *zari* work that gilds saris in heavy gold stitching and can bring their weight to almost nine kilos. Other galleries are dedicated to embroideries, *bandhani* tie-and-dye, textiles made for overseas trade and woollen shawls from Kashmir and Chamba. In addition to exhibits from other Indian regions, tribal crafts such as Kutchi silk-and-cotton *mashru* weaving are displayed in spectacular wooden *havelis* from Patan and Siddhpur in northern Gujarat. Clearly labelled models and diagrams explain the weaving, dyeing and embroidery processes. The **afternoon tour** (2.45–4.45pm) includes the galleries of *pichwais* and other temple paintings and decorations, including Jain statues housed in a replica *haveli* temple and centuries-old manuscripts and *mandalas* painted on palm leaves. There are also bronzes from South India and a room dedicated to Indian music.

SEWA

Almost ninety percent of women who work in India are self-employed. Existing outside the protection of labour laws and the minimum wage, they are particularly subject to exploitation, often at the hands of unscrupulous banks and private lenders. Ahmedabad, however, has maintained a tradition of self-help since the days of Gandhi, and has achieved world recognition as the home base of the ground-breaking **Self-Employed Womens' Association, SEWA** (Ⓣ079/2550 6444, Ⓦwww.sewa.org), founded in the early 1970s by Ela Bhatt. Originally set up to offer legal advice, provide training and child care, and to negotiate with police and local government for vendors' licences and education for members' children, it soon opened its own co-operative **Mahila Bank**, the first to offer women low-interest loans, savings and deposit accounts and insurance. Women were now able to buy basic materials and tools, and use their income to live on rather than paying off high interest rates. SEWA is now involved with projects throughout Gujarat and India, and also works closely with similar movements in Yemen, Turkey and southern Africa.

In 1984 a major textile industry slump affected 35,000 families, most of them Harijans and Muslims. Many had to resort to rag- and paper-picking, collecting grimy scraps of paper, polythene and broken glass for recycling, a task which threatened their health and brought in pathetic wages. Setting up training centres in weaving, sewing, dyeing and printing, and providing efficient machinery, SEWA helped to re-establish many women in the textile labour force, and provided an outlet for their products. SEWA (now with 319,000 members nationwide, 206,000 in Gujarat) has trained its members in a variety of skills including accountancy and office administration, and its management committee includes farmers, rag-pickers and *beedi*-makers. The organization has also responded to complaints of verbal and sexual assault in the workplace and at home. In 1987, 2000 women registered a protest against *sati* (widow burning) and a campaign to have verbal divorce and polygamy banned in Gujarat resulted in a change in the law. SEWA also strongly opposes the sex determination tests that lead to female foeticide, a particularly widespread practice in Gujarat. SEWA has two **craft shops** in Ahmedabad (both Mon–Sat 10am–7pm); one on the east side of Ellis Bridge, in the organization's reception centre; another on CG Road at the Banascraft Chandan Complex.

City Museum

Just west of Sardar Bridge in the modern Sanskar Kendra on Bhagatcharya Road, the **City Museum** (Tues–Sun 10.30am–6pm; free) is well worth a visit. The nicely laid out exhibits cover such diverse subjects as the history of the city, urban growth, sociological development and the activities of Gandhi and the freedom movement. Other displays include ancient sculpture, folk and modern art, paintings of literary figures, a colourful section on world religions, and a **Kite Museum** (same hours) in the basement.

Sabarmati (Gandhi) Ashram

At the northern end of Ashram Road, the **Sabarmati Ashram** (daily 8.30am–6.30pm; free) is where the Mahatma lived from 1917 until 1930, holding meetings with weavers and Harijans as he helped them find security and re-establish the manual textile industry in Ahmedabad. In keeping with the man's uncluttered lifestyle, the collection of his personal property is modest but poignant – wooden shoes, white seamless clothes and a pair of round spectacles. A one-hour **sound-and-light show** narrating his life story has an English-language showing three evenings a week (Sun, Wed & Fri 8.30pm; Rs5) except during monsoon. Tickets are sold at the door, or you can reserve on Ⓣ079/2755 6073.

The ashram itself is no longer operating, but many people come here simply to sit and meditate.

Other museums

Ahmedabad's museums are strong in arts and crafts. Among them, the informative **Shreyas Folk Art Museum**, way out to the west near the city limits (daily except Mon 9.30am–1pm & 1.30–5.30pm; Rs45; bus #34/2 or 34/3 from Lal Darwaja), displays the traditional work of Gujarat's many tribes. The **Tribal Museum** (daily except Mon 11am–5pm; free) in Gujarat Vidyapith, north of Income Tax Circle on Ashram Road, is also illuminating, detailing the various peoples of the state and their customs, such as the painting of "magical" pictures by Bhils to ward off disaster. The **N.C. Mehta Gallery** in the **LD Institute of Indology** in the west of town (Tues–Sun: May 1–June 15 8am–1pm, rest of the year 11am–noon & 3–5pm; free) has a superb collection of miniature paintings from all over India; an **Indology Museum** in the same complex is strong on Jain sculpture and manuscripts. Take bus #52/1 from Lal Darwaja. All these museums are in educational institutions and thus closed on public holidays.

Vishalla village

If you're unlikely to experience the genuine article, it's worth taking time to visit **Vishalla village** (daily 11am–2pm & 7–11pm; Rs15), out on Sarkhej Road, 4km south of town (bus #31). Designed by Surendra Patel, a prominent local architect and antique collector, Vishalla is an admirably authentic collection of traditionally decorated mud huts where potters, weavers and *paan*-makers demonstrate their skills. The on-site **Vechaar Utensils Museum** (daily 11am–2pm & 7–10.30pm; Rs5) houses a vast collection of Gujarati metalware, including jewellery, knives and forks, all sorts of strange nut-crackers, and odd-looking machinery for milking camels. The village atmosphere can also be taken in during a leisurely evening trip, when **dinner** is served (7.30–11pm; Rs190 including entry fee) to the accompaniment of local dance, music or puppet shows; the menu includes Gujarati dishes, super-sweet desserts and mugs of buttermilk. Lunch (Rs70 including entry) is served during the earlier session, with snacks and juices available at all times.

Eating

Ahmedabad's most popular **restaurants** are clustered around Relief Road, Salapose Road and Badhra; for **snack** food, including kebabs and mutton samosas, there are good stalls at Khas Bazaar. There are also good coffee, sandwich and ice cream places at Shri Krishna Complex on the Mithakali crossroads, and branches of American pizza chains on the nearby CG Road. A number of swanky restaurants, lively tea and coffee bars, and juice places have opened on CG Road and around Panchvati. If you are making only a brief stop in Gujarat, don't miss the opportunity to sample the state's delicious thali; *Gopi Dining Hall* is a favourite place to try it, but there are a number of good thali restaurants along Ashram Road.

Agashiye *House of Mangaldas*, opposite Sidi Sayyid's Mosque. One of Ahmedabad's classiest restaurants, on the roof of an old mansion that's now a heritage hotel. Prices are steep by Gujarati standards, but the large thalis are good and well-presented. Spacious seating on floor cushions under a tented canopy or regular dining outdoors on the terrace.

Anand Dining Hall Salapose Rd, off Relief Rd. Small, very inexpensive veg place, good for Gujarati thalis. Open for lunch and dinner daily, except Sun evening. A branch across the street serves South Indian snacks.

Chetna Dining Hall Relief Rd. Popular veg place for excellent and inexpensive South Indian dishes and sumptuous Gujarati thalis.

Gandhi Cold Drinks House Khas Bazaar. Third-generation hole-in-the-wall serving up refreshing milk and ice cream concoctions, including Indonesian-style "Royal Faluda", unique to Ahmedabad, and saffron-flavoured *kesar* milkshake.

Gopi Dining Hall Pritamrai Rd ⓣ079/657 6388. Welcoming, tourist-friendly, non-smoking veg place on the west side of Ellis Bridge, offering Gujarati and Kathiawadi thalis at unbeatable prices. Very popular, so reserve or wait in line.

Green House *House of Mangaldas*, opposite Sidi Sayyid's Mosque. Run by the same people as *Agashiye*, this street-side café, with outdoor and indoor (a/c) seating, serves Gujarati, South Indian and Punjabi dishes and snacks at far lower prices.

Kalapi Advance Cinema Rd. A/c, non-smoking restaurant cooking up the best veg food in the area at easily affordable prices.

Mahendi Rang Lagyo Fruit Juice House Relief Rd. Large stall with a wide selection of juices and shakes made to order.

Moti Mahal *Moti Mahal* hotel, Kapasia Bazaar. A stone's throw from the railway station, this non-veg restaurant and sweet centre is renowned for its good service and its great biriyanis. Don't miss the salted *lassi* with cumin.

Nishat Khas Bazaar. Smart premises with an a/c room upstairs, serving sumptuous meat dishes and veg standards.

Paramount Bhadra, near Karanj Police Station. Drab outside but imaginatively decorated inside, this a/c non-veg restaurant dishes up a wide selection of excellent Indian dishes specially tikkas and biriyanis.

Sheeba Near Telephone Exchange, CG Rd. One of the best for north Indian food, along with some western and Chinese dishes. Specialities include the Tandoori Platter (Rs200 for two, with barbecued mutton, chicken, fish and prawn curries), along with rich curries like *malai-kofta* and *chicken makhani*. There is also a take-out counter in the evening for kebabs and egg rolls.

Simran Khanpur Rd. A/c restaurant handy for those staying at the big hotels on this road. Good choices include *tawa jhinga* (shrimp/prawn curry), chicken tikka masala, mutton kebabs, *shahi raan (*tandoori leg of lamb*)* and fish curries. Also good veg and non-veg thalis from Rs45.

Tomato's Mardia Plaza, Panchwati off CG Rd. A TGIF lookalike restaurant, run by a Parsi, decorated with1950s and '1960s rock 'n' roll and Hollywood posters with music to match. Passable nachos and potato skins, good grilled chicken and other western dishes, plus great coffees and desserts; the Indian food isn't at all bad, either. If you're short on time, grab a soup, salad and sandwich at the café/cake shop upstairs.

Listings

Airlines, Domestic Air Deccan (airport ⓣ079/3092 5213); Air Sahara (airport ⓣ079/2285 8002 or 2285 8003 or 5545 5969); Indian Airlines, on the road from Sidi Sayyid's Mosque to Nehru Bridge ⓣ079/2550 3061; Jet Airways, Ashram Rd opposite Gujarat Vidyapith ⓣ079/2754 3304.

Airlines, International Air India, near the old High Court ⓣ079/2658 5622; Air France, Madhuban House near Ellis Bridge town hall ⓣ079/2644 6886; Alitalia and Kenya Airways, c/o Ajanta Travels, behind City Gold movie complex, off Ashram Rd ⓣ079/2658 5077; British Airways, Centre Point Building, Panchwati Circle, CG Rd ⓣ079/2656 5957; Cathay Pacific, Ratnanabh Complex, opposite Gujarat Vidyapith ⓣ079/2754 5421; Delta, Inter Globe, Empire Tower, CG Rd ⓣ079/646 5573; KLM, in the Shefali Centre, Paldi ⓣ079/2657 7677; Swissair, c/o Samveg, in the Abhigam Building near Parimal Railway Crossing, Ambwadi ⓣ079/656 1056; Malaysia Airlines ⓣ079/5561 3355; Singapore Airlines ⓣ079/5525 9933.

Banks and exchange Facilities for US or sterling cash and travellers' cheques are available at the Bank of India in Khas Bazaar, the Central Bank of India opposite Sidi Sayyid's Mosque, and the State Bank of India opposite Lal Darwaja bus station (all Mon–Fri 11am–3pm, Sat 11am–1pm). For Visa encashment, go to the Bank of Baroda's Ashram Rd branch on the west side of the river, 300m north of Nehru Bridge. There's a branch of Thomas Cook at 208 Sakar III, off Ashram Rd near the old High Court. CITIBank has a branch on CG Rd at B/201 Fairdeal House, near Swastik Four Rd.

Bookshops For maps, guides and books try Crossword, a megastore with a coffee shop in the Shri Krishna Complex, near the Mithakali crossroad. Also good are Sastu Kitab Ghar on Relief Rd,100m east of Salapose Rd, and People's Book House 100m further down.

Cinemas Modern multi-screen cineplexes like City Gold Cinema (ⓣ079/2658 7782), above *McDonald's* near the tourist office on Ashram Rd, Fun Republic (ⓣ079/5530 0000), west of town on the Sarkhej–Gandhinagar Highway and the nearby Wide Angle show English and Hindi films. Advance Cinema (ⓣ079/550 6580) on Salapose Rd is also very popular.

Moving on from Ahmedabad

As a main station along the Delhi–Mumbai train line, Ahmedabad sees plenty of through traffic. It's also the jumping-off point for nearly all destinations within Gujarat, and, if you're heading north, to Mount Abu, Jodhpur and Udaipur in Rajasthan. For longer hauls it's best to leave by train, but shorter hops to places like Gandhinagar or Mehsana can be made by road. See "Travel details" at the end of this chapter for more information on journey frequencies and durations.

By bus

The **ST Bus Stand** serves a variety of local destinations including Gandhinagar (every 15min; 1hr), Dholka (for Lothal, every 30min; 1hr 30min), Mehsana (every 10min; 2hr), and Dhrangadhra (every 30min; 3hr), as well as destinations in Rajasthan, Maharashtra and Madhya Pradesh. More comfortable and expensive **private buses** to various destinations both in Gujarat and inter-state are run by any of a cluster of agencies in Paldi, just west of Sardar Bridge, from where most services leave for Bhavnagar, Rajkot, Bhuj and Mumbai.

By plane

Flights to Delhi ($145) and Mumbai ($85) are operated by Indian Airlines and Jet Airways. IA also serves Bangalore ($230), Hyderabad ($175), Kolkata (Calcutta; $240) and Jaipur ($115). Ahmedabad is expanding as an **international** airport, with Air India now operating a daily flight to New York via London and, on most days, to Chicago via London or Frankfurt; Indian Airlines has flights to various Gulf states on most days, while Singapore Airlines and Malaysia Airlines operate flights to Singapore and Kuala Lumpur. A number of reliable IATA-approved travel agencies on Ashram Road and CG Road can book all tickets.

By train

The main **railway station** is in the east of town at the end of Relief Road. Gandhigram Station in the west was being upgraded to a broad-guage track at the time of research; when complete (slated for 2006), it will serve destinations across Saurashtra, including a direct train to Delwada (for Diu). There are computerized **reservation centres** (Mon–Sat 8am–8pm & Sun 8am–2pm) at both stations.

Recommended trains from Ahmedabad

The following trains from Ahmedabad main station are recommended as the fastest or most convenient for the destinations listed; all are daily services except the Shatabdi Express which does not travel on Friday. Departure times were correct at the time of writing, but check them when you buy your ticket. For **Diu**, the only possibility is to take one of the daily trains departing Ahmedabad in the morning for Veraval and then to head onwards by bus or taxi.

Destination	Name	No.	Departs	Total time
Bhavnagar	Bandra Bhavnagar Express	#9271	6.18pm	3hr 30min
Bhuj	Kutch Express	#9031	2.25am	8hr
Delhi	Ashram Express	#2915	5.45pm	16hr 30min
Dwarka	Saurashtra Mail	#9005	5.40am	10hr 40min
Jamnagar	Saurashtra Express	#9215	9.15am	7hr
	Saurashtra Mail	#9005	5.40am	7hr
Jodhpur	Suryanagari Express	#4846	10pm*	9hr
Mumbai	Shatabdi Express	#2010	1.20pm	7hr
	Lokshakti Express	#9144	9.10pm	13hr
Porbandar	Saurashtra Express	#9215	9.15am	8hr
Udaipur	Adi Dee Express	#9944	10.55pm	8hr 30min
	Mewar Fast Express	#932	7.15am	10hr

*Mon, Wed, Fri

Hospitals VS General, Ellis Bridge (☎079/657 7621) is a large government hospital; for traditional treatments, try Akhandanand Ayurvedic, Akhandanand Rd (☎079/550 7796).
Internet access Facilities available at Cyber Valley, Shri Krishna Complex near the Mithakali crossroads. Also handy is Wizard Online, 50m down an alley, just north of Income Tax Circle, on the west side of the Ashram Rd.
Photography Gujarat Mercantile Co, 100m south of the GPO on Salapose Rd; One Hour Photo, Ashram Rd, northwest corner of Income Tax Circle. For transparencies, the best is Sukruti (☎079/2658 7335) at Jaldarshan Apartments opposite Natraj Cinema.
Post office Salapose Rd (Mon–Sat 10am–8pm, Sun 10am–4pm).

Around Ahmedabad

The most obvious day-trip from Ahmedabad is north to **Adalaj**, with its impressive step-well, and perhaps on a little further to the new capital of **Gandhinagar**, which has the extraordinary Swaminarayan religious complex, but is otherwise a characterless conglomeration of landscaped grids. South of town, the lake, pavilions and mausoleums of **Sarkhej** make a pleasant break from the crowded city. Further south is **Lothal**, an excavated ancient Harappan site which dates back four thousand years and is well worth a visit, either from Ahmedabad or en route to Diu.

Adalaj Vav

One of Gujarat's most spectacular step-wells, **Adalaj Vav** (daily 8am–6pm; free), stands in lovingly tended gardens about 1km from a bus stop on the route between Ahmedabad, 19km away, and Gandhinagar. Once a Hindu sanctuary, the well is now totally out of use; local women wash clothes and cooking utensils at modern water taps nearby. The monument is best seen around noon, when sunlight penetrates to the bottom of the five-storey octagonal well shaft. Steps lead down to the cool depths through a series of platforms raised on pillars. Alive with exquisite sculptures, the walls, pillars, cornices and niches portray erotica, dancing maidens, musicians, animals and images of Shiva in his terrible aspect, Bhairava. Stone elephants, horses and mythical animals parade around the sides of the shaft, where green parrots swoop down to rest in the shade. Before descending you'll see several Sanskrit inscriptions etched into the walls just above eye level, one of which records the building of the well by Ruda, wife of a local chief, in 1498.

Gandhinagar

The second state capital after Chandigarh to be built from scratch since Independence, the uninspiring city of **GANDHINAGAR** is laid out in thirty residential sectors in an ordered style influenced by the work of **Le Corbusier**, who designed Chandigarh and had a hand in conceiving the layout of New Delhi. Its near-symmetrical numbered streets are wide and strangely quiet, lined with a total of sixteen *lakh* trees – that's 26 per head of the city's population. There's little to warrant spending much time here, but the headquarters of the Swaminarayan sect, **Akshardham** – which made international headlines in 2002 when a Muslim suicide squad went on the rampage through it and killed 33 people – is worth a look. This Hindu revivalist movement, established in 1907, promotes Vedic ideals pronounced by Lord Swaminarayan (1781–1830), who proclaimed that his presence would continue through a succession of saints: the fifth and most recent is a Gujarati named Pramukh Swami Maharaja, now in his 80s.

Swaminarayan Complex

The Akshardham may advocate simplicity and poverty, but the colossal **Swaminarayan complex** on J Road, Sector 20 (Mon–Fri 9.30am–6pm, Sat & Sun 9.30am–6.30pm; free), a centre for representing their precepts and practices, is hugely extravagant. Built of pink sandstone, all six thousand tonnes of it brought from Rajasthan, with domed roofs raised on almost one hundred profusely carved pillars, it houses the gold-leaf coated statues of Swaminarayan and two other prominent gurus. The rest of the complex is a surreal **theme park**, with a Hall of Holy Relics containing possessions of Swaminarayan and state-of-the-art audio-visual show using fourteen screens. The Sahajanand Hall relives Swaminarayan's seven-year, 12,000-kilometre journey, sweeping the enthralled visitor from the jungles to the mountains and at last the sea. Tours end with a concert played by robot musicians.

From the tone of the place, you'd never guess that Akshardham witnessed one of the most appalling massacres in recent Indian history, when 33 innocent people were killed and 72 more injured during a fourteen-hour **armed siege** by Pakistani suicide terrorists. On September 24, 2002, two men equipped with hand grenades and guns entered the compound in broad daylight and went on a shooting spree, firing on visitors and police until they themselves were shot dead the following morning; their victims included two children and a 10-week-old baby. Cyanide pills were found around their necks, as well as two letters written in Urdu which bore the name of the "Movement for Taking Revenge" – a previously unheard of group. Links were quickly made between the attack and the recent rioting in which hundreds of Muslims had died. Politicians in New Delhi were quick to blame it on the Pakistani government, but Islamabad denied involvement. Today, the only evidence that the massacre happened at all is a few scattered bullet holes, a heavy security presence at the entrance and video monitoring of visitors.

Practicalities

Regular **buses** run between Gandhinagar and Ahmedabad (45min), but there's only one train a day in each direction (1hr) and the station is rather inconveniently placed, out in Sector 14. Should you want to **stay**, the *Capital Guest House*, next to the tourist office (entrance round the back, ⓣ079/323 2651; ❷–❸), has airy but dull rooms with attached bathrooms. There's a **youth hostel** about 1km up the lane behind it (ⓣ079/322 2364; ❶) with spartan dorms (Rs50) and a discount for student ID cardholders.

Sarkhej

Just under 10km southwest of Ahmedabad (bus #31 from Lal Darwaja), the suburb of **Sarkhej** holds a complex of beautifully fashioned monuments arranged around an artificial **lake**. On the southwest side of the lake, the square **tomb** of the revered saint Sheikh Ahmed Khattu, the spiritual mentor of Ahmed Shah, who died in 1445, is the largest mausoleum in Gujarat, with scores of pillars inside supporting the domed roof. Tracery work and inlaid marble decorates the upper walls and the outer wall supports rows of arched wooden doors and brass screens. The mausoleum was constructed by Ahmed Shah's successor, Mohammed Shah, in 1446. The later Sultan Mohammed Beghada (died 1511) so deeply admired Sheikh Ahmed that he added palaces, a harem and a vast lake to the site, and finally chose to build his own tomb here as well. Sarkhej became a retreat of Gujarati Sultans, who added gardens, pavilions and tombs to the elaborate complex. While some of the buildings are falling into ruin, it remains a charming place, usually teeming with brightly dressed Gujarati holidaymakers.

Lothal

Remains of the **Harappan** (Indus Valley) civilization that once spread across what are now western India and eastern Pakistan have been discovered in more than fifty places in Gujarat. The largest excavated site is at **Lothal** (daily dawn–dusk; free), close to the mouth of the River Sabarmati, roughly 100km south of Ahmedabad, and an easy journey by bus (change at Dholka) or train (3hr). Foundations, platforms, crumbling walls and paved floors are all that remain of the prosperous sea-trading community that dwelt here between 2400 and 1900 BC, when a flood all but destroyed the settlement. A walk around the **central mound** reveals the old roads that ran past ministers' houses and through the acropolis, where you can see the remains of twelve baths and a sewer. The lower town, evident today from a scattering

The Indus Valley Civilization

Before the Mauryan empire took hold in the fourth century BC, the greatest empire in India was the **Indus Valley Civilization**. Well-planned, sophisticated settlements dating back to 2500 BC were first discovered in 1924 on the banks of the River Indus in present-day Sind (in Pakistan), at **Mohenjo Daro** (which means "mound of the dead" in Sindi). Further excavations in 1946 on the banks of the River Ravi in Punjab revealed the city of **Harappa**, dating from the same era, on which archeologists based their knowledge of the entire Indus Valley Civilization. In its prime, this great society spread from the present borders of Iran and Afghanistan to Kashmir, Delhi and southern Gujarat, covering an area larger than the Egyptian and Syrian dominions put together. It lasted until 1900 BC when a series of heavy floods swept away the towns and villages in the delta regions of major rivers in Sind, Saurashtra and southern Gujarat.

A prosperous and literate society, importing raw materials from regions as far west as Egypt and trading ornaments, jewellery and cotton cultivated in the fertile delta plains, it also had a remarkable, centrally controlled **political system**. Each town was almost identical, with separate areas for the ruling elite and the "workers", and all buildings built with bricks measured according to a system distinctly similar to that laid out in the Vedic *Shastras* (the earliest Hindu treatises). A uniform system of weights and measures, corresponding almost exactly to modern ounces, was used, and the complex, efficient drainage systems were unmatched by any other pre-Roman civilization.

Towns established on river deltas were perfectly placed for trade. **Lothal**, close to the Gulf of Cambay in southern Gujarat, was a major port, and also the source of shells which the Harappans made into jewellery. Some four thousand years later, Cambay is still the largest producer of shell jewellery in India, and southern Gujarati artisans make their wonderful beadwork using barely altered materials and techniques. Although much about this complex society remains unknown – including their impenetrable script – similarities do exist between the Indus Valley Civilization and present-day India. While their most important deity appears to have been a horned god, there was also a strong custom of worshipping a mother goddess, in the same way as Hindus. The *peepal* tree was revered as it is by Buddhists today, and there is evidence, too, of phallic worship, still strong among Shaivites. Altars bearing the remains of animal sacrifice have been discovered in Lothal and, in every settlement, large baths suggest a belief in the purifying quality of water. For more about the Indus Valley Civilization and its significance in Indian history, see p.1359.

of fragmented bricks and foundations, comprised a bazaar, workshops for coppersmiths, bead-makers and potters, and residential quarters. On the eastern edge of the site, shattered walls enclosing a rectangle indicate the existence of a dock – the only one discovered of its kind, suggesting that Lothal was probably a port serving a number of Harappan towns. Evidence has been found here of an even older culture, perhaps dating from the fourth millennium BC, known because of its red pottery as the **Red Ware Culture**. You can see remains from this period and from the Indus Valley Civilization in the illuminating site **museum** (daily except Fri 10am–5pm; free). Among the jewellery collection, a necklace made from gold beads, each a mere 25mm in diameter, provides evidence of sophisticated skills and great wealth. Seals, delicately carved with animal motifs, were used by the Harappans to mark packages; one from Bahrain, imprinted with a dragon and a gazelle, shows the extent of their trading links. A range of accurate weights and compasses testifies to the Harappans' knowledge of geometry and astronomy. From the Red Ware Culture, the museum displays bowls, jars, ceramic and terracotta pots and toys – including touchingly familiar spinning tops and marbles.

Northern Gujarat

North of Gandhinagar, the district of Mehsana was the Solanki's seat of government between the eleventh and thirteenth centuries. Some remains of their old capital – including the extraordinary **Rani-ki-Vav** step-well – still stand at **Anhilawada Patan**, just outside the modern city of **Patan**, which is home to Gujarat's last remaining *patola* weavers. From the city of **Mehsana**, at the province's centre, it's easy to get to the ancient and well-preserved sun temple at **Modhera**. A Jain temple in the hills at **Taranga** can be reached from Mehsana, or directly from Ahmedabad.

Mehsana

The crowded residential city of **MEHSANA**, less than 100km north of Ahmedabad, is the centre of huge dairy industry, one of the largest in Asia, processing 170,000 litres of milk per day. It's a dirty sprawling place without much to hold you down – the one building of any interest is the old **Rajmahal** palace, now used as government offices – but it makes an obvious night halt if you are exploring northern Gujarat. About 3km from the station on the Ahmedabad–Palanpur highway, the *Savera Guesthouse* (☎02762/256710; ❸–❹), with fixed prices, is the best **accommodation** Mehsana has to offer, with reasonably clean and spacious doubles, hot bucket water and some a/c rooms. If you're coming in from Modhera you will be on the other side of town; ask a rickshaw driver to take you to the "highway". Across the road is the flash *Navjivan* restaurant, an upscale family place with a pure-veg menu excellent sweet lassis; the a/c room upstairs is more expensive. The **budget lodges** in town, grimy and noisy, are some of the worst in Gujarat, but if you're out of options try *A-One Guesthouse* (☎02762/51394; ❶) near the station. The nearby Janta Supermarket houses a **post office** and three **banks**. **Trains** link Mehsana to Ahmedabad (2–3hr), Abu Road (2hr), Ajmer (7hr) and Jodhpur (7hr 30min). There are also very slow passenger trains to Patan (2hr). **Buses** tend to be faster and serve cities in Rajasthan and Gujarat including Bhuj.

Modhera

If you visit only one town in northern Gujarat, it should be **MODHERA**, where the eleventh-century **sun temple** (daily 7am–6pm; Rs100) is the best example of Solanki temple architecture in the state. Almost a thousand years old, the temple has survived Muslim iconoclasm and nineteenth-century earthquakes; apart from a missing *shikhara* and slightly worn carvings, it remains largely intact. The Solanki kings numbered Jains among their courtly advisers, and were probably influenced in their temple design by Jain traditions; deities and their vehicles, animals, voluptuous maidens and complex friezes adorn the sandy brown walls and pillars. Within the *mandapa*, or pillared entrance hall, twelve *adityas* set into niches in the wall portray the transformations of the sun in each month of the year – representations found only in sun temples. Closely associated with the sun, *adityas* are the sons of *Aditi*, the goddess of infinity and eternity, and represent the constraints under which the universe can exist. According to Indian convention, Modhera's sun temple is positioned so that at the equinoxes the rising sun strikes the images in the sanctuary, which at other times languish in a dim half-light.

Modhera is linked by road to Mehsana (40min) and Ahmedabad (2–3hr). If you are coming from Ahmedabad by **bus** and want to save time, ask to get out at Mehsana highway and you can head off the hourly Modhera buses at the junction without going all the way into town. The last bus from Modhera to Mehsana leaves at 5.30pm. The return fare for a **taxi** from Mehsana is Rs300. There are also direct buses from Modhera to Patan. There's nowhere to **stay** in Modhera, but the state-run *Toran Cafeteria* in the temple grounds sells thalis, **snacks** and ice cream.

If you are here in January, ask about Modhera's **dance festival**, staged against the backdrop of the Sun Temple which is dramatically illuminated for the occasion.

Patan and Anhilawada Patan

Founded in 1796, **PATAN**, roughly 40km northwest of Mehsana, has few monuments to speak of, but the streets of its older quarters are interesting enough, overlooked by the carved balconies of Muslim *havelis* and the marble domes of Jain temples. In the **Salvivad** area you can watch the complex weaving of silk *patola* saris, once the preferred garment of queens and aristocrats, and an important export of Gujarat, now made by just one extended family. Each sari, which is sold for Rs50-70,000, takes from four to six months to produce: both the warp and the weft threads are first dyed to a set pattern drawn by the weaver on graph paper before being woven on a complex loom, and the utmost care is taken to ensure completely even tension throughout the cloth. Two **trains** leave Mehsana for Patan each day at 8.30am and 1.45pm, returning at 2.30pm and 6pm.

The big-city bustle of Patan is a far cry from the old Gujarati capital at **ANHILAWADA PATAN**, 2km northwest. The original city served several Rajput dynasties, including the Solankis, between the eighth and the twelfth centuries, before being annexed by the Moghuls. It fell into decline when Ahmed Shah moved the capital to Ahmedabad in 1411. Little remains now except traces of fortifications scattered in the surrounding fields, and the stunning **Rani-ki-Vav** (daily 8am–6pm; Rs100), Gujarat's greatest **step-well**. It was built for the Solanki queen Udaimati in 1050 and extensively restored during the 1980s. The restorations, unlike those at the sun temple in Somnath, are not obtrusively modern, and re-create as perfectly as possible the original carving.

Rani-ki-Vav is extravagantly carved throughout, but its most distinctive carving lines the well shaft, dominated by sculptures of Vishnu and his various *avatars*, or incarnations. Not far from the well is **Sahastraling Talav**, the "thousand-*lingam* tank" built at the turn of the twelfth century, but razed during Moghul raids. Only a few pillars of the Shiva temples that surrounded it still stand. This is part of the same **complex** (daily 8am–6pm; free) that includes a small open-air **museum** displaying a modest collection of sculpture from the area. Sparse ruins of Rani Udaimati's house crumble nearby on a hill that affords excellent views over the surrounding plains. The mosques and tombs that you see are within easy walking distance, and make for interesting exploration; many were constructed using pillars from Hindu temples. It's a Rs25 (10min) rickshaw ride out to Rani-ki-Vav from the station. Less than a ten-minute walk from the station, the *Gujary Hotel* (ⓣ02766/230244; ❷–❸) is one of a few hotels in this neighbourhood offering reasonable rooms, some of them a/c, with attached bath, as well as a restaurant.

The Jain temple at Taranga

Although it's off the tourist trail, the **hilltop temple complex** at **TARANGA**, 60km or so northeast of Mehsana, is easily reachable by bus; the site also lies on the railway line, though the daily train chugs up from Mehsana at a snail's pace, taking almost three hours. Built during the Solanki period, the shrines are particularly striking, and better preserved than more famous sites such as Mount Abu, Girnar and Shatrunjaya. Pilgrims and white-clad monks and nuns gather here year-round to take blessings and pray. The **main temple**, built of durable sandstone, is dedicated to Ajitanath, the second of twenty-four *tirthankaras*. His image gazes out from the main sanctuary, while the rest of the temple is alive with a tangle of voluptuous maidens and musicians in smooth carved stone round the walls, pillars and ceilings. There is little in the way of tourist facilities here, although you can get a remarkably inexpensive lunch at the Jain *dharamshalas*.

Kutch

Bounded on the north and east by marshy flats and on the south and west by the Gulf of Kutch and the Arabian Sea, the province of **KUTCH** (also Kuchchh or Kachchha) is a place apart. All but isolated from neighbouring Saurashtra and Sind, the largely arid landscape is shot through with the colours of the heavily embroidered local dress. Kutchi legends can be traced in sculptural motifs, and its strong folk tradition is still represented in popular craft, clothing and jewellery designs. Although few tourists make it out to this region, those who do are invariably enchanted. With a little effort, you can head out from the central city of **Bhuj** – whose population and medieval centre were devastated by the 2001 earthquake – to villages, ancient fortresses, medieval ports and isolated monasteries. The treeless marshes to the north and east, known as the Great and Little **Ranns of Kutch**, can flood completely during a heavy monsoon, effectively transforming Kutch into an island, though it's now several years since this last happened. Home to the rare wild ass, the Ranns are also the only region in India where flamingos breed successfully, during July and August, out of reach of any but the most determined bird-watchers who can cross the marshes by camel. The southern district, known as **Aiyar Patti**, was once among India's most fertile areas, and though drier

Kutchi pastoral groups

Kutch has the most significant and conspicuous population of **pastoral communities** in Gujarat, most of whom migrated from east and west from the seventh century onwards. Each tribe can be identified from its costume, and gains its income from farming or crafts such as weaving, painting, woodcarving and dyeing. Traditionally, each has concentrated on different crafts, although the distinctions today are far less clear-cut.

The **Rabari** is the largest group in the Kutchi pastoral community. They rear cattle, buffalo and camels, sell ghee, weave, and are known for fine **embroidery**. The men, most of whom sport a white turban, wear white cotton trousers tight at the ankle and in baggy pleats above the knee, a white jacket (*kehdiyun*) with multiple folds tucked around chest level and overlong sleeves, and a blanket thrown over one shoulder. Rabari women dress in black pleated jackets or open-backed blouses, full black skirts and tie-dyed head cloths, usually black and red, and always deck themselves with heavy silver jewellery and ivory bangles around the upper arms. Typical houses made of mud or brick are decorated inside with *gargomati* – a raised pattern of whitewashed mud and dung inlaid with mirrors. Child marriages, customary among the Rabari, are performed over a four- or five-day period in the summer; immediately upon the birth of a daughter, a mother starts embroidering cloth to form the most valuable basis of her dowry. In **Bhujodi**, near Bhuj, the Rabari weave camel wool on pit looms into blankets and shawls.

Claiming descent from Krishna, the **Bharvad** tribes infiltrated Gujarat from Vrindavan, close to Mathura in Uttar Pradesh. Their dress is similar to that of the Rabaris, though the men are distinguishable by the peacock, parrot and flower motifs sewn into their *khediyun*, and the women by their bright backless shirts, *kapadun*, rarely covered by veils. Both men and women wear a thick *bori* cloth around the waist. Mass marriages take place among the Bharvad every few years, a custom originating as a form of protection in the Muslim period when single girls were frequently victims of abduction (the kidnapping of married girls was heavily punished). In the first week of each September the Bharvads gather at the Trinetresvar temple in **Tarnetar**, 65km from Rajkot, celebrating with dances and songs and sheltering under the shade of embroidered umbrellas made especially for the occasion.

The wandering **Ahir** cattle-breeders came to Gujarat from Sind, settling as farmers in Kutch and at Morvi in Saurashtra. Baggy trousers and *khediyun* are worn by the men, together with a white loosely wound headcloth; the women dress like the Rabaris, with additional heavy silver nose rings. The children's bright *topis*, or skull-caps, overlaid with neat fragments of mirrors, are like those common in Pakistan. During Diwali, Ahirs lead their cattle through the streets to be fed by other local communities, which bestows merit on the giver and is good for karma. Today the Ahirs are prospering as entrepreneurs and much of the truck-transport in Kutch is operated by them.

The **Charans**, the long-established bards of Gujarat, encompass in their clans the Maldharis, who raise prize cattle in southern Kutch and the Gir Forest, and the leather-workers known as Meghavals. They claim descent from a celestial union between Charan and a maiden created by Parvati, and many gain almost divine status after death. The women are often worshipped by other tribes, since their connection with Parvati links them closely to the mother goddess, Ashpura, who is popular in Kutch. The men's curses were once considered so powerful that they drove their opponents to kill themselves in the hope that the curse would be deflected upon the Charans: such "heroes" are remembered by stone monuments around Kutch depicting a man piercing his neck with a dagger.

Said to have migrated from Pakistan, the Kutchi **Jats** are an Islamic pastoral group. The men can be identified by their black dress, while young Jat girls have dainty plaits curving round the sides of their faces, and wear heavy nose rings. Traditionally seminomadic camel- and cattle-rearers, with houses made of reed (*pakha*) that are easily folded and carried from place to place, they have recently begun to settle more permanently.

today, still supports crops of cotton, castor-oil plants, sunflowers, wheat and groundnuts. Northern Kutch, or **Banni**, on the other hand, is semi-desert with dry shifting sands, arid grasslands and no perennial rivers; the villagers rely on their livestock and the income drawn from traditional crafts.

Some history

Remains from the third millennium BC in eastern Kutch suggest that migrating Indus Valley communities crossed the Ranns from Mohenjo Daro in modern Pakistan to Lothal in eastern Gujarat. Despite being so cut off, Kutch felt the effect of the Buddhist Mauryan empire, and later came under the control of Greek Bactrians, the Western Satraps and the powerful Guptas. The Arab invasion of Sind in 720 AD pushed refugees into Kutch's western regions, and tribes from Rajputana and Gujarat crossed its eastern borders. Later in the eighth century the region fell under the sway of the Gujarati capital Anhilawada (now Patan), and by the tenth century the Samma Rajputs, later known as the Jadejas, had infiltrated Kutch from the west and established themselves as rulers. Their line continued until Kutch was absorbed into the Indian Union in 1948. When the Muslim sultans ruled Gujarat, they made repeated unsuccessful

Kutchi handicrafts

Kutch is known for its distinctive traditional crafts, and particularly its **embroidery**, practised by pastoral groups like Hindu Rabaris and Ahirs, and Muslim Jaths and Muthwas, as well as migrants from Sind including the Sodha Rajputs and Meghwal Harijans. Traditionally, each community has its own stitches and patterns, though these distinctions are becoming less apparent as time goes on.

The northern villages of Dhordo, Khavda and Hodko are home to the few remaining communities of **leather embroiderers**, who stitch flower, peacock and fish motifs onto bags, fans, horse belts, wallets, cushion covers and mirror frames, which are then sold in villages throughout the region. Dhordo is also known for its **woodcarving**, while Khavda is one of the last villages to continue the printing method known as **ajrakh**. Cloth is dyed with natural pigments in a lengthy process similar to batik, but instead of wax, a mixture of lime and gum is used to resist the dye in certain parts of the cloth when new colours are added. Women in Khavda also **paint terracotta** pots, using cotton rags and brushes made from bamboo leaves.

Rogan painting is practised only by a few artisans at Nirona in northern Kutch. A complex process turns hand-pounded castor oil into coloured dyes which are used to decorate cushion covers, bedspreads and curtains with simple geometric patterns. Craftsmen also make melodic **bells** coated in intricate designs of copper and brass; these were once used for communication among shepherds. Silver jewellery is common, featuring in most traditional Kutchi costumes, but Kutchi **silver engraving**, traditionally practised in Bhuj, is a dwindling art form. The anklets, earrings, nose rings, bangles and necklaces are similar to those seen in Rajasthan; many of them are made by the Ahir and Rabari communities who live in both areas. The main centres for silver are Anjar, Bhuj, Mandvi and Mundra.

Kutchi clothes are distinctive not only for their fine embroidery but also their bold designs. The most common form of **cloth** printing is **bandhani**, or tie-dye, practised in most villages, but concentrated in Mandvi and Anjar. One craft unique to the area is *mushroo*-weaving (*ilacha*), a skill practised today by less than twenty artisans. The yarn used is silk, carefully dyed before it is woven in a basic striped pattern, with a complex design woven over the top in such fine detail that it seems to be embroidered. *Ilacha* cloth, made into *cholis* (blouses) and dresses, is hard to buy now; the best place to see it is Mandvi, or in the Calico Museum in Ahmedabad (see p.633).

attempts to cross into Kutch. It remained separate, however, with its own customs, laws and a thriving maritime tradition. Trade with Malabar, Mocha, Muscat and the African coast brought in spices, drugs, silks, rhino hides and elephant tusks, while connections with Africa also encouraged the slave trade, already common among the Portuguese in southern Saurashtra. African deck hands and slaves arrived with merchants and sailors, and after the abolition of slavery in 1834 a small African community settled in north Bhuj. Their crafts, dances and music have been integrated into the region's traditional arts.

Bhuj

Set in the heart of Kutch, the narrow streets and old bazaars of the walled town of **BHUJ** retained a medieval flavour unlike any other Gujarati city – until much of it was reduced to rubble in the **earthquake** of January 2001, which buried thousands of residents. The section immediately behind the famed Aina Mahal ("Palace of Mirrors") suffered the most damage, and has been cleared of buildings in preparation for redevelopment. The multi-million dollar face-lift will be dramatic – blueprints call for public gardens, wide streets and squat apartment blocks centred on spacious courtyards. Buildings higher than two stories are now outlawed and the population density will be halved. Although the clearing and re-construction will take years, Bhuj is very much up and running, in some ways more so than other Gujarati cities. The huge amount of aid workers sent in for assistance following the earthquake left an infrastructure of Internet cafés, restaurants and hotels – although much of this lies around in the new part of town and bus station, about 1km from the main historical sites: the **Prag Mahal**, **Aina Mahal** and **Hamirsar Tank**.

Bhuj was established as the capital of Kutch in the mid-sixteenth century by Rao Khengarji, a Jadeja Rajput. The one interruption before 1948 in his family's continuous rule was a brief period of British domination early in the nineteenth century. When the governance of the state was handed back to the rightful ruler, Maharao Desal, in 1834, the import of slaves from Africa was banned and Africans were given homes in the north of the city. With the establishment of the city of Gandhidham and the port of Kandla southeast of the capital, the economic centre of gravity shifted away from Bhuj, leaving it to carry on its traditions little affected by the modernizations of the twentieth century.

Arrival and information

Bhuj **airport** is 5km north of town and fifteen minutes away by auto-rickshaw. Both the new and old **railway stations** are also north of town; rickshaws wait at both. The **bus stand** is on ST Station Road on the southern edge of the old city.

Bhuj has no official tourist office, so your best bet for **information** is to consult the Aina Mahal's well-informed caretaker, Pramod Jethi, at his tourist information desk (daily except Fri 9am–1pm & 3–6pm; ⓣ02832/260094 or 222004).

Most of the **Internet** cafés are located on Hospital Road, less than 1km south of the bus stand: try Funworld (Rs20/hr) in the Jay Somnath Apartments opposite Ganatra Hospital, the nearby www.cyber.com café (Rs15/hr) or Orbitt opposite PPC Club (Rs20/hr).

You can get around town by a **bicycle** (Rs25/day) rented from Assa Cycles, Shop 40, 100m east of the *VRP Guesthouse* on Station Road. MK Auto (ⓣ02832/250077), below the *VRP Guesthouse*, rents **motorcycles** for Rs300 per 24 hours – very useful for exploring Kutchi villages, although most of them are in a poor state of repair, with less than dependable brakes and lights. The State Bank of India on Hospital Road will **change money** and travellers' cheques, as does ICICI across the street.

Bhuj is one of the cheapest places in western India to pick up **handicrafts** and there are shops all over town, especially at Shroff Bazaar and Vaniyawad near the old railway station around 1km north of town. In the old city, on Darbargadh Road near the Aina Mahal, Anand Handicrafts sells embroidered fabrics, woollen shawls, wall hangings, saris and *bandhani* (tie-dye).

Accommodation

Bhuj has a good selection of **hotels**, including a couple of options in the old town. Most places to stay are strewn along the buzzing Station Road.

Gangaram Guesthouse Behind the Aina Mahal in the old city ⓣ02832/222948, ⓔhotelgangaram@yahoo.co.in. The most welcoming, foreigner-friendly hotel in Bhuj, with an Internet connection, foreign exchange, snacks, and clean rooms with hot bucket. ❷–❸

Garha Safari Lodge 14km north of Bhuj overlooking the Gorudra Reservoir, ⓣ98250/13392, Ahmedabad ⓣ079/657 9672, ⓔgbglad1@sancharnet.in. A good option for those with their own car and a little extra cash, this camp offers accommodation inside concrete huts designed to look like a traditional *bhunga* (mud-brick and straw home). Meals are available and Jeeps can be hired to the nearby villages (Rs850 per person). ❽–❾

KBN east of the bus stand on Station Rd ⓣ02832/227251, ⓕ02832/254711. Brand new, welcoming hotel with large a/c rooms with all mod cons. ❹–❼

Prince 450m east of the bus stand on Station Rd ⓣ02832/220370, ⓔprincad1@sancharnet.in. Well-kept high-end hotel with a foreign exchange counter, two restaurants, and a permit to sell alcohol. Rooms are large and comfortable and staff generally helpful. ❺–❼

Sahara Palace Opposite the bus stand, Station Rd ⓣ02832/223419. The only mid-range option near the bus stand is reasonable, although it gets its share of street noise, including a morning racket from the chai stall across the street. ❸–❺

VRP Guesthouse 150m west of the bus stand on Station Rd ⓣ02832/221388. The best of the budget choices in this area; most rooms are scruffy, dim and depressing, but the west-facing rooms are off the street and relatively quiet. ❷

The Town

Bhuj is overlooked from the east by the old and crumbling fort on Bhujia Hill, closed to the public as it lies in a military area, while the vast **Hamirsar Tank**, with a small park on an island in its centre, stands on the western edge of town. The remnants of the **old city** form an intricate maze of streets and alleyways leading to the **palace complex**, guarded by sturdy walls and high heavy gates, which still enclose the Aina and Prag Mahals. Built in the eighteenth century during the reign of Maharao Lakho, and later turned into a museum showcasing the opulence of the royal dynasty, the **Aina Mahal** suffered much damage in the 2001 earthquake. Fortunately, despite the roof collapsing and sections of the walls being pulled down, the famed **Hall of Mirrors** (daily except Fri 9am–noon & 3–6pm; Rs10, Rs35 cameras, Rs100 video cameras) remained intact, and rebuilding will take place if and when a monetary rehabilitation package is secured. Many of the exhibits remain in situ, but the hall itself is closed pending renovation work; visitors are allowed into an adjacent gallery, from where you can peek into the hall. Curiously, the unique original design and decoration of the Aina Mahal never would have happened were it not for a shipwreck. The chief architect, Ram Singh Malam, was an Indian seafarer who studied art and architecture in Europe for seventeen years after being rescued from a shipwreck by Dutch sailors off the coast of Africa. His masterpiece was the tiled pleasure chamber at the heart of the palace where the Maharaja, soothed by an ingenious system of fountains, used to compose poetry and listen to music. It's closed these days pending repair work, but you can peer in from the adjacent apartments, where royal heirlooms include a couple of original Hogarths, a portrait of Catherine the Great and some priceless antique embroidery.

The nearby **Prag Mahal**, built in the 1860s and combining Moghul, British, Kutchi and Italian architectural styles, likewise suffered damage during the quake, but from the outside it appears only cosmetic. Visitors are allowed inside the main hall only (Mon–Sat 9am–noon & 3–6pm; Rs10, Rs30 cameras, Rs100 video cameras). Movie buffs may recognize the palace as one of the locations used in the 2001 hit crossover movie, *Lagaan*, starring Amir Khan.

Occupying the southwest corner of Hamirsar Tank, the **Sharad Bagh Palace** (daily except Fri 9am–noon & 3–6pm; Rs10, Rs20 cameras, Rs100 video cameras) came through the earthquake relatively unscathed. Built in 1867 and the retreat of the last maharao, the small porticoed buildings are delicately proportioned and include a plush drawing room, decked with hunting trophies, photographs and old clocks, and a dining room containing Maharao Madansinjhi's coffin, shipped over from England after his death in 1991. The palace's most appealing feature, however, is its well-tended garden. The **Kutch Museum** at the southeast corner of Hamirsar Tank suffered a collapsed roof in the earthquake, but is expected to re-open.

Just south of Hamirsar Tank and west of College Road, a path leads to the 250-year-old bone-dry **Ramkund tank**, made of hard grey stone and shaded by trees. Decorated with skilfully crafted images of Kali, Vishnu, Nag and Ganesh, the tank also has small niches in the walls where oil lamps would glitter in the dusk as devotees prayed at the evening puja. Nearby is a set of sixteenth-century *sati* stones.

Bhuj's private **Folk Museum**, on Mandvi Road 100m west of the Collectors' Office (Mon–Sat 9am–noon & 3–6pm; Rs10, plus Rs50 for camera), contains fine examples of Kutchi pottery, embroidery, games and wall hangings. There is also a small mock-village here complete with *bhungas* (mud-brick and straw homes).

Eating

Restaurants and **juice shops** are plentiful in Bhuj, and there is an excellent crop of both along **Station Road**. *Hotel Nilam*, across from the *Prince*, is a top-notch, attractively decorated vegetarian restaurant with a mixed menu. Station Road is also the place to pick up the local favourite **snack**, *dhabeli* (lentils and peanuts smothered with herbs and spices in a bun) available for about Rs10 each. The *Bharat Juice and Cold Drinks Shop*, 50m east of the station, and *Gopi's Parlour* on the other side of the station near the *VRP Hotel*, serve up refreshing shakes and ice-cream coffees. Opposite the bus stand, the air-conditioned, family-orientated *Green Rock* serves delicious Gujarati thalis as well as Punjabi dishes, South Indian *dosas* and pizzas. For **breakfast**, *Omelette Centre* near the bus stand is popular, dishing up eggs, cheese-toast and tea.

In the **old city**, the delightful *Green Hotel*, 200m east of the palace off Shroff Bazaar and opposite the vegetable market, has been serving since 1948. *Noor* at Danda Bazaar is locally popular for mutton and chicken dishes, biriyanis and egg curries. A popular travellers' hang-out is *Annapurna* at Bhid Gate where Kutchi thalis are available in an unpretentious dining hall with coffee-table books and maps of Kutch – the owners are friendly and well informed. In the **newer areas of town**, developed after the earthquake, *Ashapura Dining Hall* on Hospital Road is a good place for Gujarati thalis.

Moving on from Bhuj

Jet Airways has daily **flights** to Mumbai for around $110; book through their office near Bank of Baroda on Station Road (☎02832/253671) or at their airport counter (☎02832/244101). H.M. Menon & Sons (☎02832/252286), 200m west of the station opposite the *Sagar Guesthouse*, also sell international and domestic air tickets.

Bhuj is well connected to the rest of the state by **train**. For Ahmedabad, take the #2082 Jansatabdi departing at 5am and arriving at 12.15pm (Rs167/480 for second class/first class); the #9032 Kutch Express departs at 6.30pm and stops in Ahmedabad at 2.30am before continuing onto Mumbai. For Rajkot, the Anand Express departs at 3pm and arrive as 9.45pm; and for Abu Road, a train departs every Tuesday and Friday at 11.30am, arriving at midnight. Five trains a day travel to Gandhidham (5am, 7.50am, 3pm, 6.30pm & 8.10pm), but it's easier to take the bus. For updated scheduling, ring ☎02832/251315.

There are GSTC **buses** to Ahmedabad, Rajkot and Jamnagar, as well as Kutchi towns like Mandvi and Mundra. More sparse connections serve some villages in northern Kutch. Call ☎02832/220002 for timings. Private bus operators are strung along Station Road. Ashapura Travels (☎02832/252491), opposite the bus stand, has a daily bus to Barmer (Rajasthan) at 5pm, which continues to Jaisalmer every other day (Rs240). They also have a bus to Ajmer (for Pushkar) departing at 4pm (Rs300). Patel Tours and Travels (☎02832/657781), 100m west of the station, has two night sleeper buses to Ahmedabad (Rs220).

For more on transport from Bhuj see "Travel details" on p.688.

Villages around Bhuj

Bhuj is a useful base for visiting the **outlying villages**, whether by motorcycle (see p.646 for details of hiring motorbikes), bus or taxi. Exploring the area by **taxi** or **motorcycle** gives you the most freedom; public **buses** are impractical as they are slow, infrequent and only stop in each village for a few minutes, while the lack of private cars makes **hitching** difficult. Should you opt for the bus, services run from Bhuj to Nirona (9 daily; 1hr 30min), Dhordo (1.30pm & 5pm) and Khavda (7.30am, 9am, noon, 2.15pm, 4.15pm, 5.45pm & 7.45pm).

The best way to get a fix on which settlements you might want to visit is to chat with Mr Pramod Jethi at the Aina Mahal museum. He's produced an inexpensive little guide book to the region featuring a fold-out map with all the main craft villages marked on it, and can advise you on the best ways to reach them.

Earthquake damage in the places mentioned below was minimal, with the exception of the toppled Jain temples at Bhadreswar. Note, however, that you'll need a **permit** to visit many of the more outlying villages, especially those close to the Ranns and Pakistani border. These are issued at the Foreigners' Registration Office on Jubilee Ground Road. You'll need to take along your passport and photocopies of your visa pages, and go a day or two in advance.

Mandvi

The compact town of **MANDVI**, on the west bank of a wide tidal estuary 60km southwest of Bhuj, faces the Arabian Sea to the south and supports a dwindling *dhow*-building industry. In the late eighteenth century it was the docking point for a fleet of four hundred vessels exporting goods from a hinterland that encompassed Gujarat and the lands to the north as far as Jaisalmer. Merchants, seamen and later the British were all keen to settle in this flourishing port; few remained, but they left behind grand mansions, painted and carved in a style clearly influenced by European tastes.

△ *Dhow*-builder, Mandvi

Mandvi today has a leisurely feel, with several chai stalls set among the old houses, cluttered shops stretching west of the estuary, and **markets** stocked with *bandhani* and silver. The estuary is blocked on the south side by shifting sands, forming a long, uncrowded **beach** offering good swimming, although camel and horse rides are more popular with Indian tourists. Beside the estuary you can see the **dhows** being hand-built from long wooden planks, with nails up to 1m long forged by local blacksmiths. Fifty men spend two years building each ship, the largest of which cost around Rs2 crore (around £250,000); they're commissioned by wealthy Gulf Arabs for use as pleasure vessels, floating hotels or casinos.

Mandvi's neglected and little-visited **Vijay Vilas Palace** (daily 9am–1pm & 2–6pm; Rs20, Rs15 cameras, Rs200 video camera, Rs20 parking), 8km west of town (turn left after 4km), is a sandy-white domed building set in almost 700 acres of land, built as a summer retreat by Kutch's maharao in the 1940s. Inside, Belgian, British and Italian furniture fills the high-ceilinged carpeted rooms, hunting trophies deck the walls, and a grand stairway leads to the ladies' quarters on the first floor. The palace estate has a private beach (Rs50) with a royal pavilion offering unending sea views.

Practicalities

Hourly **buses** run between Bhuj and Mandvi (1hr 30min); **taxis** crammed with as many people as possible make the journey when full, for Rs25 a head. Other buses travel to Gandhidham via Mundra (hourly), to Rajkot (6am, 7.10am, 7.45am, 2pm & 9pm), Ahmedabad (6.30am and 7.15pm), and Dwarka via Jamnagar (two morning buses). Of the town's few **guesthouses**, the clean, modern *Sahara*, adjoining the city wall some 300m west of the bus stand (Ⓣ02834/220272; ❷) is the best, with a dorm (Rs50) and 24-hour check out. Alternatives are the *Maitri Guest House* (Ⓣ02834/220183; ❷), a smartly painted building 200m further west, also with a dorm (Rs70); and the cheap and cheerful *Shital* near the bridge (Ⓣ02834/221160; ❷). You can also stay in one of two guesthouses at *Vijay Vilas Palace* (Ⓣ02834/222543; ❺–❻), which although characterful are not very well kept; meals (Rs100) are served in the aristocratic dining room and there is also an expensive luxury camp with a sea-facing restaurant on the private beach. The best bet for **food** is *Zorba the Buddha Restaurant* (11am–2pm & 6–10pm) on KT Shah Road, west of the bus stand behind an old town gate, where the renowned thalis include more than ten dishes plus fresh chutneys, pickles and sweets.

Mundra

The small, lively fishing port of **MUNDRA**, 44km east of Mandvi, has few sights of particular note of its own, but it's a pleasant place to catch the sea breezes and buy local crafts – batik prints, silver jewellery, unusual woollen *namadas*, floor coverings and wall-hangings. A bus ride and a short walk will get you to several small Rabari and Jat villages nearby and, to the east, the Jain temple site at **Bhadreswar**, which was levelled in the 2001 earthquake but is set for complete reconstruction using the original stones and salvaged artwork.

Mundra is served by slow **buses** from Mandvi (hourly; 1hr 30min), and Bhuj (hourly; 1hr 30min), but hiring a **taxi** (Rs175) or **motorcycle** is far more rewarding – half the fun of travelling around southern Kutch is in taking a leisurely ride through this quiet backwater. Basic **rooms** are available at the unsigned *Saheb* (Ⓣ02838/222356; ❶) and the *Eshant* (Ⓣ02838/222737; ❶–❷), both near the central crossroads; in addition, many new hotels and restaurants are cropping up to cater to the massive new port that has been built nearby.

Southeast to Kandla

The fifty-kilometre journey southeast from Bhuj to **KANDLA**, India's busiest port, takes you past dry scrubland. In the small village of **Bhujodi**, about 7km out of Bhuj, artisans weave thick shawls and blankets on pit looms dug into the floors of squat mud houses decorated with *gargomati*. You can buy their products from the small shop run by the Bhujodi Handweaving Co-op Society, or from the Shrujan showroom, which sells a variety of Kutchi handicrafts. Further along on this road are the villages of **Paddhar,** known for Rabari embroidery, and **Dhaneti**, a centre for Ahir embroidery (ask for artisan Radhaben Ahir or for Laxmiben who runs a small cooperative). **Dhamadka** is still an important centre for Ajrakh block-printing, though after the earthquake many artisans were moved to a new village, **Ajrakhpur**, around 10km east of Bhuj on the main highway (opposite a large industrial complex).

The first main town beyond Bhuj, **ANJAR**, was the capital of Kutch until 1548. It was badly affected by the earthquake; recovery here has been much slower than in Bhuj, and traditional craftsmaking – Ahir embroidery, *bandhani*, batik and nut-crackers – seriously disrupted, although a market is still held once or twice a week. Further east is **GANDHIDHAM**, the city planned for Sind refugees who came to Kutch after Partition. It too suffered quake damage, but as an industrial centre supporting the modern port of Kandla at the mouth of the Gulf of Kutch, it recovered quickly. For tourists it serves mainly as a place to change buses or trains; it is also a good place to buy cheap handicrafts, at the market stalls along Court Road near the bus station. A state bus to Barmer (Rajasthan) passes through here daily at 3.30pm; buses run every fifteen minutes between Bhuj and Gandhidham (1hr); and the rail connections around the state include #4312 Ala Hazrat Express to Palanpur (for Abu Road), departing at 12.55pm and arriving at 11pm.

North of Bhuj

A recently resurfaced road leads north of Bhuj to the craft centres of **HODKO**, **DHORDO** and **KHAVDA**, where clusters of grass-roofed mud huts are decorated with traditional clay and whitewash patterns. Around **LUDIA** – a Rabari village where NGOs unnecessarily flexed their muscles in the wake of the earthquake, and built up expensive and unwanted modern *bhunga* housing at a site called Ghandigram – there's a fairly commercial attitude towards tourists, so expect insistent sales pitches. Embroidery centres include **BHIRENDIARA**, where some houses feature beautiful mud-work (*liponkan*) interiors, and **SUMERASER SHEIKH**, where an NGO named **Kala Raksha** (ⓣ02808/277238, ⓦwww.kala-raksha.org) maintains a collection of antique textiles, reproductions of old patterns and a handicraft shop. Originally established to preserve and foster traditional arts in Kutch, most of Kala Raksha's participants are women from marginalized communities, and this is a great place for travellers seriously interested in textile design to learn about local embroidery, tie-dyeing, patchwork and inlay techniques. Call ahead if you want them to arrange a tour of the village, where you'll be able to watch painstaking embroidery techniques like *soof* and *paako*, which create intricate symmetrical patterns, in action, as well as viewing their textile museum. The showroom sells quality local crafts at fixed prices.

Than and Dhinodar

The monastery at **THAN**, 60km northwest of Bhuj, is home to a Tantric order of Hindu *sadhus* known as Kanphata ("split-ear") after the heavy agate rings they traditionally wear in their ears. The sect was founded by the twelfth-century saint Dharamnath who travelled to Kutch from Saurashtra sometime in the seventh-century AD, and practised severe austerities for 12 years on a nearby hilltop. Surrounded by impressive walls (to protect its occupants from attack by marauding Sindhi pirates), the whitewashed complex at the foot of the hill encloses a handful of medieval temples, tombs and domed dwellings. You can spend the night in its *dharamshala* (or up on the flat rooftop) for a small donation. Facilities are extremely basic, but worth enduring for the atmosphere: the site lies deep amid idyllic Kutchi countryside, close to the Rann, and wild peacocks congregate around the main temple at dawn to be fed by the last remaining Kanphata *sadhu*.

From Than, you can walk up a rocky ravine via an ancient pilgrims' trail to the mountain top behind, where Dharamnath performed his yoga austerities. **Dhinodar** is now the site of a neatly painted little temple, home to a single Kanphata yogi, Hiranath Baba, and his acolytes; it's a popular low-key pilgrimage destination for Kutchis during the winter. Allow three hours for the round trip from Than, and take along enough water as there's little shade along the route.

Dholavira

In the far north of Kutch, on an island surrounded by snow-white salt flats, the tiny village of **DHOLAVIRA** is strewn around the remnants of a once-thriving city which, six-thousand or more years ago, maintained trade links with Persia and the Euphrates Delta. Of all the so-called "Indus Valley" or "Harappan" archeological centres so-far unearthed, only Mohenjo Daro and Harappa, in neighbouring Pakistan, outstrip this in scale and sophistication. Yet Dholavira sees barely a trickle of visitors. A bumpy 250-km trip from Bhuj (the last of them on causeway across the Rann), it requires a major effort and sense of adventure to reach, and offers little in the way of facilities when you get there. The reward, however, is the chance to see a world-class ancient site which, if it were anywhere else, would attract huge crowds.

Archeological digs started here in the 1970s after a local farmer ploughed up a small terra-cotta seal and sent it to Delhi. Work on a prominent mound just outside the village soon revealed the existence of a major planned city, which is still being painstakingly uncovered. At its centre, a citadel, complete with monumental structures, palace complex and extraordinary water management system, surveys a fortified "Middle Town" and, on its east side, a more amorphous "Lower Town". These are all laid out in a large parallelogram measuring nearly a kilometre in length. Uniquely among Indus Valley sites, a large ten-lettered **inscription** was found on a stone near the entrance to citadel, which archeologists claim is the "world's oldest signboard". Unfortunately it's covered over, though a facsimile version is on display at the nearby Survey Office.

Visits to the Dholavira site (daily 9am–dusk; admission free) are carefully managed by a resident *chowkidar* who zealously enforces the inexplicable **no photography** rule. The recently built "visitors centre" at the main gate is nothing of kind, providing accommodation only for archeologists and visiting dignitaries. Instead, most people travel up here by taxi and return the same day. **Buses** do run from Bhuj, but arrive late in the evening, in which case you'll have no option but to seek out local postmaster and farmer, Mr Sambhu Dan (the man who found the first Dholavira seal), and request a *charpoi* in his yard. As in most Kutchi villages, offers of payment will at first be refused, out of politeness, but you should persevere until they're accepted; give what you'd pay for a simple hotel room (around Rs250 per person), plus Rs100–150 for a meal.

Little Rann Wild Ass Sanctuary

Spanning 4850 square kilometres, the **Little Rann Wild Ass Sanctuary**, a vast salt-encrusted desert plain that becomes inundated during the rains (July–Sept), is home to an abundance of wildlife, including the endangered Indian **wild ass**. Usually seen in loosely knit herds that scatter when disturbed, the ass, a handsome chestnut-brown and white member of the horse family, is capable of running very fast, and despite strict penalties imposed by the forest department, some visitors still persist in chasing them in their cars for fun. The best way to approach the ass, which can only be found in this sanctuary (the closest relative is the Kiang, seen in the high altitudes of Ladakh) is on foot, walking up to them slowly; once they get accustomed to your presence they will pretty much continue their peaceful existence. The sanctuary is also home to wolves, Indian and desert foxes, jackals, jungle and desert cats, *nilgai* and blackbuck antelopes, the chinkara gazelle and a wide variety of birds. Large flocks of flamingo, pelicans and winter-visiting cranes can be seen at Bajana Lake; if you want to see the migratory birds, October to March is the best time to come. Most of the wildlife is concentrated on elevated areas called *bets*, which become islands when the Rann endures its annual flood.

The sanctuary headquarters is at Dhrangadhra in Saurashtra, but most of the tourist facilities are at **Dasada**, a bumpy six-hour bus-ride east from Bhuj and 33km from Viramgam (which is on the train line from Bhuj to Ahmedabad). From Dasada (or via the resorts below) you can rent a 4WD (Rs900 for 3–4hr) and guide to take a tour of the sanctuary. Entrance fees ($5, $5 cameras) should be paid at the entrance to the sanctuary near **Bajana** village, which is about thirty minutes' drive from Dasada. The nearest railhead to the sanctuary is 32km away at **Virangam**, on the main Ahmedabad–Mumbai line. Both of the **accommodation** options in the area are pitched at well-heeled wildlife tourists, and can arrange to pick you up at the station on arrival. *Rann Riders* (Ⓣ02757/280257 Ⓦwww.rannriders.com; ⑨), 2km from Dasada and a half-hour drive from the train line, has comfortable a/c *kooba* huts, a restaurant and swimming pool, built in local architectural styles. Their all-in package of Rs2500 per person includes all meals and two daily tours of the sanctuary and nearby villages. Another 12km on towards the sanctuary gates, *Camp Zainabad* (aka "Desert Coursers"; Ⓣ0257/241333), is in a similar mould, only slightly cheaper, with all-in packages (including accommodation, all meals and Jeep safaris) from Rs1800 per person.

Saurashtra

SAURASHTRA, also known as the **Kathiawar Peninsula**, forms the bulk of Gujarat state, a large knob of land spreading south from the hills and marshes of the north out to the Arabian Sea, cut into by the Gulf of Cambay to the east and the Gulf of Kutch to the west. This is Gujarat at its most diverse, populated by cattle-rearing tribes and industrialists, with Hindu, Jain, Buddhist and Muslim architecture, modern urban centres and traditional bazaars.

Saurashtra boasts India's finest Jain temple city at **Shatrunjaya** near **Palitana**, Krishna temples at **Dwarka** and **Somnath** and Ashoka's Buddhist capital, **Junagadh**. Lions thrive in the national park in **Gir Forest**, while in the flat yellow grassland northeast of Bhavnagar, India's largest herd of blackbuck live in a national park at **Velavadar**. Gandhi's birthplace is still honoured in **Porbandar**; he is also remembered by a museum in **Rajkot** where he spent some years. The best place to head to enjoy sun, sea, beaches and beer is the formerly Portuguese island of **Diu**, just off the south coast.

Rajkot

Founded in the sixteenth century, **RAJKOT** was ruled by the Jadeja Rajputs until merging with the Union of Saurashtra after Independence, since when it has become a successful industrial centre – a fact that greatly contributes to its high levels of pollution. Best known for its associations with **Mahatma Gandhi**, who schooled here, this quiet city has little to attract tourists except a museum and Gandhi's family home. Its central position, however, makes it a good base for trips to nearby princely towns.

Arrival and information

Three main roads radiate from the busy road junction at Sanganwa Chowk in the centre of Rajkot: **Dhebar Road** heads south, past the ST bus stand 100m away; **Lakhajiraj Road** goes east, through the old city; and **Jawahar Road** runs north, past the earthquake-damaged Alfred High School (Gandhi's former school) and Jubilee Gardens towards **Rajkot Junction station**, 2km northeast (get off here rather than at City Station if arriving by train), and the airport 4km northwest. Eagle Travels (ⓣ0281/554444) has a/c bus services to Ahmedabad, Porbandar, Baroda and Surat. Rajkot's rather redundant **tourist office** (Mon–Sat 10.30am–2pm & 2.30–6pm, closed 2nd and 4th Sat of month; ⓣ0281/223 4507) is off Jawahar Road, north of Sanganwa Chowk behind the **State Bank of Saurashtra** (Mon–Fri 11am–3pm & 3.30–4.45pm; look for the blue ATM signs as the bank's name is in Gujarati). You'll find the **post office** on Sadar Road, off Jawahar Road opposite Jubilee Gardens. I-way **Internet centres** all over Rajkot offer fast connections (Rs25/hr). You can **rent a bike** at Moke Cycles (Rs3/hr, Rs300 deposit) behind the bus stand.

Accommodation

Rajkot has a clutch of **hotels** around the bus stand; the cheapest leave much to be desired, so it's worth spending a little more to escape the noise and dirt of the city. Most places listed below are on the marginally quieter back side of the bus stand, to the east. Note that, in contrast to the rest of the state, **room rates** in Rajkot are rigidly fixed.

Babha Guest House Panchnath Rd, off Jawahar Rd just south of Alfred High School ⓣ0281/222 0861, ⓦwww.hotelbhaba.com. One of the cleanest budget options, with small rooms, some of which are a/c. 24hr checkout. 2–4

Galaxy Jawahar Rd, 100m north of Sanganwa Chowk ⓣ0281/222 2904, ⓔinfo@thegalaxyhotel.com. Spacious, cool rooms decorated with crayon drawings done by local children, on the third floor of a shopping complex accessed only by lift. High standard of hygiene and service, and a small library heavy on Agatha Christie novels. 4–6

Grand Regency Debar Rd ⓣ0281/224 0100. Rajkot's newest 3-star hotel with large, modern rooms, helpful staff, and a multi-cuisine restaurant. 7–9

Harmony Opposite Shastri Maidan, near Limda Chowk ⓣ0281/224 0950, ⓕ224 0949. Upscale hotel with spotless, well-appointed rooms and a good restaurant. Management can arrange a taxi or train and plane tickets, but also require an exchange receipt upon room payment. 6–7

Jyoti Kanak Rd, 200m north of the bus stand ⓣ0281/222 5472. The best of the scruffy and poky lodges, thanks mostly to its friendly manager. 1

Kavery Kanak Rd ⓣ0281/223 9331, ⓕ223 1107. Upmarket place round the corner from the *Jyoti*. Comfortable a/c rooms and suites. 6–7

The Town

Rajkot's most appealing area is the **old city**, where you'll see plenty of typical Gujarati wooden-fronted houses with intricately carved shutters and stained-glass windows. The Gandhis moved here from Porbandar in 1881. Tucked away in the narrow streets on Ghitaka Road, off Lakhajiraj Road about 300m east of Sanganwa

Chowk – the turning is marked by a blue signpost, but it's not easily spotted – the family house **Kaba Gandhi no Delo** (Mon–Sat 9am–noon & 3–6pm; free) has a small display of artefacts and photographs from the Mahatma's life.

The other chief tourist attraction in the city is the **Watson Museum** (daily except Sun and 2nd & 4th Sat of month, 9am–1pm & 2–6pm; Rs50), in a robust nineteenth-century building in Jubilee Bagh. The museum, named after Colonel Watson, British Political Agent from 1886 to 1893, displays relics from 2000 BC to the nineteenth century, including findings from Indus Valley sites, medieval statues, manuscripts, miniatures and Rajput bronzes. On the ground floor a vast collection of portraits of Gujarat's rulers surrounds a staunch Queen Victoria, fashioned in 1899 by Alfred Gilbert who modelled Eros in London's Piccadilly Circus.

Eating

Rajkot has a number of **restaurants** serving Gujarat's sweet-and-sour tasting thalis, including the regional Kathiawadi version, spiced with ginger and garlic. Most places, are vegetarian, including those in the hotels. Western fast food, South Indian snacks and Punjabi food are also becoming increasingly popular, and there are a number of good *dhabas* (called lodges or dining halls) near the station for snacks and inexpensive thalis. Rajkot is known for milk **sweets** like the *thabdi halwas* and saffron-flavoured *kesar pedas* – head for *Jai Siyaram*, which has outlets all over the city. Most restaurants open after 10.30am, so for **breakfast** you'll need to visit one of the hotels.

Big-Bite Race Course Circle. Popular with local students, who enjoy pizzas, grilled sandwiches, juices and ice-cream sundaes in a strip-lit interior or outdoors in a courtyard off the main road. Open11am till midnight.

Bukara *Kavery Hotel*, Kanak Rd. Smart-looking restaurant with good north Indian, South Indian and Western dishes (about Rs80 each) as well as Gujarati thali lunches. Daily 8–10am, 11am–3pm & 7–11pm.

City Fast Food 37 Karanpura. Clean café behind the bus stand serving meals and South Indian snacks, including wonderful *dosas*.

Grand Regency Debar Rd. Good multi-cuisine hotel restaurant; the glass-walled kitchen is an attraction in itself, as diners get to see Indian breads like *naans* being prepared on the spot.

Havmor Jawahar Rd, opposite Alfred High School. Good for Punjabi, Chinese and Western options (with delicious chicken tikkas) and their own-brand ice cream. The snacks are overpriced – a puny chicken sandwich costs Rs40 – but you sit in a/c comfort. Open 10am–11.30pm.

Lord's Banquet Kasturba Rd, opposite Dharam Cinema. Where locals go when they want a treat, this efficient place serves good north Indian food in a/c comfort. You can get Western and Chinese snacks at their food court on the first floor of the neighbouring building. Open 7.30–11am, 12.30–3.30pm, 4–6.30pm & 7.30–11.30pm.

Around Rajkot

The princes of Rajkot district left a rich legacy of elaborate **residences** whose architectural styles range from the delicate detail of the seventeenth century to bold 1930s Art Deco. Most of the buses from Rajkot to Ahmedabad stop at **SAYLA**, 87km beyond Rajkot, where a colonial bungalow has been converted into a heritage hotel, *Old Bell Guest House* (ⓣ02755/280017; ❸–❺) with large, comfortable a/c rooms and a good restaurant. At Sayla you can see a range of Saurashtran handicrafts, including beadwork and weaving; it is also a good base if you want to visit **Wadhwan**, known for its *bandhani* tie-dye and brassware.

Wankaner

The flamboyant **Ranjit Vilas Palace** at **WANKANER**, 39km northeast of Rajkot, is still home to the family who once ruled the old state of the same name. Built between 1899 and 1914, the symmetrical building can be seen from far across the flat Saurashtran plains. Up close, its fancy arched facade shows a frenzy of Moghul, Italianate, Moorish and Victorian Gothic styles with stained-glass windows, domed towers, chandelier-lit hallways and scores of hunting trophies looming from the walls. You can **stay** in Art Deco splendour at the family's nearby summer home, the *Royal Oasis* (Ⓣ02828/220000, Ⓕ220002; ❼). Nightly rates include a tour of the family museum, stables, garage and step-well, use of the beautiful indoor swimming pool, and all meals; at least one of which is taken with former Maharaja Pratap Singh (born 1908) and his son and heir Digvijay Sinh, a former Member of Parliament. Expect slow service. The hotel lies near the highway that leads northwest to Bhuj.

Gondal

GONDAL, 39km south of Rajkot towards Junagadh and Porbandar, was one of the most progressive of the princely states of Saurashtra, known for its wide-ranging educational and social reforms. Some of the infrastructure put in place by the late Maharaja Bhagwat Sinh who ruled Gondal state from the 1800s to the 1930s can still be seen in the concrete roads, sanitary drainage, irrigation and grand buildings. The former royal family still lives at the Huzoor Palace, and have converted their guest wing into the *Orchard Palace Hotel* (Ⓣ02825/224550, Ⓔssibal@ad1.vsnl.net.in; ❾). Facing onto groves of fruit trees, it's a great place to stay, with large high-ceilinged rooms, four-poster beds, period furniture and nice hot showers. Rates (Rs2200 per person) include delicious meals and **tours** of the beautifully carved 1748 Naulakha Palace, the Maharaja's vintage car collection, rail saloon and horse-drawn carriages, and the estate's bird-rich lakes and grasslands.

Gondal is a centre for beadwork embroidery, handloom weaving, silverware, handmade brass-boxes called *pataras* and ayurvedic medicine. Good places for **shopping** include the market on Darbargadh Road and the Udyog Bharati emporium near the palace.

Jamnagar

Close to the northwest coast of Saurashtra, the busy, noisy city of **JAMNAGAR** preserves some fabulous architectural surprises at its heart. Founded in the sixteenth century, the walled city was built to the east of Ranmal Lake, centring on the circular Lakhota Fort. **K.S. Ranjitsinhji**, the famously elegant cricketer who played for England alongside W.G. Grace, ruled Jamnagar for several years at the turn of the twentieth century, improving commercial contacts and replacing run-down buildings with attractive constructions that remain as testimony to a prosperous and efficient rule. The city is renowned for excellent *bandhani* (tie-dye), sold in the markets near the Darbargadh and in the new shopping complexes.

Arrival and information

From the ST **bus station**, it's a 2km walk or rickshaw ride west, past Ranmal Lake, to **Bedi Gate** and the **New Super Market**, the unofficial centre of town. Coming from Rajkot, your bus will pass right through town before arriving at the bus station, so ask to be dropped off at Bedi Gate; if departing to Rajkot, you can flag down a bus outside the *President Hotel*. From theHapa **railway station**, it's a six-kilometre ride southeast into town, past Teen Bati, an important square; most trains also stop at the smaller Gandhinagar railway station, just 2km from the centre of town. A number of a/c **private buses** set off from Pancheshwar

Tower near Teen Bati – Patel Tours & Travels (Ⓣ0288/255 2419) has frequent services to Ahmedabad, Gandhidham and Bhuj. For air tickets and other travel queries, try Savetime Travel (Ⓣ0288/255 3137) on Bedi Gate Road. The **airport** is 8km west of the bus stand.

The State Bank of India in New Super Market will **change cash** or travellers' cheques. **Internet** facilities are available at CyberCity (Rs25/hr) at City Point building near the *President Hotel*, or closer to the bus stand at Sky Link, on the first floor of the Sarovar Complex opposite Rathi Hospital.

Accommodation

Acceptable **accommodation** is limited in Jamnagar. The inexpensive places in and around New Super Market are noisy and sub-standard. The more expensive hotels, though more spread out, are comparatively good value.

Aram Nand Niwas, Pandit Nehru Marg Ⓣ0288/255 1701, Ⓕ255 4957. Palatial old house with a garden restaurant 2km towards the railway station from Bedi Gate. The large a/c rooms, nostalgic for the days of the Raj and filled with European antiques, have a faded charm. ❺

Ashiana Third Floor, New Super Market Ⓣ0288/255 9110, Ⓕ255 1155. Carpeted deluxe rooms and grubbier ordinary ones; all have TV and bathroom with hot water. Spacious for a downtown budget hotel. ❷–❹

Gayatri Guest House Sumer Club Rd Ⓣ0288/256 4727. A five-minute walk south of the bus stand, on the second floor across from Rathi Hospital; reasonably comfy rooms, some with a/c and TV. Good-value singles and 24hr checkout. ❸

Kama Opposite ST bus stand Ⓣ0288/255 9217, Ⓕ255 8219. Set slightly back from the mayhem, this functional concrete block has the most decent rooms in the immediate vicinity of the bus stand. The dorm (Rs100) has a locker. ❷–❺

President Teen Bati Ⓣ0288/255 7491, Ⓔpresident@wilnetonline.net. Very clean, well-managed hotel with parking, bar, restaurant and currency exchange. The owner is an excellent source of local advice. Credit cards accepted. ❹–❼

Punit Pandit Nehru Marg, just northwest of Teen Bati Ⓣ0288/255 9275, Ⓕ255 0561. Friendly, clean and popular, with a small roof terrace. More centrally placed than other mid-range options. ❸–❹

The City

The most remarkable of Ranjitsinhji's constructions is **Willingdon Crescent**, the swooping arches of its curved facade overlooking the wide streets of Chelmsford Market and the old palace, the **Darbargadh**. In the heart of town, just off Ranjit Road southwest of Bedi Gate, stands the late-nineteenth-century **Ratan Bai Mosque**. This grand domed prayer hall, its sandalwood doors inlaid with mother-of-pearl, is the unlikely neighbour to a magnificent pair of **Jain temples**, both decorated with extraordinary **murals**. The most spectacular of the two, **Shantinath Mandir**, is a maze of brightly coloured columns. The outer side of the large dome over **Adinath Mandir** is inlaid with gold and coloured mosaic and both temples have cupolas enriched with a design of mirrors above the entrance porch. The temples form the hub of **Chandni Bazaar**, an almost circular market area enlivened by carved wooden doors, mosaics and balconies.

Stretching west towards the bus stand, Ranmal Lake and **Lakhota Fort** (daily except Wed and 2nd & 4th Sat of month, 10.30am–1pm & 3–6.30pm; Rs 50) were part of an employment-generating measure during a spell of drought in Jamnagar state during the 1750s. The palace is connected to solid land in both directions by a causeway but only accessible from the north side. Thick circular walls studded with gun-holes protect the inner building. On entering you'll pass a guardroom containing muskets, swords and powder flasks; the **museum** on the upper floor used to hold a mediocre display of paintings, sculpture, folk art and coins but was being renovated and improved at the time of writing. South of the lake stands the solid **Bhujia Fort**, one of the few casualties of the earthquake in Jamnagar and closed ever since. To its northwest, on the edge of the old city, the **Bala Hanuman temple** has been the scene of round-the-clock non-stop chanting ("Shree Ram, Jay Ram, Jay Jay Ram") since 1964, for which feat it is cited in the *Guinness Book of Records*.

Eating

A fairly wide choice of good inexpensive **restaurants**, most of them clustered around Teen Bati, serve vegetarian dishes. Most places close at 10pm. Jamnagar is known for its sweets.

Brahmaniya Dining Hall Teen Bati. Dark and cool a/c restaurant, serving one of Jamnagar's most famous Gujarati thalis (Rs50). Closed Sat evening.

Fresh Point Near the Town Hall. Locally popular a/c restaurant for Punjabi and other north Indian food.

Kalpana Teen Bati. Ageing decor but great cheap veg food: South Indian, Punjabi, ice cream, fruit juice and milkshakes, but no hot drinks. Closed Mon.

Madras Teen Bati. Justly famous for its *dosas* and other South Indian snacks, coffee and set meals, it also has ice creams and juices. Opens early for breakfast. Closed Tues.

Seven Seas *Hotel President*, Teen Bati. Dimly lit, comfortable a/c restaurant dishing up Indian, Chinese and Western dishes at moderate prices. Good if you fancy a meat or fish feast – try the tandoori pomfret, prawns masala and tangri chicken.

Urvee Town Hall Road. Popular with local families for dinner, due to its good veg Punjabi and a few Western and Chinese dishes.

Dwarka

In the far west of the peninsula, fertile wheat, groundnut and cotton fields emerge in vivid contrast to the arid expanses further inland. According to popular Hindu legend, Krishna fled Mathura to this coastal region, declaring **DWARKA** his capital. A labyrinth of narrow winding streets cluttered with temples, the town resonates today with the bustle of eager saffron-clad pilgrims and the clatter of celebratory drums. Dwarka really comes to life during the major Hindu **festivals**; the most fervent are Shivratri, dedicated to Shiva (Feb/March) and Janmashtami, Krishna's birthday (Aug/Sept).

The elaborately carved tower of sixteenth-century **Dwarkadish temple** (daily 7am–12.30pm & 5–9pm) looms 50m above the town. Non-Hindus can enter the shrine only on signing a form declaring, at the very least, respect for religion. Get small change for donations from the change-wallahs at the east entrance.

When Krishna came to Dwarka with the Yadava clan, he eloped with Princess Rukmini. One kilometre east of town, the small **Rukmini temple** – which local priests may tell you is 1500 years old, but in fact dates from the twelfth century – is, if anything, more architecturally impressive than the Dwarkadish temple, with carvings of elephants, flowers, dancers and Shiva in several of his aspects covering every wall. For great **views** over the town and the sea beyond, climb to the top of the **lighthouse** (daily 4–6pm; Rs2), near the *Toran Guest House*.

Practicalities

Trains from Jamnagar arrive at the station north of town, from where tongas or auto-rickshaws ferry visitors to hotels and the temple. The **bus stand** on the road to Okha has regular services to and from Jamnagar, Porbandar and Veraval. Dwarka Darshan run **tours** (Rs30) at 8am and 2pm to the underground *jyotrilingam* at the Nageshwar temple, 16km from

Dwarka. **Internet** access is available at Shreeji Cybercafe opposite the *Hotel Uttam* (ⓣ02892/234692; Rs40/hr).

Accommodation in Dwarka is, for the most part, inexpensive and simple. *Guru Prerna* (ⓣ02892/235512; ❺–❻), just off the approach road leading from the highway to the bus stand, has clean, comfortable rooms with hot water, some of them a/c. The clean, modern *Hotel Rajdhani* on Hospital Road (ⓣ02892/234070; ❷–❸), just off the main road between the bus stand and the temple, has excellent-value rooms, all with TV. *Meera* (ⓣ02892/234031; ❷) on the approach road has simple but clean rooms along with a dining hall that does a brisk turnover in Rs25-30 **thalis**.

Porbandar

Once an international port and princely state capital, **PORBANDAR**, smack in the middle of the 200km of coastline between Veraval and Dwarka, is inextricably associated with Mahatma Gandhi, who was born here. In addition, and in common with much of the southwest coast of Saurashtra, Porbandar is linked with the legends of **Krishna** – in ancient times the settlement was called Sudampuri, after one of Krishna's comrades. Today, shrouded in a dim haze of excretions from the cement and chemical factories on its outskirts, Porbandar is grimier than ever, despite the flow of remittance cheques from its emigrants overseas; this is where most of Gujarat's **diaspora** originate, and "NRIs" (Non-Resident Indians) from Britain, Canada and East Africa are often here on visits to family and friends.

Arrival and information

Porbandar's main street, **Mahatma Gandhi (MG) Road**, runs from a fountain at its eastern end – northeast of which is the **railway station** – to a triple gateway at its western end, near Gandhiji's house. In the middle, at the **main square**, it is bisected by Arya Sumaj Road, which runs northwards across Jubilee Bridge, and southwards to the **GPO**. Just east of that is the **ST bus stand** (connected to MG Road by ST Road) and, to its south, the main beach.

Banks along MG Road change foreign currency and travellers' cheques as does Thankys Tours and Travels (see below). Below the *Indraprasth Hotel*, Shiny the Cyber Hut and Skyline (both Rs25/hr) offer **Internet** access, as do a number of centres across the road. Thankys Tours and Travels, on MG Road near Dreamland Cinema (ⓣ0286/224 4344, ⓦwww.thankys.com), can book taxis, domestic and international flights, along with tickets on the #9215 Saurashtra Express **train**, which departs at 8pm, arriving in Ahmedabad at 6am and Mumbai at 7pm. Eagle Travels (ⓣ0281/221 2089) books a/c **buses** to Rajkot, Ahmedabad and other centres. Jet Airways has a **flight** to Mumbai daily except Saturday at 1pm (Rs4555); the airport is 5km from town.

Accommodation

Porbandar has an adequate range of **hotels**. Those in town are generally better quality but noisier, while the *New Oceanic* has sea views to make up for its shortcomings. Checkout time is usually 10am.

Flamingo MG Rd, across from the State Bank of India ⓣ0286/224 7123. A good budget option in the centre of town with bright, clean rooms tended by a friendly staff. ❷–❸

Indraprasth Off ST Rd ⓣ0286/224 2681, ⓕ221 3778. The huge neon sign visible all over town makes this place hard to miss. It's a modern hotel with English speaking receptionists, smartly dressed

Mahatma Gandhi – India's great soul

Gujarat's most famous son was born **Mohandas Karamchand Gandhi** on October 2, 1869 at Porbandar on the Kathiawar peninsula. Although his family were merchants by caste – Gandhi meaning grocer – both his grandfather and father had risen to positions of political influence. Young Mohandas was shy and sickly, only an average scholar, but from early on questioned the codes of power around him and even flouted accepted Hindu practice: he once ate meat for a year believing it would give him the physical edge the British appeared to possess. As a teenager, he began to develop an interest in spirituality, particularly in the Jain principle of **ahimsa** (nonviolence).

Gandhi moved to London to study law at 19, outwardly adopting the appearance and manners of an English gentleman, but also keeping to his mother's wish that he resist meat, alcohol and women. Avidly reading the Bible alongside the *Bhagavad Gita*, he started to view different religions as a collective source of truth from which everyone could draw spiritual inheritance.

After a brief spell back in India, Gandhi left again to practise law in South Africa, where the plight of fellow Indians – coupled with his own indignation at being ejected from a first-class rail carriage – fuelled his campaigns for racial equality. His public profile grew and he gained crucial victories for minorities against the practices of indentured labour. During this time he also opted to transcend material possessions, dressing in the handspun *dhoti* and shawl of a peasant, and took a vow of celibacy. This turn to ascetic purity he characterized as *satyagraha*, which derived from Sanskrit ideas of "truth" and "firmness", and would become the touchstone of **passive resistance**. Returning to India with his messianic reputation well established – the poet Tagore named him **"Mahatma"** (Great Soul) – Gandhi travelled the country campaigning for **swaraj** (home rule). He also worked tirelessly for the rights of women and untouchables, whom he called **Harijans** (children of God), and founded an ashram at Sabarmati outside Ahmedabad where these principles were upheld. Gandhi stepped up his activities in the wake of the brutal massacre of protesters at Amritsar, leading a series of self-sufficiency drives during the 1920s, which included the public burning of imported clothes on huge pyres and culminated in the great **salt march** from Ahmedabad to Dandi in 1930. This month-long 386-kilometre journey led a swelling band of followers to the coast, where salt was made in defiance of the British monopoly on production. The march drew worldwide attention: though Gandhi was promptly imprisoned, British resolve was seen to have weakened and on release he was invited to a round-table meeting in London to discuss home rule. The struggle continued for several years and Gandhi served more time in jail – his wife Kasturba dying by his side.

As the nationalist movement gained strength, Gandhi grew more concerned about the state of Hindu–Muslim relations. He responded to outbreaks of **communal violence** by subjecting his own body to self-purification and suffering through fasting. When Britain finally guaranteed independence in 1947 and sent Lord Mountbatten to oversee transition, it seemed that Gandhi's dream of a united and free India was possible after all. But the partition of India left him with a deep sense of failure. Once more he fasted in Calcutta in a bid to stem the violence as large numbers of Hindus and Muslims flowed between the new countries. Gandhi's commitment to the fair treatment of Muslim Indians and his intention to visit and endorse Pakistan as a neighbour enraged many Hindu fundamentalists. He survived an attempt on his life on January 20, 1948, only to be shot dead from close range by a lone Hindu gunman in Delhi ten days later. Prime Minister Nehru announced the loss on national radio: "Friends and comrades, the light has gone out of our lives and there is darkness everywhere." The funeral was attended by a roll call of postwar statesmen and women. One representative of the new world order, US Senator Vandenberg, remarked that "Gandhi made humility and truth more powerful than empires".

room boys, all mod cons, and a range of rooms, some with unusually shaped beds. Tastefully decorated with original murals by a local artist. ❸–❻

Moon Palace MG Rd, 100m east of the main square ⓣ0286/224 1172, ⓕ224 3248. Smart new hotel with a range of spotless rooms from simple singles to large (overpriced) suites. The a/c doubles are good value. ❸–❻

New Oceanic Chowpatty Sea Face ⓣ0286/221 4222, ⓕ224 1298. Sizeable a/c rooms with large windows offering sea views and hot water. Not very efficiently run. ❹–❺

The Town

For foreign visitors, the town harbours little of note, save, of course, **Gandhi's birthplace** (daily 7.30am–7.30pm; free, but the guide will expect a donation), in the west of town (the rickshaw-wallahs all know how to find it). The whole place is empty, though some of the walls in the reading and prayer rooms on the upper floors bear faded traces of paintings. The Kirti Mandir, a memorial to the Mahatma and his wife erected in the 1950s, has photographs and artefacts from his life.

The former Maharajas' palaces can be seen near the Chowpatty Seaface. **Huzoor Palace** is occupied by the family when they visit from their present home in London, while the **Daria Rajmahal Palace** near the lighthouse is now a college. **Grishmabhawan**, near the bus stand, is an impressive pavilion, adorned with arches and carvings, built for the eighteenth-century poet Maharaja Sartanji. Porbandar's lake is a designated bird sanctuary, but you can actually see more **flamingos** – along with *dhow*-builders – at the creeks along the coast than here.

Eating

Although Porbandar is well known in Gujarat for its **seafood**, you'll have a job finding it. Outside the hotels, there's a fairly uninspiring choice of **restaurants**; many seem to serve only a limited number of the dishes listed on the menus. However, *dhabas* like *Raghuvanshi* and *Natraj* just off MG Road have tasty and cheap Gujarati dishes – a meal costs just Rs25–30 per person. *Aarti Sweets* on MG Road is popular for packaged nibbles and freshly made sweets.

Moon Palace MG Rd. Very popular hotel restaurant serving Gujarati thalis (Rs50–70), Punjabi dishes and Western snacks. Opens early for breakfast and stays open till 11pm, though thalis are available only 11.30am–2.45pm.

National MG Rd. Muslim-run place serving skimpy but ultra-cheap portions of meat and veg. Open 11.30am–3.30pm & 6.30–11pm.

Swagat MG Rd, 250m east of the main square. Softly lit place serving excellent, mid-priced Punjabi and South Indian veg dishes. Open 9.30am–2.45pm & 6.30–10.45pm.

Junagadh and around

The small town of **JUNAGADH** (also spelt Junagarh), around 160km from Diu (via Veraval), is an intriguing place, with a skyline broken by domes and minarets and narrow streets whose shopfronts are piled high with pyramids of spices. It's fun to amble through the town's lively bazaars, and with a mixture of Buddhist monuments, Hindu temples, mosques, bold Gothic archways and mansions – not to mention the magnificent Jain temples on **Mount Girnar** – Junagadh is an exciting city to explore for anyone with an interest in architecture and a taste for history.

From the fourth century BC to the death of Ashoka (c. 232 BC), Junagadh was the capital of Gujarat under the Buddhist Mauryas. The short reigns of the Kshatrapas and the Guptas came to an end when the town passed into the hands of the Hindu Chudasanas, who in turn soon lost out to Muslim

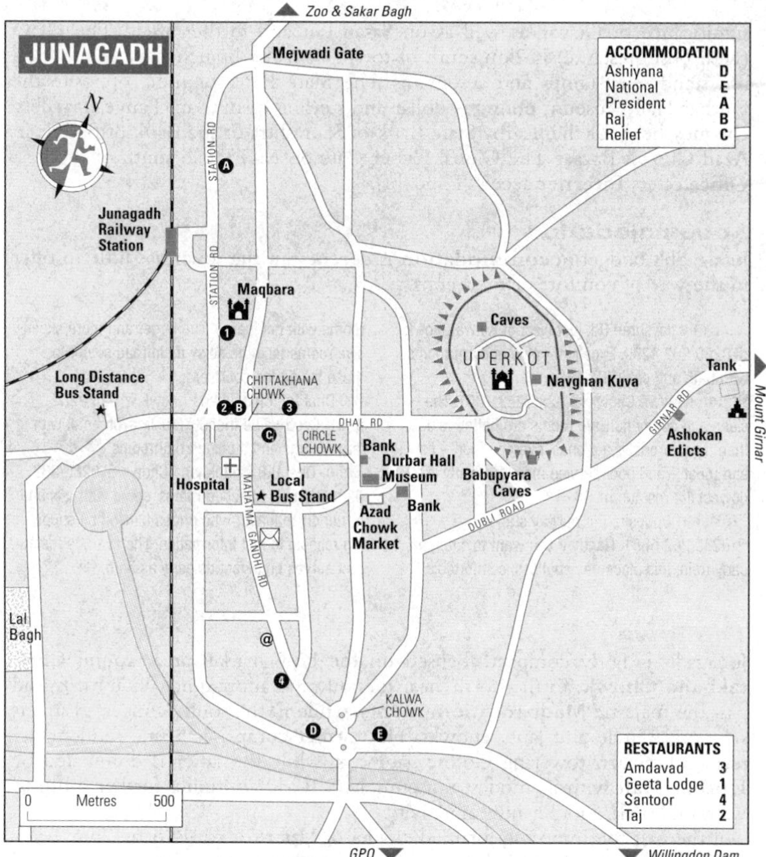

invaders. Muslim sovereignty lasted until Independence when, although the leaders planned to unite Junagadh with Pakistan, local pressure ensured that it became part of the Indian Union. Because of the sanctity of Mount Girnar, 4km away, the **Shivratri festival** (Feb/March) assumes particular importance in Junagadh, when thousands of saffron-clad *sadhus* come to camp around the town and in the surrounding hills. Fireworks, processions, chanting, chillum-smoking and demonstrations of body-torturing ascetic practices continue for nine days and nights, and performances of folk dances and Bhawai theatre are staged. Tourists arriving in Junagadh at this time are in for a memorable experience, but rooms are at a premium, so book well in advance.

Arrival and information

Arriving in Junagadh by bus or train, you're within easy walking distance of nearly all the hotels. Local transport is provided by **auto-rickshaws**, though bicycles are great for getting around; with a bit of leg-work you can even cycle to the foot of Mount Girnar. Run-of-the-mill bikes can be rented from a shop just west of Chittakhana Chowk, or from the *Relief Hotel*, where the friendly manager also gives the best **information** on the town's sites and the religious significance of Girnar, as well as on Sasan Gir and further afield. The **GPO** (with poste restante) is 2km south of town; a smaller branch next to the local bus stand sells stamps and aerograms. The State Bank of India opposite the Durbar Hall Museum **changes** dollar and sterling cash; to exchange travellers' cheques, head for the nearby State Bank of Saurashtra or the Bank of Baroda in Azad Chowk Bazaar. The Global Cyber Café on MG Road south of the Post Office offers **Internet** access (Rs30/hr).

Accommodation

Junagadh's budget **accommodation** is decent, but the town has little to offer in the way of comfort or mod cons.

Ashiyana Jayshree Rd, just west of Kalwa Chowk ☎0285/262 4299. Excellent-value uniform rooms with bath and cable TV. ❷

National Kalwa Chowk ☎0285/262 7891. The clean and comfy non-a/c rooms are better value than the overpriced a/c ones. Average food – fish and meat – and poor service mars the dimly lit downstairs restaurant. ❸–❹

President Opposite the railway station ☎0285/262 5661. Handy if you want to catch an early train, this place has spotless, comfortable rooms with hot water. The larger and more expensive rooms face the noisy main road so opt for those facing the courtyard. ❹

Raj Dhal Rd, Chittakhana Chowk ☎0285/262 3961. Good-value friendly Muslim-run hotel with large rooms and attached bathrooms. ❶–❷

Relief Dhal Rd, Chittakhana Chowk ☎0285/262 0280. Homely attached rooms, some with a/c, and a friendly manager who prides himself on supplying reliable tourist information. The average restaurant serves breakfast as early as 5am. ❷–❸

The Town

Junagadh is fairly compact, focused on the busy market area around **Chittakhana Chowk**. To the north, near the railway station, quiet wide roads lead past the majestic **Maqbara monuments**, while in the south, congested streets surround Circle and Janta chowks. The former comprises a fine semicircular terrace between towering Gothic gateways, while the latter is dominated by **Durbar Hall** with its modest museum. MG Road continues further south to Kalwa Chowk, another hub of activity.

In the east the imposing fortified citadel of **Uperkot** (daily 6am–7pm; Rs5), perched on a thickly walled mound in the northeast of the city and colonized by eagles, egrets and squirrels, is a peaceful place with a rich history. Legend dates the fort's origins to the time of the Yadavas (Krishna's clan) who fled Mathura to settle in Dwarka, but historians believe it was built by Chandragupta Maurya in 319 BC. Rediscovered and repaired in 976 AD by Muslim conquerors, it regained its defensive importance, withstanding sixteen sieges over the next eight hundred years.

A grand sequence of three high gateways cut into solid rock during the Muslim occupation stands at the entrance to the citadel, spanning a cobbled walkway that winds upwards past a *kund* (small pool) and some modern Hindu temples to the summit of the raised fort, where the **Jami Masjid** stands abandoned. Supporting the high roof, many of its 140 pillars were taken from the Chudasana palace and feature common Hindu motifs. The two fierce cannons opposite the mosque were used at Diu fort in defence against the Portuguese in 1530 and were brought here in 1538.

Heading north from the Jami Masjid, you come to a complex of small cells arranged around courtyards cut down into the rock. These **Buddhist Caves** (Rs100) were built in the third or fourth century AD – worn traces of figurines and foliage can still be made out on the columns in the lower level. Nearby, more than 170 steps descend to the well **Adi Chadi Vav**, believed to have been built in the fifteenth century. The more impressive eleventh-century **Navghan Kuva**, in the southeast of the citadel, consists of a superb staircase that winds around the well shaft to the dimly lit water level over 52m below.

Below the southern wall of the fort, the **Babupyara Caves** (Rs100), hewn from the rock between 200 BC and 200 AD, were used by Buddhists until the time of Ashoka, and then by Jains. A little to the north of Uparkot, the slightly later, plainer **Khapra Kodia Caves** remain in good condition, intersected with staircases, colonnades and passages.

West of the main entrance to Uparkot, in Janta Chowk, the **Durbar Hall Museum** (daily except Wed and the 2nd & 4th Sat of each month, 9am–12.15pm & 3–6pm; Rs50) takes up part of the former palace of the nawabs. Silver chairs in the great hall stand in regal splendour around a large carpet, valuable silver clocks encase scruffy stuffed birds and huge coloured chandeliers hang from the ceiling. Surrounding rooms contain silver *howdahs* (elephant seats), weaponry, portraits and a collection of textiles.

Junagadh's chief Muslim monuments are the boldly decorated **maqbara** – quite unlike any other in Gujarat – on MG Road opposite the High Courts. Built for Muslim rulers in the nineteenth century, these squat and square mausolea are crowned with a multitude of bulbous domes. The most opulent tomb is the 1892 sepulchre of Mahabat Khan I, but more outstanding, for its complex design, is that of Vizir Sahib Baka-ud-din Bhar, completed four years later and flanked on each corner by tall minarets hugged with spiral staircases. Next to the *muqbara* is a mosque whose multicoloured pillars and gaily painted walls are oddly reminiscent of a *cassata*.

An eighteenth-century group of **smaller memorials** to earlier nawabs stands in a peaceful graveyard shielded by shops on Chittakhana Chowk. Delicate in both size and design, they boast fine carving on the graves and stone lattice-work cut from the walls. You'll have to scramble around the back of the shops to find the entrance: the rooftop of the adjacent *Amdavad* restaurant gives good aerial views.

Ashokan edicts

Two kilometres east of town on the road to Girnar, a rock engraved with the Buddhist **edicts of Ashoka** (daily except Wed 8.30–11am & 2–6pm; Rs100), Junagadh's most famous monarch, remains where it was placed in the third century BC, its impact somewhat marred by a modern shelter and concrete platform. Written in the Prakrit dialect, the worn verses etched into the granite encourage the practice of *dharma* and equality and beseech different religious sects to live in harmony and repent the evils of war. Situated on the route taken by pilgrims to the sacred hill of Girnar, Ashoka's edicts had a lasting influence: even as late as the seventh century AD there were about three thousand Buddhists in Junagadh, and over fifty convents. Sanskrit inscriptions on the same rock were added during the reigns of King Rudraman (150 AD) and Skandagupta (455 AD).

Mount Girnar

Rising to a height of more than 1100m, **Mount Girnar** (bus #4 and #6 from the GPO, or take an auto-rickshaw for Rs35), a steep-sided extinct volcano 4km east of Junagadh, is a major pilgrimage centre for both Jains and Hindus, and has been considered sacred since before the third century BC. It's best to start the ascent, which takes at least two hours, well before 7am, when the scorching sun starts to rise from behind the peak. The path of five thousand irregular steps

Moving on from Junagadh

Trains to Rajkot, Ahmedabad and the south coast call at Junagadh. The Down #352 leaves at 6.15am every morning for Sasan Gir (2hr 30min) and Delvada (6hr) for connections to Diu. It's slow, but more comfortable than the bus. Rajkot is best serviced by the Veraval–Rajkot Mail #9837 departing at 5pm. For Ahmedabad the overnight Girnar Express #9945 departing at 9.20pm is the most convenient. There are two morning expresses to Veraval. **Buses** from the long-distance bus stand, just west of Chittakhana Chowk, serve destinations around the state, including hourly services to Diu. Mahasagar Travels (☎0285/262 6085) near the railway station sell tickets for private buses, notably to Mumbai (18hr); they have another office at Kalwa Chowk (☎0285/262 1913). See "Travel details" at the end of this chapter for more information on journey frequencies and durations.

climbs through eucalyptus forests before zigzagging across the sheer rock face, and there's a ready supply of chai and biscuits at stalls along the way.

On a plateau below the summit, roughly ninety minutes' climb from the base of the steps, the picturesque huddle of Jain temples has been slightly renovated since its erection between 1128 and 1500. Neminath, the 22nd *tirthankara* who is said to have died on Mount Girnar after seven hundred years of meditation and asceticism, is depicted as a black figure sitting in the lotus position holding a conch in the marble **Neminath temple**, the first on the left as you enter the "temple city". It's well worth making the effort to climb the final two thousand steps to the summit of Mount Girnar; the views on the way are breathtaking. At the top, a temple dedicated to the Hindu goddess **Amba Mata** attracts both Hindu and Jain pilgrims, particularly newlyweds who come here to be blessed by the mother goddess and to pray for a happy marriage. Steps lead down from this temple and then up again along a narrow ridge towards **Gorakhnath Peak**, where a small shrine covers what are supposedly the footprints of the pilgrim Gorakhnath, and further to a third peak where the imprints of Neminath's feet are sheltered by a small canopy. At the most distant point of the ridge, a shrine dedicated to the fierce Hindu goddess **Kalika**, the eternal aspect of Durga, is a haunt for near-naked **Aghora ascetics** who express their absolute renunciation of the world by ritually enacting their own funerals, living among corpses on burial grounds, and smearing themselves with ash from funeral pyres.

Eating

Kalwa Chowk is the place to head for most of Junagadh's Punjabi and South Indian restaurants and snack stalls, while **Dhal Road** has Gujarati thali restaurants and cheap non-veg *dhabas*.

Amdavad Dhal Rd, just east of Chittakhana Chowk. Limited menu of veg and non-veg favourites (try the chicken tikka) on an airy rooftop. Friendly service and good views of streetlife and tombs.

Geeta Lodge Opposite the railway station. Great-value all-you-can-eat thalis for Rs 50. Open 11am–2.45pm & 6–11pm.

Santoor North of Kalwa Chowk on MG Rd. Delicious, reasonably priced South Indian and Punjabi dishes. Open 9.45am–3pm & 5–11pm.

Taj Dhal Rd, Chittakhana Chowk. A good place for cheap mutton, chicken and fish dishes with books on Gandhi to read while you wait. Open 9am–noon for breakfast, noon–2.30pm & 7–10.30pm for meals.

Veraval and Somnath

On the Saurashtran coast, midway between Porbandar and Diu, the fishing port of **VERAVAL** is the jumping-off point for trips to **Somnath**, 5km east, whose temple is one of the twelve *jyotrilingams* of Shiva (see Contexts). Its shrines to Vishnu and connection with Krishna – who is said to have lived here with the Yadavas during the time of the *Mahabharata* – make it equally important for Vaishnavites.

Veraval practicalities

Veraval's **bus stand** (ⓣ02876/221666) is a ten-minute walk west of town. The town is well connected to Junagadh, Porbandar and Dwarka; local buses also run to Diu, but the service is slow and the roads are rough – consider hiring a taxi. Services to Sasan Gir (1hr) start at 8am and continue every two hours thereafter. Buses to Somnath (every 15–30min) terminate a few hundred metres east of the Shiva temple. **Trains** from Junagadh (2hr), Rajkot (5hr) and Ahmedabad (12hr), pull in at the station (ⓣ02876/220444) just over 1km north of town. For long journeys by train from Veraval it's best to change at Rajkot. The train for Sasan Gir departs at 9am.

Veraval has a wider choice of **accommodation** than Somnath, though the smell and dirt may be enough to dissuade you from staying. *Hotel Kaveri* in Akar Complex on ST Road (ⓣ02876/220842, ⓕ240140; ❷–❹) is the best in town, with clean, comfortable and well-appointed a/c and non-a/c rooms with TV and hot showers. The *Tourist Bungalow* on College Road (ⓣ02876/220488; ❷–❺), on the outskirts near the shore and the lighthouse, offers a dorm (Rs100) and spacious rooms, though the restaurant is pretty barren, failing even to produce bottled water. *Hotel Chirag*, a block south of the main street, 200m east of the bus stand (ⓣ02876/244205; ❷–❸), is also habitable.

Food is unremarkable but easy to come by. The comfortable a/c *Sagar* restaurant, opposite the *Chirag*, provides a varied veg menu of Indian, Chinese and some Continental dishes, while the *Prakash* nearby is popular for Gujarati thalis. Though Veraval is one of the largest fishing ports in India few places in town, except perhaps some of the cheap *dhabas* near the railway station, serve seafood. If you're hankering after a fishy feast, head for the *Park Hotel* (ⓣ02876/242703) on the approach road from Junagadh (Rs25 auto-rickshaws from ST Road), which has veg and non-veg restaurants. Call ahead to get details of the day's fresh catch.

Somnath

SOMNATH consists of only a few streets and a bus stand – even its famed sea-facing **temple** (dawn–dusk; free; photography prohibited) is little to look at, despite its many-layered history. Legend has it that the site, formerly known as **Prabhas Patan**, was dedicated to Soma, the juice of a plant used in rituals and greatly praised for its enlightening powers (and hallucinogenic effects) in the Rig Veda. The temple of Somnath itself is believed to have appeared first in gold, at the behest of the sun god, next in silver, created by the moon god, a third time in wood at the command of Krishna and, finally, in stone, built by Bhimdeva, the strongest of the five Pandava brothers from the *Mahabharata* tale. The earliest definite record, however, dates the temple to the tenth century when it became rich from devotees' donations. Unfortunately, such wealth came to the attention of the brutal iconoclast Mahmud of Ghazni who destroyed the shrine and carried its treasure off to Afghanistan. The next seven centuries saw a cycle of rebuilding and sacking, though the temple lay in ruins for over two hundred years after a final sacking by Aurangzeb before the most recent reconstruction began in 1950. Very little of the original structure remains and, although planned in the style of the Solanki period, the temple is built from unattractive modern stone. It's just possible to imagine its former glory from the height of the pillars supporting the towering *mandapa* and the fervour of the stream of devotees who pray in its airy halls. The main pujas are held at 7am, noon and 7pm. An **architectural museum** (daily except Wed and 2nd & 4th Sat of month, 9am–noon & 3–6pm) north of the temple, contains a hoard of its treasures – statues, lintels, sections of roof pillars, friezes and *toranas* from the tenth to twelfth centuries.

Somnath's new **museum** (daily except Wed and 2nd & 4th Sat of month, 9am–noon & 3–6pm; Rs50), housed inside a hideous pile of concrete across from the bus stand, is loaded up with seaworthy artefacts.

Tongas and rickshaws gather outside the bus station, ready to take pilgrims to **temple sites east of Somnath**. Most important of these is **Triveni Tirth**, at the confluence of the Hiran, Saraswati and Kapil rivers as they flow into the sea: a peaceful place with a couple of unspectacular new temples. Before reaching the confluence, the road passes the ancient **Surya Mandir**, probably built during the Solanki period and now cramped by a newer temple and concrete houses built almost against its walls.

Practicalities

Somnath's best place to **stay** is the modern *Shivam* (☎02876/233086; ❷–❸), tucked away in the side streets near the temple, where you'll get clean rooms with the option of a/c. Competing for second place are the *Mayuram* (☎02876/231286; ❸), southeast of the bus stand, with a Gujarati sign, and *Nandi* (☎02786/231839; ❷–❸) near the architectural museum. The temple trust dishes up good-value veg **thalis** at their simple dining area near the parking lot in front of the temple.

Gir National Park

The **Asiatic lion** which, thanks to hunting, forest-cutting and poaching, has been extinct in the rest of India since the 1880s, now survives in the wild in just 1150 square kilometres of the gently undulating Gir Forest. **Gir National Park** (mid-Oct or Nov to mid-June daily 7–11am & 3–5.30pm), entered from **Sasan Gir**, 60km southeast of Junagadh and 45km northeast of Veraval, holds around 325 Asiatic lions in its 260 square kilometres. They share the land with Maldhari cattle-breeders, whose main source of income is buffalo milk. Many families have been relocated outside the sanctuary, but those who remain are paid compensation by the government for the inevitable loss of buffalo to marauding lions. Gir also shelters two hundred **panthers**, which you are more likely to see here than in any other Indian park.

The best place to get acquainted with the park and its facilities is the well-presented **Gir Orientation Centre**, to the right as you enter the walled-in park headquarters. Across the road, behind the gift shop, **permits** can be obtained at the **park information centre**. Entry is $5, plus $5 extra for a camera. Further, you'll be slapped with a $10 permit for vehicles (good for three days) and a mandatory **guide fee** of $10. You'll need to hire a Jeep, available at the park gates (Rs650/2hr 30min–3hr trip; max 6 passengers). Though sightings are far from certain, the lions are accustomed to human noise, and seem not to be disturbed by Jeeps. Summer is the best time to spot them, when they gather at waterholes to drink. The guides usually know the likely spots and suggest the best routes.

For a guaranteed sighting, head for **Dewaliya** (daily dawn–dusk; $5), a partially fenced-off area of the park known as the Gir Interpretation Zone. Regular Jeeps (Rs200 return) leave from Sasan Gir; once in the centre visitors are driven in a minibus (10am & 3pm) past docile lions. You get a surprisingly

The Asiatic lion

The rare **Asiatic lion** (*panthera leo persica*) is paler and shaggier than the more common African breed, with longer tail tassles, more prominent elbow tufts and a larger belly fold. Probably introduced to India from Persia, the lions were widespread in the Indo-Gangetic plains at the time of the Buddha. In 300 BC Kautilya, the minister of Chandragupta Maurya, offered them protection by declaring certain areas *abharaya aranyas*, "forests free from fear". Later, in his rock-inscribed edicts, **Ashoka** admonished those who hunted the majestic animals – the emblem of Ashoka, printed on all Indian currency notes, shows four Asiatic lions standing back to back.

The Asiatic lion was favourite game for India's nineteenth-century rulers and by 1913, not long after it had been declared a protected species by the Nawab of Junagadh, its population was reduced to twenty. Since then, Gir Forest has been recognized as a sanctuary (1969), and a national park (1975), and their number has swelled to over 325. While this is good news for the lions, they are starting to stray from the sanctuary, and recent attacks on humans and their livestock have caused justifiable concern. If plans to create a new reserve near Porbandar come to fruition, the lions should be assured security in their natural habitat. For more info see Ⓦwww.asiatic-lion.org.

good impression of them "in the wild" here – they still have to hunt their food even if the deer have limited space to escape.

Practicalities

Buses connect Sasan Gir to Junagadh (1hr 30min), Veraval (1hr) and Una (2hr 15min). Trains leave Junagadh at 6.15am, and Veraval at 9.40am. Sasan Gir itself comprises little more than an unfriendly, litter-strewn street fronted by chai stalls and ugly concrete blocks and swarming with touts. Of the **lodges**, the *Anapurna* (Ⓣ02877/285569; ❹) has been reliable, with clean, well-kept rooms, but at the time of writing there is talk of new management taking over, so check it out before committing. The best place to stay near the bus stand is the comfortable, Taj-run *Gir Lodge* (Ⓣ02877/285521, Ⓕ285528; ❾), down a lane to the right of the Orientation Centre and backing onto the park. It has a library and offers occasional evening views of lions drinking at the nearby waterhole. Avoid the Forest Department's mediocre and overpriced *Sinh Sadan Guest House*.

If you have your own vehicle, consider heading out to one of two hotels in the mango orchards around the park. At the sanctuary's Bambaphor Gate, the *Gir Birding Lodge* (Ⓣ079/2630 2019, Ⓔnwsafaris@hotmail.com; ❼) has rooms in a main building and in cottages. There's a natural history library and a friendly naturalist-guide who takes guests for birdwatching walks along the nearby river. The restaurant, overlooking the sanctuary, serves good Indian and Continental food. *Anil Bagh* (Ⓣ02877/285590; ❺), just off the main road from Junagadh, is a farmhouse set in a large mango plantation. The excellent-value rooms are clean and comfortable with hot water, and you can enjoy all-you-can-eat meals in the unpretentious dining room for Rs100. A luxury camp in the same plantation has another, more expensive river-facing restaurant.

Note that high-season (Dec) hotel **prices** can drop by up to seventy percent in the low season (June/July).

Diu

Set a little off the southern tip of Saurashtra, the island of **DIU**, less than 12km long and just 3km wide, was still under Portuguese control only forty years

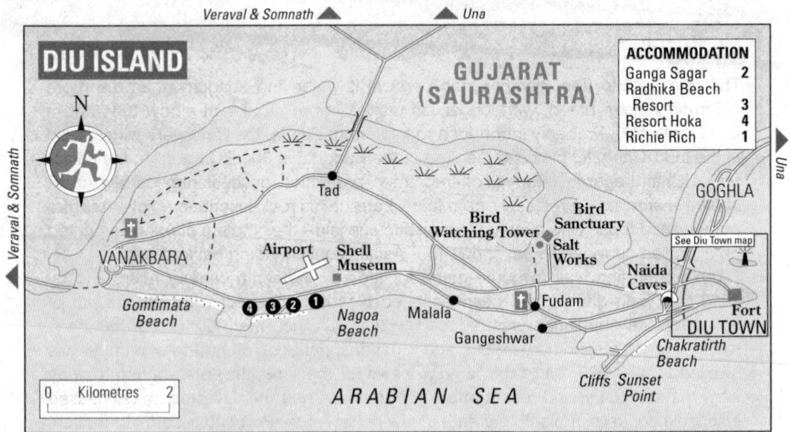

ago. Today, governed along with Daman as a Union Territory from Delhi, it has a relaxed atmosphere quite different from anywhere in central Saurashtra. Though its smallish beaches are nowhere near as idyllic as Goa's, most visitors stay longer than intended, idling in cafés, cycling around the island or strolling along the cliffs. The leisurely pace is also due in part to the lack of alcohol restrictions: the island's many bars can ply you with a vast array of beers and various hard liquors.

The island is easy to explore by bike. **Diu Town** in the east is the focus, where a maze of alleys lined with distinctive Portuguese buildings form the hub of the **old town**, where the **fort** stands on the easternmost tip of the island, looking out into the Gulf of Cambay. Along the northern coast the island's main road runs past salt pans that give way to mud flats sheltering flocks of water birds, including flamingos that stop to feed in early spring. The route skirting the south coast passes rocky cliffs and beaches, the most popular of which is **Nagoa Beach**, before reaching the tiny fishing village of **Vanakbara** in the very west of the island.

Some history

The earliest records of Diu date from 1298, when it was controlled by the Chudasana dynasty. Soon after, like most of Gujarat, it fell into the hands of invading Muslims and by 1349 was ruled by Mohammed bin Tughluq who successfully boosted the shipbuilding industry. Diu prospered as a Gujarati harbour, and in 1510 came under the government of the Ottoman Malik Ayaz, who repelled besieging **Portuguese** forces in 1520 and 1521. Well aware of Diu's strategic position for trade with Arabia and the Persian Gulf, and having already gained a toehold in Daman on the eastern edge of the Gulf of Cambay, the Portuguese did not relent. Under the leadership of **Nuno da Cunha**, they once more tried, but failed, to take the island in 1531. In 1535 Sultan Bahadur of Gujarat agreed to sign a peace accord, but when the two leaders met, Bahadur was murdered and the Portuguese took control of Diu, immediately building the fort and a strong wall around the town.

While local traders and merchants thrived under the new rule, many resented paying taxes to boost Portuguese coffers already full with profits from customs duties levied on all vessels using the port. In defiance, local seamen made a series of unsuccessful raids on Portuguese ships. Moghul and Arab attacks were resisted, too, but the Portuguese were finally forced out in 1961 by the Indian government which, after a swift bombing campaign, declared Diu part of India.

Arrival and information

The usual point of entry to Diu island is by road, via **Goghla**, the small fishing village on the mainland that forms the northern edge of Diu territory. The three hotels here are nothing special and most people head straight on to the island across the new bridge that links it to the northwestern edge of Diu Town. If arriving directly from points west, you may come across the other bridge in the centre of the island.

Buses usually pull in to the stand by the bridge, from where it's less than ten minutes' walk to the town. GSTC operates buses to Ahmedabad (7am & 7pm), Porbandar (1pm), and Veraval (5am & 2.15pm); for Palitana, take the 6.30am bus to Bhavnagar and change at Talaja. A number of private tour operators, including Shivshakti and Swaminarayan, operate more comfortable buses to Bhavnagar, Rajkot, Ahmedabad and Porbandar from the main bus stand. Better transport connections are found on the mainland, at **Una** bus stand and **Delvada** railway station, both of which are connected to Diu by *tempos*, auto-rickshaws and half-hourly buses. Jet Airways (Ⓣ02875/253542) operates a **flight** every day but Saturday to Mumbai ($100) via Porbandar; their office is at the airport.

Panchmurthi Travels (Ⓣ02875/252515) is a reliable agency for booking bus tickets, while convenient air, bus and train **bookings** can be made at Goa Travel (Ⓣ02875/252180). For air tickets you can also contact Oceanic Travels (Ⓣ02875/252180).

Diu's **tourist office** (Mon–Fri 9.30am–1.30pm & 2–6pm, Sat 9.30am–noon; Ⓣ02875/252653, Ⓦwww.diuindia.com), in the port opposite the main square, offers maps of the island but little else. The **GPO** is on the west side of the main square, upstairs, and the State Bank of Saurashtra, near the square, will **exchange money**. Deepak Cyber Café (Rs40/hr), on the main square, is one of several **Internet** access points, as is the A–Z Tourist Centre in the Old Portuguese District, which can set you up with Web access, a moped, bike and car in one fell swoop.

The most common way to get around is by **bike** (Rs40–50/day), which you can rent at shops near the main square or close to the gate on the town's western edge. The *Apana Hotel* (see below) is a good place to ask about **motorbikes** (Rs100/day). Taxis and auto-rickshaws are available, but if you're staying at Nagoa Beach and want to get back from town at night, expect high charges (Rs50).

Accommodation

The atmosphere of Diu's **hotels**, largely concentrated in Diu Town around the central open-air markets and along Fort Road on the northeast coast, is in keeping with the leisurely pace of the island. Nearly all have a restaurant and bar. The price codes below represent high-season **tariffs**; festival periods, particularly Diwali and Holi, can see the prices skyrocket, while in the off-season they can come down by as much as fifty to seventy percent. Some people, especially women, may also be put off at festival times by the rowdy atmosphere, fuelled by the freely available cheap booze.

Diu Town

Ankur Near the western gate Ⓣ02875/252388, Ⓕ253135. Clean and efficient with big airy rooms, but a bit impersonal. ❺–❻

Apana Fort Rd Ⓣ02875/252650, Ⓕ252309. Lively place where attached rooms have cable TV; the most expensive have sea-facing balconies. Tariffs are more than halved in the off-season. ❼

Jay Shankar Jallandhar Beach ☎02875/252424. By far the best budget option, with a friendly atmosphere. The upstairs restaurant is a good place to meet travellers, or to down an excellent bottle of Goan port (R120). ❶–❷

Pensão Beira Mar Fort Rd ☎02875/253031. Recently refurbished colonial mansion that is already peeling. Its six rooms, including two huge corner suites, have a common sea-facing veranda. Management gives lots of discounts. ❻–❼

Samrat Collectorate Rd ☎02875/252354, Ⓕ252754. Diu Town's most upmarket hotel. Comfortable carpeted a/c rooms with cable TV, balconies, bathrooms and constant hot water. ❹–❻

São Tome Retiro St Thomas's Church ☎02875/253137. Only five rooms of vastly different size and quality upstairs at this atmospheric church/museum. Regular barbecue and booze parties in the yard are open to non-guests. ❷–❸

The rest of the island

Ganga Sagar Nagoa Beach ☎02875/252249. Recently refurbished option right on the beach. Comfortable rooms with tile floors, most with ocean views. ❸–❺

Radhika Beach Resort Nagoa Beach ☎02875/252553, Ⓦwww.radhikaresort.com. The island's prime resort. Immaculate a/c deluxe and VIP rooms, quality restaurant, gym and residents-only swimming pool. ❼–❾

Resort Hoka Behind Nagoa Beach ☎02875/253036. The best budget place to stay outside Diu Town. Tasteful, simple rooms in a friendly rural setting. The courtyard restaurant, serving travellers' staples, is a little pricey. ❺

Richie Rich Nagoa Beach ☎02875/255355. New low-rise hotel, with eight comfortable rooms with hot showers. ❻

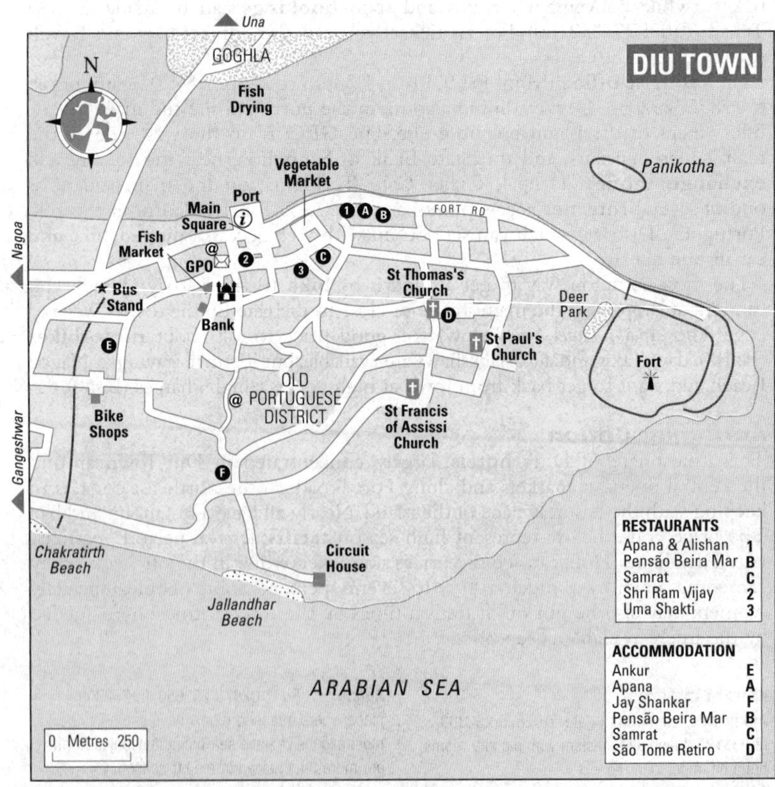

Diu Town

Little **Diu Town** is protected by the fort in the east and a wall in the west. **Nagar Seth's Haveli**, one of the grandest of the town's distinctive Portuguese mansions, is on Makata Road, hidden in the web of narrow streets that wind through the residential Old Portuguese District. Fisherfolk make daily trips from the north coast in wooden boats; women lay the silvery catch out on rugs to sell in the market near the mosque.

Although the Christian population is dwindling along with the old language, a few **churches** built by the former European inhabitants are still used. Portuguese Mass is celebrated beneath the high ceilings and painted arches of **St Paul's**, while the church of **St Thomas**, to the northwest, is now a museum (daily 8am–9pm; free), and that of **St Francis of Assisi**, to the south, is partly occupied by the local hospital.

Diu's serene **fort** (daily 8am–6pm; free) stands robust, resisting the battering of the sea on three sides and sheltering birds, jackals and the town jail. Its wide moat and coastal position enabled the fort to withhold attack by land and sea, but there are obvious scars from the Indian government's air strikes in 1961 – notice the hole above the altar of the church in the southwest corner. Now abandoned almost completely to nature, and littered with centuries-old cannonballs, it commands excellent views out to sea and over the island. Just offshore, the curious, ship-shaped **Panikotha Fort** – connected to the mainland by tunnel, according to lore – is off limits to tourists, but you can hire a fishing boat (Rs60 for up to six people) from the dock to take you over for a closer look.

Around the island

Cliffs and rocky pools make up much of the southern coast of the island, giving way to the occasional sandy stretch. South of Diu Town is an idyllic stretch of sand called **Jallandhar Beach**; the larger **Chakratirth Beach**, overlooked by a high mound, is a little to the west, just outside the city walls. In many ways this is the most attractive beach and it's usually deserted, making it the best option for an undisturbed swim, especially for female travellers. At its western end, **Sunset Point** provides the regular spectacle of a golden disc sinking into the waves. The longest and only developed beach is at **Nagoa**, 7km west of town, where there are four hotels and a restaurant, as well as stalls, camel rides and the like, but sunbathers, especially women, are more likely to get hassled here. Buses leave Diu Town at 8am, 11am and 3.30pm and return from Nagoa at 1pm, 4pm and 6pm. With a vehicle, **Gomtimata Beach**, which is between Nagoa and Vanakbara and invariably deserted, lies within reach. At the end of the road, you can watch day labourers assembling ships by hand at the Vanakbara dockyard.

Not far out of town, a turning off the Nagoa Road leads to **FUDAM**, an attractive village of Portuguese houses washed in pale yellow and sky-grey where a church has been converted into a medical clinic. One small outdoor **bar**, shaded by twisted palm fronds, stands in the centre of the village. Further along the main road, on the right just before the airport, the **Shell Museum** (daily 8.30am–6.30pm; Rs10) is the personal collection – 42 years in the making – of Captain Fulbari, an old sailor who spent a lifetime on the ocean picking up shells wherever he weighed anchor.

Eating

Sadly, the only vestige of Portuguese influence on the dining scene in Diu is the availability of **alcohol**. Most bars close in the afternoon and after 9pm, although restaurants are often open later. Stalls in Diu Town's main square sell snacks all day; look out for the break-dancing, juggling lassi-wallah.

Alishan Fort Rd. Interior design reminiscent of a 1950s diner; the food is veg, meat and fish, with Chinese options.
Apana Fort Rd, aka *The Peacock*. Slightly posher and pricier than the *Alishan* next door, with a pleasant terrace. Good tandoori chicken and lobster is usually available if ordered in advance.
Samrat Collectorate Rd. One of the best hotel restaurants, serving the earliest breakfast in town (7–11am), with pancakes and South Indian featuring on the morning menu. Tasty north Indian dishes in rich sauces and good grilled fish from 12.30-3pm & 6-11pm.
Shri Ram Vijay Just off the main square. Delicious ice creams and shakes.
Uma Shakti Behind the market. Friendly hotel rooftop with copious portions of tasty Indian, Chinese and Western food.

Bhavnagar

The coastal port of **BHAVNAGAR**, founded in 1723 by the Gohil Rajput Bhavsinghji, whose ancestors came to Gujarat from Marwar (Rajasthan) in the thirteenth century, is an important trading centre whose principal export is cotton. With few sights of its own, Bhavnagar does, however, boast a fascinating bazaar in the old city, and is an obvious place to stay for a night or two before heading southwest to the wonderful Jain temples of Palitana. For Gujarati industrialists, it serves as the jumping-off point for the massive and controversial ship-breaking yard at **Alang**, where 20,000 highly paid labourers literally tear ships apart by hand and with explosives. The yard has been strictly off-limits to foreigners since Greenpeace red-flagged it for environmental

damage, toxic spills and hazardous work – all problems tipped off by journalists posing as steel buyers.

Arrival and information

The **airport** is 5km southeast of town; auto-rickshaws into the centre cost Rs35–40. Arriving by **train**, the way into town is straight ahead along Station Road. From the ST **bus stand**, turn right up ST Station Road for the town centre. The State Bank of Saurashtra and the Bank of India have **exchange** facilities; they're on Amba Chowk between the hotels *Shital* and *Vrindavan*. The **GPO** is next to the High Court on High Court Road, with branches just off Station Road a block south of the station, and opposite the southeastern corner of Ganga Jalia Tank. You can rent **bikes** (Rs3/hr) from a shop less than 100m south of the *Mini Hotel* on Station Road. **Internet** access is not widespread but you can surf at Yahoo Cyber Café in Madhav Darshan Shopping Complex (Rs25/hr).

Accommodation

Bhavnagar has a reasonable choice of **places to stay**. There are a few budget hotels near the railway station, which also has retiring rooms; the more upmarket options are in Darbargadh, towards the bus stand, and around the bus stand itself.

Apollo ST Station Rd, opposite the bus stand ⓣ0278/242 5251, ⓕ241 2440. Carpeted clean rooms with TV, some a/c. ❹–❺

Jubilee Opposite Pil Gardens ⓣ0278/243 0045, ⓕ242 1744. Similar to the adjacent *Blue Hill*, but not quite as smart and a little cheaper. ❻–❼

Mini Station Rd ⓣ0278/242 4415, ⓦwww.hotelmini.com. The cheapest option in town offers an unkempt lobby that reflects the state of the rooms. No a/c but some rooms with TV. ❶

Nilambagh Palace ST Station Rd ⓣ0278/242 4241, ⓕ242 8072. The classiest hotel in Bhavnagar, in an old palace set in vast gardens west of the bus stand, with large luxurious rooms. ❼–❾

Satkar Station Rd ⓣ0278/241 4894, ⓕ241 4894. Small well-maintained rooms, all with attached baths, some with cable TV. The best-value place near the railway station. ❸–❹

Sun 'n' Shine ST Station Rd ⓣ0278/251 6131 ⓕ251 6130. Plush new hotel with a fountain in the lobby, well-maintained rooms, a gym and Internet access. Rates include breakfast and free airport transfer. ❻

Vrindavan Darbargadh ⓣ0278/251 8928. Immaculate, unelaborate rooms (some with TV and a/c), set in part of a massive old palace in the town centre. The dorm (Rs50) is the best bet for budget travellers. 24hr checkout. ❷–❸

The Town

The focus of interest in Bhavnagar is the **old city**, its vibrant markets overlooked by delicate wooden balconies and the plush, pillared fronts of former merchants' houses. Local handicrafts to look out for include *bandhani* and the elaborate beadwork characteristic of the region. The marble temple, **Ganga Devi Mandir**, by the Ganga Jalia Tank in the centre of town, has a large dome and intricate latticework on its walls, while the otherwise unspectacular **Takhteshwar temple**, raised on a hill in the south of town, at least affords a good view over the city to the Gulf of Cambay in the east. Southeast of the town centre, on the road to Diamond Chowk, the **Gandhi Smriti Museum** (Mon–Sat 8.30am–12.30pm & 3.30–7pm; free) exhibits old sepia photos of the Mahatma, who studied here at the Shamaldas Arts College & Sir PP Science Institute for some time – a plaque in his honour can be seen in the forecourt of the imposing 1880s building. The **Barton Museum** downstairs (Mon–Sat 9am–1pm & 2-6pm except the 2nd and 4th Saturday of the month; Rs50) haphazardly shows off Buddhist, Jain and

Moving on from Bhavnagar

The usual way to get anywhere from Bhavnagar is by **bus**. Services run from the ST bus stand to Ahmedabad (hourly; 5hr), Mumbai, Bhuj, Rajkot, Junagadh and Veraval, plus Vadodara (8 daily; 6hr) and Surat (5 daily; 9hr). There's no direct service to Diu but five to Una (6hr), where you can pick up buses to Diu every 30min. There are buses to Palitana (every 30min; 1hr 15min) but only two daily services direct to Velavadar (1hr). **Private buses**, operated by firms such as Tanna Travels (☎0278/2425218) at Crescent Circle and any of those on Waghawadi Road, serve destinations instate – a/c buses to Ahmedabad take 3hr 30min. Some pricier sleeper buses (with berths) for longer journeys are available.

The most convenient **train** is the #9271 Bandra–Bhavnagar Express, which leaves at 6.25pm, stopping at Ahmedabad at 11.30pm and goes on to arrive at Mumbai at 10.35am. **Flights** to Mumbai (50min) are operated four days a week by Indian Airlines (northwest of Ganga Jalia Tank; ☎0278/242 6503), Jet Airways (☎0278/220 2004) and Air Deccan (airport; ☎0278/309 1179). Parag Travels (☎0278/251 4700) at Madhav Hill complex near the turn for Takteshwar Temple, Tamboli Travels (☎0278/242 3400) and Tikki Tours and Travels (☎0278/243 1477) in the Prithvi Complex in Kalanala, can arrange flight tickets. See the Travel Details at the end of this chapter for more information on journey frequencies and durations.

Hindu statues, medieval bronzes and Harappan terracottas, farming implements, coins of the princely states of Saurashtra and Kutch, weapons, and a collection of handicrafts from all over India. The **Khadi Gramodyog** shop in the same building has a good selection of Gujarati cotton shirts. Bhavnagar also has a number of impressive buildings – including the government hospital, with its huge domes and arches – commissioned by the maharajas from prominent architects like Sir William Emerson whose works include the Victoria Memorial and Crawford Market in Mumbai.

Eating

Most of Bhavnagar's **restaurants** adjoin the main hotels, and offer local, national and international cuisine; the most upmarket is the *Nilambagh Palace Hotel*. An excellent unnamed place behind Police Chowk on Gandhi Road stays open all day for low-priced local **thalis**, and there are a number of fast food and **snack joints** on Waghawadi Road near Madhav Darshan. At night, foodstalls lining the streets of Godha Circle of Crescent Circle do brisk business in freshly made *dosas* and *iddlis*. Salty nibbles called *ganthias* and *farsans*, and sweets like the famous Bhavnagar *pedas*, can be bought at *Das* on the approach road from Ahmedabad and at *Khattri* on Waghawadi Road.

Blue Hill *Blue Hill Hotel*, opposite Pil Gardens. Two high-standard hotel restaurants: the *Nilgiri*, with Indian, Chinese and Western food; and the slightly cheaper *Gokul*, which serves Gujarati thalis.

Manali *Apollo Hotel*, ST Station Rd. Comfy ground-floor restaurant serving excellent meat, prawn and veg dishes. Sauces are especially rich and tasty. Open 11am–2.30pm & 7–10.30pm.

Mashoor Juice Centre Darbargadh. Excellent range of juices at this corner stall.

Mirch Masala *Jubilee Hotel*, opposite Pil Gardens. Decent pure veg place for Indian and Chinese food on a pleasant terrace. Meals 11am–3pm & 7–11pm, sandwiches round the clock.

Tulsi Kalanala Chowk. Indian, Chinese and a couple of continental dishes, as well as soup and salad. It's a calm, quiet and dimly lit place, providing respite from the noise outside.

Vrindavan *Hotel Vrindavan*, Darbargadh. Good Gujarati thalis in an a/c hall; for snacks ask to see the room service menu. Open 11am–3pm & 7–11pm.

Velavadar Blackbuck National Park

Outside the tiny village of **VELAVADAR**, 65km north of Bhavnagar, the 34-square-kilometre **Blackbuck National Park** (mid-Oct to mid-June) shelters the highest concentration of this Indian antelope anywhere in the country. Prior to Independence their number stood at some 8000, but habitat loss and hunting cut this figure down to 200 by 1966. A sanctuary was set up, which subsequently received full national park status in 1976, and the number of buck is now over 3400. You can see the elegant black-and-white males strutting, chasing and jousting with their magnificent curved horns to define and defend their territories, each accompanied by a group of fawn-coloured hornless females. The park also holds the endangered Indian wolf, *nilgai* antelopes, jackal foxes and jungle cats, as well as Indian fox along the periphery. Birdwatchers can spot rare species like the Stoicka's bushchat and a large roost of harrier-hawks.

There are no Jeeps available for hire on site, so it's best to have your own vehicle (a **taxi** costs Rs1000 for a day trip from Bhavnagar). If you arrive by bus, it is possible to walk to one of the watchtowers near the entrance and get a good view, but it's not the same. Two daily **buses** travel from Bhavnagar to Velavadar (2pm & 3.30pm; 1hr), returning the following day at 6am and 6.30am. The best time for wildlife viewing is dawn and dusk.

The park's 23-kilometre western **access road** runs via Velabhipur (on the Ahmedabad road); while its ten-kilometre eastern access road is via the tiny truck stop called Adelhai (on the road to Vadodara). **Entry** to the park is $5, plus $4 per vehicle and $5 for a still camera. On top of this you are required to take a **guide** ($10/4hr, $5 each additional hour), though none speak English and most of them are in a hurry to get back to the entrance post; their primary role is to ensure that you don't litter. Since the earthquake a crop of expensive new **cottages** (non-a/c and a/c rooms ❺–❽; tents $10, dorms $5) have emerged near the park gate; they're not very good value, but unfortunately there are no inexpensive alternatives. The food served here is likewise expensive, but it's your only option. For more **information**, contact Bhavnagar's Forest Office (Mon–Sat 10.30am–6pm, closed 2nd & 4th Sat of month; ⓣ0278/242 6425), in the cream-and-brown concrete Bahumaliya Multi-Storey Building, Annexe F/10, just west of the bus stand, or call the park directly (ⓣ0278/288 0342). Reservations are recommended.

Shatrunjaya and Palitana

For many visitors, the highlight of a trip to Saurashtra is a climb up the holy hill of **Shatrunjaya** (dawn to dusk), India's principal Jain pilgrimage site, just outside the dull town of **PALITANA**, 50km southwest of Bhavnagar. More than nine hundred temples – many made of marble – crown this hill, said in legend to be a chunk of the mighty Himalayas from where the Jains' first *tirthankara*, Adinath, and his chief disciple gained enlightenment. While records show that the hill was a *tirtha* as far back as the fifth century, the existing temples date only from the sixteenth century, anything earlier having been lost in the Muslim raids of the 1500s and 1600s.

Climbing the wide steps up Shatrunjaya takes one to two hours, depending on weather conditions and fitness, though, as with all hilltop pilgrimage centres, *dholis* (seats on poles held by four bearers) are available for those who can't make it under their own steam. The view as you ascend is magnificent; spires and towers swoop upwards, hemmed in by mighty protective walls. You should allow at least two more hours to see even a fraction of the temples. Just before entering the main courtyard, by the shoe racks, you'll come to an office selling **photography permits** (Rs40). If you intend taking photos, buy one and be prepared to flash it at any guard; violators will have their film promptly ripped out from their camera.

The individual *tuks* – temple enclosures – are named after the merchants who funded them. Together they create a formidable city, laid over the two summits and fortified by thick walls. Each *tuk* comprises courtyards within courtyards chequered in black-and-white marble and several temples whose walls are exquisitely and profusely carved with saints, birds, animals, buxom maidens, musicians and dancers. Many are two or even three storeys high, with balconies crowned by perfectly proportioned pavilions. The *shikharas* (spires) are hollow on the inside, their conical ceilings swarming with carved figures that flow in concentric circles outwards from a central lotus blossom. The largest temple, dedicated to Adinath, in the Khartaravasi *tuk* on the northern ridge is usually full of masked Svetambara nuns and monks, dressed in white and carrying white fly-whisks. The southern ridge and the spectacular Adishvara temple in its western corner are reached by taking the right-hand fork at the top of the path. On a clear day the view from the summit takes in the Gulf of Cambay to the south, Bhavnagar to the north and the mountain range which includes Mount Girnar to the west.

The **museum** (daily 8am–noon & 4pm–8.30pm; Rs5), located 400m before the start of the steps at the bottom of the hill, displays a collection of Jain artefacts, labelled in Gujarati but well worth seeing.

A path leads along the ridge and down into the valley of Adipur, 13km away; it's open for one day only, during the festival of **Suth Tera** (Feb/March), when up to 50,000 pilgrims come to Shatrunjaya for this unique display of devotion.

Practicalities

Buses to Palitana depart from Bhavnagar (hourly; 1hr–1hr 30min), Junagadh (2 daily; 6hr) and Una (1 daily; 5hr). Auto-rickshaws (Rs30) and tongas run from Palitana to the foot of Shatrunjaya (10min).

There is no **accommodation** on Shatrunjaya, so you'll have to stay in Palitana, either at one of many Jain *dharamshalas* in the old part of town (all of which oblige guests to observe strict vegetarianism) or in one of the hotels on the bus stand side of town. The comfortable GTDC *Hotel Sumeru* (Ⓣ02848/252327; ❸–❹), on Station Road between the bus stand and the railway station, has ordinary and a/c rooms and dorms (Rs75); its restaurant serves lunchtime thalis and excellent pasta. *Hotel Shavrak* (Ⓣ02848/252428; ❷–❸), opposite the bus stand, is adequate, though less spacious; it also has inexpensive men-only dorms (Rs50). *Vijay Vilas Palace Hotel* (Ⓣ02848/282371, Ⓔssibal@ad1.vsnl.net.in; ❽) at Adpur, 4km from the bus station, is a good alternative for those who have a bit of cash and their own vehicle (an auto-rickshaw costs Rs50 one way). This converted 1906 European-style palace guesthouse is run by Yashpal, great-grandson of Prince Vijay Singh of Palitana who built it, and his wife. The rooms boast four-posters, old dressers and other early-twentieth century paraphernalia, and delicious home-cooked Indian food is on offer.

For **food** outside the hotels, head for the narrow alley next to *Hotel Shavrak*, where the basic, busy and very cheap *Jagruti Restaurant* serves excellent Gujarati meals and snacks.

Southeastern Gujarat

The seldom-visited **southeastern** corner of Gujarat, sandwiched between Maharashtra and the Arabian Sea, harbours few attractions to entice you off the road or railway line to or from Mumbai. There's little to recommend **Vadodara** (Baroda), former capital of the Gaekwad rajas, other than its proximity to the old Muslim town of **Champaner** and the ruined forts and exotic Jain and Hindu temples that encrust **Pavagadh Hill**. Further south, dairy pastures gradually give way to a swampy, malaria-infested coastal strip of banana plantations and shimmering saltpans cut by silty, sinuous rivers. The area's largest city is **Surat**, a sprawling modern industrial centre sporting a handful of colonial monuments. The only place of real interest in the far south of the state is the former Portuguese territory of **Daman**. Although nowhere near as appealing as its colonial cousins Goa and Diu, the 12km-long enclave, whose main *raison d'être* is as a watering hole for alcohol-starved Gujarati men, does boast some impressive colonial architecture.

The west coast's main **transport** arteries, the NH-8 and Western Railway, run in tandem between Mumbai and Ahmedabad. The train is always more comfortable, especially between Ahmedabad and Vadodara, where the undivided highway is one of the most nail-bitingly terrifying roads in India.

Vadodara (Baroda)

The area between Ahmedabad and **VADODARA** (or Baroda) is primarily agricultural, but Vadodara itself is a congested industrial city with few tourist attractions. However, its old core does retain some interest, with beautiful *havelis* and traditional bazaars, and the city does make the most convenient place to stay for a trip to the ruined city of **Champaner**. If you are here at the time of the **Navratri** festival (late Sept/early Oct), you can join the throngs watching thousands of colourfully dressed women, men and children dancing into the small hours.

Arrival and information

The **railway station** and **bus stand** are very close together in the west of town, within easy walking distance of almost all the hotels. The airport is 6km northeast, or about Rs25 away by auto-rickshaw. **Gujarat Tourism** (Mon–Sat 10.30am–6pm, closed 2nd and 4th Sat of month; ⓣ0265/242 7487 to 7489) is a couple of kilometres from the station at C-Block, Ground floor, Narmada Bhavan, Jail Road. In addition, the Vadodara Municipal Corporation runs a tourist desk (Mon–Sat 11am–5pm; ⓣ0265/279 4456), across from the railway station near Yogikrupa Travel Service; ask about city tours. Sterling and dollars cash or **travellers' cheques** can be changed at the Bank of Baroda international services branch in Sayaji Gunj behind Kadak Bazaar (Mon–Fri 11am–3pm), the Bank of South India opposite, or the State Bank of India on RC Dutt (Racecourse) Road between the *Green* and *Welcomgroup* hotels. The Trade Wings agency behind *Hotel Amity* in Sayaji Gunj also runs an efficient exchange service and is open later than the banks. The **GPO** is off Raopura Road in the centre of town. The best **bookstore** is Crossword at Annapurna Society in Alkapuri, west of town, and there is a small selection at Book World near Sardar Patel statue. There's an abundance of **cyber cafés** around Sayaji Gunj; Jal Cybercafe (Rs25/hr) at *Hotel Jaldarshan* is open 24 hours.

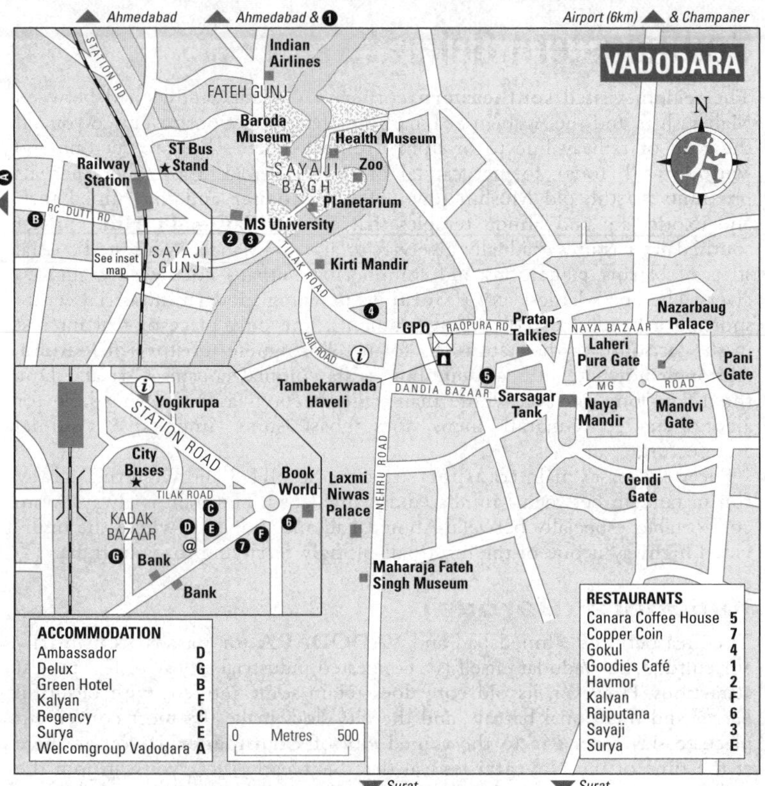

Accommodation

Vadodara's **hotels** are designed with business visitors in mind: there are several mid-range and upmarket places, and just a handful of inexpensive lodges which could all do with improved maintenance. Most of the hotels are grouped in the **Sayaji Gunj** area just south of the railway station.

Ambassador Sayaji Gunj ⓣ0265/236 2726, ⓕ236 2726. Slightly grubby but spacious rooms with TV and bath. ❸

Delux Kadak Bazaar ⓣ0265/236 2533. It hardly lives up to its name, but this small clean hotel in the heart of a lively bazaar is friendly. ❷

Green Hotel RC Dutt (Racecourse) Rd ⓣ0265/233 6111. The best low-budget option, five minutes' walk from the station. The 100-year-old house has rooms (some with TV and phone) with period furniture and character. ❷–❸

Kalyan Sayaji Gunj ⓣ0265/236 2211. Clean, efficient hotel, with reasonably priced well-furnished rooms. ❸–❹

Regency Sayaji Gunj ⓣ0265/236 1616, ⓕ236 3050. Smart, modern multi-storey with all facilities and 24hr check-out. Good value for its price range. ❺–❻

Surya Sayaji Gunj ⓣ0265/236 1361, ⓦwww.hotelsurya.com. Smart, spacious rooms with complimentary breakfast and free Internet access. ❺–❼

Welcomgroup Vadodara RC Dutt (Racecourse) Rd ⓣ0265/233 0033, ⓕ233 0050. Baroda's only five-star hotel, with predictably swanky and well-maintained rooms ($60–135) plus all services. ❾

The City

Vadodara's chief attractions are in **Sayaji Bagh**, a large green park that holds a number of museums, the planetarium, zoo and a vintage toy train; the main entrance is on Tilak Road. Leave yourself one or two hours to get round the large Indo-Saracenic **Baroda Museum and Picture Gallery** (daily 10.30am–5.30pm; Rs10), reached from University Road, which holds art and textiles from all over the world, Gujarati archeological remains and Moghul miniatures.

From Sayaji Bagh, Tilak Road continues east across the river past **Kirti Mandir** (the mausoleum of Vadodara's rulers) towards the old city, the centre of which is MG Road, bounded at its western end by **Laheri Pura Gate** and **Naya Mandir** (literally "New Temple"), a fine Indo-Saracenic building which is now a law court. There's another gate (Pani Gate) at the eastern end of MG Road, near the late nineteenth-century **Nazarbaug Palace** and, halfway between the two, the four-way **Mandvi Gate**, originally Moghul but much altered since. To the west of MG Road is an artificial lake, the **Sarsagar Tank** (check out Pratap Talkies, an over-the-top Art Deco theatre at the northeastern corner), surrounded by glorious painted *havelis* and with a huge modern statue of Shiva in the middle. Other buildings worth a look include **Laxmi Niwas Palace** in the south of town, the most extravagant ofVadodara's palaces. If you wish to tour the palace's impressive Durbar Hall, armoury and palm-filled mosaic courtyards (Rs100), head to the **Maharaja Fateh Singh Museum** (Tues–Sun 10.30am–5.30pm; Rs15) in the palace grounds; the museum itself holds a range of Japanese, Chinese, Indian and European arts collected by the Maharajas.

Eating

With a large student population and a constant influx of business people, Vadodara has a choice of **restaurants** in all price ranges. Several upmarket hotels lay on buffet spreads; fast food, snack joints, ice cream parlours and juice centres are dotted all around Sayaji Gunj and the studenty Fateh Gunj area. The cheapest places to eat are in the market and shopping centres

Moving on from Vadodara

Vadodara **railway station** is often crowded and queues for tickets can be long (the reservation office is upstairs); you can bypass the hassle for a Rs15–25 fee if you buy your ticket from Yogikrupa Travel Service opposite (daily 8.30am–8.30pm; ⓣ0265/279 4977). All trains travelling along the main Delhi–Mumbai line stop here. The fastest and most convenient train heading north is the daily Rajdhani Express #2951, serving Kota (6hr 30min) and New Delhi (12hr; overnight), while the other superfast Shatabdi Express #2009/2010 serves Ahmedabad (1hr 55min), Surat (1hr 50min) and Mumbai Central (5hr 30min) daily except Friday.

The **bus stand** on Station Road, a little north, has regular, state-run services to other Gujarati towns, including Champaner (hourly; 1hr 30min). Mumbai (14hr) is served by eight buses, all in the evening, but none start at Vadodara, so they may be full when they arrive – the train is far better. Stalls selling tickets for **private buses** (to Mumbai, Rajasthan and Madhya Pradesh) line Station Road.

Jet, Indian Airlines and Air Deccan **fly** daily to Mumbai (55min) and Delhi (1hr 25min). The IA office is in Fateh Gunj, just north of Sayaji Bagh (ⓣ0265/279 4747). Jet Airways (ⓣ0265/234 3441) is opposite *Welcomgroup Vadodara* on RC Dutt (Racecourse) Road. See "Travel details" at the end of this chapter for more information on journey frequencies and durations.

opposite Sar Sagar tank, along Dandia Bazaar and at the *dhabas* near the railway station.

Canara Coffee House Dandia Bazaar. Pukka coffee – a rarity in north India – and South Indian snacks at very low prices; a good place for breakfast.
Copper Coin World Trade Centre, Sayaji Gunj. Good, though not cheap, variety of veg and non-veg food in an octagonal a/c room with piped muzak.
Gokul Koti Char Rasta. Small snack bar serving excellent South Indian, Punjabi and Gujarati thalis, and ice cream at very low prices.
Goodies Cafe Fateh Gunj. Lively, well-lit café with Indian and Western main courses, snacks and great desserts. It also has takeways and a very large selection of cakes and puddings.
Havmor Tilak Rd. Tasty but fairly pricey Indian, Chinese and Western food with a/c and good service. Try the Havmor Platter – tandoori prawns, fish tikka, chicken tikka and mutton kebabs – with *rumali roti*, the koftas in rich Indian sauces, or the mixed grill sizzler. There is also an ice cream and juice centre facing the main road outside.
Kalyan Hotel Sayaji Gunj. Reasonably priced veg canteen extremely popular with students, and a coffee shop specializing in Mexican snacks, Chinese food and pizza.
Rajputana Sayaji Gunj. A busy pure-veg Kutch/Rajasthani restaurant that locals report serves the best food in town.
Sayaji *Hotel Sayaji* Sayaji Gunj. The rootop restaurant of this multi-storey hotel has one of the best lunch buffets in Baroda.
Surya Sayaji Gunj. Two good moderately priced veg restaurants: the *Vega*, offering filling lunch buffets with dishes from all over the world; and the cheaper *Myra*, with delicious Gujarati thalis.

Pavagadh and Champaner

The hill of Pavagadh, 45km northeast of Vadodara, rises 820m above the plains, overlooking the almost forgotten **Muslim city** of **CHAMPANER**, now a World Heritage Site. Champaner today has a strange, time-warped atmosphere. The massive city walls with inscribed gateways still stand, encompassing several houses, exquisite mosques and Muslim funerary monuments, as well as newer Jain *dharamshalas* to accommodate and feed pilgrims visiting Pavagadh. The largest mosque, the exuberant **Jami Masjid**, is east of the walls. Towering *minars* stand either side of the main entrance, and the prayer halls are dissected by almost two hundred pillars supporting a splendid carved roof raised in a series of domes. The **entry fee** is Rs100; save your ticket, as it's also good for the **Shahr-ki Matchi temple**, located inside the city wall near the bus stand.

For **Pavagadh**, take a Jeep from Champaner, or walk up the path that ascends through battered gates and past the old walls of the Chauhan Rajput fortress to a mid-point where you can get snacks, souvenirs and chai. From here you can proceed by ropeway (Rs30 one way, Rs45 return; 7min; last ride 4.45pm; services were curtailed at the time of writing after a major accident), or on foot up a well-trodden path, to the summit. On top of the hill a number of Jain temples lie below a Hindu temple dedicated to Mataji, which has a shrine to the Muslim saint Sadan Shah on its roof. The view stretches for miles over the patchwork plains of south Gujarat; you can spot the concrete barricades being built along the Narmada canal.

While the view is Pavagadh's top draw, in fact the most interesting part of the area is the ruined **fort**, located across the road from the main bus stand. In 1297 the Chauhan Rajputs made Pavagadh their stronghold, and fended off three attacks by the Muslims before eventually losing to Mohammed Begada in 1484. All the women and children committed *johar* (ritual suicide by self immolation) and the men who survived the battle were slain when they refused to embrace Islam. After his conquest, Mohammed Begada set to work on Champaner, which took 23 years to build. The town was the political capital of Gujarat until the death of Bahadur Shah in 1536, when the courts moved to Ahmedabad and Champaner fell into decline.

Buses from Vadodara leave hourly (via Halol; 1hr 30min) for Champaner. There's also a direct service from Ahmedabad every three hours. Finding a shared taxi for the ride back isn't too tough. The state-owned *Hotel Champaner* (☎02676/245667; ❷–❺), halfway up Pavagadh, has a dorm (Rs75) and adequate **rooms** with magnificent views over the vast plains of south Gujarat. The **restaurant** serves veg thalis.

Surat

Packed around a tight bend in the River Tapti, 19km before it dumps its silty waters into the Gulf of Cambay, sprawling **SURAT** was the west coast's principal port before the meteoric rise of Bombay. These days, it is one of India's fastest growing industrial centres, of real interest only to colonial history buffs, who come to inspect what few vestiges remain of the East India Company's first foothold on the subcontinent as well as some relics of Dutch and Portuguese settlers in the city before it fell to the British.

The **British** took control of what was then a minor trading post, which had been repeatedly plundered by their Portuguese rivals before being taken by Akbar, early in the seventeenth century. It might eventually have become west India's number one port had not the town ranged around it been devastated by fire and floods in 1837, forcing its Jain and Parsi merchants south to Bombay. Surat recovered from the ensuing decline to become one of Gujarat's major cities of the 1980s, thanks to help from a booming textile, chemical and diamond-cutting businesses – the latter a legacy of old Dutch tradelinks.

Arrival, information and accommodation

Surat has very good **train and bus** connections; both stations are on the eastern edge of the city centre. Private buses dump you about 50m from the railway station. The easiest way to **get around** town is to use auto-rickshaws. GTDC's **tourist office** (Mon–Sat 10.30am–6pm, closed 2nd & 4th Sat of month; ☎0261/347 6586), which can arrange visits to diamond-cutting workshops, is hidden away at 1/847 Athugar St in Nanpura. A Rs25 auto-rickshaw ride from the railway station takes you 4km up the Ring Road to the riverbank, from where you eventually curve left towards the tourist office; the State Bank of India is in the same street.

Although you are unlikely to choose to stay in Surat, there are plenty of **hotels** near the station (many of them in Sufi Baug, the street running straight ahead opposite the entrance). Surat is a major hub for business travellers and finding a room can be hard on weekdays, so phone ahead.

Hotels

Diamond Plaza 6/3014 Unapani Rd ☎0261/741 4061, Ⓕ741 3906. Five minutes' walk from the station, one block behind the main road at the far end of Sufi Baug, this spotless hotel provides compact well-furnished rooms with phone and TV. ❸–❹

Embassy To the right of Sufi Baug ☎0261/744 3170, Ⓕ744 3173. Stylish three-star, carpeted throughout, with a/c, bathtubs and "ozonated water around the clock". The best in its bracket. ❺–❼

Hospice Khand Bazaar near the railway station ☎0261/254 2424, Ⓕ0261/254 8484. Friendly, welcoming high-rise hotel with clean, comfortable rooms with cable TV and attached bathroom with hot water. ❸–❹

Omkar and **Vaibhav** Eighth Floor, Omkar Chambers, Sufi Baug, opposite the station ☎0261/741 9329. Two hotels with identical prices and a shared reception (with handy train timetable), attached or shared shower-toilets, room-service tea, lots of coming and going, great if not exactly picturesque views and optional Star TV. A good budget deal. ❶–❷

The Town

Surat's two main sights can be seen in an hour if you take an auto-rickshaw between them. Start at **Chowk**, the busy riverside intersection at the foot of Nehru Bridge, where the **castle** is the city's oldest surviving monument. Erected in 1540 by the Sultan of Gujarat, it was occupied by the Moghuls and British but these days houses government offices. You can wander in and scale the ramparts, from where there are views upriver, over the old walled town to the east and across the square with its many colonial buildings. The other historic remnant of note lies fifteen minutes northeast across town beside Kataragama Road, beyond the fortified gateway of the same name. Hemmed in by modern blocks of flats, the domed mausolea of the weed-choked **English cemetery** could easily be mistaken for an oriental tomb garden. Its most impressive sepulchre is that of General Oxinden, who defeated the Marathas. Another – that of the factor Francis Breton, at the time the East India Company's most senior representative in India – was admired by the architect John Vanbrugh when he was a young factor in Surat, and is believed to have inspired his famous domed mausolea at British country seats such as Castle Howard and Blenheim.

Eating

The station area is overloaded with **restaurants** and some excellent **drink stalls** selling juice, milkshakes and ice cream. Most of the big hotels have quality restaurants; try the *Mossam* in the *Hotel Yuvraj* near the station or *Copper Chimney* at *Lords Park Inn* on the Ring Road. *Sheer-e-Punjab*, below Omkar Chambers near the station, is one of the best non-veg options in town. Surat is known for its local shortbread cookies called *nankatai*; they're available at *Mazda* in the Lalgate area and *Dotiwala* at Nanpura, while local sweets like *ghari* are available at *Mohan-ni-Mathi* near the railway station.

Daman

Ask any Gujarati what they know about **DAMAN** and they'll probably say "liquor". As a Union Territory, independent of the dry state that surrounds it, Daman has liberal licensing laws and low duty on booze, making it something of a target at weekends for busloads of Gujarati men who drink themselves senseless and stagger around the main street. The rest of the time Daman is quieter, but disappointing on the whole, with a rather forlorn feel and a couple of uninspiring beaches. It does, however, offer excellent **seafood** and some immaculately preserved **Portuguese churches**, **houses** and **forts**.

Straddling the mouth of the **Damanganga River**, which rises in the Sahyadri Range on the Deccan plateau, Daman made an obvious target for the Portuguese, who took it in 1531 from the Sultan of Gujarat's Ethiopian governor, Siddu Bapita. The governor of Goa, Dom Constantino de Bragança, cajoled the Sultan of Gujarat into ceding the territory 28 years later, after which it became the hub of the Portuguese trans-Arabian Sea trade with East Africa. The town's economic decline was precipitated by the British occupation of Sind in the 1830s, which effectively strangled its **opium** business. Colonial rule, however, survived until 1961 when Nehru lost patience with Portuguese refusal to negotiate a peaceful handover and sent in the troops.

Today Daman is administered from New Delhi as a Union Territory, along with the nearby ex-Portuguese colonies of Diu, and Dadra and Nagar Haveli.

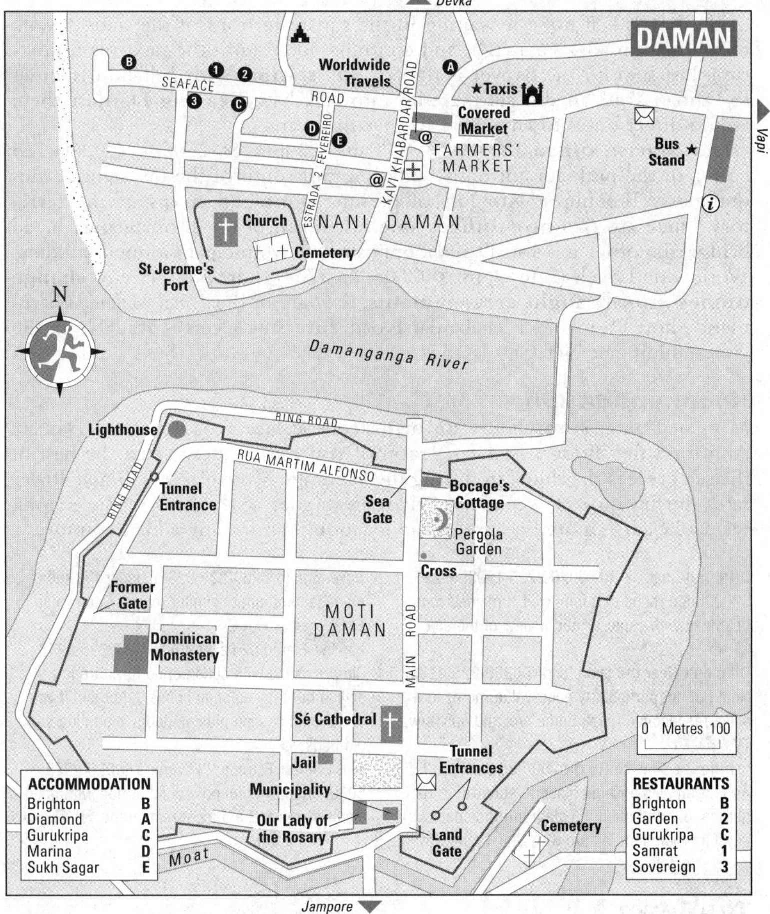

Apart from alcohol production and sales, its chief sources of income are coconuts, salt production and smuggling. In recent years, the local tourist office has also been trying to promote the area as a mini-Goa. Don't be taken in – the unbroken stretch of palm-fringed sand that runs along its twelve-kilometre coastline may look idyllic in the brochures, but is in fact rather grubby and subject to massive tides.

The town of Daman is made up of two separate districts. On the north side of the Damanganga River is **Nani** ("Little") **Daman**, where you'll find most of the hotels, restaurants, bars and markets; **Moti** ("Great") **Daman**, the old Portuguese quarter, lies to the south, its Baroque churches and Latinate mansions encircled by imposing stone battlements.

Arrival and information

The nearest **railhead** to Daman is 12km east at **Vapi** (check when you book that your train stops here). Shared Ambassador **taxis** charging Rs10 per head to Daman will drop you on Seaface Road, a five-minute walk east from most of the hotels – if none is waiting in the square in front of the station, walk to the main road, take a right and continue 500m until the next main junction. Just beyond the flyover is the ST **bus station**, with half-hourly buses to Daman. You can also get there by auto-rickshaw. **Leaving Daman**, there are no direct buses to anywhere further than Vapi.

The **tourist office** (Mon–Fri 9.30am–1.30pm & 2–6pm; ⓣ0260/225 5104), in the pink administrative building just south of the bus stand, hands out glossy brochures with lots of gushing prose and **maps** of the territory. There are two **post offices**: one just north of the Damanganga Road bridge, the other in Moti Daman, opposite the Municipal Council building. Worldwide Travels (9am–9pm; ⓣ0260/225 5734) is the best place to **change money** or make **flight arrangements**; they are in the *Hotel Maharaja* basement, Shop 11, on Kavi Khabardar Road. **Internet** access is available in the same building at Net City (Rs35/hr).

Accommodation

Most of Daman's **hotels** are on or just off Seaface Road in Nani Daman. Aim for a first floor west-facing room if you can, as these catch the best of the sea breezes that blow in during the evenings. Most places will give lower rates during quieter weekdays. Prices are higher at the resort hotels along Devka beach – more because of the location than for any added comfort.

Brighton Seaface Rd ⓣ0260/225 1208, ⓕ225 5209. Good range of comfy well-furnished rooms, nearly all with cable TV and a view of the sea. ❹–❻

Diamond Near the taxi stand ⓣ0260/225 4235. Neat but not particularly good-value rooms in a solid, respectable hotel. Some a/c, and only b/w TVs. ❹–❻

Gurukripa Seaface Rd ⓣ0260/225 5046, ⓕ225 4433. Daman's poshest place to stay with a roof garden, bar and quality restaurant; the spacious en-suite rooms are all a/c with Star TV. Nearby *Sovereign* (ⓣ0260/225 0236), under the same management, offers similar rooms. Good value. ❺–❻

Marina Estrada 2 Fevereiro ⓣ0260/225 5945. Simple rooms with solid period furniture in a stylish but tatty colonial house. A bargain if you don't mind peeling plaster, dodgy plumbing and old beds. ❷

Sukh Sagar Estrada 2 Fevereiro ⓣ0260/225 5089. Friendly hotel on a quiet street, with good clean rooms and a decent restaurant. ❷–❸

The Town

Most of the action in **Nani Daman** centres on **Seaface Road**, which runs west from the market past rows of hotels, seedy bars and IMFL (Indian Made Foreign Liquor) stores to the **beach**. Too polluted for a comfortable swim or sunbathe, Daman's dismal strand is only worth visiting around sunset. South across town, the **riverfront** area is dominated by fishing trawlers and markets. The ramparts of **St Jerome's Fort**, directly behind the quay, make a good place from which to survey the activity. Erected in the early seventeenth century to counter the threat of Moghul invasion, the citadel encircles a small *maidan*, a Catholic church and a well-kept walled Portuguese cemetery.

The town's most impressive monuments lie across the river in the leafy colonial compound of **Moti Daman**, 2km south of Seaface Road. Inside its hefty walls, elegant double-storeyed mansions with sweeping staircases, wooden shutters, verandas and colour-washed facades overlook leafy courtyards. Now used as government offices, these residences were originally the homes of Portuguese nobles or *fidalgos* – the only people allowed to live inside the fort.

Moti Daman's highlights are its **churches**, which rank among the oldest and best-preserved Christian monuments in Asia. Grandest of all is the **cathedral** (Church of Bom Jesus) on the main square. Built in 1603, its gigantic gabled Baroque facade opens onto a lofty vaulted hall. On the opposite side of the square, the **Church of Our Lady of the Rosary** is crammed with ornate woodwork, notably some fine tableaux of the life of Jesus by the altar.

Main Road links Moti Daman's two **gates**, which were installed in the 1580s following a Moghul invasion. A small cottage next to the northern ("sea") gate was once the home of the eighteenth-century Portuguese poet Bocage, while atop the bastion facing the southern ("land") gate is the cell where prisoners condemned to death in Portuguese times spent their final days. The windowless dungeons used by the Inquisition were located in chambers beneath. A vivid account of the appalling conditions in which those interred in them were kept has been preserved in the chronicle of **Charles Dellon**, an unfortunate young French physician who found himself at the mercy of the Inquisition in 1673 after the governor suspected him of having an affair with his wife. Dellon recalls how rather than endure the squalour, forty Malabar pirates hanged themselves with their own turbans. Transferred to Goa, the Frenchman survived three more years in solitary confinement before being released as a galley slave. His account of the ordeal, published in 1687 and an international bestseller in its day, remains one of the most harrowing accounts of captivity ever written.

Eating and drinking

The disproportionately large number of **places to eat** in Daman is due to the town's liquor laws, which oblige all bars to serve food with alcohol. Most of the "bar-restaurants" along Seaface Road are restaurants in name only, and best avoided. **Seafood**, on offer all year except during the monsoons, is especially good from late September to early November, when the fish market is glutted with fresh crabs, prawns and lobsters. Also seasonal is *papri*, a street snack consisting of beans baked in a pot with potatoes, sold with a special masala between January and April.

Brighton Seaface Rd. Comfortable a/c multi-cuisine restaurant, serving veg and non-veg specialities and filling set breakfasts.

Garden Seaface Rd. A bar with a large terrace out back, serving reasonably priced tandoori pomfret and lobster, as well as Goan and Damanese meat and veg specialities. Open 11am–3pm & 6–11pm.

Gurukripa Seaface Rd. The place for a slap-up meal, serving veg and non-veg tandoori, seafood, pomfret stuffed with prawns, fish curries, Chinese dishes and Goan *fenni* (coconut spirit) nips.

Samrat Seaface Rd. Spotless roadside restaurant that specializes in inexpensive, eat-till-you-burst Gujarati thalis that come with *namkeens* (salty titbits), a couple of different dhals, and mouth-watering mild veg dishes. Strictly "pure-veg" (read "no alcohol") and excellent value. Open 11am–4pm & 7–11pm.

Sovereign Seaface Rd. South Indian snacks, side dishes and beers served indoors or alfresco on a breezy balcony done up like a Gujarati village. Open 6.30–10pm only.

Travel details

Trains

Ahmedabad to: Abu Rd (7 daily; 3hr 30min–4hr 30min); Ajmer (4 daily; 7hr 5min–10hr 55min); Bangalore (6 weekly; 35hr 55min–37hr 40min); Bhavnagar (2 daily; 3hr 30min–7hr); Chennai (1 daily; 37hr 30min); Delhi (2 daily; 14hr 15min–33hr 35min); Dwarka (1 daily; 10hr 50min); Jaipur (3 daily; 9hr 5min–13hr 30min); Jamnagar (4 daily; 7hr); Jodhpur (2 daily; 9hr 5min–9hr 55min); Junagadh (1 daily, 2 nightly; 8hr 20min–9hr 55min); Kolkata (Calcutta: 1 daily; 44hr 10min); Mumbai (4 daily, 6 nightly; 7hr 10min–12hr 20min); Porbandar (1 daily; 10hr 25min); Rajkot (5–6 daily; 4hr 5min–5hr 35min); Surat (11–14 daily; 3hr 30min–4hr 30min); Thiruvananthapuram (2 weekly; 42hr 25min); Udaipur (2 daily; 8hr 45min); Vadodara (14–17 daily; 1hr 35min–2hr 25min); Varanasi (3 weekly; 41hr 40min); Veraval (3 nightly; 10hr 25min–12hr 5min).

Bhavnagar to: Ahmedabad (3 daily; 3hr 30min–7hr 5min); Veraval (1 daily, 9hr).

Dwarka to: Ahmedabad (1–2 daily; 10hr 40min); Jamnagar (2–3 daily; 2hr 20min–4hr 40min); Mumbai (1 daily; 20hr 25min); Rajkot (3–4 daily; 4hr 50min–7hr 30min).

Junagadh to: Ahmedabad (1 daily; 9hr 25min); Diu/Delvada (1 daily; 6hr); Rajkot (3 daily; 3hr 20min–5hr); Sasan Gir (1 daily; 2hr 30min); Veraval (3 daily; 2hr–3hr 30min).

Porbandar to: Ahmedabad (1–2 daily; 10hr); Jamnagar (2–3 daily; 2hr 25min–4hr); Mumbai (1 daily; 23hr 30min); Rajkot (2–3 daily; 4hr 40min– 6hr); Surat (1 daily; 16hr 40min); Vadodara (1 daily; 13hr 35min).

Rajkot to: Ahmedabad (3–5 daily; 4hr 20min–5hr 15min); Junagadh (4 daily; 3hr 30min–5hr 15min); Porbandar (2–3 daily; 4hr 30min–5hr 45min); Veraval (1 daily; 5hr 15min).

Vadodara to: Ahmedabad (14–17 daily; 1hr 55min–2hr 30min); Baruch (every 30min daily; 48min–1hr 15min); Delhi (6 daily; 12–24hr); Indore (2 daily; 8hr 18min); Jaipur (1 daily; 11hr 50min); Kolkata (Calcutta: 1 daily; 42hr); Mumbai (16–20 daily; 7hr); Porbandar (1 daily; 13hr 45min); Pune (1 daily; 10hr 20min–11hr 5min); Surat (every 30min; 1hr 50min–2hr 30min); Vapi (for Daman: 10 daily; 4hr).

Vapi to: Ahmedabad (7 daily; 6–7hr); Jamnagar (1 daily; 15hr); Mumbai (10 daily; 3–4hr); Rajkot (1 daily; 12hr 30min); Surat (9 daily; 1hr 45min–3hr); Vadodara (13 daily; 4–5hr).

Buses

Ahmedabad to: Abu Rd (5 daily; 6hr); Ajmer (1 daily; 14hr); Bhavnagar (hourly; 5hr); Bhuj (12 daily; 8–10hr); Diu (1 daily; 11hr); Dwarka (6 daily; 11hr); Indore (1 nightly; 10hr); Jaipur (1 nightly; 16hr); Jamnagar (hourly; 7hr); Jodhpur (3 daily; 12hr); Junagadh (10 daily; 8hr); Mumbai (1 nightly; 14hr); Porbandar (4 daily; 10hr); Rajkot (every 30min; 5hr); Surat (every 30min; 5hr 30min); Udaipur (hourly; 8hr); Una (4 daily; 10hr); Vadodara (every 10min; 2hr 30min); Veraval (7 daily; 10hr).

Bhavnagar to: Ahmedabad (hourly; 5hr); Bhuj (2 daily; 8hr); Junagadh (5 daily; 7hr); Mumbai (2 daily; 17hr); Palitana (hourly; 1hr 15min); Rajkot (14 daily; 4hr); Una (5 daily; 6hr); Vadodara (8 daily; 6hr).

Bhuj to: Ahmedabad (hourly; 8–10hr); Bhavnagar (2 daily; 8hr); Gandhidham (every 30min; 1hr); Jamnagar (5 daily; 7hr); Palanpur (5 daily; 8hr); Rajkot (10 daily; 7hr).

Diu to: Ahmedabad (4 daily; 11hr); Junagadh (4 daily; 5hr 30min); Rajkot (4 daily; 7hr 30min); Una (every 30min; 40min); Veraval (4 daily; 3hr).

Dwarka to: Ahmedabad (3 daily; 11hr); Jamnagar (8 daily; 3hr); Junagadh (3 daily; 5hr); Porbandar (hourly; 3hr); Veraval (hourly; 5–6hr).

Junagadh to: Ahmedabad (hourly; 8hr); Jamnagar (hourly; 5hr); Porbandar (10 daily; 3hr); Rajkot (hourly; 2hr 30min); Veraval (every 30min; 2hr).

Porbandar to: Ahmedabad (6 daily; 10hr); Dwarka (hourly; 3hr); Jamnagar (hourly; 2hr 30min); Rajkot (10 daily; 5hr).

Rajkot to: Ahmedabad (every 15min; 5hr); Jamnagar (every 30min; 2hr); Junagadh (hourly; 2hr 30min); Porbandar (10 daily; 5hr); Una (6 daily; 8hr); Vadodara (12 daily; 8hr); Veraval (hourly; 5hr).

Vadodara to: Ahmedabad (every 10min; 2hr 30min); Baruch (every 30min; 2hr); Bhopal (1 daily; 16hr); Indore (2 daily; 12hr); Mumbai (7 daily; 14hr); Pune (3 daily; 14hr); Rajkot (15–16 daily; 8hr); Surat (every 30min; 3hr).

Flights

Ahmedabad to: Bangalore (1 daily; 3hr 15min); Delhi (5 daily; 1hr 25min–2hr 35min); Hyderabad (4 weekly; 1hr 40min); Jaipur (3 weekly; 1hr); Kolkata (Calcutta: 6 weekly; 2hr 15min–3hr 35min); Mumbai (6–7 daily; 1hr); Vadodara (1 daily; 30min).

Bhavnagar to: Mumbai (2–3 daily; 50min–1hr 15min).
Bhuj to: Mumbai (1 daily; 1hr 5min).
Diu to: Porbandar (6 weekly; 45min); Mumbai (6 weekly; 2hr 45min).
Jamnagar to: Bhuj (1 daily; 40min); Mumbai (1 daily; 2hr 15min).
Porbandar to: Diu (6 weekly; 30min); Mumbai (6 weekly; 1hr 30min).
Rajkot to: Mumbai (3 daily; 50min–1hr).
Vadodara to: Delhi (1 daily; 1hr 25min); Mumbai (3–4 daily; 50–55min).

CHAPTER 10

Highlights

* **The Gateway of India** The departure-point for the last British troops leaving India, now a favourite spot for an evening stroll. See p.704

* **Chhatrapati Shivaji Museum** A fine collection of priceless Indian art, from ancient temple sculpture to Moghul armour, displayed in splendid Raj-era surroundings. See p.707

* **Maidans (parks)** Where Mumbai's citizens escape the hustle and bustle to play cricket, eat lunch and hang out. See p.709

* **CS ("Victoria") Terminus** A fantastically eccentric pile, perhaps the greatest railway station ever built by the British. See p.712

* **The bazaars** A labyrinth of packed streets selling everything from gold wedding jewellery to junk left over from the Raj. See p.715

* **Elephanta Island** A magnificent rock-cut Shiva temple on an island in Mumbai harbour. See p.717

* **Bollywood blockbusters** Check out the latest Hindi mega movie in one of the city centre's gigantic air-conditioned cinemas. See p.723

△ Gateway of India

10

Mumbai

Ever since the opening of the Suez Canal in the 1869, the principal gateway to the Indian subcontinent has been **MUMBAI** (**Bombay**), the city Aldous Huxley famously described as "the most appalling ... of either hemisphere". Travellers tend to regard time spent here as a rite of passage to be survived rather than savoured. But as the powerhouse of Indian business, industry and trade, and the source of its most seductive media images, the Maharashtran capital can be a compelling place to kill time. Whether or nor you find the experience enjoyable, however, will depend largely on how well you handle the heat, humidity, hassle, traffic fumes, relentless crowds and appalling poverty of India's most dynamic, westernized city.

First impressions of Mumbai tend to be dominated by its chronic **shortage of space**. Crammed onto a narrow spit of land that curls from the swamp-ridden coast into the Arabian Sea, the city has, in less than five hundred years since its "discovery" by the Portuguese, metamorphosed from an aboriginal fishing settlement into a sprawling megalopolis of over sixteen million people. Being swept along broad boulevards by endless streams of commuters, or jostled by coolies and hand-cart pullers in the teeming bazaars, you'll continually feel as if Mumbai is about to burst at the seams.

The roots of the population problem and attendant poverty lie, paradoxically, in the city's enduring ability to create wealth. Mumbai alone generates nearly forty percent of India's GNP, its port handles half the country's foreign trade, and its movie industry is the biggest in the world. Symbols of prosperity are everywhere: from the phalanx of office blocks clustered on Nariman Point, Maharashtra's Manhattan, to the expensively dressed teenagers posing in Colaba's trendiest nightspots.

The flip side to the success story is the city's much chronicled **poverty**. Each day, hundreds of economic refugees pour into Mumbai from the Maharashtran hinterland. Some find jobs and secure accommodation; many more (around a third of the total population) end up living on the already overcrowded streets,

Mumbai/Bombay

In 1996 Bombay was renamed **Mumbai**, as part of a wider policy instigated by the ultra-right-wing Shiv Sena Municipality to replace names of any places, roads and features in the city that had connotations of the Raj. Mumbai is the Marathi title of the local deity, the mouthless "Maha-amba-aiee" (Mumba for short), who is believed to have started her life as an obscure aboriginal earth goddess.

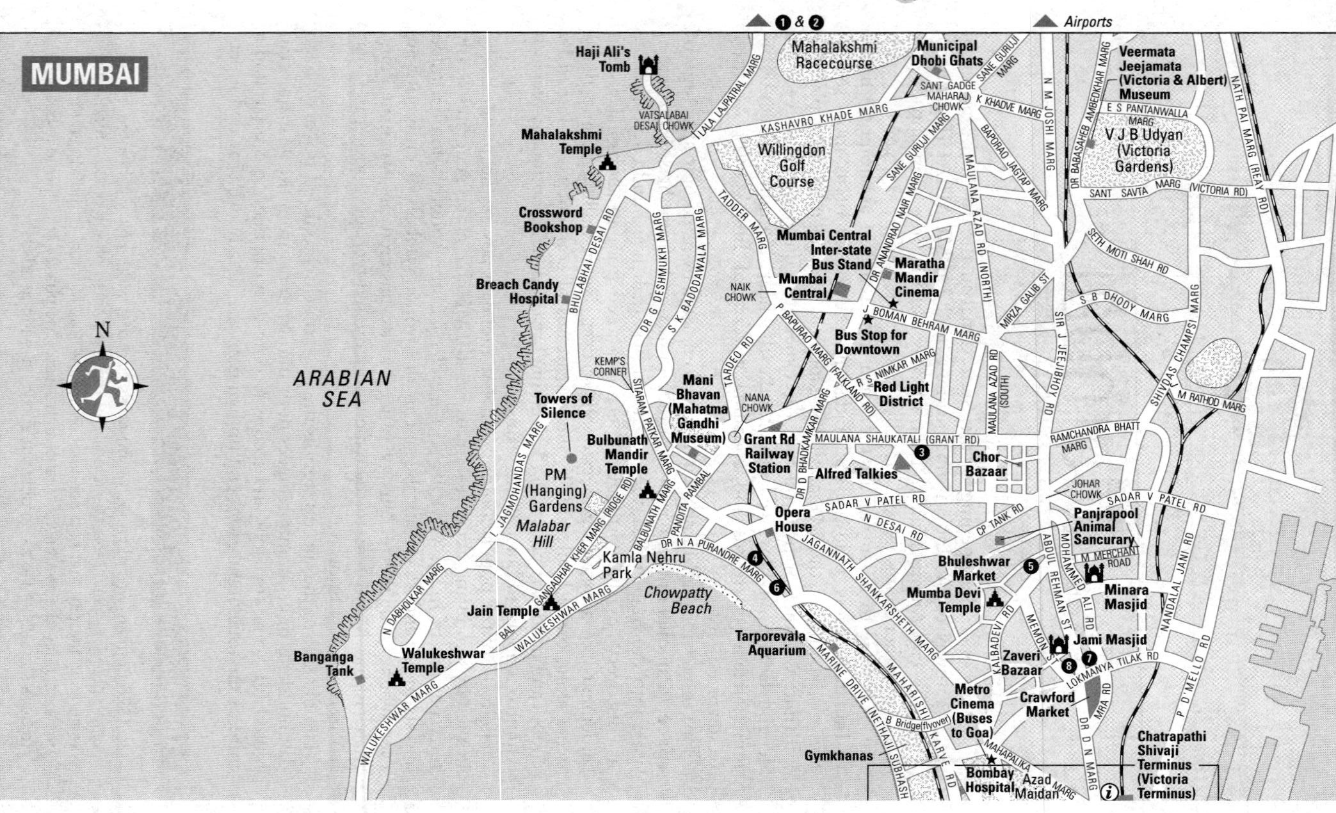
MUMBAI
1 & 2
Airports
ARABIAN SEA
N
Haji Ali's Tomb
Mahalakshmi Temple
Crossword Bookshop
Breach Candy Hospital
Towers of Silence
PM (Hanging) Gardens
Malabar Hill
Bulbunath Mandir Temple
Kamla Nehru Park
Chowpatty Beach
Jain Temple
Walukeshwar Temple
Banganga Tank
Mahalakshmi Racecourse
Willingdon Golf Course
Municipal Dhobi Ghats
Mumbai Central Inter-state Bus Stand
Mumbai Central
Maratha Mandir Cinema
Bus Stop for Downtown
Red Light District
Mani Bhavan (Mahatma Gandhi Museum)
Grant Rd Railway Station
Alfred Talkies
Chor Bazaar
Opera House
Tarporevala Aquarium
Gymkhanas
Bhuleshwar Market
Mumba Devi Temple
Panjrapool Animal Sancurary
Minara Masjid
Jami Masjid
Zaveri Bazaar
Crawford Market
Metro Cinema (Buses to Goa)
Bombay Hospital
Azad Maidan
Chatrapathi Shivaji Terminus (Victoria Terminus)
Veermata Jeejamata (Victoria & Albert) Museum
V J B Udyan (Victoria Gardens)
VATSALABAI DESAI CHOWK
KEMP'S CORNER
NAIK CHOWK
NANA CHOWK
SANT GADGE MAHARAJ CHOWK
JOHAR CHOWK
LALA LAJPATRAI MARG
KASHAVRO KHADE MARG
K KHADVE MARG
SANE GURUJI MARG
BAPORAO JAGTAP MARG
N M JOSHI MARG
DR BABASAHEB AMBEDKHAR MARG
E S PANTANWALLA MARG
SANT SAVTA MARG (VICTORIA RD)
NATH PAI MARG (REAY RD)
TADDER MARG
DR ANANDRAO NAIR MARG
MAULANA AZAD RD (NORTH)
MAULANA AZAD RD (SOUTH)
MIRZA GALIB ST
SIR J JEEJIBHOY RD
SETH MOTI SHAH RD
S B DHODY MARG
SHIVDAS CHAMPSI MARG
J M RATHOD MARG
J BOMAN BEHRAM MARG
P BAPURAO MARG (FALKLAND RD)
R S NIMKAR MARG
TARDEO RD
MAULANA SHAUKATALI (GRANT RD)
RAMCHANDRA BHATT MARG
DR D BHADKAMKAR MARG
SADAR V PATEL RD
N DESAI RD
CP TANK RD
BHULABHAI DESAI RD
DR G DESHMUKH MARG
S K BADODAWALA MARG
SITARAM PATKAR MARG
PANDITA RAMBAI
BALBUNATH MARG
GANGADHAR KHER MARG (RIDGE RD)
L JAGMOHANDAS MARG
DR N A PURANDRE MARG
JAGANNATH SHANKARSHETH MARG
N DABHOLKAR MARG
BAL
WALUKESHWAR MARG
MARINE DRIVE (NETHAJI SUBHASH
MAHARISHI KARVE RD
B Bridge(flyover)
MAHAPALIKA MARG
ABDUL REHMAN ST
MOHAMMED ALI RD
I M MERCHANT ROAD
MEMON ST
KALBADEVI RD
LOKMANYA TILAK RD
MRA RD
DR D N MARG
NANDALAL JANI RD
P D'MELLO RD

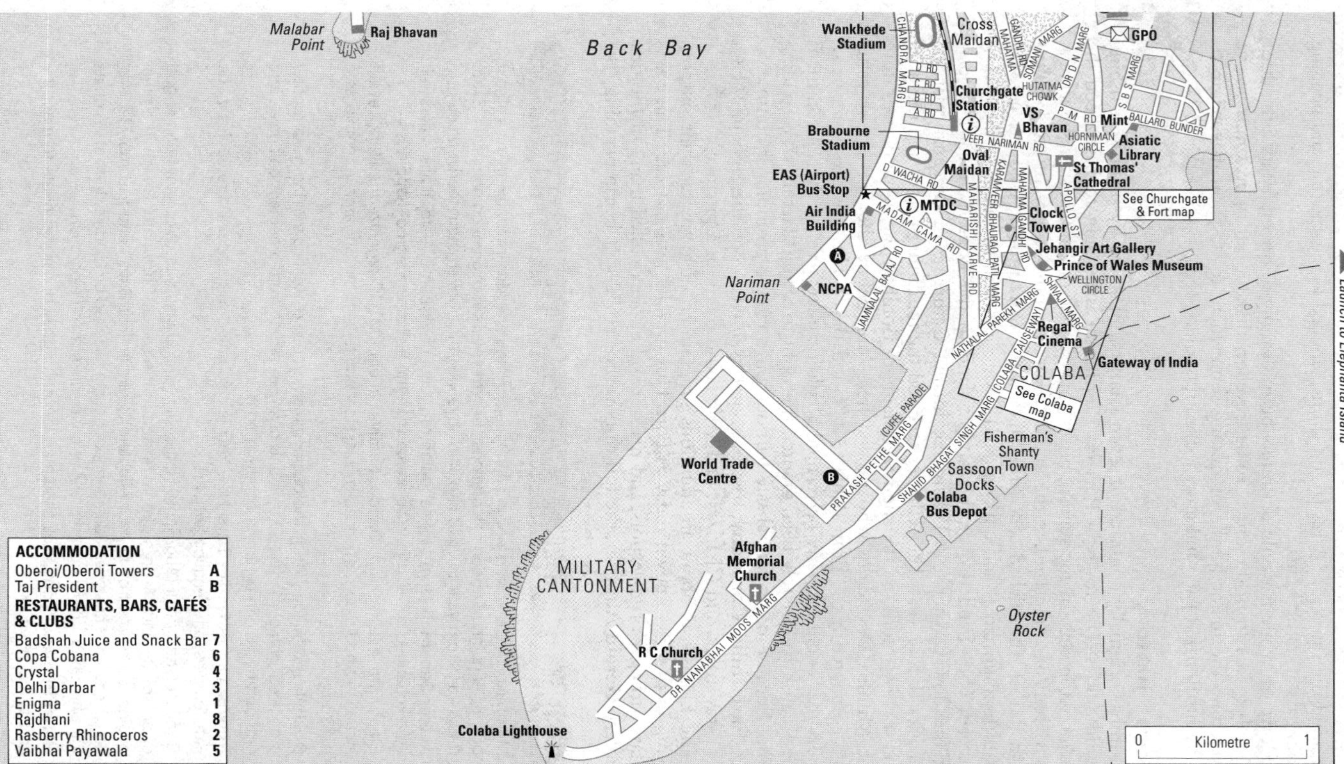
Launch to Elephanta Island
Mandve & Alibag
Malabar Point
Raj Bhavan
Back Bay
Wankhede Stadium
Cross Maidan
GPO
CHANDRA MARG
D RD
C RD
B RD
A RD
MAHATMA GANDHI RD
SOMANI MARG
DR D N MARG
S B S MARG
HUTATMA CHOWK
Churchgate Station
VS Bhavan
P M RD
Mint
BALLARD BUNDER
Brabourne Stadium
VEER NARIMAN RD
HORNIMAN CIRCLE
Asiatic Library
Oval Maidan
St Thomas' Cathedral
D WACHA RD
EAS (Airport) Bus Stop
MTDC
See Churchgate & Fort map
Air India Building
MADAM CAMA RD
MAHARISHI KARVE RD
KARAMVEER BHAURAO PATIL MARG
Clock Tower
APOLLO ST
Jehangir Art Gallery
Prince of Wales Museum
WELLINGTON CIRCLE
Nariman Point
NCPA
JAMNALAL BAJAJ RD
SHIVAJI MARG
NATHALAL PAREKH MARG
Regal Cinema
COLABA CAUSEWAY
Gateway of India
COLABA
See Colaba map
CUFFE PARADE
PRAKASH PETHE MARG
SHAHID BHAGAT SINGH MARG
Fisherman's Shanty Town
Sassoon Docks
World Trade Centre
Colaba Bus Depot
Afghan Memorial Church
MILITARY CANTONMENT
DR NANABHAI MOOS MARG
Oyster Rock
R C Church
Colaba Lighthouse
0 Kilometre 1
ACCOMMODATION
Oberoi/Oberoi Towers A
Taj President B
RESTAURANTS, BARS, CAFÉS & CLUBS
Badshah Juice and Snack Bar 7
Copa Cobana 6
Crystal 4
Delhi Darbar 3
Enigma 1
Rajdhani 8
Rasberry Rhinoceros 2
Vaibhai Payawala 5

or amid the squalor of Asia's largest slums, reduced to rag-picking and begging from cars at traffic lights.

However, while it would definitely be misleading to downplay its difficulties, Mumbai is far from the ordeal some travellers make it out to be. Once you've overcome the major hurdle of finding somewhere to stay, you may begin to enjoy its frenzied pace and crowded, cosmopolitan feel.

Some history

Mumbai originally consisted of seven **islands**, inhabited by small Koli fishing communities. The town of Puri on **Elephanta** is thought to have been the major settlement in the region, until King Bimba, or Bhima, sited his capital at Mahim on one island, at the end of the thirteenth century. In 1534, Sultan Bahadur of Ahmedabad ceded the land to the **Portuguese**, who felt it to be of little importance, and concentrated development in the areas further north instead. They handed over the largest island to the English in 1661, as part of the dowry when the Portuguese infanta Catherine of Braganza married Charles II; four years later Charles received the remaining islands and the port, and the town took on the anglicized name of Bombay (the name derives from the Mumba Devi deity who resided here long before the Portuguese came and corrupted it to "Bom Bahia", or "Good Bay"). This was the first part of India that could properly be termed a colony; elsewhere on the subcontinent the English had merely been granted the right to set up "factories", or trading posts. Because of its natural safe harbour and strategic position for commerce, the **East India Company**, based at Surat, wanted to buy the land; in 1668 a deal was struck, and Charles leased Mumbai to them for a pittance.

The English set about an ambitious programme of fortifying their outpost, living in the area known today as Fort. However, life was not easy. There was a fast turnover of governors, and malaria and cholera culled many of the first settlers. **Gerald Aungier**, the fourth governor (1672–77), began planning "the

Festivals in Mumbai

Mumbai has its own versions of all the major Hindu and Muslim **festivals**, plus a host of smaller neighbourhood celebrations imported by its immigrant communities. Exact dates vary from year to year; check in advance at the government tourist office.

Makar Sankranti (Jan). A celebration of prosperity, when sweets, flowers and fruit are exchanged by all, and kites are flown in the parks as a sign of happiness.

Elephanta Music and Dance Festival (Feb). MTDC-organized cultural event including floodlit performances by classical artists with the Shiva cave temple as a backdrop.

Gokhulashtami (July/Aug). Riotous commemoration of Krishna's birthday; terracotta pots filled with curd, milk-sweets and cash are strung from tenement balconies and grabbed by human pyramids of young boys.

Nowroz (July/Aug). The Parsi New Year is celebrated with special ceremonies in the Fire Temples, and feasting at home.

Ganesh Chathurthi (Aug/Sept). Huge effigies of Ganesh, the elephant-headed god of prosperity and wisdom, are immersed in the sea at Chowpatty Beach in a ritual originally promoted by freedom-fighters to circumvent British anti-assembly legislation. Recently it has seemed in danger of being hijacked by Hindu extremists such as the Shiv Sena, colouring it more with chauvinism than celebration.

Nariel Purnima (Sept). Koli fishermen launch brightly decorated boats to mark the end of the monsoon.

The Dons

Criminals have always been a part of Mumbai's life, but the 1980s saw an intensification of **organized crime** in the city. Previously, gangsters had confined their activities to small-scale racketeering in poor neighbourhoods. After the post-1970s real-estate boom however, many petty "landsharks" became powerful godfather figures, or **dons**, with drug- and gold-smuggling businesses as well as involvement in extortion and prostitution. Moreover, corrupt politicians who employed the gangs' muscle-power to rig elections had become highly placed political puppets with debts to pay – a phenomenon dubbed **criminalization**. The dividing line between the underworld and politics grew increasingly blurred during the 1990s – in 1992, no less than forty candidates in the municipal elections had criminal records.

The gangs have also become integral in the dirty war between India and Pakistan, with Karachi-based Dawood Ibrahim heavily implicated with the Pakistani security services – he is thought to be behind the bombings of 1993 – and Bombay's leading don, Chhota Rajan, with the Indian forces. In fact, many see the bungling of Rajan's subsequent extradition from Thailand, and escape from a guarded hospital room (he drugged his Thai police guards and climbed out of the window using his bed sheets), as payment for services rendered.

The late 1980s saw the entrance of the dons into **Bollywood**, when the rise of video and TV made regular film financiers nervous of investing in the industry. Mob money poured in and it's an open secret that the film industry is one of the favoured forms of money-laundering with the dons – rival films mysteriously put back their release dates in order to give mob-backed movies a clear run at the box office. In 2000, however, the authorities began to take action, and Bollywood mogul Bharat Shah (who usually has around ten billion rupees invested in films at any one time) was imprisoned for two years for financial links to the Dawood Ibrahim gang.

However, Mumbai is still the playground for mafia gangs, each with their own personalities and legends. If you read any newspapers while you're in the city you won't escape this phenomenon; the media revels in the shocking and bloodthirsty exploits of the gangsters, and the unfolding sagas run like a Bollywood blockbuster.

city which by God's assistance is intended to be built", and by the start of the eighteenth century the town was the capital of the East India Company. He is credited with encouraging the mix that still contributes to the city's success, welcoming Hindu traders from Gujarat, Goans, Muslim weavers, and most visibly, the business-minded Zoroastrian **Parsis**.

Much of the British settlement in the old Fort area was destroyed by a devastating fire in 1803. The arrival of the **Great Indian Peninsular Railway** half a century or so later improved communications, encouraging yet more immigration from elsewhere in India. This crucial artery, coupled with the cotton crisis in America following the Civil War, gave impetus to the great Bombay cotton boom and established the city as a major industrial and commercial centre. With the opening of the Suez Canal in 1869, and the construction of enormous docks, Bombay's access to European markets improved further. **Sir Bartle Frere**, governor from 1862 to 1867, oversaw the construction of the city's distinctive colonial-Gothic buildings; the most extravagant of all, **Victoria Terminus** railway station – now officially Chhatrapati Shivaji Terminus or CST – is a fitting testimony to this extraordinary age of expansion.

As the most prosperous city in the nation, Bombay was at the forefront of the Independence struggle; Mahatma Gandhi used a house here, now a museum, to co-ordinate the struggle through three decades. Fittingly, the first British colony took pleasure in waving the final goodbye to the Raj, when the last contingent of

British troops passed through the Gateway of India in February 1948. Since Independence, Mumbai has prospered as India's commercial and cultural capital and this period has seen the population grow tenfold to more than thirteen million.

However, the resultant overcrowding has done little to foster relations between the city's various minorities and the past two decades have seen repeated outbursts of communal tensions among the poorer classes. Strikes and riots paralysed the metropolis throughout the 1980s and early 1990s as more and more immigrants from other regions of the country poured in. The mounting discontent fuelled the rise of the extreme right-wing Maharashtran party, the **Shiv Sena**, founded in 1966 by the former cartoonist, Bal "the Saheb" Thackery, a self-confessed admirer of Hitler. Many people blamed Sena cadres for orchestrating the appalling attacks on Muslims that followed in the wake of the Babri Masjid destruction in Ayodhya in 1992–93, when thousands were murdered by mobs as the city descended into anarchy for ten days.

Just as Mumbai was regaining its composure, disaster struck again. On March 12, 1993, ten massive **bomb blasts** ripped through the heart of the city, destroying key buildings (such as the Stock Exchange and Air India HQ) and killing 260 people. No one claimed responsibility, but the involvement of Muslim godfather Ibrahim Dawood and the Pakistani secret service was suspected. The finger of blame pointed in the same direction eleven years later when – on August 25, 2003 – a **car bomb** exploded near a crowded concourse next to the **Gateway of India**; 107 people died and hundreds more were injured. Police arrested four suspects soon after, but the identity of their backers remains a subject of speculation.

After both bombing attacks, the city bounced back with characteristic ebullience, and in the popular imagination continues to be identified less with terrorist outrages than with the glamour purveyed by its movie and satellite-TV industries: Bollywood starlets, VJs and playboy heirs to industrial fortunes provide the staple for the gossip columns and fanzines lapped up across the country, while dozens of Hindi blockbusters are shot in its streets and suburban studios each month.

Arrival and information

Unless you arrive in Mumbai by train at **Chhatrapati Shivaji Terminus** (formerly Victoria Terminus), be prepared for a long slog into the centre. The international and domestic **airports** are north of the city, way off the map, and ninety minutes or more by road from the main hotel areas, while from **Mumbai Central** train or **bus station**, you face a laborious trip across town. Finding a place to stay can be even more of a hassle; phone around before you set off into the traffic.

By air

Mumbai's busy **international airport**, **Chhatrapati Shivaji** (30km north), is divided into two "modules", one for Air India flights and the other for foreign airlines. Once through customs and the lengthy immigration formalities, you'll find a 24hr State Bank of India exchange facility, government (ITDC) and state (MTDC) tourist information counters, car rental kiosks, cafés and a prepaid taxi stand in the arrivals concourse. There's also – very usefully – an **Indian Railways booking office** which you should make use of if you know your next destination; it'll save you a long wait at the reservation offices downtown. If you're on one of the few flights to land in the afternoon or early evening

Malaria warning

Due to the massive slum encampments and bodies of stagnant water around the **airports**, both Chhatrapati Shivaji and Santa Cruz are major **malaria** blackspots. Clouds of mosquitos await your arrival in the car park, so don't forget to smother yourself with strong insect repellent before leaving the terminal.

– by which time most hotels tend to be full – it can be worth paying on the spot for a room at the **accommodation booking desk** in the arrivals hall. All of the domestic airlines also have offices outside the main entrance, and there's a handy 24hr **left luggage** "cloakroom" in the car park nearby (Rs60 per day, or part thereof; maximum duration 90 days).

Many of the more upmarket hotels, particularly those near the airport, send out **courtesy coaches** to pick up their guests. **Taxis** are not too extravagant. To avoid haggling over the fare or being duped by the private taxi companies outside the airport, pay the "Pre-Paid" taxi desk in the arrivals hall. The price on the receipt, which you hand to the driver on arrival at your destination, is slightly more than the normal meter rate (around Rs350 to Colaba or Nariman Point, or Rs150 to Juhu), but at least you can be sure you'll be taken by the most direct route. Taxi-wallahs sometimes try to persuade you to stay at a different hotel from the one you ask for. Don't agree to this; their commission will be added onto the price of your room.

Internal flights land at Mumbai's **domestic airport** (26km to the north of downtown), formerly called "Santa Cruz" but, somewhat confusingly, renamed Chhatrapati Shivaji, like its international counterpart. It is divided into separate terminals: the cream-coloured one (Module 1A) for Indian Airlines, and the blue-and-white (Module 1B) for private carriers. If you're transferring directly from here to an international flight take the free "fly-bus" that shuttles every fifteen minutes between the two. The Indian government and MTDC both have 24hr information counters in the arrivals hall, and there's a foreign exchange counter and accommodation desk tucked away near the first-floor exit. The official "Pre-Paid" taxi counter on the arrivals concourse charges around Rs350 to Colaba.

Don't be tempted by the cheaper fares offered by touts outside, and avoid **auto-rickshaws** altogether, as they're not allowed downtown and will leave you at the mercy of unscrupulous taxi drivers on the edge of vile-smelling Mahim Creek, the southernmost limit of their permitted area.

By train

Trains to Mumbai from most central, southern and eastern regions arrive at **Chhatrapati Shivaji Terminus or CST** (formerly **Victoria Terminus**, or VT), the main railway station at the end of the Central Railway line. From here it's a ten- or fifteen-minute ride to Colaba; taxis queue at the busy rank outside the south exit, opposite the new reservation hall.

Mumbai Central, the terminus for Western Railway trains from northern India, is a half-hour ride from Colaba; take a taxi from the forecourt, or flag one down on the main road outside.

Some trains from South India arrive at more obscure stations. If you find yourself at **Dadar**, way up in the industrial suburbs, and don't want to shell out on a taxi (Rs500), cross the Tilak Marg road bridge onto the Western Railway and catch a suburban train into town (remembering to purchase a ticket at the hatch on platform 1 beforehand). **Kurla** station, where a few Bangalore trains pull in, is even further out, just south of the domestic airport; taking a suburban train for Churchgate is the only reasonable alternative to a taxi (Rs300). From either, it's worth asking at the station when you arrive if there is another long-distance train going to Churchgate or CST (Victoria Terminus) shortly after – it's far preferable to trying to cram into either a suburban train or bus.

By bus

Nearly all interstate **buses** arrive at **Mumbai Central** bus stand, a stone's throw from the railway station of the same name. You have a choice between municipal black-and-yellow taxis, the BEST buses (#66, #70 & #71), which run straight into town from the stop on Dr DN Marg (Lamington Road), two minutes' walk west from the bus station, or a suburban train from Mumbai Central's local platform over the footbridge.

Most **Maharashtra State Road Transport Corporation** (MSRTC) buses terminate at Mumbai Central, though those from Pune, Nasik (and surrounding areas) end up at the **ASIAD** bus stand, a glorified parking lot near the railway station in **Dadar**.

Information

The best source of **information** in Mumbai is the excellent **India Tourism** (Mon–Fri 8.30am–6pm, Sat 8.30am–2pm; ⓣ022/2203 3144, ⓦwww.india-tourism.com) at 123 M Karve Rd, opposite Churchgate station's east exit. The staff here are exceptionally helpful and hand out a wide range of leaflets, maps and brochures both on Mumbai and the rest of the country. There are also 24hr tourist **information counters** at Chhatrapati Shivaji International (ⓣ022/2682 9248) and Domestic (ⓣ022/2615 6920) airports.

The Maharashtra State Tourism Development Corporation (**MTDC**) office, on Madam Cama Road (Mon–Sat 8.30am–7pm; ⓣ022/2202 6731), opposite the LIC Building in Nariman Point, can reserve rooms in MTDC resorts and also sells tickets for city sightseeing tours (see below).

If you need detailed **listings**, the most complete source is Mumbai's *Time Out*, which carries full details of what's on and where, just like its London and New York counterparts. Alternatively, check out "The List" section of *Mid-Day* (Mumbai's main local rag), the "Metro" page in the *Indian Express*, or the "Bombay Times" section of the *Times of India*. All are available from street vendors around Colaba and the downtown area.

City transport

Transport congestion has eased slightly since the opening of the huge flyover that now scythes straight through the heart of the city from just north of CST station. During peak hours, however, gridlock is the norm and you should brace yourself for long waits at junctions if you take to the roads by taxi, bus or auto. Local **trains** get there faster, but can be a real endurance test even outside rush hours.

Tours

MTDC's "City" tour (Tues–Sun 2–6pm; Rs75, not including admission charges) is a good way to cram downtown Mumbai's touristic highlights into a half day, with stops at the Prince of Wales Museum, Marine Drive, Chowpatty Beach, the Hanging Gardens and Mani Bhavan. The trip starts at the company's main office on Madam Cama Road (see opposite), where you can also purchase tickets in advance. A more leisurely alternative, focusing on architecture and history, are the guided walks organized by the Mumbai Heritage Walks Society on the last Sunday of each month (except during the monsoons). The tours cost Rs100 (or Rs50 for students on production of a student ID card) and last ninety minutes. Get further details on ⓣ022/2281 0123 or 2834 4622, or ⓔheritagewalks@hotmail.com.

Buses

BEST (Brihanmumbai Electric Supply and Transport; ⓣ022/2285 6262; ⓦwww.bestundertaking.com) operates a **bus** network of labyrinthine complexity, extending to the furthest-flung corners of the city. Unfortunately, neither its website, route booklets, maps nor "Point to Point" guides (which you can consult at the tourist office or at news-stands) make things any clearer. Finding out which bus you need is difficult enough. Recognizing them in the street can be even more problematic, as the numbers are written in Marathi (although in English on the sides). Aim, wherever possible, for the "Limited" services, which stop less frequently, and avoid rush hours at all costs. Tickets should be bought from the conductor on the bus.

Trains

Mumbai's local **trains** carry millions of commuters each day between downtown and the sprawling suburbs in the north. One line begins at CST (VT), running up the east side of the city as far as Thane. The other leaves Churchgate, hugging the curve of Back Bay as far as Chowpatty Beach, where it veers north towards Mumbai Central, Dadar, Santa Cruz and Vasai, beyond the city limits. Services depart every few minutes from 5am until midnight, stopping at dozens of small stations. Carriages remain packed solid virtually the whole time, with passengers dangling precariously out of open doors to escape the crush, so start to make your way to the exit at least three stops before your destination. Peak hours (approximately 8.30am–10am & 4–7pm) are the worst of all. Women are marginally better off in the "ladies carriages"; look for the crowd of saris and *salwar kamises* grouped at the end of the platform.

Taxis

With rickshaws banished to the suburbs, Mumbai's ubiquitous black-and-yellow **taxis** are the quickest and most convenient way to nip around the city centre. In theory, all should have meters and a current "tariff card" (to convert the amount shown on the meter to the correct fare); in practice, particularly at night or early in the morning, many drivers refuse to use them. If this happens, either flag down another or haggle out a fare. As a rule of thumb, expect to be charged Rs8 per kilometre after the minimum fare of around Rs15, together with a small sum for heavy luggage (Rs5 per article). The latest addition to Mumbai's hectic roads is the **cool cab**, a blue taxi that boasts air conditioning, and charges higher rates for the privilege (ⓣ022/2824 6216).

Boats

Ferryboats regularly chug out of Mumbai harbour, connecting the city with the far shore and some of the larger islands in between. The most popular with visitors is the **Elephanta Island** launch (see p.717), which departs from the Gateway of India. Boats to **Mandve** (9 daily; 6.30am–6.15pm; 90min; Rs45), for Alibag, the transport hub for the rarely used **coastal route south**, leave from the Gateway of India.

Car rental

Cars with drivers can be rented per eight-hour day (Rs900–1250 for a non-a/c Ambassador, upwards of Rs1450 for more luxurious a/c cars), or per kilometre, from ITDC. They have an (occasionally) staffed counter at the Government of India tourist office and on the eleventh floor of the Nirmal Building at Nariman Point. Otherwise, go through any good travel agent (see p.728). Ramniranjan Kedia Tours and Travels (Ⓣ022/2437 1112, Ⓦwww.rnk.com) are recommended if you want to book a vehicle on arrival at Chhatrapati Shivaji international airport.

Accommodation

Finding **accommodation** at the right price when you arrive in Mumbai may be a real problem. Budget travellers, in particular, can expect a hard time: standards at the bottom of the range are grim and room rates exorbitant. The best of the relatively inexpensive places tend to fill up by noon, which can often mean a long trudge in the heat with only an overpriced fleapit at the end of it, so you should really phone ahead as soon as (or preferably well before) you arrive. Prices in upmarket places are further inflated by the state-imposed "**luxury tax**" (between four and thirty percent depending on how expensive the room is), and "**service charges**" levied by the hotel itself; such charges are included in the price symbols used in the following reviews.

Colaba, down in the far, southern end of the city, is where the majority of foreign visitors head first. A short way across the city centre, **Marine Drive**'s accommodation is generally a little more expensive, but more salubrious, with Back Bay and the promenade right on the doorstep. If you're arriving by train and plan to make a quick getaway, a room closer to **CST** (VT) station is worth considering. Alternatively, **Juhu**, way to the north near the airports, hosts a string of flashy four- and five-stars, with a handful of less expensive places behind the beach. For those who just want to crawl off the plane and straight into bed, a handful of overpriced options are also available in the suburbs around the **airports**, a short taxi ride from the main terminal buildings.

Finally, if you would like to **stay with an Indian family**, ask at the government tourist office in Churchgate, or at their information counters in the airports about the popular "**paying guest**" **scheme**. Bed and breakfast-style accommodation in family homes, vetted by the tourist office, is available throughout the city at rates ranging from Rs500 to Rs1350.

Colaba

A short ride from the city's main commercial districts, railway stations and tourist office, **Colaba** makes a handy base. It also offers more in the way of food and entertainment than neighbouring districts, especially along its busy main thoroughfare, "**Colaba Causeway**" (Shahid Bhagat Singh – SBS – Marg). The streets immediately south and west of the Gateway of India are chock-full of accommodation, ranging from grungy guesthouses to India's most famous five-star hotel, the *Taj Mahal Palace & Tower*. Avoid at all costs the nameless lodges lurking on the top storeys of wooden-fronted houses along **Arthur Bunder Road** – the haunts of touts who depend on commission to finance their heroin habits.

The hotels below are marked on the **map** of Colaba on p.705, except for the *Taj President*, which is on the main Mumbai map (pp.692–693).

Aga Bheg's & Hotel Kishan Ground & 2nd Floor, Shirin Manzil, Walton Rd ⓣ022/2284 2227. *Aga Bheg's* has lurid pink walls and little wooden blue beds, though it's clean, cool and quiet. *Hotel Kishan*'s more comfy a/c rooms are better value. ❺–❻

Ascot 38 Garden Rd ⓣ022/2284 0020 or 2287 2105, ⓦwww.ascothotel.com. One of the oldest hotels in Mumbai, now sporting a state-of-the-art designer look. Very comfortable, and a bargain for a three-star in this area. All rooms en suite and a/c. ❽

Bentley's 17 Oliver Rd ⓣ022/2284 1474, ⓦwww.bentleyshotel.com. Dependable old favourite in four different colonial tenements, all on leafy backstreets. Well maintained, secure and good value, with spacious rooms opening onto rear gardens. ❻

Fariyas 25 Arthur Rd ⓣ022/2204 2911, ⓦwww.fariyas.com. Compact luxury hotel, overlooking the Koli fishing *basti* on one side, with all the trimmings of a five-star but none of the grandeur. Doubles from $175. ❾

Godwin Jasmine Building, 41 Garden Rd ⓣ022/2287 2050, ⓦwww.cybersols.com/godwin. Top-class three-star with great views from upper floors (ask for 804, 805 or 806 when you book). The *Garden* (ⓣ022/2283 1330, ⓕ2204 4290) next door, is similar but slightly inferior. Both ❽

Gorden House 5 Battery St, Apollo Bunder ⓣ022/2287 1122, ⓦwww.ghhotel.com. Ultra-chic designer place behind the Regal cinema. Each floor is differently themed: "Scandinavian" (the easiest to live with), "Mediterranean" and "American Country"; CD players in every room, but no pool. Doubles from $150. ❾

Lawrence 3rd Floor, 33 Sri Sai Baba Marg (Rope Walk Lane), off K Dubash Marg, behind *TGI's* ⓣ022/2284 3618 or 5633 6107. Arguably Mumbai's best-value inexpensive hotel, close to the Jehangir Art Gallery. Six well-scrubbed doubles (one single) with fans, and not-so-clean shared shower-toilet. Breakfast included in the price. Advance booking essential. ❸

Moti International 10 Best Marg ⓣ022/2202 1654. British-era building that's quiet and clean, though frayed around the edges, with original painted woodwork. The rooms range from non-attached doubles (Rs650) to deluxe with a/c, fridges and TVs. ❹–❻

Red Shield Red Shield House, 30 Mereweather Rd, near the *Taj* ⓣ022/2284 1824 or 2282 4613. Rock-bottom bunk beds (Rs135) in cramped, stuffy dorms (lockers available), or larger good-value doubles (Rs600 without a/c, Rs900 with), recently refurbished and fully en suite. Rates include three meals, served in a sociable travellers' canteen. Priority given to women, but your stay is limited to one week or less. ❶–❹

Regent 8 Best Rd ⓣ022/2287 1854, ⓔhotelregent@vsnl.com. Smart, international-standard hotel on a small scale; the rooms aren't large, but good value in its bracket. ❽

Sea Palace Kerawalla Chambers, 26 PJ Ramchandani Marg ⓣ022/2284 1828, ⓦwww.seapalacehotel.com. Comfortable, recently renovated hotel at the quiet end of the harbour front. Sea views cost extra. All rooms a/c. ❽

Sea Shore 4th Floor, 1-49 Kamal Mansion, Arthur Bunder Rd ⓣ022/2287 4237. Among the best budget deals in Colaba. The sea-facing rooms with windows (Rs520) are much nicer than the airless cells on the other side. Friendly management and free, safe baggage store. Common baths only, though some rooms have a/c. If it's full try the wooden-partitioned rooms at the less salubrious *India* (ⓣ022/2283 3769; ❹–❺) or the grubby but bearable *Sea Lord* (ⓣ022/2284 5392; ❹–❻) in the same building. ❺–❼

Shelley's 30 PJ Ramchandani Marg ⓣ022/2284 0229, ⓦwww.shellyshotel.com. Charmingly old-fashioned hotel in the colonial mould despite renovations to the rooms. Worth paying the extra Rs300 for sea-facing. ❼

Taj Mahal Palace & Tower PJ Ramchandani Marg ⓣ022/5665 3366, ⓦwww.tajhotels.com. The stately home among India's top hotels (see p.706), and the haunt of Mumbai's *beau monde*, with 546 luxury rooms, shopping arcades, a huge outdoor pool, nine bars and restaurants, plus one of the city's favourite nightclubs (*Insomnia*). Views vary according to price. If your budget can stretch to it, go for a sea-facing suite in the old wing, where rates range from $400–500; in the *Tower*, count on $300–380. ❾

Taj President 90 Cuffe Parade, ⓣ22/5665 0808, ⓦwww.tajhotels.com. Modern, business-oriented five-star occupying an 18-floor skyscraper just south of Colaba. A much more competitively priced option than its sister concern, the *Taj Mahal Palace & Tower*, though lacking old-world style and atmosphere. The pool is outdoors and large, with a multi-gym and steam room adjacent. ❾

YWCA 18 Madam Cama Rd ⓣ022/2202 5053, ⓦwww.ywcaic.info. Relaxing, secure and quiet hostel with spotless dorms (Rs35 per bed), doubles (recently renovated and with windows from Rs600, or Rs900 a/c) or family rooms (sleeping 3 to 6). Rates include membership, breakfast and filling buffet dinner. One month's advance booking (by money order) advisable. ❼

Marine Drive and Nariman Point

At the western edge of the downtown area, Netaji Subhash Chandra Marg, or **Marine Drive**, sweeps from the skyscrapers of Nariman Point in the south to Chowpatty Beach in the north. Along the way, four- and five-star hotels take advantage of the panoramic views over Back Bay and the easy access to the city's commercial heart, while a couple of inexpensive guesthouses are worth trying if Colaba's cheap lodges don't appeal.

The hotels below are marked on the **map** on p.711, apart from the *Oberoi*, which is marked on pp.692–693.

Ambassador VN Rd ⓣ022/2204 1131, ⓦwww.ambassadorindia.com. Ageing four-star whose scruffy concrete exterior and slightly worn furnishings are redeemed by its choice location, close to the sea and main shopping and café strip. Even if you're not staying, pop up to the revolving *Pearl in the Orient* restaurant for the matchless city views. ❾

Bentley 3rd Floor, Krishna Mahal, Marine Drive ⓣ022/2281 5244. Not to be confused with *Bentley's* in Colaba (see p.701), this small, friendly guesthouse is across town on the corner of D Rd/Marine Drive, near the cricket stadium. It had a major face lift in 2004 and now offers great value for money. The rooms are marble-lined and most share shower-toilets, but they're kept immaculately clean. Rates (from Rs700) include breakfast. ❺

Chateau Windsor 5th Floor, 86 VN Rd ⓣ022/2204 4455, ⓦwww.chateauwindsor.com. Impeccably neat and central, with unfailingly polite staff and a choice of differently priced rooms in 1950s style. Very popular, so reserve well in advance. ❼–❽

Intercontinental 135 Marine Drive ⓣ022/3987 9999, ⓦwww.intercontinental.com. Ultra-chic "boutique" hotel that's currently one of India's most stylishly modern addresses. The rooms have huge sea-facing windows and state-of-the-art gadgets (including 42" plasma screens, DVD players, safes with laptop rechargers and broadband connections), while the bars and restaurants rank among Mumbai's most fashionable. Doubles from $335. ❾

Marine Plaza 29 Marine Drive ⓣ022/2285 1212, ⓦwww.sarovarparkplaza.com. Ritzy but small luxury hotel on the seafront, with retro-Art-Deco atrium lobby, glass-bottomed rooftop pool, and the usual 5-star facilities. Rooms from around $330. ❾

Oberoi/Oberoi Towers Nariman Point ⓣ022/2232 5757, ⓦwww.oberoihotels.com. India's largest hotel, where Bill Clinton stayed on his state visit, enjoys a prime spot overlooking Back Bay. There's little difference between the two sections, which form a single complex. Glitteringly opulent throughout, and the first choice of business travellers, though lacking the heritage character of the *Taj*. Rooms from $365 to $2500 per night. ❾

Around Victoria (Chhatrapati Shivaji) Terminus

Arriving in Mumbai at **CST** (VT) after a long train journey, you may not feel like embarking on a room hunt around Colaba. Unfortunately, the area around the station and the nearby GPO, though fairly central, has little to recommend it. The majority of places worth trying are mid-range hotels grouped around the crossroads of P D'Mello (Frere) Road, St George's Road and Shahid Bhagat Singh (SBS) Marg, immediately southeast of the post office (5min on foot from the station). CST (VT) itself also has **retiring rooms** (Rs150), although these are invariably booked up by noon. The following are all marked on the Churchgate and Fort map on p.711.

City Palace 121 City Terrace ⓣ022/2261 5515, ⓔhotelcitypalace@vsnl.net. Large and popular hotel bang opposite the station. "Ordinary" rooms are tiny and windowless, but have a/c, are perfectly clean and proudly sport "electronic push button telephone instruments". The pricier ones higher up the building have great views over Nagar Chowk. And there's a reliable left luggage facility for guests. ❻–❼

Grand 17 Shri SR Marg, Ballard Estate ⓣ022/5658 0500, ⓦwww.grandhotelbombay.com. British-era place out near the old docks and former financial district. Their rooms are huge and a bit institutional but have plenty of 1940s period feel, which some may consider worth the extra. ❽–❾

Oasis 276 SBS Marg ⓣ022/5637 6521 or 2269 7887, ⓔhoteloasis@satyam.net.in. The best-value budget place in this area. Non a/c doubles from under Rs700: good beds, clean linen, all en suite and with TVs, and very well placed for CST station. ❺

Prince 34 Walchand Hirachand Rd, near Red Gate ⓣ022/2261 2809, ⓕ2265 8049. The best fallback if *Oasis* is full: nothing special, but neat and respectable. Avoid the airless partition rooms upstairs. ❹–❼

Railway 249 P D'Mello Rd ⓣ022/2261 6705 or 2262 0775, ⓦwww.hotelrailway.com. Spacious, clean and friendly, and the pick of the mid-range bunch around CST (VT), though correspondingly pricey and with no a/c options. ❼–❽

Around the airports

Hotels in the congested area around Chhatrapati Shivaji and Santa Cruz **airports** cater predominantly for transit passengers and flight crews, at premium rates. If you can face the half-hour drive across town, head for **Juhu**, one of the city's swisher suburbs, which faces the sea and is a lot less hectic. With its palm trees, glamorous seaside apartment blocks and designer clothes stores, Juhu is Mumbai's answer to Sunset Boulevard, though sunbathing and swimming are out of the question, thanks to an oily slick of raw sewage that seeps into the Arabian Sea from the slum *bastis* surrounding Mahim Creek to the south. Wherever you stay, bookings should be made well in advance, by phone, fax or email, and re-confirmed a couple of days before your arrival. Nearly all the hotels below have courtesy buses to and from the terminal building, or at worst can arrange for a car and driver to meet you (in which case check the tariff beforehand). Travellers on lower budgets who need to overnight close to the airport might also consider one of the Government of India's Paying Guest addresses, available via email: ⓔgitobest@bom5.vsnl.net.in or ⓔindiatourism@vsnl.com.

Bawa International Vile Parle (East) ⓣ022/2611 3636, ⓔbawaintl@vsnl.com. Nothing special, but spotlessly clean, efficient, modern and right next to the domestic airport. Doubles from Rs4400. ❾

Holiday Inn Balraj Sahani Marg, Juhu ⓣ022/2693 4444, ⓦwww.holidayinnbombay.com. Formulaic five-star – exactly what you'd expect from a *Holiday Inn*, and slap on the beach, with a decent-sized swimming pool. Rooms from around $200. ❾

Lotus Suites Andheri Kurla Rd, International Airport Zone, Andheri (East) ⓣ022/2827 0707, ⓦwww.lotussuites.com. An "Eco-Four-Star at Three-Star prices" is how this environment-friendly hotel describes itself. A very comfortable option for under $100 if you book online. ❾

Midland Jawaharlal Nehru Rd, Santa Cruz (East) ⓣ022/2611 0413, ⓦwww.hotelmidland.com. Dependable, welcoming two-star with well furnished twin-bedded rooms. Rates (from Rs2300) include courtesy bus and breakfast. ❼

Orchid 70-C Nehru Rd, Vile Parle (East) ⓣ022/2616 4040, ⓦwww.orchidhotel.com. Award-winning "Eco-Five-Star", built with organic or recycled materials and non-VOC paints. Every effort is made to minimize waste of natural resources, with a water recycling plant and "zero garbage" policy. Even the coat hangers are made of compressed sawdust. Rooms from around $300. ❾

Samrat 3rd Rd, Khar, Santa Cruz (East), near Khar railway station ⓣ022/2648 5441, ⓔhotelsamrat@vsnl.com. Basic budget transit hotel in a quiet suburban backstreet. No courtesy bus. ❻

Sea Princess Juhu Tara Rd, Juhu ⓣ022/2661 1111, ⓦwww.seaprincess.com. The nicest of the five-stars overlooking Juhu beach. Cosy, recently refitted rooms (some with sea views) and a smart restaurant, in addition to a small pool. Doubles from $175. ❾

The City

Nowhere reinforces your sense of having arrived in Mumbai quite as emphatically as the **Gateway of India**, which, alongside its grandly gabled and domed neighbour, the *Taj Mahal Palace & Tower*, stands as the city's defining landmark.

Crowds of trippers congregate here on evenings and weekends, but early morning before the heat builds is the best time to be at the adjacent boat jetty if you're planning a trip across the harbour to the ancient rock-cut Shiva temple on **Elephanta Island**. Only a five-minute walk north, the **Prince of Wales Museum** (or the Chhatrapati Shivaji Vastu Sanghralaya, as it was recently re-named) should be next on your list of sightseeing priorities, as much for its flamboyantly eclectic exterior as for the art treasures inside. The museum provides a foretaste of what lies in store just up the road, where the cream of Bartle Frere's Bombay – the University and High Court – line up with the open *maidans* on one side, and the boulevards of **Fort** on the other. The commercial hub of the city, Fort is a great area for aimless wandering, with plenty of old-fashioned cafés, department stores and street stalls crammed between the pompous Victorian piles. The innumerable banks and other financial institutions at the east end of Fort around **Horniman Circle** – site of the British era's oldest buildings, **St Thomas' Cathedral** and the old **town hall** – stand as reminders of the cotton boom prosperity of the late-nineteenth century. But for the fullest sense of why the city's founding fathers declared it *Urbs Prima in Indis*, you should visit **Victoria Terminus** (now re-named Chhatrapati Shivaji Terminus), the high watermark of India's Raj architecture.

Few visitors venture much further north than here unless they have to, but teeming **central Mumbai** certainly has its appeal. Beginning at **Crawford Market**, a quirky British structure crammed with fresh produce, you can press north into the thick of the intense **bazaar** district to visit the Mumba Devi temple from which the city took its name. Beyond lie the Muslim neighbourhoods, which encompass some of Mumbai's most interesting backstreet bazaars, as well as a serene little **Jain animal sanctuary**.

When the crush of city's central districts gets too much, an evening stroll along **Marine Drive**, bounding the western edge of the downtown area, is the ideal antidote. From there you can skirt Mumbai's most affluent enclave, Malabar Hill, to reach two important religious sites, the Hindu **Lakshmi temple** and Muslim **tomb of Haji Ali**.

One incentive to break out of Mumbai altogether is the thousand-year-old **Kanheri Cave** complex, carved from a forested hillside, which you can get to within striking distance of by train.

Colaba

At the end of the seventeenth century, **Colaba** was little more than the last in a straggling line of rocky islands extending to the lighthouse that stood on Mumbai's southernmost point. Today, the original outlines of the promontory (whose name derives from the Koli who first lived here) have been submerged under a mass of dilapidated colonial tenements, hotels, bars, restaurants and handicraft emporia. If you never venture beyond the district, you'll get a very distorted picture of Mumbai. In spite of being the main tourist enclave and a trendy hang-out for the city's rich young things, Colaba has retained the sleazy feel of the port it used to be, with touts, dealers and pimps hissing at passers-by from the kerbsides.

The Gateway of India

Commemorating the visit of King George V and Queen Mary in 1911, India's own honey-coloured Arc de Triomphe, the **Gateway of India**, was built in 1924 by George Wittet, the architect responsible for many of the city's grandest constructions. Blending indigenous Gujarati motifs with high Victorian

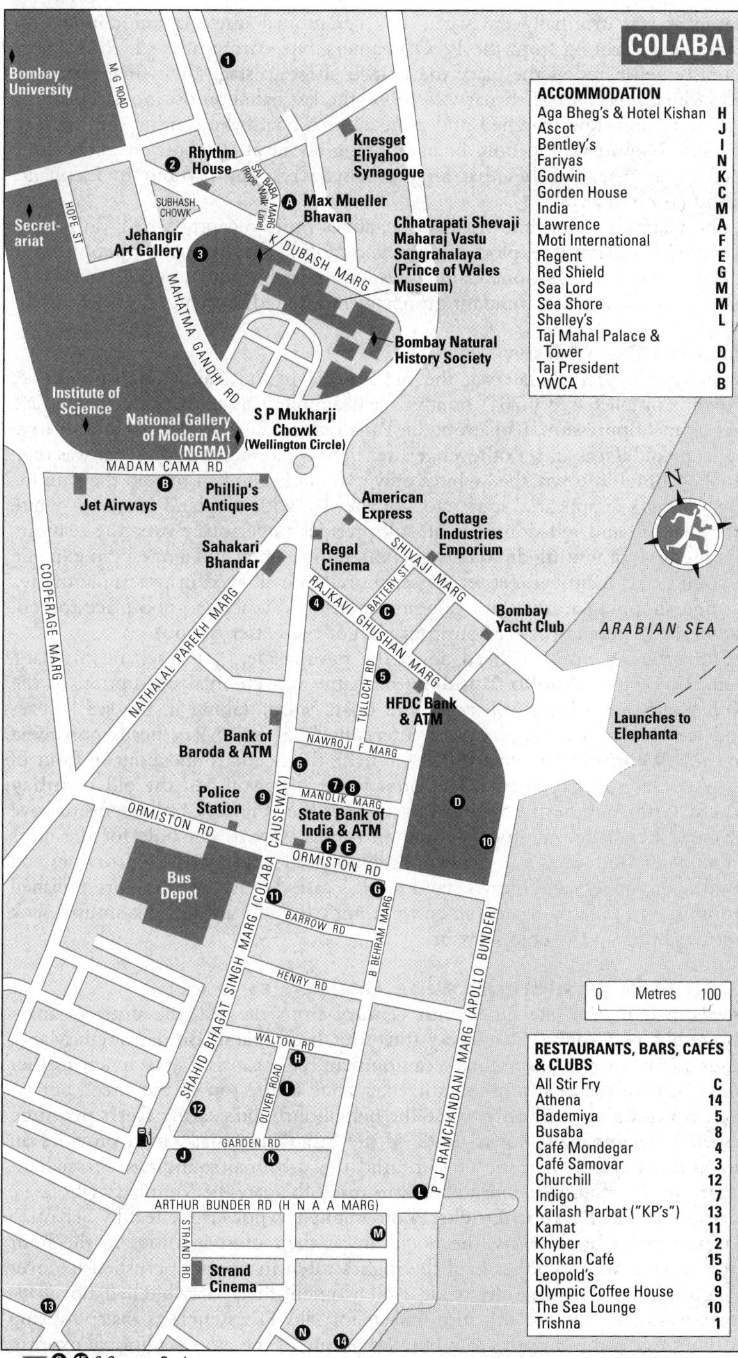

10 MUMBAI | The City

pomp, it was originally envisaged as a ceremonial disembarkation point for passengers alighting from the P&O steamers, but – ironically – is today more often remembered as the place the British chose to stage their final departure from the country. On February 28, 1948, the last battalion of troops remaining on Indian soil slow marched under the arch to board the waiting ship back to Tilbury. Nowadays, the only boats bobbing about at the bottom of its stone staircase are the launches that ferry tourists across the harbour to Elephanta Island (see p.717).

The Gateway made international headlines more recently when, on August 25, 2003, a car bomb exploded at the taxi rank in front of it; 107 people were killed in the attack. No one claimed responsibility, but four suspects believed to have links with Islamic militant groups were arrested soon after.

Behind the Gateway

Directly behind the Gateway, the older hotel in the **Taj Mahal Palace & Tower** complex (see p.701) stands as a monument to local pride in the face of colonial oppression. Its patron, the Parsi industrialist J.N. Tata, is said to have built the old *Taj* as an act of revenge after he was refused entry to what was then the best hotel in town, the "whites only" *Watson's*. The ban proved their undoing. *Watson's* disappeared long ago, but the *Taj*, with its grand grey-and-white stone facade and red-domed roof, still presides imperiously over the seafront, the preserve of visiting diplomats, sheikhs, businessmen and aircrew on expense accounts, and Mumbai's jet set. Lesser mortals are allowed in to sample the tea lounge, shopping arcades and vast air-conditioned lobby (a good place to cool down if the heat of the harbourfront has got the better of you).

From the *Taj*, you can head down the promenade, PJ Ramchandani Marg, better known as **Apollo Bunder** (the name is a colonial corruption of the Koli words for a local fish, *palav*, and quay, *bunda*), taking in the sea breezes and views over the busy harbour. Alternatively, Shivaji Marg heads northwest towards **Wellington Circle** (SPM Chowk), the hectic roundabout in front of the Art-Deco Regal cinema. The latter route takes you past the old **Bombay Yacht Club**, another idiosyncratic vestige of the Raj. Very little seems to have changed here since its smoky common rooms were a bolt-hole for the city's *burra-sahibs*. Behind its half-timbered gabled facade, dusty sporting trophies and models of clippers and dhows stand in glass cases lining the corridors, polished from time to time by bearers in cotton tunics. If you want to look around, seek permission from the club secretary.

Southwards along Colaba Causeway

Reclaimed in the late-nineteenth century from the sea, the district's main thoroughfare, **Colaba Causeway** (this stretch of Shahid Bhagat Singh Marg), leads south towards the military cantonment. Few tourists stray much further down it than the claustrophobic hawker zone at the top of the street, but it's well worth doing so, if only to see the neighbourhood's earthy **fresh produce market**, a couple of blocks south of the Strand cinema, which provides an unexpected splash of rustic colour amid the urban surroundings. From here, return to the main road and turn left to reach the gates of Mumbai's wholesale seafood market, **Sassoon Docks**. Photographed to powerful effect by Sebastião Salgado in his book, *Work*, the docks are at their most vigorous in the hour after sunrise, when coolies haul the night's catch in crates of crushed ice over gangplanks to the quayside, while Koli women, their saris hitched up *dhoti*-style, wash and pile the fish into baskets for sale. The stench, as overpowering as the noise, comes mostly from bundles of one of the city's traditional exports,

"**Bombay duck**", drying on the trawlers' rigging. Note that **photography** is strictly forbidden, as the docks are adjacent to a sensitive navy area.

Hop on any bus heading south down Colaba Causeway (#3, #11, #47, #103, #123, or #125) through the cantonment to reach the **Afghan Memorial Church of St John the Baptist**, built (1847–54) as a memorial to the British victims of the First Afghan War. With its tall steeple and tower, the pale yellow church wouldn't look out of place in Worcester or Suffolk. If the door is unlocked, take a peep inside at the battle-scarred military colours on the wall and marble memorial plaques to officers who died in various campaigns on the Northwest Frontier.

Downtown Mumbai

The critic and travel writer Robert Byron (of *Road to Oxiana* fame), although a wholehearted fan of New Delhi, was unenthusiastic about the architecture of **downtown Mumbai**, which he described as "that architectural Sodom". Today, the massive monuments of Empire and Indian free enterprise appear not so much ugly, as intriguing. Between them, you'll occasionally come across still more curious buildings, with facades flanked by what appear to be Mesopotamian griffins. These are old Zoroashtrian (Parsi) **fire temples** – or agiaries – erected by wealthy worthies in the late nineteenth century. Few attract more than a trickle of ageing worshippers, and as a non-Parsi you won't be allowed inside, but they're a definitive Mumbai spectacle.

The area immediately north of Colaba, centred on the crescent of MG Road and Subhash Chowk, is known as **Kala Ghoda** ("Black Statue"), after the large equestrian statue of King Edward VII which formerly stood in its main square. Flanked by the city's principal museum and art galleries, the district has in recent years been re-launched as a "cultural enclave" – as much in an attempt to preserve its many historic buildings as to promote the contemporary visual arts that have thrived here since the 1950s. Fancy stainless-steel interpretative panels now punctuate the district's walkways, and on Sundays in December and January, the **Kala Ghoda Fair** sees portrait artists, potters and *mehendi* painters plying their trade in the car park fronting the Jehangir Art Gallery.

Chhatrapati Shivaji Museum (Prince of Wales Museum)

Set back from Mahatma Gandhi (MG) Road in its own grounds, the **Prince of Wales Museum of Western India** (Tues–Sun 10.15am–6pm; Rs300, Rs6 for students and Indian nationals, camera Rs30 – no tripods or flash), recently renamed as the tongue-twisting **Chhatrapati Shivaji Maharaj Vastu Sangrahalaya**, ranks among the city's most distinctive Raj-era constructions. Crowned by a massive white Moghul-style dome, it houses a superb collection of paintings and sculpture that you'll need several hours, or a couple of visits, to get the most out of. The building was designed by George Wittet, of Gateway of India fame, and is the epitome of the hybrid **Indo-Saracenic** style – regarded in its day as an "educated" interpretation of fifteenth- and sixteenth-century Gujarati architecture, mixing Islamic touches with typically English municipal brickwork.

To justify the hefty entrance fee demanded from foreigners, the museum's curators recently introduced an **audio tour** (included in the ticket price), which you collect at the admissions kiosk inside. Given the haphazard nature of the exhibitions and absence of contextual information, this would have been a welcome initiative if the commentary were up to scratch, but you'll probably find it does little to enhance your visit. The heat and humidity inside the building can also be a trial. For breaks, the institutional tea-coffee kiosk in the ground-floor garden is a much less congenial option than the *Café Samovar* outside (for a review, see p.719), but to exit the museum and re-enter (which you're entitled to do) you'll have to get your ticket stamped in the admissions lobby first.

The **Key Gallery** in the central hall provides a snapshot of the collection's treasures. Highlights here include the richly bejewelled Rewa dagger, a few choice Moghul paintings, an exquisitely enamelled Lucknowi hookah and – to the right of the entrance – stucco Buddhist figures dating from the fifth century AD. These were unearthed by the archeologist Henry Cousens in 1909 at Mirapur Khas, an early Gupta stupa that was bricked over soon after construction, which explains why the pieces remain so well preserved: traces of black and red paint are still visible on some of them. The standing figure, thought to represent a donor disciple, is the most recognizable of the group, his high rank denoted by non-matching earrings and a gracefully held lotus flower (reminiscent of the Padmapani masterpiece in Ajanta's Cave 1 – see p.758).

The main **sculpture room** on the **ground floor** displays some fine fourth- and fifth-century heads and figures from the Buddhist state of Gandhara, a former colony of Alexander the Great (hence the Greek-style features). Important Hindu sculptures include a seventh-century Chalukyan bas-relief from Aihole depicting Brahma seated on a lotus, and a sensuously carved torso of Mahisasuramardini, the goddess Durga, with tripod raised ready to skewer the demon buffalo.

Once past a missable mezzanine gallery dominated by facsimiles of prehistoric artefacts and Assyrian bas reliefs, the main attraction on the **first floor** has to be the famous collection of **Indian painting**. Most of it was amassed by the Peshwa diplomat, Nana Phadnis (1741–1800), from distress sales of aristocratic heirlooms during the breakup of the Moghul empire. Featured here are pages of Akbar's own lavish edition of the *Panchatantra* – the Moghul equivalent of Aesop's fables – and an equally well known portrait of Shah Jahan in old age. More fine medieval miniatures are housed in the recently inaugurated **Karl & Meherbai Khandalavala Gallery**, on the renovated east wing of this floor. Around a contemporary mock-courtyard made of rubber and wood, objects collected by a wealthy Parsi lawyer and his wife, former curators of the museum, are displayed to great effect. They include priceless pieces of Ghandaram sculputre, a splendid devotional wall hanging from Nathdwara in Rajasthan (see p.263), Chola bronzes (see p.1169) and some of the country's finest surviving examples of medieval Gujarati wood carving.

Himalayan *thangkas*, deities and ritual objects dating from the thirteenth century onwards form the backbone of the **Buddhist gallery**, also on the first floor. The final, **second floor** showcases a vast array of Oriental ceramics and glassware, and some European art gifted by wealthy Parsi benefactors, including a minor Titian and a Constable. Finally, among the grizzly **weapons** and pieces of armour stored in a small side gallery at the top of the building are a cuirass, helmet and jade dagger which the museum only recently discovered belonged to the Moghul emperor Akbar – the Persian inscription on the breast-plate hinted at its provenance, but wasn't translated until a few years ago.

Kala Ghoda Art Galleries

Technically in the same compound as the Prince of Wales Museum, though approached from further up MG Road, the **Jehangir Art Gallery** (daily 11am–7pm; free) is Mumbai's oldest-established venue for contemporary art, with five small halls specializing in twentieth-century arts and crafts from

Dabawallahs

Mumbai's size and inconvenient shape create all kind of hassles for its working population – not least having to stew for over four hours each day in slow municipal transport. One thing the daily tidal wave of commuters does not have to worry about, however, is where to find an inexpensive and wholesome home-cooked lunch. In a city with a wallah for everything, it will find them. The members of the **Nutan Mumbai Tiffin Box Suppliers Charity Trust**, known colloquially, and with no little affection, as "**dabawallahs**", see to that. Every day, around 1000 *dabawallahs* deliver freshly cooked food from 160,000 suburban kitchens to offices in the downtown area. Each lunch is prepared early in the morning by a devoted wife or mother while her husband or son is enduring the crush on the train. She arranges the rice, dhal, *subzi*, curd and *parathas* into cylindrical aluminium trays, stacks them on top of one another and clips them together with a neat little handle. This **tiffin box**, not unlike a slim paint tin, is the lynchpin of the whole operation. When the runner calls to collect it in the morning, he uses a special colour code on the lid to tell him where the lunch has to go. At the end of his round, he carries all the boxes to the nearest railway station and hands them over to other *dabawallahs* for the trip into town. Between leaving the wife and reaching its final destination, the tiffin box will pass through at least half a dozen different pairs of hands, carried on heads, shoulder-poles, bicycle handlebars and in the brightly decorated handcarts that plough with such insouciance through the midday traffic. Tins are rarely, if ever, lost – a fact recently reinforced by the American business magazine, *Forbes*, which awarded Mumbai's *dabawallahs* a 6-Sigma performance rating, the score reserved for companies who attain a 9.99999 percentage of correctness. This means that only one tiffin box in 6 million goes astray, in efficiency terms putting the illiterate *dabawallahs* on a par with bluechip firms such as Motorola.

To catch them in action, head for **CST (VT)** or **Churchgate** stations around late morning time, when the tiffin boxes arrive in the city centre. The event is accompanied by a chorus of "lafka! lafka!" – "hurry! hurry!" – as the *dabawallahs*, recognizable in their white Nehru caps and baggy pyjama trousers, rush to make their lunch-hour deadlines. Nearly all come from the same small village near Pune and are related to one another. They collect Rs150 from each customer, or around Rs5000 per month in total – not a bad income by Indian standards. One of the reasons the system survives in the face of competition from trendy fast food outlets is that *daba* lunches still work out a good deal cheaper, saving precious paise for the middle-income workers who use the system.

around the world. You never know what you're going to find – most exhibitions last only a week and exhibits are often for sale.

On the opposite side of MG Road, facing the museum and Mukharji Chowk, stands the larger **National Gallery of Modern Art** (Tues–Sun 10am–5pm; Rs20), housed in a converted concert hall. It holds a mix of permanent and temporary exhibitions on three storeys, charting the development of modern Indian art from its beginnings in the 1950s to the present day. The installations, in particular, tend to be a lot more adventurous than those you'll find in the Jehangir across the road.

Around Oval Maidan

Some of Mumbai's most important Victorian buildings flank the eastern side of the vast green **Oval Maidan**, where impromptu cricket matches are held almost every day (foreign enthusiasts are welcome to take part, but should beware the *maidan*'s demon bowlers and less-than-even pitches). The dull yellow

Old Secretariat now serves as the City Civil and Sessions Court. Indian civil servant G.W. Forrest described it in 1903 as "a massive pile whose main features have been brought from Venice, but all the beauty has vanished in transhipment". Inside, you can only imagine the originally highly polished interior, which no longer shines, but buzzes with activity. Lawyers in black gowns, striped trousers and white tabs bustle up and down the staircases, whose corners are emblazoned with expectorated paan juice, and offices with perforated swing-doors give glimpses of textbook images of Indian bureaucracy – peons at desks piled high with dusty beribboned document bundles.

Across AS D'Mello Road from the Old Secretariat, two major buildings belonging to **Mumbai University** (established 1857) were designed in England by Sir Gilbert Scott, who had already given the world the Gothic extravaganza of London's St Pancras railway station. Access through the main gates is monitored by caretakers who only allow you in if you say you're visiting the library. Funded by the Parsi philanthropist Cowasjee "Readymoney" Jehangir, the **Convocation Hall** greatly resembles a church. The **library** (daily 10am–10pm) is beneath the 79.2-metre-high **Rajabhai Clock Tower** which is said to be modelled on Giotto's campanile in Florence. Until 1931, it chimed tunes such as *Rule Britannia* and *Home Sweet Home*. You can scale the grand staircase from the lobby to enter the magnificent vaulted reading room, whose high Gothic windows and stained glass still evoke a reverential approach to learning.

Hutatma Chowk (Flora Fountain)

A busy five-point intersection in the heart of the Fort area, the roundabout formerly known as **Flora Fountain** has been renamed **Hutatma Chowk** ("Martyr's Square") to commemorate the freedom fighters who died to establish the state of Maharashtra in the Indian Union. The chowk centres on a statue of the Roman goddess **Flora**, erected in 1869 to commemorate Sir Bartle Frere. It's hard to see quite why they bothered – the Raj architecture expert, Philip Davies, was not being unkind when he said, "The fountain was designed by a committee, and it shows."

Horniman Circle and the Town Hall

Horniman Circle, formerly Elphinstone Circle, is named after a pro-Independence newspaper editor. It was conceived in 1860 as a centrepiece of a newly planned Bombay by the then Municipal Commissioner, Charles Forjett, on the site of Bombay "Green". Forjett, a Eurasian, had something of a peculiar reputation; he was fond of disguising himself in "native" dress and prowling about certain districts of the city to listen out for seditious talk. In 1857, at the time of the First War of Independence (as it is now known by Indians; the British call it the Indian Mutiny), Forjett fired on two suspected revolutionaries from a cannon on the Esplanade (roughly the site of the modern *maidans*).

Flanking the east side of the circle, the impressive Doric Town Hall on SBS Marg houses the vast collection of the **Asiatic Society Library** (Mon–Sat 10am–7pm). Save for the addition of electricity, little has changed here since the institution was founded in the early eighteenth century. Inside the reading rooms, lined with wrought-iron loggias and teak bookcases, scholars pour over mouldering tomes dating from the Raj. Among the 10,000 rare and valuable manuscripts stored here is a fourteenth-century first edition of Dante's *Divine Comedy*, said to be worth around $3 million, which the Society famously refused to sell to Mussolini. Visitors are welcome but should sign in at the Head Librarian's desk on the ground floor.

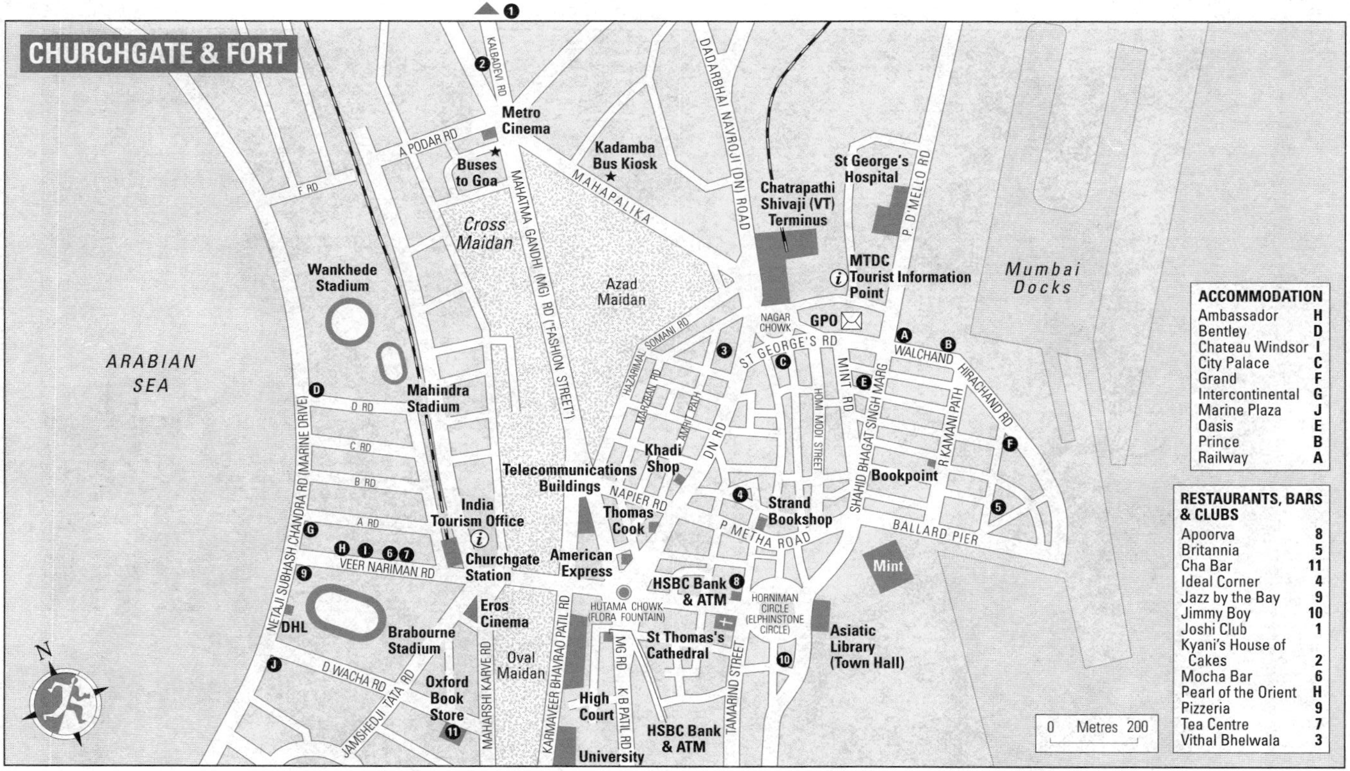

CHURCHGATE & FORT

ACCOMMODATION

Ambassador	H
Bentley	D
Chateau Windsor	I
City Palace	C
Grand	F
Intercontinental	G
Marine Plaza	J
Oasis	E
Prince	B
Railway	A

RESTAURANTS, BARS & CLUBS

Apoorva	8
Britannia	5
Cha Bar	11
Ideal Corner	4
Jazz by the Bay	9
Jimmy Boy	10
Joshi Club	1
Kyani's House of Cakes	2
Mocha Bar	6
Pearl of the Orient	H
Pizzeria	9
Tea Centre	7
Vithal Bhelwala	3

0 Metres 200

ARABIAN SEA
Mumbai Docks
KALBADEVI RD
Metro Cinema
A PODAR RD
Buses to Goa
F RD
Cross Maidan
Kadamba Bus Kiosk
MAHAPALIKA
MAHATMA GANDHI (MG) RD ("FASHION STREET")
DADARBHAI NAVROJI (DN) ROAD
Chatrapathi Shivaji (VT) Terminus
St George's Hospital
P. D'MELLO RD
MTDC Tourist Information Point
Wankhede Stadium
Azad Maidan
NAGAR CHOWK
GPO
ST GEORGE'S RD
WALCHAND
HIRACHAND RD
HAZARIMAL SOMANI RD
MARZBAN RD
AMRI PATH
DN RD
MINT RD
HOMI MODI STREET
SHAHID BHAGAT SINGH MARG
R KAMANI PATH
Mahindra Stadium
D RD
C RD
B RD
A RD
Khadi Shop
Telecommunications Buildings
NAPIER RD
Bookpoint
India Tourism Office
Thomas Cook
Strand Bookshop
P METHA ROAD
BALLARD PIER
Mint
Churchgate Station
American Express
VEER NARIMAN RD
NETAJI SUBHASH CHANDRA RD (MARINE DRIVE)
HSBC Bank & ATM
HUTAMA CHOWK (FLORA FOUNTAIN)
HORNIMAN CIRCLE (ELPHINSTONE CIRCLE)
Eros Cinema
DHL
Brabourne Stadium
St Thomas's Cathedral
Asiatic Library (Town Hall)
Oval Maidan
MG RD
TAMARIND STREET
D WACHA RD
JAMSHEDJI TATA RD
Oxford Book Store
MAHARSHI KARVE RD
KARMAVEER BHAVRAO PATIL RD
High Court
K B PATIL RD
HSBC Bank & ATM
University
N

△ Ganesh Festival

St Thomas' Cathedral

The small, simple **St Thomas' Cathedral** (daily 6.30am–6pm), on Tamarind Street, is reckoned to be the oldest British building in Mumbai, blending Classical and Gothic styles. After the death of its founding father, Governor Aungier, the project was abandoned; the walls stood 5m high for forty-odd years until enthusiasm was rekindled by a chaplain to the East India Company in the second decade of the eighteenth century. It was finally opened on Christmas Day 1718, complete with the essential "cannon-ball-proof roof". In those days, the seating was divided into useful sections for those who should know their place, including one for "Inferior Women".

St Thomas' whitewashed and polished brass-and-wood interior looks much the same as when the staff of the East India Company worshipped here in the eighteenth century. Lining the walls are memorial tablets to British parishioners, many of whom died young, either from disease or in battle.

Victoria Terminus (Chhatrapati Shivaji Terminus)

Inspired by St Pancras station in London, F.W. Stevens designed **Victoria Terminus**, the most barmy of Mumbai's buildings, as a paean to "progress". Built in 1887 as the largest British edifice in India, it's an extraordinary amalgam of domes, spires, Corinthian columns and minarets that was succinctly defined by the journalist James Cameron as "Victorian-Gothic-Saracenic-Italianate-Oriental-St Pancras-Baroque". In keeping with the current re-Indianization of the city's roads and buildings, this icon of British imperial architecture has been renamed **Chhatrapati Shivaji Terminus**, in honour of a Maratha warlord. However, the new name is a bit of a mouthful and the locals mostly still use **VT** (pronounced "vitee" or "wee tee") when referring to it.

Few of the two million or so passengers who fill almost a thousand trains every day notice the mass of decorative detail. A "British" lion and Indian tiger stand guard at the entrance, and the exterior is festooned with sculptures executed at the Bombay Art School by the Indian students of John Lockwood Kipling, Rudyard's father. Among them are grotesque mythical beasts, monkeys and plants and medallions of important personages. To minimize the sun's impact, stained glass was employed, decorated with locomotives and elephant images. Above it all, "Progress" stands atop the massive central dome.

An endless frenzy of activity goes on inside: hundreds of porters in red with impossibly oversize headloads; TTEs (Travelling Ticket Examiners) in black jackets and white trousers clasping clipboards detailing reservations; spitting checkers busy handing out fines to those caught in the act; chai-wallahs with trays of tea; trundling magazine stands; crowds of bored soldiers smoking *beedis*; and the inexorable progress across the station of sweepers bent double. Amid it all, whole families spread out on the floor, eating, sleeping or just waiting and waiting.

Marine Drive and Chowpatty Beach

Netaji Subhash Chandra Marg, better known as **Marine Drive**, is Mumbai's seaside prom, an eight-lane highway with a wide pavement built in the 1920s on reclaimed land. Sweeping in an arc from the skyscrapers at Nariman Point in the south, the route ends at the foot of Malabar Hill and Chowpatty Beach. The whole stretch is a favourite place for a stroll; the promenade next to the sea has uninterrupted views virtually the whole way along, while the apartment blocks on the land side are some of the most desirable and expensive addresses in the city.

Just beyond the huge flyover at its northern end are a series of cricket pitches known as **gymkhanas**, where there's a good chance of catching a match any day of the week. A number are exclusive to particular religious communities. The first doubles as a swanky outdoor wedding venue for Parsi marriages; others include the Catholic, Islamic and Hindu pitches, the last of which has a classic colonial-style pavilion.

Chowpatty Beach

Chowpatty Beach is a Mumbai institution, which really comes to life at night and on Saturday. People do not come here to swim (the sea is foul) but to wander, sit on the beach, let the kids ride a pony or a rusty Ferris wheel, have a massage, get ears cleaned or picnic on *bhel puri* and cups of kulfi. For the last century or so, Gupta Bhelwallas's *bhel puri* stall has satisfied the discerning Mumbai palate with a secret concoction of the sunset snack; you'll find it amid the newly constructed "shacks" to which the *bhel* wallahs were recently moved as part of the Municipality's bid to clean the beach up.

Once a year in September the **Ganesh Chathurthi** festival (see box p.694) draws gigantic crowds to participate in the immersion of idols, both huge and small, of the elephant-headed god Ganesh.

Mani Bhavan Mahatma Gandhi Museum

A ten-minute walk north from the middle of Chowpatty Beach (along P Ramabai Marg), **Mani Bhavan**, at 19 Laburnum Rd (daily 9.30am–6pm), was Gandhi's Bombay base between 1917 and 1934. Set in a leafy upper-middle-class road, the house is now a permanent memorial to the Mahatma with an extensive research library. Within the lovingly maintained polished-wood interior, the walls are covered with photos of historic events and artefacts from the man's extraordinary life – the most disarming of which is a friendly letter to Hitler suggesting world peace. Gandhi's predictably simple sitting room-cum-bedroom is preserved behind glass. Laburnum Road is a few streets along from the Bharatiya Vidya Bhavan music venue on KM Munshi Marg – if coming by taxi ask for the nearby Gamdevi Police Station.

North of Chowpatty

Two of Mumbai's most popular religious sites, one Hindu, the other Muslim, can be reached by following Bhulabhai Desai Road **north from Chowpatty** as far as Prabhu Chowk, through the exclusive suburb of Breach Candy (bus #132 from Colaba). Alternatively, make for Mumbai Central and head due northwest to Vatsalabai Desai Chowk (also bus #132).

Mahalakshmi Mandir is joined to Bhulabhai Desai Road by an alley lined with stalls selling puja offerings and devotional pictures. Mumbai's favourite *devi*, **Lakshmi**, goddess of beauty and prosperity – the city's most sought-after attributes – is here propitiated with coconuts, sweets, lengths of shimmering silk and giant lotus blooms. Gifts pile so high that the temple *pujaris* run a money-spinning sideline reselling them. Their little shop, to the left of the entrance, is a good place to buy cut-price saris and brocades infused with lucky Lakshmi-energy. While you're here, find out what your future holds by joining the huddle of devotees pressing rupees onto the rear wall of the shrine room. If your coin sticks, you'll be rich.

Occupying a small islet in the bay just north of the Mahalakshmi is the mausoleum of the Muslim saint, Afghan mystic **Haji Ali Bukhari**. The tomb is connected to the mainland by a narrow concrete **causeway**, only passable at low tide. When not immersed in water, its entire length is lined with beggars who change one-rupee pieces into ten-paise coins for pilgrims. The prime sites, closer to the snack bars that flank the main entrance, near the small mosque, and the gateway to the **tomb** itself, are allocated in a strict pecking order. If you want to make a donation, spare a thought for the unfortunates in the middle. After all the commotion, the tomb itself comes as something of a disappointment. Its white Moghul domes and minarets look a lot less exotic close up than when viewed from the shore, silhouetted against the sun as it drops into the Arabian Sea.

The central bazaars

Lining the anarchic jumble of streets north of Lokmanya Tilak (formerly Carnac) Road, Mumbai's teeming **central bazaars** are India at its most intense. You could wander around here for days without seeing the same shop front twice. In practice, most visitors find a couple of hours mingling with the crowds in the heat and din quite enough. Nevertheless, the market districts form a fascinating counterpoint to the wide and Westernized streets of downtown, even if you're not buying.

In keeping with traditional divisions of guild, caste and religion, most streets specialize in one or two types of merchandise. If you lose your bearings, the best way out is to ask someone to wave you in the direction of **Mohammed Ali Road**, the busy road through the heart of the district (now surmounted by a gigantic flyover), from where you can hail a cab.

Crawford Market

Crawford (aka Mahatma Phule) **Market**, ten minutes' walk north of CST (VT) station, is an old British-style covered market dealing in just about every kind of fresh food and domestic animal imaginable. Thanks to its pompous Norman-Gothic tower and prominent position at the corner of Lokmanya Tilak Road and Dr DN Marg, the Crawford Market is also a useful landmark and a good place to begin a foray into the bazaars.

Before venturing inside, stop to admire the **friezes** wrapped around its exterior – a Victorian vision of sturdy-limbed peasants toiling in the fields designed by Rudyard Kipling's father, Lockwood, as principal of the Bombay School of Art in 1865. The **main hall** is still divided into different sections: pyramids of polished fruit and vegetables down one aisle, sacks of nuts or oil-tins full of herbs and spices down another. Around the back of the market, in the atmospheric wholesale wing, the pace of life is more hectic. Here, noisy crowds of coolies mill about with large reed-baskets held high in the air (if they are looking for work) or on their heads (if they've found some).

One place animal-lovers should definitely steer clear of is Crawford Market's **pet** and **poultry** section, on the east side of the building. You never quite know what creatures will turn up here, cringing in rank-smelling, undersized cages.

North of Crawford Market

The streets immediately **north of Crawford Market** and west of **Mohammed Ali Road**, form one vast bazaar area. Ranged along both sides of narrow **Mangaldas Lane**, the cloth bazaar, are small shops draped with lengths of bright silk and cotton. Low doorways on the left open onto a colourful **covered market** area, packed with tiny stalls.

Eastwards along Mangaldas Lane from Carnac Road, the pale green-washed domes, arches and minarets of the **Jami Masjid**, or "Friday Mosque" (c.1800), mark the start of the Muslim neighbourhoods. **Memon Street**, cutting north from the mosque, is the site of the **Zaveri Bazaar**, the jewellery market where Mumbaikars come to shop for dowries and wedding attire.

By the time the gleaming golden spire that crowns the **Mumba Devi temple**'s cream-and-turquoise tower appears at the end of the street, you're deep in a maze of twisting lanes hemmed in by tall, wooden-balconied buildings. One of the most important centres of Devi worship in India, the temple was built early in the nineteenth century, when the deity was relocated from her former home to make way for CST (VT) station. Mumba Devi's other claim to fame is that her name is the original root of the word "Bombay", as well as the official, Maharashtran version, "**Mumbai**".

Bear left at the temple and keep heading along the main bazaar for ten or fifteen minutes and you'll arrive at another important Hindu enclave, **Bhuleshwar**. The district is famous throughout the city for its colourful **phool galli** (flower lane), where temple goers buy luxurious garlands, lotus bundles and marigolds heaped in huge baskets. Of the 85 shrines said to be crammed into its lanes the most important is the **Bhola Ishtwar Mandir**, the ancient Shiva temple around which this district is believed to have first grown up in the eighteenth century. Its odd mix of Gujarati, Rajasthani and Konkan architectural styles reflect the origins of the neighbourhood's first immigrants. Jain merchants also settled here from the northwest, erecting a pair of finely carved white marble temples – **Shantinath** and **Parshavanath** – tucked away down a narrow lane just off the nest crossroads, Jayamber Chowk. Animal lovers should ask the way here to the nearby **Panjarapool animal sanctuary**, where around four hundred beautiful brown *gir* cows are cared for, along with a menagerie of pigeons, rabbits, chickens and ducks. You can purchase donatory bowls of grain and *ladoo* balls to feed them at reception, where stern-faced Jain attendants enforce the strict no photography rule.

Chor Bazaar, Mutton Road and the red-light district

Jump in a taxi at the junction just down the lane from the Mumba Devi temple for the two-kilometre trip north to the other concentration of markets around **Johar Chowk**, just north of SV Patel Road. The most famous of these, **Chor** (literally "thieves") **Bazaar** (where vendors peevishly insist the name is a corruption of the Urdu *shor*, meaning "noisy"), is the city's largest **antiques**-cum-flea market. Friday, the Muslim holy day, is the best day to be here. From 9am onwards, the neighbourhood is cluttered with hawkers and hand-carts piled high with bric-a-brac and assorted junk. At other times, the antique shops down on **Mutton Road** are the main attraction. Once, you could hope to unearth real gems in these dark, fusty stores, but your chances of finding a genuine bargain nowadays are minimal. Most of the stuff is pricey Victoriana – old gramophones, chamber pots, chipped china – salvaged from the homes of Parsi families on the decline. The place is also awash with **fakes**, mainly small bronze votive statues, which make good souvenirs if you can knock the price down.

Press on north through Chor Bazaar and you'll eventually come out onto **Grant Road** (Maulana Shaukatali Road). Further north and west, in the warren of lanes below JB Behram Marg, lies the city's infamous **red-light district**. **Kamathipura**'s rows of luridly lit, barred shop fronts, from where an estimated 25,000 prostitutes ply their trade, are one of Mumbai's more degrading and unpleasant spectacles. Many of these so-called "**cage girls**" are young teenagers from poor tribal areas, and from across the border in Nepal, who have been sold by desperate parents into **bonded slavery** until they can earn the money to pay off family debts.

Elephanta

An hour's boat ride from Colaba, the island of **ELEPHANTA** offers one of the more atmospheric escapes from the seething claustrophobia of the city – as long as you time your visit to avoid the weekend deluge of noisy day-trippers. Populated only by a small fishing community, it was originally known as **Gharapuri**, the "city of Ghara priests", until the island was renamed in the sixteenth century by the Portuguese in honour of the carved elephant they found at the port. Its chief attraction is its unique **cave temple**, whose massive **Trimurti** (three-faced) **Shiva sculpture** is as fine an example of Hindu architecture as you'll find anywhere.

"**Deluxe**" **boats** set off from the Gateway of India (Oct–May hourly 9am–2.30pm; Rs100 return including government guide); book through the kiosks near the Gateway of India. Ask for your guide at the cave's ticket office on arrival – they take about thirty minutes. **Ordinary ferries** (Rs80 return), also from the Gateway of India, don't include guides, and are usually packed. The journey takes about an hour on either boat.

Cool drinks and souvenir stalls line the way up the hill, and at the top, the MTDC *Chalukya* restaurant offers food and beer, and a terrace with good views out to sea, but you cannot stay overnight on the island.

The Cave

Elephanta's impressive excavated eighth-century **cave** (9.30am–4pm; $5 [Rs5]), covering an area of approximately 5000 square metres, is reached by climbing more than one hundred steps to the top of the hill. Inside, the massive columns, carved from solid rock, give the deceptive impression of being structural. To the right, as you enter, note the panel of **Nataraj**, Shiva as the cosmic dancer. Though spoiled by the Portuguese who, it is said, used it for target practice, the panel remains magnificent; Shiva's face is rapt, and in one of his left hands he removes the veil of ignorance. Opposite is a badly damaged panel of Lakulisha, Shiva with a club (*lakula*).

Each of the four entrances to the simple square main **shrine** – unusually, it has one on each side – is flanked by a pair of huge fanged *dvarpala* guardians (only those to the back have survived undamaged), while inside a large *lingam* is surrounded by coins and smouldering joss left by devotees. Facing the northern wall of the shrine, another panel shows Shiva impaling the demon Andhaka, who wandered around as though blind, symbolizing his spiritual blindness. The panel behind the shrine on the back wall portrays the marriage of Shiva and Parvati. A powerful six-metre bust of **Trimurti**, the three-faced Shiva, who embodies the powers of creator, preserver and destroyer, stands nearby, and to the west a sculpture shows Shiva as **Ardhanarishvara**, half male and half female. Near the second entrance on the east, another panel shows Shiva and Parvati on **Mount Kailasha** with Ravana about to lift the mountain. His curved spine shows the strain.

The outskirts: Kanheri Caves

Overlooking the suburb of Borivli, 42km out at the northern limits of Mumbai's sprawl, are the Buddhist **Kanheri Caves** (daily 9am–5.30pm; $2 [Rs5]), ranged over the hills in virtually unspoilt forest. It's an interminable journey by road, so catch one of the many **trains** (50min) on the suburban line from Churchgate (marked "BO" on the departure boards; "limited stop" trains are 15min faster) to Borivli East. When you arrive, take the Borivli East exit, where a **bus** (for Kanheri Cave via SG Parles; Rs14), **auto-rickshaw** (about Rs75) or **taxi** (about Rs100) will take you the last 15km. Bring water and food as the stalls here only sell warm soft drinks.

Kanheri may not be as spectacular as other cave sites, but some of its sculpture is superb – though to enjoy the blissful peace and quiet that attracted its original occupants you should **avoid the weekends**. Most of the caves, which date from the second to the ninth century AD, were used simply by monks for accommodation and meditation during the four months of the monsoon, when an itinerant life was impractical. They are connected by steep winding paths and steps; engage one of the friendly local guides at the entrance to find your way about, but don't expect any sort of lecture as their English is limited. The risk of muggings in some of the remoter caves means it is not advisable to venture off the beaten track alone.

In **Cave 1**, an incomplete *chaitya* hall (a hall with a stupa at one end, an aisle and row of columns at either side), you can see where the rock was left cut, but unfinished. Two stupas stand in **Cave 2**; one was vandalized by a certain N. Christian, whose carefully incised Times-Roman graffiti bears the date 1810. A panel shows seated Buddhas, portrayed as teachers. Behind, and to the side, is the *bodhisattva* of compassion, Padmapani, while to the right the *viharas* feature rock-cut beds.

Huge Buddhas, with serenely joyful expressions and unfeasibly large shoulders, stand on either side of the porch to the spectacular **Cave 3**. Between them, you'll see the panels of "donor couples", thought to have been foreigners that patronized the community.

The sixth-century **Cave 11** is a large assembly hall, where two long "tables" of rock were used for the study of manuscripts. Seated at the back, in the centre, is a figure of the Buddha as teacher, an image repeated in the entrance, to the left, with a wonderful flight of accompanying celestials. Just before the entrance to a small cell in **Cave 34**, flanked by two standing Buddhas, an unfinished ceiling painting shows the Buddha touching the earth. There must be at least a hundred more Buddha images on panels in **Cave 67**, a large hall. On the left side, and outside in the entrance, these figures are supported by *nagas* (snakes representing *kundalini*, yogic power).

Eating

In keeping with its cosmopolitan credentials, Mumbai is crammed with interesting **eating places**, whether you fancy splashing out on a buffet lunch-with-a-view from a flashy five-star restaurant, or simply tucking into piping-hot roti kebab by gaslight in the street.

Street food

Mumbai is renowned for distinctive street foods – and especially **bhel puri**, a quintessentially Mumbai *masala* mixture of puffed rice, deep-fried vermicelli, potato, crunchy *puri* pieces, chilli paste, tamarind water, chopped onions and coriander. More hygienic, but no less ubiquitous, is **pao bhaji**, a round Portuguese-style bread roll stuffed with griddle-fried, spicy lentil stew, and **kanji vada**, savoury doughnuts soaked in fermented mustard and chilli sauce. And if all that doesn't appeal, a pit stop at one of the city's hundreds of **juice bars** probably will. There's no better way to beat the sticky heat than with a glass of cool milk shaken with fresh pineapple, mango, banana, *chikoo* (small brown fruit that tastes like a sweet pear) or custard apple. Just make sure they hold on the ice – made, of course, with untreated water.

Restaurants, bars and cafés are listed by district. **Phone numbers** have been given where we recommend you reserve a table for dinner; and beware of **service charges** levied on your bill by some of the more expensive places.

Colaba and Kala Ghoda

Colaba and Kala Ghoda's cafés, bars and restaurants encompass just about the full range of modern Mumbai's gastronomic possibilities, from no-frills kerb-side kebab joints and old Irani cafés to exclusive air-conditioned restaurants patronized by Bollywood stars and politicians. The majority – among them the popular travellers' haunts, *Leopold's* and the *Café Mondegar* – are up at the north end of the Causeway. The following all feature on our Colaba map, p.705.

All Stir Fry *Gorden House Hotel.* Build-your-own wok meal from a selection of fresh veg, meat, fish, noodles and sauces, flash-cooked in front of you (Rs250–350 per bowl). Trendy white, minimalist decor, glacial a/c, and snappy service.

Bademiya Behind the *Taj* on Tulloch Rd. Legendary Colaba kebab-wallah serving delicious flame-grilled chicken, mutton and fish steaks, wrapped in paper-thin, piping hot *rotis*, from benches on the sidewalk. Rich families from uptown drive here on weekends, eating on their car bonnets, but there are also little tables and chairs if you don't fancy a takeaway.

Busaba 4 Mandlik Marg ⓣ022/2204 3779. Sophisticated bar-restaurant specializing in Far-Eastern cuisine – Thai, Korean, Burmese, Vietnamese and Tibetan staples, with exotic salads (green mango and glass noodle). One of *the* places to be seen (if you can't quite afford to eat at *Indigo* next door). Count on Rs750–1000 per head for the works.

Café Samovar Jehangir Art Gallery, MG Rd ⓣ022/2284 8000. Very pleasant, peaceful semi-al fresco café opening onto the museum gardens, with a good-value lunch menu (Rs50) featuring *pulaos*, stuffed *parathas* and biriyanis, as well as plenty of à la carte choices (prawn curry, *roti kebabs*, and fresh salads and dhansak. They also served delicious chilled guava juice and beer (Rs90), but note no drinks served from 1–3pm.

Churchill 103 Colaba Causeway. Tiny 26-seater Parsi diner, with a bewildering choice of curious dishes, mostly meat based and served in mild gravies alongside a blob of mash and boiled veg – ideal if you've had your fill of spicy food. No alcohol. Main courses around Rs150.

Indigo 4 Mandlik Marg ⓣ022/2236 8999. Currently the city's most fashionable restaurant, and for once deserving of the hype. The cooking's Italian-based with a Konkan-Keralan twist (eg Kochi oysters with saffron ravioli). House flambée is extremely popular, as much for its head-turning potential as anything else. Count on Rs1000-plus for three courses. Reservations essential.

Kailash Parbat ("KP's") 1 Pasta Lane, near the Strand cinema. Uninspiring on the outside, but the *aloo parathas* for breakfast, pure veg nibbles, hot snacks and sweets (across the road) are worth the walk. A Colaba institution – try their famous *makai-ka* (corn) *rotis*.

Kamat Colaba Causeway. Friendly little eatery serving unquestionably the best South Indian breakfasts in the area, as well as the usual range of southern snacks (*iddli-vada-sambar*), delicious spring *dosas* and (limited) thalis for Rs30–85. The best option in the area for budget travellers with big appetites.

Khyber opposite Jehangir Art Gallery, Kala Ghoda ⓣ022/2267 3227. Opulent Arabian Nights interior and uncompromisingly rich "Northwest Frontier" cuisine, served by black-tie waiters. The chicken tikka is legendary, but their tandoori dishes and kebab platter are superb too. Count on Rs800–1000.

Konkan Café *Taj President Hotel*, Cuffe Parade ⓣ022/5665 0808. This is the place to push the boat out: a sophisticated five-star hotel restaurant serving fine regional cuisine from coastal Maharashtra, Goa, Karnataka and Kerala – at reasonable prices. You can choose from their thali platters (Rs375–475), or go à la carte: the crab in butter pepper garlic is to die for, as is the tiger prawn in *kokum* garlic and *meen pollichattu* (red snappers steamed Keralan-style in banana leaves). Quite simply some of the most mouthwatering South Indian food you'll ever eat.

Leopold's Colaba Causeway. Colaba's most famous – and overpriced – café-bar is determinedly Western, with a clientele to match. Three hundred items on the menu from scrambled eggs to "chilly chicken", washed down with cold beer (Rs120). There's also a bar upstairs.

Olympia Coffee House 1 Colaba Causeway. *Fin-de-siècle* Irani café with marble tabletops, wooden wall panels, fancy mirrors and a mezzanine floor for "ladies". Waiters in Peshawari caps and *salwar kamises* serve melt-in-the-mouth kebabs, flavoured with subtle spices and delicious curd-based dips. For dessert, go for the "custard". A quintessential Bombay experience. Inexpensive.

The Sea Lounge *Taj Mahal Hotel*. Spacious 1930s-style lounge café on the first floor of the *Taj*. Come for afternoon tea or a late breakfast with a backdrop of the Gateway and harbour. Worth splashing out on for the atmosphere. Opens at 7am for breakfast; closes at midnight. Pastries Rs200–300; coffees and teas Rs125–200.

Trishna 7 Sai Baba Marg (Ropewalk Lane), Kala Ghoda ☎022/2270 1623. Visiting dignitaries and local celebs from the President of Greece and Imran Khan to Bollywood stars have eaten here (as photos attest). Wonderful fish dishes in every sauce going, and prices to match the clientele (main courses from Rs450). Butter pepper garlic crab is their signature dish, but the pomfret stuffed with green masala is great too. Very small, so book in advance.

Downtown: Fort, CST (VT) and Dhobi Talao

Don't be discouraged by the heat and traffic from venturing outside Colaba for a meal. A short walk or taxi ride north are some of the best cafés and restaurants in the city, among them Mumbai's last surviving traditional Parsi diners, whose menus and decor have changed little over three or four generations. The places listed below are all marked on the Churchgate and Fort map on p.711.

Apoorva Vasta House (Noble Chambers), SA Brelvi Rd ☎022/2287 0335. Currently the city's most rated Mangalorean, hidden up a side street off Horniman Circle (look for the tree trunk wrapped with fairy lights). The cooking's completely authentic and the seafood – simmered in spicy coconut-based gravies – fresh off the boats each day. Try their definitive Bombay Duck or sublime prawn *gassi*, served with perfect *sanna* and *appams*. Women should note the ground floor doubles as a bloke-ish bar in the evenings.

Britannia & Co Opposite the GPO, Sprott Rd, Ballard Estate. Quirky little Parsi restaurant, famous as much for its quaint period atmosphere as its wholesome Irani food. Most people come for the sublime "berry pulao" (chicken, mutton or vegetable), made with deliciously tart dried berries imported from Tehran (Rs150, but portions are gigantic). For afters, there's the house "caramel custard". One of the city's unmissable eating experiences. Open 11.30am–3.30pm.

Ideal Corner 12 F/G Hornby View, Gunbow St ☎022/2262 1930. Another Parsi café with a cult following, but more in the thick of things than *Britannia* and less old world since its recent facelift. Go for one of their delicious homemade Parsi specialities: *kihchidi* prawn, lamb dhansak or chicken *farcha*, rounded off with the legendary *lagan* custard (a nutty crème caramel served chilled in little foil tubs). Most mains Rs45–60. Closed evenings and Sun.

Jimmy Boy 11 Bank St, Vikas Bldg, off Horniman Circle ☎022/2270 0880. Among the few places left in Mumbai where you can sample pukka Parsi wedding food (albeit in rather inauthentic a/c surroundings, to a Shania Twain soundtrack). Go for the Rs225 fixed menu (pomfret and green chilli sauce steamed in a banana leaf/mutton pulao with dhansak dhal/dessert).

Joshi Club 31-A Narottamwadi, Kalbadevi Rd ☎022/2205 8089. Also known as *The Friends Union Joshi Club*, this eccentric thali canteen serves what many aficionados regard as the most genuine and tasty Gujarati-Marwari meals in the city, dished up on unpromising Formica tables against a backdrop of grubby walls. Rs70 buys you unlimited portions of four vegetables, dhals and up to four different kinds of bread, with all the trimmings (and banana custard). Extra *farsan* and sweets cost Rs20. Finding it requires some effort: walk or catch a cab to the bottom of Kalbadevi Rd (opposite the Metro cinema; see map p.711); head north across Vardhaman Chowk, and continue up Kalbadevi Rd for 5min until you see a signboard on your right for "Bhonalaya", below a first-floor window. The locals will know where it is.

Kyani's "House of Cakes" Bakery opposite Metro cinema, Dhobi Talao. The most dated and authentic Parsi joint in the city, worth a visit more for the atmosphere than for the food – neither of which has altered in over ninety years since the café first opened. They serve freshly baked biscuits and cakes, "bun-*maska*" (basically warm buttered rolls) and good strong chai in china cups.

Vithal Bhelwala 5 AK Naik Marg (Baston Rd), close to CST (VT). Mumbai's favourite *bhel puri* outlet, open since 1875 and still doing a roaring trade. No less than 25 kinds of *bhel* are on offer, including one pitched at British palates, with "boiled veg and cornflakes". They also do delicious potato cutlets, served with crunchy *puri* and yoghurt. Handy for the movie houses and the station.

Churchgate and Nariman Point

The restaurants listed below are marked on the Churchgate and Fort map on p.711.

Cha Bar Oxford Bookstore, 3 Dinsha Vaccha Rd, Churchgate. Very chic a/c café accessed via the city's top book store, popular mainly with well-heeled students. They serve an exhaustive range of single-estate and regional teas and coffees, from high-fired Darjeeling to Kashmiri *kawa* and Ladhaki butter tea, as well as trendy ayurvedic brews and house "tea cocktails"; and there's a tempting menu of (pricy) light snacks and toasties. Open 10am–10pm.

Mocha Bar VN Rd. Chilled terrace café where swarms of north Mumbai bratpackers order American-style coffees, Mediterranean mezes and outrageously expensive New World wines, crashed out on bolster cushions smoking fruit-flavoured tobacco on a hookah pipe: very much the zeitgeist.

The Pearl of the Orient *Ambassador Hotel*, VN Rd ⓣ022/229 1131. Revolving Oriental restaurant in this four-star hotel. The cooking's nothing special (and expensive at around Rs750 for three courses), but the views over the city are extraordinary.

The Pizzeria corner of Veer Nariman and Marine Drive. Delicious, freshly baked pizzas served on newly renovated terrace overlooking Back Bay, or to take away. Plenty of choice, and moderate prices (Rs175–295 per pizza).

The Tea Centre Resham Bhavan, 78 VN Rd. Another vestige of colonial days which, despite a lavish new refit, has retained its Raj-era charm, with paddle fans, comfy furniture and waiters wearing old-style *pugris*. Fine tea is its *raison d'être*, but they also serve delicious Continental snacks (try their fluffy cheese omlettes) and cakes, as well as a good-value "Executive Lunch" (Rs200).

Crawford Market and the central bazaars

The restaurants listed below are marked on the main Mumbai map on pp.692–693.

Badshah Juice and Snack Bar Opposite Crawford Market, Lokmanya Tilak Rd. Mumbai's most acclaimed *falooda* joint also serves delicious kulfi, ice creams and dozens of freshly squeezed fruit juices. The ideal place to round off a trip to the market, though expect to have to queue for a table.

Delhi Darbar Corner of Maulana Shaukatali Rd (Grant Rd) and PB Marg (Falkland Rd), opposite Alfred Talkies. On the fringes of the red light district, but a must for lovers of authentic Mughlai cuisine. Waiters in Peshawari caps serve up superb flame-grilled chicken and mutton *sheekh* kebabs, biriyanis, *pulaos* and the house speciality, chicken tikka, rounded off with the creamiest lassis in Mumbai. Most dishes only Rs50–150.

Rajdhani Mangaldas Rd (in the silk bazaar opposite Crawford Market). Outstanding, eat-till-you-burst Gujarati thalis. Very cramped and more expensive than usual (Rs150 on weekdays, or Rs195 for the "Special" Sunday lunch), but they don't stint on quality. Closed Sun evenings.

Vaibhai Payawala 45 Guzer St, Bohri Mohalla. Aicionados of the "full English breakfast" should sample its Muslim Mumbaikar equivalent, the *bara handi*. Slow-cooked overnight in twelve pots sealed with flour dough, the dishes are all traditional meat delicacies, prepared the same way here for four generations. Enjoy them with rice or smoky-flavoured *lamba pau* bread from the adjacent bakery. Jump in a cab to Bohri Mohalla and ask the way when you get there. Inexpensive.

Chowpatty Beach

The restaurant listed below is marked on the main Mumbai map on pp.692–693.

Crystal 19 Chowpatty Seaface, near Wilson College. Chowpatty is crammed with snack joints and cheap restaurants, but this one stands out – not that you'd ever know it from the grimy decor. Homesick Punjabis and lovers of pukka north Indian home cooking travel here from across the city to eat the wholesome dhal *makhini*, *alu jeera* and other spicy vegetarian dishes, served from a soot-blackened kitchen. A hot contender for Mumbai's best budget restaurant, with most mains under Rs50. And don't miss the lightly chilled *kir* for dessert.

Nightlife and entertainment

Mumbai never sleeps. No matter what time of night you venture out, there are bound to be others going about some business or other. The city has always led the **nightlife** scene in India and there are bars and clubs to suit every taste: jazz dens compete with salsa, tabla-dance fusions and funk. Mumbai's alternative but decidedly yuppie crowd meet at the *Ghetto Bar* before heading down to the gay, glitzy or groovy clubs around Colaba and Juhu.

Of course, Mumbai is also a cultural centre, attracting the finest **Indian classical music** and **dance** artists from all over the country. There are frequent concerts and recitals at venues such as: Bharatiya Vidya Bhavan, KM Munshi Marg (ⓣ022/2363 0224), the headquarters of the international cultural (Hindu) organization; and the National Centre for the Performing Arts, Nariman Point (NCPA; ⓣ022/2288 3838).

Bars

Mumbai has an unusually easy-going attitude to **alcohol**; popping into a bar for a beer is very much accepted (for men at least) even at lunchtime. Chowpatty Beach and Colaba Causeway, where you'll find *Leopold's* and the *Café Mondegar*, form the focus of the travellers' social scene, but if you want to sample the pulse of the city's nightlife, venture up to Bandra and Juhu.

Café Mondegar Colaba Causeway (see map p.705). Draught beer by the glass or pitcher (both imported and Indian) and deliciously fruity cocktails in a small café-bar. The atmosphere is very relaxed, the music tends towards rock classics and the clientele is a mix of Westerners and students; murals by a famous Goan cartoonist give the place a cheerful ambience.

Copa Cobana 39-D Dariya Vihar, Chowpatty Beach (see map pp.692–693). A small, trendy tapas bar in a great location.

Czar Bar *Hotel Intercontinental*, 135 Marine Drive. Trendy vodka bar with chic, minimalist décor, clever lighting and 24 brands on offer (from Rs200/shot), plus a full range of other drinks and cocktails. The music's lounge until around 11pm, then picks up. Quiet on weekday nights, but popular on weekends.

Indigo 4 Mandlik Rd, Colaba (see map p.705). One of the coolest hangouts in south Mumbai, popular with young media professionals and wine buffs. Its funky, stripped-bare decor set a new trend in the city.

Leo's Square 1st Floor, *Leopold's*, Colaba Causeway. Pretty much the same menu and prices as *Leopold's* downstairs, but here you can enjoy a/c, black-lighting and a quality sound system.

Nightclubs

The **nightclub** scene in Mumbai is the best in India and the late 1990s saw the rise of a funkier, groovier scene as the moneyed jet set began to hear

Laughter clubs

On the principle that laughter is the best medicine, Mumbai doctor Madan Kataria has created a new kind of therapy: *hasya* (laughter) yoga. There are now over 300 **Laughter Clubs** in India and many more worldwide; around 50,000 people joined the Laughter Day celebrations in Mumbai in January 2003.

Fifteen-minute sessions start with adherents doing yogic breathing whilst chanting "Ho ho ha ha," which develops into spontaneous "hearty", "silent" and "swinging" laughter. Sessions mostly take place between 6am and 7am, a time that, according to the good doctor, "keeps you in good spirits throughout the day, energizes your body and charges you with happiness". There are many clubs in Mumbai itself: look for semi-circles of people holding their hands in the air and laughing on Juhu beach, or go to ⓦwww.laughteryoga.org for the full story.

Bollywood

For anyone brought up on TV, it's hard to imagine the power that **movies** continue to wield in India. Every village has a cinema within walking distance and, with a potential audience in the hundreds of millions, the Indian film industry is the largest in the world, producing around 900 full-length features each year. Regional cinema, catering for different language groups (in particular the Tamil cinema of Chennai), though popular locally, has little national impact. Only Hindi film – which accounts for one-fifth of all the films made in India – has crossed regional boundaries to great effect, most particularly in the north. The home of the Hindi blockbuster, the "all-India film", is Mumbai, famously known as **Bollywood**.

To overcome differences of language and religion, the Bollywood movie follows rigid conventions and genres; as in myth, its characters have predetermined actions and destinies. Knowing a plot need not detract from the drama, and indeed, it is not uncommon for Indian audiences to watch films numerous times. Unlike the Hollywood formula, which tends to classify each film under one genre, the Hindi film follows what is known as a "**masala format**", and includes during its luxurious three hours a little bit of everything, especially romance, violence and comedy. Frequently the stories feature dispossessed male heroes fighting evil against all odds with a love interest thrown in. The sexual element has tended to be repressed, with numerous wet sari scenes and dance routines featuring the tensest pelvic thrusts, but strictly no kissing. Other typical **themes** include male bonding and betrayal, family melodrama, separation and reunion and religious piety. Dream sequences are almost obligatory, too, along with a festival or celebration scene – typically Holi, when people shower each other with paint – a comic character passing through, and a depraved, alcoholic and mostly Western "cabaret", filled with strutting villains and lewd dancing.

Recent blockbusters have also seen the introduction of a new stock character, the returning emigrant or "NRI" (Non-Resident Indian). This is one element in a more general trend sweeping Bollywood at the moment, as the big studios seek to pull in Hindi-speaking audiences in the UK, US and Canada. Overseas tickets typically cost ten times what they do in the flashiest of Mumbai's cinemas, and together with videos and DVD sales now account for forty percent of the industry's revenues. Budgets, production standards and on-screen sauciness have all been on the rise as a result, with more and more films using foreign locations, smaller spangly miniskirts and MTV-style choreography. A memorable recent example was the big first dance sequence in the smash hit *Kal Ho Haa Ho*, starring Shahrukh Khan and Preity Zinta, which takes place on the streets of Manhattan, featuring a multicultural cast of dancers in outlandish outfits waving little American flags.

Audiences may be growing in New York and London, but there has been a thirty percent drop in cinema receipts at home with the new pro-Western trends. Many pundits now warn that in its scramble for crossover hits, Bollywood is becoming perilously detached from the tastes of its less sophisticated audiences in India.

Visitors to the city should have ample opportunity to sample the delights of a Hindi movie, traditional or otherwise. To make an educated choice, buy *Bombay* magazine, which contains extensive **listings** and reviews. Alternatively, look for the biggest, brightest hoarding, and join the queue. Seats in a comfortable air-conditioned cinema cost Rs50–75, or less if you sit in the stalls (not advisable for women). Of the two hundred or so **cinemas**, only eight regularly screen **English-language** films. The most central and convenient are the Regal in Colaba, the gloriously Art-Deco Eros opposite Churchgate station, the Sterling, the New Excelsior and the New Empire, which are all a short walk west of CST (VT) station.

the latest house, trance, fusion and funk that was hitting the decks in Goa and the West.

Most discos and clubs charge per couple on the door (with a portion of the entrance cost redeemable at the bar), and in theory have a "couples-only" policy. In practice, if you're in a mixed group or don't appear sleazy you won't have any problems. At the five-star hotels, entry can be restricted to hotel guests and members. Closing times vary; the Municipality recently slapped a 1.30am finish time on nightclubs, but – in spite of fears that this would kill Mumbai's booming nightlife – the ruling is routinely ignored.

Athena 41–44 Minoo Desai Marg, behind Radio Club, Colaba (see map p.705). Along with *Insomnia*, south Mumbai's most talked about nightspot: an all-white affair with a high-end restaurant, various lounges and a huge wine list (the owner is an Indian wine magnate). The music's mainstream R&B and Hindi pop, with the odd trance number. Rs1000 per couple. Closes at 1.30am, when there's a general exodus over to *Insomnia*.

Enigma *JW Marriott Hotel*, Juhu Tara Rd (see map pp.692–693). If you want to see what Hindi film stars and hip young Indian millionaires do for kicks, this is the place to come: the sexiest outfits, latest dance music (including plenty of *filmi* hits), most gorgeous decor and stiffest entrance cost (Rs1500 per couple).

Insomnia *Taj Mahal Palace & Tower*. Well-heeled yuppies and their NRI relatives strut their stuff in this warren of light-up bars, hardwood dance floors and chill-out spaces beneath the *Taj*, featuring one of the city's heftiest sound systems. Open to non-members, but you'll have to look your best. Cover Rs1000 per couple. Punters start arriving at 11pm and it usually stays open until 3am.

Polly Esther's *Gorden House Hotel*, Battery St, Colaba. Retro club with brightly coloured theme decor, leather upholstery and a 1990s night on Thursdays; pop, rock, disco and Motown on the weekend. Rs750 per couple.

Rasberry Rhinoceros *Juhu Hotel*, Juhu Beach (see map pp.692–693). The most famous nightspot in the city, with a live head-banging rock band on Thursdays and a heavy metal sound system the rest of the time. Rs800 per couple.

Shopping

Mumbai is a great place to shop, whether for last-minute souvenirs, or essentials for the long journeys ahead. Locally produced **textiles** and export-surplus clothing are among the best buys, as are **handicrafts** from far-flung corners of the country. With the exception of the swish arcades in the five-star hotels, prices compare surprisingly well with other Indian cities. In the larger shops, rates are fixed and **credit cards** are often accepted; elsewhere, particularly dealing with street-vendors, it pays to haggle. Uptown, the **central bazaars** – see p.715 – are better for spectating than serious shopping, although the **antiques** and Friday flea market in the Chor, or "thieves" bazaar, can sometimes yield the odd bargain. The **Zaveri** (goldsmiths') **bazaar** opposite Crawford Market is the place to head for new gold and silver jewellery. The city features a number of swish modern **shopping centres**, including India's largest, Crossroads, at 28 Pandit MM Rd near the Haji Ali mosque. **Tea** lovers should check out the *Tea Centre* on VN Road (reviewed on p.721), which sells a wide range of quality tea, including the outrageously expensive "fine tippy golden Orange Pekoe" (Rs1000 per 250g).

Opening hours in the city centre are Monday to Saturday, 10am to 7pm. The Muslim bazaars, quiet on Friday, are otherwise open until around 9pm (or through the night during Ramadan).

Antiques

The **Chor Bazaar** area, and Mutton Street in particular, is the centre of Mumbai's **antique trade**. For a full account, see p.716. Another good, if much more expensive, place is **Phillip's** famous antique shop, on the corner of Madam Cama Road, opposite the Regal cinema in Colaba, which was in the middle of a major re-fit on our last visit. Brass, bronze and wood Hindu sculpture, silver jewellery, old prints and aquatints form the mainstay of its collection. Most of the stuff on sale dates from the twilight of the Raj – a result of the Indian government's ban on the export by foreigners of items more than a century old.

In the **Jehangir Art Gallery** basement, a branch of the antiques chain Natesan's Antiqarts offers a tempting selection of antique (and reproduction) sculpture, furniture, paintings and bronzes.

Clothes, textiles and household goods

Mumbai produces the bulk of India's **clothes**, mostly the lightweight, light-coloured "shirtings and suitings" favoured by droves of uniformly attired office-wallahs. For cheaper Western clothing, you can't beat the long row of stalls on the pavement of MG Road, opposite the Mumbai Gymkhana. "**Fashion Street**" specializes in reject and export-surplus goods ditched by big manufacturers, selling off T-shirts, jeans, leggings, summer dresses, and trendy sweatshirts. Better-quality cotton clothes (often stylish designer-label rip-offs) are available in shops along **Colaba Causeway**, such as Cotton World, down Mandlik Marg.

If you're looking for **traditional Indian clothes**, head for the Khadi Village Industries Emporium at 286 Dr DN Marg, near the Thomas Cook office. As Whiteaway & Laidlaw, this rambling Victorian department store used to kit all the newly arrived *burra-sahibs* out with pith helmets, khaki shorts and quinine tablets. These days, its old wooden counters, shirt and sock drawers stock dozens of different hand-spun cottons and silks, sold by the metre or made up as vests, *kurtas* or block-printed *salwar kamises*. Other items include the ubiquitous white Nehru caps, *dhotis*, Madras-check *lunghis* and fine brocaded silk saris.

Mumbai is one of the cheapest places in the world to buy **soft furnishings** and **household goods**, and if you know where to shop you could save the cost of your flight in an afternoon. For tablecloths, cotton and silk quilts, rattan blinds and upholstery fabric, try Chunilal Mulchand & Co, at the Indian Mercantile Mansion on Madam Cama Road, close to the Prince of Wales Museum. They'll copy **loose covers** for sofas and lounge chairs in a week.

Malabar, at the *Taj Mahal Palace & Tower*, is much pricier, but stocks some exquisite beaded cushion covers and throws in traditional Indian textiles. For other designer home furnishings – everything from cutlery to curtain panels – Contemporary Arts & Crafts at 19 Jagmohandas Marg (Napean Sea Road) up in the exclusive Malabar Hill area, is a must.

Handicrafts

Regionally produced **handicrafts** are marketed in assorted state-run emporia at the World Trade Centre, down on Cuffe Parade, and along Sir PM Road, Fort. The quality is consistently high – as are the prices, if you miss out on the periodic holiday discounts. The same goes for the **Central Cottage Industries Emporium**, 34 Shivaji Marg, near the Gateway of India in Colaba, whose size and central location make it the single best all-round place to hunt for souvenirs. Downstairs you'll find inlaid furniture, wood- and metal-work, miniature paintings and jewellery, while upstairs specializes in toys, clothing and textiles – Gujarati appliqué bedspreads, hand-painted pillowcases and Rajasthani mirror-work, plus silk ties and Noel Coward dressing-gowns. **Mereweather Road**, directly behind the *Taj*, is awash with Kashmiri handicraft stores stocking overpriced papier-mâché pots and bowls, silver jewellery, woollen shawls and rugs. Avoid them if you find it hard to shrug off aggressive sales pitches.

Perfume is essentially a Muslim preserve in Mumbai. Down at the south end of Colaba Causeway, around Arthur Bunder Road, shops with mirrored walls and shelves are stacked with cut-glass carafes full of syrupy, fragrant essential oils. **Incense** is hawked in sticks, cones and slabs of sticky *dhoop* on the sidewalk nearby (check that the boxes haven't already been opened and their contents sold off piecemeal). For bulk buying, the hand-rolled, cottage-made bundles of incense sold in the Khadi Village Industries Emporium on Dr DN Marg (see p.725) are a better deal; it also has a handicraft department where, in addition to furniture, paintings and ornaments, you can pick up glass bangles, block-printed and calico bedspreads, and wooden votive statues produced in Maharashtran craft villages.

Books

Mumbai's excellent English-language **bookshops** and bookstalls are well stocked with everything to do with India, and a good selection of general classics, pulp fiction and travel writing. Indian editions of popular titles cost a fraction of what they do abroad and include lots of interesting works by lesser-known local authors. If you don't mind picking through dozens of trigonometry textbooks, back issues of National Geographic and salacious 1960s paperbacks, the **street stalls** between Flora Fountain and Churchgate station can also be good places to hunt for secondhand books.

Chetana 34 Dubash Rd (Rampart Row). Exclusively religion and philosophy.

Crossword Mahalakshmi Chambers, 22 Bhulabhai Desai Rd, Breach Candy ☎022/2492 2458. Mumbai's largest reputable retailer, a bus ride (#132) from the downtown area, near Mahalakshmi temple/Haji Ali's tomb. Open Mon–Fri 10am–8pm, Sat & Sun 10am–9pm.

Nalanda Ground floor, *Taj Mahal*. An exhaustive range of coffee-table tomes and paperback literature, though at top prices.

Oxford Bookstore Apeejay House, 3 Dinsha Vacha Rd, Churchgate. Not quite as large as Crossword, but almost, and much more easily accessible if you're staying downtown or in Colaba. It also has a very cool a/c café.

Pustak Bharati Bharatiya Vidya Bhavan, KM Munshi Marg. Excellent small bookshop specializing in Hindu philosophy and literature, plus details of Bhavan's cultural programmes.

Shankar Book-Stand Outside the *Café Mondegar*, Colaba Causeway. Piles of easy-reads, guidebooks, classic fiction, and most of the old favourites on India, at competitive rates.

Strand Next door to the Canara Bank, off PM Rd, Fort. The best value bookshop in the city centre, with the full gamut of Penguins and Indian literature, sold at amazing discounts.

Music

The most famous of Mumbai's many good **music shops** are near the Moti cinema along SV Patel Road, in the central bazaar district. Haribhai Vishwanath, Ram Singh and RS Mayeka are all government-approved retailers of traditional Indian instruments, including sitars, sarods, tablas and flutes. For **cassettes and CDs** the best outlet by far is Rhythm House, Subhash Chowk, next to the Jehangir Art Gallery. This is a veritable Aladdin's cave of classical, devotional and popular music from all over India, with a reasonable selection of Western rock, pop and jazz, as well as DVDs of classic and contemporary Hindi movies.

Listings

Airlines, domestic Indian Airlines, Air India Building, Nariman Point (Mon–Sat 8.30am–7.30pm, Sun 10am–1pm & 1.45–5.30pm; ⓣ022/2202 3031); counter at the airport ⓣ022/2682 9328; Jet Airways, Amarchand Mansion, Madam Cama Rd ⓣ022/2285 5788; Sahara Airlines, Unit 7, Ground Floor, Tulsiani Chambers, Nariman Point ⓣ022/2283 6000.

Airlines, international Aeroflot, Ground Floor, 14 Tulsiani Chambers, Free Press Journal Rd, Nariman Point ⓣ022/2285 6648; Air France, Maker Chambers VI, 1st Floor, Nariman Point ⓣ022/2202 4818; Air India, Air India Building, Nariman Point ⓣ022/2202 4142; Air Lanka, 12-D, Raheja Centre, Nariman Point ⓣ022/2282 3288; Alitalia, Industrial Insurance Building, VN Rd, Churchgate ⓣ022/5663 0800; British Airways, 202-B Vulcan Insurance Building, VN Rd, Churchgate ⓣ022/2282 0888; Cathay Pacific, Bajaj Bhavan, 3rd Floor, 226, Nariman Point ⓣ022/2202 9561; Delta, Taj Mahal, Colaba ⓣ022/2288 5652; Egypt Air, Oriental House, 7 J Tata Rd, Churchgate ⓣ022/2282 4088; Emirates, 228 Mittal Chambers, Nariman Point ⓣ022/2287 1645; Gulf Air, Maker Chamber V, Nariman Point ⓣ022/2202 4065; Japan Airlines, Raheja Centre, Nariman Point ⓣ022/2283 3136; KLM, 7th Floor, 712 Acme Plaza, Andheri–Kurla Rd, opp. Sangam cinema ⓣ022/5697 5959; Kuwait Airways, 86 VN Rd, Churchgate ⓣ022/2204 5351; Lufthansa, 1st Floor, Express Towers, Nariman Point ⓣ022/5630 1940; Qantas Airways, 2nd Floor, Godrej Bhavan, Home St ⓣ022/2200 7440; Royal Nepal Airlines, 222, Maker Chamber V, Nariman Point ⓣ022/2283 6197; SAS and Thai Airways, Oberoi Towers, 11th Floor, Room 1120, Nariman Point ⓣ022/2230 8725; Saudia, 3rd Floor, Express Towers, Nariman Point ⓣ022/2202 0199; South African Airways, Podar House, 10 Marine Drive, Churchgate ⓣ022/2284 2242; Syrian Arab Airlines, 7 Brabourne Stadium, VN Rd, Churchgate ⓣ022/2282 6043; TWA, Amarchand Mansion, M Carve Rd ⓣ022/2282 3080.

Airport enquiries Chhatrapati Shivaji International Airport ⓣ022/2682 9000. Chhatrapati Shivaji Domestic Airport ⓣ022/2615 6600.

Ambulance ⓣ101 for general emergencies; but you're nearly always better off taking a taxi. See also "Hospitals" below.

Banks and currency exchange The logical place to change money when you arrive in Mumbai is at the State Bank of India's 24hr counter in Chhatrapati Shivaji International Airport. Rates here are standard but you may have to pay for an encashment certificate – essential if you intend to buy tourist-quota train tickets or an Indrail pass at the special counters in Churchgate or CST (VT) stations. All the major state banks downtown change foreign currency (Mon–Fri 10.30am–2.30pm, Sat 10.30am–12.30pm); some (eg the Bank of Baroda) also handle credit cards and cash advances. Most now have 24hr ATMs that can handle international transactions, usually Visa, Delta and Mastercard. It's worth noting that there's often a limit on how much you can take out: it can be as low as Rs4000. For the location of large branch ATM machines downtown, see our maps. The most convenient if you're staying in Colaba is the Bank of Baroda's at the north end of SBS Marg (Colaba Causeway). The fast and efficient American Express office (daily 9.30am–6pm; ⓣ022/2204 8291), on Shivaji Marg, around the corner from the Regal cinema in Colaba, offers all the regular services (including poste restante) to travellers' cheque- and card-holders and is open to anyone wishing to change cash. Thomas Cook's big Dr DN Marg branch (Mon–Sat 9.30am–7pm; ⓣ022/2204 8556), between the Khadi shop and Hutatma Chowk, can also arrange money transfers from overseas.

Consulates and high commissions Although the many consulates and High Commissions in Mumbai can be useful for replacing lost travel documents or obtaining visas, most of India's neighbouring states, including Bangladesh, Bhutan, Burma, Nepal and Pakistan, only have embassies in New Delhi and/or Kolkata (Calcutta) – see relevant city account. All of the following are open Mon–Fri: Australia, 16th Floor, Maker Tower "E", Cuffe Parade (9am–5pm; ⓣ022/2218 1071); Canada, 41/42 Maker Chambers VI, Nariman Point (9am–5.30pm; ⓣ022/2287 6027); China, 1st floor, 11 ML Dahanukar Marg (10am–4.30pm; ⓣ022/2282 2662); Denmark, L & T House, Narottam Moraji Marg, Ballard Estate (10am–12.45pm; ⓣ022/2261 4462); France, 2nd Floor, Datta Prasad, N Gamadia Cross Rd (9am–1pm & 2.30–5.30pm; ⓣ022/2495 0948); Germany, 10th Floor, Hoechst House, Nariman Point (8–11am; ⓣ022/2283 2422); Indonesia, 19 Altamount Rd, Cumbala Hill (10am–4.30pm; ⓣ022/2380 0940); Netherlands, Forbes Bldg, Chiranjit Rai Marg, Fort (9am–5pm; ⓣ022/2201 6750); Norway, Navroji Mansion, 31 Nathelal Parekh Marg (10am–1pm; ⓣ022/2284 2042); Philippines, 61 Sakhar Bhavan, Nariman Point (10am–1pm; ⓣ022/2202 4792); Republic of

Ireland, Royal Bombay Yacht Club Chambers, Apollo Bunder (9.30am–1pm; ⓣ022/2202 4607); Singapore, 10th Floor, Maker Chamber IV, 222 Jamnal Bajaj Marg, Nariman Point (9am–noon; ⓣ022/2204 3205); South Africa, Gandhi Mansion, 20 Altamount Rd (9am–noon; ⓣ022/2389 3725); Spain, Ador House, 3rd floor, 6 K Dubash Marg, Kala Ghoda (10.30am–1pm; ⓣ022/2287 4797); Sri Lanka, Sri Lanka House, 34 Homi Modi St, Fort (9.30am–11.30am; ⓣ022/2204 5861); Sweden, 85 Sayani Rd, Subash Gupta Bhawan, Prabhadevi (10am–12.30pm; ⓣ022/2436 0493); Switzerland, Maker Chamber IV, 10th floor, Nariman Point (8am–10am; ⓣ022/2288 4563); Thailand, Malabar View, 4th floor, Dr Purandure Marg, Chowpatty Sea Face (9–11.30am; ⓣ022/2363 1404); United Kingdom, 2nd Floor, Maker Chamber IV, Nariman Point (8am–11.30am; ⓣ022/2283 0517); USA, Lincoln House, 78 Bhulabhai Desai Rd (8.30am–11am; ⓣ022/2363 3611).

Hospitals The best hospital in the centre is the private Bombay Hospital (ⓣ022/2206 7676, ⓦwww.bombayhospital.com), New Marine Lines, just north of the government tourist office on M Karve Rd. Breach Candy Hospital (ⓣ022/2363 3651, ⓦwww.breachcandyhospital.org) on Bhulabhai Desai Rd, near the swimming pool, is also recommended by foreign embassies.

Internet access A couple of cramped 24hr places (Rs40/hr) can be found in Colaba, just round the corner from *Leopold's* on Nawroji F Marg, though it's worth paying the Rs5 extra at Access Infotech, located down a small alley further down Colaba Causeway on the left, which is faster and more comfortable. At the time of writing, neither offered broadband services.

Left luggage If your hotel won't let you store bags with them, try the cloakrooms at the airports (see pp.696–697), or the one in CST (VT) station (Rs7–10 a day). Anything left here, even rucksacks, must be securely fastened with a padlock and can be left for a maximum of one month.

Libraries Alliance Française de Mumbai, Theosophy Hall, 40 New Marine Lines; Asiatic Society (see p.710), SBS Marg, Horniman Circle, Ballard Estate (Mon–Sat 10.30am–7pm); British Council (for British newspapers), A Wing, 1st Floor, Mittal Tower, Nariman Point (Tues–Sat 10am–6pm); Max Mueller Bhavan, Prince of Wales Annexe, off MG Rd (Mon–Fri 9.30am–6pm). The KR Cama Oriental Institute, 136 Mumbai Samachar Marg (Mon–Fri 10am–5pm, Sat 10am–1pm), specializing in Zoroastrian and Irani studies has a public collection of 22,000 volumes in European and Asian languages. Mumbai Natural History Society, Hornbill House (Mon–Fri 10am–5pm, Sat 10am–1pm, closed 1st & 3rd Sat of the month), has an international reputation for the study of wildlife in India. Visitors may become temporary members which allows them access to the library, natural history collection, occasional talks and the opportunity to join organized walks and field trips.

Pharmacies Bombay Chemist, 39–40 Kakad Arcade, opposite Bombay Hospital, New Marine Lines (ⓣ022/2207 6171) opens daily 8am–11pm. Kemps in the Taj Mahal also opens late.

Photographic studios and equipment The Javeri Colour Lab, opposite the Regal cinema in Colaba, stocks colour-print and slide film, as do most of the big hotels. A small boutique behind the florists in the Sahakari Bhandar covered market does instant Polaroid passport photographs.

Police The main police station in Colaba (ⓣ022/2285 6817) is on the west side of Colaba Causeway, near the crossroads with Ormiston Rd.

Postal services The GPO (Mon–Sat 9am–8pm, Sun 9am–4pm) is around the corner from CST (VT) Station, off Nagar Chowk. Its poste restante counter (Mon–Sat 9am–6pm, Sun 9am–3pm) is among the most reliable in India, although they trash the letters after four weeks. The much less efficient parcel office (10am–4.30pm) is behind the main building on the first floor. Packing-wallahs hang around on the pavement outside. DHL (ⓣ022/2850 5050) has eleven offices in Mumbai, the most convenient being the 24hr one under the *Sea Green Hotel* at the bottom of Marine Drive (turn south off the western end of VN Rd and it's a short way on your right).

Telephones and faxes STD/ISD booths abound in Mumbai. For rock-bottom phone and fax rates however, head for Videsh Sanchar Bhavan (open 24hr), the swanky government telecom building on MG Marg, where you can make reverse charge calls to destinations such as the UK, US and Australia. Receiving incoming calls costs a nominal Rs10. Numbers in the city change constantly, so if you can't get through after several attempts, try directory enquiries on ⓣ197.

Travel agents The following travel agents are recommended for booking domestic and international flights, and long-distance private buses where specified: Cox and Kings India Ltd, 271/272, Dr DN Marg ⓣ022/2207 3065, ⓦwww.coxkings.com; Sita World Travels Pvt Ltd, 8 Atlanta Building, Nariman Point ⓣ022/2286 0684, ⓔ bom@sitaincoming.com; Thomas Cook (see p.727).

Moving on from Mumbai

Most visitors feel like getting out of Mumbai as soon as they can. Fortunately, the city is equipped with "super-fast" services to arrange or confirm **onward travel**. All the major international and domestic **airlines** have offices in the city, the railway networks operate special tourist counters in the main reservation halls, and dozens of **travel agents** and road transport companies are eager to help you on your way by **bus**.

Travel within India

Mumbai is the nexus of several major internal flight routes, train networks and highways, and is the main transport hub for traffic heading towards South India. The most travelled trails lead north up the Gujarati coast to **Rajasthan** and **Delhi**; northwest into the **Deccan** via Aurangabad and the caves at Ellora and Ajanta; and south towards **Goa** and the **Malabar Coast**.

By plane

Indian Airlines and other **domestic carriers** – such as the more efficient Jet Airways and Sahara Airlines – fly out of Chhatrapati Shivaji domestic airport (formerly Santa Cruz) to destinations all over India. Availability on popular routes should never be taken for granted. Check with the airlines as soon as you arrive; **tickets** can be bought directly from their offices (see p.727), via the Internet, or through any reputable travel agent.

In theory, it is also possible to book domestic air tickets abroad when you buy your original long-haul flight. However, as individual airlines tend to have separate agreements with domestic Indian carriers, you may not be offered the same choice (or rates) as you will through agents in Mumbai. Note, too, that Indian Airlines is the only company offering 25 percent discounts (on all flights) to customers under the age of thirty.

By train

Three main networks converge on Mumbai: the **Western Railway** (Ⓦwww.westernrailway.com) runs to north and west India; the **Central Railway** (Ⓦwww.centralrailway.com) connects Mumbai to central, eastern and southern regions; and the **Konkan Railway** (Ⓦwww.konkanrailway.com) winds south down the coast to Goa, Mangalore and Kerala.

Nearly all services to Gujarat, Rajasthan, Delhi and the far north leave from **Mumbai Central** station, in the mid-town area. Second-class tickets can be booked here through the normal channels, but the quickest place for foreign nationals to make reservations is at the efficient tourist counter (no. 28) on the first floor of the **Western Railway's booking hall**, next door to the Government of India tourist office in **Churchgate** (Mon–Fri 9.30am–4.30pm, Sat 9.30am–2.30pm; Ⓣ022/2209 7577). This counter, at the far (bottom) end of the booking hall, also has access to special "tourist quotas", which are released the day before departure if the train leaves during the day, or the morning of the departure if the train leaves after 5pm. If the quota is "closed" or already used up, and you can't access the "Emergency quota" (always worth a try), you will have to join the regular queue. Periods before major national holidays (notably **Diwali**, when half of India is on the move) should be avoided at all costs. But if you do find yourself having to travel when there don't seem to be any tickets left, bear in mind you can pay extra for a special *tatkal* seat (see p.56 for full details on these) - an option well worth considering, for example, if you want to get to Goa on the oversubscribed Konkan Railway route.

Recommended trains from Mumbai

The services listed below are the most direct and/or the fastest. This list is by no means exhaustive and there are numerous slower trains that are often more convenient for smaller destinations. All the details listed below were correct at the time of writing, but departure times, in particular, should be checked when you purchase your ticket, or in advance via the Indian Railways website: ⓦwww.indianrail.gov.in.

Destination	Name	No.	From	Frequency	Departs	Total time
Agra	Punjab Mail	#2137/38	CST	Daily	7.10pm	24hr 15min
Aurangabad	Devgiri Express	#1003	CST	Daily	9.05pm	7hr 05min
Bangalore	Udyan Express	#6529	CST	Daily	8am	25hr
Bhopal	#2137 Punjab Mail	CST	Daily	7.10pm	14hr	
Chennai	Mumbai–Chennai Express	#6011	CST	Daily	2.10pm	26hr 35min
Delhi	Rajdhani Express	#2951	MC	Daily	4.55pm	17hr
	Golden Temple Mail	#2903	MC	Daily	9.25pm	21hr 35min
Goa	Mumbai–Madgaon Express	#KR0111	CST	Daily	11pm	11hr 45min
Hyderabad	Hussainsagar Express	#7001	CST	Daily	9.50pm	15hr
Jaipur	Mumbai–Jaipur Express	#2955	MC	Daily	6.50pm	18hr
Jodhpur	Ranakpur Express	#4708	Bandra	Daily	3pm	19hr 25min
Kochi* (Cochin)	Netravati Express	#6345	LTT (Kurla)	Daily	11.40am	26hr 40min
Kolkata (Calcutta/ Howrah)	Gitanjali Express	#2859	CST	Daily	6am	31hr 35min
	Mumbai–Howrah Mail	#2809	CST	Daily	8.40pm	33hr 45min
Mysore	Sharavathi Express	#1035	Dadar	Tues	10.45pm	23hr 45min
Pune	Udyan Express	#6529	CST	Daily	8.40am	3hr 35min
Thiruvananthapuram (Trivandrum)	Netravati Express	#6345	LTT (Kurla)	Daily	11.40am	31hr 40min
Udaipur	Saurashtra Express**	#9215	MC	Daily	7.55am	23hr 45min
Varanasi	Mahanagiri Express	#1093	CST	Daily	12.10pm	28hr 20min

*details also applicable for Ernakulam Junction
**change at Ahmedabad to the Delhi Sarai Rohila Express #9944

Mumbai's other "Tourist Ticketing Facility" is in the snazzy air-conditioned **Central Railway booking office** to the rear of **CST** (VT) (Mon–Sat 8am–1.30pm & 2–3pm, Sun 8am–2pm; ⓣ022/2262 2859), the departure point for most trains heading east and south. Indrail passes can also be bought here, and there's an MTDC tourist information kiosk in the main concourse if you need help filling in your reservation slips.

Tickets for seats on the **Konkan Railway** can be booked at either Churchgate or CST booking halls; for more info on getting to Goa by rail, see below.

Just to complicate matters, some Central Railway trains to **South India** – notably those running via the Konkan Railway to **Kerala** – do not depart from CST at all, but from **Kurla station** (aka Lokmanya Tilak Terminus, or **LTT**), up near the airports. Others leave from **Dadar**, also way north of the centre. Getting to either on public transport can be a major struggle, though many long-distance trains from CST (VT) or Churchgate stop there and aren't as crowded. Much the easiest way is to jump in a cab.

Wherever you're heading, a good investment for anyone planning to do much rail travel is Indian Railway's indispensable *Trains at a Glance*, available from most station bookstalls for Rs30. You can also access **timetables** via the Indian Railways website at ⓦwww.indianrail.gov.in, and even book tickets online.

By bus

The main departure point for long-distance **buses** leaving Mumbai is the frenetic **Central bus stand** on JB Behram Marg, opposite Mumbai Central railway station. States with bus company counters here (daily 8am–8pm; ⓣ022/2307 6622) include Maharashtra, Karnataka, Madhya Pradesh, Goa and Gujarat. Few of their services compare favourably with train travel on the same routes. Reliable timetable information can be difficult to obtain, reservations are not available on standard buses, and most long-haul journeys are gruelling overnighters. Among the exceptions are the deluxe buses run by MSRTC to Pune, Nasik and Kolhapur; the small extra cost buys you more leg-room, fewer stops and the option of advance booking. The only problem is most leave from the ASIAD bus stand in Dadar, thirty minutes or so by road or rail north of Mumbai Central.

Other possibilities for road travel include the "super-fast" **luxury coaches** touted around Colaba. Most are run by private companies, guaranteeing breakneck speeds and possible long waits for the bus to fill up. ITDC also operate similarly priced services to the same destinations, which you can book direct from their main offices downtown or through the more conveniently situated Government of India tourist office, 123 M Karve Rd, Churchgate. Two night buses leave Nariman Point every evening for the twelve-hour trip to **Aurangabad**, and there are morning departures to **Nasik** and **Mahabaleshwar**, which take six and seven hours respectively.

Leaving India

In spite of its prominence on trans-Asian flight routes, Mumbai is no longer the bargain basement for **international air tickets** it used to be. Discounted fares are very hard to come by – a legacy of Rajiv Gandhi's economic reforms of the 1980s. If you do need to book a ticket, stick to one of the tried and tested agents listed on p.728.

All the major airlines operating out of Mumbai have offices downtown where you can buy scheduled tickets or confirm your flight; see p.727 for a list of addresses. The majority are grouped around Veer Nariman Road, opposite the *Ambassador Hotel*, or else on Nariman Point, a short taxi ride west of Colaba.

Getting to Goa

Since the inauguration of the Konkan Railway, the best-value way to travel the 500km from Mumbai to Goa has been by **train**. However, tickets for the twelve-hour ride down the coast tend be in short supply, and virtually impossible to obtain at short notice, so it's best to try and book at home before setting off. Otherwise, you'll probably find yourself having to shell out for a **flight**. Considering how hellish the bus ride can be, and how hard getting hold of train tickets is, it's well worth paying the extra to travel by plane, which could save you days waiting around in Mumbai. Alternatively, consider heading south in stages, via Pune or southern Maharashtra.

By plane

Between ten and twelve flights shuttle daily between Mumbai and Dabolim airport in Goa. The cheapest fares, by far, are offered by low-cost airline Air Deccan (Ⓦwww.airdeccan.net/airdeccan), which sells tickets on its website from as little as Rs550, though the normal rate is more like $60. Flying with Indian Airlines (Ⓦwww.indian-airlines.nic.in) will set you back $95, or $100 with Sahara (Ⓦwww.airsahara.net) or Jet (Ⓦwww.jetairways.com). In addition, Air India (Ⓦwww.airindia.com) operates a service to Mumbai (also for $100) which few people seem to know about, so you can nearly always get a seat (the one drawback is that you have to check in three hours before departure as Air India is an international carrier). At the time of writing, two more low-cost carriers – Kingfisher Airlines (Ⓦwww.flykingfisher.com) and SpiceJet (Ⓦwww.spicejet.com) – were also poised to enter the fray, and will be worth checking for competitive fares.

Demand for seats can be fierce around Diwali and Christmas/New Year, when you're unlikely to get a ticket at short notice. At other times, one or other of the carriers should be able to offer a seat on the day you wish to travel. If you didn't pre-book when you purchased your international ticket, check availability with the airlines as soon as you arrive; tickets can be bought directly from their offices (see "Listings" on p.727), through any reputable travel agent in Mumbai (bearing bear in mind that an agent may charge you the dollar fare at a poorer rate of exchange than that offered by the airline company), by phone or direct via the Internet (the best way in the case of the low cost airlines).

All Goa flights leave from Chhatrapati Shivaji Domestic Airport, 30km north of the city centre.

By train

The Konkan Railway line runs daily express trains from Mumbai to Goa. **Fares** for the twelve-hour journey from CST start at Rs293 for standard sleeper class, rising to

Travel details

Trains

Mumbai to: Agra (4 daily; 23hr 15min–27hr); Ahmedabad (4 daily; 7hr 10min–12hr); Aurangabad (2 daily; 7hr 45min); Bangalore (3 daily; 26hr 10min); Bhopal (4 daily; 14hr); Chennai (3 daily; 24–29hr); Delhi (11 daily; 17–33hr); Hyderabad (2 daily; 15–17hr); Indore (1 daily; 14hr 35min); Jaipur (2 daily; 18–23hr); Jodhpur (1 daily; 19hr 25min; change at Ahmedabad); Kolhapur (3 daily; 11–12hr); Kolkata (Calcutta) (4 daily; 32–40hr); Nagpur (4 daily; 14–15hr); Nasik (15 daily; 4hr); Pune (25 daily; 3hr 25min–5hr); Thiruvananthapuram (2 daily; 42hr); Udaipur (1 daily; 24hr 40min; change at Ahmedabad); Ujjain (1 daily; 12hr 25 min); Varanasi (2 daily; 29–36hr).

Buses

Only state bus services are listed here; for details of private buses, see above.

ASIAD Dadar to: Kolhapur (4 daily; 10hr); Nasik (17 daily; 5hr); Pune (half-hourly; 4hr).

Mumbai Central to: Aurangabad (2 daily; 10hr); Bangalore (3 daily; 24hr); Bijapur (3 daily; 12hr); Goa (2 daily; 18–19hr); Indore (2 daily; 16hr); Ujjain (1 daily; 17hr).

Rs1242 for II class a/c or Rs2345 for luxurious I class a/c. However, these services are not always available at short notice from the booking halls at CST and Churchgate. If you're certain of your travel dates in advance (ie if you're flying into Mumbai and want to catch the train to Goa soon after arriving), consider **booking online** (at Ⓦwww.konkanrailway.com). There are downsides to this: you're only entitled to relatively expensive three-tier a/c fares (Rs1242 one-way) and must make your booking between seven and two days before your date of departure – but all in all, online reservation is a much more convenient way to secure a seat than leaving it until you arrive in Mumbai. Alternatively, you could make the reservation through an Indian Railways agent in your home country; for more on how to do this, see Basics on p.57.

Don't be tempted to travel "unreserved" class on any Konkan service as the journey as far as Ratnagiri (roughly midway) is overwhelmingly crushed. The most convenient of the Konkan services is the overnight Mumbai–Madgaon Express #KR0111 (11pm; 12hr) which departs from CST. The other, only slightly faster train is the Mandovi Express #KR0103, leaving at 7am (also from CST).

By bus

The Mumbai–Goa bus journey ranks among the very worst in India. Don't believe travel agents who assure you it takes thirteen hours. Depending on the type of bus you get, appalling road surfaces along the sinuous coastal route make eighteen to twenty hours a more realistic estimate.

Fares start at around Rs300 for a push-back seat on a beaten-up Kadamba (Goan government) or MSRTC coach. Tickets for these services are in great demand in season with domestic tourists, so book in advance at Mumbai Central or Kadamba's kiosks on the north side of Azad Maidan, near St Xavier's College (just up from CST station; Ⓣ022/2262 1043). More and more private overnight buses (around 25 daily) also run to Goa, costing around Rs375–400 for a noisy front-engined Tata bus, Rs400–450 for an a/c bus with pneumatic suspension and on-board toilet, and Rs600–675 for a service with coffin-like sleeper compartments which quickly become unbearably stuffy. Tickets should be booked at least a day in advance through a reputable travel agent (see p.728), though it's sometimes worth turning up at the car park opposite the Metro cinema, Azad Maidan, where most buses leave from, on the off-chance of a last-minute cancellation. Make sure, in any case, that you are given both your seat and the bus registration number, and that you confirm the exact time and place of departure with the travel agent, as these frequently vary between companies.

Flights

For a list of **airline addresses and travel agents,** see p.727 & p.728. In the listings below AI Air India, IA is Indian Airlines, JA Jet Airways and SA Sahara Airlines.

Chhatrapati Shivaji Domestic Airport to: Ahmedabad (AI, IA, JA 5–7 daily; 1hr); Aurangabad (IA, JA 3 daily; 45min); Bangalore (IA, AI, JA, SA 10–12 daily; 1hr 30min); Bhopal (IA, JA 2 daily; 2hr 05min); Bhubaneshwar (IA 3 weekly; 2hr); Bhuj (IA, JA daily; 1hr 15min); Chennai (AI, IA, JA 6–8 daily; 1hr 45min); Cochin (see "Kochi"); Delhi (IA, AI, JA, SA 33–36 daily; 1hr 55min); Coimbatore (SA 1 daily; 2hr); Goa (AI, IA, JA, SA 7–8 daily; 45min–1hr); Hyderabad (IA, JA, SA 8–15 daily; 1hr 15min); Indore (IA, JA 3 daily; 1hr 05min); Jaipur (IA, JA 4 daily; 1hr 35min); Jodhpur (IA, JA 2 daily; 2hr 10min); Kochi (AI, IA, SA 2–4 daily; 1hr 45min); Kolkata (Calcutta; IA, AI, JA, SA 9–10 daily; 2hr 40min); Madurai (IA 1 daily; 3hr 20min); Mangalore (JA, IA, 2–3 daily; 1hr 15min); Nagpur (IA, JA 3 daily; 1hr 55min); Pune (IA, JA, SA 5 daily; 35min); Thiruvananthapuram (AI, IA, JA 2–3 daily; 2hr); Udaipur (IA 2–3 daily; 1hr 10min); Varanasi (IA, SA 2 daily; 4hr 55min).

CHAPTER 11 Highlights

* **Ellora caves** Breathtaking Hindu, Buddhist and Jain caves carved from solid volcanic rock. See p.747

* **Ajanta caves** Chiselled from a horseshoe-shaped ravine and adorned with extraordinary Buddhist and Hindu murals. See p.754

* **Lonar** This remote lake, within a meteorite crater, is a tranquil escape, dotted with temples and surrounded by a forest rich in wildlife. See p.762

* **Nasik** One of the four holy places that host the Kumbh Mela, the city's *ghats* on the River Godavari present a lively picture of modern Hindu practices. See p.763

* **Gandhi ashram, Sevagram** Learn about the great man's life and beliefs at the last ashram he lived in. See p.769

* **Miniature train to Matheran** Fantastic views across the Western Ghats on the relaxing journey to this hill station. See p.771

* **Ganpatipule** A little-visited golden sandy beach on the Konkan Coast between Mumbai and Goa, with a lovely Ganapati temple. See p.774

△ Relief, Ellora Caves

11

Maharashtra

Vast and rugged, the modern state of **MAHARASHTRA**, the third largest in India, was created in 1960 from the Marathi-speaking regions of what was previously Bombay State. As soon as you leave its seething port capital, **Mumbai** (formerly Bombay), developed by Europeans and now the epitome of modern, cosmopolitan, polyglot India, you enter a different world with a different history.

Undoubtedly, Maharashtra's greatest treasures are its extraordinary **cave temples** and **monasteries**. The finest of all are found near **Aurangabad**, renamed after the Moghul emperor Aurangzeb and still home to a sizeable Muslim population (as well as "the poor man's Taj Mahal", the **Bibi-ka-Maqbara**). The busy commercial city is the obvious base for visits to the caves at **Ajanta**, with their fabulous and still-vibrant murals, and the monolithic temples of **Ellora**, where the Hindu **Kailash temple** may look like a regular structure but was carved in its entirety from one single rock. From the second century BC, this region was an important centre of Buddhism; artificial caves were excavated to shelter monks, and the finest artists sculpted magnificent cathedral-like halls for congregational worship. Around 100km east of Aurangabad lies fascinating **Lonar** lake, situated in a meteorite crater.

Hinduism later supplanted Buddhism as the region's principal religion, which it remains, despite the efforts of the successive Muslim rulers to introduce Islam to Maharashtra – around eighty percent of the population is Hindu. Balancing modern industry alongside ancient associations with the *Ramayana*, the main pilgrimage centre has always been **Nasik**, 187km northeast of Mumbai en route to Aurangabad. As one of the four locations of the Kumbh Mela, when up to four million devotees battle to bathe simultaneously in the holy River Godavari, the town is always a hive of devotional activity, even during less auspicious times. A short distance west, one of India's most sacred Shiva shrines lies close to the source of the Godavari, reached by a short trek from **Trimbak**.

Away from the cities, the most characteristic feature of the landscape is a plenitude of **forts** – as the western borderland between north and South India, Maharashtra's trade routes were always important, but could also bring trouble. Inland, parallel to the sea, and never further than 100km from it, the mighty **Western Ghats** rise abruptly. The areas of level ground that crowned them, endowed with fresh water, were easily converted into forts where small forces could withstand protracted sieges by large armies. Modern visitors can scale such windswept fortified heights at **Pratapgadh** and **Daulatabad**, which – briefly, bizarrely and disastrously – replaced Delhi as capital in the fourteenth century.

During the last century, the mountains found another use. When the summer proved too much for the British in Bombay, they sought refuge in nearby

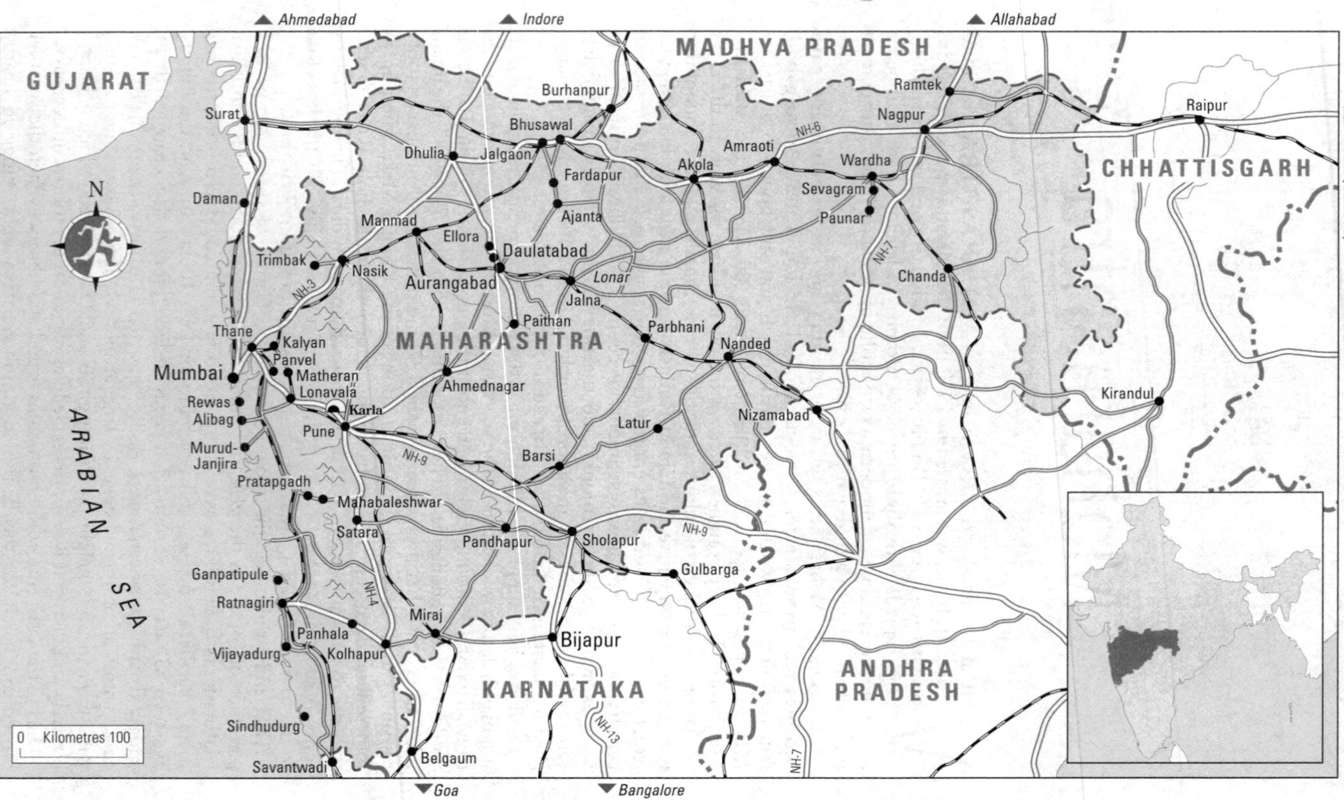
Ahmedabad
Indore
Allahabad
Kolkata (Calcutta)
Goa
Bangalore
GUJARAT
MADHYA PRADESH
CHHATTISGARH
MAHARASHTRA
ANDHRA PRADESH
KARNATAKA
ARABIAN SEA
N
Surat
Daman
Burhanpur
Bhusawal
Jalgaon
Dhulia
Fardapur
Ajanta
Manmad
Ellora
Daulatabad
Aurangabad
Trimbak
Nasik
NH-3
Lonar
Jalna
Paithan
Parbhani
Nanded
Thane
Kalyan
Panvel
Matheran
Lonavala
Karla
Mumbai
Rewas
Alibag
Murud-Janjira
Pune
Ahmednagar
NH-9
Latur
Nizamabad
Barsi
Pratapgadh
Mahabaleshwar
Satara
Pandhapur
Sholapur
Gulbarga
Ganpatipule
Ratnagiri
NH-4
Miraj
Panhala
Vijayadurg
Kolhapur
Bijapur
Sindhudurg
Savantwadi
Belgaum
NH-13
NH-7
Ramtek
Nagpur
NH-6
Raipur
Amraoti
Akola
Wardha
Sevagram
Paunar
Chanda
Kirandul
0 Kilometres 100

hill stations, the most popular of which, **Mahabaleshwar**, now caters for droves of Indian holidaymakers. **Matheran**, 108km east of Mumbai and 800m higher, has a special attraction: a rickety miniature train that twists up the hill on a sinuous track. Beyond the Ghats, the modern city of **Pune**, site of the internationally famous **Osho ashram** founded by the New Age guru Bhagwan Rajneesh, presides over a semi-arid tableland of flat-topped hills and dusty wheat fields. Maharashtra extends 900km further east across the Deccan plateau to the geographical centre of the subcontinent, an area largely populated by several different tribal groups and where Mahatma Gandhi set up his headquarters at **Sevagram** during the Independence struggle.

To the west, Maharashtra occupies 500km of the **Konkan coast** on the Arabian Sea, from Gujarat to Goa. The palm-fringed coast winds back and forth with countless inlets, ridges and valleys, studded with forts. Incentives to break the journey down to Goa include **Murud-Janjira**, an extraordinary island fort flanked by beaches, and, in the far south, the interesting little seaside Ganesh temple of **Ganpatipule**, with its almost deserted stretch of beach.

Some history

Although some Paleolithic remains have been discovered, Maharashtra enters recorded history in the second century BC, with the construction of its first Buddhist caves. These lay, and still lie, in peaceful places of great natural beauty, but could never have been created without the wealth generated by the nearby caravan trade routes between north and South India.

The region's first Hindu rulers – based in Badami, Karnataka – appeared during the sixth century. Buddhism was almost entirely supplanted throughout the country by the twelfth century, in what has been characterized as a peaceful people's revolution attributable largely to the popular songs and teachings of poet-saints. The tradition they established continued to flourish throughout the thirteenth and fourteenth centuries, even when forced underground by Islam, reaching its zenith in the simple faith of **Ramdas** (1608–81), the "Servant of Rama".

Ramdas, ascetic and political activist, provided the philosophical underpinning behind the campaigns of Maharashtra's greatest warrior, **Shivaji** (1627–80). The fiercely independent Maratha chieftain united local forces to place insurmountable obstacles in the way of any prospective invader; so effective were their guerrilla tactics that he could even take on the mighty Moghuls. Shivaji progressively fought his way northwards, at a time when the Moghuls, who had got as far as capturing Daulatabad in 1633, were embroiled in protracted family feuds. A year after he succeeded in sacking the great port of Surat (Gujarat), in 1664, he was defeated in battle and imprisoned by **Aurangzeb** in Agra. He is said to have escaped by hiding in a package which the prison guards imagined was a gift intended for local Brahmins; once outside, Shivaji simply walked away, disguised as a religious mendicant. By the time he died, in 1680, he had managed to unite the Marathas into a stable and secure state, funded by the plunder gleaned through guerrilla raids as far afield as Andhra Pradesh.

To be better placed to subdue the Marathas, Aurangzeb moved his court and capital south to the Deccan, first to Bijapur (1686) and then Golconda (1687). But after 25 years of relentless campaigns, he had still failed to subdue Shivaji's dynasty, which had meanwhile become a confederacy with a dominion extending as far east as Orissa. By the end of the eighteenth century, however, the power of both had weakened and the British were able to take full control.

Maharashtra claims a crucial role in the development of a nationalist consciousness. An organization known as the Indian National Union, originally convened in Pune, held a conference in Bombay in 1885, which was thereafter known as the **Indian National Congress**. This loose congregation of key figures from local politics around the country was to change the face of Indian politics. At first, its aim was limited to establishing a national platform to raise the status of Indians, and it remained loyal to the British. In the long term, of course, it was instrumental in the achievement of Independence 62 years later, with many of the Congress's factional leaders over the years hailing from Maharashtra. Of late, the modern Congress has reasserted its power in the state assembly, as the influence of the BJP and Shiv Sena has waned.

With Independence, the Bombay Presidency, to which most of Maharashtra belonged, became known as Bombay State. Maharashtra as such was created in 1960. Its manufacturing industries, centred on Mumbai and to a lesser extent cities such as Nagpur, Nasik, Aurangabad, Sholapur and Kolhapur, now account for a quarter of the nation's output. Textiles have long been important, but this is now also one of the premier high-tech industry regions, especially along the Mumbai–Pune corridor. However, the majority of Maharashtra's population of over 95 million are still engaged in agriculture: main crops include sugar cane, cotton, peanuts, sunflowers, tobacco, pulses, wine grapes, fruit and vegetables.

Northern Maharashtra

Beyond the seemingly endless concrete housing projects, petrochemical works and mosquito-infested swamplands of Greater Mumbai, a wall of bare bluish-brown hills dominates the horizon. The **Western Ghats** form a series of huge steps that march up from the narrow, humid coastal strip to the edge of the **Deccan** plateau in a vast, dry tableland punctuated with weathered ridges and plains dotted with scruffy villages and market towns. **Northern Maharashtra's** main transport arteries, the NH-3 and Central Railway line, wind in tandem through this stark landscape, following an ancient trade route that once linked the western ports with the prosperous cities further north. Over the centuries, a number of pilgrimage sites sprang up to take advantage of the lucrative through-traffic, and these form the principal points of interest in the region today.

The holy city of **Nasik** is a handy place to break journeys to or from Mumbai, four hours away by road. Amid impressive scenery, the town of **Trimbak**, 10km west at the start of a steep half-day hike to the source of the sacred River Godavari, makes a more relaxing overnight stop. Most foreign visitors, however, head straight for the regional capital, **Aurangabad**, the jumping-off point for the rock-cut **caves** at **Ellora** and **Ajanta**. Among **Muslim monuments** to seek out here are Aurangabad's answer to the Taj Mahal, the **Bibi-ka-Maqbara**, the dramatic hilltop fort at **Daulatabad**, and the tiny tomb town of **Khuldabad**, 5km from Ellora, where the emperor Aurangzeb is buried.

From Aurangabad, a well-beaten track cuts through the middle of Madhya Pradesh, via **Jalgaon**, towards Varanasi and Nepal. Alternatively, you could head across central India to **Wardha** and **Nagpur**, in the far northeastern corner of the state, where a couple of **Gandhi ashrams**, and the picturesque whitewashed Hindu temple complex at **Ramtek** make pleasant pauses on long cross-country hauls.

Aurangabad and beyond

It's easy to see why many travellers regard **AURANGABAD** as little more than a convenient, though largely uninteresting, place in which to kill time on the way to **Ellora** and **Ajanta**. First impressions seem to confirm its reputation as an industrial metropolis; yet, given a little effort, northern Maharashtra's largest city can compensate for its architectural shortcomings. Scattered around its ragged fringes, the dilapidated remains of fortifications, gateways, domes and minarets – including those of the most ambitious Moghul tomb garden in western India, the **Bibi-ka-Maqbara** – bear witness to an illustrious imperial past; the small but fascinating crop of **rock-cut Buddhist caves**, huddled along the flanks of the flat-topped, sandy yellow hills to the north, are remnants of even more ancient occupation.

The city, originally called **Khadke**, or "Big Rock", was founded in the early sixteenth century by **Malik Amber**, an ex-Abyssinian slave and prime

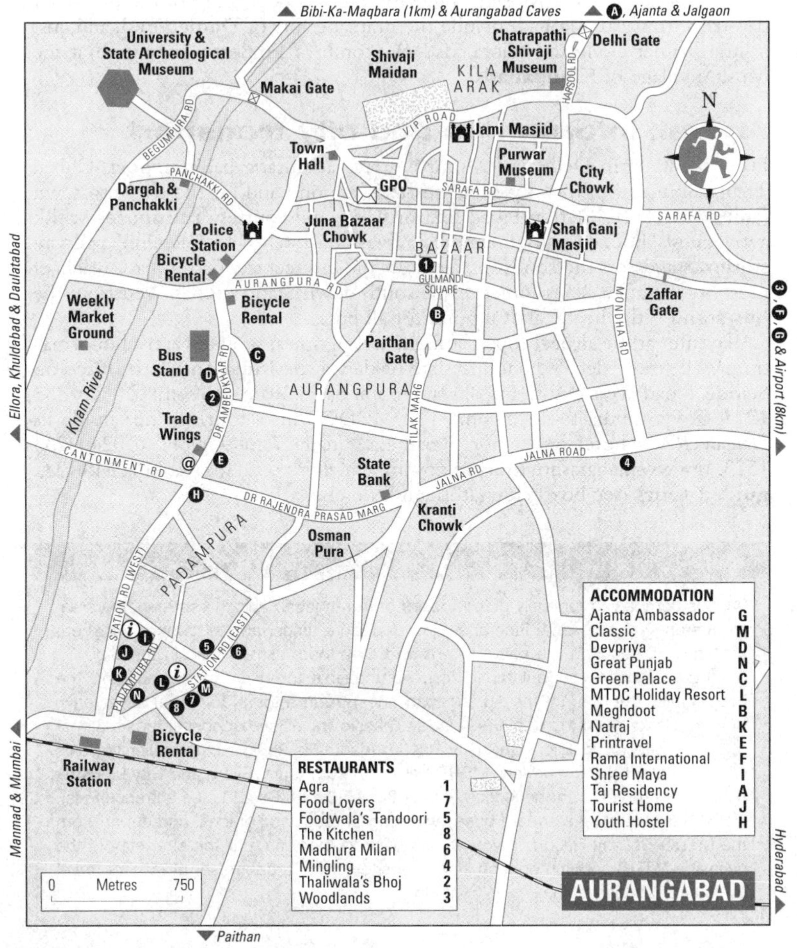

minister of the independent Muslim kingdom of the Nizam Shahis, based at Ahmadnagar, 112km southwest. It was a perfect spot for a provincial capital: on the banks of the **River Kham**, in a broad valley separating the then-forested Sahyadri Range to the north from the Satharas to the south, and at a crossroads of the region's key trade routes. Many of the **mosques** and palaces erected by Malik Amber still endure, albeit in ruins.

Aurangabad really rose to prominence, however, towards the end of the seventeenth century, when **Aurangzeb** decamped here from Delhi. At his behest, the impressive city walls and gates were raised in 1682 to withstand the persistent Maratha attacks that bedevilled his later years. Following his death in 1707, the city was renamed in his honour as it changed hands once again. The new rulers, the **Nizams of Hyderabad**, somehow staved off the Marathas for the greater part of 250 years, until the city finally merged with Maharashtra in 1956.

Today Aurangabad is one of India's fastest growing commercial and industrial centres, with the likes of Skoda moving in. It's a decidedly upbeat place, with plenty of restaurants, bars and interesting shops in the old city, and communal tensions with the large Muslim minority seem to be a thing of the past. Easy day-trips from Aurangabad include the dramatic fort of **Daulatabad**, and, just a little further along the Ellora road, the tomb of Emperor Aurangzeb at the Muslim village of **Khuldabad**.

Arrival, information and city transport

Daily flights from Delhi and Mumbai arrive at Aurangabad's **airport**, Chikal Thana, 8km east of the city. Metered **taxis** are on hand for the trip into town (around Rs180 to Station Road East or West), and courtesy **minibuses** whisk away guests booked into the nearby five-star hotels. The mainline **railway station** stands on the southwest edge of the city centre, within easy reach of most hotels, and a 2.5-kilometre ride south down Station Road West from the **bus stand** – the hectic arrival point for all buses.

A counter at the airport (open at flight arrival times) provides arrival information, while more detailed enquiries are fielded at the **India Tourism office** on Station Road West (Mon–Fri 8.30am–6pm, Sat 8.30am–1.30pm; ⓣ0240/233 1217, ⓦwww.india-tourism.com). The MTDC runs a tourist office inside its *Holiday Resort* hotel on Station Road East (daily 7am–9.30pm; ⓣ0240/233 1513, ⓦwww.maharashtratourism.gov.in), which is useful for booking MSRTC **guided tours** (see box below), though little else.

Tours

Various companies run daily guided **tours** of Aurangabad and the surrounding area, all operating to the same itineraries and departure times, and all generally rushed; the only difference is the price. **Ellora and City** tours usually take in the Bibi-Ka-Maqbara, Panchakki, Daulatabad fort, Aurangzeb's tomb at Khuldabad, and the Ellora caves (though not the Aurangabad ones). **Ajanta** tours go to the caves only, but are a long round trip to make in a day. Classic Travel (see opposite) runs the best of the private tours (Ellora and City Rs150, Ajanta Rs 230), using smaller vehicles with a greater level of comfort. MSRTC also run both tours (Ellora and City 9.30am–5.30pm, Rs100 plus entrance fees; Ajanta 8am–5.30pm, Rs 230 plus entrance fees). MSRTC tours are on standard buses with English-speaking guides, and depart from the MTDC *Holiday Resort*. If you want to spend more time at the site, stay in the caveside MTDC accommodation (see opposite), or at Fardapur (see p.761), or travel on to Jalgaon (see p.762).

A very efficient **foreign exchange** service is provided at Trade Wings (daily 8am–8pm) on Dr Ambedkhar Road, directly opposite the *Printravel* hotel, though they charge a Rs60 commission. There is also an ICICI Bank **ATM** on the opposite side of the road to the MTDC office. The **GPO** (Mon–Sat 10am–5pm, Speedpost 8am–7pm, registered mail and parcels 10am–2pm) is at Juna Bazaar Chowk, on the north side of the old city. There's an **Internet** café (Rs40/hr) opposite the *Printravel* hotel, or try the faster service inside the *Shree Maya Hotel* (Rs40/hr).

City transport

Most of Aurangabad's sights lie too far apart to take in on foot. The city is, however, buzzing with **auto-rickshaws**, which, on the whole, will happily flag their meters; longer sightseeing trips work out much cheaper if you settle on a fare in advance (usually Rs400–500). Taxis can be hailed in the street or found at the railway station and **cars with drivers** can be hired through travel agents such as the extremely friendly and efficient Classic Travel (ⓣ0240/233 5598, ⓔclassictours@vsnl.com), opposite MTDC's *Holiday Resort* on Station Road East. Expect to pay Rs800–1200 for an eight-hour day with an additional overnight charge of around Rs150. Victor Tours & Travels (ⓣ0240/562 9989), also on Station Road East, next to the *Great Punjab*, is another helpful place for making general travel arrangements.

Much the cheapest and most satisfying way to get around the city, however, is by **bicycle**. While the busy main streets and market can be hair-raising at times, a ride out to the sights in the north of town makes an enjoyable alternative to public transport. Two stalls just north of the bus stand have the best bikes (Rs3/hr), and there's another near the railway station.

Accommodation

Aurangabad's proximity to some of India's most important monuments, together with its new "boom-city" status, ensures a profusion of **hotels**. On the whole, standards tend to be high and prices very reasonable, particularly in the **budget** places, most of which are near the bus stand or the railway station. All have 24-hour checkout unless otherwise stated.

Ajanta Ambassador Chikalthana ⓣ0240/248 5211, ⓦwww.ambassadorindia.com. Luxurious, top-notch establishment near the airport, with over-the-top ersatz traditional interior. Excellent sports facilities. ⑨

Classic beside Goldie Cinema, Station Rd East ⓣ0240/562 4313, ⓦwww.aurangabadhotel.com. New, gaily-painted hotel with a splendid atrium and compact but comfy rooms with most mod cons. ④–⑥

Devpriya Near Siddharth Gardens, Dr Ambedkhar Rd ⓣ0240/233 9032, ⓕ233 6129. Neat, clean and efficiently run family hotel. ②

Great Punjab Station Rd East ⓣ0240/233 6482, ⓕ233 6131. Business-oriented hotel very near the railway station. All 42 rooms have bathrooms, balconies and TVs. Bland but very good value. ③–④

Green Palace On strip one block back from Dr Ambedkhar Rd, opposite the bus stand ⓣ0240/233 5501. Spartan but clean. Handy if you have just crawled off a bus and can't face a room hunt. There are a crop of good fall-backs such as the *Shangrila* nearby. ①–②

MTDC Holiday Resort Station Rd East ⓣ0240/233 4259, ⓕ233 1198. Spacious, comfortable rooms, if a touch shabby. Mosquito nets over the beds. 8am checkout. ⑤

Meghdoot Tilak Marg ⓣ0240/235 2310. Modern functional place with decent attached rooms, all with TV. Good spot for some comfort in the atmosphere of the old city. ③–④

Natraj Station Rd West ⓣ0240/232 4260. Very traditional lodge run by two elderly Gujarati brothers. Spacious, clean, good-value rooms with shared bathrooms around a peaceful green courtyard. Strictly no alcohol. ②

Printravel Dr Ambedkhar Rd ⓣ0240/232 9707, ⓦwww.printravel.com. Faintly 1950s building near city centre. Common balcony with easy chairs and a good restaurant. Huge rooms. ③–④

Rama International Airport Rd ⓣ0240/ 248 5441, ⓦwww.welcomehotelrama.com. Classically designed, palatial building with sculptures and landscaped grounds, 3km from the centre. Facilities include a huge health centre, swimming pool, tennis, mini-golf and croquet. ❾

Shree Maya Bharuka Complex, Padampura Rd, off Station Rd West ⓣ0240/333093, ⓔshrimay_agd@sancharnet.in. Friendly place with large cleanish rooms (some a/c), all with attached bathrooms and most with TV. Has a pleasant rooftop terrace restaurant. ❸

Taj Residency Ajanta Rd ⓣ0240/238 1106, ⓦwww.tajhotels.com. Business-orientated branch of the famous chain, about 3km north of Delhi Gate, and convenient for sights on the north side of town. Large swimming pool, tennis courts, gardens and health suite. ❾

Tourist Home Station Rd West ⓣ0240/233 7212. Congenial travellers' hostel with neat rooms, attached shower/toilets, and a sociable terrace where evening thalis are served. Excellent value. ❷

Youth Hostel Off Station Rd West ⓣ0240/233 4892. Cheapest option in town: neat and clean segregated dorms (Rs40 under 35s, Rs60 over 35s) with mosquito nets, and reasonable private rooms. Book in advance if possible. Checkout 9am, closed 11am–4pm and 10pm curfew. ❷

The City

The old walled city, laid out on a grid by Malik Amber in the sixteenth century, still forms the core of Aurangabad's large **bazaar** area. It's best approached via **Gulmandi Square** to the south, along any of several streets lined with colourful shops and stalls. The bazaar lacks the character and intensity of those in larger Indian cities, but has a pleasant, workaday feel, and you'll not be approached by too many zealous salesmen.

Keep walking north, and you'll come out on the chaotic east–west thoroughfare of Ghati Road. In a tiny backroom behind a shop on Ghati Road stands the **Purwar Museum** (open on request; donations). Housed in a beautiful old *haveli*, this impressive private collection of antiquities boasts a seventeenth-century Koran hand-painted by Aurangzeb, superb bronzes and a host of other wonderful objects. Look for the sign above a doorway and ask at the handicraft shop next door to be let in. The retired doctor who owns the collection has shifted around three thousand items into spacious new premises in the **Chatrapathi Shivaji Museum** (Tues–Sun 10.30am–1.30pm & 3–6pm; Rs5), 1km north on VIP Road. The museum is exclusively devoted to sixteenth-century artefacts, arranged in six rooms, each with a different theme.

The unremarkable eighteenth-century **Shah Ganj Masjid** that presides over the main square directly east of City Chowk is surrounded on three sides by small shops and a congested roundabout. Anyone keen to see other remnants of Aurangabad's Moghul splendour should make for the city's largest and most impressive mosque, the **Jami Masjid**, 1km northwest of Shah Ganj Masjid. Its amalgam of parts was begun by Malik Amber in 1612 and added to by Aurangzeb nearly a century later. To the east of the mosque lie the ruins of Aurangzeb's former imperial headquarters, the **Kila Arak**. Once this was a complex of palaces, battlements, gateways, tanks and gardens that housed three princes and a retinue of thousands.

On the left bank of the Kham River, on Panchakki Road, the **Dargah** of Baba Shah Muzaffar (daily sunrise–8pm; Rs5) is a religious compound built by Aurangzeb as a memorial to his spiritual mentor, a *chishti* mystic. The principal point of interest is not so much the mosque, the modest tomb or ornamental gardens nearby, pleasant as they are, but the unusual adjoining water mill known as the **Panchakki**. Water pumped underground from a reservoir in the hills 6km away collects in a tank, now teeming with enormous *khol* fish, to drive a small grindstone once used to mill flour. The whole complex was an impressive engineering feat for its time, and makes a lively place to wander around in the early evening with lots of chai shops, *mehendi* (henna hand-painting) artists and souvenir shops. South of the Panchakki, also on the left bank of the river, an excellent **weekly market** is held every Thursday. Villagers from outlying areas pour in all morning on bullock carts to buy and sell livestock and fresh produce. The market gets into its stride by noon, winding up around 5pm.

Further north, amidst the pleasantly wooded grounds of the university, hemmed in by hills, the **State Archeological Museum** (Mon–Sat 9.30am–5.30pm; Rs3) occupies the renovated seventeenth-century Sonehri Mahal. Objects on display include stone sculptures (mostly thirteenth- and fourteenth-century), more recent brass figures, and paintings, though the labelling in English is limited.

The Bibi-ka-Maqbara

Were it not so flagrantly an imitation of the Taj Mahal, Aurangabad's much-maligned Moghul tomb-garden would probably attract more admiration. In spite of being one of India's most impressive Islamic monuments, however, the **Bibi-ka-Maqbara** (daily 8am–sunset; $2 [Rs5]) is widely regarded as the definitive "also-ran".

The mausoleum, completed in 1678, was dedicated by **Prince Azam Shah** to the memory of his mother **Begum Rabi'a Daurani**, Aurangzeb's wife. Lack of resources dogged the 25-year project, and the end result fell far short of expectations. The entrance to the complex is through an enormous brass-inlaid **door**, decorated with Persian calligraphy. An inscription around its edge names the maker, the year of its installation and the chief architect, **Ata Ullah**. Looking at the mausoleum from beyond the ornamental gardens and redundant fountains in front of it, you can see why commentators have been critical. The truncated minarets and ungainly entrance arch make the Bibi-ka-Maqbara seem squat and ill proportioned compared with the elegant height and symmetry of the Taj. The impression is not enhanced by the abrupt discontinuation of marble after the first 2m as a cost-saving measure.

Of the two entrances to the main tomb, one provides access to the inner balcony while the second leads down through another beautiful door to the **vault** itself (since a suicidal student jumped from a minaret, visitors may no longer climb them). Inside, an exquisite octagonal **lattice-screen** of white marble surrounds the raised plinth supporting Rabi'a Daurani's grave. Like her husband's in nearby Khuldabad, it is "open" as a sign of humility. The unmarked grave beside it is said to be that of the empress's nurse.

The caves

Carved out of a steep-sided spur of the Sahyadri Range, directly overlooking the Bibi-ka-Maqbara, Aurangabad's own **caves** (Tues–Sun 8.30am–5pm; $2 [Rs5]) bear no comparison to those in nearby Ellora and Ajanta, but their fine **sculpture** makes a worthwhile introduction to rock-cut architecture. In addition, the infrequently visited site is peaceful and pleasant in itself, with commanding views over the city and surrounding countryside.

The caves, all Buddhist, consist of two groups, eastern and western, numbered 1 to 9 by the Archeological Survey of India. The majority were excavated between the fourth and eighth centuries, under the patronage of two successive dynasties: the **Vakatkas**, who ruled the western Deccan from Nasik, and the **Chalukyas**, a powerful Mysore family who emerged during the sixth century. All except the much earlier Cave 4, which is a *chaitya* hall, are of the *vihara* (monastery) type, belonging to the Mahayana school of Buddhism.

Unless you cycle, the only practical way of **getting to the caves** is by auto-rickshaw or taxi; you'll be expected to shell out for waiting time, or the return fare. You could also drop down on foot to the Bibi-ka-Maqbara to pick up an auto-rickshaw back into town.

Eating and drinking

Food in Aurangabad tends to be an incongruous mixture of strictly vegetarian **Gujarati** and meat-oriented north Indian Muslim dishes. Typically, "non-veg" is synonymous with dim lights, drawn curtains and a male clientele, while the veg restaurants attract families and are particularly popular on Sunday evenings, when booking is recommended. As elsewhere in Maharashtra, **drinking** is a male preserve, carried out in the many specially segregated bars (or "permit rooms"), with the exception of the larger and more tourist-oriented hotels and restaurants.

Agra Off Tilak Marg, Bazaar. Clean, no-nonsense restaurant on the southern edge of the old town, serving authentic, moderately priced Gujarati food, mainly to visiting business people. Can be hard to find on foot, but the rickshaw drivers know where it is.

Food Lovers Station Rd East, opposite MTDC office. A kitsch wonderland of bamboo, plastic waterfalls and fish tanks – all lit by candlelight – with a non-seedy bar. The mid-price Indian and Chinese food is pretty standard fare.

Foodwala's Tandoori Shyam Chambers, Station Rd East. Upmarket a/c bar/restaurant with numerous à la carte chicken and mutton dishes. Pricey but worth it.

The Kitchen Station Rd East, almost opposite MTDC office. Reasonably priced and well-run diner serving quality Indian food to a mix of Indian holidaymakers and backpackers. Features many local (mainly non-veg) dishes, a Rs35 thali and Continental or English breakfasts.

Madhura Milan Station Rd East. Smart but inexpensive veg restaurant serving Chinese, Punjabi, tandoori and South Indian snacks. Sign in Marathi only.

Mingling *Rajdoot Hotel*, Jalna Rd. Best Chinese in town, though a bit ostentatious and overpriced, with main courses upwards of Rs100.

Thaliwala's Bhoj Near Baba Petrol Pump, Dr Ambedkhar Rd. An old favourite, pure veg restaurant

Moving on from Aurangabad

Daily **flights** from Aurangabad to **Mumbai** (45min; $85) are operated by Jet Airways (8.45am & 7.55pm) and Indian Airlines (5.30pm). The Indian Airlines flight also carries on to **Delhi** (3hr 25min; $185). Their office is on Jalna Road (☎0240/248 5421), as is Jet Airways (☎0240/244 1392).

All the state transport corporation (MSRTC) buses leave from the Central bus stand, including good-value "luxury" daily **night buses** to **Mumbai**. If you feel like a little more comfort, there are a couple of companies running more expensive a/c buses to most of the larger destinations; tickets can be booked through travel agents. Getting to **Pune** is easy, on MSRTC's "express"; **Nasik** buses are also frequent, as are services to Jalgaon. A couple of private bus companies run buses to **Indore**, **Nasik**, **Pune**, **Udaipur**, **Ahmedabad** and **Jalgaon** which can be booked through most travel agents.

Trains to and from Aurangabad are very limited, as the city is not on the main line. The two most convenient services to **Mumbai** are the heavily booked Devgiri Express #1004 and Tapovan Express #7618, which leave at 11.25pm and 2.35pm respectively. You can also get direct to **Secunderabad** (for Hyderabad) on the Manmad–Kacheguda Express #7663 at 5.30pm. Otherwise, the nearest mainline station, at **Jalgaon**, 108km north, is served by far more trains to many destinations, including Mumbai, Delhi, Agra, Bhopal, Kolkata (Calcutta) and Chennai.

See "Travel details" at the end of this chapter for information on journey frequencies and durations.

at shiny, new premises. Renowned for its meticulously prepared, good-value lunchtime Rajasthani thalis.

Woodlands Jalna Rd, past the *Rama International*. Decidedly yuppie crowd but locally renowned for good, mid-priced South Indian food.

Daulatabad (Deogiri)

Dominating the horizon 13km northwest of Aurangabad, the awesome hilltop citadel of **DAULATABAD** crowns a massive conical volcanic outcrop whose sides have been shaped into a sheer sixty-metre wall of granite. The fort's forbidding appearance is further accentuated by the enormous minaret rising out of the ruins of the city that once sprawled from its base. If only for the panoramic **views** from the top of the hill, Daulatabad makes a rewarding pause en route to or from the caves at Ellora, 17km northwest.

Aside from the inevitable Buddhist and Jain hermits, occupation of the site – then known as **Deogiri**, "Hill of the Gods" – dates from its ninth-century role as bastion and capital of a confederacy of Hindu tribes. The **Yadavas** were responsible for scraping away the jagged lower slopes of the mount to form its vertical-cliff base, as well as the fifteen-metre-deep moat that still encircles the upper portion of the citadel. Their prosperity eventually aroused the interest of the acquisitive Delhi sultans, who stormed the fortress in 1294 and carried off a hoard of gold, silver and precious stones.

Muslim occupation of Deogiri began in earnest with the arrival in 1327 of Ghiyas-ud-din **Tughluq**. Convinced that the fort was the perfect base for campaigns further south, the sultan decreed that his entire court should decamp here from Tughluqabad, the "third city" of Delhi. The epic 1100-kilometre march cost thousands of lives. But within seventeen years, drought, famine and the growing threat of a full-scale Moghul invasion on his northern borders forced the beleaguered ruler to return to Tughluqabad. His governor, Zafar Khan, took the opportunity to mount a rebellion and established the **Bahmani** dynasty. Thereafter, the fortress fell to a succession of different regimes, including Shah Jahan's **Moghuls** in 1633, before it was finally taken by the **Marathas** midway through the eighteenth century.

The fortress

Daulatabad's labyrinthine **fortress** (daily 6am–6pm; $2 [Rs5]) unfolds around the **Chandminar**, or "Victory Tower", erected by Ala-ud-din Bahmani to celebrate his conquest of the fort in 1435. The Persian blue-and-turquoise tiles that once plastered it in complex geometric patterns have disappeared, but it remains an impressive spectacle.

The Jami Masjid, directly opposite, is Daulatabad's oldest Islamic monument. Built by the Delhi sultans in 1318, the well-preserved mosque comprises 106 pillars plundered from the Hindu and Jain temples which previously stood on the site. It was recently converted into a Bharatmata temple, much to the chagrin of local Muslims. Nearby, the large stone-lined "Elephant" **tank** was once a central component in the fort's extensive water-supply system. Two giant terracotta pipes channelled water from the hills into the Deogiri's legendary fruit and vegetable gardens.

Once beyond the open ground surrounding the tower, the main walkway heads through a series of interlocking bastions, fortified walls, moats and drawbridges before emerging to the **Chini Mahal**, or "Chinese Palace". The impressive ram-headed **Kila Shikan** ("Fort Breaker") cannon, inscribed with its name in Persian, rests on a stone platform nearby. From here onwards, a sequence of macabre traps lay in wait for the unwary intruder, including a moat infested with man-eating crocodiles and a maze of passageways with iron covers that could be heated to generate toxic gases.

At the end of the final tunnel, a broad flight of rock-cut steps climbs to an attractive twelve-pillared pavilion. The **Baradi** is thought to have been the residence of a Yadavi queen, though it was later used by the emperor Shah Jahan during his visits to Daulatabad. The **views** from the flat roof of the building are superb, but an even more impressive panorama is to be had from the **look-out post** perched on the summit of the hill, marked with another grand cannon and a cave that in Moghul times sheltered a famous holy man.

Practicalities

If you're not on a guided tour, it's recommended that you hire a guide, as the passages of the fort are pitch-black and hopelessly confusing otherwise. Although Daulatabad features on the guided **tours** of Ellora from Aurangabad (see p.740), you'll have more time to enjoy it by travelling there on one of the hourly shuttle **buses** between Aurangabad and the caves. From Daulatabad, it is easy to catch another bus onto Khuldabad and Ellora; the stop is directly opposite the main entrance to the fort, beside the string of chai and souvenir stalls and the good, small MTDC-run **restaurant**. Note that there's no **accommodation** in Daulatabad.

Khuldabad (Rauza)

Nestled on a saddle of high ground, 22km from Aurangabad and a four-kilometre ride from Ellora, **KHULDABAD**, also known as **Rauza**, is an old walled town famous for a wonderful crop of onion-domed **tombs**. Among the Muslim notables deemed worthy of a patch of earth in this most hallowed of burial grounds ("Khuldabad" means "Heavenly Abode"), were the emperor Aurangzeb, a couple of nizams, and a fair few of the town's *chishti* founding fathers – the seven hundred mystic missionaries dispatched by the saint Nizam-ud-din Aulia to soften up local Hindus before the Sultanate's invasion in the fourteenth century. Khuldabad's monuments are nowhere near as impressive as those in Delhi, Agra or Bijapur, but a couple harbour important **relics** and are still venerated for their miraculous properties. While they see a steady trickle of visitors, and even large crowds on festival days, the lesser mausoleums on the outskirts of the sleepy Muslim town lie deserted and all but forgotten, their old stone pavilions, domes and walled enclosures choked with weeds.

MSRTC **buses** run every half-hour from Aurangabad to Khuldabad's small bus stand, a short walk west of the walls, en route to the Ellora caves just down the hill. There is no **accommodation** in the village, nor anywhere decent to **eat**, so you'll need to bring your own supplies.

The Dargah of Sayeed Zain-ud-din

Khuldabad is encircled by tall granite battlements and seven fortified **gateways** raised by Aurangzeb before his death in 1707. The last of the great Moghuls' tomb lies inside a whitewashed **dargah** (sunrise–10pm; free), midway between the North and South gates. In keeping with the teachings of Islam, the grave itself is a humble affair decorated only by the fresh flower petals scattered by visitors, open to the elements instead of sealed in stone. The devout emperor insisted that it be paid for not out of the royal coffers, but with the money he raised in the last years of life by selling his own hand-quilted white skullcaps. The pierced-marble **screen** and walls that now surround the spot were erected much later by the British viceroy, Lord Curzon, and the Nizam of Hyderabad.

Aurangzeb chose this as his final resting place primarily because of the presence, next door, of Sayeed **Zain-ud-din**'s tomb. The mausoleum of the Muslim saint, or *pir*, occupies a quadrangle separating Aurangzeb's grave from those of his wife and second son, Azam Shah. The steps leading to it are encrusted with highly polished semiprecious stones donated by the wandering Muslim ascetics, or *fakirs*, who formerly came here on pilgrimages. Locked away behind a small door is Khuldabad's most jealously guarded relic, the **Robe of the Prophet**, revealed to the public once a year on the twelfth day of the Islamic month of Rabi-ul-Awwal (usually around November), when the tomb attracts worshippers from all over India.

The Dargah of Sayeed Burhan-ud-din

Directly opposite Zain-ud-din's tomb is the **Dargah of Sayeed Burhan-ud-din** (same hours), a *chishti* missionary buried here in 1334. The shrine is said to contain hairs from the Prophet's beard which magically increase in number when they are counted each year. At the end of the fourteenth century, when a financial crisis had left the saint's disciples unable to provide for upkeep of the *dargah*, a pair of "**silver trees**" miraculously sprouted in its central courtyard. The attendant will point out the two innocuous-looking lumps in the pavement nearby where the fabled trees once stood, and which are still said to secrete the odd drop of silver.

Ellora

Palaces will decay, bridges will fall, and the noblest structures must give way to the corroding tooth of time; whilst the caverned temples of Ellora shall rear their indestructible and hoary heads in stern loneliness, the glory of past ages, and the admiration of ages yet to come.

Captain Seely, *The Wonders of Ellora*

Maharashtra's most visited ancient monument, the **ELLORA** caves, 29km northwest of Aurangabad, may not enjoy as grand a setting as their older cousins at Ajanta, but the amazing wealth of **sculpture** they contain more than compensates, and this is an unmissable port of call if you're heading to or from Mumbai, 400km southwest. In all, 34 Buddhist, Hindu and Jain caves – some excavated simultaneously, in competition – line the foot of the two-kilometre-long Chamadiri escarpment as it tumbles down to meet the open plains. The site's principal attraction, the colossal **Kailash temple**, rears from a huge, sheer-edged cavity cut from the hillside – a vast lump of solid basalt fashioned into a spectacular complex of colonnaded halls, galleries and shrines.

The original reason why this apparently remote spot became the focus of so much religious and artistic activity was the busy **caravan route** that passed through here on its way between the prosperous cities to the north and the ports of the west coast. Profits from the lucrative overland trade fuelled a five-hundred-year spate of excavation, beginning midway through the sixth century AD at around the same time that Ajanta, 100km northeast, was abandoned. This was the twilight of the **Buddhist** era in central India; by the end of the seventh century, **Hinduism** had begun to reassert itself. The Brahmanical resurgence gathered momentum over the next three hundred years under the patronage of the Chalukya and Rashtrakuta kings – the two powerful dynasties responsible for the bulk of the work carried out at Ellora, including the

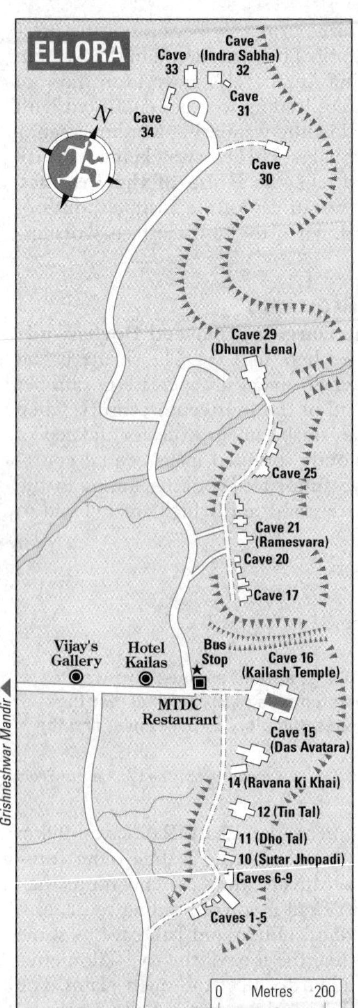

eighth-century Kailash temple. A third and final flourish of activity on the site took place towards the end of the first millennium AD, after the local rulers had switched allegiance from Shaivism to the Digambara sect of the **Jain** faith. A small cluster of more subdued caves to the north of the main group stand as reminders of this age.

Unlike the isolated site of Ajanta, Ellora did not escape the iconoclasm that accompanied the arrival of the **Muslims** in the thirteenth century. The worst excesses were committed during the reign of Aurangzeb who, in an attack foreshadowing the Taliban's 2002 destruction of the Bamiyan Buddhas in Afghanistan, ordered the demolition of the site's "heathen idols". Although Ellora still bears the scars from this time, most of its best pieces of sculpture have remained remarkably well preserved, sheltered from centuries of monsoon downpours by the hard basalt hillside.

All the **caves** are numbered, following a roughly chronological plan. Numbers 1 to 12, at the south end of the site, are the oldest, from the Vajrayana Buddhist era (500–750 AD). The Hindu caves, 13 to 29, overlap with the later Buddhist ones and date from between 600 and 870 AD. Further north, the Jain caves – 30 to 34 – were excavated from 800 AD until the late eleventh century. Because of the sloping hillside, most of the cave entrances are set back from the level ground behind open courtyards and large colonnaded verandas or porches. At the time of writing, **admission** to all but the Kailash temple was free, but fences were being erected to make the entire complex a fee-paying zone.

To see the oldest caves first, turn right from the car park where the buses pull in and follow the main pathway down to Cave 1. From here, work your way gradually northwards again, avoiding the temptation to look around Cave 16, the Kailash temple, which is best saved until late afternoon when the bus parties have all left and the long shadows cast by the setting sun bring its extraordinary stonework to life.

The Buddhist group

The **Buddhist caves** line the sides of a gentle recess in the Chamadiri escarpment. All except Cave 10 are *viharas*, or monastery halls, which the

Rock-cut caves of the northwestern Deccan

The **rock-cut caves** scattered across the volcanic hills of the northwestern Deccan rank among the most extraordinary religious monuments in Asia, if not the world. Ranging from tiny monastic cells to colossal, elaborately carved temples, they are remarkable for having been hewn by hand from solid rock. Their third-century BC origins seem to have been as temporary shelters for Buddhist monks when heavy monsoon rains brought their travels to a halt. Modelled on earlier wooden structures, most were sponsored by **merchants**, for whom the casteless new faith offered an attractive alternative to the old, discriminatory social order. Gradually, encouraged by the example of the Mauryan emperor Ashoka, the local ruling dynasties also began to embrace Buddhism. Under their patronage, during the second century BC, the first large-scale monastery caves were created at **Karla**, **Bhaja** and **Ajanta**.

Around this time, the austere **Hinayana**, or "Lesser Vehicle", school of Buddhism predominated in India. Caves cut in this era were mostly simple worship halls, or **chaityas** – long, rectangular apsed chambers with barrel-vaulted roofs and two narrow colonnaded aisles curving gently around the back of a monolithic **stupa**. Symbols of the Buddha's Enlightenment, these hemispherical burial mounds provided the principal focus for worship and meditation, circumambulated by the monks during their communal rituals.

By the fourth century AD, the Hinayana school was losing ground to the more exuberant **Mahayana**, or "Greater Vehicle", school. Its emphasis on an ever-enlarging pantheon of deities and **bodhisattvas** (merciful saints who postponed their accession to nirvana to help mankind towards Enlightenment) was accompanied by a transformation in architectural styles. *Chaityas* were superseded by lavish monastery halls, or **viharas**, in which the monks both lived and worshipped, and the once-prohibited image of the Buddha became far more prominent. Occupying the circumambulatory recess at the end of the hall, where the stupa formerly stood, the colossal **icon** acquired the 32 characteristics, or **lakshanas** (including long dangling ear-lobes, cranial protuberance, short curls, robe and halo) by which the Buddha was distinguished from lesser divinities. The peak of Mahayanan art came towards the end of the Buddhist age. Drawing on the rich catalogue of themes and images contained in ancient scriptures such as the **Jatakas** (legends relating to the Buddha's previous incarnations), Ajanta's exquisite and awe-inspiring wall **painting** may, in part, have been designed to rekindle enthusiasm for the faith, which was, by this point, already starting to wane in the region.

Attempts to compete with the resurgence of **Hinduism**, from the sixth century onwards, eventually led to the evolution of another, more esoteric religious movement. The **Vajrayana**, or "Thunderbolt" sect stressed the female creative principle, **shakti**, with arcane rituals combining spells and magic formulas. Ultimately, however, such modifications were to prove powerless against the growing allure of Brahmanism.

The ensuing shift in royal and popular patronage is best exemplified by **Ellora** where, during the eighth century, many old *viharas* were converted into temples, their shrines housing polished *shivalinga* instead of stupas and Buddhas. Hindu cave architecture, with its dramatic mythological **sculpture**, culminated in the tenth century with the magnificent **Kailash temple**, a giant replica of the freestanding structures that had already begun to replace rock-cut caves. It was Hinduism that bore the brunt of the iconoclastic medieval descent of Islam on the Deccan, Buddhism having long since fled to the comparative safety of the Himalayas, where it still flourishes.

monks would originally have used for study, solitary meditation and communal worship, as well as the mundane business of eating and sleeping. As you progress through them, the chambers grow steadily more impressive in scale and tone. Scholars attribute this to the rise of Hinduism and the need to compete for patronage with the more overtly awe-inspiring Shaivite cave-temples being excavated so close at hand.

Caves 1 to 5

Cave 1, which may have been a granary for the larger halls, is a plain, bare *vihara* containing eight small cells and very little sculpture. In the much more impressive **Cave 2**, a large central chamber is supported by twelve massive, square-based pillars while the side walls are lined with seated Buddhas. The doorway into the shrine room is flanked by two giant *dvarpalas*, or guardian figures: an unusually muscular Padmapani, the lotus-holding *bodhisattva* of compassion, on the left, and an opulent bejewelled Maitreya, the "Buddha-to-come", on the right. Both are accompanied by their consorts. Inside the sanctum itself, a stately Buddha is seated on a lion throne, looking stronger and more determined than his serene forerunners in Ajanta. **Caves 3** and **4**, slightly older and similar in design to Cave 2, are in rather poor condition.

Known as the "Maharwada" cave because it was used by local Mahar tribespeople as a shelter during the monsoon, **Cave 5** is the grandest single-storeyed *vihara* in Ellora. Its enormous 36-metre-long rectangular assembly hall is thought to have been used by the monks as a refectory, and has two rows of benches carved from the stone floor. The Buddha inside the central shrine is seated, this time on a stool, his right hand touching the ground in the *mudra* denoting the "Miracle of a Thousand Buddhas" (performed by the Master to confound a gang of heretics).

Cave 6

The next four caves were excavated at roughly the same time in the seventh century, and are mere variations on their predecessors. On the walls of the antechamber at the far end of the central hall in **Cave 6** are two of Ellora's most famous and finely executed figures. **Tara**, the female consort of the *bodhisattva* Avalokitesvara, stands to the left, with an intense, kindly expression. On the opposite side, the Buddhist goddess of learning, Mahamayuri, is depicted with her emblem, the peacock, while a diligent student sets a good example at his desk below. The parallels with Mahamayuri's Hindu counterpart, Saraswati, are strong (the latter's mythological vehicle is also a peacock), and show the extent to which seventh-century Indian Buddhism incorporated elements from its rival faith in an attempt to rekindle its waning popularity.

Caves 10, 11 and 12

Excavated in the early eighth century, **Cave 10** is one of the last and most magnificent of the Deccan's rock-cut *chaitya* halls. Steps lead from the left of its large veranda to an upper balcony, where a trefoil doorway flanked by flying threesomes, heavenly nymphs, and a frieze of playful dwarfs leads to an interior balcony. From here, you have a good view down into the long apsed hall, with its octagonal pillars and vaulted roof. The stone "rafters" carved out of the ceiling, imitations of the beams that would have appeared in earlier freestanding wooden structures, are the source of this cave's popular name, the **Sutar Jhopadi**, or "Carpenter's Workshop". At the far end, a seated Buddha is enthroned in front of a votive **stupa** – the hall's devotional centrepiece.

In spite of the rediscovery in 1876 of its hitherto hidden basement, **Cave 11** continues to be known as the **Dho Tal**, or "two floors" cave. Its top storey is a long columned assembly hall housing a Buddha shrine and, on its rear wall, images of Durga and Ganesh, the elephant-headed son of Shiva – evidence that the cave was converted into a Hindu temple after being abandoned by the Buddhists.

Cave 12 next door – the **Tin Tal**, or "three floors" – is another triple-storeyed *vihara*, approached via a large open courtyard. Again, the main highlights are on the uppermost level. The shrine room at the end of the hall, whose walls are lined with five large *bodhisattvas*, is flanked on both sides by seven Buddhas – one for each of the Master's previous incarnations.

The Hindu group

Ellora's seventeen **Hindu caves** are grouped around the middle of the escarpment, to either side of the majestic Kailash temple. Excavated at the start of the Brahmanical revival in the Deccan during a time of relative stability, the cave-temples throb with a vitality absent from their restrained Buddhist predecessors. In place of benign-faced Buddhas, huge **bas-reliefs** line the walls, writhing with dynamic scenes from the Hindu scriptures. Most are connected with **Shiva**, the god of destruction and regeneration (and the presiding deity in all of the Hindu caves on the site), although you'll also come across numerous images of Vishnu (the Preserver) and his various incarnations.

The same tableaux crop up time and again, a repetition that gave Ellora's craftsmen ample opportunity to refine their technique over the years leading up to their greatest achievement, the **Kailash temple** (Cave 16). Covered separately (see p.752), the temple is the highlight of any visit to Ellora, but you'll appreciate its beautiful sculpture all the more if you visit the earlier Hindu caves first. Numbers 14 and 15, immediately south, are the best of the bunch if you're pushed for time.

Cave 14

Dating from the start of the seventh century AD, and among the last of the early excavations, **Cave 14** was a Buddhist *vihara* converted into a temple by the Hindus. The entrance to the sanctum is guarded by two impressive river goddesses, Ganga and Yamuna, while in an alcove behind and to the right, seven heavy-breasted fertility goddesses, the **Sapta Matrikas**, dandle chubby babies on their laps. The female aspect of Shiva's elephant-headed son, Ganesh, sits to their right beside two cadaverous apparitions, Kala and Kali, the goddesses of death. Superb **friezes** adorn the cave's long sidewalls.

Cave 15

Like its neighbour, the two-storeyed **Cave 15**, reached via a long flight of steps, began life as a Buddhist *vihara* but was hijacked by the Hindus and became a Shiva shrine. Skip the largely uninteresting ground floor, and make for the upper level to find some of Ellora's most magnificent sculpture. The cave's name, **Das Avatara**, is derived from the sequence of panels along the right wall, which show five of **Vishnu**'s ten incarnations (*avatars*).

A carved panel in a recess to the right of the antechamber shows Shiva emerging from a *lingam*. His rivals, Brahma and Vishnu, stand before the apparition in humility and supplication – symbolizing the supremacy of Shaivism in the region at the time the conversion work was carried out. Finally, halfway down the left wall of the chamber as you're facing the shrine, the cave's most elegant piece of sculpture shows Shiva, as Nataraja, poised in a classical dance pose.

Caves 17 to 29

Only three of the Hindu caves strung along the hillside north of the Kailash temple are worth a visit. **Cave 21** – the **Ramesvara** – was excavated late in the sixth century. Thought to be the oldest Hindu cave at Ellora, it harbours some well-executed sculpture, including a fine pair of river goddesses on either side of the veranda, two wonderful door guardians and some sensuous loving couples, or *mithunas*, dotted around the walls of the balcony. **Cave 25**, further along, contains a striking image of the sun-god **Surya** speeding in his chariot towards the dawn.

From here, the path picks its way past two more excavations, then drops steeply across the face of a sheer cliff to the bottom of a small river gorge. Once under the seasonal **waterfall**, the trail climbs the other side of the gully to emerge beside **Cave 29**, the **Dhumar Lena**. Dating from the late sixth century, the cave boasts an unusual cross-shaped floor plan similar to the Elephanta cave in Mumbai harbour. Pairs of rampant lions guard its three staircases while, inside, the walls are covered with huge **friezes**. Left of the entrance, Shiva skewers the Andhaka demon; in the adjacent wall panel he foils the many-armed Ravana's attempts to shake him and Parvati off the top of Mount Kailash (look for the cheeky dwarf baring his bum to taunt the evil demon). On the south side, a dice-playing scene shows Shiva teasing Parvati by holding her arm back as she prepares to throw.

The Kailash temple (Cave 16)

Cave 16, the colossal **Kailash temple** (daily except Tues 9am–5.30pm; $5 [Rs10]), is Ellora's masterpiece. Here, the term "cave" is not only a gross understatement but a complete misnomer. For although the temple was, like the other excavations, hewn from solid rock, it bears a striking resemblance to earlier freestanding structures in South India. The monolith is believed to have been the brainchild of the Rashtrakuta ruler **Krishna I** (756–773). One hundred years and four generations of kings, architects and craftsmen elapsed, however, before the project was completed. Climb up the track leading along the lip of the compound's north-facing cliff to the ledge overlooking the squat main tower, and you'll see why.

The sheer scale is staggering. Work began by digging three deep trenches into the top of the hill using pickaxes and lengths of wood which, soaked with water and stuffed into narrow cracks, expanded to crumble the basalt. Once a huge chunk of raw rock had been exposed in this way, the royal sculptors set to work. In all, a quarter of a million tonnes of chippings and debris are estimated to have been cut from the hillside, with no room for improvization or error. The temple was conceived as a giant replica of Shiva and Parvati's Himalayan abode, the pyramidal **Mount Kailash** – a Tibetan peak, said to be the "divine axis" between heaven and earth. Today, all but a few fragments of the thick coat of white-lime plaster that gave the temple the appearance of a snowy mountain have flaked off, to expose elaborately carved surfaces of grey-brown stone beneath. Around the rear of the tower, these have been bleached and blurred by centuries of erosion, as if the giant sculpture is slowly melting in the fierce Deccan heat.

The temple

The main **entrance** to the temple is through a tall stone screen, intended to mark the transition from the profane to the sacred realms. After passing between two guardian river goddesses, Ganga and Yamuna, you enter a narrow passage that opens onto the main forecourt, opposite a panel showing **Lakshmi**, the goddess of wealth, being lustrated by a pair of elephants – the scene known to Hindus as "Gajalakshmi". Custom requires pilgrims to circumambulate clockwise around Mount Kailash, so descend the steps to your left and head across the front of the courtyard towards the near corner.

From the top of the concrete steps in the corner, all three principal sections of the complex are visible. First, the shrine above the entrance housing Shiva's vehicle, **Nandi**, the bull; next, the intricate recessed walls of the main assembly hall, or **mandapa**, which still bear traces of the coloured plaster that originally coated the whole edifice; and finally, the sanctuary itself, surmounted by the stumpy, 29-metre, pyramidal tower, or **shikhara** (best viewed from above). These three components rest on an appropriately huge raised platform, borne by dozens of lotus-gathering elephants. As well as symbolizing Shiva's sacred mountain, the temple also represented a giant **chariot**. The transepts protruding from the side of the main hall are its wheels, the Nandi shrine its yoke, and the two life-sized, trunkless elephants in the front of the courtyard (disfigured by marauding Muslims) are the beasts of burden.

Most of the main highlights of the temple itself are confined to its sidewalls, which are plastered with vibrant **sculpture**. Lining the staircase that leads up to the north side of the *mandapa*, a long, lively narrative panel depicts scenes from the *Mahabharata*. Below this, you may recognize episodes from the life of **Krishna**. Continuing around the temple in a clockwise direction, the majority of the panels around the lower sections of the temple are devoted to **Shiva**. On the south side of the *mandapa*, in an alcove carved out of the most prominent projection, you'll find the relief widely held to be the finest piece of sculpture in the compound. It shows Shiva and Parvati being disturbed by the multi-headed demon **Ravana**, who has been incarcerated inside the sacred mountain and is now shaking the walls of his prison with his many arms. Shiva is about to assert his supremacy by calming the earthquake with a prod of his toe. Parvati, meanwhile, looks nonchalantly on, reclining on her elbow as one of her handmaidens flees in panic.

At this point, make a short detour up the steps at the bottom (southwest) corner of the courtyard, to the "**Hall of Sacrifices**", with its striking frieze of the seven mother goddesses, the Sapta Matrikas, and their ghoulish companions Kala and Kali (shown astride a heap of corpses). The sixteen-columned assembly hall is shrouded in a gloomy half-light designed to focus worshippers on the presence of the deity within. Using a portable arc light, the *chowkidar* will illuminate fragments of painting on the ceiling, where Shiva, as **Nataraja**, performs the dance of death.

The Jain group

Ellora's small cluster of four **Jain caves** is north of the main group, at the end of a curving asphalt road. They can be reached either from Cave 29, by dropping down to the T-junction and bearing right, or directly from the Kailash temple. Either way, the two-kilometre round trip is quite a hike in the heat, and you may feel like taking a rickshaw.

Excavated in the late ninth and tenth centuries, after the Hindu phase had petered out, the Jain caves are Ellora's swansong. After the exuberance of the Kailash temple, their modest scale and subdued interiors lack vitality and inspiration, although some of the decorative carving is very fine. Only one of the group is of any real note. **Cave 32**, the **Indra Sabha** ("Indra's Assembly Hall"), is a miniature version of the Kailash temple. The lower of its two levels is plain and incomplete, but the upper storey is crammed with elaborate stonework, notably the ornate pillars and the two *tirthankaras* guarding the entrance to the central shrine. The naked figure of Gomatesvara, on the right, is fulfilling a vow of silence in the forest. He is so deeply immersed in meditation that creepers have grown up his legs, and animals, snakes and scorpions crawl around his feet.

The Grishneshwar Mandir

Rising above the small village west of the caves, the cream-coloured *shikhara* of the eighteenth-century **Grishneshwar Mandir** pinpoints the location of one of India's oldest and most sacred deities. The *lingam* enshrined inside the temple's cavernous inner sanctum is one of the twelve "self-born" **jyotirlingas** ("*linga* of light"), thought to date back to the second century BC. Non-Hindus are allowed to join the queue for *darshan*, but men have to remove their shirts before entering the shrine itself.

Ellora practicalities

Most visitors use Aurangabad as a base for day-trips to the caves, **getting to Ellora** either via the half-hourly MSRTC buses or on one of MTDC's popular guided **tours** (see p.740). These tours are very rushed, however; if you prefer to take in the caves at a more leisurely pace and climb Daulatabad Hill, either spend the night at Ellora or leave Aurangabad early in the morning. Official multilingual **guides** are on hand to take you on a tour (1–4hr) of the most interesting caves (groups of up to four people Rs550).

Ellora offers a couple of decent **places to stay**. The *Hotel Kailas* (Ⓣ02437/245443, Ⓦwww.hotelkailas.com; ❻–❼) is a small campus of self-contained chalets insensitively positioned opposite the caves, with a few cheaper rooms by the road, and a restaurant and a/c bar. They also have a limited number of **dorm beds** (Rs150) in an adjacent wing called the *Nataraj*. The only other accommodation is *Vijay's Rock Art Gallery and Restaurant* (no phone; ❷), a little down the road from the *Kailas*. The rooms and washing facilities here are very basic, but the congenial guesthouse, run by a local painter for "visiting artists, writers and thinkers", is a nice place to stay if you've come to study the caves in any detail. You can also buy wonderful reproduction paintings of the Ajanta murals.

Tasty, moderately priced **food** is available at the MTDC restaurant. In addition to the usual veg and non-veg Indian dishes, they serve Chinese, good-value lunchtime thalis and cold beer – indoors under the fan or alfresco on the shady terrace. You can also order meals and filled rolls in the *Kailas's* slightly pricier *Heritage* restaurant, but their turnover is sluggish, especially during the week. Roadside *dhabas* opposite the bus stand sell *bhajis*, pakoras and other snacks as well as inexpensive rice-plates.

Ajanta

Hewn from the near-vertical sides of a horseshoe-shaped ravine, the caves at **AJANTA** occupy a site worthy of the spectacular ancient art they contain. Less than two centuries ago, this remote spot was known only to the local Bhil tribespeople; the shadowy entrances to its abandoned stone chambers lay buried deep under a thick blanket of creepers and jungle. The chance arrival in 1819 of a small detachment of East India Company troops, however, brought the caves' obscurity to an abrupt end. Led to the top of the precipitous bluff that overlooks the gorge by a young "half-wild" scout, the tiger-hunters spied what has now been identified as the facade of Cave 10 protruding through the foliage.

The British soldiers had made one of the most sensational archeological finds of all time. Further exploration revealed a total of 28 colonnaded caves chiselled out of the chocolate-brown and grey basalt cliffs lining the River Waghora. More remarkable still were the immaculately preserved **paintings** writhing over their interior surfaces. For, in addition to the phalanxes of stone Buddhas and other **sculpture** enshrined within them, Ajanta's excavations are adorned with a swirling profusion of murals, depicting everything from battlefields to sailing ships, city streets and teeming animal-filled forests to snow-capped mountains. Even if you aren't wholly familiar with the narratives they portray, it's easy to see why these paintings rank among India's most beautiful treasures.

In spite of its comparative remoteness, Ajanta receives an extraordinary number of visitors. If you want to enjoy the site in anything close to its original serenity, avoid coming on a weekend or public holiday – it takes a fertile imagination indeed to picture Buddhist monks filing softly around the rough stone steps when riotous schoolkids and holidaymakers are clambering over

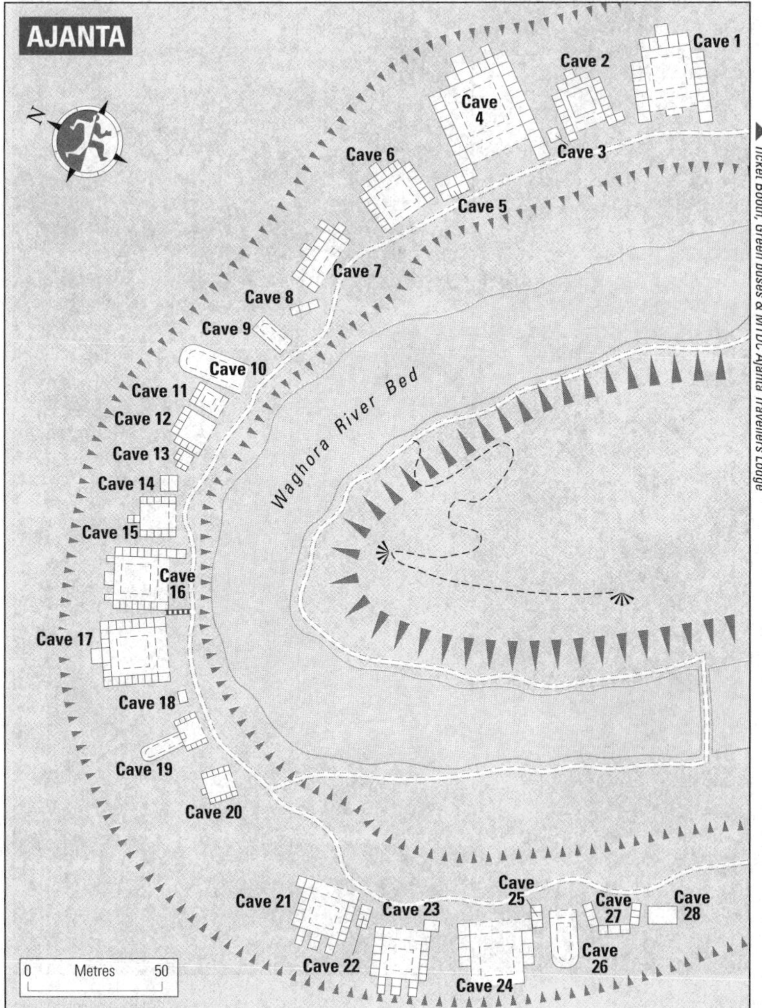

△ Cave paintings, Ajanta

them. The best **seasons to visit** are either during the monsoon, when the river is swollen and the gorge reverberates with the sound of the waterfalls, or during the cooler winter months between October and March. At other times, the relentless Deccan sun beating down on the south-facing rock can make a trip around Ajanta a real endurance test. Whenever you go, take a hat, some dark glasses, a good torch and plenty of drinking water.

Some history

Located close enough to the major trans-Deccan trade routes to ensure a steady supply of alms, yet far enough from civilization to preserve the peace and tranquillity necessary for meditation and prayer, Ajanta was an ideal location for the region's itinerant Buddhist monks to found their first permanent monasteries. Donative inscriptions indicate that its earliest cave excavations took place in the second century BC.

In its heyday, Ajanta sheltered more than two hundred monks, as well as a sizeable community of painters, sculptors and labourers employed in excavating and decorating the cells and sanctuaries. Sometime in the seventh century, however, the site was abandoned – whether because of the growing popularity of nearby Ellora, or the threat posed by the resurgence of Hinduism, no one knows. By the eighth century, the complex lay deserted and forgotten, overlooked even by the Muslim iconoclasts who wrought such damage to the area's other sacred sites during the medieval era.

Early attempts to document the amazing rediscovery of the site met with such little success that Ajanta has ever since been associated with a sinister **curse**. In 1866, after spending 27 years faithfully copying the paintings from his field-camp nearby, the artist **Robert Gill** lost his entire collection when London's Crystal Palace burned to the ground. The same fate befell another batch of facsimiles in the 1870s, which went up in smoke with London's Victoria and Albert Museum, while the efforts of a Japanese team were dramatically foiled when their rice-paper impressions of Ajanta's sculpture were crushed in an earthquake. Even **restoration** work has been dogged with misfortune. In 1920, the Nizam of Hyderabad (who then ruled the region) employed a pair of Italian experts to patch up some of the more badly damaged paintings. Unfortunately, the varnish they used to seal the flakier fragments of plaster to the cave walls darkened and cracked over time, causing further irreparable deterioration.

Nowadays, the job of restoration has fallen to the Archeological Survey of India (ASI). Among measures to minimize the impact of the hundreds of visitors who daily trudge through is a ban on **flash photography**, and strict limits on the numbers allowed into a single cave at any given time – another reason to avoid weekends. A new move to reduce the ecological impact on the area is the recent creation of the Ajanta T-junction – see "Ajanta practicalities" on p.761. For more information on the rock-cut caves of the northwestern Deccan, see p.749.

On arrival at the Ajanta **caves**, head straight to the admissions kiosk on the other side of the rise (daily 9am–5.30pm; $5 [Rs10]) to buy your entry and all-important **light-tickets** (Rs10 per group). An obvious path leads from there to the grand **Mahayana** *viharas*; if you'd prefer to see the caves in chronological order, however, start with the smaller **Hinayana** group of *chaitya* halls at the bottom of the river bend (caves 12, 10 & 9), then work your way back up, via Cave 17. If you need help getting up the steps, sedan-chair porters (around Rs150/hr), or *dhooli*-wallahs, stand in front of the stalls below. Official **guides** make two-hour tours which can be arranged through the ticket office; most deliver an interesting spiel (it's difficult to follow the pictorial stories without

Cave painting techniques

The basic **painting techniques** used by the artists of Ajanta to transform the dull rock walls into lustrous kaleidoscopes of colour changed surprisingly little over the eight centuries the site was in use, from 200 BC to 650 AD. First, the rough-stone surfaces were primed with a six- to seven-centimetre coating of paste made from clay, cow-dung, and animal hair, strengthened with vegetable fibre. Next, a finer layer of smooth white lime was applied. Before this was dry, the artists quickly sketched the outlines of their pictures using red cinnabar, which they then filled in with a coating of *terre verte*. The **pigments**, all derived from natural water-soluble substances (kaolin chalk for white, lamp soot for black, glauconite for green, ochre for yellow and imported lapis lazuli for blue), were thickened with glue and added only after the undercoat was completely dry. Thus the Ajanta paintings are not, strictly speaking, frescoes (always executed on damp surfaces), but **tempera**. Finally, after they had been left to dry, the murals were painstakingly polished with a smooth stone to bring out their natural sheen.

The artists' only sources of **light** were oil-lamps and sunshine reflected into the caves by metal mirrors and pools of water (the external courtyards were flooded expressly for this purpose). Ironically, many of them were not even Buddhists but Hindus employed by the royal courts of the day. Nevertheless, their extraordinary mastery of line, perspective and shading, which endows Ajanta's paintings with their characteristic other-worldly light, resulted in one of the great technical landmarks in Indian Buddhist art history.

them) but you may well feel like taking in the sights again afterwards at a more leisurely pace.

Cave 1

Cave 1 contains some of the finest and stylistically most evolved paintings on the site. By the time work on it began, late in the fifth century, *viharas* served not only to shelter and feed the monks, but also as places of worship in their own right. In common with most Mahayana *viharas*, the extraordinary murals lining the walls and ceilings depict episodes from the *Jatakas*, tales of the birth and former lives of the Buddha.

Left of the doorway into the main shrine stands another masterpiece. **Padmapani**, the lotus-holding form of Avalokitesvara, is surrounded by an entourage of smaller attendants, divine musicians, lovers, monkeys and a peacock. His heavy almond eyes and languid hip-shot *tribhanga* (or "three-bend") pose exudes a distant and sublime calm. Opposite, flanking the right side of the doorway, is his counterpart, **Vajrapani**, the thunderbolt holder. Between them, these two *bodhisattvas* represent the dual aspects of Mahayana Buddhism: compassion and knowledge.

The real focal point of Cave 1, however, is the gigantic sculpted Buddha seated in the shrine room – the finest such figure in Ajanta. Using portable electric spotlights, guides love to demonstrate how the expression on the Buddha's exquisitely carved face changes according to where the light is held.

On the way out, you may be able to spot this cave's other famous trompe l'oeil, crowning one of the pillars (on the third pillar from the rear as you face the shrine): the figures of four apparently separate stags which, on closer inspection, all share the same head.

Cave 2

Cave 2 is another similarly impressive Mahayana *vihara*, dating from the sixth century. Here, the ceiling, which seems to sag like a tent roof, is decorated with complex floral patterns, including lotus and medallion motifs. The design clearly takes its cue from ancient Greek art – perhaps a legacy of Alexander the Great's foray into the subcontinent half a millennium earlier. Sculpted friezes in the small subsidiary shrine to the right of the main chapel centre on a well-endowed fertility goddess, **Hariti**, the infamous child-eating ogress. When the Buddha threatened to give her a taste of her own medicine by kidnapping *her* child, Hariti flew into a frenzy (upper right), but was subdued by the Buddha's teachings of compassion (upper left). Below, a schoolroom scene shows a teacher waving a cane at a class of unruly pupils.

The side walls teem with lively **paintings** of the *Jatakas* and other mythological episodes. A frieze on the left veranda shows the birth of the Buddha, emerging from under his mother's arm, and his conception when a white elephant appeared to her in a dream (bottom left).

Caves 3 to 9

Caves 3, 4 and 7 hold little of interest, but take a quick look into **Cave 6**, a double-storeyed *vihara* with a finely carved doorjamb above its shrine room and some peeling paintings above the entrances to its cells. Cave 8 is always closed; it contains the generator for the lights.

Cave 9, which dates from the first century BC, is the first *chaitya* you come to along the walkway. Resting in the half-light shed by a characteristic *peepal*-leaf-shaped window in the sculpted facade, the hemispherical **stupa**, with its inverted pyramidal reliquary, forms the devotional centrepiece of the fourteen-metre-long hall. The fragments of painting that remain, including the procession scene on the left wall, are mostly superimpositions over the top of earlier snake-deities – *nagarajas*.

Cave 10

Though partially collapsed, and marred by the unsightly wire meshing erected by the ASI to keep out bats, the facade of **Cave 10**, a second-century BC *chaitya* hall – the oldest and most impressive of its kind in the ravine – is still a grand sight. The cave's main highlights, however, are far smaller and more subdued. With the help of sunlight reflected from a mirror held by an attendant, you may be able to pick out the fading traces of painting along the left wall (now encased in glass). The scene in which a raja and his retinue approach a group of dancers and musicians surrounding a garlanded *bodhi* tree – a symbol of the Buddha (the Hinayanas preferred not to depict him figuratively) – is believed to be the earliest surviving Buddhist mural in India. Elsewhere on the wall is graffiti scrawled by the British soldiers who rediscovered the caves in 1819.

The apsidal-ended hall itself, divided by three rows of painted octagonal pillars, is dominated by a huge monolithic **stupa** at its far end. If there's no one else around, try out the *chaitya*'s amazing acoustics.

Cave 16

The next cave of interest, **Cave 16**, is another spectacular fifth-century *vihara*, with the famous painting known as the "**Dying Princess**" near the front of its left wall. The "princess" was actually a queen named **Sundari**, and she isn't dying, but fainting after hearing the news that her husband, King Nanda (Buddha's cousin), is about to renounce his throne to take up monastic orders. The opposite walls show events from Buddha's early life as **Siddhartha**.

Cave 17

Cave 17, dating from between the mid-fifth and early sixth centuries, boasts the best-preserved and most varied paintings in Ajanta. As with caves 1 and 2, only a limited number of visitors are allowed in at any one time. While you wait, have a look at the frescoes on the **veranda**. Above the door, eight seated Buddhas, including Maitreya, the Buddha-to-come, look down. To the left, an amorous princely couple share a last glass of wine before giving their worldly wealth away to the poor. The wall that forms the far left side of the veranda features fragments of an elaborate "Wheel of Life".

Inside the cave, the murals are, once more, dominated by the illustrations of the *Jatakas*, particularly those in which the Buddha takes the form of an animal to illustrate certain virtues. Running in a continuous frieze down the left aisle, the **Vishvantara Jataka** tells the story of a prince who was banished from the court by his father for giving away a magic rain-making elephant. On the wall to the left of the main shrine is one of Ajanta's more gruesome highlights. In the **Sudasa Jataka**, a *bodhisattva* adopts the guise of a lioness to talk a prince out of eating his subjects. The artists have spared no detail, with gory illustrations of the cooking pots and chunks of human flesh being chopped up to put in them. Cannibalism is also the theme of the great **Simhala** frieze on the right-hand side of the cave. This relates the story of a merchant-adventurer and his band of mariners who, after being shipwrecked and washed ashore on a desert island, find themselves surrounded by voluptuous maidens. In a cruel twist, these beautiful women turn, by night, into a horde of blood-crazed, man-eating ogresses.

The pillar separating the *Simhala Jataka* from a smaller frieze, which shows how the Buddha tore out his eyes to give to a blind brahmin, holds an exquisite and much-celebrated portrait of a sultry, dark-skinned princess admiring herself in a mirror while her handmaidens and a female dwarf look on. The *chowkidars* will demonstrate how, when illuminated from the side, her iridescent eyes and jewellery glow like pearls against the brooding dark background.

Cave 19

Excavated during the mid-fifth century, when the age of Mahayana Buddhism was in full swing, **Cave 19** is indisputably Ajanta's most magnificent *chaitya* hall, its **facade** teeming with elaborate sculpture. On the columns flanking the walls, benign *bodhisattvas* in translucent robes are interspersed with meditating Buddhas, while on either side of the gracefully arched and pointed window, two pot-bellied, double-chinned demigods look smugly down. The penchant of the Mahayanas for theatrical luxuriance has been interpreted as a response to the concurrent rise of Brahmanism. This Hindu influence is even more manifest in the friezes that line the interior of the **porch**. On the left wall, crowned with a halo of cobra heads, the snake-king Nagaraja and his queen sit in a relaxed pose – reminiscent of the many Shiva and Parvati panels at Ellora, and of the indigenous snake-cult that formerly held sway here in the Waghora gorge.

Inside the hall, the faded frescoes are of less note than the sculpture around the tops of the pillars. The standing Buddha at the far end, another Mahayana innovation, is even more remarkable. Notice the development from the stumpier stupas enshrined within the early *chaityas* (caves 9 & 10) to this more elongated version. Its umbrellas, supported by angels and a vase of divine nectar, reach right up to the vaulted roof.

Caves 21 to 26

Caves 21 to 26 date from the seventh century, a couple of hundred years after the others, and form a separate group at the far end of the cliff. Apart from the unfinished **Cave 24**, whose roughly hacked trenches and pillars give an idea of how the original excavation was carried out here, the only one worth a close look is **Cave 26**. Envisaged on a similarly grand scale to the other large *chaitya*, Cave 19, this impressive hall was never completed. Nevertheless, the sculpture is among the most vivid and dramatic at Ajanta. In the gloomy apse at the far end, the Buddha sits in front of a large cylindrical stupa ringed with *bodhisattvas*. In the "**Temptation of Mara**" frieze to his right (your left as you enter the cave), he appears again, this time ensconced under a *peepal* tree as seven tantalizing sisters try to seduce him. Their father, the satanic Mara, watches from astride an elephant in the top left corner. The ruse to lead the Buddha astray fails, of course, eventually forcing the evil adversary and his daughters to retreat (bottom right). In contrast, the colossal image of **Parinirvarna** (Siddhartha reclining on his deathbed) along the opposite wall is a pool of tranquillity. Note the weeping mourners below, and the flying angels and musicians above, preparing to greet the sage as he drifts into nirvana. The soft sunlight diffusing gently from the doorway over Buddha's fine sensuously carved features completes the appropriately transcendent effect.

The viewpoint

The stiff thirty-minute climb to the "**viewpoint**" from where the British hunting party first spotted the Ajanta caves is well worth the effort – the panorama over the Waghora gorge and its surrounding walls of bare, flat-topped mountains is spectacular. The easiest way to pick up the path is to head through the souvenir stalls outside the entrance to the caves and ford the river; alternatively, drop down the steps below caves 16 and 17 and follow the walkway until you reach a concrete footbridge. Turn left on the far side of the river, and then right when you see steps branching uphill. A right turn at the end of the bridge will take you further into the ravine, where there's an impressive waterfall. Don't attempt this during **monsoon**, though, as water levels can be dangerously high.

Ajanta practicalities

The only way of **getting to Ajanta**, unless you have your own transport, is by **bus**. All transportation (including taxis) must now stop at **Ajanta T-junction**, 5km from the caves on the main Aurangabad–Jalgaon road. Here, you'll find a reception centre, refreshments, toilets and souvenirs. It costs Rs5 to enter the complex; once inside, eco-friendly green buses regularly ply the route to and from the caves (return fare Rs12 non-a/c, Rs20 a/c). All **MSRTC buses** between **Aurangabad**, 108km southwest, and the nearest railhead at **Jalgaon**, 58km north, stop at the T-junction on request. Provided you catch an early enough bus up here, it's possible to see the caves, grab a bite to eat, and then head off again in either direction. Alternatively, you could do the round trip from Aurangabad on one of the rushed **tours** (see p.740). There are also single daily services to and from Pune and Indore.

Limited **accommodation** is available in Ajanta proper – most visitors stay in Aurangabad, or Jalgaon, to catch a train early the following day. If you want to stay within striking distance of the caves, head for the run-down MTDC's *Ajanta Travellers Lodge* (Ⓣ02438/244226; ❸), where the green bus can deposit you and your bags. Alternatively, their more upmarket *Holiday Resort* (Ⓣ02438/244230; ❹–❺), a few kilometres down the Jalgaon road in the village of **Fardapur**, has some slightly nicer but overpriced rooms. Since the old *dhabas* at the caves were removed, the only **food** available at Ajanta is at the snack joints back at the T-junction or at the mundane restaurant of the *Ajanta Travellers Lodge*, which serves veg and non-veg Punjabi dishes and thalis, but only until 6pm.

Lonar

Few visitors reach the unique crater at **LONAR** but those who do find this **meteorite-formed lake** an amazing and tranquil place. Referred to as "Tarat-irth" in the Hindu legend that correctly claimed it was created by a shooting star, the **crater** was formed about 50,000 years ago when a lump of space rock survived its fiery descent through the atmosphere to bury itself here. The biggest of its kind in the world, the crater has a diameter of 1800m and depth of 170m. The high alkaline content of the lake's water should mean that living organisms could not develop in it but scientific experiments have identified some unicellular blue-green algae, which theoretically means that multi-cellular life could develop – evolution on earth, take two.

The steep **path** down to the lake from the rim begins almost opposite the MTDC *Tourist Bungalow* and emerges in the basin near a twelfth-century temple dedicated to Shiva after he slew the demon Lonasura. A complete circuit of the lake, surrounded by thick forest, home to scampering monkeys and a rich array of **birdlife**, takes a leisurely hour and a half. En route you will discover other seemingly lost shrines to Surya and Vishnu, as well as a stone *lingam* on an alternative path up, which marks the spot where, in the *Ramayana*, Rama and Sita are said to have bathed during their exile. On the lake itself you are likely to see flamingos, moorhens and reed warblers among the wallowing buffalo.

Practicalities

The easiest way to get to Lonar is by **taxi** from Aurangabad, which costs about Rs1500 for a day-trip; it allows you a couple of hours at the crater. There are two daily **buses** direct from Aurangabad at 7.30am and 8.30am, returning at 3pm and 4pm. These cover the 150km in four to five hours, although you can also get a later bus to Jalna and change there. The only **accommodation** is at the new MTDC *Travellers Resort* (☎07260/221602; ❹), where rooms are comfortable enough but **food** is not guaranteed if there are few guests; the only alternative are the basic chai stalls 2km away in the village.

Jalgaon

Straddling an important junction on the Central and Western Railway networks, as well as the main trans-Deccan trunk road, NH-6, **JALGAON** is a busy market town for the region's cotton and banana growers, and a key jumping-off point for travellers heading to or from the Ajanta caves, 58km south. Even though the town holds nothing of interest, you may find yourself obliged to hole up here to be well placed for a morning departure.

Practicalities

Jalgaon is well served by mainline **trains** between Delhi, Kolkata (Calcutta) and Mumbai, and convenient for most cities to the north on the Central Railway. Express services also pass through en route to join the Southeastern Railway at Nagpur. **Buses** to Indore (257km north) and Pune (336km south) leave from the busy MSRTC bus stand, a ten-minute rickshaw ride across town from the railway station. Private services to Mumbai, Indore, Pune and other towns can be booked through any travel agent, including the reliable and friendly Shivalik Tours, almost opposite the bus stand at 4 Stadium Complex (☎0257/223 8405), who can also offer tailor-made **tours**. If you're heading to Ajanta, the fastest buses are the half-hourly ones to Aurangabad, 160km south, all of which stop at the Ajanta T-junction. For withdrawing **money**, there's a UTI Bank ATM 500m towards the bus stand from the station, while for **Internet** try the Mandora Cyberpoint (Rs25/hr), near the *Arya Nivas* (see below).

You shouldn't have any difficulty finding **accommodation** in Jalgaon. If you're not too squeamish about dirty toilets and a dawn chorus of throat-clearing, you could try the retiring rooms (Rs100–150) above platform 1 at the railway station. The rest of Jalgaon's places to stay are within easy walking distance, with a number of cheap lodges around the square at the station's entrance and along the main street, Station Road. *Aram Guest House*, Station Road (Ⓣ0257/222 6549; ❷), is comfortable, with reasonably clean – if cramped – attached singles and doubles. One of the best budget hotels in India, however, has to be the very spruce *Plaza Hotel*, two minutes from the station on the left side of Station Road (Ⓣ0257/222 7354, Ⓔhotelplaza_jal@yahoo.com; ❷–❹). Its economy rooms are particularly good, brightly decorated with immaculate, tiled bathrooms; there is a spotless a/c dorm (Rs150), while pricier rooms come with cable TV, and they'll provide tea in your room if you're leaving early in the morning. The Jain owners also act as an unofficial tourist office and have a wealth of local information, including a decent map and Internet access. One kilometre further back, past the bus stand, the plush new *Royal Palace* (Ⓣ0257/223 3888; ❹–❺) is a decent mid-range place.

There's no better place to **eat** than the *Silver Palace*, next to the *Plaza Hotel*, a smart new restaurant with an a/c lounge and open terrace, serving quality Chinese and Indian veg and non-veg, including dishes from Hyderabad and Lahore; it also has the only non-seedy bar. *Anjali*, back towards the station on the other side of the road, does a good range of South Indian veg snacks and fairly spicy Punjabi meals. Another pure veg joint, the north Indian *Hotel Arya*, is a five-minute walk from the station – turn left at the roundabout at the top of Station Road, carry on past the Mandora Cyberpoint and the *Arya Nivas* (reasonable and inexpensive thalis); take the first left and it's on the left.

Nasik and around

Lying at the head of the main pass through the dark hills of the Western Ghats, **NASIK** makes an interesting stopover on the lengthy journey to or from Mumbai, 187km southwest. The city is one of the four sites of the world's largest religious gatherings, the **Kumbh Mela**, held at different locations in India every three years (see p.320); having given the 2003 event (see box, p.764), Nasik is next due to host the gathering in 2015.

Even outside festival times, the *ghat*-lined banks of the **River Godavari** are always animated. According to the *Ramayana*, Nasik was where Rama – Vishnu in human form – his brother Lakshmana and wife Sita lived during their exile from Ayodhya, and the arch-demon Ravana carried off Sita from here in an aerial chariot to his kingdom, Lanka, in the far south. The scene of such episodes forms the core of the busy pilgrimage circuit – a lively enclave packed with religious specialists, beggars, *sadhus* and street vendors touting puja paraphernalia. However, Nasik has a surprising dearth of historical buildings – even the famous temples beside the Godavari only date from the **Maratha era** of the eighteenth century. Its only real monuments are the rock-cut caves at nearby **Pandav Lena**. Excavated at the peak of Buddhist achievement on the Deccan, these two-thousand-year-old cells hark back to the days when, as capital of the

Kumbh Mela melee

As is so often the case when there is the heady mix of enormous crowds and religious fervour, the 2003 Kumbh Mela was not without its own tragedy. On one of the most auspicious bathing days of the festival a saffron-robed *sadhu* threw a handful of silver coins in the direction of the assembled throng, resulting in a stampede that killed 39 people and injured around 150. To make matters worse, many of the dead may have survived if it had not taken hours for the ambulances to reach the river through the jam-packed alleyways approaching it.

powerful **Satavahana** dynasty, Nasik dominated the all-important trade routes linking the Ganges plains with the ports to the west.

From Nasik, you can make an interesting day-trip to the highly auspicious village of **Trimbak**, where hordes of Hindu pilgrims come to seek the nectar of immortality, spilt by Vishnu whilst in battle. A steep climb up from Trimbak takes you to **Brahmagiri**, the source of the holy Godavari River. Somewhat in contrast to its religious importance, Nasik is also the centre of Maharashtra's burgeoning **wine region**; permits have been granted for around fifty wineries to open in the next few years. Of those already open, Sula has the best reputation, if you want to try a sample.

Arrival, information and accommodation

Buses from Mumbai pull in at the **Mahamarga bus stand**, a ten-minute rickshaw ride from the city centre. Aurangabad buses terminate at the chaotic central **City bus stand**, an easy walk from several cheap hotels and restaurants. Arrival by train is more problematic as the **railway station**, on Nasik Road, lies 8km southeast. Local buses regularly ply the route into town, however, and there is no shortage of shared taxis and auto-rickshaws. If you plan to leave Nasik by train, particularly on a weekend when the city booking counter (Mon–Fri 10am–5pm), off MG Road, is closed, reserve your outward ticket on arrival.

Predictably for a city that sees so few foreign visitors, the MTDC **tourist office**, near the golf course on Old Agra Road (Mon–Fri 10am–5pm; ⓣ0752/257 0059) is welcoming but not worth the trouble to find. Their daily "Darshan Tour" (7.30am–3pm; Rs90) of the city and its environs will only appeal to those with a passion for ferroconcrete temple architecture. To **change money**, the State Bank of India is just up from the City bus stand on Swami Vivekanand Road. The **GPO** is around the corner on Trimbak Road. **Internet** access is available at Matrix (Rs20/hr), down an alley beside the *Hotel Basera*.

Accommodation

Most of Nasik's **hotels** are pitched at middle-class Mumbai business travellers. The few noteworthy exceptions are the lodge-style budget places around the City bus stand *chowk*.

Basera Shivaji Rd ⓣ0253/257 5616, ⓕ257 3958. Very close to the City bus stand. Airy, comfortable rooms, all with hot water till 11.30am and some with a/c. Added attractions are astrology and palm readings. ❸–❹

Padma Sharampur Rd ⓣ0253/257 6837. Directly opposite the City bus stand. Safe, clean and convenient, with restaurant and permit room. All rooms have attached bathrooms and hot water 6am–noon. ❸

Panchavati 430 Vakil Wadi ⓣ0253/257 5771, ⓕ257 1823. Nasik's largest city-centre hotel, with three restaurants (see p.766) and a "Mexican-style" saloon bar. Also equipped with Jacuzzi, sauna, foreign exchange and room service. Great value. ❺–❻

Raj Mahal Lodge Sharampur Rd ⓣ0253/258 0501, ⓔrajmahalnsk@sancharnet.in. Across the road from the City bus stand. Rather basic, though undergoing renovations. All rooms have hot water and TV. The best-value budget hotel. ❷–❸

Shradha Nasik Rd ⓣ0253/246 5916. Best of the bunch clustered around the railway station. Rooms vary from basic to more spacious with cable TV; all have attached bath, some with a/c. Pleasant rooftop restaurant. ❷–❹

Taj Residency 12km west on Mumbai–Agra Rd ⓣ0253/560 4499, ⓦwww.tajhotels.com. Primarily a business hotel and the plushest place to stay in the area. Set in beautiful grounds, the lobby is designed in Maratha style and the restaurant is excellent. Discounts are often available. ❾

The City

Down on the riverbank, over 1km east of the bus stand, the **Ram Kund** is the reason most people come to Nasik. Surrounded by concrete viewing towers (built to alleviate the crush at the big *melas*), it looks more like an overcrowded municipal swimming pool than one of India's most ancient sacred places. Among the Ram Kund's more arcane attributes is its capacity to dissolve bones – a trick that has earned it the epithet of "**Astivilaya Tirth**" or "Bone Immersion Tank". Some of the more celebrated remains that have allegedly ended up here include those of King Dasharatha of Ayodhya (Rama's father), Jawaharlal Nehru, his daughter Indira Gandhi, her son Rajiv, and a host of saints, musicians and movie stars.

Follow the street opposite Ram Kund up the hill, past assorted ashrams and *dharamshalas*, to arrive at the city's second most important sacred site, the area around the **Kala Ram Mandir**, or "Black Rama Temple". Among the well-known episodes from the *Ramayana* to occur here was the event that led to Sita's abduction, when Lakshmana sliced off the nose of Ravana's sister after she had tried to seduce Rama by taking the form of a voluptuous princess. Sita's cave, or **Gumpha**, a tiny grotto known in the *Ramayana* as *Parnakuti* ("Smallest Hut"), is just off the square.

The Kala Ram temple itself, at the bottom of the square, houses unusual jet-black deities of Rama, Sita and Lakshmana; these are very popular with visiting pilgrims, as access is free from all caste restrictions. The best time to visit is around sunset, after evening puja, when a crowd, mostly of women, gathers in the courtyard to listen to a traditional storyteller recount tales from the *Ramayana* and other epics.

Halfway up one of the precipitous conical hills that overlook the Mumbai–Agra road, 8km southwest of Nasik, is a small group of 24 rock-cut **caves**, some dating from the first century BC. The **Pandav Lena** site is famous for its well-preserved inscriptions in the ancient Pali language, and fine ancient stone sculpture. The most straightforward way of getting to Pandav Lena without your own vehicle is by auto-rickshaw (around Rs50 each way), although the numerous local buses that go there are not too packed most of the time.

Eating and drinking

By and large, Nasik's best-value meals are to be had in its traditional "keep it coming" thali **restaurants**. While they may not always be the cheapest option,

Going doolally

In the days of the Raj, soldiers who cracked under the stresses and strains of military life in British India were packed off to recuperate at a psychiatric hospital in the small Maharashtran cantonment town of **Deolali**, near Nasik. Its name became synonymous with madness and nervous breakdown; hence the English idiom "to go doolally".

for less than the price of a beer you can enjoy carefully prepared and freshly cooked food, often including such regional specialities as *bajra* (wholemeal *rotis*) and *bakri* (hot oatmeal biscuits), together with a plethora of tasty vegetable, pulse and lentil dishes. The city's religious associations tend to mean that meat and alcohol are less easily available than elsewhere in Maharashtra, but most of the larger hotels have **bars** and restaurants with permits.

Dhaba *Panchavati Hotel*, Vakil Wadi. Classy Gujarati thalis. Popular with families. The *Khyber* is a quality non-veg terrace restaurant.

Samrat Swami Vivekanand Rd. Well-known 24hr thali joint, 2–3 minutes from the City bus stand, doing a brisk trade in moderately priced, quality Gujarati food.

Shilpa Near the *Panchavati Hotel*, Vakil Wadi. A garden restaurant that offers a small amount of peace and respite amidst the chaos; the usual range of pure veg Chinese and particularly good Punjabi tandoori items.

Suruchi Under *Basera Hotel*, Shivaji Rd. Cheap, clean, no-nonsense, South Indian fast-food café that also serves spicy snacks and cold drinks. Full of crowds of office workers at lunch. Family/ladies' room upstairs.

Tandoor Down an alley beside the *Basera*. As the name suggests, tandoori and other largely meat-based dishes are available in this small joint with a dark but wholesome interior.

Trimbak (Trimbakeshwar)

Crouched in the shadow of the Western Ghats, 28km west of Nasik, **TRIMBAK** – literally "Three-Eyed", another name for Lord Shiva, in Marathi – was the exact spot where one of the four infamous drops of immortality-giving *amrit* nectar fell to earth from the *kumbh* vessel during the struggle between Vishnu's vehicle Garuda and the Demons – the mythological origin of the Kumbh Mela (see p.320). Trimbak is also near the source of one of India's longest and most sacred rivers, the Godavari; the spring can be reached via an ancient pilgrim-trail that cuts through a cleft in an awesome, guano-splashed cliff face. En route you pass colourful wayside shrines and a ruined fort (see below).

Numbering among India's most sacred centres for Shiva worship (it houses one of the twelve "self-born" *jyotirlingas* – see Contexts), the **Trimbakeshwar Mandir** temple is unfortunately closed to non-Hindus. Its impressive eighteenth-century *shikhara* (tower), however, can be glimpsed from the backstreets nearby.

The Brahmagiri hike

The round trip to **Brahmagiri**, the source of the Godavari, takes between two and three hours. It's a strenuous walk, particularly in the heat, so make sure you take adequate water. From the trailhead at the bottom of the village, the way is paved and stepped as far as the first level outcrop, where there are some welcome chai stalls and a small hamlet. Beyond that, either turn left after the last group of huts and follow the dirt trail through the woods to the foot of the **rock-cut steps** (20min), or continue straight on, to the three **shrines** clinging to the base of the cliff above. The first is dedicated to the goddess Ganga, the second – a cave containing 108 *lingams* – to Shankar (Shiva), and the third to the sage Gautama Rishi, whose hermitage this once was.

The steps climb 550m above Trimbak to the remains of **Anjeri Fort** – a site that was, over the years, attacked by the armies of both Shah Jahan and Aurangzeb before it fell into the hands of Shaha-ji Raj, father of the legendary rebel-leader Shivaji. The **source** itself is another twenty minutes further on, across **Brahmagiri Hill**, in the otherwise unremarkable Gaumukhu ("Mouth of the Cow") temple. From its rather unimpressive origins, this paltry trickle flows for nearly 1000km east across the entire Deccan plateau to the Bay of Bengal.

Practicalities

Getting to Trimbak from Nasik is easy. Half-hourly **buses** leave from the depot opposite the main City bus stand (45min). To return, you can catch a bus (until around 8pm) or one of the shared **taxis** that wait outside Trimbak bus stand; there's no difference in price as long as the car is full.

Although Trimbak makes an easy day-trip from Nasik, it's a peaceful and atmospheric place to spend a night, with plenty of basic pilgrim **accommodation**. The MTDC *Tourist Bungalow* (Ⓣ0259/233143; ❸–❺), opposite the start of the Brahmagiri path, is in a pleasant location, with scruffy (but peaceful) doubles with attached bathrooms. More modern and comfortable rooms are to be had at the *Shri Prasad* (Ⓣ0259/233737; ❷), halfway between the bus stand and the temple.

For food, you're more or less limited to one of the two **restaurants** on the main street which both serve adequate thalis and north Indian dishes. There's also **Internet** access at RajNet Café (Rs25/hr) towards the top of the main street.

Nagpur and around

Capital of the "land of oranges" and geographically at the virtual centre of India, **NAGPUR** is the focus of government attempts to develop industry in the remote and tribal northeastern corner of Maharashtra – most foreigners in the city are there for business rather than aesthetic purposes. The trickle of visitors who do stop here tend to do so en route to the Gandhian ashrams at **Sevagram** and **Paunar**, near **Wardha** (77km southwest). The other worthwhile excursion is the ninety-minute bus ride northeast to the hilltop temple complex at **Ramtek**.

In the city itself, the most prominent landmark is the **Sitabuldi Fort**, standing on a saddle between two low hills above the railway station. Strengthened by the British in the wake of the 1857 Mutiny, its ramparts and monuments were later annexed by the Indian army and are now closed to the public. North and west of the fort, the **Civil Lines** district holds some grand Raj-era buildings and bungalows, dating from the era when this was the capital of the vast Central Provinces region.

If you have an evening to fill, take an auto-rickshaw out to the **Ambazari Bagh**, the large artificial lake and gardens 5km southwest of the railway station, for a row and a chai at its waterside cafés.

Practicalities

Nagpur's busy central mainline **railway station**, Nagpur Junction, is a short auto-rickshaw ride from the main hotel and market districts along Central Avenue. MSRTC **buses** pull in at the state bus stand, a further 1.5km southeast of the railway station. Buses to and from Madhya Pradesh use the smaller MPSRTC bus stand, five minutes' walk south down the main road outside the station. If you're in a rush to get away, Indian Airlines (Ⓣ0712/253 3962) runs **flights** to Mumbai daily, as does Jet (Ⓣ0712/561 7888), and on certain days to Delhi, Kolkata (Calcutta) and Hyderabad.

The MTDC **tourist office** (daily 10am–6pm; Ⓣ0712/253 3325), in the Sanskrutik Bachat Bhavan building, Sitabuldi, can book other MTDC accommodation but will disappoint if you're seeking specific information relating to Nagpur. At the helpful MPTDC tourist office, on the fourth floor of the

Lokmat Building, Wardha Road (Mon–Fri 10am–5pm; ⓣ0712/252 3324), you can book accommodation for Pachmarhi (see p.425) and for Kanha National Park (see p.457). The **GPO** is on Palm Road, in the Civil Lines, 4km west of the centre. **Banks** that deal in foreign exchange include the State Bank of India on Kingsway, near the railway station.

Accommodation

Most of Nagpur's **places to stay** are across the big railway bridge east of the station, along Central Avenue, or southwest of the fort around Sitabuldi, in the central bazaar. The station also has cheap **retiring rooms** (Rs100–150).

Blue Diamond 113 Central Ave, Dosar Chowk ⓣ0712/272 7460. Cheap, dingy and near the station. All rooms have cable TV, a/c, attached bathrooms and "peep-out" balconies. ❷–❹

Blue Moon Central Ave ⓣ0712/272 6061, ⓔmicron@bom3.vsnl.net.in. Nearest to the station and definitely the least seedy of the cheaper hotels; cleanish and friendly with large doubles. ❷–❸

Centre Point 24 Central Bazaar Rd ⓣ0712/252 0910, ⓔhcpngo@nagpr.net.in. The most established of Nagpur's top hotels, with all the trimmings, including a pool. ❼

Hardeo Dr Munje Margi Marg, Sitabuldi ⓣ0712/252 9115, ⓕ253 4885. Fairly new three-star hotel near the fort. Quality restaurant, spacious and comfortable a/c rooms, bar and 24hr coffee shop. Recommended. ❽

Jagson's Regency Wardha Rd ⓣ0712/222 8120, ⓕ222 4524. Modern luxury hotel next to the airport boasting a rooftop restaurant, shopping arcade, gym and pool. ❽–❾

Skylark 119 Central Ave ⓣ0712/272 4654, ⓕ272 6193. Close to railway station and best value in its class, with cable TV in all rooms and a good restaurant, though a tad grubby. Some credit cards accepted. ❹–❺

Eating

While Nagpur's swish hotels, such as the *Hardeo* and *Jagson's Regency*, boast the majority of its top gourmet **restaurants**, a number of smaller, less pretentious places to eat around Central Avenue and Sitabuldi offer excellent food at a fraction of the cost.

Continental Central Ave. Low light, lurid decor, and a good selection of inexpensive spicy (mainly meaty) Indian food and chilled beer. Some veg options too.

The Grill Ground floor of *Skylark Hotel*. Slightly more expensive than average but fine quality veg and non-veg dishes can be enjoyed in the comfy a/c dining room. Live *ghazals* every evening from 8.30pm.

Naivedhyam Off Rani Jhansi Chowk, Sitabuldi. Respectable first-floor family restaurant serving delicious veg food to a background of Hindi-Hawaiian music.

Parnakuti North Ambhajari Rd, Daga Layout, on the outskirts near the lake. Attractive restaurant noted for rustic decor and authentic, mouthwatering mid-priced Maharashtran cooking. Hard to find but well worth it.

Shivraj Central Avenue, near *Blue Moon*. Tasty and cheap South Indian snacks and thalis, especially good for breakfast as it opens at 7am.

Ramtek

The picturesque cluster of whitewashed hilltop temples and shrines at **RAMTEK**, 40km northeast of Nagpur on the main Jabalpur road (NH-7), is one of those alluring apparitions you spy from afar on long journeys through central India. According to the *Ramayana*, this craggy, scrub-strewn outcrop was the spot where Rama, Sita and Lakshmana paused on their way back from Lanka. It is also allegedly the place where the greatest-ever Sanskrit poet and playwright, **Kalidasa**, penned the fifth-century *Meghdoota*, "the Cloud Messenger". Although few traces of these ancient times have survived (most of Ramtek's temples date from the eighteenth century), the site's old paved pilgrim trails, sacred lake, tumbledown shrines and fine views across the endless plains more than live up to its distant promise.

Buses from Nagpur stop short of **Ram Mandir** (the temple complex) at Ramtek town, from whose fringes a flight of stone steps climbs steeply up the side of Ramtek hill. Built in 1740 by Raghoji I, the Bhonsla ruler of Nagpur, the temple stands on the site of an earlier structure erected between the fourth and fifth centuries, of which only three small sandstone shrines remain.

Another of Ramtek's sacred sites is **Ambala Lake**, a holy bathing tank 1500m on foot from the hilltop. To pick up the flagstone pathway that leads down to it, head along the concourse opposite the temple's main entrance porch to the edge of the plateau. From here, either turn left towards the small **Trivikarma Krishna temple**, clinging to the north slope of the hill, or continue down the main pilgrims' trail to the **lake**, which lies at the bottom of the gully, enfolded by a spur of parched brown hills. Its main attractions are the temples and *ghats* clinging to its muddy banks. More energetic visitors may wish to combine a look with a *parikrama*, or circular **tour** of the tank, taking in the semi-derelict cenotaphs and weed-choked shrines scattered along the more tranquil north and western shores. A rickshaw (around Rs25) will get you back to Gandhi Chowk – the drivers hang around by the chai shop near the entrance.

Practicalities

Direct **buses** leave Nagpur (MSRTC stand) every thirty minutes for the hour-long trip to Ramtek. Long-distance MPSRTC buses also pass by en route to and from Jabalpur, although these will dump you on the main road at Mansar, 6km from Ramtek. If you don't feel like hiking up to the temple, **auto-rickshaws** will whisk you up from the town bus stand via Ambala Lake for Rs60–80. A pleasant alternative to these is to take a **bicycle**, which are available for rent near the bus stand (Rs5/hr, no deposit). Ramtek's **railway** station, 4km from the town centre, connects with Nagpur, but this service takes longer than the bus.

Apart from the mosquito-infested pilgrims' *dharamshalas* and ashrams around Ambala Lake, the only **accommodation** near the sights is the newly privatized *Rajkamal Resort* (ⓣ07114/255620; ❸–❺), on the hill beside the main temple complex, offering simple but clean self-contained rooms, some with a/c. Otherwise, there are more basic en-suite rooms just next to the bus stand towards the centre of town (no sign in English or phone; ❶). **Food** and snacks are available at the *Rajkamal Resort* or you could try the *Shakti Restaurant* in Nehru Chowk (near Gandhi Chowk); it's primarily the town bar but can rustle up some food, though it's wise to ask what they have ready to avoid a tedious wait.

Sevagram

SEVAGRAM, Gandhi's model "Village of Service", is set deep in the serene Maharashtran countryside, 9km from the railroad town of **WARDHA**. The Mahatma moved here from his former ashram at Sabarmati in Gujarat during the monsoon of 1936, on the invitation of his friend Seth Jamnalal Bajaj. Right at the centre of the subcontinent, within easy reach of the Central Railway, it made an ideal headquarters for the national, nonviolent *Satyagraha* movement, combining seclusion with the easy access to other parts of the country Gandhi needed in order to carry out his political activities.

These days, the small settlement is a cross between a museum and living centre for the promulgation of Gandhian philosophies. Interested visitors are welcome to spend a couple of days here, helping in the fields, attending discussions and prayer meetings (daily 4.45am, 10am & 6pm; bring mosquito repellent for the last), and learning the dying art of hand-spinning. The older ashramites, or **sadhaks**, are veritable founts of wisdom when it comes to the words of their guru, Gandhiji.

Once past the **visitors' centre** (daily except Tues 10am–6pm), with its photos and documents relating to Gandhi's life, the real focal point of the ashram is the main compound. These modest rustic **huts** – among them the Mahatma's main residence – have been preserved exactly the way they were when the great man and his disciples lived here in the last years of the Independence struggle.

Practicalities

Half-hourly local **buses** run from Wardha – on the Central Railway and accessible from Mumbai (759km) – to the crossroads outside the Kasturba Gandhi Hospital, from where it's a one-kilometre walk to the ashram. There are frequent "express" buses from Nagpur's MSRTC bus stand (2hr).

Accommodation is limited to the ashram's own *Yatri Niwas* (Ⓣ07152/222172; donations), a basic but spotless hostel for those staying at the ashram; it's not really a hotel, but phone to see what they have. If you decide to stay and learn something of Gandhi and the philosophy of nonviolence, you can sleep and eat here for no charge, though you'll be expected to do a couple of hours' communal work a day. The only other place to stay nearby is *Yatri Vihar* (Ⓣ07125/284147; ❶), which has ten spartan non-attached rooms halfway to the ashram from the crossroads. Back in Wardha, the best option is to be found a ten-minute walk down Main Road at the *Hotel Gulshan* (Ⓣ07152/241026; ❸), which also has an excellent veg/non-veg restaurant.

Paunar

Vinoba **Bhave's** ashram at **PAUNAR**, 10km by road south of Wardha on the Nagpur Road, has an altogether more dynamic feel than its more famous cousin at Sevagram. Bhave, a close friend and disciple of Gandhi, best remembered for his successful Bhoodan or "**land gift**" campaign to persuade wealthy landowners to hand over farmland to the poor, founded the ashram in 1938 to develop the concept of **swarajya**, or "self-sufficiency". Consequently, organic gardening, milk production, spinning and weaving have an even higher profile here than the regular meditation, prayer and yoga sessions. Another difference between this institution and the one up the road is that the *sadhaks* here are almost all female.

In the ashram's living quarters, Bhave's old **room** is kept as a shrine. Stone steps lead down from the upper level to a small terrace looking out over the **ghats**, where two small memorials mark the spots where a handful of Gandhi's, and later Bhave's, ashes were scattered onto the river: Gandhi's is the circular plinth at the end of the long, narrow jetty, Bhave's the brass urn on the small stupa-shaped dome to the right. Every year, on January 30, the *ghats*, which are immersed by floods for four months during the monsoon, are inundated with half a million people who come here to mark the anniversary of Gandhi's death.

Practicalities

Paunar can be reached by **bus** from either Nagpur (67km) or Wardha by hopping off at the old stone bridge near the ashram. Alternatively, you can **walk** the 3km from Sevagram. The path, a cart track that runs over the hill opposite the hospital crossroads, comes out in the roadside village 1km west of the Paunar ashram.

As with Sevagram, it is possible to **stay** at Paunar in one of the visitors' rooms or dorms (donation). These are frequently booked up during conferences or seminars, so check when you arrive. Women are given preference if space is short. **Meals**, made from organic, home-grown produce, are available on request.

Southern Maharashtra

Most tourists heading south from Mumbai skip southern Maharashtra, but if you have a little time you can break up the journey. **Pune** retains its Maratha character, in the old quarter at least, and also boasts a unique museum; some may also be attracted by its much-derided Osho Commune. Hill stations such as **Matheran** and **Mahabaleshwar** provide coolness, wooded walks and fine views, while the **Konkan coast** has little-visited beaches and forts that make a pleasant journey down to Goa. From **Lonavala**, you can get to see the earliest Buddhist rock-cut art in the western Deccan, while **Kolhapur**, the last major city before Karnataka to the south, or Goa to the southwest, is a town with more traditional atmosphere than most and some striking Raj-era architecture.

Matheran

The little hill station of **MATHERAN**, 108km east of Mumbai, is set on a narrow north–south ridge, at an altitude of 800m in the Sahyadri Range. From viewpoints with such names as Porcupine, Monkey and Echo, at the edge of sheer cliffs that plunge into deep ravines, you can see way across the hazy plains – on a good day, so they say, as far as Mumbai. The town itself, shrouded in thick mist for much of the year, has, for the moment, one unique attribute: cars, buses, motorbikes and auto-rickshaws are prohibited. That, added to the journey up, on a **miniature train** that chugs its way through spectacular scenery to the crest of the hill, gives the town an agreeably quaint, time-warped feel.

Matheran (literally "mother forest") has been a popular retreat from the heat of Mumbai since the nineteenth century. These days, however, few foreign visitors venture up here, and those that do only hang around for a couple of days, to kill time before a flight or to sample one of India's most charming colonial-style hotels, **Lord's Central Hotel**. The tourist season lasts from mid-September to mid-June (at other times it's raining or misty), and is at its most hectic between November and January, in April and May, and over virtually any weekend. There's really nothing up here to do but relax, wander the woods on foot or horseback, and enjoy the fresh air and views.

Phone codes from Mumbai

Note that when phoning towns within 200km of Mumbai, such as Matheran or Murud-Janjira, you should replace the initial 0 of the area code with 95 in order to be charged a lower local rate.

As the crow flies, Matheran is only 6.5km from Neral on the plain below, but the train climbs up on 21km of track with no less than 281 curves, said to be among the sharpest on any railway in the world. After 1907, the demanding haul was handled by four complex steam engines. Sadly, they puffed their last in 1980 and were replaced by cast-off diesels from Darjeeling, Shimla and Ooty. The two-hour train ride is a treat, especially if you get a window seat, but be prepared for a squash and hard benches.

In 1974, the All India Rail Strike cut Matheran off. To combat the situation, the track from Neral was made passable for Jeeps and finally in 1984 was sealed up to Dasturi Naka, 2km from the town, though any attempts to extend it through the town have been thwarted by the encouragingly eco-friendly local authorities.

Practicalities

To reach Matheran by **train**, you must first get to **Neral Junction**, easily done by taking the hourly suburban train from **Mumbai** (CST or Dadar) to Kargat, which stops there (2hr 15min). Otherwise, the daily Deccan Express #1007 (7.15am) or Sahyadri Express #1023 (5.50pm) are both considerably quicker and also leave from CST. From **Pune** (2hr 30min–3hr), the same two trains – Sahyadri Express #1024 (7am) and Deccan Express #1008 (3.30pm) stop at Neral. Note that later services in each direction do not connect with the toy train. A good alternative from Pune is to travel to Karjat and pick up the suburban service to Mumbai.

Narrow-gauge trains up from **Neral** to **Matheran** (2hr) depart at 9am, 10.45am and 5pm (also 7.30am April to mid-June) on weekdays and there are a couple of extra services at weekends. All trains are timed to tie in with incoming mainline services, so don't worry about missing a connection if the train you're on is delayed – the toy train service should wait. Matheran **station** is in the centre of town on MG Road, which runs roughly north–south. Leaving town, there is a little halt on the miniature railway near the Dasturi Naka taxi stand, but unless you've already booked a seat, you won't be allowed on.

All **motor transport**, including shared taxis and minibuses from Neral (Rs50 per person, Rs250 for car), parks at the taxi stand next to the MTDC *Holiday Camp* at Dasturi Naka, 2km north of the town centre. From here you can walk with a porter (Rs50–60), be led by horse (Rs80), or take a hand-pulled rickshaw (Rs120). If you're happy to carry your own bags, follow the rail tracks, which cut straight to the middle of Matheran, rather than the more convoluted dirt road. However you arrive, you must pay a **toll** (Rs25) to enter the town, valid for your entire stay.

A small **tourist information** booth (daily 10am–6pm) opposite the railway station has maps and can help you get your bearings – otherwise, you can buy maps (Rs2) of the town at *Prince's Cafe*. To **change money**, The Union Bank near the station can cash travellers' cheques only but the rates are poor; the larger hotels accept credit cards.

Accommodation and eating

Matheran has plenty of **hotels**, though few could be termed cheap. Most are close to the railway station on MG Road and on the road behind it, Kasturba Bhavan. Reduced rates of up to fifty percent often apply to midweek or long stays, and during the rainy off-season (when many places close down). Most operate a 10am or 11am checkout. Virtually all the hotels provide **full** or **half board** at reasonable rates, but if you want to eat out, or are on a tight budget, try one of the numerous thali joints around the station or tasty meat dishes at *Hookahs'N'Tikkas*, also on MG Road.

Gujarat Bhavan Maulana Azad Rd ⓣ02148/230278 or Mumbai ⓣ022/2203 0876. Clean and comfortable pure-veg Jain resort hotel, with a range of rooms and cottages (some a/c with TV), playground and swimming pool. Full board only. ⑦–⑧

Hope Hall MG Rd ⓣ02148/230253, opposite *Lord's Central*. The best budget option: large, clean en-suite rooms arranged around a secluded yard with badminton and table tennis at the quiet end of town. Run by a very friendly brother-sister duo. ②

Lord's Central MG Rd ⓣ02148/230228, ⓦwww.lordsmatheran.com Matheran's most characterful landmark, near the railway station. Genteel (non-a/c) Raj-era cottages with terraces, and superb views across the Western Ghats from a relaxing garden. Excellent veg and non-veg menu including Parsi and British food. Full board only, booking recommended. ⑧–⑨

Madhumalti Just north of railway station ⓣ02148/230144. Basic but clean lodge with attached rooms among the enclave just below the tracks. Best budget option if *Hope Hall* is full. ③

MTDC Holiday Camp Dasturi Naka ⓣ02148/230540, ⓕ230566 or Mumbai ⓣ022/2202 6713. "Cottage-style" rooms in a large old colonial house, plus a simple open-air restaurant. A 40min walk from the centre of town but a good option. ④–⑥

Rugby Vithalrao Kotwal Marg ⓣ02148/230291, ⓦwww.rugbyhotel.com. Two minutes' walk up the road opposite the railway station. Old hotel, recently renovated and expanded, offering a range of rooms around a garden, with a multi-cuisine restaurant (complete with Raj-era decor) and a good bakery attached. ⑦–⑨

The Verandah in the Forest 2km southwest of station ⓣ02148/230296, ⓦwww.neemranahotels.com. Set in woods a short way above Charlotte Lake, this tastefully restored colonial house, with elegant rooms and a huge verandah, rivals *Lord's Central* as Matheran's classiest hotel. ⑧–⑨

The Konkan Coast: Murud-Janjira

Despite the recent appearance of a string of upscale resorts pitched at wealthy urbanites, the coast stretching south from Mumbai, known as the **Konkan** region, remains relatively unspoilt. Empty beaches, backed by casuarina and areca trees and coconut plantations, regularly slip in and out of view, framed by the distant Ghats, while little fortified towns preserve a distinct coastal culture, with its own dialect of Marathi and fiery cuisine. The number of rivers and estuaries slicing the coast meant that for years this little explored area was difficult to navigate, but the Konkan railway, which winds inland between Mumbai and Kerala via Goa, now renders it easily accessible.

The first interesting place to break the journey south is the quiet port of **MURUD-JANJIRA**, 165km south of Mumbai. A traditional trade centre formerly belonging to the Siddis of Janjira, it still features plenty of attractive wood-built houses, some brightly painted and fronted by pillared verandas. The gently shelving beach is wide and safe for swimming, though the sand is cleaner and softer 3km north in **Kashid**. Five kilometres south, an imposing sixteenth-century **fort**, built on an island in the river, was one of the few the Marathas failed to penetrate. You can reach it by local *hodka* boat (around Rs50) from the jetty at the southern end of town – an excellent excursion – or by tempo. The 1661 Kasa Fort sits in the open sea 2km off the beach but cannot be visited, nor can the impressive nineteenth-century palace of the last Nawab, which dominates the northern end of the bay. Fine views of the bay and surrounding countryside can be had, however, from the hilltop **Dattatreya Temple**, sporting an Islamic-style tower but dedicated to the triple-headed deity comprising Brahma, Vishnu and Shiva.

Murud-Janjira practicalities

There is a **ferry** service from the Gateway of India in Mumbai to **Rewas** (hourly 6am–5.30pm; 1hr 30min), from where you have to get a local bus that trundles through the coastal villages from Alibag to Murud. Most direct **buses** from Mumbai Central take five hours; there are two faster ASIAD services (5.45am & 11am; 4hr), which must be booked in advance. Don't jump out prematurely at the inland bus stand but continue to Murud's main street, Durbar Road, parallel to the coast, where you'll find the tiny post office, covered market, a handful of basic restaurants and the town's accommodation.

Most **hotels** are overpriced for what you get, one exception being the basic *Sea Shore Resort* (Ⓣ02144/274223; ❷–❸), which has a pleasant courtyard and one sea-facing room; it's almost directly opposite the smart, new *Club Leisure Shoreline* (Ⓣ02144/274640; ❺–❼), which has well-appointed rooms. Further north up Durbar Road are the *Mirage Holiday Homes* (Ⓣ02144/276744; ❺–❻), in an attractive colonial-style building, and the luxury concrete bungalows of the *Golden Swan Beach Resort* (Ⓣ02144/274078, Ⓦwww.goldenswan.com; ❻–❾), some only inches from the virtually deserted beach; its restaurant serves local Malvani cuisine.

Other reasonable places to **eat** on Durbar Road include the shady garden of the *Anand Vatika*, south of the *chowk*, which serves South Indian veg snacks and fuller north Indian meals, and the *Hotel Vinayak*, whose menu is more extensive in theory than practice. A row of seafront stalls south of the *chowk* dish up tasty seafood and veg snacks.

Ganpatipule

Two hundred and fifteen kilometres south of Marud-Janjira lies the Konkan coast's other commendable stopover, **GANPATIPULE**, a tiny village with a long, golden sandy beach and a very fine **Ganapati temple**. Although attracting thousands of Indian pilgrims each year, this sleepy place sees relatively few foreign visitors, with most of the tourists being honeymooners from Mumbai. The temple is built around a Ganapati *omnar*, a naturally formed – though not strictly accurate – image of the elephant god. **Accommodation** is available at the swanky MTDC *Resort* (Ⓣ02357/235248, Ⓕ235328; ❹–❽), which has very comfortable and mostly a/c rooms, as well as cheaper tent accommodation – all a stone's throw from the beach. Two cheaper options, both on the approach road to the beach and offering good discounts out of season, are the *Shri Ganesh Kripa* (Ⓣ02357/235229; ❹), with basic attached rooms, and the *Shreesagar* (Ⓣ02357/235145; ❺), which has clean compact doubles with TV. For **food**, there's decent Nepalese cooking at the MTDC resort, a Punjabi menu at the *Shri Ganesh Kripa*, or *dhabas* at the bottom of the village towards the main road.

To get to Ganpatipule, either make your way to Ratnagiri (on the Konkan railway and well connected by state and private buses) and take a local bus (10 daily; 1–1hr 30min) the last 32km, or take one of the direct MSRTC services from Mumbai, Pune or Kolhapur. All the buses stop outside the MTDC resort.

Lonavala and around

Just thirty years ago, the town of **LONAVALA**, 110km southeast of Mumbai, and 62km northwest of Pune, was a quiet retreat in the Sahyadri hills. Since then, the place has mushroomed to cope with hordes of holidaymakers and second-home owners from the state capital, and is now only of interest as a base for the magnificent **Buddhist caves** of **Karla**, **Bhaja** and **Bedsa**, some of which date from the Satavahana period (second century BC).

Frequent buses arrive at Lonavala's central **bus stand**, just off the old Mumbai–Pune Road, but the train is infinitely preferable. Lonavala is on the main railway line between Mumbai (3hr) and Pune (1hr 30min), and most express trains stop here. The **railway station** is on the south side of town, a ten-minute walk from the bus stand area; take the path right at the end of platform 1 to get there. With a car, or by taking an early train, it's just about possible to take in the caves as a day-trip from Mumbai, but it's better to allow yourself a full day to get around. There's a UTI Bank **ATM** before the bridge across the railway lines, left off the Mumbai–Pune Road, and just before the corner leading to it is the Ritz Cyber Café (Rs40/hr).

Accommodation

Lonavala has a wide range of **accommodation**, from moderately cheap to five-star; many of its hotels lower their rates out of season (Oct–March) or for longer stays or weekdays. Budget and mid-range places are concentrated in the centre, by the bus and railway stations.

Adarsh Behind the bus stand on Shivaji Rd ⓣ02114/272353. Spotless a/c and non-a/c rooms, some overlooking a central courtyard. Dependable mid-range option, but the management isn't very welcoming and early mornings are noisy. ❻–❽

Chandralok Opposite the bus stand on Shivaji Rd ⓣ02114/272294, ⓕ272921. Tucked just off the busy road, this mid-range place has comfortable rooms, some a/c, and a good Gujarati thali restaurant. ❸–❺

Duke's Retreat Mumbai–Pune Rd, Khandala ⓣ02114/269201, ⓦwww.dukesretreat.com. Superb position overlooking a ravine around 6km from town, with a prize-winning garden and a pool (Rs150 for non-residents). Comfortable rooms and cottages, with its own outdoor café, a/c restaurant and bar. Weekend packages include breakfast and dinner. ❽–❾

MTDC Karla Resort Mumbai–Pune Rd ⓣ02114/282230, ⓕ282370. On the Lonavala–Karla bus route, 3km from Malavli railway station and 7km out of town. Range of comfortable accommodation (some a/c) in cottages, suites and economy doubles in a tranquil setting. ❹–❽

Shahani Holiday Home DJ Shahani Rd, 5min walk east of the railway station ⓣ02114/272784. Lonavala's best budget option: large, immaculate rooms in a modern block tucked down a suburban backstreet. ❸

Eating

Most of Lonavala's hotels lay on full board or have very good **restaurants**, while a number of smaller restaurants and snack bars on the main street cater for the brisk through trade. You'll also come across dozens of shops selling the local sweet speciality, **chikki** – a moreish amalgam of dried fruit and nuts set in rock-solid honey toffee. Super Chikki on the main street allows you to sample the many varieties before you buy. Their main competitors, National Chikki, further down, is also recommended; this is also the best place to stock up on delicious deep-fried nibbles (*namkeen*), the other local speciality.

China Blue Before bridge over railway. Sparkling, colourfully decorated a/c lounge upstairs serving above average Chinese favourites.

Diamond Mumbai–Pune Rd, opposite the *Kumar Resort*. Garden restaurant specializing in Punjabi and Chinese food, with fairly high prices but a relaxing atmosphere.

Guru Krippa Mumbai–Pune Rd. Sparkling, clean pure-veg joint on the main street: piping-hot South Indian snacks, cheese toasties, and inexpensive thalis with Chinese and Punjabi main meals. Also a good selection of ice creams, *kulfi* and full-on *faloodas*. Recommended.

Shabri *Hotel Rama Krishna*, Mumbai–Pune Rd. The well-heeled Mumbaikar favourite. Spacious and clean, serving a wide range of north and South Indian dishes and chilled beer.

The Buddhist caves of Karla, Bhaja and Bedsa

The three cave sites of **Karla**, **Bhaja** and **Bedsa** comprise some of the finest rock-cut architecture in the northwest of the Deccan region. Though not in the same league as Ajanta and Ellora, they harbour some beautifully preserved ancient sculpture, and are definitely worth a look if you are passing.

The three sites lie some way from each other, all to the east of Lonavala. Covering Karla and Bhaja under your own steam by bus and/or train is manageable in a day, if you are prepared for a good walk, but if you want to get out to Bedsa too, the easiest option is to rent an **auto-rickshaw** (around Rs300–400) or **car** (Rs500–600 for 4hr) for the tour (usually found at Lonavala railway station). Finally, if you want to see the caves at their best, avoid the weekends, when they are inundated with busloads of rowdy day-trippers.

For a full rundown on the history and features of rock-cut cave architecture in the Deccan, see p.749.

Karla

KARLA (also Karli) is 3km north of **Karla Caves Junction** on the Mumbai–Pune Road and 11km from Lonavala. Take any bus or tempo to the junction (from where it's a Rs30 rickshaw ride), or there are five daily **buses** (6am, 9am, 12.30pm, 3pm & 6.30pm) that head for the caves directly from Lonavala, with the last bus returning from Karla at 6.30pm.

The rock-cut Buddhist **chaitya** hall at Karla (daily 8.30am–6pm; $2 [Rs5]), reached by steep steps that climb 110m, is the largest and best preserved in India, dating from the first century AD. As you approach across a large courtyard, itself hewn from the rock, the enormous fourteen-metre-high facade of the hall towers above, topped by a horseshoe-shaped window and with three entrances below, one for the priest and the others for devotees. To the left of the entrance stands a *simhas stambha*, a tall column capped with four lions.

In the porch of the cave, dividing the three doorways, are panels of figures in six couples, presumed to have been the wealthy patrons of the hall. Two rows of octagonal columns with pot-shaped bases divide the interior into three, forming a wide central aisle and, on the outside, a hall that allowed devotees to circumambulate the monolithic stupa at the back. Above each pillar's fluted capital kneels a finely carved elephant mounted by two riders, one with arms draped over the other's shoulders. Amazingly, perishable remnants survive from the time when the hall was in use. Full views of the main entrance are obscured by the much later accretion, to the right, of a Hindu shrine to **Ekviri**, a goddess-oracle revered by Koli fishing communities.

Bhaja

Although the eighteen **caves** (daily 8.30am–6pm; $2 [Rs5]) at **BHAJA** may not be as elaborate as those at Karla, they are more atmospheric. They lie 3km south of Karla Caves Junction, reached by following a path up from the village square near the railway station at Malavli, just 1.5km away. Hourly passenger **trains** call here, and are the cheapest and most convenient way to get back to Lonavala if you're not travelling by rented rickshaw or car.

The caves are among the oldest in India, dating from the late second to early first century BC, during the earliest, Hinayana, phase of Buddhism. Most consist of simple halls – *vihara* – with adjoining cells that contain plain shelf-like beds; many are fronted by rough verandas. Bhaja's apsidal *chaitya* hall, **Cave 12**, which contains a stupa, but no figures, has 27 plain bevelled pillars which lean inwards, mimicking the style of wooden buildings. Sockets in the stone of the exterior arch reveal that it once contained a wooden gate or facade. Further south, the last cave, **Cave 19**, a *vihara*, is decorated with superb carvings. Mysteriously, scholars identify the figures as the Hindu gods, **Surya** and **Indra**, who figure prominently in the *Rig Veda* (c. 1000 BC).

Bedsa

It's quite possible that you won't encounter anyone else when visiting the caves at **BEDSA** (daily 8.30am–6pm; $2 [Rs5]), which is one of its great attractions. Once you reach the village, 12km beyond Bhaja on NH-4, or a three-kilometre bus ride from Kamshet, the nearest railway station, you'll have to ask the way to the unsigned path. The village kids hanging around might scramble up the steep hillside with you, for a fee.

Bedsa's *chaitya* hall, excavated later than that at Karla, is far less sophisticated. The entrance is extremely narrow, leading from a porch which appears to be supported, though of course it is not, by four octagonal pillars more than 7m high, with pot-shaped bases and bell capitals; bulls, horses and elephants rest on inverted, stepped slabs on top. Inside, 26 plain octagonal columns lead to an unadorned monolithic stupa.

Pune (Poona)

At an altitude of 598m, **PUNE**, Maharashtra's second largest city, lies close to the Western Ghat mountains (known here as the Sahyadri hills), on the edge of the Deccan plains as they stretch away to the east. Capital of the Marathas' sovereign state in the sixteenth century, Pune was – thanks to its cool, dry climate – chosen by the British in 1820 as an alternative headquarters for the Bombay Presidency. Their military cantonment in the northwest of town is still used by the Indian army, and a number of British buildings, such as the Council Hall and Deccan College, survive. Since colonial days, Pune has continued to develop as a major industrial city and a centre for higher education. But to most outsiders, it is notorious as the home of the **Osho International Meditation Resort**, founded in 1970 by the charismatic Bhagwan Rajneesh, or Osho (1931–90), whose syncretic and, to many Indians, scandalous philosophy of life lured thousands of followers from Europe and America. The city is now linked to Mumbai by the three-lane NH-4 motorway, which is planned to extend all the way to Bangalore eventually.

Arrival and information

From Pune's Lohagaon **airport**, 10km northeast of the centre, prepaid taxis (around Rs200), auto-rickshaws (Rs120–130) and regular "Ex-Servicemen" buses (Rs25) are on hand for the fifteen-minute trip to the city centre. Pune is an important staging point on southern express-train routes from Mumbai (3hr 30min–4hr 30min); the main **railway station** is in the centre of town, south of the river. Auto-rickshaws and tourist taxis wait outside the station – locals often use shared long-distance taxis to get to Mumbai (see box p.782). Of the three main **bus stands**, the City bus stand, next to the railway station, is split into two sections, one serving the city itself (with signs and timetables only in Marathi), the other opposite serving some destinations south and west, including Goa, Lonavala and Mumbai. Swargate Bus Stand, about 5km south, close to Nehru Stadium, services Karnataka and some of the same destinations as City, while the stand next to Shivaji Nagar Railway Station, 3km west of the centre, runs buses to towns in the north, including Nasik and Aurangabad. To establish which station you require for your destination, ask at the enquiries hatch of the City bus stand.

You can get general information, make MTDC resort reservations and seek advice about bus services at the **MTDC Tourist Office** (Mon–Sat

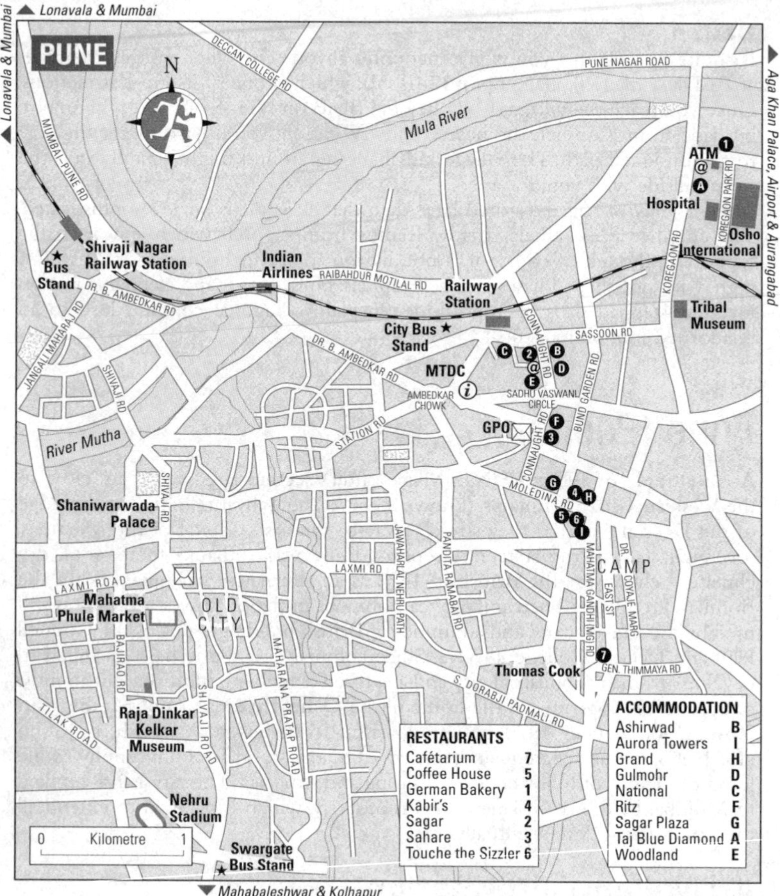

10am–5.30pm; Ⓣ0212/2612 6867, Ⓕ2611 9434), inside "I" block of Central Building (enter between Ambedkar Chowk and Sadhu Vaswani Circle). Similar services are available at the **Information Counter** (allegedly Mon–Fri 10am–6pm & Sat 10am–1pm; closed 2nd & 4th Sat of month) opposite the railway station's first-class booking office.

One of the best places to **change money** is Thomas Cook, at 13 Thacker House, just off General Thimmaya Road (Mon–Sat 9.30am–6pm; Ⓣ0212/613 8188); the State Bank of India on Laxmi Road will do the same, only more slowly and without any commission. There is a Citibank **ATM** next to the *German Bakery* near the Osho ashram. The very efficient **GPO** is on Connaught Road. The Modern Bookshop, on General Thimmaya Road, stocks an impressive array of fiction and a good selection of Indian maps and guidebooks. Manney's Booksellers, 7 Moledina Rd, Clover Centre, and Crossword, Sohrab Hall, 1st floor (behind the railway station), are two alternatives. You can access the **Internet** in many places, including the superfast Dishnet, five minutes' walk from the railway station on Connaught Road (Rs25/hr), and the Hub near the Osho ashram (Rs30/hr), which also has Net2phone facilities.

Accommodation

Pune is well supplied with **hotels**, though in keeping with most big cities prices are quite high for what you get. Most of the budget accommodation can be found in the area south of the railway station around Connaught Road. The station itself also has better-than-average **retiring rooms** (Rs100–200). For information on staying at the *Osho International Meditation Resort*, see p.780.

Ashirwad 16 Connaught Rd ⓣ0212/2612 8585, ⓔhotelash@vsnl.com. Newish hotel near the station. Some smart a/c rooms with balconies and TV. Good veg restaurant, room service, exchange and travel desk. ❼–❽

Aurora Towers 9 Moledina Rd ⓣ0212/2613 1818, ⓦwww.auroratowers.com. High-rise luxury hotel 2km from railway station, offering smart rooms with full amenities, 24hr room service and coffee shop, two good Indian and Chinese restaurants, shops and pool. ❾

Grand MG Rd, near Dr Ambedkar Statue ⓣ0212/2636 0728, opposite *Aurora Towers*. Single wood-partition rooms with common bathrooms or simple but spacious en-suite doubles in an old colonial townhouse. Relaxing veranda, beer garden, restaurant and fast-food outlet, cats and friendly management. ❸

Gulmohr 15A/1 Connaught Rd ⓣ0212/2612 2773, ⓔgulmohr@vsnl.com. Clean mid-range hotel near the railway station. Good value rooms, all with attached bathroom and cable TV, some a/c. ❹–❻

National 14 Sassoon Rd, two minutes' walk from the railway station ⓣ0212/2612 5054. Rooms, some a/c, with wooden verandas and attached bathrooms in a dilapidated old building, while others are in basic modern "cottages". Popular with budget travellers. ❸–❺

Ritz Connaught Rd ⓣ0212/2612 2995. Former travellers' hangout revamped into mostly a/c hotel with swish marble interiors and prices to match. There are two restaurants – thankfully still serving their legendary Gujarati thalis – and a travel centre. ❻–❽

Sagar Plaza 1 Bund Garden Rd ⓣ0212/2612 2622, ⓦwww.sarovarparkplaza.com. Medium-sized, flashy four-star, 1km from railway station, with ritzy restaurant, 24hr coffee shop, bar, health club, bookshop and swimming pool. ❾

Taj Blue Diamond 11 Koregaon Rd ⓣ0212/2612 5555, ⓦwww.tajhotels.com. Five-star Taj group hotel, 2km northeast of railway station near the Osho ashram. Classy rooms with plush carpets and furniture. Facilities include posh Indian and Thai restaurants, 24hr coffee shop, swimming pool, and shops. ❾

Woodland Sadhu Vaswani Circle ⓣ0212/2612 6161, ⓦwww.tghotels.com. Reasonable value rooms of decent size and comfort, mostly a/c, ten minutes' walk from the railway station. Veg restaurant, travel desk and foreign exchange. ❼–❽

The City

Pune centre is bordered on the north by the **River Mula** and to the west by the **River Mutha** – the two join in the northwest to form the Mutha-Mula, at Sangam Bridge. The principal shopping area, and the greatest concentration of restaurants and hotels, is in the streets south of the railway station, particularly Connaught and, further south, **MG Road**. The old Peshwa part of town, by far the most interesting to explore, is towards the west between the fortified **Shaniwarwada Palace** and fascinating **Raja Dinkar Kelkar Museum**; old wooden *wadas* – palatial city homes – survive on these narrow, busy streets, and the Victorian, circular **Mahatma Phule Market** is always a hive of activity.

Raja Dinkar Kelkar Museum

Dinkar Gangadhar Kelkar (1896–1990), aside from being a celebrated Marathi poet, published under the name Adnyatwass, spent much of his life travelling and collecting arts and crafts from all over the country. In 1975, he donated his collection to the Maharashtran government for the creation of a museum dedicated to the memory of his son, Raja, who had died at the age of 12. Housed in a huge old-town mansion, the **Raja Dinkar Kelkar Museum** (daily

9.30am–5.30pm; Rs100 [Rs12]) on 1378 Shukrawar Peth (buses #72 or #74 from the railway station to Mahatma Phule Market), is a wonderful pot-pourri in which beauty and interest is found in both artistic and everyday objects. Paraphernalia associated with *paan*, the Indian passion, includes containers in every conceivable design, made from silk, wood, brass and silver: some mimic animals or fish, or are egg-shaped and in delicate filigree; others are solid, heavy-duty boxes built to withstand constant use. Also on show are musical instruments, superb Marathi textiles and costumes, toys, domestic shrines and furniture, beauty accessories and a model of Shaniwarwada Palace.

Shaniwarwada Palace

In the centre of the oldest part of town, only the imposing high walls of the **Shaniwarwada Palace** (daily 8am–noon & 2–6pm; Rs100 [Rs5]) survived three fires in the eighteenth and nineteenth centuries. Founded by the Peshwa ruler Bajrao I in 1730 and the chief residence of the Peshwas until the British arrived in 1817, the building has little to excite interest today, though there's a daily **Sound and Light** show in English (7pm; Rs100). Entrance is through the Delhi gate on the north side, one of five set into the perimeter wall, whose huge teak doors come complete with nasty elephant-proof spikes. The interior of the palace is now grassed over, the seven-storey building entirely absent. Only one of the guides, usually available in the afternoons, speaks English. Bus #3 runs the 2km southwest from the railway station to the palace.

Aga Khan Palace and Gandhi Memorial

In 1942, Mahatma Gandhi, his wife Kasturba and other key figures of the freedom movement were interned at the **Aga Khan Palace** (daily 9am–5.30pm; Rs100 [Rs5]), which is set in quiet leafy gardens across the River Mula, 5km northeast of the centre (buses #1, #158 & #156). The Aga Khan donated the palace to the state in 1969, and it is now a small Gandhi museum, typical of many all over India, with captioned photos and simple rooms unchanged since they were occupied by the freedom fighters. A memorial behind the house commemorates Kasturba, who died during their imprisonment. A small *khadi* shop sells handloom cloth and products made by village co-operatives.

Tribal Museum

The Tribal Research and Training Institute, which runs the **Tribal Museum**, Koregaon Road (daily 10am–5pm; free), 2km east of the railway station, is dedicated to the protection and documentation of Maharashtra's numerous tribal groups, such as the Wagdheo, Bahiram, Danteshwari and Marai, who number more than five million. The museum's faded photos, costumes and artefacts serve as an excellent introduction to this little-known world, but the highlights are the wonderful collections of dance masks and Worli wedding paintings. Talk to the director of the museum if you're interested in guided (but culturally sensitive) **tours** to tribal areas.

Osho Commune International

Pune is the headquarters of Bhagwan Rajneesh's avowedly nonreligious **Osho International Meditation Resort**, 17 Koregaon Park Rd (Ⓣ0212/2401 9999, Ⓦwww.osho.com), 2km east of the railway station. Calling itself a "tasteful and classy resort", the commune celebrates the sniping of critics, proudly displaying the *Wall Street Journal*'s description of it as a "spiritual Disneyland for disaffected First World yuppies".

Bhagwan Rajneesh

It is more than thirty years since the first disciple was initiated into the **Bhagwan Rajneesh** cult, latterly renamed Osho Commune International, an evolving philosophy of Buddhism, Sufism, sexual liberationism, Tantric practices, Zen, yoga, hypnosis, Tibetan pulsing, disco and unabashed materialism. The first Rajneesh ashram was founded in Pune in 1974. It rapidly attracted droves of Westerners and some Indians, who adopted new Sanskrit names and a uniform of orange or maroon cottons and a bead necklace (*mala*) with an attached photo of the enlightened guru, in classic style, sporting long white hair and beard. This immediately identified the wearer as a *sannyasin* (borrowing from Shaivistic tradition, a renunciating mendicant who has attained a state of holiness).

Few early adherents denied that much of the attraction lay in Rajneesh's novel approach to fulfilment. His dismissal of Christianity ("Crosstianity") as a miserably oppressive obsession with guilt struck a chord with many, as did the espousal of liberation through sex. Rajneesh assured his devotees that material comfort was not to be shunned. Within a few years, satellite ashrams were popping up throughout Western Europe, and by 1980 an estimated 200,000 devotees had liberated themselves in 600 meditation centres across 80 countries.

To protect itself from pollution, nuclear war and the AIDS virus, the organization poured money into a utopian project, **Rajneeshpuram**, on 64,000 acres of agricultural land in Oregon, USA. It was at this point that the tabloids and TV documentary teams really got interested in Rajneesh, now a multimillionaire. Infiltrators leaked stories of strange goings-on at Rajneeshpuram and before long its high-powered female executives became subject to police interest. Charges of tax evasion, drugs, fraud, arson, and a conspiracy to poison several people in a neighbouring town to sway the vote in local elections, provoked further sensation. Although he claimed to know nothing of this, Rajneesh pleaded guilty to breaches of US immigration laws and was deported in 1985. Following protracted attempts to resettle in 21 different countries, and now suffering complications of the chronic fatigue, ME, the Valium-addicted Rajneesh returned home to Pune, where he died in 1990, aged 59.

The ashram went through a period of internal squabbles and financial trouble in the 1990s. At his death, Rajneesh appointed an inner circle to manage the group, though several departed and the Osho "brand" – with around 4 million books sold each year (supplemented by tapes, paintings and photos) – is now controlled from Zurich and New York. Pune wasn't seeing enough of this to meet its costs and consequently prices have been hiked, changing the pattern of life at the ashram; whereas in its heyday an average stay was three to six months, today people typically stay no more than two weeks and few followers live on site. This has led to a labour shortage, with non-Osho locals brought in to keep the place afloat, and a dismantling of the sense of community that was the source of its attraction.

With a considerable daily income during peak season (Dec–March) and years of dedicated help from volunteers, the commune has transformed its twenty acres into a dreamy playground of cafés, swimming pool, sauna and clinics, with a shop selling Osho's enormous list of books, videos and cassettes. The faithful have erected space-age, air-conditioned buildings, landscaped the gardens, bored tube wells for water, planted trees to improve air quality and grow organic vegetables. Courses at its Multiversity, mostly one to three days in duration (around Rs2500 per day), are offered in a variety of New Age and traditional techniques. Forty-five-minute lunchtime demos are also available if you want to try before you buy. Osho's own brand of jargon is extensive; tennis, for example, is here played as Zennis, which helps you "get out of your body's way, bring the outer and the inner together" in "a unique synthesis of tennis and meditation". There are a host of other courses ranging from primal screaming to meditation techniques and more offbeat therapies.

This eco-friendly bubble follows a strict door policy: visitors who wish to spend longer than the ten minutes of the guided tours (daily 9.45am–noon & 2–3.30pm; Rs10) must produce two passport photos and an HIV-negative certificate no less than thirty days old. If you don't have one and still want to stay there, you'll have to take an HIV test at the ashram clinic as part of your induction – the registration, HIV test and initial day-pass package costs Rs1160 for foreigners (Rs460 for

Moving on from Pune

By air

Indian Airlines runs two daily **flights** to Delhi, one travelling via Mumbai, and one flight to Bangalore via Goa; Jet Airways has two daily flights to Mumbai, one of which continues to Kolkata (Calcutta), one flight to Delhi and one to Chennai via Bangalore. Sahara operates two daily flights to Delhi, one to Bangalore and one to Kolkata via Hyderabad. IA's office is at Airline House on Dr Ambedkar Rd (℡0212/2612 6451), Jet Airways at 39 Dr Ambedkar Rd (℡0212/2613 7181) and Sahara at 21 Sassoon Rd (℡0212/2605 9003).

By train

As Pune is one of the last stops for around twenty long-distance **trains** bound for or Mumbai, rail services are excellent. Many depart early morning, however, and some terminate at Dadar, so always check first – an information service is run through the Railway Enquiries Office (℡131/133). The most convenient, if crowded, options for Mumbai CST are Deccan Queen Express #2124 (7.15am), Pragati Express #1026 (7.50am) and Deccan Express #2124 (3.30pm), which all take around four hours. Direct express trains from Pune also run to Hyderabad (Mumbai–Hyderabad Express #7031; daily 4.40pm), New Delhi (Jhelum Express #1077; daily 5.35pm), Chennai (Mumbai–Chennai Express #6011; daily 6.05pm), Bangalore (Udyan Express #6529; daily 11.40am) and Thiruvananthapuram (Kanniyakumari Express #1081; daily 3.45pm). Reservations for all trains should be made at the new **Reservation Centre** next to the station (Mon–Sat 8am–2pm & 2.15–8pm, Sun 8am–2pm).

By bus and taxi

Private luxury buses to Ahmedabad, Indore, Goa, Aurangabad and Ratnagiri can be booked through Prasanna Tours & Travels, Shivaji Nagar Terminus (℡0212/2553 9358) or Swargate Terminus (℡0212/2444 4139, Ⓦwww.prasannatours.com). Recommended **travel agents** in the centre of town for the above are Abhay Travels, 42 Karve Rd (℡0212/2543 6463), and Bulsara Tours & Travels, 14 Sadhu Vaswani Rd (℡0212/2612 3137). Seek advice from the MTDC Tourist Information Counter at the railway station or call ℡0212/2612 6218 for the latest information on **state bus** services; the bus stands display no information in English. Services from the long-distance section of the City stand next to Pune station head south and west, to Mahabaleshwar, Kolhapur, Goa and Lonavala. ASIAD buses to Mumbai also leave here every fifteen minutes between 5.30am and 11.30pm. Additional services in these directions leave from the Swargate stand 5km south. If you're heading up to Nasik or Aurangabad, you'll have to travel across the river to the Shivaji Nagar terminus. There are several excellent-value 24-hour **taxi agencies** near the City bus stand that drive the three to four hours to Dadar in Mumbai, charging per person – try Cool Cabs (℡0212/2612 1090; non-a/c Rs255, a/c Rs315)

See "Travel details" at the end of this chapter for more information on journey frequencies and durations.

Indians), after which it's Rs330 per day. You'll also need two robes (maroon for daywear, white for evenings), which cost Rs300 inside the ashram or Rs150 from stalls outside. If you want to actually stay inside the ashram, the smart but simply furnished guesthouse will set you back $60 a night for a double, $57 a single.

Eating

In addition to the hotel restaurants, there are numerous reasonably priced cafés and fast-food outlets around **Connaught** and **Moledina** roads, always busy in the evening. A sociable place to round off the day is on Dr Ambedkar Road, running east from the GPO, where, from dusk until around 10pm, a string of pavement cafés serve up spicy snacks, cold drinks and fresh juices to young punters.

Cafétarium Sunder Plaza, MG Rd. Smart coffee shop in the atrium round the corner from Thomas Cook, serving from mid-morning until 11pm. The place for a cappuccino, light lunch or cosmopolitan meal.

Coffee House 2 Moledina Rd. A relaxing, upmarket South Indian snack joint that serves the best coffee, *dosas* and breakfasts in Pune. It's also a/c, and a good spot to beat the heat.

German Bakery 291 Koregaon Park. One of the infamous chain of cafés providing safe Western meals, pastry snacks and home-made breads for homesick travellers and Oshoites.

Kabir's 6 Moledina Rd. Good selection of north Indian dishes for around Rs50–90, including lots of tasty tandoori options. Try to get a table outside in the garden. Serves beer.

Sagar Sassoon Rd, opposite the railway station. Large and busy, serving tasty, Indian and Chinese food in clean, no-smoking surroundings. The place to head for if you are staying at the *National* or have a long wait for a train.

Sahare 5 Connaught Rd. Outstanding Gujarati/Rajasthani unlimited thalis served in spotless airy surroundings opposite the GPO. Costs a little more than the average thali, but well worth it.

Touche the Sizzler 7 Moledina Rd. Great fast food: chicken and lamb "sizzlers" and burgers, and plenty of Punjabi-style veg dishes. Popular with Pune's bright young things, and a little pricey.

Mahabaleshwar and around

MAHABALESHWAR, 250km southeast of Mumbai and rivalling Matheran as the most visited hill resort in Maharashtra, is easily reached from Pune, 120km northeast. The highest point in the Western Ghats (1372m), it is subject to extraordinarily extreme **weather** conditions. The start of June brings heavy mists and a dramatic drop in temperature, followed by a deluge of biblical proportions: up to seven metres of rain can fall in the hundred days up to the end of September. As a result, tourists only come here between November and May; during April and May, at the height of summer, the place is packed. There is a Rs10 per head entry fee for visitors, collected at toll booths at each end of town.

For most foreign visitors, Mahabaleshwar's prime appeal is its location mid-way between Mumbai and Goa, but it holds enough good **hiking trails** to keep walkers here for a few days, with tracks through the woods to waterfalls and assorted vantage points overlooking the peaks and plains. You can also take **boats** out on the central **Yenna Lake**, and **shop** for strawberries, raspberries, locally made jams and honey in the lively market. One commendable short route is the walk to **Wilson's Point**, the highest spot on the ridge, which you should aim to reach well before dusk. To pick up the (driveable) trail, head south through the bazaar (away from the bus stand) and straight over the crossroads at the end past the *Mayfair* hotel; ten minutes' further up the hill, you reach a red-and-white sign pointing left off the road.

Wilson's Point lies another stiff ten minutes' up, crowned by a gigantic radio transmitter that is visible for miles. The sunset **panoramas** from here can be breathtaking.

Practicalities

The central **State bus stand** at the northwest end of the bazaar serves Pune (hourly; 3hr 30min), the most convenient railhead, as well as Kolhapur (7 daily; 7hr) and Satara (every two hours; 1hr), which is 17km from Satara Road railway station, connected to Mumbai via Pune and Goa via Miraj. There are five daily buses from Mumbai, the best option being the MSRTC semi-luxury bus which departs from the Mumbai Central bus stand at 7am (7hr). The single daily direct service to Panaji in Goa departs at 9am (12hr). There are a couple of unreliable **Internet** joints in the bazaar, where you can also **change money** at the Bank of Maharashtra.

As in many hill stations, despite an abundance of hotels, prices in Mahabaleshwar are well above average. The cheapest **places to stay** are on the Main Bazaar (officially Dr Sabne Road) and the road parallel to it, Murray Peth; with a little haggling, you can pick up rooms for under Rs300 midweek or off season. Accommodation is scarce during the monsoon (mid-June to mid-Sept), when most hotels close, and during peak times like Diwali and over Christmas and New Year, when tariffs double. Apart from the hotel restaurants and ubiquitous thali joints, two worthwhile **eateries** on the Main Bazaar are *Dragon Chinese Den* and *Tinklers-The Taste Bud*, which does excellent if slightly pricey South Indian and other snacks.

Hotels

Blue Star 114 Dr Sabne Rd ⓣ02168/260678. Plenty of peeling plaster but adequate; offers as good off-peak deals as you'll find for a basic attached room with TV. ❸–❹

Deluxe Dr Sabne Rd ⓣ02168/260202. Clean modern lodge above a fabrics shop. One of the better budget deals. ❷–❹

Dreamland Directly below the State bus stand ⓣ02168/260228, ⓦwww.hoteldreamland.com. Large, established resort hotel in extensive gardens. Rooms range from simple chalets ("cottages") to new a/c poolside apartments with stupendous views. The congenial garden café serves decent espresso and the restaurant fine Indian, Continental, Mexican and Chinese cooking. ❼

MTDC Holiday Camp 2km west of the centre ⓣ02168/260318, ⓕ260300 or Mumbai ⓣ022/2202 6713. Wide range of good-value no-frills accommodation, including cottages to sleep four, doubles and group accommodation. Better than average restaurant and beer bar. ❹–❻

Paradise International Main Rd, near bus stand ⓣ02168/260084. Ramshackle but acceptable mid-range lodge whose saving grace is a pleasant courtyard. ❹–❺

Rahil International 292 Murray Peth ⓣ02168/260639. One of a string of dependable, clean and essentially characterless places on this street. Good deals on full board. ❻

Pratapgadh

An hour's bus ride away from Mahabaleshwar, or a hike of 24km, the seventeenth-century **fort** of **PRATAPGADH** (daily dawn–dusk; free) stretches the full length of a high ridge. Reached by five hundred steps, it is famously associated with the Maratha chieftain, **Shivaji**, who lured the Moghul general Afzal Khan here from Bijapur to discuss a possible truce. Neither, it would seem, intended to keep to the condition that they should come unarmed. Khan attempted to knife Shivaji, who responded by killing him with the gruesome *wagnakh*, a set of metal claws worn on the hand. Modern visitors can see Afzal Khan's tomb, a memorial to Shivaji, and views of the surrounding hills. The easiest way to reach the fort is on MSRTC's daily half-day tour (9.30am–1.30pm; Rs60).

Kolhapur

KOLHAPUR, on the banks of the River Panchaganga 225km south of Pune, is thought to have been an important centre of the Tantric cult associated with Shakti worship since ancient times. The town probably grew around the sacred site of the present-day **Mahalakshmi temple**, still central to the life of the city, although there are said to be up to 250 other temples in the area. With a population of more than 500,000, Kolhapur has become a major industrial centre, but the city has retained enough Maharashtran character to make it worthy of a stopover.

Former capital of the Chhatrapatis (descendents of Shivaji, who made this their capital in 1708), Kolhapur later played an important role in the development of the so-called **Indo-Saracenic** style of British colonial architecture. The architect Major Charles Mant, under the auspices of the maharaja, blended Western styles with Islamic, Jain and Hindu ones, resulting in buildings that would prove profoundly influential. Mant's work, which can be seen all over the city, includes the High School and Town Hall; the General Library; the Albert Edward Hospital; and the New Palace, now a museum.

The **Mahalakshmi temple**, whose cream-painted sanctuary towers embellish the western end of town, is thought to have been founded in the seventh century by the Chalukyan king Karnadeva. However, what you see today probably dates from the early eighteenth century. It is built from bluish-black basalt on the plan of a cross, with the image of the goddess Mahalakshmi beneath the eastern and largest of five domed towers. Presiding over the square just up the road from the Mahalakshmi temple, the **Rajwada**, or Old Palace, is still occupied by members of the Chhatrapati family. Visitors can see the entrance hall (daily 10am–6pm; free) by passing under a pillared porch which extends out into the town square.

Kolhapur is famous as a centre for traditional wrestling, or *kushti*. On leaving the palace gates, turn right and head through the low doorway in front of you, from where a path picks its way past a couple of derelict buildings to the sunken *motibaug*, or **wrestling ground**. Come here between 5.30am and 5.30pm, and you can watch the wrestlers training. The main season is between June and September, the coolest time of year, but you may see them active at other times. Hindus and Muslims train together, and it's fine to take photographs.

The maharaja's **New Palace** (Tues–Sun 9.30am–1pm & 2.30–6pm; Rs20), 2km north of the centre, was built in 1884, following a fire at the Rajwada. Designed by Major Mant, its style fuses Jain and Hindu influences from Gujarat and Rajasthan and local touches from the Rajwada while remaining indomitably Victorian, with a prominent clock tower. The present maharaja lives on the first floor, while the ground floor holds an absorbing collection of costumes, weapons, games, jewellery, embroidery and paraphernalia such as silver elephant saddles.

Practicalities

Two direct express **trains** leave Mumbai CST for Kolhapur via Pune (9hr) each evening: the Mahalaxmi Express #1011 (8.25pm; 11hr 20min) and the Sahyadri Express #1023 (5.50pm; 12hr 45min). Heading in the other direction, the Mahalaxmi Express, bound for Pune and Mumbai leaves Kolhapur at 7.15pm. The **railway station** is 500m from the **bus stand** on Station Road, near the centre of town. A five-minute walk from here (turn right) brings you to the **MTDC tourist office**, in the Kedar Complex on Station Road (Mon–Sat 8.30am–6.30pm; ⓣ0231/269 2935), where you can sign up for a guided **tour** of Kolhapur (Mon–Sat 10am–5.30pm; Rs60). The only place in Kolhapur to **exchange** travellers' cheques is at the State Bank of India at Dasara Chowk Bridge, near Shahamahar railway station, though there's a UTI Bank **ATM** on Station Road. If you need to get online, Balaji Net Café (Rs20/hr), on Station Road between the bus stand and railway station, is reliable.

There's no shortage of decent, reasonably priced **accommodation** in Kolhapur, most within easy reach of the bus stand along Station Road. the *Maharaja*, 514 Station Rd (Ⓣ0231/265 0829; ❸), is a basic lodge, directly opposite the bus stand, with dozens of good-value, simple, clean rooms, and a veg restaurant. If it's full, try the *Sony* (Ⓣ0231/265 8585; ❷–❸), diagonally across the square inside the Mahalaxmi Chambers complex. Opposite the railway station, the *Rajpurush* (Ⓣ0231/266 4888, Ⓔhotelrajpurush@yahoo.com; ❷–❸) also offers good-value, clean rooms, with TV and attached bathrooms. One of the best options, though, is in a peaceful suburb a five-minute rickshaw drive away: *Hotel Woodlands*, 204E Tarabai Park (Ⓣ0231/265 0941, Ⓕ263 3378; ❺–❻), has a range of a/c and non-a/c rooms with TV, plus a 24-hour coffee shop, multi-cuisine restaurant, garden and bar.

Outside the hotels, the best **food** is to be had in *Subraya* at the top of Station Square, a comfortable a/c restaurant with a varied menu including good Maharashtran thalis, breakfast and cheaper South Indian-style snacks such as tasty *dosas*, *vada pao* and filling *pani puris*.

Travel details

Trains

Aurangabad to: Delhi (5 weekly; 24hr 5min); Mumbai (3–4 daily; 7hr 20min–8hr).
Jalgaon to: Agra (3–4 daily; 15hr–18hr 20min); Bangalore (1–2 daily; 24–25hr 50min); Bhopal (6 daily; 7hr–8hr 30min); Chennai (1–2 daily; 23hr 35min); Delhi (3 daily; 18hr 15min–22hr 50min); Gwalior (3–5 daily; 13hr 30min–16hr 20min); Kolkata (Calcutta; 3 daily; 28–34hr); Mumbai (10–12 daily; 7hr 45min–9hr 30min); Nagpur (5–7 daily; 7hr 45min–9hr 15min); Pune (2–3 daily; 9hr 30min–11hr 15min); Varanasi (2–4 daily; 19hr 25min–23hr 15min); Wardha (5–7 daily; 6hr 30min–7hr 45min).
Nagpur to: Bhopal (12–15 daily; 5hr 30min–8hr 30min); Chennai (3–5 daily; 15hr 15min–23hr 30min); Delhi (10–13 daily 13hr 45min–21hr 45min); Hyderabad (2–4 daily; 8hr 30min–14hr 45min); Indore (1 daily; 13hr 50min); Jabalpur (8 weekly; 9hr 15min–10hr 20min); Jalgaon (5–7 daily; 7hr 40min–9hr 35min); Kolkata (Calcutta; 3–5 daily; 18hr 40min–24hr 10min); Mumbai (6–8 daily; 17hr 15min–19hr); Nasik (4 daily; 11–13hr); Pune (1–2 daily; 17hr 20min–19hr); Varanasi (6 weekly; 18hr 45min–19hr 50min); Wardha (hourly; 2hr).
Nasik to: Agra (3–4 daily; 17hr 20min–21hr 15min); Bhopal (4–5 daily; 10hr–12hr 20min); Delhi (3 daily; 21hr 20min–25hr 50min); Jabalpur (5–6 daily; 12hr 20min–14hr 55min); Mumbai (8–10 daily; 4–6hr); Nagpur (4–5 daily; 11hr 10min–13hr).
Pune to: Bangalore (3–4 daily; 19hr 15min–22hr 40min); Chennai (3 daily; 20hr–25hr 45min; 55min); Delhi (3 daily; 26hr 30min–29hr 15min); Hyderabad (3–5 daily; 11hr 25min–14hr); Jalgaon (2–3 daily; 9hr 45min–11hr); Kolhapur (4 daily; 7hr 30min–7hr 50min); Mumbai (20–23 daily; 3hr 25min–5hr 10min); Nagpur (1–2 daily; 17hr 20min–19hr).

Buses

Aurangabad to: Ahmedabad (1 nightly; 14hr); Ajanta (every 30min–1hr; 3hr); Bijapur (1 daily; 12hr); Ellora (every 30min; 40min); Indore (2 daily; 12hr); Jalgaon (every 30min–1hr; 4hr); Lonar (2 daily; 4–5hr); Mumbai (6 nightly; 10–12hr); Nagpur (4 daily; 12hr); Nasik (8 daily; 5hr); Pune (10 daily; 5hr).
Jalgaon to: Ajanta (every 30min; 1hr); Aurangabad (every 30min–1hr; 4hr); Mumbai (1 daily; 10hr 30min); Nagpur (2 daily; 9hr); Pune (5 daily; 9hr).
Nagpur to: Aurangabad (4 daily; 12hr); Bhopal (1 daily; 7hr); Indore (4 daily; 11–12hr); Jabalpur (9 daily; 7–8hr); Jalgaon (2 daily; 8–9hr); Pune (5 daily; 16hr); Ramtek (hourly; 1hr).

Nasik to: Aurangabad (8 daily; 5hr); Mumbai (hourly; 4–5hr); Pune (every 30min; 3–4hr); Trimbak (hourly; 45min).
Pune to: Aurangabad (10 daily; 5hr); Bijapur (1 daily; 11–12hr); Goa (4 daily; 15–16hr); Kolhapur (4 daily; 6–7hr); Mahabaleshwar (9 daily; 3hr 30min–4hr); Mumbai (every 15min; 4hr–4hr 30min); Nasik (every 30min; 3–4hr).

Flights

Aurangabad to: Delhi (1 daily; 3hr 25min); Mumbai (3 daily; 45min–1hr).
Nagpur to: Delhi (1 daily; 1hr 25min); Hyderabad (3 weekly; 1hr); Kolkata (Calcutta; 3 weekly; 1hr 25min); Mumbai (4 daily; 1hr 15min).
Pune to: Bangalore (2 daily; 1hr 20min–2hr 25min); Chennai (1 daily; 2hr 45min); Delhi (5 daily; 2hr 5min–3hr 20min); Hyderabad (1 daily; 1hr); Kolkata (Calcutta; 2 daily; 2hr 55min–3hr 30min); Mumbai (3 daily; 30–35min).

CHAPTER 12 Highlights

✱ Old Goa The belfries and Baroque church facades looming over the trees on the banks of the Mandovi are all that remains of this once splendid colonial city. See p.804

✱ Ingo's Night Market, Arpora Cooler and less hassly than the Flea market, with better quality goods on sale and heaps more atmosphere. See p.820

✱ Flea market, Anjuna Goa's famous tourist bazaar is the place to pick up the latest party gear, shop for souvenirs, and watch the crowds go by. See p.821

✱ Nine Bar, Vagator The epicentre of hip Goa, where trance music accompanies the sunsets over the beach. See p.828

✱ Arambol An alternative resort with exquisite beaches and some of Asia's best budget restaurants. See p.834

✱ Perreira-Braganza House, Chandor The region's most extravagant colonial-era mansion, crammed with period furniture and fittings. See p.841

✱ Beach shacks Tuck into a fresh kingfish, tandoori pomfret or lobster, washed down with a *feni* cocktail or an ice-cool Kingfisher beer. See p.844 & p.850

✱ Sunset stroll, Palolem Tropical sunsets don't come much more romantic than at this idyllic palm-fringed cove in the hilly deep south. See p.846

△ Arambol beach

12

Goa

If one word could be said to encapsulate the essence of **GOA**, it would have to be the Portuguese *sossegarde*, meaning "carefree". The pace of life in this former colonial enclave, midway down India's southwest coast, has picked up over the past twenty years, but in spite of the increasing chaos of its capital, beach resorts and market towns, Goa has retained the laid-back feel that has traditionally set it apart from the rest of the country. Its 1.4 million inhabitants are unequivocal about the roots of their distinctiveness; while most of the subcontinent was colonized by the stiff-upper-lipped British, Goa's European overlords were the **Portuguese**, a people far more inclined to enjoy the good things in life than their Anglo-Saxon counterparts.

Goa was Portugal's first toe-hold in Asia, and served as the linchpin for a vast trade network for over 450 years. However, when the Lusitanian empire began to founder in the seventeenth century, so too did the fortunes of its capital. Cut off from the rest of India by a wall of mountains and hundreds of miles of un-navigable alluvial plain, it remained resolutely aloof from the wider subcontinent – while India was tearing itself to pieces in the run-up to Independence in 1947, the only machetes being wielded here were cutting coconuts. Not until 1961, after exasperated Prime Minister Jawaharlal Nehru gave up trying to negotiate with the Portuguese dictator Salazar and sent in the army, was Goa finally absorbed into India.

Those who visited in the late 1960s and 1970s, when the overland travellers' trail wriggled its way south from Bombay, found a way of life little changed in centuries: Portuguese was still very much the lingua franca of the well-educated elite, and the coastal settlements were mere fishing and coconut cultivation villages. Relieved to have found somewhere inexpensive and culturally undemanding to recover from the travails of Indian travel, the "freaks" got stoned, watched the mesmeric sunsets over the Arabian Sea and partied madly on full-moon nights, giving rise to a holiday culture that soon made Goa synonymous with hedonistic **hippies**.

Since then, the state has largely shaken off its reputation as a drop-out zone, but hundreds of thousands of visitors still flock here each winter, the vast majority to relax on Goa's beautiful **beaches**. Around two dozen stretches of soft white sand indent the region's coast, from spectacular 25-kilometre sweeps to secluded palm-backed coves. The level of development varies wildly; while some are lined by ritzy Western-style resorts, the most sophisticated structures on others are palm-leaf shacks and old wooden outriggers that are heaved into the sea each afternoon.

Wherever you travel in Goa, vestiges of former Portuguese domination are ubiquitous, creating an ambience that is at once exotic and strangely familiar.

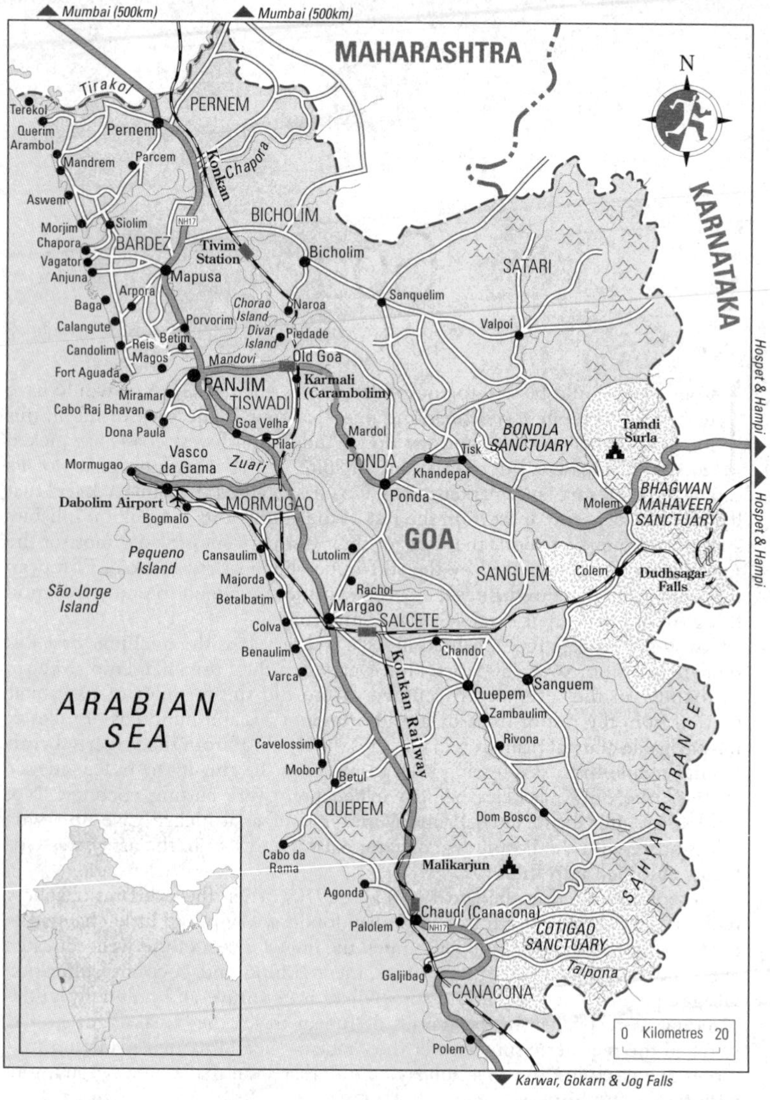

This is particularly true of Goan **food** which, blending the Latin love of meat and fish with India's predilection for spices, is quite unlike any other regional cuisine in Asia. Equally unique is the prevalence of **alcohol**. Beer is cheap, and six thousand or more bars around the state are licensed to serve it, along with the more traditional tipple, *feni*, a rocket-fuel spirit distilled from cashew fruit or coconut sap.

Travelling around the Christian heartland of central Goa, with its white-washed churches and wayside shrines, it's all too easy to forget that **Hinduism** remains the religion of more than two-thirds of the state's population. Unlike

The festivals of Goa

Some of Goa's **festivals** are on fixed dates each year; ask at a tourist office for dates of the others. The biggest celebrations take place at Panjim and Margao.

Festa dos Reis (Jan 6). Epiphany celebrations include a procession of young boys decked out as the Three Kings to the Franciscan chapel of Reis Magos, near Panjim on the north bank of the Mandovi, 3km east of Fort Aguada. Other processions are held at Cansaulim and Chandor.

Carnival (Feb/March). Three days of *feni*-induced mayhem, centring on Panjim, to mark the run-up to Lent.

Shigmo (Feb/March). The Goan version of Holi is celebrated with big parades and crowds; drum and dance groups compete and huge floats, which threaten to bring down telegraph wires, trundle through the streets.

All Saints (March). On the fifth Monday in Lent, 26 effigies of saints, martyrs, popes, kings, queens and cardinals are paraded around the village of Velha Goa, near Panjim. A fair also takes place.

Igitun Chalne (May). *Dhoti*-clad devotees of the goddess Lairya enter trances and walk over hot coals at the village of Sirigao, Bichloim.

Sanjuan (June 24). The festival of St John is celebrated all over Goa, but is especially important in the coastal villages of Arambol and Terekol. Youngsters torch straw dummies (representing St John's baptism, and thus the death of sin), while revellers in striped pants dive into wells after drinking bottles of *feni*.

International Film Festival of India (late Nov to early Dec). The powers that be haven't decided whether or not Panjim is to become the permanent venue for this Bollywood bash (see p.796), but it looks more than likely. Hundreds of movies – both foreign and Indian – are shown over a fortnight, on huge beachside screens and in Panjim's two major venues, the Innox multiplex and Kala Academy. For more, see p.803.

Christmas (Dec 24–25). Celebrated everywhere in Goa. Late-night Mass is usually followed by music, dancing and fireworks.

Siolim Zagor (first Sun after Christmas). Processions, dance dramas and satirical songs mark this unusual festival at Siolim, in northern Goa near Chapora, which is ostensibly Christian but celebrated with equal enthusiasm by local Hindus.

in many parts of the country, however, religious intolerance is rare here, and traditional practices mingle easily with more recently implanted ones. Faced by the threat of merger with neighbouring states, Goans have always put regional cohesion before communal differences at the ballot box. A potent stimulus for regional identity was the campaign through the 1980s to have **Konkani**, the language spoken by the vast majority of Goans, recognized as an official state language, which it eventually was in 1992. Since then, the **immigration** issue has come to dominate the political agenda. Considerably more prosperous than neighbouring states, Goa has been deluged over the past couple of decades with economic refugees, stirring up fears that the region's cultural distinctiveness will disappear. Among the main employers of migrant labour in recent years has been the **Konkan Railway**, completed in 1997 to form a super-fast land link with Mumbai – another conduit of economic prosperity that has brought lasting changes.

Which beach you opt for when you arrive largely depends on what sort of holiday you have in mind. More developed resorts such as **Calangute** and **Baga** in the north, and **Colva** and **Benaulim** in the south, offer more "walk-in" accommodation and tourist facilities than elsewhere. Even if you're looking for a less touristy scene, it can be worth heading for these centres first, as finding places to stay in less commercialized corners is often difficult. **Anjuna**, **Vagator**, and **Chapora**, where accommodation is generally more basic and harder to come by, are the beaches to aim for if you've come to Goa to party. However, the bulk of budget travellers taking time out from tours of India end up in **Palolem**, in the far south, or **Arambol**, both beyond the increasingly long reach of the charter buses. That said, Palolem, in particular, has become a major resort in its own right, with thousands of long-stay visitors in peak season.

Some 10km from the state capital, **Panjim**, the ruins of the former Portuguese capital at **Old Goa** are foremost among the attractions away from the coast – a sprawl of Catholic cathedrals, convents and churches that draw crowds of Christian pilgrims from all over India. Another popular day excursion is to Anjuna's Wednesday **flea market**, a sociable place to shop for souvenirs and dance wear. Further inland, the thickly wooded countryside around **Ponda** harbours numerous temples, where you can experience Goa's peculiar brand of Hindu architecture. The district of Salcete, and its main market town, **Margao**, is also littered with Portuguese mansions, churches and seminaries. Finally, wildlife enthusiasts may be tempted into the interior to visit the nature reserve at **Cotigao** in the far south.

The best **time to come** to Goa is during the dry, relatively cool winter months between mid-November and mid-March. At other times, either the sun is too hot for comfort, or the monsoon rains and clouds make life miserable. During peak season, from mid-December to the end of January, the weather is perfect, with temperatures rarely nudging above 32°C. Finding a room or a house to rent at that time, however – particularly over Christmas and New Year when tariffs double, or triple – can be a real hassle.

Some history

Goa's sheer inaccessibility by land has always kept it out of the mainstream of Indian history; on the other hand, its control of the seas and the lucrative spice trade made it a much-coveted prize for rival colonial powers. Until a century before the arrival of the Portuguese, Goa had belonged for over a thousand years to the kingdom of **Kadamba**. They, in turn, were overthrown by the Karnatakan Vijayanagars, the Muslim Bahmanis, and Yusuf Adil Shah of Bijapur, but the capture of the fort at Panjim by **Afonso de Albuquerque** in 1510 signalled the start of a Portuguese occupation that was to last 451 years.

As Goa expanded, its splendid capital (now Old Goa) came to hold a larger population than Paris or London. Though Ismail Adil Shah laid siege for ten months in 1570, and the Marathas under Shivaji and later chiefs came nail-bitingly close to seizing the region, the greatest threat was from other European maritime nations, principally Holland and France. Meanwhile, conversions to **Christianity**, started by the Franciscans, gathered pace when St Francis Xavier founded the **Jesuit** mission in 1542. With the advent of the **Inquisition** soon afterwards, laws were introduced censoring literature and banning any faith other than Catholicism. Hindu temples were destroyed, and converted Hindus adopted Portuguese names, such as da Silva, Correa and de Sousa, which remain common in the region. Thereafter, the colony, whose trade monopoly had been broken by its European rivals, went into gradual decline, hastened by the unhealthy, disease-ridden environment of its capital.

Despite a certain liberalization, such as the restoration of Hindus' right to worship and the final banishment of the dreaded Inquisition in 1820, the

Police, drugs and nudism

While the vast majority of visitors to Goa never encounter any **trouble**, tourism-related crime is definitely more prevalent here than in other parts of the country. **Theft** is the most common problem – usually of articles left unattended on the beach. Don't assume your valuables are safe in a padlocked house or hotel room, either; break-ins, particularly on party nights, are on the increase. The most secure solution is to rent a deposit box at your hotel or guesthouse, or from a private locker shop.

The other eventuality to avoid, at all costs, is getting on the wrong side of the law. **Drugs** are the most common cause of serious trouble. Many travellers imagine that, because of Goa's free-and-easy reputation, drug use is legal: it isn't. Possession of even a small amount of cannabis is a criminal offence, punishable by large fines or prison sentences. If you're approached by anyone offering you narcotics, whether foreign or Indian, ignore them; and bear in mind that numerous arrests in the past three or four years have followed tip-offs from the dealers themselves, who are paid a cut of the resulting bribe taken by the police as a reward, or have been obliged to inform on their customers in order to operate free from police interference. A couple of seasons ago, several foreigners were also admitted to Panjim hospital with life-threatening conditions resulting from having smoked *charas* (cannabis resin), bought from Kashmiri dealers, which had been cut with something very nasty.

Though violent crime is rare, women should think twice before wandering down deserted beaches and dark tracks on their own. **Sexual harassment** usually takes the form of unsubtle ogling, but there have also been several incidents of **rape** in recent years. So wherever you're staying, take the same common-sense precautions as you would at home: keep to the main roads when travelling on foot or by bicycle, avoid dirt tracks and unfrequented beaches (particularly on party nights) unless you're in a group, and when you're in your hotel or guesthouse after dark, ensure that all windows and doors are locked.

Bikinis and, increasingly, topless bathing are the norm on Westerner-dominated beaches, but expect to attract plenty of attention if you walk around under-dressed in front of Indian visitors from out of state, or in less developed parts of Goa. Such behaviour isn't likely to cause offence, but will provoke staring and possibly hassle. The best policy for women is to cover up with a sarong or *lunghi* when you see families or groups of Indian men approaching. Total **nudism** is never acceptable, and technically illegal.

nineteenth century saw widespread civil unrest. During the British Raj many Goans moved to Bombay, and elsewhere in British India, to find work.

The success of the post-Independence Goan struggle for freedom owed as much to the efforts of the Indian government, who cut off diplomatic ties with Portugal, as to the work of freedom fighters such as **Menezes Braganza** and **Dr Cunha**. After a "liberation march" in 1955 resulted in a number of deaths, the state was blockaded. Trade with Bombay ceased, and the railway was cut off, so Goa set out to forge international links, particularly with Pakistan and Sri Lanka. That led to the building of Dabolim airport, and a determination to improve local agricultural output. In 1961, Prime Minister Jawaharlal Nehru finally ran out of patience with his opposite number in Lisbon, the right-wing dictator Salazar, and sent in the armed forces. Mounted in defiance of a United Nations resolution, "**Operation Vijay**" met only token resistance, and the Indian army overran Goa in two days. Thereafter, Goa (along with Portugal's other two enclaves, Daman and Diu) became part of India as a self-governing **Union Territory**, with minimum interference from Delhi.

Getting around

White Maruti van **taxis** serve as the main means of travelling between resorts. You'll find them lined up outside most charter hotels, where a board invariably displays "fixed rates" to destinations in and around the region. These fares only apply to peak season, however, and at other times you should be able to negotiate a hefty reduction.

By ferry

Although gradually being superceded by road bridges, flat-bottomed **ferries** are Goa's quintessential mode of transport. Crammed with cars, buses, commuters on scooters, fisherwomen and clumps of overheated tourists, these rusting blue-painted hulks are incredibly cheap, and run from the crack of dawn until late in the evening. The most frequented river crossings in Goa are Panjim to **Betim**, across the Mandovi (every 15min); **Old Goa** to Divar Island (every 15min); Querim to **Terekol**, over the River Terekol (every 30min); and **Cavelossim**, in the far south of Salcete, to Assolna (every 20–30min).

By train

The **Konkan Railway** serves as Goa's principal long-distance transport artery, although it's rarely convenient for shorter journeys within the state. The relative infrequency of services and distance of the line from most of the resorts means you're invariably better off catching the bus. The one trip it really is worth catching the train for is the two-hour ride south to the temple town of Gokarna, in neighbouring Karnataka.

By bus

The Goan transport corporation, **Kadamba**, runs long-distance services throughout the state from their main stands at Panjim, Mapusa and Margao. Private buses, serving everywhere else (including the coastal resorts) are cheap, frequent and more relaxed than many in India, although you should still brace yourself for a crush on market days and when travelling to major towns and tourist centres. Details on how to get around by bus are listed in the relevant accounts, and on p.855.

By motorcycle taxi

Goa's unique pillion-passenger **motorcycle taxis**, known locally as "**pilots**", are ideal for nipping between beaches or into town from the resorts. Bona fide operators ride black bikes with yellow mudguards and white number plates. Fares, which should

Since Independence, Goa has continued to prosper, bolstered by iron-ore exports and a booming tourist industry. Dominated by the issues of statehood, the status of Konkani and the ever-rising levels of immigration, its political life has been dogged by chronic **instability**. In the 1990s, no less than twelve chief ministers held power over a succession of shaky, opportunistic coalitions, which saw standards of government plummet to depths hitherto unseen in the region.

Among the main beneficiaries of the ongoing chaos have been the extreme right-wing Hindu fundamentalists, the **BJP**. In the past, their advocacy of merger with Maharashtra made them unpopular with the Goan electorate – even Hindus – despite the party's dominance in the national arena. But with one quarter of the seats in the Goan assembly, the BJP dominated the state government between 2000 and 2004. Chief Minister **Manohar Parrikkar** made himself popular with middle class urban voters after he initiated be settled in advance, are comparable with auto-rickshaw rates: roughly Rs7 per kilometre.

By rented motorcycle

Renting a motorcycle in Goa gives a lot of freedom but can be perilous. Every season, an average of one person a day dies on the roads; many are tourists on two-wheelers. Make sure, therefore, that the lights and brakes are in good shape, and be especially vigilant at night: Goan roads can be appallingly pot-holed and unlit, and stray cows, dogs and bullock carts can appear from nowhere.

Officially, you need an **international driver's licence** to rent, and ride, anything more powerful than a 25cc moped. Owners and rental companies rarely enforce this, but some local **police** use the rule to extract baksheesh from tourists. If you don't have a licence with you, the only way around the problem is to avoid big towns such as Panjim, Margao and Mapusa (or Anjuna on market day), and only to carry small sums of money when driving. If you are stopped for not having the right papers, it's no big deal, though police officers may try to convince you otherwise; keep cool, and be prepared to negotiate. Some unlicensed operators attempt to rent out machines to unwary visitors; always make sure you get some evidence of rental and insurance.

Rates vary according to the season, the vehicle, and how long you rent it for; most owners also insist on a deposit and/or passport as security. The range is pretty standard, with the cheapest choice a step-through style scooter such as a **Honda Kinetic 100cc**, (Rs150–200 per day); with automatic gears, this is a good first-time choice and arguably the best all-rounder. To travel any significant distance, however, you should consider renting an **Enfield Bullet 350cc** (upwards of Rs250 per day), popular mainly for its pose value, or a smaller, lighter and generally more reliable **Yamaha 100cc** or **Bajaj Pulsar 180cc** (both around Rs200/250 per day respectively).

Tours

On paper, guided **tours** (daily; Rs150) run by the local tourism authority **GTDC** (Ⓦwww.goa-tourism.com) from Panjim, Margao, Calangute and Colva seem like a good way of getting around Goa's highlights in a short time. However, they're far too rushed for most foreign tourists, appealing essentially to Indian families wishing to combine a peek at the resorts with a whistle-stop puja tour of the temples around Ponda. Most also include a string of places inland that you wouldn't otherwise consider visiting. Leaflets giving full itineraries are available at any GTDC office.

improvements to buildings and roads in the capital, and brought the International Film Festival of India to Panjim. But life for him and his party became more difficult after the elections of May 2004, when Congress won a majority in the State Legislature.

Pressure started to build after a series of tit-for-tat political sackings and appointments created the Goan equivalent of a hung parliament, and sent leaders of both parties scurrying to the Governor's residence to request permission to form a government. With both Congress and the BJP trying to engineer defections from one side to the other, the situation soon spiralled into chaos. Eventually, in March 2005 – barely three hours after the Congress narrowly won a vote of confidence (the third in thirty days) – New Delhi stepped into the breach and declared **President's Rule**. At the time of writing, a new round of elections was planned to break the deadlock, but it seems unlikely that Goa's political life will stabilize in the medium to long term.

Panjim and central Goa

Stacked around the sides of a lush terraced hillside at the mouth of the River Mandovi, **PANJIM** (also known by its Marathi name, **Panaji** – "land that does not flood"), was for centuries little more than a minor landing stage and customs house, protected by a hilltop fort and surrounded by stagnant swampland. It only became state capital in 1843, after the port at Old Goa had silted up and its rulers and impoverished inhabitants had fled the plague. Although the last Portuguese viceroy managed to drain many of Panjim's marshes, and erect imposing public buildings on the new site, the town never emulated the grandeur of its predecessor upriver – a result, in part, of the Portuguese nobles' predilection for erecting their mansions in the countryside

Goan to the movies

Goa's state capital ground to a total halt for three days in February 2003 when it was commandeered by the makers of **The Bourne Supremacy**, starring Hollywood star Matt Damon. Although the chase scene that opened the movie started at a location you might recognize as Palolem beach, it cut straight to Panjim, and then to Nerul bridge, near Candolim, via a dramatic car chase through the normally sleepy streets of Fontainhas.

This brush with international cinema celebrity was the perfect preamble to the thirty-fifth **International Film Festival of India** (IFFI), held for the first time in Goa the following year. In the months leading up to the event, Panjim enjoyed a multi-crore makeover: main roads and buildings around the city were spruced up and the formerly broken walkway along the riverbank became a revamped promenade, complete with 2000 ornamental street lamps and fountains specially imported from Belgium. Three controversial lights (costing more than £27,000), were also installed to illuminate the temporary wooden jetty behind the festival's main venue, the Kala Academy, where delegates and guests alighting from launches from the *Taj Fort Aguada* hotel would arrive. The stage was thus set for superstars from across the world to pose for photocalls along Panjim's waterfront, "à la Cannes". Hollywood was conspicuous by its absence, but a bevy of Bollywood's top names, including Amir Khan, Sanjay Dutt and the "Big B" himself, Amitabh Buchchan, loyally turned up, to the obvious delight of the local dignitaries and politicians hosting the event.

In total, 169 films from 55 countries were shown over the course of the fortnight, among them the Indian premiere of *Vanity Fair*, introduced by its director, Mira Nair. But the biggest splash was reserved for *filmi* score supremo, A.H. Rahman, who performed a live outdoor concert.

Although some dissenting voices in the Goan media deemed the whole exercise a colossal waste of time and money, most people in Panjim were flattered by the profile it gave the town, and greeted the news that Goa would host the 2005 IFFI with great enthusiasm, amid hopes that the state would become a permanent venue for the event.

If it does, expect a stiff hike in hotel rates around the end of November to early December, and an acute shortage of rooms. Rather than stay in town to catch the films, therefore, consider travelling down from one or other of the resorts up the coast. In addition to the big open-air venues along the Mandovi in Campal, movies are screened in Panjim's state-of-the-art new multiplex, the Innox (see "Listings", p.803); tickets can be purchased in advance from the festival box office at the Old Goa Medical College Heritage precinct, Dayanand Bandodkar (DB) Marg. For listings and previews of the films on show, pick up a festival programme from the festival office (opposite the Inox cinema, Old Goa Medical College Heritage precinct, Dayanand Bandodkar (DB) Marg), or at the Kala Academy.

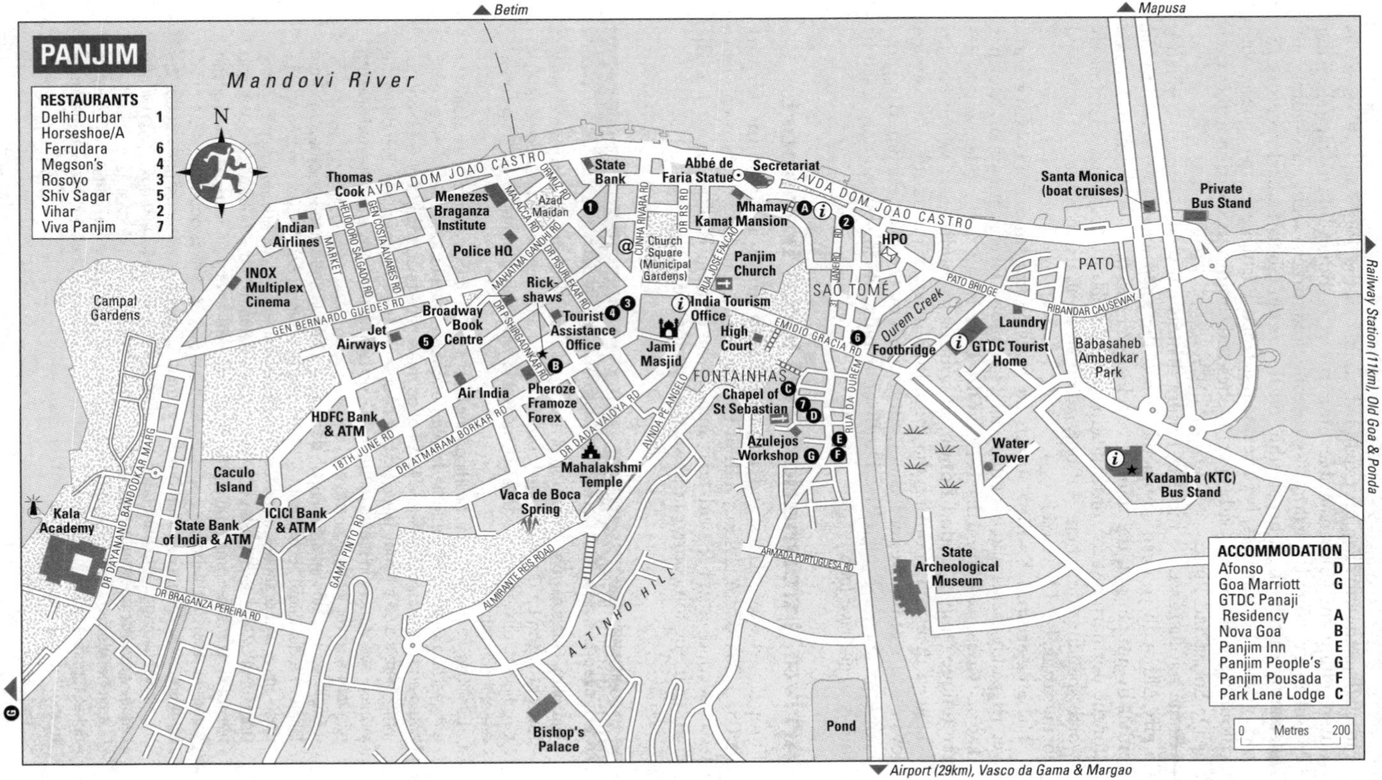

PANJIM

RESTAURANTS

Delhi Durbar	1
Horseshoe/A Ferrudara	6
Megson's	4
Rosoyo	3
Shiv Sagar	5
Vihar	2
Viva Panjim	7

ACCOMMODATION

Afonso	D
Goa Marriott	G
GTDC Panaji Residency	A
Nova Goa	B
Panjim Inn	E
Panjim People's	G
Panjim Pousada	F
Park Lane Lodge	C

Betim
Mapusa
Railway Station (11km), Old Goa & Ponda
Airport (29km), Vasco da Gama & Margao
G
Mandovi River
N
Avda Dom Joao Castro
Thomas Cook
Indian Airlines
INOX Multiplex Cinema
Campal Gardens
Menezes Braganza Institute
Police HQ
Ormuz Rd
Malacca Rd
Azad Maidan
State Bank
Abbé de Faria Statue
Secretariat
Mhamay Kamat Mansion
HPO
Santa Monica (boat cruises)
Private Bus Stand
Pato
Heliodoro Salgado Rd
Gen Costa Alvares Rd
Market
Mahatma Gandhi Rd
Dr Pisurlekar Rd
Cunha Rivara Rd
Church Square (Municipal Gardens)
Dr RS Rd
Rua Jose Falcao
31 Janeiro Rd
Panjim Church
Sao Tomé
Pato Bridge
Ribandar Causeway
Ourem Creek
Laundry
Babasaheb Ambedkar Park
Gen Bernardo Guedes Rd
Jet Airways
Broadway Book Centre
Rick-shaws
Dr P Shirgaonkar Rd
Tourist Assistance Office
India Tourism Office
Jami Masjid
High Court
Emidio Gracia Rd
Footbridge
GTDC Tourist Home
Fontainhas
Chapel of St Sebastian
Rua da Ourem
Azulejos Workshop
Water Tower
Kadamba (KTC) Bus Stand
Air India
Pheroze Framoze Forex
HDFC Bank & ATM
18th June Rd
Dr Atmaram Borkar Rd
Dr Dada Vaidya Rd
Avnda Pe Angelo
Mahalakshmi Temple
Vaca de Boca Spring
Caculo Island
ICICI Bank & ATM
State Bank of India & ATM
Kala Academy
Dr Dayanand Bandodkar Marg
Dr Braganza Pereira Rd
Gama Pinto Rd
Almirante Reis Road
Altinho Hill
Armada Portuguesa Rd
State Archeological Museum
Bishop's Palace
Pond
0 Metres 200

rather than the city. Panjim expanded rapidly in the 1960s and 1970s, without reaching the unmanageable proportions of other Indian capitals. After Mumbai, or even Bangalore, its uncongested streets seem easy-going and pleasantly parochial. Sights are thin on the ground, but the backstreets of the old quarter, **Fontainhas**, have retained a faded Portuguese atmosphere, with colour-washed houses, Catholic churches and shopfronts sporting names such as De Souza and Pinto.

Some travellers see no more of Panjim than its noisy bus terminal – which is a pity. Although you can completely bypass the town when you arrive in Goa, either by jumping off the train or coach at Margao (for the south), or Mapusa (for the northern resorts), or by heading straight off on a local bus, it's definitely worth spending time here – if only a couple of hours en route to the ruined former capital at Old Goa.

The area **around Panjim** attracts far fewer visitors than the coastal resorts, yet its paddy fields and wooded valleys harbour several attractions worth a day or two's break from the beach. **Old Goa** is just a bus ride away, as are the unique temples around **Ponda**, an hour or so southeast, to where Hindus smuggled their deities during the Inquisition. Further inland still, the forested lower slopes of the Western Ghats, cut through by the main Panjim–Bangalore highway, shelter the impressive **Dudhsagar falls**, which you can only reach by four-wheel-drive Jeep.

Arrival, information and local transport

European charter planes and domestic flights arrive at **Dabolim airport** (ⓣ0832/254 0788), 29km south of Panjim on the outskirts of Vasco da Gama, Goa's second city. Pre-paid taxis into town (45min; Rs475), booked at the counter in the forecourt, can be shared by up to four people.

Dabolim airport

Dabolim, Goa's airport, lies on top of a rocky plateau, 4km southeast of the industrial town of Vasco da Gama. A large new civilian terminal has been constructed at this naval aerodrome to accommodate Goa's rapidly increasing air traffic, but long delays are still common.

Facilities in the terminal buildings include a post office, counters for domestic airlines and State Bank of India **foreign exchange desks** (check exchange certificates and cash carefully before leaving, as there have been reports of short-changing). There's also a handy pre-paid **taxi counter** outside the main exit. Fixed fares to virtually everywhere in the state are displayed behind the desk; pay here and give the slip to the driver when you arrive.

Facilities in Dabolim's first floor **departures hall** include another pint-size State Bank of India (Mon, Tues, Thurs & Fri 10.30am–1.30pm, Sat 10.30am–noon), a sub-post-office and branches of several domestic airlines: Indian Airlines (daily 7.15am–2pm; ⓣ0832/251 2788), Sahara Airlines (daily 9.30am–5pm; ⓣ0832/251 0043) and Jet (daily 9.30am–5pm; ⓣ0832/254 0029). There's a very ordinary and overpriced cafeteria, too, but it doesn't open in time for early-morning domestic departures, so if you're looking for a filling breakfast, head across the road from the front of the terminal building to the staff canteen, where you can grab piping hot *pau bhaji* and *batata wada* for a few rupees.

Anyone **visiting** the airport, or meeting arrivals, should note that a Rs20 visitor ticket (on sale at the hatch next to the main ground-floor exit) will buy you entrance to the foyer of the air-conditioned arrivals hall.

There's no **train** station in town itself; the nearest one, on the Konkan Railway, is at **Karmali** (11km east of Panjim at Old Goa; ⓣ0832/228 5798). State buses to central Panjim await arrivals.

Long-distance and local **buses** pull into Panjim's busy Kadamba bus stand, 1km east of the centre in the district of Pato. Ten minutes' walk, across Ourem Creek to Fontainhas, brings you to several budget hotels. For the more modern west end of town, flag down a motorcycle taxi or jump into an auto-rickshaw at the rank outside the station concourse (Rs20–25).

GTDC's **information** counter, inside the concourse at the main Kadamba bus stand (daily 9.30am–1pm & 2–5pm; ⓣ0832/222 5620, ⓦwww.goa-tourism.com) is useful for checking train and bus timings, but little else. The more efficient **India Tourism office** is across town on Church Square (Mon–Fri 9.30am–6pm, Sat 9.30am–1pm; ⓣ0832/222 3412, ⓦwww.tourismofindia.com).

Auto-rickshaws are the most convenient way of **getting around** Panjim; flag one down at the roadside or head for one of the ranks around the city.

Accommodation

The majority of Goa's Indian visitors prefer to stay in Panjim rather than the coastal resorts, which explains the huge number of **hotels** and **lodges** crammed into the town centre, especially its noisy, more modern west end. Foreigners spending the night here instead of on the coast, on the other hand, tend to do so primarily to sample the atmosphere of the old quarter, Fontainhas. Finding a room is only a problem during the festival of St Francis (Nov 24–Dec 3), Dusshera (Sept/Oct) and during peak season (mid-Dec to mid-Jan); the codes below apply to October through March, excluding the above periods, when prices can double or triple. Note that **checkout times** vary wildly; find out what yours is as soon as you arrive, or your hard-earned lie-in could end up costing you an extra day's rent.

Afonso St Sebastian Chapel Square, Fontainhas ⓣ0832/222 2359. This refurbished colonial-era house in a picturesque backstreet is your best bet if you can't afford the *Panjim Inn* down the road. Spotlessly clean, cool en-suite rooms, friendly owners and rooftop terrace with views. Single occupancy available. Rates soar to Rs800 at Christmas, but are otherwise low for the level of comfort and location. ❹

Goa Marriott Miramar beach ⓣ0832/243 7001, ⓦwww.marriott.com. Huge five-star out on the edge of town, facing the mouth of the Mandovi. Predictably formulaic, and not a great location for a package holiday (despite what the brochures might suggest), but large and luxurious, with all the mod cons you'd expect, and the management hosts complimentary cocktail parties each week for guests' feedback. ❾

GTDC Panaji Residency Avda Dom Joao Castro ⓣ0832/222 4132, ⓦwww.goa-tourism.com. Spacious rooms in an amorphous government-run hotel next to the main road and river. Not at all inspiring, but good value. ❺

Nova Goa Dr Atmaram Borkar Rd ⓣ0832/227 7226, ⓦwww.hotelnovagoa.com. Panjim's brightest, newest top-class hotel in the heart of the shopping area and with the usual comforts, plus bath tubs and a pool. Popular mainly with visiting Portuguese and corporate clients. ❽

Panjim Inn E-212, 31 Janeiro Rd, Fontainhas ⓣ0832/243 5628, ⓦwww.panjiminn.com. Grand 300-year-old townhouse, now managed as a homely heritage hotel, with period furniture, sepia family photos, balconies and a common veranda where meals and drinks are served to guests. The same family runs the even more beautiful *Panjim Pousada* (same phone number; ❻), across the road, an old Hindu house which gives you the chance sample what Panjim must have felt like a century ago; ask for a room on the first floor, where a lovely wooden balcony, shaded by a breadfruit tree, overlooks the inner courtyard. ❻

Panjim Peoples 31 Janeiro Rd, Fontainhas ⓣ0832/222 1122, ⓦwww.panjiminn.com. The *Panjims Inn*'s latest "heritage" venture, opposite the original house (see above) occupies a former high school. It's more upmarket than their other two wings, but no less appealing for that. The rooms are huge, fitted with antique rosewood furniture, gilded pelmets and lace curtains, and the bathrooms feature the Sukhija family's hallmark crazy-mosaic tiling. Tariffs mid-season start at around Rs5000 per night. ❾

Park Lane Lodge near the Chapel of St Sebastian ⓣ0832/222 7154, ⓔpklaldg@sancharnet.in. Cramped but clean and friendly family guesthouse in a rambling 1930s house. Pepper and coffee plants add atmosphere to a narrow communal terrace, and there's a TV lounge upstairs; also safe deposit facilities, Internet access and a laundry service. Rates are ambitious in season, but at other times you get discounts. ❹

The Town

The leafy rectangular park opposite the India Government tourist office, known as **Church Square** or the **Municipal Gardens**, forms the heart of Panjim. Presiding over its southeast side is the town's most distinctive and photogenic landmark, the toothpaste-white Baroque facade of the **Church of Our Lady of the Immaculate Conception**. Flanked by rows of slender palm trees, at the head of a crisscrossing laterite walkway, the church was built in 1541 for the benefit of sailors arriving here from Lisbon. The weary mariners would stagger up from the quay to give thanks for their safe passage before proceeding to the capital at Old Goa – the original home of the enormous bell that hangs from its central gable.

Running north from the church, Rua José Falcao brings you to the riverside, where Panjim's main street, Avenida Dom Joao Castro, holds the town's oldest surviving building. With its sloping tiled roofs, carved-stone coats of arms and wooden verandas, the stalwart **Secretariat** looks typically colonial. Yet it was originally the summer palace of Goa's sixteenth-century Muslim ruler, the Adil Shah. Later, the Portuguese converted it into a temporary rest house for the territory's governors (who used to stay overnight here en route to and from Lisbon) and then a residence for the viceroy. Today, it accommodates the Goan State Legislature – hence shiny chauffeur-driven Ambassador cars outside and the armed guards at the door.

A hundred metres east, a peculiar statue of a man holding his hands over the body of an entranced reclining woman shows **Abbé de Faria** (1755–1819), a Goan priest who emigrated to France to become one of the world's first professional hypnotists.

Just behind the esplanade, 500m west of the Abbé de Faria statue, stands another grand vestige of the colonial era, the **Menezes Braganza Institute**. Now the town's Central Library (Mon–Fri 9.30am–1pm & 2–5.30pm), this Neoclassical building was erected as part of the civic makeover initiated by the Marquis of Pombal and Dom Manuel de Portugal e Castro in the early nineteenth century. Its entrance lobby on Malacca Road is lined with panels of blue-and-yellow-painted ceramic tiles, known as **azulejos**, depicting scenes from Luis Vaz Camões' epic poem, *Os Luisiades*.

Fontainhas

Panjim's oldest and most interesting district, **Fontainhas**, spreads from the banks of Pato creek opposite the bus stand – a dozen or so blocks of Neoclassical houses rising up the sides of leafy Altinho Hill. Many have retained their traditional coat of ochre, pale yellow, green or blue – a legacy of the Portuguese insistence that every Goan building (except churches, which had to be white) should be colour-washed after the monsoons. While some (notably the Portuguese **Fundacão Oriente** building at the south end of the neighbourhood, and the three wings of the *Panjim Inn*) have been restored, most remain in a state of charismatic decay.

The whitewashed **Chapel of St Sebastian**, still holding to the old colonial decree, stands at the centre of Fontainhas, at the head of a small square where the Portuguese-speaking locals hold a lively annual street *festa* to celebrate their patron saint's day in mid-November. The eerily lifelike crucifix inside the chapel, brought here in 1812, formerly hung in the Palace of the Inquisition in Old Goa. Unusually, Christ's eyes are open – allegedly to inspire fear in those being interrogated by the Inquisitors.

Just off the bottom of the square is a small workshop where you can watch traditional Goan *azulejos* being made. The main sales room, **Galeria Velha Goa**, is a couple of blocks away, next door to the *Panjim Inn*.

Grander colonial-era buildings are to found up on **Altinho Hill**, which can be reached via the flight of steps beginning alongside the *Park Lane Lodge*. The first one you come to at the top of the steps is the High Court of Goa, a splendid example of late-nineteenth-century Portuguese municipal architecture. Ten minutes' walk further south, occupying the highest point in Panjim, the **Archbishop's Palace**, a long, white, double-storeyed building with an imposing facade, is still occupied by Goa's highest ranking prelate, hence the whitewash.

The State Archeological Museum

The most noteworthy feature of Panjim's **State Archeological Museum** (Mon–Fri 9.30am–1.15pm & 2–5.30pm; Rs20; Ⓦwww.goamuseum.nic.in) is its impressive size, which stands in glaringly inverse proportion to the collections inside. In their bid to erect a structure befitting a state capital, Goa's bureaucrats ignored the fact that there was precious little to put in it. The only rarities to be found amid the lame array of temple sculpture, hero stones and dowdy colonial-era artefacts are a couple of beautiful Jain bronzes rescued by Customs and Excise officials from smugglers and, on the first floor, the infamous Italian-style table used by Goa's Grand Inquisitors, complete with its original, ornately carved tall-backed chairs.

The Houses of Goa Museum

Across the river, near the new hilltop suburb of **Porvorim**, renowned local architect Gerard de Cunha and colleagues recently set up the quirky **Houses of Goa Museum** (Tues–Sun 10am–7.30pm; Rs25; Ⓦwww.archgoa.org). Its general aim is to showcase the region's way of life as it used to be before the protective shield of Portuguese rule was lifted in 1961.

The triangular building itself resembles a modern ark, with themed displays divided between four levels interconnected by spiral staircases. After a whistlestop graphic résumé of Goan history, the exhibitions are largely given over to domestic houses, described as "the prime expression of Goan identity". Pieces of traditional colonial-era houses – from wonderful old doors and oyster-shell windows, to carved railings, ceramic tiles, furniture and masonry – are assembled to explain construction processes and changes in decor and style. Architectural features that were adapted in a uniquely Goan way, such as colour schemes, ornamental gateposts, verandas and false ceilings, are also highlighted, and interactive computer exhibits let you delve more deeply into the subjects covered.

Only 5km from Panjim, the House of Goa museum is most easily reached by taxi or auto-rickshaw. With your own transport, head north over the Mandovi bridge and keep going until you reach the big Alto-Porvorim Circle roundabout. Take a right here and follow the road until it forks, then bear left and head straight on for 750m or so, until you reach a second fork, where you bear left again: the museum is next to Nisha's Play School. By bus, you can travel as far as the Alto-Porvorim circle on any Panjim–Mapusa service from the Kadamba stand: get down at *O Coqueiro* restaurant (infamous as the place where international jewel thief and suspected serial killer **Charles Sobhraj** was captured by police in 1987), which is just north of the roundabout, then walk the remaining 2km, or jump in an auto if there's one hanging around.

Eating and drinking

Catering for the droves of tourists who come here from other Indian states, as well as more price-conscious locals, Panjim is packed with good **places to eat**, from hole-in-the-wall fish-curry-rice joints to swish air-conditioned restaurants serving top-notch Mughlai cuisine. In a week you could feasibly attempt a gastronomic tour of the subcontinent without straying more than five minutes from the Municipal Gardens. Vegetarians are best catered for at the numerous *udipi* canteens dotted around town, most of which open around 7am for South Indian **breakfasts**. Beer, *feni* and other spirits are available in all but the purest "pure veg" places.

Delhi Durbar behind the *Hotel Mandovi*. A provincial branch of the famous Mumbai restaurant, and the best place in Panjim – if not all Goa – to sample traditional Mughlai cuisine of mainly meat steeped in rich, spicy sauces (try their superb *rogan josh* or melt-in-the-mouth chicken tikka). Most main dishes are around Rs175–200, but this place is well worth a splurge.

Horseshoe/A Ferrudara Rua de Ourem, Fontainhas. The town's only Portuguese restaurant, serving a limited, but reasonably priced, menu of old standards such as *canja de galinha, caldo verde, feijoada*, soup, chicken piri piri, fish *balchao* and grilled sardines. The food is not as good as at *Viva Panjim*, but the decor and atmosphere make this a worthwhile option, plus it's air-conditioned. Most mains around Rs100.

Megson's 18th June Rd. The state's top deli, with a great selection of traditional Goan foods: spicy sausages, prepared meats, tangy cheese from the

Goan food and drink

Not unnaturally, after 450 years of colonization, Goan **cooking** has absorbed a strong Portuguese influence – palm vinegar (unknown elsewhere in India), copious amounts of coconut, garlic, tangy tamarind and fierce local chillies all play their part. Goa is the home of the famous *vindaloo* (from the Portuguese *vinho d'alho*, literally "garlic wine"), originally an extra-hot and sour pork curry, but now made with a variety of meat and fish. Other **pork** specialities include *chouriço* red sausages, *sorpotel*, a hot curry made from pickled pig's liver and heart, *leitao*, suckling pig, and *balchao*, pork in a rich brown sauce. Delicious alternatives include mutton *xacutti*, made with a sauce of lemon juice, peanuts, coconut, chillies and spices. The choice of **seafood**, often cooked in fragrant masalas, is excellent – clams, mussels, crab, lobster, giant prawns – while **fish**, depending on the type, is either cooked in wet curries, grilled, or baked in tandoor clay ovens. *Sanna*, like the South Indian *iddli*, is a steamed cake of fermented rice flour, but here made with palm toddy. Sweet tooths will adore *bebinca*, a rich, delicious solid egg custard with coconut.

As for **drinks**, locally produced wine, spirits and beer are cheaper than anywhere in the country, thanks to lower rates of tax. The most famous and widespread **beer** is Kingfisher, which tastes less of glycerine preservative than it does elsewhere in India, but you'll also come across pricier Fosters, brewed in Mumbai and nothing like the original. Goan **port**, a sweeter, inferior version of its Portuguese namesake, is ubiquitous, served chilled in large wine glasses with a slice of lemon. Local **spirits** – whiskies, brandies, rums, gins and vodkas – come in a variety of brand names for less than Rs30 a shot, but, at half the price, local speciality **feni**, made from distilled cashew or from the sap of coconut palms, offers strong competition. Cashew *feni* is usually drunk after the first distillation, but you can also find it double-distilled, flavoured with ginger or cumin to produce a smooth liqueur.

Nilgiris, olive oil, and the best *bebinca* you can buy (ask for *Linda* brand).

Rosoyo 18th June Rd. Run by *Megson's*, this busy little fast-food joint is *the* place to sample tasty, hygienic Mumbai-style street food: crunchy *bhel puri* or delicious *pau bhaji*. They also serve Gujarati snacks such as *thepla* – chapatis griddle-cooked with curry leaves and cumin, and served with South Indian *chatni* – plus a range of shakes and ice creams. You'll be hard pushed to spend Rs50.

Shiv Sagar Mahatma Gandhi Rd. Smarter than average snack-café that does a brisk trade with the city's middle classes, offering consistently fresh, delicious pan-Indian food and fresh fruit juices. The northern dishes aren't so great, but their South Indian menu is superb (try the delicious *palak dosa*, made with spinach). A/c "family" mezzanine upstairs. No alcohol.

Vihar 31 Janeiro Rd. Arguably the best budget *udipi* in Panjim; try their super tasty *rawa* masala dosas.

Viva Panjim 31 Janeiro Rd, Fontainhas. Traditional Goan home cooking – millet-fried mussels, *xacutis*, vindaloo, prawn *balchao*, *cafreal*, *amotik* and delicious freshly grilled fish – served by a charming local lady in atmospheric colonial-era backstreet. This place should be your first choice for dinner if you're staying in Fontainhas for a taste of old colonial Goa. Get there early for one of the half-dozen tables outside in the alley. Most mains under Rs150.

Listings

Airlines Air France, Air Seychelles, American Airlines, Biman Bangladesh, Gulf Air, Kenyan Airways, Royal Jordanian, Sri Lankan Airlines, all c/o Jetair, Rizvi Chambers, 1st Floor, H. Salgado Rd ⓣ0832/222 0122 or 222 6154; Air India, Colvakar Centaur, Campal ⓣ0832/222 4081 or 222 5172; British Airways, DKI Airlines Service, 2 Excelsior Chambers, MG Rd ⓣ0832/222 4573 or 243 8055–57; Alitalia, Globe Trotters International, G-7 Shankar Parvati Building, 18th June Rd ⓣ0832/243 8950–52; Indian Airlines, Dempo House, Dr D. Bandodkar Rd ⓣ0832/242 8787 or 223 7826; Jet Airlines, Sesa Ghor, ECD Plaza, next to GTDC *Panjim Residency*, Pato ⓣ0832/243 8792 or 222 1476; Sahara Airlines, Ground Floor, Livein Appts, General Bernard Guedes Rd ⓣ0832/223 7346 or 223 0237.

Banks and ATMs The most efficient places to change money are: Thomas Cook, near the Indian Airlines office at 8 Alcon Chambers, Devanand Bandodkar Rd (Mon–Sat 9am–6pm, Oct–March also Sun 10am–5pm); and the Pheroze Framroze Exchange Bureau on Dr P. Shirgaonkar Rd (Mon–Sat 9.30am–7pm & Sun 9.30am–1pm). The latter's rates are competitive and they don't charge commission on either currency or travellers' cheques. The HDFC Bank on 18th June Rd is one of several major banks in the centre with a handy 24hr ATM, where you can make withdrawals using Visa or Mastercard. Changing money in the regular, government-run banks tends to take a lot longer: the Bank of Baroda (where you can draw money on Visa cards at its Bobcard counter), is on Azad Maidan.

Books The best selection of Goa-related books is at the Broadway Book Centre on 18th June Rd, opposite Gulf Supermarket, which sells a great range of old stuff in facsimile editions and lots of architecture and photographic tomes in hardback at discounted prices.

British Consular Assistant The British High Commission of Mumbai has a Tourist Assistance Office in Panjim, run by Ms Shilpa Caldeira – a useful contact for British nationals who've lost passports, get into trouble with the law or need help dealing with a death. It's over near the Kadamba bus stand at 13/14 Dempo Towers, Patto Plaza ⓣ0832/243 8734, ⓔbcagoa@sancharnet.in, ⓦwww.ukinindia.com. In emergencies only, Ms Caldeira may be reached on her mobile number ⓣ9822/102428.

Cinema Panjim's swanky new multiplex, the 1272-seater Inox, is in the northwest of town on the site of the old Goa Medical College, Dayanand Bandodkar (DB) Marg (ⓣ0832/242 0999, ⓦwww.inoxmovies.com). Designed by the Kiwi architects, Walkers, and opened for the first International Film Festival of India in 2004, the complex screens all the latest Hindi blockbusters, and some English-language Hollywood movies; see the local press or the Inox website for listings and booking details (Internet ticketing was in the pipeline when we last checked).

Hospital The state's main medical facility is the new Goa Medical College, aka GMC (ⓣ0832/245 8700–07), 7km south on NH-17 at Bambolim, where there's also a 24hr pharmacy. Ambulances (ⓣ102) are likely to get you there a lot less quickly than a standard taxi. Conditions are grim by Western standards; relatives sleep in the wards to provide food for patients. Less serious cases can receive attention at the Vintage Hospital, next to Fire Brigade Headquarters in Panjim's St Inez district (ⓣ0832/564 4401–05).

Internet access Hotels and guesthouses, including the *Park Lane Lodge* and *Panjim Inn* (see p.799), offer Internet access to guests. Otherwise, the little net café on the west side of Church Square, has an ISDN connection.
Music and dance Regular recitals of classical Indian music and dance are held at Panjim's school for the performing arts, the Kala Academy in Campal (ⓦ www.kalaacademy.org), at the far west end of town on Devanand Bandodkar Rd. The building, originally designed by award-winning Goan achitect Charles Correa, enjoyed a major facelift ahead of the 2004 film festival, in the hope that it would provide a permanent venue for the event. For details of forthcoming concerts, consult the boards in front of the auditorium or the listings page of local newspapers.
Pharmacies Panjim's best pharmacy is Hindu Pharma, next to the *Hotel Aroma* on Church Square, which stocks Ayurvedic, homeopathic and allopathic medicines.
Police Police Headquarters is on Malacca Rd, central Panjim (ⓣ 0832/222 5360 or 222 4997).
Post Panjim's reliable poste restante counter (Mon–Sat 9.30am–1pm & 2–5.30pm) is in the Head Post Office, 200m west of Pato Bridge. To get your stamps franked, walk around the back of the building and ask at the office behind the second door on the right. For parcel stitching, ask at Deepak Stores on the corner of the next block north.
Travel agent AERO Mundial, Ground Floor, *Hotel Mandovi*, Dr D. Bandodkar Rd ⓣ 0832/222 3773.

Old Goa

A one-time byword for splendour with a population of several hundred thousand, Goa's erstwhile former capital, **OLD GOA**, was virtually abandoned following malaria and cholera epidemics from the seventeenth century onwards. Today you need considerable imagination to picture the once-great capital as it used to be. The maze of twisting streets, piazzas and ochre-washed villas has gone, and all that remains is a score of cream-painted churches and convents. Granted World Heritage Status by UNESCO, Old Goa today attracts busloads of foreign tourists from the coast, and Christian pilgrims from around India, in roughly equal numbers. While the former come to admire the gigantic facades and gilt altars of the beautifully preserved churches, the main attraction for the latter is the tomb of **St Francis Xavier** (see p.807), the legendary sixteenth-century missionary, whose remains are enshrined in the **Basilica of Bom Jesus**.

If you're staying on the coast and contemplating a day-trip inland, this is the most obvious and accessible option. Just thirty minutes by road from the

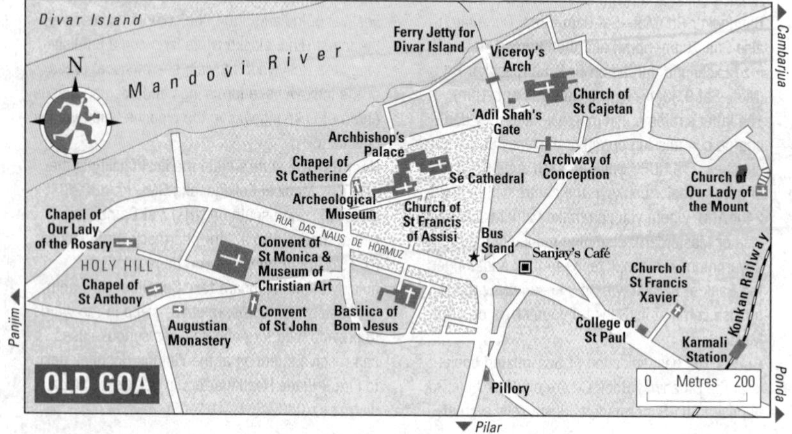

state capital, Old Goa is served by buses every fifteen minutes from Panjim's Kadamba bus stand; alternatively, hop into an auto-rickshaw (Rs75–100), or rent a taxi (Rs250-300). The best **place to eat** on the site, where all the taxi drivers go, is *Sanjay's Café*, which serves wholesome vegetarian and Goan fish-curry-rice thalis. To find it, head east along the main road through Old Goa and across the roundabout towards Karmali Station; the café is on the right (north) side of the road.

Arch of the Viceroys and the Church of St Cajetan

On arriving at the river landing stage to the north, seventeenth-century visitors passed through the **Arch of the Viceroys** (1597), constructed to commemorate Vasco da Gama's arrival in India and built from the same porous red laterite as virtually all Old Goa's buildings. Above it a Bible-toting figure rests his foot on the cringing figure of a "native", while its granite facade, facing the river, holds a statue of da Gama himself. It's hard to imagine today that these overgrown fields and simple streets with a few cool-drinks stands were once the focus of a lively market, with silk and gem merchants, horse dealers and carpet weavers. The one surviving monument, known as **'Adil Shah's Gate**, predates the Portuguese and possibly even the Muslim period. Hindu in style, it consists simply of a lintel supported by two columns in black basalt, to which are attached the remains of perforated screens. You can find it by turning left at the crossroads immediately above the Arch of the Viceroys.

A short way up the lane from the Gate, the distinctive domed **Church of St Cajetan** (1651) was modelled on St Peter's in Rome by monks from the Theatine order. While it does boast a Corinthian exterior, you can also spot certain non-European elements in the decoration, such as the cashew-nut designs in the carving of the pulpit. Hidden beneath the church is a crypt where the embalmed bodies of Portuguese governors were once kept in lead coffins before they were shipped back to Lisbon. Forgotten for over thirty years, the last batch (of three) was only removed in 1992 on the eve of the state visit to Goa of Portuguese president Mario Soares.

The Sé (St Catherine's Cathedral)

The Portuguese viceroy Redondo (1561–64) commissioned the **Sé**, or **St Catherine's Cathedral**, southwest of St Cajetan's, to be "a grandiose church worthy of the wealth, power and fame of the Portuguese who dominated the seas from the Atlantic to the Pacific". Today it stands larger than any church in Portugal, although it was beset by problems, not least a lack of funds and Portugal's temporary loss of independence to Spain. It took eighty years to build and was not consecrated until 1640.

On the Tuscan-style exterior, the one surviving tower houses the **Golden Bell**, cast in Cuncolim (south Goa) in the seventeenth century. During the Inquisition, its tolling announced the start of the gruesome *auto da fés* that were held in the square outside, when suspected heretics were subjected to public torture and burned at the stake. The scale and detail of the Corinthian-style interior is overwhelming; no less than fifteen altars are arranged around the walls, dedicated among others to Our Ladies of Hope, Anguish and Three Needs. An altar to St Anne treasures the relics of the **Blessed Martyrs of Cuncolim**, whose failed mission to convert the Moghul emperor Akbar culminated in their murder, while a chapel behind a highly detailed screen holds the **Miraculous Cross**, which stood in a Goan village until a vision of Christ appeared on it. Said to heal the sick, it is kept in a box; a small opening on the side allows devotees to touch it. The staggeringly ornate gilded main **altar** comprises nine carved frames and a splendid crucifix. Panels depict episodes from the life of St Catherine of Alexandria (died 307 AD), including an interchange of ideas with the pagan Roman emperor Maxim, who wished to marry her, and her subsequent flogging and martyrdom.

The Archbishop's Palace

Adjoining the Sé Cathedral, with which it is an exact contemporary, the **Archbishop's Palace** is unique as the last surviving civil building of colonial Goa's golden era. Though in a lamentable state of disrepair, its steeply inclined roofs and white facade still perfectly embody the solidity and imposing strength of the so-called "chã" style of architecture, derived from military constructions of the day, of which the most extreme example was the Viceroy's Fortress Palace (Palacio da Fortaleza), which has since vanished without trace. Presenting their most austere aspect to the river, these two fortified palaces formerly dominated the skyline of the waterfront, appropriately enough for a city perennially under threat of attack.

Nineteenth-century photos show that the city-facing side of the building was originally enfolded by a low wall, which surrounded a garden. This has long been dismantled, but the two grand **entrance porches** remain intact. The one on the right (as you look at the building) is original, complete with red decorative frescoes lining the side walls, among the last remaining paintings of their kind left in Goa. During the Portuguese heyday, guards in blue livery would have stood on its steps, as they did in the Viceroys' palace and most *hidalgo* (noble) houses.

The palace is officially closed to visitors so if you want to have a nose around, you'll have to persuade the ASI caretaker.

The Church of St Francis of Assisi and Archeological Museum

Southwest of the Cathedral is the ruined **Palace of the Inquisition**, in operation up until 1774, while to the west stands the **Convent of St Francis of Assisi**, built by Franciscan monks in 1517 and restored in the mid-eighteenth century. Today, the core of its **Archeological Museum** (daily except Fri 10am–5pm; Rs5) is a gallery of **portraits** of Portuguese viceroys, painted by local artists under Italian supervision. Other exhibits include coins, domestic Christian wooden sculpture, and downstairs in the cloister, pre-Portuguese Hindu sculpture. Next door, the **Church of St Francis** (1521) features fine decorative frescoes, *hidalgos'* tombstones in the floor paving, and paintings on wood showing the life of St Francis of Assisi.

Basilica of Bom Jesus

Close to the convent of St Francis, the 1605 church of **Bom Jesus**, "Good" or "Menino Jesus" (Mon–Sat 9am–6.30pm, Sun 10am–6.30pm), is known principally for the **tomb of St Francis Xavier**. In 1946, it became the first church in India to be elevated to the status of Minor Basilica. On the west, the three-storey Renaissance facade encompasses Corinthian, Doric, Ionic and Composite styles.

The interior is entered beneath the choir, supported by columns. On the northern wall, in the centre of the nave, is a cenotaph in gilded bronze to **Dom Jeronimo Mascarenhas**, the Captain of Cochin and benefactor of the church. The main altar, extravagantly decorated in gold, depicts the infant Jesus under the protection of St Ignatius Loyola (founder of the Jesuit Order); to each side are subsidiary altars to Our Lady of Hope and St Michael. In the southern

St Francis Xavier

Francis Xavier, the "Apostle of the Indies", was born in 1506 in the old kingdom of Navarre, now part of Spain. After taking a masters' degree in philosophy and theology at the University of Paris, where he studied for the priesthood until 1535, he was ordained two years later in Venice. He was then recruited by (Saint) **Ignatius Loyola** (1491–1556) along with five other priests into the new "Society of Jesus", which later became known as the **Jesuits**.

When the Portuguese king, Dom Joao III (1521–57), received reports of corruption and dissolute behaviour among the Portuguese in Goa, he asked Ignatius Loyola to despatch a priest who could influence the moral climate for the better. In 1541 Xavier was sent to work in the diocese of Goa, constituted seven years earlier, and comprising all regions east of the Cape of Good Hope. Arriving after a year-long journey, he embarked on a busy programme throughout southern India. Despite frequent obstruction from Portuguese officials, he founded numerous churches, and is credited with converting 30,000 people and performing such miracles as raising the dead and curing the sick with a touch of his beads. Subsequently he took his mission further afield to Sri Lanka, Malacca (Malaysia), China and Japan, where he was less successful.

When Xavier left Goa for the last time, it was with the ambition of evangelizing in China; however, he contracted dysentery aboard ship and died on the island of San Chuan (Sancian), off the Chinese coast, where he was buried. On hearing of his death, a group of Christians from Malacca exhumed his body – which, although the grave had been filled with lime, they found to be in a perfect state of preservation. Reburied in Malacca, it was later removed and taken to Old Goa, where it has remained ever since, enshrined in the Basilica of Bom Jesus.

However, Saint Francis' incorruptible corpse has never rested entirely in peace. Chunks of it have been removed over the years by relic hunters and curious clerics: in 1614, the right arm was dispatched to the Pope in Rome (where it allegedly wrote its name on paper), a hand was sent to Japan, and parts of the intestines to southeast Asia. One Portuguese woman, Dona Isabel de Caron, even bit off the little toe of the cadaver in 1534; apparently, so much blood spurted into her mouth, it left a trail to her house and she was discovered.

Every ten years, the saint's body is carried in a three-hour ceremony from the Basilica of Bom Jesus to the Sé Cathedral, where visitors file past, touch and photograph it. During the 2004–5 "**exposition**", around 256,000 pilgrims flocked for *darshan* or ritual viewing of the corpse, these days a shrivelled and somewhat unsavoury spectacle.

transept, lavishly decorated with twisted gilded columns and floriate carvings, stands the **Chapel and Tomb of St Francis Xavier**. Constructed of marble and jasper in 1696, it was the gift of the Medici, Cosimo III, the Grand Duke of Tuscany; the middle tier contains panels detailing the saint's life. An ornate domed reliquary in silver contains his remains; for a week around his feast day, December 3, tens of thousands of pilgrims – Hindus as well as Christians – queue for *darshan* (ritual viewing) of the casket before attending open-air Mass in the square outside.

Holy Hill

A number of other important religious buildings and a museum stand opposite Bom Jesus on **Holy Hill**. The **Convent of St Monica**, constructed in 1627, destroyed by fire in 1636 and rebuilt the following year, was the only Goan convent at the time and the largest in Asia. It housed around a hundred nuns, the Daughters of St Monica, and also offered accommodation to women whose husbands were called away to other parts of the empire. The **church** adjoins the convent on the south. As they had to remain away from the public gaze, the nuns attended mass in the choir loft and looked down upon the congregation. Inside, a **Miraculous Cross** rises above the figure of St Monica at the altar. In 1636, it was reported that the figure of Christ had opened his eyes, motioned as if to speak, and blood had flowed from the wounds made by his crown of thorns. The last Daughter of St Monica died in 1885, and since 1964 the convent has been occupied by the Mater Dei Institute for nuns.

Next door to the Chapel of the Miraculous Cross stands Goa's foremost **Museum of Christian art** (daily 9.30–5pm; Rs15), moved here from the Rachol Seminary in 2002. Exhibits include processional crosses, ivory ornaments, damask silk clerical robes and some finely sculpted wooden icons dating from the sixteenth and seventeenth centuries, among them an unusual statue of John the Baptist wearing a tiger-skin wrap (in the style of the Hindu god Shiva).

Nearby, the **Convent of St John of God**, built in 1685 by the Order of Hospitallers of St John of God to tend to the sick, was rebuilt in 1953. At the top of the hill, the **Chapel of Our Lady of the Rosary**, built in 1526 in the Manueline style (after the Portuguese king Manuel I, 1495–1521), features Ionic plasterwork with a double-storey portico, cylindrical turrets and a tower that commands fine views across the river from the terrace where Albuquerque surveyed the decisive battle of 1510. Its cruciform interior is unremarkable, except for the marble tomb of **Catarina a Piró**, believed to have been the first European woman to set foot in the colony. A commoner, she eloped here to escape the scandal surrounding her romance with Portuguese nobleman Garcia de Sá, who later rose to be governor of Goa. Under pressure from no less than Francis Xavier, Garcia eventually married her, but only *in articulo mortis* as she lay on her deathbed. Her finely carved tomb, set in the wall beside the high altar, incorporates a band of intricate Gujarati-style ornamentation, probably imported from the Portuguese trading post of Diu.

Ponda and around

Characterless, chaotic **Ponda**, 28km southeast of Panjim and 17km northeast of Margao, is Ponda district's administrative headquarters and main market town. Straddling the busy Panjim–Bangalore highway (NH-4), it's not a place to spend any time. However, scattered among the lush valleys and forests **around Ponda** are a dozen or so **Hindu temples** founded during the seventeenth and eighteenth centuries, when this hilly region was a Christian-free haven for Hindus fleeing persecution by the Portuguese. Although the temples are fairly modern by Indian standards, their deities are ancient and held in high esteem by both local people and thousands of pilgrims from Maharashtra and Karnataka.

The temples are concentrated in two main clusters: the first to the north of Ponda, on the NH-4, and the second deep in the countryside, around 5km west of the town. Most people only manage the **Shri Manguesh** and **Shri Mahalsa** (Ⓦwww.mahalsa.org), between the villages of **Mardol** and **Priol**. Among the most interesting temples in the state, they lie just a stone's throw from the main highway and are passed by regular **buses** between Panjim and Margao via Ponda. The others are farther off the beaten track, although they are not hard to find on motorbikes: locals will wave you in the right direction if you get lost.

Mardol and Priol

Although the **Sri Manguesh** temple originally stood in a secret location in Cortalim, and was moved to its present site between **MARDOL** and **PRIOL** during the sixteenth century, the structure visitors see today dates from the 1700s. A gateway at the roadside leads to a paved path and courtyard that gives onto a water tank, overlooked by the white temple building, raised on a plinth. Also in the courtyard is a seven-storey *deepmal*, a tower for oil lamps. Inside, the floor is paved with marble, and bands of decorative tiles emblazon the white walls. Flanked by large *dvarpala* guardians, embossed silver doorways with floriate designs lead to the sanctum, which houses a *shivalingam*.

Two kilometres south, the **Mahalsa Marayani** temple was also transferred from its original site, in this case Salcete *taluka* further south, in the seventeenth century. Here, the *deepmal* is exceptionally tall, with 21 tiers rising from a figure of Kurma, the tortoise incarnation of Vishnu. Original features include a marble-floored wooden *mandapa* (assembly hall) with carved pillars, ceiling panels of parakeets and, in the eaves, sculptures of the incarnations of Vishnu.

Dudhsagar waterfalls

Measuring a mighty 600m from head to foot, the famous **Dudhsagar waterfalls**, on the Goa–Karnataka border, are some of the highest in India, and a spectacular enough sight to entice a steady stream of visitors from the coast into the rugged Western Ghats. After pouring across the Deccan plateau, the headwaters of the Mandovi River form a foaming torrent that fans into three streams, then cascades down a near-vertical cliff face into a deep green pool. The Konkani name for the falls, which literally translated means "sea of milk", derives from clouds of foam kicked up at the bottom when the water levels are at their highest. Overlooking a steep, crescent-shaped head of a valley carpeted with pristine tropical forest, Dudhsagar is set amid breathtaking **scenery** that is only accessible on foot or by Jeep; the recently upgraded Margao–Castle Rock railway actually passes over the falls on an old stone viaduct, but services along it are infrequent.

One you've reached Dudhsagar, there's little to do beyond enjoying the views and clambering over the rocks below the falls in search of pools to swim in. The **best time to visit** is immediately after the monsoons, from October until mid-December, when water levels are highest, although the falls flow well into April. Unfortunately, the train line only sees two services per week in each direction, neither of them returning the same day. As a result, the only practicable way to get there and back is by four-wheel-drive **Jeep** from **Colem** (reachable by train from Vasco, Margao and Chandor, or by taxi from the north coast resorts for around Rs1250). The cost of the onward thirty- to forty-minute trip from Colem to the falls, which takes you across rough forest tracks and two or three river fords, is Rs350–400 per person; the drive ends with an enjoyable fifteen-minute hike, for which you'll need a sturdy pair of shoes. Finding a Jeep-wallah is easy; just turn up in Colem and look for the "Controller of Jeeps" near the station. However, if you're travelling alone or in a couple, you may have to wait around until the vehicle fills up, or else fork out to cover the cost of hiring the whole Jeep yourself. Note that it can be difficult to arrange transport of any kind from Molem crossroads, where regular taxis are in short supply.

North Goa

Beyond the mouth of the Mandovi estuary, the Goan coast sweeps **north** in a near-continuous string of beaches, broken only by the odd saltwater inlet, rocky headland, and three tidal rivers – the most northerly of which, the Arondem, still has to be crossed by ferry. Development is concentrated mainly behind the seven-kilometre strip of white sand that stretches from the foot of **Fort Aguada**, crowning the peninsula east of Panjim, to Baga creek in the north. Encompassing the resorts of **Candolim**, **Calangute** and **Baga**, this is Goa's prime charter belt and an area most independent travellers steer clear of.

Since the advent of mass tourism in the 1980s, the alternative "scene" has drifted progressively north away from the sunbed strip to **Anjuna** and **Vagator** – now predominantly Israeli rave enclaves boasting some of the region's loveliest beaches – and scruffier **Chapora**, a workaday fishing village on the riverside which has in the last few seasons been colonized by Russians. Further north still, **Arambol** has thus far escaped any large-scale development, despite the completion of the new road bridge across the Chapora River. What little extra traffic there is since the new road link tends to focus on the low-key resorts just south of Arambol, namely **Aswem** and **Mandrem**, where facilities remain basic by modern standards.

North Goa's market town, **Mapusa**, is this area's main jumping-off place, with bus connections to most resorts on the coast. If you're travelling here by train via the **Konkan Railway**, get off the train at **Tivim** (Ⓣ0832/229 8682), 19km west of Margao, from where you'll have to jump in a bus or taxi for the remaining leg.

Mapusa

MAPUSA (pronounced *Map*sa) is the district headquarters of Bardez *taluka*. A dusty collection of dilapidated, mostly modern buildings ranged around a busy central square, the town is of little more than passing interest, although it does host a lively **market** on Friday mornings. Anjuna's market may be a better place to shop for souvenirs, but Mapusa's is much more authentic. Local specialities include strings of spicy Goan sausages (*chouriço*), bottles of *toddy* (fermented palm sap) and large green plantains from nearby Moira.

Practicalities

Tivim, the nearest railway station to Mapusa, is 12km east in the neighbouring Bicholim district. Buses should be on hand to transport passengers into town, from where you can pick up local services to Calangute, Baga, Anjuna, Vagator, Chapora, and Arambol. These leave from the **Kadamba bus stand**, five minutes' walk west of the main square, where all state-run services from Panjim also pull in. **Motorcycle taxis** hang around the square to whisk lightly laden shoppers and travellers to the coast for around Rs40–50. **Taxis** charge considerably more (Rs125–150), but you can split the fare with up to five people.

The Konkan Railway's Konkan–Kanya Express (#KR0111) arrives in Tivim at around 9.30am, leaving plenty of time to find **accommodation** in the coastal resorts west of Mapusa. It's best to avoid staying in the town if possible, but if you can't, try GTDC's *Mapusa Residency* (Ⓣ0832/226 2794, Ⓦwww.goa-tourism.com; ❹), on the roundabout below the square, which has spacious and clean rooms and a Goa **tourist information** counter. Best of the **eating** options on or around the main square are the *Ruchira*, within the *Hotel Satyaheera* on the north side of the main square, which serves a standard multi-cuisine menu and cold beer. For quick, authentically Goan food, you won't do better than the beguilingly dated *FR Xavier* café over in the Municipal Market, which has been here (and changed little) since the Portuguese era. The waiters leave heaped baskets of fresh veg patties and beef samosas on your table, billing you for what you eat at the end.

Candolim and Fort Aguada

Compared with Calangute, 3km north along the beach, **CANDOLIM** (from the Konkani kandoli, meaning "dykes", in reference to the system of sluices that the area's first farmers used to reclaim land from nearby marshes) is a surprisingly sedate resort, attracting mainly middle-aged package tourists from the UK and Scandinavia. Over the past five years or so, however, its ribbon development of hotels and restaurants has sprouted a string of multistorey holiday complexes, and during peak season the few vestiges of authentically Goan culture that remain here are drowned in a deluge of Kashmiri handicraft stalls, luridly lit terrace cafés and shopping arcades. On the plus side, Candolim has lots of pleasant places to stay, many of them tucked away down quiet sandy lanes and better value than comparable guesthouses in nearby Calangute, making this a good first stop if you've just arrived in Goa and are planning to head further north after finding your feet.

Immediately south, **Fort Aguada** crowns the rocky flattened headland at the end of the beach. Built in 1612 to protect the northern shores of the Mandovi estuary from Dutch and Maratha raiders, the bastion encloses several natural springs, the first source of drinking water available to ships arriving in Goa after the long sea voyage from Lisbon. The ruins of the fort can be reached by road; follow the main drag south from Candolim as it bears left, past the turning for the *Taj Holiday Village*, and keep going for around 1km until you see a right turn, which runs uphill to a small car park. Nowadays, much of the site serves as a prison, and is therefore closed to visitors. It's worth a visit, though, if only for the superb views from the top of the hill where a four-storey Portuguese **lighthouse**, erected in 1864 and the oldest of its kind in Asia, looks down over the vast expanse of sea, sand and palm trees.

From the base of Fort Aguada on the northern flank of the headland, a rampart of red-brown laterite juts into the bay at the bottom of picturesque **Sinquerim Beach** (in effect the southernmost reach of Calangute beach). This was among the first places in Goa to be singled out for upmarket tourism. Taj Group's *Fort Aguada* resorts, among the most expensive hotels in India, lord over the sands from the slopes below the battlements.

Practicalities

Buses to and from Panjim stop every ten minutes or so at the stand opposite the *Casa Sea Shell*, in the middle of Candolim. A few continue south to the *Fort Aguada Beach Resort* terminus, from where services depart every thirty minutes for the capital via Nerul village; you can also flag down buses from anywhere along the main drag to Calangute. **Taxis** are ubiquitous. During the season, however, there is often a shortage of **motorcycles for rent** here, and you may find yourself having to search for a bike in Calangute.

Warning

Candolim Beach has seen a spate of **drownings** over the past couple of years. The undertow here has always been strong at certain phases of the tide, but the currents rarely proved treacherous until June 6, 2000, when the 61,000-tonne bulk carrier **MV River Princess** ran aground just off Sinquerim. Since then, the ship's owners, its insurers and the Goan government have been embroiled in a dispute over who should foot the bill for salvaging the vessel, leaving the *River Princess* to lurch deeper into the sand. Meanwhile, eddies and whirlpools whipped up around its hull claim lives each season.

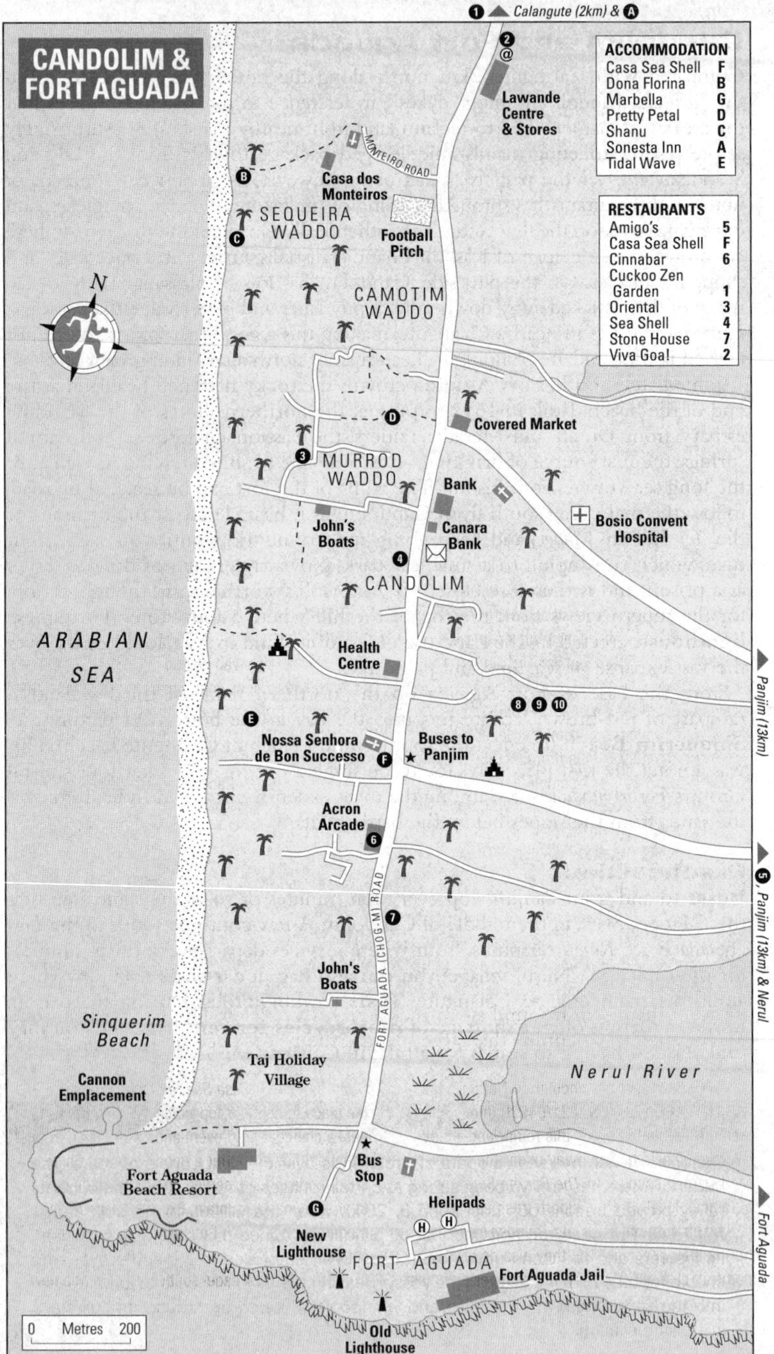

CANDOLIM & FORT AGUADA

ACCOMMODATION

Casa Sea Shell	F
Dona Florina	B
Marbella	G
Pretty Petal	D
Shanu	C
Sonesta Inn	A
Tidal Wave	E

RESTAURANTS

Amigo's	5
Casa Sea Shell	F
Cinnabar	6
Cuckoo Zen Garden	1
Oriental	3
Sea Shell	4
Stone House	7
Viva Goa!	2

1 Calangute (2km) & A
2 @
Lawande Centre & Stores
Monteiro Road
Casa dos Monteiros
Sequeira Waddo
Football Pitch
Camotim Waddo
Covered Market
Murrod Waddo
Bank
Bosio Convent Hospital
John's Boats
Canara Bank
Candolim
Arabian Sea
Health Centre
Panjim (13km)
Nossa Senhora de Bon Successo
Buses to Panjim
Acron Arcade
5, Panjim (13km) & Nerul
Fort Aguada (Chog-M) Road
John's Boats
Singuerim Beach
Taj Holiday Village
Nerul River
Cannon Emplacement
Bus Stop
Fort Aguada Beach Resort
Helipads
Fort Aguada
New Lighthouse
Fort Aguada
Fort Aguada Jail
Old Lighthouse
0 Metres 200

You can **change money** at any number of private exchange places dotted around Candolim, but their rates are unlikely to be as competitive as those on offer in Calangute. For **Internet** access, I-Way, at the north end of the village on the main road, offers a fast broadband connection.

Accommodation

Candolim is charter-holiday land, so **accommodation** tends to be expensive for most of the season. That said, if bookings are down you can find some great bargains here.

Casa Sea Shell Fort Aguada Rd, near *Bom Successo* ⓣ0832/247 9879 or 277 6131, ⓔseashellgoa@hotmail.com. A newish block with its own pool, picturesquely situated beside a small chapel. The rooms are large, with spacious tiled bathrooms, and the staff and management welcoming and courteous. If they're full ask for a room in the identical and slightly cheaper (but pool-less) *Sea Shell Inn* (ⓣ0832/228 1555) up the road. ❺

Dona Florina Monteiro Rd ⓣ0832/275051 or 227 7398. Large, ten-year-old guesthouse in a superb location, overlooking the beach in the most secluded corner of the village. Well-heeled *sanyasins* from the Rajneesh ashram in Pune have long been its mainstay, hence the higher than usual rates – worth paying if you want idyllic sea views. No car access. ❹

Marbella Sinquerim ⓣ0832/247 9551, ⓔmarbella_goa@yahoo.com. Individually styled suites and spacious rooms (from Rs1550) in a beautiful house built to resemble a traditional Goan mansion. The decor, fittings and furniture are gorgeous, especially in the top-floor "Penthouse" (Rs2500), and the whole place is screened by a giant mango tree. Unashamedly romantic and well worth splashing out on. ❼–❽

Pretty Petal Camotim Waddo ⓣ0832/276184, ⓦwww.prettypetalsgoa.com. Not as twee as it sounds: very large, modern rooms, all with fridges and balconies, and relaxing, marble-floored communal areas overlooking lawns. The top-floor apartment, with windows on four sides and a huge balcony, is the best choice, though more expensive. ❺–❻

Shanu Escrivao Waddo ⓣ0832/227 9606, ⓔshanu_goa@yahoo.com. Good-sized, well-furnished rooms with narrow balconies right on the dunes, some of them with uninterrupted views of the sea (a real rarity). Ask the hospitable owners, Shanu and Peter Mascarenhas, for #120 (or failing that #118, #111, #110 or #107). Breakfast served in your room. ❹–❺

Sonesta Inn Escrivao Waddo ⓣ0832/222 7688, ⓦwww.sonestainns.com. Smart package hotel, a 2-min walk from the sea, ranged around a large central pool. Most of the comforts of a 4-star, but on a smaller scale. ❽

Tidal Wave Vaddy Candolim, just down the lane from *Casa Sea Shell* ⓣ0832/227 6884, ⓔnewmanwarren@rediffmail.com. Lovely sea-facing rooms in a recent construction right behind the beach. Those in the newest block are more spacious and have kitchenettes for long lets. ❹

Eating and drinking

Candolim's numerous beach **cafés** are a cut above your average seafood shacks, with pot plants, posh sound systems and prices to match. The further from the *Taj* complex you venture, the more realistic the prices become.

Amigo's 3km east of Candolim at Nerul bridge ⓣ0832/240 1123, or 98221/04920 (mobile). Well off the beaten track, this rough-and-ready riverside shack, tucked away under the bridge Matt Damon sped off in *The Bourne Supremacy*, is famous locally for its superb fresh seafood, served straight off the boats. *Tamoso* (red snapper) is their speciality, but they also do stuffed pomfret, calamari chilli-fry, red snapper and, best of all, Jurassic-sized crabs in butter-garlic sauce (to order the day before). Count on Rs250 for the works, with drinks.

Casa Sea Shell *Casa Sea Shell* hotel. This is the place to head for top-notch tandoori (from a pukka charcoal-fired oven) and north Indian dishes, although they also offer a good choice of Chinese and European food, served on a hotel patio next to an illuminated fountain. Excellent service and moderate prices. Don't miss the to-die-for Irish coffee.

Cinnabar Acron Arcade, south Candolim. Hip new café, with Italian-style glass- and wood-panelled interior, stone vases and Indian curios, serving what we reckon is Goa's best cappuccino. Occasional

DJs add to the ambience. Opens at 8am for cooked breakfasts.

Cuckoo Zen Garden 1.5km north of Candolim. Authentic Taiwanese and Japanese evening meals, including melt-in-the-mouth (and scrupulously hygienic) sushi, miso and tofu, made with imported ingredients and served on Oriental porcelain against a backdrop of low light and chilled music. Go for a seat on the rooftop. It's difficult to find: turn down the lane just south of *Bob's Inn* (towards the sea), and then first right, and first left after that. Most mains Rs150–200. Closed Sat.

Oriental next to *Surfside Holiday Home*, Murrod Waddo. Sumptous Thai cuisine prepared by Master Chef Chawee, who turns out eighteen house sauces to accompany choice cuts of seafood, meat and poultry, as well as plenty of vegetarian options. Be sure to try their signature starter, *soom tham* (papaya salad). At around Rs500–600 for three courses, it's superb value for cooking of this standard.

Sea Shell at the *Sea Shell Inn*, Fort Aguada Rd. A congenial terrace restaurant in front of an old, double-fronted colonial-era *palacio* decked with green fairy lights. Sizzlers, spaghetti bolognaise and beef steaks are their specialities, but they do a range of seafood and Indian dishes, as well as delicious cocktails. Not at all as pricey as it looks, either (with most mains Rs175–300). Wine by the bottle or glass.

Stone House Fort Aguada Rd. Lively, low-lit bar-restaurant, spread in front of a gorgeous bare-laterite Goan house. Prime cuts of beef and kingfish, served with scrumptious baked potatoes, are their most popular dishes. It's run by a blues aficionado; enthusiasts will want to come just for the CD collection. Most mains under Rs200.

Viva Goa! Fort Aguada Rd. Succulent, no-nonsense Goan food fresh from the market – mussel fry, barramundi (*chonok*), lemon fish (*modso*) and sharkfish steaks fried *rechead* style in chilli paste or in millet (*rawa*) – served on a roadside terrace. Tourists are welcome, but it's essentially a locals' place – with local prices.

Calangute

In the 1970s and early 1980s, Indian visitors flocked by the busload to **CALANGUTE**, a 45-minute ride up the coast from Panjim, in order to giggle at the tribes of dreadlocked Westerners lying naked on the vast white sands. All but a handful of die-hard hippies moved off long ago, but this remains the state's busiest resort, and continues to attract streams of Indian tourists from out of state – which ensures large, noisy bus parties of paddlers on the beach (especially at weekends) and relentlessly heavy traffic during the day. As a consequence, the main drag through the village has become a shambles of hastily erected shops and market stalls, clogged with itinerant vendors, day labourers and stray animals – much to the amazement of the few package tourists who book holidays here after seeing brochure pictures of the beach (out of season).

Each year, as another crop of construction sites blossoms into resort complexes, what little charm Calangute has retained gets steadily more submerged under ferroconcrete. Its all too evident pollution problems are compounded by an absence of adequate provision for waste disposal and sewage treatment, and ever-increasing water-consumption levels. One worrying sign that the village has already started to stew in its own juices has been a dramatic rise in **malaria** cases: virex, and the more serious falciparum strain, are now both endemic here, and rife during the early part of the season.

In short, this isn't somewhere to consider for a lengthy stay, even though it does hold several outstandingly good value guesthouses. If you're staying somewhere else, the only reasons to endure the chaos are to shop for essentials in the well-stocked market, change money, and to eat: Calangute boasts some of the best **restaurants** in the whole state.

Practicalities

Buses from Mapusa and Panjim pull in at the small bus stand-cum-market square in the centre of Calangute. Some continue to Baga, stopping at the crossroads behind the beach en route.

The best place to **change money** and travellers' cheques is Wall Street Finances (Mon–Sat 8.30am–7pm, Sun 10am–2pm), opposite the petrol pump. For Visa encashments, go to the Bank of Baroda (Mon–Fri 9.30am–2.30pm, Sat 9.30am–noon, Sun 9.30am–2pm), just north of the temple and market area; a commission fee of Rs100, plus one percent of the amount changed, is levied on all Visa withdrawals. The ICICI Bank, on the main street, is one of several banks in the market with a 24-hour **ATM** (all the usual cards accepted). There are innumerable cafés scattered around town offering broadband **Internet** access, notably Sify-I-Way, marked on our map.

One of Goa's best **book shops**, The Oxford Bookstore, stands on the south side of town, directly opposite St Anthony's Chapel on the main Candolim road.

Accommodation

In spite of the encroaching mayhem, plenty of budget travellers return to Calangute year after year, staying in little family guesthouses in the fishing *waddo* where the pace of life remains remarkably unchanged.

Arabian Retreat Gauro Waddo ⓣ0832/227 9053, ⓦwww.arabianretreat.com. Swathed in greenery and shaded by areca palms, this new block has large rooms with balconies on both sides (those on the first floor are best), and some have a/c. Much loved by frequent returners are Simba the cat and Foxy the dog. Only Rs700 per double, but rising to Rs1200 from December to mid-January. ④

Camizala 5-33B Maddo Waddo ⓣ0832/227 9530 or mobile 98229/86544. Lovely, breezy little place with only four rooms, common verandas and sea views. About as close to the beach as you can get, and the *waddo* is very quiet. Cheap considering the location. ②–③

CoCo Banana 1195 Umta Waddo ⓣ0832/227 6478 or 227 9068, ⓦwww.cocobanana.com. Very comfortable, spacious chalets, all with bathrooms, fridges, mosquito nets, extra-long mattresses and verandas, around a central garden – but no a/c. Down the lane past *Meena Lobo's* restaurant, it's run by a very sorted Swiss-Goan couple, Walter and Marina Lobo, who have been here for nearly 20 years. Rates double at Christmas. ⑤

Gabriel's Gauro Waddo ⓣ0832/227 9486, ⓔfele@rediffmail.com. A congenial, quiet guesthouse midway between Calangute and Candolim, run by a gorgeous family who go out of their way to help guests. Shady garden, pleasant views from the rear side across the *toddi* dunes, a top little restaurant and very close to the beach. ③

Golden Eye Gauro Waddo ⓣ0832/227 7308, ⓦwww.hotelgoldeneye.com. Situated on the sand; no pool, but the rooms are attractively done out and some have sea views from their balconies. ⑥–⑦

Indian Kitchen behind Our Lady of Piety Church ⓣ0832/227 7555, ⓔikitchen@satyam.net.in. Jazzily decorated guesthouse with crazy mosaic tiling, brightly patterned walls and lanterns. The rooms, all en-suite, have fridges and music systems. ③–④

Kerkar Retreat Gauro Waddo ⓣ0832/227 6017, ⓦwww.subodhkerkar.com. Colour-themed "boutique hotel", artfully decorated with original paintings (by local artist and owner, Subodh Kerkar), Goan *azulejos* and designer furniture creating an effect that's modern, but definably Goan. The only downside is the roadside location. ⑦

Pousada Tauma Porba Waddo ⓣ0832/227 9061, ⓦwww.pousada-tauma.com. Small-scale luxury resort complex, comprising double-storey laterite villas ranged around a pool, near the middle of Calangute, but screened from the din by lots of vegetation. Understated decor and repro-antique furnishings, and a very exclusive atmosphere, preserved by five-star prices. Their big draw is a first-rate Keralan Ayurvedic health centre (open to non-residents). From $200 per night. ⑨

Eating and drinking

Ever since *Souza Lobo* opened on the beachfront to cater for Goan day-trippers in the 1930s, Calangute has been somewhere people come as much to eat as for a stroll on the beach, and even if you stay in resorts elsewhere you'll doubtless be tempted down here for a meal.

After Eight Gauro Waddo. Midway between Calangute and Candolim, down a lane leading west off the main road, between the Lifeline Pharmacy and a small chapel, this is a superb gourmet restaurant in a quiet garden, run by two ex-*Taj* (Mumbai) whizz kids. Steaks are their most popular dish, but seafood is equally sublime, served with original, delicate sauces blending Bengali and Italian influences (try the *rahu*, a local river fish, in balsamic vinegar and mustard); there's baby-corn milles feuilles for veggies, and they do a memorable chocolate mousse. Main courses Rs175–225.

A Reverie Gauro Waddo ⓣ0832/228 2597. Set up by the co-founders of *After Eight*, with even more romantic and extravagant menu and decor, but within reach of most budgets (around Rs500 per head, plus drinks – a steal given the quality of the food). The dishes are all original, with eclectic influences, and beautifully presented: try the cappuccino of mushrooms with marjoram and fresh parsley sauce, or chicken breast stuffed with pistachio mousseline.

Florentine's 4km inland from Calangute church at Saligao, opposite Ayurvedic Natural Health Centre. Well worth the trip inland to taste Florence D'Costa's legendary chicken *cafreal*, made to a jealously guarded family recipe that pulls in crowds of locals and tourists from across north Goa. The restaurant's a down-to-earth Goan-style place, with prices to match, serving only chicken, some seafood and vegetarian snacks.

Gabriel's *Gabriel's* guesthouse, Guara Waddo. Authentic Goan cooking (pork *sorpotel*, chicken *xacuti*, stuffed squid and prawn masala), and very popular Italian dishes (with homemade pasta) served on a cosy roof terrace well away from the main road. A tiny bit pricier than average for a budget place (most mains around Rs100) but worth it, and the espresso coffee is excellent.

Infantaria Pastelaria Baga Rd, next to St John's Chapel. Roadside terrace café run by *Souza Lobo's* that gets packed out for its stodgy croissants, freshly baked apple pie and traditional Goan sweets (such as *dodol* and house-made *bebinca*). Top of the savoury list, though, are the prawn and veg patties, which locals buy by the boxload.

Plantain Leaf near Vanessa cinema, Calangute market. The best *udipi* restaurant outside Panjim, serving the usual range of delicious *dosas* and other spicy snacks in a clean, cool, marble-lined canteen, with relentless background *filmi* music. Try their tasty *iddli*-fry – South India's answer to chips – or the filling thalis (Rs50).

Souza Lobo Beachfront. A Calangute institution, even though the food – served on gingham tablecloths by legions of fast-moving waiters in matching Madras-checked shirts – isn't always what it used to be. Stuffed crab, whole baby kingfish and crêpe Souza are the house specialities. Main dishes Rs100–150.

Nightlife

Calangute's **nightlife** is surprisingly tame for a resort of its size. All but a handful of the bars wind up by midnight, leaving punters to prolong the short evenings back at their hotels, find a shack that's open late, or else head up to Baga (see below).

Down on the south edge of Calangute in Gauro Waddo, the **Kerkar Art Gallery** (ⓣ0832/227 6017, ⓦwww.subodhkerkar.com) hosts evenings of **classical music and dance** (Tues 6.45pm; Rs300), held in the back garden on a sumptuously decorated stage, complete with incense and evocative candlelight. The recitals, performed by students and teachers from Panjim's Kala Academy, are kept comfortably short for the benefit of Western visitors, and are preceded by a short introductory talk. You can also attend performances of authentic Keralan **Kathakali** at a small venue next to the roundabout on the beach road (see map opposite); make up starts at 6pm, and the performance lasts from 7–8pm. Both their explanations of this arcane form of ritual theatre, and the dancing, get positive reviews from readers.

Baga

BAGA, 10km west of Mapusa, is basically an extension of Calangute; not even the locals agree where one ends and the other begins. Lying in the lee of a rocky, wooded headland, the only difference between this far northern end of the beach and its more congested centre is that the scenery here is marginally more varied and picturesque. A small creek flows into the sea at the top of the village below a broad spur of soft white sand, from the opposite bank of which a stoney path winds around the promontory towards Anjuna.

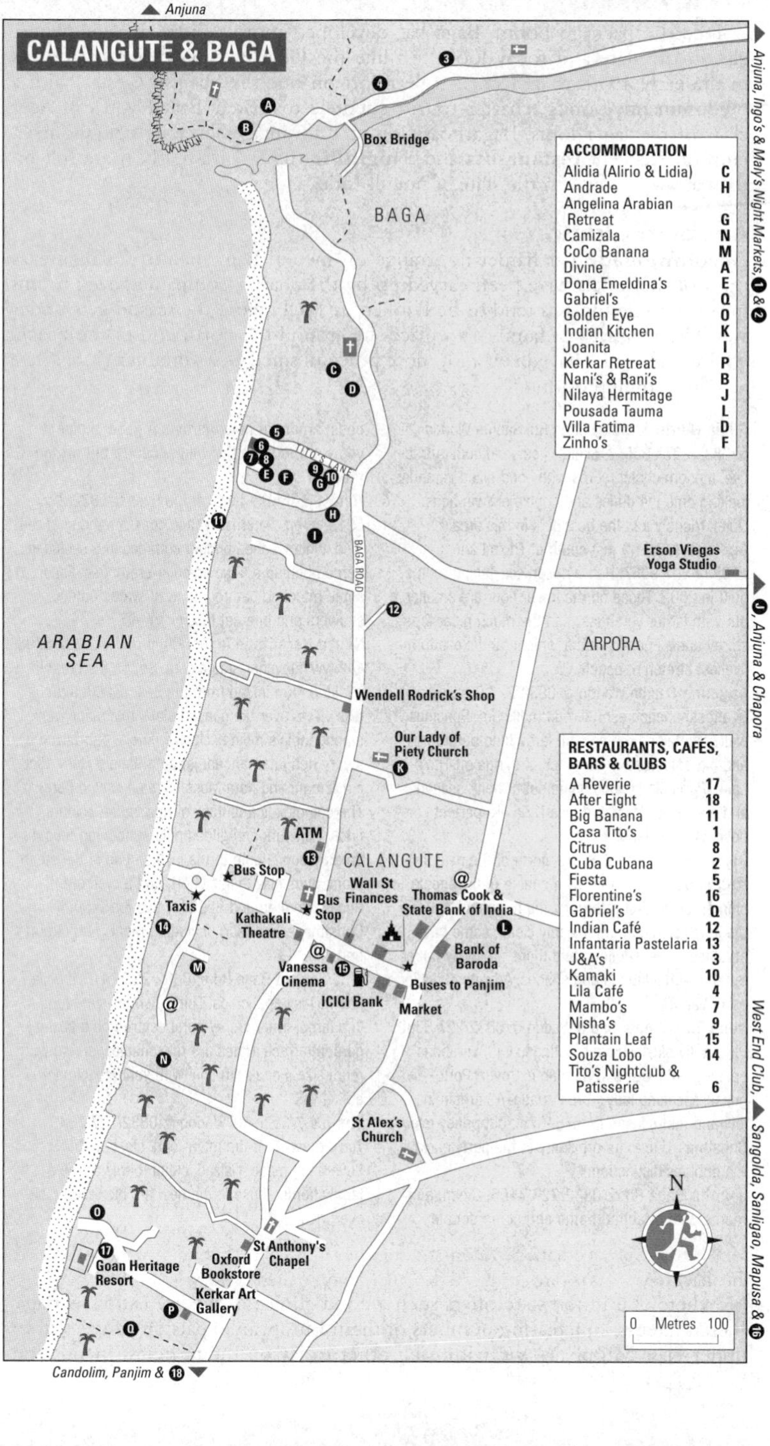

CALANGUTE & BAGA

ACCOMMODATION

Alidia (Alirio & Lidia)	C
Andrade	H
Angelina Arabian Retreat	G
Camizala	N
CoCo Banana	M
Divine	A
Dona Emeldina's	E
Gabriel's	Q
Golden Eye	O
Indian Kitchen	K
Joanita	I
Kerkar Retreat	P
Nani's & Rani's	B
Nilaya Hermitage	J
Pousada Tauma	L
Villa Fatima	D
Zinho's	F

RESTAURANTS, CAFÉS, BARS & CLUBS

A Reverie	17
After Eight	18
Big Banana	11
Casa Tito's	1
Citrus	8
Cuba Cubana	2
Fiesta	5
Florentine's	16
Gabriel's	Q
Indian Café	12
Infantaria Pastelaria	13
J&A's	3
Kamaki	10
Lila Café	4
Mambo's	7
Nisha's	9
Plantain Leaf	15
Souza Lobo	14
Tito's Nightclub & Patisserie	6

Anjuna
Anjuna, Ingo's & Maly's Night Markets, 1 & 2
Box Bridge
BAGA
Tito's Lane
Baga Road
Erson Viegas Yoga Studio
J, Anjuna & Chapora
ARABIAN SEA
ARPORA
Wendell Rodrick's Shop
Our Lady of Piety Church
ATM
CALANGUTE
Bus Stop
Wall St Finances
Thomas Cook & State Bank of India
Taxis
Bus Stop
Kathakali Theatre
Bank of Baroda
Vanessa Cinema
Buses to Panjim
ICICI Bank
Market
West End Club, Sangolda, Sanligao, Mapusa & 16
St Alex's Church
St Anthony's Chapel
Oxford Bookstore
Goan Heritage Resort
Kerkar Art Gallery
N
0 Metres 100
Candolim, Panjim & 18

Since the package boom, Baga has developed more rapidly than anywhere else in the state and today looks less like the Goan fishing village it still was in the early 1990s than a small-scale resort on one the Spanish Costas, with a predominantly young, charter-tourist clientele to match. But if you can steer clear of the lager louts, Baga boasts distinct advantages over its neighbours: a crop of excellent **restaurants** and a **nightlife** that's consistently more full-on than anywhere else in the state, if not all India.

Accommodation

Accommodation is harder to arrange on spec in Baga than in Calangute, as most of the hotels have been carved up by the charter companies; even rooms in smaller guesthouses tend to be booked up well before the season gets under way. The majority of family-run places lie around the north end of the beach, where nighttimes have been a lot more peaceful since Goa's premier club, *Tito's*, acquired soundproofing.

Alidia (Alirio & Lidia) Baga Rd, Saunta Waddo ⓣ0832/227 6835, ⓔalidia@goaworld.com. Attractive, modern chalet rooms with good-sized verandas looking onto the dunes and double or twin beds. Quiet, friendly and the best deal in this area. ❹

Andrade ("Rita") just south of Tito's Lane ⓣ0832/227 9087. Half a dozen sea-facing rooms, built in 2002. Those on the lower floor are smaller, but with larger verandas than the much nicer top-storey ones. Friendly management, and close to the liveliest stretch of beach. ❸

Angelina Saunta Waddo ⓣ0832/227 9145, ⓔangelinabeachresort@rediffmail.com. Spacious, well-maintained rooms with large tiled bathrooms and big balconies, in the thick of things off Tito's Lane. Particularly good value out of peak season, and owners Stanley and Lisa D'Sa are perfect hosts. A/c available. ❸

Divine near *Nani's & Rani's*, north of the river ⓣ0832/227 9546. Run by a couple of hospitable, animal-loving Gulf returners, the rooms are on the small side, but impeccably clean; some have attached shower-toilets; and there's a lovely upper terrace with sunbeds and shades. Advance booking essential. ❸

Dona Emeldina's Sauto Waddo ⓣ0832/227 6880. Pleasantly old-fashioned cottages with verandas opening onto lawns, run by an extrovert Portuguese-speaking lady from Canada. A bargain in low and mid-season (Rs575–675), but pricey over Christmas, due to its proximity to the party enclave – a dubious distinction. ❺

Joanita Baga Rd ⓣ0832/227 7166. Clean, airy rooms with attached baths and some double beds, around a quiet garden. A good choice if you want to be in the village centre but off the road. ❷–❸

Nani's & Rani's north of the river ⓣ0832/227 6313, ⓔgizellaferns@yahoo.com. A handful of red-tiled, whitewashed budget cottages in a secluded garden behind a huge colonial-era house. Fans, some attached bathrooms, well-water, outdoor showers and Internet facility. ❸–❹

Nilaya Hermitage Arpora Bhati ⓣ0832/227 6793, ⓦwww.nilayahermitage.com. Set on the crest of a hilltop 6km inland from the beach, with matchless views over the coastal plain, this place ranks among India's most exclusive hotels, patronized by a very rich international jet set (Richard Gere, Giorgio Armani and Kate Moss have all stayed here). The complex is a fantasy of rich Indian colours, fiddly ironwork and gilded pillars, opening onto a dreamy pool. Room tariffs include use of the steam room, gym, clay tennis court, and a restaurant. Rooms from around $295 for two (or $450 over Christmas–New Year), including meals and airport transfers. ❾

Villa Fatima Baga Rd ⓣ0832/227 7418, ⓔvilla.fatima@sympatico.ca. Thirty-two en-suite rooms in a large, three-storey hotel centred on a sociable garden terrace. Rates are reasonable, varying with room size. Popular mainly with young backpackers. ❷–❸

Zinho's 7/3 Saunta Waddo ⓣ0832/227 7383. Tucked away off the main road, close to *Tito's*. Seventeen modest-sized, clean rooms above a family home; those in the new a/c block are a bit overpriced. ❺–❻

Eating

Nowhere else in the state offers such a good choice of quality eating as Baga. Restaurateurs – increasing numbers of them European expats or refugees from upper-class Mumbai – vie with each other to lay on the trendiest menus and most romantic, stylish gardens or terraces. It's all a very far cry indeed from the rough-and-ready beach-shack culture that held sway only seven or eight years ago.

Big Banana on the beach, at the end of CSM Lane. We tend not to recommend shacks, but this one deserves a mention for its superb steaks: try the house speciality, Chateaubriand, which is enough for two. They also do the usual range of local seafood specialities.

Citrus Tito's Lane. The first pure-vegetarian fine-dining restaurant in Goa. Starters include delicious cashew rissoles with satay sauce; creamed pumpkin croquettes and roquefort brik are pick of the mains (from Rs175). Real Italian coffee is also available.

Fiesta Tito's Lane ⓣ0832/227 9894. Baga's most extravagantly decorated restaurant enjoys a perfect spot at the top of a long dune, with sea views extending from the veranda of a 1930s house. The Mediterranean–Portuguese menu is delectable – try their buffalo mozzarella salad or smoked aubergine paté for starters, followed by paella, moussaka or the wonderful house pizzas. Most mains around Rs200–250.

Indian Café Baga Rd. Traditional home-cooked South Indian snacks – *dosas*, *iddlis* and *vadas*, with fiery *sambar*, green chutney and delicious fresh fruit lassis – dished up on the veranda of an old Goan house. A lot more relaxing than the *Plantain Leaf* in Calangute, and much cheaper.

J&A's Anjuna Rd ⓣ0832/227 5274, ⓦwww.littleitalygoa.com. Mouthwatering, authentic Italian food (down to the imported Parmesan, sun-dried tomatoes and olive oil) served in the gorgeous candlelit garden of an old fisherman's cottage. There's an innovative range of salads and antipasti (the carpaccio of beef is sublime), a choice of sumptuous pasta dishes, wood-fired pizzas and tender steaks (in port and rosemary sauce) for mains, though their signature dish, seafood lasagna, is hard to beat. For dessert, go for the melt-in-the-mouth hot chocolate soufflé to round things off. Most mains Rs275–300; count on at least Rs550 per head for three courses, plus drinks.

Lila Café Baga Creek. Laid-back bakery-cum-terrace-café with white and purple decor run by a German couple who've been here for decades. Their healthy homemade breads and cakes are great, and there's an adventurous lunch menu featuring spinach à la crème, aubergine paté and smoked water buffalo ham.

Nisha's Tito's Lane ⓣ0832/227 7588. This little restaurant, occupying a sandy terrace just down from *Tito's*, can't be beaten for simply prepared seafood – snapper, kingfish, tiger prawns and lobster – flame-grilled or tandoori-baked to perfection in front of you. Freshness counts more here than fancy sauces. For starters, try calamari in chilli oil with lemon. Most mains are a reasonable Rs250–300.

Tito's Patisserie Tito's Lane. Relaxed little a/c café that couldn't be further from the headlong atmosphere of *Tito's* by night. Their chilled pastries – including toffee and apple tart, banoffi pie and lemon cheesecake – are delicious, as is the freshly ground espresso and cappuccino; and it's only a skip from the beach.

Nightlife

That Baga's **nightlife** has become legendary in India is largely attributable to one club, *Tito's*. Lured by TV images of sexy dancewear and a thumping sound-and-light system, hundreds of revellers descend on its long narrow terrace each night to drink, shuffle about and watch the action, the majority of them men from other states who've come to Goa as an escape from the moral confines of life at home. For Western women, in particular, this can sometimes make for an uncomfortably loaded atmosphere, although since a recent facelift (and a hike in door charges), *Tito's* seems to have put the era of Kingfisher-fuelled brawls behind it. New theme bars and clubs are also popping up each year, offering increasingly sophisticated alternatives.

For anyone who's been travelling around the rest of the country, Baga by night – complete with drunken karaoke, toga parties and all the garishness of a Saturday in British clubland – can come as an unpleasant shock. So, too, can the traffic congestion on Fridays and Saturdays; if you venture down here by motorbike on the weekend, park well away from Tito's Lane or you might find yourself literally jammed in until the small hours.

Saturday Night Bazaars

One of the few genuinely positive improvements to the north Goa resort strip in recent times has been the **Saturday Night Bazaar**, held on a plot midway between Baga and Anjuna. The brainchild of an expat German, it's run with great efficiency and a sense of fun that's palpably lacking these days at the Anjuna Flea Market. The balmy evening temperatures and pretty lights are also a lot more conducive to relaxed browsing than the broiling heat of mid-afternoon on Anjuna beach; moreover, the laid-back ambience is preserved with a "three-strikes-and-out" ban on hassling customers, which means you can even walk past the normally full-on Lamani women unmolested.

Although far more commercial than its predecessor in Anjuna, many old Goa hands regard this as far truer to the original spirit of the flea market. A significant proportion of the stalls are taken up by foreigners selling their own stuff, from reproduction Indian pop art to antique photos, the latest trance-party designer wear, hand-polished coconut shell art and techno DJ demos. There's also a mouthwatering array of ethnic food to choose from and a stage featuring live music from around 7pm until midnight, when the market winds up. Admission is free.

Somewhat confusingly, a **rival but inferior market** in much the same mould, called **Macy's**, has opened nearby, closer to Baga by the riverside. Spurned by the expatriate designers and stallholders, this one's not a patch on its rival, though, no matter what your taxi driver may tell you.

For more on the area's nightlife, see our accounts of Calangute (p.816) and Anjuna (p.826).

Bars and clubs

Casa Tito's Arpora, opposite Ingo's Night Market. Chic Italian gastro-lounge bar in an old Portuguese-era house, with designer furniture, cocktails and gourmet food. Perfect post-Ingo's chill-out spot.

Cuba Cubana 82 Xim Waddo, Arpora Hill ⓦwww.clubcubana.net. Glam nightclub on a forested hilltop inland from Baga, spread around an underlit open-air pool. Its high entrance charge (Rs500 for men, Rs400 for women) buys you unlimited drinks from a well-stocked bar – a policy intended to keep out the low-spending riff-raff from down on the strip. R&B, hip hop and garage (they purposely stay well away from techno) played on a twin-storey, a/c dance floor. Fri, Sat & Sun 9.30pm–5am.

Kamaki Tito's Lane, Saunta Waddo. Big screen sports and a state-of-the-art karaoke machine account for the appeal of this a/c, Brit-dominated bar just up the lane from *Tito's*. Rs100 cover charge sometimes applies.

Mambo's Tito's Lane, Saunta Waddo. Large, semi-open air bar with wooden decor and a big circular bar that gets packed out most nights in season with a lively, mixed crowd. Once again, karaoke is the big draw, though drinks cost well above average, and they slap on a Rs200 admission charge after 11pm.

Tito's Tito's Lane, Saunta Waddo. Occasional cabarets, fashion shows and guest DJs feature throughout the season at India's most famous nightclub. Red upholstery and uniformed waiters set the tone; music policy is lounge grooves till 11pm, and hip hop, house, salsa and trance thereafter. See the notice board for retro and other theme nights. Admission prices vary for men (from Rs400–450, or Rs300 for couples); no charge for women. At Christmas, prices can soar to Rs800 or more depending on the attraction. Open 8–late Nov–Dec; and until 11pm out of season.

Anjuna

With its fluorescent-painted palm trees and famous full-moon parties, **ANJUNA**, 8km west of Mapusa, is Goa at its most "alternative". Fractal patterns and day-glo lycra may have superseded cotton kaftans, but most people's reasons for coming are the same as they were in the 1970s: drugs, dancing and lying on the beach slurping

Yoga in north Goa

Whether you're a complete beginner, improver or a budding yogi, Goa is the perfect place to brush up on your yoga, as several first-rate teachers set up small schools here in the winter.

Down in **Candolim**, the **Goa Iyengar Yoga School** (☎0832/249 7245, mobile 9326/12373, Ⓦwww.yogamaggieh.com) is run by Maggie Hughes, an Iyengar-certified teacher with twenty-plus years' experience. She works from her first-floor studio, opposite *Sonesta Inn* – heading south, take the turning on the right between Davidair and *Bob's Inn* (there's a sign pointing the way). Drop-in classes start at 8am (or sometimes an hour later), last for ninety minutes, and cost Rs300. Beginners are welcome. Maggie also hosts teacher training courses in January and February, lasting ten or thirty days (for more details see her website).

Another Iyengar-qualified teacher is **Erson Viegas** (☎0832/227 7993), whose studio is a couple of kilometres inland from Calangute at Arpora. Erson charges Rs250–300 per session for individual tuition and slightly less if you attend one of his group classes.

In **Anjuna**, the **Purple Valley Yoga Centre** (☎0832/226 9643, mobile ☎098/2309 9788, Ⓦwww.yogagoa.net) specializes in Ashtanga yoga, as taught in Mysore by Sri K. Pattabhi Jois. They have world-class teachers in residence at their main studio in the garden of *Granpa's Inn* (see p.823), but all levels of ability are catered for. Drop-in classes cost Rs400, or Rs3000 if you book ten in advance, and they also offer two-week retreats in a purpose-built *shala* (yoga studio) in some nearby woods.

Between Aswem and Arambol, look out for signs advertising classes by Iyengar-qualified **Sharat** (Ⓦwww.hiyogacentre.com), a highly respected direct student of BKS Iyengar who holds five-day classes at his centre on the beach (Rs1250). Prospective students usually have to sign up by Tuesday at 2pm; courses start on Fridays. Sharat also hosts month-long intensives, as well as teacher training courses (full details on the website).

tropical fruit. Depending on your point of view, you'll find the hedonism a total turn-off or heaven-on-sea. Either way, the scene looks here to stay, despite government attempts to stamp it out, so you might as well get a taste of it while you're in the area, if only from the wings, with a day-trip to the famous **flea market**.

The season in Anjuna starts in early November, when most of the long-staying regulars show up, and peters out in late March, when they drift off again. Young Israelis – fresh out of the army and full of devil-may-care attitudes to drugs and other people's sleep – are the village's mainstay these days, much to the chagrin of the locals. Outside peak season, however, Anjuna has a surprisingly simple, unhurried atmosphere – due, in no small part, to the shortage of places to stay. Most visitors who come here on market day or for the parties travel in from other resorts.

The **beach** is no great shakes by Goan standards, with a dodgy undertow and even dodgier groups of whiskeyed-up Indian men in constant attendance. North of the market ground, the sand broadens, running in an uninterrupted kilometre-long stretch to a low red cliff. A small, pretty and better sheltered cove at its opposite southern end is where Anjuna's mostly Israeli, frisbee-throwing tourists hang out during the day, techno thumping away from the shacks behind it.

Practicalities

Buses from Mapusa and Panjim drop passengers at various points along the tarmac road across the top of the village, which turns north towards Chapora

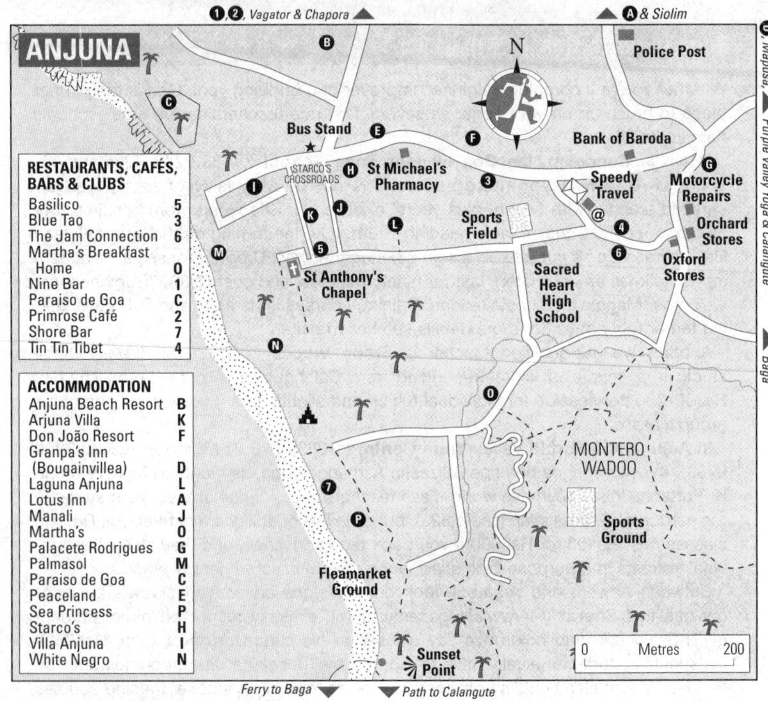

at the main Starco's crossroads. If you're looking for a room, get off here as it's close to most of the guesthouses. The crossroads has a couple of small **stores**, a **motorcycle taxi** rank, and functions as a de facto village square and **bus stand**.

The *Manali* guesthouse (see opposite) and Oxford Stores **change money** (at poor rates). The Bank of Baroda on the Mapusa Road will make encashments against Visa cards, but doesn't do foreign exchange, nor is it a good place to leave valuables, as thieves have previously climbed through an open window and stolen a number of "safe custody" envelopes. The **post office**, on the Mapusa road near the bank, has an efficient poste restante counter. The *Manali* guesthouse also offers broadband **Internet access** (Rs40/hr), as does Space Ride, next to Speedy Travel.

Accommodation

Most of Anjuna's **accommodation** consists of small unfurnished **houses**, although finding one is a problem at the best of times – in peak season it's virtually impossible. By then, all but a handful have been let to long-staying regulars who book by post several months in advance, and budget travellers hoping to find one on spec will probably have to make do with a room in a guesthouse at first. Since the recent construction of a couple of classy designer hotels, higher spending visitors are spoiled for choice.

Anjuna Beach Resort De Mello Waddo ⓣ0832/227 4499, ⓔfabjoe@sancharnet.com. Fifteen spacious, comfortable rooms with balconies, fridges, attached bathrooms and solar hot water in a new concrete building. Those on the upper floor are best. There's also a newly constructed block of

The Anjuna flea market

Anjuna's Wednesday **flea market** is the hub of Goa's alternative scene, and *the* place to indulge in a spot of souvenir shopping. A decade or so ago, the weekly event was the exclusive preserve of backpackers and the area's semi-permanent population, who gathered here to smoke chillums, and to buy and sell clothes and jewellery they probably wouldn't have the nerve to wear anywhere else: something like a small pop festival without the stage. These days, however, everything is more organized and mainstream. Pitches are rented out by the metre, drugs are banned and the approach roads to the village are choked solid all day with a/c buses and Ambassador cars ferrying in tourists from resorts further down the coast.

The range of **goods** on sale has broadened, too, thanks to the high profile of migrant hawkers and stallholders from other parts of India. Each region or culture tends to stick to its own corner. At one end, Westerners congregate around racks of fluorescent party gear and designer beachwear. Nearby, hawk-eyed Kashmiris sit cross-legged beside trays of silver jewellery and papier-mâché boxes, while trendily dressed Tibetans preside over orderly rows of prayer wheels, turquoise bracelets and sundry Himalayan curios. Most distinctive of all are the Lamani women from Karnataka, decked from head to toe in traditional tribal garb, and selling elaborately woven multicoloured cloth, which they fashion into everything from jackets to money belts, and which makes even the Westerners' party gear look positively funereal. Elsewhere, you'll come across dazzling Rajasthani mirrorwork and block-printed bedspreads, Keralan woodcarvings and a scattering of Gujarati appliqué.

What you end up paying for this exotic merchandise largely depends on your ability to **haggle**. Lately, prices have inflated as tourists not used to dealing in rupees will part with almost anything. Be persistent, though, and cautious, and you can usually pick things up for a reasonable rate. Even if you're not spending, the flea market is a great place to sit and watch the world go by. Mingling with the sun-tanned masses are bands of strolling musicians, religious mendicants, performing monkeys, snake-charmers and holy cows.

apartments for long stayers (4). Both options are very good value. 3

Anjuna Villa House #681/1 D'Mello Waddo, 4th Lane ⓣ0832/227 4590 or 227 4591, ⓔdogfreymathia@hotmail.com. Basic but pleasant budget rooms with tiled floors and high ceilings, opening on to a deep common veranda (again, those on the upper storey are much nicer). Floodlit badminton a speciality. 4

Don João Resort Soronto Waddo ⓣ0832/227 4325 or 222 2147, ⓦwww.travelingoa.com/donjoaoresorts. Large former charter hotel, slap in the middle of the village, with a pool. A bit shabby around the edges, but comfortable enough and very good value in this bracket. 4–5

Granpa's Inn Gaunwadi ⓣ0832/227 3270, ⓦwww.goacom.com/hotels/granpas. Formerly known as *Bougainvillea*, a lovely 200-year-old house set in half an acre of lush gardens, with a pool and shady breakfast terrace. The en-suite rooms are large and have high ceilings; the suites are even nicer. Ashtanga yoga on site; and there's a billiards table. Very popular, so book well ahead. 5–6

Laguna Anjuna De Mello Waddo ⓣ0832/227 4305, ⓦwww.lagunaanjuna.com. Alternative "boutique resort", comprising 25 colourfully decorated, domed laterite cottages with wooden rafters and terracotta tiles, grouped behind a convoluted pool. Restaurant, pool tables and bar. Doubles from $125 mid-season, rising to $225 for Christmas–New Year. 9

Lotus Inn Zor Waddo ⓣ0832/227 4015, ⓦwww.lotusinngoa.com. On the leafy northern limits of Anjuna, tucked away down a maze of narrow lanes: eleven swish suites (9) and six double rooms (on the small side for the Rs1500 tariff), all with a/c and centred around a good-sized pool (Rs100 for non-residents). There's also a trendy Italian poolside restaurant, and parties hosted on Sundays. 7

Manali south of Starco's Crossroads ⓣ0832/227 4421, ⓔmanali@goatelecom.com. Anjuna's best all-round budget guesthouse has simple rooms (shared toilets) opening onto a yard, fans, safe deposit, money-changing, library, Internet connection, and sociable terrace-restaurant. Good value, so book in advance. 2

Martha's 907 Montero Waddo ⓣ0832/227 4194, ⓔmpd8650@hotmail.com. Eight immaculate en-suite rooms run by a friendly family. Basic amenities include kitchen space, fans and running solar-heated water. Two pleasant houses also available. ④

Palacete Rodrigues near Oxford Stores, Mazal Waddo ⓣ0832/227 3358, ⓦwww.palaceterodrigues.com. Two-hundred-year-old residence converted into an upmarket guesthouse, with carved wood furniture and a relaxed, traditional-Goan feel. Single occupancy available. The three economy options in a separate block around the back are good value. ④–⑤

Palmasol Guest House Praia de St Anthony ⓣ0832/227 3258. Huge, comfortable rooms in an immaculately kept old house very near the beach. The larger ones have running water, verandas, cooking space and a relaxing garden; cheaper alternatives are in the back yard. ③

Peaceland Soronto Waddo ⓣ0832/227 3700. Simple en-suite rooms in two blocks, run by a charming local couple with the help of a pair of friendly dogs. All have high-clay-tiled roofs, mosquito nets, rucksack racks, hammocks, clothes hangers and other nice homely touches that make this easily the best value place in its class. ③

Sea Princess House #649 Goenkar Waddo, Dando ⓣ0832/227 4499, ⓔfabjoe@sancharnet.com. Newish guesthouse in a prime position in the middle of the beach, near the *Shore Bar*. The rooms are spacious and well maintained, and all have bathrooms with dependable plumbing. Hard to beat in terms of location and value for money in this mid-range bracket. ③–④

Starco's Starco's Crossroads. No phone. Some of the cheapest rooms in Anjuna: very basic, but well maintained, clean and screened from the racket outside. Excellent value if you're happy with bare-bones amenities. ②

Villa Anjuna near Anjuna beachfront ⓣ0832/227 3443, ⓦwww.anjunavilla.com. Modern, efficient resort hotel close to the beach-front area, on the main road through the village. Amenities include a good-sized pool and Jacuzzi. Popular with party lovers who can't afford *Laguna* as it's a short stagger from *Paradiso* (so noisy at night). ⑦

White Negro 719 Praia de St Anthony, south of the village ⓣ0832/227 3326, ⓔmjanets@goatelecom.com. A row of twelve spotless back-to-back chalets catching the sea breeze, all with attached bathrooms, tiled floors, safe lockers and mosquito nets. Quiet, efficient and good value. ⑤

Eating and drinking

Anjuna's beach shacks tend to be overpriced by comparison with those elsewhere in the state (especially on flea market days, when they hike their prices) but many will feel the location is worth paying for. Responding to the tastes of its many "alternative" visitors, the village also boasts a crop of quality wholefood **cafés** serving healthy veg dishes and juices. If you're hankering for a taste of home, call in at the **Orchard Stores** on the eastern side of the village, which, along with its rival **Oxford Stores**, directly opposite, serves the expatriate community with pricey imported delights such as digestive biscuits, Marmite and extra-virgin olive oil. They also offer delicious coffee and fresh croissants.

Basilico D'Mello Waddo ⓣ0832/227 3721. Cool, Italian-run garden restaurant, hidden away down one of the village's quieter lanes. The pizzas and pasta dishes are authentic, the service efficient and the atmosphere relaxed. Most mains around Rs150–175.

Blue Tao on the main road through the village. Another Italian-run place, this time an "alternative health restaurant" that offers some of Goa's most delicious breakfasts (sour-dough and wholemeal breads, herbal teas, tahini and spirulina spreads). In addition to a full menu of main courses (Rs100–150), they also do an excellent range of juices, including wheatgrass, ginseng and ayurvedic concoctions. Non-smoking and child-friendly.

The Jam Connection near Oxford Stores, opposite *Tin Tin Tibet*. Fresh, interesting salads (with real organic rocket and garden herbs), mocha and espresso coffee, homemade ice cream and all-day breakfasts, served in a lovely garden. You can lounge on bamboo easy chairs or on tree platforms. Daily except Wed 11am–7pm.

Martha's Breakfast Home *Martha's* guesthouse, 907 Montero Waddo. Secluded, very friendly breakfast garden serving fresh Indian coffee, crepes and delicious waffles.

Tin Tin Tibet near Oxford Stores. Well-established budget café, serving the usual budget-travellers' grub, plus Tibetan specialities (*momos* and *thukpa*), and some Israeli dishes. Worth a try if only for the fried banana with cashew nuts.

The dark side of the moon

Hedonism has figured prominently in European images of Goa from the mid-sixteenth century, when mariners and merchants returned to Lisbon with tales of unbridled debauchery among the colonists. The French traveller François Pyrard was first to chronicle this as moral decline, in a journal peppered with accounts of wild parties and sleaze scandals.

Following the rigours of the Inquisition, a semblance of morality was restored, which prevailed through the Portuguese era. But traditional Catholic life in Goa's coastal villages sustained a rude shock in the 1960s with the first influx of **hippies** to Calangute and Baga beaches. Much to the amazement of the locals, the preferred pastime of these would-be *sadhus* was to cavort naked on the sands together on full-moon nights, amid a haze of *chillum* smoke and loud rock music blaring from makeshift PAs. The villagers took little notice of these bizarre gatherings at first, but with each season the scene became better established, and by the late 1970s the **Christmas and New Year** parties, in particular, had become huge events, attracting thousands of foreign travellers.

In the late 1980s, the local party scene received a dramatic facelift with the coming of acid house and techno. Ecstasy became the preferred dance drug as the dub-reggae scene gave way to rave culture, with ever greater numbers of young clubbers pouring in for the season on charter flights. Goa soon spawned its own distinctive brand of psychedelic music, known as **Goa Trance**. Distinguished by its multilayered synth lines and sub-bass rhythms, the hypnotic style combines the darkness of hard techno with an ambient sentiment. Cultivated by artists such as Goa Gill, Juno Reactor and Hallucinogen, the new sound was given wider exposure when big-name DJs Danny Rampling and Paul Oakenfold started mixing Goa Trance in clubs and on national radio back in the UK, generating a huge following among music lovers who previously knew nothing of the place which had inspired it.

The **golden era** for Goa's party scene, and trance, was in the early 1990s, when big raves were held two or three times a week in beautiful locations around Anjuna and Vagator. UV and flouro gear appeared and for a few years no-one bothered about the growing scene. Then, quite suddenly, the plug was pulled by the local authorities. For years, drug busts and bribes had provided the notoriously corrupt Goan cops with a lucrative source of baksheesh. But after a couple of drug-related deaths, a series of sensational articles in the local press and a decision by Goa Tourism to promote upmarket over backpacker tourism, the police began to demand impossibly large bribes – sums that the organizers (many of them drug dealers) could not hope to recoup. Although the big New Year and Christmas events continued unabated, smaller parties, hitherto held in off-track venues such as "Disco Valley" behind Middle Vagator beach, started to peter out, much to the dismay of local people, many of whom had become financially dependent on the raves and the punters they pulled in to the villages.

Against this backdrop, news of the Y2K **amplified-music ban** between 10pm and 7am seemed to sound the death knell for Goa's party scene. Reports in the international media that India's rave-era was at an end were, however, premature. Five years on, the scene survives, albeit in a more mainstream style, with a batch of large new clubs – notably the **Nine Bar** and **Paradiso** (see p.826 & p.827) – providing permanent venues and big sound systems for the first time in Goa.

All the same, if you've come here expecting an Indian equivalent of Ko Pha Ngan or Ibiza-on-the-Arabian-Sea, you'll be sorely disappointed. Only over Christmas and New Year do really big parties take place, and these are a far cry from the free-and-easy events that once filled the beaches and bamboo groves of Anjuna on full-moon nights.

Nightlife

Anjuna's **nightlife** scene has calmed down considerably over the past few years (see box on p.825), but there are now a couple of pay-to-enter clubs have that, unlike illegal free parties, are above board and thus less prone to being shut down by the police. First stop for confirmed techno heads should be the **Paraiso de Goa**, aka **Paradiso**, at the far north end of Anjuna beach. Partly owned by the government, it epitomizes the new, more above-board face of Goa Trance. Presiding over a dance space surrounded by spacey statues of Hindu gods and Tantric symbols, visiting DJs spin textbook tunes for a mainly Israeli crowd.

It's all a bit commercial, but even the now-legendary Goa Gill, one of the leading free-party hosts of the 1980s and 1990s, has given the club his seal of approval by playing here. *Paradiso* keeps to a sporadic timetable, but should be open most nights from around 10pm; admission charges are Rs300–500, depending on the night. Along similar lines, but with free admission, is the **Nine Bar**, above Vagator beach, and the nearby **Primrose Café** (see p.828).

Down on the beach proper, the **Shore Bar** used to be *the* place to hang out after the flea market, attracting hundreds of people for sunset, but it has fallen out of favour over the past couple of years and now lacks the atmosphere of the Nine Bar.

Vagator

Barely a couple of kilometres of clifftops and parched grassland separate Anjuna from the southern fringes of its nearest neighbour, **VAGATOR**. Spread around a tangle of leafy lanes, this is a more chilled, undeveloped resort that appeals, in the main, to Israeli and northern European trance-heads, who hole up for the full season in ramshackle old Portuguese bungalows or cheap guesthouses.

With the red ramparts of Chapora fort looming above it, Vagator's broad sandy **beach** – known as **Big Vagator** – is undeniably beautiful. However, a peaceful swim or lie on the sand is out of the question here as it's a prime stop for bus parties of domestic tourists, which ensures a steady stream of whisky-swilling Maharashtran men. Far better, then, to head to the next cove south. Backed by a steep wall of crumbling palm-fringed laterite, **Ozran** (or "Little") **Vagator beach** is more secluded and much less accessible than either of its neighbours. To get there, walk ten minutes' south from Big Vagator, or drive to the end of the lane off the main Chapora–Anjuna road, from where a footpath drops sharply down to the wide stretch of level white sand (look for the mopeds and bikes parked at the top of the cliff). The Israeli- and Italian-dominated scene revolves around a string of large, well established shacks behind Little Vagator, at the end of which a face carved out of the rocks – staring serenely skywards – is the most prominent landmark. Relentless racquetball, trance sound systems and a particularly big herd of stray cows are this beach's other defining features.

Practicalities

Buses from Panjim and Mapusa, 9km east, pull in every fifteen minutes or so at the crossroads on the far northeastern edge of Vagator, near where the main road peels away towards Chapora. From here, it's a one-kilometre walk over the hill and down the other side to the beach, where you'll find most of the village's accommodation, restaurants and cafés. The *Primrose Café*, on the south side of the village, has a **foreign exchange** licence (for cash and travellers' cheques) but their rates are less competitive than those on offer at Jackie's Daynite shop on the south side of the village. For **Internet** access, go to *Bethany Inn* (Rs50/hr).

Petrol pumps in north Goa

The main Calangute **petrol pump** was closed down in 2000 when it was found to be bulking out its supply with solvents. As a result, you'll either have to travel up to the one between **Anjuna and Vagator** to refill, or else head into **Mapusa**. There's also a station just north of **Arambol** on the Kerim–Terekol road, but the locals claim it laces its petrol too. As ever, ensure the attendants reset the pumps to zero before serving you – they often don't, in order to overcharge and pocket the extra.

Accommodation

Accommodation in Vagator consists of family-run budget guesthouses, a couple of pricey resort hotels and dozens of small private properties rented out for long periods. **Water** is in very short supply here, and you'll be doing the villagers a favour if you use it frugally at all times.

Bethany Inn Chapora crossroads ⓣ0832/227 3731, ⓔbethany@goatelecom.com. Seven immaculately clean rooms with fridges, balconies and attached bathrooms. Tastefully furnished, and efficiently managed. ❹–❺

Boon's Ark near *Bethany Inn* ⓣ0832/227 4045. Pleasant, clean and efficient place with recently built rooms opening on to small verandas and a well tended little garden. ❹

Dolrina Vagator Beach Rd ⓣ0832/227 4896. Nestled under a lush canopy of trees near the beach, Vagator's largest budget guesthouse is run by a friendly Goan couple and features attached or shared bathrooms, a sociable garden café, individual safe deposits and roof space. Single occupancy rates, and breakfasts available. ❸

Garden Villa Vagator Beach Rd ⓣ0832/227 3571, ⓔgarden@goatelecom.com. Two categories of rooms: the older ones are better value than the ones in the newer block. All are spacious and cool, with tiled floors and large bathrooms, and there's a friendly café showing video movies daily at 7.30pm. ❸

Jolly Jolly Lester Vagator Beach Rd ⓣ0832/227 3620. Eleven pleasant doubles with tiled bathrooms set in a lovingly kept garden and surrounded by woodland. Small restaurant on site; single occupancy is possible. ❸

Jolly Jolly Roma Vagator Beach Rd ⓣ0832/227 3620. Very smart, good-sized chalet rooms with verandas; laundry, exchange facilities and a small library for guests. ❹

Julie Jolly south side of the village ⓣ0832/227 3357. Recently revamped and now one of the most pleasant places in Vagator, set on the edge of a leafy belt and within easy reach of Ozran beach. All rooms tiled and well aired; self-caterers can stay in larger suites with sitting rooms and kitchenettes. ❷–❸

L'Amour north side of village, on hillside above Chapora ⓣ0832/277 4180. Immaculately clean, tiled en-suite rooms in a block tucked away in the woods above Chapora. Quiet, well-run and fantastic value. ❷

Leoney Resort on the road to Disco Valley ⓣ0832/227 3634, ⓦwww.leoneyresortgoa.com. Comfortable option, with swish chalets and pricier (but more spacious) octagonal "cottages" on the sleepy side of village, ranged around a very nice little pool. Restaurant, laundry, lockers and foreign exchange facilities. No advance bookings Dec–Jan. ❼–❽

Eating, drinking and nightlife

Vagator boasts an eclectic batch of **restaurants**, with wildly varying menus and prices, and an equally dramatic turnover of chefs. Western tourists tend to stick to the pricier ones lining the road through the village, while Indian visitors frequent the more impersonal, cheaper places down on the beach itself. For a sundown drink, head to *Nine Bar*, encircled by a fortress-style laterite wall that opens onto a great chill-out terrace and the sea on one side. Big trance sounds attract a fair-sized crowd for sunset, especially on Wednesdays after the flea market; the dancing starts after dark and keeps going until the bar closes around 10pm. At this point, there's a general exodus over to the nearby *Primrose Café*, which offers much the same atmosphere, without the views.

Bean Me Up near the petrol pump. India's one and only American-run tofu joint – the last word in Goan gourmet healthy eating. Main courses (around Rs175–225) come with steamed spinach, fresh brown bread and hygienically washed salads; try their delicious Thai-style *tempeh* in spicy cashew sauce. There's also a tempting range of vegan desserts – the banana pudding with soya whip is a winner.

China Town Chapora Crossroads, next to *Bethany Inn*. This small roadside restaurant, tucked away just south of the main drag, is the village's most popular budget eating place, serving particularly tasty seafood dishes in addition to a large Chinese selection, as well as all the usual Goa-style travellers' grub.

Le Bluebird on the road out to *Nine Bar*. Tucked away in the most appealing corner of the village is Vagator's renowned French-run restaurant, which serves classier-than-average Gallic food – pepper steak in brandy sauce, prawns in coconut, squid in white wine and garlic – at traveller-friendly prices (around Rs300–400 for 3 courses, plus wine). Seafood is their strong point, but they offer a better range of veg dishes than you'd find in a real French restaurant, as well as crepes, Bordeaux claret and champagne (around Rs2000 per bottle).

Nine Bar above Ozran beach. Boasting a crystal trance sound system, this clifftop café enjoys a prime location, with fine sea views from its terrace through the palm canopy, where Nepali waiters serve up cold beer and the usual range of budget travellers' grub to a generally spaced-out clientele.

Primrose Café on the southern edge of the village. Goa's posiest café-bar livens up around 10pm. Tasty German wholefood snacks, light meals and cakes are on offer, as well as drinks.

Tibet O-Live Main Road. Run by a team of friendly young lads from Darjeeling, this place shuttles between Manali in the summer and Goa in the winter, and has earned a strong reputation in both for its ultra-tasty, inexpensive pizzas. There's also top-fried *momos* (the spinach and cheese ones are best).

Chapora

Huddled in the shadow of a Portuguese fort on the opposite, northern side of the headland from Vagator, **CHAPORA**, 10km from Mapusa, is a lot busier than most north coast villages. Dependent on fishing and boat-building, it has, to an extent, retained a life of its own independent of tourism. That said, the recent relaxation of Goa's drug laws combined with the influx of long-staying Russians have made a significant impact here over the past three or four years. Whereas the main street used to retain a workaday indifference to the annual invasion of foreigners, now it's largely given over to Amsterdam-style coffee shops and budget travellers' cafés, with everyone spliffing up in public at sunset time. Even so, it's unlikely Chapora will ever develop into a major resort; tucked away under a dense canopy of trees on the muddy southern shore of a river estuary, it lacks both the space and the white sand that have pulled crowds to Calangute and Colva. The main drawback to staying here, though, is the general grubbiness of the accommodation on offer, which tends to be booked for long periods to a mixture of hard-drinking, heavy-smoking hippies and dodgy-looking Muscovites with tattoos.

Chapora's chief landmark is its venerable old **fort**, most easily reached from the Vagator side of the hill. At low tide, you can also walk around the bottom of the headland, via the anchorage and the secluded coves beyond it to Big Vagator, then head up the hill from there. The red-laterite bastion, crowning the rocky bluff, was built by the Portuguese in 1617 on the site of an earlier Muslim structure (thus the village's name – from *Shahpura*, "town of the Shah"). Deserted in the nineteenth century, it lies in ruins today, although the **views** up and down the coast from the weed-infested ramparts are still superb.

Also worth a visit is the village's busy little **fishing anchorage**, where you can buy delicious calamari fresh off the boats most evenings.

Practicalities

Direct **buses** arrive at Chapora three times daily from Panjim, and every fifteen minutes from Mapusa, with departures until 7pm from various points along the

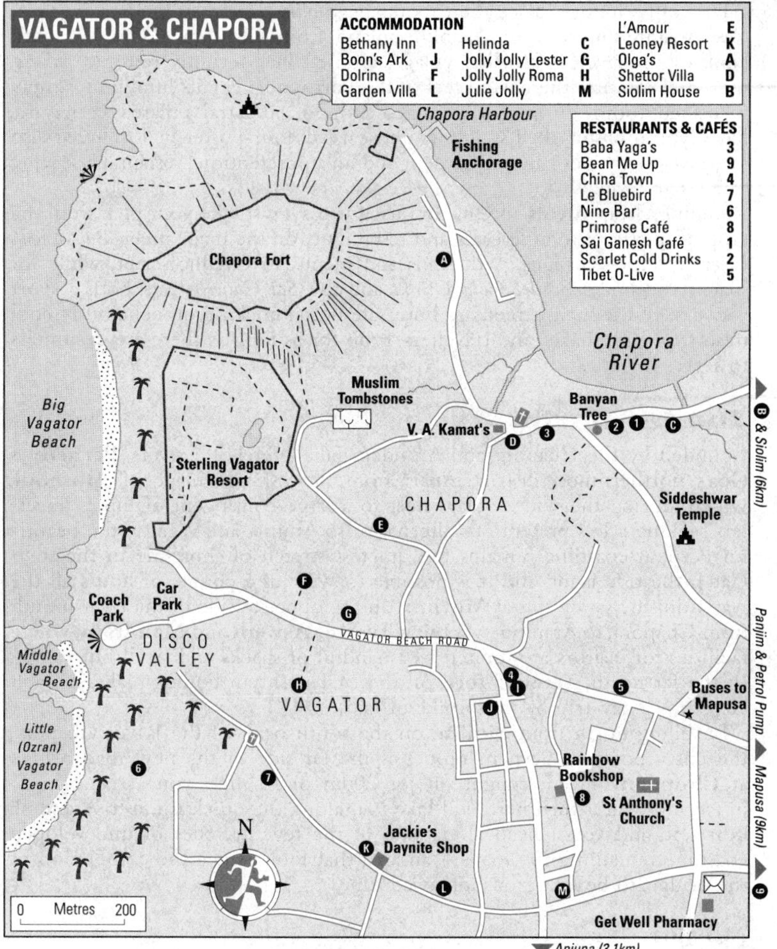

main road. **Motorcycle taxis** hang around the old banyan tree at the far end of the main street, near where the buses pull in. Air, train and bus **tickets** may be booked or reconfirmed at Soniya Tours and Travels, next to the bus stand. For **medical attention**, contact Dr Jawarhalal Henriques at Zorin, near the petrol pump (☎0832/227 4308).

If you want to check into a cheap guesthouse while you sort out more permanent **accommodation**, best bet is the basic but good-value *Shettor Villa* (☎0832/227 4335; ❷–❸), off the west side of the main street. Nearly all its rooms, ranged around a sheltered back yard, come with fans and running water. Otherwise, try the *Helinda* (☎0832/227 4345; ❷–❸), at the opposite end of the village, which has rock-bottom options and a couple of more comfortable rooms with attached shower-toilets; or *Olga's* (☎0832/227 4355; ❷), a rudimentary but clean and quiet little guesthouse on the west side of the village towards the fishing anchorage.

The only luxury place hereabouts is *Siolim House* (ⓣ0832/227 2138, ⓦwww.siolimhouse.com; ⑨), 5km inland from Chapora along the south bank of the river, in **Siolim** village. Housed in a recently restored *palacio*, the hotel captures the period feel of the Portuguese era: its luminous, simply furnished rooms (from $70), ranged around a central pillared courtyard, have typical oyster-shell windows and carved, four-poster beds. There's also a twelve-metre pool in the garden, and an unpretentious restaurant serving fine Goan food.

Finding cheap **meals** in Chapora itself is easy: just take your pick from the crop of inexpensive little cafés and restaurants on the main street. *Baba Yaga's* caters for the Russians, with signs and menus in Cyrillic script, while for snacks and juices *Scarlet Cold Drinks* and the *Sai Ganesh Café*, both a short way east of the main street, are both safe bets, knocking up deliciously cool fresh fruit milkshakes and travellers' grub for as long as there are customers to serve.

The far north

Bounded by the Chapora and Arondem (aka "Terekol") rivers, **Pernem** is Goa's northernmost district. Apart from the fishing village of **Arambol**, which, during the winter, plays host to a large contingent of hippy travellers seeking a less pretentious alternative to Anjuna and Vagator, the beautiful Pernem coastline remains the quietest stretch of shoreline in the state. Catch the tide right, and it is possible to walk in a couple of hours all the way from the sandy spit at **Morjim**, on the opposite side of the river mouth from Chapora, to Arambol, via the villages of **Aswem** and **Mandrem**, where facilities for visitors are limited to a handful of shacks and small hut camps. In the far north, **Terekol fort**, on the Maharashtran border, makes a good target for a day-trip by motorbike or taxi.

Travelling north from **Siolim**, on the south bank of the River Chapora, the entry point to Pernem proper is the far side of the new road bridge at **Chopdem**. Head straight on for 200m or so until you arrive at a T-junction. A right turn here will take you along the quick route to Arambol; bear left, and you'll head along one of the few stretches of undeveloped coastline remaining in Goa – – an area that looks, since the completion of the bridge, to be living on borrowed time.

Morjim

Viewed from Chapora fort, **MORJIM** (or **Morji**) appears as a dramatic expanse of empty sand sweeping north from a spoon-shaped spit to the river mouth – one of Goa's last remaining nesting site for Olive Ridley turtles (see box). Behind it, broken dunes are backed by a dense patch of palms and casuarina trees, sheltering a mixed Hindu-Christian village whose inhabitants still live predominantly from in-shore fishing and rice farming. Bypassed completely by the main road north, their settlement has remained a relative backwater. Only in the past three or four years, since the completion of the Siolim bridge, has it started to see many tourists, the majority of them young Russians (whose early-morning fitness routines on the beach are still regarded with puzzled amusement by the straw-hatted handnet fishers working the foreshore).

Practicalities

Half a dozen **buses** per day connect Morjim with Panjim, the first at 7am; heading the other way, you can pick up a direct bus from Panjim at 5pm, and there are frequent services from Mapusa via Siolim. They'll drop you on the main road, five minutes' walk from the beachfront area at **Vithaldas Waddo**. If you're planning to stay anywhere else, keep your eyes peeled for the roadside signboards or you could be in for a long walk – rickshaws are few and far between this far north.

The main turning for Vithaldas Waddo, 1km back from the beach, is where you'll find Morjim's **Internet café**, Amigo's; access (on a slow dial-up connection but with good new computers) costs Rs40/hour. They also have telephone and fax facilities, and are licensed to **change money** (albeit at poor rates).

For **food**, you won't do better than *Britto's*, a small, family-run shack five minutes' walk down the beach, where millet-fried mussels, clams in spicy coconut sauce, vegetable fried rice and Chapora calamari in lime are the specialities; they also serve stupendously good lassis and fresh fruit juices. The shack is decorated with **murals** by the Welsh artist Andrea Davies.

Accommodation

Most of the **accommodation** in Morjim is in private houses which get snapped up early in the season, or even the previous one by entrepreneurial Muscovites who then sublet them at inflated rates. But you can usually find vacant rooms in one or other of the small guesthouses that have opened close to the beach; and a couple of higher-end places have recently sprung up beyond the northern limits of the village, on the road to Aswem.

Britto's Vithaldas Waddo ⓣ0832/224 4245. Friendly guesthouse back in the palm grove. The rooms are a bit institutional, but cheap, and the fun family atmosphere more than compensates. To find it, turn left down a sandy track 30m before the main beachfront road swings to the right (a blue signboard marks the spot); or else walk down the beach. ❷

Camp 69 Vithaldas Waddo ⓣ0832/224 4458. The oldest established place on the beachfront, now boasting large, well spaced "log cabins", fitted with beds, sofas, fans and en-suite bathrooms. They also run a relaxing little terrace restaurant shaded by palms and flowering trees. ❹

Hard Rock ("Gilbert's") Temb Waddo ⓣ9822/581928, ⓔbobmarley_gilbert@hotmail.com. Local lad Gilbert Fernandes has converted a wing of his family home, behind the southernmost part of the beach inland from the shacks, with very stylish oxide floors and ochre-washed walls. Comfortable, secluded and retaining plenty of local Goan atmosphere. ❸

Montego Bay Vithaldas Waddo ⓣ0832/224 4222, ⓦwww.montegobaygoa.com. A dozen or so plush Rajasthani tents, stylishly equipped with driftwood beds, fans, coir mats and running-water bathrooms, at a breezy spot in the dunes under coconut trees. The most comfortable option bang on the beach, though overpriced for the area. Breakfast included. ❼

Morjim Beach Resort Temb Waddo ⓣ9822/481480. This recently built guesthouse is a long plod south down the beach, midway between the village centre and sandy spit at the end: basically, you'll need at least a bicycle to stay here. But it is perfectly situated and well set up, with proper rooms as well as leaf huts. Signposted off the road. ❸

Nifa 480 Mardi Waddo ⓣ0832/224 4635 or mobile 98221/35333, ⓔhotelnifa@yahoo.com. Charming, peaceful guesthouse on the coast road, run by a welcoming Iranian-Swiss couple. They've made a real effort with the rooms, which are spacious and have mosquito nets, floaty curtains and hot showers in the bathrooms. Also worth singling out is the restaurant and the views from their pleasant garden terrace. ❼

Papa Jolly's House #749/A, Morjim–Aswem Road, Mardi Waddo. A self-styled "Spiritual Holiday Resort", complete with ethnically furnished rooms and lovely curved pool. The new laterite building is pleasant enough, as is the location, but the tariffs – sweetened with lots of soothing New Age blurb on the website – are ludicrous: Rs6730 (roughly $125) for a double room, rising to Rs8775 at Christmas. ❾

Tequila Sunset Hideout Vithaldas Waddo ⓣ9822/588003. Large, new rooms, with attached bathrooms (closets) and big tiled balconies overlooking a beachfront plot. A first-floor café-restaurant is in the pipeline, which will have great sea views. ❹

The turtle wind

When a strong and steady on-shore breeze blows through the night in early November at Morjim – the long, empty beach west of the ferry ramp at Chopdem – the locals call it a **turtle wind** because such weather normally heralds the arrival of Goa's rarest migrant visitors: the **Olive Ridley marine turtles** (*Lepidochelys olivacea*).

For as long as anyone can remember, the spoon-shaped spit of soft white sand at **Temb**, the far southern end of the beach, has been the nesting ground of these beautiful sea reptiles. Each winter, a succession of females emerges from the surf during the night and, using their distinctive flippers, crawls to the edge of the dunes to lay their annual clutch of 105–115 eggs. Just over two months later, the fresh hatchlings clamber out and crawl blinking over their siblings to begin the perilous trek back to the water, guided into the sea by reflected moonlight. Little more is known about how these enigmatic creatures spend the rest of their long lives (turtles frequently live for over a century), but it is thought that the females return to the beaches where they were born to lay their own eggs. Some have been known to travel as far as 4500km to do this.

Once a thriving species, with huge populations spread across the Pacific, Atlantic and Indian oceans, the Olive Ridley is nowadays endangered. Aside from a wealth of traditional predators (such as crows, ospreys, gulls and buzzards, who pick off the hatchlings during their dash for the sea), the newborns and their parents are vulnerable to a host of man-made threats. In Morjim, as in most of Asia, the eggs are traditionally considered a delicacy and local villagers collect them to sell in Mapusa market. Many (perhaps as many as 35,000 worldwide) are killed accidentally by fisherman, caught up in fine shrimp nets or attracted by squid bait used to catch tuna. Floating litter, which the hapless turtles mistake for jellyfish, has also taken its toll over the past two decades, as have tar balls from oil spills, which coat the animals' digestive tracks and hamper the absorption of food. The growth of tourism poses an additional danger: electric lights behind the beaches throw the hatchlings off course as they scuttle towards to sea, and sand compressed by sunbathers' trampling feet damages nests, preventing the babies from digging their way out at the crucial time. On average, only two out of a typical clutch of more than one hundred survive into

Aswem

A solitary whitewashed crucifix rises from the rocks dividing Morjim from **ASWEM**, the next village north. Aside from the odd German nudist or two, you should have the sands pretty much to yourself until you arrive at the burgeoning cluster of shacks and hut camps midway along the beach. Huddled under the canopy of a beautiful coconut *mand*, this ad hoc tourist settlement started to snowball after a couple of French restaurateurs from Baga opened a chic beach café here (*La Plage* – see opposite). Their business excepted, amenities remain basic (leaf huts are the norm as the local council has vigorously enforced the Coastal Protection Zone building ban), but the beach is all the more appealing for that. It's clean, quiet for most of the season and, outside the full-moon period, safe for kids to swim off. Only at the far northern end, where a tidal creek periodically prevents you from continuing north towards Arambol, has package tourism made any discernable inroads: Maruti vans deposit punters here to overnight in purpose-built hut camps on the shoreline, but the setup is very low-key.

Practicalities

Sporadic **buses** from Panjim and Mapusa cover the quiet stretch of road running parallel to the beach inland, from where a five-minute walk across the paddy fields brings you to the shacks (signboards indicate the paths). Other than adulthood to reproduce. In Goa, the resulting decline has been dramatic. Of the 150 nesting females that used to return each year to Morjim, for example, only thirteen showed up in 1999.

However, under the auspices of the Forest Department, a scheme has been launched to revive turtle populations. Locals are employed to watch out for the females' arrival in November, and guard the nests after the eggs have been laid until they hatch. You'll see them camped under palm-leaf shades on the beach, with the nests fenced in and marked by Forest Department signs. One of the main reasons the fishing families at Temb have so enthusiastically espoused the initiative is that its success promises to bring about the creation of an official **nature sanctuary** at Morjim, blocking forever plans to build unwanted tourist resorts on their beach.

So far, the government-led conservation attempt seems to have been successful, although after an initial leap in hatchling figures, recent results have shown a marked dip, which the Forest Department ascribes to an increase in tourist activity. Over the winter of 2003–04, 927 eggs were laid in nine nests on Morjim, of which 558 hatched (as against a total of 2500 hatchlings in 2001–2002). A further 922 baby turtles survived at Goa's other main nesting site, Galjibag, in the south (see p.854), and 213 more in Agonda.

Watching the nesting turtles is an unforgettable experience, although one requiring a certain amount of dedication, or luck. No one knows for sure when an Olive Ridley female will turn up, but with a strong turtle wind blowing at the right time, the chances are good. Much more predictable are the appearances of the hatchlings, who emerge exactly 54 days after their mothers laid the eggs. If you ask one of the wardens looking after the nests, they can tell you when this will be.

For more on international attempts to save marine turtles, including the massive synchronized *arribida* (arrival) of around 200,000 at the Bhitarakanika Sanctuary, Orissa, on the east coast of India, visit the website of the World Wildlife Fund (Ⓦwww.wwf.org), which tells you how can join environmental groups such as the Marine Conservation Society.

the cafés, there are no facilities whatsoever here. Nearly everyone who stays rents a scooter from somewhere else to get to and around Aswem. The nearest Internet access and shops are at Morjim, an idyllic half-hour plod south.

For **food**, head to *La Plage* (Ⓣ9850/258543; closed evenings), where light Gallic-Mediterranean, heat-beating snacks and drinks (chilled asparagus soup, mint lassis, Moroccan salads, fresh strawberries and cream), along with sumptuous chargrilled seafood and barbequed main courses, are dished up by Nepalis in black *lunghis* against a diaphanous backdrop of floaty white muslin. It's a surreal counterpoint to the fishing *waddo* down the beach, but a very pleasant breakfast or lunch venue nonetheless.

Accommodation

Change Your Mind Ⓣ0832/224 4790 or 9822/389290. Basic huts and treehouses behind a lively shack. ❷–❸

Gopal Ⓣ0832/224 4431, 224 7030 or 9822/147416, Ⓔgopal@ingoa.com/258543. In much the same mould as *Change Your Mind*, at identical rates. ❷–❸

Little Goa Ⓣ9822/383795. Classier than average huts – with comfier beds and fans – and an unusually well-stocked bar, though you pay dearly for the frills. ❹

Palm Grove Ⓣ0832/224 7440. Pick of the bunch: further up the beach from the others, and with large treehouses that are not only well spaced but also have perfect sea views. The best option if you're here to escape the tourist scene. ❹

Mandrem

A magnificent, and largely empty, beach stretches north of Aswem towards Arambol, uninterrupted save for a couple of large-scale hut camps and a single package hotel. Whether or not **MANDREM** can continue to hold out against the rising tide of tourism remains to be seen, but for the time being, nature still has the upper hand. Olive Ridley marine turtles nest on the quietest stretch, and you're more than likely to catch a glimpse of one of the white-bellied fish eagles that live in the casuarina trees – their last stronghold in Pernem. If you can afford it, the best spot from which to savour this last unspoilt strip of the Goan coast is Denzil Sequeira's exclusive beachhouse *Elsewhere* (see below), nestled in the dunes just north of the creek and unquestionably the most beautiful hideaway hereabouts. The rest of this area's accommodation is tucked away inland at **Junasa Waddo**, where a handful of small guesthouses and hotels have sprung up.

Practicalities

Public transport is thin on the ground. Visitors walk or rent scooters for the five-minute ride to **Madlamaz-Mandrem**, a typically north-Goan market village straddling the main road inland. Parsekar Stores holds an Anjuna-style stock of tourist-oriented food and drink – including muesli, olive oil and Nilgiri cheese – and natural cosmetics; and there's a tiny **laundry** above a jeweller's shop in the small courtyard just to the east of the main road.

Accommodation

Dunes ⓣ0832/224 7219 or 224 7071, ⓦwww.dunesgoa.com. Huge "holiday village" of twin-bedded, yellow-painted leaf huts. They're a notch too close together for comfort and brightly lit, spoiling the aspect of the beach at night, but this is an efficiently run outfit that fills up in peak season. Pricier en-suite available. ❸–❹

Elsewhere ⓣ022/2373 8757 or 9820/037387, ⓦwww.aseascape.com. Goan fashion photographer Denzil Sequeira converted his grandfather's hot-season retreat into a dream getaway, retaining its colonial-era character with a gorgeous sea-facing veranda and traditional wood furniture, yet incorporating modern elements (a fridge, two cobalt-blue bathrooms and luminous white cotton drapes that catch the breezes). Flanked by the beach on one side and a creek on the other, it's romantic and exclusive, but affordable if you get a group together (the three bedrooms sleep six). From £670 per week; includes services of an on-site cook. ❾

Flying Carpet ⓣ0832/244 7104 or 9822/140996. A dozen neatly furnished holiday rooms in a new block on the lane through Junasa Waddo. ❸

Otter Creek ⓣ022/2373 8757 or 9820/037387, ⓦwww.aseascape.com. Three beautiful luxury tents, each with their own bamboo four-posters, bathroom, colour-washed sitout and jetty on the river; you have to cross a rickety foot bridge to get there, or walk over the dunes from the beach. Rs3320 per night. ❾

Riva Resort ⓣ0832/224 7088 or 224 7612, ⓦwww.rivaresorts.com. The other big hut camp next to *Dunes*. This one's more upmarket, with swisher huts and higher rates (Rs400–800 depending on the level of comfort, rising to a hefty Rs1500–2000 at Christmas.) The site centres on a huge bar-restaurant that hosts DJ nights and has big-screen video/DVD. ❸–❺

Villa River Cat ⓣ0822/224 7928, ⓦwww.villarivercat.com. Quirky riverside hotel, screened from the beach by the dunes, with distinctive hippy-influenced decor and furniture. The 16 rooms are all individually designed: mosaics, shells, devotional sculpture and hammocks set the tone. Some have balconies, and there's a great sunset roof terrace and rear garden for lounging in. Host Rinoo Seghal is an animal lover, so brace yourself for a menagerie of cats and dogs, which some will enjoy. ❺

Arambol (Harmal)

The largest coastal village in Pernem district is **ARAMBOL** (sometimes called **Harmal**), 32km northwest of Mapusa. If you're happy with basic amenities but

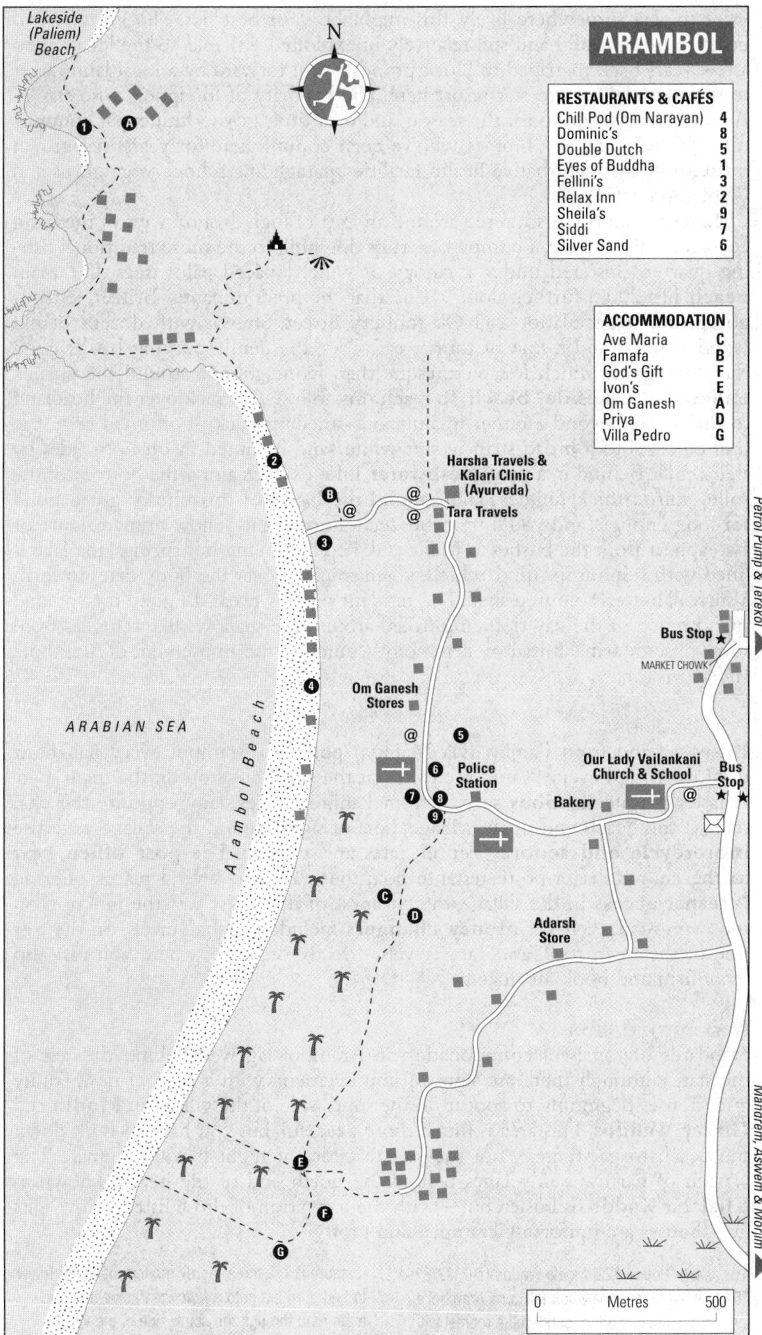

ARAMBOL
RESTAURANTS & CAFÉS
Chill Pod (Om Narayan) 4
Dominic's 8
Double Dutch 5
Eyes of Buddha 1
Fellini's 3
Relax Inn 2
Sheila's 9
Siddi 7
Silver Sand 6
ACCOMMODATION
Ave Maria C
Famafa B
God's Gift F
Ivon's E
Om Ganesh A
Priya D
Villa Pedro G
N
Lakeside (Paliem) Beach
ARABIAN SEA
Arambol Beach
Harsha Travels & Kalari Clinic (Ayurveda)
Tara Travels
Om Ganesh Stores
Police Station
Our Lady Vailankani Church & School
Bakery
Bus Stop
MARKET CHOWK
Adarsh Store
Petrol Pump & Terekol
Mandrem, Aswem & Morjim
0 Metres 500

want to stay somewhere lively, this might be your best bet. The village's two beaches are beautiful and still relatively unexploited – thanks to the locals, who a few years back managed to block proposals put forward by a local landowner to site a sprawling five-star resort here. The majority of foreigners who stay in Arambol tend to do so for the season, and over time a close-knit expat community (of mostly ageing hippies who've been coming here for years) has grown up, with its own alternative health facilities, paragliding school, yoga gurus and wholefood cafés.

Modern Arambol is scattered around an area of high ground west of the main coast road. From here, a bumpy lane runs downhill to the more traditional fishing quarter, clustered under a canopy of widely spaced palm trees. The main **beach** lies 200m further along a lane that the predominantly British, festival-going tourist population call Glastonbury Street. Strewn with dozens of old wooden boats and a line of tourist café-bars, the gently curving bay is good for bathing, but much less picturesque than its neighbour around the corner, **Paliem** or "**Lakeside**" **beach**. To reach this, follow the track over the headland to the north; beyond a rather insalubrious-smelling, rocky-bottomed cove, the trail emerges to a broad strip of soft white sand hemmed in on both sides by steep cliffs. Behind it, a small **freshwater lake** extends along the bottom of the valley into a thick jungle. Hang around the banks of this murky green pond for long enough, and you'll probably see a fluorescent-yellow human figure or two appear from the bushes at its far end. Fed by boiling hot springs, the lake is lined with sulphurous mud, which, when smeared over the body, dries to form a surreal, butter-coloured shell. The resident hippies swear it's good for you and spend much of the day tiptoeing naked around the shallows like refugees from some obscure tribal initiation ceremony – much to the amusement of Arambol's Indian visitors.

Practicalities

Buses to and from Panjim (via Mapusa) pull into Arambol every half-hour until noon, and every 90min thereafter, at the small bus stop on the main road. A faster private **minibus** service from Panjim arrives daily opposite the chai stalls at the beach end of the village. Lots of signs around the village advertise **motorcycle and scooter rental**; rates are standard. The **post office**, next to the church, has a poste restante box; there are also several places offering **Internet access** in the village, the cheapest of them just past the junction on the main road. Reliable **money changers** include Harsha Travels, on the east side of the main road, and Tara Travels, directly opposite, where you can also reconfirm and book air tickets.

Accommodation

Standards of tourist accommodation in Arambol lag well behind the rest of the state, although there are signs of improvement, with a crop of new, family guesthouses beginning to appear on the south side of the village in **Modlo** and **Girkar Waddos**. This area is much more peaceful, but you have to walk down the beach to get there – not such a great idea at night if you're female. The warren of narrow sandy lanes behind the north end of the beach, known as **Khalcha Waddo**, is busier, but – with the exception of those listed below – its guesthouses are uniformly cramped and grotty.

Ave Maria House #22, Modlo Waddo ⓣ0832/229 7674, ⓔavemaria_goa@hotmail.com. Arambol's largest guesthouse offers good-value rooms, with or without bathrooms, and a sociable rooftop restaurant in a three-storey modern building. Tricky to find: turn left onto a *kutchha* track where the main road through the south side of the village makes a sharp right bend. ❷

Famafa Khalcha Waddo ⓣ0832/229 2516, ⓦwww.travelingoa.com/famafa. Large, ugly concrete place just off Glastonbury Street; popular with Israelis, and correspondingly rowdy, but it usually has vacancies and is very close to the beach. ❸

God's Gift House #411, Girkar Waddo ⓣ0832/222 9239. Variously priced, sizeable rooms, all tiled and with comfortable verandas; some also have living rooms and kitchens. Rates are good and the proprietors friendly. ❷

Ivon's Girkar Waddo ⓣ0832/229 2672 or 9822/127398. The pick of the bunch, with immaculately clean, tiled rooms, all with attached bathroom and fronted by good-sized tiled balconies opening onto a well-groomed family compound or the dunes. ❸

Om Ganesh in the cove between the village and Lakeside beach; book at the Om Ganesh stores, near *Double Dutch Café* on the main drag ⓣ0832/229 7657 or 0832/229 7619. Nicest of the "cottages" stacked up the cliffside just south of Lakeside beach. The sea views from their verandas are superb, but some may find the Israeli chillum scene in the nearby cafés a bit of a disincentive. Rates vary wildly according to demand, and advance booking (with a deposit) is all but essential by mid-season. ❹

Priya Modlo Waddo ⓣ0832/229 2661, ⓔzdmello@hotmail.com. Welcoming ten-roomed guesthouse, that's the best fallback if nearby *Ave Maria*, is full. ❷

Villa Pedro Girkar Waddo ⓣ0832/229 7689. Small family guesthouse just beyond *God's Gift*, amid the toddy grove just in from the beach – thus well placed if you want to be near the sea, but a fair way away from the village. The rooms are clean and pleasant, and some have sea views. Good value. ❷

Eating

Thanks to its annually replenished pool of expatriate gastronomic talent, Arambol harbours a handful of unexpectedly good **restaurants** – not that you'd ever guess from their generally lacklustre exteriors. The village's discerning hippy contingent cares more about flavours than fancy decor, and prices reflect the fact that most of them eke out savings to stay here all winter. If you're on a really rock-bottom budget, stick to the "rice-plate" shacks at the bottom of the village. Tasty thalis at *Sheila's* and *Siddi* come with *puris*, and both have a good travellers' breakfast menu of pancakes, eggs and curd. *Dominic's*, also at the bottom of the village (near where the road makes a ninety-degree bend), is renowned for its fruit juices and milkshakes, while *Sai Deep*, a little further up the road, does generous fruit salads with yoghurt.

Chill Pod (aka "Om Narayan") on the beach, midway down the shacks. Great for inexpensive north-Indian vegetarian: go for the *malai kofta*, cheese *nan* and veg *makhanwala*.

Double Dutch Main Street, halfway down the on the right (look for the yellow signboard). Spread under a palm canopy in the thick of the village, this laid-back café is the hub of alternative Arambol. Renowned for its melt-in-the-mouth apple pie (possibly the best in the world), it also does a tempting range of home-baked buttery biscuits, cakes (Buddha's Dream's a winner), healthy salads and sumptuous main meals (from Rs120), including fresh buffalo steaks and the perennially popular "mixed stuff" (stuffed mushrooms and capsicums with sesame pesto).

Fellini's Glastonbury Street. Italian-run restaurant serving delicious wood-fired pizzas (Rs80–140), and authentic pasta or gnocchi with a choice of over twenty sauces. It gets horrendously busy in season, so be here early if you want snappy service.

Relax Inn Arambol beach. Top-quality seafood straight off the boats and unbelievably authentic pasta (you get even more of the expat Italians in here than at *Fellini's*). Try the vongole clam sauce. Inexpensive, but expect a wait as they cook to order.

Silver Sand opposite Arambol chapel. At the south side of the village, this is another deceptively ordinary streetside café specializing in fresh seafood (including Chapora calamari), home-made pasta, ratatouille for vegans and popular chocolate cake, baked daily. The espresso's top-notch, too, and there can be queues at breakfast for the home-made pineapple jam.

Terekol

North of Arambol, the sinuous coast road climbs to the top of a rocky, undulating plateau, then winds down through a swathe of thick woodland to join the

River Arondem (or Terekol), which it then follows for 4km through a landscape of vivid paddy fields, coconut plantations and temple towers protruding from scruffy red-brick villages. The tiny enclave of **TEREKOL**, the northernmost tip of Goa, is reached via a clapped-out car ferry (every 30min; 5min) from the hamlet of Querim, 42km from Panjim. If the tide is out and the water levels are too low for the ferry to run, you can either backtrack 5km, where there's another one, or arrange for the boatman at the jetty to run you across (for a negotiable fee).

Set against the backdrop of a filthy iron-ore complex, the old **fort** that dominates the estuary from the north – an ochre-painted building with turreted ramparts that wouldn't look out of place in coastal Portugal – was built by the Marathas at the start of the eighteenth century, but taken soon after by the Portuguese. These days, it serves as a low-key luxury heritage **hotel**, *The Fort Tiracol* (Ⓣ0832/226 8258; ⑨), created by the owners of the swish *Nilaya Hermitage* at Arpora (see p.818). The seven rooms are all decorated in traditional ochre and white, with black-oxide floors, black-tiled drench showers and rustic wood and wrought-iron furniture; tariffs start at $180 per night. Non-residents are welcome to visit the restaurant and stylish lounge bar, where you can eat chargrilled tiger prawns while enjoying what must rank among the finest seascapes in southern India.

South Goa

Beyond the unattractive port city of Vasco da Gama and its nearby airport, Goa's southern reaches are fringed by some of the region's finest **beaches**, backed by a lush band of coconut plantations, and green hills scattered with attractive villages. An ideal first base if you've just arrived in the region is **Benaulim**, 6km west of Goa's second city, **Margao**. The most traveller-friendly resort in the area, Benaulim stands slap in the middle of a spectacular 25-kilometre stretch of pure white sand. Although increasingly carved up by Mumbai time-share companies, low-cost accommodation here is plentiful and of a consistently high standard. Nearby Colva, by contrast, has degenerated over the past decade into an insalubrious charter resort. Frequented by huge numbers of day-trippers, and boasting few discernible charms, it's best avoided.

With the gradual spread of package tourism down the coast, **Palolem**, a couple of hours' south of Margao down the main highway, has emerged as the budget travellers' preferred resort, despite its relative inaccessibility. Set against a backdrop of forest-cloaked hills, its beach is spectacular and development restrained, although the numbers of visitors can feel overwhelming in high season.

Margao (Madgaon) and around

The capital of prosperous Salcete *taluka*, **MARGAO** – referred to in railway timetables and on some maps by its official government title, **Madgaon** – is Goa's second city. Surrounded by fertile farmland, the town has always been an important agricultural market, and was once a major religious centre, with dozens of wealthy temples and *dharamshalas* – however, most of these were destroyed when the Portuguese absorbed the area into their Novas Conquistas ("New Conquests") during the seventeenth century. Today, Catholic churches still outnumber Hindu shrines, but Margao has retained a cosmopolitan feel due to a huge influx of migrant labour from neighbouring Karnataka and Maharashtra.

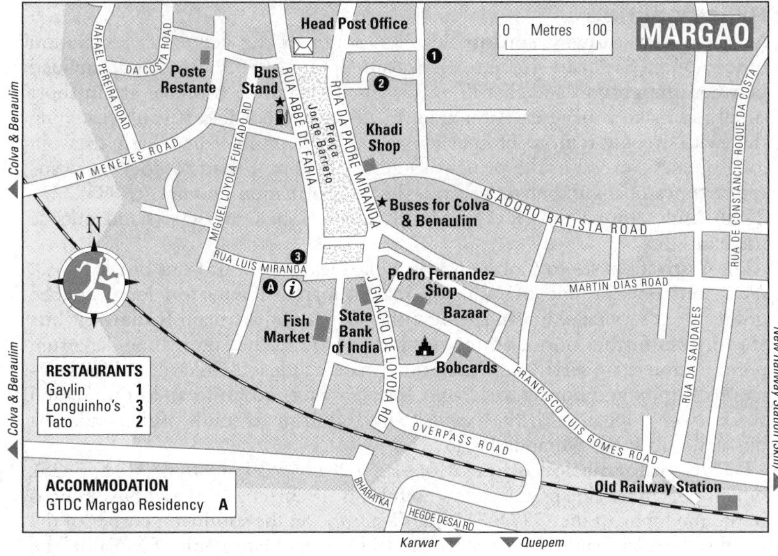

If you're arriving in Goa on the Konkan Railway from Mumbai or South India, you'll almost certainly have to pause in Margao to pick up onward transport by road. The other reason to come here is to shop at the town's **market**. Stretching from the south edge of the main square to within a stone's throw of the old railway station, the bazaar centres on a labyrinthine covered area where you'll find everything from betel leaves and sacks of lime paste to baby clothes and cheap Taiwanese toys. When the syrupy air gets too stifling, explore the streets around the market, among which is one given over to cloth merchants and tailors. Also worth checking is the excellent little government-run **Khadi Gramodyog** shop, on the main square (near the *Kamat*), which sells quality hand-spun cottons and raw silk by the metre, as well as ready-made traditional Indian garments.

A rickshaw ride north, the **Church of the Holy Spirit** is the main landmark in Margoa's dishevelled colonial enclave. Built by the Portuguese in 1675, it ranks among the finest examples of late-Baroque architecture in Goa, its interior dominated by a huge gilt reredos dedicated to the Virgin. Just north-east of it, overlooking the main Ponda road, stands one of the state's grandest eighteenth-century *palacios*, **Sat Banzam Ghor** ("Seven Gables house"). Only three of its original seven high-pitched roof gables remain, but the mansion is still an impressive sight, its facade decorated with fancy scroll work and huge oyster-shell windows.

For more of Goa's wonderful vernacular colonial architecture, you'll have to head **inland from Margao**, where villages such as **Lutolim**, **Racaim** and **Rachol** are littered with decaying old Portuguese houses, most of them empty – the region's traditional inheritance laws ensure that old family homes tend to be owned by literally dozens of descendants, none of whom are willing or can afford to maintain them.

Another reason to head into Margao is to catch a movie in South Goa's principal **cinema**, the Osia Multiplex (Ⓣ0832/270 1717), out in the north of town near the Kadamba bus stand. It screens Hollywood as well as Bollywood releases; tickets cost Rs50–70.

Practicalities

Margao's new **railway station** lies 3km south of the centre, its reservation office (Mon–Sat 8am–4.30pm, Sun 8am–2pm; ☎0832/271 2940) divided between the ground and first floor. Tickets for trains to Mumbai are in short supply, so make your reservation as far in advance as possible. If you're catching the twice-weekly train to Hospet (en route to Hampi) get here early to avoid long queues. Several of the principal trains that stop in Margao do so at unsociable times of night, but there's a 24-hour information counter (☎0832/271 2790), and a round-the-clock pre-paid auto-rickshaw and taxi stand outside the exit.

Local private buses to Colva and Benaulim leave from in front of the *Kamat Hotel*, on the east side of Margao's main square. Arriving on long-distance government services you can get off either here or at the main **Kadamba bus stand**, 3km further north, on the outskirts of town. The latter is the departure point for interstate services to Mangalore, via Chaudi and Gokarn, and for services to Panjim and north Goa. Paulo Travel's deluxe coach to and from Hampi works from a lot next to the *Nanutel Hotel*, 1km or so south of the Kadamba bus stand on Padre Miranda Road.

GTDC's **information office** (Mon–Fri 9.30am–5.30pm; ☎0832/222 5528), which sells tourist maps and keeps useful lists of current train and bus times, is inside the lobby of the *GTDC Margao Residency*, on the southwest corner of the main square. Exchange facilities are available at the State Bank of India off the west side of the square, which also has a 24-hourr **ATM**; the Bobcard office in the market sub-branch of the Bank of Baroda, on Francisco Luis Gomes Road, does Visa encashments. The GPO is at the top of the central municipal gardens, although its poste restante is in a different building, 200m west on the Rua Diogo da Costa. For the central **police** station, on the west side of the main square near the GPO, ☎0832/270 5095.

For visitors in need of medical attention, Margao's two main **hospitals** are: the Hospicio (☎0832/270 5664 or 270 5754), Rua De Miranda and the Apollo Victor Hospital, in the suburb of Malbhat (☎0832/272 8888 or 272 6272).

With Colva and Benaulim a mere twenty-minute bus ride away, it's hard to think of a reason why anyone should choose to **stay** in Margao. If you do get stuck here, however, the safest choice is the *GTDC Margao Residency* (☎0832/271 5528; ❹), a comfortable mid-range place that recently had a major face-lift.

In terms of **eating**, most visitors make a beeline for *Longuinho's* on Rua Luis Miranda. The long-established hang-out of Margao's English-speaking middle classes, it's a relaxing, old-fashioned café serving a reasonable selection of moderately priced meat, fish and veg mains, freshly baked savoury snacks (including Portuguese prawn *rissois* and veg puffs), cakes and drinks. The food isn't up to much these days, and the old Goan atmosphere has been marred by the arrival of satellite TV, but it's a pleasant enough place to catch your breath over a beer. South Indian snacks are available all over town, but the best place is *Tato*, tucked away up an alley off the east side of the Municipal Gardens square: the breakfast samosas are especially good, and they do masala dosas from midday on. *Gaylin*, behind Grace Church, serves a good selection of Cantonese and Szechuan dishes (mostly steeped in hot red Goan chilli paste) in a smart air-conditioned dining room.

Chandor

Thirteen kilometres east of Margao across Salcete district's fertile rice fields lies sleepy **CHANDOR** village, a scattering of tumbledown villas and farmhouses ranged along shady tree-lined lanes. The main reason to venture out here is the splendid **Perreira-Braganza/Menezes-Braganza house** (daily except holidays, no set hours; recommended donation Rs100), regarded as the grandest of Goa's colonial mansions. Dominating the dusty village square, the house, built in the 1500s by the wealthy Braganza family for their two sons, has a huge double-storey facade, with 28 windows flanking its entrance. Braganza de Perreira, the great-grandfather of the present owner, was the last knight of the king of Portugal; more recently, Menezes Braganza (1879–1938), a journalist and freedom fighter, was one of the few Goan aristocrats to actively oppose Portuguese rule. Forced to flee Chandor in 1950, the family returned in 1962 to find their house, amazingly, untouched. The airy tiled interiors of both wings contain a veritable feast of **antiques**.

The house is divided into two separate wings, owned by different branches of the old family. Both are open to the public, though there are no set hours as such – just turn up between 10am and noon or 3 to 5pm, go through the main entrance, up the stairs and knock at either of the doors. You'll be expected to leave a donation of at least Rs100. Furniture enthusiasts, and lovers of rare Chinese porcelain, in particular, will find plenty to drool over in the Menezes-Braganza wing (to the right as you face the building), which has preserved the famous journalist's library. Next door in the Perreria-Braganza portion, an ornate oratory enshrines St Francis Xavier's diamond-encrusted toenail, recently retrieved from a local bank vault. The house's most famous feature, however, is its ostentatiously grand ballroom, or **Great Salon**, where a pair of matching high-backed chairs, presented to the Perreira-Braganzas by King Dom Luís of Portugal, occupy pride of place.

Colva

A hot-season retreat for Margao's moneyed middle classes since long before Independence, **COLVA** is the oldest and largest – but least appealing – of south Goa's resorts. Its outlying *waddos*, or wards, are pleasant enough, dotted with colonial-style villas and ramshackle fishing huts, but the beachfront is dismal: a lacklustre collection of concrete hotels, souvenir stalls and fly-blown snack bars strewn around a bleak central roundabout. The atmosphere is not improved by heaps of rubbish dumped in a rank-smelling ditch that runs behind the beach, nor by the stench of drying fish wafting from the nearby village. Benaulim, only a five-minute drive further south, has a far better choice of accommodation and range of facilities, and is altogether more salubrious.

Benaulim

According to Hindu mythology, Goa was created when the sage Shri Parasurama, Vishnu's sixth incarnation, fired an arrow into the sea from the top of the Western Ghats and ordered the waters to recede. The spot where the shaft fell to earth, known in Sanskrit as Banali ("place where the arrow landed") and later corrupted by the Portuguese to **BENAULIM**, lies in the dead centre of Colva Beach, 7km west of Margao. Twenty years ago, this atmospheric fishing

Cobra warning

You'll rarely see a Benaulim villager crossing a rice field at night. This is because paddy is prime territory for snakes, especially **cobras**. If you do intend to cut across the fields after dark, take along a strong flashlight, make plenty of noise and hit the ground ahead of you with a stick to warn any lurking serpents of your approach.

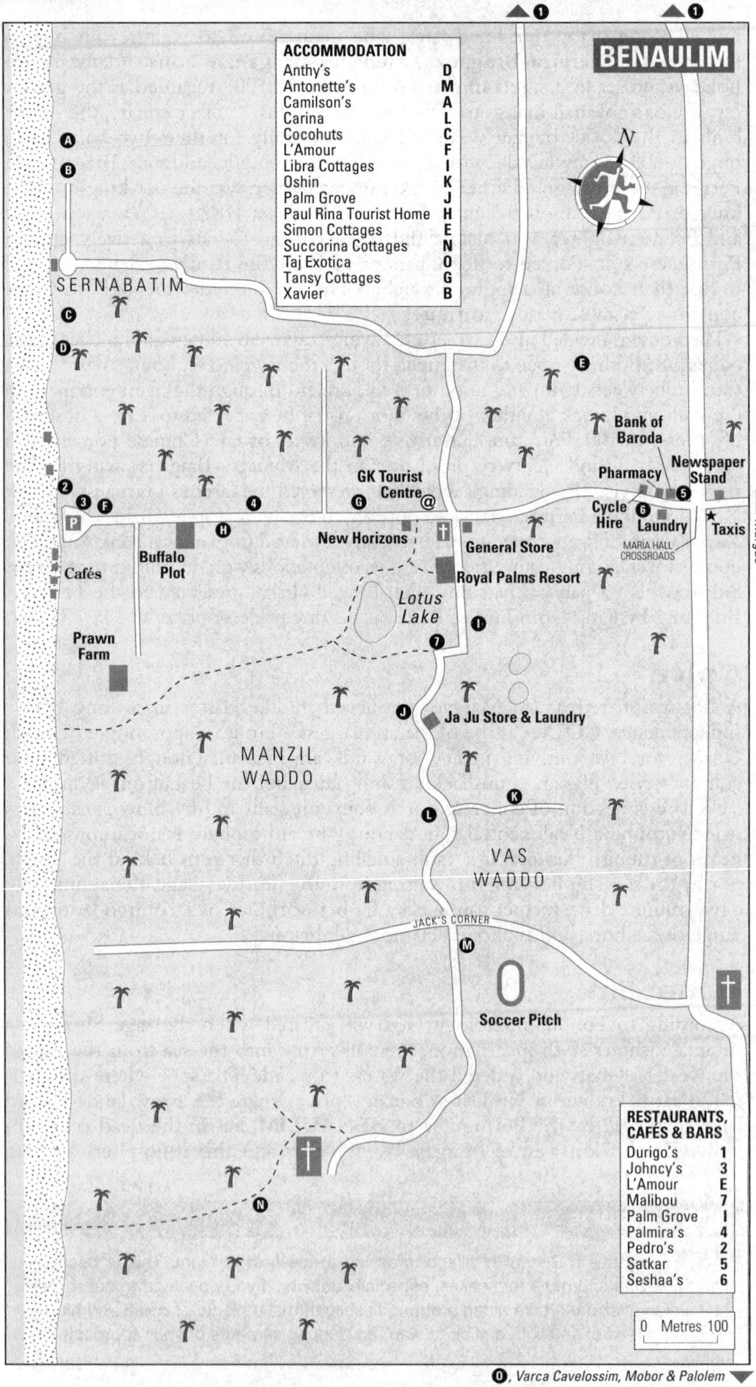

BENAULIM

ACCOMMODATION	
Anthy's	D
Antonette's	M
Camilson's	A
Carina	L
Cocohuts	C
L'Amour	F
Libra Cottages	I
Oshin	K
Palm Grove	J
Paul Rina Tourist Home	H
Simon Cottages	E
Succorina Cottages	N
Taj Exotica	O
Tansy Cottages	G
Xavier	B

RESTAURANTS, CAFÉS & BARS	
Durigo's	1
Johncy's	3
L'Amour	E
Malibou	7
Palm Grove	I
Palmira's	4
Pedro's	2
Satkar	5
Seshaa's	6

SERNABATIM
Bank of Baroda
Newspaper Stand
Pharmacy
GK Tourist Centre
Cycle Hire
Laundry
Taxis
Margao
MARIA HALL CROSSROADS
New Horizons
General Store
Buffalo Plot
Cafés
Royal Palms Resort
Lotus Lake
Prawn Farm
Ja Ju Store & Laundry
MANZIL WADDO
VAS WADDO
JACK'S CORNER
Soccer Pitch
0 Metres 100

1
O, Varca Cavelossim, Mobor & Palolem

and rice-farming village, scattered around the coconut groves and paddy fields between the main Colva–Mobor road and the dunes, had barely made it onto the backpackers' map. Since the completion of the nearby Konkan railway, however, big-spending middle-class Indians have started to holiday here, in the luxury resorts and time-share apartment complexes that have mushroomed in the rice fields. As a result, the village has lost some of its famously *sossegarde* feel. Even so, if you time your visit well (avoiding Diwali and the Christmas peak season), Benaulim is still hard to beat as a place to unwind. Its tourist scene is neither particularly "alternative" nor alcohol-driven. The seafood is superb, accommodation and motorbikes cheaper than anywhere else in the state, and the beach breathtaking, particularly around sunset, when its brilliant white sand and churning surf reflect the changing colours to magical effect. Shelving away almost to Cabo da Rama on the horizon, the beach is also lined with Goa's largest, and most colourfully decorated, fleet of wooden outriggers, and these provide welcome shade during the heat of the day.

Practicalities

Buses from Margao and Colva roll through Benaulim every fifteen minutes or so, dropping passengers at the Maria Hall crossroads. Ranged around this busy junction are two well-stocked general stores, a couple of café-bars, a bank, pharmacy, laundry and the taxi and auto-rickshaw rank, from where you can pick up **transport** to the beach, 1.5km west.

Signs offering **motorbikes** for rent are dotted along the lane leading to the sea: rates are standard, descending in proportion to the length of time you keep the vehicle. Worth bearing in mind if you're planning to continue further south is that motorbikes are much cheaper to rent (and generally in better condition) here than Palolem, where there's a relative shortage of vehicles. **Petrol** is sold by the litre from a table at the roadside, two minutes' walk south down the road leading to *Royal Palm Beach Resort*, but tends to be laced with solvent and smokes badly. Local boys will try to get you to pay them to fill your bike up in Margao, but invariably pocket half of the money in the process, so if you've a valid licence do it yourself (Margao's main petrol pump is on the west side of the Praça Jorge Barreto – see map on p.839).

Bicycles cost around Rs50 per day to rent. If you're intending to stay for a long time, it might be worth buying one. Several cycle shops in Margao sell standard Indian-style Hero models for Rs2000–25000; you can expect to re-sell it again for half the original price.

For **changing money**, the most convenient places offering the best rates are G.K. Tourist Centre, at the crossroads in the village centre, and New Horizons, diagonally opposite. It's often worth comparing the two. Down at the beachfront, *L'Amour* also has a forex counter which in principle offers the same rates as Thomas Cook. With a Visa card, you can also make encashments at the Bank of Baroda on Maria Hall crossroads. The nearest **ATMs** are in Margao and Colva. Finally, international and domestic **flights** can be booked, altered or reconfirmed at New Horizons, which also does deluxe bus and train ticketing for cities elsewhere in India.

For **Internet access**, try G.K. Tourism (Rs40/hr). New Horizons has been promising to install a broadband connection for the past couple of seasons, and may well have done so by the time you read this.

Accommodation

Most of Benaulim's **accommodation** consists of small budget guesthouses, scattered around the lanes 1km or so back from the beach. The majority are featureless annexes of spartan tiled rooms with fans and, usually, attached shower-toilets; the only significant difference between them is their location. The best way to find a vacancy is to hunt around on foot or by bicycle, although if you wait at the Maria Hall crossroads or the beachfront with luggage, someone is bound to ask if you need a room. During peak season, the village's few mid-range hotels (namely *L'Amour*, *Palm Grove* and *Carina*) tend to be fully booked, so reserve in advance if you want to stay in one of these.

Anthy's Sernabatim ⓣ0832/277 1680, ⓔanthysguesthouse@rediffmail.com. Well-maintained rooms right on the sea, with tiny bathrooms and breezy verandas; there's a Keralan ayurvedic massage centre on site too. ❸

Antonette's Jack Corner, House #1695 Vas Waddo ⓣ0832/277 0358. Not a particularly inspiring location (next to a crossroads where all the local fishermen and lads hang out), but in a peaceful corner of the village and the rooms are large for the price, plus they have fridges – a rarity in this bracket. ❷

Camilson's Sernabatim ⓣ0832/277 1582, ⓦwww.camilsons.com. Well-maintained rooms, with private terraces, in a small resort set very close to the beach amid a lush garden, well away from the village. If they don't have vacancies, try the less welcoming *Xavier's* next door (ⓣ0832/227 1489) next door. Both ❺–❻

Carina Tamdi-Mati, Vas Waddo ⓣ0832/277 0413, ⓔcarinabeachresort@yahoo.com. Good-value, if somewhat lackadaisical, upmarket hotel in a tranquil location on the south side of Benaulim, with a pool, garden and bar-restaurant. Some rooms have a/c. ❺–❻

Cocohuts Sernabatim ⓣ9822/101398. The only bona fide budget option this far north of the village, a stone's throw from the beach. Its eight leaf huts have tiled floors and attached bathrooms, but heat up in the day and the beds are a bit ropey. A better prospect are the six rooms in an adjacent block, which have high clay-tiled roofs and partition toilets. ❸

L'Amour Beach Roadⓣ0832/277 0404, ⓕ277 0578. Benaulim's oldest hotel comprises a comfortable thirty-room cottage complex, with terrace restaurant, travel agent, money-changing and some a/c rooms: No single occupancy. ❺–❻

Libra Cottages Vas Waddo ⓣ0832/277 0598. Spartan but clean budget rooms, all with fans, attached bathrooms, sound plumbing and Western toilets. Very good value. ❷

Oshin Mazil Waddo ⓣ0832/277 0069, ⓔinaciooshin@rediffmail.com. Large, triple-storey complex set well back from the road. Its rooms are spacious and clean, with en-suite bathrooms and balconies; those on the top floor afford views over the tree tops. A notch above most places in this area, and very good value, but quite a walk from the beach. ❹

Palm Grove Tamdi-Mati, 149 Vas Waddo ⓣ0832/277 0059, ⓦwww.palmgrovegoa.com. Secluded hotel surrounded by beautiful gardens, offering two classes of room (Rs600–800), some of them a/c; plus there's one of Benaulim's better restaurants on site. A bike-ride back from the beachfront, but by far the most pleasant place in its class, and the management is very helpful. ❺

Paul Rina Tourist Home Beach Rd ⓣ0832/277 0595. Nice big rooms, secluded balconies and attached shower-toilets in a modern house next to the beach road. A little better than the standard budget places, so good value. If full, try the cheaper *Caroline Guest House* (ⓣ0832/277 0590) next door. Both ❷

Simon Cottages Sernabatim Ambeaxir ⓣ0832/277 1839. Currently among the best budget deals in Benaulim: huge rooms on three storeys, all with shower-toilets and verandas, opening onto a sandy courtyard in a quiet spot at the unspoilt north side of the village. ❷

Succorina Cottages 1711/A Vas Waddo ⓣ0832/277 0365. Immaculate rooms in a newish, pink-coloured house, 1km south of the crossroads in the fishing village, offering glimpses of the sea across the fields. A perfect place to get away from the tourist scene, and a 5-min walk from the quietest stretch of beach. Telephone bookings accepted. ❷

Tansy Cottages Beach road ⓣ0832/277 0574. Various sized apartments, from rooms with self-catering kitchenettes (for Rs500) to one- and two-bedroom flats in a three-storey block (Rs700–1000). The balconies could be more private, but you get lots of space indoors for your money, plus fridges and cooking utensils, and guesthouse owner Libby Fernandes is very welcoming. ❹–❻

Eating and drinking

Benaulim's proximity to Margao market, along with the presence of a large Christian fishing community, means its **restaurants** serve some of the most succulent, competitively priced seafood in Goa. The best shacks flank the beachfront area, where *Johncy's* catches most of the passing custom. However, you'll find better food at lower prices at places further along the beach, which seem to change chefs annually; the only way to find out which ones offer the best value for money is to wander past and see who has the most customers. An enduring favourite is *Domnick's,* whose gregarious owner hosts bonfire parties one night per week (traditionally on Tuesdays), featuring a live band; prices here are on the high side. *Pedro's* on the beachfront is marginally better value and also puts on gigs, mostly on Saturday nights.

Durigo's Sernabatim, 2km north of Maria Hall. This is the locals' favourite place to eat, serving traditional Goan seafood of a kind and quality you rarely find in the shacks: try their succulent mussels, lemon fish (*modso*) or barramundi (*chonok*), marinated in spicy, sour *rechead* sauce and pan-fried in millet. They also serve delicious local coconut *feni*, as well as the usual range of bottled beers. Some may find the atmosphere a bit rough and ready, in which case follow the example of the village's middle classes and order a takeout.
L'Amour *L'Amour* hotel. Just about the slickest restaurant in Benaulim, serving an exhaustive multi-cuisine dinner menu (mains Rs100–150), as well as drinks. With background noise limited to chinking china and hushed voices, it's also a relaxing place for breakfast: fresh fruit, muesli, yoghurt and pancakes.
Malibou Vas Waddo, near *Palm Grove.* Cosy little corner café-restaurant that's also a popular late-night drinking spot. Attentive service, fresh seafood, and a tandoor to bake pomfret, kebabs and spicy chicken. Mains from Rs75.
Palmira's Beach Road. Benaulim's best tourist breakfasts: wonderfully creamy, fresh set curd, copious fruit salads with coconut, real espresso coffee, warm local bread (*bajri*) and smiling service.
Palm Grove *Palm Grove* hotel. Mostly Goan seafood, with some Indian and Continental options, served in a smart new garden pagoda, against a backdrop of illuminated trees. Main courses Rs100–150.
Satkar Maria Hall Crossroads. No-frills locals' *udipi* canteen that's the only place in the village where you can order regular Indian snacks – samosas, masala dosas, hot pakoras and spicy chickpea stew (*channa*) – at regular Indian prices. And the *pau bhaji* breakfast here is a must.
Seshaa's Maria Hall Crossroads. Gloomy and rather cramped local lads' café, but great for pukka Goan *channa bhaji* and, best of all, deliciously flaky veg or beef patties.

The far south: Canacona

Ceded to the Portuguese by the Raja of Sund in the Treaty of 1791, Goa's **far south** – **Canacona** district – was among the last parts of the territory to be absorbed into the Novas Conquistas, and has retained a distinctly Hindu feel. The area also boasts some of the state's most outstanding scenery. Set against a backdrop of the jungle-covered Sahyadri hills (an extension of the Western Ghat range), a string of pearl-white coves and sweeping beaches scoop its indented coastline, enfolded by laterite headlands and colossal piles of black boulders.

With the exception of the village of **Palolem**, whose near-perfect beach attracts a deluge of travellers during high season, coastal settlements such as **Agonda**, a short way north, remain rooted in a traditional fishing and *toddy*-tapping economy. However, the red gash of the **Konkan Railway** threatens to bring its days as a tranquil rural backwater to an end. For the last few years, it has been possible to reach Canacona by direct "super-fast" express trains from Mumbai, Panjim and Mangalore: the developers' bulldozers and concrete mixers are sure to follow.

The region's main transport artery is the NH-17, which crawls across the Sahyadri and Karmali ghats towards Karnataka via the district headquarters, **Chaudi**; travellers jump off here for Palolem, a few kilometres across the fields, and the small market is a useful source of essentials. Bus services between here and Margao are frequent; off the highway, however, bullock carts and bicycles still outnumber motor vehicles. The only way to do the area justice, therefore, is by motorcycle, although you'll have to rent one further north (Benaulim's your best bet for this) and drive it down here, as few are available in situ.

Agonda

AGONDA, 10km north of Chaudi, can only be reached along the sinuous coast road connecting Cabo da Rama with NH-17 at Chaudi. No signposts mark the turning, and few of the tourists that whizz past en route to Palolem pull off here, but the beach is superb – albeit with a strong undertow that weak swimmers should be very wary of (head for the safer cove at the far southern end of the beach, where the fishing boats are moored).

Facilities for visitors are basic, but adequate, and well spaced apart: Agonda never gets too congested, even in peak season. **Places to stay and eat** are dotted along the road behind the beach, and over the past couple of seasons a handful of small guesthouses and treehouse camps have also opened up at the northern end, beyond the church. If you're only overnighting here en route to or from Palolem, *Dercy's* should probably be your first choice, not least because its terrace restaurant offers the best seafood in the village: groaning fillets of butter-garlic rockfish straight off the boat, served with piles of chips. For a sundowner, the aptly named *Sun Set Bar*, up on a bluff just south of *Dercy's* surveying the bay, is hard to beat.

Accommodation

Dercy's south end of the beach, on the roadside ⓣ0832/264 7503. Exceptionally clean and comfortable, with tiled floors and good sized bathrooms. Those on the first floor (front side) have a common sea-facing veranda that catches the breezes; you can lie in bed and hear the waves crashing only 100m away. Proprietor Inacio also runs a couple of rows of beach huts on the opposite side of the lane. ❸

Dunhill Beach Resort A short way down the lane beyond *Dercy's* ⓣ0832/264 7604, ⓔdunhill-resort@rediffmail.com. All the rooms here are en-suite with small verandas opening onto a sandy enclosure, where you can eat locally caught fish (the pan-fried *rawa* mackerel is delicious). The family also offer Internet access for guests. ❸

Jelicia north end of the beach, 100m before *Sea View*; no phone. A couple of simple budget rooms, with coconut wood rafters and clay tile roofs, plus three huts on the beach. ❶–❷

Palm Beach Lifestyle Resort Behind *Dercy's* ⓣ0832/214 7783. Swish, purpose-built chalets that have nice wooden decks and sea views. The most comfortable option in Agonda. ❻

Maria Paul just north of *Dercy's* towards the church ⓣ0832/264 7606. Big new pink building on the roadside (look for the disconcerting "Welcome Aboard" life-ring), with six large, cool, marble-floored rooms. A bigger and slightly more anonymous guesthouse than the others in the village, which some might prefer. ❹

Sami near the church ⓣ9850/453805. Most appealing of the village's small hut camps, right on the beach. Larger than average huts that are far enough apart, with painted balconies. Bikes for rent. Also worth trying is the nearby *Madhu* (ⓣ0832/264 7116, ⓔshekhar1303@sify.com). Both ❷

Sea View at the far north end of the beach ⓣ0832/264 7548. The quietest option: three lovely mud-and-thatch huts with cow-dung floors (a lot more fragrant than they may sound) and decent beds, run by the friendly Fatima Fernandes. They're ultra basic, but clean and secluded, and slap on the sand. ❷

Palolem

Nowhere else in peninsula India conforms so closely to the archetypal image of a paradise beach as **PALOLEM**, 35km south of Margao. Lined with a swaying curtain of coconut palms, the bay forms a perfect curve of golden sand, arcing north from a giant pile of boulders to the spur of Sahyadri Ghat, which tapers into the sea draped in thick forest. For those foreigners who found their way here before the mid-1990s, however, Palolem is most definitely a paradise lost

△ Fishing boat, Palolem

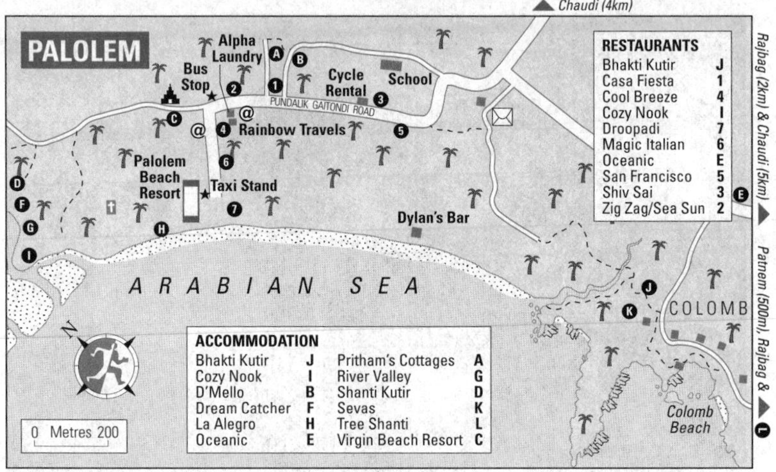

these days. With the rest of Goa largely carved up by package tourism, this is the first-choice destination of most independent travellers, and the numbers can feel overwhelming in peak season, when literally thousands of people spill across the beach. Behind them, an unbroken line of shacks and Thai-style bamboo- and palm-leaf huts provide food and shelter that grows more sophisticated (and less Goan) with each season – not least because many of the businesses here are now run, if not owned, by expatriates. Thanks to a local law forbidding the construction of permanent buildings close to the beach, development has been restrained, but it's still a far cry from the idyll of only a few years ago.

Palolem in full swing is the kind of place you'll either love at first sight or want to get away from as quickly as possible. If you're in the latter category, try smaller, less frequented **Patnem** beach, a short walk south, where the shack scene is more subdued and the sand emptier. Further south still, **Rajbag**, around half-an-hour's walk from Palolem, used to be one of Goa's last deserted beaches until a vast, seven-star luxury resort was recently built slap behind it.

Practicalities

Frequent **buses** run between Margao and Karwar (in Karnataka) via Chaudi (every 30min; 2hr), from where you can pick up an **auto-rickshaw** (Rs50) or **taxi** (Rs75) for the 2km journey west to Palolem. Alternatively, get off the bus at the Char Rastay ("Four-Way") crossroads, 1.5km before Chaudi, and walk

Water shortages in Palolem

The vast increase in Palolem's visitor numbers has led, in part, to the severe water shortages that have afflicted Canacona district over the past three years. The municipality seems unwilling or unable to do anything about the problem, so the onus falls on tourists to **use as little water as possible** during their stay. One of the most effective ways you can do this is to **avoid water toilets**, which dump a colossal quantity of untreated sewage into often poorly manufactured septic tanks below the ground. Traditional pig loos, still common in the village, are a far cleaner, greener option.

the remaining kilometre or so to the village. Hourly buses also go all the way to Palolem from Margao; these stop at the end of the lane leading from the main street to the beachfront.

The last bus from Palolem to Chaudi/Margao leaves at around 4.30pm; check with the locals for the precise times, as these change seasonally. **Bicycles** may be rented from a stall halfway along the main street for the princely sum of Rs5 per hour (with discounts for longer periods). The village has a dozen or more STD/ ISD **telephones**: avoid the one in the *Beach Resort*, which charges more than double the going rate for international calls, and head for the much cheaper booths 100m down the lane (next to the bus stop). This is also where you'll find several **Internet cafés**; others are dotted around the village, and there are three or four over in Patnem. Rates are pretty standard at around Rs40/hr.

You can **change money** at any number of agents advertising their services along the lanes through Palolem and on the beach road, though it's worth shopping around for the best rates; LKP Forex in the *Palolem Beach Resort* (on the beachfront behind the taxi stand) was the most competitive when we last checked. The nearest **ATM** (for Visa and Mastercard withdrawals) is in Chaudi. For those wishing to stash valuables, Lalita Enterprises, on the main beach road, offer lockers for Rs15 per day.

Accommodation

Local resistance to large-scale development explains why most of the village's **accommodation** consists of simple palm-leaf huts or tree houses. With the exception of the more snazzily set up places listed below, there's very little difference between most of the camps: check in to the first that takes your fancy and investigate the rest of the beach at leisure when you've found your feet. The other option is to look for a room in a family home. The majority, though not all, of these also have limited shared washing facilities, and sometimes pig toilets. The easiest way to find a place is to walk around the palm groves behind the beach with a rucksack; sooner or later someone will approach you. Rates vary depending on the size of the room, levels of comfort and the time of year.

At the time of writing, some of the best set up and situated places were at the far north end of the beach, just behind *Cozy Nook* on the banks of the estuary (see map opposite). At the southern end, there are several good places in the *waddo* of Colomb, which we cover below.

Bhakti Kutir Colomb ⓣ0832/264 3469 or 264 3472, ⓦwww.bhaktikutir.com. Eco-friendly, Indian-village-style "Eco Huts" equipped with Western amenities (including completely biodegradable chemical toilets), set amid mature gardens five minutes' walk from the south end of Palolem beach, on the headland above the fishing village. Beautifully situated, discreet and sensitively designed to blend with the landscape by its German–Goan owners. The new double-storey units (❽), aimed at families, offer more space; and there's a quality ayurvedic healing centre on site. ❻

Cozy Nook north end of the beach, near the island ⓣ0832/264 3550. One of the most attractive setups in the village, comprising 25 bamboo huts (sharing seven toilets, but with good mattresses, mosquito nets, safe lockers and fans) opening onto the lagoon on one side and the beach on the other – an unbeatable spot, which explains the higher than average tariffs. ❺

D'Mello Pundalik Gaitondi Rd ⓣ0832/264 3057. A mix of en-suite and shared-bathroom rooms on three storeys, some in a concrete annexe set back from the main road. Well maintained, and most have balconies. ❸

Dream Catcher north end of the beach behind *Cozy Nook* ⓣ0832/264 4873 or 9822/137446, ⓔlalalandjackie7@yahoo.com. Individually styled huts, with more space, better mattresses, nicer textiles, bigger windows and sturdier foundations than most, in a plum position by the riverside. The welcoming Keralan-Liverpudlian couple who run it have also built shaded yoga *shala* for classes, and there's a "chillout-ambient bar". ❹–❺

La Alegro north side of the beach ⓣ0832/264 4261. En-suite rooms right on the beach. Very basic and not all that private, but the location's great. The same owner also has five more (cheaper) identikit rooms around the back, as well as a clutch of slightly larger ones on Pundalik Gaitondi Rd. ❸

Oceanic Tembi Waddo ⓣ0832/264 3059, ⓦwww.hotel-oceanic.com. A relative newcomer that, strictly speaking, is in Colomb, a 10-min walk inland from the beach; you can also get here via the back-road to Chaudi. Owned and managed by a resident British couple, its rooms are tastefully fitted-out, with large mosquito nets, blockprinted bedspreads and bedside lamps. There's also a brand new pool on a wooded terrace behind, and a quality restaurant. ❹

Pritham's Cottages down a lane north of Pundalik Gaitondi Rd ⓣ0832/264 3320. Quiet two-storey block of budget rooms in the centre of the village: they're bigger than average (all with attached bathrooms) and share a common veranda. ❷

River Valley north end of beach behind *Cozy Nook* ⓣ9822/155502, ⓔsrmh2141@hotmail.com. This small hut camp and its hospitable young owner, Manju, consistently get rave reviews. Named after sacred Indian rivers, the ten bamboo huts (sharing three toilets) are in a nice open compound with beautiful views across the estuary to the hills and forest. Good value for the location, which is a lot more relaxing than comparable sites on the beach. A sound budget choice. ❷

Shanti Kutir north end of beach behind *River Valley* and *Dream Catcher* ⓣ9422/450392 or 9822/183631, ⓔshantikutirgoa@yahoo.co.in. Keralan-run hut camp that's pleasantly secluded and well sited on the river. Thirty comfortable huts (some en-suite) on stilts. Rates vary according to proximity to the water. ❷–❸

Sevas Colomb ⓣ0832/231 7408 or 9326/117674, %ⓔsevasmicho@yahoo.com. A cheaper, less sophisticated version of *Bhakti Kutir*, but beautifully done all the same, and the site is peaceful. The "ethnic" cabañas have traditional rice-straw roofs, mud and dung floors, hygienic squat-style loos and bucket baths. Also on offer are massages and yoga classes, and there's a pleasant restaurant serving very good thalis for only Rs50. ❹

Tree Shanti Colomb ⓣ0832/264 4460, ⓔsaritagita7@rediffmail.com. Seven basic rooms and three huts in a lovely spot under dense tree cover, ten minutes' walk south of Palolem in Colomb. Run by the feisty Komarpant sisters, this is a fun and lively place to stay with a full-on family atmosphere. ❷

Virgin Beach Resort Palolem village ⓣ0832/264 3451. Swanky new tiled rooms, in modern three-storey block near the lane. Not exactly the kind of architecture that enhances the village's natural feel, but it's an out-of-the-way spot and some may consider the comfort and security a good trade-off. ❷

Eating and drinking

Palolem's **restaurants** and **bars** reflect the cosmopolitan make-up of its visitors. Each year, a fresh batch of innovative, ever more stylish places open, most of them managed by expats – and both standards, and prices, have increased greatly as a consequence. For those on tight budgets, there are a couple of cheap and cheerful **bhaji stalls** outside the landmark *Palolem Beach Resort*, and a pair of local cafés along the road running parallel with the beach – the Hindu *Shiv Sai* and Christian *San Francisco* – which serve filling breakfasts of *pau bhaji*, fluffy bread rolls, omelettes and chai for next to nothing, and equally inexpensive fish-currry-rice meals and samosas from lunchtime. Again, you'll find several good options in the *waddo* of Colomb, just south of Palolem.

Bhakti Kutir Colomb. Laid-back terrace café-restaurant with rustic wooden tables and an Indo-European fusion menu: sunny tomato and mozzarella salad (with fresh basil), fish from the bay and north Indian vegetarian dishes, all made with local and organically produced ingredients.

Casa Fiesta Pundalik Gaitondi Rd. Funky expat-run place on the main drag, offering an eclectic menu of world cuisine: hummus, Greek salad, Mexican specialities and fish *pollichatu*; mains (mostly under Rs175) come with delicious roast potatoes.

Cool Breeze Beach Rd. This is one of the classiest restaurants in the village. The steaks, tandoori chicken and seafood, in particular, have set new standards for Palolem, and the prices are reasonable. Come early, or you could face a long wait for a table – and leave room for the banoffi pie dessert. Most mains around Rs150–200.

Cozy Nook far north end of the beach. Wholesome Goan-style cooking served on a small terrace that occupies a prime position opposite the island at the end of the bay. The filling four-course set dinners (7–9pm; Rs150) are deservedly popular, offering imaginative and carefully prepared dishes such as pan-fried fish, aubergine with shrimps and fresh beans. They also do a tasty veg equivalent (Rs100), as well as a full seafood and north Indian curry, and there's a popular, hygienic salad bar (eat all you like for Rs100).

Droopadi on the beachfront. This place enjoys both a top location and Palolem's best Indian chef, who specializes in rich, creamy Mughlai dishes and tandoori fish. Go for the superb *murg makhini* or one of the paneer options. With most main courses around Rs125, prices are low considering the quality of the cooking.

Magic Italian Beach Rd. South Goa's number one Italian restaurant, on the busy approach to the seafront, serving home-made ravioli and tagliatelle, along with scrumptious wood-fired pizzas (Rs130–175).

Oceanic Tembi Waddo, Colomb. Chilled terrace restaurant, set well back from the beach but worth the walk for the better-than-average food and background music (the owner is an ex-Womad sound man). North and South Indian dishes are the chef's forte (especially *dum aloo* Kashmiri and butter chicken), but there's also great red and green Thai curries, tempting desserts, including lemon-and-ginger cheesecake and banoffi pie, and coffee liqueur. Check the specials board for dishes of the day. Occasional live music.

Zig Zag/Sea Sun Pundalik Gaitondi Rd. A Keralan-British co-project, particularly strong on South Indian food (a rarity in Palolem), in addition to veg, meat and fish dishes prepared with light, mild sauces and fresh herbs. Mains under Rs150. Some confusion surrounds the name, so look for both.

South of Palolem: Colomb, Patnem and Rajbag

Once across the creek and boulder-covered spur bounding the south end of Palolem beach, you arrive at **COLOMB**, a largely Hindu fishing village scattered around a series of rocky coves. Dozens of long-stay rooms, leaf huts and houses are tucked away under the palm groves and on the picturesque headland running seawards from the *Boom Shankar Bar*, at the bottom of the bay. This is the best place in the village to start an accommodation hunt – the lads will know of any vacant places; but be warned that most of the rooms here are very basic indeed and may not have running water, let alone toilets. Alternatively, there are several good guesthouses reviewed along with Palolem's accommodation (pp.849–850).

A string of small hut camps and shacks line the next beach south, **PATNEM**, but the scene is altogether more subdued here than in Palolem. The beach, curving for roughly a kilometre to a steep bluff, is broad, with little shade, and shelves quite steeply at certain phases of the tide, though the undertow rarely gets dangerously strong. There are plenty of good **accommodation** options, ranging from no-frills leaf huts with shared toilets to fully en-suite rooms with verandas. At the top of the range, *Home*, in the centre of the beach (Ⓣ0832/264 3916, Ⓔhomeispatnem@yahoo.com; ❸), is a cut above your average beachfront guesthouse, run by a Swiss-English couple who've fitted out an annexe of en-suite rooms with attractive textiles, lampshades and other cosy little touches to justify higher than usual tariffs. They also run Patnem's best café-restaurant, serving *mezes*, fresh salads, Italian espresso and wonderful desserts (such as banoffi pie, warm apple tart with fresh cream, chocolate-and-walnut cake). A notch cheaper, but another place that's made an untypically Goan effort with interior design, is *Mountain Palms* (no phone; ❷), whose bargain huts are kitted out with big four-posters, pink mosquito nets, silky drapes and floral curtains. Among the string of camps behind the beach shacks, *Namaste* (Ⓣ9850/925821; ❷), is another dependable, fun budget option, run by the amiable Satay, most of whose clientele comes back season after season. He offers two categories of shack, ranging from Rs150–350 depending on size and time of year. *Magic View*, tucked at the far north end of the beach, serves the best cappuccinos for miles, chocolate pastries for breakfast, good salads and pastas, though its pizzas (evenings only) get mixed reviews. With main courses from Rs100–140, prices are a bit above average for the area, but the view over the beach is as lovely as its name suggests.

Moving on from Goa

Seats on planes from Goa can be in short supply, especially around Diwali and Christmas. Wherever possible, try and book directly through the airline, as private agents charge the dollar fare at poor rates of exchange; addresses of airline offices in Panjim are listed on p.803. Seats on all **Konkan Railway** services can be booked at the KRC reservation office on the first floor of Panjim's Kadamba bus stand (Mon–Sat 8am–8pm, Sun 8am–2pm), or at KRC's main reservation hall in Margao station (Mon–Sat 8am–4.30pm, Sun 8am–2pm; ⓣ0834/271 2780). Make bookings as far in advance as possible, and try to get to the offices soon after opening time – the queues can be horrendous (at the KRC office in Panjim, touts monopolize queue numbers early in the day, and then charge what they think they can get away with to wait on your behalf). Seats on the Konkan Railway from Goa to Mumbai are in notoriously short supply as the lion's share of the quotas goes to longer-distance travellers from Kerala, with the result that peak periods tend to be reserved up to two months in advance. One way around this is to **book online** at ⓦwww.konkanrailway.com, though bear in mind if you do you'll only be eligible for the relatively expensive three-tier a/c fares (Rs1250 one-way) and must make your booking between seven and two days before your date of departure.

Kadamba **bus tickets** can be bought in advance at their offices in Panjim and Mapusa bus stands (daily 9–11am & 2–5pm); private companies sell theirs through the many travel agents immediately outside the bus stand in Panjim, and at the bottom of the square in Mapusa. **Information** on all departures and fares is available from Goa Tourism's counter inside Panjim's bus stand (see p.799).

For a full rundown of transport from Goa, see "Travel details" p.855.

To Mumbai

If you're heading north to **Mumbai**, the quickest and easiest way is **by plane**. Between eight and ten flights leave Goa's Dabolim airport daily. One-way fares range from $60 or less with the low-cost Internet airline Deccan Air (ⓦwww.airdeccan.net) to $95 with Indian Airlines (ⓦwww.indian-airlines.nic.in), or $100 with Sahara (ⓦwww.airsahara.net) or Jet (www.jetairways.com). In addition, Air India (ⓦwww.airindia.com) operates a service to Mumbai on which, you can nearly always get a seat (the one drawback is that you have to check in three hours before departure as Air India is an international carrier).

Two services run daily on the **Konkan Railway**, the most convenient being the overnight Konkankanya Express (#0112), which departs from Margao at 6pm, arriving at CST (still commonly known as "Victoria Terminus", or "VT") at 5.50am the following day. The other fast train from Margao to Mumbai CST is the Mandvi Express (#0104), departing at 10.10am and arriving at 9.45pm.

The cheapest, though most nightmarish, way to get to Mumbai is by **night bus**, which takes fourteen to eighteen hours, covering 500km of rough road at often terrifying speeds. Fares vary according to levels of comfort, and luxury buses arrive two or three hours sooner. Book Kadamba bus tickets at their offices in the Panjim and Mapusa bus stands private companies sell theirs through the many travel agents immediately outside the bus stand in Panjim, and at the bottom of the square in Mapusa. The most popular private service to Mumbai, and the most expensive, is the 24-seater run by Paulo Travels. A cramped berth on this bus (which bizarrely you may have to share) costs Rs650, and it is worth pointing out that women travellers have complained of harassment during the journey. For tickets, contact Paulo near the Kadamba bus stand, Panjim (ⓣ0832/222 3736) or at *Hotel Nanutel*, opposite Club Harmonia, Margao (ⓣ0834/272 1516). Information on all departures and fares is available from Goa Tourism's counter inside Panjim's bus stand (see Arrival, information and local transport, p.798).

To Hampi

THe least stressful way to reach Hampi from Goa is by **train**. Three services each week leave Vasco (at 7.10am) and Margao (7.35am) on Wednesdays, Saturdays and Sundays, arriving in Hospet – the nearest railhead to Hampi – just over eight and a half hours later at 4pm. Tickets can be bought on the day at either point of departure. This is a wonderful rail journey, taking you along one of the wildest stretches of the Western Ghats, including the Dudhsagar Falls area (see p.809). Travelling in the other direction, trains leave Hospet at 8.50am on Mondays, Thursdays and Fridays, and arrive in Margao at 6.23pm. Tickets cost Rs700 for two-tier a/c, Rs450 for a/c three-tier and Rs170 in standard sleeper class.

The **bus** journey covering the same route is no cheaper than the train (sleeper class) and far more gruelling. Two or three clapped-out government services leave Panjim's Kadamba stand (platform 9) each morning for Hospet, the last one at 10.30am. Brace yourself for a long, hard slog; all being well, it should take nine or ten hours, but delays and breakdowns are frustratingly frequent. **Tickets** for Kadamba and KSRTC (Karnatakan State Road Transport Corporation) services should be booked at least one day in advance at the hatches in the bus stand.

From Margao, you can also travel to Hampi on a swish **night bus**, complete with pneumatic suspension and berths. The service, operated by Paulo Travels, leaves at 6pm from a lot next to the *Nanutel Hotel* on Margao's Rua da Padre Miranda, arriving in Hampi early the next morning. Tickets cost around Rs450 and can be bought from most reputable travel agents around the state. Although the coach is comfortable enough, the coffin-like berths can get very hot and stuffy, making sleep very difficult.

To Gokarna, Jog Falls, Mangalore and southern Karnataka

From Goa, the fastest and most convenient way to travel down the coast to Gokarna is via the **Konkan Railway**. At 2.10pm, the Verna–Mangalore Passenger leaves Margao, passing through Chaudi at 2.50pmpm en route to Gokarna Road, the town's railhead, where it arrives at around 4pm. The station lies 9km east of Gokarna itself, but a minibus shuttles passengers the rest of the way. As this is classed as a passenger service, you don't have to buy tickets in advance; just turn up at the station 30min before the departure and pay at the regular ticket counter. It's a good idea to **check timings** in advance, through any tourist office or travel agent, or via the KRC's website (Ⓦ www.konkanrailway.com).

Buses take as much as two-and-a-half hours longer to cover the same route. A direct service leaves Margao's interstate stand in the north of town daily at 1pm. You can also get there by catching any of the services that run between Goa and Mangalore, and jumping off either at **Ankola**, or at the Gokarna junction on the main highway, from where frequent private minibuses and tempos run into town.

The Konkan highway is straightforward by **motorcycle**, with a better-than-average road surface, and frequent fuel stops along the way. A rented bike also gives the option to explore some of the gorgeous beaches seen from the road. Aside from the dangers involved in motorcycling on Indian highways, the main drawback is **crossing the border**, which can involve a baksheesh transaction.

For **Jog Falls**, the easiest route is the Konkan Railway to **Honavar** (two stations south of Gokarna Road; 2hr 15min), from where seven daily buses run up the *ghats* to Jog.

To Delhi

The Konkan Railway has also improved train services to **Delhi**, which can now be reached on the superfast Rajdhani Express #2431 in a little over 26 hours (Weds & Fri only). A slower daily service, the Vasco–Nizamuddin Express (#2779) takes nearly 38 hours to cover the same distance. Alternatively, you can fly to the capital with Indian Airlines or Jet in 2hr 45min from around $249 one-way.

Most of the **buses** between Palolem and Margao pass through Patnem (roughly 20min later), stopping at regular intervals along the lane running parallel with the beach.

At low tide, you can walk around the bottom of the steep-sided headland dividing Patnem from neighbouring **RAJBAG**, another kilometre-long sweep of white sand. Sadly, its remote feel has been entirely submerged by the massive five-star *Goa Grand Intercontinental* (Ⓦwww.intercontinental.com; ❾), recently erected on the land behind it – much to the annoyance of the locals, who campaigned for four years to stop the project.

It's possible to press on even further **south from Rajbag**, by crossing the Talpona River via a hand-paddled ferry, which usually has to be summoned from the far bank (fix a return price in advance and only pay once you've completed both legs of the trip, as the boatmen are rumoured to have been holding wealthy tourists from the *Goa Grand* to ransom by refusing to paddle them back unless they hand over huge "tips"). Once across, a short walk brings you to **Talpona Beach**, backed by low dunes and a line of straggly palms. From there, assuming you haven't already succumbed to sunstorke and dehydration, you can cross the headland at the end of the beach to reach **Galjibag**, a totally wild white-sand bay that's a protected nesting site for Olive Ridley marine **turtles.** A strong undertow means swimming isn't safe here.

Cotigao Wildlife Sanctuary

The **Cotigao Wildlife Sanctuary**, 12km southeast of Palolem, was established in 1969 to protect a remote and vulnerable area of forest lining the Goa–Karnataka border. Encompassing 86 square kilometres of mixed deciduous woodland, the reserve is certain to inspire tree lovers, but less likely to yield many wildlife sightings: its tigers and leopards were hunted out long ago, while the gazelles, sloth bears, porcupines, panthers and hyenas that allegedly lurk in the woods rarely appear. You do, however, stand a good chance of spotting at least two species of monkey, a couple of wild boar and the odd gaur (the primeval-looking Indian bison), as well as plenty of exotic birdlife, including hornbills. Best visited between October and March, Cotigao is a peaceful and scenic park that makes a pleasant day-trip from Palolem. Any of the buses running south on the NH-14 to Karwar via Chaudi will drop you within 2km of the gates. However, to explore the inner reaches of the sanctuary, you really need your own transport. The wardens at the reserve's small **Interpretative Centre** at the main gate, where you have to pay your entry fees (Rs15, plus Rs75 for a car, Rs20 for motorbike; Rs40 for camera permit) will show you how to get to a 25-metre-high tree-top watchtower, overlooking a **waterhole** that attracts a handful of animals around dawn and dusk. You can also **stay** in a rather unprepossessing little room (❷) in the compound behind the main reserve gates; it's rented out on a first-come first-served basis. Food and drink may be available by prior arrangement, and there's a **shop** at the nearest village, 2km inside the park.

More inspiring accommodation is to be found at a secluded riverside location on the edge of Cotigao. Hidden away in a working spice plantation, *Pepper Valley* (Ⓣ0832/264 2370; ❸) comprises a row of simple huts on the riverbank, shaded by a canopy of areca palms, with cashew bushes and yam plants growing around. Facilities are basic for the money, but this is lovely spot to chill out for an evening. Too find it, turn left at the Cotigao Interpretative Centre then follow the road for 500m until you see a signboard indicating a motorable track off to the right.

Travel details

Trains

Margao to: Chaudi (3 daily; 50min); Colem (3 weekly; 55min); Delhi (1–2 daily; 26–35hr); Ernakulam/Kochi (4 weekly; 12–15hr 40min); Gokarna (2 daily; 1hr 50min); Hospet (3 weekly; 8hr); Hubli (3 weekly; 5hr 30min); Mangalore/Kanakadi (5 daily; 4–6hr); Mumbai (4–5 daily; 12hr); Pune (1 weekly; 13hr 40min); Thiruvananthapuram (1–2 daily; 16hr); Udupi (4 daily; 3hr 40min).

Buses

Benaulim to: Cavelossim (hourly; 20min); Colva (every 30min; 20min); Margao (every 30min; 15min); Mobor (hourly; 25min).
Chaudi to: Gokarna (2 daily; 3hr); Karwar (every 30min; 1hr); Margao (every 30min; 1hr 40min); Palolem (2 daily; 15min); Panjim (hourly; 2hr 15min).
Mapusa to: Anjuna (hourly; 30min); Arambol (12 daily; 1hr 45min); Baga (hourly; 30min); Calangute (hourly; 45min); Chapora (every 30min; 30–40min); Mumbai (6 daily; 13–17hr); Panjim (every 15min; 25min); Vagator (every 30min; 25–35min).
Margao to: Agonda (4 daily; 2hr); Benaulim (every 30min; 15min); Cavelossim (8 daily; 30min); Chandor (hourly; 45min); Chaudi (every 30min; 1hr 40min); Colva (every 15min; 20–30min); Gokarna (2 daily; 4hr 30min); Hampi (1 nightly; 10hr); Karwar (every 30min; 2hr); Mangalore (5 daily; 7hr); Mapusa (10 daily; 2hr 30min); Mobor (8 daily; 35min); Mumbai (2 daily; 16–18hr); Panjim (every 30min; 50min); Pune (1 daily; 12hr).
Panjim to: Arambol (12 daily; 1hr 45min); Aurangabad (1 daily; 16hr); Baga (every 30min; 45min); Bijapur (7 daily; 10hr); Calangute (every 30min; 40min); Candolim (every 30min; 30min); Chaudi (hourly; 2hr 15min); Gokarna (2 daily; 5hr 30min); Hampi (2 daily; 9–10hr); Hospet (3 daily; 9hr); Hubli (hourly; 6hr); Hyderabad (1 daily; 18hr); Kolhapur (hourly; 8hr); Mahabaleshwar (1 daily; 12hr); Mangalore (4 daily; 10hr); Mapusa (every 15min; 25min); Margao (every 15min; 55min); Morjim (6 daily; 1hr 30min–2hr); Mumbai (6 daily; 14–18hr); Mysore (2 daily; 17hr); Old Goa (every 15min; 20min); Ponda (hourly; 50min); Pune (7 daily; 12hr).

Flights

For a list of **airline addresses and websites,** see p.803. In the listings below **IA** is Indian Airlines, **AI** Air India, **JA** Jet Airways, **SA** Sahara Airlines and **AD** Air Deccan.
Dabolim airport (Vasco da Gama) to: Bangalore (2 daily; 1hr 30min–2hr 25min); Chennai (Madras) (2 weekly; 3hr 15min); Cochin (Kochi) (2 weekly; 1hr); Delhi (IA, SA 2 daily; 2hr 35min–3hr 45min); Hyderabad (DA, JA 2 daily; 1hr 40min–3hr 15min); Kolkota (Calcutta) (AS 2 daily; 3hr 30min); Mumbai (IA, AI, JA, SA & DA 8–10 daily; 40–50min).

CHAPTER 13

Highlights

* **Victoria Memorial** This monument to the British Empire in Kolkata is a dizzying blend of Moghul and Italian architecture. See p.876

* **Eden Gardens** Enjoy the chaos and spectacle of a match at Kolkata's famous cricket ground. See p.878

* **Sunderbans** A mangrove forest that is home to a profusion of wildlife, including Bengal tigers. See p.896

* **Shantiniketan** This tranquil university town exudes the spirit of its founder, the mystic and philosopher Rabindranath Tagore. See p.899

* **Toy Train** Small-gauge steam-driven railway, which takes nine hours to loop though stunning scenery to Darjeeling. See p.905

* **Darjeeling** A charming hill station with spectacular views and famously fine tea. See p.908

* **Singalila Trek** This Darjeeling trek features unforgettable mountain vistas, especially beautiful in April and May, when the rhododendrons are in bloom. See p.916

* **Kalimpong** Orchids grow in profusion around this backwater hill station. See p.919

△ Victoria Memorial, Kolkata

13

Kolkata (Calcutta) and West Bengal

Unique among Indian states in stretching all the way from the Himalayas to the sea, **WEST BENGAL** is nonetheless explored in depth by few travellers. That may have something to do with the exaggerated reputation of its capital, **KOLKATA (Calcutta)**, a sophisticated and friendly city that belies its popular image as poverty-stricken and chaotic. Certainly the rest of Bengal holds an extraordinary assortment of landscapes and cultures, ranging from the dramatic hill station of **Darjeeling**, within sight of some of the highest mountains in the world, to the vast mangrove swamps of the **Sunderbans**, prowled by man-eating Royal Bengal tigers. The narrow central band of the state is cut across by the huge River Ganges as it pours from Bihar into Bangladesh; the **Farrakha Barrage** controls the movement of south-flowing channels such as the River Hooghly, the lifeline of Kolkata.

At the height of British rule, in the nineteenth and early twentieth centuries, Bengal flourished both culturally and materially, nurturing a uniquely creative blend of West and East. The **Bengali Renaissance** produced thinkers, writers and artists such as Raja Ram Mohan Roy, Bankim Chandra Chatterjee, and above all **Rabindranath Tagore**, whose collective influence still permeates Bengali society a century later.

Not all of Bengal, however, is Bengali; the current Nepalese-led separatist movement for the creation of a semi-autonomous "Gurkhaland" in the Darjeeling area has highlighted sharp differences in culture. Although the Hindu Nepalese migration eastward from the nineteenth century onwards has largely displaced the indigenous tribal groups of the north, Lamaist Tibetan Buddhism continues to flourish, partly due to an influx of Tibetan refugees. In the southwest, on the other hand, tribal groups such as the Santhals and the Mundas still maintain a presence, and itinerant Baul **musicians** epitomize the region's traditions of song and dance. The Bauls are most often heard around Tagore's university at **Shantiniketan**, where his own musical form, *Rabindra Sangeet*, is a popular amalgam of influences including folk and classical. Other historical specialities of Bengal include its ornate **terracotta temples**, as seen at Bishnupur, and its **silk** production, concentrated around **Murshidabad**, the last independent capital of Bengal.

Bengal's own brand of Hinduism emphasizes the **mother goddess**, who appears in such guises as the fearsome Kali and Durga, the benign Saraswati, goddess of learning, and Lakshmi, the goddess of wealth. The most mysterious of all is Tara,

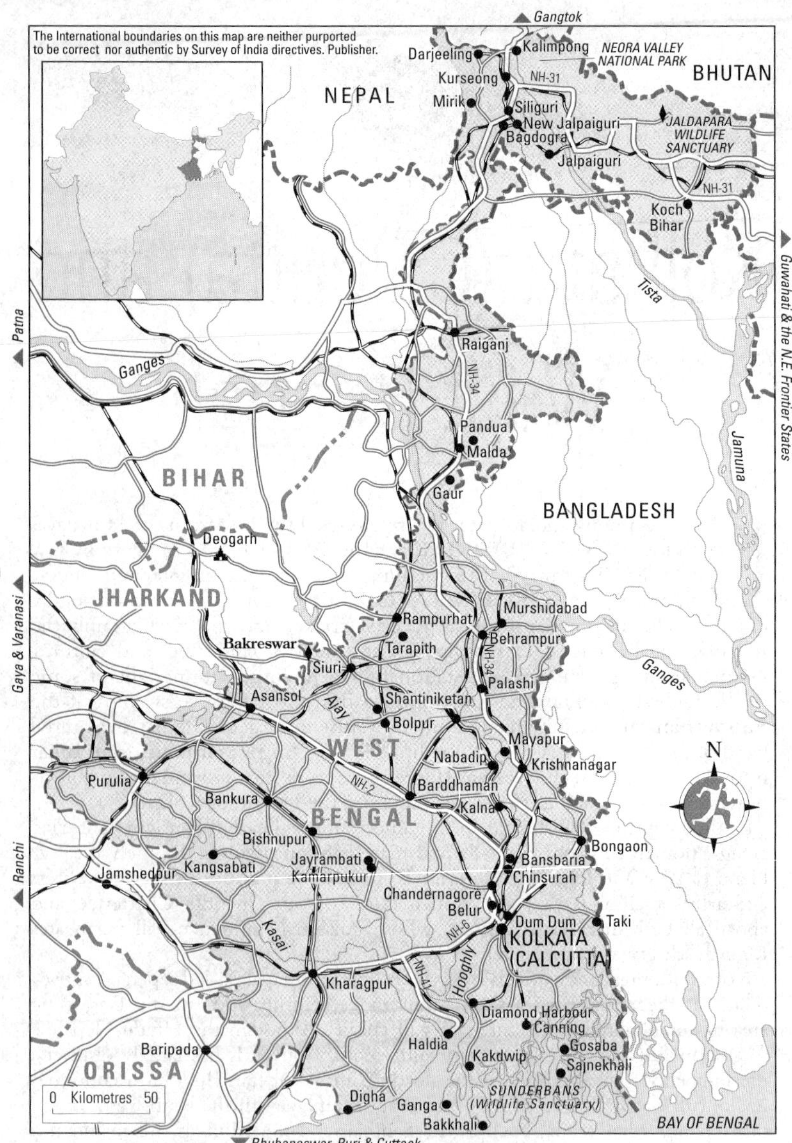

an echo of medieval links with Buddhism; her temple at Tarapith is perhaps the greatest centre of Tantrism in the entire country. In recent years, however, the prayer flags have given way to red flags, and the new religion of politics.

Some history

Although Bengal was part of the Mauryan empire during the third century BC, it first came to prominence in its own right under the Guptas in the fourth century AD. So dependent was it on trade with the Mediterranean that the fall of Rome caused a sharp decline, only reversed with the rise of the Pala dynasty in the eighth century.

After a short-lived period of rule by the highly cultured Senas, based at **Gaur**, Bengal was brought under Muslim rule at the end of the twelfth century by the first Sultan of Delhi, Qutb-ud-din-Aibak. Sher Shah Suri, who usurped power from the Moghuls in the mid-sixteenth century, achieved much in Bengal; it was thanks to him that the Grand Trunk Road took its most developed form, running all the way to the Northwest Province on the borders of his native Afghanistan. Akbar reconquered the territory in 1574, shortly before the advent of the Europeans.

The Portuguese, who were the first to set up a trading community beside the Hooghly, were soon joined by the British, Dutch, French and many others. Rivalry between them – all received some degree of sanction from the Moghul court – eventually resulted in the ascendancy of the **British**, with the only serious indigenous resistance coming from the tutelary kingdom of **Murshidabad**, led by the young Siraj-ud-Daula. His attack on the fledgling British community of Calcutta in 1756 culminated in the infamous **Black Hole** incident, when British prisoners, possibly in error, were incarcerated in a tiny space that caused many to suffocate to death. Vengeance, in the form of a British army from Madras under **Robert Clive**, arrived a year later. The defeat of Siraj-ud-Daula at the **Battle of Plassey** paved the way for British domination of the entire subcontinent. Bengal became the linchpin of the British East India Company and its lucrative trading empire, until the company handed over control to the Crown in 1854.

Up to 1905, Bengal encompassed Orissa and Bihar; it was then split down the middle by Lord Curzon, leaving East Bengal and Assam on one side and Orissa, Bihar and West Bengal on the other. The move aroused bitter resentment, and the rift it created between Hindus and Muslims was a direct cause of the second Partition, in 1947, when East Bengal became East Pakistan. During the war with Pakistan in the early 1970s that resulted in the creation of an independent **Bangladesh**, up to ten million refugees fled into West Bengal; though most returned, a steady migration from Bangladesh still continues. Shorn of its provinces, and with the capital moved from Calcutta to Delhi in 1911, the story of West Bengal in the twentieth century was largely a chronicle of decline.

Economically, the **rice** grown in the paddy fields of the lowlands remains West Bengal's most important cash crop, though **tea** – first introduced by the British from China and grown mainly on the Himalayan foothills around Darjeeling – comes a close second. The other great nineteenth-century industry, **jute**, has not fared so well, the mills along the Hooghly around Kolkata having been cut off from the main growing regions across the border in East Bengal – now Bangladesh.

The state's political life has been dominated by a protracted – and sometimes violent – struggle between the **Congress** and the major left-wing parties: the Marxist Communist Party of India, or **CPI(M)**, and the Marxist-Leninist **Naxalites** (Communist Party of India). In the 1960s and 1970s, the latter launched an abortive but bloody attempt at revolution. Bolstered by a strong rural base, the CPI(M) eventually emerged victorious under the enigmatic Jyoti Basu, weathering the collapse of world communism. However, the decades of CPI(M) rule have been dogged by decline and neglect. Despite a recent sense of optimism and growth, the party is often accused of being unable to provide a healthy environment for industrial and economic progress. To compound the economic problems, **political turmoil** has increased in recent years, with the rise of the **Trinamul Congress** under Mamata Bannerjee challenging the Communists' traditional power base.This has led to violent clashes between party activists and frequent strikes, while political elements to the north of the state are calling for independence from West Bengal.

Kolkata (Calcutta) and around

One of the four great urban centres of India, **KOLKATA (CALCUTTA)** is to its proud citizens the equal of any city in the country in charm, variety and interest. Like Mumbai and Chennai, it is not ancient, its roots lying in the European expansion of the seventeenth century – as the showpiece capital of the British Raj, it was the greatest colonial city of the Orient, and descendants of the fortune-seekers who flocked from across the globe to participate in its eighteenth- and nineteenth-century trading boom remain conspicuous in its cosmopolitan blend of communities. Despite this, there has been a recent rise in Bengali nationalism, which has resulted in the renaming of Calcutta as Kolkata – the Bengali pronunciation and official new name – which has yet to be universally embraced – leading English-language paper *The Telegraph* continues to use Calcutta.

Since Indian Independence, mass migrations of dispossessed refugees occasioned by twentieth-century upheavals within the subcontinent have tested the city's infrastructure to the limit.The resultant suffering – and the work of Mother Teresa in drawing attention to its most helpless victims – has given Kolkata a reputation for **poverty** that its residents consider ill-founded. They argue that the city's problems – the continuing influx of refugees notwithstanding – are no longer as acute as those of Mumbai or other cities across the world, and that the slum scenes familiar from the book and film *City of Joy* are distortions of the truth. In fact, though Kolkata's mighty Victorian buildings lie peeling and decaying, and its central avenues choked by traffic, the city exudes a warmth that leaves few visitors unmoved. But despite the opening of India's first underground system in 1984 – seen as the first portent of a new economic beginning – Kolkata lost much ground over the years to newly emerging commercial centres elsewhere in the country. Today, however, there's a renewed sense of optimism, especially amongst the middle-classes: the construction of new roads have allowed the city to expand and develop an explosion of new shopping arcades and restaurants are seen as proof that the city is – at last – fighting back.

The Bengalis of Kolkata like to see themselves as the **intelligentsia** of India; a long-standing maxim states that "what Bengal does today, India will do tomorrow." Artistic endeavour is held in higher esteem than political and economic success: the city is home to a multitude of **galleries** and huge Indian classical **music** festivals, with a thriving Bengali-language **theatre** scene and a tradition of **cinema** brought world renown by Satyajit Ray. Adding to the chaos and colour, Kolkata has a wonderful tradition of political posters and graffiti. Witty and flamboyant slogans compete with a forest of advertising hoardings to festoon every available surface.

Though Marxists may rule from the chief bastion of imperialism (the **Writers Building**, which has changed little over the decades), visitors still experience Kolkata first and foremost as a colonial city. Grand edifices in a profusion of styles include the imposing **Victoria Memorial** and the gothic **St Paul's Cathedral**, while the collection at the eclectic **Indian Museum**, one of the largest museums in Asia, ranges from natural history to art and archeology. Among numerous venerable Raj institutions to have survived are the racecourse, the reverence for cricket and several exclusive gentlemen's clubs.

In terms of **climate**, Kolkata is at its best during its short winter (Nov–Feb), when the daily maximum temperature hovers around 27°C, and the markets are filled with vegetables and flowers. Before the monsoons, the heat hangs unbearably heavily; the arrival of the rains in late June brings relief, but usually also floods that turn the streets into a quagmire. After a brief period of post-monsoon high temperatures, October and November are quite pleasant; this is the time of the city's biggest festival, **Durga Puja**.

Some history

By the time the remarkable **Job Charnock** established the headquarters of the **East India Company** at **Sutanuti** on the east bank of the Hooghly in 1690, the riverside was already dotted with trading communities from European countries. Besides the British, previously based at Hooghly on the west bank, there were the French at Chandernagore, the Dutch and Armenians at Chinsurah, the Danes at Serampore, the Portuguese at Bandel, and even Greeks at Rishra and Prussians at Bhadeshwar.

Supported by Armenian funds, the East India Company bought land around Sutanuti, and in 1699 completed its first fort in the area – **Fort William**. A few years later, Sutanuti was amalgamated with two other villages to form the town of **Calcutta**, whose name probably originated from *Kalikutir*, the house or temple of Kali (a reference to the **Kalighat** shrine). With trading success came ambitious plans for development; in 1715 a delegation to the Moghul court in Delhi negotiated trading rights, along with several villages and towns on both banks of the Hooghly, to create a territory that was around 15km long. The East India Company then built a moat around the perimeter, known as the **Maratha Ditch** (marked by today's Circular Road), to ward off possible Maratha attacks. Later, it became entangled in the web of local power politics, with consequences both unforeseen (as with the Black Hole; see p.859) and most assiduously desired, as when the Battle of Plassey in 1758 made the British masters of Bengal. Recognized by parliament in London in 1773, the company's trading monopoly led it to shift the capital of Bengal here from Murshidabad, and Calcutta became a clearing house for a vast range of commerce, including the lucrative export of opium to China.

At first, the East India Company brought young bachelors out from Britain to work as clerks. Known as "writers", they lived in spartan conditions in communal mud huts until the **Writers' Building** was eventually erected to accommodate them. This was the era before the arrival of the British Memsahib, when sexual relations with local women were the norm, and over time many young writers took Indian wives, giving rise to the new **Eurasian** community, now known as the **Anglo-Indians**. Merchants and adventurers – among them Parsis, Baghdadi Jews, Afghans and Indians from other parts of the

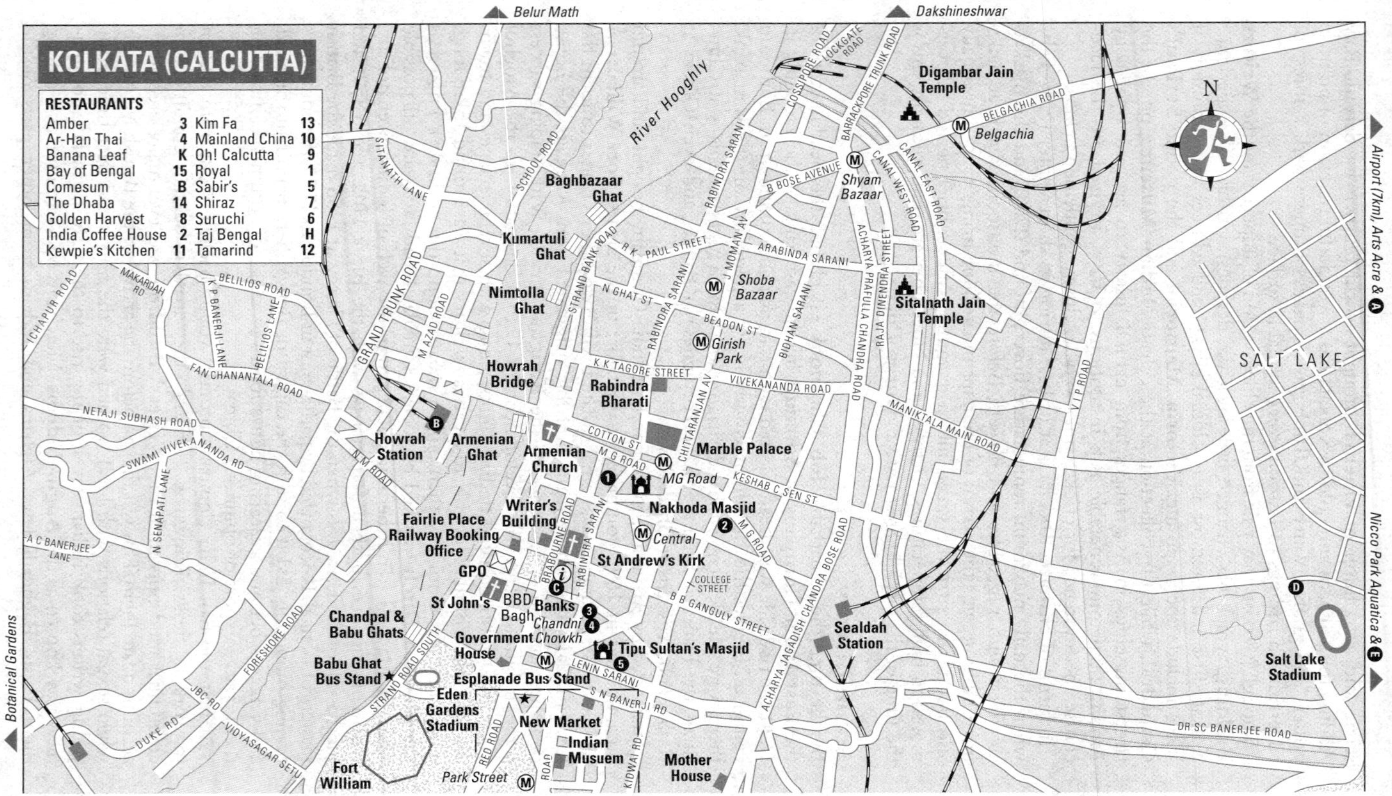

KOLKATA (CALCUTTA)

RESTAURANTS

Amber	3	Kim Fa	13
Ar-Han Thai	4	Mainland China	10
Banana Leaf	K	Oh! Calcutta	9
Bay of Bengal	15	Royal	1
Comesum	B	Sabir's	5
The Dhaba	14	Shiraz	7
Golden Harvest	8	Suruchi	6
India Coffee House	2	Taj Bengal	H
Kewpie's Kitchen	11	Tamarind	12

Belur Math
Dakshineshwar
Airport (7km), Arts Acre & A
Nicco Park Aquatica & E
Botanical Gardens
N
River Hooghly
Digambar Jain Temple
Belgachia
Belgachia Road
Shyam Bazaar
Baghbazaar Ghat
Kumartuli Ghat
Nimtolla Ghat
Howrah Bridge
Howrah Station
Armenian Ghat
Armenian Church
Rabindra Bharati
Marble Palace
Shoba Bazaar
Girish Park
Sitalnath Jain Temple
Salt Lake
MG Road
Nakhoda Masjid
Writer's Building
Fairlie Place Railway Booking Office
Central
St Andrew's Kirk
GPO
St John's
BBD Bagh
Banks
Chandni Chowkh
Government House
Tipu Sultan's Masjid
Chandpal & Babu Ghats
Babu Ghat Bus Stand
Esplanade Bus Stand
Eden Gardens Stadium
New Market
Indian Musuem
Mother House
Fort William
Park Street
Sealdah Station
Salt Lake Stadium
Ichapur Road
Makardah Rd
Belilios Road
K P Banerji Lane
Belilios Lane
Sitanath Lane
School Road
Grand Trunk Road
M Azad Road
Fan Chanantala Road
Netaji Subhash Road
Swami Vivekananda Rd
N M Road
N Senapati Lane
A C Banerjee Lane
Foreshore Road
JBC Rd
Duke Rd
Vidyasagar Setu
Strand Road South
Strand Bank Road
R K Paul Street
N Ghat St
Rabindra Sarani
Beadon St
K K Tagore Street
Cotton St
M G Road
Chittaranjan Av
Vivekananda Road
Bidhan Sarani
Arabinda Sarani
J Moman Av
B Bose Avenue
Cossipore Road
Lockgate Road
Barrackpore Trunk Road
Canal West Road
Canal East Road
Acharya Prafulla Chandra Road
Raja Dinendra Street
V I P Road
Maniktala Main Road
Keshab C Sen St
Brabourne Road
College Street
B B Ganguly Street
Acharya Jagadish Chandra Bose Road
Lenin Sarani
S N Banerji Rd
Red Road
Kidwai Rd
Dr SC Banerjee Road

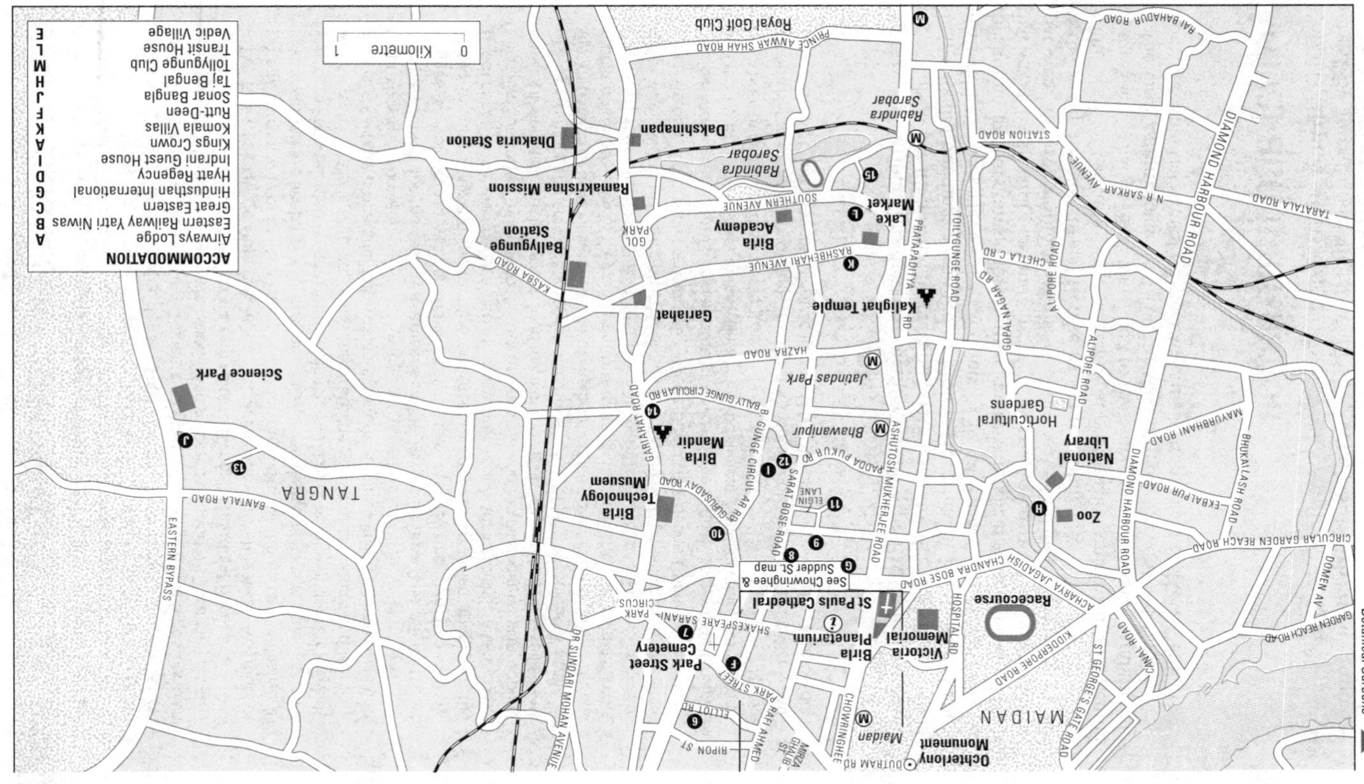

ACCOMMODATION
Airways Lodge A
Eastern Railway Yatri Niwas B
Great Eastern C
Hindusthan International G
Hyatt Regency D
Indrani Guest House I
Kings Crown A
Komala Villas K
Rutt-Deen F
Sonar Bangla J
Taj Bengal H
Tollygunge Club M
Transit House L
Vedic Village E
0 Kilometre 1
Science Park
TANGRA
BANTALA ROAD
EASTERN BYPASS
Ballygunge Station
KASBA ROAD
Ramakrishna Mission
Dhakuria Station
Dakshinapan
Rabindra Sarobar
Royal Golf Club
PRINCE ANWAR SHAH ROAD
GOL PARK
Gariahat
GARIAHAT ROAD
Birla Academy
SOUTHERN AVENUE
RASHBEHARI AVENUE
Lake Market
Kalighat Temple
PRATAPADITYA RD
TOLLYGUNGE ROAD
STATION ROAD
N R SARKAR AVENUE
TARATALA ROAD
RAI BAHADUR ROAD
DIAMOND HARBOUR ROAD
CHETLA C RD
GOPAL NAGAR RD
ALIPORE ROAD
HAZRA ROAD
Jatindas Park
Bhawanipur
BALLY GUNGE CIRCULAR RD
B. GUNGE CIRCUL AR RD
Birla Mandir
Birla Technology Musuem
GURUSADAY ROAD
PADDA PUKUR RD
SARAT BOSE ROAD
ELGIN LANE
ASHUTOSH MUKHERJEE ROAD
Horticultural Gardens
National Library
Zoo
MAYURBHANJ ROAD
EKBALPUR ROAD
BHUKAILASH ROAD
CIRCULAR GARDEN REACH ROAD
DOMEN AV
GARDEN REACH ROAD
CANAL ROAD
ST GEORGE'S GATE ROAD
KIDDERPORE ROAD
ACHARYA JAGADISH CHANDRA BOSE ROAD
Racecourse
MAIDAN
HOSPITAL RD
Victoria Memorial
Birla Planetarium
St Pauls Cathedral
See Chowringhee & Sudder St. map
SHAKESPEARE SARANI
PARK CIRCUS
Park Street Cemetery
PARK STREET
RAFI AHMED
ELLIOT RD
RIPON ST
MIRZA GHALIB ST.
CHOWRINGHEE
Maidan
OUTRAM RD
Ochterlony Monument
DR SUNDARI MOHAN AVENUE
Botanical Gardens

The festivals of Kolkata

Most of Kolkata's Hindu **festivals** are devoted to forms of the mother goddess, **Shakti**. Kolkata's own deity, the black goddess **Kali**, is an emanation of **Durga**, the consort of Shiva. Kali is most commonly depicted with four arms, standing on the prostrate Shiva after killing the demon Raktviya, her tongue protruding in horror; other forms include the terrifying Chinemasta (torn head), where Kali holds her own severed head and drinks her own blood.. The mysterious goddess **Tara** (see p.1407) embodies ancient Tantric traditions with links to Bengal's Buddhist past.

The two-week **Durga Puja** (Sept/Oct) is Kolkata's most lavish festival. A symbol of victory, **Durga**, wife of Shiva, is shown with ten arms slaying the demon Mahisasura, who assumed the shape of a buffalo and threatened the gods. Durga either sits on a lion, or is accompanied by one. Other pujas honour **Lakshmi**, the goddess of wealth, whose festival falls in autumn, and **Saraswati**, the goddess of the arts and learning, who is shown as a beautiful fair woman sitting on a lotus playing a sitar-like instrument known as the *veena*.

In preparation for the festivals, artisans in the Kumartuli area (see p.880) mould images of voluptuous women from straw, papier-maché, and *pith* (the marrow of the banana tree) and then clothe and decorate them into lavish images of the goddesses; these are then carried in noisy procession to makeshift altars called *pandals*. Supported by donations from businesses and local residents, with popular music blaring distortedly through loudspeakers, *pandals* often block off small streets on their way to immerse the images in the river after puja. The colourful scene of the immersion is best viewed via one of the boat cruises offered by the West Bengal tourist office (see p.866); they also offer bus tours that take in the best *pandals*. more traditional form of Durga Puja takes place in purpose-built halls known as *thakur dalan* within North Kolkata's old manor houses; the best of these is held at the Than Thani Rajbari, a fabulous mansion off College Street at 1 Bechu Chatterjee Street.

Jaidev Mela (early Jan) Commemorating Joydeb, the author of the *Gita Govinda* revered by Bauls, and held in the village of Kenduli near Shantiniketan; the place to hear Baul minstrels in their element.

Ganga Sagar Mela (mid-Jan) During the winter solstice of Makar Sankranti, hundreds of thousands of Hindu pilgrims travel through Kolkata for a three-day

country – contributed to the great melting pot after the East India Company's monopoly was withdrawn. The ensuing boom lasted for decades, during which such splendid buildings as the Court House, Government House and St Paul's Cathedral earned Calcutta the sobriquet "City of Palaces". In reality, however, the humid and uncomfortable climate, putrefying salt marshes and the hovels that grew haphazardly around the metropolis created unhygienic conditions that were a constant source of misery and disease. Endemic since the colony's birth, corruption, too, began to take its toll on public life.

The death of Calcutta as an international port finally came with the opening of the Suez Canal in 1869, which led to the emergence of Bombay and the end of the city's opium trade. In 1911, the days of glory drew to a definitive close when the imperial capital of India was finally transferred to New Delhi.

Arrival and information

Kolkata's **airport** (☎033/2511 8787), 20km north of the city centre, is served by international flights. Officially **Netaji Subhash Bose Interna-**

festival at Sagar Dwip, 150km south at the mouth of the Hooghly where the Ganges meets the sea. Many of the *sadhus* drawn to the *mela* stay at the Shiva temple at Nimtolla Ghat, north of Howrah Bridge.

Dover Lane Music Festival (Jan/Feb) A week-long festival in south Kolkata attracting many of the country's best musicians.

Saraswati Puja (Jan/Feb) Important *pandal* festival to the goddess of learning, celebrated throughout the city.

Chinese New Year (Jan/Feb) Celebrated with a week-long festival of dragon dances, firecrackers and fine food, concentrated around the suburb of Tangra.

Muharram (May/June) Shi'ite Muslims mark the anniversary of the martyrdom of Hussein by severe penance including processions during which they flagellate themselves.

Durga Puja (Sept/Oct) At the onset of winter, Durga Puja is the Bengali equivalent of Christmas. It climaxes on Mahadashami, the tenth day, when images are taken to the river for immersion. Elsewhere, the festival is known as Dussehra.

Laxmi Puja (Oct/Nov) Held five days after Mahadashami on the full moon, to honour the goddess of wealth.

Id ul Fitr (Oct/Nov) Celebrating the end of the fasting month of Ramadan and heralded by the new moon, the festival is a time of joyousness when people don new clothes and sample wonderful food at the restaurants and the stalls around Park Circus.

Diwali and Kali Puja (Oct/Nov) Two weeks after Lakshmi Puja, Kali Puja is held on a moonless night when goats are sacrificed. Kali Puja coincides with Diwali, the festival of light.

Christmas (Dec 25) Park Street and the New Market are adorned with fairy lights and the odd Christmas tree. Plum pudding is sold at confectioners, and Midnight Mass is well attended.

Poush Mela (late Dec) Held in Shantiniketan around Christmas, the *mela* attracts Bauls, the wandering minstrels who perform to large audiences (too large for some tastes).

tional Airport, it is still universally known by its old name of **Dum Dum** – a moniker that became infamous during the Boer War, when the notorious exploding bullet was manufactured in a nearby factory. Undergoing a long and slow facelift, the dreary **international terminal** has 24-hour **money changing** facilities including a Thomas Cook, a **prepaid taxi** booth and an India Tourism information counter. The modern **domestic terminal**, 500m to the south, has a much better range of amenities including separate government tourist offices for Kolkata, West Bengal and Tripura, an accommodation booking counter, a railway reservation desk and prepaid taxi booth. Booked here, a **taxi** to the central Sudder Street area costs around Rs200. Another alternative is to take a taxi (around Rs50) or the shuttle bus to the Dum Dum **Metro** station (5km), and then the metro (see p.867) into town; Sudder Street is a short walk from Park Street station. Bear in mind, however, that you can't take large items (bikes, sports equipment etc) onto the Metro system. The extension of the Metro is to the airport (slated for completion in early 2006; see p.867) will allow a seamless ride into town.

Of Kolkata's two main **railway stations**, neither of which is on the Metro system, **Howrah Station** – the point of arrival for major trains from the south and west, such as the Rajdhani Express from Delhi – stands on the far bank

What's in a name?

While Kolkata struggles to maintain its position as a world city, a strong parochial trend in recent years has been to replace all English names with Bengali – the most obvious result has been the **renaming** of the city as **Kolkata**. The shedding of the city's colonial past began decades ago in the Sixties and Seventies when many of the old British **street names** were officially changed, but old habits die hard and three decades or so later, some of the original names continue to be widely used in tandem. The most important of these is Chowringhee or Jawaharlal Nehru Road (which we continue to call Chowringhee). Other name changes to note are Rabindranath Tagore Street (although everyone still calls it Camac Street), BBD Bagh (still often referred to by its old name, Dalhousie Square or simply "Dalhousie"), Indira Gandhi Road (Red Road), Lenin Sarani (Dharamtala), Mirza Ghalib Street (Free School Street), Bepin Bihari Ganguly Street (Bowbazar Street), Rabindra Sarani (Chitpore Road), Ho Chi Minh Sarani (Harrington Street), Dr Mohammed Ishaque Road (Kyd Street), AJC Bose Road (Lower Circular Road), Muzaffar Ahmed Street (Ripon Street), Shakespeare Sarani (Theatre Road) and Rafi Ahmed Kidwai Street (Wellesley Street).

of the Hooghly a couple of kilometres west of the centre. To reach the central downtown area, traffic has to negotiate **Howrah Bridge** – the definitive introduction to the chaos of the city, especially during rush hours, which start late in the mornings. Avoid the touts and taxis outside the station building, and head instead straight for the **prepaid taxi booth**, from where the fare to central Sudder Street and the Park Street areas costs Rs60–80. **Minibuses** and **buses** also operate from Howrah to destinations all over the city, but tend to be very crowded. The best alternative is to follow the signs from the station gate and take a **ferry** (Rs3) across the Hooghly with great views of the bridge, to Babu Ghat or the adjacent Chandpal Ghat, close to BBD Bagh, and pick up a metered taxi, bus or minibus from there.

Sealdah Station, used by trains from the north and with its own prepaid taxi booth in the car park, is on the eastern edge of the centre, and much more convenient as you don't have to cross the river. Long-distance **buses** from the south terminate at **Babu Ghat Bus Stand**, not far from Fort William on the east bank, while some luxury buses, such as the *Rocket* from Darjeeling, arrive at **Esplanade Bus Stand**, less than 1km north of Sudder Street.

Information

The efficient and friendly **India Tourism office**, off the central Chowringhee Road at 4 Shakespeare Sarani (Mon–Fri 9am–6pm, Sat 9am–1pm; ⓣ033/2282 5813 or 2282 7731, ⓔindtour@cal2.vsnl.net.in), is your best bet for information on Kolkata, West Bengal and destinations further afield, and can assist with itineraries and booking tours; they also have a poste restante service. The **Government of West Bengal Tourist Bureau**, near the Writers' Building at 3/2 BBD Bagh East (Mon–Sat 10.30am–4.30pm; ⓣ033/2248 8271), arranges tours of Kolkata (see opposite) and package trips around West Bengal. They also issue permits and book tours and accommodation at the Sunderbans and Jaldapara wildlife parks (Mon–Fri only). **Tourist information counters** at both the domestic and international terminals of the airport and Howrah Station offer the same services.

English-language **newspapers** such as the *Statesman*, *Telegraph* and *Hindusthan Standard* remain the primary source for information on **what's on**, but the monthly *CalCalling* (Rs20), also found in some hotel rooms, is excellent for listings and general information on the city. *Calcutta This Fortnight* is a free leaflet available from both the West Bengal and India Tourism tourist offices and details exhibitions and performing arts events.

City tours

City tours are organized by the West Bengal Tourist Bureau (Rs150; 7.30am–5pm) and by India Tourism Development Corporation (ITDC), near Shakespeare Sarani at 3rd Floor, Everest House, 46C Chowringhee Rd (Ⓣ033/2288 0901; Rs130; 8.00am–5.30pm); trips leave from their respective premises. An even better way to explore the sprawl of Kolkata is to hire your own **car and guide**, arranged with the assistance of the India Tourism office. For a group of three to four people, it works out reasonably cheap (half-day tours from Rs600 and full-day tours from Rs1200. The **walking tours** (4–5hr; $20) offered by Help Tourism (Ⓣ033/2455 0917, Ⓦwww.helptourism.com) provide a great insight into the historic heart of the city: the Dalhousie Square Walking Tour is usually conducted on Sundays around BBD Bagh, while the similarly priced North Kolkata Walking Tour begins and ends at Sovabazaar Rajbari, a mansion close to College Street. The Australian-run Kali Travel Home (Ⓣ033/2558 7980, Ⓦwww.traveleastindia.com) organize tailor-made city tours (from $40 a day), ranging from Raj-themed city walks to riverside strolls that include the artisans of Kumartuli (see p.880). If you want to devise your own walking itineraries, the essential companion is *Ten Walks in Calcutta* by Prosenjit Das Gupta, available at bookshops such as Oxford.

City transport

The **Metro**, India's first and Kolkata's pride and joy, provides a fast, clean and efficient way to get around. It's also very easy to use, as it consists of just the one line running on a north–south axis. The **river** is also used for transport, with the *ghats* near Eden Gardens at the hub of a **ferry** system. You can beat the traffic by jumping on one of the frequent ferries from Chandpal Ghat to Howrah Station (Rs3); other sailings head downriver from Armenian, Chandpal or Babu *ghats* to the Botanical Gardens, although the running of this route is erratic. Of more use to commuters than tourists, a **circular railway** loops south from Sealdah station before moving upriver along the Strand and Princep Ghat, past Howrah Bridge and eventually to Dum Dum; it's currently being extended to the airport (see p.865). While using public transport, be wary of **pickpockets**, especially on crowded buses.

The Metro

Despite a few small hiccups, Kolkata's Russian-designed **Metro**, inaugurated in 1984, is every bit as good as its inhabitants proudly claim, with trains operating punctually every few minutes. Services run from 7am to 9.45pm Monday to Saturday and 3pm to 9.45pm on Sundays. Tickets are very cheap – you can travel the entire length of the line from Dum Dum near the airport to Tollygunge in the south for just Rs8. The line follows Kolkata's main arteries including Chowringhee Road, with convenient stations such as Park Street, Kalighat, Esplanade and Rabindra Sadan, and is currently being extended to the airport. For an update on the extension, contact tourist offices or visit Ⓦwww.kolmetro.com.

Buses and minibuses

Kolkata supports a vast and complicated **bus** network, in operation each day roughly between 5am and 11pm, and subject to overcrowding and pickpocketing. The profusion of bus routes, many privately run, is best explained in the dark-blue pocket guide, *Calcutta & Howrah* by DP Publications (Rs10), available through roadside magazine and book vendors and at railway station bookshops. Once the mainstay of Calcutta Transport Corporation – **CTC** – just a handful of red double-decker buses are still in service today. Useful bus routes include: **#8** from Howrah via Esplanade and Gariahat Road to Gol Park; **#S17** from Chetla near Kalighat via Esplanade; and **#5** and **#6**, which both travel via Howrah and the Esplanade-Chowringhee area, and stop at the Indian Museum at the head of Sudder Street; #5 goes to Garia in the south via Rabindra Sadan and Kalighat. The **#C6** travels via Chowringhee, passing the top of Park Street before crossing the Vidyasagar Setu (the second bridge over the Hooghly) to the Botanical Gardens. Buses with an "S" prefix denote special express buses charging marginally more. Of the six Executive (Green Line) bus routes, the **#GL1** runs from Esplanade to the airport.

In addition, private brown-and-yellow **minibuses** travel at inordinate speeds on ad-hoc routes; their destinations are usually painted boldly in Bengali and English on their sides, and conductors shout them out at bus stops or major junctions.

Taxis

Taxis in Kolkata prove to be extremely good value, especially on long journeys such as to and from the airport (around Rs180 for a twenty-kilometre ride), but a few drivers can be unwilling to go anywhere for less than Rs50, even for short journeys. Sudder Street's taxi touts are particularly averse to haggling, and you're better off walking around the corner and flagging down a cab. Alternatively, you could use the **prepaid taxi** service behind *Trincas Restaurant* on Park Street, in the parking lot of the *Park Hotel* (other such services are found at the main railway stations and the airport), or call ⓣ033/2511 8787. Most cabs have working **meters** and tend to use them in conjunction with the conversion charts they are obliged to carry. To complicate matters, there are two meter systems operating simultaneously. New digital meters (located inside the cab) start on Rs15 (plus Rs1.50 per 200m) but add on another thirty percent. Old meters (located on the outside) start on Rs5 but the fare will be charged at double what the meter says plus another thirty percent. When fare rises are announced, the Taxi Association finds it cheaper to issue the conversion charts rather than reset each and every meter. Note there is a small additional charge for placing your luggage in the boot. An ambitious project in its infancy, **Blue Arrow taxis** (ⓣ13658) are customized a/c Tata Indicabs equipped with tamper-proof meters that produce printed receipts, and complimentary mineral water. The courteous drivers (some of whom are women) are insured and trained. At the time of writing, you have to book over the phone 24 hours before travelling; charges are slightly steeper than regular taxis: meters start at Rs13.50, plus Rs10 per kilometre. There's a night-time surcharge (10pm–6am); up to two pieces of luggage are free, but there's an additional Rs10 charge for further pieces.

Trams

Kolkata's cumbersome **trams** (ⓦwww.calcuttatramways.com), barely changed save for a lick of paint since they started operating in 1873, are being phased out, but certain routes linger on. However, notwithstanding the general dilapidation, they do have an odd quirky charm and provide an interesting way of seeing the city; female travellers may well be glad of the rush-hour women-only coaches. Routes include **#20**, Howrah Bridge via Sealdah to Park Circus; **#25**, BBD Bagh to Ballygunge via Rafi Ahmed Kidwai Road, Park Circus; and **#29**, BBD Bagh to Tollygunge via the Maidan and Diamond Harbour Road, Alipore Road and Hazra Mor and Kalighat.

Rickshaws, auto-rickshaws and cycle rickshaws

Kolkata is the only city in India to have **human-drawn rickshaws**, which are only available in the central areas of the city, especially around New Market where many drivers supplement their meagre income by acting as pimps. Rickshaws come into their own during the monsoons, when the streets get flooded to hip height and the rickshaw-men can extract healthy amounts of money for their pains. If you take one, be careful not to lean back as your weight will unbalance the driver. Most of the rickshaw-pullers are Bihari pavement-dwellers, who live short and very hard lives. Haggle for a realistic price but feel free to give a handful of baksheesh too.

Auto-rickshaws, rare in the centre of town, are used as shared taxis on certain routes (such as the Rashbehari to Gariahat; Rs3.50) and link with Metro stations in suburbs; try to avoid a share of the front cab as head-on collisions are frequent. **Cycle rickshaws**, banned from much of the city, are only available in outlying suburbs.

Accommodation

As soon as you arrive in Kolkata, taxi-drivers are likely to assume that you'll be heading for central **Sudder Street**, east of Chowringhee Road, a heady mix of travellers and businessmen and Bangladeshis in transit. As the main travellers' hub in Kolkata and close to all amenities, the area is a sociable place to stay with numerous small to mid-sized hotels; in fact, many visitors spend most of their time in this one enclave. Most Sudder Street hotels are in the budget or mid-range brackets; the latter tend to be overpriced and poor value for money, and if you're after a modicum of luxury, you may have to look further afield.

The many **guesthouses** all over Kolkata – usually comfortable private houses or flats, with the use of a "cook-cum-bearer" – provide mid-budget travellers with an alternative to Sudder Street. Be sure to clarify the food arrangements and all costs at the start of your stay. The Guest Agency, a division of Travel & Cargo Service, 23 Shakespeare Sarani (Ⓣ033/2247 9662), represents guesthouses throughout the city.

Some of the city's very **top hotels** are slightly further afield; the luxurious *Taj Bengal*, for example, is in Alipore to the south, while there are some new top-end options along the EM Bypass en route to the airport. Well-heeled visitors might also consider a stay at Kolkata's most exclusive **club**, the Tollygunge, considered one of the best in the world.

Note that places under the Sudder Street, Park Street and Chowringhee headings appear on the Chowringhee and Sudder Street map (p.870); all others appear on the main Kolkata map (pp.862–863).

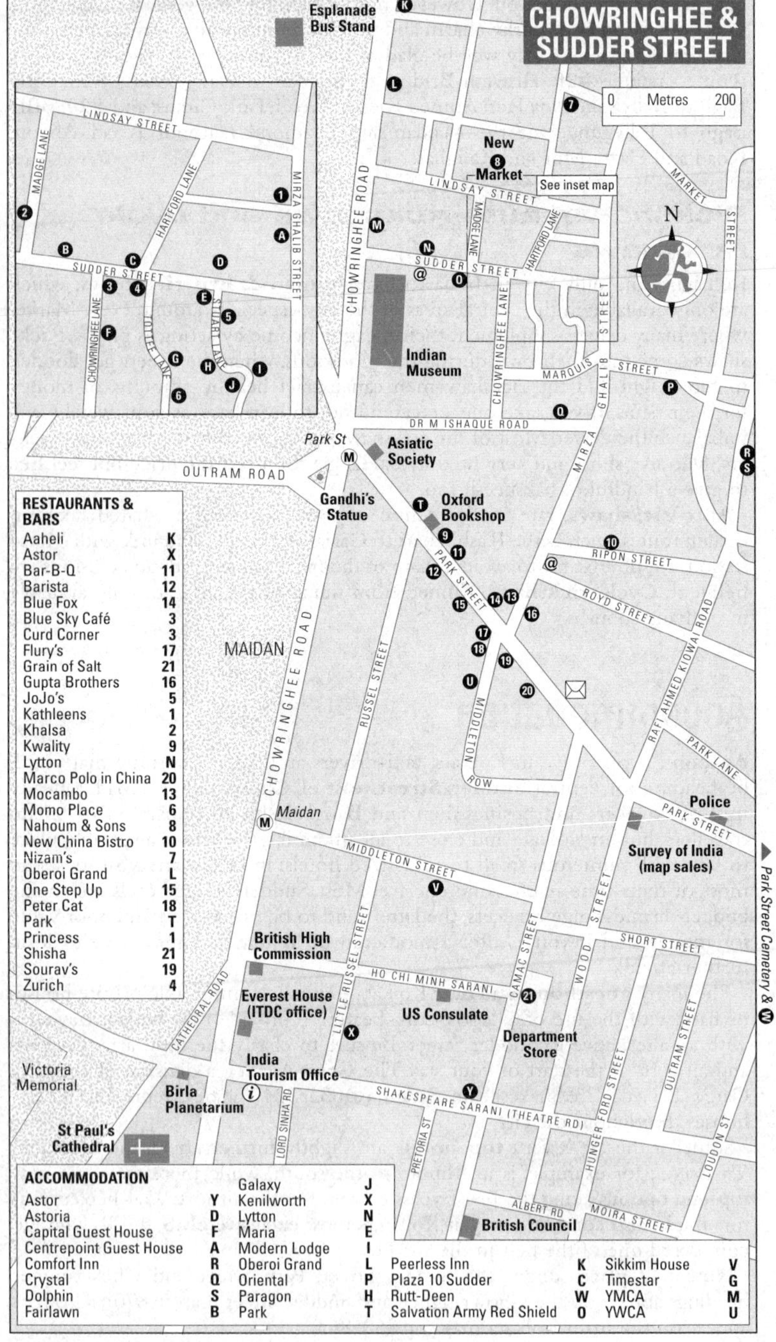
CHOWRINGHEE & SUDDER STREET
0 Metres 200
Esplanade Bus Stand
New Market
See inset map
Indian Museum
Asiatic Society
Park St
Gandhi's Statue
Oxford Bookshop
MAIDAN
Maidan
Police
Survey of India (map sales)
Park Street Cemetery & W
British High Commission
Everest House (ITDC office)
US Consulate
Department Store
India Tourism Office
Victoria Memorial
Birla Planetarium
St Paul's Cathedral
British Council
LINDSAY STREET
MADGE LANE
HARTFORD LANE
MIRZA GHALIB STREET
SUDDER STREET
CHOWRINGHEE LANE
TOTTEE LANE
STUART LANE
CHOWRINGHEE ROAD
MARKET STREET
MARQUIS STREET
DR M ISHAQUE ROAD
OUTRAM ROAD
PARK STREET
RIPON STREET
ROYD STREET
RAFI AHMED KIDWAI ROAD
PARK LANE
RUSSEL STREET
MIDDLETON ROW
MIDDLETON STREET
LITTLE RUSSEL STREET
CAMAC STREET
WOOD STREET
SHORT STREET
HO CHI MINH SARANI
CATHEDRAL ROAD
LORD SINHA RD
SHAKESPEARE SARANI (THEATRE RD)
PRETORIA ST
HUNGERFORD STREET
OUTRAM STREET
LOUDON ST
ALBERT RD
MOIRA STREET
RESTAURANTS & BARS
Aaheli K
Astor X
Bar-B-Q 11
Barista 12
Blue Fox 14
Blue Sky Café 3
Curd Corner 3
Flury's 17
Grain of Salt 21
Gupta Brothers 16
JoJo's 5
Kathleens 1
Khalsa 2
Kwality 9
Lytton N
Marco Polo in China 20
Mocambo 13
Momo Place 6
Nahoum & Sons 8
New China Bistro 10
Nizam's 7
Oberoi Grand L
One Step Up 15
Peter Cat 18
Park T
Princess 1
Shisha 21
Sourav's 19
Zurich 4
ACCOMMODATION
Astor Y
Astoria D
Capital Guest House F
Centrepoint Guest House A
Comfort Inn R
Crystal Q
Dolphin S
Fairlawn B
Galaxy J
Kenilworth X
Lytton N
Maria E
Modern Lodge I
Oberoi Grand L
Oriental P
Paragon H
Park T
Peerless Inn K
Plaza 10 Sudder C
Rutt-Deen W
Salvation Army Red Shield O
Sikkim House V
Timestar G
YMCA M
YWCA U

Budget

Sudder Street, Park Street and Chowringhee

Capital Guest House 11B Chowringhee Lane ⓣ033/2252 0598. Set in a large courtyard away from the bustle of Sudder St, rooms in this purpose-built block are plain, with hot water by the bucket; some have a/c. ❸–❹

Centrepoint Guest House 20 Mirza Ghalib St ⓣ033/2252 8184. Friendly and popular, though cramped, with a range of rooms and two cheap, clean and cramped single-sex dorms (Rs75). ❷

Dolphin 8 AK Mohammed Siddique Lane ⓣ033/2217 5135. Ten minutes' walk from Sudder St, tucked away down a tiny lane, offering small, clean rooms with TV and cold showers. ❸–❹

Galaxy 3 Stuart Lane ⓣ033/2252 4565. Small hotel with just four rooms. Clean and good value, with hot water but no a/c. ❹

Maria 5/1 Sudder St ⓣ033/2252 0860. The good-sized budget rooms in this old high-ceilinged, rather faded building are often full; there is also a dorm (Rs60), a reliable cybercafé and a pleasant terrace upstairs. ❷

Modern Lodge 1 Stuart Lane ⓣ033/2252 4960. Cramped place, with a relaxing roof terrace, that has been popular with budget travellers since the 1960s, despite the surly – sometimes downright rude – service. ❷–❸

Oriental 9A Marquis St ⓣ033/2217 4536. Clean Sikh-run establishment offering modest rooms with cable TV and hot showers (mornings only) and authorized money change. ❸

Paragon 2 Stuart Lane ⓣ033/2252 2445. Popular and very traveller-friendly place, offering dark and dingy rooms downstairs, and better ones around the rooftop courtyard; there are also dorm beds (Rs70–80). ❷

Salvation Army Red Shield Guest House 2 Sudder St ⓣ033/2252 0599. A dependable option that's changed little over the years, screened from the noise and pollution by a large gate. Dorms (from Rs80) and a few doubles including a couple of over-priced a/c ones. Book well in advance. ❷–❹

Timestar 2 Tottee Lane ⓣ033/2252 8028. The fair-sized rooms in this old villa come with fans and hot water by the bucket; some have TV, too. ❸

Elsewhere in the city

Airways Lodge No. 2 Airport Gate, Kolkata Airport ⓣ033/2512 7280. An inexpensive place in the vicinity of the airport, with basic but clean rooms. Handy for early departures and late arrivals. ❸

Eastern Railway Yatri Niwas Howrah Station ⓣ033/2660 1742. Large place with small dorms (Rs100) and a/c and non a/c doubles, for travellers holding 200km+ rail tickets only. Maximum stay one night and a 9am check out. Avoid the dull restaurant in favour of the nearby *Comesum* food hall in Howrah's South Station (see p.886). ❸–❹

Komala Villas 73 Rashbehari Ave ⓣ033/2464 1960. A clean and popular South Indian-run hotel, with a good selection of accommodation, from dorms (Rs135) to deluxe a/c rooms, and an excellent restaurant (see p.885). ❸–❻

Mid-range

Sudder Street, Park Street and Chowringhee

Astoria Sudder St ⓣ033/2252 9679. Popular with businessmen, though the old-fashioned a/c rooms are a bit overpriced. ❻–❼

Comfort Inn 63 Rafi Ahmed Kidwai Rd ⓣ033/2216 9138, ⓔcomfortinn@vsnl.net. Smart business hotel with a/c and satellite TV in all of the clean, spacious rooms. ❹–❻

Crystal 11/1 Dr Mohammed Ishaque Rd (Kyd St) ⓣ033/2226 6400, ⓔhcrystal@vsnl.net. Friendly hotel with decent sized rooms, all with cable TV and hot water; some have a/c too. ❹–❻

Plaza 10 Sudder St ⓣ033/2252 6411. Clean if pokey rooms that are popular with visiting businessmen. ❸–❺

Sikkim House 4/1 Middleton St ⓣ033/2281 5328. A well-located government guesthouse with a small selection of wonderful, very competitively-priced rooms; it tends to get booked up early, so ring in well in advance. Their *Red Panda* restaurant serves great *thukpa*. ❺

YMCA 25 Chowringhee Rd ⓣ033/2249 2192. Former grand nightclub near the Indian Museum that's now a faded but popular meeting place, offering a range of shabby rooms, some a/c, on half-board basis. Temporary membership (Rs40) allows access to a well-kept snooker table and table tennis. ❹–❻

YWCA 1 Middleton Row ⓣ033/2229 7033. Safe for women and especially good for longer stays, this clean, central option off Park St is built around a pleasant courtyard with a tennis court. Rates include breakfast. ❹–❺

Elsewhere in the city

Indrani Guest House 3B Lovelock St ⓣ033/2475 7712. A comfortable family residence offering B&B and optional home cooking in a residential part of the city off Ballygunge Circular Rd. Just three wonderful rooms so book well ahead; popular for longer stays. ❻

Kings Crown VIP Rd, near the airport ⓣ033/2573 5451. A good range of accommodation, from plain singles to comfortable a/c rooms, along with a good restaurant and bar; very convenient for early or late flights. ❹–❽

Transit House 11A Raja Basanta Roy Rd ⓣ033/2466 2700, ⓔtransit1@vsnl.net. Excellent, comfortable guesthouse with a reputation for being safe for women; away from the centre but in an interesting location close to markets and the lakes, and not far from the Metro. ⑤–⑥

Expensive

Sudder Street, Park Street and Chowringhee

Astor 15 Shakespeare Sarani ⓣ033/2282 9950. Comfortable, well-equipped old garden hotel with satellite TV, fridge and a/c in all rooms; the hotel also houses a nightclub and excellent restaurants (see p.884). Doubles from $62. ⑧

Fairlawn 13A Sudder St ⓣ033/2252 1510, ⓦwww.fairlawnhotel.com. Chock-full of memorabilia, this famous old-fashioned hotel exudes a faded, decadent and eccentric Raj atmosphere, and the homely rooms have recently been refurbished. Non-residents can sample a drink in the lush garden. Prices include all meals. Doubles from $47.50. ⑧

Kenilworth 1 & 2 Little Russell St ⓣ033/2282 3939, ⓦwww.kenilworthhotels.com. Comfortable place with opulent rooms and a pleasant garden and a convenient location that adds to its popularity. Facilities include a good restaurant, coffeeshop, two bars, a barbeque in the garden and a multigym with steam bath and sauna. From $130. ⑨

Lytton 14 Sudder St ⓣ033/2249 1872, ⓦwww.lyttonhotelindia.com. The most modern and comfortable hotel on Sudder St, lacking in character but with a/c, fridges and satellite TV in all rooms. Facilities include a bar and a couple of good restaurants. From $63. ⑧–⑨

Oberoi Grand 15 Chowringhee Rd ⓣ033/2249 2323, ⓦwww.oberoihotels.com. The white Victorian facade of this luxurious hotel, established in 1938, is very much part of the fabric of the city. The interior has been completely revamped; facilities include a swimming pool, and Thai and Indian restaurants. From $270. ⑨

Park 17 Park St ⓣ033/2249 9000, ⓦwww.theparkhotels.com. Modern five-star in a good location on a cosmopolitan street; amenities include swimming pool, health club, late checkout and good food at the three restaurants including the 24hr *Atrium*; plus a popular nightclub and a bar with live music. Comfortable if plain rooms. From $225. ⑨

Peerless Inn 12 Chowringhee Rd ⓣ033/2228 0301, ⓦwww.peerlesshotels.com. This overpriced four-star hotel exudes a very upmarket Bengali feel. The restaurant specializes in local cuisine and there's also a 24hr coffee shop, a bar, a disco and a gym. From $115 including breakfast. ⑨

Elsewhere in the city

Great Eastern 1–3 Old Court House St ⓣ033/2248 2311, ⓔgeh@vsnl.com. Now government-run, this famous old hotel near BBD Bagh was once patronized by Mark Twain, but the marble floors and wood-panelled corridors have definitely seen better days. There are a handful of cheaper, non-a/c rooms. ⑤–⑧

Hindusthan International 235/1 AJC Bose Rd ⓣ033/2280 2323, ⓦwww.hindusthan.com. Well-located but plain business hotel with a shopping arcade and travel service, restaurants, and a health club with swimming pool open to the public for a fee. From $165. ⑨

Hyatt Regency JA-1 Sector 3, Salt Lake City ⓣ033/2335 1234, ⓦwww.kolkata.regency.hyatt.com. Plush hotel on the EM Bypass, en-route to the airport and handy for the city too. It's built to impress with capacious lobbies, restaurants, a palm-fringed swimming pool and all facilities. From $140. ⑨

Rutt-Deen 21B Loudon St ⓣ033/2240 2389, ⓔruttdeen@vsnl.com. Well situated on a leafy avenue just off Park St, this place is popular with businesspeople and wedding parties alike with comfortable rooms (now showing their age) and a pleasant garden bar and restaurant, plus good amenities such as currency exchange. ⑦

Sonar Bangla EM Bypass ⓣ033/234 5545, ⓦwww.sheraton.com/calcutta. Busy hotel whose popularity rests on its convenient location between city and airport and its excellent range of restaurants, bars and nightclubs. All the comforts and services one would expect from a five-star, and a relaxed welcome, though an unflattering exterior. From $295. ⑨

Taj Bengal 24B Belvedere Rd, Alipore ⓣ033/2223 3939, ⓦwww.tajhotels.com. Opulent showpiece hotel, attempting to amalgamate Bengali features with the usual *Taj* grandeur. Excellent range of restaurants, including Chinese and Indian, a pool and a nightclub. From $275. ⑨

Tollygunge Club 120 Deshapran Sasmal Rd, at the southern end of the Metro line ⓣ033/2473 2316. The city's most exclusive club offers a choice of cottages or rooms in one of two newish blocks; rates include temporary membership and the use of an eighteen-hole golf course, plus riding, swimming, tennis and squash facilities, as well as open-air and indoor restaurants and a good bar. There's an Ayurvedic treatment centre too. You'll need to contact the secretary well in advance, as the club is extremely popular and often full. ⑧

Vedic Village Shikarpur, Rajahat ⓣ03216/263180, ⓦwww.thevedicvillage.com. A sprawling development with beautifully presented modern cottages around a lake and equally luxurious rooms in the main block. There's also a good restaurant and a swimming pool and an excellent and exclusive naturopathy health centre. It's 28km from central Kolkata, but only 12km from the airport along slow windy village roads. ❽–❾

The City

Kolkata's crumbling, weatherbeaten buildings and anarchic streets can create an intimidating first impression. Given a little time and patience, however, this huge metropolis starts to resolve itself into a fascinating conglomerate of styles and influences. The **River Hooghly**, which was until recently spanned only by the remarkable cantilever Howrah Bridge, is not all that prominent in the life of the city. Instead its heart is the green expanse of the **Maidan**, which attracts locals from all walks of life for recreation, sports, exhibitions and political rallies. At its

The Bengali Renaissance

Although a rich tradition of poetry existed in India long before the arrival of the Europeans – even scientific manuscripts were written in rhyming couplets – **prose** was all but unknown. Thus the foundation by the British of **Fort William College** in 1800 – primarily intended to assist administrators to learn Indian languages by commissioning prose in Bengali, Urdu and Hindi – had the unexpected side effect of helping to create a vital new genre in indigenous literature. **Bankim Chandra Chatterjee** (1838–99), a senior civil servant who wrote novels of everyday life, became known as the father of Bengali literature, while **Michael Madhusudan Dutt** (1829–73) introduced European conventions into Bengali poetry. Simultaneously, Westernization began to sweep Bengali middle-class society, as people grew disenchanted with their culture and religion.

A leading figure in the new intelligentsia was **Raja Ram Mohan Roy** (1774–1833). Born an orthodox Hindu, he founded the Brahmo Samaj, a socio-religious movement that believed in a single god and set out to purge Hinduism of its idol worship and rituals, advocating the abolition of *sati* and child marriage. **Keshab Chandra Sen**'s breakaway church Navabidhan (New Dispensation), a synthesis of all the world's major religions, created a split in 1866 over its emphasis on universal Unitarianism and the downplaying of the role of Hinduism.

No single figure epitomized the Bengali Renaissance more than **Rabindranath Tagore**, a giant of Bengali art, culture and letters, and a Brahmo, who received the Nobel Prize for Literature in 1913. As well as writing several hymns, he set out the principles of the Brahmo Samaj movement in *The Religion of Man*. The intellectual and cultural freedom of the Brahmo Samaj earned it an important influence over the Bengali upper classes that endures to this day, but in recent years extreme Bengali reformists have attacked the movement for having been a corrupting influence on Bengali society.

During and following the period of the Renaissance, Bengal saw a resurgence of Hindu thought through religious leaders such as **Ramakrishna** (1836–86), a great Kali devotee whose message was carried as far as North America by his disciple **Vivekananda**. A formidable spiritual intellect and once a Brahmo himself, Vivekananda went on to inspire successive generations of Hindu nationalists. After having spent some time in London as a student, **Sri Aurobindo** (1872–1950) returned to India to become a freedom fighter and, finally, emerged as one the most influential philosophers of twentieth-century India. Aurobindo went on to establish his own ashram in Pondicherry (see p.1150), preaching a return to a reformed esoteric Hinduism.

southern end stands the white-marble **Victoria Memorial**, and close by rise the tall gothic spires of **St Paul's Cathedral**. Next to the busy **New Market** area alongside looms the all-embracing **Indian Museum**. Further north, the district centred on BBD Bagh is filled with reminders of the heyday of the East India Company, dominated by the bulk of the **Writers' Building**; nearby stand **St Andrew's Kirk** and the pillared immensity of the **GPO**. A little further out, the **Armenian Church** stands on the edge of the frenetic, labyrinthine markets of **Barabazaar**, while the renowned and influential temple of **Kalighat** is away to the south. Across the river, south of the marvellous **Howrah railway station**, lies the tranquillity of the **Botanical Gardens**.

The Maidan, New Market and Park Street

One of the largest city-centre parks in the world, the **Maidan** – literally "field" – stretches from the area known as Esplanade in the north to the racecourse in the south, and is bordered by **Chowringhee Road** to the east and the Strand and the river to the west. This vast area of open space stands in utter contrast to the chaotic streets of the surrounding city, and is big enough to swallow up several clubs, including the Calcutta Ladies Golf Club and the immaculate greens of the Calcutta Bowling Club. It was created when the now-inconspicuous **Fort William** was laid out near the river in 1758, and Robert Clive cleared tracts of forest to give its guns a clear line of fire. Originally a haven for the elite, with a strictly enforced dress code, today ordinary citizens come to exercise early each morning, while shepherds graze their flocks and riders on horseback canter along the old bridleways. In the late afternoons, the Maidan plays host to scores of impromptu cricket and football matches, as well as games of kabadi (see p.890).

Esplanade, New Market and Chowringhee

The 46-metre column of **Shahid Minar** (Martyrs' Memorial) towers over busy tram and bus terminals and market stalls at the northeast corner of the Maidan, known here as Esplanade. As the **Ochterlony Monument**, it was built in 1828 to commemorate the memory of David Ochterlony, who led the East India Company troops to victory in the Nepalese Wars of 1814–16. On the east side of Esplanade, the formerly elegant colonnaded front of Chowringhee Road, with its long line of colonial villas and palaces, is now in a sorry state of decay and perpetually crowded with hawkers and shoppers. The only one of its grand institutions to survive relatively unscathed is the Victorian **Grand Hotel** which, after endless renovations and changes of management, remains a haven of colonialism, with its palm court inspired by the famous *Raffles* of Singapore.

Around the corner to the east, Chowringhee Road leads to the single-storey **New Market**, little changed since it opened in 1874 and with plenty of old world charm. Its correct name is Sir Stuart Hogg Market; supposedly, the ghost of Sir Stuart roams the corridors at night. Beneath its Gothic red-brick clock tower, the market itself stocks a vast array of household goods, luggage, ready-made garments, jewellery, curio shops, bookshops, textiles and kitchenware, as well as meat, vegetables and fruit. Among shops that stand out from the rest, **Chamba Lama** sells Tibetan curios, silver jewellery, bronzes and the occasional antique. The **Symphony** store has a good selection of classical and popular Indian music, while **Sujata's** is known for its silk, and **Nahoum & Sons** is a Jewish bakery and confectioner which does a roaring trade. Further up the corridor, condiment stalls offer cheese from Kalimpong, miniature rounds of salty Bandel cheese and *amshat*, blocks made up of sheets of dried mango; the produce poultry, fish and meat market near by is unmistakable through by its aroma. If there is even a flicker of uncertainty on the part of the shopper, eager coolies with baskets are only too happy to assist and avail of the commission offered by retailers.

Indian Museum

At the corner of Chowringhee and Sudder streets, the stately **Indian Museum** (Tues–Sun 10am–5pm; Rs150 [Rs10]) is the oldest and the largest museum in India, founded in 1814. Visitors come in their thousands, many of them villagers who bring offerings to the *jadu ghar* or "house of magic", which had its reputation blighted by a blatant theft when, in December 2004, a priceless Buddhist statue was stolen during opening hours without anyone noticing; rumour has it that pilfering from the museum is nothing new.

The main showpiece is a collection of **stone and metal sculptures** obtained from sites all over India, which centres on a superb Mauryan polished sandstone **lion capital** dating from the third century BC. One gallery houses the impressive remains of the second-century BC Buddhist **stupa from Bharhut** in Madhya Pradesh, partly re-assembled to display posts, capping stones, railings and gateways all made from red sandstone. Carvings depict human and animal figures, as well as scenes from the *Jataka* tales of the Buddha's many incarnations. There is also a huge collection of Buddhist schist sculptures, dating from the first to the third century, from the Gandhara region. You'll also see stone sculpture from **Khajuraho** and Pala bronzes, plus copper artefacts, Stone-Age tools and terracotta figures from other sites.

Along with an excellent exhibit of Tibetan *thangkas*, the museum holds Kalighat *pats* (see p.881) and paintings by the **Company School**, a group of mid-nineteenth-century Indian artists who emulated Western themes and techniques for European patrons. Finally, there's a spectacular array of fossils and stuffed animals, most of which look in dire need of a decent burial.

Park Street

Around the corner from the museum, the **Asiatic Society** at 1 Park St, established in 1784 by Orientalists including Sir William Jones, houses a huge collection of around 150,000 books and 60,000 manuscripts, some of which date back to the seventh century. The society has a **reading room** open to the public (Mon–Fri 10am–8pm, Sat 10am–5pm; free) as well as a **gallery** of art and antiquities that holds paintings by Rubens and Reynolds, a large coin collection and one of Ashoka's stone edicts.

Around 2km east along Park Street from the Maidan, the disused but recently restored **Park Street Cemetery** is one of the city's most haunting memorials to its imperial past. Inaugurated in 1767, it is the oldest in Kolkata, holding a wonderful concentration of pyramids, obelisks, pavilions, urns and headstones, under which many well-known figures from the Raj lie buried. The epitaphs make fascinating reading.

Fort William

A road leads west through the Maidan from the top of Park Street to the gates of **Fort William**. The fort functions as the military headquarters of the Eastern Command, so entry is restricted and the public only allowed into certain sections on special occasions. Built on the site of the old village of Govindapur, and commissioned by the British after their defeat in 1756, Fort William was completed in 1781 and named after King William III. A rough octagon, about 500m in diameter, whose massive but low bunker-like battlements are punctuated by six main gates, it was designed to hold all the city's Europeans in the event of attack. To one side it commanded a view of the Maidan, cleared to give a field of fire; to the other it dominated the river and the crucial shipping lanes. Water from the river was diverted to fill the surrounding moat. Eighteenth- and nineteenth-century structures inside include the Church of St Peter's (now a library), barracks and stables, an arsenal, strong rooms and a prison.

Victoria Memorial and the Calcutta Gallery

The dramatic white marble **Victoria Memorial** (Tues–Sun 10am–4.30pm; Rs150 [Rs10]) at the southern end of the Maidan, with its formal gardens and water courses, continues to be Kolkata's pride and joy. Other colonial monuments and statues throughout the city have been renamed or demolished, but the popularity of Queen Victoria seems to endure forever; thirty years of attempts to change the name of the "VM" have come to nothing. This extraordinary hybrid building, with Italianate statues over its entrances, Moghul domes in its corners, and tall elegant open colonnades along its sides, was conceived by Lord Curzon to commemorate the empire at its peak. Designed by Sir William Emerson, it was completed in 1921. A sombre statue of Queen Victoria, flanked by two ornamental tanks, gazes out towards the Maidan from a pedestal lined with bronze panels and friezes. Faced with Makrana marble from Jodhpur, the building itself is capped by a dome bearing a revolving five-metre-tall bronze figure of Victory.

The main entrance, at the Maidan end, leads into a tall chamber beneath the dome. The 25 **galleries** inside burst with mementoes of British imperialism – statues and busts of Queen Mary, King George V and Queen Victoria; paintings of Robert Clive and the Queen (again); a huge canvas of the future Edward VII entering Jaipur in 1876; French guns captured at the Battle of Plassey in 1758; and the black marble throne of a nawab defeated by Robert Clive. One chamber, converted and renamed the **Calcutta Gallery**, is dedicated to the Indians of the city and the Independence struggle. The evening **Sound and Light** show (Tues–Sun 7.45–8pm; Rs20) concentrates on the same theme.

Admission to the Victoria Memorial's popular **gardens** (daily 4.30am–6.00pm) is free during the day. After they close, the Maidan in front of the gates is transformed. A seething mass of people come to enjoy the breeze, roadside snacks, and pony and *ikka* (open carriage) rides, and to watch the garish **musical fountains**.

Galleries

Bengal has a proud and lively tradition of contemporary art, with its few **galleries** showing a high standard of work. The places below are all worth checking out.

Birla Academy of Art and Culture 108 Southern Ave ⓣ033/2466 2843. Ancient and modern art with regular exhibitions of contemporary Indian artists. Tues–Sun 3.30–6pm; Rs5.

Chemould 12 Park St ⓣ033/2229 8641. Art gallery and picture framer that stages special exhibitions from time to time. Mon–Sat 10am–7pm; free.

CIMA (Centre of International Modern Art), 2nd Floor, Sunny Towers, 43 Ashutosh Chowdhury Ave ⓣ033/2474 8717. Prestigious Ballygunge gallery, displaying work by contemporary artists. Tues–Sun 2–8pm; free.

Galerie 88 28B Shakespeare Sarani t033/2247 2274. Private gallery showing contemporary Indian paintings plus specialist exhibitions. Also stocks art supplies. Mon–Sat 10am–7pm; free.

St Paul's Cathedral and around

A little way along from the Victoria Memorial, past the Birla Planetarium, stands the gothic edifice of **St Paul's Cathedral**, erected by Major W.N. Forbes in 1847. Measuring 75m by 24m, its iron-trussed roof was then the longest span in existence. For improved ventilation, the lancet windows inside extend to plinth level, and tall fans hang from the ceiling. The most outstanding of the many well-preserved memorials and plaques to long-perished imperialists is the stained glass of the west window, designed by Sir Edward Burne-Jones in 1880 to honour Lord Mayo, assassinated in the Andaman Islands. The original steeple was destroyed in the 1897 earthquake; after a second earthquake in 1934 it was remodelled on the Bell Harry Tower at Canterbury Cathedral.

South of the cathedral, the **Academy of Fine Arts** (Tues–Sun noon–8pm; Rs5) on Cathedral Road is a showcase for Bengali contemporary arts. As well as temporary exhibitions, it holds permanent displays of the work of artists such as Jamini Roy and Rabindranath Tagore. A café and pleasant grounds add to the appealing ambience. **Rabindra Sadan**, the large auditorium close by, regularly features programmes of Indian classical music and next door, **Nandan**, designed by Satyajit Ray, is a large and lively film centre with archives, library and auditoria.

Central Kolkata

The commercial and administrative hub of both Kolkata and West Bengal is **BBD Bagh**, which die-hard Calcuttans still insist on referring to as **Dalhousie Square**. The new official name, in a fine piece of official rhetoric, commemorates three revolutionaries hanged for trying to kill Lieutenant-Governor General Lord Dalhousie.

Built in 1868 on the site of the original Fort William – destroyed by Siraj-ud-Daula in 1756 – the **GPO** on the west side of the square hides the supposed site of the **Black Hole of Calcutta**. On a hot June night in 1756, 146 English prisoners were forced by Siraj-ud-Daula's guards into a tiny chamber with only the smallest of windows for ventilation; most suffocated to death by the next morning. By all accounts, the guards were unaware of the tragedy unfolding and, on hearing the news, Siraj-ud-Daula was deeply repentant. A memorial to the victims that formerly stood in front of the Writers' Building was removed in 1940 to the grounds of St John's Church south of the GPO. When Robert Clive regained control of Calcutta, he had learned his lesson: Fort William was not rebuilt in this virtually undefendable location in a built-up area, but in its current location on the Maidan, with clear visibility in all directions.

Now the seat of the West Bengal government, the **Writers' Building** to the north of the square was built in 1780 to replace the original structure used to house the clerks or "writers" of the East India Company. No official tours take in the building, but wandering in to any department armed reveals a world of endless corridors and vast chambers, desks piled high with dusty old files and clerks in a state of advanced apathy.

West of the Writers' Building, beyond the headquarters of Eastern Railways on Netaji Subhash Road, you come to the heart of Kolkata's **commercial district**, clustered around the Royal Stock Exchange at the corner of Lyon's Range. The warren of buildings, erected along the same lines as the contemporary business districts of Shanghai, houses all sorts of old colonial trading companies; Scottish names in particular still seem to be very much in evidence.

A trio of eighteenth- and nineteenth-century British **churches** are dotted around this district, the most interesting of them **St John's**, just south of the GPO.

Erected in 1787, it houses memorials to British residents, along with an impressive painting of *The Last Supper* by Johann Zoffany, in which prominent Calcuttans are depicted as apostles. In the grounds, Kolkata's first graveyard holds the tomb of Job Charnock, the city's founding father, who earned eternal notoriety for marrying a Hindu girl he saved from the funeral pyre of her first husband.

Dominating the area south of BBD Bagh, **Government House** (closed to the general public) overlooks the north end of the Maidan and the broad, ceremonial Red Road, which was once used as an airstrip. Until 1911, this was the residence of the British governor-generals and the viceroys of India; now the official home of the Governor of Bengal, it's known as **Raj Bhavan**. Nearby, opposite the **Assembly House** (Rajya Sabha) of West Bengal's Legislative Council, are the All India Radio building, and the sports complex of **Eden Gardens**, site of the huge world-famous **cricket** ground (officially known as the Ranji Stadium). Watching a test match here is an unforgettable experience as the 100,000-seat stadium resounds to the roar of the crowd and the sound of crackers thrown indiscriminately; if you want to avoid the missiles, sit in the covered sections. The pleasant palm-fringed gardens themselves (daily dawn till dusk) with a lake and a Burmese pagoda, are free.

North Kolkata

The sprawling and amorphous area of **north Kolkata** was long part of the "native" town rather than the European sectors, and was where the city's prosperous nineteenth-century Bengali families created their little palaces, or "raj baris", some of which are now in advanced and fascinating states of decay. Its markets continue to thrive unchanged, and the occasional church stands as a reminder of days gone by.

North of BBD Bagh, the area known as **Barabazaar** has played host to a succession of trading communities; the Portuguese were here even before Job Charnock landed at the fishing village that stood close by, and it later became home to Marwari and Gujarati merchants. The small and hectic lanes south of MG Road are lined with shops and stalls that sell everything from glass bangles to textiles.

At the northwest corner of Barabazaar, near Howrah Bridge, is Kolkata's oldest church, the **Armenian Church of Our Lady of Nazareth**. Founded in 1724 by Cavond, an Armenian from Persia, it was built on the site of an Armenian cemetery in which the oldest tombstone dates to 1630. The Armenian community, drawn from both Armenia and Persia, was already highly influential at the courts of Bengal by the time the British arrived, and played an important role in the early history of the East India Company. Later they went on to help start the lucrative jute industry.

East of Barabazaar on Rabindra Sarani (formerly Chitpore Road), the huge red **Nakhoda Masjid**, whose two lofty minarets rise to 46m, is the great Jami Masjid (Friday mosque) of the city. Completed in 1942, it was modelled on Akbar's Tomb at Sikandra near Agra; its four floors can hold ten thousand worshippers. The traditional Muslim market that flourishes all around the mosque sells religious items along with clothes, dried fruit and sweets such as *firni*, made of rice.

Until relatively recently, the chaotic jumble of streets to the south along Rabindra Sarani housed a thriving **Chinatown**, opium dens and all. This has gradually disappeared, though Chinese families continue to live around Chhatawala Gully, where a small early-morning street market offers home-made pork sausages, noodles and jasmine tea.

North of MG Road, on the tiny Muktaram Babu Street off Chittaranjan Avenue, the extraordinary **Marble Palace** (closed Mon & Thurs 10am–4pm; free; no photography) preserves its lavish, sensuous treasures in somewhat cramped and dilapidated conditions. Would-be visitors should obtain passes to join a guided tour from the tourist offices at BBD Bagh or Shakespeare Sarani. Built in 1835, the palace earns its name from its ornate marble-paved chambers, which hold statues, European antiques, Belgian glass, chandeliers, mirrors, Ming vases, and paintings by Rubens, Titian, Sir Joshua Reynolds and Gainsborough. To the north of Marble Palace, **Sonagachi**'s warren of lanes comprise Kolkata's largest red-light district.

On Dwarkanath Tagore Lane, a short walk northeast of the Marble Palace, the small campus of Rabindranath Tagore's liberal arts university, **Rabindra Bharati**, preserves the house where he was born and died as the **Rabindra Bharati Museum** (Tues–Sun 10am–4.30pm; Rs50 [Rs10]), otherwise known as Tagore House. The museum holds a large collection of his paintings.

Howrah and the River Hooghly

Although **Howrah** is technically a separate town, as the home of much of Kolkata's industry, as well as **Howrah Station** – a striking red-brick building built in 1906 and used by millions of passengers each day – it forms an integral part of the city. Until recently, antiquated **Howrah Bridge** was the only road link across the River Hooghly; since the opening of the tall and elegant **Vidyasagar Setu**, the second Hooghly bridge, the west bank of the river is changing rapidly. Vidyasagar Setu (also referred to as the New or Natun Bridge) provides easy access to Shibpur and the beautiful **Botanical Gardens**, and onwards southwest to the open highways towards Orissa.

Until silting rendered it impractical for large ships, the **River Hooghly**, a tributary of the Ganges, was responsible for making Calcutta a bustling port. Unlike those at Varanasi, the *ghats* that line its east (Kolkata) bank have no great mythological significance; they simply serve as landings and places for ritual ablutions. Around 1.5km north of Howrah Bridge, **Nimtolla Ghat**, one of

Howrah Bridge

One of Kolkata's most famous landmarks, **Howrah Bridge** – officially Rabindra Setu, though few use this new name – is 97m high and 705m long, spanning the river in a single giant leap to make it the world's largest cantilever bridge. It was erected during World War II in 1943 to give Allied troops access to the Burmese front, replacing an earlier pontoon bridge that opened to let river traffic through. Looking like a giant version of something a child might make using a construction set, it was the first bridge to be built using rivets and is still the world's busiest, used by millions of commuters daily. Despite the removal of the tramlines, its eight lanes are still perpetually clogged with vehicles, and in the 1980s became so worn out that a man pushing his broken-down car is said to have fallen through a hole and disappeared. Don't let that put you off; the bridge has undergone major repairs in recent years, and joining the streams of pedestrians who walk across it each day is a memorable experience.

Vidyasagar Setu, the second Hooghly bridge, built 3km south to relieve the strain, was 22 years in the making. It's a vast toll bridge, high enough to let ships pass below, and with spaghetti-junction-style approaches. Despite the reluctance of many to use it, a one-way system that governs the use of Howrah Bridge is at last forcing traffic to swallow the Rs7 toll.

the city's main cremation grounds, is sealed off from the public gaze. The large steps alongside, and a Shiva temple, attract *sadhus* as they head through the city on their way to January's Ganga Sagar Mela (see p.864). A little further north, behind **Kumartuli Ghat**, a warren of lanes is home to a community of artisans who specialize in making the clay, straw and pith images of deities used for the major festivals. In the days leading up to the great pujas, especially that of Durga, Kumartuli is a fascinating hive of activity. As you walk north, you come next to **Baghbazaar Ghat**, where overloaded barges of straw arrive for the craftsmen of Kumartuli. Baghbazaar, the Garden Market, stands on the original site of Sutanuti, its grand but decaying turn-of-the-twentieth-century mansions epitomizing the long-vanished lifestyle of the Bengali gentry, the *bhadra log* (lampooned by Kipling in *The Jungle Book*, whose monkey troupe he called the "bandar log").

South of Howrah Bridge, but right in its shadow, the large **Armenian Ghat** is at its most animated soon after dawn, when traditional gymnasts and wrestlers, devotees of Hanuman the monkey god, do their morning practice, and a **flower market** is in full swing. As the Strand – separated from the river by the Circular Railway line – heads south, it passes several warehouses and the recently established ornamental **Millennium Park** on the way beyond Fairly Place to another cluster of *ghats*. **Babu Ghat** here, identified by its crumbling colonnade, is used for early-morning bathing, attended by *pujaris* (priests) and heavy-handed masseurs. Messy and busy, Babu Ghat's Bus Stand nearby is one of Kolkata's main cross-country terminuses, while frequent ferries (7.30am–8pm) from **Chandpal Ghat**, a couple of hundred metres north, provide an easy alternative to Howrah Bridge. Further south towards Hastings, the buildings recede and the Strand comes into its own; it's particularly pleasant during the early evenings with a pleasant café, food stalls and boat rides from the small jetty near the café (around Rs150 per hour).

Botanical Gardens

The **Botanical Gardens** (daily 7am–5pm; free) at Shibpur lie 10km south of Howrah Station on the west bank of the Hooghly. Although they were created in 1786 to develop strains of Indian tea, Calcuttans have only started to appreciate these 109 hectares since the opening of the second bridge. Populated by countless bird species, such as waders, cranes, and storks, the huge gardens are best seen in winter and spring, and early in the mornings, before the heat of the day sets in. Their single most famous feature is the world's largest **banyan tree**, 24.5m high and an astonishing 420m in circumference. The Orchid House, the Herbarium and the Fern Houses are also worth seeing, and there's an attractive riverside promenade.

The gardens are accessible as a tedious road trip from Esplanade, by minibus or the ordinary ash-coloured #C6 bus. The #T9 runs from Park Street and #6 minibus runs from Dharamtala via Howrah. Taxis from the central Sudder Street area cost around Rs80 one-way and are by far the most relaxing way to get there, unless, that is, the erratic **ferry** service is running from Chandpal or Babu Ghat.

South Kolkata

South of the Maidan and Park Street, Kolkata spreads towards **suburbs** such as Alipore and Ballygunge, both within easy distance of the centre. The thoroughfare that starts life as Chowringhee proceeds south from Esplanade past **Kalighat** to **Tollygunge**, following the Metro line which terminates near the luxurious Tollygunge Club (see p.872), the mansion of an indigo merchant now surrounded by immaculate golfing fairways and bridle paths. Northeast of Tollygunge, beyond a white-tiled mosque built in 1835 by descendants of Tipu Sultan, the vast open area around the Rabindra Sarobar lakes leads to **Ballygunge**, the home of Kolkata's Bengali middle classes.

Alipore

Around 3km south of Park Street, the crumbling nineteenth-century splendour of **Alipore** is slowly being engulfed by a forest of multistorey buildings. Elegant triple-arched gates just south of the popular **Zoo** (daily except Tues 9am–5pm; Rs5) lead to Belvedere, the former residence of the lieutenant-governor of Bengal and now serving as the **National Library** (Mon–Fri 10am–6pm; separate periodical and newspaper reading room on Esplanade Mon–Fri 9am–2pm, Sat & Sun 10am–6pm; free). Presented to Warren Hastings by Mir Jafar, the building's original simplicity was enhanced by double columns and the sweeping staircase that leads to the Durbar Hall. When the capital shifted to Delhi, this library was left behind; today it houses a huge and extensive collection of books, periodicals and reference material, as well as rare documents in an air-conditioned chamber.

Kalighat

Some 5km south of Park Street along Ashutosh Mukherjee Road (an extension of Chowringhee Road), Kolkata's most important temple, **Kalighat**, stands at the heart of a diverse and animated area, part residential, part bazaar, while the destitute hoping for charity from pilgrims line the approaches to the temple and prostitutes linger on the thoroughfares and bridges offering their services in tragic, grimy circumstances. The plain but typically Bengali temple, built of brick and mortar in 1809 but capturing the sweeping curves of a thatched roof, is dedicated to Kali, the black goddess and form of Shakti. According to legend, Shiva went into a frenzy after the death of his wife Sati, dancing with her dead body and making the whole world tremble. The gods had attempted to stop him in various ways before Vishnu took his solar discus and chopped the disintegrating corpse into 51 bits. The spot where each piece fell became a *pitha*, or pilgrimage site, for worshippers of the female principle of divinity – Shakti. The shrine here marks the place where her little toe fell.

The temple is open all hours, and is always a hive of activity. Avaricious priests will try to whisk you downstairs to confront the dramatic monolithic image of the terrible goddess in the basement, with her huge eyes and bloody tongue.

Kalighat paintings

Early in the nineteenth century, Kalighat was in its heyday, drawing pilgrims, merchants and artisans from all over the country. Among them were **scroll painters** from elsewhere in Bengal, who developed the distinctive style now known as **Kalighat pats** (paintings). Adapting Western techniques, they used paper and water-based paints instead of tempera, and gradually moved away from religious themes to depict contemporary subjects. By 1850, Kalighat *pats* had taken on a dynamic new direction, satirizing the middle classes in much the same way as today's political cartoons. As a result, their work serves as a witty record of the period, filled with images of everyday life. Kalighat *pats* can now be found in galleries and museums around the world, and in the Indian Museum (see p.875) as well as the Birla Academy in Kolkata.

Mother Teresa

Beatified by Pope John Paul II on 19 October 2003, **Mother Teresa**, Kolkata's most famous citizen (1910–97), was born Agnes Gonxha Bojaxhiu to Albanian parents, and grew up in Skopje in the former Yugoslavia. After joining the Sisters of Loreto, an Irish order, she was sent as a teacher to Darjeeling, where she took her vows in May 1931 and became Teresa. In her work at St Mary's School in Kolkata, she became aware of the incredible poverty around her; in 1948, with permission from Rome, she put aside her nun's habit to clothe herself in the simple blue-bordered white sari that became the uniform of the **Missionaries of Charity**.

The best known of their many homes and clinics is **Nirmal Hriday** at 251 Kalighat Rd, a hospice for destitutes. In the face of local resistance, Mother Teresa chose its site at Kalighat – Kolkata's most important centre of Hinduism – in the knowledge that many of the poor specifically come here to die, next to a holy *tirtha* or crossing-place. Mother Teresa's simple piety and single-minded devotion to the poor won her international acclaim, including the Nobel Peace Prize in 1979. Subsequently she also attracted a fair share of controversy, with her fierce anti-abortion stance, giving rise to accusations of fundamentalist Catholicism. She was also accused by her detractors of disregarding modern advances in medicine in favour of saving the souls of the dying and destitute. Censure, however, seems iniquitous in the light of her immense contribution to humanity.

If you're interested in working for the Missionaries of Charity, they can be contacted at Mother House, 54A AJC Bose Rd (Ⓣ033/2249 7115, closed Thurs). Although they occasionally turn casual **volunteers** away, they run orientation workshops (a brief introduction to their work) on Mondays, Wednesdays and Fridays from 3pm to 5pm. Nearby Shishu Bhavan, 78 AJC Bose Rd, is an orphanage and a dispensary for children.

The appalling poverty highlighted by Mother Teresa has led to a number of NGO charities developing in the city. Established in 1979, **Calcutta Rescue** is a non-religious organization which, with the help of worldwide support groups, runs four clinics, three schools and a creche in Kolkata, as well as an outreach programme to help those in need further afield in West Bengal. For more Information visit them online at Ⓦwww.calcuttarescue.org or call Ⓣ033/2217 5675.

The courtyard beyond the main congregational hall is used for sacrificing goats on special occasions such as Kali Puja; allegedly, humans were formerly sacrificed here to appease the fertility goddess. To the north of the compound, a *lingam* is worshipped by women praying for children, while shops all around cater for pilgrims. **Nirmal Hriday**, Mother Teresa's home for the destitute and dying, is nearby.

Eating

Although locals love to **dine out**, traditional Bengali cooking was, until recently, restricted to the home; however now with a handful of excellent restaurants now offer the chance to taste this wonderful fish-based cuisine. However the most popular option for dining out is Chinese food, spiced and cooked to local tastes: the city has a rich tradition including its own Chinatown at **Tangra** (closes early around 10pm) on the road to the airport. You'll also find several good South Indian restaurants, as well as rich Muslim cooking at places like *Royal*, and *Sabirs*; the *kathi* roll, invented at *Nizam's*, is now part and parcel of Kolkata's cuisine. Tibetan cafés around Rabindra Sadan Metro offer cheap,

△ Coffee house, College Street

plain *momos* and *thukpa*, while a crop of brash modern restaurants and cafés have sprung up all over the city, serving everything from vernacular cooking to pizzas, and numerous patisseries and confectioneries work hard to keep abreast of demand. For that special occasion, fine dining at one of Kolkata's five-star hotels doesn't have to break the bank, if you avoid the wine.

Restaurants and cafés around **Sudder Street** cater for Western travellers staying in the local hotels, while roadside chai shops and snack vendorsoffer a tasty alternative. The busy environs around **New Market** include a Muslim quarter with several good restaurants, most with an emphasis on meat.

New Market and Sudder Street

All the places below appear on the Chowringhee and Sudder Street map, p.870.

Aaheli *Peerless Inn*, 12 Chowringhee Rd ⓣ033/2288 0301. Excellent Bengali food and a friendly but refined atmosphere. No bar.

Blue Sky Café Sudder St. Budget travellers' haunt halfway down the strip on a corner, providing all the old favourites. Clean, well run and a popular meeting place.

Curd Corner Sudder St. One-table café offering curd, fresh fruit juices, coffee and street scenes.

JoJo's 6 Sudder St. Upstairs a/c restaurant that gets packed at lunchtime, with a good flexible menu including travellers' fare.

Kathleens 12 Mirza Ghalib St. Popular bakery and patisserie with several other branches throughout the city.

Khalsa Madge Lane. Simple but enduringly popular *dhaba* serving basic, inexpensive food.

Lytton 14 Sudder St. Along with a bar, this hotel has two good restaurants including the *Dynasty* serving Chinese food, and *Gaylords* serving Indian and Western fare.

Momo Palace 1B Tottee Lane. A tiny four-table café serving delicious *momos* and *thukpa*.

Nahoum & Sons F20, New Market. Legendary Jewish bakery and confectioner selling delicious fruitcake, cashew macaroons, *chala* (Jewish braided bread), cheese straws, chicken patties and bagels with cream cheese.

Nizam's 22–25 Hogg Market. Though its legendary restaurant has closed, staff have set up stalls outside on the street, specializing in the *kathi roll*, tasty *sheesh kebabs*, rolled into a *paratha* of white flour.

Oberoi Grand 15 Chowringhee Rd ⓣ033/2249 2323. Although expensive – Rs1600 per head and up – *Ban Thai* produces by far the best Thai cooking in town.

Princess 12 Mirza Ghalib St. Around the corner from Sudder St, this smart but affordable place is good for tandoori, ice cream, teas and cold beer. Closed Thurs.

Zurich 3 Sudder St. Near the *Blue Sky Café* and similarly pitched at travellers; more comfortable and restaurant-like, with good food and a relaxed atmosphere.

Around Park Street

All the places below appear on the Chowringhee and Sudder Street map, p.870.

Astor 15 Shakespeare Sarani ⓣ033/2242 9950. This hotel houses a bar and several restaurants: the multi-cuisine *Serai*; the *Banyan Tree* serving Bengali food; and, best of all, the *Kebab-e-Que* in the garden, dishing up excellent tandoori food. Try the *Moti Kebab* (mushrooms and *paneer*).

Bar-B-Q 43 Park St. An old favourite, offering Chinese and much-lauded tandoori cuisine in pleasant dimly lit surroundings with a bar downstairs.

Barista 12D Park St. The Kolkata branch of this trendy and popular nationwide chain serves up a range of snacks and good coffee, and has a tiny bookshop upstairs.

Blue Fox 55 Park St. Once a celebrated jazz nightclub, but now a plush restaurant renowned for its sizzlers and excellent seafood.

Flury's 18 Park St, on the corner of Middleton Row. A Kolkata landmark, this legendary Swiss teashop and patisserie has been completely revamped, swapping its flaky, laid-back atmosphere for a more upbeat, hectic (if chaotic) style. Still worth visiting for its cakes, patties and Swiss pastries – try the rum balls. They also make their own chocolates.

Grain of Salt Block D, 5th Floor, 22 Camac St (Pantaloons). Chic dining on the top floor of this monument to consumerism; the mixed menu is strong on Indian, but there's also Chinese and a "world" selection including the likes of Creole prawns and ratatouille.

Gupta Brothers 42A Park Mansions, Mirza Ghalib St. Excellent, clean and cheap vegetarian snack bar and sweet counter with a good Rajasthani restaurant upstairs. Try the *tandoori bharwan aloo*.

Kwality 17 Park St. A plush and airy ambience and a good range of food (including ice creams) ensures that this place remains one of best restaurants on the strip, especially good for a leisurely lunch.

Marco Polo in China 24 Park St. Expensive new restaurant with a pleasant garden theme, serving the best Cantonese and Szechuan food on the strip along, with dim sum and seafood specialities including lobster.
Mocambo 25B Park St, around the corner on Mirza Ghalib St. An old restaurant which has grown from strength to strength and is now a firm favourite for its smart but relaxed ambience, good cooking and varied menu including Chicken Kiev and pizzas.
New China Bistro 119A MA Ahmed St. A relaxed but smart new bistro a short walk away from Sudder St, specializing in Chinese cuisine but with a sprinkling of Italian too. Expect to pay around Rs250 per head.
One Step Up 18A Park St. Bright new bistro offering a range of options, from sandwiches and light meals to tandoori and pastries in smart and impeccable surroundings.
Park 17 Park St ⓣ033/2249 3121. The upmarket hotel has developed a reputation for some of the finest dining in town. The *Oriental Zen* serves dishes from Thailand, China, Japan and Indonesia; *Saffron* specializes in Indian cuisine, while the 24hr *Atrium* coffee bar also provides a good food menu.
Sourav's 20G Park St, Middleton Row ⓣ033/2249 4646. Fancy, modern complex of restaurants on four floors topped with a swanky bar and nightclub. The reasonably priced *One-Day* café serves light meals including sandwiches, *dosas* and pizzas; *Over-Boundary* is a plush and pricey multicuisine restaurant, and there's also the vegetarian *Maharaj.* Named after the illustrious former cricket captain, and a place of pilgrimage for cricket fans.

Chandni Chowk and around

All the places listed below appear on the Kolkata map, pp.862–863.
Amber 11 Waterloo St ⓣ033/2248 6520. This quality restaurant is a Kolkata landmark, serving legendary Mughlai and tandoori cuisine. Plush and dimly lit, it covers three floors, and has a bar downstairs.
Ar-Han Thai 31 Bentinck St. The good, reasonably priced Thai food here provides a welcome alternative to local fare.
India Coffee House 15 Bankim Chatterjee St (just off College St). Atmospheric historic café in the heart of the university area where students and intellectuals continue to meet.
Sabir's Chandni Chowk. Traditional, tasty but very rich Muslim cooking behind the market. Try their *razala* – an aromatic meat curry.

AJC Bose Road and around

All the places listed below appear on the Kolkata map, pp.862–863.
Golden Harvest 11/1 Sarat Bose Rd near Minto Park ⓣ033/2247 0294. Excellent Chinese and Indian food from lunchtime till late at this upmarket restaurant.
Kewpie's Kitchen 2 Elgin Lane ⓣ033/2475 9880. Private home with a restaurant annexe, offering Bengali feasts fit for a *jamai babu* (son-in-law) first entering his wife's home – try their *lucci* (*puris*) and the fish and prawn preparations including *malai chingri* (prawns in cream) and *dab-er-chingri* (prawns in a green coconut). Closed Mon.
Oh! Calcutta 4th Floor, Forum, 10/3 Elgin Rd. On the top floor of the shopping complex, offering smart dining with an emphasis on Bengali fish-based cuisine.
Shiraz 56 Park St. Good Muslim food from Mughlai to tandoori and excellent biriyani.
Suruchi 89 Elliot Rd. Run by the All Bengal Women's Union – a charity for rehabilitated prostitutes and their children – and a great place to sample simple Bengali home-cooking. Unpretentious atmosphere and very reasonable prices; highly recommended. Look out for *macher jhol* (fish stew). Closed Sat and Sun evenings.

South Kolkata

All the places listed below appear on the Kolkata map, pp.862–863.
The Dhaba Ballygunge Phari. Sikh-run café, where the core menu of good Punjabi cooking in the mid-range restaurant upstairs has been extended to cover middle-class tastes.
Banana Leaf 73 Rashbehari Ave, Lake Market. Plain decor and a fast turnaround for this extremely popular restaurant that's widely considered to offer some of the best South Indian food in town; try the lemon rice.
Bay of Bengal 6 Dr Satyananda Roy Rd, near Menoka Cinema. A good place to taste Bengali home-cooking, with an à la carte menu as well as set platters including the luxurious *Mahabhoj* set menu; specialities include *doi mach* (fish in yoghurt), *ilish* (a particularly delicate fish, best eaten in spring), *posto* (vegetable cooked with sesame seed) or *mangsho jhol* (mutton curry); end with *mishti doi* (sweet set curd).
Tamarind 64 Sarat Bose Rd ⓣ033/3095 4226. A popular family restaurant offering various South Indian cuisines, including, dosas and biriyanis, but best for its Keralan fish and prawn curries; you may want to book ahead.

Sweet shops

Milk-based sweets such as the small and dry *sandesh* are a Bengali speciality. Though the white *rosogulla*, the brown (deep-fried) *pantua* and the distinctive black *kalojam*, all in syrup, are found elsewhere in north India, the best examples are made in Kolkata. Another one to try is *lal doi* – a delicious red steamed yoghurt made with jaggery – or plain white *mishti doi*, made with sugar. Sweet shops often serve savoury snacks in the afternoons such as deep-fried light pastry strips called *nimki* (literally "salty"); *shingara*, a delicate Bengali samosa; and *dhal puri*, paratha-like bread made with lentils.

Amrita 16A Sarat Bose Rd. Excellent *mishti doi*.

Bhim Chandra Nag Surya Sen Street, off College St. Best of several good sweet shops in the area.

Ganguram 46C Chowringhee Rd. Legendary sweet shop near Victoria Memorial, with branches all over the city; try *mishti doi* and *sandesh*.

Jadab Chandra Dass 127A Rashbehari Ave. Another popular outlet in Gariahat.

KC Das 11 Esplanade East and 1/433 Gariahat Rd. One of the city's most famous sweet shops; try their *rosogolla*.

Mithai 48B Syed Amir Ali Ave. A good all-round sweetshop.

Sen Mahasay 171H Rashbehari Ave. Next to Gariahat Market, renowned for its *sandesh*.

Elsewhere in the city

All the places listed below appear on the Kolkata map, pp.862–863.

Comesum South Station, Howrah Station. A wonderful spotless food hall in Howrah's relatively placid annexe, offering sandwiches and pizzas through to South Indian and Chinese food; the *Haldiram* counter offers hot *kachori* and great sweets.

Kim Fa 47 South Tangra Rd ⓣ033/2329 2895. One of Tangra's best and most-established Chinese restaurants – try the Thai soup, garlic prawns and chilli king prawns, which can be quite potent. If full, try *Lily's Kitchen* down the road.

Mainland China 3A Gurusaday Rd ⓣ033/2287 2206. Chic Chinese restaurant with elegant service and excellent seafood; widely considered the city's finest, but perhaps a bit overdone.

Royal Near Nakhoda Masjid, Rabindra Sarani. No trip to this area is complete without a visit to this legendary Muslim restaurant for a biriyani or a chicken or mutton champ (chop) cooked in aromatic spices and accompanied by *rumali* roti (thin "handkerchief" bread).

Taj Bengal Hotel 24B Belvedere Rd, Alipore ⓣ033/2223 3939. Smart and beautifully presented, the *Chinoiserie* offers some of Kolkata's best Chinese food; *Sonargaon* serves local delicacies and north Indian food; and *The Hub* coffeeshop offers Italian food, and is open all hours.

Drinking, nightlife and entertainment

The tense all-male atmosphere of Kolkata's **bars** is slowly changing, with a recent spate of designer bars attracting a young new professional clientele. The small but lively music scene is a fraction of what it was in the 1960s, when Park Street places such as the *Moulin Rouge* were the centre of a small but thriving pop, jazz and cabaret scene; however some restaurants and bars continue to put on live music.

Kolkata's spirited **arts scene** is known for its music and Bengali theatre, though the latter is of limited interest to most tourists as performances are in Bengali. Of the many non-religious festivals each year, the **Ganga Utsav**, held over a few weeks around the end of January at Diamond Harbour, involves music, dance and theatrical events. **Rabindra Sadan** is Kolkata's theatre and concert hall district, with numerous venues including **Nandan** next door on AJC Bose Road, the city's leading art-house cinema. *Calcutta This Fortnight* (see p.867), is a useful source for **listings**, as is *CalCalling* and local papers.

Bars and clubs

As well as the places below, the big hotels are a good option for a quiet drink; some of them also have **discos**.

Amber 11 Waterloo St. On the ground floor of a superb restaurant (see p.885), with strong a/c and low lights.

Bar-B-Q 43 Park St. Below the restaurant, this is one of the better, more stylish bars on the strip.

Chowringhee Bar *Oberoi Grand*, Chowringhee Rd. Plush and traditionally styled, but pricey.

Incognito *Taj Bengal*, 24B Belvedere Rd, Alipore. Upmarket nightclub and disco that attracts the city's well-healed. Resident DJ and a lively atmosphere until late.

Peter Cat 18A Park St. Plush and pleasant ambience, with a good reputation both as a place for a drink, and for its wide-ranging menu.

Shisha 5th Floor, Block D, 22 Camac St. On the top floor of the shopping centre, the *Shisha* nightclub's *Hookah Bar* is proving the in place in Kolkata, with flavoured hookahs served by mock-Arabs and cigars for the less adventurous. There's also cocktails, mocktails and a resident DJ.

Someplace Else *Park Hotel*, 17 Park St. A pleasant, dimly lit bar which gets especially lively in the evenings when bands belt out familiar Western and Indian covers. Open every day (3pm–midnight) and longer on Saturdays (till 2am).

Sunset Bar *Lytton Hotel*, Sudder St. Friendly and relaxed bar, popular with travellers.

Tantra *Park Hotel*, 17 Park St. Still the liveliest disco in Kolkata, where the action starts at 7pm (Rs100–300, couples free on Tues) with occasional floor shows of varying degrees of taste.

Winning Streak *Hotel Hindusthan*, 235/1 AJC Bose Rd. A popular disco with resident DJ, where the action starts late (9pm–3am).

Music and dance

Kolkatan **music** audiences have a reputation as the most discerning in the country. The main concert seasons is winter to spring, with the huge week-long **Dover Lane Music Festival**, held under a marquee in south Kolkata around the end of January and early February, attracting many of India's best musicians. Other popular venues for single- and multi-day festivals include Rabindra Sadan on the junction of AJC Bose Road and Cathedral Road and Kala Bhavan on Theatre Road (Shakespeare Sarani). Sangeet Research Academy, near Tollygunge Metro Station, one of the country's leading north Indian classical music research institutes, offers long-term courses in various music forms and holds free Wednesday-evening concerts. **All India Radio Calcutta** is a good source for Indian classical music, folk music and *Rabindra Sangeet*, the songs of Rabindranath Tagore. At the time of writing the India Tourism office were holding **dance shows** (Mon–Fri 5.30pm; Rs100; ⓣ033/2571 0420 for more information) which, though clearly for tourists, give some insight into traditional Indian dance.

Cinemas

Cinemas that show English-language films three or four times each day can be found along Chowringhee near Esplanade and New Market. All are air-conditioned; some, like the Lighthouse on Humayan Place, are fine examples of Art Deco. Names to look for include Inox, at the Forum on Elgin Road; Elite, SN Banerjee Road; Globe, Lindsay Street; and Chaplin, Chowringhee Place. Nandan (ⓣ033/2223 1210), behind Rabindra Sadan on AJC Bose Road, is the city's leading art-house cinema with a library, archives and three auditoria.

Shopping

Unlike Delhi, Kolkata is not geared towards tourism – a fact which is reflected, with one or two exceptions, by its **shops**. However, it does hold many characterful **markets**, including the wide-ranging **New Market** (see pp.874–875), and local institutions such as **Barabazaar** to the north (see p.878). Modern **shopping complexes** – good for bookshops, clothes, leather and jewellery – are cropping up all over the city; these include Pantaloons, 22 Camac St; Forum, 10/3 Elgin Rd, Emami Shoppers City at Lord Sinha Road; the Metro Shopping Centre at 1 Ho Chi Minh Sarani; and the Shree Ram Arcade, opposite the Lighthouse near New Market.

Typical Bengali handicrafts to look out for include **metal** *dokra* items from the Shantiniketan region northwest of the city, in which objects such as animals and birds are roughly cast by a lost-wax process to give them a wiry look. Long-necked, pointy-eared terracotta horses from Bankura, in all sizes, have become something of a cliché. *Kantha* **fabrics** display delicate line stitching in decorative patterns, while Bengali **leatherwork** features simple patterns dyed in subtle colours.

Books

The month-long **Kolkata Book Fair**, held on the Maidan near Park Street in January and February, is now among the biggest of its kind in the country, and provides a good opportunity to pick up books at a discount. The bookshops and the roadside stalls of **College Street** are well worth a browse, with an occasional rare gem turning up.

Cambridge Books & Stationery 20B Park St. Small place packed with assorted titles; knowledgeable staff, but a limited selection.

Classical Books Middleton Row. Small, friendly and well worth a browse, with a focus on classics.

Crossword 8 Elgin Rd. Large modern bookshop on two floors, with a good selection including novels, illustrated books and travel plus a music section and a café.

Dey Bros B47 New Market. One of several bookshops in this part of the market selling popular books on India and a selection of novels.

Family Book Shop 1A Park St. On the Chowringhee end of Park St, this place is small but crammed full of books.

Landmark Emami Shoppers City, 3 Lord Sinha Rd. Modern and extensive bookshop in a popular new shopping complex.

Oxford Book & Stationery 17 Park St. Tastefully revamped with a/c and a small music section, but despite the ambience the collection of fiction, coffee-table books, maps, guides, magazines, stationery and postcards is limited.

Seagull 31A SP Mukherjee Rd ⓣ033/2476 5869 ⓦwww.seagullindia.com. Pleasant little bookshop owned by interesting and creative publishers; their resource centre a block away, has a library and holds special exhibitions and events.

Emporia

Good selections of most handicrafts, including lace, can be found in various **state emporia**, many of which are located in the large **Dakhsinapan** shopping complex south of Dhakuria Bridge near Gol Park and the lakes. Offering fixed (if slightly high) prices, these are the simplest places to start shopping.

Assam 8 Russell St. As part of Assam House, the emporium sells handicrafts and textiles from Assam including fabrics in *pat* and *moga*, two techniques of silk manufacturing.

Central Cottage Industries 7 Chowringhee Rd, Esplanade. Part of the national chain, selling handicrafts from all over India. Along with fabrics, leather, furnishings and papier mâché from Kashmir, there's a small but interesting collection of silver jewellery, with some tribal bracelets.

Gurjari Dakhsinapan complex. An outstanding selection of Gujarati textiles, including handloom and mirrored cushion covers.

Nagaland 13 Shakespeare Sarani. A fine assortment of Naga shawls, with red bands and white and blue stripes on black backgrounds. As with Scots tartan, certain patterns denote particular tribes.

Orissa Handicrafts Dakhsinapan complex, near Gol Park. Very strong on silk and *ikat* cloth.

Sasha 27 Mirza Ghalib St. This women's self-help group have a good collection of handicrafts and textiles including kantha.

Shyam Ahuja 10 Azimganj House, 7 Camac St. Upmarket ethnic and designer fabrics and furnishings and an international name in rugs.

Fabrics and clothing

Kolkata's dress sense, in general, is conservative, and the choice of ready-made garments is not very exciting. However, a wide range of fabric is available, and all outlets should be able to point you towards a very good (and very cheap) **tailor**; there are several around Mirza Ghalib Street and Sudder Street. Upmarket boutiques such as Burlingtons on Mirza Ghalib Street cater for the city's wealthy, as do department stores such as Pantaloons (see above), which have plenty of off-the-peg designer labels. Ritu's, 46A Rafi Ahmed Kidwai Rd. specializes in chic *salwar kamise*. You can still get shoes made to order at one of the many Chinese shoe shops around Chittaranjan Avenue.

Anokhi 2nd Floor, Forum, 10/3 Elgin Rd. Chic hand printed cottons from this famous chain.

Balaram Saha 14/6 Gariahat Rd. Tangail, Baluchari and Kantha saris from Bengal.

Fabindia 16 Hindusthan Park. Down a side road off Rashbehari Avenue and not far from Gariahat, this excellent chain is renowned for its handprinted ready-to-wear cottons and accessories, and is also good for furnishings.

Handloom House 2 Lindsay St. Near New Market, this government-run co-operative shop has a wide range of textiles, including cotton and raw silks at reasonable fixed prices.

Henry's New Market. One of Kolkata's better-known Chinese shoe shops.

Indian Silk House AC Market, 1 Shakespeare Sarani. Lots of printed silks.

Jaggi & Sons Lindsay St. One of several good tailors in the city, with a long tradition of formal men's tailoring.

Kolhapuri Centre College St and Gariahat Rd, Ballygunge Phari. Dedicated to selling Kolhapuri sandals and shoes – painful at first, but very comfortable if you persist.

Musical instruments

Kolkata is renowned for its sitar and sarod makers – expect to pay upwards of Rs5000 for a decent instrument. Shops around Sudder Street are strongest on Western instruments but their traditional instruments are invariably of inferior quality and may be beyond tuning; **Rabindra Sarani** (Chitpore Road) has several shops but quality is suspect. Kolkata must produce more tabla players than any other Indian city, with Anindo Chatterjee being the most highly acclaimed at present; tabla-makers can be found at **Kalighat**, next to Kalighat Bridge and at **Keshab Sen Street** off College Street.

Hemen Roy & Sons Rashbehari Ave, Triangular Park. Once master instrument-makers to Ali Akbar Khan, the sarod maestro, though they've lost out to competition in recent years. They now make sitars and *tanpuras* (the drone instruments used to accompany singing).

Hiren Roy & Son Rashbehari Ave, Gariahat. The most famous sitar-maker in the country, whose clients include Imrat Khan, the late Vilayat Khan and Ravi Shankar; off-the-shelf instruments available.

Manoj Kumar Sardar & Bros 8A Lalbazaar St, opposite Lalbazaar Police Station. Ashok Sardar makes very good sitars and sarods to order, with a small selection of off-the-shelf instruments; he also sells Indian-made guitars and will ship instruments.

Sports

Sport is enthusiastically followed in Kolkata, with **football** matches – especially those between the two leading clubs, Mohan Bagan and East Bengal – and **cricket** test matches draw huge crowds. There are two major stadium complexes, the **Ranji Stadium** at Eden Gardens and the new **Salt Lake Stadium** on the eastern edge of the city.

The **Maidan**, home to the Calcutta Bowling Club and the Ladies Golf Club, is a favourite venue for impromptu cricket and football matches, and the scene of regular race meetings in winter and spring. These are run by the Calcutta Turf Club, and bets can also be placed at their premises on Russell Street. Also in winter, army teams play **polo** at the grounds at the centre of the racecourse. The curious sport of **kabadi**, a fierce form of tag played by two teams on a pitch the size of a badminton court, can also be seen around the Maidan.

The easiest **swimming pool** for visitors to use is Calcutta Swimming Club, 1 Strand Rd (℡033/2248 2894) where you can apply for temporary membership. The *Hindusthan* hotel, 235-1 AJC Bose Rd (℡033/2247 2394), allows non-residents to use their newly renovated pool on a daily basis (Rs400). Across the road from the superbly equipped Tollygunge Club, where with the right connections you might get to use the pool and tennis courts, the elite Royal Calcutta Golf Club is the world's second-oldest golf club, after St Andrews in Scotland.

Listings

Airlines, domestic Indian Airlines, 39 Chittaranjan Ave ℡033/2211 0730 (24hr with a tourist counter); airport office enquiries ℡033/2511 9272; recorded flight enquiries: general ℡1400, arrival ℡1402, departure ℡1403. Jet Airways, 18D Park St ℡033/2229 2227 & 2229 2237; airport enquiries ℡033/2511 9894. Sahara Indian Airlines, 2A Shakespeare Sarani ℡033/2282 6118.

Airlines, international ** International airlines with flights in and out of Kolkata.* Airline/flight enquiries: ℡033/2511 8787 & 2511 9721; Aeroflot, 1st Floor, Lords Building, 7/1 Lord Sinha Rd ℡033/2282 3765; Air France, 230 AJC Bose Rd ℡033/2240 8646; Air India, 50 Chowringhee Rd ℡033/2242 2356–9*; Alitalia, 228 AJC Bose Rd ℡033/2247 1777; American Airlines, Chitrakoot Building, 230 AJC Bose Rd ℡033/2280 1335; Austrian Airlines, Vasundhara Building, 2/7 Sarat Bose Rd ℡033/2474 5091; Bangladesh Biman, 30C Chowringhee Rd ℡033/2229 2843*; British Airways, 5th Floor, L&T Chambers (above British Council), 16 Camac St ℡98313 77470*; Cathay Pacific, 1 Middleton St ℡033/2240 3211; Continental Airlines, Stic Travels, East Anglia House, 3C Camac St ℡033/2217 4913; Druk Air, 51 Tivoli Court, 1A Ballygunge Circular Rd ℡033/2240 2419*; Gulf Air, Chitrakoot Building, 230A AJC Bose Rd ℡033/2247 7783; Japan Airlines, 35A Chowringhee Rd ℡033/2246 8363; KLM Royal Dutch Airlines, Jeevan Deep, 1 Middleton St, ℡033/2240 3151*; Kuwait Airlines, Chitrakoot Building, 230 AJC Bose Rd ℡033/2247 4697; Malaysian Airlines, Stic Travels, East Anglia House, 3C Camac St ℡033/2229 2092; North West Airlines, Jeevan Deep, 1 Middleton St, ℡033/2283 0151; Qantas, 58 Chitrakoot Building, 230 AJC Bose Rd ℡033/2247 0718; Royal Brunei, East Anglia House, 3C Camac St ℡033/2229 7112*; Royal Jordanian Airlines, Vasudhara Building, 2/7 Sarat Bose Rd ℡033/2474 5094*; Singapore Airlines, 1 Lee Rd ℡033/2280 9898; Thai Airways, International 8th floor, Crescent Tower, 229 AJC Bose Rd ℡033/2280 1630*.

Ambulance Call ℡102, or the Dhanwantary Clinic ℡033/2449 7634; St Johns Ambulance Brigade ℡033/2248 5277; or Bellevue Clinic ℡033/2247 2321.

Banks and currency exchange Kolkata Airport has a 24hr branch of the State Bank of India, as well as Thomas Cook at the international terminal. Major banks, concentrated either in the vicinity of BBD Bagh or scattered around Chowringhee Rd, include Bank of America, 8 India Exchange Place; Banque Nationale de Paris, 4a BBD Bagh

East; Citibank, 43 Chowringhee Rd; Hong Kong & Shanghai, 31 BBD Bagh East; State Bank of India, 1 Stand Rd and Kolkata airport. The ATM machines at some banks (such as most UTI branches, as well as HSBC at 3A Shakespeare Sarani, HDFC at BBD Bagh East, and ICICI at 24B Camac St) take Mastercard, Visa, Cirrus and Maestro. Other currency exchange bureaus include: Thomas Cook, Chitrakoot Building, 230 AJC Bose Rd (Ⓣ033/2247 5378), and American Express, 21 Old Court House St, near the West Bengal Tourist Office (Ⓣ033/2248 6283). There are numerous private foreign exchange bureaus on Sudder St and around New Market.

Car rental Autoriders, 10A Ho Chi Min Sarani Ⓣ033/2281 3561; Avis, Oberoi Grand, 15 Chowringhee Rd Ⓣ033/2249/2323; Hertz, 219 Kamalaya Centre, 156A Lenin Sarani Ⓣ033/2221 7313, and at the airport Ⓣ033/2511 8787 (ext 4224); Car-Cab, Manook Lane, off Ezra St Ⓣ033/2235 3535; Mark Corporation, P27 Princep St Ⓣ033/2221 9412.

Consulates Bangladesh, 9 Circus Ave (Sheikh Mujib Sarani) Ⓣ033/2247 5208; Canada, Duncan House, 31 Netaji Subhash Rd Ⓣ033/2220 8515; France, 4th Floor, Sagar Estate, Clive Ghat St Ⓣ033/2220 4571; Germany, 1 Hastings Park Rd Ⓣ033/2479 1141; Italy, 3 Raja Santosh Rd, Alipore Ⓣ033/2479 2414; Nepal, 1 National Library Ave, Alipore Ⓣ033/2456 1224; Singapore, 7/1 Lord Sinha Rd Ⓣ033/2282 4106; Sri Lanka, Nicco House, 2 Hare St Ⓣ033/2248 5102; Thailand, 18B Mandeville Gardens Ⓣ033/2440 7836; UK, 1 Ho Chi Minh Sarani Ⓣ033/2242 5171 or 2288 5172; USA, 5/1 Ho Chi Minh Sarani Ⓣ033/2282 3611.

Cultural centres Cultural representatives of overseas countries in Kolkata, typically with reading rooms and facilities for performances and film shows, include: the British Council, 16 Camac St Ⓣ033/2282 5370; the Russian Gorky Sadan, Gorky Terrace, near Minto Park Ⓣ033/2247 5407; and the German Max Mueller Bhavan, 8 Pramathesh Barua Sarani Ⓣ033/2475 9398. Similar facilities can be found at the Ramakrishna Mission Institute of Culture in Gol Park Ⓣ033/4264 1303, and USIS, American Centre, 38A Chowringhee Rd Ⓣ033/2282 2336.

Homeopaths and herbal medicine Homeopaths include King & Co 90/6A MG Rd; Sterling & Co, 91-C Elliot Rd. Tibetan Medical & Astro Institute, 9 East Rd, Jadavpur, offer herbal treatments.

Hospitals Cheap, government-run hospitals are notoriously mismanaged, and private medical care, if expensive by comparison, is infinitely superior. In case of serious illness, you are best advised to contact your consulate. Good private clinics include Belle Vue, 9 Loudon St Ⓣ033/2247 2321; Ruby General, EM Bypass, Kasba Ⓣ033/2442 0291; Woodlands Nursing Home, 8/5 Alipore Rd Ⓣ033/2456 7079.

Internet Internet access (from Rs15 an hour) is easily available throughout the city. The Reliance chain are the most reliable, while the Amazone, 8 Bowbazar St, with its rainforest theme, is friendly with free tea and coffee. Of the many places around Sudder St, try Hotel Maria and Netfreaks. Around the corner on Mirza Ghalib St, Sify iway is part of a dependable chain; a short walk south, Cyberia, 8 Kyd St is also consistent.

Libraries Asiatic Society Library, 1 Park St; British Council Library, 16 Camac St (a monthly rate which includes borrowing books, use of the reference section and discounted Internet use); National Library, 1 Belvedere Rd; Ramakrishna Mission Library, Gol Park; University of Kolkata library, College Square. Seagull Arts and Media Resource Centre, 36C SP Mukherjee Rd, near the Bhowanipur police station, has a small but very pleasant and well-organised a/c library.

Opticians Lawrence & Mayo, 20E Park St Ⓣ033/2229 8310; President Optical company, 306 BB Ganguly St Ⓣ033/2236 3280.

Permits and visas The Foreigners' Registration Office is at 237 AJC Bose Rd (Ⓣ033/247 3300).

Pharmacies Deys Medical Stores 6 Lindsay St and 20A Nelly Sengupta Sarani; Angel 151 Park St (24hr); Dhanwantary Clinic, 65 Diamond Harbour Rd (24hr); Welmed, 4–1 Sambhunath Pandit St (24hr Mon & Tues).

Photography Bombay Photo Stores Private Ltd, 33–34 Park Mansions, Park St, for film processing; Camera Craft, Park Centre, 1st floor, 24 Park St, for camera repairs; Madan St between SN Banerji Rd and Dharamtala is good for all kinds of film, but non-refrigerated.

Police Ⓣ100. The central police station is on Lal Bazaar St, BBD Bagh Ⓣ033/2241 3230. Others include Park St Ⓣ033/2226 8321.

Postal services The GPO, on the west side of BBD Bagh, houses the poste restante and has a philatelic department. The Central Telegraph Exchange is nearby at 8 Red Cross Place, close to Telephone Bhavan, the headquarters for Calcutta Telephones. If you're staying in the Sudder St area, the New Market Post Office, Mirza Ghalib St, is much more convenient. Sending parcels is easiest from the large and friendly post office on Park St, where enterprising individuals will handle the entire process for you for a negotiable fee. If you need a quicker service, DHL is at 21 Camac St Ⓣ033/2281 3131. Poste restante is also available from India Tourism,

Embassy Building, 4 Shakespeare Sarani, Kolkata 700 071.

State tourist offices The most useful of the many offices representing other states in Kolkata are those that cover the northeastern states (details of permit requirements can be found on pp.982–983), and that of the Andaman and Nicobar islands. Andaman and Nicobar, 3A Auckland Place ⓣ033/2247 5084 (permits are issued on arrival, but check before you go); Arunachal Pradesh, Block CE, 109 Sector 1, Salt Lake ⓣ033/2334 1243; Assam, 8 Russell St ⓣ033/2229 5094; Manipur, 26 Rowland Rd ⓣ033/2475 8075; Meghalaya, 120 Shantipally, EM Bypass ⓣ033/2441 1932, and in the Great Eastern Hotel ⓣ033/2248 2331 ext 2224; Mizoram, 24 Old Ballygunge Rd ⓣ033/2475 7887; Nagaland, 11 Shakespeare Sarani ⓣ033/2282 5247; Orissa, 41 & 55 Lenin Sarani ⓣ033/2216 4556; Sikkim, 4/1 Middleton St ⓣ033/2281 5328; Tripura, 1 Pretoria Stⓣ033/2282 5703. Another useful tourist office is that of the Darjeeling Gurkha Hill Council, India Tourism, 4 Shakespeare Sarani ⓣ033/2282 1715.

Tour Operators Help Tourism (see p.867) offer choice accommodation in the Sunderbans and wildlife tours in north Bengal. Kali Travel Home 22/77 Raja Manindra Rd (ⓣ033/2248 7980 ⓦwww.traveleastindia.com) offer guided tours of Bengal and the northeast. Himalayan Footprints, 1st floor, 77 Netaji Subhash Rd (ⓣ033/2243 1063, ⓦwww.trekinindia.com) offer informative and flexible wildlife tours, nature treks and trips to the Sunderbans, Sikkim and Darjeeling.

Travel agents American Express Travel Related Services, 21 Court House St (ⓣ033/2248 6283), and Thomas Cook, Chitrakoot Building, 2nd Floor, 230 AJC Bose Rd (ⓣ033/2247 5378), deal with inbound tours and international flights and foreign exchange. For domestic and international flights, there are numerous travel agents around Sudder St: try Miles 'n' More opposite *Blue Sky Café*, 2/1 Sudder St (ⓣ033/2246 4991), and Star Travels, 10 Sudder St (ⓣ033/2245 1655). Chocks-Off, 1 Cockburn Lane, off Royd St (ⓣ033/2246 8780, ⓔchocks@cal3.vsnl.net.in), are very reliable and efficient. Warren Travels, 31 Chowringhee Rd (ⓣ033/2226 6178), is a well-established service dealing with international and domestic flights, hotel bookings, group tours, and travel documents; so is Sita World Travels, 3B Camac St (ⓣ033/2247 5420).

Moving on from Kolkata

Transport connections between Kolkata and the rest of India are summarized on pp.923–925. If you're short of time, consider employing one of the **travel agents** listed above to book your plane, train or bus ticket for you. For more on public transport from Kolkata, see "Travel details", p.923.

By air

For information about flights from **Kolkata Airport**, call ⓣ033/2511 8787; otherwise call the individual airlines listed on p.890 to confirm departure and arrival. Remember that return flights must be confirmed at least 72 hours in advance. Major domestic routes from Kolkata are summarized in the "Travel details" on p.923.

By rail

Centralized recorded information on **train** connections is available on ⓣ033/2220 3545; to speak to an operator, call ⓣ033/2220 3535 or ⓣ141. Making **reservations** to leave Kolkata by train is easy, with computerized booking offices throughout the city; you can also book online (see p.58). The best place to book tourist quota train tickets is at the tourist office on the first floor of the **Eastern Railways office**, in the northwest corner of BBD Bagh at 6 Fairlie Place (Mon–Sat 10am–1pm & 1.30–5pm, Sun & hols 10am–2pm; ⓣ033/2242 2789 or 2220 4025). You'll need to bring proof of encashment (an exchange or ATM receipt) to reserve a berth if paying in rupees. Reservations up to sixty days in advance can be made for most trains out of the city.

Recommended trains from Kolkata

Destination	Name	No.	From	Departs	Total time
Allahabad	Kalka Mail	#2311	Howrah	7.40pm	13hr 30min
Bhubaneswar	Dhauli Express	#2821	Howrah	6am	7hr 5min
Bolpur	Shantiniketan Express	#3015	Howrah	10.05pm	2hr 25min
Chennai	Coromandal Express	#2841	Howrah	2.25pm	28hr
Delhi	Rajdhani Express*	#2301**	Howrah	4.15pm	17hr 35min
	Rajdhani Express*	#2313	Sealdah	4.35pm	18 hr 15min
Gaya	Poorva Express	#2381***	Howrah	9.10am	5hr 30min
	Mumbai Mail	#2321	Howrah	10pm	7hr 30min
Guwahati	Saraighat Express	#2345***	Howrah	3.45pm	18hr
Kalka (for Shimla)	Kalka Mail	#2311	Howrah	7.40pm	33hr 10min
Lucknow	Amritsar Mail	#3005	Howrah	7.15pm	21hr
Mumbai	Gitanjali Express	#2860	Howrah	1.30pm	32hr
New Jalpaiguri (for Siliguri**)**	Darjeeling Mail*****	#2343	Sealdah	22.05pm	10hr 35min
	Kanchenjunga Express	#5657	Sealdah	6.25am	14hr 10min
	Kamrup Express	#5959	Howrah	5.35pm	13hr 25min
Patna	Lal Qila Express	#3111	Sealdah	8.15pm	10hr 15min
Puri	Puri Express	#8007	Howrah	22.05pm	9hr 30min
Raxaul (for Birganj in Nepal)	Mithila Express	#3021	Howrah	4pm	15hr 10min
Varanasi	Amritsar Mail	#3005	Howrah	7.15pm	14hr 40min
	Poorva Express	#2381***	Howrah	9.10am	10hr 10min

*A/c only
**Except Sun
***Wed, Thur & Sun
**** Connect here for Darjeeling, Kalimpong and Gangtok
***** Please check planned planned change in schedule to connect with the Toy Train.

There are several **other booking offices** (same hours) including the Booking Office for Eastern and South Eastern Railways, Alexandra Court, 61 Chowringhee Rd, Rabindra Sadan; Howrah Station, 1st Floor; Computerized Booking Office, 3 Koilaghat St (Ⓣ033/2248 0257); New Koilaghat, 14 Strand Rd (Ⓣ033/2220 3496); Sealdah Station, 1st Floor (Ⓣ033/2350 3496). For general reservation enquiries call Ⓣ033/2220 3496 or Ⓣ138.

By bus

The most famous of the main roads out of the city are the **Grand Trunk Road**, which runs via Varanasi and Delhi all the way to Peshawar in Pakistan, and the **Mumbai Trunk Road**. Normally, you have to reckon on an average speed on Bengal's notoriously poor highways of around 30kph, but the buses to Siliguri – handy for Darjeeling and Sikkim – cover the 560km journey overnight, if not in any great comfort (6pm; Rs280, or Rs448 a/c). ITDC (Ⓣ033/2288 0901) and Rocket Bus are a couple to try at the **Esplanade Bus**

Stand; WBTDC also runs a luxury "sleeper service" (Rs695 including food) booked through the Tourist Centre at BBD Bagh (see p.866). Other services leaving from Esplanade include Behrampur (for Murshidabad), Bishnupur, Maldah and Rampurhat (for Tarapith).

Frequent buses for Bhubaneswar and Puri in Orissa leave the **Babu Ghat Bus Stand**, where Orissa Roadways and West Bengal State Transport (☎033/241 6388) have booths. Buses from Babu Ghat also head to Namkhana, and there are frequent services to Basanti and the Sunderbans (especially early morning). Buses leave both Babu Ghat and Esplanade for Diamond Harbour.

To Bangladesh

Kolkata is the main gateway to Bangladesh from India. The **Bangladesh Consulate** is at 9 Circus Ave (Mon–Fri 9am–5pm; ☎033/2247 5208, ext. 207 for visa section). Visas must be obtained in advance and will be issued on the same day if you submit your passport before 10am.

You can reach Bangladesh by air, train or road. There are two **flights** daily from Kolkata to Dhaka with Bangladesh Biman; return flights cost around $130. Although there is no direct line from Kolkata into Bangladesh, **trains** from Sealdah take you as far as Bongaon. From here you can take an auto-rickshaw to Haridaspur, 5km away, and then a rickshaw to Benapal on the border, where you can find inexpensive accommodation. The next morning take one of the frequent buses to Dhaka via Jessore (8hr). **Buses** run from Salt Lake International Karunamoyee terminal (☎033/2359 8448), a Rs120 taxi ride from the centre, to Dhaka (Mon–Sat 6.30am and 7am; 12hr; Rs1000). Several travel agents around Sudder and Marquis streets sell tickets for private buses to Dhaka, which depart from the Esplanade stand.

To the Andaman Islands

Alliance Airways **fly to Port Blair** four times a week (Mon, Wed, Fri & Sun) and Indian Airlines flies daily. If you want to take a **ship** (there are three to four sailings a month) you'll need to book through the Shipping Corporation of India, 13 Strand Rd (☎033/2248 2354). Although theoretically you need a permit before buying your ticket, the Foreigners Regional Registration Office at 237 AJC Bose Rd (☎033/2247 3300) has informed travellers to get their permits on arrival in Port Blair; check in advance. There are four classes starting with bunk beds (from around Rs1141) to a/c dorms and deluxe cabins (Rs5241); the journey takes three to five days, so bring plenty to read and some food to supplement the dull meals. Of the three ships that sail the route, *MV Nicobar* is the most luxurious, and *MV Akbar* the cheapest.

Around Kolkata

For centuries, the River Hooghly served as a lifeline for foreign traders; north of Kolkata, its banks are dotted with the remains of tiny European settlements such as **Chandernagore**. All these sites, together with the Hindu temples of **Dakshineshwar** and **Belur Math**, and even the great Vaishnavite centres of **Nabadip** and **Mayapur** further north, can be taken in as day-trips on local trains from Kolkata's Sealdah and Howrah stations. Simple hotels are always available should you want to stay.

Dakshineshwar and Belur Math

At the outermost edge of Kolkata, 20km north of Esplanade on the east bank of the river, the popular temple of **Dakshineshwar** stands in the shadow of Bally Bridge. Built in 1855, it was a product of the Bengali Renaissance, consecrated at a time when growing numbers of middle-class Hindus were rejecting their faith. Typical Bengali motifs – a curved roof reminiscent of local village huts, nine *chhatris* and beehive cupolas – dominate the design. The mystic and influential religious philosopher, **Ramakrishna**, once officiated here and his former room, beside the main gate, now preserves a collection of personal effects. Not far from the main temple, **Yogoday Satsanga Math** is the headquarters of the Self-Realization Fellowship, founded in California in 1925 by the author of *Autobiography of a Yogi*, **Paramahansa Yogananda**.

Across Bally Bridge from Dakshineshwar, 3km south along the west bank of the Hooghly, the massive riverfront temple at **Belur Math** was founded by a disciple of Ramakrishna, Swami Vivekananda, and completed (after his death) in 1938. A symbol of the resurgence of Bengali Hinduism, it incorporates elements from several world religions; the gate is inspired by early Buddhist sculpture, the windows by Islamic architecture, and the ground plan is based on the Christian cross. Local **trains** run from Sealdah to Bally Bridge adjacent to Dakshineshwar, and from Howrah to Belur Math.

Chandernagore and Hooghly

Around 35km north of Howrah, the former French outpost of **CHANDERNAGORE** still bears traces of its colonial masters, who left in 1949 and officially ceded the town to India in 1952. Crumbling buildings along its grand riverside promenade, formerly the Quai Dupleix and now the **Strand**, include what was once the Hotel de Paris, while the Eglise du Sacré Coeur, set back from the river, houses an image of Joan of Arc. Nearby, the eighteenth-century mansion of the French administrator serves as the **Institut de Chandernagore**, with a library, a French-language school and an interesting museum of documents, antiques, art and sculpture (Mon–Wed, Fri & Sat 4–6.30pm, Sun 11am–5pm; free).

The next significant community as you continue north from Chandernagore is the former Armenian township of **CHINSURAH**. A kilometre beyond that, **HOOGHLY** was a major East India Company trading post. Packed with Islamic monuments, it was devastated in turn by the Moghuls and the Marathas before being retaken by Robert Clive. Both Chandernagore and Hooghly lie on the busy suburban **train** network from Howrah.

Nabadip and Mayapur

Pilgrims come in the thousands to the pleasant little town of **NABADIP** (or Nawadip), on the west bank of the Hooghly, around 100km north of Howrah. Although it was the eleventh-century capital of Bengal under the Sen dynasty, and the home of **Sri Chaitanya** (1486–1533), a Hindu sage, few of the many temples clustered around its Mayapur Ghat are of any great antiquity. The courtyards of virtually all, however, are alive with devotees singing *kirtan* (devotional song). A fifty-kilometre *padakrama*, or foot pilgrimage, links Chaitanya with various sites spread across nine islands. It may be a Vaishnava town, but Nabadip's most atmospheric temple is the **Kali Bari** at Poramatolla, dedicated to the goddess, tucked into the folds of one of the most impressive banyan trees you are ever likely to see.

Nabadip's twin town, **MAYAPUR**, is a short, often overcrowded ferry ride across the river. Its conspicuous, massive stupa-like temple belonging to the Hare Krishna sect ISKCON is clearly visible across the water. A symbol of the contemporary face of Vaishnavism, the labyrinthine temple stands in the middle of an ornamental park and is extremely popular, especially at weekends.

Trains from Howrah run to Nabadip, 2.5km from the main Boral *ghat* (Rs15 by cycle rickshaw), from where ferries (Rs2) leave regularly for Mayapur. Suburban trains from Sealdah serve Krishnagar with buses travelling the 18km to Mayapur; the connecting medium-gauge train to Nabadip Ghat is sporadic, but if you do get it you will need to catch a ferry to either Mayapur or Nabadip from the adjacent Swarupganja Ghat. Mayapur is also serviced by direct CSTC **buses**, departing from Esplanade in Kolkata. ISKCON (3C Albert Rd, Kolkata; ⓣ033/2247 3757) runs **day-trips** starting at 6am and leaving Mayapur at 4pm for Rs250.

A clean, friendly place **to stay** in Nabadip is the *Trimurti* (ⓣ03472/240170; ❷), which has comfortable rooms in the heart of the market. In Mayapur, ISKCON's own *Guest House* (ⓣ03472/245620 or 033/2247 3757; ❷) is a massive, well-organized complex; reservations are only accepted three days in advance. Their *prasad* is a real treat, but you'll have to join the long orderly lines.

South of Kolkata: the Sunderbans

South of Kolkata down to the coast, the Hooghly fringes one of the world's largest estuarine deltas, the **Sunderbans**, a 10,000-square-kilometre expanse of marshland, mangrove swamp and islets formed by silt swept down from the Himalayas. Its most southerly and remote districts have been designated a nature reserve to protect the region's abundant wildlife, which includes saltwater crocodiles, Gangetic dolphins, otters and the world's largest single population of **tigers**. Closer to the city, on the east bank of the Hooghly, the other obvious target for a trip out of Kolkata is **Sagardwip**, the sacred spot where the Ganges officially debouches in to the sea. An important pilgrimage place, it's reached via the former colonial port of **Diamond Harbour**.

Sajnekhali and the Sunderbans Tiger Reserve

The cluster of mangrove-covered islands known as the **Sunderbans**, or "beautiful forest", lie in the Ganges Delta, stretching east from the mouth of the Hooghly to Bangladesh. They are home to the legendary **Royal Bengal tiger**, a ferocious man-eater which has adapted remarkably well to this watery environment, swimming from island to island and covering distances of as much as 40km in one day. Other wildlife include wild boar, spotted deer, Olive Ridley sea turtles, sharks, dolphins and large estuarine crocodiles. Among the half-million or so people who find themselves sharing this delicate ecosystem with the mighty cats are honey collectors, woodcutters and fisherfolk. All, regardless of their official religion, worship Banbibi, the goddess of the forest, and her Muslim consort Dakshin Rai, supreme ruler of the Sunderbans; their occupations are so hazardous that wives take off all their marriage ornaments when their husbands go out to hunt, fish or farm, becoming widows until they return. As the tigers like to creep up from behind, the honey collectors and woodcutters wear masks at the back of their heads. Meanwhile, the women and children drag nets along the estuary shores to catch prawns – no less hazardous, considering they have to deal with crocodiles and sharks as well as tigers.

Practicalities

Foreigners require a **permit** to visit the Sunderbans; if you're travelling to the area independently (tour companies will get them for you), get your permit in advance from the WB Tourist Centre in Kolkata (see p.866). You'll also need to book accommodation in the main camp of the **Sunderbans Tiger Reserve**, at the tiny hamlet of **SAJNEKHALI**, which is sealed off from the jungle by wire fencing (though tigers still stray into the compound); permits are meticulously checked as you pass through the gates, where you are also required to pay for an additional day permit (Rs15), plus the entry fee (Rs5) and, if applicable, camera fees. The *Sajnekhali Tourist Lodge* (ⓣ03463/252699; ③–⑤) itself is a large ramshackle forest **lodge** built on stilts; the price includes meals. The adjacent Project Tiger compound has a mini zoo, a small museum and a watchtower. Food is left out for the wild animals in the late afternoons, which invariably attracts deer and monkeys but rarely tigers. However, the cats have been known to jump the fence and it's advised not to venture out after dark. Other Sunderbans watchtowers stand at Sudhannyakhali, Haldi and Netidhopani, near the ruins of a four-hundred-year-old temple that's approached via caged pathways meant to protect you from the very real threat of tiger attack.

All transport within the reserve is by **boat**; these can be rented with the help of the lodge staff for around Rs1000 per whole day – you have to take along a Project Tiger guide (Rs200). The loud diesel motors of the boats tend to scare wildlife away, but when they cut their engines the silence is awesome.

The **best times to visit** are winter and spring. As getting to the Sunderbans from Kolkata is a laborious process, you might want to opt for an all-inclusive **package tour** booked through the West Bengal Tourist Centre (ⓣ033/2248 5917). Two- and three-day packages with stays either on the boat or at the *Tourist Lodge*, start from Rs1175. The cruises can get crowded and don't expect peace and quiet. The main disadvantage of joining such large tours is that the general chatter reduces the likelihood of seeing any animals, and the cruises can get crowded. **Tailor-made tours** by private operators tend to be more peaceful and leisurely: try Australian Kali Travel Home (see p.892), or Neil Law of Himalayan Footprints (see p.892). Help Tourism (see p.867) have their own resort, a tasteful development of thatched cottages on Bali island near the reserve and employ local villagers as guides; they also have their own boat. Prices (from Rs5000 for a three-day package) are steep, but the opportunity to get deep into the forest makes it worth a splurge. The cheaper but less imaginative *Sunderbans Tiger Camp* (ⓣ033/2229 8606, ⓔsunderbanstigercamp@hotmail.com; ⑥–⑧) in Dayapur near Gosaba, is in the core area of the reserve; most guests staying here are on one of the WBTC tours from Kolkata. The range of accommodation, all in a secure compound, includes two- to four-man tents and comfortable a/c cottages. Three-day packages cost from Rs2550.

Getting to the Sunderbans using public transport is complicated, whether by **train** (from Sealdah; the route is outlined in reverse, below) or by **bus**. To go by road, start by catching a bus from Babu Ghat to **Basanti** (4 daily; 3hr); aim for the one at 7am. From Basanti, you cross by ferry to **Gosaba**, an hour-long trip through the delta – sit well away from the belching diesel engines. Sajnekhali is a six-kilometre cycle rickshaw ride from Gosaba. Finally, to reach the Project Tiger compound itself, and the *Tourist Lodge*, you have to cross the estuarine channel on a country boat from the further back and less likely looking of the two *ghats*. There isn't usually a lot of traffic around here, so you may well have to wait or appeal to local boatmen.

Returning to Kolkata, allow plenty of time to make all the connections; the last bus leaves Basanti around 4pm. Alternatively, shared auto-scooters from Basanti can take you to **Doc Ghat** (30min), to pick up a boat across the river to **Canning**, and then a local train to Sealdah via Ballygunge station. If you're unlucky enough to find that the tide is out when you get to Canning, you're faced with a laborious 500-metre wade through calf-deep squelchy mud. A short walk through the town brings you to the station, where there are taps to wash off the mud. Your reward is the train ride itself, infinitely faster and more comfortable than the bus.

Along the Hooghly to the sea

The Hooghly reaches the Bay of Bengal at **Diamond Harbour**, 50km south of Kolkata. The harbour here was used by the East India Company, and a ruined fort is said to date back to Portuguese pirates. A two-week cultural festival, the **Ganga Utsav**, is held here towards the end of January – its theatre and dance performances are advertised in *Calcutta this Fortnight* (see p.867). The trip down to Diamond Harbour from the city, by bus or train from Sealdah station, is a popular day's excursion for Calcuttans, though it's also possible to stay the night at the *Sagarika Tourist Lodge* (❷–❺), which has some a/c rooms. Book through the tourist office on BBD Bagh (Ⓣ033/2248 8271). For a lot more luxury, the *Ffort Radisson Resort* at nearby Raichak (Ⓣ033/2280 0043, Ⓦwww.ffort.com; ❾) is a popular place for a break from the, city with opulent rooms (doubles from $250), river cruises and a luxurious health spa as well as day-trip packages.

Sagardwip, at the mouth of the Hooghly and accessible by ferry or bus from Diamond Harbour, is revered by Hindus as the point where the Ganges meets the sea. The actual confluence is venerated at the **Kapil Muni Temple**, on an island that bears the brunt of the savage Bay of Bengal cyclones and is gradually being submerged. On Makar Sankranti (mid-Jan), during the **Sagar Mela**, hundreds of thousands of pilgrims from all over India descend on the island, cramming into the water to bathe. A selection of small hotels, ashrams and *dharamshalas* offer basic accommodation, while the *Larika Sagar Vihar* (Ⓣ03210/240266; ❸) provides slightly more comfort.

H2/ Central Bengal

A low-lying rural region where the pace of life is in stark contrast to that of Kolkata, **central Bengal** has a few sights to tempt tourists off the Kolkata–Darjeeling route. **Shantiniketan**, built on the site of Rabindranath Tagore's father's ashram, is a haven of peace, and a must for anyone interested in Bengali music, art and culture. The other highlights of the region include a cluster of exquisite terracotta temples in **Bishnupur**, the ruins of **Gaur**, the region's seventh-century capital, and the palaces of **Murshidabad**, capital of Bengal's last independent dynasty, supplanted by the British.

Bishnupur

BISHNUPUR, a sleepy backwater town around 150km northwest of Kolkata, is a famous centre of Bengali learning, renowned above all for its exquisite **terracotta temples**. It was the capital of the Malla rajas, under whose patronage one of India's greatest schools of **music** developed. Largely beyond the sphere of Muslim influence in Bengal, Bishnupur's long tradition of temple-building had its roots in the basic form of the domestic hut. Translated into temple architecture, built of brick (as stone was rarely available) and faced with finely carved terracotta decoration often depicting scenes from the *Ramayana*, the temples combine striking simplicity of form with vibrant texture.

Several temples (daily 9am–5pm; all Rs100 [Rs5]) stand within the enclosure of the later Muslim fort which lies around 3km east of town. **Raas Mancha**, built around 1600 by Bir Hambir in a unique pyramidal style, is used to display the images of Krishna and Radha during the annual Raas festival. The tenth-century **Mrinmoyee temple** encloses the auspicious *nababriksha*, nine trees growing as one. The **Madan Mohan**, with its domed central tower, is one of the largest, dating from the late seventeenth century. Its facade panels depict scenes from the life of Krishna.

Two express **trains** a day connect Bishnupur to Kolkata's Howrah Station. **Accommodation** is fairly limited, with the best option being the comfortable *WBTDC Tourist Lodge* (Ⓣ03244/252013, reservations Ⓣ033/2248 5917; ❸–❹), which also has a dorm (Rs80) and serves good meals. Other alternatives include *Heritage Lodge* (❷–❸) and the budget *Rangini* (❶) in the small village of Satyepirtola, a few kilometres away.

Shantiniketan and around

Despite rapid growth and the subsequent encroachment into the tribal Santhal habitat, the peaceful haven of **SHANTINIKETAN**, 136km northwest of Kolkata, remains a world away from the clamour and grime of the city. Founded by **Rabindranath Tagore** in 1921 on the site of his father's ashram, both the settlement and its liberal arts university **Vishwa Bharati** were designed to promote the best of Bengali culture. Towards the end of the Bengali Renaissance, Tagore's vision and immense talent inspired a whole way of life and art; the university and school still operate under this momentum. However, the university's image has been somewhat tarnished by the theft, in 2004, of Rabindranath Tagore's Nobel Prize from the museum, It has now been replaced, but Bengali visitors still flock in to see where the heinous crime took place.

Centred around the **Uttarayan** complex of buildings, designed by Tagore, the university remains in perfect harmony with its surroundings, despite its recent growth as Calcuttans have settled or built holiday homes nearby. Well-known graduates include Indira Gandhi and Satyajit Ray, and departments such as **Kala**

Rabindranath Tagore

The Bengali poet and literary giant **Rabindranath Tagore** (1861–1941) has inspired generations of artists, poets and musicians. He developed an early interest in theatre, and set his poems to music – now, as *Rabindra Sangeet*, one of the most popular musical traditions in Bengal. Introduced to England and the West by the painter William Rothenstein and the poet W.B. Yeats, Tagore had his collection of poems *Gitanjali* first published in translation in 1912, and the following year was awarded the Nobel Prize for Literature. Though he preferred to write in Bengali, and encouraged authors in other Indian languages, he was also a master of English prose. Not until he was in his 70s did his talent as an artist and painter emerge, developed from scribblings on the borders of his manuscripts. Tagore was an enormous inspiration to many, including his student, the illustrious painter Nandalal Bose, and later the film-maker Satyajit Ray, who based several of his films on the works of the master.

Bhavan (art) and **Sangeet Bhavan** (music) still attract students from all over the world. **Chin Bhavan** – the China Department – is the largest of its kind in India, while the Japanese Department at **Nippon Bhavan** is one of the latest additions to the university. The **Kala Bhavan Archive** (daily except Tues 10am–5pm; free, with special permission from the head of department) houses twentieth-century Bengali sculpture and painting, including works by eminent artists such as Abanendranath and Gaganendranath Tagore, Nandalal Bose and Rabindranath Tagore himself, as well as a collection of Chinese and Japanese art. The **Vichitra Museum** (daily 10am–1.30pm & 2–4.30pm, Tues open am only, closed Wed; Rs5), also known as the Rabindra Bhavan Museum, captures the spirit of Tagore's life and work with a collection of his paintings, manuscripts and personal effects.

Some 3km west, **Shriniketan** (daily 10am–4.30pm, Tues open am only, closed Wed; free) is another important subdivision of the university, established by Tagore as a rural reconstruction program fostering self-reliance, with emphasis on local crafts and agriculture. The crafts and ceramics produced here are sold through the Amarkutir outlet on the Siuri Road; the leather goods are particularly distinctive.

The large fair of **Poush Mela** (also known as Poush Utsav), is held at Shantiniketan's fairground between December 22 and 25 to commemorate the initiation of Rabindranath Tagore's father, Maharishi Debendranath Tagore, into the Brahmo Samaj. Poush Mela features Santhal sports, dances and music, but is most renowned for the Bauls, Bengal's wandering minstrels who have created their own unique style of folk music; their Muslim counterparts, fakirs, also perform here.

Practicalities

Bolpur, 3km south of Shantiniketan, is the nearest **railway** station, on the main line between Kolkata and Darjeeling, served by several trains via Burdhaman (or Burdwan). The best train to take to Bolpur **from Kolkata** is the Shantiniketan Express #3015, which leaves Howrah at 10am and terminates at Bolpur at 12.25pm, returning to Howrah half an hour later. Baul singers occasionally get on to second-class carriages and busk, and there's a resident Baul in the regular a/c first-class coach.

If you're heading on from Shantiniketan **to Darjeeling**, the best of the many express trains is the Darjeeling Mail, which is timetabled to stop at 10.34pm in Bolpur and to arrive in New Jalpaiguri (NJP) at 7.50am the next morning.

Alternatively, the Kanchenjunga Express #5657 departs at 9.30am and arrives at NJP at 6.20pm, which normally means a night's stay in the Siliguri area before moving on to Darjeeling or Sikkim. **Reservation** are available from the Shantiniketan reservations counter (Mon–Sat 10am–3pm) near the post office; **quotas** from here are tiny but do include some upper class seats – so book early. There's a computerized reservations counter at Bolpur station which links you into the national network and offers more choice. Palataka Travels, on Netaji Road in Bolpur (ⓣ03643/254148), can sometimes book difficult-to-get railway tickets, as well as arranging air tickets and car rental. The main **bus stand** is at Jamboni, 2km west towards Surul. Cycle rickshaws are the chief means of transport in the area. The best way to experience Shantiniketan is to cycle – ask at your hotel or at one of the bicycle shops along the main road. If you need **Internet access** there are a couple of slow places in Bolpur.

For **currency exchange**, there's a State Bank of India at the main crossroads in Shantiniketan, and an ATM machine on the main road midway between Bolpur and Shantiniketan.

The Shantiniketan area holds a reasonable amount of **accommodation**, with several options along the noisy main Shantiniketan–Bolpur road, and some and better places around the fringes of the campus. Though some of the better **restaurants** offer multi-cuisine menus, they tend to be strongest on local cuisine, especially fish – try the garden restaurant at the *Park Guest House*. *Ghare Baire* at the Gitanjali Complex on Siuri Road is as smart as it gets in Shantiniketan, with upmarket Bengali cuisine, while *Pancho Byangan* at Shyambati serves everything from *dosas* and wonderful *shingharas* (Bengali samosas) to Chinese and Mughlai cooking, and offers a home delivery service (ⓣ03463/262942). Well worth the excursion, *Bonolakhi* (ⓣ03463/271202), 5km on the road to Ilam Bazaar, is a co-operative that specializes in organic farming and has its own restaurant serving wholesome rice-based local cuisine and home-grown vegetables.

Accommodation

Bolpur Lodge Bolpur ⓣ03463/252662. Large, long-established and welcoming lodge, set away from the bustle of the main road with a pleasant courtyard, large plain rooms and a reasonable restaurant. ❷–❸

Bonpulak Shyambati ⓣ03463/261193. Three pleasant airy rooms in a friendly family home with a small colourful garden and meals on request. ❸

Chhuti 241 Charu Palli, Jamboni ⓣ03463/252692, ⓔchhutiholidayresort@rediffmail.com. Comfortable and well-laid-out cottages with an ethnic touch, some with a/c, and a restaurant. The most luxurious option around Shantiniketan; credit cards accepted. ❻–❼

International Guest House Shantiniketan ⓣ03463/252751. The university runs two of these large guesthouses – the *Old* and the *New*, although the old one looks newer. Large, simple rooms and a cheap restaurant. ❷

Hotel Shantiniketan Bhubandanga ⓣ03463/254434. A brash new hotel with a pleasant garden and a quiet location down a lane; the cheaper rooms are better value but hot water comes by the bucket and all doubles have twin beds. ❸–❹

Shantiniketan Tourist Lodge Bolpur Tourist Lodge Rd ⓣ03463/252699. Large, apathetically-run government place with some a/c rooms, cottages, a dorm (Rs80), a pleasant garden and a restaurant which once enjoyed a better reputation. ❸–❻

Tarapith

One of the most important centres of Tantric Hinduism, **TARAPITH**, lies 50km north of Shantiniketan. The temple and cremation ground, in a grove beside the river, are popular with Tantric *sadhus*, and it's not uncommon to witness rituals involving skulls and cremation ashes. The temple itself is a simple building dedicated to *shakti* as the mysterious and feared goddess Tara, who appears here with a silver face and large eyes; shrines litter the area, and the grove is populated by monkeys. Of Tarapith's **hotels**, the friendly *Sathi* (ⓣ03461/253287; ❹–❺) has with large en-suite rooms, while *Sonar Bangla* (ⓣ03461/253827; ❹–❻) offers slightly more comfort and a great restaurant; there's a pleasant *dharamshala* near the temple. The Rampurhat Express **train** departs Howrah at 6.05am and arrives at **Rampurhat** railway station, 8km north of Tarapith, at 10.20am; the 5.10pm train from Rampurhat arrives back in Shantiniketan at 6.35pm. **Buses**, shared Vikrams (auto rickshaw taxis) and taxis make the 10km journey between Tarapith and Rampurhat. There are occasional direct **buses** from Tarapith to Jasidih in Jharkand; otherwise change at Rampurhat.

Kendubilwa

The town of **KENDUBILWA**, also known as **Kenduli**, on the bank of a wide shallow river 42km from Shantiniketan, is the birthplace of **Jaidev**, the author of *Gita Govinda*, and the spiritual home of the Bauls. Its small terracotta temple is engulfed each year in mid-January when the **Jaidev Mela** attracts streams of pilgrims, as well as a collection of *yogis* and *sadhus* who gather amongst the banyan trees to hear the Bauls perform through the night. Over the years the *mela* has grown to include a wide range of stalls and a funfair. During the *mela*, special buses leave regularly from Bolpur (2hr).

Murshidabad

Set in the brilliant green landscape of rural Bengal, historic **MURSHIDABAD** lies close to the commercial town of **Behrampur**, 219km north of Kolkata. Several eighteenth-century monuments along the banks of the Hooghly here stand as reminders of its days as the last independent capital of Bengal. Established early in the eighteenth century by the **Nawab Murshid Quli Khan**, Murshidabad was soon eclipsed when the forces of Siraj-ud-Daula were defeated by Robert Clive at the Battle of Plassey in 1757, as a result of which the British came to dominate Bengal from the new city of Calcutta. Clive described Murshidabad as equal to London, with several palaces and seven hundred mosques; today it's not even a city and most of its past glory lies in ruins, though it is still renowned for cottage industries, especially silk weaving.

Murshidabad's intriguing mixture of cultures is reflected in its architectural styles, which range from the Italianate **Hazarduari**, the nawab's palace, designed by General Duncan Macleod of the Bengal Engineers, to the **Katra Mosque**, built by Murshid Quli Khan in the style of the mosque at Mecca. The palace, with its mirrored banqueting hall, circular *durbar* room, armoury and library of fine manuscripts, is now a museum (daily except Fri 10am–4.30pm; Rs100 [Rs15]); some of the paintings are in dire need of restoration but the portrait collection is excellent. A large oxbow lake, the **Moti Jheel** or **Pearl Lake**, guards the desolate ruins of Begum Ghaseti's palace where Siraj-ud-Daula reigned before his defeat, and which was subsequently occupied for a while by Clive. To the south, across the river, **Khushbagh**, the **Garden of Delight**, holds the tombs of many of the nawabs, including Alivardi Khan and Siraj-ud-Daula.

Practicalities

Accommodation in Murshidabad is limited, with the friendly and welcoming *Hotel Manjusha* near Hazarduari (Ⓣ03482/270321; ❷–❹) offering rooms with balconies and a colourful flower garden on the river. **Behrampur**, 12km away on the busy north–south highway and easily accessible by auto-rickshaw or bus, has far more amenities, including the *Tourist Lodge* (Ⓣ03482/250439; ❷–❹), which has some a/c rooms, and the welcoming *Behrampore Lodge*, 30/31 RN Tagore Rd (Ⓣ03482/252952; ❸–❹), which serves meals. The *Samrat* (Ⓣ03482/251147; ❸–❻), on the main highway some 3km south of the centre at Panchanantatala, handy for the Murshidabad turnoff, offers a wide range of accommodation, from dorms (Rs60) to carpeted a/c rooms, and has an a/c restaurant-bar and a garden.

A handful of **trains** run to Behrampur from Kolkata (Sealdah station; 4–6hr), including the Bhagirathi Express and the Lalgola Passenger; the latter also stops at Murshidabad. Frequent **buses** from Behrampur station depart for Kolkata's Esplanade (5–6hr), as well as Malda (3hr 30min).

Malda and around

Famous for its mangos, the large, unattractive commercial town of **MALDA**, 340km north of Kolkata, makes a good base to explore the historic sites of **Gaur** and **Pandua**, both earlier capitals of Bengal, which can be reached by either bus or tonga. Malda is on the main line between Kolkata and Darjeeling, served by **trains** such as the Gaur Express, Kanchenjunga Express and the Darjeeling Mail. **Accommodation** includes the budget *Manohar* on Station Road (Ⓣ03512/265515; ❷), which has small rooms, attached baths and a restaurant; and the more luxurious *Pratapaditya* (Ⓣ03512/268104; ❸–❻), a short distance down Station Road in a slightly quieter location, with some a/c rooms and a good restaurant. Other possibilities include a good range of rooms at the railway station (❷–❸) for those with a valid ticket. **Taxis** to both Gaur and Pandua charge around Rs900 for the day.

Gaur

Spread across a landscape of lush paddy fields, 16km south of Malda, **GAUR** was the seventh-century capital of King Sasanka, and then successively belonged to the Buddhist Pals and the Hindu Senas. The latter, the last Hindu kings of Bengal, were violently displaced by the Muslims at the start of the thirteenth century. The city was eventually sacked in 1537 by Sher Shah Sur, and its remaining inhabitants were wiped out by plague in 1575.

Guar was deserted and buried in silt for centuries, but ongoing excavations have begun to reveal the extensive remains of a city which once boasted over a million inhabitants. Recent finds include the remains of a vast brick palace dating back to the fifteenth century, complete with waterways and a mint. The presence of a *ghat* with chains for anchoring barges suggests that the River Ganges may have once flowed past the palace. Elsewhere, Guar's sites include various large tanks, such as 1.5km long **Sagar Dighi** from 1126, and the embankments of the old city, which extend for several kilometres through the rural landscape. From the Muslim period, **Dakhil Darwaza**, an impressive red-brick gateway built in 1425, leads through the embankments surrounding the **Fort**, in the southeast corner of which a colossal wall encloses the ruins of the old palace. Nearby are the **Qadam Rasul Mosque**, built in 1531 to contain the Prophet's footprint in stone, and the seventeenth-century tomb of Fateh Khan, one of Aurangzeb's generals, in Bengali hut style. Other remains of interest include the elegant **Tantipara Mosque**, with its finely detailed terracotta decoration, the Lattan or **Painted Mosque**, where visible traces remain of the enamelled bricks that gave it its name, and the massive **Bara Sona Masjid**, "Great Golden Mosque", northeast of the Fort.

Pandua

The splendid **Adina Masjid** at **PANDUA**, 18km north of Malda, built around 1370, was the largest mosque in the subcontinent in its day. It now lies in ruins but these still betray the origin of much of the building materials – carved basalt masonry from earlier Hindu temples was used to support 88 brick-built arches and 378 identical small domes, the design following that of the great eighth-century mosque of Damascus. Other monuments include the **Eklakhi mausoleum** – one of the first square brick tombs in Bengal with a carved Ganesh on the doorway; and **Qutb Shahi Masjid**, or the Golden Mosque, built to honour saint Nur Qutb-ul-Alam whose ruined shrine is nearby together with that of Saint Hazrat Shah Jalal Tabrizi.

North Bengal

NORTH BENGAL, where the Himalayas soar from the flat alluvial plains towards Nepal, Sikkim and Bhutan, holds some magnificent mountain panoramas, and also some of India's most attractive **hill stations**. Most visitors pass as quickly as possible through **Siliguri** en route to **Darjeeling**, **Kalimpong** and the small, mountainous state of Sikkim. For anyone with a bit of time on their hands, it's well worth making a detour east of Siliguri near the Bhutanese border to the sub-Himalayan forest belt that encompasses the **Jaldapara Wildlife Sanctuary**, home to the one-horned rhino, bison and wild boar.

Besides the occasional strike, few travellers will notice anything of the **political turmoil** that wracks the region. The Gurkhaland movement, centred around Darjeeling, and the Kamtapuri Liberation Front, which purports to represent most of North Bengal south to Malda, have called for a complete break from the state of West Bengal. To compound matters, Bodo and ULFA insurgents have rendered unsafe the borders with Bangladesh and the forested frontier with Assam and Bhutan in the far northeast.

Siliguri and New Jalpaiguri

A major commercial hub and Bengal's second city, ever-expanding **SILIGURI** has a thriving tea-auction centre and serves as the gateway to Darjeeling, Kalimpong, Sikkim and Bhutan. Together with its main railway station, **NEW JALPAIGURI** – commonly referred to as NJP – and the airport at **Bagdogra**,

The Darjeeling Himalayan Railway: the Toy Train

Completed in 1881, the small-gauge (2ft or 610mm) **Darjeeling Himalayan Railway** was designed as an extension of the North Bengal State Railway, climbing from **New Jalpaiguri**, via **Siliguri**, for a tortuous 88km up to **Darjeeling**. Given **World Heritage** status by UNESCO in 1999, the **Toy Train** – as it is affectionately called – follows the Hill Cart Road, crossing it at regular intervals and even sharing it with traffic. No longer an essential mode of transport, the Toy Train, pulled by endearing, ancient blue steam engines, some over 75 years old, has survived due to its unique historical importance and tourist appeal.

Weather permitting, first-class coaches with large viewing windows provide magnificent views as the six-hour journey from the plains progresses and the scenery gradually unfolds; second class can be fun but crowded. At the high pass at Jore bungalow near **Ghoom** (2438m), 7km short of Darjeeling, the dramatic panorama of the Kanchenjunga Range is suddenly revealed. Just beyond Ghoom, the train does a complete circle at the **Batasia Loop** – the most dramatic of the three loops encountered along the way; another method used to gain rapid height are the **reversing stations** where the track follows a "Z" shape.

Some travellers find this claustrophobic and painfully slow ride a real test of endurance, especially after an overnight journey from Kolkata to Siliguri. An alternative, more relaxing, way to experience the Toy Train is to take a short ride from Darjeeling to Ghoom, just 7km up the track (see box on p.917) from where you can visit a few monasteries and either walk, take a taxi, bus or even the train back to Darjeeling.

For more **information** on the Toy Train, contact the Darjeeling Himalayan Railway Society, 4 Dimsdale View East, Porthill, Newcastle-under-Lyme ST5 8HL, UK (Ⓦwww.dhrs.org; Ⓔsecretary@dhrs.org), or contact the *Windamere Hotel* (see p.912) in Darjeeling.

it forms an unavoidable link between the rail and air connections to Kolkata and Delhi, and the roads up into the mountains. The border with Nepal at **Kakarbitta** nearby is open to tourists, though the bus journey from there to Kathmandu is an arduous one.

Most tourists pass straight through Siliguri, but travel connections may mean that you have to stop overnight. Besides teeming bazaars such as Bidhan Market, there's little of interest to see. A small Tibetan enclave 1km or so beyond *Hotel Cindrella* on Sevoke Road houses the **Tashi Gomang Stupa** (daily 5am–noon & 1–5pm), established by Kalu Rinpoche. At the end of a small lane next to the *Sona Hotel*, delicious fragrances rise as Tibetan medicine-makers pound fresh herbs and spices; top quality Tibetan healing and meditation incense is available for sale here.

Practicalities

Bagdogra airport, 12km west of Siliguri, is served by flights from Delhi, Kolkata and Guwahati; there's also a helicopter service from here to Gangtok in Sikkim (weather permitting), while **taxis** run directly to Siliguri (Rs220) and Darjeeling (Rs900). Siliguri does have its own railway station, used by the Toy Train, but the **New Jalpaiguri (NJP)** station, 4km east, is the main railway junction in the region, with trains to and from Kolkata, Delhi and Assam. Cycle- and auto-rickshaws (Rs30 and Rs80) ply the route between NJP and Siliguri, battling through the often-gridlocked market; taxis follow a circuitous twelve-kilometre detour. Use the pre-paid booth outside the main station for local and long distance journeys in auto-rickshaws as well as **taxis**. A reserved taxi to Siliguri costs Rs175, or Rs900 to Darjeeling, while a seat in a Jeep to Siliguri costs Rs90. Most buses arriving at Siliguri terminate at the **Tenzing Norgay Bus Terminal** on Hill Cart Road at Pradhan Nagar, close to most hotels and taxis to Darjeeling.

Moving on from Siliguri

Both Indian Airlines and Jet Airways fly from **Bagdogra** to **Kolkata**, **Delhi** and **Guwahati**. The Indian Airlines' office is in the *Hotel Mainak* Complex, Hill Cart Road (☎0353/251 1495); Jet Airways is in the *Hotel Vinayak*, Hill Cart Road (☎0353/243 1495).

All major **trains**, most terminating or starting at Guwahati, use NJP station, not Siliguri. Reservations can be made at NJP Railway Station or the Central Railway Booking Office (daily 8am–4pm), Bidhan Road, near Kanchenjunga Stadium in Siliguri. The best train to **Kolkata** is the Darjeeling Mail #3143/3144, which terminates at Sealdah, while the most convenient for Delhi is the efficient Rajdhani Express #2435 (25hr 30min), which also passes through Patna with connections for Gaya and Bodhgaya. The Mahananda Link Express #4083/4084 stops at Mughal Sarai, convenient for Varanasi.

The easiest way to get to **Darjeeling** is by **shared Jeep**. Jeeps depart from in front of NJP station, and Tenzing Norgay Bus Terminal in Siliguri, where Jeep transport syndicates have their own ticket booths and the prices are fixed. Taxis to Darjeeling depart when full, take 3–5 hours and cost Rs80 per seat. Other options include the **Toy Train** (leaving Siliguri at 9am, arriving Darjeeling around 3pm; second class Rs38, first class Rs217), or a bus from Siliguri's Tenzing Norgay Bus Terminal. Regular buses and shared Jeeps also run to **Kalimpong** and to **Gangtok**.

Overnight **buses** to **Kolkata** (12hr), such as the Rocket Bus and ITDC (which has a ticket counter at the Tenzing Norgay Bus Terminal), are much cheaper than the train (bus tickets Rs260 non-a/c, Rs448 a/c), and have the advantage of depositing you in Esplanade, near the central Sudder Street area. WBTDC's a/c bus is by far the most comfortable, and fares (Rs595) include dinner Whatever you're promised, be it a "luxury bus" or a "two-by-two", be prepared for a severe rattling. North Bengal State Transport Corporation buses run to **Kolkata**, **Patna** and **Guwahati**.

If you're braving the journey to **Kathmandu** in **Nepal**, check the current safety situation with the helpful Tourist Service Agency (TSA), in Pradhan Nagar, the lane opposite the bus terminal (☎0353/253 1219). You can share a taxi (Rs45), arrange an auto-rickshaw (Rs220) or taxi (Rs450) or catch a bus to the border at **Kakarbitta** and make your own arrangements there. Pick up a Nepalese visa for $30 in cash on the Indian side at **Paniktanki**, from where cycle rickshaws (Rs20) travel the 2km across the border. The advantage of a pause in Kakarbitta is that it gives you a greater choice of onward buses to Kathmandu (17hrs Rs360), but at the time of writing this was not a safe option; again, check before you travel – the TSA offer bus tickets all the way through to Kathmandu if safe. For a lot more luxury take one of several **flights** from **Bhadrapur** in Nepal to Kathmandu ($120); taxis charge around Rs500 for the 45-minute journey from Kakarbitta to Bhadrapur, and airport tax is Rs150. Bookings can be made through agencies like the TSA, which also books **helicopter** flights to **Gangtok** (Rs1500) leaving from Bagdogra at 2pm, weather permitting.

Sikkim Nationalized Transport, opposite the bus terminus in Pradhan Nagar (daily 6am–4pm; ☎0353/251 1496), runs a bus service to **Gangtok** (departures 8.30am, 9.30am & 11.30am), and various other points in **Sikkim**. Sikkim **permits** (see opposite), can be obtained at SNT, and shared Jeeps are also available from here.

Buses also run to Phuntsoling, on the border of **Bhutan**, just 160km away, and to Thimpu the capital, 176km further on, as well as to **Guwahati** in Assam, although the train is far more comfortable.

The Government of West Bengal's **tourist office** (Mon–Fri 10.30am–4pm ⓣ0353/251 1974), opposite the bus station on Pradhan Nagar, provides information and organizes weekend excursions to Jaldapara Wildlife Sanctuary. Upstairs, commercial wings WBTDC (Mon–Fri 10.30am–4pm, Sat 10.30am–1pm; ⓣ0353/251 1974) are far more helpful. There are other tourist offices at NJP station (Mon–Sat 8am–9pm, Sun 8am–2pm; ⓣ0353/256 1118) and at the airport (ⓣ0353/255 1794). Siliguri's best private tour operator, Help Tourism, 143 Hill Cart Rd (ⓣ0353/253 5892; ⓦwww.helptourism.com), organize wildlife tours, village home-stays, and treks and tours off the beaten track.

Opposite the bus stand, the **Sikkim Tourist Information Centre** (ⓣ0353/251 2646), SNT Colony, in the same compound as the Sikkim Nationalized Transport stand, provides information and **Sikkim permits**. To **change money**, try the bureau at the Delhi Hotel across from the bus terminal on Hill Cart Road; the State Bank of India, Mangaldeep Building, Hill Cart Road, will also change **travellers' cheques**. There's a Centurion Bank **ATM** (Visa, Cirrus, Maestro & Mastercard) at the Bharat Petrol station opposite the *Manila Hotel* on Hill Cart Road, and others around Sevoke Mor. The main **post office** is on Kacheri Road and there are other branches on Bidhan Road, close to the **Central Railway Booking Office**, near Kanchenjunga Stadium, and near the Tenzing Norgay Bus Terminal.

The best **restaurants** are located in hotels along Hill Cart Road: the *Conclave* serves Thai food. Alternatives include the excellent café *Khana Khazana*, at Pradhan Nagar opposite the bus terminal. For Bengali cuisine, try the basic but legendary *Kalpatru*, Rani Tanki More, Sevoke Road, famous for its fish – and its sister branch, *Kalpana Paish* at Bidhan Market.

Accommodation

Apsara 18 Patel Rd, opposite Tenzing Norgay Bus Terminal ⓣ0353/251 4252. Down a lane parallel to the main road, close to all amenities and handy for transport links, this is a friendly and helpful Tibetan-run hotel with basic, clean rooms. 2–3

Chancellor Sevoke Mor, corner of Sevoke and Hill Cart roads ⓣ0353/243 2372. Welcoming and safe Tibetan-run hotel in the busy heart of town with a quieter block at the back; with plain but decent rooms, and good Tibetan, Chinese and Indian food is served in the dining hall. 2–3

Heritage Pradhan Nagar ⓣ0353/251 6511. Spotless two-star, with comfortable rooms, a good restaurant and a convenient location opposite the bus terminal; if full try the slightly cheaper *Manila* next door. 4–7

Holydon NJP Station Rd ⓣ0353/269 1335. Friendly and cheap hotel, convenient for the main railway station; the best of a handful of similar places along this road. 2–5

Marinas Naxalbari Rd, Bagdogra ⓣ0353/255 1375. Part of the Glenary's chain, and handy for both the airport (Rs100 for transfers) as well as the Nepal border at Kakarbitta. The reasonably priced rooms have attached baths, and there's a restaurant and a bar. 3

Sinclairs Pradhan Nagar ⓣ0353/251 7674, ⓦwww.sinclairshotels.com. Upmarket hotel on the edge of town, with comfortable rooms, swimming pool and a good restaurant. 8

Vinayak Hill Cart Rd ⓣ0353/243 1130. A good mid-range hotel with a choice of rooms including some a/c. The restaurant downstairs serves good Indian food. 3–5

WBTD Maniak Tourist Lodge Pradhan Nagar ⓣ0353/243 0986. Set in large grounds, with friendly, welcoming staff, reasonable rooms and a restaurant and bar. Car rental available. 4–6

Jaldapara Wildlife Sanctuary

Apart from Darjeeling and the hills, most of North Bengal is well off the beaten track, and few travellers make detours from the Darjeeling–Sikkim–Nepal road. Probably the best reason to do so is to visit the small **Jaldapara Wildlife**

Sanctuary, roughly 124km east of Siliguri, established in 1943 to help protect wildlife against the encroachment of tea cultivation. Part of a large forest corridor, Jaldapara comprises tracts of tall elephant grass on the banks of the River Torsa, and is set against the backdrop of forested foothills; it shelters around fifty highly endangered greater **one-horned rhinoceroses**, as well as wild elephants, sambar and hog deer.

Jaldapara is open from October to the end of April, with March being the best month to view animals, as they graze on new shoots. Much the best way to explore it is on elephant back (Rs140 [Rs80]). During the opening months, the WB Tourist Office in Siliguri (see p.907) organizes a daily bus to Jaldapara (Rs60), leaving NJP at 9.30am and Siliguri at 10am; departures from Jaldapara are at noon. The WB Tourist Office also offer a package tour, bookable in Siliguri, Darjeeling or Kolkata, which leaves Siliguri at noon on Saturday and returns early evening on Sunday (from Rs2250) but this tends to take in several places en route and there's not really enough time to explore the sanctuary. If you want to spend more time there, you could travel by train or bus from Siliguri to the town of **Madarihat**, 7km from the sanctuary and 1km from the sanctuary gates, from where taxis run to **Hollong** in the heart of the forest for around Rs150. **Accommodation** and **food** are available at the *Jaldapara Tourist Lodge* at Madarihat (☎03563/262230; ④–⑥), or at the *Hollong Forest Lodge* (☎03563/262228; ⑤–⑥); both must be booked through the WB tourist offices in Siliguri, Darjeeling or Kolkata. Note that there is a Rs25 entrance fee to the park, payable at the entrance.

Darjeeling

Part Victorian holiday resort, part major tea-growing centre, **DARJEELING** (from *Dorje Ling*, "the place of the thunderbolt") straddles a ridge 2200m up in the Himalayas and almost 600km north of Kolkata. Over fifty years after the British departed, the town remains as popular as ever with holidaymakers from the plains, and promenades such as the Mall and the Chowrasta still burst with life. The greatest appeal for visitors has to be its stupendous mountain vistas – with Kanchenjunga (the third-highest mountain in the world) and a vast cohort of ice-capped peaks dominating the northern horizon. However, the infrastructure created under the Raj has been unable to cope with the ever-expanding population – there are acute shortages of water and electricity, and chaos on the hopelessly inadequate roads – and despite Darjeeling's cosmopolitan atmosphere and charm, the town is slowly but surely being swamped by its rampant, uncontrolled growth. It remains a colourful and lively place, however, with good shopping and dining, plenty of walks in the surrounding countryside and attractions such as the Toy Train and the many thriving Buddhist monasteries. Darjeeling has a considerable **Tibetan** presence and like Dharamsala in Himachal Pradesh offers opportunities to study Tibetan culture. The best seasons to visit – and to attempt the magnificent trek to Sandakphu to see Everest – are after the monsoons and before winter (late Sept to late Nov), and spring (mid-Feb to May).

Until the nineteenth century, Darjeeling belonged to **Sikkim**. However, in 1817, after a disastrous war with Nepal, Sikkim was forced to concede the right to use the site as a health sanatorium to the **British**, who had helped to broker a peace settlement. Darjeeling soon became the most popular of all hill resorts, especially after the Hill Cart Road was built in 1839 to link

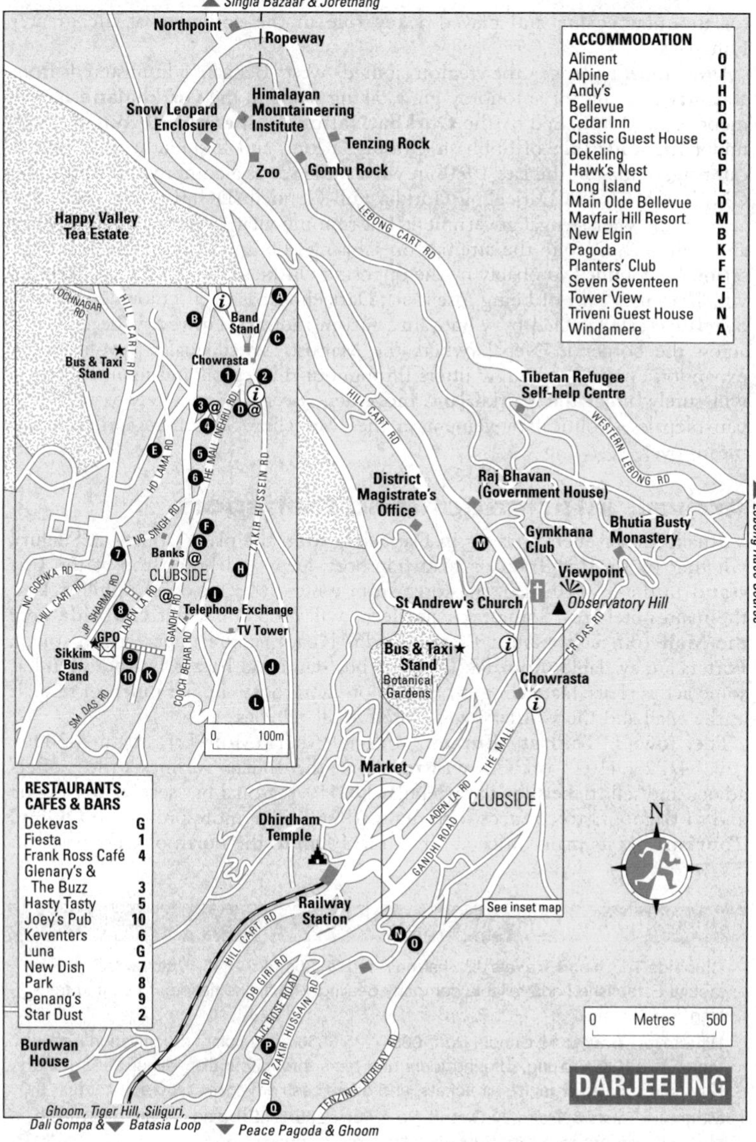

it with Siliguri. **Tea** arrived a few years later, and with it an influx of Nepalese labourers and the virtual disappearance of the forests that previously carpeted the hillsides. The town's growing economic significance led Britain to force a treaty on the Sikkimese in 1861, thereby annexing Darjeeling and Kalimpong. In the early 1900s, Darjeeling had a reputation for being one of the most glamorous and far-flung outposts of the British empire, attracting socialites and adventurers in equal numbers. Subsequently it became a centre for mountaineering and played a key role in the conquest of the greater Himalayas.

After Independence, the region joined West Bengal, administered from Calcutta, but calls for autonomy grew, taking shape in the **Gurkhaland** movement of the 1980s. Led by the **Gurkha National Liberation Front** (GNLF) under the leadership of Subhash Ghising, a long and frequently very violent campaign ended in the late 1980s in what some see as a compromise. Today, the GNLF controls the Darjeeling Gurkha Hill Council (DGHC), still under the aegis of the West Bengal government, but running vital services such as tourism and transport. Despite the attempt on Ghising's life in 2001, in which he was seriously wounded (probably by the opposing Gurkha Liberation Organization, which accuses him of being a sellout), Darjeeling has been enjoying a period of relative calm fuelled by a buoyant tourism industry. However, the civil war across the border in Nepal (where the Marxists' stated goal is revolutionary expansion), has caused a few jitters throughout the region and its implications will surely affect the Gurkhaland movement over the next few years – the pan-Nepalese political movement in the Darjeeling/Sikkim region is by no means over.

Arrival, information and transport

Virtually all travellers arriving in Darjeeling from the plains come via Siliguri, whether by the Toy Train or road transport. Jeeps and buses stop at the **bus stand** in the lower half of the town from where it's a bit of an uphill trek to the main hotel area. Some taxis and Jeeps will drop you off at **Clubside** near the **Mall** (officially Nehru Road/Gandhi Road), at the upper end of town. Porters are available (from Rs30) at the bus stand and bazaar, but be careful as some act as touts. Darjeeling is best explored on foot – in fact much of it, such as the Mall and the Chowrasta, is closed to all vehicles.

The town's **Tourist Bureau**, 1 The Mall (Mon–Fri 10am–4.30pm; ⓣ0354/225 4102), on **Chowrasta** above the Indian Airlines office, offers advice and sells tickets for the irregular DGHC seasonal bus service to Siliguri and to Bagdogra to connect with flights (Rs60). The more pro-active **DGHC Tourism** has its main office at Silver Fir, 100m to the north of Chowrasta on

Travel, trek and tour operators

Clubside Tours and Travels JP Sharma Road ⓣ0354/225 4646, ⓔclubside@satyam.net.in. Established and reliable company dealing with airline tickets, tours and trekking.

Himalayan Travels 18 Gandhi Rd ⓣ0354/225 6956. An efficient organisation run by the affable K.K. Gurung, offering tours and treks throughout Darjeeling, Sikkim and Bhutan. Can also organize air tickets, and offers cash advances on credit cards.

Magnolia Tours & Treks 20 Goodie Rd ⓣ0354/225 2852. Good option for Sandakphu treks and transport for Darjeeling and Sikkim tours.

Tenzing Kanchenjunga Tours DB Giri Road ⓣ0354/225 3058. An efficient, international organization run by Tenzing Norgay's son: excellent for trekking and mountaineering.

Trek-Mate Singalila Arcade, Nehru Road ⓣ0354/225 6611, ⓔchagpori@satyam.net.in. Very helpful agency which arranges treks to Sandakphu and west Sikkim. Also provides guides and porters and rents out sleeping bags, down jackets and day packs.

Bhanu Sarani (daily 8am–6pm; ⓣ0354/225 4879) can arrange tours, treks, transport and white-water rafting on the River Teesta (from Rs350), and also book trekkers' huts. They supply a very useful leaflet with map on the Sandakphu trails. The DGHC booths at Clubside and the railway station are of limited use.

Anyone planning to head on to **Sikkim** will have to get a **permit**. Travelling to Gangtok, you should be able to get a permit instantly at the **Rangpo** border checkpoint and extend it in Gangtok – though check beforehand to see if this will be possible (and similarly for the border crossing at Naya Bazaar for west Sikkim). Restrictions on visiting Sikkim are easing up, and from Darjeeling you can travel directly to west Sikkim on a hair-raising 27-kilometre road descending through tea plantations to Jorethang via Naya Bazaar, or via Singtam to Gangtok. If you need to get your permit in Darjeeling, pick up a form from the **District Magistrate's Office** (Mon–Fri 10am–4pm) on Hill Cart Road near Loreto Convent; take it to be stamped at the **Foreigners' Registration Office** (daily 10am–6pm) on Laden La Road, then return to the DM's office for the final stamp. The process is a formality and quite easy but it does involve legwork.

Accommodation

Darjeeling has over five hundred hotels, and new ones spring up all the time, placing further strains upon the infrastructure. The main thing to establish before you check in anywhere is the **water** situation; many cheaper places only provide water in buckets, and charge extra if you like it hot – as well as requesting that you don't do your own laundry and use their pay service instead. Off-season (late June to Sept & late Nov to April) **discounts** can be as much as fifty percent.

Budget

Aliment 40 Dr Zakir Hussein Rd ⓣ0354/225 5068. Cheap and very popular travellers' hangout with friendly management and Internet access, but plain rooms. The wonderful top-floor café has sensational views. ❸

Alpine 104/1 Rockville Rd ⓣ0354/225 6355. A good range of clean rooms which, like all the others around here, are expensive for what it is at the height of season. ❸–❺

Andy's 102 Zakir Hussein Rd ⓣ0354/225 3125. Run by a retired couple, this is the best of the ridge-top guesthouses; safe with large immaculate rooms and great views towards Kalimpong and Bhutan but no restaurant. ❷–❸

Long Island 11/A/2 Dr Zakir Hussein Rd ⓣ0354/225 2043. Just beyond the *Tower View* and above the road, with views towards Bhutan. Friendly, with a pleasant café and some of the best budget rooms on the ridge-top. Hot water by the bucket. ❷

Pagoda 1 Upper Beechwood Rd ⓣ0354/225 3498. A quiet central spot, close to Laden La Rd and the post office, with keenly priced rooms and a fire in the lounge; this area is no longer the haunt of budget travellers. Free hot water by the bucket. ❸

Tower View 8/1 Dr Zakir Hussein Rd ⓣ0354/225 4452. A friendly place near the TV tower with good views and a popular traveller's restaurant. Cheap cubbyholes plus a couple of pleasant wood-lined rooms. ❷–❸

Triveni Guest House 85/1 Dr Zakir Hussein Rd ⓣ0354/225 3878. Plain and roomier than the *Aliment* opposite, but not as popular. Friendly with a good restaurant and nice views from the sun deck. Rs10 per bucket for hot water. ❸

Mid-range

Bellevue The Mall ⓣ0354/225 4075. Above the tourist bureau, and dominating Chowrasta; not as grand as it once was, but still pleasant enough with low-key service, airy wood-lined rooms and a pleasant bar and restaurant. ❹–❻

Classic Guest House CR Das Rd ⓣ0354/225 7025. Clean comfortable rooms with bathrooms and verandahs. A couple of minutes below Chowrasta, with great views. ❺–❻

Dekeling 51 Gandhi Rd, above the popular *Dekevas* restaurant ⓣ0354/225 4159, ⓦwww.dekeling.com. A great central location, a range of comfortable rooms with running hot water – the timber rooms upstairs are warm and charming – and good off-season discounts. The Tibetan owners are especially welcoming and helpful. ❺–❻

Main Olde Bellevue Beside *Bellevue*, 1 & 5/1 Nehru Rd ⓣ0354/225 4178. A less characterful new block or the rambling old manor hotel gradually being renovated, with creaky wooden corridors, large rooms and ancient plumbing. ❹–❼

Planters' Club The Mall ⓣ0354/225 4348. A local landmark (also known as the *Darjeeling Club*) with old-fashioned rooms, coal fires, a billiard room, bar, restaurant and library. Guests have to take temporary membership (Rs50). ❹–❼

Seven Seventeen HD Lama Rd ⓣ0354/225 5099. Extensive, well-run hotel with comfortable airy rooms, despite the location just above the bazaar. Exchange facilities and credit cards are accepted for un-discounted rooms; there is a cheaper annexe up the road. ❹–❻

Expensive

Cedar Inn Jalapahar Rd (Dr Zakir Hussein Rd) ⓣ0354/225 4446, ⓔcedarinn@satyam.net.in. An unusual position high above town, though a steep 15min walk from the centre, this new mock-gothic hotel has plush rooms complete with fireplaces and grand views; there's also a pleasant terrace café and a garden. Doubles from $110. ❾

Hawk's Nest, 2 AJC Bose Rd ⓣ0354/225 3092, ⓦwww.dekeling.com. Four luxury suites with fireplaces and tasteful Tibetan decor in a delightful old Tibetan-owned colonial villa; well worth the short walk out of town. Good home cooking and a warm welcome. ❽

Mayfair Hill Resort Below Government House, The Mall ⓣ0354/225 6376, ⓔmayfair@cal2.vsnl.net.in. Once a maharaja's summer retreat, the rooms and garden cottages here offer ostentatious luxury. Good facilities and an immaculate garden. ❾

New Elgin 32 HD Lama Rd ⓣ0354/225 4114, ⓦwww.elginhotels.com. Premier hotel, opulent and well maintained, with good facilities and an old-fashioned, formal atmosphere that captures the spirit of Darjeeling. Rates include all meals. From $91. ❾

Windamere Observatory Hill ⓣ0354/225 4041, ⓦwww.windamerehotel.com. The most celebrated of Darjeeling's hotels has accommodated a pantheon of rich and famous guests in its old-fashioned self-contained cottages decked out with Raj memorabilia. Expensive, but well worth a visit for tea on the lawn or the occasional concert. From $140. ❾

The Town

The heart of Victorian Darjeeling is the **Chowrasta**, a traffic-free square above the busy bazaar on Hill Cart Road. One of the four main roads leading off it is the **Mall** (also called Nehru Road) , which descends from Chowrasta to

Darjeeling tea

Although the original appeal of Darjeeling for the British was as a hill resort with easy access from the plains, inspired by their success in Assam they soon realized its potential for growing **tea**. Today, the Darjeeling tea industry continues to flourish, producing China Jat, China Hybrid and Hybrid Assam. A combination of factors, including altitude and sporadic rainfall, have resulted in a relatively small yield – only three percent of India's total – but the delicate black tea produced here is considered to be one of the finest in the world. It is also some of the most expensive; the world record is held by a grade from Castleton, an estate near Kurseong, which sold at auction a few years ago for an astronomical Rs13,500 a kilo.

Grades such as Flowery Orange Pekoe (FOP) or Broken Orange Pekoe (BOP) are determined by quality and length of leaf as it is withered, crushed, fermented and dried. To watch the process for yourself, call in at the **Happy Valley Tea Estate** (Tues–Sat 8am–noon & 1–4.30pm, Sun 8am–noon; free); it's a 30min walk from town – follow the signs from the Hill Cart Road near the District Magistrate's office. As for **buying**, try the Castleton Shop or the Chowrasta Teas Store on the Chowrasta; R.N. Agarwal on the Mall and the informative Nathmull's on Laden La Road also have good reputations. Such vendors usually trade in unblended tea, bought directly from tea gardens. Being independent, they are able to pick and choose according to quality and do not necessarily stock tea from the same garden every year. The typical cost of a kilo of good middle-grade tea is Rs400–500.

Clubside, the area below the prestigious **Planters' Club**. Established in 1868, and otherwise known as the **Darjeeling Club**, this venerable institution was once the centre of Darjeeling high society. Not much seems to have changed since the days when tea planters from all over the territory rode here to attend social occasions. Visitors who take temporary membership are welcome to stay, and facilities such as the bar and snooker room are available for a day-use fee.

Taking the right fork of the Mall from the northern end of the Chowrasta, near the bandstand, brings you to the **viewpoint** from where you can survey the Kanchenjunga massif and almost the entire state of Sikkim. From near the *Windamere Hotel* steps, ascend the pine-covered hillside to **Observatory Hill**, another viewpoint and the site of the Bhutia Busty monastery. Decorated with streams of Buddhist prayer flags, the shrine at the summit, dedicated to the wrathful Buddhist deity Mahakala, whom Hindus equate with Shiva, has been influenced by Hinduism, creating a garish hybrid of styles. Another faded Raj-era institution, the **Gymkhana Club** (Ⓣ0354/225 4342), stands near Observatory Hill. Casual visitors can drop in to play billiards, snooker, badminton, table tennis, tennis, squash and even to roller-skate (Rs50 for day membership plus nominal game charges), or take advantage of the small library, bar and bridge tables; it's also possible to stay overnight.

Below the club, the small and little-visited **Natural History Museum** (daily except Thurs 10am–4.30pm; Rs5) holds a large collection of moths and butterflies, an assortment of stuffed animals and birds, and a natural-habitat display complete with sound effects. Further away from Chowrasta, and a steep drop down from Government House, stands the extensive **Tibetan Refugee Self-Help Centre** (closed Sun). Founded in 1959, it houses around seven hundred refugees, most of whom make carpets or Tibetan handicrafts. Tourists are welcome to watch the activity in the workshops; among items on sale are clothes, hats and leatherwork, excellent carpets, and Tibetan boots made of embroidered cloth with leather soles.

A kilometre further north towards the high mountains and just above the gothic **St Joseph's College**, you reach the **Passenger Ropeway**, a cable car providing access to the Tukvar Tea Estate halfway down to the Rangit Valley. The ropeway has been closed for a major refit since 2003, following an accident that left five people dead; check at the tourist office to see if it has reopened. On the way to the ropeway, Darjeeling's **Zoo** (daily except Thurs 8.30am–4pm; Rs50, or Rs100 [Rs10] combined with HMI ticket), with an emphasis on conservation, is well maintained and well worth a visit. The zoo's Snow Leopard Breeding Centre (closed to the public) established in 1986 is the only place in the world to have successfully bred this endangered species, while Project Panda has produced several Red Panda; endangered Tibetan wolves have also been bred here. Among the animals that visitors can see are a collection of pheasants, and cat species including Siberian tigers.

The **Himalayan Mountaineering Institute (HMI)**, reached via the zoo and covered by the same ticket, is one of India's most important training centres for mountaineers, holding numerous courses (Indians only) throughout the year. Its first director was **Sherpa Tenzing Norgay**, Sir Edmund Hillary's climbing partner on the first successful ascent of Everest, who lived and died in Darjeeling, and is buried in the Institute's grounds. In the heart of the beautiful, leafy complex, the **HMI Museum** (daily except Thurs 9am–4.30pm,; included in ticket price) is dedicated to the history of mountaineering, with equipment old and new, a relief map of the Himalayas, and a collection of costumes of different hill people. The **Everest Museum** in the annexe recounts the history of ascents on the world's highest peak, from Mallory and Irvine's ill-fated 1924 expedition, to Tenzing and Hillary's triumph in 1953 and the record breaking 20-hour and 24-minute climb by Kaji Sherpa in 1998.

Back in town, Lochnagar Road winds down from the bus stand in the bazaar to enter the **Botanical Gardens**, where pines, willows and maples cover the hillside and pleasant walks zigzag down to the slightly dilapidated central greenhouses, filled with ferns and orchids. One final prominent sight you're bound to notice is the multi-roofed **Dhirdham Temple**, below the railway station, built as a replica of the great Shiva temple of Pashupatinath on the outskirts of Kathmandu. Heading out of town on AJC Bose Road you come to the discreetly hidden **Nipponjan Myohoji Buddhist Temple** (daily 4.30am–7pm), usually referred to as the Peace Pagoda, which is a bastion of tranquillity and enjoys great views over the valley to Kanchenjunga.

Eating and drinking

Darjeeling has plenty of choice for **eating out**, with the more touristy places around the top of town. Many of the hotels, such as the *Windamere* and *New Elgin*, have good multi-cuisine restaurants; the latter has a superb tea service. The *Aliment* has an excellent budget-traveller-friendly menu and a great rooftop location (meals for Rs50–100), while *Triveni* opposite and the *Tower View* around the corner are similar. The *New Embassy* restaurant at the Chinese-owned *Valentino* is worth the splurge. For **drinks** or light meals, try *The Buzz* at *Glenary's* (see below) or *Joey's Pub* on Dr SM Das Road, with its warm, friendly ambience; *Beni's Café* on the same road does excellent snacks and Indian sweets.

Dekevas 51 Gandhi Rd. Popular with travellers and locals alike, this non-smoking restaurant with pleasant Tibetan decor offers the usual mixed menu, including a wide range of Tibetan dishes and a very good-value breakfast. *Kungas* next door is similar.

Fiesta Chowrasta. With Darjeeling's premier people-watching position, this new bistro is best for a snack or a coffee; service is languid and the main meals uninspiring.

Frank Ross Café 14 The Mall. Friendly vegetarian snack bar serving sandwiches, pizzas and a good range of *dosas*.

Glenary's The Mall. Darjeeling's most reputable eating place serves up tasty sizzlers and the best tandoori in town. There's also a great coffee shop and patisserie with an Internet café; in the basement, *The Buzz* is an American-style bar with a pool table which also serves burgers and pizzas.

Hasty Tasty The Mall. Offering Indian fast food, and very popular with Indian holidaymakers, this self-service place serves tasty cheese *dosas* and superb veg thalis. Service is hardly hasty, however.

Keventers Clubside. A landmark café serving toasted sandwiches, and fried breakfasts that

Mountaineering

Although there are plenty of opportunities for trekking around Darjeeling, you can also take things a step further by joining one of the mountaineering courses run by the **HMI** (see p.913). Lasting 28 days and costing $500, the basic and advanced **courses** are run with military precision and provide a challenging introduction to climbing in the Sikkim Himalayas. After a short preparation, you trek to their Chaurikhang Base Camp at the foot of Rathong Glacier, where a gruelling programme of acclimatization and climbing on the glacier culminates with an attempt at a sub-6000m summit. The more rewarding advanced course requires previous mountaineering experience; to join either course, you must be ages between 17 and 40. Course fees include accommodation, food, instruction, basic equipment including sleeping bags and transport to and from the start of treks. The HMI also **rents** cheap and basic equipment to those not on one of their courses; gear rented by Trek-Mate (see p.910) is of better quality.

include bacon and ham. The terrace above the crossroads is excellent for people-watching, even if the service is poor. A delicatessen downstairs sells cheese, ham and sausages.

Luna *Hotel Luna*, 51 Gandhi Rd, Clubside. This vegetarian restaurant offers great South Indian cooking – try their *dosas* – but also serves good north Indian food.

New Dish JP Sharma Rd. Darjeeling's best choice for Chinese food, though it's served up in rather dour surroundings.

Park 41 Laden La Rd. Plush place that cooks up some of Darjeeling's finest north Indian cuisine and tandoori; there's also an annexe, *Lemon Grass*, serving good Thai food.

Penang's Opposite the GPO, Laden La Rd. Cheap, grubby but popular local haunt which acts as a bar as much as a café, and serves excellent *momos* and *thukpa*.

Star Dust Chowrasta. Open-air restaurant serving coffee and snacks; the great terrace makes up for the dull food.

Listings

Banks and exchange The State Bank of India (Mon–Fri 10am–4pm, Sat 10am–1pm; Rs100 per transaction), Laden La Rd, is slow and only accepts American Express or Thomas Cook travellers' cheques in US$ and UK£. Licensed private foreign exchange vendors are a bit more flexible but charge around four percent more than the bank rate. Amongst these, the *Hotel Mohit* is marginally more expensive than *Hotel Seven Seventeen*; both are on HD Lama Rd; For currency exchange and cash advances on credit/debit cards, try Poddar's, 8 Laden La Rd; or Himalayan Travels, 18 Gandhi Rd. There is an ATM (Visa, Maestro, Mastercard & Cirrus) at the ICICI Bank, 49 Laden La Rd.

Bookshops Oxford Books & Stationery, Chowrasta, has an excellent selection of novels and coffee-table books.

Car rental Darjeeling Transport Corporation Laden La Rd (Ⓣ0354/225 2074) is one of the more established operators; numerous others are centred around Clubside.

Hospital Try Planters' Hospital, Planter's Club, The Mall Ⓣ0354/225 4327; Mariam Nursing Home, The Mall Ⓣ0354/225 4327. The Tibetan Medical & Astro Institute, *Hotel Seven Seventeen*, 26 HD Lama Rd (Ⓣ0354/225 4735), is part of the Dalai Lama's medical organization, Men-Tsee-Khang, and has a clinic and a well-stocked dispensary. There is also a Women's Clinic (Mon–Sat 1.30–5pm, Sun 10am–1pm) under *Hotel Springburn*, 70 Gandhi Rd.

Internet access Of the numerous Internet cafés, those at *Glenary's* and *Hotel Bellevue* (both Rs30/hr) are the most central and convenient.

Pharmacies Frank Ross & Co, The Mall. There are several more pharmacies clustered around Sadar Hospital above the bus stand.

Photography Das Studios and Darjeeling Photo Stores are both on the Mall.

Post office The main post office (Mon–Fri 9am–5pm & Sat 9am–noon) is on Laden La Rd.

Tibetan studies The Manjushree Centre of Tibetan Culture 8 Burdwan Rd (Ⓣ0354/225 6714, Ⓦwww.kreisels.com/manjushree), founded in 1988 to preserve and promote Tibetan culture, offers both part-time Tibetan language classes (Mon–Sat 4–6pm) and more intensive three-, six- and nine-month courses ($210, $320 and $430). The centre also has a library with lending facilities ($20 deposit), and holds regular seminars, talks, video shows and exhibitions. The Chakpori Medical School at Takdha (en route to Teesta) runs excellent long courses in Tibetan medicine; ask Manjushree.

Around Darjeeling

One really unmissable part of the Darjeeling experience is the early-morning mass exodus to **Tiger Hill**, to watch the sunrise. This can easily be combined with a visit to the old monastery of **Ghoom**, and the huge monastery at **Sonada** on Hill Cart Road towards Siliguri.

Tiger Hill

Jeeps and taxis packed with tourists leave from Clubside in Darjeeling around 4am each morning, careering 12km through Ghoom to catch the sunrise at **TIGER HILL**. This incredible viewpoint (2585m) on the eastern extremity

Singalila treks: the Maneybhanjang–Phalut trail

The single ridge of the **Singalila Range** rises near Darjeeling and extends all the way to the summit of Kanchenjunga. Unfortunately, although some longer trails have been opened in Sikkim (see p.953) for package groups armed with the right permits, there is no provision yet to link them to the relatively easy trails along the initial sections of the ridge to **Sandakphu** (3636m) and **Phalut** (3600m).

Easily accessible from Darjeeling, the later stages of the Maneybhanjang–Phalut trail provide magnificent views of the higher ranges; lightweight expeditions are possible as there are trekking huts (though the quilts provided are inadequate when it gets cold) and simple food stalls along the way. Several organizations (see p.910) arrange porters (Rs180–200 per day) as well as **guides** (Rs200–300 per day) allocated by the Wildlife Department, and can arrange all-inclusive packages (from $30 a day); DGHC Tourism and Trek-Mate in Darjeeling both **rent equipment** (sleeping bags cost Rs30, plus Rs1500 deposit). The **best time** to trek is after the monsoons (Oct & Nov), and during spring (Feb–May). It gets hot at the end of April and into May, but this is an especially beautiful season, with the rhododendrons in bloom.

Maneybhanjang, a small town and roadhead 27km from Darjeeling, is the usual starting point for the route, with the finest **views** found along the **Sandakphu–Phalut** section of the trail. The steep trail from Maneybhanjang as far as Sandakphu is wide enough for a Jeep to pass so it is possible to drive along this section – the Sandakphu Motor Syndicate at Manybhanjang supply Jeeps to shorten the walk. For the best panoramas, trek north from Sandakphu towards Phalut.

Foreigners are expected to register with the police at Sukhiapokhari and Maneybhanjang; with the civil war across the border in Nepal, security is becoming far tighter. Taking a taxi or the early-morning bus (7am; 90min) to Maneybhanjang from Darjeeling enables you to start the trek the same day, otherwise you can **stay** in the basic *Pradhans* (1), the *Goperna Lodge* (2), or the simple but comfortable rooms above *Wangdi Tibetan Restaurant* (2).

The route

DAY 1 Assuming you start from Maneybhanjang, the first day begins with a sharp

of the Singalila Range provides an unparalleled 360-degree Himalayan panorama, with the steamy plains bordering Bangladesh to the south, the Singalila ridge with Everest beyond to the west, Kanchenjunga and Sikkim to the north, and the Bhutan and Assam Himalayas trailing into the distance to the northeast. From left to right, the **peaks** include: Lhotse (which actually looks larger than Everest); Everest itself; Makalu; then, after a long gap, the rocky summit of Kang on the Sikkim–Nepal divide; the prow of Jannu in Nepal; Rathong; tent-like Kabrus south and north; Talung; Kanchenjunga main, central and south; Pandim; Simvo; horned Narsing; and the fluted pyramid of Siniolchu. As the sun rises from the plains, it lights each one in turn; not yet obscured by the haze of the day, they are bathed in pastel hues.

In peak season up to 150 Jeeps leave Darjeeling daily, transporting more than 2000 people to the viewpoint in good weather. A Jeep tour with stops briefly at Ghoom, the Gurkha War Memorial (Rs5) and the Batasia Loop, organized with one of the operators around Clubside will cost Rs650 per vehicle or around Rs65 per seat. The **viewing tower** at Tiger Hill provides a warmer but often crowded space for those who wish to see the sunrise from behind the safety of glass: it costs Rs40 for the "Super Deluxe" top floor (including coffee), Rs30 for the floor below, or Rs20 for the viewing platform. Just to get on the hill is climb to **Meghma**, then eases to the hut (①) at **Tonglu** (3070m). Trekkers used to continue from Meghma to the small town of **Jaubari** in Nepal, with its handful of lodges such as the *Everest Lodge* (①) and the hospitable *Indira Lodge* (①) but the military has closed the border. Strong walkers can press on to Gairibas, or to Kalipokhari where there are a couple of lodges including *Sherpa* (①–②); otherwise, you'll stay at the Tonglu hut.

DAY 2 From Tonglu, you meet the Jaubari trail at **Gairibas**, and head on to **Kalipokhari** and **Bikhebhanjang**. The trail then rises steeply to **Sandakphu** (3636m), which has a trekkers' hut (①) with blankets, the friendly *Sherpa Chalet* (③) and a couple of PWD bungalows.

DAY 3 The panorama opens out as you leave Sandakphu, and the trek follows the ridge to **Sabarkum**. There's no shelter or food there, but if you drop down to the right for thirty minutes to **Molley**, you'll find an inhospitable DGHC trekkers' hut (①).

DAY 4 Retrace your steps to Sabarkum and continue along the ridge to **Phalut** (3600m), where you'll find a trekkers' hut (①), which should be able to rustle you up some basic food. The panorama from here is particularly impressive.

DAY 5 Either retrace your steps to Sandakphu, or follow the trail from Phalut via **Gorkhey**, which has a trekkers' hut (①) and the *Shanti Lodge* (①–③) which also has a dorm, to **Rammam** (2560m), home of the welcoming *Sherpa Lodge* (④), a DGHC trekkers' hut (①) and several other lodges.

DAY 6 The final day leads to **Rimbik** (2286m); check with locals before setting off as the route is confusing. In Rimbik there's the friendly but cramped *Shiva Pradhan* (②), which has hot water but an unflattering location; warm and cosy *Sherpa Lodge* (③), where they'll help arrange bus tickets to Darjeeling; the *New Sherpa Tenzing* (③) with shared baths and hot water by the bucket; the comfortable *Ganga Prasad* (③); and a DGHC trekkers' hut (①). Rimbik is a roadhead served by buses and taxis heading to Darjeeling, or you can set off on another (long) day's walk to **Bijanbari**, which also has transport to Darjeeling.

Rs5. The energetic can opt to walk back from Tiger Hill visiting the *gompas* of Ghoom on the way.

Ghoom and other monasteries

Often obscured in cloud, **GHOOM** (2438m), with its charming little railway station and tiny bazaar on the edge of Jorebangla, holds several interesting monasteries. The most venerated of these is **Yiga Choling**, or the Old

The Toy Train to Ghoom

Ghoom is the highest point on the **Toy Train** railway (see p.905), just 7km from Darjeeling. The steam-driven tourist train (Rs240 return trip) leaves Darjeeling at 10.30am to travel up to Ghoom, where it stops for just fifteen minutes, not leaving enough time to view the monasteries, before returning to Darjeeling with another brief stop at Batasia Loop for views of the Himalayas. The regular 9am service from Darjeeling to Siliguri via Ghoom is far cheaper. You could take alternative transport back to Darjeeling or take the top road for a quiet, traffic-free walk back, taking in the stupendous views along the way with a visit to the **Peace Pagoda** in the woods above the Dali Gompa.

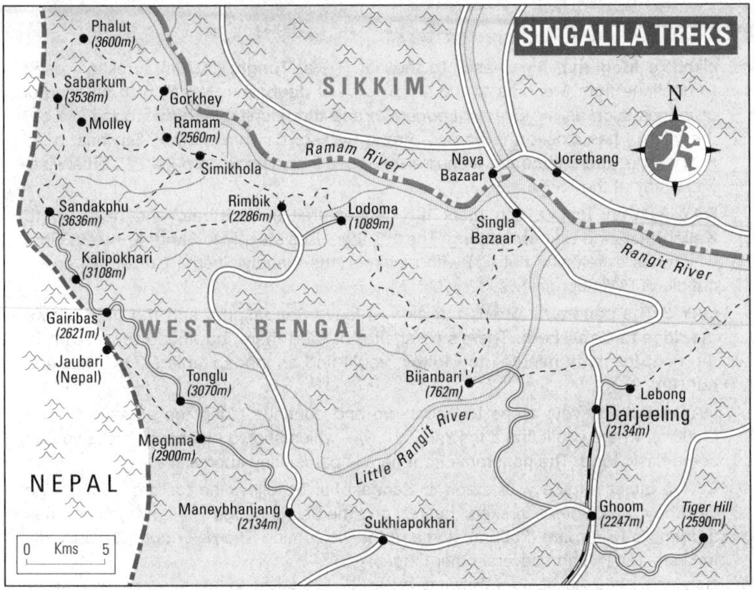

Ghoom Monastery, tucked off the main thoroughfare above the brash *Sterling Resort*. From Ghoom railway station, head back towards Darjeeling for 200m and turn left into the side road (signposted) and continue through the small market for 500m. Built in 1850 by Sharap Gyatso, a renowned astrologer, the monastery comprises a single chambered temple, with a few residential buildings and an outhouse. Inside the prayer hall is a huge figure of Maitreya, the Buddha of the future – a statue of an exceptionally high standard of workmanship, with fine detail above and around the bronze face. Back on the main road, the **Shakya Choling** *gompa* has expanded in recent years, while **Samten Choling**, a small but colourful *gompa* on a bend in the main road to Darjeeling, is sometimes included on the Jeep tours to Tiger Hill. You may prefer to spend time looking around Ghoom when the Jeeps have all returned to Darjeeling.

Halfway between Ghoom and Darjeeling on the main road stands the imposing **Thupten Sanga Choeling**, otherwise known as the **Dali Gompa**, inaugurated by the Dalai Lama in 1993. This is a very active **Drukpa Kagyu** *gompa* with two hundred monks, including several young *rinpoches*. The huge meditation hall is richly decorated with exquisite murals and ceiling mandalas.

South of Ghoom, down the Hill Cart Road towards Kurseong, the influential **Sonada Monastery**, founded in the 1960s, was the seat of **Kalu Rinpoche** who developed a large American and French following. It has recently been extensively renovated to house Kalu Rinpoche's young *tulku* or reincarnation. Rooms (1) are available for retreat and you can dine with the monks for a nominal fee.

Moving on from Darjeeling

The nearest **airport** to Darjeeling is **Bagdogra**, 100km to the south (see p.905). DGHC buses leave from Clubside at around 8am to connect with flights at Bagdogra but the service is irregular; ask at the Tourist Bureau. Indian Airlines (☎0354/225 4230) have an office on the Mall at Chowrasta, and Jet Airways tickets are available through the Clubside Tours and Travels, JP Sharma Road (☎0354/225 4646) and Himalayan Travels 18 Gandhi Rd (☎0354/225 6956). Both also handle flights (several airlines) from **Bhadrapur** in Nepal to **Kathmandu** (around $120) (see p.906).

Buses and minibuses (Rs60) run every thirty minutes or so to **Siliguri** from the bus stand; shared taxis charge Rs70. Four minibuses run each day to **Gangtok** (4–5hr; Rs80) and private buses at 7.30am, 1.30pm & 2pm (4hr 30min). One minibus leaves every day for **Kalimpong** (3hr 30min; Rs60) at 8am. Overland bus travel to **Kathmandu** is proving increasingly hazardous and you are advised to check the situation through reputable travel companies such as Himalayan Travels in Darjeeling and Siliguri before starting out.

Jeeps run to **Gangtok**, **Siliguri**, **Mirik**, **Kalimpong** and **Jorethang** (for west Sikkim), and, though slightly more expensive than buses, are by far the most efficient way to travel, especially if you pay more to book two seats in the front for yourself. Book in advance if you can at the Jeep stand (next to the bus stand); each route has its own syndicate and some have two or three. Gangtok services (4hr 30min; Rs110) run frequently between 7am and 2pm.

The **Toy Train** (see p.905) runs to **Siliguri** and **New Jalpaiguri**, weather and landslides permitting, but takes a leisurely six-and-a-half to eight hours; the train leaves at 9am and costs Rs217 for first class and Rs38 for second. **Railway reservations** (daily 8am–2pm) for selected **main-line trains** out of NJP can be made at Darjeeling's station a couple of days before departure. They have tourist quotas for trains to Delhi, Kolkata, Bangalore, Cochin and Thiruvananthapuram. If stuck, try Gupta Tours & Travel, near the station at 5 Chachan Mansion (☎0354/225 4616), who can get tickets (for a commission) when quotas are "full".

Kalimpong and around

Though it may seem quite grubby at first, the quiet hill station of **KALIMPONG**, 50km east of Darjeeling, has much to offer including an extraordinary profusion of orchids and other flowers, great views of Kanchenjunga, several monasteries and lots of potential for walks in the surrounding hills, which are still home to the tribal **Lepcha community**. Like Darjeeling, Kalimpong once belonged to Sikkim; it later fell into the hands of Bhutan. Unlike Darjeeling, however, this was never a tea town or resort, but a trading town on the vital route to Tibet – a location that rendered Kalimpong virtually out of bounds for tourists for a couple of decades after the Sino-Indian conflict of the early 1960s. Despite the large military presence, Kalimpong's recent history has been one of neglect, which has led to water shortages and a general decay in the infrastructure. A deep-rooted dissatisfaction has its political voice in the **Gurkha Liberation Organization**, a shadowy, radical movement committed to the cause of **Gurkhaland** and freeing the Darjeeling Hills from the state of West Bengal, with violence if necessary. Political uncertainties and wildcat strikes have not detracted from the charm of this underdeveloped town, and Kalimpong's leafy avenues offer a breath of fresh air after the razzmatazz of Darjeeling.

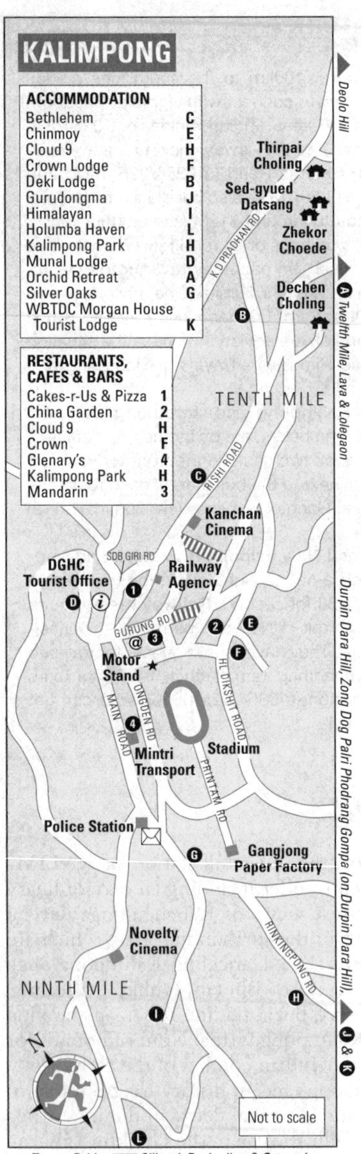

The Town

Kalimpong spreads along a curving ridge to either side of its main **market area**, known as **Tenth Mile**. Though there are few of the curio and tourist emporia so abundant in Darjeeling, there are plenty of places selling Buddhist handicrafts and religious paraphernalia, which attract wholesale buyers from all over India. Silk brocade, Tibetan incense and silver bowls predominate; Kaziratna Shakya on Rishi Road has statues, silver bowls of various degrees of purity, jewellery and *thangkas*. On Wednesdays and Saturdays, Tenth Mile gets very lively as villagers flock in from the surrounding areas for the principal weekly markets. Below the *Silver Oaks Hotel*, the **Gangjong Paper Factory** on Printam Road (Mon–Sat 9am–4.30pm) welcomes visitors to their handmade paper workshop.

Rinkingpong Hill, also known as **Durpin Dara**, looms above the town to the southwest and is firmly in the hands of the army, who allow tourists through in taxis but occasionally stop those on foot. At its highest point, entirely surrounded by the army, **Zong Dog Palri Phodrang Gompa**, also known as Durpin ("telescope") Monastery, built in 1957 to house three copper statues brought from Tibet in the 1940s, was modelled on Guru Rinpoche's mythical "pure realm" palace and consecrated by the Dalai Lama. The beautifully painted building is a scenic four-kilometre hike from the centre of town and, despite the communication masts, its roof is a great place to take in the sunrise accompanied by the chants of the monks below.

At the other end of town, half an hour's walk up Deolo Hill brings you to the **Thirpai Choling Gompa**, a breakaway Gelugpa monastery, founded in 1892 and recently renovated. Below and closer to town is **Dechen Choling Gompa**, a small Bhutanese monastery founded in 1692 and belonging to the Nyingma school; its two meditation halls are covered with beautiful murals in contrasting styles. The summit of **Deolo Hill** (1704m), is a popular picnic spot (daily 9am–6pm; Rs5) with a DGHC tourist lodge (see opposite) and restaurant, and offers superb views on a fine day. The amazing vista ranges over the town and the steamy Teesta Valley far below, and takes in the summit of Kanchenjunga, with the frontier ridge and the passes of Nathula and Jelepla into Tibet clearly visible.

Set amidst landscaped gardens to the south of town, the **Himalayan Hotel** – a "museum" and hotel as well as the home of the MacDonald family – is an impressive building with oak ceilings, teak furniture and a large collection of Tibetan artefacts and memorabilia; it's well worth a visit even if you can't afford to stay here. David MacDonald was the interpreter on Francis Younghusband's mission to Lhasa in 1904 and was later posted to Tibet as a British Trade Agent until he retired in 1924. MacDonald helped the 13th Dalai Lama to escape from Tibet in 1910, and served as British Political Officer in Sikkim where he was responsible for Britain's relations with Tibet, Bhutan and Sikkim.

Kalimpong is renowned for its **horticulture** and especially its orchid culture, with around fifty nurseries, such as L.K. Pradhan and Sri Ganesh Mani Pradhan at Twelfth Mile, specializing in new hybrids as well as cacti, amaryllis, palms and ferns. Although Kalimpong blossoms all year long, the best time to see orchids in bloom is between mid-April and mid-May, when the flower festival is usually held.

Practicalities

Kalimpong, only accessible by **road**, is served by regular buses, taxis and Jeeps from Darjeeling and Siliguri. Scheduled Jeeps and the odd bus also connect to Gangtok. You could also connect from Gangtok–Siliguri transport for local taxis or buses at the crossroads south of town near the Teesta Bridge (no photography permitted) over the fast-flowing River Teesta. A sign near the crossroads welcomes you to Kalimpong, although the town itself is 14km further on, and more than 1000m higher up.

Most transport pulls in at the **Motor Stand** in the central market area. This is the place to pick up Jeeps and buses to Darjeeling (2hr 30min–4hr; Rs80), Siliguri (2hr 30min; Rs80) and Gangtok (3hr; Rs70); each route has its own syndicate and ticket office. Moving on from Kalimpong, remember the last reliable transport links are around mid-afternoon. Mintri Transport on Main Road run a bus to Bagdogra airport (7am; Rs150). For **train tickets**, head to the railway agency on Rishi Road (daily 10am–4pm), although their quota for NJP is fairly low.

Kalimpong's **DGHC tourist office**, Damber Chowkh (daily 9.30am–5pm; Ⓣ03552/257992), is good for general information and leaflets; they also arrange **white-water rafting** on the Teesta (from Rs350). Private operators offering this increasingly popular activity include Johnny Gurkha (Ⓣ09832/074341) and White Water Action Adventure (Ⓣ09832/097676), both at Teesta, and Murmi White Water Adventures (Ⓣ03552/276071) at Melli.

Amongst local **tour operators**, Gurudongma Tours and Treks (Ⓣ03552/255204, Ⓦwww.gurudongma.com) specializes in ornithological, culinary and trekking trips throughout the northeast and has a beautiful farmhouse on the Samthar Plateau that it uses as a base. Himali Tours and Travels, near Mary's Doctor Clinic, Main Road (Ⓣ03552/258031) organizes trips to the Neora Valley, walks, cycling trips and visits to villages.

Soni Emporium on the Main Road near DGHC office **changes money**, as does its neighbour, Kaziratna Shakya. The ATM next to the State Bank of India on the Main Road accepts credit and debit cards. The **post office** is close to the centre of town, above the bazaar area just behind the police station. There are a few **Internet** cafés around; try the helpful Delta below the police station at Thana Dara on the main road.

Accommodation and eating

Kalimpong's acute water shortages are likely to influence your choice of **accommodation** – few of the lower-range options have running water. Tenth Mile and the area around the Motor Stand hold most of the budget places.

The best **restaurants** are in the *Kalimpong Park*, *Crown* and *China Garden* hotels. In a complex on SBG Road near DGHC office, there's *Cakes-r-Us* patisserie and *Pizza*, a bright little bistro with a snacky menu. Once a legendary restaurant, the *Mandarin* at the Motor Stand is now more of a bar, while the franchised *Glenary's* on SDB Giri Road is not nearly as good as its Darjeeling namesake, but is nevertheless popular for its coffee and snacks. The DGHC has a surprisingly good restaurant and bar above the tourist office. If you're after a beer, head up to *Cloud 9* or the adjacent *Park* hotels.

Accommodation

Bethlehem Rishi Rd ⓣ03552/255185. Comfortable option with hot running water and clean bathrooms; if full try *Norling* next door with its beautifully painted Tibetan restaurant. ❸

Chinmoy Below the bus stand ⓣ03552/256264. Very central with a range of pleasant, clean rooms and a quiet location despite its proximity to the taxi and bus stands. ❸

Cloud 9 Ringkingpong Rd ⓣ03552/259554. Five spacious and comfortable rooms, set above a restaurant and bar that's especially lively when the owner Binodh is around, with guitar jams and Beatles covers. ❺

Crown Lodge Below the bus stand ⓣ03552/255846. Justifiably popular place with clean rooms, hot running water and a good restaurant. Book early. ❸

Deki Lodge Tirpai Rd ⓣ03552/255095. Ten minutes' walk from the Motor Stand, this clean and very welcoming family-run hotel offers a wide choice, from budget rooms with hot water by the bucket to comfortable doubles with running hot water in the new wing at the rear. ❷–❺

Gurudongma Hill Top ⓣ03552/255204, ⓦwww.gurudongma.com. Immaculate family home, with just two rooms in the house and a tastefully recreated village cottage in the picturesque garden; book ahead. ❼

Himalayan Upper Cart Rdⓣ03552/255248, ⓦwww.himalayanhotel.biz. Historic and comfortable hotel full of Tibetan memorabilia, set amid exquisite gardens; the modern blocks are luxurious but lack the ambience. Rates (doubles from $90) include meals. ❾

Holumba Haven 8.5 Mile, near the Fire Station ⓣ03552/256936, ⓦwww.holumba.com. Comfortable, beautifully presented cottages set within a stunning orchid nursery with a menagerie of birds and animals. Some have their own kitchens, or you can have home-cooked meals with the informative and extremely welcoming owners. Recommended. ❺–❻

Kalimpong Park Ringkingpong Rd ⓣ03552/255305. An old-world hotel, without the grandeur of the *Himalayan* but more affordable, with a pleasant bar and restaurant. ❻

Munal Lodge Malli Rd ⓣ03552/255404. Airy and clean rooms with good views from the terrace. Hot water by the bucket in the cheaper rooms. ❸

Orchid Retreat Twelfth Mile ⓣ03552/274275, ⓦwww.theorchidretreat.com. Fabulous horticultural garden and nursery with comfortable rustic cottages amongst the palms and ferns; the new concrete blocks are rather unimaginative. ❼

Silver Oaks Ringkingpong Rd ⓣ03552/255296, ⓔsilveroaks@sify.com. One of the grandest addresses in town, with a central location, spacious rooms, a lovely garden and good restaurant. From $84. ❾

WBTDC Morgan House Tourist Lodge Durpin Hill ⓣ03552/255384. Grand but poorly maintained grey lodge, around 4km from town, set in fabulous gardens and built for a British jute merchant. There's an equally beautiful annexe, the *Tashiding Tourist Lodge*. ❻–❽

Around Kalimpong

Although the **Lepchas**, the original inhabitants of the area, have lost their traditional way of life in most other parts of Darjeeling and Sikkim, their lifestyle

Village tourism and homestays

Offering the chance to explore the rural landscape and experience local culture away from the hustle and bustle of towns like Darjeeling, Gangtok and Kalimpong, organised village tourism is becoming increasingly popular hereabouts. The main operators include the excellent Gurudongma (see p.921) in Kalimpong, Help Tourism (see p.907) in Siliguri and Himalayan Footprints in Gangtok (ⓣ03592/220092). Amongst the popular destinations, Gurudongma's *Farm House* (❼–❾) is a rustic but luxurious development on the beautiful Samthar Plateau, an 80km drive from Kalimpong. The family-run *Tinchuley Village House* (ⓣ0354/226 2236; ❹–❺), 28km from Kalimpong near Takdah on the Ghoom road, is in a beautiful remote setting, part forest and part tea and cardamom plantation, with plenty of wildlife including leopard and wild boar. Across the border into Sikkim, the comfortable *Turuk Village House* (ⓣ09434022580; ❻–❼), 35km from Kalimpong, dates back to the late nineteenth-century and offers an idyllic stay near the River Teesta.

has remained relatively untouched in the unspoilt forest-covered hills and deep river valleys to the south of Kalimpong. Lying on an old trade route to Bhutan, the small hamlet of **LAVA** (2184m), 35km from Kalimpong and accessible by shared Jeep, makes an ideal base for exploring the nature trails of **Neora Valley National Park**, a 880 hectare reserve stretching along a narrow river valley, with a huge variation in wildlife and abundant orchids and birds. Agents like Gurudongma and Himali Tours in Kalimpong (see p.921) can arrange the necessary guides and permits as well as transport. Lava is also convenient for approaching the **Rachela Pass** (3152m) on the Sikkim–Bhutan border, which provides excellent views of the Chola Range including Chomalhari (7314m), the sacred mountain of Bhutan on its border with Tibet. The town is also very popular with Bengali tourists who come up here directly from Siliguri. There is plenty of basic **accommodation**, including the *Forest Rest House* (❶) whose huts that should be booked through the Forest Department in Kalimpong, off Rinkingpong Road (ⓣ03552/255780, ⓦwww.wbfdc.com); the Forest department also provide permits for visiting the Neora Valley park. Of other accommodation in Lava, the *DGHC Tourist Lodge* (❹), booked through any of their bureaus, is as comfortable as it gets.

Pleasant **trails** lead west from Lava towards **Budhabare**, a weekly-market town in the Git River Valley which has a sprinkling of Lepcha, Gurkha and Bhutia villages. The track continues through forest to **Kafer**, where a comfortable DGHC *Tourist Lodge* has rooms (❺) and a dorm (Rs100). At nearby **Lolegaon**, there's the *Forest Rest House* (❶), and alternative accommodation in village houses; the trail north from here crosses the Relli River near the village of the same name and returns directly to Kalimpong.

Travel details

Trains

Kolkata to: Agra (1 daily; 30hr); Ahmedabad (1 daily; 41hr); Bhubaneswar (8–16 daily; 7–9 hr); Bishnupur (2 daily; 3hr 30min–4hr 20min); Chandernagore (20 daily; 30min); Chennai (2–7 daily; 27hr–32hr 20min); Delhi (6–8 daily; 29hr 45min–35hr 35min); Gaya (5–6 daily; 5hr 30min–7hr 30min); Guwahati (2–5 daily; 18hr–24hr 30min); Gwalior (1–3 daily; 23hr–29hr 20min); Haridwar (1–2 daily; 27hr 15min–32hr 30min); Hooghly (20 daily; 20min); Jabalpur (2 daily; 19hr 30min–27hr 45min); Kalka (Shimla) (1 daily; 33hr 10min); Krishnagar (4 daily; 2hr–3hr);

Lucknow (4–5 daily; 18–30hr); Mumbai (3 daily; 30hr–38hr); Nabadip (6–8 daily; 3hr–4hr 30min); Nagpur (4–5 daily; 17hr 40min–24hr 40min); Patna (5–6 daily; 7hr 20min–11hr 15min); Puri (2 daily; 8hr 30min–10hr); Rampurhat (4–5 daily; 4hr 10min–5hr); Raxaul (1 daily; 15hr 10min); Shantiniketan (6–7 daily; 2hr 30min–4hr); Siliguri NJP (5 daily; 10hr 20min–14hr); Thiruvananthapuram (1 weekly; 50hr 30min); Varanasi (4–5 daily; 7hr 30min–14hr 50min).

Shantiniketan (Bolpur) to: Kolkata (6–7 daily; 2hr 30min–4hr); Siliguri NJP (5–6 daily; 8hr 35min–9hr 15min).

Siliguri New Jalpaiguri (NJP) to: Delhi (4–5 daily; 21hr 40min–30hr 30min); Guwahati (8–10 daily; 7hr 30min–10hr 30min); Kolkata (6–7 daily; 10hr 25min–14hr 35min); Patna (4–5 daily; 8hr 25min–12hr 20min); Shantiniketan (Bolpur) (5–6 daily; 8hr 35min–9hr 15min); Varanasi (Mughal Sarai) (4–5 daily; 11hr 50min–19hr).

Buses

Kolkata to: Basanti (4 daily; 3hr); Behrampur (every 30 min; 5hr); Bhubaneswar (4 daily; 8–10hr); Bishnupur (3 daily; 5 hr); Bongaon (2 daily; 4hr); Dhaka (2 daily; 12hr); Diamond Harbour (12 daily; 2hr); Maldah (7 daily; 7hr); Mayapur (4 daily; 3hr 30min); Puri (2 daily; 12hr); Rampurhat (2 daily; 6hr); Siliguri NJP (4 daily; 12hr).

Siliguri to: Gangtok (4 daily; 4hr); Guwahati (4–5 daily; 9hr); Kakarbitta (12 daily; 40min); Kolkata (4 daily; 12hr); Patna (3–4 daily; 10hr); Phuntsoling (4 daily; 4hr).

Flights

Any disparities in length of flight times are due to stopovers operating on certain flights only. In the listings below, **AA** represents Alliance Airways (Indian Airlines), **AD** Air Deccan, **BB** Bangladesh Biman, **DA** Druk Air, **IA** Indian Airlines, **JA** Jet Airways, **S** is Sahara, and **TA** is Thai Airways.

Bagdogra (Siliguri) to: Delhi (IA, JA, AD 2–3 daily; 3hr–4hr); Guwahati (IA, JA, AD 2–3 daily; 45min); Kolkata (IA, JA 2 daily; 1hr).

Kolkata to: Agartala (AA, IA, JA 2–3 daily; 50min); Ahmedabad (AA 4 weekly; 2hr); Bagdogra/Siliguri (AA, IA, JA 2 daily; 1hr); Bangkok (IA, DA, TA 2 daily; 2hr 25min–3hr 45min); Bhubaneswar (AA, S 2 daily; 55min); Chennai (IA, JA, AA, S, AD 4 daily; 2hr); Delhi (AA, IA, AD, JA, S 8 daily; 2hr–2hr 15min); Dhaka (BB 2 daily; 1hr); Guwahati (IA, JA, AA, S, AD 6–7 daily; 1hr 10min); Hyderabad (AA, AD, JA, S 3–5 daily; 2hr–3hr); Imphal (AA, JA 1–3 daily; 1hr 55min–2hr 40min); Jaipur (AA 4 weekly; 2hr 20min–4hr); Kathmandu (IA 3 weekly; 1hr 30min); Lucknow (S 1 daily; 2hr 20min); Mumbai (IA, JA, S, AI 9 daily; 2hr 30min); Nagpur (AA 3 weekly; 1hr 30min); Paro (Bhutan), (DA 4 weekly; 1hr 10min); Patna (S 1 daily; 1hr–2hr); Port Blair (AA, IA 1–2 daily; 2hr); Yangon (Rangoon) (IA 2 weekly; 2hr 45min).

CHAPTER 14

Highlights

* **Sonepur Mela** Starting in early November and lasting for a whole month, this festival and cattle fair sees a great gathering of pilgrims and *sadhus*. **See p.933**

* **The Bodhi Tree** A cutting from the tree under which Buddha was enlightened provides the focus of Bodhgaya's renowned Mahabodhi Temple. **See p.938**

* **Rajgir** A dusty Buddhist pilgrimage town full of shrines and host to India's best sushi restaurant. **See p.942**

* **Palamau National Park** This national park covers 1000 square kilometres of hills in remote western Jharkhand, and offers elephant rides through tiger country. **See p.946**

△ Bodhgaya

14

Bihar and Jharkhand

BIHAR occupies the flat eastern Ganges basin, south of Nepal between Uttar Pradesh and West Bengal. To its south, the state of **JHARKHAND**, occupying the hilly Chotanagpur plateau north of Orissa, was hewn out of Bihar in 2000, following agitation by its tribal majority. This attempt by the government to arrest the spread of what the author William Dalrymple has called the "Bihar disease" continues to flounder, however, as both states remain seriously troubled by poverty, a lack of infrastructure, inter-caste violence, corruption and general lawlessness (see box, p.929).

The region's plight is all the more tragic considering its history. It was at **Bodhgaya** in the sixth century that Prince Gautama settled under a Bodhi tree and attained enlightenment, following a quest for truth that saw him wandering the kingdoms of the Ganges, including visits to **Vaishali** and **Rajgir**. Today, the region's Buddhist sites draw pilgrims from all over the world. As well as being the first centre of Buddhism in north India, Bihar was its last bastion; the university at **Nalanda** stands as a poignant reminder of the extent of the faith. During the sixth century BC, this was the heartland of the **Magadhas**, whose king, Bimbisara, was converted by the Buddha at his capital of Rajagriha (now Rajgir). Around 321 BC, shortly after the Magadhas shifted their capital to **Patna**, they were overthrown by the dynamic **Chandragupta Maurya**, who was said to have met Alexander the Great. The next major dynasty to rule the area was the **Guptas**, around the fourth century AD, whose advent marked the return of Hinduism. Extraordinarily, even after the Muslim Sultanate swept the region at the end of the twelfth century, and the Moghuls came to rule all northern India from Delhi three hundred years later, the Buddhist centre of Bodhgaya continued to thrive.

Although the ordinary visitor is usually unaffected by the frequent kidnappings, murders and acts of banditry, Buddhist pilgrims and tourists have been subject to looting and few travellers spend much time here. This is a great shame, because the region is refreshingly off the tourist trail, has some attractive lakes and waterfalls and a fascinating mix of religious history. Check the safety situation with the foreign office before travel, however, and with local press on arrival in India (Ⓦ www.patnadaily.com and Ⓦ www.bihartimes.com are both good sources). It is advisable to avoid the region during local election periods, when tensions run high and riots and violent crime are not uncommon.

Patna and around

The capital of Bihar, **PATNA**, dates back to the sixth century BC, which makes it one of the oldest cities in India. Today, it holds only the barest of indications of its former glory as the centre of the Magadhan and Mauryan empires. The sprawling metropolis hugs the south bank of the Ganges, stretching for around 15km in a shape that has changed little since Ajatasatru (491–459 BC) shifted the Magadhan capital here from Rajgir.

The first Mauryan emperor, **Chandragupta**, established himself in what was then **Pataliputra** in 321 BC, and pushed the limits of his empire as far as the Indus; his grandson **Ashoka** (274–237 BC), among the greatest of all Indian

Lalu and the caste wars: politics in Bihar

"Good, bad and Bihar" ran a magazine headline in 2001, announcing that Bihar still falls last in every index of development from literacy to GDP, with the newly formed state of Jharkhand not faring much better. Half a decade on, absolutely nothing has improved – roads are still appalling, buses and trains are ancient and jammed, and even in the capital there are few street lights. Yet Bihar is blessed with ample resources of coal and iron and large tracts of arable land. Its appalling condition is due largely to criminal misgovernance.

For most of the period since Independence, Bihar was ruled by a mafia of high-caste landowners. No lower caste was allowed to catch the eye of his social superior or to sit on a chair in his presence. All that seemed about to change in 1991 when a rabble-rouser from the lowly caste of buffalo milkers, **Lalu Prasad Yadav**, united the backward castes, the Muslims and the untouchables – seventy percent of the electorate – under the banner of social justice, and won the election by a landslide. The charismatic earthy figure, who willingly drank tea with the lowest of the low and promised "a lantern for every home", seemed like the new broom the state needed. In power, Lalu delighted with his common touch; he spontaneously unclogged traffic congestion by walking the streets with a loud-hailer and filled the grounds of his official residence with buffalo.

Unfortunately Lalu proved at least as bad as his predecessors. His cabinet of caste brethren included men wanted for murder and kidnap. Any distinction between criminals and politicians disappeared as violence became the usual route to political success. One hopeful candidate said, "Without one hundred men with guns you cannot contest an election in Bihar." Much of the countryside degenerated into civil war as the upper castes, lower castes, Maoist guerrillas, police and private armies clashed in massacre and counter-massacre, leaving their enemies beheaded, or "shortened" as the locals say.

Lalu's career looked to be over when in 1997 he was imprisoned for embezzling billions of rupees from the state's animal husbandry department. He responded by getting his illiterate wife **Rabri Devi** proclaimed chief minister and ruling through her from prison. As one despondent voter said, "You need to graduate here before you can carry bags at a hotel, but to be chief minister you don't even need to be able to write your name."

Released from jail after a short stint, however, Lalu resumed the presidency of his RJD party for another eight years, his wife continuing as chief minister. It was not until the February 2005 state elections that both were finally toppled from power when neither party nor opposition managed to secure a majority and a "President's rule" was declared by central government, with a pledge to improve Bihar's record on law and order. Biharis were jubilant. Meanwhile Lalu continued to be embroiled in scandal, and was set to face trial for numerous offences, including illegal withdrawal of money from various treasuries. However, popular opinion suggests that his political career is far from over, and that he will be part of any power sharing arrangement that evolves when popular rule is restored.

rulers, held sway over even greater domains. To facilitate Indo–Hellenic trade, the Mauryans built a Royal Highway from Pataliputra to Taxila in Pakistan, which later became the Grand Trunk Road, and similar highways reached towards the Bay of Bengal and along the east coast. The city experienced two later revivals. The first Gupta emperor, also named **Chandra Gupta**, made Patna his capital early in the fourth century AD, and a thousand years later it was rebuilt by the brilliant Afghan ruler Sher Shah Suri (1540–45), who constructed the Sher Shahi Mosque in the east of the city. Nearby, the beautiful *gurudwara* of **Har Mandir** was built to honour the birthplace of the tenth and most militant

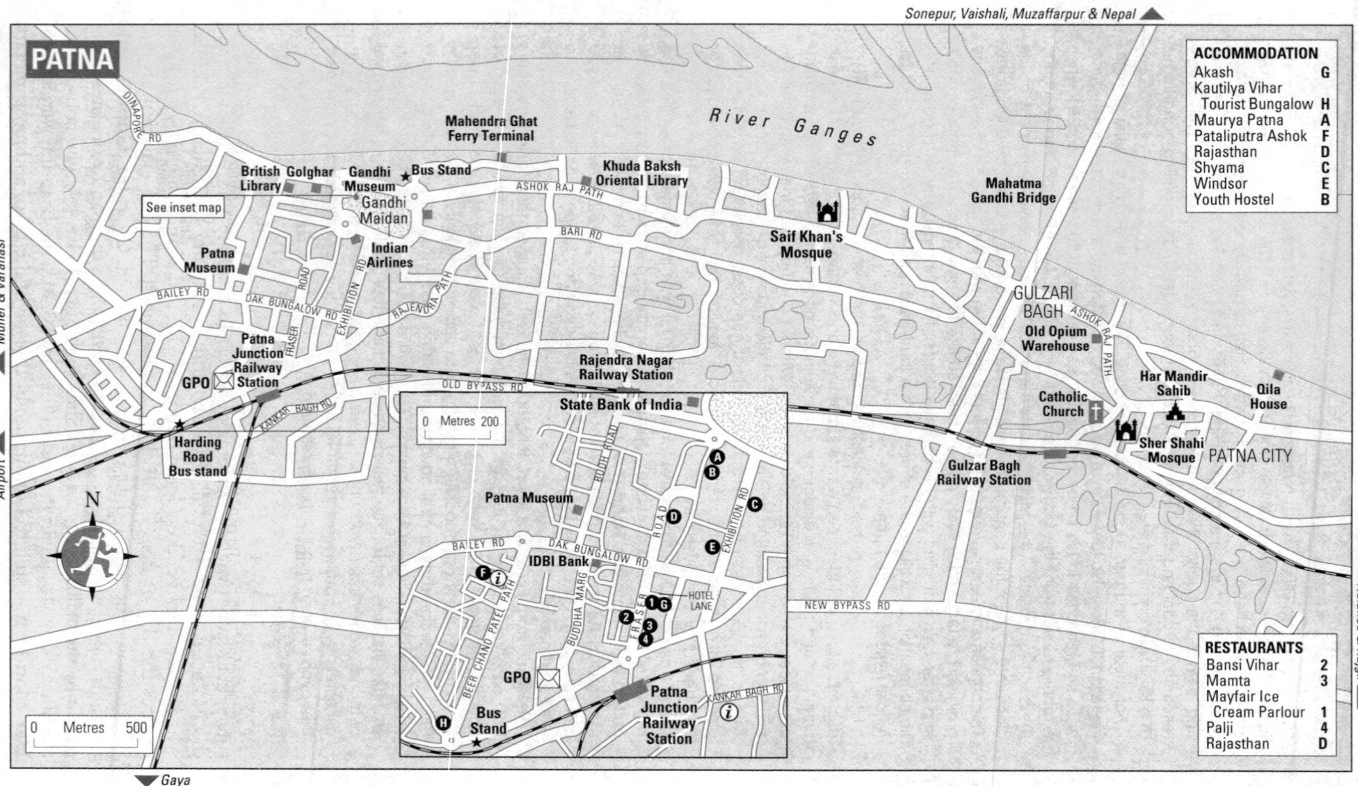
PATNA
Sonepur, Vaishali, Muzaffarpur & Nepal
Nalanda & Rajgir
Muner & Varanasi
Airport
Gaya
River Ganges
DINAPORE RD
Mahendra Ghat Ferry Terminal
British Library
Golghar
Gandhi Museum
Bus Stand
Gandhi Maidan
Khuda Baksh Oriental Library
ASHOK RAJ PATH
BARI RD
Saif Khan's Mosque
Mahatma Gandhi Bridge
See inset map
Patna Museum
Indian Airlines
BAILEY RD
DAK BUNGALOW RD
ROAD
FRASER
EXHIBITION RD
RAJENDRA PATH
Patna Junction Railway Station
GPO
OLD BYPASS RD
KANKAR BAGH RD
Harding Road Bus stand
Rajendra Nagar Railway Station
GULZARI BAGH
Old Opium Warehouse
Catholic Church
Har Mandir Sahib
Qila House
Sher Shahi Mosque
PATNA CITY
Gulzar Bagh Railway Station
NEW BYPASS RD
N
0 Metres 500
0 Metres 200
State Bank of India
BUDH ROAD
IDBI Bank
BUDDHA MARG
BEER CHAND PATEL PATH
HOTEL LANE
Bus Stand
ACCOMMODATION
Akash G
Kautilya Vihar Tourist Bungalow H
Maurya Patna A
Pataliputra Ashok F
Rajasthan D
Shyama C
Windsor E
Youth Hostel B
RESTAURANTS
Bansi Vihar 2
Mamta 3
Mayfair Ice Cream Parlour 1
Palji 4
Rajasthan D

Sikh guru – Guru Gobind Singh. In his honour, the old Patna City quarter of the city is often referred to as **Patna Sahib**.

Arrival and information

Patna has three **stations** but all main-line train services arrive at Patna Junction, in the west of the city. Fraser Road (officially Mazharul-Raq Path but many still use the old name), immediately north of the station, is the main drag, with as much glamour as the state can muster – though even here you'll see rag pickers living on the pavement. Patna's **airport** lies 5km to the west. A pre-paid taxi to Fraser Road costs about Rs180, and Indian Airlines buses are also available. A few hundred metres west of the station, the chaotic **Harding Road bus stand** runs services to and from Gaya, Varanasi, and the Nepal border at Raxaul (see "Moving on from Patna" box, p.934). North of Fraser Road, between Gandhi Maidan and the River Ganges, the **Gandhi Maidan bus stand** is the terminus for Bihar State Transport and serves destinations throughout Bihar. Cycle rickshaws and auto-rickshaws are the most common means of transport; shared Vikram auto-rickshaws cross the city east to west for around Rs10 with a change at Gandhi Maidan for Patna Sahib.

The **Bihar tourist office** in the *Pataliputra Ashok* hotel (Mon–Sat 10.30am–5pm; ⓣ0612/222 2622), provides scant information but organizes weekend tours to Patna, Nalanda, Rajgir and Pawapuri. The **Bihar State Tourism Development Corporation**, based in the *Kautilya Vihar Tourist Bungalow* on Beer Chand Patel Path (ⓣ0612/222 5411; ⓦhttp://bstdc.bih.nic.in), is worth trying for local information and can also arrange day-trips. The inconveniently located **Government of India tourist office**, close to the railway bridge at Sudama Place, Kankar Bagh Road (Mon–Fri 9.30am–6pm, Sat 9am–1pm; ⓣ0612/234 5776), runs a guide service. A number of agents (see p.934) also organize tours and arrange **car rental**, but many drivers refuse to take visitors to the more isolated areas because of bad roads and fear of banditry. The State Bank of India, West Gandhi Maidan (ⓣ0612/222 1527), handles **foreign exchange**. **ATMs** are dotted all over the town and include those at the ICICI Bank on Fraser Road and the IDBI Bank on Dak Bungalow Road (both take Visa, Mastercard, Cirrus and Maestro). The **GPO** is on Buddha Marg. For **Internet access**, the New Cyber Junction at Vishwanath Market, Musallahpur Hatt, has a/c multimedia booths (Rs5/hr) and reliable printers and scanners.

Accommodation

Patna has plenty of **accommodation**, although curiously most of it is fully booked most of the time. The cheaper hotels can be found at the station end of Fraser Road, and there is another cluster of cheap to mid-range hotels at the top end of Exhibition Road. The railway station **retiring rooms** are good value at Rs100.

Akash Hotel Lane, off Fraser Rd ⓣ0612/223 9599. Better than most in the lane, with smallish but clean good-value rooms. ❷

Kautilya Vihar Tourist Bungalow Beer Chand Patel Path ⓣ0612/222 5411, ⓦhttp://bstdc.bih.nic.in. Reasonable dorms (from Rs75) and doubles. ❹

Maurya Patna Fraser Rd, South Gandhi Maidan ⓣ0612/220 3040, ⓦwww.maurya.com. Somewhat impersonal five-star hotel but with a range of clean rooms in different styles, from colonial to oriental – the "Mauryan chamber" rooms are the best value for budget-conscious travellers. There's also a bar, multi-cuisine restaurant, café, bakery, beauty salon, travel agency and swimming pool. ❽

Pataliputra Ashok Beer Chand Patel Path ⓣ0612/222 6270, ⓦwww.theashokgroup.com. Large chain hotel, with characterless but comfortable a/c rooms with en-suite bathroom and fridge. Features include swimming pool, restaurant and coffee shop, and the state tourist office is located here. ❽–❾

Rajasthan Fraser Rd ⓣ0612/222 5102. Well-managed hotel with a travel counter, laundry service and recommended vegetarian restaurant (which also serves great ice cream), though the rooms look rather tired. ④–⑤

Shyama Exhibition Rd ⓣ0612/268 5539. One of the better budget hotels on this busy road, with cheap rooms and attached baths. ①

Windsor Exhibition Rd ⓣ0612/221 2428, ⓔhotelwindsor@vsnl.net. A good-value mid-range option, aimed primarily at businessmen. Also has a reliable 24hr Internet café. ⑤–⑥

Youth Hostel Fraser Rd ⓣ0612/221 1486, ⓦwww.yhmysore.com/patna_main.htm. The usual restrictions apply, but it's only Rs40 for a dorm bed (Rs20 if you have a YHA card). Clean and well run, it's the cheapest budget option in town and serves good food. ①

The City

Patna's most remarkable monument dates from the British era. This huge grain storage house known as **Golghar**, the "round house" – now a symbol of the city – was built in 1786 in the hope of avoiding a repetition of the terrible famine of 1770. Mercifully, it never needed to be used. Overlooking the river and the *maidan*, it is decorated with two sets of stairs that spiral their way to the summit, 29m above the road; these were designed so that coolies could carry grain up one flight, deliver their load through a hole at the top, and descend the other stairs. Constructed with stone slabs, the base of the structure is 125m wide, with 3.6-metre-thick walls. Sightseers now clamber up for views of the mighty river and the town. Within walking distance, the **Gandhi Museum** (Mon–Fri 10am–6pm; free) is worth a visit for its pictures of the Mahatma's life.

The **Patna Museum** on Budh Road (daily except Mon 10.30am–4.30pm; Rs5), though faded and run-down, has an excellent collection of sculpture. Among its most famous pieces is a polished sandstone female attendant, or *yakshi*, holding a fly-whisk, found at Didarganj in Uttar Pradesh and dating from the third century BC. There are also some Jain images from the Kushana period, and a group of Buddhist *bodhisattvas* from the Gandhara region (in northwest Pakistan), which belong to the second and third centuries AD. Amongst the natural history exhibits are several stuffed animals, including a few freakishly deformed ones, and a gigantic fossilized tree thought to be 200 million years old. The museum also houses Chinese art, and the second floor is devoted to some superb Tibetan *thangkas* (scroll paintings), in dire need of restoration.

Founded in 1900, the **Khuda Bhaksh Oriental Library** (Mon–Fri 11am–5pm; free), east of Gandhi Maidan, has a remarkable selection of books from all over the Islamic world, all gathered by one man. Besides rare Persian and Arabic manuscripts, it houses Moghul and Rajput miniatures, and manuscripts rescued from the Moorish University at Cordoba in Spain. One of its more unusual exhibits is a tiny Koran measuring just 25mm in width.

Har Mandir Sahib and beyond

In the most interesting area of Patna – the older part of town, 10km east of Gandhi Maidan – filthy congested lanes crammed with vehicles of all kinds lead to **Har Mandir Sahib**, the second holiest of the four great Sikh shrines known as *takhts* (thrones). Set in an expansive courtyard off the main road, the dazzling white onion-domed marble temple is dedicated to Guru Gobind Singh, born in Patna in 1660. Visitors are welcome to roam around the courtyard and even venture inside where more than likely there will be some devotional music playing. A free shoe locker service is provided at the edge of the courtyard; remove your shoes and cover your head before entering. Shared auto-rickshaws cost around Rs10 from Gandhi Maidan.

A little way northeast, the private **Qila House** (or Jalan Museum; call ahead for permission from the Jalan family; ⓣ0612/264 2354) on Jalan Avenue holds a fine collection of art, including Chinese paintings and Moghul filigree work in jade and silver. Among the antiques are porcelain that once belonged to Marie Antoinette, and Napoleon's four-poster bed. To the west, the **Old Opium Warehouse** at **Gulzaribagh**, now a government printing press, was where the East India Company stored opium for trade on behalf of the British government.

Midway between Har Mandir Sahib and Gandhi Maidan stands **Saif Khan's Mosque** or the "mosque of stone", built by Parwez Shah, son of the great Moghul emperor Jahangir, during his time in charge of Bihar.

Eating

Fraser Road has several good **restaurants**. The *Bansi Vihar* offers tasty and inexpensive South Indian food, with good vegetarian options, while the *Rajasthan* hotel has a quality vegetarian restaurant, and serves homemade ice cream. At *Mamta*, you'll get a good range of north and South Indian food as well as beer. Reasonably priced *Palji* at Krishna Chowk near the railway station is popular with middle-class locals for its mix of meat and veg dishes, and the *Mayfair Ice cream Parlour* at the end of Hotel Lane serves tasty *dosa* and other snacks, and is always busy and cheerful. Many of the a/c restaurants along this stretch double as bars and have two shifts – families are served earlier in the evening; later the custom is all male.

Around Patna

Patna makes a popular base for exploring Nalanda and Rajgir (see p.942), as well as Vaishali to the north (see p.934), but there are also places of interest closer at hand. The fabulous *dargah* (Sufi mausoleum) at **Muner**, on the road to Varanasi, is the prime attraction, but if you're in the area between early November and early December, don't miss the **Sonepur Mela**, an enormous month-long **cattle fair** held 25km north of Patna across the huge Gandhi Bridge – claimed to be Asia's longest river bridge – at the confluence of the Gandak and Ganges. Cattle, elephants, camels, parakeets and other animals are brought for sale, pilgrims combine business with a dip in the Ganges, *sadhus* congregate, and festivities include song and dance performances as well as a large funfair with stalls and a circus. Incidentally, Sonepur town also claims to have the longest railway platform in the world, though it's not one that would win any prizes for maintenance.

Tourist offices in Bihar (see p.931) organize tours and maintain a tourist village at Sonepur during the Mela, with a bungalow and several huts providing a range of accommodation (❶–❼).

Muner

The imposing but neglected red-sandstone **mausoleum** of the Sufi saint Yahia Muneri overlooks a lake 27km west of Patna on the busy Varanasi road, 1km west of **MUNER** – an easy bus ride from the city. The shrine itself, built in 1605 by Ibrahim Khan, the governor of Gujarat under Jahangir, stands atop a hillock; the beautifully maintained gardens below are the responsibility of the devout and traditionalist Sufi caretakers. Every year, around February, a three-day *urs* or festival in the saint's honour attracts pilgrims from far and wide, including *qawwals*, the renowned Sufi minstrels of the Chishtia of Delhi and Ajmer. If you do come to Muner, it's worth knowing that the town is famous for its **sweets**, and especially *ladoos*, made of lentils.

Moving on from Patna

Patna Junction is the most important **railway** station in the region, connected to Gaya, Delhi, Varanasi, NJP (for Darjeeling, Kalimpong and Sikkim), Kolkata, Mumbai and Chennai. There is a foreigners' reservation counter on the first floor of the booking office. The best train to **Kolkata** (Howrah) is the fast Rajdhani Express #2306 (Tues & Sat); other principal trains to Kolkata are the Poorva Express #2304 (Mon, Thurs, Fri & Sun) and the daily Howrah–Amritsar Express #3050. The Patna–Delhi Shramjeevi Express #2401 also stops at **Varanasi** and most major trains stop at **Mughal Sarai**, not far from Varanasi. Among others, the Rajdhani Express #2305 and the Poorva Express #2303 travel to **Delhi**. The Guwahati–Dadar Express #5646 travels to **Mumbai** and in the other direction, on its way to **Guwahati**, stops at **New Jalpaiguri**, handy for Darjeeling and Sikkim; more convenient trains to the northeast include the NE Express #5622. The Patna–Puri Express #8450 (Thurs) travels to **Puri** on the Orissa coast, while the #2816 New Delhi–Puri train (Tues, Thurs, Fri & Sun) is more regular, but passes through Gaya not Patna; take the 9.55am Patna–Hatia Express #8625 for the short journey to Gaya. Travelling to the deep south, the weekly Cochin–Patna Express #6310 leaves on Thursday.

Patna Airport is linked by Indian Airlines, at City Office, South Gandhi Maidan (☎0612/222 2554), to Bagdogra, Delhi, Guwahati, Kolkata, Lucknow, Mumbai and Ranchi; Air Sahara, East Gandhi Maidan (☎0612/223 0293), flies directly to Kolkata, Lucknow and Varanasi, with connections from Kolkata to Bangalore, Delhi and Mumbai. There are also daily flights with Jet Airways (☎0612/222 3046) linking Patna with Delhi.

Travel companies offer bus tickets to **Kathmandu** with a voucher for the bus across the border, although it is just as easy and often wiser to make your own arrangements. Harding Road **bus stand** is a 200-metre stretch of chaos with few signs and no central booking office, but there are plenty of vociferous touts who will guide you to your bus. Around eighteen buses a day leave for the six-hour ride to the Nepalese border at Raxaul (see p.936) from gate 6, starting at 4am and timetabled until 1am, although it's best to stick to services running during daylight hours. **Buses** to Ranchi, Bodhgaya, Gaya, Vaishali and via Muner to Varanasi leave from Harding Road; some services to Vaishali also depart from the Gandhi Maidan bus stand. There are no direct buses to Rajgir, Nalanda and Pawapuri; services run via Bihar Sharif.

Reliable **travel agents** include Ashok Travel & Tours in the *Hotel Pataliputra Ashok* (☎0612/222 3238); Inter Travel Shop, Fraser Road (☎0612/222 1337); and the Travel Corporation of India at the Maurya Patna (☎0612/222 1699).

North Bihar

The one area of Bihar capable of growing reliable crops is the fertile agricultural belt along the Himalayan foothills north of the Ganges. Other than passing through en route to Nepal, most visitors only pause to explore the remains of the abandoned Buddhist city of **Vaishali**, although the region also holds a handful of shrines and temple towns associated with the *Ramayana*.

Vaishali

Set amid paddy fields 55km north of Patna, the quiet hamlet of **VAISHALI** is significant to both Buddhists and Jains. Archeological excavations are still in progress and only a fraction of this ancient city, buried in the silt of the River Gandak and dating from the sixth century BC, has yet been unearthed. This was where the Buddha preached his last sermon before he died in Kushinagar around 483 BC.

Named after King Visala, who is mentioned in the *Ramayana*, Vaishali is believed by some historians to have been the first city state in the world to practise a democratic, republican form of government. After leaving Nepal and renouncing the world and his family, Prince Gautama studied here, but eventually rejected his master's teachings and found his own path to enlightenment and Buddhahood. He returned to Vaishali three times and on his last visit announced his final liberation – *Mahaparinirvana* – and departure from the world. One hundred years later, in 383 BC, the Second Buddhist Council was held in Vaishali and two stupas were erected. For a further thousand years, under Pataliputra (Patna) as capital, Vaishali continued to prosper.

A small but well-presented **archeological museum** (daily except Fri 10am–5pm; free) provides a glimpse into the ancient Buddhist world. A short path next to the Coronation Tank (Abhishekh Pushkarni) leads off to the remains of the **stupa**, now covered by a roof, where the supposed ashes of the Buddha were found in a silver urn.

Two kilometres north at **Kolhua** stands the remarkably well-preserved **Ashokan Pillar**, erected by the Mauryan emperor (273–232 BC) to commemorate the site of the Buddha's last sermon. Known locally as Bhimsen-ki-lathi (Bhimsen's Staff), the 18.3-metre-high pillar, made of polished red sandstone, is crowned by a lion sitting on an inverted lotus, which faces north towards Kushinagar. Jains of the Svetambara sect, who believe that the last *tirthankara*, Mahavira, was born in Vaishali in 599 BC, have erected a **shrine** in the fields 1km east of Kolhua.

Travel agents in Patna can arrange **transport** to Vaishali or you can take a bus as far as Sonepur or Hajipur, and change onto one of the overcrowded local shared taxis. Direct buses leave from Gandhi Maidan but are few and far between. Most people take in Vaishali as a day-trip from Patna, but there is a **tourist bungalow** (❶–❷) and a **youth hostel** (❶) here, both run by Bihar Tourism (Ⓣ0612/222 2622).

The road to Nepal

Some 55km north of Vaishali is **KESARIYA**, formerly known as Kessaputta. There's an impressive, five-terraced eighth-century stupa here, said to be built on top of the one erected by Buddha's Licchavi disciples after he announced his impending nirvana and gave them his begging bowl as a souvenir. To get to

Madhubani paintings

Jitwarpur, a village on the outskirts of the small town of **Madhubani**, in the district of Mithila in north Bihar, is the home of a vibrant tradition of Indian folk art. Madhubani **paintings** started out as decorations for the outside of village huts, executed by women using natural dyes. Illustrations of mythological themes, incorporating images of local deities as well as Hindu gods and goddesses, the paintings were eventually transferred onto handmade paper, often using bright synthetic primary colours to fill the strong black line drawings. You do see plain black and white pictures, but more familiar now are paintings dominated by reds, pinks and blues and offset by yellow on a white background. **Fabrics** printed with Madhubani designs have become very chic; these days they tend to be professionally made elsewhere, and are sold in the expensive boutiques of India's major cities, though you can still pick them up cheaply in Madhubani itself.

Buses connect Patna to Madhubani (5hr 30min), where there is some basic accommodation; rickshaws can take you on to Jitwarpur.

Kesariya, take a bus from Vaishali to **CHAKIA** (3hr), 20km away, then a taxi or rickshaw to the site. You could also visit as a (somewhat tiring) day-trip from Patna – buses run every hour en route to Motihari (5hr).

In 1917, **MOTIHARI**, a poor and lawless town 298km north of Patna, was the site of one of Gandhi's first acts of civil disobedience – he refused bail whilst protesting the plight of local farmers, who were being forced to grow indigo for the British textile industry. There's a small **museum** here displaying photographs and items such as Gandhi's walking stick and slippers. Motihari was also the birthplace of **George Orwell**, whose father worked here as a government opium agent. Most travellers simply pass through it on the way to Nepal, though there are local *dharamshalas* should you need to stay – ask on arrival in town.

Travellers heading from Patna towards **Nepal** have to cross the border (open 4am–8pm) at **RAXAUL**, six hours away by bus. Raxual is an unattractive, grubby town infested with mosquitoes and flies and with limited amenities – you're better off staying at Birganj across the Nepal border. If you have to spend the night, the clean **retiring rooms** are the best bet, but guests have to have a rail ticket. Otherwise, the *Ajanta* on Ashram Road (❷–❸) is the best that Raxaul has to offer, with meals prepared to order. There's a **café** along the main road at the cinema, serving a local delicacy of kebab and *muri* (puffed rice).

The border itself, between Raxaul and the Nepalese town of **Birganj**, 5km away (a Rs20 rickshaw ride), is open 24hr for foreigners, but in practice the Nepal side is often left unmanned and closes from 7pm to 5am. If you don't already have a visa, you'll be expected to pay in cash ($60). Early morning buses and one at night run from Birganj to Kathmandu (12hr) and Pokhara (10hr). Minibuses (8hr) cost slightly more – reserve a seat in advance if you can. The foreign exchange facility in Raxaul will only change Indian to Nepalese rupees, but Birganj has facilities to change travellers' cheques and US dollars.

Central Bihar

South of the Ganges and north of the hills of the Chotanagpur plateau, **Central Bihar** contains some of north India's most important Buddhist sites, including the great university at **Nalanda** and the small town of **Rajgir**. The greatest shrine of all, however, and a focus for Buddhists from around the world, is the Bodhi Tree at **Bodhgaya** where the Buddha gained enlightenment.

Gaya

The flyblown and densely packed town of **GAYA**, 100km south of Patna, serves as an essential transit point for visitors to **Bodhgaya**, 13km away. Though not an appealing town, it's of great significance to Hindus, who come here to honour their parents a year after death by offering *pind* – a gift of funeral cakes – at the massive **Vishnupad temple**, where non-Hindus are forbidden. After the monsoon, when the river is in spate, pilgrims bathe in the river and present offerings. During the dry season, they have to content themselves with holes dug into the riverbed to the water level.

Practicalities

Most people arrive at Gaya by **train** and are met by a bewildering array of touts offering rickshaws, auto-rickshaws, taxis and tongas; all of them assume that you are heading for Bodhgaya. The best option is take a cycle rickshaw to

Moving on from Gaya

Moving on from Gaya is a high priority for most foreign visitors, who usually only wish to travel 13km to the sanctuary of **Bodhgaya** (see p.940 for details of transport from Gaya to Bodhgaya). However Gaya is an important transport centre and a major junction on the main railway line between Kolkata, **Varanasi** and New Delhi. Trains to **Kolkata** include the Poorva Express #2382, the Dehra Dun Express #3010 and the faster but less convenient Rajdhani Express #2302, which departs very early in the morning. The New Delhi–Puri Express #2816 runs on Mon, Wed, Thurs and Sat to **Puri** on the Orissa coast. Trains to **New Delhi** include the Rajdhani Express #2301 (Mon, Tues, Thurs, Fri & Sat) and the Poorva Express #2381 (Wed, Thurs & Sun).

Bihar Roadways runs services from the Gandhi Maidan bus stand to **Patna**, **Ranchi**, **Varanasi** and **Kolkata**. Buses to **Rajgir** leave from the Gaurakshini bus stand across the river on the outskirts of town (hourly; 2hr 30min). Three buses to **Patna** (7am, 8am & 3pm) pick up passengers from the railway station.

Gaya's international **airport** (☎0631/428081) has flights to **Kolkata** twice a week. The schedule changes quite regularly, so check with Indian Airlines; there is an office at *Hotel Royal Residency* in Bodhgaya (☎0631/220 0124).

Kacheri bus stand from where you can continue to Bodhgaya by auto-rickshaw or bus (see p.940). If you arrive after dark, plan to stay the night in Gaya as the route between the two is dangerous bandit territory. There is precious little to do in Gaya and tourist facilities and information are appalling given the large numbers of tourists passing through.

Most of Gaya's **hotels** are along Station Road near the railway station, and there's little to choose between them: the *Ajitsatru* (☎0631/243 4584; ❷–❹) is run down and not great value, but has a good restaurant. The *Siddhartha International* on Station Road (☎0631/243 6368; ❾) is an upmarket hotel close to the railway station with reasonable if musty rooms, ISD/STD facilities and 24hr room service. The **railway retiring rooms** are clean and some offer a/c.

Bodhgaya

BODHGAYA, 13km south of Gaya beside the River Phalgu, is sacred to Buddhists as the place where the Buddha gained enlightenment. A giant Buddhist resort of international monasteries and temples has grown up around the imposing **Mahabodhi temple**, which holds the world's most revered tree, an offshoot of the original Bodhi tree under which the Buddha sat. Bodhgaya is by far the most important and significant of the four holy sites of Buddhism – the other three being Buddha's birthplace, Lumbini in Nepal; Sarnath near Varanasi, where he preached his first sermon ("The Turning of the Wheel of Dharma"); and Kushinagar near Gorakhpur, Uttar Pradesh, where he passed away.

Although the site dates back to the period immediately following the Buddha's passing, the temple complex probably began to take its present shape in the seventh century AD. Even after the sack of Nalanda and the virtual demise of Buddhism in north India, it continued to flourish during the Muslim period. After the sixteenth century it began to decline, falling into the hands of brahmin Hindu priests, who professed to be baffled by its origins when the first British archeologists turned up here early in the nineteenth century. Once excavations had shown the site's true provenance, it was rejuvenated by overseas Buddhists, and is now the most important pilgrimage site of international Buddhism, with all Buddhist nations represented in its many scattered monasteries, temples and shrines.

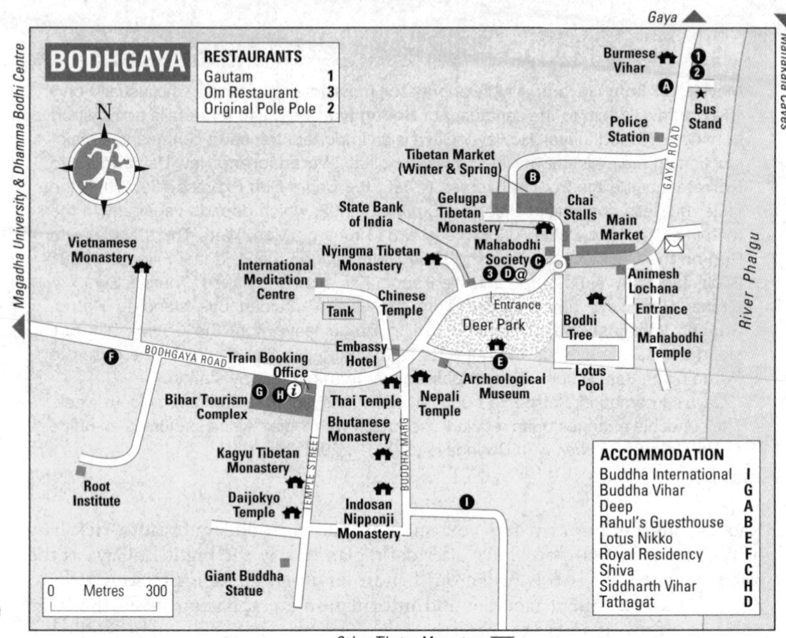

From November to February, Bodhgaya is the home of an animated community of exiled **Tibetans**, sometimes including the Dalai Lama himself, as well as a stream of shaven-headed international Tibetophiles. During this time a huge canvas city emerges on the grounds next to the Gelugpa monastery. Hinayana and Mahayana meditation courses attract others (see box, p.940), while large monasteries from places like Darjeeling bring their international followers to attend ceremonies and lectures under the Bodhi Tree, where Buddhists from around the world rub shoulders. In summer, from mid-March to mid-October, long after the Dalai Lama's official and unofficial entourage has left for the hills, the region becomes oppressively hot, and Bodhgaya returns once again to its quiet ways.

Unfortunately, all is not wholly untroubled at this holiest of holy shrines. The Mahabodhi temple is also sacred to Hindus, who see the Buddha as an incarnation of Vishnu, and, despite strong protests from the Buddhist world, the committee that looks after it is controlled by a Hindu majority. The resultant differences of approach are exacerbated by contrasting forms of worship – while the Buddhists continue a solitary inward approach, Hindus tend towards spectacle and noisy ceremony.

The Mahabodhi temple and the Bodhi Tree

The elegant single spire of the **Mahabodhi temple**, rising to the lofty height of 55m above the trees of its leafy compound at the centre of Bodhgaya, is visible from all over the surrounding countryside. Within the temple complex, which is liberally sprinkled with small stupas and shrines, the main brick temple stands in a hollow encircled by a stone railing dating from the second century BC. Only three-quarters of the railing remains in place; other sections are in the site museum and museums in Kolkata (Calcutta) and London. The area is now a World Heritage Site.

Unlike most popular temples in India, the Mahabodhi temple exudes an atmosphere of peace and tranquillity. Extensively renovated during the nineteenth century, it is supposed to be a replica of the seventh-century structure that in turn stood on the site of Ashoka's original third-century BC shrine. Its busy detail includes niches and short towers on all four corners. Inside the temple, a single chamber holds a large gilded image of the Buddha, while upstairs are a balcony and a small, plain meditation chamber.

At the rear of the temple to the west, the large **Bodhi Tree** grows out of an expansive base, in pleasant grounds that attract scholars and meditators. For all its holiness, this is in fact only a distant offshoot of the original tree under which the Buddha gained enlightenment – the actual tree was destroyed by Ashoka before his conversion to the faith. His daughter Sanghamitra took a sapling to Sri Lanka, and planted it at Anuradhapura, where its offshoots were nurtured, and a sapling was brought back and replanted here. Pilgrims tie coloured thread to its far-reaching branches, decorated by prayer flags, and Tibetans accompany their rituals with long lines of butter lamps. A sandstone slab with carved sides next to the tree is believed to be the **Vajrasana**, or "thunder-seat", upon which the Buddha sat facing east.

The small white **Animesh Lochana temple** to the right of the compound entrance – a miniature version of the main one – marks the spot where the Buddha stood and gazed upon the Bodhi Tree in gratitude. It now obscures the view of the tree, but not the long raised platform known as the **Chankramana** along the northern wall where the Buddha paced in meditation. Remains of a row of columns suggest that it may once have been covered. Numerous ornate stupas from the Pala period (seventh to twelfth centuries) are littered around the grounds. Next to the temple compound to the south is the rectangular Lotus Pool where the Buddha may have bathed.

Entry to the temple compound (daily 5am–9pm) is from the east; shoes are tolerated within the grounds but not inside the temple, and can be left here for a small donation. There is a Rs20 camera fee, Rs300 for video cameras.

Temples and monasteries

Incongruous modern monasteries and temples transform the arid landscape around the Mahabodhi temple compound into Buddhaworld. Some are very simple and others, like the **Thai** temple, complete with its unmistakeable roof, elaborate confections. They are all open from around 7am until noon and between 2pm and 6pm. The Gelugpa **Tibetan** monastery, or *gompa*, is located within the Tibetan quarter northwest of the main shrine. Built over the last four decades, the complex includes a central prayer hall, a large prayer wheel and residential buildings. Each winter, this area of Bodhgaya is transformed by its annual influx of Tibetans, who erect a small market and set up restaurants and cafés. The bigger of the two other Tibetan monasteries further west belongs to the **Kagyu** sect; its spacious main prayer hall is decorated with beautiful modern murals, Buddha images and a large *Dharma Chakra* or Wheel of Law. The other two major Tibetan schools also have monastic representation here – there's a new **Nyingma** *gompa* next to the Chinese temple and a small **Sakya** *gompa* beyond *Hotel Buddha International*.

Next to the Kagyu monastery, the **Daijokyo** monastery captures in concrete some elements of a traditional Japanese temple and belongs to the Nichiren sect. Opposite that, the **Indosan Nipponji temple** has an elegant and simple hut-like roof and a beautiful image of Buddha inside its main hall. Next door, the exquisite **Bhutanese Monastery** features finely painted murals and ceiling mandalas. In a decorative garden at the end of the road, the 25-metre Japanese-style **Giant Buddha Statue** was consecrated by the Dalai Lama in 1989.

Meditation courses in Bodhgaya

Especially during the winter high season, short- and long-term **meditation courses** are available in either of two distinct traditions of Buddhism: Mahayana (the Great Vehicle), epitomized by the various forms of Tibetan Buddhism which spread across China and Japan, evolving along the way; and Hinayana (or Theravada), as practised in Sri Lanka, Thailand and other parts of Southeast Asia. Check noticeboards in the various cafés, and ask at the Root Institute or the Burmese Vihar.

The **Root Institute for Wisdom Culture** (Ⓣ0631/220 0714, Ⓦwww.rootinstitute.com) is a real haven, a semi-monastic *dharma* centre 2km west of the main temple with pleasant gardens, a shrine room, library and accommodation, all enclosed in its own grounds. It organizes residential courses, focusing on the Mahayana tradition. There are drop-in meditation classes, one-day workshops and longer courses on Buddhism, yoga and meditation between October and March. Accommodation is in single or dorm rooms in comfortable blocks, or retreat huts, and good vegetarian food is available. A typical eight-day course, including accommodation, all meals, and course fees, ranges from Rs3745 for a dorm to Rs4970 for a double room with private bath. Practitioners can take on rooms for retreats of up to three months, but these should be booked well in advance. The institute is always looking for volunteers (minimum three months) for general tasks and to help in its charitable school and polio, TB and mobile clinics. All are funded by the Foundation for the Preservation of the Mahayana Tradition, which is also involved in the ambitious Maitreya Project to construct a 128-metre Buddha; originally this was to be built a few kilometres from Bodhgaya, but has been relocated to Kushinagar in Uttar Pradesh.

The **Dhamma Bodhi International Meditation Centre** (Ⓣ0631/220 0437), one of many Vipassana centres in India, lies a few kilometres out of town near Magadha University on Dobi Road. It organizes regular courses throughout the year. Details of all Vipassana courses are available from the International Academy in Maharashtra (Ⓣ02553/228 4076), or you can contact the Vipassana Meditation Centre in England (Harewood End, Hereford HR2 8JS; Ⓣ01989/730234, Ⓦwww.dhamma.org).

The **International Meditation Centre** (Ⓣ0631/220 0707), a couple of hundred metres behind the Chinese temple, is run by Dr Rastrapal Mahathera and holds Vipassana courses, from beginners through to advanced students. A typical day begins at 4.30am and features six hours of group meditation with various breaks in between. Donations are accepted as there are no fixed fees.

Another centre of activity is the **Burmese Vihar**. Although not currently running meditation courses they have some useful information and are involved with voluntary social work projects including schools. Western volunteers are always welcome. The **Thai monastery** runs annual meditation retreats in January and February – contact Gaia House in the UK (Ⓣ01626 333613, Ⓦwww.gaiahouse.co.uk). Friends of the Lotus Mission just behind the Chinese temple offer **Zen** instruction.

Bodhgaya's **Archeological Museum** (daily except Fri 10am–5pm; Rs2), a few hundred metres west of the Mahabodhi temple compound, holds a collection of locally discovered sculpture, and ninth-century Pala bronzes of Hindu and Buddhist deities.

Practicalities

Gaya's international **airport** (Ⓣ0631/428081) is around 12km from Bodhgaya. **Buses** connecting Bodhgaya and Gaya leave from outside Gaya railway station and more frequently from the Kacheri bus and auto-rickshaw stand a couple of kilometres south of the station. **Shared auto-rickshaws** are quicker, even more frequent and, at Rs10, cost just a little more. You'll need to travel back to Gaya to pick up most onward services from Bodhgaya, although two buses a day (7am &

2pm), departing from the Bihar Tourism Complex, run directly to Patna, and a direct bus also leaves for Varanasi from near Mahabodhi temple at 5am. For **train tickets** there's a computerized reservation office next to the Tourism Complex. All buses turn round on the main road north, by the Burmese Vihar and 600m before the pedestrianized temple zone, while auto-rickshaws drop off at the end of the road. The pedestrian area in front of the main Mahabodhi temple has numerous souvenir stalls and travel agents, a small tourist office and throngs of expectant beggars and buskers. The main **tourist office** (Mon–Sat 10am–5pm) is in the Bihar Tourism Complex a couple of hundred metres west of the Thai temple. The State Bank of India (Mon–Fri 10.30am–4pm, Sat 10.30am–1.30pm) has a tiny **foreign-exchange** room. There is also a Bank of India in the *Embassy Hotel* building, while Niranjana Tours and Travels in the pedestrianized zone changes cash and travellers' cheques but at slightly worse than bank rates.

Tours of the area and car rental can be arranged by any of the numerous **travel agents** in Bodhgaya, including Buddha Tours, Middle Way Tours and Potala Tours. The Sri Lankan-based **Mahabodhi Society** (ⓣ0631/220 0742), responsible for reviving Bodhgaya in the nineteenth century, maintains a small complex north-west of the Mahabodhi temple and has staff willing to offer advice on accommodation and **courses**. For **Internet access** try downstairs at the *Shiva Hotel* or one of the handful of places in the pedestrianized zone near the Mahabodhi Temple. For up-to-date local information, check out ⓦwww.bodhgayanews.net.

Accommodation

Bodhgaya has countless mediocre and overpriced **hotels** which, with few exceptions, cash in on the pilgrimage season, charging silly prices from November to February (highest in January); outside of these months, discounts of around fifty percent are available in all but the cheapest places.

Pilgrims usually stay in their respective temples, monasteries or pilgrim guesthouses. Most of the **monastery guesthouses** welcome tourists, but expect them to adhere to the same rules and regulations as the pilgrims, in particular no smoking, alcohol or sex. They are much cheaper than the hotels and provide opportunities to chat to the monks and join in the prayer ceremonies. Note that monasteries are not allowed to define a fixed rate for accommodation; the price codes listed below are based on recommended donations. Wherever you stay, make sure they provide a mosquito net or put up your own.

Monasteries

Bhutanese Monastery Old guesthouse next to the monastery, and full of character. Singles and family rooms, some with private bathroom and hot water ❶–❷

Burmese Monastery (Vihar) Gaya Rd. Set in a pleasant garden, this guesthouse is cramped but cheap. The absence of fans and a/c and the prevalence of biting insects will test your Buddhist indifference to personal comfort. ❶

Daijokyo Temple Near the Giant Buddha Statue ⓣ0631/220 0747. Beautifully maintained Japanese Nichiren Buddhist hotel for pilgrims and tour groups; others are allowed to stay by discretion – telephone first. An excellent kitchen specializes in Japanese cuisine. ❷–❸

Gelugpa Tibetan Monastery At the end of the pedestrian zone, this popular accommodation stands right in the heart of it all. ❷–❸

Mahabodhi Society Pilgrim Rest House ⓣ0631/220 0742. Also called the *Sri Lankan Guest House*, this Mahabodhi Society-run place is popular with pilgrims and often full. There's a dorm and a handful of rooms, plus a reasonable vegetarian canteen. ❶–❷

Root Institute See "Meditation courses in Bodhgaya box", p.940. ❷–❹

Sakya Tibetan Monastery On the edge of town past the *Buddha International* hotel. Quiet, basic and inexpensive double rooms. ❶–❷

Hotels

Buddha International ⓣ0631/220 0506. In the south of town near the Indosan Japanese temple, with an impressive lobby and lawn, and pleasant rooms. ❼–❽

Buddha Vihar Bihar Tourist Complex ⓣ0631/220 0445. Inexpensive but comfortable three-, four-, six,- and ten-bed dorm accommodation with a restaurant. ❶

Deep Guesthouse Out towards the Burmese Vihar ⓣ0631/220 0463. Fairly basic, but clean and well priced throughout the year. ❷

Lotus Nikko Near the museum, and 4km from Gaya airport – call Delhi to book, ⓣ011/2689 3502. ⓔlotusnikkohotels@yahoo.co.in. This peculiar blend of bungalow and concrete tower has attractive, comfortable rooms, some with view, mini-bar and cable TV. ❼–❽

Rahuls Guesthouse At the northwest end of the Tibetan refugee market. Friendly place with big rooms, spacious rooftop and a terrace with views over nearby hills. ❶–❷

Royal Residency Domuhan Rd ⓣ0631/220 0124, ⓕ0631/220 0181. A comfortable three-star hotel with a/c, twin-bedded rooms and more luxurious suites. 24hr room service, an Indian Airlines office and swanky "Japanese Community Bath" – a deep hot relaxing bath you can take with same-sex guests. ❽–❾

Shiva Opposite Mahabodhi Temple ⓣ0631/220 0425. Central and small with a range of comfortable rooms, a restaurant popular with Western tourists, and Internet access. ❻

Siddharth Vihar Bihar Tourist Complex ⓣ0631/220 0445. One of the few options in this price range, with rather shabby but comfortable double rooms with attached bathroom. ❸–❹

Tathagat International Opposite the deer park ⓣ0631/220 0106; ⓦwww.hoteltathagatbodhgaya.net. Clean and comfortable hotel offering decent rooms with balconies. ❹–❻

Eating

There are several small **cafés** in the Mahabodhi temple market complex. Opposite the Burmese Vihar, you'll find excellent cinnamon rolls and apple strudel at the *Gautam* tent restaurant. The various *Pole Pole* restaurants nearby have similar Western-oriented menus and all claim to have been the first; the *Original Pole Pole* is the most pleasant, with good coffee. *Om Restaurant* opposite the Deer Park has standard traveller food and does a good veg Manchurian. During the Tibetan influx (Nov–Feb), Tibetan cafés spring up in the temporary tented market area across the road from the Gelugpa Tibetan Monastery.

Around Bodhgaya: Mahakala Caves

In remote, almost desert-like surroundings on the far side of the Phalgu 18km northeast of Bodhgaya, sit the **Mahakala** (or Dungeshwari) **Caves**, where the Buddha did the severe penance that resulted in the familiar image of him as a skeletal, emaciated figure. After years of extreme self-denial at Mahakala, he realized its futility and walked down to Bodhgaya, where he eventually achieved nirvana under the Bodhi Tree.

A short climb from the base of the impressive cliff leads to a Tibetan monastery and the small caves themselves. A Buddhist shrine inside the main cave is run by Tibetans, although a Hindu priest has recently set himself up in competition. Few tourists make it here and the occasional car or bus that does arrive gets mobbed by urchins and beggars. Offers by international Buddhist communities to help build roads and some sort of infrastructure have been rejected by the Bihar government.

Rajgir

Eighty kilometres northeast of Bodhgaya, the small market town of **RAJGIR** nestles in the rocky hills that witnessed the meditations and teachings of both the Buddha and Mahavira. The capital of the Magadha kingdom before Pataliputra, this was the place where King Bimbisara converted to Buddhism. Today the picturesque and quiet environs, visited by international pilgrims, are also enjoyed as a health resort because of the local **hot springs**. The pools are always open, but can get unpleasantly crowded.

Several sites bear witness to the Buddha's many visits. A Japanese shrine at **Venuvana Vihara** marks the spot where a monastery was built for the Buddha to live in, while it was at **Griddhakuta** (Vulture's Peak) that the Buddha set in motion his second Wheel of Law. Each year, during the three-month rainy season, he preached to his disciples here. The massive modern **Peace Pagoda** built by the Japanese dominates the hill and can be reached by a rather tricky little chairlift, 3km from the centre of Rajgir, which takes fifteen minutes round-trip (daily 8.15am–1pm & 2–5pm, last ticket 4.30pm; Rs20). Griddhakuta is actually halfway down the hill, so you may prefer to wander down from here rather than climb back up to take the chair lift. Look out for the 26 Jain shrines on top of these hills, reached by a challenging trek attempted almost solely by Jain devotees. On an adjacent hill, in the **Saptaparni cave**, the first Buddhist council met to record the teachings of the Buddha after his death.

Rajgir is connected by **bus** to Gaya, Bodhgaya and Patna, which usually involves a change at Bihar Sharif, 25km away. You can also visit Rajgir as part of a long and tiring day-trip including Nalanda and Pawapuri from either Patna or Bodhgaya.

Accommodation

Ajatshatru Near the hot springs ⓣ06112/255027. A basic place run by Bihar Tourism, where it costs Rs51 to stay in a dorm. ❶

Gautam Vihar 300m from the bus station on the road to Nalanda ⓣ06112/255273. Spacious old building with large rooms and verandas run by Bihar Tourism. ❶–❹

Indo Hokke 4km from the bus station and 2km from Kund market, at the end of a dusty road leading from the hot springs ⓣ06112/255245. An ugly concrete exterior plays host to an extraordinary Japanese hotel, where the strange shape and corridors act like a giant air-conditioning unit. There are 20 Japanese-style and 6 Western-style rooms, and an 18-metre-high cylindrical shrine room. The restaurant serves superb state-of-the-art Japanese haute cuisine. ❽–❾

Rajgir Close to the bus station ⓣ06112/255266. Pleasant garden, reasonable if basic rooms and restaurant. Discounts may be available off-season. ❷

Siddharth Kund market ⓣ06112/255216. Cheerful and popular hotel, a couple of kilometres from the town centre. Rooms have carpets and attached bath. ❸–❹

Nalanda and around

The richly adorned towers and the fairy-like turrets, like the pointed hill-tops, are congregated together . . . The stages have dragon projections and coloured eaves, the pearl-red pillars carved and ornamented, the richly adorned balustrades, and the roofs covered with tiles that reflect the light in a thousand shades. These things add to the beauty of the place.

Hiuen Tsang, who spent twelve years at Nalanda as student and teacher.

Founded in the fifth century AD by the Guptas, the great monastic **Buddhist university** of **NALANDA** flourished, with thousands of international students and teachers, until it was sacked by the Afghan invader Bhaktiar Khilji in the twelfth century. Courses taught at Nalanda included the study of scriptures of the Mahayana and Hinayana Schools of Buddhism, Brahmanical and Vedic texts, philosophy, logic, theology, grammar, astronomy, mathematics and medicine. Education was provided free, supported by the revenue from surrounding villages, and by benefactors such as the eighth-century king of Sumatra.

Excavations have revealed nine levels of occupation on the site, dating back to the time of the Buddha, and the Jain founder Mahavira in the sixth century BC. Most of it is now in ruins, but the orderliness and scale of what remains is staggering evidence of the strength of Buddhist civilization in its prime. The site is strewn with the remains of stupas, temples and eleven monasteries, their thick walls impressively intact. Nalanda is now part of the modern Buddhist pilgrimage circuit, but even the casual tourist will appreciate taking the time to walk through the extensive site, or climb its massive 31-metre **stupa** for commanding views. Informative booklets available at the ticket booth render the numerous guides unnecessary. A small alfresco bar inside the grounds serves tea, coffee and soft drinks without the hassle of the touts and beggars at the entrance.

Nalanda Museum (daily except Fri 10am–5pm; Rs5) houses antiquities found here and at Rajgir, including Buddhist and Hindu bronzes and a number of undamaged statues of the Buddha. Other sculptures produced here during the eighth- to tenth-century Pala period are displayed at the Indian Museum in Kolkata, the National Museum in New Delhi and the Patna Museum. **Nava Nalanda Mahavihara**, the Pali postgraduate research institute, houses many rare Buddhist manuscripts, and is devoted to study and research in Pali literature and Buddhism.

Shared jeeps ply regularly between Rajgir and the town of Bihar Sharif, 35km to the northeast, stopping at the turning to Nalanda from where an assortment of transport, including shared tongas, is available for the remaining 2km to the gates of the site. An old colonial villa 300m past the site is run as a PWD **resthouse** (❶), offering large double rooms with veranda, lounge, gardens and simple food.

East of Nalanda

Eighteen kilometres east of Nalanda, at **PAWAPURI**, Mahavir, the founder of Jainism, is said to have gained enlightenment. He died and was cremated here around 500 BC, and the site is now a major draw for Jain pilgrims, who come to visit the **Jalamandir**, a white marble temple in the centre of a lotus pond. To reach Pawapuri from Rajgir, change at Bihar Sharif.

A further 80km east of Pawapuri, at **MUNGER**, is the **Bihar School of Yoga** (Ⓣ06344/222430; Ⓦwww.yogamag.net). Led by Swami Niranjananda Saraswati, the ashram is the world's first accredited yoga university and runs popular four-month yoga courses in English from October to January, though short stays are also possible. Buses run from Bihar Sharif, or the ashram can help arrange transport. It also has a sister school at Rikhia in Jharkhand (see p.946).

Jharkhand

On the eastern extremities of the Vindhya hills, at the northern fringes of the Deccan, lies the rugged **Chotanagpur plateau** which makes up **JHARKHAND.** An independent state since 2000 after years of agitation by its largely Adivasi population, it yields 36 percent of India's minerals, and produces some of the cheapest iron and steel in the country. The government has grand plans for its infrastructure, and for investment in IT, education and tourism. Roads are also noticeably better than in Bihar, and residents have a more upbeat attitude to their future than their neighbours to the north. Change will take a lot of time, however – in reality, Jharkhand continues to suffer from lawlessness and extreme poverty, and inefficient government has meant that the state had yet to spend its full budget five years on from secession from Bihar.

You'll need to pass through **Ranchi**, the cheerless state capital, to reach Jharkhand's prime attraction, the **Palamau National Park**. Sadly, the beautiful forests of the park have been damaged by years of drought and its tigers are now severely endangered. Other forest reserves and parks pepper the state, including

Hazaribagh National Park in the north. As bandits still patrol some of these areas, it's vital to check the security situation before venturing out, and to avoid travelling at night.

Ranchi

Once the pleasant summer capital of Bihar, **RANCHI** is now a rather ugly city, though you'll probably need to stay here on your way to Palamau National Park. There is a small museum detailing the life and history of Jharkhand's tribes at the **Jharkhand Tribal Research Institute** (Mon–Sat 10am–5pm; free). The seventeenth-century Hindu **Jagannath Temple** is just under 10km away on a hilltop, and the beautiful **Hundru Falls** and nearby **Jonha Falls** can be visited in a morning if you're after some respite from the city.

Several major **trains** connect Ranchi with Kolkata, Delhi, Patna, Daltonganj (for Palamau National Park) and Dhanbad, some terminating at Hatia, 7km from town. You can fly from Ranchi's **airport** with Indian Airlines to Kolkata, Delhi, Mumbai and Patna and Lucknow; there are plans to upgrade it to an international airport. The government **bus stand** near the railway station serves Bodhgaya, Gaya and Patna; Daltonganj is reached from the Rathu Road terminus. Services to all other destinations leave from Khadgarh bus station, 3km from the railway station. Ashok Travels run a **luxury bus** to Patna from the *Ranchi Ashok* (see below).

Ranchi's **tourist office**, at 5 Main Rd (Mon–Sat 9am–6pm; ⓣ0651/230 0646), offers little more than dusty brochures. Ashok Travels at the *Ranchi Ashok* (daily 7am–7.30pm; ⓣ0651/248 0759) and Holiday Travellers, Patel Chowk (ⓣ0651/220 2615), can arrange local sightseeing, overnight trips to Palamau National Park and chauffeur hire. Most of Ranchi's facilities can be found along Main Road including the **post office**, State Bank of India, and IDBI Bank **ATM**; there are **Internet** places on Station Road.

Most of Ranchi's **hotels** are along, or just off, the long Main Road. *Embassy* (ⓣ0651/246 0813; ❷–❸) is one of the better budget hotels in town. The Raj-style *BNR (South Eastern Railway)* (ⓣ0651/246 0584; ❹–❽) has pleasant gardens and bungalows with sizeable rooms, while the justifiably popular *Kwality Inn* (ⓣ0651/246 0128; ❻–❽) has one of the best restaurants in town – the *Nook* (see below). *Yuvaraj Palace Hotel* (ⓣ0651/248 0326; ❽–❾) in the Doranda district is Ranchi's best hotel, with 25 clean, a/c rooms and a multi-cuisine restaurant. Nearby, *Ranchi Ashok* (ⓣ0651/248 0759, ⓦwww.theashokgroup.com; ❽–❾) is an efficient exception to the generally poorly run government chain. The *Yogoda Math Ashram* on Paramahansa Yogananda Path (ⓣ0651/246 0071; ⓦwww.ranchi.com/tourism/views/yogodasatsanga.asp) is a tranquil place to stay for a few days of solitude if you're seriously interested in meditation.

There are lots of reasonable **restaurants** off Ranchi's Main Road, including *Min Min's Chinese* and the vegetarian *Vegica's*, near the Sujata cinema. *Kaveri* at the Church Complex, Main Road, is another reasonably priced vegetarian restaurant despite its upmarket ambience. *Krishna*, below it, serves cheaper food and decent Chinese in its *Maharaja* restaurant, while *Sunny Restaurant*, on Station Road, serves cheap south Indian snacks. Finally, *The Nook* at *Kwality Inn* (see above) serves inexpensive, tasty food and has friendly staff and a buzzy atmosphere.

North of Ranchi

Just over 100km north of Ranchi lies **HAZARIBAGH NATIONAL PARK**, a mix of meadow, grassland and low hills peppered with streams, and inhabited by deer, wild boar, leopards and tigers. The park entrance is 19km north of Hazaribagh, where you can **stay** in basic but clean rooms at the *Hotel Upkar* (☎06546/22246; ❷–❹) or the *Circuit House* (☎06546/22317; ❶–❸). To arrange a tourist cottage inside the park, contact the Field Director (☎06546/22339; ❷–❹). There's a **tourist information centre** in Paryatan Bhawan (in town), and daily buses run from Ranchi.

Around 190km northeast of Ranchi, **PARASNATH** is the most important Jain pilgrimage site in eastern India, with 24 temples representing the Jain *tirthankaras* clustered around the highest point in the state (1450m). You can stay at one of the pilgrims' *dharamshalas* at the site itself or there's a *Tourist Bungalow* (☎06532/232361; ❶–❷) in nearby **Madhuban**. Parasnath is connected to Patna and Kolkata by train and to Ranchi by bus.

At **DEOGARH**, further northeast, you'll find the 22 Hindu temples of **Baidyanath Dham**, a site that heaves with pilgrims during the *Shravan* festival in July and August. *Yatrik Hotel* (☎06432/232299; ❷–❹), near Tower in town, has clean rooms and a restaurant and houses Yatrik Travels, which can arrange transport and sightseeing. Jasidih Junction railway station, 10km south of Deogarh, is accessible from Delhi, Kolkata and Patna.

A twenty-minute bus or taxi ride from Deogarh town takes you to the **Bihar School of Yoga ashram** at **RIKHIA**, where Swami Satyananda Saraswati has adopted a hundred villages and educates the village girls and women. If you're interested in experiencing genuine ashram life, you can apply to stay here (☎06432/232870; write to Bihar School of Yoga, PO Rikhia, Dist Deogarh, Jharkhand, 814112).

Palamau (Betla) National Park

In a remote and lawless corner of Jharkhand, 170km west of Ranchi, the beautiful forests of the **PALAMAU NATIONAL PARK** cover around 1000 square kilometres of hilly terrain rising south towards Madhya Pradesh. Though it's part of the **Project Tiger** scheme, Palamau has been hard hit by drought and tiger sightings are rare. You are more likely to see elephants, antelope, bison and wild boar, whether from one of the park's observation towers or on the back of an elephant; starting early will increase your chances.

Practicalities

The official headquarters of the park, **Daltonganj**, are served by direct buses and a branch railway line from Ranchi. Regular buses make the 25km journey from Daltonganj to **Betla**, the park's entry point. If you're coming from Ranchi, you could try to change buses at the turn-off and get to Betla without going through Daltonganj.

Next to the Betla gates is an **information centre**, where entry tickets can be purchased (Rs100; Rs60 for a jeep) and elephant rides and **accommodation** arranged; alternatively book in advance with the Field Director (☎06562/222 650). In Betla, there's a comfortable central resthouse (❶–❷), or, if that's full of visiting civil servants, you could try the basic *Janata* and *Shyama* lodges (❶); the *Naihar* (❶–❹), 300m from the park gates, which has a decent garden and restaurant; or the *Van Vihar* (☎06562/282 2111; ❷–❹), run by Bihar Tourism, which has spacious rooms and a restaurant. Simple **cafés** can be found opposite the gates at Betla.

Travel details

Trains

Gaya to: Allahabad (4 daily; 4hr 20min–6hr 30min); Dehra Dun (1 daily; 25hr); Delhi (9 daily; 12–15hr); Haridwar (1 daily; 23hr); Kolkata; 5–6 daily; 6–13hr); Lucknow (3 daily; 12–13hr); Mughal Sarai (13 daily; 2hr 20min–5hr); Mumbai (1 daily; 31hr); Patna (4 daily; 2hr 30min); Puri (2 daily; 15hr 30min–18hr 10min); Ranchi (2 daily; 8hr 30min); Sasaram (10 daily; 1–3hr); Varanasi (3 daily; 4hr–5hr 30min).
Jasidih to: Delhi (6 weekly, 16–21hr); Kolkata (6 weekly, 5–6hr); Patna (6 weekly, 3hr 30min).
Patna to: Agra (1 daily; 18hr 30min); Allahabad (8–9 daily; 5hr–8hr 45min); Chennai (3 weekly; 38hr 30min–40hr); Delhi (8 daily; 12hr 40min–24hr); Gaya (3 daily; 2hr 30min); Guwahati (3 daily; 19–25hr); Kolkata (3–4 daily; 8hr 10min–13hr); Lucknow (4–5 daily; 5hr 30min–15hr); Mumbai (2–3 daily; 31–36hr); Puri (1 weekly; 19hr); Ranchi (3 daily; 11–13hr 35min); Varanasi (2–3 daily; 3–5hr).
Ranchi to: Allahabad (2 daily; 13–18hr); Daltonganj (3–4 daily; 5hr 30min–8hr 30min); Delhi (2 daily; 23–29hr); Dhanbad (2–3 daily; 3hr 40min–6hr 10min); Gaya (2–3 daily; 4hr–8hr 30min); Kolkata (5 weekly; 8hr 30min); Patna (3 daily; 11–13hr 30min).

Buses

Bodhgaya to: Gaya (hourly; 45min); Patna (2 daily; 5hr); Rajgir (hourly; 2hr 30min); Ranchi (1 daily; 9hr); Varanasi (1 daily; 6–7hr).
Gaya to: Bodhgaya (hourly; 45min); Mughal Sarai (6 daily; 5hr); Patna (hourly; 3hr); Ranchi (8 daily; 8hr); Sasaram (8 daily; 3hr); Varanasi (6 daily; 5hr 30min).
Patna to: Gaya (hourly; 3–4hr); Ranchi (4 daily; 12--14hr); Raxaul (18 daily; 6hr); Vaishali (2 daily; 3hr); Varanasi (4 daily; 6hr 30min).
Rajgir to: Bihar Sharif (hourly; 1hr).
Ranchi to: Bodhgaya (1 daily; 9hr); Daltonganj (4 daily; 8hr); Dhanbad (6 daily; 5hr); Gaya (8 daily; 8hr); Parasnath (hourly; 6hr); Patna (4 daily; 12–14hr).
Vaishali to: Chakia (hourly; 3hr).

Flights

Patna to: Bagdogra (3 weekly; 45min); Delhi (4 daily; 1hr 25min–2hr 30min); Guwahati (3 weekly; 2hr); Kolkata (1–2 daily; 1–2hr); Lucknow (1–2 daily; 55min); Mumbai (4 daily; 3hr 45min–5hr 40min); Ranchi (4 weekly; 45min); Varanasi (1 daily; 40min).
Gaya to: Kolkata (2 weekly; 55min).

CHAPTER 15

Highlights

* **Rumtek** One of Sikkim's most venerated monasteries, Rumtek is home to the Black Hat sect, and hosts a spectacular festival in February. See p.961

* **Maenam mountain** A day-trek through an ancient forest to the summit of the mountain; you may be lucky enough to spot deer and red panda. See p.964

* **Pemayangtse** A wonderful seventeenth-century monastery perched on a high ridge facing Darjeeling. See p.966

* **Pelling** This sleepy town has gentle walks to nearby monasteries, and stunning views of Kanchenjunga. See p.968

* **Dzongri Trail** Trek through rhododendrons and across high alpine meadows close to Kanchenjunga, the third-highest mountain in the world. See p.970

* **Tashiding** A monastic complex on a conical hill with marvellous views. See p.973

* **Varshey Rhododendron Sanctuary** Magnificent views and gentle trails through a botanical paradise. See p.974

△ Rice terraces, Sikkim

Sikkim

The tiny and beautiful state of **SIKKIM** lies just south of Tibet, sandwiched between Nepal to the west and Bhutan to the east. Measuring just 65km by 115km, its landscape ranges from sweltering deep valleys just 300m above sea level to lofty snow peaks such as Kanchenjunga (Kanchendzonga to the locals), which, at 8586m, is the third-highest mountain in the world. A small but growing network of tortuous roads penetrate this rugged Himalayan wilderness, but they take a massive battering every monsoon, with large and frequent landslides disrupting communications.

For centuries Sikkim was an isolated, independent Buddhist kingdom, until war with China in the early 1960s led the Indian government to realize the area's worth as a crucial corridor between Tibet and Bangladesh. As a result of its annexation by India in 1975, Sikkim has experienced dramatic changes. Now a fully-fledged Indian state, it is predominantly Hindu, with a population made up of 75 percent **Nepalese Gurungs**, and less than twenty percent **Lepchas**, its former rulers. Smaller proportions survive of **Bhutias**, of Tibetan stock, and **Limbus**, also possibly of Tibetan origin, who gave the state its name – *sukh-im*, "happy homeland". Nepali is now the lingua franca and the Nepalese are socially and politically the most dominant people in the state. The ruling minority in neighbouring Bhutan, having observed this transition with alarm, has adopted an intransigent and aggressive stance towards the Nepalese, with ugly violence on both sides and the final expulsion of all ethnic Nepalese from Bhutan. The civil war across the western border in Nepal has caused some jitters in Sikkim but so far the state remains unaffected. Instead, the belief that lucrative trade routes across the border into Tibet are about to re-open has fuelled a growing optimism. Sikkim continues to hold a special status within the Indian union, exempt from income tax and attracting government subsidy. Although only Sikkimese can hold major shares in property and businesses, partnerships with Indian (non-Sikkimese) entrepreneurs, and subsidies to indigenous Sikkimese light industry have led to prosperity that's evident as soon as you cross the border from West Bengal.

Historically, culturally and spiritually, Sikkim's strongest links are with **Tibet**. The main draws for visitors are the state's off-the-beaten-track **trekking** and its many **monasteries**, over two hundred in all, mostly belonging to the ancient **Nyingmapa** sect. **Pemayangtse** in west Sikkim is the most important historically, and houses an extraordinary wooden mandala depicting Guru Rinpoche's Heavenly Palace. **Tashiding**, a Nyingmapa monastery built in 1717, surrounded by prayer flags and *chortens* and looking across to snowcapped peaks, is considered Sikkim's holiest. **Rumtek** is the seat of the **Gyalwa Karmapa** – head of the **Karma Kagyu** lineage – and probably the most influential monastery in Sikkim.

The problems in Nepal have led to a tourism boom in Sikkim, with trekkers searching for alternative Eastern Himalayan routes. The capital, **Gangtok**, is home to a bewildering array of trekking agents only too happy to take your money in dollars – it's also the place to get hold of permits for Sikkim's restricted areas.

Sikkim's gigantic mountain walls and steep wooded hillsides, drained by torrential rivers such as the **Teesta** and the **Rangit**, are a botanist's dream. The lower slopes abound in **orchids**; sprays of cardamom carpet the forest floor, and the land is rich with apple orchards, orange groves and terraced paddy fields (to the Tibetans, this was **Denzong**, "the land of rice"). At higher altitudes, monsoon mists cling to huge tracts of lichen-covered forests, where countless varieties of rhododendron carpet the hillsides and giant magnolia trees punctuate the deep verdant cover. Higher still, approaching the Tibetan

Permits and restrictions

Though foreigners need to obtain an **Inner Line Permit** (ILP) to visit Sikkim, getting one is a mere, if irritating, formality. The easiest way is to request a permit when applying for your Indian visa, though it is also possible to pick up permits in India at the offices listed below. Permits are also instantly available at the **Sikkim border** at Rangpo; go to the tourist office for an application form and then cross the road to have it registered by the police. If you are picking up your permit after arrival in India, you'll need two passport photographs and photocopies of your passport and visa details.

Permits are date-specific and usually valid for two weeks from entry into the state, which allows enough time to visit the towns and villages at a fairly leisurely pace but places constraints on time if trekking. However, permits are usually renewable for a further two weeks: **extensions** can be obtained at the Foreigner's Regional Registration Office, Tibet Road, Gangtok, and are also available through the superintendents of police at Mangan, Ghezing and Namchi, the capitals of the three other districts.

Certain areas, like Tsomgo (also known as Changu or Tsangu) Lake, Yumthang and Dzongri, require **restricted area permits** (see box on p.953) and only allow entry to foreigners in groups accompanied by representatives of approved travel agents. As well as Gangtok and its surrounds in east Sikkim, the general Sikkim permit covers most areas in west and south Sikkim apart from the high-altitude treks, and areas towards the borders; some areas remain completely off-limits to foreigners. Despite the regulations, Sikkim is slowly but surely opening up and the trend looks set to continue.

Areas covered by Sikkim permit

Eastern Sikkim: Gangtok, Rumtek Phodong and Labrang..

Northern Sikkim: Mangan up to Singhik.

Western and southern Sikkim: Jorethang, Namchi, Dentam, Hilley, Varshey, Uttarey, Ravangla, Legship, Ghezing, Pelling, Pemayangtse, Tashiding, Khecheopalri and Yoksum.

Restricted areas open only to group tours

Eastern Sikkim: Tsomgo Lake.

Northern Sikkim: Chungthang, Lachung, Yumthang, Lachen, Thangu and Dzongu. For the trek to Green Lake, permission must be sought from Delhi at least three months in advance (more easily organized through a reputable Gangtok trekking agent).

Western Sikkim: Dzongri, parts of the Singalila Range.

Offices in India issuing permits

Airport immigration At the four main entry points: Delhi, Mumbai, Kolkata (Calcutta), Chennai.

Foreigners' Regional Registration Offices In Delhi, Mumbai, Kolkata (Calcutta) and Chennai. Also in Darjeeling on Laden La Road (see Darjeeling, p.911 for details).

Resident Commissioner Sikkim House, 14 Panchsheel Marg, Chanakyapuri, New Delhi ⓣ011/2611 5346.

Sikkim Tourist Centre SNTC Bus Stand, Hill Cart Road, Siliguri ⓣ0354/432646.

Sikkim Tourist Information Centre Sikkim House, 4/1 Middleton St, Kolkata (Calcutta) ⓣ033/2281 5328.

plateau, larch and dwarf rhododendron give way to meadows abundant with gentians and potentilla. Sikkim's forests and wilderness areas are inhabited by a wealth of fauna including elusive snow leopards, tahr (wild ass on the Tibet plateau), *bharal* or blue sheep, black bear, flying squirrels and the symbol of Sikkim – the endangered **red panda**.

The **best time to visit** Sikkim is between mid-March and June but especially March, April and May, when the rhododendrons and orchids bloom – although temperatures can be high at this time of year, especially in the valleys. Any earlier than that, and lingering winter snow can make high-altitude trekking arduous. During the monsoons, from the end of June until early September, rivers and roads become impassable, though plants nurtured by the incessant rain erupt again into bloom towards the end of August. October (when orchids bloom once again) and November tend to have the clearest weather of all. As December progresses, it gets bitterly cold at high altitudes, and remains that way until early March, despite long periods of clear weather.

Some history

No one knows quite when or how the **Lepchas** – or the Rong, as they call themselves – came to Sikkim, but their roots can be traced back to the animist Nagas of the Indo-Burmese border. **Buddhism**, which arrived from Tibet in the thirteenth century, took its distinctive Sikkimese form four centuries later, when three Tibetan monks of the old Nyingmapa order, disenchanted with the rise of the reformist Gelugpas, migrated south and gathered at Yoksum in western Sikkim. Having consulted the oracle, they sent to Gangtok for a certain Phuntsog Namgyal, whom they crowned as the first **chogyal** or "righteous king" of Denzong in 1642. Both the secular and religious head of Sikkim, he was soon recognized by Tibet, and set about sweeping reforms. His domain was far larger than today's Sikkim, taking in Kalimpong and parts of western Bhutan.

Over the centuries, territory was lost to the Bhutanese, the Nepalese and the **British**. Sikkim originally ceded Darjeeling to the East India Company as a spa in 1817, but was forced to give up all claim to it in 1861 when the kingdom was declared a protectorate of the British. **Tibet**, which perceived Sikkim as a vassalage, objected and invaded in 1886, but a small British force sent in 1888 to Lhasa helped the British consolidate their hold. By importing workers from Nepal to work in the tea plantations of Sikkim, Darjeeling and Kalimpong, the British sought to diminish the strong Tibetan influence and helped alter the ethnic make-up of the region, with the new migrants soon outnumbering the indigenous population.

After Indian Independence, the reforming and intensely spiritual eleventh chogyal, **Tashi Namgyal**, strove hard until his death in 1962 to prevent the dissolution of his kingdom. Officially Sikkim was a protectorate of India, and the role of India became increasingly crucial, with the Chinese military build-up along the northern borders that culminated in an actual invasion early in the 1960s. His son **Palden Thondup**, the last chogyal, married as his second wife an American, Hope Cook, whose reforms as gyalmo (queen) did not prove popular and also came to irritate the Indian government. The embattled chogyal eventually succumbed to the demands of the Nepalese majority, and Sikkim was **annexed** by India in 1975 after a referendum with an overwhelming 97-percent majority. The chogyal remained as a figurehead until his death in 1981.

The state continues to be treated with care by the Indian government, partly through a lingering sense of unease amongst the disaffected Sikkimese minority and an increasingly complex ethnic patchwork but, more importantly, because Sikkim remains a bone of contention between India and China despite huge inroads in cross border diplomacy. Today, the **Sikkim Democratic Front** forms the government of Sikkim; generous government subsidies and loans have helped to ensure that life remains generally contented, while a huge programme of road building is bringing benefits to remote communities.

Trekking in Sikkim

Although the potential is huge, **trekking** in Sikkim remains restricted, confined to certain routes in the west and recently opened areas in the north. The fact that trekking permits do not necessarily extend your total stay in Sikkim places a constraint on time, while high charges, payable in US dollars, ensure that only the well-heeled get to see certain areas.

Trekking permits (aka **protected area permits**) are only available from the Sikkim Tourism offices in Gangtok (see p.956) and Delhi (see p.951). Trekking or tour operators in Gangtok (see p.955) usually make the necessary arrangements; check papers before you set off, as the slightest error can lead to problems later on. Trekking parties consist of a minimum of two people; tour operators charge an official daily rate that ranges from $35 to $100 per head depending on the route.

The two high-altitude treks currently on offer are the **Dzongri–Goecha La** route (plus its variation starting from Uttarey) and the **Singalila ridge**, both detailed on pp.970–971 and pp.916–917. Treks from **Lachen to Green Lake** are possible, but permission must be obtained from Delhi (most easily arranged through a Gangtok agent) at least three months in advance. At the moment Dzongri still bears the brunt of the trekking industry in the state, and the pressure is beginning to tell severely on the environment (see p.973). Softer, low-level treks such as the rhododendron trails around Vershey are a pleasant alternative (and don't require special permits) and there are numerous other rewarding possibilities throughout the state.

A recent edict from the Sikkim Government states that for purposes of **mountaineering**, all peaks under 20,000 feet no longer require special permits but it is too early to tell what this really means, as the Sikkim and Central governments often seem to contradict each other. Although mountains such as Tangchung Khang (6010m) and Jopuno (5935m) were designated as "trekking peaks" years ago, bureaucratic wrangles mean that permission to climb them has never been forthcoming; contact agents such as Namgyal and Khangri in Gangtok for an update (see p.955).

The **Ecotourism and Conservation Society of Sikkim** (ECOSS), State Archives Annexe, Zero Point, Gangtok (☎03592/228211), is an independent organization seeking to develop sustainable tourism here, while protecting natural resources, the environment and traditional social customs and culture. One of their key aims is to ensure remote and marginalized communities benefit from the part they play in the process. For more information check out their website Ⓦwww.sikkiminfo.net/ecoss.

Gangtok

Capital of Sikkim, the overgrown hill town of **GANGTOK** (1870m) occupies a rising ridge in the southeast of the state, on what used to be a busy trade route into Tibet. Due to rapid development and new wealth, an ugly assortment of concrete multistorey buildings is growing virtually unchecked, and the town retains only a few traditional Sikkimese elements. However, a short amble soon leads you away from the hectic central market area, while longer walks out into the surrounding countryside provide glimpses of the full grandeur of the Himalayas. On a good day, you can see Kanchenjunga and the fluted pyramid of Siniolchu.

Although modern Gangtok epitomizes the recent changes in Sikkimese culture and politics, its Buddhist past is the root of its appeal for visitors, evident in the collection at the **Institute of Tibetology** and the charming **Enchey Monastery**, as well as the impressive **Rumtek Monastery**, 24km east of town. However, the **palace** used by the chogyals between 1894 and 1975 is now out of bounds, occupied by the new regime and not acknowledged as part of

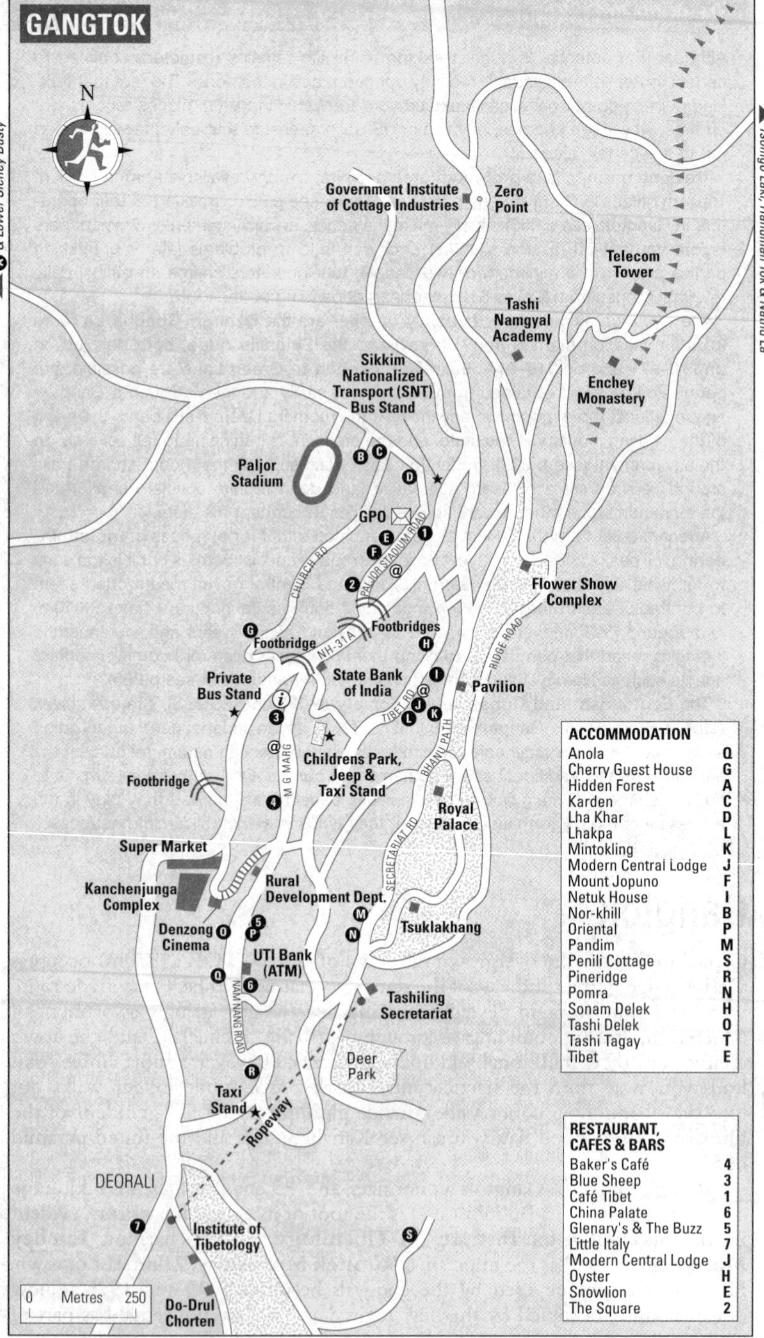
GANGTOK
N
Tashi View Point, Phodong & Mangan
A & Lower Sichey Busty
Tsomgo Laki, Hanuman Tok & Nathu La
Government Institute of Cottage Industries
Zero Point
Telecom Tower
Tashi Namgyal Academy
Enchey Monastery
Sikkim Nationalized Transport (SNT) Bus Stand
Paljor Stadium
GPO
PALJOR STADIUM ROAD
CHURCH RD
Flower Show Complex
Footbridges
Footbridge
NH-31A
RIDGE ROAD
State Bank of India
Pavilion
Private Bus Stand
TIBET RD
M G MARG
BHANU PATH
Childrens Park, Jeep & Taxi Stand
Footbridge
Royal Palace
SECRETARIAT RD
Super Market
Kanchenjunga Complex
Rural Development Dept.
Tsuklakhang
Denzong Cinema
UTI Bank (ATM)
NAM NANG ROAD
Tashiling Secretariat
Deer Park
Taxi Stand
Ropeway
DEORALI
Institute of Tibetology
Do-Drul Chorten
0 Metres 250
T, Rumtek, Darjeeling & Siliguri
ACCOMMODATION
Anola Q
Cherry Guest House G
Hidden Forest A
Karden C
Lha Khar D
Lhakpa L
Mintokling K
Modern Central Lodge J
Mount Jopuno F
Netuk House I
Nor-khill B
Oriental P
Pandim M
Penili Cottage S
Pineridge R
Pomra N
Sonam Delek H
Tashi Delek O
Tashi Tagay T
Tibet E
RESTAURANT, CAFÉS & BARS
Baker's Café 4
Blue Sheep 3
Café Tibet 1
China Palate 6
Glenary's & The Buzz 5
Little Italy 7
Modern Central Lodge J
Oyster H
Snowlion E
The Square 2

Sikkimese heritage. Sikkim's pride and joy, the **orchid**, is nurtured at several sites in and around Gangtok, and celebrated every spring in a flower show held at the Flower Show Complex near **White Hall**, the governor's residence on the ridge above town.

Arrival and information

Gangtok is not served directly by rail; most travellers arrive by **Jeep** from **Siliguri** in West Bengal (4hr 30min; see p.906), the transport centre for the railhead at **New Jalpaiguri** and for **Bagdogra** airport. Shared Jeeps also run from **Darjeeling** and **Kalimpong**. A **helicopter** service, run in conjunction with Sikkim Tourism, connects Bagdogra airport with Gangtok (Rs1500).

All **buses** run by **Sikkim Nationalized Transport** (SNT), the state carrier, use the **SNT bus stand** on Paljor Stadium Road, but passengers may prefer to be dropped off earlier at the main crossing on MG Marg near the State Bank

Trekking and tour operators

All **high-altitude treks** in Sikkim have to be conducted in groups and arranged through travel agents, who will also secure the necessary permits. Prices may vary a little between agents: high altitude treks for three to five people cost $40–100 per person per day, while low-altitude treks for three to four people cost around $35 per person per day in large groups, rising to $80 per person for small groups.

Blue Sky Tours & Travels Tourism Building, MG Marg ⓣ03592/225113. Very helpful agency which specializes in Jeep safaris and are especially good at organising north Sikkim Jeep itineraries.

Himalayan Footprints Tibet Road, Near IPR ⓣ03592/280433, ⓦwww.trekinindia.com. Exellent choice for nature tours and treks, as well as village homestays.

Khangri Tours & Treks Tibet Road ⓣ03592/226050, ⓦwww.khangri.com. Tsering Dorjee is an experienced trekking guide and a keen amateur botanist who can arrange cultural and monastic tours and treks throughout Sikkim, including the 10-day return trip to Green Lake (which requires at least three months notice for a permit).

Marcopolo World Travels PS Road ⓣ03592/204116, ⓦwww.worldmarcopolo.com. The experienced Karma Tashi runs a flexible and reliable tour operation; offerings include high-altitude treks and Jeep safaris to North Sikkim.

Namgyal Treks & Tours Tibet Road ⓣ03592/203701 or mobile ⓣ9434/033122, ⓦwww.namgyaltreks.net. Namgyal Sherpa is a Nepal specialist and a highly capable and experienced high-altitude trek and expedition operator (and there aren't many in Gangtok), recognized by both the Sikkim and Central Government tourist offices.

Sikkim Adventure 6th Mile, Tadong ⓣ03592/251250, ⓔsikkimorchid@hotmail.com. Sailesh Pradhan runs a plant nursery and is an extremely knowledgeable and enthusiastic botanist and specialist guide for trips focused around Sikkim's rich flora.

Sikkim Tours & Travels Church Road ⓣ03592/202188, ⓦwww.sikkimtours.com. The owner Lukendra is an extremely helpful and experienced travel operator who specializes in nature tours and photography, bird-watching and treks.

Tashila Tours and Travels Below TNSS School Hall ⓣ03592/229842, ⓦwww.tashila.com/sikkim.html. Experienced operator offering trekking, mountain biking and two-hour to three-day river-rafting expeditions from Singtam to Rangpo, as well as yak safaris, angling and monastery tours.

Vajra Adventure Tours Kyitsel House, Arithang Road ⓣ03592/229676, ⓔslg_vatours@sancharnet.in. A very competitively priced and reliable operator, good for transport and treks; the owner comes from Tsokha near Dzongri and specializes in treks in the area.

of India, which is more convenient for the tourist office and the hotels around the bazaar and Tibet Road. Non-SNT buses stop at the **private bus stand**, located on a small slip road just off the National Highway. Shared taxis and Jeeps from Kalimpong and Darjeeling also stop here; Jeeps and taxis from other destinations in Sikkim terminate at the **Nam Nang** taxi stand, at the far end of MG Marg. With terminals at the Secretariat, Nam Nang and Deorali, the new **ropeway** (daily 8am–6pm) provides a spectacular view of the southern city but is an expensive way to get around by local standards (Rs30 one-way, Rs50 round trip) and is not particularly useful for most accommodation. While it's scheduled to run every twelve minutes, in practice it waits to fill up before moving on. The numerous **shared local taxis** are the most common way of commuting along the main highway, with a ride from central Gangtok to the suburb of Deorali costing around Rs10 per seat. After 9pm taxis become scarce, but reserved taxis are available from stands near the SNT Bus Stand and Post Office, the Private Bus Stand, the supermarket, Nam Nang and Deorali.

Sikkim Tourism's **tourist information centre**, MG Marg (mid-March to early June & mid-Sept to Nov daily 9am–7pm; mid-June to mid-Sept & Dec–Feb Mon–Sat 10am–4pm; ⓣ03592/221634), provides maps and will advise on arranging transport. This is also the place to extend your Sikkim permit from the initial 15-days. For details of **trekking permits**, see p.953. Sikkim Tourism also sell tickets for their spectacular **helicopter flights** (Rs1200–7000) to West Sikkim, Yumthang, Gangtok and, the most breathtaking of them all, a ninety-minute Kanchenjunga trip up the Zemu Glacier. Note that cameras aren't allowed on most routes.

Changing money is limited to the State Bank of India (SBI) near the tourist office at the junction of NH-31A and MG Marg, and a couple of licensed private bureaus including Silk Route Tours & Travels at the *Green Hotel* on MG Marg, and Namgyal Treks & Tours off Tibet Road. While the SBI restricts itself to changing dollars and sterling, Namgyal and Silk Route will change several currencies. **Credit card** facilities are increasing in Gangtok: the UTI Bank on MG Marg, opposite the *Tashi Delek Hotel*, has an ATM which takes Visa, Mastercard and Maestro; there are other UTI ATMs in aNew Market, Deorali and Tadong.

The STN Memorial Hospital, on the junction of NH-31A and Paljor Stadium Road, has a 24hr emergency wing and an ambulance service (ⓣ03592/222944). The main **post office** lies further down Paljor Stadium Road just beyond *Tibet Hotel*. The town is brimming with **email** services for around Rs30 per hour – try the Web Centre, NH-31A near *Café Tibet*.

Accommodation

Gangtok's **hotels** are expensive in high season – broadly speaking April to June and September to November – but at other times offer discounted rates. Rooms with views are invariably more expensive. As the town spreads so does the choice of accommodation, with good hotels springing up along the highway at Deorali and Tadong and there are a growing number of alternatives away from the bustle but within striking distance of Gangtok.

Central Gangtok

Anola MG Marg, New Market ⓣ03592/203238. Sikkimese-run hotel with plain, if somewhat expensive, rooms and a restaurant that serves good Sikkimese food. ❺

Cherry Guest House Rai Cottage Complex, Church Rd ⓣ03592/209652, ⓔtttcherry@yahoo.com. Handy for the private bus stand, this immaculate place set in a private courtyard has beautifully presented rooms and large verandas with views. ❹–❺

Karden Paljor Stadium Rd ⓣ03592/221332. Bengali-run hotel with clean rooms and a quiet location above the stadium. ❸–❹

Lha Khar Opposite SNT, Paljor Stadium Rd ⓣ03592/225708. Clean rooms in a well-run guesthouse convenient for the bus stand; its restaurant has a reputation for good Sikkimese cooking. ❸–❹

Lhakpa Tibet Rd ⓣ03592/223002. Cheap, atmospheric hotel-restaurant above the main bazaar. A bar as much as a restaurant, it serves Indian, Tibetan and Sikkimese food with prior notice. ❷

Mintokling Bhanu Path (Tashiling Rd) ⓣ03592/224226, ⓔmintokling@hotmail.com. Sikkimese family-run guesthouse with a lovely garden, quietly situated near the palace high above the market. Most of its twelve comfortable, airy rooms have good views over the valley to the mountains. ❹–❺

Modern Central Lodge Tibet Rd ⓣ03592/224670. Popular hotel geared towards backpackers, with useful information – though some visitors feel pressured to join their tours. Boasts running hot water, a restaurant and even snooker. Dorms Rs50. ❷

Mount Jopuno Paljor Stadium Rd ⓣ03592/223502. Government-run hotel featuring twelve rooms with hot water and attached bathroom, and a rooftop terrace. Well-maintained and offers good value, and there's a good restaurant and bar. ❺

Netuk House Tibet Rd ⓣ03592/226778, ⓔreservations@windamerehotel.net. A family home with a comfortable hotel annexe: warm, atmospheric and beautifully presented with Sikkimese decor and a pleasant roof terrace. The price of Rs3700 for a double includes all meals. ❾

Nor-khill Paljor Stadium Rd ⓣ03592/225637, ⓦwww.elginhotels.com. Luxurious former guesthouse of the Chogyal. The large plush rooms come with all mod cons, and there's a good restaurant, but the location is poor, overlooking the sports stadium; prices (starting at $125) include all meals. ❾

Oriental MG Marg ⓣ03592/221180, ⓦwww.orientalsikkim.com. A homogenised oriental theme in almost doll's house proportions with a good multi-cuisine restaurant; comfortable and a cheaper alternative to *Tashi Delek* across the road. ❼

Pandim Secretariat Rd ⓣ03592/227540. Friendly and pleasant budget hotel with plain rooms but a great location high above town – the rooftop restaurant has lovely views. ❷–❸

Pineridge Nam Nang Rd ⓣ03592/220122. One of several identikit places along this strip, this is a friendly Bengali-run place with a restaurant. Just below the taxi stand, it's handy for late arrivals. ❹–❺

Pomra Secretariat Rd ⓣ03592/226648. A bit more comfy than *Pandim* next door and a similar great location, although the restaurant is not great (head to *Pandim* instead). There is also a dorm (Rs100). ❹

Sonam Delek Tibet Rd ⓣ03592/222566. High above the bazaar, with a range of comfortable, clean rooms, a good restaurant and expansive views across the valley to the mountains from the terrace café. ❹–❺

Tashi Delek MG Marg ⓣ03592/222991, ⓦwww.hoteltashidelek.com. An easily missed entrance off the market area hides one of Gangtok's legendary hotels – a plush, extensive complex in need of a revamp, with spacious, old-fashioned rooms. The multi-cuisine *Blue Poppy* restaurant and adjoining rooftop café serve Sikkimese and Tibetan dishes, and club sandwiches. ❽–❾

Tibet Paljor Stadium Rd ⓣ03592/222523 or 223468. Award-winning hotel with Tibetan decor; deluxe rooms have Kanchenjunga views but the roadside rooms are overpriced. The *Snowlion* restaurant (see p.960) is excellent. ❻–❾

Around Gangtok

Hidden Forest Lower Sichey Busty ⓣ03592/205197, ⓦwww.hiddenforestretreat.com. A 2km taxi ride from the SNT bus terminus and Paljor Stadium leads away from the bustle of Gangtok to this tranquil horticultural idyll, with organic food and comfortable cottages in a family-run nursery specializing in orchids and azaleas. ❼

Penili Cottage Upper Syari ⓣ03592/280433; A quiet family homestay below Deorali, featuring five rooms all with attached baths and views across terraced fields to Tsomgo. The owner offers day hikes. ❹

Tashi Tagey NH-31A, near State Bank of India, Tadong ⓣ03592/231631, ⓦwww.tashitagey.com. Small, welcoming Tibetan family-run hotel 5km from Gangtok. Clean, welcoming, homely atmosphere, with a good restaurant popular with locals. It's a steep fifteen-minute walk up to Do Drul *chorten*, and central Gangtok is an easy Rs10 taxi ride away; recommended. ❸–❺

The Town

Though central Gangtok – which means "the hilltop" – is concentrated immediately below the palace, its unchecked urban sprawl begins almost as soon as the road rises from the valley floor at Ranipool, 11km southwest. Most of the town itself looks west; one explanation for the lack of development east of the ridge is that tradition dictates that houses face northwest, towards Kanchenjunga, Sikkim's guardian.

The town's best shopping areas are the **Main Market**, stretching for a kilometre along MG Marg; and the local produce bazaar in the concrete **Kanchenjunga Shopping Complex**, which occupies the site of the once atmospheric Lall Market. Stalls sell dried fish, yak's cheese (*churpi*), and yeast for making the local beer (*tomba*). At the huge complex run by the **Government Institute of Cottage Industries**, on the National Highway north of the centre, visitors can watch rural Sikkimese create carpets, hand-loomed fabrics, *thangka* paintings and wooden objects, and buy their work at fixed prices. Curio shops on MG Marg and on Paljor Stadium Road sell turquoise and coral jewellery, plus religious objects such as silver ritual bowls and beads.

Right at the top of town just below a colossal telecom tower, 3km from the centre of town and reached by several roads (the most picturesque follow the west side of the ridge), **Enchey Monastery** is a small two-storey Nyingmapa *gompa*. It was built in the mid-nineteenth century on a site blessed by the Tantric master Druptob Karpo who was renowned for his ability to fly. Visitors are welcome; the best time to visit is between 7am and 8am, when the monastery is busy and the light is good. Surrounded by tall pines, and housing over a hundred monks, it's a real gem of a place. Built by the chogyal, on traditional Tibetan lines, its beautifully painted porch holds murals of protective deities and the wheel of law, while the conch shells that grace the doors are auspicious Buddhist symbols. Enchey holds an annual *chaam,* or masked lama dance, each December or January according to the lunar calendar.

The walk down from Enchey leads to the **Flower Show Complex** (daily 10am–5pm; Rs5) at the northern end of Ridge Road near White Hall, where a large well-maintained greenhouse has a good collection of orchids and other Himalayan plants laid out around a set of water features. The complex, with a shop selling seeds, plants and bulbs, comes alive in March and April during the annual flower festival.

Although in theory guards deny entry to the **Royal Palace** to anyone without permission, visitors not carrying cameras are occasionally granted access to **Tsuklakhang**, the yellow-roofed royal chapel at its far end, to see its impressive murals, Buddhist images and vast collection of manuscripts. Here too there's a lama dance, known as *kagyat*, at the end of December, during which the main gates are open to the public; some years the *kagyat* takes place in Pemayangtse instead (see p.966).

Beyond the chapel the road meanders down to the small **Deer Park** (also known as the Himalayan Zoological Park; daily 10am–4pm; free) and beyond to Deorali, 3km from the centre on the National Highway, where, set in wooded grounds, is the museum-cum-library of the **Institute of Tibetology** (daily 10am–4pm; Rs5). Here you can see an impressive collection of books and rare manuscripts, as well as religious and art objects such as exquisite *thangkas* (scrolls). You can also get here from the upper town via the new ropeway (see p.956).

A couple of hundred metres beyond the Institute on the brow of the hill, an imposing whitewashed *chorten* (see p.1455), known as the **Do-Drul Chorten** – one of the most important in Sikkim – dominates a large, lively monastery. The *chorten* is capped by a gilded tower, whose rising steps signify the thirteen steps to nirvana; the sun and moon symbol at the top stands for the union of opposites and the elements of ether and air. The 108 prayer wheels that surround it – each with the universal prayer *Om mani padme hum*, "Hail to the jewel in the lotus" – are rotated clockwise by devotees as they circle the stupa. Nearby, a prayer hall houses a large image of **Guru Rinpoche** (Padmasambhava) who brought Buddhism to Tibet at the request of King Trisong Detsen in the eighth century AD. He later travelled through Sikkim hiding precious manuscripts (*termas*) in caves, for discovery at a future date by *tertons*. Curiously, part of the head of the image projects into the ceiling protected by a raised section of roof; belief has it that the image is slowly growing.

Eating and drinking

Sikkimese food is a melange of Nepalese, Tibetan and Indian influences; rice is a staple and dhal is readily available, while *gyakho* is a traditional chimney stew served on special occasions. Sikkimese delicacies include *ningro* (fern rings), *shisnu* (nettle soup), *phing* (glass noodles) and *churpi* (yak cheese) cooked with chillies. Some of the best eating is in the restaurants of hotels like such as the *Tibet* and there are now several fast food places and patisseries, like *Baker's Café* and *Café Tibet*, to choose from.

Most restaurants serve **alcohol**. "Foreign" liquor such as brandy and beer is cheap enough, but look out for **tomba**, a traditional drink consisting largely of fermented millet, with a few grains of rice for flavour, served in a wooden or bamboo mug and sipped through a bamboo straw. The mug is occasionally topped up with hot water; once it's been allowed to sit for a few minutes, you're left with a pleasant milky beer. *Tomba* is usually found in less salubrious places where the mixture might be doctored to make it stronger; or a better-quality brew, try the better hotels. Note that the Sikkimese have alcohol-free days during full moon.

Moving on from Gangtok

The busiest route in and out of Sikkim is the road between Gangtok and Siliguri in West Bengal, site of the nearest airport and railway station (see pp.904–905). **Flights** from Bagdogra can be booked through either Josse & Josse, MG Marg (☎03592/224682), agents for Jet Airways, or through Silk Route Tours and Travels, first floor, *Green Hotel*, MG Marg (☎03592/223354), who also sell tickets for the various airlines flying from Biratnagar (2hr from Siliguri) in eastern Nepal to Kathmandu. Sikkim Tourism sell tickets for the **helicopter** flight (subject to weather conditions daily 10.30am; Rs1500) to Bagdogra to connect with Indian Airlines and Jet flights. **Train reservations** from New Jalpaiguri can be made at the SNT complex on Paljor Stadium Road (Mon–Sat 8am–2pm, Sun 8–11am; ☎03592/222016), but the reservations quota for Gangtok is highly inadequate so it is better to book in Siliguri.

Shared **Jeeps** are the most popular and efficient mode of transport, though buses are slightly cheaper. Jeeps to Siliguri (Rs100), New Jalpaiguri (Rs125), Kalimpong (Rs85) and Darjeeling (Rs100) leave from the private bus stand on NH-31A. Jeeps to Rumtek (Rs25) leave from Lall Bazaar, while Jeeps to other destinations within Sikkim such as Legship, Ghezing, Pelling and Jorethang depart from Nam Nang taxi stand above the extension to MG Marg. These services are timetabled and require **advance booking** (from the ticket booth at the taxi stand).

Those determined to suffer the **buses** – although those to Siliguri are not that bad – can choose between SNT (Sikkim Nationalized Transport) or the ever-growing number of private operators. The SNT bus stand is on NH-31A beyond the *Tibet* hotel and the private bus stand is also on NH-31A just past the *Orchid*. Buses run to Kalimpong, Darjeeling and Siliguri in West Bengal and Ravangla, Legship, Ghezing, Pelling and Jorethang in Sikkim.

Baker's Café MG Marg. A modern and spotless patisserie a short walk from the tourist office, with a tempting selection of cakes, pizzas, good filter coffee and a selection of fruit drinks; there's another outlet on the national highway near the private bus stand.

Blue Sheep MG Marg, next to the tourist information office. A relaxed and fairly priced option with good Indian, Chinese and Tibetan food and a bar.

Café Tibet NH-31A, past the hospital, run by the *Tibet Hotel*. Lively and popular with students, the café serves pizzas and burgers, croissants, cakes and ice cream.

China Palate MG Marg, New Market. A combination of a bar and a restaurant serving Tibetan and local cuisine – try their Sikkimese combo which includes *shisnu* and *ningro*.

Glenary's and **The Buzz** MG Marg. The patisserie is no longer up to the mark but the café upstairs is popular and varied, offering pizzas and pastries. On the floor above, *The Buzz* is a modern, lavishly decorated and comfortable pub.

Little Italy Deorali, upstairs next to the petrol pump. Busy, trendy bar-restaurant that serves Italian food and is especially good for pizzas.

Modern Central Lodge Tibet Rd. Good travellers' choice for hearty breakfasts, including muesli and delicious pancakes.

Oyster *Sonam Delek Hotel*, Tibet Rd. Well-reputed place whose menu includes Indian, Chinese and Sikkimese food, plus a smattering of Tex-Mex and Italian dishes.

Snowlion *Tibet Hotel*, Paljor Stadium Rd ⓣ03592/222523 or 223468. Probably the best restaurant in Gangtok. The superb Tibetan and Indian food, with a selection of Sikkimese and Japanese dishes, is highly recommended.

The Square Paljor Stadium Rd, next to *Mount Jopuno*. Bright little café-bistro which offers a small but varied menu including Thai, continental and Nepalese cuisine. There's a bar, and great views.

Around Gangtok

The most obvious destinations for day-trips from Gangtok are the great Buddhist monasteries of **Rumtek** to the southwest, and **Phodong** to the north.

Closer to Gangtok there are three popular viewing points offering panoramas of the **Kanchenjunga Range**. The most accessible is **Ganesh Tok**, a steep one- to two-hour walk from the TV tower and Enchey monastery. A small Ganesh shrine and views of Gangtok and the mountains reward those that make the climb. Opposite the shrine lies the **Himalayan Zoological Park** (daily 10am–5pm; Rs10) with large open enclosures for red panda and snow leopards. **Hanuman Tok** (2300m), 7km out of town on the road to Tsomgo Lake, is the site of a Hanuman temple, and the cremation ground of the Royal Family, with *chortens* containing relics of the deceased. On the road to Phodong, **Tashi View Point**, 6km out of Gangtok, provides views of the eastern aspects of Kanchenjunga, whose tent-like appearance here is radically different from the way it looks from Darjeeling, and the snowy pyramid of Siniolchu (6887m), which the pioneering mountaineer Eric Shipton ranked among the most beautiful in the world.

Tsomgo Lake (pronounced "Changu"), 35km northeast of Gangtok and just 20km from the Tibetan border at **Nathu La**, is a scenic spot that's especially popular with Indian visitors who flock here to sample the high-mountain environment and, hopefully, experience their first thrill of snow in the colder months. While the military dominate the place, tourism manages to thrive with yak rides, and stalls selling pelts and other curios. It's possible to visit the **Kyongnosla Alpine Sanctuary** (3350m) en route, where a profusion of wild flowers bloom between May and August and migratory birds stop over in winter on their annual pilgrimage from Siberia to India. Tsomgo Lake is now open to foreigners, but only Indians are allowed up to Nathu La, where they can gawk at bemused Chinese soldiers across the rope border marker. Many of

Gangtok's travel agents, including Vajra Adventure Tours & Travels and Sikkim Tours, run excursions to Tsmogo, and some hotels will arrange tours at the request of their guests.

Rumtek

Visible from Gangtok, and a 24-kilometre road trip southwest of the capital, the large *gompa* of **RUMTEK** is the main seat of the **Karma Kagyu** lineage – also known as the **Black Hat** sect – founded during the twelfth century by the first Gyalwa Karmapa, Dusun Khyenpa (1110–93). Dusun Khyenpa established the Tsurphu monastery in central Tibet near Lhasa, which became the headquarters of the Karma Kagyu for eight centuries until the Chinese invasion of Tibet in 1959. The sixteenth **Karmapa**, Rangjung Rigpe Dorje, fled Tibet for Sikkim where he was invited to stay at the old Rumtek *gompa*. Within a couple of years the Karmapa had begun the work of building a new monastery at Rumtek to become his new seat, on land donated by the Sikkimese king Chogyal Tashi Namgyal. One of the great Tibetan figures of the twentieth century, the sixteenth Karmapa was very influential in the spread of Tibetan Buddhism to the West, setting up over 200 Karma Kagyu centres and raising funds for the rebuilding of Tsurphu. When he died in 1981, he left behind a wealthy monastery with a huge international network, but one bitterly divided by an ugly squabble over his rightful successor. Two re-incarnate Karmapas have now emerged as the main contenders to the lucrative throne – one blessed by the Dalai Lama and ensconced in Dharamsala, the other in nearby Kalimpong.

The new Rumtek, now heavily guarded against possible raids by the feuding parties, is a large and lavish complex consisting of the main temple, golden stupa, and the Karma Shri Nalanda Institute, with a few smaller shrines and a guesthouse outside the monastery courtyard. The **main temple**, with its ornate facade covered with intricate brightly painted wooden latticework, overlooks the expansive **courtyard**. Large red columns support the high roof of the **prayer hall**, where the walls are decorated with murals and *thangkas*. Visitors can attend daily rituals here, when lines of monks sit chanting. A chamber off the hall, used for Tantric rituals, is painted with gold against a black background and depicts wrathful protective deities (no photography allowed). During Losar, the Tibetan New Year (in February), the main courtyard stages *chaam* dance spectacles, in which ceremonial **Black Hat dancers** spin to the sounds of horns, drums and clashing cymbals.

The **Karma Shri Nalanda Institute of Buddhist Studies**, behind the main temple, built in 1984 in traditional Tibetan style, is the most ornate of all the buildings of Rumtek. Monks spend a minimum of nine years studying here followed by an optional three-year period of isolated meditation. The main hall on the third floor is decorated with magnificent murals, and holds images including the Buddha Sakyamuni – the historic Buddha – and the sixteenth Karmapa.

The ashes of the sixteenth Karmapa are contained in a gilded four-metre-high *chorten* or stupa, studded with turquoise and coral, that sits in the **Golden Stupa** hall opposite the Institute. Behind the stupa is a central statue of Dorje Chang (Vajradhara) flanked by Tilopa, Naropa, Marpa and Milarepa, the four great Kagyu teachers. Statues of the previous sixteen Karmapas line the side walls. The door to the hall and *chorten* is kept closed so you will need to knock loudly or find a monk to take you in.

Half a kilometre beyond the new monastery and Rumtek village, a path leads to the simple original Rumtek *gompa*, founded in 1740 and recently renovated, in an attractive wooded clearing and surrounded by empty outbuildings in traditional Sikkimese alpine style, with latticed wooden windows. Behind the statues in the main prayer hall on the right side is a small shrine room dedicated to the Karma Kagyu protector Mahakala, an image so fierce that it is kept veiled.

Practicalities

If you don't arrange your own **transport** (Rs431 return including waiting time), the best way to get to Rumtek is by the shared Jeeps that leave Gangtok from Lall Bazaar when full and cost Rs25 per head. The one SNT bus from Gangtok leaves daily at 4pm and returns the next morning.

Rumtek has a limited choice of budget **accommodation**, and a growing number of more upscale resorts present a pleasant alternative to the crowded cityscape of Gangtok. The monastery's own hotel, *Kunga Delek* (❶–❷), opposite the entrance to the courtyard, has small, clean rooms with attached bathroom; there are good views and simple food is available. Just below the *Kunga Delek* and next to a couple of stalls is the atmospheric but no-frills *Sangay* (❶–❷), with rudimentary bathrooms and a traditional restaurant. The friendly *Sun-Gay Rumtek Guesthouse* (Ⓣ03592/252221; ❶–❷), close to the main gate of the monastery, is by far the best of the budget options, boasting clean rooms with views in a garden. A traditional smoke-blackened wooden kitchen churns out banana pancakes and other favourites. A couple of hundred metres before the main gate, the *Shambhala Mountain Resort* (Ⓣ03592/252240; ❽) is as comfortable as it gets in Rumtek, set in a pleasant garden complex with doubles and comfortable cottages, some in local ethnic style; the main block lacks character, however. Of the resorts, the *Martam Village Resort* (Ⓣ03592/223314, Ⓔmartam@dte.vsnl.net.in; ❽) is 7km beyond Rumtek in an idyllic rural setting amidst beautiful rice terraces. The landscaped complex consists of fourteen purpose-built en-suite thatched cottages with verandas and views, as well as a restaurant; staff can arrange mountain bike rental and local guides to explore the countryside. Closer to Rumtek, 1km before the monastery gates at Sajong, the friendly Swiss/Sikkimese-run *Bamboo Resort* (Ⓣ0353/2202049, mobile Ⓣ9832/061986; ❾) is pleasantly located with a herb garden, a library and a meditation room and a good pizza oven; double start at $65. In Rumtek itself, noodles and chai are available at the **teashops** clustered near the monastery gate and at the checkpoint where foreigners are requested to give passport details.

Phodong and Labrang

Phodong, 38km north of Gangtok on the Mangan road, is another living monastery, but a far less ostentatious one. Lying on a spur of the hill 1km above the main road, and commanding superb views, it consists of a simple square main temple, plus several outhouses and residential quarters. Built in the early eighteenth century, this was Sikkim's pre-eminent Kagyu monastery until the growth of Rumtek in the 1960s. It too hosts colourful lama dances, similar to the *chaam* of Rumtek, each December. A rough road leads a further 4km up to another renovated old monastery – the unusual octagonal **Labrang**. A cluster of *chortens* between these two monasteries marks the ruins of **Tumlong**, Sikkim's capital city for most of the nineteenth century.

Few stay at Phodong, preferring rather to continue to Mangan or return to Gangtok, but there are a couple of options. Two kilometres beyond the Phodong monastery turn-off in the hamlet on the main road, *Yak & Yeti* (no phone; ❷) and the slightly more comfortable *Northway* (no phone; ❷–❸) offer clean budget **accommodation** in idyllic rural settings; the latter is also a restaurant. The bus to Gangtok stops at the hamlet around 4pm; shared Jeeps also ply the route.

Southern Sikkim

Ignored by travellers en route to higher trekking trails and the great *gompas* of west Sikkim, southern Sikkim nevertheless offers a quiet charm, its lichen-covered forests draped with a stunning array of orchids and inhabited by rare animals – and now that permit restrictions have eased, it offers many more possibilities for visitors. Traditionally serving as an access point to western Sikkim via border towns like **Jorethang**, the area is dominated by the great forested peak of **Maenam**, famous for its plants and flowers, and for the tremendous view from its summit. Towering above the town of **Ravangla**, Maenam makes a challenging day trek, while high above the district capital of Namchi, the gigantic statue of **Samdruptse** is clearly visible from as far away as Darjeeling.

Jorethang

The bustling market town of **JORETHANG** lies in the very south of the state, just across the River Rangit from Singla Bazaar in West Bengal and a mere 30km north of Darjeeling, which is just visible across the tea plantations. Set on an extensive shelf, which makes it feel oddly flat despite the huge hills that rise in every direction, it's a surprisingly pleasant and well-ordered place, with a good market and a few decent budget **hotels**. The *Namgyal* (ⓣ03595/276852; ❷–❹), next to the Darjeeling taxi stand, has good-value doubles with running hot water, some with river views; it also has a decent restaurant and an a/c bar. In the middle of the market on Street No.3, the *Dzongri* (ⓣ03595/257076; ❷–❹) is a clean place, though the more expensive rooms with attached baths are a bit pokey. For **food**, try the Indian and Chinese fare at *Walk-In* on Street No.2, which also doubles as a popular bar.

Jorethang is well connected by **bus** with the rest of Sikkim, and there is a direct service to Siliguri daily at 9am. Buses for Gangtok leave at 7am and 12.30pm, for Pelling at 9.30am and 1pm, and for Ghezing at 8.30am, 9.30am and 11.15am, connecting with the 2pm departure for Tashiding and Gerathang (for Yoksum). Shared **Jeeps** make the extraordinarily steep 25-kilometre journey to Darjeeling, and go regularly to Legship (change here for Pelling, Yuksom and Tashiding); there are less frequent services to Ghezing, Namchi and Varshey. Few Jeeps leave Jorethang after 1pm and the rule of thumb is to travel early.

Samdruptse

High above the busy town of **Namchi**, 79km southeast of Gangtok and 24km to the northwest of Jorethang, the gigantic 41m statue known as **SAMDRUPTSE** ("Guru Rinpoche") sits on a high ridge gazing south towards Darjeeling. Constructed by the regional government, the huge edifice has become one of south Sikkim's most popular attractions, its sheer size as much of an attraction as its spiritual significance. Inaugurated by the Dalai Lama in 2004, the statue cost Rs67,600,000 (around US$15,558,112) to build, and contains a meeting hall as well as, somewhat ironically, a window in its back. Samdruptse lies 8km to the north of Namchi along the unfolding ridge; to get there, you'll either need to make the steep, gruelling climb past Ngadak Monastery, or take a Jeep (Rs200) to the ornamental Rock Garden and then make a 3km climb up steps to the statue; taxis directly to the car park near the statue are Rs250.

Both Ravangla (see below) and Namchi have choice of **accommodation**; in the middle of Namchi near the Jorethang taxi stand, the *Rockville* (no phone; ❷–❸) has basic rooms over a popular local restaurant and bar. For a bit more comfort try *Mayal* (☎03595/263588; ❹–❺), in a quiet location on the Jorethang road, with clean rooms and a good restaurant serving Indian and Chinese food. Namchi is well connected to all points in Sikkim as well as Siliguri and Darjeeling.

Ravangla and Maenam

Spread across a high saddle, 65km west of Gangtok and 52km east of Pelling, the sleepy market town of **RAVANGLA** (also known as Ravang and Rabang) makes for a convenient stopover, especially for those interested in trekking through one of the last remaining **rhododendron forests** in south-central Sikkim. Although threatened by deforestation, the fabulous **Maenam Sanctuary** remains a botanist's dream, covering the flanks of the gigantic forested peak which looms over the town.

The summit of **Maenam** (3235m), 10km from Ravangla bazaar, is home to a small chapel to Guru Rinpoche (Padma Sambhava) and boasts superlative views, weather permitting – the mountain's position on the watershed between the Teesta and the Rangit river systems means that overcast weather can veil the dramatic views of the distant plains to the south, and of the Kanchenjunga range and especially the horned summit of Narsing (5825m). Feasible as a day-trek, the stiff 1000-metre **ascent** of Maenam (2hr 30min–4hr) starts with steps rising from the bazaar up to the small *gompa* (usually shut) before trailing off the road and rising at first gently and then quite steeply through the sanctuary. Besides locals and the occasional Indian trekker, few come this way, and you may even be lucky enough to glimpse some wildlife including deer, the elusive red panda, black bear and a variety of birds. If you want to catch the sunrise from the summit, take a good sleeping bag, food and water, as there is a dilapidated shelter in which to huddle from the elements, but little else. Locals, who occasionally camp up here, scour the forests for firewood; deforestation is a real worry so use your discretion and bring down your rubbish. The route through the forest is not all that obvious (especially in descent when a wrong turn can dump you

Kewzing homestays

If you're interested in getting an introduction to Sikkimese rural life, you might want to try a **homestay**. While Gangtok agents will charge you in dollars for the privilege, the Kewzing Tourism Development Committee (KTDC), offers homestays (Rs1000 per night for two) in the welcoming Kewzing *busti* (village), a pleasant rural idyll surrounded by terraced fields just outside the sleepy market town of Kewzing, itself 8km east of Ravangla. Several villagers are in the process of upgrading their properties for visitors (call the number below), but at the time of writing, KTDC chairman Sonam Dadul Bhutia (mobile ☎09434/357926) was offering two very pleasant, well furnished wood-lined rooms in his home, with attached bathrooms and a common veranda with views. Don't expect fancy plumbing here (hot water by the bucket is the order of the day), though for an extra charge you can use a Bhutan-style communal hot tub heated by fired stones. Meals are taken in the traditional wooden, smoke-darkened kitchen.

on the wrong side of the mountain) and you may want to take a local **guide** (Rs300) arranged through hotels or the tourist office (see below).

Monasteries in the vicinity of Ravangla include the old and the new *gompas* at **Ralang**, 13km to the north, with shared Jeeps travelling the route on demand. The old *gompa*, Karma Rabtenling, is linked to the ninth Karmapa and was founded in 1768. The new Ralang monastery, built in 1995 in much the same style as Rumtek, and also part of the Kagyu order, is one of the largest temple buildings in Sikkim. Usually held in December, the *chaam* (lama dance) which commemorates Losung (the end of the harvest) is a particularly colourful and local affair.

In late August each year Ravangla hosts the three-day **Pang Lhabsol festival**, which celebrates the worship of Kanchenjunga and draws thousands of Sikkimese to enjoy the traditional sports and **Pangtoed Chaam**, a festival of masked dances unique in that it is performed here, not by monks, but by *zigtempas* or lay people. Local villagers come to sell their wares at Ravangla's Wednesday **market**.

Practicalities

Buses and shared **Jeeps** leave from the stand at the crossroads towards the southern end of the market, heading to Gangtok and Namchi, as well as Legship and Ghezing, where you'll need to change for Pelling; you can't be assured of transport much after midday. Two buses pass through town each day, for Ghezing at around 11am and for Gangtok at around 9am. The shortest route to Darjeeling is via Namchi, where you may have to change for a Jeep or bus to Jorethang and then change for Darjeeling. Ravangla's **tourist information office**, in the main bazaar on the Legship road was being rebuilt at the time of writing; when reopened, it should still be able to help arrange village homestays, guides and transport to local sights. The State Bank of India at the bazaar will **change money**.

There's a reasonable choice of **accommodation** on offer; all of the places listed below have attached bathrooms and running hot water. *Meanamla* (ⓣ03595/260666; ❸–❻) on Kewzing Road (the Legship Road) offers a modest degree of comfort, although the cheapest rooms are a little pokey; it also has a restaurant and bar. Near the taxi stand, *Hotel 10Zing* (ⓣ03595/260705; ❷) is a friendly place with plain rooms over a popular restaurant, while at the end of the market, the *Melody* (ⓣ03595/260817; ❹) has bright, clean rooms with attached baths and a spotless restaurant offering Chinese and Indian dishes. On the way out of town, on the Kewzing Road towards Legship, the more upmarket *Ravangla Star* (ⓣ03595/260733; ❹) has pleasant rooms and a restaurant. *Zumthang* (ⓣ03595/260870, ⓔzumthang@yahoo.com; ❺) next door offers a warm welcome and large, clean rooms in a extensive complex that's popular with Bengali tour groups. If you want to get away from it all, the stunningly located *Mt Narsing Village Resort* (ⓣ03595/260558, ⓔtakapa@sancharnet.in; ❸–❻), 3km further on, offers furnished tents and a couple of log chalets; for total solitude ask to stay in the *Annexe*, a steep twenty-minute walk (or precarious Jeep drive) up from the road, with comfortable chalets and stunning views. Most of the hotels have **restaurants**, but the best *momos* in town can be found at the *Florida* and *Karma* cafés, opposite one another on the market road.

Western Sikkim

This beautiful land, characterized by great tracts of virgin forest and deep river valleys, is home to ancient monasteries such as **Pemayangtse** and **Tashiding** and the attractive but rapidly developing hamlet of **Pelling**. The old capital,

Yoksum, lies at the start of the trail towards Dzongri and Kanchenjunga. In the far west, along the border with Nepal, the watershed of the Singalila Range rises along a single ridge, with giants such as Rathong and Kabru culminating in Kanchenjunga itself. Only two high-altitude trails are currently easily accessible, and even these are subject to restrictions and high charges; however, several low-altitude treks with numerous variations provide ample opportunities to enjoy the wonderful profusion of orchids, rhododendron forests, waterfalls and terraced hillsides with a backdrop of majestic vistas.

Permit restrictions (see p.953) mean that high-altitude trekkers can only follow well-beaten trails within a limited period of time, but there are numerous alternatives at lower altitudes. If you're coming from Darjeeling and arrange permits and itineraries in advance you could enter Sikkim at Jorethang (see p.963) and go directly to Pelling or Yoksum, saving precious permit time.

Ghezing and Legship

The bustling market town of **GHEZING** (also known as Gyalshing), 110km west of Gangtok, is the administration centre and transport hub of western Sikkim, and a good place to stock up on provisions and extend permits. There are a couple of **hotels** near the main square should you need to stay, including the basic *Kanchanjangha* (❷), above a restaurant and bar, and the more comfortable *Attri* (Ⓣ03595/250602; ❸). For a bit of luxury head for the dramatically situated *Tashigang Resort*, 3km from town at Deecheling (Ⓣ03595/250340; ❻–❽), an incongruous multi-storey building with stunning views over deep valleys; there are also attractive and comfortable cottages in a landscaped garden. Back in town, a few yards from the market on the Tashigang road, *Denkhang* is one of the best *restaurants* in Gangtok..

Shared **Jeeps** leave for Gangtok, Siliguri (tickets in advance from the counter near the playground; Ⓣ03595/250121) and Pelling (just turn up) and other local destinations from the main square; most have left by midday, with the exception of Jeeps and Maruti Omnivans to Pelling, which continue until sunset. If reserving a taxi, Omnis tend to be cheaper as they can travel up the steep short-cut to Pelling, which is closed to Jeeps. One Jeep a day leaves for Ravangla at 8.30am, and a Jeep to Dentam via Pelling leaves at noon. A Jeep to Yoksum will cost Rs1000–1500 depending on the season. There are also regular Jeeps for Jorethang, where you can change for Darjeeling. The SNT office (daily 6.30am–3.30pm) is at the bottom of town next to a small Tibetan *gompa*. A **bus** to Siliguri (via Jorethang) leaves at 7am daily; other buses to Jorethang depart at 9.30am, 1pm and 3.30pm – change there for Darjeeling and Siliguri but travel early as scheduled transport winds down early afternoon from Jorethang. The daily bus for Gangtok goes at 7am and so does the bus to Siliguri. At 2pm there's a service for Gerathang (for Yoksum), via Legship and Tashiding.

The gateway to western Sikkim, **LEGSHIP** sits in the deep and recently dammed Rangit Valley, just under 100km west of Gangtok and 14km south of Ghezing. It's an important regional road junction and one where you could find yourself with an hour or so to spare, but not an interesting destination. At the crossroads, *Trishna* (Ⓣ03595/250887; ❷) has a few rooms and a restaurant. Jeeps and buses connect Legship with Gangtok, Jorethang, Ravangla, Ghezing and Pelling as well as Yoksum via Tashiding.

Pemayangtse

Perched at the end of a ridge parallel to (and visible from) that of Darjeeling, the hallowed monastery of **PEMAYANGTSE**, 118km from Gangtok and a

△ Doorway, Pemayangtse

mere 2km from Pelling, is poised high above the River Rangit, which snakes towards its confluence with the Teesta on the West Bengal border. It's a nine-kilometre journey along the main road from Ghezing; or you can take a steep, four-kilometre short-cut through the woods past a line of *chortens* and the otherwise uninteresting remains of Sikkim's second capital, **Rabdantse**, now made into a park.

"Perfect Sublime Lotus", founded in the seventeenth century by Lhatsun Chempo, one of the three lamas of Yoksum, and extended in 1705 by his re-incarnation, is one of the most important *gompas* in Sikkim and belongs to the Nyingmapa school. Expansive views of the Kanchenjunga massif and the surrounding woods create an atmosphere of meditative solitude. Surrounded by exquisite outhouses, with intricate woodwork on the beams, lattice windows and doors, the main *gompa* itself is plain in comparison. Built on three floors, it centres around a large hall which contains images of Guru Rinpoche and Lhatsun Chempo (the latter was an enigmatic Tibetan lama who is the patron saint of Sikkim), and an exquisite display of *thangkas* and murals. On the top floor, a magnificent wooden sculpture carved and painted by Dungzin Rinpoche, a former abbot of Pemayangtse, depicts Sang Thok Palri, the celestial abode of Guru Rinpoche, rising above the realms of hell. The extraordinary detail includes demons, animals, birds, Buddhas and *bodhisattvas*, *chortens* and flying dragons, and took him just five years to complete. An annual *chaam* – masked dance – is held here during the Tibetan New Year (February), and attracts visitors from all over Sikkim.

In 1980, the **Denjong Padma Choeling Academy** was set up by the monastery to provide for destitute children and orphans; there are currently around 300 children being housed, clothed, fed and educated here. Generous donations have enabled further building and the setting up of a yak and *dri* dairy project near Dzongri, a tea garden and carpet-weaving. Volunteer teachers – more of whom are always welcome, for a minimum of two months – receive free accommodation in the monastery, and opportunities to study meditation and Buddhism and to learn local crafts. The monastery also runs **courses** at the International Heritage Meditation centre where nine well-furnished rooms are available to students of Buddhism or anyone wanting to experience monastic life. Contact Sonam Yongda at Pemayangste Gompa, West Sikkim 737 113 (Ⓣ03595/250760 or 250141).

Pelling and around

The quiet, scenic but rapidly swelling town of **PELLING**, situated 2085m above sea level only 2km beyond Pemayangtse, exists primarily for its access to the hinterland, and affords expansive views north towards the glaciers and peaks of Kanchenjunga. High above forest-covered hills, in an amphitheatre of cloud, snow and rock, the entire route from Yoksum over Dzongri La to the Rathong Glacier can be seen. Pelling itself consists of little more than a road junction and helicopter pad in Upper Pelling (which enjoys the best views), with a string of hotels running down through Middle Pelling to a strip of highly unimaginative identikit concrete blocks in Lower Pelling. Frenetic building activity is over-saturating the place with even more hotels, but, this doesn't detract from Pelling's charm, with numerous attractive walks and hotel terraces that allow you to gaze in awe at the world's third-highest peak. A four-kilometre trail rises from the playing fields just above Pelling to reach the small but highly venerated monastery of **Sanga Choling**, one of the oldest *gompas* in Sikkim. It's another of Lhatsun Chenpo's creations, and is held in high esteem among the

Nyingmapa. Gutted by fire, it has been rebuilt and houses some of the original clay statues.

A scenic low-altitude **trek** along roads and trails to Khecheopalri Lake, Tashiding and Yoksum starts in Pelling (see opposite). Public transport runs from both Yoksum and Tashiding back to Legship, from where you can continue to Ghezing and eventually back to Pelling. If you have less time on your hands, tour operators such as the reliable Simvo Tour and Travels (Ⓣ03595/258549) in Upper Pelling can arrange **day-trips** by Jeep (around Rs1600 for a Jeep holding 6–8 people).

Practicalities

Shared **Jeeps** travel regularly (6am–4pm) between Pelling and Ghezing; three times daily for Gangtok via Ravangla (6.30am, 8.30am & 12.30pm); and once a day for Siliguri (6.30am). The road from Pelling via Rimbi to Yoksum is still poor but is being slowly repaired and upgraded while the diversion to Khecheopalri has been improved. There is no direct service to Yoksum from Pelling but a daily **bus** leaves Ghezing and travels via Legship and Tashiding to Gerathang, 5km short of Yoksum; there's also a direct bus for Siliguri (6.30am). The **post office** is in Upper Pelling just above the crossroads, but note that there are no official facilities for **changing money**. For **trekking information** consult the books at *Hotel Garuda*; the new Tourist Information Centre near the helipad (daily 10am–4pm) will help with tours but is otherwise pretty useless.

Pelling's **hotels** (which now number more than 150) are spread along a 2km stretch of road between Upper, Middle and Lower Pelling, with Lower Pelling's "Bengali Boulevard" gearing itself more towards the domestic market and upper Pelling offering the finest views. New hotels of varying standards are cropping up all the time and high-season prices are steep.

Most **restaurants** are to be found in hotels and traditional Sikkimese food is getting increasingly difficult to come by due to the predominance of domestic tourists who prefer *dhal bhat*. Pelling is a good place to sample a *tomba* (warm millet bee); it's best in Sikkimese-run hotels like *Phamrong*.

Accommodation

Dubdi Near the helipad Ⓣ03595/258349. A small hotel pleasantly located in a quiet corner above town, with clean mid-range rooms and views. ❹–❺

Garuda At the crossroads Ⓣ03595/258319. A popular travellers' haunt and good meeting place, this well-run family hotel offers a range of singles, doubles and dorms (Rs60), and useful comment books have the latest trekking information. The restaurant boasts excellent food and low-key service. ❶–❸

Green Valley Upper Pelling Ⓣ03595/258348. The traditional ambience of the family-run *Sister's Guest House* has been replaced by this concrete hotel – but it's still as friendly and welcoming, with a restaurant and a dorm (Rs100). ❸–❹

Kabur 200m before the crossroads Ⓣ03595/258504. A friendly place, though not quite as atmospheric as *Garuda*. Has doubles with carpets and hot water, one cheap four-bed room and a pleasant rooftop terrace. ❷–❸

Ladakh Upper Pelling. A rapidly dying breed in Pelling – a traditional, rustic Sikkimese house with one double, two triples and a dorm (Rs50); the common bathrooms are outside but the family-run lodge is being upgraded to add comfort and two new wooden rooms; a concrete block is planned. ❷

Mount Pandim Just below Pemayangtse monastery Ⓣ03595/250756. Large, comfortable, government hotel with magnificent views and the best location in western Sikkim, but poor management. ❺–❻

Norbu Ghang Resort Near the helipad Ⓣ03595/258245, Ⓦwww.sikkiminfo.net/norbughang. With well-appointed cottages spread up the hillside and a great location at the top of the hill, this is still far and away the best that Pelling can offer. ❽

Pemachen Lower Pelling Ⓣ03595/258542. One of several Bengali-run hotels in this part of town, with friendly management and spacious, appealing rooms. ❸–❹

Phamrong Upper Pelling ⓣ03595/258218, ⓔmailphamrong@yahoo.com. A wide range of comfortable, clean rooms, running hot water and attentive service; there's a pleasant restaurant and great views from some of the more expensive rooms. Email is available. ❺–❻

Simvo Near the helipad ⓣ03595/258347. A large block in a developing area, with a terrace, good views, a restaurant and reasonable if overpriced rooms. ❹–❻

View Point Near the helipad ⓣ03595/258222. A quiet spot with comfortable doubles and running hot water; the views from the terrace are wonderful. ❸–❹

Khecheopalri Lake

Surrounded by dense forests and hidden in a mountain bowl (2000m) 33km northwest of Pelling, **Khecheopalri Lake**, known as the "Wishing Lake", is sacred to the Lepchas. Legend has it that if a leaf drops onto the lake's surface,

West Sikkim high-altitude treks

Two **high-altitude treks** are currently allowed in Sikkim. The first, from **Yoksum** to **Dzongri**, in the shadow of Kanchenjunga, passes through huge tracts of forest and provides incredible mountain vistas. The second, the **Singalila ridge**, explores the high pastures of the Singalila frontier range with breathtaking views of the massif. Trekkers for either of the two must have special **permits** (see p.951), travel in groups organized by authorized agencies (see p.955), complete with guides, and pay a daily rate of $35–80. Check your permit and the food arrangements before you set off – both should be included in the cost. Bring adequate clothing, including protective headgear to cope with the heat of the river valleys, as well as boots and sleeping bags. For general advice on trekking equipment and health issues, see Basics.

The Dzongri Trail

Although Dzongri is the junction of several trails, the prescribed route onwards leads to **Goecha La** via Zemanthang and Samiti Lake. Well-marked and dotted with basic accommodation, the trail, also used by yak herders, is at its best in May when the rhododendrons bloom.

DAY 1 It takes approximately 6hr to climb the 16km from **Yoksum** (1780m) to **Tsokha** (3048m). The trail begins gently and soon reaches deep forest cover before arriving at the Parekh Chu above its confluence with the Rathong. The next 3–4km involve a knee-grinding ascent past the rambling *Forest Rest House* at **Bakhim** (2684m). You have now entered the lichen zone and cloud forests. **Tsokha**, 1.5km further on and 300m higher, settled by Tibetan yak herders, has a couple of huts including the *Trekkers Hut*, as well as several rustic houses, where guests are offered Tibetan tea – a salty brew made with rancid butter.

DAY 2 This day can be spent acclimatizing yourself to the altitude at Tsokha, perhaps with a short trek of around 5km towards Dzongri, to a watchtower which (weather permitting) has superb views of Kanchenjunga and Pandim.

DAY 3 The 11km section from **Tsokha** to **Dzongri** (4030) takes at least 5hr, rising through beautiful pine and rhododendron forests to **Phedang Meadows** (3450m), before continuing to the hut on the meadows of Dzongri.

DAY 4 Once again, it's worth staying around Dzongri for further acclimatization. That gives you the opportunity to climb Dzongri Hill above the hut, for early-morning and early-evening views of Kanchenjunga's craggy south summit. Look out for the black tooth of Kabur, a forbidding-looking holy mountain that towers above Dzongri La pass. Several trails meet at the meadows at Dzongri – one descends to cross the Rathong Chu and rises again to the demanding pass of Kang La into Nepal; another crosses Dzongri La (4400m), descends around 450m and rises again to the HMI base camp 12km away at Chaurikhang and the Rathong Glacier.

a guardian bird swoops down and picks it up, thereby maintaining the purity of the water. From the Pelling–Yuksom road, a turnoff diverts at "zero point" to Khecheopalri (11km), with only occasional Jeeps travelling the route (landslides permitting) to the lake. If you want to trek from Pelling to Khecheopalri, there's a shortcut leading down to the river valley, steeply up to the Pelling–Yuksom road and then up to the lake (allow 5hr); you can continue the circuit to Yuksom (see p.972), but arm yourself with a handy map from *Hotel Garuda* (see p.969) before setting off.

Khecheopalri village and the *gompa* 2km from the lake on top of the ridge provide excellent views of Mount Pandim (6691m), and several sacred caves are scattered through the hills. **Guides** to these caves and to Yoksum, Tashiding and Pelling can be arranged through *Trekker's Hut* (no phone; ❶), 300m before the

DAY 5 The 8km trek from **Dzongri** to **Thangsing** (3841m) takes around 4hr, descending against an incredible backdrop of peaks to a rhododendron forest, crossing a bridge and continuing through woods to the *Trekkers Hut* at **Thangsing** at the end of a glacial valley.

DAY 6 The 10km short, sharp shock up to **Samiti Lake** (4303m) takes around 3hr. The trail follows a stream and alpine meadows past a yak herders' hut, then traverses glacial moraine, crosses meadows and a rocky landscape before arriving at the emerald-green **Samiti Lake** (local name Sungmoteng Tso). If you are still going strong, you could continue to **Zemanthang** (4453m) where there's a *Trekkers Hut*.

DAY 7 Very much the climax of the trek, and also by far its most difficult section – not because of any technicalities, but simply due to its high altitude. From **Samiti Lake** the 14km round-trip climb takes around 4hr up to **Goecha La** and 2–3hr back down again. Leaving Samiti Lake, the trail follows glacial moraine, drops to a dry lake at Zemanthang, then makes a final grinding rise alongside cairns decorated with the occasional prayer flag to the defile at **Goeche La** (5000m). Kanchenjunga South is clearly visible above the pass, while to the left glaciers tumble off Kabru Dome.

DAY 8 Most of the long 24km hike from **Samiti Lake** back to **Tsokha** is downhill and takes around 8hr, involving a short cut to avoid Dzongri. Crossing the bridge and following the path to a junction signed to the left puts you back above **Tsokha**, to rejoin the trail to Yoksum.

The Singalila ridge

Itineraries for **Singalila ridge** treks range between ten and nineteen days. The section of the ridge for trekkers stretches from the roadhead at **Uttarey** (1965m), 28km to the west of Pelling, or from **Soreng**, 30km to the west of Jorethang, and ascends to **Chewabhanjang** (3170m) on the Sikkim–Nepal frontier, offering spectacular views of the Kanchenjunga massif. Thereafter, the trail rarely descends below 3500m, crossing steep rocky hillsides and remote, high alpine meadows above the tree line; the highest point of the trail is the **Danfeybhir Tar**, a pass at 4400m or for the very fit, the optional excursion to **Kang La** (5200m). Several lakes such as **Lampokhari**, all considered holy, are encountered along the route, and here and there dwarf rhododendron forests bring a blaze of colour in season (April–May). The route dips down to **Gomathang** (3725m), a yak herders' shelter on the banks of the Boktochu; the route then passes through a delightful forest of silver fir and rhododendron before arriving at the welcome sight of the bungalow at **Dzongri**. You could descend from here via Tsokha to Yuksom or continue to **Goecha La**, thus completing a grand and rewarding traverse. The best time to do both treks is between October and mid-November, when the weather is clearest.

village, one of the few **places to stay** at Khecheopalri – a friendly but very basic option which serves simple meals. It also has some very useful information on the local area and a definitive list for bird-watchers. Tea stalls at the car park serve chai and simple meals. The trail on to Yoksum is 18km long and takes around four hours. Stock up on snacks from Ghezing market or some of the small stalls in Pelling. The *Garuda* hotel in Pelling can also provide information on the trail and a limited but useful map.

Yoksum

The sleepy, spread-out hamlet of **YOKSUM**, which occupies a large shelf at the entrance to the Rathong Chu gorge, 40km north of Pemayangtse at the end of the road, holds a special place in Sikkimese history. This was the spot where three lamas converged from different directions across the Himalayas to enthrone the first religious king of Sikkim, Chogyal Phuntsog Namgyal, in 1642. Named the "Great Religious King", he established Tibetan Buddhism in Sikkim. Lhatsun Chenpo is supposed to have buried offerings in Yoksum's large white **Norbugang Chorten**, built with stones and earth from different parts of Sikkim. From here a path branches left through the village to a small grove and the simple stone throne of the first chogyal. In front of the throne an impressive footprint embedded in a rock by one of the lamas no doubt impressed the king too. High above the town, prayer flags announce the site of the Nyingma **Dubdi Monastery**, built in 1701. From the end of the road at the hospital, a path threads past water wheels and a small river and rises through the forest to arrive at the dramatically situated *gompa*, looking out over Yoksum; however there's unlikely to be anyone around to let you have a look inside. **Kathok Lake**, a small scummy pond at the top end of town has nothing of the pristine beauty of Khecheopalri Lake, but has views of the snowcapped peaks in the distance. Above the bazaar, a small *gompa* under construction (**Kathol Wodsal Ling**) adds colour to the scene.

Yoksum's main role these days is as the start of the **Dzongri Trail**. Visitors are welcome in Yoksum itself, but unless you have a Dzongri Trek permit you're not supposed to venture any further. The police are quite vigilant, so there's not much chance of a surreptitious high-mountain trek, but so long as you're not carrying a backpack they may allow a day-trip along the main trail to the Parekh Chu and its confluence with the Rathong Chu – a 28km round trip. You won't see the high Himalayas, but you do pass through some beautiful forest scenery. Yaks – or rather *dzo*, a more manageable cross between yak and domestic cattle – travel this route, with supplies for trekking parties and isolated communities.

Practicalities

There are no **buses** to or from Yoksum itself, but a daily bus connects **Gerathang**, 5km down the road from Yoksum (a walk or Jeep-ride away), to Ghezing via Tashiding and Legship; it leaves Gerathang at 7am. **Jeeps** start to depart at around 6.30am to Legship via Tashiding, and there are unscheduled services to Ghezing and Jorethang, but you're unlikely to get shared transport after 1pm. **Internet** access is available at the Community Information Centre (Rs50 per hour) above the bazaar.

Accommodation in Yoksum is improving, with several budget options around the small market area, including *Demazong* (Ⓣ03595/241215; ❷–❸), which has dorms (Rs60) as well as some rooms with attached bath and a pleasant garden restaurant in season; *Wild Orchid* (❷), an attractive traditional house; and the plain *Dzongrila* (❶), which also has a cheap dorm (Rs50).

Conservation and the Kanchenjunga National Park

Set up in 1996 with the help of the Sikkim Biodiversity and Ecotourism Project, the **Khangchendzonga Conservation Committee** (KCC), a community-based NGO based in Yoksum, aims to promote **ecological awareness** to locals and visitors alike. The KCC's main concern is the impact of tourism on the fabric of the **Kanchenjunga National Park**, and their methods include planting trees, mobilizing local participation in the planning of ecotourism and organizing clean-up campaigns. Conservation has also been embraced by the Sikkim government, which has put in place a code of conduct, banning the use of wood for fuel in preference to kerosene; however, wood fires continue to be part and parcel of the Sikkim landscape.

One major KCC programme is the uphill battle to keep the Yoksum, Dzongri and Thangsing trails clean – volunteers regularly remove vasts amounts of litter and camping debris. Other KCC initiatives include publishing leaflets to promote eco-awareness, training local workers including porters and guides in the ecotourism industry, and educating villagers on alternative sources of income generation such as vegetable production. For more information on the KCC, contact their co-ordinator Pema Chewang Bhutia at the *Hotel Wild Orchid*, Yoksum (Ⓔkcc_sikkim@hotmail.com).

Approaching the Yuksom's tiny market, *Dragon* (Ⓣ03595/241290; ❸–❹) is a friendly new place whose clean rooms have shared; the restaurant serves good local cuisine. Next door, *Pemathang* (Ⓣ03595/241221; ❹) is a pleasant place with attached bathrooms and a small picturesque garden; neighbouring *Yangri Gang* (Ⓣ03595/241217; ❷) is not nearly as attractive but is traveller-friendly, with a restaurant. The *Tashi Gang* (Ⓣ03593/241202; ❺–❻), a large, pink building, is the plushest of Yoksum's hotels and the only place with running hot water; it also has a restaurant. At the *Tashi Gang* gates, *Pemalingpa Cottage* (Ⓣ03593/241214; ❷) is a traditional house offering basic wooden rooms with toilets outside. The *Trekker's Hut* (❶) in a field near the bazaar has plain wooden rooms, outhouse toilets and allows camping.

Besides hotel restaurants, the only other **places to eat** are the cafés – such as *Guptas* and the friendly *Yak* – along the main drag, which serve basic meals such as rice and dhal and are good for snacks.

Tashiding

Considered the holiest in Sikkim, the beautiful *gompa* of **TASHIDING** occupies the point of a conical hill 19km southeast of Yoksum, high above the confluence of the Rangit and the Rathong. "The Devoted Central Glory" was built in 1717, after a rainbow was seen to connect the site to Kanchenjunga. A wide path leaves the main road near an impressive *mani* wall (painted green and inscribed in silver paint with the mantra *Om mani padme hum*: "Hail the jewel in the lotus") and leads steeply past rustic houses and fields up to the monastery compound. The large complex consists of a motley collection of buildings, *chortens*, chapels and the unassuming main temple itself, which was recently rebuilt using some of the features and wooden beams of the original. At the far end of the temple complex, surrounded by numerous multi-coloured *mani* stones inscribed with a mantra, is an impressive array of *chortens* containing relics of Sikkim's chogyals and lamas. On the fifteenth day of the first month of the Tibetan New Year, devotees from all over Sikkim gather in Tashiding for the **Nyingmapa Bhumchu festival**, when they are blessed with the holy water from an ancient bowl said by legend never to dry up. Oracles consult the water's level to determine the future.

West Sikkim walks

The gradual relaxing of the permit system offers opportunities to walk the numerous trails which crisscross the countryside of west Sikkim, many of which take you into the heart of the Singalila forests. Best visited between mid-April and mid-May, when the rhododendrons are in full bloom, the **Varshey Rhododendron Sanctuary** covers 104 square kilometres, which range in altitude from 2840m to 4250m and are home to black bear, red panda and pheasant. The sanctuary is accessible, entry permits (see p.951), from **Hilley**, **Soreng** and **Uttarey**, and the most popular trail is the 8km round-trip from Hilley to **Varshey** (3030m), which offers spectacular views. You can extend the walk to Uttarey (3–4 days with tented accommodation), from where you can either take transport to Jorethang and points en route, or continue on foot to the small town of **Dentam**. From Dentam, a river valley trail leads to **Rinchenpong** (4–5hr), a good base for west Sikkim treks; another trail from Dentam leads east up the ridge to **Pelling** (4–5hr). There are numerous permutations and possibilities to trekking in this region including an extension, with prior arrangement with tour operators and the appropriate permits, into the long high-altitude **Singalila ridge** trek to Dzongri and beyond (see pp.970–971).

Walk practicalities

Most Gangtok tour operators (see p.955) can arrange treks and tours of this part of West Sikkim; Sailesh of Sikkim Adventure is an extremely knowledgeable and enthusiastic botanist offering specialized tours. Sikkim Tours & Travels are a good alternative. Reliable bases convenient to Varshey and Uttarey include *Yangsum Farm* (Ⓣ03595/245322, mobile Ⓣ09434/179029, Ⓦwww.yangsumfarm.com; ❽), a sylvan retreat below Rinchenpong, which can arrange all-inclusive treks including transport, food, guides and tents. Another comfortable base is the *Dhallam Farm Resort* (Ⓣ03595/254225 or mobile Ⓣ09320/620222; ❻) at Daramdin, 26km to the west of Jorethang, which can also organize tailor-made itineraries and treks in the region. Both Daramdin and Varshey are connected by Jeep services to Jorethang.

Around 2km below the *gompa*, Tashiding's tiny bazaar – also known as Senik Bazaar – is situated near a saddle that separates the mountainside from the monastery hill. Basic **accommodation** in the bazaar includes the friendly and cosy *Blue Bird* (❶) with a dorm (Rs40) and a restaurant serving simple, wholesome food, and the more spacious, slightly more expensive *Mount Siniolchu Guesthouse* (❷) further up the hill.

Leaving from the bottom of the bazaar's cobbled high street, one or two timetabled **Jeeps** and a handful of unscheduled Jeeps and trucks connect Tashiding to Yoksum (Rs30) and Ghezing (Rs50). The last shared Jeeps departs at 9am. A daily **bus** from Gerathang, 5km short of Yoksum, passes through Tashiding at around 8am and continues via Legship to Ghezing. In the other direction the bus leaves Ghezing at 8pm, passing through Tashiding (at approximately 3.30pm) on its way up to Gerathang. Trails through the forests and along stretches of the main road make trekking an alternative option to public transport; the route to Legship takes around two and a half hours.

North Sikkim

Most of spectacular **North Sikkim** is closed to visitors. Until 1993 no one was allowed to venture past Phodong, but the government is now starting to open up the area to tourism. Groups armed with special permits, arranged through travel and tour operators in Gangtok (see p.955), are allowed as far as **Thangu**, at the edge of the Tibetan plateau. Past Mangan, foreigners are only allowed up in organized tour groups inclusive of transport and accommodation, with the choice of accommodation and food – all limited in these parts – in the hands of tour operators. In general, **permits** for North Sikkim (extendable through the Superintendent of Police in Mangan) are only good for five days and a further seven for trekking. The **jeep safaris** can prove long and tedious, and due to restrictions on time and movement as well as the lack of infrastructure, the rewards are few. Although there has been a significant improvement in the roads, every year throughout the monsoon, **landslides** take out stretches of road making travel even more tedious.

The road north of Gangtok follows the deep Teesta gorge past Phodong across what is said to be the highest bridge in Asia (no photography allowed), before reaching the quiet little town of **MANGAN**, the district capital of North Sikkim. There is little of interest here other than a small bazaar and a handful of grubby hotels and cafés on the main road. The *Lachen Valley* (❷) and *Ganga* (❷) have very basic rooms and shared bathrooms, while the *Himalayan Hotel* (❸) offers a bit more comfort. The drive down to **Namprikdang**, a popular angling spot at the confluence of the Rangit and Teesta, is both spectacular and hair-raising. A small *gompa* 5km north of Mangan – the northernmost point for those tourists not travelling in a group with permits – **SINGHIK** provides incredible views, especially early in the morning, of the huge east face of Kanchenjunga and is a quiet place to chill out for a day or two. The *Tourist Lodge* (ⓣ03592/234287; ❸) at Singhik takes advantage of the location, widely considered to be the best viewpoint in all Sikkim. Only recently opened up to visitors, the magnificent valley of **Dzongu** branches northwest from Mangan towards Kanchenjunga. At the heart of the valley, the ancient *gompa* of **Tholung** is home to ancient treasures of the chogyals; these are displayed every three years to the public with the next display in January 2006. A few **homestay** options are now available, arranged, along with permits, through tour operators like Sikkim and Khangri in Gangtok (see p.955). A five-day trek starting at Lingza and passing through Tholung, Thizon and across Kyeshong La (3790m) explores the forests and meadows of this unspoilt Lepcha homeland.

A further 40km north of Mangan lies **CHUNGTHANG**, a dark and grubby town set in a deep valley at the confluence of the Lachen and Lachung rivers, with a large military presence. Basic amenities include hotels and restaurants on the main road and the large Public Works Department bungalow where tourists can stay if there's room. Beyond Chumthang the valleys fork. These are border areas and the military, who maintain the rough roads, are very sensitive – photography, even of harmless monasteries, is not tolerated. The road to the right climbs rapidly to the small settlement of **LACHUNG**, the "big pass", a mere 15km west of Tibet. Across the river, **Lachung Monastery** is a two-storey Tibetan-style *gompa* belonging to the Nyingmapa sect. The Bhotia people of Lachung and Lachen practice a unique social system known as *Dzumsa* – a sort of gathering of elders that controls everything from grazing to law and order. The **accommodation** here will be pre-booked along with all food and transport through tour operators such as Blue Sky, Marcopolo and Khangri in Gangtok (see p.955) and include the *Apple Valley Inn* and the *Lecoxy*, a large comfortable timber lodge. **Food** is basic. Twenty-four kilometres further north, the valley becomes even more spectacular. Craggy snow-bound peaks rise as high as 6000m to either side above **YUMTHANG** (3645m), which has hot sulphur springs but no accommodation. The other road from Chungthang leads 26km to **LACHEN** and a further 36km to **THANGU**, tantalizingly close to the Tibet plateau and far as foreign tourists are allowed to go. This is the route to the sacred and spectacular **Guru Dongmar Lake**, considered blessed by Guru Rinpoche and the source of the River Teesta. **Accommodation** at Lachen and Thangu is available at several basic lodges and at the height of the season over 150 tourist-laden cars a day wind their way up from Gangtok along these northern routes.

Several interesting **high-altitude treks** are now open to group tours in this isolated region, including the popular Lachen to **Green Lake** trek which takes approximately nine days there and back, and offers great views of Mount Siniolchu (6687m) across the Zemu glacier. Green Lake (4850m) is the base for climbing expeditions attempting the many 6000–7000m peaks in the region. The region abounds with possibilities such as a circuitous trail taking in Guru Dongmar and the route from Yabuk near Green Lake crossing the Zemu and Tholung glaciers, through Dzongu, to eventually cross Goecha La (4940m) into western Sikkim, an extremely challenging trek. **Trekking permits** for the north must be sought through Sikkim Tourism in Delhi (see box on p.951) or through one of the Gangtok operators; they take a minimum of three months to process and, despite all that, the final clearance rests with the army at Gangtok, who are known to refuse on a whim. Tsering Dorjee of Khangri tours in Gangtok has long experience of securing permits, so you might want to go through him. **Mountaineering** permits can be obtained through the Indian Mountaineering Foundation, also in Delhi (see p.83); now that peaks under 6000m have officially been declassified, agents such as Namgyal and Khangri in Gangtok (see p.955) will also assist with getting the necessary permits – you will need to submit six photographs and copies of your visa and passport and plan atleast three months ahead.

Travel details

Jeeps tend to go when full (less frequently after midday), except for long distance services such as the Gangtok–Ghezing and Pelling routes, with one or two scheduled departures daily. There are no train or plane services available and the helicopter service from Gangtok only operates to meet flights at Bagdogra. Buses cost a few rupees less than the Jeeps but they are much slower and tend to be a lot more uncomfortable.

Jeeps

Gangtok to: Darjeeling (5–6hr); Ghezing (4–5hr); Kalimpong (3–4hr); Pelling (5–6hr); Mangan (2–3hr); Ravangla (3hr); Rumtek (1hr); Siliguri (5–6hr).

Ghezing to: Gangtok (5–6hr); Jorethang (2hr 30min–3hr); Pelling (30min); Tashiding (1hr); Yoksum (2hr 30min–3hr).

Jorethang to: Darjeeling (2hr); Gangtok (4–5hr); Ghezing (2hr); Legship (1hr).

CHAPTER 16 Highlights

* **Kaziranga National Park, Assam** Encounter the rare one-horned rhino on a dawn elephant ride. See p.989

* **Majuli Island, Assam** Fascinating Vaishnavite *sattras* (Hindu monasteries) on the world's largest river island. See p.991

* **Khasi Hills, Meghalaya** Explore the impressive caves and dramatic waterfalls among the rolling hills of this picturesque state. See p.994

* **Tawang Monastery, Arunachal Pradesh** A spectacular Tibetan Buddhist monastery in one of the most remote locations imaginable. See p.1003

* **Namdapha National Park, Arunachal Pradesh** A remote and beautiful park in a stunning setting with clear air, prehistoric trees and pristine vegetation. See p.1005

* **Kohima, Nagaland** Proud capital of Nagaland, with a fascinating museum of Naga life and a poignant World War II memorial. See p.1008

△ Tawang Monastery

16

The Northeast

The least explored and arguably the most beautiful region of India, the **NORTHEAST** is connected to the rest of the country by a very narrow stretch of land between Bhutan and Bangladesh, and was all but sealed from the outside world until a decade or so ago. Arunachal Pradesh shares an extremely sensitive northern border with Chinese-occupied Tibet and, together with Nagaland, Manipur and Mizoram, a 1600-kilometre border with Myanmar.

Insurgency has agitated the region since Independence, with tribal groups pushing for various degrees of autonomy as well as fighting each other. A huge influx of Bangladeshis and the displacement of many tribal people has created further tension. The situation has improved in recent years, although Tripura and Manipur remain unsafe for travel (see p.1014) and Restricted or Protected Area Permits are still required for four of the seven states (see "Access, permits and tour operators" box, pp.982–983). Tourists are not a target of violence in any state, however, and following the considerable easing up of government restrictions on travel since 2000, this fascinating corner of the country continues to open up for travellers. An extraordinary diversity of peoples and spectacular landscapes make a visit worth the effort. One of the wettest monsoon belts in the world, the area also boasts an astounding array of flora and fauna, estimated at fifty percent of India's entire biodiversity.

Until the 1960s the region comprised just two states, the North East Frontier Agency (NEFA), now known as Arunachal Pradesh, and Assam, but separatist pressures further divided it into seven states, known as "the seven sisters". **Assam** consists of the flat, low-lying valley of the Brahmaputra. Its capital, **Guwahati**, boasts two of India's most important ancient temples and acts as a gateway to the entire region, while a dawn encounter with a one-horned rhino in the state's magnificent **Kaziranga National Park** is a highlight of any trip through the Northeast.

The other six states occupy the surrounding hills, and are quite distinct from the rest of India in landscape, climate and peoples. **Meghalaya** boasts beautiful lakes and is home to the wettest place on earth. Its capital, **Shillong**, retains some of the colonial atmosphere from its time as the summer capital of East India. Majestic **Arunachal Pradesh** is one of the most remote states in India, and is inhabited by a fascinating range of peoples, many of Tibetan origin. In the far northwestern corner lies the Buddhist monastery of **Tawang**, encircled by awesome mountains, while in the far northeast you'll find the remote wilderness of **Namdapha National Park**. To the south, the lush mountains of **Nagaland** are home to fourteen major tribal groups, each with a strong sense of identity and history. A progressive tourist policy has made many of its far-flung tribal

The International boundaries on this map are neither purported to be correct nor authentic by Survey of India directives. Publisher.

Travelling through the northeast

Though much of the region is still best reached through tour operators (see p.983), adventurous travellers will find it increasingly possible – and richly rewarding – to travel independently, though this demands a considerable amount of time, energy and perseverance. Be prepared for bureaucracy, language barriers, long drives on terrible roads, very basic accommodation and (except in Assam) extremes in temperature. You should consider hiring your own **Jeep and driver**, at least for part of the trip, and using public Tata **Sumos**, Jeeps which operate like shared taxis and are much quicker and more comfortable than buses. If you're travelling in winter, take your own sleeping bag and thermals, as much of the accommodation is not set up for cold weather. Be aware that people rarely drive at night because of the threat of banditry, and, since the region shares the same time zone with the rest of India despite being so far east, the sun rises and sets early and a lot of places close shop by 6pm. Outside Guwahati, **money-changing** facilities are few and far between, so bring what cash you need with you. There are regular day-long *bandhs* (strikes) throughout the region when shops, restaurants and public transport tend to shut down and state police usually require tourists to remain in their hotels – during a typical three-week trip you're likely to lose a day for a tea pickers' *bandh* and a day for a *bandh* called by insurgents.

capitals accessible to tourists. **Mizoram**, in the Lushai hills, was the most peaceful state at the time of writing. Predominantly Christian due to intensive missionary work under the British, it has one of the highest literacy rates in India.

Manipur and **Tripura** were deemed unsafe for travel at the time of writing and the sections on the two states have not been updated for this edition (see boxes, p.1018 & p.1014). Though tourists are not a direct target, both states continue to suffer from inter-tribal disputes and insurgency involving kidnapping, banditry, village raids, arson and killings. Once an independent princely kingdom, Manipur is at the cultural crossroads where the subcontinent and Southeast Asia meet, and its people are more closely related to the neighbouring Burmese than to the Aryans from the west, and speak languages quite unrelated to Hindi or Assamese. Tripura is bordered by Bangladesh on three sides but was cut off from the Bangladeshi plains during the 1947 Partition.

The recommended **time to visit** the Northeast is from November to April, although mountain areas can be extremely cold by December. It rains heavily from May to the end of September. In two weeks you could travel from West Bengal to Guwahati, Shillong and Kaziranga, while three weeks would be enough to cover the main sights of Assam and Meghalaya. A month would enable you to enjoy the two most beautiful and remote states, Arunachal Pradesh and Nagaland – to take in all the states together, including Mizoram, you'll need considerably longer.

Assam

The state of **ASSAM** is dominated by the mighty **River Brahmaputra**, whose huge, lush valley is sandwiched between the Himalayan foothills to the north and the hills and plateau of Meghalaya to the south. It's an attractive state, especially to drive through, with miles of smooth, flat roads coursing through jungle or vibrant villages. One of India's few **oil** regions, Assam also produces more than half of the nation's **tea**. Most of its eight hundred tea estates were

Access, permits and tour operators

Although the region is increasingly opening up for tourism, **regulations** can change according to the current state of security. Check with the Indian Embassy or tourist office before travelling, and again, with state representatives in India.

In terms of permits, **Assam**, **Meghalaya** and **Tripura** are completely open; you can enter by any route and travel freely within. Foreigners require **Restricted or Protected Area Permits** to visit **Arunachal Pradesh**, **Nagaland, Mizoram** and **Manipur**, with ten days currently the maximum length of time currently allowed. At the time of writing, the UK Foreign Office was advising against all travel to Tripura and Manipur, though permits were still being issued for Manipur. Arunachal is the only state which demands a fee for its permit (currently $50), though Manipur's state government charges a Rs1500 "royalty fee" when your permit is issued. It is sometimes possible to get an extension to the ten-day permit – ask on application or check with a tour operator once you're inside the region.

For all states you are officially required to travel in **groups** of at least four, with the exception of Nagaland, where married couples may be granted a permit (or sometimes friends travelling in pairs, if applied for by a tour operator, see opposite). Currently Nagaland and Arunachal Pradesh are the easiest for foreigners to get permits for – travellers to both are strongly encouraged by the government to visit with a tour operator, which can cost upwards of $50 per person per day, and it is, in any case, vital to have some contact with one, as you'll need help arranging Jeep hire, guides and permits. Independent travellers should have permits endorsed at the **Foreigners' Registration Office** (or with the Superintendent of Police) in the state capitals (see p.951). Indian nationals require Inner Line Permits for the aforementioned four states.

Be aware that permits are not date-stamped when you cross a **border**, so if, as is likely, your travels take you in and out of a state more than once, there may be some confusion as to whether you are allowed back in again. In theory, passes are eligible for the full period they are allocated for, no matter how many times you enter and exit a state, but in practice you may find yourself facing border guards demanding bribes of rupees or whisky. Stand your ground.

Permits

By far the quickest and easiest way of getting a **permit** for Mizoram, Nagaland and Arunachal Pradesh is four to six weeks in advance through a well-connected northeast tour operator (see opposite). You'll probably have to pay a small administration fee, but they may be able to help put together a group of four people. The alternative is to apply to the Foreigners' Division of the Ministry of Home Affairs, Lok Nayak Bhavan, Khan Market, New Delhi. It is also possible to obtain permits from the offices of the various state representatives in Kolkata or New Delhi (see p.154); or from Indian embassies abroad. If you choose the last option, note that all embassies have to get permission from Delhi, so apply at least two months in advance, and be prepared for a drawn-out, frustrating process. In all cases, applications (attaching two passport photos to the form) must be made at least four weeks in advance of

laid down by the British, with one golf club for every fifteen estates to relieve the tea planters' boredom and loneliness.

Sadly, the state has suffered from **political violence** since the United Liberation Front of Asom (**ULFA**) began an armed struggle for independence in 1985. In the early 1990s, Assamese nationalism sparked opposition from Bodos, Cachars and other ethnic minorities, giving rise to further insurgence. However, though bombings, *bandhs* and in-fighting still continue, the situation has vastly improved and tourists are not a target.

your proposed visit. An invitation from someone in one of the states will make the process quicker and more certain.

To obtain **Inner Line Permits**, Indian citizens should apply with two passport photographs to representatives of the state governments concerned. Applications should only take a day to process and are valid for a week in the first instance but can be extended for up to six months in the relevant state capital.

State Government representatives

Arunachal Pradesh Arunachal Bhawan, Kautilya Marg, Chanakyapuri, Delhi ⓣ011/2301 3915; Block CE-109, Sector 1, Salt Lake, Kolkata ⓣ033/2334 1243.

Manipur Manipur Bhawan, 2 Sardar Patel Marg, Chanakyapuri, Delhi ⓣ011/2687 3311; Manipur Bhawan, 26 Rowland Rd, Kolkata ⓣ033/2475 8075.

Mizoram Mizoram Bhawan, Circular Rd (behind the Sri Lankan Embassy), Chanakyapuri, Delhi ⓣ011/2301 0595; Mizoram House, 24 Old Ballygunge Rd, Kolkata ⓣ033/2475 7034.

Nagaland 29 Aurangzeb Rd, Delhi ⓣ011/2301 6411; Nagaland House, 12 Shakespeare Sarani, Kolkata ⓣ033/2242 5269.

Northeast tour operators

Ashoka Holidays Sanmati Plaza, GS Road, Guwahati, Assam ⓣ0361/245 7600, ⓔnwttghy@satyam.net.in. Guwahati-based company organizing adventurous and cultural tours throughout the northeast.

Cultural Pursuits Adventures Mawlai Nongpdeng, Shillong, Meghalaya ⓣ0364/550573, ⓦwww.culturalpursuits.com. Friendly Canadian operation based in Shillong arranging trips in Meghalaya and across the northeast, including tailor-made trips for budget travellers.

Gurudongma Tours & Treks *Gurudongma Lodge*, Hilltop, Kalimpong, West Bengal ⓣ3552/255 204, ⓦwww.gurudongma.com. Highly professional and capable team arranging tailor-made Jeep tours, trekking, mountain biking, tribal, wildlife and bird-watching holidays in Assam, Meghalaya, Nagaland and Arunachal Pradesh, with particular expertise in bird-watching trips (ⓦwww.allindiabirding.com).

Himalayan Holidays ABC Building, Main Market, Bomdila, Arunachal Pradesh ⓣ03782/222017, ⓦwww.himalayan-holidays.com. Local tour agency specialising in cultural and angling trips throughout the northeast, including Manipur, Mizoram and Tripura.

Jungle Travels GNB Road, Silpukhuri, Guwahati, Assam ⓣ0361/266 0890, ⓦwww.jungletravelsindia.com. Guwahati-based agent organizing quality group and tailor-made tours, including a four-day luxury boat cruise from Guwahati to Kaziranga.

Purvi Discovery Jalannagar, Dibrugarh, Assam ⓣ0373/230 1120, ⓦwww.purviweb.com. Dibrugarh-based tour operator with excellent guides, arranging tailor-made wildlife, fishing, golfing, horse-riding, war memorial, tribal and tea tours around Dibrugarh and throughout the northeast.

Assam's busy capital, **Guwahati** boasts one of India's most important Kali temples, **Kamakhya**, and is a hub for the whole northeast region, while within easy access of the city, the magnificent **Kaziranga** national park is renowned for its one-horned **rhinos** – the state symbol. Further along the Brahmaputra lies fascinating **Majuli**, the biggest riverine island in the world and home to unique *sattras*, or Hindu monasteries. Another 60km northeast, **Sibsagar** is unusual for its imposing Shivadol Temple, while further north still, **Dibrugarh** is slowly opening up as a second hub for the region.

Guwahati and around

The state capital **GUWAHATI** (or Gauhati), lies on the banks of the **Brahmaputra**, whose swollen sandy channel is so wide that the far shore is often invisible. It's a dirty and crowded city, but as it's the main gateway to the region you will probably need to stay here for a night or two. The busy downtown market area contrasts sharply with the rural riverside northeast of the centre, and the surrounding hills rising beyond. The main attractions are the city's temples – **Kamakhya** and **Navagraha** both occupy commanding hilltop positions, while **Umananda** sits on a small island in the middle of the Brahmaputra. The city's main business is tea, and a visit to an auction can be exciting. Northwest of Guwahati lie the famous silk village of **Sualkachi**, the prilgrimage site of **Hajo** and the beautiful **Manas National Park**.

Arrival and information

The **railway station** lies in the centre of town, with the **state bus stand**, which operates a left-luggage service (4.30am–10.30pm), right behind. The back of the railway station leads into the hectic Paltan Bazaar area, from which most of the private bus companies operate. Guwahati **airport**, 18km west of the centre, is served by taxis and airport buses, including those run by Indian Airlines. **Minibuses** for travel all over the city can be flagged down by the roadside.

The **Directorate of Tourism** for Assam on Station Road (Mon–Sat 10am–5pm; closed 2nd & 4th Sat of every month; ⓣ0361/254 4475) organizes day-trips and longer tours. The **ITDC India tourism office**, GL Publication Complex, GS Road (Mon–Fri 9am–5.30pm, Sat 9.30am–1.30pm; ⓣ0361/254 7407, ⓔindtour@asm.nic.in), provides information on the entire northeast, and has counters at the airport and the railway station.

Accommodation

Guwahati has a good range of **places to stay**. Railway station **retiring rooms** can be booked at the information desk.

Ananda Lodge MN Rd, Pan Bazaar ⓣ0361/254 4832. Basic budget option with a pleasant atmosphere but dingy rooms. ❷

Belle Vue MG Rd ⓣ0361/254 0847. Guwahati's oldest hotel, located on a wooded hill, with a good restaurant but tired rooms. ❻

Brahmaputra Ashok MG Rd ⓣ0361/254 1064, ⓔbrahmaputra@satyam.net.in. 1km from the station, with pleasant, airy rooms, some with river views, plus a beauty salon and foreign exchange facilities. ❽

Dynasty SS Rd, Fancy Bazaar ⓣ0361/251 0496, ⓔdynasty@gnl.vsnl.net.in. In the heart of the market area, with homely rooms, foreign exchange facilities and a good restaurant serving Indian, Chinese and Western fare. ❽

Landmark Stadium Complex ⓣ0361/245 5248. Good mid-range choice with reasonable rooms and a restaurant serving decent veg and non-veg dishes. ❺–❻

Nandan GS Rd, Paltan Bazaar ⓣ0361/252 1476, ⓔnandan@gwl.dot.net.in. Large hotel near the bus stand with comfortable en-suite rooms and a restaurant, bar and email facilities. ❼

Nova SS Rd, Fancy Bazaar ⓣ0361/252 3464. In the heart of the bazaar, with clean, spacious rooms and a pleasant restaurant. ❻

Raj Mahal AT Rd, Paltan Bazaar ⓣ0361/252 2478, ⓔrajmahal@gwl.vsnl.net.in. Comfortable hotel with vegetarian restaurant and a swimming pool. ❽

Suradevi MN Rd, Pan Bazaar ⓣ0361/254 5050. Good budget option with dorms (Rs80) or a choice of shared or en-suite bathrooms. There's also a popular and inexpensive restaurant. ❷–❸

Tibet AT Rd, Paltan Bazaar, opposite bus station ⓣ0361/263 9600. Good budget option with refreshingly clean rooms, though they can be noisy. ❷–❸

Vishwaratna AT Rd, close to Fancy Bazaar ⓣ0361/260 7712, ⓦwww.vishwaratnahotel.com. Upmarket hotel with clean, cool, air-conditioned rooms with Internet access points, including some deluxe suites. There's also a rooftop swimming pool, bar, coffee shop, multi-cuisine restaurant and travel agency which can book airline tickets. ❽–❾

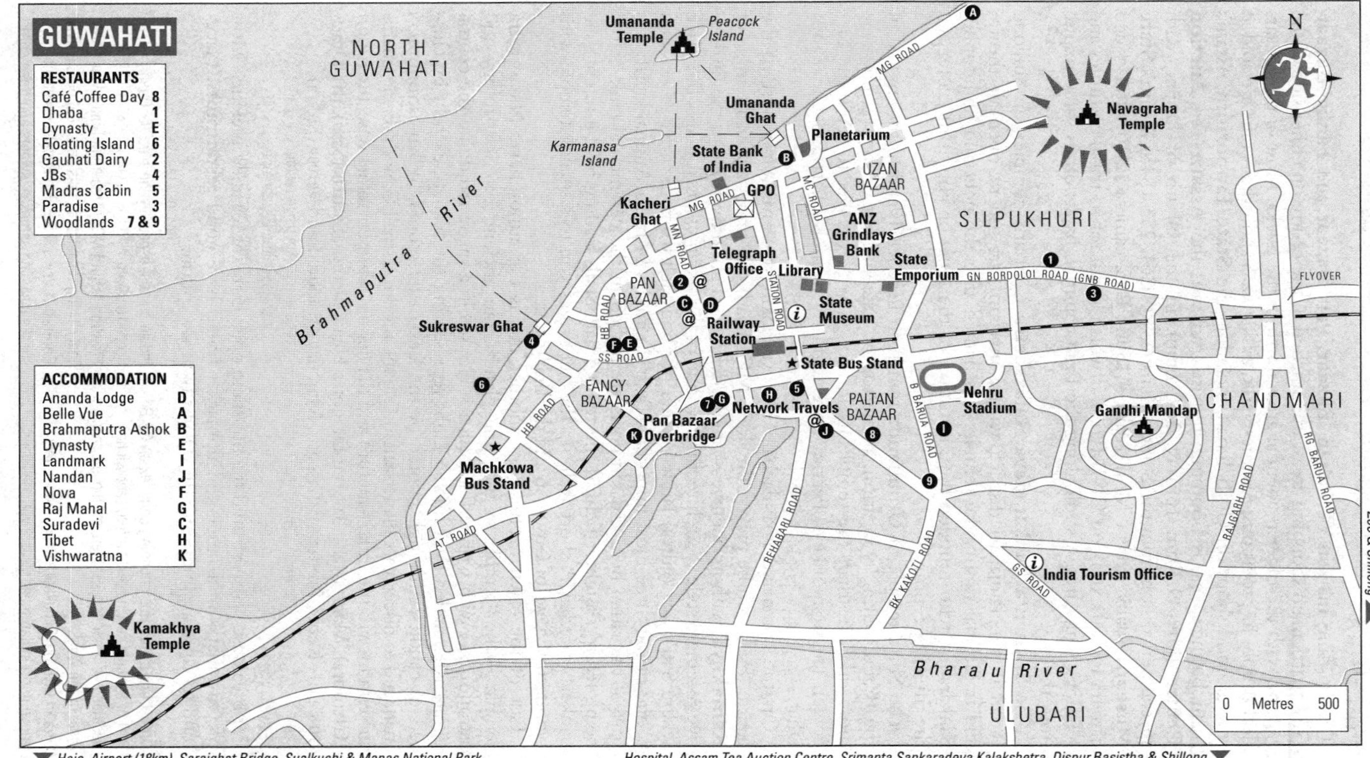
GUWAHATI
RESTAURANTS
Café Coffee Day 8
Dhaba 1
Dynasty E
Floating Island 6
Gauhati Dairy 2
JBs 4
Madras Cabin 5
Paradise 3
Woodlands 7 & 9
ACCOMMODATION
Ananda Lodge D
Belle Vue A
Brahmaputra Ashok B
Dynasty E
Landmark I
Nandan J
Nova F
Raj Mahal G
Suradevi C
Tibet H
Vishwaratna K
NORTH GUWAHATI
Umananda Temple
Peacock Island
Karmanasa Island
Brahmaputra River
Umananda Ghat
Kacheri Ghat
Sukreswar Ghat
Planetarium
State Bank of India
GPO
MG ROAD
MC ROAD
MN ROAD
HB ROAD
SS ROAD
AT ROAD
STATION ROAD
UZAN BAZAAR
PAN BAZAAR
FANCY BAZAAR
PALTAN BAZAAR
ANZ Grindlays Bank
Telegraph Office
Library
State Emporium
State Museum
Railway Station
State Bus Stand
Network Travels
Pan Bazaar Overbridge
Machkowa Bus Stand
Navagraha Temple
SILPUKHURI
GN BORDOLOI ROAD (GNB ROAD)
FLYOVER
Nehru Stadium
B BARUA ROAD
Gandhi Mandap
CHANDMARI
RG BARUA ROAD
RAJGARH ROAD
REHABARI ROAD
BK KAKOTI ROAD
GS ROAD
India Tourism Office
Bharalu River
ULUBARI
Kamakhya Temple
0 Metres 500
N
Zoo & Shillong
Hajo, Airport (18km), Saraighat Bridge, Sualkuchi & Manas National Park
Hospital, Assam Tea Auction Centre, Srimanta Sankaradeva Kalakshetra, Dispur,Basistha & Shillong

The Town

The bustling markets of **Paltan Bazaar**, **Pan Bazaar** and **Fancy Bazaar**, Guwahati's main shopping areas, are bunched in the centre on either side of the railway, with the older residential areas north of the tracks. Most of the bazaars deal simply in provisions; Assamese **silk**, basketware and other crafts are sold at several good shops on GNB Road, including the **State Emporium**. Assam's main business, tea, is booming; tourists can visit the **Assam Tea Auction Centre** (Tues 9.30am–1pm & 2.30–6pm), in the suburb of Dispur, with special permission from the Senior Manager (Ⓣ0361/233 1845). Assam's **State Museum** (daily except Mon 10am–4.15pm; Rs5, camera Rs10 extra, video camera Rs250 extra), on GNB Road, is worth a visit for its tribal costumes and religious sculptures. A stroll along the Brahmaputra's banks offers some respite from the city.

The **Srimanta Sankaradeva Kalakshetra** is an arts complex on Shillong Road in the Panjabari district, with a museum, art gallery, open-air theatre and traditional Vaishnavite temple. It is named after the poet and philosopher Sankaradev, who founded the institution of the *sattra* or Hindu monastery in the fifteenth century.

The Shiva temple of **Umananda** stands on Peacock Island in the middle of the Brahmaputra. Its location, at the top of a steep flight of steps is, however, more dramatic than the temple itself, though you may get to see some rare golden langur monkeys. Ferries leave regularly from Kachari and Umananda Ghat.

On the commanding Nilachal Hill, overlooking the river 8km west of the centre (buses can be picked up along MG Road), the important Kali temple of **Kamakhya**, with its beehive-shaped *shikhara*, is a good example of the distinctive Assamese style of architecture. As one of the *shakti pithas*, it marks the place where Sati's *yoni* (vulva) landed when her body fell to earth in 51 pieces, and is one of the three most important Tantric temples in India. Animal sacrifice is part of the ritual here and kid goats are bathed in the ceremonial tank before being led to slaughter behind the temple hall. Stalls leading to the temple sell trinkets and chai. A short walk up the hill brings you to a smaller temple with wonderful views of Guwahati and the Brahmaputra.

East of the town centre, atop another hill, is the atmospheric **Navagraha** temple – the "temple of the nine planets", an ancient seat of astrology and astronomy – with wonderful acoustics. Housed in a single red dome, the central *lingam* is encircled by a further eight representing the planets, each lit by clusters of candles. Although limited by the lack of telescopes, Indian astronomers managed to discern six planets including the moon. A small Ganesh shrine guards the entrance to the inner sanctum and the *lingams* represent, clockwise: the moon (Chandra), Mars (Mangala), the Dragon's Head (Rahu), Saturn (Sani), the Dragon's Tail (Ketu), Jupiter (Brhaspati), Mercury (Buddha) and Venus (Sukra).

Eating

For breakfast, places around the bus stand open early for tea and omelettes. Most of Guwahati's mid-range and upmarket hotels have good **restaurants**. Places tend to close around 9pm; the *Dhaba* is an exception.

Café Coffee Day Hub shopping complex on GS Rd. Part of a chain, serving real coffee, sandwiches, pastries and other snacks; ideal for those craving a taste of the West.

Dhaba GNB Rd, Silpukhuri. Good, moderately priced north Indian meat dishes, with delicious Indian breads, especially the *paratha*. Open noon–10.30pm.

Floating Island MG Rd, south of Sukreswar Ghat. Tasty, filling Rajasthani thalis on a boat on the river.

Gauhati Dairy MN Rd, Pan Bazaar. Excellent snacks including samosas, sweets and fresh curd.

JBs Near the main ferry point, MG Rd. Clean and friendly restaurant serving South and north Indian and Chinese dishes from Rs100 as well as snacks and sweets – try the tasty *halwa*.
Madras Cabin AT Rd, Paltan Bazaar. Tasty, inexpensive, South Indian food, including a range of good *sabzi*; handy for breakfast before catching an early morning bus or train.
Paradise GNB Rd, Silpukhuri. Good Assamese cuisine – pleasantly mild, with an emphasis on fish – and the only place to specialize in it. Also thalis, meat curries and Chinese food.
Woodlands GS Rd, Ulubari, and another on AT Rd near the *Raj Mahal*. South Indian veg restaurant, serving thalis, masala dosas and real coffee.

Listings

Airlines British Airways c/o Pelican Travels, *Brahmaputra Ashok Hotel* ☎0361/260 1605; Air India also in the *Brahmaputra Ashok* ☎0361/260 2281; Indian Airlines, GS Rd, Ganeshguri Charili, near Assam Assembly, Dispur ☎0361/256 4420 or 256 4421; Jet Airways, GNB Rd, Silpukhuri ☎0361/266 2202; Sahara Airlines, GS Rd, Ulubari, near Bara petrol station ☎0361/254 8676.
Banks and exchange ANZ Grindlays, GNB Rd and the State Bank of India, MG Rd, both cash travellers' cheques and change foreign currencies. There are ATMs all over town.
Bookshops There are a number of bookshops in Pan Bazaar, notably Western Book Depot, Josovanta Rd just off HB Rd, with a good selection of fiction, and titles on the northeast; the Vintage Bookshop on MN Rd opposite *Ananda Lodge*; and the Modern Book Depot on HB Rd near MN Rd.
Hospital Downtown Hospital ☎0361/233 1003; Guwahati Medical College Hospital ☎0361/252 9457.
Internet access Internet Club close to the *Ananda Lodge*; plenty of other places can be found on GNB, GS and MN roads.
Pharmacy Life Pharmacy on GS Rd, just south of B Barua Rd (daily 8am–10.30pm).
Photography New Frontier Colour Lab, SS Rd, Lakhtokia, 50m west of Pan Bazaar; S Ghoshal, HB Rd, Pan Bazaar.
Police Emergencies ☎100, Pan Bazaar ☎0361/254 0106.
Post office ARB Rd, just round the corner from the State Bank of India. The telegraph office is nearby and is open 24hr.
Travel agents Those at the *Vishwaratna*, *Dynasty*, *Raj Mahal* and *Brahmaputra Ashok* hotels can book domestic and international airline tickets. Rhino Travels, MN Rd, Pan Bazaar (☎0361/254 0666) can also book air tickets and buses run to the airport from their office. Network Travels, Paltan Bazaar (☎0361/252 2007), can arrange tours, Indian Airlines and Jet Airways air tickets and private bus tickets. Jungle Travels (see box, p.983) will book domestic and international flights, help acquire permits and arrange tours.

Around Guwahati

Every home in the village of **SUALKUCHI**, 36km from Guwahati, produces the golden-coloured *muga* **silk**, named after the rich amber colour of the *muga* cocoon exclusive to Assam. The village started to pay its women weavers the same as men in 2005, setting a precedent for other Assamese villages which rely on weaving for their main income. The silk is cheaper here than in Guwahati, and you can buy it direct from many of the villagers' homes. **HAJO**, 2km north, is a pilgrimage site for Hindus, Buddhists and Muslims, worth seeing for its mix of religious temples including the Hindu **Hayagriba-Madhava Mandir**. Muslims believe that visiting the **Poa Mecca mosque** here four times in a lifetime is equivalent to a pilgrimage to Mecca.

The beautiful **MANAS NATIONAL PARK** (Rs250, camera Rs500), a World Heritage Site, lies 80km west of Guwahati off the NH-31 on the border with Bhutan. Reopened in 2001, the park was closed for many years because of insurgency, during which time it lay open to poaching. As a result, its population of large mammals has sadly diminished and sightings of its eighty-odd tigers and wild elephants are rare. It is still worth a visit for its varied natural beauty however, with water buffalo grazing on expansive stretches of sand and grass, and Sal tree forests flanking the Manas River. The park is also home

Moving on from Guwahati

Many routes follow narrow, steep mountain roads, making progress painfully slow. **State-run buses** to destinations throughout the northeast leave from the ASTC stand on AT Rd; some routes are serviced by superfast luxury state buses. **Private buses** are a lot more comfortable than normal state buses; most have booths in Paltan Bazaar just behind the railway station.

Of the several daily **trains** linking Guwahati to Delhi – the thrice-weekly Rajdhani Express #2423 (Mon, Thurs & Fri; departs 6am; 28hr) is the fastest. For Kolkata, the daily Kanchenjunga Express #5658 to Sealdah station (departs 10pm; 22hr 35min) and the daily Kamrup Express #5960 (departs 7am; 23hr 30min) are two of the best. Within the hill states, there are services to Lumding, all of which continue to Dimapur. On the metre-gauge line, the daily Tezpur Express #5813 serves North Lakhimpur (13hr) and Murkong Selek (19hr).

There are Pawan Hans **helicopter** flights to Shillong, Tura, Naharlagun and Tawang in Arunachal Pradesh (ⓣ0361/284 0300) from Guwahati. For details of **airline** flights, see p.1021; see Guwahati listings for flight-booking travel agents.

For those with time and money to spare, the Assam Bengal Navigation Company (ⓣ0361/260 2186, ⓦwww.assambengalnavigation.com; 1st Floor, Mandovi Apartment, GNB Road) runs four- to ten-day sightseeing **cruises** on the Brahmaputra.

to four hundred species of birds, capped and golden langurs, and swamp and hog deer. The *Mathunguri Forest Bungalow* overlooking the river has three rooms (❸) but no telephone – for more information contact the Field Director (ⓣ03666/260289). Or try the *Bansbari Tourist Lodge* just outside the park – book with Jungle Travels in Guwahati (see box, p.983; ❹–❺). You'll need to hire your own transport to get here.

Tezpur and around

TEZPUR, 174km northeast of Guwahati, is a busy little town on the north bank of the Brahmaputra. Literally meaning "full of blood", it is named after a mythical battle between Vishnu and Shiva. You may need to stay here if you're heading up to Arunachal Pradesh.

Chitralekha Udyan (daily 8am–8pm; Rs5, camera Rs10 extra), with its central lake (paddleboats Rs20 for 15min), is a good place to potter, especially in the early evening when the pathways are lit up with fairy lights. Still known locally as Cole Park after its founder, the British deputy commissioner, it was established in the 1800s to house the sculptures and ruins of the Ban dynasty. The town's main market, **Chowk Bazaar**, is on MC Road; a little further north lies the ninth-century **Mahabhairav Temple**, dedicated to an incarnation of Shiva. Along the river 1km to the east, the hill of **Agnigarh** commands great views, and is known as the place where Asura, the king of the Ban dynasty, protected his beautiful daughter, Usha, from men who wanted to seduce her.

Practicalities

Tezpur's ASTC state **bus stand**, on Kabarkhana (KK) Road, serves most destinations throughout the region and is 500m north from the **tourist office** (Mon–Sat 10am–4.30pm; ⓣ03712/221016), in the *Tourist Lodge* on KP Agarwalla Road. The **GPO** is on Head Post Office Road, parallel to the main road; at the time of writing, no banks changed foreign currency in town. Indian Airlines flights from the **airport** here (see "Travel details", p.1021) can be booked through Anand Travels (ⓣ03712/230693), near the Jonaki cinema, or the Indian Airlines office is two doors down from the *Tourist Lodge*. Shambhala Tours & Travels (☎03712/252108) and Seven Sisters Safari (☎03712/223580), both on Kabarkhana (KK) Road, run daily **Sumo** 4WD services from Tezpur to Tawang (12hr).

For **accommodation**, decent budget options include *Hotel Basanth* (☎03712/230831; ❸) on MC Road, with very clean rooms, and the *Tourist Lodge* (☎03712/221016; ❷–❸), 500m south of the bus stand, which has six clean and peaceful rooms and a cheap fifteen-bed dorm (Rs75). The *Luit* (☎03712/224708; ❻), a large white building 100m north of the state bus stand down a little lane off Ranu Singh Road, is Tezpur's only mid-range hotel. Though its rooms are clean and some have balcony views, it's a rather tired and soulless place with a dingy restaurant and an unreliable power supply. For something a little different, you can stay a 30km drive north of Tezpur at the *Addabarie Tea Estate Burra Bungalow* (❼–❽), which has comfortable, quiet rooms surrounded by pretty gardens – book through *Wildgrass* in Kaziranga (see p.990).

Restaurants include *Flora*, on MC Road, which serves good Indian, continental and Chinese dishes; *Raj Chinese Hotel* on Nehru Maidan also serves decent Chinese food.

Nameri National Park

A 35km journey north of Tezpur and only reachable by taxi, the 200-square-kilometre **NAMERI NATIONAL PARK** (Nov–March daily; Rs250 [Rs20]) flanks the River Bharali and is a lovely, quiet place for fishing, rafting, bird-watching or guided walks in safe areas of the park. There are over three hundred species of birds here, including the rare white-winged wood duck, as well as fish eagles and hornbills. You may also see deer, but the park's larger wildlife – tigers, elephants and bison – are rarely sighted. Guides can be arranged at the park entrance, while fishing and walking can be arranged via the *Eco Camp* (☎03714/210533; ❻), 3km- from the park, which has ten comfortable twin-bedded tents; a dormitory was being built at the time of writing. Alternatively, stay in Bhalukpong (see p.1001), which is only 10km from the park entrance. Gurudongma Tours & Treks (see p.983) can arrange specialist bird-watching tours to Nameri, as can *Wildgrass* in Kaziranga (see p.990).

Kaziranga National Park

A World Heritage Site covering an area of 430 square kilometres on the southern bank of the Brahmaputra, the magnificent **KAZIRANGA NATIONAL PARK**, 217km east of Guwahati, occupies the vast valley floor against a backdrop of the Karbi Anglong hills. Its rivulets, shallow lakes and the semi-evergreen forested highlands blend into marshes and flood plains covered with tall elephant grass. A visit here, especially in the early morning, is an exhilarating experience and you will likely see elephants, deer, wild buffalo and the park's famous one-horned **rhino** – numbering around 1500, the largest concentration in the subcontinent. Though its estimated eighty tigers are very elusive, driving through the park's landscape of open savannah grassland interspersed with dense jungle is a wonderful experience. The abundant birdlife includes egrets, herons, storks, fish eagles, kingfishers and a grey pelican colony.

Kaziranga celebrated its centenary in 2005. Sadly, with grasslands bordering onto cultivated fields, and domestic cattle encroaching on the sanctuary and introducing epidemics, the wild animals are under increasing threat. The authorities say that poaching is now under control, though rhino horns still fetch astronomical prices as aphrodisiacs.

The rhino is best seen from the back of an elephant, first thing on a winter's morning. They seem oblivious to camera-clicking tourists, although like the unpredictable wild buffalo, they're equipped with lethal horns and are potentially ferocious. Jeeps will take you deeper into the forest than elephants but they cannot get nearly as close to the rhinos.

Kaziranga is open from November to early April. Try to avoid visiting the park on Sundays, when it gets busy with noisy groups of Indian tourists. During the monsoons (June–Sept), the Brahmaputra bursts its banks, flooding the low-lying grasslands and causing animals to move to higher ground within the park.

Kaziranga practicalities

Kaziranga is easily accessible by **bus**, with services from Tezpur (80km), Jorhat (97km), Guwahati (220km) and Dibrugarh (220km) in Assam, Itanagar in Arunachal Pradesh and Kohima in Nagaland. ASTC and private buses from all directions stop at **Kohora**, the main gate, on the NH-37 (AT Road), with Network Travels serving as the pick-up and drop-off point – you can arrange transport to and from the park here, and there's an inexpensive restaurant. The nearest town is **BOKAKHAT**, 20km east, which is good for shopping and has Internet facilities.

For **information** on the park, visit the Directorate of Tourism (Ⓣ03776/262423) in *Bonani Lodge* (see below), or contact the Field Director (Ⓣ03776/268095). Visiting Kaziranga is expensive because of the two-tier price system, with different entry costs for Indian nationals (Rs20) and foreigners (Rs250), plus camera fees (Rs 500 still, Rs10,000 video [Rs250/Rs 2500]). Both **Jeeps** (Rs500 plus Rs150 tax, Rs50 compulsory guard fees and Rs20 "viewing" fees) and one-hour **elephant rides** (5.15am, 6.15am & 7.15am; Rs750 plus Rs250 viewing fee [Rs120 plus Rs20]) can be booked in advance via hotels or the park offices in Kohora, as can guides. All vehicles also have to pay an extra toll of Rs300. Elephant rides take place in both the Kohora and Baguri ranges of the park.

Kaziranga now has a good range of **places to stay** and eat. There are four government tourist lodges clustered around the main gate at Kohora. *Aranya* (Ⓣ03776/262429; ❹) is the best of the tourist lodges, with 21 clean rooms, balconies, room service and a decent restaurant; *Bonani* (Ⓣ03776/262423; ❸) has five clean double rooms, with a/c if needed; *Bonoshree* (❷) offers eight doubles and a four-bedded room, all with bath; while *Kunjaban* is the basic budget option, with dorm beds (Rs50 or Rs75 with bed linen). Both *Bonoshree* and *Kunjaban* should be booked through *Bonani*. There are some comfortable alternatives to the tourist lodges. Set back from the main NH-37 in quiet, peaceful gardens 1km from the park entrance, *Bonhabi Resort* (book through *Bonani*; Ⓣ03776/262675; ❺–❻) is a clean and spacious place with double rooms, attractive, comfortable cottages with balconies backing onto woodland, charming, helpful staff and a pleasant restaurant. At the foot of the Karbi hills, 4km east of Kohora and 1.5km off the road, *Wildgrass* (Ⓣ0361/254 6827; Ⓕ263 0465; ❻) is an attractive and spacious eco-resort with pleasant en-suite rooms decked out with bamboo and cane furniture, a swimming pool and excellent bird-watching and wildlife guides. Both *Wildgrass* and *Bonhabi* can arrange visits to local Mising and Karbi villages. Finally, the *Soil Conservation Inspection Bungalow* (Ⓣ03776/262409; ❹), has clean rooms in a pleasant house set back from a picnic ground, though it can get noisy on Sundays. You can use the Internet at the Community Information Centre next door.

Network Travels and *Aranya Lodge* provide inexpensive **food** for those not staying at *Bonhabi* or *Wildgrass*. *Ashyana Green Resort* on the NH-37 towards the Baguri range has a spacious restaurant serving Indian and Chinese dishes and snacks.

Upper Assam

Around 310km northeast upriver from Guwahati, **Jorhat** has an airport and road connections to Kaziranga, Nagaland and northern Arunachal Pradesh, and makes a good base for exploring the unique Vaishnavite culture of **Majuli**, the largest river island in the world, and **Sibsagar**, former capital of the Ahoms and home to numerous tombs, temples and palaces. Further north, **Dibrugarh**, connected to Delhi by air, is opening up as a convenient gateway to northern Nagaland and eastern Arunachal Pradesh. On the road to Arunachal Pradesh, the **Dibru-Saikhowa National Park** is worth a visit for its birdlife and wild horses, and **Digboi**'s attractions include an interesting oil museum and war memorial.

Jorhat

Well connected by railway, **JORHAT** is not in itself of great interest but it's the nearest town to Kaziranga and makes a good base for exploring Majuli and Sibsagar. The **airport** is 5km out of town and served by Indian Airlines buses and auto-rickshaws. Indian Airlines and Jet both have offices in the *Hotel Paradise* (see below). The ASTC terminal is half a block north of the private companies' offices and bus stops. The **railway station** is 3km southeast of the bus stand. Assam Tourism's **tourist office** is at the *Tourist Lodge* on MG Road (Mon–Sat 10am–4pm, closed 2nd & 4th Sat of month; ⓣ0376/232 1579). The State Bank of India on AT Road changes cash and travellers' cheques. A number of places provide **Internet** access.

The *Tourist Lodge* (ⓣ0376/232 1579; ❷) has tired-looking but inexpensive **rooms**, or try the more comfortable *Hotel Paradise* (ⓣ0376/232 1366; ❹–❻), down a lane off AT Road. A 17km-drive south of Jorhat along the Na Ali Road at Jalukonibari lies the delightful *Thengal Manor* (ⓣ0376/233 0268, ⓔsasankasaikia@yahoo.com, ⓦwww.heritagetourismindia.com; ❽), the colonial-style former holiday home of the local Barooah family. The house has a gorgeous colonnaded veranda and spacious terraces, as well as fishing ponds and a manicured lawn, and all five rooms have four-poster beds and elegant antique furniture. The same family also run the *Sangsua Tea Estate Burra Bungalow* (booking details as *Thengal Manor*; ❼–❽) a peaceful tea planter's bungalow 25km southwest of Jorhat with a colonial-style veranda and comfortable, spacious rooms; a tea tour is available from here.

As well as the hotels, **eating** options include the *Oasis* on MG Road and *Treats* on KB Road for Indian and Chinese food, or the *Food Hut* near the *Tourist Lodge* for Assamese thalis.

Majuli

The most popular outing from Jorhat is a trip to **MAJULI**, the largest river island in the world and now a UNESCO World Heritage Site. It's a fascinating place, largely because of its unique Vaishnavite *sattras* (monasteries), and a population containing a wide mix of tribal peoples, including Ahoms, Kacharis, Mising and Deori. The island is also a haven for bird-watchers.

Ferries for Majuli leave twice a day (10am & 3pm; Rs10) from **Nimatighat**, which is accessible by public bus or taxi (Rs250; 1hr) from Jorhat. As the ferry timings only give you an hour or so on the island, it is inadvisable to visit as a day-trip – you can hire your own boat for Rs3500 return (contact monk Dulal Saikia (ⓣ03775/273037 for details) but you'll get more out of the island if you stay overnight (see p.992).

Although distances are short, public transport around the island is limited to the occasional bus – these run to the village of **Kamalabari** (6 daily; roughly

5km), and beyond to the island's "capital" at **Garamur** – there are also some taxis and auto-rickshaws. For those with plenty of time, the most relaxing way to take in the *sattras* is on foot or bicycle. **Accommodation** options include the *Natun Kamalabari Guesthouse* (Ⓣ03775/273302; ❶), which has eight rooms and offers food, or there are three basic rooms in a separate guesthouse (no name) just by the gate to the Utter Kamalabari where you can stay for a small donation. There is also a *Circuit House* (Ⓣ03775/274439; ❸) at Garamur.

There are 22 *sattras* on Majuli: the *sattra* – a temple, monastery, school and centre for the arts where poetry, folk music, literature, sculpture and dance are explored – consists of a prayer hall (*namghar*) surrounded by living quarters for devotees, and *ghats* for bathing. In a day, you could visit **Natun Kamalabari**, and 1.5km away, **Utter Kamalabari**, where Michael Palin pitched up in the BBC television series *Himalaya*. The monks will give you tea, and you can sometimes sit in on prayer meetings in their meditation hall. Four kilometres further west at **Auniati**, another *sattra* keeps royal artefacts from the Ahom kingdom and has an interesting collection of Assamese handicrafts and jewellery. **Bengenati**, 4km east of Auniati, was built in the early seventeenth century; **Shamaguri**, 6km beyond Bengenati, is renowned for the making of clay and bamboo masks. **Bongaori**, 8km beyond Shamaguri, and **Dakhinpat**, 5km further south, are also worth a visit.

There are two ferries a day (8am & 2pm) back to Nimatighat; the journey from Garamur to Jorhat takes around five hours. It is also possible to travel north from Majuli, with two daily ferries from Luhitghat, 3km north of Garamur, to Khabalughat on the north bank, from where there are buses to North Lakhimpur, and from there, buses on to Itanagar or Tezpur, and a train to Guwahati. Allow yourself plenty of time.

Sibsagar

The former capital of the Ahoms and one of the oldest towns in Assam, **SIBSAGAR** – "The Ocean of Shiva" – lies 60km northeast of Jorhat. Its cluster of monuments from six centuries of Ahom rule are still of significance to modern Assamese culture. A huge **tank**, constructed by Queen Madambika in 1734, lies at the heart of the complex. Rising from its southern shore, the massive 32-metre-high **Shivadol** is the tallest Shiva temple in India, flanked by smaller temples dedicated to Durga and Vishnu. Nearly 4km west of the centre of town is the **Rang Ghar** pavilion, from which the royal family watched traditional games such as buffalo fighting; and the ruins of the **Talatal Ghar**, the Ahom's impressive seven-storey palace.

Though best visited as a day-trip, there are **accommodation** options: *Siddhartha* on Bhuban Gogoi Road near the fire station (Ⓣ03772/222276, Ⓔe7safari@rediffmail.com; ❸–❺) has decent rooms, friendly staff, a laundry service and a bar and restaurant; there are clean and homely rooms at *Shiva Palace* (Ⓣ03772/225184; ❸–❺) on AT Road, 200 metres from the ASTC bus stand, where you can get tasty north Indian food at its in-house restaurant, *Sky Chef*. *Kareng* on Temple Road (Ⓣ03772/222713; ❷) is a clean budget option with a bar. A great cup of coffee can be had from the stalls opposite the Shivadol.

Dibrugarh and around

The dusty, little-touristed town of **DIBRUGARH**, 443km north of Guwahati, is surrounded by no fewer than nine golf courses and lies at the heart of tea-growing country. Though there's little to see in the town itself, Dibrugarh is opening up as a gateway for eastern and northern Arunachal Pradesh and northern Nagaland, especially for those who have limited time in the northeast and want to avoid Guwahati. Dibrugarh is a good place to see how Assamese **tea** is produced. Purvi Discovery (see "Access, permits and tour operators" box, p.983) offers tea tours on its working tea estate.

Practicalities

Dibrugarh's **airport**, with direct flights to Delhi, Kolkata and Guwahati, is 16km from town. Domestic air tickets can be booked at Crown Travels, Mancotta Road (ⓣ0373/232 0007). There are good rail and bus connections to Guwahati and the rest of the region. The bus stations are in the centre of town – the **government bus station** is in Chowkidinghee, the **private bus stand** nearby at Phool Bagan. There's a State Bank of India at Thanka Charali, the central commercial district, which will cash **travellers' cheques**. A **car with driver** can be hired from Monikanchan Travel Agency near Chowkidinghee (ⓣ0373/232 5879), or ask Purvi Discovery about Jeep hire (see p.983). To reach northern Arunachal Pradesh from Dibrugarh, there is a daily **ferry** from Dibrugarh to Oiramghat, near Pasighat (4–6hr; Rs96 per passenger, Rs1500 for a Jeep). The ferry leaves Dibrugarh at 9am – arrive at least an hour before departure to ensure a seat.

Places to stay in town include *Mona Lisa* on Mancotta Road (ⓣ0373/232 0416, ⓔpaneijonki@sancharnet.in; ❺), which has a pleasant courtyard, spacious rooms and a bar; or try one of the cool and airy rooms at *Indsurya* on RKB Path (ⓣ0373/232 6322; ❹–❺). The best option, 5km from the railway station and 15km from the airport, is to stay in one of the two peaceful *Chang Bungalows* (❽) on Purvi Discovery's tea estate. Built on stilts by British tea planters to protect them from floods and jungle animals, the bungalows have polished wooden floors, elegant dark wood furniture and offer excellent service. For **food**, *H_20* on the first floor of Amrit Mansion on RNC Path is a trendy bar and restaurant with English-speaking staff serving Thai, Indian, Chinese and Assamese food.

Dibru-Saikhowa National Park

About 60km north of Dibrugarh, **DIBRU-SAIKHOWA NATIONAL PARK**, is rich in birdlife and popular for its wild horses. Good railway services run to New Tinsukia Station, 10km from the park's southern entry point at **Guijan**. Information is available from the Range Officer here (ⓣ0374/233 7569). Reachable as a day-trip from Dibrugarh, you can alternatively stay in the *Inspection Bungalow* at Guijan (ⓣ0374/233 7569; ❷) or campsite (ⓣ0374/233 7666). Purvi Discovery (see p.983) has a basic bungalow which is sometimes available for independent travellers. In Tinsukia, *Highway* on AT Road (ⓣ0374/336383; ❸–❹) is 500m from the station and has adequate rooms and a vegetarian restaurant.

Digboi

DIGBOI, 80km northeast of Dibrugarh, is an interesting place to stop en route to Arunachal Pradesh, with an oil refinery established by the British in 1900, an oil museum, a peaceful World War II cemetery and an eighteen-hole golf course. If you get stuck in Digboi, the Indian Oil Corporation has a guesthouse with 22 clean and spacious rooms (ⓣ03751/64715; ❸–❺).

South Assam: Silchar

South Assam, divided from the north by the Cachar Hills, is the crossing point for the surrounding states of Meghalaya, Tripura, Mizoram and Manipur.

Nondescript **SILCHAR** acts as the region's main transport hub. A group of Tibetan traders run a small wool market on Central Road during the winter months which is worth a visit for its clothing, carpets and friendly atmosphere. If you need to stay the night, *Sudakshina* (Ⓣ03842/230156; ❸–❹), on Shillong Patty, has reasonable rooms and hot water, or the *Hotel Siddharth* (Ⓣ03842/232473; ❷–❹), just round the corner on Narshingtola, has clean rooms with showers and TV – there's no restaurant but you can order good Indian food in your room. *Geetanjali* (Ⓣ03842/231738; ❷–❹) on Club Road has adequate rooms and a good restaurant.

Silchar's **airport** is 13km from town; Moti Travels on Hospital Road (Ⓣ03842/233716) is a good ticket agent for flights. The **state bus stand**, near the Devdoot cinema, is the terminus for Assam, Meghalaya and Tripura state services; most **private bus** and **Sumo** companies also run services from here and have agents all over town. The road to Imphal is not recommended because of its bad condition and numerous army checkpoints. The **railway station** is 3km out of town in Tarapur, though at the time of writing, services to Lumding, from where you can pick up connections to Guwahati, were temporarily suspended.

Meghalaya

MEGHALAYA, one of the smallest states in India, occupies the plateau and rolling hills between Assam and Bangladesh. Its people are predominantly Christian and belong to three main ethnic groups, the Khasis, Jaintias and Garos. The state has a high literacy rate and teaching is in English.

Much of Meghalaya ("land of the rain-clouds") is covered with lush forests, rich in orchids. These "blue hills" catch the main force of the monsoon-laden winds off the Bay of Bengal, and are among the wettest places on earth. Stupendous waterfalls can be seen near the capital, **Shillong**, but the most dramatic plummet from the plateau to the south, around **Cherrapunjee**. The hills of Meghalaya rise to just under 2000m, which makes for a pleasant year-round climate, a welcome refuge from the steamy valleys of Assam. The **Jaintia Hills** in the east offer good walking and caving, and the state is laced with historical sights such as **Nartiang** near **Jowai**, which has an impressive collection of monoliths and standing stones.

On January 21, 1972, after an eighteen-year struggle for autonomy from Assam, Meghalaya became a full-fledged state. The HNLC, the rebel underground movement, regularly calls *bandhs* demanding independence from the rest of India – shops and restaurants close during such times, and it's difficult to travel anywhere by public transport.

Shillong and around

With its rolling hills and elegant pines, **SHILLONG** was known to the British as "the Scotland of the East" – an impression first brought to mind by **Barapani**, the stunning loch-like reservoir on its fringes, and the sight of the local Khasi women wearing gingham and tartan shawls. At an altitude of around 1500m, Shillong became a popular hill station for the British, who built it on the site of a thousand-year-old Khasi settlement and made it the capital of Assam in 1874.

Sadly, much of the town is now charmless and dirty, and its surrounding hills have been subjected to severe deforestation. The influx of settlers from the

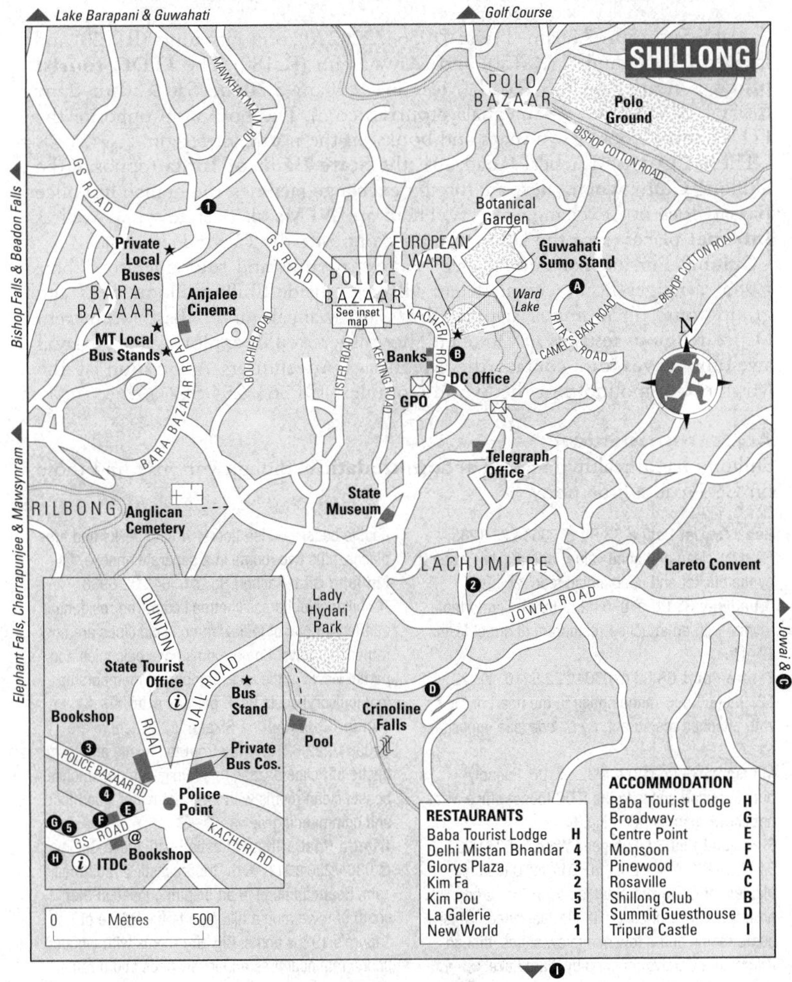

plains has placed a strain on natural resources, especially water, and a general lack of planning has resulted in haphazard growth and an invasion of rats. Much of the original Victorian town, however, is still evident, and the large gardens around the clean and well-kept **Ward Lake** and the buildings surrounding it conjure up images of a colonial past. North of the polo ground, there is an eighteen-hole golf course founded in 1898 by a group of enthusiastic British civil servants.

Arrival and information

Shillong (also known as Umroi) **airport** is 34km west of the city centre, with regular bus connections to town (1hr 30min). Buses from outside the state pull in at the **Police Bazaar** area at the heart of town. Central Shillong can easily be explored on foot, though auto-rickshaws and taxis are available. The **state tourist office**, on Jail Road opposite the main bus station (Mon–Sat

7.30am–5pm, Sun 7.30am–11am; ⓣ0364/226220), runs city tours (Rs120) and trips to Cherrapunjee (Rs150) and Mawsynram (Rs180). The **ITDC tourist office** is nearby on GS Road (Mon–Fri 9.30am–5.30pm, Sat 9.30am–2pm; ⓣ0364/225632, ⓦwww.meghalayatourism.com). The bookshop opposite the ITDC office stocks town maps and books on the northeast region.

The **GPO** is on Kacheri Road, as is the **State Bank of India** (opposite the Shillong Club), where there are foreign exchange facilities; the branch in Police Bazaar does not exchange money. There are **ATMs** all over town, as well as **Internet** places – for the latter, try *Alfies*, opposite the *Centre Point Hotel*.

Cultural Pursuits Adventures (see "Access, permits and tour operators" box, p.983) arranges homestays in Khasi villages outside Shillong, local treks and group tours, including a trip to the Garo Wangala and Khasi Nongkrem Dance religious festivals in October. Those interested in exploring Meghalaya's awesome **caves** can contact the Meghalaya Adventurers Association at the Mission Compound near the Synod Complex (ⓣ0364/254 5621).

Accommodation

Shillong has a healthy range of **accommodation**, though you may find those on GS Road a little noisy.

Baba Tourist Lodge GS Rd ⓣ0364/221 1285. Friendly, clean and good value, with a/c, hot water by the bucket and good Indian food. ❷–❸

Broadway GS Rd ⓣ0364/222 6996. Comfortable rooms, with an attached restaurant at street level. ❸–❹

Centre Point GS Rd ⓣ0364/222 5210, ⓕ222 5239. Good mid-range option in the heart of town, with attached restaurant, *La Galerie* (see opposite). ❺–❽

Monsoon GS Rd ⓣ0364/222 7106. Friendly budget option opposite the ITDC tourist office, with hot showers in the morning. ❹

Pinewood Rita Rd, European Ward ⓣ0364/222 3116, ⓕ222 4176. Built in 1917 for British tea planters, this Raj-era hotel is now rather tired, grubby and overpriced, with old-fashioned, rather damp rooms and a few bungalow suites, though it's set in attractive grounds by Ward Lake. ❺–❾

Rosaville ⓣ0364/222 1622, ⓦwww.heritagetourismindia.com. A peaceful, homely, 1930s colonial house a few kilometres east of Shillong, off the National Highway. Three large rooms with comfy double beds, wooden floors, writing desks and fireplaces, plus two rooms in a separate annexe. ❽

Shillong Club Kacheri Rd ⓣ0364/222 6938, ⓔshillongclubltdresi@hotmail.com. The residential quarters of one of India's famous old clubs are now rather run down. Some rooms have balconies and partial views of the lake. Temporary membership (compulsory) costs Rs30 per day extra. ❸–❻

Summit Guesthouse Sikandra 23 Lachumiere ⓣ0364/222 6216. Away from the hustle and bustle of Police Bazaar, this family-run guesthouse boasts clean rooms with 24hr hot water, good food and commanding views. ❹–❺

Tripura Castle Tripura Castle Road, Cleve Colony ⓣ0364/250 1111, ⓔrh_tripuracastle@rediffmail.com. Beautiful hotel in an inspiring location 3km south of town atop a hill, next to the Prince of Tripura's 1920s home. Big airy rooms with wooden floors, real coal fires and lovely beds and a range of DVDs for hire, plus a mezzanine bar and restaurant (see opposite). You can arrange to have a very good local Khasi massage in your room here with Dr Alka Kharsati. ❻–❽

The Town

Life in Shillong used to revolve around the decorative **Ward Lake** (daily except Tues) and the exclusive European Ward next to it, with its large bungalows set in generous pine-shadowed gardens, including the governor's official residence, Government House. The ambience here is in stark contrast to the narrow streets of **Police Bazaar**, packed with vendors, or, further west, **Bara Bazaar**, where Meghalaya's oldest market, **Iewduh**, is held every eight days. Meghalaya's shabby **State Museum** in Lachumiere (Mon–Sat, 10am–4pm; closed 2nd & 4th Sat of the month; free) has exhibits depicting tribal customs, though at the time of writing, a new Meghalaya Museum was planned.

Moving on from Shillong

Local buses depart from Bara Bazaar, and **Jeeps** leave from outside the Anjalee cinema for the same destinations when full. **State buses** depart from the bus stand on Jail Road, leaving hourly for Guwahati between 6am and 4pm. **Private bus** firms run services all over the northeast and there are ticket agents all around Police Point. The journey to Agartala in Tripura is a tortuous 20 hours. For Aizawl you may prefer to travel to Silchar and then continue by Jeep. Services to Nagaland and Manipur go via Guwahati. The border crossing to **Bangladesh** at Dawki, southeast of Cherrapunjee, is served by private buses from Bara Bazaar, and a fleet of Tata Sumos, which also run to Cheerapunjee and Mawsynram.

There are regular **flights** to Aizawl, Kolkata and Silchar with Indian Airlines from Shillong airport; book with Sheba Travels (Ⓣ0364/222 3015) in Police Bazaar, which can also book domestic flights with Air Sahara and Jet Airways. There are also two or three **helicopter** flights (Ⓣ0364/222 3129) a day to Guwahati (Rs 725) and four a week to Tura (Rs1525). See "Travel details" at the end of this chapter for more information.

For some respite from the city, head to *Tripura Castle* (see opposite), from which a short uphill walk takes you past some community buidings into pine-forested hills. There are great views of the city.

Eating

Police Bazaar has places to pick up a snack – there are some good cheap cafés down the road from the tourist office on Jail Road. Bara Bazaar also has a few simple restaurants.

Baba Tourist Lodge GS Rd. Inexpensive and clean, with tasty Indian food.
Delhi Mistan Bhandar Police Bazaar Rd. Classic Indian snacks and sweets. Very cheap, always full, and recommended for its excellent South Indian breakfasts.
Glorys Plaza Police Bazaar Rd. Several cheap places serving tasy Tibetan *momo* (stuffed dumplings).
Kim Fa Lachumiere. Branch of *Kim Pou*.
Kim Pou GS Rd. Good Chinese restaurant.
La Galerie *Hotel Centre Point*, Police Bazaar. Popular mid-range restaurant, serving tasty Indian and Chinese food.
New World GS Rd, at Bara Bazaar junction. A crowded local favourite, serving good Chinese food including spicy Szechuan dishes.
Tripura Castle (see opposite). A good place for lunch in a lovely setting. Book ahead for dinner, and order in advance for Khasi food – dishes on offer include banana flower with sesame seeds and red rice with wild mushrooms.

Cherrapunjee and Mawsynram

CHERRAPUNJEE, 56km south of Shillong in the Khasi Hills, achieved fame as the wettest place on earth, with an average annual rainfall of 1205cm. The highest daily rainfall ever recorded fell here in 1876 – 104cm in 24 hours – but Cherrapunjee now shares its watery crown with nearby Mawsynram, whose average annual rainfall is a staggering 11,873mm. Cherrapunjee's numerous falls are most impressive during the steamy monsoon season when awesome torrents of water plunge down to the Bangladeshi plains.

The town is divided into upper and lower sections, spread out over several kilometres. Every eight days (and four days after the Iewduh in Shillong), a market is held here, with tribal jewellery and the local orange-coloured honey on offer. The various nearby points of interest – the **Noh Kalikai waterfall**, **Bangladesh viewpoint**, and **Mawsmai village and cave** – are each a few kilometres in different directions out of Cherrapunjee. An easy way of seeing them all is to join the Meghalaya Tourism **day-trip** from the ITDC tourist office in Shillong (see p.996). Alternatively, regular state buses and Sumos run from Shillong, leaving from the Anjalee cinema bus stand from 7am, though the last bus returns early, at 2.30pm.

Good **accommodation** and food are available at the stunningly located *Cherrapunjee Holiday Resort* (Ⓣ03637/264218, Ⓦwww.cherrapunjee.com; ❹–❺), perched on the edge of the East Khasi hills with excellent views to the plains of Bangladesh below. From here you can also explore some fascinating 150-year-old living root bridges, cool springs, waterfalls, caves and Khasi villages.

You can take a day trek to Cherrapunjee along the David Scott trail from **Mawsphlang**, the site of an ancient sacred grove – try Impulse Inc at the NGO Network in Shillong's Lachumiere (Ⓣ0364/250 0587).

At **MAWSYNRAM**, 12km from Cherrapunjee, the main attraction is **Mawjinbuin cave**, where a stalagmite resembling a Shiva-lingam is perpetually bathed by water dripping from a breast-shaped stalactite above. Since there are no direct buses between Mawsynram and Cherrapunjee, you will need to hire a taxi; buses from Shillong leave from Bara Bazaar, or you can visit as part of the (somewhat rushed) Meghalaya Tourism day-trip. The only **accommodation** in Mawsynram is the Inspection Bungalow (❶); book with the Deputy Commissioner's office in Shillong (Ⓣ0364/222 4003).

Dawki

Ninety-six kilometres southeast from Shillong, **DAWKI** is the most important of the Meghalaya–Bangladesh border crossings and has excellent views of the Khasi Hills and Bangladesh. A regular Jeep service from Bara Bazaar serves Dawki. The equivalent border town in Bangladesh is **Tamabil**, just two-and-a-half hours from Sylhet. There is no Bangladesh visa office in Meghalaya, so you will need to possess a valid visa before entering the country – Kolkata has a consulate. There is also a Bangladeshi Embassy in Agartala, Tripura and a border crossing into Bangladesh from there (see p.1016). If you are arriving at Dawki from Bangladesh, the last bus to Shillong departs around 11.30am. Accommodation is available, including an Inspection Bungalow, which can be booked at the police station.

Jowai and Nartiang

The market town of **JOWAI**, 64km northeast of Shillong in the **Jaintia Hills**, holds the annual Behdienkhlam Festival every July. About 12km north of the town, at **NARTIANG**, are the remains of the Jaintia kings' summer palace and an impressive collection of monoliths and standing stones. A taxi costs about Rs400 from Jowai. There are caves throughout the area – Cultural Pursuits in Shillong can arrange visits and treks (see p.983). Two daily **buses** run from Shillong to Jowai (4hr), or take a taxi (2hr 30min).

Arunachal Pradesh

ARUNACHAL PRADESH, "the land of the dawn-lit mountains", is one of the last unspoilt wildernesses in India. Almost every major river valley is home to a different tribe, with a wealth of fascinating cultures and peoples living in a habitat that combines glacial terrain, alpine meadows and subtropical rainforests.

The state capital of **Itanagar** is located north of the Brahmaputra across from Jorhat. In the far west of the state, the road from **Bhalukpong** on the Assamese border to **Tawang** climbs steadily through rugged hills, glacial streams and dense primeval forest, crossing the bleak and dramatic **Sela Pass** (4300m) midway. Along the route lie the Buddhist towns of **Bomdila**, **Rupa** and **Chillipam**, with their colourful Tibetan monasteries. In the far northeast of Arunachal, the pristine vegetation of **Namdapha National Park** (Oct–April) is home to clouded and snow leopards, tigers and elephants. Nearby **Parasuramkund** is one of India's most important and least accessible Hindu pilgrimage sites, where a dip washes away the sins of a lifetime.

Despite its beauty, tourism in Arunachal Pradesh has been discouraged due to the extremely sensitive border with Chinese-occupied Tibet in the north and Myanmar in the east. In 1962, the Chinese invaded Arunachal Pradesh, reaching Tezpur in Assam, a 300-kilometre incursion that India has never forgotten. Since then, a strong military stance has been adopted in the area. All visitors require a **permit** to visit the state, and are strongly encouraged to visit with a **tour operator**, especially as most places are only accessible by Jeep (see box, p.983).

Be aware that during the summer months, most of the hill towns in Arunachal Pradesh can be extremely cold, and the accommodation is not geared up to cope – bring your own winter sleeping bag, and consider packing a hot water bottle.

Itanagar

Just under 400km northeast of Guwahati, **ITANAGAR**, the capital of Arunachal Pradesh holds little to interest visitors, though as it's a transport hub you may need to spend the night. Surrounded by densely forested hills, the town itself is little more than a four-kilometre stretch of road running between Zero Point, where the two top-range hotels are located, and Ganga Market, the main bazaar area where you can find cheaper accommodation around the bus stand.

If you are holed up here, the **Jawaharlal Nehru State Museum** (daily except Mon 9.30am–4pm; Rs50 [Rs2]) describes the festivals, dances, houses and lifestyles of the local tribes. Its impressive ethnographic collection on the first floor is worth a visit for its lovely wooden sculptures, musical instruments, inventive jewellery and esoteric objects such as cane penis covers. The dimly lit Government **sales emporium** above Zero Point, near *Donyi-Polo Ashok* (daily except Mon 9am–4pm), sells some interesting handicrafts and cane furniture. Ten kilometres from town, **Gyakar Sinyi** (Ganga Lake; Rs5, Rs10 for a camera) and its lush surrounding jungle provides a taste of the state's magnificent scenery, though is somewhat marred by a 2.5km concrete path. You can get good views of the surrounding countryside on the hill just above the town from the small **Tibetan Buddhist temple,** consecrated by the Dalai Lama.

Practicalities

The nearest **airport** is 67km away at **Lilabari,** just outside North Lakhimpur in Assam. There is a daily Pawan Hans **helicopter** service (☎0361/284 0300) between Itanagar and Guwahati (Rs3000), and irregular shuttle services throughout the region – flights run from **Naharlagun**, 10km away. **Trains** from Guwahati run as far as Harmuti, 33km away in Assam. Overnight **buses** connect Itanagar with Guwahati (11hr), and Arunachal State Transport runs an extensive service throughout the state. As there's no bridge across the Upper Brahmaputra, services to Dibrugarh, Tinsukia and Jorhat have to cross the Brahmaputra south of Tezpur. Taking a Tata **Sumo** will greatly reduce travel times; destinations include Hapoli (5hr), Bomdila (7hr 30min), Pasighat (6hr 30min) and Along (10hr). Several agents around Ganga Market sell tickets. In town, there's a **state tourist office** behind the Akash Deep complex.

△ Demon dancer

The most expensive **hotel** in Itanagar is the government-run *Donyi-Polo Ashok*, above Zero Point (Ⓣ0360/221 2635; Ⓔhoteldonyi@sancharnet.in; ❼). There are great views from here but its soulless and tired rooms are overpriced and there's a very noisy disco-cum-bar most evenings. A better choice is the *Arun Subansiri*, just below Zero Point (Ⓣ0360/221 2806; ❹–❺), which has a cool, marble interior, clean rooms and friendly staff. Buddhist-run *Samsara* (Ⓣ0360/221 1266; ❸–❹), in the Akash Deep complex, has adequate if shabby rooms, a relaxing rooftop space and indoor and outdoor restaurants. The *Blue Pine* on APST Road (Ⓣ0360/221 1118; ❷–❹), *Alpine* (Ⓣ0360/221 4298; ❸–❹) and *Himalaya* (Ⓣ0360/221 2590; ❶) are reasonable alternatives. Should you get stuck in **Naharlagun**, *Hotel Tosum* (Ⓣ0360/224 7228; ❹–❺) on the main road has a spacious restaurant and comfortable if musty rooms, while the *Simang* (Ⓣ0360/224 5110; ❸), near the State Bank of India, is a plant-filled, airy, budget option with clean if basic rooms and a small restaurant.

For **eating**, alternatives to the hotel restaurants in Itanagar include *Aane Hotel* on Banktinali Road for Indian and Chinese, the *Dragon Restaurant*, at 1st Floor Akash Deep, which also serves Western dishes, and *Hotel Jimsi* on the main drag at Ganga Market.

West Arunachal

Bordered by Bhutan and Tibet, the isolated hills and valleys of western Arunachal climb to some of the remotest glaciers and peaks in the Himalayas. With the exceptions of **Gori Chen** (6858m) and **Nyegi Kangsang** (7047m), most of the 6000-metre-plus mountains remain completely unknown. The solitary road serving the region runs from Tezpur in Assam through **Bhalukpong** on the Assamese border to **Tawang**, ending bone-shakingly high in the mountains at one of Asia's largest monasteries. On the way you pass through the market town of **Bomdila**, home to three Tibetan monasteries, and **Dirang**, a fortress town a couple of hours up the valley. To the west of the Tawang road lie picturesque **Rupa**, with its colourful Tibetan monastery; **Chillipam**, whose monastery and temple offer astounding views; and the fascinating Buddhist settlements of **Tenzingang** and **Kalaktang.** Beyond Tawang and very close to the border of Tibet stretches the lake district of **Bangachangsa**.

Bhalukpong

The River **Kameng** emerges from a deeply forested valley at **BHALUKPONG**. All public transport services from Tezpur, 56km away, to Bomdila stop here for border formalities and refuelling. **Accommodation** is available at the basic *Aama Yangri* (Ⓣ03782/234507; ❷), though a better option is just across the state border in Assam at the friendly and peaceful *Bhalukpong Tourist Lodge* (Ⓣ03872/234037; ❷–❹), which has four rooms and ten clean and spacious cottages overlooking the river and surrounding hills. The lodge can help arrange rafting and angling – the River Kameng is famed amongst anglers for its fighting mahseer fish. On the track leading to the lodge, *Kunki's Resort* (Ⓣ03872/234788; ❹) is a pleasant, clean, if slightly pricey guesthouse with a veranda. **Tipi**, seven kilometres north of Bhalukpong, has a small orchidarium. From here, the narrow highway winds up through dense and beautiful mountain forests to Bomdila, 100km away.

Bomdila

BOMDILA is a dirty if friendly town (2530m) set on a spur of the Thagla Ridge, the dividing line between rainforests to the south and sub-alpine valleys to the north. Its three **Tibetan Buddhist monasteries** reflect the origins and culture of the local people and its proximity to Tibet. The largest of these, a Gelugpa *gompa* high above the town, was inaugurated by the Dalai Lama in 1997, and its rooftop offers superb mountain views. The older *gompa* below houses a large blue statue of the Medicine Buddha – Sangye Menhla. A few kilometres beyond Bomdila on the Tawang road, the snow-covered peaks of Gorichen (6488m) and Kangto (7042m) come into view.

The **tourist office** (ⓣ03782/222049) is based in the *Tourist Lodge* (see below). Himalayan Holidays (ⓣ03782/222017, ⓦwww.himalayan-holidays.com), on the main market street, can arrange local **sightseeing trips** and treks, including one to Gorichen base camp. Wanges Computer World next door offers **Internet** access. The craft centre sells handicrafts by the local Monpa tribe.

There are just two **routes** out of Bomdila: onward and upward towards Tawang, and back down towards the Assamese border at Bhalukpong. State buses run from the bus station in the lower part of town to **Tezpur** (2 daily; 7–8hr); slightly faster **private buses** for Tezpur (2 daily) depart from outside Himalayan Holidays, though Tata **Sumos** are the best and most comfortable way to negotiate these steep switchback roads. Daily services run via Rupa to Tezpur, and north to Tawang.

Most of Bomdila's budget **hotels** are situated on the main market street. *Passang* (ⓣ03782/222627; ❶–❷) is the pick of the bunch, with simple clean rooms and attached bathrooms. *La*, opposite the sports ground in the upper town (ⓣ03782/222958; ❷), has small pleasant rooms with or without attached bathrooms. In the lower town, the *Dawa* (❶–❷), just up from the bus stand, has a few basic rooms with outside toilets. A better option is the *Tourist Lodge* (ⓣ03782/22049; ❷–❸), which has a pleasant garden and restaurant and big, comfy rooms, though a heater costs Rs100 extra; book ahead.

Eating options include the *Dragon*, in the centre of town, for Indian and Chinese; the *Tourist Lodge* restaurant, for simple Chinese and Indian dishes; and *Siphiyang Phong*, opposite the stadium, which serves tasty curries and soups in its rather drafty restaurant and closes later than other places at 9.30pm. There are several *dhabas* dotted around which offer simple alternatives.

Rupa and beyond

The picturesque settlement of **RUPA**, 17km below Bomdila, is the centre of the Sherdukpen people, who occupy the hills that stretch all the way to Bhutan and practise a mixture of Tibetan Buddhism and animism. Rupa has an attractive Tibetan *gompa* and a colourful riverside *lhakang* (chapel) a little further up the valley. A small roadside Guru Rinpoche cave graces the entrance to the town. Places to stay include the government Inspection Bungalow (ⓣ03782 232362; ❷) and the *Sawme* (❶–❷); both are clean with basic facilities and buckets of hot water can be provided.

About 14km beyond Rupa further off the main road, **Chillipam** has a peaceful monastery housing a community of 75 monks. An impressive new temple with astounding views is being built here, scheduled to open in 2006. A further 40km takes you to the influential Tibetan refugee settlement of **Tenzingang**. The Gelugpa monastery here houses nearly four hundred lamas, and is one of only two Tantric Gelugpa centres in India. The original monastery, founded in 1474 by Jetsun Kunga Thondrup near Xegar in central Tibet, was destroyed by the Chinese during the Cultural Revolution. It has been reconstructed here on land donated by neighbouring villages. Behind the throne is a large statue of Cho, a rare manifestation of Sakyamuni Buddha crowned by Je Tsong Khapa, who is seated on his right.

Another 15km beyond Tenzingang lies the end-of-the-road settlement of **Kalaktang**, surrounded by densely forested hills dotted with villages, and close to the Bhutanese border. The small Nyingma Zangdo Peri *gompa* houses some wacky sculptures. There is a basic government Inspection Bungalow here where you can sometimes stay; ask the tourist office in Bomdila.

Dirang and beyond

Ninety minutes beyond Bomdila and halfway to the Sela Pass, the ancient fortress town of **DIRANG** stands sentinel over the narrow valley at an altitude of 1690m. Although most of Dirang's original **fort** lies in ruins, it's worth checking out, as is the five-hundred-year-old *gompa* above the village. New Dirang is 5km further up the valley, with a **Yak Research Centre**. Nearby there's an interesting modern **monastery** (small donation requested) belonging to the Red Sect, the oldest Tibetan Buddhism sect. About 8km away, the **Sangti Valley** is the winter home of the black-necked crane and a popular place for bird-watching – *Hotel Pemaling* can arrange guides.

The best **place to stay** is the attractive *Hotel Pemaling* (Ⓣ03780/242615; Ⓔrinchinpemaling@yahoo.com; ④–⑥), halfway between Old Dirang and the new town, with wood-panelled rooms, hot showers and a restaurant with wonderful mountain views; local treks and bird-watching can be arranged here. The adjacent *Tourist Lodge* (②–③) is reasonable, with great views up the valley.

The road from Dirang to Tawang (a 12hr drive) is truly spectacular, with alpine trees, glacial waterfalls and lakes, grazing yaks and mellow villages with two-storey wooden houses. Signs along the way declare that you have reached "rough and tough country", and you'll pass quite a few army bases – one of which has an Internet connection which you can use in emergencies. En route is a war memorial dedicated to those who lost their lives during the 1962 Chinese invasion. A series of extraordinary switchbacks climbs up to the dramatic 4300m **Sela Pass**, where you can take tea in front of a *bakari* (wood-fired oven) at the tiny *Tanzing Restaurant,* a cosy wooden shack selling a range of dry foods including noodles and biscuits.

Thirteen kilometres on from Sela Pass, most buses and Sumos stop at the **Jaswant Singh Memorial**, dedicated to an Indian soldier. Conflicting stories of his actions abound, but most claim that he held off the invading Chinese army single-handedly for several days in 1962 by racing from bunker to bunker firing at Chinese positions, creating the illusion that the position was held by a substantial Indian garrison. He was eventually captured and killed by the Chinese, who continued virtually all the way to Tezpur before retreating to Tibet.

If you're feeling adventurous, stay en route at *Dzongrila Rest House* (③), in a small mountain hamlet before the last stretch to Tawang. There's no telephone here and you'll need your own sleeping bag, but there's a friendly owner and fantastic views.

Tawang

Some 180km beyond Bomdila, the great Buddhist monastery of **TAWANG**, the largest in India, dominates the land of the Monpas. Perched at around 3500m, it looks out onto a semicircle of peaks, snow-capped for much of the year. Tawang feels very much like the end-of-the-road place that it is and there are few luxuries to be enjoyed. Be warned that it is cold here most of the time – bring your thermals.

Tawang Monastery was established in the seventeenth century when this area was part of Greater Tibet, and was the birthplace of the sixth Dalai Lama.

The colourful fortress-like complex, a couple of kilometres beyond the town, is home to around five hundred monks, and is renowned for its collection of manuscripts and *thangkas*. There is a small **museum** (Rs20) filled with Buddhist ornaments and relics, including jewellery belonging to the sixth Dalai Lama's mother. The main shrine room is richly decorated and houses several statues including a beautiful thousand-armed Chenrezig (or Avalokitesvara).

Tawang is a friendly town which relishes various **festivals** throughout the year. The monastic three-day Torgya festival is held every January to protect the community from evil spirits and natural disasters – national dress is worn and the monks perform dances. The week-long Losar (or New Year) festival is held in February or early March, with more dancing and festivities.

Two *ani gompas* (nunneries) are visible from the main gate, clinging to the steep mountain slopes in the distance. They can be reached by foot in a couple of hours or by vehicle on a road that passes through a military camp and therefore requires a permit.

Beyond Tawang and very close to the border of Tibet lies the lake district of **Bangachangsa**. Dotted with pristine high-altitude lakes, small *gompas* and Guru Rinpoche caves, it is sacred to Tibetan Buddhists and also to Sikhs – Guru Nanak visited the region twice, hence the small Sikh *gurudwara*. There is no public transport but challenging treks and overnight camping can be arranged at *Hotel Pemaling* in Dirang or at the tourist office in Bomdila.

Practicalities

Daily **Sumos** and private **buses** run between Bomdila and Tawang – book in advance from ticket agents in the bus stand square. There are also twice-weekly **helicopter** flights from Guwahati and Dirang (T0361/284 0300). The small, friendly **tourist office** at the *Tourist Lodge* offers a list of places in addition to those below. *Hotel Buddha* has **Internet** access.

The best of the **hotel** options is the *Buddha*, on the main road (T03794/222107; 4–5), which has attractive rooms with wood finish and electric heaters, a vegetarian restaurant and Internet access. The *Paradise*, by the large arch on the main bazaar (T03974/222063; 4), has six large, en-suite rooms with hot water by the bucket and a small dining room – the manager can also arrange Jeep hire. The *Tourist Lodge* above the main market road (T03794/222359; 2–4) is slightly run down but it has running hot water and a restaurant and the rooms are spacious. Near the bus terminus, the *Shangri La* (T03794/222275; 1–4) has clean and basic rooms, including dorms with bathrooms attached.

In addition to the hotels, **restaurants** include *Dolphins*, in the Old Market, which offers decent Indian food, and *Hotel Snowland*, which has good Chinese. Both are on the main road, where you'll also find a number of basic eateries serving Tibetan food, including *momos* (meat or veg dumplings) and *thukpa* (thick noodle soup). As the sun sets, the temperature here plummets, and the shops and restaurants tend to close by around 6pm.

Central Arunachal

The hill station of **HAPOLI** (formerly Ziro), 1780m above sea level on the Apatani plateau, is 150km north of Itanagar. Although there is little to see in the town itself, the market area is lively. There are several villages dotted around the plateau, some of which are within walking distance, where you can still see Apatani men with impressive facial tattoos and women with bamboo nose plugs. **Old Ziro** is a scenic seven-kilometre walk from the town centre, or you can take one of the half-hourly buses. Accommodation is available in Hapoli at the pleasant *Arunachal Guest House* (ⓣ03788/224196; ❷), a couple of minutes above the main road; the *Jumalhari* (no phone; ❸) on the main road; and the *Hotel Blue Pine* (ⓣ03788/224812; ❸), 2km from the town centre. Local Sumo services run to Itanagar, Daporijo, Along and Pasighat. Peak Tour and Travels (ⓣ03788/225221) can help with local tours.

To the north and east, **ALONG** and **PASIGHAT**, the district headquarters of West and East Siang respectively, both offer trekking and angling. Near Along, there are a number of Adi villages to explore, while around Pasighat, Arunachal's oldest town, the local population is primarily Mishmi. Basic accommodation in both towns is available at the local *Circuit House* (Along ⓣ0360/222220, Pasighat ⓣ0360/222340; ❶–❷), or, in Pasighat, try the *Oman Hotel* in the Oman Complex (no phone; ❸), where the clean but basic rooms have attached bathrooms, and buckets of hot water and meals in your room can be provided. The towns can be reached from Itanagar on the NH-52 (7hr to Along, nearly 9hr to Pasighat), via **North Lakhimpur**, which has a range of interesting market stalls and shops and is a good place to break your journey.

A thirty-minute taxi drive from Pasighat is **Oiramghat**, from which you can get a daily ferry to Dibrugarh (see p.1006).

Eastern Arunachal

In eastern Arunachal, the remote valleys of the **Dibang** and **Lohit** rivers, inhabited by the Mishmi, Singhpo and Khampti tribes, descend from snow-covered passes through subtropical forests to the plains of the Brahmaputra. Highlights here include the Hindu pilgrimage centre of **Parasuramkund**, a twelfth-century fort at **Bhismaknagar**, and the pristine **Namdapha National Park**.

Parasuramkund

The sacred Hindu site of **Parasuramkund**, on the banks of the River Lohit, is mentioned in the *Kalika Purana* as the place where Parasuram washed away his act of matricide. Thousands of pilgrims make the arduous journey here on Makar Sankranti (mid-Jan), the most auspicious day of the year to take a dip as it's said to wash away all negative karma accumulated in this lifetime. The nearest town, **TEZU**, about 20 km southwest, acts as the gateway to the site, with accommodation available at the *Circuit House* (❶) and *Inspection Bungalow* (ⓣ03804/223666; ❶).

Bhismaknagar

At **BHISMAKNAGAR**, northwest of Tezu, you can see the ruins of a twelfth-century hill fort thought to have been built by the **Chutiyas**, a tribe originating in Mongolia. Made of burnt bricks, and covering ten square kilometres, it's reputedly the oldest archeological site in Arunachal. The nearest significant town is **Roing**, about 25km away, where you can stay at the *Circuit House* (ⓣ03803/222636; ❶), or, 3km outside town, *Sally Lake Guest House* (ⓣ03803/223061; ❷).

Namdapha National Park

The magnificent and remote **NAMDAPHA NATIONAL PARK** (Oct–April; Rs50 [Rs10], Jeep Rs100, cameras Rs100, video cameras Rs500), covering an area of almost 2000 square kilometres, is unique for its massive range of altitude (200–4500m). Close to the Myanmar border, Namdapha is home to tigers, leopards (clouded and snow), elephants, red pandas, deer and the endangered Hoolock gibbon, as well as over 600 species of birds. The journey here is long and uncomfortable, and stops at border posts can require a long wait, so it is advisable to visit the park with a tour operator and your own Jeep. The park's remote location, inaccessibility and the density of its forests, however, mean that vast tracts remain unexplored, and though you're highly unlikely to spot any big wildlife on a short visit, Namdapha's stunning setting, clear air and pristine prehistoric vegetation still make a visit well worth the effort required to get here. From **Deban**, the main camp, there are wonderful views over the river valley.

The park headquarters are at **Miao** (ⓣ03807/222249, ⓕ222249), where you can book to stay at the *Forest Rest House* (❷–❹) in Deban. The two top rooms with adjoining veranda are the most comfortable, and have en-suite bathrooms. At the time of writing, the nearby dormitory and tourist huts (❶–❷) were in a very sorry state – the park was awaiting funding from central government to spruce them up.

Jeeps are no longer allowed but short daytime elephant rides are available, and it's also possible to take a guided elephant trek with overnight camping inside the park – contact the Field Director at Miao. Alternatively, both Purvi Discovery and Gurudongma Tours & Treks (see p.983) arrange well-organised camping and bird-watching trips. Those with specialist interest in the environment, botany, birds or wildlife can apply for longer visits to the park in writing (Namdapha National Park, Miao, Arunachal Pradesh, India 792122). Buses to and from Miao pass through **Margherita**, 64km southwest, and **Tinsukia**, 40km further southwest in Assam, where rail services run to Guwahati (see "Travel details", p.1021). **Dibrugarh** is a further 47km beyond Tinsukia.

Nagaland

On the border with Myanmar, south of Arunachal Pradesh and east of Assam, **NAGALAND** is physically and conceptually at the very extremity of the subcontinent. Home to the fiercely independent – and very good-looking – Nagas, its hills and valleys were only opened up to tourism in 2000, and the two factions of the National Socialist Council of Nagaland (NSCN) remain locked in a battle for independence against the Indian army. It is arguably one of India's most beautiful states – a glimpse of the Naga hills in the mist is enough to give respite to any weary northeast traveller. Once renowned for their tribes of fierce head-hunters (see box, opposite), the Nagas were converted to Christianity by missionaries, and the state is now ninety percent Christian.

When the British arrived in neighbouring Assam in the mid-nineteenth-century, they initially chose to leave the fierce warrior tribes of Nagaland well alone. But after continued Naga raids on Assamese villages, the British, in their commitment to protecting colonial subjects, sought to push the Nagas back into the hills, sparking a series of battles. The Angami warriors defeated the British twice, but were finally defeated in 1879, and a truce was declared. A commissioner stationed in Khonoma toured the territories collecting taxes and sorting disputes, and came to hold a certain authority among the various tribes. The Nagas remained loyal to the British, joining the fight against the Japanese invaders during World War II. At the time of Indian Independence, the Nagas pleaded with the British to grant them an independent homeland, but instead found their land divided into two, with the larger area falling to Burma. After Independence, Gandhi asked the Nagas to remain within the new-found union for ten years, promising them choice of destiny thereafter. Gandhi was assassinated, his promise never fulfilled.

Fifty years on, the Nagas are still fighting for a homeland they believe is their inherent right. Though a ceasefire has officially been in place for the past few years, violence and infighting continue – a bomb explosion in late 2004 killed seventy people in Dimapur, and it is considered unsafe to travel at night. Though many Nagas agree that they could not survive independently of India, few feel much affinity with their neighbours in Assam and beyond, in either temperament or outlook.

A progressive tourism policy continues to open up Nagaland. Though you need a **permit** to travel here, are encouraged to travel with a tour operator and must officially either be in a group of four or a married couple, it is sometimes possible to obtain a second ten-day pass via a tour operator once inside the state. Pairs of friends have also sometimes been given permits, again if applied for by a northeast tour operator (see "Access, permits and tour operators" box, p.983).

A visit to a Naga village is a fascinating insight into a fast-disappearing way of life. Most northeast tour operators will arrange trips here, working with a network of local guides. Be warned, however, that some Nagas are tired of having their homes "on show". If you do visit (and tourism has become a vital source of income), it's a good idea to bring a gift from home and ensure that your guide speaks the relevant dialect. You should offer money for the village to the chief (or *angh*) on arrival.

Traditional Angami villages surround the regional capital of **Kohima**, including **Khonoma**. From **Mon** you can see various Konyak villages including **Shangnyu**, with its impressive fertility sculpture and opium-smoking *angh*. The Ao tribe inhabits **Mokokchung** and is surrounding villages, while **Tuensang** is home to six different tribes. Though most people visit Nagaland for its tribal culture, the state's terrain is ideal for trekking and other sports – Gurudongma Tours & Treks (see p.983) arranges excellent mountain biking trips to the state.

The Nagas

There are fourteen main tribal groups in Nagaland, most of them inhabiting villages perched high on mountain ridges. **Naga warriors** have long been feared and respected throughout the northeast and head-hunting was practised within living memory. The Nagas originally lived in northeast Tibet, then moved through southwest China into Myanmar, Malaya and Indonesia, as well as eastern Assam. They are skilful farmers, growing up to twenty different species of rice according to altitude and aspect of the terraces.

Nagas differentiate between the soul, a celestial body, and the spirit, a supernatural being. The human soul resides in the nape of the neck, while the spirit, being in the head, holds great power and brings good fortune. Heads of enemies and fallen comrades were once collected to add to those of the community's own ancestors. Some tribes decorated their faces with tattoos of swirling horns to mark success in **head-hunting**. The heads were kept in the men's meeting house (*morung*) of each village, which also served as the boys' dormitory, and was decorated with fantastic carvings of animals, elephant heads and tusks – you can still see examples in many villages. The Nagas also constructed megalithic monuments which lined the approaches to villages personifying those who erected them after death. **Menhirs** stand in pairs, or in long double rows, to honour fame and generosity or enhance the fertility of a field. Traditionally, relations between the sexes were conducted with great openness and equality. Although each tribe has its own dialect, a hybrid language drawn from various Naga languages and Assamese has developed into the common Nagamese tongue.

Kohima

The pleasant, busy town of **KOHIMA**, the capital of Nagaland, was built alongside the large Angami village of Kohima by the British in the nineteenth century for administrative purposes. Traditional Naga villages, inhabited by tribes such as the Rengma, Zeliang and Kuki as well as the Angami lie just a short drive away. They include **Khonoma**, 20km beyond Kohima, **Jakhema** and **Kigwema**.

The Town

Spread loosely over a saddle joining two large hills, Kohima forms a pass that played a strategic role during World War II. The highway from Imphal to Dimapur – the route along which the Japanese hoped to reach the plains of India – crosses the saddle at the foot of the **World War II Cemetery**, set amongst immaculate lawns in a peaceful location overlooking the town. It stands as an emotional memorial to the Allies who died at this very spot during the three-month Battle of Kohima, which ended in April 1944 after claiming the lives of over 10,000 soldiers.

Below the cemetery, on the old NST Road in central Kohima, small shops such as the Nagaland Handlooms and Handicrafts Development Corporation and the tiny Handloom Centre sell local produce and a variety of Naga shawls and wraps, spears, bags and cane and bamboo **handicrafts**. Weaving is a traditional craft here and each Naga tribe has distinctive shawls such as the black, red and green of the local Angamis. There's also a **food market** behind the bus station, selling everything from dead birds to live maggots (via banana cake). The **Cathedral**, on the way out of town towards the State Museum, contains the largest wooden crucifix in India.

The fascinating **State Museum** (Tues–Sat 9.30am–2.30pm, closed every 2nd and 4th Sat; Rs1) in Bayavu Hill Colony, a pleasant twenty-minute walk from Centre Point, is very well laid out and kept. It houses an excellent collection of Naga jewellery, costumes spears, beaded corsets and handicrafts. Outside there's an impressive gateway and a log drum, traditionally used in religious rites, during festivals and for sending messages across the hills.

The large Angami settlement of **Kohima village** is set on a high hill overlooking modern Kohima. It is now quite modernised and only a few of its buildings are traditional with pitched roof and crossed "house-horns" on the gable, but its tightly knit labyrinth of lanes and houses gives the village a definite Naga feel. Carved heads to signify family status, grain baskets in front of the houses, and troughs used to make rice beer are among the distinctive features. There are less modernised villages at **Jakhema**, a few kilometres south on the road to Manipur, and **Kigwema**, a little further on still – go with a guide from an established tour operator.

Practicalities

Most **private buses** from Imphal are through services to Dimapur and don't go into the centre of town – ask the driver to drop you off on the main highway just below the *Japfu* hotel. **State buses** arrive and leave from the bus stand in the centre of town. Taxis and minibuses are the main forms of public transport around the town, although the central area is small enough to explore on foot. The **tourist office** (Mon–Fri 10am–4pm; ⓣ0370/224 3124, ⓦwww.nagalandtourism.com) is on the National Highway, below the *Japfu*. Peak Travels (ⓣ0370/224 2993, ⓔpeaktravels@rediffmail.com) on PR Hill can arrange transport, local sightseeing and trips around Nagaland. Zinki Tours and

Moving on from Kohima

From Kohima, roads lead west to the railhead and airport at **Dimapur**, north to Mokokchung and south to Imphal. From Mokokchung, the road continues to Jorhat in Upper Assam. There are state and private **buses** in all directions: state buses run from the Nagaland State Transport stand in the centre of town; tickets for private buses can be bought from agents in the centre or on Phool Bari. State buses to Dimapur run every half-hour from 6am to 4pm, and daily to Mokokchung and Imphal. Frequent Tata **Sumo** services to Dimapur depart when full from the taxi stand 200m up from the bus station.

Adventure can also arrange local sightseeing, and is based next to the *Japfu*, as is the Indian Airlines office

Kohima has few **accommodation** choices, though standards aren't bad. Its showpiece hotel is the *Japfu* (ⓣ0370/224 0211, ⓔhoteljapfu@yahoo.co.in; ⑥–⑦), with great views from PR Hill at the top end of town; it has clean, spacious rooms with big windows, unusually powerful heaters, its own generator, friendly staff and a restaurant. The *Fira* (ⓣ0370/224 5006; ④–⑤), near the *Japfu*, is a budget hotel with adequate if somewhat old-fashioned rooms and a restaurant. *Pine*, on Phool Bari (ⓣ0370/224 3129; ④–⑤), has decent doubles but no singles; the *Valley View* (②), next to the bus station, is friendly but basic, while the *Capital* (ⓣ0370/222 4365; ②) opposite has rooms ranging from grim to good.

Naga food provides a welcome relief from the strong spices of Indian cuisine, and consists mainly of rice, boiled vegetables and lots of meat, cooked with ginger or chilli. Pomelos, a type of grapefruit, are also widely available here. Naga cuisine is available at the *Bamboo Shoot* and *Sema* hotels; *China Town*, on Old NST Road, and *Rendez Vous* serve decent Indian and Chinese. Most restaurants and *dhabas* close around 6pm – the *Japfu* restaurant stays open till around 9pm.

Khonoma and Tuophema

KHONOMA, 20km northwest from Kohima, holds a special place in Naga history as the area where Angami warriors made their final stand against the British in 1879. Magnificent rice terracing surrounds the village, irrigated by a complex system of bamboo water pipes. Its highest point, approached through a carved gate and up a flight of steps, provides excellent views of the Naga hills and neighbouring villages of Mezoma and Secuma.

Over the densely forested ridge behind the village lies the scenic Dzoukou valley, part of the Khonoma Nature Conservation and Tragopan Sanctuary, and graced with waterfalls and wonderful viewpoints. Guides can be hired in Khonoma for a popular four-day **trek** into the sanctuary.

Public buses leave three times a day to Khonoma from Kohima NST stand, or **private buses** leave every afternoon at 2pm from the TCP Gate. There is also a daily bus from Dimapur. Khonoma boasts one guesthouse, which can be booked through Peak Travels in Kohima (see opposite). Taxis are the best bet if visiting as a day-trip, as buses back can be unreliable.

Forty-one kilometres north of Kohima on the way to Mokokchung, **TUOPHEMA** is a genuine Angami village situated next to a "tourist village" built by the locals, with a small museum displaying Naga artefacts, jewellery and clothing. Guided walks in the surrounding countryside can be arranged here.

Accommodation is available in one of twelve comfortable Naga huts with hot showers (ⓣ0370/227 0786, ⓦwww.touristvillage.biz). Regular buses run from Kohima (1hr 30min) and Dimapur (2hr), though hiring a taxi is preferable if you want to visit as a day-trip.

Dimapur

DIMAPUR, the "city of the river people", 74km northwest of Kohima, is Nagaland's most industrialized town. Noisy and polluted, it bears little resemblance to the rest of Nagaland and functions for visitors primarily as a gateway to the state. If you have time to kill, visit the **Kachari ruins**, fertility symbols dating back to the Kachari Kingdom on the riverside edge of town.

The sole railhead in Nagaland, Dimapur is served by **trains** to Simaluguri (for Sibsagar), Tinsukia and Dibrugarh in Upper Assam. The best service for Guwahati is the daily overnight Kamrup Express #5960, which leaves at 12.05pm, arriving in Guwahati at 6.30am. **Buses** run to Guwahati and towns throughout the northeastern hill states. State and private buses run to Kohima (3hr) from the Nagaland bus stand as do Tata **Sumos** (2hr–2hr 30min) from the main drag outside. Private buses to Jorhat, Guwahati and Itanagar leave from the Assam bus stand in Golaghat Road across the railway tracks. Dimapur's **airport** is 6km out of town on the Kohima road.

The best **accommodation** option is the *Saramati*, the sister hotel to Kohima's *Japfu* (ⓣ03862/234761; ❻–❼); cheaper places to stay, with clean if uninspiring rooms, include the *Tourist Lodge* (ⓣ03862/226355; ❷), next to the Nagaland bus stand; the *Fantasy* (ⓣ03862/232013; ❸–❻) next door; and the *Tragopan* (ⓣ03862/2267771; ❹–❻) near the overbridge.

Mon and around

In the far northeast of Nagaland, 200km south of Dibrugarh in Assam, **MON** is the regional capital of the Konyak tribe. A friendly town with a daily fruit and vegetable market, its main attraction is as a base for visits to its surrounding Konyak villages. Organized **tours** can encompass several villages in a day (dependent on the condition of the roads). Look out on the roads between villages for older Konyaks with elaborate facial tattoos and goat-horn earrings. Sennunger Imsong, based in Mokokchung (see opposite), is a reliable young guide who can arrange day-trips.

Shangnyu is a typical village, a bumpy drive 23km from Mon, with a small museum housing fascinating village artefacts including an impressive wooden fertility sculpture. Outside the museum is a huge log drum, which the villagers used for festivals and to send messages to each other across the hills. There's also a set of eerie tall stones on which the villagers once displayed hunted heads. The friendly opium-smoking *angh* here will offer you tea in his home, the front of which is packed with horns and animal skulls to indicate his status. Locals will let you wander – look out for the lovely carved wooden benches and doors dotting the rest of the village.

Mon's only **hotel** is the *Mountain View* (ⓣ03869/221730, ⓔphejin@yahoo.com; ❹), which has large, clean rooms in an ugly building on Mon's noisy main street; tasty meals can be brought in. **Buses** to Mon run from Dibrugarh via Sibsagar in Assam, though trips to Mon are best undertaken in a Jeep with a tour operator; Jeeps take 7 hours from Dibrugarh, buses considerably longer. In late March or early April, the whole area celebrates its spring **festival** over three to six days with traditional dress and dancing.

Mokokchung and around

A vibrant hill town southwest of Mon and 160km (5hr by Jeep) north of Kohima, **MOKOKCHUNG** is a good place to soak up Naga town life. There is a small **museum** with unusual exhibits worth a quick visit, and shops here sell Naga shawls and local bamboo-woven footstools. The town provides a base for a visit to surrounding Ao villages, including **Longkhum**, 17km away, which has a small museum depicting Ao tribal culture and a guesthouse. Day-trips including to Tuensang (see below), can be arranged by Sennunger Imsong, whose aunt Apokla Imsong rents out a pleasant double room with attached bathroom in *Tongpok Abode*, her home at Dilong Ward in Mokokchung (Ⓣ0369/222 7030, Ⓔimsong2003@rediffmail.com); meals are included.

TUENSANG, 115km southeast of Mokokchung, lies at the centre of a region inhabited by six different tribes – you can visit villages belonging to the Phom, Khiamniungan, Chang, Yimchunger and Sangtam. From here it's a two-day drive to **Thanamir**, and the start of a stunning two-day trek between tribal villages to **Mount Saramati**, the highest peak in Nagaland (3826m), near the Burmese border. En route, there are basic places to stay at **Kiphere** – contact the Imsongs to arrange (see above).

WOKHA, 80km south from Mokokchung, is a good place to stop on the NH-61 route to Kohima. It's a mellow, friendly town, inhabited by Lotha people, with street stalls selling sugar cane and bamboo baskets filled with oranges. Just down the hill on the left after entering the town, the tiny *Tea Hotel* does good samosas, *momos*, omelettes and mugfuls of decent tea. Cultural and mountain biking trips in the area are run by Gurungdoma Tours & Treks (see p.983).

Mizoram

Heading south from Assam into the hills of **MIZORAM**, "the land of the highlanders", a winding mountain road takes you into forests and bamboo-covered hills. Mizoram is a gentle pastoral land, and the **Mizos** are a friendly and welcoming people who have seen very little tourism. Whitewashed Christian churches dot the landscape, giving it more of a Central American feel than a state squashed between Myanmar and the Chittagong Hill Tracts of Bangladesh.

The Mizos, who migrated to the area from the Chin hills of Burma, were regularly raiding tea plantations in the Assam Valley right into the late nineteenth century; only in 1924 did the British administration finally manage to bring about some semblance of control. They opened up what was then the **Lushai Hills** to missionaries, who, with great zeal converted much of the state to Christianity. **Aizawl**, Mizoram's busy capital, is a large sprawling city built on impossibly steep slopes which have necessitated stilted housing. In the heart of the state, traditional Mizo communities occupy the crests of a series of ridges, each village dominated by its chief's house and *zawlbuk*, or bachelors' dormitory. An egalitarian people, without sex or class distinctions, the Mizos remain proud of their age-old custom of *Tlawmgaihna*, a code of ethics which governs hospitality, and the weaving of local costumes such as the *puan*, characterized by white, black and red stripes. They enjoy a 95 percent literacy rate, and many speak both Mizo and English and are culturally more influenced by the Christian West than by India.

The uprising that ended

Mizoram's two main species of bamboo flower every fifty years (one eighteen years after the other), attracting hordes of rats and boosting their fertility rate fourfold. The rats devour crops in the fields, leaving famine in their wake. The first time this happened, in 1959, the newly independent governments in Delhi and Assam were unprepared, which led **Laldenga**, a clerk on the District Council, to found the **Mizo Famine Front** (MFF). Set up initially to combat famine, it transformed into the **Mizo National Front** (MNF), a guerrilla group fighting for secession. The government's heavy-handed response in 1967, rounding up Mizos from their homes into guarded villages under curfew, not only boosted support for the MNF, but also sought to wipe out the traditional Mizo way of life at a stroke. Bangladeshi independence was a bitter blow to the MNF, who had relied on Pakistani support, and moderates on both sides eventually brought the MNF to the negotiating table, where statehood was granted in 1986 in return for an end to the insurgency. Mizoram is now the most peaceful of the "seven sisters."

Tourism remains restricted due to the sensitive border with Myanmar, and permits are still required, but the opening of an airport at Lengpui has made the state far more accessible.

Aizawl

One of India's remotest state capitals, **AIZAWL** perches precariously on the steep slopes of a sharp ridge, straddling the watershed between the Tlawng and the Tuirial river valleys and enjoys a comfortable year-round climate by virtue of its altitude of 1250m. Although the views are of hills rather than snowy mountains, it has something of the feel of a Himalayan hill station. There's little to see in the way of monuments and temples, but the markets are interesting. Be warned that everything (including restaurants) closes on Sunday, when everyone goes to church. Aizawl's rural surroundings are within easy reach by bus or on foot.

Zarkawt is the main downtown area, where you'll find a host of inexpensive hotels on the upper of two parallel streets which form part of Aizawl's complex road network. They are connected by a series of ridiculously long and steep stairways.

Bara Bazaar (literally "big bazaar") is the main attraction in Aizawl (daily except Sun 6am–3pm). Everything from recordings of Mizo music to bespoke shoes made by Chinese cobblers is on sale.

Further up the hill, Solomon's Cave in **Zodin Square** is an indoor market selling fabrics, garments and music; traditional stuff is notably absent. The District Industries Centre in Upper Bazaar stocks local handicrafts such as shawls and bags. The **Mizoram State Museum**, on MacDonald Hill (Mon–Fri 9am–5pm, Sat 9am–1pm; free), has a small but interesting collection of Mizo costumes and implements.

Due to its precipitous setting, much of Aizawl does not see the sun for significant parts of the day, and the multi-storey concrete edifices clinging to the hillsides increase the depth of the shade. But there are many vantage points offering great views of the lush green hills surrounding the town – two of the best are **Chaltlang Hill**, high above Chandmari in the north, and the Theological College, perched above the dramatic cleft on the road into Aizawl.

The **Durtlang Hills** immediately north of Aizawl, and **Luangmual**, 7km west, provide pleasant **walking** country – both easy day-trips from the centre. There is also a handicrafts shop. Buses leave for Luangmual from outside the Salvation Army Temple.

Moving on from Mizoram

The only recommended road out of Mizoram leads to **Silchar**, 180km north in Assam. Tata **Sumos** are the quickest and most comfortable way to travel, taking around 4–6 hours. There are several Sumo agents around Zarkawt including Chungnungi (☎0389/234 4616). Several **private bus** companies also run services to Silchar (12hr), including Capital Travels (☎0389/234 0166) and Jagannath Travels (☎0389/234 2092), also based in Zarkawt. Sumo and bus services are also available direct to Shillong and Guwahati. Mizoram State Transport offer cheaper, slower and less comfortable rides.

For Manipur and Nagaland, the best option is to fly from Aizawl to Imphal. Aizawl's **airport** at **Lengpui**, ninety minutes (45km) north, handles flights to Guwahati, Imphal, Kolkata and Shillong (see p.1021). Book through Quality Tour & Travels, A–51, Chanmari (☎0389/234 1265), who also run an airport bus service. Their office is just a couple of minutes walk down from the tourist office.

Practicalities

Aizawl is reachable as a day-trip from Silchar in Assam (4hr by Jeep). The friendly staff of the basic state **tourist office**, in the Chandmari district (Mon–Fri 9am–5pm; ☎0389/231 2475), provide advice and transport, and can book tourist lodges throughout Mizoram redundant. The **post office** is on Treasury Square. The State Bank of India, near First AR Ground, has a **foreign exchange** counter, though it's best to bring what cash you need with you. Of the **minibuses** that run between central Aizawl and the suburbs, the most useful head from the top of town near the GPO and Zodin Square to Chandmari in the north – otherwise a tiring two-kilometre walk.

Several **hotels** in Aizawl are geared towards budget and mid-range travellers, and simple cafés, especially around Bara Bazaar, serve **Mizo food**. Lentils, fish, rice and bamboo shoots are popular; the mild dishes can be a welcome change from most north Indian cooking. There are several cheap and cheerful local *dhabas* on Zodin Square.

Ahimsa Zarkawt ☎0389/234 1133. One of Aizawl's better hotels. Central, with comfortable rooms, rooftop views and a popular restaurant. ❹

Berawtlang Tourist Complex Zemabawk ☎0389/235 2067. Seven hilltop cottages with great views in a rural setting. ❹

Capital Guest House Zarkawt ☎0389/234 1721. Below Capital Travels. Clean rooms and hot water by the bucket. ❸

Chawlhna Zarkawt ☎0389/234 2292. Popular budget hotel with canteen-like restaurant. ❷

Luangmual Tourist Lodge ☎0389/233 2263. 7km out of town on a bus route, very friendly with clean rooms around a garden courtyard. There are also dorms (Rs30). Recommended for its views and ambience ❶

Ritz Bara Bazaar, near Machhunga Point ☎0389/231 0409. Comfortable business hotel with some en-suite rooms. Excellent restaurant and rooftop views. ❸–❹

State Guest House Chaltlang ☎0389/234 9979. One of the smartest hotels, and its restaurant has a good reputation for Indian and Chinese cooking. ❸

Tourist Lodge Chaltlang ☎0389/234 1083. Perched on a sharp ridge with a terrace providing great views, though the rooms are very basic and quite run down. Dorms are also available (Rs30). ❸

Tripura

Tucked away in a corner of the northeast, surrounded by Bangladesh on three sides, the lush green mountains and valleys of **TRIPURA** have attracted many different peoples over the centuries. It became part of the

Indian Union in 1949; since then, its fate has been entwined with that of Bengal. The Partition of India and subsequent creation of East Pakistan (now Bangladesh) in 1948, followed by war, famine and military regimes drove millions of Bangladeshis to flee into Tripura, where they now outnumber the indigenous people by four to one, leaving many of the original inhabitants feeling that their land and resources have been stolen and exploited. Tripura is more like India proper than the other northeast hill states and its connections with the Bangladeshi plains are strong. The Tripuris are the biggest tribal group, accounting for more than half the tribal population, and the Reangs, originally from the Chittagong Hill Tracts, are the second biggest tribe.

Agartala, the state capital, is a relaxed city with a palace and a few temples, from which easy day-trips can be made to **Udaipur** and the fairy-tale palace at **Neermahal**. Tripura's **forests** were once famed for their elephants, praised by the Moghul chronicler Abul Fazal in his *Ain-e-Akbari*. Sadly, due to the widespread and uncontrolled practice of slash-and-burn agriculture, and to general pressure on the land, wildlife has come under severe threat. A handful of sanctuaries such as Gumti, Rowa, Trishna, and **Sepahijala** strive to protect the few forests that remain.

The **history** of the kingdom of Tripura and its Manikya rulers, who claimed descent from far-off Rajput *kshatriyas*, is told in a curious Bengali poem, the *Rajmala*. Udai Manikya (1585–96) founded the city of Udaipur on the site of the old capital of Rangamati, adorning it with beautiful tanks, buildings and temples. The Tripura Sundari temple here is one of India's most important *shakti pithas*. After staving off the Muslim rulers of Bengal, the Manikyas finally submitted to the Moghuls, but continued to rule the kingdom until it was eventually subsumed into British India. Maharaja Birchandra Manikya, who came to the throne in 1870 and was heavily influenced both culturally and spiritually by Bengal – and by his close relationship with Bengali poet, author and painter Rabindranath Tagore – established Bengali as the language of the court. You will also see lots of quite graphic clay sculptures of **Kali**, Bengal's favourite goddess, made by households for their monthly pujas. English is not widely spoken here.

Safety in Tripura

Although Tripura is open to tourism, **insurgency** and **ethnic conflict** remain a problem, particularly in the north. At the time of writing, travel to Tripura was deemed **unsafe**, and the UK Foreign and Commonwealth Office was advising against all visits to the state. The information in this section has therefore not been updated for this edition, and it is essential to check the security situation before you intend to travel. Buses from Silchar to Agartala travel in convoy, with a military escort from Kumarghat as far as Teliamura. Although you're unlikely to meet trouble in the tourist spots, it's sensible to heed the advice of local people.

The **NLFT** (National Liberation Front of Tripura) and the **ATTF** (All Tripura Tiger Force) are fighting for tribal rights, autonomy, independence and the expulsion of Bangladeshis. Other insurgents have a financial agenda. In the run-up to elections, kidnapping and extortion help raise large sums of money which can then buy political clout: a successful group may promise to step down from the election in exchange for payments from the competing political parties. Another common event is the mass surrender of militants after elections – followed by their appointment in well-paid jobs. The **UBLF** (United Bengal Liberation Front) has also joined the fray with vicious reprisals against tribals to quell the activities of the other two groups.

Agartala and around

AGARTALA, the capital of Tripura, is a laid-back administrative centre very reminiscent of the low-level towns of Bangladesh, whose border is just 2km away. Its main monument of interest is the gleaming white **Ujjayanta Palace**, completed in 1901. Set amid formal gardens and artificial lakes, this huge building, whose main block now houses the State Legislative Assembly, covers an area of around eight hundred acres. One of many temples nearby and open to the public, the **Jagannath Temple** with its orange tower rises from an octagonal plinth across the road. It contains some fascinating and very colourful sculptures depicting various episodes in Krishna's life.

Most of Agartala's amenities, bazaars, bus stands and administrative offices are concentrated in the centre, immediately south of the palace. Opposite the GPO, the **State Museum** displays interesting ethnographic and archeological exhibits (Mon–Sat 10am–5pm; free), with one gallery devoted to the excavations at Unakoti in the forests of northern Tripura. The Tribal Cultural Research Institute and Museum (11am–1pm; free) at Supari Bagan lies well hidden in the backstreets of Krishna Nagar district, near the Jagannath temple.

Practicalities

Arriving by bus, you'll probably be dropped off at one of the private company offices on Laxmi Narayan Bari (LN Bari) Road, or at the state bus depot at Krishna Nagar. Buses and taxis ply the 12km from the **airport** to the centre of

town. The local **tourist office** (Mon–Sat 10am–5pm, Sun 3–5pm; ⓣ0381/222 5930) can be found in a wing of the palace, which in theory is the only part of the palace open to the public, but they may be able to get you a visitor's pass for the main part if you're interested. They also organize **tours** and arrange transport for sightseeing.

Cycle **rickshaws** and auto-rickshaws are plentiful, and **Jeeps** can be chartered at the bus stand. The **post office** (Mon–Sat 7am–6pm) is at Post Office Chowmuhani. Those wishing to access the **Internet** should head to Star Graphics, on BK Road, 50m past the *Rajdhani* hotel, or to Cyber Masti on Durga Bari Road, next to the Telegraph office. There are currently no foreign exchange facilities in Agartala.

Agartala has a small but good selection of **hotels**. All places listed provide mosquito nets. Choices for **eating** are more limited: *Abhishek* on Durga Bari Road is the best in town, with indoor and garden tables; *Ambar*, next to the hotel of the same name, is another option, serving inexpensive (Rs150–350) basic, filling non-veg dishes.

Ambar SD Barman Sarani ⓣ0381/222 3587. Central location with reasonably priced rooms. ❷

Brideway JB Rd, near the west side of the palace ⓣ0381/220 7298. Friendly place. Reasonable rooms with large attached bathrooms. ❸

Deep Guest House LN Bari Rd ⓣ0381/220 4718. Small homely hotel on main road. Carpets and attached bathrooms, though the single rooms lack windows. ❷

Moonlight LNB Rd ⓣ381/220 0813. Basic and friendly, if a little noisy, with attached bathrooms and a good cheap veg restaurant. ❶

Rajarshi Badshah Airport Rd ⓣ0381/220 1034. A couple of kilometres out of town through the north gate. Pleasant, peaceful rooms, lawn, gardens and restaurant. ❸–❺

Rajdhani BK Rd, near Indian Airlines office ⓣ0381/222 3387. Friendly and comfortable mid-range hotel near the palace. ❷–❺

Royal Guest House Palace Compound West ⓣ0381/222 5652. Down a side street near the palace. Roomy and comfortable, with a good restaurant. ❸–❹

Welcome Palace HGB Rd ⓣ0381/238 4940, ⓔabanik@sancharnet.in. New hotel and the best in town. Their *Kurry Klub* restaurant serves Thai, Chinese and Indian food. ❺

Around Agartala

On the border with Bangladesh, 27km south of Agartala, the large lake of **Kamala Sagar** is overlooked by a small but important Kali Temple. Its twelfth-century sandstone image of Mahishasuramardini, a form of Durga, has a *shivalingam* in front of it. Buses leave from Battala bus stand in Agartala to the lake (5 daily; 1hr).

On the road to Udaipur, 35km south of Agartala, the nature reserve at **Sepahijala** extends over eighteen square kilometres, with a lake, zoo and botanical gardens, and is home to primates including the Hoolock gibbon and golden langur and around 150 species of birds. The beautiful *Abasarika Bungalow* (❶) offers comfortable rooms in jungle surroundings which you can book in advance at the Forestry Office (ⓣ0381/222 2224) in Agartala, 2km up Airport Road on the left. All buses to Udaipur travel past the park gate.

Udaipur

The former capital of the Manikyas, **UDAIPUR** retains an atmosphere of antiquity not found in the metropolis of Agartala. An important market town, it is surrounded by paddy fields and low forested hills. On the southwest bank of **Jagannath Dighi** tank, stand the ruins of the **Jagannath** temple, while the seventeenth-century **Moghul Masjid** marks the furthest outpost of the Moghul Empire. **Tripura Sundari**, the most important temple in the area, stands 5km outside Udaipur, on a small hillock in front of a holy lake which

Moving on from Agartala

State buses leave from the terminus on the corner of Hospital Rd and LN Bari Rd for the gruelling stop-start convoy to Silchar, Shillong and Guwahati. It's well worth paying extra for the more comfortable **private buses** run by Network, Capital, Tania, Green Valley and Sagar which depart from LN Bari Rd, 100m east of the palace. All buses heading north from Agartala have to travel in thrice-daily army-escorted convoys from Teliamura to Kumarghat, leaving at the same times – 6am, 8am and 11.30am. Buses to Udaipur (every 30min; 2hr) leave from the Battala bus stand at the western end of HGB Rd, as do shared **Jeeps**, which also serve Melaghar (for Neermahal) and Kamala Sagar. Kumarghat, seven hours away, is the nearest **railhead** to Agartala.

Agartala's **airport**, 12km north of the centre, can be reached by bus or taxi from the motor stand, by bus from the beginning of Airport Rd, or by auto-rickshaw. The Indian Airlines office is on VIP Rd, just west of BK Rd (ⓣ0381/222 5470).

See "Travel details" at the end of this chapter for more information on journey frequencies and durations.

To Bangladesh

Agartala is just 2km from the **border with Bangladesh**, and you can easily walk or take a rickshaw to the checkpoint on Akhaura Rd. Rickshaws on the Bangladeshi side can take you to Akhaura Junction, 4km away, from where there are trains to Comilla, Sylhet and Dhaka (2hr 30min). Although there are seven official border crossings from Tripura to Bangladesh, this one is the most convenient.

The **Bangladeshi Embassy** (Mon–Thurs 8.30am–1pm & 2–4.30pm, Fri 8.30am–noon; ⓣ0381/222 4807), next to the *Brideway* hotel, issues visas on the spot. Two passport photos are needed and prices vary according to nationality.

teems with carp and turtles. Built in typical Bengali-hut style with a square sanctum and large meeting hall in front, this is one of the 51 *shakti pithas* sacred to the Tantras, marking the spot where Sati's right leg is supposed to have fallen when Shiva was carrying her body from the funeral pyre. Animal sacrifices are performed here daily.

Most people visit Udaipur on a long day-trip from Agartala, but **accommodation** is available at the *Pantha Niwas Tourist Lodge* (❶–❷). There's also a small tourist office (ⓣ0381/222432). **Buses** run from Agartala every thirty minutes (2hr), and there are also frequent shared **Jeeps**.

Neermahal

The romantic water palace of **NEERMAHAL**, in the middle of **Rudrasagar Lake**, 55km south of Agartala, was built in 1930 as a summer residence for Maharaja Bir Bikram Kishore Manikya. Inspired by Moghul architecture, the palace (daily 9am–6pm) is rather derelict inside, but the exterior and gardens have been restored, and the sight of the domes and pavilions reflected in the lake, especially under the early evening floodlights, is impressive. You can rent boats to cross the lake to the palace from just opposite the tourist lodge (motorboats Rs125/hr, punts Rs60/30min), a very pleasant journey among lily pads, dragonflies, ducks and cormorants.

The lake is 1km from the town of **Melaghar**, which has bus connections with Agartala (every 30min; 2hr) and Udaipur (every 30min; 30min). Neermahal can be visited together with Udaipur as a day-trip from Agartala, provided you're steeled for a long hard day – the round trip covers 130km along seriously potholed roads. Should you prefer to break up the journey, the lakeside *Sagarmahal*

Tourist Lodge (☎0381/264418; ❸) has large rooms, some affording great views across the lake, along with seven-bedded dorms (Rs60). Food is available at the lodge and at a nearby **restaurant** run by the local fishermen's co-operative.

Manipur

The state of **MANIPUR**, stretching along the border with Myanmar, centres on a vast lowland area watered by the lake system south of its capital **Imphal**. This almost forgotten region is home to the **Meithei**, who have created in isolation their own fascinating version of Hinduism. Manipur feels closer to Southeast Asia than India, and visitors encounter the problem of a **language** barrier as many of the locals speak neither English nor Hindi.

Though the area around Imphal is now all but devoid of trees, the outlying hills are still forested, and shelter such exotic birds and animals as the spotted linshang, Blyth's tragopan, the curiously named Mrs Hume's bar-backed pheasant, slow loris, Burmese pea-fowl and the beautifully marked clouded leopard, as well as numerous unclassified varieties of orchids. The unique natural habitat of **Loktak Lake**, with its floating islands of matted vegetation, is home to the sangai deer.

Manipur's **history** can be traced back to the founding of Imphal in the first century AD. Despite periodic invasions from Burma, it enjoyed long periods of independent and stable government until the end of the Indo-Burmese war in 1826 when it was incorporated into India. It came under British rule in 1891 after the Battle of Kangla. During World War II, most of Manipur was occupied by the Japanese, with 250,000 British and Indian troops trapped under siege in Imphal for three months. Thanks to a massive RAF air-lift operation from Agartala, they held out, and when Japanese troops received the order to end the Imphal campaign, it was in effect the end of the campaign to conquer India. Manipur became a fully-fledged Indian state in 1972.

Imphal and around

Circled by distant hills, the capital of Manipur, **IMPHAL**, lies on a plain at an altitude of 785m. Though it lacks dramatic monuments, its broad avenues give it an open feel. The small centre is sandwiched between the stately avenue of Kanglapat to the east and the somewhat stagnant River Nambu to the west. The town's **Polo Ground** dominates the area; according to popular legend, the Manipuri game of *Sagol Kangjei* is the original form of the modern game of polo. In one corner, the **Shaheed Minar** memorial commemorates the Meithei revolt against British occupation in 1891, while just southeast, the **Manipur State Museum** (daily except Mon 10am–4.15pm; Rs2) focuses on tribal costumes, jewellery and weapons along with geological, archeological and natural history displays.

Safety in Manipur

Since Independence, Manipur has seen waves of violence as a result of self-rule campaigns and a brutal **conflict** between the Kukis and Nagas. Disturbances are still common. At the time of writing, the UK Foreign and Commonwealth office advised against all travel to the region, and this section has not been updated for this edition. Check the security situation before you decide to visit, and even then, tourists are advised not to venture too far from the capital. For permit requirements, see p.982.

The festivals and performing arts of Manipur

Manipuri dance, like the associated colourful traditions of Myanmar, Indonesia and Thailand, is replete with Hindu themes and influences. Now recognized as one of India's main classical dance forms, it centres around the story of Krishna cavorting with the *gopis* (milkmaids). Here the *gopis* are dressed in elaborate crinoline-like skirts, while the accompanying music includes energetic group-drumming, with large barrel drums suspended across the players' shoulders. The Jawaharlal Nehru Manipur Dance Academy, North AOC, Imphal (Ⓣ0385/222 0297), Manipur's premier dance institution, arranges occasional recitals and hosts an annual dance festival.

The **martial arts** of Manipur are currently going through something of a revival with performances by men and women being choreographed for the stage. **Thang-Ta** is a dynamic form utilizing *thang*, the sword, and *ta*, the spear. Fast, furious and seemingly extremely dangerous, performances take place each May during **Lai Haraoba**, a ritual dance festival held at Moirang (see p.1021).

Finally, the annual **Heikru Hitongba Boat Race** is held every September as part of a celebration to commemorate the founding of the two major Vaishnavite temples of Imphal, Bijoy Govinda and Govindjee. Two teams of rowers, standing in long dugout canoes, race on the Thangapat moat near the Bijoy Govinda temple

At the heart of Imphal, along Kangchup Road, the fascinating daily market of **Khwairamband** – also known as Nupi Keithel and Ima Bazaar (mothers' market) – is run by more than 3000 Meithei women, making it the largest of its kind in Asia. One section is devoted to textiles – shawls and fabrics including the *moirangphee*, the traditional Meithei dress. This striped skirt comes in two pieces, which for a small fee will be stitched together on the spot with amazing speed. Across the road, the other section of the market sells local fish, vegetables, and other provisions. Smaller markets nearby sell handicrafts, including cane and wicker. If you prefer not to haggle, there are a few fixed-price shops around, including Eastern Handloom and Handicrafts, at GM Hall, near the clock tower, and the Handloom House in Paona Bazaar.

South of the old palace complex, the golden dome of **Shri Govindjee**, Manipur's pre-eminent Vaishnavite temple, can be seen amongst the palm trees. The temple has a large prayer hall and pleasant ambience; the early morning pujas, complete with conch blowing, drumming and procession, are well worth attending – aim to be there by 7.30am. The **British War Cemetery**, 500m north of the *Tourist Lodge*, is the resting place of British and Indian soldiers killed during the Burma campaign and is beautifully maintained by the Commonwealth War Graves Commission.

Langthabal, set on a small hillock 8km south of Imphal on the road to Burma (Myanmar) overlooking the University of Manipur, has remains of an old palace, together with a few temples and ceremonial houses. The **Khonghampat Orchidarium**, 12km north of Imphal on NH-39 (the Dimapur road), displays over a hundred varieties of orchids which bloom in April and May in a riot of colours.

Practicalities

State **buses** arrive at the stand next to the Polo Ground and private buses at their individual offices, most of which are along MG Avenue, 200m north of Khwairamband Bazaar. Manipur's **tourist office** (Mon–Sat 9.30am–5pm, Oct–March 4.30pm; closed 2nd Sat of month; Ⓣ0385/222 0802) is based at *Hotel Imphal*, north of the palace on the main Dimapur road. The ITDC tourist office, on Jail Road (Mon–Sat 9.30am–5.30pm; Ⓣ0385/222 1131), provides

Moving on from Imphal

Imphal's **airport**, 6km south of town, is served by both Indian Airlines and Jet Airways. The Indian Airlines office is on MG Avenue (☎0385/222 0999), and Jet Airways is in Room 201, *Hotel Nirmala* (☎0385/223 0835), on the same road.

Bus connections with Guwahati are good, and the 579-kilometre journey takes around twelve hours. Several private bus companies operate from MG Avenue near the State Bank of India, and also have stands on DM Rd outside *Hotel Tampha*. National Highway 39 – "The Burma Road" – links Imphal to Kohima in **Nagaland** and continues to Dimapur, the nearest railhead 215km away. You will need a valid permit for Nagaland to travel this route. Buses to Dimapur (6hr) leave daily at 6am and will drop off passengers at Kohima, but on the edge of town, not at the central bus stand. For those heading to Silchar, the 200-kilometre road journey via the border point of Jiribam may look tempting, but military checkpoints and bus searches make it a nightmare trip of around fourteen hours. The twice-weekly thirty-minute flight is recommended.

See "Travel details" at the end of this chapter for more information on journey frequencies and durations.

information and maps. The **GPO** (Mon–Sat 9am–5pm) is on Secretariat Road, at the southern end of the palace complex. Individual travellers can get permits endorsed at the **Foreigners' Registration Office** along from the GPO. The State Bank of India on MG Avenue has a foreign exchange service. **Internet** facilities are easily accessible; Millennium Link in Paona Bazaar usually has good connections. Auto- and cycle-**rickshaws** are the main means of transport within Imphal.

Imphal has a few simple **hotels** in the market area, and a handful of mid-range ones further out. Similarly, the choice of **restaurants** is small – the best in town being the *Host* in the *Anand Continental* hotel. There are no **bars** – this is a dry state.

Anand Continental Khoyathong Rd ☎0385/222 3422. Best in town, with carpets, hot showers, TV in all rooms and an excellent restaurant. ③–④

ITDC Imphal North AOC, Dimapur Rd ☎0385/222 0459. Resplendent government-run hotel with large rooms, lawns and restaurant. ③–④

Mass Assembly Rd ☎0385/222 2797. Reasonable-sized doubles, some with balconies and attached bathrooms. Central location. ②–③

Nirmala MG Ave ☎0385/222 9014. A good-value option with carpeted rooms and hot showers – soap and towels provided. ③–⑤

Pintu North AOC, Dimapur Rd ☎0385/222 4172. Large pink building next to the cinema. Clean and friendly, with a restaurant whose advert declares that "slightly hurried food" is served here. ②–③

Tampha North AOC, Dimapur Rd ☎0385/222 1486. Basic accommodation near small dhabas and the bus stand. ①

White Palace MG Ave ☎0385/222 0599. Reasonable hotel with fair-sized rooms near the main markets. ①–③

Loktak Lake

South of Imphal, the huge and complex body of water known as **Loktak Lake**, fed by numerous rivers and dotted with islands, is home to a unique community of fishermen who live on large rafts made of reeds. Rare and endangered sangai, brow-antlered "dancing" deer, live on the floating vegetation that covers much of the lake, sharing their habitat with other species including the hog deer. Much of the lake is taken up by the **Keibul Lamjao National Park**, 53km from Imphal, which attracts a host of waterfowl and migratory birds between

November and March. A forty-room hilltop Tourist Bungalow (☎0385/222 0802; Rs10 per bed) on **Sendra Island**, 48km from Imphal, provides a good vantage point from which to view the lake and can be booked through the tourist office in Imphal.

On the more populated western shore of Loktak, the small town of **MOIRANG**, 45km south of Imphal, is the traditional centre of Meithei culture, with a temple devoted to the pre-Hindu deity **Thangjing**. In April 1944, the Indian National Army under Netaji Subhas Chandra Bose planted its flag here, having fought alongside the Japanese against the British Indian Army for the cause of Independence. A **memorial** and **museum** commemorating the event includes several photos and Japanese-issued rupee notes from 1943. Guided tours of Loktak, run by Imphal's tourist office, usually include Moirang, or you can take a bus (1hr) from the private stand at Keishampat on Jail Road, near the centre of Imphal. The *Moirang Tourist Home* is currently occupied by the Indian army, so travellers will have to return to Imphal for accommodation.

Travel details

Trains

Dibrugarh to: Chennai (weekly; 46hr); Delhi (daily; 52hr); Dimapur (2–3 daily; 5hr 40min–8hr); Guwahati (2–3 daily; 12hr 30min–15hr 15min); Kolkata (daily; 35hr).

Dimapur to: Dibrugarh (2–3 daily; 5hr 40min–8hr); Guwahati (5–6 daily; 5–7hr).

Guwahati to: Chennai (6 weekly; 41–56hr 30min); Delhi (4 daily; 28hr 40min–43hr); Dibrugarh (2–4 daily; 12hr–15hr 50min); Dimapur (5–7 daily; 4hr 45min–7hr); Jorhat (1 daily; 11hr); Kolkata (2–4 daily; 17hr 50min–24hr); Mughal Sarai/Varanasi (3–4 daily; 20–29hr); Mumbai (3 weekly; 30hr 20min–33hr)

Jorhat to: Guwahati (1 daily; 11 hours).

Tinsukia to: Dimapur (3 daily; 7hr); Guwahati (3 daily; 16–17hr); Lumding (3 daily 9hr–10hr 30min).

Buses

The buses listed are state services. Numerous private operators run quicker, more comfortable and therefore more expensive services, including some direct routes not covered through the state system – ask a local travel agent.

Agartala to: Guwahati (2 daily; 20hr); Neermahal (every 30min; 2hr); Shillong (1 daily; 20hr); Silchar (2 daily; 11hr); Udaipur (every 15min; 2hr).

Aizawl to: Silchar (2 daily; 12hr).

Dibrugarh to: Digboi (5–6 daily; 4hr); Dimapur (1 daily; 10hr); Guwahati (6–8 daily; 10hr); Jorhat (8–10 daily; 4hr); Kaziranga (6–8 daily; 6hr); Miao (3 daily; 6–8hr); Tezpur (4–6 daily; 7hr).

Guwahati to: Agartala (2 daily; 20hr); Imphal (2 daily; 12hr); Itanagar (3 daily; 12hr); Jorhat (6–7 daily; 7hr); Kaziranga (14 daily; 4hr); Kohima (4 daily; 10hr); Shillong (12 daily; 3–4hr); Silchar (5 daily; 12hr); Siliguri (6 daily; 12hr); Tezpur (frequent; 5hr).

Imphal to: Dimapur (2 daily; 9hr); Guwahati (1 daily; 18hr); Kohima (2 daily; 6hr).

Jorhat to: Dimapur (5–6 daily; 5hr); Guwahati (12 daily; 6–7hr); Itanagar (1 daily; 9hr); Kaziranga (frequent; 1hr 30min); Sibsagar (frequent; 1hr 30min); Tezpur (14–15 daily; 4hr); Tinsukia (frequent; 5–6hr).

Kohima to: Dimapur (10 daily; 3hr); Guwahati (1 daily; 12–14hr).

Shillong to: Agartala (1 daily; 20hr); Aizawl (3 weekly; 18hr); Cherrapunjee (2 daily; 2hr); Guwahati (12 daily; 3–4hr); Jowai (2 daily; 3-4 hr); Mawsynram (2 daily; 3hr); Silchar (2 daily; 10hr); Tura (2 daily; 12hr).

Tezpur to: Bomdila (daily; 7hr); Dibrugarh (4–6 daily; 7hr); Guwahati (frequent; 6hr); Itanagar (daily; 5hr); Jorhat (frequent; 4hr).

Flights

In the listings below, **AD** represents Air Deccan, **IA** Indian Airlines, **JA** Jet Airways and **SA** Sahara Airlines.

Agartala to: Guwahati (IA, JA 1–2 daily; 40min); Kolkata (IA, JA 1–2 daily; 50min); Silchar (IA 2 weekly; 50min).

Aizawl to: Guwahati (IA 4 weekly; 1hr); Imphal (IA 3 weekly; 30 min); Kolkata (IA daily; 55 min); Shillong (IA 2 weekly; 50 min).

Dibrugarh to: Delhi (AD, SA 4 weekly; 3hr 45 mins); Guwahati (AD, SA at least 4 weekly; 50min); Kolkata (IA 5 weekly; 1hr 30 min).

Dimapur to: Guwahati (IA 5 weekly; 50min); Jorhat (IA weekly; 30min); Kolkata (IA daily; 1hr 10min).
Guwahati to: Agartala (IA, JA 1–2 daily; 40min); Bagdogra (AD, IA, JA 6 weekly; 50min); Delhi (AD, IA, JA, SA at least 3 daily; 2hr 25min–3hr 55min); Dibrugarh (AD, SA 2 daily; 1hr); Imphal (IA, JA 7 weekly; 50min); Jorhat (JA 2 weekly; 50min); Kolkata (AD, IA, JA, SA at least 3 daily; 1hr 10min); Mumbai (JA daily; 4hr 40min).
Imphal to: Aizawl (IA 3 weekly; 30min); Delhi (IA 2 weekly; 3hr 50min); Guwahati (IA, JA 9 weekly; 50min); Kolkata (IA, JA 1–2 daily; 1hr 5min–2hr 35min); Silchar (IA daily; 30min).
Jorhat to: Guwahati (JA 2 weekly; 50min); Kolkata (IA, JA 6 weekly; 1hr 20min).
Lilabari to: Guwahati (IA 2 weekly; 1hr).
Shillong to: Aizawl (IA 2 weekly; 50min); Kolkata (IA 4 weekly; 1hr 45min); Silchar (IA 2 weekly; 35min).
Silchar to: Agartala (IA 2 weekly; 50min); Guwahati (IA 4 weekly; 45 min); Imphal (IA daily; 35 min); Kolkata (IA daily; 1hr 40min); Shillong (IA 2 weekly; 35min).
Tezpur to: Dimapur (IA 1 weekly; 30min); Jorhat (IA 1 weekly; 30min); Kolkata (IA 2 weekly; 2hr 20min).

CHAPTER 17

Highlights

* **Bhubaneswar** Hidden in the city's suburbs are five hundred or so temples, with unique architecture and elaborate sculptures. See p.1028

* **Pipli** Small village famous for its bold appliqué; the main street is a riot of colour with parasols, tablecloths and clothing in every store. See p.1038

* **Puri** Pilgrims flock to the vast temple devoted to Lord Jagannath, particularly during the frenetic midsummer Car Festival. See p.1039

* **Konarak** An elegant thirteenth-century Hindu temple sitting astride a huge stone chariot. See p.1050

* **Olive Ridley turtles** These endangered creatures find their way to Gahirmatha beach for one night in February to lay eggs – an unforgettable scene. See p.1055

△ Olive Ridley turtle

Orissa

Despite being one of India's poorest regions, **ORISSA** boasts a distinctive and rich cultural heritage. The coastal plains claim the highest concentration of historical and religious monuments – Orissa's principal tourist attractions. **Puri**, site of the famous **Jagannath temple** and one of the world's most spectacular devotional processions, the *Rath Yatra*, combines the heady intensity of a Hindu pilgrimage centre with the more hedonistic pleasures of the beach. Just a short hop off the main Kolkata (Calcutta)–Chennai road and railway, Puri sees its fair share of backpackers, who are enticed by plenty of budget accommodation near the beach and a laid-back social scene. **Konarak**, a short hop up the coast, has the ruins of Orissa's most ambitious medieval temple. Hidden for years under a gigantic sand dune, its surfaces writhe with exquisitely preserved sculpture, including some eyebrow-raising erotica. The ancient rock-cut caves and ornate sandstone temples of **Bhubaneswar**, the state capital – all too often skipped by visitors – hark back to an era when it ruled a kingdom stretching from the Ganges delta to the mouth of the River Godavari.

Away from the central "golden triangle" of sights, foreign travellers are few and far between, though you'll see plenty of Bengalis travelling in family groups throughout coastal Orissa. Visitors to these outlying districts, with their minimal infrastructure and overtaxed public transport, tend to have a specialist interest, such as bird or animal life, temples or tribal culture. The **Simlipal National Park**, deep in the *sal* forests of the far northeast, boasts some spectacular scenery, as well as tigers, elephants and hundreds of other species of animals, birds and reptiles. In winter, the small islands dotted around **Chilika Lake**, a huge salt-water lagoon south of Bhubaneswar, become a bird-watcher's paradise. Further north, in the **Bhitarakanika Sanctuary** at the end of Orissa's river delta, a remote stretch of beach is the nesting site for a school of giant Olive Ridley marine **turtles** that migrate here in February and March.

From the number of temples in Orissa, you'd be forgiven for thinking Brahmanical Hinduism was its sole religion. In fact, almost a quarter of the population are **adivasi**, or "tribal" (literally "first") people, thought to have descended from the area's pre-Aryan aboriginal inhabitants. In the more inaccessible corners of the state many of these groups have retained unique cultural traditions and languages. So-called "ethnic" tourism is the latest encroachment on the *adivasis*' way of life, following in the wake of dam builders, missionaries and "advancement programmes" initiated by the state government. In Puri you'll come across signboards advertising "tribal tours" for top dollars, few of which ever trickle down to the *adivasi* villagers themselves.

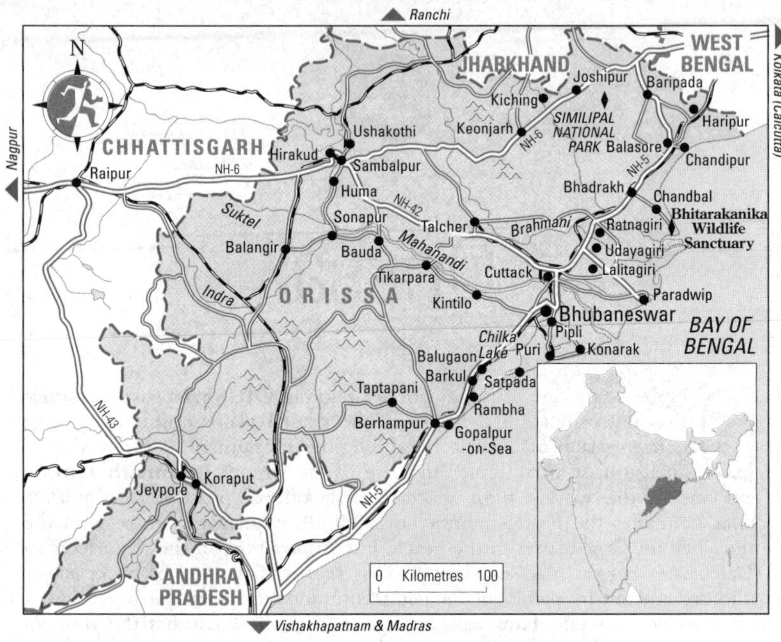

Orissa enjoys a fairly congenial **climate** for most of the year, with average temperatures ranging from 17°C between November and March, to a bearable-if-humid 32°C in summer. The monsoon blows in around mid-June, just in time for the festival of *Rath Yatra*. The cool winter months are the **best time to visit**, particularly around *Makar Sankranti*, in January, when Orissan villages celebrate the end of the harvest with colourful festivals.

Getting around presents few practical problems if you stick to the more populated coastal areas. National Highway 5 and the Southeast Railway, which cut in tandem down the coastal plain via Bhubaneswar, are the main arteries of the region. A metre-gauge branch line also runs as far as Puri, connecting it by frequent, direct express **trains** to Delhi, Kolkata (Calcutta) and Chennai. Elsewhere, **buses** are the best way to travel. Regular government and ever-expanding private services (which tend to be faster and more comfortable) cover all the main routes and most of the more remote stretches.

Some history

Other than scattered fragmentary remains of prehistoric settlement, Orissa's earliest archeological find dates from the fourth century BC. The fortified city of **Sisupalgarh**, near modern Bhubaneswar, was the capital of the **Kalinga** dynasty, about which little is known. In the third century BC, the ambitious Mauryan emperor **Ashoka** descended on ancient Kalinga with his imperial army and routed the kingdom in a battle so bloody, that the carnage was supposed to have inspired his legendary conversion to **Buddhism**. Rock edicts erected around the empire extol the virtues of the new faith, *dharma*, as well as the principles that Ashoka hoped to instil in his vanquished subjects. With the demise of the Mauryans, Kalinga enjoyed something of a resurgence. Under the

Orissan festivals

Chances of coinciding with a **festival** while in Orissa are good, since the region celebrates many of its own as well as all the usual Hindu festivals.

Makar Mela (mid-Jan). Pilgrims descend on a tiny island in Chilika Lake to leave votive offerings in a cave for the goddess Kali.

Adivasis Mela (Jan 26–Feb 1). Bhubaneswar's "tribal" fair is a disappointing cross between Coney Island and an agricultural show, though it does feature good live music and dance.

Magha Saptami (Jan & Feb). During the full moon phase of Magha, a small pool at Chandrabhaga beach, near Konarak, is swamped by thousands of worshippers in honour of Surya, the sun god and curer of skin ailments.

Panashankranti (early April). In various regions, on the first day of Vaisakha, saffron-clad penitents carrying peacock feathers enter trances and walk on hot coals.

Chaitra Parba (mid-April). Santals (the largest of Orissa's many *adivasi* ethnic groups) perform *Chhou* dances at Baripada in Mayurbhunj district, northern Orissa. Some fishing castes also hold "horse-dances" involving wooden horse costumes, drumming and processions through the streets.

Ashokastami (April & May). Bhubaneswar's own Car Festival (procession of temple chariots), when the Lingaraj deity takes a dip in the Bindu Sagar tank.

Sitalasasthi (May & June). Celebration of the marriage of Shiva and Parvati, celebrated in Sambalpur and Bhubaneswar.

Rath Yatra (June & July). The biggest and grandest of Orissa's festivals. Giant images of Lord Jagannath, his brother Balabhadra and his sister Subhadra make the sacred journey from the Jagannath temple to Gundicha Mandir in Puri.

Bali Yatra (Nov & Dec). Commemorates the voyages made by Orissan traders to Indonesia. Held at full moon on the banks of the River Mahanadi in Cuttack.

Konarak Festival (early Dec). A festival of classical dance featuring Orissan and other regional dance forms in the Sun Temple at Konarak.

imperialistic **Chedi** dynasty, which espoused the Jain faith, vast sums were spent expanding the capital and on carving elaborate monastery caves into the nearby hills of **Khandagiri** and **Udaigiri**. In the course of the second century BC, however, the kingdom gradually splintered into warring factions and entered a kind of Dark Age. The influence of Buddhism waned, Jainism all but vanished, and **Brahmanism**, disseminated by the teachings of the Shaivite zealot Lakulisha, started to resurface as the dominant religion.

Orissa's golden age, during which the region's prosperous Hindu rulers created some of south Asia's most sophisticated art and architecture, peaked in the twelfth century under the **Eastern Gangas**. Fuelled by the gains from a thriving trade network (extending as far east as Indonesia), the Ganga kings erected magnificent **temples** where Shiva worship and arcane Tantric practices adopted by earlier Orissan rulers were replaced by new forms of devotion to Vishnu. The shrine of the most popular royal deity of all, Lord Jagannath at Puri, was by now one of the four most hallowed religious centres in India.

In the fifteenth century, the **Afghans of Bengal** swept south to annex the region, with Man Singh's **Moghul** army hot on their heels in 1592. That even a few medieval Hindu monuments escaped the excesses of the ensuing iconoclasm is miraculous; thankfully some did, though **non-Hindus** have never since been allowed to enter the most holy temples in Puri and Bhubaneswar. In 1751 the **Marathas** from western India ousted the Moghuls as the dominant regional power. The East India Company, meanwhile, was also making inroads along the coast, and 28 years after Clive's victory at Plassey in 1765, Orissa finally came under **British rule**.

Since **Independence**, the state has sustained rapid **development**. Discoveries of coal, bauxite, iron ore and other minerals have stimulated considerable industrial growth and improvements to infrastructure. Despite such urban progress, however, Orissa remains essentially a poor rural state, heavily dependent on agriculture to provide for the basic needs of its 36 million inhabitants. Political instability and natural disasters have dogged the region over the past decade. Though Orissa came through the December 2004 tsunami unscathed, October 1999 saw the most devastating "super-cyclone" in recent history (see p.1050) rip through the northern and central coastal plains, leaving a trail of destruction that catapulted Orissa briefly into the glare of the world's media.

Bhubaneswar

At first impression, **BHUBANESWAR**, with its featureless 1950s architecture and rows of decaying concrete shopping arcades, may strike you as surprisingly

dull for a city with a population approaching half a million and a history of settlement stretching back over two thousand years. Beyond the confines of the modern planned city, however, the backstreets and wastegrounds of the southern suburbs harbour the remnants of some of India's finest medieval **temples**. These are indisputably the main attractions, made all the more atmospheric by the animated religious life that continues to revolve around them, particularly at festival times.

Bhubaneswar first appears in history during the fourth century BC, as the capital of ancient **Kalinga**. It was here that Ashoka erected one of the subcontinent's best-preserved rock edicts – still in place 5km south of **Dhauli**. Under the **Chedis**, ancient Kalinga gained control over the thriving mercantile trade in the region and became the northeast seaboard's most formidable power. The elaborate sculpture adorning a complex of Jain caves cut from the hillsides of **Khandagiri** and **Udaigiri**, which still overlook the capital, provides a taste of the military might and opulent royal lifestyles enjoyed by its rulers.

Bhubaneswar then went into decline, re-emerging as a regional force only in the fifth century AD, when – as home to the revolutionary Pasupati sect – it became an important Shaivite centre. Coupled with the formidable wealth of the **Sailodbhavas** two centuries later, the growing religious fervour fuelled an extraordinary spate of temple construction. Between the seventh and twelfth centuries some 7000 shrines are believed to have been erected in the sacred enclave around the **Bindu Sagar** tank. Most were razed in the Muslim incursions of the medieval era, but enough survived for it to be possible in even a short visit to trace the evolution of Orissan architecture from its small, modest beginnings to the gigantic, self-confident proportions of the **Lingaraj** – the seat of Trimbhubaneshwara, or "Lord of Three Worlds", from which the modern city takes its name. A relative backwater until after Independence, Bhubaneswar was only declared the new state capital after nearby Cuttack reached bursting point in the 1950s.

Arrival, information and city transport

There's no regular bus service from Bhubaneswar domestic **airport** into town but taxis and auto-rickshaws cover the 2–3km journey to the centre. Long-distance **buses** terminate at the inconveniently situated Baramunda bus stand, 5km out on the western edge of town, though not before making a whistle-stop tour of the centre. Ask to be dropped at **Station Square** (look for a statue of a horse in the middle of a large roundabout), which is near most hotels. If you miss the stop, frequent buses run along Raj Path and Mahatma Gandhi Marg towards the **railway station** by Station Square.

The **OTDC tourist office** on Lewis Road, next to the *Panthaniwas Hotel* (Mon–Sat 10.30am–5.30pm, closed 2nd Sat of every month; ⓣ0674/243 1299, ⓦwww.orissa-tourism.com), and the counters at the railway station (24hr) and the airport (ⓣ0674/240 4006), can arrange taxis for local sightseeing and help with hotel bookings. The Lewis Road office also offers rather rushed **tours** of the city (Tues–Sun 9am–5pm; Rs150), and a similarly hurried trip to Puri, Konarak and Pipli (daily 9am–6.30pm; Rs155, a/c Rs170). OTDC's luxury bus to Berhampur departs from this office at 6.30am (Rs75), stopping at the bus stand on Station Square at 7am. The India Tourism office behind the museum at B-21 BJB Nagar (Mon–Fri 10am–5pm; ⓣ0674/243 2203) stocks leaflets and city plans for other parts of the country.

Modern Bhubaneswar is too spread out to explore on foot and is best seen by auto- or cycle-**rickshaw**. Sights outside the city, such as Dhauli or the

Udaigiri and Khandagiri caves, can be reached by local **buses** from the old city bus stand near Capital Market, by auto-rickshaw or on one of OTDC's **luxury bus tours**. Cycle rickshaw-wallahs will also make the trip but the journey can be painfully slow. Private Ambassador **taxis** can be arranged through most travel agents and upmarket hotels (Rs800–1000 per day), although far better value are the taxis at the OTDC tourist office.

Accommodation

As state capital, Bhubaneswar offers a typical range of accommodation. While the better-class hotels are spread out all over the city, the inexpensive places tend to be grouped around the **railway station**, or near the busy **Kalpana Square** junction at the bottom of Cuttack Road, a five-minute rickshaw ride away. The railway station also has **retiring rooms** if you're really stuck. Reservations must be made in advance at the counter in the main hall.

Aristo Lodge Kalpana Square ⓣ0674/231 1093. Very basic, but friendly; some rooms have TV and all have attached bath. ❶–❷

Bhagwat Niwas 9 Buddha Nagar ⓣ0674/231 3708. Managed by an Aurobindo devotee, the hotel is safe and welcoming. A range of simple, clean rooms, some with balcony and a/c; there's an in-house ISD booth and a good restaurant. ❷–❺

Jajati MG Marg ⓣ0674/240 0352. Modern hotel at the top end of Station Square. A little frayed around the edges, but the a/c rooms are comfortable and good value. ❸–❺

Keshari Station Square ⓣ0674/253 4994, ⓕ253 5553. Friendly staff and very close to the railway station. The rooms are dark but clean and comfortable, and the restaurant serves local specialities. Also has a good travel agency. ❺–❽

Meghdoot 5-B Sahid Nagar ⓣ0674/254 5710. Some distance away in the north of town, but well appointed. All rooms, from high-quality doubles to luxurious suites, have bathtubs and colour TV. Good pool, restaurant, coffee shop and foreign exchange. ❽

New Marrion 6 Jan Path ⓣ0674/250 2689 ⓕ0674/250 3287, ⓔmarrion@sancharnet.in. Upmarket and welcoming hotel with a pool, foreign exchange, travel agent and two good restaurants, one serving Chinese food. The 24hr bar (open to non-residents) has intriguing frescos around the walls. ❼–❽

OTDC Panthaniwas Lewis Rd ⓣ0674/243 2515. Institutional government hotel close to the museum and temples. Nothing fancy, but the rooms are large and comfortable – although the non-a/c are over-priced, especially in the peak season (Oct–Feb). The hotel also has TV in the a/c rooms, room service and two restaurants. Note the 8am check-out – though negotiable if they are not too busy. ❸–❺

Padma Kalpana Square ⓣ0674/231 3330, ⓕ231 0904. A busy little place with cheap and simple rooms; a good fall-back if others are full. No restaurant. ❷

Richi Station Square ⓣ0674/253 4619, ⓔhotelrichi@sify.com. Large efficient place opposite the station, with cable TV in all rooms. The price includes breakfast. ❸–❺

Sishmo 86/A-1 Gautam Nagar ⓣ0674/243 3600, ⓕ243 3351. Plush four-star in the centre of town with pleasant rooms, a bar, pool, 24hr coffee shop and excellent restaurant. Rates include morning tea and breakfast. ❽–❾

Swosti 103 Jan Path ⓣ0674/253 4678, ⓦwww.swosti.com. Grand four-star hotel bang in the centre of town. Luxurious rooms, all with cable TV; travel agency, two top-class restaurants and a bar. Doubles from $83. ❾

Trident Bhubaneswar Nayapalli ⓣ0674/230 1010, ⓦwww.trident-hilton.com. Indisputably the city's top hotel, part of the Oberoi chain, in the north of town. Exquisitely furnished using antique textiles, stone and metalwork; facilities include an excellent restaurant, an efficient travel centre, foreign exchange, Internet access, and a pool. Doubles from $120. ❾

The temples

Of the five hundred or so **temples** that remain in Bhubaneswar, only a handful are of interest to any but the most ardent templo-phile. They all stand in the south of the city and quite spread out, but it's possible to see the highlights in a

Orissan temples

Orissan temples constitute one of the most distinctive regional styles of religious architecture in south Asia. Like their counterparts elsewhere in the subcontinent, they were built according to strict templates set down a thousand or more years ago in a body of canonical texts called the *Shilpa Shastras*. These specify not only every aspect of temple design – from the proportions of the sanctuary tower to the tiniest sculptural detail – but also the overall symbolic significance of the building. Unlike Christian churches or Islamic mosques, Hindu shrines are not simply places of worship but objects of worship in themselves – re-creations of the "Divine Cosmic Creator-Being" or the particular deity enshrined within them. For a Hindu, to move through a temple is akin to entering the very body of the god glimpsed at the moment of *darshan*, or ritual viewing, in the shrine room. In Orissa, this concept also finds expression in the technical terms used in the *Shastras* to designate the different parts of the structure: the foot (*pabhaga*), shin (*jangha*), torso (*gandi*), neck (*kantha*), head (*mastaka*) and so forth.

Most temples are made up of two main sections. The first and most impressive of these is the **deul**, or sanctuary tower. A soaring, curvilinear spire with a square base and rounded top, the *deul* symbolizes Meru, the sacred mountain at the centre of the universe. Its intricately ribbed sides, which in later buildings were divided into rectangular projections known as *raths*, usually house images of the accessory deities, while its top supports a lotus-shaped, spherical *amla* (a motif derived from an auspicious fruit used in Ayurvedic medicine as a purifying agent). Above that, the vessel of immortality, the *kalasha*, is crowned by the presiding deity's sacred weapon, a wheel (Vishnu's *chakra*) or trident (Shiva's *trishul*). The actual deity occupies a chamber inside the *deul*. Known in Oriya as the **garbha griha**, or inner sanctum, the shrine is shrouded in a womb-like darkness intended to focus the mind of the worshipper on the image of God.

The **jagamohana** ("world delighter"), which adjoins the sanctuary tower, is a porch with a pyramidal roof where the congregation gathers for readings of religious texts and other important ceremonies. Larger temples, such as the Lingaraj in Bhubaneswar and the Jagannath in Puri, also have structures that were tacked on to the main porch when music and dance were more commonly performed as part of temple rituals. Like the *jagamohana*, the roofs of the **nata mandir** (the dancing hall) and **bhoga-mandapa** (the hall of offerings) are pyramidal. The whole structure, along with any smaller subsidiary shrines (often earlier temples erected on the same site), is usually enclosed in a walled courtyard.

Over the centuries, as construction techniques and skills improved, Orissan temples became progressively grander and more elaborate. It's fascinating to chart this transformation as you move from the earlier buildings in Bhubaneswar to the acme of the region's architectural achievement, the stunning Sun Temple at **Konarak**. Towers grow taller, roofs gain extra layers, and the **sculpture**, for which the temples are famous all over the world, attains a level of complexity and refinement unrivalled before or since.

day by rickshaw: allow Rs150–200 for a tour of the main sites (including waiting time). It's a good idea to visit the temples in chronological order. Apart from giving a sense of the way styles developed over the years, this also leaves the most impressive monuments until last. The majority are active places of worship, so dress appropriately, remove your shoes (and any leather items) at the entrance and seek permission before taking photographs, particularly inside the buildings. The resident priest will expect a donation if he's shown you around, of course, but don't necessarily believe the astronomical amounts recorded in the ledgers you'll be shown. Entry is free to all temples apart from Rajrani.

The central group

The compact **central group**, just off Lewis Road, includes some of Bhubaneswar's most celebrated temples. In order to see the oldest first, follow the footpath from the main road past the more recent Muktesvara Mandir and its adjacent water tank, as far as a small square lined with cold-drink stalls and souvenir shops.

The best preserved and most beautiful of Bhubaneswar's early temples, the lavishly decorated **Parasuramesvara Mandir** stands in the shade of a large *banyan* tree just beyond the square. Dating from around 650 AD, the shrine's plain, rectangular assembly hall (*jagamohana*), simple stepped roof and squat beehive-shaped tower (*deul*) typify the style of the late seventh century. In addition to the sheer quality of the building's exterior sculpture, Parasuramesvara is significant in marking the then-recent transition from Buddhism to Hinduism. Look out for panels depicting Lakulisha, the proselytizing Shaivite saint whose sect was largely responsible for the conversion of Orissa to Hinduism in the fifth century. More graphic assertions of Hindu supremacy mark corners of the *deul*, where rampant lions crouch or stand above elephants, symbols of the beleaguered Buddhist faith.

Erected in the mid-tenth century, the **Muktesvara Mandir** is often dubbed "the gem" of Orissan architecture for its compact size and exquisite sculptural detail. It stands close to the main road in a separate walled courtyard, beside the small **Marichi Kund** tank (whose murky green waters are believed to cure infertility). The temple was constructed two hundred years after the Parasuramesvara, and represents the new, more elaborate style that had evolved in Bhubaneswar. Its *jagamohana* sports the more distinctively Orissan pyramidal roof, while the *deul*, though similar in shape to earlier sanctuary towers, places more emphasis on vertical rather than horizontal lines. Once again, the sandstone sculpture is also superb. Directly facing the main entrance, the ornamental **torana** (gateway), topped by two reclining female figures, is the Muktesvara's masterpiece. The grinning lions and dwarfs around the windows on the side of the porch, known as the *bho* motif, come a close second.

On the edge of Muktesvara's terrace stands an example of the mature phase of Orissan temple building. The unfinished **Siddhesvara** was erected at more or less the same time as the Lingaraj, in the eleventh century, but is nowhere near as imposing. The lesser deities around the tower, Ganesh and Kartikeya (Shiva's sons) are about its only remarkable features.

The eastern group

To reach the first of the more scattered **eastern group** of temples, ten to fifteen minutes' walk from Muktesvara, head back up Lewis Road as far as the crossroads, turn right down Tankapani Road, and keep going until you reach the park on the right.

Even though it was never completed, the twelfth-century **Rajrani Mandir** (daily sunrise–sunset; Rs100 [Rs5], video camera Rs25) ranks among the very finest of Bhubaneswar's later temples. From the far end of the well-watered gardens in which it stands, the profile of the *deul*, with its successive tiers of projections rising to form an elegant eighteen-metre tower, dominates first impressions. Closer up, you can make out the profusion of sculpted figures for which Rajrani is equally famous. The best surround the sides of the tower, roughly 3m off the ground, where the **dikpalas** ("guardians of the eight directions") "protect" the main shrine. Surrounded by their respective vehicles and attributes, the figures form a marked contrast to the languid and alluring poses of the exquisite female *nayikas* dividing them.

From Rajrani, a fair walk leads up Tankapani Road to the turn-off for the **Brahmesvara Mandir**, 500m on the right. Unlike most of its neighbours, the eleventh-century shrine still houses a living deity, as indicated by the saffron pennant flying from the top of the sanctuary. Here too *dikpalas* preside over the corners, with a fierce Chamunda on the western facade (shown astride a corpse and holding a trident and severed head). Curvaceous maidens admire themselves in mirrors or, in the panels around the tower, dally with their male consorts. An inscription, now lost, records that one Queen Kovalavati once made a donation of "many beautiful women" to this temple, recalling that **devadasis**, the dancers-cum-prostitutes who were to become a prominent feature of Orissan temple life in later years (see p.1051), made an early appearance here. Non-Hindus are not supposed to enter the central shrine – whose majestic Nandi bull has testicles well polished by years of propitious rubbing from worshippers.

The Bindu Sagar group

By far the largest group of temples is clustered around the **Bindu Sagar** ("ocean drop tank"), 2km south of the city centre. This small artificial lake, mentioned in the *Puranas*, is itself a place of great religious importance. Said to contain nectar, wine and water drawn from the world's most sacred rivers, the tank is the main bathing place both for pilgrims visiting the city and for the Lingaraj deity, who is taken to the pavilion in the middle once every year during Bhubaneswar's annual **Car Festival** (Ashokastami) for his ritual purificatory dip. The hours around sunrise and sunset are the most evocative time for a stroll here, when the residents of the nearby *dharamshalas* file through the smoky lanes to pray at the *ghats*.

Lingaraj Mandir

Immediately south of the Bindu Sagar stands the most stylistically evolved temple in all Orissa. Built early in the eleventh century by the Ganga kings, one hundred years before the Jagannath temple at Puri, the mighty **Lingaraj Mandir** has remained very much a living shrine. For this reason, foreign visitors are not permitted inside, but there is a **viewing platform** overlooking the north wall of the complex, around the corner from the main entrance. From this vantage-point you can see all four of the principal sections of the building. The two nearest the entrance, the *bhoga-mandapa* (Hall of Offering) and the *nata mandir* (Hall of Dance, associated with the rise of the *devadasi* system – see p.1051) are both later additions. Beautiful **sculpture** depicting the music and dance rituals that would once have taken place inside the temple adorns its walls, although these can be difficult to appreciate with the naked eye.

Even more than the huge *jagamohana*, the immense 45-metre *deul* is the literal and aesthetic high point of the Lingaraj. Notice the rampant lion projecting from the curved sides of the tower, and the downtrodden elephant beneath him – symbolizing, once again, the triumph of Hinduism over Buddhism. On the top, the typical Orissan motif of the flattened, ribbed sphere (*amla*) supported by gryphons, is crowned with Shiva's trident. As in the Brahmesvara temple, the long saffron pennant announces the living presence of the deity below.

The **shrine** inside is very unusual. The powerful 2.5-metre-thick Svayambhu (literally "self-born") *lingam* that it contains, one of the twelve *jyotirlingas* in India, is known as "Hari-Hara" because it is considered half Shiva, half Vishnu – an extraordinary amalgam that is thought to have resulted from the ascendancy of Vaishnavism over Shaivism in the twelfth and thirteenth centuries. Unlike other *lingasm*, which are bathed every day in a concoction prepared from hemlock, Svayambhu is offered a libation of rice, milk and *bhang* by the brahmins. Another peculiar feature of the shrine room is that it lacks a ceiling. Instead, the roof reaches right to the top of the tower.

Vaital Deul Mandir

From the Lingaraj viewing platform, head left and up the main street to the **Vaital Deul** temple, one of the group's oldest buildings and a real feast of Tantric art. The building was erected sometime around 800 AD in a markedly different style from most of its contemporaries in Bhubaneswar, drawing heavily on earlier Buddhist influences. Among the panels of Hindu deities encrusting its outer walls, you can make out examples of some of India's earliest erotic sculpture.

Once past the four-faced *lingam* post at the main entrance (used for tethering sacrificial offerings), your eyes soon adjust to the darkness of the **interior**, whose grotesque images convey the macabre nature of the esoteric rites once performed here. Durga, in her most terrifying aspect as **Chamunda**, peers out of the half-light from behind the grille at the far end of the hall – her withered body, garlanded with skulls and flanked by an owl and a jackal, stands upon a rotting corpse. In front of her, to the right of the door, an even more nightmarish figure of a man picks himself up from the floor, having filled his skull-cup with blood from the decapitated body nearby. The whole gruesome frieze is littered with severed heads and jackals gnawing at corpses.

Around the town

The **Orissa State Museum**, in a large modern building at the top of Lewis Road (Tues–Sun 10am–5pm; Rs50), has a collection of "tribal" artefacts, illuminated manuscripts and various archeological finds. On display in the downstairs galleries are pieces of religious sculpture, including pre-twelfth-century Buddhist statues, coins and donative inscriptions on stone and copper plates salvaged from the city's temples. The upstairs rooms feature ethnographic material from indigenous Orissan societies. As well as heavy jewellery, musical instruments, weapons, tools and moth-eaten traditional costumes, there are reproductions of **chitra muriya**, the folk murals seen on walls and floors in village houses around Puri. The museum's real highlight, however, has to be its collection of antique **painting** and illuminated **palm-leaf manuscripts** (see p.1046). Only the National Museum in New Delhi holds finer examples of this traditional Orissan art form.

Hidden away on the northwestern edge of town, close to Baramunda bus stand on NH-5, is the Tribal Research Institute's anthropological **Museum of Man** (Mon–Sat 10am–5pm; free), with exhibits on the distinctive cultures and art of the 62 different tribal groups spread throughout Orissa, mostly in the southern hinterlands. Filling the gardens outside are somewhat idealized replicas of *adivasi* dwellings, decorated with more authentic-looking murals. The **library** behind the main institute building holds all the books and journals ever compiled on the *adivasi* groups of Orissa.

Asia's largest **cactus collection** (daily 10am–5pm; free) is housed on the opposite side of the highway to the Museum of Man, in the Acharya Vihar building. No less than 1050 species of cacti are displayed at this state-funded initiative, whose resident scientists claim to have recently discovered a cure for elephantiasis, a disease that causes huge swelling in the limbs and affects a great number of the paddy farmers across Orissa.

Capital Market, situated in a residential area along Jan Path, is the place to buy typical Orissan handlooms, handicrafts and jewellery. All the material shops claim to be the official government outlet, so the prices for lengths of beautifully woven cloth and ready-made garments are very competitive.

Eating

Eating out in Bhubaneswar is basically limited to the predictable five-star food dished up in the a/c comfort of hotels such as the *Sishmo*, or the cheap and chilli-ful South Indian dishes served in rather less salubrious cafés such as the *Swosti* and the *Venus Inn*; both are open for breakfast. The one or two restaurants that make an effort to include traditional **Orissan cuisine** on their menus are worth seeking out (you will have to order at least eight hours in advance at the big hotels); seafood dishes like prawn curry or delicate pomfret (a white fish) combined with rice, fresh vegetables, coconut, yoghurt and spices are common in the coastal villages, but you rarely see them in the city. Another Orissan speciality to look out for is *chenna poda* (yummy cheesecake stuffed with almonds), and other sweets like *raswadi* (thickened milk with balls of curd) and *gajjar halwa* (a rich sweet made from grated carrots).

Bhuvanashree At the top of Station Square next to the *Jajati* hotel. Excellent, clean veg restaurant with some South Indian food, a choice of thalis and good coffee. Closed Tues.

Dalema Bhouma Nagar. Dark, simple place offering authentic Orissan dishes like *macha bhaja* (fish curry), *chengudli tarkari* (prawn curry), *dahi machho* (river fish in yoghurt sauce) and a variety of vegetables. Main courses are inexpensive at about Rs40 each.

Fahien and **Mohini** At the OTDC *Panthaniwas*, Lewis Rd. *Fahien* and *Mohini* offer identical multi-cuisine menus, but the former is more comfortable.

Hare Krishna Jan Path, just north of the junction with MG Marg, entrance up a flight of stairs in a small market. Quite expensive, with waiters in dinner jackets rather than *dhotis*, but the food is strictly ISKCON-style (the Hare Krishna movement's unique cuisine, without garlic or onions): vegetarian and delicious.

Maurya Gardens 122A Station Square, next to and part of the *Richi*. Smart interior and reasonable prices. Serves Indian and Chinese food, specializing in tandoori dishes.

Sishmo *Sishmo Hotel*. High-quality food with a wide variety of Indian tandoori dishes in classy surroundings. Pricey, but not as expensive as it looks (around Rs1000 a head with wine).

Swosti *Swosti Hotel*. Ultra-reliable place for good, moderately priced authentic Orissan dishes, such as the mouthwatering *dahi machho*); order ahead at least two or three hours ahead.

Listings

Airlines Indian Airlines' main booking office is on Raj Path, near New Market (☎0674/253 0533; airport office ☎0674/253 5743). Air Sahara has an office at the airport (☎0624/253 5729).

Banks and exchange The State Bank of India on Raj Path has an efficient foreign exchange counter and accepts all major currencies. There is an ATM accepting Visa and Cirrus at the Centurion Bank, *Hotel Arya Palace*, 126/b Ashok Nagar.

Bookshops The Modern Book Depot at the top of Station Square has a rack of pulp fiction and a section dedicated to history, dance, economy, geography and natural history of Orissa. Across the square in Ashoka Market, the Bookshop stocks a wide range of Western literature, Indian literature in translation, and books on politics, religion and history.

Dance Visits or lessons can be arranged through the Orissa Dance Academy, 64 Kharwal Nagar, Unit 3 (☎0674/240 8494). The Rabindra Mandap auditorium on Sachivalaya Marg (☎0674/241 7677) runs regular music, dance and drama events.

Hospital The Capital Hospital and Homeopathic Clinic (☎0674/240 1983) is near the airport. For casualty, call ☎0674/240 0688. There's an Ayurvedic hospital between the *Panthaniwas* hotel and the Ramesvara temple (☎0674/243 2347). For a Red Cross ambulance, call ☎0674/240 2384.

Internet access There are plenty of Internet cafés around Station Square, as well as along Cuttack Rd and Jan Path. Iway, in the building next to the *Swosti* hotel, and beside the exhibition ground near the Shri Ram Temple, charges Rs25/hr for a fast connection.

Photography Fotomakers, 28 West Tower New Market; Photo Express, 44 Ashok Nagar; Unicolor Photo Lab, 133 Ashok Nagar.

Moving on from Bhubaneswar

Bhubaneswar lies on the main **Howrah–Chennai** line with many **trains** passing through daily, including the recommended Coromandel Express #2841/42. Also heading south, the weekly Guwahati–Cochin Express #5624 (Fri) and the twice-weekly Guwahati–Bangalore Express #5626 (Tues & Sun) call here. Trains to **Delhi** include the Rajdhani Express #2421 on Wed and Sun (the fastest and most convenient), and a daily service from Puri on either the New Delhi Express #2815 or the Neelachal Express #8475 (Tues, Fri & Sun). The best train to **Kolkata (Calcutta)** is the daily Sri Jagannath Express #8410.

Buses run by Orissa State Transport depart from Baramunda bus stand. You can pick up buses to Puri, Pipli and Cuttack from Jayadev Nagar opposite the *Kalinga Ashok* hotel, and from near the railway station. **Buses** and **minibuses** run to Puri (Rs19 per person) as soon as they are full, but they become extremely overloaded and drive dangerously fast.

Indian Airlines has **flights** from Bhubaneswar airport to Mumbai, Delhi, Chennai and Hyderabad; Air Sahara has services to Kolkata (Calcutta) and Hyderabad.

See "Travel details" at the end of this chapter for more information on journey frequencies and durations.

Post office On the corner of MG Marg and Sachivalaya Marg (Mon–Sat 9am–6pm). For poste restante ask at "enquiries" on the middle counter. A pan-wallah by the main entrance packs and seals parcels.
Police station Raj Path, near the State Bank of India (Ⓣ0674/253 3732).
Travel agents The *Keshari, New Marrion, Meghdoot, Sishmo* and *Trident Bhubaneswar* hotels all have in-house travel agents. Swosti Travels (Ⓣ0674/250 8738) in the *Swosti Hotel*, 103 Jan Path, does ticketing for Indian Airlines and Jet Airways, and offers upmarket package tours of Bhubaneswar, Puri and Konarak. Prime Tours and Travels, in the Pushpak Complex on Kalpana Square, can fix up car rental, airline tickets and train reservations.

Around Bhubaneswar

A number of places around Bhubaneswar are worth combining with a day-trip to the city. Fifteen minutes by auto-rickshaw out of the centre, the second-century BC caves at **Khandagiri** and **Udaigiri** offer a glimpse of the region's history prior to the rise of Hinduism. **Dhauli**, just off the main road to Puri, boasts an even older monument: a rock edict dating from the Mauryan era, commemorating the battle of c.260 BC that gave the emperor Ashoka control of the eastern seaports, and thus enabled his missionaries to export the state religion across Asia. **Pipli**, 20km south, is famous for its appliqué work and colourful lampshades.

Udaigiri and Khandagiri caves

Six kilometres west of Bhubaneswar, a pair of low hills rise from the coastal plain. More than two thousand years ago, caves chiselled out of their malleable yellow sandstone were home to a community of **Jain monks**. Nowadays, they lie virtually deserted, left for troupes of black-faced langur monkeys and occasional parties of tourists to clamber over. Though by no means in the same league as the caves of the Deccan, **Udaigiri** and **Khandagiri** (daily 8am–5pm; Rs100 [Rs5], video camera Rs25) rank, nevertheless, among Orissa's foremost historical monuments.

Inscriptions show that the **Chedi** dynasty, which ruled ancient Kalinga from the first century BC, was responsible for the bulk of the work. There are simple monk's cells for meditation and prayer, as well as royal chambers where the hallways, verandas and facades outside several caves are encrusted with **sculpture** depicting court scenes, lavish processions, hunting expeditions, battles, dances and a host of domestic details from the daily life of Kalinga's cool set. The later additions (from medieval times, when Jainism no longer enjoyed royal patronage in the region) are more austere, showing the twenty-four heroic Jain prophet-teachers, or *tirthankaras* ("crossing-makers").

From Bhubaneswar, the caves are approached via a road that follows the route of an ancient **pilgrimage path** (leading, archeologists believe, to a now-vanished stupa). As you face the hills with the highway behind you, Khandagiri ("Broken Hill") is on your left and Udaigiri ("Sunrise Hill") on your right. It's best to begin with the latter, which has the finest of the early stonework.

Udaigiri

The **Udaigiri** caves occupy a fairly compact area around the south slope of the hill. **Cave 1** (Rani Gumpha or "Queen's Cave"), off the main pathway to the right, is the largest and most impressive of the group. A long frieze across the back wall shows rampaging elephants, panicking monkeys, sword fights and the abduction of a woman, perhaps illustrating episodes from the life of Kalinga's King Kharavela. **Caves 3** and **4** contain sculptures of a lion holding its prey and elephants with snakes wrapped around them, and pillars topped by pairs of peculiar winged animals. **Cave 9**, up the hill and around to the right, houses a damaged relief of figures worshipping a long-vanished Jain symbol. The crowned figure is thought to be the Chedi king, Vakradeva, whose donative inscription can still be made out near the roof. Inside the sleeping cells of all the caves, deep grooves in the stone wall at the back and in the floor were specially designed to carry rainwater down from the roof as an early air-conditioning system.

To reach **Cave 10**, return to the main steps and climb towards the top of the hill. Its popular name, "Ganesh Gumpha", is derived from the elephant-headed Ganesh carved on the rear wall of the cell on the right. From here, follow the path up to the ledge at the very top of Udaigiri Hill for good views and the ruins of an old **chaitya hall**, probably the main place of worship for the Jain monks who lived below.

Below the ruins are **Cave 12**, shaped like the head of a tiger, and **Cave 14**, the Hathi Gumpha, known for the long **inscription** in ancient Magadhi carved onto its overhang. This relates in glowing terms the life history of King Kharavela, whose exploits, both on and off the battlefield, brought in the fortune needed to finance the cave excavation.

Khandagiri

The caves on the opposite hill, **Khandagiri**, can be reached either by the long flight of steps leading from the road, just up from the main entrance to the Udaigiri caves, or by cutting directly across from Hathi Gumpha via the steps that drop down from Cave 17. The latter route brings you out at **Caves 1** and **2**, known as Tatowa Gumpha ("Parrot Caves") for the carvings of birds on their doorway-arches. Cave 2, excavated in the first century BC, is the larger and more interesting. On the back wall of one of its cells, a few faint lines in red *Brahmi* script are thought to have been scrawled two thousand years ago by a monk practising his handwriting. The reliefs in **Cave 3**, the Ananta Gumpha ("Snake Cave") – serpents decorate the doorways – contain the best of the sculpture on Khandagiri hill, albeit badly vandalized in places. **Caves 7** and **8**, left of the main steps, were former sleeping quarters, remodelled in the eleventh century as sanctuaries. Both house reliefs of *tirthankaras* on their walls as well as Hindu deities which had become part of the Jain pantheon by the time conversion work was done. From the nineteenth-century **Jain temple** at the top of the hill there are clear views across the sprawl of Bhubaneswar to the white dome of Dhauli.

Dhauli

The gleaming, white **Vishwa Shanti Stupa** on **Dhauli Hill**, 8km south of Bhubaneswar on the Pipli road, overlooks the spot where the Mauryan emperor **Ashoka** defeated the Kalingas in the decisive battle of 260 BC. Apart from bringing the prosperous Orissan kingdom to its knees, the victory also led the emperor, allegedly overcome by remorse at having slain 150,000 people, to renounce the path of violent conquest in favour of the spiritual path preached by Gautama Buddha. Built in 1972 by an association of Japanese Buddhists, the modern stupa, which eclipses its older predecessor nearby, stands as a memorial to Ashoka's legendary change of heart, and the massive religious sea change it precipitated. Panels around the sides illustrate episodes from the lives of Ashoka (below) and the Buddha (above), while the umbrella-like projections on the top symbolize the five cardinal Buddhist virtues of faith, hope, compassion, forgiveness and non-violence.

After his conversion, Ashoka set about promulgating the maxims of his newly found faith in **rock edicts** installed at key sites around the empire (see "History" in Contexts). One such inscription, in ancient **Brahmi**, the ancestor of all non-Islamic Indian scripts, still stands on the roadside at the foot of Dhauli Hill, etched from a rock featuring a beautifully carved figure of an elephant (symbolizing Buddhism). Having lain forgotten for centuries under a blanket of scrub, the monument was re-discovered in 1837 by a British coal prospector, Lt Markham Kittoe, who sent a facsimile to the eminent indologist James Prinsep in Calcutta. By comparing copies of similar inscriptions from across northern India, Prinsep was able eventually to decipher the script, unlocking the lost history of Ashoka and the Mauryans. The translation placed alongside this one at Dhauli gives some idea of its contents: a mixture of rambling philosophical asides, discourses on animal rights and tips on how to treat your slaves. Particularly of note are the lines claiming the Buddhist doctrine of non-violence was being recognized by "the kings of Egypt, Ptolemy and Antigonus and Magas", which proved for the first time the existence of a connection between the ancient civilizations of India and the West. The Dhauli edict also features the famous "All men are my children . . ." declaration, but diplomatically omits the account that crops up elsewhere describing how many Kalingas Ashoka had put to the sword before he finally "saw the light". If you are here in February, ask at tourist offices about the annual martial dances festival at the stupa, with performances depicting battles and the traditional martial arts of Manipur, Orissa, Maharashtra and Kerala.

If you don't have your own vehicle and are not on a tour, **getting to Dhauli** involves a two-kilometre walk. Ask to be dropped off the bus at Dhauli Chowk, the junction on the main Puri–Bhubaneswar road, and make your way along the avenue of cashew trees to the rock edict. The road to the stupa begins its short climb up the hill here, ending at a small car park surrounded by postcard and chai stalls.

Pipli

Fifteen minutes' drive or so beyond Dhauli, on the Puri road, splashes of bright colour in the shop fronts ranged alongside the main street announce your arrival in **PIPLI**, Orissa's **appliqué** capital (see box on p.1047). Much of what the artisans produce here nowadays on their hand-powered sewing machines is shoddy kitsch compared with the painstaking work traditionally undertaken for the Jagannath temple. Express enough interest and you'll be shown some of the better-quality pieces for which Pipli is justly famed. Bedspreads, wall-hangings and small *chhatris* (awnings normally hung above household and temple shrines) are about the most authentic goods on offer. The shops do not open early; the best time to wander around is in the evening, when gas lamps, devotional music and gentle bargaining make the experience much more atmospheric.

Puri

A true-hearted pilgrim does not fear to measure kingdoms with his feeble footsteps.

Old Hindu saying

As the home of Lord Jagannath and his siblings, **PURI** ranks among Hindu India's most important sacred sites, visited by a vast number of pilgrims each year. The crowds peak during the monsoons for **Rath Yatra**, the famous "Car Festival" featured on virtually all of Orissa's tourist literature, when literally millions pour in to watch three giant, multi-coloured chariots drawn up the main thoroughfare. At the centre of the maelstrom, the **Jagannath temple** soars above the town's medieval heart and colonial suburbs like some kind of misplaced space rocket. Non-Hindus aren't allowed inside its bustling precincts, but don't let this deter you; Puri's streets and beach remain the focus of intense devotional activity year round, while its bazaars are crammed with collectable religious souvenirs associated with the Jagannath cult.

Three distinct types of visitors come to Puri: middle-class Bengalis lured by the combined pleasures of puja and promenade; young Western and Japanese backpackers enjoying the low-key travellers' scene; and the thousands of pilgrims from mostly rural eastern India who flock in to pay their respects to Lord Jagannath. Over the years the three have staked out their respective ends of town and stuck to them. It all makes for a rather bizarre and intoxicating atmosphere, where you can be transported from the intensity of Hindu India to the sea and back to the relative calm of your hotel veranda at the turn of a bicycle wheel.

Some history

Until the seventh and eighth centuries, Puri was little more than a provincial outpost along the coastal trade route linking eastern India with the south. Then, thanks to its association with the Hindu reformer **Shankaracharya** (Shankara), the town began to feature on the religious map. Shankara made Puri one of his four *mathas*, or centres for the practice of a radically new, and more ascetic form of Hinduism. Holy men from across the whole subcontinent came here to debate the new philosophies – a tradition carried on in the town's temple courtyards to this day. With the arrival of the **Gangas** at the beginning of the twelfth century, this religious and political importance was further consolidated. In 1135, Anantavarman Chodaganga founded the great temple in Puri, and dedicated it to **Purushottama**, one of the thousand names of Vishnu – an ambitious attempt to integrate the many feudal kingdoms recently conquered by the Gangas. Under the Gajapati dynasty in the

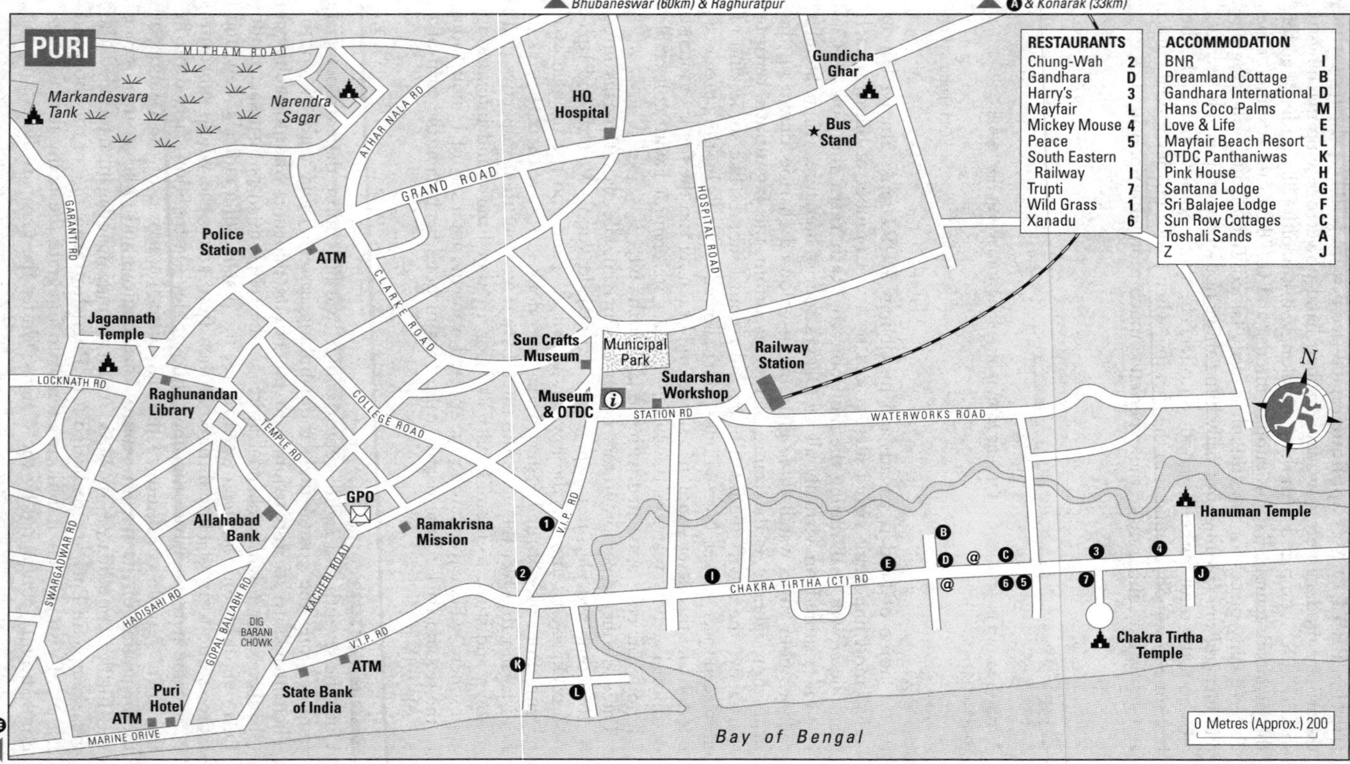
PURI
Bhubaneswar (60km) & Raghuratpur
A & Konarak (33km)
F, G, H & Sanskrit University
M
RESTAURANTS
Chung-Wah 2
Gandhara D
Harry's 3
Mayfair L
Mickey Mouse 4
Peace 5
South Eastern Railway I
Trupti 7
Wild Grass 1
Xanadu 6
ACCOMMODATION
BNR I
Dreamland Cottage B
Gandhara International D
Hans Coco Palms M
Love & Life E
Mayfair Beach Resort L
OTDC Panthaniwas K
Pink House H
Santana Lodge G
Sri Balajee Lodge F
Sun Row Cottages C
Toshali Sands A
Z J
Markandesvara Tank
Narendra Sagar
MITHAM ROAD
ATHAR NALA RD
GRAND ROAD
HQ Hospital
Gundicha Ghar
Bus Stand
HOSPITAL ROAD
GARANTI RD
Police Station
ATM
CLARKE ROAD
Jagannath Temple
LOCKNATH RD
Raghunandan Library
Sun Crafts Museum
Municipal Park
Museum & OTDC
Sudarshan Workshop
STATION RD
Railway Station
WATERWORKS ROAD
N
COLLEGE ROAD
TEMPLE RD
GPO
Ramakrisna Mission
Allahabad Bank
V.I.P. RD
SWARGADWAR RD
HADISAHI RD
GOPAL BALLABH RD
KACHERI ROAD
DIG BARANI CHOWK
V.I.P. RD
ATM
State Bank of India
Puri Hotel
ATM
MARINE DRIVE
CHAKRA TIRTHA (CT) RD
Hanuman Temple
Chakra Tirtha Temple
Bay of Bengal
0 Metres (Approx.) 200

fifteenth century Purushottama's name changed to **Jagannath** ("Lord of the Universe"). Henceforth **Vaishnavism** and the devotional worship of Krishna, an incarnation of Vishnu, was to hold sway as the predominant religious influence in the temple. Puri is nowadays one of the four most auspicious pilgrimage centres, or *dhams*, in India.

Western-style leisure **tourism**, centred firmly on the town's long sandy beach, is a comparatively new phenomenon. The British were the first to spot Puri's potential as a resort. When they left, the Bengalis took over their bungalows, only to find themselves sharing the beach with an annual migration of young, *chillum*-smoking Westerners attracted to the town by its abundant hashish. Today, few vestiges of this era remain. Thanks to a concerted campaign by the municipality to clean up Puri's image, the "scene" has dwindled to little more than a handful of cafés, and is a far cry from the swinging hippy paradise some still arrive here hoping to find.

Arrival, information and city transport

Trains arriving at Puri's end-of-line **station**, in the north of town, are greeted by fired-up cycle rickshaw-wallahs sprinting alongside in the race to catch a foreigner. You'll encounter similar "rickshaw rage" at the main bus station and the Jagannath temple, caused by competition for the commission offered by the hotels. The bus stand is further in the north of the city, a ten-minute rickshaw ride from the centre through the bumpy back-streets. The OTDC **tourist office** on Station Road (Mon–Sat 10am–5pm, closed 2nd Sat of the month; ⓣ06752/222664) is friendly and helpful; the 24-hour counter at the railway station is a waste of time. Train travel arrangements are best made or checked directly with the station itself or else through a travel agent.

Puri is fairly spread out but flat, so **bicycles** (Rs15–20 per day) are ideal for getting around and exploring the maze of streets around the Jagannath temple. There are several places to rent them on Chakra Tirtha (CT) Road, in the travellers' enclave between the *Gandhara International* and *Love and Life* – try Unique Tours opposite *Z* hotel. **Auto-rickshaws** are thin on the ground, though one or two are always hanging around the railway station and the hotels. **Mopeds** (Rs150 per day) and Enfield **motorbikes** (Rs250 per day) are rented out by a couple of travel agents and shops along CT Road for full or half-days and are useful for trips up the coast to Konarak. In-house **travel agents** at the larger hotels can help with all transport arrangements, though the most reliable all-round place for ticket booking, flights and car/motorcycle/bike rental is Heritage Tours, based at the *Mayfair Beach Resort* (ⓣ06752/223656).

Accommodation

Virtually all Puri's **hotels** stand on or near the beach, where a strict distinction is observed: the hotels pitched at domestic tourists are lined up behind Marine Drive, the promenade on the west end of the beach, while budget-conscious Westerners are sandwiched further east around CT Road between the high-rise, upmarket resort hotels and the fishing village; this backpackers' enclave is known locally as **Pentakunta**. The less expensive hotels are quiet during the summer months, but the pricier accommodation tends to be booked solid well in advance over Rath Yatra, which coincides with the Bengali holiday season – make reservations as early as possible. Checkout is 8am for most hotels in Puri due to the influx of early trains on the town, although off season this rule is less rigidly enforced.

BNR (South Eastern Railway Hotel) CT Rd ⓣ06752/222063. Nothing has changed here since it was the premier bolt-hole for Calcutta's burra- and memsahibs. Turbaned bearers with big belts pad barefoot around the wide verandas. A must for Rajophiles, even if only for dinner. ❹–❺

Dreamland Cottage off CT Rd ⓣ06752/224122. Not exactly roses around the door, but homely and relaxed, with a leafy secluded garden dotted with birdcages. Five rooms all with attached bath, but no a/c. ❶

Gandhara International CT Rd ⓣ06752/222618, ⓔgandhara@india.com. Good value for the budget traveller: cheap clean rooms and dorms (Rs40) around a courtyard, and a new upmarket block behind with a/c rooms, hot showers and TV. Two roof terraces and a restaurant serving authentic Japanese food on request. Internet, travel service, and free poste restante also available. ❷–❺

Hans Coco Palms Marine Drive ⓣ06752/230951, ⓔhanscocoplams@hotmail.com. Modern complex in a superb setting 2km west of the centre; all rooms are a/c and overlook the sea and the beach is pleasant here. Pool, bar and restaurant. ❽–❾

Love and Life CT Rd ⓣ06752/224433, ⓕ226093. Popular with the many young Japanese visitors to Puri, this place has an easy-going atmosphere and a good restaurant. The clean rooms all have an attached bath, and are either in the main block or in cottages in the garden. The dorm is Rs30 per bed. ❶–❺

Mayfair Beach Resort Off CT Rd ⓣ06752/227800, ⓕ224242. Luxury chalets and rooms looking down through palm trees to a pool and the beach. Five-star facilities, including a massage parlour, a bar and an excellent restaurant. Recommended. Doubles from $68. ❾

OTDC Panthaniwas off CT Rd ⓣ06752/222562. A good-value hotel; some of the plain but spacious rooms catch sea breezes; the old Raj-era building has more atmosphere. There is a pleasant restaurant, a bar and a garden. ❷–❻

Pink House Off CT Rd ⓣ06752/222253. Laid-back, pinky-red pad, right on the beach at the edge of the fishing village, with its very own travellers' scene and an adjacent restaurant. ❶–❷

Santana Lodge At the very end of CT Rd ⓣ06752/251491. Small, pleasant hotel geared up for travellers; especially popular with the Japanese. Prices include breakfast and communal dinner. ❶

Sri Balajee Lodge CT Rd ⓣ06752/223388. Some way beyond most of the other hotels, this small lodge has simple rooms around a colourful courtyard. ❶–❸

Sun Row Cottages CT Rd ⓣ06752/223259, ⓔchitranjan@hotmail.com. Little cottages, each with a private veranda, big cane chairs and attached bath. Rates are reduced for long stays. ❶–❷

Toshali Sands Konarak Rd ⓣ06752/250571, ⓔtsands@sancharnet.in. Self-styled "ethnic village" 9km north of town, consisting of a/c cottages grouped around a garden and pool. Good restaurant, gym and sauna; ideal for families. Doubles from $57. ❽–❾

Z CT Rd ⓣ06752/222554. An institution, the *Z* (pronounced "jed") made its name by providing cheap, clean and comfortable rooms. Prices are higher now, but the rooms are still pleasant and there are plenty of communal areas, including a large garden and a common room with TV. Women-only dorm (Rs60) also available. ❷–❸

The Jagannath temple

The mighty **Jagannath temple** in Puri is one of the four holy *dhams*, or "abodes of the divine", drawing pilgrims, or *yatris*, here to spend three auspicious days and nights near Lord Jagannath, the presiding deity. The present temple structure, modelled on the older Lingaraj temple in Bhubaneswar, was erected by the Ganga ruler Anantavarman Chodaganga, at the start of the twelfth century.

Non-Hindu visitors, despite the temple's long-standing "caste no bar" rule, are obliged to view proceedings from the flat roof of the **Raghunandan Library** (Mon–Sat 10am–noon & 4–6pm), directly opposite the main gate.

One of the librarians will show you up the stairs to the vantage point overlooking the East Gate. You should make a donation for this service – but don't believe the large sums written in the ledger. From the rooftop a fine view encompasses the immense **deul**, at 65m by far the loftiest building in the entire region. Archeologists have removed the white plaster from the tower to expose elaborate **carving** similar to that on the Lingaraj. Crowning the very top, a long

The Jagannath deities and Rath Yatra

Stand on any street corner in Orissa and you'll probably be able to spot at least one image of the black-faced **Jagannath deity**, with his brother **Balabhadra** and sister **Subhadra**. This faintly grotesque family trio, with glaring eyes, stumpy legless bodies, and undersized arms, seems to crop up everywhere – from buses and cycle rickshaws, to *bidi* wrappers and bags of nuts.

The origins of this peculiar symbol are shrouded in **legend**. One version relates that the image of Lord Jagannath looks the way it does because it was never actually finished. King Indramena, a ruler of ancient Orissa, once found the god Vishnu in the form of a tree stump washed up on Puri beach. He carried the lump of wood to the temple and, following instructions from Brahma, called the court carpenter Visvakarma to carve out the image. Visvakarma agreed – on condition that no one set eyes on the deity until it was completed. The king, however, unable to contain his excitement, peeped into the workshop; Visvakarma, spotting him, downed tools just as he had promised and cast a spell on the deity so that no one else could finish it.

These days, new versions have to be produced about every twelve years (they rot in the humidity) by specially trained temple priests in a sacred ceremony known as **Nava Kalebara**, literally "new embodiment". The culmination of this highly secret, nocturnal ritual takes place when the "divine essence" of the old Lord Jagannath is removed from his hollowed-out chest and placed inside that of the new incumbent.

Rath Yatra

The Jagannath deities are also the chief focus of Puri's annual "Car Festival", the **Rath Yatra** – just one episode in a long cycle of rituals that begins in the full moon phase of the Oriya month of Djesto (June & July). In the first of these, the **Chandan Yatra**, special replicas of the three temple deities are taken to the **Narendra Sagar** where for 21 consecutive days they are smeared with *chandan* (sandalwood paste) and rowed around in a ceremonial, swan-shaped boat. At the end of this period, in a ceremony known as **Snana Yatra**, the three go for a dip in the tank, after which they head off for fifteen days of secluded preparation for Rath Yatra.

The Car Festival proper takes place during the full moon of the following month, Asadho (July & Aug). Lord Jagannath and his brother and sister are placed in their chariots and dragged by 4200 honoured devotees through the assembled multitudes to their summer home, the **Gundicha Ghar** ("Garden House"), 1.5km away. If you can find a secure vantage point and escape the crush, it's an amazing sight. The immense chariots are draped with brightly coloured cloth and accompanied down Grand Road by elephants, the local raja (who sweeps the chariots as a gesture of humility and equality with all castes) and a cacophony of music and percussion. Each chariot has a different name and a different-coloured cover, and is built anew every year to rigid specifications laid down in the temple's ancient manuals. Balabhadra's *rath*, the green one, leads; Subhadra is next, in black; and lastly, in the thirteen-metre-tall chariot with eighteen wheels and a vivid red and yellow drape, sits Lord Jagannath himself. It takes eight hours or more to haul the *raths* to their resting place. After a nine-day holiday, the sequence is performed in reverse, and the three deities return to the temple to resume their normal lives.

Conventional wisdom has it that the procession commemorates Krishna's journey from Gokhul to Mathura; historians cite the similarity between the *raths* and temple towers to claim it's a hangover from the time when temples were made of wood. Whatever the reason for the Car Festival, its devotees take it very seriously indeed. Early travellers spoke of fanatics throwing themselves under the gigantic wheels as a short cut to eternal bliss (whence the English word "**Juggernaut**", meaning an "irresistible, destructive force"). Contemporary enthusiasts are marginally more restrained, but like most mass gatherings in India, the whole event teeters at times on the brink of complete mayhem.

△ Rath Yatra, Puri

scarlet pennant and the eight-spoked wheel (*chakra*) of Vishnu announce the presence of Lord Jagannath within.

The pyramidal roofs of the temples' adjoining halls, or *mandapas*, rise in steps towards the tower like a ridge of mountain peaks. The one nearest the sanctuary, the *jagamohana* (Assembly Hall), is part of the original building, but the other two, the smaller *nata mandir* (Dance Hall) and the *bhoga-mandapa* (Hall of Offerings) nearest the entrance, were added in the fifteenth and sixteenth centuries. These halls still see a lot of action during the day as worshippers file through for *darshan*, while late every night they become the venue for devotional music. Female and transvestite dancers (*maharis* and *gotipuas*) once performed episodes from Jayadev's *Gita Govinda*, the much-loved story of the life of Krishna, for the amusement of Lord Jagannath, his brother Balabhadra and sister Subhadra. Nowadays, piped songs have replaced the traditional theatre.

Outside the main building, at the left end of the walled compound surrounding the temple, are the **kitchens**. The food prepared here, known as *mahaprashad*, is blessed by Lord Jagannath himself before being eaten. It's said to be so pure that even a morsel taken from the mouth of a dog and fed to a brahmin by a Harijan (an "untouchable") will cleanse the body of sin. Everywhere, devotees mill around carrying pieces of broken pots full of dhal and rice; they can only offer food to the deity from an imperfect pot as Lord Jagannath is the only perfection in this world. Among the ten thousand or so daily recipients of the *mahaprashad* are the six thousand employees of the temple itself. These **servants** are divided into 96 hereditary and hierarchical orders known as *chhatisha niyoga*, and include the priests who minister to the needs of the deities (teeth cleaning, dressing, feeding, getting them ready for afternoon siesta, and so forth), as well as the teams of craftspeople who produce all the materials required for the daily round of rituals.

A good place to sample the atmosphere of the temple is the main gate on the east side. Opposite the doorway is the ceremonial **column** that once stood before the Surya temple in Konarak. Brought here in the eighteenth century by the Marathas, it is topped by a figure of Aruna, the charioteer of the sun god.

Around the temple

The crowded streets **around the Jagannath temple** are buzzing with activity – commercial as much as religious. **Grand Road**, Puri's broad main thoroughfare, is lined with a lively **bazaar**, many of its stalls specializing in *rudraksha malas* (Shaivite "rosaries" made of 108 beads), Ayurvedic cures and the ubiquitous images of Lord Jagannath. Look out too for the wonderful "religious maps" of Puri.

Leading south from the main square in the temple surrounds, the dingy **Swargadwar** ("Cremation") **Road** leads through a dingy bazaar to the main promenade. The cremation ground itself, situated well beyond the south corner of the beach, is among India's most auspicious mortuary sites, where inquisitive tourists, especially those wielding cameras, are definitely not welcome.

A more enjoyable foray from the main square is the trip up to the **sacred tanks** in the north of town (best attempted by bicycle). Follow the north wall of the Jagannath temple up to the little road junction in the far corner, then turn right and stick to the same narrow twisting backstreet for about a kilometre until you arrive at the **Markandesvara tank**. This large, steep-sided bathing place is said to have been the spot where Vishnu once resided in the form of a *neem* tree while his temple was buried deep under a sand dune. There's no sign of the tree, but the temples on the south side are worth a look, particularly the smaller of the group, which contains images of the Jagannath trio.

If you retrace your route from here back down the lane as far as the first road junction, then bear left and continue for another kilometre or so, you'll emerge at the **Narendra Sagar**, Puri's most holy tank. A small temple stands in the middle, joined to the *ghats* by a narrow footbridge. During the annual **Chandan Yatra** (swimming festival), a replica deity of Lord Jagannath, Madan Mohan, is brought here every day for his dip. The temple itself is plastered with vivid **murals** that you can photograph on payment of the set fee listed nearby. The list also advertises the range of services offered by the temple *pujaris*, including the unlikely sounding "throw of bone" and "throw of hair" – references to the tank's role as another of Puri's famous mortuary ritual sites.

Museums and the Sudarshan workshop

The **Sun Crafts Museum** (daily 6am–10pm; free), on the crossroads of VIP Road and Station Road, showcases the more commercial side of the Lord Jagannath phenomenon. Run by a Hare Krishna devotee, it houses an

Orissan art and artists

Few regions of India retain as rich a diversity of **traditional art forms** as Orissa. While a browse through the bazaars and emporia in Puri and Bhubaneswar provides a good idea of local styles and techniques, a trip out to the **villages** where the work is actually produced is a much more memorable way to shop. On the whole, different villages specialize in different crafts – a division that harks back to the origins of the caste system in Orissa. Patronage from the nobility and wealthy temples during medieval times allowed local artisans, or *shilpins*, to refine their skills over generations. As the market for arts and crafts expanded, notably with the rise of **Puri** as a pilgrimage centre, **guilds** were formed to control the handing down of specialist knowledge and separate communities established to carry out the work. Today, the demand for **souvenirs** has given many old art forms a new lease of life.

• **Stone sculpture** With modern temples increasingly being built out of reinforced concrete, life for Orissa's stone sculptors is getting tougher. To see them at work, head for Pathuria Sahi ("Stonecarvers' Lane") and the famous Sudarshan Workshop in **Puri** (see p.1039), where mastercraftsmen and apprentices still fashion Hindu deities and other votive objects according to specifications laid down in ancient manuals.

• **Painting** *Patta chitra*, classical Orissan painting, is closely connected with the Jagannath cult. Traditionally, artists were employed to decorate the inside of the temples in Puri and to paint the deities and chariots used in the Rath Yatra. Later, the same vibrant colour schemes and motifs were transferred to lacquered cloth or palm leaves and sold as sacred souvenirs to visiting pilgrims. In the village of **Raghurajpur** near Puri, where the majority of the remaining artists, or *chitrakaras*, now live, men use paint made from the local mineral stones. Specialities include devotional images of Lord Jagannath, scenes from the *Gita Govinda* and sets of **ganjiffa** – small round cards used to play a trick-taking game based on the struggle between Rama and the demon Ravana, as told in the *Ramayana*.

• **Palm-leaf manuscripts** Palm leaves, or *chitra pothi*, have been used as writing materials in Orissa for centuries, and the basic techniques have changed little. Using a sharp stylus called a *lohankantaka*, the artist first scratches the text or design onto the surface of palm leaves, then applies a paste of turmeric, dried leaves, oil and charcoal. When the residue is rubbed off, the etching stands out more clearly. On many, palm-leaf flaps are tied onto the structure so an innocent etching of an extensive collection of images of the deity and his siblings, in various forms. There is also a workshop where little wooden replicas are carved and painted, before being dispatched to ISKCON centres around the world. A more controversial image of Lord Jagannath is the one depicting him mounted on the centre of a Christian crucifix – some regard it as a symbolic demand for religious tolerance in light of recent hostility between Hindus and Christians in Orissa. You may have to ask discreetly to be shown it.

Puri's small **museum** (Tues–Sun 10am–5pm; free), tucked away above the tourist office on Station Road, houses tacky reproductions of the Jagannath deities' ceremonial garb, along with models of the *raths* used in the Car Festival, but little else of note.

Further down the road towards the railway station, close to the Shinto shrine, the **Sudarshan workshop** is one of the few traditional stone-carvers' yards left in Puri. For once, the sculptors and their apprentices seem more interested in pursuing their art than selling it to tourists, but gladly point potential customers in the direction of the factory **shop** next door. Most of the pieces here are large religious icons carved out of khondalite – the multi-coloured stone used in the Sun Temple at Konarak.

animal or deity can be lifted to reveal *Kamasutra* action. Some scholars claim that the rounded Oriya script may have developed to cope with the problems of writing on palm leaves, the straight lines of other Indian languages being more likely to pierce the leaf. Today, *Patta chitra* artists in **Raghurajpur** bind strips of palm leaves together to make canvases, and in the **Raghunandan Library** in Puri, students diligently copy old manuscripts to sell to tourists. The best places to see genuine antique palm-leaf books, however, are the National Museum in New Delhi or the state museum in Bhubaneswar.

• **Textiles** Distinctive textiles woven on handlooms are produced throughout Orissa. Silk saris from **Berhampur** and **Sambalpur** are the most famous, though **ikat**, which originally came to Orissa via the ancient trade links with Southeast Asia, is also typical. It is created using a tie-dye-like technique known as *bandha* in which bundles of thread are wrapped and dyed in different colours, and the pattern emerges automatically when they are woven together. The same principle is employed by weavers from the village of **Nuapatna**, 70km from Bhubaneswar, who produce silk *ikats* covered in verses from the scriptures for use in the Jagannath temple.

• **Appliqué** The village of **Pipli** (see p.1038), between Bhubaneswar and Puri, has the monopoly on appliqué, another craft rooted in the Jagannath cult. Geometric motifs and stylized birds, animals and flowers are cut out of brightly coloured cloth and sewn onto black backgrounds. Pipli artists are responsible for the chariot covers used in the Rath Yatra as well as for the small canopies, or *chhatris*, suspended above the presiding deity in Orissan temples.

• **Metalwork** *Tarakashi* (literally "woven wire"), or silver filigree, is Orissa's best-known metalwork technique. Using lengths of wire made by drawing strips of silver alloy through small holes, the smiths create distinctive ornaments, jewellery and utensils for use in rituals and celebrations. The designs are thought to have come to India from Persia with the Moghuls, though the existence of an identical art form in Indonesia, with whom the ancient Orissan kingdoms used to trade, suggests that the technique itself may be even older. *Tarakashi* is now only produced in any quantity in **Cuttack** and it's becoming a dying art form, thanks to a preference among Hindus for gold jewellery rather than silver, and a reluctance on the part of the artisans to change their designs with the times.

The beach

If a peaceful swim and a lie in the sun are your top priorities, you may be disappointed with **Puri beach**. It's not just the constant stream of hawkers that's the problem; the stretch of beach in front of the fishing village has become a three-kilometre-long open-air toilet and rubbish dump. For a more salubrious dip, press on beyond the Sanskrit University, 3km further east.

In the west end of town, along **Marine Parade**, the atmosphere is more akin to a British Victorian holiday resort, with a row of hotels looking across the parade to the beach. This stretch is very much the domain of the domestic tourist industry and the beach is much cleaner here. It's a pleasant place to stroll and becomes highly animated after sunset when the nightly souvenir market gets going.

Local fishermen patrol the beach as **lifeguards**; recognizable by their triangular straw hats and *dhotis*, they wade with their punters into the surf and literally hold their hands to keep them on their feet – the **undertow** claims victims every year, so weak swimmers should be careful. When not saving lives, the fishermen are busy at the CT Road end of the beach, engaged in the more traditional industries of mending nets and boats. The **fishing village** is one of the biggest in Orissa, with dozens of tiny sails tacking to and fro off the coast during the day. Once landed, the catch is transferred to baskets for women to carry to the **fish market** in the village.

Eating

Inexpensive eating options are limited to the handful of cafés and bakeries along CT Road, most of which are of the "write your own order" ilk, with typically unexciting, spiced-down travellers' menus. Most of the restaurants do thalis, some better than others, and there's good **fresh fish** to be had. Better food can be found at the nearby resort hotels. Most serve a reasonable range of veg and non-veg Indian dishes, including fish, with a few Chinese alternatives thrown in.

Chung-Wah, *Hotel Lee Garden*, VIP Rd. Run by a Chinese family from Kolkata, this is one of Puri's most popular Chinese restaurants, with fast, efficient service and a good choice of fish dishes.

Gandhara *Gandhara International Hotel*, CT Rd. Primarily for hotel guests, but non-residents can book in advance for excellent and authentic Japanese meals. Take a cold beer up onto the high roof terrace and enjoy the sea view.

Harry's CT Rd. One of the town's most popular budget places, this pure veg restaurant serves tasty Indian food made without onions or garlic in Hare-Krishna tradition, and good freshly pressed juices.

Mayfair *Mayfair Beach Resort*, off CT Rd. Sophisticated place with an a/c indoor restaurant and an air verandah dining room, this is Puri's best option for an extravagant evening away from dhal and rice and. A top-class chef whips up a delicious and unusually adventurous menu, including Orissan seafood specialities (order 8hr in advance).

Mickey Mouse CT Rd. A popular place for a late-night drink, with the loudest music and the most original lampshades. Very laid-back service and chess sets provided.

Peace CT Rd. Friendly place, with tables in the garden, serving all the usual fare but specializing in seafood.

South Eastern Railway *BNR/South Eastern Railway* hotel, CT Rd. Idiosyncratic colonial charm, with checked tablecloths, silver butter dishes and waiters in *pukka* turbans. The poor-value set menus are less memorable. Non-residents should give a couple of hours' warning.

Trupti CT Rd. Indian veg restaurant serving a good range of regional thalis. Especially busy at lunchtime. Also has a sweet counter.

Wild Grass Corner of VIP Rd and College Rd, 2km from the CT Rd ghetto. Popular with the locals, serving excellent tandoori, seafood, vegetarian and Orissan dishes at very reasonable prices, with tables spread around a beautiful leafy garden. Open for lunch and dinner. Recommended.

Xanadu CT Rd. Easily the best of the cheapies with a pleasant garden and extensive menu, including a special children's breakfast.

Moving on from Puri

Puri is joined to the main Kolkata (Calcutta)–Chennai routes by a branch line of the busy South East **Train** network and a good metalled road through Bhubaneswar, so it's well connected with most other major Indian cities. Travel agents at major hotels and on CT Rd can also book tickets.

The Puri–New Delhi Express #2815 leaves at 9.30am (Mon, Wed, Thurs & Sat), calling at **Bhubaneswar**, **Gaya** and **Mughalsarai** (for Varanasi), and arrives in **Delhi** at 5pm the following day. The slower Neelachal Express #8475 (Tues, Fri & Sun) leaves Puri at the same time stopping at the same stations, but arrives in Delhi at 9.25pm. A quick and convenient train to **Kolkata (Calcutta)** is the Jagannath Express #8410, which leaves Puri at 10.00pm for the 11hr overnight trip. For central Indian destinations such as Nagpur, take the Ahmedabad Express #8403 (Tues, Wed, Thurs & Sun) which leaves Puri at 10.15am and takes 22hr. Getting to **Mumbai** involves changing at Bhubaneswar and a total journey time of more than 40hr.

If you're heading for **South India**, it's also best to change at Bhubaneswar or Khurda Road, 44km from Puri, where you can pick up any of a number of daily trains to **Chennai** (19hr 30min–27hr), including the daily Coromandel Express #2841 or the slightly slower Kanniyakumari Express (Thurs, Sun & Mon). There are also two trains from Bhubaneswar to Thiruvananthapuram in Kerala: the Howrah–Trivandrum Express #6324 (Tues & Sun; 40hr) and the weekly Guwahati–Trivandrum Express #5628 (Wed; 40hr 45min–43hr). Computerized reservations can be made at the main station in Puri (Mon–Sat 8am–8pm, Sun 8am–2pm; ⓣ06752/222056) or through Puri's many travel agents.

There are hourly buses, although **minibuses** are the easiest way to travel, between Puri and Bhubaneswar (both Rs19). Services are fast (1hr) and frequent until 5pm, but make sure that it's "non-stop" before you get on. The same applies to Konarak minibuses (Rs12), which also leave when full from the main city bus stand in the northeast of town, near the Gundicha Ghar. **Jeeps** ply the same route hourly for the same price, departing from the bus stand when full.

If you plan to head south by road along the Orissan coast, buses to Satapada on Chilika Lake leave every thirty minutes during the day from the main bus stand, as well as some from the OTDC booking counter on Marine Drive.

See "Travel details" at the end of this chapter for more information on journey frequencies and durations.

Listings

Banks and exchange The State Bank of India beyond the *Nilachal Ashok Hotel*, on VIP Rd, will change American Express travellers' cheques and cash in US and Australian dollars and sterling, but doesn't give cash on credit cards. You can also change money at a branch of the Allahabad Bank on Temple Rd, 200m up from the GPO towards the temple, and Trade Wings above the *Travellers Inn* on CT Rd. There is an ICICI ATM near the Police Station on Grand Rd and Andhra Bank ATM near *Puri Hotel*; both take foreign cards.
Bookshops Loknath Bookshop next to *Raju's* restaurant on CT Rd. Books bought and sold, or you can use the extensive library upon paying a deposit of Rs300, with books lent at Rs10 per day.
Hospitals Puri's main "HQ" hospital (ⓣ06752/223742) is well outside the town centre on Grand Rd. Hotels such as the *Panthaniwas*, or Heritage Tours at the *Mayfair* can help find a doctor in an emergency.
Internet access There are a number of places along CT Rd and on VIP Rd, but services can be slow and unreliable; the *Gandhara* hotel is good value at Rs25/hr, while Nanako.com nearby has a better connection than most others hereabouts.
Police The main station is on Grand Rd, near the Jagannath temple. There is another branch at the Kacheri Rd, VIP Rd junction (ⓣ06952/222025)
Post office The GPO is on Kacheri Rd. For poste restante (Mon–Fri 9am–noon & 4–6pm, Sat

The Orissa cyclone

Though it wasn't affected by the December 2004 tsunami, Orissa is no stranger to tropical storms, and Orissans will never forget the appalling "**Super Cyclone**" that devastated the state in 1999, leaving thousands dead and countless without homes. For 36 hours, beginning on October 29, winds of up to 300km per hour blew in from the Bay of Bengal, generating a five-metre **tidal wave** which washed 20km inland over Paradwip and Konarak districts, drew back, and then spread over the coastal strip again. Mud and dung houses, sheltering whole families and their livestock, were swept away, along with roads, telephone lines, electricity cables and train tracks. Around twenty purpose-built cyclone shelters were each able to accommodate 1500 people standing up, though as many as 3000 squeezed into some. Many villagers refused to leave their houses, thinking this was just another monsoon storm; to leave would mean a loss of precious earnings, and their belongings would be vulnerable to looting.

On the third day the winds finally dropped and the flood-levels lowered, but many people remained stranded in trees. They were starving, in shock, without clean water, and all around them bodies of victims and livestock began to decompose. Luckily, a much-feared epidemic of cholera or typhoid was avoided, but the toll from the cyclone and the lack of immediate rescue response left a death toll close to 15,000, although the official government figure is 10,000.

Similarly affected states such as Andhra Pradesh and West Bengal, as well as Bangladesh, have suffered disasters of similar scale, although potentially huge death tolls have been significantly reduced by effective preparation, such as early warning systems in the villages and the construction of community cyclone shelters. Orissa, by contrast, paid the maximum price as its government had not implemented recommendations set out in the 1984 National Cyclone Review.

While many villages have been rebuilt and livelihoods restored, some areas around Puri and Konarak still remain little more than wasteland of fallen and stripped trees.

9am–noon), use the side door on the left side of the building.

Shopping and markets Utkalika and the other handloom emporiums, just up from the GPO on Temple Rd, stock a good range of local crafts at fixed prices. Antique India, next to the *Holiday House* on CT Rd is good for antiques and jewellery. Sudarshan on Station Rd (close to the OTDC tourist office) is the best place to buy traditional stone sculpture. For reproductions of the Jagannath deity, look in the bazaar around the temple. For classical Orissan paintings visit the Patta Chitra Centre on Nabakalebar Rd. There's a lively market on the beach off Marine Drive, south of *Puri Hotel*, open every evening until around 10pm.

Tours OTDC runs tour buses from in front of the *Panthaniwas* to nearby attractions including Bhubaneswar and environs and Konarak (Tues–Sat 6.30am–6.30pm; Rs130, a/c Rs160), and Chilika Lake (daily 7.00am–5.30pm; Rs110). Gandhara Travel, at the *Gandhara International Hotel*, does tours and ticketing and organizes trips to Konarak during the dance festival. Heritage Tours (Ⓣ06752/223656, Ⓔnamaskar@heritagetours.org), based at the *Mayfair Beach Resort*, are well established and reliable and offer 6- to 10-day tribal tours in Orissa, as well as special-interest tours such as birdwatching and archeology. Adventure Odyssey on CT Rd (Ⓔpulak_odessey@hotmail.com) arranges excellent tours of the area, including to Chilika Lake.

Konarak and around

Time runs like a horse with seven reins,
Thousand-eyed, unageing, possessing much seed. Him the poets mount; His wheels are all beings.

The *Artharva Veda*

If you visit only one temple in Orissa, it should be **KONARAK**. Standing imperiously in its compound of lawns and casuarina trees, 35km north of Puri

Odissi dance

Even visitors who don't normally enjoy classical dance cannot fail to be seduced by the elegance and poise of Orissa's own regional style, **Odissi**. Friezes in the Rani Gumpha at Udaigiri (see p.1037) attest to the popularity of dance in the Orissan courts as far back as the second century BC. By the time the region's Hindu "golden age" was in full swing, it had become an integral part of religious ritual, with purpose-built dance halls, or *nata mandapas*, being added to existing temples and corps of dancing girls employed to perform in them. **Devadasis**, literally "wives of the god", were handed over by their parents at an early age and symbolically "married" to the deity. They were trained to read, sing and dance and, as one disapproving early nineteenth-century chronicler put it, to "make public traffic of their charms" with male visitors to the temple. Gradually, ritual intercourse (a legacy of the Tantric influence on medieval Hinduism) degenerated into pure prostitution, and dance, formerly an act of worship, grew to become little more than a form of commercial entertainment. By the colonial era, Odissi was all but lost.

This would probably have heralded the end of Odissi altogether, had it not been for the rediscovery in the 1950s of the **Abhinaya Chandrika**, a fifteenth-century manual on classical Orissan dance. Like Bharatanatyam, India's most popular dance style, Odissi has its own highly complex language of poses and steps. Based on the *tribhanga* "hip-shot" stance, movements of the body, hands and eyes convey specific emotions and enact episodes from well-known religious texts – most commonly the **Gita Govinda** (the Krishna story). Using the *Abhinaya* and temple sculpture, dancers and choreographers were able to reconstruct this grammar into a coherent form and within a decade Odissi was a thriving performance art once again. Today, dance lessons with a reputed guru have become *de rigueur* for the young daughters of Orissa's middle classes – an ironic reversal of its earlier associations.

Few types of dance match Odissi for sheer style. The dancers deck themselves out in extravagant costumes of pleated silk brocades, silver jewellery, bells, jasmine flowers and distinctive *dhotis*, while in front of the stage, musicians and singers recite hypnotic *talas* – cycles of devotional poetry set to music. Unfortunately, catching a **live performance** is a matter of being in the right place at the right time. The only regular recitals take place in the Jagannath temple. If, however, you're not a Hindu, the annual **festival of dance** at Konarak, in the first week of December, is your best chance of seeing Orissa's top performers. If you're keen to learn, a number of dance academies in Bhubaneswar run **courses** for beginners (see p.1035).

on the coast road, this majestic pile of oxidizing sandstone is considered to be the apogee of Orissan architecture and one of the finest religious buildings anywhere in the world.

The temple is all the more remarkable for having languished under a huge mound of sand since it fell into neglect three hundred or so years ago. Not until early in the twentieth century, when the dune and heaps of collapsed masonry were cleared away from the sides, did the full extent of its ambitious design become apparent. In 1924, the earl of Ronaldshay wrote of the newly revealed temple as "one of the most stupendous buildings in India which rears itself aloft, a pile of overwhelming grandeur even in its decay". A team of seven galloping horses and 24 exquisitely carved wheels found lining the flanks of a raised platform showed that the temple had been conceived in the form of a colossal chariot for the sun god **Surya**, its presiding deity. Equally sensational was the rediscovery among the ruins of some extraordinary **erotic sculpture**. Konarak, like Khajuraho (see p.443), is plastered with loving couples locked in ingenious amatory postures drawn from the *Kama Sutra* – a feature that may well explain the comment made by one of Akbar's emissaries, Abul Fazl, in the sixteenth century: "Even those who are difficult to please," he enthused, "stand astonished at its sight."

Apart from the temple, a small **museum** and a fishing **beach**, Konarak **village** has little going for it. In recent years, a few cafés and hotels have mushroomed around its dusty bus stand to service the stream of bus parties that buzz in and out during the day. Sundays and public holidays are best avoided if you're hoping for some peace and quiet. Aim to be around at sunset after most of the tour groups have left, when the rich evening light works wonders on the natural colours in the khondalite sandstone.

Some history

Inscription plates attribute the founding of the temple to the thirteenth-century Ganga monarch **Narasimhadeva**, who may have built it to commemorate his military successes against the Muslim invaders. Local legend attributes its aura of power to the two very powerful magnets said to have been built into the tower, with the poles placed in such a way that the throne of the king was suspended in mid-air.

The temple's seventy-metre tower became a landmark for European mariners sailing off the shallow Orissan coast, who knew it as the "**Black Pagoda**", and the frequent incidence of shipping disasters along the coast was blamed on the effect of the aforesaid magnets on the tidal pattern. The tower also proved to be an obvious target for raids on the region. In the fifteenth century, Konarak was sacked by the Yavana army; though unable to raze the temple or destroy its deity, which had been smuggled away by the priests to Puri, the marauding Muslims nevertheless managed to damage it sufficiently to allow the elements to get a foothold. As the sea receded, sand slowly engulfed the building and salty breezes set to work on the spongy khondalite, eroding the exposed surfaces and weakening the superstructure. According to local legend, the removal of the magnets would cause the temple to crumble. Indeed, by the end of the nineteenth century, the tower had disintegrated completely, and the porch lay buried up to its waist, prompting one art historian of the day to describe it as "an enormous mass of stones studded with a few peepal trees here and there".

Restoration only really began in earnest at the start of the twentieth century. After putting an end to the activities of the local raja, who had been plundering the ruins for masonry and sculpture to use on his own temple, British archeologists set about unearthing the immaculately preserved hidden sections of the building and salvaging what they could from the rest of the rubble. Finally, trees were planted to shelter the compound from the corrosive winds, and a museum opened to house what sculpture was not shipped off to Delhi, Calcutta and London. Today, Konarak is one of India's most visited ancient monuments, and the flagship of Orissa Tourism's bid to promote the area as an alternative to the "golden triangle" of Delhi, Agra and Jaipur.

The temple

The main entrance to the **temple** complex (daily 9am–6pm; Rs250 [Rs10]) on its eastern, sea-facing side brings you out directly in front of the **bhogamandapa**, or "hall of offerings". Ornate carvings of amorous couples, musicians and dancers decorating the sides of its platform and stocky pillars suggest that the now roofless pavilion, which was a later addition to the temple, must originally have been used for ritual dance performances.

To get a sense of the overall scale and design, stroll along the low wall that bounds the south side of the enclosure before you tackle the ruins proper. As a giant model of Surya's war chariot, the temple was intended both as an offering to the Vedic sun god and as a symbol for the passage of time itself – believed to lie in his control. The seven **horses** straining to haul the sun eastwards in the direction of the dawn (only one is still intact) represent the days of the week. The **wheels** ranged along the base stand for the twelve months, each with eight spokes detailed with pictures of the eight ideal stages of a woman's day. Originally, a **stone pillar** crowned with an image of Aruna, Surya's charioteer, also stood in front of the main door, though this has since been moved to the eastern gateway of the Jagannath temple in Puri.

With the once-lofty **sanctuary tower** now reduced to little more than a clutter of sandstone slabs tumbling from the western wing, the **porch**, or *jagamohana*, has become Konarak's real centrepiece. Its impressive pyramidal roof, rising to a height of 38m, is divided into three tiers by rows of uncannily lifelike statues – mostly musicians and dancers serenading the sun god on his passage through the heavens. Among the figures on the bottom platform are a four-headed, six-armed Shiva as Nataraja, garlanded with severed heads and performing the dance of death. Though now blocked up, the huge cubic **interior** of the porch was a marvel of medieval architecture. The original builders ran into problems installing its heavy ornamental ceiling, and had to forge ten-metre iron beams as support – a considerable engineering feat for the time.

Amazingly elaborate **sculpture** embellishes the temple's exterior with a profusion of deities, animals, floral patterns, bejewelled couples, voluptuous maidens, mythical beasts and aquatic monsters. Some of Konarak's most beautiful **erotica** is to be found in the niches halfway up the walls of the porch, where a keen eye may be able to spot the telltale pointed beards of *sadhus*, clearly making the most of a lapse in their vows of chastity. Bawdier scenes also appear in miniature along the sides of the platform and around the two remaining intricate doorframes on the main building – just look for the groups of tittering teenagers. Many theories have been advanced over the years to explain the phenomenon. In Konarak's case, it seems likely that the erotic art was meant as a kind of metaphor for the ecstatic bliss experienced by the soul when it fuses with the divine cosmos – a notion central to **Tantra** and the related worship of the female principle, **shakti**, which were prevalent throughout medieval Orissa.

Moving clockwise around the temple from the south side of the main staircase, you pass the intricately carved **wheels** and extraordinary **friezes** that run in narrow bands above and below them. These depict military processions (inspired by King Narasimhadeva's tussles with the Muslims) and hunting scenes, and feature literally thousands of rampaging elephants. In the top frieze along the south side of the platform, the appearance of a giraffe is proof that trade with Africa took place during the thirteenth century.

Beyond the porch, a double staircase leads up to a shrine containing a **statue of Surya**. Carved out of top-quality green chlorite stone, this serene image – one of three around the base of the ruined sanctuary tower – is considered one of Konarak's masterpieces. Notice his characteristic tall riding boots and the little figure of Aruna, the charioteer, holding the reins of the seven horses at his feet. The other two statues in the series are also worth a look, if only to compare their facial expressions which, following the progress of the sun around the temple, change from wakefulness in the morning (south) to heavy-eyed weariness at the end of the day (north). Before working your way around the far side of the porch, you can also climb down into the remains of the **sanctum sanctorum** where the deity was once enshrined. At the foot of the western wall there's an altar-like platform covered with carving: the kneeling figure in its central panel is thought to be King Narasimhadeva, the donor of the temple.

In early December, the temple hosts one of India's premier **dance festivals**, drawing an impressive cast of both classical and folk dance groups from all over the country. For the exact dates, line-up and advance bookings, contact OTDC in Bhubaneswar (ⓣ0674/243 1299) or Delhi (ⓣ011/2336 4580).

The village and around

Some way outside the compound, near the *Yatri Niwas* hotel (see below), the **archeological museum** (daily 9am–5pm; Rs5) has lost most of its best pieces to Delhi, but has retained fragments of sculpture, much of it erotic. Outside, a small shed in the northeast corner of the enclosure houses a stone architrave bearing images of **nine planet deities**, the Navagrahas, which originally sat above one of the temple's ornamental doorways and is now kept as a living shrine.

Konarak's own **beach**, 3km down the Puri road, was once picturesque but remains thoroughly windswept and forlorn following the impact of the 1999 cyclone in October. Although far from ideal for swimming or sunbathing, it's still a good place to wander in the evening or watch the local fishing fleet at work.

Practicalities

The easiest way to get to Konarak **from Puri**, 33km down the coast, is by bus or Jeep. There are regular services in both directions and the journey only takes an hour or so, which makes it possible to do the round trip in a day – the last bus back to Puri leaves at 6.30pm. If you've got a bit more cash to spend, an auto-rickshaw will do the return journey for Rs250–300 including waiting time. Buses **from Bhubaneswar** are much less frequent and take between two and four hours to cover the 65km (with a change at Pipli), depending on whether you catch the one direct express "tourist" bus, which leaves from the town stand at 10am. Alternatively, you could join one of OTDC's tours which leave from the *Panthaniwas* in Bhubaneswar (Tues–Sun 6.30am–6.30pm; Rs130, a/c Rs160), with stops at Konarak, Bhubaneswar and Dhauli. The OTDC **tourist office** in Konarak is in the *Yatri Niwas* hotel (ⓣ06758/236821; Mon–Sat 10am–5pm); staff can help with information on local festivals and tour.

With Puri only an hour down the road, few people end up staying in Konarak. There is, however, some **accommodation** here, convenient if you want to spend the night somewhere a little more peaceful, or enjoy the temple at a more leisurely pace. Not far from the main entrance to the monuments, the OTDC *Panthaniwas* (ⓣ06758/236831; ❷–❸) offers dark but clean and reasonably priced rooms with a/c and hot water. They also run the reasonable *Travellers' Lodge* (ⓣ06758/236820; ❷–❸), tucked behind the pleasant OTDC *Yatri Niwas* (ⓣ06758/236820; ❷–❸), which has mosquito nets (essential), a restaurant and coloured fountains in the gardens. The manager here boasts an impressive knowledge of local history and the temple itself. The *Labanya Lodge* (ⓣ06758/236824, ⓔlabanyalodge1@rediffmail.com; ❶), a little out of the village on the beach road, is the most backpacker-friendly place, with a small garden and Internet access.

For **food** you have a choice between the row of thali and tea stalls opposite the temple or a more substantial meal in one of the hotel restaurants. The *Panthaniwas'* very popular and inexpensive *Geetanjali* café serves the usual range of veg and rice dishes. The *Yatri Niwas* is also open to non-residents and is likely to be packed out at lunchtime with tour parties, all tucking into a good Orissan thali. The *Sun Temple Hotel* is the best of the *dhabas*.

Northern Orissa

North of Bhubaneshwar, Orissa's second city, **Cuttack**, straddles the Mahanadi, its chaotic concrete centre packed on to an island in the river. Devoid of noteworthy historic monuments and with an uncommonly drab bazaar, it detains few travellers on the long journey to or from Kolkata (Calcutta). Once clear of Cuttack's polluted outskirts, however, you soon find yourself amid the flat paddy fields, palm groves and mud-walled villages of the **Mahanadi Delta**. The main railway line and NH-5 twisting through it follow the path of the famous pilgrim trail, the **Jagannath Sadak**, that once led from Calcutta to Puri.

Following the 1865 famine (which wiped out nearly a quarter of Orissa's population), the British were pressured into upgrading the route with a road and railway, connecting Orissa to more prosperous parts of the country. It's now one of India's busiest transport arteries.

Travelling through northern Orissa, the one attraction worth venturing off the main drag for is **Simlipal National Park**, reached via the town of **Baripada**. During the turtle nesting season, a handful of tourists also brave minimal infrastructure to reach the **Bhitarakanika Sanctuary**, 130km north of Bhubaneshwar.

Sea turtles

Every year around February and March, a strip of beach at the end of Orissa's central river delta witnesses one of the world's most extraordinary natural spectacles. Having swum right across the Pacific and Indian oceans, an average 200,000 female **Olive Ridley marine turtles** crawl onto the sand; each looks for a safe spot, then sets about digging a hole with its hind flippers in which to lay its annual batch of eggs. Twenty minutes later, after a quick breather, they're off again into the surf to begin the journey back to their mating grounds on the other side of the world.

No one knows quite why they travel such distances, but for local villagers the arrival of the giant turtles has traditionally been something of a boon. Turtle soup for breakfast, lunch and tea . . . and extra cash from market sales. Over the years the annual slaughter began to turn into something of a green gold rush, and turtle numbers plummeted drastically until a special wildlife reserve was set up to protect them at the personal behest of Indira Gandhi. Today, the Bhitarakanika Sanctuary on **Gahirmatha beach**, 130km northeast of Bhubaneswar, is a safe haven for the creatures. Weeks before the big three- or four-day invasion, coastguards monitor the shoreline and armed rangers ensure that poachers are kept at bay. For wildlife enthusiasts it's a field day.

In recent years, however, **environmental threats** have impacted on the turtles' habitat. Several hundred local families have begun to cultivate land within the sanctuary, water quality has been jeopardized by the growth of illegal prawn farms, and trawlers have been caught illegally fishing in the area without "turtle excluder devices" (TEDs). The turtles are further menaced by industrial pollution, including some mildly radioactive waste from a Paradip-based fertiliser plant, which, in spite of being ordered to close in 2002, re-opened only two months later and remains in business. The Worldwide Fund for Nature is monitoring the area, and whilst 2005 saw some 234,000 turtles come to nest at Gahirmatha, in other years none come at all.

Visits to Gahirmatha are allowed, though you should ask at the OTDC tourist office in Bhubaneswar to find out exactly when – or if – the turtles are expected. **Permits**, **transport**, **food** and **accommodation** can be a problem unless you are prepared to rough it or to pay through the nose for a rental car, as the sanctuary is well off the beaten track.

Baripada

To reach Simlipal from the coastal artery, you'll first have to pass through **BARIPADA**, headquarters of **Mayurbhunj** district (pronounced "marvunj"). Though possessing few sights to speak of, it's a good place to experience small-town Orissan life, with a tumbledown bazaar and whitewashed **Jagannath temple**. Dotted around the outskirts, quietly decaying bungalows and civic buildings survive from the days of the Raj, when Mayurbhunj was a semi-autonomous princely state (one of the last to join independent India). For centuries it remained under the **Bhanja** kings, a reputedly "progressive" ruling family favoured by the British, whose present incumbent still lives in an incongruous Neoclassical mansion overlooking the river in the north of town.

Mayurbhunj is the traditional home of the **Santal** tribe, settled agriculturalists who practise a blend of ancestor worship and Hinduism, and who comprise around seventy percent of the local *adivasi* population. Traditionally a landless under-caste, they have, like most of Orissa's minorities at one time or another, been the target of evangelical Christian missionaries. Resentment among local Hindu fundamentalists erupted in 1999 when an Australian missionary and his two young sons were murdered while attending a prayer meeting. With local support, however, the mission has survived and continues to run an impressive leprosy hospital.

Practicalities

Arriving in Baripada, **buses** pass the temple at the bottom of the broad main street and then head up the hill to the bus stand and market. From here it's a five-minute walk to the most central hotels: the simple *Bishram* (Ⓣ06792/253535; ❶) and the *Hotel Ambika* (Ⓣ06792/252557; ❷–❹) are both shabby but adequate places with variously priced rooms, all with attached baths and frames for the much-needed mosquito nets. Baripada's best restaurant is on the ground floor of the *Ambika*. The OTDC tourist office (Mon–Fri 10am–5pm; Ⓣ06792/252710) is five minutes' walk from the bus stand in the opposite direction. The manager at the *Ambika* can arrange transport to Simlipal or rent out bicycles and jeeps.

Simlipal National Park

West of Baripada, the landscape suddenly changes from open fields to the thickly wooded slopes and ridges of the Eastern Ghats. At more than 1000m, **Khairbhuru**, the peak visible from the outskirts of town, is the highest in the region and one of the last true wildernesses in eastern India. The mixed deciduous forests, perennial streams and glades of savannah grasslands draped around its flanks have allowed for an uncommonly rich diversity of flora and fauna.

In 1979 the whole area (2750 square kilometres) around the mountain was declared a wildlife sanctuary – primarily in an attempt to revive its dwindling population of **tigers** (see "Wildlife" in Contexts). Prior to this it had been the exclusive preserve of the Maharaja of Mayurbhunj, who used the woods as a private hunting ground and source of timber. Six years later **SIMLIPAL** was officially designated a **national park**, and the following year became the site of one of India's first Project Tiger reserves.

Simlipal deserves to be one of eastern India's major attractions. The fact that it isn't has less to do with the amount of wildlife within its borders than with its comparative **inaccessibility**. Unlike its counterparts in neighbouring states, transport to and around the park is a real problem and accommodation is rudimentary. If you overcome these obstacles, however, the rewards more than compensate. Apart from the elusive tigers – park rangers, perhaps a touch optimistically, claim they number almost one hundred, alongside a slightly larger number of equally secretive leopards – the reserve boasts sloth bears, sambar and spotted deer, barking deer, gaur, rhesus and langur monkeys; evening walks near the forest resthouses might yield sightings of mongoose, ratel badgers, porcupines, civets, jungle cats, foxes and jackals. Herds of wild **elephant** are also common (too common for the unfortunate villagers, who have to spend nights in tree houses waiting to scare rampaging pachyderms away from their crops), and the park's pools and lakes also support marsh crocodiles, pythons, fishing cats and monitor lizards near the water. There are reportedly 231 species of **birds** here, too, including colourful trogons, barbets, hornbills, thrushes, orioles, woodpeckers, parakeets, bee-eaters, spurfowl and jungle fowl. The landscape itself is equally rich, with a backdrop of beautiful granite hills, and a tranquil and pristine old-growth Sal forest; no less than 1076 species of plant have been recorded here, including an impressive 87 different varieties of orchid.

Park practicalities

The park is **open** from November to mid-June (daily 6am–noon; visits extended to 2pm by prior arrangement ⓣ06792/252553), but the ideal visiting season ends in February. The majority of the tigers and leopards are supposed to hang out in the 845-acre "core zone" which is mostly out of bounds. There are two main **entrances**: one at Joshipur in the west (convenient if you're driving from Kolkata (Calcutta), and close to most of the lodges), and one at Pithabata near Baripada on the eastern side. You have to pay a daily **entry fee** (Rs100 [Rs10]) plus Rs100 per vehicle and Rs100 camera charge; the fee includes the permit to enter the park. From the gates, unsurfaced but driveable roads link up the lodges with the numerous waterfalls, panoramas, grazing areas and water holes in the buffer zone.

The easiest way to visit Simlipal is on an organized **tour**. Heritage Tours in Puri (ⓣ06752/223656 or 222747) and Swosti Travels in Bhubaneswar (ⓣ0674/253 5773) can both arrange transport, accommodation and guides at very short notice and charge reasonable rates. Without your own vehicle, the only alternative way to **get around** the park is to rent a **Jeep**. This can be arranged through the manager at the *Ambika* in Baripada (see opposite), or through the less reliable taxi-wallahs hanging around the bus stand. In either case, expect to pay up to Rs1000 per day. Another way to cut costs is to use **JOSHIPUR** as an alternative base for visiting the park; closer to most of the points of interest than Baripada, it also features a couple of extremely basic lodges, and Jeeps are available for rent. For more information contact the Joshipur wildlife warden (ⓣ06797/22474).

Accommodation

Advance booking is officially required for all but one lodge (the *Aranya Niwas* – see overleaf), through the Field Director of Project Tiger, Baripada 757002, Mayurbhunj district, Orissa ⓣ06792/252593. It is not possible to pay for any accommodation using foreign currency or traveller's cheques. All are in the ❸–❹ region.

Where to go in Simlipal is largely dictated by the location of the lodges. There are six dotted around the park, but the best from the point of view of spotting wildlife is *Chahala* (83km from Baripada), one of the maharaja's former hunting lodges, situated just inside the core zone near a salt-lick where animals congregate in the evenings. As with all accommodation in the park, facilities are very basic. You have to take in your own food, though all utensils are provided and the *chowkidar* will cook for you. The other lodges are *Barheipani* (73km from Baripada), a small wooden lodge with wide verandas; it's near a waterfall and offers impressive views; *Newana* (60km), which is in a "frost-prone valley"; *Gudugudia* (25km from Joshipur), said to be particularly good for bird-watching and orchids; and *Joranda* (64km from Baripada), which has a bit of everything and a waterfall. The only lodge not requiring advance permission is the *Aranya Niwas* at Lulung, on the Baripada side (Rs150 by Jeep from Baripada). You're unlikely to see much wildlife here, but the rooms are pleasant; there's a cheap dorm (Rs80) and a restaurant, and the compound, surrounded by an elephant-proof ditch, is right in the heart of the forest.

Southern Orissa

Long stretches of dishevelled roadside settlements and rural stations along the National Highway do not inspire much excitement about the stretch of coast between Puri and Andhra Pradesh. However, there are a couple of scenic detours that may tempt you to break a long journey. Three hours south of the capital, at the foot of a barren, sea-facing spur of the Eastern Ghats – which creep up to the coast here – is India's largest salt-water lake. **Chilika**'s main attractions are the one million or so migratory birds that nest here in winter, and leisurely boat trips to its islands. Seventy kilometres further on, **Gopalpur-on-Sea** is sufficiently remote to have remained a decidedly low-key beach town. **Berhampur**, 16km inland, is southern Orissa's biggest market town, and the main transport hub for the sinuous route west through the hills to the spa station of **Taptapani** and "tribal districts" beyond.

Chilika Lake

Were it not for its glass-like surface, **CHILIKA LAKE**, Asia's largest lagoon, could easily be mistaken for the sea; from its mud-fringed foreshore you can barely make out the narrow strip of marshy islands and sand-flats that separate the 1100-square-kilometre expanse of brackish water from the Bay of Bengal. Come here between December and February, though, and you'll see a variety of **birds**, from flamingos, pelicans and painted storks to fish eagles, ospreys and kites; many of them migrants from Siberia, Iran and the Himalayas. Chilika is also one of the few places in India where the Irrawady dolphin can be seen. The best way to see the lake and the birds is via a **boat trip** (see opposite); many of these visit Chilika's **islands** (some inhabited by small subsistence fishing communities, others deserted); the best one to head for in terms of birds is Nalabana, designated a bird sanctuary.

By and large, the fishing villages and fabled island "kingdom" of **Parikud** on the eastern side of the lake are passed up in favour of the boat ride to the *devi* shrine on **Kalijai** island. Legend has it that a local girl once drowned here on the way to her wedding across the lake, and that her voice was subsequently heard calling from under the water. Believing the bride-to-be had become a goddess, local villagers inaugurated a shrine to her that over the years became associated with **Kali** (Shiva's consort Durga in her terrifying aspect). Each year at *makar sankranti*, after the harvest, pilgrims flock to the tiny island from all over Orissa and West Bengal to leave votive offerings in the sacred cave where the deity was enshrined.

Practicalities

The best **place to stay** on the lake is the excellent value *Yatri Niwas* (❶–❷) at **SATAPADA** on the coastal side, just 45km from Puri and linked by several daily buses. Some rooms have private balconies and the well-tended gardens run down to the lake; the restaurant prepares delicious thalis and fresh seafood if given advance notice. Rooms can be booked from Puri's tourist office. There's a cheap and accessible OTDC *Panthaniwas* (☎06810/278346; ❸) near the railway station at **RAMBHA**, 135km from Bhubaneswar; it's somewhat lacklustre, but well placed for walks around the more scenic southern corner of the lake and for boat rides to Parikud. The OTDC *Panthaniwas* (☎06756/222 0488; ❸–❺) at **BARKUL**, 34km north of Rambha, is a collection of shabby pink chalets, but rooms come with bath and mosquito nets (you won't get much sleep without one) and the food is reasonable. To get there, take a bus from Puri or Bhubaneswar towards Berhampur and get off at Balugaon, where you can get an auto-rickshaw for the remaining 7km to Barkul. If you plan to visit between September and March, it is best to book ahead in the Bhubaneswar OTDC tourist office. If you want to stay on an island, *Saga Camp* (☎06810/278518) at Sonakada Island, a short boat ride from Rambha, has tents with comfortable cots and attached baths, no electricity but hot water in buckets, and its own boats for trips to the coastal areas, the Nalabana Bird Sanctuary and the southern areas of the lake. Rates are Rs3500 per day for two people, and include all meals and two daily boat rides.

Gandhara Travel in Puri runs **day-trips** to Chilika on Mondays and Fridays for Rs100 per head. Note that accommodation prices at Chilika drop substantially out of season. OTDC motor launches, and rowing boats manned by local villagers, operate **boat trips** from Barkul and Satapada; it costs around Rs450 per hour to hire a seven-seater motor launch, or you can book yourself a seat on a twenty- or thirty-seat launch: the round trip to **Kalijai island**, the most popular option with domestic tourists, takes around two hours (Rs40), while a combination trip to Kalijai **Nalabana island** takes four hours (Rs175). The manager at the Barkul *Panthaniwas* can arrange seats. Rowing boats also depart from Rambha, though the fishermen who run them seem to be more intent on attending to their nets than ferrying passengers to the islands.

Gopalpur-on-Sea

Two thousand or more years ago, when the Kalingas were piling up wealth from the pearl and silk trade with southeast Asia, **GOPALPUR-ON-SEA**, formerly the ancient port of Paloura, must have been a swinging place. Today, the only time you're likely to encounter much action is during festivals and holidays, when the village is temporarily inundated with Bengali holidaymakers. For the rest of the year, its desultory collection of crumbling bungalows and seafront hotels stands idle, left to the odd backpacker blown off-course by the promise of an undiscovered beach paradise, and the armies of industrious fishermen (*katias*) hauling in hand nets on Gopalpur's endless empty shoreline, dressed in traditional pointy straw bonnets. Paradise it certainly isn't, but if you're looking for a spot along the coast to unwind and enjoy the warm sea breezes, this is as appealing a place as any. Just don't expect too much from the **beach**, which is less than ideal for swimming and sunbathing; crash out on the sands and you'll soon find yourself the centre of attention.

Practicalities

Getting here is easiest via the town of **Berhampur**, which lies on the main coastal highway and train line. From Berhampur, frequent minibuses and Jeeps depart from the central bus stand for the sixteen-kilometre trip. You'll be dumped at the top of Gopalpur's "main street", ten minutes' walk from the seafront and most of the hotels. Tourist information can be had from the friendly folk at the OTDC *Panthaniwas*.

Gopalpur's many **rooms** tend to cost considerably more than elsewhere, and you may well feel inclined to haggle. Only during holiday times, however, are they liable to be booked up in advance. The rates below all refer to the off-season between October and March. As for **eating**, there's a surprising dearth of seafood in Gopalpur, though some restaurateurs can be cajoled into cooking the odd pomfret or prawn curry, given sufficient warning. The *Seashell* shack serves up cheap and tasty meals overlooking the beach.

Holiday Inn Near the lighthouse. Couldn't be less like its North American namesake – a handful of very basic rooms around a pleasant courtyard, with a communal kitchen. ❶

Kalinga On the main road leading to the seafront ⓣ0680/224 2069. Clean, pleasant and airy rooms with balconies and TVs. ❷–❸

Mermaid On the north side of the beach ⓣ0680/224 2050. Friendly place pitched at wealthy Calcuttans, with plain rooms and private sea-facing balconies. With advance notice, non-residents can enjoy delicious Bengali thalis. ❸

OTDC Panthaniwas By the temple ⓣ0680/224 2088. Clean rooms – none sea-facing, but with attached bath – and a dorm (Rs70); the excellent chef will whip up tasty Indian dishes and breakfast on demand. ❷–❸

Rosalin On the seafront ⓣ0680/224 2071. Chaotic family-run establishment with basic small rooms around a garden courtyard and a restaurant. Cheap and cheerful. ❶

Sea Pearl On the seafront ⓣ0680/242556. A well-run hotel with clean and comfortable rooms, efficient staff and a terrace restaurant with sea views. ❹–❺

Swosti Palm Beach Near the *Holiday Inn* ⓣ0680/2242453. One of Gopalpur's best hotels, with spacious and comfortably furnished a/c rooms and gardens; no sea views, however. The restaurant is strong on Indian seafood, such as *chengudi malai* (prawns in coconut cream) and *macha tarkari* (sea-fish curry). ❼–❽

Taptapani

One possible foray from the coast, if you're tempted by the lure of the nearby hills, is the trip to the spa village of **TAPTAPANI**, nestled in the *ghats* 51km west from the town of Berhampur. Little more than a line of dingy snack stalls and mildewed bungalows deep in the forest, it's the kind of place to which government servants pray not to be posted. Pilgrims, however, come here in large numbers for the legendary **hot springs**, which are believed to cure infertility. The boiling sulphurous water bubbles out of a cleft in the mountainside and is piped into a small pool, where little rocks smeared with vermilion and hibiscus petals mark the presence of the living deities believed to reside in the water (which explains why it is prohibited to dip any part of the body in the pool).

You can also enjoy the water in the privacy of your own **hotel**; it's pumped into capacious sunken bathtubs in some of the more expensive rooms at the atmospheric and peaceful OTDC *Panthaniwas* (ⓣ06816/255031; ❷–❸), a short way down the hill from the springs. Despite the fine views it commands over the valley, the *Panthaniwas* is rarely full, which is just as well, as there's nowhere else to stay for miles around (so reserve through an OTDC office or hotel in advance). The decent restaurant at the *Panthaniwas* serves inexpensive and delicious Indian food.

Beyond Taptapani

Once over the pass above **Taptapani**, the appearance of pots attached to sago palms and windowless mud huts with low thatched roofs indicate that you've arrived in the traditional land of the **Saoras**, one of Orissa's many *adivasi* minorities. Further west around the Koraput and Jeypore area live the **Dongria Kondh**, the **Koya** and the **Bondas**.

Officially, you're not allowed into the district without first obtaining a **permit** from the local police superintendent. Paranoia about Naxalites hiding out in the forests along the Andhra Pradesh border, coupled with a marked reluctance to allow foreigners into tribal zones, make these notoriously difficult to obtain. This, coupled with the minimal infrastructure, rudimentary accommodation and infrequent transport around the region, means that if you're really keen to visit *adivasi* villages, the best – though far from cheapest – way is to arrange a **tour** through a specialist travel agent in Bhubaneswar or Puri. They'll take care of the permits, sort out food and rooms and, if they're any good, have local contacts to make sure you behave appropriately in the villages and markets. Heritage Tours (Ⓣ06752/223656) in Puri arrange six- to ten-day trips for roughly Rs1200 (or the dollar equivalent) per person per day and make every effort not to intrude where outsiders are not welcome. That said, *adivasi* villages see little or no share of the spoils, a situation they feel justifiably angry about, and you may well receive a very frosty reception. Whichever way you look at it, turning up in an isolated and culturally sensitive place with an Ambassador car and a camera has got to be a pretty unsound way of "meeting" the locals, as Norman Lewis recalls in his travelogue, *Goddess in the Stones* (see "Books" p.1435).

Travel details

Trains

Balasore to: Bhubaneswar (9–11 daily; 3hr 20min–5hr 15min); Kolkata (Calcutta: 8–9 daily; 4–6hr); Puri (5–6 daily; 4hr 40min–5hr 40min).
Bhubaneswar to: Agra (1–2 daily; 31hr 50min–34hr); Balasore (14–15 daily; 3hr 15min–4hr); Bangalore (2 weekly; 31hr); Berhampur (10–11 daily; 2hr 30min–3hr 15min); Chennai (4–6 daily; 20hr–22hr 50min); Cochin (4 weekly; 34–35hr); Cuttack (14–15 daily; 20–45min); Delhi (2–3 daily; 23hr 30min–34hr 20min); Gaya (1–2 daily; 15hr); Guwahati (1 daily; 31hr); Hyderabad (1 daily; 23hr 20min); Kolkata (Calcutta: 10–11 daily; 7hr 30min–10hr 30min); Mumbai (1 daily; 34hr 15min); Puri (7–9 daily; 1hr 25min–1hr 45min); Thiruvananthapuram (Trivandrum; 4 weekly; 42hr); Varanasi (3 weekly; 20hr).
Puri to: Ahmedabad (5 weekly; 44hr); Agra (1 daily; 36hr); Balasore (5–6 daily; 4hr 40min–5hr 40min); Bhubaneswar (7–9 daily; 1hr 25min–1hr 45min); Delhi (2 daily; 31hr 30min–36hr); Gaya (1–2 daily; 17hr); Kolkata (Calcutta: 2 daily; 10hr 25min–11hr); Mughalsarai (2–3 daily, 21hr); Nagpur (5 weekly, 23hr); Varanasi (1 daily; 22hr).

Buses

Bhubaneswar to: Balasore (every 30min; 3hr 30min–5hr); Berhampur (6–8 daily; 4hr); Cuttack (every 15min; 45min–1hr); Kolkata (Calcutta: 4 nightly; 10hr); Konarak (1 daily; 1hr 30min–2hr); Pipli (every 15min; 30min); Puri (every 15min; 2hr).
Balasore to: Baripada (every 20min; 1hr); Bhubaneswar (6–8 daily; 3hr 30min–5hr); Chandipur (5 daily; 30min); Kolkata (Calcutta: 5 daily; 5–7hr); Puri (4–6 daily; 4hr).
Berhampur to: Bhubaneswar (6–10 daily; 3hr); Gopalpur-on-Sea (every 15min; 30min); Koraput (1 daily; 8hr); Rayagada (1 daily; 3hr); Taptapani (hourly; 1hr 15min).
Puri to: Bhubaneswar (every 20min; 2hr); Kolkata (Calcutta: 2 daily; 12hr); Konarak (hourly; 40min–1hr); Satapada (every 30min; 1hr).

Flights

Bhubaneswar to: Chennai (4 weekly; 2hr 30min); Delhi (1 daily; 2hr); Hyderabad (1–2 daily; 1hr 35min); Kolkata (Calcutta: 1–2 daily; 55min); Mumbai (1–2 daily; 1hr 56 min).

CHAPTER 18

Highlights

* **Hyderabad** A predominately Islamic city offering a compelling combination of monuments, museums and lively bazaars. See p.1065
* **Golconda Fort** Set in a lush landscape just west of Hyderabad, the capital of the Qutb Shahi dynasty boasts a dramatic fort. See p.1071
* **Warangal** Features two important Hindu monuments: the medieval fort and a thousand-pillared Shiva temple. See p.1075
* **Amaravati** At this village on the banks of the Krishna, fine carvings surround the remains of a great Buddhist stupa. See p.1079
* **Tirumala Hill, Tirupati** The most visited pilgrimage centre in the world, Tirumala Hill is crowned by the Venkateshwara Vishnu temple. See p.1079
* **Puttaparthy** Sai Baba's main ashram attracts modern pilgrims from all over the world, and forms the centrepiece of a thriving community. See p.1082

△ Pilgrims, Tirupati

18

Andhra Pradesh

Although **ANDHRA PRADESH** occupies a great swathe of eastern India, stretching for more than 1200km along the coast from Orissa to Tamil Nadu and reaching far inland from the fertile deltas of the Godavari and Krishna rivers to the semi-arid Deccan Plateau, it's not a place that receives many tourists. Most foreign travellers pass through en route to its more attractive neighbours, which is understandable as places of interest are few and far between. However, the sights that Andhra Pradesh does have are absorbing and sufficiently well connected to warrant at least a few stops on a longer tour of India.

Now thriving as a major hi-tech hub, the state capital, **Hyderabad**, is an atmospheric city dating from the late sixteenth century. Its endless bazaars, eclectic Salar Jung museum and the mighty **Golconda Fort** nearby make it an enticing place to spend a day or two; by contrast, the adjacent twin city of **Secunderabad** excels only in characterlessness. **Warangal**, 150km northeast of Hyderabad, has both Muslim and Hindu remains from the twelfth and thirteenth centuries, while the region's Buddhist legacy – particularly its superb sculpture – is preserved in museums at sites such as **Nagarjunakonda** and **Amaravati**, the ancient Satavahana capital. In the east, the big city of **Vijayawada** has little to recommend it, though it makes a convenient access point for Amaravati. However, the temple town of **Tirupati** in the far southeast – best reached from Chennai in Tamil Nadu – is one of India's great Hindu phenomena, a fascinating and impossibly crowded pilgrimage site that's said to attract more pilgrims than Mecca or the Vatican. In the southwest of the state, the small town of **Puttaparthy** attracts a more international pilgrim crowd, drawn here by the prospect of *darshan* from spiritual leader Sai Baba.

Although modern industries have grown up around the capital, and shipbuilding, iron and steel are important on the coast, most people in Andhra Pradesh remain poor. Away from the Godavari and Krishna deltas, where the soil is rich enough to grow rice and sugar cane, the land is in places impossible to cultivate.

Some history

Earliest accounts of the region, dating back to the time of **Ashoka** (third century BC), refer to a people known as the Andhras. The **Satavahana dynasty** (second century BC–second century AD), also known as the Andhras, came to control much of central and southern India from their second capital at Amaravati on the Krishna. They enjoyed extensive international trade with both eastern Asia and Europe, and were great patrons of Buddhism. Subsequently, the Pallavas from Tamil Nadu, the Chalukyas from Karnataka, and the Cholas

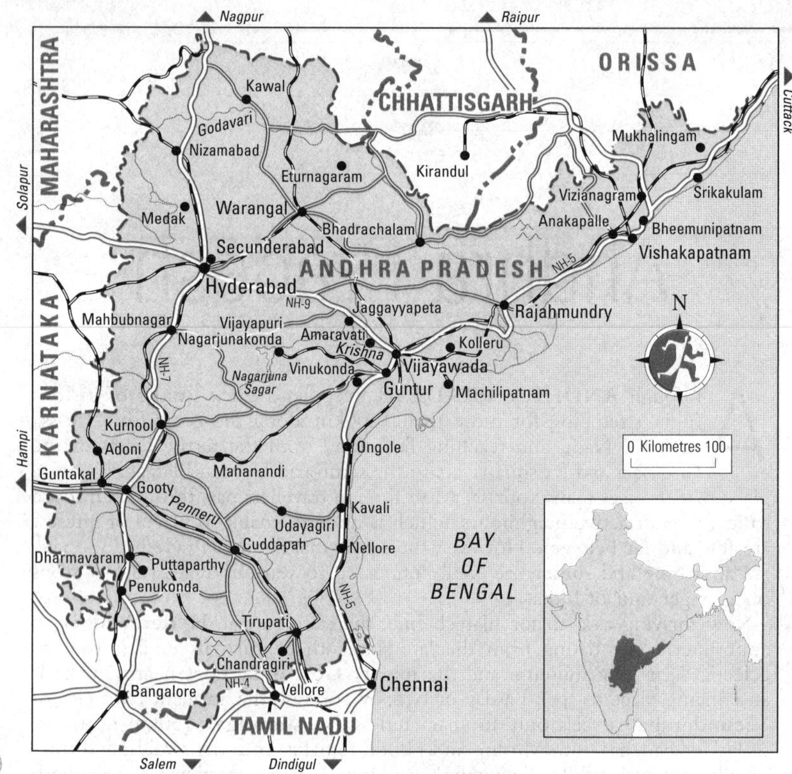

all held sway. By the thirteenth century, the Kakatiyas of Warangal were under constant threat from Muslim incursions, while later on, after the fall of their city at Hampi, the Hindu Vijayanagars transferred operations to Chandragiri near Tirupati.

The next significant development was in the mid-sixteenth century, with the rise of the Muslim **Qutb Shahi dynasty**. In 1687, the son of the Moghul emperor Aurangzeb seized Golconda. Five years after Aurangzeb died in 1707, the viceroy of Hyderabad declared independence and established the Asaf Jahi dynasty of **nizams**. In return for allying with the British against Tipu Sultan of Mysore, the nizam dynasty was allowed to retain a certain degree of autonomy even after the British had come to dominate all India.

During the struggle for Independence, harmony between Hindus and Muslims in Andhra Pradesh disintegrated. **Partition** brought matters to a climax, as the nizam desired to join other Muslims in the soon-to-be-created state of **Pakistan**. In 1949 the capital erupted in riots, the army was brought in and Hyderabad state was admitted to the Indian Union. Andhra Pradesh state was created in 1956 from Telugu-speaking regions (although Urdu is widely spoken in Hyderabad) that had previously formed part of the Madras Presidency on the east coast and the princely state of Hyderabad to the west. Today almost ninety percent of the population is Hindu, with Muslims largely concentrated in the capital. In 2004 Congress regained control of the state government, easing any lingering sectarian tensions, although the minority

TRS party is pushing for northwestern Andhra Pradesh, known as Telangana, to split off as a separate state.

Hyderabad/Secunderabad

A melting-pot of Muslim and Hindu cultures, the capital of Andhra Pradesh comprises the twin cities of **HYDERABAD** and **SECUNDERABAD**, with a combined population of nearly seven million. Secunderabad, of little interest to visitors, is the modern administrative city founded by the British, whereas Hyderabad, the old city, has plenty to offer the visitor, with teeming **bazaars**, **Muslim monuments** and the **Salar Jung Museum**. Hyderabad went into decline after Independence, with tensions often close to the surface due to lack of funding. Although the old city is still creaking with overpopulation and substandard amenities, the conurbation as a whole is booming. Recently Hyderabad has overtaken Bangalore as the south's hi-tech capital, and is now India's foremost computer and information technology centre; the industry has brought much revenue into the city and given rise to the nickname "Cyberabad".

Hyderabad was founded in 1591 by **Mohammed Quli Shah** (1562–1612), beside the River Musi, 8km east of Golconda, the fortress capital of the Golconda empire which by now was suffering from overcrowding and a serious lack of water. Unusually, this new city was laid out on a grid system, with huge arches and stone buildings that included Hyderabad's most famous monument, **Charminar**. At first it was a city without walls; these were only added in 1740, as defence against the Marathas. Legend has it that a secret tunnel linked the spectacular **Golconda Fort** with the city, dotted with dome-shaped structures at suitable intervals to provide the unfortunate messengers who had to use it with the opportunity to come up for fresh air.

For the three hundred years of Muslim reign, there was harmony between the predominantly Hindu population and the minority Muslims. Hyderabad was the most important focus of Muslim power in South India at this time; the princes' fabulous wealth derived primarily from the fine gems, particularly diamonds, mined in the Kistna Valley at Golconda. In the 1600s, Golconda was the diamond centre of the world. The famous **Koh-i-Noor** diamond was found here – the only time it was ever captured was by Moghul emperor Aurangzeb, when his son seized the Golconda Fort in 1687. It ended up, cut, in the British royal crown.

Arrival and information

The old city of **Hyderabad** straddles the River Musi. Most places of interest lie south of the river, while much of the accommodation is to the north. Further

Hyderabad addresses

Hyderabadis appear to have a deep mistrust of logical, consistent road-naming, mapping and **addresses**. One road merges into another, some addresses refer to nothing more specific than a locality and others identify themselves as being opposite buildings that no longer exist. Just as confusing are those that have very specific addresses consisting of a string of hyphenated numbers referring to house and plot numbers, incomprehensible to anybody other than town surveyors. All this is somewhat ironic in a city that is home to one of the major sections of the Survey of India.

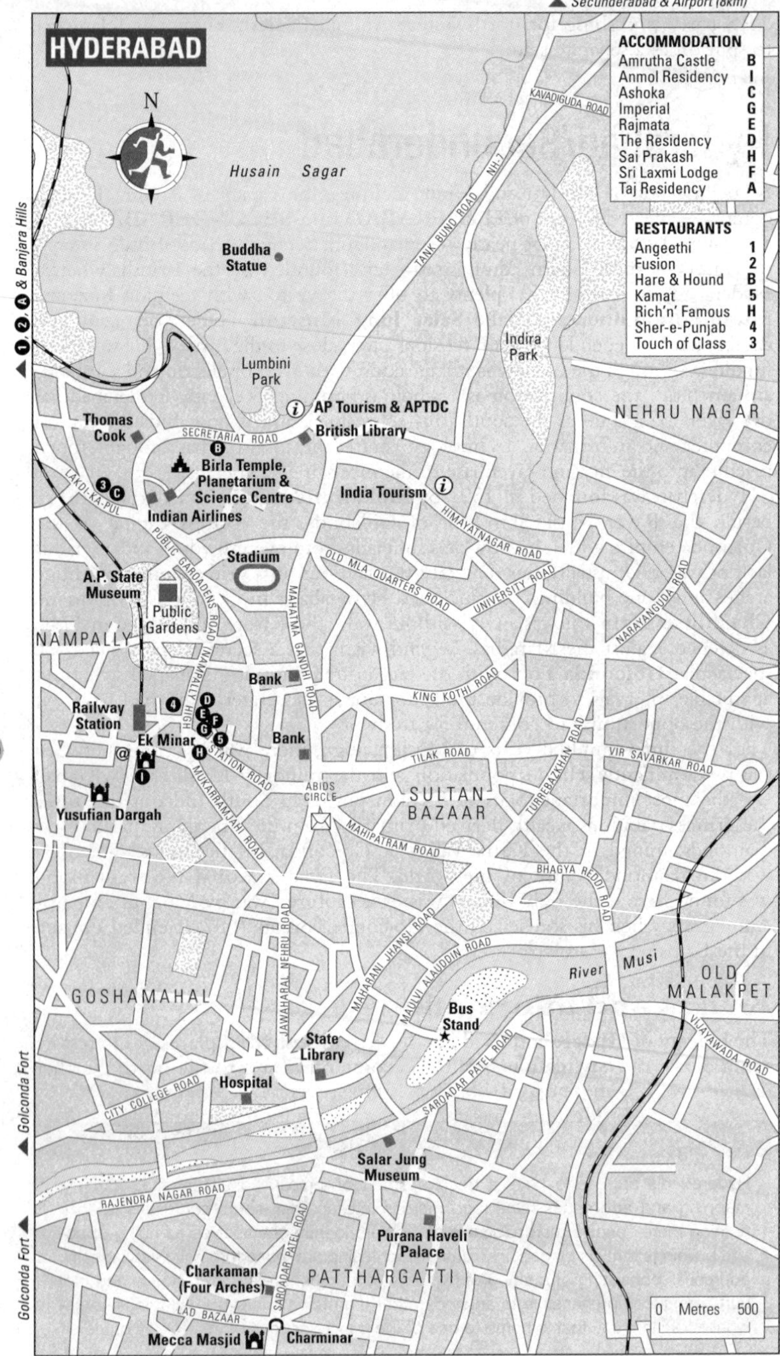
HYDERABAD
Secunderabad & Airport (8km)
1, 2, A & Banjara Hills
Golconda Fort
Golconda Fort
ACCOMMODATION
Amrutha Castle B
Anmol Residency I
Ashoka C
Imperial G
Rajmata E
The Residency D
Sai Prakash H
Sri Laxmi Lodge F
Taj Residency A
RESTAURANTS
Angeethi 1
Fusion 2
Hare & Hound B
Kamat 5
Rich'n' Famous H
Sher-e-Punjab 4
Touch of Class 3
Husain Sagar
Buddha Statue
Lumbini Park
Indira Park
AP Tourism & APTDC
British Library
Thomas Cook
Birla Temple, Planetarium & Science Centre
Indian Airlines
India Tourism
Stadium
A.P. State Museum
Public Gardens
NAMPALLY
NEHRU NAGAR
Bank
Bank
Railway Station
Ek Minar
Yusufian Dargah
ABIDS CIRCLE
SULTAN BAZAAR
GOSHAMAHAL
OLD MALAKPET
River Musi
Bus Stand
State Library
Hospital
Salar Jung Museum
Purana Haveli Palace
Charkaman (Four Arches)
PATTHARGATTI
Mecca Masjid
Charminar
KAVADIGUDA ROAD
NH-7
TANK BUND ROAD
SECRETARIAT ROAD
LAKDI-KA-PUL
PUBLIC GARDENS ROAD
HIMAYATNAGAR ROAD
OLD MLA QUARTERS ROAD
UNIVERSITY ROAD
NARAYANGUDA ROAD
MAHATMA GANDHI ROAD
NAMPALLY HIGH ROAD
KING KOTHI ROAD
TILAK ROAD
VIR SAVARKAR ROAD
TURREBAZKHAN ROAD
STATION ROAD
MUKARRAMJAHI ROAD
MAHIPATRAM ROAD
BHAGYA REDDI ROAD
MAHARANI JHANSI ROAD
MAULVI ALAUDDIN ROAD
JAWAHARAL NEHRU ROAD
VIJAYAWADA ROAD
SARODAR PATEL ROAD
CITY COLLEGE ROAD
RAJENDRA NAGAR ROAD
SARODAR PATEL ROAD
LAD BAZAAR
0 Metres 500

Guided tours

APTDC operates a number of **guided tours**. All timings quoted below relate to when the tours set off from the Secunderabad office; pick-up time in Hyderabad is 45min later.

The better of the two **city tours** (daily 8am–5.45pm; Rs190) includes Hussain Sagar, the Birla temple and planetarium, Qutb Shahi tombs (not Fri), Salar Jung Museum (not Fri), Charminar and Golconda. There are also shorter morning and afternoon city tours, and one to Golconda Fort's **sound and light show** (daily 2–9pm; Rs170 including entrance fee), which also stops at the Botanical Gardens and drives past Hi-Tech City. **Ramoji Film City**, a 2000-acre site full of wild and wonderful film sets, 35km from Hyderabad, also has its own tour (daily 7.45am–6pm; Rs375 including entry).

If the idea of a shorter **half-day city tour** appeals, AP Tourism hits most of the principal sights twice a day (9am–1pm and 2–6pm; Rs125) and offer an evening tour (daily 7–9pm), though these trips are contingent on there being sufficient demand. Tours depart from the main Hyderabad office.

APTDC's **Nagarjunakonda tour** (Sat & Sun 7am–9.30pm; Rs310, excluding entry fees) covers 360km in total, and is rather rushed, but is a convenient way to get to this fascinating area (see p.1076). The longer tours to **Tirupati/Tirumala**, more conveniently reached from Chennai and further afield in South India, are not worth considering.

north, separated from Hyderabad by the Hussain Sagar Lake, is the modern twin city of **Secunderabad**, where some long-distance trains terminate, and where all through-trains deposit passengers. If you do have to get off at Secunderabad, your ticket is valid for any connecting train to Hyderabad; and if none is imminent, many buses including #5, #8 and #20 ply between both stations. Hyderabad **airport**, 8km north of the city at Begumpet, is served by auto-rickshaws, taxis, and buses #9M or #10 via Nampally station, and a number of routes including #10, #45, #47 and #49 from Secunderabad. **Hyderabad railway station** (also known as Nampally) is close to all amenities and offers a fairly comprehensive service to major destinations. The well-organized **long-distance bus stand** occupies an island in the middle of the River Musi, 3km southeast of the railway station.

The main **tourist office** in Hyderabad is the **AP Tourism office** (daily 7am–7pm; ⓣ040/2345 3110, ⓦwww.aptourism.com), on Secretariat Road just before it becomes Tank Bund Road, near the start of the flyover. The **APTDC office** next door (daily 7am–8pm; ⓣ040/2345 3036, ⓦwww.tourisminap.com) and the other APTDC office, at Yatri Nivas, Sardar Patel Road, Secunderabad (ⓣ040/2781 6375), exist principally to book their tours. The **India Tourism office**, Sandozi Buildings, Himayatnagar Road, Hyderabad (Mon–Fri 9am–5pm; ⓣ040/2763 1360), offers a few brochures. However, the best source of local information is the monthly listings **magazine**, *Channel 6* (Rs15; ⓦwww.channel6magazine.com), available from most bookstalls.

Accommodation

The area in front of **Hyderabad railway station** (Nampally) has the cheapest accommodation, but you're unlikely to find anything basic for less than Rs250. The grim little enclave of five lodges with "Royal" in their name is usually full and best avoided. The real **bargains** are more in the mid- to upper-range hotels, which offer better facilities for lower rates than in other big cities. Little over 1km north of Secunderabad railway station, decent places can be found on **Sarojini Devi Road**, near the Gymkhana Ground.

Hyderabad

Amrutha Castle 5-9-16 Saifabad, opposite the Secretariat Ⓣ040/5663 3888, Ⓦwww.bestwestern.com. Affiliated to *Best Western*, this extraordinary hotel, designed like a fairy castle with round turret rooms, offers international facilities at fair prices. With its rooftop swimming pool, it's a good place to splash out. ❽–❾

Anmol Residency Adjacent to Ek Minar mosque, Nampally Ⓣ040/2460 8116. Friendly lower mid-range place, handily placed for the station and offering great value. The deluxe corner rooms have a lot more space and windows covering two walls. ❸–❹

Ashoka 6-1-70 Lakdi-ka-Pul Ⓣ040/2323 0105, Ⓕ5551 0220. Standard mid-range hotel with a variety of clean attached rooms, including cable TV and some a/c. ❹–❺

Imperial 5-8-107 Station Rd Ⓣ040/5582 7777, Ⓕ2320 9089. Reasonably well kept lodge, a 3min walk from the station area. Some rooms have a/c and/or TV. ❷–❹

Rajmata Nampally High Rd, opposite railway station Ⓣ040/5566 5555, Ⓕ2320 4133. Set back from the road in the same compound as the various *Royal* lodges, with large, clean non-a/c deluxe rooms. Their adjacent *Lakshmi* restaurant offers good South Indian veg food. ❹

Residency Nampally High Rd Ⓣ040/2320 4060, Ⓦwww.theresidency-hyd.com. This swish modern hotel belonging to the *Quality Inn* group is the most upmarket option near the station, but overcharges foreigners at $72–120 per double. Good veg restaurant. ❾

Sai Prakash Station Rd Ⓣ040/2461 1726, Ⓔhotelsaiprakash@rediffmail.com. Modern hotel, a 5min walk from the station, offering comfortable, carpeted rooms all with cable TV; the non-a/c rooms are good value and very popular. Good restaurants and bar on site. ❺–❻

Sri Laxmi Lodge Gadwal Compound, Station Rd Ⓣ040/5563 4200. Quiet place down a small lane opposite the *Sai Prakash*, with reasonably clean rooms. Good value, especially for singles. ❷

Taj Residency Rd No.1, Banjara Hills Ⓣ040/2666 3939, Ⓦwww.tajhotels.com. Some 4km from the centre, this is the least expensive of the three Taj hotels in the vicinity (doubles $140–160). The usual top-notch facilities, including a quality multi-cuisine restaurant and 24hr coffee shop. ❾

Secunderabad

Baseraa Sarojini Devi Rd Ⓣ040/2770 3200, Ⓦwww.baseraa.com. The comfiest hotel within walking distance (15min) of the station. Boasts 77 modern rooms and suites with all mod cons. ❼–❽

National Lodge Annexe Opposite Secunderabad railway station Ⓣ040/2770 5572. No-frills lodge amongst the motley cluster of hotels here, offering very basic rooms; most have their own bathroom. ❷

Ramakrishna St John's Rd Ⓣ040/2783 4567, Ⓕ2782 0933. With Some a/c rooms, this comfy mid-range option, in a large concrete block opposite the railway reservation complex, is the smartest place in the immediate station area. ❹–❻

Sri Vinayak off Regimental Bazaar Ⓣ040/2771 0146, Ⓕ2780 2146. Decent lower mid-range lodge tucked in a quiet lane only 3mins from the station. Some rooms are a/c or air-cooled. ❸–❺

The City

Hyderabad has three fairly distinct sectors: **Hyderabad**, the old city; **Secunderabad**, the new (originally called Hussain Shah Pura); and **Golconda**, the old fort. The two cities are basically one big sprawl, separated by a lake, **Hussain Sagar**, which was created in the 1500s and named after Hussain Shah Wali, who had helped Ibrahim Quli Qutb Shah recover from a serious illness.

The most interesting area, south of the River Musi, holds the **bazaars**, **Charminar** and the **Salar Jung Museum**. At only a tenth the width of the main bridge to the old city, the river is just a trickle, even after the rains – most of the area under the bridge is planted with palms and rice. North of the river, the main shopping malls are found around **Abids Circle** and **Sultan Bazaar** (readymade clothes, fruit, veg and silk), ten minutes' walk east of the railway station. Abids Circle is connected to MG Road, which runs north to join Tankbund Road at Hussain Sagar and runs on to Secunderabad, while to the south it metamorphoses into Jawaharal Nehru Road. Newer trendy shops, restaurants and bars are also springing up in the posh **Banjara Hills** district, on the west side of the city.

Salar Jung Museum

The unmissable **Salar Jung Museum** (daily except Fri 10am–5pm; Rs150 [Rs10]), on the south bank of the Musi, houses part of the huge collection of Salar Jung, one of the nizam's prime ministers, and his ancestors. A well-travelled man of wealth, he bought whatever took his fancy from both the East and West, from the sublime to, in some cases, the ridiculous. His extraordinary hoard includes Indian jade, miniatures, furniture, lacquer-work, Moghul opaque glassware, fabrics, bronzes, Buddhist and Hindu sculpture, manuscripts, and weapons. Avoid visiting the museum at the weekend, when it gets very crowded.

Charminar, Lad Bazaar and the Mecca Masjid

A maze of bazaars teeming with people, the old city has at its heart the **Charminar**, or Four Towers, a triumphal arch built at the centre of Mohammed Quli Shah's city in 1591 to commemorate an epidemic. As its name suggests, it features four graceful minarets, each 56m high, housing spiral staircases to the upper storeys. The (now defunct) mosque on the roof is the oldest in Hyderabad; it was built to teach the royal children the Koran. The yellowish colour of the building is due to a special stucco made of marble powder, gram and egg yolk.

Charminar marks the beginning of the fascinating **Lad Bazaar**, as old as the town itself, which leads to Mahboob Chowk, a market square featuring a mosque and Victorian clocktower. Lad Bazaar specializes in everything you could possibly need for a Hyderabadi marriage; it's full of bangle shops, old stores selling rosewater, herbs and spices, and material. You'll also find silver filigree jewellery, antiques, *bidri*-ware, hookah-paraphernalia with delicate inlay work and, in the markets near the Charminar, **pearls** – so beloved of the nizams that they not only wore them but also ground them into powder to eat. Today Hyderabad is the centre of India's pearl trade.

Southwest, behind the Charminar, **Mecca Masjid** is the sixth-largest mosque in India, constructed in 1598 by the sixth king, Abdullah Qutb Shah, from locally hewn blocks of black granite. Small red bricks from Mecca are slotted over the central arch. The mosque can hold 3000 devotees with up to 10,000 more in the courtyard; on the left of the courtyard are the tombs of the nizams. The **Charkaman**, or Four Arches, north of Charminar, were built in 1594 and once led to the parade ground of royal palaces (now long gone). The western arch, **Daulat-Khan-e-Ali** (which originally led to the palace), was at one time adorned with rich gold tapestries.

North of the river

Set in a leafy courtyard not far south of the railway station, the **Yusufian Dargah**, with its striking bulbous yellow dome, is the shrine of a seventeenth-century Sufi saint of the venerable Chishti order. You can enter (cover your head) to view the flower-decked tomb. About a kilometre north of the station, set in Hyderabad's tranquil public gardens, the **AP state museum** (daily except Fri and 2nd Sat of each month 10.30am–5pm; Rs10) displays a modest but well-labelled collection of bronzes, prehistoric tools, copper inscription plates, weapons and household utensils. There's a gallery of modern art in the extension.

The **Birla Venkateshwara temple** (daily 7am–noon & 3–9pm), on Kalapahad ("black mountain") Hill, north of the Public Gardens, is open to all.

△ Hyderabad bazaar

Constructed in Rajasthani white marble in 1976, the temple itself is not of great interest, but it affords fine views. Nearby, and built by the same organization, is the **planetarium** (shows in English: daily except Thurs 11.30am, 4pm & 6pm; Rs17) and a **science centre** (daily 10.30am–8pm; Rs15) with lots of satellite hardware and photos, machines demonstrating sensory perceptions and a small dinosaur display.

Hussain Sagar

Hussain Sagar, the large expanse of water separating Hyderabad from Secunderabad, lends a welcome air of tranquillity to the busy conurbation. The lakeside is a popular place for a stroll, especially at sunset. In the centre of the water stands a large stone statue of the **Buddha Purnima** or "Full Moon Buddha", which was erected in 1992. Regular **boats** (Rs25 return) chug out to the statue from Lumbini Park, just off Secretariat Road. Two luxury boats – the *Bhageerathi* and the *Bhagmati* – operated by APTDC, offer hour-long **cruises** of the lake (11am–3pm Rs50; 6–8pm Rs60).

Golconda Fort and the tombs of the Qutb Shahi kings

Golconda, 122m above the plain and 11km west of old Hyderabad, was the capital of the seven Qutb Shahi kings from 1518 until the end of the sixteenth century, when the court moved to Hyderabad. Well preserved and set in thick green scrubland, it is one of the most impressive forts in India. The citadel boasted 87 semicircular bastions and eight mighty gates, four of which are still in use, complete with gruesome elephant-proof spikes.

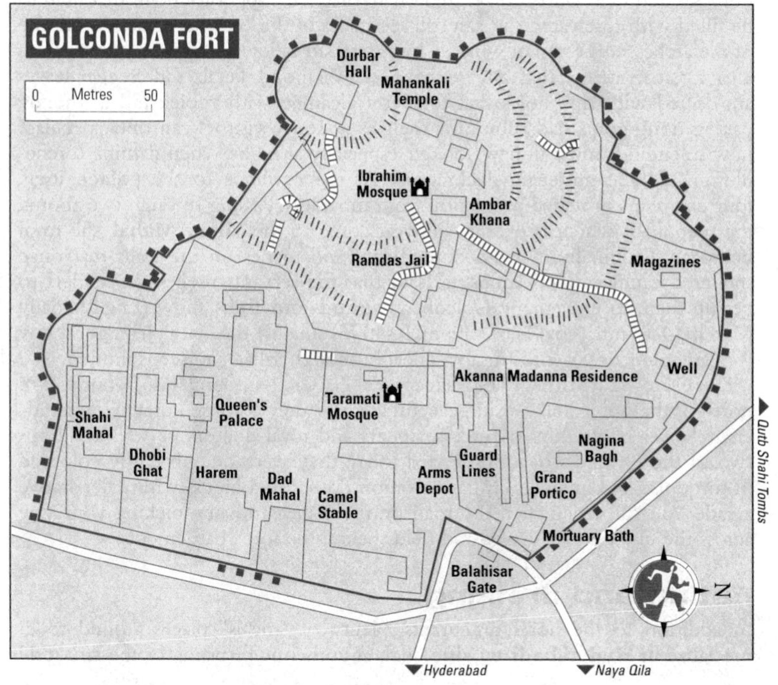

To get **to the fort**, bus #119 runs from Nampally, while the #66G direct bus from Charminar and #80D from Secunderabad stop outside the main entrance. **For the tombs**, take #123 or #142S from Charminar. From Secunderabad the #5, #5S, and #5R all go to Mehdipattanam, where you should hop onto #123. Or, of course, you could take a rickshaw and spare yourself the bother (agree a waiting fee in advance). Set aside a day to explore the fort, which covers an area of around four square kilometres.

Entering the **fort** (daily 9am–5pm; $2 [Rs5]) by the Balahisar Gate, you come into the Grand Portico, where guards clap their hands to show off the fort's acoustics; the claps can be clearly heard at the Durbar Hall. To the right is the **mortuary bath**, where the bodies of deceased nobles were ritually bathed prior to burial. If you follow the arrowed anticlockwise route, you pass the two-storey residence of ministers Akkana and Madanna before starting the stairway ascent to the Durbar Hall. Halfway along the steps, you arrive at a small, dark cell named after the court cashier **Ramdas**, who while incarcerated here produced the clumsy carvings and paintings that litter the gloomy room. Nearing the top, you come across the small, pretty mosque of Ibrahim Qutb Shah; beyond here, set beneath two huge granite stones, is an even tinier temple to Durga in her manifestation as Mahakali.

The steps are crowned by the three-storey **Durbar Hall** of the Qutb Shahis, on platforms outside which the monarchs would sit and survey their domains. Their accompaniment was the lilting strains of court musicians, as opposed to today's cacophony of incessant clapping from far below. As you head back down to the palaces and harems, you pass the tanks that supplied the fort's water system.

The ruins of the **queen's palace**, once elaborately decorated with multiple domes, stand in a courtyard centred on an original copper fountain that used to be filled with rosewater. You can still see traces of the "necklace" design on one of the arches, at the top of which a lotus bud sits below an opening flower with a cavity at its centre that once contained a diamond. Petals and creeper leaves are dotted with tiny holes that formerly gleamed with rubies and diamonds; parrots, long gone, had rubies for their eyes. Today visitors can only speculate how splendid it must all have looked, especially at night, when flaming torches illuminated the glittering decorations. At the entrance to the **palace** itself, four chambers provided protection from intruders. Passing through two rooms, the second of which is overgrown, you come to the **Shahi Mahal**, the royal bedroom. Originally it had a domed roof and niches on the walls that once sheltered candles or oil lamps; it's said that the servants used silver ladders to get up there to light them. Golconda's **sound-and-light** show (English: daily March–Oct 7pm; Nov–Feb 6.30pm; Rs40) is suitably theatrical. It's a good way for foreigners to get into the fort cheaply, though what you see is limited.

There are 82 **tombs** (daily except Fri 9.30am–4.30pm; Rs5) about 1km north of the outer wall. Set in peaceful gardens, they commemorate commanders, relatives of the kings, dancers, singers and royal doctors, as well as all but two of the Qutb Shahi kings. Faded today, they were once brightly coloured in turquoise and green; each has an onion dome on a block, with a decorative arcade. You can reach them by road or, more pleasantly, by picking your way across the quiet grassy verges and fields below the fort's battlements.

Eating and drinking

In addition to the hotel restaurants, plenty of "meals" places around town specialize in **Hyderabadi cuisine**, such as authentic biriyanis, or the famously chilli-hot Andhra cuisine. Hyderabadi cooking is derived from Moghul court cuisine, featuring sumptuous meat dishes with northern ingredients such as cinnamon, cardamom, cloves and garlic, and traditional southern vegetarian dishes with an array of flavourings like cassia buds, peanuts, coconut, tamarind leaves, mustard seeds and red chillies. Though not as abundant as in Bangalore, **bars** conducive to both sexes have started appearing, mostly along Main Road No.1 in Banjara Hills: along here, try the plush white leather couches and Indo-Euro pop at *Liquids*, the disco theme nights at *Cinnabar Redd* (above *Fusion 9*) or the basement rock sounds at *Easy Rider*, further down the road.

Hyderabad

Angeethi Main Rd No.1, Banjara Hills. Highly-rated and rather pricey north Indian restaurant, with excellent Punjabi and tandoori dishes.

Hare and Hound Secretariat Rd, Saifabad. The *Amrutha Castle* hotel's multicuisine restaurant and bar, presided over by suits of armour, has a wide-ranging à la carte menu, and there's a great-value lunchtime (12.30–3pm) buffet for Rs175 in the section next to the foyer.

Fusion 9 Main Rd No.1, Banjara Hills. Expensive but quality cuisine from nine different regions as diverse as Mexico, Europe, the Middle East and southeast Asia, served in a smart modern lounge overlooking the street through tinted windows.

Kamat Station Rd, opposite *Sai Prakash* hotel. Conveniently located branch of this extremely inexpensive and clean veggie chain.

Rich'n'Famous Station Rd. The posher and pricier of the *Sai Prakash* hotel's two restaurants, with comfy chairs and imaginative daily specials featuring crab and prawns, plus specialities from both Hyderabad and further afield; the veg *Sukha Sagara* downstairs serves cheaper South Indian snacks and north Indian dishes.

Sher-e-Punjab Corner of Nampally High Rd and station entrance. Popular basement restaurant offering tasty north Indian veg and non-veg food at bargain prices.

Touch of Class Lakdi-ka-Pul. The *Central Court* hotel's restaurant offers good Hyderabadi non-veg plus some veg options and barbecue kebabs on a small patio; also Mughlai, Western and Chinese food. There's a good-value lunch buffet (Rs175) and a midnight buffet (Rs125).

Secunderabad

Akbar 1-7-190 MG Rd. A fine range of Hyderabadi dishes – including top quality biriyanis – at moderate prices.

Paradise-Persis MG Rd. Very popular multi-restaurant complex bashing out fine Hyderabadi cuisine at little expense.

Listings

Airlines Air Canada, see Gulf Air; Air France, Gupta Estate 1st floor, Basheerbagh ⓣ040/2323 0947; Air India, 5-9-193 HACA Bhavan, opposite Public Garden Saifabad ⓣ040/2338 9719; Bangladesh Biman, see Gulf Air; British Airways, Nijhawan Travel Services, 5-9-88/4 Ainulaman Fateh Maidan Rd ⓣ040/2324 1661; Delta/Sabena/Swissair/Singapore Airlines, Aviation Travels, Navbharat Chambers, 6-3-1109/1 Raj Bhavan Rd ⓣ040/2340 2664; Emirates, Floor F, Reliance Classic Building 3 & 4, Road No.1, Banjara Hills ⓣ040/2332 1111; Gulf Air/Bangladesh Biman/Air Canada/Royal Jordanian, Jet Air Flat 202, 5-9-58 Gupta Estate, Basheerbagh ⓣ040/2324 0870; Indian Airlines, opposite Assembly Saifabad ⓣ040/2329 9333; Jet Airways, 6-3-1109/1 GF Nav Bharat Chambers, Raj Bhavan Rd ⓣ040/2340 1222; Lufthansa, 3-5-823 Shop #B1–B3, Hyderaguda ⓣ040/2323 5537; Qantas, Transworld Travels, 3A 1st floor, 5-9-93 Chapel Rd ⓣ040/2329 8495; Qatar Airways, Reliance Krishna 5-10-197197/A, B & C Hillfort Rd, Nowbat Pahad ⓣ040/5536 7333 Royal Jordanian, see Gulf Air; Sabena, see Delta Airlines; Sahara, 15 Sahara Manzil opp Secretariat, Saifabad ⓣ040/2321 2767; Singapore Airlines, see Delta Airlines; Swissair, see Delta Airlines.

Banks and exchange Surprisingly few banks do foreign exchange, two exceptions being the State Bank of Hyderabad, MG Rd, and Federal Bank, 1st floor, Orient Estate, MG Rd; both open Mon–Fri 10.30am–2.30pm, the latter also Sat 10.30am–12.30pm. It's better to head for an agency such as Thomas Cook ⓣ040/2329 6521 at Nasir Arcade, Secretariat Rd; or L.K.P. Forex ⓣ040/2321 0094 on Public Gardens Rd, only ten minutes' walk north of Nampally station; both open Mon–Sat 9.30am–5.30pm. There are an increasing number of ATMs, however, such as the SBI on Nampally High Rd,

Syndicate Bank on Station Rd and Oriental Bank at Secunderabad railway station.

Bicycle hire Bikes can be rented for Rs20 per day at a friendly stall on the right as you approach Hyderabad station from Nampally High Rd.

Bookshops A.A. Hussian & Co, 5-8-551 Arastu Trust Building, Abid Rd, Hyderabad; Akshara, 8-2-273 Pavani Estate, Road no. 2, Banjara Hills, Hyderabad; Higginbothams, 1 Lal Bahadur Stadium, Hyderabad; Gangarams, 62 DSD Rd, near *Garden Restaurant* in Secunderabad; and Kalaujal, Hill Fort Rd, opposite the Public Gardens, which specializes in art books.

Car rental Air Travels in Banjara Hills (Ⓣ040/2335 3099, Ⓕ2335 5088) and Classic Travels in Secunderabad (Ⓣ040/2775 5645) both provide a 24hr service, with or without driver.

Crafts Lepakshi, the AP state government emporium at Gunfoundry on MG Rd, stocks a wide range of handicrafts, including Bidri metalwork, jewellery and silks. Utkalika (Government of Orissa handicrafts), house no. 60-1-67, between the Ravindra Bharati building and *Hotel Ashoka*, has a modest selection of silver filigree jewellery, hand-loom cloth, *ikat* tie-dye, Jagannath papier-mâché figures and buffalo bone carvings. Cheneta Bhavan is a modern shopping complex a little south of the railway station, stuffed with hand-loom cloth shops from various states, including Andhra Pradesh. For silks and saris, try Meena Bazaar, Pochampally Silks and Sarees, and Pooja Sarees, all on Tilak Rd.

Dentist Kakade's Dentistree, opposite *Taj Banjara* hotel, Rd No.1 Ⓣ040/ 2330 2633.

Hospitals The government-run Gandhi Hospital is in Secunderabad Ⓣ040/2770 2222; the private CDR Hospital is in Himayatnagar Ⓣ040/2322 1221; and there's a Tropical

Moving on from Hyderabad

Useful daily **train** services from **Hyderabad railway station (Nampally)** include: the Charminar Express #2760 to Chennai (20.10pm; 14hr 10min); the Hyderabad–Ernakulam Express #7030 (noon; 26hr); the Andhra Pradesh Express #2723 to Delhi (6.40am; 26hr 20min); the Hyderabad–Mumbai Express #7032 (8.40pm; 16hr 15min); the East Coast Express #7046 to Kolkata (Calcutta: 6.50am; 31hr 25min) via Vijayawada (6hr 16min) and Bhubaneswar (22hr 25min); and the Rayasaleema Express #7429 to Tirupati (5.25pm; 15hr 35min). Almost all northeast-bound services call at Warangal and Vijayawada. **From Secunderabad**, there are some originating services and many through trains in all directions. Useful services include the Konark Express #1020 to Mumbai (11.45am; 16hr 10min); the Secunderabad–Bangalore Express #7085 (6.40pm; 12hr 35min); and the Secunderabad–Rajendranagar Express #7091 calling at Varanasi (Mon & Wed 10.30pm; 30hr 10min).

The **railways reservations office** at Hyderabad (Mon–Sat 8am–2pm & 2.30–8pm, Sun 8am–2pm) is to the left as you enter the station. Counter #211 (next to enquiry counter) is supposedly for tourist reservations, but it's also used for group bookings and lost tickets. Foreign visitors can make bookings at the Chief Reservation Inspector's Office on platform 1 for same-day journeys (daily 9am–5pm). The **Secunderabad reservation complex** is by the major junction with St. John's Road over 400m to the right as you exit the station. Counter 34 is for foreigners.

From the Central Bus Stand, **regular bus services** run to a host of destinations around the state and beyond. In addition, various **deluxe and video buses** depart for Bangalore, Chennai, Mumbai and other major destinations, from outside Nampally station, where you will find a cluster of private agencies, such as National Travels (Ⓣ040/2320 3614).

Between them, Indian Airlines, Jet Airways and Sahara offer regular flights to numerous cities around India. In terms of international services, Indian Airlines runs one flight daily to Dubai, as well as routes to other Gulf states; Air India has twice weekly departures to Singapore. Silk Air, the regional wing of Singapore Airlines (Ⓣ040/2340 2644), also fly three times a week to Singapore. Details of booking offices for airlines are given on p.1073.

See "Travel details" at the end of this chapter for more information on journey frequencies and durations.

Diseases Hospital in Nallakunta ⓣ040/2766 7843.

Internet access Internet outlets abound throughout both cities: try Modi Xerox opposite Ek Minar mosque (Rs20/hr). Several Net2phone facilities can be found behind the large Medwin Hospital on Nampally High Rd.

Library The British Library, Secretariat Rd (Tues–Sat 11am–7pm; ⓣ040/2323 0774) has a wide selection of books and recent British newspapers. Officially you must be a member or a British citizen to get in.

Pharmacies Apollo Pharmacy ⓣ040/2323 1380 and Health Pharmacy ⓣ040/2331 0618 are both open 24hr.

Police ⓣ040/2323 0191. In an emergency call ⓣ100.

Travel agents General agents for airline and private-bus tickets include: Travel Club Forex ⓣ040/2323 4180, Nasir Arcade, Saifabad, close to Thomas Cook; and Kamat Travels in the *Hotel Sai Prakash* complex ⓣ040/2461 2096. There's a host of private-bus agents on Nampally High Rd outside Hyderabad railway station.

Around Hyderabad

As you head north from Hyderabad towards the borders of Maharashtra and Madhya Pradesh, the landscape becomes greener and more hilly, sporadically punctuated by photogenic black-granite rock formations. There is little to detain visitors here except the small town of **Warangal**, situated on the main railway line, which warrants a stop to visit the nearby medieval fort and Shiva temple. South of the capital, vast swathes of flat farmland stretch into the centre of the state, where the Nagarjuna Sagar Dam has created a major lake with the important Buddhist site of **Nagarjunakonda**, now an island in its waters.

Warangal

WARANGAL – "one stone" – 150km northeast of Hyderabad, was the Hindu capital of the Kakatiyan empire in the twelfth and thirteenth centuries. Like other Deccan cities, it changed hands many times between the Hindus and the Muslims – something that is reflected in its architecture and the remains you see today.

Warangal's **fort** (daily 9am–5pm; $2 [Rs5]), 4km south of town, is famous for its two circles of fortifications: the outer made of earth with a moat, and the inner of stone. Four roads into the centre meet at the ruined temple of **Swayambhu** (1162), dedicated to Shiva. At its southern, freestanding gateway, another Shiva temple, from the fourteenth century, is in a much better shape; inside, the remains of an enormous *lingam* came originally from the Svayambhu shrine. Also inside the citadel is the **Shirab Khan**, or **Audience Hall**, an early eleventh-century building very similar to Mandu's Hindola Mahal (see p.469).

Some 6km north of town, just off the main road beside the slopes of Hanamkonda Hill, the largely basalt Chalukyan-style "**thousand-pillared**" **Shiva temple** (daily 10am–6pm; Rs5) was constructed by King Rudra Deva in 1163. A low-roofed building on several stepped stages, it features superb carvings and three shrines to Vishnu, Shiva and Surya, the sun god. They lead off the *mandapa*, whose numerous finely carved columns give the temple its name. In front, a polished Nandi bull was carved out of a single stone. A Bhadrakali temple stands at the top of the hill.

Practicalities

If you make an early start, it's just about possible to visit Warangal as a day-trip from Hyderabad. Frequent buses and trains run to the town (roughly 3hr).

Warangal's **bus stand** and **railway station** are opposite each other, served by local buses, auto- and cycle rickshaws. The easiest way to cover the site is to **rent a bicycle** from one of the stalls on Station Road. To get to the fort, follow Station Road from the station, turn left just beyond the post office, go under the railway bridge and left again at the next main road. For Hanamkonda, follow the same route from the station but turn right onto JPN Road at the next main junction after the post office, left at the next major crossroads onto MG Road, and right at the end onto the Hanamkonda main road. The temple and hill are on the left.

Accommodation is limited: *Hotel Ashok* on Main Road, Hanamkonda, 6km from the railway and bus stand (ⓣ08712/285491; ❸–❺), has a/c rooms, a restaurant and bar and is rather more upmarket than *Hotel Ratna* (ⓣ08712/260645, ⓕ260096; ❷–❹), 2km from the station on MG Road. Basic lodges nearer the station include *Vijaya* (ⓣ08712/225851; ❷–❸) on Station Road, which is the closest and best value, and *Urvasi* (ⓣ08712/261760; ❷–❹) at the junction of Station and JPN roads, which has some a/c rooms. Several decent **eating places** line Station Road – the upstairs *Titanic*, halfway along on the right, serves good tandoori and other non-veg dishes. Internet facilities are available at Grace@Net on JPN Road (Rs30/hr).

Nagarjunakonda

NAGARJUNAKONDA, or "Nagarjuna's Hill", 166km south of Hyderabad and 175km west of Vijayawada, is all that now remains of the vast area, rich in archeological sites, submerged when the huge Nagarjuna Sagar Dam was built across the River Krishna in 1960. Ancient settlements in the valley were first discovered in 1926; extensive excavations carried out between 1954 and 1960 uncovered more than one hundred sites dating from the early Stone Age to late medieval times. Nagarjunakonda was once the summit of a hill, where a fort towered 200m above the valley floor; now it's just a small oblong island near the middle of Nagarjuna Sagar Lake, accessible by boat from the mainland. Several Buddhist monuments have been reconstructed, in an operation reminiscent of that at Abu Simbel in Egypt, and a **museum** exhibits the more remarkable ruins of the valley. **VIJAYAPURI**, the village on the shore of the lake, overlooks the colossal dam itself, which stretches for almost 2km. Torrents of water flushed through its 26 floodgates produce electricity for the whole region, and irrigate an area of almost 800 square kilometres. Many villages had to be relocated to higher ground when the valley was flooded.

The island and the museum

Boats arrive on the northeastern edge of **Nagarjunakonda island** (daily 9am–5pm; $2 [Rs5]), unloading passengers at what remains of one of the gates of the fort, built in the fourteenth century and renovated by the Vijayanagar kings in the mid-sixteenth century. Low, damaged, stone walls skirting the island mark the edge of the fort, and you can see ground-level remains of the Hindu temples that served its inhabitants.

Well-kept gardens lie between the jetty and the museum, beyond which nine Buddhist monuments from various sites in the valley have been rebuilt. West of the jetty, there's a reconstructed bathing *ghat*, built entirely of limestone during the reigns of the Ikshvaku kings (third century AD).

The **maha-chaitya**, or stupa, constructed at the command of King Chamtula's sister in the third century AD, is the earliest Buddhist structure in the area. It was raised over relics of the Buddha – said to include a tooth – and has been reassembled in the southwest of the island. Nearby, a towering **statue** of the Buddha stands draped in robes beside a ground plan of a monastery that enshrines a smaller stupa. Other **stupas** stand nearby; the brick walls of the *svastika chaitya* have been arranged in the shape of swastikas, common emblems in early Buddhist iconography.

The **museum** (daily except Fri 9am–5pm; Rs3) houses stone friezes decorated with scenes from the Buddha's life, and statues of Buddha in various postures. Earlier artefacts include stone tools and pots from the Neolithic age (third millennium BC), and metal axe heads and knives (first millennium BC). Later exhibits include inscribed pillars from Ikshvaku times showing Buddhist monasteries and statues. Medieval sculptures include a thirteenth-century *tirthankara* (Jain saint), a seventeenth-century Ganesh and Nandi, and some eighteenth-century Shiva and Shakti statues, and there is also a model showing the excavated sites in the valley.

Practicalities

Organized **APTDC tours** from Hyderabad to Nagarjunakonda at weekends (see p.1067) – taking in the sites and museum, the nearby Ethiopothala Waterfalls (entry Rs20) and an engraved third-century Buddhist monolith known as the Pylon – can be a bit rushed: if you want to spend more time in the area you can take a bus from Hyderabad (4hr; all the regular Macherla services stop at Vijayapuri) or Vijayawada (6hr; a direct service runs daily at 11am and frequent services leave from Guntur).

Accommodation at Vijayapuri is limited, and there are two distinct settlements 6km apart on either side of the dam. Decide in advance where you want to stay and get off the bus at the best spot. The right bank jetty is more accessible – ask the bus to leave you at the launch station. The drab-looking concrete *Nagarjuna Motel Complex* (☎08642/278188; ❷–❹) has adequate rooms, some with a/c. Five hundred metres away in the village, the *Golden Lodge* (☎08642/278148; ❶) is much more basic. Both APTDC places are on the other side of the dam as you approach the lake from the direction of Hyderabad: the *Punnami Vihar* (☎08680/277361; ❹–❺) has spacious rooms with balconies and a good restaurant, and is 2km further up the hill from the *Punnami Hill Colony* (☎08680/276540; ❷–❹), which also has a dorm (Rs100).

Tickets for **boats** to the island (daily 9am & 1.30pm; 45min) are on sale 25 minutes before departure (Rs45). Each boat leaves the island ninety minutes after it arrives, which allows enough time to see the museum and walk briskly round the monuments, but if you want to take your time and soak up the atmosphere, take the morning boat and return in the afternoon (bring provisions). At weekends a twin-deck boat conducts three hour luxury cruises around the lake and to the island for Rs150 per head.

Eastern Andhra Pradesh

Perhaps India's least visited area, **eastern Andhra Pradesh** is sandwiched between the Bay of Bengal in the east and the red soil and high peaks of the Eastern Ghats in the north. Its one architectural attraction is the ancient Buddhist site of **Amaravati**, near the city of **Vijayawada**, whose sprinkling of historic temples is far overshadowed by impersonal, modern buildings. For anyone with a strong desire to explore, however, pockets of natural beauty along the coast and in the hills of eastern Andhra Pradesh can offer rich rewards. In this sleepy landscape, little affected by modernization, bullocks amble between swaying palms and the rice fields are iridescent against rusty sands. Unless you have the patience to endure the excruciatingly slow public transport system, your own vehicle is essential.

Vijayawada and around

Almost 450km north of Chennai, a third of the way to Kolkata (Calcutta), **VIJAYAWADA** is a bustling commercial centre on the banks of the Krishna delta, 90km from the coast. This mundane city, alleviated by a mountain backdrop of bare granite outcrops and some urban greenery, is seldom visited by tourists, but does, however, make the obvious stop-off point for visits to the third-century Buddhist site at **Amaravati**, 60km west.

The **Kanaka Durga** (also known as Vijaya) **temple** on Indrakila Hill in the east, dedicated to the city's patron goddess of riches, power and benevolence, is the most interesting of Vijayawada's handful of temples. Across the river, roughly 3km out of town, is an ancient, unmodified cave temple at **Undavalli**, a tiny rural village set off the main road and reachable on any Guntur-bound bus, or the local #13 service.

Practicalities

Vijayawada's **railway station**, on the main Chennai–Kolkata (Calcutta) line, is in the centre of town. Buses arriving from Guntur, Amaravati and as far afield as Hyderabad and Chennai pull into the Pandit Nehru **bus stand** 1.5km further west, on the other side of the Ryes Canal which flows through the heart of town. Specific ticket offices cater for each service, and a **tourist office** (Ⓣ0866/252 3966) has details on local hotels and sights. APTDC also has an office in the centre of town at *Hotel Ilapuram* complex, Gandhi Nagar (Ⓣ0866/257 0255). You can **change money** at Zen Global Finance, 40-6-27 Krishna Nagar in Labbipet, or use the SBI ATM at the bus stand.

Vijayawada is a major business centre, with a good selection of mid-range **hotels**, all within 1km of the railway station and bus stand. *Monika Lodge* (Ⓣ0866/257 1334; ❷), just off Elluru Road about 300m northeast of the bus stand, is one of the cheapest but a bit grubby. Two better-value places, both on Atchutaramaiah Street, which links the railway station to Elluru Road, are the *Hotel Narayana Swamy* (Ⓣ0866/257 1221; ❸–❹) and the *Sri Ram* (Ⓣ0866/257 9377; ❸–❹), both with spotless rooms, some a/c and cable TV. *Raj Towers* (Ⓣ0866/257 1311, Ⓕ556 1714; ❸–❻) on Elluru Road, is a tall modern block with good mid-range rooms and a decent **restaurant**. The fourth-floor *Palace Heights* restaurant at the *Hotel Swarna Palace*, where Atchutaramaiah Street meets Elluru Road, also provides large portions of Indian, Chinese and continental food, and has a bar. Inexpensive Andhra *thali* joints abound.

Guntur

Another sprawling and bustling commercial city 30km southwest of Vijayawada, **GUNTUR** has no merits of its own but makes an even more convenient jumping-off point for Amaravati than Vijayawada, especially if you are coming from the area of Nagarjuna Sagar. There are buses every ten to fifteen minutes to Vijayawada (45min–1hr), and every half-hour to Amaravati from the old bus stand (adjacent to the main bus stand). If you decide to spend the night here, try the **lodges** opposite the bus stands. *Annapurna Lodge* (Ⓣ0863/235 6493; ❷–❹) has decent-sized, clean rooms and some a/c; *Padmasri Lodge* (Ⓣ0863/222 3813; ❷–❹) also has a/c and cheaper singles.

Amaravati

A small village on the banks of the Krishna 30km west of Vijayawada, **AMARAVATI** is the site of a Buddhist settlement, formerly known as Chintapalli, where a stupa larger than those at Sanchi (see p.417) was erected over relics of the Buddha in the third century BC, during the reign of Ashoka. The stupa no longer stands, but its size is evident from the mound that formed its base. There was a gateway at each of the cardinal points, one of which has been reconstructed, and the meticulously carved details show themes from the Buddha's life. A two week Kalachakra initiation programme is being conducted by the Dalai Lama here in January 2006 to commemorate 2550 years since the Buddha's birth.

Exhibits at the small but fascinating **museum** (daily except Fri 10am–5pm; $2 [Rs5]) range in date from the third century BC to the twelfth century AD and include Buddha statues with lotus symbols on the feet, tightly curled hair and long ear lobes – all traditional indications of an enlightened teacher. Other stone carvings show Buddhist symbols such as the *chakra* (wheel of *dharma*), throne, stupa and *bodhi* tree. Later sculptures include limestone statues of the goddess Tara and *bodhisattva* Padmapani, showing that Mahayana teachings had taken over from the earlier Hinayana doctrines. What you see here are some of the finer pieces excavated from the site – other remains have been taken to the Chennai Government Museum and the British Museum in London.

Practicalities

Theoretically **buses** run hourly from Vijayawada to Amaravati but the service can be unreliable, so it's best to take a bus to Guntur (every 15min; 45min–1hr), where you can pick up a connection to Amaravati (1hr–1hr 30min). Buses return to Guntur every half-hour. The excavated site and museum are roughly 1km from the bus stand. Trishaws – miniature carts attached to tricycles – take tourists to the site and the riverbank, where there are several drink stalls. The APTDC *Punnami* (Ⓣ08645/255332; ❷) has reasonable rooms and a dorm (Rs50). Their canteen provides basic meals and snacks.

Southern Andhra Pradesh

The further south you travel from the fertile lands watered by the great Krishna and Godavari rivers, the less hospitable the terrain becomes, especially in the rocky southwest of the state. For Hindus, the main attraction in southern Andhra Pradesh is the tenth-century **Venkateshvara temple**, outside **Tirupati**, the most popular Vishnu shrine in India, where several thousand pilgrims come each day to receive *darshan*. **Puttaparthy**, the home town of the spiritual leader Sai Baba, is the only other place in the region to attract significant numbers of visitors. Both Tirupati and Puttaparthy are closer to Chennai in Tamil Nadu and Bangalore in Karnataka than to other points in Andhra Pradesh, and for many tourists, constitute their only foray into the state.

Tirupati and Tirumala Hill

Set in a stunning position, surrounded by wooded hills capped by a ring of vertical red rocks, the **Shri Venkateshvara temple** at Tirumala, 170km northwest of Chennai, is said to be the richest and most popular place of pilgrimage in the world, drawing more devotees than either Rome or Mecca. With its many shrines and *dharamshalas*, the whole area around Tirumala Hill, an enervating drive 700m up in the Venkata hills, provides a fascinating insight into contemporary Hinduism practised on a large scale. The hill is 11km as the crow flies from its service town of **TIRUPATI**, but double that by road.

Just a five-minute walk from the railway station, the one temple in Tirupati itself that's definitely worth a visit is **Govindarajaswamy**, whose modern grey *gopura* is clearly visible from many points in town. Begun by the Nayaks in the sixteenth century, it's an interesting complex with large open courtyards decorated with lion sculptures and some ornate wooden roofs. The inner sanctum is open to non-Hindus and contains a splendid large black reclining Vishnu, coated in bronze armour and bedecked in flowers. A visit during the *sanadarsanan* (daily 10am–8.45pm; Rs5) will let you in to glimpse the deity, and participate in fire blessings at the main and subsidiary shrines. In its own compound by the side entrance stands the fine little Venkateshvara Museum of Temple Arts (daily 8am–8pm; Rs1). The temple's impressive tank lies 200m to the east.

Between Tirupati and Tirumala Hill, the **Tiruchanur Padmavati temple** is another popular pilgrimage halt. A gold *vimana* tower with lions at each corner surmounts the sanctuary, which contains a black stone image of goddess Lakshmi with one silver eye. At the front step, water sprays wash the feet of the devotees. A Rs20 ticket allows you to jump the queue to enter the sanctuary. Photography is prohibited.

Tirumala Hill, the Venkateshvara temple and Kapilateertham

There's good reason for the small shrine to Ganesh at the foot of **Tirumala Hill**. The journey up is hair-raising and it's worth saying a quick prayer when embarking on it, but at least separate routes up and down preclude head-on crashes. Overtaking is strictly forbidden, but drivers do anyway; virtually every bend is labelled "blind" and every instruction to drive slowly is blithely ignored. The fearless sit on the left for the best views; the most devout, of course, climb the hill by foot. The **trail** starts at Alipuri, 4km from the centre of Tirupati; all the pilgrim buses pass through – look out for a large Garuda statue and the soaring *gopura* of the first temple. The first hour consists of a flight of knee-crunching concrete steps, covered in yellow, orange and red *tikka* daubed by pilgrims as they ascend. The path then mercifully levels out before the final assault some two hours on. Allow at least four hours to the top – fitter pilgrims might do it half an hour quicker. The trail is covered over for most of the way, affording protection from the blistering sun, and there are drinks stalls all along the route. An early start is recommended. When you get to the top, you will see barbers busying themselves giving pilgrims tonsures as part of their devotions.

The **Venkateshvara temple** (aka Sri Vari) dedicated to **Vishnu** and started in the tenth century, has been recently renovated to provide facilities for the thousands of pilgrims who visit daily; a rabbit warren of passages and waiting rooms wind their way around the complex in which pilgrims interminably shuffle towards the inner sanctum; weekends, public holidays, and festivals are even busier. Unless your visit is intended to be particularly rigorous, on reaching the temple you should follow the signs for the special *darshan* that costs Rs50 (daily 6–10am & noon–9pm) as this may reduce the time it takes to get inside by quite a few hours. You can also obtain these *darshan* tickets from the temple tourism office near the temple bus stand on Station Road. Once inside, you'll see the somewhat incongruous sight of brahmins sitting at video monitors, observing the goings-on in the inner sanctum; the constant to-ing and fro-ing includes temple attendants bringing in supplies, truckloads of oil and other comestibles, and huge cooking pots being carried across the courtyard. You may also catch deities being hauled past on palanquins to the accompaniment of *nageswaram* (a South Indian oboe-like double-reed wind instrument) and *tavil* drum, complete with an armed guard. At the entrance is a colonnade, lined with life-sized statues of royal patrons, in copper or stone. The *gopura* gateway leading to the inner courtyard is decorated with sheets of embossed silver; a gold *stambha* (flagstaff) stands outside the inner shrine next to a gold upturned lotus on a plinth. Outside, opposite the temple, is a small museum, the **Hall of Antiquities** (daily 8am–8pm). Your special *darshan* ticket entitles you to enter the museum via a shorter queue opposite the exit and to pick up two free *laddu* sweets. Temple funds support a university, hospital, orphanages and schools at Tirupati as well as providing cheap, and in some cases free, accommodation for pilgrims.

At the bottom of the hill, the **Sri Kapileswaraswami** temple at Kapilateertham is the only Tirumala temple devoted to Shiva, and has a small Hindu pleasure garden at the entrance and a sacred waterfall which crashes into a large tank surrounded by colonnades, where pilgrims pile in for a bath.

Chandragiri Fort

In the sixteenth century, **Chandragiri**, 11km southwest of Tirupati, became the third capital of the Vijayanagars, whose power had declined following the fall of the city of Vijayanagar (Hampi) in Karnataka. It was here that the British negotiated the acquisition of the land to establish Fort St George, the earliest settlement at what is now Chennai. The original fort (daily except Fri 10am–5pm; $2 [Rs5]), thought to date from around 1000 AD, was taken over by Haider Ali in 1782, followed by the British in 1792. A small **museum** of sculpture, weapons and memorabilia is housed in the main building, the Indo-Saracenic Raja Mahal. Another building, the **Rani Mahal**, stands close by, while behind that is a hill with two freestanding boulders that was used as a place of public execution during Vijayanagar times. A little temple from the Krishna Deva Raya period and a freshwater tank stand at the top of the hill behind the Raja Mahal. In the evening there is a 45-minute **sound and light** show (English version daily: Nov–Feb 7.30pm, March–Oct 8pm; Rs30).

Practicalities

The best way of **getting to Tirupati** is by train from Chennai; the trip can be done in a day if you get the earliest of the three daily services (3hr 30min). From Hyderabad it takes sixteen hours. The main APTDC **tourist office** is at 139 T.P. Area, 3rd Choultry (daily 6.30am–9pm; ⓣ0877/225 5385), and there's also an APTDC counter at the **railway station** accessible from the entrance hall and platform 1, where there's a 24-hour left-luggage office and a self-service veg refreshment room. Stands sell English copies of TKT Viraraghava Charya's *History of Tirupati*, and there's a Vivekananda religious bookshop next door. Tirupati's APSRTC Central **bus station** – also with 24-hour left-luggage – is about 1km east of the railway station. Frequent express services run from Chennai (4hr), but the train is far more comfortable. However, if you're travelling south and want to avoid Chennai, there are hourly buses to Kanchipuram (5hr), three of which continue to Mahabalipuram (7hr). In addition, the useful Tirupati–Nagercoil Express #6351 runs twice-weekly (departs 12.34 Wed & Sun), and stops at the Tamil Nadu temple towns of Kanchipuram, Tiruchchirapalli and Madurai. Beautifully decorated **cycle rickshaws**, and auto-rickshaws are available for travelling round town.

A special section at the back of the bus stand has services (Rs44 return) every few minutes **to Tirumala** and the Venkateshvara temple; you can also access the hill from a separate local bus stand outside the railway station. You shouldn't have to queue for long at either unless it's a weekend or festival. An easier option is to take a **taxi**, best organized through the APTDC counter at the railway station; avoid the unlicensed taxis outside the station. The tourist office runs **tours** which take in Chandragiri Fort (except Fri) and a number of temples (10am–5.30pm; Rs165 or Rs190 including Chandragiri sound & light show), but do not include Venkateshvara temple because of the queues.

There are a few **Internet** places in Tirupati, including Q Net N Play, 340 Netaji Rd, one minute from the railway station (turn left as you exit), and Net Hill in the shopping complex at the corner of the bus stand. The Syndicate and ICICI banks both have **ATMs** on Netaji Road, and there are even a couple up on Tirumala Hill.

Accommodation and eating

Unless you're a pilgrim seeking accommodation in the *dharamshalas* near the temple, all the decent **places to stay** are in Tirupati, near the railway station and bus stand: there's a vast array of hotels and lodges to suit all budgets. **Eating** is almost exclusively vegetarian, even in the hotels, and cheap "meals" places abound in town and on Tirumala Hill. If you're in need of meat and booze, head for the *Yalamuri* beer garden, off the traffic circle opposite the bus stand.

Apsara 213 TP Area ⓣ0877/557 8062. Almost opposite the bus station, this is a pretty standard place offering basic but clean attached rooms of varying sizes. ❷

Balaji Bhavan 189 Railway Station Rd ⓣ0877/222 5930. Newish place with fair-sized, clean rooms – some a/c, but all have attached bathrooms, and smarter rooms have cable TV. ❷–❺

Bhimas Deluxe 34–38 G Car St, near the railway station ⓣ0877/222 5521. Decent, comfortable rooms with central a/c, and 12hr "transit rooms" available at half price. The *Maya* veg restaurant serves north and South Indian food plus some Chinese dishes in the evenings. ❺

Indira Rest House Tiruchanur Rd ⓣ0877/222 7479. Basic, no-nonsense lodge, a few minutes' walk behind the railway lines from the bus stand, 100m beyond the *Poojith Residency*. Some new a/c rooms, and generally quieter than most places. ❷–❸

Mayura 209 TP Area ⓣ0877/222 5925, ⓔmayura@nettlink.com. Best but most expensive of a host of hotels opposite the bus station, offering average mid-range rooms with decent bathrooms and TV. ❹–❺

Raghunadha 191 Railway Station Rd ⓣ0877/222 3130. This good, simple, clean lodge is one of the better cheap places. Cable TV in all rooms and some inexpensive a/c. ❷–❸

Sindhuri Park Beside bathing tank ⓣ0877/225 6430, ⓦwww.hotelsindhuri.com. The smartest place in the centre, this all a/c hotel has excellent facilities and great views of the tank and temple. The basement *Vrinda* restaurant serves quality veg food, including a range of thalis, and has a Rs99 buffet on weekend evenings. ❺–❼

Puttaparthy

Deep in the southwest of the state, amid the arid rocky hills bordering Karnataka, a thriving community has grown up around the once insignificant village of **PUTTAPARTHY**, birthplace of spiritual leader **Sai Baba**, whose followers believe him to be the new incarnation of God. Centring on **Prasanthi Nilayam**, the ashram where Sai Baba resides from July to March, the town has schools, a university, a hospital and sports centre which offer up-to-date and free services to all. There's even a small airport. The ashram itself is a huge complex with room for thousands, with canteens, shops, a museum and library, and a vast assembly hall where Sai Baba gives *darshan* twice daily (6.40am & 3pm). Queues start more than an hour before the appointed time, and a lottery decides who

Shri Satya Sai Baba

Born on November 23, 1926 in Puttaparthy, then an obscure village in the Madras Presidency, **Satyanarayana Raju** is reported to have shown prodigious talents and unusual purity and compassion from an early age. His apparently supernatural abilities initially caused some concern to his family, who took him to Vedic doctors and eventually to be exorcized. Having been pronounced to be possessed by the divine rather than the diabolical, at the age of 14 he calmly announced that he was the new incarnation of **Sai Baba**, a saint from Shirdi in Maharashtra who died eight years before Satya was born.

Gradually his fame spread, and a large following grew. In 1950 the **ashram** was inaugurated and a decade later Sai Baba was attracting international attention; today he has millions of devotees worldwide, a considerable number of whom turn out for his birthday celebrations in Puttaparthy, when he delivers a message to his devotees. Just 5ft tall, with a startling Hendrix-style Afro, his smiling, saffron-clad figure is seen on posters, framed photos and murals all over South India. Though his **miraculous powers** reportedly include the ability to materialize *vibhuti*, sacred ash, with curative properties, Sai Baba claims this to be an unimportant activity, aimed at those firmly entrenched in materialism, and emphasizes instead his message of **universal love**. In recent years a number of ex-followers have made serious accusations about coercion and even sexual abuse on the part of the guru himself, which have been vehemently denied. Whatever your feelings about the divinity of Sai Baba, the atmosphere around the ashram is undeniably peaceful, and the growth of such a vibrant community in this once-forgotten backwater is no small miracle in itself. You can do some research on the guru at ⓦwww.saibabalinks.com.

gets to sit near the front. The museum (daily 10am–noon) contains a detailed, fascinating display on the world's major faiths with illustrations and quotations from their sacred texts, punctuated by Sai Baba's comments.

Practicalities

Puttaparthy is most accessible from Bangalore in Karnataka (see p.1292), from where seven daily **buses** (4hr) run to the stand outside the ashram entrance. The town is also connected to Hyderabad (3 daily; 10hr) and Chennai (1 nightly; 11hr). Regular buses make the 42-kilometre run to **Dharmavaram**, the nearest **railhead**, which has good services north and south. There are also three Indian Airlines **flights** a week from Bangalore (Mon, Thurs & Sat; depart 2pm; 30min), though the short distance hardly justifies the expense.

Many visitors choose to **stay** in the ashram accommodation, which is strictly segregated by sex, except for families. Costs are minimal, and though you can't book in advance, you can enquire about availability at the secretary's office (ⓣ08555/287583). Outside the ashram, many of the basic lodges are rather overpriced, but a good cheap option is the friendly *Sai Ganesh Guest House* near the police station (ⓣ08555/287079; ❷). The *Sri Sai Sadan* at the far end of the main street (ⓣ08555/287507; ❷–❹) is also great value; all rooms have fridge, TV and balcony with views of the countryside or the ashram, and there's a meditation room and rooftop restaurant. At the top end, the *Sai Towers*, near the ashram entrance (ⓣ0855/287270, ⓦwww.saitowers.com; ❺–❽), charges a lot for its smallish non-a/c and a/c rooms, but has a good **restaurant** downstairs. The ashram also has a canteen which is open to non-residents and there are simple snack stalls along the main street outside the ashram; it's also worth trying the delicious Tibetan food at the *Bamboo Nest* on Chitravathi Road.

Travel details

Trains

Hyderabad/Secunderabad to: Aurangabad (1 daily; 12hr 15min); Bangalore (2–4 daily; 12hr–15hr 55min); Bhubaneswar (4 daily; 18hr 40min–22hr 25min); Chennai (2 daily; 14hr 10min); Delhi (3–4 daily; 22hr 20min– 32hr); Kolkata (Calcutta: 2–3 daily; 26hr 45min–31hr 25min); Mumbai (3 daily; 16hr 10min–17hr); Tirupati (3–4 daily; 13hr 30min–15hr 30min); Varanasi (2 weekly; 30hr 20min); Vijayawada (12–13 daily; 5hr 30min–7hr 45min); Warangal (11–13 daily; 2hr 14min–3hr 13min).
Tirupati to: Chennai (3 daily; 2hr 55min–3hr 15min); Hyderabad/Secunderabad (3–4 daily; 12hr 50min–17hr 10min); Kanchipuram (2 weekly; 2hr 40min) Kolkata (Calcutta: 1 daily; 38hr 30min); Madurai (2 weekly; 12hr 20min); Tiruchchirapalli (2 weekly; 8hr 35min); Varanasi (1 weekly; 39hr 40min); Vijayawada (4–6 daily; 7hr–8hr 45min).
Vijayawada to: Chennai (7–12 daily; 6hr 35min–8hr 50min); Delhi (4–6 daily; 23hr 10min–32hr 40min); Hyderabad/Secunderabad (12–13 daily; 5hr 20min–8hr 15min); Kolkata (Calcutta: 5–7 daily; 21hr 15min–33hr 20min); Tirupati (4–6 daily; 6hr 30min–8hr 15min).

Buses

Hyderabad to: Amaravati (2 daily; 7hr); Bangalore (hourly; 13hr); Bidar (every 30min–1hr; 4hr); Chennai (1 daily; 16hr); Mumbai (7 daily; 17hr); Puttaparthy (3 daily; 10hr); Tirupati (8 daily; 12hr); Vijayapuri (hourly; 4hr); Vijayawada (every 15min; 6hr); Warangal (every 15–30min; 3hr).
Tirupati to: Chennai (every 15–30min; 3hr 30min–4hr); Hyderabad (8 daily; 12hr); Kanchipuram (hourly; 3hr 30min); Mahabalipuram (3 daily; 5hr 30min); Puttaparthy (1 daily at 8pm; 10hr).
Vijayawada to: Amaravati (hourly; 2hr); Guntur (every 15min; 1hr–1hr 30min); Hyderabad (every 15min; 6hr).

Flights

Hyderabad to: Ahmedabad (5 weekly; 1hr 40min); Bangalore (5 daily; 1hr–1hr 30min); Chennai (7–8 daily; 1hr–1hr 30min); Delhi (7 daily; 2hr–4hr 15min); Goa (1 daily; 3hr); Kolkata (Calcutta: 3 daily; 2hr–2hr 55min); Mangalore (1 daily; 3hr 10min); Mumbai (10 daily; 1hr 15min–3hr 45min); Pune (1 daily; 1hr); Tirupati (4 weekly; 55min); Varanasi (1 daily; 5hr 30min).
Puttaparthy to: Bangalore (3 weekly; 30min).
Tirupati to: Hyderabad (4 weekly; 55min).

CHAPTER 19

Highlights

* **Port Blair** The hilly and green capital is everybody's entry point to the Andamans, with the grim Cellular Jail standing as a reminder of the gruesome past. See p.1093

* **Wandoor** The white sandy beach and islets of the Mahatma Gandhi National Marine Park are the archipelago's most popular day-trip destination, and a good appetizer for more remote parts. See p.1100

* **Scuba-diving** The Andamans' beautiful coral reefs teem with vivid underwater life. See p.1102

* **Neill Island** Cruise by boat to Havelock's tiny neighbour, an excellent hangout, very laid-back, friendly and great for snorkelling. See p.1103

* **North Andaman** The long haul on the road from Port Blair is worthwhile for the backdrop of thick rainforest and the dazzling tropical beaches when you get there. See p.1107

△ Coral reef, Andaman Islands

The Andaman Islands

Comprising India's most remote state, the **ANDAMAN ISLANDS** are situated 1000km off the east coast in the middle of the Bay of Bengal, connected to the mainland by flights and ferries from Kolkata (Calcutta), Chennai and Vishakapatnam. Thickly covered by deep green tropical forest, the archipelago supports a profusion of wildlife, including some extremely rare species of bird, but the principal attraction for tourists lies offshore, around the pristine reefs ringing most of the islands. Filled with colourful fish and kaleidoscopic corals, the crystal-clear waters of the Andaman Sea feature some of the world's richest and least spoilt marine reserves – perfect for **snorkelling** and **scuba diving**. Potential visitors have long been faced by the quandary as to whether the expense and effort required to get there, the lack of infrastructure and certain increased health risks, as well as ethical concerns about ecological and tribal issues, outweigh the benefits of a trip. On the other hand, more islanders are becoming dependant on tourism as the Andamans' profile develops, and they could certainly use a boost to their business, which was decimated by the tsunami (see box on p.1089).

For administrative purposes, the Andamans are grouped with the **Nicobar Islands**, 200km further south but, as yet, strictly off limits to foreigners. Approximately 200 islands make up the Andaman group and nineteen the Nicobar. They are islands of varying size, the summits of a submarine mountain range stretching 755km from the Arakan Yoma chain in Burma to the fringes of Sumatra in the south. All but the most remote of these are populated in parts by **indigenous tribes** whose numbers have been slashed dramatically as a result of nineteenth-century European settlement and, more recently, rampant **deforestation**. Today new felling is supposed to be strictly controlled, confined to mature trees of certain species at least 1km from the coast, but how strictly that is adhered to is a matter for conjecture, while the situation is compounded by timber poachers and there is the additional problem of timber poachers from Burma and Thailand.

Foreign tourists are only permitted to visit certain parts of the Andaman group, separated by the deep Ten Degree Channel from the Nicobar Islands. The point of arrival for boats and planes is **South Andaman**, where the predominantly Tamil and Bengali community in the small but busy capital, **Port Blair**, accounts for almost half the total population. **Permits**, obtainable on arrival by both sea and air, are granted for a stay of one month. The most beautiful beaches and coral reefs are found on outlying islands. A healthy get-up-and-go spirit is essential if you plan to explore these, as connections and transport can be erratic, frequently uncomfortable and severely limited, especially on the less visited islands. Once away from the settlements, you'll need your own camping

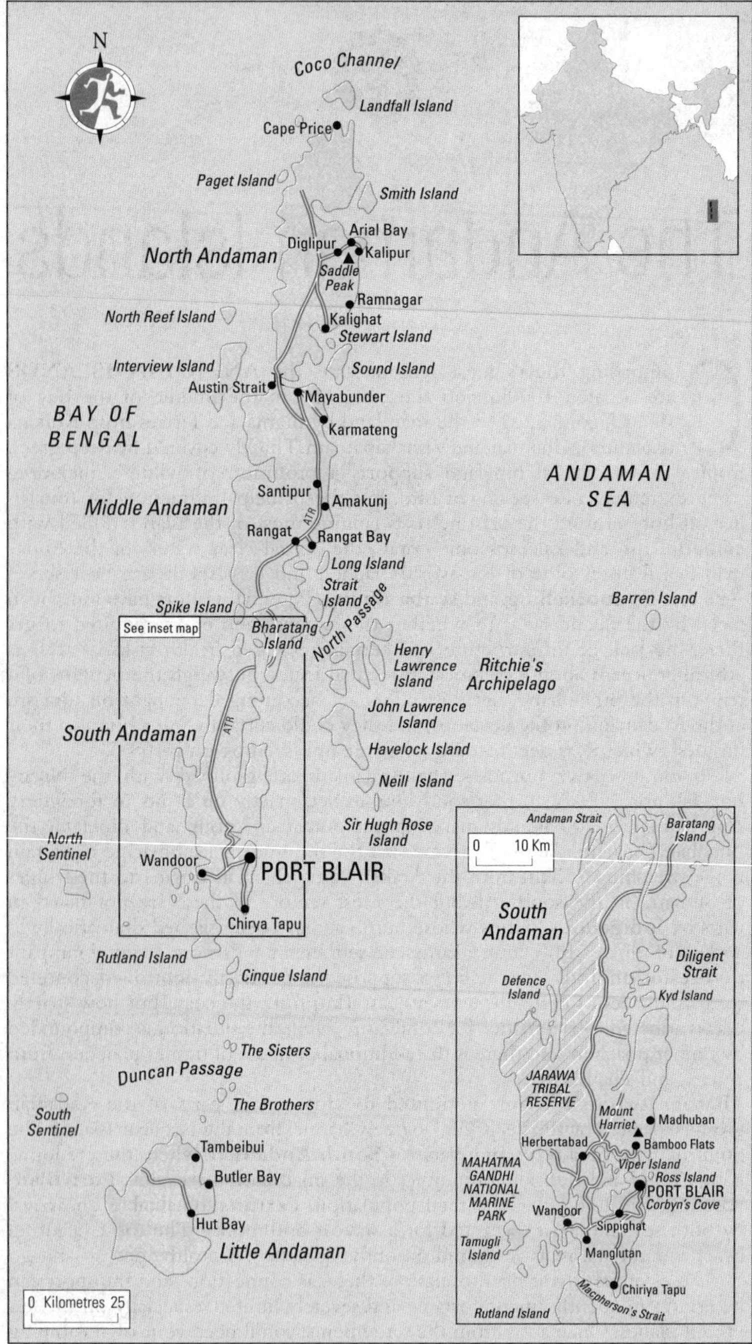

N
Coco Channel
Landfall Island
Cape Price
Paget Island
Smith Island
Arial Bay
Diglipur
Kalipur
North Andaman
Saddle Peak
Ramnagar
North Reef Island
Kalighat
Stewart Island
Interview Island
Sound Island
Austin Strait
Mayabunder
Karmateng
BAY OF BENGAL
ANDAMAN SEA
Santipur
Amakunj
Middle Andaman
ATR
Rangat
Rangat Bay
Long Island
Strait Island
North Passage
Barren Island
Spike Island
See inset map
Bharatang Island
Henry Lawrence Island
Ritchie's Archipelago
John Lawrence Island
South Andaman
ATR
Havelock Island
Neill Island
Sir Hugh Rose Island
North Sentinel
Wandoor
PORT BLAIR
Chirya Tapu
Rutland Island
Cinque Island
The Sisters
Duncan Passage
The Brothers
South Sentinel
Tambeibui
Butler Bay
Hut Bay
Little Andaman
0 Kilometres 25
Andaman Strait
Baratang Island
0 10 Km
South Andaman
Diligent Strait
Defence Island
Kyd Island
JARAWA TRIBAL RESERVE
Mount Harriet
Madhuban
Herbertabad
Bamboo Flats
MAHATMA GANDHI NATIONAL MARINE PARK
Viper Island
Ross Island
PORT BLAIR
Corbyn's Cove
Wandoor
Sippighat
Tamugli Island
Manglutan
Chiriya Tapu
Rutland Island
Macpherson's Strait

After the waves

Contrary to the rumours based on the sketchy information that emerged in the days following the devastating **tsunami** of Boxing Day 2004, the island chain did not suffer the total destruction and loss of life at first feared. Most of the damage and death took place in the Nicobars, which lie much closer to the earthquake's epicentre off Indonesia, especially the islands of Car Nicobar, Katchall and Great Nicobar. In all, around three thousand people were confirmed dead and a further four and a half thousand declared missing, presumed dead. The only island in the Andamans to suffer extensively was Little Andaman (see p.1110).

Indeed, the handful of deaths and structural damage in the Port Blair area – mainly to a few old buildings around town, and the quay and Water Sports Complex at Aberdeen Jetty – were caused by the **earthquake** rather than the ensuing tsunami. Elsewhere, the Austin Bridge connecting Middle to North Andaman also had to be closed for repairs. No foreigners on the islands at the time suffered anything more serious than a few belongings getting swept out to sea, while a few beach huts on the main touristic island of Havelock were left with some flood damage to mop up. The worst consequence of the tsunami was that the flow of domestic and foreign tourists to the islands diminished to an almost non-existent trickle in the months following the disaster, leaving those whose livelihood depends on tourism rather high and dry.

One **positive note** to emerge from the entire episode is that not a single indigenous person of those who are still allowed to live in the traditional way (see box pp.1090–1091) is said to have perished, even on islands that were badly battered. This is thought to be due to the fact that the tribal people got wind of the impending tragedy by observing the agitation amongst the wildlife and quickly shifted to higher ground. Such a powerful testament to the benefits of living so close to nature provides a sobering lesson to more "civilized" folk.

supplies and equipment. It's also worth pointing out that a surprising number of travellers fall sick in the Andamans. The dense tree cover, marshy swamps and high rainfall combine to provide the perfect breeding ground for mosquitoes, and **malaria** is endemic in even the most remote settlements. Sandflies are also ferocious in certain places and **tropical ulcer** infections from scratching the bites is a frequent hazard.

The **climate** remains tropical throughout the year, with temperatures ranging from 24°C to 35°C and humidity levels never below seventy percent. By far the best time to visit is between January and May. From mid-May to October, heavy rains flush the islands, often bringing violent cyclones that leave west-coast beaches strewn with fallen trees, while in November and December less severe rains arrive with the northeast monsoon. Despite being so far east, the islands run on Indian time, so the sun rises as early as 4.30am in summer and darkness falls soon after 5pm

Some history

The earliest mention of the Andaman and Nicobar islands is found in **Ptolemy's** geographical treatises of the second century AD. Other records from the Chinese Buddhist monk I'Tsing some five hundred years later and Arabian travellers who passed by in the ninth century depict the inhabitants as fierce and cannibalistic. **Marco Polo** arrived in the thirteenth century and could offer no more favourable description of the natives: "The people are without a king and are idolaters no better than wild beasts. All the men of the island of Angamanian have heads like dogs . . . they are a most cruel generation, and eat everybody they catch . . ." It is unlikely, however, that the Andamanese were cannibals, as

Native people of the Andaman and Nicobar Islands

Quite where the **indigenous population** of the Andaman and Nicobar islands originally came from is a puzzle that has preoccupied anthropologists since Radcliffe-Brown conducted his famous field work among the Andamanese at the beginning of this century. Asian-looking groups such as the Shompen may have migrated here from the east and north when the islands were connected to Burma, or the sea was sufficiently shallow to allow transport by canoe, but this doesn't explain the origins of the black populations, whose appearance suggests African roots. Wherever they came from, the survival of the islands' first inhabitants has long been threatened by traders and colonizers, who introduced disease and destroyed their territories by widespread felling. Thousands also died from addiction to alcohol and opium, which the Chinese, Japanese and British exchanged for valuable shells. Of perhaps 5000 aborigines in 1858, from six of the twelve native tribal groups, only five percent remain. More background information and updates on current issues concerning tribal people in the Andamans (and elsewhere) can be found at Ⓦwww.survival-international.org, Survival International's excellent website.

The indigenous inhabitants of the Andamans, divided into *eramtaga* (those living in the jungle) and *ar-yuato* (those living on the coast), traditionally subsisted as hunter-gatherers on fish, turtles, turtle eggs, pigs, fruit, honey and roots. The largest surviving population is of 30,000 or so **Nicobarese**; being horticulturalists, unlike the other tribes, they eventually assimilated more readily to modern culture and many converted to Christianity under British rule. Ironically, the loss of their traditional culture perhaps contributed to the fact that the Nicobarese were among the worst affected by the tsunami – they were taken as much by surprise as the settlers, and twelve of their villages on Car Nicobar were wiped out.

Although they comprised the largest group when the islands were first colonized, only 43 **Great Andamanese** remain on Strait Island, north of South Andaman, where they've been forcibly settled as a "breeding centre" and where they are reliant on the Indian authorities for food and shelter. After the tsunami, however, they were relocated to Port Blair, hopefully as a temporary move. In the 1860s, the Rev. Henry Corbyn set up a "home" for them to learn English on Ross Island, insisting that they wear clothes and attend reading and writing classes. Five children and three adults from Corbyn's school were taken as curiosities to Kolkata in 1864, where they were shown around the sights. The whole experience, however, proved more fascinating for the crowds who'd come to ogle the "monkey men" than for the Andamanese themselves, who, one of the organizers of the trip, ruefully remarked "...never evinced astonishment or admiration at anything which they beheld, however wonderful in its novelty we might suppose it would appear to them". From the foreign settlers the Andamanese tragically contracted diseases such as syphilis, measles, mumps and influenza, and fell prey to opium addiction. Within three years almost the entire population had died.

The **Jarawas**, who shifted from their original homes when land was cleared to build Port Blair, now live on the remote western coasts of Middle and South Andaman, hemmed in by the Andaman Trunk Road (ATR) which since the 1970s has cut them off from hunting grounds and freshwater supplies. For the final two decades of the

the most vivid reports of their ferocity were propagated by Malay pirates who held sway over the surrounding seas, and needed to keep looters well away from trade ships that passed between India, China and the Far East.

During the eighteenth and nineteenth centuries **European missionaries** and trading companies turned their attention to the islands with a view to colonization. A string of unsuccessful attempts to convert the Nicobaris to Christianity was made by the French, Dutch and Danish, all of whom were twentieth century, encroachments on their land by loggers, road builders and Bengali settlers met with fierce resistance. Dozens, possibly hundreds, of people died in skirmishes. In one incident a party of Burmese were caught poaching on Jarawa land; of the eleven men involved, six limped out with horrific injuries, two were found dead, and the other three were never seen again. Most of the incidents have occurred on or near the ATR, which is why armed escorts board the buses at several points during the journey north from Port Blair to Mayabunder. Some contact between settlers and tribals was made in the late 1990s through gift exchanges at each full moon, when consignments of coconuts, bananas and red cloth were taken to a friendly band of Jarawas on a boat, but the initiative was later cancelled due to settlers' worries that the Jarawas were becoming reliant on such benefaction. This nevertheless led to some Jarawas becoming curious about what "civilization" had to offer and starting to hold their hands out for goodies to passing vehicles and even visiting Indian settlements near their territory. When the initially generous reception waned, their visits evolved into surreptitious raids and there was an attack on a police outpost in March 1998. In the last six years the government has tried to minimize contact, which has remained peaceful, and even increased Jarawa land by 180 square kilometres but it has failed to enforce a 2002 Indian Supreme Court order to close the ATR. The tribe currently numbers around 270.

Aside from a couple of violent encounters with nineteenth-century seamen (seventy were massacred on first contact in 1867), relations with the **Onge**, who call themselves the **Gaubolambe**, have been relatively peaceful. Distinguished by their white-clay and ochre body paint, they continue to live in communal shelters (*bera*) and construct temporary thatched huts (*korale*) on Little Andaman. The remaining population of around one hundred retain their traditional way of life on two small reserves. The Indian government has erected wood and tin huts in both, dispatched a teacher to instruct them in Hindi, and encouraged coconut cultivation, but to little avail. Contact with outsiders is limited to an occasional trip into town to purchase liquor, and visits from rare parties of anthropologists. The reserves are strictly off limits to foreigners, but you can learn about the Onge's traditional hunting practices, beliefs and rituals in Vishvajit Pandya's wonderful ethnography study, *Above the Forest*.

Only very limited contact is ever had with the isolated **Shompen** tribe of Great Nicobar, whose population of around 380 manage to lead a traditional existence. The most elusive tribe of all, the **Sentinelese**, live on North Sentinel Island west of South Andaman. Some contact was made with them in 1990, after a team put together by the local administration had left gifts on the beaches every month for two years, but subsequent visits have invariably ended in a hail of arrows. Since the early 1990s, the AAJVS, the government department charged with tribal welfare, have effectively given up trying to contact the Sentinelese, who are estimated to number anywhere between fifty and two hundred and fifty. Flying in or out of Port Blair, you pass above their island, ringed by a spectacular coral reef, and it is reassuring to think that the people sitting at the bottom of the plumes of smoke drifting from the forest canopy have for so long resisted contact with the outside world.

forced to abandon their plans in the face of hideous diseases and a severe lack of food and water. Though the missionaries themselves seldom met with any hostility, several fleets of trading ships that tried to dock on the islands were captured, and their crews murdered, by Nicobari people.

In 1777 the British Lieutenant Blair chose the South Andaman harbour now known as **Port Blair** as the site for a **penal colony**, based on the deportation of criminals that had proved successful in Sumatra, Singapore and Penang.

Both this scheme, and an attempt to settle the Nicobar Islands in 1867, were thwarted by the harsh climatic conditions of the forests. However, the third go at colonization was more successful, and in 1858 Port Blair finally did become a penal settlement, where political activists who had fuelled the Mutiny in 1857 were made to clear land and build their own prison. Out of 773 prisoners, 292 died, escaped or were hanged in the first two months. Many also lost their lives in attacks by Andamanese tribes who objected to forest clearance, but the settlement continued to fill with people from mainland India, and by 1864 the number of convicts had grown to 3000. In 1896 work began on a jail made up of hundreds of tiny solitary cells, which was used to confine political prisoners until 1945. The prison still stands and is one of Port Blair's few "tourist attractions".

In 1919, the British government in India decided to close down the penal settlement, but it was subsequently used to incarcerate a new generation of freedom fighters from India, Malabar and Burma. During World War II the islands were occupied by the **Japanese**, who tortured and murdered hundreds of indigenous islanders suspected of collaborating with the British, and bombed the homes of the Jarawa tribe. British forces moved back in 1945, and at last abolished the penal settlement.

After **Partition**, refugees, mostly low-caste Hindus from Bangladesh and Bengal, were given land in Port Blair and North Andaman, where the forest was clear-felled to make room for rice paddy, cocoa plantations and new industries. Since 1951, the population has increased more than ten-fold, further swollen by repatriated Tamils from Sri Lanka, thousands of Bihari labourers, ex-servicemen given land grants, economic migrants from poorer Indian states, and the legions of government employees packed off here on two-year "punishment postings". This replanted population greatly outnumbers the Andamans' indigenous people, who currently comprise around half of one percent of the total. Contact between the two societies is limited, and is not always friendly. In addition, there exists within Port Blair a clear divide between the relatively recent incomers and the so-called "**pre-42s**" – descendants of the released convicts and freedom fighters whose families settled here before the major influx from the mainland. This small but influential minority, based at the exclusive Browning Club in the capital, has been calling for curbs on immigration and new property rules to slow down the rate of settlement. While doubtless motivated by self-interest, their demands nevertheless reflect growing concern for the future of the Andamans, where rapid and largely unplanned development has wreaked havoc on the natural environment, not to mention on the indigenous population.

With the timber-extraction cash cow now partially tethered, the hope is that **tourism** will replace tree felling as the main source of revenue. However, the extra visitor numbers envisaged are certain to overtax an already inadequate infrastructure, aggravating seasonal water shortages and sewage disposal problems. Given India's track record with tourism development, it's hard to be optimistic. Delhi has already given the go-ahead for services from Southeast Asia and eventually charter flights from Europe to land on the recently extended airport runway – indeed the first flights from Bangkok would have touched down in January 2005 had the tsunami not taken place. If only a small percentage of the tourist traffic between Thailand and India is diverted through the Andamans, the impact on this culturally and ecologically fragile region could be catastrophic.

Getting to the Andaman Islands

Port Blair, on South Andaman, is served by Indian Airlines **flights** from Kolkata (Calcutta; 1–2 daily) and daily flights from Chennai on both IA and Jet

Airways. Tickets for the two-hour flights cost $205 one way, unless you qualify for a discount (see p.1098). It's also possible to get to Port Blair by **ship**. Services to and from Chennai can be reasonably relied upon to leave in each direction once a week. Those from Kolkata (departing every two weeks; see p.1098) and Vishakapatnam (once a month; call the Shipping Office on ⓣ0891/256 5597 for more info) are still somewhat erratic. Although far cheaper than flying, the crossings are long (3–5 days), uncomfortable and often delayed by bad conditions. However you get to the islands, thirty day **permits** are obtainable on arrival in Port Blair. Permits are usually extendable for fifteen days but the authorities sometimes only allow you to stay in Port Blair for that period – not an appealing prospect.

South Andaman: Port Blair and around

South Andaman is today the most heavily populated of the Andaman Islands – particularly around the capital, **Port Blair** – thanks in part to the drastic thinning of tree cover to make way for settlement. Foreign tourists can only visit its southern and east central reaches – including the beaches at **Corbyn's Cove** and **Chiriya Tapu**, the fine reefs on the western shores at **Wandoor**, 35km southwest of Port Blair, and the environs of **Madhuban** and **Mount Harriet** on the east coast across the bay from the capital. With your own transport it's easy to find your way along the narrow bumpy roads that connect small villages, weaving through forests and coconut fields, and skirting the swamps and rocky outcrops that form the coastline.

Port Blair

A refreshingly leafy but ultimately characterless cluster of tin-roofed buildings tumbling towards the sea in the north, east and west, and petering into fields and forests in the south, **PORT BLAIR** merits only a short stay. There's little to see here – just the **Cellular Jail** and a few small **museums** – but as the point of arrival for the islands, and the only place with a bank, tourist offices and hotels, it can't be avoided. If you plan to head off to more remote islands, this is also the best place to stock up on supplies and buy necessary equipment.

Arrival and information

Port Blair has two jetties: **boats** from the mainland moor at **Haddo Jetty**, nearly 2km northwest of **Phoenix Jetty**, arrival point for inter-island ferries. The Director of Shipping Services at Phoenix Jetty has the latest information on boats and ferries, but you can also check the shipping news column of the local newspaper, the *Daily Telegrams* (Rs1.50), for details of forthcoming departures. Advice on booking ferry tickets appears in the box on p.1098.

The smart, newly extended **Veer Savarkar airport** terminal is 4km south of town at Lamba Line. **Taxis** and **auto-rickshaws** are on hand for short trips into town (Rs40–50), but if you have booked a room in any of the middle- or upper-range hotels or do so at the counter in the airport, you should find a shuttle bus waiting outside. Local **buses** also frequently ply the route to town from the main road about 300m from the terminal building.

The counter at the airport (ⓣ03192/232414) hands out a useful general brochure, but trying to get more than basic tour and hotel info from the desk in the lobby of the main **A&N Directorate of Tourism office** (Mon–Fri 10am–5pm, Sat 10am–1pm; ⓣ03192/232747 ⓦwww.andaman.nic.in),

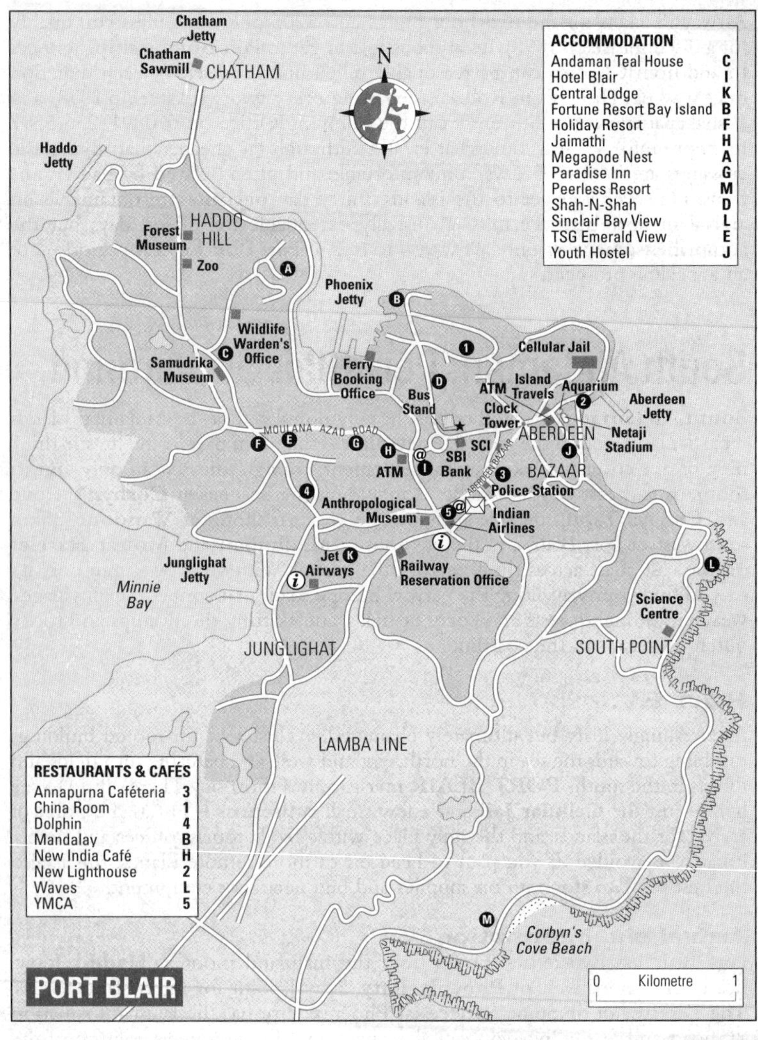

situated in a modern building diagonally opposite Indian Airlines on the southern edge of the town, can be frustrating – try to talk to someone in the hierarchy upstairs. Further southwest on Junglighat Main Road, the **India Tourism office** (Mon–Fri 8.30am–5pm; ⓣ03192/233006) is not much better. Note that if you intend to visit Interview Island (see p.1107), you must first attain a free permit from the **Chief Wildlife Warden**, whose office (ⓣ03192/233270) is next to the zoo in Haddo.

Road names are not used much in Port Blair, with most establishments addressing themselves simply by their local area. The name of the busiest and most central area is **Aberdeen Bazaar**, where you'll find the superintendent of police (for permit extensions), the SCI office for onward bookings by sea

(☎03192/233590) and the State Bank of India (Mon–Fri 9am–1pm, Sat 9–11am). Some hotels will change travellers' cheques, but you'll get faster service and better rates at Island Travels (☎03192/233034; Mon–Sat 9am–6pm), which has a licence to change money, and is just up the road from the clocktower in Aberdeen Bazaar. There's an ICICI Bank **ATM** at the lower end of Moulana Azad Road and UTI Bank one near Netaji Stadium. You can use the Internet at Cyber Point on Moulana Azad Road, Samsuras next to the post office or at the *Holiday Resort* (see p.1096; all Rs30/hr).

Local transport and tours

Walking is tiring and time-consuming in hilly Port Blair – even taking into account the minimal amount of sightseeing the place offers – making transport essential. Yellow-top **taxis** gather opposite the bus stand. They all have meters, but negotiating the price before leaving is the usual practice. Expect to pay Rs50 for a trip from the centre of town to Corbyn's Cove. In 1999 the islands received their first fleet of **auto-rickshaws**, but they tend to charge just as much as taxis.

Local **buses** run infrequently from the bus stand in central Port Blair to Wandoor and Chiriya Tapu, and can be used for day-trips, though it's best to rely on your own transport to get around South Andaman. **Bicycles** can be rented from Aberdeen Bazaar, at Rs5 per hour, but the roads to the coasts are most easily covered on a **motorbike** or **scooter**, both available for rent at TSG Travels (☎03192/232894) or GDM Tours (☎03192/232999) on Moulana Azad Road, behind Phoenix Bay. They require a licence and Rs500 deposit, while the charge itself is only Rs120–150 per day. The petrol pump is on the crossroads west of the bus stand, and there's another on the road towards the airport. Fill up before you leave town, as petrol is hard to come by elsewhere.

Most of the ANIIDCO **tours** – cramming the island's few interesting sights together with a string of dull destinations – are a complete waste of time; you're better off renting a scooter or taxi and taking in the jail and museums at your own pace. However, more worthwhile are their **harbour cruises** (daily 3–5pm; Rs65) that depart from Phoenix Jetty for fleeting visits to the floating docks and **Viper Island**, and excursions to **Ross Island** (see p.1100).

Accommodation

Port Blair boasts a fair selection of places to stay. Concentrated mainly in the centre of town, the bottom-range **accommodation** can be as dour as any port town on the mainland. More comfortable hotels occupy correspondingly more salubrious locations on the outskirts. The abundance of options means there is rarely an availability issue.

Andaman Teal House Delanipur ☎03192/234060. High on the hill above Haddo Jetty, this Directorate of Tourism place offers great views, spacious and pleasant rooms, and is very good value, although can be inconvenient without your own transport. ❸–❺

Hotel Blair HSKP Complex, 5 minutes' walk from the bus stand ☎03192/238109, Ⓔhotelblair@yahoo.com. Rather over-priced modern hotel with large clean rooms in a fairly quiet and central location. Airy rooftop restaurant. ❹–❼

Central Lodge Middle Point ☎03192/233634. Ramshackle wooden building situated in a quiet and secluded corner of town. A rock-bottom option, offering basic rooms, garden space for hammocks and a dorm (Rs60). ❶

Fortune Resort Bay Island Marine Hill ☎03192/234101, Ⓦwww.fortuneparkhotels.com. Port Blair's swishest hotel: elegant and airy with polished dark wood. All rooms have carpets and balconies overlooking Phoenix Jetty (the less expensive ones are a little cramped). There's a quality restaurant, gardens and an open-air sea-water swimming pool. The steep tariff from $134 per double includes full board. ❾

Holiday Resort Premnagar, a fifteen-minute walk from the centre ⓣ03192/230516, ⓔholidayresort88@hotmail.com. Much better value than most budget places that cost little less; all the rooms are clean and spacious, with TV. There's also a bar and computer room. ❸

Hotel Jaimathi Moulana Azad Rd ⓣ03192/230836. Popular lodge with both Westerners and Indians, offering large fairly clean rooms with communal balconies. Slightly cheaper than the *Jagannath* next door and more likely to have availability. ❷

Megapode Nest Haddo Hill ⓣ03192/232380, ⓦwww.aniidco.nic.in. ANIIDCO's upscale option has 25 comfortable rooms, and pricier self-contained "cottages", ranged around a central lawn, with good views, and a quality restaurant. ❻–❼

Paradise Inn Moulana Azad Rd ⓣ03192/245772, ⓕ233479. Compact modern lodge, all rooms with TV and phone. Great value and extra off-season discounts. ❸

Peerless Resort Corbyn's Cove ⓣ03192/229263, ⓔpblbeachinn@sancharnet.in. Lovely setting amid gardens of palms, jasmine and bougainvillea, opposite a white sandy beach but the balconied a/c rooms and cottages are a bit tatty for a starting price of Rs3650. Bar and mid-priced restaurant with an average evening buffet. ❾

Shah-N-Shah Mohanpura ⓣ03192/233696. Set between the bus stand and Phoenix Jetty, this is basic but friendly and comfortable, with en-suite rooms and a sociable terrace and restaurant. ❸

Sinclair Bayview On the coast road to Corbyn's Cove ⓣ03192/227824, ⓔpblsinbview@sancharnet.in. Clifftop hotel offering spotless carpeted rooms (from Rs3240) with balconies, en-suite bathrooms, dramatic views, bar and restaurant and airport shuttle bus. ❾

TSG Emerald View 25 Moulana Azad Rd ⓣ03192/246488. Smart new upper mid-range place with spacious, colourfully furnished rooms, some a/c, boasting all mod cons. ❸–❻

Youth Hostel Opposite Netaji Stadium ⓣ03192/232459. Run down and predictably institutional, but dorm beds are only Rs50 and there are two doubles. Often full of students or itinerant workers. ❶

The Town

Port Blair's only firm reminder of its gloomy past, the sturdy brick **Cellular Jail** (Tues–Sun 9am–noon & 2–5pm; Rs5), overlooks the sea from a small rise in the northeast of town. Built between 1896 and 1905, its tiny solitary cells were quite different and far worse than the dormitories in other prison blocks erected earlier. Only three of the seven wings that originally radiated from the central tower now remain. Visitors can peer into the cells (3m by 3.5m), and imagine the grim conditions under which the prisoners existed. Cells were dirty and ill-ventilated, drinking water was limited to two glasses per day, and the convicts were expected to wash in the rain as they worked clearing forests and building prison quarters. Food, brought from the mainland, was stored in vats where the rice and pulses became infested with worms; more than half the prison population died long before their twenty years' detention was up. Protests against conditions led to hunger strikes in 1932, 1933 and 1937, resulting in yet more deaths, and frequent executions took place at the gallows that still stand in squat wooden shelters in the courtyards, in full view of the cells. The **Sound and Light Show** (daily in English 7.15pm; in Hindi 6pm; not during the rainy season of May–Sept & Nov; Rs20) outlines the history of the prison, and a small **museum** by the entrance gate (same hours as the jail) exhibits lists of convicts, photographs and grim torture devices.

South of the jail near the Water Sports Complex, you can see tanks full of fish and coral from the islands' reefs at the **Aquarium** (daily 9am–1pm & 2–4.45pm; Rs5). Three kilometres out along the coast road towards Corbyn's Cove, Port Blair's newest attraction is the **Science Centre** (Mon–Sat 9am–5.30pm; free), which displays an array of equipment and has some interactive displays on various scientific subjects. There is also a **planetarium** within the complex, which conducts shows on demand (Rs5).

On the south side of town, close to the Directorate of Tourism, exhibits in the **Anthropological Museum** (Mon–Sat 9am–noon & 1–4pm; Rs50 [Rs10]), devoted to the Andaman and Nicobar tribes, include weapons, tools and also rare photographs of the region's indigenous people taken in the 1960s. Among the most striking of these is a sequence featuring the Sentinelese, taken on April 26, 1967, when a party of Indian officials made the first contact with the tribe. After scaring the aborigines, the visitors marched into one of their hunting camps and made off with the bows, arrows and other artefacts now displayed in the museum. The anthropologist charged with documenting the expedition noted afterwards that "the whole atmosphere was that of conquering hordes over-running conquered territory".

Further northwest in Delanipur opposite ANIIDCO's *Teal House* hotel, the **Samudrika Naval Maritime Museum** (Tues–Sun 8.30am–noon & 2–5pm; Rs10) is an excellent primer if you're heading off to more remote islands, with a superlative shell collection and informative displays on various aspects of local marine biology. One of the exhibits features a cross-section of the different corals you can expect to see on the Andamans' reefs, followed by a rundown of the various threats these fragile organisms face, from mangrove depletion and parasitic starfish to clumsy snorkellers.

Wildlife lovers are advised to steer clear of the grim little **zoo** (Tues–Sun 8am–5pm; Rs2), further down towards Haddo, whose only redeeming feature is that it has successfully bred rare crocodiles and monkeys for release into the wild. The adjoining **Forest Museum** (Mon–Sat 8am–noon & 2–5pm; free) is an equally dismal spectacle, feebly attempting to justify the Indian Forest Service's wholesale destruction of the Andamans' forests with a series of lacklustre photographs of extraction methods. However, if you really want to confront the grim reality of the local timber industry, press on north to **Chatham Sawmill** (Mon–Sat 7am–2.30pm; Rs2), at the end of the peninsula marking the northernmost edge of Port Blair. One of the oldest and largest wood-processing plants in Asia, it seasons and mills rare hardwoods taken from various islands – a sad testimony to the continued abuse of international guidelines on tropical timber production. Photography is prohibited.

Eating

Between them, Port Blair's **restaurants** offer dishes from north and South India, Burmese specialities and a wide variety of seafood. For rock-bottom budget travellers, there are roadside stalls selling plates of grilled fish at Rs15–20, in addition to the usual crop of cheap but run-of-the-mill "meals" cafés in the main bazaar: of these, the *Majestic*, *Gagan* and *Milan* on Aberdeen Bazaar are the best, but you should steer clear of the *Dhanalakshmi* hotel's notoriously dreadful canteen. **Alcohol** is increasingly easy to come by, either in the upscale hotels or a smattering of less salubrious bars such as the one underneath the *Jaimathi* hotel (see opposite).

Annapurna Cafeteria Aberdeen Bazaar, towards the post office. Far and away Port Blair's best South Indian joint, serving the usual range of huge crispy *dosas*, plus north Indian and Chinese meals, delicious coffee, and wonderful *pongal* at breakfast. The lunchtime thalis are also great. Closed Sundays.

China Room On the hill above the Phoenix Jetty ⓣ03192/230759. The most tourist-oriented restaurant in town, run by a Burmese-Punjabi couple whose roots are vividly reflected in the chilli-and-ginger-rich cuisine, which is also Chinese-influenced. Particularly recommended for seafood, which comes in a range of tasty sauces. There's a roomy courtyard, but reserve a table inside if it's rainy.

Dolphin Marthoma Church Complex, Golghar. Pleasantly decorated restaurant with cane chairs and blinds, serving carefully prepared Indian and Chinese dishes, as well as some Continental options and a few house specialities involving chicken and seafood.

Mandalay *Fortune Resort*, Marine Hill. A la carte dishes or a reasonable Rs350 dinner buffet can be

enjoyed in the airy open restaurant with great bay views. Service can be a bit lax for its class. The adjacent *Nico Bar* is fine for a drink.

New India Cafe Moulana Azad Rd. In the basement of *Jaimathi* lodge, this cheap restaurant is popular with Westerners and Indians alike. There's a wide menu of veg and meat dishes but expect to wait if you order anything that's not already prepared.

New Lighthouse Near Aberdeen Jetty. Popular place with outdoor seating, where you can catch the sea breeze while feasting on some of the cheapest lobster and other seafood in India.

Waves *Peerless Resort*, Corbyn's Cove. Slightly pricey but very congenial alfresco hotel restaurant under a shady palm grove, and one of the few places in town you can order a beer with your meal. Most dishes Rs100–150.

YMCA Near the Post Office. North and South Indian standards served on a pleasant covered terrace; the pure veg thalis are especially good.

Around Port Blair

At some point, you're almost certain to find yourself killing time in Port Blair, waiting for boats to show up or tickets to go on sale. Rather than wasting days in town, it's worth exploring the **coast** of South Andaman which, although far more densely populated than other islands in the archipelago, holds a handful of easily accessible beauty spots and historic sites. Among the latter, the ruined colonial monuments on **Viper** and **Ross islands** can be reached on daily harbour cruises or regular ferries from the capital. For **beaches**, head southeast

Moving on from Port Blair

Port Blair is the departure point for all flights and ferry crossings to the **Indian mainland**; it is also the hub of the Andamans' inter-island bus and ferry network. Unfortunately, booking tickets (especially back to Chennai, Kolkata or Vishakapatnam) can be time-consuming, and many travellers are obliged to come back here well before their permit expires to make reservations, before heading off to more pleasant parts again.

To the mainland

If you've travelled to the Andamans **by ship**, you'll know what a rough ride the three-day or more crossing can be in bunk class, and how difficult tickets are to come by. It's also a good idea to talk to fellow travellers about current conditions, which vary from year to year and vessel to vessel. The one factor you can be sure about is that the ship offers the cheapest route back, at around Rs1500. The downside is that schedules can be erratic, and accurate information about them difficult to obtain – annoying when you only have a one-month permit. For **Chennai**, whose weekly service run by the DSS is the most reliable, you'll have to head down to the ticket office at Phoenix Jetty. Basically, the only sure way of finding out when the next ship is leaving and securing a ticket to **Kolkata** and **Vishakapatnam** is to join the "queue" outside the SCI office (☎03192/233590), opposite the *Dhanalakshmi* hotel in Aberdeen Bazaar. Tickets are supposed to go on sale a week in advance of departure, but don't bank on it. Bear in mind, too, if you're reading this a couple of days' journey away from the capital, and with only a week or less left on your permit, that the local police can get heavy with foreigners who outstay their allotted time.

Returning to the mainland by **plane** in just two hours instead of seventy-two can save lots of time and hassle, but at $205 one-way ($157 student or under 30), air tickets to **Chennai** and **Kolkata** are far from cheap. With Jet Airways and Indian Airlines now both running daily flights, tickets to Chennai are usually easy to obtain at short notice apart from peak times like Diwali or Christmas. The situation has also eased in the case of Kolkata, as IA operates daily flights and an extra one on four days per week. The IA office (☎03192/234744) is diagonally opposite the ANIIDCO to **Corbyn's Cove**, or cross South Andaman to reach the more secluded **Chiriya Tapu**, both of which are easily accessible on day-trips if you rent a moped or taxi. By far the most rewarding way to spend a day out of town, however, is to catch the tourist boat from **Wandoor** to **Jolly Buoy** or **Red Skin islands** in the **Mahatma Gandhi National Marine Park** opposite, which boasts some of the Andamans' best snorkelling. The other area worth visiting is **Mount Harriet** and **Madhuban** on the central part of South Andaman, north across the bay from Port Blair.

Viper and Ross islands

First stop on the harbour cruise from Port Blair (daily 3–5pm; Rs65; see p.1100) is generally **Viper Island** (entry Rs16), named not after the many snakes that doubtless inhabit its tangled tropical undergrowth, but a nineteenth-century merchant vessel that ran aground on it during the early years of the colony. Lying a short way off Haddo Wharf, it served as an isolation zone for the main prison, where escapees and convicts (including hunger strikers) were sent to be punished. Whipping posts and crumbling walls, reached from the jetty via a winding brick path, remain as relics of a torture area, while occupying the site's most prominent position are the original gallows.

office, while Jet Airways (☎03192/236922) is on the first floor at 189 Main Rd, Junglighat, next to the GITO office.

Travellers intending to catch onward **trains** from their port of arrival on the mainland should note that Port Blair has an efficient computerized Southern Railways reservation office near the Secretariat (Mon–Sat 8.30am–1pm & 2–4pm).

Inter-island services

Buses connect Port Blair with most major settlements on South and Middle Andaman, mainly via the Andaman Trunk Road. From the mildly chaotic bus stand at the bottom of town, at least one daily government service, usually at 4.30–5am, runs via Rangat (6hr) and **Mayabunder** (9hr) to **Diglipur** (11hr). There's another daily service to Rangat at 6am. Several private companies including Geetanjali Travels (tickets at *Tillai* teashop by the bus stand) and the cheaper Ananda (☎03192/233252) run deluxe or video coach (ear-plugs essential) services, which leave from the road outside the bus stand also at 5am.

Most of the islands open to foreign tourists, including **Neill, Havelock**, **Middle** and **North Andaman**, are also accessible by **boat** from Phoenix Jetty. Details of forthcoming departures are posted in the shipping news columns of the local newspapers, but the only way to guarantee a passage is to book tickets in advance at the office by the quay between 9am and 11am the day before – this can turn into quite a scrum. Note that there are three separate queues: the left one for Hut Bay, the middle one for Diglipur and the right-hand one for Neill, Havelock, Long and Rangat. Schedules change frequently but you can expect at least one boat daily to Havelock, Neill and Rangat, four weekly to Long, three weekly to Arial Bay and every other day to Hut Bay on Little Andaman. If possible, try to travel on a newer vessel like the *Ramanujam* or *Long Island*. The journeys on older boats can be a lot longer and more uncomfortable than you might expect. From 9am onwards, the heat on board is intense, with only corrugated plastic sheets for shade, while the benches are highly uncomfortable and the toilets generally dismal. You should take adequate supplies of food and water with you; only biscuits and simple snacks are sold on the boats. More details of boat services to destinations outside the capital appear in the relevant accounts, and in "Travel details", p.1111.

No less eerie are the decaying colonial remains on **Ross Island** (entry Rs16), at the entrance to Port Blair harbour, where the British sited their first penal settlement in the Andamans. Originally cleared by convicts wearing iron fetters (most of them sent here in the wake of the 1857 Mutiny, or First War of Independence), Ross witnessed some of the most brutal excesses of British colonial history, and was the source of the prison's infamy as **Kalapani**, or Black Water. Of the many convicts transported here, distinguished by their branded foreheads, the majority perished from disease or torture before the clearance of the island was completed in 1860. Thereafter, it served briefly as the site of Rev. Henry Corbyn's "**Andaman Home**" – a prison camp created with the intention of "civilizing" the local tribespeople – before becoming the headquarters of the revamped penal colony, complete with theatre hall, tennis courts, swimming pool, hospitals and grand residential bungalows. Rather ambitiously dubbed "the Paris of the East", the settlement typified the stiff-upper-lipped spirit of the Raj at its most cruel: while the *burra-* and *memsahibs* dressed for dinner and sang hymns in church, convicts languished in the most appalling conditions only a kilometre away. In the end, the entry of the Japanese into World War II, hot on the heels of a massive earthquake in 1941, forced the British to evacuate, and in the coming years most of the buildings were dismantled by the new overlords, who themselves founded a POW camp here.

Little more than the hilltop Anglican church, with its weed-infested graveyard, has survived the onslaught of tropical creepers and vines, and the island makes a peaceful break from Port Blair. To get here, jump on one of the regular launches from Phoenix Jetty (daily departing 8.30am, 10.30am & 12.30pm and returning 8.45am, 10.45am & 12.40pm; Rs65).

Corbyn's Cove and Chiriya Tapu

The best beach within easy reach of the capital lies 6km southeast at **Corbyn's Cove**, a small arc of smooth white sand backed by a swaying curtain of palms. There's a large hotel here (see p.1096), but the water isn't particularly clear, and bear in mind that lying around scantily clothed may bring you considerable attention from crowds of local workers.

For more isolation, rent a moped or take a taxi 30km south to **Chiriya Tapu** ("Bird Island"), at the tip of South Andaman. The motorable track running beyond this small fishing village leads through thick jungle overhung with twisting creepers to a large bay, where swamps give way to shell-strewn beaches. Other than at lunchtime, when it often receives a deluge of bus parties, the beach offers plenty of peace and quiet, forest walks on the woodcutters' trails winding inland from it, and easy access to an inshore reef. However, the water here is nowhere near as clear as at some spots in the archipelago, and serious snorkellers and divers should enquire if any boats are going out from the big hotels to volcanic **Cinque Island** (see p.1110), a couple of hours' further south. It is also possible to charter your own fishing boat here; ask around the bar in the village, and expect to pay around Rs3000 per boat for the return trip.

Wandoor and the Mahatma Gandhi National Marine Park

Much the most popular excursion from Port Blair is the boat ride from **Wandoor**, 30km southwest, to one or other of the fifteen islets comprising the **Mahatma Gandhi National Marine Park**. Although set up purely for tourists, the trip is worth considering, as it provides access to one of the richest coral reefs in the region. The downside is that entry into the park for foreigners now costs Rs500 (Indians Rs50). Boats depart at 10am (daily except Mon;

Rs100–150) from Wandoor, which you can reach on A&N Tourism's **tour** (8.30am–4.30pm; Rs104) or by local bus, but it's more fun to rent a moped and ride down to meet the boat yourself.

The long white **beach** at Wandoor is littered with the dry, twisted trunks of trees torn up and flung down by annual cyclones, and fringed not with palms, but by dense forest teeming with birdlife. You should only snorkel here at high tide, as the coral is easily damaged when the waters are shallow. From the jetty, the boats chug through broad creeks lined with dense mangrove swamps and pristine forest to either **Red Skin Island** or, more commonly, **Jolly Buoy**. The latter, an idyllic deserted island, boasts an immaculate shell-sand beach ringed by a bank of superb coral. The catch is that the boat only stops for around an hour, which isn't nearly enough time to explore the shore and reef. While snorkelling off the edges of the reef, however, beware of **strong currents**.

Mount Harriet and Madhuban

The richly forested slopes of **Mount Harriet** make for decent exercise and can easily be done as a day-trip from Port Blair. You can take one of the passenger ferries (every 30min–1hr) from Chatham Jetty to **Bamboo Flats** or, if you want to have your own transport on the other side, there are eight daily vehicle ferries from Phoenix Bay between 5.30am and 8.30pm. From Bamboo Flats it's a pleasant seven-kilometre stroll east along the coast and north up a path through trees hung with thick vines and creepers to the 365-metre summit, which affords fine views back across the bay. An intermittent bus service runs between Bamboo Flats and Hope Town, where the path starts, and saves you 3km. Alternatively, Jeeps and taxis are available to take you all the way to the top, but they charge at least Rs300. There's a charge of Rs250 (Indians Rs25; students/teachers Rs5) to enter Mount Harriet National Park, but the checkpost is on the road so you probably won't be asked if you take the path. It's 2.5km from the checkpost up to the rest house and viewing tower at the summit. If you have strong legs you can reach **Madhuban** on the coast north-east of the mountain by the sixteen-kilometre round route via Kala Patthar (Black Rock) and back via the coast. There is a decent beach at Madhuban and the area is still used for training logging **elephants**, so you stand a good chance of seeing them learning their trade.

Islands north of Port Blair

Printed on the permit card you receive on arrival in the Andamans is a list of all the other **islands** you're allowed to visit in the archipelago. The majority of them are north of Port Blair. Given the great distances involved, not to mention the sometimes erratic connections between them (and the time limit imposed by the one-month permit), it definitely pays to know where to head for as soon as you arrive rather than drift off on the first promising ferry out of Phoenix Jetty. The best way of doing this is to talk to fellow travellers arriving back in the capital. The following accounts will give you a good idea of what to expect upcountry, but new islands are opened up to tourists (and occasionally one goes off-limits again) each year and these may well offer the kind of wilderness experience you're here for.

Having travelled all the way to the Andamans, it is surprising how many visitors make a beeline for the only two developed islands in the group, **Neill** and **Havelock**, both within easy reach of Port Blair. To get further north, where

Scuba diving in the Andaman Islands

The seas around the Andaman and Nicobar islands are some of the world's most unspoiled. Marine life is abundant, with an estimated 750 species of fish existing on one reef alone. Parrot, trigger and angel fish live alongside manta rays, reef sharks and loggerhead turtles. Many species of fish and coral are unique to the area and fascinating life-systems exist in ash beds and cooled lava based around the volcanic Barren Island. For a quick taste of marine life, you could start by **snorkelling**; most hotels can supply masks and snorkels, though some equipment is in dire need of replacement. The only way to get really close, however, and venture out into deeper waters, is to **scuba dive**. The experience of weaving in and out of coral beds, coming eye to eye with fish or swimming with dolphins and barracudas is unforgettable.

Dive operations have come and gone more frequently than the rains in recent years and the picture is constantly changing. At the time of writing the only fully operational and certified schools were the following two on Havelock, but it's always worth checking if any have opened up in Port Blair or elsewhere. Based at the *MS Lodge* near the jetty, the British/Indian **Andaman Dive Club** (ⓣ03192/282002 or UK 020/7538 4643, ⓦwww.andamandiveclub.com) has a smart boat, brand new equipment and offers two-dive trips (including food) for $80 as well as PADI open water courses for $340 or BSAC ocean diver certification for $400; more advanced courses are also available. Further down the coast at *Wild Orchid* hotel on beach #5, **Dive India** (ⓣ03192/282472, ⓦwww.diveindia.com) is run by friendly divemasters from the Karen community around Mayabunder; single dives cost Rs2000, while a PADI course will set you back Rs15,500. The *Jungle Resort* over on Radhnagar beach has also invested in scuba equipment and was just about to bring groups from Thailand when the tsunami put things on hold. Permit difficulties made the affable Swiss duo of the Andaman Scuba Club suspend Havelock operations some time back, but you can check ⓦwww.andamanscubaclub.com to see if they are up and running again.

Underwater in the Andamans, it is not uncommon to come across schools of reef sharks, which rarely turn hostile, but one thing to watch out for and avoid is the **black-and-white sea snake**. Though the snakes seldom attack – and, since their fangs are at the back of their mouths, would find it difficult to get a grip on any human – their bite is twenty times more deadly than that of the cobra.

Increased tourism inevitably puts pressure on the delicate marine ecosystem, and poorly funded wildlife organizations can do little to prevent damage from insensitive visitors. You can ensure your presence in the sea around the reefs does not harm the coral by observing the following **Green Coral Code** while diving or snorkelling:

- Never touch, or walk on, living coral or it will die.
- Try to keep your feet away from reefs while wearing fins; the sudden sweep of water caused by a flipper kick can be enough to destroy coral.
- Always control the speed of your descent while diving; enormous damage can be caused by divers' landing hard on a coral bed.
- Never break off pieces of coral from a reef, and remember that it is illegal to export dead coral from the islands, even fragments you may have found on a beach.

tourism of any kind has thus far had very little impact, you can take a bus or ferry from Havelock to ramshackle **Rangat**, at the south end of **Middle Andaman**, or bypass the whole east coast by catching a bus or boat from Port Blair direct to **Diglipur**'s port of Arial Bay, at the top of **North Andaman**. Either way, you'll be lucky not to be marooned from time to time in some truly ugly little settlements, interspersed with a few long hard slogs up the infamous **Andaman Trunk Road** (or "ATR"). On Middle and North Andaman, and their satellite islands, **accommodation** is scarce, to say the least. Aside from a handful of ANIIDCO hotels (bookable in advance in Port Blair), the only places to stay are a few basic and occasionally grim lodges or the preferable APWD *Rest Houses* (see box p.1106).

To escape the settled areas you have to be prepared to rough it, travelling on in-shore fishing dugouts, sleeping on beaches and cooking your own food. The rewards, however, are great. Backed by dense forest filled with colourful birds and insects, the beaches, bays and reefs of the outer Andamans teem with wildlife, from gargantuan crabs, pythons and turtles, to dolphins, sharks, giant rays and the occasional primeval-looking dugong. Essential **kit** for off-track wanderings includes a sturdy mosquito net, mats to sleep on (or a hammock), a large plastic container for water, some strong antiseptic for cuts and bites (sandflies are a real problem on many of the beaches) and, most importantly, **water purification** tablets or a water purifier – bottled water is virtually nonexistent. Wherever you end up, preserve the goodwill of local people by packing your rubbish out or burning it, and being sensitive to scruples about dress and nudity.

Neill

Tiny, triangular-shaped **Neill** is the most southerly inhabited island of **Ritchie's Archipelago**, barely two hours northeast of Port Blair on a fast ferry. The source of much of the capital's fresh fruit and vegetables, its fertile centre, ringed by a curtain of stately tropical trees, comprises vivid patches of green paddy dotted with small farmsteads and banana plantations. The beaches are mediocre by the Andamans' standards, but worth a day or two en route to or from Havelock. **Boats** leave Port Blair daily for Neill, all services connecting with Havelock and some with Rangat.

Neill boasts three **beaches**, all of them within easy cycling distance of the small bazaar just up the lane from the jetty (you can rent **cycles** from one of several stallholders for Rs20–30 per day). The best place to swim is **Neill Kendra**, a gently curving bay of white sand, which straddles the jetty and is scattered with picturesque wooden fishing boats. This blends into **Lakshmangar**, which continues for 3km north: to get there by road, head right at the ANIIDCO hotel (see below) and follow the road for around twenty minutes until it dwindles into a surfaced track, then turn right. Wrapped around the headland, the beach is a broad spur of white shell sand, with shallow water offering good snorkelling but that makes entry into the water tough at any time other than high tide. Exposed to the open sea and thus prone to higher tides, **Sitapur** beach, 6km south at the tip of the island, is also appealing and has the advantage of a sandy bottom extending into the sea. The ride there (by hourly bus or bicycle) across Neill's central paddy land is pleasant, but there are no facilities when you get there so stock up for the day.

The island has four **accommodation** options. From the jetty, a two-minute walk brings you to the ANIIDCO *Hawabill Nest* (Ⓣ03192/282630; ⑤), a dozen or so clean, carpeted rooms with sitouts, ranged around a central courtyard and restaurant; it's best booked in advance from Port Blair. The three private options are all at Lakshmangar or en route to it: the best of the bunch is *Tango Beach Resort* (Ⓣ03192/282634, Ⓔtangobeachresort@rediffmail.com; ①–③), a friendly place right on the beach, with two deluxe and ten much more basic bamboo huts. Before *Tango*, little over 500m from the jetty, you pass *Cocon Huts* (Ⓣ03192/282528, Ⓔcoconhuts@yahoo.com; ①–③), which has a similar range of huts, although the bar can attract rowdy revellers from the village. The furthest option, 1km north of *Tango*, is *Pearl Park Hotel* (Ⓣ03192/282510; ①–⑥), which has some small huts and posher but hugely overpriced a/c bungalows.

Although many people stick to the **restaurants** at the private establishments, far and away the best place to eat is the delightful and welcoming *Gyan Garden*, 500m along the road to Lakshmangar opposite the football pitch, where fresh fish and home-grown veg dishes are a speciality. Of the few tiny eateries in the bazaar, *Hotel Chand* serves up the tastiest, albeit somewhat oily, food.

Havelock

Havelock is the largest island in Ritchie's Archipelago, and the most intensively cultivated, settled like many in the region by Bengali refugees after Partition. Thanks to its regular ferry connection (1–2 daily; 2hr–4hr 30min) with the capital, it is also visited in greater numbers than anywhere else in the Andamans. In recent peak seasons, well over three hundred tourists could be holed up here, making Havelock's much-photographed Radhnagar beach – often touted as the most beautiful in India – feel overwhelmed. The tsunami just about stemmed the flow of visitors, however, and it may take two or three years for numbers to recover: bad for locals but a bonus for travellers. The boat journey here from Neill, skirting a string of uninhabited islets with shadowy views of South Andaman to the west, is wonderful, and wildlife – both on land and in the sea – remains abundant despite intensive settlement and deforestation.

Havelock's main **jetty** is on the north side of the island, at the village known as **Havelock #1**. There are three small **lodges** as you turn right from the jetty, on the mangrove-lined outskirts of the village. Best of these is the seafront *M.S. Guest House* (ⓣ03192/282439; ❸), but just about everyone heads for a more picturesque place to stay. You'll also find a handful of basic **restaurants** and **stalls** dotted around the settlement. Otherwise, rent a **moped** (Rs150 per day) or **cycle** (Rs50 per day) for a few days and head straight inland to the bazaar, 2km to the south. Here there are more stalls and shops, plus the island's only place to change money, the State Co-operative Bank (Mon–Fri 9am–1pm, Sat 9–11am). Further accommodation listed below is available at beaches #2 to #5 – really one long unbroken strand, which you get to by turning left at the main junction, or at Radhnagar (aka #7 beach), 12km southwest, reached by turning right. An intermittent bus service also covers the east coast between beaches #3 and #5, but you could find yourself waiting all day for it and missing out on a room; buses to Radhnagar are more reliable (5 daily).

The first proper place to stay on the **east coast** is *Eco Villa* (ⓣ03192/282072; ❶) at beach #2, whose ten huts are only average value but the restaurant serves tasty meals. On the other side of the bazaar at #3 is the relaxed *Café del Mar* (ⓣ03192/282343; ❶–❻), followed by the wonderful *Pristine Beach Resort* (ⓣ03192/282344; ❶–❸) – both offer a friendly atmosphere and have the advantage of lockable huts as well as some sturdier bungalows. Next up are half a dozen places backing onto #5: the best of these, in order of appearance, are *Sunrise* (ⓣ03192/282408; ❶), with basic huts set in a picturesque palm grove; *Wild Orchid* (ⓣ03192/282472, ⓦwww.wildorchidandaman.com; ❼), by far the plushest resort on this side of the island, with superbly furnished rooms, landscaped gardens and a great split-level multicuisine restaurant-bar. The operators have also opened the more budget-orientated *Emerald Gate* (same contacts; ❺), a few hundred metres down the road beyond the adequate but institutional ANIIDCO *Dolphin Resort* (ⓣ03192/282411; ❸–❼); and *Coconut Grove* (ⓣ03192/282427; ❶–❷), another sociable hangout with sturdy huts of varying sizes. Beyond these the road carries on for about 3km before petering out behind disappointing beach #6.

Heading past a string of thatched villages hemmed in by banana groves and paddy fields, the road towards **Radhnagar** drops through some spectacular woodland to a kilometre-long arc of perfect white sand, backed by stands of giant *mowhar* trees. The water is a sublime turquoise colour and, although the coral is sparse, marine life here is diverse and plentiful, especially among the rocks around the corner from the main beach (to get there on foot, back-track along the road and follow the path through the woods and over the bluff). The main drawback, which can make sunbathing uncomfortable, is a preponderance of pesky sandflies. Radhnagar has few **places to stay**: behind the beach are ANIIDCO's *Tent Camp* (no phone; ❶–❸), rows of canvas tents of varying size and comfort and a toilet block; and the upmarket *Jungle Resort* (Ⓣ03192/237656, Ⓦwww.barefootindia.com; ❶–❷), recently taken over by a large conglomerate who have revamped the luxurious wood-and-thatch cottages and have plans to bring in tour groups from Thailand and elsewhere. A kilometre inland, the *Harmony Resort* (Ⓣ03192/282421; ❸) is the only real budget-hut venture on this side of the island, but it's overpriced nonetheless. The *Jungle Resort* has a good **restaurant** or you can try the treehouse-like *Golden Sands*, next to *Tent Camp* – both serve a standard mixture of Indian, Chinese and Continental dishes. A string of basic food shacks lines the road down to the beach, of which *Arati* is the best. As the nesting site for a colony of Olive Ridley **turtles**, Radhnagar is strictly protected by the Forest Department, whose wardens ensure tourists do not light fires or sleep on the beach. Elephant "jolly rides" are available for Rs20 per person from a podium en route to the beach. Five buses daily (7.30am–5.30pm) run between Radhnagar and the jetty.

Long Island

Just off the southeast coast of Middle Andaman, **Long Island** is dominated by an unsightly plywood mill, but don't let this put you off. Served by only four boats per week from the capital and Rangat, plus two daily launches from Yeratta (7am & 2pm), it sees far fewer visitors than either Neill or Havelock, but boasts a couple of excellent beaches, at **Marg Bay** and **Lalaji Bay**. Both are most easily reached by chartering a fisherman's dinghy from the jetty (around Rs500), as they are a good couple of hours' hike from where the boat docks. The main settlement by the jetty has the island's only facilities, including a couple of tatty lodges – try *Kaniappa* (Ⓣ03192/278529; ❶). Most foreigners head for the beaches with tents, hammocks and supplies; mercifully, plans to develop the beaches into an upscale resort have been shelved, meaning the Robinson Crusoe experience remains viable.

Middle Andaman

For most travellers, **Middle Andaman** is a charmless rite of passage to be endured en route to or from the north. The sinuous Andaman Trunk Road, hemmed in by walls of towering forest, winds through miles of jungle, crossing the strait that separates the island from its neighbour, Baratang Island, by means of rusting flat-bottomed ferry. The island's frontier feeling is heightened by the presence on the buses of armed guards, and the knowledge that the impenetrable forests west of the ATR comprise the **Jarawa Tribal Reserve** (see p.1090). Of its two main settlements, the more northerly **Mayabunder**, the port for alluring **Interview Island**, is slightly more appealing than characterless inland

APWD Rest Houses

Though they are officially set aside for government officials and engineers, travellers are often allowed to stay at the **APWD Rest Houses**, which often constitute the best and sometimes the only accommodation in Middle and North Andaman. To stay in these it is best to get a letter of recommendation from the APWD office (ⓣ03192/232294), just up the road from *Hotel Blair* in Port Blair, but you have to give specific dates. Just turning up is not guaranteed to meet with success even if rooms are free, but you will stand a much better chance of getting in if you can provide staff with photocopies of your permit, Indian visa and personal details pages from your passport. Details on individual locations are given through out the text, but all *Rest Houses* have standardized prices despite varying standards of comfort: the rooms are doubles but charges are per bed (Rs200 for non-a/c, Rs400 for a/c), so you are not penalized for travelling solo.

Rangat because of its pleasant setting by the sea, but neither town gives any reason to dally for long.

Rangat and around

At the southeast corner of Middle Andaman, **RANGAT** consists of a ramshackle sprawl around two rows of insanitary chai shops and general stores divided by the ATR, which in the monsoon degenerates into a fly-infested mud slick, churned at regular intervals by overladen buses. However, as a major staging post on the journey north, it's impossible to avoid – just don't get stranded here if you can help it.

Ferries to and from Port Blair (9hr) dock at Rangat Bay (aka Nimbutala), 8km east; some stop at Havelock Island (4 weekly) and Long Island (3 weekly), and there are also two daily launches to Long Island from nearby **Yeratta**. In addition, Rangat is served by two daily government buses to Port Blair (6–7hr) as well as some private services, which pass through in the morning en route from further north. The APWD *Rest House* (ⓣ03192/274237; ❸–❺), pleasantly situated up a winding hill from the bazaar with views across the valley, is the best place to stay and eat, providing good filling fish thalis. The newish *RG Lodge* (ⓣ03192/274237; ❷–❸), just off the main road, is a decent fallback. The town's best restaurant is the *Hotel Vijay*, whose amiable proprietor serves up copious thalis and, if the boat is in, crab curry.

If you do get stuck here, rather than staying put in Rangat jump on a bus heading north, or find a Jeep to take you to **Amakunj beach**, aka Cuthbert Bay, 9km along the road to Mayabunder. On the right of the road just beyond the helipad, a Forest Department signboard saying "Sand Collection Point" marks the start of a track running the remaining 500m to the sea. The beach has little shade to speak of, but the snorkelling is good and, best of all, there's the very comfortable ANIIDCO *Hawksbill Nest* (ⓣ03192/279022; ❸–❺) **hotel** on the main road, which is invariably empty.

Mayabunder

Only 70km further north by road, perched on a long promontory right at the top of the island and surrounded by mangrove swamps, **MAYABUNDER** is the springboard for the remote northern Andaman Islands. Unfortunately the bus journey from Rangat often exceeds three hours due to continual stops on the surprisingly populated route. Home to a large minority of former Burmese

Karen tribal people who were originally brought here as cheap logging labour by the British, the village is more spread out and more appealing than Rangat, but again there is little to hold your interest for long. At the brow of the hill, before it descends to the jetty, a small hexagonal wooden structure houses the **Forest Museum/Interpretation Centre** (Mon–Sat 8am–noon & 1–4pm; free), which holds a motley collection of turtle shells, snakes in formaldehyde, dead coral, a crocodile skull and precious little information. Next door, the APWD *Rest House* (Ⓣ03192/273211; ❸–❺) is large and very comfortable, with a pleasant garden and gazebo overlooking the sea, and a dining room serving good set meals. The only other reasonable **accommodation** nearby is back in the centre of the bazaar at the *Anmol Lodge* (Ⓣ03192/262695; ❷–❸), where some of the attached rooms have TV; and nearby *S&S Lodge* (Ⓣ03192/273449; ❶), which has clean but unattached rooms; the dilapidated and cockroach-infested *Lakshminarayan Lodge* should be avoided at all costs. Further afield at **Karmateng beach**, 14km southeast, there's another ANIIDCO hotel, the *Swiftlet Nest* (Ⓣ03192/273495; ❸–❹) but nothing else. Two buses are supposed to go there daily, failing which there are taxis or auto-rickshaws. Buses from Port Blair now continue over the new bridge to Diglipur on North Andaman at least twice a day. Heading towards the capital, there are a couple of private services, such as Geetanjali Travels, as well as one government bus, all departing very early in the morning.

Interview Island

Mayabunder is the jumping-off place for **Interview Island**, a windswept nature sanctuary off the remote northwest coast of Middle Andaman – if you've come to the Andamans to watch **wildlife**, it should be top of your list. Large and mainly flat, it is completely uninhabited save for a handful of unfortunate forest wardens, coastguards and policemen, posted here to ward off poachers. Foreigners aren't permitted to spend the night on the island and to do a day-trip you must first obtain permission from the Chief Wildlife Warden in Port Blair (see p.1094). The only way to reach Interview is to charter a private fishing dinghy from Mayabunder jetty for around Rs500. Arrange one the day before and leave at first light. Try to get your boatman to pull up onto the **beach** at the southern tip of the island, which has a perennial freshwater pool inside a low cave; legend has it that the well, a nesting site for white-bellied **swifts**, has no bottom. At the forest post, where you have to sign an entry ledger, ask the wardens about the movements of Interview's feral **elephants**, descendants of trained elephants deserted here by a Kolkata-based logging company after its timber operation failed in the 1950s.

North Andaman

Shrouded in dense jungle, **North Andaman** is the least populated of the region's large islands, crossed by a single road linking its scattered Bengali settlements. Although parts have been seriously logged, the total absence of motorable roads into northern and western areas has ensured blanket protection for a vast stretch of convoluted coastline, running from Austin Strait in the southeast to the northern tip, Cape Price. Even if it were physically possible to reach this region, you wouldn't be allowed to, but it's reassuring to know at least one extensive wilderness survives in the Andamans. That said, the completion of the ATR's final section and the opening, in 2002, of the bridge from Middle Andaman may herald the start of a new settlement influx. So far, the main settlement of **Diglipur** and its nearby port of **Arial Bay** have existed in remote seclusion. Meanwhile the opening of the bridge may render the village of **Kalighat**, previously the island's entry point from Middle Andaman, virtually redundant.

Kalighat

Although you can now proceed directly to Diglipur by road across the Austin Bridge, a small ferry still chugs once daily (departs 9.30am; returns 12.30pm) through a narrowing mangrove-lined estuary from Mayabunder to **KALIGHAT**, a more relaxed, if slower, point of entry. A cluttered little bazaar unfolds from the top of the slipway, hemmed in by dense mangrove swamps, and when you arrive you should hope a bus is standing here to take you to Diglipur. If there isn't, head for one of the village's dismal little chai stalls and dig in for a wait, or turn right to see if there's space in the three-roomed APWD *Rest House* (ⓣ03192/273360; ❸–❺) on the hill overlooking the end of the street. The only **food** is at chai stalls in the bazaar.

The one worthwhile place to visit in this area is **Ramnagar**, 10km northeast of town and served by hourly buses, where there's a beautiful sandy beach backed by unspoilt forest where camping is feasible. Try to rent a **cycle** from one of the stalls in Kalighat though, as the beach is 2km outside Ramnagar bazaar, the nearest source of refreshments. In principle, four **buses** per day run north from Kalighat to **Diglipur**; they're crammed full, but the trip takes only 45 minutes.

Diglipur, Arial Bay and around

Known in the British era as Port Cornwallis, **DIGLIPUR**, North Andaman's largest settlement, is another disappointing market where you're only likely to pause long enough to pick up a local bus further north to the coast. On the hill above the main road, the APWD *Rest House* (ⓣ03192/272203; ❸–❺) offers the village's nicest **accommodation**, although the *Maa Yashoda Lodge* on the main street (ⓣ03192/272258; ❶) is a cheaper alternative. If you are peckish, reasonable veg and non-veg fare can be found at the central *Ganga Devi* **restaurant**, while *Ice Cube*, on the road north, serves Chinese and tandoori cuisine. Preferably, head 9km on to **ARIAL BAY**, where a smaller APWD *Rest House* (ⓣ03192/271230; ❸–❺) stands on a hillock overlooking the settlement's tiny bazaar. The best place to while away time with a snack or beer while waiting for a boat is the *Annu* general store. From Arial Bay, the **boat** that has made its way up from the capital returns direct to Port Blair overnight (3 weekly; 13–14hr).

Better still, continue another 9km to **Kalipur**, served by several daily buses, where the ANIIDCO *Turtle Resort* (ⓣ03192/272553; ❸–❹), occupies a perfect spot on a hilltop with superb views inland and to sea. It's an unfeasibly large hotel for such a remote location, with spacious, clean rooms with fans and a restaurant (residents only). Competition has recently sprung up in the shape of the bamboo huts of the *Pristine Beach Resort* (ⓣ03192/27220603; ❶–❸), on the opposite side of the road below. Only five minutes' walk from the *Turtle* down the path by the sharp bend in the road there's an excellent deserted beach, backed by lush forest and covered in photogenic driftwood. Swimming is best at high tide because the water recedes across rocky mudpools.

△ Kalipur

Locals claim it's possible to walk from Kalipur to **Saddle Peak**, at 737m the highest mountain in the Andamans, which rises dramatically to the south, swathed in lush jungle. Permission to make the three- to four-hour climb must be obtained from the Range Officer at the Forest Check Post near the start of the ascent, but don't attempt it without a guide and plenty of drinking water.

Many tourists who find their way up here do so in order to explore the various **islands** dotted around the gulf north of Arial Bay, particularly **Smith** and **Ross** (not to be confused with its namesake near Port Blair), whose white sandbars, coral reefs and flora are splendid. Neither island is officially listed on the arrival permit, but day-trips can be sanctioned on payment of Rs500 at the Forestry Department in Arial Bay; you will need to charter a dinghy for Rs400 to reach the islets.

Other islands

The remaining islands open to foreign tourists in the Andaman group are all hard to get to and, with the exception of **Little Andaman** – where a vestigial population of Onge tribespeople have survived a massive influx of Indian Tamils and native Nicobars – uninhabited. Two hours' boat ride south of Chiriya Tapu on South Andaman, **Cinque Island** offers superlative diving.

Cinque Island

Cinque actually comprises two islets, joined by a spectacular sand isthmus with shallow water either side that covers it completely at high tide. The main incentive to come here is the superb diving and snorkelling around the reefs. However, heaps of dead coral on the beach attest to damage wreaked by the Indian navy during the construction of the swish "cottages" overlooking the beach. Rumour has it that these were built for the visit of a Thai VIP in 1996, but local government officials now use them as bolt holes from Port Blair. Although there are no **ferries** to Cinque, it is possible to arrange dinghies from Chiriya Tapu village on the mainland (see p.1100). Currently, overnight stays are prohibited.

Little Andaman

Little Andaman is the furthest point south in the archipelago you can travel to on a standard one-month tourist permit. Located ten hours by sea from Port Blair, most of the island has been set aside as a tribal reserve for the **Onge** (see p.1091) and is thus off limits. It is also the only island open to foreigners to sustain extensive damage in the 2004 **tsunami**, and at the time of writing it was not clear how much was left standing on the whole coastal strip surrounding the port of **Hut Bay**. The most attractive beach is at **Butler Bay**, some 15km north. Boats from the capital leave for the island every other day but it is not possible to give reliable accommodation details, given the current uncertainties. The island also has a chronic problem with **malaria** and **sandflies**. If, after all that, you're still intent to go and provide some much-needed tourist cash, check thoroughly at the tourist office in Port Blair or better still with returning fellow travellers before you set off.

Travel details

Flights

Port Blair to: Chennai (2 daily; 2hr); Kolkata (Calcutta: 1–2 daily; 2hr).

Boats

Arial Bay to: Port Blair (3 weekly; 13–14hr).
Havelock to: Long Island (3 weekly; 2–3hr); Neill Island (5–6 weekly; 1hr–1hr 30min); Port Blair (1–2 daily; 2hr–4hr 30min); Rangat Bay (4 weekly; 3–5hr).
Mayabunder to: Kalighat (1 daily; 2hr 30min).
Port Blair to: Arial Bay (3 weekly; 13–14hr); Bamboo Flats (every 30min–1hr; 20min); Chennai (1 weekly; 60–72hr); Havelock Island (1–2 daily; 2hr–4hr 30min); Kolkata (Calcutta: 1 every 2 weeks; 72–96hr); Little Andaman (3–4 weekly; 9–10hr); Long Island (4 weekly; 5–8hr); Neill Island (1–2 daily; 2hr–3hr 30min); Rangat Bay (1–2 daily; 6–9hr); Vishakapatnam (1 monthly; 72–84hr).
Rangat Bay to: Havelock Island (4 weekly; 3–5hr); Long Island (2–3 daily; 1hr–1hr 30min); Neill Island (2–3 weekly; 4–6hr); Port Blair (1 daily; 6–9hr).

Buses

Diglipur to: Arial Bay (every 1–2hr; 20min); Kalighat (4 daily; 45min); Kalipur (5 daily; 40min); Port Blair (2–3 daily; 11–12hr).
Mayabunder to: Karmateng beach (2 daily; 30min); Port Blair (2–4 daily; 9–10hr); Rangat (5 daily; 2hr 30min–3hr 30min).
Port Blair to: Chiriya Tapu (3 daily; 1hr 15min); Diglipur (2–3 daily; 11–12hr) Mayabunder (3–5 daily; 9–10hr); Rangat (5 daily; 6–7hr); Wandoor (4 daily; 1hr 15min).
Rangat to: Mayabunder (5 daily; 2hr 30min–3hr 30min); Port Blair (5 daily; 6–7hr).

CHAPTER 20

Highlights

* **Mamallapuram** Stone-carvers' workshops, a long sandy beach and a bumper hoard of Pallava monuments have made this the state's principal tourist attraction. **See p.1135**

* **Pondicherry** Former French colony that has retained the ambience of a Gallic seaside town: croissants, a promenade and gendarmes wearing *képis.* **See p.1150**

* **Thanjavur** Home to some of the world's finest Chola bronzes, this town is dominated by the colossal shrine tower of the Brihadishwara Temple. **See p.1164**

* **Madurai** This major temple, the love-nest of Shiva and his consort Meenakshi, hosts a constant round of festivals. **See p.1175**

* **Kanniyakumari** The sacred meeting point of the Bay of Bengal, Indian Ocean and Arabian Sea, at the southern tip of the subcontinent. **See p.1188**

* **The Ghats** The spine of southern India, where you can trek through forested mountains and tea plantations from the refreshingly cool hill stations of Ooty, Conoor and Kodaikanal. **See p.1190**

△ Krishna's Butter Ball, Mamallapuram

Tamil Nadu

When Indians refer to "the South", it's usually **TAMIL NADU** they're talking about. While Karnataka and Andhra Pradesh are essentially cultural transition zones buffering the Hindi-speaking north, and Kerala and Goa maintain their own distinctively idiosyncratic identities, the peninsula's massive Tamil-speaking state is India's Dravidian Hindu heartland. Traditionally protected by distance and the military might of the southern Deccan kingdoms, the region has, over the centuries, been less exposed to northern influences than its neighbours. As a result, the three powerful dynasties dominating the south – the Cholas, the Pallavas and the Pandyans – were able, over a period of more than a thousand years, to develop their own unique religious and political institutions, largely unmolested by marauding Muslims. The most visible legacy of this protracted cultural flowering is a crop of astounding **temples**, whose gigantic gateway towers, or *gopuras*, still soar above just about every town large enough to merit a railway station. It is the image of these colossal wedge-shaped pyramids, high above the canopy of dense palm forests, or against patchworks of vibrant green paddy fields, which Edward Lear described as "stupendous and beyond belief". Indeed, the garishly painted gods, goddesses and mythological creatures clinging onto the towers linger long in the memory of most travellers.

The great Tamil temples, however, are merely the largest landmarks in a vast network of **sacred sites** – shrines, bathing places, holy trees, rocks and rivers – interconnected by a web of ancient pilgrims' routes. Tamil Nadu harbours 274 of India's holiest Shiva temples, and 108 are dedicated to Vishnu. In addition, five shrines devoted to the five Vedic elements (Earth, Wind, Fire, Water and Ether) are to be found here, along with eight to the planets, as well as other places revered by Christians and Muslims. Scattered from the pale orange crags and forests of the Western Ghats, across the fertile deltas of the **Vaigai** and **Kaveri** rivers to the Coromandel coast on the Bay of Bengal, these sites were celebrated in the hymns of the Tamil saints, composed between one and two thousand years ago. Today, so little has changed that the same devotional songs are still widely sung and understood in the region.

The Tamils' living connection with their ancient Dravidian past has given rise to a strong **nationalist movement**. With a few fleeting lapses, one or other of the pro-Dravidian parties have been in power here since the 1950s, spreading their anti-brahmin, anti-Hindi proletarian message to the masses principally through the medium of movies. Indeed, since Independence, the majority of Tamil Nadu's political leaders have been drawn from the state's prolific **cinema** industry. Indians from elsewhere in the country love to caricature their southern cousins as "reactionary rice growers" led by "fanatical film stars". While such stereotypes should be taken with a pinch of salt, it is undeniable that the Tamil way of life, which has evolved along a distinctive and unbroken path since prehistoric times, sets it apart from the rest of the subcontinent. This remains, after all, one of the last places in the world where a classical culture has survived well into the present.

Despite its seafront fort, grand mansions and excellence as a centre for the performing arts, the state capital **Chennai** (formerly **Madras**) is a hot, chaotic, noisy Indian metropolis that still carries faint echoes of the Raj. However, it is a good base for visiting **Kanchipuram**, a major pilgrimage and sari-weaving centre, filled with reminders of an illustrious past.

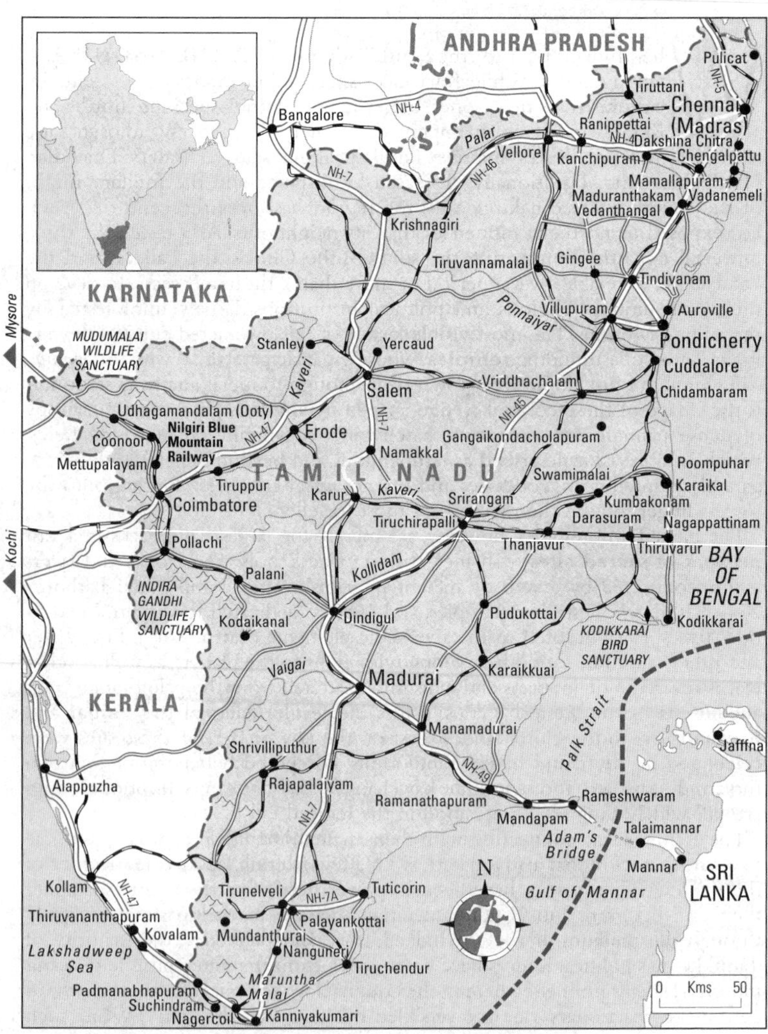

Much the best place to start a temple tour is nearby in **Mamallapuram**, a seaside village that – quite apart from some exquisite Pallava rock-cut architecture – boasts a long and lovely beach. Further down the coast lies **Pondicherry**, a former French colony that's home to the famous Sri Aurobindo ashram; nearby, the campus of **Auroville** has carved a role as a popular New Age centre. The road south from Pondicherry puts you back on the temple trail, leading to the tenth-century Chola kingdom and the extraordinary architecture of **Chidambaram**, **Gangaikondacholapuram**, **Kumbakonam** and **Darasuram**. For the best Chola bronzes, however, and a glimpse of the magnificent paintings that flourished under Maratha rajas in the eighteenth century, travellers should head for **Thanjavur**. Chola capital for four centuries, the city boasts almost a hundred temples and was the birthplace of Bharatanatyam dance, famous throughout Tamil Nadu.

In the very centre of Tamil Nadu, **Tiruchirapalli**, a commercial town just northwest of Thanjavur, held some interest for the Cholas, but reached its heyday under later dynasties, when the temple complex in neighbouring **Srirangam** became one of South India's largest. Among its patrons were the Nayaks of **Madurai**, whose erstwhile capital further south, bustling with pilgrims, priests, peddlers, tailors and tourists, is an unforgettable destination.

Rameshwaram, on the long spit of land reaching towards Sri Lanka, and **Kanniyakumari**, at India's southern tip (the auspicious meeting point of the Bay of Bengal, the Indian Ocean and the Arabian Sea) are both important pilgrimage centres, and have the added attraction of welcome cool breezes and vistas over the sea.

While Tamil Nadu's temples are undeniably its major attraction, the hill stations of **Kodaikanal** and **Udhagamandalam** (Ooty) in the west of the state are popular destinations on the well-beaten tourist trail between Kerala and Tamil Nadu. The verdant, cool hills offer mountain views and gentle trails through the forests and tea and coffee plantations. Sadly, at the time of writing the teak forests of **Mudumalai Wildlife Sanctuary** and the trekking routes of **Anamalai Sanctuary**, situated near Kodaikanal in the Palani Hills, were still closed to foreigners due to security concerns, and are not covered in this guide. To get close to any real wildlife, you'll have to head for the coast, where areas of wetland provide perfect resting places for migratory birds, whose numbers dramatically increase during the winter monsoon at **Vedanthangal**, near Chennai, and **Point Calimere**.

Visiting Tamil Nadu

Temperatures in Tamil Nadu, which usually hover around 30°C, peak in May and June, when they often soar above 40°C and the overpowering heat makes anything but sitting in a shaded café exhausting. The state is barely affected by the southwest monsoon that pounds much of India from June to September: it receives most of its **rain** between October and December, when the odd cyclone may well make an appearance. The cooler, rainy days, however, bring their own problems: large-scale flooding can disrupt road and rail links and imbue everything with an all-pervasive dampness. Note that though the Asian **tsunamis** of December 2004 hit Tamil Nadu hard (see p.1117), the area's tourist infrastructure was up and running at the time of writing, and those who depend on the industry were keen to see visitor numbers return to pre-tsunami levels.

Accommodation throughout the state is good and plentiful; all but the smallest towns and villages have something for every budget. Most hotels have their own dining halls which, together with local restaurants, usually serve sumptuous and unlimited thalis, tinged with tamarind and presented on banana leaves. **Indigenous dishes** are almost exclusively vegetarian; for north Indian or Western alternatives, head for the larger hotels or more upmarket city restaurants.

Some history

Since the fourth century BC, Tamil Nadu has been shaped by its majority **Dravidian** population, a people of uncertain origins and physically quite different from north Indians. Their language developed separately, as did their social organization; the difference between high-caste brahmins and low-caste workers has always been more pronounced here than in the north – caste divisions that continue to dominate the state's political life. The influence of the powerful *janapadas*, established in the north by the fourth and third centuries BC, extended as far south as the Deccan, but they made few incursions into **Dravidadesa** (Tamil country). Incorporating what is now Kerala and Tamil Nadu, it was ruled by three dynasties: the **Cheras**, who held sway over much of the Malabar coast (Kerala), the **Pandyas** in the far south, and the **Cholas**, whose realm stretched along the eastern Coromandel coast. Indo-Roman trade in spices, precious stones and metals flourished at the start of the Christian era, when **St Thomas** arrived in the south, but dwindled when trade links began with Southeast Asia.

In the fourth century, the **Pallava** dynasty established a powerful kingdom centred in **Kanchipuram**. By the seventh century, the successors of the first Pallava king, Simhavishnu, were engaged in battles with the southern Pandyas and the forces of the Chalukyas, based further west in Karnataka. However, the centuries of Pallava dominion are not marked simply by battles and territorial expansion; this was also an era of social development. **Brahmins** became the dominant community, responsible for lands and riches donated to temples. The emergence of *bhakti*, devotional worship, placed temples firmly at the centre of religious life, and the inspirational *sangam* literature of saint-poets fostered a tradition of dance and music that has become Tamil Nadu's cultural hallmark.

In the tenth and eleventh centuries, the Cholas experienced a period of profound expansion and revival; they soon held sway over much of Tamil Nadu, Andhra Pradesh and even made in-roads into Karnataka and Orissa. In the spirit of such glorious victories and power, the Cholas ploughed their new wealth into the construction of splendid and imposing temples, such as those at Gangaikondacholapuram, Kumbakonam and Thanjavur.

The **Vijayanagars**, who gained a firm footing in Hampi (Karnataka) in the fourteenth century, resisted Muslim incursions from the north and spread to cover most of South India by the sixteenth century. This prompted a new phase of architectural development: the building of new temples, the expansion of older ones and the introduction of colossal *gopuras*. In Madurai, the Vijayanagar governors, **Nayaks**, set up an independent kingdom whose impact spread as far as Tiruchirapalli.

Simultaneously, the south experienced its first significant wave of **Europeans**. First came the Portuguese, who landed in Kerala and monopolized Indian trade for about a century before being joined by the British, Dutch and French. Though mostly on cordial terms with the Indians, the Western powers soon found themselves engaged in territorial disputes. The most marked were between the French, based in **Pondicherry**, and the British, whose stronghold since 1640 had been Fort St George in **Madras**. After battles at sea and on land, the French were confined to Pondicherry, while British ambitions reached their apex in the eighteenth century, when the East India Company occupied Bengal (1757) and made firm its bases in Bombay and Madras.

The tsunamis and Tamil Nadu

When the Asian **tsunamis** struck India on December 26, 2004, the coastline of Tamil Nadu bore the brunt of the damage. The waves here averaged 7–10 metres in height, and travelled some 3km inland at Pondicherry, causing a huge amount of devastation; in the aftermath, some 8000 people were pronounced dead, while hotels and restaurants in popular resorts such as Mammallapuram were badly damaged. Furthermore, the fact that tourism pretty much collapsed following the waves served only to further frustrate those struggling to rebuild their livelihoods. Cleanup efforts were swift, however, and at the time of writing, the vast majority of the state's resorts and attractions were back in business, and their owners and operators hopeful that the return of tourist revenue would help to fully rebuild the region.

As well as rebellions against colonial rule, Tamil Nadu also saw anti-brahmin protests, in particular those led by the Justice Party in the 1920s and 1930s. **Independence** in 1947 signalled the need for state boundaries, and by 1956 the borders had been demarcated on a linguistic basis; Andhra Pradesh and Kerala were formed, along with Mysore state (later Karnataka) and **Madras Presidency**. In 1965, Madras Presidency became **Tamil Nadu**, the latter part of its name coming from the Chola agrarian administrative units known as *nadus*.

Since Independence, Tamil Nadu's industrial sector has mushroomed. The state was a Congress stronghold until 1967, when the **DMK** (Dravida Munnetra Kazhagam), championing the lower castes and reasserting Tamil identity, won a landslide victory. Anti-Hindi and anti-central government rule, the DMK flourished until the film star "**MGR**" (M.G. Ramachandran) broke away to form the **All India Anna Dravida Munnetra Kazhagam** (AIADMK), and won an easy victory in the 1977 elections. Virtually deified by his fans-turned-supporters, MGR remained successful until his death in 1987, when the Tamil government fell back into the hands of the DMK. Soon after, the AIADMK were reinstated, led by **Srimati Jayalalithaa Jayaram**, an ex-film star and dancer once on close terms with MGR (see p.1120), who is currently enjoying her second period in power, having been unseated on corruption charges during the mid-1990s.

Chennai (Madras)

In the northeastern corner of Tamil Nadu on the Bay of Bengal, **CHENNAI** (still commonly referred to by its former British name, **Madras**) is India's fourth largest city, with a population nudging six million. Hot, fast, congested and noisy, it is the major transportation hub of the south – the international airport makes a marginally less stressful entry point to the subcontinent than Mumbai or Delhi – and most travellers stay just long enough to book a ticket for somewhere else. The attractions of the city itself are sparse, though it does boast fine specimens of **Raj architecture**, pilgrimage sites connected with the apostle **Doubting Thomas**, superb **Chola bronzes** at its state museum, and plenty of **classical music** and **dance** performances.

As capital of Tamil Nadu, Chennai is, like Mumbai and Kolkata (Calcutta), a comparatively modern creation. It was founded by the **British East India Company** in 1639, on a five-kilometre strip of land between the Cooum and

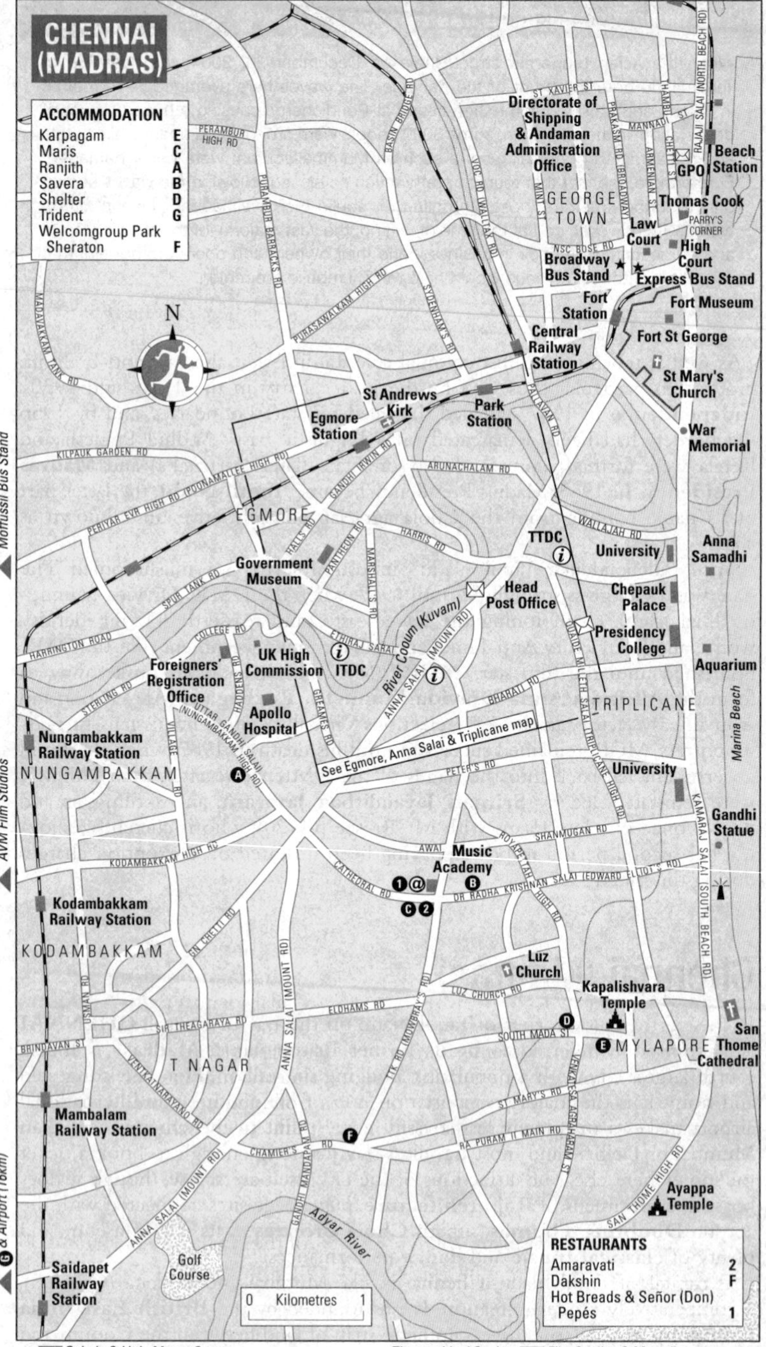

CHENNAI (MADRAS)
ACCOMMODATION
Karpagam E
Maris C
Ranjith A
Savera B
Shelter D
Trident G
Welcomgroup Park Sheraton F
RESTAURANTS
Amaravati 2
Dakshin F
Hot Breads & Señor (Don) Pepés 1
Enfield Factory
Royapuram
Moffussil Bus Stand
AVM Film Studios
& Airport (16km)
Guindy & Little Mount Caves
Theosophical Society, Film Studios & Mamallapuram
Directorate of Shipping & Andaman Administration Office
GEORGE TOWN
Beach Station
GPO
Thomas Cook
Law Court
High Court
Broadway Bus Stand
Express Bus Stand
Fort Station
Fort Museum
Fort St George
St Mary's Church
Central Railway Station
St Andrews Kirk
Park Station
Egmore Station
War Memorial
EGMORE
TTDC
University
Anna Samadhi
Government Museum
Head Post Office
Chepauk Palace
Presidency College
Aquarium
UK High Commission
ITDC
Foreigners' Registration Office
Apollo Hospital
TRIPLICANE
See Egmore, Anna Salai & Triplicane map
Nungambakkam Railway Station
NUNGAMBAKKAM
University
Gandhi Statue
Music Academy
Kodambakkam Railway Station
KODAMBAKKAM
Luz Church
Kapalishvara Temple
MYLAPORE
San Thome Cathedral
T NAGAR
Mambalam Railway Station
Ayappa Temple
Golf Course
Saidapet Railway Station
Adyar River
River Cooum (Kuvam)
Marina Beach
Kilometres

Name changes

The city's former name, "Madras", is not the only one to have been weeded out over the last few years by pro-Dravidian politicians. Several major roads in the city have also been renamed as part of an ongoing attempt to "**Dravidify**" the Tamil capital (most of the new names immortalize former nationalist politicians). However, far from all of Chennai's inhabitants are in favour of the recent changes, while some (notably a large contingent of auto-rickshaw-wallahs) seem completely oblivious to them. The confusing result of this is that both old and new names remain in use. We have used the new ones throughout the chapter. Thus Mount Road, the main shopping road through the centre of town, is now **Anna Salai**; to the east, Triplicane High Road, near *Broadlands Hotel*, has become **Quaide Milleth Salai**; Poonamallee High Road, running east–west across the north of the city, is **Periyar EVR High Road**; North Beach Road, along the eastern edge of George Town is known as **Rajaji Salai**; South Beach Road, the southern stretch of the coastal road, is **Kamaraj Salai**; running west, Edward Elliot's Road has been renamed **Dr Radha Krishnan Salai**; Mowbray's Road is also known as **TTK Road**; C-in-C Road is now **Ethiraj Salai**; and Nungabamkkam High Road **Uttamar Gandhi Salai.**

Although, for the sake of political correctness, we've adopted the new names, it's safe to say that the old ones are still more commonly understood, and that using them will not cause offence – unless, of course, you happen to be talking to a pro-Dravidian activist.

Adyar rivers, a few kilometres north of the ancient Tamil port of **Mylapore** and the Portuguese settlement of San Thome; a fortified trading post, completed on St George's Day in 1640, was named **Fort St George**. By 1700, the British had acquired neighbouring territory including **Triplicane** and **Egmore**, while over the course of the next century, as capital of the **Madras Presidency** which covered most of South India, the city mushroomed to include many surrounding villages. The French repeatedly challenged the British, and finally managed to destroy most of the city in 1746. **Robert Clive** ("Clive of India"), then a clerk, was taken prisoner, an experience said to have inspired him to become a campaigner. Clive was among the first to re-enter Chennai when it was retaken by the British three years later, and continued to use it as his base. Following this, fortifications were strengthened and the British survived a year-long French siege in 1759, completing the work in 1783. By this time, however, Calcutta was in the ascendancy and Madras lost its national importance.

The city's renaissance began after Independence, when it became the centre of the Tamil **movie industry**, and a hotbed of **Dravidian nationalism**. Rechristened as Chennai in 1997 (to reassert its precolonial identity), the metropolis has boomed since the Indian economy opened up to foreign investment under Rajiv and Rao (former prime ministers) in the early 1990s. The flip side of this rapid economic growth is that Chennai's infrastructure has been stretched to breaking point: poverty, oppressive heat and pollution are more likely to be your lasting impressions than the conspicuous affluence of the city's modern marble shopping malls.

Arrival

Chennai airport in Trisulam, 16km southwest of the city centre on NH-45, is comprehensively served by international and domestic flights; the two terminals are a minute's walk from each other. Out in the main concourse, you'll find a 24-hour post office, Thomas Cook and State Bank of India foreign-exchange

Of movie stars and ministers

One notable difference between the Chennai movie industry and its counterpart in Mumbai is the influence of **politics** on Tamil films – an overlap that dates from the earliest days of regional cinema, when stories, stock themes and characters were derived from traditional folk ballads about low-caste heroes vanquishing high-caste villains. Already familiar to millions, such Robin Hood-style stereotypes were perfect propaganda vehicles for the nascent Tamil nationalist movement, the Dravida Munnetra Kazhagam, or **DMK**. It is no coincidence that the party's founding father, **C.N. Annadurai**, was a top screenplay and script writer. Like prominent Tamil Congress leaders and movie-makers of the 1930s and 1940s, he and his colleagues used the two popular film genres of the time – "mythologicals" (movie versions of the Hindu epics) and "socials" (dramas set around caste conflicts) – to convey their political ideas to the masses. Audiences were actively encouraged by party workers to boo the villains and cheer each time the proletarian hero, or DMK icons and colours (red and black), appeared on the screen. From this tradition were born the **fan clubs**, or *rasigar manrams*, that played such a key role in mobilizing support for the nationalist parties in elections.

The most influential fan club of all time was the one set up to support the superstar actor Marudur Gopalamenon Ramachandran, known to millions simply as "**MGR**". By carefully cultivating a political image to mirror the folk-hero roles he played in films, the maverick matinee idol generated fanatical grass-roots support in the state, especially among women, and rose to become chief minister in 1977. His eleven-year rule is still regarded by liberals as a dark age in the state's history, as chronic corruption, police brutality, political purges and rising organized crime were all rife during the period. Even the fact that his bungled economic policies penalized precisely the rural poor who voted for him never dented MGR's mass appeal. When he suffered a paralytic stroke in October 1984, 22 people cut off limbs, toes and fingers as offerings to pray for his recovery, while more than a hundred followers attempted to burn themselves to death. For the next three years he was barely able to speak let alone govern effectively, yet the party stalwarts and fan club members still did not lose faith in his leadership. When he died in 1987, two million people attended his funeral

counters and a couple of snack bars. It's by no means certain that anyone will be staffing the **Government of Tamil Nadu Tourist Information Centre** booth at the arrivals exit, but if you're lucky you may be able to fix up accommodation from here, or at the "Free Fone" desk nearby. If you plan to leave Chennai by train, head for Southern Railways' computerized **ticket reservation** counter (Mon–Sat 8am–2pm & 2.15–8pm, Sun 8am–2pm), immediately outside the domestic terminal exit.

There are prepaid minibus and taxi counters at the exit in the international arrivals hall. **Taxis** cost Rs270–300 for the 35-minute ride to the main hotels or railway stations; rickshaws charge around Rs180, but you'll have to lug your gear out to the main road as they're not allowed to park inside the airport forecourt. A taxi to **Mamallapuram** costs in the region of Rs1000 (Rs1500 for a/c). Shuttle **buses** (Rs50) run to Egmore and Central stations and Thiruvalluvar (Express) bus stand, but they call at several upmarket hotels en route, and are certainly not "Express". The quickest, cheapest and most efficient way to get into town is by suburban **train**. Services run every ten to fifteen minutes (4.30am–11pm) from **Trisulam** Station, 500m from the airport on the far side of the road, to Park, Egmore and North Beach stations, taking 30-40 minutes. If you want to leave Chennai straight away by bus, catch local bus #70 or #70a to the Moffussil bus stand (see box on p.1184).

and 31 grief-stricken devotees committed ritual suicide. Even today, MGR's statue, sporting trademark sunglasses and lamb's-wool hat, is revered at tens of thousands of wayside shrines across Tamil Nadu.

MGR's political protégée, and eventual successor, was a teenage screen starlet called **Jayalalitha**, a convent-educated brahmin's daughter whom he spotted at a school dance and, despite an age difference of more than thirty years, recruited to be both his leading lady and mistress. The couple would star opposite each other in 25 hit films, and when MGR eventually moved into politics, Jayalalitha followed him, becoming leader of the AIADMK (the party MGR set up after being expelled from the DMK in 1972), after a much publicized power struggle with his widow. Larger than life in voluminous silver ponchos and heavy gold jewellery, the now portly Puratchi Thalavi ("Revolutionary Leader") has taken her personality cult to extremes brazen even by Indian standards. On her forty-sixth birthday in 1994, Rs50,000 of public money was spent on giant cardboard cut-outs depicting her in academic and religious robes, while 46 of her more fervent admirers rolled bare-chested along the length of Anna Salai. Jayalalitha's spell as chief minister, however, was brought to an ignominious end at the 1996 elections, after allegations of fraud and corruption on an appropriately monumental scale. Despite being found guilty by the High Court, she still managed to bring down the national government and force a general election in 1999 (by withdrawing AIADMK support from prime minister Vajpayee's shaky, BJP-led coalition); she later ousted her arch rival, **M. Karunanidhi**, leader of the DMK, to regain her old job as chief minister of Tamil Nadu. One of her first acts was to exact revenge on Karunanidhi, throwing him and one thousand of his supporters into prison on corruption charges.

The intermingling of Tamil politics and cinema is now so established in the state that it's almost inconceivable for anyone to attain high office without some kind of movie credentials. Distinguished among Chennai's huge roadside hoardings by his MGR-style shades and yellow shawl, the previous chief minister was another former screenwriter, while the wavy-haired megastar of the 1980s, **Rajnikanth**, ended years of speculation a few years back when he threw his lot in with Congress (I) party.

By train

Arriving in Chennai by train, you come in at one of two **long-distance railway stations**, 1.5km apart on Periyar EVR High Road, towards the north of the city. **Egmore Station**, in the heart of the busy commercial Egmore district, is the arrival point for most trains from Tamil Nadu and Kerala. On the whole, all the others pull in at **Central Station**, further east, on the edge of George Town, which has a 24-hour left-luggage office, and STD phone booths outside the exit. Information kiosks at both stations are poorly staffed and badly equipped, but both have plenty of metered taxis and auto-rickshaws.

By bus

Buses from elsewhere in Tamil Nadu and other states arrive at the huge **Moffussil** bus stand, inconveniently situated in the suburb of Koyambedu, over 10km west of the centre – the chaotic old **Express** and **Broadway** bus stands in the centre have been amalgamated and are only used for local services. Moffussil is linked to these and other parts of Chennai by a host of city buses, which depart from the well-organized platforms outside the main terminal: buses #27, #15B, #15F and #17E go to the Egmore/Central area and Parry's Corner; bus #27B also goes on to Triplicane; while bus #70 and #70A link the bus stand to the airport. Note that most buses from Mamallapuram, Pondicherry and other towns to the south of Chennai stop at Guindy suburban railway station on their way in and you will save a lot of time by connecting onto the train there.

Information

The highly efficient and very helpful **India Tourism Office** at 154 Anna Salai (Mon–Fri 9am–6pm, Sat 9am–1pm; ⓣ044/2846 0285), has maps and leaflets, and can arrange accommodation. They also keep a list of approved **guides**.

The **Tamil Nadu Tourism Development Corporation** (TTDC) is based in a smart new complex on Wallajah Road, near Anna Park in Triplicane (Mon–Sat 10am–5.30pm; ⓣ044/2538 3333), where you can also find the tourist offices of many other states including Kerala (ⓣ044/2536 9789). TTDC can book you tours or accommodation in their own hotels across the state. You can make advance bookings for ITDC hotels across the whole country, and arrange tours of the city, state and country at the **India Tourist Development Corporation** (ITDC) office at 29 Dr PV Cherian Crescent, Ethiraj Salai (Mon–Fri 10am–5.30pm; ⓣ044/2827 8884, ⓔitdc.ros@gems.vsnl.net.in).

The long-established *Hallo! Madras* (monthly; Rs10) is an accurate directory to all the city's services, with full moon dates (useful for estimating temple festivals), a guide to Tamil Nadu for tourists, exhaustive flight and train details, and an outline of Chennai bus timetables. Alternatively, the even more comprehensive quarterly directory *Madura Welcome* (Rs50) lists every bus service and route in Chennai, and from Chennai to other towns in the state. Both are available at all book and stationery shops. Unfortunately, neither have a "What's On" section; for forthcoming music and dance performances, buy the weekly *City Info* (Rs30), consult the events column on page three of the *Hindu*, or try and get hold of a copy of *Chennai: This Fortnight*, available free from all moderate to expensive hotels.

City transport

The offices, sights, railway stations and bus stands of Chennai are spread over such a wide area that it's impossible to get around without using some form of **public transport**. Most visitors jump in auto-rickshaws, but outside rush hours you can travel around comfortably by **bus**, or suburban **train**.

Buses

To ride on a bus in most Indian cities you need to be incredibly resilient and a master of the art of hanging on to open doorways with two fingers. **Buses** in Chennai, on the other hand, are regular, inexpensive, and only cramped during rush hours. On Anna Salai, buses have special stops, but on smaller streets you have to flag them down, or wait with the obvious crowd. Buses in Egmore gather opposite the railway station. Numbers of services to specific places of interest in the city are listed in the relevant accounts, or for a full directory of bus routes, buy *Madura Welcome* (see above). Buses to and from the Moffussil bus stand are listed in "Arrival" (above).

Trains

If you want to travel south from central Chennai to Guindy (Deer Park) or the airport, the easiest way to go is by **train**. Services run every fifteen minutes (on average) between 4.30am and 11pm, prices are minimal, and you can guarantee a seat at any time except rush hour (around 9am & 5pm). First-class carriages substitute padded seats for wooden slatted benches, and are a little cleaner; buy a ticket before boarding.

Tours

One good way to get around the sights of Chennai is on a TTDC **bus tour**; bookings are taken in the relevant offices. They're good value, albeit rushed, and the guides can be very helpful. The TTDC **half-day tour** (daily 8am–1pm or 1.30pm–6.30pm; Rs110non a/c, Rs160 with a/c) starts at their office on Periyar EVR High Road. It takes in Fort St George, the Government Museum, the Snake Park, Kapalishvara Temple, Elliot's Beach and Marina Beach (on Friday, the Government Museum is closed, so the tour goes to the Birla Planetarium instead). TTDC also offer good-value **day-trips**, including visits to Mamallapuram, Kanchipuram, and Pondicherry, with meals included in the tariff: check at their office for the various itineraries and prices.

City trains travel between: Beach (opposite the GPO), Fort, Park (for Central), Egmore, Nungambakkam, Kodambakkam, Mambalam (for T Nagar and silk shops), Saidapet (for Little Mount Church), Guindy, St Thomas Mount and Trisulam (for the airport).

Taxis and rickshaws

Chennai's yellow-top Ambassador **taxis** gather outside Egmore and Central railway stations, and at the airport. All have meters, but drivers often prefer to set a price before leaving, and invariably charge a return fare, whatever the destination. At around Rs150 from Central Station to Triplicane, they're practically pricing themselves out of business. For this reason more reliable and economical **radio taxis** such as Bharati Call Taxi (Ⓣ044/2814 2233) are becoming more popular.

Flocks of auto- and cycle-rickshaws wait patiently outside tourist hotels, and not so patiently outside railway stations. **Auto-rickshaw** drivers in Chennai are notorious for demanding high fares from locals and tourists alike. A rickshaw from Triplicane to either of the bus stations, plus Egmore and Central railway stations should cost no more than Rs40. All rickshaws have meters; a few drivers use them if asked, but in many cases you'll save a lot of frustrating bargaining by offering a small sub above the meter-reading (a driver may offer you a rate of "meter plus 5", meaning Rs5 above the final reading). If you need to get to the airport or station early in the morning, book a rickshaw and negotiate the price the night before (the driver may well sleep in his vehicle outside your hotel). Only take **cycle rickshaws** on the smaller roads; riding amid Chennai traffic on a fragile tricycle seat can be extremely hair-raising.

Car, motorcycle and bike rental

A great, relatively stress-free way to get about if you can afford it, **car rental**, with driver, is available at many of the upmarket hotels or through the Government of India Tourism Office. Welcome Tourrs and Travels at 150 Anna Salai (Ⓣ044/2846 0614, Ⓔwelcome@md2.vsnl.net.in) are efficient and reliable, and can arrange local sightseeing and tours throughout South India. Prices for car rental are around Rs1000–1500 per day for non a/c and a/c respectively.

Anyone brave enough to rent a **moped** or **motorcycle** for short rides around the city, or tours ofTamil Nadu, should head for U-Rent Services, at 1, 1st Main Road, Gandhinagar, Adayar (Mon–Sat 8am–7pm, Sun 9am–6pm; Ⓣ044/2491 0838). Prices range from Rs150 to Rs300 per day, and you have to pay a flat Rs200 annual membership fee regardless of how long you rent a bike for.

Accommodation

Finding a **place to stay** in Chennai can be a problem, as hotels are often full by noon. Demand has pushed prices up, with only a couple of places offering anything for less than Rs200; however, standards in the cheapies are better than in other cities. To secure a room in one of the cheapies, it's advisable to phone and book in advance, at least from the railway station or airport.

Most of the mid-range and inexpensive hotels are around the railway station in **Egmore**, and further east in **Triplicane**, a characterful, busy market and Muslim residential district. The bulk of the top hotels are in the south of the city and several offer courtesy buses to and from the airport. Almost all hotels have at least one South Indian/multi-cuisine restaurant attached to their premises. Due to frequent shortages, visitors should use **water** as sparingly as possible.

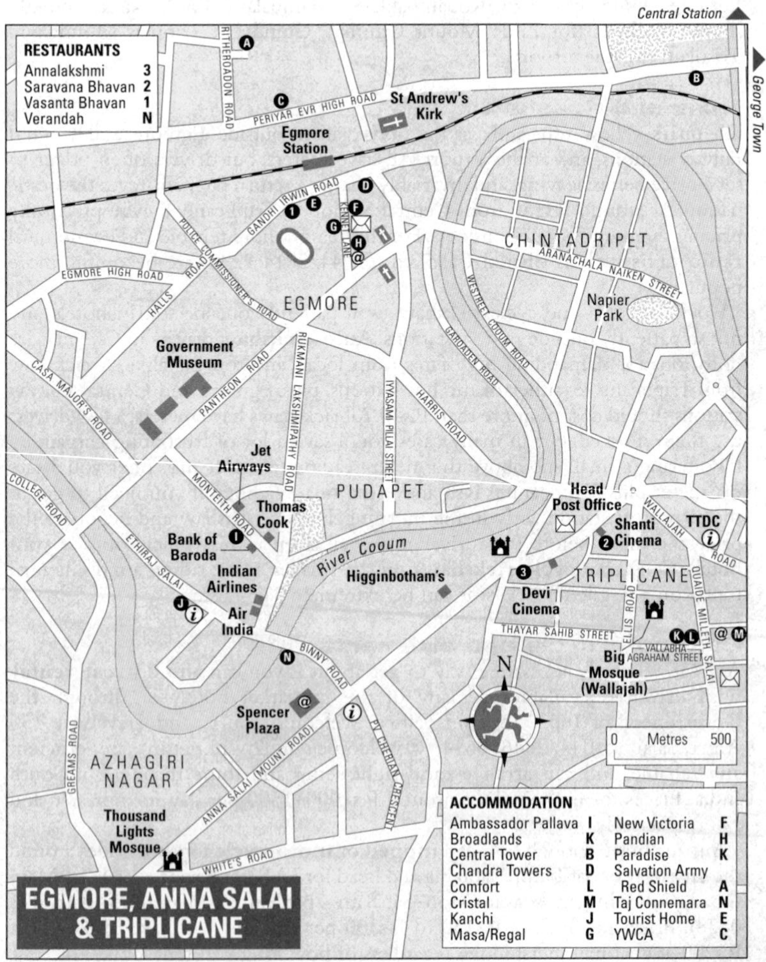

Accommodation listed under the "Outside the centre" heading appears on the main Chennai **map** (p.1118); all others are marked on the Egmore, Anna Salai and Triplicane map (opposite).

Egmore

Central Tower 17/2 Periyar EVR High Rd ⓣ044/2538 1491, ⓕ2536 0522. Ugly modern block in a busy but convenient location almost opposite Central Station. Clean, decent-sized en-suite rooms and a restaurant ❹–❺

Chandra Towers 9 Gandhi Irwin Rd ⓣ044/2514 8137, ⓕ5214 8140. Undergoing refurbishment at the time of writing, this is one of the better hotels in the area, with central a/c, foreign exchange, 24hr coffee shop, bar and rooftop restaurant. ❺–❻

Masa 15/1 Kennet Lane ⓣ044/2819 3344. Variously priced rooms with attached bathrooms and TVs in a clean, modern building, close to the station. Good value. The similar *Regal*, tacked onto the back, is marginally cheaper. ❷–❹

New Victoria 3 Kennet Lane ⓣ044/2819 3638. Egmore's smartest: all rooms have a/c and hot showers. Non-residents can use the bar (11am–11pm) and Internet centre (Rs75/hr) while waiting for a train. Rate includes breakfast. ❻–❼

Pandian 15 Kennet Lane ⓣ044/2819 1010, ⓔhotelpandian@vsnl.com. Pleasant, clean and modern mid-scale place within walking distance of the railway station. Ask for a room on the Church Park side of the building for green views. Some rooms have a/c. 24hr Net service for Rs40/hr. ❺–❻

Salvation Army Red Shield Guest House 15/31 Ritherdon Rd ⓣ044/2532 1821, ⓔredshieldguesthouse@hotmail.com. A friendly and helpful Sally Army lodge tucked away in a leafy backstreet behind the station. It's all extremely basic with several dorms (Rs70), and doubles with attached baths (some a/c). 9am checkout. ❷–❹

Tourist Home 43 Gandhi Irwin Rd ⓣ044/2819 4679. Popular hotel directly opposite the railway station that could do with a spring clean; nonetheless it's good value and often full. Rooms (some a/c) have showers and TVs, and clean linen and towels are provided; one room has three beds, another six. Back rooms suffer less from early morning noise. ❸–❹

YWCA International Guest House 1086 Periyar EVR High Rd ⓣ044/2532 4234, ⓔywca_igh@indiainfo.com. Attractive hotel in quiet gardens behind Egmore station with spotless, spacious rooms, safe-deposit and a good restaurant. A highly recommended, safe and friendly place; book in advance. Rates include a buffet breakfast. ❹–❻

Anna Salai and Triplicane

Ambassador Pallava 30 Montieth Rd ⓣ044/2855 4476, ⓔpallava@ambassadorindia.com. Colossal four-star, close to Anna Salai, with great views from its upper storeys. Amid all the gold-plated mirrors and cool white marble is a sports complex with a pool and health club. Rooms from $85. ❾

Broadlands 18 Vallabha Agraham St, Triplicane ⓣ044/2854 5573, ⓔbroadlandshotel@yahoo.com. An old whitewashed house, with crumbling stucco and stained glass, ranged around a leafy courtyard; the kind of budget travellers' enclave you either love or loathe. There's a large roof terrace and clean rooms, a few with attached bathrooms, private balconies and views of the mosque. Inexpensive left-luggage facility is available. A "No Indians" policy is strictly enforced. ❷–❹

Comfort 22 Vallabha Agraham St, Triplicane ⓣ044/2858 7661, ⓕ2852 9999. A chaotic place with yards of dimly lit corridors; rooms are clean but on the small side, all with attached bathrooms. ❸–❹

Cristal 34 CNK Rd, Triplicane ⓣ044/2858 5605. In a modern building off Quaide Milleth Salai, this is a safe and friendly place run by a team of brothers; the reception is busy all day with locals sipping coffee. Rooms are tiled and clean, all with attached showers. TVs cost Rs25 extra. As cheap as it gets in Chennai. ❶

Kanchi 28 Ethiraj Salai ⓣ044/2827 1100, ⓔreservations@hotelkanchi.com. Soulless skyscraper redeemed by spacious rooms with views, two good restaurants (one rooftop) and a bar. ❺–❻

Paradise 17/1 Vallabha Agraham St, Triplicane ⓣ044/2859 4252, ⓔparadisegh@hotmail.com. Very friendly and a dependable choice, offering inexpensive rooms with attached bathroom, TV and a choice of western or Indian loos. There's seating on a large roof terrace, and room service. Good value. ❷–❸

Taj Connemara Binny Rd ⓣ044/5500 0000, ⓦwww.tajhotels.com.vsnl.net.in. Dating from the Raj era, this whitewashed Art Deco five-star near Anna Salai is a Chennai institution. The large "heritage" rooms feature Victorian decor, dressing rooms and verandahs overlooking the pool. There is also a health club, 24hr coffee shop, two excellent restaurants (see p.1131) and a bar. Rates are $202–270. ❾

Outside the centre

Karpagam International 41 South Mada St, Mylapore ⓣ044/2495 9984, ⓕ5210 7925. Very

ordinary, slightly dingy place whose only outstanding feature is its location overlooking the Kapalishvara Temple. It's also on the right side of the city for the airport, 12km away. Inexpensive single rooms available. ❸–❹

Maris 11 Cathedral Rd ⓣ044/2811 0541, ⓕ2811 4847. A 1970s concrete block right next to the *Sheraton* and near the Music Academy. Their a/c rooms are a particularly good deal for the area, but there's a distinct lack of atmosphere. You can book TTDC city tours here. ❺–❻

Ranjith 9 Nungambakkam High Rd ⓣ044/2827 0521, ⓔhotelranjith@yahoo.com. Spotless en-suite rooms (some a/c) with cable TV; facilities include veg and non-veg restaurants, a bar and a travel agent. ❻–❼

Savera 146 Dr Radhakrishnan Rd ⓣ044/2811 4700, ⓔhotsave@md2.vsnl.net.in. Slightly older than the other upmarket hotels in the locality, but boasting all mod cons, including a pool, good pastry shop, bar and three restaurants (including an excellent South Indian, and rooftop one with great views and Mughlai cuisine). Doubles $92–118. ❾

Shelter 19–21 Venkatesa Agraharam St, Mylapore ⓣ044/2495 1919, ⓔshelter@vsnl.com. Sparklingly clean luxury hotel a stone's throw from the Kapalishvara Temple. The comfortable. clean, a/c rooms are better value than most at this price, with central a/c. Doubles $53–78. ❽–❾

Trident 1/24 GST Rd ⓣ044/2234 4747, ⓦwww.trident-hilton.com. Comfortable five-star in lovely gardens; it's near the airport (3km), but a long (12km, albeit complimentary) drive into town. Luxurious rooms (doubles start at $100), swimming pool and good restaurants, one of which serves Thai cuisine. ❾

Welcomgroup Park Sheraton 132 TTK Rd ⓣ044/2499 4101, ⓦwww.welcomgroup.com. The last word in American-style executive luxury, with bow-tied valets yet somehow not too ostentatious. Three excellent restaurants, a 24hr coffee shop and other five-star facilities. Recommended choice for business travellers; rates from $190. ❾

The City

Chennai divides into three main areas. The northern district, separated from the rest by the River Cooum, is the site of the first British outpost in India, **Fort St George**, and the commercial centre, **George Town**, which developed during British occupation. At the southern end of Rajaji Salai is **Parry's Corner**, George Town's principal landmark – look for the tall grey building labelled *Parry's* – it's a major bus stop.

Central Chennai is sandwiched between the Cooum and Adyar rivers, and crossed diagonally by the city's main thoroughfare, **Anna Salai**, the modern, commercial heart of the metropolis. To the east, this gives way to the atmospheric old Muslim quarters of **Triplicane** and a long straight **Marina** where fishermen mend nets and set small boats out to sea, and hordes of Indian tourists hitch up saris and trousers for a quick paddle. South of here, near the coast, **Mylapore**, inhabited in the 1500s by the Portuguese, boasts **Kapalishvara Temple** and **San Thome Cathedral**, both tourist attractions and places of pilgrimage.

Fort St George

Quite unlike any other fort in India, **Fort St George** stands amid state offices facing the sea in the east of the city, just south of George Town on Kamaraj Salai. It looks more like a complex of well-maintained colonial mansions than a fort; indeed many of its buildings are used today as offices, a hive of activity during the week as people rush between the Secretariat and State Legislature.

The fort was the first structure of Madras town and the first territorial possession of the British in India. Construction began in 1640, but most of the original buildings were replaced later that century, after being damaged during French sieges. The most imposing structure is the eighteenth-century colonnaded **Fort House**, coated in deep-slate-grey and white paint. Next door, in the more modestly proportioned **Exchange Building** – site of Madras' first bank – is the excellent **Fort Museum** (daily except Fri 10am–5pm; $2 [Rs5], video cameras Rs25). The collection within faithfully records the central events of the British occupation of Madras with portraits, regimental flags, weapons, East India Company coins, medals, stamps and thick woollen uniforms that make you wonder how the Raj survived as long as it did. The squat cast-iron cage on the ground floor was brought to Madras from China, where for more than a year in the nineteenth century it was used as a particularly sadistic form of imprisonment for a British captain. The first floor, once the public exchange hall where merchants met to gossip and trade, is now an **art gallery**, where portraits of prim officials and their wives sit side by side with fine sketches of the British embarking at Chennai in aristocratic finery, attended by Indians in loincloths. Also on display are etchings by the famous artist **Thomas Daniells**, whose work largely defined British perceptions of India at the end of the eighteenth century.

South of the museum, past the State Legislature, stands the oldest surviving Anglican church in Asia, **St Mary's** (daily 9am–5pm), built in 1678 and partly renovated after the battle of 1759. Constructed with thick walls and a strong vaulted roof that has withstood the city's many sieges, the church served as a store and shelter in times of war. It's distinctly English in style, crammed with plaques and statues in memory of British soldiers, politicians and their wives. The grandest plaque, made of pure silver, was presented by Elihu Yale, former governor of Fort St George (1687–96), and founder of Yale University in the USA. A collection of photographs of visiting dignitaries, including Queen Elizabeth II, is on display in the entrance porch.

George Town

North of Fort St George, the former British trading centre of **George Town** (reached on bus #18 from Anna Salai) remains the focal area for banks, offices and shipping companies. This confusing – if well-ordered – grid of streets harbours a fascinating medley of architecture: eighteenth- and nineteenth-century churches, Hindu and Jain temples, and a scattering of mosques, interspersed with grand mansions. In the east, on Rajaji Salai, the **General Post Office** occupies a robust earth-red Indo-Saracenic building constructed in 1884. George Town's southern extent is marked by the bulbous white domes and sandstone towers of the **High Court**, and the even more opulent towers of the **Law College**, both showing strong Islamic influence.

Government Museum

Unfortunately the Chennai **Government Museum** (daily except Fri 9.30am–5pm; $5 [Rs10], camera Rs200, video camera Rs500) has joined the ASI sites in charging a ridiculous rate for foreigners. It does have remarkable archeological finds from South India and the Deccan, stone sculptures from major temples, and an unsurpassed collection of Chola bronzes, but whether it's worth the exorbitant entry fee is debatable. To get there, hop on bus #11H from Anna Salai for Pantheon Road, south of Egmore railway station.

The deep-red, circular **main building**, fronted by Italian-style pillars and built in 1851, stands opposite the entrance and ticket office. The first gallery is devoted to archeology and geology; the highlight are the dismantled panels, railings and statues from the second century AD stupa complex at **Amaravati** (see p.1079). Depicting episodes from the Buddha's life and scenes from the *Jataka* stories from ancient Hinayana Buddhist texts, these sensuously carved marble reliefs are widely regarded as the finest achievements of early Indian art, outshining even the Sanchi *toranas*. To the left of here high, arcaded halls full of stuffed animals lead to the **ethnology gallery**, where models, clothes, weapons and photographs of expressionless faces in orderly lines illustrate local tribal societies, some long since wiped out. A fascinating display of wind and string instruments, drums and percussion includes the large predecessor of today's sitar and several very old tablas. Nearby, a group of wooden doors and window frames from Chettinad, a region near Madurai, are exquisitely carved with floral and geometric designs much like those found in Gujarati *havelis*.

The museum's real treasure, however, is the modern, well-lit gallery, left of the main building, which contains the world's most complete and impressive selection of **Chola bronzes** (see p.1169). Large statues of Shiva, Vishnu and Parvati stand in the centre, flanked by glass cases containing smaller figurines, including several sculptures of Shiva as **Nataraja**, the Lord of the Dance, encircled by a ring of fire, and standing with his arms and legs poised and head provocatively cocked. One of the finest models is **Ardhanarishvara**, the androgynous form of Shiva (united with Shakti in transcendence of duality); the left side of the body is female and the right male, and the intimacy of detail is astounding. A rounded breast, a delicate hand and tender bejewelled foot are counterpoints to the harsher sinewy limbs and torso, and the male side of the head is crowned with a mass of matted hair and serpents.

Elsewhere, a **children's gallery** demonstrates the principles of electricity and irrigation with marginally diverting, semi-functional models, while the magnificent Indo-Saracenic **art gallery** houses old British portraits of figures such as Clive and Hastings, plus Rajput and Moghul miniatures, and a small display of ivory carvings.

St Andrew's Kirk

Just northeast of Egmore Station, off Periyar EVR High Road, **St Andrew's Kirk**, consecrated in 1821, is a fine example of Georgian architecture. Modelled on London's St Martins-in-the-Fields, it's one of just three churches in India with a circular seating plan, laid out beneath a huge dome painted blue with gold stars and supported by a sweep of Corinthian columns. Marble plaques around the church give a fascinating insight into the kind of people who left Britain to work for the imperial and Christian cause. A staircase leads onto the flat roof, surrounding the dome, from where you can climb further up into the steeple past the massive bell to a tiny balcony affording excellent views of the city.

Marina

One of the longest city beaches in the world, the **Marina** (Kamaraj Salai) stretches 5km from the harbour at the southeastern corner of George Town, to San Thome Cathedral. The impulse to transform Chennai's "rather dismal beach" into a Marina, styled "from old Sicilian recollections" to function as a "lung" for the city, was conceived by Mountstuart Elphinstone Grant-Duff (governor 1881–86) who had otherwise won himself the reputation for being "feeble, sickly" and a "failure". Over the years, numerous buildings have sprung up, among them surreal modern memorials to Tamil Nadu's chief political heroes; the memorial to illustrious movie actor and chief minister MGR (see box on p.1120) gets pride of place. Going south, you'll pass the Indo-Saracenic **Presidency College** (1865–71), one of a number of stolid Victorian buildings that make up the **University**.

Today the **beach** itself is a sociable stretch, peopled by idle paddlers, picnickers and pony-riders; every afternoon crowds gather around the beach market. However, its location just a little downstream from the port, which belches out waste and smelly fumes, combined with its function as the toilet for the fishing community detract somewhat from its natural beauty. Unsurprisingly, swimming and sunbathing are neither recommended nor approved. Tragically, many young children playing cricket here were swept away by the 2004 tsunami. Around 200 people lost their lives on Marina Beach, and although the death toll here was lower than at other stretches of the coast (much of the city was protected by the sheer width of Marina beach), the fact that a high percentage of those who died were children added to the sense of loss.

Mylapore

Long before Madras came into existence, **Mylapore**, south of the Marina (reached by buses #4, #5 or #21 from the LIC building on Anna Salai), was a major settlement; the Greek geographer Ptolemy mentioned it in the second century AD as a thriving port. During the Pallava period (fifth to ninth centuries) it was second only to Mamallapuram.

An important stop – with Little Mount – on the St Thomas pilgrimage trail, **San Thome Cathedral** (daily 6am–8pm) marks the eastern boundary of Mylapore, lying close to the sea at the southern end of the Marina. Although the present neo-Gothic structure dates from 1896, it stands on the site of two earlier churches (the first possibly erected by Nestorian Christians from Persia during the tenth century) built over the tomb of St Thomas; his relics are kept inside.

The large **Kapalishvara temple** sits less than 1km west of the cathedral. Seventh-century Tamil poet-saints sang its praises, but the present structure, dedicated to Shiva, probably dates from the sixteenth century. Until then, the temple is thought to have occupied a site on the shore; sea erosion or demolition at the hands of the Portuguese led it to be rebuilt inland. The huge (40m) *gopura* towering above the main east entrance, plastered in stucco figures, was added in 1906. Surrounding an assortment of busy shrines, where priests offer blessings for devotees and non-Hindus alike, the courtyard features an old tree where a small shrine to Shiva's consort, Parvati, shows her in the form of a peahen (*mayil*) worshipping a *lingam*.

A little further west, before you come to TTK Road, the **Luz Church**, on Luz Church Road, is thought to be the earliest in Chennai, built by the Portuguese in the sixteenth century. Its founding is associated with a miracle; Portuguese sailors in difficulties at sea were once guided to land and safety by a light which, when they tried to find its source, disappeared. The church, dedicated to Our Lady of Light, was erected where the light left them.

Little Mount Caves

St Thomas is said to have sought refuge from persecution in the **Little Mount Caves**, 8km south of the city centre (bus #18A, #18B, or #52C from Anna Salai), now 200m off the road between the Maraimalai Adigal Bridge and the residence of the governor of Tamil Nadu. Entrance to the caves is beside steps leading to a statue of Our Lady of Good Health. Inside, next to a small natural window in the rock, are impressions of what are believed to be St Thomas' handprints, created when he made his escape through this tiny opening.

Behind the new circular church of Our Lady of Good Health, together with brightly painted replicas of the *Pietà* and Holy Sepulchre, is a natural **spring**. Tradition has it that this was created when Thomas struck the rock, so the crowds that came to hear him preach could quench their thirst; samples of its holy water are on sale.

The Theosophical Society Headquarters

The **Theosophical Society** was established in New York in 1875 by American Civil War veteran Colonel Henry S. Olcott, a failed farmer and journalist, and the eccentric Russian aristocrat Madame Helena Petrovna Blavatsky, who claimed occult powers and telepathic links with "Mahatmas" in Tibet. Based on a fundamental belief in the equality and truth of all religions, the society in fact propagated a modern form of Hinduism, praising all things Indian and shunning Christian missionaries. Needless to say, its two founders were greeted enthusiastically when they transferred their operations to Madras in 1882, establishing their headquarters near Elliot's Beach in Adyar (buses #5, #5C or #23C from George Town/Anna Salai). Even after Madame Blavatsky's psychic powers were proved to be bogus, the society continued to attract Hindus and Western visitors, and its buildings still stand today, sheltering several shrines and an excellent **library** (Mon–Sat 8.30–10am & 2–4pm) of books on religion and philosophy. The collection, begun by Olcott in 1886, comprises 165,000 volumes and nearly 200,000 palm-leaf manuscripts, from all over the world. A selection is housed in an exhibition room on the ground floor. This includes 800-year-old scroll pictures of the Buddha; rare Tibetan xylographs written on bark paper; exquisitely illuminated Korans; a giant copy of Martin Luther's *Biblia* printed in Nuremberg three hundred years ago; and a Bible in seven languages that's the size of a thumbnail.

The 270 acres of woodland and gardens surrounding the society's headquarters make a serene place to sit and restore spirits away from the noise and heat of the city streets. In the middle of the grounds, a vast 400-year-old **banyan tree**, said to be the second-largest in the world, provides shade for up to 3000 people at a time.

The Enfield factory

India's most stylish home-made motorcycle, the **Enfield Bullet**, is manufactured at a plant on the outskirts of Chennai, 18km north of Anna Salai (bus #1 from LIC Building or Parry's Corner). With its elegant tear-drop tank and thumping 350cc single-cylinder engine, the Bullet has become a contemporary classic – in spite of its propensity to leak oil and break down. Bike enthusiasts should definitely brave the long haul across town to see the **factory**, which is as much a period piece as the machines it turns out. Guided tours, which last around ninety minutes and are free (Mon–Fri 9.30am–5.30pm; Rs500; ⓣ044/2573 2622), have to be arranged in advance by telephoning the Enfield's marketing general manager, Mr K. Muralidharan. You can do this yourself, or through the India Tourism Office on Anna Salai.

Eating

Chennai runs on inexpensive indigenous fast-food **restaurants** and "meals" (**thali**) joints, in particular the legendary *Saravana Bhavan* chain, which serves superb South Indian food for a fraction of the cost of a coffee at one of the five-stars. That said, a minor splurge at *Annalakshmi* on Anna Salai or the *Park Sheraton* on TTK Road is well worth considering.

The restaurants listed below are marked on either the Egmore, Anna Salai and Triplicane **map** on p.1124 or the Chennai **map** on p.1118.

Amaravati Corner of Cathedral and TTK roads. One of four dependable options in this complex of regional speciality restaurants, south of the downtown area. This one does excellent Andhran food, including particularly tasty biriyanis.

Annalakshmi 804 Anna Salai. A nonprofitmaking venture run voluntarily by devotees of Swami Shivananda, where you can enjoy a leisurely and expensive meal in beautiful surroundings. You choose one of several set menus (each with different Ayurvedic properties), and the profits go to charitable works in the community.

Dakshin *Welcomgroup Park Sheraton*, 132 TTK Rd ⓣ044/2499 4101. One of the country's top South

Indian restaurants, this upmarket place offers an excellent choice of unusual dishes from the four southern states, including seafood and fish in marinated spices, Karnataka mutton biriyani and piping-hot *iddiappam* and *appam* made on the spot. There is live Carnatic music; expect to pay around Rs600 per head with beer.

Hot Breads Cathedral Rd. Wholewheat breads, baguettes, fresh quiches, and an impressive range of cakes, biscuits and pastries. Decent espresso coffee, too. Eat in or take away.

Saravana Bhavan Thanigai Murugan Rathinavel Hall, 77 Usman Rd, T Nagar. This famous South Indian fast-food chain is an institution among the Chennai middle class, with other branches opposite the bus stand in George Town, and in the forecourt of the Shanti cinema (at the top of Anna Salai). Try their delicious *rawa iddlis*, or range of thalis rounded off with some freshly made *ladoo* or *barfi* from the sweets counter outside.

Señor (Don) Pepés 1st floor, above *Hot Breads*, Cathedral Rd. Swish a/c Tex-Mex joint, serving a predictable menu of fajitas, enchiladas, tortillas and burritos, plus so-so pasta dishes (dubbed "Euro-Mex"). Main courses about Rs120.

Vasanta Bhavan 20 Gandhi Irwin Rd. Easily the best "meals" joint among many around Egmore station, with ranks of attentive waiters and delicious pure veg food – just Rs25 for an unlimited thali. It's busy, spotlessly clean, and their coffee and sweets are delicious.

Verandah *Taj Connemara*, Binny Rd ⓣ044/2852 0123. The ideal venue for a posh Sunday morning breakfast buffet: crisp newspapers and fresh coffee served in silver pots. The blow-out lunchtime buffets (around Rs400) are also recommended, and they serve à la carte Italian food in the evening. *The Rain Tree* is the second Taj eatery, with great Chettinad (South Indian) specialities included in the weekend dinner buffets (around Rs400). Reserve in advance.

Listings

Airline offices Air France, Thaper House, 43–44 Montieth Rd ⓣ044/2855 4916; Air India, 19 Rukmani Lakshmipathy Rd ⓣ044/2855 4477, airport ⓣ044/2256 0747; British Airways, Sigma Wing, 177 Anna Salai ⓣ044/2860 3123; Deccan, 32 92nd St, 18th Ave ⓣ044/3097 8596; Gulf Air, 52 Montieth Rd ⓣ044/2855 4417; Indian Airlines, 19 Rukhmani Lakshmipathy Rd ⓣ044/2855 5201; Jet Airways, Thaper House, 43–44 Montieth Rd ⓣ044/2841 4141; KLM, 10 Monteith Rd ⓣ044/2852 4427; Lufthansa, 167 Anna Salai ⓣ044/2854 3500; Malaysia Airlines, Arihant Nico Park, 90 Dr RK Salai ⓣ044/5219 9999; Qantas, Eldorado Building, 112 Uttar Gandhi Salai ⓣ044/2827 8680; Sahara, D-91 First Ave, Anna Nagar East ⓣ044/5208 7070; Singapore Airlines, 108 Dr Radha Krishnan Salai ⓣ044/2847 3995; Sri Lankan Airlines, Nagabrahma Towers, 76 Cathedral Rd ⓣ044/2811 1536; Swissair, 19 Hamid Building, 191 Anna Salai ⓣ044/2852 4783; Thai Airways, 31 Haddows Rd, Nungambakkam ⓣ044/5217 3311. For American, Air Canada, Biman, Philippine, Royal Jordanian and TWA, contact JetAir, Apex Plaza, 3 MG Rd ⓣ044/2859 2564. Most offices open Mon–Fri 10am–5pm, Sat 10am–1pm.

Banks and currency exchange Tourists have few difficulties changing money in Chennai: there are plenty of banks, and the major hotels offer exchange facilities to residents only. A conveniently central option is American Express, G-17, Spencer Plaza, 769 Anna Salai (Mon–Fri 9.30am–5.30pm, Sat 9.30am–2.30pm). Thomas Cook (Mon–Sat 9am–6pm) have offices at the Ceebros Centre, 45 Montieth Rd, Egmore, at the G-4 Eldorado Building, 112 Uttar Gandhi Salai and also at the airport (open to meet flights). For encashments on Visa cards, go to Bobcards, next door to the Bank of Baroda on Montieth Rd, near the *Ambassador Pallava Hotel*. There is also an increasing number of 24hr ATMs popping up around town, such as at Citibank, 766 Anna Salai.

Bookshops Higginbothams on Anna Salai is Chennai's oldest bookshop, with a vast assortment of Indian and Western titles, and a few maps at rupee rates. Landmark (First floor, Spencer Plaza, Anna Salai) has a huge selection of books, stationery, and music. Serious bookworms, however, head for the hole-in-the-wall Giggles, in the *Taj Connemara Hotel*, where, stacked in precariously high piles, you'll find a matchless stock of novels, academic tomes on the region and coffee-table books. Unlike other bookstores in the city, this one will take credit cards and post purchases abroad for you for nominal charges.

Cinemas The Abhirami and Lakshmi along Anna Salai show English-language films, but for the full-on Tamil film experience, take in a show at the Shanti, off the top of Anna Salai, which boasts the city's biggest screen and a digital stereo sound-system. Nearby, the equally massive Devi hosts the latest Bollywood blockbusters.

Consulates Canada, 3rd Floor Dhun Bldg, 827 Anna Salai ⓣ044/2852 0918; Sri Lanka, 196 TTK Rd ⓣ044/2498 7896; UK, 20 Anderson Rd,

Nungambakkam ⓣ044/2825 7422; USA, Anna Salai ⓣ044/2811 2000.

Hospitals Chennai's best-equipped private hospital is the Apollo, 21/22 Greams Rd ⓣ044/2829 3333. For an ambulance, try ⓣ044/102, but it's usually quicker to jump in a taxi.

Internet Access is widely available for Rs30–40 per hour in net cafes, more in hotel business centres. The snazziest option is Net Café, at 101/1 Kanakasri Nagar, down an alleyway off Cathedral Rd (daily 7am–midnight) – look for the neon "@" sign. SRIS Netsurfing Café on the first floor of Spencer Plaza is a cheaper, though smaller, alternative. Gee Gee Net in Triplicane, next door to *Hotel Comfort*, is open 24hr. Egmore options include the 24hr service at the *Pandian* hotel.

Left luggage Counters at Egmore and Central railway stations store bags for Rs10 per day; they usually require you to chain and padlock your baggage and you must show your train ticket. Some hotels also guard luggage at a daily rate.

Music stores For the best range of concert quality Indian instruments, including *vinas*, check out Saptaswara Music Store, on Raipetha Rd, Mylapore, or Musee Musicals at 67 Anna Salai. Music World, on the first floor of Spencer Plaza, has the best selection of contemporary Indian and Western music in the city.

Photographic equipment Dozens of stores around town offer film and developing services on modern machines (Konica studios are particularly reliable), but the only Kodak-approved Q-Lab in the city (recommended for transparency processing) is Image Park, GEE Plaza, 1 Craft Rd, Nungambakkam Reliance Opticals, at 136 Anna Salai, stocks Fuji Provia and Sensia II. For camera repair, your best bet is Camera Crafts, 325/8A Quaide Milleth Salai, Triplicane, near *Broadlands Hotel*. Delhi Photo Stores, in an arcade directly behind the big Konica shop on Wallajah Rd, is crammed with spare parts and other useful Indian-made bits and bobs for cameras.

Postal services Chennai's main post office is opposite Shanti theatre on Anna Salai (Mon–Sat 8am–8pm; Sun 10am–5pm). If you're using it for poste restante, make sure your correspondents mark the envelope "Head Post Office, Anna Salai", or your letters could well end up across town at the GPO, north of Parry's Corner on Rajaji Salai (same hours). The post office on Quaide Milleth Salai, in Triplicane (Mon–Sat 7am–3pm) is convenient if you're staying at *Broadlands*.

Souvenirs Spencer Plaza on Anna Salai has an excellent selection of boutiques, clothes shops and small souvenir stalls. Across the road at 152 Anna Salai, the Indian Arts Emporium has a good selection of handicrafts, furniture and metalwork.

Travel agents Reliable travel agents include Welcome Tourrs and Travels, 150 Anna Salai ⓣ044/2846 0908; PL World Way, G-11 Ground Floor, Spencer Plaza ⓣ044/2822 6853; Surya Travels, F-14 1st Floor, Spencer Plaza ⓣ044/2852 3934.

Moving on from Chennai

Transport connections between Chennai and the rest of India are summarized on opposite page. If you're short of time, consider employing one of the **travel agents** listed above to book your plane, train or bus ticket for you. This doesn't apply to boat tickets for the Andaman Islands, which have to be booked in person (see overleaf). For more on public transport from Chennai, see "Travel details", p.1204.

By air

Chennai's domestic airport stands adjacent to the international terminal, 16km southwest of the centre at **Meenambakkam**; for more on transport to and from it, see pp.1122–1123. Indian Airlines flies from Meenambakkam to fifteen destinations around the country, including several daily flights to Mumbai, Delhi, Hyderabad and Kolkata (Calcutta). Jet Airways operates services to twelve cities, including Ahmedabad and Bangalore. Both airlines fly daily to Port Blair.

By train

Trains to Tiruchirapalli (Trichy), Thanjavur, Kodaikanal Road, Madurai and most other destinations in south Tamil Nadu leave from **Egmore Station**, with the occasional service leaving from the suburban **Tambaram** station. All other trains leave from **Chennai Central** where, left of the main building on

Recommended trains from Chennai

Destination	Name	No.	From	Departs	Total time
Bangalore	Shatabdi Express*	#2007	Central	6am**	4hr 50min
	Chennai–Bangalore Express	#6523	Central	1pm	7hr 5min
Bhubaneswar	Coromandel Express	#2842	Central	9.05am	20hr 10min
	Howrah Mail	#6004	Central	10.30pm	22hr 55min
Coimbatore	Kovai Express	#2675	Central	6.15am	7hr 40min
	Cheran Express	#2673	Central	10.10pm	8hr 5min
Delhi	Tamil Nadu Express	#2621	Central	10pm	33hr 30min
	Grand Trunk Express	#2615	Central	4.30pm	36hr 30min
Hyderabad	Charminar Express	#2759	Central	6.10pm	14hr 15min
Kanniyakumari	Kanniyakumari Express	#2633	Egmore	5.30pm	13hr
Kochi/ Ernakulam	Chennai–Alleppey Express	#6041	Central	8.30pm	11hr 40min
	Trivandrum Mail	#2623	Central	7.30pm	11hr
Kodaikanal Road	Pandyan Express	#2637	Egmore	9.30pm	7hr 58min
Kolkata (Calcutta)	Coromandel Express	#2842	Central	9.05am	28hr
	Chennai–Howrah Mail	#6004	Central	10.30pm	31hr 10min
Madurai	Vaigai Express	#2635	Egmore	12.25pm	7hr 50min
Mettuppalayam (for Ooty)	Nilgiri Express	#2671	Central	9pm	9hr 20min
Mumbai	Mumbai Express	#6012	Central	11.45am	26hr
	Chennai–Dadar Express	#1064	Central	6.50am	23hr 15min
Mysore	Shatabdi Express*	#2007	Central	6am**	7hr
	Mysore Express	#6222	Central	9.30pm	10hr 55min
Rameshwaram	Sethu Express	#6713	Tambaram	1pm	17hr 50min
Rameshwaram Express	Tambaram–Rameshwaram Express	#6701	Tambaram	8.15pm	17hr 5min
Thanjavur	Rock Fort Express	#6177	Egmore	10.30pm	8hr 20min
Tirupathi	Saptagiri Express	#6057	Central	6.25am	3hr 5min
Thiruvananthapuram	Trivandrum Mail	#2623	Central	7.30pm	16hr 20min
Varanasi Express***	Ganga Kaveri	#6039	Central	5.30pm	38hr 40min

*A/c only

**Except Tues

***Mon & Sat only

the first floor of the Moore Market Complex, the efficient **tourist reservation counter** (Mon–Sat 8am–8pm, Sun 8am–2pm; no phone) sells tickets for trains from either station. The booking office at Egmore, up the stairs left of the main entrance (same hours), also handles bookings for both stations, but has no tourist counter.

By boat

Boats leave Chennai every week for **Port Blair**, capital of the **Andaman Islands**. However, getting a ticket can be a rigmarole, even though the schedule is now more regular. The first thing you'll need to do is head up to the Chennai Port Trust, next to the Directorate of Shipping on Rajaji (North Beach) Salai, George Town, where a small hut houses the Andaman Administration Office. A chalkboard on the wall advertises details of the next sailing, and you buy a ticket from the hatch around the corner, at the front of the main building. There are no ticket sales on the day of sailing. You no longer have to get a **permit** on the mainland, as they are available on arrival in Port Blair. For more details, see the Andaman Islands chapter pp.1098–1099.

By bus

All long-distance **buses** leave from the **Moffussil bus stand**, over 10km from the centre – see "Arrival", p.1121, for local bus connections. The six platforms are each divided into thirty-odd bays, with frequent services to destinations throughout Tamil Nadu and the neighbouring states. The first stop beyond Chennai for many people is **Mamallapuram**, for which the fastest services are #188, #188A and anything marked "East Coast Express" (every 15–30min; less than 2hr); #19A, #19C, #119 and #119A all take rather longer, and the 108b (via the airport and Chengalpattu) much longer.

The northeast

Fazed by the fierce heat and air pollution of Chennai, most visitors escape as fast as they can, heading down the Coromandel coast to India's stone-carving capital, **Mamallapuram**, whose ancient monuments include the famous Shore Temple and a batch of extraordinary rock sculptures. En route, it's well worth jumping off the bus at **Dakshina Chitra**, a folk museum 30km south of Chennai, where traditional buildings from across South India have been beautifully reconstructed. Further inland, **Kanchipuram** is an important pilgrimage and silk-sari-weaving town from where you can loop southwest to **Tiruvannamalai**, a wonderfully atmospheric temple town clustered at the base of the sacred mountain, Arunachala. On the coast, you can breakfast on croissants and espresso coffee in the former French colony of **Pondicherry**. A short way north, **Auroville**, the Utopian settlement founded by followers of the Sri Aurobindo Ghose's spiritual successor, The Mother, provides a New-Age haven for soul-searching Westerners and an economy for the local population.

Both Mamallapuram and Pondicherry are well connected to Chennai by nail-bitingly fast bus services, running along a smooth coastal highway. Take care to use state buses where possible; their safety record is far better than the private ones. You can also get to Pondicherry by train, but this involves a change at the junction town of **Villupuram**, from where services are slow and relatively infrequent.

Mamallapuram (Mahabalipuram)

Scattered around the base of a colossal mound of boulders, is the small seaside town of **MAMALLAPURAM** (aka Mahabalipuram), 58km south of Chennai. From dawn till dusk, the rhythms of chisels chipping granite resound down its sandy lanes – evidence of a stone-carving tradition that has endured since this was a major port of the Pallava dynasty, between the fifth and ninth centuries. Little is known about life in the ancient city, and it is only possible to speculate about the purpose of much of the boulder sculpture, which includes one of India's most photographed monuments, the **Shore Temple**. It does appear, however, that the friezes and shrines were not made for worship at all, but rather as a showcase for the talents of local artists. Due in no small part to the maritime activities of the Pallavas, their style of art and architecture had wide-ranging influence, spreading from South India as far north as

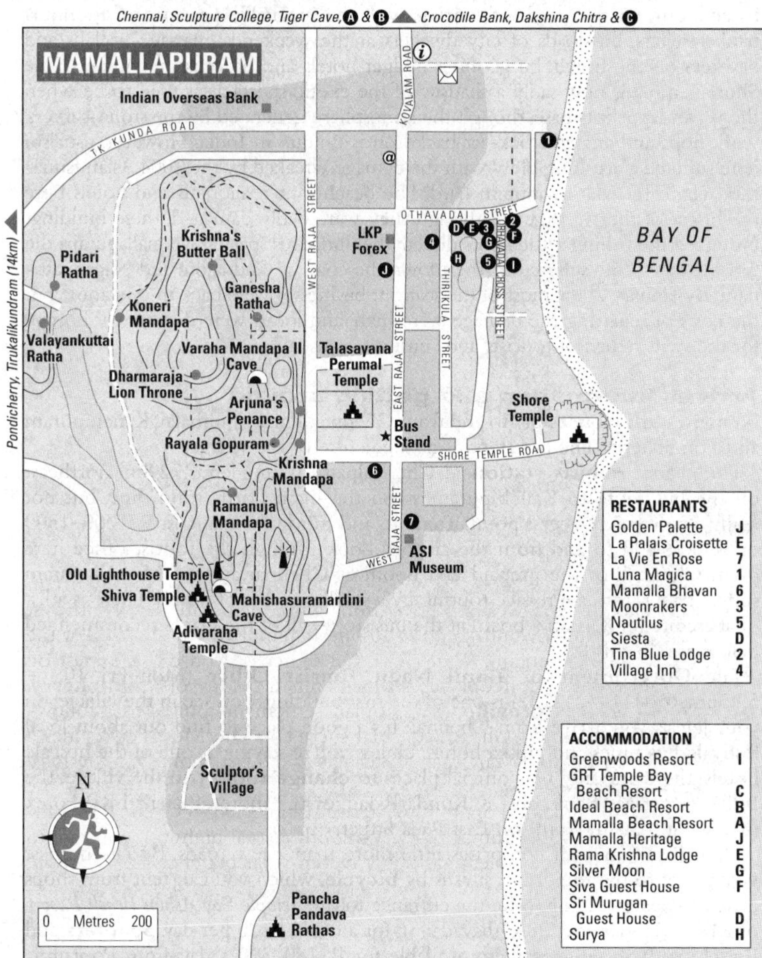

Ellora, as well as to Southeast Asia. This international cultural importance was recognized in 1995 when Mamallapuram was granted World Heritage Site status by UNESCO.

Mamallapuram's monuments divide into four categories: open-air **bas-reliefs**, structured **temples**, man-made **caves** and **rathas** ("chariots" carved *in situ* from single boulders to resemble temples or the chariots used in temple processions). The famous bas-reliefs, **Arjuna's Penance** and the **Krishna Mandapa**, adorn massive rocks near the centre of the village, while the beautiful **Shore Temple** presides over the beach. Sixteen man-made caves and monolithic structures, in different stages of completion, are scattered through the area, but the most complete of the nine *rathas* are in a group, named after the five Pandava brothers of the Mahabharata.

Given the coexistence of so many stunning archeological remains with a long white-sand **beach**, it was inevitable this would become a major destination for Western travellers. Over the past two decades, Mamallapuram has certainly oriented its economy to the needs of tourists, with the inevitable presence of Kashmiri trinket sellers, bus-loads of city dwellers at the weekends, massage-wallahs and hawkers on the beach, burgeoning budget hotels and little fish restaurants. The Shore Temple is now sadly a shadow of the exotic spectacle it used to be when the waves lapped its base, though the atmosphere generated by the stone-carvers' workshops and ancient rock-art backdrop is unique in India. However, tourism here suffered a crushing blow with the damage wreaked by the 2004 Asian tsunamis, which hit Mamallapuram hard. The beachfront restaurants and hotels bore the brunt of the waves, but although they were badly damaged, these buildings protected the fishing settlements directly behind, thus sparing Mamallapuram the terrible loss of life suffered further down the coast at Cuddalore and Nagappattinam. By January 2005, most of the seafront businesses were back in operation, but the costs of repairing the damage were high, and locals were desperately hoping for the swift return of tourists and "business as usual".

Arrival, information and getting around

Numerous daily **buses** ply to and from Chennai, Thiruvannmalai, Kanchipuram and Pondicherry. The bus stand is in the centre of the village.

The nearest **railway station**, at Chengalpattu (Chingleput), 29km northeast on the bus route to Kanchipuram, is on the main north–south line, but not really a convenient access point. **Taxis** to and from Chennai cost Rs1000–1500 or Rs600–800 to and from the airport; book through the tourist office here or in Chennai, or the prepaid taxi booth at Chennai airport. Mamallapuram suffers badly from aggressive touting by a small number of hotels. There is a list of accredited hotels on a board at the bus stop – all of the places recommended below are on this list.

The **Government of Tamil Nadu Tourist Office** (Mon–Fri 10am–5.45pm; ⓣ04114/242232) is one of the first buildings you see in the village; on your left as you arrive from Chennai. It's a good place to find out about local festivals, bus times and pukka hotels. Unless you're staying at one of the upscale hotels, there are only two official places to **change money** in the village: the Indian Overseas Bank, on TK Kunda Road, or the more efficient LKP Forex (Mon–Sat 9.30am–7pm) on East Raja Street.

Mamallapuram itself comprises little more than a few roads. By far the best way to get to the important sites is by **bicycle**, which you can rent from shops on East Raja Street, opposite the entrance to the *Temple Bay Ashok Beach Resort*, or MK Cycle Centre, 28 Othavadai St, for around Rs20 per day. **Scooters** and Enfield **motorcycles** are also available for Rs150–300 a day, from Poornima

Travels, next to *Moonraker's* restaurant, and through some guesthouses. Welcome Tourrs and Travels (Ⓣ044/2846 0908) on Othavadai Street can arrange car hire. The going rate for the increasing number of **Net facilities** is Rs30 per hour, though connection speed and reliability can vary; most of them are bunched together along Othavadai and Othavadai Cross streets. If you need **medical treatment**, the Suradeep Hospital on Thirukula Street (Ⓣ04114/242390) is highly recommended.

Accommodation

Mamallapuram is not short of **accommodation**, and reduced visitor arrivals in recent years mean that bargaining is the order of the day. The bulk of cheap and mid-range lodges are within the village, a short stroll from the beach. Many of the expensive resorts can be found along the six-kilometre stretch of coast north of the village, while the *Taj Fisherman's Cove* is located almost halfway to Chennai. Without a taxi or bike, getting to these can prove a bit of a hassle; it's easy enough to take a rickshaw out there from the village, but not in the other direction. However, the walk back into Mamallapuram along the beach is pleasant – if you're not carrying luggage.

Greenwoods Resort Othavadai Cross St Ⓣ04114/243318, Ⓔgreenwoods_resort@yahoo.com. A very friendly family-run place, a stone's throw from the beach and set in a lush garden that's lovingly tended by the numerous ladies of the house. There's a choice of a/c or non-a/c rooms, some with a private balcony. Extremely good value. ❷–❺

GRT Temple Bay Beach Resort 1km north of town, off Kovalam Rd Ⓣ04114/242251, Ⓦwww.grttemplebay.com. Great location on the beach, with views of the Shore Temple. Thatched beach-side cottages have sea-facing balconies, and there are huge rooms in the main building. There's a swimming pool and restaurant on site. Rates start at $130. ❾

Ideal Beach Resort 5km from town, Kovalam Rd Ⓣ04114/242240, Ⓦwww.resortsindia.com. Comfortable cottages near the Tiger Cave, and a large pool and pleasant alfresco restaurant on site. Popular with overland tour groups, so book well ahead during the high season. ❼–❾

Mamalla Beach Resort 108 Kovalam Rd, 2.5km north of town Ⓣ04114/242375, Ⓔmbresort@vsnl.net. Good-value resort with spacious, well-decorated a/c and non a/c chalets with attached bathrooms and verandas. Decent restaurant and games area, but no pool. ❺–❻

Mamalla Heritage 104 East Raja St Ⓣ04114/242060, Ⓕ242160. Efficient and modern hotel on the main drag through the village, with comfortable and spotless a/c rooms, with fridge and TV, overlooking a courtyard. There's a very good restaurant on site (see p.1143). ❺

Rama Krishna Lodge 8 Othavadai St Ⓣ04114/242331. Clean, well-maintained rooms in the heart of the tourist enclave, all with bathrooms but no a/c, set round a courtyard filled with pot plants; the newest rooms are on the top storey, and have sea views. There's a back-up generator, and they often have vacancies when everywhere else is full. ❶

Silver Moon 24 Othavadai Cross St Ⓣ04114/243644, Ⓔsilver_moonguesthouse@yahoo.com. Very clean and friendly lodge with cosy en-suite rooms and a small leafy courtyard. ❷

Siva Guest House 2 Othavadai Cross Rd Ⓣ04114/243234, Ⓔsivaguesthouse@hotmail.com. Clean, tidy lodge with choice of a/c and non a/c rooms. Good value. ❷–❹

Sri Murugan Guest House 42 Othavadai St Ⓣ04114/242552. Small and peaceful, with courteous service, clean non a/c rooms and a rooftop restaurant. One of the nicest options in the area. ❶–❷

Surya Thirukula St Ⓣ04114/242292, Ⓕ242492. Lakeside hotel set in an eccentric compound dotted with broken sculpture – the hotel seems rather peripheral to the sculpture school and gallery which share the same space. There's a range of rooms, some with a/c and balconies; mosquito nets are available. The pool is open to non-guests for Rs100. ❸–❺

The Krishna Mandapa and Arjuna's Penance

A little to the west of the village centre, off Shore Temple Road, the enormous bas-relief known as the **Krishna Mandapa** shows Krishna raising Mount

The temples of Tamil Nadu

No Indian state is more dominated by its **temples** than Tamil Nadu, where temple architecture catalogues the tastes of successive dynasties and testifies to the centrality of religion in everyday life. Most temples are built in honour of Shiva, Vishnu and their consorts; all are characterized not only by their design and sculptures, but by constant activity: devotion, dancing, singing, pujas, festivals and feasts. Each is tended by brahmin priests, recognizable by their *dhotis* (loincloths), a sacred thread draped over the right shoulder, and marks on the forehead. One to three horizontal (usually white) lines distinguish Shaivites; vertical lines (yellow or red), often converging into a near-V shape, are common among Vaishnavites.

Dravida, the temple architecture of Tamil Nadu, first took form in the Pallava port of **Mamallapuram**. A step-up from the cave retreats of Hindu and Jain ascetics, the earliest Pallava monuments were **mandapas**, shrines cut into rock faces and fronted by columns. The magnificent Arjuna's Penance **bas-relief** shows the fluid carving of the Pallavas at its most exquisite. This sculptural skill was transferred to freestanding temples, **rathas**, carved out of single rocks and incorporating the essential elements of Hindu temples: the dim inner sanctuary, the *garbhagriha*, capped with a modest tapering spire featuring repetitive architectural motifs. In turn, the Shore Temple was built with three shrines, topped by a **vimana** similar to the towering roofs of the *rathas*; statues of Nandi, Shiva's bull, later to receive pride of place, surmount its low walls. In the finest structural Pallava temple, the Kailasanatha Temple at **Kanchipuram**, the sanctuary stands within a courtyard enclosed by high walls carved with images of Shiva, his consort and ghoulish mythical lions, *yalis*, were the prototype for later styles.

Pallava themes were developed in Karnataka by the Chalukyas and Rashtrakutas, but it was the Shaivite **Cholas** who spearheaded Tamil Nadu's next architectural phase, in the tenth century. In **Thanjavur**, Rajaraja I created the Brihadeshvara Temple principally as a status symbol; its proportions far exceed any attempted by the Pallavas. Set within a vast walled courtyard, the sanctuary, fronted by a small *mandapa*, stands beneath a sculpted *vimana* that soars over 60m high. Most sculptures once again feature Shiva, but the *gopuras* each side of the eastern gateway to the courtyard, were an innovation, as were the lions carved into the base of the sanctuary walls, and the pavilion erected over Nandi in front of the sanctuary. The second great Chola Temple was built in **Gangaikondacholapuram** by Rajendra I. Instead of a mighty *vimana*, he brought new elements, adding subsidiary shrines and placing an extended *mandapa* in front of the central sanctuary, its pillars writhing with dancers and deities.

By the time of the thirteenth-century **Vijayanagar** kings, the temple was central to city life, the focus for civic meetings, education, dance and theatre. The Vijayanagars extended earlier structures, adding enclosing walls around a series of **prakaras**, or courtyards, and erecting freestanding *mandapas* for use as meeting halls, elephant stables, stages for music and dance, and ceremonial marriage halls (*kalyan mandapas*). Raised on superbly decorated columns, these *mandapas* became known as **thousand-pillared halls**. **Tanks** were added, doubling as water stores and washing areas, and used for festivals when deities were set afloat in boats.

Under the Vijayanagars, the *gopuras* were enlarged and set at the cardinal points over the high gateways to each *prakara*, to become the dominant feature. Rectangular in plan, and embellished with images of animals and local saints or rulers as well as deities, *gopuras* are periodically repainted in pinks, blues, whites and yellows, a sharp and joyous contrast with the earthy browns and greys of halls and sanctuaries beyond. **Madurai** is the place to check out Vijayanagar architecture. Its temples regularly come alive for festivals, in which Shiva and his "fish-eyed" consort are hauled through town on mighty wooden chariots. Outside Tiruchirapalli, the temple at **Srirangam** was extended by the Vijayanagar Nayaks to become South India's largest. Unlike that in Madurai, it incorporates earlier Chola foundations, but the ornamentation, with pillars formed into rearing horses, is superb.

△ Temple detail, Chennai

TAMIL NADU

20

Govardhana aloft in one hand. The sculptor's original intention must have been for the rock above Krishna to represent the mountain, but the seventeenth-century Vijayanagar addition of a columned *mandapa*, or entrance hall, prevents a clear view of the carving. Krishna is also depicted seated milking a cow, and standing playing the flute. Other figures are *gopas* and *gopis*, the cowboys and girls of his pastoral youth. Lions (one with a human face) sit to the left, while above them is a bull.

Another bas-relief, **Arjuna's Penance** (also referred to as the "Descent of the Ganges") is a few metres north, opposite the modern Talasayana Perumal Temple. The surface of this rock erupts with detailed carving, most notably endearing and naturalistic renditions of animals. A family of elephants dominates the right side, with tiny offspring asleep beneath a great tusker. Further still to the right, separate from the great rock, is a freestanding sculpture of an adult monkey grooming its young. On the left-hand side, Arjuna, one of the Pandava brothers and a consummate archer, is shown standing on one leg. He is looking at the midday sun through a prism formed by his hands, meditating on Shiva, who is represented by a nearby statue fashioned by Arjuna himself. The *Shiva Purana* tells that Arjuna made the journey to a forest on the banks of the Ganges to do penance, in the hope that Shiva would part with his favourite weapon, the *pashupatashastra*, a magic staff or arrow. Shiva eventually materialized in the guise of Kirata, a wild forest-dweller, and picked a fight with Arjuna over a boar they both claimed to have shot. Arjuna only realized he was dealing with the deity after his attempts to drub the wild man proved futile; narrowly escaping death at the playful hand of Shiva, he was finally rewarded with the weapon. Not far away, mimicking Arjuna's devout pose, an emaciated (presumably ascetic) cat stands on hind legs, surrounded by mice.

To the right of Arjuna, a natural cleft represents the **Ganges**, complete with *nagas* – water spirits in the form of cobras. Near the bottom, a fault in the rock that broke a *naga* received a quick fix of cement in the 1920s. Evidence of a cistern and channels remain at the top, which at one time must have carried water to flow down the cleft, simulating the great river. It's not known if there was some ritual purpose to all this, or whether it was simply an elaborate spectacle to impress visitors. You may see sudden movements among the carved animals: lazing goats often join the permanent features.

Ganesha ratha and Varaha Cave

Just north of Arjuna's Penance a path leads west to a single monolith, the **Ganesha ratha**. Its image of Ganesh dates from this century; some say it was installed at the instigation of England's King George V. The sculpture at one end, of a protecting demon with a tricorn headdress, is reminiscent of the Indus Valley civilization's 4000-year-old horned figure known as the "proto-Shiva".

Behind Arjuna's Penance, southwest of the Ganesha *ratha*, is the **Varaha Mandapa II Cave**, whose entrance hall has two pillars with horned lion-bases and a cell flanked by two *dvarpalas*, or guardians. One of four **panels** shows the boar-incarnation of Vishnu, who stands with one foot resting on the *naga* snake-king as he lifts a diminutive Prithvi – the earth – from the primordial ocean. Another is of Gajalakshmi, the goddess Lakshmi seated on a lotus being bathed by a pair of elephants. Trivikrama, the dwarf brahmin who becomes huge and bestrides the world in three steps to defeat the demon king Bali, is shown in another panel, and finally a four-armed Durga is depicted in another.

A little way north of Arjuna's Penance, precipitously balanced on the top of a ridge, is a massive, natural, almost spherical boulder called **Krishna's Butter Ball**. Picnickers and goats often rest in its perilous-looking shade.

The Shore Temple

East of the village, the distinctive, soaring silhouette of Mamallapuram's **Shore Temple** (daily sunrise–sunset; $5 [Rs10], includes Pancha Pandava *rathas* if visited on the on the same day; video camera Rs25) dates from the early eighth century and is considered to be the earliest stone-built temple in South India. The design of its two finely carved towers was profoundly influential: it was exported across South India and eventually abroad to Southeast Asia. Today, due to the combined forces of wind, salt and sand, much of the detailed carving has eroded, giving the whole temple a soft, rounded appearance.

The taller of the towers is raised above a cell that faces out to sea – don't be surprised to see mischievous monkeys crouching inside. Approached from the west through two low-walled enclosures lined with small Nandi (bull) figures, the temple comprises two *lingam* shrines (one facing east, the other west), and a third shrine between them housing an image of the reclining Vishnu. Recent excavations, revealing a tank containing a structured stone column thought to have been a lantern, and a large Varaha (boar incarnation of Vishnu) aligned with the Vishnu shrine, suggest that the area was sacred long before the Pallavas chose it as a temple site.

The lighthouses and the Mahishasuramardini Cave

South of Arjuna's Penance at the highest point in an area of steep paths, unfinished temples, ruins, scampering monkeys and massive rocks, the **New Lighthouse** affords fine views east to the Shore Temple, and west across paddy fields and flat lands littered with rocks. Next to it, the **Olakanesvara** ("flame-eyed" Shiva), or **Old Lighthouse Temple**, used as a lighthouse until the beginning of the twentieth century, dates from the Rajasimha period (674–800 AD) and contains no image.

Nestling between the two lighthouses is the **Mahishasuramardini Cave**, whose central image portrays Shiva and Parvati with the child Murugan seated on Parvati's lap. Shiva's right foot rests on the back of the bull Nandi, and Parvati sits casually, leaning on her left hand. On the left wall, beyond an empty cell, a panel depicts Vishnu reclining on the serpent, his attitude of repose contrasted with the weapon-brandishing demons, Madhu and Kaithaba. Other figures seek Vishnu's permission to chase them. Opposite, an intricately carved panel shows the eight-armed goddess Durga as Mahishasuramardini, the "crusher" of the buffalo demon Mahishasura. The panel shows Durga riding a lion, in the midst of the struggle. Accompanied by dwarf *ganas*, she wields a bow and other weapons; Mahishasura, equipped with a club, can be seen to the right, in flight with fellow demons.

The tiny **Archeological Survey of India Museum** (daily 9am–1pm & 2–5.30pm; Rs2, camera Rs10) on West Raja Street, near the lighthouse, has a rather motley collection of unlabelled Pallava sculpture found in and around Mamallapuram.

Pancha Pandava rathas

In a sandy compound 1.5km south of the village centre stands the stunning group of monoliths known for no historical reason as the **Pancha Pandava rathas** (daily sunrise–sunset; $5 [Rs10] which includes the Shore Temple on the same day; video camera Rs25) the five chariots of the Pandavas. Dating from the period of Narasimhavarman I (c.630–670 AD), and consisting of five separate freestanding sculptures that imitate structured temples plus some beautifully carved life-size animals, they were either carved from a single gigantic sloping boulder, or from as many as three distinct rocks.

The "architecture" of the *rathas* reflects the variety of styles employed in temple building of the time, and stands almost as a model for much subsequent development in the **Dravida**, or southern, style. Carving was always executed from top to bottom, enabling the artists to work on the upper parts with no fear of damaging anything below. Any unfinished elements are always in the lower areas. Intriguingly, it's thought that the *rathas* were never used for worship. A Hindu temple is only complete when the essential pot-shaped finial, the *kalasha*, is put in place – which would have presented a physical impossibility for the artisans, as the *kalasha* would have had to have been sculpted first. *Kalashas* can be seen next to two of the *rathas* (Dharmaraja and Arjuna), but as part of the base, as if they were perhaps to be put in place at a later date.

The southernmost and tallest of the *rathas*, named after the eldest of the Pandavas, is the pyramidal **Dharmaraja**. Set on a square base, the upper part comprises a series of diminishing storeys, each with a row of pavilions. Four corner blocks, each with two panels and standing figures, are broken up by two pillars and pilasters supported by squatting lions. Figures on the panels include Ardhanarishvara (Shiva and female consort in one figure), Brahma, the king Narasimhavarman I, and Harihara (Shiva and Vishnu combined). The central tier includes sculptures of Shiva Gangadhara holding a rosary with the adoring river goddess Ganga by his side, and one of the earliest representations in Tamil Nadu of the dancing Shiva, Nataraja, who became all-important in the region. Alongside, the **Bhima** *ratha*, the largest of the group, is the least complete, with tooling marks all over its surface. Devoid of carved figures, the upper storeys, like in the Dharmaraja, feature false windows and repeated pavilion-shaped ornamentation. Its oblong base is very rare for a shrine.

The Arjuna and Draupadi *rathas* share a base. Behind the **Arjuna**, the most complete of the entire group and very similar to the Dharmaraja, stands a superb unfinished sculpture of Shiva's bull Nandi. **Draupadi** is unique in terms of rock-cut architecture, with a roof that appears to be based on a straw thatched hut (a design later copied at Chidambaram)`. There's an image of Durga inside, but the figure of her lion vehicle outside is aligned side-on and not facing the image, a convincing reason to suppose this was not a real temple. To the west, close to a life-size carving of an elephant, the *ratha* named after the twin brothers **Nakula** and **Sahadeva** is, unusually, apsidal ended. The elephant may be a visual pun on this, as the Sanskrit technical name for a curved ended building is *gajaprstika*, "elephant's backside".

The road out to the *rathas* resounds with incessant chiselling from sculptors' workshops. Much of their work is excellent, and well worth a browse – the sculptors produce statues for temples all over the world and are used to shipping large-scale pieces. Some of the artists are horrifyingly young; children often do the donkey work on large pieces, which are then completed by master craftsmen.

Eating

Mamallapuram is crammed with small restaurants, most of them specializing in **seafood** – tiger prawns, pomfret, tuna, shark and lobster – usually served marinated and grilled with chips and salad. The upmarket hotels charge a lot more for the same variety of dishes, and lack the atmosphere of the village. Wherever you eat, avoid a nasty shock at the end of your meal by establishing exactly how much your fish, or lobster, is going to cost in advance.

As this is a traveller's hangout, there are also numerous places offering the usual array of pasta, pancakes, brown bread and bland Indian dishes. If you want to enjoy real Indian food – including full-on fiery fish curry – head over to the bus stand, where there are some good joints serving excellent, spicy thalis and *dosas*. Likewise, you can get a plate of steaming breakfast *iddlis* from the carts at the station for less than Rs10. **Beer** is widely available, but it's on the pricey side (Rs80–90); best place for a late-night drink is the pleasant and friendly *Globe Trotters*, on the beach beyond *Luna Magica*.

Golden Palette *Mamalla Heritage* 104 East Raja St. Blissfully cool café with a/c and tinted windows, serving the best veg food in the village – Rs55 thalis at lunchtime, north Indian tandoori in the courtyard in the evenings – and wonderful ice-cream sundaes. Worth popping in just for a coffee to beat the heat.

La Palais Croisette *Rama Krishna Hotel*, 8 Othavadai St. A popular Nepali-run rooftop German-style bakery with croissants, pancakes, set breakfasts, and variations on salads, noodles, seafood and chicken.

La Vie En Rose West Raja St. Pleasant garden location offering a Westerner-oriented menu including a few unusual salads, pasta dishes (their spaghetti's great) and chicken specialities.

Luna Magica 100m north of Othavadai St. Slap on the beach with top-notch seafood, particularly tiger prawns and lobster, which are kept alive in a tank. The big specimens cost a hefty Rs600–800, but are as tasty as you'll find anywhere, served in a rich tomato, butter and garlic sauce. They also do passable sangria, made with sweet Chennai red wine, and cold beer, as well as plenty of less expensive dishes – including a good fish curry and "sizzlers" – for budget travellers.

Mamalla Bhavan Shore Temple Rd, opposite the bus stand. Very popular pure-veg and "meals" joint that's invariably packed. Good for *iddli-wada* breakfasts, and evening *dosas* and other snacks. Unlimited thalis cost Rs22–30.

Moonrakers Othavadai St. Cool jazz and blues sounds, great fresh seafood, chess sets and slick service ensure this place is filled year round with foreign tourists; the owners will try and entice you in every single time you pass by.

Nautilus Othavadai Cross St. High quality but reasonably priced eatery, run by an amicable French chef. Features fine soups, meat, seafood and veg dishes, grilled or with an array of sauces, plus travellers' favourites.

Siesta *Sri Murugan Guest House*, Othavadai Street. Rooftop restaurant run by a Spanish chef, serving a selection of delicious *tapas* and seafood specials at moderate prices.

Tina Blue Lodge 54 Othavadai St. Reasonable Indian and continental food – try the excellent honey-banana pancakes – served on a sociable rooftop terrace.

Village Inn Thirukula St. This diminutive thatched eatery serves up seafood grilled on a charcoal fire, as well as a superb butter-fried chicken in a tomato-garlic sauce.

Around Mamallapuram

The sandy hinterland and flat estuarine paddy fields around Mamallapuram harbour a handful of sights well worth making forays from the coast to see. A short way north along the main highway, the **Government College of Sculpture** and elaborately carved **Tiger Cave** can easily be reached by bicycle. To get to the **Crocodile Bank**, where rare reptiles from across south Asia are bred for release into the wild, or **Dakshina Chitra**, a museum devoted to South Indian architecture and crafts, you'll need to jump on and off buses or rent a moped for the day.

Government College of Sculpture and the Tiger Cave

A visit to the **Government College of Sculpture**, 2km north of Mamallapuram on the Kovalam (Covelong) Road (☎04114/242261; free) gives a fascinating insight into the processes of sculpture training. You can watch anything from preliminary drawing, with its strict rules regarding proportion and iconography, through to the execution of sculpture, both in wood and stone, in the classical Hindu tradition. Contact the college office to make an appointment.

A further 3km north along Kovalam Road from the college, set amid trees close to the sea, the extraordinary **Tiger Cave** (sunrise–sunset; free) contains a shrine to Durga, approached by a flight of steps that passes two subsidiary cells.

Following the line of an irregularly shaped rock, the cave is remarkable for its elaborate exterior, which features multiple lion heads surrounding the entrance to the main cell. If you sit for long enough, the section on the left with seated figures in niches above two elephants begins to resemble an enormous owl.

Crocodile Bank

The **Crocodile Bank** (Tues–Sun 8am–6pm; Rs20, camera Rs10, video camera Rs75) at Vadanemmeli, 14km north of town on the road to Chennai, was set up in 1976 by the American zoologist Romulus Whittaker, to protect and breed indigenous crocodiles. The bank has been so successful (from fifteen crocs to five thousand in the first fifteen years) that its remit now extends to saving endangered species, such as turtles and lizards, from around the world.

Low-walled enclosures in its garden compound house hundreds of inscrutable crocodiles, soaking in ponds or sunning themselves on the banks. Breeds include the fish-eating, knobbly-nosed gharial, and the world's largest species, the salt-water *crocodylus porosus*, which can grow to 8m in length. You can watch feeding time at about 4.30pm on Monday or Thursday or have your own brief feeding session anytime for a fee of Rs20. The temptation to take photos is tempered by the sight of those hungry saurians clambering over each other to snap up the chopped flesh, within inches of the top of the wall.

Another important field of work is conducted with the collaboration of local Irula people, whose traditional expertise is with snakes. Cobras are brought to the bank for **venom collection**, to be used in the treatment of snakebites. Elsewhere, snakes are repeatedly "milked" until they die, but here at the bank only a limited amount is taken from each snake, enabling them to return to the wild. This section costs an extra Rs5.

Coastal route buses #117 and #118 stop at the entrance.

Dakshina Chitra

Occupying a patch of sand dunes midway between Chennai and Mamallapuram, **Dakshina Chitra** (daily except Tues 10am–6pm; Rs50; lunch available for Rs175), literally "Vision of the South", is one of India's best-conceived folk museums, devoted to the rich architectural and artistic heritage of Kerala, Karnataka, Andhra Pradesh and Tamil Nadu. Set up by the Chennai Craft Foundation, the museum exposes visitors to many disappearing traditions of the region which you might otherwise not be aware of, from tribal fertility cults and *Ayyannar* field deities to pottery and leather shadow puppets.

A selection of traditional buildings from across peninsular India has been painstakingly reconstructed using original materials. Exhibitions attached to them convey the environmental and cultural diversity of the south, most graphically expressed in a wonderful textile collection featuring antique silk and cotton saris from various castes and regions. To get there, catch any of the buses heading north to Chennai or rent a moped from Mamallapuram (see p.1136).

Kanchipuram

Ask any Tamil what **KANCHIPURAM** (aka "Kanchi") is famous for, and they'll probably say silk saris, shrines and saints – in that order. A dynastic capital throughout the medieval era, it remains one of the seven holiest cities in the subcontinent, sacred to both Shaivites and Vaishnavites, and among the few surviving centres of goddess worship in the south. Year round, pilgrims pour through for a quick puja stop on the Tirupati tour circuit and, if they can afford it, a spot of shopping in the sari emporia. For non-Hindu visitors, however,

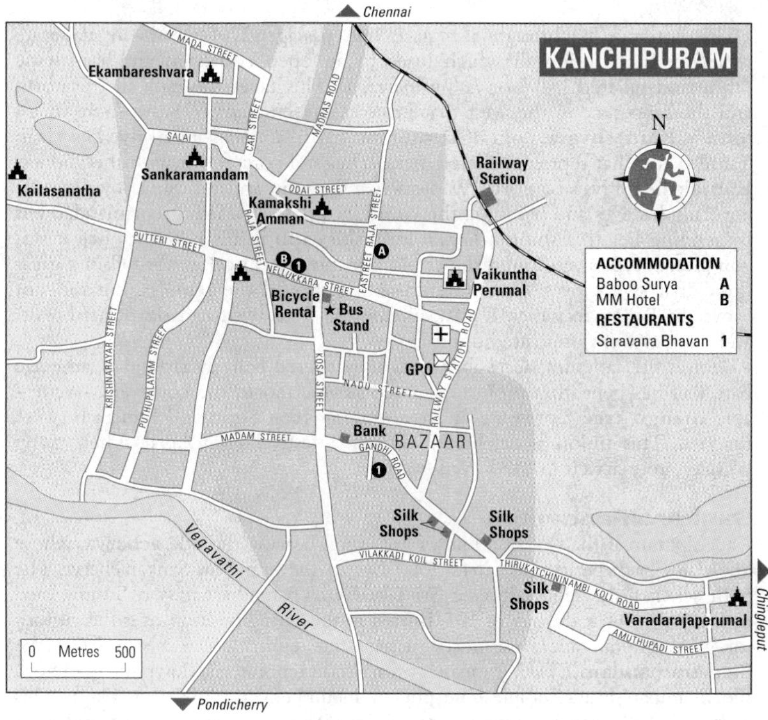

Kanchipuram holds less appeal. Although the temples are undeniably impressive, the town itself is unremittingly hot, with only basic accommodation and amenities. Some people prefer to visit Kanchipuram as a **day-trip** from Chennai or Mamallapuram, both a two-hour bus ride away.

Established by the **Pallava** kings in the fourth century AD, Kanchipuram served as their capital for five hundred years, and continued to flourish throughout the Chola, Pandya and Vijayanagar eras. Under the Pallavas, it was an important scholastic forum, and a meeting point for Jain, Buddhist and Hindu cultures. Its **temples** dramatically reflect this enduring political prominence, spanning the years from the peak of Pallava construction to the seventeenth century, when the ornamentation of the *gopuras* and pillared halls was at its most elaborate (for more on Tamil Nadu's temples, see p.1138). All can be easily reached by foot, bike or rickshaw, and shut daily between noon and 4pm. You might need to be a little firm to resist the attentions of pushy puja wallahs, who try to con foreigners into overpriced ceremonies. If you've come for silk, head for the shops that line Gandhi and Thirukatchininambi roads.

Ekambareshvara Temple

On the north side of town, Kanchipuram's largest temple and most important Shiva shrine, the **Ekambareshvara temple** – also known as Ekambaranatha – is easily identified by its colossal whitewashed *gopuras*, which rise to almost 60m. The main temple contains some Pallava work, but was mostly constructed in the sixteenth and seventeenth centuries, and stands within a vast walled enclosure beside some smaller shrines and a large fish-filled water tank.

The entrance is through a high-arched passageway beneath an elaborate *gopura* in the south wall which leads to an open courtyard and a majestic "thousand-pillared hall", or *kalyan mandapa*. This faces the tank in the north and the sanctuary in the west that protects the emblem of Shiva (here in his form as **Kameshvara**, Lord of Desire), an "earth" *lingam* (one of five *lingams* in Tamil Nadu that represent the elements). Legend connects it with the goddess **Kamakshi** (Shiva's consort, "Wanton-Eyed"), who angered Shiva by playfully covering his eyes and plunging the world into darkness. Shiva reprimanded her by sending her to fashion a *lingam* from the earth in his honour; once it was completed, Kamakshi found she could not move it. Local myths tell of a great flood that swept over Kanchipuram and destroyed the temples, but did not move the *lingam*, to which Kamakshi clung so fiercely that marks of her breasts and bangles were imprinted upon it.

Behind the sanctum, accessible from the covered hallway around it, an eerie bare hall lies beneath a profusely carved *gopura*, and in the courtyard a venerable **mango tree** represents the tree under which Shiva and Kamakshi were married. This union is celebrated during a festival each April, when many couples are married in the *kalyan mandapa*.

Sankaramandam

Kanchipuram is the seat of a line of holy men bearing the title **acharya**, whose line dates back perhaps as far as 1300 BC to the saint Adi Sankaracharya. The 68th acharya, the highly revered Sri Chandrasekharendra Sarasvati Swami, died in January 1994 at the age of 101. Buried in the sitting position, as is the custom for great Hindu sages, his mortal remains are enshrined in a *samadhi* at the **Sankaramandam**, a *math* (monastery for Hindu renouncers) down the road from the Ekambareshvara Temple. The present incumbent, the 69th acharya, has his quarters on the opposite side of a marble meditation hall to the shrine, and gives *darshan* to the public during the morning and early evening. Lined with old photographs from the life of the former swami, with young brahmin students chanting Sanskrit verses in the background, it's a typically Tamil blend of simple sanctity and garish modern glitz. The *math*'s two huge elephants are available to bestow blessings upon visiting pilgrims – just sweeten the mahout's hand with a few rupees.

Kailasanatha Temple

The **Kailasanatha Temple**, the oldest structure in Kanchipuram and the finest example of Pallava architecture in South India, is situated among several low-roofed houses just over 1km west of the town centre. Built by the Pallava king Rajasimha early in the eighth century, its intimate size and simple carving distinguish it from the town's later temples. Usually quieter than its neighbours, the shrine becomes the focus of vigorous celebrations during the **Mahashivratri festival** each March. Like its contemporary, the Shore Temple at Mamallapuram, it is built of soft sandstone, but its sheltered position has spared it from wind and sand erosion, and it remains remarkably intact, despite some rather clumsy recent renovation work.

Kamakshi Amman Temple

Built during Pallava supremacy and modified in the fourteenth and seventeenth centuries, the **Kamakshi Amman Temple**, northwest of the bus stand, combines several styles, with an ancient central shrine, gates from the Vijayanagar period, and high, heavily sculpted creamy *gopuras* set above the gateways.

This is one of India's three holiest shrines to Shakti, Shiva's cosmic energy depicted in female form, usually as his consort. The goddess Kamakshi, a local form of Parvati, shown with a sugar-cane bow and arrows of flowers, is honoured as having lured Shiva to Kanchipuram, where they were married, and thus having forged the connection between the local community and the god. In February or March, deities are wheeled to the temple in huge wooden "cars", decked with robed statues and swaying plantain leaves.

Practicalities

Kanchipuram is situated on the River Vegavathi 70km southwest of Chennai, and slightly less from Mamallapuram on the coast. **Buses** from Chennai, Mamallapuram and Chengalpattu stop at the stand in the town centre just off Kosa Street. The sleepy **railway station** in the northeast sees only four daily passenger services from Chengalpattu (two of them originating in Chennai) and two from Anakkonam.

As most of the main roads are wide and traffic rarely unmanageable, the best way to **get around** Kanchi is by **bicycle** – available for minimal rates (Rs2/hr) at stalls west and northeast of the bus stand. The town's vegetable markets, hotels, restaurants and bazaars are concentrated in the centre of town, near the bus stand.

Note that there is nowhere in the town to **change money**. Some mid-range hotels accept credit cards, but the nearest official foreign exchange places are in Chennai and Mamallapuram.

Accommodation and eating

There's not a great choice of **accommodation** in Kanchipuram, but the hotels are sufficient for a night. Best of the bunch is *MM*, 65/66 Nellukkara St (Ⓣ04112/230023, Ⓔinfo@mmhotels.com; ❸–❹), with clean, good-value rooms. Next door at 68C Nellukkara St, the marble-lined *Sri Kusal Lodge* (Ⓣ04112/222356; ❶–❷) is a good budget option with friendly staff and reasonable rooms. The *Baboo Surya,* 85 East Raja St (Ⓣ04112/222556, Ⓦwww.hotelbaboosoorya.com; ❸–❹) is an excellent-value mid-range option, with immaculate en-suite rooms (a/c and non-a/c) and its own restaurant.

The most highly rated place to **eat** in town is *Saravana Bhavan* on Gandhi Road, an offshoot of the famous Chennai chain of pure veg restaurants, which offers superb Rs30 "meals" at lunchtime, and a long list of South Indian snacks the rest of the day. There's a branch on Nellukkara Road near *Sri Kusal*, and another next to the *Jaybala* off Gandhi Road.

Vedanthangal

One of India's most spectacular bird sanctuaries lies roughly 1km east of the village of **VEDANTHANGAL**, a cluster of squat, brown houses set in a patchwork of paddy fields 30km from the east coast and 86km southwest of Chennai. It's a tiny, relaxed place, bisected by one road and with just two chai stalls.

A low-lying area less than half a kilometre square, the **sanctuary** is busiest with birdlife between December and February, when it's totally flooded. The rains of the northeast monsoon, sweeping through in October or November, bring indigenous water birds that nest and settle here until the dry season (usually April), when they leave for wetter areas. Abundant trees on mounds above water level provide perfect nesting spots, alive by January with fledglings. Visitors can watch the avian action from a path at the water's edge, or from a watchtower (fitted out with strong binoculars). Try to come at sunset, when the birds return from feeding. Common Indian species to look out for are openbill storks, spoonbills, pelicans, black cormorants, and herons of several types. You may also see ibises, grey pelicans, migrant cuckoos, sandpipers, egrets (which paddle in the rice fields), and tiny darting bee-eaters. Some migrant birds pass through and rest on their way between more permanent sites; swallows, terns and redshanks are common, while peregrine falcons, pigeons and doves are occasionally spotted.

Practicalities

Getting to Vedanthangal can present a few problems. The nearest town is Maduranthakam, 8km east, on NH-45 between Chengalpattu and Tindivanam. Head here to wait for the hourly buses to the sanctuary, or catch one of the four daily direct services from Chengalpattu. Taxis make the journey from Maduranthakam for Rs250–300, but cannot be booked from Vedanthangal.

Vedanthangal's only accommodation is the four-roomed **forest lodge** (❸) near the bus stand, school and chai stall, which has a/c and non a/c rooms, all spacious and comfortable with attached bath. It's best to book these through the Wildlife Warden, 259, 3rd Road Block, 4th Floor, DMS Compound, Teynampet, Chennai (Ⓣ044/2432 1471) but you can also try calling the lodge mobile phone directly (Ⓣ954115/200006) – if you turn up on spec, it may well be full, especially in December and January. Staff can prepare food if given enough notice.

Tiruvannamalai

Synonymous with the fifth Hindu element of fire, **TIRUVANNAMALAI**, 100km south of Kanchipuram, ranks, along with Madurai, Kanchipuram, Chidambaram and Trichy, as one of the five holiest towns in Tamil Nadu. Its name, meaning "Red Mountain", derives from the spectacular extinct volcano, **Arunachala**, which rises behind it, and which glows an unearthly crimson in the dawn light. This awesome natural backdrop, combined with the colossal **Arunachaleshvara temple** in the centre of town, make Tiruvannamalai one of the region's most memorable destinations. Well off the tourist trail, it's a perfect place to get to grips with life in small-town Tamil Nadu. The countless shrines, sacred tanks, ashrams and paved pilgrim paths scattered around the sacred mountain (not to mention the legions of dreadlocked *babas* who line up for alms outside the main sites) will keep anyone who is interested in Hinduism absorbed for weeks.

Mythology identifies Arunachala as the place where Shiva asserted his power over Brahma and Vishnu by manifesting himself as a *lingam* of fire, or **agni-lingam**. The two lesser gods had been disputing their respective strengths when Shiva pulled this primordial pyro-stunt, challenging his adversaries to locate the top and bottom of his blazing column. They couldn't (although Vishnu is said to have faked finding the head) and collapsed on their knees in a gesture of supreme submission. The event is commemorated each year at the rising of the full moon in November/December, when a vast vat of ghee and paraffin is lit by priests on the summit of Arunachala. This symbolizes the fulfilment of Shiva's promise to reappear each year to vanquish the forces of darkness and ignorance with firelight.

The sacred Red Mountain is also associated with the famous twentieth-century saint, **Sri Ramana Maharishi**, who chose it as the site for his twenty-three-year meditation retreat. A crop of small ashrams have sprung up on the edge of town below Sri Ramana's Cave, some of them more authentic than others, and the ranks of white-cotton-clad foreigners floating between them have become a defining feature of Tiruvannamalai.

Arunachaleshvara Temple

Known to Hindus as the "Temple of the Eternal Sunrise", the enormous **Arunachaleshvara Temple**, built over a period of almost a thousand years, consists of three concentric courtyards whose gateways are topped by tapering *gopuras*, the largest of which cover the east and north gates. The best spot from which to view the precinct, a breathtaking spectacle against the sprawling plains and lumpy, granite Shevaroy Hills, is the path up to Sri Ramana Maharishi's meditation cave, Virupaksha (see below), on the lower slopes of Arunachala. To enter the temple, however, head for the huge eastern gateway, which leads through the thick outer wall carved with images of deities, local saints and teachers. In the basement of a raised hall to the right before entering the next courtyard is the Parthala *lingam*, where Sri Ramana Maharishi is said to have sat in a state of Supreme Awareness while ants devoured his flesh.

The caves and Sri Ramanasram ashram

Opposite the western entrance of the temple complex, a path leads up a holy hill (15min) to the **Virupaksha Cave**, where Ramakrishna stayed between 1899 and 1916. He personally built the bench outside and the hill-shaped *lingam* and platform inside, where all are welcome to meditate in peace. When this cave became too small, constantly crowded with relatives and devotees, Ramana shifted to another, hidden away in a clump of trees a few minutes further up the hill. He named this one, and the small house built onto it, **Skandasraman**, and lived there between 1916 and 1922. The inner cave here is also set aside for meditation, and the front patio affords splendid views across the temple, town and surrounding plains.

The caves can also be reached via the pilgrims' path winding uphill from the **Sri Ramanasram ashram**, 2km south of the temple along the main road. This simple complex is where the sage lived after returning from his retreat on Arunachala, and where his body is today enshrined. The *samadhi* has become a popular place for Sri Ramana's devotees on pilgrimage, but interested visitors are welcome to stay in the dorms here (Ⓣ01475/237292, Ⓦwww.ramana-maharshi.org). There's also an excellent bookshop (daily 7.30–11am & 2.30–6.30pm) stocking a huge range of titles on the life and teachings of the guru, as well as quality postcards, calendars and religious images.

Pradakshana

During the annual Kartiggai festival, Hindu pilgrims are supposed to perform an auspicious circumambulation of Arunachala, known as the **Pradakshana** (*pra* signifies the removal of all sins, *da* the fulfilment of desires, *kshi* freedom from the cycle of rebirth, and *na* spiritual liberation). Along the way, offerings are made at a string of shrines, tanks, temples, *lingams*, pillared meditation halls, sacred rocks, springs, trees, and caves related to the Tiruvannamalai legends. Although hectic during the festival, the paved path linking them all together is quiet for most of the year, and makes a wonderful day-hike, affording fine views of the town and its environs.

Practicalities

Tiruvannamalai is served by regular buses from Bangalore via Vellore, Chennai, Pondicherry and Trichy. Coming from the coast, it's easiest to make your way there on one of the numerous buses from Tindivanam. The town bus stand is 2km north of the temple on the main road to Gingee. Half a kilometre north of there, the **railway station** is on the line between Tirupati and Madurai, with a daily service in each direction. There are a couple of places to access the **Inter-**

net including the Image Computer Centre, 52 Car St (daily 9.30am–9.30pm; Rs20/hr).

Accommodation and eating

For such an important pilgrimage place, Tiruvannamalai has surprisingly few decent **hotels**. However the two-star places are fairly comfortable, and the budget options fine for a short stay.

For **food**, you've a choice of a dozen or so typical South Indian "meals" joints just off the bottom of Car Street. Delicious hot ghee chapatis are served here all afternoon, as well as all the usual rice specialities. The *Udipi Brindhavan* and the *Deepam* on Car Street opposite the temple's east entrance are typical *udipi* restaurants, serving, amongst other dishes, excellent *parottas* for under Rs10. The latter also has an adjacent ice cream and milkshakes parlour. Of the hotels, the *Trisul* has a posh ground-floor restaurant which serves north Indian buffets for around Rs100, and tandoori in the evening, while the *Ramakrishna* does excellent lunchtime thalis and a range of north and South Indian food in the evenings.

Accommodation

NS Lodge 47 Thiruvoodal St ⓣ04175/225388. Facing the south entrance of Arunachaleshvara temple. Clean en-suite rooms (some a/c) with cable TV; great temple view from the roof. ❶–❸

Park 26 Kosmadam St ⓣ04175/222471. Reliable budget option just northeast of the main temple entrance. Basic non a/c rooms with a busy vegetarian canteen on the ground floor. ❶–❷

Ramakrishna 34-F Polur Rd ⓣ01475/250005, ⓔinfo@ramakrishna.com. Three minute walk north of the bus stand. Decent two-star hotel with large clean good-value a/c and non a/c rooms with TV. ❸–❹

Sri Durgalakshmi 73 Chinnakadai St ⓣ04175/226041. Best of the budget lodges and handy for the bus station. ❷

Trisul 6 Kanakaraya Mudali St ⓣ04175/222219, ⓔtact@vsnl.com. Near the main temple entrance. Two star hotel with huge, immaculately clean rooms (some a/c), courteous staff and a good restaurant. However, often booked for long periods by Westerners studying at the ashrams. ❹–❺

Pondicherry and Auroville

First impressions of **PONDICHERRY**, the former capital of French India, can be unpromising. Instead of the leafy boulevards and *pétanque* pitches you might expect, its messy outer suburbs and bus stand are as cluttered and chaotic as any typical Tamil town. Closer to the seafront, however, the atmosphere grows tangibly more Gallic, as the bazaars give way to rows of houses whose shuttered windows and colourwashed facades wouldn't look out of place in Montpellier. For anyone familiar with the British colonial imprint, the town can induce culture shock to see richly ornamented Catholic churches, French road names and policemen in De Gaulle-style *képis*, not to mention hearing French spoken in the street and seeing *boules* played in the dusty squares. Note, however, that although many of the seafront buildings were damaged by the 2004 Asian tsunamis, when many local people lost their lives here, Pondicherry's tourist infrastructure was quickly rebuilt.

Known to Greek and Roman geographers as "Poduke", Pondicherry was an important staging post on the second-century maritime trade route between Rome and the Far East (a Roman amphitheatre has been unearthed at nearby Arikamedu). When the Roman empire declined, the Pallavas and Cholas took control and were followed by a succession of colonial powers, from the Portuguese in the sixteenth century to the French, Danes and British, who exchanged the enclave several times after the various battles and treaties of the

Carnatic Wars in the early eighteenth century. Pondicherry's heyday, however, dates from the arrival of the French governor **Dupleix**, who accepted the governorship in 1742 and immediately set about rebuilding a town decimated by its former British occupants. It was he who instituted the street plan of a central grid encircled by a broad oblong boulevard, bisected north to south by a canal dividing the "Ville Blanche", to the east, from the "Ville Noire", to the west.

Although relinquished by the French in 1954 – when the town became the headquarters of the **Union Territory of Pondicherry**, administering the three other former colonial enclaves scattered across South India – Pondicherry's split personality still prevails. West of the canal stretches a bustling Indian market town, while to the east, towards the sea, the streets are emptier, cleaner and decidedly European. The seaside promenade, **Goubert Salai** (formerly Beach Road), has the forlorn look of an out-of-season French resort, complete with its own white Hôtel de Ville. Tanned sun-worshippers share space with grave Europeans in white Indian costume, busy about their spiritual quest. It was here that **Sri Aurobindo Ghose** (1872–1950), a leading figure in the freedom struggle in Bengal, was given shelter after it became unwise to live close to the British in Calcutta. His ashram attracts thousands of devotees from all around the world, most particularly from Bengal.

Ten kilometres north, the Utopian experiment-in-living **Auroville** was inspired by Aurobindo's disciple, the charismatic Mirra Alfassa, a Parisian painter, musician and mystic better known as "The Mother". Today this slightly surreal place is populated by numbers of expats and visited by long-stay Europeans eager to find inner peace.

The Town

Pondicherry's beachside promenade, **Goubert Salai**, is a favourite place for a stroll; there's little to do, other than watch the world go by. The Hôtel de Ville, today housing the Municipal Offices building, is still an impressive spectacle, and a four-metre-tall Gandhi memorial, surrounded by ancient columns, dominates the northern end. Nearby, a French memorial commemorates French Indians who lost their lives in World War I.

Just north of the Hôtel de Ville, a couple of streets back from the promenade, is the leafy old French-provincial-style square now named **Government Place**. On the north side, the impressive, gleaming white **Raj Nivas**, official home to the present lieutenant governor of Pondicherry Territory, was built late in the eighteenth century for Joseph Francis Dupleix.

The **Pondicherry Museum** (Tues–Sun 10am–5pm; Rs2) is on Ranga Pillai Street, opposite Government Place. The archeological collection includes Neolithic and 2000-year-old remains from Arikamedu, a few Pallava (sixth- to eighth-century) and Buddhist (tenth-century) stone sculptures, bronzes, weapons and paintings. Alongside are a bizarre assembly of French salon furniture and bric-a-brac from local houses, including a velvet S-shaped "conversation seat".

The **Sri Aurobindo Ashram**, a few blocks north on Rue de la Marine (daily 8am–noon & 2–6pm; no children under 3; photography with permission; Ⓦwww.sriaurobindosociety.org.in), is one of the best-known and wealthiest ashrams in India. Founded in 1926 by the Bengali philosopher-guru, Aurobindo Ghosh, and his chief disciple, personal manager and mouthpiece "The Mother", it serves as the headquarters of the Sri Aurobindo Society, or SAS. Today the SAS owns most of the valuable property and real estate in Pondicherry, and wields what many consider to be a disproportionate influence over the town (note how many of the shops and businesses have "auro" somewhere in their name). The **samadhi**, or mausoleum, of Sri Aurobindo and "The Mother" is covered daily with flowers and usually surrounded by supplicating devotees with their hands and heads placed on the tomb. Inside the main building, an incongruous and very bourgeois-looking Western-style room complete with three-piece suite and Persian carpet, is where "The Mother" and Sri Aurobindo chilled out. The adjacent bookshop sells a range of literature and tracts, while the building opposite hosts frequent cultural programmes

In the southwest of town, near the railway station, you can hardly miss the huge cream-and-brown **Sacred Heart of Jesus**, one of Pondicherry's finest Catholic churches, built by French missionaries in the 1700s. Nearby, the shady **Botanical Gardens**, established in 1826, offer many quiet paths to wander (daily 9.30am–6pm; free). The French planted 900 species here, experimenting to see how they would do in Indian conditions; one tree, the *khaya senegalensis*, has grown to a height of 25m. You can also see an extraordinary fossilized tree, found about 25km away in Tiravakarai.

Practicalities

All buses – long and short distance – pull into **New Bus Stand**, which lies on the west edge of town; for a summary of routes, see "Travel details", pp.1204–1205. From here, a rather precarious cycle-rickshaw ride into the main hotel district should cost about Rs20, and an auto-rickshaw or taxi Rs50. Pondicherry's **railway station** is in the south, five minutes' walk from the sea off Surbaiyah Salai.

The **Pondicherry Tourism Development Corporation** office is at 40 Goubert Salai (daily 8.45am–5pm; ⓣ0413/233 9497). The staff are extremely helpful, providing leaflets and a city map, and information about Auroville; they can also book you onto their **city tours** (half-day 2–5.30pm, Rs80; full-day 9.30am–5.30pm, Rs100) and arrange **car rental** (Rs650 per day plus fuel). Recommended places to **change money** include: the Indian Overseas Bank, in the Hôtel de Ville; the State Bank of India on Surcouf Street; and UCO Bank, Rue Mahe de Labourdonnais. The **GPO** is on Ranga Pillai Street (Mon–Sat 10am–7.30pm). **Internet access** is available throughout central Pondicherry; you'll find Net cafés on Ranga Pillai Street, Rue Nehru and on MG Road; most open daily from 10am until 10pm, and charge Rs20/hr.

Pondicherry is well served with both auto- and cycle rickshaws, but for **getting around** most tourists rent a **cycle** from one of the many stalls dotted around town (Rs20/day, plus Rs200 refundable deposit). If you're staying at the *Park Guest House*, use one of theirs (they're all immaculately maintained). For trips further afield (to Auroville, for example), you may want to rent a **moped** or **scooter**. Of the rental firms operating in town, Sri Ganesh Cycle Store, 39 Mission Street (ⓣ0413/222 2801), has new Honda Kinetics for Rs100 per day. You'll have to pay a Rs300 deposit and leave a passport or driving licence as security.

Accommodation

Pondicherry's **basic lodges** are concentrated around the main market area, Ranga Pillai Street and Rue Nehru. Guesthouses in Pondicherry belonging to the **Sri Aurobindo Ashram** (ⓦwww.sriaurobindosociety.org.in) offer fantastic value for money, but come with a lot of baggage apart from your own (regulations, curfews and overpowering "philosophy of life" notices). Although supposedly open to all, they are not keen on advertising, or on attracting misguided individuals indulging in "spiritual tourism".

Anandha Inn 154 Sardar Vallabh bhai Patel Salai (North Blvd) ⓣ0413/233 0711, ⓔcheckin@anandha.in. Seventy luxurious rooms and two restaurants in a gleaming white building. Good value and popular with tour groups, so book well in advance. ❼–❽

Aruna 3 Zamindar Garden, SV Patel Rd ⓣ0413/233 7756. Set on a quiet side street, the decent value en-suite doubles here are of varying sizes; some have a/c and/or balconies. ❸–❹

Hotel de l'Orient 17 Rue Romain Rolland ⓣ0413/234 3067, ⓕ222 7829. A beautiful, UNESCO heritage-accorded French house with sixteen rooms, individually decorated with French antiques, tiled balconies and long shuttered windows overlooking a leafy courtyard restaurant. Wonderfully romantic. ❽–❾

International Guest House 47 Gingee Salai ⓣ0413/233 6699, ⓔingh@vsnl.net. The largest Aurobindo establishment, with dozens of very large, clean rooms, some a/c. Recommended as a budget option, and safe for single women. ❶–❸

Park Guest House Goubert Salai ⓣ0413/233 4412, ⓔparkgh@sriaurobindoashram.org. Another Sri Aurobindo Society pad, with very comfortable, spotless rooms, right on the seafront, with mosquito nets and "sitouts" overlooking a well-watered garden. Cycle rental, laundry and restaurant. Strict rules. ❸

Pondicherry Ashok Chinnakalapet, 12km north of Pondicherry on the old coastal road to Mamallapuram, near Auroville ⓣ0413/265 5160, ⓔitdcpa@satyam.net.in. Comfortable rooms in a quiet, breezy location on the seashore. Children's park, restaurant, barbecue and bar. Generous discounts for stays of three days or more. ❽

Qualithe 3 Rue Mahe de Labourdonnais ⓣ0413/233 4325, ⓔrajarathnam8@engineer.com. Budget lodge with character, in a slightly rickety old French building. Upstairs, big, spotless rooms that fit four lead off a pleasant balcony with wicker chairs and great views over Government Place. There's also one cheap single room. ❸

Soorya International 55 Ranga Pillai St ⓣ0413/233 6856 Central hotel with very large, immaculate rooms. An ostentatious exterior, but the tariffs are reasonable. Rates include breakfast. ❸–❺

Surya Swastika 11 ID Koil St ⓣ0413/234 3092, ⓔsuryaswastika@sify.com. Traditional Tamil guesthouse in a quiet corner of town, with nine basic rooms around a central courtyard that doubles as a pilgrims' canteen at lunchtime. Incredibly cheap, and cleaner than most of the bazaar lodges. ❶–❸

Eating

If you've been on the road for a while and are hankering for healthy salads, fresh coffee, crusty bread, cakes and real pastry, you'll be spoilt for choice in Pondicherry. Unlike the traveller-oriented German-Bakery-style places elsewhere in the country, the Western **restaurants** here cater for a predominantly expatriate clientele with discerning palettes and fat Euro pay cheques. **Beer** is available just about everywhere (except the SAS-owned establishments) and is half the regular Tamil Nadu/India price at Rs30–40 a bottle.

Anugraha *Hotel Surguru*, 104 SV Patel Rd (North Blvd). Widely rated as the best lunchtime "meals" restaurant in town, but also serving superb *dosa-iddli* breakfasts and filter coffee, and a full tandoori menu in the evening. The only downside is the exceedingly low lighting.

Hot Breads 42 Ambour Salai. Crusty croissants, fresh baguettes, and delicious savoury pastry snacks, served in a squeaky-clean French *boulangerie*-café full of French expats.

Indian Coffee House Rue Nehru. Not their finest branch, but the coffee is good and the food inexpensive.

La Terrasse 5 Subbiah Salai (closed Wed). The most popular French restaurant for the European backpacker crew, who hang out in and devour croissants and cappuccino al fresco. Excellent prawn dishes start at Rs80 and there are crêpes, pizzas and a variety of salads on offer all day.

Le Club 33 Rue Dumas (closed Mon). Beyond the pocket of most travellers, not to mention locals, but far and away the town's top restaurant complex. The predominantly French menu features their famous coq au vin, steak au poivre, plenty of seafood options and a full wine list, rounded off with cognac at Rs200 a shot. Count on Rs300 per head (if you forsake the shorts). There is also a cheaper bistro that is great for Sunday brunch, a tapas and cocktail bar, and a Vietnamese and Southeast Asian restaurant (open Mon).

Le Rendezvous 30 Rue Suffren. Filling seafood "sizzlers", fantastic pizza and tandoori brochettes are specialities of this popular expat-oriented restaurant. They also serve fresh croissants and espresso for breakfast, indoors, or up on the more romantic thatched rooftop, where there's jazz sounds and chilled beer in discreet ceramic jugs in the evenings. Most main dishes Rs100–150.

Satsanga 30 Labourdonnais St. If you only eat once in Pondy, it should be here. Served on the colonnaded veranda of an old colonial mansion, the menu (devised by the French patron) is carefully prepared and exactly the kind of thing you dream about elsewhere in India: organic salads with fresh herbs, tzatziki and garlic bread, sauté potatoes, *tagliatelle alla carbonara*, and mouthwatering pizzas washed down with chilled Kingfisher. Check their *plat du jour* for fresh fish dishes. Around Rs300 per head for three courses, with drinks. It's also a breat spot for breakfast.

Seagulls Rue Damas. Reasonably priced, open-air rooftop restaurant in a breezy spot right next to the sea, new pier and cargo harbour. Huge, inexpensive menu, with veg dishes, meat, seafood, Indian, Chinese and even some Italian dishes (pizza, spaghetti).

Auroville

The most New Age place anywhere in India must surely be **AUROVILLE**, the planned "City of Dawn", 10km north of Pondicherry, just outside the Union Territory in Tamil Nadu. Founded in 1968, Auroville was inspired by "The Mother", the spiritual successor of Sri Aurobindo. Around 1350 people live in communes (two-thirds of them non-Indians), with such names as Fertile, Certitude, Sincerity, Revelation and Transformation, in what it is hoped will eventually be an ideal city for a population of 50,000. Architecturally experimental buildings, combining modern Western and traditional Indian elements, are set in a rural landscape of narrow lanes, deep red earth and lush greenery. Income is derived from agriculture, handicrafts, alternative technology, educational and development projects and Aurolec, a computer software company.

Considering how little there is to see here, Auroville attracts a disproportionately large number of day-trippers – much to the chagrin of its inhabitants, who rightly point out that you can only get a sense of what the settlement is all about if you stay a while. Interested visitors are welcomed as paying guests in most of the communes (see below), where you can work alongside permanent residents.

Begun in 1970, the space-age **Matri Mandir** – a gigantic, almost spherical, hi-tech meditation centre at the heart of the site – was conceived as "a symbol of the Divine's answer to man's inspiration for perfection". Earth from 126 countries was symbolically placed in an urn, and is kept in a concrete cone in the amphitheatre adjacent to Matri Mandir, from where a speaker can address an audience of 3000 without amplification. The focal point of the interior of the Matri Mandir is a seventy-centimetre crystal ball symbolising the neutral but divine qualities of light and space. Visitors are allowed in for a fleeting glimpse with strict instructions on behaviour.

Practicalities

Auroville lies 10km north of Pondicherry on the main Chennai road; you can also get there via the coastal highway, turning off at the village of Chinna Mudaliarchavadi. **Bus** services are frequent along both routes but – as Auroville is so spread out, covering some fifty or so square kilometres – it's best to come with your own transport, at the very least a bike. Most people rent a scooter or **motorcycle** from Pondicherry and ride up. Alternatively, there's Tamil Nadu Tourism's half-day **tour** from Pondicherry (daily 2–5.30pm; Rs80); book at the Pondy office (see p.1153).

For a pre-visit primer, call in at the **visitor centre** (daily 9am–5.30pm; ⓣ0413/262 2239, ⓦwww.auroville.org), in the middle of the site near the Bharat Niwas, which holds a permanent exhibition on the history and philosophy of the settlement. This is the place to get admission tickets for the grounds of the Matri Mandir (daily 10am–noon & 2–4pm), available from 9.45am–12.45pm and 1.45–4pm; before tickets are issued, you're shown a short video presentation about the village. You can also pick up some inexpensive literature on Auroville in the adjacent bookshop and check the notice board for details of **activities** in which visitors may participate (these typically include yoga, reiki and Vipassana meditation, costing around Rs100 per session). In addition, there are a couple of quality handicraft outlets and several pleasant little vegetarian cafés serving snacks, meals and cold drinks.

The information desk at the visitor centre is also the place to enquire about **paying guest accommodation** in Auroville's thirty or so communes. Officially there's no lower limit on the time you have to stay, but visitors are encouraged to stick around for at least a week, helping out on communal projects; tariffs range from Rs100–500 per day, depending of levels of comfort. Alternatively, you can arrange to stay in one of the four a/c **guesthouses**, which have rooms for Rs1500. Beds here and in the communes are always in short supply, especially during the two peak periods of December to March and July to August, when it's advisable to book well in advance (Ⓣ0413/262 2704, Ⓔavguests@auroville.org.in). Otherwise, the only rooms in the area are just outside Auroville in the village of Chinna Mudaliarchavadi. The *Palm Beach Cottage Centre* (no phone; ❶) is nothing of the kind (the sea is fifteen minutes' walk away), but has passably clean rooms with shared toilets and a small garden, where meals are served. Nearby, the *Cottage Guest House* (no phone; ❷–❸) offers a little more comfort in thatched huts or in a block of en-suite rooms. For **food**, you won't do better than the simple, filling vegetarian meals served in Auroville itself.

Central Tamil Nadu: the Chola heartland

To be on the banks of the Cauvery listening to the strains of Carnatic music is to have a taste of eternal bliss

Tamil proverb

Continuing south of Pondicherry along the Coromandel coast, you enter the flat landscape of the **Kaveri** (aka Cauvery) **Delta**, a watery world of canals, dams, dykes and rivulets that has been intensively farmed since ancient times. Only a hundred miles in diameter, it forms the verdant rice-bowl core of Tamil Nadu, crossed by more than thirty major rivers and countless streams. The largest of them, the **River Kaveri**, known in Tamil as *Ponni*, "The Lady of Gold" (a form of the Mother Goddess), is revered as a conduit of liquid *shakti*, the primordial female energy that nurtures the millions of farmers who live on her banks and tributaries. The landscape here is one endless swathe of green paddy fields, dotted with palm trees and little villages of thatched roofs and market stalls; it comes as a rude shock to land up in the hot and chaotic towns.

This mighty delta formed the very heartland of the **Chola** empire, which reached its apogee between the ninth and thirteenth centuries, an era often compared to classical Greece and Renaissance Italy both for its cultural richness and the sheer scale and profusion of its architectural creations. Much as the Cholas originally intended, every visitor is immediately in awe of their huge temples, not only at cities such as **Chidambaram**, **Kumbakonam** and **Thanjavur**, but also out in the countryside at places like **Gangaikondacholapuram**, where the magnificent temple is all that remains of a once-great city. Exploring the area for a few days will bring you into contact with the more delicate side of Chola artistic expression, such as the magnificent **bronzes** of Thanjavur.

Chidambaram

CHIDAMBARAM, 58km south of Pondicherry, is so steeped in myth that its history is hard to unravel. As the site of the *tandava*, the cosmic dance of Shiva as **Nataraja**, King of the Dance, it's one of the holiest sites in South India and a visit to the **Sabhanayaka Temple** affords a fascinating glimpse into ancient Tamil religious practice and belief. The legendary king **Hiranyavarman** is said to have made a pilgrimage here from Kashmir, seeking to rid himself of leprosy by bathing in the temple's Shivaganga tank. In thanks for a successful cure, he enlarged the temple. He also brought 3000 brahmins, of the Dikshitar caste, whose descendants, distinguishable by top-knots of hair at the front of their heads, are the ritual specialists of the temple to this day.

Few of the fifty *maths*, or monasteries, that once stood here remain, but the temple itself is still a hive of activity and hosts numerous **festivals**. The two most important are ten-day affairs, building up to spectacular finales: on the ninth day of each, temple chariots process through the four Car streets ("**car festival**"), while on the tenth, **abhishekham**, the principal deities in the Raja Sabha (thousand-pillared hall) are anointed. For exact dates (one is in May/June, the other in Dec/Jan), contact any TTDC tourist office and plan well ahead, as they are very popular. Other local festivals include fire-walking and *kavadi* folk dance (dancing with decorated wooden frames on the head) at the Thillaiamman Kali (April/May) and Keelatheru Mariamman (July/Aug) temples.

The town also has a hectic market, and a large student population, based at Annamalai University to the east, a centre of Tamil studies. Among the simple thatched huts in the surrounding countryside, the only solid-looking structures are small roadside temples, most of which are devoted to Aiyannar, the village deity who protects borders, and are accompanied by *kudirais*, brightly painted terracotta or wooden figures of horses.

Sabhanayaka Nataraja Temple

For South India's Shaivites, the **Sabhanayaka Nataraja Temple** (daily 4am–noon & 4–10pm), where Shiva is enthroned as Lord of the Cosmic Dance (Nataraja), is the holiest of holies. Its huge *gopuras*, whose lights are used as landmarks by sailors far out to sea in the Bay of Bengal, soar above a fifty-five-acre complex, divided by four concentric walls. The oldest parts now standing were built under the Cholas, who adopted Nataraja as their chosen deity and crowned several kings here. The rectangular outermost wall, of little interest in itself, affords entry on all four sides, so if you have the time the best way to tackle the complex is to work slowly inwards from the third enclosure in clockwise circles. **Guides** are readily available but tend to shepherd visitors towards the central shrine too quickly. Frequent **ceremonies** take place at the innermost sanctum, the most popular being at noon and 6pm, when a fire is lit, great gongs are struck and devotees rush forward to catch a last glimpse of the *lingam* before the doors are shut. On Friday nights before the temple closes,

Visiting Sabhanayaka Nataraja

In recent years, Sabhanayaka Nataraja has received some negative reports from tourists who experienced very aggressive **temple priests** stinging them for large amounts of rupees. Unlike most major temples in Tamil Nadu, which are funded and governed by the state, Chidambaram is a private enterprise run exclusively by the high-caste Dikshitar dynasty, and is dependent solely upon pilgrims' donations – and this reliance has led to unacceptable methods of extortion, including forceful demands for hundreds of rupees for the simple act of applying a tikka-dot to the forehead. Things came to a head in 2004, when a priestly committee agreed that aggressive priesting was to be curtailed, and since then things have calmed down somewhat. The simplest way to avoid the Sabhanayaka sting is to not offer your temple and forehead to be tikka'ed by any of the priests. Stock up on small change so you can make frequent – if modest – donations, and consider taking an official temple guide, which can be arranged either through your hotel or the Chidambaram tourist office.

during a particularly elaborate puja, Nataraja is carried on a palanquin accompanied by music and attendants carrying flaming torches and tridents. At other times, you'll hear ancient devotional hymns from the *Tevaram*.

The western *gopura* is the most popular entrance, as well as being the most elaborately carved and probably the earliest (c.1150 AD). Turning north (left) from here, you come to the colonnaded **Shivaganga tank**, the site of seven natural springs. From the broken pillar at the tank's edge, all four *gopuras* are visible. In the northeast corner, the largest building in the complex, the **Raja Sabha** (fourteenth- to fifteenth-century) is also known as "the thousand-pillared hall"; tradition holds that there are only nine hundred and ninety-nine actual pillars, the thousandth being Shiva's leg. During festivals the deities Nataraja and Shivakamasundari are brought here and mounted on a dais for the anointing ceremony, *abhishekha*.

The importance of **dance** at Chidambaram is underlined by the reliefs of dancing figures inside the east *gopura*, demonstrating 108 *karanas* (a similar set is to be found in the west *gopura*). A *karana* (or *adavu* in Tamil) is a specific point in a phase of movement prescribed by the extraordinarily comprehensive Sanskrit treatise on the performing arts, the *Natya Shastra* (c.200 BC–200 AD) – the basis of all classical dance, music and theatre in India. A caption from the *Natya Shastra* surmounts each *karana* niche. Four other niches are filled with images of patrons and *stahapatis* – the sculptors and designers responsible for the iconography and positioning of deities.

To get into the square **second enclosure**, head for its western entrance (just north of the west *gopura* in the third wall) which leads into a circumambulatory passageway. Once beyond this second wall it's easy to become disorientated, as the roofed inner enclosures see little light and are supported by a maze of colonnades. The atmosphere is immediately more charged, reaching its peak at the very centre.

The innermost **Govindaraja shrine** is dedicated to Vishnu – a surprise in this most Shaivite of environments. The deity is attended by non-Dikshitar brahmins, who, it is said, don't always get along with the Dikshitars. From outside the shrine, non-Hindus can see through to the most sacred part of the temple, the **Kanaka Sabha** and the **Chit Sabha**, adjoining raised structures, roofed with copper and gold plate and linked by a hallway. The latter houses bronze images of Nataraja and his consort Shivakamasundari; behind and to the left of Nataraja, a curtain, sacred to Shiva and strung with rows of leaves from the bilva tree, demarcates the most potent area of all. Within it lies the **Akashalingam**, known as the *rahasya*, or "secret", of Chidambaram: made of the most subtle of the elements, Ether (*akasha*) – from which Air, Fire, Water and Earth are born – the *lingam* is invisible – signifying the invisible presence of God in the human heart.

A crystal *lingam*, said to have emanated from the light of the crescent moon on Shiva's brow, and a small ruby Nataraja are worshipped in the Kanaka Sabha. They are ritually bathed in the flames of the priests' camphor fire or oil lamps six times a day. This inner area is where you're most likely to hear **oduvars**, hereditary singers from the middle, non-brahmin castes, intoning verses of ancient Tamil poetry. The songs with which they regale the deities at puja time, drawn from compilations such the *Tevaram* or earlier *Sangam*, are believed to be more than a thousand years old.

Practicalities

Chidambaram revolves around the Sabhanayaka Temple and the busy market area that surrounds it, along North, East, South and West Car streets. Though little more than a country halt, the **railway station**, just over 1km southeast of the centre, has good connections both north and south, and boasts retiring rooms and, on Platform 1, a **post office** (Mon–Sat 9am–1pm & 1.30–5pm). Frequent buses from Chennai, Thanjavur, Mamallapuram and Madurai pull in at the **bus stand**, also in the southeast, but nearer the centre, about 500m from the temple.

Staff at the TTDC **tourist office** (Mon–Fri 9.45am–5.45pm; ⓣ04144/238739), next to *Vandayar Gateway Inn* hotel on Railway Feeder Road, are charming and helpful, but only have a small pamphlet to give visitors. None of the **banks** in Chidambaram change money, although the *Saradharam* hotel, near the bus stand, will change cash and there is an ICICI Bank ATM in the forecourt. They also have an **Internet** café where you can get online for Rs30/hr.

Accommodation and eating

To cope with the influx of tourists and pilgrims, Chidambaram abounds in budget **accommodation**, but there are few upper-bracket options beyond the *Saradharam* hotel. The **railway retiring rooms** (Rs100–200) offer the best deal in town, with huge clean rooms, though the bathrooms are a little dilapidated; ask at the Station Master's Office on Platform 1.

As for **eating**, there are plenty of basic, wholesome "meals" places on and around the Car streets – the *Sri Ganesa Bhavan*, on West Car Street, gets the locals' vote. For quality, inexpensive South Indian food you can't beat the *Pallavi* at the *Saradharam* hotel, which is packed at lunchtimes for its good-value thalis. The *Anupallavi* behind it is an equally commendable, though somewhat dingy, non-veg alternative. There's also a small *Indian Coffee House*, on Venugopal Pillai Street, a pleasant breakfast venue or place to peruse the papers over coffee.

Hotels and guesthouses

Akshaya 17/18 East Car St ⓣ04144/222592, ⓔakshayhotel@hotmail.com. Pleasant, clean mid-range hotel, with a lawn backing right onto the temple wall. The rooms (a/c and non-a/c) are a decent size but the latter are cheaper and better value, and there are a couple of restaurants. ❷–❺

Mansoor Lodge 91 East Car St ⓣ04144/221072. Good, clean, friendly budget option, offering a choice of rooms with or without TV. Good value. ❶–❷

Raja Rajan 162 West Car St ⓣ04144/222690. Close to the west gate of the temple, the clean rooms here have tiled bathrooms and low tariffs; the a/c ones are good value. ❶–❸

Sabanayagam 22 East Sannathi St, off East Car St ⓣ04144/220896. Despite a flashy exterior, this is a run-of-the-mill budget place, with clean rooms off dim corridors. Some rooms are windowless, and there's a choice of a/c and non a/c rooms, and Western or Indian loos. Good veg restaurant downstairs. ❷–❹.

Saradharam 19 Venugopal Pillai St, opposite the bus stand ⓣ04144/221336, ⓔhsrcdm@vsnl.com. Large, clean and well-kept rooms, some of which have a/c and/or big balconies. There are two decent restaurants, including one serving pizzas, as well as a small garden, bar and a laundry. ❸–❻

Vandayar Gateway Inn Railway Feeder Rd, between the railway station and bus stand ⓣ04144/238056. Clean, decent-sized rooms with tiled floors. Two restaurants, an a/c bar and a tourist office are on site. ❷–❹

Kumbakonam

Sandwiched between the Kaveri (Cauvery) and Arasalar rivers is **KUMBAKONAM**, 74km southwest of Chidambaram and 38km northeast of Thanjavur. Hindus believe this to be the place where a water pot (*kumba*) of *amrita* – the ambrosial beverage of immortality – was washed up by a great deluge from atop sacred Mount Meru in the Himalayas. Shiva,

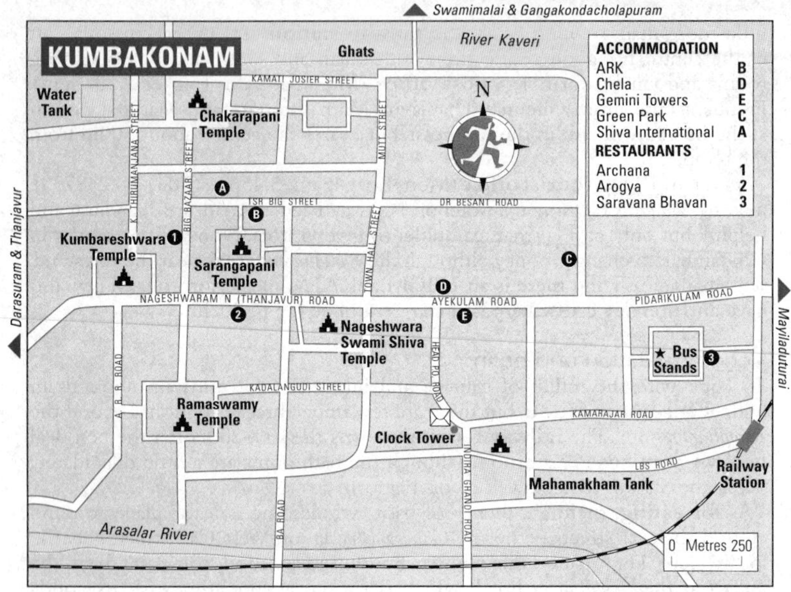

who just happened to be passing through in the guise of a wild forest-dwelling hunter, for some reason fired an arrow at the pot, causing it to break. From the shards, he made the *lingam* that is now enshrined in **Kumbareshwara Temple**, whose *gopuras* today tower over the town, along with those of some seventeen other major shrines. A former capital of the Cholas, who are said to have kept a high-security treasury here, Kumbakonam is the chief commercial centre for the Thanjavur region. The main bazaar, **TSR Big Street**, is especially renowned for its quality costume jewellery.

The main reason to stop in Kumbakonam is to admire the exquisite sculpture of the **Nageshwara Swami Shiva Temple**, which contains the most refined Chola stone carving still in situ. The town also lies within easy reach of the magnificent Darasuram and Gangaikondacholapuram temples, both spectacular ancient monuments that see very few visitors. Note that all temples in the area close between noon (or thereabouts) and 4pm. For a change, the village of Swamimalai, only a bike ride away, is the state's principal centre for traditional **bronze casting**.

The Town

Surmounted by a multicoloured *gopura*, the east entrance of Kumbakonam's seventeenth-century **Kumbareshwara Temple**, home of the famous *lingam* from which the town derived its name, is approached via a covered market selling a huge assortment of cooking pots, a local speciality, as well as the usual glass bangles and trinkets. At the gateway, you may meet the temple elephant, with a painted forehead and necklace of bells. Beyond the flagstaff, a *mandapa* houses a fine collection of silver *vahanas*, vehicles of the deities, used in festivals, and *pancha loham* (compound of five metals) figures of the 63 Nayanmar poet-saints.

The principal and largest of the Vishnu temples in Kumbakonam is the thirteenth-century **Sarangapani Temple**, entered through a ten-storey pyramidal *gopura* gate, more than 45m high. The **central shrine** dates from the late Chola period, with many later accretions. Its entrance, within the innermost court, is guarded by huge *dvarpalas*, identical to Vishnu whom they protect. Between them are carved stone *jali* screens, each different, and in front of them stands the sacred, square *homam* fireplace. During the day, rays of light from tiny ceiling windows penetrate the darkness around the sanctum, designed to resemble a chariot with reliefs of horses, elephants and wheels. A painted cupboard contains a mirror for Vishnu to see himself when he leaves the sanctum sanctorum.

The small **Nageshwara Swami Shiva Temple**, in the centre of town, is Kumbakonam's oldest, founded in 886 and completed a few years into the reign of Parantaka I (907–c.940). First impressions are unpromising, as much of the original building has been hemmed in by later Disney-coloured additions, but beyond the main courtyard, occupied by a large columned *mandapa*, a small *gopura*-topped gateway leads to an inner enclosure where the earliest Chola shrine stands. Framed in the main niches around its sanctum wall are a series of exquisite stone figures, regarded as the finest surviving pieces of **ancient sculpture** in South India. With their languid stance and mesmeric, half-smiling facial expressions, these modest-sized masterpieces far outshine the more monumental art of Thanjavur and Gangaikondacholapuram. The figures show Dakshinamurti (Shiva as a teacher; south wall), Durga and a three-headed Brahma (north wall) and Ardhanari, half-man, half-woman (west wall). Joining them are near-life-size voluptuous maidens believed to be queens or princesses of King Aditya's court.

The most famous and revered of many sacred **water tanks** in Kumbakonam, the **Mahamakham** in the southeast of town, is said to have filled with ambrosia (*amrit*) collected from the pot broken by Shiva. Every twelve years, when Jupiter passes the constellation of Leo, it is believed that water from the Ganges and eight other holy rivers flows into the tank, thus according it the status of *tirtha*, or sacred river crossing. At this auspicious time, as many as four million pilgrims come here for an absolving bathe; the last occasion was in early 2004.

Practicalities

Kumbakonam's small **railway station**, in the southeast, 2km from the main bazaar, is well served by trains both north and south, and has a left-luggage office (24hr) and decent **retiring rooms** (non a/c Rs125, a/c Rs250). The hectic bus stand is in the southeast of town, just northwest of the railway station. All the timetables are in Tamil, but there's a 24-hour enquiry office with English-speaking staff. Buses leave for Gangaikondacholapuram, Pondicherry, and Thanjavur every five to ten minutes, many via Darasuram. Frequent services run to Chennai, Trichy and several daily to Bangalore. There are a few small **Internet** places on TSR Big Street, where there is also an ICICI ATM machine, 100m east of the *Shiva International*.

Accommodation

Kumbakonam is not a major tourist location, and has limited **accommodation**, with only one upper-range hotel, the *Sterling Swamimalai*, 10km southeast of town on the outskirts of Swamimalai village (see p.1163). The good news for budget travellers is that most of the inexpensive places are clean and well-maintained.

ARK 21 TSR Big St ⓣ0435/242 1234. Fifty large, clean rooms (some a/c), on five floors, all with windows; TVs available on request. Bland, but comfortable enough, with an a/c bar serving snacks. ❸–❺

Chela 9 Ayekulam Rd ⓣ0435/243 0336, ⓕ243 1592. Large mid-range place, between the bus stand and centre, distinguished by its horrendous mock-classical facade. Soap, fresh towels and TVs are offered as standard. Two restaurants (veg and non-veg) and a bar. ❸–❺

Gemini Towers 18 Ayekulam Rd ⓣ0435/243 1559. Across the road from the *Chela*; a grand name for a very run-of-the-mill budget lodge, but it's welcoming and all the rooms are tidy and good value (though non-a/c). ❷

Green Park 10 Lakshmi Vilai St ⓣ0435/240 3912, ⓔgreenpark_hotel@rediffmail.com. Excellent-value business-oriented hotel with spotless doubles, all with TV, some a/c. There's also a coffee shop and the *Peacock* non-veg restaurant. ❸–❻

Shiva International 101/3 TSR Big St ⓣ0435/242 4013, ⓔhotelsiva@rediff.com. After the temple *gopuras*, this huge hotel complex is the tallest building in town. Their standard non-a/c is a bargain (ask for #301, which has great views on two sides) and all the spacious, airy doubles are decent value. You can climb onto the roof for incredible views of sunset and dawn behind the *gopuras*. ❸–❹

Eating

There's nothing very exciting about **eating out** in Kumbakonam, and most visitors stick to their hotel restaurant. For a change of scene, though, a few places stand out.

Archana Big Bazaar St. Right in the thick of the market, and popular among shoppers for its good-value South Indian "meals", and great *uttapams*, although it can get hot and stuffy inside. Foreigners appear to cause quite a stir here, but are made very welcome.

Arogya *Athityaa* hotel (ground floor), Nageshwaram N (Thanjavur) Rd. The best veg restaurant in town. No surprises on the menu, but their lunchtime "unlimited meals" (Rs25–35) are excellent, and they serve north Indian tandoori in the evenings. No alcohol.

Saravana Bhavan Just east of the bus stands. Cheap South Indian veg place serving lunchtime thalis and a range of veg dishes throughout the day.

Around Kumbakonam

The delta lands around Kumbakonam are scattered with evocative vestiges of the Cholas' golden age, but the most spectacular has to be the crumbling Airavateshwara Temple at **Darasuram**, 6km southwest. Across the fields to the north, the bronze-casters of **Swamimalai** constitute a direct living link with the culture that raised this extraordinary edifice, using traditional "lost wax" techniques, unchanged since the time when Darasuram was a thriving medieval town, to create graceful Hindu deities.

You can combine the two sights in an easy half-day trip from Kumbakonam. The route is flat enough to cycle, although you should keep your wits about you when pedalling the main Thanjavur highway, which sees heavy traffic. To reach Swamimalai from Darasuram, return to the main road from the temple and ask directions in the bazaar. Swamimalai is only 3km north, but travelling between the two involves several turnings, so expect to have to ask someone to wave you in the right direction at regular intervals. From Kumbakonam, the route is more straightforward; cross the Kaveri at the top of Town Hall Street (north of the centre), turn left and follow the main road west through a ribbon of villages.

Darasuram

The **Airavateshwara Temple**, built by King Rajaraja II (c.1146–73), stands in the village of **DARASURAM**, an easy five-kilometre bus or cycle ride (on the

Thanjavur route) southwest of Kumbakonam. This superb, if little-visited, Chola monument ranks alongside those at Thanjavur and Gangaikondacholapuram; but while the others are grandiose, emphasizing heroism and conquest, this is far smaller, exquisite in proportion and detail and said to have been decorated with *nitya-vinoda*, "perpetual entertainment", in mind. Shiva is called Airavateshwara here because he was worshipped in this temple by Airavata, the white elephant belonging to the king of the gods, Indra.

Darasuram's finest pieces of sculpture are the Chola black basalt images adorning wall niches in the *mandapa* and inner shrine. These include images of Nagaraja, the snake-king, with a hood of cobras, and Dakshinamurti, the "south-facing" Shiva as teacher, expounding under a banyan tree. Equally renowned is the unique series of somewhat gruesome panels, hard to see without climbing onto the base, lining the top of the basement of the closed *mandapa*. They illustrate scenes from Sekkilar's *Periya Purana*, one of the great works of Tamil literature.

Swamimalai

SWAMIMALAI, 8km west of Kumbakonam, is revered as one of the six sacred abodes of Lord Murugan, Shiva's son, whom Hindu mythology records became his father's religious teacher (*swami*) on a hill (*malai*) here. The site of this epic role reversal now hosts one of the Tamils' holiest shrines, the **Swaminatha Temple**, crowning the hilltop of the centre of the village, but of more interest to non-Hindus are the **bronze-casters**' workshops dotted around the bazaar and the outlying hamlets.

Known as **sthapathis**, Swamimalai's casters still employ the "lost wax" process perfected by the Cholas to make the most sought-after temple idols in South India. Their finished products are displayed in numerous showrooms along the main street, from where they are exported worldwide, but it is more memorable to watch the *sthapathis* in action, fashioning the original figures from beeswax and breaking open the moulds to expose the mystical finished metalwork inside. For more on Tamil bronze casting, see p.1169.

The nearby hamlet of **Thimmakkudy**, 2km back towards Kumbakonam, is the site of the area's grandest **hotel**, the *Sterling Swamimalai* (Ⓣ0435/242 0044, Ⓦwww.sterlingswamimalai.net; ❾), a beautifully restored nineteenth-century brahmins' mansion with all mod cons in its rooms. They also have an in-house yoga teacher, Ayurvedic massage room, and lay on a lively culture show in the evenings. Rooms cost $93.50.

Gangaikondacholapuram

Devised as the centrepiece of a city built by the Chola king Rajendra I (1014–42) to celebrate his conquests, the magnificent **Brihadishwara Temple** stands in the tiny village of **GANGAIKONDACHOLAPURAM**, in Trichy District, 35km northeast of Kumbakonam. The tongue-twisting name means "the town of the Chola who took the Ganges". Under Rajendra I, the Chola empire did indeed stretch as far as the great river of the north, an unprecedented achievement for a southern dynasty. Aside from the temple and the rubble remains of Rajendra's palace, 2km east at Tamalikaimedu, nothing of the city remains. Nonetheless, this is among the most extraordinary archeological sites in South India, outshone only by Thanjavur, and the fact that it's devoid of visitors most of the time gives it a memorably forlorn feel.

Buses run here from Kumbakonam every five minutes, and it's also served by some between Trichy and Chidambaram; to move on, buses back to

Kumbakonam pass through the village every ten minutes. Be sure not to get stuck here between noon and 4pm when the temple is closed. Facilities are minimal, with little more than a few cool drinks stands. Parts of the interior are extremely dark, and a torch is useful.

Brihadishwara Temple

Dominating the village landscape, the **Brihadishwara Temple** (daily 6am–noon & 4–8pm; free) sits in a well-maintained grassy courtyard, flanked by a closed *mandapa* hallway. Over the sanctuary, to the right, a massive pyramidal tower (*vimana*) rises 55m in nine diminishing storeys. Though smaller than the one at Thanjavur, the tower's graceful curve gives it an impressive refinement. At the gateway you are likely to meet the ASI caretaker, who is worth taking as a guide, especially if you'd like to climb up onto the roof for views of the vicinity and the tower.

Turning right (north) inside the courtyard, before you reach a small shrine to the goddess **Durga**, containing an image of Mahishasuramardini (the slaying of the buffalo demon), you come across a small well, guarded by a lion statue, known as Simha-kinaru and made from plastered brickwork. King Rajendra is said to have had Ganges water placed in the well to be used for the ritual anointing of the *lingam* in the main temple. The lion, representing Chola kingly power, bows to the huge Nandi respectfully seated before the eastern entrance of the temple, in line with the Shiva *lingam* contained within.

Directly in front of the eastern entrance to the temple stands a small altar for offerings. Two parallel flights of stairs ascend to the *mukhamandapa* or porch, which leads to the long pillared *mahamandapa* hallway, the entrance of which is flanked by a pair of large guardian deities. Immediately inside the temple a guide can show you the way to the tower, up steep steps. On either side of the temple doorway, sculptures of Shiva in his various benevolent (*anugraha*) manifestations include him blessing Vishnu, Devi, Ravana and the saint Chandesha. In the northeast corner, an unusual square stone block features carvings of the nine planets (*navagraha*). A number of **Chola bronzes** (see p.1169) stand on the platform; the figure of Karttikeya, the war god, carrying a club and a shield, is thought to have had particular significance.

The base of the main temple sanctuary is decorated with lions and scrollwork. Above this decoration, running from the southern to the northern entrance of the *ardhamandapa*, a series of sculpted figures in plastered niches portray different images of Shiva. The most famous is at the northern entrance, showing Shiva and Parvati garlanding the saint Chandesha, who here is sometimes identified as Rajendra I. For more on the temples of Tamil Nadu, see p.1138.

Two minutes' walk northeast along the main road (turn right from the car park), the tiny **Archeological Museum** (daily except Fri 10am–1pm & 2–5.45pm; free) contains Chola odds and ends, discovered locally. The finds include terracotta lamps, coins, weapons, tiles, bronze, bangle pieces, palm-leaf manuscripts and an old Chinese pot.

Thanjavur

As one of the busiest commercial towns of the Kaveri delta, **THANJAVUR** (aka "Tanjore"), 55km east of Tiruchirapalli and 35km southwest of Kumbakonam, is often overlooked by travellers. However, its history and treasures – among them the breathtaking **Brihadishwara Temple**, Tamil Nadu's most awesome Chola monument – give it a crucial significance to South Indian culture. The home of the world's finest Chola bronze collection, it holds

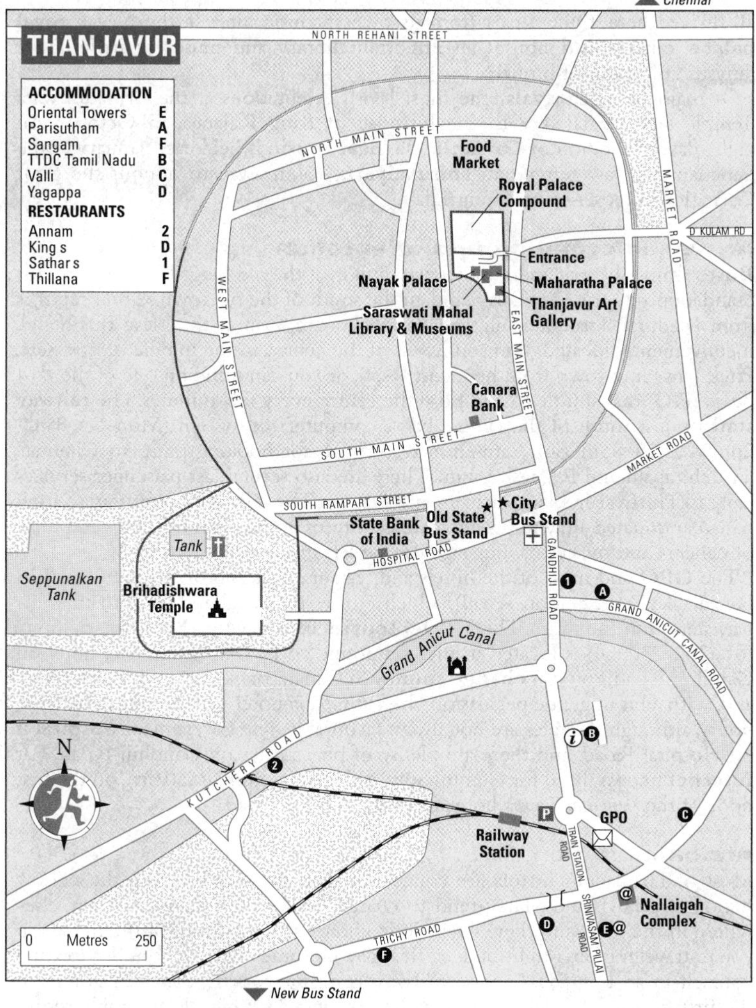

enough of interest to keep you enthralled for at least a couple of days, and is the most obvious base for trips to nearby Gangaikondacholapuram, Darasuram and Swamimalai.

Thanjavur is roughly split in two by the east–west **Grand Anicut Canal**. The **old town**, north of the canal and once entirely enclosed by a fortified wall, was chosen, between the ninth and the end of the thirteenth century, as the capital of their extensive empire by all the Chola kings save one. None of their secular buildings survive, but you can still see as many as ninety temples, of which the Brihadishwara most eloquently epitomizes the power and patronage of Rajaraja I (985–1014), whose military campaigns spread Hinduism to the Maldives, Sri Lanka and Java. Under the Cholas, as well as the later Nayaks and Marathas, literature, painting, sculpture, Carnatic classical music and Bharatanatyam dance all thrived here. Quite apart from its own intrinsic interest, the Nayak **royal palace compound** houses an important library and museums including a famous collection of bronzes.

Of major local **festivals**, the most lavish celebrations at the Brihadishwara Temple are associated with the birthday of King Rajaraja, in October. An eight-day celebration of **Carnatic classical music** is held each January at the Panchanateshwara temple at **Thiruvaiyaru**, 13km away, to honour the great Carnatic composer-saint, Thyagaraja.

Arrival, information and orientation

Buses from Chennai and Pondicherry pull in at the old long-distance State Bus Stand, opposite the City Bus Stand, in the south of the old town. Other services from Madurai, Tiruchirapalli, and Kumbakonam, stop at the New Bus Stand, inconveniently located 4km southwest of the centre, in the middle of nowhere. Rickshaws into town from here cost Rs50, or you can jump on one of the #74 buses (Rs3) that shuttle to and from the centre every few minutes. The **railway station**, just south of the centre, has a computerized system (Mon–Sat 8am–2pm & 2.15–8pm, Sun 8am–2pm & 3–5pm) for booking trains to Chennai, Tiruchirapalli and Rameshwaram. There are also several fast passenger services daily to Thiruvarur, Nagapattinam and Nagore. The red-and-cream station itself has an antiquated air, with its decorated columns in the main hall, and sculptures of dancers and musicians. Luggage can be left in the parcel office.

The **GPO** and most of the hotels and restaurants lie on or around **Gandhiji Road** (aka Train Station Road), which crosses the canal and leads to the railway station in the south. The **TTDC tourist office** (Mon–Fri 10am–5.45pm; ⓣ04362/230984) is located in the compound of TTDC *Tamil Nadu* hotel on Gandhiji Road. You can **change money** at Canara Bank on South Main Street and, with a bit of gentle persuasion, the *Parisutham* hotel – useful out of banking hours, although the rates are not always favourable. The government **hospital** is on Hospital Road, and there are plenty of pharmacies on Gandhiji Road. For **Internet access**, head for Gemini Soft (daily 9am–10pm; Rs30/hr), on the first floor of the *Oriental Towers* hotel, Srinivasam Pillai Road.

Accommodation

Most of Thanjavur's **hotels** are concentrated in the area between the railway station and bus stands. They tend to charge higher rates than you'd pay elsewhere in the state, and there's very little choice at the bottom of the market; if you're travelling on a tight budget, this may be somewhere to consider treating yourself to an upgrade. For the **railway retiring rooms**, contact Matron on the first floor of the railway station; they comprise six big, clean double rooms opening out onto a large communal veranda, overlooking the station approach. Great value, as ever, though invariably booked (Rs150).

Oriental Towers 2889 Srinivasam Pillai Rd ⓣ04362/230724, ⓔtnj._hotowers@sancharnet.in. Huge hotel-cum-shopping complex, with a small swimming pool and luxurious rooms. Although it's good value at this price and has all modern facilities, it's not as slick as the starred hotels. ❼

Parisutham 55 Grand Anicut Canal Rd ⓣ04362/231801, ⓔhotel.parisutham@vsnl.com. Plush hotel with spacious, centrally a/c rooms (from $119), a large palm-fringed pool (residents only), multi-cuisine restaurant, craft shop, foreign exchange and a travel agent. Popular with tour groups, so book ahead. ❾

Sangam Trichy Rd ⓣ04362/239451, ⓦwww.hotelsangam.com. International four-star standards at this luxury hotel with comfortable a/c rooms (from $102), an excellent restaurant, pool (Rs150 for non-residents) and beautiful Tanjore paintings – the one in the lobby is worth a trip here in itself. ❾

TTDC Tamil Nadu Gandhiji Rd, 10min from the bus and railway stations ⓣ04362/231325,

Ⓕ231970. Once the raja's guesthouse, but now a typically dilapidated state-run hotel, with more character than modern alternatives. Large, comfortable carpeted rooms (some with a/c) are set around a leafy enclosed garden. ❷–❺
Valli 2948 MKM Rd Ⓣ04362/231580. An exceptionally friendly place with super-clean rooms (some a/c) opening onto bright green corridors; there's a roof terrace and a popular restaurant on the ground floor. The best budget option in town. ❷–❺
Yagappa 1 Trichy Rd Ⓣ04362/230421. Spacious, well-appointed rooms with sitouts and large, tiled bathrooms. Staff are friendly, there's a bar and restaurant, and the reception features intriguing picture frames made from coffee roots. Good value. ❸

Brihadishwara Temple

Thanjavur's skyline is dominated by the huge tower of the **Brihadishwara Temple** (daily 6am–noon & 4–8pm; free), which for all its size lacks the grandiose excesses of later periods. The site has no great significance; the temple was constructed as much to reflect the power of its patron, King Rajaraja I, as to facilitate the worship of Shiva. Profuse **inscriptions** on the base of the main shrine provide incredibly detailed information about the organization of the temple, showing it to have been rich, both in financial terms and in ritual activity. Among recorded **gifts** from Rajaraja, from booty acquired in conquest, are the equivalent of 600lb of silver, 500lb of gold and 250lb of assorted jewels, plus income from agricultural land throughout the Chola empire, set aside for the purpose. No less than four hundred female dancers, **devadasis** (literally "slaves to the gods", married off to the deity), were employed, and each provided with a house. Other staff – another two hundred people – included dance teachers, musicians, tailors, potters, laundrymen, goldsmiths, carpenters, astrologers, accountants and attendants for all manner of rituals and processions.

Entrance to the complex is on the east, through two **gopura** gateways some way apart. Although the outer one is the larger, both are of the same pattern: massive rectangular bases topped by pyramidal towers with carved figures and vaulted roofs. At the core of each is a monolithic sandstone lintel, said to have been brought from Tiruchirapalli, over 50km away. The outer facade of the inner *gopura* features mighty fanged *dvarpala* door guardians, mirror images of each other, and thought to be the largest monolithic sculptures in any Indian temple.

Once inside, the gigantic **courtyard** gives plenty of space to appreciate the buildings. The **main temple**, constructed of granite, consists of a long pillared *mandapa* hallway, followed by the *ardhamandapa*, or "half-hall", which in turn leads to the inner sanctum, the *garbha griha*. Above the shrine, the pyramidal 61m *vimana* tower rises in thirteen diminishing storeys, the apex being exactly one-third of the size of the base. Such a design is quite different from later temples, in which the shrine towers become smaller as the *gopura* entranceways increasingly dominate – a desire to protect the sanctum sanctorum from the polluting gaze of outsiders. This *vimana* is an example of a "structured monolith", a stage removed from the earlier rock-cut architecture of the Pallavas, in which blocks of stone are assembled and then carved. As the stone that surmounts it is said to weigh eighty tonnes, there is considerable speculation as to how it got up there; the most popular theory is that the rock was hauled up a six-kilometre-long ramp. Others have suggested the use of a method comparable to the Sumer Ziggurat style of building, in which logs were placed in gaps in the masonry and the stone raised by leverage. The simplest answer, of course, is that perhaps it's not a single stone at all.

The black *shivalingam*, over 3.5m high, in the **inner sanctum** is called Adavallan, "the one who can dance well" – a reference to Shiva as Nataraja, the King of the Dance, who resides at Chidambaram and was the *ishtadevata*, chosen deity, of the king. The *lingam* is not always on view, but during puja ceremonies (8am, 11am, noon & 7.30pm), a curtain is pulled revealing the god to the devotees.

Outside, the walls of the courtyard are lined with **colonnaded passageways** – the one along the northern wall is said to be the longest in India. The one on the west, behind the temple, contains 108 *lingams* from Varanasi and (heavily graffitied) panels from the Maratha period. In the southwest corner of the courtyard, the small **Archeological Museum** (daily 9am–1pm & 4–6pm; free) houses an interesting collection of sculpture, including an extremely tubby, damaged Ganesh, before-and-after photos detailing restoration work to the temple in the 1940s and displays about the Cholas. You can also buy the excellent ASI booklet, *Chola Temples*, which gives detailed accounts of Brihadishwara and the temples at Gangaikondacholapuram and Darasuram. For more on Tamil Nadu's temples, see p.1138.

The Royal Palace Compound and around

The **Royal Palace Compound**, where members of the erstwhile royal family still reside, is on East Main Street (a continuation of Gandhiji Road), 2km northeast of Brihadishwara Temple. Dotted around the compound are several reminders of Thanjavur's past under the Nayaks and the Marathas, including an exhibition of oriental manuscripts and a superlative museum of **Chola bronzes**. The palace buildings have been in a sorry state for years; hopes were raised for their preservation when the responsibility for maintenance passed in 1993 to the Indian National Trust for Cultural Heritage (INTACH), but almost immediately some suffered extensive damage in storms. The Sarja Madi or "seven-storey" bell tower, built by Serfoji II in 1800, is closed to the public due to its unsafe condition.

Work on the palace began in the mid-sixteenth century under Sevappa Nayak, the founder of the Nayak kingdom of Thanjavur; additions were made by the Marathas from the end of the seventeenth century onwards. Remodelled by Shaji II in 1684, the **Durbar Hall**, or hall of audience, houses a throne canopy decorated with the mirrored glass distinctive of Thanjavur. Although damaged, the ceiling and walls are elaborately painted. Five domes are striped red, green and yellow, and on the walls, friezes of leaf and pineapple designs, and trumpeting angels in a night sky show European influence.

Saraswati Mahal Library Museum

The **Saraswati Mahal Library** holds one of the most important oriental manuscript collections in India, used by scholars from all over the world. The library is closed to the general public, but a small **museum** (daily except Wed 10am–1pm & 2–5pm; free) displays a bizarre array of books and pictures from the collection. Among the palm-leaf manuscripts is a calligrapher's *tour de force* in the form of a visual mantra, where each letter in the inscription "Shiva" comprises the god's name repeated in microscopically small handwriting. Most of the Maratha manuscripts, produced from the end of the seventeenth century, are on paper; they include a superbly illustrated edition of the *Mahabharata*. Sadists will be delighted to see the library managed to hang on to their copy of the explicitly illustrated **Punishments in China**, published in 1804. Next to it, full rein is given to the imagination of French artist, **Charles Le Brun** (1619–90), in a series of pictures on the subject of physiognomy. Animals such as the horse, bullock, wolf, bear, rabbit and camel are drawn in painstaking care above a series of human faces which bear an uncanny, if unlikely, resemblance to them. You can buy postcards of this scientific study and exhibits from the other palace museums in the **shop** next door.

Thanjavur Art Gallery

A magnificent collection of **Chola bronzes** – the finest of them from the Tiruvengadu hoard, unearthed in the 1950s – fills the **Thanjavur Art Gallery** (daily 9am–1pm & 3–6pm; Rs15, camera Rs30, video camera Rs200), a high-ceilinged audience hall with massive pillars, dating from 1600.

Chola bronzes

Originally sacred temple objects, **Chola bronzes** are the only art form from Tamil Nadu to have penetrated the world art market. The most memorable bronze icons are the **Natarajas**, or dancing Shivas. The image of Shiva, standing on one leg, encircled by flames, with wild locks caught in mid-motion, has become almost as recognizably Indian as the Taj Mahal, and few Indian millionaires would feel their sitting rooms to be complete without one.

The principal icons of a temple are usually stationary and made of stone. Frequently, however, ceremonies require an image of the god to be led in procession outside the inner sanctum, and even through the streets. According to the canonical texts known as *Agamas*, these moving images should be made of metal. Indian bronzes are made by the **cire-perdu** (**"lost wax"**) process, known as *madhuchchishtavidhana* in Sanskrit. Three layers of clay mixed with burned grain husks, salt and ground cotton are applied to a figure crafted in beeswax, with a stem left protruding at each end. When that is heated, the wax melts and flows out, creating a hollow mould into which molten metal – a rich five-metal alloy (*panchaloha*) of copper, silver, gold, brass and lead – can be poured through the stems. After the metal has cooled, the clay shell is destroyed, and the stems filed off, leaving a unique completed figure, which the caster-artist, or *sthapathi*, remodels to remove blemishes and add delicate detail.

Knowledge of bronze-casting in India goes back at least as far as the Indus Valley Civilization (2500–1500 BC), and the famous **"Dancing Girl"** from Mohenjo Daro. The earliest produced in the south was made by the Andhras, whose techniques were continued by the Pallavas, the immediate antecedents of the Cholas. The few surviving **Pallava** bronzes show a sophisticated handling of the form; figures are characterized by broad shoulders, thick-set features and an overall simplicity that suggests all the detail was completed at the wax stage. The finest bronzes of all are from the **Chola** period, in the late ninth to the early eleventh century. As the Cholas were predominantly Shaivite, Nataraja, Shiva and his consort Parvati (frequently in a family group with son Skanda) and the 63 Nayanmar poet-saints are the most popular subjects. Chola bronzes display more detail than their predecessors. Human figures are invariably slim-waisted and elegant, with the male form robust and muscular and the female graceful and delicate.

The design, iconography and proportions of each figure are governed by the strict rules laid down in the **shilpa shastras**, which draw no real distinction between art, science and religion. Measurement always begins with the proportions of the artist's own hand and the image's resultant face-length as the basic unit. Then follows a scheme which is allied to the equally scientific rules applied to classical music, and specifically *tala* or rhythm. Human figures total eight face-lengths, eight being the most basic of rhythmic measures. Figures of deities are *nava-tala*, nine face-lengths.

Those bronzes produced by the few artists practising today invariably follow the Chola model; the chief centre is now **Swamimalai** (see p.1163). Original Chola bronzes are kept in many Tamil temples, but as temple interiors are often dark it's not always possible to see them properly. Important **public collections** include the Nayak Durbar Hall Art Museum at Thanjavur, the Government State Museum at Chennai and the National Museum, New Delhi. Those interested in shopping for bronzes and other handicrafts should check out the Chola Art Galerie (Ⓣ04362/277355), a two-minute walk south of the palace entrance at 78/79 East Main St.

The elegance of the figures and delicacy of detail are unsurpassed. A tenth-century statue of Kannappa Nayannar (#174), a hunter-devotee, shows minutiae right down to his embroidered clothing, fingernails and the fine lines on his fingers. The oldest bronze, four cases left of the main doorway (#58) shows Vinadhra Dakshinamurti ("south-facing Shiva") who, with a deer on one left hand, would have originally been playing the *vina* – the musical instrument has long since gone. However, the undisputed masterpiece of the collection shows Shiva as Lord of the Animals (#86), sensuously depicted in a skimpy loin cloth, with a turban made of snakes. Next to him stands an equally stunning Parvati, his consort (#87), but the cream of the female figures, a seated, half-reclining Parvati (#97), is displayed on the opposite side of the hall.

Eating and drinking

For **food**, there's the usual crop of "meals" canteens dotted around town, the best of which are *Annantha Bhavan* and the *Sri Venkantan*, both on Gandhiji Road near the textile stores. The *Sangam* hotel's swish *Thillana* restaurant is a lot pricier, but worth it for the live Carnatic music. *King's* in the *Yagappa* hotel is the best choice for a quiet beer.

Annam *Pandiyar Residency*, 14 Kutchery Rd. Small, inexpensive and impeccably clean veg restaurant that's recommended for its cut-above-the-competition lunchtime thalis (Rs25), and evening South Indian snacks (especially the delicious cashew *uttapams*). A safe option for women travellers.

King's *Yagappa*, Trichy Rd. Seven kinds of beer are served in the usual dimly lit room, or on the "lawn" (read: "sandy back yard"), where decor includes stuffed lizards and plastic flowers in fish tanks. They also serve tasty chicken and *pakora* snacks.

Sathar's Gandhiji Rd. This is the town's most popular non-veg restaurant, and due to the constant turnover it's a pretty safe place to eat chicken. Seating for the predominantly male clientele is downstairs, or on a covered terrace. Dishes are Rs60–80.

Thillana *Sangam*, Trichy Rd. Swish multi-cuisine restaurant that's renowned for its superb lunchtime South Indian thalis (11am–3pm; Rs105). Evenings feature an extensive à la carte menu (their *chettinad* specialities are superb). Worth a splurge just for the live Carnatic music from 7.30–10pm featuring either veena, flute or vocals with percussion. Count on Rs250–300 per head.

Tiruchirapalli and around

TIRUCHIRAPALLI – more commonly referred to as **Trichy** – stands in the plains between the Shevaroy and Palani hills, just under 100km north of Madurai. Dominated by the dramatic Rock Fort, it's a sprawling commercial centre with a modern feel; the town itself holds little attraction, but pilgrims flock through en route to the spectacular **Ranganathaswamy Temple** in **Srirangam**, 6km north.

The precise date of Trichy's foundation is uncertain, but though little early architecture remains, it is clear that between 200 and 1000 AD control of the city passed between the Pallavas and Pandyas. The Chola kings who gained supremacy in the eleventh century embarked upon ambitious building projects, reaching a zenith with the Ranganathaswamy Temple. In the twelfth century, the Cholas were ousted by the Vijayanagar kings of Hampi, who then stood up against Muslim invasions until 1565, when they succumbed to the might of the sultans of the Deccan. Less than fifty years later the Nayaks of Madurai came to power, constructing the fort and firmly establishing Trichy as a trading city. After almost a century of struggle against the French and British, who both sought lands in southeast Tamil Nadu, the town came under British control until it was declared part of Tamil Nadu state in 1947.

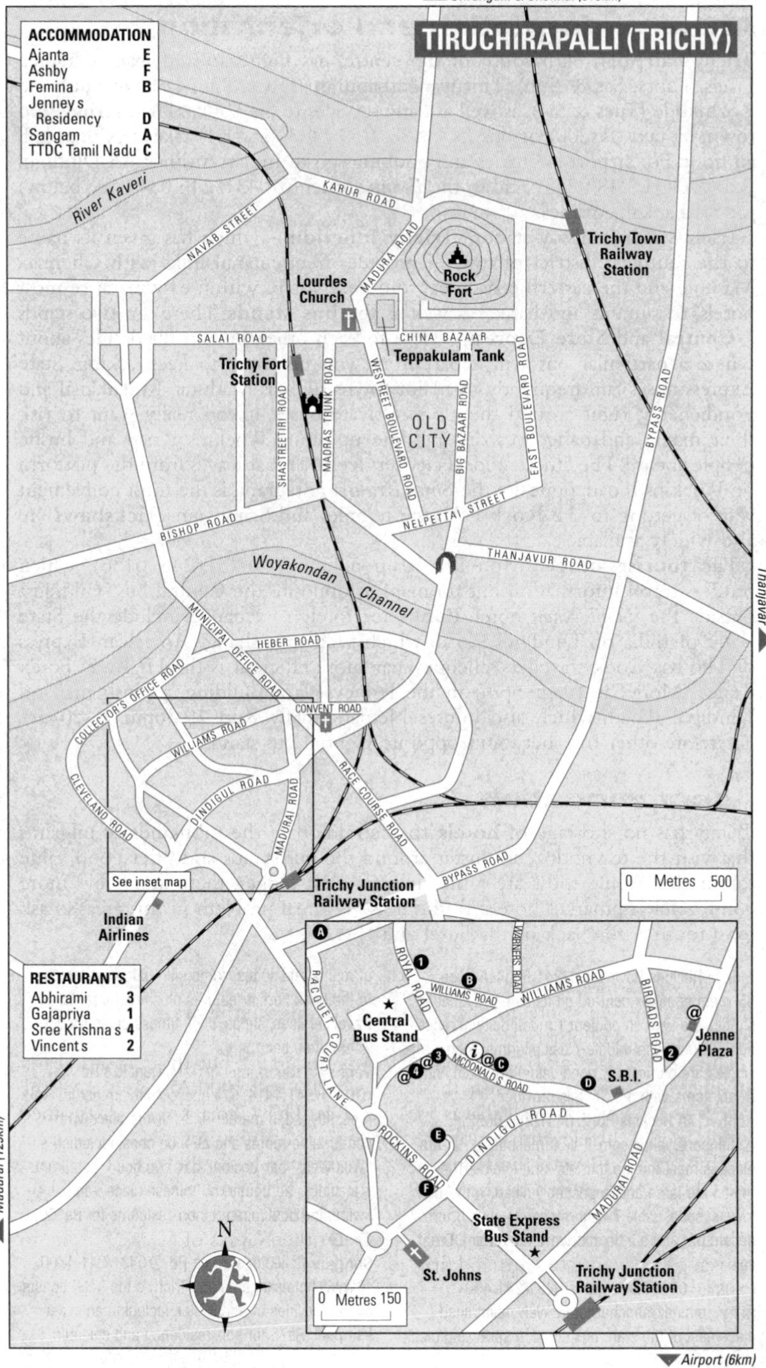

Tiruchirapalli and around

TAMIL NADU

20

Arrival, information and orientation

Trichy's **airport**, 8km south of the centre, has flights to and from Chennai (Tues, Thurs, Sat & Sun), Thiruvananthapuram (Tues, Thurs, Sat & Sun) and Kozhikode (Tues & Sat), as well as daily services to Sri Lanka. The journey into town, by taxi (Rs200) or bus (#7, #28, #59, #63, or #K1) takes less than half an hour. For airport enquiries and bookings go to Indian Airlines, 4A Dindigul Rd (Ⓣ0431/248 0233); and to the *Femina* hotel (Ⓣ0431/246 0844; see below) for Sri Lankan Airlines.

Trichy's main railway station, **Trichy Junction** – which has given its name to the southern district of town – provides frequent rail links with Chennai, Madurai and the eastern coastline. From here you're within easy reach of most hotels, restaurants and banks, as well as the **bus stands**. There are two stands – **Central** and **State Express** – close to each other, but no fixed rules about where a particular bus will depart from; you just have to keep asking. State Express buses run frequently to major towns such as Madurai, Kodaikanal and Pondicherry, right around the clock. Private buses, if you really want to risk their manic and dangerous driving, line up along Rockins Road and hustle people aboard. The efficient local city service (#1) that leaves from the platform on Rockins Road, opposite the *Shree Krishna* restaurant, is the most convenient way of getting to the Rock Fort, the temples and Srirangam. **Rickshaws** are also widely available.

The **tourist office** (Mon–Fri 10am–5.45pm; Ⓣ0431/246 0136), which proffers travel information but no maps, is opposite the Central bus stand, just outside the *Tamil Nadu* hotel. **Banks** for foreign exchange include the State Bank of India on Dindigul Road, which will only change American Express or Thomas Cook travellers' cheques. Far more efficient is the Highway Forex dealer (Mon–Sat 10am–6pm) in the Jenney Plaza Building, a plush mall on Dindigul Road, which also houses Netpark (daily 8am–10.30pm; Rs20/hr). There are other Internet joints opposite Central bus stand.

Accommodation

Trichy has no shortage of **hotels** to accommodate the thousands of pilgrims that visit the town; dozens cluster around the bus stands and offer good value for money. While most are rather characterless lodges, there are a few more comfortable upmarket hotels. Traffic noise is a real problem in this area, so ask for a room at the back of any hotel you check into.

Ajanta Rockins Rd Ⓣ0431/241 5504. A huge, 85-room complex centred on its own Vijayanagar shrine, and with an opulent Tirupati deity in reception. Popular with middle-class pilgrims; rooms (the singles are particularly good value) are plain and clean, some with a/c. Towels provided. ❸–❺

Ashby 17A Rockins Rd Ⓣ0431/246 0652, Ⓔchinoor@yahoo.com. This atmospheric Raj-era place is most foreign tourists' first choice. The rooms are large and impeccably clean, with fresh towels, soap, cable TV and mosquito coils. There's decent bar and a little courtyard restaurant. Great value. ❸–❺

Femina 109 Williams Rd Ⓣ0431/241 4501, Ⓔtry_femina@sancharnet.in. Well-maintained place east of the state bus stand. A sprawling block of rooms and suites, some with balconies looking to the Rock Fort, it features plush restaurants, travel services, shops, pool, fitness centre and a 24hr coffee bar. ❹–❼

Jenney's Residency 3/14 McDonald's Rd Ⓣ0431/241 4414, Ⓔjenneys@satyam.net.in. A slightly jaded marble-and-mirrors place with comfortable rooms and all mod cons, including a "Wild West" bar, cocktail bar, two good restaurants – including an upmarket Chinese place –and swimming pool (open to non-residents for Rs100). ❼–❽

Sangam Collector's Office Rd Ⓣ0431/241 4700, Ⓦwww.hotelsangam.com. Trichy's top hotel boasts all the facilities of a four-star, including an excellent pool (Rs75 for non-residents) and splendid restaurant with live music at weekends. Rooms from $125. ⑨

TTDC Tamil Nadu McDonald's Rd ⓣ0431/241 4346. One of TTDC's better hotels, and just far enough from the bus stand to escape the din. Best value are the non-a/c doubles, though even these are dowdier than most of the competition; all a/c rooms have cable TV. ②–⑤

The Town

Although Trichy conducts most of its business in the southern **Trichy Junction** district, the main sights are at least 4km north. The **bazaars** immediately north of the Junction heave with locally made cigars, textiles and fake diamonds made into inexpensive jewellery and used for dance costumes. Thanks to the town's frequent, cheap air connection with Sri Lanka, you'll also come across boxes of smuggled Scotch and photographic film. Head north along Big Bazaar Road and you're confronted by the dramatic profile of the **Rock Fort**, topped by the seventeenth-century Vinayaka (Ganesh) Temple.

North of the fort, the River Kaveri marks a wide boundary between Trichy's crowded streets and its more serene temples; the **Ranganathaswamy Temple** is so large it holds much of the village of Srirangam within its courtyards. Also north of the Kaveri is the elaborate **Sri Jambukeshwara Temple**, while several British **churches** dotted around town make an interesting contrast – most notable is **Our Lady of Lourdes** west of the Rock Fort, modelled on the Basilica of Lourdes. A forty-minute bus ride from town, the peaceful **Shantivanam ashram** on the banks of the River Kaveri is open to visitors year round.

The Rock Fort

Trichy's **Rock Fort** (daily 6am–8pm; Rs1, camera Rs10, video camera Rs50) is best reached by bus (#1) from outside the railway station, or from Dindigul Road; rickshaws will try to charge you Rs50 or more for the five-minute ride.

The massive sand-coloured rock on which the fort rests towers to a height of more than 80m, its irregular sides smoothed by wind and rain. The Pallavas were the first to cut into it, but it was the Nayaks who grasped the site's potential as a fort, adding only a few walls and bastions as fortifications. From the entrance, off China Bazaar, a long flight of red-and-white painted steps cuts steeply uphill, past a series of Pallava and Pandya rock-cut temples (closed to non-Hindus), to the **Ganesh Temple** crowning the hilltop. The views from its terrace are spectacular, taking in the Ranganathaswamy and Jambukeshwara temples to the north, their *gopuras* rising from a sea of palm trees, and the cubic concrete sprawl of central Trichy to the south.

Sri Ranganathaswamy Temple

The **Sri Ranganathaswamy Temple** at **Srirangam**, 6km north of Trichy, is among the most revered shrines to Vishnu in South India, and also one of the largest and liveliest. Enclosed by seven rectangular walled courtyards and covering more than sixty hectares, it stands on an island defined by a tributary of the River Kaveri. This location symbolizes the transcendence of Vishnu, housed in the sanctuary reclining on the coils of the snake Adisesha, who in legend formed an island for the god, resting on the primordial Ocean of Chaos.

Frequent **buses** from Trichy pull in and leave from outside the southern gate. The temple is approached from the south. A gateway topped with an immense and heavily carved *gopura*, plastered and painted in bright pinks, blues and yellows, and completed in the late 1980s, leads to the outermost courtyard, the latest of seven built between the fifth and seventeenth centuries. Most of the present structure dates from the late fourteenth century, when the temple was renovated and enlarged after a disastrous sacking in 1313. The outer three courtyards, or *prakaras*, form the hub of the temple community, housing ascetics, priests, and musicians.

At the fourth wall, the entrance to the temple proper, visitors remove footwear and can purchase camera and video tickets (Rs50/100) before passing through a high gateway, topped by a magnificent *gopura* and lined with small shrines to teachers, hymn-singers and sages. In earlier days, this fourth *prakara* would have formed the outermost limit of the temple, and was the closest members of the lowest castes could get to the sanctuary. It contains some of the finest and oldest buildings of the complex, including a temple to the goddess **Ranganayaki** in the northwest corner where devotees worship before approaching Vishnu's shrine. On the eastern side of the *prakara*, the heavily carved "thousand pillared" *kalyan mandapa*, or hall, was constructed in the late Chola period. The pillars of the outstanding **Sheshagiriraya Mandapa**, south of the *kalyan mandapa*, are decorated with rearing steeds and hunters, representing the triumph of good over evil.

To the right of the gateway into the fourth courtyard, a small **museum** (daily 10am–noon & 3–5pm; free) houses a modest collection of stone and bronze sculptures, and some delicate ivory plaques. For Rs10, you can climb to the roof of the fourth wall from beside the museum and take in the view over the temple rooftops and *gopuras*, which increase in size from the centre outwards. The central tower, crowning the holy sanctuary, is coated in gold and carved with images of Vishnu's incarnations, on each of its four sides.

Inside the gate to the third courtyard – the final section of the temple open to non-Hindus – is a pillared hall, the **Garuda Mandapa**, carved throughout in typical Nayak style. Maidens, courtly donors and Nayak rulers feature on the pillars that surround the central shrine to Garuda, the man-eagle vehicle of Vishnu.

The dimly lit innermost courtyard, the most sacred part of the temple, shelters the image of Vishnu in his aspect of Ranganatha, reclining on the serpent Adisesha. The shrine is usually entered from the south, but for one day each year, during the **Vaikuntha Ekadasi festival**, the north portal is opened; those who pass through this "doorway to heaven" can anticipate great merit. Most of the temple's daily festivals take place in this enclosure, beginning each morning with *vina*-playing and hymn-singing as Vishnu is awakened in the presence of a cow and an elephant, and ending just after 9pm with similar ceremonies.

For more on Ranganathaswamy and Tamil Nadu's other great temples, see p.1138.

Eating

To **eat** well in Trichy, you won't have to stray far from the bus stand, where the town's most popular "meals" joints do a roaring trade all day long.

Abhirami 10 Rockins Rd, opposite the bus stand. Trichy's best-known South Indian restaurant serves up unbeatable value lunchtime "meals", and the standard range of snacks the rest of the day. They also have a fast food counter where you can get *dosas* and *uttapams* at any time.

Gajapriya Royal Rd, on the ground floor of the *Gajapriya* hotel. Non-veg north Indian and noodle dishes are specialities of this small but blissfully cool and clean a/c restaurant. A good place to chill out over coffee.

Sree Krishna's 1 Rockins Rd, opposite the bus stand. Delicious and very filling American or South Indian "set breakfasts", unlimited banana-leaf thalis at lunch time (Rs35) and South Indian specialities in the evenings – all served with a big smile.

Vincent's Dindigul Rd, next to the bakery. An "Oriental" theme restaurant, set back from the road in its own terrace garden, with mock pagodas, concrete bamboo and a multi-cuisine menu that includes tasty chicken tikka and other tandoori dishes. A bit shabby, but it's an escape from the hectic bus stand area. No alcohol; evenings only.

Madurai

One of the oldest cities in south Asia, **MADURAI**, on the banks of the River Vaigai, has been an important centre of worship and commerce for as long as there has been civilization in South India – indeed, it has long been described as "the Athens of the East". Not surprisingly then, when the Greek ambassador Megasthenes came here in 302 BC, he wrote of its splendour, and described its queen, Pandai, as "a daughter of Herakles". Meanwhile, the Roman geographer Strabo complained at how the city's silk, pearls and spices were draining the imperial coffers of Rome. It was this lucrative trade that enabled the **Pandyan** dynasty to erect the mighty **Meenakshi-Sundareshwarar temple**. Although today surrounded by a sea of modern concrete cubes, the massive *gopuras* of this vast complex, writhing with multicoloured mythological figures and crowned by golden finials, remain the greatest man-made spectacle of the south. Any day of the week no less than 15,000 people pass through its gates; increasing to over 25,000 on Friday (sacred to the goddess Meenakshi), while the temple's ritual life spills out into the streets in an almost ceaseless round of festivals and processions. The chance to experience sacred ceremonies that have persisted largely unchanged since the time of the ancient Egyptians is one that few travellers pass up.

Madurai's urban and suburban sprawl creates traffic jams to rival India's very worst. Chaos on the narrow, potholed streets is exacerbated by political demonstrations and religious processions, wandering cows – demanding right of way with a peremptory nudge of the haunch – and put-upon pedestrians forced onto the road by ever-increasing numbers of street traders. Open-air kitchens extend from chai-shops, where competing *parota*-wallahs literally drum up custom for their delicious fresh breads with a tattoo of spoon-on-skillet signals. Given the traffic problems, it's just as well that Madurai, with a profusion of markets and intriguing corners, is an absorbing city to walk around.

Some history

Although invariably interwoven with myth, the traceable history and fame of Madurai stretches back well over 2000 years. Numerous natural **caves** in local hills, and boulders often modified by the addition of simple rock-cut beds, were used both in prehistoric times and by ascetics, such as the Ajivikas and Jains, who practised withdrawal and penance.

Madurai appears to have been the capital of the Pandyan empire without interruption for at least a thousand years. It became a major commercial city, trading with Greece, Rome and China, and *yavanas* (a generic term for foreigners) were frequent visitors to Pandyan seaports. The Tamil epics describe them walking around town with their eyes and mouths wide open with amazement, much as foreign tourists still do when they first arrive. Under the Pandya dynasty, Madurai also became an established seat of Tamil culture, credited with being the site of three **sangams**, "literary academies", said to have lasted 10,000 years and supported some 8000 poets.

The Pandyas' capital fell in the tenth century, when the **Chola** King Parantaka took the city. In the thirteenth century, the Pandyas briefly regained power until the early 1300s, when the notorious **Malik Kafur**, the Delhi Sultanate's "favourite slave", made an unprovoked attack during a plunder-and-desecration tour of the south, and destroyed much of the city. Forewarned of the raid, the Pandya king, Sundara, fled with his immediate family and treasure, leaving his uncle and rival, Vikrama Pandya, to repel Kafur. Nevertheless, the latter returned to Delhi with booty said to consist of "six hundred and twelve elephants,

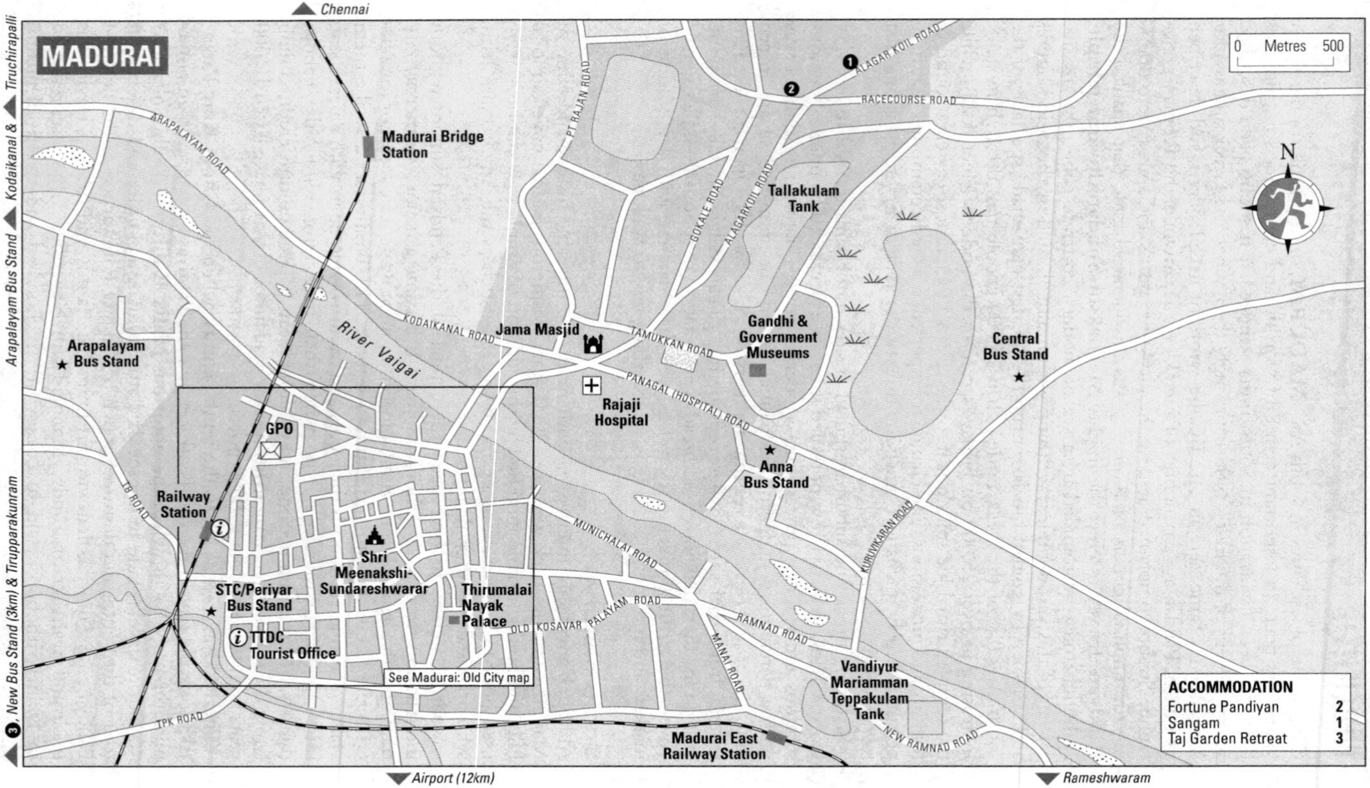

MADURAI
Chennai
Tiruchirapali
Kodaikanal &
Arapalayam Bus Stand
3, New Bus Stand (3km) & Tirupparakunram
Airport (12km)
Rameshwaram
0 Metres 500
N
ALAGAR KOIL ROAD
RACECOURSE ROAD
PT RAJAN ROAD
GOKALE ROAD
ALAGARKOIL ROAD
Tallakulam Tank
Madurai Bridge Station
ARAPALAYAM ROAD
KODAIKANAL ROAD
River Vaigai
Jama Masjid
TAMUKKAN ROAD
Gandhi & Government Museums
Central Bus Stand
PANAGAL (HOSPITAL) ROAD
Rajaji Hospital
Arapalayam Bus Stand
GPO
Anna Bus Stand
Railway Station
TB ROAD
KURUVIKARAN ROAD
MUNICHALAI ROAD
Shri Meenakshi-Sundareshwarar
STC/Periyar Bus Stand
Thirumalai Nayak Palace
OLD KOSAVAR PALAYAM ROAD
RAMNAD ROAD
MANAI ROAD
TTDC Tourist Office
See Madurai: Old City map
Vandiyur Mariamman Teppakulam Tank
TPK ROAD
NEW RAMNAD ROAD
Madurai East Railway Station
ACCOMMODATION
Fortune Pandiyan 2
Sangam 1
Taj Garden Retreat 3

ninety-six thousand *mans* of gold, several boxes of jewels and pearls and twenty thousand horses".

Shortly after this raid Madurai became an independent Sultanate; in 1364, it joined the Hindu **Vijayanagar** empire, ruled from Vijayanagar/Hampi and administered by governors, the **Nayaks**. In 1565, the Nayaks asserted their own independence. Under their supervision and patronage, Madurai enjoyed a renaissance, being rebuilt on the pattern of a lotus centring on the Meenakshi Temple. Part of the palace of the most illustrious of the Nayaks, **Thirumalai** (1623–55), survives today. The city remained under Nayak control until the mid-eighteenth century when the **British** gradually took over. A hundred years later the British de-fortified Madurai, filling its moat to create the four Veli streets that today mark the boundary of the old city.

Arrival and information

Madurai's small domestic **airport** (Ⓣ0452/269 0433), 12km south of the city, is served by flights to and from Chennai, and Mumbai. Theoretically you should be able to get information at the **Government of Tamil Nadu tourist information centre** booth by the exit, but it's not always open to meet flights. There's also a bookshop and a branch of Indian Bank which changes traveller's cheques only. **Taxis** charge fixed rates of around Rs200 for journeys within the city. City Bus #10A leaves frequently from near the exit and will drop you at Periyar Bus Stand in town.

Arriving in Madurai by **bus**, you come in at one of two stands. The **Central Bus Stand** is 7km from the centre on the east side of the river: it's connected to the centre by, among others, the dedicated city bus #700. Central is the arrival point of all services except those from towns in the west, including Kodaikanal and Coimbatore, and Kerala, which terminate at the **Arapalayam Bus Stand** in the northwest, about 2km from the railway station. In the centre, only local city buses operate from either **STC bus stand**, or **Periyar stand** next door. Both are on West Veli Street in the west of the old city, and are very close to the railway station and most accommodation. Madurai's clean and well-maintained **railway station** is just west of the centre off West Veli Street. You can leave your luggage at the 24-hour cloakroom (Rs10/24hr) next to the **reservations office** (Mon–Sat 8am–2pm & 2.15–8pm, Sun 8am–2pm) in the main hall, where you'll also find a very helpful branch of the **Tourism Department information centre** (daily 6.30am–8.30pm). There's a small veg **canteen** on Platform 1, and, unusually, a **prepaid auto-rickshaw** and **taxi booth** outside the main entrance, open to coincide with train arrivals.

The **Department of Tourism**'s main office is on West Veli Street (Mon–Fri 10am–5.45pm, plus most Saturdays 10am–1pm; Ⓣ0452/233 4757) and the staff are very helpful, as are those at the railway station tourist office (see above); both offices offer maps and general information about Madurai and the surrounding areas, and provide details of **car rental** firms. They will also arrange, with a little notice, **city tours** (7am–noon or 3–8pm; Rs100 per head) in a minibus with one of the government-approved **guides**, who can otherwise usually be found at the southern entrance to the temple. If you're hiring a guide at the temple entrance, get a list of names first from the tourist office; government-approved guides usually speak far better English than private operators and are reliable. If you want to rent a **taxi** to see the outlying sights, the rank at the main railway station abides by government set rates.

Madurai's **GPO** is at the corner of West Veli and North Veli streets (Mon–Sat 8am–7.30pm, Sun & hols 9am–4.30pm; speedpost 10am–7pm). For **poste**

restante (Mon–Sat 9.30am–7pm), go to the Philatelic Bureau on the south-west corner of the building. **Internet access** is widely available: try Net Tower, next to the *Hotel International* (daily 8am–10pm; Rs30/hr), and Friends (daily 9am–11pm; Rs20/hr), just round the corner at 13/8 Kaka Thoppu St.

The best place to **change money** is Alagendran Forex Services, opposite the GPO at 168 North Veli St (Mon–Sat 9am–6.30pm), which offers more or less the same rates as the State Bank of India, 6 West Veli Street. There are 24-hour ATMs at the SBI, one at the Canara Bank on West Perumal Maistry Street, and another at the UTI Bank at Station. **Bike rental** at low rates is available at SV, West Tower Street, near the west entrance to the temple, or the stall on West Veli Street, opposite the *Tamil Nadu* hotel.

Accommodation

Madurai has a wide range of **accommodation**, from rock-bottom lodges to good, clean mid-range places that cater for the flocks of pilgrims and tourists. There's a cluster of hotels on **West Perumal Maistry Street**; upmarket options lie a few kilometres out of the town centre, north of the Vaigai. The **railway retiring rooms** (Rs150), 1st floor, stairway on Platform 1 (turn right from the main entrance hall), are huge and cleanish, some with a/c, but are often booked.

Unless otherwise stated, the hotels listed below are marked on the Old City map (opposite).

Aarathy 9 Perumal Koil, off South Masi St ⓣ0452/233 1571. Great location overlooking the Kundalagar Temple, and often booked up. All rooms have TV, others have a/c and a balcony – some are better than others, so ask to see a range before checking in. There's an excellent a/c restaurant which extends out into the courtyard where the temple elephant is led through each morning and afternoon. ❸–❺

Duke 6 North Veli St, close to the junction with West Masi St ⓣ0452/234 1154. A modern hotel, with larger-than-average non-a/c rooms; ask for one on the "open side", with a window. Good value. ❸–❹

Fortune Pandyan Racecourse Rd, north of the river (see main Madurai map. p.1176) ⓣ0452/253 7090, ⓔmail@fortunepandiyan.com. Comfortable decent-sized a/c rooms with TV; on-site facilities include a bar, good restaurant, currency exchange, travel agency and a nice garden. $84–$107. ❾

International 46/80 West Perumal Maistry St ⓣ0452/537 7463. Mid-range hotel with laid-back service. The clean and comfortable rooms have cable TV. ❷–❹

New College House 2 Town Hall Rd ⓣ0452/234 2971, ⓔinfo@newcollegehouse.com. Recently spruced up, this is a huge maze with more than 200 rooms (a few with a/c), and one of the town's best "meals" canteens on the ground floor (see p.1186). The very cheapest rooms are decidedly grimy, but they are likely to have vacancies when everywhere else is full. ❷–❺

Padmam 1 Perumal Tank West St ⓣ0452/234 0702. Clean, comfortable modern hotel, centrally located and with a rooftop restaurant. The views from the front-side rooms, overlooking the ruined Perumal tank, are worth paying extra for. Popular with the foreign crowd, so book in advance. ❹–❺

Prem Nivas 102 West Perumal Maistry St ⓣ0452/234 2532, ⓔpremnivas@eth.net. From the outside this place looks a lot swankier than it is, but the spacious en-suite rooms (some with a/c) make it among the best deals in the city. ❸–❹

Sangam Alagar Koil Rd (see main Madurai map, p.1176) ⓣ0452/253 7531, ⓔreservation@hotelsangam.com. Plush hotel on the northern outskirts, with 24hr room service, bar, currency exchange, craft shop, swimming pool and gardens. Rooms from $125. ❾

Sree Devi 20 West Avani Moola St ⓣ0452/234 7431. Good-value, spotless non-a/c doubles right next to the temple mean this place is always filled with foreigners. For a romantic splurge, splash out on their "deluxe" a/c rooftop room, which has matchless views over the western *gopura*. No restaurant, but they will order in food and beer for you. ❷–❸

Supreme 110 West Perumal Maistry St ⓣ0452/234 3151, ⓦwww.supremehotels.com. A large, swish and central hotel, with a great rooftop restaurant (see p.1186), an a/c restaurant on the ground floor and a choice of comfortable a/c and non a/c rooms in a seven–storey block;

the more expensive have temple views. It's a little overpriced, but has good facilities including a 24hr forex desk, Internet facilities and travel counter. Book in advance. ❹–❻

Taj Garden Retreat 40 TPK Rd, Pasumalai Hills (see main Madurai map, p.1176) ⓣ0452/260 1020, ⓦwww.tajhotels.com. Madurai's most exclusive hotel; a beautifully refurbished colonial house set within 25 acres of manicured gardens in the hills overlooking the city and temples, albeit 6km out. Of the three categories of room, the superior ones in the old colonial building are the most atmospheric, but the deluxe have the best views. Facilities include a gourmet restaurant, swimming pool, tennis court and bar. $145–190. ❾

TM 50 West Perumal Maistry St ⓣ0452/234 1651, ⓔtmlodge@maduraiinfo.com. Despite the rather unfriendly reception and institutional atmosphere, this is an immaculately clean option, with spotless attached bathrooms; the top-floor rooms are the airiest. It's one of the best of the budget bunch on this street. ❸–❹

TTDC Hotel Tamil Nadu I West Veli St ⓣ0452/233 7471, ⓦwww.tamilnadutourism.org. Somewhat on a limb, away from the atmosphere of the temples and the bazaar, but with spacious rooms (some a/c) overlooking a leafy courtyard. The cheapest rooms are especially good value. ❷–❹

West Tower 42/60 West Tower St ⓣ0452/234 6908. The selling point is its proximity to the temple, and the great views from the rooftop (but not from the rooms), where there's a pleasant little thatched terrace. However, the rooms are very basic and rather overpriced; some have a/c. ❸–❺

The City

Although considerably enlarged and extended over the years, the overall layout of Madurai's **old city**, south of the River Vaigai, has remained largely unchanged since the first centuries AD, comprising a series of concentric squares centred on the massive **Meenakshi Temple**. Aligned with the cardinal points, the street plan forms a giant *mandala*, or magical diagram, whose sacred properties are believed to be activated during mass circumambulations of the central temple, always conducted in a clockwise direction.

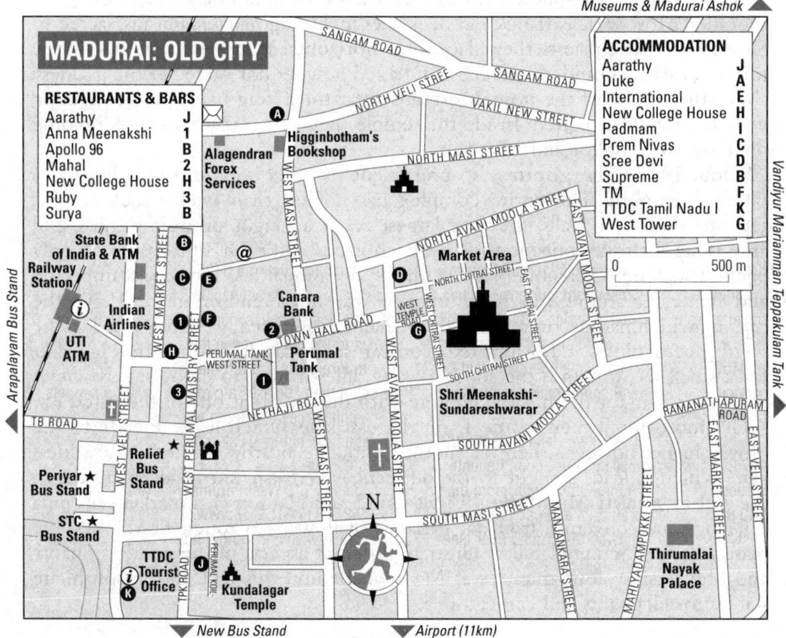

North of the river, Madurai becomes markedly more mundane and irregular. You're only likely to cross the Vaigai to reach the city's more expensive hotels or the Gandhi Museum.

Sri Meenakshi-Sundareshwara Temple

Enclosed by a roughly rectangular six-metre-high wall, in the manner of a fortified palace, the **Meenakshi-Sundareshwara Temple** (daily 6am–12.30pm & 4–9.30pm; cameras Rs30, videos not allowed) is one of the largest temple complexes in India. Much of it was constructed during the Nayak period between the sixteenth and eighteenth centuries, but certain parts are very much older. The principal shrines (closed to non-Hindus) are those to Sundareshwar (Shiva) and his consort Meenakshi (a form of Parvati); unusually, the goddess takes precedence and is always worshipped first.

For the first-time visitor, confronted with a confusing maze of shrines, sculptures and colonnades, and unaware of the logic employed in their arrangement, it's very easy to get disorientated. However, if you're not in a hurry, this should not deter you. Quite apart from the estimated 33,000 sculptures to arrest your attention, the life of the temple is absolutely absorbing, and many visitors find themselves drawn back to experience it all at different times of the day. Be it the endless round of puja ceremonies, loud *nagaswaram* and *tavil* music, weddings, brahmin boys under religious instruction in the *Vedas*, the prostrations of countless devotees, the glittering market stalls inside the east entrance, or, best of all, a festival procession, something is always going on to make this one of the most compelling places in Tamil Nadu.

Approximately fifty priests work in the temple, and live in houses close to the north entrance. They are easily identified – each wears a white *dhoti* (*veshti* in Tamil) tied between the legs; on top of this, around the waist, is a second, coloured cloth, usually of silk. Folded into the cloth, a small bag contains holy white ash. The bare-chested priests invariably carry a small towel over the shoulder. Most wear earrings and necklaces including *rudraksha* beads, sacred to Shiva. As Shaivite priests, they place three horizontal stripes of white ash on the forehead, arms, shoulders and chest and a red powder dot, sacred to the goddess, above the bridge of the nose. Most also wear their long hair tied into a knot, with the forehead shaved. Inside the temple they also carry brass trays holding offerings of camphor and ash.

Madurai takes the **gopura**, so prominent in other southern temples, to its ultimate extreme. The entire complex has no less than twelve such towers; set into the outer walls, the four largest reach a height of around 46m, and are visible for miles outside the city. Each is covered with a profusion of gaily painted stucco gods and demons, with the occasional live monkey scampering and chattering among the divine images. After a referendum in the 1950s, the *gopuras*, which had become monochrome and dilapidated, were repainted in the vivid greens, blues, and bright reds you can see today. It is sometimes possible, for a small fee, to climb the southern and tallest tower, to enjoy superb views over the town; for permission, enquire with the guards at one of the gateways.

The most popular **entrance** is on the east side, which leads directly to the Shiva shrine; however there is another entrance nearby, through a towerless gate, which is leads straight to the adjacent Meenakshi shrine deep inside. In the **Ashta Shakti Mandapa** ("Eight Goddesses Hallway"), a market sells puja offerings and souvenirs, from fat garlands of flowers to rough-hewn sky-blue plaster deities. Sculpted pillars illustrate different aspects of the goddess Shakti, and Shiva's sixty-four miracles at Madurai. Behind this hall, to the south, are stables for elephants and camels.

Meenakshi the fish-eyed goddess

The goddess **Meenakshi** of Madurai emerged from the flames of a sacrificial fire as a three-year-old child, in answer to the Pandyan king Malayadvaja's prayer for a son. The king, not only surprised to see a female, was also horrified that she had three breasts. In every other respect, she was beautiful, as her name, Meenakshi ("fish-eyed"), suggests – fish-shaped eyes are classic images of desirability in Indian love poetry. Dispelling his concern, a mysterious voice told the king that Meenakshi would lose the third breast on meeting her future husband.

In the absence of a son, the adult Meenakshi succeeded her father as Pandyan monarch. With the aim of world domination, she then embarked on a series of successful battles, culminating in the defeat of Shiva's armies at the god's Himalayan abode, Mount Kailash. Shiva then appeared at the battlefield; on seeing him, Meenakshi immediately lost her third breast. Fulfilling the prophecy, Shiva and Meenakshi travelled to Madurai, where they were married. The two then assumed a dual role, firstly as king and queen of the Pandya kingdom, with Shiva assuming the title Sundara Pandya, and secondly as the presiding deities of the Madurai temple, into which they subsequently disappeared.

Their shrines in Madurai are today the focal point of a hugely popular fertility cult; centred on the gods' coupling, temple priests maintain that it ensures the preservation and regeneration of the Universe. Each night, the pair are placed in Sundareshwara's bedchamber together, but not before Meenakshi's nose ring is carefully removed so that it won't cut her husband in the heat of passion. Their celestial lovemaking is consistently earth-moving enough to ensure that Sundareshwara remains completely faithful to his consort (exceptional for the notoriously promiscuous Shiva). Nevertheless, this fidelity is never taken for granted, and has to be ritually tested each year when the beautiful goddess Cellattamman is brought to Sundareshwara "to have her powers renewed". After she is spurned, she flies into a fury that can only be placated with the sacrifice of a buffalo – one among the dozens of arcane ceremonies that make up Madurai's round of temple rituals.

If you continue straight on from here, cross East Ati Street, and go through the seven-storey **Chitrai gopura**, you enter a passageway leading to the eastern end of the **Pottamarai Kulam** ("Golden Lotus Tank"), where Indra bathed before worshipping the *shivalingam*. From the east side of the tank you can see the glistening gold of the Meenakshi and Sundareshwarar *vimana* towers. Steps lead down to the water from the surrounding colonnades, and in the centre stands a brass lamp column. People bathe here, prior to entering the inner shrines, or just sit, gossip and rest on the steps.

The ceiling paintings in the corridors are modern, but Nayak murals around the tank illustrate scenes from the *Gurur Vilayadal Puranam* which describes Shiva's Madurai miracles. Of the two figures located halfway towards the Meenakshi shrine on the north side, one is the eighth-century king Kulashekhara Pandyan, said to have founded the temple; opposite him is a wealthy merchant patron.

On the west side of the tank is the entrance to the **Meenakshi shrine** (closed to non-Hindus), popularly known as **Amman Koyil**, literally the "mother temple". The immoveable green stone image of the goddess is contained within two further enclosures that form two ambulatories. Facing Meenakshi, just past the first entrance and in front of the sanctum sanctorum, stands Shiva's bull-vehicle, Nandi. At around 9pm, the moveable images of the god and goddess are carried to the **bed chamber**. Here the final puja ceremony of the day, the **lalipuja**, is performed, when for thirty minutes or so the priests sing lullabies (*lali*), before closing the temple for the night.

The corridor outside Meenakshi's shrine is known as the **Kilikkutu Mandapa** ("Parrot Cage Hallway"). Parrots used to be kept just south of the shrine as offerings to Meenakshi, a practice discontinued in the mid-1980s as the birds suffered due to "lack of maintenance". Sundareshwar and Meenakshi are brought every Friday (6–7pm) to the sixteenth-century **Oonjal Mandapa** further along, where they are placed on a swing (*oonjal*) and serenaded by members of a special caste, the Oduvars. The black and gold, almost fairground-like decoration of the *mandapa* dates from 1985.

Across the corridor, the small **Rani Mangammal Mandapa**, next to the tank, has a detailed eighteenth-century ceiling painting of the marriage of Meenakshi and Sundareshwar, surrounded by lions and elephants against a blue background. Sculptures in the hallway portray characters such as the warring monkey kings from the Ramayana, the brothers Sugriva (Sukreeva) and Bali (Vahli), and the indomitable Pandava prince, Bhima, from the *Mahabharata*, who was so strong that he uprooted a tree to use as a club.

Walking back north, past the Meenakshi shrine, through a towered entrance, leads you to the area of the Sundareshwarar shrine. Just inside, is the huge monolithic figure of Ganesh, **Mukkuruni Vinayaka**, believed to have been found during the excavation of the Mariamman Teppakulam tank. Chubby Ganesh is well-known for his love of sweets, and during his annual **Vinayaka Chaturthi festival** (Sept), a special *prasad* (gift offering of food) is concocted from ingredients including 300 kilos of rice, 10 kilos of sugar and 110 coconuts.

Around a corner, a small image of the monkey god **Hanuman**, covered with *ghee* and red powder, stands on a pillar. Devotees take a little with their finger for a *tilak*, to mark the forehead. A figure of Nandi and two gold-plated copper flagstaffs face the entrance to the **Sundareshwar shrine** (closed to non-Hindus). From here, outsiders can just about see the *shivalingam* beyond the blue-and-red neon "Om" sign (in Tamil).

Causing a certain amount of fun, north of the flagstaffs are figures of Shiva and Kali in the throes of a dance competition. A stall nearby sells tiny **butter balls** from a bowl of water, which visitors throw at the god and goddess "to cool them down". If you leave through the gateway here, on the east, you'll find in the northeast corner the fifteenth-century **Ayirakkal Mandapa**, or thousand-pillared hall, now transformed into the temple's **Art Museum** (daily 10am–5.30pm; Rs2, camera Rs5, no videos). In some ways the current function of this gigantic space as a gallery has detracted from its beauty, as the numerous screens and dusty educational displays prevent clear unobstructed view. However, there's a fine, if rather dishevelled, collection of wood, copper, bronze and stone sculpture, and an original nine-metre-high teak temple door. Throughout the hall, large sculptures of strange mythical creatures and cosmic deities rear out at you from the broad stone pillars, some of which startlingly metallic-like musical tones when tapped.

For more on the temples of Tamil Nadu, see p.1138.

Vandiyur Mariamman Teppakulam tank and the floating festival

At one time, the huge **Vandiyur Mariamman Teppakulam** tank in the southeast of town (bus #4 or #4A; 15min) was full with a constant supply of water, flowing via underground channels from the Vaigai. Nowadays, thanks to a number of accidents, it is only filled during the spectacular Teppam **floating festival** (Jan/Feb), when pilgrims take boats out to the goddess shrine in the centre. Before their marriage ceremony, Shiva and Meenakshi are brought in procession to the tank, where they are floated on a raft decorated with lights, which devotees pull by ropes three times, encircling the shrine. The boat trip is believed to be the overture to a seduction that reaches its passionate conclusion later that night in the temple. This traditionally makes the Teppam the most auspicious time of year to get married.

During the rest of the year the tank and the central shrine remain empty. Accessible by steps, the tank is most often used as an impromptu cricket green, and the shade of the nearby trees makes a popular gathering place. Tradition states that the huge image of Ganesh, Mukkuruni Vinayaka, in the Meenakshi Temple, was uncovered here when the area was originally excavated to provide bricks for the Thirumalai Nayak Palace.

Thirumalai Nayak Palace

Roughly a quarter survives of the seventeenth-century **Thirumalai Nayak Palace** (daily 9am–1pm & 2–5pm; Rs50 [Rs10]; includes Palace Museum), 1.5km southeast of the Meenakshi Temple. Much of it was dismantled by Thirumalai's grandson, Chockkanatha Nayak, and used for a new palace at Tiruchirapalli; what remains today was renovated in 1858 by the governor of

Shopping and markets in Madurai

Old Madurai is crowded with **textile and tailors' shops**, particularly in West Veli, Avani Moola and Chitrai streets and Town Hall Road. The tailors' shops near the temple, where locally produced textiles are generally good value, and tailors pride themselves on turning out faithful copies of favourite clothes in a matter of hours. Many souvenir shops in the immediate vicinity also offer an incentive by allowing visitors to climb up to their roofs for views over the Meenakshi complex. Swarms of touts operate in this vicinity, and are all out to sting you. Although the rooftop views are worth checking out, **be warned** that leaving these emporiums empty-handed can be difficult, due to the aggressive sales pitch you're likely to encounter. South Avani Moola Street is packed with **jewellery**, particularly gold shops, while at 10 North Avani Moola St, you can plan for the future at the Life & Lucky Number Numerology Centre.

Madurai is also a great place to pick up South Indian **crafts**. Among the best outlets are All India Handicrafts Emporium, 39–41 Town Hall Rd; Co-optex, West Tower Street, and Pandiyan Co-op Supermarket, Palace Road, for handwoven textiles; and Surabhi, West Veli Street, for Keralan handicrafts. For souvenirs such as sandalwood, temple models, carved boxes and oil lamps head for Poompuhar, 12 West Veli St, or Tamilnad Gandhi Smarak Nidhi Khadi Gramodyog Bhavan, West Veli Street, opposite the railway station, which sells crafts, oil lamps, Meenakshi sculptures and *khadi* cloth and shirts.

The old purpose-built, wooden-pillared fruit and vegetable market, between North Chitrai and North Avani Moola streets, provides a slice of Madurai life that can't have changed for centuries. Beyond it, on the first floor of the concrete building at the back, the **flower market** (24hr) is a riot of colour and fragrance; weighing scales spill with tiny white petals and plump pink garlands hang in rows. Varieties such as orange, yellow or white marigolds (*samandi*), pink jasmine (*arelli*), tiny purple spherical *vanameli* and holy *tulsi* plants come from hill areas such as Kodaikanal and Kumili. These are bought in bulk and distributed for use in temples, or to wear in the hair; some are made into elaborate wedding garlands (*kalyanam mala*). The very friendly traders will show you each and every flower, and if you've got a camera will more than likely expect to be recorded for posterity. It's a nice idea to offer to send them a copy of any photograph you take.

Chennai, Lord Napier, and again in 1971 for the Tamil World Conference. The palace originally consisted of two residential sections, plus a theatre, private temple, harem, royal bandstand, armoury and gardens.

The surviving building, the **Swargavilasa** ("Heavenly Pavilion"), is a rectangular courtyard, flanked by 18m-tall colonnades. As well as occasional live performances of music and dance, the Tourism Department arranges a nightly **Sound and Light Show** (in English 6.45–7.30pm; Rs10), which relates the story of the Tamil epic, *Shilipaddikaram*, and the history of the Nayaks. Some find the spectacle edifying, and others soporific – especially when the quality of the tape is poor. In an adjoining hall, the **Palace Museum** (same hours as the palace) includes unlabelled Pandyan, Jain and Buddhist sculpture, terracottas and an eighteenth-century print showing the palace in a dilapidated state.

Tamukkam Palace: the Gandhi and Government museums

Across the Vaigai, 5km northeast of the centre near the Central Telegraph Office (bus #1, #2, #11, #17, or #24; 20min), stands Tamukkam, the seventeenth-century multi-pillared and arched palace of Queen Rani Mangammal. Built to accommodate such regal entertainment as elephant fights, Tamukkam was taken over by the British, used as a courthouse and collector's office, and in 1955 became home to the Gandhi and Government museums. The **Gandhi Memorial Museum** (daily 10am–1pm & 2–5.30pm; free) charts the history of India since the landing of the first Europeans, viewed in terms of the freedom struggle. Generally the perspective is national, but where appropriate, reference is made to the role played by Tamils. Wholeheartedly critical of the British, it states its case clearly and simply, quoting the Englishman, John Sullivan: "We

Moving on from Madurai

By air

Indian Airlines flies daily (1.20pm) to **Mumbai** via **Chennai**; their office, at 7a West Veli St near the post office (t0452/234 1234), is efficient and helpful. Jet Airways at Madurai airport (t0452/269 0771) also have 2 daily flights (9am & 8.55pm) to Chennai. To get to the airport, catch a taxi (around Rs200), or take city bus #10A from Periyar bus stand.

By bus

Since the amalgamation of Madurai's five bus stands into two, **long-distance buses** are a straightforward prospect; if you're still unsure which one you need, ask at the tourist office in the railway station, and ignore the unscrupulous hustlers hanging around the central STC bus stand.

Services from the new **Central Bus Stand** include government buses to Chennai, and TTC or SRTC buses to Bangalore in Karnataka. Northern destinations include Thanjavur, Tiruchirapalli, Kumbakonam, Rameshwaram, Kanniyakumari and Thiruvananthapuram.

From the **Arapalayam stand**, buses depart to Coimbatore, Kodaikanal, Kumily (for Periyar Wildlife Sanctuary) Palakaad and Ernakulam/Kochi via Kottayam. There are no direct services from Madurai to Ooty.

By train

Madurai is on the main broad-gauge line and well connected to most major towns and cities in South India. To make a **reservation**, ask for a form at the enquiry counter, then join the long queues in the forecourt at the station; the best time to have denied to the people of the country all that could raise them in society, all that could elevate them as men; we have insulted their caste; we have abrogated their laws of inheritance; we have seized the possessions of their native princes and confiscated the estates of their nobles; we have unsettled the country by our exactions, and collected the revenue by means of torture." One chilling artefact, kept in a room painted black, is the bloodstained *dhoti* the Mahatma was wearing when he was assassinated. Next door to the museum, the **Gandhi Memorial Museum Library** (daily except Wed 10am–1pm & 2–5.30pm; free) houses a reference collection, open to all, of 15,000 books, periodicals, letters and microfilms of material by and about Gandhi.

It's not really worth paying the high, recently-imposed entrance fee to visit the small **Government Museum** (daily 9am–5pm; Rs100) opposite. Displays include stone and bronze sculptures, musical instruments, paintings (including examples of Tanjore and Kangra styles) and folk art such as painted terracotta animals, festival costumes and hobbyhorses. There's also a collection of shadow puppets, said to have originated in the Thanjavur area and probably exported to Southeast Asia during the Chola period. A small house in which **Gandhi** once lived stands in a garden within the compound.

Eating

As with accommodation, the range of places to eat in Madurai is gratifyingly wide, and standards are generally high whether you're eating at one of the many utilitarian-looking "meals" places around the temple, or in an upscale hotel. When the afternoon heat gets too much, head for one of the **juice bars** dotted around the centre, where you can order freshly squeezed pomegranate, pineapple, carrot or orange juice for around Rs15 per glass. To make the most of Madurai's exotic

book trains is in the evening or early morning. For **timetable** details, ask the Tourism Department Information Centre, to the right of the ticket counters.

It is possible to reach the railhead for Kodaikanal by train, but the journey is much faster by Express bus. For **Thiruvananthapuram**, **Ernakulam** and **Quilon**, head over to **Coimbatore** (see table below), and then catch the super fast Kerala Express #2626 (departs daily at 5.40am). For **Ooty**, catch any train to Coimbatore, where you can spend the night in order to pick the early morning Nilgiri Express (daily; 5.15am) to Mettapalayam, departure point for the Blue Mountain Railway (see p.1202), or connect with it via the overnight express given below. The daily Chennai–Kanniyakumari Express #2633 passes through Madurai at the rather unsociable hour of 01.55am; the #6803/6355 Howrah–Kanyakumari Express departs at the friendlier time of 7.15am (Sat, Tues & Wed).

For more on transport out of Madurai, see "Travel details", pp.1204–1205.

Recommended trains from Madurai

Destination	Name	No.	Departs	Total time
Bangalore	Tuticorin–Mysore Express	#6731	7.40pm	10hr 55min
Chennai	Vaigai Express	#2636	6.45am	7hr 45min
	Pandiyan Express	#2638	8.30pm	9hr
Coimbatore (Ooty)	Madurai–Coimbatore Express	#6716	10.45pm	6hr 15min
Trichy	Vaigai Express	#2636	6.45am	2hr 20min

skyline, though, you'll have to seek out a **rooftop restaurant** – another of the modern city's specialities. Rock-bottom-budget travellers should try the street-side stalls at the bottom of West Perumal Maistry Street, where old ladies dish up filling leaf plates of freshly steamed *iddli* and spicy fish masala for around Rs10 per portion.

Restaurants and bars

Aarathy *Aarathy Hotel*, 9 Perumalkoil, West Mada St. Tasty tiffin (*dosas*, *iddlis* and hot *wada sambar*), served on low tables in a hotel forecourt, where the temple elephant turns up twice daily. For more filling, surprisingly inexpensive and excellent lunchtime thalis, step into their blissfully cool a/c restaurant.

Anna Meenakshi West Perumal Maistry St. An upmarket branch of *New College House's* more traditional canteen, serving top tiffin to a discerning, strictly vegetarian clientele. This one's smaller and brighter, with shiny marble tables and an ornate bell metal lamp in the doorway. Arguably the most hygienic, best-value food in the centre. Delicious coconut or lemon "rice meals" and cheap banana-leaf thalis are served at lunchtime.

Apollo 96 *Supreme Hotel*, 110 West Perumal Maistry St. Boasting 75,000 flashing diodes and a punchy sound system, South India's most hi-tech bar looks like the set from a low-budget 1970s sci-fi movie. Closes at 11pm sharp. It's altogether a surreal experience.

Mahal 21 Town Hall Rd. Nicely decorated street level restaurant serving small but tasty portions of fish and chips, plus tandoori items and South Indian veg snacks.

New College House *New College House* hotel, 2 Town Hall Rd. Huge meals-cum-tiffin hall in this old-style hotel. Lunch-time, when huge piles of pure veg food are served on banana leaves to long rows of locals, is a real deep-south experience; and the coffee's pure Coorg.

Ruby West Perumal Maistry St. Officially licensed as a bar after years of moonlighting, this is a popular meeting place for foreign travellers. Cold beers are served in a leafy courtyard or in more claustrophobic compartments indoors, though the food is best avoided.

Surya *Supreme Hotel*, 110 West Perumal Maistry St. Possibly Madurai's best and breeziest rooftop restaurant, with sweeping views of the city and temple, and an eclectic multi-cuisine menu; the ideal venue for watching the sunset. Open 4pm–midnight.

Rameshwaram

The sacred island of **RAMESHWARAM**, 163km southeast of Madurai and less than 20km from Sri Lanka across the Gulf of Mannar is, along with Madurai, South India's most important pilgrimage site. Hindus tend to be followers of either Vishnu or Shiva, but Rameshwaram brings them together, being where the god Rama, an incarnation of Vishnu, worshipped Shiva in the *Ramayana*. The **Ramalingeshwara Temple** complex, with its magnificent pillared walkways, is the most famous on the island, but there are several other small temples of interest, such as the **Gandhamadana Parvatam**, sheltering Rama's footprints, and the **Nambunayagi Amman Kali Temple**, frequented for its curative properties. **Danushkodi** ("Rama's bow") at the eastern end, is where Rama is said to have bathed. The boulders that pepper the sea between here and Sri Lanka, known as "Adam's Bridge", are the stepping stones used by Hanuman in his search for Rama's wife, Sita, after her abduction by Ravana, the demon king of Lanka. The town also offers uncommercialized **beaches**, though by no means India's most stunning, where foreigners can unwind or even do a spot of snorkelling.

Rameshwaram, whose streets radiate out from the vast block enclosing the Ramalingeshwara, is always crowded with day-trippers and ragged mendicants who camp outside the Ramalingeshwara and the **Ujainimahamariamman**, the small goddess shore temple. An important part of their pilgrimage is to bathe in the main temple's sacred tanks and in the sea; the narrow strip of beach is shared by groups of bathers, relaxing cows and mantra-reciting *swamis* sitting next to sand *lingams*. As well as fishing – prawns and lobsters for packaging and export to Japan – shells are a big source of income in the coastal villages.

Ramalingeshwara Temple

The core of the **Ramalingeshwara** (or Ramanathaswamy) **Temple** was built by the Cholas in the twelfth century to house two much-venerated **shiva-lingams** associated with the *Ramayana*. After rescuing his wife Sita from the clutches of Ravana, Rama was advised to atone for the killing of the demon king – a brahmin – by worshipping Shiva. Rama's monkey lieutenant, Hanuman, was despatched to the Himalayas to fetch a *shivalingam*, but when he failed to return by the appointed day, Sita fashioned a *lingam* from sand (the *Ramanathalingam*) so the ceremony could proceed. Hanuman eventually showed up with his *lingam* and in order to assuage the monkey's guilt Rama decreed that in future, of the two, Hanuman's should be worshipped first. The *lingams* are now housed in the inner section of the Ramalingeshwara, not usually open to non-Hindus. Much of what can be visited dates from the 1600s, when the temple received generous endowments from the Sethupathi rajas of Ramanathapuram.

Ramalingeshwara temple is enclosed by high walls forming a rectangle with huge pyramidal *gopura* entrances on each side. Each gateway leads to a spacious closed ambulatory, flanked to either side by continuous platforms with massive pillars set on their edges. These **corridors** are the most famous attribute of the temple, their extreme length – 205m, with 1212 pillars on the north and south sides – giving a remarkable impression of receding perspective. Delicate scrollwork and brackets of pendant lotuses supported by *yalis*, mythical lion-like beasts, adorn the pillars.

Before entering the inner sections of the temple, pilgrims are expected to bathe at each of the 22 temple **tirthas** (tanks) in the temple – hence the groups of dripping-wet pilgrims, most of them fully clothed, making their way from one tank to the next to be doused in a bucket of water by a temple attendant. Each tank is said to have special benefits: the Rama Vimosana Tirtha provides relief from debt, the Sukreeva Tirtha gives "complete wisdom" and the attainment of *Surya Loka*, the realm of the Sun, and the Draupadi Tirtha ensures long life for women and "the love of their spouses".

Monday is Rama's auspicious day, when the Padilingam puja takes place. **Festivals** of particular importance at the temple include **Mahashivaratri** (ten days during Feb/March), **Brahmotsavam** (ten days during March/April) and **Thirukalyanam** (July/Aug), celebrating the marriage of Shiva to Parvati.

Practicalities

The NH-49, the main road from Madurai, connects Rameshwaram with Mandapam on the mainland via the impressive two-kilometre-long Indira Gandhi Bridge, originally built by the British in 1914 as a railway link, and reopened for road traffic by Rajiv Gandhi in 1988. **Buses** from Madurai (via Ramnad), Trichy, Thanjavur, Kanniyakumari and Chennai pull in at the bus stand, 2km west of the centre. The **railway station**, 1km southwest of the centre, is the end of the line for trains from Chennai, Trichy and Thiruvarur, and boasts decent **retiring rooms**, a veg restaurant and a left-luggage office (5.30am–10pm).

Red-and-white city buses run every ten minutes from the stand to the main temple; otherwise, **local transport** consists of unmetered cycle and auto-rickshaws that gather outside the bus stand. Jeeps are available for rent near the railway station, and bicycles from shops in the four Car streets around the temple. There is still no **ferry service** to and from Sri Lanka, though talk of it being reinstated abounds, perhaps initially from Tuticorin down the coast.

The main TTDC **tourist office** at the bus stand (daily 10am–5.45pm; ⓣ04573/221371) gives out information about guides, accommodation and boat trips. TTDC also have a counter at the railway station (to coincide with arriving trains; ⓣ04573/221373). The best source of local information, however, is friendly official guide R. Kannan (ⓣ04573/221277), who can also be contacted through the *TTDC Hotel Tamil Nadu* and happily gives foreigners advice, even if they do not use his services. The **post office** is on Pamban Road, the road next to the bus stand.

Accommodation

Apart from the TTDC hotels, **accommodation** in Rameshwaram is restricted to basic lodges, mostly in the Car streets around the temple. The temple authorities have a range of rooms for pilgrims; ask at the Devasthanam Office, East Car Street (ⓣ04573/221223). The **railway retiring rooms** consist of six large double and three triple rooms, generally cleaner (and quieter) than town lodges for the same price, plus a dorm (Rs30).

Chola Lodge North Car St ⓣ04573/221307. A basic but adequate pilgrim place in the quietest of the Car streets. Most rooms are non a/c, and some have TV. ❷–❹

Maharaja's 7 Middle St ⓣ04573/221271, ⓔhotelmaharajas21271@sancharnet.in. Located next to the temple's west gate, and offering comfortable, clean rooms with attached bathrooms, some a/c and all with TV. Some rooms have temple views from the balconies. There's no restaurant, but food can be ordered in. ❷–❹

Shriram Hotel Island Star 41a South Car St ⓣ04573/224172, ⓕ239332. Large hotel with pleasantly appointed a/c and non-a/c rooms, most with sea views. Non-a/c rooms are better value. ❷–❻

TTDC Hotel Tamil Nadu Near the beach, 700m northeast of main temple ⓣ04573/221277, ⓦwww.tamilnadutourism.org. The best place in Rameshwaram, in a pleasant location and with a bar and restaurant. Comfortable, sea-facing rooms, some a/c; the best ones are actually the cheaper ones in the new block, with pleasant sitouts. ❷–❺

Eating

Eating in Rameshwaram is more about survival than delighting the taste buds. Most places serve up fairly unexciting "meals" for Rs50–100.

Ashoka Bhavan West Car St. Cheap South Indian vegetarian place, which also serves a variety of regional thalis

Ganesh Mess Middle St. One of the better "meals" joints, serving lunchtime thalis as well as classic South Indian snacks throughout the day

TTDC Hotel Tamil Nadu Near the beach. Gigantic, noisy, high-ceilinged glasshouse near the sea, serving good South Indian snacks and "meals". There is a bar in the main hotel building.

Kanniyakumari

At the southernmost extremity of India, **KANNIYAKUMARI** is almost as compelling for Hindus as Rameshwaram. It's significant not only for its association with a virgin goddess, Kanya Devi, but also as the meeting point of the Bay of Bengal, Indian Ocean and Arabian Sea. Watching the sun rise and set from here is the big attraction, especially on full-moon day in April, when it's possible to see both the setting sun and rising moon on the same horizon. Although Kanniyakumari is in the state of Tamil Nadu, most foreign visitors arrive on day-trips from Thiruvananthapuram, the capital of Kerala, 86km northwest. While the place is of enduring appeal to pilgrims and those who just want to see India's tip, some may find it bereft of atmosphere, its magic obliterated by ugly concrete buildings and hawkers selling shells and trinkets. Kanniyakumari was seriously affected by the tsunami with the loss of around one thousand lives, many of whom were pilgrims doing the high-season video coach tours of Tamil Nadu's sacred places. The seafront and jetty were devastated but the enormous statue on its tiny rocky isle was sufficiently distant from the shore to escape the ferocity of the breaking waves.

The Town

The seashore **Kumari Amman Temple** (daily 4.30–11.30am & 4–8pm) is dedicated to the virgin goddess **Kanya Devi**, who may originally have been the local guardian deity of the shoreline, but was later absorbed into the figure of Devi, or Parvati, consort of Shiva. The image of Kanya Devi inside the temple wears a diamond nose stud of such brilliance that it's said to be visible from the sea. Male visitors must be shirtless and wear a *dhoti* before entering the temple; non-Hindus are not allowed in the inner sanctum. It is especially auspicious for pilgrims to wash at the bathing *ghat* here.

Resembling a prewar British cinema, the **Gandhi Mandapam** (daily 7am–7pm), 300m northwest of the Kumari Amman Temple, was actually conceived as a modern imitation of an Orissan temple. It was designed so that the sun strikes the auspicious spot where the ashes of Mahatma Gandhi were laid, prior to their immersion in the sea, at noon on his birthday, October 2.

Possibly the original sacred focus of Kanniyakumari are two rocks, about 60m apart, half-submerged in the sea 500m off the coast, which came to be known as the Pitru and Matru *tirthas*. In 1892 they attracted the attention of the Hindu reformer Vivekananda (1862–1902), who swam out to the rocks to meditate on the syncretistic teachings of his recently dead guru, Ramakrishna Paramahamsa. Incorporating elements of architecture from around the country, the 1970 **Vivekananda Memorial** (daily except Tues; 7–11am & 2–5pm), reached by the Poompuhar ferry service from the jetty on the east side of town (every 30min; same hours), houses a statue of the saint. The footprints of Kanya Devi can also be seen here, at the spot where she performed her penance. The other rock features an imposing 40m-high statue of the ancient Tamil saint Thiruvalluva.

For more on the life and teachings of Vivekananda, visit the **Wandering Monk Museum (Vivekananda Puram)**, just north of the tourist office on the main road (daily 8am–noon & 4–8pm; Rs2). A sequence of forty-one panels (in English, Tamil and Hindi) provide a meticulously detailed account of the *swami*'s odyssey around the subcontinent at the end of the nineteenth century.

Practicalities

Trains from Thiruvananthapuram, New Delhi, Mumbai and Bangalore stop at the **railway station** in the north of town, 2km from the seafront; as does the weekly #6317/6787 Kanniyakumari–Jammu Tawi Himsagar Express which departs every Friday and offers the opportunity of the longest rail journey in India (73 hours). You can leave **luggage** in the generator room behind the ticket office for Rs10 per item. The new and well-organized Thiruvalluvar **bus stand**, near the lighthouse on the west side of town, is served by regular buses from Thiruvananthapuram, Kovalam, Madurai, Rameshwaram and Chennai. Taxis and auto-rickshaws provide **local transport**.

Accommodation

As Kanniyakumari is a "must-see" for Indian tourists and pilgrims, **hotels** can fill up early and it's worth booking in advance. However, a recent spate of hotel development – many of them identikit mid-range places – has helped to relieve the pressure on space.

Lakshmi Tourist Home East Car St ⓣ04652/246333, ⓕ246627. Smart rooms, some sea-facing, with central a/c. There's an excellent non-veg restaurant. ❸–❹

Maadhini East Car St ⓣ04652/246787, ⓕ246657. Large hotel right on the seafront above the fishing village, with fine sea views, comfortably furnished rooms and one of the best restaurants in town. ❸–❻

Manickam Tourist Home North Car St ⓣ04652/246387. Spacious but simple and clean rooms, some with balconies and sea views, set in a building that faces the sunrise and the Vivekananda rock. Good value. ❸

Samudra Sannathi St ⓣ04652/246162, ⓕ246627. Smart hotel near the temple entrance, with well-furnished deluxe rooms facing the sunrise. Facilities include satellite TV in rooms and a veg restaurant. ❸–❺

TTDC Hotel Tamil Nadu Seafront ⓣ04652/246257, ⓔttdc@md3.vsnl.net.in. Cottages (some are a/c) and clean rooms (a/c on the first floor), most with sea views, as well as cheaper and very basic "mini" doubles at the back, and a dorm (Rs50). Good square meals are served in functional surroundings. ❷–❻

Eating

Aside from the usual "meals" places and hotel dining rooms, there are a few popular veg and non-veg **restaurants** in the centre of town, most attached to one of the hotels.

Archana *Maadhini Hotel*, East Car St. An extensive veg and non-veg multi-cuisine menu served inside a well-ventilated dining hall, or alfresco on a sea-facing terrace (evenings only). They also have the town's widest selection of ice cream.

Saravana North of the Kumari Amman Temple, on the main bazaar. Arguably Kanniyakumari's best "meals" restaurant, serving all the usual snacks, cold drinks, and huge Tamil thalis at lunchtime, to hoards of hungry pilgrims. Their coffee is good, too. There is another branch a little further from the temple.

The Ghats

Sixty or more million years ago, what we know today as peninsular India was a separate land mass drifting northwest across the ocean towards central Asia. Current geological thinking has it that this mass must originally have broken off the African continent along a fault line that is today discernible as a north–south ridge of volcanic mountains, stretching 1400km down the west coast of India, known as the **Western Ghats**. The range rises to a height of around 2500m, making it India's second-highest mountain chain after the Himalayas.

Forming a natural barrier between the Tamil plains and coastal Kerala and Karnataka, the *ghats* (literally "steps") soak up the bulk of the southwest monsoon, which drains east to the Bay of Bengal via the mighty Kaveri and Krishna river systems. The massive amount of rain that falls here between June and October (around 2.5m) allows for an incredible **biodiversity**. Nearly one-third of all of India's flowering plants can be found in the dense evergreen and mixed deciduous forests cloaking the *ghats*, while the woodland undergrowth supports the subcontinent's richest array of wildlife.

It was this abundance of game, and the cooler temperatures of the range's high valleys and grasslands, that first attracted the sun-sick British, who were quick to see the economic potential of the temperate climate, fecund soil and plentiful rainfall. As the forests were felled to make way for tea plantations, and the region's many tribal groups – among them the Todas – were forced deeper into the mountains, permanent **hill stations** were established. Today, as in the days of the Raj, these continue to provide welcome escapes from the fierce summer heat for the middle-class Tamils, and foreign tourists, who can afford the break.

Much the best known of the hill resorts – in fact better known, and more visited, than it deserves – is **Udhagamandalam** (formerly Ootacamund, and usually known just as "**Ooty**"), in the **Nilgiris** (from *nila-giri*, "blue mountains"). The ride up to Ooty, on the **miniature railway** via Coonoor, is fun, and the views breathtaking, but the town centre suffers from heavy traffic pollution and has little to offer. There are some scenic walks out of the town and several viewpoints which, together with boating and horse rides, make up the quintessentially Bollywood-esque activities which attract hordes of Indian tourists. Further south and reached by a scenic switchback road, the other main hill station is **Kodaikanal**. The lovely walks around town provide views and fresh air in abundance, while the bustle of Indian tourists around the lake makes a pleasant change from life in the city.

Accessed via the hill stations, the forest areas lining the state border harbour Tamil Nadu's principal **wildlife sanctuaries**, **Annamalai** and **Mudumalai** which, along with Wayanad in Kerala, and Nagarhole and Bandipur in Karnataka, form the vast **Nilgiri Biosphere Reserve**, the country's most extensive tract of protected forest. The activities of notorious sandalwood smuggler-cum-bandit "**Veerapan**" led to the closure of much of this area to the public, but following his demise in a police ambush in October 2004, some areas may re-open for tourism. However, stakes are high in the sandalwood smuggling business and it remains to be seen whether someone rises from the ranks to resume Veerapan's twenty-year rule of the region. The main route between Mysore and the cities of the Tamil plains wriggles through the Nilgiris and you may well find yourself pausing for a night or two along the way, if only to enjoy the cold air and serene landscape of the tea terraces. Whichever direction you're travelling in, a stopover at the dull textile city of **Coimbatore** is hard to avoid, even if only to change buses.

Kodaikanal

Perched on top of the Palani range, around 120km northwest of Madurai, **KODAIKANAL**, also known as **Kodai**, owes its perennial popularity to its hilltop position which, at an altitude of more than 2000m, affords breathtaking views over the blue-green reaches of the Vaigai plain. Raj-era bungalows and flower-filled gardens add atmosphere, while short walks out of the centre lead to rocky outcrops, waterfalls and dense *shola* forest. With the more northerly wildlife sanctuaries and forest areas of the *ghats* closed to visitors, Kodai's outstandingly scenic hinterland also offers South India's best **trekking** terrain. Even if you're not tempted by the prospect of the open trail and cool air, the jaw-dropping **bus ride** up here from the plains makes the detour into this easternmost spur of the *ghats* an essential one.

Kodaikanal's history, with an absence of wars, battles for leadership and princely dominion, is uneventful, and the only monuments to its past are the neat British bungalows that overlook the lake and Law's Ghat Road on the eastern edge of

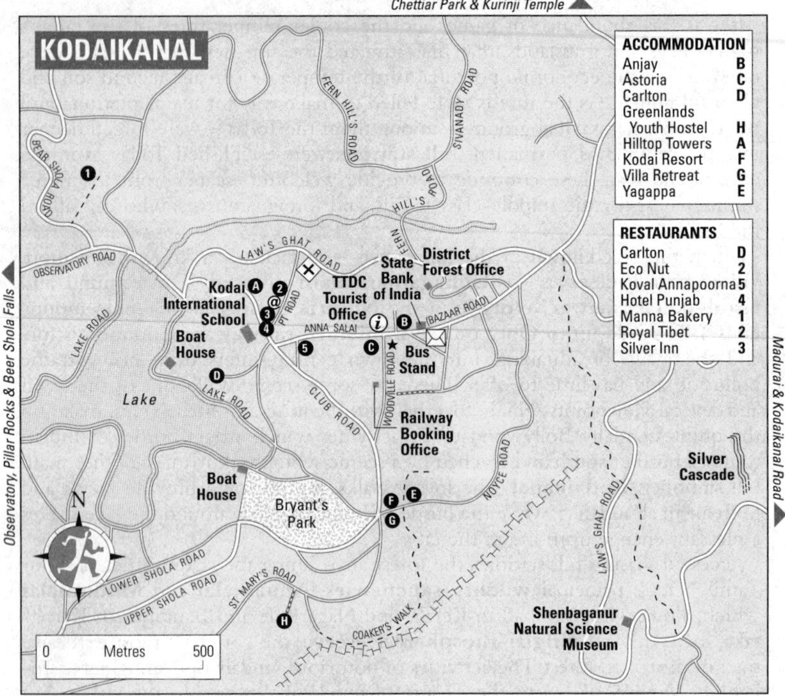

town. The British first moved here in 1845, to be joined later by members of the American Mission who set up schools for European children. One remains as Kodai International School; despite the name, it has an almost exclusively Indian student population. The school lays a strong emphasis on music, particularly guitar playing, and occasionally holds concerts on the green just east of the lake.

After a while in the South Indian plains, a retreat to Kodai's cool heights is more than welcome. However, in the height of summer (June–Aug), when temperatures compete with those in the lowlands, it's not worth the trip – nor is it a good idea to come during the monsoon (Oct–Dec), when the town is shrouded in mists and drenched by heavy downpours. In late February and early March the nights are chilly; the **peak tourist season** therefore, is from April to June, when prices soar.

Arrival, information and orientation

The **buses** from Madurai and Dindigul that climb the spectacular road up the steep hillside to Kodai pull in at the stand in the centre of town. Unless you're coming from as far as Chennai or Tiruchirapalli, the bus is much more convenient than the train: the nearest **railhead**, Kodaikanal Road – also connected to Dindigul (30min) and Madurai (50min) – is three hours away by bus. Note, too, that **the road from Palani** (65km; 3hr 30min by bus) is by far the most spectacular approach, although the least travelled (except during the monsoons when the other is invariably blocked). If you plan to spend a few days in Kodai, it's worth visiting Palani, an atmospheric destination in itself, as a day-trip just to travel this route.

Tickets for onward rail journeys from Kodaikanal Road can be booked at the Southern Railway office, down a lane beside the *Anjay Hotel* (Mon–Sat 8am–noon & 2.30–5pm, Sun 8am–noon). Nearby King Tours and Travels on Woodville Road can reserve trains, buses and planes within South India. The **tourist office** (Mon–Fri 10am–5.45pm; ⓣ04542/241675), on Anna Salai (Bazaar Road), offers little except unclear sketch maps of the area. For **email**, try Alpha Net (daily 9am–9pm; Rs40/hr), next to *Royal Tibet* restaurant, on PT Road.

Taxis line Anna Salai in the centre of town, offering sightseeing at high fixed rates. Most tourists, however, prefer to amble around at their own pace. Kodaikanal is best explored on foot, or by **bicycle**, which you can rent from a stall on Anna Salai for Rs10 per day (those on offer at the lakeside are much more expensive); it may be fun to freewheel downhill, but most journeys will involve a hefty uphill push too. If you need to **change money**, head for the State Bank of India or Canara Bank, both on Anna Salai; there is an SBI ATM near the *Carlton Hotel*.

Accommodation

Kodaikanal's inexpensive **lodges** are grouped at the lower end of Anna Salai. Always ask whether blankets and hot water are provided (this should be free, but you may be charged in budget places). **Mid-range hotels** are usually good value, especially if you get a room with a view, but they hike their prices drastically during high season (April–June). The codes below reflect rates outside of April–June.

Anjay Anna Salai ⓣ04542/241089. Simple budget lodge slap in the centre. Rooms are smarter than you'd expect from the outside (all have balconies, and the deluxe ones have views), but those at the front suffer some traffic noise. If they're full, check out the equally good-value *Jaya* behind. ❷–❸

Astoria Anna Salai ⓣ04542/240524, ⓔastoria1@eth.net. Well-kept hotel opposite the bus stand, with homely rooms and a good, mid-priced restaurant. Hardly any views, but comfortable enough. ❸–❹

Carlton Off Lake Rd ⓣ04542/240056, ⓔcarlton@krahejahospitality.com. The most luxurious hotel in Kodaikanal, this is a spacious, tastefully renovated and well-maintained colonial house overlooking the lake, with a bar and comfortable lounge. Cottages within the grounds are available (from $187) as well as rooms (from $100); rates include meals. ❾

Greenlands Youth Hostel Off St Mary's Rd ⓣ04542/241099, ⓔgreenlandsyh@rediffmail.com. Attractive old stone house offering unrivalled views and sunsets from its deep verandas. The rooms are basic with wooden beds, open fireplaces (wood Rs50) and attached bathrooms, and there's a dorm (Rs80). Book ahead. ❸–❹

Hilltop Towers Club Rd ⓣ04542/240413, ⓔhttowers@sancharnet.in. Very near the lake and school, with modern, comfortable rooms featuring arched doors. There's also a cosy and romantic honeymoon suite with a round bed. Three restaurants and good service. ❹–❺

Kodai Resort Hotel Noyce Rd ⓣ04542/241301, ⓦwww.kodairesorthotel.com. Large complex of fifty incongruous-looking but very pleasant chalets situated at the top of the hill and offering good views of the town. There's a health club and rather dull restaurant on site. ❺–❻

Villa Retreat Coaker's Walk, off Club Rd ⓣ04542/240940, ⓦwww.villaretreat.com. Comfortable old stone house, with more character than most, in lovely gardens that afford superb views. Though a touch overpriced, all rooms have great views and attached hot-water bathrooms. Wood and electric heaters are available upon request. ❹–❼

Yagappa Noyce Rd ⓣ04542/241235.This small, clean lodge in old buildings ranged around a lawn-cum-courtyard is the best budget deal in town, good views and a tiny whitewashed restaurant and a great little bar. ❷–❸

The Town

Kodai's focal point is its **lake**, sprawling like a giant amoeba over 24 hectares just west of the town centre. This is a popular place for strolls, or bike rides along the five-kilometre path that fringes the water's edge, while pedal- or rowing boats can be rented on the eastern shore (Rs20–100 for 30min, plus Rs20–40 if you require an oarsman). Horse riding is also an option here, but it's rather pricey and tame at Rs80 to be led along the lakeside. Bikes can be hired for around Rs10 per hour. Shops, restaurants and hotels are concentrated in a rather congested area of brick, wood and corrugated iron buildings east of and downhill from the lake. To the south is **Byrant's Park** (dawn–dusk; Rs5; camera Rs25, video camera Rs500), with tiered flowerbeds on a backdrop of pine, eucalyptus, rhododendron and wattle which stretches southwards to Shola Road, less than 1km from the point where the hill drops abruptly to the plains. A path, known as **Coaker's Walk** (Rs2), skirts the hill, winding from the *Villa Retreat* to *Greenland's Youth Hostel* (10min), offering remarkable views that stretch as far as Madurai on a clear day.

One of Kodai's most popular natural attractions is the **Pillar Rocks**, 7km south of town, where a series of granite cliffs rise more than 100m above the hillside. To get there, follow the westbound Observatory Road from the northernmost point of the lake (a steep climb) until you come to a crossroads; the southbound road passes the gentle **Fairy Falls** on the way to Pillar Rocks. Observatory Road continues west from the crossroads to the **Astrophysical Observatory**, perched at Kodai's highest point (2347m). Visitors can't go in, but a small **museum** (daily 10am–noon & 2–5pm; outside peak season Fri only, same hours; free) displays assorted instruments. Some 2km west of the lake **Bear Shola Falls** now sees barely a trickle of water but remains a popular picnic and photo-stop for local tourists.

East of the town centre, about 3km south down Law's Ghat Road (towards the plains), the **Shenbaganur Natural Science Museum** (Mon–Sat 9am–noon & 2–5pm; Rs2.50) has a far from inviting array of stuffed animals. However, the spectacular orchid house contains one of India's best collections, which can be viewed by appointment only. Head 2km further along Law's Ghat Road to reach **Silver Cascade** waterfall, where the overflow from Kodai Lake has created a pleasant pool for bathing.

Chettiar Park, on the very northwest edge of town, around 3km from the lake at the end of a winding uphill road, flourishes with trees and flowers all year round, and every twelve years is flushed with a haze of pale-blue **Kurinji blossoms** (the next flowering will be in 2006). These unusual flowers are associated with the god Murugan, the Tamil form of Karttikeya (Shiva's second son), and god of Kurinji, one of five ancient divisions of the Tamil country. A temple in his honour stands just outside the park.

Eating

If you choose not to eat in any of the **hotel restaurants**, head for the food stalls along **PT Road** just west of the bus stand. Menus include Indian, Chinese, Western and Tibetan dishes, and some cater specifically for vegetarians. Look out, too, for the **bakeries**, with their wonderful, fresh, warm bread and cakes each morning.

Carlton *Carlton Hotel*, off Lake Rd. Splash out on the evening veg and non-veg buffet spread (Rs330) at Kodai's top hotel, and round off with a *chhota* peg of IMFL scotch in the bar.

Eco Nut J's Heritage Complex, PT Rd. One of South India's few bona fide Western-style wholefood shops and a great place to stock up on trekking supplies: muesli, home-made jams, breads, pickles and muffins, high-calorie "nutri-balls" and delicious cheeses from Auroville.

Hotel Punjab PT Rd. Top north Indian cuisine and reasonably priced tandoori specialities; try their great butter chicken and hot naan.

Kovai Annapoorna *Golden Parks Inn*, Anna Salai. Popular restaurant serving a range of South Indian vegetarian meals, good value lunchtime thalis.

Manna Bakery Bear Shola Rd. Fried breakfasts, pizzas and home-baked brown bread and cakes served in an eccentric, self-consciously ecofriendly café-restaurant.

Royal Tibet PT Rd. One of three small Tibetan joints along this road, with dishes ranging from thick home-made bread to particularly tasty *momos* and noodles, as well as some Indian and Chinese options. Friendly service.

Silver Inn PT Rd. Western favourites such as porridge, lasagne, mashed potato and apple crumble are all adequately cooked up at this hole-in-the-wall place.

Coimbatore

Visitors tend only to use the busy industrial city of **COIMBATORE** as a stopover on the way to Ooty, 90km northwest. Once you've climbed up to

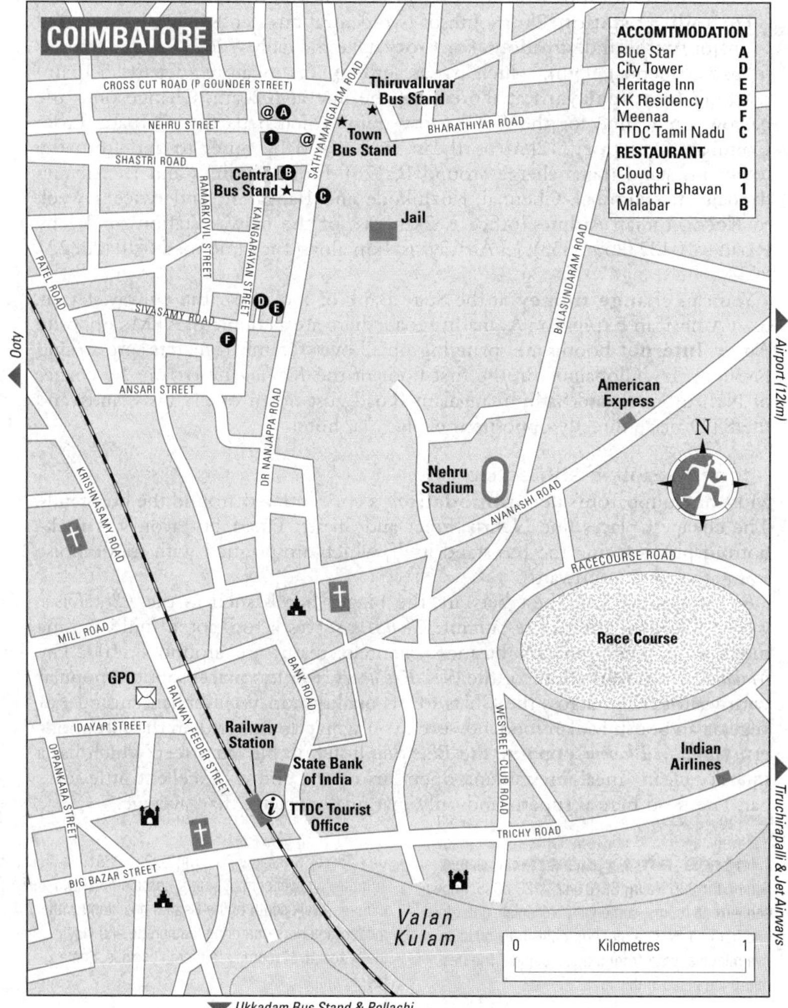

your hotel rooftop to admire the blue, cloud-capped haze of the Nilgiris in the west, there's little to do here other than kill time wandering through the nuts-and-bolts bazaars, lined with lookalike textile showrooms, "General Traders" and shops selling motor parts.

Practicalities

Coimbatore's two main **bus stands**, Central and Thiruvalluvar, are close together towards the north of the city centre; the busy Town bus stand is sandwiched in between. From Central bus stand, on Dr Nanjappa Road, buses leave for Ooty every fifteen minutes. Buses to Bangalore and Mysore from Central can be booked in advance at the **reservation office** (9am–noon & 1–8pm). There are also frequent services to and from Madurai, Chennai and Tiruchirapalli (Trichy). A third bus stand, Ukkadam, in the southwest of the city next to the lake, serves local towns and destinations in northern Kerala.

The **railway station**, 2km south of two central bus stands, is well-connected to major southern destinations. For **Ooty**, take the daily #2671 Nilgiri Express (departs Chennai 9pm), which passes through Coimbatore (departs 5.15am) reaching **Mettupalayam** at the end of the line at 6.20am. Change onto the narrow gauge line for the #662 Ooty train which departs at 7.10am. From Coimbatore **airport**, 12km northeast and served by buses to and from the town bus stand (taxis charge around Rs175), Indian Airlines and Jet Airways fly daily to Mumbai, Chennai, Kozhikode and Bangalore, and twice a week to Kochi. Indian Airlines' office is 2km east of the railway station on Trichy Road (Ⓣ0422/239 9833); Jet Airways is 4km along the same road (Ⓣ0422/221 2034).

You can **change money** at the State Bank of India near the railway station, or at American Express on Avanashi Road; there are a couple of ATM's opposite Amex. **Internet** booths are springing up all over Coimbatore; rates are around Rs30/hr. Try Globalnet, on the first floor of the *Krishna Towers*, on the corner of Nehru Street and Sathyamangalam Road, just north of the bus stands; and the STD place directly opposite the *Blue Star* hotel.

Accommodation and eating

Most of Coimbatore's **accommodation** is concentrated around the bus stands. The cheapest places line Nehru Street and Shastri Road, but avoid the rock-bottom places facing the bus stand itself, which are plagued with traffic noise from around 4am onwards.

As for **eating**, your best bets are the bigger hotels such as the *City Tower*, whose excellent rooftop restaurant, *Cloud 9*, serves a top-notch multi-cuisine menu to a predominantly business clientele; mains are around Rs100. The *Malabar*, on the first floor of the *KK Residency*, is a less pricey option, popular with visitors from across the Ghats for its quality non-veg Keralan cuisine. For vegetarian South Indian food, however, you won't do better than the ultramodern *Gayathri Bhavan*, opposite the *Blue Star* hotel on Nehru Street, which has a squeaky clean "meals" restaurant, open-air terrace, and an excellent little juice bar. The food here is superb, and only marginally pricier than average.

Hotels and guesthouses

Blue Star 369 Nehru St Ⓣ0422/223 0635. Impeccably clean rooms, some with balconies, quiet fans and bathrooms, in a modern multistorey building five minutes' walk from the bus stands. The best mid-price place in this area. ❸–❺

City Tower Sivasamy Rd Ⓣ0422/223 0681, Ⓦhotelcitytower.com. A smart, upscale hotel two minutes' walk south of the Central bus stand with modern interiors (featuring leatherette and vinyl); the "Executive" rooms are more spacious. Some rooms are a/c. ❻–❼

Heritage Inn 38 Sivasamy Rd ⓣ0422/223 1451, ⓔheritageinn@vsnl.com. Coimbatore's top hotel, featuring 63 centrally a/c rooms, a couple of quality restaurants and foreign exchange. Credit cards accepted. 7–8

KK Residency 7 Shastri Rd ⓣ0422/223 2433. Large tower-block hotel around the corner from the main bus stands; very clean rooms and a couple of good restaurants. 3–4

Meenaa 109 Kalingarayar St ⓣ0422/223 5420. Tucked away off the main drag, but handy for the bus stand and a good choice for budget travellers. The rooms are clean, with attached shower-toilets and small balconies. 2–3

TTDC Tamil Nadu Dr Nanjappa Rd ⓣ0422/230 2176. Opposite Central bus stand; convenient, clean, reliable and better than most in the chain, with a/c and non-a/c rooms. It's often fully booked, so phone ahead. 3–5

Coonoor

A scruffy bazaar and tea-planters' town 27km north of Mettupalayam and 19km south of Ooty, **COONOOR** sits at an altitude of 1858m on the southeastern side of the Dodabetta mountains at the head of the Hulikal ravine (and on the Nilgiri Blue Mountain Railway; see p.1202). Thanks to its proximity to its more famous neighbour, Coonoor has avoided Ooty's over-commercialization, and can make a pleasant place for a short stop.

Coonoor loosely divides into two sections, with the bus stand (regular services to Mettupalayam, Coimbatore and elsewhere in the Nilgiris) and railway station (four trains daily to Ooty, and one daily service to Mettupalayam) in **Lower Coonoor**, where there's also a small but atmospheric hill market specializing in leaf tea and fragrant essential oils. In **Upper Coonoor**, there's a fine sprinkling of old Raj-era bungalows along narrow lanes edged with flower-filled hedgerows. At the top lies **Sim's Park**, a fine botanical garden on the slopes of a ravine with hundreds of rose varieties (daily 8am–6.30pm; Rs5).

Around the town, rolling hills and valleys, carpeted with spongy green tea bushes and stands of eucalyptus and silver oak, offer some of the most beautiful scenery in the Nilgiris, immortalized in many a Hindi movie dance sequence. Cinema fans from across the south flock here to visit key locations from their favourite blockbusters, among them **Lamb's Nose** (5km) and **Dolphin's Nose** (9km), former British picnicking spots with paved pathways and dramatic views of the Mettupalayam plains. Buses run out here from Coonoor every two hours. It's a good idea to catch the first one at 7am, which gets you to Dolphin's Nose before the mist starts to build up, and walk the 9km back into town via Lamb's Rock – an enjoyable amble that takes you through tea estates and dense forest.

Visible from miles away as tiny orange or red dots amid the green vegetation, **tea-pickers** work the slopes around Coonoor, carrying wicker baskets of fresh leaves and bamboo rods that they use like rulers to ensure that each plant is evenly plucked. Once the leaves reach the factory, they're processed within a day, producing seven grades of tea. **Orange Pekoe** is the best and most expensive; the seventh lowest grade, a dry dust of stalks and leaf swept up at the end of the process, will be sold on to make instant tea. To visit a tea or coffee plantation, contact UPASI (United Planters' Association of Southern India), "Glenview" House, Coonoor ⓣ0423/223 0270.

Practicalities

When it comes to finding somewhere to **stay** or **eat**, there isn't much choice in Coonoor, and it's not a good idea to leave it too late in the day to be looking for a room. By and large the hotels are dotted around Upper Coonoor, within 3km of the station; you'll need an auto-rickshaw to find most of them. As ever, ignore any rickshaw-wallahs who state that the hotel you want to go to is "full" or "closed". The correct fare from the bus stand to Bedford Circle/*YWCA* is Rs20–25.

If you're staying at the *YWCA*, or one of the upmarket hotels, your best bet is to eat there. In the bazaar, the only commendable **restaurants** are *Hotel Tamizhamgam* (pronounced "Tamirangum"), on Mount Road near the bus stand, which is Coonoor's most popular vegetarian "meals"-cum-tiffin joint. For good-value non-veg north Indian tandoori and Chinese food, try the *Greenland* hotel, further up Mount Road.

The Travancore Bank, on Church Road in Upper Ooty, near Bedford Circle, **changes currency**, but not always travellers' cheques. Otherwise, the nearest place is the State Bank of India in Ooty (see p.1200).

Accommodation

The tariffs included here are for the low season, as high-season prices may increase by anywhere between twenty and a hundred percent, depending on the tourist influx.

La Barrier Inn Coonoor Club Rd ⓣ0423/223 2561. Comfortable mid-range option way up above the bazaar, with great views of surrounding hills (and cricket nets). The rooms are spotless and very large, opening onto flower-filled balconies. ❹

Taj Garden Retreat Hampton Manor ⓣ0423/223 0021, ⓦwww.tajhotels.com. Colonial-era hotel with cottage accommodation, tea-garden lawns and spectacular views, plus a good range of sports and activities including freshwater fishing. Luxurious, but way overpriced. The restaurant serves spectacular lunchtime buffets (around Rs300). Rooms from $120. ❾

Velan (Ritz) Ritz Rd, Bedford ⓣ0423/223 0784, ⓕ223 0606. Luxury hotel in a great location on the outskirts; it's very spacious with carpeted rooms, deep balconies and fine views. Much better value than the *Taj Garden Retreat* but rather lacking in charm. ❻

Vivek Tourist Home Figure of Eight Rd, near Bedford Circle ⓣ0423/223 0658. Managed by a very amiable lady, offering clean rooms (some with tiny balconies overlooking the tea terraces) and a great value dorm (Rs60). Just beware of the "monkey menace". To get there, catch a town bus to Bedford Circle and walk from there. ❷–❸

YWCA Guest House Wyoming, near the hospital ⓣ0423/223 4426. A characterful Victorian-era house on a bluff overlooking town, with a flower garden, tea terraces and fine views from the verandas. There are five double rooms and two singles; superb home-cooked meals are available at very reasonable rates. No alcohol. ❸

Udhagamandalam (Ootacamund)

When John Sullivan, the British *burrasahib* credited with "discovering" **UDHAGAMANDALAM** – still more commonly referred to by a shortened version of its anglicized name, **Ootacamund** – first clambered into this corner of the Nilgiris through the Hulikal ravine in the early nineteenth century, the territory was the traditional homeland of the pastoralist **Toda** hill tribe. Until then, the Todas had lived in almost total isolation from the cities of the surrounding plains and Deccan plateau lands. Sullivan quickly realized the agricultural potential of the area, and acquired tracts of land for Rs1 per acre from the Todas, and set about planting flax, barley and hemp, as well as potatoes, soft fruit and, most significantly of all, **tea**, which all flourished in the mild climate. Within twenty years, the former East India Company clerk had made a fortune. Needless to say, he was soon joined by other fortune-seekers, and a town was built, complete with artificial lake, churches and stone houses that wouldn't have looked out of place in Surrey or the Scottish Highlands. Soon "**Ooty**", as the town was fondly called by the *burra-* and *memsahibs* of the south, was the "Queen of Hill Stations" and had become the most popular hill retreat in peninsular India.

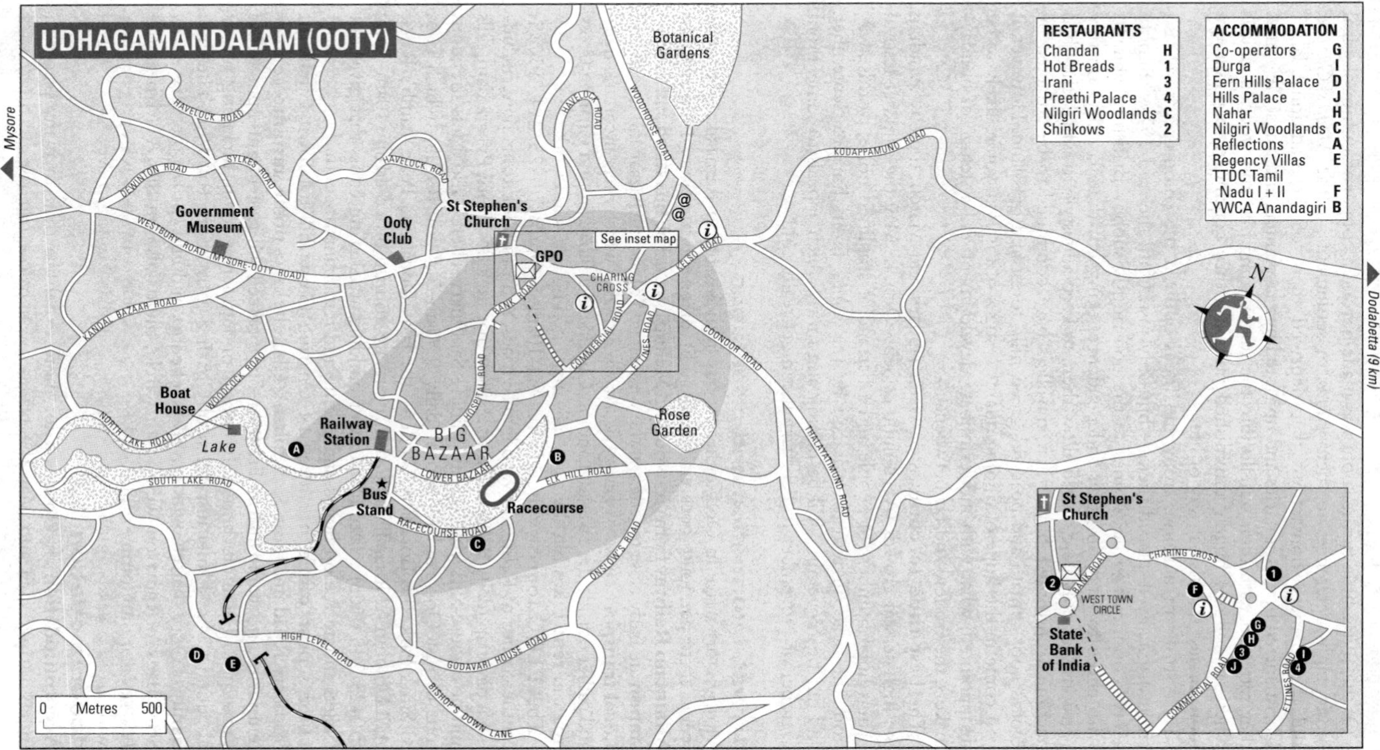
UDHAGAMANDALAM (OOTY)
RESTAURANTS
Chandan H
Hot Breads 1
Irani 3
Preethi Palace 4
Nilgiri Woodlands C
Shinkows 2
ACCOMMODATION
Co-operators G
Durga I
Fern Hills Palace D
Hills Palace J
Nahar H
Nilgiri Woodlands C
Reflections A
Regency Villas E
TTDC Tamil Nadu I + II F
YWCA Anandagiri B
Mysore
Dodabetta (9 km)
Coonoor
Botanical Gardens
Government Museum
Ooty Club
St Stephen's Church
GPO
See inset map
Charing Cross
Boat House
Lake
Railway Station
Big Bazaar
Bus Stand
Racecourse
Rose Garden
Havelock Road
Dewinton Road
Sylkes Road
Westbury Road (Mysore-Ooty Road)
Kandal Bazaar Road
Woodcock Road
North Lake Road
South Lake Road
Hospital Road
Bank Road
Commercial Road
Ettines Road
Kelso Road
Woodhouse Road
Kodappamund Road
Coonoor Road
Thalayatimund Road
Lower Bazaar
Elk Hill Road
Racecourse Road
Onslow's Road
High Level Road
Godavari House Road
Bishop's Down Lane
0 Metres 500
West Town Circle
State Bank of India

Of the Todas, little further note was made beyond a couple of anthropological monographs, references to their *munds*, or settlements, in the *Madras Gazette*, and the financial transactions that deprived them of the traditional lands. Christianized by missionaries and uprooted by tea-planters and forest clearance, they retreated with their buffalo into the surrounding hills and wooded valleys where, in spite of hugely diminished numbers, they continued to preserve a more-or-less traditional way of life.

By a stroke of delicious irony, the Todas outlived the colonists whose cash crops originally displaced them – but only just. Until the mid-1970s "Snooty Ooty" continued to be "home" to the notoriously snobby British inhabitants who chose to "stay on" after Independence, eking out their last days on tiny pensions that only here would allow them to keep a lifestyle to which they had become accustomed. Since then, travellers have continued to be attracted by Ooty's cool climate and peaceful green hills, forest and grassland. However, if you come in the hope of finding quaint vestiges of the Raj, you're likely to be disappointed; what with indiscriminate development and a deluge of holiday-makers, they're few and far between.

The **best time to come** is between January and March, thereby avoiding the high-season crowds (April–June & Sept–Oct). In May, the summer festival brings huge numbers of people and a barrage of amplified noise; worlds away from the peaceful retreat envisaged by the *sahibs*. From June to September, and during November, it'll be raining and misty, which appeals to some. From October or November to February it can get really cold.

Arrival, information and orientation

Most visitors arrive in Ooty either by bus from Mysore in Karnataka (the more scenic, if steeper, route goes via Masinagudi), or on the miniature **Nilgiri Blue Mountain Railway** from Coonoor and Mettupalayam. The **bus stand** and **railway station** are fairly close together, at the western end of the big bazaar and racecourse. **Local transport** consists of auto-rickshaws and taxis, which meet incoming trains and gather outside the bus stand and on Commercial Road around Charing Cross. You can **rent bikes** but the steep hills make cycling very hard work.

The **TTDC tourist office** (Mon–Sat 10am–5.45pm; ⓣ0423/244 3977) is on the corner of Kelso and Woodhouse roads. You can book tours here, including a day-trip (daily 9.30am–7pm; Rs200) that includes Ooty, Pykara dam, falls and boathouse and Mudumalai Wildlife Sanctuary. There's also a less strenuous tour of just Ooty and Coonoor (daily 9.30am–5.30pm; Rs125), which goes to Sim's Park, the Botanical Gardens, the lake, Dodabetta Peak, Lamb's Rock and Dolphin's Nose. There's also a private tourist office (daily 10am–7pm; ⓣ0423/245 0665) in the clocktower building at Charing Cross that gives out leaflets and advice on hotels, sightseeing and restaurants.

Ooty's **post office**, northwest of Charing Cross at West Town Circle, off Spencers Road and near St Stephen's Church, has a **poste restante** counter (enquiries and stamps Mon–Fri 9am–5pm; parcels Mon–Fri 9am–3pm & Sat 9am–2pm). There are numerous **email** outlets across town, including Cyber Link and Cyber Planet just north of Charing Cross (both Rs30/hr). The only **bank** in Ooty that changes travellers' cheques and currency is the very *pukka* State Bank of India on West Town Circle; there's also an SBI ATM near the *Hotel Nahar* on Commercial Road.

Accommodation

Accommodation in Ooty is a lot more expensive than in many places in India; during April and May the prices given below can rise by thirty to a hundred percent. It also gets very crowded, so you may have to hunt around to find what you want. The best by far are the grand old Raj-era places; otherwise, the choice is largely down to average hotels at above-average prices. In **winter** (Nov–Feb), when it can get pretty cold, most hotels provide extra blankets and buckets of hot water on request, but a check whether these services are complementary.

Co-operators Guest House Commercial Rd, Charing Cross ⓣ0423/244 4046. An L-shaped Raj-era building with clean rooms whose yellow-and-turquoise balconies look down to a courtyard; slightly back from the main road so it's relatively quiet. ❷

Durga Ettines Rd ⓣ0423/244 3837, ⓔhotel_durga@thenilgiris.com. The best deal among the many mid-range places around Charing Cross. It's clean, comfortable and central, but the constant noise of buses stopping outside creates a lot of unwelcome noise and dust. ❹–❺.

Fern Hills Palace off High Level Rd ⓣ0423/244 3097, ⓔregency@sancharnet.com. Luxury heritage hotel in what was the maharajah of Mysore's palace; the original exterior remains, but the interior has been tastefully renovated. All rooms are modern and en suite, and feature jacuzzis. $85–250. ❾

Hills Palace Commercial Rd, Charing Cross ⓣ0423/244 6483, ⓔhillspalace@sify.com. Modern place that's just below the main bazaar, but secluded, quiet and spotlessly clean inside. Great value in the low season. ❸

Nahar Commercial Rd, Charing Cross ⓣ0423/244 2173, ⓔnahar@mds.vsnl.net.in. One of Ooty's smartest hotels, offering spacious, well-furnished rooms (the best are in the modern building at the back) and two veg restaurants. A favourite with large Indian family holiday parties, so book ahead. ❻–❾

Nilgiri Woodlands Racecourse Rd, 1km from the bus stand and railway station ⓣ0423/244 2451, ⓔnilgiris_woodlands@yahoo.com. A grand Raj-era building with a wood-panelled lobby, hunting trophies and bare, clean rooms that are particularly good value off season. The little cottages around the garden are worth the extra. Friendly, helpful staff and a good restaurant. ❸–❻

Reflections Guest House North Lake Rd ⓣ0423/244 3834, ⓔreflectionsin@yahoo.co.in. Homely, relaxing guesthouse by the lake, five minutes' walk from the railway station, with rooms opening onto a small terrace. Easily the best budget option in Ooty, but it's small and fills up quickly, so book in advance. ❷–❸

Regency Villas off High Level Rd ⓣ0423/244 3097, ⓔregency@sancharnet.com. The maharaja's former guesthouse, now a rather run-down but atmospheric hotel that's perfect if you're here for faded traces of the Raj. The palatial suites (❻) in the main block are locked in a time warp, with frayed nineteenth-century furniture, original bathtubs, and sepia photos of the Ooty hunt. By contrast, the cottages are cheerless and overpriced although they have generous lawns. Even if you don't stay here, it's worth a nose around and coffee on the lawn. ❻–❼

TTDC Hotel Tamil Nadu, Unit I & II Unit I is in the northwest corner of the complex above Charing Cross, reached by a flight of stairs, and Unit II in the northeast corner ⓣ0423/244 4370, ⓕ244 4369 (same contacts for both). Two identical large, characterless complexes in the centre of town, but with good-value restaurants, a bar and billiards rooms. ❸–❺

YWCA Anandagiri Ettines Rd ⓣ0423/244 2218. Charming 1920s building set in spacious grounds near the racecourse. Seven varieties of rooms and chalets are on offer, all immaculate, with bucket hot water and bathrooms. There's a dining room. and you can while away the evening by the piano or in the cosy "English parlour". Excellent value, and very safe. An inexpensive laundry facility is available. Book ahead. ❷–❺

The Town

Ooty sprawls over a large area of winding roads and steep climbs. The obvious focal point is **Charing Cross**, a busy junction on dusty **Commercial Road**, the main, relatively flat, shopping street that runs south to the big bazaar and municipal vegetable market. Goods on sale range from fat plastic bags of cardamom and Orange Pekoe tea to presentation packs of essential oils (among them natural mosquito repellent citronella). A little way north of Charing Cross, the **Botanical Gardens** (daily 8am–6.30pm; Rs10, camera Rs30, video camera Rs500), laid out in 1847 by gardeners from London's Kew Gardens, consist of twenty hectares of immaculate lawns, lily ponds and

The Nilgiri Blue Mountain Railway

The famous narrow-gauge **Nilgiri Blue Mountain Railway** climbs up from Mettupalayam on the plains, via Hillgrove (17km) and Coonoor (27km) to Udhagamandalam, a journey of 46km passing through sixteen tunnels, eleven stations and nineteen bridges. It's a slow haul of four-and-a-half hours or more – sometimes the train moves little faster than walking pace, and always takes at least twice as long as the bus – but the **views** are absolutely magnificent, especially along the steepest sections in the Hulikal ravine.

The line was built between 1890 and 1908, paid for by the tea-planters and other British inhabitants of the Nilgiris. It differs from India's two comparable narrow-gauge lines, to Darjeeling and Shimla, for its use of the so-called **Swiss rack system**, by means of which the tiny locomotives are able to climb gradients of up to 1 in 12.5. Special bars were set between the track rails to form a ladder, which cogs of teeth, connected to the train's driving wheels, engage like a zip mechanism. Because of this novel design, only the original locomotives can still run the steepest stretches of line, which is why the section between Mettupalayam and Coonoor has remained one of South Asia's last functioning **steam routes**. The chuffing and whistle screeches of the tiny train, echoing across the valleys as it pushes its blue-and-cream carriages up to Coonoor (where a diesel locomotive takes over) rank among the most romantic sounds of South India, conjuring up the determined gentility of the Raj era. Even if you don't count yourself as a train spotter, a boneshaking ride on the Blue Mountain Railway should be a priority while traversing the Nilgiris between southern Karnataka and the Tamil plains.

Timetable details for the line appear in the account of Coimbatore (see p.1196), and in the "Moving on from Ooty" box, opposite.

beds, with more than a thousand varieties of shrubs, flowers and trees. There's a refreshment stand in the park, and shops in the small Tibetan market sell icecreams and snacks.

Northwest of Charing Cross, the small Gothic-style **St Stephen's Church** was one of Ooty's first colonial structures, built in the 1820s on the site of a Toda temple; timber for its bowed teak roof was taken from Tipu Sultan's palace at Srirangapatnam and hauled up here by elephant. The area around the church gives some idea of what the hill station must have looked like in the days of the Raj. To the right is the rambling and rather dilapidated **Spencer's store**, which opened in 1909 and sold everything a British home in the colonies could ever need; it's now a computer college. Nearby, in the same compound as the post office, gowned lawyers buzz around the red-brick **Civil Court**, a quasi-Gothic structure with leaded diamond-shaped windows, corrugated iron roofs and a clock tower capped with a weather vane. Over the next hill (west), the snootiest of Ooty's institutions, the **Club**, dates from 1830. Originally the house of Sir William Rumbold, it became a club in 1843 and expanded thereafter. Its one claim to fame is that the rules for snooker were first set down here (although the members of Jabalpur Club in Madhya Pradesh are supposed to have originated the game in the first place). Entry is strictly restricted to members and their guests or members of affiliated clubs. Further along Mysore Road, the modest **Government Museum** (daily except Fri & second Sat of month 10am–5.30pm; free) houses a few paltry tribal objects, sculptures and crafts.

West of the railway station and racecourse (races mid-April to mid-June), the **lake**, constructed in the early 1800s, is one of Ooty's main tourist attractions, despite being heavily polluted (most of the town's raw sewage gets

Moving on from Ooty

Ooty **railway station** has a reservation counter (daily 8am–12.30pm & 2.30–4pm) and a booking office (daily 6.30am–7pm), where you can buy tickets for the Nilgiri Blue Mountain Railway, as well as onwards services to most other destinations in the south. Of the four trains that run along the narrow-gauge line to Coonoor each day (9.15am, 12.15pm, 3pm and 6pm) only one (the 3pm) continues down to Mettupalayam and the main broad-gauge network. If you're heading to Chennai, take the Mettupalayam service, which links up with the daily #2672 Nilgiri Express (departs 7.45pm; arr Chennai Central 5.15am).

You can also book **buses** in advance at the bus stand, at the reservation offices for both state buses (daily 9am–12.30pm & 1.30–5.30pm) and the local company, Cheran Transport (daily 9am–1pm & 1.30–5.30pm). A combination of stop-start local and express "super-deluxe" state buses serve Bangalore and Mysore (half-hourly buses to both pass through Mudumalai), Kodaikanal, Thanjavur, Thiruvananthapuram and Kanniyakumari, as well as Kotagiri, Coonoor and Coimbatore nearer to hand. **Private buses** to Mysore, Bangalore and Kodaikanal can be booked at hotels, or agents in Charing Cross; even when advertized as "super-deluxe", many turn out to be cramped minibuses.

dumped here – worth bearing in mind if you're tempted to venture out on it). Boating (daily 9am–6pm), which you can arrange at the boathouse on North Lake Road, is very popular among Indian tourists and there is a choice of crafts and different tariffs; rowing and paddle boats cost Rs60–Rs100, and motor boats seating 8–15 Rs200–375. Horse riding (short rides Rs50–75, or Rs100 per hour) can also be arranged from outside the boathouse.

Fern Hills Palace, not far from the southeast end of the lake, and once the summer residence of the maharaja of Mysore, is now operating as a luxury heritage hotel (see p.1201). An ostentatious expression of Ooty's characteristic Swiss-chalet style, it boasts carved wooden bargeboards and ornamental cast-iron balustrades, while interior retains the original antique furniture and massive fireplaces. Even if you don't stay here, you can take tea on the lawn at the adjacent Raj-esque *Regency Villas* (see p.1201).

Eating

Many of the mid-range hotels serve up good South Indian food, but Ooty has yet to offer a gourmet **restaurant**. For an inexpensive *udipi* breakfast, head to one of the restaurants around Charing Cross for *iddli-dosa* and filter coffee.

Chandan *Nahar Hotel*, Commercial Rd, Charing Cross. Inexpensive, carefully prepared north Indian specialities (their *paneer kofta* is particularly good), and a small selection of tandoori vegetarian dishes, served inside a posh restaurant or on a lawnside terrace. They also do a full range of *lassis* and milkshakes.

Hot Breads Charing Cross. French-established franchise selling the usual range of quality pastries, cheesy and plain breads and savouries from a bakery outlet downstairs, as well as pizzas and other tasty snacks in a rather dull first-floor café.

Irani Commercial Rd. A gloomy old-style Persian joint run by Baha'ís. Uncompromisingly non-veg (the menu's heavy on mutton, liver and brains), but an atmospheric coffee stop, and a popular hang-out for both men and women.

Preethi Palace Ettines Rd. Excellent lunchtime thalis (north and South Indian) for Rs25–45, and a delicious range of pure veg food served throughout the day.

Shinkows 42 Commissioners Rd. Good-value, authentic Chinese restaurant serving up good-sized portions on the spicy and pricey side – a main meat course will set you back Rs70–140, and a veg course Rs40–80.

Travel details

Trains

* Trains from Egmore; trains from **Tamabaram; trains from ***Egmore and Tambaram; all others from Central.

Chennai to: Bangalore (7 daily; 4hr 50min–8hr 50min); Bhubaneswar (3–4 daily; 20–23hr); Coimbatore (2 daily; 8hr); Chengalpattu (9 daily***; 1hr); Delhi (2–4 daily; 33hr 30min–41hr); Dindigul (6–7 daily*; 6hr 30min–8hr); Hyderabad (2 daily; 14hr–14hr30min); Kanniyakumari (1–2 daily; 13hr–16hr 55min); Kochi (2–3 daily; 14hr10min–14hr 35min); Kodaikanal Road (3–4 daily*; 8hr–8hr 30min); Kolkata (Calcutta) (2–4 daily; 28hr–31hr 10min); Kumbakonam (2 daily***; 7hr 30min–9hr 15min); Madurai (6–8 daily*; 7hr 50min–10hr 40min); Mumbai (3 daily; 23hr 40min–28hr 45min); Mysore (1–2 daily; 7hr–10hr 55min); Pune (3 daily; 19hr–24hr 15min); Rameshwaram (2 daily**; 17hr 5min–17hr 50min); Salem (10 daily; 4hr 30min–5hr 45min); Thanjavur (1 daily*; 8hr 20min); Thiruvananthapuram (2–3 daily* & Central; 15hr 20min–18hr50min); Tiruchirapalli (9–10 daily*; 5hr 10min–6hr 35min); Tirupati (3 daily; 3hr–3hr 35min); Vijayawada (10–11 daily; 6hr 20min–9hr).

Chidambaram to: Chengalpattu (4 daily; 4hr 45min–6hr); Kumbakonam (1 daily; 2hr 12min); Rameshwaram (2 daily; 11hr 35min–12hr 16min).

Coimbatore to: Bangalore (2–3 daily; 6hr 45min–9hr); Chennai (5–6 daily; 7hr 20min–8hr 55min); Delhi (1–2 daily; 43–47hr 30min); Hyderabad (1 daily; 21hr 15min); Kanniyakumari (2–3 daily; 11hr 55min); Kochi (7–8 daily; 2hr 15min–5hr 30min); Kolkata (Calcutta) (7 weekly; 38hr 45min); Madurai (1–2 daily; 6hr 15min–6hr 35min); Mumbai (2 daily; 31hr 10min–32hr 50min); Mettupalayam, for Ooty (1 daily; 1hr 5min); Salem (10–11 daily; 2hr 35min–3hr 15min); Tiruchirapalli (2 daily; 5hr 15min–5hr 40min); Thiruvananthapuram (4–5 daily; 9hr 30min–10hr 25min).

Kanniyakumari to: Bangalore (1 daily; 19hr 40min); Chennai (2–3 daily; 13hr–15hr 25min); Coimbatore (1 daily; 11hr 15min); Delhi (Wed only; 53hr 10min); Kochi (2 daily; 6hr 15min–6hr 30min); Madurai (1–2 daily; 4hr 25min–5hr 15min); Mumbai (1 daily; 44hr 10min); Tiruchirapalli (1–2 daily; 7hr 10min–8hr 15min); Thiruvananthapuram (2 daily; 1hr 35min–2hr).

Madurai to: Bangalore (1 daily; 11hr 20min); Chengalpattu (6–7 daily; 6hr 45min–8hr 55min); Chennai (7–9 daily; 7hr 45min–10hr 15min); Coimbatore (1–2 daily; 6hr 15min); Kanniyakumari (1–2 daily; 4hr 35min–5hr 50min); Kodaikanal Road (2–4 daily; 33min–43min); Tiruchirapalli (6–8 daily; 2hr 20min–3hr 10min); Tirupati (2 weekly; 11hr 30min).

Tiruchirapalli to: Bangalore (1 daily; 10hr); Chengalpattu (6–7 daily; 4hr–5hr 28min); Chennai (7–9 daily; 5hr 20min–7hr); Coimbatore (2 daily; 4hr 55min–5hr 10min); Kanniyakumari (1–2 daily; 7h r40min–9hr 5min); Kochi (1 daily; 9hr 30min); Kodaikanal Road (2–4 daily; 1hr 50min–2hr 18min); Madurai (7–9 daily; 2hr 35min–3hr 35min); Thanjavur (2 daily; 1hr 10min–1hr 25min).

Buses

Chennai to: Bangalore (every 15–30min; 8–11hr); Chengalpattu (every 5–10min; 1hr 30min–2hr); Chidambaram (22 daily; 5–7hr); Coimbatore (9 daily; 11–13hr); Dindigul (10 daily; 9–10hr); Kanchipuram (every 20min; 1hr 30min–2hr); Kanniyakumari (10 daily; 16–18hr); Kodaikanal (1 daily; 14–15hr); Kumbakonam (33 daily; 7–8hr); Madurai (every 20–30min; 10hr); Mamallapuram (every 20–30min; 2–3hr); Pondicherry (every 20–30min; 4–5hr); Rameshwaram (1 daily; 14hr); Salem (21 daily; 5–7hr); Thanjavur (20 daily; 8hr 30min); Thiruvananthapuram (6 daily; 20hr); Tindivanam (every 30min; 3–4hr); Tiruchirapalli (every 15–30min; 8–9hr); Tirupati (9 daily; 4–5hr); Tiruvannamalai (every 20min; 4–6hr); Udhagamandalam (Ooty) (2 daily; 15hr).

Chidambaram to: Chengalpattu (22 daily; 4hr 30min–5hr); Chennai (22 daily; 5–6hr); Coimbatore (6 daily; 7hr); Kanchipuram (8–10 daily; 7–8hr); Kanniyakumari (3 daily; 10hr); Kumbakonam (every 10min; 2hr 30min); Madurai (10 daily; 8hr); Pondicherry (every 20min; 2hr); Thanjavur (every 20min; 4hr); Tiruchirapalli (every 30min; 5hr); Tiruvannamalai (16 daily; 3hr 30min).

Coimbatore to: Bangalore (10 daily; 8–9hr); Chennai (9 daily; 10–12hr); Kanchipuram (3 daily; 9–10hr); Kanniyakumari (3 daily; 14hr); Kodaikanal (2 daily; 6hr); Madurai (25 daily; 5–6hr); Mysore (3 daily; 6hr); Ooty (every 15mins; 3hr 30min–4hr); Pondicherry (8 daily; 7hr); Rameshwaram (2 daily; 14hr); Salem (every 15mins; 3hr 30min); Thiruvananthapuram (10–15 daily; 12hr); Tiruchirapalli (every 30min; 5hr).

Kanchipuram to: Chennai (every 10min; 1hr 30min–2hr); Coimbatore (3 daily; 9–10hr); Madurai (4 daily; 10–12hr); Pondicherry (15 daily; 7hr); Tiruchirapalli (6 daily; 7–8hr); Tiruvannamalai (15–20 daily; 3–4hr).

Kanniyakumari to: Chennai (10 daily; 16–18hr); Kovalam (10–12 daily; 2hr); Madurai (every

30min; 6hr); Pondicherry (10–12 daily; 12–13hr); Rameshwaram (via Madurai; 4 daily; 10hr); Thiruvananthapuram (20 daily; 2hr 45min–3hr 30min); Tiruchirapalli (every 30min; 10–12hr).
Madurai to: Bangalore (21 daily; 8–9hr); Chengalpattu (every 20–30min; 9hr); Chennai (every 20–30min; 11hr); Chidambaram (5 daily; 7–8hr); Coimbatore (every 30min; 5–6hr); Kanchipuram (4 daily; 10–12hr); Kanniyakumari (every 30min; 6hr); Kochi (8 daily; 10hr); Kodaikanal (10 daily; 4hr); Mysore (5 daily; 10hr); Pondicherry (14 daily; 11–13hr); Rameshwaram (every 30min–1hr; 4hr); Thanjavur (every 30 min; 4–5hr); Thiruvananthapuram (15 daily; 7hr); Tiruchirapalli (every 30min; 4–6hr); Tirupati (4 daily; 15hr).
Pondicherry to: Bangalore (4 daily; 10–12hr); Chennai (every 10–20min; 2hr 30min–3hr); Chidambaram (every 20min; 2hr); Coimbatore (8 daily; 10hr); Kanchipuram (8 daily; 3–4hr); Kanniyakumari (10–15 daily; 12–13hr); Madurai (hourly; 11–13hr); Mamallapuram (every 10–20min; 3hr); Thanjavur (20 daily; 5hr); Tiruchirapalli (every 30min; 5–6hr); Tiruvannamalai (every 20min; 2hr).
Tiruchirapalli to: Chengalpattu (every 20min; 7–8hr); Chennai (hourly; 8–9hr); Coimbatore (every 30min; 5hr); Kanchipuram (2 daily; 7–8hr); Kanniyakumari (15–20 daily; 10–12hr); Kodaikanal (8–10 daily; 5hr); Pondicherry (every 30min; 5–6hr); Madurai (every 30min; 4–6hr); Thanjavur (every 10min; 1hr–1hr 30min); Tiruvannamalai (5 daily; 6hr).

Flights

In the listings below **AI** is Air India, **DA** Deccan Airlines, **IA** Indian Airlines, **JA** Jet Airways and **SA** Sahara Airlines.
Chennai to: Ahmedabad (JA 1 daily; 3hr 25min); Bangalore (DA, IA, JA, SA 11–12 daily; 50min); Bhubaneswar (IA 3 weekly; 2hr 30min); Coimbatore (DA, IA, JA, SA 3–4 daily; 55min–1hr 55min); Delhi (DA, IA, JA, SA 11 daily; 2hr 30min); Hyderabad (DA, IA, JA 7–8 daily; 1hr); Kochi (IA, JA 1–3 daily; 1hr–2hr 15min); Kolkata (Calcutta) (DA, IA, JA, SA 5 daily; 2hr 5min); Kozhikode (IA 8 weekly; 1hr); Madurai (DA, IA, JA 4 daily; 55min–1hr 20min); Mumbai (AI, DA, IA, JA, SA 14–17 daily; 1hr 45min–3hr 40min); Port Blair (IA, JA 2 daily; 2hr); Thiruvananthapuram (IA 1–2 daily; 1hr 10min); Tiruchirapalli (IA 1–2 daily; 50min).
Coimbatore to: Bangalore (DA 2 daily; 40–55min); Chennai (DA, IA, JA, SA 3–4 daily; 1hr 5min–1hr 55min); Delhi (IA, SA 1 daily; 4hr 45min); Kochi (JA 2 weekly; 30 min); Kozhikode (IA daily; 30min); Mumbai (IA, JA, SA 3 daily; 1hr 45min).
Madurai to: Chennai (DA, IA, JA 4 daily; 55min–1hr 20min); Mumbai (IA 1 daily; 3hr 20min).

CHAPTER 21

Highlights

✱ **Varkala** Chill out in a clifftop café, sunbathe on the beach or soak up the atmosphere at the village's temple tank. See p.1224

✱ **The backwaters** Explore the beautiful waterways of this densely populated coastal strip on a traditional *kettu vallam* boat, following the narrow, overgrown canals right into the heart of the villages. See p.1234

✱ **Plantations** Head into the lush hills around Kumily, where the air is heady with the smell of cloves, cardamom and coffee, or Munnar, for tea. See p.1241 & p.1245

✱ **Fort Cochin** This atmospheric peninsula, strung with Chinese fishing nets, draws on Jewish, Portuguese, British and Keralan culture. See p.1247

✱ **Wildlife** Opportunities to view elephants, buffalo, boar and deer in the wildlife sanctuaries of Periyar and Erivakulam – and if you're very lucky, the elusive tiger. See p.1242 & p.1246

✱ **Kathakali performance** An essential part of the Kerala experience, this noisy and colourful ritualized drama is stunning; arrive early to watch the characters come alive as intricate make-up is applied. See p.1258

△ Fishermen hauling nets

Kerala

A sliver of dense greenery sandwiched between the Arabian Sea and the forested Western Ghats, the state of **KERALA** stretches for 550km along India's southwest coast, and is just 120km wide at its broadest point. It's blessed with unique geographical features and the lush tropical landscape, fed by two annual monsoons, together with the beautiful backwaters, intoxicate every newcomer. Equally, Kerala's arcane rituals and spectacular festivals stimulate even the most jaded imagination, continuing centuries of tradition that has never strayed far from the realms of magic.

Travellers weary of India's daunting metropolises will find Kerala's cities smaller and more relaxed. The most popular is undoubtedly the great port of **Kochi** (Cochin), where the state's long history of peaceful foreign contact is evocatively evident in the atmospheric old quarters of Mattancherry and Fort Cochin, hubs of a still-thriving tea and spice trade. In Kerala's far south, the capital, **Thiruvananthapuram** (Trivandrum), is gateway to the nearby palm-fringed beaches of **Kovalam**, and provides visitors with varied opportunities to sample Kerala's rich cultural and artistic life.

One of the nicest aspects of exploring Kerala, though, is the actual travelling – especially by **boat**, in the spellbinding Kuttanad region, around historic **Kollam** (Quilon) and **Alappuzha** (Alleppey). Cruisers and beautiful wooden barges known as *kettu vallam* ("tied boats") ply the **backwaters**, offering tourists a rare glimpse of village life in India's most densely populated state. Furthermore, it's easy to escape the heat of the lowlands by heading for the **hills**, which rise to 2695m. Roads pass through landscapes dotted with churches and temples, tea, coffee, spice and rubber plantations, and natural forests, en route to wildlife reserves such as **Peppara** or **Periyar**, where herds of mud-caked elephants roam freely.

Kerala is short on the historic monuments prevalent elsewhere in India, and the few ancient temples that remain in use are usually closed to non-Hindus (though you can of course take a look at the exteriors and soak up the surrounding atmosphere). Following an unwritten law, few of Kerala's buildings, whether houses or temples, are higher than the surrounding trees, and from high ground in urban areas this often creates the illusion that you're surrounded by forest. Typical features of both domestic and temple architecture include long, sloping tiled and gabled roofs that minimize the excesses of rain and sunshine, and pillared verandas; the definitive example is **Padmanabhapuram Palace**, in neighbouring Tamil Nadu but easily reached from Thiruvananthapuram.

Huge amounts of money are lavished upon many, varied, and often all-night **festivals** usually associated with Kerala's temples. Fireworks rend the air, while processions of gold-bedecked elephants are accompanied by some of the loudest

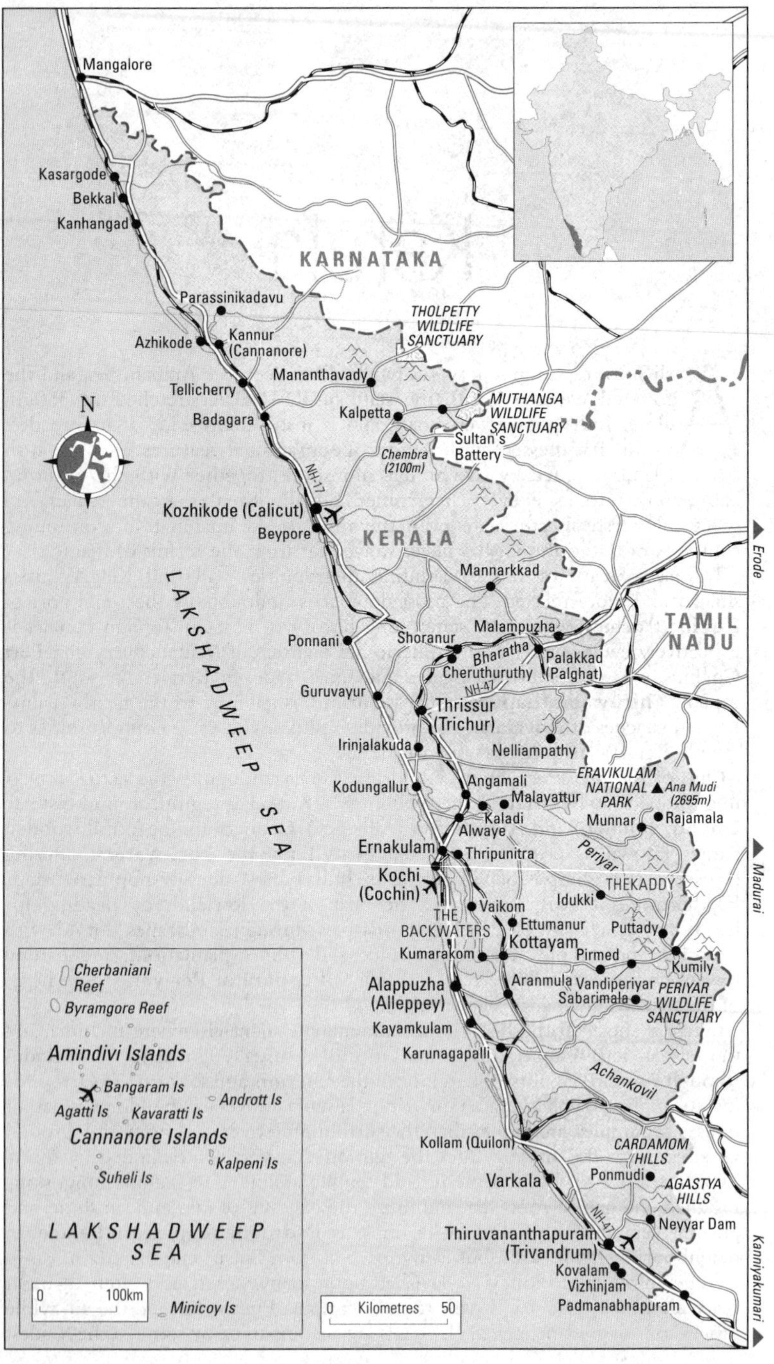

Mangalore
Kasargode
Bekkal
Kanhangad
KARNATAKA
Parassinikadavu
THOLPETTY WILDLIFE SANCTUARY
Azhikode
Kannur (Cannanore)
Mananthavady
Tellicherry
Badagara
Kalpetta
MUTHANGA WILDLIFE SANCTUARY
Sultan's Battery
Chembra (2100m)
N
NH-17
Kozhikode (Calicut)
Beypore
KERALA
Erode
LAKSHADWEEP SEA
Mannarkkad
Malampuzha
TAMIL NADU
Ponnani
Shoranur
Bharatha
Palakkad (Palghat)
Cheruthuruthy
NH-47
Guruvayur
Thrissur (Trichur)
Irinjalakuda
Nelliampathy
ERAVIKULAM NATIONAL PARK
Ana Mudi (2695m)
Kodungallur
Angamali
Malayattur
Munnar
Rajamala
Kaladi
Alwaye
Ernakulam
Thripunitra
Periyar
Madurai
Kochi (Cochin)
THEKADDY
Idukki
Vaikom
THE BACKWATERS
Ettumanur
Puttady
Kottayam
Kumarakom
Pirmed
Kumily
Alappuzha (Alleppey)
Aranmula
Vandiperiyar
Sabarimala
PERIYAR WILDLIFE SANCTUARY
Kayamkulam
Karunagapalli
Achankovil
Cherbaniani Reef
Byramgore Reef
Amindivi Islands
Bangaram Is
Andrott Is
Agatti Is
Kavaratti Is
Cannanore Islands
Kalpeni Is
Suheli Is
LAKSHADWEEP SEA
0 100km
Minicoy Is
Kollam (Quilon)
CARDAMOM HILLS
Ponmudi
Varkala
AGASTYA HILLS
NH-47
Neyyar Dam
Thiruvananthapuram (Trivandrum)
Kanniyakumari
Kovalam
Vizhinjam
Padmanabhapuram
0 Kilometres 50

(and deftest) drum orchestras in the world. The famous **Puram** festival in Thrissur (April/May) is the most astonishing, but smaller events take place throughout the state – often outdoors, with all welcome to attend. **Theatre** and **dance** styles also abound; not only the region's own female classical dance form, **Mohiniattam** ("dance of the enchantress"), but also the martial-art-influenced **Kathakali** dance drama, which has for four centuries brought gods and demons from the *Mahabharata* and *Ramayana* to Keralan villages. Its 2000-year-old predecessor, the Sanskrit drama **Kutiyattam**, is still performed by a handful of artists, while localized rituals known as **Theyyam**, where dancers wearing decorative masks and hats become "possessed" by temple deities, continue to be a potent ingredient of village life in the north. Few visitors witness these extraordinary all-night performances, but between December and March, it is possible to spend weeks hopping between these village festivals in northern Kerala, experiencing a way of life that has altered little in centuries.

Some history

Ancient Kerala is mentioned as the land of the **Cheras** in a third-century BC Ashokan edict, and in several even older Sanskrit texts, including the *Mahabharata*. Pliny and Ptolemy also testify to thriving trade between the ancient port of Muziris (now known as Kodungallur) and the Roman Empire. Little is known about the history of the region's early rulers, whose dominion covered a large area, but whose capital, Vanji, has not so far been identified. At the start of the ninth century, king Kulashekhara Alvar – a poet-saint of the Vaishnavite *bhakti* movement known as the *alvars* – established his own dynasty. His son and successor, Rajashekharavarman, is thought to have been a saint of the parallel Shaivite movement, the *nayannars*. The great Keralan philosopher **Shankaracharya**, whose *advaitya* ("non-dualist") philosophy influenced the whole of Hindu India, lived at this time.

Eventually, the prosperity acquired by the Cheras through trade with China and the Arab world proved too much of an attraction for the neighbouring **Chola** empire, who embarked upon a hundred years of sporadic warfare with the Cheras at the end of the tenth century. Around 1100, the Cheras lost their capital at Mahodayapuram in the north, and shifted south to establish a new capital at Kollam (Quilon).

Direct trade with Europe commenced in 1498 with the arrival in the capital, Calicut, of a small Portuguese fleet under **Vasco da Gama** – the first expedition to reach the coast of India via the Cape of Good Hope and Arabian Sea. After an initial show of cordiality, relations between him and the local ruler, or Zamorin, quickly degenerated, and da Gama's second voyage four years later was characterized by appalling massacres, kidnapping, mutilation and barefaced piracy. Nevertheless, a fortified trading post was soon established at Cochin from which the Portuguese, exploiting old enmities between the region's rulers, were able to dominate trade with the Middle East. This was gradually eroded away over the ensuing century by rival powers France and Holland, and in the early 1600s the East India Company entered the fray. An independent territory was subsequently carved out of the Malabar coast by Tipu Sultan of Mysore, but his defeat in 1792 left the British in control right up until Independence.

Kerala today can claim some of the most startling **radical** credentials in India. In 1957 it was the first state in the world to democratically elect a communist government, and despite having one of the lowest per capita incomes in the country it has the most equitable land distribution, due to uncompromising reforms made during the 1960s and 1970s. In 1996, the Left Democratic Front, led by CPI(M), retook the state from the Congress-led United Democratic

No Smoking

In 2003 Kerala became the first state in India to **ban smoking** from all public places, which includes streets, parks and beaches. Unlike such laws in the West, though, it does not include restaurants or bars, where it remains at the owner's discretion. There's a Rs200 on-the-spot fine for offenders, though the law seems to be more strictly enforced in larger cities than rural areas. Of course, you won't receive a ticket if busted, so it's a handy extra source of baksheesh for the Keralan peelers.

Front, who had been in power for five years, only to lose it again in 2001. Poverty is not absent, but is less acute than in other parts of India. Kerala is justly proud of its reputation for health care and education, with a literacy rate that stands, officially at least, at 100 percent. Industrial development is low, however, as potential investors are reluctant to deal with a politicized workforce. Too many graduates and too little investment has led to a significant proportion of the male workforce heading for the Gulf states, and many Keralan families are benefiting from the substantial earnings that are being sent home. As you explore the state, you'll see massive white mansions on the outskirts of every village – bought by Gulf oil-dollars – but you'll see plenty of hammer and sickle flags too.

Thiruvananthapuram

Kerala's capital, the coastal city of **THIRUVANANTHAPURAM** (still widely and more commonly known as **Trivandrum**), is set on seven low hills, 87km from the southern tip of India. Despite its administrative importance – demonstrated by wide roads, multistorey office blocks and gleaming white colonial buildings – it's a decidedly easy-going city, with a mix of narrow backstreets and traditional red-tiled gabled houses, and acres of palm trees and parks breaking up the bustle of its modern concrete centre.

Although it has few monuments as such, Thiruvananthapuram, as a window on Keralan culture, is an ideal first stop in the state. The oldest most interesting part of town is the **Fort** area in the south, around the **Shri Padmanabhaswamy temple** and **Puttan Malika palace**, while important showcases for painting, crafts and sculpture, the **Shri Chitra Art Gallery** and **Napier Museum**, stand together in a park in the north. In addition, schools specializing in the martial art Kalarippayat and the dance/theatre forms of Kathakali and Kutiyattam offer visitors an insight into the Keralan obsession with physical training and skill.

Most travellers choose to pass straight through Thiruvananthapuram, lured by the promise of Kovalam's palm-fringed beaches (see p.1218). A mere twenty-minute bus ride south, this popular resort is close enough to use as a base to see the city.

Arrival, information and tours

The international **airport** (connected to most major Indian cities, as well as Sri Lanka, the Maldives and the Middle East), with tourist information and foreign exchange facilities, is 6km southwest of town and serviced by an airport bus and bus #14 to and from the City bus stand. Auto-rickshaws will run you into the centre for around Rs50 and there's also a handy prepaid taxi service.

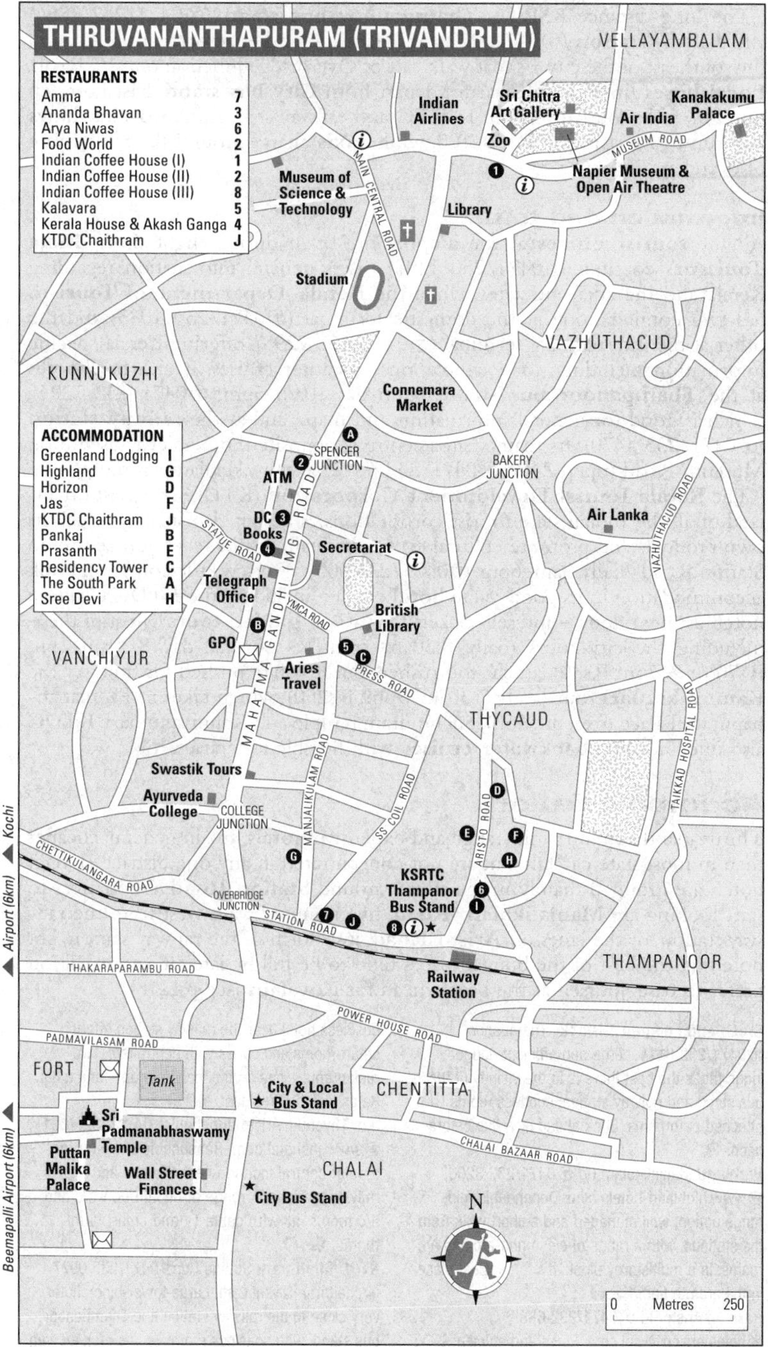

Kollam, Kochi & NH-47
THIRUVANANTHAPURAM (TRIVANDRUM)
RESTAURANTS
Amma 7
Ananda Bhavan 3
Arya Niwas 6
Food World 2
Indian Coffee House (I) 1
Indian Coffee House (II) 2
Indian Coffee House (III) 8
Kalavara 5
Kerala House & Akash Ganga 4
KTDC Chaithram J
ACCOMMODATION
Greenland Lodging I
Highland G
Horizon D
Jas F
KTDC Chaithram J
Pankaj B
Prasanth E
Residency Tower C
The South Park A
Sree Devi H
VELLAYAMBALAM
Indian Airlines
Sri Chitra Art Gallery
Kanakakumu Palace
Air India
Zoo
MUSEUM ROAD
Napier Museum & Open Air Theatre
Museum of Science & Technology
MAIN CENTRAL ROAD
Library
Stadium
VAZHUTHACUD
KUNNUKUZHI
Connemara Market
SPENCER JUNCTION
BAKERY JUNCTION
ATM
VAZHUTHACUD ROAD
Air Lanka
DC Books
STATUE ROAD
Secretariat
MAHATMA GANDHI (MG) ROAD
Telegraph Office
YMCA ROAD
British Library
GPO
VANCHIYUR
Aries Travel
PRESS ROAD
THYCAUD
TAIKKAD HOSPITAL ROAD
MANJALIKULAM ROAD
Swastik Tours
SS COIL ROAD
Ayurveda College
COLLEGE JUNCTION
ARISTO ROAD
Kochi
CHETTIKULANGARA ROAD
KSRTC Thampanoor Bus Stand
Airport (6km)
OVERBRIDGE JUNCTION
STATION ROAD
THAMPANOOR
THAKARAPARAMBU ROAD
Railway Station
POWER HOUSE ROAD
PADMAVILASAM ROAD
FORT
Tank
City & Local Bus Stand
CHENTITTA
Sri Padmanabhaswamy Temple
Beemapalli Airport (6km)
Puttan Malika Palace
CHALAI BAZAAR ROAD
Wall Street Finances
CHALAI
City Bus Stand
N
0 Metres 250
Kovalam & Kanniyakumari

The long-distance KSRTC **Thampanoor bus stand** (☎0471/232 3886) and **railway station** (☎0471/232 1622) face each other across Station Road in the southeast of the city, a short walk east of Overbridge Junction on MG Road. **Local buses** (including Kovalam) depart from **City bus stand**, East Fort, ten minutes' walk south from the KSRTC and railway stations. **Auto-rickshaws** also run to Kovalam for Rs80–100, while **taxis** charge around Rs150. Beware of overcharging scams.

Information and tours

All the **tourist offices** at the **airport** are open during flight times. **India Tourism**'s counter (☎0471/250 1498) offers general information regarding Kerala and the adjacent states, while the **Kerala Department of Tourism** has two counters, one at the domestic terminal (☎0471/250 1085) and the other at the international terminal (☎0471/250 2298), offering Kerala-specific information including, for example, on backwater cruises. It also has booths at the **Thampanoor bus stand** (Mon–Sat 10am–5pm; ☎0471/232 7224), which is good for general information and maps, and at the **railway station** (☎0471/233 4470). Its main visitor centre is opposite the Napier Museum on Museum Road (open 24hr; ☎0471/232 6812, Ⓦwww.keralatourism.org)

The **Kerala Tourist Development Corporation** (KTDC), the best organized of all the Indian state tourist corporations, is designed primarily to sell its own products and promote cultural events. Its main visitor reception centre on Station Road, (daily 8am–6pm; ☎0471/233 0031, Ⓦwww.ktdc.com), can book accommodation in its good-value **hotel** chain – including the *KTDC Chaitram* hotel just next door – and sells tickets for various **guided tours**. Most of these, including the city tours (daily 8.30am–7pm, Rs130; half-day 8.30am–1pm Rs70 or 2–7pm Rs80), are far too rushed, but if you're pushed for time try the **Kanniyakumari** tour (daily 7.30am–9pm; Rs250), which takes in Padmanabhapuram Palace (except Mon), Suchindram temple and Kanniyakumari. KTDC also offers its own **backwater cruises** with flexible itineraries.

Accommodation

Thiruvananthapuram's mid-range and expensive **hotels** are, in general, cheaper than in most state capitals, but are not concentrated in any one district. Budget hotels are grouped mainly in the streets around **Station Road**. Good areas to start looking are **Manjalikulam Road**, five minutes' walk west from the railway station, or the lanes off **Aristo Road**, just north of the railway station, but note that the best of the budget places tend to be full by late afternoon. If you prefer to base yourself at the beach, head for **Kovalam** (see p.1218).

Greenland Lodging Aristo Rd, Thampanoor ☎0471/232 8114. Large and efficient budget lodge that's the best there is in the vicinity of the bus stand and railway station; spotless rooms with attached bathrooms. Book ahead or arrive before noon. ❷

Highland Manjalikulam Rd ☎0471/233 3200, Ⓦwww.highland-hotels.com. Dependable mid-range option, well managed and a short walk from the stations, with a range of clean non-a/c and a/c rooms. In a multistorey block, it's the easiest place in the area to find. ❸–❻

Horizon Aristo Rd ☎0471/232 6888, Ⓔhotelhorizon@vsnl.com. Plush and efficient business hotel near the railway station offering smart rooms and suites with central a/c. Two restaurants – one on the leafy rooftop – and a bar. Rates include breakfast. ❼–❾

Jas Thycaud, Aristo Junction ☎0471/232 4881, Ⓦwww.jashotel.com. Reasonable two-star in a quiet central location near the bus and railway stations. A range of decent non-a/c and a/c rooms, all with cable TV and smart bathrooms. ❺–❽

KTDC Chaithram Station Rd ☎0471/233 0977, Ⓔchaithram@vsnl.com. Large tower-block hotel very close to the railway station and Thampanoor bus stand, with spacious rooms (some a/c), a/c veg restaurant, bank, travel agent, car rental, beauty parlour, cybercafé, bookshop and bar. ❹–❻

Pankaj MG Rd, opposite Secretariat ⓣ0471/246 4645, ⓦwww.hotelpankaj.com. Stylish and well-maintained three-star hotel. Some rooms have beautiful views over the trees, as does the good Keralan restaurant. Tariff includes buffet breakfast. ❼–❾

Prasanth Aristo Rd ⓣ0471/232 7180. One of a crop of rock-bottom and very basic family-run guesthouses near the station. The non-a/c rooms have attached bathrooms and are ranged around a courtyard. The *Sajin* and *Salrah* next door, are similar. ❷

Residency Tower Press Rd ⓣ0471/233 1661, ⓦresidencytower.com. A centrally located, upper-range business hotel with reasonable a/c rooms, rooftop restaurant and cocktail bar. ❽–❾

The South Park MG Rd ⓣ0471/233 3333, ⓦwww.thesouthpark.com. Comfortable, business-oriented Welcomgroup four-star with central a/c in the rooms, efficient travel agency, multi-cuisine restaurant and 24hr coffee shop. Popular with tour groups and flight crews so book in advance. ❽–❾

Sree Devi off Aristo Rd ⓣ0471/233 7195. Small budget hotel within easy reach of the railway station, offering very basic but clean en-suite rooms. ❶

The City

Thiruvananthapuram's centre can be explored easily on foot, though you might be glad of a rickshaw ride (around Rs20) back from the museums and parks, close to the top end of MG Road. The historical and spiritual heart of town is in the **Fort area**, at the southern end of **MG Road**, which encloses the Shri Padmanabhaswamy Vishnu temple. Following MG Road north leads you through the main shopping district, which is busy all day, and especially choked when one of the frequent, but generally orderly, political demonstrations converges on the grand colonial **Secretariat** building halfway along. Just north of the Station Road junction, an assortment of **craft shops** sell sandalwood, brass and Keralan bell-metal oil lamps (see p.1268), while the Gandhian **Khadi Gramodyog**, near Overbridge Junction, stocks hand-loom cloth (dig around for the best stuff), plus radios and cassette machines manufactured by the Women's Federation. **Natesan's Antique Arts**, further up, is part of a chain that specializes in paintings and temple woodcarvings. Prices are high, but they usually have some beautiful pieces, among them superb reproductions of Thanjavur paintings and traditional inlaid chests for Kathakali costumes.

Fort area

A solid but unremarkable fort gateway leads from near the Kovalam bus stand at East Fort to the **Shri Padmanabhaswamy temple**, which is still controlled by the Travancore royal family. Unusually for Kerala, it's built in the Dravidian style of Tamil Nadu, with a tall *gopura* gateway, but it's surrounded by high fortress-like walls, and is closed to non-Hindus. Most of Padmanabhaswamy's buildings date from the eighteenth century, added by Raja Marthanda Varma to a much older shrine. The area in front of the temple, where devotees bathe in a huge tank, is lined with stalls selling religious souvenirs and flower offerings. As you approach the main entrance, the red-brick CVN Kalari Sangam, a **Kalarippayat martial arts** gymnasium, is on the left. From 6.30am to 8am (Mon–Sat) you can watch the students practising Kalarippayat fighting exercises. Foreigners may join courses in the gym, arranged through the head teacher, although prior experience of martial arts and/or dance is a prerequisite; three-month courses are also available, but the fee of Rs500 does not cover accommodation. You can also come here for a traditional **Ayurvedic massage**, and to consult the gym's expert Ayurvedic doctors (Mon–Sat 10am–1pm & 5–7.30pm, Sun 10am–1pm).

Behind the temple on West Fort, set back from the road across open ground, the Margi school of **Kathakali** dance drama and **Kutiyattam** theatre is housed in Fort High School. With prior notice you can watch classes; this is the place to ask about authentic Kathakali performances.

Puttan Malika Palace

The **Puttan Malika Palace** (Tues–Sun 8.30am–12.30pm & 3–5.30pm; Rs20, Rs15 for cameras), immediately southeast of the temple, became the seat of the Travancore rajas after they left Padmanabhapuram at the end of the nineteenth century. Although much of the palace remains off limits, you can wander around some of the most impressive wings, which have been converted into a **museum**. Cool chambers, lined with delicately carved wooden screens and highly polished plaster floors, house a crop of dusty Travancore heirlooms, including a solid crystal throne given by the Dutch and some fine murals. The real highlight, however, is the typically understated, elegant Keralan architecture. Beneath sloping red-tiled roofs, hundreds of wooden pillars carved into the forms of rampant horses prop up the eaves, with airy verandas projecting onto the surrounding lawns.

Festivals of Thiruvananthapuram

The annual **Nishangandi Dance and Music festival** (Feb 22–27) is held at Kanakakannu Palace, just to the east of the public gardens, originally built as a cultural venue for the maharajas of Thiruvananthapuram. A large amphitheatre in the formal gardens is a pleasant place to take in an evening of classical dances and music by Indian artists. Ask at a KTDC office for details.

The **Arattu** festival, centred around the Shri Padmanabhaswamy temple, takes place biannually, in Meenam (March/April) and Thulam (Oct/Nov). Each time, ten days of festivities inside the temple (open to Hindus only) culminate in a procession through the streets of the city, taking the deity, Padmanabhaswamy, to the sea for ritual immersion. Five caparisoned elephants, armed guards, a *nagaswaram* (double-reed wind instrument) and *tavil* drum group are led by the maharaja of Travancore, in his symbolic role as *kshatriya*, the servant of the god. Instead of the richly apparelled figure that might be anticipated, the maharaja wears a simple white *dhoti*, with his chest bare save for the sacred thread. Rather than riding, he walks the whole way, bearing a sword. To the accompaniment of a 21-gun salute and music, the procession sets off from the east gate of the temple at around 5pm, moving at a brisk pace to reach Shankhumukham Beach at sunset, about an hour later. The route is lined with devotees, many of whom honour both the god and the maharaja. After the seashore ceremonies, the cavalcade returns to the temple at about 9pm, to be greeted by another gun salute. An extremely loud firework display rounds off the day.

For ten days in March, Muslims celebrate **Chandanakudam Maholsavam** at the Beemapalli mosque, 5km southwest of the city on the coastal road towards the airport. The Hindu-influenced festival commemorates the anniversary of the death of Beema Beevi, a woman revered for her piety, and features processions of *panchavadyam* drum-and-horn orchestras and caparisoned elephants, as well as firework displays.

The great festival of **Onam** (late Aug or Sept) takes place throughout the state over ten days during the coolest time of year, when Keralans remember the reign of King Mahabali, a legendary figure who, it is believed, achieved an ideal balance of harmony, wealth and justice during his tenure. Unfortunately, the gods became upset and envious at Mahabali's success and so Vishnu came to pack him off to another world. However, once a year the king was allowed to return to his people for ten days, and Onam is a joyful celebration of the royal visit. Families display their wealth, feasts and boat races are held and, in Thiruvananthapuram, there's a week-long cultural festival of dance and music culminating in a colourful street carnival (ask at a KTDC office for details).

The royal family have always been keen patrons of the arts, and the tradition is maintained with an open-air **Carnatic music festival**, held in the grounds during the festival of Navaratri (Oct/Nov). Performers sit on the palace's raised porch, flanked by the main facade, with the spectators seated on the lawn. For details, ask at the KTDC tourist office.

The Napier Museum and Shri Chitra Art Gallery

A minute's walk east from the north end of MG Road, opposite the KTDC Visitors' Centre, brings you to Thiruvananthapuram's **Public Gardens**. As well as serving as a welcome refuge from the noise of the city – its lawns usually filled with courting couples, students and picnicking families – the park holds an eminently missable zoo and the city's best museums. The extraordinary **Napier Museum** of arts and crafts (Tues–Sun 10am–5pm; Rs6) stands two minutes' walk east of the far northern end of MG Road. Designed at the end of the nineteenth century by architect Robert Fellowes Chisolm (1840–1915), it was an early experiment in what became known as the "Indo-Saracenic" style, with gabled roofs, garishly patterned brickwork, and, above the main entrance, a series of Islamic arches. The spectacular interior is dimly lit through stained-glass windows, and the wooden ceiling features loud turquoise, pink, red and yellow stripes which blend Keralan elements with colonial architecture. Highlights of the museum collection include fifteenth-century Keralan woodcarvings, gold necklaces and belts, minutely detailed ivory work, a carved temple chariot (*rath*), wooden models of Guruvayur temple and an oval temple theatre (*kuttambalam*), plus twelfth-century Chola and fourteenth-century Vijayanagar bronzes.

The attractive **Shri Chitra Art Gallery** (Tues–Sun 10am–5pm; Rs5) opposite, with its curved veranda and tiled roof, houses some splendid paintings from the Rajput, Moghul and Tanjore schools, as well as China, Tibet and Japan. The work by Raja Ravi Varma (1848–1906), who is widely credited with having introduced oil painting to India, have been criticized for their sentimentality and Western influence, but his treatment of Hindu mythological themes is both dramatic and beautiful. Also on display are the paintings of the Russian artist-philosopher and mystic, Nicholas Roerich, who arrived in India at the turn of the twentieth century. His spiritually oriented, strongly coloured Himalayan landscapes reflect his love of the region. Roerich lived out his latter years in Nagar (in the Kulu valley), where he died in 1947.

Nair Kalari Gymnasium

On the eastern side of town, visitors can watch classes (by arrangement) at the P.S. Balachandran Nair Kalari **martial arts gymnasium**, Kalariyil, TC 15/854, Cotton Hill, Vazhuthakad (daily 6–8am & 6–7.30pm). Built of stone in 1992 along traditional lines, the *kalari* fighting pit is overlooked from a height of 4m by a viewing gallery. Students (some as young as eight) train in unarmed combat and in the use of weapons. Traditionally, the art of battle with long razorblade-like *urumi* is only taught to the teacher's successor. The school arranges short courses in Kalarippayat, and can also provide guides for forest trekking.

Eating

Thiruvananthapuram offers menus for all tastes and budgets, although smart **restaurants** specializing in Keralan cuisine are thin on the ground. The *South Park* hotel's restaurant occasionally has live Carnatic music. For full-flavoured Keralan meals or cheap *dosa*-type snacks, eat with the locals in the numerous small *udipi* cafés dotted around town.

Moving on from Thiruvananthapuram

Thiruvananthapuram is the main transport hub for traffic along the coast and cross-country. Towns within a couple of hours of the capital – such as Varkala and Kollam – are most quickly and conveniently reached by **bus**. For longer hauls, though, you're better off travelling by **train** as buses tend to hurtle along the coastal highway at terrifying speeds; they're also more crowded. JAICO produces an excellent monthly guide with timetables and comprehensive travel details for Kerala and beyond; it's available from bookshops, Thampanoor bus stand and the railway station for Rs10. For an overview of travel services to and from Thiruvananthapuram, see "Travel details", pp.1275–1276.

By air

From Thiruvananthapuram's **airport**, there are Jet Airways, Indian Airlines and Air India flights to **Bangalore**, **Chennai**, **Delhi**, **Mumbai and Trichy**. Indian Airlines and Air Maldives also fly daily to **Malé** in the **Maldives**, with additional services on Fridays and Sundays. Sri Lankan Airlines operates one or two flights daily to **Colombo** in Sri Lanka.

By bus

From the KSRTC **Thampanoor bus stand** (☎0471/232 3886), frequent services run north through Kerala to Kollam, Allappuzha to Ernakulam/Kochi. Two buses a day go up to Thekkady for the Periyar Wildlife Reserve and there are six buses daily to Kanniyakumari. Most state buses heading eastwards or southwards are operated by the Tamil Nadu State Road Transport Corporation (TNSRTC; ☎0471/232 7756) and include ten daily buses to Chennai via Madurai. **Tickets** for all the services listed above may be booked in advance at the reservations hatch on the main bus stand concourse; note that TNSRTC has its own counter. Numerous private bus companies also run inter-state services and many of the agents are on Aristo Road near the *Greenland Hotel*.

By train

Kerala's capital is well connected **by train** with other towns and cities in the country, although getting seats at short notice on long-haul journeys can be a problem.

Amma Station Rd. Blissful a/c and conveniently near the stations, offering the usual South Indian snacks and no less than seven different types of *uttappam* (rice pancake).
Anand Bhavan MG Rd. Cheap, simple restaurant offering fresh regional veg meals.
Arya Niwas *Arya Niwas* hotel, Aristo Junction, Thampanoor. Excellent Indian vegetarian food served in a spotless dining room on the hotel's ground floor. Hugely popular with locals and justifiably so. Expect to pay Rs30–70.
Food World Anna's Arcade, Spencer Junction, MG Rd. Bakery-cum-supermarket offering tasty savoury and sweet pastries and cakes. No seating.
Indian Coffee House (I) LMS Junction. Opposite the entrance to the Public Gardens, this is a clean and busy place to down a refreshing cold coffee after visiting the museums; excellent omelettes, South Indian snacks and low-cost meals available all day.
Indian Coffee House (II) Spencer Junction, MG Rd. Small, colonial-style building, set back from the road dishing up the usual ICH fare.
Indian Coffee House (III) Station Rd. Next to the bus station and unbeatable for breakfast or a quick snack. Turbaned waiters serve *dosas*, *wadas*, omelettes and hot drinks in a bizarre spiral building. Obligatory cultural and gastronomic pit-stop and very cheap too.
Kalavara Press Rd. Situated on the same stretch as several bookshops, *Kalavara* is an upstairs restaurant which features a mixed menu and local cuisine, including pork and beef dishes. Count on around Rs60 for a main dish.
Kerala House & Akash Ganga Statue Rd. Good-value Keralan cuisine in the basement *Kerala House*, and more upmarket local

Reservations should be made as far in advance as possible from the efficient computerized booking office at the station (Mon–Sat 8am–2pm & 2.15–8pm, Sun 8am–2pm). Sleepers are sold throughout Kerala on a first-come, first-served basis, not on local stations' quotas.

The following trains are recommended as the **fastest** and/or **most convenient** from Thiruvananthapuram.

Recommended trains from Thiruvananthapuram

Destination	Name	Number	Frequency	Departs	Total time
Bangalore	Kanniyakumari–Bangalore Express	#6525	daily	12.55pm	18hr
Chennai	Triv'–Chennai Mail*	#2624	daily	2.30pm	16hr 30min
Delhi	Rajdhani Express**	#2431	Tues & Thurs	7.15pm	42hr 35min
	Kerala Express	#2625	daily	11.30am	52hr 30min
Ernakulam (Kochi)	Kerala Express	#2625	daily	11.30am	4hr
Kanniyakumari	Kanniyakumari Exp	#1081	daily	9.55am	2hr
Kollam	Kerala Express	#2625	daily	11.30am	1hr 5min
Kozhikode	Triv'–Kannur Exp	#6347	nightly	8.45pm	10hr 30min
Madgaon (Goa)	Netravati Express	#6346	daily	10am	20hr 20min
Mangalore	Parasuram Exp***	#6349	daily	6.10am	15hr
	Malabar Express***	#6329	daily	6.20pm	15hr 30min
Mumbai	Netravati Express***	#6346	daily	10.am	30hr 55min

* via Kollam, Kottayam, Ernakulam and Palakkad
** a/c only
*** via Kollam, Ernakulam, Thrissur, Kozhikode, Kannur, Kasargode

dishes and good views at *Akash Ganga* on the rooftop.

KTDC Chaithram Station Rd. Two moderately priced restaurants, one pure veg and the other Mughlai-style. The former, a tastefully decorated air-cooled place, is the better of the two, offering good-value Keralan specialities and a standard range of rice-based North Indian dishes.

Listings

Airlines Indian Airlines: Air Centre, Mascot Junction ☎0471/231 6870; airport ☎0471/250 1542. Jet Airways, Akshaya Towers, 1st Floor, Sasthamangalam Junction ☎0471/272 1018; airport ☎0471/250 0710. Air India: Museum Rd, Vellayambalam Circle ☎0471/231 0310; airport ☎0471/250 1426. Air Maldives, Spencer Rd ☎0471/24 6341. Gulf Air (for regular flights to various Gulf states), Vellayambalam ☎0471/232 8003. British Airways, Vellayambalam ☎0471/232 6604. KLM/Northwest, Spencer Junction ☎0471/246 3531. Sri Lankan Airlines, Spencer Building, Palayam, MG Rd ☎0471/247 1815.

Ayurvedic health centres Contact the Ayurvedic Medical College Hospital, MG Rd ☎0471/246 0823. For Kayachikistsa or traditional Ayurvedic massage and foot therapy, contact Agastheswara, Ayurvedic Health Centre, Jiji Nivas, Killi, Kattakkada ☎0471/229 1270.

Banks and exchange The State Bank of India, near the Secretariat on MG Rd, changes travellers' cheques and currency. The State Bank of Travancore (Mon–Fri 10am–2pm, Sat 10am–12noon), at

Statue Junction and the domestic airport terminal accepts traveller's cheques, currency, Visa and Mastercard. Thomas Cook has a counter at the airport and an office at Tourindia, MG Rd. There's a Central Reserve Bank branch and Andhra Bank ATM at the *KTDC Chaitram* hotel and an IDBI Bank ATM near the Secretariat on MG Rd.

Bookstores Continental Books on MG Rd stocks a good choice of titles in English, mostly relating to India and with a fair selection of fiction. Also worth a browse are DC Books on Statue Rd, on the first floor of a building above Statue Junction, and Higginbothams and Paico Books, also on MG Rd.

Car rental Nataraj Travels, Thampanoor ☎0471/232 3034; Swastik Travels, MG Rd ☎0471/233 1770; Travel India, opposite the Secretariat, MG Rd ☎0471/247 8208.

Dance and drama For Kathakali and Kutiyattam check with the Margi School (see p.1213), or the tourist office on Station Rd (see p.1212), which can also supply info on the Nishagandi Festival at the open-air Nishagandhi Auditorium in the first week of April.

Hospitals General Hospital, near Holy Angels Convent, Vanchiyur ☎0471/244 3870; Ramakrishna Mission Hospital, Sastamangalam ☎0471/232 2123.

Internet access Of the many outlets, the most efficient is *KTDC Chaithram* hotel on Station Rd (Rs30/hr). Alternatively, try Megabyte on MG Rd or Tandem Communications at Statue Junction.

Pharmacies Central Medical Stores, amongst others, at Statue Junction, MG Rd.

Post office The GPO, with poste restante (daily 8am–6pm), is on MG Rd, south of the Secretariat.

Travel agents Airtravel Enterprises (good for air tickets), New Corporation Building, MG Rd, Palayam ☎0471/232 3900; Aries Travels (specialists for tours to the Maldives), Ayswarya Building, Press Rd ☎0471/233 0964; Tourindia (pioneering cruise and tour operators), MG Rd ☎0471/233 0437.

Yoga The Sivananda Yoga Ashram at 37/1929 Airport Rd, Palkulangara, West Fort (☎0471/245 0942) holds daily classes at various levels, which you can arrange on spec. Better still, head for Neyyar Dam (see box on p.1224), 28km east of town, where the world-famous Dhanwanthari ashram offers excellent two-week introductory courses amid idyllic mountain surroundings.

Around Thiruvananthapuram

Although the **Keralan coast** is lined with sandy beaches, rocky promontories and coconut palms for virtually its entire 550-kilometre length, **Kovalam** is one of the only places where swimming in the sea is not considered eccentric by locals, and which offers accommodation to suit all budgets. Another easy excursion from Thiruvananthapuram is its predecessor as capital of Travancore, **Padmanabhapuram**, site of a magnificent palace.

Kovalam and around

The coastal village of **KOVALAM** may lie just 14km south of Thiruvananthapuram but, as Kerala's most developed **beach resort**, it's a world away from the rest of the state. Although hippy travellers started holing up here three decades ago, it was only in the early 1990s, with the arrival of Kerala's first charter tourists, did the boom really kick off; since then the place has changed almost beyond recognition. Prices have rocketed, construction continues apace, and in high season the beach gets packed with package tourists.

Arrival, information and getting around

Buses, marked in English, from platform #9 (the furthest south) at Thiruvananthapuram's East Fort bus stand (every 10–15min; 20min) loop through Kovalam, and stop at the gates to the *Kovalam Beach Resort* complex, on the promontory between Hawah and Kovalam beaches. If you're not intending to stay here or on Samudra Beach get off the bus just past *Hotel Blue Sea* where the road forks – the left road leads down to Hawah Beach. It's also possible to take an **auto-rickshaw** or **taxi** all the way from Thiruvananthapuram;

auto-rickshaws cost between Rs80 and Rs100 but will try to get away with a lot more, while taxis charge around Rs150. There are a lot of commission-seeking touts working in Kovalam, so if you've already got a hotel in mind, give them a wide berth – walking round the back paths is a good ploy.

The friendly **tourist facilitation centre** (daily 10am–5pm, closed Sun in low season; ⓣ0471/248 0085), just inside the *Kovalam Beach Resort* gates, has plenty of leaflets to give out and up-to-date advice about cultural events. They

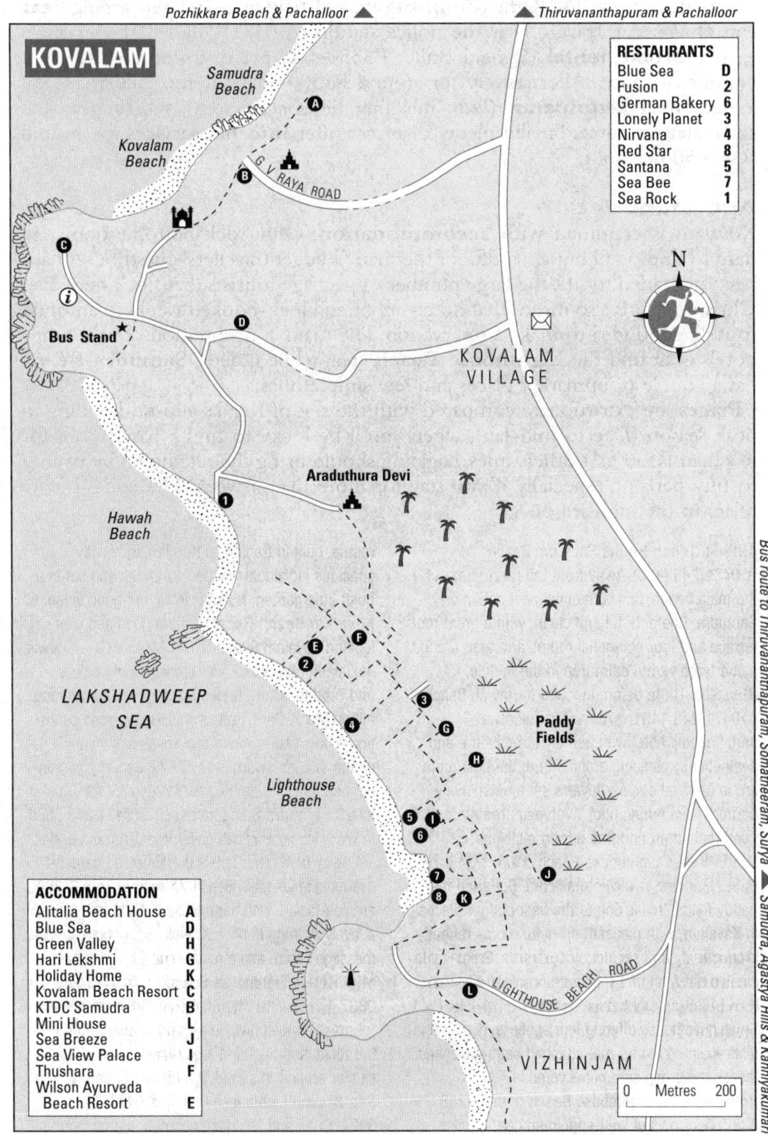

also run a small **reading room** next door (same hours) that holds British and American newspapers and novels.

There are plenty of places to **change money** in Kovalam, but private exchange rates can vary so it's best to check beforehand. The Central Bank of India is at the *Kovalam Beach Resort* and the Andhra Bank at KTDC *Samudra*. Reliable private operators include Pheroze Framroze Foreign Exchange (daily 9.30am-7pm) near the bus stand, and *Wilson's* hotel (see opposite).

Western Travels (daily 8am–8pm; ⓣ0471/248 1334) near the bus terminus is a reliable agent for flight confirmations and ticketing, and can arrange **car rental**. Voyager Travels, near the police station (ⓣ0471/248 1993) specializes in **motorbike rental** (Enfield Bullet Rs350–500 per day, scooter Rs250) at competitive rates. Alternatively, for around Rs300 you can also take a ride on a traditional **kettumaran** (*kettu* meaning tied, *maran* logs), which gave the catamaran its name. Finally, plenty of places offer **Internet** services for around Rs40–50 per hour.

Accommodation

Kovalam is crammed with **accommodation**. Only rock-bottom rooms are hard to find, as all but a handful of the many budget travellers' guesthouses have been upgraded to suit the large number of package tourists that flock here over Christmas. This also means that hotels are often block-booked weeks in advance, so it's a good idea to make a reservation. The main concentration of mid-range hotels is around the **Lighthouse Beach** area, while quieter **Samudra Beach** has a couple of upmarket places and few simple ones.

Prices are extortionate compared with the rest of Kerala, almost doubling in peak season (Dec to mid-Jan), when you'll be lucky to find a basic room for less than Rs300. At other times, haggling should bring the rate down by twenty to fifty percent, especially if you stay for more than a week. The codes below relate to the high season.

Alitalia Beach House Samudra Beach ⓣ0471/248 0042. Away from the razzmatazz of the main beach, this is the cheapest option on Samudra. Characterful and clean, with a great roof terrace and four octagonal rooms arranged around a courtyard with a palm tree in the middle. ❺

Blue Sea 100m before junction to Hawah Beach ⓣ0471/248 1401, ⓦwww.hotelbluesea.net. Friendly hotel with homely atmosphere and aesthetically pleasing architecture: the best rooms are in unusual circular towers set amidst lovely gardens. Swimming pool, Ayurvedic treatments, good restaurant and free airport pick-ups. ❸–❽

Green Valley Lighthouse Beach ⓣ0471/248 0636, ⓔindira_ravi@hotmail.com. Set amid the paddy fields, this is one of the best budget places in Kovalam, with pleasant en-suite rooms ranged around leafy and secluded courtyards. Great-value singles but a bit of a mosquito problem. ❹

Hari Lekshmi Lighthouse Beach ⓣ0471/248 1341. Small guesthouse offering four spotless, good-value white-painted rooms with attached bathrooms, and there's a relaxing communal veranda. ❸

Holiday Home Lighthouse Beach ⓣ0471/248 6382. Two rows of well-appointed cottage-like rooms, built in traditional Keralan style with spacious individual wooden verandas and set in a quiet little garden. No sea views, but good value. ❸

Kovalam Beach Resort On the headland overlooking Kovalam Beach ⓣ0471/248 0101, ⓦwww.kovalamhotel.com. Four complexes of chalets and "cottages" in Charles Correa's award-winning hilltop block. Bars, restaurants, pools, yoga centre and tennis courts make this Kovalam's swankiest option, but it's swarming with VIP security personnel and tour groups. Rooms $125–175. ❾

KTDC Samudra Samudra Beach ⓣ0471/248 0089, ⓦwww.ktdc.com. Posh government-run three-star, set away from other hotels in manicured gardens overlooking Kovalam Beach. All rooms (from Rs3000) are sea-facing, with hammocks outside, and there's a lovely swimming pool, as well as a good Ayurvedic massage centre and a restaurant. ❾

Mini House Lighthouse Beach Rd ⓣ0471/248 0867, ⓔnaswara@hotmail.com. Six large non-a/c rooms with balconies, in a great location right over the rocks and breaking sea. Nicest place of the cluster around this road, if a bit overpriced. ❺–❻

Sea Breeze Lighthouse Beach ⓣ0471/248 0024. Quiet and secluded (located in a coconut grove) with large and sunny communal balconies overlooking a tropical garden. Most of the clean and simple rooms are non a/c with attached bathrooms; a/c costs considerably more. ❶–❺

Sea View Palace Lighthouse Beach ☎0471/248 1599, ✉hotelseaviewpalace@hotmail.com. Set back from the beach but with unobstructed sea views. Eighteen identical rooms with tasteful wooden furniture and common balconies set on three floors. ❺

Thushara Behind Lighthouse Beach ☎0471/248 1694, 🌐www.hotelthushara.net. Small, smart mid-range hotel where the rooms have private balconies, but no views. There's a pool, and rates include Continental breakfast. ❻–❼

Wilson Ayurveda Beach Resort Lighthouse Beach ☎0471/248 0051. Popular place, worth the extra rupees for its spacious en-suite rooms (some a/c), balconies (some with swinging chairs), garden and friendly staff. Ayurvedic treatment available. ❸–❻

The beaches

Kovalam consists of four, fairly small, stretches of sand; the southernmost, known for obvious reasons as **Lighthouse Beach**, is where most visitors spend their time. It takes about ten minutes to walk from end to end, either along the sand or on the concrete pathway (patrolled by lots of touts) which fronts a long strip of resorts, guesthouses and restaurants. On the promontory at the southern end of the beach, the red-and-white **lighthouse** is the area's most prominent landmark, but is closed to the public.

On the other side of a small rocky headland, **Hawah Beach** functions as a base for local fishermen, who hand-haul their massive nets through the shallows each morning, singing and chanting as they work – the *Sea Rock* terrace (see p.1222) is the best vantage point to watch them in action. North of the headland which holds the *Kovalam Beach Resort*, and in full view of its distinctive sloping terraces, is **Kovalam Beach**. It's also used by local fishermen and is the preferred domain of domestic tourists. The next beach north, **Samudra**, is very small, especially at high tide, with a glut of new package-tour resorts surrounding the tiny temple.

Eating, drinking and nightlife

Lighthouse Beach is lined with identikit cafés and restaurants specializing in **seafood**: you pick from the fresh fish (such as blue marlin, sea salmon, barracuda and delicious seerfish), lobster, tiger prawns, crab and mussels on display, which are then weighed, grilled over a charcoal fire or cooked in a tandoor (traditional clay oven), and served with rice, salad or chips. Meals are **pricey** by Indian standards – typically around Rs150 per head for fish, and double that for lobster or prawns – and service is often painfully slow, but the food is generally very good and the ambience of the beachfront terraces convivial. Beer, spirits and local *feni* are served, albeit very discreetly due to tight liquor restrictions, to a background of reggae or Pink Floyd. For **breakfast** you can chose from any number of typical budget-traveller cafés with the usual brown-bread, fruit-salad menus, or search out a traditional breakfast of *iddli* and *sambar* at one of the cheap cafés along the main road and near the bus stand.

Warning: swimming safety

Due to unpredictable rip currents and a strong undertow, especially during the monsoons, **swimming** from Kovalam's beaches is not always safe. The introduction of blue-shirted lifeguards has reduced the annual death toll, but at least a couple of tourists still drown here each year, and many more get into difficulties. Follow the warnings of the safety flags at all times and keep a close eye on children. There's a first-aid post midway along Lighthouse Beach.

Nightlife in Kovalam is pretty laid-back, and revolves around the beach, where Westerners chill when the restaurants close. Several restaurants now run **movie nights**, screening pirate copies of just-released hits. The *Kingfisher*, at the northern end of Lighthouse Beach, occasionally hosts classical Indian music, as does the *Blue Sea* hotel. The *Hotel Neptune*, behind the mid-point of the beach, has regular **Kathakali** performances (Mon, Wed & Sat; make-up 5pm; dance 6.45pm).

During your stay in Kovalam you may be offered *charas*, but bear in mind cannabis is illegal in Kerala, as everywhere else in India, and that the local police occasionally conduct raids.

Blue Sea 100m before junction to Hawah Beach. Well worth the 5-min walk up the hill to sample excellent garlic prawns or tandoori chicken and to enjoy the Escher-esque architecture.

Fusion Lighthouse Beach. Currently the funkiest place in Kovalam, with three menus (Eastern, Western, and fusion), a fine selection of drinks, the best music on the beach and a toilet that has to be seen to be believed.

German Bakery Lighthouse Beach. Rooftop terrace serving tasty Western food, lots of tempting cakes (try the waffles with chocolate sauce) and fruit lassis. Breakfasts include a "full English" and "French" (croissants with espresso and a cigarette).

Lonely Planet Lighthouse Beach. Congenial, generally inexpensive, veg restaurant tucked away in the paddy fields and overlooking a pond (bring mozzie repellent in the evening). Wide selection of Indian food, including breakfast *iddli*. Thursday evenings see a cultural show with all-you-can-eat buffet (7–9pm; Rs150).

Nirvana Lighthouse Beach. Relaxed seafront restaurant with a wide variety of fish, as well as other Indian, Chinese and Continental dishes.

Red Star Lighthouse Beach. Small shack near the lighthouse that's popular with budget travellers. Inexpensive breakfasts, South Indian snacks, lassis and Keralan meals including fiery fish curries.

Santana Lighthouse Beach. One of the best seafood joints with a great barbecue, tandoori fish and chicken, and better music than most.

Sea Bee Lighthouse Beach. Nice ambience and some of the best Indian fusion music as a background to the tasty curries and seafood on offer. Strong beer usually available too.

Sea Rock Hawah Beach. Superb seafront location, best enjoyed in the morning when the local fishermen are gathered on the sand.

Pozhikkara Beach and Pachalloor village

If you're in need of a break from the rampant commercialism of Kovalam, there are nearby alternatives. Heading north along Samudra beach for around 4km, you'll pass through a string of fishing hamlets before eventually arriving at a point where the sea merges with the backwaters to form a salt-water lagoon. Although only thirty minutes' walk from the *Kovalam Beach Resort*, the sliver of white sand, known as **Pozhikkara Beach**, is a world away from the headlong holiday culture of Kovalam. Here, the sands are used primarily for landing fish and fixing nets, while the thick palm canopy shelters a mixed community of Hindu fishermen and Christian coir makers.

The tranquil village of **PACHALLOOR**, behind the lagoon, is a good alternative base to Thiruvananthapuram or Kovalam. There are two guesthouses here, including the idyllic *Lagoona Davina* (Ⓣ0471/238 0049, Ⓦwww.lagoonadavina.com; ❾), whose twenty individually decorated en-suite rooms ($77–137) are all close to the water. The **food** served in the restaurant – a fusion of authentic Keralan village dishes and European *nouvelle cuisine* – is exceptional, and they organize **backwater trips** (Rs350 per head for 2hr). Book in advance and you'll be met at the airport; otherwise jump in a cab or auto-rickshaw.

Vizhinjam

A tightly packed cluster of thatched fishers huts overlooked by a modern pink mosque, **VIZHINJAM** (pronounced "Virinyam"), on the opposite (south) side of the headland from Lighthouse Beach, was once the capital of the Ay kings, the earliest dynasty in south Kerala. A number of simple small shrines survive from those times, and can be made the focus of a pleasant afternoon's stroll through the coconut groves, but brace yourself for the sharp contrast between hedonistic tourist resort and simple fishing village.

On the far side of the fishing bay in the village centre, 50m down a road opposite the police station, a small unfinished eighth-century rock shrine features a carved figure of Shiva with a weapon. The **Tali Shiva** temple nearby, reached by a narrow path from behind the government primary school, may mark the original centre of Vizhinjam. The simple shrine is accompanied by a group of *naga* snake statues, a reminder of Kerala's continuing cult of snake worship that survives from pre-brahminical times.

Toward the sea, ten minutes' walk from the village's main road along Hidyatnagara Road, the grove known as **Kovil Kadu** ("temple forest") holds a square Shiva shrine and a rectangular one dedicated to the goddess **Bhagavati**. Thought to date from the ninth century, these are probably the earliest structural temples in Kerala, although the Bhagavati shrine has been renovated.

Padmanabhapuram

Although now officially in Tamil Nadu, **PADMANABHAPURAM**, 63km southeast of Thiruvananthapuram, was the capital of Travancore between 1550 and 1750, and maintains its historic links with Kerala, from where it is still administered. For anyone with even a minor interest in Keralan architecture, the small **Padmanabhapuram Palace** (Tues–Sun 9am–4.30pm; Rs50 [Rs20], cameras Rs20), whose design represents the high watermark of regional building, is an irresistible attraction. However, **avoid weekends**, when the complex gets overrun with bus parties.

Above the palace's entrance hall is the **mantrasala** (council chamber) whose highly polished black floor is made from an age-old concoction of burnt coconut, sticky sugar-cane extract, egg whites, lime and sand. The oldest part of the complex is the **Ekandamandapam** – "the lonely place" – which was built in 1550 and used for rituals for the goddess Durga that featured elaborate *kalam ezhuttu* floor paintings.

The Pandya-style stone-columned **dance hall** stands directly in front of a shrine to the goddess of learning, Saraswati. The women of the royal household had to watch performances through screens on the side, and the staff through holes in the wall from the gallery above. Typical of old country houses, steep wooden ladder-like steps, ending in trapdoors, connect the floors. Belgian mirrors and Tanjore miniatures of Krishna adorn the chamber forming part of the **women's quarters**, where a swing hangs on plaited iron ropes. A four-poster bed, made from sixteen kinds of medicinal wood, dominates the **raja's bedroom**. Its elaborate carvings depict a mass of vegetation, human figures, birds and as the central motif, the snake symbol of medicine, associated with the Greek physician Asclepius.

The **murals** for which the palace is famous – alive with detail, colour, graceful form and religious fervour – adorn the walls of the **meditation room** directly above the bedroom, used by the raja and the heirs apparent. Unfortunately, this is now closed to preserve the murals, which have been severely damaged by generations of hands trailing along the walls. Further points of interest in the palace include a **dining hall** intended for the free feeding of up to 2000 brahmins, and a 38-kilo stone which, it is said, every new recruit to the raja's army had to raise above his head 101 times.

Practicalities

Frequent **buses** run to Padmanabhapuram from Thiruvananthapuram's Thampanoor station; hop on any service heading south towards Nagercoil or Kanniyakumari and get off at **Thakkaly** (sometimes written Thuckalai). If you're determined to see Padmanabhapuram and Kanniyakumari (see p.1188) in one day, leave the city early to arrive when the palace opens at 9am. Note that two express buses leave Thakkaly at 2.30pm and 3.30pm for Thiruvananthapuram. Another way to see Padmanabhapuram is on KTDC's Kanniyakumari tour from Thiruvananthapuram (daily 7.30am–9pm; Rs250).

The small stalls inside the outer walls of the palace are the best place to get **snacks** and **drinks**, as the area around the bus station is noisy and dirty.

Varkala

Long renowned by Hindus as a place of pilgrimage, **VARKALA**, 54km northwest of Thiruvananthapuram, with its beautiful sands and cliffs, is a considerably more appealing beach destination these days than Kovalam. Centred on a clifftop row of budget guesthouses and palm-thatch cafés, the tourist scene is somewhat less full on, although the arrival in recent years of the first charter groups and luxury hotels may well be the harbinger of full-scale development and building inland and at both ends is already proceeding apace. The best time to visit is from October to early March; during the monsoons the beach is virtually unusable.

Arrival and information

Varkala's railway station, 2.5km east of the village, is served by express and mail **trains** from Thiruvananthapuram, Kollam (hourly; 45min), and most other

Sivananda Yoga Vedanta Dhanwantari

Located amid the serene hills and tropical forests around **Neyyar Dam**, 28km east of Thiruvananthapuram, the **Sivananda Yoga Vedanta Dhanwantari** (Ⓦwww.sivananda.org) is one of India's leading **yoga** ashrams. It was founded by Swami Sivananda – dubbed the "Flying Guru" because he used to pilot light aircraft over war-stricken areas of the world, scattering flowers and leaflets calling for peace – as a centre for meditation, yoga and traditional Keralan martial arts and medicine. Sivananda was a renowned exponent of Advaitya Vedanta, the philosophy of non-duality, as espoused by the Upanishads and promoted later by Shankara in the eleventh century.

Aside from training teachers in advanced raja and hatha yoga, the ashram offers excellent **introductory courses** for beginners. These comprise four hours of intensive tuition per day (starting at 5.30am), with background lectures that provide helpful theory and a good practical start. During the course, you have to stay at the ashram and comply with a regime that some Western students find fairly strict (no sex, drugs, rock'n'roll, no smoking, pure veg diet and early morning starts), as well as join in Hindu devotional worship. Some people have also noted strained relations with the local villagers, whom ashramites are discouraged from mixing with or even buying goods from. However, if you are keen to acquire the basic techniques and knowledge of yoga, this is a great place to start. For more details, contact the ashram itself (Ⓣ0471/229 0493), or its branch in Thiruvananthapuram (37/1929 Airport Rd, West Fort Ⓣ0471/245 0942). For more information look at its publication, *Sivananda Yoga Life*, published by the Sivananda Yoga Vedanta Centre, 51 Felsham Rd, London SW15 1AZ (Ⓣ020/8780 0160).

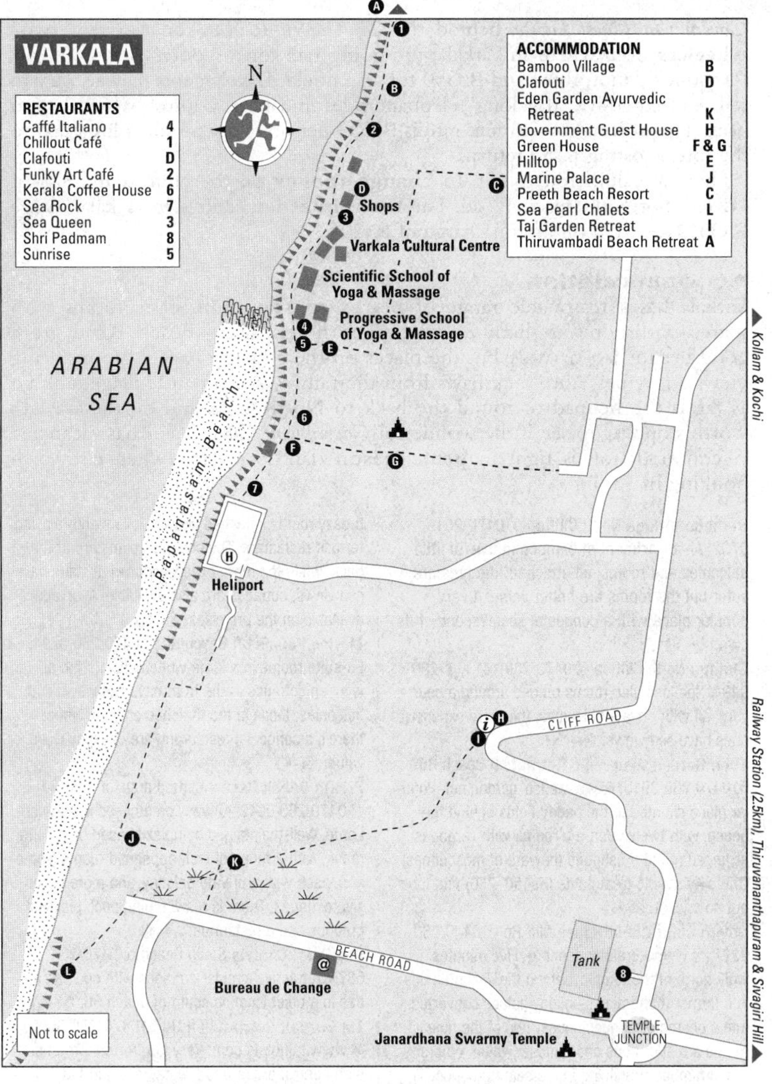

Keralan towns on the main line. An auto-rickshaw to the beach costs around Rs40. Regular **buses** also run from Thiruvananthapuram's Thampanoor stand, and from Kollam (1hr 30min). A few go all the way to the beach, but most stop in the village centre, a five-minute auto-rickshaw ride away. If you can't get a direct bus, take any "superfast" or "limited stop" bus along the main NH-47 highway to Kallamballam, from where you can get a local bus to Varkala (15km), or an auto-rickshaw (Rs80–100) or taxi (Rs120–150).

The new **Kerala Department of Tourism** office (Mon–Sat 10am–5pm; ⓣ0470/260 2227, ⓦwww.keralatourism.org) is in the same complex as its

Government Guest House, behind the *Taj Garden Retreat*. You can rent **two-wheelers** everywhere in Varkala; the going rate for a scooter is Rs200–250, Rs300 for a motorbike and Rs350 for an Enfield. Travel agents may also try to sell you expensive "day-long" elephant rides in a nearby forest, which last an hour. The official government rate is Rs350 per hour per person, plus a taxi to the forest costing Rs50 return.

There are numerous places to **change money** on the clifftop and also at *Nikhil's* hotel on Beach Road. The many **Internet** centres in Varkala charge Rs35–40, with a minimum charge of Rs20.

Accommodation

Varkala has a reasonable range of **places to stay**, from basic rooms with shared bathrooms to luxury resorts. The hotels along Beach Road are a good bet for late arrivals, but the places on the cliff-top have more inspiring views and vibes. Auto-rickshaws from the railway station and village tank go as far as the helipad or round the back to North Cliff, and on the way it's worth stopping to see if the wonderful *Government Guest House* has vacancies. Accommodation is tight in **peak season** (late Nov–Jan), when it's worth booking in advance.

Bamboo Village North Clifftop ⓣ0470/261 0732. An assortment of bamboo huts with little balconies and rooms, all attached; the huts are cuter but the rooms are better value. A very popular place with a congenial social scene of its own. ❷–❸

Clafouti North Clifftop ⓣ0470/260 1414, Ⓕ260 0494. Spotless tiled rooms ranged around a courtyard, all with private balconies; the more expensive ones have sea views. ❸–❹

Eden Garden Ayurvedic Retreat off Beach Rd ⓣ0470/260 3910, Ⓦwww.eden-garden.net. Popular place situated in the paddy fields behind the beach, with twelve non-a/c rooms with verandas, arranged round a fishpond (beware of mosquitoes). Offers Ayurvedic treatments (Rs450–750) and food but no cricket. ❸–❻

Government Guest House Cliff Rd ⓣ0470/260 2227, Ⓦwww.keralatourism.org. Five minutes' walk north of the temple, behind the *Taj* hotel, this is a former maharajah's holiday palace converted into a characterful guesthouse. Two of the nine rooms are enormous and fantastic value; others are in a modern building in the same grounds. Meals available on request. ❷–❸

Green House Clifftop ⓣ0470/260 4659, Ⓔgreenhousecliff@hotmail.com. Only two minutes' walk from the cliff edge, behind a small temple in an unhurried and friendly hamlet. The rooms are basic and the cheapest ones share a common bathroom. Nice vibe and popular with backpackers. A small new block right on the clifftop (❺) offers more comfortable rooms. ❷

Hilltop North Clifftop ⓣ0470/260 1237, Ⓦwww.hilltopvarkala.com. A great spot, with pleasant, breezy rooms, attached shower-toilets and relaxing terrace restaurant. The cheaper rooms are at the back, while the more expensive ones upstairs have sea views; cottages are also available. Ayurveda is available on the premises. ❸–❼

Marine Palace Off Beach Rd ⓣ0470/260 3204. En-suite rooms in a large white building; the pricier wooden cottages at the front have sea views and balconies; those in the thatched annexe, where there's a congenial restaurant, are cheaper. Good value. ❷–❺

Preeth Beach Resort Clifftop area, off Cliff Rd ⓣ0470/260 0942, Ⓦwww.preethbeachresort.com. Large, well-maintained complex shaded by a palm grove, with a range of well-appointed rooms (some a/c), each with a private balcony, and more expensive cottages. There is a swimming pool, pleasant grounds and a restaurant. ❹–❽

Sea Pearl Chalets South Beach ⓣ0470/260 5875. Attractive circular cottages with good amenities in a quiet location south of Beach Rd. ❸–❺

Taj Garden Retreat Cliff Rd ⓣ0470/260 3000, Ⓦwww.tajhotels.com. Very comfortable rooms with central a/c, a good restaurant and bar, fitness and Ayurveda centre, terraced gardens and a pleasant swimming pool, but it's all a bit ostentatious for a laid-back place like Varkala. The tariff includes breakfast and dinner buffets. $125–160. ❾

Thiruvambadi Beach Retreat North Clifftop ⓣ0470/260 1028. Set back from the cliffs in a palm grove at the quiet northern end of Varkala, with four sea-facing rooms and cheaper inner rooms, hammocks in garden and a restaurant. Expensive for non a/c. ❺–❻

The beach and village

Known in Malayalam as Papa Nashini ("sin destroyer"), Varkala's beautiful white-sand **Papanasam beach** is backed by sheer red-laterite cliffs and drenched by rolling waves off the Arabian Sea. It's imposingly scenic and still a relatively peaceful place to soak up the sun, though the "hello pineapple" hawkers can irritate at first. Bear in mind that the town is quite conservative and nudity, or topless bathing for women, are not acceptable.

The expanding string of chilled travellers' cafés, hotels and souvenir shops of the **clifftop** area feels a world apart from the village a short way inland. The beach is reachable via several sets of very steep sandy steps cut into the cliffs from the beach, as well as along a gentler path up starting behind the *Marine Palace* restaurant, or the metalled road from the village. Beware that the rope cordoning off the precipitous cliff edge is flimsy and actually extends beyond the edge in places where it has crumbled. Two **yoga schools** on North Clifftop, the Scientific School of Yoga & Massage and the Progressive School, offer **Ayurvedic massage**, and courses in meditation, massage and yoga; the former also runs the small Prakrithi Stores, selling honey, essential oils, herbs, handmade soaps and books.

Back in the **village**, the tank at Temple Junction is a hive of activity in the early mornings, when pilgrims come to bathe. Nearby is the **Janardhana Swamy** temple, said to be more than 2000 years old; devotees bring the ashes of departed relatives here for "final rest". Unlike many temples in Kerala, non-Hindus are welcome into the temple courtyard but not into the small shrines. At the eastern edge of the village, Sivagiri Hill harbours a traditional **ashram** that attracts pilgrim devotees of Shri Narayana Guru, a saint who died here in 1922. Born into the low *ezhava* caste, he fought orthodoxy with a philosophy of social reform ("one caste, one religion, one God for man") which included the consecration of temples with an open-door policy to all castes, and had a profound effect on the "upliftment" of the untouchables.

Aimed unashamedly at the tourist market, the **Varkala Cultural Centre** (Ⓣ0470/608793), behind the *Sunrise* restaurant on North Clifftop, holds daily **Kathakali** and **Bharatanatyam** dance performances (make-up 5pm; performance 6.30–8pm; Rs150). It's a pleasant enough introduction to the art, especially if you're not going to make it to Kochi.

Eating

Seafood lovers will enjoy Varkala's crop of clifftop **café-restaurants**, which dish up delicious baked, steamed or coconut-curried freshly caught shark, marlin or butterfish, as well as pasta, pizza and, if you're lucky, some Indian dishes too. Prices are fairly high: expect to pay around Rs50 for a simple veggie curry, Rs50–100 for pizza or pasta and over Rs100 for a fresh fish dish. Service, though, can be very slow here, but the superb location more than compensates, especially in the evenings when the sea twinkles with the lights of distant fishing boats.

Due to Kerala's antiquated licensing laws, which involve huge amounts of tax, a lot of cafés choose to serve **beer** discreetly; a teapot-full costs Rs75–90. The *Taj Garden Retreat*'s licensed bar is nice but far more expensive.

Caffé Italiano Clifftop. Authentic Italian menu starring several varieties of pizza and pasta, and very good – but pricey – cappuccino.

Chillout Café North Clifftop. Simple thatched café with a limited menu but you can't beat the Rs40 breakfast specials.

Clafouti North Clifftop. Wonderful French bakery offering real croissants, pain aux raisins, baguettes and sweet pies, served at little tables under rustling palm trees. There's a range of moderately priced multi-cuisine options, including seafood dishes, and a set three-course evening menu (Rs150).

Funky Art Café North Clifftop. Trendiest place at

the northern end, with a good musical vibe and a selection of Indian and Western fare.

Kerala Coffee House Clifftop. The funkiest place on this stretch of clifftop, pleasingly close to the edge, with great music, a friendly vibe and with a more extensive Indian menu than at many places hereabouts. Expect to pay Rs50–100 for a main course.

Sea Rock Clifftop, next to heliport. A fairly standard range of Indian and Continental cuisine. Plays good Indian music and shows films.

Sea Queen North Clifftop. Good views and plenty of fish, calamari, mussel and prawn dishes amongst the pizza and pasta – only the wine is missing. The adjacent *Gnosh* is a very similar alternative.

Shri Padmam Varkala village. This grubby-looking café might seem unpromising, but the veg food is cheap and delicious, and the location is very atmospheric, with a large rear terrace affording views of the temple tank.

Sunrise North Clifftop. Great-value Israeli, French, Italian, English and South Indian set breakfasts, good fruit juices and an evening Keralan speciality of fish with coconut and spices, steamed in a banana leaf and served with rice.

Kollam (Quilon) and around

One of the Malabar coast's oldest ports, **KOLLAM** (pronounced "Koillam" and previously known as Quilon), 74km northwest of Thiruvananthapuram and 85km south of Alappuzha, was once at the centre of the international spice trade. The sixteenth-century Portuguese writer Duarte Barbossa described it as a "very great city with a right good haven", which was visited by "Moors, Heathen and Christians in great numbers", and stated that "a great store" of pepper was to be found there. In fact, the port flourished from the very earliest times, trading amicably with the Phoenicians, Arabs, Persians, Greeks, Romans and Chinese.

Nowadays, Kollam is chiefly of interest as one of the entry or exit points to the backwaters of Kerala (see p.1234), and most travellers simply stay overnight en route to or from Alappuzha. The **town** itself, sandwiched between the sea and Ashtamudi ("eight inlets") Lake, is less exciting than its history might suggest. It's a typically sprawling Keralan market community, with a few old tiled wooden houses and winding backstreets, kept busy with the commercial interests of coir, cashew nuts (a good local buy), pottery, aluminium and fishery industries. The missable ruins of **Tangasseri** fort (3km from the centre) are the last vestiges of colonial occupation.

Practicalities

The **railway station** is east of the clocktower which marks the centre of town. Numerous daily trains run from Ernakulam and Thiruvananthapuram and beyond. On platform 4, the tiny **District Tourism Promotion Council** (DTPC) tourist information counter will book hotels; you have to pay one night in advance, but but the only extra charge is for the phone calls. It also has a tourist office (daily 9am–6pm; ⓣ0474/274 5625, ⓦwww.dtpckollam.com) at the **boat jetty** on the edge of Ashtamudi Lake, but only provides details on its own tourist ferry service. The local **Allapuzha Tourism Development Council** (ATDC; daily 7am–9pm; ⓣ0474/276 7440) office on the opposite side of the road also has information on tourist and local ferry services. The two alternate daily **cruises** from Kollam to Alappuzha, which depart at 10.30am and take eight hours (Rs300), with stops for lunch and tea. While the cruise is popular, you may find that you get a far better impression of backwater life by hopping between villages on the very cheap local ferries. Tickets for both the DTPC and ATDC ferries can be bought on the morning of the trip from any agent and some of the hotels; tickets for the local ferries are purchased at the booth on the jetty. Both companies also offer exclusive overnight *kettu vallam* cruises (see box pp.1234–1235 for details), and the DTPC organizes half-day trips to nearby **Monroe island**

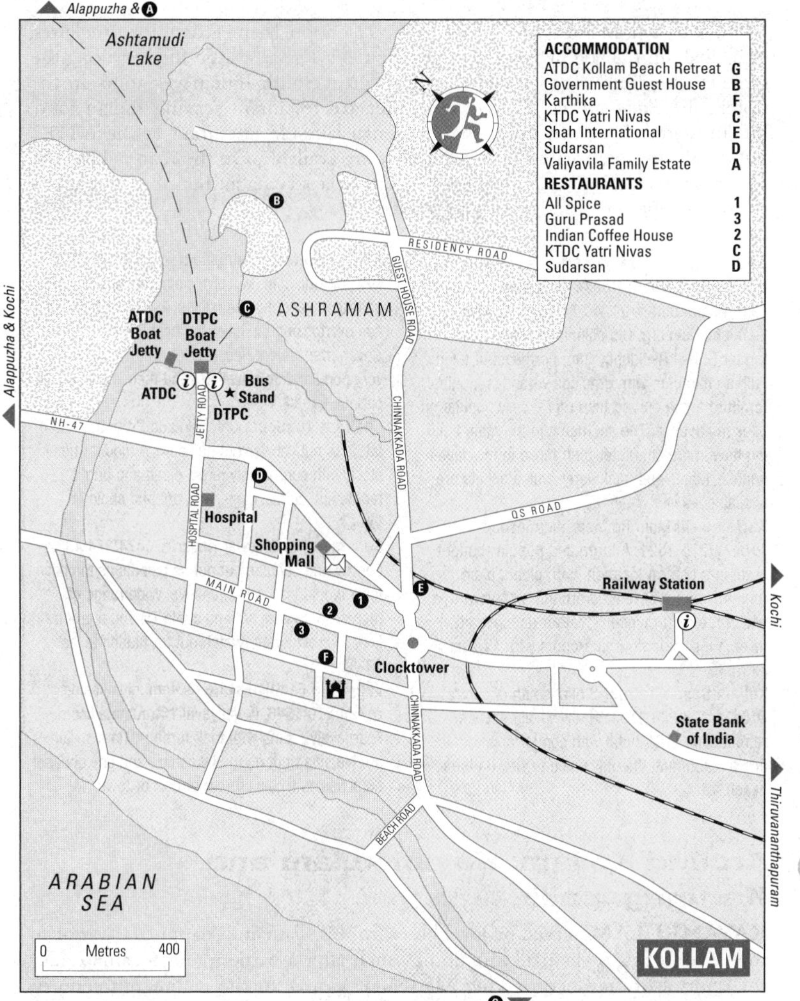

(9am–1pm & 2–6.30pm; Rs300), which provide a fascinating glimpse of village life in this unique – and very scenic – waterlogged region.

The KSRTC **bus stand** is next to the DTPC jetty. Bookable express **buses** run south to Thiruvananthapuram (1hr 30min) and north to Kochi (3hr) via Alappuzha (1hr 15min). Useful **facilities** such as exchange bureaux, ATMs and Internet outlets are to be found in the smart modern shopping mall, just south of the main road between the jetty and the clocktower.

Accommodation and eating

The most congenial **places to stay** are outside the town, across Ashtamudi Lake from the boat jetty; they're reachable by ferry (Rs20), or auto-rickshaws (Rs15) which go around the lake.

Places to **eat** include the *Indian Coffee House* on Main Road, for omelettes, rice, dhal, simple veg dishes and coffee, or *Guru Prasad*, a little further along the same road, which serves a wide range of great South Indian veg food. In the hotels, the *Sudarsan* has a good, upmarket a/c restaurant serving Indian food, but most travellers end up at the congenial lakeside restaurant at the KTDC *Yatri Niwas*, where various tasty fish dishes are available. On the road behind the shopping mall, *All Spice* is a brightly lit cafeteria serving authentic Chinese and reasonable Western food, above a good bakery.

Hotels and guesthouses

Government Guest House Ashtamudi Lake, Ashramam ⓣ0474/274 3620, ⓦwww.keralatourism.org. Old colonial building and former British Residency 3km northeast of town. Full of character, with gracious verandas, original furniture and a curved tiled roof – very popular so book in advance. The six rooms in the main building have more character than those in the newer annexe. Meals and backwater cruise tickets are available. ❷–❸

Karthika Off Main Rd, near the mosque ⓣ0474/275 1821. A large and popular budget hotel in a central location, with clean, plain rooms (some a/c) ranged around a courtyard in which the centrepiece is, rather unexpectedly, three huge nude figures. Rooms with TV cost extra. ❷–❹

Kollam Beach Retreat 3.5km south of centre ⓣ0474/275 276 3793, ⓦwww.kollambeachretreat.com. ATDC hotel with comfortable rooms and a restaurant, the only place to stay on the town beach. ❸–❹

KTDC Yatri Nivas Ashramam ⓣ0474/274 5538, ⓦwww.ktdc.com. Modern, clean rooms with bathrooms and nice balconies, in a great location overlooking the lake; the best fall-back if the *Government Guest House* is full. The restaurant is very popular with travellers, and there's also a beer parlour. ❸–❺

Shah International Chinnakkada Rd ⓣ0474/274 2362, ⓔhotelshah@hotmail.com. A modern hotel block with surprisingly large, clean and bright rooms and suites, some with a/c and cable TV. ❸–❻

Sudarsan Parameswar Nagar ⓣ0474/274 4322. Central and popular, but not as palatial as the posh foyer would lead you to believe. Wide range of rooms, some with a/c and cable TV, and a ground floor a/c restaurant (watch out for hidden taxes). ❸–❽

Valiyavila Family Estate Ashtamudi Lakeside ⓣ474/270 1546, ⓔvaliyavali1@rediffmail.com. Four lovely rooms with teak furniture, in a stylish marble villa right on the lakeshore and one cheaper outhouse. Will collect from airport or town. ❺–❽

Around Kollam: Kayamkulam and Karunagapalli

KAYAMKULAM, served by local buses from Kollam and Alappuzha, was once the centre of its own small kingdom, which after a battle in 1746 came under the control of Travancore's king Marthanda Varma. In the eighteenth century, the area was famous for its spices, particularly pepper and cinnamon. The Abbé Reynal claimed that the Dutch exported some two million pounds of pepper each year, one-fifth of it from Kayamkulam. At this time, the kingdom was also known for the skill of its army, made up of 15,000 Nayars (Kerala's martial caste).

Set in a tranquil garden, the eighteenth-century **Krishnapuram Palace** (Tues–Sat 10am–4.30pm; Rs3, camera Rs15) is imbued with Keralan grace, constructed largely of wood with gabled roofs and rooms opening out onto internal courtyards. It's now a museum, but unlike the palace at Padmanabhapuram (see p.1223), with which it shares some similarities, the whole place is in need of restoration and the collection inside is poorly labelled and neglected. A display case contains puja ceremony utensils and oil lamps, some of which are arranged in an arc known as a *prabhu*, placed behind a temple deity to provide a halo of light. Fine miniature *panchaloha* ("five-metal" bronze alloy, with gold as one ingredient) figures include the water god Varuna and several Vishnus. The prize exhibit is a huge **mural** of the classical Keralan school, in muted ochre-reds and blue-greens, which covers more than fourteen square metres. It depicts **Gajendra Moksha** – the salvation of Gajendra, king of the elephants. The centre of the painting is dominated by a dynamic portrayal of Garuda about to land, with huge spread wings and a facial expression denoting *raudra* (fury), in stark contrast to the compassionate features of the multi-armed Vishnu.

In **KARUNAGAPALLI**, 23km north of Kollam on NH-47 towards Alappuzha, it's possible to see the traditional **kettu vallam** ("tied boats") being made. These long cargo boats, a familiar sight on the backwaters, are built entirely without the use of nails. Each jackwood plank is **sewn** to the next with coir rope, and then the whole is coated with a caustic black resin made from boiled cashew kernels. With careful maintenance they last for generations. If you want to buy a *vallam* you'll need around two *lakh* (200,000) rupees; a far cheaper alternative is to rent these boats by the day or on longer overnight trips (see p.1235).

Karunagapalli is best visited as a day-trip from Kollam; regular **buses** pass through on the way to Alappuzha. One daytime **train**, #6525, leaves Kollam at 2.25pm, arriving in Karunagapalli half an hour later, but you have to get a bus back. On reaching the bus stand or railway station, ask an auto-rickshaw to take you to the boatyard of the *vallam asharis*, the boat carpenters (4km northwest).

Alappuzha

Under its former appellation of Alleppey, **ALAPPUZHA**, roughly midway between Kollam (85km south) and Kochi (64km north) was one of the best-known ports along the Malabar coast. Contemporary tourist literature is fond

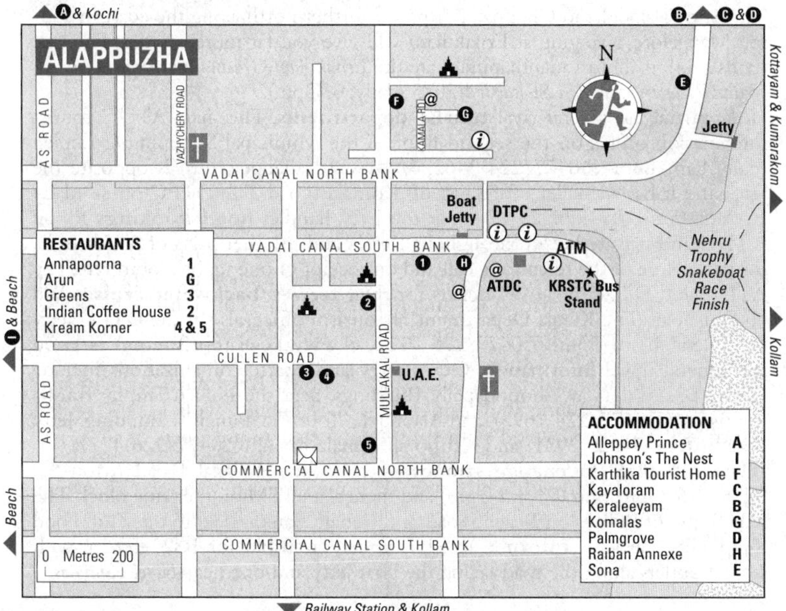

of referring to the town as "Venice of the East", but while it may be full of interconnecting **canals**, there the resemblance ends. Alappuzha has a bustling, messy centre of ramshackle wood and corrugated iron-roofed houses, although some suburban parts are quiet and leafy. The town is chiefly significant in the coir industry, which accounts for much of the traffic on its sludgy waterways.

The town is prominent on the tourist trail as one of the major centres for **backwater boat trips**, served by ferries to and from Kollam and Kottayam. Most visitors stay just one night, catching a boat or bus out early the next morning. A commendable time-killing walk takes you about 1km northeast of the centre to the **lakeside**, shaded under a canopy of palm trees.

Alappuzha really comes alive on the second Saturday of August, in the depths of the rainy season, when it serves as the venue for one of Kerala's major spectacles – the **Nehru Trophy snakeboat race**. This event, first held in 1952, is based on the traditional Keralan enthusiasm for racing magnificently decorated longboats, with raised rears designed to resemble the hood of a cobra. More than enthusiastically powered by up to 150 singing and shouting oarsmen, scores of boats take part, and Alappuzha is packed with thousands of spectators. Similar races can be seen at Aranmula (p.1239), and at Champakulam, 16km by ferry from Alappuzha. The ATDC information office (see below) will be able to tell you the dates of these events, which change every year.

Practicalities

The KSRTC **bus stand**, on the east of town, is served by half-hourly buses to Kollam, Thiruvananthapuram and Ernakulam; less frequent buses run to Kottayam, Thrissur and Palakkad. The **boat jetty** is just one minute's walk west from the bus stand. Few **trains** continue south beyond Alappuzha, and the most useful services north from the **railway station**, 3km southwest of the jetty, include the *Jan Shatabdi Express* #2076 at 8.20am to Ernakulam Junction, and the *Alleppey–Chennai Express* #6042 at 3pm, which stops at Ernakulam Junction before continuing to Thrissur, Palakkad and Chennai. For points further north along the coast including Mangalore, changing at Ernakulam will give you far more options. The best trains south to Thiruvananthapuram are the *Ernakulam–Trivandrum Express* #6341 (daily; 7.20am) and *Jan Shatabdi* #2075 (daily; 6.33pm).

Alappuzha has several rival **tourist departments**. The main ATDC tourist information office, on the second floor of the Municipal Shopping Complex (daily 8am–8pm; ⓣ0477/224 3462, ⓦwww.atdcalleppey.com) is opposite the jetty, and it has a smaller office just off Komala Road. The DTPC office (daily 7.30am–9pm; ⓣ0477/225 1796), at the jetty, handles **hotel bookings** for all KTDC and private hotels throughout Kerala and in other parts of South India for the charge of the telephone call and on receipt of one night's room rate. The ATDC and DTPC both sell tickets for their **ferries**, **backwater cruises** and charter boats. The Kerala Department of Tourism office, also at the DTPC jetty (Mon–Sat 10am–5pm; ⓣ0477/226 0722, ⓦwww.keralatourism.org) is good for general travel information. Other ferry and charter organizations include Kerala Backwaters at Choondapally Buildings, near the Nehru Trophy finishing point (ⓣ0477/224 1693), and Alappuzha Tour Co, Punchiri Building, Jetty Road (ⓣ0477/226 2931) and Cruisors, Komala Road (ⓣ0477/226 4777).

The best place to **change money** is UAE on Mullakal Road (Mon–Sat 9.30am–6.30pm, Sun 9.30am–1pm) and there is an ATM on the same block. The State Bank of India is on Beach Road, and Canara Bank is next to the Zion Food Shop, near the jetty. **Internet** access is widely available, for Rs25–35/hr, with several outlets along the road facing the boat jetty and one near *Hotel Komalas*.

Accommodation

Alappuzha's town centre **lodgings** are uninspiring, but there are some great places to stay if you're willing to travel into the outskirts.

Alleppey Prince AS Rd (aka Ernakulam Rd or NH-47), 2km north of the jetty ⓣ0477/224 3752, ⓔprincehotel@satyam.net.in. Though past its prime, the poshest option close to the town centre: all rooms are a/c. Private backwater trips, and classical music or Kathakali staged by the pool. ❻–❽

Johnson's The Nest Lalbagh, Convent Square ⓣ0477/224 5825, ⓔjohnsongilbertlk1@hotmail.com. Wonderful and extremely friendly homestay in an attractive colonial building 2km west of the centre and a 10-min walk from the beach. Huge rooms with spacious balconies and some smaller ones in the house opposite. Home-cooked food on request. ❷–❹

Karthika Tourist Home Mullakal Rd, across the canal and opposite the jetty ⓣ0477/224 5524. Plain rooms, some with attached bathrooms and wicker chairs; no. 31, with its large bay windows, is particularly good value. There's also a budgie aviary. ❷

Kayaloram Punnamada Kayal ⓣ0477/223 2040, ⓕ225 2918. An incredible location in a grove of palms with views onto the lake; the twelve cool wood cottages are built in Keralan style and have open-air showers. Ayurvedic treatment courses and daily sunset cruises are available, and there's a pool. Book through its city office at Punchiri Buildings, Jetty Rd (ⓣ0477/226 2931) and you'll be taken there by boat from the Nehru Trophy jetty. $70 including breakfast. ❾

Keraleeyam Nehru Trophy Rd, Thathampally ⓣ0477/223 1468, ⓦwww.keraleeyam.com. Situated on the Nehru Trophy channel (and reachable by boat from the jetty), this traditional Keralan house with oodles of character has been an Ayurvedic centre for sixty years; tailor-made rejuvenation courses are available. Elegant rooms arranged around a communal living area, as well as lovely cottages (some with a/c). ❻–❽

Komalas Zilla Court Ward ⓣ0477/224 3631. A 5-min walk across the canal from the bus stand, with a good range of clean rooms (some with a/c) and a decent South Indian restaurant. ❷–❺

Palmgrove Punnamada Kayal, Punnamada ⓣ0477/223 5004. Some 2.5km from the jetty, and reachable by bus or boat. Quaint and very simple bamboo huts dotted around a manicured palm grove, with attached open-air bathrooms. The restaurant is in an open hut, serving South Indian food only. This place isn't in the same league as some other "resorts" along the backwaters, but then it is a lot more affordable. ❺

Raiban Annexe Vadai Canal South Bank ⓣ0477/226 1017. Budget hotel set back from the canal in a communal courtyard. Small rooms but reasonable value. ❷–❸

Sona Lakeside, Thathampally ⓣ0477/223 5211, ⓦwww.sonahome.com. Lovely old Keralan home set in a beautiful garden; four rooms with mosquito nets, plenty of family atmosphere and home cooking. The warm and hospitable owners love to share their knowledge of local history of the town and backwaters. ❸–❹

Eating

Alappuzha has plenty of decent, inexpensive places to eat, but for a splurge, catch a rickshaw out to the *Alleppey Prince*, whose a/c *Vembanad* restaurant offers the town's classiest menu, and beer by the pool. The KTDC *Aaram* round the corner is a lot cheaper and also serves beer.

Annapoorna Vadai Canal South Bank. A very good, inexpensive veggie restaurant whose menu highlights include delicious Keralan coconut curries.

Arun *Komalas Hotel*, Zilla Court Ward. Tasty Chinese noodles and Indian veg (including delicious dhal *makhini*, *malai kofta* and *subzis*) at reasonable prices, but avoid the Continental food. One of the most popular places in town; if it's busy, settle in for a wait.

Greens Cullen Rd. Popular restaurant, cheap and clean with a little garden out front. Fresh South Indian snacks and all-you-can-eat thalis, mainly veg but some meat and fish.

Indian Coffee House Mullakal Rd. Part of the all-India chain of co-operatives with a predictable, inexpensive menu of reliable filter coffee, omelettes, *dosas* and *iddlis*, but with the addition of meat dishes.

Kream Korner Mullakal Rd. Non-veg restaurant-cum-ice-cream parlour. Mains centre on chicken and mutton, and there's a selection of snacks, milkshakes and ice creams. A second, smaller branch has opened next to *Greens*.

Kuttanad: the backwaters of Kerala

One of the most memorable experiences for travellers in India – even those on the lowest of budgets – is the opportunity to take a boat journey on the **backwaters of Kerala**. Immortalized as the setting for Arundhati Roy's Booker-prize-winning novel *The God of Small Things*, the area known as **Kuttanad** stretches for 75km from Kollam in the south to Kochi in the north, sandwiched between the sea and the hills. This bewildering labyrinth of shimmering waterways, composed of lakes, canals, rivers and rivulets, is lined with dense tropical greenery, and preserves rural Keralan lifestyles that are completely hidden from the road.

Views change from narrow canals and dense vegetation to open vistas and dazzling green paddy fields. Homes, farms, churches, mosques and temples can be glimpsed among the trees, and every so often you might catch the blue flash of a kingfisher, or the green of a parakeet. Pallas fishing eagles cruise above the water looking for prey and cormorants perch on logs to dry their wings. Daily life continues both on the water and the palm-fringed shorelines. Families subsist on tiny pockets of land, with just enough room for a simple house, yard and boat, and bathe and wash their clothes – sometimes their buffaloes, too – at the water's edge. Powered both by gondolier-like boatmen with poles and by sail, *kettu vallams* glide past laden with heavyweight cargoes, and fishermen work from rowing boats or operate massive Chinese nets on the shore.

Coconut trees at improbable angles form shady canopies, and occasionally you pass under simple curved bridges. Here and there, basic drawbridges can be raised on ropes, but major bridges are few and far between; most people rely on boatmen to ferry them across the water to connect with roads and bus services, a constant criss-crossing of the waters from dawn until dusk (a way of life beautifully represented in the visually stunning film *Piravi*, by Keralan director Shaji). Poles sticking out of the water indicate dangerous shallows.

The **African moss** that often carpets the surface of the narrower waterways may look attractive, but it is actually a menace to small craft traffic and starves underwater life of light. It is also a symptom of the many serious **ecological problems** currently affecting the region, whose population density ranges from between two and four times that of other coastal areas in southwest India. This has put growing pressure on land, and hence a greater reliance on fertilizers, which eventually work their way into the water causing the build up of moss. Illegal land reclamation, however, poses the single greatest threat to this fragile ecosystem. In a little over a century, the total area of water in Kuttanad has been reduced by two-thirds, while mangrove swamps and fish stocks have been decimated by pollution and the spread of towns and villages around the edges of the backwater region. Unfortunately, tourism is now adding to the problem, as the barely perceptible film of oil from motorized ferries and houseboats spreads through the waters. This kills yet more fish and the number of bird species found in the region has been reduced by over fifty percent to under one hundred. Some of the tourist agencies are trying to lessen the impact by introducing more eco-friendly vessels and you can always play your part by asking for one.

Routes and practicalities

There are numerous backwater **routes** to choose from, on vessels ranging from local ferries, through chauffeur-driven speedboats offered by the KTDC, to customized *kettu vallam* and rice boat cruises. The most popular excursion is the full-day journey between **Kollam** and **Alappuzha**. All sorts of private hustlers offer their services, but the principal boats are run on alternate days by the Alleppey Tourism Development Co-op (ATDC) and the District Tourism Promotion Council (DTPC) – see p.1232 for contact details. The double-decker boats leave from both Kollam and Alappuzha daily, departing at 10.30am (10am check-in); tickets cost Rs300 and can be bought in advance or on the day, at the ATDC/DTPC counters, other agents and some hotels. Both companies make three stops during the 8hr journey, including one for lunch, and another at the renowned **Mata Amritanandamayi Mission** at Amritapuri, around three hours north of Kollam. Foreigners are welcome to stay at the ashram (Ⓣ0476/289 6399, Ⓦwww.amritapuri.org; 1), which is the home of the renowned female guru, Shri Amritanandamayi Devi, known as the "hugging Mama" because she gives each of her visitors and devotees a big, power-imparting hug during the daily *darshan* sessions. The Rs150 a night includes a basic room in the startling high-rise block and simple meals.

Although it is by far the most popular backwater trip, many tourists find the Alappuzha–Kollam route too long and at times uncomfortable, with crowded decks and intense sun. There's also something faintly embarrassing about being cooped up with a crowd of fellow tourists madly photographing any signs of life on the water or canal banks, while gangs of kids scamper alongside the boat screaming "one pen, one pen". You can sidestep the tourist scene completely by catching **local ferries**. These are a lot slower and more crowded, but you'll gain a more intimate experience of life on the backwaters. The trip from Alappuzha to Kottayam (5 daily; Rs10) is particularly recommended. The first ferry leaves at 7.30am; arrive early to get a good place with uninterrupted views. There are also numerous daily ferries that ply routes between local villages, allowing you to hop on and off as you like. The scenery on these routes is often more varied than between Alappuzha and Kollam, beginning with open lagoons and winding up on narrow canals through densely populated coconut groves and islands; furthermore the tickets cost a fraction of the tourist boats. Whichever boat you opt for, take a sun hat and plenty of water. **Check the departure times** in advance, as these can vary from year to year.

Groups of up to ten people can charter a *kettu vallam* moored at **Karunagapalli** for a day's **cruise** on the backwaters. Boats have comfortable cane chairs and a raised central platform where passengers can laze on cushions; there are bathrooms on board plus food and drinks are available. Whether powered by local gondoliers or by sail, the trip is as quiet and restful as you could possibly want. Starting at Rs4000 for the day, including lunch, the luxury is well worth it.

Almost every mid- to top-range hotel situated near the backwaters has its own private *kettu vallam* boat available for residents to rent, while DTPC and ATDC (see p.1232) also offer trips. Of the many private *kettu vallam* operators who can arrange a trip if you turn up on spec, Southern Backwaters (Ⓣ0474/274 6037, Ⓦwww.southernbackwaters.com) in Kollam and Tharavad Boats (Ⓣ0477/224 4599, Ⓔalleppeytharavad@sify.com) in Alleppey are two reliable names. However, these overnight *kettu vallam* cruises are not cheap – expect to pay Rs4000–10,000 for two people for a 24hr cruise, depending on the distance travelled, though you may be able to haggle the price down in the low season.

Although backwater life may seem idyllic, there have been recent reports of theft, especially during the night when the crew sleep on land and windows are left open – so take care of your belongings at all times; lock them away if possible, or at the very least, keep them away from the windows. Also insist your boat is not moored near one with a generator that may run all night.

△ Kerala backwaters

Kottayam and around

The busy commercial centre of **KOTTAYAM** is strategically located between the backwaters to the west and the spice, tea and rubber plantations, forests, and the mountains of the Western Ghats to the east, 76km southeast of Kochi and 37km northeast of Alappuzha. Most visitors come here on the way somewhere else – foreigners take short backwater trips to Alappuzha or set off to Periyar Wildlife Sanctuary, while Ayappa devotees pass through en route to the forest temple at Sabarimala (see p.1244).

Kottayam's long history of **Syrian Christian** settlement is reflected by the presence of two thirteenth-century churches on a hill 5km northwest of the centre, which you can get to by rickshaw. Two eighth-century Nestorian stone crosses with Pahlavi and Syriac inscriptions, on either side of the elaborately decorated altar of the **Valliapalli** ("big") church, are probably the earliest solid evidence of Christianity in India. The visitors' book contains entries from as far back as the 1890s, including one by the Ethiopian king, Haile Selassie, and a British viceroy. The interior of the nearby **Cheriapalli** ("small") church is covered with lively, unskilled paintings, thought to have been executed by a Portuguese artist in the sixteenth century. If the doors are locked, ask for the key at the church office (9am–1pm & 2–5pm).

Practicalities

Kottayam's KSRTC **bus stand**, 500m south of the centre on TB Road (not to be confused with the private stand for local buses on KK Road, aka Shastri Road), is an important stop on routes to and from major towns in South India. Four of the frequent buses to Kumily/Periyar (3–4hr) each day go on to Madurai, in Tamil Nadu (7hr), and there are regular services to Thiruvananthapuram, Kollam and Ernakulam. The **railway station**, 2km north of the centre, sees a constant flow of traffic between Thiruvananthapuram and points north. **Ferries** from Alappuzha and elsewhere dock at the weed-clogged jetty, 2km south of town.

There is a tiny DTPC tourist office at the jetty (daily 9am–5pm; ⓣ0481/256 0479). The best place to **change money** is Muthoot Bankers (Mon–Sat 9.30am–1pm & 1.30–5pm) on KK Road and there's a CorpBank ATM near the corner of KK Road and Gandhi Square. **Internet** facilities are available at Intimacy (Rs25/hr) on KK Road and Brain Net (Rs15/hr), just north of the bus stand.

Accommodation and eating

Kottayam has a good choice of mid-range **hotels**; if you're in search of utter luxury, head out to one of the five-star resorts that nestle on the banks of the nearby Vembanad lake (see p.1238) in Kumarakom.

There are basic **restaurants** in the centre of Kottayam, especially around the bus station on TB Road, and an *Indian Coffee House* on TB Road, while the best spot for non-veg grub such as burgers or Indian/Chinese favourites is *JobGees* on MC Road. Hotel eateries include the *Vembanad Lake Resort*, where you eat Indian, Western and Chinese dishes, including seafood, either in a lakeside garden or on a moored *kettu vallam*, making for a special evening out.

Hotels and guesthouses

Aida TB Junction, MC Rd ⓣ0481/256 8391, ⓦwww.aidahotel.com. Large, friendly hotel with a wide range of rooms, including some a/c and reasonably priced singles. Facilities include a good restaurant, bar, money changing and travel agency. ❹–❺

Ambassador KK Rd ⓣ0481/256 3293. A well-run economy hotel with clean rooms, some with big TV and balcony. Chocolate delicacies for sale in reception. ❷–❹

Green Park Kurian Uthup Rd, Nagampadam, near the railway station ⓣ0481/256 3311,

Ⓔ greenparkhotel@yahoo.com. Modern and efficient business hotel, with decent non-a/c and a/c rooms, a bar and two restaurants. Good value. ❸–❺

Vembanad Lake Resort Kodimatha, 5min walk from ferry and nearly 3km from the centre of town Ⓣ 0481/236 0866, Ⓦ www.vembanadlakeresort.com. Western-style motel beside an inlet of Lake Vembanad. The ten old rooms are close to the noisy road but newer wing near the water is pleasant. ❹–❺

Windsor Castle/Lake Village Kodimatha, just before *Vembanad Lake Resort* Ⓣ 0481/230 3622, Ⓦ www.thewindsorcastle.com. Two distinct sections: a white tower-block of characterless luxury rooms (the "castle" part), or the far nicer "Lake Village" of comfortable, a/c chalets ($135) on a lagoon, with a pool and a very pleasant open-air restaurant specializing in Keralan cuisine. ❽–❾

Around Kottayam

Some of Kerala's most attractive scenery lies within easy access of Kottayam. The beautiful **Kumarakom** bird sanctuary is in the backwaters to the west, while **Aranmula** to the south is one of the last villages still making *kannady* metal mirrors, and has a Krishna temple that organizes a ritual "non-competitive" boat race. The Mahadeva temple at **Ettumanur**, a short way north of Kottayam, is known to devotees as the home of a dangerous and wrathful Shiva, and to art-lovers as a sublime example of temple architecture, adorned with woodcarvings and murals.

Kumarakom

KUMARAKOM, 16km west of Kottayam, is technically an island on Vembanad Lake. Although right in the thick of a tangle of lush tropical waterways, it can be reached quite easily by bus from Kottayam (every 10min). The peak time to visit the **Bird Sanctuary** (daily dawn–dusk; Rs45) is between November and March when it serves as a winter home for many migratory birds, some from as far away as Siberia. Species include the darter or snake bird, little cormorant, night heron, golden-backed woodpecker, crow pheasant, white-breasted water hen and tree pie. Dawn is the quietest and best time for viewing, when the first rays of sunlight fall through the lush tropical canopy. Although the island is quite small, a guide is useful; you can arrange one through the KTDC *Water Scapes* (see below) or the other luxury hotels.

Next to the sanctuary, set in waterside gardens, a refurbished colonial bungalow that once belonged to a family of Christian missionaries and rubber planters forms the nucleus of a luxury **hotel**, the *Taj Garden Retreat* (Ⓣ 0481/252 5711, Ⓦ www.tajhotels.com; ❾), which consists of eighteen cottages ($190–230) in a landscaped garden around a private lagoon, and also a *kettu vallam* houseboat ($250–300). However, it's not nearly as impressive as the *Coconut Lagoon Hotel* (Ⓣ 0481/252 4491, Ⓕ 252 4495; ❾), 1km northwest on the edge of Vembanad Lake and reached by launch (you can telephone for the boat from a kiosk at the canalside). Superbly crafted from fragments of ruined Keralan palaces, with beautiful woodcarvings and brass work, the building alone merits a visit. It was designed in traditional Keralan style, and even if you can't afford to stay here (rooms start at $230), you could try the wonderful Keralan specialities at the **restaurant**. Another alternative for those with deep pockets is the *Kumarakom Lake Resort* (Ⓣ 0481/252 4900, Ⓦ www.klresort.com; ❾), 3km from the village and just before the *Taj*. This is an ostentatious place – two beautiful 300-year-old palaces recovered and reconstructed on site, and ultra-luxurious cottages ($210–280) made up from bits of old Keralan houses, each with an outdoor bathroom in the lush tropical garden. The Ayurveda centre has two doctors and four massage rooms; the swimming pool boasts a Jacuzzi, its water lapping the edge of the lake. Nearby, KTDC *Water Scapes* (☎0481/252 5861, Ⓦwww.ktdc.com; ⑨) is right on the lake, and consists of comfortable a/c cottages (from Rs5500) built on stilts; few have a decent view over the lake and the ugly metal walkways further detract, but it's significantly cheaper than its competitors and convenient for the bird sanctuary. You can drift across the lake on one of the luxury *kettu vallams* moored here. If you're on a budget, take advantage of the excellent *Moolappura Guest House* (☎0481/252 5980; ⑤) just 200m before the bus stand at the *Taj*, which has just three rooms with attached bathrooms. The family is very warm and welcoming – they offer rides on their dugout boats and personal tours in the bird sanctuary, and have a professional chef, who conjures up Keralan and Continental dishes.

Besides the hotels, the only other place to **eat** is KTDC's uninspiring café at the *Tourist Complex* near where the bus from Kottayam pulls in, close to the *Taj* hotel gates.

Aranmula

The village of **ARANMULA** offers another appealing day-trip – so long as you start early – from Kottayam, 30km south of the town and 10km beyond Chengannur. Its ancient temple is dedicated to Parthasarathy, which was the name under which Krishna acted as Arjuna's charioteer during the bloody Kurekshetra war recorded in the *Mahabharata*. Each year towards the end of the Onam festival (Aug/Sept), when a **Snakeboat Regatta** is celebrated as part of the temple rituals, crowds line the banks of the River Pampa to cheer on the thrusting longboats (similar to those seen at Alappuzha; see p.1232).

Aranmula is also known for the manufacture of extraordinary *kannady* **metal mirrors**, produced, using the "lost wax" technique, with an alloy of copper, silver, brass, lead and bronze. Once a prerequisite of royal households, these ornamental mirrors are now exceedingly rare and only a few master craftsmen continue making them. Modest models cost around Rs300, while custom-made mirrors can cost up to Rs50,000.

Ettumanur

The magnificent Mahadeva temple at **ETTUMANUR**, 12km north of Kottayam on the road to Ernakulam, features a circular shrine, fine woodcarving and one of the earliest (sixteenth-century) and most celebrated of Keralan **murals**. The deity is Shiva in one of his most terrible aspects, described as *vaddikasula vada*, "one who takes his dues with interest" and is "difficult to please". His predominant mood is *raudra* (fury). Although the shrine is open to Hindus only, foreigners can see the courtyard murals, which may be photographed after obtaining a camera ticket (Rs20; video Rs50) from the counter on the left in the temple courtyard. The four-metre mural depicts Nataraja – Shiva – executing a cosmic *tandava* dance, trampling evil underfoot in the form of a demon. Musical accompaniment is courtesy of Krishna on flute, three-headed Brahma on cymbals, and, playing the ancient sacred Keralan *mizhavu* drum, is Shiva's special rhythm expert Nandikesvara.

Ettumanur's ten-day **annual festival** (Feb/March) reflects the wealth of the temple, with elaborate celebrations including music. On the most important days, the eighth and tenth, priests bring out figures of elephants, fashioned from gold and collectively weighing over 700kg, presented in the eighteenth century by Marthanda Varma, the raja of Travancore.

Periyar Wildlife Sanctuary and around

One of the largest and most visited wildlife reserves in India, the **Periyar Wildlife Sanctuary** occupies 777 square kilometres of the Cardamom hills region of the Western Ghats. The majority of its visitors come in the hope of seeing **tigers** and **leopards** – and most leave disappointed, as the few that remain, very wisely keep their distance, and there's only a slight chance of a glimpse even at the height of the dry season (April/May). However, there are plenty of other animals: elephant, sambar, Malabar giant squirrel, gaur, stripe-necked mongoose, wild boar and over 260 species of birds including Nilgiri wood pigeon, purple-headed parakeet, tree pie and flycatchers. Located close to the Kerala–Tamil Nadu border, the park makes a convenient place to break the long journey across the Ghats between Madurai and the coast. It's also a good base for day-trips into the Cardamom hills, with a couple of tea factories, spice plantations, the trailhead for the Sabarimala pilgrimage (see p.1244), and viewpoints and forest waterfalls within striking distance.

Just over 100km east of Kottayam, and centred on a vast artificial **lake** created by the British in 1895 to supply water to the drier parts of neighbouring Tamil Nadu, Periyar lies at altitudes of 900m to 1800m and is correspondingly cool: temperatures range from 15°C to 30°C. The royal family of Travancore, anxious to preserve favourite hunting grounds from the encroachment of tea plantations, declared it to be a Forest Reserve, and built the Edapalayam Lake Palace to accommodate their guests in 1899. It expanded as a wildlife reserve in 1933, and once again when it became part of **Project Tiger** in 1979 (see Contexts).

Seventy percent of the protected area, which is divided into core, buffer and tourist zones, is covered with evergreen and semi-evergreen forest. The **tourist zone** – logically enough, the part accessible to casual visitors – surrounds the lake, and consists mostly of semi-evergreen and deciduous woodland interspersed with grassland, both on hilltops and in the valleys. Although excursions on the lake are the standard way to experience the park, you can get much more out of a visit by **walking** with a local guide in a small group, or, especially, staying in basic accommodation in the sanctuary (see p.1242) away from the crowd. However, avoid the period immediately after the monsoons, when **leeches** make hiking virtually impossible. The **best time to visit** is from December until April, when the dry weather draws animals from the forest to drink at the lakeside.

Getting to Periyar

The base for exploring Periyar is the village of **Kumily**, 1.5km north of the main park entrance at **Thekkady**. **Buses** from Kottayam (every 30min; 4hr), Ernakulam (10 daily; 6hr), and Madurai in Tamil Nadu (frequent service; 5hr 30min) pull in to the scruffy bus stand east of Kumily bazaar. **Auto-rickshaws** will run you the 4km from the bus stand to the visitor centre inside the park for around Rs35, stopping at the park entrance for you to pay the fee. Remember the gates close at 6pm, after which you will have to show proof of accommodation booking before they will let you in. If you are staying at the KTDC *Lake Palace*, the last boat is officially at 4pm but the hotel will arrange a boat during daylight hours.

The **entrance fee** to the park is Rs12 for Indians and Rs150 for foreigners for the first day, Rs50 on subsequent days. If you're staying inside the park you must buy a new pass for each day you stay, either from the entrance gate or from the Forest Information Centre by the jetty.

KTDC's hectic and uncomfortable **weekend tours** to Periyar from Kochi, calling at Kadamattom and Idukki Dam en route (Sat 7.30am–Sun 8pm), are not recommended unless you're really pushed for time.

Kumily

As beds inside the sanctuary are in short supply, most visitors stay in **KUMILY**, which is now built up all the way to the park gates. Here tourism runs side by side with the spice trade as the main source of income. Almost every shop on the town's main street sells freshly collected spices; just walking along the street and breathing in air filled with the scent of cloves, nutmeg, cinnamon and cardamom is a heady experience. In the middle of the bazaar stands the main **cardamom sorting** area, where you can watch tribal women sifting through the fragrant green pods in heart-shaped baskets.

There's a new Idduki State **tourist office** (Mon–Sat 10am–5pm; ⓣ04869/222620) just south of the bus stand. Besides offering information on the district itself, it organizes conducted tours, including a *Spice Valley* trip (daily 6.30am–9.30pm; Rs250) that takes in Munnar and several spice plantations. The other source of information is the **TTDC office** inside the *Rolex Tourist Home* (ⓣ04869/222081).

As well as the attraction of the wildlife sanctuary – one of the best in India for seeing elephants – **tea factory** and **spice plantation tours** are a big draw here: every hotel and tourist agency in Kumily offers similar packages at very competitive rates. Unfortunately, some places have become heavily commercialized and expensive, so it's worth shopping around. Expect to pay Rs250–500 per person (depending on numbers; maximum group size is five) for a three-hour tour with guide and vehicle.

Both the State Bank of Travancore, near the bus stand, and the Muthoot bureau on Thekkady Road can **change money** and there's an ATM at the former. **Internet** facilities are available around Thekkady Junction for around Rs40/hr. Although hilly, this is good cycling territory and **bicycle rental** is available from stalls in the market. For entertainment, Mudra Kathakali, near *Woodlands* hotel, puts on daily shows at 4pm and 7pm.

Accommodation and eating

Kumily has **accommodation** to suit all pockets, and new hotels and resorts emerge each season. Thankfully, most places are well outside the noisy bazaar area, dotted along the Thekkady Road leading to the park. **Homestays** are popular options; some hosts will cook for you, while others provide kitchen facilities. Most of them are around By-pass Road, ten minutes' walk south from the bus stand.

Ambadi Next to turn-off for Mangaladevi temple, Thekkady Rd ⓣ04869/222193, ⓦwww.hotelambadi.com. Pleasant hotel with decent rooms sporting coir mats and wood carvings, and some cottages. The *Adhithi* restaurant serves good chicken. ❺–❻

Coffee Inn Thekkady Rd ⓣ04869/222763, ⓔcoffeeinn@sancharnet.in. A handful of simple rooms (one en-suite) around a covered terrace and garden. The "Wild Huts" annexe, in an attractive enclosed garden just along the road, has a small but eclectic selection of accommodation, including tree houses and huts, all with shared showers and toilet. ❶–❸

Green View By-pass Rd ⓣ04869/211015. Pleasant homestay, consisting of several rooms, each with attached bathrooms. Quiet and great value. ❷–❸

Kumily Gate Behind the bus stand ⓣ04869/222279. Modern block with large, clean rooms, and a restaurant and popular, noisy bar on site. Expensive for what it is, but good for late arrivals. Try for a discount. ❺

Mickey's Cottage By-pass Rd ⓣ04869/222196, ⓦwww.mickeyscottage.com. One of the best homestays with lovely rooms and cottages, all with balconies and some with swinging basket chairs. ❷–❸

Rolex Tourist Home Thekkady Rd ⓣ04869/222465, ⓦwww.thekkadytours.com. Smart new block with a range of attached rooms and good views from the upper floors. ❷–❹

Spice Village Thekkady Rd ⓣ04869/222315, ⓦwww.cghearth.com. Thatched huts and traditional Keralan wood cottages (from $220) in immaculate grounds boasting every imaginable spice and species of tree. Great restaurant and a pool, Keralan cookery classes available, and lots of activities on offer. Book ahead. ❾

Taj Garden Retreat Amalambika Rd ⓣ04869/222273, ⓦwww.tajhotels.com. Luxurious, pseudo-rustic cottages ($165) built to emulate a jungle lodge with great views. There's an elegant restaurant and a pool. ❾

Woodlands Prime Castle Thekkady Rd ⓣ04869/222077. Two separate blocks which share a reception. The *Tourist Bhavan* on the left is cheap and very rudimentary, although clean enough for a short stay; includes Rs75 dorm. The main block is a good mid-range option, with en-suite rooms and some a/c. ❶–❻

Eating

Nearly every Kumily hotel has its own **café-restaurant**, ranging from the *Taj Garden Retreat*'s smart à la carte, to the more traveller-oriented *Coffee Inn*.

Aayam *Lake Queen* hotel, Main Rd. Good veg restaurant in the basement, better than the non-veg *Ginger* upstairs.

Coffee Inn Thekkady Rd. Well-established café serving delicious but slightly overpriced homemade backpacker nosh. With a pleasant wooden terrace and garden, it's a popular place for a lingering breakfast after the early morning boat ride in the sanctuary.

Pepper Garden Coffee House By-pass Rd. Wonderful coffees and teas (both grown in the garden), lassis and excellent breakfasts. Inexpensive and good thalis, and some Chinese and South Indian dishes.

Spice Village Thekkady Rd. Superb restaurant that caters primarily for the tour groups and rich Indian visitors who stay at the hotel; the accent is on multi-cuisine but the chef's speciality is Keralan food. During peak season the dinner buffet (7.30–9.30pm) will cost a whopping Rs500.

Into the sanctuary

Vehicles are allowed in to the Periyar sanctuary from 7am to 6pm. Tickets for the **boat trips** on the lake (daily 7am, 9.30am, 11.30am, 2pm & 4pm; 2hr; Rs55 for lower deck, Rs100 for upper deck) are sold through the Forest Department at their hatch just above the main **visitor centre** (daily 7am–6pm; ⓣ04869/222027, ⓦwww.periyartigerreserve.org) at the end of the road into the park. Those on a tight budget should ask at the centre for spaces on the Forestry Commission boat (same times; Rs15) – but if there are seats, they'll be on the lower deck.

Although it is unusual to see many animals from the boats – engine noise and the presence of a hundred other people make sure of that – you might spot a family group of elephants, wild boar and sambar by the water's edge. Upper decks are best for game viewing, although the seats are often block-booked by the upmarket hotels. To maximize your chances of seeing wildlife, take the 7am boat (wear warm clothing) – the early morning mist is very atmospheric too. Chances of good sightings lessen after heavy rain, as the animals only come to the lake when water sources inside the forest have dried up.

Trekking in the sanctuary (3hr; Rs500 per group, maximum five people) is arranged through the visitor centre (7am, 11am & 1pm). Private guides, who operate on a more flexible time basis, will approach you in Kumily or near the park gates at Thekkady, but some have proven to be unreliable, so it's best to go by word of mouth. The Forest Department also offers full-day treks (8am–6pm; Rs750 per person) and the night Jungle Patrol (7pm, 10pm & 1am; Rs500 per person) around the forest fringe, though this one is more attractive for the atmosphere than the chance of seeing anything other than the odd watchful eye reflecting your torch beam. **Elephant rides** into the park are a bargain at Rs30 for two people (30min) but the pachyderms are often out of commisson.

Accommodation and eating in the sanctuary

Unfortunately, at the time of writing it was not possible to stay in the Forest Department's dilapidated watchtowers, long a star attraction, and there were no immediate plans to reopen them but it's worth checking. For the KTDC properties you should book in advance at its offices in Thiruvananthapuram or Ernakulam – essential if you plan to come on a weekend, a public holiday, or during peak season (Dec–March), when rooms are often in short supply.

Bamboo Grove & Jungle Inn Reserve in advance at the Forest Department's visitor centre in Thekkady. These too are rather overpriced and cramped, but have slightly more facilities and the price includes supper, breakfast, boating and trekking. 7

Forest Department Rest Houses Reserve in advance at the Forest Department's visitor centre in Thekkady. Fairly basic and overpriced accommodation in the woods on the far side of the lake, either at Edappalayam (6 rooms) or Mankavala (2 rooms). Bring your own food. An unforgettable experience – you'll be lucky to get in on a weekend or in December. 5

KTDC Aranya Niwas Near the boat jetty, Thekkady ⓣ04869/222023, ⓦwww.ktdc.com. Plusher than *Periyar House*, a colonial manor with some huge rooms ($100–160), a pleasant garden, a great swimming pool, an excellent multi-cuisine restaurant, a cosy bar and plenty of marauding wild monkeys to keep you entertained. Full board and upper-deck tickets for two boat trips are included in the tariff. 9

KTDC Lake Palace Across the lake from the visitor centre ⓣ04869/222023, ⓦwww.ktdc.com. The sanctuary's most luxurious hotel, with six suites in a converted maharajah's game lodge surrounded by forest, with wonderful views. Charming old-fashioned rooms, great dining and a lovely lawn. This has to be one of the few places in India where you stand a chance of spotting tiger and wild elephant while sipping tea on your own veranda. Full board only at $190 per double room. 9

KTDC Periyar House Midway between the park gates and the boat jetty, Thekkady ⓣ04869/222026, ⓦwww.ktdc.com. Close to the lake, with a restaurant, bar and balcony overlooking the monkey-filled woods leading down to the waterside. Not as nice a location as the neighbouring *Aranya Niwas*, but a lot cheaper. Ask for a lake-facing room. 5–7

Around Periyar and Kumily: the Cardamom hills

Nestled amid mist-covered mountains and dense jungles, Periyar and Kumily are convenient springboards from which to explore Kerala's beautiful **Cardamom hills**. Guides will approach you at Thekkady with offers of trips by jeep; if you can get a group together, these are good value. Among the more popular destinations is the **Mangaladevi temple**, 14km east of Kumily. The rough road to this tumbledown ancient ruin deep in the forest is sometimes closed due to flood damage, but when it is open the round trip takes about five hours. With a guide, you can also reach remote waterfalls and mountain viewpoints, offering panoramic vistas of the Tamil Nadu plains. Rates vary according to the season, but expect to pay around Rs500 for the taxi, and an additional Rs150 for the guide.

High Range Tea Factory

Of places that can be visited under your own steam, the fascinating **High Range Tea Factory** (ⓣ04868/277038) at Puttady (pronounced "Poo-*tee*-dee"), 19km north is a rewarding diversion on the road to Munnar. Regular buses leave from Kumily bus stand; get down at Puttady crossroads, and pick up a rickshaw from there to the factory. Driven by whirring canvas belts, old-fashioned English-made machines chop, sift, and ferment the leaves, which are then dried by wood-fired furnaces and packed into sacks for delivery to the tea auction rooms in Kochi. You can usually be shown around and don't have to arrange the visit, but it's a good idea to phone ahead to check if they are open.

Sabarimala

The other possible day-trip from Kumily, though one that should not be undertaken lightly (or, because of Hindu lore, by pre-menopausal women), is to the Sri Ayappan forest shrine at **Sabarimala**. This remote and sacred site can be reached in a long day, but you should leave with a pack of provisions, as much water as you can carry, and plenty of warm clothes in case you get stranded. Jeep

The Ayappa cult

During December and January, huge crowds of men wearing black or blue *dhotis*, make their way to the Shri Ayappa forest temple (also known as Hariharaputra or Shasta) at **Sabarimala**, in the Western Ghat mountains, around 200km from both Thiruvananthapuram and Kochi. The **Ayappa devotees** can seem disconcertingly ebullient, chanting "*Swamiyee Sharanam Ayappan*" (give us protection, god Ayappa) in a call-and-response style reminiscent of English football fans.

Although he's primarily a Keralan deity, Ayappa's appeal has spread phenomenally in the last thirty years across South India, to the extent that this is said to be the **second largest pilgrimage in the world**, with as many as a million devotees visiting every year. Pilgrims are required to remain celibate, abstain from intoxicants, and keep to a strict vegetarian diet for a period of 41 days prior to setting out on the four-day walk through the forest from the village of **Erumeli** (61km, as the crow flies, northwest) to the shrine at Sabarimala. Rather less devoted devotees take the bus to the village of Pampa, and join the five-kilometre queue. When they arrive at the modern temple complex – a surreal spread of concrete sheds and walkways in the middle of the jungle – pilgrims who have performed the necessary penances may ascend the famous eighteen **gold steps** to the inner shrine. There they worship the deity, throwing donations down a chute that opens onto a subterranean conveyor belt, where the money is counted and bagged for the bank. In recent years, the mass appeal of the Ayappa cult has brought an abundance of rupees to the temple, which now numbers among India's richest, despite being open for only a few months each year. Funds also pour in from the shrine's innumerable spin-off businesses, such as the sale of coconut oil and milk (left by every pilgrim) to a soap manufacturer.

The pilgrimage reaches a climax during the festival of **Makara Sankranti** when massive crowds of over 1.5 million congregate at Sabarimala. On January 14, 1999, 51 devotees were buried alive when part of a hill crumbled under the crush of a stampede. The devotees had gathered at dusk to catch a glimpse of the final sunset of *makara jyoti* (celestial light) on the distant hill of Ponnambalamedu.

Although males of any age and even of any religion can take part in the pilgrimage, females between the ages of nine and fifty are barred. This rule, still vigorously enforced by the draconian temple oligarchy, was contested in 1995 by a bizarre court case. Following complaints to local government that facilities and hygiene at Sabarimala were substandard, the local collector, a 42-year-old woman, insisted she be allowed to inspect the site. The temple authorities duly refused, citing the centuries-old ban on women of menstrual age, but the High Court, who earlier upheld the gender bar, was obliged to overrule the priests' decision. The collector's triumphant arrival at Sabarimala soon after made headline news, but she was still not allowed to enter the shrine proper.

For advice on how to visit Sabarimala, via a back route beginning at Kumily near the Periyar Wildlife Sanctuary, see p.1240.

taxis wait outside Kumily bus stand to transport pilgrims to the less frequented of Sabarimala's two main access points, at a windswept mountain top 13km above the temple (2hr; Rs50 per person if the jeep is carrying ten passengers). Peeling off the main Kumily–Kottayam road at **Vandiperiyar**, the route takes you through tea estates to the start of appallingly rutted forest track. After a long and spectacular climb, this emerges at a grass-covered plateau where the jeeps stop. You proceed on foot, following a well-worn path through superb old-growth jungle – complete with hanging creepers and monkeys crashing through the high canopy – to the temple complex at the foot of the valley. Allow at least two hours for the descent, and an hour or two more for the climb back up to the roadhead, for which you'll need plenty of drinking water. Given the very real risks involved with missing the last jeep back to Kumily (the mountain is prime elephant and tiger country), it's advisable to get a group together and rent a 4WD for the day (about Rs800 plus waiting time).

Munnar and around

MUNNAR, 130km east of Kochi and four-and-a-half hours by bus north of Periyar, is the centre of Kerala's principal tea growing region. Although billed as a "hill station", it is less a Raj-style resort than a scruffy settlement of corrugated iron-roofed cottages and factories, surrounded by vast swathes of rolling green **tea plantations**. All the same, it's easy to see why the pioneering Scottish planters who first developed this hidden valley in the 1900s felt so at home here. At an altitude of around 1600m, the town enjoys a refreshing climate, with crisp winter mornings and relentlessly heavy rain during the monsoons. Hemmed in by soaring mountains – including peninsular India's highest peak, **Ana Mudi** (2695m) – it also boasts a spectacular setting; when the river mist clears, the surrounding summits form a wild backdrop to the carefully manicured plantations carpeting the valley floor and sides.

Munnar's greenery and cool air draw mainly well-heeled honeymooners from Mumbai and Bangalore. However, more and more foreigners are stopping here for a few days, enticed by the spellbinding bus ride from Periyar across the high ridges and through the lush tropical forests of the Cardamom hills, or by the equally spectacular climb across the Ghats from Madurai. The town itself has little of interest, although **hiking** and **cycling** possibilities in the surrounding hills are excellent, with a range of gradients available. One of the best hikes is from Rajamala, 17km north of Munnar, to the **Eravikulam National Park**, home to endangered Nilgiri tahr as well as sambar, macaques and langurs.

The Town and around

Rajophiles will enjoy the prospect of verandaed British bungalows clinging to the side of the shallow valleys, and the famous **High Range Club** on the southeast edge of town, with its manicured lawns and golf course (open to non-residents). Beyond the club sprawl some of the valley's 37 thousand-acre plantations, most of which are owned by the industrial giant, Tata. You can wander freely among the plantations and visit the **Tea Museum** (Tues–Sun 9am–4pm; Rs50), 2km northwest of the centre on Nallathany Road, which contains lots of machinery and information on production techniques.

Munnar has become popular with the young **off-road cycling** posse. There are no official routes, just miles and miles of hills to climb up and speed down. You can **rent** gearless bicycles (Rs10/hr) in the market or proper mountain bikes from either the DTPC office (around Rs250 per day) or KTDC *Tea County* (see opposite) – their top-notch bikes are officially for residents but its worth enquiring if any are available.

Eravikulam National Park and Top Station

Encompassing 100 square kilometres of moist evergreen forest and grassy hill-tops in the Western Ghats, the **Eravikulam National Park** (daily 7am–5pm; Rs50 [Rs10]) 13km northeast of Munnar is the last stronghold of one of the world's rarest mountain goats, the **Nilgiri tahr**. Its innate friendliness made the tahr pathetically easy prey during the hunting frenzy of the colonial era. During a break in his campaign against Tipu Sultan in the late 1790s, the future Duke of Wellington reported that his soldiers were able to shoot the unsuspecting goats as they wandered through his camp. By Independence, the tahr was virtually extinct; today, however, numbers are healthy, and the animals have regained their tameness. To protect the creatures during their calving season, the park is closed for around six weeks from mid-January.

Another popular excursion is the 34-kilometre uphill climb by bus through the subcontinent's highest tea estates to **Top Station**, a tiny hamlet on the Kerala–Tamil Nadu border with superb views across the plains. It's renowned for the very rare **Neelakurunji plant** (*Strobilatanthes*), which grows in profusion on the mountainsides but only flowers once every twelve years, when crowds descend to admire the cascades of violet blossom spilling down the slopes. The next flowering is due in October–November 2006. Top Station is accessible by **bus** from Munnar (10 daily starting at 5.30am; 1hr 30min), and Jeep-taxis will do the round trip for Rs700.

Practicalities

Munnar can be reached by **bus** from Kochi, Kottayam, Kumily and Madurai. State-run and private services all pull into the stand in the modern main bazaar, near the river confluence and Tata headquarters before the state ones terminate at the bus stands nearly 3km south. For most hotels you should ask to be dropped off at Old Munnar, 2km south of the centre, near the ineffectual DTPC **tourist office** (daily 8.30am–7pm; ⓣ04865/231516). A better source of **information** on transport, accommodation and day-trips, including to Eravikulam, is the helpful **Joseph Iype**, who runs the Tourist Information Service (no set hours; ⓣ04865/230349) from a small office in the main bazaar. Immortalized in Dervla Murphy's book *On a Shoestring to Coorg*, this self-appointed tourist officer has become something of a legend. He has some useful **maps** and newspaper articles, can arrange **transport** for excursions, and may well bombard you with background on the area. His office is just south of the independent Munnar Tourist Information Centre (daily 10am–8pm; ⓣ04865/230552), only much use for local tours. You can **change money** at the State Bank of Travancore, the State Bank of India or the two ATMs facing each other on Gandhi Road. **Internet** access is available from a couple of places around town, such as Alpha Computer Centre (Rs50/hr), next to the Tamil Nadu bus stand.

Accommodation and eating

Munnar has plenty of **accommodation**, although budget options are limited and are unfortunately too close to the bazaar bus stand for a peaceful sleep. The *Royal Retreat* and *KTDC Tea County* have highly recommended restaurants with eclectic menus and attentive service, while *Gurus*, in the old bazaar opposite the government high school, is a characterful old-style coffee shop serving South Indian snacks. *Saravana* in the main market serves good vegetarian food while *East End*'s plush mid-priced restaurant is the best in the town centre, with an extensive Indian menu. For a tasty pastry or cake, check out the *Krishna* fast food outlet on Gandhi Street.

East End Temple Rd, across the river from the bus stand ⓣ04865/230451, ⓦwww.edasserygroup.com. Immaculate upmarket hotel close to the centre of town, with Raj-style "cottages" in a big garden, and a recommended restaurant. ❼–❽

Government Guest House Mattupatty Rd ⓣ04865/230385. Near the main bazaar, on the far side of the river, this is a characterful old British bungalow with just six well-refurbished and comfortable rooms; meals are provided by arrangement. Nice garden and location. ❻

High Range Club Kannan Devan Hills ⓣ04865/230253, ⓔhrcmunnar@sify.com. A renowned members' club for a hundred years, now offering cosy rooms in the large Raj-era clubhouse hung with hunting trophies. Knock back the gins, play billiards, golf, tennis, squash, or just read a good book in the beautiful gardens. Full board only. ❺–❼

Hilltop Lodge Corner of Temple Rd and Thekkady Rd ⓣ04865/230655. One of Munnar's best budget deals: small, clean rooms with attached bathrooms (blankets and hot water extra), but with a constant racket of traffic outside. ❷

JJ Cottage Near KSRTC bus stand ⓣ04865/230104. Excellent and very friendly homestay with rooms of varying sizes, the posh two front ones with stunning views of the hills. ❸–❹

KTDC Tea County Off Mattupathy Rd ⓣ04865/230460, ⓦwww.ktdc.com. The grandest address in Munnar, with a range of luxurious chalet style rooms and suites ranged along a hilltop, affording views across the valley. There's a good Indian restaurant, a bar, and a range of sporting and adventure activities, including paragliding and rock climbing. $90–140. ❾

Poopada Kannan Devan hills, on the Manukulam Rd ⓣ04865/230223 ⓦwww.poopada.com. The front looks a bit dilapidated but the good-sized en-suite rooms are clean. Secluded location, fine valley views and a good cheap restaurant. Booking recommended on weekends. ❺–❻

Shree Narayana ("SN") Tourist Home Kannan Devan hills, on the main road near the tourist office ⓣ04865/230212. A popular and cheerful lodge by a river, offering slightly shabby en-suite rooms with hot water. ❹

Kochi (Cochin) and around

The venerable city of **KOCHI** (long known as Cochin), is Kerala's prime tourist destination, spreading across islands and promontories in a stunning location between the Arabian Sea and the backwaters. Its main sections – modern **Ernakulam** and the old peninsular districts of **Mattancherry** and **Fort Cochin** to the west – are linked by a complex system of ferries, and distinctly less romantic bridges. Although some still opt for more convenient Ernakulam, with increased accommodation options, more and more visitors stay in Fort Cochin , where Kochi's complex history is reflected in an assortment of architectural styles. Exotic spice markets, Chinese fishing nets, a synagogue, Portuguese palace, India's first European church, Dutch homes, and a village green that could have been transported from England's Home Counties can all be found within an easy day's walk. Kochi is also one of the few places in Kerala where you are guaranteed **Kathakali dance** performances, both authentic and abridged tourist versions. Around Kochi, a 12km auto-rickshaw or bus ride southeast of Ernakulam, the colonial-style hill palace at **Thripunitra** is now an eclectic museum that stages a music and dance festival in October or November.

Kochi was founded in 1341, when a flood created a natural safe port, replacing Muziris (or Kodungallur, 50km north) as the chief harbour on the Malabar coast. In 1405, the royal family made it their new base, after which the city expanded rapidly, attracting Christian, Arab and Jewish settlers from the Middle East. Its name probably derives from *kocchazhi*, meaning new, or small, harbour.

European involvement in Kochi began in the early 1500s with the Portuguese – followed by the Dutch and British, all wanting to control the port and its lucrative spice trade. In 1800, the state of Cochin became part of the British Madras Presidency and from 1812 until Independence in 1947, was administered by a succession of *diwans*, or finance ministers. In the 1920s, the British expanded the port to make it suitable for modern ocean-going ships and Willingdon Island, between Ernakulam and Fort Cochin, was created by extensive dredging.

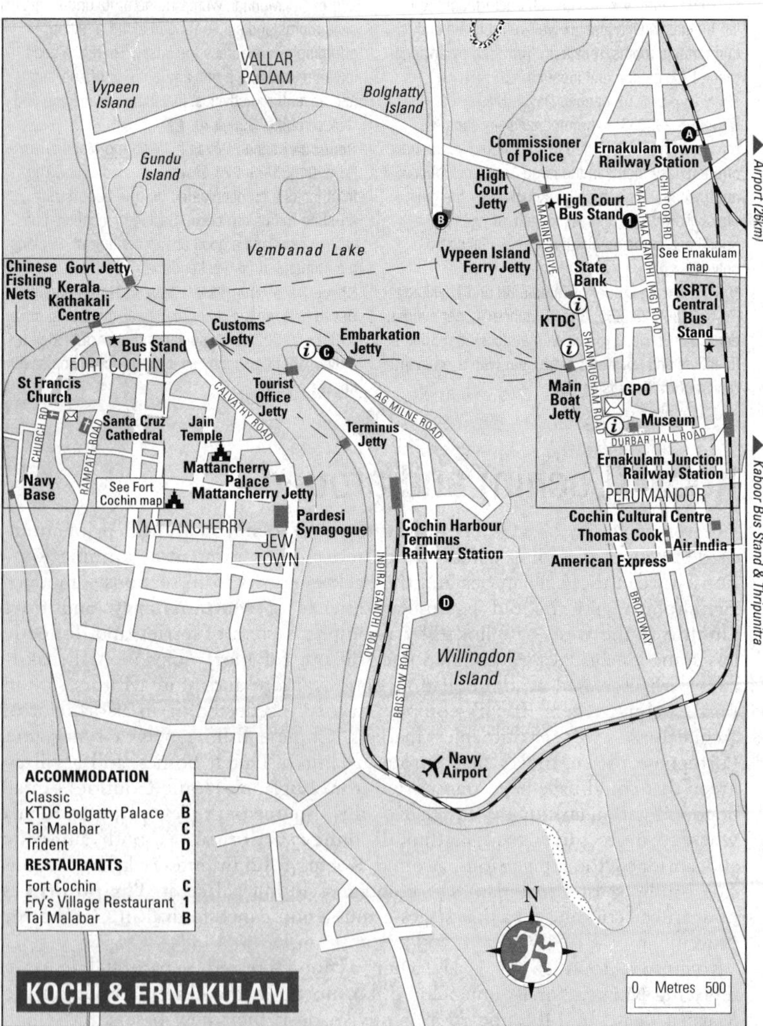

Arrival and local transport

Kochi's **international airport** is at Nedumbassery, near Alwaye (aka Alua), 26km to the north of Ernakulam – a pre-paid taxi into town costs Rs350–375. There are two main **railway stations** – Ernakulam Junction (Ⓣ0484/237 6131) near the centre, and Ernakulam Town (Ⓣ0484/239 5198), 2km further north. No trains run to Fort Cochin or Mattancherry. The Cochin Harbour Terminus, on Willingdon Island, serves the luxury hotels on the island.

The KSRTC **central bus stand** (Ⓣ0484/237 2033), beside the rail line east of MG Road and north of Ernakulam Junction, is for state-run long-distance services. There are also two private bus stands (see box on p.1260): the **Kaloor stand** (rural destinations to the south and east) is across the bridge from Ernakulam Town railway station on the Alwaye Road; while the **High Court stand** (buses to Kumily, for Periyar Wildlife Reserve, and north to Thrissur, Guruvayur and Kodungallur) is opposite the High Court ferry jetty. The Fort Cochin bus stand serves tourist buses and local services to Ernakulam.

Although **auto-rickshaws** are plentiful and reliable in Ernakulam, expect to pay well over the odds across the water in Mattancherry and Fort Cochin. Kochi's excellent **ferry system** (see p.1250) provides a relaxing way to reach the various sectors of town. **Bicycles** can be rented from many of the hotels and guesthouses in Fort Cochin (see p.1252).

Tours and backwater trips

KTDC's half-day **Kochi boat cruise** (daily 9am–12.30pm & 2–5.30pm; Rs100) is a good way to orient yourself. However, it doesn't stop for long in either Mattancherry or Fort Cochin, so give it a miss unless you're pushed for time. Departing from the Sealord Jetty on Shanmugham Road, Ernakulam, it calls at Willingdon Island, the synagogue, Mattancherry Dutch Palace, St Francis Church, the Chinese fishing nets and Bolghatty Island. There is also a daily sunset tour (5.30–7pm; Rs40). Book at the KTDC Reception Centre on Shanmugham Road (Ⓣ0484/235 3234).

The KTDC tourist office and a couple of private companies also operate popular all-day **backwater trips** (see below) out of Kochi. Taking in a handful of coir-making villages north of the city, these are a leisurely and enjoyable way to experience rural Kerala from small hand-punted canoes. KTDC's daily tours cost Rs350, including the car or bus trip to the departure point, 30km north, and a knowledgeable guide. Better value is the excellent trip run by the **tourist desk** (see below) at the Main Boat Jetty (daily 8.30am–5pm; Rs550), which includes hotel pick-up, transfer, a morning cruise on the open backwaters, a village tour, excellent Keralan lunch buffet on board the *kettu vallam* and an afternoon trip through narrow waterways in a much smaller boat.

Information

If you're based on Willingdon Island, head for the helpful **India Tourism** office (Mon–Fri 9am–5.30pm, Sat 9am–noon; Ⓣ0484/266 8352, Ⓦwww.india-tourism.com), between the *Taj Malabar Hotel* and Tourist Office Jetty. It offers information on Kerala and beyond, and can provide reliable guides; it also has a desk at the airport. KTDC's **reception centre**, on Shanmugham Road, Ernakulam (daily 8am–7pm; Ⓣ0484/235 3234, Ⓦwww.ktdc.com) reserves accommodation in its hotel chain and organizes sightseeing and backwater tours (see above); it also has a counter at the airport. The **Kerala Department of Tourism** has a new office (Mon–Sat 10.15am–5pm; no phone, Ⓦwww.keralatourism.com),

Kochi by ferry

Half the fun of visiting Kochi is getting about on the cheap **local ferries**, which depart from the four jetties marked on the map on p.1248. Theoretically, the routes below should work in reverse – however, play safe, and don't rely on getting the last boat. A pamphlet giving the exact ferry timings is available from the ticket hatches by the jetties, and from the helpful tourist desk at the Main Boat Jetty in Ernakulam.

Ernakulam to Fort Cochin

From Ernakulam (Main Jetty) to Fort Cochin (Customs Jetty). Pick up a free timetable at the tourist desk for exact times. First boat 5.55am, every 20–55min until 9.30pm. Journey time 15min. A less frequent express service runs from Ernakulam's High Court Jetty to the Government Jetty in Fort Cochin.

Ernakulam to Mattancherry

From Ernakulam (Main Jetty), via Fort Cochin (Customs Jetty), for Chinese fishing nets, St Francis Church, Dutch Cemetery; Willingdon Island (Terminus Jetty); and Mattancherry Jetty for Jewish Synagogue and Dutch Palace. Journey time 20min. First boat 7.10am, every 90min until 5.40pm.

Ernakulam to Vypeen

From Ernakulam (Main Jetty). This service has two routes: one via Willingdon Island (Embarkation Jetty; 25min), and a fast one to Vypeen (Govt Jetty; 15min); fewer services since the bridge opened. First boat 7am, every 30min–1hr until 9.30pm.

Fort Cochin to Vypeen

From Fort Cochin (Government Jetty) to Vypeen (Government Jetty). Journey time 10min. First boat 6.30am, every 10min until 9pm.

Willingdon Island to Fort Cochin

From the Tourist Office Jetty (Willingdon Island) to Customs Jetty (Fort Cochin). Journey time 10min. First boat 6.30am, every 30min until 6.15pm.

Ernakulam to Bolghatty Island

From Ernakulam (High Court Jetty). Journey time 10min. First boat 6.30am, last 9pm; there are also speedboat taxis (Rs25; free if you are staying at *Bolgatty Palace* hotel)

which hands out excellent maps of the town and backwaters, by the Government Jetty in Fort Cochin. The tiny, independent, award-winning **tourist desk** (daily 8am–6.30pm; ⓣ0484/237 1761, ⓔtouristdesk@satyam.net.in) at the entrance to the Main Boat Jetty in Ernakulam is very friendly and helpful and the best place to check ferry and bus times or pick up free city and state maps. A mine of information on ritual theatre and temple festival dates around the state, the office also publishes a useful South India information guide, arranges daily boat tours, accommodation on houseboats, and runs two excellent guesthouses, one near Kannur (see p.1274) and the other in Wayanad, which should be booked in advance through this office. It has a subsidiary office (same hours; ⓣ0484/221 6129) on Tower Road in Fort Cochin.

Useful local **publications** include the monthly *Jaico Timetable* (Rs10) and the bimonthly *Hello Cochin* (free), which both give comprehensive details of bus, train, ferry and flight times. KTDC publishes an excellent walking tour map and guide to Fort Cochin (free; available from all KTDC tourist offices), which includes a brief history of the area and most important buildings in the Fort area.

Accommodation

The romantic atmosphere of **Fort Cochin** is being rashly exploited, and the growing number of budget guesthouses and upmarket hotels is altering the face of this quaint area. The biggest crisis however, is the **shortage of clean water** that has hit the locals very hard, especially in the high season; if you do stay in Fort Cochin, keep your daily water consumption to a minimum. To help preserve the Fort area, you could opt to stay in **Ernakulam**, which lacks the old-world ambience, but is far more convenient for travel connections and has lots of choice; however its guesthouses and hotels often fill up by late afternoon, so book in advance. The eighteenth-century Dutch palace on the tip of **Bolghatty Island** is a congenial three-star complex, although after years of endless renovation it now possesses little of its once grand charm.

Hotels in Ernakulam and Fort Cochin are marked on their respective maps (p.1255 & p.1257); those on Willingdon and Bolghatty islands appear on the main Kochi/Ernakulam map (p.1248).

Ernakulam

Abad Plaza MG Rd ⓣ0484/238 1122, ⓦwww.abadhotels.com. Comfortable and pleasant business-style high-rise in the centre of Ernakulam, with restaurant and bar, swimming pool and health club. Rs150 for non-residents. ❼–❽

Avenue Regent MG Rd ⓣ0484/237 7977, ⓦwww.avenueregent.com. Very comfortable four-star Best Western affiliate, close to the railway station and main shopping area, with a restaurant, 24hr coffee shop and bar. Expect only the highest standards, as this place doubles as a well-respected hotel-management training college. ❽–❾

Basoto Lodge Press Club Rd ⓣ0484/235 2140, ⓔtouristplanet@yahoo.com. Dependable backpackers' lodge with twelve basic non-a/c rooms. Useful information on offer, but no restaurant. ❶

Bharat Gandhi Square, Durbar Hall Rd ⓣ0484/235 3501, ⓦwww.bharathotel.com. Large, modern hotel with comfortable rooms (non-a/c ones are relatively inexpensive). Two restaurants and Internet access. The *Sulabh* restaurant has tribal decor and excellent cheap food, and there's a 24hr coffee shop. ❺–❼

Cochin Tourist Home Chavar Rd ⓣ0484/237 7577, ⓔcthcochin@sify.com. Cleanest of the cheap hotels lined up outside Ernakulam Junction station, but often full of noisy family and pilgrim groups. There's a dingy organic restaurant in the basement. ❷–❸

Grand MG Rd ⓣ0484/238 2061, ⓦwww.grandhotelkerala.com. Smart hotel, recently upgraded to three-star, where the spacious rooms have wooden flooring, a/c and cable TV. There is a multi-cuisine restaurant and bar on site. ❼–❽

Hakoba Shanmugham Rd ⓣ0484/236 9839. Convenient location midway between Main and High Court Jetties. Dowdy, but all rooms have cable TV, making these harbourside (front) a/c and non-a/c rooms fair value. There's a trendy new coffee bar below the hotel on the ground floor. ❸–❺

Maple Guest House XL/271 Cannonshed Rd ⓣ0484/235 5156. This is the best deal in the district, with cheap, clean non-a/c rooms; the more expensive ones are only slightly bigger. Good location, very close to the main boat jetty. ❷

Metropolitan Chavar Rd ⓣ0484/237 5412, ⓦwww.metropolitancochin.com. Smart business hotel near Ernakulam Junction station that's good for late night arrivals or early morning departures. Multi-cuisine restaurant, 24hr coffee shop and bar. ❻–❼

Modern Guest House XL/6067 Market Rd ⓣ0484/235 2130. Popular place above a (noisy) Keralan veg restaurant, with simple non-a/c rooms with attached bathrooms. If full try the annexe, the *Modern Rest House* (ⓣ0484/236 1407), which has sixteen plain but pleasant rooms that are slightly more expensive. ❷

Saas Tower Cannonshed Rd ⓣ0484/236 5319, ⓦwww.saastower.com. Dependable four-storey block, handy for the Main Jetty, with average a/c and non-a/c rooms. ❸–❺

Yuvarani Residency Jos Junction, MG Rd ⓣ0484/237 7040, ⓦwww.yuvaraniresidency.com. Comfortable, central, well-managed three-star hotel with a choice of carpeted or tiled rooms, all with TV. Excellent seafood restaurant, a well-stocked bar and a street-level coffee shop. 5–7

Fort Cochin

Adams Old Inn Burgher St ⓣ0484/221 7595, ⓔadamsoldinn@hotmail.com. Great family-run guesthouse in a well-restored period building; the rooms are modern and one has a/c and a balcony. There is a decent rooftop dorm (Rs100) and a small rooftop terrace. 2–3

Brunton Boatyard Bellar Rd, next to Fort Cochin Jetty ⓣ0484/221 8221, ⓦwww.cghearth.com. Luxury chain hotel, built on the site of an eighteenth-century British boatyard; the look is Keralan carved wood and whitewash, with beautifully designed, breezy a/c rooms and balconies overlooking the bay. Three speciality restaurants and a pool edging onto the lake. $200–275. 9

Chiramel Residency 1/296 Lilly St ⓣ0484/221 7310, ⓦwww.chiramelhomestay.com. A great seventeenth-century heritage homestay, with five carefully restored rooms around a congenial communal sitting room; the lofty non-a/c rooms all have big wooden beds, teak floors and modern bathrooms; some have balconies. The welcoming and warm owners live downstairs. 5–6

Delight Ridsdale Rd, opposite the Parade Ground ⓣ0484/221 7658, ⓦwww.delightfulhomestay.com. Another attractive homestay, with distinctive white latticework, run by a friendly, helpful and eco-conscious family. Seven spacious, comfortable and airy rooms (a couple a/c) and a pleasant, leafy courtyard garden. Breakfast available. 3–7

Elite Princess St ⓣ0484/221 5733. Several floors of basic but clean and cheap non-a/c rooms and a few a/c, all attached. Very popular restaurant and pleasant rooftop garden. Foreign exchange. 2–5

Fort House 2/6A Calvathy Rd ⓣ0484/221 7103, ⓦwww.forthousecochin.com. Pleasant non a/c rooms and bamboo huts ranged around an interesting if eccentric compound, littered with pots and statues. Café serving delicious seafood, and a waterfront jetty, though none of the rooms overlooks the lake. Mosquito screens and nets. 6

Malabar House Residency 1/268 Parade Rd ⓣ0484/221 6666, ⓦwww.malabarhouse.com. Beautiful, historic mansion renovated with a highly successful mix of old-world charm and delightful European designer chic. The Keralan temple-style pool in the minimalist courtyard is stunning, and there's an excellent restaurant. Tariff includes breakfast. $150–250. 9

Spencer Home 1/298 Parade Rd ⓣ0484/221 5049. Characterful place set in an old, rambling Portuguese house, with eleven large and spotless a/c and non-a/c rooms, all facing the pretty communal garden. 4–6

Walton's Homestay Princess St ⓣ0484/221 5309, ⓔcewalton@rediffmail.com. Excellent homestay run by an interesting and philosophical gentleman in a centuries-old Dutch house. One cheaper single available. Facilities include an exchange library and communal breakfast for Rs50 pp. 5–6

Willingdon and Bolghatty islands

KTDC Bolgatty Palace Bolghatty Island ⓣ0484/275 0500, ⓦwww.ktdc.com. Extensively renovated palace in a beautiful location, a short hop from High Court Jetty. The main building, built by the Dutch in 1744 and later home of the British Resident, is now a three-star hotel with twenty deluxe rooms; there are also six "honeymoon" cottages on stilts right at the water's edge. Reserve through any KTDC tourist office, and come armed with mosquito repellent. At weekends, the adjacent KTDC canteen and bar is noisy with day-trippers. 8–9

Taj Malabar Willingdon Island, by Tourist Office Jetty ⓣ0484/266 6811, ⓦwww.tajhotels.com. Pinky-orange tower block in a superb location on the tip of the island with sweeping views of the bay; the old "heritage" wing, waterfront gardens and pool have been extensively refurbished, and the whole place oozes *Taj* style and quality. $170–220. 9

Trident Bristow Rd, Willingdon Island ⓣ0484/266 6816, ⓦwww.tridentcochin.com. Despite the grey dockyard environs, this new hotel is the most intimate and congenial of the five-stars on the island, with interesting displays of Keralan tribal and household artefacts, a pool in a tropical oasis, a restaurant, bar and a range of luxurious rooms. Officially $120–170 but discounts often available. 9

Mattancherry and Fort Cochin

With high-rise development restricted to Ernakulam, across the water, the old-fashioned character of **Mattancherry** and **Fort Cochin** remains intact, with glimpses of Kochi's past greeting you at virtually every turn. Approaching Mattancherry jetty by ferry, the shoreline, with its tiled roofs and pastel-coloured buildings, offers a view that can't have changed for centuries.

Despite the revenue brought in by tourism, traditional trade is still the most important activity here. Barrows loaded with sacks of produce trundle between *godowns* (warehouses), and there are numerous little shops where you can negotiate prices for tea, jute, rubber, chillies, turmeric, cashew, ginger, cardamom and pepper.

Jew Town

The road heading left from Mattancherry Jetty leads into the district known as **Jew Town**, where N.X. Jacob's tailor shop and the offices of J.E. Cohen, advocate and tax consultant, serve as reminders of a once-thriving Jewish community. The area is now occupied by a sizeable population of Kashmiris, entrepreneurial as always and quite aggressive in their touting for trade. The hassle-factor is partially defused by the sheer variety of goods on sale: antiques, Hindu and Christian wood-carvings, oil lamps, masks, spice boxes and other bric-a-brac, plus some tempting coffee-table books.

Turning right at the India Pepper & Spice Trade Building, usually resounding with the racket of dealers shouting the latest prices, and then right again, brings you into Synagogue Lane. The **Pardesi (White Jew) Synagogue** (Mon–Thurs & Sun 10am–noon & 3–5pm; Rs2) was founded in 1568, and rebuilt in 1664. Its interior is an attractive, if incongruous, hotchpotch; note the floor, paved with hand-painted eighteenth-century blue and white tiles from Canton, each unique, depicting a love affair between a mandarin's daughter and a commoner. Opposite the entrance, an elaborately carved Ark houses four scrolls of the *Torah* (the first five books of the Old Testament), encased in silver and gold, on which are placed gold crowns presented by the maharajas of Travancore and Cochin, testifying to good relations with the Jewish community.

An attendant is usually available to show visitors around and answer questions, and his introductory talk features as part of the KTDC guided tour (see p.1249).

The Jews of Kochi

According to tradition, the **Myuchasim Jews**, who were the first to arrive on the Malabar coast, were fleeing from the occupation of Jerusalem by Nebuchadnezzar, in 587 BC. However another legend claims that the first Jews arrived in the eleventh century BC, as part of King Solomon's trading fleet. Whatever the truth, the Jews settled in Cranganore, just north of Cochin, to trade in spices. They remained respected members of Keralan society and even had their own ruler until the arrival of the Portuguese Inquisition in the early sixteenth century.

At that time, when Jews were being burned at the stake in Goa, and evicted elsewhere along the coast, the raja of Cochin gave them a parcel of land adjoining the royal palace in Mattancherry. A new Jewish community was created and a synagogue built. The Jews were in demand as they spoke Malayalam, and trading was in their blood; the community thrived during the great trading period under the more liberal and supportive Dutch and later British rule.

There were three distinct groups of Jews in Kerala. The **Black** Jews were employed as labourers in the spice business, and their community of thousands resulted from the earliest Jewish settlers marrying and converting Indians; **Brown** Jews are thought to have been slave converts. **White** Jews considered both groups inferior to themselves; they were orthodox and married only among their number. However, by the early 1950s, most of Kochi's Jews emigrated when they were given free passage to Israel. The White Jews' traditional ways of life are on the verge of disappearing as only seven families survive, and their ideals and values have inevitably moved with the times.

Outside, in a small square, several antique shops are worth a browse – but don't expect a bargain.

Draavidia, on Jew Street, is a small but active art **gallery** with an emphasis on contemporary work. Live "Sadhana" Indian **classical music** concerts are staged here daily (6–7pm); admission Rs100.

Mattancherry Palace

Mattancherry Palace (daily except Fri 10am–5pm; Rs2) stands on the left side of the road a short walk from the Mattancherry Jetty in the opposite direction to Jew Town. The gateway on the road is, in fact, the back entrance, but the most accessible way from the ferry. In the walled grounds behind the gate stands a circular, tiled Krishna temple (closed to non-Hindus).

Known locally as the **Dutch Palace**, the two-storey building was actually erected by the Portuguese, as a gift to the Cochin raja, Vira Keralavarma (1537–61) – though the Dutch did add to the complex. While its squat exterior is not particularly striking, the interior is captivating. The **murals** that adorn some of its rooms are among the finest examples of Kerala's much underrated school of painting; friezes illustrating stories from the *Ramayana*, on the first floor, date from the sixteenth century. Packed with detail and gloriously rich colour, the style is never strictly naturalistic; the treatment of facial features is pared down to the simplest of lines for the mouths, and characteristically aquiline noses. Downstairs, the women's bedchamber holds several less complex paintings, possibly dating from the 1700s.

While the paintings are undoubtedly the highlight of the palace, the collection also includes interesting Dutch maps of old Cochin, coronation robes belonging to past maharajas, royal palanquins, weapons and furniture. Without permission from the Archeological Survey of India, **photography** is strictly prohibited.

Jain temple

A few hundred metres west of the palace, on Gujarati Road, the **Jain temple** is open to all. It's a peaceful place, except at noon when one devotee religiously (and loudly) rings a bell to announce the daily feeding of the local pigeons. At this point the courtyard becomes a mini Trafalgar Square and anyone around is encouraged to help dish out grain to the hungry birds. There are two airy marble sanctuaries with some delicate carving to admire in the compound and the office staff are glad to supply information about Jainism.

Fort Cochin

The heart of the fort area is some three kilometres from Mattancherry Palace, reachable by foot, ferry or auto-rickshaw. The architecture in this historic enclave is strongly European, with fine houses built by wealthy British traders, and Dutch cottages with split farmhouse doors. Photogenic Chinese fishing nets line the waterside on the northwestern tip and Princess Street.

Tourism development has inevitably led to the construction of more guesthouses, so altering the face of the area, while the added water demand is threatening the community's fragile infrastructure. For a while Fort Cochin was being protected as a "**Heritage Zone**", by way of a grant from USAID, but this was unfortunately cut following India's nuclear tests in 1998.

Fort Cochin has a small but active **arts scene** based around the *Kashi Art Café* (daily 8.30am–7.30pm) on Burgher Street, which has a gallery exhibiting contemporary art, occasional musical performances, news of eco-events and a relaxed café space.

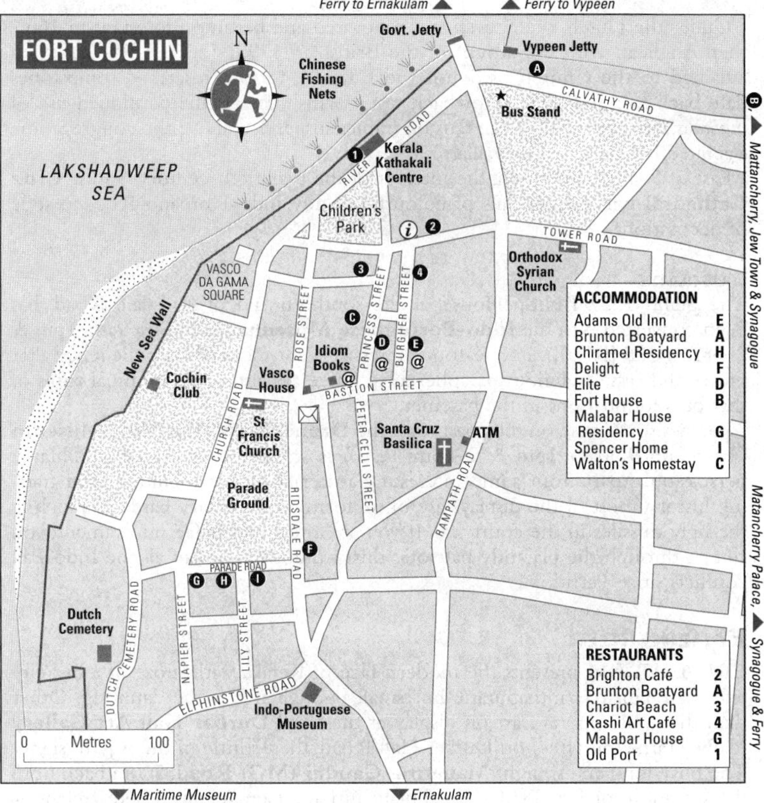

Chinese fishing nets

The huge, elegant **Chinese fishing nets** that line the northern shore of Fort Cochin add grace to an already characterful waterside view, and are probably the single most familiar photographic image of Kerala. Traders from the court of Kublai Khan are said to have introduced them to the Malabar region. Known in Malayalam as *cheena vala*, they can also be seen throughout the backwaters further south. The nets, which are suspended from arced poles and operated by levers and weights, require at least four men to control. You can buy fresh fish from the tiny market here and have it grilled at the adjacent stalls, often a safer bet than the fried fish on display, which may have been cooked in old oil.

St Francis Church and around

South of the Chinese fishing nets on Church Road, the continuation of River Road, stands the church of **St Francis**, the first built by Europeans in India. It overlooks the large typically English village green, known locally as the **Parade Ground**. The exact age of the church is not known, though the stone structure dates back to the early sixteenth century; the land was a gift of the local raja, and the title deeds, written on palm leaf, are still kept inside. The facade, with its multi-curved sides, became the model for most Christian churches in India. Vasco da Gama was buried here in 1524, but his body was later removed to Portugal.

Under the Dutch, the church was renovated and became Protestant in 1663, then Anglican with the advent of the British in 1795; since 1949 it has been attached to the Church of South India. Inside, various inscribed tombstones date back to 1562. One throwback from British days is the continued use of *punkahs*, large swinging cloth fans on frames suspended above the congregation, operated by the "punkah-wallah".

East of St Francis church, the interior of the twentieth-century **Santa Cruz Cathedral** will delight fans of colourful, gaudy Indo-Romano-Rococo style of decoration.

Museums

The grand 1557 Bishop House, at the southern end of Ridsdale Road, has been converted into the **Indo-Portuguese Museum** (Tues–Sun 9am–1pm & 2–6pm; Rs25 [Rs10]), a none-too-impressive assortment of Catholic relics, altar pieces and other religious paraphernalia. There are also some minimal ruins of the fort's foundations in the basement.

Further southwest, on the coast road, the **Dronacharya Maritime Museum** (Tues–Sun 9.30am–1pm & 2–6pm; Rs10) is strictly for those of a militarist persuasion. Apart from some interesting material on early cultural and trading history, most of the displays are of uniforms and military hardware, such as the ugly missiles in the courtyard. If you are a real sucker for punishment, you can sit through the blatantly patriotic thirty-minute video of all the Indo-Pak conflicts since Partition.

Ernakulam

ERNAKULAM presents the modern face of Kerala, with more of a big-city feel than Thiruvananthapuram, but small enough not to be daunting. Other than the contemporary art on display at the small **Durbar Hall Art Gallery** (daily 11am–7pm; free) on Durbar Hall Road, there's little in the way of sights. The busy, long and straight **Mahatma Gandhi (MG) Road**, 500m back from the sea, more or less divides Ernakulam in half; main activities here are shopping, eating and movie-going. Here you can email and phone to your heart's content, and choose from an assortment of great places to eat excellent Keralan food.

An eight-day annual **festival** (Jan/Feb) at the Shiva temple, on Durbar Hall Road in Ernakulam, features elephant processions and *panchavadyam* (drum and trumpet groups) out in the street. As part of the festival, there are usually night-time performances of Kathakali, and the temple is decorated with an amazing array of electric lights: banks of coloured tubes and sequenced bulbs imitating shooting stars.

Thripunitra

Some 12km southeast of Ernakulam and a short bus or auto-rickshaw ride from the bus stand MG Road just south of Jos Junction, the small suburban town of **THRIPUNITRA** is worth a visit for its dilapidated colonial-style **Hill Palace** (Tues–Sun 9am–5pm; Rs10), now an eclectic museum. The royal family of Cochin at one time maintained around forty palaces – this one was confiscated by the state government after Independence, and has slipped into dusty decline over the past decade.

One of the museum's finest exhibits is an early-seventeenth-century wooden *mandapa* removed from a temple in Pathanamthitta, featuring excellent carvings of the coronation of the monkey king Sugriva and other themes from the

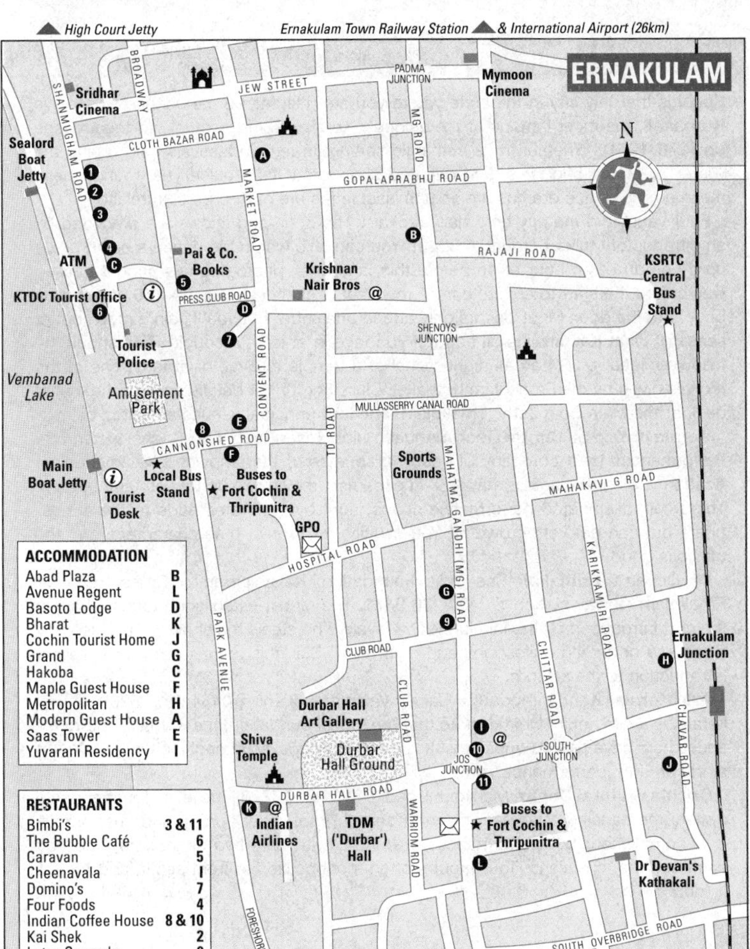

Ramayana. Sculpture, ornaments and weapons in the bronze gallery include a *kingini katti* knife, whose decorative bells belie the fact that it was used for beheading, and a body-shaped cage in which condemned prisoners would be hanged while birds pecked them to death. Providing the place isn't crowded with noisy school groups here to see the nearby deer park, the garden behind the palace is a peaceful spot to picnic beneath the cashew trees.

Performances of theatre, classical music and dance, including consecutive all-night **Kathakali** performances, are held over a period of several days during the annual festival (Oct/Nov) at the **Shri Purnatrayisa temple** on the way to the palace. Inside the temple compound, both in the morning and at night, massed drum orchestras perform *chenda melam* in procession with fifteen caparisoned elephants. At night, the outside walls of the sanctuary are covered with thousands

Kathakali in Kochi

Kochi is the only city in the state where you are guaranteed the chance to see live **Kathakali**, the most famous of the uniquely Keralan forms of ritualized theatre (see pp.1270–1271). Whether in its authentic setting, in temple festivals held during the winter or at the shorter tourist-oriented shows that take place year-round, these mesmerizing dance dramas are an unmissable feature of Kochi's cultural life.

Four venues in the city hold daily recitals. The hour-long shows are preceded by an introductory talk at around 6.30pm. You can also watch the dancers being made up if you arrive an hour or so before this, and keen photographers should turn up well before the start to ensure a front-row seat. Tickets cost Rs100–150 and can be bought at the door. Most visitors only attend one show, but you'll gain a much better sense of what Kathakali is all about if you take in at least a couple. This should be followed, ideally, with an all-night recital at a temple festival, or at least one of the recitals given by the Ernakulam Kathakali Club. For further details contact the tourist desk at the Main Boat Jetty, Ernakulam. The four principal venues are listed below:

Kerala Kathakali Centre Cochin Aquatic Club, River Road, Fort Cochin waterfront. Performances by a company of young graduates of the renowned Kalamandalam Academy. What the actors may lack in expertise, they make up for with enthusiasm. The small, dilapidated performance space, right by the water, adds to the atmosphere but can get very crowded. You usually get to see three characters, and the music is good.

Dr Devan's Kathakali See India Foundation, Kalathiparambil Cross Rd, near Ernakulam railway station ⓣ0484/236 9471. The oldest-established tourist show in the city, introduced by the inimitable Dr Devan, who steals the show with his lengthy discourse on Indian philosophy and mythology. Still, this constitutes and excellent introduction to the art form.

Art Kerala Kannanthodathu Lane, Valanjambalam ⓣ0484/237 5238 ⓔart_kerala@satyam.net.in. Next door to the See India Foundation, the Kathakali performances here have proved popular with large tour groups, so expect a crowd. Make-up starts at 6pm, performance 7pm.

Cochin Cultural Centre Manikath Road ⓣ0484/236 7866. The least commendable option: the dancing at this a/c theatre ("sound-proof, insect-proof, and dust-proof") is accomplished, but performances are short, with only two characters, and you can't see the musicians. Tour groups often monopolize the front seats, and the PA is loud.

of tiny oil lamps. Although the temple is normally closed to non-Hindus, admittance to appropriately dressed visitors is usually allowed at this time.

Continuing eastwards from Thripunitra, the road leads through Muvattupuzha to **KADALIKAD**, 55km east of Kochi in the direction of Munnar. Here, the **Haritha Farms** homestay (ⓣ04865/260216, ⓦwww.harithafarms.com; ❻–❼), an organic farm practising permaculture, makes a relaxing base for exploring the surrounding countryside. Accommodation is in four en-suite cottages, and vegetarian meals are included in the price; Keralan vegetarian cooking classes are offered from June to August.

Eating

Unusually for Keralan cities, Kochi offers a wide choice for **eating out**, from the delicious fresh-cooked fish by the Chinese fishing nets at Fort Cochin to the sophistication of the *Brunton Boatyard*. Between the two extremes, various popular and modestly priced places in Ernakulam include authentic Keralan dishes on their menus. If you're eating out across the water from your hotel, make sure you are familiar with the ferry timings back to your accommodation (see box p.1250).

Unless otherwise stated, restaurants under the "Ernakulam" and "Fort Cochin" headings are marked on their relevant maps (see p.1257 & p.1255); all others appear on the main Kochi and Ernakulam map (p.1248).

Ernakulam

Bimbi's Shanmugham Rd and Jos Junction. Indian-style fast food joints. Hugely popular for inexpensive Udupi, north Indian and Chinese snacks and meals, and the tangiest *wada-sambars* in town. They also do a great selection of shakes and ice creams.

The Bubble Café *Taj Residency*, Marine Drive. Luxury coffee shop in a vast conservatory, serving pricey snacks and a particularly good range of Western cakes (Dundee, plum, palmettes and fudge).

Caravan Broadway, near the KTDC tourist office. Air-conditioned ice-cream parlour that's a good place to chill out over a banana split or milkshake. Open until midnight so you can nip in for a late dessert.

Cheenavala *Yuvarani Residency*, MG Rd. Restaurant specializing in seafood dishes. The excellent food is accompanied by gentle live fusion music every night except Tuesday.

Domino's Esplanade Complex, Canal Rd ⓣ1600/111 123. Pizzas here all come with extra chilli and topping options that reflect Keralan cuisine, and deliveries to hotels are free.

Four Foods Shanmugham Rd. Busy, clean and popular roadside restaurant serving veg and non-veg meals, including generous thalis, fish dishes and a good-value "dish of the day". For dessert, try the Mumbai-style *faloodas*, vermicelli steeped in syrup with dried fruits and ice cream.

Fry's Village Restaurant Chittoor Rd, adjacent to Mymoor cinema (see main Kochi map). Moderately priced, ultra-spicy Keralan and "ethnic" specialities served in style, including the Calicut Muslim delicacy *patthri*, wafer-thin rice pancakes, *iddliappam* dumplings, and *puthoo* (steamed rice cakes).

Indian Coffee House Corner of Cannonshed Rd/Park Ave, and Jos Junction. The usual excellent coffee, veg and non-veg meals and simple snacks such as *dosa* and omelettes.

Kai Shek Shanmugham Rd. Very smart upmarket restaurant owned and managed by the Casino Group of hotels. Excellent Keralan fish dishes, crab specialities, good north Indian cuisine and some Continental food.

Lotus Cascade *Woodlands Hotel*, Woodlands Junction, MG Rd. Classy veg Indian food, with plenty of tandoori options, at bargain prices. Great service too.

Sayanna *Sealord* hotel, Shanmugham Rd. Reasonably priced rooftop restaurant serving good Chinese, Indian and sizzlers. The harbour view is not what it was since the shopping centre opposite was built, but it's still a great spot for a chilled beer.

Utsav *Taj Residency*, Marine Drive. Expensive à la carte Indian restaurant. The Rs320 lunchtime buffets (noon–2.45pm) are better value and you get a matchless view over the harbour and bay at noon. At night, the twinkling lights make this the place for a very romantic dinner.

Fort Cochin

Brighton Café Tower Rd. Fair fish'n'chips and cheap curries in this simple eatery. No peppermint rock though.

Brunton Boatyard Calvathy Rd, next to Fort Cochin Jetty. The expensive menu comprises a broad selection of dishes designed to reflect all the cultural influences that have played a part in the history of Kochi, including Lebanese, Portuguese, British Raj, Dutch, Jewish and, of course, Keralan. Unfortunately, it is à la carte and you end up just wanting to try everything.

Chariot Beach Princess St. Huge variety of seafood and Chinese dishes at reasonable prices, and you can eat alfresco on the small terrace.

Kashi Art Café Burgher St. Great café and exhibition space in a restored old building, with chilled vibes and music. Healthy light meals, cakes, and excellent breakfasts and coffees served all day. Check the noticeboards for details of events and festivals.

Malabar House 1/268 Parade Rd. Superb restaurant where you can wine and dine to live classical music every evening, either at the poolside or at indoor tables. The seafood platter is tastefully arranged and tastes sensational. Not cheap, but excellent value.

Old Port River Rd. Great location for a relaxing night right by the Chinese fishing nets. Offers a good range of fish, seafood, beef, pork and veg, both Indian and Western style. Surreptitious beer possible.

Willingdon Island

Fort Cochin *Casino Hotel* ⓣ0484/266 8221. This seafood restaurant is considered to create some of the best fish dishes in India. You select from a

Moving on from Kochi/Ernakulam

For an overview of travel services to and from Kochi/Ernakulam, see "Travel details" on pp.1275–1276.

By air

The international airport (☎484/261 0113) at **Nedumbassery**, near Alwaye (aka Alua), is 26km north of Ernakulam and caters predominantly for flights to and from the Gulf States like **Doha**, **Sharjah**, **Kuwait** and **Muscat**. Jet Airways, Indian Airlines and Air India also operate domestic flights from here to **Bangalore**, **Chennai**, **Delhi**, **Goa**, **Mumbai** and **Thiruvananthapuram**. For flights to the **Lakshadweep Islands** contact *Casino Hotel*, Willingdon Island (see p.1259). For details of airlines and travel agents, see Listings on p.1263.

By bus

Buses leave Ernakulam's KSRTC Central bus stand for virtually every town in Kerala, and some beyond; most, but not all, are bookable in advance at the bus station (reservation enquiries ☎0484/237 2033). Travelling south, dozens of buses each day run to **Thiruvananthapuram**; most go via **Alappuzha** and **Kollam**, but a few go via **Kottayam**. It's also possible to travel all the way to **Kanniyakumari** (9hr). However, for destinations further afield in Karnataka and Tamil Nadu, you're much better off on the train, although KSRTC's "super express" and private "luxury" buses travel to these destinations. Agents include Sharma Travels, *Grand Hotel*, Jos Junction, MG Road (☎0484/235 0712); Indira Travels, also near Jos Junction (☎0484/236 0693); Sona Travels (☎0484/262 3984); and SMP Travels (☎0484/235 3080).

By train

Kochi lies on Kerala's main broad-gauge line, and sees frequent trains down the coast to Thiruvananthapuram, via Kottayam, Kollam and Varkala. Heading north, there are plenty of services to Thrissur, and thence northeast across Tamil Nadu to Chennai, but only a couple run direct to Mangalore. Since the opening of the Konkan Railway, however, a few superfast trains travel along the coast to Goa and Mumbai, stopping close to Mangalore.

Although most long-distance express and mail trains depart from **Ernakulam Junction**, a couple of key services leave from **Ernakulam Town**. To confuse matters further, a few also start at Cochin Harbour station, so be sure to check the departure point when you book your ticket. The main reservation office, good for trains leaving all three stations, is at Ernakulam Junction (☎131 for general enquiries). For more on Kochi's railway stations, see p.1249.

The trains listed below are recommended as the fastest and/or most convenient services from Kochi. If you're heading to **Alappuzha** for the backwater trip

display of the catch of the day, and then choose the style of preparation, which is all done in front of you. Absolutely delicious, but very expensive and the decor is dull.

Taj Malabar Willingdon Island ☎0484/266 6811. Two restaurants: the *Jade Pavilion* for Chinese and *Rice Boats* serving Western, north Indian and Keralan dishes in a beautiful waterside location. The food is excellent and prices reflect this; the Rs250 lunchtime buffet includes veg and non-veg dishes and is good value.

Listings

Airlines, domestic: Indian Airlines, Durbar Hall Rd ☎0484/237 1141, ⓦwww.indian-airlines.com; Jet Airways, Bab Chambers, Atlantis, MG Rd ☎0484/235 9212, ⓦwww.jetairways.com.

Airlines, international: Air India, 35/1301 MG

to Kollam, take the bus, as the only train that can get you there in time invariably arrives late.

Recommended trains from Kochi/Ernakulam

Destination	Name	Number	Station	Frequency	Departs	Total time
Bangalore	Kanniyakumari–Bangalore Express	#6525	ET	daily	5.55pm	13hr
Mumbai	Netravati Express	#6346	EJ	daily	2.10pm	26hr 50min
Chennai	Trivandrum–Chennai Mail	#2624	ET	daily	7.05pm	11hr 55min
Delhi	Rajdhani Express*	#2431	EJ	Tues & Thurs	10.50pm	39hr
	Kerala Express	#2625	EJ	daily	3.40pm	48hr 20min
Madgaon/Margao (Goa)	Rajdhani Express*	#2431	EJ	Tues & Thurs	10.50pm	12hr 35min
	Mangala–Lakshadweep Express	#2617	EJ	daily	12.45pm	14hr 25min
Mangalore	Malabar Express	#6029	ET	daily	11.30pm	10hr 45min
	Parasuram Express	#6349	ET	daily	11.00am	10hr 30min
Thiruvananthapuram	Parasuram Express	#6350	ET	daily	1.50pm	5hr 5min
	Ernakulam–Trivandrum Express	#6341	EJ	daily	6.15am	4hr 10min
Varkala	Parasuram Express	#6350	ET	daily	1.50pm	3hr 43min

EJ = Ernakulam Junction
ET = Ernakulam Town
* = a/c only, meals included.

Rd, Ravipuram ☎0484/235 1295; British Airways, c/o Nijhwan Travels, MG Rd ☎0484/236 4867; Air France, Old Thevara Rd ☎0484/237 0250; Egypt Air, c/o ABC International, Sreekandath Rd ☎0484/235 3457; Gulf Air, c/o Jet Air, Atlantic Junction, MG Rd ☎0484/235 9242; Kuwait Airways, c/o National Travel Service, MG Rd ☎0484/235 9114; Saudi Arabian Airlines, c/o Arafaath Travels, MG Rd ☎0484/235 2689; Singapore Airlines/Silk Air, Aviation Travels, 35/2433 MG Rd, Ravipuram ☎0484/235 8129; Sri Lankan Airlines, Trans Lanka Ltd, MG Rd ☎0484/236 1215; Air Maldives, Cathay Pacific and KLM/Northwest c/o Spencer & Co, Arya Vaidya Sala Buildings, 35/718 MG Rd ☎0484/238 0517.

Ayurvedic treatment Although widely advertized, the following two come highly recommended: Kerala Ayurveda Pharmacy, Warriom Rd, off MG Rd ☎0484/236 1202 (Rs350–400 for 1hr 30min massage); and PNVM Shanthigiri, Thrikkakara ☎0484/255 8879 (Rs300 per session), on the northern outskirts.

Banks Branches on MG Rd in Ernakulam include: ANZ Grindlays; State Bank of India (which also has a branch opposite the KTDC Tourist Reception Centre); and Andhra Bank. To exchange travel-

The Lakshadweep Islands

Visitors to Kochi in search of an exclusive tropical paradise may well find it in **LAKSHADWEEP** (ⓦwww.lakshadweep.nic.in), the "one hundred thousand islands" which lie between 200km and 400km offshore in the deep blue of the Arabian Sea. The smallest Union Territory in India, Lakshadweep's 27 tiny, coconut-palm-covered **coral islands** are the archetypal tropical hideaway, edged with pristine white sands and surrounded by calm lagoons where average water temperature stays around 26°C all year. Beyond the lagoons lie the coral **reefs**, home to sea turtles, dolphins, eagle rays, lionfish, parrotfish, octopus and predators like barracudas and sharks. Devoid of animal and bird life, only ten of the islands are inhabited, with a total population of just over 50,000, the majority of whom are Malayalam-speaking Sunni Muslims said to be descended from seventh-century Keralan Hindus who converted to Islam.

The main sources of income are fishing and coconuts. Fruit, vegetables and pulses are cultivated in small quantities but staples such as rice and many other commodities have always had to be imported. The Portuguese, who discovered the value of **coir rope**, spun from coconut husk, controlled Lakshadweep during the sixteenth century; when they imposed an import tax on rice, locals retaliated by poisoning some of the forty-strong Portuguese garrison – and terrible reprisals followed. As Muslims, the islanders enjoyed friendly relations with Tipu Sultan of Mysore, which naturally aroused the ire of the British, who moved in at the end of the eighteenth century and remained until Independence, when Lakshadweep became a Union Territory.

Visiting Lakshadweep

Concerted attempts are being made to minimize the ecological impact of tourism in Lakshadweep. At present, accommodation is available for **non-residents of India** on only two of the islands – Bangaram and Kadmat. Indian tourists are also allowed to visit the neighbouring islands of Kavarattu and Minicoy (both closed to foreigners).

All visits to **Kadmat** must be arranged in Kochi through the Society for Promotion of Recreational Tourism and Sports (SPORTS) on IG Road, Willingdon Island (ⓣ0484/266 8387, ⓦwww.lakshadweeptourism.com). SPORTS offers a six-day package cruise to Kadmat ($450 per person for non-a/c, $500 for a/c) on one of their

lers' cheques, the best places are: Thomas Cook (Mon–Sat 9.30am–6pm), near the Air India Building at Palal Towers, MG Rd; or Surana Financial Corporation next door. Among the increasing number of ATMs are: in Ernakulam Syndicate Bank, opposite *Hotel Hakoba*, Shanmugham Rd, and South India Bank, outside *Yuvarani Residency*, MG Rd; in Fort Cochin SBI, at *Fort Avenue* homestay, and South India Bank, next to Santa Cruz Basilica.

Bookstores Idiom, opposite the Synagogue, Jew Town, Mattancherry and on Bastion St near Princess St, Fort Cochin are wonderful places to browse for books on travel, Indian and Keralan culture, flora and fauna, religion and art; there's also an excellent range of non-fiction.

Cinemas Sridhar Theatre, Shanmugham Rd, near the *Sealord* hotel, screens English-language movies daily; check the listings pages of the *Indian Express* or *Hindu* (Kerala edition) to find out what's on. For the latest Malayalam and Hindi releases, head for the comfortable a/c Mymoon cinema at the north end of Chitoor Rd, or the Saritha Savitha Sangeetha, at the top of Market Rd.

Handicrafts On MG Rd, try: Kairali; Khadi Bhavan; Khataisons Curio Palace; Surabhi Kerala State Handicrafts; Coirboard Showroom (for coir carpets). For good quality Keralan, Portuguese and Dutch antiques, head over to Jew St, although you'll have to bargain extremely hard.

Hospitals General, Hospital Rd (ⓣ0484/236 0002); City, MG Rd (ⓣ0484/236 1809); Government, Fort Cochin (ⓣ0484/221 6444).

Internet access There are numerous outlets in travel agencies and hotel receptions along Princess St in Fort Cochin; in Ernakulam, head for Net Park on Convent Rd or Mathsons on Durbar Hall Rd. Access costs around Rs15–30/hr.

Music stores Sargam, XL/6816 GSS Complex, Convent Rd, opposite the Public Library, stocks the best range of music tapes ships; you spend two days at sea and four lying on the beach. All food is included, and permits are taken care of.

The uninhabited, teardrop-shaped 128-acre islet of **Bangaram** welcomes a limited number of foreign tourists at any one time, and expects them to pay handsomely for the privilege. *Bangaram Island Resort* (9), bookable in Kochi (see below), accommodates up to thirty couples in thatched cottage rooms, each with a veranda. Cane tables and chairs sit outside the restaurant on the beach, and a few hammocks are strung up between the palms. There's no air conditioning, TV, radio, telephone, newspapers or shops, let alone discos. Facilities include scuba diving (again expensive at $65 per day, plus $30 per dive or $50 for two), glass-bottomed boat trips to neighbouring uninhabited islands, and deep-sea fishing (Oct to mid-May; $50–75). Kayaks, catamarans and a sailing boat are available free, and it's possible to take a day-trip to Kadmat.

Getting to the islands

At present, the only way for foreigners to reach Bangaram are the expensive flights on small aircraft run by Indian Airlines out of **Kochi** (one daily, except Sun; 1hr 35min), bookable through the *Casino Hotel* on Willingdon Island (see p.1259). Foreigners pay around $300 for the round trip, which takes an hour and a half. Flights arrive in Lakshadweep at the island of **Agatti**, 8km southwest from where the connecting boat journey to Bangaram takes two hours, picking its way through the shallows to avoid the corals. During the monsoon (May 16–Sept 15), helicopters are used to protect the fragile coral reefs that lie just under the surface. All arrangements, including flights, accommodation and the necessary entry permit, are handled by the *Casino Hotel*, Willingdon Island, Kochi (Ⓣ0484/266 8221, Ⓔcasino@vsnl.net). Some foreign tour operators, however, offer all-in packages combining Lakshadweep with another destination, usually Goa.

Theoretically, it's possible to visit Lakshadweep all year round; the hottest time is April and May, when the temperature can reach 33°C; the **monsoon** (May–Sept) attracts approximately half the total rainfall seen in Kerala, in the form of passing showers rather than a deluge, although seas are rough.

in the state, mostly Indian (Hindi films and lots of Keralan devotional music), with a couple of shelves of Western rock and pop. Music World, MKV Building, MG Rd is Kochi's answer to a music superstore with Western pop, classical, compilations, world music and Indian *filmi* music. Sound of Melody, DH Rd, near the Ernakulam Junction station, also has a good selection of traditional South Indian and contemporary Western music.

Musical instruments Manuel Industries, Banerji Rd, Kacheripady Junction is the best for Indian classical and western instruments. For traditional Keralan drums, ask at Thripunitra bazaar (see below).

Photography City Camera, Lovedale Building, Padma Junction, MG Rd, repairs and sells cameras; Krishnan Nair Bros, Convent Rd, stocks the best range of camera film, including black and white, Kodachrome and Fujichrome and professional colour transparency; Royal Studio, Shanmugham Rd, is also worth a try.

Police The city's tourist police have a counter at the railway station. There is also a counter next to the KTDC Tourist Office at the southern end of Shanmugham Rd.

Post office The GPO is on Hospital Rd, not far from the Main Jetty; the city's poste restante is at the post office behind St Francis Church in Fort Cochin.

Tour and travel agents Clipper Holidays, 40/6531 Convent Rd (Ⓣ0484/236 4443), are experienced agents good for wildlife and adventure tours in Kerala and Karnataka. Sita World Travels (Ⓣ0484/236 1101) and Travel Corporation of India, MG Rd (Ⓣ0484/235 1646), specialize in tours and air-ticketing. The Tourist Desk, Main Jetty (Ⓣ0484/237 1761), offers backwater and wildlife tours as well as accommodation in a couple of beautiful locations.

Thrissur

The pleasant town of **THRISSUR** (Trichur), between Kochi (74km south) and Palakkad (79km northeast) on NH-47, is a convenient base for exploring the cultural riches of central Kerala. Near the Palghat (Palakkad) Gap – an opening in the natural border made by the Western Ghat mountains – it presided over the main trade route into the region from Tamil Nadu and Karnataka. For years Thrissur was the capital of Cochin State, controlled at various times by both the zamorin of Kozhikode and Tipu Sultan of Mysore. Today, it prides itself on being the cultural capital of Kerala and is home to several influential art institutions. Kerala's largest temple complex, **Vadakkunatha**, surrounded by a *maidan* (green), is the focal point of town and home of the state's most extravagant, noisy and sumptuous festival, **Puram**.

Arrival and information

Thrissur's **railway station** is 1km southwest of Round South, near the KSRTC **long-distance bus stand**. **Priya Darshini** (also known as "North", "Shoranur" and "Wadakkancheri") bus station, close to Round North, serves Shoranur (for the Kalamanadalam Academy). The **Shakthan Thampuran** stand, on TB Road, just over 1km from Round South, serves local destinations south such as Irinjalakuda, Kodungallur and Guruvayur.

The DTPC **tourist office** (Mon–Sat 10am–5pm; ⓣ0487/232 0800) is on Palace Road, opposite the Town Hall (five minutes' walk off Round East). Run on a voluntary basis, its primary purpose is to promote the Puram elephant festival, but they also give out maps of Thrissur. KTDC have a small information counter at the *Yatri Niwas* hotel, Stadium Road (ⓣ0487/233 2333). The best place for **change money** and travellers' cheques is UA Exchange & Financial Services (Mon–Sat 9.30am–6pm, Sun 9.30am–1.30pm) in the basement of the *Casino Hotel* building. The State Bank of India and the Canara Bank on South Road also change money and travellers' cheques, plus there's a UTI Bank ATM on Palace Road. The **GPO** is on the southern edge of town, near the *Casino Hotel* off TB Road. **Internet** facilities are available at the excellent Internet Thrissur.Com, Second Floor, City Centre Shopping Complex, Round West (daily 9am–10pm) and SS Consultants near the *Luciya* hotel (daily 9am–11pm); rates are around Rs30/hr.

Accommodation

Thrissur has a fair number of mid-price **hotels**, but only a couple of decent budget places. The best deal is the palatial *Ramanilayam Government Rest House*, which offers star-hotel comfort at economy lodge rates, but the constant stream of government officials gets priority. Almost all of Thrissur's hotels follow a 24-hour checkout policy. If you're planning to be here during **Puram**, book well in advance and bear in mind that room rates soar – some of the more upmarket hotels charge up to ten times their normal prices.

Casino TB Rd, near the railway station ⓣ0487/242 4699, ⓦwww.casinotels.com. Once Thrissur's poshest hotel, but has seen better days; the rooms are decent (non-a/c and a/c) and there's a multi-cuisine restaurant, cocktail bar, lawn and kiddies park, and foreign exchange (residents only). ❸–❻

Elite International Chembottil Lane, off Round South ⓣ0487/242 1033, ⓔhoteleliteinternational@yahoo.co.in. Pronounced "Ee-light". A big tower block of standard and deluxe rooms, some with balconies overlooking the green. Friendly staff, a good restaurant and a great garden. ❸–❼

Gurukripa Lodge Chembottil Lane, off Round South ⓣ0487/242 1895. A variety of rooms (including several great-value singles) in a large compound; those without a/c are large and simple with cool tiled floors and attached bathrooms. Some rooms with TV. ❷–❸

KTDC Yatri Niwas Off Museum Rd ⓣ0487/233 2333, ⓦwww.ktdc.com. Friendly motel-type place with spotless rooms (some a/c and with cable TV), a beer parlour and a restaurant. ❷–❹

Ramanilayam Government Rest House Palace Rd ⓣ0471/233 2016. Very good value, extremely popular, and often full: huge, clean, comfortable suites with balconies, and non-a/c and a/c doubles. It's officially for VIPs, and they're not obliged to give you a room, but smart clothes will help. Breakfast is served daily; other meals by advance order only. ❷–❸

Siddartha Regency Veliyannur Rd, Kokkalai ⓣ0487/242 4773, ⓔsregency@md5.vsnl.net.in. In the southwestern corner of town, near all the transport hubs, this is a comfortable hotel geared toward Indian visitors, with central a/c and suites with bathtubs. Swimming pool, health club, restaurant, bar and gardens. ❺–❻

The Town

The principal point of orientation in Thrissur is the **Round**, a road subdivided into North, South, East and West, which circles the Vadakkunatha temple complex and *maidan*. Once you've established which side of the Round you're on, you can make short-cuts across the green.

The **State Art Museum** and **Zoo** (both Tues–Sun 10am–5pm; Rs6) stand together on Museum Road, ten minutes' walk from Round East, in the northeast of town. Although small, the museum has excellent local bronzes, jewellery, fine woodcarvings of fanged temple guardians and a profusion of bell-metal oil lamps. The zoo predictably houses a rather depressing set of tenants, although the snakes – king cobra, krait, and viper – are well enough to spit. The peculiar **Multi-Purpose Museum** (same hours; free) stands in the same compound, with its odd hoard of skeletons, stuffed animals, minerals, weapons and costumes.

Next door to the *Yatri Niwas* hotel, the **Kerala Sangeet Natak Academy** (ⓣ0487/233 2134) features a large auditorium that hosts occasional music and dance concerts as well as Keralan theatre, which has an enthusiastic following and tends to be heavily political. Around the corner is the **Kerala Lalitha Kala Akademi** (ⓣ0487/233 3773), which often exhibits contemporary Indian art.

Vadakkunatha temple

Vadakkunatha temple (shrines closed to non-Hindus), is a walled complex of fifteen shrines, dating from around the twelfth century and dedicated to Shiva. Inside the walls, the grassy compound is surprisingly quiet and spacious, with a striking apsidal shrine dedicated to Ayappa (see p.1244). The long, sloping-roofed **Kuttambalam theatre** (also closed to non-Hindus) with carved panels and lathe-turned wooden pillars is the venue for the ancient Sanskrit performance forms Chakyar Kuttu and Kutiyattam.

Shopping

Thrissur is a good place to pick up Keralan crafts. The main shopping area is on the Round; on Round West, the Kerala State Handicraft Emporium specializes in wood; a one-minute walk from Round East at the top of Palace Road, Co-optex sells a good range of hand-loom cloth. At Chemmanur's, Round South, near the *Elite Hotel*, you'll find the usual carved wooden-elephant-type souvenirs, and, on the ground floor, a high-kitsch Aladdin's Cave of nodding dogs, Jesus clocks, Mecca table ornaments and parabolic nail-and-string art. Alter Media at Utility Building, Nehru Bazaar, Nayarangadi is a small but interesting bookshop devoted to women's studies, while Cosmos, on Round West, is a treasure-trove of novels, academic tomes and books on art, drama and culture.

Puram

Thrissur is best known to outsiders as the venue for Kerala's biggest festival, **Puram**, which takes place on one day in April/May. Introduced by the Kochi (Cochin) Raja, Shaktan Tampuran (1789–1803), Puram is today the most extreme example of the kind of celebration seen on a smaller scale all over Kerala, whose main ingredients invariably include **caparisoned elephants**, **drum music** and **fireworks**.

On this day, at the hottest time of year, the centre of Thrissur fills to capacity with people gravitating towards Round South, where a long path leads to the southern entrance of the **Vadakkunatha temple** complex. Two processions, representing the Tiruvambadi and Paramekkavu temples in Thrissur, compete to be the most impressive, and eventually meet, facing each other at either end of the path. Both sides present fifteen tuskers sumptuously decorated with gold ornaments, each ridden by three Brahmins clutching objects symbolizing royalty: silver-handled whisks of yak hair, circular peacock-feather fans and patterned silk umbrellas fringed with silver pendants. At the centre of each group, the principal elephant carries an image of the temple's deity.

Known as **chenda melam**, this quintessentially Keralan music, featuring as many as a hundred loud, hard-skinned, cylindrical *chenda* drums, crashing cymbals and wind instruments, mesmerizes the crowd while its structure marks the progress of the procession. Each kind of *chenda melam* is named after the rhythmic cycle (*tala* or, in Malayalam, *talam*) in which it is set. Drummers stand in ranks, the most numerous at the back often playing single beats. At the front, a line of master drummers, the stars of Keralan music, try to outdo each other with their speed, stamina, improvisational skills and showmanship. Facing the drummers, musicians play long double-reed, oboe-like *kuzhals* (similar to the north Indian *shehnai*) and C-shaped *kompu* bell-metal trumpets. The fundamental structure is provided by the *elatalam* – medium-sized, heavy, brass hand-cymbals that resolutely and precisely keep the tempo, essential to the cumulative effect of the music. Over an extended period, the *melam* passes through four phases of tempo, each a double of the last, from a majestic dead slow through to a frenetic pace.

The arrival of the fastest tempo is borne on a wave of aural and visual stimulation. Those astride the elephants stand at this point, to manipulate their feather fans and hair whisks in co-ordinated sequence while behind, unfurled umbrellas are twirled in flashes of dazzling colour. Meanwhile, the cymbals crash furiously, often raised above the head, requiring extraordinary stamina (and causing weals on the hands). The master drummers play at their loudest and fastest, frequently intensified by single players, one after another; a chorus of trumpets make an ancient noise.

All this is greeted by firework explosions and roars from the crowd; many people punch the air, some fairly randomly, while others are clearly *talam branthans*, rhythm "madmen", who follow every nuance of the structure. When the fastest speed is played out, the slowest tempo returns and the procession edges forward, the *mahouts* leading the elephants by the tusk. Stopping again, the whole cycle is repeated. At night, the Vadukannatha temple entrances are a blaze of coloured lights and a spectacular firework display takes place in the early hours of the morning.

If you venture to Thrissur for Puram, be prepared for packed buses and trains. Needless to say, accommodation should be booked well in advance. An umbrella or hat is recommended for protection from the sun. Unfortunately, Puram has become an excuse for groups of Indian men to get very drunk; women are advised only to go in the morning, or to watch with a group of Indian women.

Similar but much smaller events take place in town, generally from September onwards, with most during the summer (April & May). Enquire at a tourist office or your hotel, or ask someone to check a local edition of the newspaper, *Mathrabhumi*, for local performances of *chenda melam*, and other drum orchestras such as *panchavadyam* and *tyambaka*.

Kuruppam Road, which leads south towards the railway station from the western end of Round South, is one of the best places in Kerala to buy **bell-metal** products, particularly oil lamps made in the village of Nadavaramba, near Irinjalakuda (see p.1268). **Nadavaramba Krishna & Sons** and **Bell-metal Craft** both specialize in brass, bronze and bell metal. Lamps cost Rs80–25,000, and "superfine" bell metal is sold by weight, at over Rs250 per kilo. Continuing south on Kuruppam Road to the next junction with Railway Station Road, you'll find a number of small shops selling cheap Christian, Muslim and Hindu pictures etched on metal, and festival accessories, including umbrellas similar to those used for Puram (see box opposite).

Eating and drinking

Thrissur's big **hotels** offer Indian, Western and Chinese food, and Keralan lunches, while several quality, inexpensive places are clustered near the **Round**. Late at night, on the corner of Round South and Round East, opposite the Medical College Hospital, you'll find a string of chai and omelette stalls, frequented by auto-rickshaw-wallahs, hospital visitors, itinerant mendicants, Ayappa devotees and student revellers.

AFC Round West. Upstairs fast-food joint with Asian as opposed to Kentucky fried chicken. Also serves tasty burgers and pizza.

Bharath Lodge Chembottil Lane, next door to *Elite Hotel*. Excellent South Indian breakfasts, evening snacks and fixed-price "all you can eat" Keralan meals at lunch time. Inexpensive.

Chick City Round West. Bright ice-cream parlour featuring an astounding array of sundaes, with names like Cold Duck or Parrot Attack, and Western music.

Indian Coffee House Round South. The better of two in town (the Station Rd branch is very run-down); this cheap and very popular restaurant serves snacks, Indian meals and excellent filter coffee.

Luciya Palace Marar Rd, just off the southwest corner of the Round ☎0487/424731. Hotel restaurant serving Indian and Chinese dishes; dinner is served in a pleasant garden illuminated by fairy lights.

Ming Palace Pathan Building, Round South. Inexpensive "Chindian", serving chop suey, noodles and lots of chicken and veg dishes; dim lighting and cheesy muzak.

Pathan's Round South. Deservedly popular veg restaurant, with a cosy a/c family annexe and a large canteen-like dining hall. Generous portions and plenty of choice, including *koftas*, kormas and lots of tandoori options, as well as Keralan thalis and wonderful Kashmiri naan.

Around Thrissur

The chief appeal of exploring the area **around Thrissur** is the opportunity to get to grips with Kerala's cultural heritage. Countless festivals, at their peak before the monsoon hits in May, enable visitors to catch some of the best drummers in the world, **Kathakali** dance drama and **Kutiyattam**, the world's oldest surviving theatre form.

Irinjalakuda

The village of **IRINJALAKUDA**, 20km south of Thrissur, has a unique temple, five minutes' walk west from the bus stand, dedicated to **Bharata**, the brother of Rama. Visitors are usually permitted to see inside (men must wear a *dhoti*), but as elsewhere, the inner parts of the temple are closed to non-Hindus. It boasts a superbly elegant tiled *kuttambalam* **theatre** within its outer courtyard, built to afford an unimpeded view for the maximum number of spectators (drawn from the highest castes only), and known for its excellent acoustics. A

Nadavaramba bell-metal oil lamps

Keralan nights are made more enchanting by the use of **oil lamps**; the most common type, seen all over, is a slim floor-standing metal column surmounted by a spike that rises from a circular receptacle for coconut oil, and using cloth or banana plant fibre wicks. Every classical theatre performance keeps a large lamp burning centre-stage, all night. The special atmosphere of temples is also enhanced by innumerable lamps, some hanging from chains; others, *deepa stambham*, are multi-tiered and stand metres high.

The village of **Nadavaramba**, near Irinjalakuda, is an important centre for the manufacture of oil lamps and large cooking vessels, known as *uruli* and *varppu*. Alloys made from brass, copper and tin are frequently used, but the best are from bell metal, said to be eighty percent copper, and give a sonorous chime when struck. Shops in Thrissur that specialize in Nadavaramba-ware arrange visits to see the craftsmen at work.

profusion of painted woodcarvings of mythological animals and stories from the epics decorate the interior. On the low stage, which is enclosed by painted wooden columns and friezes of female dancers, stand two large copper *mizhavu* drums, for use in the Sanskrit drama Kutiyattam, permanently installed in wooden frames into which a drummer climbs to play. Traditionally, *mizhavus* were considered sacred objects; Nandikeshvara, Shiva's rhythm-man, was said to reside in them. The drama for which they provided music was a holy ritual, and in the old days the instrument was never allowed to leave the temple and was only played by members of a special caste, the Nambyars. Since then, outsiders have learned the art of *mizhavu* playing, but the orthodox authorities do not allow them to play inside.

Natana Kairali is an important cultural centre dedicated to the performance, protection and documentation of Kerala's lesser-known – but fascinating and vibrant – theatre arts, including Kutiyattam, Nangiar Koothu (female mono-acting), shadow and puppet theatres. Left of the Bharata temple as you leave, it is based in the home of one of Kerala's most illustrious acting families, Ammanur Chakyar Madhom (cite this name when you ask for directions). Natana Kairali's director, Shri G. Venu (Ⓣ0488/282 5559), is a mine of information about Keralan arts, and can advise on forthcoming performances.

Irinjalakuda is best reached by **bus** from the Shakthan Thampuran stand at Thrissur rather than by train, as the railway station is an inconvenient 8km east of town.

Guruvayur

Kerala's most important Krishna shrine, the high-walled temple of **GURUVAYUR**, 29km northwest of Thrissur, attracts a constant flow of pilgrims, second only in volume to Ayappa's at Sabarimala (see p.1244). Its deity, **Guruvayurappan**, has inspired numerous paeans from Keralan poets, most notably Narayana Bhattatiri, who wrote the *Narayaniyam* during the sixteenth century, when the temple, whose origins are legendary, seems to have first risen to prominence.

Guruvayar temple (3am–1pm & 4–10pm; closed to non-Hindus) is one of the richest in Kerala and hosts 24 **annual festivals**, the most important of which are Ekadashi and Ulsavam. In the month of Vrischikam (Nov/Dec), during the eighteen days of Ekadashi – marked by processions of caparisoned elephants outside the temple – the exterior of the building is decorated with the tiny flames of innumerable oil lamps. On certain days (check with a KTDC office), programmes staged in front of the temple attract the cream of South Indian classical-music artists.

During Ulsavam, in the month of Kumbham (Feb/March), when tantric rituals are conducted inside, an **elephant race** is run outside on the first day and elephant processions take place during the following six days.

The Punnathur Kotta Elephant Camp

When not involved in races and other arcane temple rituals, Guruvayur's tuskers are chained at the **Punnathur Kotta Elephant Camp** (daily 9am–6pm; Rs5; cameras Rs25), 4km north of town. Around fifty elephants, aged from 8 to 95, live here, munching for most of the day on specially imported piles of fodder and cared for by their three personal *mahouts*, who wash and scrub them several times a week. Only approach an elephant if a *mahout* allows you.

All the animals are the personal possession of Lord Guruvayur, given to the temple by wealthy patrons from as far afield as Bihar and Assam; apart from the most elderly, who are allowed an honourable retirement, the elephants are gainfully employed in local temples, especially at the Guruvayur temple itself. All temples demand pretty elephants for their elaborate festivals, and the competition to rent a particularly favoured beast can become a bitter auction between villages: the standard daily charge of Rs3500 per elephant once reached a record Rs75,000.

Practicalities

Buses from Thrissur (40min) arrive at the main **bus stand** at the top end of East Nada Street, five minutes east of the temple, and the home of most of the **accommodation**. Try the pilgrim-oriented KTDC *Mangalya*, near the entrance of the Krishna temple (Ⓣ0487/255 2408; ❸), which has large rooms for up to six people and a devotional atmosphere; or the one-star deluxe KTDC *Nandanam* near the railway station (Ⓣ0487/255 6266; ❸–❹), which has some a/c rooms.The town is crammed with veg **restaurants**, and there's an *Indian Coffee House* on the southern side of E Nada Street that serves South Indian snacks.

Cheruthuruthy

The village of **CHERUTHURUTHY** – an easy day-trip 32km north of Thrissur through gently undulating green country – is famous as the home of **Kerala Kalamandalam**, the state's flagship training school for Kathakali and other indigenous Keralan performing arts. Founded in 1927 by the revered Keralan poet Vallathol (1878–1957) and patronized at first by the Raja of Cochin, the school has been instrumental in the large-scale revival of interest in Kathakali and other unique Keralan art forms. Despite conservative opposition, it followed an open-door recruitment policy, based on artistic merit, which produced "scheduled caste", Muslim and Christian graduates along with the usual Hindu castes, something that was previously unimaginable. Kalamandalam artists perform in the great theatres of the world. Nonetheless, many of these trained artists are still excluded from entering, let alone performing in, temples, which are popular venues for Hindu art forms, and in particular music.

Non-Hindus can see Kathakali, Kutiyattam and other minor art forms performed in the school's superb **theatre**, which replicates the wooden, sloping-roofed traditional theatres, known as *kuttambalams*, found in Keralan temples. If you're interested in how this extraordinary technique is taught, don't miss the chance to sit in on the training sessions (Mon–Fri 4.30am–5pm; closed on public

Keralan ritual and ritualized theatre

Among the most magical experiences a visitor to Kerala can have is to witness one of the innumerable ancient rituals, ritualized theatre or dance styles that play such an important and unique role in the cultural life of the region. The dance drama **Kathakali** is the best known; other less publicized forms, which clearly influenced its development, include the classical Sanskrit **Kutiyattam** and the village hero-worship ritual **Theyyam**.

Many Keralan forms share broad characteristics. A prime aim of each performer is to transform the mundane to the world of gods and demons; his preparation is highly ritualized, involving other-worldly costume and mask-like make-up. In Kathakali and Kutiyattam, this preparation is a rigorously codified part of the classical tradition, whereas the much wilder appearance of Theyyam differs from village to village. One-off **performances** of various ritual types take place throughout the state, building up to fever pitch during April and May before pausing for the monsoon (June–Aug). Finding out about such events requires a little perseverance, but it's well worth the effort; enquire at tourist offices, or buy a Malayalam daily paper such as *Mathrabhumi* and ask someone to check the listings for **temple festivals**, where most of the action invariably takes place. Tourist Kathakali is staged daily in Kochi (see p.1258) but to find authentic performances, contact **performing arts schools** such as Thiruvananthapuram's Margi (see p.1213) and Cheruthuruthy's Kerala Kalamandalam; Kutiyattam artists work at both, as well as at Natana Kairali at Irinjalakuda (see p.1268).

Kathakali

Here is the tradition of the trance dancers, here is the absolute demand of the subjugation of body to spirit, here is the realization of the cosmic transformation of human into divine.

Mrinalini Sarabhai, classical dancer

Kathakali dance drama, Kerala's most popular theatre form, is recognized as one of the four major classical Indian styles. The image of a Kathakali actor in a magnificent costume with extraordinary make-up and a huge gold crown has become Kerala's trademark, seen on anything from matchboxes to TV adverts for detergents. Traditional performances, of which there are still many, usually take place on open ground outside a temple, beginning at 10pm and lasting until dawn, illuminated by the flickers of a large brass oil lamp centre stage. Virtually nothing about Kathakali is naturalistic, because it depicts the world of gods and demons; both the male and female roles are played by men.

Standing at the back of the stage, two musicians play driving rhythms, one on a bronze gong, the other on heavy bell-metal cymbals; they also sing the dialogue. Actors appear and disappear from behind a hand-held curtain and never utter a sound, save the odd strange cry. Learning the elaborate hand gestures, facial expressions and choreographed movements, as articulate and precise as any sign language, requires rigorous training which can begin at the age of 8 and last ten years. At least two more drummers stand left of the stage; one plays the upright **chenda** with slender curved sticks, the other plays the *maddalam*, a horizontal barrel-shaped hand drum. When a female character is "speaking", the *chenda* is replaced by the hourglass-shaped *ettaka*, a "talking drum" on which melodies can be played. The drummers keep their eyes on the actors, whose every gesture is reinforced by their sound, from the gentlest embrace to the gory disembowelling of an enemy.

Although it bears the unmistakeable influences of Kutiyattam and indigenous folk rituals, Kathakali, literally "story-play", is thought to have crystallized into a distinct theatre form during the seventeenth century. The plays are based on three major sources: the Hindu epics the *Mahabharata*, *Ramayana* and the *Bhagavata Purana*. While the stories are ostensibly about god-heroes such as Rama and Krishna, the most popular characters are those that give the most scope to the actors – the villainous, fanged, red-and-black-faced *katti* ("knife") anti-heroes; these types, such as the kings Ravana and

Duryodhana, are dominated by lust, greed, envy and violence. David Bolland's *Guide to Kathakali*, widely available in Kerala, gives invaluable scene-by-scene summaries of the most popular plays and explains in simple language a lot more besides.

When attending a performance, arrive early to get your bearings before it gets dark, even though the first play will not begin much before 10pm. (Quiet) members of the audience are welcome to visit the dressing room before and during the performance. The colour and design of the mask-like make-up, which specialist artists take several hours to apply, reveal the character's personality. The word *pacha* means both "green" and "pure"; a green-faced *pacha* character is thus a noble human or god. Red signifies *rajas*, passion and aggression, black denotes *tamas*, darkness and negativity, while white is *sattvik*, light and intellect. Once the make-up is completed, elaborate wide skirts are tied to the waist, and ornaments of silver and gold are added. Silver talons are fitted to the left hand. The transformation is complete with a final prayer and the donning of waist-length wig and crown. Visitors new to Kathakali will almost undoubtedly get bored during such long programmes, parts of which are very slow indeed. If you're at a village performance, you may not always find accommodation, so you can't leave during the night. Be prepared to sit on the ground for hours, and bring some warm clothes. Half the fun is staying up all night to witness, just as the dawn light appears, the gruesome disembowelling of a villain or a demon *asura*.

Kutiyattam

Three families of the Chakyar caste and a few outsiders perform the Sanskrit drama **Kutiyattam**, the oldest continually performed theatre form in the world. Until recently it was only performed inside temples and then only in front of the uppermost castes. Visually it is very similar to its offspring, Kathakali, but its atmosphere is infinitely more archaic. The actors, eloquent in sign language and symbolic movement, speak in the compelling intonation of the local brahmins' Vedic chant, unchanged since 1500 BC.

A single act of a Kutiyattam play can require ten full nights; the entire play takes forty. A great actor, in full command of the subtleties of expression through gestures, can take half an hour to do such a simple thing as murder a demon, berate the audience, or simply describe a leaf fall to the ground. Unlike Kathakali, Kutiyattam includes comic characters and plays. The ubiquitous **Vidushaka**, narrator and clown, is something of a court jester, and traditionally has held the right openly to criticize the highest in the land without fear of retribution.

Theyyam

In northern Kerala, a wide range of ancient ritual "performances", loosely known as **Theyyam**, are performed between October and May. They might include *bhuta* (spirit or hero worship), trance dances, the enactment of legendary events, and oracular pronouncements. The role of the Theyyam performer passes from father to son; they are usually from low castes, but during the ritual, a brahmin will honour the deities they represent, so the status of each individual is reversed and they become the priests. During a performance several dancers will be involved, but only one at a time may sit on the chair of the deity and become possessed.

Although Theyyam performances can now be seen in government-organized cultural festivals, the powerful effect is best experienced in an all-night ceremony in the courtyard of a house or temple, in a village setting. Some figures, with intricately painted faces and bodies, are genuinely terrifying; costumes include metres-high headgear, sometimes doubling as a mask, and clothes of banana leaves and bark. You may be lucky enough to stumble upon a very rare performance involving fire rituals. Amid frantic drumming, a dancer will volunteer to demonstrate the demonic power temporarily held within him, either by walking on red-hot coals or by rapidly dancing around the fire and throwing himself on it, an auspicious 52 times. Each time he allows the demon to drive his body onto the fire, the temple brahmins pull the possessed figure back.

holidays). A handful of foreigners also come to the Kalamandalam academy each year to attend full-time **courses** in Kathakali and other traditional dance and theatre forms. Short courses last for a minimum of one month, condensed courses for three to six months and full courses from four to six years. Foreign students with the correct visas can attend a maximum of four years. Applications may be made from abroad (write to the Secretary, Kerala Kalamandalam, Vallathol Nagar, Cheruthuruthy, Thrissur District, Kerala 679531), but it's a good idea to visit before committing yourself, as the training is rigorous. A good time to visit is during their annual week-long festival starting on Christmas Day. For information contact the school office (Ⓣ04884/262418).

A short walk past the old campus leads to a small but exquisite **Shiva temple** built in classic Keralan style. During evening pujas the candle-lit exterior further adds to the atmosphere.

Practicalities

Cheruthuruthy's **accommodation** is limited, with some students staying as guests in private accommodation (phone school for details). Otherwise, the village has a couple of simple guesthouses, and the atmospheric *Government Guest House* (Ⓣ04884/262760; ❷–❸), a short distance along the Shoranur road from Kalamandalam, has eight huge but basic rooms, some with Western-style toilets, and all sharing a veranda. For a touch of a/c luxury try the *River Retreat* on Palace Road (Ⓣ04884/262922; ❾).

Buses from Thrissur pass through, and the nearest **railway** station is Shoranur Junction, 3km south, served by express trains to and from Mangalore, Chennai and Kochi.

Kozhikode (Calicut)

Formerly one of Asia's most prosperous trading capitals, the coastal city of **KOZHIKODE** (Calicut), 225km north of Kochi, occupies an extremely important place in Keralan legend and history. It is also significant in the history of European involvement on the subcontinent, as Vasco da Gama landed nearby in 1498. Nowadays, with precious few historical remnants, there's little of interest here, and the few foreigners who do come are either lost or merely breaking the long journey between Mysore and Kochi. All the same, Kozhikode remains a busy commercial centre, not least because of the huge amounts of money pouring in from expatriates working in the Gulf states.

Practicalities

The **railway station** (Ⓣ0495/270 1234), close to the centre of town, is served by coastal expresses and slower passenger trains; superfast express trains from Delhi, Mumbai, Kochi and Thiruvananthapuram stop here. There are three **bus stands**. All services from destinations as far afield as Bangalore, Mysore, Ooty, Madurai, Coimbatore and Mangalore pull in at the **KSRTC stand**, on Mavoor Road (aka Indira Gandhi Road). Private long-distance buses stop at the **New Mofussil private stand** (Ⓣ0495/272 2823), 500m away on the other side of Mavoor Road – there's a row of agents for booking them on MM Ali Road. The **Palayam stand** just serves city buses.

Kozhikode's **airport** is at Karippur, 23km south of the city. A taxi into town will cost around Rs300, but you can save a few rupees by taking an **auto-rickshaw** to the Kozhikode–Palakkad highway and then catching a bus.

The friendly **KTDC tourist information** booth (daily 9am–7.30pm; ⓣ0495/270 0097) at the railway station has info on travel connections and sites around Kozhikode but its hours are erratic. The KTDC tourist office (daily 9am–6pm; ⓣ0495/272 2391) in the *Malabar Mansion* hotel at the corner of SM Street, can supply only limited information about the town and area. There is a **24-hour left luggage** facility at the railway station but, as is always the case, they only accept locked luggage. With so much Gulf money floating around, you shouldn't have any difficulty **changing currency** in Kozhikode. A good place for cash or travellers' cheques is PL Worldways, 3rd Floor, Semma Towers, Mavoor Road. The Standard Chartered Bank on Town Hall Road and the State Bank of India at Manachira Park also change money, while the Corp Bank on Town Hall Road and Federal Bank on Kallai Road both have ATMs. **Internet** facilities are available at The Hub, on the first floor of the block to the right of *Nandhinee Sweets*, MM Ali Road, and Internet Zone near *KTDC Malabar Mansion* (both Rs30/hr).

Accommodation and eating

Kozhikode's reasonably priced city-centre **hotels** mostly operate a 24-hour check-out but can still be full later in the day; the beach area is a quiet alternative. Your best bet for a proper **meal** is to eat at your hotel, though you can get South Indian snacks and great omelette and coffee breakfasts at the dependable *Indian Coffee Houses* on Kallai Road and GH Road. The *Tandoor Prince* on GH Road is a no-nonsense, hole-in-the-wall, principally non-veg restaurant. *Nandhinee Sweets*, on MM Ali Road, is an ultra-hygienic sweets, nuts and savoury snacks pit-stop, where you can also get great fresh fruit cocktails, *badam* milk and *falooda* shakes.

Hotels and guesthouses

Alakapuri Guest House MM Ali Rd, near the railway station, 1km from KSRTC bus stand ⓣ0495/272 3451, ⓦwww.alakapurihotels.com. Built around a courtyard, the a/c rooms here have huge bathtubs, polished wood and easy chairs; the cheaper, non-a/c options are rather spartan. Bar, restaurant and lovely lawn. Single rates available. ❹–❺

Imperial Kallai Rd ⓣ0495/270 1291. Large hotel around a courtyard with basic, very cheap rooms and a branch of *India Coffee House* on the ground floor. ❷

KTDC Malabar Mansion SM St ⓣ0495/272 2391, ⓦwww.ktdc.com. Modern high-rise hotel near the railway station. Huge a/c suites with cable TV, reasonable non-a/c rooms, beer parlour and a good South Indian restaurant. Good value. ❷–❹

Sasthapuri MM Ali Rd ⓣ0495/272 3281, ⓦwww.sasthapuri.com. Small budget place with well-maintained non-a/c and a/c rooms and a decent roof garden restaurant and a bar. It's set back 20m from the main road. Good value. ❷–❺

Sea Queen Beach Rd ⓣ0495/236 6604, ⓔseaqueenclt@sify.com. Quiet, comfortable but ageing middle-class hotel overlooking a rather grim part of the beach. The a/c and non-a/c rooms are a little dim and stuffed with furniture; there's a popular South Indian restaurant and bar on the ground floor. ❹–❻

Taj Residency PT Usha Rd ⓣ0495/276 5354, ⓦwww.tajhotels.com. The grandest hotel in town but it lacks the ubiquitous *Taj* style; nonetheless, the centrally a/c rooms ($80–110) are very comfortable and there's a pool, coffee shop, multi-cuisine restaurant, and health and Ayurvedic centre. ❾

The far north

The beautiful coast **north of Kozhikode** is a seemingly endless stretch of coconut palms, wooded hills and virtually deserted beaches; the towns, though, hold little of interest for visitors, most of whom bypass the area completely. However, this would mean missing out on the chance to see **Theyyam**, the extraordinary masked trance dances and oracle readings that take place in villages throughout the region between November and May.

Kannur (Cannanore)

KANNUR (Cannanore), 92km north of Kozhikode, was for many centuries the capital of the Kolathiri rajas, who prospered from the thriving maritime spice trade through its port. In the early 1500s, after Vasco da Gama passed through, the Portuguese took it and erected an imposing bastion, **St Angelo's fort**, overlooking the harbour, but today this is occupied by the Indian army and closed to visitors. In Kannur itself, the popular town beach can get quite crowded; for a bit more quiet head down to the small **Baby Beach** (4km) in the army's cantonment area (daily access 9am–5pm).

Most visitors use Kannur as a base while they search out **Theyyam** (also known loosely as Teyyattam), spectacular spirit-possession rituals (see box p.1271), an important feature of town and village life in the area. There are over 400 different varieties of Theyyam, so you could spend days and nights enthralled in it, and never see the same ritual twice. Locating these events is exciting and an essential part of the whole experience – you can often hear the loud and frenetic drumming miles away, but the temple where the *theyyam* is performed may be hidden deep within the forest or coconut groves. The best way to find them is to ask at the local tourist office or at *Costa Malabari* (see below), which is also a great place to hole up for idyllic beaches. If you're short of time, try the daily rituals at **Parassinikadavu** (see opposite).

Practicalities

Straddling the main coastal transport artery between Mangalore and Kochi/ Thiruvananthapuram, Kannur is well connected by **bus** and **train** to most major towns and cities in Kerala, as well as Mangalore. In addition, buses from here travel to Mysore turning inland at Thalassery (aka Tellycherry) and climb the beautiful wooded ghats to Virajpet in Kodagu. The railway station is just over five minutes by foot southwest of the bus stand. The State Bank of India on Fort Road will **change money** and travellers' cheques, as will UAExchange in KVR Tower, 500m east of the bus stand. There is a **DTPC** office near Civil Station (Mon–Sat 10am–5pm; ☎0497/270 6336), and a tourist information centre at the railway station (Mon–Sat 10am–5pm; ☎0497/270 3121). **Internet** access is widely available; try Asianet (Rs20/hr), in an arcade near the station end of Fort Road, or Cyber Valley (Rs30/hr), just beyond KVR Tower.

Accommodation

Costa Malabari 10km south near Tottada village (book through the Tourist Desk in Kochi ☎0484/237 1761, Ⓦwww.costamalabari.com. Hidden deep in cashew and coconut groves, this warm and welcoming guesthouse has five airy and comfortable rooms, and serves up huge portions of excellent Keralan food. There are five pristine golden beaches within a 10-min walk. Price includes full board, and the owners can pick up from Kannur for Rs120 by prior arrangement. ❻–❼

Government Guest House Cantonment area ☎0497/270 6426. On a cliff overlooking the sea, with huge, simple non-a/c rooms that catch the breezes; it's primarily for visiting VIPs but there are usually a few spare rooms. ❷–❸

Malabar Residency Thavakkara Rd ☎0497/276 5456, Ⓦwww.malabarresidency.com. Smart, central hotel with comfortable en-suite a/c rooms, two restaurants, including the multi-cuisine *Grand Plaza*, and 24hr coffee shop. ❻–❼

Mascot Beach Resort 300m before Baby Beach ☎0497/270 8445, Ⓔmascot_beach_resort@vsnl.com. Perched on the rocky shoreline, offering large well-appointed a/c rooms with views across the cove to the lighthouse. Swimming pool, foreign exchange and a good restaurant – but no bar. ❹–❼

Sweety International 200m north of railway station ☎0497/270 8283. Standard budget business high-rise with ordinary, executive and a/c rooms, all pretty decent value. ❷–❸

Parassinikadavu

The only place you can be absolutely guaranteed a glimpse of **Theyyam** is the village of **PARASSINIKADAVU**, 20km north of Kannur beside the River Valapatanam, where the head priest, or *madayan*, of the **Parassini Madammpura** temple performs every day during winter before assembled devotees. Elaborately dressed and accompanied by a traditional drum group, he becomes possessed by the temple's presiding deity – Lord Muthappan, Shiva in the form of a *kiratha*, or hunter – and enacts a series of complex offerings. The two-hour ceremony culminates when the priest/deity dances forward to bless individual members of the congregation. Even by Keralan standards, this is an extraordinary spectacle, and well worth taking time out of a journey along the coast for. The dawn performance is guaranteed but you can call the temple office (ⓣ0497/278 0722) to see if the regular 6pm ritual is also taking place.

Regular local buses leave Kannur **for Parassinikadavu** from around 7am, dropping passengers at the top of the village, ten minutes on foot from the temple. However, if you want to get there in time for the dawn Theyyam, you'll have to splash out on one of the Ambassador taxis that line up outside Kannur bus stand (around Rs400 round trip). The cabbies sleep in their cars, so you can arrange the trip on the spot by waking one up; you can also arrange a taxi through one of the more upmarket hotels. Either way, you'll have leave around 4.30am. There is also a snake park in Parassinikadavu (daily 8.30am–5.30pm) with demonstrations of snake-handling.

Travel details

For details of ferry services on the backwaters – primarily between Alappuzha and Kollam – see p.1228 & p.1232.

Trains

Kochi/Ernakulam to: Alappuzha (5–7 daily; 1hr 5min–1hr 40min); Bangalore (1–2 daily; 13hr–13hr 15min); Chennai (4–5 daily; 11hr 55min–16hr 20min); Delhi (2–4 daily; 39hr–48hr 20min); Kanniyakumari (2–3 daily; 7hr 25min–7hr 50min); Kollam (13–16 daily; 2hr 50min–4hr 25min); Kottayam (10–12 daily; 1hr 2min–1hr 20min); Kozhikode (5–6 daily; 4hr 25min–5hr 30min); Mumbai (2–3 daily; 26hr 50min–37hr 35min); Thiruvananthapuram (12–16 daily; 4hr 10min–5hr 35min); Thrissur (15–18 daily; 1hr 15min–2hr 30min).

Kozhikode to: Kannur (10–12 daily; 1hr 30min–2hr 10min); Kochi/Ernakulam (5–6 daily; 4hr 15min–5hr 40min); Mangalore (2-4 daily; 5hr 10min–5hr 30min); Mumbai (1 daily; 21hr 35min); Thiruvananthapuram (4–6 daily; 8hr 20min–10hr 30min); Thrissur (7–8 daily; 2hr 40min–3hr 30min).

Thiruvananthapuram to: Alappuzha (3–5 daily; 2hr 30min–3hr 15min); Bangalore (1–2 daily; 18hr–19hr 40min); Chennai (3–4 daily; 16hr 30min–18hr 45min); Delhi (1–3 daily; 42hr 35min–56hr 40min); Kanniyakumari (3–4 daily; 2hr); Kochi/Ernakulam (12–16 daily; 3hr 45min–5hr 20min); Kolkata (Calcutta: 4 weekly; 47hr 40min–47hr 55min); Kollam (13–16 daily; 55min–1hr 30min); Kozhikode (4–6 daily; 8hr 40min–10hr 15min); Madgaon (Goa: 1–3 daily; 16hr 20min–20hr 20min); Mumbai (2–3 daily; 30hr 55min–42hr 20min); Thrissur (10–12 daily; 5hr 45min–7hr); Varkala (8–10 daily; 33min–55min).

Thrissur to: Chennai (4–5 daily; 10hr–13hr 15min); Kochi/Ernakulam (15–18 daily; 1hr 20min–2hr 15min); Thiruvananthapuram (11–13 daily; 6hr 5min–7hr 10min).

Buses

Kochi/Ernakulam to: Alappuzha (every 30min; 1hr 30min); Kanniyakumari (6 daily; 9hr); Kollam (every 30min; 3hr); Kottayam (every 30min; 1hr 30min–2hr); Kozhikode (hourly; 5hr); Kumily (10 daily; 6–7hr); Thiruvananthapuram (every 30min; 5–6hr); Thrissur (every 30min; 2hr).

Kozhikode to: Kannur (every 30min; 2–2hr 30min); Kochi/Ernakulam (hourly; 5hr); Mysore (2 daily; 9–10hr); Ooty (4 daily; 6–7hr);

Thiruvananthapuram (12–15 daily; 11–12hr); Thrissur (hourly; 3hr 30min–4hr).
Kumily to: Kochi/Ernakulam (10 daily; 6–7hr); Kottayam (every 30min; 3–4hr); Madurai (10 daily; 5hr); Munnar (4 daily; 4hr); Thiruvananthapuram (6 daily; 8–9hr).
Munnar to: Kochi/Ernakulam (6 daily; 4hr 30min–5hr); Kottayam (5 daily; 5hr); Kumily (4 daily; 4hr); Madurai (6 daily; 5hr); Thiruvananthapuram (5 daily; 8–9hr).
Thiruvananthapuram to: Alappuzha (every 30min; 3hr–3hr 30min); Chennai (8 daily; 16–18hr); Kanniyakumari (every 30min–1hr; 2hr); Kochi/Ernakulam (every 30min; 5–6hr); Kollam (every 30min; 1hr 30min–2hr); Kottayam (every 30min; 4hr); Kumily (6 daily; 8hr); Madurai (10 daily; 7hr); Ponmudi (4 daily; 2hr 30min); Varkala (hourly; 1hr 30min).
Thrissur to: Guruvayur (10 daily; 40min); Kochi (every 30min; 2hr); Mysore (2 daily; 10–11hr); Palakkad (hourly; 2hr); Thiruvananthapuram (hourly; 7–8hr).

Flights

Kochi/Ernakulam to: Bangalore (3 daily; lhr 15min–2hr 15min); Chennai (1–3 daily; 1hr–1hr 55min); Delhi (3 daily; 4hr 25min); Goa (2 weekly; 1hr 10min); Hyderabad (1 daily; 3hr 30min) Lakshadweep (6 weekly; 1hr 35min); Mumbai (5–6 daily; 1hr 45min–3hr); Thiruvananthapuram (1 daily; 30min).
Kozhikode to: Chennai (8 weekly; 1hr–2hr 25min); Goa (3 weekly; 1hr 5min); Kochi (1–2 daily; 30min); Mumbai (3 daily; 1hr 40min–3hr); Tiruchirapalli (2 weekly; 55min).
Thiruvananthapuram to: Bangalore (1 daily; 1hr 5min); Chennai (1–2 daily; 1hr 10min–2hr 20min); Colombo (Sri Lanka) (l daily; 1hr 25min); Delhi (1 daily; 3hr); Malé (Maldives) (1 daily; 40min); Mumbai (2 daily; 1hr 55min–2hr); Tiruchirapalli (4 weekly; 50min).

CHAPTER 22

Highlights

* **Mysore** The sandalwood city has bundles of old-fashioned charm and lots to see, including the opulent Maharaja's Palace. See p.1294

* **Halebid & Belur** Two wonderfully ornate Hoysala temples, set in the slow-paced Karnataka countryside. See p.1307 & p.1309

* **Jog Falls** India's highest waterfalls offer fresh air, superb views and the chance to take a dip after the downhill hike. See p.1323

* **Gokarna** A quiet Hindu holy town, blessed with a series of exquisite crescent beaches, ideal for serious unwinding. See p.1325

* **Hampi** The remains of the Vijayanagar kingdom, scattered among fertile plantations bisected by the Tungabadra and punctuated by weird rock formations. See p.1331

* **Bijapur** Known as the "Agra of the South" for its splendid Islamic architecture, most famously the vast dome of the Golgumbaz. See p.1344

* **Bidar** Rarely visited Muslim outpost in the remote north-east of the state, famed for its *bidri* metalwork and magnificent medieval monuments. See p.1351

△ The Golgumbaz, Bijapur

22

Karnataka

Created in 1956 from the princely state of Mysore, **KARNATAKA** – the name is a derivation of the name of the local language, Kannada, spoken by virtually all of its 53 million inhabitants – marks a transition zone between northern India and the Dravidian deep south. Along its border with Maharashtra and Andhra Pradesh, a string of medieval walled towns, studded with domed mausoleums and minarets, recall the era when this part of the Deccan was a Muslim stronghold, while the coastal and hill districts that dovetail with Kerala are quintessential Hindu South India, profuse with tropical vegetation and soaring temple *gopuras*. Between the two are scattered some of the peninsula's most extraordinary historic sites, notably the ruined Vijayanagar city at Hampi, whose lost temples and derelict palaces stand amid an arid, boulder-strewn landscape of surreal beauty.

Karnataka is one of the wettest regions in India, its **climate** dominated by the seasonal monsoon, which sweeps in from the southwest in June, dumping an average of 4m of rain on the coast before it peters out in late September. Running in an unbroken line along the state's palm-fringed coast, the **Western Ghats**, draped in dense deciduous forests, impede the path of the rain clouds east. As a result, the landscape of the interior – comprising the southern apex of the triangular Deccan trap, known here as the **Mysore Plateau** – is considerably drier, with dark volcanic soils in the north, and poor quartzite-granite country to the south. Two of India's most sacred rivers, the Tungabhadra and Krishna, flow across this sun-baked terrain, draining east to the Bay of Bengal.

Broadly speaking, Karnataka's principal attractions are concentrated at opposite ends of the state, with a handful of lesser-visited places dotted along the coast between Goa and Kerala. Road and rail routes dictate that most itineraries take in the brash state capital, **Bangalore**, a go-ahead, modern city that epitomizes the aspirations of the country's new middle classes, with glittering malls, fast-food outlets and a nightlife unrivalled outside Mumbai. The state's other major city, **Mysore**, appeals more for its old-fashioned ambience, nineteenth-century palaces and vibrant produce and incense markets. It also lies within easy reach of several important historical monuments. At the nearby fortified island of **Srirangapatnam** – site of the bloody battle of 1799 that finally put Mysore State into British hands, with the defeat of the Muslim military genius **Tipu Sultan** – parts of the fort, a mausoleum and Tipu's summer palace survive.

A clutch of other unmissable sights lie further northeast, dotted around the dull railway town of **Hassan**. Around nine centuries ago, the Hoysala kings sited their grand dynastic capitals here, at the now middle-of-nowhere villages of **Belur** and **Halebid**, where several superbly crafted temples survive intact. More impressive still, and one of India's most extraordinary sacred sites, is the

22

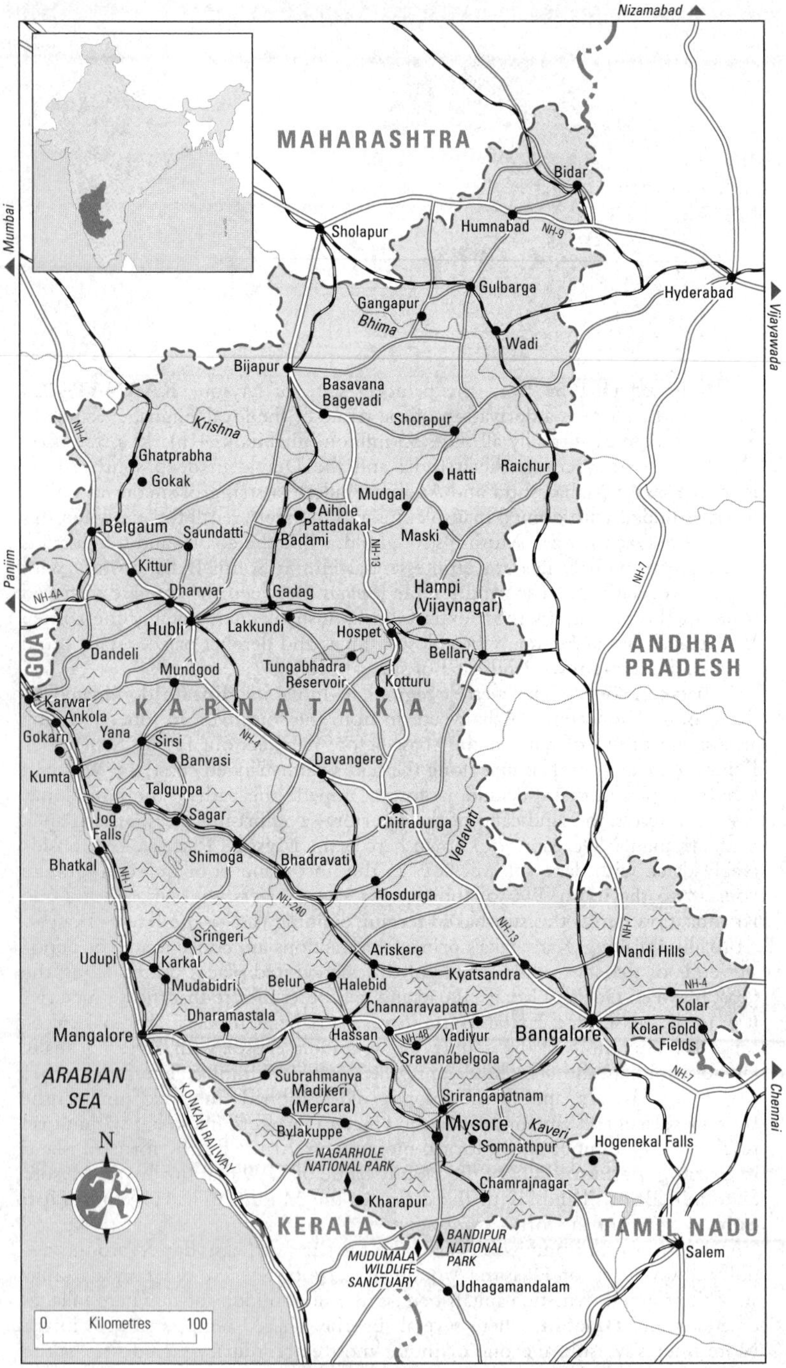

Nizamabad
MAHARASHTRA
Mumbai
Bidar
Humnabad
NH-9
Sholapur
Gulbarga
Hyderabad
Vijayawada
Gangapur
Bhima
Wadi
Bijapur
Basavana
Bagevadi
Krishna
NH-4
Shorapur
Ghatprabha
Gokak
Hatti
Raichur
Mudgal
Aihole
Pattadakal
Belgaum
Saundatti
Badami
Maski
NH-13
Kittur
Panjim
NH-4A
Dharwar
Gadag
Hampi
(Vijaynagar)
NH-7
Hubli
Lakkundi
Hospet
GOA
Dandeli
Bellary
ANDHRA
PRADESH
Mundgod
Tungabhadra
Reservoir
Kotturu
Karwar
Ankola
K A R N A T A K A
Gokarn
Yana
Sirsi
NH-4
Banvasi
Kumta
Davangere
Talguppa
Jog
Falls
Sagar
Chitradurga
Vedavati
Shimoga
Bhatkal
NH-17
Bhadravati
Hosdurga
NH-240
NH-13
NH-7
Sringeri
Udupi
Karkal
Ariskere
Nandi Hills
Mudabidri
Belur
Halebid
Kyatsandra
NH-4
Kolar
Channarayapatna
Dharamastala
Mangalore
Hassan
NH-48
Yadiyur
Bangalore
Kolar Gold
Fields
Sravanabelgola
ARABIAN
SEA
Subrahmanya
NH-7
Chennai
KONKAN RAILWAY
Madikeri
(Mercara)
Srirangapatnam
Bylakuppe
Mysore
Kaveri
N
Somnathpur
Hogenekal Falls
NAGARHOLE
NATIONAL PARK
Chamrajnagar
Kharapur
KERALA
TAMIL NADU
BANDIPUR
NATIONAL
PARK
MUDUMALA
WILDLIFE
SANCTUARY
Salem
Udhagamandalam
0 Kilometres 100
Ernakulam/ Kochi

eighteen-metre Jain colossus at **Sravanabelagola**, which stares serenely over idyllic Deccani countryside.

West of Mysore, the Ghats rise in a wall of thick jungle cut by deep ravines and isolated valleys. You can either traverse the range by rail, via Hassan, or explore some of its scenic backwaters by road. Among these, the rarely visited coffee- and spice-growing region of **Kodagu (Coorg)** has to be the most entrancing, with its unique culture and lush vistas of misty wooded hills and valleys. Most Coorgi agricultural produce is shipped out of **Mangalore**, the nearest large town, of little interest except as a transport hub whose importance can only increase now the Konkan Railway is more or less operating to its full potential. Situated midway between Goa and Kerala, it's also a convenient – if uninspiring – place to pause on the journey along Karnataka's beautiful **Karavali coast**. Interrupted by countless mangrove-lined estuaries, the state's 320-kilometre-long red-laterite coast has always been difficult to navigate by land, and traffic along the recently revamped highway remains relatively light. Although there are plenty of fine beaches, facilities are, with rare exceptions, nonexistent, and locals often react with astonishment at the sight of a foreigner.

Few Western tourists visit the famous Krishna temple at **Udupi**, an important Vaishnavite pilgrimage centre, and fewer still venture into the mountains to see India's highest waterfall at **Jog Falls**, set amid some of the region's most spectacular scenery. However, atmospheric **Gokarna**, further north up the coast, is an increasingly popular beach hideaway for budget travellers. Harbouring one of India's most famous *shivalinga*, this seventeenth-century Hindu pilgrimage town enjoys a stunning location, with a high headland dividing it from a string of exquisite beaches.

Winding inland from the mountainous Goan border, NH-4A and the rail line comprise sparsely populated **northern Karnataka**'s main transport artery, linking a succession of grim industrial centres. This region's undisputed highlight is the ghost city of Vijayanagar, better known as **Hampi**, scattered around boulder hills on the south banks of the River Tungabhadra. The ruins of this once splendid capital occupy a magical site, while the ancient bazaar is a great spot to hole up for a spell. The jumping-off place for Hampi is **Hospet**, from where buses leave for the bumpy journey north across the rolling Deccani plains to **Badami**, **Aihole** and **Pattadakal**. Now lost in countryside, these tiny villages were once capitals of the **Chalukya** dynasty (sixth to eighth centuries). The whole area is littered with ancient rock-cut caves and finely carved stone temples.

Further north still, in one of Karnataka's most remote and poorest districts, craggy hilltop citadels and crumbling wayside tombs herald the formerly troubled buffer zone between the Muslim-dominated northern Deccan and the Dravidian-Hindu south. **Bijapur**, capital of the Bahmanis, the Muslim dynasty that oversaw the eventual downfall of Vijayanagar, harbours South India's finest collection of Islamic architecture, including the world's second-largest free-standing dome, the Golgumbaz. The first Bahmani capital, **Gulbarga**, site of a famous Muslim shrine and theological college, has retained little of its former splendour, but the more isolated **Bidar**, where the Bahmanis moved in the sixteenth century, definitely deserves a detour en route to or from Hyderabad, four hours east by bus. Perched on a rocky escarpment, its crumbling red ramparts harbour Persian-style mosaic-fronted mosques, mausoleums and a sprawling fort complex evocative of Samarkand and the great silk route.

Some history

Like much of southern India, Karnataka has been ruled by successive Buddhist, Hindu and Muslim dynasties. The influence of Jainism has also been marked;

India's very first emperor, **Chandragupta Maurya**, is believed to have converted to Jainism in the fourth century BC, renounced his throne, and fasted to death at Sravanabelagola, now one of the most visited Jain pilgrimage centres in the country.

During the first millennium AD, this whole region was dominated by power struggles between the various kingdoms who controlled the western Deccan. From the sixth to the eighth centuries, the **Chalukya** kingdom included Maharashtra, the Konkan coast on the west, and the whole of Karnataka. The **Cholas** were powerful in the east of the region from about 870 until the thirteenth century, when the Deccan kingdoms were overwhelmed by General Malik Kafur, a convert to Islam.

By the medieval era, Muslim incursions from the north had forced the hitherto warring and fractured Hindu states of the south into close alliance, with the mighty **Vijayanagars** emerging as overlords. Their lavish capital, Vijayanagar, ruled an empire stretching from the Bay of Bengal to the Arabian Sea and south to Cape Comorin. The Muslims' superior military strength, however, triumphed in 1565 at the Battle of Talikota, when the **Bahmanis** laid siege to Vijayanagar, reducing it to rubble and plundering its opulent palaces and temples.

Thereafter, a succession of Muslim sultans held sway over the north, while in the south of the state, the independent **Wadiyar rajas** of Mysore, whose territory was comparatively small, successfully fought off the Marathas. In 1761, the brilliant Muslim campaigner Haider Ali, with French support, seized the throne. His son, Tipu Sultan, turned Mysore into a major force in the south before he was killed by the British at the **battle of Srirangapatnam** in 1799.

Following Tipu's defeat, the British restored the Wadiyar family to the throne. They kept it until riots in 1830 led the British to appoint a Commission to rule in their place. Fifty years later, the throne was once more returned to the Wadiyars, who remained governors until Karnataka was created by the merging of the states of Mysore and the Madras Presidencies in 1956. Since Independence, the political scene has largely been dominated by the Congress party, which was routed in the Nineties – first by a reunited Janata Dal and subsequently by a fundamentalist BJP alliance – but returned to power in the most recent state elections.

Bangalore

Once across the Western Ghats, the cloying air of Kerala and the Konkan coast gradually gives way to the crisp skies and dry heat of the dusty **Mysore Plateau**. The setting for E.M. Forster's acclaimed Raj novel, *A Passage to India*, this southern tip of the Deccan – a vast, open expanse of gently undulating plains dotted with wheat fields and dramatic granite boulders – formed the heartland of the region's once powerful princely state. Today it remains the political hub of the region, largely due to the economic importance of **BANGALORE**, Karnataka's capital, which, with a population racing towards eight million, is one of the fastest growing cities in Asia. A major scientific research centre at the cutting edge of India's technological revolution, Bangalore has a trendy high-speed self-image that ensures it is quite unlike anywhere else in South India.

In the 1800s, Bangalore's gentle climate, broad streets, and green public parks made it the "Garden City". Until well after Independence, senior figures, film stars and VIPs flocked to buy or build dream homes amid this urban idyll, which offered such unique amenities as theatres, cinemas and a lack of restrictions on

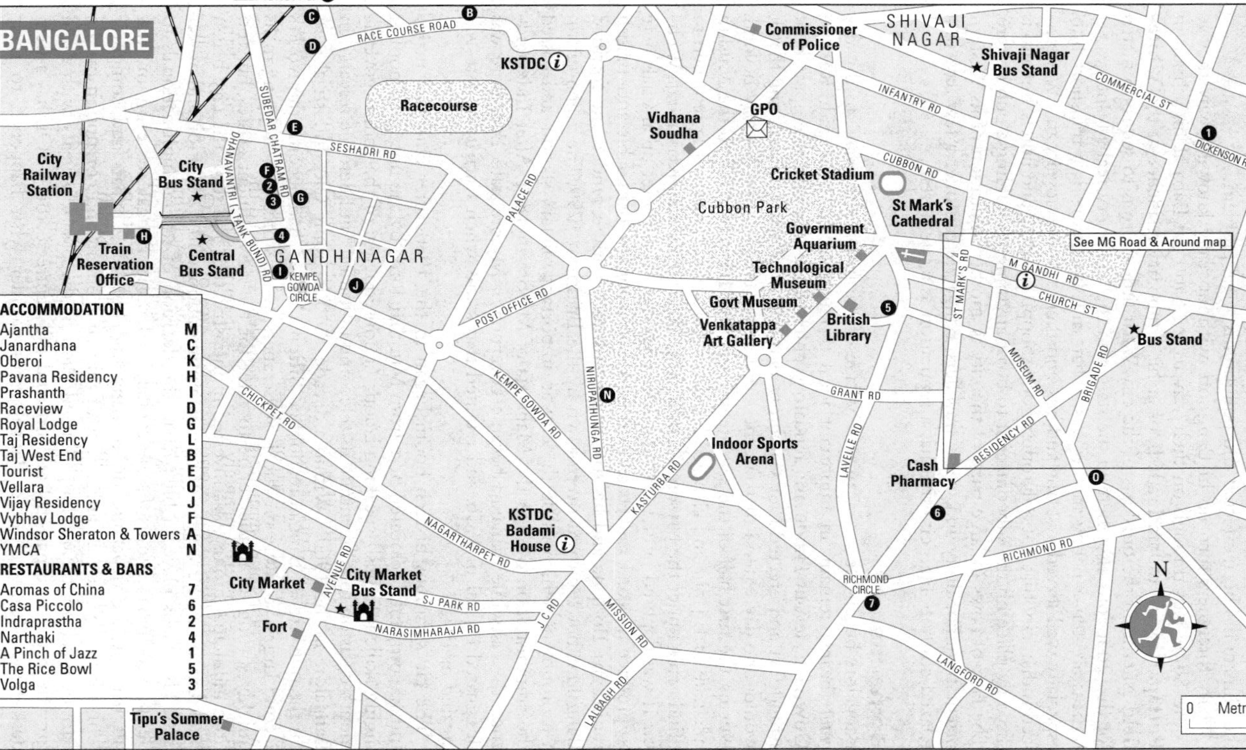
BANGALORE
ISKON & A
L & Whitefield Ashram
Chennai & Airport (13km)
Mysore
Bull Temple & Gandhi Market
Lalbagh Gardens
Lalbagh Botanical Gardens
ACCOMMODATION
Ajantha M
Janardhana C
Oberoi K
Pavana Residency H
Prashanth I
Raceview D
Royal Lodge G
Taj Residency L
Taj West End B
Tourist E
Vellara O
Vijay Residency J
Vybhav Lodge F
Windsor Sheraton & Towers A
YMCA N
RESTAURANTS & BARS
Aromas of China 7
Casa Piccolo 6
Indraprastha 2
Narthaki 4
A Pinch of Jazz 1
The Rice Bowl 5
Volga 3
City Railway Station
Train Reservation Office
City Bus Stand
Central Bus Stand
GANDHINAGAR
KEMPE GOWDA CIRCLE
Racecourse
KSTDC
Vidhana Soudha
GPO
Cubbon Park
Cricket Stadium
Commissioner of Police
SHIVAJI NAGAR
Shivaji Nagar Bus Stand
St Mark's Cathedral
Government Aquarium
Technological Museum
Govt Museum
Venkatappa Art Gallery
British Library
Indoor Sports Arena
KSTDC Badami House
Cash Pharmacy
City Market
City Market Bus Stand
Fort
Tipu's Summer Palace
Bus Stand
See MG Road & Around map
Ulsoor Lake
RICHMOND CIRCLE
RACE COURSE ROAD
SUBEDAR CHATRAM RD
DHANAVANTRI (TANK BUND) RD
SESHADRI RD
PALACE RD
POST OFFICE RD
CHICKPET RD
KEMPE GOWDA RD
NIRUPATHUNGA RD
KASTURBA RD
NAGARTHARPET RD
AVENUE RD
SJ PARK RD
NARASIMHARAJA RD
J C RD
MISSION RD
LALBAGH RD
LANGFORD RD
RICHMOND RD
LAVELLE RD
GRANT RD
RESIDENCY RD
MUSEUM RD
BRIGADE RD
CHURCH ST
M GANDHI RD
ST MARK'S RD
ULSOOR RD
CUBBON RD
INFANTRY RD
COMMERCIAL ST
DICKENSON RD
N
0 Metres 500

alcohol. However, for well over a decade, Bangalore has undergone a massive transformation. The wide avenues, now dominated by tower blocks, are teeming with traffic, and water and electricity shortages have become the norm. Even the climate has been affected and pollution is a real problem.

Many foreigners turn up in Bangalore without really knowing why they've come. Some pass through on their way to see Satya Sai Baba at his ashram in **Puttaparthy** in Andhra Pradesh, or at his temporary residence at the **Whitefield** ashram on the outskirts of the city. What little there is to see is no match for the attractions elsewhere in the state, and the city's very real advantages for Indians are ten-a-penny in the West. That said, Bangalore is a transport hub, especially well served by plane and bus, and there is some novelty in a Westernized Indian city that not only offers good shopping, eating and hotels, but also is the only place on the subcontinent to boast anything resembling a pub culture. The lack of cows in large parts of the city is another indication of its Western orientation. For dusty and weary travellers, Bangalore can offer a few days in a relaxed cosmopolitan city that has a reputation as a safe haven.

Some history

Bangalore began life as the minor "village of the half-baked *gram*"; to this day *gram* (beans) remain an important local product. In 1537, Magadi **Kempe Gowda**, a devout Hindu and feudatory chief of the Vijayanagar empire, built a mud fort and erected four watchtowers outside the village, predicting that it would, one day, extend that far; the city now, of course, stretches way beyond. During the first half of the seventeenth century, Bangalore fell to the Muslim sultanate of Bijapur and changed hands several times before being returned to Hindu rule under the Mysore Wadiyar rajas. In 1758, Chikka Krishnaraja Wadiyar II was deposed by the military genius Haider Ali, who set up arsenals here to produce muskets, rockets and other weapons for his formidable anti-British campaigns. Both he and his son, **Tipu Sultan**, greatly extended and fortified Bangalore, but Tipu was overthrown by the British in 1799. They then set up a cantonment, which made the city an important military station, and passed the administration over to the Maharaja of Mysore in 1881. After Independence, the erstwhile maharaja became governor of Mysore state. Bangalore was designated capital in 1956, and retained that status when Karnataka state was created in 1973.

The city's famous hi-tech boom began in the 1980s after clutch of major Indian companies relocated here from Mumbai, lured by the untapped pool of highly skilled, English-speaking labour (a consequence of the Indian government's decision to concentrate its telecommunications and defence research in Bangalore in the 1960s). Within a decade, the Electronic City Industrial Park on the outskirts of Bangalore, dubbed **Silicon Valley**, had become the world's second largest software producer. Skyscrapers, swish stores and shopping malls quickly sprung up in the centre to cater for the new affluent classes, but too little municipal money was invested in infrastructure and soon the city began buckling under the weight of massive immigration, traffic pollution and power cuts. The chaos played a bit part in the decision of several multinationals to decamp to India's latest software capital, Hyderabad. Bangalore's economy was hit hard by the departure of so many high-spending expats and computer whizz kids, but, despite allegations of mismanagement and corruption on the part of local politicians, has bounced back in the past few years with rapid growth in the international telecom and call centre sector – AOL has a help desk here. Meanwhile, old Bangaloreans wonder what happened to their beloved "Garden City".

Arrival, information and city transport

Bangalore airport, 13km north of the city centre, serves cities throughout South India and beyond; for details of departures, see p.1354. The **KSTDC desk** in the arrivals hall (daily 7.30am–1.30pm & 2–7.30pm; ⓣ080/2526 8753) stocks leaflets on Karnataka and can book hotel rooms. Branches of the State Bank of Mysore (daily 8am–7pm) and Vijaya Bank (daily 8.30am–12.30pm) both **change money**. You can get into the city by **taxi** (Rs160–200; book at the prepaid desk), by the **auto-rickshaws** (Rs80–100) that gather outside, or by **bus** – numerous local services run along the main road only several hundred metres from the terminal.

Bangalore City railway station is east of the centre, near Kempe Gowda Circle, and across the road from the main bus stands (for the north of the city, get off at Bangalore Cantonment station). As you come into the entrance hall from the platforms, the far left-hand corner holds an **ITDC booth** (daily 8am–4pm; ⓣ080/2220 4277), where you can rent cars and book tours; staff will book you a hotel for a fee of ten percent of the day's room rate. The **KSTDC tourist information office** (daily 7am–8pm; ⓣ080/2287 0068), to the right, also books tours and can provide useful advice. To hire an auto-rickshaw it is best to pay the Rs1 fee at the prepaid booth to guarantee the proper fare – a typical charge is Rs25–40 to MG Road, depending on the time of day.

Innumerable **long-distance buses** arrive at the big, busy **Central** (KSRTC) **stand**, opposite the railway station. There is a comprehensive timetable in English in the centre of the concourse. A bridge divides it from **City stand**, used by local services.

Information

For information on Bangalore, Karnataka and neighbouring states, go to the excellent **India Tourism Office** (Mon–Fri 9.30am–6pm, Sat 9am–1pm; ⓣ080/2558 5417, ⓦwww.india-tourism.com), in the KSFC Building, 48 Church St (parallel to MG Road between Brigade and St Mark's roads). You can pick up a free city map here and the staff will help you put together tour itineraries.

Apart from the desks at the City railway station and airport, **Karnataka State Tourist Development Corporation** has two city offices: one at Badami House, NR Square (daily 6.30am–10pm; ⓣ080/2227 5883), where you can book the tours outlined above; and the head office on the second floor of Khanija Bhavan, Race Course Road (Mon–Sat 10am–5.30pm, closed second

Tours

KSTDC operates a selection of guided **tours** from Bangalore. Though rushed, these can be handy if you're short of time. The twice-daily **City Tour** (7.30am–1.30pm or 2–7.30pm; Rs105), calls at the museum, Vidhana Soudha, Ulsoor Lake, Lalbagh Gardens, Bull Temple and Tipu Sultan's palace and winds up with a long stop at the Government handicrafts emporium. The New Bangalore tour (Wed–Sun 7.15am–8pm; Rs185) gets you to the "seven new wonders" of the city, including the ISKCON temple, planetarium and musical fountain. **"Outstation" tours** include a long day-trip to Srirangapatnam/Mysore and another to Belur/Halebid/Sravanabelagola but they are not recommended unless you're happy to spend at least eight hours on the bus.

Sat of month; ⓣ080/2235 2901–3, ⓦwww.kstdc.nic.in). It shares its smart new offices with Karnataka Tourism, which does not provide face-to-face information for visitors but has a decent website (ⓦwww.karnatakatourism.com). For up-to-the-minute information about **what's on**, plus restaurants and shops, check the ad-sponsored listings magazine *City Info* (ⓦwww.explocity.com), distributed free at the larger hotels and the India Tourism Office.

If you're planning to visit any of Karnataka's **national parks**, call at the Wildlife Office, Forest Department, Aranya Bhavan, Malleswaram (ⓣ080/2334 1993) for information, or approach Jungle Lodges & Resorts, Floor 2, Shrungar Shopping Centre, (off) MG Road (ⓣ080/2559 7021, ⓦwww.junglelodges.com). A quasi-government body, Jungle Lodges promotes "ecotourism" through a number of upmarket forest lodges including the much lauded *Kabini River Lodge* near Nagarhole.

City transport

The easiest way of getting around Bangalore is by metered **auto-rickshaw**; fares start at Rs10 for the first kilometre and Rs5 per kilometre thereafter. Most meters do work and drivers are usually willing to use them, although you will occasionally be asked for a flat fare, especially during rush hours.

Bangalore's extensive **bus** system, run by the Bangalore Metropolitan Transport Corporation, radiates from the City (Kempe Gowda) bus stand (ⓣ080/222 2542), near the railway station. Most buses from platform 17 travel past MG Road. Along with regular buses, BMTC also operates a deluxe express service, Pushpak, on a number of set routes (#P109 terminates at Whitefield ashram) as well as a handful of night buses. Other important city bus stands include the KR Market bus stand (ⓣ080/670 2177) to the south of the railway station and Shivaji Nagar (ⓣ080/286 5332) to the north of Cubbon Park – the #P2 Jayanagar service from here is handy for the Lalbagh Botanical Gardens.

You can book **chauffeur-driven cars and taxis** through several agencies including the Cab Service, Sabari Complex, 24 Residency Rd (ⓣ080/2558 6121) and the 24-hour Dial-a-Car service (ⓣ080/2526 1737, ⓔdialacar@hotmail.com). Typical rates for car rental are around Rs150 per hour, Rs400 for four hours (which includes 40km) and Rs550 for eight hours (80km); the extra mileage charge is around Rs5 per kilometre. Most taxi companies start calculating their time and distances from when the car leaves their depot. If you need a taxi for a one-way journey, be prepared to pay for the return fare as well. A metered taxi system is planned for the future which will make hiring a cab simpler. See Listings, p.1291, for details of self-drive car rental.

Accommodation

Rooms in Bangalore often fill up, especially the smarter places, and though the 24-hour checkout system operated by most hotels means openings always crop up there's no harm in phoning ahead. **Budget accommodation** is concentrated around the railway station (which itself has good-value, but often full, retiring rooms; dorm Rs125, rooms Rs300–400) and the Central bus stand. Standards in this area can be very low; the better options are on the east side, dotted around Dhanavanthri (Tank Bund) Road and parallel Subedar Chatram Road. **Mid-range** and **expensive hotels** are more scattered; most are near MG Road, and some are around the racecourse, a short rickshaw trip northeast of the station. All hotels in the first two sections are on the main map, while all those in the third section are on the MG Road map, except where stated.

Around the railway station and Central bus stand

Pavana Residency 88 RBDGT Charities Building ⓣ080/2228 6681, ⓔhotelpavan@hotmail .com. Rather overpriced but as close to the railway station as you can be, yet quiet. Sizeable rooms of varying comfort, some a/c. 4–6

Prashanth 21 E Tank Bund Rd ⓣ080/2287 4041, ⓦwww.prasanth_hotel.com. Among the better hotels opposite the Central bus stand. All rooms have windows and shower-toilets. The *Mayura* nearby is the best fall-back. 3–4

Royal Lodge Subedar Chatram Rd ⓣ080/2226 3740–2. Large, clean and efficient lodge. Most rooms are compact attached doubles with cable TV. 2–3

Tourist Ananda Rao Circle ⓣ080/2226 2381–8. A short walk from the station, one of Bangalore's best all-round budget lodges, with small rooms, long verandas, and friendly family management. No reservations and it fills up quickly. 2

Vijay Residency 18 3rd Cross, Main Road ⓣ080/2220 3024, ⓦwww.vijayresidency.net. A Comfort Inn franchise that's plush and comfortable, if a bit ostentatious. Within striking reach of the railway station, with central a/c, foreign exchange and quality restaurant. 7–8

Vybhav Lodge 60 Subedar Chatram Rd ⓣ080/2287 3997. Good clean budget lodge offering small attached rooms with TV, dotted around a little courtyard. Decent value, especially for singles. 3

Around the racecourse and Cubbon Park

Janardhana Kumara Krupa Rd ⓣ080/2225 4444, ⓕ2225 8708. Neat, clean and spacious rooms with balconies and baths. Well away from the chaos and good value at this price (despite hefty service charges). 3–5

Raceview 25 Race Course Rd ⓣ080/2220 3401. Run-of-the-mill mid-range hotel whose upper front rooms overlook the racecourse. Safe deposit, foreign exchange and some a/c. 4–5

Taj West End Race Course Rd ⓣ080/2225 5055, ⓦwww.tajhotels.com. Dating back to 1887 with fabulous gardens and long colonnaded walkways. The most characterful rooms, which start at $260 a night, are in the old wing, where deep verandas overlook acres of grounds. 9

Windsor Sheraton & Towers 25 Golf Course Rd ⓣ080/2226 9898, ⓦwww.sheraton.com. Ersatz palace run by Starwood as a luxurious five-star, mainly for overseas businesspeople with rates from $270. Facilities include voicemail, modems, gym, jacuzzi and pool. 9

YMCA Nirupathanga Rd, Cubbon Park, midway between the bus stand and MG Rd ⓣ080/2221 1848. Large, clean rooms and cheaper dorm beds for students only. Economical rates, but often full. 3

Around MG Road

Ajantha 22-A MG Rd ⓣ080/2558 4321, ⓕ2558 4780 (main map). Best value in this area, with larger than average en-suite rooms and some a/c cottages, located down a quiet lane but close to shops. Often booked up days in advance. 3–5

Brindavan 40 MG Rd ⓣ080/558 4000. Old-style budget to mid-range hotel with some a/c rooms, set slightly off the main road. Good value, especially for singles. 3–5

Empire International 36 Church St ⓣ080/2559 3743, ⓦwww.hotelempireinternational.com. Smart

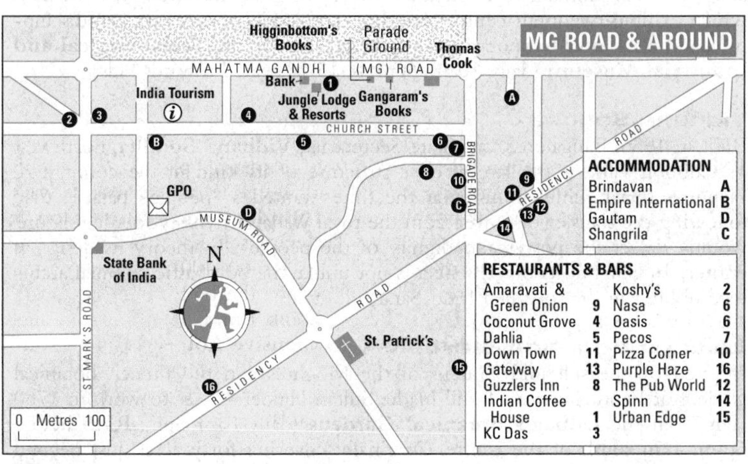

new hotel with very comfortable rooms boasting modern decor and good facilities. ❻–❼

Gautam 17 Museum Rd ⓣ080/558 8764. Large, characterless concrete block of standard rooms, but there's lots of space so it's a good fallback if other places are full. The quiet street is a bonus. ❹

Oberoi 37–39 MG Rd ⓣ080/2558 5858, ⓦwww.oberoiblr.com (main map). Ultra-luxurious five-star, with a clutch of swish restaurants, beautiful landscaped garden and a pool. Rooms range from $260–780. ❾

Shangrila 182 Brigade Rd ⓣ080/5112 1622. Tibetan-run lodge right in the thick of things but welcoming; the comfy standard rooms are as decent value as anywhere in the area. ❹–❻

Taj Residency 41/3 MG Rd ⓣ080/2558 4444, ⓦwww.tajhotels.com (off main map). Not quite in the same league as the *Oberoi* or *Taj West End* but a fully fledged five-star, with all the trimmings. ❾

Vellara 283 Brigade Rd, opposite Brigade Towers ⓣ080/2536 9116, ⓕ2536 9775 (main map). Rather overpriced rooms range from simple "standard", to light and airy "deluxe" on the top floor (with sweeping city views). ❺–❻

The City

The centre of modern Bangalore lies about 4km east of Kempe Gowda Circle and the bus and railway stations. On **MG Road** you'll find most of the mid-range accommodation, restaurants, shops, tourist information and banks. Leafy **Cubbon Park**, and its less than exciting museums, lie on its eastern edge, while the oldest, most "Indian" part of the city extends south from the railway station, a warren of winding streets at their most dynamic in the hubbub of the **City** and **Gandhi markets**. Bangalore's tourist attractions are spread out: monuments such as **Tipu's Summer Palace** and the **Bull Temple** are some way south of the centre. Most, if not all, can be seen on a half-day tour but if you explore on foot, be warned that Bangalore has some of the worst pavements in India.

Cubbon Park and museums

A welcome green space in the heart of the city, shaded by massive clumps of bamboo, **Cubbon Park** is entered from the western end of MG Road, presided over by a statue of Queen Victoria. On Kasturba Road, which runs along its southern edge, the poorly labelled and maintained **Government Museum** (Tues–Sun 10am–5pm; Rs4) features prehistoric artefacts, Vijayanagar, Hoysala and Chalukya sculpture, musical instruments, Thanjavur paintings and Deccani and Rajasthani miniatures. It includes the adjacent **Venkatappa Art Gallery**, which exhibits twentieth-century landscapes, portraits, abstract art, wood sculpture, and occasional temporary art shows. Next door, the **Technological and Industrial Museum** (daily 10am–6pm; Rs15) is geared towards kids.

Vidhana Soudha

Built in 1956, Bangalore's vast State Secretariat, **Vidhana Soudha**, northwest of Cubbon Park, is the largest civic structure of its kind in the country. K. Hanumanthaiah, chief minister at the time, wanted a "people's palace" that, following the transfer of power from the royal Wadayar dynasty to a legislature, would "reflect the power and dignity of the people". In theory its design is entirely Indian, but its overall effect is not unlike the bombastic colonial architecture built in the so-called Indo-Saracenic style.

Lalbagh Botanical Gardens

Inspired by the splendid gardens of the Moghuls and the French botanical gardens at Pondicherry in Tamil Nadu, Sultan Haider Ali set to work in 1760 laying out the **Lalbagh Botanical Gardens** (daily 8am–8pm; Rs15 before 6pm), 4km south of the centre. Originally covering forty acres, just beyond his fort – where one of Kempe Gowda's original watchtowers can still be seen – the gardens were expanded under Ali's son Tipu, who introduced numerous exotic species of plants, and today the gardens house an extensive horticultural seedling centre. The British brought in gardeners from Kew in 1856 and – naturally – built a military bandstand and a glasshouse, based on London's Crystal Palace, which hosts wonderful flower shows. Now spreading over 240 acres, the gardens are pleasant to visit during the day, but tend to attract unsavoury characters after 6pm. Great sunsets and views of the city to the north are to be had from the central hill of very old rock, topped by a small shrine.

Tipu's Summer Palace

A two-storey structure built in 1791, mostly of wood, **Tipu's Summer Palace** (daily 9am–5pm; $2 [Rs5]), southwest of the City Market and 3km from MG Road, is similar to the Daria Daulat Palace at Srirangapatnam (see p.1301), but in a far worse state, with most of its painted decoration destroyed. Next door, the **Venkataramanaswamy temple**, dating from the early eighteenth century, was built by the Wadiyar rajas. The *gopura* entranceway was erected in 1978.

Bull Temple

Lying 6km south of the City bus stand (bus #34 & #37), in the Basavanagudi area, Kempe Gowda's sixteenth-century **Bull Temple** (open to non-Hindus; daily 7.30am–1.30pm & 2.30–8.30pm) houses a massive monolithic Nandi bull, its grey granite made black by the application of charcoal and oil. The temple is approached along a path lined with mendicants and snake charmers; inside, for a few rupees, the priest will offer you a string of fragrant jasmine flowers.

ISKCON temple

A hybrid of ultramodern glass and vernacular South Indian temple architecture, ISKCON's (International Society of Krishna Consciousness) gleaming new temple – **Sri Radha Krishna Mandir**, Hare Krishna Hill, Chord Road (daily 7am–1pm & 4–8.30pm), 8km north of the centre, is a lavish showpiece crowned by a gold-plated dome. Barriers guide visitors on a one-way journey through the huge, well-organized complex to the inner sanctum with its images of the god Krishna and his consort Radha. Collection points throughout, and inescapable merchandizing on the way out, are evidence of the organization's highly successful commercialization. Regular **buses** to the temple depart from both the City and Shivaji Nagar bus stands.

Eating

With unmissable sights thin on the ground, but tempting cafés and restaurants on every corner, you could easily spend most of your time in Bangalore **eating**. Nowhere else in South India will you find such gastronomic variety. Around **MG Road**, pizzerias (including *Pizza Hut*), ritzy ice-cream parlours and gourmet French restaurants stand cheek by jowl with regional cuisine from Andhra Pradesh and Kerala, Mumbai *chaat* cafés and snack bars where, in true Bangalorean style, humble thalis from as little as Rs30 masquerade as "executive mini-lunches". The places below are marked on the MG Road map unless stated otherwise.

Amaravati Residency Road Cross, MG Rd. Excellent Andhra cooking with "meals" served on banana leafs and specialities including biriyanis and fried fish. Hectic at lunchtime but well worth any wait.

Aromas of China G3–4 Shiva Shankar Plaza, 19 Lalbagh Rd, Richmond Circle (main map). Among the city's top Chinese restaurants. Delicacies include quality dim sum, duck and sharkfin soup, as well as above-average versions of all the favourites. Fairly pricey.

Casa Piccolo Devata Plaza, 131 Residency Rd (main map). A dozen different tasty pizzas and big portions of *wiener schnitzel*, steaks, fried chicken and ice cream but no alcohol. Tables outside on the basement patio and flower baskets give the place a European ambience.

Coconut Grove Church St. Mouthwatering and moderately priced gourmet Keralan coastal cuisine: vegetarian, fish and meat preparations served in traditional copper thalis on a leafy terrace. Try the tender coconut juice cocktail, *thala chickory bom*. Recommended.

Dahlia Brigade Gardens, Church St. Japanese café tucked in a modern business complex, serving authentic dishes from further east at not unreasonable prices.

Gateway 66 Residency Rd ⓣ080/2558 4545. The *Northern Gate* serves a fairly undistinguished selection of Mughlai and other north Indian dishes, while the *Karavalli* specializes in west coast dishes from Goa to Kerala, including seafood and veg. Very attractive room in traditional southern style with wooden ceiling – plus tables outside under an old tamarind tree. Reservations essential. Expensive.

Green Onion Next door to the *Amaravati*, this small modern triangular-shaped establishment offers a tasty range of kebabs, curries, Chinese and sweets at fair prices in a café-style atmosphere.

Indian Coffee House MG Rd. The usual cheap South Indian snacks, egg dishes and good filter coffee, served by waiters in turbans and cummerbunds. Best for breakfast.

Indraprastha Subedar Chatram Rd (main map). Excellent cheap South Indian snacks, including their wonderful special masala dosa, and a fuller veg menu available. One of the best options in the vicinity of the train and bus stations.

KC Das 38 Church St (corner of St Mark's Rd). Part of the legendary chain of Bengali sweet shops serving traditional steam-cooked sweets, many soaked in syrup and rosewater. Try their definitive *rasgullas*. Eat in or take away.

Koshy's St Mark's Rd. Spacious old-style café with cane blinds, pewter teapots and cotton-clad waiters. Bangalore's most congenial meeting place. Serves full meals, snacks and alcohol.

Narthaki just off Subedar Chatram Rd (main map). The best restaurant in the station/bus stand area. Filling Andhra meals are served on the first floor, while on the second there is a restaurant-bar with a full menu of Indian and Chinese dishes. The chicken chilli is a belter.

Pizza Corner Brigade Rd. The most central location of this popular chain. Quality pizza (with curry toppings available of course) and other fast food items.

Rice Bowl 40/2 Lavelle Rd. Plush a/c Chinese restaurant; try the chop suey, followed by lychees and ice cream. Evenings only.

Volga Subedar Chatram Rd (main map). Revamped restaurant with bright plastic downstairs and more ambient breezy roof garden. Serves good portions of the usual Indian and Chinese fare.

Nightlife

The big boom may be over, but Bangalore's bright young things still have money to spend, and **nightlife** in the city is thriving. A night on the town generally kicks off with a bar crawl along **Brigade Road**, **Residency Road** or **Church Street**, where there are scores of swish **pubs**, complete with MTV, lasers and thumping sound systems. If you persevere, you can get away from the noise and have a quiet drink. Drinking alcohol does not have the seedy connotations here it does elsewhere in India; you'll even see young Indian women enjoying a beer with their mates. Pubs close at 11pm but once in you generally get served till later. For quiet, elegant drinking head for the bars of five-star **hotels** such as the *Jockey Club* at the *Taj Residency* or its competition, the *Polo Club* at the *Oberoi* and, for a taste of colonial grandeur, the *Colonnade* at the *Taj West End*.

Check the listings magazines to catch Bangalore's small but steady stream of **live music** and **theatre**, some of which is home-grown, and there are a handful of **clubs**, which usually follow a couples-only policy.

Bangalore is also a major centre for **cinema**, with a booming industry and dozens of theatres showing the latest releases from India and abroad. Check the listings page of the *Deccan Herald*, the *Evening Herald*, the free listings monthly *Trail Blazer* and *City Info*, to find out what's on. Western movies are often dubbed into Hindi, although their titles may be written in English; check the small print in the newspaper. Cinema fans should head for **Kempe Gowda Circle**, where the Majestic and Triveni cinemas are crammed with posters, hoardings and larger-than-life cardboard cut-outs of the latest stars, strewn with spangly garlands. To arrange a visit to a **movie studio** phone Chamundeshwari Studio (ⓣ080/2226 8642).

Pubs and clubs

Down Town next to Galaxy cinema, Residency Rd. Large pub that also serves food and wine, and has a couple of pool tables at the back.
Guzzlers Inn 48 Rest House Rd, off Brigade Rd. Popular and established pub offering MTV, Star Sport, snooker, pool and draught beer.
Nasa 1/4 Church St. Karaoke and sci-fi decor with lasers in a mock space shuttle. The usual combination of big-screen MTV and in-your-face music.
Oasis Church St, adjacent to *Nasa*. Low light and an unobtrusive sound system: the chill-out option.
Pecos Rest House Rd, off Brigade Rd. Small and relaxed pub on two floors with 1960s and 1970s music; popular with a mixed arty set.
A Pinch of Jazz The Central Park, 47 Dickenson Rd. Upmarket jazz café serving Cajun cuisine and live soft-jazz covers.
The Pub World opposite Galaxy Cinema, Residency Rd. A well-presented newish place popular with trendy young professionals. Actually four pubs from different regions under one roof. The usual high-volume music and sports on TV.
Spinn 80 3rd Cross, Residency Rd. Funk house and other dance music in old colonial house with hi-tech add-ons. No shorts. Open late.
Urban Edge 131 Brigade Rd. Hopping disco with an E-zone, games and regular theme nights.

Listings

Airlines domestic Air Deccan, mobile phone only ⓣ98457 77008; Indian Airlines, Cauvery Bhavan, Kempe Gowda Rd ⓣ080/2297 8423, airport 2522 6233, enquiry ⓣ1407; Jet Airways, 1–4 M Block, Unity Building, JC Rd ⓣ080/2522 1929, airport 2522 0688; Sahara Airlines, 35 Church St ⓣ080/2558 3957, airport 2522 0065.
Airlines international Air France, Sunrise Chambers, 22 Ulsoor Rd ⓣ080/2558 9397; Air India, Unity Building, JC Rd ⓣ080/2227 7747; Alitalia, 44 Safina Plaza, Infantry Rd ⓣ080/2559 1936; American/Austrian/Biman Bangladesh/Royal Jordanian, 22 Sunrise Chambers, Ulsoor Rd ⓣ080/2559 4240; British Airways, 7 Sophia's Choice, St Mark's Rd ⓣ080/2227 1205; Delta/Sabena/Swiss Air/Singapore Airlines, Park View, 17 Curve Rd, Tasker Town ⓣ080/2286 7873; Gulf Air, Sunrise Chambers, 22 Ulsoor Rd ⓣ080/2558 4702; KLM/Northwest Airlines *Taj West End*, Race Course Rd ⓣ080/2226 5562; Lufthansa, 44/2 Dickenson Rd ⓣ080/2558 8791; Malaysian Airlines, Richmond Circle ⓣ080/2212 2991; Pakistan International Airlines, 108 Commerce House, 911 Cunningham Rd ⓣ080/2226 0667; Qantas, Westminster, Cunningham Rd ⓣ080/2226 4719; Thai Airways, G-5 Imperial Court, Cunningham Rd ⓣ080/5112 4333; United Airlines, 17–20 Richmond Towers, 12 Richmond Rd ⓣ080/2224 4620.
Banks and exchange A reliable place to change money is Thomas Cook, 55 MG Rd, on the corner of Brigade Rd, though if it's busy Weizmann Forex Ltd, 56 Residency Rd, and Wall Street Finances, 3 House of Lords, 13/14 St Mark's Rd, are just as efficient and quieter (all Mon–Sat 9.30am–6pm). Better rates are still to be had at banks, of which the State Bank of Mysore (usual hours) on MG Rd is most convenient. There is now an increasing number of ATMs dotted around the city, especially in the MG Rd area.
Bookstores The first floor of Gangarams, 72 MG Rd, offers a wide selection on India (coffee-table art books and academic) plus the latest paperback fiction, and a great selection of Indian greetings cards. Higginbotham's, 68 MG Rd, is also good, while you can browse amongst a wide range of subjects in a/c comfort at LB Publishers, 91 MG Rd. The Sapna Book House in the Thunga Complex opposite Tribhuvan cinema, Gandhinagar, is a massive 32,000 sq ft bibliophile's paradise.
The shop belonging to renowned publishers Motilal Banarsidas, 16 St Mark's Rd, close to the junction with MG Rd, offers a superb selection of heavyweight Indology and philosophy titles.
Car rental You can find self-drive car rental at Avis, the *Oberoi* hotel, 37–39 MG Rd ⓣ080/2558 5858, ⓦwww.avis.com; and Hertz, Unit 12 Raheja Plaza, 17 Commissariat Rd ⓣ080/2559 9408, ⓦwww.hertz.com; both have airport outlets. Charges are from around Rs1000 per day. For long-distance car rental and tailor-made itineraries,

Moving on from Bangalore

Bangalore is South India's principal transport hub. Fast and efficient computerized booking facilities make **moving on** relatively hassle-free, although availability of seats should never be taken for granted; book as far in advance as possible. For an overview of travel services to and from Bangalore, see "Travel details" on p.1354.

Bangalore's modern **airport** is the busiest in South India, with international and domestic departures and plans for more. The most frequent flights are to **Mumbai**, **Delhi** and **Chennai**, with about ten daily flights to each operated by Air Deccan, Air India, Jet Airways, Indian Airlines and Sahara. For a full rundown of destinations, see Travel details p.1355; addresses of airline offices and recommended travel agents appear in Listings on p.1291.

Most of the wide range of long-haul **buses** from the Central stand can be booked in advance at the computerized counters near Bay 13 (7.30am–7.30pm). Aside from KSRTC, state bus corporations represented include Andhra Pradesh, Kerala, Maharashtra, Tamil Nadu and the Kadamba (Goa) Transport Corporation. Timings and ticket availability for the forthcoming week are posted on a large board left of the main entrance. For general enquiries, call ⓣ080/2287 3377. Several private bus companies run luxury coaches to destinations such as Mysore, Bijapur, Ooty, Chennai, Kochi/Ernakulam, Thrissur, Kollam and Thiruvananthapuram. Agencies opposite the bus stand sell tickets for private coach companies such as Sharma (ⓣ080/2652 1924), National (ⓣ080/2225 7202) and Shama (ⓣ080/2670 3186), which all advertise overnight deluxe buses to **Goa** (Rs350) as well as sleeper coaches (Rs450) and services to **Mumbai** for Rs550 and **Chennai** for Rs250–450. The most reliable of the private bus companies is Vijayanand Travels, with a branch at *Sri Saraswathi Lodge*, 3rd Main 2nd Cross, Gandhinagar (ⓣ080/2228 7222) and several others throughout the city; its distinctive yellow-and-black luxury coaches run to destinations such as Mangalore and Hospet for Hampi.

While Southern Railways complete the conversion to broad gauge, the **line** from Hassan to Mangalore remains closed. Check the situation when you arrive. Bangalore City station's reservations office (Mon–Sat 8am–2pm & 2.15–8pm, Sun 8am–2pm; reservations ⓣ132) is in a separate building, east of the main station (to the left as you approach). Counter 14 is for foreigners. If you have an Indrail Pass,

try Gullivers Tours & Travels, South Black 201/202 Manipal Centre, 47 Dickenson Rd ⓣ080/2558 8001; Clipper Holidays, 406 Regency Enclave, 4 Magrath Rd ⓣ080/2559 9032; any KSTDC office; and the ITDC booth at the railway station.

Hospitals Victoria, near City Market ⓣ080/2670 1150; Sindhi Charitable, 3rd Main St, S R Nagar ⓣ080/2223 7318.

Internet access At the last count Bangalore had a staggering 700 email/Internet bureaux – they generally charge Rs10–30 per hour and open for most if not all 24 hours of the day. The Cyber Café, 13–15 Brigade Rd, is one of the most popular; there is coffee, but they don't encourage more than one person per computer. Alternatives include Cyber Craft, 33 Rest House Rd; and Cyber Den, first floor, S112A Manipal Centre, Dickenson Rd. There is a superfast DSL service at Hub, in the forecourt of Bangalore City railway station.
A number of Internet joints have Net2Phone facilities, such as the one outside *Hotel Brindavan*, off MG Rd.

Libraries The British Council (English-language) library, 23 Kasturba Rd Cross (Mon–Sat 10.30am–6.30pm; ⓣ080/2221 3485), has newspapers and magazines that visitors are welcome to peruse in a/c comfort, as does the Alliance Française (French), 16 GMT Rd (ⓣ080/2225 8762), and Max Mueller Bhavan (German), 3 Lavelle Rd (ⓣ080/2227 5435).

Music stores The best music shops in the city centre, selling Indian, Western and World music, are Music World and Planet M, both on Brigade Rd, or Rhythms, at 14 St Mark's Rd, beneath the *Nahar Heritage* hotel; look out for the excellent box-set introducing South Indian or Carnatic music.

Pharmacies Open all night: Al-Siddique Pharma Centre, opposite Jama Masjid near City Market; Janata Bazaar, in the Victoria Hospital, near City go to the Chief Reservations Supervisor's Office on the first floor (turn left at the top of the stairs), where "reservations are guaranteed". There are two 24-hour telephone information lines; one handles timetable enquiries (Ⓣ131), the other reels off a recorded list of arrivals and departures (Ⓣ133).

Box Recommended trains from Bangalore

The following trains are recommended as the fastest and/or most convenient from Bangalore:

Destination	Name	No.	Departs	Total time
Delhi	Rajdhani Express*	#2429	4 weekly 6.35pm	34hr 40min
	Karnataka Express	#2627	daily 6.30pm	41hr 40min
Chennai	Shatabdi Express*	#2008	daily except Tues 4.25pm	5hr
	Lalbagh Express	#2608	daily 6.30am	5hr 30min
Hospet (for Hampi)	Hampi Express	#6592	daily 10.05pm	9hr 35min
Hyderabad (Secunderabad)	Rajdhani Express*	#2429	4 weekly 6.35pm	12hr 5min
Ernakulam (for Kochi)	Kanniyakumari Express	#6526	daily 9.45pm	11hr 50min
Mumbai	Udyan Express	#6530	daily 8pm	23hr 55min
Mysore	Shatabdi Express*	#2007	daily except Tues 11am	2hr
	Tipu Express	#6206	daily 2.15pm	2hr 30min
	Chamundi Express	#6216	daily 6.15pm	3hr
Thiruvananthapuram	Kanniyakumari Express	#6526	daily 9.45pm	17hr

*= a/c only

Market; Sindhi Charitable Hospital, 3rd Main SR Nagar. During the day, head for Santoshi Pharma, 46 Mission Rd.

Photographic equipment Adlabs, Mission Rd, Subbaiah Circle, stocks transparency film. GG Welling, 113 MG Rd and GK Vale, 89 MG Rd, sell transparency and Polaroid film.

Police Ⓣ100.

Post office On the corner of Raj Bhavan Rd and Cubbon St, at the northern tip of Cubbon Park, about ten minutes' walk from MG Rd (Mon–Sat 10am–7pm, Sun 10.30am–1.30pm).

Swimming pools The only five-star hotel pool open to non-residents (including sauna, jacuzzi and health club) is at the *Taj West End* (Rs500).

Travel agents For flight booking and reconfirmation and other travel necessities, try Gullivers Tours & Travels, South Black 201–202 Manipal Centre, 47 Dickenson Rd Ⓣ080/2558 8001; Merry Go Round Tours, 41 Museum Rd, next to the *Empire International* hotel Ⓣ & Ⓕ080/2558 6946; Marco Polo Tours, Janardhan Towers, 2 Residency Rd Ⓣ080/2227 4484, Ⓕ2223 6671; and Sita Travels, 1 St Mark's Rd Ⓣ080/2558 8892.

Around Bangalore

Many visitors to Bangalore are on their way to or from Mysore. The **Janapada Loka Folk Arts Museum**, between the two, gives a fascinating insight into Karnatakan culture, while anyone wishing to see or study classical dance in a rural environment should check out **Nrityagram Dance Village**.

Janapada Loka Folk Arts Museum

The **Janapada Loka Folk Arts Museum** (daily 9am–6pm; free), 53km southwest of Bangalore on the Mysore road, includes an amazing array of Karnatakan agricultural, hunting and fishing implements, weapons, ingenious household gadgets, masks, dolls and shadow puppets, carved wooden *bhuta* (spirit-worship) sculptures and larger-than-life temple procession figures, manuscripts, musical instruments and *Yakshagana* theatre costumes. In addition, 1600 hours of **audio and video recordings** of musicians, dancers and rituals from the state are available on request. To get to the museum, take one of the many slow Mysore buses (not the nonstop ones) from Bangalore. After the town of Ramanagar, alight at the 53-kilometre stone by the side of the road. A small **restaurant** serves simple food, and dorm **accommodation** (❶) is available. For more details contact the Karnataka Janapada Trust, 7 Subramanyaswami Temple Rd, 5th Cross, 4th Block, Kumara Park West, Bangalore.

Nrityagram Dance Village

NRITYAGRAM DANCE VILLAGE (Tues–Sun 10am–5.30pm; Rs20) is a delightful, purpose-built model village, 30km west of Bangalore, designed by the award-winning architect Gerard de Cunha and founded by the late Protima Gauri, who tragically died in an avalanche during a pilgrimage to Kailash in Tibet in 1998. Gauri, who had left Nrityagram sometime before her death, had a colourful career in media and film, and eventually came to be renowned as an exponent of Odissi dance (see p.1051). The school continues without her and attracts pupils from all over the world. It hosts regular performances and lectures on Indian mythology and art, and also offers courses in different forms of Indian dance. **Guided tours** of the complex cost Rs850 per person (minimum 6), including lunch and a demonstration. **Accommodation** for longer stays (❼) promises "oxygen, home-grown vegetables and fruits, no TV, telephones, newspapers or noise". Contact its Bangalore office (Ⓣ080/2846 6313).

Mysore

A centre of sandalwood-carving, silk and incense production, 159km southwest of Bangalore, **MYSORE**, the erstwhile capital of the Wadiyar rajas, is one of South India's most popular attractions. Considering the clichés that have been heaped upon the place, however, first impressions can be disappointing. Like anywhere else, you are not so much greeted by the scent of jasmine blossom or gentle wafts of sandalwood when you stumble off the bus or train, as by a cacophony of careering auto-rickshaws and noisy buses, bullock carts and tongas. Nevertheless, Mysore is certainly a charming, old-fashioned and undaunting town, dominated by the spectacular **Maharaja's Palace**, around which the boulevards of the city radiate. Nearby, the city centre with the colourful and frenetic **Devaraja Market** makes for an inviting stroll. Just up the road from Mysore, **Srirangapatnam** still harbours architectural gems from the days of the great Indian hero, Tipu Sultan, and the magnificent Hoysala temple of **Somnathpur** lies little more than an hour's drive away.

In the tenth century Mysore was known as "Mahishur" – "the town where the demon buffalo was slain" (by the goddess Durga). Presiding over a district of many villages, the city was ruled from about 1400 until Independence by the Hindu **Wadiyars**, its fortunes inextricably linked with those of Srirangapatnam, which became headquarters from 1610. Their rule was only broken from 1761, when the

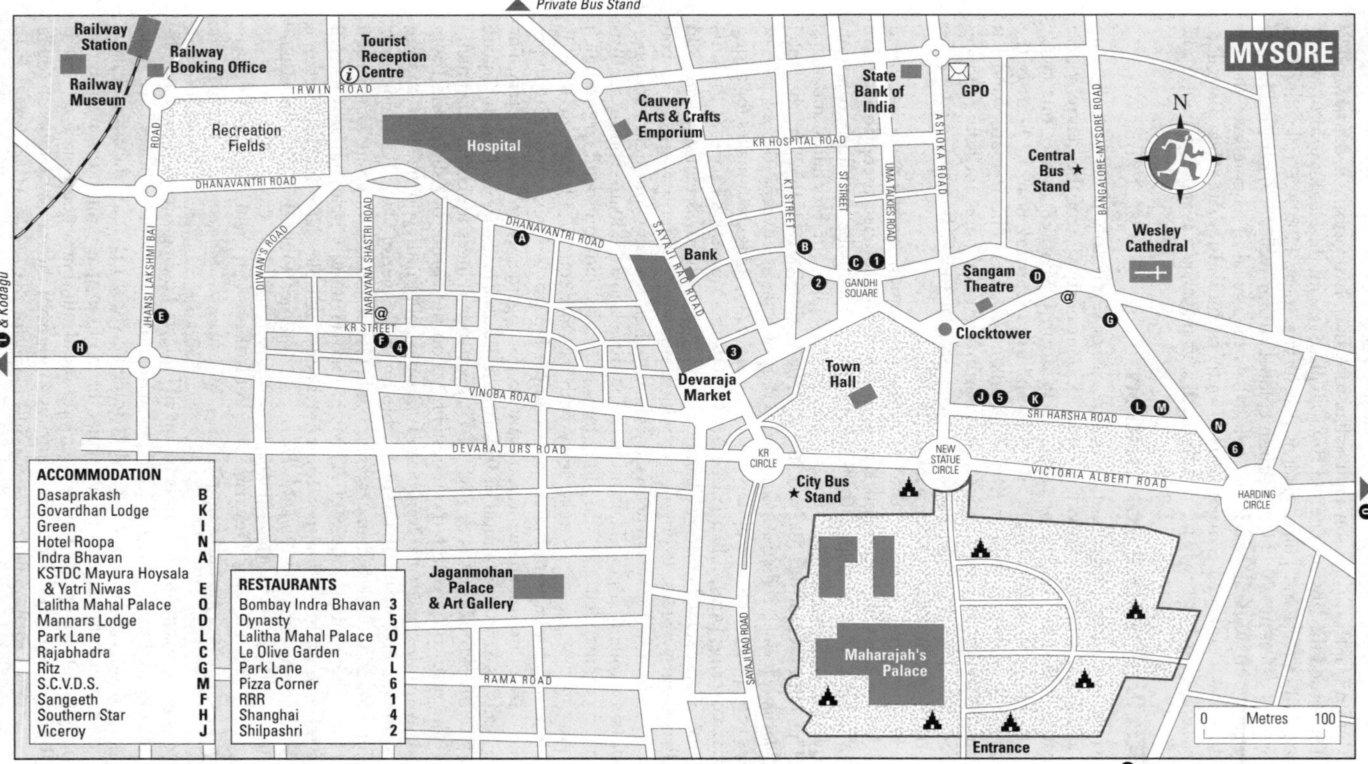
MYSORE
N
Private Bus Stand
Railway Station
Railway Booking Office
Railway Museum
Tourist Reception Centre
IRWIN ROAD
ROAD
Recreation Fields
Hospital
DHANAVANTRI ROAD
Cauvery Arts & Crafts Emporium
KR HOSPITAL ROAD
State Bank of India
GPO
ASHOKA ROAD
UMA TALKIES ROAD
ST STREET
KT STREET
Central Bus Stand
BANGALORE-MYSORE ROAD
Wesley Cathedral
SAYAJI RAO ROAD
Bank
GANDHI SQUARE
Sangam Theatre
Clocktower
DIWAN'S ROAD
NARAYANA SHASTRI ROAD
KR STREET
JHANSI LAKSHMI BAI
Devaraja Market
Town Hall
SRI HARSHA ROAD
VINOBA ROAD
DEVARAJ URS ROAD
KR CIRCLE
NEW STATUE CIRCLE
VICTORIA ALBERT ROAD
HARDING CIRCLE
City Bus Stand
Jaganmohan Palace & Art Gallery
RAMA ROAD
SAYAJI RAO ROAD
Maharajah's Palace
Entrance
0 Metres 100
1 & Kodagu
Fort Mohalla
7 Chamundi Hill
0
ACCOMMODATION
Dasaprakash B
Govardhan Lodge K
Green I
Hotel Roopa N
Indra Bhavan A
KSTDC Mayura Hoysala & Yatri Niwas E
Lalitha Mahal Palace O
Mannars Lodge D
Park Lane L
Rajabhadra C
Ritz G
S.C.V.D.S. M
Sangeeth F
Southern Star H
Viceroy J
RESTAURANTS
Bombay Indra Bhavan 3
Dynasty 5
Lalitha Mahal Palace O
Le Olive Garden 7
Park Lane L
Pizza Corner 6
RRR 1
Shanghai 4
Shilpashri 2

Muslim Haider Ali and son Tipu Sultan took over. Two years later, the new rulers demolished the labyrinthine old city to replace it with the elegant grid of sweeping, leafy streets and public gardens that survive today. However, following Tipu Sultan's defeat in 1799 by the British colonel, Arthur Wellesley (later the Duke of Wellington), Wadiyar power was restored. As the capital of Mysore state, the city thereafter dominated a major part of southern India. In 1956, when Bangalore became capital of newly formed Karnataka, its maharaja was appointed governor.

Arrival and information

Mysore's nearest airport is at Bangalore. Six or seven daily trains from the state capital arrive at the **railway station**, 1500m northwest of the centre, where there's a KSTDC booking counter on Platform 1. Mysore has three **bus** stands: major long-distance KSRTC services pull in to **Central**, near the heart of the city, where there's another KSTDC booking counter. The **Private** stand has moved to a new location about 1km northwest. Local buses, including services for Chamundi Hill and Srirangapatnam, stop at the **City** stand, next to the northwestern corner of the Maharaja's Palace.

Five minutes' walk southeast of the railway station, on the corner of Irwin Road in the Old Exhibition Building, the helpful **tourist reception centre** (Mon–Sat 10am–5.30pm; ⓣ0821/242 2096) will make an effort to answer queries and can arrange transport, as well as give out brochures and maps. The **KSTDC office** (daily 6.30am–8.30pm; ⓣ0821/242 3652), at the hotel *Mayura Hoysala*, 2 Jhansi Laxmi Bai Rd, is of little use except to book one of its **tours**. The whistle-stop city tour (7.30am–8.30pm; Rs160) makes for a long day, covering Jaganmohan Palace Art Gallery, the Maharaja's Palace, St Philomena's Cathedral, the Zoo, Chamundi Hill, Somnathpur, Srirangapatnam and Brindavan Gardens. It only leaves with a minimum of ten passengers, so you may not know for sure whether it will run when you buy your ticket. Its long-distance tour to Belur, Halebid and Sravanabelagola (7.30am–9pm; Rs250) is not recommended as it is too long for a single day and you spend far too much time on the bus; it's a similar story with its Ooty tour (7.30am–9pm; Rs300). However, its **car rental** rates, at Rs4.50 per km (for a minimum of 250km per day), are quite reasonable if you want to put together your own itinerary. The private Tourist Corporation of India inside *Rajabhadra Lodge* on Gandhi Square (ⓣ0821/526 0294) acts as a KSTDC agent and arranges tours and car rental.

The main **post office** (poste restante) is on the corner of Ashoka and Irwin roads (Mon–Sat 10am–7pm, Sun 10.30am–1.30pm). If you need to **change money**, there's a State Bank of Mysore on the corner of Sayaji Rao and Sardar Patel roads, and the Indian Overseas Bank, Gandhi Square, opposite *Dasaprakash Hotel*. There are a couple of **ATMs** around Harding Circle and an Oriental Bank one at the station. For **Internet access**, reliable places include Netzone (Rs20), opposite the *Sangeeth Hotel*, and Internet Online (Rs30) on Chandragupta Road near *Mannars Hotel*.

Accommodation

Mysore boasts plenty of **hotels** to suit all budgets. Finding a room is only a problem during Dussehra (see p.1298), by which time the popular places have been booked up weeks in advance. Most foreigners stay near the Maharaja's Palace, on or around Sri Harsha Road, which has a range of accommodation to suit all budgets. Other pricier hotels are more spread out, but a good place to start is **Jhansi Laxmi Bai Road**, which runs south from the railway station. If you're looking for total opulence, then head straight for the *Lalitha Mahal Palace*.

Inexpensive

Govardhan Lodge Opposite the Opera cinema, Sri Harsha Rd ⓣ0821/243 4118, ⓦwww.hotelgovardhan.com. Basic budget rooms (some a/c) close to the palace. Frayed around the edges, but clean enough. ❷–❹

Indra Bhavan Dhanavantri Rd ⓣ0821/242 3933, ⓔhotelindrabhavan@rediffmail.com. Dilapidated and characterful old lodge popular with Tibetans, with en-suite singles and doubles. The "ordinary" rooms are a little grubby, but the good-value "deluxe" have clean tiled floors and open onto a wide common veranda. ❷

KSTDC Yatri Niwas 2 Jhansi Laxmi Bai Rd ⓣ0821/242 3492, ⓦwww.kstdc.nic.in. The government-run *Mayura Hoysala*'s economy wing: simple rooms around a central garden and dorm beds for Rs75. ❷

Mannars Lodge Chandragupta Rd ⓣ0821/244 8060. Budget hotel near the bus stand and Gandhi Square. No frills, though the "deluxe" rooms have TV. Deservedly popular with backpackers. ❷

Park Lane Sri Harsha Rd ⓣ0821/243 4340, ⓕ242 8424. Eight pleasant clean rooms backing onto a popular beer-garden/restaurant. Just about the best deal going, but can get noisy and has some dodgy plumbing. Avoid room 8 (it's next to the generator). ❶

Rajabhadra Gandhi Square ⓣ0821/526 0152. Best value of several lookalike lodges on the square. The front rooms are great if you don't mind being in the thick of things. Some singles. ❶

Ritz Bangalore–Nilgiri Rd ⓣ0821/242 2668, ⓔhotelritz@rediffmail.com. Wonderful colonial-era hotel, a stone's throw from the KSRTC bus stand. Only four rooms, so book ahead. ❸

Sangeeth 1966 Narayana Shastry Rd, near the Udipi Krishna temple ⓣ0821/242 4693. One of Mysore's best all-round budget deals: bland and a bit boxed in, but friendly and very good value, with a new rooftop restaurant. ❷

Moderate to expensive

Dasaprakash Gandhi Square ⓣ0821/244 2444, ⓔhoteldasaprakash@sancharnet.in. Slightly faded large hotel complex round a spacious courtyard: busy, clean and efficient, though lacking character. Some a/c rooms, cheap singles and a veg restaurant. ❸–❺

Green Chittaranjan Palace, 2270 Vinoba Rd, Jayalakshmipuram ⓣ0821/251 2536, ⓦwww.greenhotelindia.com. On the western outskirts, a former royal palace refurbished as an elegant, eco-conscious two-star, in large gardens. Spacious rooms, lounges, verandas, a croquet lawn and well-stocked library. All profits go to charities and environmental projects. Their auto-rickshaw will pick you up with prior arrangement; can also be contacted through the Charities Advisory Trust in London ⓣ020/7794 9835. ❼–❾

KSTDC Mayura Hoysala 2 Jhansi Laxmi Bai Rd ⓣ0821/242 5349, ⓦwww.kstdc.nic.in. Reasonably priced rooms and suites in a colonial-era mansion. Terrace restaurant and beer garden. Good value but the food is uninspiring. ❸–❺

Lalitha Mahal Palace T Narasipur Rd ⓣ0821/247 0470, ⓦwww.lalithamahalpalace.com. On a slope overlooking the city in the distance, and visible for miles around, this white, Neoclassical palace was built in 1931 to accommodate the maharaja's foreign guests. Now it's a Raj-style fantasy, popular with tour groups and film crews. Tariffs are astronomical by Indian standards, ranging from $70 turret rooms to $750 per night for the "Viceroy Suite". The tea lounge, restaurant and pool (Rs150) are open to non-residents. Free snooker table in bar. ❾

Hotel Roopa 2724c Bangalore–Nilgiri Rd ⓣ0821/244 3770, ⓦwww.hotel-roopa.com. Sparkling new hotel block with compact but comfy rooms at surprisingly reasonable prices. Very handy for the palace. ❸–❺

SCVDS Sri Harsha Rd ⓣ0821/242 1379, ⓕ242 7580. Newish lodge with cable TV in most rooms and some a/c. Very friendly and offers Rs50 discount to foreigners. ❸–❹

Southern Star Vinobha Rd ⓣ0821/242 6426, ⓦwww.ushashriramhotels.com. Modern and comfortable monolithic hotel, affiliated to *Quality Inn* with all facilities, including two restaurants, a bar and a swimming pool. Rooms from Rs4200. ❾

Viceroy Sri Harsha Rd ⓣ0821/242 8001, ⓦwww.theviceroymysore.com. Snazzy new business-oriented hotel, with most mod cons and views over the park to the palace from front rooms. Mostly a/c but generally rather overpriced. Quality restaurant on ground floor. ❻–❼

The City

In addition to its official tourist attractions, chief amongst them the **Maharaja's Palace**, Mysore is a great city simply to stroll around. The characterful, if dilapidated, pre-Independence buildings lining market areas such as **Ashok Road** and **Sayaji Rao Road** lend an air of faded grandeur to the busy centre, teeming with vibrant street life. Souvenir stores spill over with the famous

sandalwood; the best place to get a sense of what's on offer is the Government Cauvery Arts and Crafts Emporium on Sayaji Rao Road (closed Thurs), which stocks a wide range of local crafts that can be shipped overseas. The city's famous **Devaraja Market** on Sayaji Rao Road is one of South India's most atmospheric produce markets: a giant complex of covered stalls groaning with bananas (the delicious *nanjangod* variety), luscious mangoes, blocks of sticky *jaggery*, and conical heaps of lurid *kumkum* powder.

Maharaja's Palace

Mysore centre is dominated by the walled **Maharaja's Palace** (daily 10am–5.30pm; Rs12), a fairytale spectacle topped with a shining brass-plated dome. It's especially magnificent on Sunday nights and during festivals, illuminated by no less than 5000 lightbulbs. It was completed in 1912 for the twenty-fourth Wadiyar raja, on the site of the old wooden palace that had been destroyed by fire in 1897. After a lengthy judicial tussle, in 1998 the courts decided in favour of formally placing the main palace in the hands of the Karnataka state government but the royal family, who still hold a claim, are set to appeal. Twelve temples surround the palace, some of them of much earlier origin. Although there are six gates in the perimeter wall, entrance is on the south side only. Shoes and cameras must be left at the cloakroom inside.

An extraordinary amalgam of styles from India and around the world crowds the lavish **interior**. Entry is through the Gombe Thotti or **Dolls' Pavilion**, once a showcase for the figures featured in the city's lively Dussehra celebrations and now a gallery of European and Indian sculpture and ceremonial objects. Halfway along, the brass **Elephant Gate** forms the main entrance to the centre of the palace, through which the maharaja would drive to his car park. Decorated with floriate designs, it bears the Mysore royal symbol of a double-headed eagle, now the state emblem. To the north, past the gate, stands a ceremonial wooden elephant *howdah* (frame to carry passengers). Elaborately decorated with 84kg of 24-carat gold, it appears to be inlaid with red and green gems – in fact the twinkling lights are battery-powered signals that let the *mahout* know when the maharaja wished to stop or go.

Walls leading into the octagonal **Kalyana Mandapa**, the royal wedding hall, are lined with a meticulously detailed frieze of oil paintings illustrating the great Mysore Dussehra festival of 1930, executed over a period of fifteen years by four Indian artists. The hall itself is magnificent, a cavernous space featuring cast-iron pillars from Glasgow, Bohemian chandeliers and multicoloured Belgian stained glass arranged in peacock designs in the domed ceiling.

Mysore Dussehra festival

Following the tradition set by the Vijayanagar kings, the ten-day festival of **Dussehra** (Sept/Oct), to commemorate the goddess Durga's slaying of the demon buffalo, Mahishasura, is celebrated in grand style at Mysore. Scores of cultural events include concerts of South Indian classical (Carnatic) music and dance performances in the great Durbar Hall of the **Maharaja's Palace**. On Vijayadasmi, the tenth and last day of the festival, a magnificent procession of mounted guardsmen on horseback and caparisoned elephants – one carrying the palace deity, Chaamundeshwari, on a gold *howdah* – marches 5km from the palace to Banni Mantap. There's also a floating festival in the temple tank at the foot of **Chamundi Hill**, and a procession of chariots around the temple at the top. A torchlit parade takes place in the evening, followed by a massive firework display and much jubilation on the streets.

Climbing a staircase with Italian marble balustrades, past an unnervingly realistic life-size plaster of Paris figure of Krishnaraja Wadiyar IV, lounging comfortably with his bejewelled feet on a stool, you come into the **Public Durbar Hall**, an orientalist fantasy like something from *A Thousand and One Nights*. A vision of brightly painted and gilded colonnades, open on one side, the massive hall affords views out across the parade ground and gardens to Chamundi Hill. The maharaja gave audience from here, seated on a throne made from 280kg of solid Karnatakan gold. These days, the hall is only used during the Dussehra festival, when it hosts classical concerts. The smaller **Private Durbar Hall** features especially beautiful stained glass and gold-leaf painting. Before leaving you pass two embossed silver doors – all that remains of the old palace.

Nearby, behind the main palace building but within the same compound, a line of tacky souvenir shops leads to a small **museum** (same hours; Rs20) run by the royal family which shows paintings from the Thanjavur and Mysore schools, some inlaid with precious stones and gold leaf.

Jaganmohan Palace: Jayachamarajendra Art Gallery

Built in 1861, the **Jaganmohan Palace** (daily 8am–5pm; Rs10; no cameras), 300m west of the Maharaja's Palace, was used as a royal residence until it was turned into a picture gallery and museum in 1915 by Maharaja Krishnaraja Wadiyar IV. Most of the "contemporary" art on show dates from the 1930s, when a revival of Indian painting was spearheaded by E.B. Havell and the Tagore brothers, Rabrindrath and Gaganendranath, in Bengal.

Nineteenth- and twentieth-century **paintings** dominate the first floor; amongst them the work of the pioneering oil painter Raja Ravi Varma who, although not everyone's cup of tea, has been credited for introducing modern techniques to Indian art. Games on the upper floor include circular *ganjifa* playing cards illustrated with portraits of royalty or deities, and board games delicately inlaid with ivory. There's also a cluster of musical instruments, among them a brass *jaltarang* set and glass xylophone. Another gallery, centring on a large wooden Ganesh seated on a tortoise, is lined with paintings, including Krishnaraja Wadiyar sporting with the "inmates" of his *zenana* (women's quarter of the palace) during Holi.

Chamundi Hill

Chamundi Hill, 3km southeast of the city, is topped with a temple to the chosen deity of the Mysore rajas – the goddess Chamundi, or Durga, who slew the demon buffalo Mahishasura. It's a pleasant, easy bus trip (#201 from the City stand) to the top; the walk down, past a huge Nandi, Shiva's bull, takes about thirty minutes. Pilgrims, of course, make the trip in reverse order. Take drinking water to sustain you, especially in the middle of the day – the walk isn't very demanding, but by the end of it, after more than 1000 steps, your legs are likely to be a bit wobbly.

Seats to the left of the bus give the best views of the plain surrounding Mysore. Don't be surprised if, at the top of the hill, dominated by the temple's forty-metre *gopura*, you're struck by a feeling of déja vu – one of the displays at the **Godly Museum** states that "5000 years ago at this time you had visited this place in the same way you are visiting now. Because world drama repeats itself identically every 5000 years." You can proceed along a path from the bus stand to the temple square. Immediately to the right, at the end of this path, are four bollards painted with a red stripe; return here for the path down the hill.

Non-Hindus can visit the twelfth-century **temple** (daily 7am–2pm, 3.30–6pm & 7–9pm). The Chamundi figure inside is solid gold; outside, in the courtyard, stands a fearsome, if gaily coloured, statue of the demon Mahishasura. Overlooking the path down the hill, the magnificent five-metre **Nandi**, carved from a single piece of black granite in 1659, is an object of worship himself, adorned with bells and garlands and tended by his own priest. Minor shrines, dedicated to Chamundi and the monkey god Hanuman among others, line the side of the path; at the bottom, a little shrine to Ganesh lies near a chai shop. From here it's usually possible to pick up an auto-rickshaw or bus back into the city, but at weekends the latter are often full. If you walk on towards the city, passing a temple on the left, with a big water tank (the site of the floating festival during Dussehra), you come after ten minutes to the main road between the *Lalitha Mahal Palace* and the city; there's a bus stop, and often auto-rickshaws, at the junction.

Eating

Mysore has scores of **places to eat**, from numerous South Indian "meals" joints dotted around the market to the opulent *Lalita Mahal Palace*, where you can work up an appetite for a gourmet meal by swimming a few lengths of the pool. To sample the renowned Mysore *pak*, a sweet, rich crumbly mixture made of ghee and maize flour, queue at *Guru Sweet Mart*, a small stall at KR Circle, Savaji Rao Road, which is considered the best sweet shop in the city. Another speciality from this part of the world is *malligi iddli*, a delicate light fluffy *iddli* usually served in the mornings and at lunch at several of the downtown "meals" restaurants.

Bombay Indra Bhavan Savaji Rao Rd. Comfortable and popular veg restaurant that serves both south and north Indian cuisine and sweets. Its other branch on Dhanavantri Road (see p.1295) is equally, if not more, popular and also has an a/c section.

Dynasty *Palace Plaza* hotel, Sri Harsha Rd. Dark but nicely decorated restaurant/bar, serving Indian, Chinese and Continental veg and non-veg dishes. There's also a roof garden, where the same menu is available.

Lalitha Mahal T Naraispur Rd. Sample the charms of this palatial five-star with an expensive hot drink in the atmospheric tea lounge, or an à la carte lunch in the grand dining hall, accompanied by live sitar music. The old-style bar also boasts a full-size billiards table.

Le Olive Garden near base of Chamundi Hill, 2km southeast. Leafy garden restaurant with water features, serving tandoori, Chinese and Continental dishes. Occasional live entertainment; moderately expensive.

Park Lane Sri Harsha Rd. Congenial courtyard restaurant-cum-beer garden, with moderately priced veg and non-veg food (meat sizzlers are a speciality), pot plants and live Indian classical music every evening. Ladies and family balcony upstairs. Popular with travellers and Indians alike.

Pizza Corner Bangalore–Nilgiri Rd, near Harding Circle. Newish branch of the Bangalore chain serving high-quality pizza in bright plastic Western decor.

RRR Gandhi Square. A plain "meals" restaurant in front with a small but plush a/c room at the back which gets packed at lunchtimes and at weekends. Well worth the wait for its excellent set menus on banana leaves, chicken biriyani and fried fish.

Shanghai 1487 Shivrampet. Fine Chinese fare available in an elongated dining room. *Teppan yaki* dishes are featured among the better known favourites.

Shilpashri Gandhi Square. Quality north Indian-style food, with particularly tasty tandoori (great chicken tikka). Plenty of good veg options, too, including lots of dhals and curd rice. Serves alcohol.

Around Mysore

Mysore is a jumping-off point for some of Karnataka's most popular destinations. At **Srirangapatnam**, the fort, palace and mausoleum date from the era of Tipu Sultan, the "Tiger of Mysore", a perennial thorn in the side of the British. Twitchers will enjoy a visit to the nearby **Ranganathittu Bird Sanctuary**,

Moving on from Mysore

If you're contemplating a long haul, the best way to travel is by **train**, usually with a change at **Bangalore**. Six or seven express services and six passenger trains leave Mysore each day for the Karnatakan capital. The fastest of these, the a/c Shatabdi Express #2008 (daily except Tues 2.20pm; 1hr 55min), continues on to Chennai; most of the others terminate in Bangalore, where you can pick up long-distance connections to a wide range of Indian cities (see p.1292). **Reservations** can be made at Mysore's computerized booking hall inside the station (Mon–Sat 8am–2pm & 2.15–8pm, Sun 8am–2pm). There are four services daily to **Hassan**, of which the Shimoga Express #268 (10.15am; 2hr 5min) is substantially faster than the other passenger trains.

As there are so many trains between Mysore and Bangalore, you shouldn't ever have to do the trip by **bus**, which takes longer and is a lot more terrifying. Most destinations within a day's ride of Mysore can only be reached by road. Long-distance services operate out of the Central bus stand, where you can book computerized tickets up to three days in advance. English timetables are posted on the wall inside the entrance hall, and there's a helpful enquiries counter in the corner of the compound. Regular buses leave here for **Hassan** (3–4hr), jumping-off place for the Hoysala temples at **Belur** and **Halebid**, for Channarayapatna/**Sravanabelagola** (2hr 30min–3hr) and for **Hubli** (for Hospet/**Hampi**). Heading south to **Ooty** (5hr), there's a choice of eight buses, all of which stop at **Bandipur National Park**. Direct services to several cities in Kerala, including **Kannur**, **Kozhikode** and **Kochi**, also operate from Mysore. The only way to travel direct to **Goa** is on the 4pm or 5pm overnight buses that arrive at **Panjim** at 9am and 10am respectively. Most travellers, however, break this long trip into stages, heading first to **Mangalore** (7hr), and working their way north from there, usually via **Gokarna** – which you can also reach by direct bus (14hr) – or **Jog Falls**. Mangalore-bound buses and coaches tend to pass through **Madikeri**, capital of Kodagu (Coorg), which is also served by hourly buses, most of which travel through the Tibetan enclave of **Bylakuppe**. For details of services to **Somnathpur** and **Srirangapatnam**, see the relevant accounts below. A host of agents can make booking for **private buses** to many destinations – the Tourist Corporation of India at the *Rajabhadra Lodge* is one of the best.

Mysore doesn't have an **airport** (the nearest one is at Bangalore), but you can confirm and book Indian Airlines flights at the office in the KSTDC *Mayura Hoysala* (Mon–Sat 10am–1.30pm & 2.15–5pm; ⓣ0821/242 1846).

while the superb **Hoysala temple** (see p.1309) of **Somnathpur** is an architectural masterpiece.

If you're heading south towards Ooty, **Bandipur National Park**'s forests and hill scenery offer another possible escape from the city, although your chances of spotting any rare animals are slim. The same is true of **Nagarhole National Park**, three hours southwest of Mysore towards the Kerala border.

Srirangapatnam

The island of **Srirangapatnam**, in the River Kaveri, 14km northeast of Mysore, measures 5km by 1km. Long a site of Hindu pilgrimage, it is named after its tenth-century Sriranganathaswamy Vishnu temple. The Vijayanagars built a fort here in 1454, and in 1616 it became the capital of the Mysore Wadiyar rajas. However, Srirangapatnam is more famously associated with **Haider Ali**, who deposed the Wadiyars in 1761, and even more so with his son **Tipu Sultan**. During his seventeen-year reign – which ended with his death in 1799, when the future Duke of Wellington took the fort at the bloody battle of "Seringapatnam" – Tipu posed a greater threat than any other Indian ruler to British plans to dominate India. Born in 1750, of a Hindu mother, he inherited his father Haider Ali's considerable military skills, but was also an educated, cultured man, whose lifelong desire to rid India of the hated British invaders naturally brought him an ally in the French. He obsessively embraced his popular name of the **Tiger of Mysore**, surrounding himself with symbols and images of tigers; much of his memorabilia is decorated with the animal or its stripes, and, like the Romans, he is said to have kept tigers for the punishment of criminals.

The former summer palace, the **Daria Daulat Bagh** (daily except Fri 9am–5pm; $2 [Rs5]), literally "wealth of the sea", 1km east of the fort, was used to entertain Tipu's guests. At first sight, this low, wooden colonnaded building set in an attractive formal garden fails to impress. However, the superbly preserved interior, with its ornamental arches, tiger-striped columns and floral decoration on every inch of the teak walls and ceiling, is remarkable. A much-repainted mural on the west wall relishes every detail of Haider Ali's victory over the British at Pollilore in 1780. Upstairs, a small collection of Tipu memorabilia, European paintings, Persian manuscripts on handmade paper and a model of Srirangapatnam are on show.

An avenue of cypresses leads from an intricately carved gateway to the **Gumbaz mausoleum** (daily except Fri 9am–5pm; free), 3km further east. Built by Tipu Sultan in 1784 to commemorate Haider Ali, and later also to serve as his own resting place, the lower half of the grey-granite edifice is crowned by a dome of whitewashed brick and plaster, spectacular against the blue sky. Ivory-inlaid rosewood doors lead to the tombs of Haider Ali and Tipu, each covered by a pall (tiger stripes for Tipu), and an Urdu tablet records Tipu's martyrdom.

At the heart of the fortress, the great temple of **Sriranganathaswamy** still stands proud and virtually untouched by the turbulent history that has flowed around it, and remains, for many devotees, the prime draw. Developed by succeeding dynasties, the temple consists of three distinctive sanctuaries and is entered via an impressive five-storeyed gateway and a hall that was built by Haider Ali. The innermost sanctum, the oldest part of the temple, contains an image of the reclining Vishnu.

Practicalities

Frequent **buses** from Mysore City bus stand (including #313 & #316) and all the Mysore–Bangalore **trains** pull in near the temple and fort. Srirangapatnam is a small island, but places of interest are quite spread out; tongas, auto-rickshaws and bicycles are available on the main road near the bus stand. The KSTDC **hotel**-cum-restaurant, *Mayura River View* (Ⓣ08236/252114; ❹–❺), occupies a pleasant spot beside the Kaveri, 3km from the bus stand, and another good option is the smart and elegant *Fort View Resorts* (Ⓣ08236/252777; ❺–❻), set in its own grounds not far from the fort entrance.

The Ranganathittu Bird Sanctuary

Some 2km southwest of Srirangapatnam, the **Ranganathittu Bird Sanctuary** (daily 8.30am–6pm; Rs60 [Rs20]) is a must for ornithologists, especially during October/November, when the lake, fed by the River Kaveri, attracts huge flocks of migrating birds. At other times it's a tranquil spot to escape the city, where you can enjoy boat rides through the backwaters to look for crocodiles, otters and dozens of species of resident waders, wildfowl and forest birds. The easiest way to get there is by rickshaw from Srirangapatnam.

Somnathpur

Built in 1268 AD, the exquisite **Keshava Vishnu temple** (daily 9am–5pm; $2 [Rs5]), in the sleepy hamlet of **SOMNATHPUR**, was the last important temple to be constructed by the Hoysalas; it is also the most complete and, in many respects, the finest example of this singular style (see p.1309). Somnathpur itself, just ninety minutes from Mysore by road, is little more than a few neat tracks and some attractive simple houses with pillared verandas.

Like other Hoysala temples, the Keshava is built on a star-shaped plan. ASI staff can show you around and also grant permission to clamber on the enclosure walls, so you can get a marvellous bird's-eye view of the modestly proportioned structure. It's best to do this as early as possible, as the stone gets very hot to walk on in bare feet.

The temple is a *trikutachala*, "three-peaked hills" type, with a tower on each shrine. Its high plinth (*jagati*) provides an upper ambulatory, which on its outer edge allows visitors to approach the upper registers of the profusely decorated walls. Among the many superb images here are an unusually high proportion of Shaivite figures for a Vishnu temple. As at Halebid, a lively frieze details countless episodes from the *Ramayana*, *Bhagavata Purana* and *Mahabharata*. Intended to accompany circumambulation, the panels are "read" (there is no text) in a clockwise direction. Unusually, the temple is autographed; all its sculpture was the work of one man, named Malitamba. Outside the temple stands a *dvajastambha* column, which may originally have been surmounted by a figure of Vishnu's bird vehicle Garuda.

Practicalities

There are no direct **buses** from Mysore to Somnathpur. Buses from the Private stand run to T Narasipur (1hr), served by regular buses to Somnathpur (20min). Everyone will know where you want to go, and someone will show you which scrum to join. Alternatively, join one of KSTDC's guided tours (see p.1296).

There is nowhere to stay near the temple and the only **food** available is in the shape of biscuits or maybe a samosa at one of the chai stalls or fruit from a street-seller; you'll have to go back to the cheap "meals" hotels at T Narasipur for anything more substantial. Tucked in the backwaters of a dammed section of the Cauvery, a further 25km southeast, the exquisite *Talakadu Jaladhana* resort (Ⓣ08227/271196, Ⓔjaladhana@hotmail.com; ⑨) offers secluded cottages, some with rooftop hot tubs and herb gardens, and full board for Rs1770 per person. Boating and sports activities are available and it can be reached by direct private bus from Mysore.

National Parks around Mysore: Bandipur and Nagarhole

Mysore lies within striking distance of three major wildlife sanctuaries – **Bandipur**, **Nagarhole** and **Mudumalai**, across the border in Tamil Nadu – all of which are part of the vast **Nilgiri Biosphere Reserve**, one of India's most extensive tracts of protected forest. The parks are once again fully open to tourists, since the bandit Veerapan who terrorized the region for years was killed in October 2004 (see p.1191 for more). A few upmarket private "resorts" on the edge of the parks and one or two tourist complexes allow visitors to experience the delights of an area renowned for its **elephants**. Forest Department accommodation at Bandipur (see below) and Nagarhole (see p.1305) must be booked as far in advance as possible through its offices at Aranya Bhavan, Ashokapuram (Ⓣ0821/248 0901), 6km south of the centre of Mysore, on bus #61 from the City stand, or at Aranya Bhavan, 18th Cross, Malleswaram, Bangalore (Ⓣ080/2334 1993). For information on Mudumalai see p.1191.

Bandipur National Park

Situated among the broken foothills of the Western Ghat mountains, **Bandipur National Park**, 80km south of Mysore, covers 880 square kilometres of dry deciduous forest, south of the River Kabini. Created in the 1930s from the local maharaja's hunting lands and expanded in 1941, Bandipur, in spite of its good accommodation and well-maintained metalled jeep tracks, is a disappointment as a wildlife-viewing destination. Glimpses of anything more exciting than a langur or spotted deer are rare outside the core area, which is off limits, while the noisy diesel bus laid on by the Forest Department to transport tourists around the accessible areas of park scares off what little fauna remains.

On the plus side, Bandipur is one of the few reserves in India where you stand a good chance of sighting wild **elephants**, particularly in the wet season (June–Sept), when water and forage are plentiful and the animals evenly scattered. Later in the monsoon, huge herds congregate on the banks of the River Kabini, in the far north of the park, where you can see the remnants of an old stockade used by one particularly zealous nineteenth-century British hunter as an elephant trap. Bandipur also boasts some fine scenery: at **Gopalswamy Betta**, 9km from the park HQ and open to visitors, a high ridge looks north over the Mysore Plateau and its adjoining hills, while to the south, the **Rolling Rocks** afford sweeping views of the craggy, 260-metre-deep **Mysore Ditch**.

Practicalities

The **best time to visit** is during the rainy season (June–Sept); unlike neighbouring parks, Bandipur's roads do not get washed out by the annual deluge, and elephants are more numerous at this time. By November/December, however, most of the larger animals have migrated across the state border into Mudumalai, where water is more plentiful in the dry season. **Avoid weekends**, as the park attracts busloads of noisy day-trippers.

Getting to Bandipur by bus is easy; all the regular KSRTC services to Ooty from Mysore's Central bus stand (12 daily; 2hr 30min) pass through the reserve (the last one back to Mysore leaves at 5pm), stopping outside the Forest Department's reception centre (daily 9am–4.30pm). If you miss the last bus from Mysore you can change at Gundulapet, 18km away, from where you can also take a taxi to the main reception centre (Rs220). There is a Rs150 [Rs50] entrance fee plus Rs20 per camera.

You can confirm **accommodation** bookings (see above) within the sanctuary at the Forest Department's reception centre. Comfort varies from beds in large, institutional dorms to the "VIP" *Gajendra Cottages*, which have en-suite bathrooms and verandas. Upmarket options include *Tusker Trails*, a **resort** run by members of the royal family of Mysore, at Mangala village, 3km from Bandipur (bookable through its office at Hospital Cottage, Bangalore Palace, Bangalore; Ⓣ080/2353 0748, Ⓕ2334 2862; ➒), which has cottages, a swimming pool and a tennis court and organizes trips into the forest; *Bush Betta*, off the main Mysore highway (booked through Gainnet, Raheja Plaza, Richmond Road, Bangalore; Ⓣ080/2551 2631; ➒), offers comfortable cottages and guided tours; and Jungle Lodges & Resorts' *Bandipur Safari Lodge* (Ⓣ080/2559 7021, Ⓦwww.junglelodges.com; ➒), where foreigners pay $50 each per night.

Unless you have your own vehicle or are booked onto an upmarket hotel tour, the only **transport around the park** is the hopeless Forest Department bus, which makes two tours daily (6–9am & 4–6pm; Rs25). You may see a deer or two, but nothing more, on the half-hour **elephant ride** (Rs50) around the reception compound. Visitors travelling to Gopalswamy Betta should note that car rental is not available at Bandipur, but at Gundulapet, from where they will try and charge a lot more than the official Rs500. You must exit the park before nightfall.

Nagarhole National Park

Bandipur's northern neighbour, **Nagarhole** ("Snake River") **National Park**, extends 640 square kilometres north from the River Kabini, dammed to form a picturesque artificial lake. During the dry season (Feb–June), this perennial water source attracts large numbers of animals, making it a potentially prime spot for sighting wildlife. The forest here is of the moist deciduous type – thick jungle with a thirty-metre-high canopy – and more impressive than Bandipur's drier scrub.

However, disaster struck Nagarhole in 1992, when friction between local pastoralist "tribals" and the park wardens over grazing rights and poaching erupted into a spate of arson attacks. Thousands of acres of forest were burned to the ground. The trees have grown back in places, but it will be decades before animal numbers completely recover. An added threat to the fragile jungle tracts of the region is a notorious female gang of wood smugglers from Kerala, who have developed a fearsome and almost mythical reputation. Meanwhile, Nagarhole is only worth visiting at the height of the dry season, when its muddy riverbanks and grassy swamps, or *hadlus*, offer better chances of sighting gaur (Indian bison), elephant, *dhole* (wild dog), deer, boar, and even the odd tiger or leopard, than any of the neighbouring sanctuaries.

Practicalities

Nagarhole is open year-round, but avoid the monsoons, when floods wash out most of its dirt tracks, and leeches make hiking impossible. To get there from Mysore, catch one of the two daily **buses** from the Central stand to **Hunsur** (3hr), 10km from the park's north gate, where you can pick up transport to the Forest Department's two rest houses (2–5). The **rest houses** have to be booked well in advance through the Forest Department offices in Mysore or Bangalore (see intro, above). It is also essential to arrive at the park gates well before dusk, as the road through the reserve to the lodges closes at 6pm, and is prone to "elephant blocks". The Nagarhole **visitor centre** charges a Rs150 [Rs50] entrance fee plus Rs20 per camera. It organizes elephant rides (Rs50) and schedules bus tours round the sanctuary (6–9am & 3.30–6pm; Rs50).

Other **accommodation** around Nagarhole includes the highly acclaimed and luxurious *Kabini River Lodge* (book through Jungle Lodges & Resorts in Bangalore; ⓣ080/2559 7021; ⑨), approached via the village of Karapura, 3km from the park's south entrance. Set in its own leafy compound on the lakeside, this former maharaja's hunting lodge offers expensive all-in deals for $110 per person per night that include meals and transport around the park with expert guides. It's impossible to reach by public transport, so you'll need to rent a car to get there and you will also have to book well in advance. Another upmarket option but not quite in the same league, the *Jungle Inn* at Veerana Hosahalli (ⓣ08222/252781; ⑨; bookable through its Bangalore office ⓣ080/2224 3172), is close to the park entrance and arranges wildlife safaris, with a very hefty surcharge for foreign visitors. Some tour groups prefer the luxury of *Orange County* (see p.1316) near the town of Siddapura in Kodagu 75km to the north, despite the long drive.

Hassan and around

The unprepossessing town of **HASSAN**, 118km northwest of Mysore, is visited in large numbers because of its proximity to the Hoysala temples at **Belur** and **Halebid**, both northwest of the town, and the Jain pilgrimage site of **Sravanabelagola** to the southeast. Some travellers end up staying a couple of nights, killing time in neon-lit thali joints and dowdy hotel rooms, but with a little forward planning you shouldn't have to linger here for longer than it takes to get on a bus somewhere else. Set deep in the serene Karnatakan countryside, Belur, Halebid and Sravanabelagola are much more congenial places to stay.

Practicalities

Hassan's **KSRTC bus stand** is in the centre of town, at the northern end of Bus Stand Road which runs south past the post office to **Narsimharaja Circle**. Near the bus stand is Shenoy Tours & Travels (☎08172/269729), where you can change money, but not Thomas Cook travellers' cheques, and also most of the town's accommodation. Local auto-rickshaws operate without meters and charge a minimum of Rs10. The newly relocated **tourist office** is under five minutes' walk from the bus stand at AVK College Road (Mon–Sat 10am–5.30pm; ☎08172/268862) and is both friendly and informative. The **railway station**, served by one express and three slow passenger trains a day from Mysore, is a further 2km down the road. Note that the route from here across the Ghats to Mangalore on the coast is still suspended due to engineering work involved with gauge conversion.

Accommodation

In recent years the quality of **accommodation** in Hassan has improved dramatically. Many of the budget options are still of a pitiful standard but the

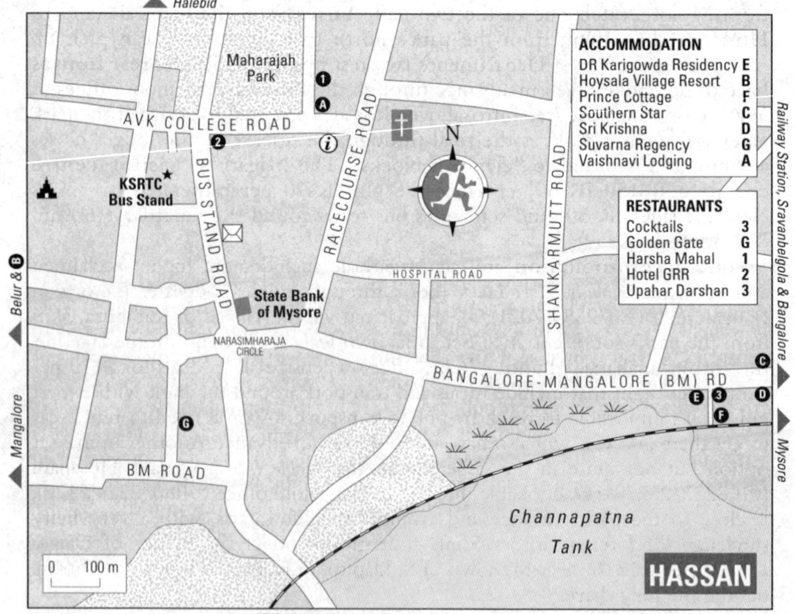

few exceptions are within walking distance of the bus stand. By contrast, there are a number of good mid-range hotels. Wherever you stay, call ahead, as most hotels tend to be full by early evening.

DR Karigowda Residency BM Rd, 1km from railway station ⓣ08172/264506. Immaculate budget hotel: friendly, comfortable and amazing value. Single occupancy possible; no a/c. ❷
Hoysala Village Resort Belur Rd, 6km northwest of the centre ⓣ08172/256764, ⓦwww.karnatakatourism.com. Government-run luxury cottages in a peaceful rural setting. Fine multi-cuisine restaurant and the only pool in the area open to non-residents (Rs75/hr). ❼–❽
Prince Cottage BM Rd, behind Bhanu Theatre ⓣ08172/234740. Small, neat guesthouse tucked away off the main road. Very cheap and handy for the railway station. ❶
Southern Star BM Rd, 500m from train station ⓣ08172/251816, ⓦwww.ushashriramhotels.com. New hotel with all mod cons belonging to the *Quality Inn* chain, but better value than most. Smartest place in town. ❻–❼
Sri Krishna BM Rd ⓣ08172/263240, ⓕ260195. A large newish hotel with some a/c rooms. The spacious non-a/c rooms are a great deal and the restaurant downstairs produces excellent South Indian cooking. ❸–❺
Suvarna Regency PB 97, BM Rd ⓣ08172/264006, ⓦwww.hotelsuvarna.com. Swish place with lots of lights, shiny marble lobby, comfortable rooms and a rooftop barbecue. Great value – as good as the Mysore's *Lalitha Mahal Palace* for half the price. Some a/c. ❸–❹
Vaishnavi Lodging Harsha Mahal Rd ⓣ08172/263885. Hassan's best budget lodge, with big clean rooms (all with phone and TV) and a veg restaurant. Reservations essential. Turn left out of the bus stand, right onto Church Rd and it's on the corner of the first left turn. ❷

Eating

Most of the **hotels** listed above have commendable restaurants, or you can take your pick from the string of cheap snack bars and thali joints outside the bus stand.

Cocktails BM Rd near *Krishna*. A new multistorey development with a terraced restaurant and bar offering a run-of-the-mill but varied menu.
Golden Gate *Suvarna Regency*, PB 97, BM Rd. Plush restaurant and bar with a garden extension, and the best Hassan has to offer; the varied menu is not cheap.
Harsha Mahal below *Harsha Mahal Lodge*, Harsha Mahal Rd. No-nonsense veg canteen that serves freshly cooked *iddli* and *dosa* breakfasts from 7.30am.
Hotel GRR opposite the bus stand. Traditional, tasty and filling "mini-meals" served on plantain leaves, with a wide choice of non-veg dishes and some ice creams.
Upahar Darshan BM Rd. A cheap South Indian restaurant serving good "meals" and fresh *dosas* and *iddlis*.

Halebid

Now little more than a scruffy hamlet of brick houses and chai stalls, **HALEBID**, 32km northwest of Hassan, was once the capital of the powerful Hoysala dynasty, who held sway over south Karnataka from the eleventh until the early fourteenth centuries. Once known as **Dora Samudra**, the city was renamed *Hale-bidu*, or "Dead City", in 1311 when Delhi sultanate forces under the command of Ala-ud-din-Khalji swept through and reduced it to rubble. Despite the sacking, several large Hoysala temples (see box) survive, two of which, the **Hoysaleshvara** and **Kedareshvara**, are superb, covered in exquisite carvings. A small **archeological museum** (daily except Fri 10am–5pm), next to the Hoysaleshvara temple, houses a collection of Hoysala art and other finds from the area.

The Hoysaleshvara temple

The **Hoysaleshvara** temple (daily sunrise–sunset; free) was started in 1141, and after some forty years of work remained incomplete; this possibly accounts for

Moving on from Hassan

Apart from taking a tour, the only way to see Sravanabelgola (53km), Belur (37km) and Halebid (30km) in one day is **by car**, which some visitors share; most of the hotels can fix this up (around Rs1000 per day or Rs4.50 per kilometre for a minimum of 250km). Travelling **by bus**, you'll need at least two days. Belur and Halebid can be comfortably covered in one day; it's best to take the first (6am) of the hourly buses to Halebid (1hr) and move on to Belur (30min; 16km), from where services back to Hassan during the evening are more frequent (6.30am–6.15pm; 1hr 10min). **Sravanabelgola**, however, is in the opposite direction, and not served by direct buses; you have to head to **Channarayapatna** aka "CR Patna" (from 6.30am; 1hr) on the main Bangalore highway and pick up one of the regular buses (30min) or any number of minibuses from there. If you want to get to Sravanabelagola in time to visit the site and move on the same day (to Mysore or Bangalore), aim to catch one of the private luxury buses to Bangalore that leave from the road just below the *Vaishnavi Lodge* before dawn (5.30–6am); they all stop briefly in Channarayapatna. Bear in mind, too, that there are places to stay in both Belur and Halebid; arrive in Hassan early enough, and you can travel on to the temple towns before nightfall, although you should phone ahead to check rooms are available.

the absence here of the type of towers that feature at Somnathpur, for example. It is no longer known which deities were originally worshipped, though the double shrine is thought to have been devoted at one time to Shiva and his consort. In any event, both shrines contain *shivalinga* and are adjoined by two linked, partly enclosed *mandapa* hallways in which stand Nandi bulls.

Hoysaleshvara also features many Vaishnavite images. The **sculptures**, which have a fluid quality lacking in the earlier work at Belur, include Brahma aboard his goose vehicle Hamsa, Krishna holding up Mount Govardhana, another where he plays the flute, and Vishnu (Trivikrama) bestriding the world in three steps. One of the most remarkable images is of the demon king **Ravana** shaking Shiva's mountain abode, Mount Kailash, populated by numerous animals and figures with Shiva and Parvati seated atop. Secular characters, among them dancers and musicians, occupy the same register as the gods, and you'll come across the odd erotic tableau featuring voluptuous, heavily bejewelled maidens. A narrative frieze, on the sixth register from the bottom, follows the length of the Nandi *mandapas* and illustrates scenes from the Hindu epics.

The Jain bastis and the Kedareshvara temple

Some 600m south of the Hoysaleshvara, a group of Jain *bastis* (temples) stand virtually unadorned; the only sculptural decoration consists of ceiling friezes inside the *mandapas* and elephants at the entrance steps, where there's an impressive donatory plaque. The thirteenth-century temple of **Adi Parshwanatha** is dedicated to the twenty-third *tirthankara*, Parshvanath, while the newer **Vijayanatha** built in the sixteenth century is dedicated to the sixteenth *tirthankara*, Shantinath. The *chowkidar* at the Parshwanatha temple will demonstrate various tricks made possible by the carved pillars' highly polished surfaces; some are so finely turned they sound metallic when struck.

To the east, there's a smaller Shiva temple, Kedareshvara (1217–21), also built on a stellate plan. Unfortunately, due to instability, it's not possible to go inside. Many fine images decorate the exterior, including an unusual stone Krishna dancing on the serpent demon Kaliya.

Hoysala temples

The **Hoysala** dynasty, who ruled southwestern Karnataka between the eleventh and thirteenth centuries, built a series of distinctive temples centred primarily at three sites: **Belur** and **Halebid**, close to modern Hassan, and **Somnathpur**, near Mysore. At first sight, and from a distance, the buildings, all based on a star-shaped plan, appear to be modest structures, compact and even squat. On closer inspection, however, their profusion of fabulously detailed and sensuous sculpture, covering every inch of the exterior, is astonishing. Detractors are prone to class Hoysala art as decadent and overly fussy, but anyone with an eye for craftsmanship is likely to marvel at these jewels of Karnatakan art.

The intricacy of the carvings was made possible by the material used in construction: a soft steatite soapstone that on oxidization hardens to a glassy, highly polished surface. The level of detail, similar to that seen in sandalwood and ivory-work, became increasingly freer and more fluid as the style developed, and reached its highest point at Somnathpur. Beautiful bracket figures, often delicate portrayals of voluptuous female subjects, were placed under the eaves, fixed by pegs top and bottom. A later addition (except possibly in the Somnathpur temple), these serve no structural function.

Another technique more usually associated with wood is the unusual treatment of the massive stone **pillars**: lathe-turned, they resemble those of the wooden temples of Kerala. They were probably turned on a horizontal plane, pinned at each end, and rotated with the use of a rope. It may be no coincidence that, to this day, wood turning is still a local speciality. Only the central shaft of each pillar seems to have been turned; in the base and capitals, a less precise, presumably handworked imitation of turning is evident.

Practicalities

Frequent **buses** run between Halebid (the last at 8.30pm) and Hassan, and to Belur (the last at 8pm). The private minibuses that leave from the crossroads outside the Hoysaleshvara temple take a lot longer and only leave when crammed to bursting.

The monuments lie within easy walking distance of each other, but if you fancy exploring the surrounding countryside, rent a **bicycle** from the stalls by the bus stand (Rs3 per hour). The road running south past the temples leads through some beautiful scenery, with possible side-hikes to hilltop shrines, while the road to Belur (16km) makes for another pleasant bicycle ride. **Accommodation** in the village is limited to the KSTDC *Mayura Shantala* (Ⓣ08177/773224; ❷) opposite the main temple and set in a small garden by the road. It offers two comfortable doubles with verandas, plus a four-bedded room – all should be booked in advance. This is also the only place to eat after 6pm, when the chai stalls at the crossroads have shut up.

Belur

BELUR, 37km northwest of Hassan, on the banks of the Yagachi, was the Hoysala capital prior to Halebid, during the eleventh and twelfth centuries. Still active (daily 7.30am–8.30pm; free) the **Chennakeshava temple**, a fine and early example of the singular Hoysala style, was built by King Vishnuvardhana in 1117 to celebrate his conversion from Jainism, victory over Chola forces at Talakad and his independence from the Chalukyas. Today, its grey-stone *gopura*, or gateway tower, soars above a small, bustling market town – a popular pilgrimage site from October to December, when busloads of Ayappan devotees stream through en route to Sabarimala (see p.1244). The **car festival** held around March or April takes place over twelve days and has a pastoral feel, attracting farmers from the surrounding countryside who conduct a bullock cart procession through the streets to the temple. If you have time to linger, Belur, with marginally better facilities than those found at Halebid, is a far better place to base yourself in order to explore the Hoysala region.

Chennakeshava stands in a huge walled courtyard, surrounded by smaller shrines and columned *mandapa* hallways. Lacking any form of superstructure, it appears to have a flat roof. If it ever had a tower, it would have disappeared by the Vijayanagar (sixteenth-century) period. Both the sanctuary and *mandapa* are raised on the usual plinth (*jagati*). Double flights of steps, flanked by minor towered shrines, afford entry to the *mandapa* on three sides; this hallway was originally open, but in the 1200s, pierced stone screens, carved with geometric designs and scenes from the *Puranas*, were inserted between the lathe-turned pillars. The main shrine opens four times a day for worship (8.30–10am, 11am–1pm, 2.30–5pm & 6.30–8.30pm) and it's worth considering using one of the guides who offer their services at the gates (Rs40) to explain the intricacies of the carvings. The quantity of **sculptural decoration**, if less mature than in later Hoysala temples, is staggering.

Within the same enclosure, the **Kappe Channigaraya temple** has some finely carved niche images and a depiction of Narasimha (Vishnu as man-lion) killing the demon Hiranyakashipu. Further west, fine sculptures in the smaller **Viranarayana** shrine include a scene from the *Mahabharata* of Bhima killing the demon Bhaga.

Practicalities

Buses from Hassan and Halebid arrive at the small bus stand in the middle of town, ten minutes' walk along the main street from the temple. Some through buses do not bother to pull into the bus stand, but stop on the highway next to it. There are auto-rickshaws available, but a good way to explore the area, including Halebid, is to rent a **bicycle** (Rs3 per hour) from one of the stalls around the bus stand. The **tourist office** (Mon–Sat 10am–5pm) is located within the KSTDC *Mayuri Velapuri* compound near the temple. It has all the local bus times, and sometimes the tourist officer is available as a guide.

The KSTDC *Mayuri Velapuri* (Ⓣ08177/722209; ❷) is the best **place to stay**, with immaculately clean and airy rooms in its new block, or dingy ones in the older wing. The two dorms are rarely occupied (Rs35 per bed), other than between March and May, when the hotel tends to be block-booked by pilgrims. Down the road, the *Annapurna* (Ⓣ08177/722039; ❷) has adequate if dull rooms over an uninspiring restaurant; the *Swagath Tourist Home* (Ⓣ08177/722159; ❶), further up the road towards the temple, is extremely basic, boxed in and does not have hot water, but is fine as a fall-back. Of the hotels around the bus stand, the *Vishnu Lodge* (Ⓣ0817/722263; ❷–❸) above a restaurant and sweet shop, is the best bet, with spacious rooms (some with TV) but tiny attached bathrooms where hot water is only available in the mornings.

The most salubrious **place to eat** is at *Mayuri Velapuri*'s restaurant, but the menu is limited. There are several other options, many located beneath hotels strung along the main road, in addition to the veg *dhabas* by the temple, and the *Indian Coffee House* on the main road by the temple gates.

Sravanabelagola

The sacred Jain site of **SRAVANABELAGOLA**, 49km southeast of Hassan and 93km north of Mysore, consists of two hills and a large tank. On one of

Gomateshvara and Mahamastakabhisheka

Gomateshvara, or Bahubali, who was the son of the legendary King Rishabdev of Ayodhya (better known as Adinath, the first *tirthankara*), had a row with his elder brother, Bharat, over their inheritance. After a fierce fight, he lifted his brother above his head, and was about to throw him to the ground when he was gripped by remorse. Gently setting Bharat down, Gomateshvara resolved to reject the world of greed, jealousy and violence by meditating until he achieved *moksha*, release from attachment and rebirth. This he succeeded in doing, even before his father.

Gomateshvara achieved *kevalajnana*, "sole knowledge" acquired through solitude, austerity and meditation. While engaged in this nonactivity, he stood "body upright" in a forest. So motionless was he that ants built their nest at his feet, snakes coiled happily around his ankles, and creepers began to grow up his legs.

Every twelve years, at an auspicious astrological conjunction of certain planets, the Gomateshvara statue is ritually anointed in the **Mahamastakabhisheka ceremony** – the next one is scheduled for some time between September and December of 2005 (the precise date has yet to be announced). The process lasts for several days, culminating on the final morning when 1008 *kalashas* (pots) of "liberation water", each with a coconut and mango leaves tied together by coloured thread, are arranged before the statue in a sacred diagram (*mandala*), on ground strewn with fresh paddy. A few priests climb scaffolding, erected around Gomateshvara, to bathe him in milk and *ghee*. After this first bath, prayers are offered. Then, to the accompaniment of temple musicians and the chanting of sacred texts, a thousand priests climb the scaffold to bathe the image in auspicious unguents including the water of holy rivers, sandalwood paste, cane juice, saffron and milk, along with flowers and jewels. The ten-hour 1993 ceremony reached a climax when a helicopter dropped 20kg of gold leaf and 200 litres of milk on the colossus, along with showers of marigolds, gemstones and multi-hued powders. The residue formed a cascade of rainbow colours down the statue's head and body, admired by *lakhs* of devotees, Jain *sadhus* and *sadhvis* (female *sadhus*), and the massed cameras of the world. A satellite township, Yatrinagar, provides accommodation for 35,000 during the festival, and eighteen surrounding villages shelter pilgrims in temporary *dharamshalas*.

the hills, Indragiri (also known as Vindhyagiri), stands an extraordinary eighteen-metre-high monolithic statue of a naked male figure, **Gomateshvara**. Said to be the largest freestanding sculpture in India, this tenth-century colossus, visible for miles around, makes Sravanabelagola a key pilgrimage centre, though surprisingly few Western travellers find their way out here. Spend a night or two in the village, however, and you can climb Indragiri Hill before dawn to enjoy the serene spectacle of the sun rising over the sugar cane fields and outcrops of lumpy granite that litter the surrounding plains – an unforgettable sight.

Sravanabelagola is linked in tradition with the Mauryan emperor Chandragupta, who is said to have starved himself to death on the second hill in around 300 BC, in accordance with a Jain practice. The hill was renamed Chandragiri, marking the arrival of Jainism in southern India. At the same time, a controversy regarding the doctrines of Mahavira, the last of the 24 Jain **tirthankaras** (literally "crossing-makers", who assist the aspirant to cross the "ocean of rebirth"), split Jainism into two separate branches – *svetambara*, "white-clad" Jains, are more common in north India, while *digambara*, "sky-clad", are usually associated with the south. Truly ascetic *digambara* devotees go naked, though few do so away from sacred sites.

The monuments at Sravanabelagola probably date from no earlier than the tenth century, when a General Chamundaraya is said to have visited

Chandragiri in search of a Mauryan statue of Gomateshvara. Failing to find it, he decided to have one made. From the top of Chandragiri he fired an arrow across to Indragiri Hill; where the arrow landed he had a new Gomateshvara sculpted from a single rock.

Indragiri Hill

Gomateshvara is approached from the tank between the two hills by 620 steps, cut into the granite of **Indragiri Hill**, which pass numerous rock inscriptions on the way up to a walled enclosure. Shoes must be deposited at the stall to the left of the steps, and you can leave bags at the site office nearby. Take plenty of water especially on a hot day, as there is none available on the hill. Entered through a small wagon-vaulted *gopura*, the **temple** is entirely dominated by the towering figure of Gomateshvara. With elongated arms and exaggeratedly wide shoulders, his proportions are decidedly non-naturalistic. The sensuously smooth surface of the white granite "trap" rock is finely carved: particularly the hands, hair and serene face. As in legend, ant-hills and snakes sit at his feet and creepers appear to grow on his limbs.

Bhandari Basti and monastery (math)

The road east from the foot of the steps at Chandragiri leads to two interesting Jain buildings in town. To the right, the **Bhandari Basti** (1159), housing a shrine with images of the 24 *tirthankaras*, was built by Hullamaya, treasurer of the Hoysala Raja Narasimha. Two *mandapa* hallways, where naked *digambara* Jains may sometimes be seen discoursing with devotees clad in white, lead to the shrine at the back.

At the end of the street, the *math* (monastery) was the residence of Sravanabelagola's senior *acharya*, or guru. Thirty male and female monks, who also "go wandering in every direction", are attached to the *math*; normally a member of staff will be happy to show visitors around. Among the rare palm-leaf manuscripts in the library, some more than a millennium old, are works on mathematics and geography, and the *Mahapurana*, hagiographies of the *tirthankaras*. Next door, a covered walled courtyard is edged by a high platform on three sides, on which a chair is placed for the *acharya*. A collection of tenth-century bronze *tirthankara* images is housed here, and vibrant murals detail the various lives of Parshvanath. The hills where the *tirthankaras* stood to gain *moksha* are represented in a model, somewhat resembling a jelly mould, with tacked-on footprints.

Chandragiri Hill

Leaving your shoes with the keeper at the bottom, take the rock-cut steps to the top of the smaller **Chandragiri Hill**. Miraculously, the sound of radios and rickshaws down below soon disappears. Fine views stretch south to Indragiri and, from the north on the far side, across to a river, paddy and sugar cane fields, palms and the village of **Jinanathapura**, where there's another ornate Hoysala temple, the Shantishvara *basti*.

Rather than a single large shrine, as at Indragiri, Chandragiri holds a group of *bastis* in late Chalukya Dravida style, within a walled enclosure. Caretakers will take you around and open up the closed shrines. Save for pilasters and elaborate parapets, all the temples have plain exteriors. Named after its patron, the tenth-century **Chamundaraya** is the largest of the group, dedicated to Parshvanath. Inside the **Chandragupta** (twelfth century), superb carved panels in a small shrine tell the story of Chandragupta and his teacher Bhadrabahu. Traces of painted geometric designs survive and the pillars feature detailed carving. Elsewhere in the enclosure stands a 24-metre-high *manastambha*, "pillar of fame", decorated with images of spirits, *yakshis* and a *yaksha*. No fewer than 576 inscriptions dating from the sixth to the nineteenth century are dotted around the site, on pillars and the rock itself.

Practicalities

Sravanabelagola, along with Belur and Halebid, features on **tours** from Bangalore and Mysore (see p.1285 & p.1296). However, if you want to look around at a civilized pace, it's best to come independently. The **tourist office** (Mon–Sat 10am–5.30pm; ☎08176/657254) at the bottom of the stairs has little to offer and the management committee office next door only serves to collect donations and hand out tickets for the *dolis*.

If you want **accommodation**, there are plenty of **dharamshalas**, managed by the temple authorities, offering simple, scrupulously clean rooms, many with their own bathrooms and sitouts, ranged around gardens and courtyards, and most costing under Rs150 per night. The 24-hour accommodation office (☎08176/657258), where you will be allocated a room, is located inside the *SP Guest House*, next to the bus stand (look for the clock tower). The *Yatri Niwas* (❸), close by and also booked through the accommodation office, is about as expensive as it gets but is only marginally better than the best of the guesthouses. *Hotel Raghu*, opposite the main tank, houses the best of the many small local **restaurants**.

Crisscrossed by winding back roads, the idyllic (and mostly flat) countryside around Sravanabelagola is perfect cycling terrain. **Bicycles** are available for rent (Rs3 per hour) at Saleem Cycle Mart, on Masjid Road, opposite the northeast corner of the tank or stalls on the main road. If you're returning to Hassan, you'll have to head to **Channarayapatna** aka "CR Patna" by bus or in one of the shared vans that regularly ply the route and depart only when bursting; change at CR Patna for a bus to Hassan or Mysore.

Kodagu (Coorg)

The hill region of **Kodagu**, formerly known as **Coorg**, lies 100km west of Mysore in the Western Ghats, its eastern fringes merging with the Mysore Plateau. Comprising rugged mountain terrain interspersed with cardamom jungle, coffee plantations and swathes of lush rice paddy, it's one of South India's most beautiful areas. Little has changed since Dervla Murphy spent a few months here with her daughter in the 1970s (the subject of her classic travelogue, *On a Shoestring to Coorg*) and was entranced by the landscape and people, whose customs, language and appearance set them apart from their neighbours.

Today tourism is still virtually nonexistent, and the few travellers that pass through rarely venture beyond **Madikeri** (Mercara), Kodagu's homely capital. However, if you plan to cross the Ghats between Mysore and the coast, the route through Kodagu is definitely worth considering. Some coffee plantation owners open their doors to visitors – to find out more contact the Codagu Planters Association, Mysore Road, Madikeri (☎08272/229873). A good time to visit is during the festival season in early December or during the **Blossom Showers** around March and April when the coffee plants bloom with white flowers – some people, however, find the strong scent overpowering.

Kodagu is relatively undeveloped, and "sights" are few, but the countryside is idyllic and the climate refreshingly cool, even in summer. With the help of local

The Kodavas

Theories abound as to the origins of the **Kodavas**, or **Coorgis**, who today comprise less than one sixth of the hill region's population. Fair-skinned and with their own language and customs, they are thought to have migrated to southern India from Kurdistan, Kashmir and Rajasthan, though no one knows exactly why or when. One popular belief holds that this staunchly martial people, who since Independence have produced some of India's leading military brains, are descended from Roman mercenaries who fled here following the collapse of the Pandyan dynasty in the eighth century; some even claim connections with Alexander the Great's invading army. Whatever their origins, the Kodavas have managed to retain a distinct identity apart from the freed plantation slaves, Moplah Muslim traders and other immigrants who have settled here. More akin to Tamil than Kannada, their language is Dravidian, yet their religious practices, based on ancestor veneration and worship of nature spirits, differ markedly from those of mainstream Hinduism. Land tenure in Kodagu is also quite distinctive: women have a right to inheritance and ownership and are also allowed to remarry.

Spiritual and social life for traditional Kodavas revolves around the **Ain Mane**, or ancestral homestead. Built on raised platforms to overlook the family land, these large, detached houses, with their beautiful carved wood doors and beaten-earth floors, generally have four wings and courtyards to accommodate various branches of the extended family, as well as shrine rooms, or **Karona Kalas**, dedicated to the clan's most important forebears. Key religious rituals and rites of passage are always conducted in the *Ain Mane*, rather than the local temple. However, you could easily travel through Kodagu without ever seeing one, as they are invariably away from roads, shrouded in thick forest.

You're more likely to come across traditional Kodava **costume**, which is donned for all auspicious occasions. The men wear flat-bottomed turbans, dapper knee-length coats called *kupyas*, bound at the waist with a scarlet and gold cummerbund, and daggers (*peechekathis*) with ivory handles. Kodava women's garb of long, richly coloured silk saris, pleated at the back and with a *pallav* draped over their shoulders, is even more stunning, enlivened by heaps of heavy gold and silver jewellery, and precious stones. Women also wear headscarves, in the fields as well as for important events, tying the corners behind the head, Kashmiri style.

operators, there is now a growing trickle of visitors who come to Kodagu to **trek** through the unspoilt forest tracts and ridges that fringe the district. On the eastern borders of Kodagu on the Mysore Plateau, large **Tibetan settlements** around Kushalnagar have transformed a once barren countryside into fertile farmland dotted with busy monasteries, some housing thousands of monks.

Some history

The first concrete evidence of the kingdom dates from the eighth century, when it prospered from the salt trade passing between the coast and the cities on the Deccan Plateau. Under the Hindu **Haleri rajas**, the state repulsed invasions by its more powerful neighbours, including Haider Ali and his son Tipu Sultan, the infamous Tiger of Mysore (see p.1302). A combination of hilly terrain, absence of roads (a deliberate policy on the part of defence-conscious Kodagu kings) and the tenacity of its highly trained army, ensured Kodagu was the only Indian kingdom never to be conquered.

In 1834, however, after ministers appealed to the British to help depose their despotic king, Vira Rajah, Kodagu became a princely state with nominal independence, which it retained until the creation of Karnataka in 1956. **Coffee** was introduced during the Raj and, despite plummeting prices on the international market, this continues to be the linchpin of the local economy, along with pepper and cardamom. Although Kodagu is Karnataka's wealthiest region, and provides the highest tax revenue, it does not reap the rewards – 53 percent of villages are without electricity – and this, coupled with the distinct identity and fiercely independent nature of the Kodavas, has given rise to an autonomy movement known as **Kodagu Rajya Mukti Morcha**. Methods used by the KRMM include cultural programmes and occasional strikes; violence is very rare.

Madikeri (Mercara) and around

Nestling beside a curved stretch of craggy hills, **MADIKERI** (**Mercara**), capital of Kodagu, undulates around 1300m up in the Western Ghats, roughly midway between Mysore and the coastal city of Mangalore. The gradually increasing number of foreigners who travel up here find it a pleasant enough town, with red-tiled buildings and undulating roads that converge on a bustling bazaar.

The **Omkareshwara Shiva** temple, built in 1820, features an unusual combination of red-tiled roofs, Keralan Hindu architecture, gothic elements and Islamic-influenced domes. The fort and palace, worked over by Tipu Sultan in 1781 and rebuilt in the nineteenth century, now serve as offices and a prison. Within the complex, **St Mark's Church** holds a small **museum** of British memorabilia, Jain, Hindu and village deity figures and weapons (Tues–Sun 9am–5pm, except second Sat; free). Also worth a look are the huge square **tombs of the rajas** which, with their Islamic-style gilded domes and minarets, dominate the town's skyline. At the western edge of town, **Rajas' Seat**, close to the *Hotel Valley View*, is a belvedere, said to be the Kodagu kings' favoured place to watch the sunset.

Madikeri is the centre of the lucrative coffee trade, and although auto-rickshaws will take you there and back for around Rs185, a walk to **Abbi Falls** (8km) is a good introduction to coffee-growing country. The pleasant road, devoid of buses, winds through the hill country past plantations and makes for a good day's outing. At the litter-strewn car park at the end of the road, a gate leads through a private coffee plantation, sprinkled with cardamom sprays and pepper vines, to the bottom of the large stepped falls that are most impressive during and straight after the monsoons.

Practicalities

You can only reach Madikeri by road, but it's a scenic three-hour **bus** ride via **Kushalnagar** from **Mysore**, 120km southeast (unless you mistakenly get on one of the few buses that goes via Siddapura, which take more than an hour longer). Regular services, including deluxe buses, also connect Madikeri with **Mangalore**, 135km northwest across the Ghats. The KSTRC state **bus stand** is at the bottom of town, below the main bazaar; private buses from villages around the region pull into a parking lot at the end of the main street.

The small local **tourist office** (Mon–Sat, except second Sat of month 10.30am–5.30pm; ⓣ08272/228580) stands five minutes' walk along the Mysore road, below Thimaya Circle, next to the *PWD Travellers' Bungalow*, and can suggest itineraries, but is otherwise quite limited. If you're thinking of **trekking** in Kodagu, contact Ganesh Aiyanna at the *Hotel Cauvery* (see below) who is very helpful and organizes itineraries and trips for various budgets. Coorg Travels next to *Rajdarshan Lodge* (ⓣ08272/225817) is also flexible and friendly and will help put together a tour. For information on Kodagu's **forests** and forest bungalows contact the Conservator of Forests, Deputy Commissioner's

Office at the fort (☎08272/225708). Netraiders.com and Paramount Cyber Zone (both Rs30/hr), near Chowk in the heart of the bazaar, offer Internet access.

Accommodation and eating

Accommodation in Madikeri is not usually hard to come by, except occasionally in the budget range, most of which is concentrated around the bazaar and bus stand. The better-class and some of the budget hotels generally have **restaurants** and some have bars. The *Choice Hotel* on School Road is a restaurant only, serving breakfast items and a decent range of veg and non-veg dishes. *Tao*, up near the fort, is an authentic Chinese place, while the adjacent *Sri Ambica* serves wholesome veg snacks and meals. Traditional Kodagu food is very meat orientated, with scrumptious dishes like *pandi curry* (rich, spicy pork), although *akki otti* (rice flour *puris*) and the sweet *tambittu* should appeal to vegetarians.

Anchorage Guest House Kohinoor Rd ☎08272/228939. Absolutely no frills in the attached rooms but on a quiet sidestreet close to the bus stand. ❷

Capitol Village ☎08272/225975. Six kilometres east of the centre and booked through the *Cauvery* in Madikeri, this is the best place to stay in the area, but you'll need your own transport. The "village" consists of a cottage complex surrounded by splendid flowerbeds on the edge of a coffee plantation. It's quiet and secluded and excellent value, with a lakeside dorm (Rs250). ❺

Cauvery School Rd ☎08272/225492, Ⓕ225735. Below the private bus stand, this large and friendly place is almost hidden behind their excellent *Capitol* restaurant. ❸

Chitra School Rd ☎08272/225372, Ⓕ225191. Best value in town. Neat well-kept rooms, the slightly pricier ones with cable TV. Excellent non-veg restaurant-cum-bar downstairs. ❸

Coorg International Convent Rd ☎08272/228071, Ⓕ228073. Ten minutes by rickshaw west of the centre, this is one of the few upmarket options. It's a large but slightly characterless hotel with comfortable Western-style rooms, a multi-cuisine restaurant, exchange facilities, and shops. ❽–❾

East End General Thimaya Rd (aka Mysore Rd) ☎08272/229996. A large, plain, tiled-roof colonial bungalow turned into a hotel with a hint of character, but more renowned for its popular bar and restaurant. ❹

KSTDC Hotel Mayura Valley View ☎08272/228387. Well away from the main road, past Rajas' Seat, and with excellent views. The rooms are huge and the restaurant serves beer. Hail a rickshaw to get there, as it's a stiff twenty-minute uphill walk from the bus stand. ❸

Orange County Karadigodu, nr Siddapura, 32km south of Madikeri ☎08274/258485, replace 0 in code with 91 from Madikeri. Upscale resort at the edge of a wealthy coffee estate that's the most luxurious place to stay in the whole of Kodagu. Accommodation comprises mock-Tudor cottages set in manicured grounds. Trekking and horse riding can be arranged, and there's a pleasant pool (for residents only) and restaurant serving Kodava dishes. Book in advance through its Bangalore office (☎080/2558 2380). $100 and up. ❾

Rajdarshan ☎08272/229142. A modern and salubrious place with a landscaped garden, good restaurant and bar, just below Raja's Seat. ❺–❻

Mangalore

Many visitors only come to **MANGALORE** on their way somewhere else. As well as being fairly close to the Kodagu (Coorg) hill region, it's also a stopping-off point between Goa and Kerala, and is the nearest coastal town to the Hoysala and Jain monuments near Hassan, 172km east.

Mangalore was one of the most famous ports of South India. It was already famous overseas in the sixth century, as a major source of pepper, and the fourteenth-century Muslim writer Ibn Batuta noted its trade in pepper and ginger

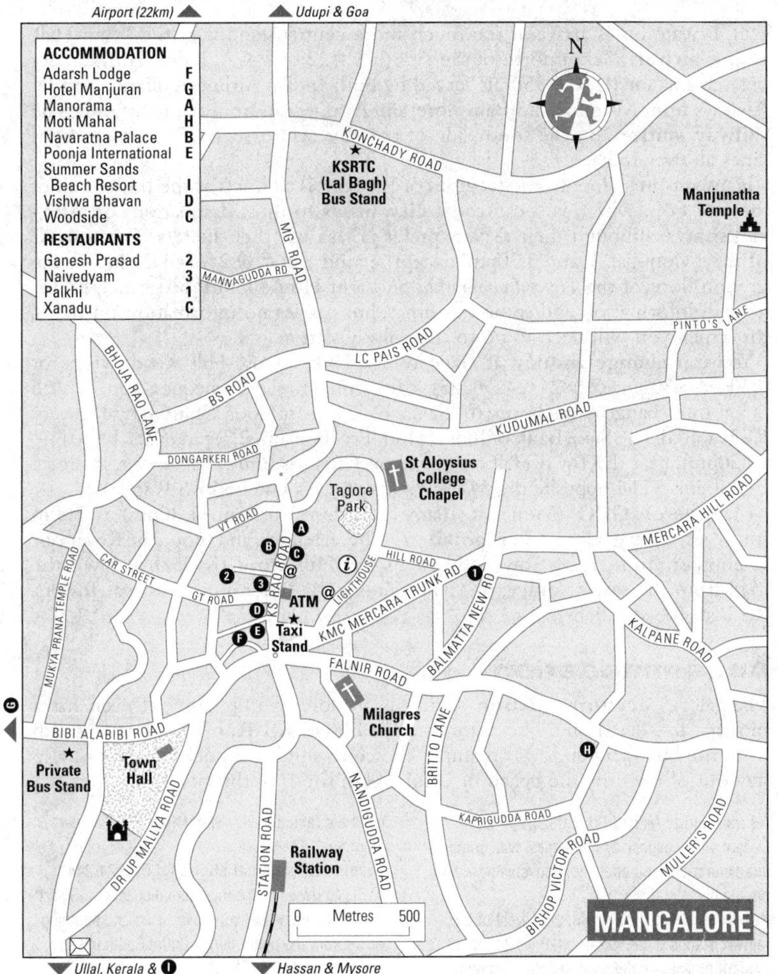

and the presence of merchants from Persia and the Yemen. In the mid-1400s, the Persian ambassador Abdu'r-Razzaq saw Mangalore as the "frontier town" of the Vijayanagar empire (see p.1333) – which was why the Portuguese captured it in 1529. Nowadays, the modern port, 10km north of the city proper, is principally known for the processing and export of coffee and cocoa (much of which comes from Kodagu), and cashew nuts (from Kerala). It is also a centre for the production of *beedi* cigarettes. Mangalore's ethnic mix lived more or less in harmony until 1998, when communal riots saw sections of the city's large Christian community attacked by right-wing Hindu fundamentalists.

Arrival, information and city transport

Mangalore's busy KSRTC **bus stand** (known locally as the "Lal Bagh" bus stand) is 2km north of the town centre, Hampankatta, at the bottom of Kadri

Hill. Private buses arrive at the much more central stand near the Town Hall. **Bajpe airport**, 22km north of the city (bus #22 or #47A, Indian Airlines city bus or taxis for Rs300–350), is served by both Indian Airlines/Alliance and Jet Airways from Mumbai and Bangalore, and Air Deccan from the latter only. The **railway station**, on the south side of the city centre, sees daily services from cities all over India.

Hampankatta, close to the facilities of KS Rao Road, acts as the traffic hub of the city from where you can catch **city buses** to most destinations or **auto-rickshaws**, although their drivers prefer not to use their meters. The **tourist office** (Mon–Sat 10am–5.30pm, except second Sat; Ⓣ0824/244 2926) on the ground floor of the *Hotel Indraprashta* on Light House Hill Road is helpful for general information and some bus times, but carries no information on trains, for which you will need to go to the railway station.

You can **change money** at Trade Wings, Light House Hill Road (Mon–Sat 9.30am–5.30pm; Ⓣ0824/242 6225) who cash travellers' cheques, and at Wall Street Interchange (same hours; Ⓣ0824/242 1717), 1st Floor, Utility Royal Towers, KS Rao Rd. The State Bank of India (Mon–Fri 10.30am–2.30pm & Sat 10.30am–12.30pm), near the Town Hall on Hamilton Circle, is somewhat slower. There's a CorpBank ATM opposite the *Mangalore International* hotel on KS Rao Road.

Mangalore's **GPO** (Mon–Sat 10am–7pm, Sun 10.30am–1.30pm) is 500m south of Shetty Circle. For **email** try the friendly and popular Kohinoor Computer Zone, Plaza Towers, Light House Hill Road (Rs25/hr) down the road from the tourist office, or Cyber Zoom, 1st Floor, Utility Royal Towers, KS Rao Road (20/hr).

Accommodation

Mangalore's **accommodation** standards are forever improving; it even has a modern five-star hotel. The main area for hotels, **KS Rao Road**, runs south from the bus stand and has an ample choice to suit most pockets. You can also stay out of town by the beach in **Ullal**, 10km south of the city.

Adarsh Lodge Market Rd Ⓣ0824/244 0878. Decent value, especially for singles, with compact but clean rooms, all attached. Convenient for the private bus stand. ❷

Hotel Manjuran Old Port Rd, 2km west of the railway station Ⓣ0824/242 0420, Ⓕ242 0585. Modern business hotel, belonging to Taj group; some rooms with sea view and all a/c. Travel desk, exchange, pool, bar, two classy restaurants and 24hr coffee shop. ❻–❾

Manorama KS Rao Rd Ⓣ0824/244 0306. A 65-room concrete block with spartan, large and very clean rooms (some a/c). Good value but there are better central options. ❸–❺

Moti Mahal Falnir Rd Ⓣ0824/244 1411. Large hotel (some a/c) with 24hr room service and coffee shop, bar, pool, shops, exchange and travel desk. *Mangala* non-veg and *Madhuvan* veg restaurants serve Indian, Chinese and Western food. ❹–❻

Navaratna Palace KS Rao Rd Ⓣ0824/244 1104, Ⓔnish77772000@yahoo.com. Preferable to its adjacent older sister *Navaratna*, it has better rooms (some a/c) for little extra cost. Also two good a/c restaurants: *Heera Panna* and *Palimar* (pure veg). ❸–❺

Poonja International KS Rao Rd Ⓣ0824/244 0171, Ⓦwww.hotelpoonjainternational.com. Smart mostly a/c high-rise with all facilities and stunning views from the upper floors. Buffet South Indian breakfast included. ❹–❽

Summer Sands Beach Resort Chota Mangalore, Ullal Ⓣ0824/246 7690, Ⓦwww.summer-sands.com. Spacious rooms and cottages (some a/c) near the beach, originally built as a campus for expats, with a pool, and a bar-restaurant serving local specialities, Indian and Chinese food. Foreign exchange for guests. Recommended. Take bus #44A from town. ❺–❾

Vishwa Bhavan KS Rao Rd Ⓣ0824/244 0822. Cheap, plain rooms, some with attached baths, around a courtyard close to all amenities. Best of the real cheapies. ❶

Woodside KS Rao Rd Ⓣ0824/244 0296. Old-fashioned hotel offering a range of rooms (the economy doubles are the best deal), but "no accommodation for servants". Some a/c. ❸–❺

The City and beaches

Mangalore's strong Christian influence can be traced back to the arrival further south of St Thomas (see p.1412). Some 1400 years later, in 1526, the Portuguese founded one of the earliest churches on the coast close to the old port. Today's **Most Holy Rosary Church**, however, with a dome based on St Peter's in Rome, dates only from 1910. Fine restored fresco, tempera and oil murals by an Italian artist, Antonio Moscheni, adorn the Romanesque-style **St Aloysius College Chapel**, built in 1885 on Lighthouse Hill, near the centre.

At the foot of Kadri Hill, 3km north, reached by a host of city buses, Mangalore's tenth-century **Manjunatha temple** is an important centre of the Shaivite and tantric **Natha-Pantha cult**. Thought to be an outgrowth of Vajrayana Buddhism, the cult is a divergent species of Hinduism, similar to certain cults in Nepal. Enshrined in the sanctuary, a number of superb **bronzes** include a 1.5-metre-high seated Lokeshvara (Matsyendranatha), made in 958 AD and considered the finest southern bronze outside Tamil Nadu. To see it close up you'll have to visit at *darshan* times (6am–1pm & 4–8pm), although the bronzes can be glimpsed through the wooden slats on the side of the sanctuary. If possible, time your visit to coincide with *mahapooja* at 8am, noon or 8pm, when the priests give a fire blessing to the accompaniment of raucous music. Opposite the east entrance, steps lead via a laterite path to a curious group of minor shrines. Beyond this complex stands the **Shri Yogishwar Math**, a hermitage of tantric *sadhus* set round two courtyards.

If you're looking to escape the city for a few hours, head out to the village of **ULLAL**, 10km south, whose long sandy **beach**, backed by wispy fir trees, stretches for miles in both directions. It's a deservedly popular place for a stroll, particularly in the evening when Mangaloreans come out to watch the sunset, but a strong undertow makes swimming difficult, and at times unsafe. You're better off using the pool at the excellent *Summer Sands Beach Resort* (see

Kambla

If you're anywhere between Mangalore and Bhatkal from October to April and come across a crowd gathering around a waterlogged paddy field, pull over and spend a day at the races – Karnatakan style. Few Westerners ever experience it, but the spectacular rural sport of **Kambla**, or **bull racing**, played in the southernmost district of coastal Karnataka (known as Dakshina Kannada), is well worth seeking out.

Two contestants, usually local rice farmers, take part in each race, riding on a wooden plough-board tethered to a pair of prize bullocks. The object is to reach the opposite end of the field first, but points are also awarded for style, and riders gain extra marks – and roars of approval from the crowd – if the muddy spray kicked up from the plough-board splashes the special white banners, or *thoranam*, strung across the course at a height of 6 to 8m.

Generally, race days are organized by wealthy landowners on fields specially set aside for the purpose. Villagers flock in from all over the region, as much for the fair, or *shendi*, as the races themselves: men huddle in groups to watch cockfights (*kori-katta*), women haggle with bangle sellers, and the kids roam around sucking sticky *kathambdi goolay*, the local bonbons. It is considered highly prestigious to be able to throw such a party, especially if your bulls win any events or, better still, come away as champions. Known as *yeru* in Kannada, racing bulls are thoroughbreds who rarely, if ever, are put to work. Pampered by their doting owners, they are massaged, oiled and blessed by priests before big events, during which large sums of money are often won and lost.

p.1318), immediately behind the beach (Rs100 for non-residents). A further 2km past the *Summer Sands*, a banyan-lined road leads to the Shiva temple of **Someshwar**, built in Keralan style, overlooking a rocky promontory, and another popular beach. Towards the centre of Ullal, and around 700m from the main bus stand, is the *dargah* (burial shrine) of **Seyyid Mohammad Shareeful Madani**, a sixteenth-century saint who is said to have come from Medina in Arabia and floated across the sea on a handkerchief. The extraordinary nineteenth-century building with garish onion domes houses the saint's tomb, which is one of the most important Sufi shrines in southern India. Visitors are advised to follow custom and cover their heads and limbs and wash their feet before entering. Local **buses** (#44A) run to Ullal from the junction at the south end of KS Rao Road. As you cross the River Netravathi en route, look out for the brick chimney stacks clustered on the banks at the mouth of the estuary. Using quality clay shipped downriver from the hills, these factories manufacture the famous terracotta red **Mangalorean roof tiles**, which you see all over southern India.

Eating

The best **places to eat** are in the bigger hotels. If you're on a tight budget, try one of the inexpensive café-restaurants opposite the bus stand, or the excellent canteen inside the bus stand itself, which serves great *dosas* and other South Indian snacks. Also recommended for delicious, freshly cooked and inexpensive "meals" is the *Ganesh Prasad*, down the lane alongside the *Vasanth Mahal*. The rooftop *Palkhi* on Mercara Trunk Road is an airy family restaurant with a wide menu. For something a little more sophisticated, head for the a/c *Xanadu*, at the

Moving on from Mangalore

Mangalore is a major crossroads for tourist traffic heading along the Konkan coast between Goa and Kerala, and between Mysore and the coast. The city is also well connected **by air** to **Mumbai**, **Bangalore** and **Chennai**. The Indian Airlines office is at Airlines House, Hathill Rd, Lalbagh (Ⓣ0824/245 1046) and the Jet Airways office at DS Ram Bhavan Complex, Kodiabail (Ⓣ0824/244 1181). Air Deccan can only be contacted by mobile or online (Ⓣ98457 77008, Ⓦwww.airdeccan.net)

With the inauguration of the single-track coastal **Konkan Railway**, services have opened up to Goa and Mumbai and all planned trains are now operating, although it should be noted that through services do not pass via the city terminus. A better choice of train connections for the Konkan Railway in both directions can be had from **Kankanadi**, around 10km north, or **Kasargode**, an easy bus ride across the Kerala border. From Mangalore itself, the fast #KR2 *Verna Passenger* departs Mangalore at 7.10am, travels north along the coast and takes 6hr 10min to get to **Margao (Goa)** via Udupi and **Gokarna** (3hr 50min). The *Matsyagandha Express* (#2620), which departs at 2.40pm, is slightly faster to Gokarna (3hr 5min) and Goa (5hr 45min), and continues to Mumbai (Lokmanya Tilak station; 13hr 55min). The service south is good and, if you're travelling to Kerala, far quicker and more relaxing than the bus. Two services leave Mangalore station every day for **Thiruvananthapuram**, via **Kozhikode**, **Ernakulam/Kochi**, **Kottayam** and **Kollam**. Leaving at the red-eyed time of 4.15am, the *Parsuram Express* (#6350) is the faster of the two but the *Malabar Express* (#6330), which leaves at 5.50pm, is convenient as an overnight train to Thiruvananthapuram, arriving there at 9.25am. For those travelling to **Chennai**, the overnight Mangalore–Chennai mail (#6602) departs at 12.30pm and follows the Kerala coast till Shoranur where it turns east to **Palakaad** before journeying on to **Erode** and arriving at Chennai at 6.25am.

Woodside Hotel, also on KS Rao Road, which offers classy non-veg cuisine and alcohol. It's too dingy for lunch, but fine for dinner, when its kitsch fish tanks and resident ducks are illuminated. One of the best of the hotel restaurants, however, is the pure veg *Naivedyam* at the *Mangalore International* also on KS Rao Road, which has both a plush a/c and a comfortable and non-a/c section.

North of Mangalore: coastal Karnataka

Whether you travel the **Karnatakan (Karavali) coast** on the newly operational Konkan Railway or along the busy NH-14, southern India's smoothest highway, the route between Goa and Mangalore ranks among the most scenic anywhere in the country. Crossing countless palm- and mangrove-fringed estuaries, the railway line stays fairly flat, while the recently upgraded road, dubbed by the local tourist board as "The Sapphire Route", scales several spurs of the Western Ghats, which here creep to within a stone's throw of the sea, with spellbinding views over long, empty beaches and deep blue bays. Highlights are the pilgrim town of **Udupi**, site of a famous Krishna temple, and **Gokarna**, another important Hindu centre that provides access to exquisite unexploited beaches. A couple of bumpy back roads wind inland through the mountains to **Jog Falls**, India's biggest waterfall, more often approached from the east.

Udupi

UDUPI (also spelt Udipi), on the west coast, 60km north of Mangalore, is one of South India's holiest Vaishnavite centres. The Hindu saint **Madhva**

Note that conversion work on the line inland to Hassan for Mysore and Bangalore has been further delayed but there's no harm checking on its progress.

The traditional way to travel on to **Goa** was always by **bus**, though that is being usurped by the Konkan Railway. Now only two buses leave the KSRTC Lal Bagh stand daily, taking around 10hr 30min to reach Panjim. You can jump off at Chaudi (for Palolem) en route. Tickets should be booked in advance (preferably the day before) at KSRTC's well-organized computer booking hall (daily 7am–8pm), or from the Kadamba office on the main concourse. KSRTC also has a central office (daily 8.30am–8.30pm) on the ground floor of Utility Royal Towers, KS Rao Road. The Goa buses are also good for **Gokarna**; hop off at **Kumta** on the main highway, and catch an onward service from there. The only direct bus to Gokarna leaves Mangalore at 1.30pm. There are plenty of state buses heading north to **Udupi** and south along the coast towards **Kerala**, though it is easier to pick up the more numerous private services to those places.

For **Mysore**, **Bangalore** and **Hassan**, you are restricted to the bus until the railway line reopens but there are plenty of services, both state and private. **Madikeri** is only reachable by road: the hourly buses to Mysore stop there, as do some luxury services to Bangalore. The best private bus service to Bangalore is on the distinctive yellow luxury coaches of VRL; two buses leave at night (10pm; 7–8hr; Rs250) and tickets are available through Vijayananda Travels, PVS Centenary Building, Kodiyabail, Kudmulranga Rao Rd (☎0824/249 3536). Agents along Falnir Road include Anand Travels (☎0824/244 6737) and Ideal Travels (☎0824/242 4899) which also runs luxury buses to Bangalore (6–7hr; Rs 240) and two buses to **Ernakulam** (8 & 9pm; 9–10hr; Rs340).

(1238–1317) was born here, and the **Krishna temple** and *maths* (monasteries) he founded are visited by *lakhs* of pilgrims each year. The largest numbers congregate during the late winter, when the town hosts a series of spectacular **car festivals** and gigantic, bulbous-domed chariots are hauled through the streets around the temple. Even if your visit doesn't coincide with a festival, Udupi is a good place to break the journey along the Karavali coast. Thronging with *pujaris* and pilgrims, its small sacred enclave is wonderfully atmospheric, and you can take a boat from the nearby fishing village of **Malpé beach** to **St Mary's Island**, the deserted outcrop of hexagonal basalt where Vasco da Gama erected a crucifix prior to his first landing in India.

Incidentally, Udupi also lays proud claim to being the birthplace of the nationally popular **masala dosa**; these crispy stuffed pancakes, made from fermented rice flour, were first prepared and made famous by the Udupi brahmin hotels.

Practicalities

Udupi's three **bus stands** are dotted around the amorphous square in the centre of town: the KSRTC and private stands form a practically indistinguishable gathering spot for the numerous services to Mangalore and more long-distance buses to Mysore, Bangalore, Gokarna, Jog Falls, and other towns between northern Kerala and Goa. The City stand is down some steps to the north and handles private services to nearby villages, including Malpé. Udupi's **railway station** is at Indrali on Manipal Road 3km from the centre, and there are at least five trains in each direction daily. The modest tourist office is near the temple in the Krishna Building, Car Street (Mon–Sat 10am–5.30pm; ⓣ0820/252 9718). Money can be **exchanged** at the KM Dutt branch of Canara Bank on the main road just south of the bus stands, UAEXchange (Mon–Sat 9.30am–6pm, Sun 9.30am–1pm; ⓣ0820/228 6655) or the Corp-Bank ATM on the south side of the square, while **email** facilities are available at nearby Netpoint (Rs30/hr), one of several such outlets.

Accommodation and eating

Udupi has a good choice of **places to stay** to suit all budgets, most within a few minutes' walk of the temple and city centre. As you might expect of the masala dosa's birthplace, there are many fine, simple South Indian **restaurants** where you can sample these and other veg favourites, such as *Adarsha*, below the *Janardhana*. For non-veg or alcohol, you'll have to try a posh hotel, such as the *Pisces* at the *Sriram Residency*.

Durga International just west of City bus stand ⓣ0820/253 6977, ⓔdurga-hotel@yahoo.com. Airy and efficient lodge with a variety of rooms, all attached with TV and some a/c, on the upper storeys of a modern block. ❸–❻

Janardhana south of the KSRTC bus stand ⓣ0820/252 3880, ⓕ252 3887. Fairly mundane hotel with simple attached rooms of different sizes, most with cable TV. ❷–❹

Hotel Sharada International 2km out of town on the NH-17 ⓣ0820/252 2910. Mid-price place with a range of rooms from singles to carpeted a/c, as well as veg and non-veg restaurants and a bar. ❸–❻

Sriram Residency opposite Head Post Office ⓣ0820/253 0761, ⓔsriramresidency@indiatimes.com. Plushest place in the centre with a smart lobby, comfortable a/c rooms, two restaurants and a bar. ❸–❼

Sri Vidyasamudra Choultry opposite Krishna temple ⓣ0820/252 0820. Basically for pilgrims but foreigners are welcome in this ultra-basic lodge. The front rooms overlooking the temple and bathing tank are incredibly atmospheric ❶

Vyavahar Lodge Kankads Rd ⓣ0820/252 2568. Basic but friendly and clean lodge between the bus stands and temple. ❷

The Krishna temple and maths

Udupi's **Krishna temple** lies five minutes' walk east of the main street, surrounded by the eight **maths** founded by Madhva in the thirteenth century. Legend has it that the idol enshrined within was discovered by the saint himself after he prevented a shipwreck. The grateful captain of the vessel concerned offered Madhva his precious cargo as a reward, but the holy man asked instead for a block of ballast, which he broke open to expose a perfectly formed image of Krishna. Believed to contain the essence (*sannidhya*) of the god, this deity draws a steady stream of pilgrims, and is the focus of almost constant ritual activity. It is cared for by *acharyas*, or pontiffs, from one or other of the *maths*. They perform pujas (5.30am–8.45pm) that are open to non-Hindus; men are only allowed into the main shrine bare-chested.

At the **Regional Resources Centre for the Performing Arts** in the MGM College, staff can tell you about local festivals and events that are well off the tourist trail; the collection includes film, video and audio archives. The pamphlet *Udupi: an Introduction*, on sale in the stalls around the sacred enclave, is another rich source of background detail on the temple and its complex rituals.

Malpé, St Mary's Island and Thottam

Udupi's weekend picnic spot, **Malpé beach**, 5km northwest of the centre, is disappointing, marred by a forgotten concrete block that was planned to be a government-run hotel. After wandering around the smelly fish market at the harbour you could haggle to arrange a boat (Rs800) to take you out to **St Mary's Island**, an extraordinary rockface of hexagonal basalt. Vasco da Gama is said to have placed a cross here in the 1400s, prior to his historic landing at Kozhikode in Kerala. From a distance, the sandy beach at **Thottam**, 1km north of Malpé and visible from the island, is tempting; in reality it's an open sewer.

Jog Falls

Hidden in a remote, thickly forested corner of the Western Ghats, **Jog Falls**, 240km northeast of Mangalore, are the highest **waterfalls** in India. These days, they are rarely as spectacular as they were before the construction of a large dam upriver, which impedes the flow of the River Sharavati over the sheer red-brown sandstone cliffs. However, the surrounding scenery is stunning at any time, with dense scrub and jungle carpeting sparsely populated, mountainous terrain. The views of the falls from the opposite side of the gorge is also impressive, unless, that is, you come here during the monsoons, when mist and rain clouds envelop the cascades. Another reason not to come here during the wet season is that the extra water, and abundance of leeches at this time, make the excellent **hike** to the floor valley a trial. So if you can, head up here between October and January. The trail starts just below the bus park and winds steeply down to the water, where you can enjoy a refreshing dip. To enhance the area's appearance, the whole patch opposite the falls where the facilities are has been landscaped to provide appealing viewing platforms and provided with its own impressive entrance gate (Rs2 per person; rate varies for vehicles) and attractively designed reception centre.

Practicalities

Getting to and from Jog Falls by **bus** is now a lot easier thanks to the completion of the NH-206 across the Ghats, which has cut the journey time to **Honavar** (6 daily; 2hr 30min), on the Konkan Railway, and on to **Kumta** (4 daily; 3hr),

△ Jog Falls

where you can connect to Gokarna. Currently there are two buses daily from the Falls to **Udupi** and on to **Mangalore** (8.30am & 8.30pm; 7hr) and hourly services to **Shimoga**, from where you can change onto buses for Hospet and Hampi. A service to **Panaji** pulls through around midnight. Better connections can be had at nearby Sagar (30km southeast) with buses to Shimoga, Udupi, Mysore, Hassan and Bangalore. Of the two direct buses to **Bangalore** from Jog Falls, the "semi-deluxe" departs at 7.30pm (9hr) and the ordinary at 8.30am. With a car or motorbike, you can approach the Falls from the coast along one of several scenic routes through the Ghats. The **tourist office** (Mon–Sat 10am–1.30pm & 2–5pm), upstairs at the new reception centre, opens rather erratically but can supply information on transport and vehicle rental.

Accommodation is limited in the settlement and largely a KSTDC monopoly (Ⓣ08186/244732); it runs the ugly concrete *Mayura Shraravathi* (❸), which has vast rooms with fading plaster and bathrooms with rickety plumbing but good views, and the humbler *Tunga Tourist Home* nearer the reception centre, with basic attached doubles (❷). On the opposite side of the road the Karnataka Power Corporation also lets its four comfy a/c rooms (Ⓣ08186/244742; ❹) when available, as does the Shimoga District *PWD Inspection Bungalow* (Ⓣ08186/244333; ❸), whose a/c rooms are nicely situated on a hillock about 400m west. The youth hostel (Ⓣ08186/244251; ❶), ten minutes' walk down the Shimoga road, has undergone renovation but is still very basic. If you can get in, the *PWD Inspection Bungalow*, on the north side of the gorge, has great views from its spacious, comfortable rooms, but is invariably full and has to be booked in advance from the Assistant Engineer's office in Siddapur (Ⓣ08389/222103; ❶–❷).

Apart from the KSTDC *Jaladarshini* canteen next to the *Tunga Tourist Home*, which offers the usual adequate but uninspiring fare, the only other **food** options are at the enclave of small chai stalls and shops that have been relocated to the reception centre – *Hotel Rashmita* is the best of the bunch.

Gokarna

Set behind a broad white-sand beach, with the forest-covered foothills of the Western Ghats forming a backdrop, **GOKARNA** (also spelled Gokarn), seven hours by bus north of Mangalore, is among India's most scenically situated sacred sites. Yet this compact little coastal town – a Shaivite centre for more than two millennia – remained largely "undiscovered" by Western tourists until the early 1990s, when it began to attract dreadlocked and didjgeridoo-toting travellers fleeing the commercialization of Goa. Now, it's firmly on the tourist map, although the Hindu pilgrims pouring through still far outnumber the foreigners that flock here in winter.

Even if you're not tempted to while away weeks on isolated beaches, Gokarna is well worth a short detour from the coastal highway. Like Udupi, it is an old-established pilgrimage place, with a markedly traditional feel.

Arrival and information

The KSRTC **bus stand**, 300m from Car Street and within easy walking distance of Gokarna's limited accommodation, means that buses no longer have to negotiate the narrow streets of the bazaar. You may well find that your bus, especially coming from major tourist points like Goa and Hampi, deposits you at the new police checkpost on the way into town, where you have to register; this is a new measure against beach crime and nothing to get het up about. Gokarna Road **railway station**, served by at least two daily trains in each direction, is 9km inland but buses and auto-rickshaws are available to take you into town.

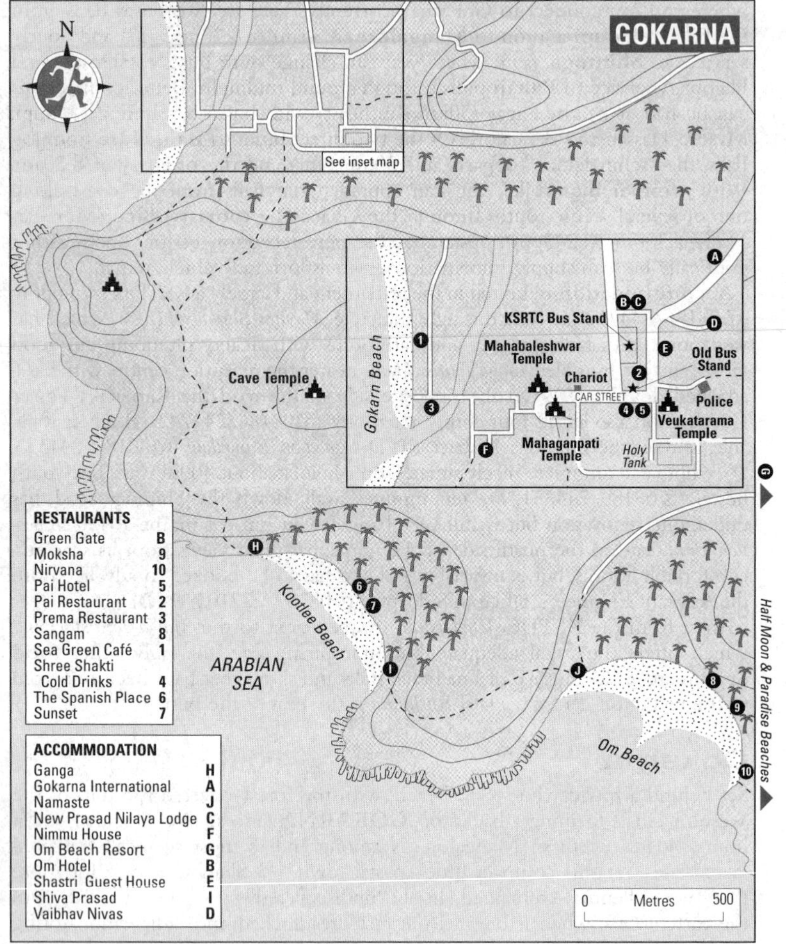

You can **change money** at the *Om Hotel* near the bus stand but the best rates to be had are at the Pai STD booth on the road into town near the bus stand, one several licensed dealers. The tiny Om bureau almost opposite is the best of the various **Internet** joints (all Rs40/hr) but none have very reliable connections. **Bicycles** are available for rent from a stall next to the *Pai Restaurant*, for Rs3 per hour or Rs30 for a full day. However, due to the roughness of the tracks you will find it near impossible to cycle to beaches other than the town beach, or along the long route to Om beach. If you become ill, English-speaking Dr Shastri (Ⓣ08386/256220) is highly recommended by long-stay visitors.

Accommodation

Gokarna has a couple of bona fide **hotels** and a small but reasonable choice of **guesthouses**. As a last resort, you can nearly always find a bed in one of the pilgrims' hostels, or **dharamshalas**, dotted around town. With dorms, bare, cell-size rooms and basic washing facilities, these are intended mainly for Hindus, but Western tourists are welcome if there are vacancies: try the *Prasad Nilaya*, just down the lane from *Om Hotel*. After staying in the village for a couple of days, however, many visitors strike out for the **beaches**, where there is very limited accommodation (see p.1328). Some people end up sleeping rough on the beaches, but the nights can be chilly and robberies are common. Leave your luggage and valuables behind in Gokarna (most guesthouses will store your stuff for a small fee), and if you plan to spend any time on the beaches, consider investing in a cheap mattress from the bazaar – you can always sell it on when you leave.

Gokarna International On the main road into town ⓣ08386/256622, ⓔhotelgokarn@yahoo.com. Gokarna's newest and smartest hotel, which is friendly and offers unbeatable value. Good range of rooms from cheap singles to deluxe a/c; some have bathtubs, TV and balconies overlooking the palms. The restaurants, one with bar, are more mediocre. ❷–❹

New Prasad Nilaya Lodge Near the new bus stand ⓣ08386/257135. A relatively new place consisting of clean, bright spacious rooms with attached baths. Very reasonable. ❶–❷

Nimmu House A minute's walk from the temples towards Gokarna beach ⓣ08386/256730, ⓔnimmuhouse@yahoo.com. Gokarna's best budget guesthouse, run by the friendly and helpful lady whose name it bears, with clean rooms (some attached). The new block has very reasonable doubles; there are reliable left-luggage and Internet facilities and a peaceful yard to sit in. ❶–❷

Om Hotel Near the new bus stand ⓣ08386/256445. Conventional economy hotel pitched at middle-class Indian pilgrims, with plain, good-sized en-suite rooms, overpriced a/c and two restaurants, one mainly a bar. ❷–❺

Shastri Guest House 100m from the new bus stand ⓣ08386/256220. Tucked behind the Shastri Clinic on the main road, this is a quiet place offering some rooms with attached bath, and rock-bottom single occupancy rates. ❷

Vaibhav Nivas Off the main road, under 5min from the bus stand ⓣ08386/256714. Friendly, cheap and justifiably popular place despite some tiny rooms. Undergoing renovations to render all rooms with attached bathrooms. Internet and left-luggage facilities available. ❶–❸

The Town

Gokarna **town**, a hotchpotch of wood-fronted houses and red terracotta roofs, is clustered around a long L-shaped bazaar, its broad main road – known as **Car Street** – running west to the town beach, a sacred site in its own right. Hindu mythology identifies it as the place where Rudra (another name for Shiva) was reborn through the ear of a cow from the underworld after a period of penance. Gokarna is also the home of one of India's most powerful *shivalinga* – the **pranalingam**, which came to rest here after being carried off by Ravana, the evil king of Lanka, from Shiva's home on Mount Kailash in the Himalayas.

The *pranalingam* resides in Gokarna to this day, enshrined in the medieval **Shri Mahabaleshwar temple**, at the far west end of the bazaar. It is regarded as so auspicious that a mere glimpse of it will absolve a hundred sins, even the murder of a brahmin. Local Hindu lore also asserts that you can maximize the *lingam*'s purifying power by shaving your head, fasting, and taking a holy dip in the sea before *darshan*, or ritual viewing of the deity. For this reason, pilgrims traditionally begin their tour of Gokarna with a walk to the beach, guided by their family *pujari*. Next, they visit the **Shri Mahaganpati temple**, a stone's throw east of Shri Mahabaleshwar, to propitiate the elephant-headed god Ganesh. Sadly, owing to some ugly incidents involving insensitive behaviour by a minority of foreigners, tourists are now banned from the temples, though you can still get a good view of proceedings in the smaller Shri Mahaganpati from the entrance.

The beaches

Notwithstanding Gokarna's numerous temples, shrines and tanks, most Western tourists come here for the beautiful **beaches** situated south of the more crowded town beach, beyond the lumpy laterite headland that overlooks the town. Many lounge for weeks, taking advantage of relatively lax attitudes towards the smoking of herb and imbibing of potent *bhang* lassis.

To pick up the trail, head along the narrow alley opposite the south entrance to the Mahaganpati temple, and follow the path uphill through the woods. After twenty minutes, you drop down from a rocky plateau to **Kootlee beach** – a wonderful kilometre-long sweep of golden-white sand sheltered by a pair of steep-sided promontories. Despite appearances, locals consider the water here to be dangerous. The palm-leaf chai stalls and seasonal cafés that spring up here during the winter offer some respite from the heat of the midday sun, and some of them offer very basic accommodation in bamboo shacks. Two places have more solid, lockable brick or mud huts but are likely to be booked out by long-term visitors: the *Ganga*, to the right as you first approach the beach (Ⓣ08386/257195; ❶); and *Shiva Prasad* at the far end (Ⓣ08386/257150; ❶). *The Spanish Place* (owned by a woman from Spain), set behind a line of neatly planted palms midway down the beach, serves good pasta, sandwiches, sweets and creamy lassis in a relaxed atmosphere, and nearby *Sunset* offers seafood, tasty sizzlers and other more basic meals. Fresh water has been a perennial problem but bottled water is widely available. A couple of places even have (slow) Internet connections these days.

It takes around twenty minutes more to hike over the headland from Kootlee to exquisite **Om beach**, so named because its distinctive twin crescent-shaped bays resemble the auspicious Om symbol. The advent of a dirt road from town means the coves are now frequented by a more diverse crowd than the hardcore hippy fringe whose exclusive preserve it used to be until the late-1990s. Hammocks and basic huts still populate the palm groves and about a dozen laid-back chai houses such as *Sangam*, *Nirvana* and *Moksha* provide ample food and drink, but the nicely landscaped *Namaste* (Ⓣ08386/257141; ❶–❷) has the best restaurant and only solid accommodation until Cgh Earth opens up its luxury resort behind the beach. Five kilometres inland on the hills, the new *Om Beach Resort* (Ⓣ08386/257052, Ⓔombeachresort@info.com; ❽) costs Rs1500 per person for full board in smart air-conditioned suites with sitouts.

Aforementioned developments notwithstanding, it's unlikely the concrete mixers will ever reach Gokarna's two most remote beaches, which lie another twenty- to forty-minute walk over the hill. **Half-Moon** and **Paradise** beaches, are, despite the presence of one or two chai houses on each and the occasional shack, mainly for intrepid sun-lovers happy to pack in their own supplies. If you're looking for near-total isolation, this is your best bet.

Eating and drinking

Gokarna town offers a good choice of **places to eat**, with a string of busy "meals" joints along Car Street and the main road.

Being Karnataka, **beer** is freely available and fairly cheap, both in town and on the beaches. Look out for the local sweet speciality *gad-bad*, several layers of different ice creams mixed with chopped nuts and chewy dried fruit.

Green Gate *Om Hotel*, near the new bus stand. The more pleasant of the hotel's two eateries offers a range of Mexican, Italian and Israeli dishes, as well as fish and sizzlers. The restaurant downstairs is more of a drinking den serving good spicy Indian but the courtyard is OK.

Pai Hotel Car St. Tiny food-only joint but its veg snacks are excellent, and the milky coffee delicious. A favourite meeting spot for travellers.

Moving on from Gokarna

Gokarna is well connected by direct daily **bus** to Goa (5hr), and several towns in Karnataka, including Bangalore (13hr), Hospet/Hampi (10hr) and Mysore (14hr), via Mangalore (7hr) and Udupi (6hr). Although there are only three direct buses north along the coast to Karwar (2hr) close to the border with Goa, you can change at Ankola on the main highway for more services. For more buses to Hospet and Hampi and the best connections to Jog Falls, change at Kumta; **tempos** regularly ply the route between Gokarna and Kumta (32km) as well as Ankola. The KSRTC counter in the new bus stand is helpful for current bus timings.

You'll get the best **train** connections to Goa, Mangalore, Udupi and Kerala by going first to either Kumta or Ankola, Gokarna Road now has at least two daily stopping trains in each direction; the *Verna Passenger* #KR2 to Margao at 11.14am and #KR1 to Mangalore at 3.29pm, while the *Matsyagandha Express* #2620 to Goa and Mumbai leaves at 6.15pm and #2619 to Mangalore at an inconvenient 1.45am. A couple of weekly expresses also call here.

Pai Restaurant Main Rd. Excellent spot for fresh and tasty veg thalis, masala dosas, crisp *wadas*, teas and coffees until late.

Prema Restaurant Near the beach end of Car St. Standard traveller-friendly menu of pasta, sandwiches and bland Indian but this is where you'll find the best *gad-bad* in town.

Sea Green Café Just behind the main town beach. Tibetan and Nepali food in a breezy courtyard, where you can enjoy sunset over a beer while waiting to be served.

Shree Shakti Cold Drinks Car St. Has its home-made peanut butter and fresh cheese, both made to American recipes and the latter served with rolls, garlic and tomato. Also available are filling toasties, ice cream and creamy lassis.

Hospet

Charmless **HOSPET**, about ten hours from both Bangalore and Goa, is of little interest except as a transport hub: in particular, it is the jumping-off place for the extraordinary ruined city of Hampi (Vijayanagar), 13km northeast. If you arrive late, or want somewhere fairly comfortable to sleep, it makes sense to stay here and catch a bus or taxi out to the ruins the following morning. Otherwise, hole up in Hampi, where the setting more than compensates for the basic facilities.

Hospet's **railway station**, 1500m north of the centre, is served by the overnight Hampi Express #6592 from Bangalore and services from Hyderabad, via Guntakal Junction. The line continues west to Hubli for connections to the coast and Goa. For connections to Badami and Bijapur, travel to Gadag and change onto the slow single track running north, but check first that it's operational as conversion is in progress. Auto-rickshaws are plentiful or you can get into town by cycle rickshaw (Rs10) or by foot if unencumbered.

The **long-distance bus stand** is in the centre, just off MG (Station) Road, which runs south from the railway station. For a summary of services see Travel details on p.1354. **Bookings** for long-distance routes can be made at the ticket office on the bus stand concourse (daily 8am–noon & 3–6pm), where there's also a **left-luggage** facility.

The **tourist office** at the Rotary Circle (Mon–Sat: June–March 10am–5.30pm; April & May 8am–1.30pm; ⓣ08394/228537) offers limited information and sells tickets for the KSTDC conducted tours (see p.1331). You can **exchange** travellers' cheques and cash at the State Bank of Mysore (Mon–Fri 10.30am–2.30pm & Sat 10.30am–12.30pm), next to the tourist office, and cash

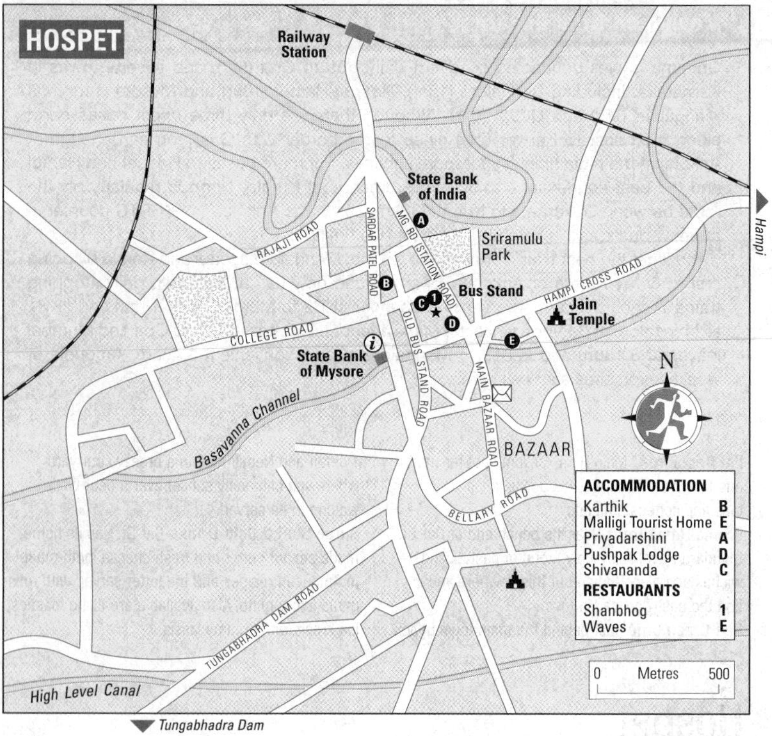

HOSPET

Railway Station
State Bank of India
Sriramulu Park
Bus Stand
Jain Temple
State Bank of Mysore
BAZAAR
Rajaji Road
Sardar Patel Road
MG Rd (Station Road)
Hampi Cross Road
College Road
Old Bus Stand Road
Main Bazaar Road
Bellary Road
Tungabhadra Dam Road
Basavanna Channel
High Level Canal
Hampi
Tungabhadra Dam

ACCOMMODATION	
Karthik	B
Malligi Tourist Home	E
Priyadarshini	A
Pushpak Lodge	D
Shivananda	C
RESTAURANTS	
Shanbhog	1
Waves	E

0 Metres 500

only at the State Bank of India (same hours) on Station Road. Full exchange facilities are available at the *Hotel Malligi*, while Sneha Travels (☎08394/225838) at the Elimanchate Complex, next to the *Hotel Priyadarshini* on MG Road, also changes any currency and travellers' cheques, and advances money on credit cards. This last also has branches in Hampi, books airline and train tickets and cars, and runs private **luxury buses to Goa**, which are actually operated by Paulo Travels (☎08394/225867) next door; the sleeper coach departs at 7pm, costs Rs450 and takes ten hours. Luxury buses are also available for Bangalore (10hr; Rs200) departing between 10pm and 11pm at night. Cybernet (Rs40/hr), next to the *Shivananda* hotel, can get you online.

Accommodation and eating

Accommodation in Hospet, concentrated around MG Road, ranges from budget to mid-price. By far the most popular place to stay is the incredibly versatile *Malligi Tourist Home*, with something to suit most budgets, but the *Priyadarshini* is also reasonable value and nearer the railway station.

There's little to do in Hospet, so you'll probably pass a fair amount of time **eating** and **drinking**. Many of the hotels have good dining rooms, but in the evening, the upscale though affordable *Waves*, a terrace restaurant in the *Malligi* complex, is the most congenial place to hang out, serving tandoori and chilled beer from 7pm to 11pm (bring lots of mosquito repellant). *Shanbhog*, an excellent little Udupi restaurant next to the bus station, is a perfect pit stop before heading to Hampi, and opens early for breakfast.

Karthik Pampa Villa, off MG Rd ⓣ0839/424938, ⓕ420028. A new, characterless block featuring unremarkable rooms but with a surprise around the back in the form of an extraordinary nineteenth-century stone villa housing two huge suites. ❸–❼

Malligi Tourist Home 6/143 Jambunatha Rd, a 2min walk east of MG Rd (look for the signs) and the bus stand ⓣ0839/428101, ⓔmalligihome@hotmail.com. Friendly, well-managed hotel with cheaper, clean, comfortable rooms (some a/c) in the old block and two new wings across the immaculate lawn, with luxurious a/c rooms. There is also a great new swimming pool (Rs25/hr for non-residents) in its Waves complex beneath the restaurant/bar plus billiards and massage facilities. The alfresco *Madhu Paradise* restaurant/bar in the old block serves great veg food and there's an efficient travel service. ❷–❽

Priyadarshini MG Rd, up the road from the bus stand, towards the railway station ⓣ0839/428838, ⓦwww.priyainnhampi.com. Rooms from rock-bottom singles to doubles with TV and a/c (some balconies). Large and bland, but spotless and very good value. Two good restaurants: the veg *Naivedyam* and, in the garden, non-veg *Manasa*, which has a bar. ❸–❻

Pushpak Lodge Near the bus stand, MG Rd ⓣ0839/421380. With basic but clean attached rooms, this is the best rock-bottom lodge. ❷

Shivananda Beside the bus stand, ⓣ0839/420700. Well-maintained hotel with spotless rooms, all attached with cable TV and some a/c. Very good value. ❷–❸

Getting to Hampi

KSTDC's daily guided **tour** only stops at three of the sites in Hampi and spends an inordinate amount of time at the far less interesting Tungabhadra Dam. It leaves from the tourist office at Rotary Circle (Taluk Office Circle), east of the bus station (9.30am–5.30pm; Rs100 including lunch).

Frequent **buses to Hampi** run from the bus stand between 6.30am and 7.30pm; the journey takes around thirty minutes. If you arrive late, either stay in Hospet, or take a taxi (Rs120–150) or one of the rickshaws (Rs60–80) that gather outside the railway station. It is also possible to catch a bus to **Kamalapuram**, at the south side of the site, and explore the ruins from there, catching a bus back to Hospet from Hampi Bazaar at the end of the day. **Bicycles** are available for rent at several stalls along the main street, but the trip to, around, and back from the site is a long one in the heat. Auto-rickshaws, best arranged through hotels such as the *Malligi* or *Priyadarshini*, will also take you to Hampi and back and charge around Rs50–60 per hour, but be warned that the roads are extremely bumpy. For the adventurous, Bullet **motorbikes** are available to rent (or sale) from Bharat Motors (ⓣ08394/224704) near *Rama Talkies*. Finally, some hotels in Hospet can also organize for you to hook up with **trained guides** in Hampi; ask at the *Malligi* or *Priyadarshini*.

Hampi (Vijayanagar)

The ruined city of **Vijayanagar**, "the City of Victory" – better known as **HAMPI**, the name of the main local village – spills from the south bank of the River Tungabhadra, littered among a surreal landscape of golden-brown granite boulders and leafy banana fields. According to the Ramayana, the settlement began its days as Kishkinda, ruled by the monkey kings Bali and Sugriva and their ambassador, Hanuman. The weird rocks – some balanced in perilous arches, others heaped in colossal, hill-sized piles – are said to have been flung down by their armies in a show of strength.

Between the fourteenth and sixteenth centuries, this was the most powerful Hindu capital in the Deccan. Travellers such as the Portuguese chronicler Domingo Paez, who stayed for two years after 1520, were astonished by its size and wealth, telling tales of markets full of silk and precious gems, beautiful, bejewelled courtesans, ornate palaces and joyous festivities. However, in the second half of the sixteenth century, the dazzling city was devastated by a six-month Muslim siege. Only stone, brick and stucco structures survived the ensuing sack – monolithic deities, crumbling houses and abandoned temples dominated by towering *gopuras* – as well as the sophisticated irrigation system that channelled water to huge tanks and temples.

Thanks to the Muslim onslaught, most of Hampi's monuments are in disappointingly poor shape, seemingly a lot older than their four or five hundred years. Yet the serene riverine setting and air of magic that lingers over the site, sacred for centuries before a city was founded here, make it one of India's most extraordinary locations. Even so, mainstream tourism has thus far made little

impact: along with busloads of Hindu pilgrims, and *sadhus* who hole up in the more isolated rock crevices and shrines, most visitors are budget travellers straight from Goa. Many find it difficult to leave, and spend weeks chilling out in cafés, wandering to whitewashed hilltop temples and gazing at the spectacular sunsets.

The **best time to come** to Hampi, weather-wise, is from late October to early March, when daytime temperatures are low enough to allow long forays on foot through the ruins. It does start to get busy over Christmas and New Year, however, and from early January for a month or so the site is invaded by an exodus of travellers from Goa, though the general tourist downturn means it has been less crowded in recent years than during the late 1990s peak; still, if you want to enjoy Hampi at its best, come outside peak season.

Some history

The rise of the **Vijayanagar empire** seems to have been a direct response, in the first half of the fourteenth century, to the expansionist aims of Muslims from the north, most notably Malik Kafur and Mohammed-bin-Tughluq. Two Hindu brothers from Andhra Pradesh, Harihara and Bukka, who had been employed as treasury officers in Kampila, 19km east of Hampi, were captured by the Tughluqs and taken to Delhi, where they supposedly converted to Islam. Assuming them to be suitably tamed, the Delhi sultan despatched them to quell civil disorder in Kampila, which they duly did, only to abandon both Islam and allegiance to Delhi shortly afterwards, preferring to establish their own independent Hindu kingdom. Within a few years they controlled vast tracts of land from coast to coast. In 1343 their new capital, Vijayanagar, was founded on the southern banks of the River Tungabhadra, a location long considered sacred by Hindus. The city's most glorious period was under the reign of **Krishna Deva Raya** (1509–29), when it enjoyed a near monopoly of the lucrative trade in Arabian horses and Indian spices passing through the coastal ports.

Thanks to its natural features and massive fortifications, Vijayanagar was virtually impregnable. In 1565, however, following his interference in the affairs of local Muslim sultanates, the regent Rama Raya was drawn into a battle with a confederacy of Muslim forces, 100km away to the north, which left the city undefended. At first, fortune appeared to be on the side of the Hindu army, but there were as many as 10,000 Muslims in their number, and loyalties may well have been divided. When two Vijayanagar Muslim generals suddenly deserted, the army fell into disarray. Defeat came swiftly; although members of his family fled with untold hoards of gold and jewels, Rama Raya was captured and suffered a grisly death at the hands of the sultan of Ahmadnagar. Vijayanagar then fell victim to a series of destructive raids, and its days of splendour were brought to an abrupt end.

Arrival and information

Buses from Hospet terminate close to where the road joins the main street in Hampi Bazaar, halfway along its dusty length. A little further towards the Virupaksha temple, the **tourist office** (daily except Fri 10am–5.30pm; ⓣ08394/241339) can put you in touch with a **guide** for Rs500 per day but not much else. Most visitors coming from Hospet organize a guide from there (see p.1331).

Rented **bicycles**, available from stalls near the lodges, cost Rs5 per hour or Rs30–40 for a 24-hour period. Pedal bikes can be hard work on the bumpy roads so consider a motorized two-wheeler. **Motorbikes and scooters** can be rented for around Rs150 per day from the Raju stall, round the corner from the tourist office. Sneha Travels, whose main office is at D131/11 Main St (daily 9am–9pm; ⓣ08394/241590), can **change money** (albeit at lowish rates), advance cash on credit cards and book airline and **train tickets**. It also runs **luxury buses** to Bangalore and sleeper coaches to Goa and Gokarna; although these drop people off right in Hampi Bazaar, you have to pick them up from Hospet thanks to the powerful taxi/rickshaw mafia. Note, too, that whatever you are told, the Gokarna bus involves a transfer at Ankola in the wee hours.

Run by Shri Swamy Sadashiva Yogi, the Shivananda Yoga Ashram overlooking the river, past the site of the new footbridge and coracle crossing, offers courses in **yoga** and **meditation** as well as homeopathic treatment, magnetotherapy and **Ayurvedic treatment**, in particular for snakebites. Finally, there are at least a dozen **Internet** outlets in Hampi, which have fixed a universally high rate of Rs60/hr.

Accommodation

If you're happy to make do with basic amenities, Hampi is a far more enjoyable place to stay than Hospet, with around fifty congenial **guesthouses** and plenty of cafés to hang out in after a long day in the heat. Staying in the village also means you can be up and out early enough to catch the sunrise over the ruins – a mesmerizing spectacle. Some travellers shun Hampi Bazaar for the fast-growing community of lodges at **Virupapuradadda** across the river, where there are now so many Israeli settlers it bears more resemblance to the west bank of the Jordan. Outside of **high season**, which lasts for six weeks starting around Christmas, you may well get a substantial discount on the room rates quoted below. Note there is generally a 10am check-out.

Garden Paradise Far east end of village ⓣ08394/241954. Four cramped but cute huts in an excellent riverside location. Shared bathrooms and a chilled-out restaurant. ❷

Goan Corner 500m east of coracle crossing, Virupapuragadda ⓣ94487 18951. Large complex amidst the paddy fields and near the rocks with a range of rooms, and huts, some with attached bathrooms. Lively restaurant. ❶–❷

Gopi Guest House A short walk down the lanes behind *Shanti* ⓣ08394/241695, ⓔgopiguesthouse93@yahoo.co.in. There's a pleasant rooftop café with temple view here, and all ten rooms have attached baths but they cost more than most in peak season. ❸

KSTDC Mayura Bhuvaneshwari Kamalapuram, 2.5km from Hampi Bazaar ⓣ08394/241574. The only remotely upscale place to stay within reach of the ruins, with clean en-suite rooms and competitively priced a/c rooms; fixed government rates mean no peak-season hikes. There's a pleasant garden, a good restaurant and a bar serving cold beers, but it feels detached from Hampi Bazaar and the village lacks charm. ❷–❸

Rahul Guest House South of Main St, near the bus stand ⓣ08394/241648. Now has some new attached rooms in addition to the small and spartan old ones, which share rudimentary washing and toilet facilities, along with a pleasant shaded café. ❶–❸

Sai Plaza Virupapuragadda ⓣ08533/287017, ⓔsantoshgvt@yahoo.com. Attractive double attached huts, set around a pleasant landscaped garden, with swing beds outside. ❷

Shanti Guest House Just north of the Virupaksha temple ⓣ08394/241568. This is a real favourite, comprising a dozen or so twin-bedded cells ranged on two storeys around a leafy inner courtyard. It's basic (showers and toilets are shared), but spotless, and all rooms have fans and windows. ❶

Shri Rama Guest House Next to the Virupaksha temple ⓣ08394/241219, ⓔvenkannaj@yahoo.com. Rock-bottom attached rooms mainly for Hindu pilgrims, but foreigners are also welcome. Now has rooftop restaurant. ❶

Sudha Guest House At the east end of the village ⓣ08394/241451. Very friendly and pleasantly situated family operation, with cool attached rooms downstairs and smaller non-attached upstairs. Good value and mosquito nets are provided. ❶–❸

Sunny Guest House Virupapuragadda ⓣ08533/287005. Nicely landscaped gardens with a row of compact rooms and somewhat roomier huts. ❷–❸

Umashankar Lodge Virupapuragadda ☎08533/287067. One of the better places to stay across the river. Small but clean attached rooms, the upstairs ones rather overpriced, set round a leafy courtyard. ❶–❸

Vikky At the end of the lane furthest northeast from the temple ☎08394/241694. Small clean rooms, some attached. Friendly and especially popular for its rooftop restaurant. ❷–❸

The site

Although spread over 26 square kilometres, the ruins of Vijayanagar are mostly concentrated in two distinct groups: the first lies in and around **Hampi Bazaar** and the nearby riverside area, encompassing the city's most sacred enclave of temples and *ghats*; the second centres on the **royal enclosure** – 3km south of the river, just northwest of **Kamalapuram** village – which holds the remains of palaces, pavilions, elephant stables, guardhouses and temples. Between the two stretches a long boulder-choked hill and swathe of banana plantations, fed by ancient irrigation canals.

Frequent buses run from Hospet to Hampi Bazaar and Kamalapuram, and you can start your tour from either; most visitors prefer to set out on foot or bicycle from the former. After a look around the soaring **Virupaksha temple**, work your way east along the main street and riverbank to the beautiful **Vitthala temple**, and then back via the **Achyutaraya** complex at the foot of Matanga Hill. From here, a dirt path leads south to the royal enclosure, but it's easier to return to the bazaar and pick up the tarred road, calling in at **Hemakuta Hill**, a group of pre-Vijayanagar temples, en route.

On KSTDC's whistle-stop **guided tour** (see p.1331), it's possible to see most of the highlights in a day. If you can, however, set aside at least two or three days to explore the site and its environs, crossing the river to **Anegondi** village, with a couple of side hikes to hilltop viewpoints: the west side of Hemakuta Hill, overlooking Hampi Bazaar, is best for sunsets, while **Matanga Hill** offers what has to be one of the world's most exotic sunrise vistas.

Hampi Bazaar, the Virupaksha temple and riverside

Lining Hampi's long, straight main street, **Hampi Bazaar**, which runs east from the eastern entrance of the Virupaksha temple, you can still make out the

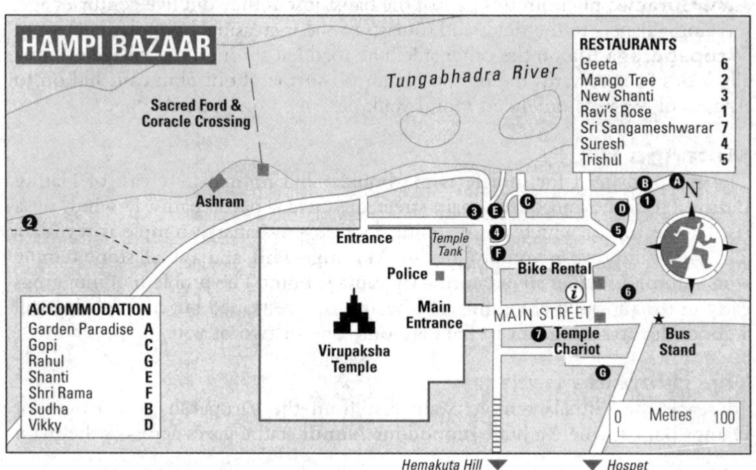

Festivals in Hampi

Vijayanagar's main **festivals** include, at the Virupaksha temple, a **Car Festival** with street processions each April, and in December the marriage ceremony of the deities, which is accompanied by drummers and dances. The **Hampi Festival**, organized by the tourist department, takes place between November the 3rd and the 5th and involves classical music and dance from both Carnatic and Hindustani (north Indian) traditions performed on temple stages and at Anegondi. The festival, which is beginning to attract several well-known musicians and dancers, has been growing in size and prestige, and hotels in the area can get booked well in advance. The national **Shivaratri** festival in February or March also draws thousands of pilgrims to the Virupaksha temple.

remains of Vijayanagar's ruined, columned bazaar, partly inhabited by today's lively market. Landless labourers live in many of the crumbling 500-year-old buildings.

Dedicated to a local form of Shiva known as Virupaksha or Pampapati, the functioning **Virupaksha temple** (daily 8am–12.30pm & 3–6.30pm; Rs2) dominates the village, drawing a steady flow of pilgrims from all over southern India. Also known as **Sri Virupaksha Swami**, the temple is free for all who come for *arati* (worship; daily 6.30–8am & 6.30–8pm) when the temple has the most atmosphere, and for a rupee you can receive a blessing from the temple elephant, Lakshmi. The complex consists of two courts, each entered through a towered *gopura*.

A colonnade surrounds the inner court, usually filled with pilgrims dozing and singing religious songs. On entering, if the temple elephant, Lakshmi, is around, you can get her to bless you by placing a rupee in her trunk. In the middle the principal temple is approached through a *mandapa* hallway whose carved columns feature rearing animals. Rare Vijayanagar-era paintings on the *mandapa* ceiling include aspects of Shiva, a procession with the sage Vidyaranya, the ten incarnations of Vishnu, and scenes from the *Mahabharata*.

The sacred **ford** in the river is reached from the Virupaksha's north *gopura*; you can also get there by following the lane around the impressive temple **tank**. A *mandapa* overlooks the steps that originally led to the river, now some distance away. **Coracles** ply from this part of the bank, just as they did five centuries ago, ferrying villagers to the fields and tourists to the increasingly popular enclave of **Virupapuragadda** on the other side. The road left through the village eventually loops back towards the hilltop Hanuman shrine, about 5km east, and on to Anegondi – a recommended round walk described on opposite page.

Matanga Hill

The place to head for sunrise is the boulder hill immediately east of Hampi Bazaar. From the end of the main street, an ancient paved pathway winds up a rise, at the top of which the magnificent Tiruvengalanatha temple is revealed. The views improve as you progress up **Matanga Hill**, and a small stone temple at its summit provides an extraordinary vantage point. The problem of muggings early in the morning along this path seems to have waned but it's probably still a good idea to be vigilant if there are only one or two of you.

The riverside path

To reach the Vitthala temple, walk east from the Virupaksha, the length of Hampi Bazaar, where a huge monolithic **Nandi** statue gazes across at the main temple from its shrine. You can also nip into the Cauvery crafts shop and small photo gallery on the left-hand side of the colonnade. Just before you reach these, a path on the left, staffed at regular intervals by conch-blowing *sadhus* and an assortment of other ragged mendicants, follows the river past a couple of cafés and numerous shrines, including a Rama temple – home to hordes of fearless monkeys. Beyond at least four Vishnu shrines, a paved and colonnaded **bazaar** leads due south to the **Achyutharaya temple**, whose beautiful stone carvings – among them some of Hampi's famed erotica – are being restored by the ASI. Back on the main path again, make a short detour across the rocks leading to the river to see the little-visited waterside **Agni temple**; next to it, the Kotalinga complex consists of 108 (an auspicious number) tiny *lingas*, carved on a flat rock. As you approach the Vitthala temple, to the south is an archway known as the **King's Balance**, where the rajas were weighed against gold, silver and jewels to be distributed to the city's priests.

Vitthala temple

Although the area of the **Vitthala temple** (daily 6am–6pm; $5 [Rs10]; ticket also valid for the Lotus Mahal on the same day) does not show the same evidence of early cult worship as Virupaksha, the ruined bridge to the west probably dates from before Vijayanagar times. The bathing *ghat* may be from the Chalukya or Ganga period, but as the temple has fallen into disuse it seems that the river crossing (*tirtha*) here has not had the same sacred significance as the Virupaksha site. Now designated a World Heritage Monument by UNESCO, the Vitthala temple was built for Vishnu, who according to legend was too embarrassed by its ostentation to live there.

The open *mandapa* features slender monolithic granite musical **pillars** which were constructed so as to sound the notes of the scale when struck. Today, due to vandalism and erosion from being repeatedly beaten, heavy security makes sure that no one is allowed to touch them. Guides, however, will happily demonstrate the musical resonance of other pillars on an adjacent structure. Outer columns sport characteristic Vijayanagar rearing horses, while friezes of lions, elephants and horses on the moulded basement display sculptural trickery – you can transform one beast into another simply by masking one portion of the image.

In front of the temple, to the east, a stone representation of a wooden processional **rath**, or chariot, houses an image of Garuda, Vishnu's bird vehicle. Now cemented, at one time the chariot's wheels revolved.

Anegondi and beyond

With more time, and a sense of adventure, you can head across the Tungabhadra to **ANEGONDI**, a fortress town predating Vijayanagar and the city's fourteenth-century headquarters. The most pleasant way to go is to take a *putti*, a circular rush-basket coracle, from the ford 1500m east of the Vitthala temple; the coracles, which are today reinforced with plastic sheets, also carry bicycles. At the time of writing a new road bridge was nearing completion, which will almost certainly put this coracle crossing out of business.

Forgotten temples and fortifications litter Anegondi village and its quiet surroundings. The ruined **Huchchappa-matha temple**, near the river gateway, is worth a look for its black stone lathe-turned pillars and fine panels of dancers. **Aramani**, a ruined palace in the centre, stands opposite the home of the descendants of the royal family; also in the centre, the **Ranganatha temple** is still active. A huge wooden temple chariot stands in the village square. The only **accommodation** here is in village houses but and you can get basic snacks at the *Hoova Café*.

To complete a five-kilometre loop back to Hampi from here (the simplest route if you have wheels), head left (west) along the turning just north of the village, which winds through sugar cane fields and eventually comes out near Virupapuragadda. En route you can visit the sacred **Pampla Sarovar**, signposted down a dirt lane to the left. The small temple above this square bathing tank, tended by a *swami* who will proudly show you photos of his pilgrimage to Mount Kailash, is dedicated to the goddess Lakshmi and holds a cave containing a footprint of Vishnu. If you are staying around Anegondi, this quiet and atmospheric spot is best visited early in the evening during *arati* (worship).

Another worthwhile detour from the road is the hike up to the tiny whitewashed **Hanuman temple**, perched on a rocky hilltop north of the river, from where you gain superb views over Hampi especially at sunrise or sunset. The steep climb up to it takes around half an hour An alternative walking route back involves following the path a further 2km until you reach an impressive old **stone bridge** dating from Vijayanagar times. The bridge no longer spans the river but just beyond it to the west, another coracle crossing returns you to a point about halfway between the Vitthala temple and Hampi Bazaar. This rewarding round walk can, of course, be completed in reverse. Whichever loop you choose and especially if you attempt it on foot, which requires at least three hours, take plenty of water.

Hemakuta Hill and around

Directly above Hampi Bazaar, **Hemakuta Hill** is dotted with pre-Vijayanagar temples that probably date from between the ninth and eleventh centuries (late Chalukya or Ganga). Aside from the architecture, the main reason to clamber up here is to admire the **views** of the ruins and surrounding countryside. Looking across the boulder-covered terrain and banana plantations, the sheer western edge of the hill is Hampi's number-one sunset spot, attracting a crowd of blissed-out tourists most evenings, along with a couple of entrepreneurial chai-wallahs and little boys posing for photos in Hanuman costumes.

A couple of interesting monuments lie on the road leading south towards the main, southern group of ruins. The first of these, a walled **Krishna temple complex** to the west of the road, dates from 1513. Although dilapidated in parts, it features some fine carving and shrines.

Hampi's most-photographed monument stands just south of the Krishna temple in its own enclosure. Depicting Vishnu in his incarnation (*avatar*) as the Man-Lion, the monolithic **Narashima** statue, with its bulging eyes and crossed legs strapped into yogic pose, is one of Vijayanagar's greatest treasures.

The southern and royal monuments

The most impressive remains of Vijayanagar, the city's **royal monuments**, lie some 3km south of Hampi Bazaar, spread over a large expanse of open ground. Before tackling the ruins proper, it's a good idea to get your bearings with a visit to the small **Archeological Museum** (daily except Fri 10am–5pm; free) at Kamalapuram, which can be reached by bus from Hospet or Hampi. Turn right out of the Kamalapuram bus stand, take the first turning on the right, and the museum is on the left – two minutes' walk. Among the sculpture, weapons, palm-leaf manuscripts and painting from Vijayanagar and Anegondi, the highlight is a superb scale model of the city, giving an excellent bird's-eye view of the entire site.

To walk into the city from the museum, go back to the main road and take the nearby turning marked "Hampi 4km". After 200m or so you reach the partly ruined massive **inner city wall**, made from granite slabs, which runs 32km around the city, in places as high as 10m. The outer wall was almost twice as long. At one time, there were said to have been seven city walls; coupled with areas of impenetrable forest and the river to the north, they made the city virtually impregnable.

Just beyond the wall, the **citadel area** was once enclosed by another wall and gates of which only traces remain. To the east, the small *ganigitti* ("oil-woman's") fourteenth-century **Jain temple** features a simple stepped pyramidal tower of undecorated horizontal slabs. Beyond it is **Bhima's Gate**, once one of the principal entrances to the city, named after the Titan-like Pandava prince and hero of the *Mahabharata*. Like many of the gates, it is "bent", a form of defence that meant anyone trying to get in had to make two 90° turns. Bas-reliefs depict such episodes as Bhima avenging the attempted rape of his wife, Draupadi, by killing the general Kichaka. Draupadi vowed she would not dress her hair until Kichaka was dead; one panel shows her tying up her locks, the vow fulfilled.

Back on the path, to the west, the plain facade of the fifteen-metre-square **Queen's Bath** belies its glorious interior, open to the sky and surrounded by corridors with 24 different domes. Eight projecting balconies overlook where once was water; traces of Islamic-influenced stucco decoration survive. Women from the royal household would bathe here and umbrellas were placed in shafts in the tank floor to protect them from the sun. The water supply channel can be seen outside.

Continuing northwest brings you to **Mahanavami-Dibba** or "House of Victory", built to commemorate a successful campaign in Orissa. A twelve-metre pyramidal structure with a square base, it is said to have been where the king gave and received honours and gifts. From here he watched the magnificent parades, music and dance performances, martial arts displays, elephant fights and animal sacrifices that made celebration of the ten-day Dussehra festival famed throughout the land (the tradition of spectacular Dussehra festivals is continued at Mysore; see p.1298). Carved reliefs decorate the sides of the platform. To the west, another platform – the largest at Vijayanagar – is thought to be the basement of the **King's Audience Hall**. Stone bases of a hundred pillars remain, in an arrangement that has caused speculation as to how the building could have been used; there are no passageways or open areas.

The two-storey **Lotus Mahal** (daily 6am–6pm; $5 [Rs10]; ticket also valid for the Vitthala temple on the same day), a little further north and part of the **zenana enclosure**, or women's quarters, was designed for the pleasure of Krishna Deva Raya's queen: a place where she could relax, particularly in summer. Displaying a strong Indo-Islamic influence, the pavilion is open on the ground floor, whereas the upper level (no longer accessible by stairs) contains windows and balcony seats. A moat surrounding the building is thought to have provided water-cooled air via tubes.

Beyond the Lotus Mahal, the **Elephant Stables**, a series of high-ceilinged, domed chambers, entered through arches, are the most substantial surviving secular buildings at Vijayanagar – a reflection of the high status accorded to elephants, both ceremonial and in battle.

Walking west of the Lotus Mahal, you pass two temples before reaching the road to Hemakuta Hill. The rectangular enclosure wall of the small **Hazara Rama** ("One thousand Ramas") temple, thought to have been the private palace shrine, features a series of medallion figures and bands of detailed friezes showing scenes from the *Ramayana*.

Eating

Hampi has a plethora of traveller-oriented chai stalls and **restaurants**, delivering safe options rather than haute cuisine. Many of the most popular are attached to guesthouses, such as *Rahul*, *Gopi*, *Vikki* and *Sudha*, all in the Bazaar, or among the growing row of joints in Virupapuragadda. As a holy site, the whole village is supposed to be strictly vegetarian and alcohol-free but one or two places bend the rules for inveterate carnivores and even more are happy to supply a surreptitious beer or two.

Geeta On main Bazaar. Old favourite not far from the bus stand, serving wholesome Western snacks, Indian veg, momos and ravioli.
Mango Tree 300m beyond sacred ford. Wonderfully relaxed riverside hangout – a great place to linger over a simple snack or drink.
Mowgli Virupapuragadda. At the far west end of the strip, this popular lodge restaurant has plenty of space to lounge on mattresses beside the rice paddies bordering the river. Mostly bland Indian, Israeli and Western food.
New Shanti On the path from Virupaksha temple down to river. Best known for its delicious cakes and breads but also does standard Indian and Continental dishes.
Ravi's Rose East end of the village. Fairly new rooftop restaurant that can actually make spicy dishes, with good sounds and a line in special lassis.
Shiv Moon Riverside path, east of the village. Good place to break the journey to or from the Vitthala temple, serving pastas and standard curries.
Sri Sangameshwarar On main Bazaar. One of the more genuine Indian places, where you can get the best thalis and masala dosas, as well as the odd Western snack.
Suresh On the path from Virupaksha temple down to the river. Established joint whose specialities are tuna, Goan dishes and momos.
Trishul On the lane from beside the tourist office. Offers one of Hampi's widest menus, featuring chicken, tuna, lasagne, pizza and desserts such as scrumptious apple crumble. Beer readily available too.

Monuments of the Chalukyas

Now quiet villages, **Badami**, **Aihole** and **Pattadakal**, in northwest Karnataka, were once the capital cities of the **Chalukyas**, who ruled much of the Deccan between the fourth and eighth centuries. The astonishing profusion of **temples** in the area beggars belief. Most visitors use Badami, which can offer a few basic lodges, as a base; Aihole boasts a single rest house, and no rooms are available at Pattadakal. The **best time to visit** is between late-October and early March; in April and May, most of this part of northwest Karnataka becomes much too hot and all government offices only work between 8am and 1pm.

Badami and Aihole's cave temples, stylistically related to those at Ellora (see p.747), are some of the most important of their type. Among the many structural temples are some of the earliest in India, and uniquely, it is possible to see both northern (*nagari*) and southern (Dravida) architectural styles side by side.

Although some evidence of Buddhist activity around Badami and Aihole exists, the earliest cave and structural temples are assigned to the period of the Chalukya rise to power in the mid-sixth century, and are mostly Hindu, with a few Jain examples. The first important Chalukyan king was Pulakeshin I (535–66), but it was Pulakeshin II (610–42) who captured the Pallava capital of Kanchipuram in Tamil Nadu and extended the empire to include Maharashtra to the north, the Konkan coast on the west and the whole of what is now Karnataka. Much of this territory (including the capital, Badami) was subsequently re-taken, but the Chalukyas recovered it and continued to reign until the mid-eighth century. Some suggest that the incursion of the Pallavas accounts for the southern elements seen in the structural temples.

Badami and around

Surrounded by a yawning expanse of flat farm land, **BADAMI**, capital of the Chalukyas from 543 AD to 757 AD, extends east into a gorge between two red sandstone hills, topped by two ancient fort complexes. The south is riddled with cave temples, and on the north stand early structural temples. Beyond the village, to the east, is an artificial lake, Agastya, said to date from the fifth century. Its small selection of hotels and restaurants makes Badami an ideal base from which to explore the Chalukyan remains at Mahakuta, Aihole and Pattadakal as well as the temple village of **Banashankari** 5km to the southeast. Dedicated to Shiva's consort Parvati, the shrine, accompanied by a large bathing tank, is the most important living temple of the region and attracts a steady stream of devotees, especially during the chariot festival held according to the lunar calendar sometime between January and February each year. Although of little architectural interest, but worth a visit for the atmosphere, the temple is supposed to date back to the sixth century; much of it, however, was built during the Maratha period of the eighteenth century. The whole Badami area is also home to numerous troupes of monkeys, especially around the monuments, and you are likely to find the cheeky characters all over you if you produce any food.

Practicalities

Badami **bus stand** – in the centre of the village on Main (Station) Road – sees frequent daily services to Gadag (2hr), Hospet (5hr), Hubli (3hr), Bijapur (4hr) and Kolhapur, and local buses to Aihole and Pattadakal. The **railway station** is 5km north, along a road lined with *neem* trees; tongas (Rs30 or Rs5 per head shared) as well as buses and auto-rickshaws are usually available for the journey into town. The slow metre-gauge line connecting Badami to Bijapur in the north, and to Gadag in the south was being converted at the time of writing and only the sector from Bagalkot via Badami to Gadag was operating with three trains daily.

The new and friendly **tourist office** (Mon–Sat: June–March 10am–5.30pm; April–May 8am–1pm; ⓣ08357/220414) on Ramdurg Road next to KSTDC *Hotel Mayura Chalukya*, can put you in touch with a **guide**. For those who need to **change money**, *Hotel Mookambika* opposite the bus stand will change US dollars and sterling at low rates, but no travellers' cheques; the other place to try is the *Hotel Badami Court*.

Ambika Tours & Travels at *Hotel Mookambika* runs **tours** taking in Badami, Mahakuta, Aihole and Pattadakal in Ambassador taxis for a reasonable Rs700. One of the best ways of exploring the closer sites, including Mahakuta and the temple village of Banashankari, is to rent a **bicycle**, available at Rs3 per hour from stalls in front of the bus stand, but cycling to Aihole and Pattadakal will prove challenging.

Accommodation and eating

Of Badami's handful of **places to stay** and **eat**, by far the most comfortable is the *Hotel Badami Court* (ⓣ08357/220230, ⓔbadamicourt@nivalink.com; ❻–❽), 2km north of town towards the railway station. Ranged around a garden on two storeys, its 27 en-suite rooms are plain, but spacious; it serves meals and expensive beer, and its swimming pool is open to non-residents for Rs80 per hour. Far cheaper, the KSTDC *Hotel Mayura Chalukya* (ⓣ08357/220046; ❷), at the south side of town on Ramdurg Road, has ten basic rooms with decrepit plumbing and peeling plaster but, despite fearless scavenging monkeys, the gardens are pleasant and there's a restaurant. Opposite the bus stand, the *Mookambika Deluxe* (ⓣ08357/220067, ⓕ220106; ❸–❻) is the best option in the centre of town, with simple doubles on the ground floor and comfortable new air-conditioned rooms upstairs. Other options include the recently upgraded *New Satkar Delux* (ⓣ08357/220417; ❷–❺) and the extremely basic *Shri Laxmi Vilas* (☎08357/220077; ❶), which has a reasonable restaurant.

For food and especially breakfast, try the *Geetha Darshini* (closed Sun), 100m south of the bus stand; it's a South Indian joint, whose *iddlis*, *vadas* and *dosas* are out of this world. Otherwise the *Mookambika Deluxe*'s plain upstairs restaurant and livelier *Kanchan* bar and restaurant next door share the same kitchen and provide a wide menu of excellent veg and non-veg Indian and Chinese food.

Southern Fort cave temples

Badami's earliest monuments, in the Southern Fort area, are a group of sixth-century **caves** (daily sunrise to sunset; $2 [Rs5]) cut into the hill's red sandstone, each connected by steps leading up the hillside. About 15m up the face of the rock, **Cave 1**, a Shiva temple, is probably the earliest. Entrance is through a triple opening into a long porch raised on a plinth decorated with images of Shiva's dwarf attendants, the *ganas*. Outside, to the left of the porch, a *dvarpala* door guardian stands beneath a Nandi bull. On the right is a striking 1.5m-high image of a sixteen-armed dancing Shiva. He carries a stick-zither-type *vina*, which may or may not be a *yal*, a now-extinct musical instrument, on which the earliest Indian classical music theory is thought to have been developed.

A little higher, the similar **Cave 2**, a Vishnu shrine, holds some impressive sculpture and painting. Steps and slopes lead on upwards, past a natural cave containing a smashed image of the Buddhist *bodhisattva*, Padmapani (he who holds the lotus), and steps on the right in a cleft in the rock lead up to the fort. **Cave 3** (578 AD) stands beneath a thirty-metre-high perpendicular bluff. The largest of the group, with a facade measuring 21m from north to south, it is also considered to be the finest, for the quality of its sculptural decoration. Treatment of the pillars is extremely elaborate, featuring male and female bracket figures, lotus motifs and medallions portraying amorous couples.

To the east of the others, a Jain temple, **Cave 4**, overlooks Agastya Lake and the town. It's a much simpler shrine, dating from the sixth century. Figures, both seated and standing, of the 24 *tirthankaras*, mostly without their identifying emblems, line the walls. Here, the rock is striped.

After seeing the caves it is possible to climb up to the fort and walk east where, hidden in the rocks, a carved panel shows Vishnu reclining on the serpent Adisesha, attended by a profusion of gods and sages. Continuing, you can skirt the gorge and descend on the east to the Bhutanatha temples at the lakeside.

North Fort

North of Agastya Lake a number of structural temples can be reached by steps. The small **Archeological Museum** (daily except Fri 10am–5pm; Rs2) nearby contains sculpture from the region. Although now dilapidated, the **Upper Shivalaya temple** is one of the earliest Chalukyan buildings. Scenes from the life of Krishna decorate the base and various images of him can be seen between pilasters on the walls. Only the sanctuary and tower of the **Lower Shivalaya** survive. Perched on a rock, the **Malegitti Shivalaya** (late seventh century) is the finest southern-style early Chalukyan temple. Its shrine is adjoined by a pillared hallway with small pierced stone and a single image on each side: Vishnu on the north and Shiva on the south.

Aihole

No fewer than 125 temples, dating from the Chalukyan and the later Rashtrakuta periods (sixth–twelfth centuries), are found in the tiny village of **AIHOLE** (Aivalli), near the banks of the River Malaprabha. Lying in clusters within the village, in surrounding fields and on rocky outcrops, many of the temples are remarkably well preserved, despite being used as dwellings and cattle sheds. Reflecting both its geographical position and spirit of architectural experimentation, Aihole boasts northern (*nagari*) and southern (Dravida) temples, as well as variants that failed to survive subsequent stylistic developments.

Two of the temples are **rock-cut caves** dating from the sixth century. The Hindu **Ravanaphadigudi**, northeast of the centre, a Shiva shrine with a triple entrance, contains fine sculptures of Mahishasuramardini, a ten-armed Nateshan (the precursor of Shiva Nataraja) dancing with Parvati, Ganesh and the Sapta Matrikas ("seven mothers"). A two-storey cave, plain save for decoration at the entrances and a panel image of Buddha in its upper veranda, can be found partway up the hill to the southeast, overlooking the village. At the top of that hill, the Jain **Meguti** temple, which may never have been completed, bears an inscription on an outer wall dating it to 634 AD. You can climb up to the first floor for fine views of Aihole and surrounding country.

The late seventh- to early eighth-century **Durga temple** (daily 6am–6pm; $2 [Rs5]), one of the most unusual, elaborate and large in Aihole, stands close to others on open ground in the Archeological Survey compound, near the centre of the village. It derives its name not from the goddess Durga but from the Kannada *durgadagudi*, meaning "temple near the fort". A series of pillars – many featuring amorous couples – forming an open ambulatory continue from the porch around the whole building. Other sculptural highlights include the decoration on the entrance to the *mandapa* hallway and niche images on the outer walls of the now-empty semicircular sanctum. Nearby, a small **Archeological Museum** (daily except Fri 10am–5pm; free) displays early Chalukyan sculpture and sells the booklet *Glorious Aihole*, which includes a site map and accounts of the monuments.

Further south, beyond several other temples, the **Ladh Khan** (the name of a Muslim who made it his home) is perhaps the best known of all at Aihole. Now thought to have been constructed at some point between the end of the sixth century and the eighth, it was dated at one time to the mid-fifth century, and was seen as one of the country's temple prototypes. Inside stands a Nandi bull and a small sanctuary containing a *shivalingam* is next to the back wall. Both may have been later additions, with the original inner sanctum located at the centre.

Practicalities

Six daily **buses** run to Aihole from Badami (1hr 30min) via Pattadakal (45min) from 5.30am to 9pm; the last bus returns around 6pm. The only place to **stay and eat** (apart from a few chai shops) in Aihole is the small, clean and spartan KSTDC *Tourist Rest House* (Ⓣ08351/234541; ❷) about five minutes' walk up the main road north out of the village, next to the ASI offices. It has a "VIP" room, two doubles with bath plus two doubles and four singles without. Simple, tasty food is available by arrangement – and by candlelight during frequent power cuts. The *Kiran Bar* on the same road, but in the village, serves beer and spirits and has a restaurant.

Pattadakal

The village of **PATTADAKAL**, on a bend in the River Malaprabha 22km from Badami, served as the site of Chalukyan coronations between the seventh and eighth centuries; in fact it may only have been used for such ceremonials.

Like Badami and Aihole, the area boasts fine Chalukyan architecture, with particularly large mature examples; as at Aihole, both northern and southern styles can be seen. Pattadakal's main group of monuments (daily 6am–6pm; $5 [Rs10]) stand together in a well-maintained compound, next to the village, and have recently attained the status of a World Heritage Site.

Earliest among the temples, the **Sangameshvara**, also known as **Shri Vijayeshvara** (a reference to its builder, Vijayaditya Satyashraya; 696–733), shows typical southern features. To the south, both the **Mallikarjuna** and the enormous **Virupaksha**, side by side, are in the southern style, built by two sisters who were successively the queens of Vikramaditya II (733–46). Along with the Kanchipuram temple in Tamil Nadu, the Virupaksha was probably one of the largest and most elaborate in India at the time. Interior pillars are carved with scenes from the *Ramayana* and *Mahabharata*, while in the Mallikarjuna the stories are from the life of Krishna.

The largest northern-style temple, the **Papanatha**, further south, was probably built after the Virupaksha in the eighth century. Outside walls feature reliefs (some of which, unusually, bear the sculptors' autographs) from the *Ramayana*, including, on the south wall, Hanuman's monkey army.

About 1km south of the village, a fine **Rashtrakuta** (ninth–tenth century) **Jain temple** is fronted by a porch and two *mandapa* hallways with twin carved elephants at the entrance. Inexplicably, the sanctuary contains a *lingam*.

Pattadakal is connected by regular state **buses** and hourly private buses to Badami (45min) and Aihole (22km, 45min). Aside from a few teashops, cold drinks and coconut stalls, there are no facilities. For three days at the end of January, Pattadakal hosts an annual **dance festival** featuring dancers from all over the country.

Bijapur and the north

Boasting some of the Deccan's finest Muslim monuments, **BIJAPUR** is often billed as "The Agra of the South". The comparison is partly justified: for more than three hundred years, this was the capital of a succession of powerful rulers, whose domed mausoleums, mosques, colossal civic buildings and fortifications recall a lost golden age of unrivalled prosperity and artistic refinement. Yet there the similarities between the two cities end. A provincial market town of just 210,000 inhabitants, modern Bijapur is a world away from the urban frenzy of Agra. With the exception of the mighty **Golgumbaz**, which attracts busloads of day-trippers, its historic sites see only a slow trickle of tourists, while the ramshackle town centre is surprisingly laid-back, dotted with peaceful green spaces and colonnaded mosque courtyards. The best **time to come** here is between November and early March because in summer the town gets unbearably hot. In the first week of February the town hosts an annual **music festival** which attracts several renowned musicians from both the Carnatic (South Indian) and the Hindustani (north Indian) classical music traditions.

Some history

Bijapur began life in the tenth century as **Vijayapura**, the Chalukyas' "City of Victory". Taken by the Vijayanagars, it passed into Muslim hands for the first time in the thirteenth century with the arrival of the sultans of Delhi. The Bahmanis administered the area for a time, but it was only after the local rulers, the **Adil Shahis**, won independence from Bidar by expelling the Bahmani

BIJAPUR

RESTAURANTS	
New Empire	F
Priyadarshini	2
Shrinidhi Hotel	1

ACCOMMODATION	
Godavari	A
Kanishka International	E
KSTDC Mayura Adil Shahi Annexe	C
Madhuvan	D
Pearl	F
Sagar Deluxe	B
Sanman	G

garrison and declaring this their capital that Bijapur's rise to prominence began.

Burying their differences for a brief period in the late sixteenth century, the five Muslim dynasties that issued from the breakdown of Bahmani rule – based at Golconda, Ahmednagar, Bidar and Gulbarga – formed a military alliance to defeat the Vijayanagars. The spoils of this campaign, which saw the total destruction of Vijayanagar (Hampi), funded a two-hundred-year building boom in Bijapur during which the city acquired its most impressive monuments. However, old enmities between rival Muslim sultanates on the Deccan soon resurfaced, and the Adil Shahi's royal coffers were gradually squandered on fruitless and protracted wars. By the time the British arrived on the scene in the eighteenth century, the Adil Shahis were a spent force, locked into a decline from which they and their capital never recovered.

Arrival, information and city transport

State and interstate **buses** from as far afield as Mumbai and Aurangabad pull into the KSRTC bus stand on the southwest edge of the town centre; ask at the enquiries desk for exact timings, as the timetables are all in Kannada. For a full rundown of destinations, see "Travel details", p.1354. Most visitors head off to their hotel in (unmetered) auto-rickshaws, though there are also horse-drawn tongas for about the same price. Just a stone's throw away from the Golgumbaz, outside the old city walls, the **railway station**, 3km northeast of the bus stand, is a more inspiring point of arrival. Since the line north has been converted to broad guage, there are now three trains weekly from both Mumbai and Yesvantpur (Bangalore), as well as a daily passenger service to Hyderabad and three more as far as Solapur, for more connections. The line south was still being converted at the time of writing.

Besides the usual literature, the **tourist office** (Mon–Sat 10am–5.30pm; ⓣ08352/250359) behind the *Hotel Adil Shahi* annexe on Station Road, can help with arranging itineraries and guides. For **changing money** (or travellers' cheques), the most reliable service is at Girikand Tours and Travels (ⓣ08352/220510) on the first floor at Nishant Plaza, Rama Mandir Road; you can also use the Canara Bank, on nearby Azad Road, but you will need to take photocopies of the relevant pages of your passport. **Internet** services are available at the adjacent Friends Cyber Zone and Cyber Park (both Rs25/hr), opposite the post office.

Bijapur is flat, relatively uncongested, and generally easy to negotiate by **bicycle**; rickety Heros are available for rent from several stalls outside the bus stand for Rs3 per hour. **Auto-rickshaws** don't have meters and charge a minimum of Rs10; although most of Bijapur is covered by a fare of Rs30, they are a much more expensive way of getting around the monuments, when they charge around Rs200 for a four-hour tour. **Taxis**, available from near the bus stand, charge Rs5.50 per kilometre.

Moving on from Bijapur is getting easier with efficient private companies such as VRL, recognizable by its distinctive yellow-and-black luxury coaches, travelling to Bangalore (3 buses from 7pm) and operating other overnight services to Mangalore via Udupi and Mumbai. VRL can be booked through Vijayanand Travel, Terrace floor, Shastri Market, Gandhi Circle (ⓣ08352/251000) or its other branch just south of the bus stand. KSRTC also runs deluxe buses to Bangalore, Hubli, Mumbai and Hyderabad (via Sholapur). Heading to Badami, it is often quicker to take the first bus to Bagalkot and change there. For train information, see arrival above and "Travel details", p.1354.

Accommodation and eating

Accommodation standards are pretty low in Bijapur, although finding a room is rarely a problem. Such hotels as exist are also fairly widely spread out, so it's not a bad idea to decide in advance. **Eating** is largely confined to the hotels – try the *New Empire* at the *Pearl* – with the odd independent establishment, although at these you'll be restricted to pure veg unless you brave a dingy drinking den. At Gandhi Chowk, the *Shrinidhi Hotel* serves good South Indian vegetarian food, as does the *Priyadarshini*, across the main road from the Gagan Mahal.

Godavari Athani Rd ⓣ08352/253105, ⓕ256225. This monolithic modern but fading hotel is something of a landmark; its prices have been pegged back to reflect its very average status. ❷–❺
Kanishka International Station Rd ⓣ08352/223788, ⓦwww.kanishkabijapur.com. One of the better value places providing comfy rooms with most mod cons and good service at decent rates. Fine veg and non-veg restaurants. ❸–❺
KSTDC Mayura Adil Shahi Annexe Station Rd ⓣ08352/250401. The only surviving state-run establishment in town with large but dowdy rooms, some a/c, and no restaurant. ❸–❹
Madhuvan Station Rd ⓣ08352/255571, ⓕ256201. The smartest place in town, with a variety of rooms, from overpriced ordinary doubles to more comfortable a/c "deluxe" options. The restaurant, however, serves good-value thalis at lunchtime. Can change money for residents. ❺–❻
Pearl Station Rd ⓣ08352/256002, ⓕ243606. Bright modern hotel with clean, sizeable rooms. The front ones have balconies and those at the top views of Golgumbaz. Better value than the *Madhuvan* and with an excellent restaurant. ❸–❺
Sagar Deluxe Next to *Bara Kaman*, Busreshwar Chowk ⓣ08352/259234. Centrally located hotel with unremarkable but cheap doubles and some deluxe and a/c rooms. ❶–❸
Sanman Opposite the Golgumbaz, Station Rd ⓣ08352/251866. Best value among the budget places, and well placed for the railway station. Good-sized rooms, some now with a/c, and all with mosquito nets and clean bathrooms. The Udupi canteen is a stop for the bus parties, so its South Indian snacks are all freshly cooked. ❷–❹

The Town and monuments

Unlike most medieval Muslim strongholds, Bijapur lacked natural rock defences and had to be strengthened by the Adil Shahis with huge **fortified walls**. Extending some 10km around the town, these ramparts, studded with cannon emplacements (*burjes*) and watchtowers, are breached in five points by *darwazas*, or strong gateways, and several smaller postern gates (*didis*). In the middle of the town, a further hoop of crenellated battlements encircled Bijapur's **citadel**, site of the sultans' apartments and durbar hall, of which only fragments remain. The Adil Shahis' **tombs** are scattered around the outskirts, while most of the important **mosques** lie southeast of the citadel.

It's possible to see Bijapur's highlights in a day, although most people stay for two or three nights, taking in the monuments at a more leisurely pace. Our account covers the sights from east to west, beginning with the Golgumbaz – which you should aim to visit at around 6am, before the bus parties descend – and ending with the exquisite Ibrahim Rauza, an atmospheric spot to enjoy the sunset.

The Golgumbaz

The vast **Golgumbaz** mausoleum (daily 6am–6pm; $2 [Rs5]), Bijapur's most famous building, soars above the town's east walls, visible for miles in every direction. Built towards the end of the Adil Shahis' reign, the building is a fitting monument to a dynasty on its last legs – pompous, decadent and ill-proportioned, but conceived on an irresistibly awesome scale.

The cubic tomb, enclosing a 170-square-metre hall, is crowned with a single hemispherical **dome**, the largest in the world after St Peter's in Rome (which is only 5m wider). Spiral staircases wind up the four, seven-storey octagonal towers that buttress the building to the famous **Whispering Gallery**, a three-metre-wide passage encircling the interior base of the dome from where, looking carefully down, you can get a real feel of the sheer size of the building. Arrive here just after opening time and you can experiment with the extraordinary acoustics; by 7am, though, the cacophony generated by busloads of whooping and clapping tourists means you can't hear yourself think, let alone make out whispering 38m away. A good antidote to the din is the superb **views** from the mausoleum's ramparts, which overlook the town and its monuments to the dark-soiled Deccan countryside beyond, scattered with minor tombs and ruins.

Set on a plinth in the centre of the hall below are the gravestones of the ruler who built the Golgumbaz, **Mohammed Adil Shahi**, along with those of his wife, daughter, grandson and favourite courtesan, Rambha. At one corner of the grounds stands the simple gleaming white shrine to a Sufi saint of the Adil Shahi period, **Hashim Pir** which, around February, attracts *qawwals* (singers of devotional *qawwali* music) to the annual *urs*, which lasts for three days.

The Jami Masjid

A little under 1km southwest of the Golgumbaz, the **Jami Masjid** (Friday Mosque) presides over the quarter that formed the centre of the city during Bijapur's nineteenth-century nadir under the Nizam of Hyderabad. It was commissioned by Ali Adil Shahi, the ruler credited with constructing the city walls and complex water supply system, as a monument to his victory over the Vijayanagars at the battle of Talikota in 1565, and is widely regarded as one of the finest mosques in India. As it is a living place of worship, you should not enter improperly dressed.

Simplicity and restraint are the essence of the colonnaded prayer hall below, divided by gently curving arches and rows of thick plaster-covered pillars. Aside from the odd geometric design and trace of yellow, blue and green tile work, the only ornamentation is found in the mihrab, or west- (Mecca-) facing prayer niche, which is smothered in gold leaf and elaborate calligraphy. The marble floor of the hall features a grid of 2500 rectangles, known as *musallahs* (after the *musallah* prayer mats brought to mosques by worshippers). These were added by the Moghul emperor Aurangzeb, allegedly as recompense for making off with the velvet carpets, long golden chain and other valuables that originally filled the prayer hall.

The Mithari and Astar Mahals

Continuing west from the Jami Masjid, the first monument of note is a small, ornately carved gatehouse on the south side of the road. Although of modest size, the delicate three-storey structure, known as the **Mithari Mahal**, is one of Bijapur's most beautiful buildings, with ornate projecting windows and minarets crowning its corners. Once again, Ali Adil Shahi erected it, along with the mosque behind, using gifts presented to him during a state visit to Vijayanagar. The Hindu rajas' generosity, however, did not pay off. Only a couple of years later, the Adil Shahi and his four Muslim allies sacked their city, plundering its wealth and murdering most of its inhabitants.

The lane running north from opposite the Mithari Mahal brings you to the dilapidated **Asar Mahal**, a large open-fronted hall fronted by a large stagnant step-well. Built in 1646 by Mohammed Adil Shahi as a Hall of Justice, it was later chosen to house hairs from the Prophet's beard, thereby earning the title **Asar-i-Sharif**, or "place of illustrious relics". In theory, women are not permitted inside to view the upper storey, where fifteen niches are decorated with mediocre, Persian-style pot-and-foliage murals, but for a little baksheesh, one of the girls who hang around the site will unlock the doors for you.

The citadel

Bijapur's **citadel** stands in the middle of town, hemmed in on all but its north side by battlements. Most of the buildings inside have collapsed, or have been converted into government offices, but enough remain to give a sense of how imposing this royal enclave must once have been.

The best-preserved monuments lie along, or near, the citadel's main north–south artery, Anand Mahal Road, reached by skirting the southeast wall from the Asar Mahal, or from the north side via the road running past the defunct KSTDC *Mayura Adil Shahi Hotel*. The latter route brings you first to the **Gagan Mahal**. Originally Ali Adil Shahi's "Heavenly Palace", this now-ruined hulk later served as a durbar hall for the sultans, who would sit in state on the platform at the open-fronted north side, watched by crowds gathered in the grounds opposite. West off Anand Mahal Road, the five-storeyed **Sat Manzil** was the pleasure palace of the courtesan Rambha, entombed with Mohammed Adil Shahi and his family in the Golgumbaz. In front stands an ornately carved water pavilion, the **Jal Mandir**, now left high and dry in an empty tank.

Malik-i-Maidan and Upli Buruj

Guarding the principal western entrance to the city is one of several bastions (*burje*) that punctuate Bijapur's battlements. This one, the Burj-i-Sherza ("Lion Gate") sports a colossal cannon, known as the **Malik-i-Maidan**, literally "Lord of the Plains". It was brought here as war booty in the sixteenth century, and needed four hundred bullocks, ten elephants and an entire battalion to haul it up the steps to the emplacement. Inscriptions record that the cannon, whose muzzle features a relief of a monster swallowing an elephant, was cast in Ahmednagar in 1551.

A couple more discarded cannons lie atop the watchtower visible a short walk northwest. Steps wind around the outside of the oval-shaped **Upli Burj**, or "Upper Bastion", to a gun emplacement that affords unimpeded views over the city and plains.

The Ibrahim Rauza

Set in its own walled compound less than 1km west of the ramparts, the **Ibrahim Rauza** represents the high watermark of Bijapuri architecture (daily 6am–6pm; $2 [Rs5]). Whereas the Golgumbaz impresses primarily by its scale, the appeal of this tomb complex lies in its grace and simplicity. Beyond the reach of most bus parties, it's also a haven of peace, with cool colonnaded verandas and flocks of iridescent parakeets careening between the mildewed domes, minarets and gleaming golden finials.

Opinions differ over whether the tomb was commissioned by Ibrahim Adil Shah (1580–1626), or his favourite wife, Taj Sultana, but the former was the first to be interred here, in a gloomy chamber whose only light enters via a series of exquisite pierced-stone (*jali*) windows. Made up of elaborate Koranic inscriptions, these are the finest examples of their kind in India. More amazing stonework decorates the exterior of the mausoleum, and the equally beautiful **mosque** opposite, the cornice of whose facade features a stone chain carved from a single block. The two buildings, bristling with minarets and domed cupolas, face each other from opposite sides of a rectangular raised plinth, divided by a small reservoir and fountains. Viewed from on top of the walls that enclose the complex, you can see why its architect, Malik Sandal, added a self-congratulatory inscription in his native Persian over the tomb's south doorway, describing his masterpiece as " . . . A beauty of which Paradise stood amazed".

Gulbarga

GULBARGA, 165km northeast of Bijapur, was the founding capital of the Bahmani dynasty and the region's principal city before the court moved to Bidar in 1424. Later captured by the Adil Shahis and Moghuls, it has remained a staunchly Muslim town, and bulbous onion domes and mosque minarets still soar prominently above its ramshackle concrete-box skyline. The town is also famous as the birthplace of the *chishti*, or saint, Hazrat Bandah Nawaz Gesu Daraz (1320–1422), whose tomb, situated next to one of India's foremost Islamic theological colleges, is a major shrine.

In spite of Gulbarga's religious and historical significance, its **monuments** pale in comparison with those at Bijapur, and even Bidar. Unless you're particularly interested in medieval Muslim architecture, few are worth breaking a journey to see. The one exception is the tomb complex on the northeast edge of town, known as **the Dargah**. Approached via a broad bazaar, this marble-lined enclosure, centres on the tomb of Hazrat Gesu Daraz, affectionately known to his devotees as "**Bandah Nawaz**", or "the long-haired one who brings comfort to others". The saint was spiritual mentor to the Bahmani rulers, and it was they who erected his beautiful double-storeyed mausoleum, now visited by hundreds of thousands of Muslim pilgrims each year. Women are not allowed inside, and must peek at the tomb. The same gender bar applies to the neighbouring tomb, whose interior has retained its exquisite Persian paintings. The *Dargah*'s other important building, open to both sexes, is the **Madrasa**, or theological college, founded by Bandah Nawaz and enlarged during the two centuries after his death.

After mingling with the crowds at the *Dargah*, escape across town to Gulbarga's deserted **fort**. Encircled by sixteen-metre-thick crenellated walls, fifteen watchtowers and an evil-smelling stagnant moat, the great citadel now lies in ruins behind the town's large artificial lake. Its only surviving building is the beautiful fourteenth-century **Jami Masjid**. Thought to have been modelled by a Moorish architect on the great Spanish mosque of Córdoba, it is unique in India for having an entirely domed prayer hall.

Practicalities

Daily KSRTC **buses** from Bijapur, Bidar and Hospet pull in to the state bus stand on the southwest edge of town. Private minibuses work from the roadside opposite, their conductors shouting for passengers across the main concourse. Don't be tempted to take one of these to Bidar; they only run as far as the fly-blown highway junction of Humnabad, 40km short, where you'll be stranded for hours. Gulbarga's main-line **railway station**, with services to and from Mumbai, Pune, Hyderabad, Bangalore and Chennai, lies 1.5km east of the bus stand, along **Mill Road**. **Station Road**, the town's other main artery, runs due north of here past the lake to the busy **Chowk** crossroads, at the heart of the bazaar.

Gulbarga's main sights are well spread out, so you'll need to get around by **auto-rickshaw**; fix fares in advance. There is a Syndicate Bank ATM on Station Road, where you can **change money**.

Accommodation and eating

Gulbarga is well provided with good-value **accommodation**, and even travellers on tight budgets should be able to afford a clean room with a small balcony. All the hotels listed below have **restaurants**, mostly pure-veg places with a no-alcohol rule. *Kamat*, the chain restaurant, has several branches in Gulbarga including a pleasant one at Station Chowk, specializing in vegetarian "meals" as well as *iddlis* and *dosas*; try *joleata roti*, a local bread cooked either hard and crisp or soft like a chapati. On the road up from the station several hole-in-the-wall spots sell freshly fried chicken and fish.

Adithya 2-244 Station Rd, opposite Public Gardens ⓣ08472/224040, ⓕ235661. Has gone more upmarket, with the posher a/c rooms costing hardly more than the non-a/c ones. Its impeccably clean pure-veg Udupi restaurant, *Pooja*, on the ground floor, does great thalis and snacks. ❹–❺

Pariwar Station Rd, a 10-min walk from the station ⓣ08472/221522, ⓔhotelpariwar@yahoo.com. One of the town's more established hotels, but not especially great value. The *Kamakshi Restaurant* serves quality vegetarian South Indian food, but no beer. Some a/c. ❸–❺

Hotel Prashant First lane on the right leaving the station ⓣ08472/221456. Decent rooms of varying size and amenities, surprisingly quiet. ❷–❹

Preetam Lodge Mill Rd ⓣ08472/221673. Head and shoulders above the rest in the vicinity of the bus stand. Clean, spacious rooms in a new block. ❷–❹

Raj Rajeshwari Vasant Nagar, Mill Rd ⓣ08472/225881. Just 5min from the bus stand, friendly and better value than the comparable *Pariwar*. Well-maintained modern building with large en-suite rooms with balconies, plus a reasonable veg restaurant. Strictly no alcohol. ❸–❹

Southern Star Near the Fort, Super Market ⓣ08472/224093. New and comfortable with two restaurants and a bar and some a/c rooms; the rooms at the back look onto the ramparts of the fort but across the stagnant and putrid moat. ❷–❺

Bidar

In 1424, following the break-up of the Bahmani dynasty into five rival factions, Ahmad Shah I shifted his court from Gulbarga to a less constricted site at **BIDAR**, spurred, it is said, by grief at the death of his beloved spiritual mentor, Bandah Nawas Gesu Daraz. Revamping the town with a new fort, splendid palaces, mosques and ornamental gardens, the Bahmanis ruled from here until 1487, when the Barid Shahis took control. They were succeeded by the Adil Shahis from Bijapur, and later the Moghuls under Aurangzeb, who annexed the region in 1656, before the Nizam of Hyderabad finally acquired the territory in the early eighteenth century.

Lost in the far northwest of Karnataka, Bidar, 284km northwest of Bijapur, is nowadays a provincial backwater, better known for its fighter-pilot training base than the monuments gently decaying in, and within sight of, its medieval walls. Yet the town, half of whose 140,000 population is still Muslim, has a gritty charm, with narrow red-dirt streets ending at arched gates and open vistas across the plains. Littered with tile-fronted tombs, rambling fortifications and old mosques, it merits a visit if you're travelling between Hyderabad (150km east) and Bijapur, although expect little in the way of Western comforts, and more than the usual amount of curious approaches from locals. Lone women travellers, especially, may find the attention more hassle than it's worth.

Bidar's sights are too spread out to be comfortably explored on foot. However, auto-rickshaws tend to be thin on the ground away from the main streets, and are reluctant to wait while you look around the monuments, so it's a good idea to rent a **bicycle** for the day (Rs3 per hour) from Rouf's, only 50m east of the bus stand next to the excellent *Karnatak Juice Centre*.

Practicalities

Bidar lies on a branch line of the main Mumbai–Secunderabad–Chennai rail route, and can only be reached by slow passenger **train**. The few visitors that come here invariably arrive **by bus**, at the KSRTC bus stand on the far northwestern edge of town. There is no tourist office or exchange facility but there are signs of Bidar's entry into the twenty-first century (and proximity to Hyderabad) in the shape of several **Internet** outlets such as Cyber Park (Rs15/hr), 100m southeast of the bus stand on Udgir Road.

Most **places to stay** are an auto-rickshaw ride away in the centre, so it makes sense to opt for the new *Hotel Mayura* (Ⓣ08482/228142; ❷–❹) opposite the bus stand, which is one of the two best in Bidar and has large rooms with optional air conditioning. The other decent hotel is its older sister, the *Ashoka* (Ⓣ08482/227621; ❷–❹), 1500m from the bus stand past Dr Ambedkar Chowk, which is comfortable with good-value deluxe rooms, some with air conditioning. If you don't mind some grubbiness, a real budget option is *Hotel Kailash* (Ⓣ08482/227727; ❶) on Udgir Road, in the centre of town.

Finding somewhere good to **eat** is not a problem in Bidar, again thanks to the restaurants at the *Mayura* and *Ashoka*, which both offer a varied selection of north Indian veg and meat dishes (try the *Mayura*'s pepper chicken) and serve cold beer. Also recommended, and much cheaper, is the popular *Udupi Krishna* restaurant, overlooking the *chowk*, which serves up unlimited pure-veg thalis for lunch; it has a "family room" for women, too, and opens early (around 7.30am) for piping hot South Indian breakfasts. The *Jyothi Udupi*, opposite the new bus stand, is another classic South Indian joint.

The old town

The heart of Bidar is its medieval **old town**, encircled by crenellated ramparts and eight imposing gateways (*darwazas*). This predominantly Muslim quarter holds many Bahmani-era mosques, *havelis* and *khanqahs* – "monasteries" set up by the local rulers for Muslim cleric-mystics and their disciples – but its real highlight is the impressive ruins of **Mahmud Gawan's Madrasa**, or theological college, whose single minaret soars high above the city centre. The distinctively Persian-style building, originally surmounted by large bulbous domes, once housed a world-famous library. However, this burnt down after being struck by lightning in 1696, while several of the walls and domes were blown

Bidri

Bidar is renowned as the home of a unique damascene metalwork technique known as **bidri**, developed by the Persian silversmiths that came to the area with the Bahmani court in the fifteenth century. These highly skilled artisans engraved and inlaid their traditional Iranian designs onto a metal alloy composed of lead, copper, zinc and tin, which they blackened and polished. The resulting effect – swirling silver floral motifs framed by geometric patterns and set against black backgrounds – has since become the hallmark of Muslim metalwork in India.

Bidri objets d'art are displayed in museums and galleries all over the country. But if you want to see pukka *bidri*-wallahs at work, take a walk down Bidar's **Siddiq Talim Road**, which cuts across the south side of the old town, where skull-capped artisans tap and burnish vases, goblets, plates, spice boxes, betel-nut tins, and ornamental hookah pipes, as well as less traditional objects – coasters, ashtrays and bangles – that crop up (at vastly inflated prices) in silver emporiums as far away as Delhi and Kolkata (Calcutta).

away when gunpowder stored here by Aurangzeb's occupying army caught fire and exploded. Today, the *madrasa* is little more than a shell, although its elegant arched facade has retained large patches of the vibrant Persian glazed tile-work that once covered most of the exterior surfaces.

The fort

Bidar's **fort**, at the far north end of the street running past the *madrasa*, was founded by the Hindu Chalukyas and strengthened by the Bahmanis in the early fifteenth century. Despite repeated sieges, it remains largely intact, encircled by 10km of ramparts that drop away in the north and west to 300-metre cliffs. The main southern entrance is protected by equally imposing man-made defences: gigantic fortified gates and a triple moat formerly crossed by a series of drawbridges. Once inside, the first building of note (on the left after the third and final gateway) is the exquisite **Rangin Mahal**. Mahmud Shah built this modest "Coloured Palace" after an unsuccessful uprising of Abyssinian slaves in 1487 forced him to relocate to a safer site inside the citadel. The palace's relatively modest proportions reflect the Bahmanis' declining fortunes, but its interior comprises some of the finest surviving Islamic art in the Deccan, with superb woodcarving above the door arches and Persian-style mother-of-pearl inlay on polished black granite surfaces. If the doors to the palace are locked, ask for the keys at the nearby ASI **museum** (daily 8am–1pm & 2–5pm; free), which houses a missable collection of Hindu temple sculpture, weapons and Stone Age artefacts.

Opposite the museum, an expanse of gravel is all that remains of the royal gardens. This is overlooked by the austere **Solah Khamb** mosque (1327), Bidar's oldest Muslim monument, whose most outstanding feature is the intricate pierced-stone *jali* calligraphy around its central dome. From here, continue west through the ruins of the former royal enclosure – a rambling complex of half-collapsed palaces, baths, *zenanas* (women's quarters) and assembly halls – to the fort's west walls. You can complete the round of **the ramparts** in ninety minutes, taking time out to enjoy the views over the red cliffs and across the plains.

Ashtur: the Bahmani tombs

As you look from the fort's east walls, a cluster of eight bulbous white domes floats alluringly above the trees in the distance. Dating from the fifteenth century, the mausoleums at **Ashtur**, 3km east of Bidar (leave the old town via Dulhan Darwaza gate), are the final resting places of the Bahmani sultans and their families, including the son of the ruler who first decamped from Gulbarga, Alauddin Shah I. His remains by far the most impressive tomb, with patches of coloured glazed tiles on its arched facade, and a large dome whose interior surfaces writhe with sumptuous Persian paintings. Reflecting sunlight onto the ceiling with a small pocket mirror, the *chowkidar* picks out the highlights, among them a diamond, barely visible among the bat droppings.

The tomb of Allaudin's father, the ninth and most illustrious Bahmani Sultan, Ahmad Shah I, stands beside that of his son, decorated with Persian inscriptions. Beyond this are two more minor mausoleums, followed by the partially collapsed tomb of Humayun the Cruel (1458–61), cracked open by a bolt of lightning. Continuing along the line, you can chart the gradual decline of the Bahmanis as the mausoleums diminish in size, ending with a sad handful erected in the early sixteenth century, when the sultans were no more than puppet rulers of the Barid Shahis.

The Badrid Shahi tombs

The **tombs of the Badrid Shahi** rulers, who succeeded the Bahmanis at the start of the sixteenth century, stand on the western edge of town, on the Udgir road, 200m beyond and visible from the bus stand. Although not as impressive as those of their predecessors, the mausoleums, mounted on raised plinths, occupy an attractive site. Randomly spaced rather than set in a chronological row, they are surrounded by lawns maintained by the ASI. The most interesting is the tomb of **Ali Barid** (1542–79), whose Mecca-facing wall was left open to the elements. A short distance southwest lies a mass-grave platform for his 67 concubines, who were sent as tribute gifts by vassals of the Deccani overlord from all across the kingdom. The compound is only officially open for afternoon promenading (daily 4.30–7.30pm; $2 [Rs5]) but the gateman may let you in earlier if he's around.

Travel details

Trains

When this book went to press, the changeover from metre- to broad-gauge track was largely completed but the Mangalore–Hassan and Bijapur–Gadag sections were still not fully operational; check the current situation with Indian Railways.

Bangalore to: Chennai (5–7 daily; 5hr–7hr 40min); Delhi (2–4 daily; 34hr 40min–49hr 40min); Gulbarga (2–3 daily; 11hr 35min–12hr 20min); Hospet (1 daily; 9hr 35min); Hubli (2–4 daily; 7–13hr); Hyderabad (Secunderabad) (1–3 daily; 12hr 15min–14hr 10min); Kochi (Ernakulam) (1–2 daily; 12hr–13hr 5min); Kolkata (Calcutta) (3 weekly; 37hr 10min); Mumbai (2–3 daily; 23hr 25min–25hr); Mysore (6–7 daily; 2–3hr 15min); Pune (2–4 daily; 19hr 20min–21hr 30min); Thiruvananthapuram (1–2 daily; 17hr–17hr 55min).

Hassan to: Mysore (4 daily; 2hr 10min–3hr 55min).

Hospet to: Bangalore (1 daily; 10hr 30min); Gadag (3 daily; 1hr 15min–1hr 35min); Hubli (3 daily; 2hr 30min–3hr 20min).

Mangalore to: Chennai (1 daily; 17hr 55min); Kochi (Ernakulam) (2 daily; 9hr 30min–10hr 5min); Kollam (2 daily; 12hr 50min–13hr 30min); Margao, Goa (2 daily; 5hr 45min–6hr 10min); Gokarna (2 daily; 3hr 5min–3hr 50min); Thiruvananthapuram (2 daily; 14hr 40min–15hr 35min).

Mysore to: Bangalore (6–7 daily; 1hr 55min–3hr 30min); Hassan (4 daily; 2hr 10min–4hr).

Buses

Bangalore to: Bidar (2 daily; 16hr); Bijapur (4 daily; 13hr); Chennai (hourly; 8hr); Coimbatore (2 daily; 9hr); Goa (4 daily; 14hr); Gokarna (2 daily; 13hr); Gulbarga (6 daily; 15hr); Hassan (every 30min; 4hr); Hospet (3 daily; 8hr); Hubli (3 daily; 9hr); Hyderabad (6 daily; 16hr); Jog Falls (1 daily; 8hr); Karwar (3 daily; 13hr); Kodaikanal (1 nightly; 13hr); Kochi (Ernakulam) (6 daily; 12–13hr); Madikeri (hourly; 6hr); Madurai (2 daily; 12hr); Mangalore (every 30min–1hr; 10hr); Mumbai (2 daily; 24hr); Mysore (every 15min; 3hr); Ooty (6 daily; 7hr 30min); Pondicherry (2 daily; 9–10hr).

Bijapur to: Aurangabad (4 daily; 12hr); Badami (4 daily; 4hr); Bangalore (5 daily; 13hr); Bidar (4 daily; 8hr); Gulbarga (hourly; 4hr); Hospet (12 daily; 5hr); Hubli (hourly; 6hr); Hyderabad (6 daily; 10hr); Mumbai (10 daily; 12hr); Pune (10 daily; 8hr).

Hassan to: Channarayapatna, for Saravanabelgola (hourly; 1hr); Halebid (hourly; 1hr); Hospet (1 daily; 10hr); Mangalore (hourly; 4hr); Mysore (every 30min; 3hr).

Hospet to: Badami (3 daily; 5hr); Bangalore (3 daily; 8hr); Bidar (2 daily; 10hr); Gokarna (2 nightly; 9–10hr); Hampi (every 30min; 20min); Hyderabad (4 daily; 12hr); Margao (4 daily; 9hr); Mysore (2 daily; 10–11hr); Panjim (4 daily; 10hr); Vasco da Gama (4 daily; 10–11hr).

Mangalore to: Bangalore (every 30min–1hr; 8hr); Bijapur (1 daily; 16hr); Chaudi (2 daily; 8hr); Gokarna (1 daily; 7hr); Kannur (hourly; 3hr); Karwar (9 daily; 8hr); Kasargode (every 30min–1hr; 1hr); Kochi (Ernakulam) (1 daily; 9hr); Madikeri (hourly; 3hr 30min); Mysore (hourly; 7hr); Panjim (2 daily; 10–11hr); Udupi (every 10 min; 1hr).

Mysore to: Bangalore (every 15min; 3hr); Channarayapatna (every 30min; 2hr); Jog Falls (via Shimoga) (every 90min; 7hr); Kannur (8 daily; 7hr); Kochi (6 daily; 12hr); Kozhikode (6 daily; 5hr); Madikeri (hourly; 3hr); Mangalore (hourly; 7hr); Ooty (10 daily; 5hr); Srirangapatnam (every 15 min; 20min).

Flights

Bangalore to: Chennai (11–12 daily; 45min–1hr); Delhi (11–12 daily; 2hr 30min–3hr 30min); Goa (3 daily; 1hr–2hr 30min); Hyderabad (7–9 daily; 1hr–1hr 30min); Kochi (Ernakulam) (3 daily; 55min–1hr 20min); Kolkata (Calcutta) (4–5 daily; 2hr 20min–3hr 30min); Mangalore (1 daily; 1hr 5min); Mumbai (15–17 daily; 1hr 30min–1hr 45min); Pune (3 daily; 1hr 20min); Thiruvanthapuram (1 daily; 2hr).
Mangalore to: Bangalore (2 daily; 1hr 5min–1hr 15min); Mumbai (3 daily; 1hr 15min).

Contexts

Contexts

History

India is the product of a complex and tumultuous past. Its climate and fertile soil, which have supported settled agriculture for at least 9000 years, have also given rise to countless regional dynasties, perennially covetous of their neighbours' land and wealth. For as long as written histories of India have existed this same fecundity has also lured invaders across the deserts, oceans and mountains that border the subcontinent. Successive waves of armed colonists, from the Aryan tribes to the British, have poured down the peninsula, assimilating indigenous traditions and implanting their own. Scholars of history, archeology and religion are still trying to make sense of the extraordinary wealth of historic monuments they left behind, and what follows is necessarily only the broadest of outlines. For a fuller overview, dip into one of the recent histories of India recommended in "Books", p.1432.

Prehistory

The earliest human activity in the Indian subcontinent can be traced back to the Early, Middle and Late **Stone Ages** (400,000–200,000 BC). Implements from all three periods have **been** found around the country, from Rajasthan and Gujarat in the west to Bihar in the east, from the northwest of what's now Pakistan to the tip of the peninsula; and rock paintings of hunting scenes can be seen in the Narmada Valley and elsewhere in central India.

These **Paleolithic peoples** were seminomadic **hunters and gatherers** for many millennia. Indeed, some isolated hill tribes continued to be hunters and gatherers or to practise the transitional "slash and burn" type of agriculture into the twentieth century. Five main peoples are known to have been present when the move to an agricultural lifestyle took place, in the middle of the eighth millennium BC: the **Negrito** race, believed to be the earliest; the **Proto-Australoid**; the **Mediterranean** peoples; the **Mongoloid** elements (confined to the north and northeast); and the western **Brachycephals** or **Alpine** peoples.

The first evidence of **agricultural settlement**, at Mehrgarh on the western plains of the Indus, is roughly contemporaneous with similar developments in Egypt, Mesopotamia and Persia. Village settlements in western Afghanistan, Baluchistan and the Sind gradually developed over the next five thousand years as their inhabitants began to use copper and bronze, domesticate animals, make pottery and trade with their western neighbours.

The distinct styles of pottery discovered at Nal and Zhob in the Brahui hills of Baluchistan, Kulli on the Makran coast and the lower Indus, and Amri in the Sind indicate the development of several independent cultures. **Terracotta figurines** of goddesses, bulls and phallic emblems echo the fertility cults and Mother Goddess worship found in early agricultural communities in the Mediterranean region and the Middle East; they also prefigure elements which were to re-emerge as aspects of the religious life of India.

The first great Indian civilization

From the start of the fourth millennium BC, the individuality of early village cultures began to be replaced by a more homogeneous style of pottery at a large number of sites throughout the **Indus Valley**; by the middle of the third millennium, a uniform culture had developed at settlements spread across nearly 1,280,000 square kilometres, including parts of the Punjab, Uttar Pradesh, Gujarat, Baluchistan, the Sind and the Makran coast. Two great cities on the Indus, **Harappa** in the north and **Mohenjo Daro** in the south, were supported by the agricultural surplus produced by such settlements. Recent archeological research has unearthed further sites, almost as large as the first two and designed on the same plan, at Kalibangan, on the border of India and Pakistan, at Kot Diji east of Mohenjo Daro, at Chanhu Daro further south on the Indus, and at Lothal in Gujarat.

The emergence of the first great Indian civilization, around 2500 BC, is almost as remarkable as its stability for nearly a thousand years. All the cities were built with baked bricks of the same size; the streets were laid out in a grid with an elaborate system of covered drains; and the houses, some with more than one storey, are large. Vast granaries and a citadel built on higher ground with a gigantic adjoining bath at Mohenjo Daro, together with the absence of royal palaces and the large numbers of religious figurines, suggest that it was a theocratic state of priests, merchants and farmers.

By now, farmers had domesticated various **animals**, including hump-backed (Brahmani) cattle, goats, water buffaloes and fowls. They cultivated wheat, barley, peas and sesamum, and were also probably the first to grow and make clothes from **cotton**. Excavations at Lothal have uncovered a **harbour**; merchants were certainly involved in extensive trading by both sea and land, for they imported metals, including gold, silver and copper, and semiprecious stones from the Indian peninsula, Persia, Afghanistan, Central Asia and Mesopotamia. While the main export was probably cotton yarn or cloth, they may have exported surplus grain as well. Indus seals found at Ur confirm the continuity of trading links with Sumer between 2300 and 2000 BC.

The sheer quantity of **seals** discovered in the Indus cities suggests that each merchant or mercantile family had its own. They're usually square, and made of steatite (a kind of soapstone), engraved and then hardened by heating. All bear inscriptions, which remain undeciphered, although nearly 400 different characters have been identified. The emblems beneath the inscriptions – iconographic scenes and animals, such as the bull, buffalo, goat, tiger and elephant – are more enlightening. One of the most notable depicts a horned deity sitting cross-legged in an ithyphallic posture, surrounded by a tiger, an elephant, a rhinoceros, a water buffalo and two deer. He appears on two other seals, and it seems certain that he was a fertility god; indeed, he has been called a "**proto-Shiva**" because of the resemblance to Pashupati, the Lord of the Beasts, a major representation of the fully developed Hindu god, Shiva. Other seals provide evidence that certain trees, especially the peepal, were worshipped, and thus anticipate their sacred status in the Hindu and Buddhist religions.

No monumental sculpture survives, but large numbers of human figurines have been discovered, including a steatite bust of a man thought to be a priest, a striking bronze "dancing girl", brilliantly naturalistic models of animals, and countless terracotta statuettes of a Mother Goddess. This goddess is thought to have been worshipped in nearly every home of the common people, but the crude style of modelling suggests that she was not part of the cult of the priestly elite.

The sudden demise of the Indus civilization in the last quarter of the second millennium BC used to be explained by invasions of barbarian tribes from the northwest; but recent research has established that tectonic upheavals in about 1700 BC caused a series of floods, and these are now considered primarily to blame.

The Vedic Age 1500–600 BC

The written history of India begins with the invasions of the charioteering **Indo-European** or **Aryan** tribes, which spelt the final collapse of the Indus civilization. This period takes its name from the earliest Indian literature, the **Vedas**, collections of hymns (*samhitas*) composed in Vedic Sanskrit. Though composed between 1500 and 1000 BC, the *Rig Veda* was not written down until as late as 900 or 800 BC. Essentially a religious text, in use to this day, it sheds great light on the social and political life of the period.

The Aryans belonged to the barbarian tribes, who broke out of the vast steppeland that stretches from Poland to Central Asia to maraud and eventually colonize Europe, the Middle East and the Indian subcontinent from the start of the second millennium BC. They probably entered the Punjab via the Iranian plateau in successive waves over several hundred years; the peaceful farmers of the Indus would have been powerless against their horse-drawn chariots. Aryan culture was diametrically opposed to the Indus civilization, and Vedic literature relates how their war god, Indra, destroyed hundreds of urban settlements.

Seminomadic hunters and pastoralists when they first reached the region between Kabul and the Thar desert (known as the *Sapta-Sindhu* or seven "Induses"), the Aryans adopted the techniques of settled farming learned from the peoples they conquered as they spread eastwards into the plain between the upper Ganges and the Yamuna (known as the "Doab"). The tribes began to organize themselves into village communities, governed by tribal councils (*sabha* and *samiti*) and warrior chiefs (*raja*), who offered protection in return for tribute; the sacrifices of the chief priest or *purohita* secured their prosperity and martial success.

The Aryans' hymns describe the intertribal conflicts characteristic of the period, but there was an underlying sense of solidarity against the indigenous peoples, known as **Dasas**. Originally a general term for "enemies", it came to denote "subjects" as they were colonized within the land of the Aryans (*arya-varta*). The Dasas are described as Negroid phallus worshippers, who owned many cattle and lived in fortified towns or villages (*pur*). The Aryans began to emphasize purity of blood as they settled among the darker aboriginals, and their original class divisions of nobility and ordinary tribesmen were hardened to exclude the Dasas. At the same time, the priests, the sole custodians and extrapolators of the increasingly complex oral traditions of the sacrificial religion, began to claim high privileges for their skill and training.

By 1000 BC, a fourfold division of society had been given religious sanction in a hymn, which describes how the four classes (**varnas**, literally "colour") emanated from the mouth, arms, thighs and feet of the primeval man (*purusha*). The *varnas* of priest, warrior, peasant and serf (brahmin, *kshatrya*, *vaishya* and *shudra*) have persisted as the fundamental structure of society to the present day. The first three encompassed the main divisions within the Aryan tribes, which later assumed the status of "twice-born" (*dvija*); the Dasas and other non-Aryan peoples became the *shudras*, who served the three higher classes.

During the later Vedic period, between 1000 and 600 BC, the centre of Aryan culture and power shifted from the Punjab and the northwest to the Doab, whence their influence continued to spread eastwards and southwards. The sacred texts of the *Sama*, *Yajur* and *Atharva Vedas*, the *Brahmanas* and the *Upanishads* all originate in this period. Like the *Rig Veda*, they tell us much about developments in religious life, but only offer glimpses of the Aryanization of the subcontinent.

The great epic poems, the **Mahabharata** and the **Ramayana**, and the *Puranas* claim to relate to this period. Though they are unreliable as historical sources, being overlaid with accretions from later centuries, it's possible to extract some of the facts entwined with the martial myths and legends.

The great battle of **Kurukshetra** – the central theme of the *Mahabharata* – is certainly historical, and took place near modern Delhi some time in the ninth and eighth centuries BC. It was the culmination of a dynastic dispute among the Kurus, who, with their neighbours the Panchalas, were the greatest of the Aryan tribes. Archeological evidence has been found of the two main settlements mentioned in the epic: Indraprastha (Delhi) and Hastinapura, further north on the Ganges; the latter was the capital of the Kurus, two of whose kings, Parikshit and Janamejaya, are described as mighty conquerors in the Vedic literature.

By the time of Kurukshetra, the Aryans had advanced into the mid-Gangetic valley to establish **Kosala**, with its capital at **Ayodhya** – according to the *Ramayana*, the realm of Rama, the god-hero. Vedic literature mentions neither Rama nor his father Dasharatha, but does refer to Rama's father-in-law, Janaka of Videha. Certainly the extension of Aryan influence to South India, reflected in the myth of Rama's invasion of Sri Lanka to rescue Sita, did not occur until much later. At this time, the megalithic cultures of Madras, Kerala and Mysore remained untouched by the Aryan invaders. The Aryanization of north India, however, continued throughout the period, and began to penetrate central India as well.

The migrating tribes pushed east beyond Kosala to found the kingdoms of **Kashi** (the region of Varanasi), **Videha** (east of the River Gandak and north of the Ganges), and **Anga** on the border of Bengal. The **Yadava** tribe settled around Mathura, on the Yamuna; a branch of the Yadavas is said later to have colonized Saurashtra in modern Gujarat. Further east, down the Yamuna, the **Vatsa** kingdom established its capital at Kaushambi. Other tribes pushed southwards down the River Chambal to found the kingdom of **Avanti**; some penetrated as far as the Narmada, and by the end of the period Aryan influence probably extended into the northwest Deccan.

This territorial expansion was assisted by significant developments in Aryan civilization. When they arrived in India Aryan knowledge of **metallurgy** was limited to gold, copper and bronze, but later Vedic literature mentions tin, lead, silver and iron. The use of iron, together with the taming of elephants, facilitated the rapid clearance of the forests and jungles for settlement. They now grew a large range of crops, including rice; specialized trades and crafts grew considerably, and merchants re-established trade with Mesopotamia, curtailed since the days of the Indus civilization.

Vedic culture and society was transformed by mutual acculturation between the Aryans and indigenous peoples. By the end of the Vedic period, the Aryan tribes had consolidated into little kingdoms, each with its capital city. Some were republics, but generally the power of the tribal assemblies was dwindling, to be replaced by a new kind of politics centred on a **king**, who ruled a geographical area. His relatives and courtiers formed a rudimentary administrative system – known as "Jewel Bearers" (*ratnins*), they included the chief priest, the chamberlain and palace officials.

Kingship was becoming more absolute, limited only by the influence of the priesthood – a relationship between temporal and sacred power that became

The account of **Hinduism** on p.1395 includes more about the *Mahabharata*, the *Ramayana*, and the development of caste divisions.

crucial. The *Brahmana* literature, compiled by the priests, contains instructions for the performance of sacrifices symbolizing royal power, such as the royal consecration ceremonies (*rajasuya*) and the horse sacrifice (*ashvamedha*). Thus, the priests sustained belief in the association of kingship with divinity through their rituals and assisted new political institutions to emerge.

Not all religious specialists were committed to these political developments, and the evolution of Aryan civilization in the late Vedic period also involved a degree of introspection and pessimism. The disintegration of tribal identity created a profound sense of insecurity, which combined with doubts as to the efficacy of sacrificial rituals led to the emergence of nonconformists and ascetics. Their teachings were set down in the metaphysical literature of the *Upanishads* and the *Aranyakas*, which laid the foundations for the various philosophical systems developed in later periods.

The age of the Buddha 600–321 BC

The age of the **Buddha** was marked by great intellectual endeavour and spiritual agitation. Though mystics and ascetics rejected the norms of Vedic society, major political and commercial developments continued; the emergence of kingdoms and administrative systems encouraged rulers to think in terms of empire.

By 600 BC, the association of tribes with the territories they had colonized had resulted in the consolidation of at least sixteen republics and monarchies, known as **mahajanapadas** (territories of the great clans). Some, like **Kuru** and **Panchala**, represented the oldest and earliest established kingdoms; others, like **Avanti**, **Vatsa** and **Magadha** had come into existence more recently. The hereditary principle and the concept of divinely ordained kings tended to preserve the status quo in the monarchies, while the republics provided an atmosphere in which unorthodox views were able to develop. The **founders** of the "heterodox" sects of **Buddhism** and **Jainism** were both born in small republics of this kind.

The consolidation of the *mahajanapadas* was based on the growth of a stable agrarian economy and the increasing importance of **trade**, which led to the use of coins and a script (*Brahmi*, from which the current scripts of India, Sri Lanka, Tibet, Java and Myanmar derive) and encouraged the emergence of towns, such as Kashi (Varanasi), Ayodhya, Rajagriha (first capital of Magadha), Kaushambi in the Ganges Valley, and Ujjain on the Narmada. The resultant prosperity stimulated conflict, however, and by the fifth century BC the four great kingdoms of Kashi, Koshala, Vatsa and Magadha and the republic of the Vrijjis between them held sway over all the others.

Eventually, **Magadha** emerged supreme, under Bimbisara (543–491 BC), a resolute and energetic organizer, and Ajatashatru (491–461 BC), who conquered Kashi and Koshala, broke up the Vrijji confederacy, and built a strong administration. Both kings set out to control the trade in the Ganges Valley with its rich deposits of copper and iron.

Magadha expanded over the next hundred years, moving its capital to **Pataliputra** (Patna) and annihilating the other kingdoms in the Ganges Valley or reducing them to the status of vassals. In the middle of the fourth century BC, the **Nanda** dynasty usurped the Magadhan throne; Mahapadma Nanda conquered Kalinga (Orissa and the northern coastal strip of Andhra Pradesh) and gained control of parts of the Deccan. The disputed succession after his death coincided with significant events in the northwest; out of this confusion the first and perhaps greatest of India's empires was born.

Darius I, the third Achaemenid emperor of Persia, had claimed Gandhara in the northwest as his twentieth satrapy, and advanced into the Punjab near the end of the sixth century BC; but a second invasion in the fourth century BC was more significant. **Alexander the Great** defeated Darius III, the last Achaemenid, crossed the Indus in 326 BC, and overran the Punjab. He was in India for just two years and although he left garrisons and appointed satraps to govern the conquered territories, his death in 323 BC made their position untenable. Chandragupta Maurya was quick to take advantage of the political vacuum.

The Mauryan Empire 321–184 BC

The accession to the throne of **Chandragupta Maurya**, who overthrew the last of the Nanda dynasty of Magadha about 321 BC, marked the beginnings of the first Indian empire. He is said to have met Alexander the Great and was probably inspired by his exploits; his 500,000-strong army drove out the Greek garrisons in the northwest, and annexed all the lands east of the Indus, and when Seleucus Nicator, Alexander's general, attempted to regain control of Macedonian provinces in India, Chandragupta defeated him too, and forced the surrender of territories in what is now Afghanistan as a reward.

According to tradition, Chandragupta was assisted by an unscrupulous brahmin adviser called Kautilya or Chanakya, the reputed author of the *Arthashastra*, a famous treatise on political economy. The Mauryan empire developed a highly bureaucratic state administration, which controlled economic life and employed a very thorough secret service system.

From about 297 BC onwards, Chandragupta's son Bindusara extended the empire as far south as Mysore, before being succeeded in around 269 BC by his son, **Ashoka** – the noblest ruler of India, whom the Buddhists called a universal emperor (*chakravartin*). Ashoka's political pragmatism and imperial vision, complemented by his humanity, practical benevolence and tolerance, mark him out as a statesman and reformer far ahead of his time. He ruthlessly consolidated his power for the first eight years of his reign, before invading and subduing the tribal kingdom of Kalinga (Orissa), his last campaign of violent conquest, in 260 BC. Two and a half years later, his conversion to **Buddhism** caused Ashoka to espouse non-violence (*ahimsa*), and consequently to abandon territorial aggression in favour of conquest by the **Law of Righteousness** (*dharma*). The fourteen **edicts** in which he laid down its principles were engraved in the *Brahmi* script on eighteen great rocks and thirty polished sandstone pillars throughout the empire, the most famous and accessible of which can be found at Sarnath in Uttar Pradesh (see p.344) and Dhauli in Orissa (see p.1038).

Ashoka sought to neutralize the regional pluralism within the empire by his proclamation of the *dharma*, a code of conduct designed to counteract the social tensions created by the *varna* distinctions of class, sectarian conflicts and economic differences. It inculcated social responsibility, encouraged socio-religious harmony, sought to ensure human dignity and expressed a paternal concern for his subjects' wellbeing and happiness. His social reforms included the restriction of animal slaughter and the prohibition of animal sacrifices in Pataliputra – which encouraged vegetarianism, the cultivation of medicinal herbs and the establishment of healing centres. The system of communications was improved by planting roadside fruit trees and by the construction of wells and rest houses. He also replaced the annual royal hunt with a pilgrimage of righteousness (*dharma yatra*), which gave him the opportunity to visit the distant corners of the empire personally and exhibit himself as the living symbol of imperial unity.

His adoption of Buddhism and this new ethical system, however, did not interfere with his imperial pragmatism, and despite his avowed remorse after the Kalinga campaign he continued to govern the newly acquired territory, retained his army without reduction and warned the wilder tribesmen that he would use force to subjugate them if they continued to raid the civilized villages of the empire.

Ashoka's empire extended from Assam to Afghanistan and from Kashmir to Mysore; only the three Dravidian kingdoms of the Cholas, Cheras and Pandyas in the southernmost tip of the subcontinent remained independent. Diplomatic relations were maintained with Syria, Egypt, Macedonia and Cyrene, and all the states on the immediate borders. The Mauryan empire was built on military conquest and a centralized administration – its well-organized revenue department ensured a strong fiscal base – but Ashoka's imperial vision, his shrewdness, and above all the force of his personality and the loyalty he inspired, held it all together.

After Ashoka's death in 232 BC, the empire began to fall apart. While princes contested the throne, the provincial governors established their independence. Interregional rivalries and further invasions from Central Asia exacerbated matters, and in 184 BC the last of the Mauryans, Brihadratha, was assassinated by his brahmin general, Pushyamitra Shunga. The Mauryans had ruled India for nearly 140 years; Ashoka's importance was recognized more than two thousand years later, when Nehru adopted the lion capital of his Sarnath pillar as the emblem of the newly independent India.

The age of invasions 184 BC–320 AD

Although economic prosperity and cultural enrichment endured for five hundred years after the death of Ashoka, India became politically fragmented. Successive **invasions**, and the emergence of regional monarchies in the south, reduced Magadha to one of many quasi-feudal kingdoms struggling for regional power. Though it still included Bengal, Bhopal and Malwa within its boundaries, the Punjab and the northwestern territories had been lost. A dynasty founded by Pushyamitra Shunga, an orthodox brahmin under whose Shunga successors Buddhism continued to be generously patronized, with elaborate stone stupas being erected at Sanchi and Bharhur, ruled Magadha until 72 BC, when the last Shunga monarch was deposed by his servant Vasudeva Kanva.

The **Bactrian Greeks**, who had asserted their independence from the Seleucids of Syria and recaptured Gandhara (the Peshawar region of Pakistan) in 190 BC, were the first invaders. When the Mauryan empire collapsed, the Indo-Greek rulers occupied the Punjab and extended their control as far as Mathura in Uttar Pradesh. One Indo-Greek king, Milinda or Menander, who ruled the Swat Valley and the Punjab from Sagala (Sialkot) between 155 and 130 BC, became famous for his conversion to Buddhism by the philosopher Nagasena. Another example of acculturation is found on the Garuda pillar at Besnagar (Bhilsa), by Heliodorus, the Greek envoy to the Shunga court, to commemorate the Bactrian conquests of northwestern India. Its inscription proclaimed Heliodorus to be a worshipper of Vasudeva, a god later identified with Krishna, the Lord of the *Bhagavad Gita*.

The next wave of invasions, in the first centuries BC and AD, saw Parthians (Pahlavas) from Iran take control of Bactria. Soon large-scale movements of Central Asian Yueh-Chi nomads had precipitated the migration of the Scythians (Shakas) from the Aral Sea area, who displaced the Parthians. During the first century AD, the Kushan branch of the Yueh-Chi in turn drove the Shakas out of northwestern India into Gujarat and Malwa around Ujjain, where they settled and became Indianized, while Kujula Kadphises established the **Kushan** dynasty in the northwest.

The third and greatest of the Kushan kings, **Kanishka**, who reigned for more than twenty years around 100 AD, extended his rule as far east as Varanasi and as far south as Sanchi. Kanishka's empire prospered through control of trade routes between India, China and the West, and his court attracted artists and musicians as well as merchants. Ashvaghosha, one of the first classical Sanskrit poets, wrote a *Life of the Buddha* (*Buddha Charita*) and is credited with converting the emperor to Buddhism.

The south

While the tribal republics of northern and central India absorbed invaders from the northwest, and the kingdoms of Ayodhya and Kaushambi continued to be important in the Gangetic valley, the first great kingdom of **southern India** was flexing its muscles. Between the second century BC and the second century AD the **Andhra** or **Satavahana** dynasty, which originated in the region between the rivers Godavari and Krishna, spread its control across much of south and central India.

Having unsuccessfully challenged the Shakas in Malwa and Gujarat, they brought the northwest Deccan under their control and created a capital at Paithan on the Godavari, northeast of Pune in Maharashtra. The Satavahanas overthrew the Kanva dynasty of Magadha in 27 BC and pushed south to the Tungabhadra and Krishna rivers. Their second capital, at **Amaravati** on the Krishna, prospered on trade with Rome and Southeast Asia, but by the middle of the third century the Satavahana kingdom had collapsed. The Pallavas took control of their territories in Andhra Pradesh, while the Vakatakas gained supremacy in the central and northwestern regions of the Deccan in the latter half of the third century, only to be subsumed within the Gupta empire by the end of the fourth century.

Further south, the three kingdoms of the **Cheras** on the Malabar coast in the west, the **Pandyas** in the central southern tip of the peninsula, and the **Cholas** on the east coast of Coromandel – together comprising much of present-day Tamil Nadu and Kerala – had been developing almost completely independently of north India. **Madurai**, the Pandyan capital, and still one of the major temple cities of the south, had become a centre of Tamil culture. Between 300 BC and 200 AD, colleges or academies (**sangam**) of poets produced a body of literature which describes an indigenous Tamil culture and society only gradually being influenced by the Aryan traditions of the north. The early kingdoms were matriarchal, and the Dravidian kinship system was endogamous, being based on cross-cousin marriage, in sharp contrast to the Indo-Aryan system of exogamy, which prescribed marriage to outsiders. Society was divided into groups based on the geographical domains of hills, plains, forest, coast and desert rather than class or *varna*, though brahmins did command high status. Although agriculture, pastoralism and fishing were the main occupations, trade in spices, gold and jewels with Rome and Southeast Asia underpinned the region's prosperity.

The three kingdoms initially balanced individual struggles for political hegemony with alliances to withstand the aggression of their northern neighbours; but after the middle of the first century BC conflicts between themselves became more frequent. This enervating warfare rendered them vulnerable; early in the fourth century AD, the **Pallavas** overran the Chola capital of Kanchipuram, and by 325 AD they were in control of Tamil Nadu. The Pallavas remained a dominant power in the south until the ninth century AD, and thus became one of the longest ruling dynasties in Indian history.

Trade and society

Despite the disintegration of the Mauryan empire and the proliferation of fiercely rival kingdoms from 200 BC to 300 AD, this was also a period of unprecedented economic wealth and cultural development. The growing importance of the mercantile community encouraged the monetization of the economy and stimulated the growth of urban centres all over India. Merchants and artisans organized themselves into guilds (*shreni*), which, along with the ruling dynasties, minted their own coins.

External **trade**, overland and maritime, opened up lines of communication with the outside world. The main highway from Pataliputra to Taxila gave India access to the old **Silk Road**, the most important trade route of the time, linking China to the Mediterranean via Central Asia. Maritime trade traversed the coastal routes between the seaports in Gujarat and southern India and as far as south Arabia; and Indian merchants established trading communities in various parts of south Asia.

The invasion of foreign peoples, the growth of trade and urbanization together had a considerable impact on the structure of society. Foreign conquerors and traders, who had to be integrated within the *varna* system; the burgeoning importance of the *vaishya* class of merchants and artisans; and the influence of urban liberalism, all presented serious challenges to law and social order. The Law Books (*Dharma Shastras*) were composed in this period in an attempt to accommodate these changes and redefine social, economic and legal rights and duties. Important developments in India's religions can also be linked to socio-economic changes. Radical schisms occurred in both Buddhism and Jainism, and may be attributed to the increasing participation and patronage of the *vaishyas*; while the Vedic religion, which had been the exclusive domain of the brahmins and *kshatryas*, underwent fundamental transformations to widen its social base.

The Classical Age 320–650

The era of the imperial Guptas (320–550 AD) and the reign of Harsha Vardhana (606–647 AD) of Kanauj, during which north India was reunified, comprises the **Classical Age** of Indian history.

Chandra Gupta I (no relation to the Mauryan Guptas) struck coins in 320 AD to celebrate his coronation and marriage to Princess Kumaradevi of the Licchavi tribe, which had re-established itself in the neighbouring territory of Vaishali, north of the Ganges. Chandra Gupta I thus established a powerful kingdom, centred on Magadha, Koshala and Ayodhya, in the Gangetic plain, which controlled the vital East–West trade route, and claimed the title of Great King of Kings (Maharajadhiraja).

His son and heir, Samudra Gupta (c.335–376 AD), expanded the frontiers of the realm from Punjab to Assam; an inscription in Allahabad claimed that he "violently uprooted" nine kings of northern India, humbled eleven more in the south and compelled another five to pay tribute as feudatories. The martial tribes of Rajasthan and the Shakas, who had ruled Malwa and Gujarat for over two hundred years, never did more than pay homage; but Samudra had built the foundations for the second largest empire in pre-medieval India, which reached its apogee under his successor.

Chandra Gupta II (376–415 AD) finally subjugated the Shakas in Gujarat to secure access to the trade of the western coast at the end of the fourth century AD, and reunified the whole of northern India, with the exception of the northwest. He extended his influence by marrying Kuvera, a queen of the Nagas, and marrying his daughter Prabhavati to Rudrasena II of the Vakatakas, whose kingdom included parts of modern Madhya Pradesh, Maharashtra and northwestern Andhra Pradesh.

Fa Hsien, a Chinese Buddhist monk who visited India during the reign of Chandra Gupta II, noted the palaces and free hospitals of Pataliputra and the fact that all respectable Indians were vegetarian. He also mentions discrimination against the Untouchables, who carried gongs to warn passers-by of their polluting presence; but generally, he describes the empire as prosperous, happy and peaceful. The Guptas performed Vedic sacrifices to legitimize their rule, and patronized popular forms of Hinduism, such as devotional religion (*bhakti*) and the worship of images of Vishnu, Shiva and the goddess Shakti in temples, which were crystallizing during the period; but Buddhism continued to thrive and Fa Hsien mentions thousands of monks dwelling at Mathura as well as hundreds in Pataliputra itself.

Patronage of art and literature under the Guptas facilitated the development of a classical idiom that became the exemplar for subsequent creative endeavours. Secular **Sanskrit literature** reached its perfection in the works of Kalidasa, the greatest Indian poet and dramatist, who was a member of Chandra Gupta II's court. The cave paintings of **Ajanta** and **Ellora** inspired Buddhist artists throughout Asia, and Yashodhara's detailed analysis of painting in the fifth century prescribed the classical conventions for the new art form. In **sculpture**, the images of the Buddha produced in Sarnath and Mathura embodied the simple and serene quality of classicism, while there were also the voluptuous mother goddesses of Hinduism.

The formative stages of the northern style of **Hindu temple**, which became India's classic architectural form, also occurred in this era; a fine example survives at **Deogarh**, near Jhansi in central India. Early Hindu temples were comparatively small and simple: an inner sanctuary (*garbha griha*) housing the deity was connected to a larger hall (*mandapa*), where the devotees could congregate to worship. This prototype of the northern Hindu temple has persisted from Gupta times to the present day, but these humble origins subsequently evolved into extravagantly ornate structures.

The era of the Guptas produced great thinkers as well: six systems of **philosophy** (*Nyaya*, *Vaisheshika*, *Sankhya*, *Yoga*, *Mimamsa* and *Vedanta*) evolved, which refuted Buddhism and Jainism. **Vedanta** has continued as the basis of all philosophical studies in India to this day. In the fifth century, the great **astronomer**, Aryabhata, argued that the earth rotated on its own axis while revolving around the sun, and his terse commentary on an anonymous mathematical text assumes an understanding of the decimal system of nine digits and a zero, with place notation for tens and hundreds. The Arabs acknowledged their debt to the "Indian art" of mathematics, and many Western European discoveries and inventions would have been impossible if they had remained encumbered by the Roman system of numerals.

Though the Gupta empire remained relatively peaceful during the long reign of Kumara Gupta, who succeeded Chandra Gupta II, by the time Skanda Gupta came to the throne in 454 AD, western India was again threatened by invasions from Central Asia. Skanda managed to repel White Hun raids, but after his death their disruption of Central Asian trade seriously destabilized the empire. By the end of the fifth century, the Huns had wrested the Punjab from Gupta control, and further incursions early in the sixth century were the death blow to the empire, which had completely disintegrated by 550 AD. Also in the sixth century another wave of Central Asian tribes, including the Gurjaras, displaced the older tribes in Rajasthan and became the founders of the **Rajput** dynasties.

After the demise of the Guptas, northern India again split into rival kingdoms, but the Pushpabhutis of Sthanvishvara (Thanesvar, north of Delhi) had established supremacy by the time **Harsha Vardhana** came to the throne in 606 AD. He reigned for 41 years over an empire that ranged from Gujarat to Bengal, including the Punjab, Kashmir and Nepal, and moved his capital to **Kanauj** in the wake of his eastern conquests. Even the king of Assam acknowledged his influence, but his attempts to advance into the Deccan were emphatically repulsed by Pulakeshin II of the Chalukyas. Harsha possessed considerable talent as well as untiring energy; in addition to his martial achievements and ceaseless touring, he wrote three dramas and found time to indulge a love of philosophy and literature. The life of Harsha (*Harshacharita*) by Bana, his court poet, is the first historically authentic Indian biography.

Harsha's empire was essentially feudal, with most of the defeated kings retaining their thrones as vassals, and when he died without heirs in 647 AD north India once again fragmented into independent kingdoms.

Kingdoms of central and South India 500–1250

After the collapse of Harsha's empire, significant events took place in the Deccan and Tamil Nadu. Aryan influences were assimilated into Dravidian culture throughout the era of the **Pallavas**, which began when they captured Kanchipuram early in the fourth century and lasted until they were overthrown by a revived Chola dynasty in the ninth century. The upper strata of society increasingly adopted Aryan ideas, but as the indigenous culture reacted to assert itself among the lower strata, a distinctive Tamil culture emerged from the synthesis.

The history of the period was dominated by conflicts between three major kingdoms. The **Pandyas** of Madurai had their own regional kingdom by the sixth century; the **Chalukyas** of Vatapi (Badami in Mysore) had expanded their kingdom into the Deccan when the Vakataka dynasty collapsed in the middle of the sixth century; and the **Pallavas** had supplanted the Satavahanas in the Andhra region and made Kanchipuram their capital.

Under Mahendravarman I, a contemporary of Harsha at the start of the seventh century, the Pallavas came into conflict with the Chalukyas over the region of Vengi in the Krishna-Godavari valley. They remained at war until the middle of the eighth century, intermittently harassed by the Pandyas further south. Both the Pallavas and the Chalukyas enlisted the support of other kingdoms at different times during the protracted struggle – the **Cheras** of Kerala, who made alliances with both sides, avoided direct involvement in the conflict – but their military strength was so evenly matched that neither was able to gain the ascendancy. Eventually the Chalukya dynasty was overthrown in 753 by a feudatory, Dantidurga, the founder of the Rashtrakuta kingdom. The Pallavas survived their archenemies by about a hundred years, then succumbed to a combined attack of the Pandyas and the Cholas.

The **Rashtrakutas** exploited the instability in the north by attempts to capture the trade routes of the Ganges Valley, and Indra III gained possession of Kanauj for a brief period, but ultimately the campaigns drained the kingdom's resources.

Meanwhile, the **Cholas** were gaining ground in Tamil Nadu; they conquered the region of Thanjavur in the ninth century, and Parantaka I, who came to power in 907 AD, captured Madurai from the Pandyas. The Cholas were defeated by the Rashtrakutas in the middle of the tenth century, who were themselves replaced by the revived "Later" Chalukyas in 973 AD, allowing the Cholas to regain lost territories and expand further during the eleventh and twelfth centuries.

Rajaraja I campaigned against the allied powers of Kerala, Ceylon and the Pandyas to break their control of western trade and combat competition from the Arab traders, who were supported by Kerala. **Rajendra I**, who succeeded his father in 1014 AD, annexed the southern territories of the Chalukyas, renewing the campaigns against Kerala and Ceylon, and initiating a northern offensive, which reached the banks of the Ganges. Rajendra did not hold his northern conquests for long, but was successful in protecting Indian commercial interests in southeast Asia.

By the end of the eleventh century the Cholas were supreme in the south, but incessant campaigning had exhausted their resources. Ironically, their destruction of the Chalukyas laid the seeds of their own downfall. Former Chalukya feudatories, such as the **Yadavas** of Devagiri in the northern Deccan and the **Hoysalas**, around modern Mysore, set up their own kingdoms; the latter attacked the Cholas from the west while the Pandyas directed a new offensive from the south. By the thirteenth century, the **Pandyas** had superseded the Cholas as South India's major power; the Yadavas and the Hoysalas controlled the Deccan until the advent of the Turkish sultans of Delhi in the fourteenth century.

Despite constant political conflicts this period was very much the classical age of the south. The ascendancy of the Cholas was complemented by the crystallization of Tamil culture; the religious, artistic, and institutional patterns of this period dominated the culture of the south and influenced developments elsewhere in the peninsula. In the sphere of religion for instance, the great philosophers **Shankara** and Ramanuja, as well as the Tamil and Maharashtrian saints, had a significant impact on Hinduism in north India.

Regional kingdoms in north India 650–1250

In north India, Harsha's death was followed by a century of confusion, with assorted kingdoms competing to control the Gangetic valley. In time, the **Pratiharas**, descendants of the Rajasthani Gurjaras, and the **Palas** of Bihar and Bengal emerged as the main rivals.

The Pala king Dharmapala (770–810) was the first to gain the initiative, by taking Kanauj; however, the Pratiharas wrested it back soon after his death. They remained in the ascendant during the ninth century, but were weakened by repeated incursions from the Deccan by the **Rashtrakutas**, who briefly occupied Kanauj in 916. The Pratiharas regained their capital, but the tripartite struggle sapped their strength and they were unable to repel the Turkish invasion of Kanauj in 1018. At the start of the eleventh century the Palas again pushed west as far as Varanasi, but had to abandon the campaign to defend their homelands in Bengal against the Chola king Rajendra.

The struggle for possession of Kanauj depleted the resources of the three competing powers and resulted in their almost simultaneous decline. In northern India, just as in the south, the tendency of feudatories of large kingdoms to assert their independence brought several small states into being. Kingdoms such as Nepal, Kamarupa (Assam), Kashmir, Orissa, the eastern Chalukyas and the Gangas of the east coast developed their own cultural identities. Regional histories and dynastic genealogies were written, local customs and literature were patronized, and the kingdoms competed to outdo each other in building temples.

In **Orissa**, small kingdoms in the Mahanadi and Brahmani valleys had co-existed for nearly five hundred years when the Somavamshi dynasty united western and central Orissa in the eleventh century, and established its capital at **Bhubaneswar**. The temples they constructed demonstrate a notable continuity from the earliest days in the eighth century, to the magnificent Lingaraja temple, dated around 1000 AD. The royal cult of Jagannath (Vishnu), with its "juggernaut" car festival and the gigantic temple at **Puri**, were cultural manifestations of the political unification completed by the eastern Gangas of Kalinga in the twelfth century. The stunning chariot temple dedicated to the sun god Surya at **Konarak** in the thirteenth century represents the aesthetic climax of these regional developments.

The **Rajputs**, so influential in the culture and politics of medieval India, were descended from the sixth-century Central Asian invaders. They attained respectability in keeping with the Puranic traditions by acquiring solar or lunar genealogies and adopting *kshatrya* status. By the tenth century, the most important clans, like the Pariharas (a branch of the Pratiharas) of south Rajasthan, the Chamanas or Chauhans of Shakambhari and Ajmer, and the Chalukyas or Solankis of Kathiawar, had all established regional kingdoms. Rajput clans in western and central India included the **Chandellas** of Bundelkhand, who produced the magnificent group of temples at **Khajuraho**, the Guhilas of Chittaurgarh, the Tomaras in Haryana, and the Kalachuris of Tripuri near Jabalpur.

The Rajputs fought among each other incessantly, however, and failed to grasp the significance of a new factor, which entered the politics of north India at the start of the eleventh century. **Mahmud**, a Turkish chieftain who had established a powerful kingdom at Ghazni in Afghanistan, made seventeen plundering raids into the plains of India between 1000 and 1027. Mathura, Thanesvar, Kanauj and Somnath in Saurashtra were all looted to enhance the greatness of Ghazni and only the astuteness of the Chandellas of Bundelkhand, who agreed to pay tribute, saved the temples of Khajuraho from destruction.

The three most powerful Rajputs of northern India, Prithviraja Chamana, Jahacchandra Gahadavala and Paramardideva Chandella, were in a state of three-way war when Mohammed of Ghur supplanted the line of Mahmud, seized the Ghaznavid possessions in the Punjab at the end of the twelfth century, and focused his attention on the wealthy lands further east. **Prithviraja III**, the legendary hero of the Chauhans, patched together an alliance to defeat the Turkish warlord at **Tarain** (near Thanesvar) in 1191; but Mohammed returned the next year with a superior force, defeated the Rajputs; he had Prithviraja executed before returning home, leaving his generals to complete the conquest and establish what became known as the **Slave Dynasty**.

The Delhi Sultanate 1206–1526

The **Delhi Sultanate** was to be the major political force in north India from the thirteenth to the sixteenth century, its power and territories fluctuating with the abilities of successive rulers. Although it never succeeded in welding together an all-India empire, the impact of Islam on Indian culture reverberated for centuries throughout the subcontinent.

Mohammed was assassinated in 1206 within a few years of his return to Ghur. His empire disintegrated, to leave his Turkish slave general, **Qutb-ud-din-Aiback**, as the autonomous ruler of the Indian territories and founder of the first "slave dynasty" of the sultanate. Aiback died four years later – before the Qutb Minar, his victory tower, in Delhi could be completed – and his son-in-law **Iltutmish** (1211–36) inherited the task of securing the sultanate's tenuous hold on northern India. When Genghis Khan annihilated the world from which the ancestors of Iltutmish had come, it gave him an added incentive to consolidate his power base in India. Iltutmish had extended the sultanate's territories from the Sind to Bengal by the time he died in 1236, but the subsequent three decades were critical. His daughter, Sultana Raziyya, succeeded but was murdered in 1240, and not until Balaban, Raziyya's chief huntsman and member of her father's palace guard, took control in 1266 did the sultanate attain any degree of stability.

Meanwhile, the **Mongols** had returned in 1241. Although internecine strife within the Mongol empire from 1260–61 offered a temporary reprieve, the accession of the Khalji dynasty in 1290 coincided with a renewed threat from the Chaghatai Mongols. Their raids extended beyond the Punjab and they even laid siege to Delhi for two months in 1303. Nevertheless, **Ala-ud-din-Khalji** (1296–1315) energetically enforced Islamic rule over the autonomous Hindu states, which were a constant source of aggravation. Having conquered Gujarat and the Rajput fortresses of Ranthambor, Chittaurgarh, Sevana and Jalor in a series of expeditions between 1299 and 1311, he turned his attention to the Deccan and the south where he exacted tribute from the Yadavas of Devagiri, the Kakatiyas of Telengana, and the Pandyas. His aspirations to build a stable empire were dashed, however, when Gujarat, Chittaurgarh and Devagiri all re-asserted their independence before his death in 1315.

A fresh imperial impetus came from the **Tughluq** dynasty, which succeeded the Khaljis in 1320. Under **Mohammed bin Tughluq** (1325–51), the sultanate reached its maximum extent, comparable in size to Ashoka's empire. Unfortunately, Mohammed weakened the empire by his attempts to finance his ambitions. He provoked a peasant uprising in the Doab by increasing the revenue demand to pay for an expedition to Khurasan in Central Asia, and later tried to introduce a token currency to pay the troops, which had to be withdrawn. He then made a controversial and abortive attempt to relocate his capital in a more central position at Devagiri (renamed Daulatabad) in the Deccan. Revolts signalled the first phase in the collapse of the Delhi Sultanate: Malabar, Bengal and Telengana all seceded between 1334 and 1339. The Bahmani dynasty became the autonomous rulers of the Deccan in 1347, and the new Hindu kingdom of **Vijayanagar** took advantage of the decline of the sultanate's authority to extend its influence. From its capital near Hampi, Vijayanagar dominated the region south of the Krishna and Tungabhadra rivers between the middle of the fourteenth century and 1565, when an alliance of Muslim kingdoms brought it down.

Firoz Shah Tughluq (1351–88), who re-established the capital at Delhi, stemmed the tide to some extent with the comparative mildness of his rule. He is credited with an impressive list of public works, including the building of mosques, colleges, reservoirs, hospitals, public baths, bridges and towns – especially **Jaunpur**, near Varanasi, which became a major centre of Islamic culture. However, by reverting to a decentralized administrative system he fostered the rise of semi-independent warlords, who became increasingly antagonistic under the last of the Tughluqs.

Family squabbles over the throne after Firoz Shah's death in 1388 further weakened the sultanate, and the degeneracy of his successors made it vulnerable to external predators. After **Timur**, the Central Asian conqueror known to the West as Tamburlaine, sacked Delhi in 1398, autonomous sultanates emerged in Jaunpur, Malwa and Gujarat; the Hindu kingdoms of Marwar and Mewar were established in Rajasthan; and small principalities even nearer the capital appeared at Kalpi, Mahoba and Gwalior. The Delhi Sultanate had been reduced to just one of several competing Muslim states in northern India.

After the death of the last Tughluq, Delhi was seized by Khizr Khan (1414–21), who had been an officer of the governor of Multan and Lahore appointed by Timur before he left India. In 37 years, Khizr's **Sayyid** dynasty lost Multan and was repeatedly harassed by the Sharqi sultans of Jaunpur. The sultanate experienced a modest revival under the more energetic rule of the Afghan Lodis, especially **Sikander Lodi** (1489–1517), who annexed Jaunpur and Bihar; but his successor, Ibrahim, was unable to overcome the dissension among his Afghan feudatories. Eventually, one enlisted the support of Babur, the ruler of Kabul, who defeated Ibrahim at Panipat in 1526.

By the time of the sultanate, India had considerable experience of assimilating foreigners; Greeks, Scythians, Parthians and Huns had all been politically, socially and culturally absorbed over the centuries. However, the sultanate brought its own theologians and social institutions. **Islam** presented a new pattern of life, far less easy for the xenophobic Hindu social system to accommodate. Nonetheless, a process of mutual acculturation did slowly evolve. Despite the Muslims' iconoclastic zeal, Hinduism found common ground with some aspects of Islam: elements of Sufi mysticism and Hindu devotionalism were combined in the teachings of many saints. **Kabir** (1440–1518), in particular, denied any contradiction between Muslim and Hindu conceptions of god, preached social egalitarianism and was claimed by adherents of both creeds as their own. The replacement of Sanskrit by Persian as the official language of the administration encouraged regional languages; **Urdu** resulted from a fusion of Hindi and Persian using an Arabic script. A stylistically unified architecture began to develop, which flourished under the **Moghuls**; and new social ideas were introduced which became integral to Indian life.

The Moghul Empire 1526–1761

Babur, a descendant of both Timur and Genghis Khan, had gained control of Delhi and Agra by defeating Ibrahim, but found his position threatened by the Rajput confederacy, led by Rana Sanga of Mewar, south of Agra, and the Afghan chiefs, who had united under the Sultan of Bengal. Babur reacted vigorously by declaring a religious war (*jihad*) against the rana, annihilating the Mewar forces at the battle of Kanwaha in 1527, before turning his attention to the Afghan uprisings in the east. Although he crushed the allied armies of the Afghans and the Sultan of Bengal in 1529, his failing health forced him to retire to Lahore, where he died in 1530.

Babur possessed many talents: as well as a brilliant military campaigner, he was a skilful diplomat, a poet and a man of letters. He constructed a loosely knit empire, extending from Badakshan and Kabul to the borders of Bengal, in just four years – his personal magnetism commanding loyalty and inspiring his warrior chiefs to fresh endeavours when they yearned to depart the hot and dusty plains of India for the cool mountains of their homeland. His very readable memoirs reveal a man of sensibility, taste and humour, who loved music, poetry, sport and natural beauty.

Humayun, his son and successor, was by contrast a volatile character, alternating between bursts of enthusiastic activity and indolence. He subdued Malwa and Gujarat, only to lose both while he "took his pleasure" in Agra. **Sher Khan Sur** of south Bihar soon assumed the leadership of the Afghan opposition and after two resounding defeats Humayun had to seek refuge in Persia in 1539. A much cleverer politician than the hot-headed Humayun, Sher Shah was quick to consolidate his territorial gains in the northwest, setting up an administrative centre in Delhi, from where he waged audacious and successful campaigns in Punjab and Sind. He later subjugated several of the Rajput dynasties which had proved troublesome for the Moghuls, and it was during a siege against the toughest of these at Kalinjar that the Afghan was killed, when a rocket rebounded off the fort's walls and exploded a pile of weapons next to him. With Sher Shah's death in 1545 Humayun took advantage of the ensuing chaos to stage a return. His armies, led by Bairam Khan and Prince Akbar, crushed Sikander Sur at Sirhund in 1555; but Humayun died the following year after a fall in the Purana Qila in Delhi leaving **Akbar**, his major contribution to the Moghul empire, to succeed where he had failed.

Akbar, aged only 13, was lucky to have Bairam Khan as guardian and regent to help him survive the crisis of the first four years. Bairam, a loyal general and an experienced politician, overcame the challenge of the Hindu general Hemu at the second battle of Panipat in 1556, recovered Gwalior and Jaunpur, and handed over a consolidated kingdom of north India to Akbar in 1560. The young emperor quickly established his own control of the government in dramatic fashion. First Bairam Khan was provoked into a revolt by religious adversaries of the Moghuls and killed. Then challenges to Akbar's rule by a group centred around Adham Khan, the son of his former wet nurse, were systematically snuffed out. In 1562 the emperor discovered Adham Khan himself attempting to murder the chief minister, and executed his young adversary by throwing him from the palace walls.

Securing the empire

Akbar's first military campaigns were against the **Rajputs**; and within a decade he had secured the flank of the Moghul bases at Delhi and Agra by subduing all the Rajput domains except Mewar (Udaipur). Akbar possessed the personal magnetism of his grandfather and was a brilliant general, who above all had the gift of rapid mobilization. In 1573 he marched his army 1000 kilometres in nine days to defeat astonished insurgents in Gujarat. He had secured Bengal, the richest province, by 1576, and by the end of his reign in 1605 he controlled a broad sweep of territory north of the River Godavari, which reached from the Bay of Bengal to Kandahar and Badakshan, with the exception of Gondwana and Assam.

Akbar was as clever a politician and administrator as he was a successful general. After subduing the Rajputs, he diplomatically bestowed imperial honours on their chiefs by making them military commanders and provincial governors. By giving them autonomy within their own states, he made the Rajputs partners in the empire and thereby secured the acquiescence of the whole Hindu community; his marriage to a Jaipur princess was an important symbolic statement of this partnership.

The imperial service, in which Akbar involved both Moghuls and Rajputs, was carefully crafted to ensure that the nobility were hereditary as an aristocratic class but not as individuals. His officers – *mansabdars*, holders of commands – were arranged in grades that indicated how many troops they were obliged to maintain for imperial service. A commander of 5000 was both an important state official and a noble; but the titles were not hereditary, being conferred by appointment and promotion, and the *mansabdars*' salaries were paid in cash so that they lacked a territorial basis for insurrection.

The creation of an administrative framework, which sustained the empire by its efficient collection of revenue, was one of Akbar's most enduring achievements.

He collected information about local revenue, productivity and price variations to arrive at a schedule, acceptable to the peasant farmers but also generating maximum profit for the state. Akbar recruited leaders of local communities and holders of land rights (*zamindars*) to collect the revenue in cash.

In addition to involving Hindu *zamindars* and nobles in economic and political life, Akbar adopted a conscious policy of religious toleration aimed at widening the base of his power. In particular, he abolished the despised poll tax on non-Muslims (*jizya*), and tolls on Hindu pilgrimages. A mystical experience in about 1575 inspired him to instigate a series of discussions with orthodox Muslim leaders (*ulema*), Portuguese priests from Goa, Hindu brahmins, Jains and Zoroastrians at his famous house of worship (*ibadat khana*) in Fatehpur Sikri. The discussions culminated in a politico-religious crisis and a revolt, organized by the alienated *ulema*, which Akbar ruthlessly crushed in 1581. He subsequently evolved a theory of divine kingship incorporating the toleration of all religions, and thereby restored the concept of imperial sanctity with which the early Hindu emperors had surrounded themselves, while declaring his nonsectarian credentials.

Akbar was a liberal patron of the arts and his eclecticism encouraged a fruitful Muslim-Hindu dialogue. Music, which he loved, was especially enriched by this mutual appreciation. Akbar ranks alongside Ashoka as one of the great statesmen of the world, and his reign laid the foundations for a century of stable government under the succeeding Moghuls.

The height of Moghul power

The reigns of **Jahangir** (1605–27) and **Shah Jahan** (1628–57) together represent the great age of the Moghuls, whose reputation for magnificence, pomp and luxury did not escape the notice of Europe and is recorded in the writings of Bernier and Dryden. It was a time of brisk economic activity notable for artistic and architectural splendour, as well as the excesses of imperial indulgence.

Despite his reputation for drunken cruelty, Jahangir was a connoisseur of art. It was under his patronage that the art of the **miniature**, imported from Persia, reached its perfection in Moghul painting before being further evolved and enriched by Hindu artists, especially in Rajasthan. Jahangir is best remembered for his great devotion to his wife Nur Jahan, which he celebrated with a special issue of gold coins (*mohur*). Nur Jahan commissioned the building of the beautiful Itmad-ud-Daulah, a magnificent tomb for her parents in Agra, sometimes said to be the blueprint for the Taj Mahal.

In the political sphere, Jahangir settled the conflict with Mewar, extended the empire by subjugating the last of the Afghan domains in east Bengal and Orissa, and restrained the threat from the Deccan by defeating the combined forces of the Nizamshahi kingdom and the Adil Shahis of Bijapur in 1620. However, the combination of failing health and political intrigues involving his beloved Nur Jahan prevented him from completing his Deccan campaign, and Persia's capture of Kandahar in 1622 dented the empire's prestige.

When Shah Jahan, Jahangir's son, came to power in 1628, he ruthlessly executed all the male descendants of his brothers and uncles. He displayed all the imperial qualities of administrative and military ability and, like his predecessors, was a great lover and patron of the arts, especially architecture. Delhi's **Red Fort** and **Jami Masjid**, Agra Fort, and the splendid **Taj Mahal**, the mausoleum he created for his wife Mumtaz, are the results of his personal inspiration and artistic direction. Thus he actively participated in the apogee of Indo-Persian culture, although his political achievements were less notable.

Shah Jahan attempted to deal with the ascendancy of the Marathas in the Deccan by conquering the Nizamshahi kingdom in 1636. Six years later, he sent his third son **Aurangzeb** to govern the province. Regarding territorial gains in the region as the most promising route to the Moghul throne, the ambitious young prince (a devout Muslim and experienced military campaigner in his mid-thirties), forged an alliance with the wealthy Persian adventurer **Mir Jumla** to mount an attack on the latter's former employer, the sultan of **Golconda**. The two-pronged invasion met with quick success, overwhelming Hyderabad. However, just as Aurangzeb's army was poised to storm the great fort, word came from Delhi to withdraw. Behind the scenes, **Dara Shikoh**, Shah Jahan's eldest son, had persuaded his father to thwart his brother's venture, recognizing that it could impede his chances of succession. Exactly the same thing happened the following year, when Aurangzeb laid siege to Bijapur.

The battle lines were now drawn for an eventual **civil war** between the two brothers, which erupted in 1657 when Shah Jahan fell seriously ill. He recovered, but not before Aurangzeb had seen off Dara Shikoh, wiping out his army in a series of encounters that culminated in a rout at Ajmer, and eliminated a son and nephew. The thirty-year reign of the ailing emperor ended ignominiously. Aurangzeb had him incarcerated in Agra fort, where he lived out his remaining days in an opium-induced stupor gazing wistfully down the Yamuna at the mausoleum of his beloved Mumtaz.

Though lacking the charisma of Akbar or Babur, Aurangzeb evoked an awe of his own and proved to be a firm and capable administrator, who retained his grip on the increasingly unsettled empire until his death at the age of 88. In contrast to the pomp of the other Moghuls, his lifestyle was pious and disciplined. In later life the ruthless statesman became an austere sage, who fasted and spent long hours in prayer.

In the first 23 years of his rule, Aurangzeb maintained a continuity with Shah Jahan's administration and ostensibly contained disruptive elements; but he failed to solve the problems which eventually erupted after his death and caused the dissolution of the empire. The **Maratha** chief, **Shivaji**, who humiliated the Moghul army early in Aurangzeb's reign, was a constant threat. Although defeated by the Rajput Jai Singh and forced to visit the Moghul court in 1666, Shivaji made a daring escape from Agra, rallied his resources, and was soon again the master of a compact and well-organized kingdom in western India, to which the Muslim kingdoms of Bijapur and Golconda were eager to ally themselves against the imperialism of Aurangzeb.

The militant separatism of the **Sikhs** was brutally suppressed when Guru Tegh Bahadur was executed in 1675 for refusing to embrace Islam; but his son, Guru Gobind, transformed the religious community into a military sect which became increasingly powerful in the Punjab. Aurangzeb's confrontation with the Rajputs over the Jodhpur succession in 1678 resulted in another war, and the alienation of most of the Rajput partners in the empire.

Meanwhile, religious and economic discontent turned the passive support of the Hindu community, cultivated by Akbar, into indifference, disdain and even armed conflict. Aurangzeb aligned himself with the orthodox Sunni Muslims of the *ulema*, who rejected the syncretism encouraged by Akbar's nonsectarian policies. Hindu places of worship were again the object of iconoclasm, the tax on non-Muslims (*jizya*) was reintroduced, religious fairs were banned, and discriminatory duties were imposed on Hindu merchants. The Jats and the Satnamis of the Agra-Delhi region rebelled over insufferable increases in land revenue demands, and elsewhere peasant farmers rallied behind Maratha, Sikh and Rajput landholders to oppose imperial exploitation.

Aurangzeb crushed the agrarian rebellions and turned his attention to expansion. He transferred his base to the Deccan in 1681 and spent the rest of his life overseeing the subjugation of the Bijapur and Golconda kingdoms and trying to contain the Maratha rebellion. In 1689, he succeeded in capturing and executing Shivaji's son, Shambhuji, and by 1698 the Moghuls had overrun almost the whole of the peninsula. The Marathas had been suppressed, but they re-emerged under the Peshwa leadership in the eighteenth century to harass the remnants of Moghul power and even to challenge the political ambitions of the British.

Aurangzeb did manage to extend the empire during his long reign of over 48 years, but the newly acquired lands in the south were difficult to administer, his nobles were divided by factionalism, and the disruptive consequences of his policies were to be critical in the eighteenth-century collapse of the empire.

The decline of the Moghuls

Bahadur Shah, Aurangzeb's son, succeeded in 1707 and briefly restored the situation, but after his death in 1712 the disintegration of the empire and power struggles between would-be successors dominated events. By the 1720s the nizam of Hyderabad and the nawabs of Avadh and Bengal were effectively independent; the Marathas overwhelmed the rich province of Malwa in 1738; Hindu landholders everywhere were in revolt; and Nadir Shah of Persia dealt a serious blow to the empire's prestige when he invaded India, defeated the Moghul army and sacked Delhi in 1739.

The **Maratha** kingdom had by now been transformed into a confederacy under the leadership of a hereditary brahmin minister, called the Peshwa. By 1750 the Marathas had spread right across central India to Orissa, had attacked Bengal, and were insinuating themselves into the imperial politics of Delhi. When Delhi was again looted in 1757, this time by an independent Afghan force led by Ahmad Shah Abdali, distraught Moghul ministers called in the Marathas to rescue the situation. The Marathas drove the Afghans back to the Punjab; but Ahmad Shah advanced again in 1761 and overwhelmed them at the third battle of Panipat. Any designs he had on the imperial throne were dashed, however, when his soldiers mutinied over arrears of pay.

New centres of Moghul culture developed, notably at Murshidabad, Lucknow, Hyderabad, and Faizabad, but the political strength of the empire had fragmented and north India was left in a power vacuum for the next forty years. It was against this background that the European trading companies, and the East India Company in particular, were able to establish their trading posts and develop their ambitions.

The East India Company 1600–1857

The prosperity of foreign trade in India attracted European interest as early as 1498, when **Vasco da Gama** landed on the Malabar coast. During the ensuing hundred years Portuguese, Dutch, English, French and Danish companies all set up coastal trading centres, exporting textiles, sugar, indigo and saltpetre.

The **East India Company**, established by eighty London merchants in 1599 and chartered by Queen Elizabeth I on December 31, 1600, arrived in Surat in 1608. Within thirty years 27 trading posts had been established, including **Fort George** on the Coromandel coast, out of which Madras developed. The enclave of Bombay, part of Catherine of Braganza's dowry in her marriage to Charles II, became crown property in 1665, was leased to the Company from 1668, and soon replaced Surat as its headquarters. The Moghul emperor permitted the Company to establish a new settlement at **Fort William**, which grew into Calcutta, and in 1701 the British received a grant of the revenues of the Twenty-Four Parganas near Calcutta from Aurangzeb, in recognition of the growing importance of their trade in the economy of Bengal.

It was in the **south**, however, that European trading initiatives first took on a political significance, after the onset of the War of the Austrian Succession in 1740. Armed conflict between the French and English trading companies along the Carnatic coast developed into a war over the succession of the nizam of Hyderabad. The British victory and the Peace of Paris in 1763 eclipsed French ambitions in India. Meanwhile, **Robert Clive**'s defeat of the rebellious young nawab of Bengal at Plassey in 1757 had decisively augmented British power; by 1765 the enervated Moghul emperor legally recognized the Company as an Indian potentate by granting the revenue management (*diwani*) of Bengal, Bihar and Orissa to Lord Clive.

The governor-generals

Ironically, the East India Company's mastery of the rich province soon brought it to the brink of bankruptcy, provoking parliamentary intervention in its affairs. The **Regulating Act** of 1773 appointed a **governor-general** of the Company's three provinces in Calcutta, Bombay and Madras; and in 1784 the India Act established a President of the Board of Control in London to oversee the governor-general in Calcutta.

Warren Hastings, the first governor-general, made the Company's colony in Bengal politically viable, successfully defending it against the jealous governors of Bombay and Madras, and the internal dissent of his Council in England. His major achievement was to protect Bombay and Madras against the assaults from a coalition of Marathas, the nizam of Hyderabad and Haidar Ali, the sultan of Mysore; but he also laid the foundations of British administration in India by replacing the Indian revenue-collecting deputies with a Board of Revenue in Calcutta and English collectors in the districts. **Lord Cornwallis** completed the reforms by fixing the land revenues in the Permanent Land Settlement of 1793; by dividing Company service into separate political and commercial branches; and by a further Europeanization of the administration.

The governor-generals were charged with nonaggression and administrative reform until the end of the eighteenth century, but the Napoleonic Wars allowed **Lord Wellesley** to follow his imperial instincts. His swift defeat of **Tipu Sultan** of Mysore, the company's best-organized and most resolute enemy, a confrontation with the Marathas, and the subjugation of the nizam of Hyderabad resulted in the annexation of considerable territories in Andhra Pradesh, Tamil Nadu, Mysore, the Upper Doab, Gujarat and Maharashtra; nearly all the other rulers in India recognized British suzerainty by 1805. There was a brief respite in the expansion until Napoleon's defeat in 1815, but the last vestiges of Maratha opposition were crushed by 1823, and the absorption of Sind, the Sikh kingdom of the Punjab, Kashmir, Assam, Chittagong and Lower Burma by 1852 established **British supremacy** in India.

The new British colony, however, was in a state of social and economic collapse as a result of the almost incessant conflicts of the previous hundred years. High revenue assessments had depressed the condition of both peasants and *zamindars*; peasants deserted their lands, land revenue receipts were falling, and there were local revolts and grain riots in the 1830s. Gangs of robbers (*dacoits*) had reached epidemic proportions, and their activities curtailed commerce between states and towns. The cult of the **thugs**, who robbed and murdered in honour of the goddess Kali, spread terror all over central and northern India.

Inspired by Burke's ideas, Utilitarianism and the Radical Humanism in Europe, **Lord William Bentinck**'s reforms as governor-general did little, however, to alleviate the situation. The campaign against the thugs received general approval, but his suppression of the practice of widows joining their husbands on funeral pyres (*sati*) was seen as an attack on the values of traditional Hindu society.

The Company's policy of government patronage for Indian learning was replaced after 1835 by a resolution to promote "European literature and science". Schools and colleges imparting Western knowledge through the medium of the English language were established, and English replaced Persian as the official state language. The educated elite and intellectuals like Ram Mohan Roy had already adopted Western ideas, but such cultural imperialism aggravated the unrest and distrust of the majority.

James Andrew Broun Ramsey, governor-general between 1848 and 1856, was a firm believer in the benefits of **Westernization**. He promoted Western education by initiating plans for the first three Indian universities with Sir Charles Wood, and embarked on a series of public works, including the development of the railway and telegraph systems. These were commendable achievements, but their Westernizing influence increased social tension. His controversial policy of annexing dependent but autonomous states, which brought **Oudh**, two Maratha kingdoms and five other states under direct administration, caused considerable resentment among the dispossessed and alarm among the Indian ruling classes.

The First War of Independence

Against this general background of unease, discontent had been growing in the army, which had been increasingly deployed overseas during the previous two decades – a practice resented on religious grounds by the many brahmins it contained. The cows' and pigs' grease on the cartridges of the new Enfield rifle, polluting to both Hindus and Muslims, convinced the soldiers that there was a conspiracy against their religious beliefs and sparked the revolt. The **Indian Mutiny** – the "First War of Independence" – started with a rising at Meerut on May 10, 1857, and Delhi was seized the next day. The last Moghul emperor Bahadur Shah in Delhi, the dispossessed court at Lucknow, and the exiled members of the Maratha court at Kanpur all supported the cause and some landlords participated in the rebellion.

The British authorities were caught by surprise. The Crimean War had reduced the number of their regiments in India, and their forces were concentrated around Calcutta or the Punjab. However, the revolt failed to cut their lines of communication, and crucially the **Sikh** regiments in the Punjab remained loyal. Delhi was retaken by a column from the Punjab in late September, **Kanpur** (Cawnpore) was relieved in the same month, and the final recapture of **Lucknow** in March 1858 effectively broke the back of the Mutiny. The rebels fought on under the leadership of Tantia Topi, and the valiant rani of Jhansi in central India, until they too were crushed in June 1858. The governing powers of the East India Company were abolished and the British crown assumed the administration of India through an appointed viceroy in the same year. Henceforth, British India was no longer merely a massive trade operation, but a fully fledged independent kingdom, or **Raj** – the term which would over time come to denote the period of British rule in the subcontinent.

The Raj and Indian nationalism 1857–1947

India played a key role in the politics of **British imperialism**, especially in the rivalry with France and Russia during this period. Its army became an instrument of British foreign policy: in the Afghan Wars, attempting to create a buffer state to block Russia's advance in Central Asia, and in the Anglo-Burmese Wars to check the French expansion in Indo-China. It was also used to protect British interests beyond the Indian subcontinent as far afield as Abyssinia and Hong Kong.

As a British colony, India assumed a new position in the world economy. Its trade benefited from the British development of the railways, and Indian businessmen began to invest in a range of industries, including the manufacture of textiles, iron and steel. However, India subsidized the British economy as a source of cheap raw materials and as a market for manufactured goods – its own economy and agriculture remained underdeveloped, and the growth of the gross national product was outstripped by increases in population.

British civil servants dominated the higher echelons of the administration, imposing Western notions of progress on the indigenous social structure. Tenurial systems based on ownership rather than land use, irrigation schemes, the suppression of social customs offensive to humanist ideals, the railways and the introduction of a Western judiciary often involved policies contrary to existing Indian interests. At the same time, the propagation of the English language and the Western knowledge to which it gave access resulted in the emergence of a new **middle class** of civil servants, landlords and professionals, whose consciousness of an Indian national identity steadily increased.

Within thirty years of the Mutiny, the history of the British in India becomes essentially a chronicle of the struggle for **Independence**. By the start of the twentieth century the British conception of empire involved a contradiction between liberal rhetoric and the fact of territorial, economic and intellectual expansion. By World War I, the imperial incentive had been swept away by the realization that Indian independence was unavoidable; the only problem remaining was how to relinquish suzerainty.

Awareness of national identity first found expression in local associations and public demonstrations about specific issues; but when the liberalism of Gladstone was confronted by a growing Indian disaffection while Lord Ripon was viceroy, the British showed their willingness to conciliate the Indian educated classes by giving their official blessing to the foundation of the first all-India political organization, the **Indian National Congress**, in 1885. It began modestly with only seventy affluent public men as delegates, who advocated limited reforms and a consolidation of union with Britain; but by 1900 Gopal Krishna **Gokhale** and Bal Gangadhar **Tilak**, both Maratha brahmins, had emerged as leaders of the moderates and the extremists respectively. By 1905 Tilak had persuaded Congress to adopt self-government as a political aim.

A romantic imperialist who believed that it was Britain's duty to protect India's past and educate it for the future, **Lord Curzon** began his second term of office as viceroy by sending the Younghusband expedition to Lhasa in 1904. When he decided on the equally controversial partition of Bengal in 1905, it precipitated the first major confrontations with the government. There were widespread protests: Tilak proposed a no-tax campaign and a boycott of British goods, and when the government crushed the protests Bengali terrorists employed even more radical tactics including bombings and assassinations.

In 1906, concerns about the predominantly Hindu interests of Congress led to the foundation of the **All-India Muslim League** to represent the Muslims, who made up a quarter of India's population. A Liberal landslide in Great Britain produced the Morley-Minto Reforms in 1909, which paved the way for Indian participation in provincial executive councils and made allowance for separate Muslim representation. Tilak was imprisoned that year for incitement to violence. The reversal of the partition of Bengal was announced at the **Great Durbar** of 1911, held in honour of the new king George V and his queen, and the capital was moved to **Delhi**.

During World War I, the British conflict with the sultan of Turkey – still considered to be the spiritual head (*khalifa*) of Indian Muslims – provoked further demonstrations. Tilak returned to found a **Home Rule League** in 1916, and made the Lucknow Pact with the Muslims in support of their *khalifa* movement. The British responded with the Royal Proclamation of 1917, which promised a gradual development of dominion-style self-government; and two years later the Montagu-Chelmsford Reforms attempted to implement the declaration. However, legislation authorizing internment without trial, also passed in 1919, seemed to contradict these promises; the Muslim population were alarmed by the collapse of Turkey and the masses were becoming more restless.

Gandhi and Independence

At this point, **Mohandas Karamchand Gandhi** – hailed as the Mahatma or "Great Soul" – took up the initiative. The Indian-style one-day strike (*hartal*) he proposed was organized in all the major cities, but feelings ran so high that there were riots, which were mercilessly crushed by the government. In particular, General Dyer dispersed the Jallianwalla Bagh meeting in **Amritsar** on April 13, 1919 by firing on the unarmed crowd, killing 379 and wounding 1200 (see p.614 for more details). The racial bitterness invoked by the atrocity inspired Gandhi's **Non Co-operation Movement**, but by 1922 further acts of violence induced him to call off the campaign just before he was imprisoned.

Born in Porbander in Gujarat, Mahatma Gandhi had been educated as a lawyer in England. Over the years he was influenced by Christian, Hindu, Jain, liberal and humanitarian ideas; but the doctrine of non-violence (*ahimsa*) and the pursuit of truth (*satya*) became the philosophical cornerstones of his endeavours to achieve a united independent India. His belief in the rights of man, and especially his championing of the Untouchables, whom he renamed the Children of God (*Harijan*), put him in opposition to brahmin orthodoxy; but he won the hearts of the people when he discarded European clothes for the homespun cotton *dhoti* and shawl, to identify with the masses. His personal charisma and all-India appeal inspired the Independence movement throughout the period, whether he was in prison, organizing the rejection of imported cloth in his *swadeshi* campaign, leading acts of civil disobedience, or fasting to bring about the cessation of Hindu-Muslim community violence.

Gandhi was released from prison in 1924. Despite liberal concessions by the British, by 1928 Congress was demanding complete Independence (*purna swaraj*). The government offered talks, but the more radical elements in Congress, now led by the young **Jawaharlal Nehru**, were in a confrontational mood. Their declaration of Independence Day on January 26, 1930 forced Gandhi's hand; he responded with a well-publicized 240-mile march from his ashram in Sabarmati to make **salt** illegally at Dandi in Gujarat. This demonstration of nonviolent civil disobedience (**satyagraha**) caught the people's imagination, leading to more processions, strikes, and the imprisonment of 100,000 of his followers by the end of the year. Abortive round-table talks, the Irwin-Gandhi truce, Gandhi's trip to London for further talks, and more civil disobedience culminated in the **Government of India Act** in 1935, which still fell short of aspirations for complete Independence. Congress remained suspicious of British intentions, and despite Gandhi's overtures refused to accommodate Muslim demands for representation.

The idea of a **separate Muslim state** was first raised in 1930 by the poet Sir Mohammed Iqbal and Chaudhuri Rahmat Ali, and a group of fellow students at Cambridge coined the name **Pakistan**, literally meaning "Land of the Pure". **Mohammed Ali Jinnah**, a lawyer from Bombay who assumed the leadership of the Muslim League in 1935, initially promoted Muslim-Hindu co-operation, but he soon despaired of influencing Congress and by 1940 the League passed a resolution demanding an independent Pakistan.

Confrontations between the government, Congress and the Muslim League continued throughout World War II. Mahatma Gandhi introduced the "**Quit India**" slogan and proposed another campaign of civil disobedience; the government immediately responded by imprisoning the whole Working Party of Congress in Pune. Jinnah, meanwhile, preached his "two nations" theory to the educated, and inspired mass Muslim support with his rhetoric against "Hinduization". A spate of terrorist activities left 1000 dead and 60,000 imprisoned; by the end of the war, the government accepted that complete Independence would have to be negotiated.

British attempts to find a solution that would preserve a united India and allay Muslim fears after the war disintegrated in the face of continued intransigence from both sides, and they gradually realized that Partition was inevitable. In 1946 Jinnah provoked riots in Calcutta with his call for Direct Action, and Hindus retaliated with atrocities against Muslims in Bihar and Uttar Pradesh. The British cabinet appointed **Lord Mountbatten** as viceroy to supervise the handover of power in 1948; Mahatma Gandhi desperately sought to avert the escalating Hindu-Muslim violence and find a resolution to secure a united India; and Nehru was persuaded that a separate Pakistan would be preferable to the anarchy of communal killings.

Lord Mountbatten brought Independence forward, the subcontinent was **partitioned** on August 15, 1947 and Pakistan came into existence, even though several princely states had still to decide which of the two new countries they would join. The new boundaries cut through both Bengal and the Punjab; Sikhs, Muslims and Hindus who had been neighbours became enemies overnight. Five million Hindus and Sikhs from Pakistan, and a similar number of Muslims from India, were involved in the ensuing two-way exodus, and the atrocities cost half a million lives. Mahatma Gandhi, who had devoted himself to ending the communal violence after Partition, was **assassinated** in January 1948 by Hindu extremists antagonized by his defence of the Muslims. India had lost its "Great Soul", but the profound shock of the Mahatma's last sacrifice at least contributed to the gradual cessation of the violence.

Independent India

Jawaharlal Nehru, India's first and longest-running prime minister, proved to be a dynamic, gifted and extremely popular leader during his seventeen years of premiership. He built the foundations of a democratic, secular state, and guided the first stages of its agricultural and industrial development. Nehru's first task, however, was to consolidate the Union.

His able deputy prime minister, **Sardar Vallabh bhai Patel**, was made responsible for incorporating the 562 princely states within the federal Union. The nizam of **Hyderabad**, who resisted even though the majority of the state's population was Hindu, had to be persuaded by an invasion of Indian troops. The Hindu maharaja of **Kashmir** also prevaricated, as three quarters of his subjects were Muslims, and by October 1947 he had to appeal to India for help against a tribal invasion supported by Pakistan. Kashmir's accession to India resulted in the first outbreak of hostilities between the two countries; the United Nations intervened in 1949 to enforce a ceasefire line. The **French** enclaves at Pondicherry and Chandernagar were incorporated in the 1950s, but the **Portuguese** refused to accept the new situation and in 1961 Nehru had to annex **Goa**. The **Naga** people were brought within the federal Union as the Nagaland state in the same year.

The Constitution for India's "Sovereign Democratic Republic and Union of States" became law on January 26, 1950, the twentieth anniversary of "Independence Day". The franchise was made universal for all adults, and with 173 million eligible to vote in 1951 India became the **world's largest democracy**. Hindi was designated the "official language of the Union"; but South India, in particular, was adamant in its opposition to Hindi, and Nehru realigned the several state borders on linguistic principles. By 1961 the Union consisted of sixteen states and six centrally administered territories. The Punjabi-speaking Sikhs had to wait until 1966 for their state to be separated from Hindu-dominated Haryana.

Nehru sought to achieve the constitutional aims of justice, liberty, equality and fraternity with a vigorous programme of social and economic reforms. He redressed the iniquities of caste by abolishing "Untouchability" in 1955 and radically improved the status of women. National average literacy was increased to 23.7 per cent by 1961 and free elementary education became more readily available, although it still fell short of aspirations.

On the **economic** front, Nehru engineered the first three of India's **Five-Year Plans** to improve production capability and eradicate poverty. Population growth and the failures of the monsoon in 1952 and 1953 eroded the mainly agricultural aims of the first plan (1951–56), but food grain production increased from 52 million to over 65 million tons by 1956, and to 80 million tons by the end of the second plan (1956–61), which also injected capital into industry. Under the third plan (1961–66), a nuclear energy programme was inaugurated, and foreign aid and technical assistance secured to speed up industrialization.

Foreign policy was Nehru's biggest disappointment. He adopted a policy of nonaligned peaceful coexistence, but **China** threatened his aim of promoting Asian unity. He attempted to dispel the tensions created by the Chinese invasion of Tibet in 1950 by concluding a trade treaty with China in 1954, which included a declaration of mutual respect for each other's territories; but this did not deter the Chinese from building a road across a remote area of Ladakh in 1957, and India sustained losses during a confrontation in 1959. In 1962, sporadic conflicts in the Northeast Frontier Agency (**Assam**) escalated into a war; the Chinese army proved to be far superior and advanced unhindered over India's northeast frontier. Their unilateral decision to withdraw, on November 21, 1962, added humiliation to defeat and spelt the end of India's policy of nonalignment. Nehru immediately made a defence treaty with the US, and set about creating a new elite Border Security Force.

Indira Gandhi 1966–1984

The whole nation, loyal throughout the China crisis, mourned Nehru's death in 1964, which prevented him from witnessing the restoration of India's military prestige in the **Second Indo-Pakistan War** of 1965. Indian tanks had advanced to within five kilometres of a virtually defenceless Lahore when the UN ceasefire was agreed on September 23. **Lal Bahadur Shastri**, who had led the interim government, died shortly after in January 1966, leaving Nehru's daughter **Indira Gandhi** to establish her superiority as leader of the Congress left, over Morarji Desai's right wing of the party.

Mrs Gandhi swiftly secured American financial support for India's fourth Five Year Plan (1966–71), but her devaluation of the rupee in June 1966 aroused considerable opposition and elections the next year radically reduced her majority. Two years later, Congress split under the pressure of internal dissent. Mrs Gandhi embraced the socialist principle by nationalizing the banks, and enlisted the support of the Communists, the Sikhs and the Dravidian Progressive Federation (DMK) to form a coalition government. By this time, India had made a spectacular agricultural breakthrough with its **Green Revolution**, as a result of the introduction of high-yield grains, and in 1969 industrial growth was over seven percent. Mrs Gandhi pressed on with her socialist reforms, abolishing the former maharajas' privy purses and privileges after she had consolidated her mandate in fresh elections in 1971.

Meanwhile, Yahya Khan's brutal repression of the struggle for independence in **East Pakistan** had caused a mass exodus of refugees, and by April 1971 Bengali civilians were pouring across into India at the rate of 60,000 a day. Mrs Gandhi astutely waited until she had the moral support of the international community, signed a Treaty of Peace, Friendship and Co-operation with the Soviet Union, and launched simultaneous attacks in West and East Pakistan on December 4. India had total air superiority, as well as the support of the East Pakistan population, and by December 15 the Pakistani general capitulated and signed the Instrument of Surrender of "all Pakistan armed forces in Bangla Desh".

If the liberation of Bangla Desh was the crowning glory of Mrs Gandhi's premiership, her abandonment of the democratic ideals so dear to her father was its lowest ebb. After widespread agrarian and industrial unrest against the rate of inflation and corruption within the Congress in 1974, the clamour of protest rose to a crescendo in June 1975, and when the opposition coalition under the joint leadership of J.P. Narayan and Morarji Desai threatened to oust India's "iron lady", she declared a **State of Emergency** on June 26, which suspended all civil rights, including habeas corpus, and silenced all opposition by internment and strict censorship of the press.

Her administrative and economic reforms had the desired effect of cutting inflation and curbing corruption, but the enforced sterilization of men with two or more children, and brutal slum-clearances in Delhi supervised by her son **Sanjay**, alienated millions of her supporters. When she finally released her opponents and called off the Emergency in January 1977, the bitterness she had engendered resulted in her ignominious defeat in the March elections. The ensuing **Janata** coalition under **Morarji Desai** fell apart within two years, and his premiership was terminated by a vote of no confidence in 1979. Mrs Gandhi, who had rebuilt her Congress (I) Party with Sanjay's help, swept back into office in January 1980. Sanjay died in a plane crash a few months later; four years afterwards, Mrs Gandhi made the second, fatal, mistake of her career.

A group of terrorists demanding a separate "nation" – Khalistan – for Sikhs, took control of the **Golden Temple** in Amritsar early in 1984, and organized a campaign of violence from its precincts. Hundreds of Hindus and moderate Sikhs fell victim to terrorist attacks, and the whole nation was calling for positive action to end the atrocities. Indira sent in her tanks in June 1984, but two days of raging combat desecrated the Sikhs' holiest shrine as well as generating the first martyrs of Khalistan. In October that year, her Sikh bodyguards avenged their brotherhood and faith by assassinating Mrs Gandhi at her house in Delhi.

Communal conflict 1984–1995

Leaving his former career as an airline pilot, **Rajiv Gandhi**, Indira's son, entered Indian politics in his mother's place and came to power in December 1984 on a wave of sympathy boosted by his reputation as "Mr Clean". His victory was given added resonance by the **Bhopal** gas tragedy just two weeks before the elections (see p.412). The honeymoon was short-lived; the political accords he reached with the Punjab, Assam and Mizoram deteriorated into armed conflict; more than two years of "peacekeeping" by the Indian army failed to disarm Tamil guerrillas in Sri Lanka; and allegations of corruption tarnished his image. By the end of the 1980s the opposition had rallied under the leadership of **V.P. Singh**, a former Congress minister. The December 1989 elections did not give V.P. Singh's Janata Party a majority, but he managed to form a coalition government with the support of the "Hindu first" Bharatiya Janata Party (**BJP**), led by **L.K. Advani**.

Singh was immediately confronted by problems in the Punjab and Kashmir, as well as upper-caste Hindu protests against his planned implementation of proposals for a sixty percent reservation of civil service jobs for lower castes and former "Untouchables"; but it was an even more emotive issue which brought down his government in less than a year. Advani had assumed the leadership of a popular Hindu revivalist movement, which was demanding that the Babri Masjid mosque in **Ayodhya**, built by Babur in the sixteenth century, should be replaced by a Hindu temple on the supposed site of the birthplace of Rama, god-hero of the epic *Ramayana*.

Singh, utterly committed to secularism, pleaded with Advani to desist but, undeterred, Advani set off towards Ayodhya in October 1990, seated on a golden chariot pushed by his followers and thousands of devout Hindus, with the avowed intention of destroying the mosque. Singh ordered Advani's arrest and the inevitable withdrawal of the BJP from his coalition government resulted in a vote of no confidence on November 7, 1990. Rajiv Gandhi declined the offer to form an interim government, hopeful that he could improve his party's position in an election. His campaign went well and it was assumed that Congress would win, until on a tour of Tamil Nadu in May 1991, he was assassinated by Tamil Tigers seeking revenge for India's active opposition to their "freedom fight" in Sri Lanka.

P.V. Narasimha Rao skilfully steered the Congress Party through the elections, and formed a government with the support of the Muslim League, the Communist "Left Front" and Tamil Nadu's most powerful party (AIADMK). At the same time, the BJP ominously increased its seats in the Lok Sabha (the Lower House of Parliament) from 80 to 120, Advani became leader of the opposition, and the enormous popular support for the rebuilding of Rama's temple in Ayodhya encouraged the Vishwa Hindu Parishad to take up the crusade. V.P. Singh countered by leading a march of five hundred secularists to Ayodhya, but the BJP had won control of the Uttar Pradesh state government, making them responsible for law and order, and this time it was Singh who found himself arrested and imprisoned.

In December 1992, when the situation came to a head again, the central government could not prevent extremists inciting the crowds of fanatical devotees to tear down the mosque in a blaze of publicity. The demolition of the Babri Masjid was followed by terrible **riots** in many parts of the country, especially Bombay and Gujarat, where Muslim families and businesses were targeted. A few months later, in retaliation against the extreme Hindu violence, **bombs** were planted in Bombay by underground Muslim groups. As a result of the Babri Masjid episode, the BJP-led state governments of UP, Himachal Pradesh, Madhya Pradesh, Rajasthan and Delhi were suspended. Elections in these states in late 1993 showed that the popularity of the BJP, and its call for the creation of **Hindutva**, a Hindu homeland, was fading. They re-asserted control

Jammu and Kashmir

The main, if not only, reason why India and Pakistan remain bitter enemies after more than fifty years of Independence is **Kashmir**. This tiny region in the far north of the country has been gripped by a bloody civil war that has, since its escalation in the late 1980s, claimed an estimated 40,000–60,000 lives. With both countries now fully fledged nuclear states, Kashmir has become one of the world's most dangerous geo-political flashpoints.

The **roots of the conflict** go back to Independence in 1947. Threatened by aggressive Baluchi and Pathan tribals from the west, the Hindu maharaja of Kashmir decided at the eleventh hour to throw his lot in with India instead of the Islamic homeland carved out by Jinnah, in spite of the fact that ninety percent of his subjects were Muslims. Since then, Pakistan has regarded Kashmir as the "unfinished business of Partition".

Agitation for the autonomy guaranteed to Kashmir under Article 370 of the Indian Constitution has intensified gradually over time, but all-out violence may have been averted had it not been for a series of blunders by New Delhi, foremost among them Indira Gandhi's decision to depose the Kashmiri chief minister, **Farooq Abdullah**, for petty political reasons in 1984. Congress-led **election rigging** further inflamed opposition to Indian rule, as Pakistani-backed paramilitary groups began to target government buildings and personnel, as well as army and police posts.

The catalyst that converted political dissent into full-scale insurgency, however, occurred in 1990, when unarmed Kashmiris protesting against the heavy-handed tactics of security forces in the valley were gunned down from both sides of the **Gawakadal Bridge** in the capital, Srinagar. A hundred people died in the massacre, watched by the world's press. By the following year violence and human rights abuses had become endemic, both in the valley and further south around Jammu. Armed and trained by Libya and Pakistan, guerrillas from at least nineteen Muslim countries flooded in to fight what was now regarded as *jihad*, or Holy War. Total curfews became routine, and thousands of suspected militants were detained without trial, amid innumerable accusations of torture, systematic rape of Kashmiri women by troops, disappearances of countless boys and men, and summary executions.

The war intensified through the 1990s, with a series of bloody clashes between the militants and Indian forces. The first of these was the **Sopone massacre**, when security forces, in retaliation for a grenade attack on an army barracks, shot dead fifty militants. Then, in November 1993, a rerun of the Golden Temple fiasco seemed inevitable as heavily armed militants occupied one of the region's holiest shrines, the **Hazratbal mosque**. This siege, however, ended with a government climb-down (the militants were allowed safe passage out of the mosque), although 22 protesters were shot by the army in its wake.

After the Hazratbal siege, there ensued a period of relative calm; curfews were suspended and the Jammu & Kashmir Liberation Front (JKLF)'s leader, Javed Mir, was captured. With pressure being brought to bear on India by the US for a speedy resolution of the crisis, the peace seemed likely to result in long-awaited elections, until yet another stand-off between troops and militants stalled negotiations. In May 1995, a Muslim shrine near Srinagar, the **Char-e-Sharief**, was burned down while surrounded by the army, killing twenty Kashmiris and sparking off riots in the capital. For the first time tourists were targeted as a means of internationalizing the independence struggle. An attempt to abduct and incarcerate three Westerners in Delhi was foiled by police but, shortly afterwards, a group of foreign Muslim extremists, **Al-Faran**, kidnapped five tourists; one, a Norwegian, was beheaded and it's assumed that the other four suffered a similar fate. A return to relative stability finally allowed Jammu and Kashmir to hold **elections** to the Lok Sabha in December 1997, but the results were inconclusive due to widespread boycotting.

Less than two years later, the crisis brought India and Pakistan to the verge of yet another all-out war. While the world was preoccupied with NATO's bombing of Belgrade, at least 800 Pakistani-backed *jehadis* crept across the so-called Line of Control (the de facto border) overlooking the Srinagar–Leh road near **Kargil** and Dras. India's response was to move thousands of troops and heavy artillery into the area, swiftly followed up with an aerial bombardment. Within days the two countries were poised on the brink of all-out war, only months after both had successfully tested long-range nuclear missiles. In the event the conflict was contained, but Pakistan took a bloody nose from the encounter, and by July 1999 the Indian army had retaken all the ground previously lost to the militants. An estimated 700 Pakistani and 330 Indian soldiers died before Pakistani premier, Nawaz Sharif, bowed to international pressure and withdrew his forces.

Kashmir was top of President Clinton's agenda when he visited India in March 2000, but the start of his five-day tour was marred by the massacre of 36 unarmed Sikhs in the village of **Chattisingpora**, the first attack on the region's Sikh minority since the start of the troubles. Following a now predictable formula, Hizbul Mujhedin, the main militant group in the valley, denied responsibility for the killings, claiming it was a "preplanned act of Indian intelligence to defame the Kashmiri freedom struggle". The Indian cabinet, for its part, saw the Sikh massacre as a "Pakistan-backed attempt to internationalize the Kashmir conflict" at a time when the world's media attention was focused on the subcontinent.

The same pattern of allegations and counter-allegations accompanied the dramatic upsurge in violence in Kashmir the following August, when a series of appalling massacres were sparked off by the gunning down of 32 Hindu pilgrims by a so-called "suicide squad" at **Pahalgam**, during the annual Amarnath Yatra. The ensuing army crackdown effectively dashed all hopes that the unilateral ceasefire, announced by **Hizbul Mujhedin** only ten days before, would pave the way for peace talks.

Bombings, ambushes, suicide raids and further killings of both soldiers and civilians punctuated the troubled year of 2000, and there was little cause for optimism when, under pressure from the US, Prime Minister Vajpayee and Pakistan's President Musharraf held a summit on Kashmir in Agra in July. Far from resulting in a joint statement, the talks broke down when India refused to support the Pakistanis' assertion that Kashmir was the chief problem dividing the two countries (India preferred to cite "cross-border terrorism" as the source of their differences).

Despite repeated reassurances to the contrary from Islamabad (Pakistan's capital), Pakistani-backed guerrillas continued to infiltrate the Kashmir Valley in ever greater numbers. The extent of the problem was emphasized by a dramatic broad-daylight suicide car bomb destroying the State Assembly building in Srinagar. Pakistan made an unprecedented condemnation of the outrage and did not try to shift the blame onto the Indian security forces. Similar protestations, however, failed to convince many Indians the following December, when armed Islamic commandos stormed the Indian **Parliament building** in New Delhi. Vajpayee was furious and wished to declare war on Pakistan, but cooler heads prevailed, with Musharraf issuing orders to his military to crackdown on the movement of Islamic *jehadis* across Pakistan's porous border. However, with an election pending and public opinion firmly against his support for America in the war against the Taliban in Afghanistan, Musharraf had to do something to appease the hardliners in his country, and in January he granted **amnesty** to hundreds of religious extremists imprisoned in Pakistan – a move that further infuriated New Delhi.

With relations between the two countries tenser than ever, the time was ripe for Islamic militants to mount another de-stabilising "spectacular". This duly came on May 14, 2002, with the attack by a *fedayin* suicide squad on an army base near Jammu; dozens of military personnel and civilians were gunned down, many of them

Jammu and Kashmir *continued*

women and children. This time Vajpayee's patience reached breakpoint. An order for a massive military build up was issued from New Delhi, and within a month one million soldiers were facing each other across the Indo-Pak border, watched with baited breath by the world's media. Full-scale war between Asia's two nuclear superpowers was only narrowly averted after intense diplomatic pressure was brought to bear on both sides by the US, which dispatched Colin Powell as an emissary.

Meanwhile, armed Islamic factions in the valley itself stepped up operations to take advantage of the increased attention. For the past year, **Kashmiri Pandits** – native Hindus who had fled the valley over the preceding decade-and-a-half of violence – had been encouraged by the Indian government to re-settle, and they provided a soft target for the terrorists. The worst in a string of atrocities directed against them in the summer of 2002 was the massacre of 27 Pandits in the village of **Nandimarg** and the storming by *jehadis* of the **Raghunath temple** in **Jammu**, the region's most holy Hindu shrine.

Nevertheless, renewed peace talks got under way in late 2002, although these caved in the following spring after a series of provocative missile tests (by both sides). Yet another round of negotiations were held in May 2003, which 78-year-old Vajpayee declared would be his last chance to make headway on Kashmir – which, indeed, it was. Few commentators held out much hope of a breakthrough, but at the time of writing – with a Congress government in power and an altogether more concilliatory tone prevailing from both New Delhi and Islamabad – the divisions separating the two South Asian powers appear to be surmountable for the first time in decades. That said, in the valley itself, public opposition to the Indian government's treatment of Kashmir is stiffer than ever. All sections of Kashmiri society, from poor farmers to judges, now support the armed struggle in some form, which in its early days was waged essentially by extremists lacking popular support. Whether or not the state and national leaders can win public support for the much touted Indo-Pak **Peace Road Map** remains to be seen.

Hanging over all high-level negotiations, of course, is a harsh realpolitik: that a bullish stance on Kashmir is a vote-winner for the beleaguered leaders of both India and Pakistan. Manmohan and Musharraf's grip on power depends on their being able, on the one hand, to placate the extremists whom they rely on for their political survival, and – on the other – avoid drawing their countries into an unwinnable war.

of Delhi, which has always been a stronghold of the Hindu right, barely hung on in Rajasthan, and lost the rest.

The electoral results provided a much needed boost for Narasimha Rao, whose grip over the leadership of the Congress Party seemed to be slipping. Accused by the opposition and press of lacking decisive policies, and dogged by allegations that he had accepted a suitcase of money as a bribe from a prominent businessman (the so-called "Harsha scandal"), the prime minister was under increasing pressure to step down. However, he weathered an unsuccessful no-confidence motion mounted by the BJP, and the surprise election victories in November temporarily silenced his rivals, among them minister Arjun Singh, who would later engineer a split in the Congress Party in an attempt to wrest power from Rao.

National morale during this post-Ayodhya period was shaky. After a year blighted by bomb blasts, riots and the rise of religious extremism, it seemed as if India's era as a secular state was doomed. To rub salt in the wounds, 15,000 people died in a massive **earthquake** around the northwestern Maharashtran city of Latur, and soon after, Surat, in southern Gujarat, was at the centre of an outbreak of a disease ominously resembling bubonic **plague**. Thousands fled the city and the international community panicked, cancelling export orders and axing flights. The "plague" turned out to be a flash in the pan, but the damage to India's self-image was done.

Against this backdrop of uncertainty, the rise of right-wing Hindu-fundamentalist parties gathered pace. Temporarily cowed by the Babri Masjid debacle, the BJP took advantage of the power struggle in the Congress Party to rekindle regional support. Expediently sidelining the contentious *Hindutva* agenda, the new rallying cry was **Swadeshi** – a campaign against the Congress-led programme of **economic liberalization** and, in particular, the activities of multinationals such as Coca Cola, Pepsi and KFC (one of whose branches was forced to close by the BJP-controlled Delhi municipality). Bal Thackeray's proto-fascist **Shiv Sena** party also made ground in Maharashtra, eventually winning the State Assembly elections there in March 1995.

The rise of the BJP 1996–1999

After the **general election** of May 1996, the political landscape altered at national level, too. Polling 194 of the Lok Sabha's 534 seats, the BJP emerged as the single largest party and attempted to form a government. Despite much behind-the-scenes wheeling and dealing, however, they were unable to muster a majority and were ousted a couple of weeks later, outmanoeuvred by a hastily formed coalition, the **Unified Front**, led by **H.D. Deve Gowda**. Ironically, the UF had to rely on the support of the Congress (I) Party – the principal opponent of many of its thirteen constituent parties – to establish a working majority. The shaky coalition could not last, and by April 1997, Gowda lost a no-confidence vote over his leadership and was speedily replaced by his foreign minister, **I.K. Gujral**. Despite maintaining good relations with America and leading the Indian market away from socialism, Gujral was much criticized by conservatives for his leftist leanings and for sporting a Lenin-style goatee.

Gujral led the United Front until its defeat in the **general election** of March 1998, after which the **BJP** struggled to power as the head of a new conservative coalition government under **Atal Behari Vajpayee**. This time, the party managed to stay in office for thirteen months, as opposed to the thirteen days of its previous spell in government. The BJP had promised change and the restoration of national pride, and one of its early acts in government was to conduct five underground **nuclear tests** in May 1998, provoking Pakistan to respond in kind. There was a chorus of world criticism, and US-led financial **sanctions** were imposed on both nations. BJP activists blamed the West for being hypocritical over the whole affair while in many people's eyes, the tests made the Kashmir issue more of a flashpoint – and now a potentially nuclear one. Within a couple of months of the tests, the Americans were leading the way in trying to persuade both countries to sign up to nuclear nonproliferation in the Comprehensive Test Ban Treaty (CTBT). In sharp contrast to increased tension over security issues, Vajpayee visited Pakistan in person in early March 1999, the first time an Indian prime minister had crossed the border in a decade. However, this atmosphere of seemingly warming relations between the two countries received a jolt when the Indian government tested an **Agni II missile**, capable of carrying nuclear warheads into Pakistan. Again, Pakistan matched this within days, testing their own long-range, nuclear-capable missiles.

Following its defeat in the 1998 elections, the Congress Party emerged as a stronger political force with **Sonia Gandhi**, the Italian-born widow of the former prime minister Rajiv Gandhi, at the helm. Congress collaborated with the Jayalalitha's AIADMK to bring about the downfall of the BJP in April 1999 (see "Of Movie Stars and Ministers", p.1120), but were unable to form a coalition government. As a consequence, India faced a third **general election** in as many years.

The 1999 election

At the start of the campaign, Congress hopes were high that, with a Gandhi once again as party leader, it could revive the popular support lost after years of infighting and corruption scandals. Moreover, to compound the BJP's problems, Vajpayee's caretaker government was saddled with a worsening financial deficit, deteriorating relations with Pakistan and a welter of domestic difficulties, foremost among them the political fallout from an horrific **train crash** in West Bengal, in which 260 people died.

The wave of **patriotism** that swept India after the Kargil victory (see box on pp.1386–1388) was a godsend for Vajpayee (cynics argued it may well have been the hidden policy behind the army's uncompromising response to the crisis). Riding high on the feelgood factor, his party inflicted the biggest defeat Congress had sustained since it first came to power in 1947. Vajpayee's majority was far from as large as he might have hoped, and the BJP-led National Democratic Alliance (NDA) coalition was fractured and tenuous, but Sonia's second election defeat seemed to herald, at last, the end of dynastic politics in India (in spite of the entrance onto the political stage of her charismatic 26-year-old daughter, Priyanka).

The election results also showed a clear swing of public support away from New Delhi towards smaller regional parties. Tired of corrupt police, unsafe drinking water, and inadequate rubbish disposal, electricity provision and sewer and road maintenance, the emerging middle classes voted out almost half of their incumbent MPs in a spirit of exasperation which led the news magazine *Outlook* to run a lead story questioning whether India actually needs a central government at all.

The NDA's post-election party was short lived. On October 30, 1999, a massive **super-cyclone** with 175mph winds struck the north coast of Orissa. Estimates of the death toll ranged from 10,000 to 20,000, around 1.5 million villagers lost their homes and thousands more died in the following weeks from cholera, typhoid and other diseases. International aid agencies were quick to criticize the Indian government, saying the relief operation was hampered by poor co-ordination and bickering between New Delhi and the state government in Orissa.

The new millennium

The start of the new millennium saw no let-up in headline-making events. **South India** was gripped by a dramatic news story which, in spite of its relative geopolitical irrelevance, attracted massive media attention. On July 30, the Tamil sandalwood smuggler and notorious bandit, **Veerapan**, kidnapped 72-year-old matinee idol, **Raj Kumar**. Following a succession of failed negotiations for his release, riots broke out in the Kumar's home state, Karnataka, and one ardent fan even set himself on fire in protest at the abduction. He was eventually freed after nearly four months of secret talks – rumours surrounding the release deal included the payment of a vast ransom. The South Indian police finally caught up with Veerapan in October 2004. By then wanted for the murder of 130 people and for butchering some 2000 elephants, he was lured into an ambush and gunned down on a deserted jungle road – the end of a manhunt which had, by its conclusion, cost the government an estimated Rs1.5 billion (£19m). The Veerapan scandal once again reaffirmed the extent of political corruption in Tamil Nadu where, the previous February, the larger-than-life AIADMK leader, former film starlet **Jayalalitha**, was imprisoned for accepting bribes from businessmen. Some 5000 demonstrators were arrested in the riots that followed, as supporters set fire to a bus full of students, killing three innocent women – an incident filmed and broadcast by Star TV news.

India's political problems, however, were temporarily eclipsed by a succession of catastrophic **natural disasters** which wracked the country in mid-2000. In the arid zones of Rajasthan and Gujarat, high May temperatures compounded the third failure of the monsoons in as many years, forcing tens of thousands of poor farming families off their land in search of fodder and drinking water. Once again, the government was heavily criticized for failing to respond quickly enough, and only after pictures of emaciated refugees and their bony cattle appeared on TV did Vajpayee make a televised appeal for donations and announce a Rs9.5 billion relief package for **drought** victims.

While the 2000 monsoon, when it finally broke, made little impact on the parched northwest, **record rainfalls** wreaked havoc in Andhra Pradesh, West Bengal and low-lying areas of Uttar Pradesh, leaving an estimated 12 million marooned or homeless as river levels rose by as much as four metres. With transport and communications at a standstill for weeks, food distribution and rescue efforts all but ground to a halt. Riots broke out in camps set up by the army for **flood** victims, as supplies of food and plastic sheets ran out.

Republic Day Quake to the attack on Parliament

An even worse natural disaster lay in store for millions of Gujaratis when, in the morning of January 26, 2001, a massive **earthquake** measuring 7.9 on the Richter scale levelled a vast area in the northwest of the state. And while rescue workers were hauling bodies from what remained of Bhuj and Bachau in Gujarat, some 70 million Hindu pilgrims were converging in Uttar Pradesh, where the **Maha Kumbh Mela** (see p.320) became largest gathering in a single place in human history. Appropriately enough, figures from the **decennial census** the following month revealed that the population of India stood at around 1.1 billion (with a literacy rate of 66 percent and an average life expectancy of 68 years).

Meanwhile in Delhi, a string of **corruption scandals** were piling pressure onto the fractious BJP-led coalition, the National Democratic Alliance (NDA). Posing as arms dealers, undercover journalists from the investigative website, **Tehelka.com**, succeeded in bribing defence minister George Fernandes, as well as senior army officers, civil servants, and even the president of the BJP, who was caught on camera shovelling cash into his desk. The scandal deeply embarrassed the prime minister, who sacked Mr Fernandes and ordered a commission of inquiry. Tehelka was the toast of ordinary Indians tired of high-level corruption, and boasted thirty million hits a week until a campaign of victimization by government departments forced it to close. (It has since re-launched – see p.37 – and continues its mission to harass corrupt officialdom.)

The assassination of the former "Bandit Queen", MLA (member of parliament) **Phoolan Devi**, drew the media's attention for a while, but Vajpayee's party came in for more flak for yielding ground to its regionalist coalition partners when the prime minister announced the **creation of three new states**: Jharkhand, Chhattisgarh and Uttaranchal, made up of remote parts of Bihar, Madhya Pradesh and Uttar Pradesh.

Towards the end of summer 2001, **Indo-Pak relations** and **Kashmir** returned to the fore as India entered one of the most volatile periods in its modern history. Tensions in the Kashmir Valley were already running high prior to the landmark **Indo-Pak summit** in July 2001. But if India felt it occupied the moral (as well as strategic) ground in the wake of the Kargil conflict, the **storming of the Indian parliament** by three Muslim gunmen the following December seemed to further vindicate its determination to bring Pakistan to account for the militancy originating across the border. The sense of indignation grew in the following weeks – Pakistani involvement was inevitably suspected, and Vajpayee announced he was in favour of declaring war immediately. Only after some intense US and British diplomacy, and more conciliatory announcements from Islamabad, were New Delhi's ruffled feathers temporarily smoothed.

A similar pronouncement followed the destruction in October 2002 of the **State Assembly building in Srinagar** by Islamic suicide car bombers. On this occasion, however, Islamabad swiftly condemned the attack – the first time in history it had done so.

To the brink of war

Following a string of major electoral setbacks in the regions and a steady decline in the patriotic fervour whipped up by the nuclear tests and Kargil war, flagging support for the prime minister and BJP seemed to revive as a wave of **communal tension** engulfed the country in the spring of 2002. The catalyst was the massacre by a Muslim mob in **Godhra**, Gujarat, of a train load of Hindu pilgrims returning from the disputed temple site in Ayodhya: 38 died and 74 were injured, but this paled in comparison with the reprisal killings that followed, in which around 2000 (mostly Muslims) were slaughtered. The BJP chief minister of Gujarat, Narendra Modi, was accused of colluding in the massacres when it emerged that his police force seemed to be following a policy of non-intervention, actually standing back on several occasions to allow Hindu mobs to go about their gruesome business.

Anti-Muslim sentiment in India was further fuelled only a month after Godhra when an Islamist suicide squad commandeered a tourist bus and used it to attack the **Kaluchak** army cantonment near **Jammu**; thirty people were killed, including several women and ten children, before the militants were themselves shot dead. Coming only four months after the attack on the Indian parliament, and hot on the heels of yet another promise by Pakistan to clamp down on the militants crossing its border, the atrocity provoked outrage in Delhi. Vajpayee, bowing to the hawks on the right of his own party, called for a "decisive battle", initiating a massive build up of troops on the border. An estimated million men at arms were involved in the ensuing stand off as India and Pakistan edged to the brink of all-out **war**. Once again, however, US diplomacy diffused the crisis and the armies stood down by the end of the monsoons.

Not even another series of massacres of Hindus in Kashmir in March and April, nor the September attack by Islamic gunmen on the headquarters of the Swaminarayan sect, **Akshardam**, in Gujarat (in which 33 people were killed and 72 more injured) could derail the **peace talks** that followed.

Peace Talks and the Mumbai bombings

Indo-Pak talks over Kashmir lasted until March 2003, but were suspended by India after Islamabad announced the successful testing of its Shaheen missile, capable of delivering nuclear warheads over a distance of 750km (as far as Delhi). The negotiations, however, resumed in May, when Vajpayee made a **declaration of peace**, announcing that the Delhi–Lahore bus connection would recommence and that hundreds of Pakistanis detained in Indian prisons since the Kargil war would be released. Pakistan responded with more "confidence building measures", announcing that it would ease trade restrictions, improve travel and sporting links and, later, by declaring a ceasefire along the Line of Control.

The most significant concessions made by the two sides in recent times, these moves paved the way for a full-blown summit, eventually held in Islamabad in early 2004. Watched by the world's press, President Pervez Musharaf and Atal Bihari Vajpayee posed for an historic handshake and even managed an hour-long discussion in which plans to strengthen diplomatic ties and re-open the Kashmir Highway (between Srinagar and Muzaffarabad) were mooted.

In tandem with these formal dialogues, Indian officials also held behind-the-scenes talks with Kashmiri separatist leaders, from which both sides emerged optimistic and committed to a non-violent Road Map. Not since the start of the troubles had a rapprochement between looked so likely to result in a definitive end to hostilities. Nevertheless, relations between Hindus and Muslims in some parts of India remained as strained as ever. As the first trials of suspects accused of atrocities in the wake of the Godhra massacres reached court in Ahmedabad, the Archeological Survey of India released its long-awaited **report on Ayodhya**. Since the destruction of the Babri Masjid by Hindu extremists in 1992, debate had raged as to whether there had in fact ever been a Rama temple beneath the mosque. To no-one's surprise, the ASI panel of "experts", appointed by the right-wing BJP government (prominent members of which had incited the Babri Masjid destruction in the first place), declared they'd found evidence to show there had been a temple, in effect condoning the tearing down of the mosque.

Rubbing salt in old wounds, the ruling did little to quell post-Godhra tensions; and when, on August 25, 2003 (the day after the Ayodhya report was published), two **bombs** ripped through the centre of downtown Mumbai, commentators were quick to identify the Babri Masjid dispute as the provocation. One exploded in a taxi next to the **Gateway of India**, Mumbai's main tourist hub, killing 107 people. No-one has ever claimed responsibility, but four suspects believed to have links with Islamic militant groups were arrested soon after.

The 2004 elections to the present

With India booming as never before and peace on the horizon in Kashmir, prime minister Vajpayee and his BJP-led coalition decided to cash in the perceived feelgood factor and call a snap **election** in **May 2004**. "India Shining" was their slogan, but the campaign strategy boomeranged badly. India was experiencing a period of unparalleled economic growth; the boom, however, was based largely on technology, and had had little impact on the vast majority of the population. Congress leader Sonia Gandhi was quick to seize the initiative, appealing directly to poor rural voters to show the government what they thought of Vajpayee's vision of the country. She also played the dynastic card, introducing her son Rahul and daughter Priyanka to the campaign and so capturing the imagination of younger voters (one in two of the Indian electorate are aged under 35).

Far from increasing his majority, as he'd expected, Vajpayee and his government were thrown out in the most dramatic political turnaround of recent times. Congress gained the largest share of the vote and **Sonia Gandhi** was duly invited to form a government. However, she stunned supporters by "humbly declining" the invitation and stepped down. The announcement caused clamorous scenes in parliament, provoking the worst losses ever seen in the 129-year history of India's stock market. Eventually, former finance minister, 71-year-old **Manmohan Singh**, stepped into the breach and was named as prime minister, the first Sikh ever to lead the country.

Kashmir quickly shot to the top of the new government's agenda, as random separatist attacks intensified in the valley. In November 2004, Manmohan made a rare prime-ministerial visit to the troubled region. Ahead of his arrival, Kashmiri militants called a general strike as a show of force, but this did not deter the PM from ordering the first of several planned troop withdrawals – key landmarks on the Indo-Pak Peace Road Map.

Meanwhile, calls for greater autonomy were also intensifying in the **north-east**, where old ethnic tensions pose a perennial threat of insurgency – even normally peaceful Darjeeling has been plagued by civil unrest in recent years, as Gurkha factions compete for power. The violence peaked in October 2004, when a wave of bombings and shootings killed more than 100 people. In Assam, an oil pipeline was attacked, cutting off power supplies, while in Dimapur, the capital of Nagaland, three explosions (including one on a crowded railway station) killed 28.

Unrest in the northeast hill states is only one manifestation of a steadily strengthening, pan-Indian pull away from the centre. Underpinning the rise of "regionalism", as it's been dubbed by the local press, has been the increased dependence of the BJP-led NDA on its lesser coalition partners, drawn from provincial state-based parties. Other factors too have led to a general weakening of the national capital's grip on the country. Incapable of raising adequate tax revenue, and rotten to its core with corruption, New Delhi no longer commands the respect and economic power it used to. Chronic political instability has also taken its toll. The absence of consistent policies has meant that big business and the affluent classes have increasingly had to look after themselves, which has conspicuously widened the gap between the haves and the have-nots.

As it struggles to balance the ambitions of its privileged elite with the basic needs of its poor, Indian society at the start of the twenty-first century is rife with ironies. The country chosen by Bill Gates as the site of Microsoft's new Hi-Tech City, and a place capable of launching satellites, nuclear rockets and manned-space programmes, India is unable to provide clean drinking water, adequate nutrition and basic education for millions of its inhabitants. Its capacity to close this yawning gap will depend on the extent to which the country's politicians are able to deliver stable government, and curb the corruption and self-interest which have come to dominate public life.

The tsunamis

Although southeast India was 2000km away from the epicentre of the Indonesian earthquake, much of its coast lay in the direct path of the **tsunamis**, and on the morning of December 26, 2004, three giant waves, measuring between 30 and 40 feet, swept ashore from the Bay of Bengal. The areas worst hit, in order of severity, were the Nagappattinam–Karaikal and Cuddalore districts of **Tamil Nadu**, **Kanyakumari** on the southern extremity of the peninsula, the **Andaman and Nicobar Islands**, and a small stretch of coastline west of the Kollam-Allapuzha backwaters in **Kerala**. Official estimates placed the death toll at around 11,000, with as many as ten times that homeless. The real figure, however, is probably much higher and will never be known.

A massive clear-up operation ensued, with rehabilitation efforts focussing on the subsistence fishing communities who lost their homes and livelihoods in the disaster. Countless houses, boats, nets and tools were destroyed, and few of their owners can afford replacements. Inland, vast swaths of formerly fertile paddy were badly salinated; it is unclear as yet whether much of this land will ever be productive again. In terms of tourism, however, most of the businesses that suffered damage were up and running at the time of writing, and people making their living from the industry were encouraging visitors not to stay away from affected areas – a continued influx of tourist dollars will doubtless help to rebuild what was lost.

Religion

For the majority of Indians, Hinduism permeates every aspect of life, from commonplace daily chores to education and politics. The vast pantheon of Hindu deities is manifest everywhere – not only in temples, but in shops, rickshaws and even on *beedi* packets and matchboxes. Beside Hindus, Muslims are the most prominent religious group; they have been an integral part of Indian society since the twelfth century, and mosques are almost as common as temples. Though Jains and Buddhists now make up a tiny fraction of the population, their impact is still felt, and their magnificent temples are among the finest in India. Both these ancient faiths, like the more recently established Sikh community, were formed in reaction to the caste laws and ritual observances of Hinduism. In addition, there are small communities of Zoroastrians, descended from Iranians, and Christians, here since the first century. Hindu practices, such as caste distinction, have crept into most religions, and many of the festivals that mark each year with music, dance and feasting, are shared by all communities. Each has its own pilgrimage sites, heroes, legends and even culinary specialities, which all combine to give India its unique religious diversity.

Hinduism

Contemporary **Hinduism** – the religion of over 85 percent of Indians – is the product of several thousand years of evolution and assimilation. It has no founder or prophet, no single creed, and no single prescribed practice or doctrine; it takes in hundreds of gods, goddesses, beliefs and practices, and widely variant cults and philosophies. Some are recognized by only two or three villages, others are popular right across the subcontinent. Hindus (from the Persian word for Indians) call their beliefs and practices **dharma**, which envelops natural and moral law to define a way of living in harmony with a natural order, while achieving personal goals and meeting the requirements of society.

Early developments

The foundations of Hinduism were laid by the **Aryans**, semi-nomads who entered northwest India during the second millennium BC, and mixed with the indigenous Dravidian population. With them they brought a belief in gods associated with the elements, including **Agni**, the god of fire and sacrifice, **Surya**, the sun-god, and **Indra**, the chief god. Most of these deities faded in later times, but Indra is still regarded as the father of the gods, and Surya, eternally present in his magnificent chariot-temple in **Konarak** (Orissa), was widely worshipped until the medieval period.

Aryan beliefs were set out in the **Vedas**, scriptures "heard" (*shruti*) by "seers" (*rishis*). Transmitted orally for centuries, they were finally written, in Sanskrit, between 1000 BC and 500 AD. The earliest were the *Samhitas*, or hymns; later came the *Brahmanas*, sacrificial texts, and *Aranyakas*, or "forest treatises".

The earliest and most important *Samhita*, the **Rig Veda**, contains hymns to deities and *devas* (divine powers), and is supplemented by other books detailing rituals and prayers for ceremonial use. The **Brahmana** stress correct ritual performance, drawing heavily on concepts of **purity and pollution** that persist today, and concentrating on sacrificial rites. Pedantic attention to ritual soon supplanted the importance of the *devas*, and they were further undermined by a search for a single cosmic power thought to be their source, eventually conceived of as **Brahma**, the absolute creator, personified from earlier mentions of Brahman, an impersonal principle of cosmic unity.

The **Aranyakas** focused upon this all-powerful godhead, and reached their final stage in the **Upanishads**, which describe in beautiful and emotive verse the mystic experience of unity of the soul (*atman*) with Brahma, ideally attained through asceticism, renunciation of worldly values and meditation. In the *Upanishads* the concepts of **samsara**, a cyclic round of death and rebirth characterized by suffering and perpetuated by desire, and **moksha**, liberation from *samsara*, became firmly rooted. Fundamental aspects of the Hindu world view, both are accepted by all but a handful of Hindus today, along with the belief in **karma**, the certainty that one's present position in society is determined by the effect of one's previous actions in this and past lives.

Hindu society

The stratification of Hindu society is rooted in the **Dharma Shastras** and **Dharma Sutras**, scriptures written from "memory" (*smriti*) at the same time as the *Vedas*. These defined four hierarchical classes, or **varnas**, each assigned specific religious and social duties known as **varnashradharma**, and established Aryans as the highest social class. In descending order the *varnas* are: **brahmins** (priests and teachers), **kshatryas** (rulers and warriors), **vaishyas** (merchants and cultivators) and **shudras** (menials). The first three classes, known as "twice-born", are distinguished by a sacred thread worn from the time of initiation, and granted full access to religious texts and rituals. Below all four categories, groups whose jobs involve contact with dirt or death (such as undertakers, leather-workers and cleaners) were classified as "**Untouchables**". Though discrimination against Untouchables is now a criminal offence, in part thanks to the campaigns of Gandhi, the lowest stratum of society has by no means disappeared.

Within the four *varnas*, social status is further defined by **jati**, classifying each individual by family and precise occupation (for example, a *vaishya* may be a jewellery seller, cloth merchant, cowherd or farmer). A person's *jati* determines his **caste**, and lays restrictions on all aspects of life from food consumption, religious obligations and contact with other castes, to the choice of marriage partners. In general, Hindus marry members of the same *jati* – marrying someone of a different *varna* often results in ostracism from both family and caste, leaving the couple stranded in a society where caste affiliation takes primacy over all other aspects of individual identity. There are almost 3000 *jatis*; the divisions and restrictions they have enforced have become, time and time again, the subject of reform movements and the target of critics.

A Hindu has three aims in life: **dharma**, fulfilling one's duty to family and caste and acquiring religious merit (*punya*) through right living; **artha**, the lawful making of wealth; and **karma**, desire and satisfaction. These goals are linked with the four traditional stages in life. The first is as a child and student, devoted to learning from parents and guru. Next comes the stage of householder, expected to provide for a family and raise children, especially sons. That accomplished, he or she may then take up a life of celibacy and retreat into the forest to meditate alone, and finally renounce all possessions to become a homeless ascetic, hoping to achieve the ultimate goal of *moksha*. The small number of Hindus, including some women, who follow this ideal life assume the final stage as **sannyasis**, saffron-clad **sadhus** who wander throughout India, begging for food, and retreat to isolated caves, forests and hills to meditate. They're a common feature in most Indian towns, and many stay for long periods in

The Ramayana

The **Ramayana** epic is the story of **Rama**, the seventh of **Vishnu's** ten incarnations. Although possibly based on a historic figure, Rama is seen essentially as a representation of Vishnu's heroic qualities.

Rama is the oldest of four sons born to Dasaratha, the king of **Ayodhya**, and heir to the throne. At the time of Rama's coronation, **Kaikeyi**, one of the king's three wives, seizes the moment to ask the king to grant her two favours, as he had promised in a moment of rash appreciation. Her first request is for her son **Bharata** to be crowned instead of the rightful Rama; her second is for Rama to be banished to the forest for fourteen years. In an exemplary show of filial piety, Rama accepts the demands and leaves the city with his wife **Sita** and brother **Laksmana**.

One day, **Suparnakha**, the sister of Rama's bitter enemy **Ravana**, spots Rama in the woods and instantly falls in love with him. Being a virtuous, loyal husband, Rama rebuffs her advances, but Suparnakhi attempts to avenge herself on Sita, seeing her as the obstacle to Rama's heart. Laksmana intervenes, cutting off Suparnakha's nose and ears in retaliation. She then flees to her demon brother, who mobilizes fourteen giants against Rama. After Rama destroys them single-handedly, Ravana dispatches a further 14,000 warriors, who are dealt with in similar fashion. Thwarted by Rama's prowess, Ravana's advisers suggest that he should kidnap Rama's beloved Sita instead, causing him to die of a broken heart. Sita is successfully captured and flown by chariot to one of Ravana's palaces on the island of **Lanka**.

Determined to find Sita, Rama enlists the help of **Hanuman**, the monkey god. Hanuman leaps across the strait to Lanka and makes his way surreptitiously into Ravana's palace, where he hears the evil king trying to persuade Sita to marry him. If not, he threatens, "my cooks shall mince thy limbs with steel and serve thee for my morning meal" – a choice of consummation or consumption. Hanuman reports back to Rama, who gathers an army and prepares to attack. Monkeys form a bridge across the straits allowing the invading army to cross; after much fighting, Sita is rescued and reunited with her husband.

On the long journey back to Ayodhya, Sita's honour is brought into question. To prove her innocence, she asks Laksmana to build a funeral pyre and steps into the flames, praying to Agni, the fire god. Agni walks her through the fire into the arms of a delighted Rama. They march into Ayodhya guided by a trail of lights laid out by the local people. Today, this illuminated homecoming is commemorated by Hindus all over the world during **Diwali**, the festival of lights. At the end of the epic, Rama's younger brother gladly steps down, allowing Rama to be crowned as the rightful king.

particular temples. Not all have raised families: some assume the life of a *sadhu* at an early age as *chellas*, pupils, of an older *sadhu*.

The popular deities

Alongside the *Dharma Shastras* and *Dharma Shutras*, the most important works of the *smriti* tradition, thought to have been completed by the fourth century AD at the latest, were the **Puranas** – long mythological stories focused on the Vedic gods and their heroic actions – and Hinduism's two great epics, the **Mahabharata** and **Ramayana**. Through these texts, the main gods and goddesses became firmly embedded in the religion. Alongside **Brahma**, the creator, **Vishnu** was acknowledged as the preserver, and **Shiva** ("auspicious, benign"), referred to in the *Rig Veda* as Rudra, was recognized for his destructive powers. The three are often depicted in a trinity, *trimurti*, but in time Brahma's importance declined, and Shiva and Vishnu became the most popular deities.

The Mahabharata

Eight times as long as the *Iliad* and *Odyssey* combined, the **Mahabharata** is the most popular of all Hindu texts. Written around 400 AD, it tells of a feuding *kshatrya* family in upper India (Bharata) during the fourth millennium BC. Like all good epics, the *Mahabharata* recounts a gripping tale, using its characters to illustrate moral values. In essence it attempts to elucidate the position of the warrior castes, the *kshatryas*, and demonstrate that religious fulfilment is as accessible for them as it is for brahmins.

The chief character is **Arjuna**, a superb archer, who with his four brothers – Yudhishtra, Bhima, Nakula and Sahadeva – represents the **Pandava** clan, upholders of righteousness and supreme fighters. Arjuna won his wife **Draupadi** in an archery contest, but wishing to avoid jealousy she agreed to be the shared wife of all five brothers. The Pandava clan are resented by their cousins, the evil **Kauravas**, led by Duryodhana, the eldest son of Dhrtarashtra, ruler of the Kuru kingdom.

When Dhrtarashtra handed his kingdom over to the Pandavas, the Kauravas were far from happy. Duryodhana challenged Yudhishtra (known for his brawn but not his brain) to a gambling contest. The dice game was rigged; Yudhishtra gambled away not only his possessions, but also his kingdom and his shared wife. The Kauravas offered to return the kingdom to the Pandavas if they could spend thirteen years in exile, together with their wife, without being recognized. Despite much scheming, the Pandavas succeeded, but on return found that the Kauravas would not fulfil their side of the bargain.

Thus ensued the great battle of the *Mahabharata*, told in the sixth book, the **Bhagavad Gita** – immensely popular as an independent story. Vishnu descends to earth as **Krishna**, and steps into battle as Arjuna's charioteer. The *Bhagavad Gita* details the fantastic struggle of the fighting cousins, using magical weapons and brute force. Arjuna is in a dilemma, unable to justify the killing of his own kin in pursuit of a rightful kingdom for himself and his brothers. Krishna consoles him, reminding him that his principal duty, his *varnashradharma*, is as a warrior. What is more, Krishna points out, each man's soul, or *atman*, is eternal, and transmigrates from body to body, so Arjuna need not grieve the death of his cousins. Krishna convinces Arjuna that by fulfilling his *dharma* he not only upholds law and order by saving the kingdom from the grasp of unrighteous rulers, he also serves the gods in the spirit of devotion (*bhakti*), and thus guarantees himself eternal union with the divine in the blissful state of *moksha*.

The Pandavas finally win the battle, and Yudhishtra is crowned king. Eventually Arjuna's grandson, Pariksit, inherits the throne, and the Pandavas trek to Mount Meru, the mythical centre of the universe and the abode of the gods, where Arjuna finds Krishna's promised *moksha*.

Depicted in human or semihuman form and accompanied by an animal "**vehicle**", other gods and goddesses who came alive in the mythology of the *Puranas* are still venerated across India. River goddesses, ancestors, guardians of particular places, and protectors against disease and natural disaster are as central to village life as the major deities.

Philosophical trends

The complications presented by Hinduism's view of deities, *samsara*, *atman* (the human soul) and *moksha* naturally encouraged philosophical debate, and led eventually to the formation of six schools of thought, known as the **Darshanas**. Each presented a different exposition of the true nature of *moksha* and how to attain it.

Foremost among these was the **Advaita Vedanta** school of **Shankara** (c.788–850 AD), a religious teacher and reformer who interpreted Hinduism as pure monotheism verging on monism (the belief that all is one: in this case, one with God). Drawing on Upanishadic writings, he claimed that they identified the essence of the human soul with that of God (*tat tvam asi*, "that thou art"), and that all else – the phenomenal world and all *devas* – is an illusion (*maya*) created by God. Shankara is revered as saint-philosopher at the twelve **jyotirlingas**: sacred Shaivite sites associated with the unbounded *lingam* of light, which as a manifestation of Shiva once persuaded both Brahma and Vishnu to acknowledge Shiva's supremacy.

Another important Darshana centred around the age-old practice of **yoga** (literally "the action of yoking [to] another"), elucidated by **Patanjali** (second century BC) in his *Yoga Sutras*. Interpreting yoga as the yoking of mind and body, or the yoking of the mind with God, Patanjali detailed various practices, which used in combination may lead to an understanding of the fundamental **unity** of all things. The most common form of yoga known in the West is *hatha* yoga, whereby the body and its vital energies is brought under control through physical positions and breathing methods, with results said to range from attaining a calm mind to being able to fly through the air, enter other bodies or become invisible. Other practices include *mantra* yoga, the recitation of formulas and meditation on mystical diagrams (*mandalas*), *bhakti* yoga (devotion), *jnana* yoga (knowledge) and *raja*, or royal, yoga, the highest form of yoga when the mind is absorbed in God.

Practice

The primary concern of most Hindus is to reduce bad karma and acquire merit (*punya*), by honest and charitable living within the restrictions imposed by caste, and by worship, in the hope of attaining a higher status of rebirth. Strict rules address purity and pollution, the most obvious of them requiring high-caste Hindus to limit their contact with potentially polluting lower castes. All bodily excretions are polluting (hence the strange looks Westerners receive when they blow their noses and return their handkerchiefs to their pockets). Above all else, **water** is the agent of purification, used in ablutions before prayer, and revered in all rivers, especially Ganga (the Ganges).

In most Hindu homes, a chosen deity is worshipped daily in a shrine room, and scriptures are read. Outside the home, worship takes place in temples, and consists of **puja**, or devotion to god – sometimes a simple act of prayer, but more commonly a complex process when the god's image is circumambulated, offered flowers, rice, sugar and incense, and anointed with water, milk or sandalwood paste (which is usually done on behalf of the devotee by the temple priest, the *pujari*). The aim in *puja* is to take **darshan** – glimpse the god – and thus receive his or her blessing. Whether devotees simply worship the deity in prayer, or make requests – for a healthy crop, a son, good results in exams, a vigorous monsoon or a cure for illness – they leave the temple with *prasad*, an offering of food or flowers taken from the holy sanctuary by the *pujaris*.

Communal worship and get-togethers en route to pilgrimage sites are celebrated with *kirtan* or *bhajan*, singing of hymns, perhaps verses in praise of Krishna taken from the *Bhagavad Purana*, or repetitive cries of "Jai Shankar!" (Praise to Shiva). Temple ceremonies are conducted in Sanskrit by *pujaris* who tend the image in daily rituals that symbolically wake, bathe, feed and dress the god, and finish each day by preparing the god for sleep. The most elaborate is the evening ritual, **arati**, when lamps are lit, blessed in the sanctuary, and passed around devotees amid the clanging of drums, gongs and cymbals. In many villages, shrines to *devatas*, village deities who function as protectors and may bring disaster if neglected, are more important than temples.

Hindu gods and goddesses

Vishnu

The chief function of **Vishnu**, "pervader", is to keep the world in order, preserving, restoring and protecting. With four arms holding a conch, discus, lotus and mace, Vishnu is blue-skinned, and often shaded by a serpent, or resting on its coils, afloat on an ocean. He is usually seen alongside his half-man-half-eagle vehicle, Garuda. **Vaishnavites**, often distinguishable by two vertical lines on their foreheads, recognize Vishnu as supreme lord, and hold that he has manifested himself on earth nine times. These incarnations, or *avatars*, have been as fish (Matsya), tortoise (Kurma), boar (Varaha), man-lion (Narsingh), dwarf (Vamana), axe-wielding brahmin (Parsuram), Rama, Krishna and Balaram (though some say that the Buddha is the ninth *avatar*). Vishnu's future descent to earth as Kalki, the saviour who will come to restore purity and destroy the wicked, is eagerly awaited.

The most important *avatars* are Krishna and Rama. **Krishna** is the hero of the Bhagavad Gita, in which he proposes three routes to salvation (*moksha*): selfless action (*karmayoga*), knowledge (*jnana*), and devotion to god (*bhakti*), and explains that *moksha* is attainable in this life, even without asceticism and renunciation. This appealed to all castes, as it denied the necessity of ritual and officiating brahmin priests, and evolved into the popular *bhakti* cult that legitimized love of God as a means to *moksha*, and found expression in emotional songs of the quest for union with the divine. Through *bhakti*, Krishna's role was extended, and he assumed different faces: most popularly he is the playful cowherd who seduces and dances with cowgirls (*gopis*), giving each the illusion that she is his only lover. He is also pictured as a small, chubby, mischievous baby, known for his butter-stealing exploits, who inspires tender motherly love in women. Like Vishnu, Krishna is blue, and often shown dancing and playing the flute. Popular legend has it that Krishna was born in **Mathura**, today a major pilgrimage centre, and sported with his *gopis* in nearby **Vrindavan**. He also established a kingdom on the far western coast of Gujarat, at **Dwarka**.

Rama, Vishnu's seventh incarnation, is the chief character in the **Ramayana**, the epic detailing his exploits in exile (see p.1397).

Shiva

Shaivism, the cult of **Shiva**, was also inspired by *bhakti*, requiring selfless love from devotees in a quest for divine communion, but Shiva has never been incarnate on earth. He is presented in many different aspects, such as **Nataraja**, Lord of the Dance, **Mahadev**, Great God, and **Maheshvar**, Divine Lord, source of all knowledge. Though he does have several terrible forms, his role extends beyond that of destroyer, and he is revered as the source of the whole universe.

Shiva is often depicted with four or five faces, holding a trident, draped with serpents, and bearing a third eye in his forehead. In temples, he is identified with the *lingam*, or phallic symbol, resting in the *yoni*, a representation of female sexuality. Whether as statue or *lingam*, Shiva is guarded by his bull-mount, Nandi, and often accompanied by a consort, who also assumes various forms, and is looked upon as the vital energy, **shakti**, that empowers him. Their erotic exploits were a favourite sculptural subject between the ninth and twelfth centuries, most unashamedly in carvings on the temples of **Khajuraho** in Madhya Pradesh.

While Shiva is the object of popular devotion all over India, as the terrible **Bhairav** he is also the god of the Shaivite **ascetics**, who renounce family and caste ties and perform extreme meditative and yogic practices. Many, though not all, smoke ganja, Shiva's favourite herb; all see renunciation and realization of God as the key to *moksha*. Some ascetic practices enter the realm of **Tantrism**, in which confrontation with all that's impure, such as alcohol, death, and sex, is used to merge the sacred and the profane, and bring about the profound realization that Shiva is omnipresent.

Other gods and goddesses

Chubby and smiling, elephant-headed **Ganesh**, the first son of Shiva and Parvati, is invoked before every undertaking (except funerals). Seated on a throne or lotus, his image is often placed above temple gateways, in shops and houses; in his four arms he holds a conch, discus, bowl of sweets (or club) and a water lily, and he's always attended by his vehicle, a rat. Credited with writing the *Mahabharata* as it was dictated by the sage Vyasa, Ganesh is regarded by many as the god of learning, the lord of success, prosperity and peace.

Durga, the fiercest of the female deities, is an aspect of Shiva's more conservative consort, Parvati (also known as Uma), who is remarkable only for her beauty and fidelity. Among Durga's many aspects, each a terrifying goddess eager to slay demons, are Chamunda, Kali and Muktakeshi, but in all her forms she is Mahadevi (Great Goddess). Statues show her with ten arms, holding the head of a demon, a spear, and other weapons; she tramples demons underfoot, or dances upon Shiva's body. A garland of skulls drapes her neck, and her tongue hangs from her mouth, dripping with blood – a particularly gruesome sight on pictures of Kali. Durga is much venerated in Bengal; in all her temples, animal sacrifices are a crucial element of worship, to satisfy her thirst for blood and deter her ruthless anger.

The comely goddess **Lakshmi**, usually shown sitting or standing on a lotus flower, and sometimes called Padma (lotus), is the embodiment of loveliness, grace and charm, and the goddess of prosperity and wealth. Vishnu's consort, she appears in different aspects alongside each of his *avatars*; the most important are Sita, wife of Rama, and Radha, Krishna's favourite *gopi*. In many temples she is shown as one with Vishnu, in the form of Lakshmi Narayan.

Though some legends claim that his mother was Ganga, or even Agni, **Karttikeya** is popularly believed to be the second son of Shiva and Parvati. Primarily a god of war, he was popular among the northern Guptas, who worshipped him as Skanda, and the southern Chalukyas, for whom he was Subrahmanya. Usually shown with six faces, and standing upright with bow and arrow, Karttikeya is commonly petitioned by those wishing for male offspring.

India's great monkey god, **Hanuman**, features in the *Ramayana* as Rama's chief aide in the fight against the demon-king of Lanka. Depicted as a giant monkey clasping a mace, Hanuman is the deity of acrobats and wrestlers, but is also seen as Rama and Sita's greatest devotee, and an author of Sanskrit grammar. As his representatives, monkeys find sanctuary in temples all over India.

The most beautiful Hindu goddess, **Saraswati**, the wife of Brahma, with her flawless milk-white complexion, sits or stands on a water lily or peacock, playing a lute, sitar or *vina*. Associated with the River Saraswati, mentioned in the *Rig Veda*, she is revered as the goddess of music, creativity and learning.

Closely linked with the planet Saturn, **Sani** is feared for his destructive powers. His image, a black statue with protruding blood-red tongue, is often found on street corners; strings of green chillies and lemon are hung in shops and houses each Saturday (*Saniwar*) to ward off his evil influences.

Mention must also be made of the **sacred cow**, Kamdhenu, who receives devotion through the respect shown to all cows, left to amble through streets and temples all over India. The origin of the cow's sanctity is uncertain; some myths record that Brahma created cows at the same time as brahmins, to provide *ghee* (clarified butter) for use in priestly ceremonies. To this day cow dung and urine are used to purify houses (in fact the urine keeps insects at bay), and the killing or harming of cows by any Hindu is a grave offence. The cow is often referred to as mother of the gods, and each part of its body is significant: its horns symbolize the gods, its face the sun and moon, its shoulders Agni (god of fire) and its legs the Himalayas.

Each of the **great stages** in life – birth, initiation (when boys of the three twice-born *varnas* are invested with a sacred thread, and a mantra is whispered into their ear by their guru), marriage, death and cremation – is cause for fervent prayer, energetic celebration and feasting. The most significant event in a Hindu's life is **marriage**, which symbolizes ritual purity, and for women is so important that it takes the place of initiation. Feasting, dancing, and singing among the bride and groom's families, usually lasting for a week or more before and after the marriage, are the order of the day all over India. The actual marriage is consecrated when the couple walk seven times round a sacred fire, accompanied by sacred verses read by an officiating brahmin. Despite efforts to reduce the importance of a **dowry**, a valuable gift from the bride's family to the groom, these are still demanded, and among wealthier families may include televisions, videos, and cars in addition to the more common items of jewellery and money. Deaths in "kitchen accidents" of wives whose dowry is below expectations are still known to occur.

Festivals and pilgrimages

Life transitions are by no means the only cause for celebration among Hindus, whose year is marked by **festivals** devoted to deities, re-enacting mythological stories and commemorating sacred sites. The grandest festivals are held at places made holy by association with gods, goddesses, miracles, and great teachers, or rivers and mountains; throughout the year these are important **pilgrimage** sites, visited by devotees eager to receive *darshan*, glimpse the world of the gods, and attain merit. The journey, or *yatra*, to a pilgrimage site is every bit as significant as reaching the sacred location, and bands of Hindus (particularly *sadhus*) often walk from site to site. Modern transport, however, has made things easier, and every state lays on pilgrimage tours, when buses full of chanting families roar from one temple to another, filling up with religious souvenirs as they go.

Perhaps India's single most sacred place is the ancient city of **Varanasi** (also known as Benares or Kashi), on the banks of the Ganges. The river has been sacred since the time of the earliest Aryan settlements, and is personified as the beneficent goddess Ganga. At Varanasi it holds the redeeming quality common to all rivers, but bathing in its waters, and more particularly, dying or being cremated there, guarantees entering heaven (*svarga*) and achieving release from rebirth. *Ghats*, steps leading to the water's edge, are common in all river- or lakeside towns, the abode of priests who offer puja to a devotee's chosen deity.

The source of the Ganges, high in the mountains of western Uttar Pradesh at **Gangotri**, is also held in great reverence, as are the five ancient temples nearby, known as **Panch Kedar**, deep in the Himalayas. Equally important are **sangams**, or **tirthas**, the points where two rivers meet. Every twelve years, when India's largest festival, the **Kumbh Mela**, is held at Allahabad, the *sangam* of the Ganges and the Yamuna, the *ghats* turn into a seething mass of bodies, overrun by near-naked ascetics who are the first of millions to bathe in the holy waters. Lesser *melas* are held at three-yearly intervals at the *tirthas* of Haridwar, Nasik and Ujjain.

Not only river confluences are auspicious: at Kanniyakumari, the southern tip of India, the waters of the Indian Ocean, the Bay of Bengal and the Arabian sea are thought to merge. Pilgrimages here are often combined with visits to the great temples of **Tamil Nadu**, where Shaivite and Vaishnavite saints established cults, and India's largest temples were constructed. Madurai, Thanjavur, Chidambaram and Srirangam are major pilgrimage centres, representing the pinnacle of the architectural development that began at Mamallapuram. Their festivals often involve the tugging of deities on vast wooden chariots through the streets, a practice most vigorously played out at **Puri**, in Orissa, when Lord Jagannath is taken from the temple during *Rath Yatra* for a foray through the town.

As well as specific temples sacred to particular gods – Brahma in **Pushkar**, Kali at **Kolkata** (Calcutta), or Shiva at the twelve *jyotirlingas* – historical sites, such as the caves of **Ellora**, and the former Vijayanagar capital at **Hampi**, remain magnets for pilgrims. More than a common ideology, it is this sacred geography, entwined with popular mythology, that unites hundreds of millions of Hindus, who have also been brought together in nationalistic struggles, particularly in response to Christian missionaries and Muslim and British domination.

Islam

Indian society may be dominated by Hindus, but **Muslims** – some twelve percent of the population – form a significant presence in almost every town, city and village. The belief in only one god, Allah, the condemnation of idol worship, and the observance of their own strict dietary laws and specific festivals set Muslims apart from their Hindu neighbours, with whom they have coexisted for centuries. Such differences have often led to communal fighting, most notably during Partition in 1947, the riots that followed the destruction by Hindus of the Babri Masjid mosque in Ayodhya in 1993 and the massacre of pilgrims at Godhra, Gujarat, in 2002.

Islam, "submission to God", was founded by **Mohammed** (570–632 AD), who is regarded as the last in a succession of prophets and who transmitted God's final and perfected revelation to mankind through the writings of the divinely revealed "recitation", the **Koran** (Qur'an). This, the authoritative scripture of Islam, contains the basis of Islamic belief: that there is one god, Allah (though he is attributed with 99 names), and his prophet is Mohammed.

The true beginning of Islam is dated at 622 AD, when Mohammed and his followers, exiled from Mecca, made the *hijra* (migration) north to Yathrib, later known as Medina, "City of the Prophet". The *hijra* marks the start of the Islamic lunar calendar: the Gregorian year 2000 was for Muslims 1421 AH (*Anno Hijra*).

From Medina, Mohammed ordered raids on caravans heading for Mecca and, inspired by *jihad*, or "striving" on behalf of God and Islam, led his community in battles against the Meccans. This concept of holy war was the driving force behind the incredible expansion of Islam – by 713 Muslims had settled as far west as Spain, and on the banks of the Indus in the east. When **Mecca** was peacefully surrendered to Mohammed in 630, he cleared the sacred shrine, the Ka'ba, of idols, and proclaimed it the pilgrimage centre of Islam.

Mohammed was succeeded as leader of the *umma*, the Islamic community, by Abu Bakr, the prophet's representative, or caliph, the first in a line of caliphs who led the orthodox community until the eleventh century AD. However, a schism soon emerged when the third caliph, Uthman, was assassinated by followers of Ali, Mohammed's son-in-law, in 656 AD. This new sect, calling themselves **Shi'as**, "partisans" of Ali, looked to Ali and his successors, infallible imams, as leaders of the *umma* until 878 AD, and thereafter replaced their religious authority with a body of scholars, the *ulema*.

By the second century after the *hijra* (ninth century AD), orthodox, or **Sunni**, Islam had assumed the form in which it endures today. A collection of traditions about the prophet, **Hadith**, became the source for ascertaining the **Sunna**, customs, of Mohammed. From the Koran and the Sunna, seven major **items of belief** were laid down: the belief in God, in angels as his messengers, in prophets (including Jesus and Moses), in the Koran, in the doctrine of predestination by

God, in the Day of Judgement, and in the bodily resurrection of all people on this day. Religious practice was also standardized under the Muslim law, **Sharia**, in the **Five Pillars of Islam**. The first "pillar" is the confession of faith, *shahada*, that "There is no god but God, and Mohammed is his messenger". The other four are prayer (*salat*) five times daily, almsgiving (*zakat*), fasting (*saum*), especially during the month of Ramadan, and, if possible, pilgrimage (*haj*) to Mecca, the ultimate goal of every practising Muslim.

The first Muslims to settle in India were traders who arrived on the south coast in the seventh century, probably in search of timber for shipbuilding. Later, in 711, Muslims entered Sind, in the northwest, to take action against Hindu pirates, and dislodged the Hindu government. Their presence, however, was short-lived. Much more significant was the invasion of north India under **Mahmud of Ghazni**, who rampaged through the Punjab in search of temple treasures, and in the spirit of *jihad*, engaged in a war against infidels and idolaters. More Turkish raids followed in the twelfth century, resulting in the colonization of India and the provision of a homeland for refugees pushed out of Persia by the Mongols. The Turks set themselves up in Delhi as **sultans**, the forerunners of the **Moghuls** (see pp.1373–1377).

Many Muslims who settled in India intermarried with Hindus, Buddhists and Jains, and the community spread. A further factor in its growth was missionary activity by **Sufis**, who emphasized abstinence and self-denial in service to God, and stressed the attainment of inner knowledge of God through meditation and mystical experience. In India, Sufi teachings spread among Shaivites and Vaishnavites, who shared their passion for personal closeness to God. Their use of music (particularly *qawwali* singing) and dance, shunned by orthodox Muslims, appealed to Hindus, for whom *kirtan* (singing) played an important role in religious practice. One *qawwali*, relating the life of the Sufi saint Waris Ali Shah, draws parallels between his early life and the childhood of Krishna – an outrage for orthodox Muslims, but attractive to Hindus, who still flock to his shrine in Deva Sharief near Lucknow. Similar shrines, or *dargars*, all over India bridge the gap between Islam and Hinduism.

Muslims are enjoined to pray five times daily, following a routine of utterances and positions. They may do this at home or in a **mosque** – always full at noon on Friday, for communal prayer. (Only the Druze, an esoteric sect based in Mumbai, hold communal prayers on Thursdays.) Characterized by bulbous domes and high minarets, from which a *muezzin* calls the faithful to prayer, mosques always contain a mihrab, or niche indicating the direction of prayer (to Mecca), a *mimbar* or pulpit, from which the Friday sermon is read, a source of water for ablutions, and a balcony for women. Firm reminders of Muslim dominance, mosques all over India display a bold linear grandeur quite different to the delicacy of Hindu temples. India's largest mosque is the Jama Masjid ("Friday Mosque") in **Delhi**, but magnificent structures, including tombs, schools and substantial remains of cities are scattered throughout north India and the Deccan, with especially outstanding examples in Hyderabad, Jaunpur, Agra and Fatehpur Sikri.

Muslim women

The position of **women** in Islam is a subject of great debate. It's customary for women to be veiled, though in larger cities many women don't cover their heads, and in strictly orthodox communities most wear a *burkha*, usually black, that covers them from head to toe. Like other Indian women, Muslim women take second place to men in public, but in the home, where they are often shielded from men's eyes in an inner courtyard, they wield great influence. In theory, education is equally available to boys and girls, but girls tend to forgo learning soon after sixteen, encouraged instead to assume the traditional role of wife and mother. Contrary to popular belief, polygamy is not widespread; while it does occur, and Mohammed himself had several wives, many Muslims prefer monogamy, and several sects actually stress it as a duty. In marriage, women receive a dowry (Hindu women must provide one) as financial security.

Buddhism

For several centuries, **Buddhism** dominated India, with adherents in almost every part of the subcontinent. However, having reached its height in the fifth century AD, it was all but eclipsed by the time of the Muslim conquest. Today Buddhists are a tiny fraction of the population, but superb monuments such as the caves of Ajanta and Ellora in Maharashtra, the remarkable stupas of Sanchi in Madhya Pradesh and Tawang Monastery in Arunachal Pradesh are fine reminders of this once flourishing culture. Outside the numerous Tibetan refugee camps, only Ladakh and Sikkim now preserve a significant Buddhist presence.

The founder of Buddhism, **Siddhartha Gautama**, known as the **Buddha**, "the awakened one", was born into a wealthy *kshatrya* family in Lumbini, north of the Gangetic plain in present-day Nepal, around 566 BC. Brought up in luxury as a prince and a Hindu, he married at an early age, and renounced family life when he was thirty. Unsatisfied with the explanations of worldly suffering proposed by Hindu gurus, and convinced that asceticism did not lead to spiritual realization, Siddhartha spent years in meditation, wandering through the ancient kingdom, or *janapada*, of Magadha. His enlightenment (*bodhi*) is said to have taken place under a *bodhi* tree in **Bodhgaya** (Bihar), after a night of contemplation during which he resisted the worldly temptations set before him by the demon, Mara. Soon afterwards he gave his first sermon in **Sarnath**, now a major pilgrimage centre. For the rest of his life he taught, expounding **Dharma**, the true nature of the world, human life and spiritual attainment. Before his death (c.486 BC) in Kushinagar (UP), he had established the **Sangha**, a community of monks and nuns who continued his teachings.

Although frequently categorized as a religion, many scholars and practitioners understand Buddhism to be the science of mind. Buddhism has no god in the monotheistic sense; the deities of Tibetan Buddhism and the Buddha statues in temples are not there for worship as such – but rather as symbols to aid and deepen spiritual awareness. The Buddha's view of life incorporated the Hindu concepts of *samsara* and karma, but remodelled the ultimate goal of religion, calling it **nirvana**, "no wind". Indefinable in worldly terms, since it is by nature free from conditioning, nirvana represents a clarity of mind, pure understanding and unimaginable bliss. Its attainment signals an end to rebirth, but no communion of a "soul" with God; neither has independent existence. The most important concept outlined by the Buddha was that all things are subject to the inevitability of **impermanence**. There is no independent inherent self due to the interconnectedness of all things, and our egos are the biggest obstacles on the road to enlightenment.

Practice

Disregarding caste and priestly dominance in ritual, the Buddha formulated a teaching open to all. His followers took refuge in the three jewels: Buddha, Dharma, and Sangha. The teachings became known as **Theravada**, or "Doctrine of the Elders". By the first century BC the **Tripitaka**, or "Three

Baskets" (a Pali canon in three sections), had set out the basis for early Buddhist practice, proposing *dana*, selfless giving, and *sila*, precepts which aim at avoiding harm to oneself and others, as the most important guidelines for all Buddhists, and the essential code of practice for the lay community.

Carried out with good intentions, *sila* and *dana* maximize the acquisition of good karma, and minimize material attachment, thus making the individual open to the more religiously oriented teachings, the **Four Noble Truths**. The first of these states that all is suffering (*dukkha*), not because every action is necessarily unpleasurable, but because nothing in the phenomenal world is permanent or reliable. The second truth states that *dukkha* arises through attachment, the third refers to nirvana, the cessation of suffering, and the fourth details the path to nirvana. Known as the **Eightfold Path** – right understanding, thought, speech, action, livelihood, effort, mindfulness and concentration – it aims at reducing attachment and ego and increasing awareness, until all four truths are thoroughly comprehended, and nirvana is achieved. Even this should not be clinged to – those who experience it are advised by the Buddha to use their understanding to help others to achieve realization.

The Sanskrit word **bhavana**, referred to in the West as **meditation**, translates literally as "bringing into being". Traditionally meditation is divided into two categories: **Samatha**, or calm, which stills and controls the mind, and **Vipassana**, or insight, during which thought processes and the noble truths are investigated, leading ultimately to a knowledge of reality. Both methods are taught in Buddhist centres across India.

At first, Buddhist iconography represented the Buddha by symbols such as a footprint, *bodhi* tree, parasol or vase. These can be seen on stupas (domed monuments containing relics of the Buddha) built throughout India from the time of the Buddhist emperor Ashoka, and in ancient Buddhist caves, which served as meditation retreats and *viharas* (monasteries). The finest are at **Ellora** and **Ajanta**; like the remarkable stupas at **Sanchi**, they incorporate later designs which depict the Buddha in human form, standing and preaching or sitting in meditation, distinguished by characteristic marks, and indicating his teaching by hand gestures, or *mudras*.

This artistic development coincided with an increase in the devotional side of Buddhism, and a recognition of **bodhisattvas** – those bound for enlightenment who delayed self-absorption in nirvana to become teachers, spurred by selfless compassion and altruism.

The importance of the *bodhisattva* ideal grew as a new school, the **Mahayana**, or "Great Vehicle", emerged. By the twelfth century it had become fully established and, somewhat disparagingly, renamed the old Theravada school "**Hinayana**" (Lesser Vehicle). Mahayanists proposed emptiness, *sunyata*, as the fundamental nature of all things, taking to extremes the belief that nothing has independent existence. The **wisdom** necessary to understand *sunyata*, and the **skilful means** required to put wisdom into action in daily life and teaching, and interpret emptiness in a positive sense, became the most important qualities of Mahayana Buddhism. Before long *bodhisattvas* were joined in both scripture and art by female consorts who embodied wisdom.

Theravada Buddhism survives today in Sri Lanka, Myanmar, Thailand, Laos and Cambodia. Mahayana Buddhism spread from India to Nepal and Tibet and from there to China, Korea and ultimately Japan. In many places further evolution saw the adoption of magical methods, esoteric teachings, and the full use of sensory experience to bring about spiritual transformation, resulting in a separate school known as **Vajrayana** based on texts called *tantras*. Vajrayana encourages meditation on *mandalas* (symbolic diagrams representing the cosmos and internal spiritual attainment), sexual imagery, and sometimes sexual practice, as a means of raising energies and awareness for spiritual goals.

Tibetan Buddhism

Buddhism was introduced to **Tibet** in the seventh century, and integrated to a certain extent with the indigenous **Bon** cult, before emerging as a faith considered to incorporate all three vehicles – Hinayana, Mahayana and Vajrayana. Practised largely in Ladakh, along with parts of Himachal Pradesh, Arunachal Pradesh and Sikkim, Tibetan Buddhism recognizes a historical Buddha, known as Sakyamuni, alongside previous Buddhas and a host of *bodhisattvas* and protector deities. These "gods" are not worshipped as such, rather they represent various emotions or states of being. The various **pujas** (ceremonies) are not so much prayers as ways of confronting or manifesting these states. For instance, to develop the quality of compassion in one's own life one may meditate and make offerings to Chenrezig (Avalokitesvara in Sanskrit), the Buddha of compassion, or to Tara, the equivalent female embodiment. Many pujas involve elaborate rituals, and incorporate music and dance. There is a heavy emphasis on teachers, lamas (similar to gurus), and reincarnated teachers, known as *tulkus*. The **Dalai Lama**, the head of Tibetan Buddhism, is the fourteenth in a succession of incarnate *bodhisattvas*, the representative of Avalokitesvara, and the leader of the exiled Tibetan community whose headquarters are in Dharamsala (HP). With over 100,000 Tibetan **refugees** now living in India, including the Dalai Lama and Tibetan government in exile, Tibetan Buddhism is probably the most accessible and flourishing form of Buddhism in India, and there are numerous opportunities for study (see Basics, p.85).

For Buddhist monks and nuns, and some members of the lay community, meditation is an integral part of religious life. Most lay Buddhists concentrate on *dana* and *sila* and, on auspicious days such as *Vesak* (marking the Buddha's birth, enlightenment and death), make **pilgrimages** to **Bodhgaya**, **Sarnath**, **Lumbini** and **Kushinagar**. After laying offerings before Buddha statues, devotees gather in silent meditation, or join in chants taken from early Buddhist texts. *Uposathas*, full-moon days, are marked by continual chanting through the night when temples are lit by glimmering butter lamps, often set afloat on lotus ponds, among the flowers that represent the essential beauty and purity to be found in each person in the thick of the confusing "mud" of daily life.

Among Tibetan communities, devotees hang prayer flags, turn prayer wheels, and set stones carved with mantras (religious verses) in rivers, thus sending the word of the Buddha with wind and water to all corners of the earth. Prayers and chanting are often accompanied by horns, drums and cymbals.

Jainism

Though the **Jain** population in India is relatively small – accounting for less than one percent of the population – it has been tremendously influential for at least 2500 years. A large proportion of Jains live in Gujarat, and all over India they are commonly occupied as merchants and traders. Similarities to Hindu worship, and a shared respect for nature and non-violence, have contributed to the decline of the Jain community through conversion to Hinduism, but there is no antagonism between the two sects.

Focused on the practice of **ahimsa** (non-violence), Jains follow a rigorous discipline to avoid harm to all **jivas**, or "souls", which exist in humans, animals, plants, water, fire, earth and air. They assert that every *jiva* is pure, omniscient, and capable of achieving liberation, or *moksha*, from existence in this universe.

However, *jivas* are obscured by **karma**, a form of subtle matter that clings to the soul, is born of action, and binds the *jiva* to physical existence. For the most orthodox Jain, the only way to dissociate karma from the *jiva*, and thereby escape the wheel of death and rebirth, is to follow the path of asceticism and meditation, rejecting passion, attachment, carelessness and impure action.

The Jain doctrine is based upon the teachings of **Mahavira**, or "Great Hero", the last in a succession of 24 **tirthankaras** ("crossing-makers") said to appear on earth every 300 million years. Mahavira (c.599–527 BC) was born as Vardhamana Jnatrputra into a *kshatrya* family near modern Patna in northeast India. Like the Buddha, Mahavira rejected family life at the age of thirty, and spent years wandering as an ascetic, renouncing all possessions in an attempt to conquer attachment to worldly values. Firmly opposed to sacrificial rites and caste distinctions, after gaining complete understanding and detachment, he began teaching others, not about Vedic gods and divine heroes, but about the true nature of the world, and the means required for release, *moksha*, from an endless cycle of rebirth.

His teachings were written down in the first millennium BC, and Jainism prospered throughout India, under the patronage of kings such as Chandragupta Maurya (third century BC). Not long after, there was a schism, in part based on linguistic and geographical divisions, but mostly due to differences in monastic practice. On the one hand the **Digambaras** ("sky-clad") believed that nudity was an essential part of world renunciation, and that women are incapable of achieving liberation from worldly existence. The ("white-clad") **Svetambaras**, however, disregarded the extremes of nudity, incorporated nuns into monastic communities, and even acknowledged a female *tirthankara*. Today the two sects worship at different temples, but the number of naked Digambaras is minimal. Many Svetambara monks and nuns wear white masks to avoid breathing in insects, and carry a "fly-whisk", sometimes used to brush their path; none will use public transport, and they often spend days or weeks walking barefoot to a pilgrimage site.

Practising Jain householders vow to avoid injury, falsehood, theft (extended to fair trade), infidelity and worldly attachment. Jain **temples** are wonderfully ornate, with pillars, brackets and spires carved by *silavats* into voluptuous maidens, musicians, saints, and even Hindu deities; the *swastika* symbol commonly set into the marble floors is central to Jainism, representing the four states of rebirth as gods, humans, "hell beings", or animals and plants. Worship in temples consists of prayer and puja before images of the *tirthankaras*; the devotee circumambulates the image, chants sacred verses and makes offerings of flowers, sandalwood paste, rice, sweets and incense. It's common to fast four times a month on *parvan* (holy) days, the eighth and fourteenth days of the moon's waxing and waning periods. While reducing attachment to the body, this emulates the fast to death (while in meditation), or *sallekhana*, accepted by Jain mendicants as a final rejection of attachment, and a relatively harmless way to end worldly life.

To enter a monastic community, lay Jains must pass through eleven *pratimas*, starting with right views, the profession of vows, fasting and continence, and culminating in renunciation of family life. Once a monk or nun, a Jain aims to clarify understanding through meditational practices, hoping to extinguish passions and sever the ties of karma and attachment, entering fourteen spiritual stages, *gunasthanas*, to emerge as a fully enlightened, omniscient being. Whether pursuing a monastic or lay lifestyle, however, Jains recognize the rarity of enlightenment, and religious practice is, for the most part, aimed at achieving a state of rebirth more conducive to spiritual attainment.

Pilgrimage sites are known as **tirthas**, but this does not refer to the literal meaning of "river crossing", sacred to Hindus because of the purificatory nature of water. At one of the foremost Svetambara *tirthas*, **Shatrunjaya** in Gujarat, over nine hundred temples crown a single hill, said to have been visited by the first *tirthankara*, Rishabha, and believed to be the place where Rama, Sita and the Pandava brothers (incorporated into Jain tradition) gained deliverance. An important Digambara *tirtha* is **Shravanabelagola** in Karnataka, where a seventeen-metre-high image of Bahubali (recognized as the first human to attain liberation), at the summit of a hill, is anointed in the huge *abhisheka* festival every twelve years.

In an incredibly complicated process of philosophical analysis known as **Anekanatavada** (many-sidedness), Jainism approaches all questions of existence, permanence, and change from seven different viewpoints, maintaining that things can be looked at in an infinite number of valid ways. Thus it claims to remove the intellectual basis for violence, avoiding the potentially damaging result of holding a one-sided view. In this respect Jainism accepts other religious philosophies, and it has adopted, with a little reinterpretation, several Hindu festivals and practices.

Sikhism

Sikhism, India's youngest religion, remains dominant in the Punjab, while its adherents have spread throughout northern India, and communities have grown up in Britain, America and Canada.

Guru Nanak (1469–1539) was the movement's founder. Born into an orthodox Hindu *kshatrya* family in Talwandi, a small village west of Lahore (in present-day Pakistan), he was among many sixteenth-century poet-philosophers, sometimes referred to as *sants*, who formed emotional cults, drawing elements from both Hinduism and Islam. Nanak declared "God is neither Hindu nor Muslim and the path which I follow is God's"; he regarded God as **Sat**, or truth, who makes himself known through gurus. Though he condemned ancestor worship, astrology, caste distinction, sex discrimination, auspicious days and the rituals of brahmins, Nanak did not attack Islam or Hinduism – he simply regarded the many deities as names for one supreme God, and encouraged his followers to shift religious emphasis from ritual to meditation.

In common with Hindus, Nanak believed in a cyclic process of death and rebirth (*samsara*), but he asserted that liberation (*moksha*) was attainable in this life by all women and men regardless of caste, and religious practice can and should be integrated into everyday practical living. He contested that all people are characterized by *humai*, a sense of self-reliance that obscures an understanding of dependence on God, encourages attachment to temporal values (*maya*), and consequently results in successive rebirths. For Sikhs, the only way to achieve release from human existence is to conquer *humai*, and become centred on God (*gurmukh*). God is seen as both absolute (*nirgun*) and personal (*sargun*), and besides being the creator of all things, is truth, beauty and eternal goodness. In their embodiment of *sargun*, the Sikh gurus are the only beings who have realized the ultimate truth, and as such, provide essential guidance to their disciples.

Guru Nanak was succeeded by a disciple, Lehna, known as **Guru Angad** ("limb"), who continued to lead the community of Sikhs ("disciples"), the **Sikh Panth**, and wrote his own and Nanak's hymns in a new script, **Gurumukhi**, which is today the script of written Punjabi.

After Guru Angad's death in 1552, eight successive gurus acted as leaders for the Sikh Panth, each introducing new elements into the faith and asserting it as a separate and powerful religious movement. Guru Ram Das (1552–74) founded the sacred city of **Amritsar**; his successor, Guru Arjan Dev, compiled the gurus' hymns in a book called the **Adi Granth**, and built the Golden Temple to house it; Arjan Dev became Sikhism's first martyr when he was executed at the hands of Jahangir. Throughout their history, the Sikhs have had to battle to protect their faith and their people, especially against the Moghuls; Guru Teg Bahadur was beheaded by Aurangzeb in 1675, an event that heralded the era of his son and successor, **Guru Gobind Singh**, who was to revolutionize the entire movement.

Gobind Singh, the last leader, was largely responsible for moulding the community as it exists today. In 1699, he founded the brotherhood of the **Khalsa** by baptizing five disciples using a sword dipped in *amrit* (the nectar of immortality). The aims of the Khalsa, as defined by Guru Gobind Singh, are to assist the poor and fight oppression, to have faith in one god and abandon superstition and dogma, to worship God, and to protect the faith with steel. The Khalsa requires members to renounce tobacco, halal meat and sexual relations with Muslims, and to adopt the **five Ks**: *kesh* (unshorn hair), *kangha* (comb), *kirpan* (sword), *kara* (steel wristlet) and *kachcha* (short trousers). This code, assumed at initiation, together with the replacement of caste names with Singh ("lion") for men and Kaur ("princess") for women, and the wearing of turbans by men, created a distinct cultural identity.

Guru Gobind Singh also compiled a standardized version of the *Adi Granth*, which contains the hymns of the first nine gurus as well as poems written by Hindus and Muslims, and installed it as his successor, naming it **Guru Granth Sahib**. This became the Sikh's spiritual guide, while political authority rested with the Khalsa, or *sangat*.

Demands for a separate Sikh state – **Khalistan** – and fighting in the eighteenth century, and later after Independence, have burdened Sikhs with a reputation as military activists, but Sikhs regard their religion as one devoted to egalitarianism, democracy and social awareness. Though to die fighting for the cause of religious freedom is considered to lead to liberation, the use of force is officially sanctioned only when other methods have failed. Due to their martial traditions and emphasis on valour, Sikhs continue to provide an essential element of the Indian army.

Practice

The main duties of a Sikh are *nam japna*, *kirt karni* and *vand chakna*; keeping God's name in mind, earning by honest means, and giving to charity. Serving the community (*seva*) is a display of obedience to God, and the ideal life is uncontaminated by the **five evil impulses**: lust, covetousness, attachment, anger and pride.

Sikh **worship** takes place in a **gurudwara** ("door to the guru") or in the home, providing a copy of the *Adi Granth* is present. There are no priests, and no fixed time for worship, but congregations often meet in the mornings and evenings, and always on the eleventh day (*ekadashi*) of each lunar month, and on the first day of the year (*sangrand*). During **Kirtan**, or hymn singing, a feature of every Sikh service, verses from the *Adi Granth* or *Janam Sakhis* (stories of Guru Nanak's life), are sung to rhythmic clapping. The communal meal, *langar*, following prayers and singing, reinforces the practice laid down by Guru Nanak that openly flaunted caste and religious differences. The egalitarian nature of Sikhism is nowhere better exemplified than in the **Golden Temple** in Amritsar, the holiest of all Sikh shrines. The four doors are open to the four cardinal directions, welcoming both devotees and visitors from other faiths.

Gurudwaras – often schools, clinics or hostels as well as houses of prayer – are generally modelled on the Moghul style of Shah Jahan, considered a congenial blend of Hindu and Muslim architecture; usually whitewashed, and surmounted by a dome, they are always distinguishable by the *nishan sahib*, a yellow flag introduced by Guru Hargobind (1606–44). As in Islam, God is never depicted in pictorial form. Instead, the representative symbol Il Oankar is etched into a canopy that shades the *Adi Granth*, which always stands in the main prayer room. In some *gurudwaras* a picture of a guru is hung close to the *Adi Granth*, but it's often difficult to distinguish between the different teachers: artistically they are depicted as almost identical, a tradition that unites the ten gurus as vehicles for God's words, or *mahalas*, and not divine beings.

Important occasions for Sikhs, in addition to naming of children, weddings and funerals, are **Gurpurbs**, anniversaries of the birth and death of the ten gurus, when the *Adi Granth* is read continuously from beginning to end.

Zoroastrianism

Of all India's religious communities, Western visitors are least likely to come across – or recognize – **Zoroastrians**, who have no distinctive dress, and few houses of worship. Most live in Mumbai, where they are known as **Parsis** (Persians) and are active in business, education and politics. Zoroastrian numbers – roughly 90,000 – are rapidly dwindling due to a falling birth rate and absorption into wider communities.

The religion's founder, **Zarathustra** (Zoroaster), lived in Iran around the sixth or seventh century BC, and was the first religious prophet to expound a dualistic philosophy, based on the opposing powers of good and evil. For him, the absolute, wholly good and wise God, **Ahura Mazda**, together with his holy spirit and six emanations present in earth, water, the sky, animals, plants and fire, is constantly at odds with an evil power, **Angra Mainyu**, who is aided by **daevas**, or evil spirits.

Mankind, whose task on earth is to further good, faces judgement after death, and depending on the proportion of good and bad words, thoughts and actions, will find a place in heaven, or suffer the torments of hell. Zarathustra looked forward to a day of judgement, when a saviour, **Saoshyant**, miraculously born of a seed of the prophet and a virgin maiden, will appear on earth, restoring Ahura Mazda's perfect realm and expelling all impure souls and spirits to hell.

The first Zoroastrians to enter India arrived on the Gujarati coast in the tenth century AD, soon after the Arabian conquest of Iran, and by the seventeenth century most had settled in Bombay. Zoroastrian practice is based on the responsibility of every man and woman to choose between good and evil, and to respect God's creations. Five daily prayers, usually hymns (*gathas*), uttered by Zarathustra and standardized in the **Avesta**, the main Zoroastrian text, are said in the home or in a temple, before a fire, which symbolizes the realm of truth, righteousness and order. For this reason, Zoroastrians are often, incorrectly, called "fire-worshippers".

Members of other faiths may not enter Zoroastrian temples, but one custom that is evident to outsiders is the method of disposing of the dead. A body is laid on a high open rooftop (or isolated hill) known as *dakhma* (often referred to as a "tower of silence"), for the flesh to be eaten by vultures, and the bones cleansed by sun and wind. Recently, some Zoroastrians, by necessity, have adopted more common methods of cremation or burial; in order not to bring impurity to fire or earth, they only use electric crematoria, and shroud coffins in concrete before laying them in the ground.

No Ruz, or "New Day", held in mid-March, celebrating the creation of fire and the ultimate triumph of good over evil, is the most popular Zoroastrian festival; the oldest sacred fire in India, in **Udwada**, just north of Daman in south Gujarat, is an important pilgrimage site.

Christianity

For many, the diminutive figure of Mother Teresa was the quintessential icon of **Christianity** in India, but foreign nuns, however revered, are far from the only Christians in the country. In total, Christians are reckoned to number around two million people, the majority among *adivasi* (tribal) and *dalit* (Untouchable) peoples.

Early history

The **Apostle Thomas** is said to have arrived in Kerala in 54 AD to convert itinerant Jewish traders living in the flourishing port of Muziris, following the death of Jesus. There are many tales of miracles by "Mar Thoma", as he is known in Malayalam. One legend tells how he approached a group of brahmins from Palur (now Malabar) who were trying to appease the gods by throwing water into the air. If the gods had accepted the offerings, the saint said, the droplets would have remained suspended. Throwing water in the air himself, it miraculously hung above him, leading most of the brahmins to convert to Christianity. The southern tradition holds that Thomas was martyred on December 21, 72 AD at Mylapore in **Madras** (the name comes from the Syriac *madrasa*, meaning "monastery"). The tomb has since become a major place of pilgrimage, and in recognition of this, the Portuguese built the Gothic **San Thome Cathedral** on the site in the late nineteenth century. By oral tradition, the Church of San Thome is the oldest Christian denomination in the world, but documentary evidence of Christian activity in the subcontinent can only be traced to the sixth century, when immigrant Syrian communities were granted settlement rights by royal charter.

Arrival of the Europeans

From the sixteenth century onwards, the history of the Church in India is linked to the spread of foreign Christians across the subcontinent. In 1552, St Francis Xavier arrived in the Portuguese trading colony of **Goa** to establish missions to reach out to the Hindu "Untouchables"; his tomb and alleged relics are retained in the Basilica of Bom Jesus in Old Goa to this day. In 1559, at the behest of the Portuguese king, the Inquisition arrived in Goa. Jesuit missionaries carried out a bloody and brutal campaign to "cleanse" the small colony of Hindu and Muslim religious practice. Early British incomers took the attitude that the subcontinent was a heathen and polytheistic civilization waiting to be proselytized. Later, they were less zealous in their conversion efforts, being content to provide social welfare and build very English-looking churches in their own cantonments.

The proximity of the entry-port at Calcutta to the **tribal regions** of the northeastern hill states drew the attention of Protestant missionaries during the Raj, whose fervent evangelism covered virtually all of Mizoram, Nagaland and much of Meghalaya. Muslim immigrants from Bangladesh have changed the balance in bordering areas, while other tribal districts, in Madhya Pradesh, Bihar, Karnataka and Gujarat in particular, have drawn both Catholic and Protestant missionaries. As Christianity is intended to be free of caste stigmas, it can be attractive to those seeking social advancement.

In early 1999, Christian communities in some areas, notably in Gujarat and Orissa, were subject to forced "reconversions" and attacks. These were allegedly carried out by Hindu extremists incensed by proselytizing evangelists targeting low-caste Hindus. Following an international outcry, some states passed laws banning "forced conversions", but in December 2002, a riot was only narrowly averted after police acted to prevent 1500 dalit ("Untouchable") people from attending a mass-conversion in Chennai (Madras).

The strong sense of regional history and culture has distinctly influenced the appearance of **Indian churches**. The St Thomas Christians of the south congregate in small white churches decorated with colourful pictures and statues of figures from the New Testament. The great twin-steepled churches of Goa and Chennai (Madras) are very different, with their heavy gold interiors and candlelit shrines to the Virgin Mary. Other churches are more syncretistic: **St John's** in south Delhi has an Anglican nave, a Hindu *chhapra* (tower) and monastic cloisters spanning out from each side. In the Himalayan part of Bengal, the influence of Buddhism is very strong. Beautiful wooden chapels are painted with scenes from the life of Christ using Buddhist symbols and Nepali-looking characters.

The Hindu influence

The **Hindu influence** on Christianity is marked too. Christian festivals in Tamil Nadu are highly structured along caste lines, and Christians there never eat beef or pork, which are considered polluting. By contrast, Christians in Goa eat both beef and pork as a feature of their Portuguese heritage. In many churches you can see devotees offering the Hindu *arati* (a plate of coconut, sweets and rice), and women wearing *tilak* dots on their foreheads. In the same way that Hindus and Muslims consider pilgrimage to be an integral part of life's journey, Indian Christians have numerous devotional sites, including St Jude's Shrine in **Jhansi** and the Temple of Mother Mary in **Mathura**. On anniversaries of the death of a loved one, Christians carry plates of food to the graves, in much the same manner as Hindus. This sharing of traditions works both ways however. At Christmas you can't fail to notice the brightly coloured paper stars and small Nativity scenes glowing and flashing outside schools, houses, shops and churches throughout India.

Wildlife

From the Himalayas to the swamps of Bengal, and from the deserts of Rajasthan to the tropical backwaters of Kerala, the breadth of India's range of habitats is only equalled by the biodiversity that it supports. Around 65,000 species of fauna are to be found here, among them 2000 different kinds of fish, 1200 birds and 340 mammals, while a staggering 13,000 varieties of flowering plants have been recorded. India is also the only country in the world where you can see both wild lions and tigers.

The Himalayas run across the breadth of the north, providing a wealth of intermingling ecosystems. Bears and black bucks range the lush deodar and rhododendron forests of the foothills, while the fabled snow leopard and yak inhabit the higher mountains. In the hills and forests of the extreme northeast, the tiger and the one-horned rhinoceros struggle to survive in beautiful – and rarely visited – sanctuaries, pitted against a biannual monsoon, severe floods and inadequate funding for protection from poachers. Down on the Gangetic Plain, a rich array of birdlife is sustained by the warm climate, the forests and the many rivers and lakes. The Ganges falls away through paddy fields in the heart of India to the Sunderbans mangrove swamps in the east, famous for their population of tigers that – most unusually – swim. Camels, both wild and domesticated, can be found in the parched Thar desert in Rajasthan; elsewhere in the west, the dry climate supports spotted deer, wild asses, and the famous Asiatic lion in its last bastion of the Gir Forest. Further south, the dry Deccan plateau is thick with sandalwood forests, the home of wild elephants, while on the weathered cliffs of the Western Ghats the civet cat prowls in the abundant fern growth. In the very southern tip of India you'll find elephants, butterflies and jewel-like birds under the canopy of the teak and rosewood rainforest.

Animals

Distinguished from its African cousin by its long front legs and smaller ears and body, the Indian **elephant** is still widely used as a beast of burden in the great teak and mahogany forests. Though they have worked and been tamed in India for three thousand years, it's through the battle legends of the sixteenth and seventeenth centuries that elephants earned their loyal and stoic reputation, both as great mounts in the imperial armies of the Moghuls and as bejewelled bearers of rajas and nawabs. Elephants are also of religious significance – they're a common sight in temple processions and ceremonies, often sporting a brightly painted trunk and forehead, and throughout the subcontinent, stone elephants stand guard with bells in their trunks as a sign of welcome in medieval forts and palaces. The popular Hindu elephant-headed god Ganesh, who represents success and prosperity, is supposed to have written the *Mahabharata* epic.

In the wild, there is still a sizeable population of roughly 19,000 elephants, but they have been included under the **Endangered Species Protection Act** due to the huge reduction of their natural forest habitat. Disaster still looms for the hulking animals: each adult eats roughly two hundred kilos of vegetation and drinks a hundred litres of water a day, and their search for sustenance often brings them into conflict with neighbouring rural communities. The wild elephant is now only naturally found in four areas – the southern tip of Tamil Nadu; the central zone of Orissa, Bihar and West Bengal; the Himalayan lowlands of Uttar Pradesh; and the Northeastern Hill States.

Another pachyderm, the lumbering **one-horned rhinoceros**, retains a tenuous foothold in the northeast of the country. Due to deforestation and the depredations of unhindered poachers cashing in on widespread oriental beliefs in the spiritual and healing properties of various parts of the rhino's anatomy, the rhino population had dropped to barely one hundred by the 1960s. Since then, numbers have risen again, and around 1100 live in the protected Manas and Kaziranga wildlife sanctuaries in Assam.

Indian tigers are fast becoming extinct in the wild (see box), but you still stand a reasonable chance of coming across one in a national park. Sightings are regularly recorded at Kanha and Bandhavgarh in Madhya Pradesh (Bandhavgarh p.457/Kanha p.460); Ranthambore in Rajasthan (see p.201); Corbett and Dudhwa in Uttar Pradesh (see p.390); Manas and Kaziranga in Assam (see p.989); and Bandipur in Karnataka (see p.1236).

Big cats

The other **big cats** have fared worse than the tiger. Once the maharaja of Indian wildlife, the **Asiatic lion** (see box on p.1416) now clings on in just one tiny patch of Gujarat, even though the proud three-headed lion emblem of the Ashokan period is still the national symbol of India. The ghostly grey- and black-spotted **snow leopard** of the Himalayas is so rare as to be almost legendary. Only the plains-dwelling **leopard** (also known as the panther) can still be commonly found, especially in forested places near human settlement where domestic animals make easy prey. Other indigenous felines include the rare multicoloured marbled cat, the miniature leopard cat, the jungle cat (with a distinct ridge of hair running down its back), the fishing cat, and a kind of lynx called the caracal. The cheetah is now extinct in India.

Deer

Deer and antelope, the larger cats' prey, are much more abundant. The often solitary sambar is the largest of the **deer**, weighing up to 300kg and bearing antlers known to reach 120cm long. Smaller and more gregarious are chital (spotted deer), usually seen in herds skulking around langur monkey or human habitats looking for discarded fruit and vegetables. In a tiger reserve you may hear the high-pitched call of the chital and the gruff reply bark of the langur warning of the presence of a tiger in the vicinity. Other deer include the elusive mountain-loving muntjac (barking deer) and the para (hog deer), which fall victim annually to flooding in the low grasslands. The smallest deer in India is the nocturnal chevrotain, known from its size (only 30cm high) as the mouse deer. The swamp deer is rarer, while the hangul (Kashmiri red deer) and musk deer are now endangered species. **Antelopes** include the nilgai ("blue cow"), the endangered black buck, revered by the Bishnoi caste who inhabit the fringes of the Thar desert around Jodhpur in central Rajasthan, and the unique forest-dwelling four-horned chowsingha (swamp deer), which has successfully been saved from near-extinction. The desert-loving gazelle is known as the *chinkara* ("the one who sneezes") due to the sneeze-like alarm call it makes.

Monkeys

The most common **monkeys** are the feisty red-bottomed Rhesus macaque and the black-faced "Hanuman" langurs, often found around temple areas. Monkeys are protected by the Hindu belief in their divine status as noble servants of the gods, a sentiment that derives from the epic *Ramayana*, where the herculean Hanuman leads his monkey army to assist Rama in fighting the demon Ravana. Wild monkeys live in large troupes in the forests. The Assamese

The Indian tiger: survival or extinction?

Feared, adored, immortalized in myth and used to endorse everything from breakfast cereals to petrochemicals, few animals command such universal fascination as the **tiger**. India is one of the very few places where this rare and enigmatic big cat can still be glimpsed in the wild, stalking through the teak forests and terai grass – a solitary predator, with no natural enemies save one.

As recently as the turn of the last century, up to 100,000 tigers still roamed the subcontinent, even though *shikar* (**tiger hunting**) had long been the "sport of kings". An ancient dictum held it auspicious for a ruler to notch up a tally of 109 dead tigers, and nawabs, maharajas and Moghul emperors all indulged their prerogative to devastating effect. But it was the trigger-happy British who brought tiger hunting to its most gratuitous excesses. Photographs of pith-helmeted, bare-kneed *burra-sahibs* posing behind mountains of striped carcasses became a hackneyed image of the Raj. Even Prince Philip (now President Emeritus of the Worldwide Fund for Nature) couldn't resist bagging one during a royal visit.

In the years following Independence, **demographic pressures** nudged the Indian tiger perilously close to extinction. As the human population increased in rural districts, more and more forest was cleared for farming, depriving large carnivores of their main source of game and of the cover they needed to hunt. Forced to turn on farm cattle as an alternative, tigers were drawn into direct conflict with humans; some animals, out of sheer desperation, even turned man-eater and attacked human settlements.

Poaching has taken an even greater toll. The black market has always paid high prices for live animals – a whole tiger can fetch up to $100,000 – and for the various body parts believed to hold magical or medicinal properties. The meat is used to ward off snakes, the brain to cure acne, the nose to promote the birth of a son and the fat of the kidney – applied liberally to the afflicted organ – as an antidote to male impotence.

By the time an all-India moratorium on tiger shooting was declared in the 1972 Wildlife Protection Act, numbers had plummeted to below 2000. A dramatic response geared to fire public imagination came the following year, with the inauguration of **Project Tiger**. At the personal behest of Indira Gandhi, nine areas of pristine forest were set aside for the last remaining tigers. Displaced farming communities were resettled and compensated, and armed rangers employed to discourage poachers.

macaque and the pig-tailed macaque prefer the northern hills, while the bonnet macaque dwells in the steamy tropical jungles of the south. Langurs, such as the noisy Nilgiri langur and the extremely rare golden langur, are more elusive, preferring to remain hidden in treetop foliage.

Other mammals

Among other wild animals you might hope to see in India, the shaggy **sloth bear** is hard to spot in the wild, although you may see it being forced to dance on busy roadways near tourist sites. Other bears include the black and brown varieties, distinguishable by the colour of their fur. Of the **canines**, the scavenging striped hyena and the small pest-eating Indian fox are fairly common. The Indian wolf lives in the plains and deserts, and is under threat of extinction due to vigorous culling by humans protecting their domestic animals. The wild **buffalo** has a close genetic relationship with the common domesticated water buffalo: wild male buffalo prefer to mate with domestic females. More exotic members of the cow family are the hill-loving **gaur**, an Indian bison which stands 2m across at the shoulders, and the nimble, mountain-dwelling **yak**. Asia's answer to the

Demand for tiger parts did not end with Project Tiger, however, and the poachers remained in business, aided by organized smuggling rings. Undercover investigators repeatedly come across huge hauls of tiger bones and skins, and over the past few years, the discovery of tiger carcasses rotting in several reserves indicate that poachers have been resorting to new, more random killing methods: four tigers (a tigress and three cubs) were killed in May 2003 after they stumbled across a live electricity cable laid for the purpose in the jungles of Kerala, while three more tiger bodies were found in northern Maharashtra the previous year after a waterhole had been poisoned. In October that same year, the **largest ever haul of tiger skins** was found by police in Lhasa, Tibet: 31 in total, along with 587 leopard and 778 otter skins.

One of the probelms facing conservationists is that even if they are caught, the perpetrators of such outrages are unikely to by adequately punished – the maximum fine for tiger poaching is $125, or one year in prison. Well-organized guerrilla groups thus operate with virtual impunity out of remote national parks, where inadequate numbers of poorly armed and poorly paid wardens offer little more than token resistance, particularly as increased use of poison is making it more and more difficult to track poachers. Project Tiger officials are understandably reluctant to jeopardize lucrative tourist traffic by admitting that sightings are getting rarer, but the prognosis looks very gloomy indeed. In April 2005, for example, a team of detectives and conservationists in Rajasthan announced that the entire tiger population of Sariska National Park had been wiped out by poachers; moreoever, eighteen known individual tigers had disappeared from Ranthambore, and nine from Panna in Madhya Pradesh, with eighteen more unaccounted for. A task force headed by the Wildlife Protection Soceity of India, headed by broadcaster Valmik Thapar, declared that these figures from high profile reserves suggested the situation in less well known ones would be even more catastrophic. By mid 2005, India was in the midst if its third major **tiger crisis**.

Official figures optimistically claim a countrywide **population** of 3000–3500, but independent evidence is more pessimistic, putting the figure at well under 2000. The population rise indicated by counts based on pug marks – thought to be like human fingerprints, unique to each individual – that gave such encouragement in the early 1990s has been declared inaccurate. Experts today claim that at the present rate of destruction, India's most exotic animal could face extinction by the end of the decade.

armadillo is a scaly anteater called a **pangolin**, whose tough plate-like scales run the length of its back and tail; this armour is believed to contain magical healing properties, for which the pangolin is hunted. Around urban environments, you're likely to see the triple-striped **palm squirrel**, said to have been marked as such by the gentle stroke of Rama. Like European squirrels, they are very common, and always busy running up trees and carrying food from place to place. **River dolphins** can be seen leaping in the Ganges, especially at Varanasi.

Reptiles

The 238 species of **snake** in India (of which fifty are poisonous) extend from the 10-centimetre-long worm snake to nest-building king cobras and massive pythons. While the mangy and languid cobra or python wrapped around the snake-charmer's neck is tame and nonvenomous, poisonous snakes you might meet in the wild are the majestically hooded cobra, the yellow-brown Russel's viper, the small krait (especially common in South India) and the saw-scaled viper. **Lizards** are common, with every hotel room seeming to have a resident gecko to keep the place free of insects. The colourful garden lizard and Sita's lizard are both found throughout India. Freshwater Olive Ridley **turtles** (see box on p.1055) nest at remote beaches along the east and southwest coasts, the most famous being Bhitarakanika Sanctuary on **Gahirmatha beach**, 130km north of Bhubaneswar, where 200,000 females come each year to lay their eggs. Similar, though much smaller, nesting sites are to be found at Morjim and Galjibag in Goa. **Crocodiles** are common throughout the subcontinent.

Birds

You don't have to be an aficionado to enjoy India's abundant **bird-life**. Travelling around the country, you'll see breathtaking birds regularly flash between the branches of trees or appear on overhead wires at the roadside. The spectacular varieties, both resident and migratory, can be attributed to the diverse range of climates and habitats sweeping down the Indian peninsula. The extremely rare **Siberian crane** makes an annual pilgrimage to Bharatpur in Rajasthan and a wealth of different aquatic feeding and nesting habitats draws exotic waterfowl such as flamingoes, spoonbills and pelicans. Stately **eagles** swoop among the Himalayas and peacocks flounce around forts and palaces.

Three common species of **kingfisher** frequently crop up amid the paddy fields and wetlands of the coastal plains. Other common and brightly coloured species include the grass-green, blue and yellow **bee-eaters** (*Merops*), the stunning **golden oriole** (*Oriolus oriolus*), and the **Indian roller** (*Coracias bengalensis*), famous for its brilliant blue, flight feathers and exuberant aerobatic mating displays. **Hoopoes** (*Upupa epops*), recognizable by their elegant black-and-white tipped crests, fawn plumage and distinctive *hoo...po...po* call, also flit around fields and villages, as do several kinds of **bulbuls**, **babblers** and **drongos** (*Dicrurus*), including the fork-tailed black drongo (*Dicrurus adsimilis*) – a winter visitor that can often be seen perched on telegraph wires. If you're lucky, you may also catch a glimpse of the **paradise flycatcher** (*Tersiphone paradisi*), which is widespread and among the subcontinent's most exquisite birds, with a thick black crest and long silver tail streamers.

Paddy fields, ponds and saline mud flats are teeming with water birds. The most ubiquitous of these is the snowy white **cattle egret** (*Bubulcus ibis*), which can usually be seen wherever there are cows and buffalo, feeding off the grubs, insects and other parasites that live on them. Look out too for the mud-brown **paddy bird**, India's most common heron, distinguished by its pale green legs, speckled breast and hunched posture.

Common birds of prey such as the **brahminy kite** (*Haliastur indus*) – recognizable by its white breast and chestnut head markings – and the **pariah kite** (*Milvus migrans govinda*) – a dark-brown buzzard with a fork tail – are widespread around towns and fishing villages, where they vie with raucous gangs of house **crows** (*Corvus splendens*) and **white-eyed jackdaws** (*Corvus monedulal*) for scraps. Gigantic pink-headed **king vultures** (*Sarcogyps clavus*) and the **white-backed vulture** (*Gyps bengalensis*), which has a white ruff around its bare neck and head, also show up whenever there are carcasses to pick clean, although in recent years a mysterious virus has decimated numbers.

Among India's abundant **forest birds**, one species every enthusiast hopes to glimpse is the magnificent **hornbill**, with its huge yellow beak with a long curved casque on top. Several species of **woodpecker** also inhabit the interior woodlands, among them the rare Indian great black woodpecker, which makes loud drumming noises on tree trunks between December and March.

A bird whose call is a regular feature of the Western Ghat forests, particularly in teak areas, is the wild ancestor of the domestic chicken – the **jungle fowl**.

The more common variety is the secretive but vibrantly coloured, red jungle fowl (*Gallus gallus*), which sports golden neck feathers and a metallic black tail. You're most likely to come across one of these scavenging for food on the verges of forest roads.

Wildlife viewing

Although you can expect to come across many of the species listed above on the edges of towns and villages, a spell in one or other of India's nature reserves offers the best chance of **viewing wild animals**. Administered by poorly funded government bodies, they're a far cry indeed from the well-organized and well-maintained national parks you may be used to at home. Information can be frustratingly hard to come by and the staff manning them can be less than helpful.

That said, at the larger, more easily accessible wildlife reserves a reasonable infrastructure exists to **transport** visitors around, whether by Jeep, minibus, coach or, in some cases, boat. Don't, however, expect to see much if you stick to these standard excursion vehicles laid on by the park authorities, as most of the rarer animals wisely keep well away from noisy groups of trippers. Wherever possible, try to organize **walking safaris** with a reliable, approved guide in the forest, while bearing in mind that not all guides may be as knowledgeable and experienced as they claim, and that an untrained, unconfident guide may actually lead you into life-endangering situations; before parting with any money, ask to see recommendation books.

Accommodation is generally available at all but the most remote sanctuaries and reserves, although it may not always be very comfortable. Larger parks tend to have a batch of luxurious, Western-style resort campuses for tour groups. In all cases, you'll find reviews of the accommodation on offer in the descriptions of individual parks featured in the Guide section of this book, along with full details of how to travel to, from and around the site. Our accounts will also advise you on the best times of year to visit in each case, and indicate the kind of wildlife present.

Myth and religion

The early **Harappa** civilization of the Indus Valley portrayed mythical creatures, bulls, elephants and tigers on their terracotta seals, amulets and toys. The itinerant **Aryan tribes** that subsequently settled in India worshipped Brahma the bull, who lay with his bovine consort to create horned **cattle** to farm the earth.

The imagery of gentle, yet strong and fertile cows and oxen is still central to the **Hindu** religion: Shaivite temples usually sport a well-reddened statue of a bull to represent Nandi, Shiva's vehicle (*vahan*), and Krishna is often depicted as a cow-herder. The *Mahabharata* epic warns that the eating of beef or wearing of leather is taboo; transgressions of this law can only be absolved by the gift of a cow to a temple. Another sin may be harder to avoid – you'll notice cows wandering freely around towns, usually when your bus swerves to avoid hitting one. Often, these are injured or old animals which the owner has released so that they can die a natural death. To touch the rump of a cow ensures fertility and prosperity.

As Brahmanical Hinduism gradually absorbed India's countless indigenous regional deities and cults, animals became a more important part of the Hindu pantheon: **Vishnu** emerged as a fish, a tortoise and a boar, an elephant head

Websites

www.5tigers.org
Everything you ever wanted to know about tigers, and more besides.

www.camacdonald.com/birding/asiaindia.htm
Exhaustive reviews of India's birdwatching hotspots, plus online resources and printed material, with dozens of pretty pics and reports from recent field trips by bona fide enthusiasts.

www.wpsi-india.org
The Wildlife Protection Society of India was set up to provide support in the struggle against poaching, and its site holds a wealth of information, links and news on everything connected to tigers in India.

www.indianwildlifeportal.com
Portal devoted to Indian wildlife, whose links you can browse by species, destination or theme.

tigersincrisis.com
US-based tiger conservation group.

www.eia-international.org
One of the best sources for up-to-date news, facts and figures on India's poaching crisis.

was placed on **Ganesh** (when he was mistakenly beheaded by his father, Shiva), and **Hanuman** was the loyal monkey-servant of Rama. The hooded cobra was revered as a god of the northeastern **Naga** tribe, and was later absorbed into the more mainstream mythological realm as the protector of Shiva and Vishnu. In fact, there are few animals and birds that do not have a spiritual association, as each of the millions of deities have to mount an animal **vahan** (vehicle) to travel between earth and heaven. Brahma rides a swan, Kartika, the god of war, sits astride a proud peacock, Ganesh is carried by a rat and Indra rides an elephant. The close link between vehicles and animals is most obvious on the roads of modern-day India, where every truck and rickshaw is liberally covered with garishly painted peacocks, cows, snakes or other animals.

The natural habitat has also played a significant role in **Buddhist** legend. Most Mahayana Buddhists recognize the ten principal Hindu deities, their animal forms and traditional *vahana*. Buddha himself is believed to have been conceived when a four-tusked white elephant entered his mother's dreams. Some legends even hold that the Buddha took on the forms of different animals during his life.

As animals, plants and geographical features have come to be symbolically associated with the characteristics they display, the landscape of India and its produce have become imbued with **sacred associations** through offerings and festivals. Coconuts yield milk and succulent flesh given as a symbolic food offering (*prasad*) at the beginning of a *puja* ceremony. The unchanging womb-like form of the lotus (*padma*) has led to its strong association with "mother creation". In yoga, the "lotus position" promotes health and wisdom, while lotus flowers bearing candles are set afloat on the Ganges as a sunset *arati* offering to summon divine blessing.

The common **deer** is sacred to both Hinduism and Buddhism. The Buddha is supposed to have preached his first sermon in a deer park, and according to Hindu law, the docile and graceful creature is so holy that even the ground that it treads should be worshipped. The **peacock** is symbolically associated with fertility for its instinctive ability to sense and dance at the approach of rain.

Music

The origin of north Indian (Hindustani) classical music is shrouded in obscurity. There is a tendency in India to attribute the invention of any ancient art form to one of the many Hindu deities, and the resulting synthesis of myth and legend is often taken as literal truth. But in reality north Indian classical music as it exists today is the result of a long process of integrating many diverse cultural influences. Not only is there a rich and varied tradition of regional folk music, but all through its history, India has absorbed the culture and traditions of foreign invaders, the most influential being the Muslim Moghuls.

The introduction of Turko-Persian musical elements is what primarily distinguishes north Indian classical music from its predecessor, Carnatic, now restricted to southern India. The latter is a complex, rich and fascinating musical tradition in its own right, and even an untrained ear can usually distinguish between the two.

Teachers and pupils

In the north, both Hindu and Muslim communities have provided outstanding artists. While music recognizes no religious differences – indeed it is something of a religion in its own right – distinguished musicians of Hindu origin customarily take the title of *pandit* (and become known as gurus), while their Muslim counterparts add the prefix *ustad* (meaning "master") to their names. An *ustad* may teach anything – not only his own particular art or instrument. It is not unusual for sitar maestros to teach sarod or vocal techniques to their pupils.

The **teaching** of north Indian classical music is a subject in itself. One thing that strikes a Westerner is the spiritual link between teacher and pupil. Quite often the two may be blood relations anyway, but where they are not, a spiritual relationship is officially inaugurated in a ceremony in which the teacher ties a string to the wrist of the pupil to symbolize the bond between them.

Apart from actual musical form and content, north Indian music has various extra-musical traditions and rituals, usually taught through musical families or **gharanas**. Traditionally, Indian music is taught on a one-to-one basis, often from father to son. Many academies and colleges of music now follow the modern style, but traditionalists still adhere to the *gharana* system, and great importance is still attached to membership of a musical family or an impressive lineage. A *gharana*, which may be for singing, for any or all kinds of instruments, or for dance, is more a school of thought than an institution. It suggests a particular belief, or a preference for a certain performance style. *Gharanas* differ not only in broad terms, but also in minute details: how to execute a particular combination of notes, or simply the correct way to hold

Features on **music**, **dance** and **performing arts**, scattered throughout this book, include:

Qawwali p.138
The Performing Arts of Lucknow p.312
Bollywood p.723
Odissi Dance p.1051

an instrument. They are usually founded by musicians of outstanding ability, and new styles and forms are added by exceptionally talented musicians who may have trained with one particular *gharana* and then evolved a style of their own.

Scales of purity and imagination

Singing is considered to be the highest form of classical music, after which instruments are graded according to their similarity to the human voice. The two main vocal traditions are *dhrupad*, the purest of all, devoid of all embellishment and entirely austere in its delivery, and *khayal*, which has a more romantic content and elaborate ornamentation and is the more popular today. Less abstract vocal forms include the so-called light classical *dadra*, *thumri* and *ghazal* as well as *qawwali*, the religious music of the Sufi tradition. The degree of musical purity is assigned according to a scale which has music at one extreme and words at the other. As words become more audible and thus the meaning of lyrics more important, so the form is considered to be musically less pure.

Musical instruments

String instruments

The best-known instrument is the **sitar**, invented by Amir Khusrau in the thirteenth century and played with a plectrum. Of the six or seven main strings, four are played and the other two or three supply a drone or a rhythmic ostinato (*chikari*). There can also be between eleven and nineteen sympathetic strings. The two sets of strings are fitted on different bridges. Twenty brass frets fastened to the long hollow neck can be easily moved to conform to the scale of a particular *raag*, and their curvature allows the player to alter the pitch by pulling the string sideways across the fret to provide the gliding portamento so characteristic of Indian music.

The **surbahar** ("spring melody"), effectively a bass sitar, is played in the same way. Developed by Sahibdad Khan, the great-grandfather of Vilayat and Imrat Khan, it produces a deep, dignified sound. The neck is wider and longer than that of the sitar but its frets are fixed. Thanks to its size and longer strings, the sound can be sustained for longer, and the range of the portamento is wider.

The **sarod** is a descendant of the Afghani rebab. Smaller than a sitar, it has two resonating chambers, the larger made of teak covered with goatskin, and the smaller, at the other end of the metal fingerboard, made of metal. Ten of its 25 metal strings are plucked with a fragment of coconut shell. Four of these carry the melody; the others accentuate the rhythm. The rest are sympathetic strings, underneath the main strings. The sarod was hugely improved by Ustad Allaudin Khan, whose pupils Ustad Ali Akbar Khan and Ustad Amjad Ali Khan are now its best-known exponents.

The **sarangi** is a fretless bowed instrument with a very broad fingerboard and a double belly. The entire body of the instrument – belly and fingerboard – is carved out of a single block of wood and the hollow covered with parchment. There are three or four main strings of gut and anything up to forty metal sympathetic strings. Some claim it is the most difficult musical instrument to play in the world. Certainly the technique is highly unusual. While the right hand wields the bow in the normal way, the strings are stopped not by the fingertips of the left hand, but by the nails. The *sarangi* is capable of a wide range of timbres and its sound is likened to that of the human voice, so it is usually used to accompany vocal recitals. Originally this was its only function, but in recent years it has become a solo instrument in its own right, thanks mainly to the efforts of Ustad Sultan Khan and Pandit Ram Narayan.

The **santoor**, a hammered zither of trapezoid shape and Persian origin, has only recently been accepted in classical music. It has over a hundred strings, pegged and

Indian musicologists talk about two **kinds of sound** – one spiritual and inaudible to the human ear, the other physical and audible. The inaudible sound is said to be produced from the ether, and its function is to liberate the soul. But to feel it requires great devotion and concentration which the average person can never really attain. Audible sound, on the other hand, is actually "struck" and is said to have an immediate and pleasurable impact.

Indian music always has a **constant drone** in the background, serving as a reference point for performer and listener alike. In north Indian music this drone is usually played on the four-stringed tambura. The privilege of accompanying a teacher's performance on the tanpura is often accorded to advanced students.

Indian music does not so much describe a mood (as some European music does) as help to create that mood, and then explore it to its depths. Where Western classical music starts at a particular point and then progresses from it, Indian classical music revolves around the point, probing it from every angle, yet maintaining a dignified restraint. It's this restraint that distinguishes Indian classical music from the carefree abandon of Indian pop and film music.

stretched in pairs, parallel to each other. Each pair passes over two bridges, one on each side of the instrument. The strings are struck by two curving wooden sticks. Its most notable exponent is Pandit Shiv Kumar Sharma.

The **surmandal** resembles a zither, and is used by vocalists to accompany themselves in performance. Even though its primary function is to provide the drone, singers sometimes also play the basic melody line on this instrument.

Wind instruments

The **shehnai**, traditionally used for wedding music, is a double-reed, oboe-type instrument with up to nine finger holes, some of which are stopped with wax for fine tuning to the scale of a particular *raag*. It demands a mastery of circular breathing and enormous breath control. A drone accompaniment is provided by a second *shehnai*.

The word **bansuri** refers to a wide variety of bamboo (*banse*) flutes, most end-blown, but some, such as Krishna's famous *murli*, are side-blown. Despite offering a range of less than two octaves, it now appears as a solo concert instrument.

Drums

The **tabla** is a set of two small drums played with the palms and fingertips to produce an incredible variety of sounds and timbres, in a range of one octave. Its name is short for tabla-*bayan* – the tabla is on the right and the *bayan* ("left") on the left. Its invention is attributed to Amir Khusrau, creator of the sitar. Both drum heads are made of skin, with a paste of iron filings and flour in the centre, but while the body of the tabla is all wood, the *bayan* is usually made of metal. The tabla is tuned to the tonic, dominant or subdominant notes of the *raag* by knocking the tuning-blocks, held into place by braces on the sides of the instrument.

Predating the tabla, the **pakhavaj** is nearly a metre long and was traditionally made of clay, although now wood is more popular. It has two parchment heads, each tuned to a different pitch, again by knocking the side blocks into place. A paste of boiled rice, iron filings and tamarind juice is applied to the smaller head and a wheat flour paste on the larger helps produce the lower notes.

The *pakhavaj* has a deep mellow sound and is used to accompany *dhrupad* singing and *kathak* dancing. A smaller version of the *pakhavaj*, the **mridangam**, is widely used in South Indian music.

Raags and rhythms

The mainstay of all north Indian classical music is the **raag** (or *raga*), an immensely intricate system of scales and associated melodic patterns. Each of the 200 main *raags* is defined by its unique combination of scale-pattern, dominant notes, specific rules to be obeyed in ascending or descending and associated melodic phrases. While Indian classical music is renowned for improvisation, this only takes place within the strictly defined boundaries of a particular *raag*. If the improviser wanders away from the main musical form of the *raag*, his or her performance ceases to be regarded as "classical" music. The mark of a good performer is the ability to improvise extensively without abandoning the set of defining rules.

Some *raags* are linked with particular seasons; there is a *raag* for rain, and one for spring; *raags* can be "masculine" or "feminine"; and musicologists may categorize them according to whether they are best suited to a male or female voice. Each *raag* is allotted a time of day, a time identified with the spiritual and emotional qualities of the *raag*. *Raags* are specifically allocated to early morning (either before or after sunrise), mid-morning, early afternoon, late afternoon, early evening (either before or after sunset), late evening, late night and post-midnight. This system causes a few problems in northern latitudes, for there is some argument as to whether a *raag* should be heard by clock-time or sun-time. Purists adhere to the archaic tradition of a "*raag* timetable" even if they're only listening to CDs.

The performance of a *raag*, whether sung or played on a sitar, sarod or *sarangi*, follows a set pattern. First comes the *alaap*, a slow, meditative "mood-setter" in free rhythm which explores the chosen *raag*, carefully introducing the notes of the scale one by one. The *alaap* can span several hours in the hands of a distinguished performer, but may only last a matter of minutes; older aficionados allege that most present-day listeners cannot sustain the attention required to appreciate a lengthy and closely argued *alaap*. As a result, performers have felt under pressure to abbreviate this section of the *raag*, to reach the faster middle and end sections as soon as possible. This became customary in the recording studio, although the advent of the CD, which does not force the music to fit into 25 minutes as the LP did, has initiated a move back to longer performances.

In the next two sections, the *jorh* and the *jhala*, the instrumentalist introduces a rhythmic element, developing the *raag* and exploring its more complex variations. Only in these and the final section, the *gath*, does the percussion instrument – usually the tabla or *pakhavaj* – enter. The soloist introduces a short, fixed composition to which he or she returns between flights of improvisation. In this section rhythm is an important structural element. Both percussionist and soloist improvise, at times echoing each other and sometimes pursuing individual variations of rhythmic counterpoint, regularly punctuated by unison statements of a short melody known as "the composition". The *gath* itself is subdivided into three sections: a slow tempo passage known as *vilambit*, increasing to a medium tempo, called *madhya*, and finally the fast tempo, *drut*.

Just as the *raag* organizes melody, so the rhythm is organized by highly sophisticated structures expressed through cycles known as *taals*, which can be clapped out by hand. A *taal* is made up of a number of beats (*matras*), each beat defined by a combination of rhythm pattern and timbre. It is the unique set of patterns (*bols*) available within a particular *taal* that defines it. There are literally hundreds of *taals*, but most percussionists use the same few favourites over and over again, the most common being the sixteen-beat *teentaal*.

The most unfamiliar aspect of *taal* to the Western ear is that the end of one cycle comes not on its last beat, but on the first beat of the following one, so that there is a continual overlap. This first beat is known as *sum*, a point of culmination which completes a rhythmic structure, and performers often indicate it by nodding to each other when they arrive at it. Audiences do the same to express satisfaction and appreciation.

Among smaller, more discerning audiences, verbal applause such as "Wah!" (Bravo!), or even "Subhan-Allah" (Praise be to God!), is considered the standard form of appreciation. Only in Western-style concert halls, where such exclamations would be inaudible, has hand-clapping come to replace these traditional gestures of approval.

Light classical music

Many concerts of classical music end with the performance of a piece in one of the styles collectively referred to as "**light classical**". Although they obey the rules of classical music with respect to *raag* and *taal*, they do so less rigorously than is required for a performance of *dhrupad*, *khayal* or other pure classical styles. The *alaap* is short or nonexistent, and the composition is frequently derived from a folk melody. Indeed, it could be said that light classical music is essentially a synthesis of folk and classical practice. The two most important and widespread types are *thumri* and *ghazal*.

Thumri

The origin of **thumri** is popularly ascribed to Nawab Wajid Ali Shah, who governed Lucknow (Avadh) from 1847 to 1856. Although little interested in matters of state, he was a great patron of the arts and during his reign, music, dance, poetry, drama and architecture flourished. *Thumri* employs a specific set of *raags* and is particularly associated with *kathak* dance; the graceful movements of the dancer are echoed in the lyricism of the musical style. Although classical instrumentalists in concert frequently perform a *thumri* to relax from the intensity of the pure classical style, most *thumri* is vocal, and sung in a language known as Braj Bhasha, a literary dialect of Hindi. The singer is always accompanied by the tabla, as well perhaps as the tambura, the *sarangi* or the *surmandal*, and sometimes the violin or harmonium.

The lyrics of *thumri* deal with **romance**. Love songs, written from a female perspective, they stress themes like dressing up for a tryst, the heartache of absence and betrayal, quarrels and reconciliation, and the joyful return from a meeting with a husband or lover. Such themes are often expressed metaphorically, with references in the lyrics to the (suggestive) flute-playing of the god Krishna, the symbol of young love. Despite the concentration on the woman's point of view, some of the greatest singers of *thumri* have been men, notably Ustad Bade Ghulam Ali Khan. As male singers are frequently middle-aged and overweight, there is a certain initial incongruity about the spectacle of this depiction of the gentle and delicate emotions of a beautiful young woman. Yet a fine artist, fat and balding though he may be, can make a song like this one infinitely affecting: "My bracelets keep slipping off/My lover has cast a spell on me/He has struck me with his magic/What can a mere doctor do?" Her bracelets have slipped off because, while pining for her absent lover, she has starved herself to the point of emaciation.

Ghazal

Still more song-like than the *thumri* is the **ghazal**. In some ways the Urdu counterpart of *thumri*, the *ghazal* was introduced to India by Persian Muslims and is mainly a poetic rather than a musical form. Although some *ghazal* tunes are based on the *raag* system, others do not follow any specific mode. The *taals* are clearly derived from folk music; at times the *ghazal* shades into the area of sophisticated pop song. Indeed, at the more commercial end of the scale – the so-called film *ghazal* – sophistication gives way to mere charm. The *ghazal* has played an important part in the cultures of India, Pakistan and Afghanistan since the early eighteenth century, when it was one of the accomplishments required of a courtesan. Modern *ghazal* singers usually come from a more "respectable" background.

While *thumri* singers take on a female persona, emotions in the *ghazal* are almost always expressed from the male point of view. Some of the finest performers of *ghazals* are women – Begum Akhtar and Shobha Gurtu among them. Many favourite *ghazals* are drawn from the works of great Urdu poets.

A patriotic poem by Faiz Ahmed Faiz, *Mujhse Pehli Si Muhabbat Mere Mehboob Na Maang* ("Do not ask me my love, to love you the way I used to love you"), proved a milestone in the advance of art poetry into the realm of the film *ghazal*. Sung by the popular Pakistani singer Noor Jehan in her inimitable style, her interpretation is said to have so impressed the poet Faiz that he formally relinquished all claims to it in her favour.

Sound of the south

Southern India's **Carnatic** classical music is essentially similar to Hindustani classical music in outlook and theoretical background but differs in many details, usually ascribed to the far greater Islamic influence in the north. To the Western ear, Carnatic music is emotionally direct and impassioned, without the sometimes sombre restraint that characterizes much of the north's music. For instance the **alaapaana** section, although it introduces and develops the notes of the *raag* in much the same way as the *alaap* of north Indian music, interrupts its stately progress with sparkling decorative flourishes. Often, too, the *alaapaana* is succeeded by a set of increasingly complex elaborations of a basic melody in a way that is more easily grasped than the abstract, sometimes severe improvisations of the Hindustani masters. Compositions, both of "themes" and the set variations upon them, play a much greater role in Carnatic musical practice than in Hindustani.

The *raags* of Carnatic music, like those of Hindustani music, are theoretically numbered in the thousands and musicians are expected to be familiar with them all. In practice, however, there are only two hundred main *raags* ever played, and probably only fifty or sixty in common use.

Song is at the root of South Indian music, and forms based on song are paramount, even when the performance is purely instrumental. The vast majority of the texts are religious, and the temple is frequently the venue for performance. The most important form is the *kriti*, a devotional song, hundreds of which were written by the most influential figure in the development of Carnatic music, the singer **Thyagaraja** (1767–1847). He was central to the music, not only for his compositions but also for the development of techniques of rhythmic and melodic variations. Southern India's biggest music festival, held annually near Thanjavur on the banks of the River Kaveri, is named after him.

Although the vocal tradition is central to this music, its singers are perhaps less well known in the West than instrumentalists. M.S. Subbulakshmi and Dr M. Balamurali Krishna are among the famous names, but the most celebrated is probably Ramnad Krishnan, who has taught in America.

The instruments of Carnatic music include the **vina**, which resembles the sitar but has no sympathetic strings (Carnatic musicians appear not to like the somewhat hollow timbre that they give to the instrument), the **mridangam** double-headed drum, and the enormous **nadasvaram**, a type of oboe just over a metre long which takes great experience and delicacy to play. The **violin** is widely used – listen to the playing of Dr L. Subramaniam or his brother L. Shankar, better known for his fusion experiments with guitarist John McLaughlin than for his classical recordings. The **mandolin** is growing in popularity and the **saxophone** has made a strikingly successful appearance in the hands of Kadri Gopalnath. Among *vina* players look out for S. Balachander and K.S. Narayanaswami.

Percussion is very important, perhaps more so than in Hindustani music, and percussion ensembles frequently tour abroad. In addition to the *mridangam*, percussion instruments include the **ghatam**, a clay pot played with tremendous zest and sometimes tossed into the air in a burst of high spirits. "Vikku" Vinayakram is its best-known player.

New paths

In earlier times the job of musician was more or less hereditary: would-be musicians began their musical education at the age of four, and music (as a profession) was considered beneath the dignity of the well-to-do and the academic classes. However, in recent years traditional restrictions have been relaxed, and music is no longer the province of a few families. Many educated Indians are becoming involved in both performance and composition, and as public performance loses its stigma the requirement for musicians to begin their training at a very early age becomes less forceful. Women instrumentalists are also making their mark – a startling innovation in a male-dominated musical culture. Two women with particularly high reputations are violinist Sangeeta Rajan and tabla player Anuradha Pal, both of whom have recorded in India. Several *gharanas* have been set up abroad, notably the one in California run by sarod player **Ali Akbar Khan**, who is probably Indian music's most influential living figure, and there is a steady trickle of Westerners who are willing to subject themselves to the disciplines of study.

However, the importance of the old families is barely diminished. Among the younger generation of players are such names as sarod player Brij Narayan, son of Ram Narayan; Nikil Banerjee, who studied sitar with his father Jitendra Nath Banerjee; and Krishna Bhatt, who studied with Ravi Shankar and also comes from a family of musicians. Ravi Shankar's own daughter, Anoushka, also created a stir when she made her debut in 2001 at the age of 19, although her film-star looks were greeted with greater critical acclaim than her playing. Other important figures to listen out for are sitar player Rais Khan and vocalist Rashid Khan. These, like the other names mentioned, bear witness to the remaining vitality and richness of the classical music tradition in India and abroad.

Folk music of India

There are many kinds of **Indian folk music**, but the main regional strands are those of Uttar Pradesh, Rajasthan, the Punjab (spread across both India and Pakistan), and Bengal (including Bangladesh). Kashmir produces its own distinctive folk sound, and the music of many of India's tribal peoples more closely resembles that of Southeast Asia or even Borneo than anything else in the subcontinent. Apart from obvious linguistic differences, the folk songs of each region have their own distinct rhythmic structures and are performed on or accompanied by different musical instruments. Some classical instruments are used, but the following are mostly associated with less formal folk occasions.

Discography

Hindustani music

Nikhil Banerjee *The Hundred-minute Raga: Purabi Kalyan* (Raga Records, US). Banerjee, one of the finest sitar players of recent years, is famed for the purity and elegance of his style. This recording finds him on top form.

Vishwa Mohan Bhatt *Guitar à la Hindustan* (Original Music Impressions, India). One of Hindustani music's most famous sons, Bhatt reworked and redesigned the Spanish guitar until it emerged as a new hybrid instrument cannily called the "Mohanvina". Along with Water Lily Acoustics *Gathering Rain Clouds*, this is a perfect place to begin an exploration of Bhatt's classical repertoire.

Debashish Bhattacharya *3: Calcutta Slide Guitar* (Riverboat, UK). This Bengali slide-guitar maestro first attracted the attention of international audiences after his superb collaboration with Bob Brozman, and here he demonstrates his extraordinary virtuoso technique in the Indian classical idiom. The "3" of the album title refers to a trinity of specially designed instruments: the *anandi* (like a ukulele), the 14-string *ghandarvi*, and 29-string *chaturangui*, from which he conjures music deeply imbued with spirituality.

Hariprasad Chaurasia *Hari-Krishna: In Praise of Janmashtami* (Navras, UK). North Indian flautist Chaurasia is one of th country's most successful ambassadors on any instrument. This three-album set captures an intimate annual tradition when the maestro, joined by his family and a few close associates, plays through the night in front of a Krishna altar in his Mumbai home. A quietly momentous album.

Kushal Das *Raga Marwa – Surbahar*. A *surbhahar* is a kind of rarely played "bass sitar", which produces a sound comparable to the ancient *vina*. Calcutta-based Kushal Das here uses its dignified and sombre voice to great effect, playing an intensely atmospheric rendition of Marwa which is melancholic and uplifting.

Ali Akbar Khan *Signature Series Volumes 1 and 2* (AMMP, US). Sarod player and master melodist Ali Akbar Khan is hailed as one of the greatest musicians on the planet, irrespective of genre. Accompanied here by one of the finest tabla players of his generation, Mahapurush Misra.

Bismillah Khan *Live in London Volumes 1 and 2* (Navras, UK). Two marvellous albums recorded in London in 1985. One of Hindustani music's foremost virtuosi, Bismillah Khan is the acknowledged master of the *shehnai*.

Imrat Khan *Ajmer* (Water Lily Acoustics, US). This 1990 recording features Khan's virtuoso performances on the sitar and its bass-voiced equivalent, the *surbahar*.

Sultan Khan *Sarangi* (Navras, UK). *Sarangi* player Sultan Khan first came under the international spotlight touring with Ravi Shankar and George Harrison, and consolidated his international career with work on the soundtrack to Gandhi. This 1992 release from a dizzy-making London concert in 1990 reveals eloquent insights that few can match.

Vilayat Khan *Sitar* (India Archive Music, US). Studio recording from the greatest living sitar player alongside – not after – Ravi Shankar. Performed with such flair and compassion that the senses tingle.

Kamalesh Maitra Tabla *Tarang – Melody on Drums* (Smithsonian Folkways, US). Compelling performance by the acknowledged master of the rare tabla tarang, a set of tablas tuned to play *raags*.

Ram Narayan *The Art of the Sarangi* (Ocora, France). "I cannot separate the *sarangi* from Ram Narayan, so thoroughly fused are they, not only in my memory but in the fact of this sublime dedication of the great musician to an instrument which is no longer archaic because of the matchless way he had made it speak." (Yehudi Menuhin)

Alla Rakha *Maestro's Choice* – Tabla (Music Today, India). A recital with Zakir Hussain illustrating the potency of Hindustani rhythm, exploring *matta taal* (a 9-beat cycle) and *jai taal* (a 13-beat cycle) with a concluding number in pashto (7 beats).

Sultan Khan supports melodically on *sarangi*. Their 67-minute Tabla *Duet* (Moment, US), with Ramesh Misra on *sarangi* is also highly recommended.

Ravi Shankar *Ravi Shankar & Ali Akbar Khan in Concert 1972* (Apple, UK). Sitar and sarod pyrotechnics and profundity recorded in New York. The concert took place weeks after the death of their mutual guru Allauddin Khan, and was dedicated to him.

Various *Call of the Valley* (EMI/Hemisphere, UK). Probably the most influential Hindustani album ever made, using various time-related *raags* to depict the passage of a Kashmiri day.

Various *Inspiration – India* (EMI, UK). A selection of instrumental and tabla duos and *jugulbandi* duets giving a varied introduction to Hindustani music.

Various *The Rough Guide to the Music of India and Pakistan* (World Music Network, UK). A digestible introduction to the music of north India, with flautist Dr N. Ramani the only southerner represented. A good survey of classical, semi-classical and folk styles.

Carnatic music

Kadri Gopalnath *Sax Melodies – Naadagaambheeryam* (Sangeetha, India/US). Golpanath typifies the duality of Carnatic music in playing a modern instrument in a tradition that goes back centuries. The saxophone harks back to the older sound of the *nagaswaram*. On this album Gopalnath is accompanied by violin, *ghatam*, *mridangam* and *morsing*.

The Karnataka College of Percussion *River Yamuna* (Music of the World, US). Despite the ensemble's name, KCP also features the voice of Ramamani and melody instruments such as *vina*, violin and solos. This 1997 album, a reworked version of their classic *Shiva Ganga* (1995), ranks among the most accessible introduction for beginners to the deep space of Carnatic music.

Shankar *Raga Aberi* (Music of the World, US). A spectacular *ragam-tanam-pallavi* performance featuring the growling low notes of Shankar's extraordinary ten-string double violin. The performance also features spectacular vocal percussion and solos.

L. Subramaniam *Electric Modes* (Water Lily Acoustics, US). A two-CD set, one volume of which consists of original compositions, the second of which focuses on traditional *raags*. Subramaniam is one of the most recorded Carnatic artists in the West and has regularly played in non-Carnatic contexts.

Song forms

Najma Akhtar *Qareeb* (Triple Earth). Having one track on the soundtrack of acclaimed British film *Sammy And Rosie Get Laid* assisted, but it is the lyrical gift, innovative arrangements and fine instrumental playing (including violin, sax and *santur*) that sets *Qareeb* ("Nearness") apart. A modern *ghazal* classic.

Asha Bhosle *Legacy* (AMMP/Triloka, US). A remarkable collaboration of Bhosle and great sarod player Ali Akbar Khan in a collection of classical and light-classical vocal gems.

Mehdi Hassan *Live in Concert* (Navras, UK). This triple CD, recorded live in London in 1990, captures the feel of a classical *ghazal* concert, or *mushaira* (gathering), with interjections of *thumri*, *dadra* and folk song for variety.

Bade Ghulam Ali Kham *Raga Piloo, Raga Bhairavi* & *Raga Rageshree* (Multitone Prestige, UK). These live *thumri* recordings have *sarangi*, tabla and tambura accompaniment, and the artist's son as the second vocalist.

Jagjit & Chitra Singh *The Golden Collection* (Gramophone Company of India, India). The names of this husband-and-wife team are synonymous with *ghazal*. These 29 solo and duo tracks over two CDs are terrific, with tasteful *sarangi* and tabla work.

Discography *continued*

Folk

Fanfare de Calcutta (Mehbooba Band) *Signature* (France Musiques). Recorded in a Calcuttan back alley, this 2001 album perfectly captures the anarchic sound of the north Indian wedding brass band, complete with wailing clarinets, bumpy euphonium bass, raucous cornet and trumpet calls, big cymbal clashes, and jaunty, Punjabi *Bhangra*-influenced folk rhythms.

Purna Das Baul *Bauls of Bengal* (Cramworld, Belgium). A compelling introduction to the wild devotional music of the *bauls*, mystical wayfaring minstrels from Bengal whose ecstatic sounds have inspired figures as diverse as Rabindranath Tagore, Alan Ginsberg and Bob Dylan. Lutes, flutes and driving *khamak* percussion underscore the joyful vocals on this, India's top-selling folk release.

Various *Bauls of Bengal* (Cramworld, Belgium). An appealing and representative introduction to the music of the *bauls*, with good instrumental playing. Recorded in Belgium in the early 90s.

Various *Inde: Rajasthan* (Ocora, France). The most varied compilation to date of folk music from north and west Rajasthan, featuring a cross-section of the region's specialist music castes.

Various *Ganga: The Music of the Ganges* (EMI/Virgin Classics, France). A wonderful introduction to Indian folk and devotional music, evoking the location and context. The three CDs trace the course of the river from the Himalayas to the Bay of Bengal and feature sounds of the river alongside performances beautifully recorded in temples, at the water's edge, on boats and so on. Much of the music is devotional, but other highlights include snake charmer's music, a festival percussion ensemble, a virtuoso toy-seller's song, *bauls* and a great *shehnai dhun* performance at dawn.

In **Rajasthan**, music is always played for weddings and theatre performances, and often at local markets or gatherings. There is a whole caste of professional musicians who perform this function, and a wonderful assortment of earthy-sounding stringed instruments like the *kamayacha* and *ravanhata* that accompany their songs. The *ravanhata* is a simple, two-stringed fiddle that, skilfully played, can produce a tune of great beauty and depth. Hearing it played by a fine street musician behind the city walls of Jaisalmer, it seems the perfect aural background for this desert citadel.

The *satara* is the traditional instrument of the desert shepherds. A double flute, it has two pipes of different lengths, one to play the melody, the other to provide the drone, rather like bagpipes without the bag. The bag is the musician himself, who plays with circular breathing. Local cassettes of these instruments are available in small stores across Rajasthan.

As well as drums, India boasts a variety of tuned **percussion instruments**. The most popular in this category is the *jaltarang* – a water-xylophone – consisting of a series of porcelain bowls of different sizes, each containing a prescribed amount of water. The bowls are usually struck with a pair of small sticks, but sometimes these are abandoned as the player rubs the rims of the bowls with a wet finger. The small brass, dome-shaped cymbals called *manjira* or *taal* are the best known of the many kinds of bells and gongs.

Filmi and Bhangra

There are songs for all kinds of work and play in India, and almost every activity is represented in song, and there is an extensive repertoire of dance music.

Marching bands

Spend any time in northern India, particularly during the winter wedding season, and you're almost certain to come across at least a couple of **marching bands**. First introduced to India by the British Army in the early nineteenth century and later adopted as a folk idiom right across the north and centre of the country (where they replaced the old *shehnai*-and-drum *naubat* troupes of the Moghul era), brass bands have become an essential ingredient of working-class weddings and religious processions. Decked out in ill-fitting, mock-military uniforms (complete with tinsel epaulettes, plastic-peaked caps and buckled gaiters), the musicians (band-wallahs) are most often called upon to accompany a bridegroom's party (*baraat*) in its procession to the bride's house. The music itself – a cacophony of squealing clarinets and crowd-stopping blasts of brass played over snare and *dholak* tattoos – is invariably at odds with the mood of the groom, sitting astride a hired white horse on his way to married life with a stranger. But no one seems to care, least of all the members of the *baraat*, hip-thrusting and strutting along like Bollywood's best, to the stream of Hindi film hits, folk tunes, popular *raags* and patriotic songs.

Inevitably, **film music** has drawn heavily from this folk tradition, but sadly has also become a relatively effortless substitute for most of it. In some instances, "pop" adaptations of traditional folk music have served to revitalize and add a fresh lease of life to the original form – *bhangra*, the folk music of Punjab, is a very good example of this. British "*bhangra*-rock" has created a fresh interest in the original *bhangra* of the Punjabi farmers.

Folk music is now beginning to awaken greater interest, particularly with non-Indian record companies, and largely as a result of the growing Western interest in different kinds of Indian music. Perhaps this overseas interest has come just in time, for although it is still practised in the old way in more traditional settings and for particular rituals – weddings, births, harvest time and so on – folk music on the whole, if it is to be defined as the "music of the people", has largely been eclipsed by the output of the Indian film industry.

Whereas in the past traditional wedding songs would have been sung by the neighbourhood women all through the festivities, it is now more usual to hear film songs blaring away at Indian weddings. Nonetheless, fears that traditional music is vanishing altogether seem unwarranted: in Pakistan the unique sound of the *sohni* bands – clarinet-led brass bands which play at weddings – fills the air with wild melody, and in Rajasthan, members of the traditional musicians' castes still make their living by playing at ceremonies and for entertainment. The radio and cassette player are by no means all-conquering.

This piece, by Jameela Siddiqi, David Muddyman, Ken Hunt, David Abram and Kim Burton, was taken from the *Rough Guide to World Music*.

Books

The following list is a personal selection of the books that proved most useful or enjoyable during the preparation of this guide. Most of them are available on websites such as ⓦwww.amazon.com or ⓦwww.amazon.co.uk, and in India itself, as are countless inexpensive editions of Indian and English classics. Books tagged with the ★ symbol are particularly recommended.

History

Jad Adams and Phillip Whitehead *The Dynasty: The Nehru-Gandhi Story*. A brilliant and intriguing account of India's most famous – or infamous – family and the way its various personalities have shaped post-Independence India, although Sonia Gandhi's recent prominence rather begs an update.

A.L. Basham *The Wonder That Was India*. A veritable encyclopedia by India's foremost authority on his country's ancient history. Every page of this masterpiece bristles with the author's erudition. A companion volume by S.A. Rizvi brings it up to the arrival of the British.

David Burton *The Raj at Table*. Few books evoke the quirky world of British India quite as vividly as this unlikely masterpiece – commendable both for its extraordinary recipes and as a marvellous piece of social history, compiled over years of travel, archival research and interviews.

Larry Collins and Dominique Lapierre *Freedom at Midnight*. Readable, if shallow, account of Independence, highly sympathetic to the British and, particularly, to Mountbatten, who was the authors' main source of information.

★ **William Dalrymple** *White Mughals*. In the course of five years' research into the lives of early European colonials who adopted "native" customs (and married Indian women), William Dalrymple stumbled apon the forgotten story of James Achilles Kirkpatrick, British Resident at Hyderabad at the end of the eighteenth century, who fell in love with, and subsequently married, the great niece of the Nizam's prime minister. Both it, and the author's account of how he pieced the picture together, make an extraordinary tale, told with relish, erudition and an impeccable sense of pace in a book that grips like a great nineteenth-century novel.

Mike Davis *Late Victorian Holocausts*. A pull-no-punches account of how British self-interest and economic policy caused the deaths of millions of Indians in the famines of the nineteenth and early twentieth centuries. Essentially an academic book, but one which puts the achievements of the Raj in a dark perspective.

Patrick French *Liberty or Death*. The definitive account (and a damning indictment) of the last years of the British Raj. Material from hitherto unreleased intelligence files shows how Churchill's "florid incompetence" and Atlee's "feeble incomprehension" contributed to the debacle that was Partition.

★ **Bamber Gascoigne** *The Great Moghuls*. By far the most interestingly written account of lives of the first six Great Moghuls, richly illustrated with photos of the surviving monuments and details from original art works. Essential reading if you plan to explore Agra and Delhi in any depth.

Christopher Hibbert *The Great Mutiny*. The sieges, battles and bloody aftermath of the "First War of Independence" in 1857, brought to life by Hibbert's easy prose and a huge amount of compelling first-hand material.

Dilip Hiro *The Rough Guide History of India*. No other book crams so much background material on India into such a small format – this pocket history fleshes out a bare-bones time-line with contextual boxes, literary extracts, potted biographies, quotations and black-and-white photos. An ideal travelling companion.

Lawrence James *Raj: the Making and Unmaking of British India*. A door-stopping 700-page history of British rule in India, drawing on recently released official papers and private memoirs. The most up-to-date, erudite survey of its kind, and unlikely to be bettered as a general introduction.

★ **John Keay** *India: A History*. In this, the most recent of his five consistently excellent books on India, John Keay manages to coax clear, impartial and highly readable narrative from 5000 years of fragmented events, spiced up with a liberal dose of fascinating snippets. Arguably the best single-volume history currently in print.

John Keay *The Honourable East India Company*. In characteristically fluent style, Keay strikes the right balance between those who regard the East India Company as a rapacious institution with malevolent intentions and others who present its acquisition of the Indian empire as an unintended, almost accidental process.

★ **John Keay** *India Discovered*. Until midway through the nineteenth century virtually nothing was known about India's ancient history. This book recounts how the secrets of such monuments as Sanchi, Ajanta and the Ashokan edicts were unlocked by a colourful band of Raj-era Indologists whose lives were, in many cases, as fascinating as their subjects. A great contexualizer for anyone planning to visit the famous archeological sites.

Dominique Lapierre and Javier Moro *Five Past Midnight in Bhopal*. The definitive account of the world's worst industrial disaster, weaving together portraits of its victims, heroes and villains to create a compelling narrative that also stands as an outstanding piece of investigative journalism.

Geoffrey Moorhouse *India Britannica*. A balanced, lively survey of the rise and fall of the British Raj, with lots of illustrations. Recommended if this is your first foray into the period, as it's a lot more concise and readable than Lawrence James' *Raj* (though correspondingly less detailed).

Romila Thapar *History of India Volume I*. Concise paperback account of early Indian history, ending with the Delhi Sultanate. Percival Spear's *History of India Volume II* covers the period from the Moghul era to the death of Gandhi.

Society

Trevor Fishlock *India File*. The latest edition of this now classic analysis of contemporary Indian society includes essays on the Golden Temple siege and the rise of Rajiv Gandhi. Recommended as an all-round introduction.

B.K.S. Iyengar *Yoga: the Path to Holistic Health*. The definitive guide to yoga by the world's leading teacher, recommended by practitioners from across the yoga spectrum. Some 1900 colour photos illustrate the postures, and there's a copious introduction giving the philosophical background and history. Too heavy to cart around India with you, but indispensable as a reference tool. A lighter (and much less expensive) version – fully endorsed by the great man, though modelled and written by three of his senior pupils – is *Yoga: the Iyengar Way*, by Silva, Mira and Shyan Mehta.

Zia Jaffrey *The Invisibles*. An investigation into the hidden world of Delhi's *hijras*, or eunuchs. Using anthropological and journalistic research techniques, Jaffrey unravels the layers of myth and mystique surrounding this secretive subculture.

John Keay *Into India*. As an all-round introduction to India, this book – originally written in 1973 but re-issued in 1999 – is the one most often recommended by old hands (including Mark Tully and William Dalrymple). Region by region, it presents a wide spread of history and cultural background, spliced with lucid personal observations.

Gita Mehta *Karma Cola*. Satirical look at the psychedelic 1970s freak scene in India, with some hilarious anecdotes, and many a wry observation on the wackier excesses of spiritual tourism. The later *Snakes and Ladders* is a brilliant overview of contemporary urban India in the form of a pot-pourri of essays, travelogues and interviews.

Prafulla Mohanti *Changing Village, Changing Life*. Entertaining portrait of life in an east Indian village through the eyes of an anglicized expat. Essential reading if you plan to visit Orissa.

Geoffrey Moorhouse *Calcutta, the City Revealed*. Fascinating, if politically out of date, anatomy of the great city in the early 1970s.

★ **V.S. Naipaul** *A Million Mutinies Now*. A superbly crafted mosaic of individual lives from around the subcontinent, producing a sympathetic and rounded portrait of the country in one of the best books on India ever written. In sharp contrast, his earlier work, *A Wounded Civilisation*, is a bleak political travelogue, researched and written during and shortly after the Emergency.

Christopher Pinney *Photos of the Gods*. In this history of the printed image in Indian popular culture, Pinney focuses on political, cultural and religious themes, and traces the importance that the visual arts – in the form of posters, postcards and other printed images – have had on India's history since the 1870s. A fascinating book illustrated with 80 colour and 87 black-and-white pictures.

★ **Mark Tully** *No Full Stops in India*. Earnest but highly readable dissection of contemporary India by the former BBC correspondent, incorporating anecdotes and first-hand accounts of political events over the past twenty years. His most recent book, *India in Slow Motion*, covers a similarly diverse range of subjects, from Hindu extremism, child labour and Sufi mysticism to the crisis in agriculture and the persistence of political corruption to the problem of Kashmir. Both challenge preconceptions foreigners often hold about India, and those held by Indians about their own country.

Various *India*. To commemorate the fiftieth anniversary of Indian Independence, Granta published this mixed bag of new fiction, comment, poetry, reportage and memoirs from an impressive cast of Indian and foreign contributors. Among its many highlights are notes from the diary of V.S. Naipaul and Sebastião Salgado's photographic essay on Mumbai.

Travel

★ **William Dalrymple** *City of Djinns*. Dalrymple's award-winning account of a year in Delhi sifts through successive layers of the city's past. Each is vividly brought to life with a blend of inspired historical sleuth work and encounters with living vestiges of different eras: Urdu calligraphers, Sufi clerics, eunuchs, Persian-style pigeon fanciers and the last surviving descendant of the Moghul emperors. A real gem. *The Age of Kali* (published in India as *In the Court of the Fish-Eyed Goddess*) is a collection of essays drawn from ten years' travel.

Trevor Fishlock *Cobra Road*. Former *Times* correspondent Fishlock's 1999 travelogue is a classic all-round introduction to the subcontinent. Sympathetic yet balanced, it looks at many of the ironies and absurdities inherent in modern India, whilst retaining a sense of humour and adventure.

Alexander Frater *Chasing the Monsoon*. Frater's wet-season jaunt up the west coast and across the Ganges plains took him through an India of muddy puddles and grey skies: an evocative account of the country as few visitors see it, and now something of a classic of the genre.

Justine Hardy *Bollywood Boy*. Sassy, chick-lit-style travelogue through the larger-than-life world of the Bombay film industry, following the author's quest to interview heart-throb Hrithik Roshan at the height of his fame. Along the way, she brushes shoulders with a lurid cast of has-been movie stars, Grant Road prostitutes, gangsters and some formidable regulars at her local beauty salon. Much of the book's appeal lies in the fact that its author finds all the glamour as seductive as she does shallow.

Norman Lewis *A Goddess in the Stones*. Veteran English travel writer's typically idiosyncratic account of his trip to Kolkata (Calcutta) and around the backwaters of Bihar and Orissa, with some vivid insights into tribal India.

Geoffrey Moorhouse *Om*. Not Moorhouse's strongest offering, but absorbing nevertheless. Following the death of his daughter, the author journeys round South India's key spiritual centres, providing typically well-informed asides on history, politics, contemporary culture and religion.

Dervla Murphy *On a Shoestring to Coorg*. Murphy stays with her young daughter in the little-visited tropical mountains of Coorg, Karnataka. Arguably the most famous modern Indian travelogue, and a manifesto for single-parent budget travel.

★ **Eric Newby** *Slowly down the Ganges*. Newby has always regarded his mammoth journey from Haridwar to the mouth of the Hooghly as the most memorable of his many adventures. Though dated in places – it was written in the 1960s – his elegant prose and wry humour evoke the timeless allure of the subcontinent's holiest river.

★ **Tahir Shah** *Sorcerer's Apprentice*. A journey through the weird underworld of occult India. Travelling as an apprentice to a master conjurer and illusionist, Shah encounters hangmen, baby renters, skeleton dealers, *sadhus* and charlatans.

★ **Mark Shand** *Travels on My Elephant*. Award-winning account of a 600-mile ride on an elephant from Konarak in Orissa to Bihar, accompanied by a drunken mahout, among others; full of incident, humour and pathos. For the sequel, *Queen of the Elephants*, Shand teams up with an Assamese princess who's the country's leading elephant handler.

Eric Shipton and H.W. Tilman *Nanda Devi*. Two classics of Himalayan mountaineering literature published in a single volume, recounting the famous expeditions of 1934 and 1936, which blazed a trail up the Rishi Gorge and British India's highest peak. Shipton's, in particular, is a masterpiece of the genre: beautifully written and enthralling from start to finish.

★ **Michael Wood** *The Smile of Murugan*. An erudite and affectionate portrait of Tamil Nadu and its people in the mid-1990s, centred on a video-bus pilgrimage tour of the state's key sacred sites. One of the most inspiring books on South India ever written, and an ideal companion to travelling in the region.

Fiction

Anita Desai *Feasting and Fasting*. This, the most recent novel by one of India's leading female authors, eloquently portrays the frustration of a sensitive young woman stuck in the stifling atmosphere of home while her spoilt brother is packed off to study in America.

E.M. Forster *A Passage to India*. Forster's most acclaimed novel, a withering critique of colonialism set in the 1920s. Memorable as much for its sympathetic portrayal of middle-class Indian life as for its insights into cultural misunderstandings.

Amitav Ghosh *The Hungry Tide*. A complex and involving story woven around the mysterious, watery world of the Sunderbans. The vivid descriptions of local history and mythology, in precarious balance with extraordinary natural events, bring this unique environment to life.

Ruth Prawer Jhabvala *Out of India*. One of many short-story collections that shows India in its full colours: amusing, shocking and thought-provoking. Other titles include *How I Became a Holy Mother*; *Like Birds, Like Fishes*; *Heat and Dust*; and *In Search of Love and Beauty*.

Rudyard Kipling *Kim*. Cringingly colonialist at times, of course, but the atmosphere of India and Kipling's love of it shine through in this subtle story of an orphaned white boy. Kipling's other key works on India are two books of short stories: *Soldiers Three* and *In Black and White*.

Dominique Lapierre *City of Joy*. Melodramatic story of a white man's journey into Kolkata's (Calcutta) slums, loaded with anecdotes about Indian religious beliefs and customs.

Rohinton Mistry *A Fine Balance*. Two friends seek promotion from their low-caste rural lives to the opportunities of the big smoke. A compelling and savage triumph-of-the-human-spirit novel detailing the evils of the caste system and of Indira Gandhi's brutal policies during the Emergency. Mistry's *Such a Long Journey* is an acclaimed account of a Bombay Parsi's struggle to maintain personal integrity in the face of betrayals and disappointment.

★ **R.K. Narayan** *Gods, Demons and Others*. Classic Indian folk tales and popular myths told through the voice of a village storyteller. Many of Narayan's beautifully crafted books, full of touching characters and subtle humour, are set in the fictional South Indian territory of Malgudi.

★ **Arundhati Roy** *The God of Small Things*. Haunting Booker Prize-winner about a well-to-do South Indian family caught between the snobberies of high caste tradition, a colonial past and the diverse personal histories of its members. Seen through the eyes of two children, the assortment of scenes from Keralan life are as memorable as the characters themselves, while the comical and finally tragic turn of events say as much about Indian history as the refrain that became the novel's catchphrase: "things can change in a day".

★ **Salman Rushdie** *Midnight's Children.* This story of a man born at the very moment of Independence, whose life mirrors that of modern India itself, won Rushdie the Booker Prize and the enmity of Indira Gandhi, who had it banned in India. Set in Kerala and Bombay, *The Moor's Last Sigh* was the subject of a defamation case brought by Shiv Sena leader Bal Thackeray.

★ **Vikram Seth** *A Suitable Boy.* Vast, all-embracing tome set in UP shortly after Independence; wonderful characterization and an impeccable sense of place and time make this an essential read for those long train journeys.

Khushwant Singh *Train to Pakistan.* A chillingly realistic portrayal of life in a village on the Partition line, set in the summer of 1947. Singh's other works include *Delhi: A Novel*, a series of voices from the city's past interrupted by an old man's quest for sexual satisfaction in the present, and *Sex, Scotch and Scholarship*, a collection of wry short stories.

William Sutcliffe *Are You Experienced?* Easy-read sendup of a "typical" backpacker trip round India.

Biography and autobiography

J.R. Ackerley *Hindoo Holiday.* During the 1920s, a gay and eccentric pal of E.M. Forster steps into the bizarre world of an even more gay and eccentric maharaja seeking a tutor for his eighteen-month-old son.

Charles Allen *Plain Tales from the Raj.* First-hand accounts from erstwhile *sahibs* and *memsahibs* of everyday British India, organized thematically.

James Cameron *An Indian Summer.* Affectionate and humorous description of the veteran British journalist's visit to India in 1972, and his marriage to an Indian woman. Somewhat dated, but an enduring classic.

Louis Fischer *The Life of Mahatma Gandhi.* First published in 1950, this biography has been re-issued several times since, and quite rightly – veteran American journalist Louis Fischer knew his subject personally, and his book provides an engaging account of Gandhi as a man, politician and propagandist.

★ **M.K. Gandhi** *The Story of My Experiments with Truth.* Gandhi's fascinating records of his life, including the spiritual and moral quests, changing relationship with the British Government in India, and gradual emergence into the fore of politics.

Paramahansa Yogananda *Autobiography of a Yogi.* Uplifting account of religious awakening and spiritual development by one of the most influential Hindu masters to leave India and bring her teachings to the West.

Women

★ **Elizabeth Bumiller** *May You Be the Mother of a Hundred Sons.* Lucid exploration of the Indian woman's lot, drawn from dozens of first-hand encounters by an American journalist.

Shashi Deshpande *The Binding Vine.* Disturbing story of one woman's struggle for independence, and her eventual acceptance of the position of servitude traditionally assumed by an Indian wife.

Anees Jung *The Night of the New Moon.* Revealing and poetic stories woven around interviews with Muslim women from all sectors of Indian society. Jung's *Unveiling India* is a compelling account of the life of a Muslim woman who has chosen to break free from orthodoxy.

Sarah Lloyd *An Indian Attachment.* Life in a Punjabi plains village through the eyes of a young Western woman, whose relationship with an opium-addicted Sikh forms the essence of this honest and enlightening book.

★ **Vrinda Nabar** *Caste as Woman.* Conceived as an Indian counterpart to Greer's *The Female Eunuch*, a wry study of the pressures brought to bear during the various stages of womanhood. Drawing on scripture and popular culture, Nabar looks at issues of identity and cultural conditioning.

Sakuntala Narasiman *Sati: A Study of Widow Burning in India.* Definitive exploration of *sati* and its significance throughout history, including an account of the infamous Roop Kanwar case.

Mala Sen *Death By Fire.* This is the second book by a London-based author better known for her biography of Phoolan Devi, *India's Bandit Queen*, which was later made into a controversial movie. It uses the story of an 18-year-old Rajasthani girl who was burned alive on her husband's funeral pyre in 1987 as a springboard to explore some of the wider and more representative issues affecting women in contemporary Indian society – a bleak read, but one that shows up the hollow triumphalism of the country's right-wing politicians in its true colours.

Virama, Josiane Racine & Jean-Luc Racine *Virama: Life of an Untouchable.* Unique autobiography of an Untouchable woman told in her own words (transcribed by French anthropologists) over a fifteen-year period, offering frank, often humorous insights into India, the universe and everything.

Development and the environment

Julia Cleves Mosse *India: Paths to Development.* Concise analysis of the economic, environmental and political changes affecting India, focusing on the lives of ordinary poor people and the exemplary ways in which some have succeeded in shaping their own future. The best country brief on the market, though somewhat out of date.

★ **Helena Norberg-Hodge** *Ancient Futures: Learning From Ladakh.* An overview of Ladakh's traditional, ecologically balanced way of life, followed up by an analysis of the ways in which modern developments (notably tourism) have impinged upon it.

Palagummi Sainath *Everybody Loves a Good Drought.* A classic report on India's poorest districts, telling the stories of individual villages that are usually lost in a maze of development statistics. Its harrowing case studies caused uproar in the capital, galvanizing the government into some drastic aid programmes. A polished view on an India few visitors see.

★ **Jeremy Seabrook** *Notes from Another India.* Life histories and interviews – compiled over a year's travelling and skilfully contextualized – reveal the everyday problems faced by Indians from a variety of backgrounds, and how grassroots groups have tried to combat them. One of the soundest, and most engaging, overviews of Indian development issues ever written.

The arts and architecture

Roy Craven *Indian Art.* Concise general introduction to Indian art, from Harappan seals to Moghul miniatures, with lots of illustrations.

Rachel Dwyer & Divia Patel *Cinema India: The Visual Culture of Hindi Film.* Definitive guide to Bollywood, tracing its development from 1913, with richly illustrated chapters charting the changes in costumes, sets and advertising trends.

Mohan Khokar *Traditions of Indian Classical Dance.* Detailing the religious and social roots of Indian dance, this lavishly illustrated book, with sections on regional traditions, is an excellent introduction to the subject.

George Michell *The Hindu Temple.* A fine primer, introducing Hindu temples, their significance and architectural development.

George Michell and Antonio Martinelli *The Palaces of India.* Now available in affordable paperback, this overview of India's royal architecture is an essential coffee-table tome, memorable less for its lacklustre prose than magnificent images of decaying architectural treasures. Photographer Antonio Martinelli frames the buildings from novel perspectives, highlighting their natural backdrops and revealing the interiors in natural light.

Bonnie C. Wade *Music in India: The Classical Traditions.* A scrupulous catalogue of Indian music, outlining the most commonly used instruments, with illustrations and musical scores.

Stuart Cary Welch *India: Art and Culture 1300–1900.* Originally produced for an exhibition at New York's Metropolitan Museum, this exquisitely illustrated and accessibly written tome covers every aspect of India's rich and varied culture. Highly recommended.

Religion

Diana L. Eck *Banaras – City of Light.* Thorough disquisition on the religious significance of Varanasi; a good introduction to the practice of Hindu cosmology. Her latest book, *Encountering God*, uses Christianity as a reference point for an exploration of the common ground between Hinduism and Buddhism.

Dorf Hartsuiker *Sadhus: Holy Men of India.* The weird world of India's itinerant ascetics exposed in glossy colour photographs and erudite but accessible text.

J.R. Hinnelle (ed) *A Handbook of Living Religions.* The beliefs, practices, iconography and historical roots of all India's major faiths explained in accessible language, with full bibliographies to back up each chapter. Deservedly the most popular book of its kind in print, and an ideal in-depth introduction.

Roger Housden *Travels through Sacred India.* A gazetteer of holy places, listings of ashrams and lively essays on temples, *sadhus*, gurus and sacred sites. Hudson derives much of his material from personal encounters, which bring the subjects to life. Includes sections on all India's main faiths, and an excellent bibliography.

Christmas Humphries *Buddhism.* Dated, and short on rituals and practices, but still the clearest, most readable work on the philosophy and beliefs of the various strands of Buddhism.

★ **Stephen P. Huyler** *Meeting God*. This acclaimed introduction provides an unrivalled overview of the beliefs and practises of contemporary Hinduism. Accompanied by text that evokes general principles by focusing on individual acts of worship, Huyler's photographs are in a class of their own, suffused with sublime colours, magical light, and an intimate sense of spirituality.

Sarah McDonald *Holy Cow*. Very readable account of how a young Aussie journalist grew to love India and how it eventually "made her", concentrating particularly on her personal brushes with the various spiritual traditions of the country. Prone to hyberbole at times but consistently perceptive and occasionally hilarious.

Wendy O'Flaherty (transl.) *Hindu Myths*. Translations of key myths from the original Sanskrit texts, providing an insight into the foundations of Hinduism.

Charlie Pye-Smith *Rebels and Outcasts: A Journey through Christian India*. An Englishman's encounters with clerics, congregations and NGOs from the full gamut of denominations. The most up-to-date survey on the subject, although unlikely to appeal to non-Christians.

Language

Language

Language

No less than eighteen major languages, officially recognized by the constitution, numerous minor ones and over a thousand dialects are spoken across India. When independent India was organized, the present-day states were largely created along linguistic lines, which at least helps the traveller make some sense of the complex situation. Considering the continuing prevalence of English, there is rarely any necessity to speak a local language but some theoretical knowledge of the background and having at least a few words of one or two can only enhance your visit.

The main languages of northern India, including the country's eastern and western extremities, are all Indo-Aryan, the easternmost subgroup of the Indo-European family that is thought to have originated somewhere between Europe and Central Asia several millennia BC, before tribal movements spread its progeny in all directions. The oldest extant subcontinental language is Sanskrit, one of the three "big sisters" (along with Latin and Greek) upon which philologists have created the model of proto-Indo-European language. It's known to have been spoken early in the second millennium BC, although it was not written down until much later, and is the vehicle for all the sacred texts of Hinduism. Sanskrit remained the language of the educated until around 1000 AD and is still spoken to some extent by the priestly class today, but over the centuries it gradually developed into the modern tongues of northern India: Hindi, Urdu, Bengali, Gujarati, Marathi, Kashmiri, Punjabi and Oriya.

North India

Hindi, the first language of over 200 million natives of north India, and **Urdu**, predominant among Muslims and across the border in Pakistan, are very closely related and prime examples of New Indo-Aryan languages. They developed in tandem around the markets and army camps of Delhi (the term Urdu derives from the Turkish word for "camp") during the establishment of Muslim rule around the start of the second millennium AD. Whereas Hindi later returned to the Sanskrit roots of its Hindu speakers, however, and adopted the classical **Devanagari** syllabary, Urdu became culturally more closely linked with Islam and is written in **Perso-Arabic** script. The vocabulary of each also reflects these cultural and religious ties. The scripts of Punjabi, Bengali and Gujarati are among those that have developed out of Devanagari and still bear some resemblance to it.

South India

In **South India** the picture changes completely. The four most widely spoken languages, Tamil (Tamil Nadu), Telugu (Andhra Pradesh), Kannada (Karnataka) and Malayalam (Kerala) all belong to the **Dravidian** family, the world's fourth largest group. These and related minor languages grew up quite separately among the non-Aryan peoples of southern India over thousands of years, and the earliest written records of **Tamil** date back to the third century AD. The exact origins of the Dravidian group have not been established, but it is possible that proto-Dravidian was spoken further north in prehistoric times before the people were driven south by the Aryan invaders. The beautiful flowing scripts, especially the exquisite curls of **Kannada**, add a constant aesthetic quality to any tour of the south.

Post Independence

With **Independence** it was decided by the government in Delhi that Hindi should become the **official language** of the newly created country. Interestingly, the idea of using Hindustani, a more recent colloquial hybrid of Hindi and Urdu, popular with Gandhi and others in an effort to encourage communal unity during the fight for freedom, was never pursued; this was due to a mixture of political reasons following Partition and the fact that the language lacked the necessary refinement. A drive to teach Hindi in all schools followed and over half the country's population are now reckoned to have a decent working knowledge of the language. However, there has always been strong **resistance** to the imposition of Hindi in certain areas, especially the **Tamil-led** Dravidian south, and the vast majority of people living below the Deccan plateau have little or no knowledge of it.

This is where English, the language of the ex-colonists, becomes an important means of communication. Not surprisingly, given India's rich linguistic diversity – there are also minority tribal languages and dialects of Sino-Tibetan that do not belong to the main groups mentioned above – **English** remains a **lingua franca** for many people. It is still the preferred language of law, higher education, much of commerce and the media, and to some degree political dialogue; and for many educated Indians, not just those living abroad, it is actually their first language. All this explains why the Anglophone visitor can often soon feel surprisingly at home despite the huge cultural differences. It is not unusual to overhear everyday contact between Indians from different parts of the country being conducted in English, and stimulating conversations can often be had, not only with students or businesspeople, but also with chai wallahs or shoeshine boys.

Useful Hindi words and phrases

Greetings

Greetings	**Namaste** (said with palms together at chest height as in prayer – not used for Muslims)
Hello	**Namaskar** (not used for Muslims)
Greetings	(to a Muslim) **Aslaam alequm**
	(in reply) **ale qum aslaam**
We will meet again	**phir milenge** (goodbye)
Goodbye (to a Muslim)	**Khudaa Haafiz** (may god bless you)
How are you?	**Ap kaise hain** (formal)
How are you?	**Kya hal hai** (familiar)
Brother (common address to a stranger)	**bhaaii** or **bhaiyaa**
Sister	**didi**
Sir	**Hazur** (Muslims only)
Sir (Sahib)	**Saaheb**

Basic words

haan	Yes
achhaa	OK
nahin	No

main	Me
aap	You (formal)
tum	You (familiar)
aur	And/More
kaise	How
kitna	How much
dhanyavad/shukriya	Thank-you
achhaa	Good
kharaab	Bad
baraa	Big
chhotaa	Small
garam	Hot
thandaa	Cold
mirchi	Hot (spicy)
saaf	Clean
gandaa	Dirty
khulaa	Open
mehngaa	Expensive
aao	Come
aaiiye	Please come
jaao	Go
bhaago	Run (also "take a run" or "scram")

Basic phrases

Mera nam . . . hai	My name is . . .
Aapka naam kya hai	What is your name? (formal)
Tumhara naam kya hai	What is your name? (familiar)
Main . . . se aa rahaa hun	I (male) come from . . .
Main . . . se a rahii hun	I (female) come from . . .
Kahan se aate hain	Where do you come from?
Maalum nahin	I don't know
Samaj nahin aayaa	I don't understand
Samaj gayaa	I understand
Main Hindi nahin bol sakta hun	I don't speak Hindi
Aaiste se boliye	Please speak slowly
Mujhe maaf kiijiiye	Please forgive me (I am sorry)
Thiik hai	It is OK
Kitna paisa?	How much?
Iskaa daam kyaa hai?	How much is this?
Kya kaam karte hain?	What work do you do?
Bhaai behan hai?	Do you have any brothers or sisters?

Getting around

. . . kahaan hai?	Where is the . . . ?
Main . . . jaanaa chaataa hun	I want to go to . . .
Kahaan hai?	Where is it?
Kitnaa duur?	How far?
Gwalior kaa bas kahaan hai?	Which is the bus for Gwalior?
Gaarii kab jayegi?	What time does the train leave?
ruko	Stop
thero	Wait

Accommodation

Mujhe kamraa chaahiye	I need a room
Kamraa kaa bhaaraa kyaa hai?	How much is the room?
Main ek raat ke liiye theroonga	I am staying for one night

Medicinal

Sir me dard hai	I have a headache
Mere pet me dard hai	I have a pain in my stomach
Dard yahaan hai	The pain is here
Daaktarkhaanaa kahaan hai?	Where is the doctor's surgery?
Haspitaal kahaan hai?	Where is the hospital?
Dawaiikhaanaa kahaan hai?	Where is the pharmacy?
dawaaii	Medicine
bimar	Ill
dard	Pain
pet	Stomach
aank	Eye
naakh	Nose
kaan	Ear
piith	Back
paao	Foot

Numbers and time

Shunya	Zero
ek	One
do	Two
tin	Three
char	Four
panch	Five
chhe	Six
saat	Seven
aath	Eight
nau	Nine
das	Ten
gyaarah	Eleven
baarah	Twelve
terah	Thirteen
chaudah	Fourteen
pandrah	Fifteen
solah	Sixteen
satrah	Seventeen
athaarah	Eighteen
unniis	Nineteen
biis	Twenty
tiis	Thirty
chaaliis	Forty
pachaas	Fifty
saath	Sixty
sathar	Seventy
assii	Eighty
nabbe	Ninety
ek sau	One hundred
ek hazaar	One thousand
ek lakh	One hundred thousand
ek crore	Ten million
aaj	Today
kal	Tomorrow/yesterday
din	Day
dopahar	Afternoon
shaam	Evening
raat	Night
haftaah	Week
mahiinaa	Month
saal	Year
somvaar	Monday
mangalvaar	Tuesday
budhvaar	Wednesday
viirvaar	Thursday
shukravaar	Friday
shanivaar	Saturday
ravivaar	Sunday

General eating terms and requests

bhat	cooked rice
chamach	spoon
chawal	uncooked rice
cheeni	sugar
cheeni mat dalna	do not put sugar (eg in tea)
cheeni nehin	no sugar!
chhoori	knife
dahi	yoghurt
dudh	milk
garam	hot
gosht	meat, usually mutton
hath dhoney ka pani	hands water for washing
jaggery	unrefined sugar
mirchi	chilli hot
kala mirch	black pepper
mirchi kam or kamti	less – eg (less hot)
kanta	fork
khaana	food
lal mirch	red pepper
macchi	fish
methi	fenugreek
mirch	pepper
murgi	chicken
namak	salt
pani	water
peeney ka pani	drinking water (not mineral water)
plate	plate
sabji	any vegetable curry
thandaa	cold
ziadah or awr	more

Vegetables

adrak	ginger
alu	potatoes
baingan	eggplant (aubergine) or brinjal
bhindi	okra (ladies finger)

chana	chick peas (garbanzo beans)
dhal	lentils
gaajar	carrot
gobi	cauliflower
kaddoo	pumpkin
karela	bitter gourd
lasoon	garlic
mattar	peas
paneer	Indian cheese
piaz	onions
sabzi	literally greens; used for all vegetables
tamatar	tomato

Dishes and cooking terms

alu baingan	potato and aubergine; mild to medium
alu methi	potato with fenugreek leaves, usually medium-hot
baingan bharta	baked and mashed aubergine mixed with onion, best with dhal and *roti*
bhindi bhaji	fried okra; gently spiced
bhuna	roasted first and thickened-down medium-strength curry
biriyani	rice baked with saffron or turmeric, whole spices, and meat (sometimes vegetables), and often hard-boiled egg; rich
Bombay duck	dried bummelo fish
chingri	prawns
chop	minced meat or vegetable surrounded by breaded mashed potato
cutlet	cutlet – often minced meat or vegetable – fried in the form of a flat cake
dahi maach	fish curry with yoghurt, ginger and turmeric; a mild Bengali dish
dhal gosht	meat cooked in lentils; hot
dhansak	meat and lentil curry, a Parsi speciality; medium-hot
dopiaza	with onions added at two different stages of cooking; medium-mild
dum	steamed in a casserole; the most common dish is *aloo dum* with potatoes
jalfrezi	with tomatoes and green chilli; medium-hot
jeera	cumin; a masala so described will usually be medium-hot
karahi	cast-iron wok which has given its name to a method of cooking meat with dry masala to create dishes of medium strength
karhi	a dhal-like dish made from *dahi* and gram flour; popular in the north, especially in Punjab and Gujarat
keema	minced meat
kofta	balls of minced vegetables or meat in a curried sauce
korma	meat braised in yoghurt sauce; mild
maacher jhol	mild fish stew, often made with the entire fish – a Bengali delicacy
malai kofta	vegetable kebabs in a rich cream sauce; medium-mild

molee	curry with coconut, usually fish, originally Malay (hence the name), now a speciality of Kerala; hot
mulligatawny	curried vegetable soup, a classic Anglo-Indian dish rumoured to have come from "Mulligan Aunty" but probably South Indian; medium-strength
pathia	thickened curry with lemon juice; hot
pomfret	a flatfish popular in Mumbai and Kolkata (Calcutta)
pulau	rice, gently spiced and pre fried
rogan josh	deep red lamb curry, a classic Mughlai dish; medium-hot
sambar	soupy lentil and vegetable curry with asafoetida and tamarind
stew or **estew**	stew with a distinct Keralan twist (contains chilli and coconut); there's also a north Indian Muslim version)
subje	white coconut chutney often served with vada
tarka dhal	lentils with a masala of fried garlic, onions and spices
vindaloo	Goan vinegared meat (sometimes fish) curry, originally pork; very hot (but not as hot as the kamikaze UK version)

Breads and pancakes

appam*	rice pancake speckled with holes, soft in the middle; a speciality of the Malabar coast of Kerala

Indian English

Over the period of the British Raj, **Indian English** developed its own characteristics, which have survived to the present day. The lilting stress and intonation patterns are owing to crossover from the Indian languages, as is the sometimes bewildering pace of delivery. Likewise, certain **vowel sounds**, for example the lack of distinction between the pronunciation of "cot" and "caught", and the utterance of some consonants, such as the common retroflex nature of "p" and "t" with the tongue touching the soft palate, are also due to strong local linguistic features.

Indian languages have contributed a good deal of **vocabulary** to everyday English as well, including words like veranda, bungalow, sandal, pyjamas, shampoo, jungle, turban, caste, chariot, chilli, cardamom and yoga. The traveller to India soon becomes familiar with other terms in common usage that have not spread so widely outside the subcontinent: *dacoit*, *dhoti*, *bandh*, *panchayat*, *lakh* and *crore* are but a few (see Glossary, p.1450, for definitions).

Perhaps the most endearing aspect of Indian English is the way it has preserved forms now regarded as highly **old-fashioned** in Britain. Addresses such as "Good sir" and questions like "May I know your good name?" are commonplace, as are terms like "tiffin", "cantonment" or "top-hole". This type of usage reaches its apogee in the more flowery expressions of the media, which regularly feature in the vast array of daily newspapers published in English. Thus headlines often appear such as "37 perish in mishap", referring to a train crash, or passages like this splendid report of a bank robbery: "The miscreants absconded with the loot in great haste. They repaired immediately to their hideaway, whereupon they divided the iniquitous spoils before vanishing into thin air."

bhatura	soft bread made of white flour and traditionally accompanying *chana*; common in Delhi
chapati	unleavened bread made of wholewheat flour and baked on a round griddle-dish called a *tawa*
dosa*	rice pancake; should be crispy; when served with a filling it is called a masala *dosa* and when plain, a *sada dosa*
iddli*	steamed rice cake, usually served with *sambar*
kachori	small thick cakes of salty deep-fried bread; especially good in Varanasi and Kolkata (Calcutta)
loochi	delicate *puri* often mixed with white flour; cooked in Bengal
nan	white leavened bread kneaded with yoghurt and baked in a tandoor
papad or **poppadum**	crisp, thin, chick-pea flour cracker
paratha or **parantha**	wholewheat bread made with butter, rolled thin and griddle-fried; a little bit like a chewy pancake, sometimes stuffed with meat or vegetables
phulka	A chapati that has been made to puff out by being placed directly on the fire
puri	crispy, puffed-up, deep-fried wholewheat bread
roti	loosely used term; often just another name for chapati, though it should be thicker, chewier, and baked in a tandoor
uttapam*	thick rice pancake often cooked with onions
vada*	doughnut-shaped, deep-fried lentil cake

**South Indian terminology; all other terms are either in Hindi or refer to north Indian cuisine.*

Glossary

AARTI evening temple puja of lights
ACHARYA religious teacher
ADIVASI official term for tribal person
AGARBATI incense
AHIMSA non-violence
AKHANDPATH continuous reading of the Sikh holy book, the Adi Granth
AMRITA nectar of immortality
ANGREZ general term for Westerners
ANNA coin, no longer minted (16 annas to one rupee)
APSARA heavenly nymph
ARAK liquor distilled from rice or coconut
ASANA yogic seating posture; small mat used in prayer and meditation
ASHRAM centre for spiritual learning and religious practice
ASURA demon
ATMAN soul
AVATAR reincarnation of Vishnu on earth, in human or animal form
AYAH nursemaid
AYURVEDA ancient system of medicine employing herbs, minerals and massage
BABA respectful term for a *sadhu*
BAGH garden, park
BAITHAK reception area in private house
BAKSHEESH tip, donation or alms, occasionally means a bribe
BANDH general strike
BANDHANI tie-dye
BANIYA another term for a *vaishya*; a moneylender
BANYAN vast fig tree, used traditionally as a meeting place, or shade for teaching and meditating. Also, in South India, a cotton vest
BASTEE slum area
BAUL Bengali singer
BAZAAR commercial centre of town; market
BEGUM Muslim princess; Muslim women of high status
BETEL leaf chewed in paan, with the nut of the areca tree; loosely applies to the nut, also
BHAJAN song in praise of god
BHAKTI religious devotion expressed in a personalized or emotional relationship with the deity
BHANG pounded marijuana, often mixed in lassis
BHOTIA Himalayan people of Tibetan origin
BHUMI earth, or earth goddess
BEEDI tobacco rolled in a leaf; the "poor man's puff"
BINDU seed, or the red dot (also *bindi*) worn by women on their foreheads as decoration
BODHI TREE/BO TREE peepal tree (*ficus religiosa*), associated with the Buddha's enlightenment
BODHI enlightenment
BODHISATTVA Buddhist saint
BRAHMIN a member of the highest caste group; priest
BUGYAL summer meadow
BUNDH general strike
BURKHA body-covering shawl worn by orthodox Muslim women
BURRA-SAHIB colonial official, boss or a man of great importance
CANTONMENT area of town occupied by military quarters
CASTE social status acquired at birth
CHAAT snack
CHADDAR large head-cover or shawl
CHAKRA discus; focus of power; energy point in the body; wheel, often representing the cycle of death and rebirth
CHANDAN sandalwood paste
CHANDRA moon
CHANG Ladakhi beer made from fermented millet, wheat or rice
CHAPPAL sandals or flip-flops (thongs)
CHARAS hashish

Note that a separate glossary of **architectural terms** appears on p.1455; many **religious** terms are explained in detail in the section which begins on p.1395; and **musical** instruments on p.1421 onwards.

CHARPOI string bed with wooden frame

CHAURI fly whisk, regal symbol

CHELA pupil

CHIKAN Lucknow embroidery

CHILLUM cylindrical clay or wood pipe for smoking charas or ganja

CHOLI short, tight-fitting blouse worn with a sari

CHOR robber

CHOULTRY quarters for pilgrims adjoined to South Indian temples

CHOWGAN green in the centre of a town or village

CHOWK crossroads or courtyard

CHOWKIDAR watchman/caretaker

COOLIE porter/labourer

CRORE ten million

DABBA packed lunch

DACOIT bandit

DALIT "oppressed", "out-caste". The term, introduced by Dr Ambedkar, is preferred by so-called "untouchables" as a description of their social position

DANDA staff, or stick

DARSHAN vision of a deity or saint; receiving religious teachings

DAWAN servant

DEG cauldron for food offerings, often found in *dargahs*

DEVA god

DEVADASI temple dancer

DEVI goddess

DEVTA deity from Himachal Pradesh

DHABA food hall selling local dishes

DHAM important religious site, or a theological college

DHARAMSHALA rest house for pilgrims

DHARMA sense of religious and social duty (Hindu); the law of nature, teachings, truth (Buddhist)

DHOBI laundry

DHOLAK double-ended drum

DHOLI sedan chair carried by bearers to hilltop temples

DHOOP thick pliable block of strong incense

DHOTI white ankle-length cloth worn by males, tied around the waist, and sometimes hitched up through the legs

DHURRIE woollen rug

DIGAMBARA literally "sky-clad": a Jain sect, known for the habit of nudity among monks, though this is no longer commonplace

DIKPALAS guardians of the four directions

DIWAN (dewan) chief minister

DOWRY payment or gift offered in marriage

DRAVIDIAN of the south

DUPATTA veil worn by Muslim women with *salwar kamise*

DURBAR court building; government meeting

DZO domesticated half-cow half-yak

EVE-TEASING sexual harassment of women, either physical or verbal

FAKIR ascetic Muslim mendicant

FENI Goan spirit, distilled from coconut or cashew fruits

GADA mace

GADI throne

GANDA dirty

GANDHARVAS Indra's heavenly musicians

GANJ market

GANJA marijuana buds

GARI vehicle, or car

GHAT mountain, landing platform, or steps leading to water

GHAZAL melancholy Urdu songs

GHEE clarified butter

GONCHA ankle-length woollen robe worn by Ladakhi women

GOONDA ruffian

GOPI young cattle-tending maidens who feature as Krishna's playmates and lovers in popular mythology

GURU teacher of religion, music, dance, astrology etc

GURUDWARA Sikh place of worship

HAJ Muslim pilgrimage to Mecca

HAJJI Muslim engaged upon, or who has performed, the *Haj*

HARIJAN title – "Children of God" – given to "untouchables" by Gandhi

HARTAL one-day strike

HIJRA eunuch or transvestite

HINAYANA literally "lesser vehicle": the name given to the original school of Buddhism by later sects

HOOKAH water pipe for smoking strong tobacco or marijuana

HOWDAH bulky elephant-saddle, sometimes made of pure silver, and often shaded by a canopy

IDGAH area laid aside in the west of town for prayers during the Muslim festival Id-ul-Zuha

IMAM Muslim leader or teacher

IMFL Indian-made foreign liquor

ISHWARA God; Shiva

JAGIRDAR landowner

JANAPADAS small republics and monarchies; literally "territory of the clan"

JATAKAS popular tales about the Buddha's life and teachings

JATI caste, determined by family and occupation

JAWAN soldier

JHUTA soiled by lips: food or drink polluted by touch

-JI suffix added to names as a term of respect

JIHAD striving by Muslims, through battle, to spread their faith

JINA another term for the Jain *tirthankaras*

JOHAR old practice of self-immolation by women in times of war

JYOTIRLINGA twelve sites sacred by association with Shiva's unbounded lingam of light

KAILASA or KAILASH A mountain in western Tibet: Shiva's abode and the traditional source of the Ganges and Brahmaputra; the earthly manifestation of the "world pillar", Mount Meru

KALAM school of painting

KAMA satisfaction

KARMA weight of good and bad actions that determine status of rebirth

KATCHA the opposite of pukka

KAVAD small decorated box that unfolds to serve as a travelling temple

KHADI home-spun cotton; Gandhi's symbol of Indian self-sufficiency

KHAN honorific Muslim title

KHEJRI small tree found in the Thar desert in Rajasthan

KHOL black eye-liner, also known as *surma*

KHUD valley side

KIRTAN hymn-singing

KOTWALI police station

KSHATRYA the warrior and ruling caste

KUMKUM red mark on a Hindu woman's forehead (widows are not supposed to wear it)

KUND tank, lake, reservoir

KURTA long men's shirt worn over baggy pajamas

LAKH one hundred thousand

LAMA Tibetan Buddhist monk and teacher

LATHI heavy stick used by police

LINGAM phallic symbol in places of worship representing the god Shiva

LOKA realm or world, eg *devaloka*, world of the gods

LUNGHI male garment; long wraparound cloth, like a *dhoti*, but usually coloured

MADRASA Islamic school

MAHA- great or large

MAHADEVA literally "Great God", and a common epithet for Shiva

MAHALLA neighbourhood

MAHARAJA (Maharana, Maharao) king

MAHARANI queen

MAHATMA great soul

MAHAYANA "Great Vehicle": a Buddhist school that has spread throughout southeast Asia

MAHOUT elephant driver or keeper

MAIDAN large open space or field

MALA necklace, garland or rosary

MANDALA religious diagram

MANDI market

MANDIR temple

MANI STONE stone etched with Buddhist prayers by Tibetans and laid in piles or set in streams

MANTRA sacred verse, often repeated as an aid to meditation

MARG road

MASJID mosque

MATAJI female *sadhu*

MATH Hindu or Jain monastery

MAUND old unit of weight (roughly 20kg)

MAYUR peacock

MEHENDI henna

MELA festival

MEMSAHIB respectful address to European woman

MITHUNA sexual union, or amorous couples in Hindu and Buddhist figurative art

MOKSHA blissful state of freedom from rebirth aspired to by Hindus and Jains

MOR peacock

MUDRA hand gesture used in Vedic rituals, featuring in Hindu, Buddhist and Jain art and dance, and symbolizing teachings and life stages of the Buddha

MUEZZIN man behind the voice calling Muslims to prayer from a mosque

MULLAH Muslim teacher and scholar

MUTT Hindu or Jain monastery

NADI river

NAGA mythical serpent; alternatively a person from Nagaland

NALA stream gorge in the mountains

NATAK dance

NATYA drama

NAUTCH performance by dancing girls

NAWAB Muslim landowner or prince

NILGAI blue bull

NIRVANA (aka NIBBANA) Buddhist equivalent of *moksha*

NIZAM title of Hyderabad rulers

NULLAH stream gorge in the mountains

OM (aka AUM) symbol denoting the origin of all things, and ultimate divine essence, used in meditation by Hindus and Buddhists

PAAN betel nut, lime, calcium and aniseed wrapped in a leaf and chewed as a digestive. Mildly addictive

PADMA lotus; another name for the goddess Lakshmi

PAISE there are a hundred paisa in a rupee

PAJAMA men's baggy trousers

PALI original language of early Buddhist texts

PANCHAYAT village council

PANDA pilgrims' priest

PARIKRAMA ritual circumambulation around a temple, shrine or mountain

PARSI Zoroastrian

PIND mourning ceremony on the thirteenth day after the death of a parent

PIR Muslim holy man

POL residential quarters, common in Gujarat

PRANAYAMA breath control, used in meditation

PRASAD food blessed in temple sanctuaries and shared among devotees

PRAYAG auspicious confluence of two or more rivers

PUJA worship

PUJARI priest

PUKKA correct and acceptable, in the very English sense of "proper"

PUNYA religious merit

PURDAH seclusion of Muslim women inside the home, and the general term for wearing a veil

PURNIMA full moon

PUROHIT priest

QAWWALI devotional singing popular among Sufis

RAAG or RAGA series of notes forming the basis of a melody

RAJ rule; monarchy; in particular the period of British Imperial rule 1857–1947

RAJA king

RAJPUT princely rulers who once dominated much of north and west India

RAKSHASA demon (demoness: *rakshasi*)

RANGOLI geometrical pattern of rice powder laid before houses and temples

RAWAL chief priest (Hindu)

RINPOCHE literally "precious one", a highly revered Tibetan Buddhist lama, considered to be a reincarnation of a previous teacher

RISHI "seer"; philosophical sage or poet

RUDRAKSHA beads used to make Shiva rosaries

RUMAL handkerchief, particularly finely embroidered in Chamba state (HP)

SADAR "main"; eg sadar bazaar

SADHAK a person who is engaged in an all-encompassing course in spirituality to achieve realization of the self and God

SADHU Hindu holy man with no caste or family ties

SAGAR lake

SAHIB respectful title for gentlemen; general term of address for European men

SALABHANJIKA wood nymph

SALWAR KAMISE long shirt and baggy ankle-hugging trousers worn by Indian women

SAMADHI final enlightenment; a site of death or burial of a saint

SAMBAR a small Asian deer

SAMSARA cyclic process of death and rebirth

SANADARSANAN special time for *darshan*

SANGAM sacred confluence of two or more rivers, or an academy

SANGEET music

SANNYASIN homeless, possessionless ascetic (Hindu)

SARAI resting place for caravans and travellers who once followed the trade routes through Asia

SARI usual dress for Indian women: a length of cloth wound around the waist and draped over one shoulder

SATI one who sacrifices her life on her husband's funeral pyre in emulation of Shiva's wife. No longer a common practice, and officially illegal

SATSANG teaching given by a religious figurehead

SATYAGRAHA Gandhi's campaign of nonviolent protest, literally "grasping truth"

SCHEDULED CASTES official name for "untouchables"

SEPOY an Indian soldier in European service

SETH merchant or businessman

SEVA voluntary service in a temple or community

SHAIVITE Hindu recognizing Shiva as the supreme god

SHANKHA conch, symbol of Vishnu

SHASTRA treatise

SHIKAR hunting

SHISHYA pupil

SHLOKA verse from a Sanskrit text

SHRI respectful prefix; another name for Lakshmi

SHUDRA the lowest of the four *varnas*; servant

SHULAB public toilet

SINGHA lion

SITOUT veranda

SOMA medicinal herb with hallucinogenic properties used in early Vedic and Zoroastrian rituals

STHALA site sacred for its association with legendary events

SURMA black eyeliner, also known as *khol*

SURYA the sun, or sun god

SUTRA (aka sutta) verse in Sanskrit and Pali texts (literally "thread")

SVETAMBARA "white-clad" sect of Jainism, that accepts nuns and shuns nudity

SWAMI title for a holy man

SWARAJ "self rule"; synonym for independence, coined by Gandhi

TALA rhythmic cycle in classical music; in sculpture a tala signifies one face-length

TALUKA district

TANDAVA vigorous, male form of dance; the dance of Shiva Nataraja

TANDOOR clay oven

TANPURA The twangy drone which accompanies all classical music

TAPAS literally "heat": physical and mental austerities

TEMPO three-wheeled taxi

TERMA precious manuscript (Tibetan Buddhist term)

TERTON one who discovers a terma. Usually an enlightened being who will be able to understand the benefit of the terma in the era of its discovery (Tibetan Buddhist term)

THAKUR landowner

THALI combination of vegetarian dishes, chutneys, pickles, rice and bread served, especially in South India, as a single meal; the metal plate on which a meal is served

THANGKA Tibetan religious scroll painting

THERAVADA "Doctrine of the Elders": the original name for early Buddhism, which persists today in Sri Lanka and Thailand

THUG member of a north Indian cult of professional robbers and murderers

TIFFIN light meal

TIFFIN CARRIER stainless steel set of tins used for carrying meals

TILAK red dot smeared on the forehead during worship, and often used cosmetically

TIRTHA river crossing considered sacred by Hindus, or the transition from the mundane world to heaven; a place of pilgrimage for Jains

TIRTHANKARA "ford-maker" or "crossing-maker": an enlightened Jain teacher who is deified – 24 appear every 300 million years

TOLA the weight of a silver rupee: 180 grains, or approximately 116g

TONGA two-wheeled horse-drawn cart

TOPI cap

TRIMURTI the Hindu trinity

TRISHULA Shiva's trident

TULKU reincarnated teacher of Tibetan Buddhism

UNTOUCHABLES members of the lowest strata of society, considered polluting to all higher castes

URS Muslim saint's day festival

VAHANA the "vehicle" of a deity: the bull Nandi is Shiva's *vahana*

VAISHYA member of the merchant and trading caste group

VARNA literally "colour"; one of four hierarchical social categories: brahmins, *kshatryas*, *vaishyas* and *shudras*

VEDAS sacred texts of early Hinduism

WADDO South Indian term meaning ward or sub-division of a district

-WALLAH suffix implying occupation, eg: *dhobi*-wallah, rickshaw-wallah

WAZIR chief minister to the king

YAGNA Vedic sacrificial ritual

YAKSHA pre-Vedic folklore figure connected with fertility and incorporated into later Hindu iconography

YAKSHI female *yaksha*

YALI mythical lion

YANTRA cosmological pictogram, or model used in an observatory

YATRA pilgrimage

YATRI pilgrim

YOGI *sadhu* or priestly figure possessing occult powers gained through the practice of yoga (female: *yogini*)

YONI symbol of the female sexual organ, set around the base of the lingam in temple shrines

YUGA aeon: the present age is the last in a cycle of four yugas, *kali-yuga*, a " black-age" of degeneration and spiritual decline

ZAMINDAR landowner

Architectural terms

AMALAKA repeating decorative motif based on the fluted shape of a gourd, lining and crowning temple towers: a distinctive feature of north Indian architecture

ANDA literally "egg": the spherical part of a stupa

BAGH garden

BAOLI step-well in Gujarat and western India

BHAWAN (also bhavan) building, house, palace or residence

BHUMIKA storey

BIRADIRI summer house; pavilion

CELLA chamber, often housing the image of a deity

CENOTAPH ornate tomb

CHAITYA Buddhist temple

CHARBAGH garden divided into quadrants (Moghul style)

CHAUMUKH image of four faces placed back to back

CHHATRI tomb; domed temple pavilion

CHORTEN monument, often containing prayers, texts or relics, erected as a sign of faith by Tibetan Buddhists

CUPOLA small delicate dome

DARGAH tomb of a Muslim saint

DARWAZA gateway; door

DEUL Orissan temple or sanctuary

DIWAN-I-AM public audience hall

DIWAN-I-KHAS hall of private audience

DU-KHANG main temple in a gompa

DUKKA tank and fountain in courtyard of mosque

DURBAR court building, hall of audience, or government meeting

DVARPALA guardian image placed at sanctuary door

FINIAL capping motif on temple pinnacle

GARBHA GRIHA temple sanctuary, literally "womb-chamber"

GARH fort

GODOWN warehouse

GO-KHANG temple in a gompa devoted to protector (gon) deities

GOMPA Tibetan, or Ladakhi, Buddhist monastery

GOPURA towered temple gateway, common in South India

HAMMAM sunken hot bath, Persian style

HAVELI elaborately decorated (normally wooden) mansion, especially in Rajasthan

IMAMBARA tomb of a Shi'ite saint

INDO-SARACENIC overblown Raj-era architecture that combines Muslim, Hindu, Jain and Western elements

IWAN the main (often central) arch in a mosque

JAGAMOHANA porch fronting the main sanctuary in an Orissan temple

JALI latticework in stone, or a pierced screen

JANGHA the body of a temple

KABUTAR KHANA pigeon coop

KALASHA pot-like capping stone characteristic of South Indian temples

KANGYU LANG book house in a gompa storing sacred Tibetan texts and manuscripts

KOT fort

KOTHI residence

KOTLA citadel

KOVIL term for a Tamil Nadu temple

LIWAN cloisters in a mosque

MAHAL palace; mansion

MAKARA crocodile-like animal featuring on temple doorways, and symbolizing the River Ganges. Also the vehicle of Varuna, the Vedic god of the sea

MANDAPA hall, often with many pillars, used for various purposes: eg *kalyana mandapa* for wedding ceremonies and *nata mandapa* for dance performances

MEDHI terrace

MIHRAB niche in the wall of a mosque indicating the direction of prayer (to Mecca). In India the mihrab is in the west wall

MIMBAR pulpit in a mosque from which the Friday sermon is read

MINARET high slender tower, characteristic of mosques

PADA foot, or base, also a poetic meter

PAGODA multistoreyed Buddhist monument

POLE fortified gate

PRADAKSHINA PATHA processional path circling a monument or sanctuary

PRAKARA enclosure or courtyard in a South Indian temple

QABR Muslim grave

QILA fort

RATH processional temple chariot of South India

REKHA DEUL Orissan towered sanctuary

SHIKHARA temple tower or spire common in northern architecture

STAMBHA pillar, or flagstaff

STUPA large hemispherical mound, representing the Buddha's presence, and often protecting relics of the Buddha or a Buddhist saint

TALA storey

TANK square or rectangular water pool in a temple complex, for ritual bathing

TORANA arch, or freestanding gateway of two pillars linked by an elaborate arch

TUK fortified enclosure of Jain shrines or temples

VAV step-well, common in Gujarat

VEDIKA railing around a stupa

VIHARA Buddhist or Jain monastery

VIMANA tower over temple sanctuary

ZENANA women's quarters; segregated area for women in a mosque

Travel store

Rough Guides travel...

UK & Ireland
Britain
Devon & Cornwall
Dublin DIRECTIONS
Edinburgh DIRECTIONS
England
Ireland
Lake District
London
London DIRECTIONS
London Mini Guide
Scotland
Scottish Highlands & Islands
Wales

Europe
Algarve DIRECTIONS
Amsterdam
Amsterdam DIRECTIONS
Andalucía
Athens DIRECTIONS
Austria
Baltic States
Barcelona
Barcelona DIRECTIONS
Belgium & Luxembourg
Berlin
Brittany & Normandy
Bruges DIRECTIONS
Brussels
Budapest
Bulgaria
Copenhagen
Corfu
Corsica
Costa Brava DIRECTIONS
Crete
Croatia
Cyprus
Czech & Slovak Republics
Dodecanese & East Aegean
Dordogne & The Lot
Europe
Florence & Siena
Florence DIRECTIONS
France
French Hotels & Restos
Germany
Greece
Greek Islands
Hungary
Ibiza & Formentera DIRECTIONS
Iceland
Ionian Islands
Italy
Italian Lakes
Languedoc & Roussillon
Lisbon
Lisbon DIRECTIONS
The Loire
Madeira DIRECTIONS
Madrid DIRECTIONS
Mallorca & Menorca
Mallorca DIRECTIONS
Malta & Gozo DIRECTIONS
Menorca
Moscow
Netherlands
Norway
Paris
Paris DIRECTIONS
Paris Mini Guide
Poland
Portugal
Prague
Prague DIRECTIONS
Provence & the Côte d'Azur
Pyrenees
Romania
Rome
Rome DIRECTIONS
Sardinia
Scandinavia
Sicily
Slovenia
Spain
St Petersburg
Sweden
Switzerland
Tenerife & La Gomera DIRECTIONS
Turkey
Tuscany & Umbria
Venice & The Veneto
Venice DIRECTIONS
Vienna

Asia
Bali & Lombok
Bangkok
Beijing
Cambodia
China
Goa
Hong Kong & Macau
India
Indonesia
Japan
Laos
Malaysia, Singapore & Brunei
Nepal
The Philippines
Singapore
South India
Southeast Asia
Sri Lanka
Taiwan
Thailand
Thailand's Beaches & Islands
Tokyo
Vietnam

Australasia
Australia
Melbourne
New Zealand
Sydney

North America
Alaska
Boston
California
Canada
Chicago
Florida
Grand Canyon
Hawaii
Honolulu
Las Vegas DIRECTIONS
Los Angeles
Maui DIRECTIONS
Miami & South Florida
Montréal
New England
New Orleans DIRECTIONS
New York City
New York City DIRECTIONS
New York City Mini Guide
Orlando & Walt Disney World DIRECTIONS
Pacific Northwest
Rocky Mountains
San Francisco
San Francisco DIRECTIONS
Seattle
Southwest USA
Toronto
USA
Vancouver
Washington DC
Washington DC DIRECTIONS
Yosemite

Caribbean & Latin America
Antigua & Barbuda DIRECTIONS
Argentina
Bahamas
Barbados DIRECTIONS
Belize
Bolivia
Brazil
Cancùn & Cozumel DIRECTIONS
Caribbean
Central America
Chile
Costa Rica
Cuba
Dominican Republic
Dominican Republic DIRECTIONS
Ecuador
Guatemala
Jamaica

TRAVEL STORE

small print and

Index

A Rough Guide to Rough Guides

In the summer of 1981, Mark Ellingham, a recent graduate from Bristol University, was travelling round Greece and couldn't find a guidebook that really met his needs. On the one hand there were the student guides, insistent on saving every last cent, and on the other the heavyweight cultural tomes whose authors seemed to have spent more time in a research library than lounging away the afternoon at a taverna or on the beach.

In a bid to avoid getting a job, Mark and a small group of writers set about creating their own guidebook. It was a guide to Greece that aimed to combine a journalistic approach to description with a thoroughly practical approach to travellers' needs – a guide that would incorporate culture, history, and contemporary insights with a critical edge, together with up-to-date, value-for-money listings. Back in London, Mark and the team finished their Rough Guide, as they called it, and talked Routledge into publishing the book.

That first *Rough Guide to Greece*, published in 1982, was a student scheme that became a publishing phenomenon. The immediate success of the book – with numerous reprints and a Thomas Cook Prize shortlisting – spawned a series that rapidly covered dozens of destinations. Rough Guides had a ready market among low-budget backpackers, but soon also acquired a much broader and older readership that relished Rough Guides' wit and inquisitiveness as much as their enthusiastic, critical approach. Everyone wants value for money, but not at any price.

Rough Guides soon began supplementing the "rougher" information about hostels and low-budget listings with the kind of detail on restaurants and quality hotels that independent-minded visitors on any budget might expect, whether on business in New York or trekking in Thailand.

These days the guides – distributed worldwide by the Penguin Group – offer recommendations from shoestring to luxury and cover more than 200 destinations around the globe, including almost every country in the Americas and Europe, more than half of Africa, and most of Asia and Australasia. Our ever-growing team of authors and photographers is spread all over the world, particularly in Europe, the USA, and Australia.

In 1994, we published the *Rough Guide to World Music* and *Rough Guide to Classical Music*, and a year later the *Rough Guide to the Internet*. All three books have become benchmark titles in their fields – which encouraged us to expand into other areas of publishing, mainly around popular culture. Rough Guides now publish:

- Travel guides to more than 200 worldwide destinations
- Dictionary phrasebooks for 22 major languages
- History guides ranging from Ireland to Islam
- Maps printed on rip-proof and waterproof Polyart™ paper
- Music guides running the gamut from Opera to Elvis
- Restaurant guides to London, New York and San Francisco
- Reference books on topics as diverse as the Weather and Shakespeare
- Sports guides from Formula 1 to Man Utd
- Pop culture books from *Lord of the Rings* to Cult TV
- World Music CDs in association with World Music Network

Visit **www.roughguides.com** to see our latest publications.

Rough Guide credits

Text editors: Polly Thomas, Sam Cook, Ann-Marie Shaw, Ed Aves
Layout: Ajay Verma
Cartography: Rajesh Chhibber
Picture editor: Jj Luck
Production: Katherine Owers
Proofreader: Madhulita Mohapatra
Editorial: London Kate Berens, Claire Saunders, Geoff Howard, Ruth Blackmore, Gavin Thomas, Richard Lim, Clifton Wilkinson, Alison Murchie, Sally Schafer, Karoline Densley, Andy Turner, Ella O'Donnell, Keith Drew, Edward Aves, Nikki Birrell, Helen Marsden, Joe Staines, Duncan Clark, Peter Buckley, Matthew Milton **New York** Andrew Rosenberg, Richard Koss, Steven Horak, AnneLise Sorensen, Amy Hegarty, Hunter Slaton
Design & Pictures: London Simon Bracken, Dan May, Diana Jarvis, Mark Thomas, Harriet Mills, Chloë Roberts; **Delhi** Umesh Aggarwal, Jessica Subramanian, Amit Verma, Ankur Guha
Production: Julia Bovis, Sophie Hewat
Cartography: **London** Maxine Repath, Ed Wright, Katie Lloyd-Jones; **Delhi** Manish Chandra, Jai Prakash Mishra, Ashutosh Bharti, Rajesh Mishra, Jasbir Sandhu, Karobi Gogoi, Animesh Pathak
Online: **New York** Jennifer Gold, Suzanne Welles, Kristin Mingrone; **Delhi** Manik Chauhan, Narender Kumar, Manish Shekhar Jha, Rakesh Kumar, Lalit K. Sharma, Chhandita Chakravarty
Marketing & Publicity: London Richard Trillo, Niki Hanmer, David Wearn, Demelza Dallow, Louise Maher; **New York** Geoff Colquitt, Megan Kennedy, Milena Perez; **Delhi** Reem Khokhar
Custom publishing and foreign rights: Philippa Hopkins
Manager India: Punita Singh
Series editor: Mark Ellingham
Reference Director: Andrew Lockett
PA to Managing and Publishing Directors: Megan McIntyre
Publishing Director: Martin Dunford
Managing Director: Kevin Fitzgerald

Publishing information

This sixth edition published October 2005 by
Rough Guides Ltd,
80 Strand, London WC2R 0RL
345 Hudson St, 4th Floor,
New York, NY 10014, USA
14 Local Shopping Centre, Panchsheel Park,
New Delhi 110017, India.
Distributed by the Penguin Group
Penguin Books Ltd,
80 Strand, London WC2R 0RL
Penguin Putnam, Inc.
375 Hudson St, NY 10014, USA
Penguin Group (Australia)
250 Camberwell Road, Camberwell,
Victoria 3124, Australia
Penguin Books Canada Ltd,
10 Alcorn Avenue, Toronto, ON,
M4V 1E4 Canada
Penguin Group (New Zealand),
Cnr Rosedale and Airborne Roads,
Albany, Auckland, New Zealand

Typeset in Bembo and Helvetica to an original design by Henry Iles.
Printed in Italy by LegoPrint S.p.A

1480pp includes index
A catalogue record for this book is available from the British Library.
ISBN-13: 978-1-84353-501-0
ISBN-10: 1-84353-501-7

1 3 5 7 9 8 6 4 2

Help us update

We've gone to a lot of trouble to ensure that this sixth edition of the **Rough Guide to India** is accurate and up to date. However, things change – places get "discovered", opening hours are notoriously fickle, restaurants and rooms raise prices or lower standards. If you feel we've got it wrong or left something out, we'd like to know, and if you can remember the address, the price, the time and the phone number, so much the better.

We'll credit any contributions, and send a copy of the next edition (or any other Rough Guide if you prefer) for the best letters. Everyone who writes to us and isn't already a subscriber will receive a copy of our full-colour thrice-yearly newsletter. Please mark letters "**Rough Guide to India Update**" and send to: Rough Guides, 80 Strand, London WC2R 0RL, or Rough Guides, 4th Floor, 345 Hudson St, New York, NY 10014. Or send an email to **mail@roughguides.com**.
Have your questions answered and tell others about your trip at
www.roughguides.atinfopop.com

Acknowledgements

Thank you from all the authors and contributors to everyone at Rough Guides who has helped make this edition of India the best to date, particularly editor Polly Thomas, who managed the sprawling project with great tact and efficiency to the end. Also, thanks to Ann-Marie Shaw, Sam Cook and Ed Aves, who pitched in the help with the editing at short notice; to Claire Saunders, who got the thing up and running in the first place (again); and to Jj Luck, for considerably improving the book's photographic content.

David Abram: Thank you to Rohinton Commissariat and the Taj Group; Denzil Sequeira; Sarah Britto and family; Nick Edwards; and Ruth French.

Nick Edwards: Thanks for invaluable help in making a smooth trip to: Rohinton Commissariat in Mumbai; the Taj hotel staff in Nasik and Pune; all those at the tourist offices of Maharashtra, Karnataka, Kerala, AP and the Andamans, especially Mr Yadav in Aurangabad and Mr Varghese in Kochi; the good folk at the following establishments: Anand of *Classic Tours and Hotel*, Aurangabad; Arjun at the *Shree Maya*, Aurangabad; all at the *Plaza*, *Jalgaon*, *Costa Malabari* and *Pachyderm Palace*, Kerala; Benny and Linda of *Wild Orchid*, Havelock Island; kindly Gyan on Neill Island; Johnson of *The Nest*, Allepey; scholarly Mr Walton in Fort Kochi. Cheers to Antonia and Jemila for company in Munnar; Kathleen and Bethany for high times in Hampi; and Noam for making the Arial Bay to Port Blair boat trip a pleasure. Fair play to Paul and Jess for Xmas frolics and them plus Graham (completing his hat-trick) for the Kerala tour; yiasou to Sylvia for the last few days in Mamallapuram; thanks to Ashok and Anita for Madras hospitality. Last but not least, much love to Maria for enduring another long absence and not changing the locks! Finally, a prayer for all those lost and affected by the tsunami.

Mike Ford: A very big thank you to the following: Mr Karunanidhi of Welcome Tourrs and Travels in Chennai for your help with transport in Tamil Nadu; to my fearless and excellent driver Mr Ramesh; to Mrs Anu John at TTDC Kerala Office in Chennai for information, connections, friendship and a wonderful Keralan meal; to Mr Varghese at the Tourist Desk in Ernakulam for contacts; to the *Taj Connemara* in Chennai, *Greenwoods* in Mamallapuram and the *Sangam* hotel in Trichy; to Polly Thomas for excellent editing. Finally, a very big thank you to friends in Bristol – too many to name – for inspiration, support, drinks and technical support during computer traumas; and heartfelt sympathy for those in Tamil Nadu who suffered during the tsunami.

Devdan Sen: Thanks to everyone who assisted, especially Vivek Angra and India Tourism; Jai Chand, Bunny Mahtab and family; Sangela and Norbu Dekevas; Norden, Thinley Pempahishey and family; Norden's father Karma; Neil Law; Thendup and Pema; and Nima and Dorji Bhutia.

Joshua Goodman: Thanks to Erika Abrams and Jim Myers; Gwendolyn Ross; Hannah Mulder; Jora Lal from Jaisalmer; and Mr and Mrs Singh in Jaipur.

Daniel Jacobs: Thanks to Punita, Madhu, Manish and all the team at Rough Guides Delhi.

Anil Mulchandani: Thanks to Anil Bhagia in Ahmedabad; Mustak Mepani in Jamnagar; Kishore Joshi in Porbandar; Sikander Rai in Diu; Raghuvendra Singh of Fort Amla near Ujjain; Rajendra Singh in Orchha; Pushpendra Singh in Bandhavgarh; Mr Tomar in Kanha; Swosti Travels in Orissa; and Naresh Bhasin, Praveen Shelley and Mr Soni of Expert Tours in Agra.

Laura Stone: Thanks to Phuntsok and family at the *Oriental GH* in Leh; the two-wheeled Raju Sharma of Kullu; Neelu of Trek Himalaya Tours for the rock-climbing and bottles of Bagpiper; and Urgain Loondup of J&K Tourism. Cheers to travellers along the way for tips, rants and for being fun; in particular, Brad Carlisle; Chrissi Dietsche (we will cycle soon!); and Reik, my "husband", for turning up in the most unusual places. Finally thanks to Martin Dunford and Claire Saunders at Rough Guides for returning me to the Indian Himalaya, my favourite part of the world.

Caroline Sylge: A huge thank you to Manoj, Vineeta, Ranjeet and Hemanta at Purvi Discovery, Dibrugarh, Assam; to Jimmy at Gurudongma Tours and Treks, Kalimpong, WB; and to Vivek Angra, director of the India Tourism office in London.

Readers' letters

Thanks to all those readers of the fifth edition who took the time to write in with amendments and additions. Apologies for any misspellings or omissions.

Florence Acworth; Kate Allen; Andreas Augustin; Wendy Backhouse; Michael Bastow; Lucy Beck; Hugh Begbie; Chris Berger; Anna Bibra; Ujjwal Borkataki; Heather Bowen; Jon Braham; Diana Care; David Carle-Ellis; Howard Carter; Heather and Michael Carver; Terrie Chilvers; Annie Clark; Antonio Claver; Paul Compton; Joy Cook; Clive Collins; James Coupland; Joel Cranshaw; Liz Curran; Jacqueline Deley; Roos Derks; Vanessa Dupin; Tina Ealovega; Ceryn Evans; Ms D. Faithfull; Faiz Farooqi; Raphael Fasko; Betty Gardiner; Amorey Gethin; Jennifer Gold; Tony Gomm; Mark Goodman; Don Grisbrook; Evelin Grofield; Gavin and Samantha Gross; Yorsten Haggenmiller; Bridget Hauserman; Alan Hickey; Jeffrey Hobbs; Sally Holmes; Mr Howell; Benjamin Hughes; Rohin S. Jaisinghani; Rafael Kampel; Vinod Kaistha; Thomas Keenan; Katja Kerl; Dr Sandeep Kesavan; Andy Kiley; Sarah Kline; Michael Knowles; Josh Krinsky; Philipe Labbey; Cari Lawley; Leanne and Mark; Marie Lippens; Chris Lucas; Nadine Maddaford; Geerdt Magiels; Tony Maisnam; Sandra Markow; Linde Maroudi; Curtis Marr; Craig McAvinue; Asha Rani Mathur; Les Medcroft; Thorsten Meyer; Patricia Moore; Julie Morrisey; Peter Nelson; Bill New; Amar Niwas; Barbara O'Callayhan; Yumi Onishi; I.H. Page; Sarah Parker; Margie Parsons; Victoria Peacock; Matthys de Pee; Remy Pigois; Pirashanthie; Martin Pitcher; Bettina Preussler; Singh Prithviraj; Robin Ray; Dominique Renn; Daniella Reif; Anita Reinhardt; Asya Reznikov; Wayne Richardson; Blair Robertson; Nikki Robilliard; Jenny Ross; Yair Sagi; Sajid Sait; Nicholas Sardi; Andrew Savage; Mr P.A. Shah; Edward Simpson; Professor Rana P.B. Singh; Trevor Skingle; David Smithson; Carol Smurthwaite; Natasha and Sven Sommer; See Stanley; Daniele Stewart; Dr Birender Thakur; Marie Thureau; Colin Todhunter; Michael Tsan; Uma; Lisa Verity and Kelly; Brenda Walker; Darren Walker; Joanna Westcombe; Julie White; Mike White; Kelly Woods; Isabel Wright; Melanie J. Wynne; Martin York; Randy Yuen; Kira Zielinski.

Photo credits

Cover
Main front picture: Pushkar Festival, Rajasthan © Alamy
Small top picture: Thar desert village © Getty
Small front lower picture: Marigolds, Madurai © Alamy
Back top picture: Taj Mahal © Alamy
Back lower picture: Lantern festival, Varanasi © Getty

Title page
Leh © Laura Stone

Full page
Indian priest, Ujjain © Dinodia Images/Alamy

Introduction
Figures © Mike Ford
Decorated truck, Trivandrum © David Sanger photography/Alamy
Arambol beach © Mike Jones
Umbrella seller, Calcutta © Reuters/Corbis
Kanchenjunga with prayer flags © Mike Jones
Ghat on the Ganges, Varanasi © Terry Harris/Alamy
Nilgiri Blue Mountain Railway © Sylvia Cordaiy Photo Library Ltd/Alamy

Things not to miss
01 Meherangarh Fort, Jodhpur © David Abram
02 Ustad Ali Akbar Khan © Gurinder Osan/Alamy
03 Chauragarh, Pachmarhi © Beth Woodlridge
04 Hats of Buddhist monks, Dharamsala © David Samuel Robbins/Corbis
05 Yoga, Rishikesh © Michael Freeman/Corbis
06 Erotic sculpture, Khajuraho Temple © Jerry Dennis
07 Hampi © Dave Abram
08 Siberian crane, Bharatpur © Roger Tidman/Corbis
09 Ajanta caves, Maharashtra © Mike Ford
10 Ghats, Varanasi © Mike Ford
11 Golden Temple, Amritsar © Mike Ford
12 Zanskar © Mike Ford
13 Kathakali performer putting on makeup © Mike Ford
14 Haveli, Jaisalmer © Jerry Dennis
15 Camels, Rajasthan © Images of India Picture Agency
16 Cricket match on the Oval Maiden, Mumbai © Nick Whitney/Images of India Picture Library
17 Durga Puja festival in New Delhi © Amit Bhargava/Corbis
18 Ellora Caves, Maharashtra © Robert Leon/Alamy

19 Rajasthani handicrafts © Dave Abram
20 Bollywood on the set © Image Solutions/ Alamy
21 Tourists on elephants, Kaziranga National Park © Paul Harris
22 Hauling in nets, Palolem, Goa © Alan Lewis/ Travel Ink
23 Gokarna © Dave Abram
24 Tiger, Bandhavgarh National Park © R.A. Acharya/Images of India picture Agency
25 Mysore market © Sheldan Collins/Corbis
26 Manali–Leh highway © David Abram
27 Boating in Kerala © Mike Ford
28 Tikse © David Abram
29 Chinese fishing nets, Kochi © Paul Harris
30 Thrissur Puram © Images of India Picture Agency
31 Gangotri Ganga © Images of India Picture Agency
32 Taj Mahal © Paul Harris
33 View from the Palace at Orchha © Elvele Images/Alamy
34 Pushkar camel mela © Jerry Dennis
35 Lake Palace Hotel across Lake Pichola © Jerry Dennis
36 Rath Yatra, Puri © Jayanta Shaw/Reuters/ Corbis
37 Fatehpur Sikri © Apex News and Pictures Agency/Alamy
38 Mamallapuram © David Abram
39 Varkala, Kerala © Images of India Picture Agency
40 Madurai © Mike Ford
41 Konarak © Mike Ford
42 River Indus, Ladakh © Images of India Picture Agency

Black and whites

p.108 Street scene, Old Delhi © David Abram
p.160 Jaisalmer Fort © Dave Abram
p.253 Doorway and tiled wall, Udaipur © Claire Edwards/Images of India Picture Agency
p.267 Ganges, Varanasi © Mike Ford
p.315 Hussainabad Imambara, Lucknow © Jerry Dennis
p.352 Gangotri © Brand X Pictures/Alamy
p.392 Bengal tigers in temple, Corbett National Park © Gallo Images/Corbis
p.404 Orchha © Chris Lisle/Corbis
p.441 Jahangir Mahal, Orchha © Jerry Dennis
p.480 Spiti Valley © Mike Ford
p.548 Mudh, Pin Valley © Michael Kohn
p.554 Alcchi monastery © Mike Ford
p.590 Lamayuru © Mike Ford
p.598 Golden Temple, Amritsar © Mike Ford
p.606 Chandigarh rock garden © Mike Ford
p.620 Palitana, Gujarat © Ilay Cooper/Images of India Picture agency
p.650 Dhow-builder © Dave Abram
p.690 Gateway of India © Jon Arnold Images/ Alamy
p.712 Ganesh Festival © Images of India Picture Agency
p.734 Relief, Ellora caves © Dave Abram
p.756 Ajanta caves © Mike Ford
p.788 Arambol beach © Dave Abram
p.847 Fishing boat on Palolem Beach © Greg Evans
p.586 Victoria Memorial © Mike Ford
p.883 College Street coffee house, Kolkata © Jerry Dennis
p.926 Bodhgaya, Bihar © Mike Ford
p.948 Rice terrace, Sikkim © Mike Ford
p.967 Window, Pemayangtse © Devdan Sen
p.978 Tawang Monastery © Tony Howard
p.1000 Demon dancer © Mike Ford
p.1024 Olive Ridley turtle © Matthew Hancock
p.1044 Rath Yatra, Puri © Images of India
p.1062 Pilgrims, Tirupati © Mike Ford
p.1070 Hyderabad bazaar © Mike Ford
p.1086 School of Moorish Idols © Jane Gould/ Alamy
p.1109 Kalipur Beach, Andaman Islands © Nick Edwards
p.1112 Krishna's Butter Ball, Mamallapuram © David Abram
p.1139 Parathasarathy Temple, Chennai © Steve Davey/La belle Aurore
p.1206 Fishermen hauling nets © Andrew Morris
p.1236 Kerala backwaters, Thelavadi © Paul Harris
p.1278 Golgumbaz Tomb © Devdan Sen
p.1324 Jog Falls, Karnataka © M. Amirtham/ Images of India picture Agency

Index

Map entries are in colour

Key to index		
Andaman Islands **(AI)**	Himachal Pradesh **(HP)**	Mumbai **(MI)**
Andhra Pradesh **(AP)**	Karnataka **(Kar)**	Northeast **(NE Hills)**
Bihar and Jharkhand **(B&J)**	Kerala **(Ker)**	Orissa **(Ori)**
Delhi **(D)**	Kolkata and West Bengal **(K&WB)**	Rajasthan **(Raj)**
Goa **(Goa)**	Ladakh **(L)**	Sikkim **(Sik)**
Gujarat **(Guj)**	Madhya Pradesh **(MP)**	Tamil Nadu **(TN)**
Haryana and Punjab **(H&P)**	Maharashtra **(M)**	Uttar Pradesh **(UP)**
		Uttaranchal **(U)**

A

B

C

D

E

F

G

H

I

J

K

L

M

N

S

T

U

V

W

Y

Z

Map symbols

Maps are listed in the full index using coloured text

REGIONAL MAPS

- Motorway
- Main road
- Minor road
- Railway
- Track/trail
- Coastline/river
- Ferry
- International boundary
- State boundary
- Chapter boundary
- Mountains
- Peak
- Rocks
- Cave
- Pass
- Waterfall
- Viewpoint
- Airport
- Domestic airport
- Point of interest
- Church
- Bugyal
- Hut
- Lighthouse
- Palm trees
- Hill shading
- Swamp
- Glacier
- Forest
- Beach
- Mudflats

STREET MAPS

- Main road
- Secondary road
- Track
- Steps
- Railway
- Path
- Wall
- Tourist office
- Post office
- Internet access
- Petrol station
- Hospital
- Bus/taxi stand
- Metro station
- Stadium
- Accommodation
- Restaurant
- Building
- Church
- Cemetery
- Muslim cemetery
- Cliff
- Pagoda
- Helipad

COMMON SYMBOLS

- Mosque/Muslim monument
- Buddhist temple
- Hindu/Jain temple
- Haveli
- Palace
- Shrine
- Monastery
- Ghat
- Park